Medical Negligence

Fifth Edition

Medical Negligence

Fifth Edition

Michael A. Jones B.A., LL.M., Ph.D.,
Solicitor of the Supreme Court
Emeritus Professor of Law of the University of Liverpool

SWEET & MAXWELL  **THOMSON REUTERS**

First Edition	1991
Second Edition	1996
Third Edition	2003
Fourth Edition	2008
Fifth Edition	2018

Published in 2018 by Thomson Reuters, trading as Sweet & Maxwell. Registered in England & Wales, Company No.1679046. Registered Office and address for service: 5 Canada Square, Canary Wharf, London, E14 5AQ.

For further information on our products and services, visit *www.sweetandmaxwell.co.uk*

Typeset by Letterpart Limited, Caterham on the Hill, Surrey, CR3 5XL.

Printed and bound in Great Britain by CPI Group (UK) Ltd, Croydon, CR0 4YY.

No natural forests were destroyed to make this product: only farmed timber was used and re-planted.

A CIP catalogue record of this book is available from the British Library.

ISBN: 978-0-414-02848-7

Thomson Reuters, the Thomson Reuters Logo and Sweet & Maxwell ® are trademarks of Thomson Reuters.

Crown copyright material is reproduced with the permission of the Controller of HMSO and the Queen's Printer for Scotland.

FOR ANNIE

Preface to the 5th edition

It is now some nine years since the last edition of this book and in that time there have been some important changes in the landscape of medical negligence claims. In practical terms the most significant change has probably been the shift in funding arrangements for claimants. With legal aid all but abolished (except for limited types of brain-damaged baby cases) the overwhelming majority of medical negligence actions are now funded by insurance-backed conditional fee agreements, placing the financial risk of failed actions on claimant lawyers. One obvious effect of this has been for claimant lawyers to place stringent filters on the claims taken on, a process that is likely to be exacerbated by current proposals to introduce fixed fees for so-called "small claims". The abolition of the right of successful claimants to recover success fees from defendants means that even successful claimants are "undercompensated" because part of the damages award has to be set aside for costs.

The General Medical Council now imposes a professional "duty of candour" requiring doctors to inform patients when injuries have been inflicted accidentally (whether negligently or non-negligently). There is a corresponding statutory duty of candour imposed on NHS organisations (by the Health and Social Care Act 2008 (Regulated Activities) Regulations 2014), but it is too early to know whether this will have an impact on the number of claims. Doctors have always been worried that telling patients that they have been the victim of an error will lead to more claims, but there is some evidence that in the past patients have had to resort to litigation in order to find out what went wrong with their treatment, and that honesty with patients at the outset may reduce the inclination of patients to litigate.

One of the changes that was anticipated in 2008 but has not come to fruition was the implementation of a scheme of "redress" through the NHS Redress Act 2006. Although the Act remained conceptually grounded in the common law of negligence, it could have provided a swifter and more inclusive mechanism for obtaining compensation in lower value claims. The Act, which set out the bare structure of a redress scheme, remains on the statute book, but the Regulations that would have created the detail of the scheme for injured NHS patients in England have never been issued (although Wales now has its own system of redress).

The ability of the NHS to learn from errors appears to remain rather limited. NHS England publishes a list of serious errors so obvious and avoidable that they should not occur called, without any sense of irony, "never events". It collects data and publishes information about the number of these events. For 2016–2017 there were 424 never events, and from April to September 2017 a further 179. These include incidents that would be indefensible if a claim for negligence were made, such as "wrong site surgery" and "retained foreign objects post procedure". At times the NHS looks not so much like an organisation with a memory but an organisation suffering from amnesia.

The number of claims has undoubtedly risen since 2008. In the four years preceding the publication of the 4th edition the number of new claims for medical negligence had been steady at around 5,500 per annum. Since then there has been an increase in claims to just under 12,000 in 2013–2014, though this has dropped to 10,686 in 2016–2017. The annual cost of claims for medical negligence has also risen from £633 million in 2007–2008 to £1,707 million in 2016–2017. To put these figures into some context, in 2000 the Department of Health estimated that there were 850,000 adverse events in NHS hospitals each year, resulting in £2 billion direct cost (at that time) in additional hospital days alone. A large proportion of the overall cost of litigation is attributable to a few very high value claims, particularly brain-damaged baby cases. Looked at from a different end of the telescope the "problem" of medical malpractice litigation is not the number of claims or overall cost to the NHS but the difficulty faced by claimants in obtaining compensation for what are often life-changing events. It is not the fault of claimants, lawyers, or the courts that governments have systematically failed to introduce alternative, more efficient compensation schemes for the victims of medical accidents. Nor is it their fault that so much iatrogenic harm appears to be the inevitable consequence of a modern healthcare system. Injured patients needing compensation have to work with the system that is available. The alternative, relying on the social security system and/or social care, is not an appealing prospect.

In some respects a book on medical negligence represents a catalogue of the myriad ways in which mistakes can be made in the provision of healthcare. In 1999 Sir Cyril Chantler observed that "Medicine used to be simple, ineffective and relatively safe. It is now complex, effective and potentially dangerous" (*The Lancet*, vol. 353, pp.1178–1181). Most of the danger stems from the inherent difficulty of what health professionals are trying to do to preserve the health and welfare of their patients, but some of it is attributable to avoidable errors by professionals who, acting entirely in good faith, are trying but sadly failing to do their best. This should not blind us to the undoubted fact that for most patients most of the time the NHS succeeds in providing excellent healthcare for grateful recipients.

The basic law on establishing breach of duty has not changed since the 4th edition, though there have been numerous cases illustrating, and in some instances refining, the application of the *Bolam* test. Causation issues, as always, have continued to trouble the courts. The stand-out development has undoubtedly been the 2015 decision of the Supreme Court in *Montgomery v Lanarkshire Health Board* to reverse *Sidaway v Bethlem Royal Hospital Governors*, thereby establishing a patient's right to be appropriately informed before giving consent to treatment. *Montgomery*, following earlier developments in Australia and Canada, has given patients a much greater say over the medical procedures that they are willing to accept.

In 2008 authority on the Mental Capacity Act 2005 was sparse, but this has developed almost exponentially, particularly on the test for capacity and the meaning of "best interests". This accounts for a large part of the expansion of Chapter 6 on consent to treatment. Additionally, the courts have fashioned a new tort of "misuse of private information" out of the law on confidentiality and article 8 of the European Convention on Human Rights. Although this new tort seems mostly to have been used by celebrity figures to combat intrusions into their private lives by the media, there is nothing to prevent a patient from resorting to the tort, particularly as awards of damages for misuse of private information have been significantly greater than for breach of confidentiality.

As with previous editions the book seeks to provide a comprehensive statement of the law of medical negligence in England and Wales, with appropriate reference to Commonwealth jurisdictions. The basic structure of the book has remained the same, though I have included more headings and subheadings with a view to making it easier for readers to navigate the text. References to professional guidance, particularly from the General Medical Council, have been updated. The GMC issued new guidance on maintaining patient confidentiality earlier this year (*Confidentiality: good practice in handling patient information*, January 2017). This complements the GMC's more general guidance, *Good Medical Practice*, which was revised in 2013. Clearly, professional guidance is not the law but its significance for the potential development of the law should not be underestimated. The GMC's document on consent to treatment (*Consent: patients and doctors making decisions together*, June 2008, which remains the current guidance on this subject), was influential in persuading the Supreme Court in *Montgomery* that professional practice, and social values, had moved on and that it was time for a change in the law on informed consent.

I would like to extend a warm welcome to John McQuater who has brought his extensive experience to bear on Chapter 13. John is a partner at Atherton Godfrey, where he is head of litigation with overall responsibility for the Personal Injury and Clinical Negligence teams. Amongst many professional distinctions he is a solicitor-advocate with rights of audience, and a senior fellow of the Association of Personal Injury Lawyers. John is the author of *Model Letters for Personal Injury Lawyers*, the APIL *Guide to Personal Injury Claims Procedure*, and a contributor to the APIL *Guide to Clinical Negligence*. He also makes regular contributions to the *Journal of Personal Injury Law*. I am very grateful for his input to the procedural issues of medical negligence litigation.

I am extremely grateful to the team at Sweet & Maxwell for their continued support, encouragement and, above all, patience. In particular, I would like to thank Lindsay Emerson and Greg Smith, who must at times have wondered whether they would ever get to see the manuscript. Special thanks go to my wife, Anne, without whose forbearance the book would never have been completed.

The law is stated on the basis of the materials available to me at mid-September 2017, though I have been able to make some changes after that date at proof stage.

Michael A. Jones
Liverpool
November 2017

TABLE OF CONTENTS

2. THE BASIS OF LIABILITY

3. STANDARD OF CARE—GENERAL PRINCIPLES

7. INFORMED CONSENT

9. LIABILITY OF HOSPITALS AND CONTRIBUTION

13. PRACTICE AND PROCEDURE

CONTENTS

TABLE OF CASES

TABLE OF STATUTES

TABLE OF STATUTORY INSTRUMENTS

TABLE OF CIVIL PROCEDURE RULES

TABLE OF PRACTICE DIRECTIONS

TABLE OF PROTOCOLS

TABLE OF NATIONAL LEGISLATION

TABLE OF EUROPEAN AND INTERNATIONAL CONVENTIONS AND TREATIES

TABLE OF EUROPEAN LEGISLATION

CHAPTER 1

MEDICAL NEGLIGENCE IN CONTEXT

Medical negligence is an emotive term: emotive for doctors and for patients. **1–001**
Lawyers, however, have to take a more dispassionate view about the rights and
wrongs of medical accidents. The tort of negligence applies an objective standard
as a measure of professional conduct, and though it is known as "fault liability"
there is no necessary correlation between a finding that a doctor was negligent in
law and a judgment that his conduct was morally blameworthy. Mistakes are
made in all areas of professional life. Some are negligent, some are not; some
cause harm, most probably do not. When Lord Denning insisted that in order to
reach the conclusion that a doctor was negligent his conduct should be deserving
of censure or inexcusable, he clearly took the view that it should be more difficult
to prove negligence against a doctor.[1] The converse of this proposition, however,
is that whenever a doctor is held liable in negligence his conduct deserves
censure. This has probably made it more difficult to view negligence in the
context of medical practice in terms of the inadvertent slip, the error which
almost anyone could have (and probably has) made, and which though careless
does not say anything about the defendant's general competence in the practice of
medicine. On another occasion Lord Denning sought to characterise such
mistakes as errors of clinical judgment and, accordingly, not negligent. This view
was categorically rejected by the House of Lords on the ground that to state that
the defendant made an error of judgment, whether clinical or otherwise, tells one
nothing about whether the error was negligent or not.[2] One consequence, perhaps,
of judicial attitudes such as that of Lord Denning is that a claim for compensation
by an injured patient is often perceived by doctors to be accompanied by
denigration of the defendant's professional competence. This may partly explain
why the medical profession, of all the professions, is most sensitive to allegations
of negligence.

The process of identifying individual fault through the tort of negligence tends to **1–002**
overlook the wider issues involved in dealing with medical accidents. While on
the one hand it may be acknowledged that some accidents are inevitable, and
indeed that some accidents through carelessness will always occur, on the other
hand the tort action is not well-suited to identifying those accidents attributable
"organisational errors", or methods of delivering healthcare which equate

---

[1] *Hucks v Cole* (1968), [1993] 4 Med. L.R. 393 at 396; *Hatcher v Black, The Times,* 2 July 1954. See
further para.3–178.
[2] The disagreement occurred in *Whitehouse v Jordan* [1980] 1 All E.R. 650, CA; [1981] 1 All E.R.
267, HL; see para.3–015.

handling clinical negligence litigation relate to the overall cost to the NHS of dealing with claims for compensation, the relatively high administrative costs of the tort system, and the consequences for the financial management of NHS bodies, principally NHS Trust hospitals which bear the brunt of negligence claims. These concerns were reflected in *Making Amends*. The government's response to *Making Amends* was the NHS Redress Act 2006, which provides for an administrative scheme of compensation, based on existing principles of liability, for comparatively small claims, but which falls significantly short of the recommendations of *Making Amends*. Even that limited reform has not been implemented, though a functioning scheme of NHS Redress does apply in Wales.[20]

1–006   This book seeks to describe, analyse and, where appropriate, criticise the law of medical negligence in its widest sense.[21] Before embarking on that task, however, it may be helpful to identify the main themes and problems surrounding medical malpractice litigation to enable practitioners, whether lawyers or doctors, to see the wider context within which the law operates. The first section of this chapter considers the available information on the number of claims and the cost of medical malpractice litigation. Since the establishment of the NHS Litigation Authority in 1995 data on the numbers and cost of medical malpractice litigation has improved significantly, and information on the prevalence of medical accidents has also become more accessible. Putting the two categories together highlights the huge disparity between the number of injuries occurring and the numbers of patients receiving compensation. Not only does this provide a context for the legal framework of medical negligence, it also allows for an assessment of claims that are sometimes put forward that there is a "malpractice crisis", at least in terms of the financial cost of compensating for medical negligence. The next section deals with an argument that has often plagued the debate about litigation, namely that doctors practise defensive medicine in response to the perceived litigation crisis. Section 3 addresses another perennial issue, that is whether a system of no-fault compensation specifically for the victims of medical accidents would both solve the malpractice crisis and provide a fairer and more efficient method of compensating injured patients. Section 4 discusses the proposals from the CMO in *Making Amends* for reform of the compensation mechanisms, and is followed by an outline of the NHS Redress Act 2006. The chapter concludes with a brief consideration of the implications of the Human Rights Act 1998 for the future development of the law of medical negligence.

---

[20] See paras 1–102–1–107.
[21] And so it is not limited to an exposition of the tort of negligence, but also includes discussion of other forms of liability that arise in the context of medical care, such as consent to treatment, confidentiality and product liability.

1. MEDICAL ACCIDENTS AND CLAIMS DATA

There is a widespread perception, particularly in the medical literature and the **1–007** popular press, that the UK is in the grip of a medical malpractice "crisis".[22] In the past that sense of crisis came, not from the realisation that large numbers of patients were suffering serious injury in the course of their medical treatment, but from the fact that claims for negligence and the cost of meeting those claims was increasing.[23] But there has also been some recognition, certainly within the NHS if not the general public, that litigation is probably a symptom of the underlying problem of iatrogenic injury attributable to "adverse events" in healthcare.[24] It makes no sense to talk of a crisis in malpractice litigation, which sometimes leads to criticism of the victims of medical negligence and their lawyers for having the temerity to sue, without addressing the prior question of the size of the problem of accidental injury (whether attributable to fault or not) in healthcare. In the absence of reliable information about how many *injuries* occur each year as a result of medical negligence it is impossible to identify what the "appropriate" level of litigation should be. All the evidence suggests that there are far fewer claims than the incidence of negligently inflicted harm would warrant.[25] From the patients' perspective it could be argued that the malpractice "crisis" arises from too few patients being able to litigate, rather than too many doctors becoming defendants. In this arena perceptions are everything.

(a) How many medical injuries occur?

It is not known with any precision how many accidental injuries attributable to **1–008** healthcare occur each year in the UK. In *An Organisation with a Memory* the Department of Health estimated that 850,000 adverse events could occur in NHS hospitals each year, resulting in £2 billion direct cost in additional hospital days

---

[22] The sense of a litigation "crisis" has not been confined to medical negligence litigation, but can be seen in assertions that the UK has developed a "compensation culture" whereby individuals are all too ready to resort to litigation, with damaging social consequences. For consideration of the validity of these claims see: R. Lewis and A. Morris "Challenging Views of Tort" [2013] J.P.I.L. 69 and [2013] J.P.I.L. 137; R. Lewis and A. Morris, "Tort Law Culture: Image and Reality" (2012) 39 J. Law & Soc. 562; J. Ilan, "The Commodification of Compensation: Personal Injury Claims in an Age of Consumption" (2011) 20 Soc. & Leg. Stud. 39; J. Hand, "The Compensation Culture: Cliché or Cause for Concern?" (2010) 37 J. Law & Soc. 569; A. Morris, "Spiralling or Stabilising? The Compensation Culture and Our Propensity to Claim Damages for Personal Injury" (2007) 70 M.L.R. 349; R. Lewis, A. Morris, and K. Oliphant, "Tort personal injury claims statistics: Is there a compensation culture in the United Kingdom?" [2006] J.P.I.L. 87; K. Williams, "State of fear: Britain's 'Compensation Culture' Reviewed" (2005) 25 L.S. 499; K. Williams, "Politics, the Media and Refining the Notion of Fault: Section 1 of the Compensation Act 2006" [2006] J.P.I.L. 347.

[23] The sense of crisis seems to come in "waves", in response to whether there has been a significant percentage increase, year on year, in the costs of handling medical malpractice claims, as published by the NHS Litigation Authority.

[24] See, in particular, *An Organisation with a Memory*, 2000 (available at *http://www.aagbi.org/sites/default/files/An%20organisation%20with%20a%20memory.pdf*).

[25] The National Audit Office report, *Managing the costs of clinical negligence in trusts* (September 2017), HC 305 Session 2017–2019, para.2.6 stated that: "The number of claims as a percentage of harmful incidents reported remains small, at less than 4%."

for Trusts (i.e. post-31 March 1995 incidents),[52] but this figure fell significantly to 2,068 in 2001–2002.[53] For 2002–2003, the first year when the NHS Litigation Authority would have received notification of all claims under both the Existing Liabilities Scheme and the Clinical Negligence Scheme for Trusts (therefore covering both pre-April 1995 and post-March 1995 incidents), a total of 6,797 claims were received.[54] The NHS Litigation Authority reported reductions in claims in 2001–2002 and 2002–2003.[55]

1–013   Figures taken from the NHS Litigation Authority[56] *Annual Report and Accounts* for 2004 to 2017[57] show that the number of new claims[58] per annum was fairly steady until 2008, rose gradually between 2008 and 2010 but then rose sharply to a peak in 2014. Since then there would appear to have been a small, but steady, decline in the number of new claims notified,[59] though the figure for 2016–2017 is almost double that of 2004–2005:

- 2004–2005: 5,602 new claims;
- 2005–2006: 5,697 new claims;
- 2006–2007: 5,426 new claims;
- 2007–2008: 5,469 new claims;
- 2008–2009: 6,217 new claims;
- 2009–2010: 6,652 new claims;
- 2010–2011: 8,655 new claims;
- 2011–2012: 9,143 new claims;
- 2012–2013: 10,129 new claims;
- 2013–2014: 11,945 new claims;
- 2014–2015: 11,497 new claims;
- 2015–2016: 10,965 new claims;
- 2016–2017: 10,686 new claims.

---

[52] *NHS (England) Summarised Accounts 2000–2001*. The NHS (England) Summarised Accounts are available from the National Audit Office at *http://www.nao.gov.uk*.
[53] *NHS (England) Summarised Accounts 2001–2002*, para.6.9.
[54] *Making Amends*, p.58, para.32.
[55] *Making Amends*, p.58, para.32.
[56] Note that the operating name of the NHS Litigation Authority since April 2017 is now "NHS Resolution", though the NHSLA's formal status has not changed.
[57] The data is taken from the *NHSLA Annual Report and Accounts* for the respective years, except for 2014–2015 where it is taken from *NHSLA Factsheet 3: information on claims* 2014–15. From 2016–2017 the annual report is referred to as the *NHS Resolution Report and Accounts*.
[58] This covers both the Clinical Negligence Scheme for Trusts and the Existing Liabilities Scheme, though the numbers for ELS are small.
[59] This is possibly attributable to changes in entitlement to legal aid, and the bar against recovery of success fees from defendants under a conditional fee agreement, brought about by the Legal Aid, Sentencing and Punishment of Offenders Act 2012; on which see C. Klage, S. Trask and J. Wheeler "Legal Aid—But Not As We Knew It: A Guide to the New Legal Aid Scheme for Personal Injury Practitioners Following LASPO" [2014] J.P.I.L. 30, 34.

In addition, the medical defence organisations (the Medical Defence Union and the Medical Protection Society) settle approximately 700 new claims per annum arising from incidents in primary care.[60]

It can be seen that, even allowing for a doubling of claims between 2005 and 2017, these figures bear no relationship to the estimated number of patients who suffer a *preventable* adverse event (425,000 patients) in NHS hospitals each year. Of course, not all preventable adverse events would necessarily be categorised as negligent by the legal system, and most of them would lead to only temporary or minor impairment or disability which may not justify litigation. Nonetheless, and notwithstanding the comparatively poor success rates for claimants in medical malpractice litigation, it seems likely that there are many more patients with a genuine potential claim who do not litigate than there are patients with a spurious claim who do.[61]

1–014

(c) How many claims are successful?

The success rate for claims depends upon how they are measured. In 1978 the Pearson Commission estimated that for all personal injury claims brought the success rate for claimants was about 85 to 90 per cent, but for medical negligence claims it was only 30 to 40 per cent.[62] The Review of Legal Aid expenditure, *Eligibility for Civil Legal Aid*,[63] estimated that for legally aided litigation the success rate for medical negligence claims was 42 per cent, whereas for road traffic claims it was 84 per cent, and 79 per cent for work accident claims. Other studies put the overall success rate for medical negligence claims at around 25 per cent[64] to 30 per cent.[65] Figures for clinical negligence claims handled by the

1–015

---

[60] *An Organisation with a Memory*, para.4.39; cf. the figures in *Making Amends*, June 2003, pp.62–63, indicating that the Medical Protection Society *receives* between 400 and 500 claims against general practitioners per annum, and the number of claims *received* by the Medical Defence Union ranged between about 1,400 and 1,800 per annum between 1995 and 2000. This data is old but the defence organisations do not systematically publish information on the annual number of claims.

[61] The National Audit Office report, *Managing the costs of clinical negligence in trusts* (September 2017), HC 305 Session 2017–2019, para.2.6 noted that: "Only a small proportion of people who experience something going wrong currently choose to make a claim against the NHS. The number of claims as a percentage of harmful incidents reported remains small, at less than 4%. ... A small change in patient attitudes to making a claim, particularly from older people, could have a large impact on the number of claims." See also P. Pleasance, N. Balmer, H. Genn, A. Buck and A. O'Grady, "The experience of clinical negligence within the general population" (2003) 9 *Clinical Risk* 211 found that respondents reporting a clinical negligence problem did nothing about resolving the problem 51 per cent of the time, compared to 18 per cent for other types of problem.

[62] *Royal Commission on Civil Liability and Compensation for Personal Injury*, Cmnd.7054 (1978), Vol.I, paras 78 and 1326.

[63] (1991) HMSO.

[64] Hawkins and Paterson, "Medicolegal audit in the West Midlands: Analysis of 100 Cases" (1987) 295 B.M.J. 1533; Fenn, Hermans and Dingwall, "Estimating the cost of compensating the victims of medical negligence" (1994) 309 B.M.J. 389.

[65] P. Fenn et al., "Current cost of medical negligence in NHS hospitals: analysis of claims database" (2000) 320 B.M.J. 1567.

£1,086.3 million).[75] One other feature of the cost of claims worth noting is how skewed awards are across the range of successful claims. The National Audit Office reported that:

"In 2016–17, there were 590 claims with a value above £250,000, representing 8% of the total number of successful claims but accounting for 83% of the total damages awarded. Between 2006–07 and 2016–17, these claims accounted for 85% of the increase in costs of damages awarded (£0.9 billion out of £1.0 billion)."[76]

1–019 **Provisions in the accounts** The amounts actually paid out in settlement of claims should be distinguished from the sums set out in the accounts as provisions for claims. Estimates of future expenditure include both (1) claims that are known about, and (2) claims that it is anticipated will be made in the future in respect of incidents that have already occurred, but the patient is either unaware of the damage or has yet to make a claim (incurred but not reported ("IBNR") claims). The first category involves estimating the total potential cost of all outstanding claims where it is estimated that there is a better than 50 per cent chance of the claim succeeding, plus cases where a periodical payments order is in place.[77] The figure involves making assumptions about the likely success rate of claims and the damages awarded. The latter category of provisions (IBNR claims) is clearly an estimate that involves a high degree of speculation, both as to the number of successful future claims and their overall value. IBNR claims make up over 60 per cent of the provisions in the accounts.[78] The figures for provisions in the accounts[79] for the last 10 years are:

- 2007–2008: £11.9 billion[80];
- 2008–2009 : £13.4 billion;
- 2009–2010: £14.9 billion;
- 2010–2011: £16.6 billion;

---

[75] See para.1–013.

[76] NAO, *Managing the costs of clinical negligence in trusts* (September 2017), HC 305 Session 2017–2019, para.2.11. A large proportion of these claims are related to birth injury.

[77] In the case of periodical payments orders the annual cost will generally be known, but the claimant's life expectancy will be uncertain. The National Audit Office report, *Managing the costs of clinical negligence in trusts* (September 2017), HC 305 Session 2017–2019, para.1.15 found that: "By the end of 2016–17, there were 1,300 clinical claims agreed with outstanding periodical payments, with an estimated future cost of £9 billion at present value, included in the provision. These costs may be settled over a long time period, depending on a claimant's life expectancy." NHS Resolution's *Annual Report and Accounts 2016–2017* noted, at p.20, that: "the costs of meeting these annual payments are increasing, as around 200 new cases a year are compensated in this way. At this point in time, more cases are being committed to such a payment regime than are leaving."

[78] NAO, *Managing the costs of clinical negligence in trusts* (September 2017), HC 305 Session 2017–2019, para.1.13

[79] These figures are taken from the *NHSLA Report and Accounts* for 2008 and 2009, and then from the *NHSLA Factsheet 2, Financial Information*, published along with the Annual Report, for the years 2010 to 2017.

[80] £1.5 billion of this was a consequence of allowing for the effects of the decision of the Court of Appeal in *Tameside and Glossop NHS Trust v Thompstone* [2008] EWCA Civ 5; [2008] 1 W.L.R. 2207 that when indexing periodical payments in respect of future pecuniary loss for the costs of care the court does not have use the retail prices index but can use an index of earnings (which is likely to increase more than RPI). See paras 12–024 to 12–027.

- 2011–2012: £18.6 billion;
- 2012–2013: £22.7 billion;
- 2013–2014: £25.7 billion;
- 2014–2015: £28.3 billion;
- 2015–2016: £56.0 billion;
- 2016–2017: £64.7 billion.

The figures for provisions in the accounts are strongly influenced by two discount rates applied to claims. If the discount rates go down, the figure for future provisions will go up, sometimes by a large amount. The increase from 2015 to 2016 (£28.3 billion to £56 billion) was almost entirely due to a change in HM Treasury's discount rate used when estimating future provisions in government accounts, to reflect the general principle that money is worth more the sooner it is received. In 2015–2016 this rate was changed from 2.2 per cent to minus 0.8 per cent, and that alone accounted for £25.5 billion of the increase in provisions.[81] The figures are also affected by the discount rate used by the courts to assess the present value of a future sum when calculating damages in personal injury cases. In March 2017 that rate was reduced from 2.5 per cent to minus 0.75[82] and that change added £4.7 billion to provisions.[83]

1–020

These very large sums for provisions in the accounts do not bear much resemblance to the actual sums paid out per annum by the NHS for clinical negligence claims.[84] It is important to appreciate that the provisions in the accounts are an accounting figure that represents the total potential liability of the NHS (in England) in respect of clinical negligence claims (including possible but as yet unidentified future claims in relation to past events—IBNR claims) if all of those claims were paid today (or, rather, at the end of the relevant accounting period). But in reality they will be paid over many years in the future and some may never crystallise into real liabilities. They do not represent the annual cost to the NHS of medical negligence litigation, and the sums can vary dramatically depending upon the actuarial assumptions used.

1–021

(e) Delay and lawyers' costs

The tort system is notoriously slow to achieve compensation for injured claimants, at least compared to administrative systems of compensation such as no-fault schemes and social security. For claims under the Clinical Negligence Scheme for Trusts (CNST) in 2001–2002 the average time was 1.27 years from notification of the claim to settlement or discontinuance of the claim.[85] This

1–022

---

[81] *NHSLA Annual Report and Accounts 2015–2016*, p.22. The change in the year of £25.5 billion was "an accounting adjustment rather than a measure of harm": at p.5.
[82] See para.12–091.
[83] *NHS Resolution Annual Report and Accounts 2016–2017* at p.9.
[84] See para.1–017.
[85] *NHS (England) Summarised Accounts 2001–2002*, fig.17. This figure subsequently fell to 1.19 years: *Making Amends*, June 2003, p.92, para.11.

figure has gradually crept up, with average time to settlement for CNST in 2007–2008 being 1.5 years[86] and in 2016–2017, 1.57 years.[87]

1–023   Although there are legitimate complaints about the cost of bringing claims through the tort system, and legal costs remain high in medical negligence cases, as a percentage of the damages awarded there has been a reduction over the past 10 years. For 2007–2008 overall costs were 43.2 per cent of the sum paid out,[88] whereas in 2016–2017 overall legal costs were 37 per cent of the sum paid out.[89] The big change has come in the distribution of those legal costs between claimant and defence lawyers. In 2007–2008 defence costs represented approximately a third, and claimant costs approximately two thirds, of the overall costs, whereas in 2016–2017 defence costs came to approximately a fifth and claimant costs approximately four fifths of the overall costs. The disparity between compensation awards and legal costs is particularly acute in low value claims, with costs, on average, exceeding the claimant's compensation in claims up to £100,000.[90]

(f)   The distribution of claims

1–024   The distribution of claims by specialty is highly skewed. It is known that cases involving brain damage to babies at birth are particularly expensive to compensate.[91] In 2000, *An Organisation with a Memory* estimated that the average amount of compensation in such cases is around £1.5 million, with some awards as high as £4 million, and that such claims accounted for 50 per cent of the NHS £400 million litigation bill per annum.[92] *Making Amends* reported that the average payment of compensation for birth related cerebral palsy claims handled by the NHS Litigation Authority to the end of September 2002 was £670,000 for claims relating to incidents since 1995, and £1,225,000 for older cases, with the highest payment being £5.5 million in February 2003.[93] More

---

[86] *NHS Litigation Authority Annual Report and Accounts* 2008.

[87] *NHS Resolution Factsheet 3—Claims Information 2016–2017.* There is a significant difference between the time taken resolve cases where proceedings have been commenced (800 days) compared to cases that are resolved before proceedings are issued (303 days): NAO, *Managing the costs of clinical negligence in trusts* (September 2017), HC 305 Session 2017–2019, Fig.18 (figures are for 2016–2017).

[88] *NHS Litigation Authority Annual Report and Accounts 2008.*

[89] Percentage calculated by the author from *NHS Resolution Annual Reports and Accounts 2016–2017*, Table A: damages awarded to claimants £1,083.0 million; claimant legal costs £498.5 million; and defendant legal costs £125.7 million.

[90] *NHS Resolution Annual Reports and Accounts 2016–2017*, Figure 15. Average claimant legal costs as a percentage of damages, for compensation awards of up to £100,000, rose in every year from 2004–2005 to 2015–2016 (from 32.3 per cent to 54.8 per cent) with a slight reduction in 2016–2017 (53.5 per cent): Figure 17. The National Audit Office, *Managing the costs of clinical negligence in trusts* (September 2017), HC 305 Session 2017–2019, para.2.17, observed that: "Between 2006–07 and 2016–17, the number of claims where the claimants' legal costs were higher than the damages awarded increased from 990 (35% of all successful claims) to 4,420 (61% of all successful claims)."

[91] The NAO report *Handling Clinical Negligence Claims in England*, 2001, concluded that, at that time, cerebral palsy and brain damage cases accounted for 80 per cent of outstanding claims by value and 26 per cent of claims by number in the Existing Liabilities Scheme (i.e. for claims arising out of incidents that occurred before 1 April 1995).

[92] *An Organisation with a Memory*, para.4.34.

[93] *Making Amends*, p.50, para.52.

recent evidence suggests that the average settlement for a severe neurological birth injury case equates to a value of £6.25 million, including costs paid out over the injured person's lifetime.[94] *Making Amends* concluded that in only a third of claims did the claimants receive damages. Figures from the NHS Litigation Authority for the total number of claims by speciality for CNST as at 31 March 2017[95] indicate that obstetrics and gynaecology gives rise to 18.14 per cent of claims by number, but 50.47 per cent of the total cost:

	Number of claims by specialty	%	Percentage of total cost	%
Surgery	50,432	39.07	Obstetrics and gynaecology	50.47
Medicine	23,899	18.51	Surgery	19.20
Obstetrics and gynaecology	23,415	18.14	Medicine	15.40
A&E	15,808	12.25	A&E	7.22
Psychiatry/mental	3,306	2.56	Radiology	1.71
Radiology	2,922	2.26	Anaesthesia	1.58
Anaesthesia	2,680	2.08	Psychiatry/mental	1.38
Pathology	1,813	1.40	Pathology	0.99
Ambulance	1,499	1.16	Ambulance	0.95
Paramedical support	1,354	1.05	Primary care	0.35
Nursing	801	0.62	Paramedical support	0.29
Primary care	727	0.56	Nursing	0.17
Public health	435	0.34	Public health	0.14

The figures cited in *Making Amends* for the financial year 2002/2003 were even more stark. At that time birth-related brain damage (including cerebral palsy) in the NHS accounted for just over 5 per cent of all cases of medical litigation in

---

[94] Department of Health, *A Rapid Resolution and Redress Scheme for Severe Avoidable Birth Injury: a Consultation* (March 2017), para.3.13. See para.1–060.

[95] That is the total number of claims since CNST began in April 1995 to 31 March 2017 (excluding "below excess" claims that were previously handled by NHS Trusts; excesses were abolished from 1 April 2002). Data is taken from *NHS Resolution Factsheet 3—Claims Information 2016–2017*. Percentages were calculated by the author from data in this Factsheet.

which damages were paid, and 60 per cent of all expenditure on medical litigation.[96] The implications for priority setting in developing risk management procedures are self-evident.[97]

2. DEFENSIVE MEDICINE

1–025   Defensive medicine has to be viewed in terms of a reaction by doctors to the perceived threat of litigation. In *Whitehouse v Jordan* Lawton LJ said that defensive medicine consists of:

> "…adopting procedures which are not for the benefit of the patient but safeguards against the possibility of the patient making a claim for negligence."[98]

This has two aspects: positive defensive medicine, which involves undertaking additional procedures, such as diagnostic tests and X-rays, which in the doctor's professional judgment are unnecessary; and negative defensive medicine, which involves avoiding procedures, which in the doctor's professional judgment are necessary in the patient's best interests, because of the risk of something going wrong. Positive defensive medicine, it is said, is wasteful of time and resources and possibly increases the risk to patients of medical intervention, and negative defensive medicine deprives patients of potentially beneficial treatment. It is important to appreciate that the term "defensive medicine" is used in a pejorative sense, to indicate that the risk of liability induces doctors to adopt practices which are not medically required or justified. The charge is that the law dictates medical practice, indeed, dictates bad medical practice.

1–026   The difficulty with the argument about defensive medicine is that as a legal concept defensive medicine does not make sense. The standard of care required by the *Bolam* test[99] is that of a reasonably competent medical practitioner exercising and professing to have that skill. This is essentially a medical test requiring medical evidence as to proper professional practice.[100] If a defendant's fellow professionals agree that a specific procedure was unnecessary and wasteful, a doctor cannot be held negligent for omitting to carry it out. On this basis it is difficult to see how doctors can *protect* themselves from a claim in negligence by carrying out an unnecessary test or procedure. If they could not be held liable for failing to do something, they could not protect themselves from

---

[96] *Making Amends*, June 2003, p.47, para.43.

[97] There have been various initiatives to address the specific problem of birth-related injury. For the most recent see the National Maternity Review, *Better Births—Improving outcomes of maternity services in England* (2016) (available at *http://www.england.nhs.uk/wp-content/uploads/2016/02/national-maternity-review-report.pdf*); Department of Health, *A Rapid Resolution and Redress Scheme for Severe Avoidable Birth Injury: a Consultation* (March 2017) (available at *http://www.gov.uk/government/consultations/rapid-resolution-and-redress-scheme-for-severe-birth-injury*), paras 1–059–1–062; and M. Magro and D. Fellow, *Five years of cerebral palsy claims—A thematic review of NHS Resolution data* (September 2017).

[98] [1980] 1 All E.R. 650 at 659.

[99] *Bolam v Friern Hospital Management Committee* [1957] 2 All E.R. 118; see paras 3–007 et seq.

[100] This remains the case notwithstanding the decision of the House of Lords in *Bolitho v City and Hackney Health Authority* [1998] A.C. 232 that the courts should subject medical judgments to "logical analysis"; see para.3–034.

liability by doing it. Indeed, to the extent that the procedure carries additional risk to the patient a doctor increases the risk of a claim if something goes wrong precisely *because* the procedure was unnecessary. Moreover, under the *Bolam* test it does not matter that some doctors do regard the procedure as essential provided that there is a responsible body of medical opinion that takes a contrary view. The same argument applies to negative defensive medicine. If the procedure would have been performed by a responsible body of professional opinion, doctors cannot be negligent for performing it (even where a responsible body of opinion would not have undertaken the procedure), and so they cannot "protect" themselves by declining to undertake it, and they may increase the risk of a finding of negligence on the basis that they have failed to perform a procedure which responsible medical opinion considers to have been necessary.

Although the existence of defensive medicine as a sociological fact appears to have achieved some acceptance in the English courts,[101] and indeed in Parliament,[102] there is very little empirical, as opposed to anecdotal, evidence to support the theory that doctors do practise defensively.[103] Doctors may *say* that they practise defensively, but there is considerable scope for confusion as to what, precisely, "defensive" means and, indeed, whether it is detrimental to patients.[104] Some doctors use the term "defensive" simply to mean treating patients conservatively or even "more carefully". What to one doctor may seem defensive may to another doctor be good practice. Moreover, from the point of view of the individual patient defensive practice, such as over-testing, may be positively beneficial if it discovers something previously unsuspected or even if it simply sets the patient's mind at rest, although it is arguably prejudicial to the NHS

1–027

---

[101] See para.3–134.

[102] It was assumed both to exist and to be detrimental to the consumers of NHS care in the National Health Service (Compensation) Bill 1991 Sch.2 para.4. The Compensation Act 2006 s.1 now provides that: "A court considering a claim in negligence or breach of statutory duty may, in determining whether the defendant should have taken particular steps to meet a standard of care (whether by taking precautions against a risk or otherwise), have regard to whether a requirement to take those steps might (a) prevent a desirable activity from being undertaken at all, to a particular extent or in a particular way, or (b) discourage persons from undertaking functions in connection with a desirable activity." Although this is of general application to all negligence actions, the assumption underpinning the provision is that the threat of potential liability detrimentally alters people's conduct. See further para.3–130. See also the Social Action, Responsibility and Heroism Act 2015, para.3–131.

[103] A commonly cited example of defensive practice is an increased rate of Caesarean section deliveries as a consequence of obstetricians fearing that claims in respect of birth injuries could arise from forceps deliveries or allowing a difficult labour to progress too long. Caesarean section rates have been increasing, however, in many developed countries with very different systems of healthcare provision and different patterns of litigation, and may be explained by factors which have very little to do with litigation: Ham, Dingwall, Fenn and Harris, *Medical Negligence: Compensation and Accountability*, 1988, p.14.

[104] Jones and Morris (1989) 5 J. of the MDU 40; Tribe and Korgaonkar (1991) 7 P.N. 2; Summerton (1995) 310 B.M.J. 27. M.J. Powers in R.V. Clements (ed.) *Safe Practice in Obstetrics and Gynaecology* (London: Churchill Livingstone, 1994), p.15, comments that: "...it should be appreciated that 'defensive medicine' is a figment of the paranoid medical profession's imagination... Often what is regarded as 'defensive' medicine is simply the prevailing view of safe and prudent practice." Black (1990) 335 *The Lancet* 35, 37 concluded that litigation does not seem to be damaging the quality of medical care, although "the cost of medical litigation may yet prove to be damaging to the quality of care". For discussion of defensive medicine in Canada see Dickens (1991) 41 Univ. of Toronto L.J. 168.

because of the extra costs involved. It is unfortunate, to say the least, that such an important document as the Chief Medical Officer's report on the review of the system of handling compensation claims and complaints in the NHS, *Making Amends*, referred uncritically to the existence of "defensive medicine" without citing a single piece of empirical evidence to support its existence in the NHS.[105]

1–028 In any event, defensive medicine can only be relevant to certain types of medical negligence. There is a difference between on the one hand, the negligence involved in leaving a swab in a patient or removing the wrong kidney or prescribing the wrong dosage of a drug and, on the other hand, the conscious assessment of risk as between alternative procedures or the risk in not doing certain things. Inadvertent errors (which probably constitute the bulk of medical accidents) cannot be the subject of defensive medicine in its pejorative sense, since the doctor has not made a conscious decision to do or avoid something due to the risk of liability. Indeed, if he had thought about it he would have avoided the error. Moreover, insofar as the threat of litigation may lead to the introduction of procedures which are specifically designed to avoid inadvertent errors the law serves an important function in promoting good practice and preventing accidents.[106] Indeed, it is arguable that one of the purposes of tort law is to reduce accidents by deterring careless behaviour.[107] By definition, defensive medicine implies that doctors respond to liability rules, i.e. they modify their behaviour in response to the risk of liability.[108] If the threat of liability were to be removed, as

---

[105] *Making Amends*, June 2003, p.27, para.17; p.76, para.5; p.108, para.61; p.110, para.6; p.118, para.8, where there is a reference to "the rising tide of defensive medicine". No explanation is offered as to how "potentially hazardous and costly investigations" carried out "not for the benefit of the patient but for the sole purpose of fending off a successful lawsuit" are likely to achieve this particular objective.

[106] For an argument that the way to reduce defensive medicine and the costs of medical malpractice is to shift the burden of liability from the individual doctor to the hospital and to change the standard of liability from negligence to strict liability; see Chapman (1990) 28 Osgoode Hall L.J. 523. See also T. Keren-Paz, "Liability regimes, reputation loss, and defensive medicine" (2010) 18 Med. L. Rev. 363 arguing that, from the perspective of doctors' reputation loss attributable to findings of liability, strict liability might be preferable as a means of reducing defensive medicine "since it serves as an insurance mechanism for reputation loss".

[107] In *Scout Association v Barnes* [2010] EWCA Civ 1476 at [34] Jackson LJ commented that: "It is the function of the law of tort to deter negligent conduct and to compensate those who are the victims of such conduct." Smith LJ agreed, at [36]. Note, however, that it has been argued that the law does not contribute to the promotion of patient safety: O. Quick, "Patient safety and the problem and potential of law" (2012) 28 P.N. 78, 98 ("it is more likely that the threat of litigation is counterproductive by discouraging an open and learning culture in healthcare"); contrast L. Mulcahy "The market for precedent: shifting visions of the role of clinical negligence claims and trials" (2014) 22 Med. L. Rev. 274 on the standard-setting function of litigation.

[108] It is arguable that it was the upsurge in medical malpractice litigation which produced a greater emphasis on clinical risk management which is designed to identify the factors that can lead to medical accidents and identify ways of reducing accidents. This is clearly in the interests of patients, but there is a strong element of seeking to reduce the cost of accidents to the NHS driving this development. The whole concept of risk management simply reiterates the point that acting in the interests of patients, by reducing the risk of accidental harm, is also in the interests of doctors in that it reduces the risk of being sued, and in the interests of the NHS which has to meet both the cost of claims and the cost of treating those patients who suffer accidental injury even if they do not sue. It is in this context that the comment in *Making Amends*, June 2003, p.117, para.2, about the effect of litigation on individual doctors is entirely misplaced: "Few neutral observers would try to argue that quality and safety of health care are improving because health care professionals are behaving more

a consequence of, say, the introduction of a scheme of no-fault compensation, would doctors become less careful, or even careless? This is at least one implication of the evidence that was presented to the Pearson Commission by the medical profession.[109]

It is sometimes suggested that a sense of public duty is what motivates individuals working in the public sector, and that therefore the imposition of a duty of care on health professionals would not lead to higher standards of medical care[110]; whereas the profit motive is what drives individuals in the private sector. This rather oversimplifies the situation in the real world. It suggests that somehow professionals working in the public sector always achieve high levels of competence from motives of altruism, professionalism or a sense of public duty, whereas private sector defendants (solicitors, accountants, surveyors, etc.) need a sharp prod from the law of tort in order to achieve an acceptable level of competence. There may be situations where the profit motive leads individuals to cut corners and thereby increase the risk of damage to others, but the risk of cutting corners is not exclusive to the private sector. Indeed, the need to keep the paying client happy may produce higher standards of care, whereas the public sector employee has a "captive market", and clients who, as a general rule, cannot take their business elsewhere, a situation that may lead to complacency rather than high standards. Moreover, linking the statement that imposing a duty of care in negligence would not lead to higher standards of care with the statement that it could lead to defensive practices[111] is logically incoherent. It asserts that, on the one hand, public sector professionals are not likely to respond to the threat of liability for carelessness by improving their performance, whereas, on the other hand, they are likely to respond to the threat of liability by indulging in defensive practices. Either they do respond as rational individuals to liability rules or they do not, but it seems highly improbable that they do both at the same time. Of course, the views of the judiciary on this subject are not necessarily uniform. Indeed, some judges take the view that imposing a duty of care "may have the healthy effect of securing that high standards are sought and secured".[112]

1–029

conscientiously clinically as a result of having watched their colleagues being sued." There are two responses to this point: (1) no-one, whether neutral or not, has produced any evidence to show that the quality and safety of health care has deteriorated because healthcare professionals are aware that they can be sued; (2) there is abundant evidence that one consequence of the growth in litigation, and its rising cost to the NHS, has been to persuade policy-makers in the NHS to appreciate the pressing need for much greater safety in the delivery of health care.

[109] *Royal Commission on Civil Liability and Compensation for Personal Injury*, Cmnd.7054 (1978), Vol.I, paras 1342–1343; see para.1–031. "Liability and Compensation in Health Care," J.R.S. Prichard, *A Report to the Conference of Deputy Ministers of the Federal/Provincial/Territorial Review of Liability and Compensation Issues in Health Care* (1990) found that malpractice litigation had a net positive effect on the quality of health care in Canada, including systematic risk reduction in areas of recurrent injury, and the introduction of quality assurance, risk management and audit. On the other hand, the threat of potential liability resulted in greater stress and anxiety in the medical profession.

[110] For example, in *Palmer v Tees Health Authority* [1998] Lloyd's Rep. Med. 447 at 460 Gage J said: "As Lord Keith pointed out in *Hill*'s case, on the whole public duty motivates police forces. The same applies to doctors. There is a considerable danger that doctors, to avoid being sued, might lean towards defensive medicine."

[111] As Gage J did in *Palmer v Tees Health Authority* [1998] Lloyds Rep. Med. 447.

[112] See the comments of Lord Clyde in *Phelps v Hillingdon London Borough Council* [2001] 2 A.C. 619, 672, quoted more fully at para.3–141; *Michael v Chief Constable of South Wales* [2015] UKSC

1–030   The claim that it is the law that is positively detrimental to the practice of medicine in this country cannot be accepted. When the rhetoric is stripped away, it is the tort of negligence that provides the bottom line: the *minimum* standard of acceptable professional conduct. In practice, medical negligence is a failure to live up to proper medical standards, and those standards are set, not by lawyers, but by doctors.

3.   No-Fault Compensation

(a) Rationale

1–031   Until the Department of Health review of the system of handling compensation claims and complaints in the NHS[113] there had not been a serious consideration of whether to introduce no-fault compensation for the victims of medical accidents. The Pearson Commission considered, and rejected, the idea of no-fault compensation specifically for medical accidents, although it was accepted that a change of circumstances might shift the balance of the arguments in favour of such a proposal.[114] The evidence from the medical profession to the Commission was overwhelmingly in favour of retaining the tort action. It was argued that:

> "Liability was one of the means whereby doctors could show their sense of responsibility and, therefore, justly claim professional freedom. If tortious liability were abolished, there could be some attempt to control doctors' clinical practice to prevent mistakes for which compensation would have to be paid by some central agency. It was said that this could lead to a bureaucratic restriction of medicine and a brake on progress. It was further argued that the traditions of the profession were not sufficient in themselves to prevent all lapses which, though small in number, might have disastrous effects. Some penalty helped to preserve the patient's opportunity to express disapproval and obtain redress."[115]

The Medical Defence Union commented that, although they paid the compensation, their investigation into the circumstances brought home to the doctor the part he had played and encouraged a sense of personal responsibility.[116]

1–032   The growth of medical malpractice litigation in the 1980s led the medical profession to reconsider its position. By 1987 the British Medical Association had come to the view that what was needed was a non-statutory scheme of compensation which "within defined limits would provide compensation without apportionment of blame". The opening paragraph of the BMA Report put the case succinctly:

2; [2015] A.C. 1732 at [179] per Lord Kerr: "arguably, the risk of litigation improves professional standards." See also *Barrett v Enfield London Borough Council* [1997] 3 All E.R. 171 at 181 per Evans LJ; *Capital and Counties plc v Hampshire County Council* [1997] Q.B. 1004 at 1043–1044, CA.

[113] See para.1–076.

[114] *Royal Commission on Civil Liability and Compensation for Personal Injury*, Cmnd.7054 (1978), Vol.I, paras 1348–1371.

[115] *Royal Commission on Civil Liability and Compensation for Personal Injury* at para.1342.

[116] *Royal Commission on Civil Liability and Compensation for Personal Injury* at para.1343.

"As a caring profession we wish to see adequate arrangements to provide compensation and support to those who suffer personal injury, given according to need and not to cause. It is clear that patients with similar disabilities may receive different benefits under current provisions. A child may remain brain damaged following (a) encephalitis, (b) vaccine inoculation, (c) traumatic birth delivery. The needs of all three children may be similar. There will be great sympathy for all three sets of parents. However, the available compensation will range through no compensation at all, through £20,000, to some hundreds of thousands of pounds. This cannot be legal, fair or sensible."[117]

While the moral force of this argument is undeniable, the statement was misleading since a no-fault compensation scheme would probably not have changed the outcome of this particular example. The child with encephalitis would not be compensated under any current no-fault scheme since illness and/or disease and congenital disability are excluded, and even the child with vaccine damage would probably not receive compensation under some no-fault schemes. This highlights a major concern with any no-fault scheme for the victims of medical accidents, namely who would be eligible to claim? The BMA returned to the issue of compensation in its *No Fault Compensation Working Party Report 1991*, and in that year a private members bill, the National Health Service (Compensation) Bill 1991, was introduced in Parliament but was opposed by the government.

The problems with the action in tort as a means of compensating for injury or disease are well-documented.[118] They include the following: **1–033**

(i)   delay, which appears to be endemic in the adversarial system.[119] The procedural reforms introduced by the Civil Procedure Rules have had some impact in improving on the speed at which disputes are resolved;

(ii)   the cost of bringing an action, which is notoriously high, at least in relation to the sums recovered in damages.[120] *Handling Clinical Negligence Claims in England* found that in 65 per cent of settlements in 1999–2000 below £50,000 the legal and other costs of settling claims exceeded the damages

---

[117] *Report of the BMA No Fault Compensation Working Party*, 1987. The same point was made in the Report of the Royal College of Physicians, *Compensation for Adverse Consequences of Medical Intervention*, 1990, para.3.3.

[118] See the *Royal Commission on Civil Liability and Compensation for Personal Injury*, Cmnd.7054 (1978); the *Civil Justice Review*, Cmnd.394, 1988; and *Access to Justice*, 1996.

[119] *The Civil Justice Review*, Cmnd.394, 1988, para.421 put the average time from accident to trial at over five years in the High Court and almost three years in the County Court. For a later analysis of the relationship between costs and delay see *Access to Justice—Final Report*, Annexe 3, 1996. Delay in medical negligence cases tends to be greater, on average, than in other types of personal injuries action (*Royal Commission on Civil Liability and Compensation for Personal Injury*, Cmnd.7054 (1978), Vol.II, Table 129 and para.242), and individual cases of over 10 years' duration are not unknown.

[120] The *Royal Commission on Civil Liability and Compensation for Personal Injury*, Cmnd.7054 (1978), Vol.I, para.83 put the administrative costs of the tort system at 85 per cent of the amounts paid in damages, whereas the cost of running the social security system came to 11 per cent of the total paid out (para.121). *The Civil Justice Review*, Cmnd.394 (1988), paras 427–432, estimated that legal costs alone amounted to up to 75 per cent of the sums recovered in the High Court and up to 175 per cent of the sums recovered in the County Court. The NHS Litigation Authority reported that in 2008 average legal costs as a percentage of the compensation payments in clinical negligence cases were approximately 43.2 per cent: *NHS Litigation Authority Annual Report and Accounts* 2008. In 2016–2017 the comparable ratio was 37 per cent: see para.1–023.

and the question of whether the doctor ought to have done something involves a judgment about the reasonableness of his conduct, hence whether he was negligent. As Todd comments:

> "Where there is a failure to treat and the patient's condition gets worse, or treatment does not alleviate a condition, how do we determine whether the continuing injury is caused by the treatment or by the underlying condition? Seemingly in each case a claimant must establish on the balance of probabilities that treatment, or different treatment, would have improved the patient's condition or prevented it from getting worse. The [Accident Compensation Corporation] is no longer required to find fault, but the need to show that it was treatment or failure to treat rather than an existing condition which caused injury is likely to involve the claimant having to show that the health professional was negligent in making his or her decisions about treatment."[141]

Similarly, the exclusion of injuries that are a necessary part of, or an ordinary consequence of, the treatment creates problems of demarcation. Are the recognised side effects of treatment excluded on the basis that they are an "ordinary consequence"? Clearly, a patient undergoing surgery will expect to have an incision of some kind with a resulting scar, and this must be a "necessary part of" the treatment. But if the surgery carries, say, a known 2 per cent risk of paralysis which materialises is this an ordinary consequence of the treatment?[142] The fundamental problem, as Todd observes, is that:

> "Medical injury frequently lies near the dividing line between accident and illness. For as long as the accident compensation scheme provides cover for accidents but not illness ... it will remain necessary to search for an unexpected accident or event which can separate a medical injury from the ordinary progress of an illness or disease. For this reason, questions of negligence are not simply going to disappear."[143]

1–041 For those who do meet the statutory criteria compensation is designed to meet pecuniary losses, rather than non-pecuniary losses. Claimants are entitled to medical expenses and loss of earnings up to 80 per cent of pre-accident earnings, subject to a maximum figure linked to a multiple of national average earnings.

---

[141] S. Todd, "Twenty Years of Professional Negligence in New Zealand" (2005) 21 P.N. 257, 260. The same point was also made in S. Todd, "Accidental conception and accident compensation" (2012) 28 P.N. 196 at 199: "... the introduction of the concept of treatment injury does not remove the need to search for an unexpected accident or event or for some medical negligence which can separate a medical injury from ordinary treatment of a condition, illness or disease." J. Manning, "Plus ça change, plus c'est la même chose: Negligence and treatment injury in New Zealand's accident compensation scheme" (2014) 14 Med. Law Int. 22 at 35 notes that: "Lapsing into negligence thinking seems to arise particularly in respect of omissions and failures in the treatment process ... such as misdiagnoses or delayed diagnoses, failures to give treatment or timely treatment, failure to refer to a specialist or hospital or to give the proper information to enable informed consent to be given."

[142] Todd (2005) at 260–261.

[143] Todd (2005) at 261. For further discussion of these issues see K. Oliphant, "Beyond Misadventure: Compensation for Medical Injuries in New Zealand" (2007) 15 Med. L. Rev. 357; J. Manning, "Plus ça change, plus c'est la même chose: Negligence and treatment injury in New Zealand's accident compensation scheme" (2014) 14 Med. Law Int. 22.

(ii) Sweden[144]

The Swedish Patient Insurance Plan was introduced as non-statutory scheme in 1975 and was put on a statutory basis in 1996 by the Patient Injury Act 1996. This scheme is probably more comprehensive in its coverage than the New Zealand scheme, and there is no explicit reference to the claimant having to prove negligence by the healthcare provider. All persons who conduct any form of healthcare and medical services are required to take out patient insurance. There is a separate scheme of pharmaceutical insurance which is a voluntary agreement largely financed by the pharmaceutical companies.[145] The 1996 Act applies in respect of personal injuries caused in the course of healthcare and medical services provided in Sweden. The scheme compensates for injuries independently of whether the healthcare provider has been seriously negligent or the action was intentional. "Patient injuries" are largely defined in accordance with the principles that applied to the voluntary patient insurance schemes, though the term now also includes purely psychological injuries. There is a threshold requirement in terms of the seriousness of the injury: the patient must have been sick for a minimum of 30 days or been hospitalised for at least 10 days or suffered permanent disability or died. Claimants are compensated on a similar basis to that of the tort system, including awards for non-pecuniary loss,[146] but the overall cost of the scheme is relatively low because payments are used to top-up relatively generous social security benefits.[147]

1–042

Eligibility   Patient injuries are divided into six different types of injuries[148]:

1–043

(1)   *treatment injuries* which include:

> "...an examination, care, treatment or similar measure provided that the injury could have been avoided either through a different performance of the chosen procedure or through the choice of another available procedure which according to an assessment made retroactively from a medical point of view would have satisfied the need for treatment in a less hazardous manner."

Treatment which is unable to halt the progression of a disease or illness is not a basis for compensation. The treatment must have caused an injury separate from the underlying disease or illness for which it was given;

(2)   *defective equipment*—compensation is payable for injuries caused by

---

[144] There are similar schemes in Finland, Denmark and Norway, based on the Swedish model. See E. Strömbäck "Personal Injury Compensation in Sweden Today", Stockholm Institute for Scandinavian Law 1957–2009 (available at *http://www.scandinavianlaw.se/pdf/38-16.pdf*). For comparison of the Swedish and New Zealand schemes see J. Manning, "Plus ça change, plus c'est la même chose: Negligence and treatment injury in New Zealand's accident compensation scheme" (2014) 14 Med. Law Int. 22 at 37–41.

[145] See *http://lff.se/a-unique-type-of-insurance/for-patients*.

[146] Approximately 12 per cent of the total compensation awarded relates to pain and suffering: Fallberg and Borgenhammar, "The Swedish No-Fault Patient Insurance Scheme" (1997) 4 Eur. J. Health Law 279, 284.

[147] There is also a limit on the maximum award per claim. In 1998 the maximum award was 5 million SEK (approximately £350,000), but this level is rarely reached.

[148] Patient Injury Act 1996 s.6 (Sweden).

"defects in the medical-technical products or hospital equipment used in the performance of an examination, care, treatment or similar measure, or improper use of the same";

(3) *diagnostic errors*—where a diagnostic injury has occurred as the result of an incorrect diagnosis; diagnostic injuries may be the consequence of the underlying illness or disease and can also occur where treatment was delayed or was incorrect either because actual visible symptoms were not observed, or because those observations were incorrectly evaluated;

(4) *infection injuries*—compensation is payable for injuries caused as the result of the "transfer of a contagious substance leading to infection in connection with an examination, care, treatment, or similar measure". There is no compensation where the infection is a complication which must be tolerated: e.g. the patient has decreased immunity level, the surgery/treatment was performed in a part of the body with reduced vitality, or the treatment itself entailed an increased risk of infection;

(5) *accidents*—accidental injuries caused "in connection with an examination, care, treatment or similar measure or during a patient transport or in connection with a fire or other damage to healthcare premises or equipment"; this means bodily injury that a person suffers involuntarily due to a sudden, outer event;

(6) *incorrect use of medicines*—injury arising through the use of medicines can be indemnified, but only if the injury has been caused because the medical or pharmaceutical staff have incorrectly used, prescribed or dispensed, or otherwise incorrectly handled pharmaceuticals.

1–044 **Exceptions** There are a number of specific exceptions to entitlement. Compensation will not be paid to a claimant:

"...if (1) the damages are a consequence of a necessary procedure for the diagnosis or treatment of an illness or injury which without treatment is directly life threatening or leads to severe disability, or (2) the damages are caused by pharmaceuticals in cases other than those mention in section 6."[149]

This refers to a situation where a patient's need for medical care is so acute that treatment must be commenced even though it has not been possible to undertake the normal preparations, for example, in an emergency, or where it is necessary, knowingly, to take major risks in order to prevent the development of serious complications in the patient's disease or injury. This exception only applies in cases where the treatment relates to an injury or disease which is directly life threatening or can result in serious disability if treatment is not commenced.

---

[149] Patient Injury Act 1996 s.7 (Sweden).

(iii)   USA—Brain-damaged babies

Virginia   Two states in the USA, Virginia and Florida, have schemes of   1–045
no-fault compensation in respect of birth-related injuries. In Virginia[150] a claim
can be made in respect of birth-related neurological injury, namely:

> "...injury to the brain or spinal cord of an infant caused by the deprivation of oxygen or
> mechanical injury occurring in the course of labor, delivery or resuscitation in the immediate
> post-delivery period in a hospital."

The disability must be serious, causing the infant to be permanently in need of
assistance in all activities of daily living. Pain and suffering is not compensated.
Eligible children qualify for two categories of benefits.[151] First, they are entitled
to compensation for "necessary and reasonable costs of [lifetime] care" which in
practice have been broadly defined.[152] This includes payment for medical
expenses, rehabilitation costs, special equipment or facilities, and travel and
residential expenses, provided that these costs are not reimbursable through any
other state or federal governmental programme or private insurance. They can
also recover the reasonable expenses incurred in filing a claim, including
lawyers' fees.[153] The expenses are paid as they are incurred, not in a lump sum.
Secondly, at the age of 18, they become eligible for monetary benefits to replace
lost wages payable until age 65. This is conclusively presumed to be "fifty per
cent of the average weekly wage in the Commonwealth of workers in the private,
non-farm sector". The number of successful claims is small. As of 16 October
1997, applications had been pursued for just 45 children. 31 of these claims had
been successful, four unsuccessful, five claimants had withdrawn their
applications and five claims were still pending.[154] The scheme is funded by levies
on health professionals and hospitals in the state, but participation in the scheme

---

[150] Birth-Related Neurological Injury Compensation Act 1987 Va. Code Ann. § 38.2–5000–5021
(available   at   *http://law.lis.virginia.gov/vacodepopularnames/virginia-birth-related-neurological-
injury-compensation-act*). For a general overview of the no-fault scheme in Virginia, see D.G. Duff,
"Compensation for Neurologically Impaired Infants: Medical No-Fault in Virginia" (1990) 27(2)
Harv. J. Leg. 391; A. Stein, "The Scope of Virginia's Birth–Related Neurological Injury
Compensation Program" (2015) (available at *http://blogs.harvard.edu/billofhealth/2015/03/08/the-
scope-of-virginias-birth-related-neurological-injury-compensation-program*).
[151] See Gallup, "Can No-Fault Compensation of Impaired Infants Alleviate the Malpractice Crisis in
Obstetrics" (1989) 14(4) J. Health Politics, Policy and Law 691, 692, who asserted that no-fault
compensation "may decrease the amount of reimbursement these neurologically damaged children
receive". Gallup also suggests that obstetricians are more likely to benefit financially from the
Virginia Act than neurologically damaged children: Gallup (1989) at p.700.
[152] The Virginia Act ss.38.2–5009 set out the benefits authorised by law. See Board of Directors for
the Virginia Birth-Related Neurological Injury Compensation Program, *Study to Increase the Scope
and Magnitude of the Virginia Birth-Related Neurological Injury Compensation Program*, 1998, at
p.19.
[153] See Sloan et al., "No-Fault System of Compensation for Obstetric Injury: Winners and Losers"
(1998) 91 Obstet. Gynecol. 437, 440, who state that legal expenses paid on behalf of no-fault
claimants have fallen dramatically. In 1989 legal expenses paid on behalf of a no-fault claimant
averaged $24,000. Contrast this to the estimated payment to claimants' attorneys of $151,000 per tort
case from 1989–1991.
[154] Board of Directors for the Virginia Birth-Related Neurological Injury Compensation Program,
Study to Increase the Scope and Magnitude of the Virginia Birth-Related Neurological Injury

which is not directly related to the damage suffered by the individual. The Vaccine Damage Payments Act 1979 currently provides for compensation of £120,000[162] for claims made on or after 12 July 2007 for an individual who is shown to have suffered injury due the administration of a vaccine against a specified list of diseases,[163] and as a result is, or was immediately prior to their death, "severely disabled". This term means at least 60 per cent disabled,[164] as assessed for the industrial injuries scheme.[165] A compensation payment may also be made where: (1) the disabled person was severely disabled because his or her mother was vaccinated against one of the diseases in the list while she was pregnant; or (2) they have been in close physical contact with someone who has been vaccinated against poliomyelitis with vaccine that was given orally. Children must be two years old or more before they can get a payment. The vaccination must have been before the person's 18th birthday unless it was against poliomyelitis or rubella, or during an outbreak of the disease in the UK (i.e. England, Scotland, Wales and Northern Ireland) or the Isle of Man. The claim has to be made: (a) on or before the vaccinated person attained the age of 21 (or if the person has died, the date they would have reached age 21); or (b) within six years of the vaccination to which the claim relates, whichever is the later.[166] Payment under the scheme, which is funded out of general taxation, is not tailored to the financial needs of the individual. The payment is tax free, but it can affect entitlement to means-tested welfare benefits. The burden of proof, on the balance of probabilities, that the disability was caused by vaccination against one of the specified diseases lies with the claimant. Proving causation is the major problem for applicants. There are few successful claims. Over the five

---

[162] The amount has been changed several times since the Act came into force on 22 March 1979. For claims made on/after 22 March 1979 the sum was £10,000. For claims made on/after 16 August 1985—£20,000. For claims made on/after 15 April 1991—£30,000. For claims made on/after 1 July 1998—£40,000. For claims made on/after 22 July 2000—£100,000. The sum of £120,000 from 12 July 2007 was introduced by the Vaccine Damage Payments Act 1979 Statutory Sum Order 2007 (SI 2007/1931).

[163] The specified diseases are: diphtheria, tetanus and whooping cough (triple); diphtheria; tetanus; whooping cough; poliomyelitis; measles, mumps, rubella (mmr); meningitis C (meningococcal group C); measles; mumps; rubella; tuberculosis; Hib (haemophilus influenzae type B); pneumococcal infection; human papillomavirus; rotavirus (for vaccinations from 1st July 2013); influenza, except for influenza caused by a pandemic influenza virus (for vaccinations from 1 September 2013); pandemic influenza A (H1N1) 2009 (swine flu; but only for vaccinations administered up to 31 August 2010); meningococcal group W (for vaccinations from 1 August 2015) and meningococcal group B (for vaccinations from 1 September 2015).

[164] Vaccine Damage Payments Act 1979 s.1(4) as amended by the Regulatory Reform (Vaccine Damage Payments Act 1979) Order 2002 (SI 2002/1592). Originally, the claimant had to be 80 per cent disabled. When assessing the degree of disablement the decision maker should take into account the applicant's prognosis; the assessment should not be limited to the applicant's current level of disablement: *Secretary of State for Work and Pensions v G* [2017] EWCA Civ 61; (2017) 154 B.M.L.R. 100.

[165] Social Security Contributions and Benefits Act 1992 s.103. Within the industrial injuries scheme 100 per cent relates to that level of disablement for which 100 per cent of the benefit is payable, which does not necessarily equate to total disability. In physical terms, 80 per cent disablement equates to, for example, amputation below the hip or below the shoulder, or to deafness so severe that the sufferer cannot hear a shout beyond a distance of 1m (see the Social Security (General Benefit) Regulations 1982 (SI 1982/1408) Sch.2).

[166] Vaccine Damage Payments Act 1979 s.3(1)(c) as amended by the Regulatory Reform (Vaccine Damage Payments Act 1979) Order 2002 (SI 2002/1592).

years to the end of 1999–2000 an average of 110 claims a year were received and an average of four awards a year were made.[167]

(c)   Proposed no-fault schemes

(i)   General issues

Problems associated with medical accident no-fault schemes   The examples   **1–050**
of limited "no-fault" schemes for industrial injuries, disability benefits and vaccine damage suggest that a scheme of no-fault compensation for medical accidents would not necessarily be a revolutionary step in the UK. Whether it would be a "solution" to the problem of medical accidents, however, depends very much on the detail of such a scheme. For example, the proposals put forward by the BMA in 1991 would have excluded significant categories of accidental medical injury, namely: (a) injuries which are a consequence of the progress of the disease under treatment; (b) diagnostic error which could only have been avoided by hindsight; (c) unavoidable complications, however carefully and competently the procedure was carried out; (d) infections arising under circumstances which made them difficult to avoid; and (e) complications of drug therapy carried out in accordance with the drug manufacturer's instructions.[168] These restrictions on eligibility would have excluded injuries which can truly be said to be accidental, and raised the question of whether such a scheme would compensate for accidental injury or would look for something equivalent to negligence. If "unavoidable complications", for example, are excluded then the test for eligibility is that the complication must have been avoidable, which might well be interpreted to mean avoidable with the exercise of reasonable care. The result would be that:

> "... the scheme would do little more than convert the negligence test into a statutory formula, thereby making it easier for the victims of negligence to obtain compensation, but doing nothing for those suffering medical injury from other causes."[169]

Causation   Even more fundamental is the problem of proving causation, which   **1–051**
is frequently the major hurdle facing a claimant bringing an action for medical

---

[167] *Amending the Vaccine Damage Payments Act 1979*, Consultation Paper, Department of Work and Pensions, July 2001, para.47; cf. the figures quoted in *Making Amends*, June 2003, p.104, para.48: "Since the scheme began, approximately 5,000 claims have been received and 910 awards made to June 2003." As at 8 December 2014, 6,026 claims had been received and 931 awards made, totalling about £73 million (reply to a freedom of information request to the Department of Health, available at *http://www.whatdotheyknow.com/request/242813/response/599844/attach/html/2/Reply%20 DE904995.pdf.html*). For discussion of the no-fault compensation scheme set up by the government for the victims of CJD and their families see Melville Williams [2004] J.P.I.L. 39; A. Boggio, "The Compensation of the Victims of the Creutzfeldt-Jacob Disease in the United Kingdom" (2005) 7 Med. Law Int. 149.
[168] *No Fault Compensation Working Party Report*, 1991. The Report of the Royal College of Physicians, *Compensation for Adverse Consequences of Medical Intervention*, 1990, did not identify any eligibility criteria.
[169] *Royal Commission on Civil Liability and Compensation for Personal Injury*, Cmnd.7054 (1978), Vol.I, para.1366.

negligence. A scheme limited to medical accidents must inevitably distinguish between injuries which are *caused* by a medical accident (however widely or narrowly this may be defined) and those which are not. Unlike road traffic accident or work accident victims, patients are usually receiving treatment because there is already something wrong with them. The process of identifying a medical accident necessarily involves attributing damage to medical treatment (or the lack of it), which necessarily involves separating the consequences of the injury or disease for which the patient was receiving treatment from the consequences of the medical treatment. This, in turn, requires the patient to show that the harm about which she is complaining could have been avoided. How could it have been avoided? By an "appropriate" or "standard" or "normal" medical intervention. But how can one establish what was "appropriate" or "standard" or "normal", except by asking whether what the healthcare professionals did complied with the common practice of the profession or was reasonable in the circumstances? In other words, to some extent, the causation question (the question: what is caused by the treatment and what is caused by the disease?) forces one to ask whether the treatment was reasonable in the circumstances. As the New Zealand accident compensation scheme has illustrated, for medical accidents it is very difficult to get away from a fault standard. Questions of eligibility, or who would qualify for compensation under a no-fault scheme, are not the only issues that have to be weighed in the balance when considering the potential ramifications of such a radical change to the compensation mechanism. There is the relationship between the medical profession and patients to consider (would a no-fault compensation scheme reduce professional accountability? would it reduce concerns about "defensive medicine"?); crucial issues of detail such as what would be compensated for and at what level; the question of the overall cost of a no-fault scheme (is it affordable?); and despite the inherently practical nature of problem (who should be compensated for what losses) there are also issues of principle in deciding who should be the beneficiaries of a scheme to which all taxpayers contribute in some shape or form.

(ii)   Scotland

1–052   In 2009 the Scottish government established a No-fault Compensation Review Group to consider whether a no-fault compensation scheme for injured patients should be introduced in addition to the existing common law action for clinical negligence. The Review Group published its report in February 2011.[170] Having considered various no-fault compensation schemes, focussing in particular on the New Zealand and Swedish models, the Review Group considered that the essential criteria for a compensation scheme were:

- the scheme provides an appropriate level of compensation to the patient, their family or carers;
- the scheme is compatible with the European Convention on Human Rights;

---

[170] See *http://www.scotland.gov.uk/Topics/Health/Policy/No-Fault-Compensation*.

- the scheme is easy to access and use, without unnecessary barriers, for example created by cost or the difficulty of getting advice or support;
- people are able to get the relevant specialist advice in using the scheme;
- decisions about compensation are timely;
- people who have used the scheme feel that they have been treated equitably;
- the scheme is affordable;
- the scheme makes proportionate use of time and resources;
- the scheme has an appropriate balance between costs of administration (e.g. financial or time) and the level of compensation awarded;
- decisions about compensation are made through a robust and independent process;
- the scheme has an independent appeal system;
- the scheme treats staff and patients fairly/equitably;
- a reasonable time limit is set for compensation claims.

In its response to a consultation exercise on the Review Group's recommendations the Scottish government added the following essential criteria:

- the scheme discourages frivolous or speculative claims;
- the scheme encourages responsible behaviour from patients and staff;
- the public (and the professions, NHS staff and others) trust the scheme to deliver a fair outcome (moved from desirable);
- the scheme encourages transparency in clinical decision-making (moved from desirable).[171]

The Review Group concluded that the Swedish model satisfied more of these criteria than any other system. It was recommended that consideration be given to the establishment of a no-fault scheme for medical injury in Scotland, along the lines of the Swedish model, but that eligibility for compensation should not be based on the "avoidability" test as used in Sweden.[172] Rather there should be a clear description of which injuries are *not* eligible for compensation under the no-fault scheme. The scheme should cover all medical treatment injuries that occur in Scotland (i.e. it would include injuries caused by the treatment itself or by a failure to treat, as well as by faulty equipment) and should extend to all registered healthcare professionals in Scotland, not simply to those employed by the NHS in Scotland. Compensation would be based on need rather than on a tariff-based system. The right to litigate would be retained, and a claimant who failed in litigation would have a residual right to claim under the no-fault scheme and vice versa. Any compensation awarded under the no-fault scheme would be deducted from any damages awarded as a result of litigation. Appeal from a decision under the no-fault scheme would lie to a court of law on a point of law or fact.

1–053

---

[171] See *Consultation on Recommendations for No-Fault Compensation in Scotland for injuries resulting from clinical treatment* (2014) para.6.4.2 (available at *http://www.gov.scot/Resource/0044/00447863.pdf*).

[172] See para.1–043.

1-062   There are major limitations to this proposed compensation scheme. Clearly, if the "reasonable care" test were to be adopted as the threshold for the second stage it could not be labelled a "no-fault" compensation scheme. It might be considered a streamlined system of fault compensation, but for claimants overall would involve a reduction in the level of compensation awarded (90 per cent rather than 100 per cent). The "experienced specialist" test would come close to a no-fault compensation scheme by moving to what is in effect a causation test (in hindsight, could the harm have been avoided by optimal care?). But in both instances the numbers of potentially successful claims would be very small, and there is no obvious rationale (other than an unspoken assumption about cost) for such a narrow range of potential beneficiaries.

(d)   Accountability and no-fault

1-063   Lack of accountability, and a doctor's sense of individual responsibility, were the principal reasons given by the medical profession for opposing the introduction of a no-fault scheme in its evidence to the Pearson Commission. Although there have been a number of changes to NHS complaints procedures,[188] and to the powers of the Health Service Commissioner[189] and the General Medical Council, the question of accountability has remained problematic.[190] The General Medical Council, which is the only body to exercise a disciplinary jurisdiction over all doctors whether in the NHS or private practice, may discipline a registered medical practitioner whose fitness to practise is impaired.[191] In the past, a persistent criticism of the way in which the GMC exercised its disciplinary powers was that it failed to deal with what by any standard was culpable conduct in the treatment of patients because it could not be categorised as *serious professional misconduct*. That issue has, to some extent, been addressed by a

---

[188] See paras 13–004 et seq.

[189] The Health Service Commissioner has the power to investigate clinical complaints: Health Service Commissioners Act 1993, as amended. For consideration of the limits on the Health Service Commissioner's powers of investigation see *R. (on the application of Cavanagh) v Health Service Commissioner* [2005] EWCA Civ 1578; [2006] 1 W.L.R. 1229. The Commissioner's functions are limited to the investigation of complaints. There is no power of investigation at large; nor may the Commissioner expand the ambit of a complaint beyond what it contains, nor the investigation of it beyond what the complaint warrants (per Sedley LJ at [16]). For consideration of the appropriate standard to be applied by the Health Service Commissioner when adjudicating on a complaint involving clinical practice see *R. (on the application of Attwood) v Health Service Commissioner* [2008] EWHC 2315 (Admin); [2009] 1 All E.R. 415.

[190] For discussion see Kennedy & Grubb, *Medical Law*, 3rd edn (London: Butterworths, 2000), pp.247–268; Longley (1997) 5 Med. L. Rev. 172; Harpwood (1996) 3 Eur. J. Health Law 207. The House of Commons Health Committee, Session 1998–99, Sixth Report, *Procedures Related to Adverse Clinical Incidents and Outcomes in Medical Care*, Vol.I, October 1999, paras 72 to 106 found that there was extensive criticism of NHS complaints procedures, despite changes to the procedures introduced in 1996. See also *Making Amends*, June 2003, p.78, para.12.

[191] Medical Act 1983 s.35C. Doctors' fitness to practise may be impaired by reason of: (a) misconduct; (b) deficient professional performance; (c) a conviction or caution for a criminal offence; (d) adverse physical or mental health; (e) not having the necessary knowledge of English; or (f) a determination of another regulatory body that their fitness to practise is impaired. See also the GMC guide, *Good Medical Practice* (April 2013) (available at *http://www.gmc-uk.org/Good_medical_practice___English_1215.pdf_51527435.pdf*).

series of reforms to the GMC's regulatory powers though the question of full accountability through the General Medical Council has remained problematic.[192]

Despite the evidence given to the Pearson Commission the BMA subsequently questioned whether a system of no-fault compensation "importantly diminishes the accountability of doctors".[193] This was not the view of the Royal College of Physicians, which accepted that a no-fault scheme could remove a source of medical accountability.[194] The Royal College recommended that a no-fault scheme should be accompanied by:

1–064

> "...a separate mechanism for the scrutiny of each claim in which doctors were involved to ensure that appropriate care had not been transgressed. If transgression is demonstrated, questions of professional discipline should be pursued."

Although this recognises that the principle of medical accountability is important, it fails to address the point that the mechanisms for accountability, although improving, remain less than ideal in all but the most serious of cases. If transgression of "appropriate care" would result in the doctor being referred to the GMC, it would only be the most flagrant instances of negligence that would be subject to accountability. Moreover, it has been claimed that the introduction of a no-fault compensation scheme would remove the deterrent effect of possible litigation, thereby tending to lower rather than raise healthcare standards.[195]

(e) Defensive medicine and no-fault

A no-fault compensation scheme would probably not change a doctor's defensive reaction to medical errors. The present tort system has no direct financial effect on a doctor, since damages are paid by the NHS Trust or a defence organisation, and a negligent doctor is not penalised financially. Thus, the deterrent effect of

1–065

---

[192] P. de Prez, "Self-Regulation and Paragons of Virtue: The Case of 'Fitness to Practice'" (2002) 10 Med. L. Rev. 28; P. Case, "The good, the bad and the dishonest doctor: the General Medical Council and the 'redemption model' of fitness to practise" (2011) 31 L.S. 591; A. Morris, "Fitness to practise and the ethics of decision-making at the end of life: Dr Michael Munro" (2007) 23 P.N. 228.

[193] Report of the *BMA Working Party on No Fault Compensation*, 1991. It is argued that the tort action does not produce accountability because the worst cases of negligence never get to court, but are settled in private, with only the marginal claims being fought. The result is that there may be an unfair burden of publicity on doctors who may well have acted perfectly properly. This misses the point about accountability, however, which enables individual patients to hold doctors to account for their actions in law, whether this results in a settlement or a trial. The payment of compensation may be completely irrelevant.

[194] Report of the Royal College of Physicians, *Compensation for Adverse Consequences of Medical Intervention*, 1990, p.21.

[195] Andrew Morrison, a Royal Society of Medicine Council member of the Medical Defence Union, in Mann and Havard, *No Fault Compensation in Medicine*, 1989, p.156. In New Zealand, where since 1974 the action in tort has been unavailable if the patient receives compensation under the no-fault scheme, complaints to the equivalent of the GMC between 1974 and 1987 increased by 1800 per cent: Dr J.A. Wall in Mann and Havard (1989), p.72. There has been concern in New Zealand about the lack of accountability of doctors in the absence of tort litigation: Ham, Dingwall, Fenn and Harris, *Medical Negligence: Compensation and Accountability*, 1988, p.23; McGregor Vennell, "Medical Misfortune in a No Fault Society" in Mann and Havard (1989), p.40. See further Brown (1985) 73 Cal. L. Rev. 976.

tort must be linked to the perceived consequences of litigation on the doctor's reputation. No-fault compensation seeks to remove the link between proving fault and obtaining compensation[196]; it does not remove "fault" from the practice of medicine. Separating compensation from proof of fault does not reduce the risk to a doctor's reputation if there is to be genuine accountability. If a suitable system of accountability was introduced along with no-fault, in which doctors who have been guilty of blameworthy conduct are held accountable for their actions, some doctors would, presumably, still be inclined to practise "defensively" in order to protect their reputation and avoid disciplinary proceedings. In other words, no-fault compensation has no relevance to a debate about "defensive medicine", and it seems unlikely that a reduction in "defensive" practice could be said to be a potential benefit of introducing a no-fault compensation scheme.

(f)   Levels of compensation

1–066   The levels of compensation for patients under the no-fault schemes in operation in Sweden and New Zealand are very different. The Swedish system opts for broadly the same levels of compensation as tort damages, but payments are comparatively modest because social security benefits are high and the scheme is frequently merely topping up the patient's pecuniary losses. The New Zealand scheme does not attempt to replicate tort damages, but concentrates on compensating economic losses subject to capping the loss of earnings element. The BMA *No Fault Compensation Working Party Report*, 1991, envisaged compensation for loss of income up to a limit of twice the national average wage, but overall aimed at "awards about half the size of those which a court would make in a successful action". From a patient's point of view the value of a no-fault compensation scheme would relate both to the ease with which a claim could be made and the amount of compensation available. If the levels of compensation were comparable with social security benefits, for example, many people might prefer the tort action, with all its vagaries, for the chance of substantial compensation.

(g)   Cost

1–067   Estimates of the overall cost of a no-fault scheme limited to medical accidents are little more than guesswork. There are three variables: (i) how many successful claimants there will be; (ii) how much the average payment of compensation will be; and, (iii) how much the system will cost to administer. There is virtually no information about either of the first two variables, and thus costings are extremely speculative.[197] Administration costs would certainly be lower, at least in terms of the percentage of compensation paid out, than under the tort system.[198]

---

[196] Although, arguably, this can never be fully achieved: see para.1–051.

[197] Ham, Dingwall, Fenn and Harris, *Medical Negligence: Compensation and Accountability*, 1988, p.31 estimated between £177 million and £235 million, at 1988 prices. The BMA *No Fault Compensation Working Party Report*, 1991, paras 7.1 and 7.2, estimated a cost of £100.4 million, at

The number of successful claimants would depend upon a whole range of variables, some of which depend upon the scope of the scheme and some of which it would be almost impossible to predict (e.g. how many more claimants than currently resort to the tort system would be encouraged to claim as a result of the existence of the scheme). The scope of the scheme depends upon what constitutes a compensatable event (would it be limited to, in effect, negligently caused harm?[199]) and what exclusionary criteria are adopted (e.g. would certain events fall outside the scheme, perhaps because they are regarded as part of the risk of treatment; how severe must the patient's damage be to qualify?[200]).

1–068

The level of compensation is entirely within the control of those establishing the no-fault scheme. The range of options goes from: (1) the full equivalent of tort damages; (2) limiting claims to financial losses; (3) compensating for a part of the financial losses (e.g. New Zealand compensates loss of earnings up to 80 per cent of pre-accident earnings, subject to a maximum figure linked to a multiple of national average earnings); (4) excluding the costs of private medical care, except where that care is not available on the NHS; to (5) adopting a social security approach which awards a specific weekly sum according to degree of disability without direct reference to the claimant's financial loss or needs (e.g. as under the industrial injuries scheme). There are numerous intermediate positions or combinations that could be considered. The levels of compensation chosen would clearly have an effect on the success of the scheme, which may also be linked to other issues, such as whether claimants would remain entitled to bring a tort claim. Combining relatively low levels of compensation with retention of the right to sue in tort would do little to address the problems associated with the litigation system. On the other hand, a denial of tort remedies without reasonable levels of compensation might fall foul of art.6 of the European Convention on Human Rights.

1–069

The administrative cost of running the system would depend upon precisely how the scheme was run. In any event, it is likely to be significantly lower than the tort system. In New Zealand the cost of running the Medical Misadventure Account comes to 17 per cent of the total expenditure of the Account (though the cost of running the whole New Zealand no-fault scheme was about 9.4 per cent). In 1998 administration costs for the Swedish scheme amounted to approximately 7.8 per cent of the total expenditure for the scheme. By any measure this is significantly below the 37 per cent for legal costs associated with medical negligence litigation.[201]

1–070

1990 prices, for the whole UK. This was on the basis of awards at half the level of tort damages, following a survey of claims rates in 10 per cent of district health authorities in 1988. The report did not attempt to quantify the possible increase in claims rates, but conceded that it was probable that there would be an exponential rise in the number of claims during the first decade of operating a no-fault scheme.

[198] See para.1–033, n.120 above. The administrative costs of the Swedish system are put at 16 per cent of the premiums.

[199] See para.1–051.

[200] All no-fault schemes exclude minor injuries. The question would be "how minor?"

[201] See para.1–023.

(h) Questions of principle

1–071   The deficiencies of the tort system are well documented. Much of the criticism which can be directed at the action in negligence as a means of compensating the victims of medical accidents applies with equal force to claims arising out of other types of accidents. It is not clear why no-fault compensation should be adopted for one category of accident victims to the exclusion of others with equally serious injuries sustained in other ways. In theory, the tort of negligence provides a conceptual basis for distinguishing between patients who are entitled to compensation and those who are not, in that negligence "identifies" individuals (or their employers) who are responsible in law for the infliction of the patient's injury, and so in fairness ought to recompense the patient for that loss. This is not how the system works in practice, because it may not be possible to establish fault, and insurance (through NHS indemnity in hospitals and through the medical defence organisations in primary care) removes a large element of individual responsibility. On the other hand, the conceptual underpinning of a scheme of no-fault compensation rests on a theory of social responsibility for the victims of misfortune, namely those who suffer injury by "accident". It is not apparent why the victims of a particular type of accident (medical accidents) should receive compensation on a no-fault basis when other accident victims have to prove fault. This is particularly the case when only certain types of medical accident, those which qualify under the eligibility criteria, would be compensated under such a scheme. These issues become especially important when it is proposed to fund a no-fault scheme from general taxation to which everyone must contribute, whether they fall into the favoured category of accident victim or not.

1–072   The argument that the principle of no-fault compensation selects its beneficiaries on a fairer basis (namely "need" not "fault") than the tort of negligence is questionable. It selects them on a *different* basis but it still draws arbitrary distinctions between those who will be compensated and those who will not. Clearly, the needs of a child with brain damage are no different whether caused by congenital disability or medical intervention at birth. On the one hand, a no-fault compensation scheme would probably provide compensation for more patients (depending upon how strict the eligibility criteria were), more quickly and more efficiently than the tort system. It could provide readier access to compensation for patients who may not be in a financial position to sue; and it would provide for periodic payments so that the compensation reflects the patient's actual loss. On the other hand, if the problem is that too few patients succeed in recovering compensation because of the difficulties of proving fault, it would be possible to improve claimant success rates under the tort system by introducing strict liability and reversing the burden of proof.[202] This would also separate the question of compensation from the proof of fault. The argument for a

---

[202] The European Commission did consider a proposal which would have had the effect of reversing the burden of proof in respect of the liability of suppliers of services for personal injuries: [1991] O.J. C12/8, 18 January 1991. It seemed likely that the construction industry and the medical profession would have been excluded from the effect of this Directive (*The Times*, 6 January 1992), but in any event the proposal was not pursued.

no-fault compensation scheme limited to the victims of medical accidents must be based on pragmatic justifications, rather than principle. Under the tort system:

- the victims of medical accidents have much lower success rates in terms of obtaining some compensation than other accident victims;
- the victims of medical accidents, on average, suffer the longest delays of all personal injury victims in obtaining compensation;
- there is skewed access to the legal system for the victims of medical accidents, attributable to the cost of making a claim—even the moderately well-off may be unable to afford to bring a claim;
- there is some evidence that the effect on health professionals of dealing with claims for negligence can be detrimental to their clinical performance (though this is not necessarily the phenomenon of so-called "defensive medicine")[203];
- perhaps most crucially, the high cost of running the tort system is a very inefficient way of transferring money to accident victims, and it would be better to reduce transaction costs and compensate more accident victims or spend any cost savings on the provision of healthcare.[204]

A carefully constructed no-fault compensation scheme would go some way to addressing most of these issues.

The relationship between a no-fault scheme and the tort system is an issue that would also have a profound effect on the success, or otherwise, of the scheme. Should a tort claim be barred for anyone falling within the terms of the scheme (as in New Zealand), or would a tort claim remain an option (as in Sweden)? Barring the tort remedy might fall foul of arts 6 and 14 of the European Convention on Human Rights, since it would prevent access to the legal system for a particular category of accident victim. This argument would be stronger if the amount of compensation available under the scheme bore little relationship the accident victim's real loss. On the other hand, certain employment rights (with capped levels of compensation) have to be pursued in an employment tribunal rather than in the courts, and it has not yet been suggested that this constitutes a breach of art.6. Allowing tort claims to run alongside (or as a backup to) the scheme (as in Sweden or the industrial injuries scheme, which does not prevent an injured employee from suing the employer for negligence), would avoid a possible conflict with art.6, but would not address the failings of the tort system, in particular the administrative cost. The result could be that there is no reduction in litigation, but that some injured patients whose tort claim currently fails, might receive compensation under the no-fault scheme, thereby significantly increasing the overall cost of paying for accidental injury to patients. Another option would be to require injured patients to "elect" either for the no-fault scheme or for tort. Once having elected for the scheme, any tort claim is barred. The problem with this approach is that if there are comparatively short

1–073

---

[203] Genn, "Effects of claims on doctors" (1996) 2 *Clinical Risk* 181; Hirst, "Supporting staff during litigation—managerial aspects" (1996) 2 *Clinical Risk* 189; *Making Amends*, June 2003, p.43.
[204] This argument is not unique to medical accidents, of course.

time limits for bringing a claim for no-fault compensation, it will effectively create a situation where the patient is forced to opt for the scheme.

1–074   Any consideration of the merits of a no-fault compensation scheme should also take into account the potential negative effects of a such a scheme, particularly if the right to sue in tort were removed. If, as rational individuals, health professionals and NHS organisations respond to the threat of negligence claims by modifying their behaviour (and all claims that doctors practise defensive medicine are claims that doctors do respond to the deterrent effect of liability rules, though with "defensive medicine" the claim is that they *overreact* to the risk of liability by doing things that are potentially detrimental to patients[205]) then there is a risk that removing the threat of litigation would have adverse consequences for patient safety. Individuals and organisations might have less of an incentive to adopt measures which improve patient safety by reducing risk. Without litigation, there would be no need for CNST and therefore no direct financial incentive to reduce risk (unless NHS Trusts were required to pay into the no-fault compensation fund). This type of argument is difficult to test empirically. It could be observed that if tort is meant to act as a deterrent to risky conduct it does not have a particularly good record, given the staggering numbers of adverse clinical incidents that occur in modern hospitals. On the other hand, it could be said that it was the significant rise in the number and cost of claims that persuaded the NHS to take the question of patient safety seriously through a number of initiatives linked to quality of service and risk management.

1–075   A no-fault compensation scheme cannot stop doctors from acting negligently, nor would it stop patients seeking to hold doctors to account for blameworthy conduct. Indeed, it would be strange if doctors were the only profession to be unaccountable in the courts. The Pearson Commission commented that:

> "... there would have to be a good case for exempting any profession from legal liabilities which apply to others, and we do not regard the special circumstances of medical injury as constituting such a case."[206]

The fact that since the early 1980s patients have sued their doctors in larger numbers than ever before can hardly be considered a "good case", since this is true of every other professional group. Ultimately, the arguments for no-fault compensation have to be grounded in improving the position of patients injured by the healthcare system in which they placed their trust. If no-fault compensation is seen as a solution to defendants' problems (by reducing cost, or reducing the opportunity to "blame" healthcare professionals who are already stressed) it will fail to address the real crisis of medical accidents, which is that there are so many patients injured by their medical treatment and so few who manage to obtain compensation for those injuries.

---

[205] Although no one has yet managed to explain how doing something that is potentially harmful to patients can be a sensible strategy for avoiding litigation.
[206] *Royal Commission on Civil Liability and Compensation for Personal Injury*, Cmnd.7054 (1978), Vol.I, para.1344.

4. MAKING AMENDS

The Chief Medical Officer's report, *Making Amends*,[207] considered many of the   1–076
issues that have already been touched on in this chapter. Although it is some 14
years since this report was published, most of the issues that it highlighted are
still with us. Indeed, it is arguable that some of the drivers for that report are even
more acute, not least the rising cost of dealing with the consequences of medical
error. The need to take systematic steps to reduce error and accidental harm is
self-evident. A health system that, in attempting to alleviate suffering, and with
the best will in the world, kills and injures so many of its patients needs to ask
itself some serious questions. That would be true whatever the arrangements
adopted for compensating the victims of those errors. Forty years ago the Pearson
Commission highlighted many of the problems with tort as a means of
compensating for personal injury, though shied away from recommending any
root and branch reform. Despite attempts to improve the efficiency of the
litigation process, it remains a relatively slow, expensive, inefficient and
sometimes capricious means of transferring money from a negligent defendant to
an injured claimant. Medical malpractice litigation tends to accentuate the flaws
in that process. But, though it is easy to criticise the present system, it is not as
easy to come up with an alternative that fits within perceptions of what is
affordable. If the steadily growing overall cost to the NHS of litigation is seen as
the problem, the criticism that tort is expensive and inefficient, while true, is
likely to redound if the solution is to put in place a much more efficient
compensation system, when combined with the knowledge that the vast majority
of the victims of medical accidents currently go uncompensated by the tort
system. In other words, the solution to a problem depends on what the problem is
perceived to be. If it is that the overall cost of compensating for medical error is
too high, then one will look for ways of cutting the cost. If it is that there is far
too much medical error, and far too many injured patients who go uncompensated, then one would look for ways to reduce error and improve the mechanisms
for paying compensation to include a wider pool of accident victims. Both
outcomes may be desirable, but they are probably incompatible objectives.

Options for reform *Making Amends*, while recognising the need to improve   1–077
risk management in the NHS (reiterating the points made three years earlier in *An
Organisation with a Memory*), opted for measures to reduce, or at least attempt to
contain the overall cost. *Making Amends* identified four options for reform: (1)
continue with reforms to the tort system; (2) introduce no-fault compensation; (3)
introduce a system of fixed tariffs for particular types of injury administered by a
national tribunal; (4) introduce a composite package of reform. The first three
options were rejected.

Tort reform   Change based solely on continued tort reform was rejected,   1–078
because:

---

[207] *Making Amends*, Department of Health, June 2003 (available at *http://webarchive.
nationalarchives.gov.uk*).

high proportion of small payments. The Commission recommended that no damages should be recoverable for non-pecuniary loss suffered during the first three months after the date of the injury.[214] At that time, this would have eliminated many small claims altogether, with a consequent saving of administration costs, and reduced by about 20 per cent the total tort compensation for personal injury

1–081   **Fixed tariffs**   *Making Amends* also rejected a system of fixed tariffs administered through a national tribunal, as under the Criminal Injuries Compensation scheme. Levels of awards under the Criminal Injuries scheme are significantly lower than the sums awarded in tort damages and bear little relationship to the actual losses of victims. If the goal was to put the patient back in the position they would have been in (as far as that is possible), a fixed tariff scheme, which would have involved the administrative cost of setting up a national tribunal, was never likely to be a serious option.

(a)   A composite package of reform?

1–082   The CMO's recommendations for reform (which applied to England only) constituted what the report called a composite package. They would provide "redress" for patients harmed as a result of "seriously substandard" NHS hospital care in relatively low value claims, and a compensation package for brain-damaged babies who suffered severe neurological impairment related to or resulting from birth, irrespective of the proof of fault. The process was to be based on the concept that the patient should be returned to the condition they would have been in had the injury not occurred.[215] In all cases where harm to a patient had arisen from an adverse event, the response should be: (1) an investigation of the incident which is alleged to have caused harm and of the harm that has resulted; (2) provision of an explanation to the patient of what has happened and why, and the action proposed to prevent repetition; (3) the development and delivery of a package of care, providing remedial treatment, therapy and arrangements for continuing care where needed. In "suitable cases" there would be consideration of whether payment for pain and suffering, for out of pocket expenses and for care or treatment which the NHS could not provide should be made. A decision on the case would be made within six months from the initial approach from the patient. This redress scheme would initially be available only to patients treated in hospital and community health settings. Consideration would be given to whether it should be extended to primary care at a later stage. *Making Amends* recognised that, initially at least, the capacity of the NHS to provide packages of care may be limited and therefore financial recompense may be offered as an alternative. However, the aim would be to develop this capacity over time. These proposed reforms were said to be intended to be fair to individual patients and meet their needs, while making care safer for

---

[214] *Royal Commission on Civil Liability and Compensation for Personal Injury*, Cmnd.7054 (1978), Vol.I, para.388.
[215] Which of course is the basis upon which tort damages are assessed: see para.12–002.

all NHS patients.[216] On the other hand, it is not obvious that there is a need to change the litigation system *in order to* make healthcare safer. There is no evidence that the litigation process makes healthcare less safe, but there is plenty of evidence that the less safe healthcare is, the more litigation there will be (which is not to suggest that this is the only factor at work in the increase in litigation). Moreover, under the tort system there is nothing to prevent a full investigation of the incident, nor to prevent healthcare professionals from giving patients an explanation of what has happened. This is something that patients' organisations, such as Action against Medical Accidents, have been calling for, for many years.

Under the proposals there would have been effectively three parallel compensa-   1–083
tion schemes, one providing "NHS Redress" for low value claims, and one for cases involving brain-damaged babies. All other claims would still have to be resolved through the tort system, though *Making Amends* made recommendations designed to reduce the cost to the NHS of the tort system.

(b)   Low value claims

Making Amends recommended that for claims not involving brain-damaged   1–084
babies, successful claimants would be entitled to a "package of care" from the NHS to deal with the effects of the injury and possible financial compensation. The financial element of the compensation would be limited to: (1) the notional cost of the episode of care or other amount as appropriate, at the discretion of the local NHS Trust; (2) up to £30,000 where authorised by the national body managing the new scheme.[217] Access to the package of care and *possible* financial compensation for an adverse outcome of NHS care would follow: a local investigation of the adverse event or of a complaint; an independent review of a complaint by the Commission for Healthcare Audit and Inspection[218]; a recommendation by the Health Services Commissioner; or an investigation of a claim made directly by a patient or relatives to the NHS Litigation Authority.[219] The criteria for receiving payment would be that: (1) there were serious shortcomings in the standards of care; (2) the harm could have been avoided; (3) the adverse outcome was not the result of the natural progression of the illness.

"Serious shortcomings" in the standards of care (also referred to in the report as   1–085
"substandard care") would seem to be a negligence standard by another name. The requirement that the harm could not have been avoided clearly involves a causation test, which combined with a negligence standard would effectively be no different from the entry criteria set by the tort of negligence. What was entirely novel under this system was the proposal for "the development and delivery of a package of care, providing remedial treatment, therapy and

---

[216] *Making Amends*, June 2003, p.117, para.4.
[217] *Making Amends* recommended that, subject to evaluation, consideration should be given to extending the scheme to a higher monetary threshold (recommendation 4).
[218] A new statutory health inspectorate which would inspect the quality of local NHS services and investigate complaints not resolved at local level.
[219] *Making Amends*, June 2003, p.119.

arrangements for continuing care where needed". Providing compensation in kind, rather than in cash, would probably have been less expensive to the NHS, though since this part of scheme was limited to relatively low value claims it would seem to be aimed at the less serious cases where long-term care would not necessarily have been needed. Also novel was a requirement to reach a decision within six months from the initial approach of the patient.

(c)   Brain-damaged babies

1–086   **No-fault compensation for brain-damaged babies**   *Making Amends* proposed that the NHS Redress scheme "should encompass care and compensation for severely neurologically impaired babies, including those with severe cerebral palsy". Given that under the tort system brain-damaged babies accounted, at that time, for about 60 per cent of the total costs, this was always going to be the pivotal issue. It was proposed that in order to qualify for "redress" under the scheme there would have to be: (1) birth under NHS care; (2) severe neurological impairment (including cerebral palsy) related to or resulting from the birth; (3) a claim made to the scheme within eight years of the birth; (4) the care package and compensation would be based on a severity index judged according to the ability to perform the activities of daily living; (5) genetic or chromosomal abnormality would be excluded.[220] Crucially, under this part of the scheme there was no reference to "serious shortcomings in the standards of care" or "substandard care" as a qualifying criterion. This would have been truly revolutionary. It would have constituted a form of no-fault compensation for brain-damaged babies.

1–087   It was recommended that compensation be provided in both cash and in kind, according to the needs of the child for assistance with the tasks of daily living resulting from the severity of impairment. This would include: (1) a managed care package; (2) a monthly payment for the costs of care which could not be provided through a care package (in the most severe cases this could be up to £100,000 per annum); (3) lump sum payments for home adaptations and equipment at intervals throughout the child's life (up to £50,000); (4) an initial payment in compensation for pain, suffering and loss of amenity capped at £50,000.

1–088   The benefits of such a scheme, as the report noted, were that compensation and support would be available to a wider range of severely disabled babies and children without the need to establish negligence or fault, although perhaps more importantly for the NHS "it would also control costs to the NHS by meeting the actual care needs as they arose".[221] Unfortunately, this element of the NHS Redress scheme was not adopted in the NHS Redress Act 2006 (which itself has not been put into effect). The government's response to the recommendation was that there should be improved resources to care for all children with serious disabilities, whether caused by brain damage or not. Of course, whether those resources are actually available is another matter. The suspicion must be that,

---

[220] *Making Amends*, June 2003, p.121.
[221] *Making Amends*, June 2003, p.121.

having looked at the potential costs of a no-fault compensation scheme for brain-damaged babies, the government decided that it was not affordable.

(d) The right to litigate

The right to litigate under the tort system would have remained for patients or families who chose not to apply for packages of care and payment under the NHS Redress scheme, but patients who accepted compensation under the scheme would not subsequently be able to litigate for the same injury. Before accepting an offer "a small amount of money would be made available to patients to allow them to seek independent advice on the fairness of the offer". This apparently preserved the right of patients to choose, but exercising that right to litigate would have been severely curtailed because it was proposed that where a claimant was seeking legal aid to pursue a claim for clinical negligence, the Legal Services Commission should take into account whether or not the case had already been pursued through the scheme in order to protect the public purse "from the unnecessary expenditure on legal aid".

1–089

(e) Other recommendations

Making Amends made a number of other recommendations, some to the way in which the NHS should respond to patients injured by an adverse event, and some to the legal system.

1–090

*   Adverse events and complaints should have a full and objective investigation, commensurate with the severity of the harm, so that patients are given a full explanation, an apology where something has gone wrong, and a specification of the action (local and national) being taken to reduce the risk of a similar event happening to future patients (recommendation 6). NHS Trusts should also offer remedial treatment or rehabilitation measures, to improve after care. This would reduce suffering and the long-term effects of any harm, "with obvious benefits to the patient and savings to the NHS".
*   The initial response to a local complaint should be an automatic investigation, which may have indicated that compensation under the NHS Redress scheme was appropriate. Even if patients decided to pursue litigation, the complaints process should continue to provide the explanations which patients and families sought (recommendation 8).
*   Effective rehabilitation services for personal injury, including that caused by medical accidents, should be developed (recommendation 10).
*   The Department of Health should consider the scope for providing more accessible high quality but lower cost facilities for severely neurologically impaired and physically disabled children, regardless of cause (recommendation 11).
*   A duty of candour should be introduced together with exemption from disciplinary action when reporting incidents with a view to improving patient safety (recommendation 12). This would be a statutory duty

requiring all healthcare professionals and managers to inform patients where they become aware of a possible negligent act or omission. This should include exemption from disciplinary action for those reporting adverse events except where the healthcare professional has committed a criminal offence or it would not be safe for the professional to continue to treat patients.[222]

• Documents and information collected for identifying adverse events should be protected from disclosure in court (recommendation 13). This would be so that such documents could not be compelled to be produced in a court so reducing the disincentive to the reporting of errors. But the protection would only apply to reports of adverse events where full information on the event was also included in the medical records.

1–091   Two crucial recommendations were designed to reduce the cost to the NHS of compensating those tort claims that remain outside the system of NHS Redress. The first was that in paying damages for future care costs and losses in clinical negligence cases the expectation should be that periodical payments will be used (recommendation 16). This recommendation was overtaken by events since the courts now have the power to order periodical payments in place of lump sum awards where appropriate.[223]

1–092   The second recommendation is far more controversial. This was that the costs of future care included in any award for clinical negligence made by the courts should no longer reflect the cost of private treatment (recommendation 17). Section 2(4) of the Law Reform (Personal Injuries) Act 1948 provides that in an action for personal injuries, in determining the reasonableness of any expenses the possibility of avoiding those expenses, or part of them, by taking advantage of facilities available under the NHS is to be disregarded. The claimant can insist on damages to cover the cost of private medical treatment even though that treatment is available free under the NHS.[224] The rule applies to all personal injury claims, including claims against the NHS, with the result that the NHS may have to fund private medical treatment at much higher cost than the NHS could itself provide that treatment. *Making Amends* recommended that clinical negligence cases arising from NHS treatment should be exempted from this provision. The NHS defendant would undertake to fund "a specified package of care or treatment to defined timescales". Initially, the report acknowledges, the costs would probably be similar to providing a sum of money to purchase private care, because the NHS would have to fund some elements of the care package privately.

---

[222] See now the Health and Social Care Act 2008 (Regulated Activities) Regulations 2014 (SI 2014/2936); para.4–055. The Regulations do not include an exemption from disciplinary action for those reporting adverse events.

[223] See paras 12–020 et seq.

[224] The converse proposition is also true. A patient who has received an award of damages which includes compensation for the cost of medical care is entitled to receive free NHS treatment. An NHS Trust cannot refuse to provide treatment to a patient simply because the patient has the means to fund a privately provided care package out of an award of damages: *R. (on the application of Booker) v NHS Oldham* [2010] EWHC 2593 (Admin); [2011] Med. L.R. 10; para.12–064.

The recommendation that s.2(4) of the Law Reform (Personal Injuries) Act 1948   **1–093**
should be abolished was made by the Pearson Commission,[225] but not in the
context of a particular type of accident or defendant. The problem with this
proposal, which if anything has become more acute with the passage of time, is
that there is no guarantee that the care the claimant needs will be provided by the
NHS when it is needed. It is all very well stating that "the NHS defendant should
undertake to fund a specified package of care or treatment to defined timescales".
What happens if the NHS fails to deliver? Does the claimant have to go back to
court to enforce the "undertaking"? The report identified the objections of
claimant and patient groups to removing a patient's right to the cost of private
medical treatment: (1) it would be inequitable to remove them only from those
suffering medical injury; (2) there was insufficient capacity in the NHS to
provide care for everyone who might need it if provision for private care costs
was removed from all personal injury cases; (3) injured patients would not be
able to access the full range of treatments and care needed though the NHS; (4)
injured patients would not wish to have an ongoing relationship with the
organisation which had injured them; (5) rehabilitation services available to the
NHS were inadequate to meet the need for either rapid and intensive or long-term
support.[226] There is much force in these criticisms of the proposal. The response
of the report was the assertion that:

> "...it can be argued that the NHS itself should be under an obligation to put right the damage
> caused. Although money is now the traditional response, a comprehensive care package (i.e.
> 'non-financial compensation'), promptly provided and efficiently delivered, is an obvious
> alternative."[227]

If the care package was comprehensive, and if it was delivered promptly and
efficiently, this would be a perfectly reasonable response to the criticisms, but
these are two very big "ifs".

(f)   Conclusion

Making Amends asserted that the proposed "new NHS Redress Scheme is centred   **1–094**
on the needs of NHS patients".[228] This claim was only partly true. It would have
taken out of the tort system the relatively low value claims, which are
disproportionately expensive to litigate, and it extended the possibility of some
form of compensation in low value claims for all patients. The qualifying criteria
for compensation would have remained proof of fault and causation, as under the
tort system, though the scope of that compensation was unclear. The proposed
scheme for brain-damaged babies, by removing proof of fault, was truly
revolutionary, but was not implemented.[229] Moreover, the NHS Redress scheme

---

[225] *Royal Commission on Civil Liability and Compensation for Personal Injury*, Cmnd.7054 (1978),
Vol.I, para.342.
[226] *Making Amends*, June 2003, pp.83–84.
[227] *Making Amends*, June 2003, para.33.
[228] *Making Amends*, June 2003, p.119.
[229] Though note that a potential no-fault scheme for some, but by no means all, brain-damaged babies
is currently under consideration again: see paras 1–060–1–062.

offered nothing for the patients who had sustained more serious injuries. Is the NHS concerned only about patients who have suffered less serious injuries? Why are the patients who suffer the greatest harm at the hands of the NHS to be left to the lottery of the tort system (which is rightly criticised in the report), though also having their rights to compensation curtailed in comparison with other accident victims? That did not look particularly patient-centred. Rather it looked as though the primary concern that prompted the CMO's review, the cost of medical negligence litigation, had strongly influenced the recommendations.

5. NHS REDRESS

(a) England

1–095   Some of the recommendations of the Chief Medical Officer in *Making Amends* were put into statutory form in the NHS Redress Act 2006.[230] The Act provides for the establishment of a scheme of NHS Redress, which would probably have been limited to claims for financial compensation up to £20,000.[231] The proposal in *Making Amends* for a no-fault compensation scheme for brain-damaged babies was not enacted. The Act created framework powers to enable the Secretary of State to create (in Regulations) a scheme for "redress to be provided without recourse to civil proceedings". Regulations have not been issued and it is widely assumed that NHS Redress has been dropped as a policy option in England, though the 2006 Act remains in place. It is only possible to provide a broad outline of the scheme for NHS Redress in England, since much of the substance depends on detail that would have been contained in the Regulations. However, a form of redress has been implemented in Wales.[232]

1–096   The intention was that NHS Redress would apply where a "qualifying liability in tort" arose in connection with the provision, as part of the health service in England, of qualifying services.[233] By s.1(4) a "qualifying liability in tort" means:

>   "(a)   in respect of or consequent upon personal injury or loss arising out of or in connection with breach of a duty of care owed to any person in connection with the diagnosis of illness, or the care or treatment of any patient, and
>   (b)   in consequence of any act or omission by a health care professional."

Strictly speaking, this would appear not to cover claims based on an absence of consent to treatment, since the tort of trespass to the person does not involve "breach of a duty of care". It seems improbable, however, that such claims were deliberately excluded from the scope of NHS Redress. What is clear, however, is

---

[230] The NHS Redress scheme was intended to apply only to claims arising from treatment provided by the English NHS (though not necessarily confined to treatment provided in the geographic area of England).

[231] For comment on the Act see A-M. Farrell and S. Devaney "Making Amends or making things worse? Clinical negligence reform and patient redress in England" (2007) 27 L.S. 630.

[232] See paras 1–102–1–107.

[233] NHS Redress Act 2006 s.1(2).

that entitlement to redress under the scheme was to be fault-based. It was clearly not intended to be a system of no-fault compensation.

The scheme applied initially to injuries sustained in a hospital (in England or elsewhere), but there is power to extend the scheme by regulations.[234] The scheme did not apply to primary medical services (i.e. general practitioners), primary dental services, general ophthalmic services, and pharmaceutical services.[235]

1–097

The scheme does not apply where a liability is or has been the subject of civil proceedings.[236] Section 6(5) provides that the scheme must provide for a settlement agreement under the scheme to include a waiver of the right to bring civil proceedings in respect of the liability to which the settlement relates; and under s.6(6) the scheme must provide for the termination of proceedings under the scheme if the liability to which the proceedings relate becomes the subject of civil proceedings. Thus, although the NHS Redress scheme did not remove the claimant's right to litigate as a condition of seeking redress, the two systems were intended effectively to be mutually exclusive. Instituting civil proceedings would have the effect of terminating the right to redress, and accepting an offer of settlement under the scheme would have the effect of preventing subsequent litigation. Where the claimant rejected the offer of redress, the option of litigation remained.

1–098

Under s.3(2) the scheme *must* provide for redress ordinarily to comprise:

1–099

(a)   the making of an offer of compensation in satisfaction of any right to bring civil proceedings in respect of the liability concerned,;
(b)   the giving of an explanation;
(c)   the giving of an apology; and
(d)   the giving of a report on the action which has been, or will be, taken to prevent similar cases arising;

but may specify circumstances in which one or more of those forms of redress is not required. Section 3(3) provides that a scheme *may*:

(a)   make provision for the compensation that may be offered to take the form of entry into a contract to provide care or treatment or of financial compensation, or both;
(b)   make provision about the circumstances in which different forms of compensation may be offered.

Where financial compensation is offered the scheme may: (a) make provision about the matters in respect of which financial compensation may be offered; and (b) make provision with respect to the assessment of the amount of any financial

---

[234] NHS Redress Act 2006 s.1(5) (by virtue of the definition of "qualifying services").
[235] NHS Redress Act 2006 s.1(6); though see s.1(7) enabling the Secretary of State by regulations to provide that services of a specified description are not to be regarded as primary dental services or primary medical services for this purpose.
[236] NHS Redress Act 2006 s.2(2).

compensation.[237] Section 3(5) provides that the scheme: (a) may specify an upper limit on the amount of financial compensation that may be included in an offer under the scheme; (b) if it does not specify a limit under paragraph (a), must specify an upper limit on the amount of financial compensation that may be included in such an offer in respect of pain and suffering; (c) may not specify any other limit on what may be included in such an offer by way of financial compensation. Under s.6(2) the scheme could also make provision:

(a)   about the investigation of cases under the scheme;
(b)   about the making of decisions about the application of the scheme;
(c)   for time limits in relation to acceptance of an offer of compensation under the scheme;
(d)   about the form and content of settlement agreements under the scheme;
(e)   for settlement agreements under the scheme to be subject in cases of a specified description to approval by a court;
(f)   about the termination of proceedings under the scheme.

1–100   The scheme must (a) make provision for the findings of an investigation of a case under the scheme to be recorded in a report, and (b) make provision for a copy of the report to be provided on request to the individual seeking redress,[238] except that the scheme may provide that no copy of an investigation report need be provided (a) before an offer is made under the scheme or proceedings under the scheme are terminated, or (b) in such other specified circumstances.[239]

1–101   There must be provision for the period during which a liability is the subject of proceedings under the scheme to be disregarded for the purposes of calculating whether any relevant limitation period has expired.[240] There must also be provision for legal advice without charge to individuals seeking redress under the scheme and for other services, including the services of medical experts,[241] and legal advice without charge in relation to the offer of redress and any settlement agreement.[242] The operation of the scheme for legal advice may be by reference to whether a potential provider is included in an authorised list[243]; and the provision of the services of medical experts must provide for such experts to be instructed jointly by the scheme authority and the individual seeking redress under the scheme.[244] Individuals seeking, or intending to seek, redress under the scheme must be provided with assistance, by way of representation or otherwise, to do so.[245] The scheme authority and the members of the scheme, in carrying out

---

[237] NHS Redress Act 2006 s.3(4).
[238] NHS Redress Act 2006 s.6(3).
[239] NHS Redress Act 2006 s.6(4).
[240] NHS Redress Act 2006 s.7(1).
[241] NHS Redress Act 2006 s.8(1).
[242] NHS Redress Act 2006 s.8(2).
[243] NHS Redress Act 2006 s.8(3).
[244] NHS Redress Act 2006 s.8(4). The intention was that the NHS Litigation Authority would act as the scheme authority.
[245] NHS Redress Act 2006 s.9(1).

their functions under the scheme, must have regard to the desirability of redress being provided without recourse to civil proceedings.[246]

(b) Wales

From 1 April 2011 the devolved administration in Wales brought into effect a NHS Redress scheme for Wales, which in many respects follows the structure of the scheme provided for in the NHS Redress Act 2006. The framework legislation is the NHS Redress (Wales) Measure 2008 with the detail set out in the National Health Service (Concerns, Complaints and Redress Arrangements) (Wales) Regulations 2011.[247] The legislation uses the term "concern" which is meant to cover any complaint, claim or reported patient safety incident in a single and more consistent system. The Redress element is set out in Pt 6 of the Regulations. It applies to a "qualifying liability" which means a liability in tort owed in respect of, or consequent upon, personal injury or loss arising out of or in connection with breach of a duty of care owed to any person in connection with the diagnosis of illness, or in the care or treatment of any patient (a) in consequence of any act or omission by a healthcare professional; and (b) which arises in connection with the provision of qualifying services.[248] This applies to a Welsh NHS body, which means a Local Health Board or NHS Trust managing a hospital or other establishment or facility wholly or mainly in Wales (i.e. it does not apply to general practitioners or independent providers of healthcare).

1–102

Compensation Where a concern is being investigated by a Welsh NHS body and it determines that a qualifying liability exists or may exist, it must decide whether or not an offer of redress should be made to the patient.[249] Redress can consist of: (a) the making of an offer of compensation in satisfaction of any right to bring civil proceedings in respect of a qualifying liability; (b) the giving of an explanation; (c) the making of a written apology; and (d) the giving of a report on the action which has been, or will be, taken to prevent similar cases arising.[250] Compensation can take the form of entry into a contract to provide care or treatment or financial compensation, or both.[251] An offer of redress by way of financial compensation cannot exceed £25,000,[252] but where this financial limit

1–103

---

[246] NHS Redress Act 2006 s.12.

[247] SI 2011/704 (W108). The Welsh government's guidance on NHS Redress, *Putting Things Right*, November 2013 provides a more detailed discussion of the scheme (available at *http://www.wales. nhs.uk/sites3/page.cfm?orgid=932&pid=50738* under the heading "Guidance for NHS on dealing with concerns about the NHS—Revised guidance version 3").

[248] National Health Service (Concerns, Complaints and Redress Arrangements) (Wales) Regulations 2011 reg.2(1).

[249] National Health Service (Concerns, Complaints and Redress Arrangements) (Wales) Regulations 2011 reg.25.

[250] National Health Service (Concerns, Complaints and Redress Arrangements) (Wales) Regulations 2011 reg.27(1).

[251] National Health Service (Concerns, Complaints and Redress Arrangements) (Wales) Regulations 2011 reg.27(2).

[252] The Regulations are silent on the question of the value of the "contract to provide care or treatment", but the reference to "financial compensation" not exceeding £25,000 suggests that the value of any "contract" should be disregarded. In any event, the NHS would normally have to provide

will be exceeded, if there is a qualifying liability, the Welsh NHS body may give consideration to making an offer of settlement outside the provisions of the Regulations.[253]

1–104   **Civil proceedings**   Redress is not available in relation to a liability that is or has been the subject of civil proceedings, and if the patient resorts to litigation during the process in which the NHS body is considering whether to make an offer of redress that consideration must cease.[254] During the period in which a claim is being considered for redress, the limitation period for bringing a common law action is suspended.[255]

1–105   **Investigation report and legal advice**   The findings of the investigation of a concern must be recorded in an investigation report, which must contain: (a) a copy of any medical evidence that has been commissioned in order to determine whether or not there is a qualifying liability or which has been commissioned to determine condition and prognosis; (b) a statement by the Welsh NHS body confirming whether or not, in its opinion, there is a qualifying liability; and (c) an explanation for that opinion.[256] There is also a requirement placed on the Welsh NHS body to ensure: (a) that legal advice (from firms of solicitors who have a recognised expertise in the field of clinical negligence) is available to the person seeking redress; and (b) if a medical expert needs to be instructed that instruction must be carried out jointly by the Welsh NHS body and the person who has notified the concern.[257] That legal advice should cover: (a) the joint instruction of medical experts; (b) any offer that is made; (c) any refusal to make an offer; and (d) any settlement agreement that is proposed. The cost of the legal advice and the costs arising from the instruction of medical experts must be borne entirely by the Welsh NHS body. An offer of redress, or a decision not to make an offer on the basis that there is no qualifying liability, must normally be notified within 12 months. The claimant has six months in which to reply.[258]

1–106   **Waiver of right to bring common law action**   An agreement to accept an offer of redress requires the claimant to waive any right to bring civil proceedings in respect of the qualifying liability. In the case of a child, or an adult who lacks capacity within the meaning of the Mental Capacity Act 2005, a settlement

---

treatment to a patient, so the contract may not be providing any more in the way of medical services than the NHS body would have had to provide anyway (though social care and some forms of rehabilitation would not necessarily fall within the NHS's remit).

[253] National Health Service (Concerns, Complaints and Redress Arrangements) (Wales) Regulations 2011 reg.29(3).
[254] National Health Service (Concerns, Complaints and Redress Arrangements) (Wales) Regulations 2011 reg.28.
[255] National Health Service (Concerns, Complaints and Redress Arrangements) (Wales) Regulations 2011 reg.30.
[256] National Health Service (Concerns, Complaints and Redress Arrangements) (Wales) Regulations 2011 reg.31, subject to exceptions listed in reg.31(4).
[257] National Health Service (Concerns, Complaints and Redress Arrangements) (Wales) Regulations 2011 reg.32.
[258] National Health Service (Concerns, Complaints and Redress Arrangements) (Wales) Regulations 2011 reg.33.

agreement will be subject to the approval of the court, but the NHS body must pay the reasonable legal costs associated with obtaining approval.[259]

In many respects the Welsh scheme of NHS Redress mirrors the proposals **1–107** contained in the unimplemented English scheme. Bringing together complaints and claims into a single, consistent process and seeking to develop a more open response to adverse events is laudable. Redress provides potential access to compensation for patients with small claims that they may not otherwise be able to afford to bring, though the £25,000 limit on access to the scheme may look somewhat arbitrary to the patient with a claim valued at £25,100. On the other hand, the process lacks independence; the NHS is, in effect, investigating itself, and there is no mechanism for an appeal against a refusal of compensation.[260]

6. HUMAN RIGHTS

The incorporation of the European Convention for the Protection of Human **1–108** Rights and Fundamental Freedoms into domestic law through the Human Rights Act 1998 has had some, though limited, impact on the way in which the courts deal with claims for medical negligence. A conventional common law action for medical negligence involves three elements. It must be shown that: (1) the defendant owed a duty of care to the claimant; (2) that there was breach of that duty; and (3) that this breach caused the claimant's damage. The vast majority of claims involve disputes about the last two elements: breach and causation. The Human Rights Act has not had a significant effect on these two "bread and butter" issues for medical negligence litigation. But there is some room for human rights jurisprudence to influence judicial perceptions of the scope of the duty of care in negligence. The interplay between the law of torts and human rights principles can shape the courts' understanding of and approach to arguments about the duty of care.

In some instances the courts have used Convention Rights effectively to sidestep **1–109** the limitations of the common law principles of negligence. The decision that a claimant's human rights have been breached is not directly equivalent to a finding that the defendant is liable in tort,[261] and the criteria for breach of a Convention right and breach of a common law duty of care are different, as are the rules on awards of damages.[262] Nonetheless, where claimants have established a breach of

---

[259] National Health Service (Concerns, Complaints and Redress Arrangements) (Wales) Regulations 2011 reg.33.

[260] For further discussion of Welsh NHS Redress see: M. Rosser, "The Changing Face of Clinical Negligence in Wales" [2010] J.P.I.L. 162; A-L. Ferguson and E. Braithwaite, "Putting Things Right in Wales" (2012) 18 Clinical Risk 6; M. Rosser "The Welsh NHS Redress Arrangements—Are they putting things right for Welsh patients?" (2014) 20 Clinical Risk 144.

[261] Although there is an argument that the Human Rights Act 1998 creates a new form of tort action for breach of statutory duty: see the Law Commission, *Damages under the Human Rights Act 1998*, Law Com. No.266, 2000, para.4.20.

[262] See Fairgrieve [2001] P.L. 695. For discussion of the principles to be applied to the assessment of damages for breach of the European Convention on Human Rights when patients detained under the Mental Health Act 1983 were denied speedy hearings to review their detention, contrary to art.5.4 of the Convention, see *R. (on the application of KB) v Mental Health Review Tribunal, Secretary of State for Health* [2003] EWHC 193 (Admin); [2004] Q.B. 936. See also *Anufrijeva v Souhwark London*

their Convention rights in circumstances where tort claims have previously failed, the courts may be willing to reconsider the common law position, or at least to weigh the balance more carefully between claimants' rights and defendants' interests.[263]

1–110 The clearest example is *JD v East Berkshire Community Health NHS Trust*[264] where the Court of Appeal concluded that the jurisprudence of the European Court of Human Rights meant that the decision of the House of Lords in *X (Minors) v Bedfordshire County Council; M (A Minor) v Newham London Borough Council*[265] could not survive the Human Rights Act 1998.[266] It would, said the Court of Appeal:

> "...no longer be legitimate to rule that, as a matter of law, no common law duty of care is owed to a child in relation to the investigation of suspected child abuse and the initiation and pursuit of care proceedings."[267]

The House of Lords confirmed the Court of Appeal's decision to depart from *X v Bedfordshire County Council*, holding that doctors and social workers who suspected that a child had been the victim of abuse do owe a duty to the child to exercise reasonable care in making judgments about the child's welfare (whether it be doctors making a diagnosis of non-accidental injury or the social workers deciding whether to take the child into care).[268] Their Lordships accepted the logic of the Court of Appeal's argument that the jurisprudence emanating from the European Court of Human Rights meant that *X v Bedfordshire County Council* could not survive the Human Rights Act, and it was irrelevant that the events in question had occurred before the Act came into force. On the other hand, the fact that the parents might have a claim under the Convention for breach of art.8 did not persuade their Lordships that a duty of care should be

---

Borough Council [2003] EWCA Civ 1406; [2004] Q.B. 1124 for discussion of the principles to be applied to the assessment of damages for infringement of art.8.

[263] For example, the decision of the House of Lords in *Arthur JS Hall & Co. (A Firm) v Simons* [2002] 1 A.C. 615 to abolish the common law immunity from suit of advocates for negligence in the conduct of trials appears to have been significantly influenced by the prospect that a "blanket immunity" would not be consistent with art.6 of the Convention. In the medical context, it is clear that the decision of the Supreme Court in *Montgomery v Lanarkshire Health Board* [2015] UKSC 11; [2015] A.C. 1430 to change the law on "informed consent" in favour of a more patient-oriented test was at least influenced by decisions of the European Court of Human Rights (per Lords Kerr and Reed at [80]).

[264] [2003] EWCA Civ 1151; [2004] Q.B. 558.

[265] [1995] 2 A.C. 633, in which the House of Lords held that a psychiatrist conducting an interview for the purpose of identifying whether a child had been abused, and if so the identity of the abuser, owed no duty of care in negligence to the child or her mother. See paras 2–092 et seq.

[266] In *TP and KM v UK* [2001] 2 F.L.R. 549 it was held that, on the facts of *M (A Minor) v Newham London BC*, the failure of the social services authority properly to involve the child's mother in the decision-making process which would have avoided the authority's error, constituted a breach of art.8 of the Convention, the right to respect for private and family life. See also *Z v UK* [2001] 2 F.L.R. 612, ECtHR, awarding damages for breach of Convention rights on the same facts as *X (Minors) v Bedfordshire County Council* (negligent failure to take into local authority care children who were subject to abuse and neglect).

[267] [2003] EWCA Civ 1151 at [84].

[268] *JD v East Berkshire Community Health NHS Trust* [2005] UKHL 23; [2005] 2 A.C. 373.

owed to the parents of a child who is suspected to be the victim of abuse, because the parents' interests are in potential conflict with the child's interests.[269]

Subsequently, in *L v Pembrokeshire County Council*[270] the claimant argued that the court should depart from the majority decision in *JD v East Berkshire Community Health NHS Trust* against the imposition of a duty of care owed to the parents, on facts that occurred after the coming into force of the Human Rights Act 1998. The trial judge, Field J, rejected the argument, suggesting that if the common law considered that the public interest required that there be no duty of care owed to the parents, then that should be taken into account when considering whether there had been any breach of the parents' Convention rights by applying art.8(2) "so as to give effect to the public interest identified" in *JD*.[271] On this approach, far from the common law responding to the demands of the Convention, the Convention would be interpreted in a manner to make it consistent with the common law. The Court of Appeal agreed that the imposition of a duty of care owed to the parents:

> "…would fundamentally distort the law of negligence in this area, putting at risk the protection for children which it provides in its present form. Article 8, with its wholly different legal construct of engaging liability without reference to a duty of care, complements it in facilitating a similar protection through mechanism for justification. The provision of a discrete Convention remedy through the medium of the HRA, does not, on that account, necessitate change of the common law in the manner proposed."[272]

The cogency of the reasoning in *JD v East Berkshire Community Health NHS Trust* remained untouched by art.8.[273]

It seems likely that the potential for tension between the common law and the human rights jurisprudence will continue to trouble the courts. On one view, the common law should seek to adjust to the demands of the Convention. After all,

1–111

1–112

---

[269] Lord Bingham, in a dissenting speech on this point, took the logic of the human rights jurisprudence a step further, considering that since the parents have Convention rights which may also be breached, they should also have a common law remedy for negligence. For Lord Bingham, although the two rights would not necessarily be co-extensive, if potential defendants had to worry about breaching the parents' Convention rights, they would still have an "apparent" conflict of duties.

[270] [2007] EWCA Civ 446; [2007] 1 W.L.R. 2991; (2007) 96 B.M.L.R. 158.

[271] [2006] EWHC 1029 (QB); [2007] P.I.Q.R. P1; [2006] Lloyd's Rep. Med. 383.

[272] [2007] EWCA Civ 446; [2007] 1 W.L.R. 2991; (2007) 96 B.M.L.R. 158 at [55]. Art.8 of the Convention also allows for public authorities to intervene in family life in order to protect children from possible abuse. See e.g. *K v United Kingdom* (38000/05) [2009] 1 F.L.R. 274; (2009) 48 E.H.R.R. 29 *at [36]*, ECtHR: "The authorities, medical and social, have duties to protect children and cannot be held liable every time genuine and reasonably-held concerns about the safety of children vis-à-vis members of their families are proved, retrospectively, to have been misguided." This point was reiterated in *MAK v United Kingdom* (45901/05) [2010] 2 F.L.R. 451; (2010) 51 E.H.R.R. 14 at [69].

[273] [2007] EWCA Civ 446; [2007] 1 W.L.R. 2991; (2007) B.M.L.R. 158 at [41], where Auld LJ also observed that "the advent of Article 8 to our domestic law, bringing with it a discrete right to children and parents of respect for their family life, does not undermine or weaken as a matter of public policy the primacy of the need to protect children from abuse, or the risk of abuse, from, among others, their parents. Nor, when those interests are or may be in conflict, does Article 8 so enhance the status of family life as, in the balancing exercise involved, would require the development of the common law by the introduction of a duty of care to parents suspected of abusing their children, a duty precluded by that public policy."

the common law may appear in a somewhat unfavourable light if it cannot be regarded as consistent with basic principles of human rights. On the other hand, since claimants have a domestic remedy for breach of their Convention rights in the form of an action under the Human Rights Act 1998, it is arguable that there is no need to bring the two systems into harmony. The claimant can have a common law action in tort or for breach of contract and a parallel action for any breach of her Convention rights. These different perspectives were on display in *Smith v Chief Constable of Sussex*.[274] The claimant brought an action in negligence alleging that the police had failed to act to prevent his former partner from attacking him, despite having been informed of previous attacks and death threats to the claimant. The problem for the claimant was that there were two decisions of the House of Lords to the effect that the police will normally owe no duty of care to a potential victim of crime.[275] The House of Lords held that no duty of care in negligence was owed by the police to the claimant.[276]

1–113   On the question of the interaction between the common law and Convention rights, Lord Bingham, in a dissenting speech, agreed with the comments of Pill LJ and Rimer LJ in the Court of Appeal.[277] Although the existence of a Convention right could not call for the "instant manufacture of a corresponding common law right where none exists" nonetheless:

> "...one would ordinarily be surprised if conduct which violated a fundamental right or freedom of the individual did not find a reflection in a body of law ordinarily as sensitive to human needs as the common law, and it is demonstrable that the common law in some areas has evolved in a direction signalled by the Convention."[278]

On the other hand, Lord Hope considered that:

> "...the common law, with its own system of limitation periods and remedies, should be allowed to stand on its own feet side by side with the alternative remedy."[279]

If there were gaps in the common law, they could be dealt with in domestic law under the Human Rights Act. Lord Brown also rejected the argument that, in a case such as *Smith*, the common law should develop "to reflect the Strasbourg jurisprudence". Given that the Human Rights Act provided for claims to be brought, it was "quite simply unnecessary now to develop the common law to

---

[274] [2008] UKHL 50; [2009] 1 A.C. 225.
[275] See *Hill v Chief Constable of West Yorkshire* [1989] A.C. 53 and *Brooks v Commissioner of Police of the Metropolis* [2005] UKHL 24; [2005] 1 W.L.R. 1495; and more recently see *Michael v Chief Constable of South Wales* [2015] UKSC 2; [2015] A.C. 1732.
[276] [2008] UKHL 50; [2009] 1 A.C. 225, applying *Hill v Chief Constable of West Yorkshire* [1989] A.C. 53 and *Brooks v Commissioner of Police of the Metropolis* [2005] UKHL 24, [2005] 1 W.L.R. 1495.
[277] [2008] EWCA Civ 39; [2008] P.I.Q.R. P12. Pill LJ had commented, at [53], that: "there is a strong case for developing the common law action for negligence in the light of Convention rights"; and Rimer LJ said, at [45]: "where a common law duty covers the same ground as a Convention right, it should, so far as practicable, develop in harmony with it."
[278] [2008] UKHL 50; [2009] 1 A.C. 225 at [58], citing *JD v East Berkshire Community NHS Trust*.
[279] [2008] UKHL 50; [2009] 1 A.C. 225 at [82].

provide a parallel cause of action".[280] Convention claims had "very different objectives from civil actions". Whereas civil actions were designed to compensate claimants for their losses, Convention claims were intended to uphold minimum human rights standards and to vindicate those rights.[281] In *Michael v Chief Constable of South Wales*,[282] a case with similar facts to *Smith v Chief Constable of Sussex*, Lord Toulson, delivering the majority judgment of the Supreme Court, applied the same reasoning to reject the claimant's argument that where there was a breach of Convention rights the common law should reflect that by providing an additional remedy in the tort of negligence. If there was no basis, applying orthodox common law principles, for a claimed duty of care then there was no rationale:

"...for gold plating the claimant's Convention rights by providing compensation on a different basis from the claim under the Human Rights Act 1998."[283]

Prisoners   There are some areas where there is a clear overlap between a   1–114
common law duty of care and a breach of Convention rights. For example, in *Keenan v UK*[284] it was held that the suicide of a prisoner, who was a known suicide risk, in police custody could give rise to a breach of art.3 ("No one shall be subjected to torture or to inhuman or degrading treatment or punishment"), arising out of a failure to provide adequate medical supervision. But a duty of care would be held to exist at common law in these circumstances, although there might be some debate as to the precise measures necessary to meet that duty.[285] Similarly, in *McGlinchey v UK*[286] (where a common law negligence action had been abandoned) the European Court of Human Rights held that inadequate medical treatment in prison could give rise to a breach of art.3. A prisoner with a long history of heroin abuse and asthma, in a poor state of general health, suffered serious weight loss and dehydration which was due to a week of uncontrolled vomiting symptoms and an inability to eat or hold down fluids. She collapsed and was rushed to hospital where she subsequently had a heart attack. She died three weeks' later. The Court held that the prison authorities' failure to provide accurate means of establishing her weight loss, and the failure to take more effective steps to treat her condition such as admission to hospital to ensure

---

[280] [2008] UKHL 50; [2009] 1 A.C. 225 at [136]. See also *Jain v Trent Strategic Health Authority* [2009] UKHL 4; [2009] 1 A.C. 853 at [136] per Lord Scott rejecting the suggestion that it was appropriate to develop the common law of negligence so as to be consistent with the Convention since breaches of the Convention could now be remedied under domestic law (though on the facts of *Jain* the claimants did not have a domestic Convention remedy because the events occurred before the Human Rights Act 1998 came into force).
[281] [2008] UKHL 50; [2009] 1 A.C. 225 at [138].
[282] [2015] UKSC 2; [2015] A.C. 1732.
[283] [2015] UKSC 2; [2015] A.C. 1732 at [125].
[284] (2001) 10 B.H.R.C. 319.
[285] cf. *Knight v Home Office* [1990] 3 All E.R. 237, para.4–152.
[286] [2003] Lloyd's Rep. Med. 264; (2003) 72 B.M.L.R. 168.

the intake of medication and fluids intravenously or to obtain more expert assistance in controlling vomiting, constituted a breach of art.3.[287]

1-115   **Duties owed to third parties?**   There are also some situations where the existence of a duty of care would be the subject of considerable debate, where Convention rights could influence the balance of the argument. For example, it is not clear that English law would conclude that doctors owe a duty to a third party to warn that their patient is potentially dangerous to that third party (e.g. a psychiatric patient who has made genuine threats to harm others or a patient with a highly infectious condition[288]). It might be argued that the failure to warn someone known to be at risk of a life-threatening condition constitutes a breach of art.2 ("Everyone's right to life shall be protected by law"). Similarly, in appropriate circumstances art.3 can impose a positive obligation on a public authority to prevent harm to individuals caused by other private individuals.[289] Thus, although the court may take the line from *Smith v Chief Constable of Sussex* and *Michael v Chief Constable of South Wales* that there is no need for a tort claim if the claimant already has a Convention claim, it is at least arguable that Convention rights could be called in aid to point the common law in a particular direction.

1-116   **Consent to treatment and breach of confidentiality**   Beyond claims based in negligence, it is apparent that some forms of medical treatment without consent may breach human rights principles. Although the European Court of Human Rights has held that the compulsory treatment of a psychiatric patient does not necessarily breach art.3, because a measure which is a therapeutic necessity is not to be regarded as inhuman or degrading, that medical necessity must be convincingly shown to exist.[290] This has led the Court of Appeal to modify the traditional approach to challenges by patients to compulsory treatment under the Mental Health Act 1983.[291] In *Montgomery v Lanarkshire Health Board*[292] the Supreme Court clearly took account of decisions of the European Court of Human Rights in deciding to adopt a "prudent patient" standard for information disclosure in place of the *Bolam* test. It would also be arguable that to enrol a patient into a therapeutic programme of medical research without informing the patient that the treatment was experimental would constitute "inhuman or

---

[287] See also *Şenturk v Turkey (13424/09)* (2013) ECHR 107; [2013] E.H.R.L.R. 439 where the Court held that denial of access to appropriate emergency treatment because the patient did not have the money to pay a deposit towards her treatment amounted to a breach of art.2 (the patient died in the course of transfer to another hospital).
[288] See paras 2–165 et seq. and paras 2–145 et seq.
[289] See *Z v UK* [2001] 2 F.L.R. 612.
[290] *Herczegfalvy v Austria* (1992) 15 E.H.R.R. 437.
[291] See para.6–094.
[292] [2015] UKSC 11; [2015] A.C. 1430 at [80]: "Under the stimulus of the Human Rights Act 1998, the courts have become increasingly conscious of the extent to which the common law reflects fundamental values. ... these include the value of self-determination ... As well as underlying aspects of the common law, that value also underlies the right to respect for private life protected by article 8 of the European Convention on Human Rights." See generally paras 7–015 et seq. In *Csoma v Romania* [2013] ECHR 8759/05, ECtHR, the failure to involve a patient in the choice of medical treatment by not informing her of the risks so that she could not make an informed choice was held to constitute a breach of the patient's art.8 rights.

degrading treatment" contrary to art.3, no matter how medically necessary the treatment, and even if the patient has expressly consented to the specific procedure. Similarly, human rights arguments have been invoked in the context of claims based on breach of confidentiality, though in practice art.8 (the right to respect for private and family life) has not proved to be significantly easier for claimants to use than the law of confidentiality.[293]

Test for breach of Convention rights   Where claimants do rely on the Convention, the courts are faced with determining the appropriate threshold test to determine whether there has been a breach, and the test may vary depending upon the nature of the state obligation that is challenged, even under the same article of the Convention. In the case of an ordinary patient in hospital "simple negligence" resulting in the death of the patient is not in itself a breach of art.2.[294] However, in the case of a compulsorily detained patient under the Mental Health Act 1983 the position may be different. In *Savage v South Essex Partnership NHS Foundation Trust*[295] a detained patient who was a known suicide risk absconded from hospital and committed suicide. The House of Lords accepted that since detained patients are, like prisoners, vulnerable due both to their mental state and because they are under the control of the hospital authorities art.2 was engaged. Whilst recognising that medical staff have to make a judgment balancing the potentially adverse effect of too much supervision on the patient's mental health condition and the risk of suicide, the test for whether there had been a breach of art.2 was whether members of the hospital staff knew or ought to have known that there was "a real and immediate risk of a patient committing suicide". If so, then art.2 imposes an operational obligation on the medical staff to do all that can reasonably be expected of them to prevent it.[296] This test imposes a higher threshold for the claimant to meet and so it is more difficult to establish a breach of this art.2 duty than "mere negligence".[297] In *Rabone v Pennine Care NHS Foundation Trust*[298] the Supreme Court held that the same principles applied to voluntary (i.e. non-detained) psychiatric patients in hospital.

1–117

In many of the cases where human rights arguments have been raised the court has concluded that the European Convention has added nothing to the existing

1–118

---

[293] Though the courts have used art.8 to develop the new tort of misuse of private information, which may provide a parallel cause of action to an allegation of breach of patient confidentiality: see paras 8–020 to 8–029.

[294] *Powell v UK* (2000) 30 E.H.R.R. CD 152; [2000] Inquest L.R. 19, ECtHR—something in the nature of "gross negligence" is required. In *R. (on the application of Takoushis) v HM Coroner for Inner North London* [2005] EWCA Civ 1440; [2006] 1 W.L.R. 461 at [96] Sir Anthony Clarke MR commented that gross negligence meant "the kind of negligence which would be sufficient to sustain a charge of manslaughter".

[295] [2008] UKHL 74; [2009] 1 A.C. 681.

[296] [2008] UKHL 74; [2009] 1 A.C. 681 at [66] and [72]. The case was referred back to the High Court for a trial on whether there had been a real and immediate risk of suicide and whether the hospital had done all that could reasonably have been expected to avoid it: see *Savage v South Essex Partnership NHS Foundation Trust* [2010] EWHC 865 (QB); [2010] P.I.Q.R. P14; [2010] Med. L.R. 292.

[297] See paras 4–185 and 4–186.

[298] [2012] UKSC 2; [2012] 2 A.C. 72; see para.4–184. *Rabone* was approved by the European Court of Human Rights in *Reynolds v United Kingdom* (2694/08) (2012) 55 E.H.R.R. 35.

law, but it would be over-optimistic to think that the common law has nothing to learn from the human rights jurisprudence. Where questions of human rights have been raised they are dealt with in this book in the context of the substantive issues that the cases address.

CHAPTER 2

THE BASIS OF LIABILITY

The nature of the relationship between doctors and patients is determined largely   **2-001**
by the practice of the medical profession, and shaped by a strong commitment to
long-standing principles of medical ethics. The law plays a significant role,
however, in providing a structure within which the doctor–patient relationship is
conducted. Whether it is the civil law or the criminal law which is invoked, legal
rules can only set the outer limits of acceptable conduct—a minimum standard of
professional behaviour—leaving the question of "ideal" standards of practice to
the profession itself. Some doctors seem to believe that the law sets too high a
standard, which does not take account of the realities of medical practice, but the
courts apply the same principles, whether they be from the law of tort, contract or
equity, that are used for any other section of the community when disputes
between individuals arise. Accordingly, the professional liability of medical
practitioners is determined by the rules of tort, contract or equity.[1]

In practice most claims for medical malpractice are brought in tort, and of these   **2-002**
the vast majority are for the tort of negligence. This is reflected in the structure of
this chapter, the bulk of which deals with the circumstances in which a doctor
will be held to owe a duty of care in the tort of negligence. The chapter begins
with a section on contractual liability which, in theory, governs the respective
rights and responsibilities of patients and doctors in the private sector. It will be
seen, however, that in practical terms there is very little difference between the
obligations undertaken by medical practitioners in private practice and those
imposed on colleagues working in the NHS. All doctors owe a duty to their
patients to exercise reasonable care in carrying out their professional skills of

---

[1] This book is concerned with civil liability, although there are occasions when a doctor's conduct
could give rise to liability under both the civil and the criminal law. For example, instances of gross
negligence could lead to a charge of manslaughter: *R. v Bateman* (1925) 94 L.J.K.B. 791; *R. v
Adomako* [1994] 5 Med. L.R. 277. The defendant's negligence will be "gross" where it was "truly
exceptionally bad" and demonstrated "a high degree of indifference to an obvious and serious risk to
the patient's life": *R. v Misra* [2004] EWCA Crim 2375; [2005] 1 Cr.App.R. 21; *R. v Sellu* [2016]
EWCA Crim 1716; [2017] 4 W.L.R. 64. For an argument that it is inappropriate to use a test based on
gross negligence in the medical context see O. Quick, "Medicine, mistakes and manslaughter: a
criminal combination?" (2010) 69 C.L.J. 186. A surgeon who performed unnecessary breast surgery
on numerous patients was sentenced to 20 years' imprisonment for wounding and wounding with
intent: *http://www.bbc.co.uk/news/uk-england-40815668*; and a surgeon who, knowing that he was a
Hepatitis B carrier, but nonetheless continued to practise surgery, infecting 19 patients and putting
hundreds of others at risk, was jailed having been convicted of the offence of public nuisance: *The
Times*, 30 September 1994; see Mulholland (1995) 11 P.N. 70. In some circumstances a breach of
patient confidentiality may give rise to a criminal offence: see Health and Social Care Act 2008
ss.76–77.

diagnosis, advice and treatment,[2] and the situations in which a stricter duty will be applied are quite rare. In addition to the contractual or tortious duty to exercise reasonable care, medical practitioners are subject to a duty of confidentiality in respect of information about patients acquired in their capacity as doctors. This obligation is dealt with in Ch.8.

1. CONTRACT

2–003
Most patients treated under the National Health Service do not enter into a contractual relationship with their doctor or the hospital where they receive treatment, although it had been suggested that there is a contract between a patient and his general practitioner, since the addition of the patient's name to the general practitioner's list increases the doctor's remuneration under his terms of service and this might constitute consideration by the patient.[3] An argument of this nature was accepted in the Canadian case of *Pittman Estate v Bain*[4] in which a hospital claimed that there was no contractual relationship with a patient because there was no consideration, the payment to the hospital for the patient's care coming not from the patient but from the government through universal health care plans. It was held that patients provide indirect or non-monetary consideration for their hospital care. They contributed indirectly through taxes and health premiums, and they also conferred a benefit on a hospital by providing the hospital with patients, without which the hospital would not operate. A hospital benefited in terms of government financial compensation and enhancement of its reputation when patients chose it for their care. Lang J concluded that by agreeing to submit himself for treatment at the hospital, the claimant conferred a benefit on the hospital, which received funding for its cardiac services as a result of its overall patient care. This was sufficient consideration to support a contract between the hospital and the patient.[5]

2–004
In theory, the same rationale would apply to patients receiving hospital treatment in the NHS, but in *Reynolds v The Health First Medical Group*[6] the argument was rejected. The increased remuneration to a general practitioner arising from the patient permitting her name to be added to the practitioner's list did not constitute consideration for a contract. Rather, the position was exactly parallel with

---

[2] The meaning of "reasonable care" is considered in Chs 3 and 4.

[3] Earlier editions of *Jackson & Powell on Professional Liability* had argued that this might be a possibility, but in the 5th edn (London: Sweet & Maxwell, 2002), paras 12.005–12.007 the editors concluded that it is no longer tenable, particularly in light of *Reynolds v The Health First Medical Group* [2000] Lloyd's Rep. Med. 240, below. See now *Jackson & Powell on Professional Liability*, 8th edn (London: Sweet & Maxwell, 2017), para.13–002. See also the *Royal Commission on Civil Liability and Compensation for Personal Injury*, Cmnd.7054 (1978), Vol.I, para.1313, stating that there is no contract where treatment is provided under the NHS. Patients who pay a prescription charge for medicinal products supplied on prescription under the NHS do not obtain the products under a contract of sale, but by virtue of the pharmacist's statutory duty to supply them: *Pfizer Corpn v Ministry of Health* [1965] A.C. 512. Presumably, the position of patients who make a partial payment for services under the NHS (e.g. for dental treatment) is similar.

[4] (1994) 112 D.L.R. (4th) 257, Ont Ct, Gen Div.

[5] (1994) 112 D.L.R. (4th) 257, Ont Ct, Gen Div at 334.

[6] [2000] Lloyd's Rep. Med. 240, Hitchin County Court.

prescription charges.[7] Moreover, the statutory context in which a general practitioner's services were provided to patients (including the National Health Service (General Medical Services) Regulations 1992[8]) left no room for bargaining between doctor and patient, and negated any suggestion that the parties intended to enter into contractual relations.

The claimant in *Reynolds v The Health First Medical Group*[9] had sought to put her claim in contract in order to avoid the effect of the House of Lords' decision in *McFarlane v Tayside Health Board*[10] that the financial costs of raising a healthy child were not recoverable in the tort of negligence. In that case Lord Slynn had suggested that if a client wants to be able to recover such costs "he or she must do so by an appropriate contract". It is not clear what an appropriate contract would consist of. Even if it could be established that the doctor had warranted the outcome[11] it would not necessarily follow that the scope of liability extended to the child-rearing costs, applying the normal rules of remoteness of damage in contract. Thus, in *Rees v Darlington Memorial Hospital NHS Trust*[12] Lord Scott considered that, in a case like *McFarlane*, the "same result must be reached whether the claimant was a private patient or an NHS patient".[13]

2–005

In *Dow v Tayside University Hospitals NHS Trust*[14] it was held that it would be possible under Scots law (which has no requirement of consideration as part of the formation of a contract) for a doctor providing treatment under the National Health Service (Scotland) Act 1978 to enter into a contractual relationship with a patient, but only where it was clear that the doctor concerned was, exceptionally, entering into a contract and was not relying on the statutory relationship alone.[15] Such a contractual obligation would have to be expressed in clear terms, demonstrating an intention to create an additional liability on the doctor's part in order to correspond with the requirements for a unilateral promise.

2–006

In *Wylie v Grosset*[16] it was held that a doctor had entered into a contractual relationship with a patient in the context of a clinical drugs trial. The claimant had

2–007

---

[7] Applying *Pfizer Corpn v Ministry of Health* [1965] A.C. 512.
[8] See now the National Health Service (General Medical Services Contracts) Regulations 2015 (SI 2015/1862) and the National Health Service (Personal Medical Services Agreements) Regulations 2015 (SI 2015/1879).
[9] [2000] Lloyd's Rep. Med. 240, Hitchin County Court.
[10] [2000] 2 A.C. 59. See paras 2–055 et seq.
[11] Which is particularly difficult to prove: see paras 2–017 to 2–018.
[12] [2003] UKHL 52; [2004] 1 A.C. 309; [2003] 4 All E.R. 987.
[13] [2003] UKHL 52; [2004] 1 A.C. 309; [2003] 4 All E.R. 987 at [133]; see also *ARB v IVF Hammersmith* [2017] EWHC 2438 (QB) and para.2–078.
[14] 2006 S.L.T. (Sh. Ct) 141; 2006 S.C.L.R. 865.
[15] As Sheriff Fletcher observed (2006 S.L.T. (Sh. Ct) 141; 2006 S.C.L.R. 865 at [19]): "Having said that, it is not easy to envisage a situation in which a doctor providing services under the National Health Service would consider it appropriate to enter into an additional contract in relation to the services. The question arises as to why and in what circumstances the doctor would do so? Perhaps he might find himself being asked by a patient whom he had advised to undergo specific treatment, to guarantee its success before the patient would accept the advice, and in order to persuade the patient to follow the advice he might find himself unwisely guaranteeing it. Clearly that would not be an appropriate response to the patient's misgivings when it might result in its being held that that was a unilateral promise of success."
[16] [2011] CSOH 89; 2011 S.L.T. 60.

early stage Parkinson's disease and was recruited by his doctor into a clinical trial of a drug for treatment of that disease produced by Schwarz Pharma AG. The doctor was the principal investigator of the trial. It was alleged that the drug led some patients to develop serious compulsive behaviour, which included gambling, and that the claimant developed an uncontrollable urge to gamble and had lost £85,000. There was no question of negligence, since the issue of the drug causing compulsive behaviour only became apparent after the claimant's problem gambling, and so not foreseeable. There was no agreement or undertaking that the claimant could enforce against Schwarz Pharma. Thus the claim relied on a contractual relationship between the claimant and his doctor and the hospital where he received treatment. Judge Wise QC held that the patient information sheet setting out information about the clinical trial constituted an offer by the defendants and the consent form signed by the claimant was the acceptance. The whole arrangement was bilateral and involved the co-operation of the patient in the trial to which he had agreed.[17] The judge accepted that, unlike *Dow v Tayside University Hospitals NHS Trust*, the claimant had entered into a contractual relationship in addition to and quite separate from the statutory relationship for NHS treatment. However, the judge went on to hold that the contract did not create a legally enforceable right to compensation for injury sustained as a result of participation in the clinical trial in the absence of fault by the defendants. The patient information sheet stated that:

"Compensation for any injury caused by taking part in this study will be in accordance with the guidelines of the Association of the British Pharmaceutical Industry (ABPI). Broadly speaking the APBI guidelines recommend that the sponsor without legal commitment, should compensate you without you having to prove that it is at fault."

Those words, said the judge, did not amount to a guarantee that compensation would actually be paid. They might have created an expectation of compensation in appropriate circumstances but they did not impose a legally enforceable obligation. They did no more than assure the recipient that there was an appropriate system for compensation but did not say that compensation "will be paid".[18]

2–008 **Who is a party to the contract?** Beyond the context of the NHS, as a general rule, where there is a contract it will be perfectly obvious who the parties to that contract are, and therefore to whom any contractual obligation is owed. In *West Bromwich Albion Football Club Ltd v El-Safty*,[19] however, a patient who did not pay for his medical treatment, and who did not consider that he had entered into a

---

[17] [2011] CSOH 89; 2011 S.L.T. 60 at [20].
[18] [2011] CSOH 89; 2011 S.L.T. 60 at [22]. The judge explained why she came to this conclusion: "The three caveats contained within the second sentence reinforce this. The words 'broadly speaking', 'recommend', and 'should', all suggest that while the sponsor really ought to pay compensation for any injury caused by taking part in the study, it is not bound to do so. The knowledge available to the pursuer was all that contained in the Patient Information Sheet which runs to some eight pages. A reasonable person having read through the document would not assume that compensation would always be available without proving fault. He would understand that the applicable guidelines contained a recommendation that that would be the case, but no guarantee."
[19] [2006] EWCA Civ 1299; [2007] P.I.Q.R. P7; [2007] LS Law Med. 50.

contractual relationship with the defendant orthopaedic surgeon, was found to have a contractual relationship with the surgeon. West Bromwich Albion FC Ltd ("WBA"), a Premiership football club, sought damages from the defendant, who had negligently treated one of its players, Michael Appleton, with the result that the player was unable to play professionally again. The player's contract with WBA required him to submit to such medical examinations and treatment as might be indicated by the club's medical advisers, at no expense to the player. WBA arranged an appointment for the player with the defendant, and WBA's representative went with the player to see the defendant. They accepted the defendant's negligent advice that the player should undergo reconstructive surgery. WBA had insurance cover from BUPA to cover the cost of medical treatment of its players, and WBA had referred many players to the defendant for advice and treatment in the past. The defendant's fees were paid direct by BUPA. WBA sued the defendant in both contract and tort,[20] claiming damages for the loss of the value of the player's contract, the cost of replacing him, and lost wages. The trial judge, Royce J, had accepted the defendant's argument that there was no intention to create legal relations and therefore no contract.[21] The Court of Appeal rejected this, however, concluding that there was a contract, or retainer, for medical services for reward, and the real issue was: with whom had the contract been made?[22] As Mummery LJ put it, Mr El-Safty expected to be paid by someone for the treatment, even if there was no insurance cover: "He was not operating a pro bono private medical service."[23]

There was no express contract between the defendant and WBA, so the question was whether a contract could be implied. For Rix LJ the natural objective interpretation of WBA, through its senior physiotherapist, booking a consultation with the defendant to see the player was the making of a contract for the patient himself, i.e. Michael Appleton. Although the player was entitled, given his contract with WBA, to consider that he would not have to meet the cost of the treatment, that did not prevent him from:

2–009

> "…having the natural contractual relationship with a doctor which a patient enjoying private medical services should objectively be regarded as entering into."[24]

The player's subjective view that he had no contractual relationship with the defendant was irrelevant. As Rix LJ observed, there was no evidence that the defendant knew of the terms of the player's contract with WBA, and if Mr El-Safty had invoiced the player for his fees it was difficult to see what answer, other than non-performance or mis-performance, Michael Appleton would have had. Could a contract between WBA and Mr El-Safty be implied? The test was whether it could be shown that it was necessary to imply such a contract. The strongest argument for an implied contract was the history of the relationship between WBA and the defendant whereby other players at the club had been referred to him for treatment, and invoices in respect of the treatment had been

---

[20] See para.2–185 for consideration of the tort action.
[21] See [2005] EWHC 2866 (QB); [2006] P.N.L.R. 324.
[22] [2006] EWCA Civ 1299; [2007] P.I.Q.R. P7 at [35]–[38] per Rix LJ; and at [73] per Mummery LJ.
[23] [2006] EWCA Civ 1299; [2007] P.I.Q.R. P7 at [74].
[24] [2006] EWCA Civ 1299; [2007] P.I.Q.R. P7 at [41].

submitted to WBA. For Rix LJ the history was simply the background to the specific transaction, and did not take the argument into the "realms of necessity":

> "...it seems to me to be unnecessary to imply a contract between Mr. El-Safty and WBA when it is sufficient to imply a contract between him and his patient, Mr. Appleton, and to say that the invoicing just represents a machinery of payment in circumstances where Mr. Appleton was a member of the BUPA scheme entered into by WBA and his relevant medical expenses were to be paid for him by WBA. Therefore, even the fact that on an occasion or occasions in the past, WBA paid where BUPA did not, or, before the change in 1998, paid first and recovered payment from BUPA, does not take the matter further than that."[25]

Nor could it be said that there would be no consideration for a contract between Mr El-Safty and a player, simply because the club agreed to meet the surgeon's fees:

> "The player would remain liable to pay his fees, and even if he did not, would provide consideration by agreeing to attend upon him and to submit to his care and treatment."[26]

It is not entirely clear, however, how merely submitting to a doctor's care and treatment could constitute consideration for a contract. Given the basic proposition of contract law that consideration must be sufficient, but need not be adequate, if the player had provided sufficient consideration by submitting to treatment would the doctor have been entitled to claim further consideration in the shape of his fees? If not, then he would effectively have been providing a "pro bono private medical service". If submitting to a doctor's care and treatment constitutes consideration for a contract, the argument that NHS patients could have a contractual relationship with their general practitioners does not seem so far-fetched.

2–010   Once the Court of Appeal had concluded that there was a contract between Mr El-Safty and the player, there was no necessity to imply a contract between Mr El-Safty and WBA. Moreover, Rix LJ considered that there was a potential conflict of interest between the club and the player:

> "...the danger of a conflict of interest between a sports employer and a sportsman, all the more important where the sportsman may think that his principal interest is tied up in his soonest possible availability to his employer, must loom large. It militates against implying a contract with the employer rather than with the patient, or with the employer as well as with the patient."[27]

Thus, the conclusion was that the surgeon's contract was with the patient, not the club, even though neither the player nor the surgeon thought that they had entered into a contractual relationship, and the player had been assured (by virtue of his contract with the club) that he would not have to pay for his medical treatment. The point, ultimately, of this conclusion is that the doctor's contractual duty to the patient was effectively the same as his tortious duty to the patient, but a

---

[25] [2006] EWCA Civ 1299; [2007] P.I.Q.R. P7 at [43].
[26] [2006] EWCA Civ 1299; [2007] P.I.Q.R. P7 at [44] per Rix LJ.
[27] [2006] EWCA Civ 1299; [2007] P.I.Q.R. P7 at [46].

contractual duty owed to the club would have created an entirely different regime of obligations for the doctor, falling well beyond the usual undertakings of a professional providing medical services.

Private medical services   Patients receiving private medical treatment clearly do have contractual rights and may sue for breach of a relevant term. Since a doctor providing private treatment also owes a concurrent duty in tort to the patient, the patient's claim may be pleaded in both contract and tort, but in practice it is rare for much to turn on this, because the doctor's contractual obligations are usually no greater than the duties owed in tort.[28] The courts are understandably reluctant to draw a sharp distinction between the rights of patients treated privately and under the NHS. For example, in *Hotson v East Berkshire Area Health Authority* Sir John Donaldson MR said that:

2–011

> "... I am quite unable to detect any rational basis for a state of the law, if such it be, whereby in identical circumstances Dr. A who treats a patient under the National Health Service, and whose liability thereby falls to be determined in accordance with the law of tort, should be in a different position from Dr. B who treats a patient outside the service, and whose liability therefore falls to be determined in accordance with the law of contract, assuming, of course, that the contract is in terms which impose upon him neither more nor less than the tortious duty."[29]

Where there are differences between contract and tort they tend to be minimised, which may partially explain the courts' attitude to strict contractual warranties in the medical context.[30]

---

[28] See, e.g. *Thake v Maurice* [1986] Q.B. 644 and *Eyre v Measday* [1986] 1 All E.R. 488 (where on appeal the claim in tort had been abandoned). In *Silverstone v Mortensen* [2012] EWHC 2706 (QB); [2013] Med. L.R. 300 at [36] Thirlwall J commented that: "Although this was a private contract the standard of care expected of Professor Mortensen would be the same as that required in his NHS practice"; *Giles v Chambers* [2017] EWHC 1661 (QB) at [1]. *Edwards v Mallan* [1908] 1 K.B. 1002 provides an early example of concurrent liability in the medical context. In *Henderson v Merrett* [1995] 2 A.C. 145 the House of Lords held that where a defendant owes concurrent duties in contract and the tort of negligence, the claimant is entitled to pursue the action which will give him a practical advantage for the purposes of the law of limitation.

[29] [1987] A.C. 750 at 760; see also, per Croom-Johnson LJ. at 768; and Sir John Donaldson MR in *Naylor v Preston Area Health Authority* [1987] 2 All E.R. 353 at 360; *Gold v Essex County Council* [1942] 2 K.B. 293 at 297, per Lord Greene MR In *Lee v Taunton and Somerset NHS Trust* [2001] 1 F.L.R. 419 at 423 which concerned a negligent failure by a radiologist to identify neural tube defects in a foetus following a scan, thereby depriving the claimant of an opportunity to terminate the pregnancy under the Abortion Act 1967, Toulson J commented that: "In the present case the relationship between Mrs Lee and the defendants was equivalent to contract. It should not make any difference in a civilised system of law whether Mrs Lee underwent the scan as an NHS patient or a private patient. The radiologist possessed a special skill. He undertook to report on what the scan revealed and, by necessary implication, to exercise a proper degree of professional skill in so doing."

[30] See para.2–017. Nonetheless some technical differences between actions in contract and tort do remain, e.g. different rules on limitation periods (though special rules apply to actions for personal injuries in both contract and tort: see Ch.11); different measures of damages; possibly different tests for remoteness of damage; possibly different approaches to claims involving "loss of a chance" following the House of Lords' ruling in *Hotson v East Berkshire Area Health Authority* [1987] A.C. 750, see paras 5–101 et seq. Moreover, there may be practical differences between the NHS and private medicine which have legal consequences. See, e.g. the comments of Finlay J in *Dryden v Surrey County Council* [1936] 2 All E.R. 535 at 539 on the different levels of staffing that could legitimately be expected in public and private hospitals.

(a) Reasonable care

2–012   In the absence of an express term, a term will be implied into a contract to provide a service that the service will be performed with reasonable care and skill.[31] The standard of care required to satisfy this obligation is the same as in the tort of negligence.[32] The surgeon who contracts to perform an operation undertakes to carry out the operation with reasonable care; he does not guarantee that it will prove to be a success.[33] If, however, he agrees to give the case his personal attention this means that he will perform the operation personally and pay such subsequent visits as are necessary for the supervision of the patient until the discharge of the patient.[34] Delegation of the operation to another doctor would constitute a breach of contract. Contractual duties of care are "non-delegable", so the doctor is liable for a failure to exercise reasonable care by the person who performs the service, notwithstanding that reasonable care has been taken in

---

[31] Supply of Goods and Services Act 1982 s.13; Consumer Rights Act 2015 s.49(1). The term implied by s.49 cannot be excluded: s.57(1). From 1 October 2015 the Consumer Rights Act applies to consumer contracts, whereas the Supply of Goods and Services Act is confined to non-consumer contracts.

[32] *Roe v Minister of Health* [1954] 1 W.L.R. 128 at 131, per McNair J. In *Sidaway v Bethlem Royal Hospital Governors* [1985] A.C. 871 at 904, Lord Templeman said that: "The relationship between doctor and patient is contractual in origin, the doctor performing services in consideration for fees payable by the patient. The doctor . . . impliedly contracts to act at all times in the best interests of the patient." It is difficult to see how a duty to act in the patient's "best interests" can differ in any substantive way from a doctor's duty to exercise reasonable care in practising the skills of medicine. The Canadian courts have taken the view that the doctor–patient relationship is a fiduciary relationship, which may give rise to obligations on the part of the doctor which are more extensive than would be the case under either contract or tort: see *McInerney v MacDonald* (1992) 93 D.L.R. (4th) 415, SCC; *Norberg v Wynrib* (1992) 92 D.L.R. (4th) 449, SCC, particularly the judgment of McLachlin J; *Taylor v McGillivray* (1993) 110 D.L.R. (4th) 64, NBQB. In *Sidaway v Bethlem Royal Hospital Governors* [1984] 1 All E.R. 1018, CA, however, both Dunn and Browne-Wilkinson LJJ, at 1029 and 1032 respectively, said that in English law the relationship of doctor and patient was not fiduciary in character, a view with which Lord Scarman agreed: at [1985] A.C. 871 at 884. In *Breen v Williams* (1996) 138 A.L.R. 259 the Australian High Court held that the doctor–patient relationship is not fiduciary in character, but based on the doctor's contractual/tort duty to exercise reasonable care, and a doctor does not owe a general duty to act with the utmost good faith and loyalty. The Court expressly declined to adopt the Supreme Court of Canada's analysis in *McInerney v MacDonald*. Commenting on Lord Templeman's dictum in *Sidaway,* Gaudron and McHugh JJ. said, at 282, that a "doctor does not impliedly promise that he or she will always act in the 'best interests' of the patient. The primary duty that a doctor owes a patient is the duty 'to exercise reasonable care and skill in the provision of professional advice and treatment'." For further discussion of the doctor as fiduciary see Grubb [1994] C.L.P. 311; Bartlett (1997) 5 Med. L. Rev. 193.

[33] The statement by a surgeon that an operation will be "well done" does not have the effect of imposing a higher standard of care in contract than in tort: *Dove v Jarvis* [2013] Med. L.R. 284 (QBD). See para.2–017 below.

[34] *Morris v Winsbury-White* [1937] 4 All E.R. 494 at 500, although Tucker J doubted whether this obligation depended upon a specific undertaking by the surgeon; rather, it was part of the retainer in the ordinary case. In any event, the consent to treatment given by the patient is consent to surgery by a *specific* doctor (see *Michael v Molesworth* (1950) 2 B.M.J. 171), unless he specifies otherwise. To deal with this problem the standard NHS consent form contained a clause stating that: "I understand that you cannot give me a guarantee that a particular person will perform the procedure. The person will, however, have appropriate experience." The forms are available at *http://webarchive. nationalarchives.gov.uk/20130107105354/http://www.dh.gov.uk/en/Publichealth/ Scientificdevelopmentgeneticsandbioethics/Consent/Consentgeneralinformation/DH_4015950.* The forms have not been updated since October 2009. See further para.6–018.

selecting a competent person.[35] Even if the procedure was a success the patient would still be entitled to nominal damages for the breach.

NHS contracts   Within the NHS doctors are under an obligation to provide   2–013
personal treatment to their patients, by virtue of the contract of employment in the case of hospital doctors, and under the terms of service in the case of general practitioners.[36] A patient would not be entitled to sue on that contract, but it does allow the health authority[37] to place reasonable limits on the use of a deputising service.[38] Although health authorities may owe non-delegable duties to their "patients"[39] it is unlikely that a general practitioner would be held to owe a non-delegable duty to ensure that reasonable care has been taken by a deputising doctor if sued in tort. The general practitioner terms of service provide, inter alia, that a doctor must not sub-contract any duties under the contract in relation to clinical matters without taking reasonable steps to see that it is reasonable in all the circumstances to do so, and that the person is qualified and competent to provide the service.[40] This is the language of liability for negligence on the part of the general practitioner in selecting a sub-contractor, not the language of non-delegable duties. Moreover, the contracts/agreements entered into under the

---

[35] Dugdale and Stanton, *Professional Negligence*, 3rd edn (London: Butterworths, 1998), para.16.20.
[36] National Health Service (General Medical Services Contracts) Regulations 2015 (SI 2015/1862) reg.17, and the National Health Service (Personal Medical Services Agreements) Regulations 2015 (SI 2015/1879) Sch.2 para.1.
[37] In this context the term "health authority" is used in a generic sense. "Health Authorities" no longer exist within the NHS. The current entity dealing with primary care services is the Clinical Commissioning Group introduced by the Health and Social Care Act 2012 (which abolished Primary Care Trusts, which had replaced Family Health Services Authorities, which in turn had replaced Family Practitioner Committees).
[38] *R. v Secretary of State for Health, ex p. Spencer* [1990] 1 Med. L.R. 255. In *Roy v Kensington and Chelsea and Westminster Family Practitioner Committee* [1992] 1 A.C. 624 the House of Lords doubted, without deciding, whether the relationship between a general practitioner and the health authority was contractual in nature. There were "contractual echoes in the relationship". But, irrespective of whether there is a contract or not the general practitioner has a "bundle of rights" which are individual private law rights against the health authority, arising from the statute and regulations (now the National Health Service Act 2006, the National Health Service (General Medical Services Contracts) Regulations 2015 (SI 2015/1862), and the National Health Service (Personal Medical Services Agreements) Regulations 2015 (SI 2015/1879)); Mulholland (1993) 9 P.N. 154. In *North Essex Health Authority v Dr. C. David-John* [2003] Lloyd's Rep. Med. 586 the Employment Appeal Tribunal held that a general medical practitioner was not in a contractual relationship with the health authority, but that the relationship was statutory. On the other hand, if that view was incorrect and the relationship was contractual, it was a contract for services rather than a contract of service, i.e. the general practitioner was an independent contractor, not an employee. An "honorary clinical contract" can be a binding contract of employment, even though the services rendered under it are not in return for pay: *R. v North Thames Regional Health Authority, Chelsea and Westminster NHS Trust, ex p. L* [1996] 7 Med. L.R. 385.
[39] See paras 3–120 to 3–122, 9–026 et seq.
[40] National Health Service (General Medical Services Contracts) Regulations 2015 (SI 2015/1862) Sch.3 para.44(1) and National Health Service (Personal Medical Services Agreements) Regulations 2015 (SI 2015/1879) Sch.2 para.43(1) (which also provides that the contractor must be satisfied that the sub-contractor holds adequate insurance).

Regulations do not create any right enforceable by any person who is not a party,[41] and the Regulations clearly do not purport to set out the common law position.

2–014   The National Health Service Act 2006 s.9 permits one health service body to "contract" to provide goods or services to another health service body as part of the "internal market" of the NHS, but such "contracts" do not give rise to any contractual rights or liabilities.[42] Although it is undoubtedly the case that the health service body providing the treatment will be liable to the patient if the treatment is negligent, it has been suggested that a purchasing authority could also be liable if it placed a "contract" which did not provide for an adequate standard of treatment or there was reason to believe that the providing authority was not reasonably able to perform the "contract".[43] The liability to the patient would be in tort, however, not contract.[44] It is unlikely that this argument will ever be tested, since if the patient can establish negligence against the health service body providing the treatment, there would be no practical reason for the patient to claim against the "purchaser". The issue of the liability of a health service body which provides services by "contracting out" to a non-NHS body remains important, however, though this situation is covered by the general rules applicable to the delegation of duties, not s.9.

2–015   In most cases of private medical treatment the existence of a contract does not affect the duties owed by the doctor in practical terms, since the same duties are owed in tort. There are, however, some circumstances in which the liabilities under the contract do differ from those in tort.

(b)   Express and implied warranties

(i)   Supply of professional services

2–016   The usual position where a professional enters into a contract with a client is that the professional agrees to exercise reasonable care in performing the professional service supplied:

> "The law does not usually imply a warranty that [a professional] will achieve the desired result, but only a term that he will use reasonable care and skill. The surgeon does not warrant that he will cure the patient. Nor does the solicitor warrant that he will win the case."[45]

---

[41] National Health Service (General Medical Services Contracts) Regulations 2015 (SI 2015/1862) reg.95; and National Health Service (Personal Medical Services Agreements) Regulations 2015 (SI 2015/1879) reg.87.

[42] National Health Service Act 2006 s.9(5); on which see *Pitalia v NHS Commissioning Board* [2014] EWCA Civ 474; (2014) 138 B.M.L.R. 89 and *NHS Commissioning Board v Bargain Dentist.com* [2014] EWHC 1994 (QB); [2014] Med. L.R. 301.

[43] Jacob [1991] P.L. 255 at 264.

[44] The analogy that Jacob draws is with the liability that used to apply to voluntary hospitals in employing consultants as independent contractors, where the obligation was to exercise reasonable care in the selection of competent staff: Jacob (1991), citing *Hillyer v Governors of St. Bartholemews Hospital* [1909] 2 K.B. 820.

[45] *Greaves & Co. (Contractors) Ltd v Baynham Meikle & Partners* [1975] 3 All E.R. 99 at 103–104, per Lord Denning MR.

Commenting on this dictum in *Platform Funding Ltd v Bank of Scotland plc* Moore-Bick LJ observed:

> "I am inclined to think that the reason why the law does not ordinarily construe the contract in such cases as giving rise to an unqualified obligation owes more to the nature of the services themselves, the context in which they are to be provided and the fact that the desired result is not one which any professional person can reasonably guarantee, than to the fact that the provision of the services involves the exercise of special skill. In other contexts the law has no difficulty in implying an unqualified obligation to achieve the desired result."[46]

Although there is a presumption that a person providing professional services will undertake only to exercise reasonable care, there is nothing to stop them undertaking an unqualified obligation to achieve a particular outcome, and whether this has been done will depend on the terms of the contract between the parties.[47]

Thus, it is theoretically possible for doctors to give a contractual warranty that they will achieve a particular result, but the court will be slow to infer such a warranty in the absence of an express term because the context is such that one would not normally expect a doctor to give a guarantee of success: medicine is an inexact science and it is unlikely that a responsible doctor would intend to give such a warranty. This point was demonstrated by decisions of the Court of Appeal in two cases involving failed sterilisations. In *Eyre v Measday*[48] the claimant underwent a sterilisation operation performed by the defendant. The defendant had explained the nature of the operation (a laparoscopic sterilisation), emphasising that it was irreversible, but he did not inform the claimant that there was a less than one per cent risk of pregnancy occurring following such a procedure. Both the claimant and her husband believed that the operation would render the claimant completely sterile. The claimant subsequently became pregnant. She issued proceedings claiming that the defendant was in breach of a contractual term that she would be rendered irreversibly sterile and/or a collateral warranty to that effect which induced her to enter the contract. It was common ground that the contract was embodied partly in oral conversations and partly in the written consent form signed by the claimant. It was also common ground that the appropriate test as to the nature and terms of the contract was objective not subjective. This does not depend upon what the claimant or the defendant thought were the terms of the contract, but on what the court objectively considers the words used by the parties must be reasonably taken to have meant. The Court of

2–017

---

[46] [2008] EWCA Civ 930; [2009] P.N.L.R. 4 at [18]. As Moore-Bick LJ comments, context is crucial. So, although the surgeon may reasonably say "I operate on very sick patients; sometimes I manage to cure them, sometimes they do not survive", no one would think it appropriate for an engineer to say "I build bridges; sometimes they stay up, sometimes they fall down". And though litigation lawyers may win some cases and lose others whilst still exercising reasonable care, onveyancers would not be acting reasonably if sometimes they managed to obtain good title for the client but on other occasions they did not.

[47] [2008] EWCA Civ 930; [2009] P.N.L.R. 4 at [30]. In *Platform Funding Ltd v Bank of Scotland plc* itself, a firm of surveyors and valuers who were fraudulently persuaded to inspect and value the wrong property for the purpose of an application for a mortgage were held to have warranted that they had provided a valuation of the correct property. They had undertaken an unqualified obligation to inspect the particular property and were in breach of contract in failing to do so.

[48] [1986] 1 All E.R. 488.

Appeal held that it was a contract to perform a particular operation, not a contract to render the claimant sterile. Additionally, there was neither an express nor an implied warranty that the procedure would be an unqualified success. Although the claimant could reasonably have concluded from the defendant's emphasis on the irreversible nature of the operation that she would be sterilised, it was not reasonable for her to have concluded that he had given her a guarantee that she would be absolutely sterile.[49]

2–018 In *Thake v Maurice*[50] the Court of Appeal (Kerr LJ dissenting) reversed the decision of Peter Pain J that the defendant had contracted to make the male claimant irreversibly sterile following a vasectomy operation. The defendant had given the claimants a graphic demonstration of the nature of the procedure and its effects, but had failed to give his usual warning that there was a slight risk that the male claimant might become fertile again. Both Neill and Nourse LJJ concluded that, on an objective interpretation, the defendant had not guaranteed the outcome, relying on the observation that medicine is not an exact science and results are to some extent unpredictable.[51] Nourse LJ said that a doctor cannot be objectively regarded as guaranteeing the success of any operation or treatment unless he says as much in clear and unequivocal terms.[52]

2–019 By contrast, in the Canadian case of *La Fleur v Cornelis*[53] a plastic surgeon contracted to reduce the size of the claimant's nose, and drew a sketch to show the changes that would be made. After the operation the claimant had some scarring and deformity. Barry J held the defendant strictly liable for breach of contract, stating that whilst there is usually no implied warranty of success, there is no law preventing a doctor from contracting to do that which he is paid to do. The defendant had said to the claimant that there would be: "...no problem. You will be very happy." This was held to constitute an express warranty of success.

---

[49] See also *Dendaas v Yackel* (1980) 109 D.L.R. (3d) 455, BCSC where there was similar confusion between doctor and patient, the patient believing that the doctor's emphasis on the "irreversible" and permanent nature of the sterilisation procedure meant that there was no chance of a future pregnancy. Bouck J held that since there was no clear meeting of minds on this essential term the claim in contract must fail; *Grey v Webster* (1984) 14 D.L.R. (4th) 706 at 713; see paras 7–162 et seq. on the question of the failure to disclose the risk of future pregnancy.

[50] [1986] Q.B. 644.

[51] "Medicine, though a highly skilled profession, is not, and is not generally regarded as being, an exact science. The reasonable man would have expected the defendant to exercise all the proper skill and care of a surgeon in that speciality; he would not in my view have expected the defendant to give a guarantee of 100 per cent. success": [1986] Q.B. 644 at 685, per Neill LJ.

[52] [1986] Q.B. 644 at 688. However, the claim that the defendant was liable in negligence for failing to warn about the small risk that the male claimant would become fertile again succeeded. See para.7–165. In *ter Neuzen v Korn* (1995) 127 D.L.R. (4th) 577 at 599, SCC an argument that the information sheet about the proposed treatment (artificial insemination) given by a doctor to a patient provided the basis for a finding of an express warranty was rejected. The purpose of the information sheet was to provide information; there was no intention that the statements in it would constitute an express warranty. See also *Dow v Tayside University Hospitals NHS Trust*, 2006 S.L.T. (Sh. Ct) 141; 2006 S.C.L.R. 865 where it was held that a statement by a doctor that a "surgical termination" of a pregnancy was required (as opposed to a "medical termination") did not amount to a warranty of the success of the surgery in terminating the pregnancy.

[53] (1979) 28 N.B.R. (2d) 569, NBSC.

Accordingly, while it may be possible to establish that a doctor has guaranteed a particular result,[54] this is likely to be a rare occurrence.[55] Indeed, the converse, a statement by the doctor that he could not guarantee the outcome, would seem to be a more likely event in practice.[56] It must be borne in mind, however, that some contractual terms have nothing to do with the exercise of reasonable care. If a defendant contracts to perform a specific act, such as attend upon the patient,[57] or use a particular procedure,[58] then he is liable for failing to carry it out irrespective of whether he exercised reasonable care.

2–020

(ii)   Supply of goods

Where the contract involves a transfer of goods there will be implied terms as to the quality and fitness for purpose of the goods supplied.[59] For example, in *Samuels v Davis*[60] the defendant dentist agreed to make a set of dentures for the claimant, but the dentures did not fit. It was held that there was an implied term that the dentures would be reasonably fit for their purpose. Similarly, in *Dodd v Wilson*[61] an injection of a vaccine into a herd of cattle by a veterinary surgeon resulted in some of the cattle becoming ill. There was held to be an implied term in the contract between the vet and the farmer that the vaccine would be reasonably fit for its purpose. There is no reason why the same proposition should not apply to injections given to patients. This principle could apply to many forms of treatment, such as the supply of drugs, prosthetics, heart pacemakers or artificial heart valves.[62]

2–021

---

[54] Both Pain J and Kerr LJ came to this conclusion in *Thake v Maurice*.

[55] It may be that with elective procedures such as sterilisation operations and cosmetic surgery the courts will be more willing to find express warranties of a successful outcome. For example, in *La Fleur v Cornelis* (1979) 28 N.B.R. (2d) 569 at 577 Barry J said that a cosmetic surgeon was in a different position from an ordinary physician; he was selling a special service and was more akin to a businessman.

[56] But if the doctor went further than this by suggesting that she does not accept liability if something goes wrong this would be caught by statutory rules governing attempts to exclude liability in both contract and tort: see paras 11–029 et seq. There is an important difference between telling the patient that treatment is risky and is not always successful and a statement that the doctor does not accept responsibility even if the failure of the procedure is due to a negligent error.

[57] *Morris v Winsbury-White* [1937] 4 All E.R. 494. See also the comments of Oliver J in *Midland Bank Trust Co. Ltd v Hett, Stubbs & Kemp* [1979] Ch. 384 at 434: "A contract gives rise to a complex of rights and duties of which the duty to exercise reasonable care and skill is but one."

[58] A dentist who contracts to employ his painless process of tooth extraction will be strictly liable for breach of contract if he fails to employ his painless process, but an allegation that the tooth was unskilfully extracted is a claim that the defendant failed to exercise reasonable care, which in substance may be treated as an action in tort: *Edwards v Mallan* [1908] 1 K.B. 1002 at 1005, CA.

[59] Supply of Goods and Services Act 1982 s.4; and, from 1 October 2015, in the case of a consumer the Consumer Rights Act 2015 ss.9 and 10. From that date the 1982 Act applies only to non-consumer contracts.

[60] [1943] 1 K.B. 526.

[61] [1946] 2 All E.R. 691.

[62] It has been suggested, for example, that the circumstances of *Roe v Minister of Health* [1954] 2 Q.B. 66 (see para.3–079) might be covered by the proposition: see Nathan, *Medical Negligence* (London: Butterworths, 1957), pp.18–19. Pharmacists who supply non-prescription products or who supply products under a private prescription will be liable in contract to the purchaser if the product is not of satisfactory quality or fit for its intended purpose; see paras 10–005 to 10–008.

(iii)   Supply of biomedical products

2–022   In Canada it has been held to be inappropriate to imply a contractual warranty as to fitness for purpose in a contract for artificial insemination where the donated semen was infected with HIV, on the basis that it was a contract for the supply of medical services, not goods, which should be confined to a claim in negligence.[63] Similarly, in *Pittman Estate v Bain*[64] Lang J concluded that because blood used for transfusions, in the form of cryoprecipitate, is not a manufactured product in the nature of other equipment and supplies it was not reasonable to imply a contractual term that a hospital warranted that the blood would be free from disease.[65] Blood, as a biological product, might be "unavoidably unsafe". Moreover, different considerations applied to the supply of blood, taking it out of the usual chain of commercial manufacture and distribution, because of the nature of the collection and distribution of blood, and society's need for a product for which there is no feasible alternative. The hospital would have no contractual claim against the suppliers, the Canadian Red Cross Society, or against the donor for latently defective blood, since the blood was donated free of charge, and provided by the suppliers to the hospital free of charge. Thus, it would not be possible for the hospital to pass on liability for breach of a contractual warranty up a chain of distribution by suing on the contracts, as would normally be the case with other products and which provided the rationale for the ordinary common law rules on implied warranties.[66] There were additional factors to take into account in the case of blood transfusions:

> "… it is not in the best interests of our health care system to impose absolute liability on the hospital in these circumstances. When a patient may be in need of a transfusion, society wants the hospital or physician to make the decision to transfuse or not on the basis of its skilled perception of the patient's best interests, after balancing the risks of transfusion against the risks of the presenting problem. To hold a hospital or physician to strict liability for a product such as blood may operate to discourage those responsible for our health care from exercising their professional judgment, because they are concerned about their own liability."[67]

2–023   The same issue arose in the Australian case of *E v Australian Red Cross Society*[68] where the Federal Court of Appeal held that the trial judge had been correct to find that there was no contract with the hospital for the supply of blood plasma to

---

[63] *ter Neuzen v Korn* (1993) 103 D.L.R. (4th) 473 at 517, BCCA: "In the face of the American experience, we are unable to identify any policy reason why a physician should face stricter liability for 'goods' which are furnished to a patient in the course of medical service than he or she would be for any lack of professional care and skill which must be brought to every healing or treating engagement." This statement was specifically approved on appeal by the Supreme Court of Canada: (1995) 127 D.L.R. (4th) 577, 609.

[64] (1994) 112 D.L.R. (4th) 257, Ont Ct, Gen Div.

[65] Not all blood products are used in "unmanufactured" form, and therefore a different approach might apply to products that had undergone some form of "manufacturing process".

[66] This issue was also considered to be an important factor by the Supreme Court of Canada in *ter Neuzen v Korn* (1995) 127 D.L.R. (4th) 577 at 607 in declining to imply a warranty in the case of donated semen.

[67] (1994) 112 D.L.R. (4th) 257 at 354.

[68] (1991) 105 A.L.R. 53, Aus Fed CA; aff'g (1991) 99 A.L.R. 601; [1991] 2 Med. L.R. 303.

the claimant when he received a blood transfusion in the course of treatment.[69] It was a contract for services, namely the provision of hospital, medical and nursing services for the purpose of treating the claimant for his medical condition. The blood was intended to be supplied, if necessary, free of charge. Lockhart J said that:

> "To the extent that goods were provided to him such as food, sleeping tablets, antibiotics, dressings and things of this nature, they were provided as an incident to the contract for the provision of services. There was no contract for the supply of goods. The contract ... was one for services and is not divisible into a contract for services and for the supply of goods. I leave open, however, the question whether in an appropriate case a contract between a patient and a hospital may be divisible in other circumstances. But the provision on the facts of this case of medicines, drugs and blood cannot be severed into concepts of the provision of services on the one hand and of purchase and sale of goods on the other."[70]

The distinction between a contract for the sale of goods and a contract for the performance of services, which is often a fine one, was the central issue on the contractual claim in *E v Australian Red Cross Society*, as indeed it is in the American courts.[71] But, as Lang J noted in *Pittman Estate v Bain*, the American cases have taken a different route from the English and Canadian cases, since they do "not seem to consider implying common law warranties to material in a hybrid contract that provides both services and material".[72] In *ter Neuzen v Korn*[73] and *Pittman Estate v Bain* the question was whether at common law there should be implied into the contract for the supply of services and goods a warranty that the semen and blood, respectively, would be fit for their purpose and free from latent defects. It may be that the Supply of Goods and Services Act 1982 s.4 or (from 1 October 2015 in the case of a consumer) the Consumer Rights Act 2015 ss.9 and 10, makes this argument redundant by implying a statutory term as to the quality and fitness for purpose of the goods where the contract involves "a transfer of goods" or, in the case of the 2015 Act, a supply of goods. Thus, it is arguable that in English law the question of whether there could be a warranty that bodily products such as blood or semen are fit for their purpose, i.e. not contaminated in some potentially harmful manner, would depend upon whether it could be said that there had been a transfer of goods. Does blood

2–024

---

[69] A finding that the giving of blood to the claimant was a "supply of goods" under a contract for the supply of goods within the meaning of s.71 of the Trade Practices Act 1974 (which is in similar terms to the English Sale of Goods Act 1979 s.14; see now the Consumer Rights Act 2015, ss.9 and 10) would have resulted in the conclusion that there were implied conditions that the goods were of merchantable quality and fit for their purpose.

[70] (1991) 105 A.L.R. 53 at 59. Query whether the distinction here is between consumables, such as food and drugs, and more durable products, such as artificial joints or heart valves.

[71] The leading case is *Perlmutter v Beth David Hospital*, 123 N.E. (2d) 792 (1954) in which the New York Court of Appeals held that the essence of the contractual relationship between a patient and a hospital was a contract for services which was not divisible into a contract for the provision of services and the transfusion of blood. Not all jurisdictions have followed *Perlmutter*, however, see: *Cunningham v MacNeal Memorial Hospital*, 266 N.E. (2d) 897, SC of Illinois (1970), holding that there was a contract to supply goods to the patient.

[72] (1994) 112 D.L.R. (4th) 257 at 351.

[73] (1993) 103 D.L.R. (4th) 473 at 517, BCCA; aff'd (1995) 127 D.L.R. (4th) 577, SCC.

or semen constitute "goods"?[74] In *E v Australian Red Cross Society* the trial judge specifically left open the question of whether blood was "goods" within the meaning of the Trade Practices Act 1974, as did Lockhart J on appeal.[75] In *PQ v Australian Red Cross Society*,[76] however, McGarvie J appears to have assumed, without comment, that a "blood product" constituted "goods" for the purpose of the legislation, observing that a blood product contaminated by HIV infection could not be regarded as being of merchantable quality. The issue arose in the context of determining whether the claimant's cause of action in contract was statute-barred, but nonetheless, the judge proceeded on the basis that such a claim was correctly conceived and that blood did constitute "goods". On the other hand, the defendant to the contractual claim was a manufacturer of blood concentrate (such as Factor VIII), not the Red Cross in respect of its supply of cryoprecipitate. The blood had gone through a manufacturing process, and it may be easier to categorise the end result of a manufacturing process as "goods" or a "product".[77]

2–025   The issue remains unresolved in English law, though in practice it has less significance since the decision in *A v The National Blood Authority*[78] that blood can be treated as a product for the purpose of the regime of strict liability under the Consumer Protection Act 1987, a position that had been recommended by the Pearson Commission.[79] In any event, it is arguable that the difficulty that the courts perceived with implying a warranty in these cases stems from the fact that the "goods" consisted of a biological product. Where the item that is transferred to the patient is in the nature of an artificial medical device which is manufactured, the courts may be more willing to approach the issue in terms of contractual warranties.[80]

(iv) Supply of design

2–026   It is possible that the contractual obligations as to fitness for purpose and satisfactory quality would apply to the design of an article, so that there may be a warranty that the design is fit for its intended purpose.[81] When it does apply the

---

[74] Note that in *Yearworth v North Bristol NHS Trust* [2009] EWCA Civ 37; [2010] Q.B. 1 the Court of Appeal held that frozen semen could constitute property; see para.2–242.

[75] (1991) 99 A.L.R. 601; [1991] 2 Med. L.R. 303 at 326 and (1991) 105 A.L.R. 53 at 58, respectively.

[76] [1992] 1 V.R. 19 at 41–42.

[77] See also *Pittman Estate v Bain* (1994) 112 D.L.R. (4th) 257 at 318 where Lang J drew a distinction between cryoprecipitate and fractionated blood products, which do undergo a manufacturing process.

[78] [2001] 3 All E.R. 289. See paras 10–091 et seq.

[79] *Royal Commission on Civil Liability and Compensation for Personal Injury*, Cmnd.7054, (1978), Vol.I, para.1276.

[80] In *ter Neuzen v Korn* (1993) 103 D.L.R. (4th) 473 at 514 the British Columbia Court of Appeal did not rule out the possibility that cases could arise where common law contractual warranties could have a role to play in medical malpractice actions (a view apparently accepted by the Supreme Court of Canada, on appeal: (1995) 127 D.L.R. (4th) 577, though not for biological products such as blood and semen, which carry "inherent risks"), and in *E v Australian Red Cross Society* (1991) 105 A.L.R. 53 at 59 Lockhart J left this option open.

[81] *Independent Broadcasting Authority v EMI Electronics Ltd and BICC Construction Ltd* (1980) 14 Build. L.R. 1 at 47–48, per Lord Scarman. This strict design duty only applies where the defendant has supplied or manufactured the article as well as designing it: *George Hawkins v Chrysler (UK) Ltd*

obligation is strict, in that the exercise of reasonable care is not a defence. If the goods are not of satisfactory quality or fit for their purpose there is a breach of contract. This does not mean, however, that the product must be effective in preventing the illness or producing a cure, which would be the equivalent of giving a guarantee of successful treatment. Rather the implied term is that the goods will be fit for their intended purpose, which they may not be if they cause harm. Moreover, a product such as a drug may be of satisfactory quality and fit for its purpose even though it carries an inherent risk of an adverse reaction from known "side-effects".[82]

(c) Misrepresentation

A false representation made by a party to a contract which induces the other party to enter into the contract may be actionable as a misrepresentation.[83] The representee may be entitled to damages or to rescind the contract. In *Webster v Liddington*[84] the claimants had all undergone a cosmetic procedure intended to rejuvenate skin. The process involved taking a skin sample from each of the patients and sending it to a company for culture in a bovine product. The cultured material was sent back to the clinicians for injection into the claimants. The company which devised and marketed the procedure produced brochures explaining the process. Some of the participating clinics gave the brochures to the patients, and other clinics produced their own brochures based on the information provided by the company. The brochures indicated that the injectate contained only the patient's cells. However, it was not possible to eradicate the bovine product entirely, and it constituted somewhere between 0 per cent and 0.02 per cent of the injectate. When patients discovered that the injectate could contain very small amounts of bovine products they brought claims against the clinics (the company having gone into administration) on the basis of misrepresentation. The Court of Appeal held that the clinics could be responsible for the accuracy of statements in the brochures, and that the statements that the injectate contained only the patients' own cells amounted to a misrepresentation. Jackson LJ observed that when a person (X) passes information produced by another (Y) to someone with whom X is hoping to contract (Z), a range of possibilities exist:

2-027

---

and Burne Associates (1986) 38 B.L.R. 36; see Dugdale and Stanton, *Professional Negligence*, 3rd edn (London: Butterworths, 1998), paras 4–008–4–009. The circumstances in which this type of strict design liability might apply in a medical context are somewhat limited, but it could be relevant in appropriate circumstances to claims arising out of cosmetic surgery, for example. An allegation of *negligent* design in the conduct of breast reduction surgery was made in *White v Turner* (1981) 120 D.L.R. (3d) 269, 279, but failed on the facts; see also *La Fleur v Cornelis* (1979) 28 N.B.R. (2d) 569, NBSC, para.2–019, above.

[82] See para.10–006, n.22. The rupture of an artificial breast implant, from some unidentified cause, does not establish as a matter of law that it was not reasonably fit for its purpose: *Hollis v Dow Corning Corp.* (1993) 103 D.L.R. (4th) 520 at 556, BCCA; aff'd (1995) 129 D.L.R. (4th) 609, SCC.

[83] See generally *Treitel, The Law of Contract*, 14th edn (London: Sweet & Maxwell, 2015), Ch.9. As a general rule the misrepresentation must be a false statement of fact, though the modern position is that in some circumstances it may extend to statements of law.

[84] [2014] EWCA Civ 560; [2014] P.N.L.R. 26.

"(i)   X may warrant to Z that the information is correct. X may thereby assume contractual liability to Z for the accuracy of the information. That liability may exist under the main contract or a collateral contract.

(ii)   X may adopt the information as his own, thereby taking on such responsibility as he would have if he were the maker of the statement.

(iii)   X may represent that he believes, on reasonable grounds, the information supplied by Y to be correct. That involves a lesser degree of responsibility than scenario (ii).

(iv)   X may simply pass on the information to Z as material coming from Y, about which X has no knowledge or belief. X then has no responsibility for the accuracy of the information beyond the ordinary duties of honesty and good faith."[85]

2–028   Applying that approach to the facts of *Webster* Jackson LJ pointed to a number of factors that were significant: the claimants were consumers and the defendants were qualified clinicians, with a stark imbalance of knowledge between the parties; the defendants were offering to sell both a product and service to the claimants and the relationship between the parties was that of clinician and patient, as well as vendor and purchaser; none of the claimants was ill or in need of the treatment for medical or therapeutic purposes, it was purely elective; and the defendants did not stipulate any disclaimer or express any reservations about the accuracy of the information.[86] A reasonable person standing in the shoes of any of the claimants would conclude that the clinician was adopting the contents of the brochure which he handed over, and therefore the case fell into scenario (ii). For scenarios (iii) or (iv) to apply the clinicians would have had to issue a disclaimer to the effect that the brochures were stating the manufacturer's view and the clinicians had no direct knowledge and could not confirm details.

2–029   As to whether there was a misrepresentation, the defendants argued that a content of between 0 per cent and 0.02 per cent of bovine product in the injectate was so small that the statements in the brochures were substantially true, and that for all material purposes the injectate did consist only of the patient's own cells. However, there was evidence that between 3 per cent and 10 per cent of the population has a propensity to suffer an allergic reaction to bovine products, and could have a mild or a severe reaction to a small trace.[87] Against that background the small traces of bovine product in the injectate were a material matter, and statements that the injectate contained only the patient's own cells and nothing else were incorrect in a material respect. This could have affected the patients' decision to accept the treatment, and that would not have been unreasonable.[88]

2–030   **Misrepresentation Act 1967**   Under s.2(1) of the Misrepresentation Act 1967 where a person has entered into a contract after a misrepresentation has been made to him by another party to the contract, and has suffered loss as a result, if the person making the misrepresentation would be liable to damages had the misrepresentation been made fraudulently, that person shall be so liable notwithstanding that the misrepresentation was not made fraudulently, unless he proves that he had reasonable grounds to believe and did believe up to the time

---

[85] [2014] EWCA Civ 560; [2014] P.N.L.R. 26 at [46].

[86] [2014] EWCA Civ 560; [2014] P.N.L.R. 26 at [51].

[87] None of the patients had actually suffered any physical harm, and it was accepted that the claims would largely be limited to recovering the costs of the treatment, somewhere between £3,500 and £4,000 per patient: [2014] EWCA Civ 560; [2014] P.N.L.R. 26 at [17].

[88] [2014] EWCA Civ 560; [2014] P.N.L.R. 26 at [64].

the contract was made that the facts represented were true. This action is more advantageous to a claimant than a claim in negligent misrepresentation because there is no question of whether a duty of care was owed and the defendant bears the burden of proof. Moreover, damages are measured under tortious rather than contractual principles, but the measure is that for the tort of deceit rather than for negligence, and so includes unforeseeable losses.[89]

2. TORT

The vast majority of claims for medical malpractice are brought in the tort of negligence, where the issue will usually be whether the defendant was in breach of a duty of care and/or whether the breach caused damage to the patient.[90] Normally, there will be no difficulty in finding a duty of care owed by the doctor to his patient, at least where the claim is in respect of personal injuries, and this is true even where there is a contractual relationship.[91] The practitioner may also owe a duty of care to the patient in respect of pure financial loss. In addition, there are a number of circumstances where the doctor may owe a duty of care to a third party arising out of the treatment given to the patient, but the incidence and extent of such duties is more problematic.

2–031

In some instances an action for trespass to the person may be available, particularly in the form of the tort of battery. Battery is an intentional tort which requires "the actual infliction of unlawful force on another person".[92] The action is potentially relevant to any medical treatment or examination which involves a touching of the patient, since, with the exception of certain forms of unavoidable or socially accepted contacts (such as jostling in a busy street or engaging someone's attention), any unwanted touching without lawful excuse will constitute a battery. So the surgeon who performs an operation without the patient's consent commits a battery, even though his intention is to benefit the patient.[93] Consent by the patient exculpates the doctor, and thus, invariably, the question turns upon whether the requirements for a valid consent have been satisfied or whether the case falls within the circumstances in which consent may be dispensed with. These issues are considered in Ch.6.

2–032

The remainder of this chapter deals with the tort of negligence and in particular the duty of care owed by health professionals. The tort of negligence consists of a legal duty to take reasonable care, and breach of that duty by the defendant

2–033

---

[89] *Royscot Trust Ltd v Rogerson* [1991] 2 Q.B. 297.
[90] On this see Chs 3 to 5.
[91] See para 2–011, n.28, above. In some circumstances the patient may be owed a duty of care by the institution providing the healthcare, such as a hospital or health authority, in addition to the duties owed by individual healthcare professionals. This form of "direct" liability is discussed in Ch.9.
[92] *Collins v Wilcock* [1984] 3 All E.R. 374 at 377. It is the act that constitutes the trespass (the touching) that must be intentional; an intention to cause the harm is not necessary: *Wilson v Pringle* [1987] Q.B. 237.
[93] *Re F. (Mental Patient: Sterilisation)* [1990] 2 A.C. 1 at 73, per Lord Goff; *T. v T.* [1988] 1 All E.R. 613 at 625, per Wood J. It is assumed throughout this book that the doctor is acting in good faith, although there are occasional examples to the contrary: see *Appleton v Garrett* [1996] P.I.Q.R. P1, para.6–067.

causing damage to the claimant.[94] The duty of care determines as a matter of policy whether the type of loss suffered by the claimant in the particular manner in which it occurred can ever be actionable, whereas breach of duty deals with the standard of care required of a defendant in the circumstances in order to satisfy the duty of care, and whether the defendant's conduct fell below that standard; in other words, whether the defendant was careless/negligent.

2–034 The usual starting point for any discussion of the duty of care in the tort of negligence is the landmark decision of *Donoghue v Stevenson*,[95] and the famous dictum of Lord Atkin.[96] Its significance in the context of medical negligence is somewhat limited, however, at least in the context of the paradigm case of physical injury caused to the patient during the course of treatment, since the duty of care owed by doctors to their patients long ante-dates *Donoghue v Stevenson*, and the relationship between doctor and patient clearly satisfies any test based upon foreseeability of harm, proximity of the relationship between claimant and defendant, or, indeed, a requirement that it be just and reasonable to impose a duty of care.[97] In addition to the "tripartite test", a number of other tests for the existence of a duty of care have emerged, including "voluntary assumption of responsibility" by the defendant, an "incremental" approach, and whether the imposition of liability satisfies the "requirements of distributive justice". It is arguable that these different approaches are simply different ways of looking at the same issue, and that if they are applied correctly they should produce the same result.[98] Even if it can be said that the defendant owes a duty of care to the claimant the defendant is not necessarily responsible for all the consequences that flow from that negligence. The limits of liability are often set by the concepts of causation and remoteness of damage, but sometimes the court may restrict a defendant's responsibility by reference to the scope of the duty.[99] Of course, ultimately, these issues involve policy judgments about the appropriate limits of a defendant's responsibility for the consequences of his negligence.

---

[94] *Lochgelly Iron Co. v M'Mullan* [1934] A.C. 1 at 25, per Lord Wright.
[95] [1932] A.C. 562.
[96] "You must take reasonable care to avoid acts or omissions which you can reasonably foresee would be likely to injure your neighbour. Who, then, in law is my neighbour? The answer seems to be—persons who are so closely and directly affected by my act that I ought reasonably to have them in contemplation as being so affected when I am directing my mind to the acts or omissions which are called in question": [1932] A.C. 562 at 580.
[97] This tripartite test for the existence of a duty of care derives from a series of appellate court decisions in the 1980s: see *Peabody Donation Fund v Sir Lindsay Parkinson & Co. Ltd* [1985] A.C. 210; *Yuen Kun-yeu v A.-G. of Hong Kong* [1988] A.C. 175; *Smith v Bush* [1990] 1 A.C. 831 at 865, per Lord Griffiths; *Caparo Industries plc v Dickman* [1990] 2 A.C. 605. These cases (and others) represented a retreat from what was perceived to be the unacceptable implications of a wide formulation of the test for the duty of care by Lord Wilberforce in *Anns v Merton London Borough Council* [1978] A.C. 728 at 751–2, a process that culminated in the overruling of that decision by the House of Lords in *Murphy v Brentwood District Council* [1991] 1 A.C. 398. Although these decisions deal with the duty of care in general terms, they are virtually exclusively concerned with liability for pure economic loss and have little relevance in the context of medical malpractice litigation.
[98] See *Clerk & Lindsell on Torts*, 22nd edn (London: Sweet & Maxwell, 2018), para.8–104, citing Sir Brian Neill in *Bank of Credit and Commerce International (Overseas) Ltd v Price Waterhouse (No.2)* [1998] P.N.L.R. 564, 583–587. See also the comments of Brooke LJ in *Parkinson v St James and Seacroft University Hospital NHS Trust* [2001] EWCA Civ 530; [2002] Q.B. 266 at [17] to [27].
[99] See para.2–043.

It is rare for the courts expressly to invoke policy as a ground for denying a   2–035
patient a right of action against a negligent medical practitioner, although certain
"policy" considerations may have a subtle influence at other points.[100] Some
types of claim have been barred on policy grounds, most of them arising from
congenital injury to unborn children. Thus, "wrongful life" claims on the part of a
child whose congenital disabilities the defendant negligently failed to diagnose
are not actionable.[101] On the other hand, the parents may have an action in these
circumstances for being deprived of the opportunity to have the pregnancy
terminated, though generally not where the child is born healthy.[102] But if the
termination of the pregnancy would not be lawful under the Abortion Act 1967,
the action for loss of opportunity to have an abortion will be denied on policy
grounds.[103] The basis for barring such actions seems to rest on the maxim ex turpi
causa non oritur actio or some analogous principle, but a denial of a duty of care
simply on the ground of "policy" is equally effective in practice. Thus, where
potential claims arise out of the negligent performance of procedures which are
unlawful the likelihood is that they will be barred on the grounds of policy.[104]

3. DUTY TO THE PATIENT

From ancient times medical practitioners have been held accountable for a failure   2–036
to exercise reasonable care in treating their patients, independently of any
contractual relationship with those patients. The surgeon, like the inn keeper or
common carrier, exercised a "common calling" which gave rise to a duty to
exercise proper care and skill.[105] Today the duty arises from the tort of
negligence, but it does not depend upon a doctor's status, qualifications or
expertise. Rather it is imposed by law when a doctor undertakes the task of
providing advice, diagnosis or treatment. It is irrelevant who called the doctor to
the patient or who pays the bill.[106] In *R. v Bateman* Lord Hewart CJ said:

> "If a person holds himself out as possessing special skill and knowledge and he is consulted, as
> possessing such skill and knowledge, by or on behalf of a patient, he owes a duty to the patient
> to use due caution in undertaking the treatment. If he accepts the responsibility and undertakes
> the treatment and the patient submits to his direction and treatment accordingly, he owes a

---

[100] In particular, in the form of an unquantifiable reluctance on the part of the courts to make findings
of negligence against doctors, possibly due to fears about defensive medicine or the effects of such a
finding on the defendant's professional reputation: see paras 1–025 to 1–030 and 3–134 to 3–146 and
3–178 to 3–179.

[101] *McKay v Essex Area Health Authority* [1982] Q.B. 1166; see para.2–141.

[102] See para.2–055 et seq.

[103] *Rance v Mid-Downs Health Authority* [1991] 1 Q.B. 587.

[104] See para.11–028. The principle of public policy that would preclude the cause of action applies
equally to claims in contract or tort.

[105] Holdsworth, *History of English Law*, Vol.III, pp.385–386; Winfield (1926) 42 L.Q.R. 184,
186–187; cf. Fifoot, *History and Sources of the Common Law*, pp.157–158.

[106] *Gladwell v Steggal* (1839) 5 Bing. (N.C.) 733: "...this is an action *ex delicto*", per Tindal CJ;
Pippin v Sheppard (1822) 11 Price 400; *Edgar v Lamont*, 1914 S.C. 277 at 279.

duty to the patient to use diligence, care, knowledge, skill and caution in administering the treatment. No contractual relation is necessary, nor is it necessary that the service be rendered for reward."[107]

2–037   It follows that, although as a general rule there is no legal obligation upon a doctor to play the "good Samaritan" and render assistance to a stranger who has been involved in an accident,[108] a doctor who chooses to do so will owe a duty of care to the "patient".[109] The duty arises from the performance of the act. In *Everett v Griffiths*[110] Atkin LJ said that the duty of medical practitioners to the people whom they undertake to treat is not based on contract or implied contract:

> "It would apply to a doctor treating a member of the household of the other party to the contract, as it would, in my judgment, apply to a doctor acting gratuitously in a public institution, or in the case of emergency in a street accident; and its existence is independent of the volition of the patient, for it would apply though the patient were unconscious or incapable of exercising a conscious volition."[111]

2–038   Moreover, the person who does not possess the relevant qualifications, expertise or skill comes under the same duty of care, since by undertaking the treatment he effectively represents that he does have these attributes.[112] In an emergency, such as a road accident, the position may well be different since a layman does not profess any specialist skill. It is doubtful, however, whether a court would conclude that no duty of care was owed in this situation; rather it may be that the standard required to satisfy the duty would be quite low. For example, a trained volunteer who offers first-aid medical help, such as a St. John's Ambulance volunteer, owes a duty of care to those to whom he renders first aid.[113] The duty

---

[107] (1925) 94 L.J.K.B. 791 at 794; *Lindsey County Council v Marshall* [1937] A.C. 97 at 121. In *Cassidy v Ministry of Health* [1951] 2 K.B. 348 at 359 Denning LJ said that: "If a man goes to a doctor because he is ill, no one doubts that the doctor must exercise reasonable care and skill in his treatment of him: and that is so whether the doctor is paid for his services or not."

[108] But see *Lowns v Woods* (1996) Aust. Torts Rep. 81–376, NSWCA, and *Kent v Griffiths, Roberts and London Ambulance Service* [2001] Q.B. 36, CA, discussed at paras 2–119 to 2–120 below.

[109] Though in these circumstances the precise scope of that duty remains unresolved. On one view the duty is limited to not to making the victim's condition worse: *Capital and Counties plc v Hampshire County Council* [1997] Q.B. 1004 at 1035. See below para.2–117. Of course, in an emergency less may be expected of the doctor to achieve the *standard* of reasonable care; see paras 3–093 to 3–096.

[110] [1920] 3 K.B. 163 at 213; *Banbury v Bank of Montreal* [1918] A.C. 626 at 657, per Lord Atkinson.

[111] See also *Goode v Nash* (1979) 21 S.A.S.R. 419: doctor liable for negligence in the course of conducting a public screening for the detection of glaucoma, notwithstanding that he "was engaged in a valuable community service, entirely on a voluntary basis".

[112] *R. v Bateman* (1925) 94 L.J.K.B. 791 at 794, per Lord Hewart CJ: "the unqualified practitioner cannot claim to be measured by any lower standard than that which is applied to a qualified man"; *Pippin v Sheppard* (1822) 11 Price 400 at 409. See *Ruddock v Lowe* (1865) 4 F. & F. 519 and *Jones v Fay* (1865) 4 F. & F. 525 (which were both cases against alleged quacks) where it was said that it was not necessary that the defendant held himself out as a qualified doctor; the question is whether the defendant undertook the treatment of the claimant and did so negligently. With one or two notable exceptions, such as the Abortion Act 1967 s.1(1), the Nursing and Midwifery Order 2001 (SI 2002/253) art.45 (attendance on a woman in childbirth), and the Dentists Act 1984 s.38 (prohibition on practising dentistry unless a registered dentist or a registered medical practitioner) there is no prohibition on the unregistered practice of medicine, although it is a criminal offence for an unregistered person to represent himself as a registered medical practitioner: Medical Act 1983 ss.49, 49A; or a nurse or midwife: Nursing and Midwifery Order 2001(SI 2002/253) art.44.

[113] *Cattley v St John's Ambulance Brigade* [1988] Lexis Citation 1703, QBD.

derives from the fact that he holds himself out as someone competent to render first aid, and he undertakes a legal responsibility to that extent. Thus, the standard of care required of a first aider is not that of a doctor but the standard of an ordinary skilled first aider exercising and professing to have the special skill of a first aider.[114] There must be a distinction, however, between a lay person who embarks upon "treatment", and one who merely gives "advice" (such as "take an aspirin and go to bed") in circumstances where it is clear that no responsibility is undertaken. Only if the circumstances are such as to indicate a genuine undertaking of responsibility for the patient's medical care will a duty arise.[115]

When does the doctor–patient relationship begin?   Although it may be trite   2–039
to state that doctors owe a duty of care to their patients, it is not so simple to state precisely when the relationship of doctor and patient begins. This is important because it is equally true to say that a doctor is not normally under a legal obligation (whatever the moral or ethical position) to render assistance by way of examination or treatment to a stranger. This stems from the "mere omissions" rule: one who chooses to act must do so carefully so as to avoid inflicting harm on others; but, as a general rule, the tort of negligence does not compel a person to take positive steps to confer a benefit on others. Generally, there is no legal obligation to rescue someone in danger, even if rescue would involve little or no effort and no danger to the rescuer,[116] although there are some signs that this overly rigid rule may be relaxed in some cases of medical emergency.[117] A "stranger" for these purposes is a person with whom the doctor is not and has never been in a professional doctor–patient relationship. Clearly, if such a relationship does exist a doctor may be liable for failing to attend or treat the patient, just as much as for careless treatment.[118]

Once a patient is accepted for treatment a duty of care will arise.[119] This, to some   2–040
extent, begs the question of what is meant by the term "accepted for treatment". A person accepted onto a general practitioner's list is clearly the doctor's patient, even if the practitioner has never seen that person in a professional capacity. Moreover, in an emergency, general practitioners may have an obligation to treat

---

[114] See para.3–118.
[115] See Nathan, *Medical Negligence*, 1957, pp.14–15. There is an analogy here with liability under *Hedley Byrne & Co. Ltd v Heller & Partners Ltd* [1964] A.C. 465.
[116] For discussion of the rule see Linden (1971) 34 M.L.R. 241; Weinrib (1980) 90 Yale L.J. 247; Smith and Burns (1983) 46 M.L.R. 147; Logie [1989] C.L.J. 115.
[117] See para.2–119 et seq.
[118] See paras 4–004 to 4–009.
[119] *Jones v Manchester Corporation* [1952] Q.B. 852 at 867, per Denning LJ. The duty would, of course, apply to any member of the medical team providing the treatment. There may sometimes be an issue as to what constitutes *medical* treatment. In the Canadian case of *Ayana v Skin Klinic* (2009) 68 C.C.L.T. (3d) 21; 179 A.C.W.S. (3d) 481 (Ont SC) the claimant suffered burns to her skin having attended a dermatology clinic for laser hair removal. Although the clinic was run by a dermatologist, she did not see the claimant after an initial conversation, and took no part in the treatment and did not provide any supervision. There were no statutory requirements for operators of laser hair removal devices to have medical qualifications, training or a licence. Price J concluded that laser hair removal was not a medical procedure: "The procedure could just as easily have been done in a beauty salon." The fact that it was conducted in a dermatologist's office did not, of itself, render it healthcare. Accordingly, the standard of care to be applied was not that of medical malpractice but was to be determined on ordinary principles of negligence.

persons who are not on their list.[120] Similarly, where a person presents himself at a hospital casualty department complaining of illness or injury, the staff in the department will owe a duty of care to that person even before he is treated or received into the hospital wards,[121] though this does not apply to a "civilian" receptionist in an Accident & Emergency department who gives incorrect information about waiting times with the result that the patient decides to leave.[122] On the other hand, "patients" are not entitled to demand that they be given particular treatment where a doctor has decided that it would be inappropriate,[123] or where a health authority does not have the resources to provide the treatment.[124]

2–041   **Consultants**   The position of consultants is less clear cut. Within the NHS patients are normally referred to a consultant through their general practitioner (though a patient admitted to hospital through the Accident & Emergency department may well be seen by a consultant without any involvement of the patient's general practitioner). It is uncertain whether the doctor–patient relationship can be said to begin when the consultant "accepts" the patient for treatment, e.g. by letter, or whether some contact between doctor and patient, in the form of a consultation, is necessary. It may also be unclear precisely when the doctor–patient relationship ends. If the treatment has been completed, but

---

[120] For the provision of services to "any person" following an accident or emergency see the National Health Service (General Medical Services Contracts) Regulations 2015 (SI 2015/1862) reg.17(7) and (8); and the National Health Service (Personal Medical Services Agreements) Regulations 2015 (SI 2015/1879) Sch.2 para.1, which by reference to the definition of "essential services" in reg.3 includes the provision of services to "any person" following an accident or emergency as set out in reg.17(7) of the National Health Service (General Medical Services Contracts) Regulations 2015. In *Barnes v Crabtree, The Times*, 1 and 2 November 1955 counsel for the defendant general practitioner conceded that the doctor's duty under the NHS was to treat any patient in an emergency, whether his own patient or not.

[121] *Barnett v Chelsea and Kensington Hospital Management Committee* [1968] 1 All E.R. 1068 at 1072. See also the comments of O'Halloran JA in *Fraser v Vancouver General Hospital* (1951) 3 W.W.R. 337 at 340, BCCA; aff'd [1952] 3 D.L.R. 785, SCC, cited in para.4–006.

[122] *Darnley v Croydon Health Services NHS Trust* [2017] EWCA Civ 151; [2017] P.I.Q.R. P14; [2017] Med. L.R. 245; discussed by J. Goudkamp [2017] J.P.I.L. C142; see para.3–098. Arguably, the position would be different if, e.g., the receptionist failed to pass on important information to the medical staff with the result that the patient was not seen promptly by a doctor or nurse. Sales LJ suggested, at [85], that "if a receptionist told someone seeking medical assistance that the A&E department was closed, without reasonable grounds for doing so, that might well be capable of founding a claim in tort".

[123] *R. v Ethical Committee of St. Mary's Hospital, ex p. Harriott* [1988] 1 F.L.R. 512; *Re J. (A Minor)(Wardship: Medical Treatment)* [1992] 4 All E.R. 614, C.A., where the Court of Appeal said that the court should not order a medical practitioner to treat a minor contrary to the practitioner's clinical judgment; cf. *Airedale NHS Trust v Bland* [1993] A.C. 789 at 858 where Lord Keith said that doctors may be in breach of duty to their patients if they cease to provide treatment in circumstances where continuance of it would confer some benefit on the patient.

[124] *R. v Secretary of State for Social Services Ex p. Hincks* (1979) 123 S.J. 436, aff'd (1980) 1 B.M.L.R. 93, CA; *R. v Central Birmingham Health Authority Ex p. Walker* (1987) 3 B.M.L.R. 32, CA; *R. v Central Birmingham Health Authority Ex p. Collier* [1988] Lexis Citation 1301, CA; *R. v Cambridge Health Authority Ex p. B.* [1995] 1 W.L.R. 898, CA; Newdick (1993) 1 Med. L. Rev. 53; *R. (on the application of Longstaff) v Newcastle NHS Primary Care Trust* [2003] EWHC 3252 (Admin); [2004] Lloyd's Rep. Med. 400. For consideration of whether a lack of resources can be a "defence" to an allegation of negligence see paras 4–151 et seq.

problems recur at a later date, is the relationship a continuing one, or is a new relationship entered into when a patient re-presents with the complaint? Moreover, in the case of specialists there must be an implied limitation to the scope of the duty created by the doctor–patient relationship. An orthopaedic surgeon, for example, would not normally be responsible for failing to diagnose a patient's heart condition. On the other hand, there are potential dangers in doctors construing their briefs too narrowly. Thus, the duty of a visiting consultant physician who is asked to conduct a physical examination of a psychiatric patient with a view to identifying a physical cause for the patient's mental condition is not limited to examining the patient predominantly in relation to his cerebral condition. By accepting an invitation to give an opinion the physician entered a doctor–patient relationship and was subject to a continuing duty of care towards the patient, which included carrying out a full examination based on the patient's history, regardless of the remit given by the psychiatrists.[125]

Private practice   The position of doctors engaged in private practice is even more problematic, because there is no equivalent to the general practitioner's "list" of NHS patients. The extent of the doctor's responsibility would depend upon the terms, whether express or implied, of the contract of retainer.[126]   2–042

(a) Scope of the duty

The doctor's duty to the patient is not necessarily limited to an obligation not to cause harm to the patient. In the case of patients with a psychiatric condition it can extend to an obligation to exercise reasonable care to prevent the patient from harming himself.[127] Moreover, in some circumstances the duty may encompass an obligation to prevent harm inflicted by others. For example, in the Canadian case of *Brown v University of Alberta Hospital*[128] it was held that the doctors at a hospital owed a duty of care to a child to report the suspicion that its injuries were non-accidental. The child was admitted to hospital by its father who claimed that the injuries were the result of a fall. A radiologist was found to have been negligent in failing to pass on to the doctors treating the child the suspicion that injuries observed on a CT scan of the child's brain could be indicative of non-accidental injury (the result of "shaken baby syndrome"). The baby was discharged from hospital without any warning to the mother or notifying the child protection authorities. The child was subsequently shaken again, sustaining severe brain damage. It was held that the hospital was vicariously liable, on the   2–043

---

[125] *Panther v Wharton* unreported, 29 March 2001, QBD, where the defendant failed to identify a serious vascular problem because he considered that he had been given a "limited brief" to exclude a brain condition or viral infection as a cause of the patient's mental state.

[126] See Nathan, *Medical Negligence* (London: Medical Negligence, 1957), pp.39–40, suggesting that with general practitioners in private practice, at least, the question might turn upon whether according to ordinary usage the person could be regarded as a patient.

[127] See para.4–165. Though this duty is generally limited to preventing physical or psychiatric harm to the patient. The doctor does not normally owe a duty to protect a patient from the legal consequences of the patient's criminal conduct: see *Clunis v Camden and Islington Health Authority* [1998] Q.B. 978, para.2–158 below.

[128] (1997) 145 D.L.R. (4th) 63, Alta QB.

basis that the radiologist owed a duty of care to the child.[129] Similarly, in *C v Cairns*[130] it was assumed that a general practitioner could come under a duty to a child patient to report to the relevant authorities (the police or social services) that the child had been sexually abused by a member of her family.[131]

2–044 Both of these cases appeared to sit uncomfortably, at least from the perspective of English law, with the decision of the House of Lords in *X v Bedfordshire County Council*[132] that no duty of care was owed by a doctor or social worker when advising a local authority about whether to exercise its statutory child-protection functions by taking a child into local authority care. However, in *JD v East Berkshire Community Health NHS Trust*[133] the House of Lords affirmed the decision of the Court of Appeal[134] to depart from *X v Bedfordshire County Council*, holding that doctors and/or social workers who suspect that a child has been the victim of abuse owe a duty of care to the child to exercise reasonable care in making judgments about the child's welfare. Although *JD v East Berkshire* involved, inter alia, allegations of negligence by doctors in making a diagnosis of non-accidental injury where none had occurred (thereby causing psychiatric harm to the child as a result of being unnecessarily separated from the family), there is no logical basis for suggesting that the duty does not extend to negligence in failing to diagnose non-accidental injury, with the result that the child suffers further harm at the hands of the person committing the abuse. There is no duty of care owed to the child's parents in this situation, however, because there is a potential conflict between the interests of the child and those of the parents.[135]

2–045 There are also limits to the scope of a doctor's duty when providing advice to a patient. The fact that had the doctor's advice been different the claimant could have avoided the loss that he has sustained does not necessarily mean that the doctor will be held liable, even if that advice was negligent. In *South Australia Asset Management Corp. v York Montague Ltd*[136] Lord Hoffmann gave an example of a doctor who negligently advises a mountaineer that his knee is fit. As a result the mountaineer goes on an expedition which he would not have undertaken if he had known the true state of his knee. He suffers an injury which is a foreseeable consequence of mountaineering but has nothing to do with his knee. Although the doctor has been negligent and clearly owed a duty to the mountaineer when advising about his knee and it can be said that the injury would not have occurred but for the negligent advice, Lord Hoffmann considered

---

[129] Although the discussion of the basis for the duty of care and its nature was extremely brief and rather lacking in analysis. See (1997) 145 D.L.R. (4th) 63 at 106.

[130] [2003] Lloyd's Rep. Med. 90.

[131] The action failed on the basis that the defendant had acted as many other general practitioners would have done at the time (1975), i.e. he accepted the child's mother's assurance that the abuse was a "one-off" event, and considered himself bound by an obligation of confidentiality, so that there was no breach of duty. The judge, Stuart Brown QC, emphasised that this reflected standards at the time, and not modern standards which reflect a greater knowledge and understanding of child sexual abuse.

[132] [1995] 2 A.C. 633.

[133] [2005] UKHL 23; [2005] 2 A.C. 373.

[134] [2003] EWCA Civ 1151; [2004] Q.B. 558.

[135] See further para.2–101.

[136] [1997] A.C. 191 at 213–214.

that the doctor would not be liable in this hypothetical example, because he was asked for information on only one of the considerations which might affect the safety of the mountaineer on the expedition. There was:

"...no reason of policy which requires that the negligence of the doctor should require the transfer to him of all the foreseeable risks of the expedition."

In *Less v Hussain*[137] the defendant was negligent in the advice that she gave to the claimant about certain specific risks of pregnancy. The claimant conceived but the child was stillborn, though the stillbirth was unrelated to the risks about which the defendant had given advice. Judge Cotter QC, distinguishing Lord Hoffmann's mountaineer example, rejected (obiter) the defendant's argument that, apart from a specific complication arising from the risks about which the defendant advised, the other consequences of the pregnancy, including the stillbirth and psychiatric injury, were outside the scope of the defendant's duty:

2–046

"Given that this was advice about conception ... loss of the baby during term was a kind of loss in respect of which a duty was owed and it makes no difference that the precise mechanism was not foreseen."[138]

It might have been different if the claim had been to recover damages because, without any previous problems, the claimant had hurt her back when heavily pregnant. In those circumstances it would have been strongly arguable that the loss would have been outwith the scope of the defendant's duty.[139]

(b) Psychiatric harm

Where a claimant has sustained physical injury and suffers psychiatric damage as a result of that physical injury there is no question of whether a duty of care in respect of the psychiatric damage is owed. It is then regarded as a matter of causation and remoteness, so that even if the claimant commits suicide as a result of depression brought on by physical injury the death may be actionable, being regarded as caused by the initial injury.[140] Emotional distress or anguish are also compensatable where the claimant has sustained physical injuries, and will be dealt with through the award of non-pecuniary damages for pain and suffering. These principles apply equally to injured patients as to any other accident victim.

2–047

The courts have had greater difficulty with claims for "pure psychiatric damage", where the claimant has not suffered any physical injury. Although most of the problematic cases have involved claims for psychiatric harm sustained by third parties as a result of witnessing traumatic events to others, some have involved claims by individuals arising out of events in which they were participants. In the medical context this could include, for example, psychiatric damage resulting from medical treatment where the patient has not yet sustained any physical

2–048

---

[137] [2012] EWHC 3513 (QB); [2013] Med. L.R. 383; (2013) 130 B.M.L.R. 51.
[138] [2012] EWHC 3513 (QB); [2013] Med. L.R. 383; (2013) 130 B.M.L.R. 51 at [174].
[139] [2012] EWHC 3513 (QB); [2013] Med. L.R. 383; (2013) 130 B.M.L.R. 51 at [172].
[140] *Pigney v Pointer's Transport Services Ltd* [1957] 1 W.L.R. 1121; *Corr v IBC Vehicles Ltd* [2008] UKHL 13; [2008] 1 A.C. 884; see para.5–157.

injury or the receipt of distressing news. The issues that such cases raise are so closely linked to the broader question of how the courts react to claims for pure psychiatric damage generally, that these cases are discussed along with those involving claims for psychiatric damage by third parties, below.[141]

(c) Financial loss

2-049 Whilst it is clear that a doctor normally owes a duty of care to the patient in respect of physical or psychological harm that may result from negligent diagnosis, advice or treatment, the position with respect to purely financial loss sustained by the patient as a result of negligent diagnosis or advice[142] is less clear. In *Stevens v Bermondsey and Southwark Group Hospital Management Committee*[143] the claimant was involved in an accident for which he had a claim against the local authority. He visited hospital and was seen by a casualty officer, who considered that there was nothing much wrong with him. On the strength of this the claimant settled his action against the local authority for a small sum. It was subsequently discovered that he was suffering from spondylolisthesis, a congenital condition activated by the accident. He sued the defendants, alleging that if the doctor's diagnosis had not been negligent he would have claimed and received a larger sum from the local authority. Paull J held that a doctor's duty was limited to the sphere of medicine and had nothing to do with the sphere of legal liability unless he conducted the examination with an eye to liability. In the absence of special circumstances, a doctor was not required to contemplate any question connected with a third party's liability to his patient.[144] On the other hand, in *Hughes v Lloyds Bank plc*[145] the claimant alleged that her general practitioner had negligently provided misleading information as to her prognosis, following a road traffic accident, as a result of which she had settled her action against the negligent motorist for much less than it was worth. The Court of Appeal took the view that the general practitioner owed the claimant a duty to take reasonable care to describe her condition accurately and make, so far as possible, a reliable prognosis. *Hughes* would appear to differ from *Stevens*, in that

---

[141] See para.2–187 et seq.

[142] Negligent *treatment* will usually give rise to physical injury or psychological harm, though it is possible for the consequences of physiological changes to a person's body caused by negligence to give rise to pure financial loss. For example, in *Greenway v Johnson Matthey plc* [2016] EWCA Civ 408; [2016] 1 W.L.R. 4487 employees who had been sensitised to platinum salts without developing any symptoms, and who would not develop symptoms unless they were further exposed platinum salts, were held not to have suffered compensatable personal injury. The financial loss they sustained as a result of no longer being able to work with platinum salts constituted pure economic loss which did not fall within the scope of their employers' duty to exercise reasonable care for the health, safety and welfare of employees.

[143] (1963) 107 S.J. 478.

[144] The decision apparently rested on the view that the claim against the council was either a novus actus interveniens or severed the chain of causation. See also *Pimm v Roper* (1862) 2 F. & F. 783, where the claimant was examined by a surgeon employed by a railway company, following a train collision. The surgeon said that his injuries were slight, and relying on this the claimant accepted £5 in compensation from the railway company. The claimant subsequently claimed that his injuries were much more serious, but his action against the doctor failed on the basis that the examination did not cause any injury to the claimant.

[145] [1998] P.I.Q.R. P98. See further the discussion of this case at para.2–111.

in *Hughes* the claimant had asked for a letter from the doctor for the express purpose of settling her claim against the motorist.

A *Hedley Byrne* duty?   If a doctor gives negligent advice or information about   **2–050**
prognosis where the patient or a third party is clearly relying on that advice for the purpose of coming to some financial arrangement this would seem to fall directly under the principle of *Hedley Byrne & Co. Ltd v Heller & Partners Ltd*.[146] Where the defendant is so placed that others could reasonably rely upon his judgment or his skill or upon his ability to make careful enquiry, and the defendant takes it upon himself to give information or advice to, or allows the information or advice to be passed on to, a person that he knows or should know will place reliance upon it, then a duty of care will arise.[147] In *Hedley Byrne* Lord Devlin considered that if the law were not developed to allow recovery for pure economic loss consequent upon a negligent statement relied upon by the claimant the consequences would be very odd. To illustrate this he gave the example of a doctor who advised the patient wrongly that his medical condition was such that he should give up work, it subsequently being discovered that there was no need for this.[148] It would be absurd, said his Lordship, that the fee-paying patient should have an action in these circumstances if the NHS patient had none. There is no reason in principle why the medical profession alone should be immune from claims under *Hedley Byrne*.[149] It may be that the distinction, if any, between Lord Devlin's example, which surely would be the subject of a *Hedley Byrne* duty, and *Stevens v Bermondsey and Southwark Group Hospital Management Committee* is that a hospital casualty officer does not undertake to give advice to a patient with regard to his financial position, and so it would not be reasonable for the patient to rely on the advice for that purpose.[150] The difficulty with this argument is that it is clearly reasonable for a patient to "rely" on a casualty officer's diagnosis where a negligent diagnosis causes personal injury. Both forms of loss are foreseeable. To take a different view of the proximity of the relationship when the loss is purely financial is to resort to a distinction which the House of Lords considered to be untenable in *Hedley Byrne* itself. Nor, arguably, does it help to speak in terms of what a casualty officer "voluntarily undertakes"

---

[146] [1964] A.C. 465.
[147] [1964] A.C. 465 at 503, per Lord Morris. Note that in *Caparo Industries plc v Dickman* [1990] 2 A.C. 605 the House of Lords restated the duty of care that may arise under *Hedley Byrne* in more restricted terms. See in particular the speeches of Lord Bridge and Lord Oliver at 621 and 638 respectively. On the other hand, in *Henderson v Merrett Syndicates Ltd* [1995] 2 A.C. 145 their Lordships took a broader view of liability under *Hedley Byrne*, which was said to rest on the principle of a voluntary undertaking of responsibility; see para.2–051.
[148] [1964] A.C. 465 at 517.
[149] In *Allen v Bloomsbury Health Authority* [1993] 1 All E.R. 651 Brooke J regarded a claim limited to the financial costs associated with the upbringing of the unwanted child to be a straightforward *Hedley Byrne* claim for foreseeable economic loss caused by negligent advice or misstatement. See, however, paras 2–052 et seq. for discussion of this type of action.
[150] cf. where a medical report is prepared for the purpose of litigation: *McGrath v Kiely and Powell* [1965] I.R. 497.

to do, since an undertaking of responsibility is in reality the imposition of a duty of care by law where the defendant behaves in a particular manner.[151]

2–051 However, in *Henderson v Merrett Syndicates Ltd*[152] and *White v Jones*[153] both Lord Goff and Lord Browne-Wilkinson suggested that some of the criticism of the concept of a voluntary assumption of responsibility was misplaced. Lord Browne-Wilkinson said that the criticism had proceeded on the basis that "assumption of responsibility" refers to the defendant having assumed legal responsibility rather than responsibility for the task, but the assumption of responsibility referred to is the defendant's assumption of responsibility for the task, not the assumption of legal liability. Even in cases of ad hoc relationships, it is the undertaking to answer the question posed which creates the relationship. If the responsibility for the task is assumed by the defendant he thereby create a special relationship between himself and the claimant in relation to which the law (not the defendant) attaches a duty to carry out carefully the task so assumed. With respect, this appears to be a matter of semantics. If it is a question of the law attaching legal responsibility to the defendant's conduct it is difficult to see what the concept of assumption of responsibility adds to the notion that the courts simply decide when and in what circumstances a duty of care in respect of financial loss will be owed. This is simply a restatement of the proposition that if the defendant chooses to act, and does so negligently, the law deems him to be liable, just as when someone chooses to drive a motor car and does so carelessly the law holds him liable for the resulting damage. In *Phelps v Hillingdon London Borough Council*[154] Lord Slynn said that assumption of responsibility:

> "...means simply that the law recognises that there is a duty of care. It is not so much that responsibility is assumed as that it is recognised or imposed by the law."[155]

---

[151] In *Smith v Bush* [1990] 1 A.C. 831 at 862, Lord Griffiths said that in the context of liability under *Hedley Byrne & Co. Ltd v Heller & Partners Ltd* [1964] A.C. 465 a voluntary assumption of responsibility "can only have any real meaning if it is understood as referring to the circumstances in which the law will *deem* the maker of the statement to have assumed responsibility to the person who acts upon the advice" (emphasis added). See also *Banbury v Bank of Montreal* [1918] A.C. 626 at 657, where Lord Finlay LC said that: "There is in point of law no difference between the case of advice given by a physician and advice given by a solicitor or banker in the course of his business. By undertaking to advise he makes himself liable for failing to exercise due care in the discharge of his duty to the person who has entrusted him, and the fact that he undertook it gratuitously is irrelevant."

[152] [1995] 2 A.C. 145.

[153] [1995] 2 A.C. 207. See also Lord Steyn in *Williams v Natural Life Health Foods Ltd* [1998] 1 W.L.R. 830, commenting that: "the general criticism is overstated".

[154] [2001] 2 A.C. 619 at 654. See also *Dean v Allin & Watts* [2001] EWCA Civ 758; [2001] 2 Lloyd's Rep 249 at [47] per Sedley LJ.

[155] Note that in respect of claims for financial loss the courts now draw a distinction between cases where the defendant's duty is merely a duty to *provide information* to the claimant to enable him to decide upon a course of action, and cases where the scope of the defendant's duty encompasses a duty to *advise* the claimant as to what course of action he should take. In the case of advice the adviser must take reasonable care to consider all the potential consequences of that course of conduct, and if he is negligent he will be responsible for all the foreseeable losses. But if the duty is only to supply information he must take reasonable care to see that the information is correct, and if he is negligent he will be responsible only for the foreseeable consequences of the information being wrong. See *South Australia Asset Management Corp. v York Montague Ltd* [1997] A.C. 191, HL. However, in *Hughes-Holland v BPE Solicitors* [2017] UKSC 21; [2017] 2 W.L.R. 1029 at [39] Lord Sumption doubted whether drawing clear-cut distinctions between giving advice and passing on information

(d)   Wrongful conception and wrongful birth

There are a number of situations in which following negligence by medical staff   **2–052**
a child is born who would not otherwise have been born. This may be the result
of a failed sterilisation procedure, or a failure to inform the patient(s) about the
risks of a sterilisation operation not achieving complete sterility. It may be the
result of negligence in the performance of an abortion, where the mother has
decided to undergo a termination of pregnancy, or it may be the result of a failure
to give appropriate advice about the risks of continuing with a pregnancy (usually
the risk of foetal abnormality) thereby depriving the mother of the opportunity of
having a termination of the pregnancy as she would be entitled to do under the
Abortion Act 1967. Typically, in the latter situation, it will be due to negligence in
failing to carry out appropriate tests, carrying out the tests negligently, or
negligently failing to report the results of those tests. Whilst the child has no
claim in these circumstances, the action being one for "wrongful life",[156] the
question arises as to potential claims by the parents. A claim by the parents is
compendiously called an action for "wrongful birth" distinguishing it from a
"wrongful life" claim by the child. Some commentators distinguish between
claims for "wrongful conception" and claims for "wrongful birth", which
respectively describe the situation where the negligence precedes conception and
those cases where the negligence occurs after conception but before birth.

Whilst these distinctions may be descriptively accurate, and the nature of the act   **2–053**
of negligence clearly differs,[157] it would appear that the same legal analysis
applies to both sets of circumstances, and therefore there is no real advantage in
seeking to separate them. In *Parkinson v St James and Seacroft University
Hospital NHS Trust*[158] Brooke LJ had suggested that cases involving post-
conception negligence were different from failed sterilisation cases because the
opportunity that is lost to the parents in "wrongful birth" cases was the
opportunity to terminate a pregnancy which they would have had if the
professional services had not been negligently performed, and:

---

was feasible. Confusion had arisen because of: "...the descriptive inadequacy of these labels. On the
face of it they are neither distinct nor mutually exclusive categories. Information given by a
professional man to his client is usually a specific form of advice, and most advice will involve
conveying information." When classifying the material as information or advice every case was likely
to depend on the range of matters for which the defendant assumed responsibility and no more exact
rule could be stated ([2017] UKSC 21; [2017] 2 W.L.R. 1029 at [44]).

[156] See *McKay v Essex Area Health Authority* [1982] Q.B. 1166 and the Congenital Disabilities (Civil
Liability) Act 1976 s.1(2)(b) limiting actions under the Act to occurrences where the child is born with
disabilities "which would not otherwise have been present". See para.2–140.

[157] Wrongful conception encompasses failed sterilisation procedures and claims based on the failure
to provide appropriate advice about the risks of a sterilisation operation failing, as well as negligent
genetic counselling; whereas a claim arising from negligence following conception would encompass
negligent performance of an abortion or negligent advice (including an absence of advice) about an
abortion, following, for example, negligent screening procedures for foetal handicap.

[158] [2001] EWCA Civ 530; [2002] Q.B. 266 at [46] to [48].

"…[b]ecause the policy issues in wrongful birth cases are different, I do not think it helpful to dwell any longer on that line of authority."[159]

Subsequently, in *Groom v Selby*[160] Brooke LJ explained that, with the wrongful birth cases, because in the case of a risk of foetal handicap a termination of pregnancy under s.1(1)(d) of the Abortion Act 1967 can take place at any time, "the issues relating to causation and to what is fair, just and reasonable in such circumstances are very much more straightforward". Hale LJ accepted that "the principles applicable in wrongful birth cases cannot sensibly be distinguished from the principles applicable in wrongful conception cases".[161]

(i) The healthy child

2–054   The legal rules applicable to wrongful birth claims have undergone significant re-evaluation. After some initial reluctance to award damages for the birth of a healthy child following a failed sterilisation operation for reasons of policy,[162] in *Emeh v Kensington and Chelsea and Westminster Area Health Authority*[163] the Court of Appeal held that damages for the birth of a child following a negligent sterilisation were recoverable, reasoning that since a sterilisation operation is lawful there were no good policy reasons for denying a claimant's action for the financial loss resulting from a negligent failure to perform the operation properly, whether or not the child was healthy (though in fact the child in *Emeh* was disabled).

2–055   This issue has been considered by the House of Lords on two occasions, first in the Scottish case of *McFarlane v Tayside Health Board*,[164] and subsequently in *Rees v Darlington Memorial Hospital NHS Trust*.[165] In *McFarlane*, following a sterilisation operation, the male claimant was wrongly and negligently informed that he was no longer fertile. He and his wife stopped taking contraceptive precautions and she became pregnant, giving birth to a healthy baby. Although their Lordships were agreed that the failure of the parents to have a termination of the pregnancy or put the child up for adoption did not break the causal link between the alleged negligence and the child-rearing costs, or constitute a failure to mitigate their loss, the House held that no duty of care was owed to the parents in respect of the financial cost of bringing up a healthy child following negligent

---

[159] His Lordship referred to *Rand v East Dorset Health Authority* [2000] Lloyd's Rep. Med. 181; *Hardman v Amin* [2000] Lloyd's Rep. Med. 498; and *Lee v Taunton and Somerset NHS Trust* [2001] 1 F.L.R. 419; [2001] Fam. Law 103, all of which involved negligent failures to detect foetal abnormality following routine testing in pregnancy, resulting in the failure to offer the mother the opportunity of a termination.
[160] [2001] EWCA Civ 1522; [2002] P.I.Q.R. P201; [2002] Lloyd's Rep. Med. 1 at [19].
[161] [2001] EWCA Civ 1522; [2002] P.I.Q.R. P201; [2002] Lloyd's Rep. Med. 1 at [28]. See further A. Whitfield (2002) 18 P.N. 234, 239. In this book, unless the context indicates otherwise, references to "wrongful birth" includes cases of both pre-conception and post-conception negligence.
[162] *Udale v Bloomsbury Area Health Authority* [1983] 2 All E.R. 522, Jupp J.
[163] [1985] Q.B. 1012.
[164] [2000] 2 A.C. 59.
[165] [2003] UKHL 52; [2004] 1 A.C. 309; [2003] 4 All E.R. 987.

advice about, or the negligent performance of, a sterilisation operation.[166] The reasons given by their Lordships for excluding the cost of rearing a healthy child varied significantly: (1) the doctor does not assume responsibility for this economic loss and it is not fair, just or reasonable to impose liability (Lord Slynn); (2) principles of distributive justice do not permit such losses to be recovered (Lord Steyn)[167]; (3) the benefits to the parents of having a healthy child are incalculable and therefore it cannot be established that the costs of rearing the child will exceed the value of the benefits (Lord Hope); (4) the extent of the alleged liability was disproportionate to the duties undertaken by the defendants (Lord Clyde and Lord Hope); (5) it was not reasonable for the pursuers to be relieved of the financial obligations of caring for their child (Lord Clyde); (6) the law must treat the birth of a normal, healthy baby as a blessing, not a detriment (Lord Millett). Indeed, Lord Millett considered that it was "morally offensive to regard a normal, healthy baby as more trouble and expense than it is worth", and given that the advantages and disadvantages of parenthood are inextricably bound together it would be:

"…subversive of the mores of society for parents to enjoy the advantages of parenthood while transferring to others the responsibilities which it entails."[168]

---

[166] Though note that, following the decision of the House of Lords in *Rees v Darlington Memorial Hospital NHS Trust* [2003] UKHL 52; [2004] 1 A.C. 309, the parents of a healthy child can claim a "conventional sum" of £15,000 for loss of the right to limit the size of one's family. See para.2–072.

[167] Lord Steyn acknowledged that from the perspective of "corrective justice", where someone has harmed another without justification he is normally liable to indemnify the other, and on this approach the McFarlanes' case must succeed: "But one may also approach the case from the vantage point of distributive justice. It requires a focus on the just distribution of burdens and losses among members of a society. If the matter is approached in this way, it may become relevant to ask commuters on the Underground the following question: Should the parents of an unwanted but healthy child be able to sue the doctor or hospital for compensation equivalent to the cost of bringing up the child for the years of his or her minority, i.e. until about 18 years? My Lords, I am firmly of the view that an overwhelming number of ordinary men and women would answer the question with an emphatic 'No.' And the reason for such a response would be an inarticulate premise as to what is morally acceptable and what is not . . . It is my firm conviction that where courts of law have denied a remedy for the cost of bringing up an unwanted child the real reasons have been grounds of distributive justice": [2000] 2 A.C. 59 at 82. Of course, Lord Steyn does not identify what particular conception of distributive justice he would favour (and there are many to choose from) and his mechanism for arriving at a conclusion (ask commuters on the underground) is fundamentally flawed. Even if one could be confident that these commuters could articulate a conception of distributive justice, they will not in fact be asked their opinions. As Hale LJ observed in *Parkinson v St James and Seacroft University Hospital NHS Trust* [2001] EWCA Civ 530; [2002] Q.B. 266 at [82]: "The traveller on the Underground is not here being invoked as a hypothetical reasonable man but as a moral arbiter. We all know that London commuters are not a representative sample of public opinion. We also know that the answer will crucially depend upon the question asked and the amount of relevant information and argument given to help answer it. The fact that so many eminent judges all over the world have wrestled with this problem and reached different conclusions might suggest that the considered response would be less emphatic and less unanimous."

[168] [2000] 2 A.C. 59 at 114. *McFarlane* has been followed in Ireland: *Byrne v Ryan* [2007] IEHC 207; [2009] 4 I.R. 542; *Ahern v Moore and The Southern Health Board* [2013] IEHC 72; [2013] 1 I.R. 205. In *Cattanach v Melchior* [2003] HCA 38; (2003) 199 A.L.R. 131; [2003] Lloyd's Rep. Med. 447 a bare majority of the High Court of Australia held that, in circumstances identical to those of *McFarlane v Tayside Health Board*, the claimants did have an action in negligence in respect of the costs of raising a healthy child. But in *Rees v Darlington Memorial Hospital NHS Trust* [2003] UKHL 52; [2004] 1 A.C. 309; [2003] 4 All E.R. 987 at [103] Lord Millett, commenting on *Cattanach*, said

2–056   The different views expressed in *McFarlane* as to the reasons for excluding the cost of raising a healthy child are indicative of the subjective value-judgments brought to bear on this issue by their Lordships, who were at pains to suggest that it was not a decision based on "policy".[169] It is difficult, however, to see what else, apart from "policy", underlies the decision, particularly when in the context of a claim against any other professional person, patently foreseeable financial loss arising from the defendant's negligence would be held actionable under the principle of *Hedley Byrne & Co. Ltd v Heller & Partners Ltd*.[170] The suspicion was that the unarticulated policy underlying *McFarlane* was that the NHS should not have to be burdened with the financial cost of such claims when it has other calls on its resources.[171]

2–057   In *Rees v Darlington Memorial Hospital NHS Trust*[172] there was general agreement that applying the ordinary principles of tort law, the claim in *McFarlane* would have succeeded.[173] Nonetheless, despite an invitation to reconsider *McFarlane* their Lordships were unanimous that it had been correctly decided. There was greater unanimity in *Rees* as to the basis for the decision in *McFarlane* than was apparent in the speeches of *McFarlane* itself (although three

---

that: "Despite the diversity of opinion, the judgments cover familiar ground and contribute no new insight." For comment on *Cattanach* see P. Cane, "The Doctor, the Stork and the Court: A Modern Morality Play" (2004) 120 L.Q.R. 23. In New South Wales the legislature has reversed the effect of *Cattanach*, providing that damages cannot be awarded for the costs of rearing or maintaining the child or for any loss of earnings while the claimant rears or maintains the child (Civil Liability Amendment Act 2003 (NSW) inserting a new s.71 into the Civil Liability Act 2002 (NSW)). This does not prevent an award of damages in respect of any additional costs associated with rearing or maintaining a disabled child (on which see para.2–061). See further *Bevilacqua v Altenkirk* 2004 BCSC 945; (2004) 242 D.L.R. (4th) 338; [2005] 4 W.W.R. 87 for a thoughtful analysis by Groberman J of the alternative bases for awarding damages following a failed sterilisation.

[169] See [2000] 2 A.C. 59 at 76, 83, 95, 100 per, respectively, Lord Slynn, Lord Steyn, Lord Hope, and Lord Clyde; cf. Lord Millett at 108 who distinguished between legal policy and public policy.

[170] [1964] A.C. 465.

[171] Consider, however, the comments of Ward LJ in *Walters v North Glamorgan NHS Trust* [2002] EWCA Civ 1792; [2003] P.I.Q.R. P232 at [44] in the rather different context of a claim for psychiatric damage following the death of her child: "I understand the concern of the Health Authority, and their insurers if there are any, that the drain on National Health resources having to meet claims for medical negligence is already sufficiently alarming as not to encourage claims being advanced by secondary victims of that clinical negligence. If I had to make the choice between redressing a wrong to an injured claimant and protecting the pocket of negligent defendants for economic reasons, then I would unrepentantly prefer to do justice than to achieve fiscal expediency. Fortunately, however, I am not called upon to make that choice. Policy does not govern findings of fact. The facts are either there or they are not. The judge was right to find the facts in the claimant's favour and having found those facts he was bound to apply the principles of law to them, especially since there was no real dispute that those principles applied. Considerations of policy do not enter this case. If the law needs to be changed, Parliament must do it." For comment on *McFarlane* see Norrie (2000) 16 P.N. 76; Weir [2000] C.L.J. 238; Maclean [2000] 3 Web J.C.L.I. 1; Jones (2000) 9 Tort L. Rev. 14; Radley-Gardner (2002) 118 L.Q.R. 11.

[172] [2003] UKHL 52; [2004] 1 A.C. 309. See P. Cane, "Another Failed Sterilisation" (2004) 120 L.Q.R. 189; A. Morris, "Another fine mess . . . The aftermath of *McFarlane* and the decision in *Rees v Darlington Memorial Hospital NHS Trust*" (2004) 20 P.N. 2; V. Chico, "Wrongful Conception: Policy, Inconsistency and the Conventional Award" (2007) 8 Med. Law Int. 139.

[173] [2003] UKHL 52; [2004] 1 A.C. 309 per Lord Bingham at [4]; per Lord Nicholls at [12]; per Lord Millett at [104]; per Lord Scott at [138].

of their Lordships in *Rees* were also in *McFarlane*—Lord Steyn, Lord Millett, and Lord Hope). Lord Steyn commented that he did:

> "...not propose to undertake the gruesome task of discussing the judgments in *McFarlane* ... There was undoubtedly divergence between the reasoning in the speeches ... [but] there was unanimity on the outcome of the principal claim for the cost of bringing up the child. There is a clear ratio."[174]

With great respect to Lord Steyn, what was clear from *McFarlane* was the decision itself—the financial cost of raising a healthy child following a negligent sterilisation or negligent advice about sterilisation is not recoverable in tort. But the ratio of a case involves both an appreciation of the decision and the reasons for the decision. The reasons for the decision emerged with greater clarity in *Rees*, but curiously included one, policy, that was expressly disavowed by their Lordships in *McFarlane*. An attempt by Hale LJ in *Parkinson v St James and Seacroft University Hospital NHS Trust*[175] to explain the decision in *McFarlane* as a case where their Lordships had created a "deemed equilibrium" whereby, in the case of a healthy child, the burdens of parenthood were deemed to be cancelled out by the benefits was said to be wrong. The emphasis, said Lord Steyn, was "squarely on the impossibility of undertaking a process of weighing the advantages and disadvantages".[176] Lord Hope commented that:

> "No calculation of that kind was attempted or even contemplated. It was considered that a calculation aimed at achieving a fair result, taking everything into account, was impossible."[177]

Three factors emerged as the basis of *McFarlane*. First, the impossibility of calculating the benefits of having a healthy child. Secondly, **2–058**

> "...a sense that for the parents to recover the costs of bringing up a healthy child ran counter to the values which [their Lordships] held and which they believed that society at large could be expected to hold."[178]

Lord Hutton considered that:

> "...the fundamental principle underlying the speeches in *McFarlane* is that it would not be fair, just or reasonable to award damages for the cost of bringing up a healthy child."[179]

Lord Scott said that different reasons were given by different members of the court in *McFarlane*. His Lordship was not in disagreement with those reasons, and reached the same conclusion on the basis of:

---

[174] [2003] UKHL 52; [2004] 1 A.C. 309 at [28].
[175] [2001] EWCA Civ 530; [2002] Q.B. 266.
[176] [2003] UKHL 52; [2004] 1 A.C. 309 at [28].
[177] [2003] UKHL 52; [2004] 1 A.C. 309 at [59]; see also per Lord Hutton and Lord Millett at [94] and [111] respectively.
[178] [2003] UKHL 52; [2004] 1 A.C. 309 at [109] per Lord Millett, citing Sir Roger Toulson; see also per Lord Steyn at [28]; cf. Lord Hope at [51]: "I did not base my decision [in *McFarlane*] on a belief that it was morally repugnant to award damages for the birth of a healthy child."
[179] [2003] UKHL 52; [2004] 1 A.C. 309 at [85].

"...a recognition of the unique nature of human life, a uniqueness that our culture and society recognise and that the law, too, should recognise."[180]

The third factor is policy. In *McFarlane* their Lordships had expressly rejected "policy" as a basis of their decision. However, in *Rees*, Lord Steyn argued that *McFarlane* was based not on public policy, but on legal policy:

"In considering this question the House was bound, in the circumstances of the case, to consider what in their view the ordinary citizen would regard as morally acceptable. Invoking the moral theory of distributive justice, and the requirements of being just, fair and reasonable, culled from case law, are in context simply routes to establishing the legal policy."[181]

Lord Bingham considered that despite the differences in reasoning in *McFarlane*, all of their Lordships reached the decision for reasons of legal policy. Those policy reasons were:

"...an unwillingness to regard a child (even if unwanted) as a financial liability and nothing else, a recognition that the rewards which parenthood (even if involuntary) may or may not bring cannot be quantified and a sense that to award potentially very large sums of damages to the parents of a normal and healthy child against a National Health Service always in need of funds to meet pressing demands would rightly offend the community's sense of how public resources should be allocated. Kirby J was surely right to suggest (in paragraph 178 of his judgment in *Melchior*) that: 'Concern to protect the viability of the National Health Service at a time of multiple demands upon it might indeed help to explain the invocation in the House of Lords in *McFarlane* of the notion of "distributive justice"'. It is indeed hard to think that, if the House had adopted the first solution discussed above [i.e. allowing full damages against the tortfeasor for the cost of rearing the child], its decision would have long survived the first award to well-to-do parents of the estimated cost of providing private education, presents, clothing and foreign holidays for an unwanted child (even if at no more expensive a level than the parents had provided for earlier, wanted, children) against a National Health Service found to be responsible, by its negligence, for the birth of the child."[182]

2-059 A problem that arose from the disparity in the reasoning of their Lordships in *McFarlane* and the difficulty of identifying a clear ratio from the case has been

---

[180] [2003] UKHL 52; [2004] 1 A.C. 309 at [139].

[181] [2003] UKHL 52; [2004] 1 A.C. 309 at [29].

[182] [2003] UKHL 52; [2004] 1 A.C. 309 at [6]. In *Cattanach v Melchior* [2003] HCA 38; (2003) 199 A.L.R. 131; [2003] Lloyd's Rep. Med. 447 at [178] Kirby J referred to Jones, "Bringing up Baby" (2000) 9 Tort L. Rev. 14 at 19 for this hypothesis, and this was one of the factors enabling His Honour to distinguish *McFarlane*, since structural arrangements for the provision of healthcare in Australia differ from the UK's NHS. The curious feature of *McFarlane*, however, was that not one of their Lordships referred to the financial position of the NHS as a factor in their decision, and indeed it was not raised by other members of the panel in *Rees* (although Lord Nicholls did suggest, at [16], "that the negligent doctor or, in most cases, the National Health Service should pay all the costs of bringing up the child seems to me a disproportionate response to the doctor's wrong"). Indeed, it is difficult to see how or why the fact that a particular defendant or category of defendant, may end up with less in the way of resources if liability is imposed can form the basis for a decision as to whether liability *ought* to be imposed. By definition, any decision to impose liability creates costs for defendants. But if healthcare provision in the UK was organised and paid for privately (through private insurance, for example) a decision that a private healthcare company ought to compensate for the financial consequences of negligent treatment might seem less controversial (and to have considerably less to do with vague notions of "distributive justice"). Of course, the courts might take into account the possibility that imposing liability might make provision of the service or insurance against the risk of liability particularly expensive, which could have implications for consumers. But this would be no different from the position of any other provider of professional services.

considerable confusion and disagreement, both at High Court level and in the Court of Appeal, as to its implications, particularly as to what can be recovered and in what circumstances in wrongful birth cases.[183] This is not simply a question of assessment of the quantum of the loss,[184] but goes to the scope of the defendant's duty of care. In *McFarlane* itself, though the parents could not claim for the economic costs involved in bringing up a healthy child, it was accepted that the mother did have a claim in respect of her losses, including general damages for the pain, discomfort and inconvenience of the unwanted pregnancy and birth, and special damages, which would encompass any additional medical expenses, clothes for herself during pregnancy, equipment on the birth of the baby and, in principle, compensation for loss of earnings due to the pregnancy and birth.[185] It would also follow that if the mother suffered any additional personal injury as result of the pregnancy, through complications in the pregnancy itself or immediately after the birth (including postnatal depression), she would be entitled to compensation for this harm as an ordinary incident of a claim for personal injuries.[186]

Where, however, a mother gives up work to look after a healthy child she is not entitled to compensation for loss of earnings. This, said the Court of Appeal in *Greenfield v Irwin*,[187] is equivalent to the costs of raising the child. The Court treated the damage as economic loss, not physical damage (the pregnancy).[188] There was no difference between this case (which involved a failure to detect that the claimant was pregnant before administering a course of contraception by injection) and *McFarlane*. But in any event in *McFarlane* Lord Steyn had refused to treat the distinction between economic loss and physical damage as relevant to the outcome, and Lord Millett had agreed that:

2–060

"...it should not matter whether the unwanted pregnancy arises from the negligent supply of incorrect information or from the negligent performance of the operation itself."

Buxton LJ observed that the claim in *McFarlane* was not rejected on the narrow ground that related to the economic nature of the loss, but on grounds of very

---

[183] See Hoyano (2002) 62 M.L.R. 883; Whitfield (2002) 18 P.N. 234.

[184] See paras 12–135 et seq. for further discussion of quantum issues.

[185] This statement is taken from the speech of Lord Slynn. Their Lordships were not, however, unanimous in their views as to what the mother could claim for. For further discussion see paras 12–137 to 12–140.

[186] This, of course, is subject to the qualification that she would have to prove a causal link between the defendant's negligence and her damage. Thus, in the case of post-conception negligence in failing to identify foetal handicap and offer the opportunity of a termination of the pregnancy, it would have to be shown that the damage was caused by the *continuation* of pregnancy, rather than the pregnancy itself.

[187] [2001] EWCA Civ 113; [2001] 1 W.L.R. 1279; Grubb (2001) 9 Med. L. Rev. 54.

[188] This was despite the ruling in *Walkin v South Manchester Health Authority* [1995] 4 All E.R. 132 that for the purpose of the law of limitation such damage is physical. See also *McLelland v Greater Glasgow Health Board* 2001 S.L.T. 446 at [28] per Lord Prosser, stating that the law to be applied to claims in relation to the cost of raising a (disabled) child was "the law governing claims for pure economic loss". cf. *Hardman v Amin* [2000] Lloyd's Rep. Med. 498 where Henriques J concluded that for the purposes of the Law Reform (Personal Injuries) Act 1948 s.2(4) (which, in a personal injuries action, requires the court to disregard the possibility that the claimant can avoid expenses by taking advantage of facilities under the NHS) the claim was an action for personal injuries.

broad principle—which was why the claim for the mother's loss of earnings in bringing up the child should also fail.[189] It was not a claim for physical damage with contingent economic loss. The loss was not caused by the pregnancy, but by the existence of the child.[190]

(ii)   The disabled child

2–061   An issue that was left untouched by the House of Lords in *McFarlane* was whether the rejection of the claim for the cost of raising a child also applied where the child happened to have disabilities. Immediately after *McFarlane* a number of decisions at first instance concluded that, though the case prohibited claims for the cost of raising a healthy child, the position was different where the child was disabled.[191] The issue came before the Court of Appeal in *Parkinson v St James and Seacroft University Hospital NHS Trust*[192] where it was held that the parents of a disabled child born following a negligently performed sterilisation operation were entitled to the additional costs of raising that child, i.e. the additional costs attributable to the disability itself, over and above the costs of raising a healthy child. Drawing on Lord Steyn's speech in *McFarlane* Brooke LJ suggested that applying the principles of distributive justice:

> "...ordinary people would consider that it would be fair for the law to make an award in such a case, provided that it is limited to the extra expenses associated with the child's disability."[193]

---

[189]   [2001] EWCA Civ 113; [2001] 1 W.L.R. 1279 at [28].

[190]   [2001] EWCA Civ 113; [2001] 1 W.L.R. 1279 at [28] at [29]. See also per May LJ at [42].

[191]   *Rand v East Dorset Health Authority* [2000] Lloyd's Rep. Med. 181 (failure to inform the mother that the child she was carrying had Down's Syndrome); *Hardman v Amin* [2000] Lloyd's Rep. Med. 498 (failure to diagnose rubella, and inform the mother of the risks of the child being seriously disabled); *Groom v Selby* [2001] Lloyd's Rep. Med. 39 (failure to conduct a pregnancy test before sterilisation); *Lee v Taunton and Somerset NHS Trust* [2001] 1 F.L.R. 419 (failure to diagnose spina bifida from an ultrasound scan).

[192]   [2001] EWCA Civ 530; [2002] Q.B. 266; see Quick (2002) 10 Tort L. Rev. 5.

[193]   [2001] EWCA Civ 530; [2002] Q.B. 266 at [50]. See also per Hale LJ at [95]. This had also been the approach of Henriques J in *Hardman v Amin* [2000] Lloyd's Rep. Med. 498 at 505: "If the commuters on the underground were asked whether the costs of bringing up Daniel (which are attributable to his disability) should fall on the claimant or the rest of the family, or the state, or the defendant, I am satisfied that the very substantial majority, having regard to the particular circumstances of this case, would say that the expense should fall on the wrongdoer." See also per Toulson J in *Lee v Taunton and Somerset NHS Trust* [2001] 1 F.L.R. 419 at 430: "I do not believe that it would be right for the law to deem the birth of a disabled child to be a blessing, in all circumstances and regardless of the extent of the child's disabilities; or to regard the responsibility for the care of such a child as so enriching in the ordinary nature of things that it would be unjust for a parent to recover the cost from a negligent doctor on whose skill that parent had properly relied to prevent the situation. If the matter were put to an opinion poll among passengers on the Underground, I would be surprised if a majority would support such a view. More importantly, Parliament has provided by s.1(1)(d) of the Abortion Act 1967 ... that a pregnancy may be terminated if two registered medical practitioners are of the opinion formed in good faith that 'there is a substantial risk that if the child were born it would suffer from such physical or mental abnormalities as to be seriously handicapped'. Parliament must therefore have considered it to be in the public good that a mother should be able to choose to have a termination in those circumstances. I cannot reconcile that provision with the argument that public mores nevertheless require the courts to regard it as a blessing that Mrs. Lee was

Hale LJ considered that the effect of the decision in *McFarlane* was that in the case of a healthy child the benefits of parenthood were to be treated as cancelling out the burdens.[194] But this approach only dealt with the ordinary costs of the ordinary child. The disabled child needed extra care and extra expenditure. He may be deemed to bring as much pleasure and as many advantages as a normal healthy child (though in practice this was much less likely) and this treated a disabled child as having exactly the same worth as a non-disabled child. "It simply acknowledges that he costs more."[195]

Hale LJ's "deemed equilibrium" approach was expressly rejected by their Lordships in *Rees v Darlington Memorial Hospital NHS Trust*,[196] where, strictly speaking, the question of whether the parents of a disabled child should be permitted to maintain an action in respect of the additional costs associated with a child's disabilities did not arise for determination (the child was healthy and it was the mother who had a disability in *Rees*). Nonetheless, their Lordships did comment on *Parkinson*. Lords Steyn, Hope and Hutton considered that the decision in *Parkinson* was correct.[197] Lord Steyn said:

2–062

> "While not wishing to endorse everything said in the detailed judgments of Brooke and Hale LJJ, I agree with the decision. The legal policy on which *McFarlane* was based is critically dependent on the birth of a healthy and normal child. That policy does not apply where the child is seriously disabled physically and/or mentally. In such cases normal principles of corrective justice permit recovery of compensation for the costs of providing for the child's needs and care relating to his disability but not for the basic costs of his maintenance."[198]

Lord Bingham doubted whether *Parkinson* was correct.[199] Lord Nicholls did not expressly refer to *Parkinson*, but the implication of his speech is that *Parkinson* is wrong, since he was critical of the anomalies that can arise if an exception to *McFarlane* was allowed "when either the child or the mother is disabled".[200] Lord Millett expressly left the correctness of *Parkinson* open. Although it would not be "morally offensive" to award compensation in the case of a disabled child, the process of separating out the additional costs attributable to the child's disability "may prove difficult to achieve without introducing nice distinctions and unacceptable refinements of a kind which tend to bring the law into

---

not able to exercise her right under the Act, when the purpose of the statutory provision (and of the scan) was to enable her to avoid the unhappy and burdensome situation in which she now finds herself."

[194] Though note that Hale LJ believed that there were: "many who would challenge that assumption. They would argue that the true costs to the primary carer of bringing up a child are so enormous that they easily outstrip any benefits" [2001] EWCA Civ 530; [2002] Q.B. 266 at [88]. Indeed, the "notion of a child bringing benefit to the parents is itself deeply suspect, smacking of the commodification of the child, regarding the child as an asset to the parents", [2001] EWCA Civ 530; [2002] Q.B. 266 at [88] at [89].

[195] [2001] EWCA Civ 530; [2002] Q.B. 266 at [90].

[196] [2003] UKHL 52; [2004] 1 A.C. 309.

[197] [2003] UKHL 52; [2004] 1 A.C. 309 at [35], [57] and [91] respectively.

[198] [2003] UKHL 52; [2004] 1 A.C. 309 at [35].

[199] "While I have every sympathy with the Court of Appeal's view that Mrs. Parkinson should be compensated, it is arguably anomalous that the defendant's liability should be related to a disability which the doctor's negligence did not cause and not to the birth which it did", [2003] UKHL 52; [2004] 1 A.C. 309 at [9].

[200] [2003] UKHL 52; [2004] 1 A.C. 309 at [18].

disrepute."[201] Lord Scott also expressly left the question of the correctness of the decision in *Parkinson* open, but considered that a distinction might have to be drawn:

> "...between a case where the avoidance of the birth of a child with a disability is the very reason why the parent or parents sought the medical treatment or services to avoid conception that, in the event, were negligently provided and a case where the medical treatment or services were sought simply to avoid conception. *Parkinson* was a case in the latter category. In such a case, where the parents have had no particular reason to fear that if a child is born to them it will suffer from a disability, I do not think there is any sufficient basis for treating the expenses occasioned by the disability as falling outside the principles underlying *McFarlane*. The striking of the balance between the burden of rearing the disabled child and the benefit to the parents of the child as a member of their family seems to me as invidious and impossible as in the case of the child born without any disability."[202]

The fact that the possibility of the child having a congenital abnormality is present in every pregnancy, and therefore foreseeable, was not a sufficient reason for holding the negligent doctor liable for the extra costs attributable to the abnormality:

> "Foreseeability of a one in 200 to 400 chance does not seem to me, by itself, enough to make it reasonable to impose on the negligent doctor liability for these costs. It might be otherwise in a case where there had been particular reason to fear that if a child were conceived and born it might suffer from some inherited disability. And, particularly, it might be otherwise in a case where the very purpose of the sterilisation operation had been to protect against that fear. But on the facts of *Parkinson* I do not think the Court of Appeal's conclusion was consistent with *McFarlane*."[203]

2–063 Lord Scott did not address the question of what the position might be if the parent(s) had mixed motives for seeking to avoid the birth of a child, which is probably not an uncommon situation. For example, a mother with four children, as Mrs McFarlane had, may seek a sterilisation on the basis that: (1) her family is complete and she does not want any more children in the household; (2) having "completed" her family she cannot or does not want to afford the cost of raising another child; (3) she is aware that with her own increasing age, there is a higher risk that any child she does conceive may have a congenital abnormality. Moreover, would the parent(s) have to convey their reasons for wanting to avoid the birth of a child to the doctor? Lord Millett, on the other hand, would not "distinguish between the various motives which the parties might have for desiring to avoid a pregnancy".[204]

2–064 The result of *Rees* is that the status of *Parkinson* is now uncertain, though, not having been overruled, it remains good law. The uncertainty stems from doubt as to the outcome if a case involving a claim for the additional costs associated with raising a disabled child were to reach the Supreme Court, though in any court below the Supreme Court *Parkinson* would still be binding authority. In *Farraj v King's Healthcare NHS Trust*[205] Swift J noted the doubt cast upon the authority of

---

[201] [2003] UKHL 52; [2004] 1 A.C. 309 at [112].
[202] [2003] UKHL 52; [2004] 1 A.C. 309 at [145].
[203] [2003] UKHL 52; [2004] 1 A.C. 309 at [147].
[204] [2003] UKHL 52; [2004] 1 A.C. 309 at [112].
[205] [2006] EWHC 1228 (QB); [2006] P.I.Q.R. P29; (2006) 90 B.M.L.R. 21.

Parkinson by the speeches in *Rees*, and Lord Scott's suggestion that a duty might be owed in cases where avoidance of a disabled child, rather than merely the use of contraception to avoid conceiving, was the specific reason for the treatment, but concluded that "for the present, the decision in *Parkinson* represents the law".[206]

(iii)   How disabled must the child be?

In *Parkinson* the Court of Appeal touched on the question of how disabled a child must be before account can be taken of the additional costs of the disability. Children vary enormously in their abilities, and some may need additional support due to perceived disabilities (such as additional tuition for public examinations). Brooke LJ referred to "significant disabilities". Hale LJ said that:

> "The answer is that the law has for some time distinguished between the ordinary needs of ordinary children and the special needs of a disabled child. Thus, for the purposes of the services to be provided under Part III of the Children Act 1989, a child is taken to be in need if, among other things, he is disabled: see s.17(10)(c). For this purpose, a child is disabled if he is blind, deaf or dumb or suffers from mental disorder of any kind or is substantially and permanently handicapped by illness, injury or congenital deformity or such other disability as may be prescribed: see s.17(11). This or very similar definitions have been used since the legislation establishing the welfare state in the late 1940s to identify those whose special needs require special services. Local social services authorities are used to operating it, for example when maintaining the register of disabled children required by Sched. 2, para. 2 of the 1989 Act. I see no difficulty in using the same definition here."[207]

In *Lee v Taunton and Somerset NHS Trust*[208] the defendants argued that since disabilities can vary infinitely in degree, it would be offensive for the courts to have to draw a line between children who are sufficiently normal to be deemed a blessing and others who are not. Toulson J considered, however, that the mother's entitlement to have a termination under the Abortion Act 1967 provided the measure of the relevant disability. Thus:

> "If a scan showed, or should have showed, evidence of such abnormality that the mother would have been entitled under s.1(1)(d) of the Act to have her pregnancy terminated, and if she would have exercised that right, but was deprived of the opportunity to do so as a result of clinical negligence, those facts should provide a sufficient foundation for her claim."[209]

(iv)   The causal connection

A further problem in applying the distinction between healthy and disabled children arising from *Parkinson* is the nature of the causal link between the

2–065

2–066

---

[206] [2006] EWHC 1228 (QB); [2006] P.I.Q.R. P29; (2006) 90 B.M.L.R. 21 at [39]; *Farraj v King's Healthcare NHS Trust* [2008] EWHC 2468 (QB) at [2] (reversed on other grounds: [2009] EWCA Civ 1203; [2010] P.I.Q.R. P7, see para.2–080 and para.9–043).
[207] [2001] EWCA Civ 530; [2002] Q.B. 266 at [91].
[208] [2001] 1 F.L.R. 419, QBD.
[209] [2001] 1 F.L.R. 419, at 431. The ground for a termination of pregnancy under s.1(1)(d) of the Abortion Act 1967 is that: "there is a substantial risk that if the child were born it would suffer from such physical or mental abnormalities as to be seriously handicapped." The Act does not define "seriously handicapped", which is a matter normally left to the judgment of the medical profession.

defendant's negligence and the child's disability.[210] The defendant's negligence results in the birth of the child, not the disabilities themselves, and though the connection between the birth and the disabilities is more obvious where the negligence consists of "negligent screening"[211] it is nonetheless causally relevant where it consists of negligently failing to prevent conception (as, e.g. with a failed sterilisation) even where there was no apparent reason to anticipate that the child would be disabled. In the latter case, the fact that the child has disabilities is simply an unfortunate coincidence, but it is this very coincidence which gives rise to the parents' claim for the costs of the disability. In *Parkinson* Brooke LJ indicated that he was only concerned with losses arising when the child's disabilities flow foreseeably from the unwanted conception. Foreseeable incidents during the mother's pregnancy and the time leading up to the birth which caused the child's disabilities would not ordinarily break the chain of causation. But there could be cases in which a child's disabilities, discernible at birth, were caused by a new intervening cause. Thus:

> "A negligent surgeon should not, without more, be held liable for the economic consequences of the birth of a child with significant disabilities if the child's disabilities were brought about between conception and birth by some ultroneous cause (for which see Lord Wright in *The Oropesa* [1943] P. 32, 39). Similarly, the ordinary rules relating to contributory negligence will be applied in an appropriate case to limit recovery."[212]

2–067   The point arose in *Groom v Selby*,[213] where the negligence consisted of a failure to perform a pregnancy test before carrying out a sterilisation, with the result that the claimant was unaware that she was pregnant until she was 15 weeks pregnant. Had she known about the pregnancy sooner she would have opted for a termination. The child was born apparently healthy, but some four weeks later she was found to be suffering from salmonella meningitis, producing long-term disabilities. This was caused by exposure to bacteria from the mother's birth

---

[210] The House of Lords made it clear in *McFarlane* itself that, in a failed sterilisation case, the failure of the mother to have a termination of the pregnancy or to put the child up for adoption did not break the causal link between the alleged negligence and the child-rearing costs. On the other hand, in the case of post-conception negligent screening for a foetal abnormality it is clear that the mother would have to prove that had she been informed about the risk or the fact of the child's disability she would have had a lawful termination of the pregnancy under the terms of the Abortion Act 1967. If, for personal reasons, she would not have had a termination (or if in the circumstances a termination would have been unlawful: *Rance v Mid-Downs Health Authority* [1991] 1 Q.B. 587), there is no causal link between the negligence and the birth of the disabled child. In Canada, where the negligence relates to non-disclosure of the risk that the child will be handicapped, the causation test is objective (applying *Reibl v Hughes* (1980) 114 D.L.R. (3d) 1; para.7–026), and therefore the question is not whether the claimant would have had an abortion, but whether a reasonable woman in her circumstances would have had an abortion: *Mickle v Salvation Army Grace Hospital* (1998) 166 D.L.R. (4th) 743 at 758–761, Ont Ct.

[211] The failure to identify or warn about the risk that the foetus may be disabled—which can arise pre-conception, from negligent genetic counselling, and post-conception, from a negligently conducted scan or test.

[212] [2001] EWCA Civ 530; [2002] Q.B. 266 at [54]. See also per Hale LJ at [92]: "I conclude that any disability arising from genetic causes or foreseeable events during pregnancy (such as rubella, spina bifida, or oxygen deprivation during pregnancy or childbirth) up until the child is born alive, and which are not *novus actus interveniens*, will suffice to found a claim."

[213] [2001] Lloyd's Rep. Med. 39, QBD; aff'd [2001] EWCA Civ 1522; [2002] P.I.Q.R. P201; [2002] Lloyd's Rep. Med. 1.

canal and perineal area during the delivery. The defendants argued that the causal proximity between the negligence and the damage was not as close in this case as in cases of failing to detect a foetal abnormality during pregnancy (as, e.g. in *Rand v East Dorset Health Authority* or *Hardman v Amin*). The negligence consisted of allowing the pregnancy to continue when the claimant did not want to be pregnant at all. The risk of giving birth to a disabled child was foreseeable, but it was mere chance that the child happened to have a disability. Moreover, the child was healthy at birth. The Court of Appeal held that this was irrelevant to the defendants' liability. It could not be said that the infection constituted an intervening event. The child's handicap arose from the normal incidents of conception, intra-uterine development and birth:

"All the causes of her meningitis were in place when the umbilical cord was severed: all that remained was for the bacterium to penetrate a weak point in the child's skin or mucous membranes and the damage was done."[214]

It followed that *Parkinson* applied. However:

"... the longer the period before the disability is triggered off, the more difficult it may be to establish a right to recover compensation, particularly because new intervening causes are likely to be at work."[215]

The question remains, therefore, as to what the outcome should be if the child's disability arose from a discrete subsequent event unconnected with her condition at birth, such as accidentally catching meningitis in the hospital. Would this break the causal link? Even the negligent conduct of a subsequent actor does not necessarily break the chain of causation,[216] so accidental harm should not necessarily break the link either. In *Groom v Selby* Hale LJ suggested that in *Parkinson* she and Brooke LJ were agreed that the child's disability must be genetic or arise from the processes of intra-uterine development and birth.[217] This would seem to exclude postnatal accidental events, and has led one commentator to suggest that negligently caused damage to the foetus in utero would also preclude the parent from recovering in respect of the costs of the disability. Rather, those costs could be claimed by the child under the Congenital Disabilities (Civil Liability) Act 1976.[218] But in a case where a claimant who never wanted to be pregnant at all gives birth to a healthy child who subsequently

2–068

---

[214] [2001] EWCA Civ 1522; [2002] P.I.Q.R. P201; [2002] Lloyd's Med. Rep. 1 at [23] per Brooke LJ.
[215] [2001] EWCA Civ 1522; [2002] P.I.Q.R. P201; [2002] Lloyd's Med. Rep. 1 at [26].
[216] See, e.g. *Webb v Barclays Bank* [2001] EWCA Civ 1141; [2002] P.I.Q.R. P61; [2001] Lloyd's Rep. Med. 500 and *Rahman v Arearose* [2001] Q.B. 351 where the Court of Appeal held that subsequent medical negligence did not break the causal link between a defendant's original negligence and the claimant's loss. See paras 5–142 and 5–143.
[217] [2001] EWCA Civ 1522; [2002] Lloyd's Rep. Med. 1 at [32].
[218] See Whitfield (2002) 18 P.N. 234, 242. Query whether different rules as to intervening conduct should apply in this category of case from other categories of negligence, given that subsequent medical negligence does not necessarily break the causal link between a defendant's original negligence and the claimant's loss. Of course, overlap between the parents' claim for the financial costs of the disability and the child's claim for the consequences of the disability should be avoided, but it is not immediately apparent that the child's claim would subsume all of the additional costs to the parents.

Millett and Lord Scott considered that the Court of Appeal's approach in *Rees* was wrong. Lord Millett, approving the dissenting judgment of Waller LJ, commented that:

> "In my opinion, principle mandates the rejection of the parent's claim. But in this case principle also marches with justice. The decision of the majority of the Court of Appeal is destructive of the concept of distributive justice. It renders the law incoherent and is bound to lead to artificial and indefensible distinctions being drawn as the courts struggle to draw a principled line between costs which are recoverable and those which are not."[227]

Lord Steyn, on the other hand, considered that:

> "...the injustice of denying to such a seriously disabled mother the limited remedy of the extra costs caused by her disability outweighs the considerations emphasised by Waller L.J."[228]

For Lord Hutton there was a clear distinction between a disabled mother and a mother in normal health. *McFarlane* was the exception to the general rule, and that exception should not apply to a disabled child or a disabled mother. The fact that one could point to hard cases very close to the line which divides recovery from non-recovery did not invalidate the principle itself.[229] Nonetheless, the result of *Rees* is that where the child is born healthy *McFarlane* applies and the parents cannot recover damages in respect of the cost of raising the child, irrespective of the parents' personal or family circumstances.

(vi) Damages for loss of the right to limit the size of one's family (or autonomy)

2–072   Perhaps the most controversial aspect of *Rees v Darlington Memorial Hospital NHS Trust*[230] was the majority decision to award a conventional sum in respect of the claimant's loss of "the right to limit the size of one's family". Although raised as a possibility in *McFarlane* by Lord Millett (who would have excluded the mother's claim arising out of the pregnancy[231] altogether as "the price of parenthood" and made a conventional award of £5,000 in respect of the loss of freedom to limit the size of their family) this was not commented on by the other members of the House of Lords in *McFarlane*. In *Rees*, Lord Bingham, while accepting that *McFarlane* was correct, indicated that this was "subject to one gloss". Even though the financial costs of bringing up an unwanted child were not recoverable, nonetheless, the fact remained that the parent of a child born following a negligently performed vasectomy or sterilisation, or negligent advice on the effect of such a procedure "is the victim of a legal wrong". Thus:

> "I can accept and support a rule of legal policy which precludes recovery of the full cost of bringing up a child in the situation postulated, but I question the fairness of a rule which denies

---

[227] [2003] UKHL 52; [2004] 1 A.C. 309 at [121].

[228] [2003] UKHL 52; [2004] 1 A.C. 309 at [39].

[229] [2003] UKHL 52; [2004] 1 A.C. 309 at [97] and [98]. See also per Lord Hope, at [63], who would have upheld the majority decision of the Court of Appeal provided the mother's disability was "serious".

[230] [2003] UKHL 52; [2004] 1 A.C. 309.

[231] See para.12–137.

the victim of a legal wrong any recompense at all beyond an award immediately related to the unwanted pregnancy and birth. The spectre of well-to-do parents plundering the National Health Service should not blind one to other realities: that of the single mother with young children, struggling to make ends meet and counting the days until her children are of an age to enable her to work more hours and so enable the family to live a less straitened existence; the mother whose burning ambition is to put domestic chores so far as possible behind her and embark on a new career or resume an old one. Examples can be multiplied. To speak of losing the freedom to limit the size of one's family is to mask the real loss suffered in a situation of this kind. This is that a parent, particularly (even today) the mother, has been denied, through the negligence of another, the opportunity to live her life in the way that she wished and planned. I do not think that an award immediately relating to the unwanted pregnancy and birth gives adequate recognition of or does justice to that loss. I would accordingly support the suggestion favoured by Lord Millett in *McFarlane* (at p.114) that in all cases such as these there be a conventional award to mark the injury and loss, although I would favour a greater figure than the £5,000 he suggested (I have in mind a conventional figure of £15,000) and I would add this to the award for the pregnancy and birth. This solution is in my opinion consistent with the ruling and rationale of *McFarlane*. The conventional award would not be, and would not be intended to be, compensatory. It would not be the product of calculation. But it would not be a nominal, let alone a derisory, award. It would afford some measure of recognition of the wrong done. And it would afford a more ample measure of justice than the pure *McFarlane* rule."[232]

Lord Nicholls agreed with this proposal, as did Lord Millett on the basis that the parents had been denied an important aspect of their personal autonomy.[233] Lord Scott also favoured an award of £15,000 for the claimant in *Rees* because she was owed a duty of care by the defendant doctor, and it was "open to the court to put a monetary value on the expected benefit of which she was, by the doctor's negligence, deprived".[234] With respect to Lord Scott, it is arguable that the expected benefit of which the claimant was deprived in *Rees* (and *McFarlane*) was probably far in excess of £15,000, if it was simply a question of monetary valuation. Lord Bingham, on the other hand, was very careful to state that the sum was not compensatory—it was not something to which a financial calculation should be applied. It was meant as recognition of the commission of a wrong, and was intended to be more than nominal, but it was not intended as compensation.

Both Lord Steyn and Lord Hope were strongly critical of this new conventional award (Lord Hutton did not comment on this aspect of *Rees*). Lord Steyn pointed out that there was no UK authority for such a novel award, and none in the decisions from many foreign jurisdictions. It was "heterodox", "contrary to principle" and "a backdoor evasion of the legal policy enunciated in *McFarlane*". It was beyond the limit of permissible creativity for judges: "In my view the majority have strayed into forbidden territory."[235] Lord Hope agreed. There was no consistent or coherent ratio in support of the proposition in the speeches of the majority, and the examination of the issue at the oral hearing was cursory and unaccompanied by research.[236] The figure of £15,000 would:

2–073

---

[232] [2003] UKHL 52; [2004] 1 A.C. 309 at [8].
[233] [2003] UKHL 52; [2004] 1 A.C. 309 at [17] and [123] respectively.
[234] [2003] UKHL 52; [2004] 1 A.C. 309 at [148].
[235] [2003] UKHL 52; [2004] 1 A.C. 309 at [45] and [46].
[236] [2003] UKHL 52; [2004] 1 A.C. 309 at [74].

> "...in many cases, and especially in this one, fall well short of what would be needed to satisfy Lord Millett's aim, which Lord Scott adopts, of compensating the parents for the wrong that has been done to them."[237]

The creation of such a power for the judges should have been left to Parliament, with the benefit of a report by the Law Commission.

2–074 One effect of the decision to award £15,000 to all parents, irrespective of their disability or the child's disability, is that rather than limiting compensation claims in relation to healthy children to those cases where the parent is seriously disabled (which would probably be a small minority of cases) defendants (normally the NHS) will now have to find £15,000 in every case of a negligently performed sterilisation or negligent advice about sterilisation, so that the policy concern articulated by Lord Bingham about the financial consequences for the NHS of such claims may be undermined. It would seem, however, that where negligent advice results in the conception of a child but the child is stillborn there will be no award for loss of autonomy.[238]

(vii)   The position of the father

2–075 One of the assumptions that has underpinned the cases of wrongful birth is that, at least in relation to the financial costs associated with raising the disabled child, the child's father is in the same position as the mother. Once the child is born, the burden of caring for the child, in theory, is shared between the parents, and the father is on an equal footing to the mother. Indeed, the legal obligation to support the child rests with both parents. The cases have tended not to distinguish between the mother and father in this respect,[239] and their Lordships in *Rees v Darlington Memorial Hospital NHS Trust* drew no distinction between a mother and father in respect of the award of a conventional sum of £15,000 for interference with the parents' autonomy. In *Whitehead v Hibbert Pownall & Newton*[240] counsel for the defendants argued that there can be no claim for damages for wrongful birth by a father, in any circumstances. Although the matter did not have to be resolved, Laws LJ noted that the possibility of a claim by the father was "certainly not ruled out in the learning" but it:

> "...would be beset by important difficulties. It would be viable, if at all, only as a secondary claim: it would critically depend upon evidence that had the mother known of the foetus' defect she would have chosen to undergo a termination. Mixed questions of policy and causation would arise ..."[241]

---

[237] [2003] UKHL 52; [2004] 1 A.C. 309 at [77].
[238] *Less v Hussain* [2012] EWHC 3513 (QB); [2013] Med. L.R. 383; (2013) 130 B.M.L.R. 51 at [180] per Judge Cotter QC (obiter—the claim failed on causation).
[239] So in *Parkinson v St James and Seacroft University Hospital NHS Trust* [2001] EWCA Civ 530; [2002] Q.B. 266 at [93] Hale LJ commented that: "My tentative view is, however, that, if there is a sufficient relationship of proximity between the tortfeasor and the father who not only has but meets his parental responsibility to care for the child, then the father too should have a claim."
[240] [2008] EWCA Civ 285; [2009] 1 W.L.R. 549. The case concerned an action against a firm of solicitors in respect of the allegedly negligent conduct of a claim against a hospital for damages for "wrongful birth" relating to the cost to the mother of raising a disabled child limited to the period between the child's birth and the mother's later death by suicide.
[241] [2008] EWCA Civ 285; [2009] 1 W.L.R. 549 at [51].

Rix LJ commented that though it may be "ultimately a House of Lords point" it could not be said that there was no real chance of a father showing that a duty of care was owed to him as well as to the mother at the time when the negligence resulting in a wrongful birth occurred:

"After all, imagine a wrongful birth case where the mother dies in childbirth and the father bears all the care costs of the child thereafter."[242]

His Lordship did not spell out the obvious implication that to deny the father a claim in respect of the costs of caring for a disabled child in such a case, where had the mother lived an action would have been permitted, would create patent injustice.[243]

In *McDonald v Sydney South West Area Health Service*[244] the New South Wales Supreme Court held that a duty of care was owed to the father of a child where there had been a negligent sterilisation of the mother. Harrison AsJ distinguished *Goodwill v British Pregnancy Advisory Service*[245] on the basis that in *McDonald* the father was actually present at one of the consultations between the doctor and the mother at which a sterilisation was discussed and so the doctor:

2–076

"...knew or ought to have known that if he did not perform the tubal ligation properly that Ms Foster and her partner may suffer the financial detriment of having to raise an additional child."[246]

The claimant was an existing partner of the mother, and there was no conflict between the duty owed to the mother and one owed to the father.[247] Such a claim

---

[242] [2008] EWCA Civ 285; [2009] 1 W.L.R. 549. at [63]. See also *Schumann v Veale Wasbrough; Chinnock v Rea* [2013] EWHC 3730 (QB); [2014] P.N.L.R. 14; (2014) 136 B.M.L.R. 214 at [61] where Dingemans J commented that: "the gratuitous care provided by a father in a wrongful birth case has been recovered in actions by some fathers. It appears that recoveries have been made by mothers for the gratuitous care provided by fathers, who then hold any such sums recovered on trust for the father." Dingemans J considered (at [68]) that it was "likely" that if the mother had a viable claim for wrongful birth damages would have been recoverable for the gratuitous care provided by the father to the child. The decision was upheld on appeal without any discussion of this point (*Chinnock v Veale Wasbrough* [2015] EWCA Civ 441; [2015] Med. L.R. 425; [2015] P.N.L.R. 25).

[243] In *Ahern and Ahern v Moore and The Southern Health Board* [2013] IEHC 72; [2013] 1 I.R. 205 at [82] Ryan J held that a father (unlike the mother) was not entitled to damages for "severe distress and emotional anguish" following the birth of a baby with severe physical defects (unrelated to the failed sterilisation) which died at six months of age. There could be no damages for distress in the absence of a defined psychiatric injury (see para.2–188). Nor could the father recover any financial expenses, since that fell into the category of pure economic loss, unconnected to any physical harm to the father.

[244] [2005] NSWSC 924. The case was concerned with the costs of raising a healthy child, which are recoverable in Australia: *Cattanach v Melchior* [2003] HCA 38; (2003) 199 A.L.R. 131. The facts of *McDonald* pre-dated the coming into force in New South Wales of s.71 of the Civil Liability Act 2002 (NSW) providing that damages cannot be awarded for financial loss arising from rearing or maintaining a healthy child.

[245] [1996] 2 All E.R. 161; see para.2–181. See also *Freeman v Sutter* [1996] 4 W.W.R. 748, Man CA at para.2–182, n.581.

[246] [2005] NSWSC 924 at [69].

[247] Harrison AsJ also clearly had in mind a similar situation to that considered by Rix LJ in *Whitehead v Hibbert Pownall & Newton*, commenting on the potential anomaly of denying a father's claim where he has actual responsibility for raising the child: "For example if a father has the sole

by the father did not have to be a joint claim brought by both parents,[248] but, given that both parents were responsible for the costs, each parent was entitled to a proportion of the quantified loss, to avoid double recovery.

2–077   In *Less v Hussain*[249] a woman sought advice privately from the defendant about whether it was safe for her to conceive, given her medical history. The advice was negligent, and she became pregnant but the child was stillborn for reasons entirely unconnected with the negligent advice. The claim failed on causation (on the evidence, the claimants would have gone ahead with the pregnancy even if given non-negligent advice), but the father claimed to be entitled to recover damages for mental distress falling short of a recognised psychiatric illness[250] given that there was a contractual relationship between the parties and it was akin to a contract which had as its object the provision of enjoyment, comfort, peace of mind or other non-pecuniary personal or family benefits.[251] Judge Cotter QC accepted that the object or dominant purpose of the contract was to secure peace of mind with regard to proceeding to a pregnancy, given the risks to the health of mother and baby, and that the defendant knew that in broad terms this was the object to be achieved. However, it was a necessary element of the claim that the existence or identity of the partner intended to benefit from the contract must have been identified or identifiable from the information provided at the time of either entering into or performing the contract. The mother had attended the consultation with the defendant on her own, and there was nothing that put the defendant on notice of the intended wider nature of the benefit. The defendant had no reason to believe that she was contracting with, and as a result advising, anyone other than the person in front of her.[252] Although these observations were obiter, if this approach is correct it opens up the possibility that where both prospective parents were present at the consultation with the defendant, and the defendant knew that she was contracting with and advising both parents, a contractual relationship could give rise to a claim for mental distress on the part of the father.

---

responsibility for raising the child and is estranged from the mother, should that circumstance dictate that he is not able to claim damages?" ([2005] NSWSC 924 at [75]).

[248] The mother had already brought a claim against the doctor which had been settled.

[249] [2012] EWHC 3513 (QB); [2013] Med. L.R. 383; (2013) 130 B.M.L.R. 51.

[250] It was unclear whether his bereavement reaction amounted to a recognised psychiatric illness, though the judge concluded that, even if it was, it was not caused as result of shock, namely the sudden appreciation by sight or sound of the distressing events he witnessed, applying *Alcock v Chief Constable of the South Yorkshire Police* [1992] 1 A.C. 310; see para.2–208.

[251] Applying *Farley v Skinner* [2001] UKHL 49; [2002] 2 A.C. 732 and *Johnson v Unisys Ltd* [2001] UKHL 13; [2003] 1 A.C. 518 as considered in *Yearworth v North Bristol NHS Trust* [2009] EWCA Civ 37; [2010] Q.B. 1; para.2–242.

[252] [2012] EWHC 3513 (QB); [2013] Med. L.R. 383; (2013) 130 B.M.L.R. 51 at [200]. The judge recognised, at [201], that: "there was the biological necessity of fertilisation to consider, however in the modern world this need not have been necessarily equated to a relationship *a fortiori* an existing relationship with a partner who was to share the advice."

(viii) A contractual claim?

In *McFarlane v Tayside Health Board*[253] Lord Slynn commented that the doctor **2–078**
does not assume responsibility for the economic costs of raising a healthy child,
and that "if a client wants to be able to recover such costs he or she must do so by
an appropriate contract". His Lordship did not specify what an "appropriate
contract" might consist of. Lord Clyde indicated[254] that special considerations
might arise in contract which were not relevant to the tort of negligence, though
the only obvious distinction was that between a contractual warranty and an
obligation to exercise reasonable care, whether contractual or non-contractual.
This leaves open the possibility that the position is different where the parties are
in a contractual relationship, at least if the defendant has given a warranty as to
the outcome.[255] On the other hand, the factors which led their Lordships to
exclude the cost of raising a healthy child would seem to be just as relevant to
contractual claims as to tort claims. If, for example, the law must treat the birth of
a normal, healthy baby as a blessing, not a detriment (per Lord Millett), or the
benefits to the parents of having a healthy child are incalculable and therefore it
cannot be established that the costs of rearing the child will exceed the value of
the benefits (per Lord Hope), or distributive justice does not permit such losses to
be recovered (per Lord Steyn), then the existence of a contractual relationship
between the parties would not obviously alter the outcome of such an approach,
whether the obligation was to exercise reasonable care or to achieve a specific
result. Subsequently, in *Rees v Darlington Memorial Hospital NHS Trust*[256] Lord
Scott considered that, in the context of cases based on professional advice or
services given by professionals, the differences between claims in contract and
tort were irrelevant:

> "In the case, for example, of a doctor working in the National Health Service and advising or
> treating an NHS patient, the advice or services are provided by the doctor pursuant to his
> contractual arrangements with the NHS, not pursuant to any contract with the patient. But the
> intention and purpose of those arrangements is that the doctor's services be made available to
> NHS patients. That being so, the extent of the duty of care owed to each NHS patient and the
> extent of the doctor's liability, and his NHS employer's vicarious liability, if the doctor is in
> breach of that duty, cannot in my opinion be any different from the extent of the duty and of
> the liability for any breach of duty that would apply in the case of a private patient with whom
> the doctor had a contractual relationship. The NHS patient is entitled to the benefit of the
> contractual duty owed by the doctor pursuant to his contract with his NHS employers."

It followed, said his Lordship, that in a case like *McFarlane*, the "same result
must be reached whether the claimant was a private patient or an NHS

[253] [2000] 2 A.C. 59 at 76.
[254] [2000] 2 A.C. 59 at 99.
[255] As had been argued in *Eyre v Measday* [1986] 1 All E.R. 488 and *Thake v Maurice* [1986] Q.B.
644; see paras 2–017 et seq. If the claimants were receiving fertility treatment privately and the
defendants, contrary to the agreement with the claimants, implanted three embryos in the woman
instead of two, could it be argued that this is, in effect, a warranty that a third child will not be born?
See Grubb (2001) 9 Med. L. Rev. 170, 173, commenting on *Thompson v Sheffield Fertility Clinic*
unreported 2000, QBD.
[256] [2003] UKHL 52; [2004] 1 A.C. 309 at [131].

the doctor may be found to owe a duty of care to third parties who are clearly not the doctor's patient, but the duty to the third party arises out of the relationship that the doctor has with a patient.

(a) Reports on the claimant for purposes other than treatment

2–083   There are a number of situations in which a doctor may be involved in preparing a report on an individual for use by others, where negligence in carrying out that function may lead to harm to that individual. Broadly, they can be divided into those cases where the doctor is examining an individual, or providing information or advice about an individual to a third party, for private purposes, such as a report for employment or insurance purposes, and those cases where a doctor examines an individual in the context of legal proceedings or in connection with statutory functions. There may be some overlap between these situations. As a matter of basic principle, it is self-evident that a doctor carrying out a physical examination should owe a duty of care to the examinee not to cause any additional physical injury to the examinee. The fact that the doctor is carrying out the examination for a purpose other than treatment of the examinee is irrelevant to this issue, and doctors should not be in a better a position with respect to the positive infliction of physical damage to the claimant than any other potential defendant. Thus, in *Re N*[268] Clarke LJ said, obiter, that:

> "It seems to me that [the forensic medical examiner] must have owed a duty of care to carry out any examination with reasonable care, and thus, for example, not to make matters worse by causing injury to the plaintiff."

The problem areas concern: (1) claims in respect of economic loss; and (2) cases involving failure to identify a serious medical condition for which the claimant could have obtained more prompt treatment.

(i)   Reports for private purposes

2–084   Where a doctor conducts a medical examination at the request of an employer, prospective employer or insurance company it is arguable that, in addition to the duty owed to the person making the request, the doctor owes a duty of care to the subject of the examination. There are two aspects to this. First, a negligent statement about the state of the examinee's health may result in the employer or insurance company refusing to enter into a contract with the examinee thereby causing financial loss. Secondly, if the doctor negligently misses a condition which if properly diagnosed and disclosed to the examinee could have enabled the examinee to seek appropriate treatment, the examinee may suffer otherwise avoidable physical harm. The position that the English courts have taken appears to exclude a duty of care in each of these situations, though the cases are fact-dependent and could be challenged.

---

[268] [1999] Lloyd's Rep. Med. 257 at 263; also reported as *N v Agrawal* [1999] P.N.L.R. 939, CA.

Employment   In *Baker v Kaye*[269] Robert Owen QC held that a doctor who   **2–085**
carried out a pre-employment medical assessment on behalf of a company could
owe a duty of care to the prospective employee in respect of the financial loss to
the prospective employee arising from a negligent report to the company
(although, on the facts, there had been no breach of duty). The duty of care
applied because the loss was clearly foreseeable, there was sufficient proximity
between the parties (the claimant provided detailed medical information to the
defendant, who regarded himself as under a duty of confidentiality and under a
duty to advise the claimant to seek further medical advice if his assessment
revealed a medical condition which required treatment), and it was just and
reasonable to impose the duty because there was no conflict between such a duty
and the duty that the defendant owed to the company. Indeed, the duty owed to
the claimant could be couched in virtually identical terms to the duty the
defendant owed to the company. In *Kapfunde v Abbey National plc*,[270] however,
the claimant applied for a job and filled in a medical questionnaire, which was
considered by a doctor who took the view that the claimant would have a higher
than average level of absence from work. The claimant was not offered the job.
The Court of Appeal held that there was no proximity of relationship between the
doctor and the claimant because the doctor had never seen the claimant, the loss
was purely economic, and the prospective employer did not owe a duty to
exercise reasonable care in selecting employees. Clearly, there is a distinction
between *Kapfunde* and *Baker v Kaye*, in that the claimant was not physically
examined in *Kapfunde*. Nonetheless, the Court of Appeal expressed a firm view
that *Baker v Kaye* was wrongly decided on the question of the duty of care.[271]

Insurance   There has been no case in English law in which the court has had to   **2–086**
determine the precise scope of a doctor's duty to the examinee when conducting
a medical examination of the individual for the purpose of advising an insurance
company. In *M (A Minor) v Newham London Borough Council*[272] a majority of
the Court of Appeal concluded, obiter, that in these circumstances the doctor
would owe no duty to the individual in the advice he gave to the insurers, even
though for the purpose of confidentiality he may treat the individual as a
patient.[273] Staughton LJ commented that the doctor's duty was "to use reasonable
skill and care so as not to cause harm in the course of examination or treatment",
but the "general duty" to perform the task with reasonable skill and care was

---

[269] [1997] I.R.L.R. 219.
[270] [1999] I.C.R. 1; [1999] Lloyd's Rep. Med. 48.
[271] In the light of comments made by the House of Lords in *X (Minors) v Bedfordshire County Council* [1995] 2 A.C. 633 at 753. See para.2–086.
[272] [1995] 2 A.C. 633.
[273] On the doctor's duty of confidentiality in these circumstances see the General Medical Council's guidance, *Confidentiality: good practice in handling patient information*, January 2017, para.115, (available at *http://www.gmc-uk.org/Confidentiality2017.pdf_69037815.pdf*) which requires the *patient's* consent to the disclosure of information for insurance or employment purposes. The GMC has also published more detailed guidance on this subject: *Confidentiality: disclosing information for employment, insurance and similar purposes* (2017).

owed to the person who engaged the doctor to perform the task, namely the insurance company.[274] Similarly, in *E (A Minor) v Dorset County Council*[275] Evans LJ commented (also obiter) that:

> "The insurance company's doctor undertakes by contract to examine and report upon the physical condition of the applicant. He does not undertake by contract or otherwise to treat the applicant, and it may well be the case—I do not know the answer to this—that it would be a breach of professional etiquette towards the applicant's own doctor if he was to offer or undertake any form of treatment, including professional advice. In these circumstances, there clearly is a limited relationship between him and the applicant and this is reflected in the limited scope of the duty of care which he owes to the applicant in tort."[276]

When *M (A Minor) v Newham London Borough Council* reached the House of Lords their Lordships agreed that a doctor does not, by examining an applicant for insurance, come under any general duty of care to the applicant:

> "He is under a duty not to damage the applicant in the course of the examination: but beyond this his duties are owed to the insurance company and not to the applicant."[277]

2–087   **Failing to report physical problems to the examinee**   In *R. v Croydon Health Authority*[278] a radiologist examining a chest X-ray as part of a pre-employment medical examination failed to spot a significant abnormality. If the abnormality had been identified the claimant would have been referred to a cardiologist who would have diagnosed primary pulmonary hypertension (PPH), an untreatable condition which limits life expectancy and which is particularly dangerous if the patient becomes pregnant. Shortly afterwards the claimant did become pregnant, and gave birth to a healthy child, although there were complications in her own health, some of which could have been avoided if the diagnosis had been made earlier. She claimed damages in respect of the effects on her own health and the cost of the pregnancy and raising the child, on the basis that if she had known about the PPH she would have taken steps to avoid conceiving. The Court of Appeal held that where the mother wanted both the pregnancy and the child there was no loss which could give rise to a claim in respect of the cost of the pregnancy and rearing the child.[279] Moreover, the duty of care owed by the radiologist did not extend to the claimant's private life and her decision to become pregnant, since the examination was conducted in the context of a pre-employment medical. But the claimant was awarded damages for the exacerbation to her ill health that could have been avoided with an earlier diagnosis of the PPH. This award was based on an admission by the defendants

---

[274] [1995] 2 A.C. 633 at 674.
[275] [1995] 2 A.C. 633.
[276] [1995] 2 A.C. 633 at 715. Though note that his Lordship was using the analogy of the insurance medical in order to distinguish the Court of Appeal's decision in *M (A Minor) v Newham London Borough Council* that a doctor examining a child for the purpose of deciding whether the child had been the victim of abuse owed no duty of care to the child.
[277] *sub. nom. X (Minors) v Bedfordshire County Council* [1995] 2 A.C. 633 at 753.
[278] [1998] P.I.Q.R. Q26; [1998] Lloyd's Rep. Med. 44.
[279] The claim in respect of the cost of rearing the healthy child would now be excluded, in any event, on the basis of the decision of the House of Lords in *McFarlane v Tayside Health Board* [2000] 2 A.C. 59.

that they owed such a duty of care to the claimant in the circumstances, though it is not clear that the Court of Appeal would have accepted this proposition if the matter had been contested.

Despite these reservations and the decision in *Kapfunde*,[280] it is strongly arguable that a doctor examining a patient for life insurance or employment purposes does owe a duty of care in negligence to that individual which extends beyond simply not causing injury to the examinee: if the doctor discovers something seriously wrong with the individual then he should come under a duty at least to alert the individual to the problem. In *Sims v MacLennan*[281] Judge Simpkiss held that a doctor carrying out a medical examination of an individual for the purpose of advising the DVLA whether that person is fit to drive does not owe a duty of care to that individual to inform his general practitioner that the person has raised blood pressure, though he was under a duty to inform the individual that his blood pressure was high and advise him that he should have it checked out by his general practitioner.[282] The issue was also considered in *Thomsen v Davison*,[283] where it was held that a doctor who, in a situation in which the relationship of doctor and patient did not exist, undertakes the examination of a person in order to assess his state of health has a duty of care not only to his employer but also to that person to conduct the examination competently, and not do or omit anything in the course of performing the examination which is likely to cause the latter damage.[284] This included a duty to inform himself of the results of pathological tests and advise the person to undergo investigation and treatment if they were adverse.

2–088

The Canadian courts have tended to conclude that where a doctor undertakes a medical examination for a third party, such as an employer or insurer, a doctor–patient relationship arises between the doctor and the person being examined. Thus, in *Leonard v Knott*[285] Kirke Smith J held that where employees underwent annual health checks conducted by a doctor who was engaged by their employer for the purpose, the relationship of doctor–patient existed between the

2–089

---

[280] And the *obiter* comments in the Court of Appeal and House of Lords in *M (A Minor) v Newham London Borough Council*, see para.2–086.
[281] [2015] EWHC 2739 (QB) at [39].
[282] Judge Simpkiss seemed to reach this conclusion on the basis of the expert general practitioner evidence that they would have expected the individual to be advised to consult his general practitioner. The claim failed on the facts, the defendant having complied with the duty to advise the deceased to consult his general practitioner about his high blood pressure.
[283] [1975] Qd R. 93. See also *Betesh v United States* 400 F. Supp. 238 (1974), DC District Ct in which a man drafted for military service expected to fail his medical examination because of a disability. The draft board doctors found him unfit for service because they discovered that he had cancer, but they did not inform him or his doctor of their diagnosis. Early treatment could have extended his life. His widow's claim against the government succeeded, notwithstanding that the court accepted that there was no doctor–patient relationship created by the medical examination. The doctors were said to be in a professional relationship, which was fiduciary in nature, which gave rise to a duty to disclose the information they had discovered in the "patient's" interests.
[284] A similar duty is arguably owed to persons whom a doctor certifies to be of unsound mind for the purpose of involuntary admission to hospital under the Mental Health Act 1983: see paras 2–161 to 2–164.
[285] [1978] 5 W.W.R. 511, 513, BCSC.

doctor and the examinees; and in *Parslow v Masters*[286] Hunter J concluded that a doctor–patient relationship was created between a doctor who examined a person for the purpose of providing a medical report on that person to an insurance company and the subject of the report. Although the insurers paid for the report, the subject was required to disclose private and personal information about herself to enable the defendant to prepare the report. This gave rise to a physician–patient relationship, even though the purpose of the consultation was not to enable the doctor to advise the patient and prescribe a course of treatment for her. There was only a difference of degree, not of substance, between the situation where a patient attended a physician for a third party medical rather than for professional services.[287] The defendants argued that the doctor did not assume or undertake responsibility for the claimant's interests as a patient nor did he expressly or impliedly undertake to exercise any power over the claimant for her benefit or assume responsibility for her interests. The assessment was completed for the benefit of the insurer. In response to this argument Hunter J commented that:

> "In my view, this construes the nature of the obligation on the physician who conducts a third party medical too narrowly. Surely, such a physician undertakes the responsibility to complete a proper examination of the patient, draw conclusions from the examination and report the results of the examination and the conclusion. Such examination is for the benefit of the patient as well as the insurance company. The patient is required by the terms of the policy to submit to such an examination at the request of the insurance company. Failure to submit to such an examination may result in a discontinuance of benefits to the insured. The reported conclusion of the physician to the insurance company affects the interests of the insured person. The physician assumes the responsibility to carry out a proper examination and exercises the power over the patient to the extent that the medical report may impact on disability benefits to the patient. In some cases, the physician may even recommend a treatment program which a patient should undertake in an effort to rehabilitate and become re-employable. Accordingly, there is a fiduciary obligation to [the claimant] in respect of the contents of the medical report prepared for [the insurers]."[288]

2–090   English law has no difficulty in holding that a doctor who is aware of a risk of individuals developing a serious medical condition has a duty to take steps to monitor their condition and give an appropriate warning. Thus, in *Stokes v Guest, Keen and Nettlefold (Bolts and Nuts) Ltd*[289] Swanwick J held that a factory medical officer was under a duty to institute six-monthly medical examinations of

---

[286] [1993] 6 W.W.R. 273, Sask QB.

[287] "In both instances, the patient must disclose personal and private information to allow the physician to make a proper assessment of his/her condition. In addition, the patient may be required to undergo physical examination as well as some tests to assist in such an assessment. In both cases the physician may make certain observations and draw conclusions about the condition of the patient," [1993] 6 W.W.R. 273 at 281.

[288] [1993] 6 W.W.R. 273 at 282. The fact that the Canadian courts regard the doctor–patient relationship as giving rise to a fiduciary relationship (see para.2–012, n.32) does not mean that the criteria for establishing the relationship should be different under English law.

[289] [1968] 1 W.L.R. 1776. In *Spring v Guardian Assurance plc* [1995] 2 A.C. 296 the House of Lords held that where A gives advice to B about C (in this case a reference on a former employee), A owes a duty to C to exercise reasonable care in giving that advice. Although the decision is concerned with the financial consequences for C of A carelessly giving information or advice to B about C, it would be strange if, in the analogous situation where a doctor is advising a third party about the state of the claimant's health, it were to be held that there was no duty of care owed to the claimant at least to

certain employees, given his knowledge of the risk to those employees of contracting cancer from the work in which they were engaged, and notwithstanding that strictly speaking they were not his patients. This situation is not substantially different from that which occurred in *Thomsen v Davison*. Even if one takes the view that a doctor should owe no duty of care in respect of pure financial loss to the examinee (though it is not clear why a doctor should be in any better position than a person writing a reference, who may owe a duty to the subject of the reference[290]), it by no means follows that the doctor should owe no duty in respect of a negligent failure to identify and report to the examinee a serious medical condition that requires treatment. As a general proposition physical harm is in a different category from pure economic loss, when it comes to the existence of a duty of care. In *Re N*[291] Clarke LJ considered that it was arguable that if the doctor discovered something seriously wrong with the individual then he should come under a duty at least to alert the individual to the problem. On the facts of *Kapfunde* there was no physical examination of the claimant, so that the question of what the doctor ought to have discovered and reported to the claimant about her state of health did not arise. Moreover, it is clear that, in some circumstances, a doctor may owe a duty of care to third parties arising out of treatment or advice given to someone who is undoubtedly a patient,[292] and it might seem strange that a court could conclude that no duty is owed to someone in a "quasi-patient" relationship with an examining doctor.

Reports for the purpose of private litigation   It is commonplace for claimants pursuing personal injury litigation to be medically examined by doctors acting both for the claimant and the defendant with a view to providing expert medical reports for use in the litigation. In the case of a report provided by an expert acting for the defendant, the claimant can be regarded as a "third party", given that the expert is instructed by the defendant and will owe duties to the defendant and to the court, but not to the claimant. Where the expert is instructed by the claimant it does not make sense to describe the claimant as a "third party", since the expert will owe a duty to the claimant and to the court, though the report on the claimant is for purposes other than medical treatment. The duties owed by the doctors in this situation are inextricably linked to the broader issue of the immunity of witnesses in legal proceedings and accordingly will be considered below.[293]

2–091

---

inform them of any problems that had been discovered as a result of the medical examination. The courts are usually more willing to protect a claimant's interest in physical wellbeing than his financial interests.

[290] *Spring v Guardian Assurance plc* [1995] 2 A.C. 296. See also *Cox v Sun Alliance Life Ltd* [2001] EWCA Civ 649; [2001] I.R.L.R. 448; *Legal & General Insurance Ltd v Kirk* [2001] EWCA Civ 1803; [2002] I.R.L.R. 124.

[291] [1999] Lloyd's Rep. Med. 257 at 263.

[292] See, e.g. paras 2–145 to 2–153, 2–165 et seq.

[293] See para.2–108 et seq.

(ii) Reports for "public" purposes

2–092 **Child protection and education** Doctors are also asked to prepare reports in connection with legal proceedings or with the exercise of the statutory functions of a public authority, for example the child protection functions of a local authority (though such a "report" is not necessarily a formal written report, but could include, for example, an oral statement of a diagnosis of non-accidental injury). In *M (A Minor) v Newham London Borough Council*[294] a child and her mother brought an action for negligence against a psychiatrist and social worker in respect of the manner in which they conducted an interview with the child for the purpose of identifying whether, and if so by whom, the child had been sexually abused. The psychiatrist and social worker were negligent in ascertaining the identity of the abuser, with the result that the child was needlessly removed from her mother's home for a lengthy period. Both mother and child alleged that this had caused them psychiatric harm. A majority of the Court of Appeal held that the psychiatrist and social worker did not owe a duty of care to a child when advising the social services authority, partly on the basis that the psychiatrist should not owe the child a duty of care when the child was not strictly speaking the psychiatrist's "patient".[295] Peter Gibson LJ said that since the psychiatrist was involved by the local authority in order to advise it in relation to its decision whether or not to intervene, it was inapt to regard the psychiatrist as under the same duty of care as if the child had been referred to the psychiatrist in order that advice or treatment be given for the child or her mother. It was true that the advice related to and foreseeably affected the child and her mother, and therefore for some limited purposes, such as a duty of confidentiality, the child was properly to be regarded as the psychiatrist's patient. But the psychiatrist did not owe the child or the mother a duty of care in relation to the advice given to the local authority "as it was never intended that the psychiatrist should give that advice to the child or her mother".[296] In principle, however, there is in no

---

[294] [1995] 2 A.C. 633; Dugdale (1994) 10 P.N. 82; Jones (1994) 6 J. of Child Law 161.

[295] cf. the dissenting judgment of Sir Thomas Bingham MR who accepted that the relationship between the child and the psychiatrist was not a normal doctor–patient relationship, but it was a very direct and personal relationship, and thus the child was the psychiatrist's patient in the sense that it was for the child alone that she was being invited to exercise her professional skill and judgment. That, said his Lordship, would ordinarily lead to the conclusion that the psychiatrist owed the child a duty of care.

[296] [1995] 2 A.C. 633 at 684. For discussion of the policy factors which the majority considered also supported the conclusion that no duty of care should be owed see paras 3–137 to 3–140. The majority also held that the local authority did not owe a duty of care when deciding whether, and if so how, to exercise its powers under the child protection legislation; cf. *T (A Minor) v Surrey County Council* [1994] 4 All E.R. 577, where a local authority was held liable in negligence for negligently advising a parent that there was no reason why a child not should be placed with a particular childminder, when the authority knew or ought to have known that there was a significant risk, because the childminder in question could well have previously inflicted a serious non-accidental injury to another child. See also *W v Essex County Council* [1999] Fam. 90 where a local authority placed a 15-year-old boy, who was a known sexual abuser, with a foster family without informing the parents of his full history, and despite oral assurances from the local authority that a suspected or known sexual abuser would not be placed with them, with the result that the family's children were sexually abused. The Court of Appeal held that the local authority had "assumed a responsibility" for the accuracy of the statements that they gave about the boy placed with the family, and therefore the claims of the children should not be

objection to holding that A can owe a duty to B in respect of advice given to C in circumstances where the advice was never intended to be communicated to B, as both the Court of Appeal and the House of Lords have concluded.[297] Staughton LJ emphasised that neither the child nor her mother had sought the doctor's services; they had been thrust upon them. With respect, having services thrust upon one gives no indication that the individual is not entitled to have those services performed with reasonable care. For example, the services of a psychiatrist are thrust upon a person who is compulsorily admitted to hospital for treatment under the Mental Health Act 1983, and yet no one would suggest that for this reason the psychiatrist does not owe a duty of care in negligence to that person. As Lord Slynn observed in *Phelps v Hillingdon London Borough Council*,[298] a case involving a claim in respect of alleged negligence by an educational psychologist:

> "The fact that the educational psychologist owes a duty to the authority to exercise skill and care in the performance of his contract of employment does not mean that no duty of care can be or is owed to the child."

In *E (A Minor) v Dorset County Council*[299] a differently constituted Court of Appeal (though including Sir Thomas Bingham MR) distinguished *M (A Minor) v Newham London Borough Council* in a case where claims for damages were brought by children against education authorities alleging negligence in the assessment of their need for special educational provision. It was held that the actions should not be struck out as disclosing no reasonable cause of action since it was arguable that a doctor, educational psychologist or head teacher could owe a duty of care to a child when assessing the child's educational needs. The basis for the duty owed to the child was not the contract under which the professional person was consulted, said Evans LJ, nor the statutory requirement that the local authority should consult the professional, but the relationship which is brought about between them:

2–093

> "Put another way, the consultant owes a duty in tort to the child as his patient, *or as the person in whose interests his professional advice is sought and given.*"[300]

The doctor in *E (A Minor) v Dorset County Council* was engaged not merely to report but to advise on the best interests of the child. The advice was a form of treatment, and the child and its parents, as well as the local authority, were entitled to expect that the advice would be carefully and competently given. As

---

struck out as disclosing no reasonable cause of action. The authority were not exercising any statutory function in respect of these children. The claims of the parents in respect of psychiatric damage were struck out, but the House of Lords reversed the Court of Appeal on this point: [2001] 2 A.C. 592.

[297] *Spring v Guardian Assurance* [1995] 2 A.C. 296; *White v Jones* [1993] 3 W.L.R. 730, CA; [1995] 2 A.C. 207, HL; see also *Gorham v British Telecommunications plc* [2000] 1 W.L.R. 2129, CA. These cases concern the somewhat different matter of liability for economic loss, but normally the courts show a greater willingness to protect a claimant from personal injury than economic loss. The analogy of *White v Jones* was specifically rejected, however, by the House of Lords in *M v Newham*: see *X (Minors) v Bedfordshire County Council* [1995] 2 A.C. 633, 752.
[298] [2001] 2 A.C. 619 at 654.
[299] [1995] 2 A.C. 633.
[300] [1995] 2 A.C. 633 at 714, emphasis added.

Evans LJ put it, the doctor owed a duty in tort to the child as his patient, "or as the person in whose interests his professional advice is sought and given". Arguably, that principle applied equally to the child in *M v Newham*: the child's interests were essentially the *only* interests at stake in that case, and therefore it was distinctly odd that a doctor could be said to owe a duty to exercise reasonable care in advising the local authority, but not to the child, when the very purpose of the duty owed to the local authority was to enable it to act in the best interests of the child.

2–094 In *X (Minors) v Bedfordshire County Council*[301] the appeals to the House of Lords in the cases of *M (A Minor) v Newham LBC* and *E (A Minor) v Dorset County Council* were considered together, along with several other actions brought against social services authorities and education authorities. Their Lordships agreed with the majority of the Court of Appeal in *M (A Minor) v Newham London Borough Council* that the psychiatrist and social worker were retained by the local authority to advise the local authority, not the claimants. The fact that the carrying out of the retainer involved contact with and a relationship with the child did not alter the extent of the duty owed by the professionals under the retainer from the local authority. The social worker and the psychiatrist, said their Lordships, did not assume any general professional duty of care to the child. In considering whether the local authority could owe a direct duty of care to the claimants (as opposed to vicarious liability for the negligence of individuals) in *X (Minors) v Bedfordshire County Council* it was accepted that there was the requisite foreseeability and proximity of relationship, but their Lordships concluded that no duty should exist because of policy considerations, applying the third limb of the *Caparo* test,[302] namely that it should be "just and reasonable" to impose a duty of care.[303] The same policy factors applied with equal force to the question of whether the psychiatrist or social worker should owe a duty of care as individuals in *M (A Minor) v Newham London Borough Council*.[304]

2–095 Somewhat puzzlingly, their Lordships accepted that in the case of *E (A Minor) v Dorset County Council* the local authority could be both directly liable in negligence and vicariously liable for the negligence of an educational psychologist in assessing a child's special educational needs. The direct duty of care arose because the authority held itself out as offering a specialist service (psychological advice) to the public:

---

[301] [1995] 2 A.C. 633.

[302] *Caparo Industries plc v Dickman* [1990] 2 A.C. 605.

[303] Lord Brown-Wilkinson identified a whole raft of policy considerations that militated against the imposition of a duty of care, including that: a common law duty of care would "cut across" the statutory system for the protection of children at risk and it would be difficult to disentangle the respective responsibilities of the different agencies for a particular decision found to be negligent; the task of dealing with children at risk is "extraordinarily delicate"; local authorities would adopt a more cautious and defensive approach to their duties; the relationship between a social worker and the child's parents is frequently one of conflict and "fertile ground in which to breed ill feeling and litigation"; there were alternative remedies in the form of a statutory grievance procedure.

[304] See [1995] 2 A.C. 633, 754, per Lord Browne-Wilkinson. See para.3–141.

"By opening its doors to others to take advantage of the service offered, it comes under a duty of care to those using the service to exercise care in its conduct. The position is directly analogous with a hospital conducted, formerly by a local authority now by a health authority, in exercise of statutory powers."[305]

The educational psychologist owed a duty of care because there was no potential conflict of duty between the professional's duties to the claimant and his duty to the education authority. Nor was there any obvious conflict, said Lord Browne-Wilkinson, between the professional being under a duty of care to the claimant and the discharge by the authority of its statutory duties. It remains something of a mystery why, in *M (A Minor) v Newham*, their Lordships considered that there was such a conflict between the duty owed by the psychiatrist to the local authority and a potential duty of care owed to the child. The psychiatrist could only discharge the duty owed to the local authority by acting with reasonable care in conducting the examination, which was being conducted in the interests and for the benefit of the child. It could not be in the interests of either the child or the local authority that the authority should act upon negligent advice (whether the careless advice is to the effect that the child has been abused or that it has not been abused). There is simply no conflict between these duties.

In *Phelps v Hillingdon London Borough Council*[306] the House of Lords had no difficulty in concluding that an educational psychologist could be liable in negligence when making an assessment of a pupil's educational needs for failing to diagnose dyslexia, as a result of which the claimant's education was seriously prejudiced, and that the local authority could be vicariously liable for the psychologist's negligence. The fact that the acts which were claimed to be negligent were carried out within the ambit of a statutory discretion was not a reason why a claim for negligence should not be permitted. Although it was important that those engaged in the provision of educational services under statute should not be hampered by the imposition of liability, it was unlikely that the existence of such duties would lead to that result, because "the recognition of the duty of care does not of itself impose unreasonably high standards".[307] The obligation was merely to exercise reasonable care in the circumstances. As Lord Clyde expressed the point:

2–096

---

[305] *X (Minors) v Bedfordshire County Council* [1995] 2 A.C. 633 at 763, per Lord Browne-Wilkinson.
[306] [2001] 2 A.C. 619.
[307] [2001] 2 A.C. 619 at 655 per Lord Slynn. See also the comments of Buckley J in *A and B v Essex County Council* [2002] EWHC 2707 (QB); [2003] 1 F.L.R. 615 at [25] where the local authority was held to have been negligent in failing to provide full information to prospective adopters about a child who was placed with them for adoption: "I cannot see how such a duty would detract from the importance of a child's interests or in any way interfere with the statutory regime. On the contrary, as has been pointed out in some of the cases, it might encourage those involved to perform their tasks better. It is clearly in the public interest that professionals and those with special skills who are paid to offer their services to the public should act to the appropriate standard and, at least in the context of this case, I can see no danger of such a duty encouraging unacceptably defensive behaviour. Indeed such action, if displayed here, might well have avoided the problems." The Court of Appeal upheld Buckley J's decision, but on different grounds: see *A v Essex County Council* [2003] EWCA Civ 1848; [2004] 1 F.L.R. 749; [2004] 1 F.C.R. 660 at [51].

case the potential conflict of duties is more apparent than real. As Lord Bingham pointed out in his dissenting speech,[321] where the parent is not the abuser there is no conflict, because the parent will want a correct diagnosis of the child's condition. Moreover, the duty:

> "...would be no different if a parent were the abuser, since the duty of the health care professional is to serve the lawful and not the criminal interests of the parent; in any event, an undetected abuser could never be heard to complain."

Lord Bingham also considered that since the parents have Convention rights which may also be breached, the parents should have a common law remedy for negligence. Although the two rights would not necessarily be co-extensive, if potential defendants have to worry about breaching the parents' Convention rights, they would still have an "apparent" conflict of duties.[322]

2–103 The facts of each of the cases in *JD v East Berkshire Community Health NHS Trust* had occurred before the Human Rights Act 1998 came into force. In *Lawrence v Pembrokeshire County Council*[323] the issue was whether, on facts that occurred after the coming into force of the Human Rights Act 1998, art.8 of the European Convention on Human Rights should change the courts' approach to the existence of a duty of care owed to the parent of a child who is the suspected victim of abuse. Although the parent clearly had a potential art.8 claim, the argument was that the Human Rights Act had also changed the policy balance in relation to the common law claim, and the court should depart from the majority decision in *JD v East Berkshire Community Health NHS* Trust that no duty of care was owed to the parent. Field J held that the existence of a potential claim by

---

(2004) 12 Tort L. Rev. 12. See also *Fairlie v Perth and Kinross Healthcare NHS Trust*, 2004 S.L.T. 1200, OH (no duty of care owed to suspected abuser by psychiatrist dealing with an adult patient who made allegations of serious abuse (subsequently retracted) following "recovered memory therapy").

[321] [2005] UKHL 23; [2005] 2 A.C. 373 at [37].

[322] See further on this issue Jones, "Child Abuse: When the Professionals Get It Wrong" (2006) 14 Med. L. Rev. 264. In *K v United Kingdom* (38000/05) [2009] 1 F.L.R. 274; (2009) 48 E.H.R.R. 29 the European Court of Human Rights found that in the case of *MK v Oldham NHS Trust* there had been no breach of the parents' art.8 rights. The Court, at [36], reiterated that: "mistaken judgments or assessments by professionals do not per se render child-care measures incompatible with the requirements of art.8. The authorities, medical and social, have duties to protect children and cannot be held liable every time genuine and reasonably-held concerns about the safety of children vis-à-vis members of their families are proved, retrospectively, to have been misguided." (This point was also emphasised in in *MAK v United Kingdom* (45901/05) [2010] 2 F.L.R. 451; (2010) 51 E.H.R.R. 14 at [69]). The baby had suffered a serious and unexplained fracture, and brittle bone disease was a very rare condition which was difficult to diagnose in very small infants. The authorities could not be faulted for not reaching a correct diagnosis immediately, nor for acting on the basis that the injury could have been caused by the parents. The measures were proportionate to the aim of protecting the child and gave due account and procedural protection to the parents' interests. However, there had been a breach of art.13 (failure to provide an effective remedy for the parents' complaints, in relation to events that occurred before the Human Rights Act 1998 came into force). Similarly, in *MAK v United Kingdom* (45901/05) [2010] 2 F.L.R. 451; (2010) 51 E.H.R.R. 14 it was held that on the facts of *RK v Dewsbury Health Care NHS Trust* the decision to prevent the father from visiting the child in hospital and a delay in consulting a dermatologist after it was recognised that the child could be suffering from a skin condition, rather than being the victim of abuse, constituted a breach of both the father's and the child's art.8 rights. *MAK v UK* is commented on by Greasley (2010) 73 M.L.R. 1026.

[323] [2007] EWCA Civ 446; [2007] 1 W.L.R. 2991.

a parent for breach of Convention rights against the professionals involved was not a basis for arguing that the professionals should owe a common law duty of care to the parent.[324] If anything, for Field J the absence of a common law duty of care was a basis for interpreting the parent's art.8 rights restrictively, when weighing up the factors that might justify an interference with the parent's art.8(1) right under art.8(2). The decision was affirmed by the Court of Appeal.[325] Auld LJ commented that:

> "...the advent of Article 8 to our domestic law, bringing with it a discrete right to children and parents of respect for their family life, does not undermine or weaken as a matter of public policy the primacy of the need to protect children from abuse, or the risk of abuse, from, among others, their parents. Nor, when those interests are or may be in conflict, does Article 8 so enhance the status of family life as, in the balancing exercise involved, would require the development of the common law by the introduction of a duty of care to parents suspected of abusing their children, a duty precluded by that public policy. In that respect the cogency of the reasoning of the Court of Appeal and of the majority of the House of Lords in *East Berkshire* remains untouched ..."[326]

For Auld LJ the claimant's proposed extension of the duty of care to parents would "fundamentally distort the law of negligence in this area", putting at risk the protection of children.[327]

It makes no difference whether a parent alleges that a local authority or NHS Trust is vicariously liable for the negligence of its employees or whether there is an allegation of breach of a "direct duty" owed to the parent (on the basis of an inadequate system, instructions, management or supervision). In either case there has to be a breach of duty by an employee and there is a potential conflict between the interests of the parent and the interests of the child suspected of being abused such that the reasoning in *JD v East Berkshire Community Health NHS Trust* precludes a duty of care being owed to the parent.[328]

2–104

On the other hand, there is no general principle that where a local authority owes a duty of care to a child, it cannot as a matter of law at the same time owe a duty of care to the parents of that child. In *Merthyr Tydfil CBC v C*[329] the claimant brought an action against the local authority in respect of psychiatric harm that she suffered due to the alleged failure of the local authority properly to investigate her concerns that her children had been abused by an older neighbouring child. The defendants sought to strike out the claim on the basis that *D v East Berkshire NHS Trust* was authority for the proposition that a local authority could not owe a duty of care to the parent of a child who had been, or who was suspected of having been, abused, either because of the potential conflict of interest or because the parent was a "third party" whose claim was parasitic on the duty owed to the child. Hickinbottom J, distinguishing *JD v East Berkshire Community Health NHS Trust*, rejected the argument that just because

2–105

---

[324] [2006] EWHC 1029 (QB); [2007] P.I.Q.R. P1; [2006] Lloyd's Rep. Med. 383.
[325] [2007] EWCA Civ 446; [2007] 1 W.L.R. 2991.
[326] [2007] EWCA Civ 446; [2007] 1 W.L.R. 2991 at [41].
[327] [2007] EWCA Civ 446; [2007] 1 W.L.R. 2991 at [55].
[328] *B v Reading Borough Council, Wokingham District Council* [2007] EWCA Civ 1313; [2008] 1 F.C.R. 295; [2008] LS Law Med. 182.
[329] [2010] EWHC 62 (QB); [2010] P.I.Q.R. P9; [2010] 1 F.L.R. 1640.

a local authority owe a duty of care to the child they can never owe a duty to the parents.[330] What *JD v East Berkshire* held, said his Lordship:

> "...was that the usual consonancy of interests between parents and children is displaced, as a matter of law, where the parent is suspected of abusing the child. It does not hold that, whenever there is any bare potential for some future conflict of interest between a child and his/her parents, then an authority is immune from owing any duty of care to the parents and from any negligence suit at the hands of the parents."[331]

Nor was this a "third party" case. The mother's claim was not parasitic on the duty owed by the local authority to her children. The claimed duty had a different basis and was of a different scope from that owed to her children.

2–106   **Forensic medical examinations**   In *Re N*[332] the Court of Appeal held that a doctor who carries out a forensic medical examination does not owe a duty of care to the person examined, other than not to cause further damage during the examination. Thus, where the defendant examined the claimant following a complaint to the police that the claimant had been raped by a third party, there was no duty of care upon the defendant to attend court to give evidence at the prosecution of the third party, even though it was foreseeable that if there was an acquittal the claimant would suffer further psychiatric harm. There is no duty to give evidence, since this would be inconsistent with the immunity of witnesses.[333] Thus, the claim was that there was a duty to take reasonable steps to attend the trial. This, however, missed the point. As Stuart-Smith LJ pointed out the duty must be a duty to take reasonable care to prevent the claimant from suffering damage of the type in question, i.e. psychiatric injury. A failure to attend to give evidence could be a breach of such a duty, but it was not the duty itself. The forensic examination at the request of the police or the Crown Prosecution Service did not create a doctor–patient relationship, and the doctor did not assume responsibility for the claimant's psychiatric welfare. The duty was simply to take reasonable care not to make the patient's condition worse during the examination.[334] The doctor was in the same position as the psychiatrist in *X v Bedfordshire County Council*.[335] Mere attendance at the trial achieved nothing without the defendant also giving evidence consistent with her earlier examination and report—but there could be no duty in relation to any evidence the doctor would give in the witness box.

---

[330] Citing *A v Essex CC* [2003] EWCA Civ 1848; [2004] 1 W.L.R. 1881; *Lambert v Cardiff CC* [2007] EWHC 869; [2007] 3 F.C.R. 148; (2007) 97 B.M.L.R. 101; and *W v Essex CC* [2001] 2 A.C. 592.

[331] [2010] EWHC 62 (QB); [2010] P.I.Q.R. P9; [2010] 1 F.L.R. 1640 at [27].

[332] [1999] Lloyd's Rep. Med. 257, also reported as *N v Agrawal* [1999] P.N.L.R. 939, CA.

[333] See para.2–108 below.

[334] Though note that Clarke LJ considered, obiter, that it was "at least arguable that where [a forensic medical examiner] carries out an examination and discovers that the person being examined has, say, a serious condition which needs immediate treatment, he or she owes a duty to that person to inform him or her of the position": [1999] Lloyd's Rep. Med. 257 at 263.

[335] Though note that this has changed following the ruling of the House of Lords in *JD v East Berkshire Community Health NHS Trust* [2005] UKHL 23; [2005] 2 A.C. 373 that a doctor examining a child for the purpose of determining whether the child is a victim of abuse owes a duty of care to the child. See para.2–099.

If, on the other hand, a witness *was* under a duty to attend and give evidence on   **2–107**
the lines of his or her witness statement, the position might be different. There
were cases where a claimant in a civil action had issued a witness summons and
the witness failed to attend where the claimant would have an action on the case
against the witness, though the older cases limited the damages to the costs of the
abortive hearing.[336] It might also be arguable that the claimant could have an
action against the witness for loss of a chance of succeeding in the litigation,[337]
although if a material witness failed to attend upon subpoena a trial judge ought
to grant an adjournment.[338] In such a case the recoverable damage would be the
costs thrown away by the adjournment. Moreover: "A similar position would
arise if the witness was contractually bound to attend."[339] Clarke LJ also
considered that:

> "...where a duty to attend court and give evidence is established, as for example by a contract
> between a party to civil proceedings and an expert..."

a claimant may be able to:

> "...recover substantial damages for any loss which he could establish as a result, no doubt
> assessed as the loss of a chance of success",

though this was "a point which can be considered when it arises for decision".[340]
Obviously, a contractual obligation to attend court to give evidence will not arise
in the context of criminal law or child protection proceedings, but could be
relevant in civil litigation.

(iii)   Witness immunity

An issue that is closely related to the question of whether a doctor conducting an   **2–108**
examination in the context of the statutory functions of public bodies owes a duty
of care to the examinee, is the question of the immunity of witnesses, though this
cuts across both public law and private law proceedings. A witness of fact in legal
proceedings (whether civil or criminal) has immunity from suit with respect to
evidence given in those proceedings,[341] and this immunity applies to the
collection and preparation of evidence such as a proof or a report prepared for
trial by a witness.[342] The immunity is based on public policy in protecting the
proper administration of justice so that witnesses are able to be frank when giving

---

[336] See *Couling v Coxe* (1848) 6 Dow & L 399; *Roberts v J & F Stone Lighting and Radio Ltd* (1945)
172 L.T. 240 at 242.
[337] Applying *Allied Maples Group Ltd v Simmons & Simmons* [1995] 4 All E.R. 907; para.5–108.
[338] [1999] Lloyd's Rep. Med. 257 at 259, at [11] per Stuart-Smith LJ.
[339] [1999] Lloyd's Rep. Med. 257 at 259. Chadwick LJ appears to have accepted that the position
could be different if there was a contractual relationship: "In the absence of contract, it cannot be said
that the defendant owed to the plaintiff a duty to take care to provide evidence or to attend a trial."
[1999] Lloyd's Rep. Med. 257 at 262.
[340] [1999] Lloyd's Rep. Med. 257 at 263.
[341] *Watson v M'Ewan* [1905] A.C. 480; *Rondel v Worsley* [1969] 1 A.C. 191 at 268; *Jones v Kaney*
[2011] UKSC 13; [2011] 2 A.C. 398 at [65].
[342] *Evans v London Hospital Medical College* [1981] 1 W.L.R. 184; *Smart v Forensic Science Service
Ltd* [2013] EWCA Civ 783; [2013] P.N.L.R. 32 at [26].

evidence free from the threat of civil proceedings, and to avoid a multiplicity of actions in which the truth of their evidence would be tried over again.[343] The immunity does not apply to the investigation of offences, as opposed to the preparation of evidence, nor does it apply to the fabrication of false evidence.[344]

2–109   **Expert witnesses: private law proceedings**   Formerly, expert witnesses enjoyed the same immunity from suit as witnesses of fact. The immunity applied to oral evidence and to those matters that could fairly be said to be preliminary to giving evidence in court, and so covered the production of a report for disclosure to the other side, but work done for the principal purpose of advising the client as to the merits of the claim fell outside the immunity.[345] However, in *Jones v Kaney*[346] the Supreme Court held that witness immunity should no longer apply to an expert witness sued by the person who had instructed them in the initial proceedings. In a personal injury claim a clinical psychologist (K) instructed as an expert for the claimant prepared a report which indicated that the claimant was suffering from post-traumatic stress disorder. An expert for the defendant considered that the claimant was exaggerating his symptoms. Following a telephone discussion between the experts the defendant's expert produced a draft joint statement, which K signed, concluding that the claimant did not have a psychiatric disorder. When the claimant's solicitors queried this with K she stated that the joint statement was not an accurate reflection of what she had agreed, but she was under pressure to sign it. The claimant settled the claim and sued K in negligence on the basis that he had had to settle the claim for much less than it was worth because K had signed the joint statement. The judge struck out the claim against K on the basis that she enjoyed witness immunity, but the Supreme Court concluded that there was no longer justification for permitting expert witnesses to rely on immunity for things said in court or for views expressed in anticipation of proceedings.[347] Part of the rationale for this was that advocates no longer had immunity from negligence claims by their client,[348] and the "expert witness has far more in common with the advocate than he does with the witness of fact".[349] The starting point was that where there is a wrong there should be a remedy, and that an exception to the rule (in the form of an immunity) had to be justified as being necessary in the public interest. The majority of the Supreme Court concluded that arguments that abolishing the immunity would discourage potential expert witnesses from acting, or discourage them from expressing their

---

[343] *Watson v M'Ewan* [1905] A.C. 480; *Evans v London Hospital Medical College* [1981] 1 W.L.R. 184; *Smart v Forensic Science Service Ltd* [2013] EWCA Civ 783; [2013] P.N.L.R. 32.

[344] *Darker v Chief Constable of West Midlands Police* [2001] 1 A.C. 435; *Smart v Forensic Science Service Ltd* [2013] EWCA Civ 783; [2013] P.N.L.R. 32 (evidence held by a forensic science laboratory tampered with).

[345] *Palmer v Durnford Ford* [1992] 1 Q.B. 483 at 488.

[346] [2011] UKSC 13; [2011] 2 A.C. 398; considered by S. Carr and H. Evans, "The Removal of Immunity for Expert Witnesses" (2011) 27 P.N. 128.

[347] Overruling *Stanton v Callaghan* [2000] Q.B. 75.

[348] *Arthur JS Hall & Co. (A Firm) v Simons* [2002] 1 A.C. 615.

[349] *Jones v Kaney* [2011] UKSC 13; [2011] 2 A.C. 398 at [50] per Lord Phillips, and at [64] per Lord Brown.

opinions frankly, or place them in the position of having a conflict of duties owed both to the court and the client,[350] did not justify retaining the immunity. Lord Dyson observed that:

"Professional indemnity insurance is available. Professional persons engage in many activities where the possibility of being sued is more realistic than it is in relation to undertaking the role of an expert in litigation."[351]

Lord Brown suggested that the most likely broad consequence of removing the immunity:

"...will be a sharpened awareness of the risks of pitching their initial views of the merits of their client's case too high or too inflexibly lest these views come to expose and embarrass them at a later date."[352]

Limits of the expert's potential liability   The Supreme Court made it clear   **2–110** that the absolute immunity of witnesses would still apply to claims in defamation,[353] nor can an action for negligence be used to mount a collateral attack on a criminal conviction.[354] *Jones v Kaney* removes an immunity. It does not create a duty of care, and though it was common ground that an expert witness instructed by a party to proceedings owes a duty of care to that party[355] an expert witness will not owe a duty of care to an opposing party and, moreover, would also be entitled to rely on the immunity.[356] Lord Brown considered that the

---

[350] "There is no conflict between the duty owed by an expert to his client and his overriding duty to the court. His duty to the client is to perform his function as an expert with the reasonable skill and care of an expert drawn from the relevant discipline. This *includes* a duty to perform the overriding duty of assisting the court. Thus the discharge of the duty to the court cannot be a breach of duty to the client", per Lord Dyson, [2011] UKSC 13; [2011] 2 A.C. 398 at [99].

[351] [2011] UKSC 13; [2011] 2 A.C. 398 at [117].

[352] [2011] UKSC 13; [2011] 2 A.C. 398 at [67].

[353] *Jones v Kaney* [2011] UKSC 13; [2011] 2 A.C. 398 at [62] (per Lord Phillips), at [72] (per Lord Collins), and at [179] (per Baroness Hale, in a dissenting judgment). Though note that the immunity for defamation should be limited to the "core immunity", so that though it applies to something said by a witness it does not apply where the complaint is not about the content of the statement but the means by which it was procured: *Singh v Reading BC* [2013] EWCA Civ 909; [2013] 1 W.L.R. 3052.

[354] [2011] UKSC 13; [2011] 2 A.C. 398 at [60] per Lord Phillips. Where the initiation of proceedings is for the purpose of mounting a collateral attack on a final decision against the intending claimant, which has been made by another court of competent jurisdiction in previous proceedings, in which the intending claimant had a full opportunity of contesting the decision the court has the power to strike out the claim as an abuse of process: *Hunter v Chief Constable of West Midlands* [1982] A.C. 529. See e.g. *Ridgewood Properties Group Ltd v Kilpatrick Stockton LLP* [2014] EWHC 2502 (Ch); [2014] P.N.L.R. 31 where, in a claim for professional negligence, a particular head of loss was struck out as a collateral attack on a previous judgment of the court.

[355] [2011] UKSC 13; [2011] 2 A.C. 398 at [95] per Lord Dyson: "an expert who acts in civil litigation owes his client a duty to act with reasonable skill and care. ... He holds himself out as a skilled and competent person. The client relies on his advice in determining whether to bring or defend proceedings, in considering settlement values and in appraising the risks at trial. The client also relies on him to give the court skilled and competent expert opinion evidence."

[356] "Nor of course is there anything in the present decision which affects the position of the adverse expert. It is not sufficient to say that the adverse expert presents no problem because the expert owes no duty to the client on the other side. There are wider considerations of policy which ought to prevent adverse experts from being the target of disappointed litigants, even if the scope of duty in tort were to be extended in the future", [2011] UKSC 13; [2011] 2 A.C. 398 at [73] per Lord Collins. Thus, Lord

removal of the immunity applied only to a witness selected, instructed and paid by a party to litigation for his expertise and permitted on that account to give opinion evidence in the dispute.[357] His Lordship specifically excluded a treating doctor or forensic pathologist who gave factual evidence as well as being asked for their professional opinions upon it without having been initially retained by either party to the dispute.

2–111 Lord Brown's reservation for a "treating doctor" can only apply, however, where the doctor is called upon to give evidence or has prepared a report for the specific purpose of giving evidence in the litigation. In *Hughes v Lloyds Bank plc*[358] the claimant sustained injuries in a road traffic accident for which she brought a claim against the other motorist. She telephoned her general practitioner, the defendant, requesting that he prepare a report on her injuries for service on the motorist's insurers. The general practitioner wrote two letters, the first stating that the claimant had been X-rayed, that her back was normal and that her symptoms would settle down in a few weeks, and the second setting out the history and observing that though the claimant's back and neck were still causing discomfort, this would "settle down in time". He also referred to her painful foot and problems sleeping at night. The claimant settled the claim for £600 general damages three months after the accident. Subsequently she found that her injuries were more serious than had been indicated, and brought an action against the general practitioner. She alleged that the defendant's prognosis had been negligent with the result that she suffered financial loss by settling her claim for less than she would have done, had she known the true position. The Court of Appeal rejected the defendant's argument that he was entitled to rely on witness immunity. The proceedings had not been issued and the evidence from the general practitioner had been supplied in the context of negotiations:

> "The doctor received a request from the client, not her solicitors, to provide a letter. He did not judge it necessary to examine the claimant. There was no indication that his report, if supplied, would form part of any pleading. He was not asked to prepare a proof or give evidence. It seems plain that he provided the letters which he did in order that the claimant (his patient, whom he had treated) might negotiate a fair settlement of her claim on the basis of an accurate statement of her medical condition since the accident and a sound prognosis of her future recovery. It is clear that he would have appreciated in all probability that if no settlement could be negotiated, proceedings might well follow."[359]

The letters written by the general practitioner could not be regarded as preliminary to giving evidence as an expert. The documents were not supplied for disclosure to the other side in the context of proceedings but purely in the context of negotiation. The probability was that, had there been a trial on quantum, the general practitioner would not have been the witness relied on by the claimant as

---

Collins considered that even if the law developed to the point where a duty of care was owed to an opposing party there would still be grounds for applying the immunity. See also *Baxendale-Walker v Middleton* [2011] EWHC 998 (QB) at [94] per Supperstone J: "the decision in *Jones v Kaney* does not touch on the immunity of a witness (whether they be a witness of fact or expert opinion) or a party to proceedings in respect of things said or done in the ordinary course of proceedings in respect of claims brought against him by an opposing party."

[357] *Jones v Kaney* [2011] UKSC 13; [2011] 2 A.C. 398 at [64].
[358] [1998] P.I.Q.R. P98.
[359] [1998] P.I.Q.R. P98 at 104, per Lord Bingham CJ.

her expert medical witness, and it was unlikely that the general practitioner, if giving what was likely to become a proof of evidence, would not have wished to make a further detailed examination of the claimant. Thus, the doctor's letters were not covered by the immunity of a witness.[360]

Expert witnesses: public law proceedings   In *M (A Minor) v Newham London*   **2–112**
Borough Council[361] the defendants claimed that they were protected by witness immunity because when interviewing the child for the purpose of determining whether she had been sexually abused, and advising on future action, the psychiatrist would have known that, if she concluded that there had been abuse and that separation was desirable, there were likely to be proceedings in which she would be a witness. This argument was rejected, however, by Sir Thomas Bingham MR and Staughton LJ, on the ground that witness immunity does not apply to those who have never become involved in the administration of justice, even though at the time of the interview the psychiatrist would have appreciated that there might very well be court proceedings in which she would be a witness. The defendants' argument would extend the immunity too far. The House of Lords concluded, however, that witness immunity should apply to the psychiatrist. The policy considerations which applied to witnesses in criminal proceedings were equally applicable to a local authority's investigation, in the performance of a public duty, of whether or not there is evidence on which to bring proceedings for the protection of children from child abuse.[362] The psychiatrist knew that if abuse was discovered, proceedings by the local authority for the protection of the child would ensue and that her findings would be the evidence on which those proceedings would be based. The investigations had an immediate link with possible proceedings in pursuance of a statutory duty, and therefore could not be made the basis of subsequent actions.

Subsequently, in *JD v East Berkshire Community Health NHS Trust*[363] the Court   **2–113**
of Appeal held that, in light of the decision of the House of Lords in *Darker v Chief Constable of West Midlands Police*,[364] where the question of witness immunity was given careful consideration, there was a distinction to be drawn between the investigation of offences and the preparation of evidence. Witness immunity did not attach simply to the investigation process. Although it might not be easy in some cases of suspected child abuse to draw the line between investigation and the preparation of evidence, in the *Newham* case "the activities of the social workers probably fell into the category of investigations".[365] When the combined appeals in *JD v East Berkshire Community Health NHS Trust*[366]

---

[360] [1998] P.I.Q.R. P98 at 106. Although this case pre-dates *Jones v Kaney*, the decision on the facts would clearly still be the same.
[361] [1995] 2 A.C. 633; see para.2–092 above.
[362] *sub. nom. X (Minors) v Bedfordshire County Council* [1995] 2 A.C. 633 at 755. Lord Browne-Wilkinson expressed "no view as to the position in relation to ordinary civil proceedings".
[363] [2003] EWCA Civ 1151; [2004] Q.B. 558.
[364] [2001] 1 A.C. 435.
[365] [2003] EWCA Civ 1151; [2004] Q.B. 558 at [116]
[366] [2005] UKHL 23; [2005] 2 A.C. 373.

reached the House of Lords there was no appeal from the Court of Appeal's ruling on the question of witness immunity. Lord Brown touched on the subject tangentially:

> "Another related situation to that presently under consideration is where a doctor prepares evidence with a view to appearing in a child abuse case as a witness. In this event, of course, an absolute immunity or privilege attaches to his evidence. Not for a moment do I suggest that that was the position in any of these cases."[367]

The Court of Appeal had rejected the suggestion that witness immunity would have been open to the doctor responsible for making the allegations of child abuse in the case of *JD v East Berkshire Community Health NHS Trust* itself.[368] The Court commented that it was:

> "...certainly far from clear that it would be open to Professor Southall to invoke witness immunity in relation to the view he expressed at the end of 1994 and we would not have been prepared to rule that the action was bound to fail because of the protection afforded by witness immunity."[369]

2–114   Similarly, in the combined appeal of *RK v Dewsbury Health Care NHS Trust* the Court of Appeal also rejected the application of witness immunity on the facts. RK suffered from Schamberg's disease, which produces bruising on the skin. When aged nine she injured herself in the genital area while riding her bicycle and was referred to a consultant paediatrician whose provisional diagnosis was that the marks did not appear to be the result of skin disease but were suggestive of abuse. Social services were informed and a further examination was carried out. The child's father and elder brother were told that they should not sleep at home when RK was discharged from hospital. In the hospital, in front of other patients and visitors to the ward, the father was told that he was not allowed to see her. RK remained in hospital for several days and her father did not visit during that time. By the time that she was discharged the correct diagnosis had been made. The trial judge held that the social workers involved in the case had been potential witnesses in criminal or child protection proceedings that might result from their investigations and were entitled to witness immunity, though left open the question of whether witness immunity applied to the hospital doctors. The Court of Appeal, noting that *Darker v Chief Constable of West Midlands Police* had not been cited to the judge, held that he was wrong to find that witness immunity protected the social workers from a civil action, bearing in mind the distinction between the investigation of offences and the preparation of evidence.[370]

---

[367] [2005] UKHL 23; [2005] 2 A.C. 373 at [136].
[368] Professor Southall, though not a psychiatrist, had formed the view that JD was suffering from Munchausen's Syndrome by Proxy, and that her child's condition (multiple severe allergies—for which JD had been seeking to obtain treatment) had been fabricated by her.
[369] [2003] EWCA Civ 1151; [2004] Q.B. 558 at [103].
[370] [2003] EWCA Civ 1151; [2004] Q.B. 558 at [116]. See also *L (A Child) v Reading Borough Council* [2001] EWCA Civ 346; [2001] 1 W.L.R. 1575 at 1593 where the Court of Appeal, applying *Darker v Chief Constable of West Midlands Police* (where it was held that witness immunity does not apply to the fabrication of evidence), held that witness immunity would not apply to the investigation of alleged child abuse where the basis of the claim was that the child had been pressurised into

It may be that for now the important distinction in the context of public law   2–115
proceedings (such as proceedings to take into local authority care a child whom it
is suspected is the victim of abuse) is that between (i) investigation of the
circumstances and (ii) the preparation of evidence for the purpose of proceedings
where it is known that the case will go to court. Witness immunity will apply in
the latter situation but not in the former. Strictly speaking the decision of the
Supreme Court in *Jones v Kaney* does not apply in public law or quasi-public law
proceedings, since the case was concerned with the position of an expert witness
instructed by a party to an ordinary civil law claim for damages, though Lord
Dyson did comment that he could see no reason to treat expert witnesses who are
engaged in criminal and family litigation any differently from those engaged in
civil litigation.[371] The uncertainty as to whom the immunity does and does not
apply, and in what circumstances, was highlighted in the dissenting judgment of
Baroness Hale in *Jones v Kaney*, though she conceded that in the context of
investigations into child abuse there may be a relatively clear dividing line
between conducting the examinations and investigations, on the one hand, and
preparing for and giving evidence, on the other.[372]

Disciplinary proceedings   Witness immunity does not apply in disciplinary   2–116
proceedings against an expert witness in respect of evidence given by the expert
witness in court.[373] If the conduct or evidence of an expert witness at or in
connection with a trial, whether civil or criminal, raises the question whether that
expert is fit to practise in his particular field, the regulatory authorities should be
entitled (and may be bound) to investigate the matter for the protection of the
public.[374]

(b)   A duty to rescue?

General—the Good Samaritan   As a general proposition the tort of   2–117
negligence does not impose a duty to rescue. The failure to intervene to prevent
harm to another (as opposed to causing damage by some positive act) does not
give rise to liability. There are quite a few exceptions to this rule, giving rise to a
positive duty to act, including situations based on particular relationships, such as
parent and child, employer and employee, or the doctor–patient relationship.
Moreover, where defendants hold themselves out as providing particular services,
they may be taken to have undertaken a responsibility for negligence in failing to
provide that service which leads to harm to an individual who has relied on that

---

making false complaints "and thereafter creating a dishonest document pretending that she had made
a complaint of sexual abuse when she had not". Moreover, it was "also arguable that the immunity
should not be available to give the police the protection for matter which, on one view of the facts,
was designed to defeat the ends of justice rather than to serve them by initiating or causing to be
initiated the family proceedings based on groundless allegations of child abuse of L" (per Otton LJ).
[371] *Jones v Kaney* [2011] UKSC 13; [2011] 2 A.C. 398 at [125].
[372] [2011] UKSC 13; [2011] 2 A.C. 398 at [186]. But Baroness Hale also considered that in many
family cases, there will be some professional witnesses who enjoy immunity in respect of their
evidence and some who do not: [2011] UKSC 13; [2011] 2 A.C. 398 at [187].
[373] *Meadow v General Medical Council* [2006] EWCA Civ 1390; [2007] Q.B. 462.
[374] [2006] EWCA Civ 1390; [2007] Q.B. 462 at [45], per Sir Anthony Clarke MR.

undertaking. It is on this basis that a hospital casualty department can owe a duty of care to a patient who is turned away unseen.[375] But as a general rule, there is no duty to play the "Good Samaritan" where the doctor–patient relationship does not exist.[376] In *Powell v Boladz*[377] the Court of Appeal commented that:

"...a doctor who goes to the assistance of a stranger injured in an accident ... does not, as a rule, undertake the patient-doctor relationship so as to make him liable for lack of care, but only a duty not to make the condition of the victim worse."

On this basis, a doctor who comes across a man who is bleeding to death, who could easily prevent this but is careless in his attempts, is not liable in negligence for the man's death, unless his intervention prevented other, more effective, aid reaching the deceased. In these circumstances, it is said, there is no practical difference between the negligent doctor and a doctor who simply ignores the deceased and passes by, and imposing liability on the former but not the latter could be seen as deterring medical intervention.

2–118   This view has been strongly criticised by Kennedy and Grubb, who assert that:

"There is no basis for stating this as a matter of law and there is no English authority for so limiting the content of the doctor's duty ... A doctor who allows a road accident victim to die by failing to deal with his injuries does not make the victim's condition 'worse'—even assuming he would not have died with immediate treatment. Yet, there can be no doubt that medical evidence will in many circumstances suggest that the doctor could reasonably have done something to improve, or prevent a deterioration in, the victim's condition. Such a doctor is in breach of his duty to act reasonably in preventing foreseeable injury to the victim and should be liable in negligence."[378]

The basis in law for the Court of Appeal's statement in *Powell v Boladz* is the "no duty to rescue" principle, which has been applied in a number of contexts. The statement by Kennedy and Grubb that "there is no English authority for so limiting the content of the doctor's duty" assumes that the duty is held to exist, as does the assertion that "such a doctor is in breach of his duty to act reasonably in preventing foreseeable injury". It is trite law that in the absence of a duty of care the unreasonableness of the defendant's conduct is irrelevant, no matter how foreseeable or catastrophic the damage. Of course, the assertion that the doctor should be liable in negligence is a normative judgment about what the law ought

---

[375] *Barnett v Chelsea and Kensington Hospital Management Committee* [1968] 1 All E.R. 1068; cf. *Darnley v Croydon Health Services NHS Trust* [2017] EWCA Civ 151; [2017] P.I.Q.R. P14; [2017] Med. L.R. 245 (no duty owed by receptionist to give patients accurate information about waiting times); see para.3–098. Where a Turkish hospital turned a pregnant woman away because she was unable to pay the costs of her admission and the surgery she needed, and she died without receiving any medical assistance whilst being transferred by ambulance to another hospital, it was held that the denial of access to appropriate emergency treatment amounted to a violation of the substantive aspect of art.2 of the ECHR: *Şenturk v Turkey (13424/09)* (2013) ECHR 107; [2013] E.H.R.L.R. 439.

[376] So there is generally no legal duty upon doctors to volunteer their services in an emergency, e.g. in reply to the call "is there a doctor in the house?": *In Re F (Mental Patient: Sterilisation)* [1990] 2 A.C. 1, 77 per Lord Goff.

[377] [1998] Lloyds Rep. Med. 116 at 124, citing the statement of the Court of Appeal in *Capital and Counties plc v Hampshire County Council* [1997] Q.B. 1004 at 1035: "If he volunteers his assistance, his only duty as a matter of law is not to make the victim's condition worse."

[378] *Medical Law*, 3rd edn, 2000, at pp.297–298.

to be, a judgment with which many commentators would agree.[379] Unless it can be said that the doctor rendering Good Samaritan services has undertaken a responsibility to the claimant[380] the mere omissions rule provides the logic, if not the moral justification, for limiting the doctor's duty. This is that if the doctor would not be liable for simply walking past the injured victim, it would be irrational to hold him liable for failing to improve the victim's position (as opposed to making it worse), not least because of the risk that this would discourage doctors from volunteering assistance in an emergency.[381] It would seem that in practice, however, there is little evidence that the risk of liability does deter doctors from rendering assistance.[382]

Ambulance service   The "no duty to rescue" principle has been applied to most emergency services, including the police,[383] the coastguard,[384] and the fire service,[385] although there have been some cases where an undertaking of responsibility has been found to have occurred on the particular facts.[386] The position of the ambulance service was considered by the Court of Appeal in *Kent*

2–119

---

[379] See also the comment of Atkin LJ in *Everett v Griffiths* [1920] 3 K.B. 163 at 213, cited above at para.2–037; and Williams (2001) 21 O.J.L.S. 393. Certainly, the vast majority of both public (98 per cent) and the medical profession (96 per cent) consider that a doctor who comes across a road traffic accident ought to render some assistance: Zwitter et al. (1999) 318 B.M.J. 251. For an argument that a doctor should be held responsible for damage caused by a careless rescue, when in the absence of intervention the rescuee would have died, see Stapleton (1997) 113 L.Q.R. 257, 277 et seq.; and for criticism of Stapleton's argument see Smith (1997) 113 L.Q.R. 426.

[380] It is better not to call the accident victim a patient, since this assumes what one is seeking to prove, namely that the doctor–patient relationship has arisen.

[381] Which is the justification often given for "Good Samaritan" legislation in North America, conferring various degrees of immunity from claims in relation to altruistic medical intervention. See McInnes (1992) 26 U.B.C.L. Rev. 239.

[382] See Williams (2001) 21 O.J.L.S. 393, 405–406. See, however, the British Medical Association (BMA) report, *The Impact of Flying on Passenger Health: A Guide for Healthcare Professionals*, May 2004, which suggests that there is evidence from airline data that there is an increasing reluctance to volunteer to assist during in-flight medical emergencies, with a steady fall in the percentage of occasions when a health care professional responds to a crew announcement seeking a volunteer. As the report notes, the General Medical Council considers that doctors have an ethical duty to assist in an emergency (see para.2–125), while also advising that a doctor must "recognise and work within the limits of your professional competence". The BMA report comments that from an insurance point of view, the Medical Defence Union, the Medical Protection Society and the Medical and Dental Defence Union of Scotland have confirmed that members are insured for all "Good Samaritan" acts in an emergency where they are a bystander, anywhere in the world. See further M. Wong, "Doctor in the sky: medico-legal issues during in-flight emergencies" (2017) 17 Med. L. Int. 65.

[383] *Hill v Chief Constable of West Yorkshire* [1989] 1 A.C. 53; *Alexandrou v Oxford* [1993] 4 All E.R. 328; *Smith v Chief Constable of Sussex* [2008] UKHL 50; [2009] 1 A.C. 225; *Michael v Chief Constable of South Wales* [2015] UKSC 2; [2015] A.C. 1732.

[384] *Skinner v Secretary of State for Transport*, The Times, 3 January 1995; *OLL Ltd v Secretary of State for Transport* [1997] 3 All E.R. 897.

[385] *Capital and Counties plc v Hampshire County Council* [1997] Q.B. 1004. The position is similar in Scotland: see *AJ Allan (Blairnyle) Ltd v Strathclyde Fire Board* [2016] CSIH 3; 2016 S.C. 304; 2016 S.L.T. 253.

[386] Usually involving police officers who have failed to go to the assistance of a fellow officer. See: *Costello v Chief Constable of Northumbria Police* [1999] 1 All E.R. 550; *Mullaney v Chief Constable of West Midlands Police* [2001] EWCA Civ 700; [2001] Po. L.R. 150; cf. *Cowan v Chief Constable of Avon & Somerset Constabulary* [2001] EWCA Civ 1699; [2002] H.L.R. 44, where it was held that

v Griffiths, Roberts and London Ambulance Service,[387] where the issue was whether the ambulance service owed a duty of care to an individual when the service is summoned to render assistance to that individual. A general practitioner telephoned the ambulance service to take his patient, the claimant, to hospital because she was experiencing breathing difficulties. It was clearly an emergency. After 12 minutes the claimant's husband telephoned again, to be told that the ambulance was on its way. After another 16 minutes the doctor telephoned again. The ambulance eventually arrived 38 minutes after the original call, and had taken 34 minutes to travel a distance (six and a half miles) that would normally have taken about nine minutes. No explanation for this was ever given by the defendants.[388] On the way to the hospital the claimant suffered respiratory arrest which resulted in brain damage. If she had been taken to the hospital sooner the brain damage could have been avoided. The defendants argued that, by analogy with the fire service, they were an emergency service and should not owe a duty of care to those whom they were summoned to assist. It was conceded that the risk of harm was foreseeable, and the defendants did not rely on public policy arguments to exclude a duty of care. Rather it was argued that there was no proximity between the defendants and the claimant: their duty was limited to taking reasonable care not negligently to create an additional danger causing injury to the individual. The Court of Appeal rejected this approach and held that the ambulance service does owe a duty of care to those whom it is summoned to assist. This duty arises once the service "accepts the call" for assistance. The analogy was not with the emergency services, but with the medical services provided by a hospital. A hospital Accident & Emergency department owes a duty of care to those who seek its assistance, and cannot simply turn patients away without accepting responsibility in the tort of negligence. Thus, the ambulance service is in a different category from other emergency services, and by accepting a call for assistance undertakes a positive obligation to exercise reasonable care.[389] An alternative basis upon which the decision could be justified is that the defendants' negligence did actually worsen the claimant's position, since it was clear on the facts that if her husband or the doctor had known that there was going to be such a long delay they would have transported the claimant to hospital in a private vehicle. However, the duty as expressed in *Kent* would seem to apply even where there is no other means of obtaining the medical assistance that the claimant needs.

---

merely turning up at the scene of a disturbance did not create an assumption of responsibility to a claimant who was being unlawfully evicted from his home.

[387] [2001] Q.B. 36.

[388] Indeed, the ambulance crew tried to falsify the log to suggest that the journey took nine minutes.

[389] In *Watson v British Boxing Board of Control Ltd* [2001] Q.B. 1134 at [54]–[57] Lord Phillips MR regarded *Kent* as an instance of a case where there was an assumption of responsibility by the defendant to exercise reasonable care to safeguard a victim from the consequences of an existing injury or illness. See also *Michael v Chief Constable of South Wales* [2015] UKSC 2; [2015] A.C. 1732 at [138] where the majority of the Supreme Court distinguished *Kent* on the basis that the call handler in *Kent* gave misleading assurances that an ambulance would be arriving shortly, whereas the call handler in *Michael* gave no advice to the caller requesting police assistance and no promise about how quickly the police would respond. The distinction being made here is between misfeasance and nonfeasance, i.e. between a positive act that worsens the claimant's position and a pure omission.

Situations could arise in which the ambulance service might have to make a   2–120
judgment about which of a number of individuals should be given priority. But
that was not a reason for saying that no duty should be owed, since the
requirement to prove that there had been negligence would provide the
ambulance service with protection.[390] The situation might be different if the
effect of the negligence action was to challenge the allocation resources, for
example by arguing that the damage would not have been sustained but for the
failure to provide sufficient ambulances, or sufficient drivers or paramedics:

> "There then could be issues which are not suited for resolution by the courts. However, once
> there are available, both in the form of an ambulance and in the form of manpower, the
> resources to provide an ambulance on which there are no alternative demands, the ambulance
> service would be acting perversely 'in circumstances such as the present,' if it did not make
> those resources available. Having decided to provide an ambulance an explanation is required
> to justify a failure to attend within reasonable time."[391]

In *Aitken v Scottish Ambulance Service*[392] Lord Mackay refused the defendants'   2–121
application to strike out a claim that the ambulance service was liable for the
death of child from a prolonged epileptic fit. It was alleged that following an
emergency phone call there was a delay of 21 minutes before the ambulance was
dispatched. An employee at the emergency medical dispatch centre ascertained
the child's medical history and condition and said that an ambulance had been
dispatched together with a rapid response unit. That unit arrived promptly but did
not have the means to transport the child to hospital. After a further call to the
dispatch centre an ambulance arrived some 23 minutes after the rapid response
unit. The child was then transferred to hospital but died later. In denying that they
owed a duty of care to the pursuer the defendants argued that: (1) the failure to
arrive promptly amounted to a pure omission for which there is duty at common
law; (2) there was no statutory duty (under the National Health Service
(Scotland) Act 1978) to attend to an emergency call; (3) the ambulance service
was in the same position as other emergency services and *Kent* should not be
followed in Scotland; (4) there was no relationship of proximity between the
child and the ambulance service, nor any voluntary assumption of responsibility
prior to the arrival of the ambulance; and (5) it would not be fair, just and
reasonable to impose a duty of care on the ambulance service prior to the
attendance of ambulance staff at the scene.

---

[390] [2001] Q.B. 36 at [46] per Lord Woolf MR: "The result would depend on the facts. I would be
resistant to a suggestion that the ambulance service could be regarded as negligent because by an error
of judgment a less seriously injured patient was transported to hospital leaving a more seriously
injured patient at the scene who, as a result, suffered further injuries. In such a situation, on the facts,
it is most unlikely that there would be conduct which could be properly regarded as negligent."
[391] [2001] Q.B. 36 at [47] per Lord Woolf MR. For discussion of the effect of *Kent v Griffiths* on the
liability of ambulance services see K. Williams, "Litigation against English NHS Ambulance Services
and the Rule in *Kent v Griffiths*" (2007) 15 Med. L. Rev. 153. Note that in some circumstances a
patient's rights under the European Convention on Human Rights may be engaged if there is a delay
in an ambulance attending an emergency: see *Daniel v St George's Healthcare NHS Trust* [2016]
EWHC 23 (QB); [2016] 4 W.L.R. 32 where it was alleged that there had been a delay in an ambulance
attending a prisoner who had suffered a cardiac arrest, but it was held, on the facts, that the ambulance
service had taken all reasonable steps to respond to the emergency call and did so within a reasonable
period of time.
[392] [2011] CSOH 49; 2011 S.L.T. 822.

believe that such person is in need of urgent attention by a registered medical practitioner but shall not be guilty under this paragraph of such conduct if he causes another registered medical practitioner to attend as aforesaid."

As Kirby P acknowledged, the statute did not impose a duty giving rise to a claim for damages in respect of its breach—it was concerned with professional discipline. But it did reflect the expectations which were accepted as appropriate and proper amongst medical practitioners in responding to a call to the aid of a "person … in need of urgent attention". This was a high standard, going beyond what was expected of other professions. But it was a standard expressed by Parliament and accepted by the medical profession. Secondly, the defendant, Dr Lowns, had himself accepted that he should have attended the claimant. His case at trial had been that he had never been requested to attend, and that a conversation which the claimant alleged had taken place had not taken place (which had been rejected by the trial judge on the facts). He had conceded that if he had received the alleged request for assistance, he would and should have gone to the child. It followed that a relationship of proximity between claimant and defendant was established, notwithstanding the absence of any previous professional link between them. The decision raises the question of when it is legitimate to convert an ethical duty into a legal duty, based on general expectations that the defendant would act when called upon to do so. In the UK the General Medical Council's guidance to doctors, *Good Medical Practice*, states that:

"You must offer help if emergencies arise in clinical settings or in the community, taking account of your own safety, your competence and the availability of other options for care."[399]

It remains to be seen whether a court could be persuaded that this statement of an appropriate professional standard can be translated into a legal obligation sounding in damages for breach.

2–126   **Genetic information and conflicting duties**   The concept of a duty to rescue is not confined to cases where the defendant could have intervened physically to save the claimant from harm. It encompasses situations where the harm could have been avoided by the giving of advice or a warning.[400] An example of this arises where a doctor has genetic information about the patient which has implications for the genetic health status of other family members. Are there circumstances where the doctor could be held to owe a duty of care to the family

---

[399] *Good Medical Practice* (April 2013), para.26 (available at *http://www.gmc-uk.org/Good_medical_practice___English_1215.pdf_51527435.pdf*). Note also the duty of a general practitioner to treat "any person" who is not on the general practitioner's list following an accident or emergency. See the National Health Service (General Medical Services Contracts) Regulations 2015 (SI 2015/1862) reg.17(7) and (8) and the National Health Service (Personal Medical Services Agreements) Regulations 2015 (SI 2015/1879) Sch.2 para.1, which by reference to the definition of "essential services" in reg.3 includes the provision of services to "any person" following an accident or emergency as set out in reg.17(7) of the National Health Service (General Medical Services Contracts) Regulations 2015. See para.2–040.

[400] As, e.g., where a patient is known to be infectious and there is a foreseeable risk that others could be infected, or where the patient has a psychiatric condition which makes it foreseeable that others might be harmed: see paras 2–145 et seq. and 2–165 et seq., respectively.

members to disclose information about the patient's genetic health status, notwithstanding the doctor's duty of confidentiality to the patient? The issue arose in *ABC v St George's Healthcare NHS Foundation Trust*.[401] The claimant's father, who had been convicted of the manslaughter of the claimant's mother on the grounds of diminished responsibility and was subject to a hospital order and a restriction order under the Mental Health Act 1983, was diagnosed with Huntington's disease. This is a genetic condition, with a 50 per cent chance that it will be transmitted to a child. It is incurable, progressive and invariably fatal. The claimant was pregnant at the time and it was alleged that the defendant hospital trusts were aware of this and that the claimant would be concerned about having child who could develop Huntington's disease. The father refused his permission for the claimant to be informed about his medical condition, although he had told his own brother.[402] The defendants complied with the father's wishes, but after the baby was born the claimant was inadvertently informed by one of the doctors about her father's Huntington's disease. The claimant was subsequently diagnosed with the disease. Her claim was that if she had known about her father's condition when she was pregnant she would have undergone tests and when diagnosed she would have terminated the pregnancy. She alleged that she had suffered psychiatric harm and that if her child had the disease she would be put to additional expense. Nicol J struck out the claim as disclosing no reasonable cause of action. The action was based on an omission in circumstances where there was no special relationship between the defendants and the claimant and there had been no assumption of responsibility by the defendants to the claimant. The defendants clearly owed a duty of confidence to the father and, though the duty of confidentiality was not absolute, it would not be fair, just or reasonable to impose on the defendants a duty of care towards the claimant.[403]

Counsel for the defendants had advanced nine reasons why it was not fair, just or reasonable to impose a duty of care namely: (i) there was no public interest in disclosure, the claimant was relying on a private interest; (ii) the claimant was arguing for a *duty* to disclose not simply a defence to disclosure, and this might encourage doctors to breach confidence where it might not otherwise have been justified; (iii) doctors would be subject to conflicting duties (a duty of confidence to the patient and a duty to disclose information to a third party); (iv) a duty to disclose information in some circumstances would undermine trust and confidence in the doctor/patient relationship, leading to some patients being less candid with their doctors; (v) a duty owed to third parties would result in doctors

2–127

---

[401] [2015] EWHC 1394 (QB); [2015] P.I.Q.R. P18. The High Court decision is discussed by R. Gilbar and C. Foster, "Doctors' Liability to the Patient's Relatives in Genetic Medicine: *ABC v St George's Healthcare NHS Trust*" (2016) 24 Med L. Rev. 112; V. Chico, "Non-disclosure of genetic risks: The case for developing legal wrongs" (2016) 16 Med. Law Int. 3; M. Fay, "Negligence, genetics and families: a duty to disclose actionable risks" (2016) 16 Med. L. Int. 115.
[402] As Nicol J noted [2015] EWHC 1394 (QB); [2015] P.I.Q.R. P18 at [19], it was "of little importance that [the father] had apparently told his brother of his condition. This did not strip the information of its confidential character".
[403] Applying the third limb of the *Caparo* tripartite test for a duty of care. Counsel for the defendants had been prepared to concede, for the purposes of the strike out application, that the claimant would be able to establish at trial that harm to the claimant was foreseeable and that there was a sufficient relationship of proximity between the claimant and the defendants for a duty of care to arise.

putting pressure on their patients to agree to disclosure to avoid the risk of being sued by third parties; (vi) some third parties may not want to receive the information or in extreme cases may suffer harm as a result of being given the information, but a doctor would be unable to assess this with someone who is not a patient without effectively imparting the information itself; (vii) there was a possibility that the third party may suffer psychiatric harm if told the information in question, and the doctor would be in a dilemma as to how to explore whether this was the case when the third party is not or may not be his patient; (viii) doctors receive a great deal of confidential information and a duty to consider whether any of it should be disclosed to third parties would impose a burden such that the time and resources committed to this would be a distraction from treating patients; and (ix) a duty to disclose the information would be a significant extension of a doctor's duty of care and would be contrary to the incremental way in which the law of negligence ought to progress. Nicol J noted that whilst individually there might be scope for debate about these reasons:

"...cumulatively they provide a formidable argument as to why it would not be fair, just or reasonable to find a duty of care."[404]

2–128   On appeal the Court of Appeal reversed the decision to strike out the claim.[405] Irwin LJ (with whom Underhill and Gloster LJJ agreed) stressed at various points in the judgment that this did not necessarily mean that the defendants would be held to owe a duty of care to the claimant, merely that it was at least arguable that such a duty was owed, and that the decision should not have been made in the absence of evidence. Nonetheless, Irwin LJ considered each of the defendants' nine reasons and provided a rationale for dismissing or disagreeing with each of them. The claimant (and Irwin LJ) placed great emphasis on professional guidance which indicates that in some cases it is acceptable to breach a patient's confidentiality in order to prevent harm to others.[406] The defendants pointed out that this guidance was permissive, i.e. the doctor may be justified (in terms of having a defence) in breaching the patient's confidentiality, but does not impose a

---

[404] [2015] EWHC 1394 (QB); [2015] P.I.Q.R. P18 at [30]. Nicol J did not specify which of the nine reasons he found compelling and which he found unpersuasive. An argument that the claimant's rights under art.8 of the European Convention on Human Rights had been breached was also rejected. In Smith v University of Leicester NHS Trust [2016] EWHC 817 (QB) Judge McKenna followed Nicol J's decision in ABC v St George's Healthcare NHS Foundation Trust, holding that the defendants' genetic counselling service did not owe a duty of care to two second cousins of a patient to diagnose the patient's genetic condition promptly. It was argued that there was no issue of confidentiality in Smith because if the patient had been diagnosed earlier he would have brought the diagnosis to the attention of his wider family. Judge McKenna concluded that this was irrelevant. It was not "fair just and reasonable" to impose a duty on the defendants to the patient's relatives arising out of the failure to diagnose the patient's genetic condition.

[405] ABC v St George's Healthcare NHS Foundation Trust [2017] EWCA Civ 336; [2017] P.I.Q.R. P15; [2017] Med. L.R. 368; discussed by R. Geraghty [2017] J.P.I.L. C125.

[406] Royal College of Physicians, the Royal College of Pathologists and the British Society of Human Genetics, Consent and Confidentiality in Genetic Practice, Guidance on Genetic Testing and Sharing Genetic Information (2006). The current edition is from 2011 (available at http://www.bsgm.org.uk/media/678746/consent_and_confidentiality_2011.pdf). See also GMC, Confidentiality: Protecting and Providing Information (2004). The current edition of the GMC guidance is Confidentiality: good practice in handling patient information, January 2017.

duty to do so. The claimant argued that this created a professional "obligation" to breach confidentiality, a view with which Irwin LJ appeared to agree.[407] Having established that there can be a professional "obligation", the issue then became whether breach of that obligation was actionable in tort. In response to the argument that doctors would be subject to conflicting legal duties (a duty of confidence to the patient and a duty to disclose information to a third party) Irwin LJ said that geneticists already faced such conflicts in the relevant professional guidance and the question for the court was whether they should be protected from a common law duty of care.[408] With respect, this overstates the claims made in the professional guidance. The 2006 version of the joint report *Consent and Confidentiality in Genetic Practice* states that:

"In special circumstances it may be justified to break confidence where the aversion of harm by the disclosure substantially outweighs the patient's claim to confidentiality."[409]

It does not refer to a professional *duty* to break a patient's confidence. The Court also considered that the case of *Tarasoff v Regents of the University of California*,[410] in which the Supreme Court of California held that a psychologist owed a duty of care to a woman murdered by the psychologist's patient after the patient made threats to kill her, held "parallels with the instant case".[411] It remains unclear whether if a case with similar facts to *Tarasoff* arose in this country the court would conclude that a duty of care was owed to the victim,[412] but in any event *ABC v St George's Healthcare NHS Foundation Trust* is at some remove from *Tarasoff*, where it was the patient himself who was the threat to the deceased. In *ABC* the father was not threatening to harm his daughter or her baby. The risk of harm came from the genetic condition itself. If doctors owe a duty of care to breach patients' confidentiality in these circumstances then it would seem that no patient diagnosed with a genetic condition would be entitled have this medical information treated as confidential.

In *Liss v Watters*[413] the Quebec Court of Appeal came to a similar conclusion to that of Nicol J in *ABC v St George's Healthcare NHS Foundation Trust*, in a case where a doctor diagnosed a genetic neurological disorder in a young child. The disorder was sex-linked in that it is inherited by 50 per cent of male children born of women who carry the gene. Reversing the trial judge, it was held that the doctor was not under a duty to alert members of the child's extended family about this genetic risk. The effect of imposing such a duty would be that:

2–129

"...pushed to its logical limit, a doctor in like circumstances might be obliged to seek out and inform all third persons within a radius of contact, beyond his or her patient, whether or not he or she had met them or knew their names and irrespective of foreseeability of risk on a

---

[407] [2017] EWCA Civ 336; [2017] P.I.Q.R. P15; [2017] Med. L.R. 368 at [23], [26], [31], [35], [47], [56] include references to the doctors' obligation.
[408] [2017] EWCA Civ 336; [2017] P.I.Q.R. P15; [2017] Med. L.R. 368 at [48].
[409] The 2011 edition states: "In special circumstances, it may be justified to break confidence where in doing so a serious harm can be avoided."
[410] 551 P. 2d 334; Sup., 131 Cal. Rptr. 14 (1976).
[411] [2017] EWCA Civ 336; [2017] P.I.Q.R. P15; [2017] Med. L.R. 368 at [56].
[412] See paras 2–166 et seq. below.
[413] 2012 QCCA 257; (2012) 92 C.C.L.T. (3d) 1.

professional measure, where a reasonable non-physician thought that right. The social costs of such a duty could prove to be prohibitive. It could serve as a disincentive to undertake medical work in fields where genetic risks are present. Moreover, the duty to warn as announced by the judge could transform the doctor–patient relationship as it is currently understood."[414]

It would also involve a breach of confidentiality, which was particularly important in the context of genetic disorders, because it had implications for the present and future consequences of the patient's autonomy and private life. Whether or not others knew of the child's disorder was, in principle, the child's and the parents' private affair. Moreover, said the Court, care must be taken not to overstate the exceptions to the fundamental duty of confidentiality a physician owes to his patient. There was a narrow category of exception whereby non-consensual disclosure could be justified by considerations of public health, urgency or imminent danger, but this case did not fall within that exception.[415]

(c) The duty owed to rescuers

2–130   As a general rule a person is not obliged to undertake a rescue, but the courts are likely to be favourably disposed to a claimant who does attempt to rescue someone endangered by the defendant's negligence and who is injured in the process.[416] Thus, a duty of care is owed to a person who is foreseeably likely to intervene to assist a person put in danger by the defendant, provided the rescuer did not act with wanton disregard for his own safety. Foreseeability of the particular emergency that arose is unnecessary, provided some emergency is foreseeable,[417] or, alternatively, provided the emergency is of the same "kind or class" as that which is foreseeable.[418]

2–131   The circumstances in which this principle can be applied in the context of medical negligence will probably be rare. The issue did arise, however, in the Canadian case of *Urbanski v Patel*.[419] The defendant removed an ectopic kidney from his patient during the course of a sterilisation operation, mistakenly believing it to be an ovarian cyst. It was then discovered that the patient had only one kidney, and the effect of removing it was much more serious than would have been the case had she had the normal complement of two. Her father, Mr Urbanski, donated one of his kidneys for transplant ("as what father would not?" remarked the trial judge, Wilson J) in what turned out to be an unsuccessful

---

[414] 2012 QCCA 257; (2012) 92 C.C.L.T. (3d) 1 at [86].

[415] 2012 QCCA 257; (2012) 92 C.C.L.T. (3d) 1 at [111].

[416] "Danger invites rescue. The cry of distress is the summons to relief. The law does not ignore these reactions of the mind in tracing conduct to its consequences. It recognises them as normal. It places their effects within the range of the natural and probable. The wrong that imperils life is a wrong to the imperilled victim; it is a wrong also to his rescuer . . . The risk of rescue, if only it be not wanton, is born of the occasion. The emergency begets the man. The wrongdoer may not have foreseen the coming of a deliverer. He is accountable as if he had," per Cardozo J in *Wagner v International Railway Co.*, 232 N.Y. 176 at 180 (1921), cited with approval by Willmer LJ in *Baker v T.E. Hopkins & Son Ltd* [1959] 3 All E.R. 225 at 241, and by Lord Wright in *Bourhill v Young* [1943] A.C. 92 at 108–109.

[417] *Videan v British Transport Commission* [1963] 2 Q.B. 650 at 669.

[418] *Knightley v Johns* [1982] 1 All E.R. 851 at 860.

[419] (1978) 84 D.L.R. (3d) 650, Manitoba QB.

attempt to alleviate his daughter's condition. In an action by the father for the expenses of and the pain and suffering involved in the operation the doctor was held liable by analogy to the rescue principle. An argument that the donation was unforeseeable was rejected, as was the suggestion that the claimant's conduct was voluntary and intentional, and so broke the chain of causation.[420]

It is probable that an English court would follow the approach adopted in *Urbanski v Patel*, although it may be that claims would be limited to donations by close family members who are clearly more foreseeable as potential donors, and who would feel a greater sense of moral obligation to the patient.[421] Moreover, it is probably the element of moral compulsion that undermines the argument that the claimant was a volunteer or that the decision to donate broke the chain of causation. One issue that might have to be addressed is the possibility that if the first transplantation proved to be unsuccessful further donations could take place. Is the defendant liable to all the donors? Possibly there would come a point at which the damage would be regarded as too remote or the donation would be treated as a novus actus interveniens, but there is nothing in either principle or logic which would dictate this, since if the first donation is both a foreseeable and reasonable consequence of the defendant's negligence then subsequent donations merit the same categorisation.

2–132

(d) Congenital disability

(i) Common law duty to the unborn child

For many years there was no case in the United Kingdom in which it was decided that a duty of care at common law was owed to an unborn child,[422] although the principle had been accepted in other common law jurisdictions.[423] The

2–133

---

[420] This type of argument has been consistently rejected in rescue cases: see, e.g. *Haynes v Harwood* [1935] 1 K.B. 146; *Baker v TE Hopkins & Son Ltd* [1959] 3 All E.R. 225. The claim in *Urbanski* was in respect of the foreseeable loss arising from the decision to donate the kidney. Clearly, if the operation to remove the kidney from the donor is performed negligently the surgeon will be responsible for the donor's injuries and their consequences, as in *XYZ v Portsmouth Hospital NHS Trust* [2011] EWHC 243 (QB); (2011) 121 B.M.L.R. 13, where liability was admitted.

[421] See Spencer [1979] C.L.J. 45; Robertson (1980) 96 L.Q.R. 19. See also Giesen, *International Medical Malpractice Law*, 1988, para.1331, discussing a similar German case in which the donor succeeded in an action against the doctor. Curiously, in the United States the courts have denied claims by organ donors against the original tortfeasor: *Sirianni v Anna*, 285 N.Y.S. 2d 709 (1969); *Moore v Shah*, 458 N.Y.S. 2d 33 (1982); *Petersen v Farberman*, 736 S.W. 2d 441 (1987). Note that s.33 of the Human Tissue Act 2004 makes the transplantation of a human organ or part of a human organ from a living donor prima facie unlawful unless the requirements of reg.11 of the Human Tissue Act 2004 (Persons Who Lack Capacity to Consent and Transplants) Regulations 2006 (SI 2006/1659) are complied with. See further para.7–152.

[422] The point was conceded by counsel for the defendant in *Williams v Luff* (1978) 122 S.J. 164; *The Times*, 14 February 1978, and in *McKay v Essex Area Health Authority* [1982] Q.B. 1166. A duty was assumed to exist in the thalidomide cases: *Distillers Co. (Biochemicals) Ltd v Thompson* [1971] A.C. 458, and in *Whitehouse v Jordan* [1981] 1 All E.R. 267.

[423] See *Montreal Tramways v Leveille* [1933] 4 D.L.R. 339; *Duval v Seguin* (1972) 26 D.L.R. (3d) 418; *Liebig v Guelph General Hospital* 2010 ONCA 450; (2010) 321 D.L.R. (4th) 378 (Canada); *Watt v Rama* [1972] V.R. 353 and *Pratt v Pratt* [1975] V.R. 378; *X. and Y. v Pal* (1991) 23 N.S.W.L.R. 26; [1992] 3 Med. L.R. 195, NSWCA (Australia); *Presley v Newport Hospital* (1976) 365 A. 2d 748

is or would, if sued in time, have been liable in tort to the parent, and it is no answer that the parent has suffered no actionable injury.[432] Thus, the child's action is derivative, in that it depends on a tortious duty owed to the parent, except that it is not necessary to show that the parent suffered any actionable injury. A child damaged by a drug taken by its mother during pregnancy, for example, can sue the manufacturer even though the mother did not suffer any harm, if there was a breach of a duty of care owed to the mother. Conversely, if the prescription of the drug to the mother was appropriate, given her medical condition, there is no breach of a duty owed to the mother, and so no claim by the child.[433]

2–136   **Infertility treatment**   Section 1A, which was added by the Human Fertilisation and Embryology Act 1990 s.44, effectively extends the provisions of s.1 of the Act to children born disabled as a result of damage to an embryo or to gametes in the course of infertility treatment, by the placing in a woman of an embryo, or of sperm and eggs or of artificial insemination. Where the disability results from an act or omission in the course of the selection, or the keeping or use outside the body, of the embryo carried by the woman or of the gametes used to bring about the creation of the embryo, and a person is answerable under the section to the child in respect of the act or omission, the child's disabilities are to be regarded as damage resulting from the wrongful act of that person. A person is answerable under s.1A if he was, or would if sued in due time have been, liable in tort to one or both of the parents, and it is no answer that the parent suffered no actionable injury.[434] But the defendants' negligence must result in actionable damage. In *A v A Health and Social Services Trust*[435] the claimants had been born following a

---

for what a mother does (or does not do) during pregnancy." See further *Dobson v Dobson* (1999) 174 D.L.R. (4th) 1 where the Supreme Court of Canada held that at common law no duty of care was owed by the mother to a foetus injured in a road traffic accident, on grounds of policy; McInnes (2000) 116 L.Q.R. 26. It follows that a defendant sued in respect of damage to the child cannot seek contribution from the mother in respect of her alleged prenatal negligence which may have contributed to the child's damage: *Preston v Chow* (2002) 211 D.L.R. (4th) 758, Man CA.

[432] Congenital Disabilities (Civil Liability) Act 1976 s.1(3).

[433] See, e.g. *Lacroix (Litigation Guardian of) v Dominique* [2001] MBCA 122; (2001) 202 D.L.R. (4th) 121, Man CA, where the child's disabilities were caused in utero by a drug prescribed for her mother's epilepsy. The Manitoba Court of Appeal commented, at [39], that imposing a duty of care on the doctor owed to a future child not to prescribe medication for the mother which he knew carried the risk of injuring a foetus: "would immediately create an irreconcilable conflict between the duty owed by the doctor to the child and that owed to the mother. The medication was properly prescribed to treat the mother's epilepsy. Without it, any foetus she might conceive would be at even greater risk from a seizure than from the medication. Surely the doctor cannot withhold the medication from the mother, and put her at risk, for the sake of avoiding risk to a yet unconceived foetus which might be at even greater risk if the mother's epilepsy went uncontrolled." See also *Pozdzik (Next Friend of) v Wilson* 2002 ABQB 351; (2002) 11 C.C.L.T. (3d) 96 on the problem of the conflict between the mother's need for treatment for epilepsy during pregnancy and the interests of the foetus. In *Paxton v Ramji* 2008 ONCA 697; (2008) 299 D.L.R. (4th) 614; (2008) 92 O.R. (3d) 401 the Ontario Court of Appeal held that a doctor did not owe a duty of care to a future child when prescribing a teratogenic drug to the mother because of the potential conflict of duties that could be owed to mother and child even though (unlike *Lacroix)* there was no benefit to the child from the drug.

[434] For discussion of some of the difficulties that may arise under this section see Lee and Morgan, *Human Fertilisation & Embryology*, 2000, pp.258–260.

[435] [2011] NICA 28; [2012] N.I. 77.

process of in vitro fertilisation carried out by the defendants. They were normal, healthy children. However, they had a different skin colour from that of their parents as a result of the defendants' negligence in the selection of gametes for the in vitro fertilisation. The Court of Appeal of Northern Ireland held that being born with a different skin colour from one's parents did not constitute actionable damage. The claimants could not point to:

"...any physical or mental defect as a result of the process which led to their existence. As the judge correctly pointed out, they have no claim under the [Congenital Disabilities (Civil Liability) Act 1976] because they are healthy and normal children. Having a different skin colour from the majority of the surrounding population and their parents' cannot sensibly be regarded as damage or disability . . ."[436]

Conflict of duties   The fact that a duty to the child depends upon a duty owed   2–137
to the parent may create difficulties in some circumstances. Where, for example, there is a conflict between the interests of the mother and those of the child during labour a doctor will owe a duty to the mother to exercise reasonable care for her health and safety. It is irrelevant that what has to be done in the mother's interests involves a risk of harm to the child, since if the doctor has exercised reasonable care there is no tort against the mother (whether damage is caused or not), and so the child can have no claim under the Act.[437] This would also be the position where the mother refused to accept recommended treatment, a Caesarean section for example, since she is entitled to refuse to give her consent to any treatment and the doctor commits no tort by accepting her decision. Indeed, there is no legal mechanism by which the mother's rights could be overridden, and the doctor who attempted to do so would commit the tort of battery.[438] Even where there is no conflict of interest between mother and child there may be circumstances where there is no breach of a duty owed to the mother, but there has been negligence with respect to the child.[439]

Defences   The derivative nature of the duty is also apparent from the defences   2–138
available. The child is bound by a contractual exclusion or limitation clause that would have applied to the parents' action.[440] Damages may be reduced to take account of the parent's share of the responsibility for the child being born

---

[436] [2011] NICA 28; [2012] N.I. 77 at [9]. The case is discussed by S. Sheldon, "Only skin deep? The harm of being born a different colour to one's parents" (2011) 19 Med. L. Rev. 657.

[437] See Eekelaar and Dingwall [1984] J.S.W.L. 258.

[438] There is no power to make a foetus a ward of court: *Re F (In utero)* [1988] Fam. 122. See also *St. George's Healthcare NHS Trust v S* [1999] Fam. 26, para.6–186.

[439] Cane (1977) 51 A.L.J. 704 at 708 gives an example of a drug manufacturer who warns the mother of adverse side effects which might cause her injury but negligently fails to warn about potential harm to the foetus. If the mother takes the drug and suffers no injury, but the child is injured, the child has no claim under the Act because, although the manufacturer owes a duty to the mother, there is no breach of duty against her (because a warning may discharge the manufacturer's duty: see paras 10–042 et seq.). As Cane comments, this is "unfortunate".

[440] Congenital Disabilities (Civil Liability) Act 1976 s.1(6). However, a contractual exclusion clause which sought to exclude liability for death or personal injury caused by negligence would be ineffective: see paras 11–030 and 11–033.

disabled.[441] Finally, where the disability is the result of an occurrence preceding the time of conception which affects the parents' ability to have a normal, healthy child, the defendant is not responsible to the child if either or both of the parents knew of the risk of disability, except that if the child's father is the defendant and he knew of the risk but the mother did not he will be answerable to the child.[442] Under this provision the parents' knowledge apparently defeats the child's claim even where objectively it would be reasonable for them to attempt to have a normal, healthy child (e.g. if the defendant's negligence has created a 1 per cent chance of them producing a disabled child).

2–139   **Causation**   Probably the most difficult aspect of bringing an action under the Congenital Disabilities (Civil Liability) Act 1976 is the problem of proving causation. The Pearson Commission, for example, considered that only a "minute proportion" of children born with congenital defects would succeed in proving both negligence and causation.[443]

(iii)   Wrongful life

2–140   The Congenital Disabilities (Civil Liability) Act 1976 applies only to children born alive, the claim effectively crystallising at birth. If the defendant's negligence causes the death of the foetus in utero there can be no claim by the child, though either or both parents may have an action in appropriate circumstances.[444] Moreover, the action is limited to "disabilities which would not

---

[441] Congenital Disabilities (Civil Liability) Act 1976 s.1(7); except where the mother causes the damage in the course of driving a motor vehicle: s.2. If a woman discovers during the course of the pregnancy that the child is likely to be born disabled it is not unreasonable for her to refuse to undergo an abortion: *Emeh v Kensington and Chelsea and Westminster Area Health Authority* [1985] Q.B. 1012; *McFarlane v Tayside Health Board* [2000] 2 A.C. 59 at 74, 81, 104, 113. Moreover, the mother's decision to decline an abortion does not contribute to the child's disabilities; rather it results in the birth of the child. This is not a ground for saying that the mother "shares responsibility" for the child's disabilities.

[442] Congenital Disabilities (Civil Liability) Act 1976 s.1(4). A specific version of this defence applies to actions arising out of errors in the course of assisted conception. By s.1A(3) a defendant is not answerable to the child if at the time the embryo, or the sperm and eggs, are placed in the woman, or at the time of her insemination, either or both parents knew the risk of their child being born disabled, i.e. the particular risk created by the act or omission. See further Lee and Morgan, *Human Fertilisation and Embryology* (Oxford: Blackstone Press, 2000), at p.259. The other defences in the Act apply to actions under s.1A: s.1A(4).

[443] *Royal Commission on Civil Liability and Compensation for Personal Injury*, Cmnd.7054 (1978), Vol.I, para.1452, and Annexes 12 and 13; Law Com. No.60, Cmnd.5709 (1974), para.28. See, e.g. *Reay v British Nuclear Fuels plc* [1994] 5 Med. L.R. 1; [1994] P.I.Q.R. P171, where the claimants were unable to prove that paternal pre-conception irradiation of the gonads had caused the claimants' cancer; *X and Y v Pal* (1991) 23 N.S.W.L.R. 26; [1992] 3 Med. L.R. 195, NSWCA, in which the claimant was unable to prove that negligent exposure to congenital syphilis in the womb caused dysmorphia and brain damage; *De Martell v Merton and Sutton Health Authority* [1995] 6 Med. L.R. 234, QBD, where the claimant was unable to prove that negligent mismanagement of his birth was probably the cause of his disabilities.

[444] See, e.g. *Kralj v McGrath* [1986] 1 All E.R. 54; *Bagley v North Hertfordshire Health Authority* (1986) 136 N.L.J. 1014 where damages were awarded to a mother in respect of a stillborn child, although Simon Brown J held that there can be no claim for damages for bereavement under the Fatal Accidents Act 1976 s.1A(2), which provides a fixed statutory sum for the parents of an unmarried minor child (a foetus cannot be said to be a "minor child" since it only attains the status of a legal

otherwise have been present". This wording was intended to exclude so-called "wrongful life" actions in which a child who is born with non-tortiously inflicted disabilities claims that, due to the defendant's negligence in failing to diagnose that the child was likely to be born disabled, the child has been permitted to be born in circumstances where, had the true position been known, the parent(s) would not have had the child either because the mother would have undergone a termination of pregnancy or the child would not have been conceived (hence "wrongful entry into life").

Common law   This issue arose for resolution under the common law in *McKay v Essex Area Health Authority*.[445] Tests conducted on a pregnant woman failed to disclose that she had contracted rubella, and her child was born severely disabled. The Court of Appeal held that a doctor did not owe a duty of care to the child to advise the mother of the serious consequences for the child of exposure to rubella and of the desirability of an abortion, although such a duty was owed to the mother.[446] The child's action claimed a right to be aborted (effectively a right not to enter the world with disabilities), and this was contrary to public policy as a violation of the sanctity of human life. This view overstates the nature of the child's claim somewhat, since the doctor could not compel a pregnant woman to have an abortion. At its highest, the child's claim is that through the defendant's negligence the mother has been deprived of the opportunity to make a choice on the child's behalf as to whether it would be in the child's interests either to be born with disabilities or not to be born at all (a point apparently accepted by Griffiths LJ). This is an interest which is implicitly recognised by the Abortion Act 1967 itself, which permits abortion where there is a substantial risk that the child would have disabilities which would cause it to be seriously handicapped.[447] Moreover, Stephenson LJ did concede that there might be some "extreme cases" where it could be said that it would be better for the child not to be born.[448] Thus, this policy argument against wrongful life actions is by no means clear cut.[449]

         2–141

---

person at birth, not before: *C v S* [1987] 1 All E.R. 1230 at 1234, per Heilbron J.); cf. *Kerby v Redbridge Health Authority* [1993] 4 Med. L.R. 178; [1994] P.I.Q.R. Q1, where Ognall J held that there should be no award for the "dashed hopes" of bringing a pregnancy to a successful conclusion, because this was either the same as bereavement, or an award for grief, sorrow or distress attendant on the loss of a loved one, which is not actionable in negligence. See further *McWilliams v Lord Advocate*, 1992 S.L.T. 1045, where the parents of a child that died shortly after birth as a result of the alleged negligence of the defendant were held entitled to maintain a claim for loss of society under the Damages (Scotland) Act 1976, despite the fact that the injuries to the child occurred before he was born, and therefore at a time when he was not a "person" in law. On claims by parents arising out of in vitro fertilisation see Hill (1985) 25 Med. Sci. and Law 270.

[445] [1982] Q.B. 1166. The child was born before the Act came into force.

[446] See also *Arndt v Smith* (1997) 148 D.L.R. (4th) 48, SCC, on the duty owed to the mother.

[447] Abortion Act 1967 s.1(1)(d), as amended. This point was acknowledged by Stephenson LJ in *McKay* at 1179–1180.

[448] His Lordship cited the example of *Croke v Wiseman* [1981] 3 All E.R. 852; see also *Re B (A Minor) (Wardship: Medical Treatment)* [1981] 1 W.L.R. 1421 at 1424 where Templeman LJ said that the court, in exercising its wardship jurisdiction, might refuse to authorise life saving medical treatment where the child's life would be demonstrably awful, an exercise that involves weighing the

2-144   Section 1(2)(a) of the Act provides that an "occurrence" includes one which "affected either parent of the child in his or her ability to have a normal healthy child", which allows for the possibility of an action by the child in respect of pre-conception negligence. This appears to recognise a form of legal interest in not being conceived.[458] However, this would probably be limited to claims arising from physical harm to one or both of the parents.[459] Negligent genetic counselling, for example, in which parents are wrongly advised that it is safe for them to conceive, because the risk of bearing a child with a genetic disability is minimal, would normally give rise to a wrongful life claim by the child since if the correct advice had been given (and acted upon) the result would have been that the parents would not have conceived, i.e. the child would not have been born at all. The correct advice would not have resulted in the child being born without disabilities. Where the negligence concerns not simply the question of whether to conceive or not but the precautions required to conceive a healthy child, the position is more complicated. If precautions would have prevented damage to *that* child then there could be a claim under the Act, but if the precautions (such as recommending an amniocentesis test) would simply have revealed that the foetus had an abnormality and the mother would have had an abortion, the child has no claim because this is a wrongful life claim.[460] There is, of course, no reason why a parent should not have an action in respect of negligent genetic counselling, with the damages reflecting the additional cost of raising a handicapped child over and above the cost of raising a healthy child, or if an abortion is carried out damages for the disappointment of being unable to complete the pregnancy, and pain and suffering.[461]

---

[458] See Pace (1977) 40 M.L.R. 141, 153. See also Whitfield (1993) 1 Med. L. Rev. 28, 42–49.

[459] Examples of this type of injury would include exposure of the mother or father to radiation causing gene mutations; a congenital disease, such as syphilis, caused by a blood transfusion negligently given to the mother before conception or the negligent failure to diagnose syphilis in the mother prior to conception: *X and Y v Pal* (1991) 23 N.S.W.L.R. 26; [1992] 3 Med. L.R. 195, NSWCA; or the supply of contaminated sperm for artificial insemination: see Law Com. No.64, Cmnd.5709, 1974, para.77. Brazier and Cave, *Medicine, Patients and the Law*, 4th edn (Manchester: Manchester University Press, 2007), p.300 cites the example of mismanagement of a previous pregnancy with the result that Rhesus incompatibility goes undiscovered and untreated, causing damage to a subsequent foetus. In *Roberts v Johnstone* [1989] Q.B. 878 a mother who was Rhesus negative was given a Rhesus positive blood transfusion, and this created a real risk that any subsequent child would suffer from haemolytic disease without appropriate treatment during pregnancy, which was not given. The defendants, who were aware of these facts throughout, admitted liability.

[460] See Brazier and Cave, *Medicine, Patients and the Law*, 4th edn (Manchester: Manchester University Press, 2007), pp.307–308, which points out that realistic examples of the former circumstance are difficult to identify.

[461] See *Anderson v Forth Valley Health Board* 1998 S.L.T. 588; (1997) 44 B.M.L.R. 108, Court of Session, Outer House. See paras 2–052 et seq. for discussion of the nature of the doctors' duty of care to the parents; and paras 12–134 et seq. for consideration of the assessment of damages.

(e) Patients with infectious disease

(i) Claims against a doctor or hospital

Where a doctor has negligently permitted a person to come into contact with a   2–145
contagious disease there should be no difficulty in establishing a duty of care,
whether that person was the doctor's patient or not. In *Lindsey County Council v
Marshall*[462] the House of Lords held the defendants liable for negligently failing
to warn the claimant of the risk of infection by puerperal fever when she was
admitted to their maternity home, following a recent outbreak of the disease.
Similarly, if a doctor negligently discharged an infectious patient from hospital
and, as a result, a third party contracted the disease, the doctor would probably
owe a duty of care to the third party.[463]

In *X and Y v Pal*[464] the example was given of a doctor who negligently failed to   2–146
diagnose a child's illness as German measles (rubella) so that the child attending
school passed on the infection to another child whose mother was pregnant, with
the result that she gave birth to a child suffering from disabilities as a result of
exposure to the rubella in utero. Could the disabled child sue the doctor? Without
purporting to answer this question Clarke J.A. commented that:

> "Given the undemanding nature of the test of foreseeability it may well be that that chain of
> events was foreseeable. On the other hand it is clear that there was no element of reliance by
> either the pregnant mother or her child on the doctor and it would be difficult to suppose that
> he would have had such persons in contemplation when tending his own patient."[465]

With respect, the question of reliance is not the issue here. Clearly, the child
cannot in any meaningful sense have "relied" on anything. The question whether
a doctor should be liable to a pregnant patient in respect of the failure to diagnose
rubella with the result that her child suffers disabilities does not depend upon
whether the patient relied upon the doctor. Of course, all patients rely in some
sense on their doctors to act with reasonable care, just as all road users "rely" in
some sense on other motorists to drive carefully, and it might be said that the
public "rely" on doctors and hospitals not negligently to permit dangerously

---

[462] [1937] A.C. 97; *Heafield v Crane*, *The Times*, 31 July 1937. See also *McDaniel v Vancouver General Hospital* (1934) 152 L.T. 56, where the claimant was a patient being treated for diphtheria in the defendant hospital, and contracted smallpox by cross-infection from other patients. The hospital was held not liable because, having conformed to accepted practice, there was no negligence.

[463] See *Evans v Liverpool Corporation* [1906] 1 K.B. 160, where on essentially similar facts a claim against the hospital authority failed on the ground that, as the law then stood, the defendants were not vicariously liable for the acts of the physician. In the United States this form of liability is commonplace: *Hofmann v Blackmon* 241 So. 2d 752 (1970), where there was a failure to diagnose tuberculosis in the father and the doctor was held liable to the daughter infected by the patient; *Fosgate v Corona* 330 A. 2d 355 (1974), where there was liability for the discharge of infectious tuberculosis patients without warnings to persons identifiable as at risk (i.e. relatives). See also *Bradshaw v Daniel*, 854 S.W. 2d 865 (1993) where a doctor was held liable for negligently failing to warn the spouse of a patient who had died from Rocky Mountain Spotted Fever of the risk of contracting the disease, despite the fact that it is not a contagious disease, because it tends to occur in clusters arising from infected ticks which transmit the disease to people.

[464] (1991) 23 N.S.W.L.R. 26; [1992] 3 Med. L.R. 195, NSWCA.

[465] (1991) 23 N.S.W.L.R. 26; [1992] 3 Med. L.R. 195, at 43.

[171]

infectious people unwittingly to spread disease. But this is not the basis for imposing liability in negligence where that negligence has resulted in physical damage to the claimant. Liability derives from the fact that the defendant has undertaken to perform the act (of driving, or diagnosis) and comes under a corresponding duty to exercise reasonable care, imposed by law.[466] The issue that Clarke JA's example identifies is how extensively the scope of any duty of care owed by the doctor should be drawn. Foreseeability cannot place sensible limits on the potential claims that could arise from the spread of disease by infectious patients. Indeed, the existence of statutory reporting provisions[467] makes the foreseeability issue virtually a foregone conclusion in respect of certain diseases. The issue is one of the "proximity" of the relationship between the defendant and the claimant, an admittedly artificial device[468] by which the courts, as a matter of judicial policy, exclude from the ambit of compensation claims which do not satisfy the required degree of "directness" or "closeness" of relationship.[469] Possibly claims of this nature would be limited to relatives or close friends who are more foreseeably at risk of contracting an infection.

2–147   **Sexually transmitted disease**   By analogy it is arguable that a doctor, such as a general practitioner, might be under a duty of care to warn the sexual partner(s) of a patient who has AIDS or who is diagnosed as HIV positive about the patient's condition and the potential risk to their health, if the patient refused to consent to the disclosure. If the sexual partner was also the doctor's patient there would probably be little difficulty in finding a duty of care, since a "duty to inform" could be seen as part and parcel of the doctor's more general duty to exercise reasonable care to safeguard the health of his patient. It would be somewhat arbitrary, however, if the doctor's liability in this situation turned upon whether the sexual partner happened also to be one of his patients. Arguably the duty would arise irrespective of the sexual partner's status, on the basis that serious physical harm was foreseeable as a real risk.[470] In *Pittman Estate v Bain*[471] a

---

[466] See para.2–036.

[467] See the Public Health (Control of Disease) Act 1984 Pt IIA, and the Health Protection (Notification) Regulations 2010 (SI 2010/659) which impose a duty on registered medical practitioners to notify the local authority of cases where a patient is suspected of having a notifiable disease, of having an infection which presents or could present significant harm to human health, or is contaminated in a manner which presents or could present significant harm to human health.

[468] In *Caparo Industries plc v Dickman* [1990] 2 A.C. 605 at 633, 651 Lord Oliver said that "proximity" was simply a label which described the circumstances from which the courts conclude that a duty of care exists; see also per Lord Bridge and Lord Roskill at 618 and 628 respectively.

[469] The same issues arise in relation to whether a psychiatrist can be held liable for injuries inflicted on a third party by a psychiatric patient who is known to be dangerous: see para.2–165.

[470] This view is not unproblematic, however, since disclosure would be a breach of the doctor's duty of confidence to the patient which would have to be justified by the public interest defence; see Jones (1990) 6 P.N. 16, 22, and paras 8–059 et seq.; Casswell (1989) 68 Can. Bar Rev. 225. The GMC advises doctors that where it is not practicable to seek the patient's consent and, in exceptional circumstances, where the patient has refused consent "disclosing personal information may be justified in the public interest if failure to do so may expose others to a risk of death or serious harm. The benefits to an individual or to society of the disclosure must outweigh both the patient's and the public interest in keeping the information confidential": *Confidentiality: good practice in handling patient information*, January 2017, para.64; see further para.8–060. The National Health Service (Venereal Diseases) Regulations 1974 (SI 1974/29) create a specific statutory duty of confidence with

general practitioner was held liable in negligence to the wife of a patient who had contracted HIV from a blood transfusion. The doctor was negligent in failing to inform the patient of his HIV status with the result that the patient did not take any precautions to protect his wife from infection with the virus through sexual intercourse. The question of whether there was an independent duty upon the doctor to inform the patient's wife of the risk to her did not arise, since it was found as a question of fact that had the general practitioner informed the patient, the patient would certainly have informed his wife and they would have taken appropriate precautions. Moreover, it was assumed that the doctor owed a duty of care in negligence to the patient's wife, the only issues being whether the doctor had been negligent and whether the failure to inform the patient had caused any damage.

In *BT v Oei*[472] the defendant doctor was held to owe a duty of care to the sexual   **2–148** partner (BT) of a patient (AT) who had contracted HIV. The doctor was found to have been negligent in failing to diagnose AT's HIV status, by failing to recommend that AT undergo an HIV test when the patient's symptoms indicated that this would have been a reasonable precaution. BT contracted HIV from sexual contact with AT. Bell J found that had AT been diagnosed as HIV positive he would have informed BT of his status (given medical evidence that the vast majority of patients in this situation agree to disclosure after counselling) and that this would have enabled AT and BT to take steps to avoid BT contracting the infection. In considering the doctor's duty to BT, Bell J commented that *Pittman Estate v Bain* did not involve an analysis of the basis of the decision that a duty of care was owed to the patient's wife, and therefore was of little guidance. The defendant argued that no duty of care was owed to BT because: BT was not a patient of the defendant; AT did not disclose to the defendant the existence of a sexual relationship between himself and BT; AT did not seek treatment for or advice about his HIV status; AT's HIV positive status was not caused by any action or inaction on the defendant's part. In effect, said the defendant, BT's argument sought to impose a duty to rescue, a duty to save the claimant from harm not caused by the defendant himself. Bell J rejected the rescue analogy. This was not a case where the defendant was being held responsible for a "failure to rescue" BT. Nor was it a case where there was a potential conflict between the doctor's duty of confidentiality to AT and a duty of care in tort being owed to BT. Since it was accepted that, if he had known about his HIV status, AT would have informed BT, there was no conflict of duties.

Bell J drew on two American authorities. In *Reisner v Regents of the University*   **2–149** *of California*[473] the California Court of Appeal held that a doctor had a duty to warn a 12-year-old patient that she was HIV positive (following a contaminated blood transfusion) and to take appropriate precautions in any future sexual relationship. The Court accepted that a duty of care was owed to her later sexual

---

respect to sexually transmitted disease, which may apply to AIDS patients: *X v Y* [1988] 2 All E.R. 648 at 656. AIDS is not a notifiable disease under the Health Protection (Notification) Regulations 2010 (SI 2010/659).

[471] (1994) 112 D.L.R. (4th) 257, Ont Ct, Gen Div, para.4–060.
[472] [1999] NSWSC 1082.
[473] 37 Cal. Rptr. 2d 518 (1995).

partner who contracted HIV, even though his identity was neither known to nor ascertainable by the doctor at the time. In *Di Marco v Lynch Homes-Chester County Inc*[474] a healthcare worker who suffered a needle-stick injury was given incorrect advice about appropriate precautions when engaging in a sexual relationship. Both the healthcare worker and her sexual partner were subsequently diagnosed as suffering from Hepatitis B. The Supreme Court of Pennsylvania held that a duty of care was owed to the sexual partner on the basis that:

> "...the class of persons whose health is likely to be threatened by the patient includes anyone who is physically intimate with the patient"

which included those who engage in "casual sex".[475] The argument that it was unforeseeable that a patient would engage in sexual activity outside a marital relationship exalted "an unheeded morality over reality".

2–150   In *BT v Oei* Bell J held that:

> "I do not consider that the fact that the members of the class may not be known or be capable of ready identification by the defendant is determinative of there being no duty of care."[476]

In reaching the conclusion that the defendant doctor did owe a duty of care to BT, Bell J took into account the following factors: (1) the Public Health Act 1991 (NSW) required a medical practitioner who reasonably believes his patient to have HIV to inform the patient of the public health implications of the condition and of the means of protecting others. The practitioner must also inform the patient of the patient's statutory responsibility to warn prospective sexual partners of his condition. These provisions had "some bearing" on whether it was appropriate to impose a common law duty of care; (2) there was no conflict between the duty owed by the defendant to AT and BT; the two duties were coincident; it was not a case where it was alleged that the defendant had a duty to warn BT despite AT's objections; (3) BT was a sexual partner of AT; (4) it was reasonably foreseeable that AT, if HIV positive, would transmit the virus to a sexual partner; (5) AT was unaware of his HIV status; (6) the defendant's specialist knowledge and training equipped him to identify the risk that AT had contracted HIV; (7) failure to diagnose and adequately counsel AT to undertake an HIV antibody test exposed AT's sexual partner(s) to the real risk of contracting a fatal disease. It was:

> "...the combination of these factors, together with a consideration of public policy reflected in the statutory obligations placed upon medical practitioners with respect to the treatment of and supply of information to patients with sexually transmissible medical conditions, which to my mind makes the imposition of the duty appropriate in the circumstances of this case."[477]

---

[474] 583 A. 2d 422 (1990).
[475] 583 A. 2d 422 (1990) at 425.
[476] [1999] NSWSC 1082 at [87], distinguishing *Goodwill v British Pregnancy Advisory Service* [1996] 2 All E.R. 161 on this issue, on the basis that that was a claim for pure economic loss; see para.2–181.
[477] [1999] NSWSC 1082 at [98].

In *Idameneo (No 123) Pty Ltd v Gross*[478] a patient underwent testing for sexually   **2–151**
transmitted disease. The test result was ambiguous, and so a letter was sent to the
patient to advise her to return for re-testing, but in the meantime the patient had
changed address. The medical centre that kept the medical records did not make
adequate efforts to trace the patient. The patient had unprotected sexual
intercourse with her partner who contracted HIV. A claim by the patient's partner
against the doctors for negligence was settled, and the doctors then brought a
contribution claim against the medical centre that had assumed responsibility for
maintaining patient records. Approving the approach of Bell J in *BT v Oei*, the
New South Wales Court of Appeal held that there was no difference in principle
between a doctor owing a duty of care to the sexual partner of a patient and a
medical centre, with its control of patient records in a medical practice, owing a
similar duty of care. The foreseeability of serious harm eventuating if patient
records were not kept up to date was clear, and the medical centre's own
documentation concerning the maintenance of accurate patient records demonstrated actual foresight and knowledge of an ascertainable class of vulnerable
persons, which included both patients and persons "who might come in contact
with a patient who unknowingly was the carrier of a communicable disease".[479]

In *Harvey v PD*[480] the claimant and her partner, FH, attended a clinic together to   **2–152**
request HIV tests because they were proposing to get married. At the time of the
consultation they had a sexual relationship but practised protected sex. The
pathology report for PD was negative for both Hepatitis B and HIV. FH's
pathology report was positive for both Hepatitis B and HIV. They were given
their results separately, and FH lied to PD about his positive result (indeed, he
subsequently forged a negative test certificate). When PD asked at the clinic
about FH's result she was told by a receptionist that the result was confidential
and could not be disclosed to her. Section 17(2) of the New South Wales Public
Health Act 1991 provides that a doctor who acquires information that another
person is or has been infected with, inter alia, HIV or AIDS, must take all
reasonable steps to prevent disclosure of the information to another person, and
s.17(4) of the Act makes contravention of the section a criminal offence.
Information can be disclosed, inter alia, with the consent of the patient. PD
married FH and subsequently contracted HIV as a result of unprotected sexual
intercourse. The New South Wales Court of Appeal upheld a finding that the
doctor had been negligent in conducting the pre-test counselling and that the
negligence caused PD to contract HIV.[481] The negligence in respect of pre-test
counselling consisted of the failure to advise PD and FH at the initial joint
consultation of the need for them both to consent to the disclosure of their results

---

[478] [2012] NSWCA 423; (2012) 83 N.S.W.L.R. 643.
[479] [2012] NSWCA 423; (2012) 83 N.S.W.L.R. 643 at [56], rejecting the argument that the sexual
partners of patients infected with a communicable disease constituted an "indeterminate group" of
potential claimants and that imposing a duty of care would create indeterminate liability.
[480] [2004] NSWCA 97; (2004) 59 N.S.W.L.R. 639.
[481] The Court also considered that there were inadequacies in the post-test counselling (for example,
that PD was given her results by a receptionist and that there was inadequate follow-up of FH, given
his positive test) which the trial judge (Cripps AJ at [2003] NSWSC 487) held constituted breach of a
duty of care, but the Court of Appeal considered that it was unnecessary to decide on these alternative
findings of breach.

"...simply not arguable in law that by promulgating these quasi-legislative standards to hospitals and health care workers, Ontario created a relationship of proximity with the plaintiff sufficient to give rise to a private law duty of care."[488]

Moreover, the Province had to balance a number of competing policy concerns when making decisions about public health, which had to be made in the general public interest rather than on the basis of the interests of a narrow class of individuals:

"Restrictions limiting access to hospitals or parts of hospitals may help combat the spread of disease, but such restrictions will also have an impact upon the interests of those who require access to the hospital for other health care needs or those of relatives and friends. Similarly, a decision to lift restrictions may increase the risk of the disease spreading but may offer other advantages to the public at large including enhanced access to health care facilities. The public officials charged with the responsibility for imposing and lifting such measures must weigh and balance the advantages and disadvantages and strive to act in a manner that best meets the overall interests of the public at large."[489]

The Court reiterated the conclusion reached in *Eliopoulos v Ontario* that imposing a duty of care would create an unreasonable burden that would interfere with public health decision-making; public health authorities should be able to make decisions without the fear of lawsuits.[490]

(f) Patient's medical condition creating other hazards to third parties

2–156   There may well be other circumstances in which it is foreseeable that a patient could be a potential hazard to third parties where a doctor would be held to owe a duty of care. If, for example, a patient's medical condition (such as epilepsy) or the side effects of a drug that the doctor has prescribed render certain conduct (such as driving a motor vehicle) hazardous, the doctor will be under a duty to warn the patient. If he fails to do so and as a result the patient causes an accident injuring others there could be little doubt that the doctor would owe a duty of care to the patient and arguably to the third parties.[491] In *Spillane v Wasserman*[492] the

---

[488] 2009 ONCA 378; (2009) 310 D.L.R. (4th) 710; (2009) 66 C.C.L.T. (3d) 193 at [28] per Sharpe JA.

[489] 2009 ONCA 378; (2009) 310 D.L.R. (4th) 710; (2009) 66 C.C.L.T. (3d) 193 at [31].

[490] 2009 ONCA 378; (2009) 310 D.L.R. (4th) 710; (2009) 66 C.C.L.T. (3d) 193 at [35]. In *Abarquez v Ontario* 2009 ONCA 374; (2009) 310 D.L.R. (4th) 726 the Court reached a similar conclusion in relation to claims brought against Ontario by nurses and the family members of nurses who contracted SARS during the outbreak. Although nurses were, by virtue of their profession, in the eye of the SARS storm, they had no higher claim to have their health protected by Ontario than any other resident of the province. A private law duty of care to safeguard the health of the nurses would conflict with the overriding public law duty to pronounce standards that were in the interest of the public at large.

[491] See Giesen, *International Medical Malpractice Law*, 1988, para.255; *Freese v Lemmon*, 210 N.W. 2d 576 (1973), SC of Iowa. See also the GMC guidance to doctors in *Confidentiality: patients' fitness to drive and reporting concerns to the DVLA or the DVA*, January 2017 (available at http://www.gmc-uk.org/Confidentiality___Patients_fitness_to_drive_and_reporting_concerns_to_ DVLA_or_DVA.pdf_70063275.pdf).

[492] (1992) 13 C.C.L.T. (2d) 267, Ont HC.

defendant W suffered an epileptic seizure while driving a heavy goods vehicle, passed through a red light, and killed a cyclist. W had a long history of epileptic seizures and should not have been driving at the time of the accident. He frequently neglected to take the medication prescribed for his condition and misrepresented his medical condition when renewing his driver's licence. Two doctors had been involved in treating W's epilepsy for years, but had failed to conduct periodic tests to monitor and control patient compliance with the medication regime. These tests would have revealed W's lax attitude to taking the medication. Neither doctor had warned W not to drive commercial vehicles, or not to drive at all except in specified circumstances, as the Canadian Medical Association's Guide required them to do. Neither doctor reported W's condition to the Registrar of Motor Vehicles as required by legislation. The doctors were held liable in negligence to the deceased's estate, being found 40 per cent responsible, with W being 60 per cent responsible.[493] Similarly, in *MacPhail v Desrosiers*[494] the defendants failed to warn a patient who had just undergone an abortion, and had been given a sedative, against driving a motor vehicle. There was an accident when the patient's vehicle crossed the highway and hit an oncoming vehicle, caused, said the Nova Scotia Court of Appeal, by the patient either fainting or a moment of inattention. The clinic treating the patient was held to have been negligent and that negligence was found to be the sole cause of the collision.[495]

(g)   Psychiatric patients

There can be no doubt that doctors, such as psychiatrists or clinical psychologists, will owe a duty of care to their psychiatric patients,[496] and that this duty may require them to take reasonable steps to protect patients from harming themselves, including, in some instances, the prevention of suicide attempts.[497] A hospital authority may also be responsible for injuries inflicted on a patient by a fellow patient where the injuries are the result of a failure to provide adequate

2–157

---

[493] See also *Toms v Foster* (1994) 7 M.V.R. (3d) 34 (Ont CA)—doctors who were aware that a patient's condition (cervical spondylosis) made it inadvisable for him to drive and failed to take steps to prevent him from driving by failing to report him to the Registrar of Motor Vehicles held liable to third parties injured by patient's driving. The duty of the doctors to report was a duty owed to members of the public: it was clearly designed to protect not only the patient but people he might harm if permitted to drive.

[494] (1998) 170 N.S.R. (2d) 145, NSCA.

[495] The negligence consisted of proceeding with the abortion when they knew the patient intended to drive home herself immediately afterwards, contrary to the clinic's own policy, when she was foreseeably at risk of having an accident. It is clear from the law report that the clinic were held liable for the injuries to the occupants of the other vehicle, as well as the patient's injuries, although there was no discussion in the judgment of the duty of care owed to the third parties.

[496] Although a psychiatrist (or indeed, any other health professional) will owe a duty of care to a child who is being examined for the purpose of determining whether the child has been the victim of abuse, no duty of care is owed to the parents of the child because of the potential conflict of interest between parent and child: *JD v East Berkshire Community Health NHS Trust*; *K v Dewsbury Healthcare NHS Trust*; *K v Oldham NHS Trust* [2005] UKHL 23; [2005] 2 A.C. 373. See para.2–101.

[497] See paras 4–166 et seq.

control and supervision.[498] The same principle applies to injuries to employees caused by a violent patient where there has been negligence in managing the risk of harm to the employees.[499]

2–158   **No duty to protect patients from consequences of their criminal acts**   The duty owed to psychiatric patients does not encompass protecting them from the consequences of their own criminal actions, at least where they are found to bear some degree of responsibility for their actions. In *Clunis v Camden & Islington Health Authority*[500] the claimant was a man with a history of mental disorder and seriously violent behaviour. He had been detained under the Mental Health Act 1983 and following his discharge from hospital the defendants came under a duty, by virtue of s.117 of that Act, to provide aftercare services, but he did not receive any aftercare. Three months after his discharge from hospital the claimant killed a stranger in a sudden and completely unprovoked attack. He was charged with murder, but a plea of manslaughter on the ground of diminished responsibility was accepted by the prosecution and he was ordered to be detained in a special hospital. He brought an action against the defendants alleging that they were in breach of a common law duty of care to treat him with reasonable professional care and skill, arguing that if he had received an appropriate assessment he would not have gone on to commit the crime because he would either have consented to become a voluntary patient or would have been detained under the Act. As a result of the alleged negligence he would now be detained for much longer than he would otherwise have been. The Court of Appeal struck out the claim as disclosing no reasonable cause of action, on the grounds that: (1) the action was based the claimant's own illegal act, and therefore the maxim ex turpi causa non oritur actio applied; and (2) the statutory obligation to provide aftercare created by s.117 of the Mental Health Act 1983 did not give rise to a duty of care at common law. The fact that the claimant was found guilty of manslaughter is most obviously relevant to the defence of ex turpi causa, but it appears also to have influenced the Court's view of the duty of care—it was not fair or reasonable to hold the health authority responsible for the consequences of the claimant's criminal act. Although it was accepted that the claimant's mental responsibility

---

[498] *Wellesley Hospital v Lawson* (1977) 76 D.L.R. (3d) 688 in which the Supreme Court of Canada proceeded on the basis that such a common law duty existed, though the case was concerned with the interpretation of a provision in the Ontario Mental Health Act 1970; *Stewart v Extendicare Ltd* [1986] 4 W.W.R. 559, Sask QB, where a nursing home was held liable for injuries caused by a patient to another patient; *Wenden v Trikha* (1991) 8 C.C.L.T. (2d) 138 at 155–156, Alta QB; aff'd (1993) 14 C.C.L.T. (2d) 225, Alta CA, where Murray J pointed out that the duty owed by a hospital to exercise control and supervision over mentally ill patients to see that they do not harm other patients is "confined to reasonable and foreseeable dangers". An analogous case is *Ellis v Home Office* [1953] 2 All E.R. 149 in which the prison authorities were held to owe a duty of care to a prisoner assaulted by another prisoner. On the facts the defendants were not found negligent since the attack was unforeseeable. See also *Stenning v Home Office* [2002] EWCA Civ 793.

[499] Although the hospital has to take into account its duty of care to the patient in determining what is reasonable in relation to protecting its employees, the issue is not simply whether the hospital is in breach of duty to its patient: see *Buck v Nottinghamshire Healthcare NHS Trust* [2006] EWCA Civ 1576; (2007) 93 B.M.L.R. 28; *Cook v Bradford Community Health NHS Trust* [2002] EWCA Civ 1616.

[500] [1998] Q.B. 978.

was substantially impaired, nonetheless a plea of diminished responsibility did not remove liability for his criminal act. He had to be taken to have known what he was doing and that it was wrong:

"...public policy would ... preclude the court from entertaining the plaintiff's claim unless it could be said that he did not know the nature and quality of his act or that what he was doing was wrong."[501]

Nor does breach of s.117 of the Mental Health Act 1983 give rise to a common law action for breach of statutory duty. In *Clunis* the Court of Appeal held that the primary means of enforcing s.117 was by way of complaint to the Secretary of State, and a common law duty of care in respect of an allegedly negligent failure to provide aftercare was inconsistent with the statutory context in which s.117 functioned.[502] However, in *K v Central and North West London Mental Health NHS Trust*[503] King J distinguished *Clunis* when refusing to strike out an allegation of negligence based on s.117. *Clunis* was concerned, said his Lordship, with an alleged duty in respect of the defendants' administrative function of arranging for aftercare services, whereas in *K v Central and North West London Mental Health NHS Trust* it was alleged that there had been negligence in performing the defendants' "treatment duty" arising out of s.117. On a narrow reading of *Clunis*, it was authority only for the proposition that simply because a person is cared for under s.117, no general common law duty of care to provide aftercare services automatically arises and a claimant cannot claim the benefit of such a duty simply because he is a member of the particular class.[504] It was at least arguable that if the defendant actually undertook to provide treatment services and was negligent in doing so, the relationship between the parties was closer than that in *Clunis*, and it may be just and reasonable to impose a duty of care. Moreover, King J also considered it to be arguable that if *Clunis* is authority for the view that a common law duty of care in the exercise of the statutory duty under s.117 is absolutely excluded in all cases, then "such a wide proposition is

2–159

---

[501] [1998] Q.B. 978 at 989. Note, however, that in *Hunter Area Health Service v Presland* [2005] NSWCA 33; (2005) 63 N.S.W.L.R. 22 a majority of the New South Wales Court of Appeal, on very similar facts to *Clunis*, held that the negligent hospital authority did not owe a duty of care to a psychiatric patient who had been prosecuted for murder but found not guilty by reason of insanity. Although the plaintiff lacked moral culpability by reason of his insanity, his act remained an unlawful and wholly unreasonable act. It was not "justifiable homicide" but unlawful homicide for which he was not criminally responsible. Spigelman CJ dissented, on the basis that where a person has been held not to be criminally responsible for his actions on the grounds of insanity, the common law should not deny that person the right to a remedy, and the acts which would otherwise constitute a crime do not break the causal chain. In *Ellis v Counties Manukau District Health Board* [2007] 1 N.Z.L.R. 196 a health authority was held not to owe a duty of care to a psychotic patient in respect of failing to take steps to prevent him from killing his father, applying *Clunis*. The claimant argued that the defendants had a duty properly to assess, treat and take all steps to detain the patient against his wishes, to prevent him causing harm to himself or others. The defendants' lack of control over the claimant was an important factor in reaching the conclusion that no duty of care existed.
[502] Applying the view expressed by Lord Browne-Wilkinson in *X (Minors) v Bedfordshire County Council* [1995] 2 A.C. 633, 739 that a common law duty of care cannot be superimposed on a statutory duty if the observance of the common law duty of care would be inconsistent with or have a tendency to discourage the due performance by the public authority of its statutory duties.
[503] [2008] EWHC 1217 (QB); [2008] P.I.Q.R. P19.
[504] [2008] EWHC 1217 (QB); [2008] P.I.Q.R. P19 at [49].

no longer tenable in the light of subsequent legal developments".[505] His Lordship had in mind the developing jurisprudence on human rights, and the fact that the reasoning in *X v Bedfordshire County Council*,[506] upon which the Court of Appeal in *Clunis* had founded its approach, was no longer regarded as being entirely definitive.[507]

2–160   There are two situations in which a duty of care may arise which is owed to someone other than the doctor's patient. First, where a doctor certifies that a person meets the statutory criteria for compulsory admission to hospital under the mental health legislation, and secondly, possibly, where a psychiatric patient has injured a third party in circumstances in which the damage was foreseeable.

(i)   Certificates for the purpose of compulsory admission to hospital

2–161   Applications to commit individuals compulsorily to hospital under Pt II of the Mental Health Act 1983[508] must be supported by the recommendations of (normally) two doctors, one of whom must be an approved specialist in mental disorder, although an approved specialist will not necessarily be a qualified psychiatrist.[509] Under s.2 of that Act a person may be detained for 28 days for assessment, during which time he may receive some treatment without his consent. The doctors must certify that the patient is suffering from a mental disorder of a nature or degree which warrants detention for assessment, and that he ought to be detained in the interests of his own health or safety or for the protection of other persons.[510] In an emergency the application for admission for assessment needs the support of only one doctor, who does not have to be an

---

[505] [2008] EWHC 1217 (QB); [2008] P.I.Q.R. P19 at [55].

[506] [1995] 2 A.C. 633.

[507] King J cited *Barrett v Enfield LBC* [2001] 2 A.C. 550, but had also referred, inter alia, to *JD v East Berkshire Community Health NHS Trust* [2005] UKHL 23; [2005] 2 A.C. 373 and *Phelps v Hillingdon London Borough Council* [2001] 2 A.C. 619. See paras 2–096 to 2–100 above for discussion of the extent to which *X v Bedfordshire County Council* has been overtaken by subsequent developments. Note, however, that King J also cited, at [54], the decision of the Court of Appeal in *Smith v Chief Constable of Sussex* [2008] EWCA Civ 39; [2008] P.I.Q.R. P12 as authority for the proposition that "*the very proximity of the parties on particular facts* may lead to a different conclusion being reached than hitherto, and that that which may have been regarded as definitive expositions of principle at the highest level as to when a common law duty of care might or might not arise, have to be reconsidered in the light of that proximity" (original emphasis). The Court of Appeal in *Smith* had departed from the ruling of the House of Lords in *Hill v Chief Constable of West Yorkshire* [1989] 1 A.C. 53 that no duty of care could be owed by the police to the victim of a criminal offence, but the House of Lords reversed the decision in *Smith*, albeit accepting that some of statements of principle in *Hill* may have been expressed in terms that would now be considered to be too wide: *Smith v Chief Constable of Sussex* [2008] UKHL 50; [2009] 1 A.C. 225. See also *Michael v Chief Constable of South Wales* [2015] UKSC 2; [2015] A.C. 1732.

[508] Pt II of the Mental Health Act 1983 provides a complete code for the compulsory admission to hospital of non-compliant mentally incapacitated patients for the purpose of assessment and treatment of their mental disorder. There is no residual common law power, under the doctrine of necessity, to justify a patient's detention; nor can the Mental Capacity Act 2005 be relied on for this purpose: *R. (on the application of Sessay) v South London and Maudsley NHS Foundation Trust* [2011] EWHC 2617 (QB); [2012] Q.B. 760.

[509] See Hale, *Mental Health Law*, 5th edn (London: Sweet & Maxwell, 2010), pp.98–100.

[510] Mental Health Act 1983 s.2(2).

approved specialist.[511] Under s.3 a person may be compulsorily detained for treatment, initially for up to six months. The doctors must certify:

(i)   that the person is suffering from mental disorder of a nature or degree which makes medical treatment in hospital appropriate;
(ii)   it is necessary for the health or safety of the patient or for the protection of other persons that he should receive such treatment which cannot be provided unless he is detained; and
(iii)   appropriate medical treatment[512] is available for him.[513]

These procedures clearly contemplate that the person detained will not necessarily be a patient of the doctor(s) supporting admission, since the Act specifies that one of the doctors must, if practicable, have "previous acquaintance" with the person.[514] It is strongly arguable, however, that the doctors owe a duty of care to that person in giving the certificate and may be liable in an action for negligence.[515] In *De Freville v Dill*[516] McCardie J was apparently opposed to the existence of such a duty but felt compelled to hold that a duty of care did exist on the balance of authority, particularly the majority decision of the Court of Appeal in *Everett v Griffiths*.[517] On the other hand, in *Everett v Griffiths*[518] the House of Lords held that the defendant doctor was not liable on the facts, without expressing a concluded view on the decision of Crompton J in *Hall v Semple*[519] in which a duty had been held to exist. In *X (Minors) v Bedfordshire County Council*[520] Lord Browne-Wilkinson pointed out that the question whether a doctor owes a duty of care to a patient when certifying that a patient is fit to be detained under the Mental Health Acts was left undecided in *Everett v Griffiths* and remains open for decision in an appropriate case.

2–162

If a doctor owes a duty not to issue a certificate negligently, it would also follow that there may be liability for negligently failing to issue a certificate if the person

2–163

---

[511] Mental Health Act 1983 s.4.
[512] References to appropriate medical treatment "are references to medical treatment which is appropriate in his case, taking into account the nature and degree of the mental disorder and all other circumstances of his case": Mental Health Act 1983 s.3(4).
[513] Mental Health Act 1983 s.3. See also s.7 of the Mental Health Act 1983 on reception into guardianship; and, in Wales only, the National Assistance Act 1948 s.47 and the National Assistance (Amendment) Act 1951 which require medical evidence in support of compulsory removal procedures.
[514] Mental Health Act 1983 ss.12(2), 4(3).
[515] *Hall v Semple* (1862) 3 F. & F. 337; *De Freville v Dill* (1927) 96 L.J.K.B. 1056; *Everett v Griffiths* [1920] 3 K.B. 163, CA; [1921] 1 A.C. 631, HL; *Harnett v Fisher* [1927] A.C. 573; *Buxton v Jayne* [1960] 1 W.L.R. 783; [1962] C.L.Y. 1167. On the procedural restrictions to bringing such an action see Mental Health Act 1983 s.139, paras 4–191 et seq.
[516] (1927) 96 L.J.K.B. 1056.
[517] [1920] 3 K.B. 163.
[518] [1921] 1 A.C. 631.
[519] (1862) 3 F. & F. 337.
[520] [1995] 2 A.C. 633, 753.

is in fact of unsound mind and through the absence of certification and restraint inflicts injury on himself. This point was acknowledged by McCardie J, obiter, in *De Freville v Dill*.[521]

2–164   On the other hand, in *X v A, B and C and the Mental Health Act Commission*[522] Morland J held that where a registered medical practitioner and two laypersons consider whether to grant or withhold a certificate that a detained patient is competent to, and has in fact, consented to treatment under the provisions of s.57 of the Mental Health Act 1983,[523] they are performing quasi-judicial, public law duties, and accordingly they do not owe a private law duty of care in negligence to the patient, even if the decision could legitimately be challenged on public law principles. His Lordship distinguished the situation where a doctor is acting as a doctor and giving medical opinions, for example for the purpose of compulsory admission under s.3 or for the purpose of giving electro-convulsive therapy under s.58(3)(b) of the Mental Health Act 1983. In those circumstances it was possible that a doctor could be in breach of a common law duty in private law, because the doctor, qua doctor, is giving a medical opinion about a patient, albeit not his patient.

(ii)   Injury to third parties

2–165   Is a doctor who is aware or ought reasonably to be aware that a psychiatric patient constitutes a serious risk of harm to others under a duty of care to the third parties to take steps to prevent the harm or minimise the risk? If, for example, a patient has threatened to kill someone does the doctor have a duty to warn either that person or the police, or to initiate the compulsory detention procedures under the Mental Health Act 1983?[524] If so, the doctor could be liable in damages to a victim of the patient if he negligently failed to take the appropriate steps.

2–166   In *Tarasoff v Regents of the University of California*[525] the Supreme Court of California held that a psychologist owed a duty of care to a woman murdered by the psychologist's patient. The patient had expressed an intention to kill the woman, who was a former girlfriend. The court accepted that there was a balance to be drawn between the public interest in effective treatment of mental illness and the consequent requirement of protecting confidentiality, and the public interest in safety from violent assault. Nonetheless, the protection of confidentiality must end where the public peril begins.[526]

---

[521] (1927) 96 L.J.K.B. 1056 at 1060–1061. In *Everett v Griffiths* [1920] 3 K.B. 163 at 196 Scrutton LJ, in a dissenting judgment, considered that the prospect of such a duty being owed was a reason for *not* imposing a duty generally in the granting of certificates.

[522] (1991) 9 B.M.L.R. 91, Q.B.D.

[523] See para.6–087.

[524] Note that there is a difference between saying that the statutory grounds for compulsory detention are satisfied, and that the doctor owes a common law duty of care to a third party to detain the patient.

[525] 551 P. 2d 334; Sup., 131 Cal. Rptr. 14 (1976); see de Haan (1986) 2 P.N. 86.

[526] "In this risk-infected society we can hardly tolerate the further exposure to danger that would result from a concealed knowledge of the therapist that his patient was lethal. If the exercise of reasonable care to protect the threatened victim requires the therapist to warn the endangered party or

This duty of care is not as wide as might at first appear. First, in *Tarasoff* it was recognised that the nature of the "psychotherapeutic dialogue" may lead patients to express threats of violence, few of which are ever executed, and a therapist should not be encouraged routinely to reveal such threats. Secondly, the California Supreme Court has subsequently distinguished *Tarasoff* in a case where a patient made general threats of violence against children, on the basis that *Tarasoff* involved a known and specifically foreseeable and identifiable victim.[527]

2–167

It remains debatable whether *Tarasoff* would be followed in this country. In *Holgate v Lancashire Mental Hospitals Board*[528] a hospital was held liable for negligently releasing on licence a dangerous patient who had been compulsorily detained following convictions for violent offences. The patient entered the claimant's home and assaulted her. The trial judge seemed to assume that a duty of care existed and the report deals largely with the question of whether there had been negligence. The case could have been justified on the basis of the degree of control exercised by the defendants over the dangerous patient, a control analogous to the relationship between gaoler and prisoner which may give rise to a duty of care.[529] This is the basis upon which a hospital authority may be held liable for injuries to a patient inflicted by a fellow patient as a result of negligent supervision, and there is no obvious reason why this duty should be owed only to patients, and not, for example, to visitors to the hospital.[530] However, in *Home Office v Dorset Yacht Co. Ltd*[531] Lord Diplock specifically reserved his opinion on *Holgate v Lancashire Mental Hospitals Board* though Lord Morris considered that in a situation comparable to *Holgate* "a duty of reasonable care would be owed to those whose safety, as reasonable foresight would show, might be in jeopardy".[532] In *Palmer v Tees Health Authority*[533] the Court of Appeal dismissed *Holgate* as a case of unsatisfactory authority where little attention was paid to the question of the defendants' duty of care. The case could not be reconciled with *Hill v Chief Constable of West Yorkshire*[534] on the question of proximity.[535]

2–168

---

those who can reasonably be expected to notify him, we see no sufficient societal interest that would protect and justify concealment. The containment of such risks lies in the public interest," 551 P. 2d 334 at 347, per Tobriner J.

[527] *Thompson v County of Alameda*, 614 P. 2d 728 (1980); see also *Brady v Hopper*, 751 F. 2d 329 (1984); cf. *Jablonski v U.S.*, 712 F. 2d 391 (1983). See also *Peterson v State of Washington* 671 P. 2d 230 (1983) and *Taggart v State of Washington* 822 P. 2d 243 (1992), both in the Supreme Court of Washington, where the requirement of an identifiable victim was rejected.

[528] [1937] 4 All E.R. 19.

[529] See *Home Office v Dorset Yacht Co. Ltd* [1970] A.C. 1004; *Ellis v Home Office* [1953] 2 All E.R. 149; *Stenning v Home Office* [2002] EWCA Civ 793; *S(J) v Clement* (1995) 122 D.L.R. (4th) 449, Ont Ct Gen Div.

[530] See *Wellesley Hospital v Lawson* (1977) 76 D.L.R. (3d) 688, SCC, where the duty was said to be owed to "third persons", not simply patients. See also *Partington v Wandsworth London Borough Council* [1990] Fam Law 468; *The Independent*, 8 November 1989.

[531] [1970] A.C. 1004 at 1062–1063.

[532] [1970] A.C. 1004 at 1041. Lord Reid said that *Holgate* "could only be supported if it could be said that the release was authorised so carelessly that there had been no real exercise of discretion", [1970] A.C. 1004 at 1031–1032.

[533] [1999] Lloyd's Rep. Med. 351.

[534] [1989] 1 A.C. 53.

[535] [1999] Lloyd's Rep. Med. 351 at 358–359, per Stuart-Smith LJ.

disclosing no reasonable cause of action. The parents had relied on oral assurances from the local authority that a suspected or known sexual abuser would not be placed with them, and in answer to a specific question about the boy were told, wrongly, that he was not known or suspected of being a sexual abuser. Thus, the local authority had assumed a responsibility for the accuracy of the statements that they gave about the boy placed with the family.[544] There are clearly differences between the factual situation in *W v Essex County Council* and *Palmer* in that there was an element of misrepresentation in the former case. Another distinction is that in *W v Essex County Council* the defendants were active in placing the perpetrator in a situation where he was able to inflict the harm on the children, whereas in *Palmer* the defendants merely failed to prevent him from causing harm in general. Nonetheless, it is arguable that *W v Essex County Council* goes some way to supporting the proposition that a duty of care could arise where there is a known, identifiable victim.

2–172   **Canada**   In the Canadian case of *Wenden v Trikha*[545] Murray J considered the circumstances in which a duty of care might be imposed upon a hospital or psychiatrist, taking into account both the decision in *Tarasoff* and the English cases, particularly *Home Office v Dorset Yacht Co. Ltd.* A voluntary psychiatric patient left the hospital in which he was receiving treatment and drove a vehicle in a trance state, causing an accident in which the claimant was injured. Murray J accepted that a hospital treating mentally ill patients did owe a duty of care to a person or class of persons other than its staff or patients if it could be said that it was foreseeable that harm would be likely to occur to such a person or persons as a result of the behaviour of a mentally ill patient, provided that there was some further ingredient which established a relationship between the hospital and that third party. That "further ingredient" consisted of exposing the claimant to a particular risk of danger due to "the nature of the patient" which was different in its incidence from the general risk shared with all members of the public.[546] The learned judge acknowledged that:

> "A psychiatrist treating an out-patient or a voluntary admittee to a hospital may not have the degree of control which one encounters in a prison-like setting or in those cases where the patient has been certified or confined. It depends upon the evidence whether or not one can say that the future pattern of behaviour of the patient would or would not be more or less accurate than predicting the behaviour of an escaped prisoner ... However, as Tobriner J pointed out [in *Tarasoff*], the psychiatrist does have the necessary special relationship involving at least the care of the patient and as such may become privy to information by which he or she knows that the patient poses a serious danger of causing damage to a third person or to a class of third parties. The psychiatrist is also highly trained in assessing mentally ill people, at least to the degree possible given today's technology, which, by its very nature, is at best an imprecise and problematic science."[547]

---

[544] The case reached the House of Lords on the question of whether the parents could claim in respect of psychiatric harm. See para.2–198.

[545] (1991) 8 C.C.L.T. (2d) 138, Alta QB; aff'd (1993) 14 C.C.L.T. (2d) 225, Alta CA.

[546] (1991) 8 C.C.L.T. (2d) 138 at 156–157, citing Lord Diplock in *Home Office v Dorset Yacht Co. Ltd* [1970] A.C. 1004.

[547] (1991) 8 C.C.L.T. (2d) 138 at 160.

It was not correct, said the judge, that only one of the two special relationships identified in *Tarasoff* need exist to except the psychiatrist/patient relationship from the general rule that one person does not owe a duty to control the conduct of another nor to warn those endangered by such conduct. In any given case there must be such a relationship between a psychiatrist and his patient that there is imposed upon the psychiatrist a duty to control the conduct of his patient, but in addition, when deciding whether or not a third party should be given a warning of the danger or whether steps should be taken to confine or restrain the patient, one must decide whether or not the requisite proximity of relationship exists between the psychiatrist and the third party:

> "... it is a logical application of the reasoning in the *Dorset Yacht* decision that it is only fair and reasonable that both a hospital and a psychiatrist who becomes aware that a patient presents a serious danger to the well-being of a third party or parties owe a duty to take reasonable steps to protect such a person or persons if the requisite proximity of relationship exists between them ... However, as pointed out by Lord Diplock, whether or not a person or persons fall within the necessary category will depend upon the particular nature of the risk posed by the patient, the predictability of future behaviour giving rise to the risk, and the ability to identify the person or class of persons at risk."[548]

On the facts of the case there had been no negligence by the hospital, and therefore Murray J did not decide whether a duty of care was owed by the hospital to the particular claimant. Nonetheless, on the stated test it would have been difficult to conclude that a duty of care was owed in the circumstances of this case, since there was nothing to indicate that the harm which the claimant sustained was the product of a risk which was different in its incidence from the general risk shared with all members of the public using public roads. The "further ingredient" required to establish the relationship of proximity between the hospital and the claimant was missing.[549]

Australia   In *Hunter and New England Local Health District v McKenna*[550] a   2–173
patient was compulsorily detained in hospital under mental health legislation. A psychiatrist consulted with the patient, the patient's mother and the patient's friend, as a result of which it was agreed that the patient would stay overnight in the hospital and the following day travel home with his friend. On that journey the patient killed his friend. The deceased's relatives brought an action against the health authority responsible for the hospital and its staff. The High Court of Australia held that the hospital authority did not owe a duty of care to the

---

[548] (1991) 8 C.C.L.T. (2d) 138 at 161.
[549] In *Ahmed v Stefaniu* (2006) 275 D.L.R. (4th) 101 the Ontario Court of Appeal upheld a jury's award of damages against a psychiatrist in relation to a murder committed by a psychiatric patient. The psychiatrist had changed the patient's status from that of a compulsorily detained patient under Ontario's mental health legislation to one of a voluntary patient. As Armstrong JA pointed out, however, the question of the existence, nature or scope of the psychiatrist's duty of care was not raised as an issue in the appeal, which dealt with matters going to breach of duty and causation. cf. *Kines Estate v Lychuk* [1996] 10 W.W.R. 426, Man QB, where a claim by the estate of a victim of a psychiatric patient that psychiatrists had negligently failed compulsorily to detain and treat the patient, who had subsequently killed the victim, was struck out as disclosing no reasonable cause of action on the basis that a doctor did not owe a duty of care to a third party who received neither treatment nor advice from the doctor.
[550] [2014] HCA 44; (2014) 314 A.L.R. 505.

such a finding. So in *Mitchell v Glasgow City Council*[560] the House of Lords held that a social landlord did not owe a duty of care to a tenant to warn him that another tenant, about whom he had made a number of complaints, had threatened to kill him. Lord Brown said that:

> "... there will be very few occasions on which a bare duty by A to warn B of possible impending violence by C will arise. Given ... that A cannot in any meaningful sense be said to have created the risk of injury that foreseeably arose here, or to have assumed specific responsibility for B's safety from C, the contention that he was under a positive duty to warn B and that he is liable for B's death because of a mere omission to do so appears to me plainly unsustainable."[561]

In *Michael v Chief Constable of South Wales*[562] the Supreme Court held that the police did not owe a duty of care to a woman killed by her ex-partner when she had made an earlier 999 call to the police complaining that her ex-partner had assaulted her and had threatened to kill her. Lord Toulson JSC, for the majority, considered that the emergency call made by the victim did not give rise to an undertaking of responsibility by the police. The call handler had given no assurance about how quickly they would respond. Telling her that the police would want to call back and to keep her phone free did not amount to advising or instructing her to remain in her house; nor did the call handler's inquiry whether the victim could lock the house amount to advising or instructing her to remain there. The case was "very different from *Kent v Griffiths* where the call handler gave misleading assurances that an ambulance would be arriving shortly".[563] The duty of the police was owed to the public at large and did not involve the kind of close or special relationship necessary for the imposition of a private law duty of care.[564]

2–177   One comparatively recent case in which it was held that a hospital could, at least arguably, owe a duty to provide a warning of threats made by a mental patient is

---

[560] [2009] UKHL 11; [2009] 1 A.C. 874; C. Ettinger [2009] J.P.I.L. C115.

[561] [2009] UKHL 11; [2009] 1 A.C. 874 at [83]. See also per Lord Hope at [29]: "as a general rule ... a duty to warn another person that he is at risk of loss, injury or damage as the result of the criminal act of a third party will arise only where the person who is said to be under that duty has by his words or conduct assumed responsibility for the safety of the person who is at risk."

[562] [2015] UKSC 2; [2015] A.C. 1732.

[563] [2015] UKSC 2; [2015] A.C. 1732 at [138]. Though as Lord Kerr noted at [165], in a dissenting judgment, the possibility (apparently accepted by the majority) that the police could be found to have undertaken responsibility to someone who called for emergency assistance, depending on what the call handler happened to say to the caller, creates the risk of arbitrary distinctions being drawn.

[564] [2015] UKSC 2; [2015] A.C. 1732 at [120]. Note that in *Michael* the Supreme Court allowed a claim based on art.2 of the European Convention on Human Rights to proceed to trial. See also *Thomson v Scottish Ministers* [2013] CSIH 63; 2013 S.C. 628—no duty of care owed by the prison service to a member of the public killed by a prisoner on short term leave, where the risk to the general public, even if grave, was not enough to satisfy the requirement of proximity; there had to be a special risk of harm to the claimant greater than that to which the general public were exposed. In *X v Hounslow LBC* [2009] EWCA Civ 286; [2010] H.L.R. 4 at [60] the Court of Appeal observed that: "a public authority will not be held to have assumed a common law duty merely by doing what the statute requires or what it has power to do under a statute, at any rate unless the duty arises out of the relationship created as a result, such as in Lord Hoffmann's example of the doctor patient relationship" (referring to Lord Hoffmann's speech in *Gorringe v Calderdale Metropolitan Borough Council* [2004] UKHL 15; [2004] 1 W.L.R. 1057 at [38]; see para.2–261, n.812 below).

the Court of Appeal decision in *Selwood v Durham CC*.[565] The claimant was a social worker employed by a local authority who was attacked and seriously injured by a mental health patient. Two NHS Trusts and the local authority sought to provide integrated health and social care, and had set out their working arrangements in a lengthy policy document. The claimant had worked closely with the two NHS Trusts in implementing these arrangements. The mental patient was known to have a history of violent behaviour and posed a risk of harm to others. Employees of the Trusts became aware that he had expressed his intention to kill the claimant if he saw her, but she was not warned about these threats. Smith LJ held that it was possible to infer an assumption of responsibility from the circumstances, and in particular the close working relationship:

> "...to do what was reasonable in the circumstances to reduce or avoid any foreseeable risk of harm to which an employee of a co-signatory was exposed in the course of their joint operations."[566]

Since the defendants, as employers, would owe a duty of care to their own employees, it was not a big step to suggest that they could owe a duty of care in respect of the actions of a third party to someone in the claimant's position, since:

> "...the force of some of the policy considerations which render a wider duty undesirable is much less than if the duty is said to be owed to the world at large."[567]

Selwood is a case where the focus of the duty of care is on the nature of the relationship between the defendant and the victim of violence, and that relationship arose out of a close working relationship between the parties. In *Mitchell v Glasgow City Council* the relationship between the defendant and claimant was that of landlord and tenant, and there is nothing in the normal incidents of such a relationship that would place responsibility on a landlord to protect a tenant from violence by a third party. *Michael v Chief Constable of South Wales* differs in that the normal expectation is that the police do come under a duty to provide a protective function, but the concern of the majority of the Supreme Court was that this should normally be confined to a public law duty owed to the public at large, and should not be converted into a private law duty of care, not least because of the potential financial implications.[568] However, Lord Toulson acknowledged in *Michael* that on appropriate facts, i.e. where it can be said that there has been a representation by the defendant and reliance on that representation by the claimant, the police could come under a duty of care to a victim of third party violence.[569] The situation in a case like *Tarasoff* differs yet

2–178

---

[565] [2012] EWCA Civ 979; [2012] P.I.Q.R. P20; [2012] Med. L.R. 531.
[566] [2012] EWCA Civ 979; [2012] P.I.Q.R. P20; [2012] Med. L.R. 531 at [52].
[567] [2012] EWCA Civ 979; [2012] P.I.Q.R. P20; [2012] Med. L.R. 531 at [53].
[568] See e.g. the comment of Lord Toulson J.S.C. in *Michael* [2015] UKSC 2; [2015] A.C. 1732 at [114] that: "It does not follow from the setting up of a protective system from public resources that if it fails to achieve its purpose, through organisational defects or fault on the part of an individual, the public at large should bear the additional burden of compensating a victim for harm caused by the actions of a third party for whose behaviour the state is not responsible. To impose such a burden would be contrary to the ordinary principles of the common law."
[569] This prompted Lord Kerr JSC, in his dissenting judgment, to point to some of the anomalies that could arise from drawing fine distinctions of fact: [2015] UKSC 2; [2015] A.C. 1732 at [165].

again, in that the critical relationship is probably that between the defendant doctor and the mental health patient, not the victim and the defendant doctor, yet it is the proximity of the relationship between the victim and the defendant doctor which the court will focus upon. If the doctor were in a position of some "control" over the patient, where for example the patient was detained under the Mental Health Act 1983 and was allowed out of hospital on short term leave in circumstances where the doctor knew or should have known that the patient had made credible threats to harm the specific claimant (not simply a broad class of the public[570]), the case for imposing a duty of care would probably be at its strongest.

(h)   Financial loss to third parties

(i)   Negligent reports

2–179   There is, in theory, no reason why a doctor should not owe a duty of care to a third party in respect of purely financial loss when giving advice to that third party as to a person's medical condition, under the principle in *Hedley Byrne & Co. Ltd v Heller & Partners Ltd*.[571] For example, a doctor who prepared a medical report on a patient for the purpose of an insurance company that was contemplating issuing a life policy on the patient would clearly owe a duty of care to the insurance company under this principle, whether or not the doctor was paid for the service.[572] The position would be similar where the report was for an employer or prospective employer of the patient as to his medical fitness to perform his job.[573] Whatever the position of the person about whom the report is made,[574] it is difficult to see how the insurance company or prospective employer does not fall squarely within the *Hedley Byrne* principle, subject to any exclusion of liability.[575]

---

[570] As in *Thomson v Scottish Ministers* [2013] CSIH 63; 2013 S.C. 628 or *Palmer v Tees Health Authority* [1999] Lloyd's Rep. Med. 351.

[571] [1964] A.C. 465; see para.2–050.

[572] See *X (Minors) v Bedfordshire County Council* [1995] 2 A.C. 633, at 753, para.2–086. Although, since a contract of insurance is a contract *uberrimae fidei*, the insurers would have a right to avoid the contract if the patient/insured had failed to disclose a material fact about his medical history, and in these circumstances would suffer no loss. The action against the doctor would only be relevant if the patient was unaware of his medical condition.

[573] See *Spring v Guardian Assurance plc* [1995] 2 A.C. 296, HL, where it was held that an employer owes a duty of care to an employee or former employee when providing a reference about the individual to a prospective employer, and it would seem to follow from this that he also owes a duty to the prospective employer.

[574] See para.2–085, above.

[575] See the comments of Millett LJ in *Kapfunde v Abbey National plc* [1999] I.C.R. 1; [1999] Lloyd's Rep. Med. 48, at [44]: "The doctor is taken to assume responsibility for his advice, but only to the employer or insurer who commissioned [the report] and not to the 'patient' who is the subject of the advice."

(ii) Failed sterilisation

The effect of *McFarlane v Tayside Health Board*[576] is that there can be no claim   **2–180**
in respect of the financial cost of raising a healthy child following negligent
advice about, or the negligent performance of, a sterilisation operation, although
the parents of a healthy or a disabled child are entitled to claim a "conventional
sum" of £15,000 for loss of the right to limit the size of their family.[577] But there
remains the question of the mother's losses arising out of an unwanted pregnancy
and entitlement to the financial costs of raising a disabled child. In the case of a
husband and wife, the courts (or defendants) have not taken the point that the
parent who did not undergo the surgery was not the doctor's patient and therefore
was seeking to recover for pure economic loss in a situation where the
doctor–patient relationship did not arise.[578] The claim of the parents for the
financial losses involved in raising the disabled child is treated as a single loss.

The position may be different, however, where the parties were not in a   **2–181**
relationship at the time of the sterilisation. In *Goodwill v British Pregnancy
Advisory Service*[579] the Court of Appeal held that a woman who knew and relied
on the fact that her sexual partner had undergone a vasectomy did not have a
cause of action in negligence against the person who performed the surgery or
advised her partner about the effects of the surgery, if she became pregnant as a
result of the failure of the vasectomy to achieve complete sterility. The man (M)
had been assured that the vasectomy had been successful and that he did not need
to use contraception in the future. Four years later the claimant began a sexual
relationship with M and he told her that he had been sterilised. The claimant also
consulted her doctor who assured her that the chances of becoming pregnant by
M were minute. Following this neither the claimant nor M used any form of
contraception. The claimant became pregnant and subsequently gave birth to a
daughter. She claimed damages from the defendants for the expenses of the birth,
the cost of bringing up the child and loss of earnings. The Court of Appeal held
that there was no duty of care owed to the claimant because the defendants could
not have known that their advice to M would be communicated to the claimant
and acted on by her as a warranty of M's sterility without independent inquiry.
They could know nothing about the likely conduct of M's future sexual partners,
and had not voluntarily assumed any responsibility to the claimant. It would have
been different if the claimant had been M's current sexual partner at the time of
the advice, and that advice had been given directly to both of them.[580]

It is arguable that *Goodwill* was based on unexpressed policy concerns about   **2–182**
compensating for the costs of raising a healthy child (which are no longer an

---

[576] [2000] 2 A.C. 59. See paras 2–055 et seq.
[577] See *Rees v Darlington Memorial Hospital NHS Trust* [2003] UKHL 52; [2004] 1 A.C. 309; [2003]
4 All E.R. 987; para.2–072.
[578] Though see the Irish case of *Ahern and Ahern v Moore and The Southern Health Board* [2013]
IEHC 72; [2013] 1 I.R. 205 at [82] where Ryan J held that the father was not entitled to claim his
financial expenses, since that fell into the category of pure economic loss, unconnected to any
physical harm to the father.
[579] [1996] 2 All E.R. 161; see Davies (1996) 12 P.N. 54.
[580] [1996] 2 All E.R. 161 at 168 per Peter Gibson LJ.

5.   PSYCHIATRIC HARM

2–187   Claims in respect of "pure" psychiatric harm, that is psychiatric harm which is not linked to physical harm sustained by the claimant, have always been problematic and continue to arouse controversy.[596] In theory different rules apply to cases involving claims by patients from those involving claims by third parties, but the distinctions between categories of claimants can become very blurred at the margins, and at times the general rules appear not to apply in the medical context. Therefore, in this section, the distinction between the duty of care owed to patients and the duty owed to third parties has not been followed. Rather, the exposition considers the courts' general approach (it would be misleading to call them "principles") to claims for "pure" psychiatric harm, and then attempts to put that general approach into the medical context (though some of the cases illustrating the general rules do involve cases of medical negligence).

(a)   Psychiatric illness not emotional distress

2–188   In *McLoughlin v O'Brian* Lord Bridge noted that "the first hurdle which a plaintiff claiming damages of the kind in question must surmount is to establish that he is suffering, not merely grief, distress or any other normal emotion, but a positive psychiatric illness."[597] There is no claim for emotional distress, anguish or grief unless this leads to a positive psychiatric illness (such as an anxiety neurosis or reactive depression) or physical illness (such as a heart attack).[598]

---

[596] "Nervous shock" was the term that was used in the past by lawyers to describe a medically recognised psychiatric illness, although it has been described as a "misleading and inaccurate expression", per Bingham LJ in *Attia v British Gas* [1988] Q.B. 304 at 317. Although in some cases the courts still require a "shocking" event as one of the criteria to establish liability, it is better to refer to the resulting injury as psychiatric harm or psychiatric damage. "Psychiatric damage" encompasses "all relevant forms of mental illness, neurosis and personality change": [1988] Q.B. 304 at 317. On post-traumatic stress disorder see Weller (1993) 143 N.L.J. 878; O'Brien [1994] J.P.I.L. 257; Turnbull [1997] J.P.I.L. 234; Lipsedge (1999) 5 *Clinical Risk* 155. See generally Teff, *Causing Psychiatric and Emotional Harm* (Oxford: Hart Publishing, 2008); Mullany and Handford, *Tort Liability for Psychiatric Damage*, 2nd edn (Sydney, Australia: The Law Book Company Limited, 2006); and Wheat, *Napier and Wheat's Recovering Damages for Psychiatric Injury*, 2nd edn (Oxford: Oxford University Press, 2002).

[597] [1983] 1 A.C. 410 at 431. Contrast the decision of the Supreme Court of Canada in *Saadati v Moorhead* 2017 SCC 28; (2017) 409 D.L.R. (4th) 395 holding that, in Canadian law, there was no requirement that a claimant prove that he was suffering from a condition that would be diagnosed as a psychiatric illness by the medical profession. It was sufficient that the defendant could have foreseen mental injury, and the claimant did not have to demonstrate that he was suffering from a psychiatric illness to which the medical profession had attached a particular "label". Note also that psychiatry's identification of what constitutes a psychiatric illness has expanded considerably over the years. The first edition of the American Psychiatric Association's *Diagnostic and Statistical Manual of Mental Disorders*, listed 106 psychiatric disorders whereas the 5th edition (2013) (DSM-V) listed 297. DSM-V has been widely criticised as "medicalising" normal human experiences. See A. Langford and N. Barry, "Clinical and medico-legal risk implications of psychiatric diagnostic reclassification" (2013) 19 Clinical Risk 109; R. Orr, "Speaking with different voices: the problems with English law and psychiatric injury" (2016) 36 L.S. 547.

[598] [1983] 1 A.C. 410 per Lord Bridge; *Alcock v Chief Constable of the South Yorkshire Police* [1992] 1 A.C. 310 at 409, per Lord Oliver; *Hinz v Berry* [1970] 2 Q.B. 40 at 42; *Tame v New South Wales*; *Annetts v Australian Stations Pty Ltd* [2002] HCA, 35; (2002) 191 A.L.R. 449 at [44] and [193] High

Anxiety at the risk of future harm is not, in itself, actionable injury, even when combined with symptomless physiological changes to the body.[599] Nor is there any duty to protect a claimant's self-esteem.[600]

In *Vernon v Bosley (No.1)*[601] the Court of Appeal held that where the claimant has developed a mental illness which has been contributed to partly by the defendant's negligence (the claimant witnessing the death of a loved one caused by the defendant's negligence) and partly by pathological grief attributable to the death itself, the claimant was entitled to damages for the mental illness, with no discount for the consequences of the grief and the consequences of bereavement, even though the mental illness was partly caused by the grief.[602] On the other hand, in *Calascione v Dixon*[603] the Court of Appeal did draw a distinction between post-traumatic stress disorder, which was held to be compensatable since it was attributable to the events the claimant had witnessed, and a pathological grief disorder which could not be causally linked to the immediate aftermath of the accident. In principle, if the courts are going to continue to distinguish between psychiatric harm attributable to the events witnessed by the claimant and

2–189

Court of Australia; *van Soest v Residual Health Management Unit* [2000] 1 N.Z.L.R. 179, NZCA; commented on by Mullany (2001) 117 L.Q.R. 182; Teff (2001) 9 Tort L. Rev. 109; Todd (2001) 17 P.N. 230. In *Reilly v Merseyside Regional Health Authority* [1995] 6 Med. L.R. 246 the Court of Appeal held that normal human emotions, together with their normal physical consequences, did not constitute either psychiatric illness or physical injury. If, however, the claimant's mental distress or grief exacerbates other injuries which the claimant sustained in the same incident, preventing the claimant from making a recovery as quickly as would otherwise have occurred, this can be reflected in the award of damages in respect of the other injuries. In *Kralj v McGrath* [1986] 1 All E.R. 54 at 62, Woolf J said: "...if the situation is one where the plaintiff's injuries have on her a more drastic effect than they would otherwise because of the grief which she is sustaining at the same time in relation to the death of a child who died in the circumstances in which Daniel died, that is something which the court can take into account." See also *Bagley v North Hertfordshire Health Authority* (1986) 136 N.L.J. 1014. *Kralj v McGrath* was approved by the Court of Appeal in *AB v South West Water Services Ltd* [1993] Q.B. 507. For criticism of the law's distinction between psychiatric disorder and "ordinary suffering" from a psychiatrist see Lipsedge (1999) 5 Clinical Risk 155; see also R. Mulheron, "Rewriting the Requirement for a 'Recognized Psychiatric Injury' in Negligence" (2012) 32 O.J.L.S. 77. J. Ahuja, "Liability for psychological and psychiatric harm: the road to recovery" (2015) 23 Med. L. Rev. 27 at 35 comments that: "Psychiatric diagnosis is not simplistically based upon a quantification of distress, and the law may be drawing the wrong conclusion from the wrong evidence when it assumes that a psychiatric diagnosis confirms the intensity of the claimant's suffering."

[599] *Rothwell v Chemical & Insulating Co Ltd* [2007] UKHL 39; [2008] 1 A.C. 281. In the Court of Appeal in this case Lord Phillips C.J. said that: "Anxiety is a form of psychiatric prejudice that is less serious than one of the recognised forms of psychiatric injury. The law does not recognise a duty to take reasonable care not to cause anxiety": [2006] EWCA Civ 27; [2006] 4 All E.R. 1161; [2006] I.C.R. 1458 at [63].

[600] *Younger v Dorset and Somerset Strategic Health Authority* [2006] Lloyd's Rep. Med. 489, Southampton County Court—defendants negligently diagnosed the claimant as suffering from coeliac disease and advised that she would need to remain on a gluten-free diet for the rest of her life. The misdiagnosis was discovered 16 years later. The claimant alleged that she had suffered psychological injury falling short of a recognised psychiatric illness, namely reduced self-esteem and loss of amenity. The claim was dismissed. Distress or mental harm falling short of a recognised psychiatric illness was not compensatable in the absence of physical injury or a specific duty upon the defendant to avoid causing mental stress or anxiety.

[601] [1997] 1 All E.R. 577.

[602] Applying *Bonnington Castings Ltd v Wardlaw* [1956] A.C. 613, see para.5–033.

[603] (1993) 19 B.M.L.R. 97.

psychiatric harm attributable to the consequences of those events (grief at the death of a loved one, which may become pathological grief—itself a recognised psychiatric condition) then the approach adopted in *Calascione v Dixon* would seem to be correct. Moreover, it is arguable that in the light of the Court of Appeal decision in *Holtby v Brigham & Cowan (Hull) Ltd*,[604] where it is possible to identify the extent of the contribution made by the defendant's negligence to the claimant's psychiatric damage, then the defendant is only liable to that extent and no more.[605] This would suggest that unless the psychiatric harm was indivisible in *Vernon v Bosley (No.1)* the outcome in that case was incorrect.

(b) Distinguish gradual onset of psychiatric harm from "sudden" events

2–190 A distinction is drawn between cases involving the gradual onset of psychiatric harm and psychiatric harm which flows from sudden, traumatic events. As will be seen, in the case of sudden traumatic events, claims based on the gradual onset of symptoms are specifically excluded. Where, however, there is an existing legal relationship between the claimant and defendant (which may be contractual or tortious) then it may be possible to claim in respect of the gradual onset of psychiatric harm. The typical example of this is the employer–employee relationship, where in appropriate circumstances it may be possible for an employee to claim in respect of psychological damage attributable to "occupational stress".[606] The existence of a duty of care in such cases is not problematic because it arises from the existing relationship between the parties, and the legal problems usually centre on breach of duty and causation. This type of claim has been extended to the solicitor–client relationship[607]; but it also explains why an action by a patient against a psychiatrist in respect of psychiatric harm negligently inflicted in the course of the psycho-therapeutic relationship does not raise an issue about the duty of care in respect of pure psychiatric damage.[608] Despite the existence of a relationship between the parties which would normally give rise to a duty of care, the courts have still attempted to apply some of the

---

[604] [2000] 3 All E.R. 421, see para.5–037.

[605] *Rahman v Arearose Ltd* [2001] Q.B. 351. See the discussion of this point in *Hatton v Sutherland* [2002] EWCA Civ 76; [2002] 2 All E.R. 1 at [36] to [41]. In *Barber v Somerset County Council* [2004] UKHL 13; [2004] 1 W.L.R. 1089; [2004] 2 All E.R. 385 at [63] Lord Walker approved the exposition and commentary by the Court of Appeal in *Hatton v Sutherland* at [1] to [42] as a valuable contribution to the development of the law, though not having heard argument on the section dealing with apportionment and quantification of damage (i.e. paragraphs [36] to [42]) thought it better to "express no view on those topics". Contrast *Dickins v O2 plc* [2008] EWCA Civ 1144; [2009] I.R.L.R. 58 (see para.5–044) where the Court of Appeal doubted whether apportionment was appropriate in a case of psychiatric harm (specifically questioning the approach taken by Hale LJ in *Hatton*).

[606] *Walker v Northumberland County Council* [1995] 1 All E.R. 737; *Hatton v Sutherland* [2002] EWCA Civ 76; [2002] 2 All E.R. 1; affirmed in *Barber v Somerset County Council* [2004] UKHL 13; [2004] 1 W.L.R. 1089; [2004] 2 All E.R. 385; Teff (2002) 10 Tort L. Rev. 161.

[607] *McLoughlin v Jones* [2001] EWCA Civ 1743; [2002] Q.B. 1312—solicitors liable for psychiatric illness suffered by their client who was wrongly convicted of an offence and sent to prison as a result of their negligent failure to investigate the case.

[608] *Landau v Werner* (1961) 105 S.J. 257, and 1008, CA.

language and legal categories that are applied in the context of claims arising out of sudden events, particularly the so-called "primary" victim or "secondary" victim labels. This tends to confuse, rather than illuminate, the picture.

The problems caused by seeking to analyse claims for pure psychiatric harm in terms of "primary" and "secondary" victims are highlighted by cases which simply do not "fit" the categories. Moreover, there are signs that the courts will sometimes simply ignore the categorisations, particularly where the nature of the relationship between claimant and defendant would normally give rise to a duty of care in respect of physical harm. For example, in *Butchart v Home Office*[609] the claimant was a prisoner who alleged that he had suffered psychiatric harm as a result of being placed in the same cell as another remand prisoner, known to be a suicide risk, who committed suicide. The claimant witnessed the suicide, was blamed by a prison officer for the suicide, and subsequently was placed in a cell with another suicidal prisoner. The Home Office applied to strike out the claim, on the basis that the claimant did not satisfy the criteria for being a "secondary victim".[610] The Court of Appeal held that this was not a "nervous shock" case. The allegation was that the claimant's psychiatric injury was the result of a breach of a primary duty of care owed to him. On the alleged facts, the Home Office knew or ought to have known that the claimant was vulnerable to psychiatric harm, and owed a duty to take reasonable steps to minimise the risk of psychiatric harm.

2–191

(c)   Sudden events

It is now well established, medically, that where individuals are exposed to the risk of injury or death, or witness injury to or the death of others, there is a real prospect that they may suffer a psychiatric reaction to the events, even though they have not sustained any physical harm. The issue that the courts have struggled with for over a century now is in what circumstances a defendant who has negligently brought about the events should be held responsible for that psychiatric harm. Scepticism about the nature of psychiatric damage and the danger of fraudulent claims led, initially, to a stark refusal to contemplate any claims for pure psychiatric harm. Then it was held that someone who had been put in fear of losing her own life as a result of the defendant's negligence was entitled to recover for psychiatric harm.[611] A quarter of a century later, the Court of Appeal extended the category of claimants to those who had not been personally endangered, but had witnessed the events themselves.[612] There was no need for any direct impact to the claimant or fear of immediate personal injury to the claimant.

2–192

The potential for opening up liability to a wide range of claimants who happened to witness the events caused by the defendant's negligence led the courts to impose a number of specific requirements, particularly in those cases arising out

2–193

---

[609] [2006] EWCA Civ 239; [2006] 1 W.L.R. 1155.
[610] See paras 2–202 to 2–208.
[611] *Dulieu v White & Sons* [1901] 2 K.B. 669.
[612] *Hambrook v Stokes Bros* [1925] 1 K.B. 141.

believed that he had been exposed to such a risk,[635] or someone who, as a result of the defendant's negligence, reasonably believes that he has been the cause of injury to another.[636] Claimants suing their employers in respect of occupational stress are also referred to as "primary" victims,[637] although these cases do not typically involve the exposure of the employee to a risk of physical harm.

2–200   The identification of a claimant as a "primary" or "secondary" victim has taken on enormous significance because of the different rules now applied to the two categories.[638] A claimant exposed to the risk of foreseeable physical injury, unlike a "secondary" victim, does not have to prove that psychiatric harm was foreseeable.[639] Thus, the claimant does not have to demonstrate reasonable fortitude (that is that a person of reasonable fortitude would also have succumbed

---

harm feared by the claimant was not of the kind that he actually suffered: *Donachie v The Chief Constable of the Greater Manchester Police* [2004] EWCA Civ 405; [2004] Po. L.R. 204. Nor is it necessary that the foreseeable physical harm be foreseeable *imminent* physical harm: per Auld LJ at [19].

[635] That belief must not be irrational: *McFarlane v E.E. Caledonia Ltd* [1994] 2 All E.R. 1 and *Hegarty v EE Caledonia Ltd* [1997] 2 Lloyd's Rep. 259.

[636] Note also that a claimant may be classified as a "primary" victim where there is no-one else who could be categorised as a "victim" to whom the claimant could be related as a "secondary" victim: *Farrell v Avon Health Authority* [2001] Lloyd's Rep. Med. 458 at 471; *AB v Leeds Teaching Hospital NHS Trust* [2004] EWHC 644 (QB); [2005] Q.B. 506 at [199]; *Wild v Southend University Hospital NHS Foundation Trust* [2014] EWHC 4053 (QB); [2016] P.I.Q.R. P3 at [22]; *Wells v University Hospital Southampton NHS Foundation Trust* [2015] EWHC 2376 (QB); [2015] Med. L.R. 477 at [83]. This is most likely to arise in the context of a claim for medical negligence. See also the comments of Lord Stewart in *Holdich v Lothian Health Board* [2013] CSOH 197; 2014 S.L.T. 495 at [88], quoted at para.2–211, n.674 below.

[637] See *Hatton v Sutherland* [2002] EWCA Civ 76; [2002] 2 All E.R. 1; affirmed by *Barber v Somerset County Council* [2004] UKHL 13; [2004] 1 W.L.R. 1089; [2004] 2 All E.R. 385.

[638] It seems likely that Lord Oliver in *Alcock* was merely identifying two descriptive categories of claimant which might help to explain some of the previous cases. The distinction between "primary" and "secondary" victims is not a *justification for* the present legal structure. A "primary" victim has suffered psychiatric illness *as a* consequence of what he has witnessed/experienced, just as the relatives in *Alcock* suffered psychiatric illness as a result of what they had witnessed/experienced. The *mechanism* by which the psychiatric illness was caused is essentially the same in each case. The categorisation merely states a conclusion rather than a basis for the distinction. See Jones [1995] 4 Web J.C.L.I. (available at *http://www.bailii.org/uk/other/journals/WebJCLI/1995/issue4/jones4.html*) where this argument is developed in more detail. For an extended discussion of why recovery for negligently inflicted psychiatric harm should be put on a more rational basis see Teff [1998] C.L.J. 91. See also J. Ahuja, "Liability for psychological and psychiatric harm: the road to recovery" (2015) 23 Med. L. Rev. 27 at 40 who observes that: "There is no evidence to suggest that fear of *any* physical injury to oneself is necessarily more traumatic than knowing of the terrible suffering of a loved one in their final moments." Indeed, the empirical evidence suggests that "serious physical injury or illness requiring hospital treatment" does not rank even among the first ten most stressful life events, whereas the death of a spouse is ranked as the single most stressful life event ((2015) 23 Med. L. Rev. 27 at 42).

[639] *Page v Smith* [1996] A.C. 155; *McLoughlin v Jones* [2001] EWCA Civ 1743; [2002] Q.B. 1312; unless the risk of foreseeable physical harm to which the claimant was exposed was of physical harm in the future, in which case he must demonstrate that his psychiatric harm was foreseeable: *Rothwell v Chemical & Insulating Co. Ltd* [2007] UKHL 39; [2008] 1 A.C. 281. In such a case the claimant has to demonstrate reasonable fortitude, and a person of reasonable fortitude would not develop a psychiatric condition as a result of becoming aware of a small risk of developing future disease.

to psychiatric harm—a test designed to exclude claimants who are particularly susceptible to suffering psychiatric harm[640]). For a "primary" victim, the:

> "...question of what might be foreseen in a person of ordinary phlegm does not arise. The question of foreseeability must be considered in relation to this particular claimant, and what the defendants knew or ought to have known about him."[641]

Moreover, the "primary" victim who is exposed to the risk of physical harm can recover for the resulting psychiatric damage, even if that damage was not produced by the fear of injury to himself, but rather was caused by witnessing the injuries of others.[642] In other words, the risk of physical injury is a "threshold test" for categorising such claimants as "primary" victims, it is not necessary as a *causal* mechanism.

For those claimants who can qualify as a "primary" victim in circumstances where physical injury to the claimant was not foreseeable, it must be demonstrated that the psychiatric damage was foreseeable, but, again, in assessing the foreseeability of the psychiatric reaction the claimant does not have to prove that he was a person of "reasonable fortitude". As a general rule, the question of what is foreseeable is normally assessed ex post facto, on the basis of what a hypothetical reasonable man would say it was proper to foresee.[643] This principle works in the case of an action where the claimant and defendant were strangers before the incident giving rise to the claim. Where, however, the parties are in a contractual relationship and the alleged breach of duty is a breach of a contractual term, or a breach of a duty of care arising out of the parties' contractual relationship which gives rise to a concurrent claim in tort, the rule does not apply.[644] Most commonly this arises in actions by employees in respect occupational stress claims, but it is not limited to such claims as *McLoughlin v Jones* demonstrates. In such cases, in assessing the question of what is foreseeable, the court will take account of "all those features of [the claimant's] personal life and disposition of which the defendants were aware".[645] It is not yet

2–201

---

[640] *Bourhill v Young* [1943] A.C. 92 at 110.
[641] *McLoughlin v Jones* [2001] EWCA Civ 1743 at [56] per Hale LJ.
[642] *White v Chief Constable of the South Yorkshire Police* [1999] 2 A.C. 455.
[643] *Bourhill v Young* [1943] A.C. 92 at 110.
[644] *McLoughlin v Jones* [2001] EWCA Civ 1743; [2002] Q.B. 1312 at [26] per Brooke LJ.
[645] [2001] EWCA Civ 1743; [2002] Q.B. 1312 at [46]. Notwithstanding this more relaxed approach to the more vulnerable claimant, the foreseeability requirement (plus the need to prove the causal connection between the defendant's breach of duty and the psychiatric harm) often results in claims by employees in respect of occupational stress failing: see *Hatton v Sutherland* [2002] EWCA Civ 76; [2002] 2 All E.R. 1; *Garrett v London Borough of Camden* [2001] EWCA Civ 395; *Petch v Customs and Excise Commissioners* [1993] I.C.R. 789, CA; *Fraser v State Hospitals Board for Scotland*, 2001 S.L.T. 1051; *Bonser v UK Coal Mining Ltd (formerly RJB Mining (UK) Ltd)* [2003] EWCA Civ 1296; [2004] I.R.L.R. 164; *Pratley v Surrey County Council* [2003] EWCA Civ 1067; [2004] I.C.R. 159; [2004] P.I.Q.R. P252; *Vahidi v Fairstead House School Trust Ltd* [2005] EWCA Civ 765; [2005] E.L.R. 607; *Pratt v Scottish Ministers* [2011] CSOH 86; 2011 S.C.L.R. 446; *MacLennan v Hartford Europe Ltd* [2012] EWHC 346 (QB); *Coventry University v Mian* [2014] EWCA Civ 1275; [2014] Med. L.R. 502; *Yapp v Foreign and Commonwealth Office* [2014] EWCA Civ 1512; [2015] I.R.L.R. 112; *Olulana v Southwark LBC* [2014] EWHC 2707 (QB); *Daniel v Secretary of State for the Department of Health* [2014] EWHC 2578 (QB); *Easton v B&Q Plc* [2015] EWHC 880 (QB). In the landmark decision of *Walker v Northumberland County Council* [1995] 1 All E.R. 737, the claimant

clear whether this principle applies to those "primary" victims who fall into the category on the basis that, as a result of the defendant's negligence, they believed that they were responsible for causing harm to another. The judgment as to what is foreseeable is a matter for the court, not expert psychiatrists, but this should be done on the basis of "informed judicial opinion".[646] In other words, judicial opinion must be "informed" by the expert evidence of psychiatrists.[647]

(e) "Secondary" victims

2–202   The second category of case identified by Lord Oliver in *Alcock v Chief Constable of the South Yorkshire Police*[648] was where the psychiatric injury was attributable simply to witnessing the misfortune of another person in an event by which the claimant was not personally threatened or in which he was not directly involved as an actor. The claimant was a "mere witness" of the event. The potential number of claimants who could fall into this category of "secondary" victim is much larger than those who were in the zone of physical danger or were participants in the event, and therefore there are stricter limits on who can claim. Psychiatric harm to the claimant must be foreseeable,[649] and when applying the test of foreseeability to "secondary" victims it has to be demonstrated that the claimant is a person of reasonable fortitude or "customary phlegm" and is not

---

succeeded on the basis of his *second*, and therefore entirely foreseeable, nervous breakdown. See also *Young v Post Office* [2002] EWCA Civ 661; [2002] I.R.L.R. 660 where the defendants were held liable for the claimant's breakdown because (as in *Walker*) they were aware of his vulnerable mental condition and failed to implement agreed measures on his return to work. Claimants have also succeeded in *Barber v Somerset County Council* [2004] UKHL 13; [2004] 1 W.L.R. 1089; [2004] 2 All E.R. 385 (where a majority of the House of Lords held the defendants liable in one of the three conjoined appeals in *Hatton v Sutherland*); *Hartman v South Essex Mental Health and Community Care NHS Trust* [2005] EWCA Civ 6; [2005] I.C.R. 782; [2005] I.R.L.R. 293; *Hone v Six Continents Retail Ltd* [2005] EWCA Civ 922; [2006] I.R.L.R. 49; *Daw v Intel Corporation UK Ltd* [2007] EWCA Civ 70; [2007] 2 All E.R. 126; *Dickins v O2 Plc* [2008] EWCA Civ 1144; [2009] I.R.L.R. 58. The outcomes in such cases are highly fact-sensitive.

[646] *McLoughlin v O'Brian* [1983] 1 A.C. 410 at 432 per Lord Bridge. See *AB v Leeds Teaching Hospital NHS Trust* [2004] EWHC 644 (QB); [2005] Q.B. 506, where, at [253], Gage J held that the action of one of the three claimants failed on the basis that it was not foreseeable that she would suffer psychiatric harm as a result of discovering some years after the event that the organs of a deceased child had been removed and retained at a post-mortem. The claimant "was a robust person and someone who [the defendant doctor] would have regarded as unlikely to collapse under the strain". The standard of foreseeability by which the defendant was to be judged was the standard of the ordinary reasonable man in the circumstances of the defendant, namely a consultant paediatrician, not someone who was a consultant psychiatrist.

[647] *Farrell v Avon Health Authority* [2001] Lloyd's Rep. Med. 458 at 473 per Bursell J. In a case involving a "primary" victim where the parties' relationship stems from contract it is open to the court to accept evidence from expert witnesses "about the statistical incidence of the occasions when people who are not immediately identifiable as vulnerable personalities suffer psychiatric illness of different kinds as a result of being exposed to events comparable to those experienced by the claimant": *McLoughlin v Jones* [2001] EWCA Civ 1743 at [44] per Brooke LJ.

[648] [1992] 1 A.C. 310; [1991] 4 All E.R. 907.

[649] In *White v Lidl UK GmbH* [2005] EWHC 871 (QB) it was held that it was not foreseeable that the claimant would suffer psychiatric harm following his wife's suicide, which was caused by a deterioration in her mental state as a result of an accident, for which the defendants were responsible. The accident had caused minor physical injuries. The sequence of events had not been foreseeable, even with hindsight.

unduly susceptible to some form of psychiatric reaction.[650] This excludes persons who are abnormally sensitive to psychiatric harm. If, however, a person of ordinary fortitude would have sustained psychiatric harm in the circumstances, a claimant who was particularly sensitive can also recover[651]; and, moreover, he is entitled to damages for the full extent of his injuries, even if they are exacerbated by a predisposition to mental illness or disorder and thus are more severe than an ordinary individual would have experienced.[652] Once the foreseeability of psychiatric damage in a person of reasonable fortitude is established, the defendant must take the claimant as he finds him, and it is not necessary for the claimant to prove that the precise psychiatric condition which he has developed was foreseeable.[653] In other words, the "eggshell skull" rule applies to psychiatric damage in the same way as it applies to physical harm.[654]

In addition to foreseeability, in *Alcock* Lord Oliver identified four factors that had to be considered: (1) the nature of the relationship between the claimant and the accident victim; (2) the proximity of the claimant to the accident or its immediate aftermath; (3) the means by which the claimant perceived the events or received the information; (4) the manner in which the psychiatric illness was caused. | **2–203**

(i)   The nature of the relationship between the claimant and the accident victim

There must be a close relationship between the accident victim and the claimant. | **2–204**
The class of persons to whom a duty could be owed was not limited by reference to a particular relationship, such as husband and wife or parent and child, but it must be within the defendant's contemplation as foreseeable. The crucial factor was the existence of a relationship between the accident victim and the claimant which involved close ties of love and affection, a tie that would have to be proved by the claimant. There was a rebuttable presumption that such ties would exist between spouses and in the parent–child relationship, though they could be present in other family relationships[655] or those of close friendship, and may be

---

[650] *Bourhill v Young* [1943] A.C. 92 at 110; *McLoughlin v O'Brian* [1983] 1 A.C. 410 at 429; *Tame v New South Wales*; *Annetts v Australian Stations Pty Ltd* [2002] HCA 35; (2002) 191 A.L.R. 449 (High Court of Australia); *Mustapha v Culligan of Canada Ltd,* 2008 SCC 27; (2008) 293 D.L.R. (4th) 29 (Supreme Court of Canada).

[651] *Jaensch v Coffey* (1984) 54 A.L.R. 417.

[652] *Brice v Brown* [1984] 1 All E.R. 997; *Benson v Lee* [1972] V.R. 879; *Bechard v Haliburton* (1991) 84 D.L.R. (4th) 668; *Tame v New South Wales*; *Annetts v Australian Stations Pty Ltd* [2002] HCA 35; (2002) 191 A.L.R. 449 at [117] and [279] per McHugh and Hayne JJ respectively.

[653] *Mustapha v Culligan of Canada Ltd,* 2008 SCC 27; (2008) 293 D.L.R. (4th) 29 at [16]; *Frazer v Haukioja* 2010 ONCA 249; (2010) 317 D.L.R. (4th) 688; (2010) 101 O.R. (3d) 528 at [53] (Ontario Court of Appeal)—not necessary for claimant to establish that it was reasonably foreseeable that a person of normal fortitude would have suffered anxiety disorder, depression and agoraphobia.

[654] See para.5–181.

[655] In *Shorter v Surrey and Sussex Healthcare NHS Trust* [2015] EWHC 614 (QB); (2015) 144 B.M.L.R. 136 the defendants conceded that a relationship between sisters which on the evidence was almost like mother and daughter was sufficiently close and loving to satisfy this element of the test for a "secondary" victim; and in *RE (A Minor) v Calderdale and Huddersfield NHS Foundation Trust* [2017] EWHC 824 (QB); [2017] Med. L.R. 390 at [48], the defendants conceded that a grandmother who was present at the traumatic birth of her grandchild was in a sufficiently close relationship. See

stronger in the case of engaged couples than in that of persons who have been married to each other for many years.[656] Psychiatric injury to a bystander unconnected with the accident victim is not ordinarily reasonably foreseeable, although Lords Keith, Ackner and Oliver contemplated the possibility that a bystander who suffered psychiatric harm after witnessing a particularly horrific catastrophe close to him might be entitled to claim damages from the person whose negligence caused the catastrophe, if a reasonably strong-nerved person would have been so affected, but the circumstances in which this exception could apply would have to be extreme.[657]

(ii)   The proximity of the claimant to the accident or its immediate aftermath

2–205   The claimant has to be in close physical proximity to the accident. In *McLoughlin v O'Brian* the requirement that the claimant be at the scene of the accident was extended to the "immediate aftermath", which was held to include seeing the victims at the hospital two hours later before they had been properly attended to by medical staff. In *Jaensch v Coffey*[658] Deane J said that the "aftermath" extended to the hospital to which the injured person was taken, and persisted for so long as he remained in the state produced by the accident up to and including immediate post-accident treatment. In *Alcock* their Lordships refused to extend the meaning of "immediate aftermath" to include the identification of a victim's

---

also *King v Philcox* [2015] HCA 19; (2015) 320 A.L.R. 398 where the High Court of Australia held that at common law a motorist could owe a duty of care to the brother of a passenger killed in an accident caused by the motorist's negligence, where the brother did not witness the accident but came upon the aftermath. Nettle J observed, at [88], that: "although the relationship between siblings might be presumed not to be as close as it is between husband and wife, the ordinary expectation as to ties between siblings makes it just as foreseeable that the death of one brother could impact severely on the mental health of the other as it is that the death of a husband may impact upon the mental health of his wife."

[656] *Alcock v Chief Constable of the South Yorkshire Police* [1992] 1 A.C. 310 at 397, per Lord Keith. In *Attia v British Gas* [1988] Q.B. 304 the Court of Appeal held that where a claimant sustained psychiatric harm as a result of witnessing a fire which caused extensive damage to her home, the shock could not be regarded as unforeseeable *as a matter of law*, although there were no personal injuries to anyone else and the claimant had not been at risk of physical injury to herself. Rather it was a question of fact on the medical evidence whether psychiatric damage was reasonably foreseeable. The status of this decision is unclear after *Alcock*, since although it was cited in argument their Lordships did not refer to it in their speeches. Clearly, the claimant did not satisfy the "relationship" requirement of *Alcock*. The Court of Appeal in *Attia* treated the issue as a matter of remoteness of damage rather than duty of care, since the defendants undoubtedly owed the claimant a duty of care not to inflict physical damage to her house.

[657] See *McFarlane v EE Caledonia Ltd* [1994] 2 All E.R. 1, CA, where it was held that no duty was owed to a person of ordinary fortitude who witnessed at close range the "horrific catastrophe" of the "Piper Alpha" oil rig disaster; a fortiori where the claimant was not a person of ordinary fortitude, though the same result was reached in *Hegarty v EE Caledonia Ltd* [1997] 2 Lloyd's Rep. 259, where the claimant, who was on the same support vessel as Mr McFarlane and witnessed similar events, was found to be a person of ordinary fortitude. For comment on *McFarlane* see Tan Keng Feng (1995) 111 L.Q.R. 48; Oughton and Lowry (1995) 46 N.I.L.Q. 18. Note that no duty of care is owed by the negligent victim of self-inflicted injuries towards a claimant who suffers psychiatric injury as a result of witnessing the event which caused the injury or its aftermath: *Greatorex v Greatorex* [2000] 1 W.L.R. 1970.

[658] (1984) 54 A.L.R. 417 at 462–463, HC of Aus.

body at a mortuary some eight or nine hours after death. This failed the test on the ground that even if the identification could be described as part of the "aftermath", it could not be described as part of the "immediate aftermath".[659] Lord Jauncey said that to attempt a comprehensive definition of the "immediate aftermath" would be a fruitless exercise. His Lordship emphasised that in *McLoughlin v O'Brian* the victims were waiting to be attended to, and were in very much the same condition as they would have been had the claimant found them at the scene of the accident.[660] Moreover, the visits to the mortuary were not made for the purpose of rescuing or giving comfort to the victim but purely for the purpose of identification.

In most instances the event that causes injury to the victim will be relatively close in time and space to the occurrence of the injury itself, often almost instantaneous. But in some cases there may be a delay between the initial accident and the physical consequences of the accident to the accident victim. The question then arises as to which event, the initial accident or the later occurrence of injury, a "secondary" victim must witness in order to satisfy the requirements of physical and temporal proximity. In *Taylor v A Novo (UK) Ltd*[661] the Court of Appeal held that in order to qualify as a "secondary" victim the claimant must witness the original accident or its immediate aftermath. The claimant's mother was injured at work when a stack of racking boards was negligently tipped over on top of her. Three weeks later she suddenly and unexpectedly collapsed and died at home as a result of deep vein thrombosis and pulmonary emboli, which had been caused by the accident at work. The claimant did not witness the accident at work, but she did witness her mother's death and developed post traumatic stress disorder. The defendants argued that the claimant was not present at the scene of the accident which caused the death or its immediate aftermath. The Court of Appeal rejected the claimant's argument that the relevant "event" to which she must be proximate in time and space was not the initial accident but her mother's collapse and death caused by the accident. Lord Dyson MR did not accept that there were two events; there was a single accident or event which had two consequences, the first of which was the injury to the claimant's mother's head, and the second, three weeks later, was her death. To allow the claimant to recover as a "secondary" victim in such circumstances

2–206

---

[659] [1992] 1 A.C. 310 at 405, per Lord Ackner. *McLoughlin v O'Brian* was a case "upon the margin" of what was acceptable as the aftermath. But as Teff (1992) 12 O.J.L.S. 440, 446 comments: "Invidious distinctions are inevitable when the 'immediate aftermath' is treated in isolation, as a crude notion of temporal proximity." Even more problematic is the point made by J. Ahuja, "Liability for psychological and psychiatric harm: the road to recovery" (2015) 23 Med. L. Rev. 27 at 44 pointing out that: "The proximity requirement views trauma as resulting primarily from the sight of the mutilated body of the loved one, and assumes that the pain is less when the body is not witnessed. This is, however, contrary to research evidence. Studies suggest that bereaved relatives who are denied the choice to view the body of their loved one may suffer more than those who were given the opportunity."

[660] Arguably, the emphasis on the fact that in *McLoughlin v O'Brian* the victims had not been cleaned up or attended to by medical staff when the claimant saw them makes too much hang on an entirely arbitrary circumstance. Should liability for psychiatric harm depend upon a race between the claimant and the ambulance? See the comment of Brennan J in *Jaensch v Coffey* (1984) 54 A.L.R. 417 at 439.

[661] [2013] EWCA Civ 194; [2014] Q.B. 150; applied in *RS v Criminal Injuries Compensation Authority* [2013] EWCA Civ 1040; [2014] 1 W.L.R. 1313.

"would be to go too far".[662] If the claimant's argument were accepted, said his Lordship, she would be able to succeed even if her mother's death had occurred months and possibly years after the accident. On the other hand if her mother had died in the accident and the claimant had not witnessed the accident but had come on the scene shortly *after* the immediate aftermath she would not have qualified as a "secondary" victim. For policy reasons the right of action of "secondary" victims was subject to strict control mechanisms, and "any further substantial extension . . . should only be done by Parliament". For Lord Dyson, the paradigm "secondary" victim case is one involving an accident which (i) more or less immediately causes injury or death to a primary victim and (ii) is witnessed by the claimant: "In such a case, the relevant event is the accident. It is not a later consequence of the accident."[663]

(iii)   The means by which the claimant perceived the events or received the information

2–207   *Alcock* confirmed that a claimant must either see or hear the event or its immediate aftermath. Psychiatric harm induced by communication of events by a third party was outside the ambit of liability. The scenes broadcast on television did not depict the suffering of recognisable individuals (this being excluded by the broadcasting code of ethics, a fact known to the defendant), and therefore the viewing of these scenes could not be equated with the claimant being within sight or hearing of the event or its immediate aftermath. Although the television pictures certainly gave rise to feelings of the deepest anxiety and distress, this was equivalent to being told about the events by a third party.[664]

(iv)   The manner in which the psychiatric illness was caused

2–208   The older cases on liability for psychiatric harm referred to claims for "nervous shock". The term nervous shock itself tends to suggest that the claimant's

---

[662] [2013] EWCA Civ 194; [2014] Q.B. 150 at [29].

[663] [2013] EWCA Civ 194; [2014] Q.B. 150 at [32]. *Taylor v A Novo (UK) Ltd* is commented on by D. Nolan, "Horrifying events and their consequences: clarifying the operation of the *Alcock* criteria" (2014) 30 P.N. 176.

[664] Both Lord Ackner and Lord Oliver agreed that simultaneous broadcasts of a disaster could not always be ruled out as providing the equivalent of the actual sight or hearing of the event or its immediate aftermath. The requirement that the claimant perceive the event with his own unaided senses appears to have been dropped by the High Court of Australia: *Tame v New South Wales*; *Annetts v Australian Stations Pty Ltd* [2002] HCA 35; (2002) 191 A.L.R. 449, where the claimants in *Annetts* recovered for psychiatric harm essentially in respect of what they had been told about the disappearance and death of their son. *Tame v New South Wales* and *Annetts v Australian Stations Pty Ltd* were applied by the High Court of Australia in *Gifford v Strang Patrick Stevedoring Pty Ltd* [2003] HCA 33; (2003) 198 A.L.R. 100, holding that the defendant employers could owe a duty of care to the children of an employee killed as a result of the employers' negligence, when they allegedly developed psychiatric illness as a result of being told about their father's death. *Gifford* is commented on by Handford (2003) 11 Tort L. Rev. 127. The New Zealand Court of Appeal has reserved its position on whether the requirement that the claimant perceive the event with his own unaided senses ought to apply in such cases: *van Soest v Residual Health Management Unit* [2000] 1 N.Z.L.R. 179; Mullany (2001) 117 L.Q.R. 182; Teff at (2001) 9 Tort L. Rev. 109; Todd (2001) 17 P.N. 230.

psychiatric illness must be caused by a single event, which in colloquial terms can be regarded as "shocking", notwithstanding that medical understanding of the mechanisms by which psychiatric injury may occur does not correspond with this approach. In *Alcock* Lord Keith said that the scenes witnessed on television could not reasonably be regarded as giving rise to shock, in the sense of a sudden assault on the nervous system. Lord Ackner agreed that:

> "Even though the risk of psychiatric illness is reasonably foreseeable, the law gives no damages if the psychiatric injury was not induced by shock. Psychiatric illnesses caused in other ways, such as from the experience of having to cope with the deprivation consequent upon the death of a loved one, attracts no damages. Brennan J in Jaensch's case (1984) 54 A.L.R. 417 at 429 gave as examples: the spouse who has been worn down by caring for a tortiously injured husband or wife and who suffers psychiatric illness as a result, but who, nevertheless, goes without compensation; a parent made distraught by the wayward conduct of a brain-damaged child and who suffers psychiatric illness as a result also has no claim against the tortfeasor liable to the child."[665]

Accordingly, "secondary" victims must suffer psychiatric harm as a result of a "shocking" event, involving the sudden appreciation by sight or sound of a horrifying event, which violently agitates the mind. Psychiatric illness caused by the accumulation over a period of time of more gradual assaults on the nervous system is excluded.[666] The requirement that a "secondary" victim's psychiatric harm be "shock-induced" is based on an outmoded scientific view about the causal mechanism for suffering psychiatric harm and, given that the legal expression "nervous shock" has been described as inaccurate and misleading, it is artificial to reintroduce the notion of "shock" as an element in the chain of causation.[667] It certainly leads to apparently arbitrary outcomes. [668]

---

[665] [1992] 1 A.C. 310 at 400. Thus, psychiatric damage, clinical depression for example, which is simply attributable to the claimant having to live with the fact that a loved one is permanently disabled as a result of the defendant's negligence will not be actionable following *Alcock*; cf. *Beecham v Hughes* (1988) 52 D.L.R. (4th) 625, where the British Columbia Court of Appeal contemplated such a claim. The claimant suffered from reactive depression which commenced some time after a motoring accident which had rendered his common law wife permanently brain damaged. The claimant failed to prove a causal connection between the events and his depression, but the majority took the view that if the claimant's depression had resulted from the stress of seeing his wife, day after day, in a condition utterly unlike her condition before the accident, the damage would have been foreseeable.

[666] [1992] 1 A.C. 310 at 401; see also *Rhodes v Canadian National Railway* (1990) 75 D.L.R. (4th) 248 at 298, BCCA; *Campbelltown City Council v Mackay* (1989) 15 N.S.W.L.R. 501 at 503, NSWCA; *Spence v Percy* [1992] 2 Qd R. 299, Qd CA. On the other hand, it has been said that this requirement is based on an "outmoded scientific view" about the causal mechanism for suffering psychiatric harm: *Campbelltown City Council v Mackay* (1989) 15 N.S.W.L.R. 501 at 503, per Kirby P. It would seem that the High Court of Australia has now abandoned the "sudden shock" requirement: see *Tame v New South Wales*; *Annetts v Australian Stations Pty Ltd* [2002] HCA 35; (2002) 191 A.L.R. 449 at [18] per Gleeson CJ, [66] per Gaudron J and [206], [213] per Gummow and Kirby JJ; *Wicks v State Rail Authority of New South Wales* [2010] HCA 22; (2010) 241 C.L.R. 60 (a "shocking" event, in this case a rail crash, was not necessarily measured in minutes, but could last for hours: "A person is put in peril when put at risk; the person remains in peril . . . until the person ceases to be at risk", which was when they had been rescued by being taken to a place of safety (at [50])).

[667] See Teff (1996) 4 Tort L. Rev. 44 for cogent criticism of the "sudden shock" requirement. See also Teff (1992) 12 O.J.L.S. 440,442 who points out that generally speaking it is the closeness of the *actual* bond between claimant and accident victim which is the key indicator of whether psychiatric illness will ensue. Focusing on precisely how the shock is experienced is "artificial". For a penetrating

(f) Human Rights

2–209   In *Walters v North Glamorgan NHS Trust*[669] an argument that the restrictions on recovery for psychiatric damage in English law constituted an immunity which could not be justified in pursuit of a legitimate aim and was not proportionate for the purpose of art.6 of the European Convention on Human Rights was rejected. In the light of *Z v United Kingdom*,[670] there was no breach of art.6 where the court was dealing with substantive, as opposed to procedural, rights.[671]

(g) Reform

2–210   The Law Commission has recommended legislative reform of liability for the negligent infliction of psychiatric harm.[672] The Commission considered that the problematic issues concerned "secondary victims", and did not see a need for legislation in relation to recovery by rescuers, involuntary participants, employees, bystanders, in respect of occupational stress, for psychiatric illness suffered as a result of damage or danger to property, or for psychiatric illness suffered as a result of the negligent communication of distressing news.[673] In order to improve the position of "secondary" victims the Commission proposed that there should be a new statutory duty of care in the tort of negligence, leaving the common law to supply the remaining features such as the necessary requirements for breach of that duty, remoteness of damage, and any defences. Under the proposed statutory duty of care, a claimant who suffered a reasonably foreseeable psychiatric illness as a result of the death, injury or imperilment of a person with whom he had a close tie of love and affection would be entitled to recover damages from the negligent defendant, regardless of the claimant's closeness in time and space to the accident, or its aftermath, or the means by which the claimant learned of it. Thus, it would no longer be a requirement that the claimant be close to the accident in time and space and directly perceive the event. There would be a fixed list of relationships covered by the statutory duty of care, creating an irrebuttable presumption that there was a close tie of love and

---

critique of the gap between medical understanding of psychiatric illness and the legal rules for obtaining compensation see J. Ahuja, "Liability for psychological and psychiatric harm: the road to recovery" (2015) 23 Med. L. Rev. 27.

[668] Contrast, e.g. *Taylorson v Shieldness Produce Ltd* [1994] P.I.Q.R. P329, CA with *Calascione v Dixon* (1993) 19 B.M.L.R. 97, CA, both cases arising out of the parents' reaction to the consequences of road traffic accidents involving their children.

[669] [2002] EWHC 321 (QB); [2002] Lloyd's Rep. Med. 227; [2003] P.I.Q.R. P15.

[670] [2001] 2 F.L.R. 612.

[671] This ruling was not appealed when the case reached the Court of Appeal: [2002] EWCA Civ 1792; [2003] P.I.Q.R. P232 at [18].

[672] *Liability for Psychiatric Illness*, Law Com No.249, 1998. For discussion of the Report see Teff (1998) 61 M.L.R. 849; Tan Keng Feng (1999) 7 Tort L. Rev. 165.

[673] However, the law has moved on since the Law Commission reported its views. The ability of rescuers to claim as "primary" victims has been significantly narrowed as a result of *White v Chief Constable of the South Yorkshire Police* [1999] 2 A.C. 455, which has arguably also limited claims by "involuntary participants" in the event to those exposed to the risk physical injury (though cf. *W v Essex County Council* [2001] 2 A.C. 592). On the other hand, liability for the negligent communication of distressing news would appear to have broadened.

affection. It would be open to a claimant outside the list to prove that a close tie of love and affection did in fact exist between himself and the immediate victim. The one recommendation that would cover all types of claimant was that the proposed legislation should remove the requirement that psychiatric illness be induced by "shock". This would apply to both cases governed by the new statutory duty of care and those continuing to be covered by the common law duty of care (i.e. the there would no longer be any need to demonstrate a "sudden assault on the nervous system", whether the claimant was a "primary" victim or a "secondary" victim).

(h)   Psychiatric harm in the context of medical negligence

The general rules on the recovery of pure psychiatric harm provide the framework for considering cases arising in the medical context. One difficulty has been that the distinctions between "primary" and "secondary" victims do not always readily fit the circumstances in which psychiatric harm arises from medical negligence.[674] It might be thought that patients are "primary" victims, but they sometimes suffer psychiatric harm in circumstances where they have not been exposed to a risk of physical harm (e.g. where they have been given negligent information). Relatives will rarely be in a position to witness events as they occur, and therefore will often have difficulty in qualifying as a "secondary" victim.

2–211

(i)   Parents in the delivery room

Mothers   In *Kralj v McGrath*[675] the claimant suffered physical injuries as a result of "horrific treatment" by the defendant in the course of delivering a baby. She also suffered shock on being told about the baby's injuries and seeing the child for the eight weeks that it survived. Woolf J held that she was entitled to be compensated for this "nervous shock", although no specific psychiatric illness was identified. This would seem to fall into the first of Lord Oliver's two categories in *Alcock*, namely a case in which the injured claimant was involved, either mediately or immediately, as a participant: the claimant was undoubtedly

2–212

---

[674] See Handford, "Psychiatric Injury Resulting from Medical Negligence" (2002) 10 Tort L. Rev. 38, who argues that the rules on recovery of damages for psychiatric harm have developed principally for cases where the parties were strangers (as in a road traffic accident) and are not necessarily appropriate to cases where the claim arises out of the provision of a service where the parties were in a pre-existing relationship of care, such as that between doctor and patient. See also the observations of Lord Stewart in *Holdich v Lothian Health Board* [2013] CSOH 197; 2014 S.L.T. 495 at [88]: "I remain unconvinced ... that the primary/secondary distinction has more than illustrative value in cases where there is only one victim. The primary/secondary issue should not arise in sole victim cases where the allegation is of wrong done directly to the injured party's interests, where the injured party's identity, as an individual or possibly as a member of a class, is known in advance to the wrongdoer and where the wrongdoer has a duty of care by virtue of pre-existing legal proximity to safeguard the interest in question."
[675] [1986] 1 All E.R. 54. In the American case of *Molien v Kaiser Foundation Hospitals* 616 P. 2d 813 (1980) a doctor was held liable for a negligent diagnosis which led to the break up of the claimant's marriage.

owed a duty of care, as the doctor's patient, and she also suffered physical injury, and therefore could be regarded as a "primary" victim of the defendant's negligence.[676]

2–213   Similarly, in *Farrell v Merton, Sutton and Wandsworth Health Authority*,[677] where a mother did not see her severely disabled child for more than 24 hours after the birth, Steel J considered that, since the delay in the mother seeing her child was wholly attributable to the defendants' conduct in not taking her to see the child (who had been moved to another hospital) and choosing not to tell her about her baby's condition, the sight of her child on the following day constituted the "immediate aftermath" of the birth. The trauma of the birth included not only the events in the operating theatre, but also the situation up to and including the first sight of her baby and the realisation that he was severely disabled. But in any event, the mother was held to be a "primary" victim, though she had also suffered separate physical injury and therefore it might be thought that she readily fell within the "primary" victim category as someone who was not only exposed to the risk of physical harm but who actually sustained physical harm. A claimant who satisfies the threshold test of being exposed to the risk of foreseeable physical harm qualifies as a "primary" victim and does not have to prove that the psychiatric harm was caused by the physical injury. Indeed, a "primary" victim who was exposed to the risk of physical injury does not even have to prove that psychiatric harm was foreseeable,[678] although there must be some temporal

---

[676] The case thus resembles *Schneider v Eisovitch* [1960] 2 Q.B. 430 where the claimant was told that her husband had been killed, but she herself was directly involved as a victim suffering physical injuries in the accident in which her husband was killed. In *M (A Minor) v Newham London Borough Council* [1995] 2 A.C. 633, para.2–092, the defendants argued that the psychiatric disorder suffered by the child and the mother as a result of their separation was not actionable in law, since it was not the product of some sudden, shocking event, relying on Lord Ackner's speech in *Alcock*. This argument was misplaced, however, since both claimants were "primary" victims of the defendants' negligence. They were not claiming on the basis of witnessing an event, rather it was for the enforced separation which had been inflicted as a result of the defendants' alleged negligence. They fell into Lord Oliver's first category as persons directly involved as participants in the events (a point acknowledged by Staughton LJ in *Sion v Hampstead Health Authority* [1994] 5 Med. L.R. 170 at 173). Accordingly, the test should have been simply whether their psychiatric injury was a foreseeable consequence of the defendants' negligence. As Sir Thomas Bingham MR observed, at 664: "It would be little short of absurd if the child were held to be disentitled to claim damages for injury of the very type which the psychiatrist should have been exercising her skill to try and prevent." Neither Staughton nor Peter Gibson LJJ expressed an opinion on this issue in *M. v Newham*, and it was not dealt with by the House of Lords: *sub. nom. X (Minors) v Bedfordshire County Council* [1995] 2 A.C. 633.

[677] (2000) 57 B.M.L.R. 158. Contrast *Speirs v St. George's Healthcare NHS Trust*, unreported 10 December 2014, QBD, where the claimant mother alleged that she had suffered psychiatric harm on seeing her child in the neonatal intensive care unit some 15 hours after the birth. She was treated as a "secondary" victim, given that the child was "out of view as she was being delivered and was immediately taken by a nurse to an incubator". In any event the judge did not accept that she had suffered psychiatric harm as a result of what she had witnessed (as opposed to postnatal depression due to multiple other causes). Simon Brown QC considered that this was a classic case where the claimant's "memory has become fainter whilst her imagination has become more active with the passage of time and the onset of litigation".

[678] *Page v Smith* [1996] A.C. 155; unless the risk of physical harm to which the claimant was exposed is a risk of harm in the future, in which case the psychiatric harm must be foreseeable: *Rothwell v Chemical & Insulating Co Ltd* [2007] UKHL 39; [2008] 1 A.C. 281.

connection between the events.[679] It would seem that, in any event, where the child has not yet been born when the shocking events occur the mother will qualify as a "primary" victim. In *RE (A Minor) v Calderdale and Huddersfield NHS Foundation Trust*[680] Goss J concluded that where a child had become stuck in the birth canal due to shoulder dystocia the mother qualified as a "primary" victim on the basis that the baby's head:

> "...had crowned but her body remained in the birth canal. At this point she was not a separate legal entity from her mother and, in law, they are to be treated as one."

Fathers   The fact that fathers are often present in the delivery room means that   2–214
when something goes wrong with the delivery of a child there is a possibility of the father qualifying as a "secondary" victim. In the county court decision of *Tredget v Bexley Health Authority*[681] negligence by medical staff at a delivery resulted in the child dying two days later. There came a point in the labour where the mother should have been strongly advised to undergo a Caesarean section, but this was not done. The parents claimed for psychiatric illness, which it was alleged was the result of their involvement in or proximity to the traumas of the birth. HH Judge White held that they were both entitled to recover for psychiatric harm. The defendants disputed that the parents' psychiatric illness was the result of shock, as opposed to stress, strain, grief, or sorrow from either a gradual or a retrospective realisation of events. The death did not take place until two days after the birth, and during this time there would have been a gradual realisation by the parents of the child's situation. The judge found that the actual birth, with its "chaos" or "pandemonium", the difficulties that the mother had had during the delivery, the sense in the room that something was wrong, and the arrival of the child in a distressed condition requiring immediate resuscitation, was frightening and horrifying for the parents. Both parents were directly involved in and with the event of the delivery. They were participants in the events rather than passive witnesses. On this basis both parents established liability, even though a full appreciation of the gravity of the child's condition only came during the following 48 hours. It was unrealistic to isolate the delivery as an event from the other sequence of happenings from the onset of labour to the child's death two days later. Although lasting for over 48 hours from the onset of labour to the death, "this effectively was one event".[682]

---

[679] In *Page v Smith* the event giving rise to the psychiatric injury was contemporaneous with the claimant's exposure to the risk of physical harm.

[680] [2017] EWHC 824 (QB); [2017] Med. L.R. 390 at [40]; discussed by A. Morris [2017] J.P.I.L. C170. See also *Wells v University Hospital Southampton NHS Foundation Trust* [2015] EWHC 2376 (QB); [2015] Med. L.R. 477 at [83] where Dingemans J took the view that the mother of a child born alive which died 35 minutes after birth as a result of aspiration of meconium prior to birth would have been a "primary" victim because the alleged negligence occurred when the child and the mother were still one person. The claim failed on the basis that there had been no breach of duty.

[681] [1994] 5 Med. L.R. 178, Central London County Court.

[682] Distinguishing *Sion v Hampstead Health Authority* [1994] 5 Med. L.R. 170, para.2–219 below, by the degree of involvement in and the immediacy of the parents to the birth of the child in *Tredget*. In *X and Y v Pal* (1991) 23 N.S.W.L.R. 26; [1992] 3 Med. L.R. 195 the New South Wales Court of Appeal awarded $15,000 damages for the psychiatric harm suffered by a mother on discovering that

2–215   It would seem, however, that the more likely response to a father's presence in the delivery room is to find that the events were not sufficiently shocking for the father to qualify as a "secondary" victim. In *Wild v Southend University Hospital NHS Foundation Trust*[683] the claimant was present with his wife when she was due to give birth but it was discovered that the baby had already died in utero due to the defendants' prior negligence. It was held that he did not qualify as a "secondary" victim. He experienced a growing and acute anxiety as the medical staff tried to identify a foetal heartbeat, which developed to the point where he realised that the baby had died, but this was not the equivalent of witnessing a horrific event leading to death or serious injury.[684] Similarly, in *Less v Hussain*[685] Judge Cotter QC acknowledged that being present when one's son is born dead was *capable* of giving rise to psychiatric injury induced by shock, but on the evidence the claimant had not established that any psychiatric illness was caused by shock (i.e. the sudden appreciation by sight or sound of the hugely distressing events he witnessed), as opposed to a bereavement reaction to the death of his child. Again, in *Wells v University Hospital Southampton NHS Foundation Trust*[686] Dingemans J considered, obiter, that a father who was present when his pregnant partner underwent a Caesarean section and the baby was taken away for attempts at resuscitation which failed did not qualify as a "secondary" victim because he had not witnessed a shocking event. There had been:

> "...no sudden appreciation of an event, or perhaps the gradual dawning of realisation that her child's life had been put in danger."[687]

---

her three-month-old child was suffering from congenital syphilis. Query, however, whether under English law this would be considered to be a sufficiently "shocking" event, given that the reaction was to an oral communication.

[683] [2014] EWHC 4053 (QB); [2016] P.I.Q.R. P3; on which see Allen [2015] J.P.I.L. 1.

[684] An argument that the claimant could not succeed as a "secondary" victim because there was no "primary" victim, given that a stillborn child never acquires legal personality, was rejected since it would create a legal "black hole" in which a father could never succeed in a claim for psychiatric harm arising out of a stillbirth. In this situation the mother could be treated as the "primary" victim on the basis that in law the foetus and the mother should be treated as one person: [2014] EWHC 4053 (QB); [2016] P.I.Q.R. P3 at [22]. See also *RE (A Minor) v Calderdale and Huddersfield NHS Foundation Trust* [2017] EWHC 824 (QB); [2017] Med. L.R. 390 at [40] and *Wells v University Hospital Southampton NHS Foundation Trust* [2015] EWHC 2376 (QB); [2015] Med. L.R. 477 at [83] (para.2–213, n.680 above).

[685] [2012] EWHC 3513 (QB); [2013] Med. L.R. 383; (2013) 130 B.M.L.R. 51 at [187] to [191].

[686] [2015] EWHC 2376 (QB); [2015] Med. L.R. 477 at [86].

[687] See also the county court decision in *Tan v East London and the City Health Authority* [1999] Lloyd's Rep. Med. 389 (Chelmsford County Court) where the negligence of the hospital resulted in the death in utero of a child. The father was informed about this, and he attended the hospital and comforted his wife while a Caesarean section was carried out to deliver the child, some four hours after it had died. He held the dead child briefly, kept vigil overnight and saw her being placed in a metal box. It was held that the death in utero of the child was an accident/event at which the claimant was required to have been present. The death, stillbirth, overnight vigil and removal of the baby were not all one event. The event did not give rise to "shock" because there was foreknowledge, and planning of the stillbirth, and the subsequent stillbirth was not part of the immediate aftermath. In addition, the claimant's depression did not amount to a recognised psychiatric illness, because it was not categorised as clinical depression; cf. *Farrell v Avon Health Authority* [2001] Lloyd's Rep. Med. 458 discussed at para.2–230 below; and *Farnworth v Wrightington Wigan and Leigh NHS Foundation Trust*, unreported 21 December 2016, Manchester County Court (where the events resulting in his

Grandparents   Some medical emergencies in the delivery room may well   2–216
qualify as sufficiently shocking to establish a claim by a relative. In *RE (A Minor)
v Calderdale and Huddersfield NHS Foundation Trust*[688] during delivery the
child became "stuck" due to shoulder dystocia, which one of the defendants'
expert witnesses described as "one of the most frightening of medical
emergencies". Goss J held that both the mother and the child's grandmother (who
was present throughout) had experienced a sufficiently sudden, shocking and
objectively horrifying event by reference to persons of ordinary susceptibility to
qualify as "secondary" victims.[689]

(ii)   *The relatives of patients in other contexts*

Two of the *Alcock* criteria create particular problems for the relatives of patients   2–217
seeking to recover in respect of psychiatric harm. The first is the extent to which
the requirement of proximity in time and space to the events can be stretched by
the concept of the "aftermath"—does a relative who sees the injured patient in
hospital after the events which caused the patient's injuries fall within the
"immediate aftermath"? Where the claimant is present at the hospital and actually
witnesses the traumatic events there should, in theory, be less difficulty in
recovering for resulting psychiatric illness, although the claimant will still have to
establish the causal link between the events witnessed and the resulting
psychiatric harm.[690] The second is the requirement that there be a sudden,
shocking event, and it is this criterion on which most of the claims seem to fail.

Immediate aftermath   In *McLoughlin v O'Brian* some emphasis was placed   2–218
on the fact that the claimant saw her family at the hospital in a distressed state,
before they had been fully attended to by the medical staff. This is unlikely to be
the case in most instances of medical negligence, at least where the injuries occur
in the hospital itself. In *Taylor v Somerset Health Authority*[691] the claimant's
husband suffered a fatal heart attack at work. He was taken to hospital and, at
about 3.00pm, found to be dead. Having been informed that her husband had
been taken to hospital, the claimant arrived at about 3.20pm. Fifteen minutes or
so later she was informed that her husband was dead. Shortly afterwards she
identified his body in the mortuary, partly because she was requested to do so but
mainly because she could not believe that he had died. The sight of his body

---

daughter's death following emergency Caesarean section witnessed by the child's father were found
to be sufficiently shocking for the father to qualify as a secondary victim).
[688] [2017] EWHC 824 (QB); [2017] Med. L.R. 390; A. Morris [2017] J.P.I.L. C170.
[689] [2017] EWHC 824 (QB); [2017] Med. L.R. 390 at [47] and [48]. In any event the mother had
qualified as a "primary" victim (at [40]).
[690] In *Dube (Litigation Guardian of) v Penlon Ltd* (1994) 21 C.C.L.T. (2d) 268, Ont Court of Justice,
the parents of a three-year-old child claimed damages for psychiatric harm having seen the aftermath
of a catastrophic overdose of anaesthetic administered during the course of minor surgery. The child
suffered serious and permanent brain damage. Although the parents had undoubtedly suffered
psychiatric damage, their claims were rejected on the basis that there was no evidence that their
illnesses were caused by a reaction to the shock of witnessing the immediate aftermath as opposed to
being worn down by the depression, grief and constant demands of caring for their disabled child. See
para.2–208.
[691] [1993] 4 Med. L.R. 34; [1993] P.I.Q.R. P262, QBD.

caused further shock and distress, and the claimant suffered a psychiatric illness. It was admitted that there had been negligence on the part of the health authority (in the form of an earlier failure to diagnose and treat the deceased's serious heart condition) and that this caused the death. Auld J held that the claimant did not witness the "immediate aftermath" of the events resulting in the death of her husband. The doctor's communication to the claimant of her husband's death did not fall within the "aftermath" principle, and the purpose of the visit to the mortuary was to confirm the information that her husband was dead, and settle her disbelief.[692] It was concerned with the fact of death rather than the circumstances in which death came about.

2–219   A more flexible approach to what constitutes the immediate aftermath was apparent in the comments of Lord Slynn in *W v Essex County Council*,[693] though this case did not involve an allegation of medical negligence. His Lordship indicated that the concept of the immediate aftermath of an incident had to be assessed in the particular factual situation. Parents claimed that they suffered a psychiatric reaction to the realisation that, due to the defendants' negligence, they felt responsible for the fact that their children had been sexually abused by a foster child placed with the family by the defendants. His Lordship did not rule out the possibility that the parents could establish that they fell within the immediate aftermath:

> "I am not persuaded that in a situation like the present the parents must come across the abuser or the abused 'immediately' after the sexual incident has terminated. All the incidents here happened in the period of four weeks before the parents learned of them. It might be that if the matter were investigated in depth a judge would think that the temporal and spatial limitations were not satisfied. On the other hand he might find that the flexibility to which Lord Scarman referred [in *McLoughlin v O'Brian*] indicated that they were."

This case is at some remove, however, from the typical factual scenario in a clinical negligence action, and it is the requirement that there be a sudden shocking event on which most claims by relatives falter.

2–220   **No sudden shocking event**   In *Sion v Hampstead Health Authority*[694] the claimant was alleged to have suffered psychiatric illness as a result of negligence by the hospital caring for his son, aged 23, who had been injured in a road traffic accident. The claimant stayed by his bedside for 14 days, as his son gradually deteriorated and eventually died. It was alleged that there was a negligent failure to diagnose internal bleeding from the son's left kidney. The Court of Appeal held that there was no sudden "shocking" event, in the sense of a "sudden appreciation

---

[692] cf. *Galli-Atkinson v Seghal* [2003] EWCA Civ 697; [2003] Lloyd's Rep. Med. 285 where the Court of Appeal held that the immediate aftermath of the claimant's daughter's death had extended from the moment of the accident (a road traffic accident) until the moment the claimant left the mortuary. That had been an uninterrupted sequence of events. Contrast *Young v MacVean* [2015] CSIH 70; 2016 S.C. 135; 2015 S.L.T. 729—mother of deceased walked past scene of an accident and thought someone must have died; when her son did not turn up for an arranged meeting she began to think that the accident could have involved her son, which was confirmed not long after by the police; held that she did not qualify as a "secondary" victim because the events did not involve the sudden appreciation by direct sight or sound of a horrifying event or of the immediate aftermath.
[693] [2001] 2 A.C. 592 at 601.
[694] [1994] 5 Med. L.R. 170.

by sight or sound of a horrifying event, which violently agitates the mind", and accordingly there was no cause of action, applying *Alcock*. There was a process which continued for some time, from first arrival in the hospital to the appreciation, after the inquest, that there may have been medical negligence. The son's death, when it occurred, was not surprising but expected, and therefore the claimant suffered no sudden and unexpected shock to his nervous system. His psychiatric problems were due to an abnormal grief reaction to the son's death. Peter Gibson LJ commented that in such a claim it was the sudden awareness, violently agitating the mind, of what is occurring or what has occurred that was the crucial ingredient of shock. It was not the violence or suddenness of the incident causing injury to the accident victim that mattered. Accordingly:

"I see no reason in logic why a breach of duty causing an incident involving no violence or suddenness, such as where the wrong medicine is negligently given to a hospital patient, could not lead to a claim for damages for nervous shock, for example where the negligence has fatal results and a visiting close relative, wholly unprepared for what has occurred, finds the body and thereby sustains a sudden and unexpected shock to the nervous system."[695]

However, simply observing a loved one's death in hospital will not, in itself, be sufficient. In *Ward v Leeds Teaching Hospitals NHS Trust*[696] the claimant's adult daughter died in hospital two days after undergoing an operation under general anaesthetic for the removal of wisdom teeth, having never recovered consciousness after the operation. The claimant saw her daughter, unconscious, for about 10 minutes in the recovery room. Subsequently she remained with her daughter in the intensive care unit all night and throughout the following day. She saw her again for a short time after the ventilator was switched off, and again at the mortuary. The claimant brought an action against the hospital in respect of post-traumatic stress disorder. Judge Hawkesworth QC, sitting as a deputy judge of the High Court, held that the claimant had not satisfied the diagnostic criteria for post-traumatic stress disorder, which, on the evidence, required a shocking event of a particularly horrific nature:

2–221

"An event outside the range of human experience, sadly, does not it seems to me encompass the death of a loved one in hospital unless also accompanied by circumstances which were wholly exceptional in some way so as to shock or horrify. Mrs. Ward's own descriptions of these incidents did not strike me as shocking at the time in that sense, although undoubtedly they were distressing. To describe an event as shocking in common parlance is to use an epithet so devalued that it can embrace a very wide range of circumstances. But the sense in which it is used in the diagnostic criteria for PTSD must carry more than that colloquial meaning."[697]

Thus, there was no medical basis for a finding that the events at the hospital and the mortuary constituted events which had induced a post-traumatic stress disorder in the claimant.

---

[695] [1994] 5 Med. L.R. 170 at 176.
[696] [2004] EWHC 2106 (QB); [2004] Lloyd's Rep. Med. 530.
[697] [2004] EWHC 2106 (QB); [2004] Lloyd's Rep. Med. 530 at [21]. This observation was cited with approval by Tomlinson LJ in *Liverpool Women's Hospital NHS Foundation Trust v Ronayne* [2015] EWCA Civ 588; [2015] P.I.Q.R. P20 at [14]. See also *Brock v Northampton General Hospital NHS Trust* [2014] EWHC 4244 (QB) at [95] where parents saw their brain-dead daughter in hospital but this could not be categorised as "wholly exceptional", following the view expressed in *Ward*.

2–222   In *Palmer v Tees Health Authority*[698] a mother's claim for severe post-traumatic stress disorder and pathological grief reaction following the abduction and murder of her four-year-old daughter by a psychiatric patient failed. She alleged that the defendants had been negligent in failing to diagnose that the patient posed a serious risk to children. Within 15 minutes of discovering that her daughter was missing she believed that she had been abducted, and she said that this produced an immediate shock to her nervous system. The child's body was discovered three days later, and the claimant was in the vicinity at the time of the discovery although she was not allowed to see the body at that time. She claimed that the psychiatric illness was caused by her presence at the scene and the immediate aftermath of her daughter's abduction, and the search for and discovery of the body, which she later identified. The Court of Appeal held that she had not witnessed the events herself (i.e. the abduction and murder) and the events which she had witnessed did not constitute a "sudden shocking event". Mrs Palmer was in the same position as the relatives in *Alcock* who, on learning about the unfolding tragedy at the Hillsborough football ground, underwent a period of grave worry and anxiety before, some hours later, having their worst fears confirmed. They did not satisfy the "immediate aftermath" test. Moreover, her imagination of what had happened, subsequently confirmed by events, did not constitute "the sudden appreciation by sight or sound of the horrifying event".

2–223   **A single shocking event**   Some cases have taken a slightly more relaxed approach to the question of what constitutes a single, shocking event. In *Walters v North Glamorgan NHS Trust*[699] a mother attending her baby son in hospital where his acute hepatitis was negligently misdiagnosed, leading to his death, was held to be entitled to claim for psychiatric harm. She was sleeping in her son's room in hospital when she was awoken in the night by the sound of him choking. His body was stiff and she found blood. She was told that he was having a fit and it was unlikely that he would have any serious damage, but in fact he had suffered a major epileptic seizure causing a coma and brain damage. He was transferred to a London hospital to undergo a liver transplant, where she was told that he had suffered severe brain damage and was on life support. His brain was so seriously damaged that he would not have had any quality of life, so she agreed to the withdrawal of life support and he died in her arms, 36 hours after the initial fit. Thomas J held that she was not a "primary" victim. There was no risk of physical injury to her and she had not played any causative role in her son's death, so she was not a "participant" in the events. Rather, the claimant was a "secondary" victim. The only issue was whether her psychiatric illness (pathological grief reaction) was caused by shock as a result of a sudden appreciation of a horrifying event or its immediate aftermath. Thomas J held that the period of 36 hours from the time of the epileptic fit to the time of the child's death was a horrifying event, the sudden appreciation of which had caused her psychiatric illness. The waking to see the child's fit was not on its own a horrifying event, but the court should look realistically at what happened, and an event extending over a period of 48 hours could be treated as a single shocking event. On the psychiatric evidence it

---

[698] [1999] Lloyd's Rep. Med. 351.
[699] [2002] EWHC 321 (QB); [2002] Lloyd's Rep. Med. 227; [2003] P.I.Q.R. P15.

was impossible to isolate the causative effect of each incident over the 36 hours.[700] Everything that happened in that period had contributed to cause the psychiatric illness. The period of 36 hours from the moment of the epileptic fit, the misdiagnosis by the hospital, the correct diagnosis by the London hospital, and the decision to turn off the life support machine could be looked on in law as a horrifying event. The claimant's appreciation of the horrifying event was sudden within that temporal context, in contradistinction to more gradual assaults on her mind, and it was that sudden appreciation of the event that caused the pathological grief reaction.

The Court of Appeal affirmed the ruling of Thomas J.[701] Ward LJ said that the court should take a realistic view of what constitutes the necessary "event". The word should not be construed as if it were in a statute, but could be given a wide meaning to refer to a:

2–224

> "...series of events which make up the entire event beginning with the negligent infliction of damage through to the conclusion of the immediate aftermath whenever that may be."[702]

This would depend on the on the facts and circumstance of each case. In this case:

> "...there was an inexorable progression from the moment when the fit occurred as a result of the failure of the hospital properly to diagnose and then to treat the baby, the fit causing the brain damage which shortly thereafter made termination of this child's life inevitable and the dreadful climax when the child died in her arms. It is a seamless tale with an obvious beginning and an equally obvious end. It was played out over a period of 36 hours, which for her both at the time and as subsequently recollected was undoubtedly one drawn-out experience."[703]

Ward LJ also rejected the defendant's argument that the court could not take account of what the claimant was told about her son's condition from time to time. There was a distinction between a case where the claim was founded upon merely being informed of, or reading, or hearing about the accident and directly perceiving by sight or sound the relevant event:

> "Information given as the events unfold before one's eyes is part of the circumstances of the case to which the court is entitled to have regard."[704]

Clarke LJ commented that the *Alcock* control mechanisms should not be applied too rigidly or mechanistically.[705]

---

[700] Note that the medical evidence was to the effect that the psychiatric impact of the extended period over which the claimant was exposed to the event was more severe than if the child had died suddenly.

[701] *Walters v North Glamorgan NHS Trust* [2002] EWCA Civ 1792; [2003] P.I.Q.R. P232.

[702] [2002] EWCA Civ 1792; [2003] P.I.Q.R. P232 at [34].

[703] [2002] EWCA Civ 1792; [2003] P.I.Q.R. P232 at [34].

[704] [2002] EWCA Civ 1792; [2003] P.I.Q.R. P232 at [35].

[705] [2002] EWCA Civ 1792; [2003] P.I.Q.R. P232 at [48]. See also the Irish case of *Courtney v Our Lady's Hospital Ltd* [2011] IEHC 226 where a mother was with her two-year-old daughter at the hospital for all but half an hour from midnight to 10.30 the following morning when the child died, the defendants having failed to diagnose meningitis until it was too late; liability was admitted, and the judge was able to draw a clear distinction between the claimant's psychiatric reaction to the events she witnessed and a "normal grief reaction" to the death of a child; cf. *Ward v Leeds Teaching*

2–225   In *Shorter v Surrey and Sussex Healthcare NHS Trust*[706] Swift J distinguished *North Glamorgan NHS Trust v Walters* in a case of clinical negligence on the basis that what happened could not properly be described as a "seamless single horrifying event". The claimant's 37-year-old sister suffered a subarachnoid haemorrhage which was not diagnosed by the defendants for a week. She died as a result of a further bleed in the brain. The claimant was a senior sister in a Neuro-intensive Care Unit and she was very familiar with the condition and of the possible outcome if treatment was unsuccessful. Swift J acknowledged that decisions about what constitutes an "event" or the "immediate aftermath" or whether the claimant's experience can be described as "horrifying" or "shocking" were not easy, and the exercise was "somewhat artificial". Cases of clinical negligence, as opposed to the paradigm case of an ordinary accident, were particularly difficult, given the variety of, often complex, factual backgrounds. In *Shorter* the negligence had started a week before it became apparent and the consequences started to manifest themselves. In the hours after the patient's second bleed much of the information that the claimant received about her sister's condition was by telephone. The claimant saw her sister twice at the hospital, first when she was plainly unwell, in pain, and fearful about the news of the bleed but:

> "…not in such a condition that to see her could be described as a 'horrifying event' or to cause 'violent agitation of the mind'."[707]

Her sister's condition was fluctuating, she did not have obvious injuries, and she did not appear to be in any obvious or immediate danger at that point. She saw her sister again some nine hours or so later on a life support machine. There had been four telephone conversations about her sister's deteriorating condition in the interim, and before the claimant saw her on the life support machine her brother-in-law had told her that they had "lost her". Seeing her sister on the life support machine was not "a sudden or unexpected shock".[708] Swift J concluded that the facts did not amount to a "seamless single horrifying event", but were a series of events over a period of time which gave rise to an accumulation of gradual assaults on the claimant's mind. Swift J rejected the claimant's submission that, because of her own professional background and knowledge about her sister's condition, she would be more likely to be sensitive to the events and therefore more likely to find them "horrifying":

> "[The] 'event' must be one which would be recognised as 'horrifying' by a person of ordinary susceptibility; in other words, by objective standards."[709]

Hospitals NHS Trust [2004] EWHC 2106 (QB); [2004] Lloyd's Rep. Med. 530 at [24] where Judge Hawkesworth QC distinguished *Walters* on the basis that the psychiatric evidence in *Walters* was clear that the claimant's illness had been caused by shock, whereas in *Ward* the evidence was that the overwhelming factor in the claimant's psychiatric illness was the fact of her daughter's death, rather than any shock at the events that the claimant had witnessed.

[706] [2015] EWHC 614 (QB); (2015) 144 B.M.L.R. 136.
[707] [2015] EWHC 614 (QB); (2015) 144 B.M.L.R. 136 at [213].
[708] [2015] EWHC 614 (QB); (2015) 144 B.M.L.R. 136 at [217].
[709] [2015] EWHC 614 (QB); (2015) 144 B.M.L.R. 136 at [214].

In *Liverpool Women's Hospital NHS Foundation Trust v Ronayne*[710] Tomlinson LJ agreed with Swift J in *Shorter* that the question whether an event is "horrifying" must be judged by objective standards and by reference to persons of ordinary susceptibility. In *Ronayne* the claimant, who was employed as an ambulance driver, observed the rapid deterioration of his wife in hospital due to the defendants' negligence. He saw her connected to drips and monitors before an emergency operation, and saw her the following day when she was unconscious and connected to a ventilator being given intravenous antibiotics. Her arms, legs and face were very swollen, a condition which the claimant described to a psychiatrist as resembling the "Michelin Man". The claimant alleged that he had suffered post-traumatic stress disorder as a result of what he had witnessed. The Court of Appeal held that these circumstances, over a period of approximately 36 hours, did not constitute a single shocking event. The facts were not comparable to *North Glamorgan NHS Trust v Walters*. There was, said Tomlinson LJ:

2–226

> "...a series of events over a period of time. There was no 'inexorable progression' and the claimant's perception of what he saw on the two critical occasions was in each case conditioned or informed by the information which he had received in advance and by way of preparation".[711]

There was no sudden appreciation of an event. Rather, there was a series of events which gave rise to an accumulation of gradual assaults on the claimant's mind. Moreover, what the claimant saw was not horrifying by objective standards since the appearance of the claimant's wife was as would ordinarily be expected of a person in hospital in her particular circumstances. Though her appearance would have been both alarming and distressing to the claimant it was not exceptional.[712] Tomlinson LJ noted that it was:

> "...telling that there is, so far as the experienced counsel who appeared before us were aware, only one reported case in which a claimant has succeeded at trial in a claim of this type in consequence of observing in a hospital setting the consequences of clinical negligence. That is in my view unsurprising. In hospital one must expect to see patients connected to machines and drips, and ... expect to see things that one may not like to see. A visitor to a hospital is necessarily to a certain degree conditioned as to what to expect, and in the ordinary way it is also likely that due warning will be given by medical staff of an impending encounter likely to prove more than ordinarily distressing."[713]

The one reported exceptional case was *North Glamorgan NHS Trust v Walters* but, said his Lordship, that case had the unusual feature of a mother witnessing at

---

[710] [2015] EWCA Civ 588; [2015] P.I.Q.R. P20 at [13]. The case is commented on by A. Burrows and J. Burrows, "A Shocking Requirement in The Law on Negligence Liability for Psychiatric Illness" (2016) 24 Med. L. Rev. 278; and Wheeler [2015] J.P.I.L. C219.

[711] [2015] EWCA Civ 588; [2015] P.I.Q.R. P20 at [36]. Sullivan and Beatson LJJ. agreed with Tomlinson LJ.

[712] [2015] EWCA Civ 588; [2015] P.I.Q.R. P20 at [40] and [41].

[713] [2015] EWCA Civ 588; [2015] P.I.Q.R. P20 at [17]. In *Owers v Medway NHS Foundation Trust* [2015] EWHC 2363 (QB); [2015] Med. L.R. 561 Stewart J applied *Ronayne* in a case where a husband witnessed the effects of his wife suffering a stroke, which the defendants had negligently failed to diagnose and treat. The events were "very distressing. However they were not 'horrifying' as judged by objective standards and by reference to persons of ordinary susceptibility. They were not wholly exceptional" and there was "no sudden appreciation of a 'horrifying' event" (at [151]).

first hand her infant child undergoing a fit as a result of negligence, and the circumstance that thereafter she was unprepared for the sequelae because she had been reassured by further incorrect medical advice.

2–227   The decision of Forbes J in *Froggatt v Chesterfield and North Derbyshire Royal Hospital NHS Trust*[714] now looks increasingly anomalous. It was held that the spouse and child of a woman who underwent a mastectomy following a negligent misdiagnosis of cancer were entitled to recover for their psychiatric injury as "secondary" victims. In the case of the husband he had had a sudden appreciation of the trauma suffered by his wife as a result of the defendant's negligence when he saw her undressed for the first time after the mastectomy. "He was quite unprepared for what he saw and he was profoundly and lastingly shocked by it."[715] In the child's case, the sudden appreciation came as a result of overhearing a telephone conversation that his mother was having:

> "...and his immediate belief, based on the negligent advice that had been given to his mother and that she felt obliged to repeat to him, that she had cancer and was likely to die. He was completely unprepared for such a shock and, as a result, he suffered a moderate Post Traumatic Stress Disorder."[716]

These "shocking" events, though clearly foreseeable consequences of the defendants' negligence, would seem to be at some temporal remove from the defendant's negligence, and it is not clear how this decision can be reconciled with, for example, *Sion v Hampstead Health Authority* and *Liverpool Women's Hospital NHS Foundation Trust v Ronayne*, even allowing for the comments of Lord Slynn in *W v Essex County Council* and the flexibility applied in *Walters v North Glamorgan NHS Trust*. When the patient's husband saw his wife undressed for the first time after the surgery, it could hardly be said that he was unaware that she had undergone a mastectomy. The "event" (seeing his wife without a breast) was just as expected as the son's death in *Sion*. It was simply that the husband in *Froggatt* reacted badly to the sight. Does this mean that a husband who reacts badly to the first sight of a wife's scars following a road traffic accident would recover for psychiatric harm against the negligent motorist, even though that event was days or even weeks after the accident? This would seem to stretch the "immediate aftermath" of an event far beyond what was contemplated in *McLoughlin v O'Brian*, and certainly beyond the point drawn by the House of Lords in *Alcock*.[717]

---

[714] [2002] All E.R. (D) 218 (Dec.) QBD, 13 December 2002.
[715] [2002] All E.R. (D) 218 (Dec.) QBD, 13 December 2002 at [79].
[716] [2002] All E.R. (D) 218 (Dec.) QBD, 13 December 2002 at [80].
[717] In *Wild v Southend University Hospital NHS Trust Foundation Trust* [2014] EWHC 4053 (QB); [2016] P.I.Q.R. P3 at [51] Michael Kent QC (sitting as a judge of the High Court) commented that: "It seems to me that had *Froggatt* been cited in *Taylor v A Novo* (it was not apparently) the Master of the Rolls would have been likely to comment that it was not supported by the authorities." See para.2–206 for consideration of *Taylor v A Novo (UK) Ltd* [2013] EWCA Civ 194; [2014] Q.B. 150.

(iii)   Communicating bad news

A further question concerns the potential liability of the person who   **2–228**
communicates information to the claimant, as a result of which the claimant
sustains psychiatric harm. It has been said that if the statement is true there is no
obligation to break bad news gently, even if it is foreseeable that the person will
be shocked by it.[718] This proposition is debatable, however, at least where the
circumstances are such that the impact of the news is needlessly exacerbated.[719]
Doctors frequently have to give bad news, both to patients and relatives. It is at
least arguable that in some cases the claimant who develops psychiatric harm as a
result of what he or she is told will be a "primary" victim of a negligent
statement, where in theory the test is simply foreseeability of psychiatric damage.
In *AB v Tameside & Glossop Health Authority*[720] the defendants conceded that
they owed a duty of care to break distressing, though truthful, news to patients in
a manner which reduced the risk of patients developing psychiatric illness in
response to the news, though the defendants were held not to have been negligent
in choosing to inform patients that there was a small risk that they might have
contracted HIV from a doctor by letter rather than face to face. It is not clear on
what basis the defendants' concession was made, given the traditional view that a
duty does not arise simply from the manner in which accurate information is
given.[721]

Negligently communicating inaccurate information   In *Allin v City &*   **2–229**
Hackney Health Authority,[722] as a result of the defendants' negligence, the
distressing information was inaccurate and the claimant alleged that she had
suffered psychiatric harm from this distressing "news", subsequently corrected,
although the incorrect information had been imparted in a sensitive and
appropriate manner (i.e. if it had been correct). The claimant had undergone a

---

[718] *Mount Isa Mines Ltd v Pusey* (1970) 125 C.L.R. 383 at 407.
[719] In *Furness v Fitchett* [1958] N.Z.L.R. 396 it was accepted that a doctor may be under a duty of
care to his *patient* not to inform her about her medical condition. The defendant was held liable for
harm to the claimant's psychiatric health even though the information was true.
[720] [1997] 8 Med. L.R. 91.
[721] See Dziobon and Tettenborn (1997) 13 P.N. 70; cf. Mullany (1998) 114 L.Q.R. 380. In *Anderson
v Wilson* (1999) 175 D.L.R. (4th) 409, Ont CA, a group of patients had been exposed to the risk of
contracting hepatitis B, but had been tested and found to be negative. The Ontario Court of Appeal
held that it was at least arguable that the notice to patients would produce psychiatric harm, and given
the uncertain state of the law on liability for psychiatric harm, it could not be said to be unarguable
that a claim in respect of mental distress alone, without a recognised psychiatric illness, would fail; cf.
Healey v Lakeridge Health Corp 2011 ONCA 55; (2011) 103 O.R. (3d) 401; (2011) 328 D.L.R. (4th)
248 in which it was alleged that patients who had been negligently exposed to the possibility of
contracting tuberculosis and then advised that they should be tested for the disease, but had tested
negative, had nonetheless suffered psychiatric harm in the form of mental anxiety, suffering and
distress. The Ontario Court of Appeal held that the claim had rightly been struck out on the basis that
the claimants had not suffered a recognisable psychiatric illness, but that even if the decision of the
Supreme Court of Canada in *Mustapha v Culligan of Canada Ltd*, 2008 SCC 27; (2008) 293 D.L.R.
(4th) 29 had loosened this requirement the claimants had not suffered harm of sufficient gravity and
duration to qualify for compensation. The harm did not amount to more than upset, disgust, anxiety,
agitation or other mental states that fall short of injury.
[722] [1996] 7 Med. L.R. 167.

very difficult labour and was told by the medical staff that her baby was dead when in fact it had not died. She only began to appreciate that the child was alive the following day when a doctor spoke to her about the baby's condition. Again, counsel for the defendants conceded the existence of a duty of care, but in this case the defendants were held liable on the facts. Again, the basis of this concession of a duty of care is not clear,[723] but if it is correct the somewhat odd consequence would be that a claimant who is correctly informed about the death of a loved one killed by the defendant's negligence has no claim against the person who killed that loved one for the psychiatric damage which results (applying *Alcock*), whereas a person who is incorrectly, and negligently, informed that a loved one has died may have a claim for psychiatric harm against the careless informant, even though no one has died and there was no negligence in respect of the loved one. On the other hand, Mullany comments that:

> "It is unquestionably right for the common law to insist that those who communicate objectively distressing (indeed, potentially life-shattering) news take all reasonable precautions to ensure that such news is accurate."[724]

While there is much force in this statement as a matter of principle, given the present structure of English law (and particularly the restrictions imposed by *Alcock*), as matter of consistency between claimants *Allin* looks distinctly out of line.[725]

2–230   In *Farrell v Avon Health Authority*,[726] without reference to *Allin*, Bursell J held that the father of a newborn baby who was wrongly told that his baby had died, and then given the body of a dead baby to hold, was owed a duty of care as a "primary" victim. He was informed 20 minutes later that there had been a mistake, and that his baby was still alive. He visited the baby, but stayed only a few minutes. Although he had not had contact with the mother before the birth and did not see the child again, the claimant alleged that the experience had caused a psychiatric reaction. Bursell J held that he was a "primary" victim on the basis that he was physically involved in the incident, and the only victim of the incident was the claimant himself: "How can there be a secondary victim if there is no other person who was physically involved as a potential victim?"[727] The

---

[723] See Jones (1997) 13 P.N. 111. See also *Guay v Sun Publishing Co.* [1953] 4 D.L.R. 577 where a newspaper was held not liable for the psychiatric harm suffered by the claimant on reading a false report of her family's death published negligently by a newspaper.

[724] (1998) 114 L.Q.R. 380, 385.

[725] Consistency between different categories of claimant was an important factor in the decision of the House of Lords in *White v Chief Constable of the South Yorkshire Police* [1999] 2 A.C. 455 to deny the claims for psychiatric damage brought by police officers at the Hillsborough disaster. The objection was to allowing the police officers' claims to succeed simply because they fell into the category of "rescuer", having denied the relatives' claims in *Alcock*.

[726] [2001] Lloyd's Rep. Med. 458; see Case (2002) 18 P.N. 248.

[727] [2001] Lloyd's Rep. Med. 458 at 471. See also *AB v Leeds Teaching Hospital NHS Trust* [2004] EWHC 644 (QB); [2005] Q.B. 506 at [199], where Gage J held that the parents of deceased children who discovered that their child's organs had been removed at post-mortem and retained by the hospital were "primary" victims since the children could not be primary victims (in the sense of someone to whom the defendants owed a duty of care not to injure, since the doctors and pathologists could not owe them a duty after they were dead). Thus, if the claimants were victims at all, "they must be primary victims." See further paras 2–248 et seq.

significance of finding that the claimant was a "primary" victim was that he merely had to prove that psychiatric damage was foreseeable—and if it was foreseeable it mattered not that the claimant had a vulnerable personality because the defendants had to take the claimant as they found him. This looks odd when compared with the position of an employee suing his employer in respect of occupational stress, where it is clear that if the employee has a vulnerable personality which is unknown to the employer the employee's action will fail for want of foreseeability.[728] However, in applying the foreseeability test the judge held that foreseeability had to be judged by reference to the circumstances at the time of the negligence, including the defendants' knowledge at that time. On the facts, the defendants were unaware of the claimant's lack of contact with the mother, and therefore of the lack of pre-natal bonding with the child, and so foreseeability of the risk of psychiatric harm had to be assessed on the basis of an ordinary parental relationship with the unborn child. Since, the judge concluded, it was foreseeable that an ordinary father could suffer a psychiatric reaction in such circumstances, it was irrelevant that the claimant was not an ordinary father or had a vulnerable personality. Of course, this does not address the more general issue of why a claimant should succeed in such circumstances. It is true that the claimant was the only "victim", but that was because he was told, erroneously as it turned out, that there was an accident victim, his "dead" son. His psychiatric reaction was the result of what he thought had happened to his son, and what he perceived, wrongly, as the consequences of that, namely the baby's dead body. Is there any difference (other than the length of time that elapsed) between this situation and seeing a dead body to identify it at the mortuary (as occurred to some of the claimants in *Alcock*)? If the claimant's baby had in fact been killed by the defendants' negligence, and the father had simply been told about this some hours later, he would probably not have recovered because he would have been treated as a "secondary" victim.

(iv)   Communicating (accurate) bad news where the defendant is responsible for the event itself

Where the defendant has been negligent in the diagnosis and/or treatment of the patient there will usually come a point at which the patient discovers that something has gone wrong. Ideally, this will be when the defendant, having realised the error, fulfils the duty of candour to explain to the patient the unintended outcome and its cause(s).[729] Psychiatric conditions which arise as a consequence of physical injury do not constitute "pure" psychiatric harm and damages for any psychiatric harm will be assessed as part of the claim for physical injury, subject to proving a causal link between the patient's psychiatric condition and the defendant's breach of duty. On the other hand, in the case of a missed or delayed diagnosis the patient's psychiatric response may arise from the patient learning of the delay and the potential implications for the patient's future

2–231

---

[728] See *Hatton v Sutherland* [2002] EWCA Civ 76; [2002] 2 All E.R. 1. The statements of legal principle in *Hatton v Sutherland* were approved by the House of Lords in *Barber v Somerset County Council* [2004] UKHL 13; [2004] 1 W.L.R. 1089; [2004] 2 All E.R. 385.
[729] See para.4–054 et seq. on the duty of candour.

treatment and prognosis. For example, a missed diagnosis of cancer may not only reduce the patient's prospects of a cure and increase the severity of the therapeutic interventions required to treat the condition, it may also result in the patient developing a psychiatric condition. Provided that this is causally linked to the negligently delayed diagnosis, and not simply the fact of the diagnosis itself, the patient will be entitled to damages for the foreseeable psychiatric harm.[730]

2–232   **Information about the risk of future harm**   Where the claimant has not suffered any physical harm but is informed that as a result of the defendant's negligence there is a risk that at some point in the future he may suffer physical injury and/or death, the position is more complex. In *CJD Litigation: Group B Plaintiffs v Medical Research Council*[731] the claimants had been injected with human growth hormone (HGH) which can carry the agent that causes Creutzfeldt-Jakob Disease (CJD), an extremely unpleasant and invariably fatal condition. None of the claimants had developed CJD by the time of the claim but they were aware that they were at risk of developing the disease in the future. Crucially, the risk of the claimants developing a psychiatric condition as a result of receiving information about the risk of developing CJD, and its effects, was found to be reasonably foreseeable and had actually been foreseen by the defendants. Morland J held that any claimant who could prove that he developed a genuine psychiatric illness caused by awareness of the risk of developing CJD was entitled to compensation for the psychiatric damage "whether of normal phlegm and ordinary fortitude or having a vulnerable personality".[732] The psychiatric injury was not triggered by a physical event which involved some physical impact on the claimants (injections of potentially contaminated human growth hormone), but from the subsequent knowledge that that event created a risk of developing the disease in the future.

2–233   Morland J held that the claimants were not "primary" victims, because of the ramifications of such a ruling in other cases (and they were clearly not "secondary" victims). If the claimants were "primary" victims, then so would individuals exposed to asbestos or radiation who subsequently learned of the exposure and developed a psychiatric reaction in response to knowledge of the risk of developing cancer in the future. The potentially huge number of claims in similar situations would make insurance difficult or impossible to obtain. It could involve all manner of products and a huge range of potential tortfeasors. It could inhibit the producers, prescribers and suppliers of a product from warning the public of the danger of a product. For example, if a potentially lethal substance had been introduced into a production batch of canned food:

---

[730] See, e.g., *Lodge v Fitzgibbon* 2011 NBQB 226; (2011) 973 A.P.R. 202; (2011) 378 N.B.R. (2d) 202 where there was medical evidence that a significant minority of patients who receive a diagnosis of cancer develop post-traumatic stress disorder. The judge took the view that a patient who had received a previous negative diagnosis of cancer was more likely to develop PTSD when she received a cancer diagnosis that contradicted an earlier one.

[731] (1997), [2000] Lloyd's Rep. Med. 161; (1997) 41 B.M.L.R. 157. See J. O'Sullivan, "Liability for Fear of the onset of future Medical Conditions" (1999) 15 P.N. 96.

[732] (1997), [2000] Lloyd's Rep. Med. 161 at 168.

"...it would be disastrous if a supplier or producer were inhibited from warning the public of danger for fear that some who of those who had already eaten the canned food might bring a claim as a 'primary' victim for psychiatric injury triggered by the warning. Against such a claim the producer could not raise defences either that the psychiatric injury was unforeseeable to a person of normal fortitude or that the law insists upon certain control mechanisms to limit the number of potential claimants."[733]

The relationship between the defendants and the recipients of the injection was akin to that of doctor and patient, said his Lordship, one of close proximity. That, combined with the fact that the cohort of potential victims of psychiatric damage was small, and the very serious nature of the potential disease which causes terrible suffering for the victim and cannot be treated or ameliorated by medical treatment, was sufficient to establish a duty of care.

"Although it may not be reasonably foreseeable that the man of ordinary fortitude would develop psychiatric illness if the information that he was at slight theoretical risk of CJD was given to him by a doctor or counsellor who would no doubt give the information with optimistic stress, in the case of a special therapeutic trial or programme as the HGH programme, it should have been reasonably foreseeable to the defendants by 1 July 1977 that, when news of the potential risk of CJD broke to those who were or had been children when treated, the news would reach Group B plaintiffs not only from considerate and skilled clinicians and counsellors but also from the media which foreseeably would tend to highlight or sensationalise the risk of the potential terrible outcome and from anxious and perhaps angry relations and friends who would be ignorant of scientific knowledge and likely to use unhelpful language."[734]

The defendants had actually foreseen this risk. It was irrelevant, said Morland J, whether the news of the risk of developing CJD produced a sudden shock or the news was received over a period of time from various sources. There was no logical reason to limit the foreseeability to an area of time contemporaneous or almost contemporaneous to the negligent physical event, i.e. the injection. Nor should the delay between the shock of the news of the first cases of CJD and the onset of psychiatric injury defeat the claims.

"A psychiatric injury can be readily induced by an accumulative awareness or drip-feed of information over a prolonged period of time although the court will scrutinise rigorously a claim so based."[735]

Similarly, in *A.P.Q. v Commonwealth Serum Laboratories Ltd*[736] Harper J refused to strike out as disclosing no reasonable cause of action a claim in respect of psychiatric harm arising from the knowledge that the claimant had been exposed to the risk of developing CJD, following treatment with human pituitary gonadtrophins manufactured by the defendants:

2–234

"...a person who suffers psychiatric illness when informed that medical treatment undergone by her may leave her with a horrible and terminal disease probably has a good cause of action

---

[733] (1997), [2000] Lloyd's Rep. Med. 161 at 165.
[734] (1997), [2000] Lloyd's Rep. Med. 161 at 166.
[735] (1997), [2000] Lloyd's Rep. Med. 161 at 168.
[736] [1999] 3 V.R. 633, Vict SC.

against the manufacturer of a drug used in the [claimant's] treatment where its manufacture (and its subsequent distribution) was conducted negligently and where that negligence exposed the [claimant] to that risk."[737]

The defendant's argument that no duty of care arose because the claimant's psychiatric condition did not arise from the sudden perception of a shocking event was rejected. The claimant was a "primary" victim, with her psychiatric illness resulting from her awareness of the possibility of her own death following an unpleasant disease:

> "The shock suffered by someone who is informed without any prior warning that she (or he) might contract a particularly undesirable disease could seldom if ever be said to arise from a 'sudden sensory perception of a person, thing or event.' Yet it might well be so distressing that it affronts or insults the mind and thereby causes a recognisable psychiatric illness. This being so, it is difficult to understand why the absence of the sudden sensory perception of a person, thing or event should make the difference between a cause of action on the one hand and no cause of action on the other, where in each instance psychiatric harm has been caused. Unless I have sadly mistaken the present [claimant's] claim, this case is not analogous to that of the worn-out spouse or the parent of the brain-damaged child."[738]

2–235   In both of these cases the judges were anxious to sidestep the normal requirement that the claimant sustained the psychiatric harm as a result of a sudden shocking event. This can be done simply by categorising the claimants as "primary" victims. It is arguable that *Page v Smith* renders any individual who has been exposed to the risk of foreseeable physical injury a "primary" victim, even if they have not suffered physical injury and the psychiatric injury was unforeseeable. For example, a patient who as a result of negligence received inappropriate treatment and thereby might expect in due course to suffer physical injury (e.g. an overdose of radiation therapy), and, being aware of the error, developed a psychiatric illness as a reaction to the events, would appear to fall within the principle of *Page v Smith* even if ultimately the physical injury did not materialise. Since the physical injury was foreseeable, so was the psychiatric injury.

2–236   It is clear that Morland J wanted to avoid the conclusion that patients given HGH were "primary" victims, because his Lordship was anxious to distinguish the CJD claimants (involving an extremely unpleasant and invariably fatal disease) from other cases where a claimant has been exposed to the risk of future disease (such as cancer arising from exposure to radiation or asbestos). It is not obvious, however, that this distinction will hold. The seriousness of the consequences is, after all, only a matter of degree. For example, workers who contract mesothelioma as a result of having been exposed to asbestos at work will almost invariably die within two years of diagnosis. The disease is extremely unpleasant and painful. It may be a nice question whether, given the option, one would chose to die from mesothelioma or CJD. Why should those who have been exposed to the risk of developing CJD as a result of a defendant's negligence have a claim for psychiatric damage arising out of their fear of the future, when those who have been exposed to the risk of mesothelioma due to inhaling asbestos particles

---

[737] [1999] 3 V.R. 633 at 635 per Harper J.
[738] [1999] 3 V.R. 633 at 639.

do not?[739] The fact that there are potentially far more claimants, a point of concern to Morland J, hardly provides a principled justification. Indeed, it might suggest that such claimants should have a stronger case in that the risk of developing mesothelioma may be higher,[740] and therefore the psychiatric reaction to the risk correspondingly more foreseeable and reasonable. Moreover, *Page v Smith* is authority for the proposition that claimants have an action for their unforeseeable psychiatric illnesses provided they were exposed to the risk of foreseeable physical injury, even though the physical injury did not occur and never will occur. Mr Page was never going to develop a physical injury from the minor traffic accident in which he was involved. But his exposure to the risk of such injury was a threshold test, which was sufficient to establish the defendant's duty of care with respect to the psychiatric harm.[741]

No risk of future harm   Where there is *no* risk that the claimants will develop   2–237
a serious condition in the future, the claimants should not be entitled to claim in respect of a genuine psychiatric illness which is an irrational response. In *The Creutzfeldt-Jakob Disease Litigation*[742] a different group of claimants who had received HGH that had been processed by a different method, which the judge considered carried no risk of CJD, argued that they should be entitled to claim for psychological injury from the news that they were at risk of CJD. Morland J held that this claim was bound to fail, commenting:

"Every man and woman will receive bad news about himself or herself or a loved one, bad news of death, fatal illness or disabling injury or accident or other disaster. It is the inevitable experience of life. Naturally, such bad news will cause grief, stress, worry, concern, unhappiness, a feeling of being depressed. Such reactions are normal. Their severity will vary from person to person. Every man and woman is expected to face such situations with such fortitude as he or she can muster. In my judgment, it would be an unhealthy society that thought it was entitled to monetary compensation in such situations. Indeed, the existence of the belief to such entitlement might well create the psychological injury which otherwise would not have occurred. ... Unless such bad news comes into the public domain, advances in medicine and public health will be inhibited. Scientific advance will inevitably lead from time to time to the discovery of new risks and side-effects, both from well-tried and experimental drugs. Full, well-informed and frank debate about the problem is required for further progress. Once a new risk is known, the recipient of the drug should be informed in a sensitive and balanced manner, preferably before lurid scare stories appear in the media. The recipient of the news of the risk should then be expected foreseeably to be able to cope and live with that news."[743]

---

[739] The answer, according to the House of Lords in *Rothwell v Chemical & Insulating Co. Ltd* [2007] UKHL 39; [2008] 1 A.C. 281, is that the risk of developing a psychiatric condition from contemplating the prospect of contracting CJD is foreseeable, whereas the risk of developing a psychiatric condition from contemplating the prospect of contracting mesothelioma after exposure to asbestos is not. See para.2–238 below.

[740] There are about 1,500 cases of mesothelioma as a result of exposure to asbestos diagnosed each year (see the figures quoted in *Fairchild v Glenhaven Funeral Services Ltd* [2002] UKHL 22; [2003] 1 A.C. 32, para.5–050). By 1998 there were 27 confirmed cases of CJD due to human growth hormone since 1985: see para.3–069, n.167. It is impossible to compare the relative risk, however, since the population of individuals given human growth hormone is far lower than the population exposed to asbestos fibres.

[741] Subsequently, the House of Lords held that exposure to the risk of foreseeable physical injury was also a *necessary* condition: *White v Chief Constable of the South Yorkshire Police* [1999] 2 A.C. 455.

[742] (1996) 54 B.M.L.R. 79.

[743] (1996) 54 B.M.L.R. 79 at 83.

Thus, it was not in the public interest that the ambit of the litigation be extended to this category of claimants.

2–238   **Small risk of future harm but risk of psychiatric harm unforeseeable**   In *Rothwell v Chemical & Insulating Co Ltd*[744] the House of Lords distinguished Morland J's judgment in *CJD Litigation: Group B Plaintiffs v Medical Research Council. Rothwell* was concerned with a number of consolidated appeals where employees had been negligently exposed to asbestos at work and had developed pleural plaques on their lungs. Their Lordships held that symptomless pleural plaques which were merely a marker of exposure to asbestos and produced no physical disability did not constitute physical damage entitling the claimants to maintain an action for negligence.[745] Nor did anxiety about the possibility of developing an asbestos-related condition in the future give rise to any claim. One of the appellants, Mr Grieves, had developed a recognised psychiatric condition (depression) as a result of contemplating the possibility that he might develop a serious physical illness (the fatal cancer, mesothelioma) in the future as a result of his exposure to asbestos. He relied on *Page v Smith*, arguing that where the defendant's negligence has exposed the claimant to the foreseeable risk of developing a serious physical condition in the future a claimant is entitled to compensation for a psychiatric condition which develops as a result of his fear or anxiety about this occurring. He had been exposed to the foreseeable risk of physical harm (as in *Page v Smith*), which had not yet materialised (as in *Page v Smith*, though in that case, unlike Mr Grieves', it was known that the physical harm would never actually materialise) and had developed a recognised psychiatric condition as a consequence (as in *Page v Smith*). The House of Lords rejected Mr Grieves' argument, concluding that he could not rely on the proposition that a "primary" victim does not have to demonstrate that he is a person of "ordinary fortitude" or that he possesses the "customary phlegm". It was not reasonably foreseeable that a person of ordinary fortitude would develop a psychiatric condition as a result of being informed that there was a small risk of developing even a serious medical condition (such as mesothelioma).

2–239   Lord Hoffmann endorsed the view expressed by Hale LJ in *Hatton v Sutherland*[746] that in the absence of knowledge of an employee's particular vulnerability to psychiatric harm, employers are entitled to assume that their employees are persons of ordinary fortitude. Since an employer was unlikely to have any specific knowledge of how a particular employee was likely to react to the risk of asbestos-related illness more than 30 years after he had left the employment, an assumption of ordinary fortitude was "inevitable".[747] Foreseeability was not a question of what a psychiatrist might foresee but what a judge, as an "educated layman", taking into account the evidence of psychiatrists, would foresee. Moreover, a test of foreseeability must also determine what it is that has to be foreseen. As Lord Hoffmann commented, in the case of psychiatric illness:

---

[744] [2007] UKHL 39; [2008] 1 A.C. 281.
[745] See para.12–001 n.1.
[746] [2002] EWCA Civ 76; [2002] I.C.R. 613.
[747] [2007] UKHL 39; [2008] 1 A.C. 281 at [25] and [26] per Lord Hoffmann.

"...the standard description of what should have been foreseen, namely that *the event which actually happened* would have caused psychiatric illness to a person of 'sufficient fortitude' or 'customary phlegm', has been part of the law since the speech of Lord Porter in *Bourhill v Young* [1943] A.C. 92, 117. It was plainly intended to make the test more difficult to satisfy than whether it was foreseeable that something might happen which would cause someone (or even a person of reasonable fortitude) to suffer psychiatric injury. The latter test would not be hard to satisfy, as is evidenced by the opinion of the majority of the House in *Page v Smith*."[748]

But the latter test, said his Lordship, applied only in the special circumstances of *Page v Smith*. The general rule still required a test of whether it was reasonably foreseeable that the event which actually happened (i.e. the creation of a risk of an asbestos-related disease) would cause psychiatric illness to a person of reasonable fortitude.[749]

The distinction between *Page v Smith* and *Grieves*, said Lord Hoffmann, was that **2–240** Mr Grieves' psychiatric illness had been caused by apprehension that the event may occur *in the future*. Since the creation of such a risk was not in itself actionable, it would be an unwarranted extension of the principle in *Page v Smith* to apply it to psychiatric illness caused by apprehension of the possibility of an unfavourable event which had not actually happened.[750] Lord Hope also considered that the causal chain between inhalation of asbestos dust and the psychiatric harm was stretched far beyond that envisaged in *Page v Smith*, which concerned an immediate response to a sudden alarming event. Mr Grieves' depression did not occur until 20 years after his inhalation of asbestos dust when told about the results of his X-ray. His depression was the result of the information he was given, not because of anything that happened or was done to him by his employers, who had exposed him to risk, not to stress.[751] On Lord Hope's analysis it is arguable that the claimants in the *CJD Litigation* should also have failed, since their psychiatric reaction was caused by what they were told, which was some years after they had been injected with human growth hormone which created a risk of developing CJD. The only realistic distinction was Morland J's specific finding that the psychiatric harm was foreseeable. Indeed, it was not only foreseeable, but had actually been foreseen by the defendants. Thus, the difference between *Page v Smith* and *Rothwell* appears to be that in *Page* the claimant's psychiatric condition was characterised as a reaction to an immediate or sudden, alarming event, whereas in *Rothwell*, Mr Grieves' depression was the product of ruminating, over a period of time, on the possibilities of an unpleasant death from mesothelioma. The difference between *Rothwell* and the *CJD Litigation* appears to be that in the latter case there was a specific finding that

---

[748] [2007] UKHL 39; [2008] 1 A.C. 281 at [30] (original emphasis).

[749] See also the comment of Lord Hope ([2007] UKHL 39; [2008] 1 A.C. 281) at [58]: "The question of what was reasonably foreseeable is approached with the benefit of hindsight, in the light of what actually happened: *Page v Smith* [1994] 4 All E.R. 522 at 549, per Hoffmann LJ. But that does not mean that everything that happened afterwards can be taken, with the benefit of hindsight, to be reasonably foreseeable."

[750] [2007] UKHL 39; [2008] 1 A.C. 281 at [33].

[751] [2007] UKHL 39; [2008] 1 A.C. 281 at [55]. See also per Lord Rodger at [95] distinguishing *Page v Smith* from *Grieves* on the basis that in *Page* the claimant developed his psychiatric illness as an immediate response to a past event, whereas in *Grieves* the claimant developed his illness on learning of a risk that he might possibly develop asbestosis or mesothelioma at some uncertain date in the future.

psychiatric harm was actually foreseen by the defendants, whereas in Mr Grieves' case the employers could not reasonably have been expected to foresee such a reaction in an individual of normal fortitude.[752]

2–241   **Bad news about destruction of claimant's property—liability in bailment**
As a general proposition, it might be thought that witnessing the destruction of one's property would not give rise to a claim in negligence for psychiatric harm, unless the claimant was also at risk of physical injury thereby qualifying as a "primary victim". If the claimant cannot qualify as a "secondary victim" without a close tie of love and affection to a person endangered or killed by the defendant's negligence, one might ask why a claimant should be able to succeed having witnessed the destruction of his property, no matter how cherished. How close a tie of love and affection can a claimant reasonably have with an item of property? The case of *Attia v British Gas*[753] is somewhat anomalous in this respect, but it can possibly be explained on the basis that the defendants were in a proximate relationship with the claimant and owed a duty of care to the claimant not to burn her house down. The question of whether they should also be liable for the claimant's resulting psychiatric harm was treated as a matter of causation and remoteness of damage.[754]

2–242   The issue arose, but was not resolved, in the medical context in *Yearworth v North Bristol NHS Trust*.[755] The claimants were six men who had undergone treatment for cancer. This carried a risk of damaging their fertility, and so prior to treatment they provided samples of sperm for storage for possible future use in fertility treatment. It was alleged that the stored sperm was effectively destroyed due to the defendants' negligence. Five of the claimants alleged that they had developed a psychiatric condition as a result of being informed that their sperm had been destroyed (the sixth claimed that he suffered mental distress). The Court of Appeal noted that in *Attia v British Gas* the claimant had actually witnessed the destruction of her home, but that the claimants in *Yearworth* had only learned of the destruction of their sperm after the event, and queried whether this distinction between witnessing the event and being informed about its consequences was

---

[752] For further discussion see Jones, "Liability for fear of future disease?" (2008) 24 P.N. 13.

[753] [1988] Q.B. 304; see para.2–204, n.656.

[754] This explanation is not without its difficulties. A motorist is under a duty of care not to damage another vehicle on the road, a duty owed to the owner of the vehicle. If A witnesses (from a safe distance) the destruction of his parked car due to the negligence of B, and suffers a psychiatric reaction to the event, the question of whether B is liable for A's psychiatric condition should arguably not turn simply on causation and remoteness of damage. If A's sister, with whom he has a normal, though not necessarily "close", sibling relationship was in the parked car at the time, A would probably not qualify as a "secondary victim" under the *Alcock* criteria. It might be thought distinctly odd that A could possibly recover damages for witnessing the damage to his car (applying *Attia v British Gas*) but not for witnessing the injury to his sister.

[755] [2009] EWCA Civ 37; [2010] Q.B. 1. The case is commented on by Hawes, "Property interests in body parts: *Yearworth v North Bristol NHS Trust*" (2010) 73 M.L.R. 130; Harmon and Laurie, "*Yearworth v North Bristol NHS Trust*: Property, Principles, Precedents and Paradigms" (2010) 69 C.L.J. 476; Priaulx, "Managing novel reproductive injuries in the law of tort: the curious case of destroyed sperm" (2010) 17 E.J.H.L. 81.

tenable.[756] However, the issue did not have to be determined because the Court concluded that, though the destruction of the claimants' sperm did not constitute "personal injury", the stored sperm was property capable of being owned by the men who had provided it and that this could give rise to an action in bailment.[757] Each claimant would have to establish that his psychiatric injury or distress was a reasonably foreseeable consequence of the breach of duty.[758] In bailment the measure of any damages to be awarded to the men was said to be more akin to that referable to breach of contract than to tort. So the question arose: if the loss of the sperm had occurred as a result of breach of a contract to store it, could the men have recovered damages for psychiatric injury or distress foreseeably suffered as a result of the breach? Under the law of contract, recovery for mental distress (and a fortiori for psychiatric injury) caused by breach of contract may be available where the contracts are:

"...are not purely commercial but which have as their object the provision of enjoyment, comfort, peace of mind or other non-pecuniary personal or family benefits."[759]

The arrangements between the claimants and the defendants were closely akin to contracts and should fall within this principle:

"The reference to peace of mind admirably fits the object of arrangements designed to preserve the ability of men to become fathers notwithstanding an imminent threat to their natural fertility. The arrangements were not in any way commercial and their object was, only too obviously, the provision to the men of non-pecuniary personal or family benefits. Any award of damages should reflect the realities behind these arrangements and their intended purpose."[760]

There was a specific promise by the defendants to the claimants. It followed that the law of bailment provided a remedy to the claimants for any foreseeable psychiatric injury, or actionable distress, caused by the breach.

In *Holdich v Lothian Health Board*,[761] on similar alleged facts to *Yearworth*, Lord **2–243** Stewart considered the position in Scots law and allowed a proof before answer for the pursuer's claims for mental distress, depression and loss of the chance of fatherhood (characterised as "loss of autonomy"). Lord Stewart clearly had some reservations about the property analysis adopted by the Court of Appeal in *Yearworth*, and acknowledged that an approach based on the notion of

---

[756] [2009] EWCA Civ 37; [2010] Q.B. 1 at [55]. Though, as the Court noted, this simply replicated the distinction applied to the recovery of foreseeable psychiatric harm by a "secondary victim" as a result of personal injury to another.

[757] See also *Lam v University of British Columbia* 2013 BCSC 2094; [2014] 5 W.W.R. 795 where claimants about to undergo chemotherapy treatment were given the opportunity to have their sperm stored in exchange for payment of an annual fee, so that there was a bailment for reward. Butler J held that the frozen sperm was the property of the claimants (and therefore satisfied the description of "goods" in the Warehouse Receipt Act 1996 (British Columbia) with the consequence that the defendants could not rely on an exclusion clause in the contract).

[758] [2009] EWCA Civ 37; [2010] Q.B. 1 at [54].

[759] [2009] EWCA Civ 37; [2010] Q.B. 1 at [56], citing *Johnson v Unisys Ltd* [2001] UKHL 13; [2003] 1 A.C. 518, at [70], per Lord Millett.

[760] [2009] EWCA Civ 37; [2010] Q.B. 1 at [57].

[761] [2013] CSOH 197; 2014 S.L.T. 495.

"witnessing the event or its immediate aftermath" was not readily applicable to the facts. His Lordship appeared to have greater confidence in the pursuer's claim in delict/tort being ultimately successful on the basis that, if legal proximity were to exist anywhere outside contractual and doctor–patient relationships, there was as good an argument for the existence of such a relationship between statutory cryostorage providers and individual service users trusting to the cryostore for fertility preservation as anywhere else. If that relationship gave rise to a duty of care not to cause reasonably foreseeable harm then the question was not whether the defenders owed a duty to avoid causing mental injury: the question was whether mental injury to the pursuer was reasonably foreseeable by the defenders as a consequence of any breach of their duty of care.[762]

(v) Deliberately misleading information

2–244   If a doctor can be liable for negligently providing false information then arguably there is an even stronger case where the defendant tells deliberate lies. In *Jinks v Cardwell*[763] a doctor who falsely told a wife that her husband had committed suicide by drowning in a bath because it would look better for the hospital was held liable for her "physical and emotional distress". At best he was negligent, said the judge, at worst callous and unfeeling. In *Frazer v Haukioja*[764] the defendant was held liable for a patient's psychiatric harm which developed as result of the defendant's decision not to get in touch with the patient to inform him that he had failed to diagnose a fracture of the patient's ankle. When the defendant did finally inform the patient of the error at a routine follow-up appointment some weeks later he misrepresented the severity of the fracture. The Ontario Court of Appeal held that the nature of the relationship between doctor and patient made it foreseeable that:

> "...a breach of that trust as blatant as the one that occurred in this case could have severe ramifications for his patient's mental health."[765]

2–245   In *Powell v Boladz*[766] the defendants admitted liability in respect of the death of a child following a failure to diagnose the child's condition. The parents alleged that a general practitioner had removed or falsified medical records concerning the child's death as part of a "cover up", and brought an action in respect of psychiatric damage allegedly caused as a result of the cover up. The Court of Appeal held that, though the parents of a child might be on a general practitioner's list of patients, nonetheless when the general practitioner is treating a child, the only patient seeking medical advice and treatment is the child, and it is to the child that the general practitioner owes a duty of care. The discharge of that duty in the case of a young child would usually involve giving advice and instructions to the parents, so that they can administer the appropriate medication, observe relevant symptoms and seek further medical assistance if need be, and in

---

[762] [2013] CSOH 197; 2014 S.L.T. 495 at [92] to [94].
[763] (1987) 39 C.C.L.T. 168, Ont HC.
[764] 2010 ONCA 249; (2010) 317 D.L.R. (4th) 688; (2010) 101 O.R. (3d) 528.
[765] 2010 ONCA 249; (2010) 317 D.L.R. (4th) 688; (2010) 101 O.R. (3d) 528 at [57].
[766] [1998] Lloyd's Rep. Med. 116, CA.

giving such advice, the doctor obviously owed a duty be careful. "But the duty is owed to the child, not to the parents."[767] Any duty owed by doctors to the parents would depend upon whether they were called upon to undertake treatment of the parents as patients. But a doctor who has been treating a patient who has died, who tells relatives what has happened, does not thereby undertake a doctor–patient relationship with the relatives. The mere fact that the person communicating the bad news is a doctor, does not, without more, mean that he undertakes the doctor–patient relationship.[768] The doctor might realise, on passing on bad news, that the shock was so great that some immediate treatment was necessary, but that situation was more akin to the doctor giving emergency treatment to an accident victim.[769] The fact that the relatives happened to be on the doctor's register as patients would make no difference, except to the extent that the doctor ought to have realised that they needed counselling or medical treatment in their own right as patients.[770] In that situation the doctor–patient relationship would exist in relation to the advice and treatment given and so a duty of care would arise. But on the alleged facts no duty of care was owed to the parents. Psychiatric harm was not foreseeable as a consequence of the claimants discovering the alleged "cover up" by alteration of the medical records following the death of their son.

An alternative approach might be to argue that a deliberate lie which causes psychiatric damage could be actionable under the principle of *Wilkinson v Downton*,[771] but in *Powell v Boladz* a claim based on the intentional infliction of psychological harm, relying on *Wilkinson v Downton*, was also rejected. Stuart-Smith LJ suggested that *Wilkinson v Downton* was authority for two propositions:

2–246

---

[767] [1998] Lloyd's Rep. Med. 116 at 123, per Stuart-Smith LJ. His Lordship drew an analogy with the duty said to be owed by the psychiatrist in *X (Minors) v Bedfordshire County Council* [1995] 2 A.C. 633 when examining a child and interviewing a parent for the purposes of discharging the local authority's care responsibilities, and an examination of a claimant by a doctor on behalf of an insurance company. "In neither of these cases does the doctor undertake to treat the person as a patient and his only duty is not to damage him in the course of the examination": [1998] Lloyd's Rep. Med. 116 at 123–124. Note, however, that the position of a psychiatrist examining a child whom it is suspected is a victim of abuse has changed following *JD v East Berkshire Community Health NHS Trust; K v Dewsbury Healthcare NHS Trust; K v Oldham NHS Trust* [2005] UKHL 23; [2005] 2 A.C. 373. Contrary to the ruling in *X v Bedfordshire County Council* the psychiatrist now owes a duty of care *to the child* (though not to the parents) in conducting such an examination, which would encompass more than simply not damaging the patient during the course of the examination. See paras 2–099 to 2–101.

[768] cf. *AB v Leeds Teaching Hospital NHS Trust* [2004] EWHC 644 (QB); [2005] Q.B. 506 where, at [201] to [203] Gage J distinguished *Powell v Boladz*, holding that a doctor could owe a duty of care to a parent when obtaining consent to the performance of a post-mortem on a child, on the basis that the purpose of carrying out the post-mortem was to enable the doctor to advise the parent about future pregnancies. See also the Scottish case of *Stevens v Yorkhill NHS Trust* [2006] CSOH 143; 2006 S.L.T. 889; (2006) 95 B.M.L.R. 1 where Temporary Judge CJ Macaulay QC held that a duty of care may be owed to a parent in these circumstances even if a doctor–patient relationship was not established. See further the discussion of these cases at paras 2–247 to 2–253.

[769] [1998] Lloyd's Rep. Med. 116 at 124.

[770] [1998] Lloyd's Rep. Med. 116 at 124.

[771] [1897] 2 Q.B. 57.

"…first, that making a statement known to be false with the intention that it should be believed and with the intention of causing injury, which in fact results, is actionable; and, secondly, that where the defendant's act is plainly calculated to produce some effect of the kind which was produced, an intention to produce it ought to be imputed to the defendant, regard being had to the fact that the effect was produced on a person in an ordinary state of health and mind. Another way of putting the second proposition is to say that a man, who foresees the consequences of his act, is to be taken to intend those consequences, even if he does not desire them."[772]

On this analysis, the facts of *Powell v Boladz* did not support the necessary degree of foresight for the imputed intent required under *Wilkinson v Downton*.

(vi)   Post-mortems and retained organs

2–247   Where a relative discovers, after the event, that a post-mortem examination has been carried out on a deceased loved one the relative may suffer significant distress. Distress is not sufficient, of course, to found a cause of action[773] but if that distress develops into a psychiatric condition the question arises whether the relative would have any claim in respect of that psychiatric reaction.[774] This issue was given particular emphasis by the "retained organs" scandal, which focused initially on two hospitals,[775] but was subsequently found to be a widespread

---

[772] [1998] Lloyds Rep. Med. 116 at 125. The second of these propositions can no longer be regarded as correct. In *Wainwright v Home Office* [2003] UKHL 53; [2004] 2 A.C. 406 at [45] Lord Hoffmann said that "imputed intention" will not suffice: "The defendant must actually have acted in a way which he knew to be unjustifiable and intended to cause harm or at least acted without caring whether he caused harm or not". In *Rhodes v OPO* [2015] UKSC 32; [2016] A.C. 219 the Supreme Court held that the necessary mental element for a claim under *Wilkinson v Downton* should no longer include imputed intention *as a matter of law*. This does not prevent a court from inferring an intention *as a matter of fact*: "There are statements (and indeed actions) whose consequences or potential consequences are so obvious that the perpetrator cannot realistically say that those consequences were unintended" (per Lord Neuberger at [112]). But recklessness is not sufficient to establish the required intention (at [87] and [113]). On the other hand, although *Wilkinson v Downton* does not provide a remedy for mere emotional distress which does not amount to recognised psychiatric injury, if the recognised psychiatric illness is the product of severe mental or emotional distress (as occurred in *Wilkinson v Downton* itself) it is not necessary for the defendant to have intended to cause the psychiatric illness; it is sufficient that he intended to cause the severe distress which in fact results in a recognised psychiatric illness ([2015] UKSC 32; [2016] A.C. 219 at [83], [87]). See further the discussion in *Clerk & Lindsell on Torts*, 22nd edn (London: Sweet & Maxwell, 2018), paras 15–14 to 15–17.

[773] See, e.g., the Irish case of *O'Connor v Lenihan* [2005] IEHC 176 where parents had suffered anger, distress and grief on learning that their children's organs had been retained after post-mortem, but had not developed a recognised psychiatric condition. Their claim was dismissed on the basis that they had not suffered any compensatable loss. Though see the discussion of the Scottish case of *Stevens v Yorkhill NHS Trust* [2006] CSOH 143; 2006 S.L.T. 889; (2006) 95 B.M.L.R. 1, below para.2–252.

[774] Norrie (1985) 34 I.C.L.Q. 442, 463 discussed the possibility of claims for psychiatric harm following unauthorised post-mortems, and, by extension, following the unauthorised removal of organs for transplantation contrary to the Human Tissue Act 1961. There is no duty of care owed to the relatives of a deceased person to store organs or tissue removed in a post mortem examination on the basis that it might be evidence in civil litigation in the future: *Dobson v North Tyneside Health Authority* [1997] 1 W.L.R. 596.

[775] Alder Hey Children's Hospital in Liverpool and Bristol Royal Infirmary. The report of the Inquiry at Alder Hey can be found at *http://www.gov.uk/government/publications/the-royal-liverpool-childrens-inquiry-report*. For a general discussion of proprietary rights in bodies and body parts in the

practice, whereby organs removed at post-mortem were, unknown to the relatives, retained for research purposes. The difficulty for relatives seeking to bring claims arising out of this knowledge, leaving aside the matter of demonstrating that they had developed a recognised psychiatric condition, is that they do not fit into the standard analysis of "primary" and "secondary" victims. They are not "primary" victims because they have not been exposed to the foreseeable risk of physical injury, and they are not "secondary" victims because, inter alia, they have not witnessed the events with their own unaided senses.

These issues were considered in *AB v Leeds Teaching Hospital NHS Trust*[776] which involved three lead claims in group litigation arising out of the retained organs cases (the Nationwide Organ Group Litigation). The three claims all involved organs removed from children (in one case a stillborn child) at post-mortems and retained in the hospitals where the post-mortems were carried out until they were disposed of by the hospitals. The claimants were parents of the deceased children. It was claimed that the organs were removed, retained and subsequently disposed of without the knowledge and consent of the claimants, and that as a result of this they had sustained psychiatric injury. In none of the cases had the organs been retained for the purposes of medical research. Two of the cases involved hospital post-mortems, and one a coroner's post-mortem. The difference between the two types of post-mortem in essence was that for a hospital post-mortem the relatives had to be asked if they objected to the post-mortem being carried out (usually referred to as a requirement to obtain consent) by virtue of the Human Tissue Act 1961.[777] A coroner's post-mortem does not require the consent (or non-objection) of the relatives. In the case of the hospital post-mortems the claimants had consented but alleged that either they had insisted that all organs and tissue should be returned with the body, or had they known that organs would be retained they would have opted to delay the child's funeral. Gage J accepted that the Human Tissue Act 1961 provided for no criminal sanctions nor any civil remedies for its breach. Section 2 of the Act required no more than a consent to a post-mortem being obtained without any further explanation having to be given. Thus:

2–248

> "There may be little conceptual difference between consent and non-objection, but the latter in my view implies a more passive approach than a requirement for consent."[778]

Wrongful interference   Gage J rejected a claim based on the tort of wrongful interference. There is no property in the body of a deceased person[779] but a part of a body may acquire the character of property which can be the subject of rights of possession and ownership where the body part has been the subject of the application of skill such as dissection or preservation techniques.[780] This

2–249

context of the Alder Hey Inquiry and the Bristol Royal Infirmary Inquiry see Skene (2002) 22 L.S. 102. See also Ellis [2001] J.P.I.L. 264; Austin (2002) 8 *Clinical Risk* 185.
[776] [2004] EWHC 644 (QB); [2005] Q.B. 506.
[777] Note that the Human Tissue Act 1961 was repealed by the Human Tissue Act 2004. See para.7–160.
[778] [2004] EWHC 644 (QB); [2005] Q.B. 506 at [127].
[779] *R. v Kelly* [1999] Q.B. 621 at 630.
[780] [2004] EWHC 644; [2005] Q.B. 506 at [148].

exception applies to the work and skill applied to body parts removed at post-mortem. The claimants had no right of burial and possession of organs lawfully removed at post-mortem and retained, and therefore there could be no action for wrongful interference with the body of the child.[781] On the other hand, said his Lordship, if a parent, when consenting to a post-mortem, specifically asked for the return of an organ, in certain circumstances it might be arguable that a cause of action based on conversion exists, but:

> "...in the absence of such a cause of action in respect of the body of a deceased person being recognised by an English court I am not prepared to hold that one does exist."[782]

Moreover, where a parent had stipulated that his or her consent to an hospital post-mortem was conditional on all organs removed being put back in the body this would give rise to a duty of care by the doctor to pass on that condition to the pathologist. It was conceded by the defendants that failure by the doctor to do this or by a pathologist to heed such a condition would prima facie amount to a breach of that duty of care:

> "In those circumstances, where a claim for negligence can arise, I see no reason or justification for constructing another cause of action which is not subject to the various common law controls inherent in any claim in negligence."[783]

2–250 **Negligence** The claim based on negligence only arose in the context of the hospital post-mortems, on the basis that the doctor owed a duty of care to the parents when seeking consent to a post-mortem (no consent being required for a coroner's post-mortem). The claims were for psychiatric harm, and therefore the question arose as to whether the claimants were "primary" or "secondary" victims. If they were classified as "secondary" victims, it was conceded that they would not be able to satisfy all of the *Alcock* criteria, and therefore the claims would fail. The problem was that the claimants did not fall into the conventional category of a "primary" victim (they were not exposed to a foreseeable risk of physical harm). Gage J commented that:

> "In my judgment, these claims do not fit easily into any of the descriptions given to primary and secondary victims. Tempting as it is to regard the primary/secondary victim dichotomy as not relevant in these claims the House of Lords has made it clear that those claiming solely for psychiatric injury must be placed in one or other category in order to determine whether or not the necessary control mechanisms come into play."[784]

Since, in his Lordship's view, Lord Oliver's categorisation of "secondary" victims involved a situation where, "as a pre-requisite, there was a primary victim to whom the defendant owed a duty of care"[785] the claimants could not be "secondary" victims. The question of whether a claimant was a "primary" or "secondary" victim was a question of fact, and the claimants fell into the "primary" victim category because:

---

[781] [2004] EWHC 644; [2005] Q.B. 506 at [161].
[782] [2004] EWHC 644; [2005] Q.B. 506 at [161].
[783] [2004] EWHC 644; [2005] Q.B. 506 at [161].
[784] [2004] EWHC 644; [2005] Q.B. 506 at [197].
[785] [2004] EWHC 644; [2005] Q.B. 506 at [198].

"First, unlike the secondary victims in *Alcock* and *Frost* the foreseeability test in these claims can be applied before the event, the event being the obtaining of consent for a post-mortem by the doctors. They are not cases where that test can only be conducted *ex post facto*. The claimants, at all times before and after that event are readily identifiable. Secondly, in my view there is force in the argument that the children were not primary victims. Neither the clinicians nor the pathologists could possibly have owed any duty of care to them after their death. In my opinion, it follows that if the claimants are victims at all they must be primary victims. Thirdly, if, but for this argument, there would exist a doctor–patient relationship, in my judgment, these claims fit more clearly into category 1 of Hale L.J.'s four categories [in *Hatton v Sutherland* [2002] EWCA Civ 76; [2002] 2 All E.R. 1 at [21]] than any of the other three. The nature of the doctor–patient relationship has frequently been described as akin to a contractual relationship. In these claims, the alleged negligence of the clinicians in obtaining consent from the claimants, is the very thing which, it is alleged, caused the psychiatric injury."[786]

Having concluded that the claimants were "primary" victims, nonetheless the question remained whether the claimants were owed a duty of care, and this in turn depended upon whether there was a doctor–patient relationship between the clinicians and the parents when the consent to post-mortem was obtained. Gage J held that a duty of care could be owed, on the basis that the purpose of carrying out the post-mortem on a baby was to enable the doctor to advise about future pregnancies, and whether, for example the abnormalities of the child were genetic. The most informed advice to the parents would involve obtaining results from a post-mortem:

2–251

"In my opinion taking consent for a post-mortem was not just an administrative matter bringing a doctor into contact with a mother. It was ... part of the continuing duty of care owed by the clinicians to the mother following the death of a child. In the circumstances, in my judgment, the necessary test of proximity between the claimants and clinicians is established."[787]

The defendants' argument that the taking of a consent to a post-mortem did not extend to a duty to protect the parents from subsequent psychiatric injury (since the Human Tissue Act 1961 s.2 made no reference to informed consent nor to a requirement that the nature of the post-mortem examination be explained) was rejected. Once the doctor–patient relationship was established the clinician owed a duty of care when seeking consent to a post-mortem:

"Although the statutory duty is to ensure non-objection, that must, in my judgment, involve some explanation of to what the parents are being asked not to object. Again, in my opinion, that must involve some explanation of the procedures of a post-mortem of which the removal and retention of organs is a relevant part. In the circumstances, I hold that the duty of care extended to giving the parents an explanation of the purpose of the post-mortem and what it involved including alerting them to the fact that organs might be retained."[788]

The requirement that there be a doctor–patient relationship means that many potential claimants who were not in the position of needing to know the cause of death in order to make a therapeutic judgment about a future course of action will probably fail to establish a duty of care.[789]

---

[786] [2004] EWHC 644; [2005] Q.B. 506 at [199].
[787] [2004] EWHC 644; [2005] Q.B. 506 at [203].
[788] [2004] EWHC 644; [2005] Q.B. 506 at [206].
[789] See *Powell v Boladz* [1998] Lloyd's Rep. Med. 116, para.2–245.

2–252   **Scotland**   The position in English law, as stated by Gage J, can be contrasted with the Scottish approach. In *Stevens v Yorkhill NHS Trust*[790] Temporary Judge Macaulay QC concluded that Scottish law supports a common law action in respect of the unauthorised removal and retention of organs from the body of a deceased person as an independent legal wrong, actionable by the surviving relatives, on the basis that it demonstrated such an insensitivity to the feelings of the relatives that it constituted an affront to their dignity and gave rise to a claim for damages. That common law action had not been affected by the passage of either the Human Tissue Act 1961 or the Human Tissue (Scotland) Act 2006. Rather, if anything, the Human Tissue (Scotland) Act 2006 reinforced:

> "...the legal policy underlining the existence in Scots law of the independent legal wrong of the unauthorised removal and retention of organs."[791]

Judge Macaulay acknowledged that English law had taken a different stance on the existence of an independent wrong.[792] His Lordship went on to consider a claim in negligence on the basis of the claimant's allegation that, though she had agreed to a post-mortem on her baby, the defendants had not explained what a post-mortem entailed, and in particular had not explained that organs would or might be removed, or that organs would or might be retained, and therefore she did not give informed permission for the post-mortem examination. Judge Macaulay concluded that there were no allegations of fact that would support a doctor–patient relationship. A relationship of proximity between a doctor and a parent who was not a patient would not in itself create a doctor–patient relationship.[793] His Lordship went on to conclude, however, that (contrary to the view expressed by Gage J in *AB v Leeds Teaching Hospital NHS Trust*) a doctor–patient relationship was not necessary to establish a duty of care owed to a parent where that parent had been jointly involved with the treating doctor in the decision to turn off the child's life support system, allowing the child to die. This was:

> "...an important background when posing the question as to whether or not, at the time consent for the post mortem was requested, there existed sufficient proximity between the pursuer and the treating doctor as to give rise to a duty of care."[794]

The process of seeking consent took place against a background of the claimant's previous reliance on the medical staff for advice in connection with her child's treatment. The defendants' decision to withhold the "precise details" of the post-mortem tended to indicate that the doctor was assuming responsibility

---

[790] [2006] CSOH 143; 2006 S.L.T. 889; (2006) 95 B.M.L.R. 1 at [39] to [62], relying in particular on *Conway v Dalziel* (1901) 3 F. 918; 1901 9 S.L.T. 86, IH; *Hughes v Robertson*, 1913 S.C. 394; 1912 2 S.L.T. 503. The case involved an application to strike out the claim on the basis that the pleadings disclosed no reasonable cause of action.

[791] [2006] CSOH 143; 2006 S.L.T. 889; (2006) 95 B.M.L.R. 1 at [58]. Whether a claimant would have to demonstrate that she suffered from a recognised psychiatric injury or could claim merely for "hurt feelings" was left open by Judge Macaulay, though his Lordship appeared to prefer the latter possibility: see at [63].

[792] [2006] CSOH 143; 2006 S.L.T. 889; (2006) 95 B.M.L.R. 1 at [62].

[793] [2006] CSOH 143; 2006 S.L.T. 889; (2006) 95 B.M.L.R. 1 at [67].

[794] [2006] CSOH 143; 2006 S.L.T. 889; (2006) 95 B.M.L.R. 1 at [78].

towards the claimant to convey only what he wanted to disclose, in the knowledge that she would rely upon what was communicated to her in deciding whether or not to consent.[795] Given the foreseeability of injury to the claimant, and the policy underlying the Human Tissue Act 1961 of contact with relatives in some circumstances in connection with the removal and retention of organs, it was at least arguable, said his Lordship, that the relationship between the claimant and the doctor seeking consent was sufficiently proximate to give rise to a duty of care.

Judge Macaulay was aware that Gage J had taken a different approach in *AB v Leeds Teaching Hospital NHS Trust*, requiring a doctor–patient relationship as the basis for a duty of care. However, Gage J had appeared to accept that if a parent had consented to a post-mortem being carried out on her child on condition that any removed organs were put back in the body before burial, the doctor could owe a duty of care to ensure that the condition was communicated to the pathologist.[796] Judge Macaulay concluded that Gage J would have found that there was a duty of care in such circumstances even in the absence of a doctor–patient relationship. His Lordship considered, however, that the existence of a duty of care should not depend on the parent's state of knowledge as to what may happen at a post-mortem. There was:

2–253

"...a certain unfairness in saying that a duty of care arises when a parent is fully informed as to what may happen, and consequently is able to impose conditions, but no such duty arises to the parent who gives consent in ignorance, without being offered the opportunity of imposing conditions. It does not seem to me that a relationship of proximity should depend upon whether the parent, in such circumstances, is aware or ignorant of important facts that the doctor does not volunteer."[797]

There is considerable force in this reasoning. If a parent with relevant knowledge can impose conditions on her consent and as a consequence the doctor assumes responsibility to that parent to take reasonable care to see that the conditions are met, it would look odd if the doctor could avoid the imposition of a duty of care by declining to inform the parent without the relevant knowledge about the possibility of organs being retained, which is the very matter about which the parent subsequently complains.

Human Tissue Act 2004   The Human Tissue Act 2004 repealed the Human Tissue Act 1961 and provides a detailed statutory framework for the removal, storage and use of human organs and other tissue, including a requirement for "appropriate consent" of patients or persons who stood in a "qualifying relationship" with a deceased person. The Act creates specific criminal offences for breach of its provisions, but does not expressly provide any civil remedy.[798] It seems likely that any claim by relatives of a deceased person in respect of psychiatric harm attributable to breach of the consent provisions of the Act will

2–254

---

[795] [2006] CSOH 143; 2006 S.L.T. 889; (2006) 95 B.M.L.R. 1 at [79].
[796] [2004] EWHC 644 (QB); [2005] Q.B. 506 at [183].
[797] [2006] CSOH 143; 2006 S.L.T. 889; (2006) 95 B.M.L.R. 1 at [82].
[798] See further para.7–161. The Act is commented on by D. Price (2005) 68 M.L.R. 798.

face similar difficulties to those that featured in *AB v Leeds Teaching Hospital NHS Trust* and *Stevens v Yorkhill NHS Trust.*

6. DUTY OWED BY THIRD PARTIES TO PREVENT HARM BY DOCTOR

2–255   Doctors do not practise medicine in a vacuum. They function in the context of a regulatory system laid down by the Medical Act 1983 and regulations made under that Act, administered by the General Medical Council (GMC). The GMC maintains a register of doctors and has the power to suspend a doctor or strike a doctor from the register if they are considered unfit to practise. Thus, an issue arises as to whether a negligent failure by the GMC to deal with an errant doctor, thereby permitting the doctor to continue to practise and harm patients, could give rise to an action against the GMC at the instance of injured patients.

2–256   The common law has always drawn a distinction between the infliction of harm through some positive action and merely allowing harm to occur by failing to prevent it. This is the distinction between misfeasance and nonfeasance. An omission is characterised by passive inaction, and the general rule is that there is no liability for nonfeasance. In other words there is no general obligation to take positive steps to confer a benefit on others, by preventing harm befalling them. The usual example is that there is no obligation to rescue someone in danger. Public bodies that exercise regulatory functions are effectively placed in the position of statutory "rescuers" in the sense that they are charged with regulating those who, unregulated, might abuse their position and cause harm to the public. The reaction of the common law to claims against regulatory bodies has generally been to deny the existence of a duty of care owed to members of the public who have suffered loss due to the actions of the regulated organisations or individuals.[799] This is often on the basis that their regulatory functions were exercisable in the interest of the public as a whole rather than for the benefit of individuals; that they had insufficient control over the day-to-day activities of the those being regulated, and that the alleged duty would be owed to an unlimited class. Moreover, the claims have generally arisen in the context of purely economic losses. Where a claimant has suffered personal injury it might be thought that there is a stronger case for redress against a regulatory body.[800]

---

[799] See, e.g. *Yuen Kun-yeu v A-G of Hong Kong* [1988] A.C. 175—commissioner of deposit-taking companies in Hong Kong regulated deposit-taking businesses and had wide discretionary powers to refuse to register or revoke the registration of a company considered to be unfit to take deposits. No duty of care owed to claimants who deposited money with a registered deposit-taking company which subsequently went into liquidation; *Davis v Radcliffe* [1990] 1 W.L.R. 821—statutory regulator of banks on the Isle of Man did not owe a duty of care to depositors who lost money when a bank's licence was revoked and it was wound up with substantial debts.

[800] See, e.g., *Health and Safety Executive v Thames Trains Ltd* [2003] EWCA Civ 720; (2003) 147 S.J.L.B. 661 where the Court of Appeal refused to strike out as disclosing no reasonable cause of action a claim in negligence by a train operator against the Health and Safety Executive (HSE) arising out of the Ladbroke Grove train accident. The accident was caused by a faulty signalling system. The train operator sought contribution from HSE on the basis that HSE owed a duty of care to the passengers. The Court of Appeal held that, though it was clear that there was no arguable case for breach of statutory duty, it was not possible to say that the HSE did not owe a duty of care to passengers until there had been a hearing with a full finding of facts. There were allegations that the

The question of whether the GMC could be held responsible for failing   **2–257**
appropriately to exercise its disciplinary functions over a doctor, with the result
that the doctor was permitted to continue to practise and thereby harm the
claimant, has not arisen in the UK, but the issue has been addressed in Canada. In
McClelland v Stewart[801] the claimants alleged that they were sexually assaulted
by a doctor during the course of medical treatment. They brought an action
against the College of Physicians and Surgeons of British Columbia for
negligence and misfeasance in public office, alleging that the College had
knowledge of specific circumstances relating to the sexual assaults and had failed
in its statutory duty to investigate the doctor and take appropriate action. The
College had a statutory duty to serve and protect the public and was mandated to
investigate breaches of standards of competence and to discipline members. The
statute provided immunity from an action for damages for anything done or
omitted in good faith in the performance of any duty or power under the statute
by the College. The College sought to strike out the claims on the basis that they
did not disclose a cause of action. L. Smith J struck out the claim for misfeasance
in public office but refused to strike out the claim based on negligence. It could
not be said that it was plain and obvious that the College did not owe a duty of
care to the claimants. If the College had notice that the doctor was sexually
assaulting patients during the course of medical examinations and failed to take
reasonable steps to prevent such assaults in the future it was reasonably
foreseeable that patients might be assaulted. The relationship between the College
and the patients, including expectations, reliance and the nature of the interests
involved (i.e. personal injury) was such that it was at least arguable that a prima
facie duty of care could be owed. The policy considerations pointing against a
duty of care did not necessarily require a conclusion that there was no duty of
care. Moreover, it was possible that a private law duty of care could co-exist with
the College's general obligation to protect the public interest. Although the
College had a defence if it had acted in good faith, there was an allegation of bad
faith in the pleadings, and the immunity would not apply if the claimants were
able to establish an absence of good faith.

L.Smith J distinguished two decisions of the Supreme Court of Canada in which   **2–258**
regulatory agencies were held not to owe a duty of care. In *Cooper v Hobart*[802]
the Supreme Court held that the Registrar of Mortgage Brokers, a statutory
regulator, did not owe a duty of care to investors who lost money as a result of the
conduct of a mortgage broker; and in *Edwards v Law Society of Upper Canada*[803]

HSE had assumed responsibility by their involvement in the design or positioning of the signal, or the
safety of the track generally, in other words that they had permitted an unsafe signalling system, not
simply that they did nothing. It was also arguable that passengers relied on the HSE performing their
duty: "In the context of a track run by Railtrack with individual rail companies profiting from its use,
the outside and independent regulator ensuring safety is arguably an important safeguard on which
rail users rely", per Waller LJ at [25]. See also *Perrett v Collins* [1998] 2 Lloyd's Rep. 255; [1999]
P.N.L.R. 77 where the Court of Appeal held that an inspector and a regulatory body which had
negligently issued a certificate of airworthiness for a light aircraft could owe a duty of care to a
passenger injured when the aircraft crashed.
[801] (2003) 229 D.L.R. (4th) 342, BCSC; aff'd (2004) 245 D.L.R. (4th) 162, BCCA.
[802] (2001) 206 D.L.R. (4th) 193.
[803] (2001) 206 D.L.R. (4th) 211, SCC.

it was held that the Law Society did not owe a duty of care to claimants who lost money as a result of the alleged failure of the Society, after it had started an investigation into the improper use of a solicitor's trust account, to monitor the trust account or warn the claimants that it had failed to do so. The British Columbia Court of Appeal upheld the judge's refusal in *McClelland v Stewart* to strike out the negligence claim, though commenting that before the decision of the Supreme Court of Canada in *Barreau du Québec v McCullock-Finney*[804] the outcome may well have been different.[805] In *Barreau du Québec v McCullock-Finney* the Supreme Court of Canada held that a regulator could owe a duty of care to a member of the public adversely affected by its failure adequately to deal with a member of the profession being regulated, in this case a lawyer. Though it had to be demonstrated that the professional regulator had acted in bad faith, the concept of bad faith should be given a broader meaning than simply malice or intention to harm, and so could encompass serious carelessness or recklessness. There had been a virtually complete absence of diligence by the Barreau in investigating and disciplining the claimant's former lawyer, which amounted to gross carelessness and serious negligence. Given that the fundamental mandate of the Barreau was to protect the public, and the claimant (as a client of the lawyer that the Barreau had failed to discipline) was a clearly identified victim, the Supreme Court upheld the Québec Court of Appeal's award of $25,000 damages.

2–259   *Cooper v Hobart* and *Edwards v Law Society of Upper Canada* are broadly consistent with the approach of the English courts to actions against regulatory agencies in respect of losses sustained by members of the public, allegedly as the result of the negligent failure by the regulatory agency to control the conduct of the person who was meant to be subject to regulation for the protection of the public interest.[806] All of these cases involved claims for economic loss. It remains to be seen whether a claim based on personal injury or death would meet the same fate, though in *X (Minors) v Bedfordshire County Council*[807] Lord Browne-Wilkinson, in holding that a social services authority owed no duty of care to protect children at risk from injury caused by others, commented that:

> "…a common law duty of care would cut across the whole statutory system set up for the protection of children at risk."

2–260   The authority of *X (Minors) v Bedfordshire County Council* has been undermined to some extent by the decision of the House of Lords in *JD v East Berkshire Community Health NHS Trust*[808] upholding the decision of the Court of Appeal that, in the light of the Human Rights Act 1998, the decision that no duty of care could be owed to children suspected of being abused when carrying out the statutory investigation could no longer stand. The combined appeals in *JD v East*

---

[804] (2004) 240 D.L.R. (4th) 410.

[805] (2004) 245 D.L.R. (4th) 162 at [14].

[806] See, e.g. *Yuen Kun-yeu v A.-G. of Hong Kong* [1988] A.C. 175; *Davis v Radcliffe* [1990] 1 W.L.R. 821; *Rowling v Takaro Properties Ltd* [1988] A.C. 473; *Minories Finance Ltd v Arthur Young* [1989] 2 All E.R. 105; *Mills v Winchester Diocesan Board of Finance* [1989] Ch. 428; *Harris v Evans* [1998] 1 W.L.R. 1285; [1998] 3 All E.R. 522.

[807] [1995] 2 A.C. 633 at 749.

[808] [2005] UKHL 23; [2005] 2 A.C. 373.

Berkshire did not concern the question of a regulatory authority's responsibility for failing to prevent harm by a professional, but the argument that a duty of care cannot be owed if it would "cut across the whole statutory system set up for the protection of children at risk" was clearly rejected in *JD v East Berkshire*. There is no obvious reason why a statutory regulatory regime for the protection of "children" should be any different from a statutory regulatory regime for the protection of "patients". Moreover, it is unclear how a duty of care imposed, say, on the GMC would "cut across" its regulatory role, which is explicitly for the protection of the public. It is difficult to see how the GMC can protect the public from seriously incompetent doctors without protecting the individual patients of such a doctor. In other words, imposing a duty of care would be entirely consistent with the GMC's statutory role. However, whether it would be appropriate to impose a duty of care on a regulatory body involves wider considerations, not least whether a regulatory body should be required to fund compensation for patients.[809] In most instances, a claim against the doctor would be dealt with by the NHS Trust for which he or she worked, or, in the case of a general practitioner or a doctor engaged in private practice, by the doctor's medical defence organisation. The problem would become significant, however, in any case where the doctor was not covered by professional indemnity "insurance", whether because none had been taken out or because the defence organisation had refused cover (which would be likely in the case of deliberate harm by the doctor).[810]

---

[809] cf. *Schubert Murphy v The Law Society* [2017] EWCA Civ 1295 where the Court of Appeal held that it was at least arguable that the Law Society could owe a duty of care to the claimant solicitors, who were acting for a purchaser of property, if it had negligently listed an imposter as a solicitor on the official Roll of solicitors published on its website, because solicitors and members of the public relied on the accuracy of the Roll. The claimants had relied on a "solicitor's undertaking" given by the imposter to discharge a mortgage on the property from the purchase monies, but the fraudster disappeared with the client's purchase money without discharging the mortgage. It was inappropriate, said the Court of Appeal, to come to a conclusion about a duty of care without findings of fact.

[810] The medical defence organisations are not insurance companies, and though they may grant a member indemnity, members do not have a right to indemnity, only a right to have an application for indemnity considered fairly: *Medical Defence Union Ltd v Department of Trade* [1980] Ch. 82; *Whetstone (t/a Welby House Dental Practice) v Medical Protection Society Ltd* [2014] EWHC 1024 (QB) (permission to appeal refused: [2015] EWCA Civ 127). Nor does a patient with a valid claim against a member of a defence organisation have a right to seek judicial review of the defence organisation's decision to refuse indemnity: *R. (on the application of Moreton) v Medical Defence Union Ltd* [2006] EWHC 1948 (Admin); [2007] LS Law Med. 180. Although there is a "public interest" in patients who have received negligent treatment being indemnified, there is no guarantee of indemnification: "There is no form of safety net for those who are negligently treated by practitioners who have no insurance at all", [2006] EWHC 1948 (Admin); [2007] LS Law Med. 180 at [26] per Newman J. Note that the Medical Act 1983 s.44C requires a person who holds a licence to practise to have in force an adequate and appropriate indemnity arrangement which provides cover in respect of liabilities which may be incurred in carrying out work as a medical practitioner. Breach of this provision, however, does not give rise to a civil action. See also, in relation to general practitioners' responsibility to have indemnity arrangements in place, the National Health Service (General Medical Services Contracts) Regulations 2015 (SI 2015/1862) reg.91 and the National Health Service (Personal Medical Services Agreements) Regulations 2015 (SI 2015/1879) reg.83. In relation to other healthcare professions see the Health Care and Associated Professions (Indemnity Arrangements) Order 2014 (SI 2014/1887) amending (and in some instances for the first time imposing) statutory provisions requiring indemnity arrangements to be in place.

2–261   In *Godden v Kent and Medway Strategic Health Authority*[811] the claimants argued that the defendant health authority owed a common law duty of care to take steps to protect them from a general practitioner who had been convicted of a number of indecent assaults on patients, arising from the National Health Service Act 1977 s.29. This section conferred authority to make arrangements for the provision of general medical services in a particular locality. The claimants accepted that it did not create an action for breach of statutory duty "simpliciter". Gray J struck out the claim as disclosing no reasonable cause of action, since s.29 did not provide that the defendants were responsible for the provision of medical services in their locality (which was the responsibility of medical practitioners); rather it was concerned with the structure and administration of the NHS. However, his Lordship refused to strike out an allegation that a common law duty of care owed to patients at risk of abuse from the general practitioner arose from the knowledge that employees of the health authority had acquired of his actions (for which the health authority could be vicariously liable), since there was nothing in the Act which could be said to have excluded the existence of such a duty of care.[812]

---

[811] [2004] EWHC 1629 (QB); [2004] Lloyd's Rep. Med. 521.
[812] See the comment of Lord Hoffmann in *Gorringe v Calderdale Metropolitan Borough Council* [2004] UKHL 15; [2004] 1 W.L.R. 1057 at [38]: "A hospital trust provides medical treatment pursuant to the public law duty in the National Health Service Act 1977, but the existence of its common law duty is based simply upon its acceptance of a professional relationship with the patient no different from that which would be accepted by a doctor in private practice. The duty rests upon a solid, orthodox common law foundation and the question is not whether it is created by the statute but whether the terms of the statute (for example, in requiring a particular thing to be done or conferring a discretion) are sufficient to exclude it."

CHAPTER 3

STANDARD OF CARE—GENERAL PRINCIPLES

The standard of care, and whether the defendant has failed to meet that standard, are normally the central issues in an action for medical negligence. Essentially, the question is: was the defendant careless? In law, the test for breach of duty in the tort of negligence is whether the defendant's conduct was reasonable in all the circumstances of the case. If it was reasonable he was not negligent; if it was unreasonable he was. At this level of abstraction the test is almost meaningless, since it begs all the important questions, namely what *is* reasonable and which circumstances of the case have to be considered. It is only when the general is applied to the particular that the term "reasonable care in all the circumstances" acquires any significance.

3–001

Within the blanket term "reasonable care" it is possible to identify some general principles which the courts have employed in the decision-making process about what constitutes negligence. They are, however, in practical terms, no more than guidelines, and as often as not competing principles point to different outcomes. The question of where the balance between negligence and due care is to be drawn can only be appreciated by developing a common-sense "feel" for the way in which the courts use these guidelines. This chapter deals with the general principles applied to the issue of breach of duty, and Ch.4 looks at specific types of medical negligence. There is, inevitably, some overlap between these two chapters, because they seek to provide different perspectives on the case law.

3–002

Medical evidence is invariably a vital element in an action for medical negligence, but the importance attached to expert opinion should not obscure the underlying basis for a finding that the defendant has been negligent, or not (as the case may be). This is that, in the light of the expert evidence, the defendant has taken an unjustified risk, for example, or has failed to keep up to date, or has undertaken a task beyond his competence, or conversely that the risk was justified by the potential benefit to the patient, or the harm was unforeseeable, and so on. In other words, expert opinion about the defendant's conduct (whether favourable or unfavourable) should itself be measured against the general principles applied to the question of breach of duty. This point was emphasised by the House of Lords in *Bolitho v City and Hackney Health Authority*[1] where Lord Browne-Wilkinson made it clear that the court has to weigh expert evidence in a form of risk-benefit analysis:

3–003

---

[1] [1998] A.C. 232 at 241–242.

"...the court has to be satisfied that the exponents of the body of opinion relied upon can demonstrate that such opinion has a logical basis. In particular in cases involving, as they so often do, the weighing of risks against benefits, the judge before accepting a body of opinion as being responsible, reasonable or respectable, will need to be satisfied that, in forming their views, the experts have directed their minds to the question of comparative risks and benefits and have reached a defensible conclusion on the matter."

1. THE BASIC PRINCIPLE

3–004   When jury trials were the norm in civil litigation the issue of whether the defendant had been negligent was for the jury to decide, and so it was treated as a question of fact. There are two stages, however, in this process. First, there must be an assessment by the court of how, in the circumstances, the defendant *ought* to have behaved—what standard of care should he have exercised? This enquiry necessarily involves a value judgment which should be made by the court. That judgment may be conditioned, but should not necessarily be determined, by the evidence. It is here that the hypothetical "reasonable man" is employed, partly as a measure of careless conduct and partly as a device to obscure the policy element of a judicial decision.[2] In a famous dictum Alderson B said:

"Negligence is the omission to do something which a reasonable man, guided upon those considerations which ordinarily regulate the conduct of human affairs, would do, or doing something which a prudent and reasonable man would not do."[3]

This judicial abstraction has also been described as the ordinary man, the average man, or the man on the Clapham omnibus.[4] The standard of care expected of the reasonable man is objective. It does not take account of the subjective attributes of the particular defendant.[5] Nor, despite references to the average man, is it necessarily determined by the average conduct of people in general if that conduct is routinely careless. Similarly, there is no concept of an "average" standard of care by which a defendant might argue that he has provided an adequate service on average and should not be held liable for the occasions when his performance fell below the norm. No matter how skilled the defendant's conduct was, he will be responsible for even a single occasion when he fell below the standard of reasonable care.[6]

---

[2] See, e.g. P. Cane, *Atiyah's Accidents, Compensation and the Law*, 8th edn (Cambridge: Cambridge University Press, 2013), pp.32–36.

[3] *Blyth v Birmingham Waterworks Co.* (1856) 11 Exch. 781 at 784.

[4] *Hall v Brooklands Auto Racing Club* [1933] 1 K.B. 205 at 217.

[5] *Glasgow Corporation v Muir* [1943] A.C. 448 at 457. This includes both the individual's physical attributes and his mental state, so that a mental disorder which prevents a defendant from appreciating the nature of his conduct or its consequences is irrelevant: *Dunnage v Randall* [2015] EWCA Civ 673; [2016] Q.B. 639 (defendant suffering from undiagnosed florid paranoid schizophrenia held liable for burn injuries to claimant who attempted to rescue the defendant when he set himself alight). It is only where it can be said that the defendant has done nothing himself to cause the injury that he escapes liability: [2015] EWCA Civ 673; [2016] Q.B. 639 at [133] per Vos LJ. For discussion of the case see J. Goudkamp and M. Ihuoma, "A tour of the tort of negligence" (2016) 32 P.N. 137.

[6] *Wilsher v Essex Area Health Authority* [1987] Q.B. 730 at 747, per Mustill LJ. The courts have not accepted a distinction between "ordinary" negligence and "gross" negligence. In *Wilson v Brett* (1843) 11 M. & W. 113 Rolfe B said that there was no difference: "it was the same thing with the addition of

The second stage requires a decision about whether on the facts of the case (as determined from the evidence) the defendant's conduct fell below the appropriate standard. This is truly a question of fact. Although these two stages are logically discrete, in practice it may be difficult to separate findings of "fact" and value judgments about the defendant's conduct.

3–005

(a) The reasonable doctor

Since the ordinary or average person would be ill-equipped to judge the competence of a professional, a person who professes a special skill is judged, not by the standard of the man on the Clapham omnibus, but by the standards of his peers. Thus, for the "reasonable man" is substituted the "reasonable professional", be it doctor, lawyer, accountant, architect, etc.[7]

3–006

The *Bolam* test   The classic statement of the test of professional negligence is the direction to the jury of McNair J in *Bolam v Friern Hospital Management Committee*.[8] Now widely known as the "*Bolam* test", this statement of the law has been approved by the House of Lords on a number of occasions as the touchstone of liability for medical negligence.[9] Moreover, the Court of Appeal has confirmed that the test is not restricted to doctors, but is of general application to any profession or calling which requires special skill, knowledge or experience.[10]

3–007

McNair J explained the law in these terms:

3–008

"But where you get a situation which involves the use of some special skill or competence, then the test whether there has been negligence or not is not the test of the man on the Clapham omnibus, because he has not got this special skill. The test is the standard of the ordinary skilled man exercising and professing to have that special skill. A man need not possess the highest expert skill at the risk of being found negligent ... it is sufficient if he exercises the ordinary skill of an ordinary competent man exercising that particular art."[11]

---

a vituperative epithet." Thus, any failure to meet the standard of reasonable care constitutes a breach of duty: Dugdale and Stanton, *Professional Negligence*, 3rd edn (London: Butterworths, 1998), para.15.03.
[7] "The public profession of an art is a representation and undertaking to all the world that the professor possesses the requisite ability and skill. An express promise or express representation in the particular case is not necessary", per Willes J in *Harmer v Cornelius* (1858) 5 C.B. (N.S.) 236 at 246.
[8] [1957] 2 All E.R. 118.
[9] *Whitehouse v Jordan* [1981] 1 All E.R. 267: treatment; *Maynard v West Midlands Regional Health Authority* [1984] 1 W.L.R. 634: diagnosis; *Bolitho v City and Hackney Health Authority* [1998] A.C. 232: failure to attend. See also *Chin Keow v Government of Malaysia* [1967] 1 W.L.R. 813, Privy Council. Note, however, that a different standard is applied to information disclosure: *Montgomery v Lanarkshire Health Board* [2015] UKSC 11; [2015] A.C. 1430; para.7–015.
[10] *Gold v Haringey Health Authority* [1988] Q.B. 481 at 489: "I can see no possible ground for distinguishing between doctors and any other profession or calling which requires special skill, knowledge or experience," per Lloyd LJ. In *Whitehouse v Jordan* [1981] 1 All E.R. 267 at 276j Lord Edmund-Davies prefaced his restatement of the *Bolam* test with the comment that "doctors and surgeons fall into no special category".
[11] [1957] 2 All E.R. 118 at 121.

[255]

"Not every error of judgment, of course, but only those errors which a reasonably competent professional man, acting with ordinary care, might commit. So explained I stand by every word I used in *Whitehouse v Jordan*. It is of the first importance so that 'medical malpractice' cases should not get out of hand here as they have done in the United States of America."

So explained, the term "error of judgment" is redundant as a guide to what constitutes negligence. It merely represents the conclusion that, applying the *Bolam* test, the defendant has not been negligent.

3–018   The Canadian courts have apparently accepted that an "error of judgment" may excuse the defendant. In *Wilson v Swanson*[30] Rand J said that:

"An error of judgment has long been distinguished from an act of unskilfulness or carelessness or due to lack of knowledge … [T]he honest and intelligent exercise of judgment has long been recognised as satisfying the professional obligation."

It has been treated as a specific defence,[31] although it may be that the term is used as a post hoc explanation of a finding that the doctor exercised reasonable care notwithstanding the occurrence of injury to the patient.[32] On this basis it stands in the same category as statements that doctors cannot guarantee results, that they are not insurers, and so on.

2.   COMMON PROFESSIONAL PRACTICE

3–019   As a general rule within the tort of negligence where the defendant has acted in accordance with the common practice of others in a similar situation this will be strong evidence that he has not been negligent.[33] People do not normally adopt systematic practices that pay careless disregard for the safety of others. Following a common practice is only *evidence*, however, it is not conclusive, since the court may find that the practice is itself negligent.[34] There may be many reasons, such as convenience, cost or habit, why a particular practice is commonly followed, which have nothing to do with reasonable prudence against potential harm to others. In the graphic words of Lord Tomlin: "Neglect of duty does not cease by repetition to be neglect of duty."[35]

3–020   A central feature of medical negligence claims is the importance that is attached to compliance with common or accepted practice. It will be recalled that in *Bolam v Friern Hospital Management Committee* McNair J directed the jury that:

---

[30] (1956) 5 D.L.R. (2d) 113 at 120, SCC; approved by Ritchie J in *Vail v MacDonald* (1976) 66 D.L.R. (3d) 530 at 535, SCC; *Lapointe v Hôpital Le Gardeur* (1992) 90 D.L.R. (4th) 7 at 14, SCC.

[31] Picard and Robertson, *Legal Liability of Doctors and Hospitals in Canada*, 4th edn (Canada: Thomson Reuters, 2007), pp.364–367.

[32] Thus, where defendants have made a "judgment call" they are not necessarily negligent simply because damage has occurred: *Pilon v Bouaziz* [1994] 1 W.W.R. 700, BCCA.

[33] *Morton v William Dixon Ltd* 1909 S.C. 807 at 809; *Morris v West Hartlepool Steam Navigation Co. Ltd* [1956] A.C. 552 at 579.

[34] See, e.g. *Lloyds Bank Ltd v E.B. Savory & Co.* [1933] A.C. 201; *Cavanagh v Ulster Weaving Co. Ltd* [1960] A.C. 145; *General Cleaning Contractors v Christmas* [1953] A.C. 180 at 193, per Lord Reid; *Roberge v Bolduc* (1991) 78 D.L.R. (4th) 666, 710, SCC.

[35] *Bank of Montreal v Dominion Gresham Guarantee and Casualty Co.* [1930] A.C. 659, 666; *Carpenters' Co. v British Mutual Banking Co. Ltd* [1937] 3 All E.R. 811 at 820, per Slesser LJ.

"A doctor is not guilty of negligence if he has acted in accordance with a practice accepted as proper by a *responsible* body of medical men skilled in that particular art ... Putting it the other way round, a doctor is not negligent, if he is acting in accordance with such a practice, merely because there is a body of opinion that takes a contrary view."[36]

There is no reason why the general approach taken by the courts to accepted practice should not also apply to actions for medical negligence. Within the *Bolam* test attention would then focus on whether the practice which the defendant had followed was accepted by *responsible* medical opinion, with the court deciding whether on the evidence before it the body of opinion which approved of the defendant's conduct could be said to be responsible. There are, however, some older judicial statements which appear to take the view that the practice of the medical profession is determinative of the issue, and that it is not open to the court to condemn as negligence a commonly adopted practice. It may be that such statements reflected the inherent ambiguity in the *Bolam* test itself, the conflation of the normative judgment of what *ought* to have happened with the factual judgment of what usually *does* happen. But as the House of Lords made clear in *Bolitho v City and Hackney Health Authority*[37] the courts must be careful to distinguish these elements of the test. What usually happens is evidence of what ought to have happened, but it is not conclusive.

(a) Complying with professional practice

In *Vancouver General Hospital v McDaniel*[38] Lord Alness said that a defendant charged with negligence can "clear his feet" if he shows that he has acted in accordance with general and approved practice. This view was repeated by Maugham LJ in *Marshall v Lindsey County Council*:   3–021

"An act cannot, in my opinion, be held to be due to a want of reasonable care if it is in accordance with the general practice of mankind. What is reasonable in a world not wholly composed of wise men and women must depend on what people presumed to be reasonable constantly do."[39]

There are many cases in which actions for medical negligence have been dismissed on the basis that the doctor conformed to an accepted practice of the profession.[40]

Where there is more than one common practice, as the *Bolam* test contemplates, compliance with one of the practices will normally excuse the defendant. In   3–022

---

[36] [1957] 2 All E.R. 118 at 122, emphasis added; *Holmes v Board of Hospital Trustees of the City of London* (1977) 81 D.L.R. (3d) 67 at 91, per Robins J, Ont HC: "Where in the exercise of his judgment a physician selects one of two alternatives, either of which might have been chosen by a reasonable and competent physician, he will not be held negligent"; *Darley v Shale* [1993] 4 Med. L.R. 161, NSWSC.

[37] [1998] A.C. 232 at 241–242; see para.3–034.

[38] (1934) 152 L.T. 56 at 57–58.

[39] [1935] 1 K.B. 516 at 540.

[40] e.g. *Vancouver General Hospital v McDaniel* (1934) 152 L.T. 56; *Whiteford v Hunter* [1950] W.N. 553; *Bolam v Friern Hospital Management Committee* [1957] 2 All E.R. 118; *Gold v Haringey Health Authority* [1988] Q.B. 481.

Maynard v West Midlands Regional Health Authority[41] Lord Scarman, delivering the judgment of the House of Lords, expressed the position in the following terms:

> "A case which is based on an allegation that a fully considered decision of two consultants in the field of their special skill was negligent clearly presents certain difficulties of proof. It is not enough to show that there is a body of competent professional opinion which considers that theirs was a wrong decision, if there also exists a body of professional opinion, equally competent, which supports the decision as reasonable in the circumstances ... Differences of opinion and practice exist, and will always exist, in the medical as in other professions. There is seldom any one answer exclusive of all others to problems of professional judgment. A court may prefer one body of opinion to the other: but that is no basis for a conclusion of negligence."[42]

3–023   This statement is unexceptional. In a later passage, however, Lord Scarman appeared to take the view that compliance with accepted practice will, without more, absolve a doctor from liability:

> "...a judge's 'preference' for one body of distinguished professional opinion to another also professionally distinguished is not sufficient to establish negligence in a practitioner whose actions have received the seal of approval of those whose opinions, truthfully expressed, honestly held, were not preferred. If this was the real reason for the judge's finding he erred in law even though elsewhere in his judgment he stated the law correctly. For in the realm of diagnosis and treatment negligence is not established by preferring one respectable body of professional opinion to another. Failure to exercise the ordinary skill of a doctor (in the appropriate specialty, if he be a specialist) is necessary."[43]

3–024   Here, the "seal of approval" of a distinguished body of professional opinion, held in good faith, acquits the defendant of negligence. Lord Scarman seems to equate a *competent* (or "responsible") body of professional opinion with "distinguished" or "respectable" in fact. He thus conflates accepted practice with the absence of negligence. This interpretation is supported by Lord Scarman's speech in *Sidaway v Bethlem Royal Hospital Governors* where he said:

> "The *Bolam* principle may be formulated as a rule that a doctor is not negligent if he acts in accordance with a practice accepted at the time as proper by a responsible body of medical opinion even though other doctors adopt a different practice. *In short, the law imposes the duty of care; but the standard of care is a matter of medical judgment.*"[44]

---

[41] [1984] 1 W.L.R. 634; *Belknap v Meakes* (1989) 64 D.L.R. (4th) 452 at 473–475, BCCA.

[42] [1984] 1 W.L.R. 634 at 638; *Ratty v Haringey Health Authority* [1994] 5 Med. L.R. 413 at 416, CA, where Kennedy LJ said that it was important "once it was accepted that [the defendants' expert witnesses] represented a responsible and respectable body of colo-rectal opinion, to accept without qualification their [evidence] when evaluating the conduct of the second defendant"; *Dunne v National Maternity Hospital* [1989] I.R. 91 at 109 (Supreme Court of Ireland); *Kaban v Sett* [1994] 1 W.W.R. 476 at 479–480, Man QB; aff'd [1994] 10 W.W.R. 620, Man CA. On the other hand, where there has been not been a considered clinical judgment, but rather "a catalogue of errors", the approach in *Maynard* to competing bodies of professional opinion is not relevant: *Le Page v Kingston and Richmond Health Authority* [1997] 8 Med. L.R. 229 at 240, QBD.

[43] [1984] 1 W.L.R. 634 at 639.

[44] [1985] A.C. 871 at 881, emphasis added; cf. Sir John Donaldson MR in the Court of Appeal, [1984] 1 All E.R. 1018 at 1028: "The definition of the duty of care is a matter for the law and the courts. They cannot stand idly by if the profession, by an excess of paternalism, denies its patients a real choice. In a word, the law will not permit the medical profession to play God."

It is also apparent from earlier passages in his Lordship's speech in *Sidaway* that   **3–025**
he considered the *Bolam* test required the determination of whether there has
been a breach of a doctor's duty of care to be conducted "exclusively by
reference to the current state of responsible and competent professional opinion
and practice at the time".[45] As Lord Scarman himself recognised:

> "…the implications of this view of the law are disturbing. It leaves the determination of a legal
> duty to the judgment of doctors."

It was this point which led Lord Scarman to dissent in *Sidaway* on the question of
the standard to be applied to the disclosure of information to patients about the
risks of treatment, but he was apparently content to apply the standard of
"responsible medical judgment" (as his Lordship had identified it) to diagnosis
and treatment.[46]

This was an interpretation of the *Bolam* test that was not accepted by Lord Bridge   **3–026**
in *Sidaway* who said:

> "… the issue whether non-disclosure in a particular case should be condemned as a breach of
> the doctor's duty of care is an issue to be decided primarily on the basis of expert medical
> evidence, applying the *Bolam* test … Of course, if there is a conflict of evidence whether a
> responsible body of medical opinion approves of non-disclosure in a particular case, the judge
> will have to resolve that conflict. But, even in a case where, as here, no expert witness in the
> relevant medical field condemns the non-disclosure as being in conflict with accepted and
> responsible medical practice, I am of opinion that the judge might in certain circumstances
> come to the conclusion that disclosure of a particular risk was so obviously necessary to an
> informed choice on the part of the patient that no reasonably prudent medical man would fail
> to make it."[47]

In other words, the court could condemn even a universally followed practice as
to risk disclosure as negligent on the basis that the hypothetical reasonable doctor
would not have adopted it.[48]

Other contexts   Beyond the context of medical negligence the courts have had   **3–027**
no difficulty with the notion that commonly adopted practices may themselves be

---

[45] [1985] A.C. 871 at 876.
[46] [1985] A.C. 871 at 882.
[47] [1985] A.C. 871 at 900. See also Sir John Donaldson MR in *Sidaway v Bethlem Royal Hospital Governors* [1984] 1 All E.R. 1018 at 1028: "…in an appropriate case, a judge would be entitled to reject a unanimous medical view if he were satisfied that it was manifestly wrong and that the doctors must have been misdirecting themselves as to their duty in law." Thus, a practice must be "rightly" accepted as proper by the profession. His Lordship drew a specific analogy with the cases in which the courts had held the common practice of employers to be negligent: see n.49, below. See further the comment of Farquharson LJ in *Bolitho v City and Hackney Health Authority* [1993] 4 Med. L.R. 381 at 386, cited below, para.3–045, n.99.
[48] A majority of their Lordships in *Sidaway v Bethlem Royal Hospital Governors* said that the *Bolam* test applied to all aspects of the doctor's duty of care (diagnosis, advice and treatment), and so there was no particular reason to confine Lord Bridge's dictum to cases of information disclosure. The Supreme Court has now ruled that a different test applies to the disclosure of information about the risks of treatment: see *Montgomery v Lanarkshire Health Board* [2015] UKSC 11; [2015] A.C. 1430; para.7–015.

negligent. This has been most apparent in cases of employers' liability,[49] but it is also evident in some cases involving professional liability. In *Lloyds Bank v Savory & Co.*,[50] for example, Lord Wright rejected the proposition that a bank is not negligent if it takes all the precautions usually taken by bankers:

> "...in cases where the ordinary practice of bankers fails in making due provision for a risk fully known to those experienced in the business of banking."

In *Edward Wong Finance Co. Ltd v Johnson, Stokes and Masters*[51] the Privy Council held that a particular conveyancing practice widely followed in Hong Kong was negligent because the practice had an inherent risk which would have been foreseen by a person of reasonable prudence, and there was no need to take this risk. The fact that virtually all other solicitors adopted the same practice was not conclusive evidence that it was prudent, nor did it make the risk less apparent or unreal.

3–028   It might be added that condemning accepted practice does not depend upon the risks being "fully known to those experienced" in the profession, but may extend to those risks which ought reasonably to have been known, but were simply not addressed by the profession as a whole. This point may be illustrated by *Re The Herald of Free Enterprise: Appeal by Captain Lewry*[52] which concerned an appeal by the captain of the *Herald of Free Enterprise* against the revocation of his master's certificate following the disaster at Zeebrugge harbour. The ferry had set sail with both the inner and outer doors to the main deck open, and capsized soon after leaving the harbour with a substantial loss of life. The Divisional Court found that the practice of failing to check that the doors had been closed was prevalent in respect of most, if not all, of the masters who commanded ferries of that class. The court concluded, however, that this was not evidence of the required standard of care, but rather of a general and culpable complacency, born perhaps of repetitive routine, and fostered by the shortcomings of the ships' owners and managers. There had been a failure to apply common sense in respect of elementary precautions required for the safety of the ship.

3–029   **Canada**   In other common law jurisdictions the courts have been careful to ensure that, ultimately, decisions as to what constitutes negligence remain for the court to determine. In *Anderson v Chasney*[53] Coyne JA commented that if following general practice was a conclusive defence:

---

[49] As, e.g. in *Cavanagh v Ulster Weaving Co. Ltd* [1960] A.C. 145; *Morris v West Hartlepool Steam Navigation Co. Ltd* [1956] A.C. 552; *Stokes v Guest, Keen & Nettlefold (Bolts & Nuts) Ltd* [1968] 1 W.L.R. 1776 at 1783.
[50] [1933] A.C. 201 at 203.
[51] [1984] A.C. 296. See also *Nye Saunders & Partners v Bristow* (1987) 37 Build. L.R. 92, CA, where it was held that no responsible body of architects would have failed to warn clients about the risks of inflation when undertaking a building project; *Roberge v Bolduc* (1991) 78 D.L.R. (4th) 666, SCC, where a notary was held liable in negligence despite following a general notarial practice because the practice was simply not reasonable.
[52] *The Independent*, 18 December 1987, D Ct.
[53] [1949] 4 D.L.R. 71, 85, Man CA; aff'd [1950] 4 D.L.R. 223, SCC. See also *Hajgato v London Health Association* (1982) 36 O.R. (2d) 669 at 693, per Callaghan J: the courts have "a right to strike down substandard approved practice when commonsense dictates such a result. No profession is

"...a group of operators by adopting some practice could legislate themselves out of liability for negligence to the public by adopting or continuing what was an obviously negligent practice, even though a simple precaution, plainly capable of obviating danger which sometimes might result in death, was well known."

Thus, expert evidence from doctors as to a general or approved practice could not be accepted as conclusive on the issue of negligence, especially where the conduct in question did not involve a matter of technical skill and experience. Similarly, in *Crits v Sylvester*[54] Schroeder JA commented that:

"Even if it had been established that what was done by the anaesthetist was in accordance with 'standard practice', such evidence is not necessarily to be taken as conclusive on an issue of negligence, particularly where the so-called standard practice related to something which was not essentially conduct requiring medical skill and training either for its performance or a proper understanding of it ... If it was standard practice, it was not a safe practice and should not have been followed."[55]

Australia   King CJ explained the justification for this in the Australian case of *F v R*:   3–030

"... professions may adopt unreasonable practices. Practices may develop in professions, particularly as to disclosure, not because they serve the interests of the clients, but because they protect the interests or convenience of members of the profession. The court has an obligation to scrutinise professional practices to ensure that they accord with the standard of reasonableness imposed by the law. A practice as to disclosure approved and adopted by a profession or a section of it may be in many cases the determining consideration as to what is reasonable ... The ultimate question, however, is not whether the defendant's conduct accords with the practices of his profession or some part of it, but whether it conforms to the standard of reasonable care demanded by the law. That is a question for the court and the duty of deciding it cannot be delegated to any profession or group in the community."[56]

---

above the law and the courts on behalf of the public have a critical role to play in monitoring and precipitating changes where required in professional standards".

[54] (1956) 1 D.L.R. (2d) 502; aff'd (1956) 5 D.L.R. (2d) 601.

[55] (1956) 1 D.L.R. (2d) 502; aff'd (1956) 5 D.L.R. (2d) 601 at 514; *Reynard v Carr* (1983) 30 C.C.L.T. 42, 68, BCSC: "If that was the standard practice at the time, it was not good enough because it was 'inconsistent with provident precautions against a known risk'. Simply because it was 'usual and long established' is not a sufficient justification," per Bouck J; *Winrob v Street* (1959) 28 W.W.R. 118 at 122, BCSC; *Hajgato v London Health Association* (1982) 36 O.R. (2d) 669 at 693; *Roberge v Bolduc* (1991) 78 D.L.R. (4th) 666 at 710, SCC, per L'Heureux-Dubé J: "The fact that a professional has followed the practice of his or her peers may be strong evidence of reasonable and diligent conduct, *but it is not determinative*. If the practice is not in accordance with the general standards of liability, i.e., that one must act in a reasonable manner, then the professional who adheres to such a practice can be found liable, depending on he facts of each case" (original emphasis); *ter Neuzen v Korn* (1995) 127 D.L.R. (4th) 577 at 591, SCC; *Comeau v Saint John Regional Hospital* [2001] NBCA 113; (2001) 9 C.C.L.T. (3d) 223, NBCA (doctors held liable despite following "accepted" practice, which was inconsistent with measures that a reasonable, prudent practitioner would take in the same circumstances).

[56] (1982) 33 S.A.S.R. 189 at 194, SC of S Aus, approved by Zelling J in *Battersby v Tottman* (1985) 37 S.A.S.R. 524 at 537; and Lockhart, Sheppard and Pincus JJ in *E. v Australian Red Cross Society* (1991) 105 A.L.R. 53 at 68, 82–83, 87, Aus Fed CA. See also *Goode v Nash* (1979) 21 S.A.S.R. 419 at 422, SC of S Aus; *Albrighton v Royal Prince Alfred Hospital* [1980] 2 N.S.W.L.R. 542 at 562–563, per Reynolds JA, NSWCA: "...it is not the law that, if all or most of the medical practitioners in Sydney habitually fail to take an available precaution to avoid foreseeable risk of injury to their patients, then none can be found guilty of negligence." In Australia, following publication of the Ipp Report (*Review of the Law of Negligence*, 2002) state legislatures have largely codified the law of

This approach was approved by the High Court of Australia in *Rogers v Whitaker*,[57] where it was accepted that, while evidence of acceptable medical practice might be regarded as a useful guide, it was for the court to determine whether the defendant's conduct conformed to the standard of reasonable care demanded by the law. The duty of deciding on this standard could not be delegated to the medical profession. This view was reiterated by the High Court of Australia in *Naxakis v Western General Hospital*[58] where it was said that the test for medical negligence is not what other doctors say they would or would not have done in the same or similar circumstances. To treat what other doctors do or do not do as decisive was to adopt a variant of the *Bolam* test, but the *Bolam* test had been rejected in *Rogers v Whitaker*.[59]

3–031   **Ireland**   In *Dunne v National Maternity Hospital*[60] the Supreme Court of Ireland said that although a medical practitioner may rely on a general and approved practice of the profession, this will not exculpate him if the claimant establishes that the practice has "inherent defects which ought to be obvious to any person giving the matter due consideration".[61] In *Gottstein v Maguire and Walsh*[62] Johnson J held that the failure of the intensive care unit of a hospital to have a nurse or doctor skilled in the replacement of a tracheostomy tube if it should become dislodged, which was the common practice in Ireland, was:

"...an inherent defect in what appears to be the practice, which ought to be obvious to any person giving the matter due consideration and having given it due consideration, it is obvious to me."

---

negligence. One consequence has been that "peer professional opinion" (the proposition that a professional is not negligent if it is established that the professional acted in a manner that was widely accepted in Australia by a significant number of respected practitioners in the field) now operates as a *defence*, which it is for the defendant to prove, rather than setting the content of the standard of care which the claimant has to prove the defendant failed to meet: *Sydney South West Area Health Service v MD* [2009] NSWCA 343; (2009) 260 A.L.R. 702; *Dobler v Halverson* [2007] NSWCA 335; (2007) 70 N.S.W.L.R. 151; *Brakoulias v Karunaharan* [2012] VSC 272; *Grinham v Tabro Meats Pty Ltd* [2012] VSC 491.
[57] (1992) 109 A.L.R. 625; [1993] 4 Med. L.R. 79; Trindade (1993) 109 L.Q.R. 352; McDonald and Swanton (1993) 67 A.L.J. 145; Malcolm (1994) 2 Tort L. Rev. 81.
[58] [1999] HCA 22; (1999) 162 A.L.R. 540 at [18].
[59] [1999] HCA 22; (1999) 162 A.L.R. 540 at [19] per Gaudron J.
[60] [1989] I.R. 91 at 109.
[61] See also *Collins v Mid-Western Health Board* [2000] 2 I.R. 154 (Supreme Court of Ireland): "...a lay tribunal will be reluctant to condemn as unsafe a practice which has been universally approved in a particular profession. The defects in a practice universally followed by specialists in the field are unlikely to be as obvious as the test requires: if they were, it is a reasonable assumption that it would not be so followed. But the principle, which was first stated by the court in *O'Donovan v Cork County Council* [1967] I.R. 173, is an important reminder that, ultimately, the courts must reserve the power to find as unsafe practices which have been generally followed in a profession" per Keane J at 156. In *O'Donovan v Cork County Council* [1967] I.R. 173 at 193, Walsh J commented that: "If there is a common practice which has inherent defects, which ought to be obvious to any person giving the matter due consideration, the fact that it is shown to have been widely and generally adopted over a period of time does not make the practice any the less negligent. Neglect of duty does not cease by repetition to be neglect of duty."
[62] [2004] IEHC 416; [2007] 4 I.R. 435 at [32].

The hospital was held to have been negligent notwithstanding its claim to be "the leading hospital in the country" and that it was following standard practice.

England and Wales pre-*Bolitho* On some occasions the English courts have found that compliance with common practice was negligent. In *Clarke v Adams*[63] the claimant was being treated for a fibrositic condition of the heel and he was warned by the physiotherapist to say if he felt anything more than a "comfortable warmth". He suffered a burning injury resulting in the leg being amputated below the knee. Slade J held the defendant liable for giving an inadequate warning to enable the claimant to be safe, although it was the very warning that the defendant had been taught to give. In *Hucks v Cole* Sachs LJ said that:

3–032

> "When the evidence shows that a lacuna in professional practice exists by which risks of grave danger are knowingly taken, then, however small the risks, the courts must anxiously examine that lacuna—particularly if the risks can be easily and inexpensively avoided. If the court finds, on an analysis of the reasons given for not taking those precautions that, in the light of current professional knowledge, there is no proper basis for the lacuna, and that it is definitely not reasonable that those risks should have been taken, its function is to state that fact and where necessary to state that it constitutes negligence. In such a case the practice will no doubt thereafter be altered to the benefit of patients."[64]

His Lordship added that the fact that other practitioners would have done the same thing as the defendant was a weighty factor to be put in the scales on his behalf, but it was not conclusive. The court had to be vigilant to see whether the reasons given for putting a patient at risk were valid the light of any well-known advance in medical knowledge, or whether they stemmed from a residual adherence to out of date ideas.

Commenting on *Hucks v Cole* in *Bolitho v City and Hackney Health Authority*[65] Dillon LJ said that the court could only adopt the approach of Sachs LJ and reject medical opinion on the ground that the reasons of one group of doctors do not really stand up to analysis:

3–033

> "...if the court, fully conscious of its own lack of medical and clinical experience, was nonetheless clearly satisfied that the views of that group of doctors were *Wednesbury* unreasonable, i.e. views such as no reasonable body of doctors could have held."

With respect, there is no need to import the restrictive public law principles applied on applications for judicial review into the private law concept of negligence. On applications for judicial review the courts are anxious not to undermine the principle of Parliamentary sovereignty by substituting their own view as to how a public body charged by Parliament with exercising a discretion

---

[63] (1950) 94 S.J. 599; see also *Jones v Manchester Corpn* [1952] Q.B. 852 at 863–864, per Singleton LJ citing Oliver J, the trial judge. Some commentators consider *Clarke v Adams* to be of questionable authority on the basis that it predates *Bolam v Friern Hospital Management Committee* [1957] 2 All E.R. 118: see Montgomery (1989) 16 J. of Law and Soc. 319, 323; Dugdale and Stanton, *Professional Negligence*, 3rd edn (London: Butterworths, 1998), para.15.26, n.6. The *Bolam* test, however, was not new, it simply encapsulated earlier statements of the law. This, at least, was Lord Diplock's interpretation: *Sidaway v Bethlem Royal Hospital Governors* [1985] A.C. 871 at 892.
[64] (1968), [1993] 4 Med. L.R. 393 at 397.
[65] [1993] 4 Med. L.R. 381 at 392; [1993] P.I.Q.R. P334.

"It is only where a judge can be satisfied that the body of expert opinion cannot be logically supported at all that such opinion will not provide the bench mark by reference to which the defendant's conduct falls to be assessed."[72]

(ii)   Applying Bolitho to reject common practice

3–037   In *Marriott v West Midlands Health Authority*[73] the claimant sustained a head injury in a fall and was unconscious for about half an hour. He was admitted to hospital, and, after X-rays and neurological observations he was discharged the next day. At home he was lethargic, had headaches and no appetite. He did not improve. Eight days after the fall his general practitioner visited the claimant at home, but the neurological tests he carried out showed no abnormality. The general practitioner advised the claimant's wife to telephone him if the claimant deteriorated and suggested analgesics for the headaches. Four days later the claimant's condition suddenly deteriorated, and following emergency surgery on a skull fracture he was left paralysed and with a speech disorder. At the trial, the defendant's expert considered that whilst other general practitioners might have referred the claimant back to hospital, nonetheless it was reasonable in the circumstances to leave the claimant at home with the guidance the defendant had given. The claimant's expert said that, in the circumstances, a general practitioner ought to have referred the patient to hospital for a comprehensive neurological examination. The trial judge held that if there was a body of professional opinion which supported the course of leaving a patient at home in these circumstances, then it was not a reasonable body of opinion. The risk might be small, but the consequences if something went wrong would be disastrous for the patient:

> "In such circumstances, it is my view that the only reasonably prudent course in any case where a general practitioner remains of the view that there is a risk of an intracranial lesion such as to warrant the carrying out of neurological testing and the giving of further head injury instructions, then the only prudent course judged from the point of view of the patient is to re-admit for further testing and observation."[74]

The Court of Appeal held that the trial judge was entitled reject the defendant's expert evidence. She had subjected the body of opinion to analysis to see whether it was properly regarded as reasonable, applying *Bolitho*. She had considered the small risk of something going wrong, but had weighed that against the seriousness of the consequences for the claimant if the risk did materialise, and the fact that the facilities available in modern hospitals for carrying out scans and other diagnostic procedures were readily available.[75]

---

[72] As Tugendhat J observed in *Zarb v Odetoyinbo* [2006] EWHC 2880 (QB); (2007) 93 B.M.L.R. 166 at [33] there is a certain asymmetry in the burden placed on claimant and defendant respectively. For the claimant to succeed she must satisfy the court that the defendant's experts' views cannot withstand logical analysis, whereas the defendant does not have to demonstrate that the claimant's experts' opinions cannot be logically supported; merely that her own experts' views are capable of withstanding logical analysis.

[73] [1999] Lloyd's Rep. Med. 23; Jones (1999) 15 P.N. 117.

[74] [1999] Lloyd's Rep. Med. 23 at 26–27, cited by Beldam LJ.

[75] An expert's views which are based on a mistaken diagnosis are likely to be condemned as illogical: *Drake v Pontefract Health Authority; Wakefield and Pontefract Community NHS Trust* [1998] Lloyd's Rep. Med. 425 at 445, QBD. See also *Hunt v NHS Litigation Authority* unreported 28 July 2000,

In *AB v Leeds Teaching Hospital NHS Trust*[76] Gage J considered that a practice   **3–038**
universally adopted by clinicians for many years of not informing the parents of
deceased children that at a post-mortem their child's organs could be removed
and may be retained was not acceptable:

> "Looked at objectively, from a common-sense point of view, in my judgment, a significant
> number, if not all, bereaved mothers of recently deceased children would want to know if
> organs from their deceased child were to be retained following a post-mortem examination."[77]

Although the expert evidence was that doctors were taught to respect a dead
body, and that the parents' wishes with respect to the body of a deceased child
were to be respected and complied with, these views simply did not fit with a
failure to explain to parents that a post-mortem might well involve the removal
and retention of an organ, particularly a heart or a brain.[78] Although the doctors
agreed that parents were entitled to have their wishes respected and complied
with, those wishes could not be complied with unless it was explained to the
parents what was involved in a post-mortem examination. The practice of the
profession was a "blanket practice" carried out by virtually all physicians, and
therefore it could not have involved a case by case therapeutic judgment.

Although in *Bolitho v City and Hackney Health Authority* Lord Browne-   **3–039**
Wilkinson considered that it would be "rare" for the court to reach a conclusion
that professional opinion is not capable of withstanding logical analysis, the
modern judicial approach of analysing expert evidence with some care means that
it is less uncommon for expert evidence to be rejected as illogical than it once
was,[79] and the frequency with which the *Bolitho* "exception" is or is not applied
is arguably simply not relevant to the court's task in weighing the expert

---

QBD, where the defendant's expert's view that the circumstances for the administration of the drug
syntocinon to a mother in the course of labour (in order to speed up contractions) had not changed in
a 47-minute period during which there were signs of foetal distress on the CTG trace was rejected as
"without logical support", not least because it was inconsistent with other answers that the witness
had given in evidence. See further *Reynolds v North Tyneside Health Authority* [2002] Lloyd's Rep.
Med. 459, discussed at para.3–090, where the defendants' argument that it was reasonable to ignore a
small risk of catastrophic consequences, when the burden of precautions was minimal, was rejected as
indefensible; *Hutchinson v Leeds Health Authority* unreported 6 November 2000, at [78], where
Bennett J held an expert's evidence to be "less than helpful (putting it tactfully) and illogical". In
Mellor v Sheffield Teaching Hospitals NHS Trust [2004] EWHC 780 (QB); [2004] All E.R. (D) 195
(Apr) at [245] Gross J said that discharging from hospital a patient who was at high risk of a coronary
event without undertaking further investigations "would not be logically sustainable", given the
potentially serious consequences if the event should occur; and in *Dowson v Sunderland Hospitals
NHS Trust* [2004] Lloyd's Rep. Med. 177, QBD at [18] it was held that a "wait and see" policy in a
situation where the foetus could suffer possible brain damage following mismanagement in the use of
syntocinon was not capable of withstanding logical analysis.
[76] [2004] EWHC 644 (QB); [2005] Q.B. 506.
[77] [2004] EWHC 644 (QB); [2005] Q.B. 506 at [230].
[78] [2004] EWHC 644 (QB); [2005] Q.B. 506 at [232].
[79] See R. Mulheron, "Trumping *Bolam*: a critical legal analysis of *Bolitho's* 'gloss'" (2010) 69 C.L.J.
609 who identifies seven factors by which to assess whether expert evidence can be categorised as
"illogical" or "irrational", namely does the expert evidence: (1) ignore a clear and simple precaution
which was not followed but which would have avoided the adverse outcome; (2) consider conflicts of
duties among patients, and resource limitations governing the medical practice; (3) weigh the
comparative risks/benefits of the medical practice, as compared to other courses of conduct; (4) take

evidence.[80] In *Shortall v Mid Essex Hospital Services NHS Trust*[81] the claimant underwent laparoscopic bowel surgery. There were complications when the anastomosis leaked and, after emergency surgery, the claimant ended up with a permanent colostomy. The defendant surgeons had not performed a "bicycle tyre" test on the bowel during the operation, which was a simple, risk-free test to check that there were no leaks. An expert for the defendants argued that if the donuts obtained after construction of the anastomosis were complete, this provided good evidence that the anastomosis was complete throughout its circumference and:

> "...therefore a responsible body of surgeons relies on the inspection of the donuts to confirm that the anastomosis is technically sound. In these circumstances a responsible body of surgeons does not carry out a bicycle tyre test to further assess the anastomosis."

Judge Cooke QC pointed out that this involved a non-sequitur:

> "...the availability of 'good evidence' does not excuse a responsible surgeon from taking advantage of the obtaining of potentially better information when it can be obtained easily and risk-free with the effect of enabling the prompt avoidance for very dangerous complications."[82]

The fact that there was in 2008 a group of surgeons who, for whatever reason, had failed to adopt what by then had been established to have been an important safeguard against devastating consequences could not assist the defendants.[83]

---

account of public expectations of acceptable medical practice; (5) take into account the whole factual context; (6) is the evidence internally consistent; and (7) does it adhere to the correct legal test governing the requisite standard of care.

[80] *Lane v Worcestershire Acute Hospitals NHS Trust* [2017] EWHC 1900 (QB) at [16] per Judge Pepperall QC: "There was some argument before me as to the rarity of what has often been referred to as the *Bolitho* exception. In my judgment, such argument is sterile. No doubt counsel saw some forensic advantage in seeking to persuade me that a *Bolitho* finding is rare (as Mr Coughlan emphasised) or rather more common since 1998 (as Dr Fox suggested), but my task is properly to apply the *Bolam* test as further explained in *Bolitho* to this case without worrying about whether that approach leads me to a commonplace conclusion."

[81] [2014] EWHC 246 (QB).

[82] [2014] EWHC 246 (QB) at [35].

[83] [2014] EWHC 246 (QB) at [61]. One study in the medical literature had shown that the risk of a leak and associated problems was 77 per cent lower when the test was done routinely. Where the defendant has not put forward any articulated or logical reason for adopting a surgical technique that increases the risk to the patient, and there has been no risk assessment, a finding of breach of duty is likely: see *Brown v Scarborough & North East Yorkshire Healthcare NHS Trust* [2009] EWHC 3103 (QB) (relatively inexperienced surgeon used a 20cm incision instead of the more usual 15cm incision when performing an hysterectomy). Judge Thornton QC at [47] observed that: "No surgeon can reasonably operate using a method which significantly increases the risk of harm unless that method is necessary for the greater good of the patient and unless there is no other reasonable way of achieving the desired results which would also reduce the risk of ancillary or collateral harm." In *Taaffe v East of England Ambulance Service NHS Trust* [2012] EWHC 1335 (QB); [2013] Med. L.R. 406; (2012) 128 B.M.L.R. 71 an expert's evidence that the response of paramedics not to advise a patient with chest pain and a family history of coronary heart disease to attend hospital fell within the range of reasonable responses by paramedics was held to be neither reasonable nor logical because it was inconsistent with the need to look at all relevant information by taking a full clinical history before making the decision. See also *Webb v Liverpool Women's NHS Foundation Trust* [2015] EWHC 133 (QB), para.4–121; *Ireland v Secretary of State for Health* [2016] EWHC 194 (QB) at [61].

Similarly, in *Ganz v Childs*[84] Foskett J held that a general practitioner who has even a relatively minor suspicion that a child may be suffering from pneumonia should refer the child to hospital for tests, given that pneumonia can give rise to life-threatening consequences and that in children its development can be unpredictable and rapidly progressive. Any weighing of the risks and benefits of investigating further if there was a suspicion of pneumonia came down in favour of further investigation, and a contrary approach:

"…would not have demonstrated the necessary weighing of the risks and benefits that a court would require to see before accepting it as a reasonable and responsible view."[85]

Given the seriousness of the risks there could have been no logical justification for delaying the relevant tests.

(iii)   The judge's role in determining whether expert opinion is "logical"

In *Smith v Southampton University Hospitals NHS Trust*[86] the Court of Appeal was critical of a deputy High Court judge for relying "exclusively on the *Bolam* test", in the sense that the judge had accepted the evidence of an expert witness for the defendant on the basis that the witness was:

"…highly reputable and that it had not been suggested that he did not represent the view of a responsible body of … surgeons…"

in his field. Wall LJ (with whom Leveson LJ and Sir Mark Potter P agreed) commented that:

"With great respect to the deputy judge, I do not think this is good enough. Where there is a clear conflict of medical opinion, the court's duty is not merely to say which view it prefers, but to explain why it prefers one to the other. This, in my judgment, is all the more so when the expert whose view is preferred accepts a substantial element of what the less favoured expert describes as basic good practice—in this case, keeping your scissors shut unless you can see what you are doing. In such circumstances, it is not sufficient, in my view, simply to say that [the defendant's expert] is representative of a responsible body of medical opinion and that, as a consequence, [the defendant] was not negligent."[87]

It is open to a judge to raise the question of whether the expert evidence stands up to logical scrutiny, even if the claimant does not seek to attack the evidence in this way, but the judge must give the experts an opportunity to address this issue in their evidence. In *Burne v A*[88] the Court of Appeal ordered a re-trial when the judge concluded that agreed expert evidence as to the nature of questions that should be put to a patient by a general practitioner in order to elicit information about symptoms had "no reasonable or logical basis", given the patient's known condition and history. The problem was that the judge had come to this view

3–040

3–041

---

[84] [2011] EWHC 13 (QB); [2011] Med. L.R. 113 (leave to appeal granted: [2012] EWCA Civ 1966).
[85] [2011] EWHC 13 (QB); [2011] Med. L.R. 113 at [94]–[96].
[86] [2007] EWCA Civ 387; (2007) 96 B.M.L.R. 79.
[87] [2007] EWCA Civ 387; (2007) 96 B.M.L.R. 79 at [44].
[88] [2006] EWCA Civ 24.

himself. The claimant had not argued the case on this basis, and it had not been put to the expert witnesses when giving their evidence. Sedley LJ commented that:

> "Judges are required to try questions of medical negligence on the evidence, not on what they themselves know or think they know. It would, for example, have been improper for Judge Harris simply to decide that Dr Burne had been negligent whatever the experts said. But judges are there to exercise judgment, and their judgment cannot be entirely dictated by expert evidence, even where the evidence is unopposed. The question always remains (provided a party raises it) whether the expert evidence makes sense."[89]

It was incumbent on the judge to ask the claimant's counsel whether he was invited to consider whether the expert evidence in support of the defendant doctor made sense, and, if counsel said yes, to ensure that the defendant had a proper opportunity to respond. Ward LJ, though having sympathy with the judge's reasoning on the evidence, said that the court was not:

> "...entitled to rely on what seems common sense to judges and consequently dismiss the views of the experts as illogical. At least we should not do so unless the *Bolitho* point has been properly taken in the court below and the experts given an opportunity to explain and justify their practice."[90]

(iv)   When is evidence of common practice relevant?

3–042   Where the case does not involve difficult or uncertain questions of medical or surgical treatment, or abstruse or highly technical scientific issues, but is concerned with whether obvious and simple precautions could have been taken, the question of the practice of experts should be largely irrelevant. The courts do not rely on expert rally drivers, for example, to say whether a motorist was negligent.[91] On the other hand, in a case where there are difficult, uncertain, highly technical scientific questions requiring information not ordinarily expected of a practitioner, and where the state of medical knowledge was highly variable between scientists, public health authorities and different medical communities, it is not appropriate for the court to find a practice which conformed to what other

---

[89] [2006] EWCA Civ 24 at [10].
[90] [2006] EWCA Civ 24 at [63].
[91] "Ordinary common sense dictates that when simple methods to avoid danger have been devised, are known, and are available, non-user, with fatal results, cannot be justified by saying that others also have been following the same old, less-careful practice; and that when such methods are readily comprehensible by the ordinary person, by whom, also, the need to use them or not is easily apprehended, it is quite within the competence of Court or jury, quite as much as of experts to deal with the issues; and that the existence of a practice which neglects them, even if the practice were general, cannot protect the defendant surgeon," per Coyne JA in *Anderson v Chasney* [1949] 4 D.L.R. 71 at 86–87, Man CA; aff'd [1950] 4 D.L.R. 223, SCC. Similarly, in *Chapman v Rix* (1959) 103 S.J. 940 Morris LJ, in a dissenting judgment, said that: "The question whether the omission was negligent was one on which expert technical guidance was not needed. Medical witnesses had . . . stated that if similarly placed their conduct would have been no different from that under review. But the duty still remained with the court to decide whether such conduct amounted in law to negligence." See further para.3–061 below.

similarly situated practitioners were following was negligent.[92] In these circumstances the court should confine itself to the prevailing standards of practice.

Although this principle is easy to state there can be significant differences of opinion as to whether a judgment about negligence involves highly technical matters, requiring expert opinion, or is simple and obvious. For example, in *Nattrass v Weber*[93] following surgery on the claimant's leg he was prescribed Heparin (a drug to thin the blood). A blood platelet count was done, and another ordered for two days later but this was not carried out. The claimant developed pain in both legs and was transferred to an emergency doctor, who suspected he had deep vein thrombosis, and treated him aggressively with Heparin. Due to complications from the Heparin the claimant had to have both legs amputated. The trial judge found both of the orthopaedic surgeons liable on the basis that they had prescribed Heparin without continuing to monitor the claimant's platelet count, notwithstanding that they had conformed to a standard orthopaedic practice: the case fell into the *ter Neuzen v Korn* exception where the standard practice could be found to be negligent because it did not adopt obvious precautions readily apparent to an ordinary trier of fact. In the Alberta Court of Appeal McFadyen and Slatter JJA concluded that the trial judge had "second guessed" the standard practice in 1998 for orthopaedic surgeons, which was not to perform routine platelet counts when prescribing Heparin:

3–043

> "The *ter Neuzen* exception does not anticipate the lay trier of fact second-guessing the medical profession based on the trier of facts' own interpretation of the scientific literature available."[94]

The orthopaedic medical literature at the time had not reached a consensus on the need to monitor platelet levels, and it was not for the judge to resolve the debate. This was beyond the ordinary experience and understanding of a trier of fact. Sulyma J, dissenting, took the view that the issue was not what was standard practice amongst *orthopaedic* surgeons but the standard of care to be expected of any medical doctor who chooses to prescribe a medication, irrespective of specialty or particular expertise in pharmacology or haematology. A doctor prescribing medication should have an understanding of the potential side effects and adverse reactions to that medication, particularly where administration of the medication could pose a grave or serious risk, and be aware of and utilise any monitoring that should be done to identify adverse reactions. Platelet counts were routine, commonly done in hospitals, and were virtually risk free. The concept that it would be prudent to monitor the effects of a prescription was easily understood by an ordinary person with no particular expertise in the practice of medicine, and so fell into the *ter Neuzen* exception.

---

[92] *ter Neuzen v Korn* (1993) 103 D.L.R. (4th) 473, 506, BCCA; aff'd (1995) 127 D.L.R. (4th) 577 at 595, SCC.
[93] 2010 ABCA 64; (2010) 316 D.L.R. (4th) 666; [2010] 12 W.W.R. 36.
[94] 2010 ABCA 64; (2010) 316 D.L.R. (4th) 666; [2010] 12 W.W.R. 36 at [39].

(v) What evidence counts?

3–044 Before any question of complying with accepted practice can arise the court must be satisfied on the evidence presented to it that there is a responsible body of professional opinion which supports the practice. Evidence which amounts simply to an expression of opinion by an expert witness of what he thinks he would have done had he been placed, hypothetically and without the benefit of hindsight, in the position of the defendant, is of little assistance in determining whether there was a responsible practice.[95] Moreover, it is always open to the court to reject expert evidence applying the ordinary principles of credibility that would be applied in any courtroom, for example, that the evidence is internally contradictory, or that the witness was acting as an advocate rather than an impartial and objective expert.[96]

(vi) How many experts?

3–045 In *Hills v Potter* Hirst J denied that the *Bolam* test allows the medical profession to set the standard of care:

> "In every case the court must be satisfied that the standard contended for ... accords with that upheld by a substantial body of medical opinion, and that this body of medical opinion is both respectable and responsible, and experienced in this particular field of medicine."[97]

In *De Freitas v O'Brien*[98] the claimant argued that Hirst J's reference to a "substantial body of medical opinion" meant that the defendant could not simply rely on a small number of experts in the field as supporting a particular practice. The Court of Appeal rejected this argument. The test was whether there was a "responsible body" of opinion, which could not be measured in purely quantitative terms. On the facts, a body of 11 doctors who specialised in spinal surgery, out of a total of well over 1,000 orthopaedic and neurosurgeons in the country, could represent a responsible body of opinion. Thus, the question of

---

[95] *J.D. Williams & Co. Ltd v Michael Hyde & Associates Ltd* [2000] Lloyd's Rep. P.N. 823 at 831, per Ward LJ, citing Oliver J in *Midland Bank Trust Co. Ltd v Hett Stubbs & Kemp* [1979] Ch. 384 at 402. In *Chapman v Rix* (1960), [1994] 5 Med. L.R. 239 at 247 Lord Goddard said that a doctor cannot avoid a finding of negligence merely by finding two doctors to say that they would have acted as he did, provided there was evidence the other way.

[96] See para.3–187. In *Dowdie v Camberwell Health Authority* [1997] 8 Med. L.R. 368 at 375, Kay J observed that: "The mere fact that two distinguished expert witnesses have testified that it was within the range of acceptable practice to proceed in that way does not oblige me to accept their evidence and, on this issue, I accept the evidence of the plaintiff's experts ..."

[97] [1983] 3 All E.R. 716 at 728. See also per Lord Diplock in *Sidaway v Bethlem Royal Hospital Governors* [1985] A.C. 871 at 895, stating that the court must be satisfied by the expert evidence that a body of opinion qualifies as a "responsible" body of medical opinion. In *Gascoine v Ian Sheridan & Co.* [1994] 5 Med. L.R. 437 at 444 Mitchell J said that "as a matter of common sense ... simply because a number of doctors gave evidence to the same effect, that does not automatically constitute an established and alternative 'school of thought' if, for example, the reasons given to substantiate the views expressed do not stand up to sensible analysis: see *Hucks v Cole* above (per Sachs LJ)."

[98] [1995] P.I.Q.R. P281; [1995] 6 Med. L.R. 108.

what constitutes a responsible body of professional opinion is not a "numbers game". The issue is whether the evidence supporting the defendant's conduct is reasonable and logically defensible.[99]

(vii)   The limits of complying with professional practice

Following accepted practice, or one of several such practices, is strong evidence   3–046
of the exercise of reasonable care, but ultimately it is for the court to determine
what constitutes negligence.[100] Although it is comparatively rare for the court to
conclude that a common practice was negligent, when this does happen it will be
through a finding that the practice was not "responsible". Once the practice
followed by the defendant is acknowledged to be a "responsible" practice it is not
open to the court to hold that it was negligent, even where another body of
"responsible" professional opinion is critical of the practice.

The inherent danger in the *Bolam* test is that if the courts defer too readily to   3–047
expert evidence medical standards could decline, since where there are competing
views within the medical profession *Bolam* opts for the lowest common
denominator. Thus, it has been cogently argued that the *Bolam* test should be
restricted to those cases where an adverse result follows a course of treatment
which has been intentional and has been shown to benefit other patients
previously. It should not be extended to certain kinds of medical accident merely
on the basis of how common they are: "To do this would set us on the slippery
slope of excusing carelessness when it happens often enough."[101]

(b)   Departing from professional practice

Just as compliance with accepted practice is good evidence that the defendant has   3–048
acted with reasonable care, a departure from accepted practice may be evidence
of negligence,[102] but in neither case is the evidence conclusive.[103] If deviation
from a common professional practice was considered proof of negligence then no

---

[99] In *Bolitho v City and Hackney Health Authority* [1993] 4 Med. L.R. 381 at 386, Farquharson LJ commented that: "There is of course no inconsistency between the decisions in *Hucks v Cole* and *Maynard's* case. It is not enough for a defendant to call a number of doctors to say what he had done or not done was in accord with accepted clinical practice. It is necessary for the judge to consider that evidence and decide whether that clinical practice puts the patient unnecessarily at risk."

[100] See *Jackson & Powell on Professional Liability*, 8th edn (London: Sweet & Maxwell, 2017), para.2.132; Dugdale and Stanton, *Professional Negligence*, 3rd edn (London: Butterworths, 1998), paras 15.25–15.26; Norrie [1985] J.R. 145.

[101] Scott (1991) 2 AVMA Medical & Legal Journal (No.3), p.16. For example, the fact that posterior dislocation of the shoulder is a rare condition in which the diagnosis is very often missed, does not necessarily mean that it is reasonable or competent to miss the diagnosis. See also the comment of Harris, (1991) 2 AVMA Medical & Legal Journal (No.3), describing the missed diagnosis in such cases as "inexcusable" because the classical signs are always present: "the problem arises because the examining doctor fails to think of the possibility and does not look for the signs."

[102] *Robinson v Post Office* [1974] 2 All E.R. 737 at 745. In *Thake v Maurice* [1986] Q.B. 644 the defendant surgeon carelessly forgot to give his own usual warning that there was a slight risk that the claimant might become fertile again after a sterilisation operation. In the absence of any other expert evidence the Court of Appeal held that the defendant's usual practice was evidence of what constituted "responsible" practice, and held him negligent for failing to comply with it.

3–052 Some instances of departure from accepted practice are quite clearly negligent even where they are performed consciously and routinely. For example, in *Chin Keow v Government of Malaysia*[112] a doctor gave a patient an injection of penicillin without making any enquiry about the patient's medical history. Had he done so he would have discovered that she was allergic to penicillin. The patient died due to an allergic reaction to the drug. The doctor was aware of the remote possibility of this risk arising but he carried on with his routine practice of not making any enquiry because he had had no mishaps before. All the medical evidence was to the effect that enquiries, which would have taken no more than five minutes, were necessary. The Privy Council held the doctor liable.

3–053 In *Landau v Werner*[113] a psychiatrist engaged in social contact with a female patient who had developed a strong and obsessive emotional attachment to him. This was a departure from recognised standards in the practice of psychiatry and led to a serious deterioration in the patient's mental health. Barry J said that although the defendant had acted from the best of intentions he had made a tragic mistake; there was no body of professional opinion which would have adopted this course of conduct with a patient in these circumstances, indeed, the medical evidence was all one way in condemning social contacts. Accordingly the defendant was liable. This was upheld on appeal. Sellers LJ said that:

> "... a doctor might not be negligent if he tried a new technique but if he did he must justify it before the court. If his novel or exceptional treatment had failed disastrously he could not complain if it was held that he went beyond the bounds of due care and skill as recognised generally. Success was the best justification for unusual and unestablished treatment."

3–054 In *Coughlin v Kuntz*[114] the defendant adopted a method of performing an operation which was experimental, unsupported by clinical study, and favoured by no other orthopaedic surgeon. The procedure was under investigation by the College of Physicians and Surgeons, which had urged the defendant to undertake a moratorium on the procedure. The defendant was held to have been negligent. Similarly, in *Cryderman v Ringrose*[115] the defendant took a biopsy at a time when there was a "presumptive pregnancy". The normal practice would have been to alert the claimant to the possibility of pregnancy and wait until a more certain diagnosis could be made. In the circumstances the biopsy was not medically justified since it could cause an abortion, and the defendant was liable.

---

[112] [1967] 1 W.L.R. 813.
[113] (1961) 105 S.J. 257 and 1008, CA.
[114] (1987) 42 C.C.L.T. 142, BCSC; aff'd [1990] 2 W.W.R. 737, BCCA.
[115] [1977] 3 W.W.R. 109; aff'd [1978] 3 W.W.R. 481, Alta SC Appellate Division. See also *Zimmer v Ringrose* (1981) 124 D.L.R. (3d) 215 at 223 on a doctor's duty to inform the patient that a new procedure or technique had not been approved by the medical profession. Reasonable practitioners would have disclosed this since they would realise that the information would be likely to influence the patient's decision whether to undergo the procedure.

(c)   Codes of practice

Codified standards of professional conduct may constitute significant evidence of   **3–055**
what constitutes reasonable care. In *Lloyd Cheynham & Co. Ltd v Littlejohn &
Co.*[116] Woolf J said of accounting and audit standards that:

> "While they are not conclusive, so that a departure from their terms necessarily involves a
> breach of a duty of care, and they are not … rigid rules, they are very strong evidence as to
> what is the proper standard which should be adopted and unless there is some justification, a
> departure from this will be regarded as constituting a breach of duty."[117]

Such standards are not, however, determinative of negligence. Thus, in *Johnson v
Bingley*[118] it was held that breach of the *Guide to Professional Conduct of
Solicitors* published by the Law Society was not per se proof of negligence. The
Guide was proper and accepted practice for solicitors, but negligence was a legal
concept, and neither the Law Society nor any other professional body could, by
issuing rules or codes of conduct, alter the law.[119] Moreover, compliance with a
Code of Practice, though usually evidence of the exercise reasonable care, may in
some circumstances not be sufficient to exculpate a defendant. So in *Baker v
Quantum Clothing Group*[120] the Supreme Court held that a government Code of
Practice issued in 1972 on occupational exposure to noise levels set the standard
for the reasonable and prudent employer without specialist knowledge until the
late 1980s, so that the "average" employer was not in breach of duty in following
the guidance. However, the Code did not provide an excuse to large employers
with *actual* knowledge of the risks of exposure to particular noise levels, since
they had come to the conclusion that the limits identified by the Code were no
longer acceptable.[121]

---

[116] (1985) 2 P.N. 154.

[117] See Gwilliam (1986) 2 P.N. 175. See also *Bevan Investments Ltd v Blackhall and Struthers (No.2)*
[1973] 2 N.Z.L.R. 45, 66 on engineering codes of practice; *Ward v The Ritz Hotel (London) Ltd*
[1992] P.I.Q.R. P315, CA—failure to comply with the British Standards Institution's recommendation
as to the height of a balustrade on a balcony was strong evidence of negligence.

[118] [1997] P.N.L.R. 392, Q.B.D.

[119] See also *Green v Building Scene Ltd* [1994] P.I.Q.R. P259, where the Court of Appeal held that
although a failure to comply with Building Regulations or the British Standards Institution's
recommendations about the safety of a staircase was evidence which the court should take into
account, because it represented current professional opinion as to what was desirable to avoid
accidents, it was not conclusive. There was a difference between laying down standards and defining
what is reasonably safe in all the circumstances of the case. In *Caldwell v Maguire and Fitzgerald*
[2001] EWCA Civ 1054; [2002] P.I.Q.R. P45 it was held that the fact that the defendants had been
found guilty of "careless riding" under Jockey Club rules by the stewards after a horserace did not
establish that an error of judgment or a momentary lapse of skill in the stress of a competitive race
constituted a breach of duty owed to a fellow rider.

[120] [2011] UKSC 17; [2011] 1 W.L.R. 1003; discussed by McCarthy [2011] J.P.I.L. C122.

[121] Lord Dyson commented, [2011] UKSC 17; [2011] 1 W.L.R. 1003 at [101], that: "There is no rule
of law that a relevant code of practice or other official or regulatory instrument necessarily sets the
standard of care for the purpose of the tort of negligence… Thus to follow a relevant code of practice
or regulatory instrument will often afford a defence to a claim in negligence. But there are
circumstances where it does not do so. For example, it may be shown that the code of practice or
regulatory instrument is compromised because the standards that it requires have been lowered as a
result of heavy lobbying by interested parties; or because it covers a field in which apathy and

3–056   **Departing from professional guidelines**   In the context of healthcare, the introduction of medical audit and NHS clinical governance has, in a number of instances, led to the development of treatment protocols and practice guidelines, providing a consensus view of experts in the field as to the proper standards.[122] It has been argued that it could become increasingly difficult for a doctor to argue that the protocol was rejected in favour of some alternative method, even if there are some doctors prepared to state that they disagree with the protocol produced by the experts.[123] The courts are prepared to consider, and accept as highly persuasive, guidelines produced by the medical profession on appropriate standards of conduct.[124] In *Pierre v Marshall*,[125] for example, the defendant was held to have been negligent for failing to follow the recommendations of the Alberta Medical Association and the Society of Obstetricians and Gynaecologists of Canada that there should be universal screening of pregnant women for gestational diabetes, notwithstanding that there was still controversy about the cost-effectiveness of universal screening. Even some experts who believed that universal screening was not cost-effective considered that doctors should heed

---

fatalism has prevailed amongst workers, trade unions, employers and legislators . . .; or because the instrument has failed to keep abreast of the latest technology and scientific understanding."
[122] One consequence of the introduction of clinical governance has been a proliferation of agencies of the Department of Health issuing guidance, some of which is directly relevant to patient safety. See, e.g. NHS England (*http://www.england.nhs.uk/patientsafety*), the National Institute for Health and Care Excellence (*http://www.nice.org.uk*), and the Care Quality Commission (*http://www.cqc.org.uk*).
[123] See A. Samanta, M. Mello, C. Forster, J. Tingle and J. Samanta, "The Role of Clinical Guidelines in Medical Negligence Litigation: A Shift from the *Bolam* Standard?" (2006) 14 Med. L. Rev. 321; Harpwood (1994) 1 Med. Law Int. 241, 250, 251. Instructive here is the National Confidential Inquiry into Patient Outcome and Death (at *http://www.ncepod.org.uk*). CEPOD has published a number of reports, going back to 1989, which have identified certain systematic errors and made recommendations for future practice (the reports are archived at the website). For example, the NCEPOD report, *Who operates when? II* (2003), looked at when operations are carried out and the grade of surgeon and anaesthetist involved, indicating that there are still too many emergency operations involving junior grades of medical staff without the supervision of a consultant. One of the authors of some of the early reports, commenting on the effects of the CEPOD reports, suggested that: "Guidelines or standards generated by competent professional and academic bodies will be included into clinical contracts and become benchmarks for the outcome expected," Devlin (1993) 4 AVMA Medical & Legal Journal (No.2) pp.8, 11. Moreover, the techniques for measuring clinical activity "challenge the individual autonomy of consultants and probably render the traditional *Bolam* definition of negligence obsolete," Devlin (1993) at p.9. See also Devlin (1995) 1 Clinical Risk 97. On the other hand, rigid adherence to guidelines can be inappropriate. Guidelines and protocols vary in their validity, and attempts to reach professional "consensus" can result in inadequate and biased guidelines: Hurwitz (1995) 1 Clinical Risk 142; Hurwitz (1999) 318 B.M.J. 661.
[124] See *W v Egdell* [1990] Ch. 359 in the context of confidentiality; and *Airedale NHS Trust v Bland* [1993] A.C. 789 in the context of the treatment for patients in a persistent vegetative state. The General Medical Council publishes extensive codes of practice for doctors, ranging from general statements of good practice (e.g. *Good Medical Practice*, 2013) to specific advice on how to proceed in particular circumstances. These codes are available from the GMC website *http://www.gmc-uk.org/guidance/ethical_guidance.asp*. In *Hayes v South East Coast Ambulance Service* [2015] EWHC 18 (QB), *Taaffe v East of England Ambulance Service NHS Trust* [2012] EWHC 1335 (QB); [2013] Med. L.R. 406; (2012) 128 B.M.L.R. 71; para.3–099, and *A v East Midlands Ambulance Service NHS Trust* [2015] EWHC 3930 (QB) the failure of ambulance crews to follow guidance contained in the UK Ambulance Service Clinical Practice Guidelines 2006, was held, in the circumstances, to constitute a breach of duty.
[125] [1994] 8 W.W.R. 478, Alta QB.

the guidelines until the controversy was settled.[126] In *Spencer v Hillingdon Hospital NHS Trust*[127] Judge Collender QC noted that although the question of whether a given practice was in accordance with guidelines issued by the National Institute for Clinical Excellence was not of itself determinative of negligence, it was "highly relevant". Similarly, in *R v Lanarkshire Health Board*[128] Lord Brailsford, whilst acknowledging that professional guidelines were intended to provide clinical guidance not to set down mandatory rules, pointed out that judgments about whether to depart from guidelines had to be informed by the clinician's level of experience. Thus, where a less experienced doctor departed from a guideline it would be prudent to consult a more experienced colleague for advice, and a failure to do so would be more likely to result in a finding of negligence.[129] On the other hand, in *Darnley v Croydon Health Services NHS Trust*[130] Judge Robinson concluded that the NICE Guidelines on the maximum time to be taken in an Accident & Emergency department to see a patient with a head injury could not be applied rigidly, since triage within 15 minutes was not necessarily achievable.

Complying with professional guidelines   The issue of reliance on professional guidelines can cut both ways, so that where the defendant has complied with guidance it will be difficult to establish that there has been negligence. In *Zarb v Odetoyinbo*[131] the Royal College of General Practitioners had issued guidelines on the management of acute low back pain, identifying certain symptoms as warning signs for the emergency referral for surgery of patients at risk of developing Cauda Equina Syndrome. The claimant's symptoms did not fit the guidelines for emergency referral. One of the experts for the claimant considered that the RCGP guidelines were simply wrong, and that a patient with bilateral sciatica should be referred for surgery immediately even in the absence of other symptoms. As Tugendhat J commented: **3–057**

---

[126] The Canadian courts have made it clear that clinical guidelines or protocols are merely evidence of the standard of care expected of a defendant; they do not in themselves set the standard in law: *Bafaro v Dowd* (2008) 169 A.C.W.S. (3d) 437 at [34]–[35] (Ont SC); *Cooper v Valiulis* 2012 ONSC 664; 211 A.C.W.S. (3d) 471 at [199] per Shaughnessy J: "clinical guidelines are only one relevant consideration for the court with respect to determining the legal standard of care."
[127] [2015] EWHC 1058 (QB) at [73]; para.4–070.
[128] [2016] CSOH 133; 2016 G.W.D. 31-556; see C. Hart, "Clinical guidelines and conflicting expert opinion in medical negligence" (2016) 32 P.N. 267.
[129] [2016] CSOH 133; 2016 G.W.D. 31-556 at [129]: "The more experienced clinician may in certain circumstances feel it appropriate to depart from the terms of a guideline, albeit that when such a clinician adopts this practice he must not only be careful but aware that in so doing his actions may be examined and indeed no doubt criticised in some circumstances. By contrast the less experienced clinician should in my view be aware that he or she, lacking the knowledge which can be acquired only from practice, is required to follow the distilled experience of other doctors more experienced which a guideline represents."
[130] [2015] EWHC 2301 (QB); [2016] P.I.Q.R. P4; [2015] Med. L.R. 506; effectively approved on appeal: *Darnley v Croydon Health Services NHS Trust* [2017] EWCA Civ 151; [2017] P.I.Q.R. P14; [2017] Med. L.R. 245 at [37], [38]; para.3–098.
[131] [2006] EWHC 2880 (QB); (2007) 93 B.M.L.R. 166.

"It is in principle possible that the Guidelines of the Royal College might fail the *Bolam* test. But it is difficult to envisage the circumstances in which a judge would be bound to reach that conclusion."[132]

In light of the approach of Lord Brown-Wilkinson in *Bolitho v City and Hackney Health Authority*[133] to the *Bolam* test, namely that where the defendant's actions are supported by a body of professional opinion the judge is entitled to hold that the body of opinion is not reasonable or responsible only where it is not capable of withstanding logical analysis, it would be exceptional for the court to conclude that the defendant was negligent if he has complied with the relevant guidelines, since, though there may be reasonable disagreement as to the content of professional guidelines, it will be very difficult to demonstrate that they are completely illogical. It is, of course, possible that a health organisation such as a NHS Trust or even an individual professional, might have greater knowledge than the "average" that a particular Code of Practice or Guidance failed to provide reasonable protection for patients, because, for example, it "has failed to keep abreast of the latest technology and scientific understanding".[134] In practice, however, even where there is substantive evidence that is critical of the professional guidance the claimant will have an uphill task to establish that the guidance was entirely illogical.[135]

(d) When the *Bolam* test does not apply

(i) When the dispute between expert witnesses concerns a question of fact

3–058   The *Bolam* test encompasses two limbs. The first is the requirement of a professional person to exercise reasonable care in undertaking the tasks

---

[132] [2006] EWHC 2880 (QB); (2007) 93 B.M.L.R. 166 at [110]. See also *Ministry of Justice v Carter* [2010] EWCA Civ 694 where the failure of doctors to refer a woman complaining of pain and a lump in her breast for further investigation when no lump was palpable on examination was held not to be negligent since it was consistent with professional guidelines issued by the National Institute for Clinical Excellence (commented on by Tomkins [2010] J.P.I.L. C169); *Wake v Johnson* [2015] EWHC 276 (QB), para.4–026, where Judge Collender QC noted that compliance with NICE guidelines did not absolve the doctor from responsibility to apply clinical judgment given the patient's circumstances, but there was no breach of duty in the circumstances; *C v North Cumbria University Hospitals NHS Trust* [2014] EWHC 61 (QB); [2014] Med. L.R. 189 at [84] per Green J: "*prima facie* a midwife who acts in accordance with the guidelines should be safe from a charge of negligence", and complying with the guidelines was "a factor militating against negligence", though it was common ground that the guidelines were in some respects unsatisfactory and adhering to the guidelines was not itself a sufficient basis for a conclusion that there was no breach of duty.
[133] [1998] A.C. 232; see paras 3–035 and 3–036.
[134] *Baker v Quantum Clothing Group* [2011] UKSC 17; [2011] 1 W.L.R. 1003, per Lord Dyson at [101]; see para.3–055.
[135] See, e.g., *Wells v University Hospital Southampton NHS Foundation Trust* [2015] EWHC 2376 (QB); [2015] Med. L.R. 477 at [70]–[72], para.4–115, where an expert's opinion that evidence from the "Cochrane Collaboration" rendered NICE Guidance on the appropriate response to a foetal CTG trace wrong, and that no responsible body of professional opinion would have followed the NICE Guidance, was rejected by Dingemans J. As the judge noted, the claimant's expert was willing to condemn as negligent all doctors who accepted and followed the NICE Guidance.

associated with the particular professional calling. The second, and more commonly invoked, is the assertion that a defendant will not be liable under the first limb if he has complied with a responsible professional practice, allowing always for the possibility that there may be more than one such practice. This is essentially a question of proof, since battle is usually joined between expert witnesses as to whether the defendant has followed a professional practice and, if so, whether it was a "responsible" practice. At this point, the requirement to subject the evidence of expert witnesses to logical scrutiny, applying the approach in *Bolitho v City and Hackney Health Authority*,[136] can be invoked. If, having undertaken that scrutiny, the court concludes that there is more than one *responsible* practice, it cannot then choose between them and find the defendant negligent on the basis that though his practice was responsible there was another practice that was better or more responsible. Thus, at this stage the court is precluded from choosing between expert evidence.

It is important, however, to keep this limitation in its proper perspective. Where there is a difference of opinion between expert witnesses about a question of fact, the court has a duty to resolve that dispute and reach a finding about the facts. In *Penney, Palmer and Cannon v East Kent Health Authority*[137] the claimants alleged that there had been negligence in the screening of cervical smear tests, in that some of the smears were falsely reported as negative, resulting in delay in obtaining treatment for cervical cancer. Screening was carried out by biomedical scientists or by qualified cytology screeners. They did not diagnose, they merely reported what they saw on the slides. If there was an abnormality or if there was doubt as to what was seen, the slide was passed on to a senior screener (a checker). If the checker agreed with the categorisation it was passed on to a pathologist. If the pathologist confirmed the abnormality the patient was referred to a gynaecologist for a colposcopy or a biopsy. The expert witnesses (five pathologists) agreed that if a screener was in doubt about what was seen on the slide, he should not classify it as negative. In each case the claimants' smears were reported as normal or negative, but they all developed cervical cancer. The trial judge had held that the *Bolam* test did not apply, and found the defendants to have been negligent. The Court of Appeal held that the *Bolam* test did apply, subject to the *Bolitho* proviso that expert evidence as to the defendants' conduct had to stand up to logical analysis. The *Bolam* test did not apply, however, to questions of fact, including the question of what could be seen on the individual slides. Thus, the questions that had to be asked were: (i) what could be seen on each slide; (ii) could a reasonably competent cytoscreener have failed to see what was on the slide; (iii) could a reasonably competent cytoscreener, bearing in mind what he or she should have observed, have treated the slide as negative? The answer to the first question required expert evidence, but if there was a dispute amongst the experts as to what was visible on the slides the judge had to make his own finding of fact, on the balance of probabilities, a finding which might inevitably involve the rejection of some of the expert evidence. Once the judge

3–059

---

[136] [1998] A.C. 232.
[137] [2000] Lloyd's Rep. Med. 41; Faulks (2000) 6 Clinical Risk 153. *Penney* was applied in *Conway v Cardiff & Vale NHS Trust* [2004] EWHC 1841 (QB)—cytogeneticist negligent in failing to identify a congenital defect in cells taken by amniocentesis for prenatal screening.

justified, namely where the past record of success of the established treatment is small. However, his Lordship also appeared to suggest that the *Bolam* test protects the doctor in this situation by acknowledging that there may be a number of different accepted practices at any particular time. This view is open to question. There is likely to be a time-lag between the development of new methods and their acceptance by the profession.[152] Where the new treatment is not yet established as a practice accepted as proper by a responsible body of medical opinion a defendant will have to justify his decision simply by reference to the "reasonable doctor". This will depend to a large extent on the relative risk of the treatment in comparison to the alternative treatments and the nature of the illness for which it is prescribed. Where the patient's condition is very serious and the standard treatment is ineffective, a doctor will be justified in taking greater risks in an attempt to provide some effective treatment. On the other hand, the patient should not be exposed to excessive risk and there should be some attempt to provide scientific validation for a new technique. For example, in *Hepworth v Kerr*[153] the defendant anaesthetist adopted a new hypotensive anaesthetic technique which he knew had never been attempted routinely before, in order to provide a blood-free field for the operating surgeon. He knew that he was experimenting, but did not embark upon any proper scientific validation of his technique in some 1,500 patients by the time of the claimant's operation. It was not a minor adjustment to well-established techniques, but a step completely outside conventional wisdom which was right at the margins of safety and effectively took patients "to the very edge of existence". McKinnon J held the defendant liable for the condition of anterior spinal artery syndrome (spinal stroke) which the claimant was subsequently found to have developed, despite the fact that this amounted to a condemnation of the defendant's "life-time work".

3–066   **Canada**   The question of experimental procedures has been considered by the Canadian courts. The use of an innovative technique will not be treated as negligence per se. In *Zimmer v Ringrose* Prowse JA said that:

> "A physician is entitled to decide that the situation dictates the adoption of an innovative course of treatment. As long as he discharges his duty of disclosure, and is not otherwise in breach of his duties of skill and care, *e.g.*, has not negligently adopted the procedure given the circumstances, the doctor will not be held liable for implementing such a course of treatment."[154]

The defendant's method of sterilisation was "experimental and quite unsupported by clinical study as a method acceptable for human beings".[155] He was held to have been negligent in failing to inform the claimant that the technique had not been approved by the medical profession, although this aspect of the claim failed on the grounds of causation (the claimant would have undergone the procedure in

---

[152] As, e.g., in *Crawford v Charing Cross Hospital, The Times*, 8 December 1953.

[153] [1995] 6 Med. L.R. 139; discussed at (1996) 2 Clinical Risk 73–87.

[154] (1981) 124 D.L.R. (3d) 215 at 223–224, Alta CA; aff'g in part (1978) 89 D.L.R. (3d) 646. See also *Waters v West Sussex Health Authority* [1995] 6 Med. L.R. 362 where the novel surgical technique of a neurosurgeon was found to accord with the standards of responsible medical opinion.

[155] (1978) 89 D.L.R. (3d) 646 at 652, per MacDonald J; see also at 655–656; see also *Coughlin v Kuntz* (1987) 42 C.C.L.T. 142, BCSC; aff'd [1990] 2 W.W.R. 737, BCCA, above para.3–054.

any event). In *Cryderman v Ringrose*[156] the claimant agreed to be sterilised by the same defendant by the same experimental procedure, which involved introducing silver nitrate into the fallopian tubes through the uterus. The claimant was not informed that the procedure was unreliable or that it might damage the uterus. The claimant believed that she was sterile, although the defendant knew that the procedure had not been successful and he did not inform her. She became pregnant and later underwent an abortion. The trial judge rejected the claimant's argument that the defendant was negligent because there was a usual and normal practice which had been not followed, on the ground that it would impede medical progress. He also distinguished *Halushka v University of Saskatch-ewan*[157] on the basis that that was a case of "pure medical experimentation", where different considerations would apply:

> "When an experimental procedure is employed the common law requires a high degree of care and also disclosure to the patient of the fact that the treatment is new and risky."[158]

The standard of care was, nonetheless, that of a reasonable doctor considering all the circumstances, including the seriousness of the condition, the risks, the patient's capacity to comprehend and decide the question involved and the likely effect on her of the knowledge of the risks involved. Moreover, the court should be alert to the risk of a conflict of interest between the patient's welfare and the interests of the doctor, particularly when the doctor is prescribing *his* new process (as distinct from the objectivity that was to be presumed in the use of someone else's new process).

Care required commensurate with risks   A similar approach would probably **3–067** be taken in this country. A degree of care is expected which is commensurate with the risk involved, and innovative treatment would be regarded as inherently "risky" until it has become tried and tested. In *Independent Broadcasting Authority v EMI Electronics Ltd and BICC Construction Ltd*[159] the House of Lords held that a defendant employed to design an experimental television mast had to demonstrate that he had exercised a high degree of care both in assessing the risks of the venture and the possible alternatives. He could not justify his actions simply by saying "we were taking a step into the unknown and so the risks were unforeseeable". There was an obligation to think things through and to assess the dimensions of the "venture into the unknown".[160]

---

[156] [1977] 3 W.W.R. 109; aff'd [1978] 3 W.W.R. 481, Alta SC Appellate Division.
[157] (1965) 53 D.L.R. (2d) 436; see further para.7–130.
[158] [1977] 3 W.W.R. 109 at 118; *Crossman v Stewart* (1977) 82 D.L.R. (3d) 677 at 686; *Poole v Morgan* [1987] 3 W.W.R. 217 at 254, per Cawsey J, Alta QB stating that "...where the risks involved in the treatment are great, or the treatment is a new one, the standard of care increases." It is submitted that the standard of care, does not change, rather the precautions required to satisfy the standard of "reasonable care in all the circumstances" are greater.
[159] (1980) 14 B.L.R. 1.
[160] (1980) 14 B.L.R. 1 at 31, per Lord Edmund-Davies. Dugdale and Stanton, *Professional Negligence*, 3rd edn (London: Butterworths, 1998), para.16.07 comment that: "In law the burden of proving lack of reasonable care in such circumstances remains on the plaintiff, but, in practice, once the plaintiff has shown that the work has proved to be faulty and that it diverged from the accepted professional approach to such issues, it will be for the defence to justify their actions."

3–068   **Research projects**   This proposition would also apply to claims arising out of a systematic research project, whether therapeutic or non-therapeutic.[161] An allegation of negligence in conducting research would involve proving that the design, the performance or the follow-up of the experimental procedure was negligent, or that the disclosure of information concerning risks was inadequate.[162] A researcher has a duty fully to investigate the possible consequences of the research using existing published literature and animal experiments where appropriate, prior to conducting research on human subjects.[163] The research should be well designed, and should seek to minimise the risks to the research subjects. This would include: the provision of a "stopping rule" by which the project would be halted if a serious risk of harm became apparent; provision for emergencies; and careful periodic observation of the subjects.[164] It is also arguable that a research project which failed to comply with national or international ethical codes on medical experimentation could be found to have been conducted negligently, on the basis that the codes constitute evidence of what is reasonable care, by reference to the accepted practice of the profession.[165]

3–069   The one English case which has involved a finding of negligence against a major clinical trial is *The Creutzfeldt-Jakob Disease Litigation, Plaintiffs v United Kingdom Medical Research Council*,[166] which concerned the transmission of the "slow virus" which causes Creutzfeldt-Jakob Disease (CJD) from human growth hormone (HGH) extracted from the pituitaries of cadavers. Between 1959 and 1985 almost 2,000 children were treated with HGH. The claimants had all been treated with HGH when they were children. Since 1985, 16 of the recipients had

---

[161] Therapeutic research is an activity which has a therapeutic intention, as well as a research intention, towards the subjects of the research; the subjects are also patients. Non-therapeutic research is an activity which does not have a therapeutic intention. This is normally carried out on healthy volunteers, who are not patients. See further paras 7–116 et seq. The Royal College of Physicians, *Guidelines on the Practice of Ethics Committees in Medical Research with Human Participants*, 4th edn, 2007 and *Research Involving Patients*, 1990, distinguish *research*, which is designed to develop or contribute to generalisable knowledge, from *innovative therapy*, where a clinician departs significantly from standard practice entirely for the benefit of a particular patient. The latter may not constitute research, although it may be described as experimental in the sense that it is novel and unvalidated.

[162] See generally Giesen (1995) 3 Med. L. Rev. 22. On the disclosure of information to research subjects see paras 7–120 to 7–125, 7–130 to 7–131.

[163] *Vacwell Engineering Co. Ltd v BDH Chemicals* [1971] 1 Q.B. 88, where the defendant was negligent in failing to check all relevant publications dealing with a little known chemical prior to marketing it.

[164] *Zimmer v Ringrose* (1978) 89 D.L.R. (3d) 646 at 656.

[165] See para.3–055. See also Dugdale and Stanton, *Professional Negligence*, 3rd edn (London: Butterworths, 1998), para.15.23. Both therapeutic and non-therapeutic medical research are governed by the guidelines of the *Declaration of Helsinki* (available at *http://www.wma.net/policies-post/wma-declaration-of-helsinki-ethical-principles-for-medical-research-involving-human-subjects*). See further the Royal College of Physicians, *Guidelines on the Practice of Ethics Committees in Medical Research Involving Human Subjects*, 4th edn, 2007 and Royal College of Physicians *Research Involving Patients*, 1990. On the potential liability of Research Ethics Committees see Brazier (1990) 6 P.N. 186. The decisions of ethics committees may, in some circumstances, be subject to judicial review: *R. v Ethical Committee of St. Mary's Hospital, Ex p. Harriott* [1988] 1 F.L.R. 512 at 518–519.

[166] (1996) 54 B.M.L.R. 8; [1996] 7 Med. L.R. 309.

died of CJD and a further three were expected to do so.[167] Eleven claimants (the group A claimants) had developed CJD as a consequence of receiving HGH contaminated with the CJD virus. There were a further 87 claimants in Group B who had received HGH who had not, as yet, been diagnosed with CJD. Until 1 July 1977 responsibility for the collection and processing of pituitaries and the allocation of HGH to nominated recipients was that of the Medical Research Council (MRC). Thereafter, it was the responsibility of the Secretary of State for Health (the Department). Treatment of those children who received HGH was under the auspices of the MRC. Under the MRC, the HGH programme had been a clinical trial but by 1976, because of the numbers receiving HGH, it had effectively become a therapeutic programme. Until 1980, the safety of HGH had remained the responsibility of the MRC, while the Department prepared for the programme's takeover. In June 1977 the Department of Health Services Human Growth Hormone Committee (HSHGHC) was responsible for the safety of HGH, but the committee believed that it was not concerned with slow viruses, a belief which had permeated the Department's staff and, through them, the professional staff at the MRC and then upwards to the chair of the committee. Morland J found that information about the risk of slow virus infection was conveyed in a cursory manner. HSHGHC had not had the appropriate expertise to make an informed decision of the risk of slow virus infection. From 1976 to 1980, the collection of pituitaries and the production of HGH had continued in the same way, despite evidence pointing to the potential risks which emerged in 1976. The HSHGHC had been deliberately kept in the dark about the details of slow viruses, despite its responsibility for the safety of the treatment.

Morland J held that the defendants had been negligent in permitting the programme to continue. From 1 July 1977 the treatment programme should have been partially suspended. New patients should not have been started on the programme after that date, unless they were suffering from hypocalcaemia and would otherwise have suffered serious ill health. However, it would not have been negligent to continue treatment for patients who had already started the treatment, since the risk was considered to be low, the cessation of treatment for ongoing recipients would have had psychological and physical disadvantages, and a synthetic product was still a few years off. Prior to October 1976, although knowledge of transmissibility of the CJD agent and slow viruses was growing, it was not established that the defendants had been guilty of negligence in failing to undertake a thorough reappraisal of the HGH programme or in failing to have imposed more stringent criteria with regard to the collection of pituitaries. Prior to 1976 CJD had been mistakenly assumed to be much rarer than it was. The claimants had not established that, before 1976, the method used to process pituitaries was negligent, although a purer HGH could have been produced by a different method. Nowhere in the world in which HGH was in production was CJD regarded as a risk through contaminated HGH. However, there was no good reason why the changes in production methods of HGH which were made in 1980 should not have been made in early 1977 if proper advice had been sought.

3–070

---

[167] Two years later there were 27 confirmed cases of CJD: see *The Creutzfeldt-Jakob Disease Litigation, Andrews and others v Secretary of State for Health (Damages Assessments)* (1998) 54 B.M.L.R. 111 at 113.

Finally, in respect of the standard of care that could be expected of an advisory committee Morland J concluded that:

> "The standard of care ... to be imposed in respect of a committee is that of a reasonably competent and carefully inquiring group of professionals in the relevant disciplines, of sufficient standing to be entrusted with the membership of that committee, bearing in mind it is a committee which is not merely advisory but is carrying out executive and administrative functions."[176]

This applied as much to the scientific and technical staff advising the committee. While a committee which was not properly briefed could not reasonably be faulted for not requesting scientific material from its staff, those staff could be. The medical and scientific staff of both the MRC and the Department had a dual role, one administrative, the other in the use of their professional skills. In servicing the HGH committees, they were under a duty to alert the members to current medical and scientific knowledge. Committee members, though experts within their own fields, could not have been expected to have had all current knowledge about CJD and transmissible slow viruses. It was the failure of the committees to be provided with that information and their failure to seek it which gave rise to negligence.[177]

3–073   **Compensation in the absence of negligence**   The Pearson Commission recommended that a volunteer for medical research or a clinical trial who suffers severe damage as a result should have a cause of action on the basis of strict liability.[178] This proposal has not been implemented, although ex gratia compensation may be available to a volunteer injured in a study sponsored by the Medical Research Council, or during drug trials.[179] It is also possible that a patient may have a contractual remedy if it is possible to demonstrate a valid contract between the patient and the doctor/hospital or the company sponsoring the research, although whether the contract provides for compensation in the absence of negligence will depend on the precise wording of the contract.[180] In an appropriate case a research subject might have an action against a drug manufacturer under Pt I of the Consumer Protection Act 1987, but the chances of such a claim succeeding are small given the difficulty that the claimant would

---

[176] (1996) 54 B.M.L.R. 8 at 24.

[177] The government subsequently set up a no-fault compensation scheme for the victims of CJD and their families. See Melville Williams [2004] J.P.I.L. 39; A. Boggio, "The Compensation of the Victims of the Creutzfeldt-Jacob Disease in the United Kingdom" (2005) 7 Med. Law Int. 149.

[178] *Royal Commission on Civil Liability and Compensation for Personal Injury*, Cmnd.7054 (1978), paras 1339–1441.

[179] See the Association of the British Pharmaceutical Industry, *Clinical trial compensation guidelines*, 2014 (available at *http://www.abpi.org.uk/our-work/library/guidelines/Pages/ct-compensation.aspx*). See also Department of Health, HSG (96)48, *Arrangements for Handling Clinical Negligence Claims Against NHS Staff*, Annex B (in App.1 to this book). J. Manning, "Does the Law on Compensation for Research-Related Injury in the UK, Australia, and New Zealand Meet Ethical Requirements?" (2017) 25 Med. L. Rev. 397 argues that the compensation arrangements for individuals injured in the course of medical research fall below ethical expectations.

[180] See, e.g., *Wylie v Grosset* [2011] CSOH 89; 2011 S.L.T. 609, para.2–007.

have in proving that the drug was defective, and the fact that the manufacturer could rely on the development risks defence.[181]

4. KEEPING UP TO DATE

Professional practice may change over time so that what was once accepted as the correct procedure is no longer considered to be respectable or responsible. In *Bolam v Friern Hospital Management Committee* McNair J pointed out that a medical practitioner cannot:

> "...obstinately and pig-headedly carry on with some old technique if it has been proved to be contrary to what is really substantially the whole of informed medical opinion."[182]

3–074

Thus, there is an obligation on doctors to keep up to date with new developments in their particular field. This principle is easy enough to state, but it is more difficult to determine precisely when a new development will render adherence to the old method negligent. In the same passage McNair J illustrated his point in this way:

> "Otherwise you might get men today saying: 'I don't believe in anaesthetics. I don't believe in antiseptics. I am going to continue to do my surgery in the way it was done in the eighteenth century'. That would clearly be wrong."

No doubt patients will be relieved to know that they should not be subjected to the surgical methods of the 18th century, but this still leaves considerable scope for debate about when practices become outdated.

In *Crawford v Charing Cross Hospital*[183] the claimant developed brachial palsy in an arm following a blood transfusion. At first instance the defendants were held liable on the basis that the anaesthetist had failed to read an article published in *The Lancet* six months earlier, concerning the best position of the arm when using a drip. The Court of Appeal reversed this decision, taking the view that it would be too great a burden on doctors to say that they have to read every article appearing in the current medical press.[184] Moreover, it was wrong to suggest that a practitioner was negligent simply because he did not immediately put into operation the suggestions made by a contributor to a medical journal,[185] although the time might come when a recommendation was so well proved and so well

3–075

---

[181] See paras 10–087, 10–122.
[182] [1957] 2 All E.R. 118, 122.
[183] *The Times*, 8 December 1953.
[184] See also *Dwan v Farquhar* [1988] 1 Qd R. 234, where an article in a journal concerning the risks of contracting the AIDS virus from blood transfusions was published in March 1983, and a patient contracted HIV from a blood transfusion performed in May 1983; it was held that there was no negligence.
[185] "The dissemination of new literature takes some time, and a medical doctor is not expected to react immediately, or change standard practices, in response to every new article that is published. Often new studies and recommendations are received with some scientific scepticism, while replication of the results is awaited. Immediate response to every publication is unrealistic": *Nattrass v Weber* 2010 ABCA 64; (2010) 316 D.L.R. (4th) 666; [2010] 12 W.W.R. 36 at [31].

accepted that it should be adopted. In *Gascoine v Ian Sheridan & Co.*[186] Mitchell J commented that a "shop floor gynaecologist" had a responsibility to keep himself generally informed on mainstream changes in diagnosis, treatment and practice through the mainstream literature, such as the leading textbooks and the *Journal of Obstetrics and Gynaecology*. Equally, it was unreasonable to suppose that he had an opportunity to acquaint himself with the content of the more obscure journals.[187]

3–076   Once the risks associated with the old procedure become generally known, so that it can be said that ordinary and reasonably competent practitioners would have changed their practice, it will be negligent to continue with that procedure.[188] But as Ebsworth J commented in *Newbury v Bath District Health Authority*,[189] changes in technique or the use of particular instruments may sometimes simply be a matter of fashion:

> "[T]he fact that new methods become available does not make the continued use of the old negligent unless and until they are shown to be wrong or to carry an unacceptably higher risk to the patient than the new. A competent consultant surgeon will keep abreast of his field and in the light of the information he acquires thereby adjust his procedures as appropriate but he remains entitled to keep the old tried method in his armoury for use where properly judged to be suitable. The fact that other surgeons, however distinguished, may use other methods with success does not render the use of a well tried method negligent. The very extent to which a surgeon is skilled in a technique is a factor to be weighed in the balance."[190]

The problem is to identify precisely when it can be said that an unacceptable risk has become generally known. For example, there may be a difference of knowledge and understanding between research scientists and clinicians, since research scientists are usually better informed about new discoveries in discrete areas of their discipline than practitioners, who have to rely on researchers and professional publications to keep them informed.[191] The obligation is to make a reasonable effort to keep up to date. A doctor cannot realistically be expected to

---

[186] [1994] 5 Med. L.R. 437 at 447.

[187] See, e.g. the comment of John Leighton Williams QC in *Bellarby v Worthing and Southlands Hospitals NHS Trust* [2005] EWHC 2089 (QB); (2005) 86 B.M.L.R. 1 at [15]: "I have been referred to textbook extracts and many papers in this case ... They tell me what was available to be read, not that I consider it would be realistic or reasonable to expect treating clinicians in a district general hospital to read every publication traceable. Their contents are frequently conflicting."

[188] See, e.g. *Roe v Minister of Health* [1954] 2 Q.B. 66; *McLean v Weir* [1977] 5 W.W.R. 609; aff'd [1980] 4 W.W.R. 330, below, para.3–079; *McCormick v Marcotte* (1971) 20 D.L.R. (3d) 345, SCC, where a surgeon was held liable for using an obsolete method of treating a broken bone (plate and screw) notwithstanding a specialist orthopaedic surgeon recommended a different procedure (the insertion of an intramedullary nail); *Reynard v Carr* (1983) 30 C.C.L.T. 42 at 67–68; rev'd in part on other grounds (1986) 38 C.C.L.T. 217, where the defendant was ignorant about the serious side effects of a drug he was prescribing, although this was general knowledge within the profession. On the other hand, where the old technique is still described as an alternative to the new technique in the leading textbooks it will be difficult to persuade the court that it cannot be logically supported: see *Ecclestone v Medway NHS Foundation Trust* [2013] EWHC 790 (QB).

[189] (1998) 47 B.M.L.R. 138, QBD.

[190] (1998) 47 B.M.L.R. 138 at 162.

[191] *ter Neuzen v Korn* (1993) 103 D.L.R. (4th) 473 at 497–498, BCCA. Moreover, there may be a lack of effective communication between public health officials and practitioners, again producing a "time lag" in the knowledge of the profession.

read every article in every learned medical journal,[192] but where a particular risk has been highlighted on a number of occasions practitioners will ignore it at their peril.

Practices adopted in other countries are not necessarily evidence of the appropriate standard here. In *Whiteford v Hunter*[193] the defendant mistakenly diagnosed prostate cancer without performing a biopsy or using a cystoscope, procedures which were both standard practice in the United States. The instrument was rare in England at the time and the defendant did not have one. Moreover, the evidence indicated that it was against approved practice in England to use a cystoscope where, as with the claimant, there was acute urinary retention. The House of Lords held that the defendant was not negligent.[194] In *Ndri v Moorfields Eye Hospital NHS Trust*[195] Sir Douglas Brown commented that in assessing the standard of care to be applied to an eye bank in its methods of decontamination and infection control, the standard of care to be applied was the acceptable standard of care in an eye bank within the UK of similar standing to the defendants, but because there are so few eye banks in the UK, it was permissible to look elsewhere. Given that the methods used by the defendants

3–077

---

[192] Although it is acknowledged that "where there is developing knowledge, [the defendant] must keep reasonably abreast of it and not be too slow to apply it": *Stokes v Guest, Keen & Nettlefold (Bolts & Nuts) Ltd* [1968] 1 W.L.R. 1776 at 1783, per Swanwick J; on the other hand, where the defendant's omission involves an absence of initiative in seeking out knowledge of facts which are not in themselves obvious "the court must be slow to blame him for not ploughing a lone furrow": *Thompson v Smith Shiprepairers (North Shields) Ltd* [1984] 1 All E.R. 881 at 894, per Mustill J. In the context of developing knowledge of the risks to employees' hearing within the industry, a reasonable employer should demonstrate "proper but not extraordinary solicitude for the welfare of his workers". See also *Baker v Quantum Clothing Group* [2011] UKSC 17; [2011] 1 W.L.R. 1003, para.3–055 above.

[193] [1950] W.N. 553; *ter Neuzen v Korn* (1993) 103 D.L.R. (4th) 473, BCCA; aff'd (1995) 127 D.L.R. (4th) 577, SCC, where knowledge of the risk of transmission of HIV by artificial insemination was available in Australia in late 1984, but not generally known in British Columbia until mid-1985. The claimant contracted HIV from an artificial insemination procedure carried out in January 1985. The Supreme Court of Canada upheld the decision of the British Columbia Court of Appeal that it was not open to a jury to find the common practice of Canadian practitioners to be negligent; the issue was whether the defendant acted as a reasonable doctor by reference to the prevailing standards. Note, however, that the Court of Appeal considered, at 501, that published guidelines in a specialised field of medicine in the United States would be admissible evidence, because it was reasonable for Canadian physicians practising within that specialty to be aware of them.

[194] In *Ritchie v Chichester Health Authority* [1994] 5 Med. L.R. 187, QBD, an article in the medical literature submitted as part of the evidence ("The wrong drug problem in anaesthesia—An analysis of 2,000 incident reports") found that of 2,000 incidents reported anonymously to the Australian Incident Monitoring Study, 7.2 per cent involved cases of the wrong drug being administered. The American experience was approximately 6 per cent. No UK figures were available, but as the judge said, at 208–209, "it would be wholly unrealistic to assume that it could not and does not happen here". This was important because it assisted the finding that the accident should not simply be attributed to "medical mystery" (an argument advanced by the defendants) and supported the conclusion that the anaesthetist had injected a neurotoxic substance into the claimant when administering an epidural anaesthetic, despite the fact that for this to have happened there would have to have been a series of errors.

[195] [2006] EWHC 3652 (QB).

the possibility that an alternative diagnosis would explain the symptoms, especially where the consequences of the alternative diagnosis, if correct, would be very serious.[217]

3–086   **Claimant's particular susceptibility**   A similar principle applies where the claimant's peculiar susceptibility makes the risk of harm occurring greater than would be the case with a normal individual. For example, a person who digs a hole in the pavement must take reasonable precautions to avoid the risk that a blind person might fall into the hole. Precautions that would protect the fully sighted will not necessarily protect the blind.[218] Accordingly:

> "...a measure of care appropriate to the inability or disability of those who are immature or feeble in mind or body is due from others, who know of or ought to anticipate the presence of such persons within the scope and hazard of their own operations."[219]

3–087   **Defendant's purpose in taking the risk**   The purpose of the defendant's conduct will also be taken into account in assessing what is reasonable. If sufficiently important, it will justify the assumption of abnormal risk.[220] In *Watt v Hertfordshire County Council*[221] it was held that it was not negligent to transport a heavy lifting jack on a vehicle that was not designed to carry it to an emergency where a woman was trapped under a lorry. A fireman was injured when the jack slipped. The risk had to be balanced against the end to be achieved and, said Denning LJ, the saving of life and limb justifies taking considerable risk. This proposition is of obvious importance to the medical profession, who, when entering upon a treatment will be seeking to improve the patient's health, even if life or limb are not at stake. This does not mean, however, that the purpose of saving life and limb can justify taking any risk. It is a matter of balancing the risk against the consequences of not taking the risk. If, for example, the patient's condition is such that he will almost certainly die without some form of medical intervention, then treatment with a high degree of risk will be justified, unless, of course, there is an equally effective alternative treatment that carries less risk. Difficulty in assessing the reasonableness of the defendant's conduct may arise

---

[217] *Lankenau v Dutton* (1986) 37 C.C.L.T. 213 at 232, BCSC; aff'd (1991) 79 D.L.R. (4th) 707, BCCA, where a doctor failed to reassess his initial diagnosis of the cause of the patient's paralysis following major surgery, with the result that it became permanent; *Bergen v Sturgeon General Hospital* (1984) 28 C.C.L.T. 155, Alta QB; *Law Estate v Simice* (1994) 21 C.C.L.T. (2d) 228 at 236, BCSC; aff'd [1996] 4 W.W.R. 672, BCCA, where it was said that once cerebral aneurism was included in a differential diagnosis there was a duty to rule it out or treat it as soon as possible because of its potentially life-threatening consequences. See further paras 4–036 to 4–038.

[218] *Haley v London Electricity Board* [1965] A.C. 778.

[219] *Glasgow Corporation v Taylor* [1922] 1 A.C. 44 at 67, per Lord Sumner, approved by Lord Reid in *Haley v London Electricity Board* [1965] A.C. 778 at 793.

[220] *Daborn v Bath Tramways Motor Co. Ltd* [1946] 2 All E.R. 333 at 336, per Asquith LJ, where the need for ambulances during wartime justified the use of a left-hand-drive vehicle, although it created greater risk of road accidents due to inadequate hand signals. See also the comments of Lang J in *Pittman Estate v Bain* (1994) 112 D.L.R. (4th) 257 at 313, Ont Ct, Gen Div: "In the case of blood, the societal need for the component produces different considerations. This is not a product that should be removed from the market if inherently dangerous. Blood is an essential source of life to many. Although a biologic, and, therefore, dangerous, the need for the product outweighs the risk."

[221] [1954] 1 W.L.R. 835.

where the alternative treatment is less risky or has less debilitating consequences, but is possibly a less effective form of treatment.

Practicability of precautions A further factor to be considered in assessing whether the taking of a foreseeable risk was justified is the practicability (or cost) of taking precautions. The practicability of taking precautions should be measured on an objective basis: the defendant's impecuniosity is not a defence if objectively a precaution was reasonably required.[222] If the risk can be avoided at small cost or with a trivial expenditure of time and effort it will be unreasonable to run the risk.[223] Conversely, some risks can only be eliminated or reduced at great expense. A reasonable person would only neglect a risk if he had a valid reason for doing so, for example, "that it would involve considerable expense to eliminate the risk. He would weigh the risk against the difficulty of eliminating it". But a reasonable person would not ignore even a small risk "if action to eliminate it presented no difficulty, involved no disadvantage and required no expense".[224]

3–088

This principle applies to cases of medical negligence. For example, in *Hucks v Cole*[225] Sachs LJ said that when risks of great danger are knowingly taken as a matter of professional practice then, however small the risks, the court must carefully examine the practice, particularly where the risks can be easily and inexpensively avoided. In *Coles v Reading and District Management Committee*[226] it was held to be negligent not to have given the patient an anti-tetanus

3–089

---

[222] In *PQ v Australian Red Cross Society* [1992] 1 V.R. 19, Vict SC, the claimant, who was a haemophiliac, alleged negligence against the Red Cross in failing to protect him from HIV infection from a transfusion of blood products. McGarvie J held that the actual resources of the defendants was not an issue that was relevant to the practicability of any precautions required. Whether the Red Cross "fell short of the required standard of care is to be tested, not by reference to a reasonable person with the defendant's actual resources of staff facilities and finance, but by reference to a reasonable person with adequate resources available to conduct the enterprise in which the Red Cross was engaged" ([1992] 1 V.R. 19 at 33). In *Pittman Estate v Bain* (1994) 112 D.L.R. (4th) 257, Ont Ct, Gen Div, on the other hand, Lang J held that when assessing the conduct of a blood bank it should be measured against that of other blood banks, not by reference to commercial organisations, on the basis that it was a "professional service" not a commercial service. It would follow from this, that if other "responsible" blood banks were unable or unwilling through lack of resources to take such precautions, the defendant would probably not be liable for failing to take the same precautions.
[223] For example, in *Leon v Tu* 2012 BCSC 1600; (2012) 223 A.C.W.S. (3d) 722 a hospital doctor injected anaesthetic into the claimant's injured hand causing significant pain. The doctor then told the claimant to stand at a sink holding his hand under running water, and left him unattended. The claimant fainted and struck his head on the floor, fracturing his skull and sustaining brain damage. Saunders J held that the doctor had been negligent by leaving the claimant unattended in a standing position given that the risk of fainting following a painful stimulus (vasovagal syncope), though small, was foreseeable: "the risk of [the patient] fainting may have been small, but it would have cost nothing to eliminate that risk. Balancing the risk of vasovagal syncope, if a course of action is pursued, against no risk at all if that course is avoided, does not require medical expertise. It is a matter of common sense" (at [74]).
[224] *Overseas Tankship (U.K.) Ltd v Miller Steamship Co. Pty Ltd, The Wagon Mound (No.2)* [1967] 1 A.C. 617 at 642; and in the medical context see *Chin Keow v Government of Malaysia* [1967] 1 W.L.R. 813, PC, para.3–052; *Leonard v Knott* [1978] 5 W.W.R. 511 at 516, BCSC.
[225] (1968), [1993] 4 Med. L.R. 393, 397.
[226] (1963) 107 S.J. 115.

injection, since it was a simple precaution, and the consequences of the infection are serious.[227] Again, in *Anderson v Chasney* McPherson CJM commented that:

> "It is not sufficient for the surgeon to say: 'I never adopted the use of either of such precautions in operations of this nature'. By doing so he took an unnecessary risk, as both were available for his use on that occasion and he assumed full responsibility for the lack of use of the same, and I would hold that he was negligent in so doing."[228]

3–090 In *Reynolds v North Tyneside Health Authority*[229] a mother was admitted to hospital for the birth of her child, having had a spontaneous rupture of the membranes and with the baby's head 3/5 palpable. In these circumstances there was a foreseeable risk of a cord prolapse, which was put at between 1 in 250 and 1 in 500. This was described as low risk, but the potential consequences from foetal hypoxia extended to death or brain damage. The alleged negligence of the defendants consisted of an omission by the midwife to carry out an immediate vaginal examination given the foreseeable risk of a cord prolapse. A vaginal examination was neither difficult nor costly. The defendants argued that the risk of cord prolapse was so slight that it could be ignored. Gross J held that the defendants were not entitled simply to ignore the risk. Although the risk was low, it was not far-fetched or fanciful. It was not a case where a nice clinical balance had to be struck. The relevant considerations pointed overwhelmingly to the conduct of an immediate vaginal examination.

> "Set against the low risk of cord prolapse were (i) the gravity of the consequences should the risk materialise and (ii) the ease and economy of undertaking an immediate [vaginal examination]."[230]

The argument against an immediate vaginal examination was that it created a risk of infection. But, a vaginal examination was likely to be conducted at some point during labour and the risks of infection would have been the same whenever it was performed; and in any event, the risk of infection was heavily outweighed by the risk of cord prolapse. In terms of the gravity of the consequences they were not "in the same league". Following this analysis of the respective risks, the question remained whether the defendants' omission could be supported on the basis that there was a responsible body of professional opinion which took the view that an immediate vaginal examination was not called for in the circumstances. Gross J was not convinced, on the evidence before the court, that

---

[227] The patient died. See also *Robinson v Post Office* [1974] 2 All E.R. 737 at 745, per Orr LJ: "It was, in our judgment, a very relevant consideration that, although the risks of tetanus having developed in the wound did not amount to any high probability, they could not be dismissed as unreal, and the consequence, if they had materialised, would be likely to be fatal unless ATS were administered."

[228] [1949] 4 D.L.R. 71 at 75, aff'd [1950] 4 D.L.R. 223, SCC; see further para.4–108; *Crits v Sylvester* (1956) 1 D.L.R. (2d) 502 at 511; aff'd (1956) 5 D.L.R. (2d) 601.

[229] [2002] Lloyd's Rep. Med. 459.

[230] [2002] Lloyd's Rep. Med. 459 at [43]. See also *McDonnell v Holwerda* [2005] EWHC 1081 (QB); [2005] Lloyd's Rep. Med. 423, para.4–027, where the seriousness of the consequences of failing to diagnose meningitis in a young child and the speed with which the infection can develop heightened the significance of the risk of failing to refer the patient to hospital for tests.

there was a body of professional opinion which supported the view that the risk so slight that it could be ignored. But, in any event:

> "…even if there was any such contrary practice, or body of opinion, then the only reason articulated in its support for not conducting an immediate [vaginal examination], namely the risk of infection, does not withstand scrutiny. Where the sole reason relied upon in support of a practice is untenable, it follows (at least absent very special circumstances) that the practice itself is not defensible and lacks a logical basis. That is the case here. The suggested contrary practice (or body of opinion) is neither defensible nor logical. Having carefully examined the evidence, this is one of those rare cases where it is appropriate to conclude that there is a lacuna in the practice for which there is no proper basis. Put another way, insofar as any such contrary practice turns on the risk of infection, I would be unable to accept that its proponents had (i) properly directed their minds to the comparative risks and benefits and (ii) reached a defensible conclusion."[231]

Moreover, since the conclusion that the defendants were negligent was also supported by medical and midwifery evidence, the decision did not impose unrealistic standards on the relevant professionals.

Unavoidable risks   Some risks are unavoidable. In this situation the risks of proceeding have to be weighed against the disadvantages of not proceeding, also taking into account the expected benefits to the patient's health. Where the consequences of not treating the patient are potentially very serious then the doctor will normally be justified in taking greater risks.[232] Conversely, where the treatment is for a minor ailment even small risks should not be disregarded[233]; a fortiori, where a diagnostic test which carries a real risk of an adverse reaction is conducted when there are no clinical indications for performing such a test.[234]   3–091

This balancing exercise must take account of the individual patient. So, for example, the risks of a general anaesthetic are greater for an elderly patient than for a young, and otherwise fit, patient, and a surgeon or anaesthetist would have to take this into account in making a decision as to whether the risks involved in   3–092

---

[231] [2002] Lloyd's Rep. Med. 459 at [47].

[232] *Davidson v Connaught Laboratories* (1980) 14 C.C.L.T. 251, where the patient suffered an allergic reaction to a rabies vaccine, having come into contact with a rabid animal. Rabies is almost invariably fatal. Linden J said, at 270, that: "Although the risk was only slight that the plaintiff might contract the disease as a result of that contact, the doctor was not negligent in advising caution when the consequences of not doing so were potentially so severe." See also *H v Royal Alexandra Hospital for Children* [1990] 1 Med. L.R. 297, NSWSC, where it was held that even when the risk of transmitting HIV through contaminated blood products became known it would not have been a practical or reasonable measure to recall or withdraw the products, given the level of risk and the need for the products.

[233] The obvious example would be cosmetic surgery, although there may well be room for disagreement as to the importance to the individual patient of removing certain cosmetic defects. In *La Fleur v Cornelis* (1979) 28 N.B.R. (2d) 569 at 573, NBSC, Barry J commented that cosmetic surgeons do not treat illnesses in the ordinary sense, and accordingly a "doctor who undertakes to operate on the nose of a healthy person for cosmetic purposes has a very high duty indeed". On the performance of breast reduction surgery see *MacDonald v Ross* (1983) 24 C.C.L.T. 242, NSSC; *White v Turner* (1981) 120 D.L.R. (3d) 269; (1982) 12 D.L.R. (4th) 319; and on cosmetic surgery that resulted in the death of a seven-year-old boy, see Dyer (1986) 293 B.M.J. 686. The General Medical Council advises doctors practising cosmetic surgery on appropriate standards of practice: see GMC, *Guidance for all doctors who offer cosmetic interventions*, April 2016 (available at *http://www.gmc-uk.org/guidance/ethical_guidance/28688.asp*).

[234] *Leonard v Knott* [1978] 5 W.W.R. 511, BCSC, see para.4–012.

severity of the patients' medical problems. The role of a triage nurse (or doctor) is to make an initial assessment of a patient's presentation for the purpose deciding how urgent the need is for treatment and to whom the patient should be sent. It is not the function of a triage nurse to make a definitive diagnosis.[247] Moreover, any assessment of the conduct of a triage nurse has to take account of the context in which the function is performed, usually that of a busy A&E department where the task is to make a quick judgment call as to where next to send the patient:

> "There is no opportunity for a triage nurse to devote a great deal of time to the taking of a detailed history or the performance of an extensive diagnosis. Such an exercise would be beyond the minimum necessary to enable that nurse to form a decision as to how to stream the patient. The reasonable nurse is one who operates in a busy A&E which has a procedure which the nurse will follow for streaming and which does not contemplate an exhaustive diagnosis being formed."[248]

By the same token, what can reasonably be expected of a doctor in A&E must take account of the context in which they function, which will often be a pressurised environment where decisions have to be taken at short notice: "the standard of care owed by an A&E doctor must be calibrated in a manner reflecting reality."[249] It will normally be reasonable for the A&E doctor to accept the conclusions of other healthcare professionals who have seen the patient before, unless the decision looks obviously wrong.[250]

---

[247] *Mulholland v Medway NHS Foundation Trust* [2015] EWHC 268 (QB); (2015) 144 B.M.L.R. 50 at [87].

[248] *Mulholland v Medway NHS Foundation Trust* [2015] EWHC 268 (QB); (2015) 144 B.M.L.R. 50 at [90] (obiter). In *Jaciubek v Gulati* [2016] EWHC 269 (QB) at [130] Foskett J observed that: "there is, in my view, even less scope for minute and detailed analysis of a triage nurse's brief notes than there is in relation to an A&E doctor's notes. There would be a massive incentive to adopting a defensive technique (by referring virtually everyone who presents to an A&E department to a senior clinician) if such became the norm." See also *Crammond v Medway NHS Foundation Trust* [2015] EWHC 3540 (QB) at [39] (triage nurse in A&E acted reasonably in obtaining short history from patient complaining of chest pain, performing an ECG and then reporting the findings to the doctor on duty). Note that not all triage will take place in the context of an A&E department: see, e.g., *Pringle v Nestor Prime Care Services Ltd* [2014] EWHC 1308 (QB), para.4–021.

[249] *Mulholland v Medway NHS Foundation Trust* [2015] EWHC 268 (QB); (2015) 144 B.M.L.R. 50 at [101].

[250] *Mulholland v Medway NHS Foundation Trust* [2015] EWHC 268 (QB); (2015) 144 B.M.L.R. 50 at [96]. On that basis in *Mulholland* an A&E doctor was found not to have been negligent in failing to diagnose a patient as having suffered a stroke when a specialist stroke team had previously come to the conclusion, correctly, that the patient had not suffered a stroke. In fact the patient had a brain tumour, which it was accepted could not reasonably have been diagnosed by the doctor. The claimant's argument was that his symptoms were indicative of a stroke and that if he had been sent to the stroke unit he would have been referred for a CT scan which would have identified the tumour. Green J pointed out that the very reason for locating a specialist stroke team in or proximate to A&E was to inject specialism into the assessment process, and to enable A&E doctors to rely upon that specialist assessment. Contrast *Crammond v Medway NHS Foundation Trust* [2015] EWHC 3540 (QB) where the A&E doctor relied on a normal electrocardiogram result on a patient with chest pain and referred the patient to a same-day treatment centre staffed by general practitioners. The A&E doctor was held to have been negligent in failing to take an adequate history from the patient, which could have been obtained relatively quickly, and would have identified several risk factors for acute coronary syndrome. Had this been done further tests would have been ordered which would have identified the patient's existing cardiac condition.

A&E receptionists   A patient presenting at an Accident & Emergency   **3–098**
department may have to negotiate a receptionist who has no medical training,
before being seen by a triage nurse. In *Darnley v Croydon Health Services NHS
Trust*[251] the claimant attended A&E, having been attacked and struck on the head.
He was told by a receptionist that he would be seen in four or five hours, contrary
to the usual practice of telling patients that they would be seen by the triage nurse
within 30 minutes. He left the hospital after 19 minutes without being seen by a
health professional, but his condition deteriorated and he suffered a left
hemiplegia. Had he been told that he would be seen within 30 minutes he would
not have left the hospital, the deterioration in his condition would have occurred
while he was still there and prompt medical treatment would have avoided any
permanent disability. NICE Guidelines stated that all patients presenting to an
emergency department with a head injury should be assessed by a trained
member of staff within a maximum of 15 minutes of arrival at hospital in order to
establish whether they are high or low risk for clinically important brain injury
and/or cervical spine injury. At first instance Judge Robinson held that the
claimant's presentation would not have alerted non-clinical reception staff to the
need to bring it to the triage nurse's attention. The standard to be applied was that
of "a member of the public exercising common sense".[252] Moreover, the NICE
Guidelines could not be applied rigidly, because triage within 15 minutes was not
always achievable, depending on the level of activity in A&E and other clinical
priorities. The failure to meet the 15-minute target by four minutes did not
amount to a breach of duty. Judge Robinson accepted that there had to be "a
longstop, or the target becomes meaningless", and the consensus among the
experts was that the longstop should be 30 minutes which seemed "entirely
appropriate". But in any event the judge went on to hold that though it was
foreseeable that some patients will use information about waiting times to make a
decision about whether to wait to be seen by a doctor or nurse, and that in some
cases they would suffer harm as a consequence of leaving, receptionists in A&E
departments are not under a duty to guard patients against such harm, even if it
could have been prevented by giving full and accurate information about waiting
times. A majority of the Court of Appeal agreed. Jackson LJ said that telling the
patient that there was a potential wait of four or five hours did not amount to an
assumption of responsibility for the consequences which the claimant might
suffer if he walked out of the hospital.[253] It was not fair, just and reasonable to
impose upon the receptionist a duty not to provide inaccurate information about
waiting times. It would add a new layer of responsibility to clerical staff and a

---

[251] [2017] EWCA Civ 151; [2017] P.I.Q.R. P14; [2017] Med. L.R. 245; see J. Goudkamp [2017]
J.P.I.L. C142.
[252] [2015] EWHC 2301 (QB); [2016] P.I.Q.R. P4; [2015] Med. L.R. 506 at [50].
[253] [2017] EWCA Civ 151; [2017] P.I.Q.R. P14; [2017] Med. L.R. 245 at [52], distinguishing at [51]
the decision of the Court of Appeal in *Kent v Griffiths, Roberts and London Ambulance Service*
[2001] Q.B. 36; see para.2–119. McCombe LJ, in a dissenting judgment, did not accept that on the
particular facts of *Darnley* there was a meaningful distinction between the two cases. McCombe LJ
considered that the functions of the hospital could not be divided up into those of receptionists and
medical staff. The duty of the hospital had to be considered in the round and, if the hospital had a duty
not to misinform patients, the duty was not removed by interposing non-medical reception staff as a
first point of contact ([2017] EWCA Civ 151; [2017] P.I.Q.R. P14; [2017] Med. L.R. 245 at
[70]–[71]).

new head of liability for NHS hospitals.[254] This conclusion was based, in part at least, on the view that patients must accept some responsibility for their own actions.[255]

3–099 **Ambulance service** The test for breach of duty to be applied to the ambulance service is the same as that applied to medical professionals, namely the *Bolam* test as explained in *Bolitho*. Of course, what can reasonably be expected of an ambulance crew will differ from that to be expected of a doctor, and will be tailored to their level of expertise, which may vary with the type of crew.[256] Some are trained as ambulance technicians and some are trained as paramedics (which will require a higher level of expertise than that applied to ambulance technicians). In *Taaffe v East of England Ambulance Service NHS Trust*[257] an ambulance was called to attend a 50-year-old woman suffering from severe chest pain. She had a history of hypertension, and a family history of cardiac disease but no history of significant indigestion. She described pain which sounded like it could have been indigestion, but it had subsided by the time the paramedics arrived. They carried out two ECGs which appeared normal, though a computer-generated report on the printed record on one of them stated "Abnormal ECG, T-Wave abnormalities, consider inferior ischaemia". The paramedics did not advise her to go to hospital but to attend an appointment with her general practitioner the following day. Their diagnosis was a panic attack. Five days later she suffered a fatal heart attack. It was conceded that if she had been admitted to hospital on the day she was seen by the paramedics her

---

[254] [2017] EWCA Civ 151; [2017] P.I.Q.R. P14; [2017] Med. L.R. 245 at [53]. Sales LJ agreed, pointing out, at [84], that one consequence of imposing such a duty would be a further duty to update the information about waiting times previously given if there were a sudden increase in the demand for available A&E resources, where patients with more urgent medical conditions were given priority. That tended to show that it was not fair, just or reasonable to impose a duty of care in the circumstances. Sales LJ accepted that a duty of care could be owed if, e.g., a receptionist told someone seeking medical assistance that the A&E department was closed, without reasonable grounds for doing so; but providing information about how long things might take to occur once an individual was admitted was peripheral to the core function of a civilian receptionist which was to admit presenting individuals into A&E ([2017] EWCA Civ 151; [2017] P.I.Q.R. P14; [2017] Med. L.R. 245 at [85]).

[255] [2017] EWCA Civ 151; [2017] P.I.Q.R. P14; [2017] Med. L.R. 245 at [57] per Jackson LJ, though this may seem a little harsh given that the claimant based his actions on the misinformation he had been given by the receptionist; cf. *Macaulay v Karim* [2017] EWHC 1795 (QB) where Foskett J distinguished *Darnley* where the claimant had been in an A&E department for six hours and left the hospital under the impression that nothing further was required. There had been a negligent "system failure" on the part of the hospital in failing to carry out a blood test that had been requested. Moreover, in the circumstances, when it was realised that he had left without the blood test being performed, the hospital were under a duty to telephone the claimant to advise him of the desirability of returning for the test: "Only then could it truly be said that he had made an informed decision about ceasing to place reliance on the hospital that day for finding out what was wrong with him. If that had happened, the decision in *Darnley* may have prevented him from pursuing a claim" ([2017] EWCA Civ 151; [2017] P.I.Q.R. P14; [2017] Med. L.R. 245 at [186]).

[256] See e.g. *Moied v South Central Ambulance Service NHS Trust* [2012] Lexis Citation 42 where a crew of ambulance technicians were found not negligent when called to see to a woman who was 33 weeks' pregnant who had collapsed. They had followed a practice which would be accepted as proper by a responsible body of ambulance technicians and it could not be said that there was no logical support for what they did or did not do.

[257] [2012] EWHC 1335 (QB); [2013] Med. L.R. 406; (2012) 128 B.M.L.R. 71.

condition would have been diagnosed and she would have avoided the cardiac arrest. Sir Robert Nelson held that the paramedics had been negligent. They had been trained to disregard the computer generated printed report on the ECGs because they could be unreliable. They were trained to look at the ECG trace and look in particular for ST wave elevation. There was no ST wave elevation on the traces, so the paramedics concluded that the ECGs were normal. However, the absence of ST wave elevation does not rule out a coronary event, as was made clear in the UK Ambulance Service Clinical Practice Guidelines 2006. It was held that the paramedics had failed to take a full history from the patient (a history of hypertension and a family history of cardiac disease), had ignored the printout of "abnormal ECG" when it was a factor to be considered with other signs and symptoms, and had relied on the absence of ST wave elevation as ruling out a cardiac infarction when it did not do so. The defendants argued that the decision confronting the paramedics was difficult because the patient did not present as a classic cardiac infarction case (some of the classic signs were absent and some were present) and so the decision not to refer her to hospital was within the range of reasonable responses by a paramedic team given the symptoms. Sir Robert Nelson concluded that the argument was unsustainable. The fact that the judgment may be difficult in some cases did not mean that whichever decision the paramedic reaches was bound to be reasonable. The defence expert's view that it was a reasonable response was inconsistent with the need for paramedics to look at all the relevant information in making the decision, and was neither reasonable nor logical.[258]

7. SPECIALISTS

A specialist is expected to achieve the standard of care of a reasonably competent specialist in that field. He must "exercise the ordinary skill of his specialty".[259] This is inherent in the *Bolam* test itself, as Lord Bridge recognised in *Sidaway v Bethlem Royal Hospital Governors*:

3–100

---

[258] [2012] EWHC 1335 (QB); [2013] Med. L.R. 406; (2012) 128 B.M.L.R. 71 at [70] applying *Bolitho v City and Hackney Health Authority* [1998] A.C. 232. See also *Hayes v South East Coast Ambulance Service* [2015] EWHC 18 (QB) where the failure of an ambulance crew to make and record basic observations on a patient suffering a life-threatening asthma attack and the consequent failure to administer appropriate medication, in breach of the UK Ambulance Service Clinical Practice Guidelines 2006, was held to be negligent; *A v East Midlands Ambulance Service NHS Trust* [2015] EWHC 3930 (QB) where ambulance technicians were held to be negligent having failed to comply with guidance given in the UK Ambulance Service Clinical Practice Guidelines 2006 and the "Blue Book", Ambulance Service Paramedic Training, to get a pregnant woman suffering from hypovolaemic shock to the nearest obstetric unit without delay; *Griffiths v Secretary of State for Health* [2015] EWHC 1264 (QB) where it was admitted that a paramedic crew were negligent when they moved a patient who had fallen down stairs without immobilising his neck, having assumed that he had suffered a stroke when in fact he had broken his neck in the fall (commented by J. McQuater [2015] J.P.I.L. C241); *Leigh v London Ambulance Service NHS Trust* [2014] EWHC 286 (QB); [2014] Med. L.R. 134 where a 17-minute delay in arriving at the scene of an accident, which amounted to about a third of the total time taken to arrive (50 minutes), was admitted to have been negligent. Globe J held that the negligent delay had materially contributed to the claimant developing post-traumatic stress syndrome.

[259] *Maynard v West Midlands Regional Health Authority* [1984] 1 W.L.R. 634 at 638, per Lord Scarman.

"The language of the *Bolam* test clearly requires a different degree of skill from a specialist in his own special field than from a general practitioner. In the field of neuro-surgery it would be necessary to substitute for the ... phrase 'no doctor of ordinary skill', the phrase 'no neuro-surgeon of ordinary skill'. All this is elementary, and ... firmly established law."[260]

3–101   References to "a doctor" in the *Bolam* test are simply shorthand for "a doctor undertaking this type of act or procedure". Thus, a general practitioner must be judged by the standards of general practitioners and not specialists,[261] and a doctor in an Accident & Emergency department will be measured against the standards of doctors practising accident and emergency medicine, not a more specialised discipline.[262] On the other hand, if general practitioners were to undertake something that was considered a specialist task they would be judged by the standards of the specialty. If they are unable meet those standards then they will be held negligent for undertaking work beyond their competence.[263]

3–102   The standard of care within a specialist field is that of the ordinary competent specialist, not the most experienced or most highly qualified within the specialty:

"A medical practitioner who holds himself out as being a specialist in a particular field is required to attain the ordinary level of skill amongst those who specialise in the same field. He is not required to attain the highest degree of skill and competence in that particular field."[264]

---

[260] [1985] A.C. 871 at 897. See also per Lord Fraser in *Whitehouse v Jordan* [1981] 1 All E.R. 267 at 280: negligence meant "a failure ... to exercise the standard of skill expected from the ordinary competent specialist having regard to the experience and expertise that the specialist holds himself out as possessing". See also *Crits v Sylvester* (1956) 1 D.L.R. (2d) 502 at 508; aff'd (1956) 5 D.L.R. (2d) 601, SCC; *Wilson v Swanson* (1956) 5 D.L.R. (2d) 113 at 119, per Rand J, SCC: "What the surgeon by his ordinary engagement undertakes with the patient is that he possesses the skill, knowledge and judgment of the generality or average of the special group or class of technicians to which he belongs and will faithfully exercise them." *Carlsen v Southerland* 2006 BCCA 214; (2006) 40 C.C.L.T. (3d) 1—a judge should not focus only on the result of surgery, but on the manner in which it is alleged the defendant failed to meet the appropriate standard of care, otherwise he risks imposing a standard of excellence amounting to perfection, a standard that would amount to a guarantee; cf. *Hernandez v Ho* 2006 BCCA 302; (2006) 54 B.C.L.R. (4th) 67 at [23] and [29], where the British Columbia Court of Appeal distinguished *Carlsen v Southerland* on the basis that, though it may be an error of law for a trial judge to draw an inference of negligence solely from a surgical result, it is not an error of law for a medical expert to do so where the expert's opinion is based on the application of specialised knowledge, skill and experience to observation of the result of the surgery and an examination of the patient and the medical records.
[261] *Langley v Campbell, The Times*, 5 November 1975; *Sa'd v Robinson* [1989] 1 Med. L.R. 41; *Thornton v Nicol* [1992] 3 Med. L.R. 41; *Gordon v Wilson* [1992] 3 Med. L.R. 401, Court of Session; *Stockdale v Nicholls* [1993] 4 Med. L.R. 190; *Durrant v Burke* [1993] 4 Med. L.R. 258; *Stacey v Chiddy* [1993] 4 Med. L.R. 216, NSWSC; aff'd [1993] 4 Med. L.R. 345, NSWCA.
[262] *Mulholland v Medway NHS Foundation Trust* [2015] EWHC 268 (QB); (2015) 144 B.M.L.R. 50.
[263] See para.3–114. This has important implications for the question of expert testimony on the appropriate standard of care to be expected of a specialist practitioner: see para.3–184.
[264] *O'Donovan v Cork County Council* [1967] I.R. 173 at 190, per Walsh J, Supreme Court of Ireland; *Giurelli v Girgis* (1980) 24 S.A.S.R. 264 at 277, per White J; *F. v R.* (1983) 33 S.A.S.R. 189 at 205, per Bollen J. On the other hand, in *M (CP) (Guardian ad litem of) v Martin* 2006 BCCA 333; (2006) 40 C.C.L.T. (3d) 11 at [24] the defendant was "very experienced in his field, to the point of having input into the applicable guidelines. He held a high opinion of his own expertise in comparison to that of his colleagues". That made it reasonable to expect him to be fully up to date on developments in his area of expertise, but this did not mean applying a higher standard than that of a "competent specialist".

Defendant's greater knowledge   If the defendant has knowledge of some fact   **3–103**
that makes harm to the claimant more likely than would otherwise be the case,
then as a reasonable person he must take account of that fact. A greater than
average knowledge of the risks will entail more than the average or standard
precautions.[265] The specialist must take greater precautions than the average
doctor when undertaking the same task, if the specialist's actual *knowledge* and
experience gives him a greater knowledge of risks that ought to be guarded
against.[266] His conduct should not be judged by reference to lesser knowledge
than in fact he had.

Defendant's greater skill   On the other hand, they do not have to use a higher   **3–104**
degree of *skill* than comparable specialists: particularly skilled defendants only
have to conform to the standard to be expected of the reasonably skilled person in
the relevant situation. There may come a point, of course, where a sub-discipline
develops within a specialty such that it can be said that a practitioner undertaking
that form of work must achieve the standards of the new "specialty".[267]
Conversely, where it can be said that a new specialty has developed the question
of whether the defendant has conformed to the practice of a responsible body of
professional opinion will be judged by reference to the standards of that specialty
rather than the standards of doctors engaged in a more generalised practice. This
may make it reasonable, for example, for a specialist surgeon to undertake
intricate exploratory surgery, on the basis that this conforms to a practice
accepted as proper by a responsible body of surgeons in the specialty, in
circumstances where surgeons in other fields might consider the procedure to be
too risky.[268]

Applying a higher standard?   In *Duchess of Argyll v Beuselinck*[269] Megarry J   **3–105**
questioned the proposition that a uniform standard of care would always apply to
specialists:

> "But if the client employs a solicitor of high standing and great experience, will an action for
> negligence fail if it appears that the solicitor did not exercise the care and skill to be expected
> of him, though he did not fall below the standard of a reasonably competent solicitor? If the
> client engages an expert, and doubtless expects to pay commensurate fees, is he not entitled to
> expect something more than the standard of the reasonably competent? I am speaking not
> merely of those expert in a particular branch of the law, as contrasted with a general
> practitioner, but also of those of long experience and great skill as contrasted with those
> practising in the same field of the law but being of a more ordinary calibre and having less
> experience."[270]

---

[265] *Baker v Quantum Clothing Group* [2011] UKSC 17; [2011] 1 W.L.R. 1003; *Stokes v Guest, Keen & Nettlefold (Nuts & Bolts) Ltd* [1968] 1 W.L.R. 1776 at 1783, per Swanwick J; *Wilson v Brett* (1843) 11 M. & W. 113 at 115, per Rolfe B: "If a person more skilled knows that to be dangerous which another not so skilled as he does not, surely that makes a difference in the liability."

[266] A point accepted as correct by Webster J in *Wimpey Construction UK Ltd v Poole* [1984] 2 Lloyd's Rep. 499 at 506–507.

[267] See, e.g. *Poole v Morgan* [1987] 3 W.W.R. 217.

[268] *De Freitas v O'Brien* [1993] 4 Med. L.R. 281 at 296; aff'd [1995] P.I.Q.R. P281; [1995] 6 Med. L.R. 108, identifying a separate specialism of spinal surgeons, comprising both orthopaedic and neurosurgeons engaged wholly or mainly in spinal surgery.

[269] [1972] 2 Lloyd's Rep. 172.

[270] [1972] 2 Lloyd's Rep. 172 at 183.

3–106   This higher standard would be based on an implied term in the contract of retainer to the effect that solicitors will use the care and skill that they actually possess rather than the care and skill of the average solicitor specialising in that field of law. There is no reason in principle why a client should not be able to purchase a higher standard of care,[271] though this justification would confine the higher duties to actions in contract. Megarry J distinguished contractual duties from the tort of negligence, where:

> "…the unusually careful and highly skilled are not held liable for falling below their own high standards if they nevertheless do all that a reasonable man would have done."

Clearly, if this distinction was accepted, and applied to the medical profession, it could lead to different duties being owed to patients in contract and tort, a position that the courts have been reluctant to countenance,[272] though in *FB v Rana* Jackson LJ left open the possibility of a higher standard of care being applied in contract.[273] In *Wimpey Construction U.K. Ltd v Poole*,[274] however, Webster J considered Megarry J's dictum and concluded that the *Bolam* test had been approved by the House of Lords and the Privy Council without qualification, and so should be applied without this gloss. Subsequently, in *Matrix-Securities Ltd v Theodore Goddard*[275] Lloyd J held that the mere fact that the defendants were an established firm of City solicitors who professed very high levels of skill and experience did not increase their duty or lead to an inference that a higher duty had been undertaken by them. Their obligation, in advising on a complex tax avoidance scheme, was to exercise that standard of care which could be expected from a reasonably competent firm of solicitors with a specialist tax department. In other words, a solicitor advising in tax matters must exercise the standard of care appropriate to that sector of the profession specialising in tax matters. This is the same test as that applied to specialist doctors.

---

[271] Though if a solicitor has agreed to accept a fee which turns out to be too low then "generally speaking" he is "obliged to complete the work, to the ordinary standard of care, even if it has become unremunerative": *Inventors Friend Ltd v Leathes Prior* [2011] EWHC 711 (QB); [2011] P.N.L.R. 20 at [76] per Cranston J.

[272] See para.2–011.

[273] [2017] EWCA Civ 334; [2017] P.I.Q.R. P17; [2017] Med. L.R. 279 at [62]: "I do not wish this judgment to be taken as accepting that in contractual professional negligence claims the particular experience and CV of the defendant should be ignored, as they must be in tortious claims. In a contractual case, the claimant may have selected and retained the defendant precisely because of their experience and CV. In a tortious claim, however, such as the present case, the claimant and her parents may play no part in the choice of doctor."

[274] [1984] 2 Lloyd's Rep. 499 at 506.

[275] [1998] P.N.L.R. 290.

8. INEXPERIENCE

(a) The inexperienced doctor

It is axiomatic that the standard of care expected of the reasonable man is   3–107
objective, not subjective. It eliminates the personal equation and takes no account
of the particular idiosyncrasies or weaknesses of the defendant.[276] Thus, the
defendant who is inexperienced or who is just learning a particular task or skill
must come up to the standards of the reasonably competent and experienced
person. His "incompetent best" is not good enough.[277] This principle applies with
as much force to an inexperienced doctor as it does to an inexperienced motorist.
In *Jones v Manchester Corporation*[278] a patient died from an excessive dose of
anaesthetic administered by a doctor who had been qualified for five months. In
an action which was concerned with the respective responsibilities of the junior
doctor and the hospital authority, the Court of Appeal made it clear that it was no
defence to an action by a patient to say that she did not have sufficient experience
to undertake the task, or to say that the surgeon in charge was also to blame:

> "The patient was entitled to receive all the care and skill which a fully qualified and
> well-experienced anaesthetist would possess and use. If Dr. Wilkes failed to exercise that care
> and skill, she would be liable to the patient or his widow for the consequences, no matter that
> the hospital authorities knew that she had not sufficient experience for the task and were much
> to blame for asking her to do it without proper supervision."[279]

This issue arose in *Wilsher v Essex Area Health Authority*.[280] A premature baby in   3–108
a special care baby unit received excess oxygen due to an error in monitoring its
supply of oxygen. A junior and inexperienced doctor inserted a catheter (by
which the blood oxygen pressure was to be measured) into a vein rather than an
artery. This in itself was not negligent, since it was the sort of mistake that any
reasonably competent doctor might have made in the circumstances. The position
of the catheter in the body can be checked, however, by means of an X-ray. This
was done and the doctor failed to spot that the catheter was mispositioned, though
he did ask a senior registrar in the unit to check the X-ray. The registrar failed to
notice the mistake. The baby was subsequently discovered be suffering from
retrolental fibroplasia[281] which causes blindness, possibly as a result of the

---

[276] *Glasgow Corporation v Muir* [1943] A.C. 448 at 457, per Lord Macmillan. There remains,
however, a subjective element in that it is left to the individual judge to decide what is reasonable and
what could have been foreseen: "What to one judge may seem far-fetched may seem to another both
natural and probable" ([1943] A.C. 448 at 457).
[277] *Nettleship v Weston* [1971] 2 Q.B. 691 at 698, 710; *Imbree v McNeilly* [2008] HCA 40; (2008) 236
C.L.R. 510; (2008) 248 A.L.R. 647 (learner driver held to same standard of care as experienced
driver).
[278] [1952] Q.B. 852.
[279] [1952] Q.B. 852 at 868, per Denning LJ. See also at 871: "Errors due to inexperience or lack of
supervision are no defence as against the injured person . . ."
[280] [1987] Q.B. 730.
[281] This term is somewhat dated. The condition is now known as retinopathy of prematurity. For
discussion of the appropriate medical management of the condition see (1997) 3 Clinical Risk 35–51;
Clements (1995) 1 AVMA Medical & Legal Journal 215.

3–115 **Satisfying the duty placed on inexperienced professionals** Inexperienced doctors will discharge their duties of care by seeking the assistance of their superiors to check their work, even though they may themselves have made a mistake.[304] It was on this basis that the junior doctor was found not to have been negligent in *Wilsher v Essex Area Health Authority*, although the registrar was held negligent.[305]

3–116 **Failing to provide supervision** An experienced doctor should also recognise and exercise caution against the inexperience of colleagues.[306] In *Drake v Pontefract Health Authority; Wakefield and Pontefract Community NHS Trust*[307] a consultant psychiatrist was found to have been negligent in allowing an inexperienced Senior House Officer to interview and treat the claimant without immediate supervision from a more experienced psychiatrist, when the patient had been expressly referred as a suicide risk.

3–117 **Negligent supervision** Of course, it is possible for both the inexperienced and the supervising doctor to be held negligent. In *Greenhorn v South Glasgow*

BCCA; aff'd [1952] 3 D.L.R. 785, SCC; *Payne v St Helier Group Hospital Management Committee, The Times*, 12 July 1952, where a casualty officer was held to be negligent in failing to detain a patient for examination by a doctor of consultant rank. See para.4–047. In *Dillon v Le Roux* [1994] 6 W.W.R. 280, BCCA, a family physician, who was working as a relief doctor in a hospital emergency room but had no training as an emergency room physician, was held liable for failing to call an experienced hospital doctor to assist with the diagnosis of a patient's medical condition.

[304] This is particularly the case where there are professional guidelines: *R v Lanarkshire Health Board* [2016] CSOH 133; 2016 G.W.D. 31-556 at [129] per Lord Brailsford: if a less experienced clinician considers the application of a guideline in a particular clinical situation to be inappropriate, it would be prudent to consult with a more experienced professional colleague.

[305] See also *Junor v McNicol, The Times*, 26 March 1959 where the House of Lords held that a house surgeon who had acted on the instructions of a consultant orthopaedic surgeon was not liable; *Tanswell v Nelson, The Times*, 11 February 1959, where McNair J said that a dentist was entitled to rely on a doctor's opinion about a patient's response to antibiotics, unless that opinion was clearly inconsistent with the observed facts; *Anderson v Queen Elizabeth II Health Sciences Centre* 2012 NSSC 360; (2012) 97 C.C.L.T. (3d) 51, where a first-year resident doctor was held not negligent for puncturing the claimant's jugular artery during an unsuccessful attempt to insert a catheter into her internal jugular vein, whereas the second-year resident who was supervising the more junior doctor, and was aware of his inexperience with the procedure, was held to have been negligent; *Leonard v Knott* [1978] 5 W.W.R. 511, BCSC, where it was held that a radiologist is entitled to rely on the judgment of the referring physician as to whether a radiological investigation is required, unless there is some obvious problem; *Weir v Graham* [2002] EWHC 2291 (QB) at [55]—a general practitioner who has referred a patient to hospital for diagnostic tests is entitled to assume that the hospital is taking reasonable care of the patient and it is not for a general practitioner to go through hospital notes to check that the hospital has done what it should have done (held to be reasonable for a general practitioner to assume that the hospital doctors were aware of the test results and were taking them into consideration in their diagnostic investigations); cf. *Davy-Chiesman v Davy-Chiesman* [1984] 1 All E.R. 321 at 332, 335, stating that solicitors should not rely blindly on the advice of counsel, although in this case the solicitor had failed to detect an "obvious error"; *Matrix-Securities Ltd v Theodore Goddard* [1998] P.N.L.R. 290—a solicitor is entitled to rely on counsel's advice, and would be negligent for failing to do so unless that advice was obviously wrong; *FirstCity Insurance Group Ltd v Orchard* [2002] Lloyd's Rep. P.N. 543 at [82]; *Regent Leisuretime Ltd v Skerrett* [2006] EWCA Civ 1184; [2007] P.N.L.R. 9.

[306] *Comeau v Saint John Regional Hospital* [2001] NBCA 113; (2001) 9 C.C.L.T. (3d) 223, NBCA.

[307] [1998] Lloyd's Rep. Med. 425.

University Hospitals NHS Trust[308] the claimant suffered serious blood loss following damage to an artery in the course of a colposuspension operation, a procedure designed to cure urinary leakage arising from genuine stress incontinence. The operation was performed by a specialist registrar in obstetrics and gynaecology (L) under the supervision of an associate specialist in obstetrics and gynaecology (H). It was argued that L was negligent in carrying out the operation, that she lacked the necessary experience to perform it, and that H failed to supervise her properly during the course of the procedure. Lord Uist held that an arterial bleed was not a recognised complication of the procedure, and that once the claimant had proved there was damage to an artery, that raised a prima facie inference of negligence on the part of the defendants which it was for them to rebut, which they had failed to do.[309] Lord Uist found that H had no clear idea about the nature of L's experience in performing colposuspensions, how recent that experience was, how many colposuspensions she had carried out as lead surgeon and when she had done them (she had done only one colposuspension as lead surgeon in the previous five to six years). H had made an unfounded assumption about L's experience and surgical ability. His failure to satisfy himself that L had sufficient recent experience was negligent, and though that in itself did not cause the injury it was "clearly a relevant background against which to consider the events which occurred at the operation". The inference was that H must have been negligent in his supervision of the performance of the operation by L since had H been exercising reasonable care, L would not have been allowed to execute the manoeuvre which damaged the artery.

Emergencies In an emergency it may well be reasonable for a practitioner inexperienced in a particular treatment to intervene, or indeed for someone lacking medical qualifications to undertake some forms of treatment. For example, a bystander who renders assistance at a road accident does not necessarily hold himself out as qualified to do so. He would be expected to achieve only the standard that could reasonably be expected in the circumstances, which would probably be very low.[310] This approach is clearly born of the emergency since if there was no urgency, the unqualified person who undertook treatment which was beyond his competence would be held to the standard to expected of the reasonably competent and experienced practitioner. A person who holds himself out as trained in first aid must conform to the standards of "the ordinary skilled first-aider exercising and professing to have that special skill of a first-aider".[311] This will obviously be greater than the standard of a layman performing first aid, and would be relevant, for example, in a claim against paramedically trained ambulance crew.

3–118

---

308 [2008] CSOH 128; (2008) 104 B.M.L.R. 50.

309 Applying *Cassidy v Ministry of Health* [1951] 2 K.B. 343; para.3–158 below.

310 On the difficulties of laymen diagnosing mental illness see *Ali v Furness Withy* [1988] 2 Lloyd's Rep. 379, where the question was the standard applicable to a ship's master diagnosing insanity in a crewman.

311 *Cattley v St John's Ambulance Brigade* unreported 25 November 1988, QBD, per Judge Prosser QC: "...the true test for establishing negligence in a first-aider is whether he has been proved to be guilty of such failure as no first-aider of ordinary skill would be guilty of, if acting with ordinary care..."

3–119   **Other factors**   The rule that inexperience is not a defence is a consequence of the objective nature of the standard of care in negligence, and applies to other factors as well as inexperience. If the defendant is unable to measure up to the objectively required standard for any reason, be it stress, overwork, tiredness or ill health, he will nonetheless be found negligent.[312] In *Barnett v Chelsea and Kensington Hospital Management Committee*[313] a casualty officer, who was himself unwell, refused to see three nightwatchmen who had presented themselves in the casualty department of a hospital, telling them to go home and call in their own doctors. One of the men subsequently died. Nield J held that the doctor's failure to see and examine the deceased was negligent:

> "It is unfortunate that Dr. Banerjee was himself at the time a tired and unwell doctor, but there was no-one else to do that which it was his duty to do."[314]

(b)   The hospital authorities

3–120   Whatever the position of the inexperienced doctor, it is possible that a health authority could be in breach of a primary duty of care to the patient if they allow inexperienced staff to practise without adequate supervision. In *Jones v Manchester Corporation*[315] a majority of the Court of Appeal held that the hospital board was liable to make contribution to the inexperienced doctor whose negligence caused the patient's death. Indeed, the board bore the brunt of the blame (80 per cent), even though counsel for the doctor admitted that she had been negligent to a degree which was inexcusable even in an inexperienced

---

[312] Old age or infirmity is not a defence for a negligent driver of a motor vehicle: *Roberts v Ramsbottom* [1980] 1 All E.R. 7 at 15; cf. *Mansfield v Weetabix Ltd* [1999] 1 W.L.R. 1263 where the Court of Appeal held that a driver who becomes unable to control a vehicle will not be liable for damage caused by his loss of control if he is unaware of the disabling condition from which he is suffering, whether the disabling event is sudden or gradual. On this point, *Roberts v Ramsbottom* had been wrongly decided, though the decision could be supported on the alternative ground that the defendant continued to drive when he was unfit to do so, and when he should have been aware of his unfitness. To apply an objective standard in a way which did not take account of the defendant's condition (of which he was unaware) would be to impose strict liability (per Leggatt LJ in *Mansfield*; but see *Dunnage v Randall* [2015] EWCA Civ 673; [2016] Q.B. 639, para.3–004, n.5). A defendant who knows that he is susceptible to such attacks will be liable for harm resulting from a loss of control: *Hill v Baxter* [1958] 1 Q.B. 277; and similarly if he ought to have known that he was subject to a condition rendering him unfit: *Waugh v James K. Allan Ltd* [1964] 2 Lloyd's Rep. 1. In *Nickolls v Ministry of Health, The Times*, 4 February 1955 the surgeon who operated on the claimant was suffering from cancer. The question was whether he was in a fit condition to have undertaken the operation. It was held that, on the facts, he was and therefore he was not negligent. Clearly, if the conclusion had been that he was unfit, it would have been negligent to operate.
[313] [1968] 1 All E.R. 1068.
[314] [1968] 1 All E.R. 1068 at 1073. It is not uncommon for junior hospital doctors to have to work long hours. If this was a factor in an error made by the doctor the health authority may also be responsible: see para.3–121. It is doubtful that overwork or the fact that resources are stretched would fall within the notion of "battle conditions" which Mustill LJ has suggested could influence the court's assessment of negligence: see *Wilsher v Essex Area Health Authority* [1987] Q.B. 730 at 749, para.3–093. The term seems to indicate something in the nature of an emergency, rather than the everyday circumstances in which doctors have to work, even if they themselves feel "embattled".
[315] [1952] Q.B. 852.

person. The hospital board should not leave patients in inexperienced hands without proper supervision, said Denning LJ:

> "It would be in the highest degree unjust that the hospital board, by getting inexperienced doctors to perform their duties for them, without adequate supervision, should be able to throw all the responsibility on to those doctors as if they were fully experienced practitioners."[316]

This point was reiterated in *Wilsher v Essex Area Health Authority*.[317] Sir Nicolas Browne-Wilkinson V-C recognised that applying a subjective standard of care to inexperienced junior doctors might mean that the rights of a patient would depend on the experience of the doctor who treats him. This would not be the case, said his Lordship, because the health authority could be directly liable:

3–121

> "In my judgment, a health authority which so conducts its hospital that it fails to provide doctors of sufficient skill and experience to give the treatment offered at the hospital may be directly liable in negligence to the patient."[318]

There was no reason why, in principle, the health authority should not be directly liable if its organisation was at fault. Arguably, this proposition would apply with equal, if not greater, force to other organisational failures which expose patients to serious risk of injury, such as requiring junior hospital doctors to work excessive hours, with the result that they become so fatigued that their judgment or competence becomes impaired. Whilst a claim that the doctor was overworked would not provide a defence for the doctor in an action by the patient, it is a good reason to place the burden of responsibility upon the health authority.[319]

There is, however, a problem with this line of argument. The standard of care applicable to a NHS Trust in determining whether it has been at fault in failing to

3–122

---

[316] [1952] Q.B. 852 at 871; *Murphy v St. Catharines General Hospital* (1963) 41 D.L.R. (2d) 697, Ont HC, where a hospital was held to have been negligent in failing to give instruction to and supervision of junior doctors in the use of a new method of inserting an intravenous catheter. In *Brus v Australian Capital Territory* [2007] ACTSC 83 a hospital was held to be in breach of duty by holding out a doctor as a level 3 registrar when it knew that she was a level 2 registrar who had been rated as unsatisfactory for surgical skills at level 2. They had allowed the doctor "to perform a procedure that was clearly beyond the capacity of a second year trainee with adverse training assessments for surgical skills" (per Connolly J at [59]). On the other hand, there was no general duty on a public hospital to provide public patients with a choice of doctor, or to inform a patient as to the academic standing of a registrar (at [62]).

[317] [1987] Q.B. 730.

[318] [1987] Q.B. 730 at 778; see also per Glidewell LJ at 775. See further the comments of Lord Browne-Wilkinson in *X (Minors) v Bedfordshire County Council* [1995] 2 A.C. 633 at 740. In *Dryden v Surrey County Council* [1936] 2 All E.R. 535 at 539 Finlay J commented that it could not possibly be held that the mere presence of probationary nurses was evidence of negligence. Although, as it stands the statement is clearly correct, this must, presumably, be a matter of degree. Note that, in Wales, Local Health Boards and NHS Trusts have a statutory duty ensure "that there are sufficient nurses to allow the nurses time to care for patients sensitively": Nurse Staffing Levels (Wales) Act 2016, amending the National Health Service (Wales) Act 2006. The statute does not create any private law remedy for breach of this duty, though it could be relevant to an assessment of whether a particular level of staffing was reasonable in the circumstances.

[319] Note that a health authority which requires a doctor to work an excessive number of hours, so damaging the doctor's health, may be liable to the doctor in its capacity as an employer: see *Johnstone v Bloomsbury Health Authority* [1992] Q.B. 333; Dolding and Fawlk (1992) 55 M.L.R. 562; Weir [1991] C.L.J. 397. This action was subsequently settled: (1995) 310 B.M.J. 1155.

such herbal remedies gave rise to a risk of liver damage. The defendant did not read orthodox medical journals, but believed the remedy to be completely safe in the light of Chinese medical textbooks. The judge, Bernard Livesey QC, held that the defendant should not be judged by the standards of orthodox medicine, since he did not hold himself out as practising orthodox medicine, and his patient had rejected the orthodox approach. But in assessing the standard of care to be applied the court should also have regard to the fact that he was practising his art alongside orthodox medicine, and he had to take account of the implications of that fact. The fact that the defendant believed the medication not to be harmful was irrelevant. He had a duty to ensure that it was not actually or potentially harmful. He also had an obligation to check that there had not been any adverse report on the remedy in an orthodox medical journal.[330] In assessing this the judge considered that an appropriate benchmark was that of a general practitioner of orthodox medicine. On the facts, a general practitioner would not have been negligent if he had not noticed the letters and warnings in the orthodox medical literature; and even if he had seen them, the reasonably competent general practitioner would not have been put on notice that the remedy was too hazardous to prescribe since the warnings were equivocal and did not paint a consistent picture of serious risk. If a general practitioner would not have been negligent in failing to identify the risk, then the defendant had conformed to the standard of care appropriate to traditional Chinese herbal medicine, practised in accordance with standards required in the UK.[331]

10. STATUTE

3–127 The focus of the tort of negligence is generally on corrective justice. This involves considering the relationship between the parties, and asking whether, in all the circumstances, the defendant has caused harm to the claimant by taking an unreasonable risk vis-à-vis the claimant. If the answer is yes, the defendant is ordered to pay compensation to restore the claimant to his pre-tort position (in so far as the payment of money can do this). The consequences for others, particularly other potential future defendants, are simply not part of the equation in determining whether *this* defendant has taken an unreasonable risk with respect to *this* claimant on the facts of *this* individual case. Of course, there are policy judgments to be made about the boundaries of the tort of negligence when considering whether a duty of care should be imposed, and these judgments do take into account the potential impact of a general liability rule, particularly

[330] Alternative practitioners are not thereby required to subscribe to a range of orthodox medical journals. It was sufficient if they subscribed to an association which arranged to search the relevant literature and promptly report any material publication to them.

[331] The Medicines & Healthcare products Regulatory Agency found a number of dangerous and illegal ingredients in traditional Chinese medicines, including mercury, lead, arsenic and Aristolochia (which can cause kidney failure and cancer): *The safety and quality of unlicensed traditional Chinese medicines on the UK market* (2004). Traditional herbal medicines are now subject to a more stringent regulatory regime. See the Human Medicines Regulations 2012 (SI 2012/1916) Pt 7 (revoking and replacing the Medicines (Traditional Herbal Medicinal Products for Human Use) Regulations 2005 (SI 2005/2750) which implemented the EU Directive on Traditional Herbal Medicinal Products, Directive 2004/24/EC (which amended Directive 2001/83/EC)).

where the potential defendants are public authorities.[332] But once the decision has been taken that it is appropriate to impose a duty of care, broader policy issues are not invoked to deny a claimant compensation that would otherwise have been granted.

The assessment of what constitutes reasonable care depends on the all the circumstances of the case, and may well involve a value judgment about the standards of safety that one can reasonably expect. For example, in determining what precautions it is reasonable for an occupier to take for the protection of entrants under the Occupiers' Liability Acts 1957 and 1984, the court will have regard to the ordinary risks of life which individuals entering the land can be expected to encounter as result of their own activities. In *Tomlinson v Congleton Borough Council*[333] Lord Hoffmann said that:

3–128

> "...it will be extremely rare for an occupier of land to be under a duty to prevent people from taking risks which are inherent in the activities they freely choose to undertake upon the land. If people want to climb mountains, go hang gliding, or swim or dive in ponds or lakes, that is their affair."

However, this approach represents a judgment about the underlying values of a system of fault liability, whereby defendants will be held to be at fault, and therefore liable to pay compensation, only where the risks that they have taken in relation to someone else's safety are unreasonable—if claimants choose to take risks with their own safety, whether out of a sense of adventure or foolhardiness, they should not expect someone else to compensate them if those risks materialise. This is not an argument about the limited defence of volenti non fit injuria,[334] but about personal responsibility, and what it is *reasonable* to expect potential defendants to do to protect claimants from harm.

Over the last 20 years or so, media reports of some high profile compensation claims have tended to induce an element of "moral panic" about the law of negligence, with assertions that a "compensation culture" has developed that is undermining basic values of personal responsibility.[335] Potential defendants (usually in the public sector), it is said, terrified at the prospect of litigation, have so curtailed their activities with overly-cautious risk assessments that they no longer undertake such benign activities as taking children on school trips or organising church bazaars,[336] and doctors are said to practise "defensive

3–129

---

[332] Some, but by no means all, of these issues are touched on in Ch.2.

[333] [2003] UKHL 47; [2004] 1 A.C. 46 at [45].

[334] See para.11–020.

[335] See D. De Saulles "The Media Circus—How Injuries Make the News" [2007] J.P.I.L. 209.

[336] For consideration of the validity of these arguments see: A. Morris, "Spiralling or Stabilising? The Compensation Culture and Our Propensity to Claim Damages for Personal Injury" (2007) 70 M.L.R. 349; R. Lewis, A. Morris, and K. Oliphant, "Tort personal injury claims statistics: Is there a compensation culture in the United Kingdom?" [2006] J.P.I.L. 87 (and also at (2006) 14 T.L.J. 158); K. Williams, "State of fear: Britain's 'Compensation Culture' Reviewed" (2005) 25 L.S. 499; K. Williams, "Politics, the Media and Refining the Notion of Fault: Section 1 of the Compensation Act 2006" [2006] J.P.I.L. 347; R. Lewis and A. Morris "Challenging Views of Tort (Part 1)" [2013] J.P.I.L. 69; R. Lewis and A. Morris "Challenging Views of Tort (Part 2)" [2013] J.P.I.L. 137; R. Lewis, "Compensation Culture Reviewed: Incentives to Claim and Damages Levels" [2014] J.P.I.L. 209; J. Spencer, "An Unethical Personal Injury Sector" [2014] J.P.I.L. 226.

the existence of a duty of care.[349] This essentially involves a judgment that imposing liability for negligence will tend to "over-deter" potential defendants, damaging the service in question, rather than contributing to an improvement in standards of conduct, though this is an intuitive judgment rather than being based on empirical evidence.[350] Logically, the same argument would apply to any defendant who is held accountable in the tort of negligence, but no one suggests that imposing a duty of care on, say, motorists makes them drive *too* carefully. Clearly, the option of denying the existence of a duty of care is not available in the vast majority of medical negligence cases, since doctors undoubtedly owe a duty of care to their patients.[351] In *Barker v Nugent*[352] counsel for the defendant doctor argued that as a matter of public policy, to avoid an escalation of defensive medicine, the courts should be slower to impute negligence to the medical profession than to others. Rougier J rejected the argument, pointing out that comparisons with the position in the United States of America are not entirely sound. Moreover, his Lordship added:

"I can think of only one thing more disastrous than the escalation of defensive medicine and that is the engendering of a belief in the medical profession that certain acts or omissions which would otherwise be classed as negligence can, in a sense, be exonerated."

3–136   Similarly, in *Wilsher v Essex Area Health Authority* Mustill LJ responded to his own acknowledgement of the risks of defensive practice with the comment that :

"...the proper response cannot be to temper the wind to the professional man. If he assumes to perform a task, he must bring to it the appropriate care and skill."

This was immediately followed, however, by the statement that the courts must constantly bear in mind that the fact that in retrospect the choice actually made can be shown to have turned out badly is not in itself a proof of negligence, and that the duty of care is not a warranty of a perfect result. Whilst this is perfectly accurate as a statement of the law, the linking of comments about defensive

---

[349] *Hill v Chief Constable of West Yorkshire* [1989] A.C. 53; *Rowling v Takaro Properties Ltd* [1988] A.C. 473 at 502; *Yuen Kun-yeu v A.-G. of Hong Kong* [1988] A.C. 175; *Saif Ali v Sydney Mitchell & Co.* [1980] A.C. 198; *Elguzouli-Daf v Commissioner of Police of the Metropolis* [1995] 1 All E.R. 833; *Marc Rich & Co. v Bishop Rock Marine Co. Ltd* [1996] A.C. 211; *Brooks v Commissioner of Police of the Metropolis* [2005] UKHL 24; [2005] 1 W.L.R. 1495 at [30]. On the other hand, in *Michael v Chief Constable of South Wales* [2015] UKSC 2; [2015] A.C. 1732 counsel criticised statements in *Hill v Chief Constable of West Yorkshire* that the imposition of a duty of care would inevitably lead to an unduly defensive attitude by the police, and Lord Toulson acknowledged, at [121], that "Those criticisms have force". But his Lordship considered that it would equally be wrong to assume, on the basis of intuition, that imposing a duty of care would lead to an improvement in the police response to domestic violence; cf. Lord Kerr at [179]: "arguably, the risk of litigation improves professional standards".

[350] See Hartshorne, Smith and Everton (2000) 63 M.L.R. 502 pointing out that the courts rarely have any empirical evidence to justify assertions about "defensive" practices.

[351] Though see *Darnley v Croydon Health Services NHS Trust* [2017] EWCA Civ 151; [2017] P.I.Q.R. P14; [2017] Med. L.R. 245 at [88] where Sales LJ stated that imposing a duty of care on an A&E receptionist not to misinform patients about waiting times "would be likely to lead to defensive practices on the part of NHS trusts to forbid their receptionists to provide any information about likely waiting times".

[352] Unreported 18 March 1987, QBD.

medicine, however vague and imprecise that notion may be, to the frequent reminders that the courts feel constrained to give themselves about the inherent risks of medical treatment suggests that "defensive medicine" does sometimes play a role in medical litigation, as part of the judicial "mind set" which creates an additional, though unquantifiable, hurdle that claimants have to overcome. This may be reflected in the standard of proof that claimants have to achieve in practice, although the formal standard of proof remains the same. But as Kilner Brown J observed in *Ashcroft v Mersey Regional Health Authority*[353]:

> "...the medical and social consequences of medical men being found guilty of negligence on insufficient evidence may be appropriate as a statement of probable consequences, but beg the question which has to be decided."

In other words, the question remains as to what constitutes "sufficient" evidence.

In *M (A Minor) v Newham London Borough Council*[354] a majority of the Court of Appeal was strongly influenced by arguments about defensive practice in holding that a psychiatrist and a social worker did not owe a duty of care to a child or its parents when advising a social services authority whether the child had been physically or sexually abused, and as to the identity of the abuser.[355] The child had been needlessly removed from its home into local authority care, and both the child and her mother claimed that they had suffered psychiatric harm as result. The defendants argued that imposing a duty of care in these circumstances would have serious adverse consequences, particularly in terms of: (a) the financial implications for local authorities; and (b) the reaction of social workers and doctors working the field of child protection to the risk of liability.

3–137

Both Peter Gibson and Staughton LJJ took the view that if a new duty of care was established many claims would be brought and a major diversion of resources to defending actions would occur, placing further strain on an already overstretched system of child protection. Time, trouble and expense would be required for the investigation of claims, to the prejudice of the defendants' budget for their proper functions.[356] In his dissenting judgment Sir Thomas Bingham MR accepted that, to a greater or lesser extent, the overstretched resources of local authorities would be diverted from the function of looking after children and wasted on litigation:

3–138

> "But this is an argument frequently (and not implausibly) advanced on behalf of doctors: it has not prevailed. Other professions resist liability on the ground that it will in the end increase the cost to the paying customer; that resistance has not on the whole been effective either. Save in

---

[353] [1983] 2 All E.R. 245 at 247.

[354] [1995] 2 A.C. 633.

[355] Note, however, that a doctor or social worker now owes a duty of care to children (but not their parents) when investigating suspected child abuse: *JD v East Berkshire Community Health NHS Trust* [2005] UKHL 23; [2005] 2 A.C. 373.

[356] Staughton LJ even went so far as to suggest that many claims with little or no prospect of success would be financed by the legal aid fund; and that many cases would be decided in favour of a claimant whose misfortunes attract sympathy, although there has been no more than an error of judgment: [1995] 2 A.C. 633 at 675. It is remarkable that his Lordship should think it appropriate to deny the existence of a duty of care partly on the basis that otherwise the legal aid fund would, in breach of its statutory duty, finance actions which have *no* prospects of success, or that judges would, out of sympathy, decide cases in favour of claimants where negligence has not been proved.

> "Not only would the child in fact being abused be prejudiced by such delay: the increased workload inherent in making such investigations would reduce the time available to deal with other cases and other children."[361]

This was a factor in persuading their Lordships that a duty of care should not be imposed for reasons of policy.[362] With respect, this argument carries weight when the assumption is made that "the child in fact is being abused". It looks less persuasive if the premise is that the child may or may not be being abused, and the local authority has a responsibility to carry out reasonable investigation of the facts to determine the truth of the matter. It is not in the interests of children that they be wrongly taken into local authority care as a result of negligence, any more than it is in the interests of children that they be negligently left at risk of abuse. In other words, the exercise of reasonable care by all those engaged in child protection, including doctors, is in the interests of all children, whether they are the victims of abuse or not. As long as it is remembered that the obligation in negligence is only to exercise reasonable care, not to achieve perfection, and that difficult decisions taken in circumstances of some urgency will not lightly be condemned as careless, a duty to exercise reasonable care should hold no terrors for the professional person. Negligence sets a minimum standard of conduct below which individuals should not be permitted to fall without being called to account. Thus, in *Phelps v Hillingdon London Borough Council*,[363] a case involving allegations of negligence against an educational psychologist in failing to diagnose dyslexia when making an assessment of a pupil's educational needs, Lord Clyde, observed:

> "I am not persuaded that the recognition of a liability upon employees of the education authority for damages for negligence in education would lead to a flood of claims, or even vexatious claims, which would overwhelm the school authorities, nor that it would add burdens and distractions to the already intensive life of teachers. Nor should it inspire some peculiarly defensive attitude in the performance of their professional responsibilities. On the contrary it may have the healthy effect of securing that high standards are sought and secured."[364]

---

[361] *sub. nom. X (Minors) v Bedfordshire County Council* [1995] 2 A.C. 633 at 750, per Lord Browne-Wilkinson.

[362] There were several other matters that contributed to this policy judgment: a common law duty would cut across the statutory system for the protection of children at risk; the task of dealing with these issues was "extraordinarily delicate"; the conflict between social workers and parents was fertile ground in which to breed ill-feeling and vexatious litigation, the cost of which would be diverted from child protection services; regulatory agencies charged with the task of protecting society from the wrongdoings of others should not normally be held liable in negligence. See [1995] 2 A.C. 633 at 749–751. See also the comments of Lord Hoffmann in *Stovin v Wise* [1996] A.C. 923 at 958: "I think that it is important, before extending the duty of care owed by public authorities, to consider the cost to the community of the defensive measures which they are likely to take in order to avoid liability."

[363] [2001] 2 A.C. 619 at 672. See also *Reynolds v North Tyneside Health Authority* [2002] Lloyd's Rep. Med. 459, where Gross J commented, at [43], that: "in a fault based system, it is indeed necessary both (i) to exclude hindsight and (ii) to recognise the social costs of inadvertently encouraging 'defensive' medicine by setting unrealistic standards." His Lordship concluded, however, that a finding that it was negligent to ignore a small risk of catastrophic consequences (death or brain damage) was neither unfair nor unrealistic.

[364] In *Michael v Chief Constable of South Wales* [2015] UKSC 2; [2015] A.C. 1732 at [179] Lord Kerr commented that: "arguably, the risk of litigation improves professional standards". See also the comment of Lady Clark in *Miller v Greater Glasgow Health Board* [2008] CSOH 71; 2008 S.L.T. 567

The "debate" about the risk that potential liability may lead to defensive practices   **3–142**
continued to rumble along in the House of Lords. In *JD v East Berkshire
Community Health NHS Trust*[365] the House of Lords departed from *X v
Bedfordshire County Council*,[366] and held that doctors and social workers who
suspected that a child had been the victim of abuse owed a duty *to the child* to
exercise reasonable care in making judgments about the child's welfare. In
reaching this conclusion, which in reality was simply an endorsement of the
Court of Appeal decision based on the incompatibility of the common law's "no
duty" stance with the human rights jurisprudence,[367] there was no discussion by
their Lordships of the problem of defensive practice. Presumably, in the 10 years
since the decision in *X v Bedfordshire* those engaged in child protection, whether
social workers or doctors, had developed a more robust approach to the risk of
litigation and were therefore able to perform their jobs without resorting to
defensive measures? On the other hand, a majority of their Lordships in *JD v
East Berkshire Community Health NHS Trust* held that no duty of care was owed
to the parents of a child suspected of being the victim of abuse when
investigating that suspected abuse, on the basis that imposing a duty of care owed
to the parents would produce a conflict of duties, which might adversely affect
the manner in which a doctor went about the business of examining the child and
offering a diagnosis of the child's injuries. Thus Lord Nicholls commented:

> "A doctor is obliged to act in the best interests of his patient. In these cases the child is his
> patient. The doctor is charged with the protection of the child, not with the protection of the
> parent. The best interests of a child and his parent normally march hand-in-hand. But when
> considering whether something does not feel 'quite right', a doctor must be able to act
> single-mindedly in the interests of the child. He ought not to have at the back of his mind an
> awareness that if his doubts about intentional injury or sexual abuse prove unfounded he may
> be exposed to claims by a distressed parent."[368]

It was not that doctors or other health professionals would be consciously swayed
by this consideration, said Lord Nicholls, for they are "surely made of sterner
stuff".[369] Lord Brown, on the other hand, considered that it was:

> "...impossible to see how such a duty could fail to impact upon the doctor's approach to his
> task and create a conflict of interest."[370]

---

at [55], responding to the defendants' argument that recognising a duty of care in relation MRSA
infections contracted in hospital would lead to a flood of actions: "Even if there were numerous
claims in which sufficient evidence existed to enable the pursuer to make relevant averments, I do not
consider that the number of claims would be a reason for denying a remedy. If numerous claims
existed, there may be merit in enabling litigation to be pursued to encourage hospitals to take
reasonable care for patients to prevent infection with MRSA."
[365] [2005] UKHL 23; [2005] 2 A.C. 373.
[366] [1995] 2 A.C. 633.
[367] See para.2–099.
[368] [2005] UKHL 23; [2005] 2 A.C. 373 at [85]; see also per Lord Rodger at [110] and Lord Brown at
[129].
[369] [2005] UKHL 23; [2005] 2 A.C. 373 at [86].
[370] [2005] UKHL 23; [2005] 2 A.C. 373 at [129].

The reasoning process may not be conscious on the part of the doctor, since a duty to the parents would have an "insidious" effect, "subtly tending to the suppression of doubts and instincts which in the child's interests ought rather to be encouraged."[371]

3–143   But as Lord Bingham pointed out in his dissenting speech the notion that there is a conflict of interest between child and parent in this situation is more apparent than real. The scope of any duty owed to the parent could be no more than an obligation to exercise reasonable care in taking a history, making a diagnosis (following appropriate diagnostic tests, where needed) and providing treatment for the child. This duty would be the same whether or not the parent has actually committed abuse. For a parent who is not an abuser, though suspected of being so, his interests are identical to those of his child. If no abuse has been committed, it is in both the child's and the parent's interests that reasonable care is taken accurately to identify the cause of the child's injuries or illness. If abuse has been committed, it is still in the interests of both parent and child to identify the fact of abuse and to commence the process of identifying the abuser. Only where the parent is the abuser can it realistically be suggested that there is a potential conflict of interest. But even here there is, in reality, no conflict, for as Lord Bingham pointed out:

> "[The duty] would be no different if a parent were the abuser, since the duty of the healthcare professional is to serve the lawful and not the criminal interests of the parent; in any event, an undetected abuser could never be heard to complain."[372]

There is simply no dilemma here for the doctor. There is but one means of discharging the obligation: to exercise reasonable care in taking a history, making a diagnosis and providing treatment for the child, which is the same obligation owed to any patient.

3–144   The argument accepted by the majority in *JD v East Berkshire Community Health NHS Trust* is that a doctor will not be able to discharge his duties appropriately if he has at the back of his mind:

> "…an awareness that if his doubts about intentional injury or sexual abuse prove unfounded he may be exposed to claims by a distressed parent."

But, doctors cannot be liable in negligence for having "unfounded doubts", only for failing to exercise reasonable care in all the circumstances (which includes the circumstance that there may be genuine doubts about a diagnosis). All professionals, if they think about it all, will have at the back of their minds an awareness that if they fail to exercise reasonable care in discharging their professional responsibilities, they may be exposed to claims for damages. This is hardly a basis for granting them an immunity from action. As Lord Bingham expressed the point:

---

[371] [2005] UKHL 23; [2005] 2 A.C. 373 at [137], per Lord Brown.
[372] [2005] UKHL 23; [2005] 2 A.C. 373 at [37].

"To describe awareness of a legal duty as having an 'insidious effect' on the mind of a potential defendant is to undermine the foundation of the law of professional negligence."[373]

Lord Nicholls' approach in *JD v East Berkshire Community Health NHS Trust* can be contrasted with the dismissive view of the "defensive medicine" argument that his Lordship expressed in *Gregg v Scott*,[374] a case where he was in favour of imposing liability on a doctor in respect of the lost opportunity of successful treatment for cancer:

3-145

> "Nor can I accept a further submission to the effect that the approach set out above will encourage wasteful defensive practices. Doctors, it was said, will become aware they may be sued whenever their negligence significantly diminishes a patient's prospects, whereas at present liability can arise only if the patient's pre-existing recovery prospects exceeded 50%. Accordingly, so the argument runs, doctors will be encouraged to conduct tests or make referrals in circumstances where at present they would not do so.
>   This argument is not impressive. Every doctor is fully aware he may be sued if he is negligent. There is no reason to believe that adopting the approach set out above will affect the practices followed by doctors."

The debate about the potential for defensive responses to the imposition of liability was considered again in *Jones v Kaney*,[375] in which the Supreme Court decided that immunity from negligence claims by the clients of expert witnesses was no longer defensible. It was suggested in argument that professionals would refuse to act as experts if they were open to an action by a disappointed client, a view that was expressly rejected by Lord Collins and Lord Dyson. Lord Collins commented that a conscientious expert would not be deterred by the danger of civil action, any more than the same expert would be deterred from providing services to any other client. Rather, the practical reality was that if the removal of the immunity were to have any effect at all on the process of preparation and presentation of expert evidence, it would tend to ensure a greater degree of care in the preparation reports.[376] Lord Dyson pointed out that:

3-146

> "Professional indemnity insurance is available. Professional persons engage in many activities where the possibility of being sued is more realistic than it is in relation to undertaking the role of an expert in litigation. Thus, for example, it is a sad fact of life that births sometimes 'go wrong' and when that happens, parents sometimes look for someone to blame. But that does not stop people from practising as obstetricians."[377]

---

[373] [2005] UKHL 23; [2005] 2 A.C. 373 at [33].
[374] [2005] UKHL 2; [2005] 2 A.C. 176 at [55] to [56]; see paras 5–112 to 5–126.
[375] [2011] UKSC 13; [2011] 2 A.C. 398.
[376] [2011] UKSC 13; [2011] 2 A.C. 398 at [85].
[377] [2011] UKSC 13; [2011] 2 A.C. 398 at [117].

discussion of *McGhee v National Coal Board* in *Wilsher v Essex Area Health Authority* centred upon the issue of the location of the burden of proving causation, it may be that the crucial, and largely unanswered, question is in what circumstances the court will draw inferences of fact which support the claimant's version of events in the absence of direct evidence. An inference is a deduction from the evidence, which, if it is a reasonable deduction, may have the validity of legal proof, as opposed to conjecture which, even though plausible, has no value, "for its essence is that it is a mere guess".[392] However, other instances of incompetence by the defendant, such as the fact that he has been the subject of a number of complaints by other patients, that he has been criticised by the Health Care Commission, and that he has been found guilty of misconduct by a GMC Fitness to Practice Panel, do not necessarily give rise to an inference that he was negligent in performing a specific operation on the claimant, unless it can be said to constitute similar fact evidence.[393]

(b) Res ipsa loquitur

3–151   The principle of res ipsa loquitur is, in essence, an evidential principle, which, in certain instances, allows the court to draw an inference of negligence. Although in some cases it has been suggested that the principle has the effect of reversing the burden of proof, the better view would seem to be that this is incorrect. The burden of proof remains with the claimant, but the defendant must adduce evidence to rebut the inference of negligence, in order to avoid a finding of liability.[394]

3–152   The maxim applies where an accident occurs in circumstances in which accidents do not normally happen unless there has been negligence by someone. The fact of the accident itself may give rise to an inference of negligence by the defendant which, in the absence of evidence in rebuttal, would be sufficient to impose

---

[392] *Jones v Great Western Railway Co.* (1930) 47 T.L.R. 39 at 45, per Lord Macmillan. Note that where it is the defendant's conduct that has made it more difficult for the claimant to prove breach of duty adverse inferences may be drawn: *Keefe v Isle of Man Steam Packet Co Ltd* [2010] EWCA Civ 683 at [19] per Longmore LJ: "a defendant who has, in breach of duty, made it difficult or impossible for a claimant to adduce relevant evidence must run the risk of adverse factual findings"; applied in *Raggett v Kings College Hospital NHS Foundation Trust* [2016] EWHC 1604 (QB) at [131]. Poor recordkeeping by a health professional gives a claimant the opportunity to submit that adverse inferences should be drawn against the defendant, though inferences will not be drawn where there is other evidence supporting the defendant's position: *Hall v Thomas* [2014] EWHC 1625 (QB) at [106]. See also *Wisniewski v Central Manchester Health Authority* [1998] P.I.Q.R. P324; [1998] Lloyd's Rep. Med. 223, CA, para.5–016, on when adverse inferences may be drawn from the failure of a witness to give evidence. In *Manzi v King's College Hospital NHS Foundation Trust* [2016] EWHC 1101 (QB); [2016] Med. L.R. 294; (2016) 151 B.M.L.R. 188 at [63xvii] Nicol J observed that in *Wisniewski* the issue was whether the trial judge was *entitled* to draw an adverse inference, whereas the claimant was suggesting that the court was *obliged* to draw such an inference, "but *Wisniewski* does not go so far and it would be surprising if it had. The fact finding process is more nuanced than that".

[393] *Laughton v Shalaby* [2014] EWCA Civ 1450; [2015] P.I.Q.R. P6; [2015] Med. L.R. 1 (criticism of defendant surgeon's conduct of knee, foot and wrist operations did not constitute similar fact evidence where the alleged negligence concerned a hip replacement operation). The case is discussed by Tavares [2015] J.P.I.L. C9.

[394] See para.3–171 below.

liability. There is no magic in the phrase res ipsa loquitur—"the thing speaks for itself". It is simply a submission that the facts establish a prima facie case against the defendant.[395] The value of this principle is that it enables a claimant who has no knowledge, or insufficient knowledge, about how the accident occurred to rely on the accident itself and the surrounding circumstances as evidence of negligence, and prevents a defendant who does know what happened from avoiding responsibility simply by choosing not to give any evidence.[396] In Canada res ipsa loquitur has been abolished as a distinct maxim for establishing a defendant's breach of duty.[397]

(i)   When does res ipsa loquitur apply?

Res ipsa loquitur is intended to assist claimants who, through no fault of their own, are unable to adduce evidence as to how the accident occurred. If all the facts about the cause of the accident are known the maxim does not apply. Rather, the question then is whether, on the known facts, negligence by the defendant can be inferred.[398]

3–153

The principle derives from the case of *Scott v London & St. Katherine Docks Co.*[399] in which several bags of sugar fell from a hoist onto the claimant below. Erle CJ said that:

3–154

"... where the thing is shown to be under the management of the defendant or his servants, and the accident is such as in the ordinary course of things does not happen if those who have the management use proper care, it affords reasonable evidence, in the absence of explanation by the defendants, that the accident arose from want of care."[400]

There are two main elements to this; first, the defendant, or someone for whom he is responsible, must have been in "control" of the thing or circumstances that caused the damage; and secondly, the accident must be such as "in the ordinary course of things" does not happen without negligence.

---

[395] *Roe v Minister of Health* [1954] 2 Q.B. 66 at 87–88, per Morris LJ; *Ballard v North British Railway Co.* 1923 S.C. 43 at 56, per Lord Shaw: "If that phrase had not been in Latin, nobody would have called it a principle."

[396] For example, patients under a general anaesthetic are not aware of what is going on about them, and the facts are peculiarly within the knowledge of the anaesthetist and others attending them: *Crits v Sylvester* (1956) 1 D.L.R. (2d) 502 at 510, per Schroeder JA, Ont CA; see also *Mahon v Osborne* [1939] 2 K.B. 14 at 50, per Goddard LJ: "The surgeon is in command of the operation, it is for him to decide what instruments, swabs and the like are to be used, and it is he who uses them. The patient, or if he dies, his representatives, can know nothing about this matter ... If, therefore, a swab is left in the patient's body, it seems to me clear that the surgeon is called on for an explanation ..." Note that the court has the power at any time to require a party to give additional information in relation to any matter which is in dispute in the proceedings: see CPR Pt 18.

[397] *Fontaine v British Columbia (Official Administrator)* (1997) 156 D.L.R. (4th) 577, SCC. It follows that the Canadian cases cited in the following paragraphs should be read in that light. See para.3–174.

[398] *Barkway v South Wales Transport Co. Ltd* [1950] 1 All E.R. 392; *Johnston v Wellesley Hospital* (1970) 17 D.L.R. (3d) 139 at 146, Ont HC.

[399] (1865) 3 H. & C. 596.

[400] (1865) 3 H. & C. 596 at 601; cited with approval by Singleton LJ in *Cassidy v Ministry of Health* [1951] 2 K.B. 343 at 353–354.

Similarly, operating on the wrong patient, or the right patient in the wrong place (commonly referred to as "wrong site surgery") will almost invariably raise an inference of negligence. This is not an uncommon problem in NHS hospitals.[427]

3–165   In *Saunders v Leeds Western Health Authority*[428] a child suffered cardiac arrest lasting 30 to 40 minutes while undergoing an operation, suffering quadriplegia. The evidence was that the heart of a fit child does not arrest under anaesthesia if proper care is taken in the anaesthetic and surgical processes. The defendants accepted that prima facie this was correct, but sought to explain the accident by suggesting that the child's normal pulse had suddenly stopped. This evidence was rejected as mistaken, and the inevitable inference was that proper monitoring of the pulse would have given a forewarning of the arrest, and that in those circumstances the anaesthetic procedure, or the system for monitoring it or the execution of it was performed negligently. Similarly, in *Holmes v Board of Hospital Trustees of the City of London*[429] an anaesthetist who administered an anaesthetic requiring a method of artificial ventilation which involved injecting jets of high pressure oxygen through a needle into the trachea produced massive tissue emphysema in the patient. This was a known danger of the procedure if the needle was not in the trachea but it did not normally happen with the exercise of due care. The anaesthetist was held liable on the basis of res ipsa loquitur.

3–166   The maxim has been held to apply in the following cases:

- where a patient sustained a burn from a high frequency electrical current used for "electric coagulation" of the blood[430];
- where gangrene developed in the claimant's arm following an intra-muscular injection[431];
- when a patient underwent a radical mastoidectomy and suffered partial facial paralysis[432];

---

agreed (at 38) that res ipsa loquitur was applicable, although he agreed with Scott LJ that the verdict against the defendant must be set aside. Scott LJ was opposed (at 21–24) to applying res ipsa loquitur.
[427] Wrong site surgery is also on the list of "never events" published by NHS England (*http://www.england.nhs.uk/patientsafety/never-events*). See further P. Thomas and C. Evans, "An identity crisis? Aspects of patient misidentification" (2004) 10 Clinical Risk 18; Giles, S.J., et al., "Experience of wrong site surgery and surgical marking practices among clinicians in the UK" (2006) 15 Qual. Saf. Health Care 363. The National Patient Safety Agency reported that between February 2006 and January 2007 it had received 24,382 reports of patients being mismatched with their care. The functions of the NPSA were transferred to the NHS Commissioning Board Special Health Authority on 1 June 2012. As of 1 April 2016 patient safety falls under the remit of NHS Improvement (*https://improvement.nhs.uk*).
[428] (1984), [1993] 4 Med. L.R. 355. See also *Glass v Cambridge Health Authority* [1995] 6 Med. L.R. 91, where it was held that res ipsa loquitur applied to a case where the heart of a healthy man went into cardiac arrest while under general anaesthesia.
[429] (1977) 81 D.L.R. (3d) 67, Ont HC.
[430] *Clarke v Warboys, The Times*, 18 March 1952, CA.
[431] *Cavan v Wilcox* (1973) 44 D.L.R. (3d) 42, NBCA; rev'd on the facts (1974) 50 D.L.R. (3d) 687, SCC; *Cox v Saskatoon* [1942] 1 D.L.R. 74, Sask KB, in which the claimant's arm was badly damaged during the course donating blood for an operation. The procedure took up to three quarters of an hour when normally it took 10 minutes, and the hospital had 100 similar operations that week without such a disastrous result. Held that res ipsa loquitur.
[432] *Eady v Tenderenda* (1974) 51 D.L.R. (3d) 79, SCC.

- where the defendant failed to diagnose a known complication of surgery on the patient's hand for Paget's disease[433];
- where there was a delay of 50 minutes in obtaining expert obstetric assistance at the birth of twins when the medical evidence was that at the most no more than 20 minutes should elapse between the birth of the first and the second twin[434];
- where, following an operation under general anaesthetic, a patient in the recovery ward sustained brain damage caused by hypoxia for a period of four to five minutes[435];
- where, following a routine appendisectomy under general anaesthetic, an otherwise fit and healthy girl suffered a fit and went into a permanent coma[436];
- when a needle broke in the patient's buttock while he was being given an injection[437];
- where a spinal anaesthetic became contaminated with disinfectant as a result of the manner in which it was stored causing paralysis to the patient[438];
- where an infection following surgery in a "well-staffed and modern hospital" remained undiagnosed until the patient sustained crippling injury[439];
- where an explosion occurred during the course of administering anaesthetic to the patient when the technique had frequently been used without any mishap;[440]

---

[433] *Rietze v Bruser (No.2)* [1979] 1 W.W.R. 31, Man QB.

[434] *Bull v Devon Area Health Authority* (1989), [1993] 4 Med. L.R. 117 at 131, CA, per Slade LJ. However, Mustill LJ doubted, at 142, whether res ipsa loquitur would assist because "all the facts that are ever going to be known are before the court", but in the absence of a proved explanation for the "inordinate delay", the judge had no choice, said his Lordship, but to find the defendants liable.

[435] *Coyne v Wigan Health Authority* [1991] 2 Med. L.R. 301, QBD.

[436] *Lindsay v Mid-Western Health Board* [1993] 2 I.R. 147 at 181, Supreme Court of Ireland per O'Flaherty J: "...it seems to me that if a person goes in for a routine medical procedure, is subject to an anaesthetic without any special features, and there is a failure to return the patient to consciousness, to say that that does not call for an explanation from defendants would be in defiance of reason and justice."

[437] *Brazier v Ministry of Defence* [1965] 1 Ll. Law Rep. 26 at 30.

[438] *Roe v Minister of Health* [1954] 2 Q.B. 66. See also *Brown v Merton, Sutton and Wandsworth Area Health Authority* [1982] 1 All E.R. 650 where the claimant developed quadriplegia following the administration of an epidural anaesthetic, in the course of preparation for giving birth. The defendants, in their stock defence, initially denied that res ipsa loquitur was applicable, but on a request for further and better particulars of the facts that they would rely on to show that "this type of accident happens in the ordinary course of epidural anaesthesia when proper care is used" the defendants conceded that the maxim did apply.

[439] *Hajgato v London Health Association* (1982) 36 O.R. (2d) 669 at 682; aff'd (1983) 44 O.R. (2d) 264, Ont CA, although the mere occurrence of infection did not give rise to an inference of negligence.

[440] *Crits v Sylvester* (1956) 1 D.L.R. (2d) 502, Ont CA; aff'd (1956) 5 D.L.R. (2d) 601, SCC; cf. *McFadyen v Harvie* [1942] 4 D.L.R. 647, SCC; aff'g [1941] 2 D.L.R. 663, Ont CA.

- where the patient suffered serious blood loss following damage to an artery in the course of a colposuspension procedure, which was not a recognised complication.[441]

3–167 Conversely, res ipsa loquitur has been held not to apply in the following circumstances:

- when a dentist left part of the root of a tooth behind during an extraction and broke the claimant's jaw[442];
- when a dental drill broke and was left embedded in the jaw resulting in a fracture[443];
- where the claimant became incontinent following a prostate operation[444];
- where a patient suffered permanent partial paralysis of the legs following anaesthesia[445];
- when the patient suffered neurological complications leading to partial paralysis of his hand following the performance of an aortagram[446];
- where a patient died from haemorrhage during the course of spinal disc surgery when the surgeon pierced an artery with a surgical instrument[447];
- where paralysis occurred following a cervical laminectomy[448] or following arteriography[449];
- where a baby suffered cerebral palsy following a forceps delivery[450];
- where a sterilisation operation failed to render the claimant sterile[451];
- where a patient was infected with HIV from a blood transfusion at a time when the virus had not been identified and there was no test available to show whether a particular blood product was contaminated[452];

---

[441] *Greenhorn v South Glasgow University Hospitals NHS Trust* [2008] CSOH 128; (2008) 104 B.M.L.R. 50.

[442] *Fish v Kapur* [1948] 2 All E.R. 176; *Carter v Higashi* [1994] 3 W.W.R. 319, Alta QB; cf. *Lock v Scantlebury*, *The Times*, 25 July 1963 where the dentist was found negligent for failing to discover that he had dislocated the patient's jaw during an extraction.

[443] Fletcher v Bench (1973) 4 B.M.J. 17, CA; Keuper v McMullin (1987) 30 D.L.R. (4th) 408.

[444] *Considine v Camp Hill Hospital* (1982) 133 D.L.R. (3d) 11, Nova Scotia SC. For discussion of the complications that can arise from prostate surgery see Moore (1995) 1 AVMA Medical & Legal Journal 121.

[445] *Girard v Royal Columbian Hospital* (1976) 66 D.L.R. (3d) 676, BCSC: " . . .medical science has not yet reached the stage where the law ought to presume that a patient must come out of an operation as well or better than he went into it", per Andrews J at 691; *Lindsay v Mid-Western Health Board* [1993] 2 I.R. 147 at 182, Supreme Court of Ireland.

[446] *O'Malley-Williams v Board of Governors of the National Hospital for Nervous Diseases* (1975) 1 B.M.J. 635.

[447] *Kapur v Marshall* (1978) 85 D.L.R. (3d) 566, Ont HC.

[448] *Rocha v Harris* (1987) 36 D.L.R. 410, BCCA.

[449] *Ferguson v Hamilton Civic Hospitals* (1983) 144 D.L.R. (3d) 214.

[450] *Whitehouse v Jordan* [1980] 1 All E.R. 650 at 658, 661; *Goguen v Crowe* (1987) 40 CCLT 212, Nova Scotia SC.

[451] *Grey v Webster* (1984) 14 D.L.R. (4th) 706; nor where the patient's ureter was damaged in the course of a tubal ligation operation: *Hobson v Munkley* (1976) 74 D.L.R. (3d) 408; *Videto v Kennedy* (1980) 107 D.L.R. (3d) 612; rev'd on other grounds (1981) 125 D.L.R. (3d) 127, Ont CA, perforation of the bowel during the course of a laparoscopic sterilisation held not to be a case of res ipsa loquitur.

[452] *Dwan v Farquhar* [1988] 1 Qd R. 234.

- where perforation of the globe of the eye occurred in the course of administering a local anaesthetic prior to cataract surgery[453]; and
- where the treatment is under the control of several people.[454]

As a general rule, the maxim will not apply where the injury sustained by the claimant is of a kind recognised as an inherent risk of the treatment, since such accidents can occur without negligence.[455] In *Kapur v Marshall*[456] Robins J said that res ipsa loquitur only comes into play when common experience or the evidence in the case indicates that the happening of the injury itself may be considered as evidence that reasonable care had not been used, and this will not be the case where the complication is a recognised, even if rare, risk inherent in the operation.[457]

(iii)   Defendant adduces evidence that rebuts the inference of negligence

It does not follow that simply because claimants are in a position to invoke res ipsa loquitur their action will necessarily succeed. The inference of negligence may be rebutted by evidence adduced by the defendant which explains how the accident occurred without negligence on his part.[458] Indeed, it is not incumbent

3–168

---

[453] *Fischer v Waller* [1994] 1 W.W.R. 83, Alta QB.

[454] *Morris v Winsbury-White* [1937] 4 All E.R. 494, 499; cf. *Cassidy v Ministry of Health* [1951] 2 K.B. 343.

[455] *O'Malley-Williams v Board of Governors of the National Hospital for Nervous Diseases* (1975) 1 B.M.J. 635; *Guertin v Kester* (1981) 20 C.C.L.T. 225, on complications following plastic surgery on the patient's eyelids; *Considine v Camp Hill Hospital* (1982) 133 D.L.R. (3d) 11, Nova Scotia SC, where the medical evidence indicated that the operation could produce incontinence in one per cent to 4 per cent of cases; *Videto v Kennedy* (1980) 107 D.L.R. (3d) 612 at 618; rev'd on other grounds (1981) 125 D.L.R. (3d) 127—statistics demonstrated that perforation injuries are an inherent risk of a laparoscopic sterilisation. Statistical evidence of this kind does not show, of course, how many of the cases in which complications ensue are the result of a lack of reasonable care (see, e.g. *Dendaas v Yackel* (1980) 109 D.L.R. (3d) 455 at 463, per Bouck J). On the other hand, where the risk is known but does not normally occur in the absence of negligence res ipsa loquitur will apply: *Holmes v Board of Hospital Trustees of the City of London* (1977) 81 D.L.R. (3d) 67, Ont HC.

[456] (1978) 85 D.L.R. (3d) 566 at 574, Ont HC.

[457] In *Chubey v Ahsan* (1977) 71 D.L.R. (3d) 550 at 552 Freedman CJM (in a dissenting judgment) took a robust approach to the occurrence of remote risks: "If in 7,000 operations of this kind, 6,999 are performed without damage to the aorta one may safely conclude that the surgeons attained this happy result by the exercise of due care. What can successfully be done in 6,999 cases ought to have been also done in the 7,000th. That it was not done in the 7,000th case must be ascribed to lack of due care." A majority of the Manitoba Court of Appeal took the view that the injury was simply the result of an inherent risk of the operation for which the surgeon was not liable. In *Fischer v Waller* [1994] 1 W.W.R. 83 at 86, Alta QB, the majority approach was applied: "The rarity of the occurrence does not change the fact that this unfortunate result may occur without negligence", per Deyell J.

[458] See, e.g. *Roe v Minister of Health* [1954] 2 Q.B. 66, where an anaesthetic was contaminated by the passage of phenol through invisible cracks in the glass ampoules in which the anaesthetic was stored, and this risk was unknown at the time; *Brazier v Minister of Defence* [1965] 1 Ll. Law Rep. 26, where a needle broke in the patient due to a latent defect in the needle rather than negligence in administering the injection; *Moore v Worthing District Health Authority* [1992] 3 Med. L.R. 431, QBD, where bilateral ulnar nerve lesions during the course of a mastoidectomy were found to be attributable to the claimant's abnormal susceptibility to this type of injury; *Kyriakou v Barnet and Chase Farms Hospitals NHS Trust* [2006] EWHC 2131 (QB), where the absence of the claimant's

on the defendant to explain how the accident happened at all, provided there is evidence to show that he exercised reasonable care. In *Delaney v Southmead Health Authority*,[459] following otherwise successful surgery, the claimant sustained a lesion of the brachial plexus which she alleged was due to her left arm having been hyper-abducted and externally rotated by the anaesthetist. The claimant argued that res ipsa loquitur should have been applied by the judge, because it was found as a fact that the claimant had suffered an injury to the brachial plexus, the injury had occurred during the course of the operation, and that there was no explanation for the claimant's injury other than that the arm had been hyper-abducted and/or externally rotated. There was no direct evidence as to what the defendant had actually done on this particular occasion, but the trial judge accepted his evidence that he had probably acted in accordance with his usual practice, which did not involve hyper-abduction or external rotation of the arm. This depended on the judge's assessment of the defendant in the witness box as a careful and conscientious professional, from which he inferred that, on the balance of probabilities, it was unlikely that the defendant had departed from his normal practice. The Court of Appeal held that a defendant was entitled to rely on evidence as to his normal practice to rebut an inference of negligence. The defendant had not succeeded in giving an explanation of what had happened to the claimant which was inconsistent with negligence, but he had proved to the judge that he had exercised reasonable care. The result was that, as far as the court was concerned there was no explanation as to how the claimant's injury was sustained, notwithstanding that there was evidence in the medical literature from 1942 onwards, backed up by expert evidence for the claimant, which, it was argued, demonstrated that there were effectively only two possible explanations for brachial plexus palsy, namely a narrowing of the thoracic outlet (which the trial judge found had not occurred) and hyper-abduction and external rotation of the arm.[460]

---

endometrium following an evacuation of the retained products of conception under anaesthetic with the use of a sharp, rather than a blunt, curette raised an inference of negligence; but the inference was rebutted by an histology report of the removed tissue stating that no endometrium was included in the specimen, leading to the conclusion that the endometrial layer of the claimant's uterus had disappeared as a result of an intrauterine infection in the three or four-day period after giving birth; *Lindsay v Mid-Western Health Board* [1993] 2 I.R. 147, Supreme Court of Ireland, where the patient failed to regain consciousness from a general anaesthetic administered in the course of a routine operation, but the defendants were able to show that they had exercised reasonable care and were not negligent. They were not required to take the further step of proving how the claimant had sustained brain damage; *Wilcox v Cavan* (1974) 50 D.L.R. (3d) 687, SCC; *Hajgato v London Health Association* (1982) 36 O.R. (2d) 669; aff'd (1983) 44 O.R. (2d) 264, Ont CA.
[459] [1995] 6 Med. L.R. 355.
[460] For further comment on *Delaney*, see Jones (1998) 14 P.N. 174. Contrast *Rowley v King's College Hospital NHS Foundation Trust* unreported 20 November 2016, London County Court, where it was held that the claimant had given a credible explanation, consistent with negligence, for the brachial plexus injury sustained whilst under general anaesthetic whereas the defendants had not adduced credible evidence to rebut the inference of negligence.

(iv) Care in performing a procedure is not evidence of skill in interpreting the results

In some cases, even though res ipsa loquitur does not, strictly speaking, apply to the circumstances, the evidence is such that the defendant will have to come up with a credible explanation for the events or risk a finding of negligence. For example, in *Lillywhite v University College London Hospitals NHS Trust*,[461] following a tertiary referral for investigation after an abnormal foetal ultrasound scan where the sonographer had been unable to detect certain structures in the foetus' brain, the defendant, on conducting further ultrasound scans, had identified three structures of the brain as being present which were absent (with the result that he advised, incorrectly, that the scan results were normal). Though the Court of Appeal considered that res ipsa loquitur did not apply, Latham LJ emphasised that the defendant had a "heavy burden" to reconcile the fact that he had incorrectly identified structures of the foetus' brain that were not present in the ultrasound scan with the exercise of reasonable skill and care. The problem for the defendant was that though it may have been possible, if difficult, to come up with a plausible explanation for misidentifying the individual structures, for Latham LJ what was "insurmountable is the hurdle of establishing that there were plausible explanations for all three".[462] The trial judge had accepted that the defendant had carried out the ultrasound scan with reasonable care. However, unlike the cases of *Ratcliffe v Plymouth and Torbay Health Authority*[463] and *Delaney v Southmead Health Authority*,[464] that was not a complete answer to the issue:

3–169

> "The mere fact that the examination had, in mechanical terms, been carried out with scrupulous care was a necessary condition of the examination not having been negligent, but it was not sufficient for that purpose."[465]

This was because there was an obligation on the defendant not merely to exercise reasonable care in performing the scan, but also to exercise skill in interpreting the results of the scan, and thus the issue was whether a reasonably competent sonologist, dealing with a tertiary referral where it was known that there was a possible problem from the initial ultrasound scan, could reasonably have come to the conclusion that he did. Buxton LJ pointed out the difference between *Ratcliffe* and *Delaney* on the one hand, and the situation in *Lillywhite*, on the other:

> "A case of *professional* negligence can therefore only be concluded by a finding of care alone when the facts are of the unusual nature of those in *Ratcliffe*, and in *Delaney v Southmead Health Authority* (1995) 6 Med LR 355 which preceded it: where a routine, orthodox and in effect mechanical procedure, in *Ratcliffe* the administration of a spinal anaesthetic, produces entirely unexpected damage. In such a case, there are only two possible explanations: either the doctor was physically careless in performing the operation; or there is some underlying condition, unknown to medicine, on which a properly performed operation reacts adversely

---

[461] [2005] EWCA Civ 1466; [2006] Lloyd's Rep. Med. 268.
[462] [2005] EWCA Civ 1466; [2006] Lloyd's Rep. Med. 268 at [39].
[463] [1998] Lloyd's Rep. Med. 162; see para.3–161.
[464] (1995) 6 Med. L.R. 355; see para.3–168.
[465] [2005] EWCA Civ 1466; [2006] Lloyd's Rep. Med. 268 at [83] per Buxton LJ; see also per Latham LJ at [33].

and for which the doctor plainly is not responsible. A finding that the operation was performed with due care leaves the latter as the only explanation. That is what this court held in *Ratcliffe*, and that is the category of case addressed by Brooke LJ in his observations cited above."[466]

Lillywhite was not, however, such a case:

> "The reading of ultrasound images requires not just care, but also skill and judgment. The complaint in this case is that the requisite level of skill and judgment simply could not have been exercised, given that the results produced were so disastrously wrong; and given that an earlier reader, in the person of Mrs Wright, had not made the same errors. As my Lord says, this is not a case of res ipsa loquitur. But it is a case in which the outcome that Dr Rodeck attributed to his reading called for an explanation."[467]

3–170   This does not involve reversing the burden of proof. When the defendant claimed to have been able to observe structures in the brain that were not present, and had not been observed by the referring sonographer, with the consequence that his advice to the mother was that the scan was normal, it would be reasonable to draw an inference of negligence unless there was some explanation of how that interpretation could have been made in the absence of negligence. The explanation has to be "plausible", in the sense of "possible", but it does not have to be shown to be the probable or likeliest answer. Thus: "An explanation to that modest standard has to be reasonably available on the evidence taken in the round."[468] However, mere assertion that the defendant exercised reasonable care, or is an internationally renowned expert in the field, is not sufficient. On the evidence:

> "...the defendant did not pass the test of plausibility or possibility, as it did not succeed in adducing explanatory material that put the initial assumption of negligence under question."[469]

(v)   Effect of invoking res ipsa loquitur

3–171   There are two possible views as to the consequences in law of a successful plea of res ipsa loquitur. The first is that it raises a prima facie inference of negligence which requires the defendant to offer some reasonable explanation as to how the accident could have occurred without negligence by them. In the absence of such evidence the prima facie case is established, and he will be found liable. If the defendant does adduce evidence that is consistent with the absence of negligence on his part, then the inference of negligence is rebutted, and the claimant has to produce positive evidence that the defendant has acted without reasonable care.[470] In practice, it is unlikely that the claimant will be able to do this, since he would not have relied on res ipsa loquitur if he had positive evidence of the defendant's carelessness. On this basis, the burden of proof does not shift to the defendant. If the probabilities are equally balanced that the defendant was or was not negligent, the claimant's action fails. So, for example, in *Colevilles Ltd v*

---

[466] [2005] EWCA Civ 1466; [2006] Lloyd's Rep. Med. 268 at [85].
[467] [2005] EWCA Civ 1466; [2006] Lloyd's Rep. Med. 268 at [86].
[468] [2005] EWCA Civ 1466; [2006] Lloyd's Rep. Med. 268 at [89] per Buxton LJ.
[469] [2005] EWCA Civ 1466; [2006] Lloyd's Rep. Med. 268 at [89].
[470] *Ballard v North British Railway Co.* 1923 S.C. 43 at 54, per Lord Dunedin.

Devine[471] it was said that the defendants had to show that the accident was just as consistent with their having exercised reasonable care as with negligence. It was not suggested that their explanation had to be more likely than the inference of negligence raised by applying the maxim, which would be the position if the burden of proof was reversed. This interpretation treats res ipsa loquitur as:

"...no more than an exotic, although convenient, phrase to describe what is in essence no more than a common sense approach, not limited by technical rules, to the assessment of the effect of the evidence."[472]

The alternative view is that when res ipsa loquitur applies it has the effect of reversing the burden of proof, so requiring defendants to show that the harm was not the product of their carelessness. The case which provides the strongest support for this proposition is the decision of the House of Lords in *Henderson v Henry E. Jenkins & Sons*[473] in which both Lord Reid and Lord Donovan specifically stated that the burden of proof lay with the defendants, and the effect of the majority finding that the defendants were liable was clearly that they had failed to discharge the burden of proof which lay upon them. A similar result was achieved in *Ward v Tesco Stores Ltd*[474] where the only evidence before the court was that the claimant had slipped on some yoghurt in the defendants' store. There was no evidence as to how long the spillage had been there or as to whether the defendants had been careless in failing to clean it up. As Ormrod LJ pointed out, in a dissenting judgment, the accident might have occurred no matter how careful the defendants had been.[475]

3–172

In *Ng Chun Pui v Lee Chuen Tat*[476] the Privy Council explicitly stated that the burden of proof does not shift to the defendant, but rests throughout the case with the claimant. Lord Griffiths, delivering the opinion of the Board, said that in an appropriate case the claimant can establish a prima facie case by relying upon the fact of the accident. However, the:

3–173

---

[471] [1969] 1 W.L.R. 475 at 479, per Lord Donovan.
[472] *Lloyde v West Midlands Gas Board* [1971] 1 W.L.R. 749 at 755, per Megaw LJ, approved by the Privy Council in *Ng Chun Pui v Lee Chuen Tat* [1988] R.T.R. 298 at 301; see also the same judge in *Ward v Tesco Stores Ltd* [1976] 1 W.L.R. 810 at 816. In *Bergin v David Wickes Television* [1994] P.I.Q.R. P167 at 168, CA, Steyn LJ observed that: "It is in truth not a doctrine, nor a principle, nor a rule. It is simply a convenient label for a group of situations in which an unexplained accident is, as a matter of common sense, the basis for an inference of negligence."
[473] [1970] A.C. 282.
[474] [1976] 1 W.L.R. 810; *Moore v R. Fox & Sons* [1956] 1 Q.B. 596; Atiyah (1972) 35 M.L.R. 337; see also per Goddard LJ in *Mahon v Osborne* [1939] 2 K.B. 14 at 50 stating that the defendant is required to show that he exercised due care.
[475] See also *Hall v Holker Estate Co Ltd* [2008] EWCA Civ 1422; [2008] N.P.C. 143 at [33] per Sir Mark Potter P: "The judgments in *Ward v Tesco* do not of course relieve the claimant of the overall burden of proof. He must show that the occurrence of the accident is *prima facie* evidence of a lack of care on the part of the defendant in failing to provide or implement a system designed to protect the claimant from risk of accident or injury. In such circumstances, as made clear by Lawton LJ... : 'Such burden of proof as there is on defendants... is evidential, not probative.'"
[476] [1988] R.T.R. 298.

"...so-called doctrine of res ipsa loquitur ... is no more than the use of a Latin maxim to describe the state of the evidence from which it is proper to draw an inference of negligence."[477]

If the defendant adduces no evidence there is nothing to rebut the inference of negligence and the claimant will have proved his case. But if the defendant does adduce evidence, that evidence must be evaluated by the court:

"Loosely speaking this may be referred to as a burden on the defendant to show he was not negligent, but that only means that faced with a prima facie case of negligence the defendant will be found negligent unless he produces evidence that is capable of rebutting the prima facie case."[478]

The duty of the court is to examine all the evidence and decide whether on the proved facts and legitimate inferences negligence has been established. Thus, the defendant's position is no different from that which arises when he is faced with positive evidence from the claimant raising an inference of negligence.

3–174 Certainly, this was the view taken by the Canadian courts on the effect of res ipsa loquitur in medical malpractice cases. In *Holmes v Board of Hospital Trustees of the City of London* Robins J explained the position in these terms:

"The fact of the happening is, as I view res ipsa loquitur, simply a piece of circumstantial evidence justifying an inference of the defendant's negligence. The weight to be given that inference, like that to be given any other circumstantial evidence, will depend on the particular factual circumstances of the case. The strength of the inference may vary: it may be very strong or it may be sufficiently potent only to present a prima facie case and prevent the plaintiff from being non-suited ... What evidence, if any, the defendant need adduce will depend on the strength of the inference raised against him. The burden of proof remains with the plaintiff throughout; res ipsa loquitur does not shift the onus to the defendant or create a legal presumption in favour of the plaintiff which the defendant must disprove before he can escape liability."[479]

In *Fontaine v British Columbia (Official Administrator)*[480] the Supreme Court of Canada considered that res ipsa loquitur no longer served any useful purpose:

"After all, it was nothing more than an attempt to deal with circumstantial evidence. That evidence is more sensibly dealt with by the trier of fact, who should weigh the circumstantial

---

[477] [1988] R.T.R. 298 at 300. See also *Lindsay v Mid-Western Health Board* [1993] 2 I.R. 147 at 183–184, Supreme Court of Ireland.
[478] [1988] R.T.R. 298 at 301. This is sometimes referred to as the defendant's "evidential burden", meaning that faced with a prima facie case of negligence he has a burden to give an explanation of the accident which is consistent with the absence of negligence.
[479] (1977) 81 D.L.R. (3d) 67 at 79, Ont HC; *Crits v Sylvester* (1956) 1 D.L.R. (2d) 502 at 510, Ont CA; *Kapur v Marshall* (1978) 85 D.L.R. (3d) 566 at 574, Ont HC; *Girard v Royal Columbian Hospital* (1976) 66 D.L.R. (3d) 676 at 691, BCSC; *MacDonald v York County Hospital* (1972) 28 D.L.R. (3d) 521 at 542; rev'd in part 41 D.L.R. (3d) 321, Ont CA; aff'd *sub. nom. Vail v MacDonald* (1976) 66 D.L.R. (3d) 530, SCC. In *Wilcox v Cavan* (1974) 50 D.L.R. (3d) 687 at 695 the Supreme Court of Canada said that: "...in medical cases where differences of expert opinion are not unusual and the sequence of events often appears to have brought about a result which has never occurred in exactly the same way before to the knowledge of the most experienced doctors, great caution should be exercised to ensure that the rule embodied in the maxim res ipsa loquitur is not construed so as to place too heavy a burden on the defendant."
[480] (1997) 156 D.L.R. (4th) 577, SCC.

evidence with the direct evidence, if any, to determine whether the plaintiff has established on a balance of probabilities a *prima facie* case of negligence against the defendant. Once the plaintiff has done so, the defendant must present evidence negating that of the plaintiff or necessarily the plaintiff will succeed."[481]

In any event, an explanation of how the events could have occurred without negligence will not *necessarily* rebut the inference of negligence, particularly where the explanation is a remote or unusual eventuality.[482] The claimant does not have to disprove every theoretical explanation, however unlikely, that might be devised to explain what happened in a way which absolves the defendant.[483] Just as the claimant is not entitled to rely on conjecture or speculation to establish his case on the balance of probabilities, so the defendant cannot resort to this when he is called upon for an explanation of events. Where an inference of negligence does arise from the circumstances of the accident, a general denial by way of defence will not be sufficient to rebut the inference of negligence.[484]

3–175

The differences between the two views of the effect of res ipsa loquitur have probably been exaggerated. It is a fine line between the probabilities being equally balanced and tipping the scale one way or the other. The issue turns upon the cogency that the court attributes to particular pieces of evidence, and this is necessarily a subjective judgment which it is virtually impossible to quantify.

3–176

(c) Standard of proof

The standard of proof in cases of medical negligence is, in theory, the same as for any other case of negligence, i.e. the general standard applicable in civil cases, namely "on the balance of probabilities". This standard tends to conceal the fact that the cogency of the evidence that the courts require in order to satisfy the test can vary with the issues at stake.[485] It is more difficult, for example, to establish that the defendant has behaved fraudulently than to prove that he was negligent.[486] It has been suggested that cases of professional negligence create

3–177

---

[481] (1997) 156 D.L.R. (4th) 577 at [27]. See also *Bencharski v Hindmarsh* [2005] SKQB 23; (2005) 260 Sask. R. 41 at [62], applying *Fontaine* in the context of medical negligence.

[482] *Holmes v Board of Hospital Trustees of the City of London* (1977) 81 D.L.R. (3d) 67 at 82; *Glass v Cambridge Health Authority* [1995] 6 Med. L.R. 91, where the defendant's explanation for the claimant's cardiac arrest under general anaesthetic, namely that he had suffered from gas embolism caused by oxygen entering the bloodstream as a result of the use of hydrogen peroxide in the cleansing and irrigation track of the claimant's wound, was rejected as "at best a highly unlikely possibility".

[483] *Bull v Devon Area Health Authority* (1989), [1993] 4 Med. L.R. 117 at 138, CA, per Dillon LJ; *Ballard v North British Railway Co.* 1923 S.C. 43 at 54, per Lord Dunedin, that the defendant's explanation must be a reasonable one; cf. *Lindsay v Mid-Western Health Board* [1993] 2 I.R. 147 at 185, Supreme Court of Ireland, where it was said that "it was legitimate... for the defendant to adduce evidence of possibilities, remote though they might be, as an explanation; in contradistinction to saying that it could not offer *any* explanation of any description whatsoever" (original emphasis).

[484] *Bergin v David Wickes Television* [1994] P.I.Q.R. P167 at 168, CA.

[485] See Pattenden (1988) 7 C.J.Q. 220.

[486] *Hornal v Neuberger Products Ltd* [1957] 1 Q.B. 247; and an allegation of murder made in civil proceedings requires the criminal standard of proof: *Halford v Brookes* [1992] P.I.Q.R. P175.

particular problems for the courts and, in practice, this may result in what is effectively a higher standard of proof than for "ordinary" cases of negligence. In *Dwyer v Roderick* May LJ said that:

> "Professional men ... are entitled to no special preference before the law, to no rule requiring a higher standard of proof on the balance of probabilities than any other. But it is to shut one's eyes to the obvious if one denies that the burden of achieving something more than that mere balance of probabilities is greater when one is investigating the complicated and sophisticated actions of a qualified and experienced lawyer, doctor, accountant, builder or motor engineer than when one is enquiring into the momentary inattention of the driver of a motor car in a simple running-down action."[487]

3–178   The disclaimer that professionals are entitled to no special treatment clearly belies what follows in this passage. There is, however, a suspicion that this judicial attitude is largely confined to the medical profession.[488] Most prominent amongst the judges taking this approach to the medical profession was Lord Denning, who was concerned both for the effect that findings of negligence might have on the reputation of individual defendants, and with the more general consequences of medical malpractice litigation for the conduct of medicine.[489] In *Hucks v Cole* these concerns were reflected in his view of the standard of proof:

> "A charge of negligence against a medical man, a solicitor or any other professional man, stands on a very different footing from a charge of negligence against a motorist or employer. The reason is because the consequences for the professional man are far more grave. A finding of negligence affects his standing and reputation. It impairs the confidence which his clients have in him. The burden of proof is correspondingly greater. The principle applies that: 'In proportion as the charge is grave, so ought the proof to be clear': see *Hornal v Neuberger Products Ltd* [1957] 1 Q.B. 247 ... A doctor is not to be held negligent simply because something goes wrong ... He is not liable for mischance, or misadventure. Nor is he liable for an error of judgment ... He is only liable if he falls below the standard of a reasonably competent practitioner in his field—so much so that his conduct may fairly be held to be—I will not say deserving of censure, but, at any rate, inexcusable."[490]

---

487 *The Times*, 12 November 1983; (1983) 127 S.J. 806.
488 *Jackson & Powell on Professional Negligence*, 5th edn (London: Sweet & Maxwell, 2002), para.12.086: "In England, the medical profession seems to fare better before the courts than most other professions. The defence of 'non-negligent mistake' succeeds more often." The editors attributed this to the *Bolam* test as it has been applied to the medical profession, and the greater degree of deference which the courts show to expert witnesses in medical negligence actions. However, the comment is omitted from later editions. See also Robertson (1981) 44 M.L.R. 457, 459 commenting on the "strong pro-defendant policy" evident in many medical negligence cases; and Montgomery (1989) 16 J. of Law and Soc. 319 for an insight into why this happened. Giesen (1993) 1 Med. Law Int. 3,5 observed that "decisions in England and Scotland betray an unusual deference to doctors' interests" in contrast to the standards expected of doctors in all other member states of the European Community and all the major common law jurisdictions. See also Giesen (1993) 9 J. of Contemp. Health Law and Policy 273. Maclean (2002) 5 Med. Law Int. 205 argued that judges are more willing to question the views of experts on issues of fact, but that this does not extend to the question normative standard-setting. Lord Woolf suggested that courts' excessive deference to the medical profession was in the process of changing: (2001) 9 Med. L. Rev. 1.
489 See *Roe v Minister of Health* [1954] 2 Q.B. 66 at 86–7; *Hatcher v Black, The Times*, 2 July 1954; *Whitehouse v Jordan* [1980] 1 All ER 650 at 658; *Hyde v Tameside Area Health Authority* (1981) reported at (1986) 2 P.N. 26.
490 (1968), [1993] 4 Med. L.R. 393 at 396. This virtually repeats his Lordship's direction to the jury in *Hatcher v Black, The Times*, 2 July 1954, where he said that a doctor should not be found negligent unless his conduct was deserving of censure. Similarly, in *Whitehouse v Jordan* [1980] 1 All E.R. 650

This approach to allegations of negligence against doctors is also apparent in the   **3–179**
frequent reiteration of the point that medical procedures often carry unavoidable
risks, not all errors connote negligence, there is no liability for mere "errors of
judgment", judgment with hindsight should be avoided, doctors are not insurers
of a favourable result, and so on. The law reports are replete with such comments.
It may be that the difference between motorists and doctors is that in a medical
negligence action the doctor's professional reputation is perceived to be in issue,
and the courts hesitate before impugning the conduct of a member of a highly
respected profession. On the other hand, some judges have taken a more robust
attitude to this issue. In *Ashcroft v Mersey Regional Health Authority* Kilner
Brown J doubted the validity of such an approach:

> "Furthermore, the suggestion that a greater burden rests on a plaintiff alleging negligence
> against a doctor is plainly open to question ... If there is an added burden, such burden does
> not rest on the person alleging negligence; on the contrary, it could be said that the more
> skilled a person is the more care that is expected of him."[491]

The question for consideration, said his Lordship, was whether on a balance of   **3–180**
probabilities it has been established that a professional person has failed to
exercise the care required of a person possessing and professing special skill in
circumstances which require the exercise of that special skill. Similarly, in
Whitehouse v Jordan,[492] Donaldson LJ pointed out that very few professionals
can claim never to have been negligent, and that often the only difference
between those who are sued and their colleagues is that the error happens to have
caused harm to the claimant.

Some instances of negligence are so glaring that they do warrant censure, but   **3–181**
many departures from the standard of reasonable care can be attributed to
understandable human error. The fact that errors are understandable does not
mean, however, that they should be condoned, nor that patients should face a
higher standard of proof in order to protect a defendant's professional reputation.
It may be that these concerns reflect the attitudes of an earlier age when deference
to professional status and reputation was more prevalent.[493]

Delay in bringing proceedings   It is not permissible to adopt a different   **3–182**
standard of proof to allow for the prejudice to the defendant of a long delay by

---

at 659 Lawton LJ commented that: "The more serious the allegation the higher the degree of
probability that is required. In my opinion allegations of negligence against medical practitioners
should be considered as serious."
[491] [1983] 2 All E.R. 245 at 247.
[492] [1980] 1 All E.R. 650 at 666 (see para.3–110, n.285); see also *Clark v MacLennan* [1983] 1 All
E.R. 416 at 433; *Thake v Maurice* [1986] Q.B. 644 at 663.
[493] See, e.g., the comments of Rafferty LJ in *Burnett v Lynch* [2012] EWCA Civ 347 at [25], noting
that the case was a "routine" clinical negligence claim which did not require "heightened
examination" of the evidence (a reference to the speech of Lord Carswell in *Re D* [2008] UKHL 33;
[2008] 1 W.L.R. 1499 at [27] where his Lordship suggested that a heightened examination of the
evidence may be required due to the inherent unlikelihood of the event taking place, the seriousness of
the allegation to be proved or, in some cases, the consequences which could follow from acceptance
of proof of the relevant fact). But in any event, even if a "heightened examination" was required "a
different standard of proof or a specially cogent standard of evidence before the trial judge can be
satisfied of the matter to be established" was not.

the claimant in bringing proceedings within the limitation period. In *Bull v Devon Area Health Authority*[494] an action was brought on behalf of a child which suffered brain damage at birth. The consequence of s.28 of the Limitation Act 1980 in these circumstances is that effectively there is no limitation period. The defendants argued that in a case involving long delay there should be a variation in the standard of proof, so that allegations of "ancient negligence" should be more strictly proved than allegations of negligence a few years ago, and where ordinarily the judge would approach the matter on the footing that the defendants have something to explain, the burden of proof should be reversed so as to rest on the claimant. While Mustill LJ expressed sympathy for this argument, he could not see how it could be sustained either in theory or in practice. The doctrine of res ipsa loquitur was just a summary of the obvious:

> "A barrel does not fall out of a first floor opening on the head of a passer-by without something having gone wrong: and that something, according to the ordinary rules of life, is liable to be connected with the conduct of those who have control of the barrel and the warehouse. By what intellectual process can it be said that the plain inference of fault in such a case is to be displaced just because the event occurred fifteen rather than two years ago? I can see none. So also where the burden is acknowledged to be upon the plaintiff. If the balance of probabilities will suffice in a recent case, why should some other standards be required if the case is old; though not so old that the court will not allow it to be pursued at all? Again, I can see no answer."[495]

The defendant's argument was also unworkable in practice, said his Lordship, since it would require a standard of proof that varied with the length of the delay and this could not be operated fairly in practice. Slade LJ commented that if the law permitted the claimant, who was himself without fault, to bring the claim after a long lapse of time, his case could not be treated as prejudiced by the delay, save only in so far as the lapse of time might render more difficult the task of proving, on the available evidence and on the balance of probabilities, those facts in respect of which the onus fell on the claimant at the trial.[496]

(d) Expert evidence and the role of the court[497]

3–183   Expert witnesses have a vital function in medical negligence actions, but the emphasis that is sometimes placed on accepted professional practice can obscure their true role, which is to provide the evidence upon which the court decides whether there has been negligence or not. This is not for the witnesses to determine. This was forcefully expressed by Bollen J in the Australian case of *F v R*:

> "Expert evidence will assist the court. But in the end it is the court which must say whether there was a duty owed and a breach of it. The court will have been guided and assisted by the expert evidence. It will not produce an answer merely at the dictation of the expert evidence. It will afford great weight to the expert evidence. Sometimes its decision will be the same as it would have been had it accepted dictation. But the court does not merely follow expert

---

[494] (1989), [1993] 4 Med. L.R. 117, CA.
[495] (1989), [1993] 4 Med. L.R. 117 at 139.
[496] (1989), [1993] 4 Med. L.R. 117 at 126.
[497] See also paras 13–097 et seq.

evidence slavishly to a decision. The court considers and weighs up all admissible evidence which it has received. If the court did merely follow the path apparently pointed by expert evidence with no critical consideration of it and the other evidence, it would abdicate its duty to decide, on the evidence, whether in law a duty existed and had not been discharged."[498]

In *Sidaway v Bethlem Royal Hospital Governors*[499] Lord Diplock said that in matters of diagnosis and treatment the court has to rely on and evaluate expert evidence remembering, however, that it is no part of its task of evaluation to give effect to any preference it may have for one responsible body of professional opinion over another, provided it is satisfied by the expert evidence that both qualify as responsible bodies of medical opinion. This is a consequence of the *Bolam* test, a point which was made abundantly clear in *Maynard v West Midlands Regional Health Authority*.[500] Lord Diplock's proviso, however, is crucial. The court must be satisfied that the experts' view constitutes a "responsible" body of professional opinion, experienced in the particular field of medicine concerned.[501] Thus, on questions of liability it is important to obtain expert opinion in the appropriate specialty, and conversely the evidence of a specialist may be of little assistance in an action against a general practitioner.[502] Where conflicting bodies of opinion are not "equally competent" or responsible the court is entitled to prefer the evidence of one body of professional opinion over another.[503]

3–184

The court may accept or reject in whole or in part the evidence of any witness on the grounds of credibility or plausibility. On the other hand, on complicated technical matters, where acquaintance with and experience of matters such as anatomy and physiology are essential, the court may not be justified in disregarding expert testimony or reaching conclusions contrary to those of the experts.[504] Conversely, where the case does not involve such considerations it will be easier for the court to form its own view of the circumstances. Where the medical evidence is equivocal, or where, for example, there is a conflict of evidence whether a responsible body of medical opinion supports a particular practice, the judge has to resolve that conflict.[505] In resolving the conflict the

3–185

---

[498] (1982) 33 S.A.S.R. 189 at 201; see also *Anderson v Chasney* [1949] 4 D.L.R. 71 at 81–82; aff'd [1950] 4 D.L.R. 223, SCC; *Goode v Nash* (1979) 21 S.A.S.R. 419 at 422, SC of S Aus.

[499] [1985] A.C. 871 at 895.

[500] [1984] 1 W.L.R. 634; see para.3–022.

[501] *Hills v Potter* [1983] 3 All E.R. 716 at 728; *Bolitho v City and Hackney Health Authority* [1993] 4 Med. L.R. 381 at 386, per Farquharson LJ.

[502] For example, in *Wilson v Swanson* (1956) 5 D.L.R. (2d) 113 at 119, the claimant's expert's evidence was described as "a collection of elementary views on the diagnosis of cancer by one who is a virtual stranger to the exercise of such a medical and surgical judgment". See the comments of Brooke J in *Scott v Bloomsbury Health Authority* [1990] 1 Med. L.R. 214 on the use of expert witnesses who have retired from practice.

[503] *Poole v Morgan* [1987] 3 W.W.R. 217 at 253.

[504] *Anderson v Chasney* [1949] 4 D.L.R. 71 at 81–82, per Coyne JA; *McLean v Weir* [1977] 5 W.W.R. 609 at 620, per Gould J, BCSC; aff'd [1980] 4 W.W.R. 330; *ter Neuzen v Korn* (1993) 103 D.L.R. (4th) 473 at 506, BCCA; aff'd (1995) 127 D.L.R. (4th) 577, SCC.

[505] *Sidaway v Bethlem Royal Hospital Governors* [1985] A.C. 871 at 900, per Lord Bridge; *Fincham v Anchor Insulation Co. Ltd, The Times*, 16 June 1989, QBD, stating that the judge has a duty to make a legal diagnosis where the medical experts were unable to agree on whether the claimant was suffering from asbestosis.

judge should not invent his own version of the facts which is not based on the evidence.[506] Of course, all expert evidence must be tested by reference to the criteria laid down in *Bolitho v City and Hackney Health Authority*.[507] It must be demonstrated that it has a logical basis, and where the issue depends upon whether a risk taken by the defendant was reasonable, the experts must have directed their minds to the question of comparative risks and benefits and have reached a defensible conclusion.[508]

3–186 In *Coopers Payen Ltd v Southampton Container Terminal Ltd*[509] the Court of Appeal held that where an expert's evidence is on a question of fact (such as the cause of an accident) and is in conflict with direct and credible evidence from a witness of fact, there is no rule of law requiring the court to favour the evidence of either the expert or the witness of fact. The judge must consider whether he can reconcile the evidence, and if that is not possible he must consider whether there is an explanation for the conflict and make a considered choice which evidence to accept. On the evidence in this case, the judge should have accepted the expert evidence because there was no alternative explanation for the accident. The evidence of the defendant's witness, though credible, would have left the accident totally inexplicable.

3–187 The cogency of the expert evidence can be affected by a number of factors such as the unimpressive demeanour of the witness or the defective logic of an argument advanced by the witness.[510] In *Caldeira v Gray*[511] the Privy Council had no doubt that in assessing the value of the testimony of expert witnesses their demeanour, their personality and the impression they make upon the trial judge, e.g. whether they confined themselves to giving evidence or acted as advocates, may powerfully and properly influence the mind of the judge who sees and hears them in deciding between them. Again, in *Joyce v Yeomans*, speaking of the advantage that a trial judge has over an appellate court in seeing a witness, even an expert witness, give evidence, Brandon LJ observed that:

> "Sometimes expert witnesses display signs of partisanship in a witness box or a lack of objectivity. This may or may not be obvious from the transcript, yet it may be quite plain to the

---

[506] *McLean v Weir* [1977] 5 W.W.R. 609 at 620, per Gould J, BCSC; aff'd [1980] 4 W.W.R. 330; *Hajgato v London Health Association* (1982) 36 O.R. (2d) 669 at 683; cf. *Hotson v Fitzgerald* [1985] 3 All E.R. 167 where Simon Brown J appeared to adopt a compromise theory about causation.
[507] [1998] A.C. 232.
[508] [1998] A.C. 232 at 241–242.
[509] [2003] EWCA Civ 1223; [2004] 1 Lloyd's Rep. 331.
[510] *Maynard v West Midlands Regional Health Authority* unreported 21 December 1981, CA, per Sir Stanley Rees. See, e.g. *Hotson v Fitzgerald* [1985] 3 All E.R. 167 at 173; *Hucks v Cole* (1968), [1993] 4 Med. L.R. 393 at 398, where Sachs LJ commented that the reasons given by the *four* experts for the defence for failing to take the simple precaution of prescribing penicillin did "not stand up to analysis"; *McAllister v Lewisham and North Southwark Health Authority* [1994] 5 Med. L.R. 343, where Rougier J rejected the evidence of one defence expert witness concerning the appropriate level of risk disclosure as inherently contradictory.
[511] [1936] 1 All E.R. 540 at 542.

trial judge. Sometimes an expert witness may refuse to make what a more wise witness would make, namely, proper concessions to the viewpoint of the other side. Here again this may or may not be apparent from the transcript."[512]

On the other hand, where the crucial issue of negligence turns upon an inference drawn from the primary facts which depends on the evidentiary value that the trial judge gave to the witnesses' evidence and not on their credibility or demeanour, an appellate court is in just as good a position as the judge to determine the proper inference to be drawn and is entitled to form its own view.[513]

3–188

There is a, not unnatural, tendency for defendants to rely not on their recollection of what they actually did or said in the case, because with the passage of time they are unable to remember, but on what was their usual practice in similar cases. In some instances the court will be willing to accept this as cogent evidence, drawing an inference (since there is no direct evidence) that the defendant did what he normally does.[514] The Supreme Court of Canada, however, has taken a more sceptical approach to this form of evidence. In *Martel v Hotel-Dieu St.-Vallier*[515] Pigeon J took the view that the defendant's testimony was not convincing:

3–189

"...because he did not have an exact recollection of this particular case. It was not because he remembered exactly what he had done that he swore that he had not committed an error, but it was only because he was convinced that he did what he always does."

---

[512] [1981] 1 W.L.R. 549 at 556, cited with approval in *Maynard v West Midlands Regional Health Authority* [1984] 1 W.L.R. 634 at 637.
[513] *Whitehouse v Jordan* [1981] 1 All E.R. 267, HL. For criticism of the manner in which this principle was applied to the facts of *Whitehouse v Jordan* see Robertson (1981) 44 M.L.R. 457. See also per Lord Bridge in *Wilsher v Essex Area Health Authority* [1988] A.C. 1074 at 1091, speaking of a conflict of expert evidence on the question of causation: "Where expert witnesses are radically at issue about complex technical questions within their own field and are examined and cross-examined at length about their conflicting theories, I believe that the judge's advantage in seeing them and hearing them is scarcely less important than when he has to resolve some conflict of primary fact between lay witnesses in purely mundane matters." See further *Lapointe v Hôpital Le Gardeur* (1992) 90 D.L.R. (4th) 7 for the view of the Supreme Court of Canada on the role of an appellate court. See also *Hay v O'Grady* [1992] 1 I.R. 210 at 217, Supreme Court of Ireland per McCarthy J: "It may be that the demeanour of a witness in giving evidence will, itself, lead to an appropriate inference which an appellate court would not draw. In my judgment, an appellate court should be slow to substitute its own inference of fact where such depends upon oral evidence or recollection of fact and a different inference has been drawn by the trial judge. In the drawing of inferences from circumstantial evidence, an appellate tribunal is in as good a position as the trial judge."
[514] See, e.g. *Sidaway v Bethlem Royal Hospital Governors* [1985] A.C. 871; *Chatterton v Gerson* [1981] Q.B. 432; *Hills v Potter* [1983] 3 All E.R. 716; *Belknap v Meakes* (1989) 64 D.L.R. (4th) 452 at 465–466, BCCA. For an alternative inference to be drawn from the defendant's failure to recall events see *Holmes v Board of Hospital Trustees of the City of London* (1977) 81 D.L.R. (3d) 67, 92, Ont HC, where it was said that in an unusual case where almost immediately the possibility of litigation was recognised and proceedings were commenced within six months, the details of the treatment given to the particular patient should be more memorable. The failure to testify, and to remember, left the impression that "the whole story has not been told and requires that more inferences be drawn than should be necessary in a case involving professional standards of care".
[515] (1969) 14 D.L.R. (3d) 445 at 449, SCC; cf. *Wilcox v Cavan* (1974) 50 D.L.R. (3d) 687, 694; rev'g (1973) 44 D.L.R. (3d) 42 at 54, NBCA.

Conversely, the claimant, for whom the incident is unique and therefore far more memorable, may have a better recollection of events.[516] Against this has to be set the fact that claimants may not recall the details because they were distressed at the time, lacked the necessary technical knowledge, or may simply have no knowledge of the crucial facts because, for example, they were under anaesthetic at the time. Where the claimant's case is inherently improbable, with little or no objective evidence supporting her account of how the injury occurred, and where there is a risk that she may have subsequently persuaded herself of a history of the incident which does not reflect what actually occurred, the judge should not approach the fact-finding process on the basis simply of whether the claimant was a credible witness; rather the judge should test the evidence by reference to independently proved, objective facts.[517]

---

[516] In *Rhodes v Spokes and Farbridge* [1996] 7 Med. L.R. 135 at 139, Smith J criticised a general practitioner's medical notes as "scanty in the extreme", then commented: "The failure to take a proper note is not evidence of a doctor's negligence or of the inadequacy of treatment. But a doctor who fails to keep an adequate note of a consultation lays himself open to a finding that his recollection is faulty and someone else's is correct. After all, a patient has only to remember his or her own case, whereas the doctor has to remember one case out of hundreds which occupied his mind at the material time." See also *Skelton v Lewisham and North Southwark HA* [1998] Lloyd's Rep. Med. 324 at 329 where Kay J commented of poor medical notes that "the significance of the poor notetaking is not that it was negligent in the legal sense but that it is indicative of an unexplained carelessness, whether in breach of a duty of care or not". In *Gray v Southampton and South West Hampshire Health Authority* [2001] EWCA Civ 855; (2001) 67 B.M.L.R. 1 at [29], the Court of Appeal refused to draw an inference from the defendants' poor record keeping that the claimant's brain damage had been caused by negligence; and in *Beech v Timney* [2013] EWHC 2345 (QB); [2013] Med. L.R. 369 a general practitioner's failure to spot a "red flag" indicator for the risk of stroke, and inadequate recordkeeping, were not taken to demonstrate that he had negligently mis-recorded and failed to act upon a very high blood pressure (the claimant's case rested upon proving that the general practitioner had measured the claimant's blood pressure correctly at a very high level but had subsequently recorded it inaccurately at a relatively low level). See further para.4–076 for consideration of the importance of the medical records.
[517] *Gow v Harker* [2003] EWCA Civ 1160; [2003] All E.R. (D) 12 (Aug), per Brooke LJ at [54] to [55], applying the approach of Robert Goff LJ in *The Ocean Frost* [1985] 1 Lloyd's Rep. 1 at 57: "I have found it essential in cases of fraud, when considering the credibility of witnesses, always to test their veracity by reference to the objective facts proved independently of their testimony, in particular by reference to the documents in the case and also to pay particular regard to their motives and to the overall probabilities." Although Robert Goff LJ was referring to cases of fraud, that approach is also applicable to cases of negligence where one party's version of events is inherently improbable (per Brooke LJ). See also *Synclair v East Lancashire Hospitals NHS Trust* [2015] EWCA Civ 1283; [2016] Med. L.R. 1 on the approach to be taken when there is a direct conflict between the claimant's evidence and the medical records. Tomlinson LJ commented, at [12], that: "Some documents are by their nature likely to be reliable, and medical records ordinarily fall into that category." Nonetheless, on the available evidence in that case the Court of Appeal accepted the claimant's account of events over that recorded in the medical notes. In *Welch v Waterworth* [2015] EWCA Civ 11; [2015] Med. L.R. 41, in a reversal of the usual position, the defendant surgeon argued unsuccessfully that his own post-operative note was inaccurate because, if correct, it was indicative of negligence. The Court concluded that the note provided very significant evidence of what had actually occurred and the trial judge had been justified in concluding that there had been a breach of duty.

In *National Justice Compania Naviera SA v Prudential Assurance Company Ltd,*   **3–190**
"The Ikarian Reefer"[518] Cresswell J set out the duties and responsibilities of
expert witnesses in civil cases:

(i)   expert evidence presented to the court should be, and should be seen to be,
the independent product of the expert uninfluenced as to form or content by
the exigencies of litigation[519];

(ii)   an expert witness should provide independent assistance to the court by
way of objective unbiased opinion in relation to matters within his
expertise. An expert witness should never assume the role of an
advocate[520];

(iii)   An expert witness should state the facts or assumptions upon which his
opinion is based. He should not omit to consider material facts which could
detract from his concluded opinion;

(iv)   an expert witness should make it clear when a particular question or issue
falls outside his expertise;

(v)   if an expert's opinion is not properly researched because they consider that
insufficient data is available, then this must be stated with an indication that
the opinion is no more than a provisional one. In cases where an expert
witness, who has prepared a report, cannot assert that the report contains
the truth, the whole truth and nothing but the truth without some
qualification, that qualification should be stated in the report;

(vi)   if, after exchange of reports, an expert witness changes his view on a
material matter having read the other side's expert's report or for any other
reason, such change of view should be communicated (through legal
representatives) to the other side without delay and when appropriate to the
court;

(vii)   where expert evidence refers to photographs, plans, calculations, analyses,
measurements, survey reports or other similar documents, these must be
provided to the opposite party at the same time as the exchange of reports.

---

[518] [1993] 2 Lloyd's Rep. 68 at 81–82, QBD. This guidance has been approved and expanded upon
by the Supreme Court in the Scottish case of *Kennedy v Cordia (Services) LLP (Scotland)* [2016]
UKSC 6; [2016] 1 W.L.R. 597 at [38]–[61].

[519] See C. Pugh and M. Pilgerstorfer, "Expert Evidence: The Requirement of Independence" [2008]
J.P.I.L. 224.

[520] See the comments of Sir Nicolas Browne-Wilkinson V.-C. in *Cemp Properties (UK) Ltd v
Dentsply Research & Development Corporation* [1991] 34 E.G. 62 at 67 lamenting the "sad feature of
modern litigation" that expert witnesses enter into the arena as advocates: "If experts do this, they
must not be surprised if their views carry little weight with the judge." Expert medical evidence may
be specifically rejected on this ground: see, e.g. *Early v Newham Health Authority* [1994] 5 Med. L.R.
214 at 216; *Parry v North West Surrey Health Authority* [1994] 5 Med. L.R. 259 at 264–265;
Hepworth v Kerr [1995] 6 Med. L.R. 139 at 165; *Murphy v Wirral Health Authority* [1996] 7 Med.
L.R. 99 at 104; *El-Morssy v Bristol and District Health Authority* [1996] 7 Med. L.R. 232 at 240;
Wiszniewski v Central Manchester Health Authority [1996] 7 Med. L.R. 248 at 254, 262, where
Thomas J pointed to the unwillingness of an expert for the defendants to criticise the defendants'
conduct where criticism was merited, which reflected a "general disinclination to say much that might
be adverse to the defendants' case".

In *Sharpe v Southend Health Authority*[521] Cresswell J added a further guideline to this list:

> "(viii)   An expert witness should make it clear in his/her report (if it be the case) that although the expert would have adopted a different approach/practice, he/she accepts that the approach/practice adopted by the defendant was in accordance with the approach/practice accepted as proper by a responsible body of practitioners skilled in the relevant field."

These duties and responsibilities are the subject of express rules of court designed to ensure the independence and impartiality of expert witnesses, and to make it clear that the expert's overriding duty is to assist the court on matters within his expertise.[522]

3–191   In *EXP v Barker*[523] it became apparent during cross-examination at the trial that the key defence expert witness (M) had worked with the defendant for a substantial period of time, had mentored him and helped him to obtain overseas placements and a consultant post, that they had written a paper together, and that they had been officers together on a professional body. None of this had been disclosed. M had also been aware that a study relied on by another expert for the defendant (who did not give oral evidence) had been largely discredited, but he did not draw this to anyone's attention. Kenneth Parker J pointed out that M's clear conflict of interest was not only contrary to the Civil Procedure Rules but was also in breach of professional guidance from the General Medical Council on expert witnesses giving evidence in court.[524] Despite this, in the exercise of his discretion the judge decided to admit M's evidence, but when it came to evaluating the rival expert evidence for claimant and defendant the court's confidence in M's independence and objectivity had been "very substantially undermined" and the evidence of the claimant's experts was, perhaps unsurprisingly, preferred.

---

[521] [1997] 8 Med. L.R. 299 at 303. See also *C v North Cumbria University Hospitals NHS Trust* [2014] EWHC 61 (QB); [2014] Med. L.R. 189 at [25] per Green J on the court's approach to the weighing of expert evidence in the context of the *Bolam* test.

[522] See CPR Pt 35. For a graphic illustration of the problems created when experts fail to remain impartial see *Vernon v Bosley (No.1)* [1997] 1 All E.R. 577 at 601 and 611; *Vernon v Bosley (No.2)* [1999] Q.B. 18; Dwyer (1998) 6 Tort L. Rev. 91.

[523] [2015] EWHC 1289 (QB); aff'd on appeal: [2017] EWCA Civ 63; [2017] Med. L.R. 121; (2017) 155 B.M.L.R. 18.

[524] GMC, *Acting as a witness in legal proceedings*, 2013 (available at *http://www.gmc-uk.org/static/ documents/content/Acting_as_a_witness_in_legal_proceedings.pdf*). The GMC states that: "Serious or persistent failure to follow this guidance will put your registration at risk."

CHAPTER 4

STANDARD OF CARE—SPECIFIC INSTANCES

The circumstances which can give rise to a claim for medical negligence are as diverse as the practice of medicine itself. It is possible for any diagnosis or treatment to be performed in a careless fashion, or for some essential step to be negligently omitted. Some situations seem to recur, however, on a regular basis and it may be helpful to discuss the law in terms of these "types" of error. This chapter attempts to translate into legal categories the wide variety of forms of negligence that may arise in practice. It must be remembered, however, that these specific instances of error must always be measured against the general test for negligence embodied in the *Bolam* test. It does not follow that simply because in one case a doctor has been held negligent for omitting to take a particular precaution, that it will always be negligent to omit that precaution. The test is whether the defendant has acted as a reasonably competent doctor in all the circumstances of the case, and this is essentially a question of fact.[1] There must be some precedential value in previous cases, however, and where a particular practice has been found to be negligent in the past a defendant who has adopted that practice should at least be required to indicate how the circumstances of this case differ from that of the earlier case. In addition, practices change over time and what was once accepted and proper practice may now be negligent in the light of new knowledge.[2]

4–001

The doctor's duty to his patient encompasses diagnosis, advice and treatment, but these components can be further divided.[3] Thus, diagnosis should be preceded by the taking of a full history from the patient, a physical examination, and, where necessary, diagnostic tests. It is obvious that this may be difficult if the doctor fails to attend the patient—"remote" diagnosis is a potentially risky exercise. Diagnosis should also be kept under review if the patient is failing to respond to the treatment. Diagnosis will normally be followed by advice, which may range from an assurance that there is nothing wrong with the patient, through the prescription of medication together with a suggestion that the patient take the

4–002

---

[1] See *Qualcast (Wolverhampton) Ltd v Haynes* [1959] A.C. 743, where the House of Lords cautioned against relying too heavily on previous cases as precedents for what constitutes negligence.
[2] *Roe v Minister of Health* [1954] 2 Q.B. 66.
[3] See *Sidaway v Bethlem Royal Hospital Governors* [1985] A.C. 871 at 896, per Lord Bridge. This division is for the purpose of exposition; it is not to imply that different criteria apply to the different components: see [1985] A.C.871 at 893, per Lord Diplock. However, note that a doctor's single duty of care owed to a patient can give rise to separate causes of action: *Golski v Kirk* (1987) 72 A.L.R. 443, Fed Court of Aust where it was held that a failure to give appropriate information to a patient before surgery is a different cause of action from an allegation of negligence in performing the surgery.

This is illustrated by *Barnett v Chelsea and Kensington Hospital Management Committee*[12] in which three nightwatchmen had become ill after drinking some tea. They attended hospital, clearly appearing ill, and a nurse was informed that they had been vomiting. The nurse telephoned the casualty officer, who did not see the men, but said that they should go home and see their own doctors. They left, and about five hours later one of the men died from arsenic poisoning. Nield J held that in these circumstances the casualty officer should have seen and examined the deceased, and was negligent in failing to do so.[13] The deceased should have been admitted for observation and diagnosis. It could not be said, however, that a casualty officer must always see a caller at the department. If, for example, the receptionist discovered that the visitor was already attending his own doctor and merely wanted a second opinion, or if the caller had a small cut which could be dressed by a nurse, the casualty officer need not be called. Moreover, the position of a receptionist in A&E is different from that of a member of the medical staff. There is no duty to provide an accurate estimate of the patient's likely waiting time, and so a hospital is not vicariously liable for a receptionist who gave misinformation about the length of the wait to be seen by medical staff, as a result of which the patient decided to leave and suffered harm as a consequence.[14]

4–007   **System for responding to foreseeable emergencies**   A hospital which offers obstetric services has a duty to provide an adequate system for securing the attendance, within a reasonable time, of doctors with sufficient expertise to deal with an emergency during the course of delivery.[15] There is no reason, of course, why this duty should be limited to obstetric services.[16] It will apply to any service offered by a hospital in which a foreseeable emergency may arise. And it may be negligent to arrange a further appointment to see the patient too long into the future, where the patient's condition is such that an earlier review of the situation is indicated.[17]

---

of access to appropriate emergency treatment amounted to a violation of art.2 of the ECHR. See also *Aydogdu v Turkey* (*40448/06*) (death of premature baby due to failure to provide access to emergency treatment, resulting from lack of neonatal facilities, and lack of coordination between health professionals constituted a breach of art.2). The case is considered at (2016) 6 E.H.R.L.R. 684.

[12] [1968] 1 All E.R. 1068.

[13] The action failed, however, on the ground that the negligence did not cause the death, since there was no effective treatment that could have been given in time to prevent it: see para.5–005.

[14] *Darnley v Croydon Health Services NHS Trust* [2017] EWCA Civ 151; [2017] P.I.Q.R. P14; [2017] Med. L.R. 245 (see para.3–098) distinguishing, at [51], *Kent v Griffiths* [2001] Q.B. 36, CA, para.2–119. On *Darnley* see J. Goudkamp [2017] J.P.I.L. C142.

[15] *Bull v Devon Area Health Authority* (1989), [1993] 4 Med. L.R. 117, C.A. In *Bolitho v City and Hackney Health Authority* [1998] A.C. 232 it was conceded by the defendants that the failure of a doctor to respond to an emergency "bleep" call for assistance by a nurse on a paediatric ward was negligent. The action failed on causation: see paras 5–011 to 5–014.

[16] Although the question of which foreseeable emergencies must be catered for will depend on the rarity of the occurrence and the resources available to the hospital: *Garcia v St Mary's NHS Trust* [2006] EWHC 2314 (QB); [2011] Med. L.R. 348 at [95]–[96].

[17] *Lowe v Havering Hospitals NHS Trust* (2001) 62 B.M.L.R. 69, where the patient had a dangerously high and unstable blood pressure, but the doctor arranged a further appointment to see him eight weeks later. He was held liable in respect of the patient's stroke, which could probably have been avoided if the medication had been changed in time. Cf. *Beech v Timney* [2013] EWHC 2345 (QB);

Post-operative emergencies   The duty to treat extends to post-operative   4–008
treatment. In *Corder v Banks*[18] a plastic surgeon who allowed the claimant to go
home after an operation on the claimant's eyelids, but failed to make any
arrangements for the claimant to contact him if bleeding occurred during the first
48 hours after the operation, was found to have been negligent. The duty to
provide post-operative attendance does not extend, however, to supervising
routine procedures carried out by nursing staff.[19]

Known risks and screening   In some circumstances the duty to examine   4–009
and/or treat the patient may arise independently of any request by or on behalf of
the patient. For example, in *Stokes v Guest, Keen and Nettlefold (Bolts and Nuts)
Ltd*[20] it was held that a factory medical officer should have instituted six-monthly
medical examinations, given his knowledge of the risk to employees of
contracting cancer from their working conditions and the fact that early diagnosis
gave a significantly better chance of successful treatment. The employers were
held vicariously liable for the medical officer's negligence in failing to
implement a system of screening employees for the disease. In this case the duty
arose out of the relationship between the employer and employee, and the fact
that the doctor's function was partially to discharge the employer's duty to the
employees. It might be more difficult, however, to establish a general duty to
engage in preventive medicine, on the part of general practitioners for example,
giving rise to a claim in negligence. If it became standard practice for general
practitioners to conduct screening exercises for a particular disease, such as
cervical cancer, then it would be easier to argue that the failure to do so
constituted negligence.[21] In *Ellsworth v Jablonski*[22] Jerke J held that a family

---

[2013] Med. L.R. 369, where the evidence was that treatment for high blood pressure tends to make
no difference to the risk of any given patient suffering a stroke until at least some months have passed,
after which the beneficial effect of medication increases but the level of reduction of risk does not
approach 50 per cent until three to five years of taking the medication.

[18] *The Times*, 9 April 1960. See also *Ocloo v Royal Brompton and Harefield NHS Trust* (2001) 68
B.M.L.R. 89, QBD, where the failure to provide clear advice to the patient about a follow-up
appointment was held to have been negligent (though the claim failed on causation); *Less v Hussain*
[2012] EWHC 3513 (QB); [2013] Med. L.R. 383; (2013) 130 B.M.L.R. 51, where the claimant
underwent a scan but was not told to arrange a further appointment with the defendant to discuss the
results of the scan and did not receive a follow-up letter; held that the failure to advise the claimant of
the need for a second appointment was negligent (though the claim failed on causation); *McLintock v
Alidina* 2011 ONSC 137; (2011) 80 C.C.L.T. (3d) 289, where the defendant doctor failed to make
sufficient efforts to contact the patient regarding a follow-up appointment to discuss the results of
routine mammogram (though, again, the claim failed on causation); *Videto v Kennedy* (1980) 107
D.L.R. (3d) 612 at 616–617; rev'd on other grounds (1981) 125 D.L.R. (3d) 127, Ont CA, where the
arrangements made by the defendant doctor for post-operative care in the event of complications were
"just about non-existent". The defendant had a duty to "ensure that his patient would get attention in
an emergency situation and, if he did not make those arrangements, to himself communicate with the
plaintiff or her relatives as to her condition", per Grange J, Ont HC; and *Cherewayko v Grafton* [1993]
3 W.W.R. 604, 626, Man QB, on the failure to provide for follow-up.

[19] *Morris v Winsbury-White* [1937] 4 All E.R. 494.

[20] [1968] 1 W.L.R. 1776.

[21] The terms of service of general practitioners include an element of "preventive medicine": see the
National Health Service (General Medical Services Contracts) Regulations 2015 (SI 2015/1862)
Sch.1. On liability in respect of the failure to identify patients at risk of developing cervical cancer
where the patients had actually participated in a screening programme see *Penney, Palmer and*

prompt the patient to give answers that the patient thinks the doctor is looking for. The trial judge, however, considered that in the case of the particular patient (a child with a ventriculo-peritoneal shunt designed to drain excess fluid from the skull, where there was a risk of a blockage of the shunt) this was not a reasonable course of conduct and that in the light of *Bolitho v City and Hackney Health Authority*,[37] there was no good reason for the general practitioner not to have asked two or three specific questions, the answers to which could have indicated whether symptoms of a blocked shunt were present. The Court of Appeal were sympathetic to the judge's approach. Thus, Sedley LJ commented that:

> "I can entirely understand why Judge Harris thought it unacceptable that the culture of general medical practice should be so suspicious of self-serving reportage that it encouraged doctors to ask nothing specific even where the caller was the mother of a child whom the doctor knew to have a shunt in place and the child might have symptoms caused by a blockage."[38]

Nonetheless, the case was remitted for a re-hearing on the basis that, though a judge is entitled to reject expert evidence on the basis that it is illogical (applying *Bolitho*), he can only do so when the experts have had an opportunity to comment on this view.[39]

4–017 **A duty to listen** The duty to take a full history obviously requires the doctor to *listen* to what the patient is saying. Sometimes, particularly if the patient is considered to be "difficult", a doctor may disregard or discount what the patient is telling him and this can colour the diagnosis. A failure to listen to a patient who is describing symptoms which would affect diagnosis and treatment will amount to negligence, where harm results.[40] The Australian case of *Giurelli v Girgis*[41] provides a vivid illustration. The claimant sustained a broken leg which was operated on by the defendant orthopaedic surgeon, who fixed a steel plate to the front outer surface of the tibia. The claimant complained on a number of occasions about serious pain in the leg and an inability to put any weight on the leg. The surgeon took the view that the claimant was a difficult patient, with a propensity for histrionics, who exaggerated his complaints. When the steel plate was removed and the claimant attempted to put weight on the leg, it gave way. A further operation was required to repair the fracture. White J held that the surgeon was liable, because he had failed to take into account the possibility that the fracture was not uniting satisfactorily and had dismissed the claimant's complaints without making any proper investigation. The claimant was not believed or given sufficient time or opportunity to describe his symptoms, or the defendant did not ask sufficient questions. He had allowed only 5–10 minutes for consultations, but "pressure of time did not justify the risks of not listening and

---

[37] [1998] A.C. 232.

[38] [2006] EWCA Civ 24 at [30]; see also the comments of Ward LJ at [63].

[39] The *Bolitho* argument had not been raised by the claimant, but had been raised and resolved by the judge when he came to give judgment.

[40] In some cases a judgment that the patient's description of physical symptoms is probably attributable to a psychiatric condition may mislead a doctor into failing to spot a genuine physical problem. See, e.g. *Panther v Wharton* unreported 29 March 2001, QBD, where both a general practitioner and a consultant physician fell into this trap.

[41] (1980) 24 S.A.S.R. 264.

inquiring".[42] Complaint of serious pain is a significant indicator of movement at the fracture site and the possibility of non-union, and the full facts were vital to a correct diagnosis. As White J observed:

> "I do not think that it was disputed that listening to the patient's history is as much a part of the art of medicine as clinical examination. Modern aids to diagnosis no doubt assist the medical practitioner in varying degrees depending upon the circumstances, but they can hardly take the place of listening to the patient's history."[43]

The patient's responses to questions   Of course, the patient also bears some   4–018
responsibility to give truthful and frank replies when questioned by a doctor. Fraser J made this telling point in the Canadian case of *Rose v Dujon*:

> "To be effective, communication must be bilateral. Doctors are not mind readers and it would be unrealistic and unfair to treat the doctor–patient relationship as one in which the doctor were constantly being tested to see if he could solve the patient's medical problems with limited or no relevant information from the key source—the patient. Diagnostic testing in a vacuum is time-consuming, costly and inefficient."[44]

If the information given by the patient is misleading the doctor will not be held accountable for acting upon it, at least where it is reasonable to rely upon the information.[45] It may not be reasonable where what the patient says is clearly contradicted by the symptoms, or where the patient may not understand the significance of the information or may not remember it,[46] or where it is contradicted by information provided by others, such as a spouse or family member.[47] Seeking information from family members or friends may be

---

[42] (1980) 24 S.A.S.R. 264 at 270.
[43] (1980) 24 S.A.S.R. 264 at 276–277; see also *Cassidy v Ministry of Health* [1951] 2 K.B. 343 at 349 on the question of medical staff ignoring the claimant's complaints of intense and excessive pain; *Saumarez v Medway and Gravesend Hospital Management Committee* (1953) 2 B.M.J. 1109; *Rietze v Bruser (No.2)* [1979] 1 W.W.R. 31, where it was held that a doctor should not attribute the claimant's complaints of pain to "anxiety" until all the possible causes of the symptoms have been explored.
[44] (1990) 108 A.R. 352; (1990) 22 A.C.W.S. (3d) 1175 at [148] (Alta QB). See also *Zeb v Frimley Health NHS Foundation Trust* [2016] EWHC 134 (QB) where, notwithstanding the defendants' admission of a breach of duty in failing to diagnose tuberculosis meningitis, the claimant's application for an interim payment was refused on the basis that, at trial, the claimant's action could fail on causation and/or contributory negligence. The defendants alleged that the claimant had not been truthful about her medical history and had failed to provide crucial information about previous visits to hospital overseas and the diagnosis and medical advice she had been given.
[45] See, e.g. *Venner v North East Essex Area Health Authority, The Times*, 21 February 1987, where the claimant assured the defendant gynaecologist immediately before a sterilisation operation that she could not be pregnant. The defendant did not perform a dilatation and curettage (D and C) which probably would have terminated any pregnancy. The claimant was in fact pregnant at the time of the sterilisation operation, and subsequently gave birth to a healthy child. Tucker J held that the defendant was not negligent in not performing a D and C as a matter of course.
[46] *Loraine v Wirral University Teaching Hospital NHS Foundation Trust* [2008] EWHC 1565 (QB); [2008] LS Law Med. 573, para.4–082 below (system of relying on pregnant patient to recall problems with previous pregnancies when medical records were available to the hospital held to be negligent).
[47] *Collins v Mid-Western Health Board* [2000] 2 I.R. 154 at 165 (Supreme Court of Ireland) per Barron J: "Where, as here, information is supplied by someone other than the patient whether in arranging the consultation or before or after a visit, it should be taken into account and, if necessary, further questions asked. This is particularly so when, as here, there is a discrepancy between what is said by the patient on the on hand and the family member on the other." It was held that a severe

4–027   **Seriousness of risks of meningitis**   On the other hand, a general practitioner should take into account the seriousness of the risk involved when dismissing the possibility of meningitis. In *McDonnell v Holwerda*[77] the defendant general practitioner was held to have been negligent in failing to refer a young child with meningitis to hospital, having concluded that he was suffering from gastroenteritis. Newman J considered that the defendant appeared to have been too certain of her diagnosis of gastroenteritis:

> "...in an area in which it is acknowledged by all the experts that diagnosis is fraught with difficulty because of the uncertainties which prevail when assessing young children with high temperatures and rashes."[78]

It was not the case that a general practitioner should refer every child with a high temperature to hospital. However, in cases of suspected meningitis referral should be made without waiting for the illness to develop to the point where specific symptoms and signs have developed. There was a balance to be drawn, taking into account the seriousness of the consequences of meningitis and the speed at which the infection can progress:

> "Between the proposition that all children with a high temperature should be sent to hospital and the proposition that one awaits the development of symptoms and signs, there is a requirement that general practitioners should assess the aggregate set of symptoms and signs which exist, even if they can be individually capable of being assessed as non-indicative of meningococcal infection. A doctor should consider whether, by reason of their aggregate presence or their totality, when taken with the general condition of the child, a decision not to refer to hospital would involve a calculable risk of harm to the child. Ultimately, as the defendant herself accepted, it is the extent and depth of the general practitioner's suspicion which must come into play. The speed with which the infection can take over so heightens the significance of the risk that referral should take place upon the basis of a properly formed and carefully assessed suspicion."[79]

The defendant had "left insufficient room for suspicion" when she conducted her examination.

4–028   Similarly, in *Large v Waldron*[80] a general practitioner was held liable for having failed to refer a child suffering from meningococcal septicaemia to hospital, on the basis that he had failed to carry out a thorough physical assessment (he had not tested specifically for photophobia and did not measure the child's temperature, relying instead on his handling of the child while on his mother's lap to assess it) and had not obtained a full and accurate history, particularly given that the child had been seen by another general practitioner earlier in the day and had been brought back by his mother due to her concern about his symptoms. Acknowledging the difficulty of making a diagnosis of meningitis, Cox J considered that the duty of a general practitioner in such cases was to carry out a careful assessment of the totality of the signs and symptoms which exist, even if

---

[77] [2005] EWHC 1081 (QB); [2005] Lloyd's Rep. Med. 423. On the negligent failure to diagnose meningitis see also: *Langdon v Williams* [2008] EWHC 741 (QB); *Dale v Munthali* (1976) 78 D.L.R. (3d) 588; aff'd (1978) 90 D.L.R. (3d) 763, para.4–034 below.
[78] [2005] EWHC 1081 (QB); [2005] Lloyd's Rep. Med. 423 at [46].
[79] [2005] EWHC 1081 (QB); [2005] Lloyd's Rep. Med. 423 at [53].
[80] [2008] EWHC 1937 (QB).

each symptom individually can be regarded as non-specific, which should include a full and accurate history and an assessment of the level of parental concern. Only at that point is the doctor in a position to exercise a judgment as to whether not referring the child to hospital involves an unacceptable risk of serious harm to the child. It was common ground, said the judge, that a doctor:

> "...should not be deterred from referring a child to hospital because there is a good chance, even a 93% chance, that the child will ultimately be found not to have serious bacterial infection. It is, therefore, acceptable practice that for every child referred who is found to be seriously infected, 16 should have been referred who did not."[81]

No reasonable general practitioner would have failed to refer the child to hospital had he elicited the information that the defendant ought to have elicited.[82]

In *Coakley v Rosie*[83] a 42-year-old patient presented to her general practitioner with purpuric and petechial rashes, a stiff neck and a severe pressure headache, which were characteristic and diagnostic of meningococcal meningitis. The claimant asked the doctor whether it could be meningitis; the doctor diagnosed a respiratory infection and told her to rest. A few hours later the claimant was found in a coma and rushed to hospital. The general practitioner had failed to identify the rash, failed to examine the claimant's neck for stiffness, and failed to make any proper enquiry about the complaints of a headache. It was held that no reasonably competent general practitioner would have diagnosed a respiratory infection, but would have diagnosed or had a high suspicion of bacterial meningitis and would, accordingly, have treated the claimant with penicillin and made an urgent referral to hospital.

4–029

Missed fractures   A number of cases in which doctors have been held responsible for negligent diagnosis concern missed fractures. In *McCormack v Redpath Brown & Co. Ltd*[84] a casualty officer who failed to discover a depressed

4–030

---

[81] [2008] EWHC 1937 (QB) at [114] referring to an article by A. Van den Bruel et al. "Signs and Symptoms for Diagnosis of Serious Infections in Children" in the British Journal of General Practice, July 2007.

[82] See also *Goby v Ferguson* [2009] EWHC 92 (QB); (2009) 106 B.M.L.R. 120 where liability turned on whether the general practitioner had been told about headaches that the five-year-old child had been suffering. Sir Robert Nelson found that he had, and that the headaches and the absence of any viral symptoms history should have led the general practitioner to refer the child to hospital. Alternatively, even if headaches had not been mentioned, the absence of any signs of a viral illness together with the length of time that the condition had lasted mandated a careful exploration of the history: "The information was there to be elicited and had the further probing which should have taken place been carried out the information would have been revealed" ([2009] EWHC 92 (QB); (2009) 106 B.M.L.R. 120 at [140]).

[83] [2014] EWHC 1790 (QB).

[84] *The Times*, 24 March 1961; see also *Newton v Newton's Model Laundry, The Times*, 3 November 1959, on a failure to diagnose a compound fracture of the patella of the left knee after the claimant had fallen 12 feet onto a concrete floor; the defendant was held to be negligent; *Saumarez v Medway and Gravesend Hospital Management Committee* (1953) 2 B.M.J. 1109, on a fracture of the distal phalanx of the left middle finger. The defendant, who ignored the patient's complaints about pain in the finger, was held to be negligent; *Fraser v Vancouver General Hospital* (1951) 3 W.W.R. 337, BCCA; aff'd [1952] 3 D.L.R. 785, SCC, on the failure to identify a dislocated fracture of the neck apparent on the X-rays; *Arkless v Betsi Cadwaladr University Local Health Board* [2016] EWHC 330 (QB)—failure to diagnose scaphoid fracture of the wrist; *Hotson v East Berkshire Area Health*

transferred to another hospital and seen by a specialist who diagnosed a staphylococcal and/or streptococcal infection. The infection was so serious that a few days later the claimant's leg had to amputated below the knee. Rowbotham J held that the general practitioners were negligent on the basis that they had failed to reconsider their diagnosis or treatment, or both, and had failed to consult with or refer the patient to a specialist. In the light of the patient's prolonged period of hospitalisation and the obviously rapid deterioration of his overall medical condition, they should have been willing to revise their diagnosis. The need to explore all the alternative diagnoses was especially important when it became increasingly evident that the original diagnosis may have been incomplete or erroneous.[104]

4–036   **Keeping alternative diagnoses in mind**   The need to consider alternatives was stressed by Hewak J in *Rietze v Bruser (No.2)*:

> "It is not sufficient in my view for a medical practitioner to say 'of the two or three probable diagnoses I have chosen diagnosis (A) or diagnosis (B) or (C)'. It must be expected that the practitioner would choose diagnosis (A) over (B) or (C) because *all* of the facts available to that practitioner and *all* of the methods available to check the accuracy of those facts and that diagnosis had been exercised with the result that diagnosis (A) remains as the most *probable* of all. For example, if there were symptoms of persistent pain and puffiness associated with a limb encased in a cast and if that cast was split in an attempt to eliminate the cast as the source and cause of the pain and puffiness then if the symptoms of pain and puffiness still persisted an alternative procedure or check would be indicated to determine an alternative cause."[105]

This point becomes even more important where the consequences of the alternative diagnosis, if it turns out to be the correct diagnosis, are likely to be serious.[106] The doctor should keep in mind that patients may suffer from concurrent complaints and that lesser complaints may, on occasion, mask more serious concerns.[107] Moreover, in making a differential diagnosis the doctor must take into account the degree of risk faced by the patient and the seriousness of the consequences of the risk should it materialise:

---

[104] Tunnel vision was also in evidence in *Panther v Wharton* unreported 29 March 2001, QBD, where a general practitioner had formed the view that the patient's symptoms were largely psychiatric in origin, and referred her for a psychiatric assessment, and a consultant physician at the hospital, asked to advise the psychiatric team, failed to approach his physical examination of the patient with an open mind, and so failed to identify a serious vascular problem. Both the general practitioner and the consultant were held to have been negligent.

[105] [1979] 1 W.W.R. 31 at 47 (original emphasis).

[106] In *Bova v Spring* [1994] 5 Med. L.R. 120, 129, QBD, a general practitioner was held negligent not for the initial diagnosis, but in being "unjustifiably sanguine about it and failing to take proper professional care to verify or falsify it in time to protect the patient if . . . the diagnosis should prove faulty". In *Rhodes v Spokes and Farbridge* [1996] 7 Med. L.R. 135 at 145 a consultant neurologist was too concerned with questions about the patient's psychiatric state, and failed to explore the possibility of organic explanations for her symptoms. In *Hutton v East Dyfed Health Authority* [1998] Lloyd's Rep. Med. 335, QBD, a consultant physician was held negligent in failing to revise an initial diagnosis of myopericarditis in a patient with chest pain, having received normal test results for that condition, and in failing to include in his differential diagnosis the risk of pulmonary embolus, despite the real risk of disastrous consequences if a further pulmonary embolus occurred.

[107] *Mellor v Sheffield Teaching Hospitals NHS Trust* [2004] EWHC 780 (QB); [2004] All E.R. (D) 195 (Apr) at [228(1)(iii)(c)].

"As to the degree of risk, this extends to both 'absolute' risk (i.e. the percentage risk faced by the individual in question, in the light of his/her particular characteristics) and 'relative' risk (i.e. how the patient compares with others of the same sex and age). Because the consequences of a coronary event, should one materialise, may be so serious (extending, obviously, to death), these stand as an obvious pointer to the general practitioner and cardiologist, respectively, erring on the side of caution."[108]

In *Lankenau v Dutton*[109] the medical evidence was that a surgeon confronted with a patient with paralysis after major surgery should not only attempt to diagnose the cause but also:

4–037

"...should make a differential diagnosis, that is to say that he should consider other likely causes of her condition and test them against her symptoms and be ready with an alternative theory to direct her treatment if his first diagnosis and treatment should fail to produce an improvement in her condition."[110]

The defendant had diagnosed an aortic dissection occurring during surgery, which initially was a reasonable diagnosis. As the patient's symptoms progressed, however, he failed to reassess the diagnosis, which resulted in the paralysis becoming permanent. He clung to the original diagnosis although the symptoms should have made him question it; he failed to test his theory by X-ray, and he failed to seek the assistance of neurological experts quickly enough. The surgeon was held negligent.

Similarly, in *Bergen v Sturgeon General Hospital*[111] a female patient was admitted to hospital complaining of pains in her abdomen. The provisional diagnosis was acute gastroenteritis, with appendicitis to be checked out. A general surgeon made a tentative diagnosis of pelvic inflammatory disease and referred the patient to a gynaecologist, who confirmed this diagnosis. The patient did not respond to treatment, and indeed deteriorated. She died from a ruptured appendix, following an emergency operation which was too late to save her. The defendants were held to have been negligent, not for the wrong diagnosis itself "for everyone will make mistakes", but for failing take account of the fact that there was no improvement in the patient's condition after 48 hours of massive doses of penicillin (for the pelvic inflammation), and for failing to take any steps to rule out appendicitis when it explained all the symptoms and they had the facilities to do so by means of an exploratory laparotomy, bearing in mind that appendicitis is life-threatening. Indeed the evidence was that where there is doubt as to whether or not a person has appendicitis, it is such a dangerous condition that an

4–038

---

108 [2004] EWHC 780 (QB); [2004] All E.R. (D) 195 (Apr) at [228(1) (iii)(c)], per Gross J. See also *Bowe v Townend* [2005] EWHC 198 (QB) at [36], where the defendant claimed to have made a differential diagnosis, but, as the judge found, "chose what he considered the most likely diagnosis and then confirmed his choice by asking a leading question". The defendant was held to have been negligent in making a diagnosis of migraine instead of a transient ischaemic attack, which was unusual for someone of the patient's young age (26) and would have warranted referral for further investigations. The patient subsequently suffered a stroke. See further *M (CP) (Guardian ad litem of) v Martin*, 2006 BCCA 333; (2006) 40 C.C.L.T. (3d) 11—defendant negligent in removing genital herpes from his differential diagnosis list when there were simple steps that would confirm or exclude the presence of genital herpes.
109 (1986) 37 C.C.L.T. 213, BCSC; aff'd (1991) 79 D.L.R. (4th) 707, BCCA.
110 (1986) 37 C.C.L.T. 213, BCSC at 231, per Spencer J; aff'd (1991) 79 D.L.R. (4th) 707, BCCA.
111 (1984) 28 C.C.L.T. 155, Alta QB.

instances patients' conditions may be such that they should be admitted to hospital for observation and tests,[122] or, once admitted, should not be discharged from hospital without further investigation or tests.[123] The expectation where a patient has been admitted to hospital via the A&E department is that an appropriate process of triage has been conducted,[124] that suitable observations of the patient are made, and that relevant tests will be undertaken.[125]

4–041   In *Pierre v Marshall*[126] a general practitioner who failed to screen a pregnant woman for gestational diabetes, contrary to the recommendations of the Alberta Medical Association and the Society of Obstetricians and Gynaecologists of

---

[1990] 1 Med. L.R. 205, where the defendant dismissed the possibility that the claimant, who was overweight and had a history of amenorrhoea, was pregnant; *Tucker v Tees Health Authority* [1995] 6 Med. L.R. 54, where the defendant was held negligent for performing a laparotomy to remove a presumed ovarian cyst without first conducting an ultrasound scan to check whether the claimant was pregnant; *Bagley v North Hertfordshire Health Authority* (1986) 136 N.L.J. 1014, on the failure to perform blood tests during pregnancy when it was known that the claimant suffered from blood incompatibility; *Zhang v Kan* 2003 BCSC 5; (2003) 15 C.C.L.T. (3d) 1 where the defendant negligently failed to refer a 36-year-old pregnant patient for an expedited amniocentesis given the risk of the baby having a genetic defect.

[122] *Dale v Munthali* (1976) 78 D.L.R. (3d) 588; aff'd (1978) 90 D.L.R. (3d) 763, Ont CA; *Barnett v Chelsea and Kensington Hospital Management Committee* [1968] 1 All E.R. 1068 at 1073.

[123] *Mellor v Sheffield Teaching Hospitals NHS Trust* [2004] EWHC 780 (QB); [2004] All E.R. (D) 195 (Apr) at [244]—43-year-old female patient with chest pain and a profound reduction in exercise tolerance discharged by consultant cardiologist, despite the relatively high risk of a coronary event and the potentially serious consequences if the event should occur. Gross J commented, at [245], that even if the *Bolam* test applied, a practice of discharging a patient in such circumstances "would not be logically sustainable". In *Haywood v University Hospitals of North Midlands NHS Trust* [2017] EWHC 335 (QB) Holroyde J came to the conclusion that no reasonable body of doctors would have discharged the claimant from hospital without carrying out further tests to exclude the possibility of post-operative infection following an emergency Caesarean section (where the risk of infection was around 5–10 per cent), given the patient's symptoms (persistent tachycardia and elevated white blood cell count). It had not been safe to view the claimant's pulse rate as having returned to the normal range.

[124] See para.3–097.

[125] See *Gardner v Northampton General Hospital NHS Trust* [2014] EWHC 4217 (QB) at [22] where a catalogue of errors were made which were admitted to have been negligent, though the hospital denied that there had been negligence in failing to diagnose the patient's sepsis, despite the fact that the missing observations and test results would have assisted in the diagnosis. The patient died from necrotising fasciitis, which was diagnosed too late for a life-saving operation. Sir David Eady held that the failure to diagnose necrotising fasciitis in time was negligent and that this had caused the patient's death (either on the basis that the patient could probably have been successfully operated upon but for the negligent treatment, or on the basis that the negligence made a material contribution to the fact that it became too late to operate with any reasonable prospect of survival, applying *Bailey v Ministry of Defence* [2008] EWCA Civ 883; [2009] 1 W.L.R. 1052, see para.5–084). See also *Macaulay v Karim* [2017] EWHC 1795 (QB) where the claimant was in an A&E department for six hours but a blood test which had been requested and which would have identified an infection was not carried out due to what Foskett J described as a "system failure", as a result of which the claimant "fell through the net". The claimant, under the impression that nothing further was required, left the hospital. In addition to the negligent system failure Foskett J held that the failure of hospital to telephone the claimant after it was realised that he had left was also negligent. The hospital had a duty "to check that there was a good reason for him not being there to provide the specimen and then to warn him of the risk of not having done so" ([2017] EWHC 1795 (QB) at [186], distinguishing *Darnley v Croydon Health Services NHS Trust* [2017] EWCA Civ 151; [2017] P.I.Q.R. P14; [2017] Med. L.R. 245; para.3–098).

[126] [1994] 8 W.W.R. 478, Alta QB.

Canada, was held to have been negligent. Moreover, the defendant also failed to do an ultrasound scan to confirm the expected size of the baby, despite his suspicion that the foetus was slightly larger than it should have been at 36 weeks. Screening for gestational diabetes is not routine practice in the UK, however, and a doctor is not necessarily negligent for failing to undertake the standard test for that condition (a glucose tolerance test). The question of whether a pregnant woman should be tested for gestational diabetes is a matter of clinical judgment involving a number of factors.[127] In *X and Y v Pal*[128] it was accepted that an obstetrician who failed to test a patient for syphilis during her pregnancy was negligent. On the other hand, a doctor should not be criticised for a refusal to offer a CT scan, or any other diagnostic procedure, which he considered inappropriate just because the patient was willing to pay and wanted reassurance.[129]

Errors in performing, interpreting or reporting diagnostic tests   Where   4–042
tests are required there may be negligence in carrying out the tests,[130] in failing to interpret the results properly,[131] in mislaying or mixing up the samples, or where the pathologist fails to inform the doctor properly or at all of the test results,[132] where the doctor fails to read the report,[133] or in failing to arrange a further

---

[127] *Hallatt v North West Anglia Health Authority* [1998] Lloyd's Rep. Med. 197, CA.

[128] (1991) 23 N.S.W.L.R. 26; [1992] 3 Med. L.R. 195, NSWCA.

[129] *Rhodes v Spokes and Farbridge* [1996] 7 Med. L.R. 135 at 146.

[130] *Robertson v Nottingham Health Authority* [1997] 8 Med. L.R. 1, CA—the failure of midwives to check cardiotacograph scans of foetal heart rate at regular 15–30 minute intervals resulted in poor quality traces, making interpretation of the results difficult, and caused culpable delay in proceeding to a Caesarean section delivery.

[131] See, e.g. *Fraser v Vancouver General Hospital* (1951) 3 W.W.R. 337, BCCA; [1952] 3 D.L.R. 785, SCC, and *R. v Croydon Health Authority* [1998] P.I.Q.R. Q26; [1998] Lloyd's Rep. Med. 44 on the negligent interpretation of X-rays; *Briffett v Gander & District Hospital Board* (1996) 29 C.C.L.T. (2d) 251, Newfd CA—negligent misreading of electrocardiogram; *Rance v Mid-Downs Health Authority* [1991] 1 Q.B. 587, on an allegedly negligent failure to interpret an ultrasound scan of a foetus, which was subsequently discovered to be suffering from spina bifida; *Penney, Palmer and Cannon v East Kent Health Authority* [2000] Lloyd's Rep. Med. 41, CA—failure to interpret smear tests for cervical cancer accurately; *McGlone v Greater Glasgow Health Board* [2011] CSOH 63—failure to interpret smear tests for cervical cancer accurately (negligence was admitted; the issue was whether earlier diagnosis would have resulted in conservative treatment rather than the radical hysterectomy that the pursuer underwent; the case is discussed by D. McKee, "The Curious Case of Helen McGlone—Part 1" [2012] J.P.I.L. 145); *Conway v Cardiff & Vale NHS Trust* [2004] EWHC 1841 (QB)—cytogeneticist negligent in failing to identify a congenital defect in cells taken by amniocentesis for prenatal screening; *Manning v King's College Hospital NHS Trust* [2008] EWHC 1838 (QB); aff'd [2009] EWCA Civ 832; (2009) 110 B.M.L.R. 175—pathologist negligent in interpretation of biopsy for rare form of cancer of the tongue; *Muller v King's College Hospital NHS Foundation Trust* [2017] EWHC 128 (QB); [2017] 2 W.L.R. 1595; [2017] P.I.Q.R. P10—failure to diagnose malignant melanoma from a biopsy.

[132] Allegations to this effect were made in *McKay v Essex Area Health Authority* [1982] Q.B. 1166; see also *Thomsen v Davison* [1975] Qd. R. 93 and *Lodge v Fitzgibbon* 2010 NBQB 63; (2010) 919 A.P.R. 100; (2010) 356 N.B.R. (2d) 100 on the pathologist's duty to communicate the results of testing to the doctor; *Gregory v Pembrokeshire Health Authority* [1989] 1 Med. L.R. 81, CA, on the doctor's duty to communicate results to the patient (see para.4–058, n.192).

[133] *Fredette v Wiebe* [1986] 5 W.W.R. 222, BCSC; see also *Braun Estate v Vaughan* [2000] 3 W.W.R. 465; (2000) 48 C.C.L.T. (2d) 142, Man CA, where the defendant doctor performed a smear test but failed to examine the cytology report which showed evidence of abnormality; the patient subsequently died from cervical cancer.

appointment with the patient to discuss the results of the test.[134] The level of care required will vary with the nature and purpose of the test being conducted. In *P v Leeds Teaching Hospitals NHS Trust*[135] the defendants were held to have been negligent in failing to interpret an ultrasound scan of a foetus when the mother had been specifically referred for specialist investigation. The obligation on a hospital dealing with a tertiary referral for investigation of a suspected anomaly was said to be a high one because this was "a scan with a focus". Similarly, in *Lillywhite v University College London Hospitals NHS Trust*,[136] where there was a tertiary referral for an ultrasound scan of a foetus because the initial scans had been unable to detect normal brain structures, but the scans carried out on referral were interpreted (incorrectly as it turned out) as showing normal brain structures, Latham LJ said that:

> "...the duty of care owed by Professor Rodeck demanded a high standard of care and skill in the context of a focused referral based upon the concerns"

raised by the sonographer.[137] Although the principle of res ipsa loquitur did not apply there was nonetheless a "heavy burden" on the defendant to reconcile the fact that he had incorrectly identified structures of the foetus' brain that were not present in the ultrasound scan with the exercise of reasonable skill and care. The defendant's problem, said Latham LJ, was that to establish a plausible explanation:

> "...a plausible explanation had to be found for all three of the absent structures. It may be that a judge could have concluded that the mistake as to the extent of the falx, or the presence of a CSP, on the anterior ventricle was not, of itself, sufficient to establish negligence. In the light of the evidence to which I have referred, the respondent would however have faced considerable difficulty in relation to each. But what seems to me to be insurmountable is the hurdle of establishing that there were plausible explanations for all three."[138]

4–043 In some circumstances a consultant physician may have a responsibility actively to seek out the results of blood tests, rather than leaving a general instruction to junior staff to inform them if any of the results are abnormal.[139] On the other

---

[134] *Less v Hussain* [2012] EWHC 3513 (QB); [2013] Med. L.R. 383; (2013) 130 B.M.L.R. 51; *McLintock v Alidina*, 2011 ONSC 137; (2011) 80 C.C.L.T. (3d) 289.

[135] [2004] EWHC 1392 (QB); [2004] Lloyd's Rep. Med. 537. See also *McGuinn v Lewisham and Greenwich NHS Trust* [2017] EWHC 88 (QB) where the claimant underwent 10 ultrasound scans during her pregnancy. The defendants were held to have been negligent with respect to two of the scans which provided evidence that the foetus was at risk of suffering from microcephaly and should have resulted in a referral to a tertiary centre for further investigation and assessment.

[136] [2005] EWCA Civ 1466; [2006] Lloyd's Rep. Med. 268.

[137] [2005] EWCA Civ 1466; [2006] Lloyd's Rep. Med. 268 at [31].

[138] [2005] EWCA Civ 1466; [2006] Lloyd's Rep. Med. 268 at [39]; cf. *B v South Tyneside Health Care NHS Trust* [2004] EWHC 1169 (QB); [2004] Lloyd's Rep. Med. 505 where, on the facts, it was unlikely that a spinal deformity would have been observable on an ultrasound scan carried out at 19 weeks' pregnancy, and in any event, even if an abnormality had been visible, a sonographer exercising reasonable care could still have failed to see the abnormality.

[139] *Panther v Wharton* unreported 29 March 2001, QBD: "In the abstract, the proposition that a consultant is entitled to rely on junior staff fulfilling his instructions may be unobjectionable. However, in my judgment, the instruction in this case has to be considered in the context of what should have been in Dr Wharton's mind at the conclusion of his examination ... Given my finding that he should have at least suspected severe vascular compromise, the cause of which was unknown,

hand, a misleading pathology report may result in a finding that a surgeon was not negligent in embarking on radical surgery in a case of suspected cancer.[140] Where a hospital sends the results of blood tests to a general practitioner it is a reasonable assumption that the hospital doctors are aware of the information that has been sent, and that in sending the information the hospital is sharing information and not indicating that the responsibility for acting upon it is being passed to the general practitioner. In these circumstances, it is reasonable for the general practitioner to assume that the hospital doctors will take the test results into consideration in conducting their diagnostic investigations.[141]

Testing for potential allergic reaction or side effects   In addition to diagnostic tests, the nature of the treatment or medication being given to the patient may require that the patient be tested in advance for an allergic reaction or that the patient be carefully monitored for an adverse drug reaction. In *Robinson v Post Office*,[142] for example, a doctor who departed from standard practice at the time by giving the claimant an anti-tetanus injection without first administering a test dose for an allergic reaction was held to have been negligent, although the action failed on the issue of causation. Similarly, in *Male v Hopmans*[143] the claimant became deaf due to a side effect of a drug administered to treat an infection in his knee. The manufacturer's instructions warned the doctor that the drug was particularly dangerous in the presence of impaired renal function, and the claimant exhibited some evidence of kidney dysfunction which, it was held, should have been investigated further by testing. The manufacturer also suggested that audiometric tests of hearing should be made prior to and during the course of therapy, because evidence of impairment to hearing can be detected by the audiometer before clinical signs develop. This precaution was particularly important when excessive doses were being given. The doctor was found negligent in failing prescribe such tests either before or during the course of treatment, even though facilities for conducting them were readily available at the hospital.[144] On the other hand, where a risk associated with the treatment is remote it will probably not be negligent to omit to test for the condition.[145]

4–044

---

his investigation was, without the outstanding test results, incomplete. The test results were important . . . The decision as to whether the results or any of them were abnormal was his decision as consultant, not that of junior colleagues", per Peter Heppel QC (sitting as judge of the High Court).
[140] *Abbas v Kenney* [1996] 7 Med. L.R. 47.
[141] *Weir v Graham* [2002] EWHC 2291 (QB).
[142] [1974] 2 All E.R. 737. For a discussion of allergic reactions associated with anaesthesia, see Fisher (1990) 6 J. of the MDU 4, stating that test dosing in this context is inherently invalid, though the availability of resuscitation facilities and drugs may affect the patient's chance of survival to such a reaction.
[143] (1967) 64 D.L.R. (2d) 105 at 113–115, Ont CA.
[144] See also *Marshall v Rogers* [1943] 4 D.L.R, 68, BCCA, para.4–067; cf. *Battersby v Tottman* (1985) 37 S.A.S.R. 524, where following a failure to monitor the known side effects of a drug (a risk of serious and permanent eye damage) the defendant was held not negligent in the circumstances.
[145] *Warren v Greig* (1935) *The Lancet*, Vol.1, 330, where a patient who was suffering from acute myeloid leukaemia, which was a rare disease, died from excessive bleeding following an operation to remove his teeth. The defendants were not liable for not testing the patient's blood prior to the operation.

(f) Failure to consult or refer patient to a specialist

4–045   **Duty to refer or seek advice**   Where doctors are unable to diagnose or treat patients they will normally be under a duty either to seek advice from appropriate specialists or refer patients to specialists.[146] If they attempt to diagnose or treat patients themselves they are, in effect, undertaking work beyond their competence, for which they will be held liable if harm results.[147] For example, in *Poole v Morgan*[148] the defendant ophthalmologist was inadequately trained in the use of a laser, although he had often used it in his practice. The treatment that he gave to the claimant was usually performed by a retina vitreous specialist. The defendant had to come up to the standard of that specialty, and since he was unable to do so he had a duty to refer the claimant to such a specialist. It has also been said that where a doctor suspects cancer he should immediately refer the patient to a specialist or arrange for an immediate biopsy. A failure to do so was held to be negligent.[149] The consequences of missing a malignant growth are so serious that a low threshold of referral should be adopted.[150] Similarly, there is a low threshold for a general practitioner to refer a premature baby back to hospital

---

[146] In *Jaglowska v Kreml* 2003 MBCA 113; [2005] 3 W.W.R. 485 the Manitoba Court of Appeal held that the duty of a general practitioner to refer a patient to a specialist when a definitive diagnosis cannot be made is not absolute. In some circumstances a "watchful waiting" approach may be acceptable.

[147] See para.3–112. It may well be a nice question whether a doctor does have sufficient experience in the relevant field: see, e.g. *Mose v North West Hertfordshire Health Authority* unreported 26 November 1987, CA.

[148] [1987] 3 W.W.R. 217; *Layden v Cope* (1984) 28 C.C.L.T. 140 at 148, para.4–035 above, per Rowbotham J: "Their most critical error in judgment was their failure, when faced with a medical problem they were unable to resolve, to consult with or refer the patient to a medical specialist until it was too late to save the patient's foot"; *Lankenau v Dutton* (1986) 37 C.C.L.T. 213; (1991) 79 D.L.R. (4th) 707, BCCA.

[149] *Wilson v Vancouver Hockey Club* (1983) 5 D.L.R. (4th) 282 at 288; aff'd (1985) 22 D.L.R. (4th) 516, BCCA. On the failure to diagnose cancer see *Sutton v Population Services Family Planning Programme Ltd, The Times*, 7 November 1981; *Judge v Huntingdon Health Authority* [1995] 6 Med. L.R. 223; *Taylor v West Kent Health Authority* [1997] 8 Med. L.R. 251—negligent failure to interpret a cytology report correctly; doctors should have sought clarification of the report, and should have been alerted to the need for further investigations; *Penney, Palmer and Cannon v East Kent Health Authority* [2000] Lloyd's Rep. Med. 41, CA; *Manning v King's College Hospital NHS Trust* [2008] EWHC 1838 (QB); aff'd [2009] EWCA Civ 832; (2009) 110 B.M.L.R. 175; *Stacey v Chiddy* [1993] 4 Med. L.R. 216, NSWSC; aff'd [1993] 4 Med. L.R. 345, NSWCA; *Gordon v Wilson* [1992] 3 Med. L.R. 401, Court of Session, where an allegation that a general practitioner, having noted and recorded certain clinical symptoms, failed to recognise the need for urgent specialist investigation which would have revealed that the patient needed surgery to remove a benign brain tumour, was rejected on the facts.

[150] This was the view of the medical experts in *Official Solicitor v Allinson* [2004] EWHC 923 (QB) where a general practitioner who failed to refer a patient with a lump in her breast for specialist investigation was held to have been negligent. On the other hand, in *Ministry of Justice v Carter* [2010] EWCA Civ 694 the Court of Appeal held that it was not negligent to fail to refer a woman who had approached doctors three times complaining of pain and a lump in her breast for further investigation when no lump was palpable on examination. This was consistent with professional guidelines issued by the National Institute for Clinical Excellence that: "In patients presenting solely with breast pain, with no palpable abnormality, there is no evidence to support the use of mammography as a discriminatory investigation for breast cancer. Therefore its use in this group of patients is not recommended. Non-urgent referral may be considered in the event of failure of initial treatment and/or unexplained persistent symptoms." Sir Scott Baker commented, at [31], that: "where

when the child was exhibiting respiratory problems.[151] Even a consultant in a specialist field may come across a problem that he has never previously encountered and accordingly may have a responsibility to seek advice.[152] In *Manning v King's College Hospital NHS Trust*[153] Stadlen J held that a consultant pathologist had been negligent in failing to consult a colleague in order to seek a second opinion as to the correctness of his diagnosis of a biopsy, in circumstances where the interpretation of the results was difficult and the consequences of a mistake were a matter of life and death.[154]

In *MacDonald v York County Hospital*[155] the claimant sustained a severe fracture of the ankle in a road traffic accident. The defendant, a general surgeon, performed a closed reduction of the fracture and put the leg in a cast as a temporary measure, intending to perform an open reduction at a later stage. At the time of the emergency treatment there was no pulse in the ankle, and this was put down to a spasm of the artery resulting from the trauma which was expected to clear up in a few hours. The next day the condition of the claimant's foot and toes caused concern to the nurses, which they expressed to the defendant when he visited the claimant on two occasions. The defendant did nothing about the condition of the foot, which ultimately had to be amputated because it became gangrenous as a result of circulatory impairment. The conclusion was that the defendant knew that he did not know the cause of the impairment and he should have taken the advice of a cardiovascular specialist or had the claimant attended by a specialist:

4-046

---

a general practitioner has found nothing potentially sinister, the law does not require routine referral for specialist investigation." The case is commented on by Tomkins [2010] J.P.I.L. C169.

[151] *Fallon v Wilson* [2010] EWHC 2978 (QB).

[152] *Gascoine v Ian Sheridan & Co.* [1994] 5 Med. L.R. 437 at 447, per Mitchell J, where a consultant gynaecologist was faced with an unexpected finding of an invasive carcinoma following the performance of a simple hysterectomy. His obligation was to seek specialist advice because he had no specific postgraduate specialist training in the field of gynaecological cancer, and none of the other consultants at the hospital had any particular interest in gynaecological cancer; *Robinson v Jacklin* [1996] 7 Med. L.R. 83, QBD—consultant paediatrician failed to refer a child to another hospital with a specialist neurosurgical team who would have been better placed to make a diagnosis; *Gouldsmith v Mid Staffordshire General Hospitals NHS Trust* [2007] EWCA Civ 397; [2007] LS Law Med. 363—breach of duty in failing to refer patient to a specialist tertiary hospital for surgical treatment of a lesion which produced a deterioration in the condition of her hand leading, ultimately, to amputation of the digits. For consideration of the causation consequences of a failure to refer the patient see para.5–017.

[153] [2008] EWHC 1838 (QB) at [313]–[316]; aff'd [2009] EWCA Civ 832; (2009) 110 B.M.L.R. 175.

[154] The "duty to consult a colleague and seek a second opinion cannot depend on the subjective confidence of a pathologist in the rightness of his diagnosis. There is no necessary correlation between the degree of a pathologist's confidence that he has got it right and the objective question whether he has in fact got it right. It would be surprising and in my view afford inadequate protection to the patient if, in a case where no reasonably competent pathologist could allay his suspicions as to malignancy, a duty to seek a second opinion would only arise if the pathologist had in fact not allayed his suspicions", per Stadlen J, [2008] EWHC 1838 (QB) at [314].

[155] (1973) 41 D.L.R. (3d) 321, Ont CA; aff'd sub nom *Vail v MacDonald* (1976) 66 D.L.R. (3d) 530, SCC.

disabilities. The Manitoba Court of Appeal held that the general practitioner had been negligent in failing to consult with a specialist immediately to obtain advice as to the patient continuing on the drug once he knew she was pregnant, because the general practitioner was uncertain as to foetal age and was aware of the risk of foetal abnormalities if a mother took the drug during the first trimester of the pregnancy. He was also aware of the risk to the mother of sudden withdrawal of the drug and the need for consultation with a specialist. This should have alerted any prudent and diligent general practitioner to the need for the consultation to be immediate and for disclosure to the mother of both the risks involved and the treatment options available.[165]

(g) Overtesting

4–050   Claims that are sometimes made about defensive medicine suggest that defensive practices tend to be manifested in the form of unnecessary diagnostic tests. If a diagnostic test or procedure is unnecessary by reference to the standards of the medical profession, i.e. according to the standards of the reasonably competent doctor exercising and professing to have that skill, it will be negligence to perform it, and it will be actionable if the patient suffers injury as a consequence.[166] This was the essence of the claimant's action in *Maynard v West Midlands Regional Health Authority*,[167] namely that the defendants had undertaken an unnecessary diagnostic operation during which an inherent risk of the procedure materialised, causing her injuries. The action failed because on the evidence a responsible body of professional opinion agreed that the operation was justified in the circumstances. It was not suggested in *Maynard* that the doctors were acting "defensively", but ultimately the issue of "defensive medicine" is merely a question of the doctor's motive for performing the procedure, and motives may be mixed.[168] It matters not whether the doctor was misguidedly seeking to protect himself from litigation or whether he simply misjudged the nature of the patient's symptoms; if no doctor of ordinary skill and acting with ordinary care would have considered the procedure to be called for it is

---

[165] See also *Hutchinson v Leeds Health Authority* unreported 6 November 2000, QBD, where an expert haematological team treating a teenager for leukaemia where held to have been negligent in failing to call in a surgical team to investigate the patient's highly abnormal bowel function.

[166] *Leonard v Knott* [1978] 5 W.W.R. 511, BCSC (see para.4–012); *Mellor v Sheffield Teaching Hospitals NHS Trust* [2004] EWHC 780 (QB); [2004] All E.R. (D) 195 (Apr) at [228(1)(iii)], per Gross J: "there is the risk that advising unnecessary and inappropriate investigations or treatment may, in some circumstances, itself amount to a breach of duty."

[167] [1984] 1 W.L.R. 634.

[168] See, e.g. *Robinson v Post Office* [1974] 2 All E.R. 737 at 743–744. Orr LJ said, at 745, that it would be "asking too much of human nature" that the doctor should have excluded the possibility of being sued from his mind when he decided to give the patient an anti-tetanus injection, but he also weighed up the competing medical considerations in reaching his decision. In *Schanczi v Singh* [1988] 2 W.W.R. 465, Alta QB, the defendant was held negligent for failing to attempt conservative treatment before resorting to spinal surgery. The operation was "unnecessary" in the circumstances, but this was not attributed to defensive practice.

negligence to perform it. This would apply with as much force to unnecessary diagnostic tests, such as X-rays, as it would to unnecessary operations, such as caesaerean sections.[169]

3. FAILURES OF ADVICE AND COMMUNICATION

A lack of communication is often said to be at the heart of many medical **4–051** negligence actions. This comment is usually directed to the fact that a patient who has suffered a medical accident may initiate proceedings because following the incident healthcare professionals have refused to discuss the circumstances frankly with the patient or his family. This results in a breakdown of the doctor–patient relationship, and the patient is left with the feeling that the only way to find out what happened is to resort to the courts.[170] Failures of communication, however, whether between doctor and patient or between practitioners, may frequently be the source of the initial injury.

(a)   Failure to warn about risks

It is axiomatic that patients will normally need some information about the nature **4–052** of their medical conditions and the form of treatment that doctors propose in order to decide whether to accept the treatment. This is required both for the purpose of the patient giving a valid consent to treatment and as part of the doctor's duty of care to advise of the inherent risks of the proposed treatment, so that the patient can make an informed decision. The legal consequences of this type of communication failure are considered in Chs 6 and 7. In some circumstances, the nature of the "treatment" is such that it simply involves advice to the patient for the purpose of enabling the patient to make certain decisions, such as whether it is safe to become pregnant or whether to terminate a

---

[169] For example, the Healthcare Commission reported on a number of incidents in which patients had been exposed to radiation unnecessarily or to levels of radiation that were excessive. As the Commission noted, unnecessary doses of radiation can cause distress and in extreme cases has the potential to cause harm. The most common error was X-raying the wrong patient, followed by operator error, X-raying the wrong part of the body, and procedures being unnecessarily repeated. See Healthcare Commission, *Ionising Radiation (Medical Exposure) Regulations 2000, A report on regulation activity from 1 November 2006 to 31 December 2007*, March 2008 (available at *http://www.cqc.org.uk/sites/default/files/documents/irmer_ar_2006_7.pdf*). In an earlier report the Royal College of Radiologists and the National Radiological Protection Board estimated that unnecessary X-rays caused between 100 and 250 deaths a year: see *Patient dose reduction in diagnostic radiology*, HMSO, 1990; Gifford (1990) 301 B.M.J. 451. Poor management, excessive dosages and unnecessary repeat X-rays were blamed. Hoyte (1994) 1 Med. Law Int. 261, 266 commented that: "it can only be a matter of time before 'unnecessary' exposure to investigative radiation becomes a cause for claim in its own right."

[170] For example, in *Stamos v Davies* (1985) 21 D.L.R. (4th) 507 at 519 Krever J commented that: "...the underlying cause of both the misadventure and of the litigation is a less than satisfactory physician-patient relationship arising out of the failure on the part of the physician to take the patient into his confidence...." See further, Simanowitz, "Medical Accidents: The Problem and the Challenge" in Byrne (ed.), *Medicine in Contemporary Society: King's College Studies* 1986–87, p.117.

pregnancy.[171] It is important to stress, however, that a doctor's duty when giving information is to advise the patient about the options for treatment and the risks involved. It is not a duty to persuade the patient to take a particular course of action.[172] Nor is there any duty to provide the treatment insisted on by the patient if, in the doctor's clinical judgment, it would not be appropriate.[173]

(b)   Failure to inform about errors

4-053   In addition to a duty to inform patients about the risks and benefits associated with particular courses of action in advance of treatment, it is arguable that there is a corresponding duty to inform patients that something has gone wrong with their treatment after the event. It might be thought that the ethical imperative that doctors should "Do no harm" to their patients would entail at least a moral duty to tell patients about errors in their treatment. In the past, there was a noticeable reluctance to tell a patient that something had gone wrong, no doubt in part because of concern that doing so might prompt litigation, though in practice openness about mistakes tends to reduce the propensity to sue, at least where the resulting harm is comparatively minor.[174] Where an error does not, and cannot in the future, result in any injury there will be no prospect of a claim for negligence (given that damage is the gist of a negligence action) but doctors may still be wary of having to deal with complaints, whether formal or informal. Whatever a doctor's personal concerns about the risk of litigation or complaints may be there is a clear professional duty to inform patients about errors, at least where they have suffered harm or distress.

4-054   **The professional duty—General Medical Council (GMC) guidance on the duty of candour**   The GMC gives explicit guidance to doctors on the issue of informing patients when something has gone wrong with treatment. Paragraph 55 of *Good Medical Practice* states that:

---

[171] See *Anderson v Forth Valley Health Board* 1998 S.L.T. 588; (1997) 44 B.M.L.R. 108, Court of Session, Outer House, where the allegation of negligence was that the doctors had failed to give advice and information about genetic risks and had failed to refer the pursuers to genetic counselling. See also *Enright v Kwun and Blackpool Victoria Hospital NHS Trust* [2003] EWHC 1000 (QB); *The Times*, 20 May 2003—negligent omission to counsel a pregnant woman of 37 to undergo an amniocentesis test; *Zhang v Kan* 2003 BCSC 5; (2003) 15 C.C.L.T. (3d) 1—negligent failure of doctor to refer a 36-year-old pregnant patient for an expedited amniocentesis given her age and the risk of the baby having a genetic defect.

[172] See *Attwell v McPartlin* [2004] EWHC 829 (QB); [2004] All E.R. (D) 111 (Mar) at [60] per Jonathan Playford QC, sitting as deputy judge of the High Court: "It would, in my opinion, be a novel and serious departure from established practice throughout a wide range of professional relationships, including those of lawyer and client and financial adviser and client in addition to that of doctor and patient, to hold that a doctor is under a legal duty, not just to advise and warn fairly and appropriately but to persuade or . . . to express his wishes in such a way as to secure compliance."

[173] *Holdsworth v Luton and Dunstable University Hospital NHS Foundation Trust* [2016] EWHC 3347 (QB); (2017) 154 B.M.L.R. 172 at [38] per Judge Freedman: "But I stress (and it needs to be stressed) that the mere fact that a patient is insistent about receiving a certain type of treatment does not and cannot, of itself, justify such treatment being provided. The mode of treatment must always be a clinical decision based upon a clinical assessment as well, of course, of taking into account the patient's wishes."

[174] See para.1–003.

"You must be open and honest with patients if things go wrong. If a patient under your care has suffered harm or distress, you should:
    (a)   put matters right (if that is possible)
    (b)   offer an apology
    (c)   explain fully and promptly what has happened and the likely short-term and long-term effects."[175]

Of course, this guidance does not create an entitlement to damages for its breach, though a doctor could be found guilty of professional misconduct if he failed to comply.[176] It is also arguable that the GMC's guidance sets the standard for professional conduct by doctors and is therefore evidence of what constitutes reasonable care for the purposes of the tort of negligence. To be actionable in negligence a breach of *this* duty would have to cause damage to the patient, and it will be comparatively rare for this to occur (as opposed to the damage caused by the initial error in diagnosis or treatment).

Statutory duty of candour   The Health and Social Care Act 2008 (Regulated Activities) Regulations 2014[177] reg.20 introduced a statutory duty of candour, which from 1 April 2015 applies to all providers of health and social care services. This provides that as soon as reasonably practicable after becoming aware that a notifiable safety incident[178] has occurred a registered person[179] must (a) notify the relevant person[180] that the incident has occurred, and (b) provide

4–055

---

[175] *Good Medical Practice* (2013) (available at *http://www.gmc-uk.org/guidance/good_medical_ practice.asp*). This guidance is supplemented by the document *Openness and honesty when things go wrong: the professional duty of candour* (June 2015) published jointly by the General Medical Council and the Nursing & Midwifery Council (available at *http://www.gmc-uk.org/DoC_guidance_ englsih.pdf_61618688.pdf*). Note that the Compensation Act 2006 s.2 provides that: "An apology, an offer of treatment or other redress, shall not of itself amount to an admission of negligence or breach of statutory duty." The policy underlying this provision is to make it clear to potential defendants that they have nothing to lose by offering an apology. See also the Apologies (Scotland) Act 2016 which renders an apology inadmissible as evidence of anything relevant to the determination of liability.

[176] Compare the position of a solicitor: where a solicitor discovers an act or omission which would justify a claim against them they have a duty to inform their client and advise that the client seek independent legal advice: Solicitors' Code of Conduct 2011, O(1.16) and IB(1.12) (available at *http://www.sra.org.uk/solicitors/handbook/welcome.page*). This professional duty may also translate into a duty of care in negligence: see, e.g. *Gold v Mincoff Science & Gold (A Firm)* [2001] Lloyd's Rep P.N. 423 at [98] to [102].

[177] SI 2014/2936.

[178] In relation to a health service body a "notifiable safety incident" means "any unintended or unexpected incident that occurred in respect of a service user during the provision of a regulated activity that, in the reasonable opinion of a healthcare professional, could result in, or appears to have resulted in (a) the death of the service user, where the death relates directly to the incident rather than to the natural course of the service user's illness or underlying condition, or (b) severe harm, moderate harm or prolonged psychological harm to the service user": SI 2014/2936 reg.20(8). The definition of a "notifiable safety incident" is somewhat different in relation to any other registered person (i.e. other than a health service body): see reg.20(9). "Moderate harm" and "severe harm" are both defined in reg.20(7).

[179] A "registered person" means, in respect of a regulated activity, a person who is the service provider or registered manager in respect of that activity: SI 2014/2936 reg.2. Regulated activities are set out in Sch.1 of the Regulations (subject to the exclusions in Sch.2). An activity is only a regulated activity if it is carried on in England: SI 2014/2936 reg.3(3).

[180] The "relevant person" means the service user or a person lawfully acting on their behalf (a) on the death of the service user, (b) where the service user is under 16 and not competent to make a decision

reasonable support to the relevant person in relation to the incident, including when giving such notification. The notification must (a) be given in person by one or more representatives of the registered person, (b) provide an account, which to the best of the registered person's knowledge is true, of all the facts the registered person knows about the incident as at the date of the notification, (c) advise the relevant person what further enquiries into the incident the registered person believes are appropriate, (d) include an apology,[181] and (e) be recorded in a written record which is kept securely by the registered person. This must be followed by a written notification given or sent to the relevant person containing (a) the account of all the facts known about the incident, (b) details of any enquiries to be undertaken, (c) the results of any further enquiries into the incident, and (d) an apology. The Regulations make breach of reg.20(2)(a) (requirement to notify that a notifiable safety incident has occurred) and reg.20(3) (the terms in which a notification must be made) a criminal offence.[182] The duty under the Regulations is imposed on the organisation providing the healthcare (through the registered person) and creates a criminal offence rather than imposing a tortious obligation on the health professional(s) concerned, but it is likely to be a highly relevant issue when considering whether a common law duty of candour giving rise to a claim in damages should be imposed. If both Parliament and the GMC have concluded that patients are entitled to be informed when something has gone wrong with their treatment it is a small step to conclude that they should also be entitled to damages if they suffer further harm as a consequence of not being told what has gone wrong and its implications.

4–056   **Common law duty of candour**   In some circumstances the practitioner will come under a common law duty to inform the patient that something has gone wrong with the treatment. In *Gerber v Pines*[183] Du Parcq J said that as a general rule a patient was entitled to be told at once if the doctor had left some foreign object in his body. Although this view was disapproved in the Irish case of *Daniels v Heskin,*[184] this reflects the attitudes of an earlier age, when medical paternalism was more widely accepted.[185] The English courts have stated that patients do have a right to know what has been done to them, particularly where something has gone wrong, just as they have the right to know what is going to be

---

in relation to their care or treatment, or (c) where the service user is 16 or over and lacks capacity in relation to the matter: SI 2014/2936 reg.20(7). A "service user" is a person who receives services provided in the carrying on of a regulated activity: SI 2014/2936 reg.2.

[181] This means "an expression of sorrow or regret in respect of a notifiable safety incident": SI 2014/2936 reg.20(7).

[182] SI 2014/2936 reg.22. The offence is punishable only by a fine: reg.23.

[183] (1934) 79 S.J. 13.

[184] [1954] I.R. 73 at 87, Supreme Court, where Kingsmill Moore J said that there was no abstract duty to tell patients what is wrong with them, or in particular to say that a needle had been left in their body, since everything depended upon the circumstances—the character of the patient, her health, her social position, her intelligence, the nature of the tissue in which the needle is embedded, the possibility of subsequent infection, the arrangements made for future observation and care, and so on.

[185] In *Walsh v Family Planning Services Ltd* [1992] 1 I.R. 496 at 520, Supreme Court of Ireland, McCarthy J commented that the observations of Kingsmill Moore J on matters such as the social position of the patient or the class and standard of education of the patient and her husband were difficult to understand as relevant criteria: "The learned judge may well have been offending against the very principle that he was seeking to uphold."

done to them prior to treatment. For example, in *Lee v South West Thames Regional Health Authority*[186] Sir John Donaldson MR pointed out that following *Sidaway v Bethlem Royal Hospital Governors*[187] a doctor has a duty to answer a patient's questions about proposed treatment, and he could see no reason why the position should be any different where the patient asks what treatment they have in fact had. Why, asked his Lordship, is the duty different before the treatment from what it is afterwards?[188] Subsequently, in *Naylor v Preston Area Health Authority*[189] his Lordship said that:

> "I personally think that in professional negligence cases, and in particular in medical negligence cases, there is a duty of candour resting on the professional man ... In my judgment, still admittedly and regretfully *obiter*, it is but one aspect of the general duty of care, arising out of the patient/medical practitioner or hospital authority relationship and gives rise to rights both in contract and in tort."

In Canada the courts have treated this issue as part and parcel of the doctor's duty   4-057
of care to the patient. In *Stamos v Davies*[190] the defendant, while performing a lung biopsy, punctured the claimant's spleen. The claimant asked what the defendant had obtained from the biopsy, and the defendant said simply that he had not obtained what he wanted, but he did not inform the claimant of the ruptured spleen. The claimant was discharged from hospital but had to be admitted as an emergency three days later, due to the bleeding into his abdominal cavity. The spleen was removed surgically, and the claimant recovered uneventfully. Krever J said that he found the reasoning of Sir John Donaldson MR in *Lee* compelling, and held that the defendant was under a duty to inform the claimant that the spleen had been punctured. The defendant's failure to be candid was a breach of that duty. Similarly, in *McCann v Hyndman*,[191] a surgeon who was aware that two parts of a medical device had become detached and migrated into the claimant's abdomen decided that the risks of attempting to locate and remove them in the course of the surgery were greater than leaving them in the abdominal cavity, but he did not inform the patient about the situation or the risk to the patient of subsequently developing a bowel obstruction. The defendant was held negligent in failing to inform the patient about this risk, depriving him of the opportunity to monitor the situation and choosing whether or not to undergo further surgery to have the material removed.

Duty of candour: the causation problem   Even in the context of a legal duty   4-058
to disclose that something has gone wrong with the treatment, the difficulty is in

---

[186] [1985] 2 All E.R. 385.
[187] [1985] A.C. 871.
[188] [1985] 2 All E.R. 385 at 389; see the quotation in para.13–064. It might be thought that this argument is even stronger given that in *Montgomery v Lanarkshire Health Board* [2015] UKSC 11; [2015] A.C. 1430 the Supreme Court adopted a more stringent test for the doctor's duty to disclose information prior to treatment than that of *Sidaway v Bethlem Royal Hospital Governors*. See para.7–015.
[189] [1987] 2 All E.R. 353 at 360.
[190] (1986) 21 D.L.R. (4th) 507, Ont HC; Robertson (1987) 25 Alberta L. Rev. 215.
[191] 2004 ABCA 191; [2004] 11 W.W.R. 216, Alta CA.

4-061   Cases in which, due to the defendant's negligence, the claimant is unaware that she is or might become pregnant, do not present causation difficulties. For example, in *Scuriaga v Powell*[200] the defendant performed a lawful abortion on the claimant, but failed to terminate the pregnancy. She subsequently gave birth to a healthy child. After the abortion operation the defendant assured the claimant that all was well, although he had found no evidence of foetal parts and believed that she had a potentially dangerous disorder. When the claimant became aware that she was still pregnant the defendant told her that the operation had failed because she had a structural defect. "In fact," said Watkins J:

> "...the doctor botched the operation, then seized on a speculative and dangerous explanation for his failure. He should have placed the matter before a consultant without delay."

If he had told the claimant the true position within two or three weeks she would have agreed to a second operation, but the delay had increased the risk to her health. She refused a second termination and gave birth to a healthy child.[201] The defendant was held liable for the claimant's loss of earnings, loss of marriage prospects and pain and suffering.[202]

4-062   Similarly, in *Cryderman v Ringrose*[203] the defendant doctor failed to inform the claimant that a sterilisation operation had not succeeded, and she believed she was sterile. She subsequently became pregnant and underwent an abortion by hysterectomy. If the claimant had been aware of the unreliability of the procedure used by the defendant, and had been told that the treatment had not rendered her sterile (as the defendant knew) she could have tried other methods of contraception or sterilisation. The defendant was held liable for this omission.

---

counselling about the ramifications. See (1994) 112 D.L.R. (4th) 257 at 377. The negligence of the hospital consisted of: failing to consider alternative methods to the lengthy and cumbersome lookback procedure that they adopted; failing to follow up in writing a telephone conversation with the patient's general practitioner informing him of the patient's possible HIV status; and failing to ensure that the general practitioner had sufficient information to give an adequate warning to the patient. See (1994) 112 D.L.R. (4th) 257 at 381–383.

[200] (1979) 123 S.J. 406; aff'd unreported 24 July 1980, CA.

[201] Note that following *Mcfarlane v Tayside Health Board* [2000] 2 A.C. 59 damages will not be awarded for the costs associated with bringing up a healthy child, though following *Rees v Darlington Memorial Hospital NHS Trust* [2003] UKHL 52; [2004] 1 A.C. 309 the parents of a healthy or a disabled child can claim a "conventional sum" of £15,000 for loss of the right to limit the size of one's family. See paras 2–055 et seq.

[202] *Fredette v Wiebe* [1986] 5 W.W.R. 222, BCSC, is another example, where the claimant was unaware that an abortion operation had failed to terminate her pregnancy, and subsequently decided to continue with the pregnancy. The defendant doctor was also unaware that the abortion had not succeeded because she negligently failed to examine a post-operative pathologist's report; *Roe v Dabbs* 2004 BCSC 957; [2004] 10 W.W.R. 478 (to the same effect). In *Cherry v Borsman* (1991) 75 D.L.R. (4th) 668; aff'd (1992) 94 D.L.R. (4th) 487, BCCA, the defendant performed an abortion operation but negligently failed to terminate the claimant's pregnancy. He also negligently failed to identify the fact that the claimant was still pregnant, and by the time this was discovered it was too late for a legal therapeutic abortion. The defendant was held liable both to the mother in respect of the pain and suffering and the costs of raising an "unwanted" child, and to the child for the injuries inflicted upon it during the course of the failed termination.

[203] [1977] 3 W.W.R. 109; aff'd [1978] 3 W.W.R. 481, Alta SC Appellate Div; cf. *McLennan v Newcastle Health Authority* [1992] 3 Med. L.R. 215, QBD, where it was held not to be negligent to let the claimant leave hospital with the impression that she had undergone a successful sterilisation.

(c) Failure to give proper instructions to the patient

A doctor will frequently need the patient's co-operation, in performing an examination, for example, or administering the treatment. This may be as simple as requiring the patient to keep still or instructing the patient about taking medication in the right quantity and at the right times of day. It may also be necessary to give the patient a warning as to any danger signs that he should look out for (e.g. as to the side effects of a drug or the symptoms that indicate that his condition is deteriorating) with instructions as to what should be done if they occur, such as stopping the medication or seeking medical assistance immediately.[204] Sometimes this will be absolutely vital. In these circumstances the doctor will be under a duty to take special care in giving the patient instructions in comprehensible terms, and making sure that the patient understands both the instructions and the importance of strictly adhering to them,[205] though if there is nothing in the patient's demeanour or presentation to alert the doctor to the possibility that the patient has misunderstood simple instructions it will not be negligent to fail to enquire into the patient's psychiatric history.[206]

4–063

Advice about risks of patient's lifestyle This obligation to give the patient appropriate instructions is not limited to advice about treatment, but can extend to advice about the risks that the patient's lifestyle poses to his health. Thus, it can be negligent to fail to advise a patient who is a heavy drinker and at serious risk of developing fatal cirrhosis of the liver, to stop drinking alcohol,[207] or to fail to advise an epileptic patient not to drive a motor vehicle,[208] or to fail to warn a patient who has just undergone an invasive procedure, such as an abortion, and been given a sedative, against driving a motor vehicle.[209] In some instances the doctor's duty may extend beyond simply giving a warning to encompass active steps in the face of a patient's poor lifestyle choices.[210]

4–064

---

[204] See, e.g. *Crossman v Stewart* (1977) 82 D.L.R. (3d) 677 where the defendant doctor was held negligent for failing to identify the indications of side effects. For the position where the risk of further injury is the result of something having gone wrong with the patient's treatment see para.4–057.

[205] See Karp (1993) 9 J. of the MDU 26.

[206] *Nathanson v Barnet & Chase Farm Hospitals NHS Trust* [2008] EWHC 460 (QB).

[207] *Hutchinson v Epson & St Helier NHS Trust* [2002] EWHC 2363 (QB). It has to be demonstrated, of course, that the deceased would probably have heeded the warning, which in an appropriate case may have to be in rather stark terms, such as: "If you do not stop drinking you will be dead in 12 months."

[208] *Spillane v Wasserman* (1992) 13 C.C.L.T. (2d) 267, Ont HC; *Joyal v Starreveld* [1996] 4 W.W.R. 707, Alta QB—defendant reduced patient's dosage of anti-epilepsy medication but failed to warn patient of the increased risk of seizures on the reduced dose.

[209] *MacPhail v Desrosiers* (1998) 170 N.S.R. (2d) 145, NSCA—the defendants had been negligent in proceeding with the abortion when they knew the patient intended to drive home herself immediately afterwards, contrary to the clinic's own policy, when she would foreseeably be at risk of having an accident.

[210] *Almario v Varipatis (No.2)* [2012] NSWSC 1578—a reasonable general practitioner would have referred a morbidly obese patient with a history of failed to attempts to lose weight permanently by conservative means directly to a bariatric surgeon for consideration for surgery. It was not sufficient simply to make the option known to the patient and then leave him to take it or leave it. More proactive involvement was required (at [96]).

advised by her general practitioner not to become pregnant in her medical condition, but was not informed that the drug could damage a foetus. She had indicated that she would take care of contraception, but subsequently became pregnant. It was held that the general practitioner was negligent in failing to inform the mother of the risks to the unborn child if she remained on the drug. She was not aware that she should seek immediate medical advice if she became pregnant or of the significance of failing to do so.

4-069   **Incomplete treatment**   If the patient's treatment has not been completed he should be told of this and advised to return for further treatment or to seek treatment elsewhere. Doctors have a responsibility to bring home to patients the importance of obtaining further treatment and the dangers involved in failing to do so.[224]

4-070   **Advice about post-operative risks**   In addition to the doctor's duty of care to warn patients in advance of the risks of treatment in order to enable the patient to decide whether to consent to treatment, in some instances there will be a duty to advise the patient about the possible post-treatment complications that the patient should look out for. For example, in *Spencer v Hillingdon Hospital NHS Trust*[225] the claimant underwent surgery for an inguinal hernia. Almost two months after his discharge from hospital he developed bilateral pulmonary emboli. On discharge he had been told that if he had any problems he should contact the hospital or his general practitioner, but he had not been informed that there was a small risk that he could develop a deep vein thrombosis or pulmonary embolism as a consequence of the surgery; nor was he given any information as to the signs and symptoms that he should look out for. The claimant had developed pain in his calves but did not appreciate the significance of the symptoms for the diagnosis of this complication. The defendants were held to have been negligent. The advice to contact the hospital if he had "any problems" was inadequate to alert him to the particular risk. Judge Collender QC considered the test adopted by the Supreme Court in *Montgomery v Lanarkshire Health Board*[226] for the duty of disclosure for the purposes of the patient giving an informed consent to treatment, namely that:

> "The doctor is … under a duty to take reasonable care to ensure that the patient is aware of any material risks involved in any recommended treatment, and of any reasonable alternative or variant treatments. The test of materiality is whether, in the circumstances of the particular case, a reasonable person in the patient's position would be likely to attach significance to the risk, or the doctor is or should reasonably be aware that the particular patient would be likely to attach significance to it."

Although the ratio of *Montgomery* was confined to cases involving the adequacy of information given to a patient when deciding whether or not to undergo a

---

[224] *Coles v Reading and District Hospital Management Committee* (1963) 107 S.J. 115, where the patient should have been warned of the importance of having an anti-tetanus injection.
[225] [2015] EWHC 1058 (QB).
[226] [2015] UKSC 11; [2015] A.C. 1430; see para.7–015.

particular type of treatment, there was force in the argument that the basic principles were likely to be applied to all aspects of the provision of advice to patients by medical and nursing staff:

> "Insofar as the judgment in *Montgomery* emphasises the need for a court to take into account a patient's as well as their doctor's point of view as to the significance of information for a patient I consider it relevant to a consideration of the facts of this case."[227]

It followed that the correct approach to the issue was to apply the *Bolam* test with an added gloss, paying regard to what the ordinary sensible patient would expect to have been told. The test was:

> "…would the ordinary sensible patient be justifiably aggrieved not to have been given the information at the heart of this case when fully appraised of the significance of it?"[228]

Moreover, in *Spencer* there were also available NICE Guidelines on *Reducing the risk of venous thromboembolism (deep vein thrombosis and pulmonary embolism) in patients admitted to hospital.*[229] The claimant fell into one of the categories of patient covered by the Guidelines ("patients admitted to a hospital bed for day-case medical or surgical procedures"), which indicated that as part of the discharge plan, patients should be given information on the signs and symptoms of deep vein thrombosis and pulmonary embolism. Judge Collender QC noted that it would have been easy and practical to give the information, and that giving the information would be very likely to improve the prospects of early and therefore more favourable treatment for patients who in fact developed signs and symptoms of deep vein thrombosis and pulmonary embolism. Although the question of whether a given practice was in accordance with the NICE Guidelines was not of itself determinative of negligence, it was "highly relevant".[230] Overall, the evidence indicated that it was known to, and accepted by, the medical profession that there is a cadre of patients who, following a surgical procedure under general anaesthetic develop deep vein thrombosis/pulmonary embolism and who may be saved from suffering or death if the early well known markers of those conditions are picked up. The claimant was in that category of patient. The judge concluded that in those circumstances the ordinary sensible patient would feel justifiably aggrieved not to have been given, on discharge, the information about the signs and symptoms of deep vein thrombosis and pulmonary embolism if appraised of the significance of the information.[231]

4–071

---

[227] [2015] EWHC 1058 (QB) at [32].

[228] [2015] EWHC 1058 (QB) at [68]

[229] National Institute for Health and Clinical Excellence, Clinical Guideline 92, January 2010 (*http://www..nice.org.uk/guidance/cg92*).

[230] [2015] EWHC 1058 (QB) at [73]. See also *Hearne v Royal Marsden Hospital NHS Hospital Trust* [2016] EWHC 117 (QB) for consideration of the NICE Guidelines (defendants held to be in breach of duty in failing to administer prophylactic heparin which would have prevented the claimant from developing a pulmonary embolism).

[231] The judge noted, [2015] EWHC 1058 (QB) at [77], that there was an apparent inconsistency if, as was accepted, there was no duty to warn of the risk of deep vein thrombosis or pulmonary embolism pre-operation to obtain a properly informed consent but there was a duty to inform about symptoms and signs indicative of it post-operatively. However, the argument was unpersuasive because different considerations were in play. The subject matter of the first duty was a warning of a remote risk;

(e) Failures of communication with other health professionals

4–075 A breakdown in essential communication between healthcare professionals with responsibility for the patient can have dangerous consequences for the patient. These errors may be the result of isolated acts of carelessness[242] or they may be the product of some organisational failure. The system of communication may be so poor that mistakes are almost inevitable, or the methods adopted may fail to take into account the risks of human error by providing some mechanism for checking.

4–076 **Medical records** Keeping accurate and reasonably full medical records is an essential part of medical practice. Errors, omissions and ambiguities can have serious consequences for the patient when incorrect information is subsequently relied on for the purposes of diagnosis or treatment. For example, in *Gemoto v Calgary Regional Health Authority*[243] a seven-month-old child died from acute peritonitis as a result of a ruptured appendix. Martin J held that though a paediatrician's initial differential diagnosis of dehydration due to flu was reasonable, she had been negligent in failing to record in the medical notes that the child's abdomen was distended. The effect was that other members of the healthcare team were not alerted to a change in his condition, continuing to operate on the incorrect belief that his stomach size was normal because that was the last recorded entry concerning his abdomen. The paediatrician was the only member of the healthcare team who had been with the child since he was admitted to the emergency department and she was going off shift. The error produced a significant lapse of communication between members of the healthcare team, such that her negligence produced consequences after she left the hospital. Martin J observed that:

> "Serious and foreseeable consequences flow from inadequate charting, especially when the hospital chooses a team based approach to care. Necessary information may not be available to the physician and other members of the health care team. There may be insufficient data to establish the trends and patterns to diagnose correctly, treat properly or monitor a patient's overall health and response to treatment. The evidence of how busy the nurses were suggests it is not reasonable to assume that the nurses will, absent charting, convey all necessary

---

[242] As, e.g. in *Law Estate v Simice* (1994) 21 C.C.L.T. (2d) 228, BCSC; aff'd [1996] 4 W.W.R. 672, BCCA, where, in referring the patient to an ophthalmologist, a doctor failed to pass on significant findings that she had identified in the course of a physical examination, which would have pointed to the possibility of an intracranial lesion; *Adams v Taylor* 2012 ONSC 4208; (2012) 94 C.C.L.T. (3d) 144, where a dermatologist who referred a patient to a plastic surgeon was held negligent in the manner in which he reported his findings about a growth, having said nothing about the growth's characteristics in the referral note. In *Starcevic v West Hertfordshire Health Authority* [2001] EWCA Civ 192; (2001) 60 B.M.L.R. 221 the claimant's husband died from a pulmonary embolism due to a deep vein thrombosis (DVT) during the course of minor surgery on his leg. It was held that the failure of an occupational therapist and a nurse to pass on information they had been given by the patient and the claimant about the condition of the patient's leg to the surgeon, which would have alerted the doctor to the risk of DVT, constituted negligence. See also *Antoniades v East Sussex Hospitals NHS Trust* [2007] EWHC 517 (QB); (2007) 95 B.M.L.R. 62 where a paediatric registrar failed to report a blockage that he had discovered in an endotracheal tube being used to clear the airway of a newborn baby, which contributed to a lack of understanding by the other doctors as to the nature and extent of the airway problem.
[243] 2006 ABQB 740; [2007] 2 W.W.R. 243.

information by oral report. Important information may be missed or forgotten or the opportunity to discuss a patient may be lacking. As a result, it is foreseeable that without adequate charting, patients will likely lose continuity of care."[244]

In *Hamed v Mills*[245] the claimant, a 17-year-old footballer who had just signed a professional contract with a Premiership football club, suffered a cardiac arrest resulting in catastrophic brain damage whilst playing for the club's youth team. He had had an electrocardiogram which suggested possible cardiac disease and the cardiologist recommended a scan and a clinical review. The scan did not show signs of hypertrophic cardiomyopathy, the most common cardiac disorder, but the cardiologist was still worried about the ECG results and a small risk of underlying heart disease (the expert evidence was that the ECG was "unequivocally abnormal"). The cardiologist recommended annual screening, but the clinical review that he had recommended was never carried out. Following a conversation between the club physiotherapist and the cardiologist's secretary the club doctor concluded that the claimant was not at risk if he continued to train and play football. The cardiologist accepted that was in breach of duty by failing to make specific reference to the clinical review in subsequent correspondence with the club. Hickinbottom J held that the club were liable for the club doctor's negligence since a reasonably competent sports physician would know (and the doctor actually knew) that there was a small chance that the claimant suffered from some pathology other than hypertrophic cardiomyopathy. She had relied on a third-hand telephone message to reach the conclusion that the claimant was not at risk of a cardiac event, which reflected "a quite shocking failure of communication". Moreover, the claimant's medical records at the club fell far short of the acceptable. Had they been adequate for their purpose it would have been apparent from them that there had been no clinical review, and there was a high likelihood that another doctor within the department would have spotted this and would have arranged the clinical review. It was unlikely that anyone reviewing the records would have fallen into the same error as that committed the club doctor in considering there was no cardiac risk for the claimant.

4–077

Forensic consequences of poor medical records   In addition to creating a foreseeable risk of harm to the patient, inadequate medical records can also have important consequences for the resolution of subsequent litigation. In *FE v St. George's University Hospitals NHS Trust*[246] McGowan J commented that the:

4–078

    "...shambolic state of the [operating] theatre records show that timings have been altered and no signatures or initials have been applied, so no explanations can be given for the appalling state of record keeping when it was obvious to all by 03.16 that the events of the night and their precise timing would be of great significance. It would be difficult not to be somewhat cynical about the nature of that piece of record keeping were it not for the fact that it is so generally awful."

Although McGowan J did not infer that the poor state of the medical notes was directly responsible for the claimant's damage, it seems likely that it contributed

[244] 2006 ABQB 740; [2007] 2 W.W.R. 243 at [345].
[245] [2015] EWHC 298 (QB).
[246] [2016] EWHC 553 (QB) at [24].

4–081 Breakdowns in communication between doctors, or doctors and nurses can also occur within hospitals if there is an inadequate system of consultation between them.[257] A doctor who fails to read the nursing notes may well be found negligent.[258] Similarly, the failure of nurses to read the medical notes, particularly on a change of staff at the start of a new shift, can also constitute negligence. In *Robertson v Nottingham Health Authority*[259] the Court of Appeal held that there had been a negligent breakdown in the communication of instructions between a hospital's medical staff and its nursing and midwifery staff. A senior house officer gave oral instructions to the midwives about the use of a stethoscope when carrying out a cardiotacograph (CTG) trace, to monitor foetal heart rate in conjunction with the timing of the mother's contractions. This had become necessary because previous scans had not produced reliable information. The doctor also recorded these instructions in the medical notes which were kept beside the nursing station so that the midwives would have access to both sets of notes, nursing and medical. The process of hand over from one nursing shift to the next involved using the nursing cardex, but not the doctors' notes. The stethoscope was not used, with the result that the information obtained from the CTG trace was difficult to interpret, and this resulted in "culpable delay" in proceeding to a Caesarean section delivery of the child. There was no evidence as to the systems in place at the hospital for ensuring that there was not such a breakdown in communication between the medical staff and the nursing staff. The Court of Appeal held that the paucity of evidence on this issue was irrelevant. If an effective system was in place to see that such breakdowns in communication did not occur, then the health authority would be vicariously liable for the negligence of any employee who did not take reasonable care to ensure that the system worked efficiently. If, on the other hand, there were no effective systems in place, the authority would be directly liable on the basis of a breach of a non-delegable duty to establish a proper system of care. Thus:

> "...if a patient is injured by reason of a negligent breakdown in the systems for communicating material information to the clinicians responsible for her care, she is not to be denied redress merely because no identifiable person or persons are to blame for deficiencies in setting up and monitoring the effectiveness of the relevant communication systems."[260]

---

done by the first doctor. Otherwise the patient is being deprived of the full skill, knowledge and aid in diagnosis that the second doctor could otherwise apply to his case", per Lord Keith at [1994] 5 Med. L.R. 239 at 245. Lord Denning said that: "Misleading information is a very dangerous thing to throw about. There is no telling where it will finish up": [1994] 5 Med L.R. 239 at 248.

[257] See, e.g. *King v South Eastern Area Health Service* [2005] NSWSC 305—hospital responsible for the negligence of a doctor in failing to disseminate information to colleagues about significant revisions to a treatment protocol of which he was, or should have been, aware.

[258] *Holmes v Board of Hospital Trustees of the City of London* (1977) 81 D.L.R. (3d) 67 at 94, Ont HC. Patients attending an A&E department may tend to assume that information communicated to a nurse will be passed on to the doctor, which provides an additional reason for the doctor to review the nurses' notes and to clarify any discrepancies which exist between the symptoms recorded in the nurses' notes and those the patient subsequently discloses to an emergency doctor: *Rose v Dujon* (1990) 108 A.R. 352; (1990) 22 A.C.W.S. (3d) 1175 at [142] (Alta QB) Fraser J.

[259] [1997] 8 Med. L.R. 1. See also *SXX v Liverpool Women's NHS Foundation Trust* [2015] EWHC 4072 (QB) (midwife held negligent in failing to refer discussion of the mode of delivery to the consultant where the mother had repeatedly requested an elective Caesarean section).

[260] [1997] 8 Med. L.R. 1 at 13 per Brooke LJ, applying *Bull v Devon Area Health Authority* (1989), [1993] 4 Med. L.R. 117. The claimant failed on causation. See also *FE v St. George's University*

Relying on the patient to recall information   In *Loraine v Wirral University*   **4–082**
Teaching Hospital NHS Foundation Trust[261] the practice of the defendant hospital
when booking in a pregnant woman was to rely on her to identify any problems
she had experienced in previous pregnancies and to obtain the medical records of
earlier pregnancies only if she flagged up a problem. If the defendants had
consulted the mother's medical records they would have appreciated first, that
there was a history of a footling presentation in a previous pregnancy, and
secondly that there was a possibility of a fibroid in the uterine wall. Steps would
then have been taken to confirm whether this was still the case and, if so, the
mother would have been admitted to hospital as a precaution because of the risk
of an obstructed delivery. The mother was at home when she suffered a placental
abruption. She was rushed to hospital and the baby was born by emergency
Caesarean section but suffered brain damage due to foetal asphyxia. If the mother
had been in hospital at the time the baby would have been delivered much sooner
and the damage would have been avoided. Plender J held that the system of
relying on the patient to alert medical staff to possible complications was flawed
because the patient may have been unaware of the significance of the medical
issues previously identified, or may have forgotten them, or remembered them
incorrectly. Although this was not a case of a failure of communication between
medical staff as occurred in *Robertson v Nottingham Health Authority*, it was a
flawed system that exposed the patient to avoidable risk.

Relying on casual professional exchanges   Relying too heavily on casual   **4–083**
exchanges can also cause problems, and this was criticised in the Canadian case
of *Bergen v Sturgeon General Hospital*:

> "There appears to be an accepted practice of what is referred to as 'Curbstone Consultations'.
> This appears to happen when doctors casually meet in such places as hospital corridors and
> discuss a patient. In my opinion, this is bad practice and to be discouraged. It seems to me that
> when an attending physician calls in a specialist for a 'consultation' the least that might be
> expected is for those physicians to have a meaningful discussion between them, or among
> them, as the case may require, whereby each advises the other of what they did, when they did
> it, and what should be done. In this way each would be fully aware of the procedure of the
> other, the findings of the other and the reasons for the diagnosis arrived at by the other. In this
> case, such a consultation did not take place which, in my opinion, contributed to the bad
> result."[262]

Mishearing or misreading instructions   Communication errors can occur   **4–084**
from simply mishearing or misreading an instruction, sometimes with catastrophic consequences. This may be attributable to a single lapse of concentration
by a doctor or nurse, but the further question may then arise as to whether there

---

Hospitals NHS Trust [2016] EWHC 553 (QB) where "Notwithstanding the pressures of a busy labour
ward, the system of communication and the response to messages sent between the teams was
inadequate"; *Colwill v Oxford Radcliffe Hospitals NHS Trust* [2007] EWHC 2881 (QB) at [59], where
there was either a breakdown in the system of recording the insertion of a cannula into the patient's
arm or the hospital had been negligent in failing to draw the attention of the doctors to the hospital
policy on the recording and removal of cannulae.
[261] [2008] EWHC 1565 (QB); [2008] LS Law Med. 573; commented on by McQuater [2008] J.P.I.L.
C186.
[262] (1984) 28 C.C.L.T. 155 at 175, per Hope J.

was any system for checking for such errors given that it is known that mistakes do sometimes happen. In *Collins v Hertfordshire County Council*[263] a patient died after being injected with cocaine instead of procaine as a local anaesthetic. The surgeon had told a junior, unqualified medical officer over the telephone his requirements for the operation the next day, and the word "procaine" was misheard for "cocaine". The pharmacist dispensing the drug at the hospital pharmacy did not question the order for an "unheard of dosage" of a dangerous drug, and the surgeon did not check prior to injecting the solution that he was in fact injecting what he had ordered. It was held that both the surgeon and the medical officer were liable, as was the hospital authority for having an unsafe system for dispensing.[264]

4–085   **Clarity in writing and interpreting medical notes**[265]   A doctor who prepares a report or medical notes which he is aware may be relied upon by others for the treatment of the patient has a duty to exercise reasonable care in writing the report.[266] The duty cuts both ways, so that the doctor interpreting medical notes written by others may have a responsibility to seek clarification. For example, where a medical term has a strict technical meaning, but also a looser, colloquial meaning, then it is incumbent on a doctor who is relying on the term as found in the patient's medical notes as the basis for a medical judgment to clarify with the person who used the term in which sense it was meant. A failure to do so will be regarded as negligent.[267] Similarly, if there is something in the patient's notes which is undecipherable, but its meaning is crucial to the judgment that the doctor has to make, then it may be negligence simply to ignore the note when it would have been a simple task to contact the person who made the note in order to have

---

[263] [1947] 1 K.B. 598; see also *Strangeways-Lesmere v Clayton* [1936] 2 K.B. 11, where a nurse who misread her instructions and gave an excess dose was held to be negligent.

[264] cf. *Fussell v Beddard* (1942) 2 B.M.J. 411 in which a patient received a fatal overdose of anaesthetic because the nurse misheard the anaesthetist's instructions about the strength of the dose. The patient received a 1 per cent solution of decicaine instead of 0.1 per cent. Lewis J said that when the nurse is inexperienced the surgeon and the anaesthetist should take care to see that she is carrying out or is competent to carry out the duties assigned to her, but when the nurse is experienced they are entitled to rely on her to carry out their instructions. His Lordship held that neither the anaesthetist nor the nurse had been negligent, but that an unfortunate mistake had been made. It would be difficult to support such a remarkable conclusion on negligence today.

[265] In one study involving four Irish hospitals the overall percentage of doctors' handwriting samples rated as illegible was 22 per cent: S. Murray, G. Boylan, S. O'Flynn, C. O'Tuathaigh and K. Doran, "Can you read this? Legibility and hospital records: a multi-stakeholder analysis" (2012) 18 Clinical Risk 95.

[266] *Everett v Griffiths* [1920] 3 K.B. 163 at 213. See the observations of Sir Thomas Bingham MR on *Everett v Griffiths* in *X (Minors) v Bedfordshire County Council* [1995] 2 A.C. 633 at 664–665; though see also the comments of Lord Browne-Wilkinson [1995] 2 A.C. 633 at 753, on these observations, when *X (Minors)* reached the House of Lords. In *Trustees of London Clinic v Edgar* unreported 19 April 2000, QBD, a surgeon who failed to record that the results of his post-operative tests for the patient's limb movement, following spinal surgery, were normal was held to have been negligent, because the nursing staff with responsibility for the patient's post-operative care then assumed (also negligently) that the surgeon was aware that the patient's response was not normal. The consequence was that the surgeon was not called to deal with the patient's deteriorating condition until it was too late.

[267] *Scheck v Dart* [2004] EWHC 2336 (QB) at [15] per Wilkie J.

it deciphered, and if necessary further explained.[268] This common sense principle also applies to the writing of a prescription, which should be reasonably legible.

Prescription errors   Prescription errors can result in both the prescribing   **4–086**
doctor being held responsible for the initial mistake and the pharmacist being held responsible for failing to spot or check the error. For example, in *Prendergast v Sam and Dee Ltd*[269] the defendant general practitioner wrote a prescription for Amoxil for the claimant's chest infection. The pharmacist misread the doctor's writing, taking the word Amoxil for Daonil, a drug used to control diabetes. The claimant suffered symptoms of hypoglycaemia as a result of taking Daonil, since he was not a diabetic, and he was left with permanent brain damage. It was held that both the doctor and the pharmacist were negligent. A doctor has a duty to his patients to write a prescription clearly,[270] and must allow for some mistakes or carelessness on the part of a busy pharmacist. Standing on its own the prescription could reasonably have been read incorrectly, and thus the doctor was liable, notwithstanding that there were other factors which should have alerted the pharmacist to the possibility of error. The pharmacist has a duty to give some thought to the prescriptions he is dispensing and should not dispense them mechanically; if there is doubt he should contact the doctor for clarification. If he had been paying attention he would have realised that there was something wrong with the prescription, since the dosage and the small number of tablets were unusual for Daonil; moreover, the claimant paid for the prescription whereas drugs for diabetes were free under the NHS.[271]

Communicating test results   A pathologist who has been given specimens for   **4–087**
testing or analysis owes a duty to the patient not only to conduct the tests in a proper manner but also to take reasonable steps to communicate the results to the referring doctor, and it is irrelevant that the doctor also has a corresponding duty

---

[268] [2004] EWHC 2336 (QB) at [16].

[269] [1989] 1 Med. L.R. 36, CA.

[270] Though most prescriptions these days are probably printed rather than handwritten, at least in general practice. Nonetheless, prescription or monitoring errors in general practice occur in around one in 20 of all prescription items: *Investigating the prevalence and causes of prescribing errors in general practice: The PRACtICe Study* (GMC, May 2012). See also R. Spencer, A. Avery, B. Serumaga and S. Crowe, "Prescribing errors in general practice and how to avoid them" (2011) 17 Clinical Risk 39.

[271] In *Horton v Evans* [2006] EWHC 2808 (QB); [2007] P.N.L.R. 17; [2007] LS Law Med. 212 a pharmacist was held to have been negligent in not questioning the prescription of a drug by a general practitioner, the dosage of which was eight times higher than previous prescriptions for the same patient. The pharmacist had failed to comply with standards laid down by the Royal Pharmaceutical Society of Great Britain and the branch procedures manual of the chemist. Such a significant increase in the strength of the dose raised the possibility that the prescription might be a mistake, and the pharmacist should have checked with the general practitioner. For similar cases of negligence by a pharmacist failing to spot prescription errors see *Collins v Hertfordshire County Council* [1947] 1 K.B. 598 and *Dwyer v Roderick, The Times*, 12 November 1983; McKevitt (1988) 4 P.N. 185. In *Wootton v J Docter Ltd* [2008] EWCA Civ 1361; [2009] LS Law Med. 63 the claimant was negligently given the wrong contraceptive drug by the pharmacist (Logynon instead of Microgynon), which she took for two days before realising the error. The claimant became pregnant at about the same time, but was unable to prove any causal link between the different pill and the conception. *Wootton* is commented on by J. McQuater [2009] J.P.I.L. C65. See generally on the pharmacist's liability: Crawford (1995) 2 J. Law and Med. 293.

to find out the results.[272] In *Farraj v King's Healthcare NHS Trust*[273] a hospital sent a foetal tissue sample to a private cytogenetics laboratory for the sample to be cultured and sent back to the hospital for a DNA test. A technician at the laboratory had doubts about whether the sample contained foetal cells but these doubts were not reported to the hospital and the DNA test was negative for an inherited blood disorder. The claimants gave birth to a child with the blood disorder and brought a claim for wrongful birth against the hospital and the laboratory. The Court of Appeal held that the laboratory had been negligent, but the hospital had not since it was reasonable to rely on an established working practice with the laboratory and it was entitled to assume, unless it heard from the laboratory to the contrary, that the sample had provided some foetal material suitable for culture and that, when the cultured cells were returned to the hospital, they could be relied on as comprising foetal cells. There was no onus on the hospital to enquire whether the sample it had sent to the laboratory was satisfactory for its purpose.[274]

4-088 A general practitioner who is sent the results of a blood test by the hospital is entitled to assume that the hospital doctors are aware of those results and are taking them into account in their investigation of the patient's symptoms; it is not for the general practitioner to go through hospital notes to check that the hospital has done what it should have done.[275] Similarly, it was not negligent for a general practitioner to fail to advise parents that there was an alternative means of providing immunisation of a child against measles, when immunisation was not imminent and the general practitioner was aware that the parents would be being advised by another doctor at another practice in 12 to 18 months about the

---

[272] *Thomsen v Davison* [1975] Qd R. 93; *Lodge v Fitzgibbon* 2010 NBQB 63; (2010) 919 A.P.R. 100; (2010) 356 N.B.R. (2d) 100 at [123] per Grant J: "...if a pathologist reading a slide which has potential life and death implications has concerns that are recorded in the microscopy it is not sufficient to simply say 'see microscopy please'. He or she owes a duty to the patient to ensure that those concerns are clearly communicated to the doctor in charge of the patient's care so that they will be acted upon and not left buried in the microscopy while the family doctor is lulled into inaction by an unequivocal diagnosis." See also *McKay v Essex Area Health Authority* [1982] Q.B. 1166 on an alleged omission to communicate test results; *Gregory v Pembrokeshire Health Authority* [1989] 1 Med. L.R. 81 CA; *Fredette v Wiebe* [1986] 5 W.W.R. 222. In *O'Gorman v Jermyn* [2006] IEHC 398 it was held that a surgeon was entitled to rely on a pathology report indicating, wrongly, that the patient had stomach cancer when deciding to perform a total gastrectomy.

[273] [2009] EWCA Civ 1203; [2010] 1 W.L.R. 2139.

[274] For discussion of the types of error that can arise in a pathology laboratory see T. Wreghitt, "Microbiological laboratory errors and dealing with patients" (2013) 19 Clinical Risk 64.

[275] *Weir v Graham* [2002] EWHC 2291 (QB). A general practitioner will normally be entitled to rely on the diagnosis provided in a pathology report without having to scour the report for signs of uncertainty in the pathologist's conclusions: *Lodge v Fitzgibbon* 2010 NBQB 63; (2010) 919 A.P.R. 100; (2010) 356 N.B.R. (2d) 100 at [183] where Grant J commented: "...the law does not require a general practitioner to question the unequivocal diagnosis of a specialist practising in his field of specialty. If there is uncertainty in the diagnosis, it is the pathologist ... not the family doctor, who should clearly say so and not just recommend further investigation but obtain a second opinion." Conversely, where a patient has been advised by her general practitioner about the risks to her unborn child from exposure to chickenpox it is not incumbent on a hospital doctor to probe the nature of the advice in order to check whether it was accurate or complete, at least where the patient does not ask questions: *Wyatt v Curtis* [2003] EWCA Civ 1779.

options for immunisation.[276] The general practitioner was entitled to assume that appropriate advice would be given at the relevant time.

(f) Medico-legal reports

Doctors who prepare medical reports for use in legal proceedings clearly come under a duty to exercise reasonable care in preparing those reports.[277] In many instances the doctor's medical skills, as to diagnosis, causation of symptoms and prognosis will be called into play, to which the *Bolam* test would be applicable. In other cases, however, the negligence may be of a more mundane nature and judgments about whether the defendant exercised appropriate professional skill by reference to the standards of his peers are irrelevant. This was the view of the Alberta Court of Appeal in *Kelly v Lundgard*[278] where it was held that the standard of care required of doctors expressing opinions in medico-legal reports was to exercise such care as the circumstances required to ensure that the representations made in the report are accurate and not misleading. It was not simply a matter of asking what the doctor should have disclosed, because the doctor may go further than required and make positive, but misleading statements, i.e. a negligent misrepresentation. Two doctors (including the claimant's general practitioner) provided medico-legal reports for the purpose of the claimant's action against a negligent motorist, advising that she would make a full recovery from her injuries. In fact, she was rendered sterile. The settlement with the motorist did not include compensation for infertility. When the claimant subsequently discovered the infertility she sued the doctors, on the basis that their negligent reports had led to her settling her claim for less than it was worth. The general practitioner was held to have been negligent in that she had failed to obtain a report on the surgery undertaken by the surgeon before writing her report. She had also failed to disclose in her report that she had not seen the surgery report. Had she seen the report she should have been alerted to the real risk of infertility developing as a result of the injuries sustained in the road traffic accident (though if the risk had been merely "speculative" there would have been no liability for failing to report it).

4–089

Conrad JA said that the standard of care in writing medico-legal reports did not require expert evidence. It was a question of common sense and fairness on which the court was competent to rule.[279] The preparation of a medico-legal report involved ordinary communication skills. A doctor may fail to exercise reasonable care in different ways. A statement may be a negligent misrepresentation because the doctor did not exercise proper care in diagnosing the subject's condition. The lack of care is the improper diagnosis, which is a technical issue requiring expert evidence:

4–090

---

[276] *Thompson v Blake-James* [1998] P.I.Q.R. P286; [1998] Lloyd's Rep. Med. 187, CA. The action also failed on causation because the claimant's mother was fully aware of the options for immunisation after subsequent discussions with other doctors.
[277] See paras 2–108 et seq. Witness immunity applies to witnesses of fact, but not to expert witnesses where the claim is brought by the party for whom the expert's report was prepared.
[278] (2001) 202 D.L.R. (4th) 385, Alta CA.
[279] (2001) 202 D.L.R. (4th) 385 at [115].

post-operative treatment[294]; unnecessary and gross cosmetic distortion following breast reduction surgery[295]; administering the wrong anaesthetic[296]; or too much anaesthetic[297]; prescribing the wrong dosage of a drug[298]; or injecting the wrong dosage by mistake[299]; damaging a nerve while administering an injection[300]; treating the wrong patient[301]; allowing an elderly patient to fall off a trolley[302]; or failing to check the position of a catheter monitoring the blood oxygen level of a premature baby.[303]

---

damage to the left femoral nerve during the course of an abdominal operation was the result of a negligent error; *Heath v West Berkshire Health Authority* [1992] 3 Med. L.R. 57, QBD, where damage to the patient's lingual nerve during the course of an operation to remove wisdom teeth was held to be negligent, on the ground that although it was possible to cause unavoidable damage to the nerve, on a balance of probabilities the injury occurred as a result of the retractor being incorrectly positioned in front of the nerve, or incorrectly adjusted to the drill in front of the nerve, or through inadvertent mis-application of the drill. On negligently inflicted damage to the lingual nerve during removal of wisdom teeth see also: *Christie v Somerset Health Authority* [1992] 3 Med. L.R. 75 and *Tomkins v Bexley Health Authority* [1993] 4 Med. L.R. 235. In *Smith v Salford Health Authority* [1994] 5 Med. L.R. 321, QBD, it was held that the defendant's technique in using an aneurism needle in performing a particular type of spinal fusion was inappropriate for the site of the spine at which he was operating, because it was inherently likely to intrude too far into the spinal canal.
[294] *Powell v Streatham Manor Nursing Home* [1935] A.C. 243, where a patient's bladder was punctured by a catheter inserted by a nurse; see also *Cassidy v Ministry of Health* [1951] 2 K.B. 343 at 355 on post-operative care.
[295] *MacDonald v Ross* (1983) 24 C.C.L.T. 242, NSSC; see also *White v Turner* (1981) 120 D.L.R. (3d) 269; (1982) 12 D.L.R. (4th) 319 on breast reduction surgery. See Ward (1992) 3 *AVMA Medical & Legal Journal* (No.1) p.2, for discussion of the possible complications arising from breast augmentation surgery; and Balen (2002) 8 *Clinical Risk* 177. See also *La Fleur v Cornelis* (1979) 28 N.B.R. (2d) 569 at 573, NBSC, on a negligently performed rhinoplasty.
[296] *Collins v Hertfordshire County Council* [1947] 1 K.B. 598; *Ritchie v Chichester Health Authority* [1994] 5 Med. L.R. 187, QBD.
[297] *Jones v Manchester Corporation* [1952] Q.B. 852.
[298] *Dwyer v Roderick, The Times*, 12 November 1983; *Horton v Evans* [2006] EWHC 2808 (QB); [2007] P.N.L.R. 17; [2007] LS Law Med. 212. On drug errors generally see (1998) 4 *Clinical Risk* 103–109,173–183; Rolfe and Harper (1995) 310 B.M.J. 1173. See further para.4–137.
[299] *Strangeways-Lesmere v Clayton* [1936] 2 K.B. 11; *Davies v Countess of Chester Hospital NHS Foundation Trust* [2014] EWHC 4294 (QB); [2015] Med. L.R. 141—patient in A&E with ventricular tachycardia given an injection of 8mg of magnesium, four times the intended dose, and immediately suffered a fatal cardiac arrest (the claim failed on causation; the patient's condition was such that he would probably have died shortly afterwards in any event).
[300] *Caldeira v Gray* [1936] 1 All E.R. 540; *Hammond v North West Hertfordshire Health Authority* (1991) 2 *AVMA Medical & Legal Journal* (No.1) p.12.
[301] Patient misidentification is a widespread problem in the NHS leading, inter alia, to errors in drug administration, blood transfusion, and surgical interventions: P. Thomas and C. Evans "An identity crisis? Aspects of patient misidentification" (2004) 10 *Clinical Risk* 18; Giles, S.J., et al., "Experience of wrong site surgery and surgical marking practices among clinicians in the UK" (2006) 15 Qual. Saf. Health Care 363. Wrong site surgery is one of the NHS's so-called "never events", i.e. "serious incidents that are wholly preventable as guidance or safety recommendations that provide strong systemic protective barriers are available at a national level and should have been implemented by all healthcare providers" (definition taken from NHS England website: *http://www.england.nhs.uk/ patientsafety/never-events*). The *Never Events List 2015/16* is available at: *https://www.england.nhs. uk/wp-content/uploads/2015/03/never-evnts-list-15-16.pdf*. There were 143 recorded instances of wrong site surgery in the NHS between April 2016 and January 2017: see NHS Improvement, *Provisional publication of never events reported as occurring between 1 April 2016 and 31 January 2017*, February 2017 (available at *https://improvement.nhs.uk/uploads/documents/Never_events_ April_2016-Jan_2017.pdf*).

(a) Operations

Difficulties may arise in assessing negligence in performing operations because   **4–096**
of the number of people involved (surgeon(s), anaesthetist, nurses) each with
their own duties and responsibilities. In the case of operations under the NHS,
from patients' points of view it does not matter if they cannot identify the
particular person at fault, provided they can prove fault on the part of someone
for whom the hospital authorities will be vicariously liable.[304] With private
treatment, where the patient has contracted with a specific surgeon for whom the
hospital is not vicariously responsible, it may be more important for the patient to
be able to identify the person at fault. Moreover, from the defendants' perspective
it will always be relevant to determine who was to blame.

The negligence of others   Normally, a doctor will not be responsible for the   **4–097**
negligence of others, such as nurses, in carrying out the instructions that have
been given with regard to the patient's treatment.[305] Nursing staff remain the
employees of the hospital:

> "… the true ground on which the hospital escapes liability for the act of a nurse who, whether
> in the operating theatre or elsewhere, is acting under the instructions of the surgeon or doctor
> is, not that *pro hac vice* she ceases to be the servant of the hospital, but that she is not guilty of
> negligence if she carries out the orders of the surgeon, however negligent those orders may
> be."[306]

The fact that a nurse acts under the instructions of a doctor, however, does not
mean that the doctor is excused from making any professional judgment. There
may be circumstances where a nurse could be negligent even though following a
doctor's instructions. For example, if a doctor ordered an obviously incorrect and
dangerous dosage of a drug a nurse who administered it without obtaining
confirmation from the doctor or higher authority might well be found

---

[302] *Smith v Lewisham Group Hospital Management Committee* (1955) 2 B.M.J. 65; *Posca v Sotto*
(1997) 34 O.R. (3d) 703, where a patient fell from a sitting position on an operating table after
complaining of feeling dizzy following the suturing of a scalp laceration, but the defendant doctor left
the patient unattended having failed to call a nurse or to advise the patient to lie down; cf. *Robertson
v Smyth* (1979) 20 S.A.S.R. 184, where it was held that there is no duty to assist a patient descending
from an examination table.
[303] *Wilsher v Essex Area Health Authority* [1987] Q.B. 730.
[304] *Cassidy v Ministry of Health* [1951] 2 K.B. 343.
[305] *Perionowsky v Freeman* (1866) 4 F. & F. 977; *Morris v Winsbury-White* [1937] 4 All E.R. 494 at
498. In *Wilsher v Essex Area Health Authority* [1987] Q.B. 730 at 749–750, Mustill LJ said that the
law does not recognise the concept of "team negligence", (although this comment was directed at the
standard of care to be expected from individual members of the team).
[306] *Gold v Essex County Council* [1942] 2 K.B. 293 at 299, per Lord Greene MR.

negligent.[307] Similarly, a pharmacist has been held to be negligent for failing to check a request for an "unheard of dosage" of cocaine.[308]

4–098   **Correcting the negligence of others**   Conversely, doctors may be negligent if they know or ought reasonably to have known that another person in the team, whether it be the anaesthetist or a nurse, has done something which puts the patient at risk but fails to take any steps to remedy the error.[309] They will also have a responsibility to take into account the possibility of error by another, for example, by making some check of what they are about to inject into a patient.[310] Moreover, it is negligent for doctors to rely on information provided by nurses whom they know or ought to know are overconfident in their own abilities and not qualified to make the clinical judgment in question.[311]

4–099   **No guaranteed outcomes to surgery**   The courts have long recognised that the mere fact that something has gone wrong during the course of an operation is not per se indicative of negligence. Thus, where a surgeon accidentally cut the patient's retina in the course of an operation on his eye this was held not to be negligent, because the surgeon was working within an extremely small margin of error.[312] There are no guaranteed outcomes in cosmetic surgery and the need for

---

[307] [1942] 2 K.B. 293 at 313, per Goddard LJ, although his Lordship added that: "In the stress of an operation, however, I should suppose that the first thing required of a nurse would be an unhesitating obedience to the orders of the surgeon." See also the analogous case of *Davy-Chiesman v Davy-Chiesman* [1984] 1 All E.R. 321 at 332, 335, stating that solicitors should not rely blindly on the advice of counsel; though a solicitor will normally be entitled to rely on counsel's advice unless the advice was obviously wrong: *Matrix-Securities Ltd v Theodore Goddard* [1998] P.N.L.R. 290.

[308] *Collins v Hertfordshire County Council* [1947] 1 K.B. 598. See also *Glyn (t/a Priors Farm Equine Veterinary Surgery) v McGarel-Groves* [2006] EWCA Civ 998; *The Times*, 22 August 2006, where a vet (G) was held partly liable, having attended an examination of a horse at the owner's request, when another vet administered a drug overdose to the horse. G gave evidence that he considered that he had a duty to observe the treatment and intervene if the proposed or actual treatment was inappropriate. He had failed to identify the drugs and dosages proposed to be administered by the other vet.

[309] *Perionowsky v Freeman* (1866) 4 F. & F. 977 at 982; *Wilsher v Essex Area Health Authority* [1987] Q.B. 730, where the registrar was held to have been negligent in failing to spot the senior house officer's error. In *Jones v Manchester Corporation* [1952] Q.B. 852 the Court of Appeal took the view that the inexperienced doctor who administered the fatal injection was not as culpable as the experienced doctor who supervised her: "She administered the pentothal under his very eyes and to his entire approval. In these circumstances it seems to me that her share in the responsibility is much less than his", per Denning LJ at 871.

[310] *Collins v Hertfordshire County Council* [1947] 1 K.B. 598; see para.4–084.

[311] *Wiszniewski v Central Manchester Health Authority* [1996] 7 Med. L.R. 248 at 256, a finding that was not challenged on appeal: [1998] P.I.Q.R. P324; [1998] Lloyd's Rep. Med. 223 at 229, CA; cf. *Briante (Litigation guardian of) v Vancouver Island Health Authority* 2017 BCCA 148; [2017] 6 W.W.R. 465 where it was held that, in the absence of "red flags", an emergency doctor was entitled to rely on an initial psychiatric assessment of the patient by a psychiatric nurse.

[312] *White v Westminster Hospital Board of Governors*, *The Times*, 26 October 1961; see also *Chubey v Ahsan* (1977) 71 D.L.R. (3d) 550, Man CA, where an orthopaedic surgeon who inadvertently pierced the aorta and vena cava during spinal surgery was held not negligent because this was recognised as an inherent risk of the procedure, albeit a remote risk; *Kapur v Marshall* (1978) 85 D.L.R. (3d) 567 at 573, per Robins J (Ont HC): "That the accident happened in this case, when it so rarely does happen, does not compel, as in effect was argued, a finding of negligence. An unfavourable result is not synonymous with negligence. A surgeon is not an insurer"; cf. the comments of Freedman CJM (dissenting) in *Chubey v Ahsan* (1977) 71 D.L.R. (3d) 550 at 552, cited at para.3–167, n.457. The fact that the margin for error is small does not necessarily preclude a finding

revision surgery is not in itself an indicator of negligence.[313] Placing an artificial hip joint outside the optimal range of angles during the course of total hip replacement is not necessarily negligent.[314] Similarly, the fact that a patient sustained damage to a facial nerve does not indicate that the surgeon used excessive force in removing granulated tissue from the eardrum.[315] On the other hand, a surgeon who accidentally knocked out four of patient's teeth during a tonsillectomy had fallen below a proper standard of care.[316]

The failure to perform a risk-free test to check that the anastomosis (the surgical connection between two structures) was complete during the performance of bowel surgery has been held to be negligent.[317] In *R (by her litigation friend) v Royal National Orthopaedic Hospital NHS Trust*[318] the claimant suffered permanent damage to the spine during the course of surgery to correct spinal

4-100

---

of negligence: see *Telles v South West Strategic Health Authority* [2008] EWHC 292 (QB); [2013] Med. L.R. 272 (surgeon carrying out paediatric heart surgery in a baby negligent in using a shunt that was too long and therefore likely to form a kink, reducing or halting the blood flow and the supply of oxygen).

[313] *Zahir v Vadodaria* [2016] EWHC 1215 (QB) at [60] (surgeon who performed rhinoplasty found not to have been negligent simply because of an undesirable outcome). For the GMC's advice to doctors who practise cosmetic surgery on appropriate standards see GMC, *Guidance for all doctors who offer cosmetic interventions*, April 2016 (available at *http://www.gmc-uk.org/guidance/ethical_guidance/28688.asp*).

[314] *Dove v Jarvis* [2013] Med. L.R. 284. Contrast *Royal Wolverhampton Hospitals NHS Trust v Evans* [2015] EWCA Civ 1059; (2016) 147 B.M.L.R. 136 where, during the course of hip replacement surgery, a large blob of cement used to secure the acetabular cup in position had come away from the rim of the cup and come into contact with the sciatic nerve, causing permanent damage. The Court of Appeal held that the surgeon had been negligent in failing to exercise sufficient vigilance at the point in the procedure when the rim was capable of being visualised to ensure that all the extruded cement was removed. The case is commented on by Lyons [2016] J.P.I.L. C4. In *Pullen v Basildon and Thurrock University Hospitals NHS Foundation Trust* [2015] EWHC 3134 (QB) a surgeon was held to have been negligent during the course of performing a hip replacement operation, in that the acetabular cup (into which the ball of the new hip is placed) was not properly fixed, resulting in a dislocation of the hip and further surgery to correct the problem. In *Thorburn v South Warwickshire NHS Foundation Trust* [2017] EWHC 1791 (QB) the defendant surgeon conceded, at the conclusion of the evidence, that there had been excessive malrotation in the course of knee replacement surgery.

[315] *Ashcroft v Merseyside Regional Health Authority* [1983] 2 All E.R. 245; aff'd [1985] 2 All E.R. 96.

[316] *Munro v United Oxford Hospitals* (1958) 1 B.M.J. 167; *Gagnon v Stortini* (1974) 4 O.R. (2d) 270, where a dentist who removed a wrong tooth was held liable in negligence.

[317] *Shortall v Mid Essex Hospital Services NHS Trust* [2014] EWHC 246 (QB) at [57]: "a reasonably competent colorectal surgeon would have been aware of the benefits of routine intra-operative bicycle tyre testing and would have carried out such a test when operating upon the claimant." No responsible body of colorectal surgeons would have failed to carry out the test, given that it was easily performed and risk-free, and could reduce the very serious risk of complications arising from a leak. In *McEwan v Ayrshire & Arran Acute Hospitals NHS Trust* [2009] CSOH 22 a surgeon was held to have been negligent when performing an operation on the claimant's small bowel in failing to failing to identify that part of the tissue was not viable, with the result that the claimant developed a major infection. The surgeon had failed to describe the condition of the bowel, or the steps taken to check its viability, in the operation note, an omission that would not have been made by a responsible medical practitioner. Lord Matthews was not impressed by the suggestion that it was implicit that the tissue *was* viable because it was not said not to be. If that was right it was difficult to see the need for an operation note at all, unless something particularly wrong was discovered or happened. For Lord Matthews the omission was significant. Moreover, the speed with which the infection developed suggested that the tissue had not been viable when the surgeon performed the operation.

[318] [2012] EWHC 492 (QB); permission to appeal refused: [2013] EWCA Civ 83.

scoliosis, leading to paralysis and quadriplegia. It was alleged that the surgical team had failed to respond properly to spinal monitoring signals which indicated that spinal damage was occurring, and were negligent to continue with the operation in the face of such signals. The defendants argued that the monitoring signals were not registering a true neurological event, and that they were "false positive" signals of nerve compromise, as had been commonly experienced in a number of other cases. McCombe J held that whether or not the signals were monitoring "real" events in the spinal cord, this could not have been known by the surgeons at the time and that the risk that they took in continuing the operation without a pause to assess the situation was unacceptable and constituted a breach of duty.

4–101 Perforation of the uterus during the course of performing a Dilatation and Curettage is relatively common, and not in itself indicative of negligence, but damage to the small bowel during the operation is so rare as to be outside the range of normal practice and is indicative of negligence.[319] In *Hendy v Milton Keynes Health Authority (No.2)*,[320] during the course of an abdominal hysterectomy, a suture was unintentionally passed around the right ureter, ultimately causing the occluded ureter to burst from a build-up of pressure. The evidence indicated that it is possible for ureteric damage to occur despite the use of a competent surgical technique, but these rare instances of non-culpable ureteric damage were attributable to anatomical variations that were outside the normal range. Most cases of ureteric damage where the anatomy was normal were due to poor technique. Thus, the likeliest explanation of ureteric damage in such cases, in the absence of evidence of an abnormal position of the ureter, was that the bladder was not sufficiently pushed down at the sides during surgery, and in the absence of pathology or other abnormality a competent surgeon should make a sound visual assessment of the position of the bladder to see that the ureters are in a position of safety. Jowitt J held that the failure to do so amounted to a negligent misjudgment.[321] Similarly, in *Smith v Southampton University*

---

[319] *Bovenzi v Kettering Health Authority* [1991] 2 Med. L.R. 293, QBD.

[320] [1992] 3 Med. L.R. 119, QBD. See also *Chiphase v Marsh* [2010] EWHC 3956 (QB) where the defendant surgeon was held to have been negligent in placing a suture around the patient's ilio-inguinal nerve during the course of an operation to repair a tear in the groin muscle. Such an event could occur in the absence of negligence if the nerve was in an unusual anatomical position, where it was largely or wholly obscured by tissue or scarring, or where it blended in unusually with its surroundings, but on the evidence the claimant's ilio-inguinal nerve was plainly visible.

[321] In *Ratty v Haringey Health Authority* [1994] 5 Med. L.R. 413 the Court of Appeal upheld a finding of negligence where there was damage to the claimant's ureters during the course of colo-rectal surgery (an abdomino-perineal resection). The negligence consisted, not in the initial damage to the ureters, which could occur even with the exercise of reasonable care, but in failing to discover and correct the damage before the end of the operation. See also *Bouchta v Swindon Health Authority* [1996] 7 Med. L.R. 62—damage to the ureter during the course of an hysterectomy found to be negligent; cf. *Hooper v Young* [1998] Lloyd's Rep. Med. 61, CA, where there was an explanation for the damage to a ureter which did not involve negligence, and the claimant failed to prove that the explanation which involved negligence by the defendant was the correct one; *Hannigan v Lanarkshire Acute Hospitals NHS Trust* [2012] CSOH 152; 2013 S.C.L.R. 179 where the defendants were held not to have been negligent in damaging the claimant's ureter during a total abdominal hysterectomy and left salpingo-oophorectomy. The patient's anatomy was abnormal, but more importantly Lord Tyre concluded that a body of professional opinion which supported the surgeons in proceeding on the basis of "confidence" that the patient's ureter was not about to be clamped or cut represented a

Hospitals NHS Trust[322] the claimant suffered damage to her right obturator nerve during the course of a radical hysterectomy, probably caused, as the Court of Appeal held, by the surgeon's scissors being partially open when not in the surgeon's view as he attempted dissection. It was held that damage to the nerve caused by a cut from partially opened scissors in this type of operation was "sub-standard surgery" and thereby negligent.

The timing of an operation   A doctor may be liable for proceeding to an operation too quickly without considering the alternative treatments available. In *Schanczi v Singh*[323] the defendant surgeon was held negligent for failing to attempt conservative treatment before resorting to spinal surgery:

4–102

> "For a specialist to plunge ahead and operate in the circumstances was exercising entirely undue haste ... [A] surgeon is retained to perform surgery, but also to avoid performing surgery in the appropriate circumstances."[324]

In *Doughty v North Staffordshire Health Authority*[325] the claimant was born with an extensive birth mark on her face. She underwent a series of 11 to 13 operations between the age of 5 and 17, performed by a plastic surgeon. Ultimately, she was left with a considerable area of scarring, and the birth mark remained and could not be concealed by make-up. Henry J held the defendants liable because in 1963 there was no body of competent, professional opinion which would have accepted surgical procedures spanning the claimant's life from 5 to 17 as proper treatment for the birth mark, and the surgeon was negligent to embark on that course of surgery. On the other hand, in *Defreitas v O'Brian*[326] the defendant's decision to resort to spinal surgery, despite the absence of definite clinical and radiological evidence of nerve compression, was held not to have been negligent. Judge Byrt observed that:

---

responsible body of professional opinion, notwithstanding another responsible body of professional opinion that considered a surgeon should only proceed when "certain" that the ureter was not about to be damaged.
[322] [2007] EWCA Civ 387; (2007) 96 B.M.L.R. 79. See also *Brown v Scarborough & North East Yorkshire Healthcare NHS Trust* [2009] EWHC 3103 (QB)—damage to the ilio-inguinal nerve during a hysterectomy held to be negligent on the basis that an initial 20cm straight incision (as opposed to a 15cm incision curved at each end) created an unnecessary risk of damage. No articulated or logical reason had been put forward by the defendant to extend the length of the incision and no risk assessment was carried out to balance the risk of harm that could arise from a normal length incision against the risk of harm to nerves generally, including the ilio-inguinal nerve, from the longer incision. Judge Thornton QC commented at [47] that: "No surgeon can reasonably operate using a method which significantly increases the risk of harm unless that method is necessary for the greater good of the patient and unless there is no other reasonable way of achieving the desired results which would also reduce the risk of ancillary or collateral harm."
[323] [1988] 2 W.W.R. 465, Alta QB.
[324] [1988] 2 W.W.R. 465 at 472, per Marshall J; see also *Coughlin v Kuntz* (1987) 42 C.C.L.T. 142, BCSC; aff'd [1990] 2 W.W.R. 737, 744, BCCA, on a failure to try conservative treatment before surgery; *Haughian v Paine* (1987) 37 D.L.R. (4th) 625 at 629–635, Sask CA; *Mann v Judgeo* [1993] 4 W.W.R. 760, Sask QB, on the performance of aggressive surgery when "first treatment surgery" was appropriate; *Cherewayko v Grafton* [1993] 3 W.W.R. 604 at 619, Man QB, on an "unnecessary" operation.
[325] [1992] 3 Med. L.R. 81, QBD.
[326] [1993] 4 Med. L.R. 281; aff'd [1995] P.I.Q.R. P281; [1995] 6 Med. L.R. 108, CA.

"To say that every operation in spinal surgery for nerve root compression must always, to be reasonable, supported by clear and unequivocal clinical and/or radiological evidence is in my judgment a counsel of caution which if applied across the board to those specialising in spinal surgery, too, would deprive many a patient of help when they had been given up as a lost cause by everyone else."[327]

4-103   Conversely, a delay in recommending surgery may also be negligent. In *Powell v Guttman*[328] the claimant developed a condition of avascular necrosis following an operation on her leg performed by the defendant orthopaedic surgeon. The defendant failed to advise the claimant to undergo an arthoplasty operation to correct this. A year after the first operation another surgeon performed the operation, and during the course of that operation the claimant sustained a rotary fracture of the femur. Due to the delay, the condition of the bone had deteriorated as a result of osteoporosis, and this was a "significant cause" of the fracture that occurred. The defendant was held liable on the basis that the delay in the second operation was attributable to his negligence, and this had caused an increase in the osteoporosis which rendered the femur more susceptible to the fracture. This "materially increased the risk of the very fracture which did occur".[329]

4-104   Whether a decision to adopt a conservative, "wait and see", approach is reasonable will depend on an assessment of the balance of the risks of the various options, and this is often dependent on clinical judgment.[330] It will also require

---

[327] [1993] 4 Med. L.R. 281 at 297. cf. *O'Neill v Rawluk* [2013] IEHC 461 where the defendant was held to have been negligent in performing a cervical discectomy without taking account of the absence of clinical symptoms supporting a diagnosis of nerve root compression. Although the MRI scans showed herniation to the C5/C6 vertebra, if there was nerve root compression it would have been expected to cause pain and impair the patient's reflexes but there was no significant pain and the patient presented with increased reflex response, thus the symptoms could not have been attributable to nerve root compression at the C5/C6 vertebra (at [46] per Moriarty J). In *Goguen v Crowe* (1987) 40 C.C.L.T. 212, Nova Scotia SC, it was alleged that the defendant obstetrician had intervened prematurely with the use of forceps to deliver a baby who sustained cerebral palsy; this was found, with hindsight, to have been an "error of judgment" but not, on the facts, negligent; *Knight v West Kent Health Authority* [1998] Lloyd's Rep. Med. 18 at 23—an obstetrician who elects to use forceps does not know that it will involve "a long and difficult pull" of a baby with an "enormous head" until it becomes difficult.

[328] (1978) 89 D.L.R. (3d) 180, Man CA.

[329] (1978) 89 D.L.R. (3d) 180 at 188; see further para.5–091 on the causation aspects of this decision.

[330] For example, in *XYZ v Warrington and Halton NHS Foundation Trust* [2016] EWHC 331 (QB); [2016] Med. L.R. 147 an orthopaedic surgeon was found not to have been negligent in deciding to perform a lumbar microdiscectomy on a 17-year-old who suffered from back pain and serious psychological problems. The surgeon had tried to manage the patient's condition with pain relief, physiotherapy and steroid injections, over a period of three years. He considered it best to delay surgery until her mental health improved because the patient's psychological problems could adversely affect the outcome of the surgery, but decided to proceed after receiving a letter from the patient's psychiatrist stating that "any surgery should not be delayed because of her mental health problems as the limitation to her activities imposed by her back problems is in itself making her mental health problems worse". Dove J held that there was no breach of duty in failing to discuss the case further with the psychiatrist. Although the patient's psychiatric condition was the main contra-indication to surgery, it was reasonable for the surgeon to take the psychiatrist's letter as a "green light" to go ahead. Nor was the surgeon negligent in failing to obtain a second opinion, since the decision whether or not to operate was a question of clinical judgment and the defendant was entitled to conclude that he was the surgeon best placed to make that judgment given his detailed knowledge of the claimant's case.

appropriate monitoring and assessment of the patient.[331] In some instances a responsible body of professional opinion may support both a judgment to "wait and see" or a decision to proceed to surgery, so that either option would be non-negligent.[332]

(i) Burns

Where a patient sustains burns in an operating theatre this is usually indicative of negligence. Thus, anaesthetists have been held liable for an explosion caused by a spark igniting a mixture of ether and oxygen,[333] and for knocking a bottle of ether over onto an electric fire.[334] It is negligence to allow a patient's arm to hang over the side of the operating table and come into contact with a hot water can,[335] and where alcohol used to sterilise the patient's body is ignited on the application of a diathermy electrode.[336] In *Clarke v Warboys*[337] the claimant was undergoing an operation in which extensive bleeding was anticipated, and so electric coagulation was applied. This involved passing a high frequency electrical current through her body, and for this purpose a pad was placed on her buttock. She sustained a severe burn at the site of the pad. The Court of Appeal held the defendants liable, applying res ipsa loquitur. Such an accident did not normally happen if reasonable care was exercised. A patient who sustained burns on her

4–105

---

[331] "It is only reasonable to wait and see if there is adequate monitoring and assessment. Otherwise, waiting and seeing may slip into neglect": *Gemoto v Calgary Regional Health Authority* 2006 ABQB 740; [2007] 2 W.W.R. 243 at [301] per Martin J.

[332] *Mackenzie v Chelsea & Westminster Hospital NHS Foundation Trust* [2012] EWHC 4176 (QB); *Murray v NHS Lanarkshire Health Board* [2012] CSOH 123; *Michael v Royal Free Hampstead NHS Trust* (QB) unreported 12 May 2014. In the somewhat unusual case of *Crossman v St George's Healthcare NHS Trust* [2016] EWHC 2878 (QB); (2017) 154 B.M.L.R. 204 the defendant hospital conceded that there had been negligence in arranging for the claimant to undergo surgery, when the surgeon's intention had been to follow a conservative plan of treatment for three months and, if that was not successful, review the patient with a view to surgery. An inherent risk of the surgery materialised and the negligence was held to be a cause of the damage. See para.7–112, n.314.

[333] *Crits v Sylvester* (1956) 1 D.L.R. (2d) 502; aff'd (1956) 5 D.L.R. (2d) 601, SCC.

[334] *Paton v Parker* (1942) 65 C.L.R. 187. For discussion of anaesthetic practice in the course of a difficult intubation see *Chambers v Southern Health and Social Services Board* [1990] 1 Med. L.R. 231; *Early v Newham Health Authority* [1994] 5 Med. L.R. 214; and (1995) 1 *Clinical Risk*, No.4.

[335] *Hillyer v Governors of St Bartholomew's Hospital* [1909] 2 K.B. 820, although the case turned on the question of the hospital authority's liability for the negligence of its professional staff. A similar case is *Hall v Lees* [1904] 2 K.B. 602 where a nurse negligently placed a hot water bottle against a patient still under the influence of anaesthetic. The report deals with the question of the liability of the nursing association who employed the nurse.

[336] *Crysler v Pearse* [1943] 4 D.L.R. 738, where the excess alcohol should have been swabbed off or allowed to evaporate; cf. *Mcfadyen v Harvie* [1941] 2 D.L.R. 663; aff'd [1942] 4 D.L.R. 647 where, in the process of cauterising an ulcer on the claimant's body, there was a flash. Alcohol had been applied to the site to sterilise it. A jury held that there was no evidence of how the accident occurred.

[337] *The Times*, 18 March 1952. Burns to the buttocks following surgery are, apparently, a common type of claim: Medical Defence Union, *Annual Report 1990*, p.45; (1993) 9 J. of the MDU 95. The Department of Health has issued specific warning to hospitals about the danger of inflammable liquids igniting during surgery: H.C. (Hazard) (90) 25.

Webster[360] the claimant's claim was unsuccessful because the evidence showed that a failed sterilisation can occur without negligence and the procedure adopted by the defendant was approved by expert evidence. But as Bouck J commented in *Dendaas v Yackel*,[361] referring to failure rates of 3 to 17 per 1,000 for tubal ligation:

> "...there was of course no indication as to how many of these resulted from improper or negligent technique and how many came about because of matters beyond the control of the surgeon."

In that case the defendant was held liable for the negligent performance of the operation itself, because in a subsequent tubal ligation performed on the claimant the surgeon found inadequate cauterisation of the fallopian tubes, and the judge was able to conclude that, on the balance of probabilities, for reasons unknown, the defendant did not properly cauterise the tubes. In *McLennan v Newcastle Health Authority*[362] it was held that the defendants were not negligent in failing to offer the claimant an HSG (hysterosalpingogram) to check that a sterilisation by tubal ligation had been successful. Such procedures were not performed routinely, they were uncomfortable, carried a risk of infection, and there was a possibility of re-opening an occluded tube. Nor was the test foolproof.

(iv)   Obstetric errors[363]

4–113   Obstetric errors are frequently the subject of litigation, partly because the consequences for the child can be extremely serious, and partly because the parents' expectation is to have a normal, healthy child. Obstetrics is rightly regarded as a high risk specialty for doctors. Birth-related brain damage claims constitute a hugely disproportionate element of NHS litigation costs, reflecting the high costs of compensation for brain-damaged babies.[364] Human error is

---

in order to effect complete occlusion the Filshie clip should be placed on the isthmic portion of the Fallopian tube, the surgeon's duty was to completely occlude the tubes thereby sterilising the patient, and if occlusion was achieved the doctor had fulfilled his duty.

[360] (1984) 14 D.L.R. (4th) 706, NBQB; *Videto v Kennedy* (1980) 107 D.L.R. (3d) 612 at 618, Ont HC. Similarly, an allegation that the sterilisation had been negligently performed was rejected by the trial judge in *Gold v Haringey Health Authority* [1988] Q.B. 481, and abandoned by the claimant in *Eyre v Measday* [1986] 1 All E.R. 488.

[361] (1980) 109 D.L.R. (3d) 455, BCSC.

[362] [1992] 3 Med. L.R. 215, QBD.

[363] "Obstetric practice is not a science but a human art upon which a great deal of science is brought to bear, and there are few complete certainties": *Bruce v Kaye* [2005] NSWCA 206 per Bryson JA at [23].

[364] In 2002–2003 birth-related brain damage (including cerebral palsy) in the NHS accounted for just over 5 per cent of all cases of medical litigation in which damages were paid, but 60 per cent of all expenditure on medical litigation: *Making Amends*, June 2003, p.47, para.43. A NHSLA study of maternity claims with an incident date between 1 April 2000 and 31 March 2010 found that there had been 5,087 claims with a total value of £3.1 billion. Overall, obstetrics and gynaecology claims account for 20 per cent of the number of all clinical negligence claims notified to the NHSLA and 49 per cent of the total value: NHSLA, *Ten Years of Maternity Claims: An Analysis of NHS Litigation Authority Data*, October 2012, p.6 (discussed by A. Anderson (2013) 19 Clinical Risk 24). For the 20 years since the introduction of the Clinical Negligence Scheme for Trusts (i.e. April 1995 to March 2015) obstetrics and gynaecology claims constituted 21.1 per cent of all claims and 47.4 per cent of

frequently implicated in obstetric accidents, many of which are avoidable,[365] but the causal link between any negligence and the child's injuries is often more difficult to establish.[366]

Failing to proceed to Caesarean section   Many of the cases[367] concern allegations that during labour the obstetrician has failed to proceed to a Caesarean section delivery quickly enough when there were signs of foetal distress, with the result that the baby's oxygen supply has been compromised.[368] The cases are

4–114

---

the total value of all claims (excluding "below excess" claims handled by Trusts) (figures calculated by the author from data contained in NHSLA *Factsheet 3: information on claims 2014–15*, August 2015).

[365] Ennis and Vincent (1990) 300 B.M.J. 1365. This reflected a number of general problems, including inadequate training and supervision of junior and middle ranking staff in the labour ward. For discussion of the general practitioner's responsibility in shared obstetric care see Burton (1995) 1 *Clinical Risk* 148.

[366] *De Martell v Merton and Sutton Health Authority* [1995] 6 Med. L.R. 234; *Robertson v Nottingham Health Authority* [1997] 8 Med. L.R. 1, CA; *Corley v North West Herefordshire Health Authority* [1997] 8 Med. L.R. 45; *Evans v Birmingham & Black Country Strategic Health Authority* [2007] EWCA Civ 1300; (2007) 100 B.M.L.R. 68—claimant unable to establish that mother's excessive contractions during labour (produced by too high a dose of Syntocinon) resulting in the depletion of her foetal reserves had either caused or contributed to a serious hypoxic event which resulted in brain damage; *Dowson v Sunderland Hospitals NHS Trust* [2004] Lloyd's Rep. Med. 177, QBD—claimant unable to establish causal link between hypoxia during birth and neonatal stroke; *Garcia v East Lancashire Hospitals NHS Trust* [2006] EWHC 2062 (QB)—claimant unable to establish that her disabilities were caused by chronic partial hypoxia rather than a perinatal stroke which had probably occurred before the defendant's breach of duty (a 26-hour delay in delivering the claimant); *Constable v Salford and Trafford Health Authority* [2005] EWHC 2967 (QB); *Baynham v Royal Wolverhampton Hospitals NHS Trust* [2014] EWHC 3780 (QB); aff'd [2016] EWCA Civ 1249; [2017] Med. L.R. 1 (claimant unable to establish causal link between 25-minute delay in proceeding to Caesarean section and her injuries, her mother having suffered a partial placental abruption). For discussion of the connection between cerebral palsy and events during labour see Moore (1993) 4 *AVMA Medical & Legal Journal* (No.3) p.3; Campbell (1995) 1 *Clinical Risk* 28. The general view amongst clinicians is that "no more than 15% of children born at term, subsequently demonstrated to have one of the cerebral palsy syndromes, can have this attributed to perinatal asphyxial damage": Rosenbloom (1996) 2 *Clinical Risk* 43. The so-called "international consensus statement" on the causal relationship between acute intrapartum events and cerebral palsy (published in the *British Medical Journal*: (1999) 319 B.M.J. 1054) has been strongly criticised both in terms of scientific and legal causation: see (2000) 6 *Clinical Risk* 135–144.

[367] But by no means all. Some, for example, involve simply the infliction of injury with the misuse of instruments: *Fotedar v St George's Healthcare NHS Trust* [2005] EWHC 1327 (QB) (use of a Ventouse, or suction, cap to deliver the claimant when the claimant's mother had not reached the second stage of labour was held to be negligent); *Townsend v Worcester and District Health Authority* unreported 10 October 1994, QBD, (where the defendant was held to have been negligent in pulling too hard with a ventouse, causing traumatic injuries to the child's brain); *Smith v Sheridan* [2005] EWHC 614 (QB); [2005] 2 F.C.R. 18 (excessive use of force with Wrigley's forceps in completing a planned Caesarean section delivery, causing brain damage, held to be negligent); *Zhang v Homerton University Hospitals NHS Foundation Trust* [2012] EWHC 1208 (QB) (unreasonable and unnecessary force used by obstetrician in attempting to disimpact baby's head from mother's pelvis in the course of conducting a Caesarean section); *JRM v King's College Hospital Foundation Trust* [2017] EWHC 1913 (QB) (use of excessive force with forceps when child was in occipito-lateral position).

[368] It is usually said that Caesarean delivery is safer for the foetus than natural delivery, although the risks of harm to the mother are greater. It should not be assumed, however, that Caesarean section operations carry no risk for the foetus: see Roberts (1993) 9 J. of the MDU 76.

extremely fact-sensitive. In *Whitehouse v Jordan*,[369] one of the earliest and still the most prominent, an allegation that the defendant had pulled too long and too hard in the course of a forceps delivery, and thus was negligent in failing to proceed to a Caesarean section delivery, was ultimately rejected on the facts.[370] In *Parry v North West Surrey Health Authority*,[371] on the other hand, the defendant was held liable for attempting to deliver a child by forceps when it was too high in the mother's pelvis, and thus for failing to undertake a Caesarean section delivery. The reasons for delay in proceeding to a Caesarean section can be various. In addition to the obstetrician having to make a fine judgment as to how long it is reasonable to allow the attempt at delivery by forceps to proceed, delay may be caused by a midwife negligently failing to summon the obstetric registrar,[372] or the obstetrician failing to attend when summoned,[373] a failure to monitor the progress of labour,[374] failing to respond to signs of foetal distress,[375]

---

[369] [1981] 1 All E.R. 267. For discussion of the "obstetric nemesis" which it is claimed that *Whitehouse v Jordan* has precipitated see Symonds (1989) 5 J. of the MDU 52.

[370] Cases in which a delay in performing or a failure to perform a Caesarean section have been found, on the facts, not to be negligent include: *Knight v West Kent Health Authority* [1998] Lloyd's Rep. Med. 18, CA; *Hinfey v Salford Health Authority* [1993] 4 Med. L.R. 143; *James v Camberwell Health Authority* [1994] 5 Med. L.R. 253; *Burke v Gillard* [2003] EWHC 2362 (QB); [2003] All E.R. (D) 255 (Oct); *Gerrard v Edinburgh NHS Trust Royal Infirmary*, 2005 1 S.C. 192; *DA v North East London Strategic Health Authority* [2005] EWHC 950 (QB). See also *Hallatt v North West Anglia Health Authority* [1998] Lloyd's Rep. Med. 197, CA (failure to undertake a glucose tolerance test for gestational diabetes, which is an indication for a Caesarean section delivery, not negligent on the facts); *Morris v Blackpool Victoria Hospital NHS Trust* [2004] EWCA Civ 1294 (defendants not negligent in failing to conduct an ultrasound scan which would have revealed baby's intra uterine growth retardation because there were insufficient indications of the need for a scan). For consideration of the potential problems arising from a breech delivery see *W (A Child) v North Durham Acute Hospital NHS Trust* unreported 24 January 2001, QBD; *Smithers v Taunton and Somerset NHS Trust* [2004] EWHC 1179 (QB) (defendant not liable for failing to proceed to a "breech extraction", i.e. actively pulling the baby out through the birth canal using traction with the baby in the breech position, which the evidence indicated was a highly dangerous procedure); *Ireland v Secretary of State for Health* [2016] EWHC 194 (QB) (defendant negligent in failing to offer the mother external cephalic version, a method by which the baby might have been turned prior to delivery, where the baby was a breech presentation, though the claim failed on causation). For discussion of the appropriate management of breech presentations see Thorpe-Beeston (2002) 8 *Clinical Risk* 99.

[371] [1994] 5 Med. L.R. 259. See also *Bowers v Harrow Health Authority* [1995] 6 Med. L.R. 16; *De Martell v Merton and Sutton Health Authority* [1995] 6 Med. L.R. 234; *Robertson v Nottingham Health Authority* [1997] 8 Med. L.R. 1 (see para.4–081); *Hill v West Lancashire Health Authority* [1997] 8 Med. L.R. 196; *Briody v St Helen's & Knowsley Health Authority* [1999] Lloyd's Rep. Med. 185; *Ogwang v Redbridge Healthcare NHS Trust* unreported 4 July 2003, QBD.

[372] *Khalid v Barnet and Chase Farm Hospital NHS Trust* [2007] EWHC 644 (QB); (2007) 97 B.M.L.R. 82; *Goncalves v Newham University Hospital Trust* unreported 24 November 2010, QBD; *Coyle v Lanarkshire Health Board* [2013] CSOH 167 (decision on causation upheld on appeal, no appeal on breach of duty: [2014] CSIH 78; 2015 S.C. 172); *OX v Derby Teaching Hospitals NHS Foundation Trust* unreported 16 September 2016, QBD.

[373] *L v West Midlands Strategic Health Authority* [2009] EWHC 259 (QB); (2009) 107 B.M.L.R. 104. This may be due to a breakdown in communication between the midwife and the doctors, but it is unnecessary to decide precisely who was responsible for the breakdown: *FE v St George's University Hospitals NHS Trust* [2016] EWHC 553 (QB) at [36].

[374] *Murphy v Wirral Health Authority* [1996] 7 Med. L.R. 99 (failure of a midwife to monitor the progress of labour by conducting regular vaginal examinations); *Reynolds v North Tyneside Health Authority* [2002] Lloyd's Rep. Med. 459, QBD (midwife failed to undertake a vaginal examination

an excessive time taken to prepare the anaesthetic in an emergency,[376] and attempting a forceps delivery in the delivery room rather than in the operating theatre.[377] In some instances there has been a negligent failure to admit the mother to hospital in anticipation of a potential complication which would require an emergency response.[378]

Interpreting the cardiotacograph (CTG) trace A relatively common issue is whether the medical staff have interpreted a cardiotacograph (CTG) trace[379] monitoring the foetal heart rate and uterine contractions correctly, and/or responded appropriately to signs of foetal distress evident in the CTG trace. This in turn may depend on whether guidance from the Royal College of Obstetricians and Gynaecologists or the National Institute for Health and Care Excellence (NICE) on the interpretation of CTG traces has been followed.[380] As *Wells v University Hospital Southampton NHS Foundation Trust*[381] demonstrates, where the defendant has complied with the guidance it will be extremely difficult to persuade the court that there has been negligence. The NICE Guidance in that

4–115

despite the existence of circumstances in which the risk of cord prolapse was foreseeable; see para.3–090); cf. *Corley v North West Herefordshire Health Authority* [1997] 8 Med. L.R. 45 (no negligence, on the facts).

[375] *Wisniewski v Central Manchester Health Authority* [1998] P.I.Q.R. P324; [1998] Lloyd's Rep. Med. 223 (SHO failed to attend a patient in labour despite having been informed of signs of foetal distress); *Simms v Birmingham Health Authority* (2000) 58 B.M.L.R. 66 (SHO failed to report the presence of undiluted meconium to the registrar, and left the midwife to interpret the CTG trace in a high-risk situation); *Hunt v NHS Litigation Authority* unreported 28 July 2000, QBD (obstetric registrar failed to respond soon enough to signs of foetal distress from the CTG trace); *Khalid v Barnet and Chase Farm Hospital NHS Trust* [2007] EWHC 644 (QB); (2007) 97 B.M.L.R. 82 (registrar negligently failed to identify a fall in the rate of the mother's contractions on the CTG trace); *Boustead v North West Strategic Health Authority (City Maternity Hospital Carlisle)* [2008] EWHC 2375 (QB); [2008] LS Law Med. 471 at [53] (see para.5–082).

[376] *Nation v King's Healthcare NHS Trust* [2003] EWHC 2542 (QB); [2003] All E.R. (D) 35 (Nov); cf. *T v Lothian NHS Board* [2009] CSOH 132 (delay in administering general anaesthetic following failed attempt to administer spinal anaesthetic to mother not a breach of duty, and in any event the delay did not alter the timing of the baby's delivery).

[377] *Gentleman v North Essex Health Authority* unreported 27 June 2001, QBD. In *Cox v Secretary of State for Health* [2016] EWHC 924 (QB) Garnham J held that there was no well-established practice in hospitals without integral operating theatres to maintain in the delivery suite a room which could rapidly be converted for use for Caesarean sections in emergency cases. The decision to transfer the mother to an operating theatre to perform a Caesarean section (which it was alleged had caused an "unacceptable delay" of 10 minutes in delivering the baby) had not been negligent.

[378] *Loraine v Wirral University Teaching Hospital NHS Foundation Trust* [2008] EWHC 1565 (QB); [2008] LS Law Med. 573; *Campbell v Borders Health Board* [2012] CSIH 49.

[379] Also known as an electronic foetal monitor.

[380] For example, in *Reeve v Heart of England NHS Trust* [2011] EWHC 3901 (QB) variations in the CTG trace were considered satisfactory in accordance with NICE Guidelines published in 2001, *The use of electronic fetal monitoring: The use and interpretation of cardiotocography in intrapartum fetal surveillance*, May 2001, and so there was no breach of duty; but in *Tasmin v Barts Health NHS Trust* [2015] EWHC 3135 (QB) the obstetrician misinterpreted the CTG trace, wrongly concluding that the traces were "suspicious" rather than "pathological" applying RCOG Guidelines on the *Use of Electronic Foetal Heart Rate Monitoring*, 2001, and it was accepted that this constituted a breach of duty.

[381] [2015] EWHC 2376 (QB); [2015] Med. L.R. 477.

case[382] recommended that where the trace was pathological the correct response was to obtain a foetal blood sample, which is what the defendant did. The claimant's expert witness was extremely critical of the decision to obtain a foetal blood sample on the basis that evidence from the "Cochrane Collaboration" demonstrated that obtaining a foetal blood sample made no difference to the outcome. Dingemans J acknowledged that *Bolitho v City and Hackney Health Authority*[383] permits a judge to conclude that a body of practitioners, acting in accordance with accepted standards, are negligent, but this was only where the accepted standards had no logical basis, or were not based on a proper understanding of risks and benefits, or had come to an indefensible conclusion. There was a logical reason for taking a foetal blood sample since it gave the doctors some idea of the actual condition of the foetus, so that the best decision could be made. The fact that the "Cochrane Collaboration" showed that outcomes were not very different did not make it an unreasonable practice, and the fact that the NICE Guidance in 2007 and the same Guidance in 2014 had suggested a foetal blood sample should be taken was strong evidence of its reasonableness.[384]

4–116   **Time taken to perform Caesarean section**   Some of the cases focus specifically on the time taken to carry out a Caesarean section once the decision has been taken to undertake surgery. In *Richards v Swansea NHS Trust*[385] a failure to perform a Caesarean section within a target time of 30 minutes from decision was held to be negligent.[386] Field J commented that:

> "…once the decision had been taken to deliver Jac by emergency Caesarean section, a decision which in the circumstances a reasonably competent obstetric registrar was entitled to make, the defendant owed a duty of care to Jac to deliver him as quickly as possible with the aim of trying to deliver him within 30 minutes. The reason for [the] decision was presumed foetal

---

[382] NICE quick reference guide *Intrapartum care: Care of healthy women and their babies during childbirth*, September 2007. The current NICE Guidance is [CG190], *Intrapartum care for healthy women and babies*, December 2014, "1.10 Monitoring during labour" (available at *http://www.nice. org.uk/guidance/cg190/chapter/1-recommendations*).

[383] [1998] A.C. 232; see para.3–034.

[384] [2015] EWHC 2376 (QB); [2015] Med. L.R. 477 at [70]. In *Tasmin v Barts Health NHS Trust* [2015] EWHC 3135 (QB) although the obstetrician was negligent in misinterpreting the CTG trace the claim failed on causation because the RCOG guidance recommended that the appropriate response to a pathological trace was to obtain a foetal blood sample, not go to an immediate Caesarean section, and on the evidence a foetal blood sample would have been in the normal range. See also *McCoy v East Midlands SHA* [2011] EWHC 38 (QB); [2011] Med. L.R. 103; (2011) 118 B.M.L.R. 107 where there was negligence in the assessment of a CTG trace but the claim failed on causation. See further the cases listed in para.4–114, n.375 above.

[385] [2007] EWHC 487 (QB); (2007) 96 B.M.L.R. 180.

[386] Relying, in part, on Thomas, Paranjothy and James, "National cross sectional survey to determine whether the decision to delivery interval is critical in emergency Caesarean section" (2004) 328 B.M.J. 665. The authors state that the "generally accepted standard in the United Kingdom and elsewhere [for decision to delivery interval] is 30 minutes" but also conclude that, after adjusting for other clinical factors, maternal and baby outcomes for delivery intervals of less than 30 minutes were no better than intervals over 30 minutes, though delays of more than 75 minutes were associated with poorer maternal and baby outcomes. Note, however, that the authors use a statistical model for calculating their results with a 95 per cent confidence interval, which is a much higher standard of proof than the balance of probabilities.

distress. This meant that although there was no indication of immediate danger there was a risk that Jac could deteriorate at any time and with disastrous consequences."[387]

The practical difficulties of meeting such a target might provide a justification for taking longer, but "the onus [was] on the defendant to adduce evidence of exculpatory reasons for why it took 55 minutes to deliver Jac".[388] The defendants had produced no exculpatory evidence "not even any notes or other records evidencing what else was going on in the [delivery unit]". In the absence of any evidence that there were logistical constraints that prevented the baby from being delivered within 45 minutes, Field J inferred that there were no such constraints and concluded that there was a negligent failure to deliver the claimant as fast as possible.[389]

Trial of forceps   It is not uncommon for an attempt to be made to deliver the baby with the assistance of forceps, on the basis that there may come a point at which this has to be abandoned and the baby delivered by surgery. This is known as a "trial of forceps".[390] In *Kingsberry v Greater Manchester Strategic Health Authority*[391] an obstetric registrar made an unsuccessful attempt to deliver the claimant on the ward by use of forceps, when the CTG trace showed signs of foetal distress. McKinnon J accepted expert evidence that a trial of forceps, which was an accepted and established obstetric management technique in 1985, should have been employed:

> "'Trial by forceps' is a procedure carried out in an operating theatre: it is a procedure designed so that if delivery is not obtained by use of the forceps, there can be a rapid switch to delivery by caesarean section."[392]

The senior registrar was called and he eventually managed to deliver the claimant by use of forceps, but the claimant had suffered an extended period of bradycardia, causing brain damage. McKinnon J held the defendants liable on the basis that the registrar should not have attempted a forceps delivery on the ward when the CTG trace indicated the presence of complicated tachycardia and foetal distress, should not have proceeded without calling the senior registrar, and should have attempted a trial of forceps in theatre with the senior registrar in attendance (and therefore in a position to switch to a Caesarean section quickly if the trial of forceps was not successful). It was accepted wisdom, said his Lordship, that it was possible for a foetus to survive 10 minutes of bradycardia without brain damage. In the absence of negligence the senior registrar would

4–117

---

[387] [2007] EWHC 487 (QB) at [28].
[388] [2007] EWHC 487 (QB) at [30].
[389] Applying *Bull v Devon Area Health Authority* (1989) [1993] 4 Med. L.R. 117; see para.4–154.
[390] See R. Clements, "Trial of forceps" (2008) 14 *Clinical Risk* 49. The Royal College of Obstetricians and Gynaecologists provides guidance on the circumstances in which this will be appropriate: RCOG, *Operative Vaginal Delivery (Green-top Guideline No.26)*, 2011 (available at *http://www.rcog.org.uk/en/guidelines-research-services/guidelines/gtg26*).
[391] [2005] EWHC 2253 (QB); (2005) 87 B.M.L.R. 73. See M. Spencer, "Trial of forceps—legal aspects" (2008) 14 *Clinical Risk* 54, discussing both *Kingsberry and Purver v Winchester and Eastleigh Healthcare NHS Trust* [2007] EWHC 34 (QB); [2007] L.S. Law Med. 193 (para.4–118 below).
[392] [2005] EWHC 2253 (QB); (2005) 87 B.M.L.R. 73 at [3].

probably have attended and would have conducted a trial of forceps, in which case it was probable that the claimant would have been delivered within 10 minutes of the onset of bradycardia.

4–118   Subsequently, in *Purver v Winchester and Eastleigh Healthcare NHS Trust*[393] David Foskett QC, sitting as a deputy judge of the High Court, concluded that if an obstetrician is considering a "trial of forceps" both the medical staff and the mother should be fully prepared to undergo an emergency Caesarean section if it becomes necessary. When minutes mattered there was no logical reason for staff to delay "scrubbing up" until the decision to operate was made, nor was there any logic in waiting for the decision to abandon the forceps before topping up the mother's epidural anaesthetic for the purpose of the Caesarean section. Given the:

> "…whole rationale of 'trial of operative delivery in theatre', the logic suggests that the *objective* of the reasonably competent and well-informed obstetrician carrying out such a process in 1997 (and, I am sure, today) would be to deliver the child well within the period of 10 minutes from the time he or she identifies either the onset of, or the serious risk of the onset of, a significant foetal bradycardia provided that to do so did not expose the mother to untoward risk."[394]

A reasonably efficient and competent obstetric team should be able achieve a decision-to-delivery time of less than 10 minutes in the case of a "trial of operative delivery in theatre".[395] This did not mean that a failure to do so in a particular case would necessarily be negligent "but any suggestion that 'in the real world' the objective is not reasonably achievable is, in my judgment, unsustainable".[396] The senior registrar in attendance had been unaware of the implications of the 10-minute rule, and this had affected his approach which the judge held to have been negligent.[397]

4–119   **Premature delivery**   Although many of the allegations of obstetric negligence concern the failure to deliver the baby quickly enough (usually by Caesarean section), sometimes the claim is that the baby was born too soon. In *French v Thames Valley Strategic Health Authority*[398] the allegation was that the baby was delivered prematurely by Caesarean section, but the obstetrician was held not to have been negligent given that the mother was suffering from deteriorating pre-eclampsia. In *Lyons v Greater Manchester Strategic Health Authority*[399] it was alleged that the defendant obstetrician's decision to induce the claimant's

---

[393] [2007] EWHC 34 (QB); [2007] L.S. Law Med. 193.
[394] [2007] EWHC 34 (QB); [2007] L.S. Law Med. 193 at [62].
[395] [2007] EWHC 34 (QB); [2007] L.S. Law Med. 193 at [67] and [81].
[396] [2007] EWHC 34 (QB); [2007] L.S. Law Med. 193 at [81].
[397] Delays in delivering the baby can be catastrophic because they can lead to a compromise of the oxygen supply to the brain, but this potential problem does not necessarily end once the baby is born. For cases involving negligence in failing to deal with a baby's breathing problems immediately following birth see: *Macey v Warwickshire Health Authority* [2004] EWHC 1198 (QB) (defendants failed to summon expert assistance to a baby suffering from respiratory distress for 45 minutes after birth); *Antoniades v East Sussex Hospitals NHS Trust* [2007] EWHC 517 (QB); (2007) 95 B.M.L.R. 62 (paediatric registrar failed to report blockage that he had discovered in an endotracheal tube being used to clear the airway of a newborn baby).
[398] [2005] EWHC 459 (QB).
[399] [2007] EWHC 1430 (QB).

birth had been negligent, a view which was rejected on the facts. Grigson J noted that the test to be applied by an obstetrician contemplating a pre-term induction of labour involved a balancing of risk:

"In every induction of labour there is a balance between the perceived risk of the foetus remaining in uterus, the perceived risk of the induction process and the perceived risk to the baby of premature delivery."[400]

A reasonable obstetrician would carry out an induction at 36 weeks' gestation if their perception of the risks to the foetus of remaining undelivered outweighed the risks of the complications of delivery at 36 weeks gestation.

In *Cowley v Cheshire and Merseyside Strategic Health Authority*[401] it was held **4–120** that a hospital's policy of administering corticosteroid therapy, as a means of preventing respiratory distress syndrome and periventricular haemorrhage in premature births, between 24 hours and seven days prior to delivery was not negligent. The claimant's mother was admitted to hospital at 28 weeks' gestation for observation. She had a history of two previous premature deliveries, but was not in pre-term labour. The hospital's policy was to administer steroids and tocolytic medication only in the presence of pre-term labour. The mother went into labour the next day, and at that point steroids were administered, but the claimant was delivered less than six hours later. The evidence was that the greatest benefit from the medication was achieved if it was administered between 24 hours and seven days prior to delivery. The claimant developed respiratory distress and cerebral palsy. The claimant argued that the policy restricting the use of steroids to cases of established pre-term labour, as opposed to cases of threatened pre-term labour, was not justified and negligent. Forbes J held that the hospital's policy fell within the range of reasonable policies in 1991.[402]

Shoulder dystocia   Shoulder dystocia,[403] whereby one, and sometimes both, of   **4–121** the baby's shoulders become stuck in the mother's pelvis is not a rare occurrence, but it is "the most frightening and threatening obstetric emergency",[404] and the consequences can be very serious. It is not necessarily an unavoidable accident,

---

[400] [2007] EWHC 1430 at [95].

[401] [2007] EWHC 48 (QB); [2007] L.S. Law Med. 160.

[402] See also *Rich v Hull and East Yorkshire Hospitals NHS Trust* [2015] EWHC 3395 (QB); [2016] Med. L.R. 33 where Jay J held that although the hospital policy was to administer corticosteroids in the case of an expected pre-term delivery this would be done where it was anticipated that the birth would be within one to seven days. It was not negligent to fail to administer corticosteroids where there was no clinical suspicion of delivery within one to seven days.

[403] For a summary and explanation of shoulder dystocia see *Croft (A Child) v Heart of England NHS Foundation Trust* [2012] EWHC 1470 (QB) at [4]–[10].

[404] D. Gibb, "The obstetrics" (1995) 1 *Clinical Risk* 49. Its incidence was said to vary from 0.2 per cent to 1.2 per cent, depending on whether it is defined to include "difficulty with the shoulders". The Royal College of Obstetricians and Gynaecologists' Guideline No.42, *Shoulder Dystocia*, 2nd edn, 2012 (available at *http://www.rcog.org.uk/globalassets/documents/guidelines/gtg42_25112013.pdf*), notes that: "There is a wide variation in the reported incidence of shoulder dystocia. Studies involving the largest number of vaginal deliveries (34,800 to 267,228) report incidences between 0.58% and 0.70%." The Guideline adds that brachial plexus injury is one of the most important foetal complications of shoulder dystocia, complicating 2.3 per cent to 16 per cent of such deliveries.

per cent to 2 per cent), given her particular circumstances,[414] and the option of a Caesarean section, though the claim failed on causation.[415]

(b)   Causing or failing to prevent infection[416]

4-124   The commonest type of case falling into this category is that of a patient who acquires an infection during a stay in hospital. More rarely a patient may be discharged from hospital in an infectious condition and infect someone else with whom he comes into contact. About eight per cent of patients pick up infections while they are in hospital, and this costs the NHS up to £1 billion a year in additional treatment.[417] Cases may arise from cross-infection, with patients acquiring a disease from another patient, or they may result from surgical intervention, or poor hygiene techniques by staff.

4-125   In *Lindsey County Council v Marshall*[418] the claimant was admitted to the defendants' maternity home notwithstanding an outbreak of puerperal fever in the home a week earlier. Neither the claimant nor her doctor was informed of the outbreak. The House of Lords held the defendants liable on the basis of a breach

---

[414] Taking into account an instance of shoulder dystocia in a previous birth, the size of the mother's previous two babies, and the mother's obesity.

[415] Nicol J concluded that the mother would have declined the option of a Caesarean section given that the obstetrician would have given strong advice in favour a vaginal delivery, in 1992 it would have been "very unusual for a woman in Mrs Jones' position to go against the advice of her consultant", the mother would have "put her trust in the doctor", and she was also a Jehovah's Witness and a Caesarean created a much higher risk of bleeding and the possible need for a blood transfusion would be correspondingly greater. Contrast *FM v Ipswich Hospital NHS Trust* [2015] EWHC 775 (QB) where the defendants conceded that in view of the mother's obstetric history there should have been a discussion about the risk of shoulder dystocia and the option of a Caesarean section delivery, but denied causation. Judge McKenna held that the claimant's mother would have opted for a Caesarean section because she would have wanted to avoid a traumatic delivery (which she had experienced with a previous child).

[416] See NICE, *Healthcare associated infections* (available at *http://www.nice.org.uk/guidance/conditions-and-diseases/infections/healthcare-associated-infections*); *Healthcare-associated infections: prevention and control*, NICE guidelines [PH36], November 2011 (available at *http://www.nice.org.uk/guidance/ph36*); *Healthcare-associated infections: prevention and control in primary and community care*, NICE guidelines [CG139], March 2012 (available at *http://www.nice.org.uk/guidance/cg139*); *The Health and Social Care Act 2008, Code of Practice on the prevention and control of infections and related guidance*, July 2015 (available at *http://www.gov.uk/government/uploads/system/uploads/attachment_data/file/449049/Code_of_practice_280715_acc.pdf*); and Royal College of Nursing, *Infection prevention and control within health and social care: commissioning, performance management and regulation arrangements (England)* (2015) (available at *http://www.rcn.org.uk/professional-development/publications/pub-004741*). For the factors to be taken into account when considering the possibility of a diagnosis of sepsis see *Gardner v Northampton General Hospital NHS Trust* [2014] EWHC 4217 (QB) particularly at [34] to [37].

[417] National Audit Office, *Reducing Healthcare Associated Infections in Hospitals in England*, 2009, HC 560 Session 2008–2009 (available at *http://www.nao.org.uk/report/reducing-healthcare-associated-infections-in-hospitals-in-england*). This report noted that in 2004, the Department of Health stated that 300,000 was the best estimate of the number of healthcare associated infections per year. There is plenty of advice available as to what health bodies should be doing to reduce the incidence of infection. See the guidance documents listed in n.416. See further Ormonde-Walsh and Newham, "Proving hospital-acquired infection" (2003) 9 Clinical Risk 61.

[418] [1937] A.C. 97.

of the general duty owed by occupiers of premises to entrants to ensure that premises are reasonably safe. Lord Wright said that he did:

"...not put the obligation as high as that of a warranty; but the gravity of the risk must emphasise the gravity of the precautions proper to be taken to guard against it."[419]

In *Miller v Greater Glasgow NHS Board*[420] following an operation the pursuer contracted MRSA which she alleged was due to the hospital failing to exercise reasonable care to ensure that adequate hygiene measures were adopted and enforced. The defenders contended that this was a non-justiciable allegation on the basis that the hospital authority had to exercise discretion in relation to the allocation of resources and the fixing of priorities, which matters might affect the extent to which protection might be available against the spread of infection. The Inner House of the Court of Session rejected the argument. The claim did not amount to criticism of the exercise of a discretion, but the management of the hospital's infection control policy. It related specifically to:

"...the institution and enforcement in the hospital of adequate hygiene measures in a context in which MRSA infection was a foreseeable risk. In our view, the making of such a case cannot be seen as an attack upon a discretionary decision relating to priorities on the part of the [hospital]. However, having said that, if the [hospital] were of the view that the implementation of some precaution desiderated by the [pursuer] would be disproportionately expensive, as compared with any benefit that it might confer, no doubt averments to that effect might have been made by the [hospital]."[421]

In *Vancouver General Hospital v McDaniel*[422] the claimant went into a hospital for infectious diseases for the treatment of diphtheria, and contracted smallpox. She claimed that the defendants were negligent in the system that they adopted, which involved the juxtaposition of smallpox patients to the claimant, and the attendance on the claimant by nurses who also nursed smallpox patients. On appeal to the Privy Council it was held that the defendants had not been negligent to adopt a new system for managing infectious patients by sterilisation rather than isolation, because they had conformed to a practice accepted as proper by a responsible body of professional opinion. At the time of this decision the claimant would have been unable to proceed against the hospital on the basis that it was vicariously liable for the negligence of the staff in implementing the system of sterilisation that had been adopted.[423] Today, however, such a claim could be made and it would be irrelevant that the claimant was unable to identify which

4–126

---

[419] [1937] A.C. 97 at 121. In *Heafield v Crane, The Times*, 31 July 1937 the claimant was admitted to a cottage hospital for her confinement. After the birth she was moved from the maternity ward to a general ward where a patient was suffering from puerperal fever, and the claimant caught the infection from this patient. Singleton J held that the hospital authorities were negligent in placing the claimant in a ward where there was a gravely suspicious case of infection, and in failing to warn the claimant. The claimant's doctor was negligent because he ought to have isolated the other patient (he was her doctor too) and when he found that the claimant had been placed in the same ward he should have had her moved to prevent her becoming infected.
[420] [2010] CSIH 40; 2011 S.L.T. 131.
[421] [2010] CSIH 40; 2011 S.L.T. 131 at [41].
[422] (1934) 152 L.T. 56.
[423] Applying *Hillyer v Governors of St. Bartholemews Hospital* [1909] 2 K.B. 820; see para.9–008.

employee was at fault.[424] Moreover, the stronger the evidence that the defendants' system was foolproof, the easier it is to infer that if cross-infection occurred it must have been caused by the negligence of one of the hospital staff in applying the system.[425] This point is illustrated by *Voller v Portsmouth Corporation*[426] in which the claimant developed meningitis after the administration of a spinal anaesthetic. It was admitted that the illness must have been caused either by contamination of the anaesthetic or by an infection occurring during its administration. The court found that the anaesthetic was not contaminated, and the staff had taken the usual precautions to disinfect themselves prior to the operation, but nonetheless held the hospital liable. It could not be said precisely how the accident occurred but there must have been some failure to follow the appropriate sterilisation procedure resulting in contamination from the equipment used.[427]

4–127   **Post-operative infection**   In the case of post-operative infection, the infection itself cannot be treated as evidence of negligence, because no-one can guarantee that post-operative infection will not occur.[428] On the other hand, it is not unreasonable to expect that specialists should be quick to recognise the development of complications following surgery, such as infection, at the earliest possible moment and to treat them accordingly.[429] Thus, it may be negligent to

---

[424] *Cassidy v Ministry of Health* [1951] 2 K.B. 343. See *Swift v Fred Olsen Cruise Lines* [2016] EWCA Civ 785 where the operators of a cruise liner were held responsible for an outbreak of norovirus on one of its vessels on the basis that there had been negligence in the implementation of its "norovirus outbreak and control plan". Although the plan itself was appropriate and conformed to industry standards there had been negligence in putting the plan into practice.

[425] There is an analogy here with the inference that may be drawn as to negligence by an employee where a product has a construction defect and the manufacturer claims that the manufacturing or quality control system is designed to be foolproof: see para.10–066.

[426] (1947) 203 L.T.J. 264.

[427] See also *Sutcliffe v Aintree Hospitals NHS Trust* [2008] EWCA Civ 179; [2008] LS Law Med. 230; (2008) 101 B.M.L.R. 113—patient developed chronic adhesive arachnoiditis caused by contamination of a spinal anaesthetic with a cleansing agent at some stage during the anaesthetic procedure. The Court of Appeal held that the judge was entitled to conclude on the evidence that this must have been due to a breach of duty on the part of the anaesthetist or her assistant. See further *Colwill v Oxford Radcliffe Hospitals NHS Trust* [2007] EWHC 2881 (QB), where the claimant developed a serious infection from an intravenous cannula inserted into the crook of her right forearm. The cannula was only used once and should have been removed much sooner than it was, but there was a failure of communication between the hospital staff due to an inadequate record in the medical notes. Dobbs J was unable to identify whether there was negligence on the part of the staff in not knowing about a form to record the insertion of the cannula or whether it was negligence on the part of the hospital in not drawing the attention of the doctors to the hospital policy on the removal of cannulae and the form (at [59]). The hospital was also held liable for the negligence of a doctor in failing to address his mind to the possibility of an infection and commencing antibiotics sooner.

[428] *Hajgato v London Health Association* (1982) 36 O.R. (2d) 669 at 681, Ont HC. See further Eykyn (1991) 2 *AVMA Medical & Legal Journal* (No.4) p.6; Mann (1993) 1 J. Law and Med. 91, discussing the difference between cases where the claimant is unlikely to succeed and cases where the claimant has some prospect of succeeding; and Sanderson (1995) 310 B.M.J. 1452 on hospital acquired urinary and respiratory infection.

[429] *Rietze v Bruser (No.2)* [1979] 1 W.W.R. 31, at 49–50, per Hewak J, Man QB: "The fault lies not with the risk or development of infection but with the failure to recognise that it is present as quickly as possible and to take steps to treat it"; *Hajgato v London Health Association* (1982) 36 O.R. (2d) 669, at 682, where failure to detect and treat a post-operative infection before crippling injury

discharge a patient from hospital without conducting a blood test for post-operative infection where there is a known risk of 5–10 per cent of developing an infection and the patient's symptoms are abnormal.[430] Discharging an infectious patient from hospital prematurely, with the result that others who come into contact with the patient contract the disease may be negligent.[431]

Infected healthcare professionals   Surgeons who are infected with HIV or   **4–128**
hepatitis B or C and who knowingly continue to practise surgery expose their patients to a foreseeable and unacceptable risk of infection, given the seriousness of the consequences, notwithstanding that the risk of passing on infection is comparatively small. This would almost certainly be deemed to be negligent if a patient were infected in this way. The GMC guidance, *Good Medical Practice*,[432] advises doctors who have, or suspect that they might have a serious condition that could be passed on to patients, or if their judgment or performance could be affected by a condition or its treatment, to consult a suitably qualified colleague and ask for and follow their advice about investigations, treatment and changes to the doctor's practice that they consider necessary. Doctors should not rely on their own assessment of the risks they pose to patients. One surgeon, a hepatitis B carrier who had infected 19 patients and put hundreds of others at risk, was convicted of the offence of public nuisance and jailed.[433]

(i)   The Control of Substances Hazardous to Health Regulations[434]

In *Ndri v Moorfields Eye Hospital NHS Trust*[435] it was alleged that there had been   **4–129**
negligence in the decontamination process of a corneal graft taken from a dead

---

resulted, in a well-staffed and modern hospital, was held to be evidence of negligence, but on the facts the defendants' evidence rebutted the inference of negligence; *Mangelana v Mcfadzen* [2006] NWTCA 6; (2006) 275 D.L.R. (4th) 178. See also *Hucks v Cole* (1968), [1993] 4 Med. L.R. 393, CA, where the claimant developed fulminating septicaemia following the normal delivery of a child, and the defendant general practitioner was held negligent in failing to prescribe penicillin when he was aware that, in the circumstances, there was a risk of this potentially fatal infection developing. The fact that the risk was small was irrelevant given the very serious consequences of the infection; *Olbourne v Wolf* [2004] NSWCA 141—doctor did not see the patient before her discharge from hospital, despite being informed that she had a raised temperature following surgery, and so "took the risk that there was nothing that would go wrong, even though he had some signs to the contrary."
[430] *Haywood v University Hospitals of North Midlands NHS Trust* [2017] EWHC 335 (QB).
[431] *Evans v Liverpool Corporation* [1906] 1 K.B. 160. The hospital authority was held not liable for the doctor's negligence on the basis that, as the law then stood, it was not vicariously liable for his negligence.
[432] (2013) para.28 (available at *http://www.gmc-uk.org/guidance/good_medical_practice.asp*). See also Mulholland (1993) 9 P.N. 79 for discussion of the position of healthcare workers who are HIV positive; Public Health England, *The Management of HIV infected healthcare workers who perform exposure prone procedures* (2014), and *Assessments on the risk of bloodborne infection transmission to patients from healthcare workers* (2012) (both available at *http://www.gov.uk/government/groups/ uk-advisory-panel-for-healthcare-workers-infected-with-bloodborne-viruses#publications*).
[433] *The Times*, 30 September 1994 (news report); see Mulholland (1995) 11 P.N. 70. See also *R. v Thornton* (1991) 1 O.R. (3d) 480, Ont CA; aff'd (1993) 13 O.R. (3d) 744, SCC, and Bronitt (1994) 1 J. Law and Med. 245 on liability for the crime of public nuisance of persons who knowingly donate HIV-infected blood.
[434] See D. Bennet, "Litigating Hospital Acquired MRSA as a Disease" [2004] J.P.I.L. 197.
[435] [2006] EWHC 3652 (QB).

donor who had died of cancer. Sir Douglas Brown held that, on the facts, the claimant had failed establish any breach of duty. In addition to an allegation of negligence the claimant had also argued that the Control of Substances Hazardous to Health Regulations 1999[436] applied to a patient in hospital. Sir Douglas Brown rejected that contention, on the basis that reg.5(1)(c) excluded the operation of the Regulations where the risk to health was "a risk to the health of a person to whom the substance is administered in the course of his medical treatment". The wording of this exclusion appears to be such as to preclude a claim under the Regulations where a patient is given a substance that could be hazardous to health, for example a drug that has potentially serious side effects, but it is judged to be in the patient's best interests to have the treatment. It is not obvious that it is intended to exclude the operation of the Regulations where a noxious substance is inadvertently administered to a patient. Nonetheless Sir Douglas Brown concluded that it was clear:

"...from the whole structure of the Regulations that patients in hospital are not to be included amongst the persons to be protected."[437]

It was "inconceivable" that it was the intention of Parliament to impose absolute liability in the circumstances of the case.[438]

4–130   On the other hand, in *Miller v Greater Glasgow Health Board*,[439] a case in which the claimant alleged that she had been infected post-operatively with MRSA (meticillin resistant staphylococcus aureus) probably by the transmission of the organism to her via the hands of a member of staff at the hospital, Lady Clark refused to strike out the claim based on breach of the Control of Substances Hazardous to Health Regulations. The obligation created by reg.3 to "any other person" did not create an absolute obligation since it was qualified by the words "so far as reasonably practicable". Lady Clark was "not persuaded" that a hospital patient who contracted MRSA was beyond the protection of the Regulations. Moreover, although the exception in reg.5(1)(c) was wide enough to cover a situation where the risk to health was a risk to the health of a person to whom the substance is administered in the course of examination or treatment by a healthcare professional, the learned judge found it:

"...difficult to envisage that this exception is intended to cover a situation where infection is transferred unintentionally and negligently by hands on treatment."[440]

---

[436] SI 1999/437.
[437] [2006] EWHC 3652 (QB) at [43].
[438] The 1999 Regulations were revoked and replaced by the Control of Substances Hazardous to Health Regulations 2002 (SI 2002/2677), but the issue remains because reg.3 of the 2002 Regulations imposes on an employer a duty not only to employees but to any other person, whether at work or not, who may be affected by the work carried out by the employer (except in relation to health surveillance, monitoring, information and training and dealing with accidents). Regulation 5(1)(c) then provides for the same exception "where the risk to health is a risk to the health of a person to whom the substance is administered in the course of his medical treatment."
[439] [2008] CSOH 71; 2008 S.L.T. 567; commented on by Tomkins [2009] J.P.I.L. C7.
[440] [2008] CSOH 71; 2008 S.L.T. 567 at [89].

Dismissing *Ndri v Moorfields Eye Hospital NHS Trust* "in which there was no analysis or reasoning given" Lady Clark held that:

"…the regulations envisage circumstances in which biological agents may be administered in the course of medical treatment and specific exception is provided for that. There may be medical treatments which involve in some way the use of biological agents or exposure thereto. I find it more difficult to construe this exception to cover a situation where there is no intention to administer the substance and the substance is not intended to be any part of the medical treatment … the regulations are not intended to provide an exception where the biological agent is unknowingly and negligently transferred to a patient and forms no part of the medical treatment."[441]

On appeal the Inner House of the Court of Session agreed (though with some hesitation) that the claim based on the 1999 Regulations could not be said to have no prospect of success and therefore it was not appropriate to strike out the claim.[442] The Court had reservations about the application of the Regulations in the context of patient infection; in particular it would not be appropriate to impose liability from the mere presence of an infective agent within the hospital environment.[443]

(ii) Post-operative infection and causation

One of the most difficult aspects of claims in respect of post-operative infection is establishing causation. In *Anderson v Milton Keynes General NHS Trust, Oxford Radcliffe Hospital NHS Trust*[444] the claimant suffered a serious fracture of his left ankle and underwent major orthopaedic reconstructive surgery. The wound was subsequently found to have been colonised by MRSA (meticillin resistant staphylococcus aureus). The defendant admitted negligence in failing to communicate the results of tests for infection, with the consequence that the claimant was not given MRSA specific antibiotics. It was held, however, that the claimant had failed to prove that the negligence had made any difference to the outcome, because the probabilities were that by the time the antibiotics should have been administered, the bacteria had entered the bone, and would have been immune from antibiotic attack. Similarly, in *Aristorenas v Comcare Health Services*[445] the claimant developed an infection following a Caesarean delivery. Over a two-week period she was treated by the defendant doctor, and several home-care nurses employed by Comcare. Her condition deteriorated and ultimately she was diagnosed with necrotising fasciitis. The judge held that the

4–131

---

441 [2008] CSOH 71; 2008 S.L.T. 567 at [89].

442 [2010] CSIH 40; 2011 S.L.T. 131 at [53] to [55].

443 [2010] CSIH 40; 2011 S.L.T. 131 at [56]. See also *Billington v South Tees Hospitals NHS Foundation Trust*, Bristol County Court, 6 January 2015 where Judge Denyer QC held that a claim on behalf of a deceased patient infected with MRSA based on the 2002 Regulations failed: "MRSA is not a 'substance arising out of or in connection with work at the workplace,' the bacteria is not manufactured by the hospital, it is not deliberately created by the hospital; it is a completely different situation from that which might arise in a chemical factory or indeed a research facility where experiments with dangerous bacteria or viruses are carried on" (at [24]). A claim in negligence was also unsuccessful.

444 [2006] EWHC 2249 (QB).

445 (2006) 274 D.L.R. (4th) 304; (2006) 83 O.R. (3d) 282.

defendants' delay in treating the infection had probably materially contributed to the claimant's injury, applying the Supreme Court of Canada's "robust and pragmatic approach" to establishing causation in medical negligence cases.[446] The reasoning was that delay in treating an infected wound is likely to lead to complex and unpredictable consequences, and there was no evidence that the claimant would otherwise have developed necrotising fasciitis but for the delay. Moreover, the defendant had to take the claimant as they found her. It was foreseeable that an untreated, infected wound would develop complications, and one of those complications had a name, necrotising fasciitis, but the claimant was not required to establish that the precise nature of the complication would be necrotising fasciitis. On appeal, the defendants argued that there was no scientific evidence that the negligent delay in treatment had led to the onset of the necrotising fasciitis, and therefore no evidence linking the negligence to the damage. A majority of the Ontario Court of Appeal accepted the defendants' argument: "Eschewing scientific certainty does not eliminate the need for any evidence to support causation."[447] Even if there was assumed to be a link between delay in the treatment of an infection and contracting necrotising fasciitis, there was no evidence from any witness as to the effect of the negligent delay. The claimant could not rely simply on the loss of a chance of avoiding the condition, nor treat an increase of risk as equivalent to a material contribution to the damage.[448]

(iii) Infection from transplantation and transfusions

4–132   Some cases of infection arise from the transplantation of human organs or the transfusion of bodily fluids from a donor who carried the infection.[449] In *Sumners v Mid-Downs Health Authority*[450] the claimant developed cancer following the transplantation of a cancerous kidney. He alleged that there had been negligence in failing to ensure that the kidney was healthy, failing to communicate the cause of the donor's death to the hospital where the transplant was performed, and failing to remove the kidney when it was discovered that the donor had suffered from cancer. The defendants ultimately conceded that it was negligent not to have removed the kidney once its cancerous condition was discovered after a post-mortem of the donor. Another potential source of infection stems from the

---

[446] See *Snell v Farrell* (1990) 72 D.L.R. (4th) 289, para.5–092.

[447] (2006) 274 D.L.R. (4th) 304; (2006) 83 O.R. (3d) 282 at [76] per Rouleau JA.

[448] (2006) 274 D.L.R. (4th) 304; (2006) 83 O.R. (3d) 282 at [78] applying *Cottrelle v Gerrard* (2003) 233 D.L.R. (4th) 45, Ont CA; see para.5–063, n.168. See, however, S. Plowden and H. Volpé, "*Fairchild* and *Barker* in MRSA Cases" [2006] J.P.I.L. 259 arguing that the *McGhee/Fairchild* principle could apply to cases of infection with MRSA in English law.

[449] See Norrie (1985) 34 I.C.L.Q. 442 for discussion of both the principles of liability in negligence and the question of consent. As to whether the doctor who performs a blood transfusion can rely on the blood having been screened by the blood bank see *Norrie (1985)* at 446. See further Giesen (1994) 10 P.N. 2. In *Ndri v Moorfields Eye Hospital NHS Trust* [2006] EWHC 3652 (QB) it was alleged that there had been negligence in the decontamination process of a corneal graft taken from a dead donor who had died of cancer, but the claimant failed to prove breach of duty.

[450] [1996] C.L.Y. 2366.

transfusion of bodily fluids, such as blood.[451] In *Re HIV Haemophiliac Litigation*[452] haemophiliacs treated with imported HIV infected blood products commenced proceedings against the Department of Health, the Blood Products Laboratory and the National Blood Transfusion Service, alleging inter alia negligence in screening donors, failing to treat the blood products to minimise the risk of infection, failing to warn donors, and failing to achieve a self-sufficiency in blood products within the NHS.[453] Although the litigation was subsequently settled, the Court of Appeal accepted that the claimants had made out at least an arguable case for the existence of a duty of care. Similarly, in *Brown v Alberta*[454] the claimants alleged that the government had negligently failed to pass regulations and adopt policies relating to the safe collection and distribution of blood products, and had negligently failed to provide funding for the implementation of a system of testing for HIV contamination in donated blood. The government sought to have the actions struck out as disclosing no reasonable cause of action, but it was held that the pleadings raised difficult and important issues which needed to be tried, since it could not be said that the actions were doomed to fail. If the proximity of relationship was sufficiently close then it could very well raise a duty of care.[455]

Blood banks and liability for infected blood   A number of cases have arisen   **4–133**
in Australia and Canada concerning the liability of a blood bank for the infection of patients with HIV from blood transfusions, at a time before a test for HIV had been developed, in 1985. The allegations of negligence consist essentially of the failure to adopt adequate screening methods to exclude as donors those from groups known to be at high risk of being infected with HIV, and the failure to introduce "surrogate testing".[456] In addition, there may be allegations that the

---

[451] The Law Commission identified an example of a successful claim in the German Supreme Court in respect of pre-natal injury for congenital syphilis caused by a negligent blood transfusion given to the mother before conception: Law Com. No.60 Cmnd.5709, 1974, para.77. In *Morgan v Gwent Health Authority, The Independent*, 14 December 1987, CA, a young unmarried woman was negligently given a transfusion of Rhesus positive blood instead of Rhesus negative blood following an operation, which raised the level of antibodies in her blood and put at risk any future pregnancy. She was awarded £20,000 in damages. For a case involving a negligent failure to carry out blood tests during pregnancy when it was known that the patient suffered from blood incompatibility see *Bagley v North Hertfordshire Health Authority* (1986) 136 N.L.J. 1014; see also *Fairhurst v St. Helens and Knowsley Health Authority* [1994] 5 Med. L.R. 422; and *Scrimshaw v Harrow Health Authority* (1992) 3 *AVMA Medical & Legal Journal* (No.3) p.15 on known Rhesus incompatibility.
[452] (1990), [1996] P.I.Q.R. P220.
[453] The Department of Health published a review of how patients were infected with Hepatitis C and HIV through contaminated blood in the 1970s and early 1980s: *Self-Sufficiency in Blood Products in England and Wales—A Chronology from 1973 to 1991* (2006) (available at *webarchive.nationalarchives.gov.uk/20130107105354/http://www.dh.gov.uk/en/ Publicationsandstatistics/Publications/PublicationsPolicyAndGuidance/DH_4130917*).
[454] [1994] 2 W.W.R. 283, Alta QB.
[455] "A question that must be answered, based on evidence that can only be assessed at trial, is whether or not the defendants were entitled to rely on the [Canadian Blood Committee] and the Crown as a member of the CBC to ensure the safety of the public in relation to the blood supply in Alberta", [1994] 2 W.W.R. 283 at 289 per Moore CJQB.
[456] *H v Royal Alexandra Hospital for Children* [1990] 1 Med. L.R. 297, NSWSC; *E v Australian Red Cross Society* (1991) 105 A.L.R. 53, Aus Fed CA; aff'g (1991) 99 A.L.R. 601; [1991] 2 Med. L.R. 303; *PQ v Australian Red Cross Society* [1992] 1 V.R. 19, Vict SC; *Pittman Estate v Bain* (1994) 112

blood bank or the hospital where the transfusion took place failed to warn doctors and/or patients of the risk of contracting HIV from blood transfusions.[457] Clearly, where the risk of infection was unknown or unforeseeable it will not be negligent to fail to take precautions against the risk.[458] Once the risk of transmission of HIV through blood products became recognised the question of negligence becomes a matter of whether reasonably practicable steps could have been taken to eliminate or reduce the risk. Negligence actions based on the failure to adopt adequate screening or surrogate testing have not been successful, bearing in mind the fact that negligence must be judged, not with the benefit of hindsight, but by reference to the state of knowledge at the time, which between 1982 and 1984 was in constant flux as scientists and health authorities sought to discover the causes of the newly identified condition of AIDS.[459] Surrogate testing, for example, namely testing blood for hepatitis B core antibodies (the anti-HBc test) on the basis that there was an association between those who tested positive and those in high risk groups for AIDS, was highly controversial. It was not particularly effective as a surrogate test,[460] and there were fears that introducing surrogate testing could lead to a reduction in the blood supply by three to five per cent, because a positive test would result in the discarding of blood that might be perfectly safe to use.[461] There was also the possibility of a "magnet effect" whereby those who were at risk of having contracted the "AIDS virus" donated blood for the specific purpose of having the surrogate test performed on them. Given that a positive surrogate test had at best a 50 per cent coincidence with HIV infection, this could have had the effect of increasing the number of undetected donations of HIV-infected blood in the blood supply, rather than reducing it. The fact that the defendants decided against surrogate testing could not be considered negligent

---

D.L.R. (4th) 257, Ont Ct, Gen Div. On infection with hepatitis from blood products see *Kitchen v McMullen* (1989) 62 D.L.R. (4th) 481, NBCA. On the question of whether the identity of blood donors should be revealed for the purpose of litigation see paras 13–094 to 13–096.

[457] *H v Royal Alexandra Hospital for Children* [1990] 1 Med. L.R. 297, NSWSC; *PQ v Australian Red Cross Society* [1992] 1 V.R. 19, Vict SC.

[458] Thus, in *H v Royal Alexandra Hospital for Children* [1990] 1 Med. L.R. 297 it was not negligent to fail to give a warning of the risk to doctors or patients in 1982, though by 1983 the situation had changed.

[459] See, e.g. the comments of Sheppard J in *E v Australian Red Cross Society* (1991) 105 A.L.R. 53 at 82, Aus Fed CA: "In cases such as this, where the facts involve a question at the cutting edge of medical and scientific knowledge concerning the development, the identification and the effects of a horrendous disease and the precautions necessary to safeguard the community against its consequences, the law will not lightly reach the conclusion, high though the duty of care may be, that institutions such as the Society here were required to do something about which there is disagreement amongst experienced persons in medical science and which may or may not have obviated the risk. Where, as here, the suggested course which the defendant should have followed runs counter to a body of medical and scientific opinion genuinely held by highly qualified and experienced persons with front line responsibility for combating the grave problem which AIDS has posed for the community, the court will not easily find that another course, advocated by other medical and scientific experts though it may be, should have been followed." See also per Pincus J at 87.

[460] A positive anti-HBc test does not establish that the donor is HIV positive, and a negative test does not establish negative HIV. A positive surrogate test had about a 50 per cent coincidence with HIV infection, according to the evidence in *E v Australian Red Cross Society* (1991) 105 A.L.R. 53. In *Pittman Estate v Bain* (1994) 112 D.L.R. (4th) 257 this figure was put at 80 per cent.

[461] A positive anti-HBc test did not mean that the blood was infectious for hepatitis, merely that the donor had previously had the infection.

when no more than 10 of the 2,000 blood banks in the United States ever adopted surrogate testing, and no blood banking or government organisation ever recommended the adoption of surrogate testing. Moreover, the standard of care to be expected of a blood bank should reflect the fact that it was neither a commercial organisation operating for a profit nor a public health organisation, with a duty to monitor, investigate and control the spread of disease.[462]

On the other hand, in *Walker Estate v York-Finch General Hospital*[463] the Canadian Red Cross Society was held to have been negligent in the method of screening blood donors for HIV, in that it had asked potential donors about their general health instead of asking about symptom specific conditions. The Supreme Court of Canada held that the trial judge was entitled to reject expert evidence that the screening procedures were reasonable, because he was not asked to assess complex scientific or highly technical matters. The issue was simply whether the general health question was sufficient to deter an HIV infected donor from donating blood. The issue was not how an expert would respond to the donor screening questions, but how a lay person would respond.[464]

4–134

Product liability for infected blood In this country the question of whether any NHS body could owe a duty of care in negligence to patients in respect of infected blood has been rendered largely redundant by the ruling of Burton J in *A v The National Blood Authority*[465] that contaminated blood is a defective product to which the strict liability rules of Pt 1 of the Consumer Protection Act 1987 apply.[466] Liability under the Act is strict, in that it does not depend on the proof of fault. The fact that the risk of infection (with hepatitis C) was unavoidable, the impracticability and the cost of identifying the potentially harmful virus and

4–135

---

[462] *Pittman Estate v Bain* (1994) 112 D.L.R. (4th) 257 at 313 at 318–319. Lang J commented that the social need for a continued supply of blood created different considerations. It was not a product that could simply be removed from the market if inherently dangerous because it is an essential source of life to many. The need for the product outweighs the risk. This did not mean that the collector of the blood did not have a duty to exercise reasonable care, but it did suggest that the calculation of what was reasonable had to be approached with some sensitivity to these issues. Note, however, the claimants' actions in this case succeeded on the basis that there had been negligence both by the Canadian Red Cross Society and the hospital where the patient had received his transfusion in implementing a suitable "lookback" program to identify those patients whom it was subsequently discovered had received HIV-infected blood, see para.4–060.

[463] (2001) 198 D.L.R. (4th) 193, SCC.

[464] (2001) 198 D.L.R. (4th) 193 at [82] per Major J. Contrast the decision of the Ontario Court of Appeal in the rather different factual context of *Robb Estate v Canadian Red Cross Society* (2001) 9 C.C.L.T. (3d) 131, where it was held that the Canadian Red Cross Society had not been negligent in failing to take positive steps to accelerate the regulatory process to allow heat-treated blood products (as a means of destroying the HIV virus) to be used for the treatment of haemophiliacs. Their duty was limited to not impeding, and so not delaying, the regulatory process of approval, and they had done nothing to delay that process. The trial judge's statement of the test, that the Society had a duty to do "everything possible" to introduce heat-treated blood products, placed the standard of care at too high a level, a level that ignored "regulatory reality". Moreover, there was no evidence as to what steps could have been taken by the Society effectively to hasten the regulatory process.

[465] [2001] 3 All E.R. 289.

[466] Burton J actually applied the European Community Directive on Liability for Defective Products (85/374/EEC) which has direct effect in English Law. The Consumer Protection Act 1987 was enacted in order to comply with the Directive.

taking appropriate precautions, and the fact that blood was supplied by the defendants as a service to society, were all irrelevant to the defendants' liability.[467]

4–136 **Infected donor semen** Similar issues arise from the possibility of transmitting infection through the donor insemination of semen.[468] In *ter Neuzen v Korn*[469] the claimant contracted HIV from artificial insemination in January 1985. The risk of infection from artificial insemination was not widely known in North America until mid-1985, although in Australia it was known by November or December 1984 that HIV could be transmitted through blood transfusion, and there was a decision to impose a moratorium on all bodily fluid and tissue transfers, because it was known that the Elisa test for HIV was being developed in the United States, was already being used in a research setting, and would soon be available for clinical use. The defendant and North American experts did not learn of the Australian moratorium until after September 1985. It was held that this was not a case in which the jury, acting judicially, could find the common practice of competent Canadian doctors to be negligent. The proper test was whether the defendant conducted himself as reasonable doctor, and this required the jury to confine itself to prevailing standards of practice.[470]

(c) Miscalculating drug reactions

4–137 Doctors must take account of manufacturers' instructions and known side effects when prescribing drugs, although they should not necessarily rely on the manufacturers' information unthinkingly, since it is known that manufacturers are not always entirely frank about the contra-indications or risks associated with their product.[471] But a decision to exceed manufacturers' guidelines or the dosages indicated in MIMMS in prescribing a drug is not necessarily

---

[467] For a more detailed discussion of *A v The National Blood Authority* see paras 10–091 and 10–092. See also the Blood Safety and Quality Regulations 2005 (SI 2005/50) (as amended) which impose safety and quality requirements on human blood collection and storage. The Regulations implement EU Directive 2002/98/EC setting out standards of quality and safety for the collection, testing, processing, storage and distribution of human blood and blood components. The Regulations do not impose civil liability for breach, but clearly may be evidence of the standards reasonably to be expected for the processing, storage and use of blood products.

[468] For discussion of the risks of sexually transmitted disease and HIV infection associated with donor insemination see Barratt and Cooke (1989) 299 B.M.J. 1178, 1531. Stern (1994) 2 Med. L. Rev. 261 discussed the possibility of strict liability under the Consumer Protection Act 1987 in respect of donated gametes. In the light of *A v The National Blood Authority* [2001] 3 All E.R. 289 it seems likely that infected gametes would fall within the Act. The analogy between donated blood and donated gametes is very close.

[469] (1993) 103 D.L.R. (4th) 473, BCCA; aff'd (1995) 127 D.L.R. (4th) 577, SCC.

[470] A new trial was ordered to consider the question of whether the defendant had exercised reasonable care in selecting and screening the semen donors for sexually transmitted diseases. It was accepted that HIV was within the same class of injury as other sexually transmitted diseases, so that the defendant could be liable for the damage caused notwithstanding that he did not foresee that a failure to undertake appropriate screening could result in HIV infection.

[471] See, e.g. *Buchan v Ortho Pharmaceuticals (Canada) Ltd* (1986) 25 D.L.R. (4th) 658, Ont CA, paras 10–047 and 10–048.

negligent.[472] Where a doctor ignores the manufacturer's instructions and warnings, it is the doctor who is responsible for any adverse reactions[473]; the manufacturer will not be liable since a warning addressed to the doctor will normally discharge the manufacturer's duty of care to the patient in the case of prescription drugs.[474] It is arguable that the standard of care that should be applied to the prescription of medication is unrelated to the specialisation of the doctor writing the prescription.[475]

Three types of case will tend to arise. First, where doctors are simply unaware of the known side effects. If they ought reasonably to have known then they are negligent.[476] Secondly, where doctors are generally aware of the dangers but make an isolated error and give an overdose or prescribe the wrong drug.[477]

4–138

---

[472] *Vernon v Bloomsbury Health Authority* (1986), [1995] 6 Med. L.R. 297, where the doctors were treating a life-threatening condition. See, however, the comments on the evidence in this case at [1995] 6 Med. L.R. 434.

[473] For a case in which it was alleged that a general practitioner had ignored the manufacturer's statement of contra-indications for giving a combined vaccination against cholera and typhoid see *King v King* unreported 1987, CA. The action was successful at first instance, but reversed on appeal. See also *Newman v Hounslow & Spelthorne Health Authority* unreported 17 April 1985, QBD, where the claimant suffered chronic adhesive arachnoiditis, a known reaction to myodil, a contrast agent used in myelography. The defendants negligently failed to spot this complication, and so failed to take the remedial measures indicated in the manufacturer's warning of adverse reactions; Herxheimer and Young (1990) 140 N.L.J. 859 on the adverse effects of minoxidil, including excessive hair growth and skin pigmentation.

[474] See para. 10–043.

[475] Contrast *Nattrass v Weber* 2010 ABCA 64; (2010) 316 D.L.R. (4th) 666; [2010] 12 W.W.R. 36, para.3–043, where the majority of the Alberta Court of Appeal, McFadyen and Slatter JJA, held that the standard of care to be applied to orthopaedic surgeons prescribing the drug heparin should be measured by reference to other orthopaedic surgeons. Sulyma J, dissenting, concluded that any doctor who chooses to prescribe a medication, irrespective of his or her qualifications as a specialist or a general practitioner, should understand the benefits of the medication to the patient as well as the potential side effects and adverse reactions (particularly where the side effects can pose a grave or serious risk), and be aware of any monitoring of the drug's effects that should be done. It is suggested that Sulyma J had the better of the argument and that, given that the potential adverse effects of medication are likely to be the same for a patient whoever prescribes the drug (subject to dosage), a single standard of care would seem to be more appropriate.

[476] In *Reynard v Carr* (1983) 30 C.C.L.T. 42, BCSC, the defendant was ignorant of the risks of avascular necrosis associated with prolonged use of prednisone, and apparently indifferent even to its other well-known side effects. For a case of osteoporosis resulting from long-term use of prednisolone see (1990) 1 *AVMA Medical & Legal Journal* (No.3) p.10. "Side-effects" can include the risk of the patient becoming dependent upon the drug, as occurred with some patients taking benzodiazepines: (1988) 4 J. of the MDU 46. See *Rowan or Kennedy v Steinberg* [1997] 8 Med. L.R. 30, Court of Session, OH, where general practitioners were held not to have been negligent in failing to withdraw the tranquiliser Equanil from the claimant, who was addicted to the drug.

[477] See, e.g. *Dwyer v Roderick*, (1983) 127 S.J. 806; *The Times*, 12 November 1983 where a general practitioner negligently directed the patient to take an overdose in the prescription, and a pharmacist failed to spot the error; *Horton v Evans* [2006] EWHC 2808 (QB); [2007] P.N.L.R. 17; [2007] LS Law Med. 212—to similar effect; *Davies v Countess of Chester Hospital NHS Foundation Trust* [2014] EWHC 4294 (QB); [2015] Med. L.R. 141—overdose of magnesium administered to patient suffering ventricular tachycardia resulting in fatal cardiac arrest; *McCaffrey v Hague* [1949] 4 D.L.R. 291, where a doctor miscalculated the dosage of X-rays. The miscalculation of drug doses through arithmetic error is apparently not uncommon: see Rolfe and Harper (1995) 310 B.M.J. 1173; (1998) 4 *Clinical Risk* 103–109,173–183. Taxis and Barber (2003) 326 B.M.J. 684 found that errors occurred in about half of the intravenous drug doses observed in a hospital setting. See also the Guidance issued by the Department of Health, *Building a Safer NHS for Patients—Improving Medication Safety*

injection in the buttocks was found to have been caused by negligence, but in *Wilcox v Cavan*[485] the Supreme Court of Canada held that where gangrene had developed in the claimant's arm following an intra-muscular injection, the nurse who administered the injection was not liable under the principle of res ipsa loquitur. Although there was no explanation as to how the injection had found its way into the claimant's circumflex artery, the defendant's version of events was consistent with the absence of negligence. It has been held that an injection into the patient's surrounding tissues instead of a vein is not necessarily negligent if the vein is difficult to find.[486] On the other hand, administering an excessive dose of a drug having misread the instructions is clearly negligent,[487] as is an excessive dose of anaesthetic given through misjudgment attributable to inexperience.[488] Contamination of the contents of a needle by a cleansing agent may also result in a finding of negligence.[489]

4–144   **Responsibility for the contents of the syringe**   In *Collins v Hertfordshire County Council*[490] a patient died following an injection of cocaine instead of procaine as a local anaesthetic, due to a misunderstanding between the surgeon and the inexperienced doctor who had been requested to prepare the anaesthetic. Hilbery J said that all surgeons must take responsibility for what they inject into a patient as an infiltration or injection for a local anaesthetic, and this requires reasonable steps to make sure that they are injecting that which they ordered. Even allowing for the fact that the person to whom the request was given was skilled in such things and that the solution was made up in a hospital pharmacy:

> "...still there remains in him a residuum of obligation and duty as the surgeon who will make the injection ... to make an efficient check to see that he is getting what he ordered, whoever has mixed it or however it has been mixed."[491]

CSOH 34; 2015 S.C.L.R. 676—puncture of an artery in the process of fixing a cannula in the patient's arm held to be negligent when the radiographer who carried out the cannulation ignored a spurt of blood on removing the cannula, and so failed to obtain medical assistance to deal with the arterial puncture.

[485] (1974) 50 D.L.R. (3d) 687, SCC; rev'g (1973) 44 D.L.R. (3d) 42, NBCA; *Fischer v Waller* [1994] 1 W.W.R. 83, Alta QB, where it was held that perforation of the globe of the eye during the course of administering a local anaesthetic prior to cataract surgery was a rare but recognised risk of the procedure which could occur in the absence of negligence.

[486] *Williams v North Liverpool Hospital Management Committee, The Times*, 17 January 1959; *Prout v Crowley* (1956) 1 B.M.J. 580; *Gent v Wilson* (1956) 2 D.L.R. (2d) 160, where an allegation of negligence in selecting a site for vaccination of a child failed on the evidence.

[487] *Strangeways-Lesmere v Clayton* [1936] 2 K.B. 11; *Smith v Brighton and Lewes Hospital Management Committee, The Times*, 2 May 1958; *Sellers v Cooke* [1990] 2 Med. L.R. 16 at 19, where a "virtually barbaric" dosage of an intravenous drip was used in the performance of an abortion. For discussion of some of the problems that can arise from the use of intravenous drips see Marcovitch (1991) 2 *AVMA Medical & Legal Journal* (No.3) p.14.

[488] As, e.g. in *Jones v Manchester Corporation* [1952] Q.B. 852; *Skelton v Lewisham and North Southwark Health Authority* [1998] Lloyd's Rep. Med. 324 at 332, QBD.

[489] *Sutcliffe v Aintree Hospitals NHS Trust* [2008] EWCA Civ 179; [2008] LS Law Med. 230; (2008) 101 B.M.L.R. 113.

[490] [1947] 1 K.B. 598.

[491] [1947] 1 K.B. 598 at 607; see also Medical Defence Union, *Annual Report 1990*, p.19 on a mix up with an unlabelled syringe; Hill (1990) 6 J. of the MDU 10; cf. *Fussell v Beddard* (1942) 2 B.M.J. 411, above, para.4–084, n.264; and *Bugden v Harbour View Hospital* [1947] 2 D.L.R. 338 where, in the course of an operation, a doctor asked for novocaine, was handed a bottle by a nurse, and without

In *Ritchie v Chichester Health Authority*[492] the treatment protocol for the administration of an epidural anaesthetic to a woman in the course labour required both the midwife and the anaesthetist to check that the correct drug had been selected for injection by reading the name on the ampoule. Despite the fact that there would have to have been a series of errors on the part of the medical staff involved, the defendants were held liable on the basis that the anaesthetist had injected a neurotoxic substance into the claimant when administering the epidural anaesthetic. This type of error is not uncommon. An article referred to in evidence in *Ritchie* suggested that administering the wrong drug can occur in over seven per cent of adverse anaesthetic incidents. The article commented that:

> "All anaesthetists should be aware that errors are common, and that they occur both with
> ampoules and with syringes. It may help if they are also aware that slips are usually caused by
> failure to monitor a highly routine action, and that this failure is much more likely when
> limited cognitive resources are compromised by haste, inattention, distraction or fatigue."[493]

Broken needles It is not uncommon for needles to break in the course of giving an injection, but this is not necessarily an indication of negligence. In *Brazier v Ministry of Defence*[494] the court accepted that a needle which broke in a patient's buttock was caused by a latent defect in the needle for which the defendant was not responsible.[495] By contrast, in *Cardin v City of Montreal*[496] a doctor administered a vaccine by hypodermic needle to a child who was struggling against his mother's efforts to keep him still. The doctor insisted on proceeding with the injection despite the mother's protestations and her offer to return another day when the child was calmer, and the needle broke in the child's arm with serious consequences. The Supreme Court of Canada held that the

4–145

4–146

---

examining the label he injected it into the patient. The solution was adrenalin and the patient died. It was held the doctor was not negligent in failing to look at the label since it was a routine matter and there was nothing about the circumstances to put him on inquiry, and he was entitled to rely on experienced nurses. The nurse was negligent. This decision is difficult to reconcile with *Collins*.
[492] [1994] 5 Med. L.R. 187, QBD.
[493] [1994] 5 Med. L.R. 187 at 210. See also Dr J. Lunn, "The Role of the Anaesthetist", in Action for the Victims of Medical Accidents, *Risk Areas in Medical Practice*, 1993, pp.128–136; and Dr Hannington-Kiff, "Overview of Obstetric Lumbar Epidural Blocks" (1993) 4 *AVMA Medical & Legal Journal* (No.1) p.2; "Clinical Focus: Managing Anaesthetic Risk" (2004) 10 *Clinical Risk* 85–96. See *Hepworth v Kerr* [1995] 6 Med. L.R. 139; (1996) 2 *Clinical Risk* 73–87 for a case where the anaesthetist was held negligent for adopting a novel, and unvalidated, method of hypotensive anaesthesia; *Glass v Cambridge Health Authority* [1995] 6 Med. L.R. 91, where the anaesthetist failed adequately to monitor the patient's transition from automatic to spontaneous ventilation at the end of an operation under general anaesthetic; *Muzio v North West Herts Health Authority* [1995] 6 Med. L.R. 184, where an anaesthetist was found not negligent when, in the course of inserting a needle for a spinal anaesthetic, she penetrated the dura, leading the claimant to develop severe spinal headaches.
[494] [1965] 1 Lloyd's Rep. 26.
[495] See also *Gerber v Pines* (1935) 79 S.J. 13; *Galloway v Hanley* (1956) 1 B.M.J. 580; *Daniels v Heskin* [1954] I.R. 73: "It is certainly not open to a jury ... to hold that the breaking was caused by imperfection of technique on the ground that say in 60 per cent of cases of broken needles it is so caused ..." per Lavery J at 79.
[496] (1961) 29 D.L.R. (2d) 492, SCC. See also *Murphy v St. Catharines General Hospital* (1963) 41 D.L.R. (2d) 697, Ont HC, where a junior doctor's negligence in inserting an intravenous catheter resulted in severing the catheter which was left in the patient's vein.

doctor was negligent in not postponing the injection until the child was in a less agitated state, since complete immobilisation of the arm was an essential precaution.

4–147 The fact that an instrument, such as a needle, has broken may indicate that the instrument itself was defective in which case there may be an action against the manufacturer either in negligence or under the Consumer Protection Act 1987. In *G v Fry Surgical International Ltd*[497] the blade of a pair of arthroscopy scissors fractured during the course of an operation and a fragment was lost in the claimant's knee. An action under the Consumer Protection Act 1987 against the importers of the scissors, on the basis that the scissors were defective, was settled by the defendants.[498]

(e) Failure to monitor treatment

4–148 A doctor has a duty to monitor the treatment given to the patient, particularly where the treatment carries a high risk of an adverse reaction.[499] Where a doctor has made an initial differential diagnosis the patient's symptoms will need careful monitoring to see whether they remain consistent with that diagnosis or whether the doctor's initial judgment should be revised.[500] The standard for post-operative care must depend on all the circumstances, including nature the treatment and the problems and needs of the particular patient. In *Matthews Estate v Hamilton Civic Hospitals* Spiegel J commented that:

> "A continuing duty rests upon a surgeon to provide adequate postoperative care or to give adequate advice and direction as to such care. The degree of care the surgeon must provide and the extent of the advice he or she must give, will depend on a long list of variables. They may include: the gravity of the operation, the age and general health of the patient, the particular problems of the patient, the nature of the postoperative medication and treatment required, the degree of isolation of the patient, the availability of medical care and hospital facilities and the degree of risk to which the patient is susceptible either from postoperative complications or subsequent medication and treatment."[501]

---

[497] (1992) 3 *AVMA Medical & Legal Journal* (No.4) p.12.

[498] For definition of an importer see the Consumer Protection Act 1987 s.2(2)(c); and for definition of when a product is defective see Consumer Protection Act 1987 s.3(1). See further paras 10–082, 10–087.

[499] *Marshall v Rogers* [1943] 4 D.L.R. 68, where a doctor who changed a diabetic's diet and reduced his insulin dosage should have conducted daily urine tests on the patient and have watched the patient very carefully; *Male v Hopmans* (1967) 64 D.L.R. (2d) 105 at 113–115, Ont CA, where a doctor was held negligent in failing prescribe audiometric tests during the course of treating a patient with a drug for which the manufacturers recommended such testing; *Wilsher v Essex Area Health Authority* [1987] Q.B. 730, on negligence in monitoring the blood oxygen levels of a premature baby in a special care baby unit; *Chan v Tang* 2012 ONSC 2050; 213 A.C.W.S. (3d) 215—negligent failure of general practitioner to monitor whether the patient's dose of warfarin (prescribed to thin the blood) was within the therapeutic range, given that the patient was at high risk of suffering a stroke from blood clotting (he had both atrial fibrillation and mechanical heart valves).

[500] *Gemoto v Calgary Regional Health Authority* 2006 ABQB 740; [2007] 2 W.W.R. 243 at [302], para.4–038, n.113 above.

[501] (2008) 170 A.C.W.S. (3d) 650 (Ont SC) at [123].

Asking the patient to monitor the effects of medication and report back to the   **4-149**
doctor may be a perfectly reasonable way for the doctor to monitor the treatment,
although this may depend up on the doctor's assessment of the patient's ability to
do so.[502] In *Bayliss v Blagg*[503] the defendants were held negligent for failing to do
anything about a marked deterioration in the condition of the patient's leg
following the application of a plaster cast, and in *Poole v Morgan*[504] it was held
that a patient who had received laser treatment on his eye should be examined as
soon as possible after the treatment. A delay of one month was too long, and
negligent. Where a defendant had performed an "innovative" sterilisation
procedure he was found negligent for failing to follow the patient's progress by
conducting regular medical examinations.[505] In *McCann v Hyndman*[506] the
defendant surgeon knew that two parts of a medical device which were part of an
artificial urinary sphincter (a balloon and tubing) had become detached and
migrated into the claimant's abdomen, or elsewhere. He replaced the artificial
sphincter, but did not locate and remove the balloon and tubing because there
were risks associated with attempting to do so, though there were also risks of
bowel obstruction in leaving the balloon and tubing in the abdomen. It was held
that the defendant's failure to monitor the situation by an X-ray, CT scan or MRI
was negligent. The defendant had failed to follow up the situation in any
meaningful way. He gave the patient no instructions as to what follow-up might
be necessary and did not suggest any further check ups. Although the risk of
bowel obstruction was small, the consequences were potentially very serious,
including, if infection occurred, peritonitis and death.

---

[502] *Mellor v Sheffield Teaching Hospitals NHS Trust* [2004] EWHC 780 (QB); [2004] All E.R. (D)
195 (Apr) at [228(1)(iv)] per Gross J.
[503] (1954) 1 B.M.J. 709; see also *Ares v Venner* (1970) 14 D.L.R. (3d) 4, SCC, and *Harrington v
Essex Area Health Authority, The Times,* 14 November 1984, QBD, on plaster casts; and on
post-operative infection see *Rietze v Bruser (No.2)* [1979] 1 W.W.R. 31 at 49–50. In *Lee v O'Farrell*
(1988) 43 C.C.L.T. 269, BCSC, the defendant was negligent in relying on an inadequate
post-operative X-ray of the patient's femur. During the course of the operation the femur had been
inadvertently broken at the base of the femoral neck. This could easily have been repaired at the time,
but because the X-ray did not show the head and neck of the femur it was not spotted and, left
untreated for several weeks, avascular necrosis set in.
[504] [1987] 3 W.W.R. 217; *Cavanagh v Bristol and Weston Health Authority* [1992] 3 Med. L.R. 49,
QBD, where the defendants were held negligent for failing to follow up and monitor the patient's
condition, which deteriorated following an operation on his eye; *Chaunt v Hertfordshire Area Health
Authority* unreported 19 February 1982, QBD, where there was a negligent failure to keep adequate
records of the patient's progress, with the result that there was a failure to detect intra-peritoneal
bleeding leading to peritonitis; *Rehman v University College London Hospitals NHS Trust* [2004]
EWHC 1361 (QB), where a nurse was negligent in failing to summon a doctor to give medical advice,
and to institute six-hourly observations, given that the patient was suffering from abdominal pain after
a laparotomy, with the result that the patient was discharged from hospital too soon. On the duty of a
midwife to conduct regular vaginal examinations during the course of labour, see *Murphy v Wirral
Health Authority* [1996] 7 Med. L.R. 99.
[505] *Zimmer v Ringrose* (1981) 125 D.L.R. (3d) 215 at 225–226, Alta CA, aff'g (1978) 89 D.L.R. (3d)
646. See also *Braun Estate v Vaughan* [2000] 3 W.W.R. 465; (2000) 48 C.C.L.T. (2d) 142, Man CA,
where the defendant doctor performed smear test but failed to examine the cytology report which
showed evidence of abnormality; the patient subsequently died from cervical cancer. The Manitoba
Court of Appeal held that the defendant was under a duty to see that there was a reasonably effective
"follow-up" system for dealing with cytology reports in place.
[506] [2004] 2 W.W.R. 353; aff'd 2004 ABCA 191; [2004] 11 W.W.R. 216, Alta CA.

Given the structure of hospital medicine within the NHS, in which very junior and overworked doctors are often stretched to the limit of their endurance and professional capacity, this is not in the least a far-fetched example. Such a claim, however, as his Lordship recognised, would raise "awkward" questions:

> "To what extent should the authority be held liable if (*e.g.* in the use of junior housemen) it is only adopting a practice hallowed by tradition? Should the authority be liable if it demonstrates that, due to the financial stringency under which it operates, it cannot afford to fill the posts with those possessing the necessary experience?"[516]

4–154   Both of these questions were touched upon in *Bull v Devon Area Health Authority*[517] in which the health authority were held liable for implementing an unsatisfactory and unreliable system for calling expert assistance to an obstetric emergency. Either there was negligence in the operation of the system, or it was inadequate to cope with even minor hitches which fell short of the kind of major breakdown against which no system could be invulnerable. Counsel for the claimant did not argue that the levels of staffing were inadequate in terms of obstetric cover because the response would have been that the levels of staffing should be judged according to professional standards at the time, and the medical evidence was that the standards did not compare unfavourably with those that existed at other split-site hospitals in the provinces at the time.[518] Mustill LJ was disturbed by the implications of this reply which at one and the same time put the foetus at risk and claimed to be good enough to be "par for the course".[519] It was not a question of highly specialist techniques or advanced equipment which it might be unrealistic to expect in provincial hospitals,[520] but simply a matter of

---

there are sufficient nurses to allow the nurses time to care for patients sensitively": Nurse Staffing Levels (Wales) Act 2016, amending the National Health Service (Wales) Act 2006. The statute does not create any private law remedy for breach of this duty, though it could be relevant to an assessment of whether a particular level of staffing was reasonable in the circumstances.

[516] [1987] Q.B. 730 at 778.

[517] (1989) [1993] 4 Med. L.R. 117, CA.

[518] And see *Garcia v St Mary's NHS Trust* [2006] EWHC 2314 (QB); [2011] Med. L.R. 348 at [94]–[96] where it was held not to have been negligent not to have a surgical registrar on site to deal with a cardiac emergency following coronary bypass surgery when such an emergency was rare (one in a thousand) and, given the resources available at the hospital, an on-call surgical registrar might, in any event, have been dealing with another emergency. The case is commented on by J. Beswick, "A First Class Service? Setting the Standard of Care for the Contemporary NHS" (2007) 15 Med. L. Rev. 245.

[519] See further the decision of the Supreme Court of Ireland in *Collins v Mid-Western Health Board* [2000] 2 I.R. 154 where a hospital was held to have been negligent in adopting an admissions system whereby a comparatively inexperienced junior doctor was allowed to substitute his own judgment as to whether the patient required admission and investigation as an emergency for the judgment arrived at by an experienced general practitioner. Keane J stated, at 156–157, that the court was not concerned with "a medical practice as such" and therefore the claim that the hospital was negligent in operating such a system could not be refuted "simply by demonstrating that it is a system in use in at least some other hospitals in these islands".

[520] In some situations facilities for specialist treatment which are available at a large teaching or specialist hospital may not available in a district hospital, but that could not, in itself, form the basis of an allegation of negligence where the patient has suffered harm as result of the lack of specialist treatment: *Ball v Wirral Health Authority* [2003] Lloyd's Rep. Med. 165, QBD. The issue of negligence will turn on whether there was any fault in not referring the patient to the specialist centre. See further *Koerber v Kitchener-Waterloo Hospital* (1987) 62 O.R. (2d) 613, Ont HC, on the question

getting the right people together in the right place at the right time. Mustill LJ was also unhappy about the (hypothetical) argument that the hospital was doing the best that could be expected with its limited resources:

"I have some reservations about this contention, which are not allayed by the submission that hospital medicine is a public service. So it is, but there are other public services in respect of which it is not necessarily an answer to allegations of unsafety that there were insufficient resources to enable the administrators to do everything which they would like to do. I do not for a moment suggest that public medicine is precisely analogous to other public services, but there is perhaps a danger in assuming that it is completely *sui generis*, and that it is necessarily a complete answer to say that even if the system in any hospital was unsatisfactory, it was no more unsatisfactory than those in force elsewhere."

His Lordship acknowledged that these matters "raise important issues of social policy, which the courts may one day have to address." Dillon LJ was content to observe that the level of staffing should be "reasonably sufficient for the foreseeable requirements of the patient". This leaves open the possibility of arguing that the provision of inadequate resources for a particular service constitutes negligence in itself.

Difficulty with a direct liability claim   There would be formidable obstacles, **4–155** however, in mounting such a claim. From the perspective of the common law, there is a distinction to be drawn between undertaking a task with inadequate resources and being found negligent for failing to perform the task properly (which would be the form of an action in a situation analogous to *Bull v Devon Area Health Authority*), and, on the other hand, not having the resources to perform the task at all, where the claimant claims that the failure to provide the service constitutes negligence. In the former circumstances a finding of negligence on the basis of inadequate resources would create the risk that, in

---

of the different standards that might be expected in community hospitals as compared with a teaching hospital or a specialist hospital. In *Bateman v Doiron* (1991) 8 C.C.L.T. (2d) 284, NBQB; aff'd (1993) 18 C.C.L.T. (2d) 1, NBCA, a patient died having been admitted to an emergency department of a hospital that was staffed only by a part-time general practitioner (with specialist doctors on call). Despite the defendant doctor doing all that could be reasonably expected of a general practitioner in the circumstances, the evidence indicated that if the patient had been attended to by a specialist in emergency medicine he would not have died. It was held that it was not negligent for the hospital to staff its emergency facility with part-time general practitioners, given that it was a small urban community in a Maritime Province. Creaghan J said that a hospital has an obligation to meet standards reasonably expected by the community it serves in the provision of competent personnel and adequate facilities and equipment and with respect to the competence of physicians to whom it grants privileges to provide medical treatment: "However, to suggest that the defendant Moncton Hospital might be reasonably expected by the community to staff its emergency department with physicians qualified as expert in the management of critically ill patients does not meet the test of reality, nor is it a reasonably expected community standard. The non-availability of trained and experienced personnel, to say nothing of the problems of collateral resource allocation, simply makes this unrealistic, albeit desirable", (1991) 8 C.C.L.T. (2d) 284 at 292. The hospital had to be judged by the standards reasonably expected by the community it served, "not communities served by large teaching facilities". There is an element, here, of applying a "locality rule" which permits different standards of care to prevail in different localities. Although still found in some US jurisdictions, it was thought that the locality rule had effectively disappeared in Canada following *McCormick v Marcotte* (1971) 20 D.L.R. (3d) 345, SCC, where the defendant was held liable, despite practising in a rural community, because he was within easy reach of large centres of population. The objection to the locality rule is that inferior standards of heath care are deemed to be acceptable.

response, a service might be withdrawn altogether, and the courts would hesitate long and hard before taking such a step.[521] The latter situation would almost certainly fall foul of the "mere omissions" rule, since there could be no common law duty to provide medical services, as opposed to acting carefully if one chooses to provide such services.[522] Moreover, decisions about the allocation of resources to a public service are normally taken in pursuance of statutory powers which confer a discretion on the decision-making body. An allegation that such a decision has been taken negligently must first establish that the discretion was exercised ultra vires the statutory power, applying public law principles.[523] The courts have demonstrated an extreme reluctance to become directly involved in resource allocation issues in the health service, and they are likely to take a highly sympathetic view of the health authority's or NHS Trust's position.[524] In

[521] In *Dryden v Surrey County Council* [1936] 2 All E.R. 535 at 539, Finlay J said that it would be: "most dangerous to hold that, because an increase of staff was recommended, therefore negligence by understaffing was established." His Lordship commented that it was impossible to receive in a public hospital the attention which a person will receive who is fortunate enough to be able to pay for the undivided attention of one or even two nurses. This remark predates the foundation of the NHS, but nonetheless it may still be accurate in practical terms.

[522] So, e.g. a casualty department of a hospital that opens its doors to the public "undertakes" the task of providing an emergency service and will be liable for negligently failing to do so: *Barnett v Chelsea and Kensington Hospital Management Committee* [1968] 1 All E.R. 1068 at 1073. If, on the other hand, it simply shuts down, there would be no liability.

[523] See *Anns v Merton London Borough Council* [1978] A.C. 728 at 754; *Dorset Yacht Co. Ltd v Home Office* [1970] A.C. 1004 at 1067; *X (Minors) v Bedfordshire County Council* [1995] 2 A.C. 633 at 736–737, though for Lord Browne-Wilkinson it was not a question of whether the decision was ultra vires, but whether it was outside the ambit of the public authority's discretion. In *Mitchell Estate v Ontario* (2004) 242 D.L.R. (4th) 560; (2004) 71 O.R. (3d) 571 the claimants alleged that their child had died in hospital because she did not receive proper treatment quickly enough, and the overcrowded conditions at the hospital had contributed to her death. They argued that these conditions were caused by reductions in hospital funding and restructuring decisions made by the premier of Ontario and the Minister of Health. The Ontario Divisional Court struck out as disclosing no reasonable cause of action the claim that the funding and restructuring decisions were actionable in negligence. The legislative framework gave the Minister the power to act in the public interest and in doing so her duty was to the public as a whole, not to a particular individual: the statutes did not give rise to a duty of care owed to a particular patient. Decisions about funding and restructuring were policy decisions which were not actionable in negligence.

[524] See, e.g. *R. v Secretary of State for Social Services, Ex p. Hincks* (1979) 123 S.J. 436, aff'd (1980), 1 B.M.L.R. 93, CA; *R. v Central Birmingham Health Authority Ex p. Walker* (1987), 3 B.M.L.R. 32, CA; *R. v Central Birmingham Health Authority Ex p. Collier* unreported 6 January 1988, CA; *R. v Cambridge Health Authority Ex p. B.* [1995] 1 W.L.R. 898; [1995] 2 All E.R. 129, CA. See, however, *Re HIV Haemophiliac Litigation* (1990), [1996] P.I.Q.R. P220, which involved allegations about the negligent allocation of resources, including a failure to achieve self-sufficiency in the supply of blood products within the NHS. This report of the case deals with disclosure of documents, not the substantive issue of negligence. Cases in which the applicant establishes that a health authority or NHS Trust has failed to establish a policy for the allocation of resources, contrary to Department of Health recommendations, or where the health authority has fettered its discretion as to the implementation of a policy may be successfully challenged on judicial review: see *R. v North Derbyshire Health Authority Ex p. Fisher* [1997] 8 Med. L.R. 327; *North West Lancashire Health Authority v A, D and G* [2000] 1 W.L.R. 977; *R. (on the application of Rogers) v Swindon NHS Primary Care Trust* [2006] EWCA Civ 392; [2006] 1 W.L.R. 2649; [2006] Lloyd's Rep. Med. 364—policy of refusing to fund a drug for treatment of early stage cancer except in exceptional circumstances was unlawful because, on the evidence, it was not possible to envisage what such exceptional circumstances might be, and therefore the policy amounted to a blanket refusal of funding, though it purported to be a policy of funding in some (exceptional) cases. This is not to say,

Hardaker v Newcastle Health Authority & the Chief Constable of Northumbria[525]
Burnton J accepted that a health authority's duty of care to the claimant was
qualified by the resources available to them. It was not negligent to fail to devote
the resources to deal with the claimant's comparatively rare condition
(decompression illness). Moreover, the claimant had not suggested any specific
alternative procedure that could have been adopted by the Health Authority:

> "In my view, it is not sufficient for a claimant to criticise a system as negligent without
> identifying what would have been an adequate system. I am not satisfied that a better system
> was available that did not involve significant additional resources; and I am in no position to
> criticise the Authority's allocation of its doubtlessly limited resources."[526]

Evidence of resource constraints   On the other hand, if defendants want to   **4–156**
rely on the argument that they could not have done more in the circumstances
because of constraints on their resources they will have to adduce some evidence
to support the contention. In *Richards v Swansea NHS Trust*[527] Field J held the
defendants to have been negligent in taking 55 minutes from the decision to
undertake an emergency Caesarean section to delivery, when the "target time"
was 30 minutes, or at the very least 45 minutes. Field J commented that if the
failure to effect the delivery within 45 minutes:

> "...had been shown to be due to the limited resources of the defendant or ... e.g. the need to
> deal with other pressing cases, the primary claim would have failed"[528]

---

however, that such decisions will necessarily give rise to private law actions for negligence. See
generally Newdick (1993) 1 Med. L. Rev. 53; Schwehr [1994] J.P.I.L. 192.
[525] [2001] Lloyd's Rep. Med. 512 at [54]. In *Ball v Wirral Health Authority* [2003] Lloyd's Rep.
Med. 165 at [32] Simon J commented that: "In the field of medicine where resources are limited and
the demands on those resources are many, it may be necessary to make difficult decisions as to how
resources are to be allocated. In general, English public and private law leaves such decisions to those
who have the legal responsibility for making such decisions. The fact that an area of medicine may be
underfunded (for example, neonatal care in the 1970s) or that a particular hospital may not have the
facilities that another hospital has, may give rise to a concern among the general public and the
experts in the field; but it does not necessarily provide the basis of a claim in negligence by a patient
who may suffer from the effects of the underfunding or the lack of facilities..."
[526] [2001] Lloyd's Rep. Med. 512 at [57]. It has been argued that the acknowledged under-funding of
the NHS should lead the courts to adopt a lower standard of care so as to "ensure that hospitals and
their staff are less vulnerable to findings of negligence for systematic failures in care which cannot
reasonably be attributed to them": Witting (2001) 21 O.J.L.S. 443, 444. The logic of this argument is
that the worse the service provided the less likely it is that a claim for negligence will succeed when
a patient is injured by that service. It seems doubtful that such an approach would be considered
tolerable in any other sphere of service provision, whether public or private. Even if it is
acknowledged that many errors are due to "systems failures" (as it is by the Department of Health: *An
organisation with a memory* (2000), available at *http://webarchive.nationalarchives.gov.uk/
20130107105354/http://www.dh.gov.uk/prod_consum_dh/groups/dh_digitalassets/@dh/@en/
documents/digitalasset/dh_4065086.pdf*), some of which may be associated with a scarcity of
resources, there will almost invariably be an individual at the end of a "chain of error" who makes the
final mistake. It will probably rarely be possible to demonstrate that the claimant's damage was
attributable *exclusively* to under-funding, as opposed to avoidable human error. On the other hand, as
Hardaker demonstrates, the *Bolam* test takes account of what is reasonable in the circumstances,
including whether, objectively, precautions against a small risk are reasonably required given the cost
of taking those precautions and the degree of risk.
[527] [2007] EWHC 487 (QB); (2007) 96 B.M.L.R. 180.
[528] [2007] EWHC 487 (QB); (2007) 96 B.M.L.R. 180 at [36].

4–160 **Court cannot require doctor to treat contrary to clinical judgment** On the other hand, in *Re J (A Minor) (Wardship: Medical Treatment)*[535] the Court of Appeal overturned an order that a doctor and a health authority should continue to treat a seriously handicapped child in a particular way, since it would be an abuse of the power of the court directly or indirectly to require a doctor to act contrary to the doctor's fundamental duty to the patient, which was to treat the patient in accordance with the doctor's best clinical judgment. Moreover, the order, to the effect that the health authority were required to use intensive therapeutic measures for so long as they were capable of prolonging the child's life, did not adequately take account of the fact that health authorities may find that they have too few resources to treat all the patients whom they would like to treat in the way in which they would like to treat them. It was the health authority's duty to make choices, and the court had no knowledge of competing claims to a health authority's resources and was in no position to express any view as to how it should elect to deploy them.[536] Admittedly, these cases are at some remove from the question of whether a doctor has been negligent in consciously implementing a cost-containment procedure which has adversely affected a patient's treatment, but to the extent that they identify the nature of the doctor's duty to the individual patient they are instructive.[537] The comments in *Bland* suggest that failing to provide resources for treatment simply because other patients might benefit from those resources is a breach of the doctor's duty to act in the patient's best interests; whereas *Re J* suggests that this is a matter within the discretion of the doctor's "clinical judgment" (which, presumably, may well be constrained by the health authority's allocation of resources). The effect of the *Bolam* test is that provided a responsible body of professional opinion would support the doctor's decision to use more "cost-effective" (i.e. resource-constrained) methods the doctor cannot be held negligent, notwithstanding that a responsible body of professional opinion would disagree. In this sense the medical profession acts as the "gatekeeper" for access to healthcare resources, and the *Bolam* test means that the patient is only ever entitled to the lowest common denominator. If pressure on resources pushes standards down *in fact*, the minimum acceptable standard *in law* will also decline.[538]

---

[535] [1993] Fam. 15.

[536] [1993] Fam. 15 at 28, per Lord Donaldson MR.

[537] *Kangas v Parker* [1976] 5 W.W.R. 25 at 43; aff'd [1978] 5 W.W.R. 667, Sask CA, in which the patient died from inhaling blood while under general anaesthetic in the defendant's office, demonstrates a slightly different point. In deciding not to refer the patient to hospital for the removal of his teeth, where there would have been better facilities in an emergency, the defendant dentist put his own financial interests over the best interests of the patient. The defendant was held negligent on this and numerous other grounds. Thus, in choosing a facility for the patient the doctor must do so with the best interests of the patient in mind.

[538] The comments by Spencer J in *Law Estate v Simice* (1994) 21 C.C.L.T. (2d) 228 at 240, BCSC; aff'd [1996] 4 W.W.R. 672, BCCA, cited above, para.4–157, can be seen as an attempt to place limits in law on the extent to which standards may decline due to resource constraints. It seems likely, however, that such an attempt is bound to fail under the present test for medical negligence. On the other hand, it must be recognised that as new medical techniques develop patients may be entitled to the benefit of a higher standard of care if the new technique is regarded by the profession as the minimum standard. Thus, in *Pierre v Marshall* [1994] 8 W.W.R. 478, Alta QB, the Alberta Medical Association and the Society of Obstetricians and Gynaecologists of Canada recommended screening

Liability of third party funders of medical treatment   The central issue that   **4–161**
the case of *Wickline v State of California* raised was the potential liability of a
third party that made a decision about the allocation of resources which caused
the patient harm that would not otherwise have occurred. The Court took the view
that a third-party decision-maker could be held liable for an allocation decision:

> "The patient who requires treatment and who is harmed when care which should have been
> provided is not provided should recover for the injuries suffered from all those responsible for
> the deprivation of such care, including, when appropriate, health care payers. Third party
> payers of health care services can be held legally accountable when medically inappropriate
> decisions result from defects in the design or implementation of cost containment mechanisms
> as, for example, when appeals made on a patient's behalf for medical or hospital care are
> arbitrarily ignored or unreasonably disregarded or overridden."[539]

Thus, *Wickline* recognises that decisions about funding for medical treatment
may attract the same liability as medical decisions themselves. Indeed, for
patients with limited economic resources a funding decision *is* a medical
decision. It also acknowledges that economic pressure by third parties can
influence doctors' medical decisions to the point of amounting to negligence.[540] If
resources are explicitly rationed by a third party then the doctor may simply have
no control over the use of a facility (e.g. if it has been withdrawn). But *Wickline*
also accepts that more subtle economic pressure may be enough to "persuade"
doctors to do something that would be against their clinical judgment, and this
may also be enough to establish liability against the third party. The
circumstances in which this type of argument could be employed in the UK are
probably limited, given the courts' general reluctance to get involved in resource
allocation issues.[541]

Causation issues   In any event, an action based on an allegation that the   **4–162**
defendant failed to provide the "best" available treatment or diagnostic procedure
(i.e. the more expensive drug or test or surgical technique) on the ground of
resource constraints, as opposed to allegations that the resource or facility had
been completely withdrawn, may well run into problems in proving causation.
Given that medical advances tend to come in comparatively small increments,
rather than in great leaps, the use of, say, a new, more expensive, drug might
produce a better result in 10 or even 20 per cent of cases. Even if the claimant can
prove that it was negligent for a doctor to prescribe the cheaper, standard
medication, the claimant still has to prove that the negligence caused the injury,
or, rather, failed to prevent a deterioration in his condition. The claimant would
have to prove, on a balance of probabilities, that he would have been one of the

---

pregnant women for gestational diabetes, despite the fact that there was controversy as to whether
universal screening was cost-effective. The defendant was held negligent for failing to comply with
these recommendations.
[539] 228 Cal. Rptr. 661 at 670–671 (1986), Cal CA.
[540] Caulfield (1994) Alberta L. Rev. 685 at 715. See also Kryworuk, Butler and Otten, "Liability in
the Allocation of Scarce Health Care Resources" (1996) 16 *Health Law in Canada* 65.
[541] See paras 9–033 to 9–036. For an argument that distributing healthcare resources on the basis of
ageism (effectively withholding treatment from the elderly because of lack of resources) could
constitute a breach of the European Convention on Human Rights see Sayers and Nesbitt (2002) 9
Eur. J. Health Law 5.

10 or 20 per cent of patients who would have had an improved result, and that this improvement would have avoided the harm. He cannot argue simply that he lost the chance of a better outcome, and on the balance of probabilities the statistics are against him.[542]

4–163 **Distinguish mismanagement of available resources**   The one situation in which a claim apparently based on a lack of resources would succeed is where a vital piece of equipment, which is normally available and should have been available, is absent or has gone missing with the result that the patient sustains avoidable harm.[543] An instrument which is essential for resuscitation in an emergency, for example, may have been negligently mislaid.[544] This is not a true example of a shortage of resources, rather it is mismanagement of the available resources.

5.   MENTAL HEALTH

4–164 Psychiatrists or clinical psychologists owe a duty of care to their psychiatric patients, which, as with any doctor–patient relationship covers diagnosis, advice and treatment in all its forms.[545] Generally, there are no special rules applicable to psychiatric patients and the *Bolam* test will apply.[546] Thus, a psychiatrist was held negligent where he engaged in social contact with a female patient who had developed a strong and obsessive emotional attachment to him, leading to a serious deterioration in the patient's mental health.[547] This was a departure from recognised standards in the practice of psychiatry which no body of professional opinion would have supported. In some instances, however, the nature of

---

[542] See Irvine (1994) 21 C.C.L.T. (2d) 259 at 260; and paras 5–100 et seq.

[543] "[M]aintaining the physical plant and equipment at a level capable of meeting the patients' needs is the hospital's responsibility": *Goodwin v Olupona* 2013 ONCA 259; (2013) 228 A.C.W.S. (3d) 524 at [38].

[544] As, e.g. in *Meyer v Gordon* (1981) 17 C.C.L.T. 1 at 15; cf. *Koerber v Kitchener-Waterloo Hospital* (1987) 62 O.R. (2d) 613, Ont HC, where the doctor had to leave the patient in order to check on the availability of a piece of equipment in the main operating room and the claimant's injury occurred while the doctor was absent. The defendants were held not to have been negligent.

[545] A doctor (including a psychiatrist) who is involved in advising a social services authority whether a child has been the victim of physical or sexual abuse owes a duty to the child to exercise reasonable care in making judgments about the child's welfare, though no duty is owed to the child's parents in this situation: *JD v East Berkshire Community Health NHS Trust* [2005] UKHL 23; [2005] 2 A.C. 373; [2005] 2 All E.R. 443. See paras 2–099 to 2–103.

[546] The claimant in *Bolam v Friern Hospital Management Committee* [1957] 2 All E.R. 118 itself was a psychiatric patient who sustained serious physical injuries in the course of electro-convulsive therapy administered to treat depression. The defendant did not use relaxant drugs or strap the claimant down before administering the treatment. There were, however, two schools of thought about the use of relaxant drugs, which reduced the danger from fractures but carried a small risk of death. There were also two schools of thought about the degree of physical restraint that should be used, one taking the view that it reduced the risk of fractures the other taking the view that it increased the risk. A jury acquitted the defendant of negligence, following the direction of McNair J (see para.3–008); *Hibbert v Ministry of Defence* [2008] EWHC 1526 (QB); (2009) 105 B.M.L.R. 1—military psychiatrist not negligent in not diagnosing a soldier with post-traumatic stress disorder, given the claimant's symptoms at the time; defendant's response to claimant's symptoms fell within a range acceptable to a reasonable and responsible body of military psychiatrists.

[547] *Landau v Werner* (1961) 105 S.J. 257, and 1008, CA.

patients' illnesses makes them dangerous, either to themselves or to others, and claims can arise out of an alleged failure to exercise control over the patient.

(a) Failing to control the patient: self-harm

Doctors undoubtedly have a duty to take reasonable steps to protect psychiatric patients from harming themselves, and in an institutional setting a hospital authority may be responsible for injuries inflicted on a patient by himself,[548] or by a fellow patient where the injuries are the result of a failure to provide adequate control and supervision.[549] But there will normally be no duty to protect psychiatric patients from the legal consequences of their own actions in causing injury to others, at least where the patient continues to have some degree of responsibility for their actions. In *Clunis v Camden & Islington Health Authority*[550] the Court of Appeal rejected a claim in negligence by a patient who had attacked and killed an innocent bystander. He alleged that had he received proper psychiatric treatment he would not have committed the offence and therefore he would not have been convicted of a criminal offence and sent to prison. The claim was struck out as contrary to public policy, because his plea of manslaughter by reason of diminished responsibility still required some degree of personal responsibility, even though it was accepted that his mental responsibility was substantially impaired. The Court of Appeal did, however, contemplate that there could be liability in negligence in such a case if it could be proved that the claimant did not know the nature and quality of his act or that what he had done was wrong.

4–165

Suicide attempts   The duty owed to the psychiatric patient can include an obligation to make reasonable efforts to prevent suicide attempts.[551] The risk of suicide must be foreseeable for the duty of care to exist, though with certain categories of claimant, such as prisoners in custody,[552] it is known that there is an increased risk of suicide which will give rise to a specific obligation to assess whether or not a prisoner presents a suicide risk. But a duty to exercise reasonable care to prevent a prisoner from committing suicide arises only where

4–166

---

[548] *Jinks v Cardwell* (1987) 39 C.C.L.T. 168, Ont HC, where there was negligent supervision of a schizophrenic patient who was known to be prone to fainting spells as a reaction to his medication; the patient drowned accidentally in a bath; *Kelly v Board of Governors of St. Laurence's Hospital* [1988] I.R. 402, Supreme Court of Ireland, where the claimant was in hospital specifically for observation, for the purpose of which he had been taken off all medication, but was permitted to leave the ward unobserved and fell out of a window.

[549] *Wellesley Hospital v Lawson* (1977) 76 D.L.R. (3d) 688 where the Supreme Court of Canada assumed that such a common law duty existed. In *Ellis v Home Office* [1953] 2 All E.R. 149 prison authorities were held to owe a duty of care to a prisoner assaulted by another prisoner, although on the facts the defendants were held not to have been negligent. See also *Stenning v Home Office* [2002] EWCA Civ 793.

[550] [1998] Q.B. 978. See also *Hunter Area Health Service v Presland* [2005] NSWCA 33; (2005) 63 N.S.W.L.R. 22; see para.2–158, n.501.

[551] Jones (1990) 6 P.N. 107. See also Hill, "Suicide risk and its management" (1997) 3 *Clinical Risk* 178.

[552] Or persons detained at an immigration removal centre pending deportation: *Nyang v G4S Care and Justice Services Ltd* [2013] EWHC 3946 (QB).

the defendant knew (following an appropriate assessment[553]), or ought to have known, that the individual prisoner presented such a risk.[554] There is no duty to treat every prisoner as a potential suicide risk.[555] In the common law context there will generally be two types of case: (i) where the patient is a known suicide risk; and (ii) where it is alleged that the medical staff ought to have realised that he was a suicide risk, but failed to do so. In the case of both prisoners and psychiatric patients at risk of suicide the patient's rights under the European Convention for the Protection of Human Rights may also be engaged.[556]

(i)   The known suicide risk

4–167   Here, the issue may turn upon how much supervision the patient should have been given, and this may in turn depend upon the degree of risk—how serious is the threat, and so, in legal terms, how foreseeable was the patient's behaviour?

4–168   In *Thorne v Northern Group Hospital Management Committee*[557] the nursing staff on a medical ward of a general hospital were aware that a patient, who was a suspected depressive, had threatened suicide. The patient walked out of the hospital, went home and committed suicide while mentally ill but not legally insane. Her husband sued the hospital alleging that a failure to provide adequate supervision of his wife was negligent. Edmund-Davies J held that there had been no negligence since in the circumstances constant supervision was not appropriate. His Lordship did comment, however, that the degree of care and supervision required of hospital staff in relation to a patient with known or, perhaps, even suspected suicidal tendencies was greater than that called for in relation to patients generally.

4–169   By contrast, in *Selfe v Ilford and District Hospital Management Committee*[558] it was accepted that reasonable care demanded reasonable supervision of a patient at risk of committing suicide, which included continuous observation by a nurse on duty in the ward. The claimant, when aged 17, was admitted to hospital

---

[553] So, a failure to carry out a sufficiently thorough mental state examination can amount to a breach of duty: *Nyang v G4S Care and Justice Services Ltd* [2013] EWHC 3946 (QB).

[554] *Orange v Chief Constable of West Yorkshire Police* [2001] EWCA Civ 611; [2002] Q.B. 347 at [41] to [43].

[555] *Smiley v Home Office* [2004] EWHC 240 (QB).

[556] See paras 4–183 et seq.

[557] (1964) 108 S.J. 484.

[558] (1970) 114 S.J. 935; *Hay v Grampian Health Board* [1995] 6 Med. L.R. 128, Court of Session, where the regime for supervising a known suicide risk broke down; *Mahmood v Siggins* [1996] 7 Med. L.R. 76, QBD, where a general practitioner was held liable for failing to refer a known manic depressive to a community mental health team for assessment, treatment and supervision; *Drake v Pontefract Health Authority; Wakefield and Pontefract Community NHS Trust* [1998] Lloyd's Rep. Med. 425, QBD, where an inexperienced psychiatrist was held negligent in failing to diagnose the claimant's condition correctly, failing to assess the risk of suicide, and failing to provide appropriate treatment, though the patient had been referred by the general practitioner as a suicide risk; *Webley v St George's Hospital NHS Trust* [2014] EWHC 299 (QB); (2014) 138 B.M.L.R. 190—seriously disturbed patient in A&E who was known to be likely to abscond and so placed under the supervision of two security guards nonetheless escaped through a side door of the room in which he was detained; patient suffered serious head injuries in a fall in making his escape; defendant NHS Trust held vicariously liable for the negligence of the security guards.

following an attempted suicide by overdose of sleeping tablets. The staff knew that he was a serious suicide risk, and he was put in a ground floor ward with 27 patients, four of whom were suicide risks. The expert evidence was that with four such patients a minimum of three nurses was required. There were three nurses on duty, but two of them were briefly absent from the ward, and the third was assisting a patient at the far end of the ward. The claimant climbed out of a window and jumped off a roof, causing serious injuries. Hinchcliffe J held the defendants liable. The degree of care required was proportionate to the degree of risk, and in this case there had been a breakdown in proper nursing supervision, which had caused the accident.

In *Villemure v L'Hôpital Notre Dame*[559] a patient was admitted on an emergency basis to the psychiatric section of a hospital (where the windows were barred) following an attempted suicide, but was subsequently moved to a semi-private room in the medical section (where the windows were not barred). The patient's pleas to be allowed to return to the psychiatric ward were ignored and no supervision or other precautions were taken to prevent a recurrence. The patient leapt to his death from the window of his room. The Supreme Court of Canada concluded that the defendants had been negligent. On the other hand, where the suicide attempt is unforeseeable there will be no liability.[560]   **4–170**

How much supervision or restraint?   Another factor which may have to be   **4–171**
considered in the case of a known suicide risk is the degree of restraint or supervision appropriate in the light of the patient's mental condition. A psychiatrist, for example, may take the view that imposing restraint on a patient may exacerbate the patient's condition, or at least inhibit effective treatment. If it is against the patient's wishes it might undermine the trust between doctor and patient. This judgment has to balance competing risks to the patient's health, including the risk of suicide. In *Haines v Bellissimo*,[561] Griffiths J said that a therapist must weigh the advantages and disadvantages of hospitalisation against the advantages of continuing out-patient treatment. If there is a real risk of suicide or if the therapist is in doubt about this, said the judge, he should opt for hospitalisation. On the other hand, close observation, restrictions, and restraint of the patient may be anti-therapeutic and aggravate the patient's sense of worthlessness, which in itself can increase the risk of suicide. On the facts, the defendants had not been negligent because hospitalisation, whether voluntary or involuntary, would have been a blow to the patient's self-esteem and pride, interfered with his long-term rehabilitation, and, most significantly, would have destroyed the strong therapeutic bond which had developed.

---

[559] (1972) 31 D.L.R. (3d) 454.
[560] *Orange v Chief Constable of West Yorkshire Police* [2001] EWCA Civ 611; [2002] Q.B. 347; *Smiley v Home Office* [2004] EWHC 240 (QB); *Lepine v University Hospital Board* (1966) 57 D.L.R. (2d) 701, SCC, where a leap out of a hospital window by a patient suffering from post-epileptic automatism was found to be unforeseeable, and reasonable care did not demand that the claimant be either physically restrained or kept at ground level; *Stadel v Albertson* [1954] 2 D.L.R. 328, Sask CA, where the defendant was not liable for the suicide of a patient whose symptoms did not suggest that he was a danger either to himself or anyone else.
[561] (1977) 82 D.L.R. (3d) 215, Ont HC; *Holan Estate v Stanton Regional Health Board* [2002] NWTSC 26; (2002) 11 C.C.L.T. (3d) 34.

4–172   In *Dunn v South Tyneside Health Care NHS Trust*[562] a patient with a history of mental health problems was compulsorily detained under the Mental Health Act 1983. The hospital recognised that there was a risk that she would abscond and there was a danger that she could harm herself "through poor judgment". A level of observation was specified, initially, requiring a nurse or other responsible person to be present continuously. This was later reduced to observation every 15 minutes. The claimant absconded on a number of occasions, and the police were involved several times in bringing her back to the hospital, though she had also returned voluntarily several times. Later she was discharged to her home, but was re-admitted under s.3 of the 1983 Act because she had failed to take her medication at home and her condition had deteriorated. In the following days her mental health fluctuated and at times she refused her medication. She was placed on hourly observation. Subsequently she absconded again and went home where she took a large overdose of her mother's anti-asthma medication and suffered permanent brain damage. The claimant alleged that the hospital were negligent in failing to have her placed under 15-minute observation, and that if that had been done her absence would have been noticed sooner, the police would have been notified and the overdose would have been prevented. The Court of Appeal held that the hospital had not been negligent in adopting a regime of hourly observation, since this was supported by a responsible body of professional opinion. The implementation of a 15-minute regime of observation had to be balanced against the potential adverse impact on the claimant's willingness to co-operate with her treatment. Nor was it negligent to fail to call the police immediately, since the policy adopted by the hospital of communicating with the claimant's family and giving her a chance to return to the hospital voluntarily was reasonable.[563]

4–173   Similarly, in *G v Central & North West London Mental Health NHS Trust*[564] Swift J held that the defendants had not been negligent in allowing a patient in a mental health unit unescorted leave. The patient, who was seriously depressed, had made many suicidal threats and gestures, but had not made any serious attempt on her life. On one occasion, when on unescorted leave, she went to a tube station and got on to the line in front of a train, and, although she avoided death or very serious injury by rolling into a pit on the track, she suffered physical and psychological consequences. It was common ground between the parties that the granting of leave away from the unit where a patient was being treated was an integral part of the process of rehabilitating the patient. Swift J concluded that the decision to grant unescorted leave was neither unreasonable nor illogical. The claimant's argument that it had been negligent ignored the potential benefits of leave and the potential risks associated with the denial of leave.

---

[562] [2003] EWCA Civ 878; [2004] P.I.Q.R. P150.
[563] The claim also failed on causation, since the probability was that even if the police had been called, it was unlikely that they would have arrived at the right time to prevent the claimant from taking the overdose.
[564] [2007] EWHC 3086 (QB); [2008] M.H.L.R. 24.

(ii)   The undiagnosed suicide risk

Where it is claimed that the medical staff negligently failed to appreciate that the   **4–174**
patient was a suicide risk the question may be cast in terms of whether
non-specialist (i.e. non-psychiatric) staff (whether doctors or nurses) ought to
have realised that the patient's mental condition was such that there was a
genuine risk of a suicide attempt. This will not be judged by reference to whether
a psychiatrist could have made this diagnosis, unless the patient is receiving
psychiatric treatment, but whether in the defendant's position a reasonable doctor
or nurse would have identified the risk.[565]

In *Hyde v Tameside Area Health Authority*[566] the claimant was admitted to   **4–175**
hospital with a painful shoulder. Twelve days later he jumped from a third floor
window in an attempt to kill himself having convinced himself, erroneously, that
he had cancer. The attempt failed, but he suffered catastrophic injuries. The
alleged negligence consisted of a failure by the medical staff to identify the
claimant's mental distress, and a failure to realise "that the hospital had a serious
psychiatric case on its hands which called for psychiatric treatment". At first
instance the defendants were held liable. The Court of Appeal reversed this
decision, finding that on the particular facts of the case there was no negligence,
merely, in the words of Watkins LJ, a "forgivable failure to achieve a standard
approaching perfection".

The court will make allowance for the fact that a decision to introduce psychiatric   **4–176**
treatment for patients who are not being treated for a psychiatric illness or
disorder is one that involves competing considerations. In *Hyde v Tameside Area
Health Authority* Watkins LJ pointed out that many patients in hospital suffer
from anxiety, and worry about their medical condition. They may need
reassurance; sometimes they need drugs to ease pain or stress, but to tell patients
who require surgery that they also need psychiatric help may be counter-
productive. As Watkins LJ put it:

> "A decision to use psychiatry may do more harm than good. An over eager resort to, and an
> excessive use of, this branch of medicine in hospitals other than those where the mentally ill
> are treated could have unfortunate and unsettling consequences."[567]

Policy concerns   In *Hyde v Tameside Area Health Authority* Lord Denning MR   **4–177**
was hostile to actions based on suicide or attempted suicide:

---

[565] For discussion of the difficulties involved in predicting suicide risk for psychiatric in-patients see
D. Baldwin, A. Mayers and R. Elgie, "Suicide in psychiatric in-patients" (2003) 9 *Clinical Risk* 229.
Of course, if the patient was seen by mental health professionals the standard of care will be that
applied to mental health professionals. See e.g. *Nyang v G4S Care and Justice Services Ltd* [2013]
EWHC 3946 (QB) where a doctor and a mental health nurse failed to carry out a thorough mental
state examination, having failed to ask the claimant specific questions about suicidal intent or intent to
self-harm, about mood, and about core symptoms of depression. The claim failed on causation: see
para.4–180 below.
[566] (1981), reported at (1986) 2 P.N. 26.
[567] (1986) 2 P.N. 26 at 30.

"I feel it is most unfitting that the personal representatives of a suicide should be able to claim damages in respect of his death. At any rate, when he succeeds in killing himself. And I do not see why he should be in any better position when he does not succeed. By this act—in self-inflicting this grievous injury—he has made himself a burden on the whole community. Our hospital services and our social welfare services have done, and will do, all they can to help him and his family—in the grievous injury that he has inflicted on himself and them. But I see no justification whatever in his being awarded, in addition, the huge sum of £200,000 because he failed in his attempt. Such a sum will have to be raised, in the long run, by society itself—a sum which it cannot well afford. The policy of the law should be to discourage these actions. I would disallow them altogether—at the outset—rather than burden the community with them."[568]

This view was clearly based on considerations of policy, and in particular Lord Denning's belief that "'medical malpractice' cases should not get out of hand here as they have done in the United States of America". In *Kirkham v Chief Constable of Greater Manchester Police*[569] Lloyd LJ said that he did not share this view, noting that neither Watkins nor O'Connor LJJ expressed agreement with Lord Denning's comments.

4–178   **Causation issues**   It has been argued that, quite apart from the question of breach of duty, claims for negligence based on suicide or attempted suicide should not be permitted, on the grounds of causation, volenti non fit injuria and ex turpi causa non oritur actio. The causation argument states that the defendant's negligence merely provided the opportunity for the deceased's act of suicide, which amounted, in effect, to a novus actus interveniens, so breaking the chain of causation. In *Kirkham v Chief Constable of Greater Manchester Police*[570] Tudor Evans J rejected the causation argument on the basis that the suicide was the very thing that the defendants had a duty to take precautions against,[571] and concluded that on the evidence the suicide would probably have been prevented.[572] His Lordship seemed to regard the deceased's state of mind as relevant to the question of causation:

"Although the act of suicide was in a sense a conscious and deliberate act, the deceased's mental balance was, I am satisfied, affected at the time."[573]

This left open the question whether, if the deceased's mind was not "affected", the suicide could be regarded as a novus actus interveniens.[574]

---

[568] (1986) 2 P.N. 26 at 29–30.

[569] [1990] 2 Q.B. 283 at 292.

[570] [1989] 3 All E.R. 882; aff'd [1990] 2 Q.B. 283.

[571] Where the intervening conduct is the very thing that the defendant was under a duty to guard against, he cannot avoid liability by arguing that the conduct constituted an intervening act: *Haynes v Harwood* [1935] 1 K.B. 146 at 156; *Perl (Exporters) Ltd v Camden London Borough Council* [1984] Q.B. 342 at 353. See also per Farquharson LJ in *Kirkham v Chief Constable of Greater Manchester Police* [1990] 2 Q.B. 283 at 295 in relation to the defence of volenti non fit injuria.

[572] See also *Funk Estate v Clapp* (1986), reported at 68 D.L.R. (4th) 229, and (1988) 54 D.L.R. (4th) 512, BCCA, where it was held that novus actus interveniens was not a defence to a claim following the suicide of a prisoner.

[573] [1989] 3 All E.R. 882 at 889.

[574] Thus, in *Wright Estate v Davidson* (1992) 88 D.L.R. (4th) 698, BCCA the deceased's suicide was held to constitute a novus actus interveniens where there was no evidence of disabling mental illness; cf. *Costello v Blakeson* [1993] 2 W.W.R. 562, BCSC.

In *Reeves v Commissioner of Police for the Metropolis*[575] a case which also   **4–179**
involved the suicide of a prisoner who was a known suicide risk, though not
found to be mentally ill, the House of Lords held that the suicide did not
constitute a novus actus. The damage arose from breach of a duty to prevent just
such an act and thus did not obliterate the defendants' wrongdoing. It was not a
new act, but the very harm that the defendants were under a duty to try to prevent.
Lord Hoffmann commented that in cases where the law imposes a duty to guard
against loss caused by the free, deliberate and informed act of a human being:

> "...it would make nonsense of the existence of such a duty if the law were to hold that the
> occurrence of the very act which ought to have been prevented negatived causal connection
> between the breach of duty and the loss."[576]

Though a duty to protect people of full understanding from causing harm to
themselves was very rare, once it was accepted that such a duty was owed, it was
self-contradictory to say that the breach could not have been a cause of the harm
because the victim caused it to himself.[577] Moreover, the deceased's mental state
was irrelevant, since the defendant's duty arose out of the fact that the deceased
was a known suicide risk, not from any particular mental state.

Of course, it is possible that a claim may fail applying standard principles of   **4–180**
causation where the conclusion is that the breach of duty would not have
prevented the claimant's act of self-harm. In *Nyang v G4S Care and Justice
Services Ltd*[578] the claimant had become depressed, with instances of paranoia
and acute agitation and stress, while detained in an immigration removal centre.
He had made threats to harm himself and others. Whilst under constant
supervision by two officers he suddenly ran head first into a concrete wall. He
broke his spine and was rendered tetraplegic. Lewis J found that there had been
two instances of negligence: an inadequate mental health assessment carried out
seven days earlier and a failure to institute the defendants' "assessment, care in
detention and teamwork process" (ACDT) the day before the event. However,
neither breach of duty would have prevented the claimant's self-harm. Even if he
had been prescribed medication following the mental health assessment the
evidence indicated that the medication would not have had a beneficial effect on
the claimant's mood for 14 days. Nor would instituting the ACDT have made any
difference. He had refused medication on the day, and administering medication
to sedate him could only have been done if he had been assessed as lacking
capacity and sedation was in his best interests, but there was no consultant
psychiatrist available in the few minutes between the claimant's agitation
returning and the act of self-harm. Even if a consultant psychiatrist had been
available, it would not have been realistically possible to assess the claimant as
lacking capacity and compulsorily administrating sedation in the few minutes
between the agitation returning and the self-harm occurring, and it was

---

[575] [2000] 1 A.C. 360.
[576] [2000] 1 A.C. 360 at 367–368.
[577] [2000] 1 A.C. 360 at 368.
[578] [2013] EWHC 3946 (QB).

unrealistic, said Lewis J, to suggest that if a psychiatrist had seen the claimant on the previous day events would have taken a different course.[579]

4–181   **Volenti non fit injuria**   In *Kirkham v Chief Constable of Greater Manchester Police* Lloyd LJ had suggested that there was no reason why volenti non fit injuria should not provide a complete defence where a person "of sound mind" committed suicide or was injured in an unsuccessful attempt, though it was unclear precisely what the term "of sound mind" meant. In *Kirkham*, although the deceased was legally sane and his suicide was a deliberate and conscious act, nonetheless he "was suffering from clinical depression. His judgment was impaired ... [H]e was not truly *volens*".[580] Thus, insanity was not essential in order to defeat the volenti defence; some impairment of judgment sufficed,[581] but that left open the possibility that suicides and attempted suicides by patients who could not be categorised as suffering from some form of mental illness would be met with the volenti defence. However, in *Reeves v Commissioner of Police for the Metropolis*[582] the House of Lords held that, as with novus actus interveniens, volenti did not apply where the claimant's act was the very thing that the defendant was under a duty to take reasonable care to prevent, irrespective of the patient's mental state. Once it was accepted that the defendant owed a duty to take reasonable care to prevent a suicide attempt he could not be permitted to argue that the very act which he was under a duty to prevent gave rise to the defence of volenti. The argument would undermine the purpose of imposing the duty in the first place. Since the duty arose because the deceased was a known suicide risk (or the defendants reasonably should have known of the risk), not because of his mental state, it would be wrong to distinguish between different mental states when applying volenti.

4–182   **Ex turpi causa**   The defendant in *Kirkham* also relied on the principle ex turpi causa non oritur actio. The Court of Appeal accepted that the ex turpi causa defence was not confined to criminal conduct, but could apply to illegal or immoral conduct by the claimant:

> "...if in all the circumstances it would be an affront to the public conscience to grant the plaintiff the relief which he seeks because the court would thereby appear to assist or encourage the plaintiff in his illegal conduct or to encourage others in similar acts."[583]

---

[579] Similarly, in *Briante (Litigation guardian of) v Vancouver Island Health Authority* 2017 BCCA 148; [2017] 6 W.W.R. 465 a psychiatric nurse was held to have been in breach of duty with the result that the patient was discharged from hospital without being referred to an on-call psychiatrist, but on the balance of probabilities if the patient had been seen by the psychiatrist this would not have prevented a suicide attempt six days later. The best that could be said was that a referral "might" have made a difference.

[580] [1990] 2 Q.B. 283 at 290, per Lloyd LJ. Farquharson LJ said, at 295, that it was "quite unrealistic" to suggest that Mr. Kirkham was truly volens: "His state of mind was such that, through disease, he was incapable of coming to a balanced decision even if his act of suicide was deliberate."

[581] cf. *Robson v Ashworth* (1987) 40 C.C.L.T. 164 Ont CA, where the fact that the deceased took his life "knowingly and deliberately while he was sane" barred the action by his widow.

[582] [2000] 1 A.C. 360.

[583] *Euro-Diam Ltd v Bathurst* [1990] 1 Q.B. 1 at 35, per Kerr LJ, cited by Lloyd LJ in *Kirkham*.

The question, then, was whether awarding damages following a suicide would "affront the public conscience, or, as I would prefer to say, shock the ordinary citizen".[584] Their Lordships concluded that the answer should be "No". Thus, said Lloyd LJ, the defence of ex turpi causa is not available in suicide cases "at any rate where, as here, there is medical evidence that the suicide is not in full possession of his mind".[585] Farquharson LJ said that an action could hardly be said to be grounded in immorality where "grave mental instability" on the part of the victim has been proved, although "the position may well be different where the victim is wholly sane". However, in *Reeves v Commissioner of Police of the Metropolis*[586] the Court of Appeal held that the defence of ex turpi causa should not apply in a case where the claimant's conduct was the very act that the defendant was under a duty of care to prevent, whether or not the claimant was of sound mind.[587] There was no distinction between persons suffering from a mental illness and persons who were not, since the claimant recovered damages, not because of his mental state, but because he was a suicide risk and had not received the care that he should have. In the House of Lords, the deceased was held to have been 50 per cent contributorily negligent, however, on the basis that where the deceased was of sound mind at the time he killed himself he bore at least partial responsibility for his death.

(iii) Suicide and human rights

Patients detained under the Mental Health Act 1983   Where prisoners are known to be mentally ill and an identified suicide risk then inadequate medical treatment and a lack of effective monitoring may constitute a breach of their rights under art.3 of the European Convention for the Protection of Human Rights.[588] In *Savage v South Essex Partnership NHS Trust*[589] a patient who was

4–183

---

[584] [1990] 2 Q.B. 283 at 291 per Lloyd LJ. Note, however, that there has been criticism of the "public conscience" test for ex turpi causa on the basis that it confers too much discretion on the court. See *Clerk & Lindsell on Torts*, 22nd edn (London: Sweet & Maxwell, 2018), para.3–08. The ex turpi causa rule is now based on two policy reasons, namely that people should not be allowed to profit from their own wrongdoing, and that the law should be coherent and not self-defeating in condoning illegality "by giving with the left hand what it takes with the right hand": *Patel v Mirza* [2016] UKSC 42; [2017] A.C. 467 at [99]; see para.11–026.

[585] [1990] 2 Q.B. 283 at 291; see also *Funk Estate v Clapp* (1986), reported at 68 D.L.R. (4th) 229, and (1988) 54 D.L.R. (4th) 512 where it was held that ex turpi causa was not a defence to an action by the widow of a prisoner who committed suicide, although there was no negligence on the facts.

[586] [1999] Q.B. 169.

[587] [1999] Q.B. 169 at 185 per Buxton LJ. There was no appeal on the issue of ex turpi causa in the House of Lords. cf. *Clunis v Camden & Islington Health Authority* [1998] Q.B. 978 where the Court of Appeal held that the defence of illegality would only be inappropriate if it could be said that the claimant did not know the nature or quality of his act or that it was wrong. cf. *Hunter Area Health Service v Presland* [2005] NSWCA 33; (2005) 63 N.S.W.L.R. 22 where, on very similar facts to *Clunis*, a majority of the New South Wales Court of Appeal held that no duty of care was owed to the claimant psychiatric patient even though he had been found not guilty of murder by reason of insanity (and, presumably, was not aware of the nature and quality of his actions). Although he lacked moral culpability, his act remained an unlawful and wholly unreasonable act.

[588] *Keenan v UK* (2001) 10 B.H.R.C. 319, ECtHR. See also *McGlinchey v UK* [2003] Lloyd's Rep. Med. 264; (2003) 72 B.M.L.R. 168 (inadequate medical treatment in prison could give rise to a breach of art.3); see further para.1–114. In *Daniel v St George's Healthcare NHS Trust* [2016] EWHC 23 (QB); [2016] 4 W.L.R. 32 an allegation of inadequate medical treatment of a prisoner was rejected on

being treated for paranoid schizophrenia in an open psychiatric ward, absconded and threw herself in front of a train. The House of Lords held that in the case of a patient detained in a NHS hospital under the Mental Health Act 1983, art.2 of the European Convention may be engaged, with the result that the relatives of the deceased may be entitled to damages where there has been a culpable failure to prevent the patient's suicide. Lord Rodger explained that a public body, such as a NHS hospital, is under an obligation to adopt general measures for protecting the lives of patients in hospitals, including recruiting competent staff, seeing that high professional standards are maintained and that suitable systems of working are put in place.[590] If this has been done then casual acts of negligence by members of staff do not give rise to a breach of art.2.[591] On the other hand, a failure to have such systems in place for preventing patients who were known to be suffering from mental illness from committing suicide could give rise to liability in both common law negligence and under art.2. Furthermore, detained patients are, like prisoners detained by the State, vulnerable due both to their mental state and because they are under the control of the hospital authorities. It followed that the principles applied to prisoners should also apply to detained patients. In deciding what level of supervision is appropriate medical staff have to exercise clinical judgment in assessing the risk of suicide in the individual patient, and to balance the potentially adverse effect of too much supervision on the patient's condition and the possible positive benefits from a more open environment.[592] But where members of staff know or ought to know that there is "a real and immediate risk of a patient committing suicide" then art.2 imposes an operational obligation on the medical staff to do all that can reasonably be expected of them to prevent it.[593] This duty is distinct from, and additional to, the hospital's more general obligations under art.2, and comparable to the duty owed to prisoners under *Keenan v UK*. It is a more stringent test than the duty to

---

the facts. The prisoner died from a heart attack, but he had no history of heart disease and the only medical condition of which the prison officers and the emergency duty nurse were aware was asthma. In the circumstances the nurse had acted reasonably and in accordance with nursing professional standards.

[589] [2008] UKHL 74; [2009] 1 A.C. 681. The case is commented on by N. Allen, "Saving Life and Respecting Death: A Savage Dilemma" (2009) 17 Med. L. Rev. 262; Lyons [2009] J.P.I.L. C1.

[590] [2008] UKHL 74; [2009] 1 A.C. 681 at [45] and [69].

[591] Citing *Powell v United Kingdom* (2000) 30 EHRR CD362, 364 where the European Court of Human Rights said that if the State has made adequate provision for securing high professional standards among health professionals and the protection of the lives of patients then "matters such as error of judgment on the part of a health professional or negligent co-ordination among health professionals in the treatment of a particular patient" were not themselves sufficient to amount to a breach of art.2. Though, of course, the hospital could be vicariously liable for the negligence of a member of staff, at common law: [2008] UKHL 74; [2009] 1 A.C. 681 at [70]–[71].

[592] [2008] UKHL 74; [2009] 1 A.C. 681 at [50] per Lord Rodger. Baroness Hale commented, at [100], that steps taken to prevent the risk of suicide must be proportionate, taking into account the liberty and autonomy rights of patients protected by art.5 and art.8. The court also has to take into account the problem of resources: "The facilities available for looking after people with serious mental illnesses are not unlimited and the healthcare professionals have to make the best use they can of what they have."

[593] [2008] UKHL 74; [2009] 1 A.C. 681 at [66] and [72]. The case was sent back to the High Court for a trial on whether there had been a real and immediate risk of suicide and whether the hospital had done all that could reasonably have been expected to avoid it: see *Savage v South Essex Partnership NHS Foundation Trust* [2010] EWHC 865 (QB); [2010] P.I.Q.R. P14; [2010] Med. L.R. 292.

exercise reasonable care and it is therefore more difficult to establish a breach of the duty than "mere negligence".[594] Despite this, a claim for breach of Convention rights has the advantage that a wider range of claimants may be able to claim as "victims" than at common law, and the test for causation is easier to satisfy.[595]

Voluntary psychiatric patients: vulnerable patients In *Rabone v Pennine Care NHS Foundation Trust*[596] the Supreme Court extended the principles of *Savage* to voluntary (i.e. non-detained) psychiatric patients in hospital. The patient had been admitted to hospital following a suicide attempt and was assessed as at high risk of making a further suicide attempt. She was allowed home on leave and whilst on leave she hanged herself. The hospital admitted negligence but denied that they were in breach of art.2. Lord Dyson noted that the existence of a "real and immediate risk" to life was a necessary but not a sufficient condition for the existence of the duty. One factor which ran through the jurisprudence of the European Court of Human Rights on art.2 was the vulnerability of the individual. In circumstances of sufficient vulnerability the Court had been prepared to find a breach of the operational duty even where there had been no assumption of control by the State. The differences between an informal psychiatric patient and one who is detained under the Mental Health Act were in many ways more apparent than real.[597] In theory, informal patients were free to leave hospital at any time, but in practice their "consent" to remaining in hospital may only be as a result of a fear that they will be detained. The position of a voluntary psychiatric patient at risk of suicide was in reality much closer to that of a detained psychiatric patient than that of a non-psychiatric patient suffering from a life-threatening physical illness who was in an ordinary hospital setting. Given the patient's mental disorder, her capacity to make a rational decision to end her life was likely to be impaired, and the very reason she was admitted to hospital was because there was a risk of suicide from which she needed to be protected.[598] Lord Dyson concluded that the hospital owed the operational duty to take reasonable steps to protect the patient from the real and immediate risk of suicide:

4–184

---

[594] [2008] UKHL 74; [2009] 1 A.C. 681 at [66] per Lord Rodger, and [99] per Baroness Hale. See also *Rabone v Pennine Care NHS Foundation Trust* [2012] UKSC 2; [2012] 2 A.C. 72 at [37] per Lord Dyson: "I accept that it is more difficult to establish a breach of the operational duty than mere negligence. This is not least because, in order to prove negligence, it is sufficient to show that the risk of damage was reasonably foreseeable; it is not necessary to show that the risk was real and immediate." Though note that once the duty to protect a patient from a real and immediate risk that she would commit suicide arises then "simple negligence in failing to identify or to guard appropriately against such a risk appears sufficient to establish breach of the duty": per Lord Mance in *Rabone* at [118].
[595] See para.4–185, n.601 below and para.5–021.
[596] [2012] UKSC 2; [2012] 2 A.C. 72. See N. Poole, "Claiming damages under the Human Rights Act: *Rabone v Pennine Care NHS Foundation Trust*" [2012] J.P.I.L. 127; Wheeler [2012] J.P.I.L. C63; M. Andenas, "Leading from the front: human rights and tort law in *Rabone* and *Reynolds*" (2012) 128 L.Q.R. 323.
[597] [2012] UKSC 2; [2012] 2 A.C. 72 at [28].
[598] [2012] UKSC 2; [2012] 2 A.C. 72 at [30]. See also per Baroness Hale at [106].

"She had been admitted to hospital because she was a real suicide risk. By reason of her mental state, she was extremely vulnerable. The trust assumed responsibility for her. She was under its control. Although she was not a detained patient, it is clear that, if she had insisted on leaving the hospital, the authorities could and should have exercised their powers under the MHA to prevent her from doing so."[599]

The difference between the patient's position and that of a hypothetical detained psychiatric patient who was in similar circumstances was one of form, not substance.

4–185   **Real and immediate risk**   In *Rabone* Lord Dyson agreed that the risk of the deceased committing suicide was "real", given that it was described in evidence as "a substantial or significant risk and not a remote or fanciful one".[600] It did not have to be shown that there was a "likelihood or fairly high degree of risk". It was also an "immediate" risk because it was "present and continuing" at the time of the alleged breach of duty, and was not a risk that would arise at some time in the future.[601] In *Savage v South Essex Partnership NHS Foundation Trust*[602] Mackay J came to the conclusion that on the facts the patient, who had been detained under the Mental Health Act 1983, presented a real and immediate risk of absconding from the hospital ward and that this also involved a similar risk of suicide.[603]

4–186   **All that can reasonably be expected**   Once it has been determined that there was a real and immediate risk, the court must then consider whether the defendant failed to do all that could reasonably have been expected to avoid or prevent that risk. Again, on the facts of *Savage*, the defendants had not done all that could reasonably have been expected:

"... all that was required to give her a real prospect or substantial chance of survival was the imposition of a raised level of observations, which would not have been an unreasonable or unduly onerous step to require of the defendant in the light of the evidence in this case."[604]

---

[599] [2012] UKSC 2; [2012] 2 A.C. 72 at [34]. *Rabone* was subsequently approved by the European Court of Human Rights in *Reynolds v United Kingdom* (2694/08) (2012) 55 E.H.R.R. 35.

[600] [2012] UKSC 2; [2012] 2 A.C. 72 at [38].

[601] [2012] UKSC 2; [2012] 2 A.C. 72 at [39]. Note that in *Rabone* the Supreme Court held that the deceased patient's parents qualified as "victims" for the purpose of maintaining a claim under the Convention arising out of their adult daughter's death, and did not lose their victim status as a result of settling a negligence action on behalf of their daughter's estate. They were entitled to financial redress for breach of their art.2 rights, though they would not have been entitled to damages for bereavement under the Fatal Accidents Act 1976 (which limits such claims to cases involving the death of a minor child). For criticism of this see A. Tettenborn, "Wrongful Death, Human Rights and the Fatal Accidents Act" (2012) 128 L.Q.R. 327.

[602] [2010] EWHC 865 (QB); [2010] P.I.Q.R. P14; [2010] Med. L.R. 292; discussed by D. Horton, "'Making Sense' of Risk in a Mental Health Facility" (2010) 18 Med. L. Rev. 578; Ettinger [2010] J.P.I.L. C119.

[603] "There was little or no risk of that while she was on the ward, or at home with her family. But once she was out in the world on her own such was her psychotic state of mind it truly was the case that anything could happen at any moment and the risk of suicide must be assessed as both real and immediate", [2010] EWHC 865 (QB); [2010] P.I.Q.R. P14; [2010] Med. L.R. 292 at [88]. The patient had absconded from the ward and thrown herself in front of a train.

[604] [2010] EWHC 865 (QB); [2010] P.I.Q.R. P14; [2010] Med. L.R. 292 at [89]. Note that the test for causation in an ECHR case is not the "but for" test, but whether the patient has lost a "substantial

There has to be an element of clinical judgment in assessing the risk of suicide and drawing a balance between the negative effects on the patient of too close a regime of supervision and the benefits to the patient of a less restrictive regime, and the available resources may have to be factored in to what it is reasonable to expect.[605] On the other hand, as Lord Rodger noted in *Savage*, where there is a real and immediate risk to life:

> "...the immediacy of the danger to life means that, for the time being, there is, in practice, little room for considering other, more general, matters concerning his treatment. There will be time enough for them, if and when the danger to life has been overcome. In the meantime, the authorities' duty is to try to prevent the suicide."[606]

(b) Failing to control the patient: harm to third parties

It remains uncertain whether, in this country, a psychiatrist or psychologist could **4–187** be held responsible for foreseeable harm inflicted by a patient on a third party. Even if it were possible to identify reasonably practicable steps that a doctor could have taken (such as requesting compulsory admission for assessment or treatment under the Mental Health Act 1983) it is not clear that a duty of care would be held to exist.[607] It may be that there is a distinction to be drawn between a failure to exercise powers to admit a potentially dangerous patient to hospital compulsorily and a decision to release from compulsory detention a patient who has already been detained in hospital.[608] On one view, where the patient is compulsorily detained the greater degree of control exercised over the patient may be sufficient to tip the balance in favour of a duty of care.[609] On the other hand, most psychiatric patients admitted to hospital are not compulsorily detained but are voluntary patients, and it might seem strange that the hospital's responsibility in tort should rest upon the technical issue of whether the patient

---

chance" of avoiding the harm, in this case the patient's death. See [2010] EWHC 865 (QB); [2010] P.I.Q.R. P14; [2010] Med. L.R. 292 at [82], applying the approach of Lord Brown in *Van Colle v Chief Constable of the Hertfordshire Police* [2008] UKHL 50; [2009] 1 A.C. 225 at [138]; see para.5–021.

[605] *Savage v South Essex Partnership NHS Trust* [2008] UKHL 74; [2009] 1 A.C. 681 [2008] UKHL 74; [2009] 1 A.C. 681 at [50] and [100] per Lord Rodger and Baroness Hale respectively.

[606] [2008] UKHL 74; [2009] 1 A.C. 681 at [42].

[607] See para.2–168.

[608] See *Ahmed v Stefaniu* (2006) 275 D.L.R. (4th) 101 where the Ontario Court of Appeal upheld a jury's award of damages against a psychiatrist in relation to a murder committed by a psychiatric patient. The psychiatrist had changed the patient's status from that of a compulsorily detained patient under the mental health legislation to one of a voluntary patient, and seven weeks later he murdered his sister. However, there was no discussion of the duty of care in this case, which turned entirely on issues of breach of duty and causation. In *Kines Estate v Lychuk* [1996] 10 W.W.R. 426, Man QB, on the other hand, a similar action against psychiatrists was struck out as disclosing no reasonable cause of action on the basis that a doctor owed no duty of care to a third party who received neither treatment nor advice from the doctor, and where the claim was not derivative to a claim by the patient (though the allegation of negligence was that the doctors had negligently failed compulsorily to detain the psychiatric patient).

[609] By analogy with the position of a prisoner who is negligently allowed to escape and causes harm during the course of the escape: see *Home Office v Dorset Yacht Co. Ltd* [1970] A.C. 1004, although in this case the House of Lords was careful to limit the potential duty to damage caused during the escape. There would be no liability for the escapee's subsequent criminal activity.

had been formally detained under the Mental Health Act 1983 and then released, as opposed to whether there had been failure formally to detain the patient in the first place.

4–188 In *Palmer v Tees Health Authority*[610] a young child was abducted and killed by a mental patient who had previously stated, while a hospital in-patient, that he had sexual feelings towards children and that a child would be murdered after his discharge. The Court of Appeal held that no duty of care was owed by the defendant health authority either to the child herself or the child's mother, in respect of an alleged negligent failure to diagnose that the patient constituted a serious risk to children. The threats made by the patient in *Palmer* were of a general nature. It would at least be arguable that, if a psychiatric patient were to make threats against a specific individual or individuals, where there was a real risk of such threats being carried out, then a duty of care on the part of a psychiatrist or psychologist might arise.[611]

(c) Negligent certification

4–189 The Mental Health Act 1983 provides that an application for a patient to be admitted to hospital and detained there for assessment or for treatment must be founded on the written recommendations of (normally) two registered medical practitioners which include a statement that in the opinion of the practitioner the grounds for compulsory admission are satisfied.[612] It is strongly arguable, though it has not been definitively settled, that doctors who provide written recommendations supporting the compulsory admission of a patient under Pt II of the Act owe a duty of care to that patient and therefore must exercise reasonable care.[613] This necessarily requires that doctors examine the patient,[614] and that they should make such further enquiries as are necessary.[615] On the one hand, the court must make due allowance for the difficulty in making an accurate diagnosis in some cases of mental illness, and on the other hand, they should require "very considerable care" where a person is being deprived of his liberty.[616]

---

[610] [2000] P.I.Q.R. P1; [1999] Lloyd's Rep. Med. 351; para.2–169. See further Jones (2000) 16 P.N. 3.

[611] As in *Tarasoff v Regents of the University of California* 551 P. 2d 334; Sup., 131 Cal. Rptr. 14 (1976); para.2–166.

[612] Mental Health Act 1983 ss.2(3) and 3(3) respectively. In an emergency the recommendation of one doctor will suffice: s.4(3). The grounds for admission for assessment and for treatment are set out in s.2(2) and s.3(2) respectively. See para.2–161.

[613] *Hall v Semple* (1862) 3 F. & F. 337; *De Freville v Dill* (1927) 96 L.J.K.B. 1056; *Everett v Griffiths* [1921] 1 A.C. 631; *Harnett v Fisher* [1927] A.C. 573; *Buxton v Jayne* [1960] 1 W.L.R. 783; [1962] C.L.Y. 1167. See para.2–162. Differing views were expressed in the Court of Appeal in *Everett v Griffiths* as to whether a duty of care was owed. In *X (Minors) v Bedfordshire County Council* [1995] 2 A.C. 633 at 664–665 Sir Thomas Bingham MR found the judgment of Atkin LJ in the Court of Appeal in favour of imposing a duty of care persuasive. However, Lord Browne-Wilkinson in *X (Minors) v Bedfordshire County Council* [1995] A.C. 633 at 753, pointed out that though there were dicta in the House of Lords in *Everett v Griffiths* in favour of a duty of care, the issue had not been finally decided by their Lordships.

[614] Mental Health Act 1983 s.12(1).

[615] *Hall v Semple* (1862) 3 F. & F. 337 at 354, per Crompton J.

[616] (1862) 3 F. & F. 337 at 355–356.

The importance that the common law attaches to individual liberty is reinforced by the fact that decisions compulsorily to detain a patient under the Mental Health Act 1983 will also engage the patient's art.5 rights under the European Convention on Human Rights.[617] This is reflected in the courts' insistence on strict adherence to the statutory requirements for compulsory detention under the Act.[618] Failure to comply with the statute's procedural requirements will render the patient's detention unlawful, giving rise to potential claims in trespass to the person and for breach of art.5.[619] However, if it turns out that notwithstanding the failure to abide by the procedural protections in the Act the patient could have been lawfully detained (whether by the actions of the defendant or those of a third party) the claimant will be entitled to nominal damages only.[620] In contrast, if there has been negligence in the process of compulsorily detaining a patient causing personal injuries (e.g. where as a result of the unlawful detention the claimant has suffered psychiatric harm or physical injury) nominal damages will be inappropriate. The claimant would be entitled to damages to reflect the actual harm sustained.[621]

4–190

(d) Procedural bars

(i) Acts done in good faith or with reasonable care

Section 139(1) of the Mental Health Act 1983 provides that no person shall be liable to any civil or criminal proceedings in respect of any act purporting to be done under the mental health legislation unless the act was done in bad faith or

4–191

---

[617] The right to liberty and security of person. An exception is made, inter alia, for the detention of persons of unsound mind, but any detention must be "in accordance with a procedure prescribed by law", which requires adherence to the procedural requirements of the Mental Health Act 1983.

[618] As, e.g., in *S-C (Mental Patient: Habeas Corpus)* [1996] Q.B. 599 and *TW v Enfield LBC* [2014] EWCA Civ 362; [2014] 1 W.L.R. 3665 insisting on a strict interpretation of s.11(4) requiring consultation with a patient's nearest relative by an approved mental health professional.

[619] There is no residual common law power, under the doctrine of necessity, to justify a patient's detention; nor can the Mental Capacity Act 2005 be relied on for this purpose. The Mental Health Act 1983 Pt II provides a complete code for the compulsory admission to hospital of non-compliant mentally incapacitated patients for the purpose of assessment and treatment of their mental disorder: *R. (on the application of Sessay) v South London and Maudsley NHS Foundation Trust* [2011] EWHC 2617 (QB); [2012] Q.B. 760; see para.6–118.

[620] *Bostridge v Oxleas NHS Foundation Trust* [2015] EWCA Civ 79; [2015] Med. L.R. 113, applying *Lumba v Secretary of State for the Home Department* [2011] UKSC 12; [2012] 1 A.C. 245 and *R. (on the application of Kambadzi) v Secretary of State for the Home Department* [2011] UKSC 23; [2011] 1 W.L.R. 1299.

[621] See, e.g., the extraordinary Canadian case of *X v Everson* 2013 ONSC 6134; (2013) 4 C.C.L.T. (4th) 205 where the defendant decided that the claimant, who was a doctor who had become concerned about the health of her newborn child and had consulted several doctors at the hospital where she worked, should be compulsorily detained for the purpose of a psychiatric assessment. The claimant had contacted the defendant, who was an administrator at the hospital and also a doctor, to seek her assistance in getting a referral for the child to another specialist. The defendant had obtained the views of the other doctors that the claimant had consulted and had concluded even before seeing the claimant that an involuntary psychiatric assessment was required. She failed conspicuously to comply with the relevant statutory procedures. The defendant was held liable in both trespass to the person and negligence for the psychiatric harm suffered by the claimant as a result of her detention.

without reasonable care.[622] The section does not apply to an application for judicial review, so that proceedings for judicial review of a decision purportedly taken in the exercise of powers conferred by the Mental Health Act 1983 can be brought even though the applicant does not allege that the decision was made negligently or in bad faith.[623] Nor does s.139 refer to omissions, so that a negligent failure compulsorily to detain someone would not fall within s.139.[624] It is, however, arguable that a private law action brought under s.7 of the Human Rights Act 1998 would require leave under s.139(2) of the Mental Health Act 1983.[625]

4–192   **Institutional defendants**   Section 139(4) of the Act provides that s.139 does not apply to certain institutional NHS defendants,[626] with the result that in a claim against these defendants the s.139(1) requirement to prove that the act was done in bad faith or without reasonable care does not apply.[627] Nor does the requirement to obtain the leave of the High Court to commence proceedings apply to these defendants.[628]

4–193   **Justification**   The rationale for a provision protecting individuals who have to make decisions under the mental health legislation has been said to be that:

> "...patients under the Mental Health Act may generally be inherently likely to harass those concerned with them by groundless charges and litigation, and may therefore have to suffer modification of the general right of free access to the courts."[629]

---

[622] See Jaconelli [1998] J.S.W.F.L. 151.

[623] *Re Waldron* [1986] Q.B. 824 (also reported as *R. v Hallstrom Ex p. W* [1985] 3 All E.R. 775). It was conceded in this case that s.139 would not apply to a writ of habeas corpus. On judicial review of a decision involving the forcible treatment of a detained patient there must be an assessment of the substantive merits of the decision, involving the finding of primary facts following oral evidence, if necessary: *R. (on the application of W) v Broadmoor Hospital* [2001] EWCA Civ 1545; [2002] 1 W.L.R. 415.

[624] Since the claimant would in any event still have to prove lack of reasonable care the practical consequence of this is simply that the requirement to obtain leave of the High Court under s.139(2) would not apply. Claimants would nonetheless face formidable hurdles in establishing a duty of care. See paras 2–165 et seq.

[625] *R. (on the application of W) v Broadmoor Hospital* [2001] EWCA Civ 1545; [2002] 1 W.L.R. 419 per Brooke LJ at [54] and Hale LJ at [61]. For discussion of s.139(2) see para.4–195.

[626] The current s.139(4) lists the following: the Secretary of State, the National Health Service Commissioning Board, a clinical commissioning group, a local health board, a special health authority, an NHS Trust (established under the National Health Service Act 2006 or the National Health Service (Wales) Act 2006), an NHS Foundation Trust, the Department of Justice in Northern Ireland, and a person who has functions under the Mental Health Act by virtue of s.12ZA in so far as the proceedings relate to the exercise of those functions.

[627] This is relevant to claims for trespass to the person. Clearly, if the action is for negligence the claimant will have to demonstrate that there was a failure to exercise reasonable care as part of the process of establishing the tort itself.

[628] See para.4–195.

[629] *Pountney v Griffiths* [1976] A.C. 314 at 329, per Lord Simon. See also per Scrutton LJ in *Everett v Griffiths* [1920] 3 K.B. 163 at 197–198: "Very few lunatics think they are properly incarcerated, and most of them would enjoy an action in which the individual has always a better chance of getting the sympathy of the jury than the officers of the state who are performing the unpleasant duty of incarcerating him . . . To leave the person who has to decide this difficult question as to the exact degree of unsoundness of mind which justifies immediate restraint, when he has acted honestly in

This justification has been strongly criticised on the grounds that only a minority of patients, even of those compulsorily detained, are suffering from disorders which make it likely that they will harass others with groundless accusations, and rather more of them are suffering from disorders which makes it likely that they will not complain at all, even where complaint would be justified.[630] Baroness Hale has commented that: "There is no evidence that the floodgates would open if section 139 were entirely repealed."[631]

Compatibility of s.139 with human rights?   Whatever its policy justification, **4–194** it is arguable that s.139 is not compatible with the Human Rights Act 1998. In *TTM v Hackney LBC*[632] an approved mental health professional (AMHP) employed by the local authority applied under the Mental Health Act 1983 to detain the claimant believing, incorrectly, that the claimant's nearest relative had withdrawn his objection to the application. Although the application was made in good faith it was unlawful by virtue of s.11(4) of the Act. The NHS Trust which actually detained the claimant acted lawfully by virtue of s.6(3), since it did so on the basis of an application that "appears to be duly made", but this did not cure the underlying unlawfulness of the AMHP's application.[633] The detention constituted false imprisonment at common law and contravened the claimant's art.5 rights under the European Convention on Human Rights (since the AMHP had not complied with the safeguards for the patient's liberty prescribed by Parliament and that had been the direct cause of the claimant's loss of liberty). It was common ground that the AMHP had acted in good faith and therefore, on the face of it, the local authority could rely on the s.139(1) defence. The claimant argued that s.139(1) was either incompatible with art.5, or should be "read down" (under s.3 of the Human Rights Act 1998) to avoid any incompatibility. Counsel for the Secretary of State for Health was anxious to avoid a declaration that s.139(1) was incompatible with art.5, and since the defendants did not dispute the claimant's argument that s.139(1) could be read down Toulson LJ was:

> "...happy to proceed on the basis that it is open to the court to read s.139(1) in that way without further consideration of the matter."[634]

---

forming his judgment, exposed to the threat of an action by the person restrained, to be decided by persons who did not see the alleged lunatic at the time he was incarcerated, but do see him when his condition may be different, by persons who may be struck by his cleverness without appreciating how near it may be to deranged intellect, seems to me calculated to hinder his properly executing the duty he owes to the community. This exemption is not giving him a licence to be negligent; it is removing from him the threat of harassing actions."

[630] Hale, *Mental Health Law*, 5th edn (London: Sweet & Maxwell, 2010), pp.343–344.

[631] Hale, *Mental Health Law* at p.344. See her more forthright judicial comments on s.139 in *Seal v Chief Constable of South Wales Police* [2007] UKHL 31; [2007] 1 W.L.R. 1910, quoted at para.4–195, below.

[632] [2011] EWCA Civ 4; [2011] 1 W.L.R. 2873.

[633] Applying *Re S-C (Mental Patient: Habeas Corpus)* [1996] Q.B. 599. Toulson LJ commented that "in matters affecting individual liberty the law is strictly applied" ([2011] EWCA Civ 4; [2011] 1 W.L.R. 2873 at [100]), and described the defendant local authority's argument that the lawfulness of the hospital's detention of the claimant rendered the original application lawful as "a back to front argument, reminiscent of the world of Alice Through The Looking-glass" ([2011] EWCA Civ 4; [2011] 1 W.L.R. 2873 at [62]).

[634] [2011] EWCA Civ 4; [2011] 1 W.L.R. 2873 at [66].

to the damage. The claimant contracted pneumoconiosis from inhaling air which contained silica dust at his workplace. The main source of the dust was from pneumatic hammers for which the employers were not in breach of duty (the "innocent dust"). Some of the dust (the "guilty dust") came from swing grinders for which they were responsible by failing to maintain the dust-extraction equipment. There was no evidence as to the proportions of innocent dust and guilty dust inhaled by the claimant, but such evidence as there was indicated that much the greater proportion came from the innocent source. On the evidence the claimant could not prove "but for" causation, in the sense that it was more probable than not that had the dust-extraction equipment worked efficiently he would not have contracted the disease. Nonetheless, the House of Lords drew an inference of fact that the guilty dust was a contributory cause, holding the employers liable for the full extent of the loss. The claimant did not have to prove that the guilty dust was the sole or even the most substantial cause if he could show, on a balance of probabilities, the burden of proof remaining with the claimant, that the guilty dust had materially contributed to the disease. Anything which did not fall within the principle de minimis non curat lex would constitute a material contribution.[79] Subsequently, in *Nicholson v Atlas Steel Foundry & Engineering Co. Ltd*,[80] on virtually identical facts, the House of Lords held the defendants liable for an employee's pneumoconiosis, even though, in the words of Viscount Simonds, it was "impossible even approximately to quantify" the respective contributions of guilty and innocent dust.

5–034 These cases were significant in easing the claimant's burden of proof for two reasons. First, they were a departure from "but for" causation—the claimants did not have to prove that they would not have suffered the "damage" (i.e. the injury or illness) but for the breach of duty. What had to be proved was redefined as a "material contribution" to the injury or illness, and, notwithstanding this redefinition of the "damage" to which the claimant must establish a causal link in more limited terms than the outcome, the claimant still recovered *damages* for the whole loss, i.e. the outcome, having proved causation in respect of a part only of that loss.[81] Secondly, the courts were willing to draw an *inference* of fact that there had been a material contribution when it was in reality impossible to say whether there had been any such contribution, or even to make a statistical guess.

---

[79] In *Carder v Secretary of State for Health* [2016] EWCA Civ 790; [2017] I.C.R. 392 the defendant conceded that a 2.3 per cent contribution to the claimant's asbestosis was a material contribution, but argued that it made no measurable difference to the symptoms and so damages should not be awarded because the claimant was no worse off. The Court of Appeal held that the defendant's concession was critical and so the judge had been correct to award damages on the basis that the claimant was slightly worse off as a result of the 2.3 per cent exposure. The defendant's argument that the claimant was no worse off could not be reconciled with the concession that the defendant had made a material contribution to the claimant's asbestosis.

[80] [1957] 1 All E.R. 776. See also *Clarkson v Modern Foundries Ltd* [1958] 1 All E.R. 33, applying *Bonnington Castings Ltd v Wardlaw* [1956] A.C. 613. "As long as a defendant is *part* of the cause of an injury, the defendant is liable, even though his act alone was not enough to create the injury. There is no basis for a reduction of liability because of the existence of other preconditions: defendants remain liable for all injuries caused or contributed to by their negligence": *Athey v Leonati* [1997] 1 W.W.R. 97, 103, SCC (original emphasis).

[81] See Stapleton (1988) 104 L.Q.R. 389, 404–405.

There has to be an element of clinical judgment in assessing the risk of suicide and drawing a balance between the negative effects on the patient of too close a regime of supervision and the benefits to the patient of a less restrictive regime, and the available resources may have to be factored in to what it is reasonable to expect.[605] On the other hand, as Lord Rodger noted in *Savage*, where there is a real and immediate risk to life:

> "...the immediacy of the danger to life means that, for the time being, there is, in practice, little room for considering other, more general, matters concerning his treatment. There will be time enough for them, if and when the danger to life has been overcome. In the meantime, the authorities' duty is to try to prevent the suicide."[606]

(b)   Failing to control the patient: harm to third parties

It remains uncertain whether, in this country, a psychiatrist or psychologist could   **4–187**
be held responsible for foreseeable harm inflicted by a patient on a third party. Even if it were possible to identify reasonably practicable steps that a doctor could have taken (such as requesting compulsory admission for assessment or treatment under the Mental Health Act 1983) it is not clear that a duty of care would be held to exist.[607] It may be that there is a distinction to be drawn between a failure to exercise powers to admit a potentially dangerous patient to hospital compulsorily and a decision to release from compulsory detention a patient who has already been detained in hospital.[608] On one view, where the patient is compulsorily detained the greater degree of control exercised over the patient may be sufficient to tip the balance in favour of a duty of care.[609] On the other hand, most psychiatric patients admitted to hospital are not compulsorily detained but are voluntary patients, and it might seem strange that the hospital's responsibility in tort should rest upon the technical issue of whether the patient

---

chance" of avoiding the harm, in this case the patient's death. See [2010] EWHC 865 (QB); [2010] P.I.Q.R. P14; [2010] Med. L.R. 292 at [82], applying the approach of Lord Brown in *Van Colle v Chief Constable of the Hertfordshire Police* [2008] UKHL 50; [2009] 1 A.C. 225 at [138]; see para.5–021.

[605] *Savage v South Essex Partnership NHS Trust* [2008] UKHL 74; [2009] 1 A.C. 681 [2008] UKHL 74; [2009] 1 A.C. 681 at [50] and [100] per Lord Rodger and Baroness Hale respectively.

[606] [2008] UKHL 74; [2009] 1 A.C. 681 at [42].

[607] See para.2–168.

[608] See *Ahmed v Stefaniu* (2006) 275 D.L.R. (4th) 101 where the Ontario Court of Appeal upheld a jury's award of damages against a psychiatrist in relation to a murder committed by a psychiatric patient. The psychiatrist had changed the patient's status from that of a compulsorily detained patient under the mental health legislation to one of a voluntary patient, and seven weeks later he murdered his sister. However, there was no discussion of the duty of care in this case, which turned entirely on issues of breach of duty and causation. In *Kines Estate v Lychuk* [1996] 10 W.W.R. 426, Man QB, on the other hand, a similar action against psychiatrists was struck out as disclosing no reasonable cause of action on the basis that a doctor owed no duty of care to a third party who received neither treatment nor advice from the doctor, and where the claim was not derivative to a claim by the patient (though the allegation of negligence was that the doctors had negligently failed compulsorily to detain the psychiatric patient).

[609] By analogy with the position of a prisoner who is negligently allowed to escape and causes harm during the course of the escape: see *Home Office v Dorset Yacht Co. Ltd* [1970] A.C. 1004, although in this case the House of Lords was careful to limit the potential duty to damage caused during the escape. There would be no liability for the escapee's subsequent criminal activity.

had been formally detained under the Mental Health Act 1983 and then released, as opposed to whether there had been failure formally to detain the patient in the first place.

4–188   In *Palmer v Tees Health Authority*[610] a young child was abducted and killed by a mental patient who had previously stated, while a hospital in-patient, that he had sexual feelings towards children and that a child would be murdered after his discharge. The Court of Appeal held that no duty of care was owed by the defendant health authority either to the child herself or the child's mother, in respect of an alleged negligent failure to diagnose that the patient constituted a serious risk to children. The threats made by the patient in *Palmer* were of a general nature. It would at least be arguable that, if a psychiatric patient were to make threats against a specific individual or individuals, where there was a real risk of such threats being carried out, then a duty of care on the part of a psychiatrist or psychologist might arise.[611]

(c)   Negligent certification

4–189   The Mental Health Act 1983 provides that an application for a patient to be admitted to hospital and detained there for assessment or for treatment must be founded on the written recommendations of (normally) two registered medical practitioners which include a statement that in the opinion of the practitioner the grounds for compulsory admission are satisfied.[612] It is strongly arguable, though it has not been definitively settled, that doctors who provide written recommendations supporting the compulsory admission of a patient under Pt II of the Act owe a duty of care to that patient and therefore must exercise reasonable care.[613] This necessarily requires that doctors examine the patient,[614] and that they should make such further enquiries as are necessary.[615] On the one hand, the court must make due allowance for the difficulty in making an accurate diagnosis in some cases of mental illness, and on the other hand, they should require "very considerable care" where a person is being deprived of his liberty.[616]

---

[610] [2000] P.I.Q.R. P1; [1999] Lloyd's Rep. Med. 351; para.2–169. See further Jones (2000) 16 P.N. 3.

[611] As in *Tarasoff v Regents of the University of California* 551 P. 2d 334; Sup., 131 Cal. Rptr. 14 (1976); para.2–166.

[612] Mental Health Act 1983 ss.2(3) and 3(3) respectively. In an emergency the recommendation of one doctor will suffice: s.4(3). The grounds for admission for assessment and for treatment are set out in s.2(2) and s.3(2) respectively. See para.2–161.

[613] *Hall v Semple* (1862) 3 F. & F. 337; *De Freville v Dill* (1927) 96 L.J.K.B. 1056; *Everett v Griffiths* [1921] 1 A.C. 631; *Harnett v Fisher* [1927] A.C. 573; *Buxton v Jayne* [1960] 1 W.L.R. 783; [1962] C.L.Y. 1167. See para.2–162. Differing views were expressed in the Court of Appeal in *Everett v Griffiths* as to whether a duty of care was owed. In *X (Minors) v Bedfordshire County Council* [1995] 2 A.C. 633 at 664–665 Sir Thomas Bingham MR found the judgment of Atkin LJ in the Court of Appeal in favour of imposing a duty of care persuasive. However, Lord Browne-Wilkinson in *X (Minors) v Bedfordshire County Council* [1995] A.C. 633 at 753, pointed out that though there were dicta in the House of Lords in *Everett v Griffiths* in favour of a duty of care, the issue had not been finally decided by their Lordships.

[614] Mental Health Act 1983 s.12(1).

[615] *Hall v Semple* (1862) 3 F. & F. 337 at 354, per Crompton J.

[616] (1862) 3 F. & F. 337 at 355–356.

The importance that the common law attaches to individual liberty is reinforced **4–190** by the fact that decisions compulsorily to detain a patient under the Mental Health Act 1983 will also engage the patient's art.5 rights under the European Convention on Human Rights.[617] This is reflected in the courts' insistence on strict adherence to the statutory requirements for compulsory detention under the Act.[618] Failure to comply with the statute's procedural requirements will render the patient's detention unlawful, giving rise to potential claims in trespass to the person and for breach of art.5.[619] However, if it turns out that notwithstanding the failure to abide by the procedural protections in the Act the patient could have been lawfully detained (whether by the actions of the defendant or those of a third party) the claimant will be entitled to nominal damages only.[620] In contrast, if there has been negligence in the process of compulsorily detaining a patient causing personal injuries (e.g. where as a result of the unlawful detention the claimant has suffered psychiatric harm or physical injury) nominal damages will be inappropriate. The claimant would be entitled to damages to reflect the actual harm sustained.[621]

(d)   Procedural bars

(i)   Acts done in good faith or with reasonable care

Section 139(1) of the Mental Health Act 1983 provides that no person shall be **4–191** liable to any civil or criminal proceedings in respect of any act purporting to be done under the mental health legislation unless the act was done in bad faith or

---

[617] The right to liberty and security of person. An exception is made, inter alia, for the detention of persons of unsound mind, but any detention must be "in accordance with a procedure prescribed by law", which requires adherence to the procedural requirements of the Mental Health Act 1983.

[618] As, e.g., in *S-C (Mental Patient: Habeas Corpus)* [1996] Q.B. 599 and *TW v Enfield LBC* [2014] EWCA Civ 362; [2014] 1 W.L.R. 3665 insisting on a strict interpretation of s.11(4) requiring consultation with a patient's nearest relative by an approved mental health professional.

[619] There is no residual common law power, under the doctrine of necessity, to justify a patient's detention; nor can the Mental Capacity Act 2005 be relied on for this purpose. The Mental Health Act 1983 Pt II provides a complete code for the compulsory admission to hospital of non-compliant mentally incapacitated patients for the purpose of assessment and treatment of their mental disorder: *R. (on the application of Sessay) v South London and Maudsley NHS Foundation Trust* [2011] EWHC 2617 (QB); [2012] Q.B. 760; see para.6–118.

[620] *Bostridge v Oxleas NHS Foundation Trust* [2015] EWCA Civ 79; [2015] Med. L.R. 113, applying *Lumba v Secretary of State for the Home Department* [2011] UKSC 12; [2012] 1 A.C. 245 and *R. (on the application of Kambadzi) v Secretary of State for the Home Department* [2011] UKSC 23; [2011] 1 W.L.R. 1299.

[621] See, e.g., the extraordinary Canadian case of *X v Everson* 2013 ONSC 6134; (2013) 4 C.C.L.T. (4th) 205 where the defendant decided that the claimant, who was a doctor who had become concerned about the health of her newborn child and had consulted several doctors at the hospital where she worked, should be compulsorily detained for the purpose of a psychiatric assessment. The claimant had contacted the defendant, who was an administrator at the hospital and also a doctor, to seek her assistance in getting a referral for the child to another specialist. The defendant had obtained the views of the other doctors that the claimant had consulted and had concluded even before seeing the claimant that an involuntary psychiatric assessment was required. She failed conspicuously to comply with the relevant statutory procedures. The defendant was held liable in both trespass to the person and negligence for the psychiatric harm suffered by the claimant as a result of her detention.

without reasonable care.[622] The section does not apply to an application for judicial review, so that proceedings for judicial review of a decision purportedly taken in the exercise of powers conferred by the Mental Health Act 1983 can be brought even though the applicant does not allege that the decision was made negligently or in bad faith.[623] Nor does s.139 refer to omissions, so that a negligent failure compulsorily to detain someone would not fall within s.139.[624] It is, however, arguable that a private law action brought under s.7 of the Human Rights Act 1998 would require leave under s.139(2) of the Mental Health Act 1983.[625]

4–192   **Institutional defendants**   Section 139(4) of the Act provides that s.139 does not apply to certain institutional NHS defendants,[626] with the result that in a claim against these defendants the s.139(1) requirement to prove that the act was done in bad faith or without reasonable care does not apply.[627] Nor does the requirement to obtain the leave of the High Court to commence proceedings apply to these defendants.[628]

4–193   **Justification**   The rationale for a provision protecting individuals who have to make decisions under the mental health legislation has been said to be that:

> "...patients under the Mental Health Act may generally be inherently likely to harass those concerned with them by groundless charges and litigation, and may therefore have to suffer modification of the general right of free access to the courts."[629]

---

[622] See Jaconelli [1998] J.S.W.F.L. 151.

[623] *Re Waldron* [1986] Q.B. 824 (also reported as *R. v Hallstrom Ex p. W* [1985] 3 All E.R. 775). It was conceded in this case that s.139 would not apply to a writ of habeas corpus. On judicial review of a decision involving the forcible treatment of a detained patient there must be an assessment of the substantive merits of the decision, involving the finding of primary facts following oral evidence, if necessary: *R. (on the application of W) v Broadmoor Hospital* [2001] EWCA Civ 1545; [2002] 1 W.L.R. 415.

[624] Since the claimant would in any event still have to prove lack of reasonable care the practical consequence of this is simply that the requirement to obtain leave of the High Court under s.139(2) would not apply. Claimants would nonetheless face formidable hurdles in establishing a duty of care. See paras 2–165 et seq.

[625] *R. (on the application of W) v Broadmoor Hospital* [2001] EWCA Civ 1545; [2002] 1 W.L.R. 419 per Brooke LJ at [54] and Hale LJ at [61]. For discussion of s.139(2) see para.4–195.

[626] The current s.139(4) lists the following: the Secretary of State, the National Health Service Commissioning Board, a clinical commissioning group, a local health board, a special health authority, an NHS Trust (established under the National Health Service Act 2006 or the National Health Service (Wales) Act 2006), an NHS Foundation Trust, the Department of Justice in Northern Ireland, and a person who has functions under the Mental Health Act by virtue of s.12ZA in so far as the proceedings relate to the exercise of those functions.

[627] This is relevant to claims for trespass to the person. Clearly, if the action is for negligence the claimant will have to demonstrate that there was a failure to exercise reasonable care as part of the process of establishing the tort itself.

[628] See para.4–195.

[629] *Pountney v Griffiths* [1976] A.C. 314 at 329, per Lord Simon. See also per Scrutton LJ in *Everett v Griffiths* [1920] 3 K.B. 163 at 197–198: "Very few lunatics think they are properly incarcerated, and most of them would enjoy an action in which the individual has always a better chance of getting the sympathy of the jury than the officers of the state who are performing the unpleasant duty of incarcerating him ... To leave the person who has to decide this difficult question as to the exact degree of unsoundness of mind which justifies immediate restraint, when he has acted honestly in

This justification has been strongly criticised on the grounds that only a minority of patients, even of those compulsorily detained, are suffering from disorders which make it likely that they will harass others with groundless accusations, and rather more of them are suffering from disorders which makes it likely that they will not complain at all, even where complaint would be justified.[630] Baroness Hale has commented that: "There is no evidence that the floodgates would open if section 139 were entirely repealed."[631]

Compatibility of s.139 with human rights?   Whatever its policy justification,   **4–194** it is arguable that s.139 is not compatible with the Human Rights Act 1998. In *TTM v Hackney LBC*[632] an approved mental health professional (AMHP) employed by the local authority applied under the Mental Health Act 1983 to detain the claimant believing, incorrectly, that the claimant's nearest relative had withdrawn his objection to the application. Although the application was made in good faith it was unlawful by virtue of s.11(4) of the Act. The NHS Trust which actually detained the claimant acted lawfully by virtue of s.6(3), since it did so on the basis of an application that "appears to be duly made", but this did not cure the underlying unlawfulness of the AMHP's application.[633] The detention constituted false imprisonment at common law and contravened the claimant's art.5 rights under the European Convention on Human Rights (since the AMHP had not complied with the safeguards for the patient's liberty prescribed by Parliament and that had been the direct cause of the claimant's loss of liberty). It was common ground that the AMHP had acted in good faith and therefore, on the face of it, the local authority could rely on the s.139(1) defence. The claimant argued that s.139(1) was either incompatible with art.5, or should be "read down" (under s.3 of the Human Rights Act 1998) to avoid any incompatibility. Counsel for the Secretary of State for Health was anxious to avoid a declaration that s.139(1) was incompatible with art.5, and since the defendants did not dispute the claimant's argument that s.139(1) could be read down Toulson LJ was:

> "...happy to proceed on the basis that it is open to the court to read s.139(1) in that way without further consideration of the matter."[634]

---

forming his judgment, exposed to the threat of an action by the person restrained, to be decided by persons who did not see the alleged lunatic at the time he was incarcerated, but do see him when his condition may be different, by persons who may be struck by his cleverness without appreciating how near it may be to deranged intellect, seems to me calculated to hinder his properly executing the duty he owes to the community. This exemption is not giving him a licence to be negligent; it is removing from him the threat of harassing actions."

[630] Hale, *Mental Health Law*, 5th edn (London: Sweet & Maxwell, 2010), pp.343–344.

[631] Hale, *Mental Health Law* at p.344. See her more forthright judicial comments on s.139 in *Seal v Chief Constable of South Wales Police* [2007] UKHL 31; [2007] 1 W.L.R. 1910, quoted at para.4–195, below.

[632] [2011] EWCA Civ 4; [2011] 1 W.L.R. 2873.

[633] Applying *Re S-C (Mental Patient: Habeas Corpus)* [1996] Q.B. 599. Toulson LJ commented that "in matters affecting individual liberty the law is strictly applied" ([2011] EWCA Civ 4; [2011] 1 W.L.R. 2873 at [100]), and described the defendant local authority's argument that the lawfulness of the hospital's detention of the claimant rendered the original application lawful as "a back to front argument, reminiscent of the world of Alice Through The Looking-glass" ([2011] EWCA Civ 4; [2011] 1 W.L.R. 2873 at [62]).

[634] [2011] EWCA Civ 4; [2011] 1 W.L.R. 2873 at [66].

It followed that the claimant was unlawfully detained, both as a matter of domestic law and under art.5, as a result of the AMHP's contravention of s.11(4), and the claimant would be given leave under s.139(2) to pursue a claim for compensation against the local authority. Although this avoided a declaration of incompatibility by the Court of Appeal, the implication is that in any case where the defendant's conduct amounts to a breach of art.5 (and most cases of unlawful detention in breach of the procedural requirements of the Mental Health Act will do so) s.139 will probably not provide a defence.[635]

(ii)   Requirement for leave

4–195   **Leave to bring proceedings required**   In addition to the defence under s.139(1), s.139(2) provides that civil proceedings may not be instituted in respect of an act purporting to be done under the mental health legislation without leave of the High Court. In *Seal v Chief Constable of South Wales Police*,[636] by a three to two majority, the House of Lords held that the failure to obtain leave of the High Court under s.139(2) renders the proceedings a nullity, it is not merely a procedural error that the court can rectify. The effect of this is that a claimant has to issue fresh proceedings and then seek leave. In most cases this will not be a problem, but it becomes a significant issue where, as in *Seal*, the proceedings were issued within the limitation period but by the time the error in not applying for leave had been discovered the limitation period had expired. Claimants making claims in respect of personal injuries after the three-year limitation period has expired can issue proceedings and request that the court exercise its discretion under the Limitation Act 1980 s.33 to allow the action to proceed.[637] The application for leave under the Mental Health Act 1983 s.139(2) could be made at the same time. So, claims in negligence or claims in trespass to the person based on lack of the patient's consent, will not necessarily be barred if the claimant has failed to apply for leave under s.139(2), provided they involve personal injuries. But an action based on false imprisonment not involving any personal injury to the claimant will be governed by s.2 of the Limitation Act 1980, with a six-year limitation period and no discretion to extend time. Many of the claims brought in relation to detention under the Mental Health Act 1983 will be for false imprisonment (as was Mr Seal's claim), so unless the claimant can point to some personal injury as a consequence of the detention (psychiatric harm, for example) someone in the position of Mr Seal will still be caught by the interaction of s.139(2) and the Limitation Act 1980 s.2. In strongly worded

---

[635] Although there was no declaration of incompatibility in *TTM v Hackney LBC*, and it remains open to a defendant to rely on s.139(1), the same arguments would no doubt be raised. If s.139 is to be read so as to be compatible with Convention rights then acting in good faith or exercising reasonable care when applying to detain a patient will not excuse a failure to comply with the strict requirements of the Mental Health Act 1983 because "the liberty of the subject is at stake in a case of this kind, and that liberty may be violated only to the extent permitted by law and not otherwise": per Toulson LJ, [2011] EWCA Civ 4; [2011] 1 W.L.R. 2873 at [41], citing Sir Thomas Bingham MR in *Re S-C (Mental Patient: Habeas Corpus)* [1996] Q.B. 599 at 603.
[636] [2007] UKHL 31; [2007] 1 W.L.R. 1910.
[637] See paras 11–121 et seq. This would apply to an action in trespass to the person, as well as negligence, where the claimant has sustained personal injury, in light of the decision of the House of Lords in *A v Hoare* [2008] UKHL 6; [2008] 1 A.C. 844.

speeches, both Lord Woolf and Baroness Hale dissented in *Seal*. Baroness Hale went so far as to suggest that a rule producing the result that claimants who have suffered a wrong were deprived of their remedy merely because of a procedural failure which no-one noticed at the time was "an affront to justice".[638] Defendants, she said, "deserve protection from vexatious claims. They do not deserve protection from meritorious claims" and if that was Parliament's intention it was "an irrational and disproportionate interference in the Convention right to access to justice".[639]

Detained patients and informal patients   The long-established view was that the requirement for leave applies only to patients who are formally detained under the Act; voluntary patients need not seek leave to bring an action.[640] On the other hand, it is clear that s.139(1) covers acts *"purporting* to be done in pursuance of this Act" so that if a doctor bona fide and reasonably believed that an informal patient was in fact detained, it would seem that s.139(1) would apply. It is not apparent, then, why s.139(2) would not also apply to the informal patient since that subsection requires leave of the High Court for any civil proceedings "in respect of any such act", i.e. the act purporting to be done referred to in s.139(1). In *Labrooy v Hammersmith and Fulham London Borough Council*[641] Cox J held that s.139 is not limited to patients who have been formally detained under the Mental Health Act but can also apply to informal patients. Cox J relied on the decision of the House of Lords in *Pountney v Griffiths*[642] to the effect that s.141 of the Mental Health Act 1959 applied:

4–196

> "...to any act, provided it has been carried out in purported pursuance of the Act, and that its scope is not limited to acts done or purported to be done in pursuance of functions specifically provided for in the terms of the Act itself."

The issue in *Pountney*, however, was not whether the protection of s.141 extended to a patient who had *not* been detained under the Mental Health Act (the patient had been compulsorily detained in Broadmoor special hospital). Rather, *Pountney* held that s.141 was not limited to the protection of individuals who signed certificates, made orders for detention and disposed of the property of patients under the Act, but also covered acts done by staff in special hospitals in discharging their day-to-day duties in the control, or the purported control, of the

---

[638] [2007] UKHL 31; [2007] 1 W.L.R. 1910 at [53].
[639] [2007] UKHL 31; [2007] 1 W.L.R. 1910 at [61]; cf. Lord Bingham, at [20], rejecting the argument that s.139(2) infringes a claimant's art.6 right of access to the court (relying on *Ashingdane v United Kingdom* (1985) 7 E.H.R.R. 528). The European Court of Human Rights agreed that s.139(2) does not contravene art.6: *Seal v UK* (50330/07) (2012) 54 E.H.R.R. 6; [2011] M.H.L.R. 1. The general aim of protecting those exercising powers under the Mental Health Act 1983 from vexatious claims was a legitimate aim, and striking out the claimant's action was not disproportionate in the circumstances, given that the claimant had delayed bringing an action and the failure to obtain leave under s.139(2) was the claimant's fault and that of his solicitors.
[640] *R. v Runighian* [1977] Crim. L.R. 361 where it was held that acts done to an informal patient are not done in pursuance of the Mental Health Act. This case is concerned with the earlier provision requiring leave, s.141 of the Mental Health Act 1959, but the differences in the wording of the section do not affect the point.
[641] [2006] EWHC 1976 (QB); [2006] M.H.L.R. 253 at [15].
[642] [1976] A.C. 314.

patients. This is not authority for the proposition that what is now s.139 of the Mental Health Act 1983 applies to *any* conduct in relation to voluntary mental health patients.[643] Acts which are *purportedly* done under the provisions of the Mental Health Act 1983 to an informal patient would be covered, but there should at least be an onus upon defendants seeking to rely on s.139 to identify which provisions of the Act they were purportedly relying on when performing the acts in question. Most things done to an informal patient would not normally involve any reliance on the Act, but on the patient's voluntary consent, and therefore there should be no requirement for leave under s.139(2) before an informal patient could bring an action based on such acts.

4–197   **Leave not required for claims against institutional defendants**   Section 139(4) of the Mental Health Act 1983 provides that s.139 does not apply to certain institutional defendants[644] so that not only does the defence in s.139(1) not apply, the requirement to obtain leave under s.139(2) before commencing proceedings also does not apply to these defendants.[645] But in *C v South London and Maudsley Hospital NHS Trust*[646] McCombe J held that, having refused to grant leave under s.139(2) to bring proceedings against the individual doctors, the proceedings against the defendant NHS Trust would be bound to fail if begun, for the same reasons as given under s.139(2), and therefore it was inevitable that they would either be struck out under the court's case management powers (Civil Procedure Rules 1998 Pt 3) or judgment would be given in favour of the defendants on the basis that the claim had no real prospect of succeeding. In practice this would seem to undermine the effect of s.139(4), if whenever leave to bring a claim against individuals is refused under s.139(2) it is probable that other procedural rules will be applied to strike out the claim against the institutional defendants.

4–198   Moreover, it had been thought that one consequence of s.139(4) was that, irrespective of the substantive defence provided to an individual doctor by s.139(1), the hospital employing that doctor would be vicariously liable for his actions (e.g. in the tort of battery) even if the doctor was held not liable because he acted in good faith and with reasonable care.[647] But in *R. (on the application of W) v Broadmoor Hospital*[648] Hale LJ suggested that a health authority or NHS Trust could only be held vicariously liable for the actions for which the individual doctors would themselves be liable, which would indirectly confer the benefit of s.139(1) on the employers. Brooke LJ[649] even suggested, provisionally, that a hospital may not be vicariously liable at all for the actions a responsible medical officer (RMO) in making treatment decisions under ss.57 or 58 of the Mental Health Act, on the basis that the Act vests the duty to carry out the specified

---

[643] *R. v Runighian* [1977] Crim. L.R. 361 was not cited in *Labrooy*.

[644] See para.4–192, n.626 above for the list of defendants.

[645] Accordingly, it did not apply to the Mental Health Act Commission, which was a special health authority: *X v A, B and C and the Mental Health Act Commission* (1991) 9 B.M.L.R. 91, 97, QBD.

[646] [2001] M.H.L.R. 269.

[647] See *R. (on the application of W) v Broadmoor Hospital* [2001] EWCA Civ 1545; [2002] 1 W.L.R. 419 at [24] per Simon Brown LJ and [58] per Hale LJ.

[648] [2001] EWCA Civ 1545; [2002] 1 W.L.R. 419 at [58] per Hale LJ.

[649] [2001] EWCA Civ 1545; [2002] 1 W.L.R. 419 at [42] and [43].

functions in the RMO personally.[650] It was not the hospital, through the agency of one of its medical staff, in whom was vested the power to direct treatment without consent, but the RMO himself.

The test for granting leave   Under s.141 of the Mental Health Act 1959 the court could not grant leave unless it was:

> "...satisfied that there is a substantial ground for the contention that the person to be proceeded against has acted in bad faith or without reasonable care."[651]

4–199

The requirement that there be a "substantial ground" was omitted from s.139 of the Mental Health Act 1983.[652] In *Winch v Jones*[653] the Court of Appeal accepted that this was intended to be a change of substance, reducing the protection given to persons purporting to act under the legislation. Otton J had held that although the claimant's application was neither frivolous nor vexatious, nor an abuse of the process of the court, he should not grant leave under s.139 unless there was a prima facie case of negligence against the defendant. The Court of Appeal, allowing the claimant's appeal, rejected this approach because it would lead to a full dress-rehearsal of the action which is inappropriate to an application for leave to commence proceedings, and at that stage an applicant who has a reasonable suspicion that there has been negligence may be quite unable to put forward a prima facie case before disclosure. Sir John Donaldson MR said that s.139 is sui generis and the question that has to be resolved is whether on the materials immediately available to the court:

> "...the applicant's complaint appears to be such that it deserves the fuller investigation which will be possible if the intended applicant is allowed to proceed."[654]

Parker LJ took the view that if an action is neither frivolous nor vexatious it is prima facie fit to be tried, and if it is fit to be tried leave ought to be given. The purpose of the section, said his Lordship, was to prevent harassment by clearly hopeless actions, it was not to see that only those actions which could be seen to be likely to succeed should go ahead. Defendants would still have some

---

[650] For consideration of ss.57 and 58 see paras 6–087 to 6–088.

[651] "Hesitancy in accepting medical opinions, particularly in the difficult discipline of psychiatry and in relation to the controversial subject of psychopathy, provides no evidence of bad faith", per Lawton LJ in *Kynaston v Secretary of State for Home Affairs* (1981) 73 Cr. App. R. 281 at 285 (a decision on s.141(2) of the Mental Health Act 1959).

[652] Mental Health Act 1959 s.141(2) having been repealed and replaced by the Mental Health (Amendment) Act 1982 s.60, now consolidated in the Mental Health Act 1983 s.139.

[653] [1986] Q.B. 296.

[654] [1986] Q.B. 296 at 305. It is arguably inappropriate to invoke the *Bolam* test when considering whether to grant leave to proceed, because this could involve adjudicating on the merits in advance, before all the evidence has been considered and before matters which arguably require investigation have been resolved: *O'Neill v Morrison* unreported 26 May 1993, CA, per Hirst LJ.

protection under the section, however, in comparison to the procedure for striking out frivolous and vexatious claims, because the claimant has to take the initiative by obtaining leave.[655]

4–200   In *James v London Borough of Havering*,[656] however, Farquharson LJ distinguished *Winch v Jones* and refused the applicant leave under s.139(2) because it was "virtually unarguable" to say that the doctor and the social worker concerned in an emergency compulsory admission for assessment could have acted without reasonable care. On the facts, there were ample grounds for them to take the course that they did, and even if they were wrong an action by the applicant would be bound to fail. His Lordship commented that:

> "What one has to look at in deciding whether they are entitled to the protection of section 139 is what appeared to the social worker and the doctor at the time and how they reacted to it. When one discovers that, to the extent which it is agreed, one decides whether there is a prima facie case of their acting without reasonable care."[657]

4–201   This would appear to be inconsistent with the views expressed by the Court of Appeal in *Winch v Jones*, in that it requires the claimant to establish a prima facie case on the application for leave. Indeed, Farquharson LJ disagreed with the approach of Sir John Donaldson MR, on the ground that the object of s.139 was to protect a social worker or doctor from the consequences of a wrong decision made in purported compliance with the Mental Health Act, particularly in circumstances where decisions have to be made quickly for the safety of the patient or others:

> "Section 139 ... is designed to protect a witness making that decision, provided they act in good faith and with reasonable care. To that extent it seems to me that the section goes beyond the effect referred to by Sir John Donaldson M.R. in *Winch v Jones* ... It is not only protection against frivolous claims; it is also a protection from error in the circumstances set out in the subsection."[658]

With great respect, it is not clear why social workers or doctors need this particular "protection from error" when it is well established that the tort of negligence does not condemn reasonable errors, particularly those made in an emergency, as carelessness for which a defendant should be held liable. Requiring a claimant to establish a prima facie case, before discovery, and in circumstances where facts are in dispute (which was the case in *James v London Borough of Havering*) arguably sets the procedural hurdle for claimants too high, a point that had been accepted in *Winch v Jones*.[659] In *Seal v Chief Constable of*

---

[655] The fact that an application for leave under s.139(2) has been successful does not preclude a judge from subsequently concluding, following further investigation, that the action should be struck out as disclosing no reasonable cause of action: *X v A, B and C and the Mental Health Act Commission* (1991) 9 B.M.L.R. 91, QBD.

[656] (1992) 15 B.M.L.R. 1.

[657] (1992) 15 B.M.L.R. 1 at 4.

[658] (1992) 15 B.M.L.R. 1 at 4.

[659] Since the decision in *James v London Borough of Havering* was of a single judge of the Court of Appeal, on an application for leave to appeal, and the decision in *Winch v Jones* was of a two judge Court on a full appeal, it is the latter which should be preferred.

South Wales Police[660] obiter comments in the House of Lords seem to have approved the standard set by the Court of Appeal in *Winch v Jones* for obtaining leave under s.139(2). Lord Bingham said that "an applicant with an arguable case will be granted leave"[661] and Lord Brown said that: "... the test now is simply whether the case deserves further investigation by the court".[662] In *Johnston v Chief Constable of Merseyside*[663] Coulson J said that it would be wrong to modify in any significant way the test propounded by Sir John Donaldson MR in *Winch v Jones*, first because it had been expressly approved by Lord Bingham in *Seal*,[664] and secondly because the test remained the correct and fair approach to s.139(2) applications. However, his Lordship suggested that the test should be modified to take account of CPR Pt 24 (allowing claims to go to trial only where they have a real prospect of success). Thus, on an application under s.139(2) it was also necessary for the court to ask whether or not the proposed claim has a real prospect of success.[665] In *DD v Durham CC*[666] the Court of Appeal stated that "the threshold under s.139 is a low one".

In *C v South London and Maudsley Hospital NHS Trust*[667] McCombe J refused leave under s.139(2) where the claimant argued that the doctors had used the procedure for compulsory admission for assessment (under s.2) in order to avoid the statutory requirements associated with compulsory admission for treatment (under s.3) because it was known that the claimant's mother objected. There was no reason why doctors could not reasonably and in good faith take the view that the grounds for admission under s.2 were met, even if they thought that in the end a s.3 admission for a longer period would almost inevitably follow. The decision to admit under s.2 was taken on the day the claimant was admitted, on the basis of his condition on that day. His Lordship added that, when considering the question of granting leave under s.139(2), the question of the overriding objective under the Civil Procedure Rules has no application. That concept directs how decisions to be taken under the Rules are to be approached, but the Civil Procedure Rules did not direct how a discretion arising under an entirely different statute was to be exercised.

4–202

---

[660] [2007] UKHL 31; [2007] 1 W.L.R. 1910.

[661] [2007] UKHL 31; [2007] 1 W.L.R. 1910 at [20].

[662] [2007] UKHL 31; [2007] 1 W.L.R. 1910 at [70]. See also per Baroness Hale at [47]. In *Labrooy v Hammersmith and Fulham London Borough Council* [2006] EWHC 1976 (QB); [2006] M.H.L.R. 253 (a case which pre-dated the decision of the House of Lords in *Seal v Chief Constable of South Wales Police*) Cox J, at [21], said that a claim did not "merit fuller investigation" if it could be said that it had "no reasonable prospect of success".

[663] [2009] EWHC 2969 (QB); [2009] M.H.L.R. 343 at [12].

[664] Though note that in *TW v Enfield LBC* [2014] EWCA Civ 362; [2014] 1 W.L.R. 3665 at [33] Aikens LJ commented that: "There might be argument on whether the expressions of Lord Donaldson and Lord Bingham import different tests."

[665] On the evidence available Coulson J concluded that the proposed claim satisfied the threshold test: it was not frivolous, vexatious or an abuse and had a real prospect of success. One factor in that assessment was that there was legitimate debate about whether the defendant police officer had even mentioned s.136 of the Mental Health Act 1983 under which he purported to have acted when restraining the claimant and spraying him with CS gas.

[666] [2013] EWCA Civ 96; [2013] M.H.L.R. 85 at [23], citing *Winch v Jones* [1986] Q.B. 296 and *Johnston v Chief Constable of Merseyside Police* [2009] EWHC 2969 (QB); [2009] M.H.L.R. 343.

[667] [2001] M.H.L.R. 269, QBD.

CHAPTER 5

CAUSATION AND REMOTENESS OF DAMAGE

In the tort of negligence damage is the gist of the action. If claimants cannot show that they sustained injury as a result of the defendant's breach of duty, there is no tort and the action fails.[1] In contract a claimant who proves that the defendant was in breach of contract is entitled to nominal damages, but, again, will not be awarded substantial damages unless a causal link between the breach and the loss can be established. A similar principle applies to a claim in battery, which, as an action in trespass to the person, is actionable per se.[2]

5–001

This chapter is divided into three main sections: causation in fact; causation in law; and remoteness of damage. Factual causation is concerned with the physical connection between the defendant's negligence and the claimant's damage. No matter how egregious the defendant's negligence he is not liable if, as a question of fact, his conduct did not cause the damage. Thus, there must be a causal link between the defendant's breach of duty and the damage sustained by the claimant.[3] This is essentially an explanatory inquiry: how, in fact, did the damage occur? In medical malpractice litigation this issue is largely a matter of medical and scientific evidence, for example, about the pathology of a particular disease and the prospects for successful treatment with proper care. The question is normally dealt with by the "but for" test. In some instances there may be several causal factors involved and the precise aetiology may be unknown. This can leave a claimant with virtually insuperable difficulties of proof. Much of the modern case law is concerned with the extent to which it is acceptable to adopt exceptions to the basic "but for" test in order to address the perceived unfairness of placing the burden of causal uncertainty on the claimant.

5–002

Even where the claimant has overcome the problem of proving factual causation, so that it can be said that the defendant's negligence is *a* cause of the damage,

5–003

---

[1] *Rothwell v Chemical & Insulating Co Ltd* [2007] UKHL 39; [2008] 1 A.C. 281; *Saunderson v Sonae Industria (UK) Ltd* [2015] EWHC 2264 (QB) at [179] per Jay J: "A transient, trifling, self-limiting, reversible reaction to an irritant is not 'actionable injury' for the purposes of the law of tort." In *Carder v Secretary of State for Health* [2016] EWCA Civ 790; [2017] I.C.R. 392 at [22] Lord Dyson MR said that it was unprofitable to use words such as "disease", "impairment", "injury", or "disability": "the use of labels to describe a medical condition may be convenient; but it must not distract attention from the only relevant question, namely whether the claimant is materially worse off as a result of the alleged tort, i.e. whether he has suffered damage."
[2] *Allan v New Mount Sinai Hospital* (1980) 109 D.L.R. (3d) 634 at 643, Ont HC. For discussion of causation in the context of battery see para.7–081.
[3] See, generally, Hart and Honoré, *Causation in the Law*, 2nd edn (Oxford: Oxford University Press, 1985); Green, *Causation in Negligence* (Oxford: Hart Publishing, 2015); Steel, *Proof of Causation in Tort Law* (Cambridge: Cambridge University Press, 2015).

there are some situations where there were other events that could have been sufficient to cause the damage or the defendant's negligence may form part of a sequence of events which led to the claimant's injury. The court has to choose whether to allocate causal responsibility to the defendant's breach of duty or to the other cause, which may be treated as a supervening event or an intervening act which "breaks the chain of causation". This type of causation problem is categorised as causation in law.

5–004   Remoteness of damage is concerned with those situations where the defendant has undoubtedly caused the claimant's loss, but the damage is not of the same type as would normally be anticipated in similar circumstances, or the damage occurred in an unusual manner. There has to be some limit, it is said, to a defendant's responsibility and it is considered to be unfair to hold people liable for all the consequences of their negligence, however bizarre or freakish those consequences might be.[4] In practice, while proof of factual causation can be a very real problem, questions of remoteness of damage are comparatively rare in medical negligence actions.

1.   CAUSATION IN FACT

(a)   The "but for" test

5–005   If damage to the claimant would not have occurred "but for" the defendant's negligence then the negligence is *a* cause of the damage. It is not necessarily *the* cause because there may well be other events which are causally relevant. Putting this another way, if the loss would have occurred in any event, the defendant's conduct is not a cause. Two cases, both involving medical negligence, illustrate this point. In *Barnett v Chelsea and Kensington Hospital Management Committee*[5] three nightwatchmen attended hospital, clearly appearing ill, and they informed a nurse that they had been vomiting. The nurse telephoned the casualty officer, who did not see the men, but said that they should go home and see their own doctors. They left, and about five hours later one of the men died from arsenic poisoning. Nield J held that in these circumstances the casualty

---

[4] The term "remoteness" is also sometimes used to describe a causation problem, rather than being confined to setting the limits of actionability for damage which was clearly caused by the defendant's negligence. Where there has been an intervening event, for example, and the question is whether the defendant's negligence can still be treated as a cause of the claimant's loss, the damage may be described as "too remote". This is simply a way of saying that the defendant's conduct was not a cause in law of the damage.

[5] [1968] 1 All E.R. 1068. In *Kerry v England* [1898] A.C. 742, PC, the defendants' negligence accelerated the death of the patient, "but not to any appreciable extent". It was held, in effect, that there was no causal connection because it was within the principle de minimis non curat lex; *Davies v Countess of Chester Hospital NHS Foundation Trust* [2014] EWHC 4294 (QB); [2015] Med. L.R. 141 where a patient with ventricular tachycardia was given an overdose of magnesium and immediately suffered a fatal cardiac arrest, but the patient's condition was such that he would probably "not have survived for any significant time" in any event; *Stamos v Davies* (1985) 21 D.L.R. (4th) 507, Ont HC, where the defendant failed to tell the claimant that during the course of performing a lung biopsy the claimant's spleen had been punctured. The failure to be candid was held to be a breach of duty, but there was no causal connection between the breach and the damage, namely the loss of the spleen, because the spleen "was doomed from the moment it was injured".

officer was negligent in failing to have seen and examined the deceased. It could not be said, however, that but for the doctor's negligence the deceased would have lived, because the medical evidence indicated that even if the patient had received prompt treatment it would not have been possible to diagnose the condition and administer an antidote in time to save him. Thus, the negligence did not cause the death.

Similarly, in *Robinson v Post Office*[6] a doctor was found to have been negligent in the manner in which he administered a test dose to test for an allergic reaction to an anti-tetanus vaccination. He waited only a minute after giving the test before giving the patient the injection, although the standard procedure at the time was to wait half an hour. Nine days after being injected with the vaccine the claimant suffered a serious allergic reaction to the vaccine, which caused encephalitis and brain damage. The Court of Appeal held that the failure to administer a proper test was not causally related to the claimant's damage, because the test was not, in any event, a complete guarantee against a subsequent reaction, and the circumstances of the claimant's reaction were such that a test involving a delay of half an hour would probably not have produced a reaction in time to alert the doctor to the danger.

5–006

Where the defendant has made an error in diagnosis, but the correct diagnosis would not have produced any difference in the treatment or management of the patient, the error has not caused any damage for which the defendant is responsible, even if he was negligent.[7]

5–007

(i) Where causation depends on hypothetical human conduct

In many cases, though not all, it may be easier to determine what would have happened in the absence of negligence by the defendant where events depend upon physical reactions which are amenable to objective scientific proof. Where the question depends upon how a person would have behaved the issue is to some extent more speculative, but this will not prevent the court from drawing an inference of fact. In *McWilliams v Sir William Arroll & Co. Ltd*,[8] for example, a steel erector who was not wearing a safety belt fell to his death. His employers were in breach of a duty to supply a safety belt for his use, but the deceased had rarely, if ever, used a belt in the past, and the natural inference, said the House of

5–008

---

[6] [1974] 2 All E.R. 737.
[7] *Fish v Kapur* [1948] 2 All E.R. 176 at 178, where a dentist who failed to diagnose a patient's broken jaw was not liable because there was no treatment that could have been given in the circumstances, and thus the claimant did not suffer any additional pain or discomfort as a result of the failure to diagnose the fracture. See also *Stockdale v Nicholls* [1993] 4 Med. L.R. 190, where the admission of a baby to hospital three hours earlier than she was in fact admitted would not have changed the observation or treatment that she received, or resulted in a diagnosis of septicaemia any earlier; *Stacey v Chiddy* [1993] 4 Med. L.R. 345, NSWCA, where the negligent failure to examine the patient did not cause her diminished life expectancy from contracting breast cancer, since on the balance of probabilities the abnormalities in the claimant's breast were not at that time malignant. Note, however, that even where a delayed diagnosis does not result in any different treatment for the patient's physical problems the negligent defendant may be responsible for the patient's psychiatric condition if that is attributable to the delayed diagnosis: *Scaddon v Morgan* [2017] EWHC 1481 (QB).
[8] [1962] 1 W.L.R. 295.

Lords, was that he would not have used one on this occasion if it had been available. Thus, the breach of duty did not cause the death which would have occurred in any event.

5–009   **Claimant's hypothetical conduct**   This type of causation problem arises in a medical context whenever claimants allege that but for the doctor's negligence they would have opted for an alternative course of treatment. Where, for example, the claimant alleges that he was not properly informed about the risks of the treatment he has received and/or of the alternatives, he still has to show that had he been given the information he would not have accepted the treatment which he received. This may be difficult for the claimant to establish because the courts are wary of disappointed patients forming judgments about what they would have done with the benefit of hindsight.[9] Similarly, where the claimant alleges that the defendants negligently failed to communicate to her the test results following an amniocentesis test during her pregnancy, she must prove to the satisfaction of the court that, had she been informed that the test indicated that the foetus would be handicapped, she would have undergone an abortion.[10]

5–010   **Negligent omissions**   This issue is not limited to circumstances where the question is what the claimant would have done, but for the breach of duty. In the case of a negligent omission the outcome may turn upon the answer to the hypothetical question of what the defendant would have done or what a third party would have done, but for the breach of duty. Where the issue turns upon what the defendant would have done the approach to causation is the same: the claimant must still prove that but for the negligence the damage would not have occurred. Where, however, the outcome depends upon what a third party would have done in hypothetical circumstances the correct approach is to assess the value of the chance of benefit (or avoiding a detriment) that the claimant has lost.[11]

5–011   **Defendant's hypothetical conduct**   In *Bolitho v City and Hackney Health Authority*[12] a two-year-old boy suffered brain damage as a result of cardiac arrest caused by an obstruction of the bronchial air passages. The claimant was in hospital at the time for the treatment of croup. The defendants admitted that there

---

[9] *Chatterton v Gerson* [1981] Q.B. 432 at 445; *Hills v Potter* [1983] 3 All E.R. 716; see further para.7–090.

[10] See *Gregory v Pembrokeshire Health Authority* [1989] 1 Med. L.R. 81, CA, where the claimant's action failed on this ground. The test had failed to produce a result, and so the claimant had to show both that if she had known about this she would have insisted on a further test, and that if that test were positive she would have had the abortion. The difficulties inherent in this exercise in speculation about hypothetical events were highlighted by Nicholls LJ, who commented that: "this unhappy case turns on Mrs Gregory's hypothetical response to Mr. Davies's hypothetical advice given at a hypothetical consultation." See also *Arndt v Smith* [1994] 8 W.W.R. 568, BCSC; aff'd (1997) 148 D.L.R. (4th) 48, SCC, where the mother was not warned about the most serious, though most remote, risks to the foetus of exposure to chickenpox, but the fact that the parents did not want an ultrasound scan of the developing foetus indicated "less concern with risks in foresight than in hindsight"; Honoré (1998) 114 L.Q.R. 52.

[11] See *Allied Maples Group Ltd v Simmons & Simmons* [1995] 1 W.L.R. 1602, discussed below at para.5–108.

[12] [1993] 4 Med. L.R. 381; [1993] P.I.Q.R. P334, CA; [1998] A.C. 232, HL.

[512]

had been negligence, in that a doctor had not attended to the claimant in response to calls for assistance by nursing staff following two earlier episodes of respiratory failure. It was common ground that had the claimant been seen by a doctor and intubated, thus clearing the obstruction, the tragedy could have been avoided. There were two schools of thought, however, as to whether in the claimant's circumstances it was appropriate to intubate. The doctor who failed to attend said that had she attended the claimant she would not have intubated, and therefore the cardiac arrest and subsequent brain damage would have occurred in any event.[13] There was evidence that a responsible body of professional opinion would have supported a decision not to intubate, although five medical experts for the claimant said that he should have been intubated, and it was agreed that this was the only course of action that would have prevented the damage. A majority of the Court of Appeal held that the action failed on the ground of causation. In a case of breach of duty by omission it was necessary to decide what course of events would have followed had the defendant's duty been discharged. Whether the doctor's failure to appear would have made any difference in the event depended upon what she would have done had she been present. The claimant had to prove that she would probably have intubated, and that if she did not do so her failure to do so was contrary to accepted medical practice.[14]

On appeal to the House of Lords[15] it was argued on behalf of the claimant that the *Bolam* test had no relevance in determining questions of causation. Lord Browne-Wilkinson agreed that, as a general proposition, that was correct. In all cases the primary question is one of fact: did the wrongful act cause the injury? But in cases where the breach of duty consists of an omission to do an act which ought to have been done (such as the failure of a doctor to attend the patient) the factual enquiry is necessarily hypothetical. The question is what would have happened if an event, which by definition did not occur, had occurred? The first question is: what would have happened—either the doctor would have intubated, had she attended, or she would not. The *Bolam* test was not, and could not, be relevant to that question. The defendant doctor said that she would not have intubated, and therefore the claimant would in any event have sustained the brain damage. But she could not escape liability by proving that she would have failed to act as any reasonably competent doctor would have acted in the circumstances:

5–012

> "A defendant cannot escape liability by saying that the damage would have occurred in any event because he would have committed some other breach of duty thereafter."[16]

---

[13] Although as Simon Brown LJ pointed out in his dissenting judgment in the Court of Appeal, [1993] 4 Med. L.R. 381 at 388: "... it would seem to me unsatisfactory to place much reliance upon any doctor's evidence in these circumstances as to what he or she would have done had they complied with their duty to attend (or arranged for someone else to attend) a patient. Inevitably, if unconsciously, any doctor would in that situation tend to believe and suggest that their attendance could and would have made no difference."

[14] [1993] 4 Med. L.R. 381 at 386, per Farquharson LJ.

[15] [1998] A.C. 232.

[16] [1998] A.C. 232 at 240. See *Wright (A Child) v Cambridge Medical Group* [2011] EWCA Civ 669; [2013] Q.B. 312 at [56]–[61] per Lord Neuberger MR for discussion of the underlying rationale for this proposition. See para.5–146. Similarly, defendants cannot rely on a wrong which they have committed in order to reduce the damages that would otherwise flow from a tort or breach of contract.

5–013 Lord Browne-Wilkinson adopted the reasoning of Hobhouse LJ in *Joyce v Merton, Sutton and Wandsworth Health Authority*[17] in explaining the majority decision of the Court of Appeal in *Bolitho*. In *Joyce* the claimant underwent an operative procedure which resulted in a partially occluded artery, leading three months later to an upper brain stem infarction causing almost total paralysis. Although the procedure was not necessarily negligent, the immediate follow-up care that the claimant had received was negligent, in that he was discharged from hospital without proper instructions and advice. It was accepted that the only thing that could have prevented the damage was if within the first 48 hours the claimant had been seen by a vascular surgeon and the surgeon had decided to operate to deal with the occlusion. The Court of Appeal held that to succeed on causation the claimant had to prove either that had the vascular surgeon at the hospital been summoned he would in fact have re-operated or that it would have been negligent for him not to do so. Hobhouse LJ said that where the negligence consisted of an act which is alleged to have had physical consequences, the question to be asked is straightforward even though its answer may not be: was the act a cause of the injury? Where the negligence consists of an omission, or an act which does not in itself have physical consequences, identifying the correct question is less easy. These cases could be further subdivided into cases where the question is what steps would have been taken if proper care had been taken and cases where the question is what would have been the outcome of any further steps that ought to have been taken. In *Joyce* the facts fell into the first of these categories, which was the same type of question that *Bolitho* raised. Hobhouse LJ summarised the position in the following terms:

> "Thus a plaintiff can discharge the burden of proof on causation by satisfying the court *either* that the relevant person would in fact have taken the requisite action (although she would not have been at fault if she had not) *or* that the proper discharge of the relevant person's duty towards the plaintiff required that she take that action. The former alternative calls for no explanation since it is simply the factual proof of the causative effect of the original fault. The latter is slightly more sophisticated: it involves the factual situation that the original fault did not itself cause the injury but that this was because there would have been some further fault on the part of the defendants; the plaintiff proves his case by proving that his injuries would have been avoided if proper care had continued to be taken … Properly viewed, therefore, this rule is favourable to a plaintiff because it gives him two routes by which he may prove his case—either proof that the exercise of proper care would have necessitated the relevant result, or proof that if proper care had been exercised it would in fact have led to the relevant result."[18]

5–014 In *Bolitho* Lord Browne-Wilkinson, having cited Hobhouse LJ, concluded that there were two questions for the judge to decide on causation: (1) what would the doctor have done, or authorised to be done, if she had attended the claimant? and

---

This stems from a principle of public policy that a person should not be entitled to rely on their own wrong in order to secure a benefit: *Normans Bay Ltd v Coudert Brothers* [2004] EWCA Civ 215; *The Times*, 24 March 2004 at [46] per Waller LJ.

[17] [1996] P.I.Q.R. P121; [1996] 7 Med. L.R. 1.

[18] [1996] P.I.Q.R. P121 at 152, original emphasis. See also *S (A Minor) v North Birmingham Health Authority* (1998) 40 B.M.L.R. 103, CA, where it was held that a senior house officer was negligent in failing to consult a senior registrar about a patient's deteriorating condition, but that even if the senior registrar been notified about the deterioration sooner he would not have arranged a transfer to the intensive therapy unit at that time, and this would not have been negligent.

(2) if she would not have intubated, would that have been negligent? The *Bolam* test had no relevance to first question but was central to the second. Another way of putting this is to say that causation is about *what in fact happened*, which in turn depends upon the hypothetical question of what would have happened had there been no negligence ("but for" the negligence would the damage have occurred?). In *Bolitho* the claim was that had the doctor not been negligent and attended he would not have suffered brain damage, because the doctor would have intervened to prevent it. The doctor denied that she would have intervened, so that the damage would have occurred in any event (no "but for" causation). The claimant alleged that a hypothetical failure to intervene would itself have been negligent, and a defendant cannot avoid a finding of causation by arguing that, in the hypothetical situation being considered, she would have acted negligently. The defendant then replies that a failure to intervene would not have been negligent because it was supported by a responsible body of professional opinion. Thus, in these circumstances the causation issue *appears* to turn on a question of negligence and the *Bolam* test. In reality *Bolitho* is about whether the failure to intubate, for whatever reason (non-attendance or conscious professional judgment), was negligent. The defendant's evidence that she would not have intubated simply moved the focus of the argument about negligence, i.e. breach of duty, from the non-attendance to the non-intubation.

(ii)   Weighing the effect of multiple hypothetical events

In some cases involving a negligent omission, there may be more than one hypothetical event that would have had to have occurred in order to avoid harm to the claimant. A question then arises as to what weight is to be attached to the cumulative probabilities of these hypothetical events. In *Bright v Barnsley District General Hospital NHS Trust*[19] the issue was whether a negligent omission to carry out an ultrasound scan on a foetus at 32 weeks' gestation to check on her growth caused the claimant's subsequent brain damage. The defendants argued that if the scan that was omitted at 32 weeks had been performed there was only a 60 per cent chance that it would have revealed foetal intrauterine growth retardation. If that had occurred a repeat scan would have been performed, but that had only an 80 per cent chance of showing a growth restricted foetus, and that the correct management of the pregnancy in this situation (a carefully controlled delivery at about 37 weeks' gestation with foetal monitoring and a readiness to move to a Caesarean section delivery) had only an 80 per cent chance of delivering an undamaged child. The cumulative chance of delivering an undamaged child was therefore only 38.4 per cent (i.e. 60 per cent × 80 per cent × 80 per cent), argued the defendants, and therefore causation had not been proved on the balance of probabilities. Recorder Burrell QC, sitting as a deputy judge of the High Court, rejected this argument. In deciding whether something in the past did or did not happen, the court approaches the issue on the

5–015

---

[19] [2005] Lloyd's Rep. Med. 449.

failed on causation because there was a minority of specialist units that would not have operated, and this minority view was *Bolam*-compliant (i.e. it would not have been negligent not to operate). A majority of the Court of Appeal[29] held that the judge had only addressed the second causation question set out by Lord Browne-Wilkinson in *Bolitho*, namely would the failure to intervene have been negligent? There is a prior question to be considered, namely what would probably have happened if the defendant had not been in breach of duty? If the claimant had been referred to a specialist vascular unit would the operation have been carried out? As Pill LJ commented:

> "If the answer to the question is that appropriate surgery would probably have been conducted, the second question: 'Would it have been negligent not to operate?' does not arise."[30]

Pill and Wilson LJJ accepted that the evidence that most specialist units would have operated was sufficient to establish, on the balance of probabilities, that had the claimant been referred it was probable that the surgery would have taken place. Maurice Kay LJ dissented on this point, on the basis that a claimant had to establish that she would have been referred to one of the majority specialist units which would have carried out the operation.[31] Wilson LJ considered that this placed too heavy an evidential burden on the claimant for which there was no logical justification in a case where the defendants have been found to be in breach of duty in failing to refer a patient, but had chosen to lead no evidence as to which particular specialist they would have referred the claimant to. Thus:

> "The fact established by the [claimant], namely that most specialists would be likely to have operated upon her, *prima facie* justified the conclusion that the specialist to whom the [defendants] should have referred her would be likely to have done so."[32]

If the defendants had produced evidence that, if they had not been in breach of duty, they would have referred the patient to a specialist centre that probably would not have operated, the result on causation would have been different.

5–018   However, *Gouldsmith* is not entirely analogous with *Bolitho* on the causation question. The issue in *Gouldsmith* was not "what would the *defendant* have done had she not failed to attend the patient?" but "what would the surgeon at the specialist vascular unit have done had the patient been referred?" In other words, the outcome depended upon the actions, not of the defendant, but of a third party (on the assumption that the defendant hospital and the specialist vascular unit are different entities). In such cases the usual approach is not to ask what the third party would probably have done, on the balance of probabilities, but to assess the chances that the third party would have acted in a manner that would have produced a benefit or avoided a detriment.[33]

---

[29] Pill and Wilson LJJ; Maurice Kay LJ dissenting.
[30] [2007] EWCA Civ 397; [2007] L.S. Law Med. 363 at [29].
[31] [2007] EWCA Civ 397; [2007] L.S. Law Med. 363 at [49].
[32] [2007] EWCA Civ 397; [2007] L.S. Law Med. 363 at [60].
[33] See *Allied Maples Group Ltd v Simmons & Simmons* [1995] 4 All E.R. 907; [1995] 1 W.L.R. 1602, para.5–108. *Allied Maples* was not referred to in the judgments in *Gouldsmith*.

(iv)   Limits to the "but for" test

The "but for" test operates as a preliminary filter to exclude events which did not **5–019** affect the outcome. It cannot, however, resolve all the problems of factual causation. For example, in the case of two simultaneous wrongs to the claimant, each of which would have been sufficient to cause the damage, the test produces the ludicrous conclusion that neither wrong caused the harm.[34] The only sensible solution here is to say that both caused the damage, but it should be recognised that this decision involves a policy judgment.[35] As Basten JA expressed it in the Australian case of *Elayoubi v Zipser*:

> "If the negligence of two tortfeasors each contributes to the indivisible harm suffered by the victim, each is liable for the harm suffered. If neither were negligent, no harm would have been caused. If either one were negligent and the other not, in each case the negligence would have caused the harm. But a conclusion that if both were negligent and the harm eventuated, neither was responsible for that harm, invites a question as to whether the reasoning process has gone awry. ... A normative element, requiring appropriate allocation of responsibility for tortious conduct should be accepted as part of the assessment of causal connection..."[36]

In that case, the negligence of the two defendants was not simultaneous, but a negligent error by both of them was necessary for the damage to the claimant to have occurred. In the course of giving birth to her fifth child the mother's uterus ruptured, as a result of which the baby was starved of oxygen and suffered serious disabilities. The New South Wales Court of Appeal held that a doctor's negligent failure to enquire about the mother's prior obstetric history did not break the causal link between the negligence of the mother's previous obstetricians (in failing to warn her that with any future pregnancy she should not attempt vaginal delivery) and the damage suffered by the claimant. Both defendants were responsible. Basten JA observed that:

> "On one view, the case could be analysed as involving independent acts of negligence, each of which gave rise to a risk, which risk in fact materialised."[37]

The avoidance of the risk which each act of negligence created required non-negligent conduct by both parties. The negligence of each party was a

---

[34] The classic illustration is that of two fires started simultaneously by A and B, each of which spreads to C's house. But for A's act, would the house have been destroyed? Yes, because B's fire would have destroyed it. Therefore A's fire is not a "but for" cause. But the same reasoning applies to B's fire, and therefore B's fire was not a "but for" cause. In a medical context, if a surgeon, A, made a negligent error in the operating theatre and at the same time the anaesthetist, B, made a different negligent error, and each error was itself sufficient to kill the patient, the "but for" test produces the conclusion that neither error was a cause of the patient's death. Despite A's error, the patient would still have died because B's error would have killed him. Therefore A's error is not a "but for" cause. The same reasoning applies to B's error, and thus the "but for" test produces the result that B's error was also not a "but for" cause.

[35] See e.g. *Kuwait Airways Corp v Iraq Airways Co* [2002] UKHL 19; [2002] 2 A.C. 883 at [74] where, in the context of the tort of conversion, Lord Nicholls said: "In this type of case, involving multiple wrongdoers, the court may treat wrongful conduct as having sufficient causal connection with the loss for the purpose of attracting responsibility even though the simple 'but for' test is not satisfied. In so deciding the court is primarily making a value judgment on responsibility."

[36] [2008] NSWCA 335; [2008] Aust Torts Reports 81–895 at [57].

[37] [2008] NSWCA 335; [2008] Aust Torts Reports 81–895 at [52].

contributing factor to the harm suffered and so each had materially contributed to that harm. Although this was not a case of simultaneous wrongs each of which was sufficient to cause the harm, it illustrates a court's refusal to permit defendants to rely on the "but for" test to shift responsibility to another culpable defendant.

5-020   Policy issues can also be apparent in the courts' attitude to the proof of causation. In *Cook v Lewis*,[38] for example, two people on a hunting trip simultaneously discharged their guns and the claimant was hit by one of them, but he was unable to prove which one. The Supreme Court of Canada held that in these circumstances the burden of proof was reversed, and it was for the defendants to prove that they did not cause the damage. If neither could do so then both would be liable. The defendants' combined negligence had removed the claimant's opportunity to prove which of them had shot him, and it would be unjust to deprive him of a remedy through the operation of the burden of proof. The difficulty (or impossibility) that a claimant may have in establishing "but for" causation has led the courts, in some limited instances, to develop less stringent tests for causation based on whether the defendant's breach of duty made a material contribution to the claimant's damage or (in even more limited instances) whether the breach of duty made a material contribution to the risk that the claimant would suffer damage.[39]

(v)   Human rights claims

5-021   An action for breach of a claimant's rights under the European Convention on Human Rights does not apply the same standard as a common law claim for negligence. In *Van Colle v Chief Constable of the Hertfordshire Police*,[40] where the claim was for an alleged breach of art.2, the Court of Appeal held that the test was:

> "...whether the protective measures that were reasonably open [to the defendant] *could have had a real prospect of altering the outcome* and avoiding the death."

In the House of Lords Lord Brown acknowledged that a:

> "looser approach to causation is adopted under the Convention than in English tort law. Whereas the latter requires the claimant to establish on the balance of probabilities that, but for the defendant's negligence, he would not have suffered his claimed loss... under the Convention it appears sufficient generally to establish merely that he lost a substantial chance of this."[41]

---

[38] [1952] 1 D.L.R. 1.
[39] See para.5–033 and para.5–046 respectively.
[40] [2007] EWCA Civ 325; [2007] 1 W.L.R. 1821 at [83], emphasis added.
[41] *Chief Constable of the Hertfordshire Police v Van Colle; Smith v Chief Constable of Sussex Police* [2008] UKHL 50; [2009] 1 A.C. 225 at [138]. This approach was applied in *Savage v South Essex Partnership NHS Foundation Trust* [2010] EWHC 865 (QB); [2010] P.I.Q.R. P14; [2010] Med. L.R. 292.

(b)   Proof of causation[42]

In an action for negligence it is for the claimant to prove,[43] on the balance of probabilities, that the defendant's breach of duty caused the damage. So where there are conflicting explanations for the claimant's condition, neither of which are wholly satisfactory, defendants do not have to prove that their explanation is the correct one, though failure to prove it may be a factor in deciding whether the claimant's explanation of the cause should be accepted.[44] In some instances the precise cause of the damage may be unknown, and this tends to be a particular problem with some types of medical injury, where the pathology of the patient's condition may be surrounded in mystery or be the subject of intense scientific dispute.[45]

5–022

Generic causation   If it cannot be shown, on a balance of probabilities, that the causal agent implicated is capable of causing the type of harm sustained by the claimant the claim will fail on causation. In *Kay v Ayrshire and Arran Health Board*,[46] for example, the claimant was unable to prove that an overdose of penicillin could ever cause deafness. The claimant was a child suffering from

5–023

---

[42] Many of the issues raised in the following paragraphs of this chapter (paras 5–022 to 5–130), including "loss of a chance", are considered by Lara Khoury, *Uncertain Causation in Medical Liability* (Oxford: Hart Publishing, 2006).

[43] Where the claimant has obtained a default judgment in the absence of a defence the defendant will still be entitled to contest causation in the context of an assessment of damages. The default judgment establishes that the defendant is in breach of duty and that the claimant has sustained *some* damage as a consequence, but it does not entail that a defendant has to accept that all the losses claimed by the claimant have been caused by the breach of duty: *Symes v St George's Healthcare NHS Trust* [2014] EWHC 2505 (QB); [2014] Med. L.R. 449; commented on by J. McQuater [2015] J.P.I.L. C54.

[44] *Pickford v Imperial Chemical Industries plc* [1998] 1 W.L.R. 1189, where the claimant, a secretary, alleged that cramp in her hand was a work-induced "repetitive strain injury". It was agreed that her symptoms were genuine (i.e. she was not malingering) but there was a dispute about their cause. The claimant alleged an organic, physical cause, whereas the defendant alleged that it was psychogenic, due to conversion hysteria. The House of Lords held that where a claimant alleges that her condition has a physical cause she must go on to prove, on the balance of probabilities, that her injury could be attributed to the physical origin that she alleged, which she had failed to do on the somewhat equivocal medical evidence. It was not for the defendant to prove that his explanation was the correct one. In *Lyons v Greater Manchester Strategic Health Authority* [2007] EWHC 1430 (QB), following an induced birth, the claimant was found to have suffered a cerebral deep venous thrombosis. The claimant alleged that the decision to induce the birth had been negligent and had caused the thrombosis. There were competing theories from the expert witnesses as to when the thrombosis had occurred. Those theories were genuinely held and were not unreasonable, but there was no actual evidence as to when the thrombosis occurred. Grigson J held that, given the lack of evidence as to when the claimant suffered the thrombosis, he had simply "failed to establish that his thrombosis was associated with the induction of labour" (applying *Pickford v Imperial Chemical Industries plc* [1998] 1 W.L.R. 1189).

[45] The Pearson Commission reported that: "The Medical Research Council said that while future research was likely to establish more causal relationships it would also reveal increasingly complex interactions which would heighten the problems of proving causation in the individual case": *Royal Commission on Civil Liability and Compensation for Personal Injury*, Cmnd.7054 (1978), Vol.I, para.1364; see also para.1449: "As the boundary of knowledge increases, so does the area of uncertainty." See, e.g. *Dowson v Sunderland Hospitals NHS Trust* [2004] Lloyd's Rep. Med. 177, QBD, para.5–177.

[46] [1987] 2 All E.R. 417. See also *Dingley v Chief Constable of Strathclyde Police* 2000 S.C. (H.L.) 77; (2000) 55 B.M.L.R. 1, HL, where there was insufficient evidence to establish whether as a general

meningitis who was negligently injected with 30 times the correct dose of penicillin. He recovered from the short term toxic effects of the overdose but was subsequently found to be deaf. One consequence of meningitis can be deafness, and the overwhelming weight of medical opinion was to the effect that penicillin did not cause deafness.[47] Similarly, in *Loveday v Renton*[48] the claimant failed to show, on a balance of probabilities, that pertussis vaccine could cause brain damage in young children, although it was "possible" that it did because the contrary could not be proved either. Medical and expert opinion was deeply divided on this issue. The evidence from the National Childhood Encephalopathy Study supported the conclusion that the vaccine sometimes caused febrile convulsions, but did not provide evidence that such convulsions following the vaccine caused permanent brain damage. Stuart-Smith LJ identified several factors that might explain a close temporal association between administration of the vaccine and subsequent neurological damage, without establishing a causal link.[49]

5–024   **Individual causation**   Even where it is possible in principle to establish a connection between the type of harm suffered by the claimant and a specific hazard, it may still be very difficult to show that the individual claimant's condition was *caused* by exposure to that hazard rather than some other factor for which the defendant was not responsible.[50] For example, it is well-understood that increased exposure to tobacco smoke will lead to an increase in the number of cases of lung cancer in a *population*, but it may be virtually impossible for an *individual* affected by exposure to tobacco smoke to prove that the disease was caused by that exposure.[51] Another example is the problem of proving that an

---

proposition multiple sclerosis can ever be triggered by trauma, and therefore the claimant was unable to establish the specific issue that there was a connection between his injury in an accident and the subsequent onset of multiple sclerosis.

[47] For criticism of the approach of the House of Lords to the medical evidence in *Kay* see Logie 1988 S.L.T. 25. In *Marsden v Bateman* [1993] 4 Med. L.R. 181 it was alleged that a general practitioner had failed to diagnose the symptoms of hypoglycaemia, but it was held that the claimant's brain damage probably occurred during gestation. There was no evidence that, in the absence of coma, convulsions or apnoea, significant brain damage is capable of resulting from hypoglycaemia; *X and Y v Pal* (1991) 23 N.S.W.L.R. 26; [1992] 3 Med. L.R. 195, NSWCA, where the claimant was unable to prove that dysmorphia and brain damage were probably caused by congenital syphilis to which she had been exposed in utero.

[48] [1990] 1 Med. L.R. 117. The Ontario High Court came to the same conclusion on pertussis vaccine in *Rothwell v Raes* (1988) 54 D.L.R. (4th) 193; aff'd (1990) 76 D.L.R. (4th) 280, Ont CA.

[49] cf. *Best v Wellcome Foundation Ltd* [1993] 3 I.R. 421; [1994] 5 Med. L.R. 81; (1992) 17 B.M.L.R 11, Supreme Court of Ireland, where the defendants were held to have been negligent in distributing a faulty batch of pertussis vaccine, and an inference of causation was drawn from the temporal connection between the administration of the vaccine and the claimant's brain damage. It was accepted that there was a possibility that pertussis vaccine could, in rare cases, cause brain damage.

[50] In *Plater v Sonatrach* [2004] EWHC 146 (QB) the claimant was unable to prove, on a balance of probabilities, that his HIV infection was caused by a contaminated syringe when he was given an intravenous injection at the defendant's clinic, because, on the evidence, he was unable to exclude other potential causes of HIV infection.

[51] "Observing that a small percentage of cases of cancer were probably caused by exposure to asbestos does not identify whether an individual is one of that group. And given the small size of the percentage, the observation does not, without more, support the drawing of an inference in a particular case": *Amaca Pty Ltd v Ellis* [2010] HCA 5; (2010) 263 A.L.R. 576 at [70] (where the issue was

individual contracted cancer as a result of exposure to radiation, rather than other causes, although it is well known that radiation can cause cancer.[52] As the Federal Court of Australia expressed this in *Merck Sharp & Dohme (Australia) Pty Ltd v Peterson*:

"...proof of what may be expected to happen in the usual case is of no value unless it is proved that the particular applicant is indeed 'the usual case'."[53]

(i)   Statistics and scientific standards of proof[54]

Neither the claimant nor the court has to apply scientific standards of proof (statistical validity to 95 per cent confidence level) when determining causation on the balance of probabilities, and, moreover, the court should also be conscious of the possibility that an expert witness may have difficulty "in readjusting his focus from the 95% confidence limit approach to the balance of probabilities test".[55] As the Supreme Court of Canada has expressed this point:

5–025

---

whether exposure to asbestos, as opposed to the deceased's smoking habit, had caused his lung cancer). See further *Heneghan v Manchester Dry Docks Ltd* [2016] EWCA Civ 86; [2016] 1 W.L.R. 2036 at [8] and [9]. The difficulty of using epidemiological evidence to draw conclusions about the cause of disease in an individual (in this case lung cancer allegedly caused by smoking) was emphasised in *McTear v Imperial Tobacco Ltd*, 2005 2 S.C. 1, Court of Session (OH).

[52] In *Reay v British Nuclear Fuels plc* [1994] 5 Med. L.R. 1; [1994] P.I.Q.R. P171 the claimants were unable to prove, on the balance of probabilities, that paternal pre-conception irradiation (radiation injury to the gonads resulting in mutation of spermatagonia causing a predisposition to either acute lymphatic leukaemia or non-Hodgkin's lymphoma) had caused the claimants' cancer. See also *B v Ministry of Defence* [2010] EWCA Civ 1317; (2011) 117 B.M.L.R. 101; para.5–035. On the problems of establishing causation in cases of man-made, usually industrial, disease see Stapleton, *Disease and the Compensation Debate* (Oxford, Oxford University Press, 1986), Ch.3.

[53] [2011] FCAFC 128; (2011) 284 A.L.R. 1 at [106], citing King CJ in *State Government Insurance Commission (SA) v Laube* (1984) 37 S.A.S.R. 31 at 33: "the statistical fact that a particular proposition is true of the majority of persons cannot of itself amount to legal proof on the balance of probabilities that the proposition is true of any given individual."

[54] For discussion of the relationship between statistics used in epidemiology and the various legal tests applied to determine causation questions when faced with scientific uncertainty see C. Miller, "Causation in personal injury: legal or epidemiological common sense?" (2006) 26 L.S. 544; and Sir R. Jay, "Standards of Proof in Law and Science: Distinctions Without a Difference?" [2016] J.P.I.L. 1. In *Sienkiewicz v Greif (UK) Ltd* [2011] UKSC 10; [2011] 2 A.C. 229 the Supreme Court was extremely cautious about the circumstances in which the use of epidemiological data to establish causation would be appropriate. Epidemiology deals with populations rather than individuals, and it would be inappropriate to reason from statistical data about causal effects within a population to a causal mechanism in an individual, unless there is something in the particular facts of the case which would enable the court to infer a causal link in relation to the individual claimant. But see C. McIvor, "Debunking Some Judicial Myths about Epidemiology and Its Relevance to UK Tort Law" (2013) 21 Med. L. Rev. 553 who argues that judicial caution is misplaced and that epidemiology is capable of providing a scientifically robust foundation for conclusions about causation in complex disease and medical negligence cases.

[55] *Carter v Basildon and Thurrock University Hospitals NHS Foundation Trust* [2007] EWHC 1882 (QB); [2007] LS Law Med. 657 at [92] and [97]. See also *Fairhurst v St Helens and Knowsley Health Authority* [1994] 5 Med. L.R. 422 where the judge was faced with a stark conflict of expert evidence as to whether the particular disabilities of which the claimant complained had been caused by kernicterus as a result of Rhesus incompatibility. In accepting the evidence of the claimant's expert, Judge Clark QC commented that the approach of the defendant's expert "was more akin to that of the scientist seeking scientific certainty".

"...a judge will be influenced by expert scientific opinions which are expressed in terms of statistical probabilities or test samplings, but he or she is not bound by such evidence. Scientific findings are not identical to legal findings."[56]

On the other hand, in *Vadera v Shaw*[57] the Court of Appeal accepted that the trial judge had been right to accept the findings of a statistical study which had failed to establish a statistical causal link between the oral contraceptive Logynon and strokes:

"Such evidence cannot be ignored by a judge. It is as common sense a conclusion as one could wish to say that if the connection between A and B cannot be shown with confidence to be other than coincidence, then it cannot be held on a balance of probabilities that A caused B. This is not to allow scientists or statisticians to usurp the judge's function, but rather to permit him to use their skills to discern a connection, or a lack of connection, between two phenomena."[58]

5–026   The Court of Appeal has suggested that with a rare medical condition it may be that greater attention should be paid to the medical literature than to the personal experience of individual expert witnesses, who may not have come across the claimant's medical condition very often.[59] But it should also be remembered that the medical literature upon which expert witnesses may rely will take a "scientific" rather than a "legal" approach to questions of proof.

5–027   **Individual causation where the statistics support the claimant's case**
Where the statistics point strongly in favour of the causal link, where, e.g. in the vast majority of similar cases the claimant's medical condition is usually treated successfully, the bare statistics, while not in themselves proving the causal link between the negligence and the claimant's damage, form part of the background against which the medical evidence on causation must be critically assessed. In *Demery v Cardiff and Vale NHS Trust*[60] there was a negligent delay in diagnosing and treating the claimant's ruptured ankle ligaments. The claimant had an ongoing disability to her ankle. The evidence was that in the great majority of cases in which prompt surgery is carried out to such injuries the outcome is successful. The trial judge said that the "statistical rarity of such failures is of no

---

[56] See *Snell v Farrell* (1990) 72 D.L.R. (4th) 289 at 301–302 and *Laferrière v Lawson* (1991) 78 D.L.R. (4th) 609 at 656–657. See also *Dingley v Chief Constable of Strathclyde Police* 2000 S.C. (H.L.) 77 at 89 per Lord Hope: "there is an important difference between the exacting standards of thought and analysis which the academic will expect of medical scientists and the task of a judge when he is considering whether the essential elements in a pursuer's case have been established on a balance of probabilities. ... when it comes to the point of exercising his judgment on [the expert evidence], he must be careful to avoid applying the standard of proof which the expert would apply to them."
[57] (1998) 45 B.M.L.R. 162 at 174.
[58] For criticism of this approach see Goldberg (2000) 8 Med. L. Rev. 316.
[59] *Roughton v Weston AHA* [2004] EWCA Civ 1509 at [17]–[18]. In *Breeze v Ahmed* [2005] EWCA Civ 223; [2005] C.P. Rep. 29 the Court of Appeal emphasised that where expert witnesses rely on medical literature to support their opinions, that medical literature should be made available to the court. The defendant's expert had referred to two articles in his oral evidence, and, from memory, had not summarised their contents accurately.
[60] [2006] EWCA Civ 1131.

assistance to me in itself" in establishing a causal link between the delay and the disability. Neuberger LJ considered that the judge's approach on this issue was correct:

> "It seems to me that, if there was no other reason for believing that the six to 10 days' delay was responsible for the failure of the operation in this case, the fact that the operation was normally successful and was very rarely unsuccessful, is not of itself of any assistance in resolving the issue between the parties. The appellant's case in this connection could be said to be a classic example of *post hoc propter hoc* reasoning."[61]

On the other hand, Pill LJ took the view that the expert evidence should have been considered against the background in which most such cases have a successful outcome:

> "The situation here is that in the great majority of cases ... the outcome is a successful one. The judge needed to consider what evidence there was of factors present which allowed a very unusual result—that is failure—to occur in this case. Such explanations as were given he rejected."[62]

The proposition that in addressing issues of causation one should consider the particular case rather than the general statistics per se, can also work against a claimant where the statistics, on their own, might suggest that the claimant should succeed on the balance of probabilities. In *Wardlaw v Farrar*[63] counsel for the claimant argued that because there was evidence that 85 per cent of patients diagnosed with a pulmonary embolus survive, the court should look at the probabilities of survival at the time of the negligent examination. Her chances of survival were said to have been reduced by the defendant general practitioner's negligent diagnosis and the resulting delay in referring the patient to hospital for treatment. Counsel suggested that the fact that it subsequently became apparent that the patient did not respond to the usual beneficial effects of anti-coagulation therapy when she received treatment in hospital should not be taken into account in assessing the probability that prompt referral to hospital would have prevented her death. Brooke LJ confessed that he did not understand the argument. The judge had to consider whether, on the balance of probabilities, the general practitioner's negligence had caused the death, and had to take into account all the relevant evidence in making this judgment. The failure of anti-coagulant therapy given at the hospital to prevent the formation of a massive pulmonary embolism was "inevitably a material piece of evidence". It tended to indicate that the patient fell into the category of 15 per cent of patients who do not survive, despite treatment, for reasons that are not well-understood by medical science. As Brooke LJ pointed out:

5–028

---

[61] [2006] EWCA Civ 1131 at [48].
[62] [2006] EWCA Civ 1131 at [35]. The case was remitted for a rehearing because the judge had failed to consider whether on the balance of probabilities the delay had turned what was a routine and normally successful operation into one of those very rare procedures in which the outcome was unsuccessful: [2006] EWCA Civ 1131 at [36].
[63] [2003] EWCA Civ 1719; [2003] 4 All E.R. 1358.

"While judges are of course entitled to place such weight on statistical evidence as is appropriate, they must not blind themselves to the effect of other evidence which might put a particular patient in a particular category, regardless of the general probabilities."[64]

On the medical evidence available in *Wardlaw v Farrar* that was a reasonable conclusion to draw. The courts should be careful, however, not to take the logic of this reasoning too far in the opposite direction. If the evidence is that, say, 80 per cent of patients survive with prompt treatment, but 20 per cent die even with prompt treatment, the fact that the patient died following delayed treatment does not establish that he probably fell into the 20 per cent category at the outset and therefore the delay did not contribute to the death. The assessment of causation turns upon the detailed medical evidence, both as to the overall statistical chances of survival and the particular condition and circumstances of the patient.

(ii) A mathematical approach to discrete causes?

5–029 In a case where there is only one defendant and the damage is not cumulative but is attributable to a single event, and there are multiple events that could have caused the damage some of which are in breach of duty but others are "innocent", and it is not possible to identify which event caused the claimant's damage, then it may be possible to use a mathematical approach to proof of causation, applying the balance of probabilities. In *The Creutzfeldt-Jakob Disease Litigation, Groups A and C Plaintiffs*[65] the claimants had all developed Creutzfeldt-Jacob Disease (CJD) as a consequence of receiving human growth hormone (HGH) treatment contaminated with the CJD virus. The treatment, consisting of an injection, was given on a regular basis over a period of time. Although there was some uncertainty, the accepted scientific view was that the CJD was caused by a single injection or dose containing a sufficient titre of the CJD agent. There was no issue of a cumulative cause nor that some individuals were more susceptible to developing CJD. The defendants were found to have been in breach of duty from 1 July 1977 by failing to give appropriate information to clinicians treating the claimants about the risks of transmitting CJD. The claimants had received injections of HGH both before and after 1 July 1977, but it was not scientifically possible to identify whether they had received a contaminated dose before or after that date. The claimants argued that if a victim received more doses after the cut-off date than before it then it was more likely than not that the contaminated dose was received after the cut-off date. For example, if a pack of cards was divided into two piles containing 27 and 25 cards respectively there is a higher probability that the pile of 27 cards contains the ace of spades. The defendants argued that this was a simplistic, mechanistic approach. There was a likelihood or possibility that a victim received a number of contaminated doses, although only

---

[64] [2003] EWCA Civ 1719; [2003] 4 All E.R. 1358 at [35]. See, e.g. the comments of Judge Eccles QC in *Anderson v Heatherwood and Wexham Park Hospitals NHS Trust* [2005] EWHC 1325 (QB) at [27]: "I am also conscious of the danger that if a patient is held to be likely to die on a balance of probabilities because he or she falls into a category where the risk of mortality is 51%, then all those falling within that category will be predicted to die, even though 49% will live. So I recognise that the studies provide a context within which to assess the gravity of Mrs Anderson's condition, but not much more, unless the probability of a particular outcome is very high indeed."
[65] (1998) 54 B.M.L.R. 100.

one would prove fatal. If there were a number of potential aces of spades in the pack then the analogy of the pack of cards was inappropriate. Morland J rejected the defendants' argument that causation was only established if the preponderance of doses were given after the cut-off date, and that a preponderance should be substantial (possibly three-quarters or two-thirds). That argument, said his Lordship, would alter the civil standard of proof from the balance of probabilities to a standard of substantially probable or very probable.[66] Thus, any "straddler victims" (someone who received doses both before and after 1 July 1977) would succeed on causation if it was proved that they received the majority of doses after the cut-off date.[67]

(iii) Drawing inferences

Where the scientific evidence is equivocal, the crucial issue from the claimant's point of view is whether the court will be prepared to draw an appropriate inference that there must have been some causal connection, since proof of causation in the medical sphere rests inevitably on the drawing of an inference of fact. In *Jones v Great Western Railway Co*. Lord Macmillan put the matter in this way:

5–030

> "The dividing line between conjecture and inference is often a very difficult one to draw. A conjecture may be plausible, but it is of no legal value, for its essence is that it is a mere guess. An inference in the legal sense, on the other hand, is a deduction from the evidence, and if it is a reasonable deduction it may have the validity of legal proof. The attribution of an occurrence to a cause is, I take it, always a matter of inference. The cogency of a legal inference of causation may vary in degree between practical certainty and reasonable probability. Where the coincidence of cause and effect is not a matter of actual observation there is necessarily a hiatus in the direct evidence, but this may be legitimately bridged by an inference from the facts actually observed and proved."[68]

The burden of proof, is, ultimately, a burden of persuading the court to attribute legal responsibility for the claimant's injuries to the defendant. This is patent in

---

[66] But contrast *Nulty v Milton Keynes BC* [2013] EWCA Civ 15; [2013] 1 W.L.R. 1183 where Toulson LJ said: "The civil 'balance of probability' test means no less and no more than that the court must be satisfied on rational and objective grounds that the case for believing that the suggested means of causation occurred is stronger than the case for not so believing ... Sometimes the 'balance of probability' standard is expressed mathematically as '50+ % probability', but this can carry with it a danger of pseudo-mathematics ... the process is not scientific (although it may obviously include evaluation of scientific evidence) and to express the probability of some event having happened in percentage terms is illusory." Toulson LJ rejected, at [37], an argument that if there is a closed list of possible causes, and if one possibility is more likely than the other, by definition that has a greater probability than 50 per cent. This was "over-formulaic" and "intrinsically unsound". The question to be asked is: "on an overall assessment of the evidence (i.e. on a preponderance of the evidence) whether the case for believing that the suggested event happened is more compelling than the case for not reaching that belief."
[67] The converse must also be true, namely that if the claimant received the majority of doses before the cut-off date the claim would fail on the balance of probabilities. Query whether in this situation a claimant could argue that the "minority" doses administered after the cut-off date had materially increased the risk of contracting CJD, applying *Fairchild v Glenhaven Funeral Services Ltd* [2002] UKHL 22; [2003] 1 A.C. 32; see para.5–050. This seems unlikely, in part because it smacks of claimants getting "two bites of the cherry" on causation.
[68] (1930) 47 T.L.R. 39, 45.

the case of causation in law, where the court must select from a number of causative factors the event or events that it considers to have been decisive. This is also the position, although maybe less obviously so, with the proof of causation in fact. The readiness of the court to draw an inference of fact, assisted where appropriate by principles of law, depends to some extent on the court's subjective assessment of the evidence, which in turn may be influenced by the underlying policy objectives of the law.[69]

(iv)   Improbable causes and legitimate inferences

5–031   Judges are not required to choose between two theories as to how an accident occurred, both of which they regard as extremely improbable, or one of which they regard as extremely improbable and the other of which they regard as virtually impossible. The third option is to conclude that the evidence left them in doubt as to the cause of the damage, and that in these circumstances the claimant has failed to discharge the burden of proving causation.[70] In *Ide v ATB Sales Ltd*; *Lexus Financial Services (t/a Toyota Financial Services (UK) Plc v Russell*[71] Thomas LJ commented that:

> "In the vast majority of cases where the judge has before him the issue of causation of a particular event, the parties will put before the judges two or more competing explanations as to how the event occurred, which though they may be uncommon, are not improbable. In such cases, it is . . . a permissible and logical train of reasoning for a judge, having eliminated all of the causes of the loss but one, to ask himself whether, on the balance of probabilities, that one cause was the cause of the event. What is impermissible is for a judge to conclude in the case of a series of improbable causes that the least improbable or least unlikely is nonetheless the cause of the event."

On the other hand, where there are only two competing causes, neither of which is improbable (even if they are uncommon events), then once one cause has been eliminated the judge is entitled to conclude that the other was the probable cause of the damage.[72] In *Nulty v Milton Keynes BC*[73] it was argued that if there is a closed list of possible causes, and one possibility is more likely than the other, then by definition that has a probability greater than 50 per cent; and that if there is a closed list of more than two possible causes, the court should ascribe a probability factor to them individually in order to determine whether one had a probability greater than 50 per cent. Toulson LJ rejected the argument as "intrinsically unsound". There was no rule of law that if possible causes A and B

---

[69] For extensive discussion of the issues involved in establishing factual causation, including the normative judgments that are made in terms of allocating responsibility for particular outcomes, which touches on many of the issues discussed in paras 5–033 to 5–130, see J. Stapleton, "Cause-in-Fact and the Scope of Liability for Consequences" (2003) 119 L.Q.R. 388.

[70] *The Popi M.* [1985] 2 Lloyd's Rep. 1 at 6, HL. For example, in *O'Callaghan v Dowling* [2014] IEHC 211 O'Neill J was unable to accept either the claimant's or the defendant's explanation of the cause of the claimant's neurological deterioration. The cause remained "shrouded in mystery" and so the claimant had failed to discharge the burden of proving that his explanation of causation was correct.

[71] [2008] EWCA Civ 424; [2008] P.I.Q.R. P13 at [4].

[72] [2008] EWCA Civ 424; [2008] P.I.Q.R. P13 at [19]–[20].

[73] [2013] EWCA Civ 15; [2013] 1 W.L.R. 1183.

are very much less likely than possible cause C then possible cause C becomes the probable cause. Rather the question is:

"...on an overall assessment of the evidence (i.e. on a preponderance of the evidence) whether the case for believing that the suggested event happened is more compelling than the case for not reaching that belief."[74]

(v) Relevance of the Bolam test to proof of factual causation

The *Bolam* test, with its injunction that the court cannot choose between competing bodies of *responsible* medical opinion, has very limited application in the context of causation. It can apply in a case of breach of duty by omission where the question of what would have happened had the defendant's duty been discharged arises. Here, the claimant has to prove either that what the doctor would have done would have prevented the damage (which is a pure question of fact to which the *Bolam* test does not apply) or that the failure to adopt such a course of action was negligent, applying the *Bolam* test.[75] In such a case, if a responsible body of professional opinion supports the defendant's version of what she would, hypothetically, have done (and this would not have avoided the damage) the claimant will fail to prove causation, notwithstanding that another responsible body of professional opinion would have taken action that would have avoided the damage. Where, however, the issue is simply whether the claimant's medical condition would or would not have deteriorated with appropriate treatment, it is not a question of opting for the view of the majority of experts or of a reasonable body of medical opinion, since "that would be to import the well-known *Bolam* test into the issue of causation, where it has no proper place".[76] Thus, where what the judge is required to do is to make findings of fact, the *Bolam* test does not apply. This is so, even where those findings of fact are subject to conflicting expert evidence. Accordingly, if there is a dispute amongst the experts about a question of fact (such as what was visible on a laboratory slide) the judge is entitled to prefer one group of experts over the other.[77]

5–032

(c) Material contribution to the damage

The courts have gone some way to relieving a claimant from the rigours of the "but for" test where the difficulty of establishing causation has been a product of scientific uncertainty. In *Bonnington Castings Ltd v Wardlaw*[78] the House of Lords held that the claimant does not have to establish that the defendant's breach of duty was the main cause of the damage provided that it materially contributed

5–033

---

[74] [2013] EWCA Civ 15; [2013] 1 W.L.R. 1183 at [37]; see also at [42].
[75] See *Bolitho v City and Hackney Health Authority* [1998] A.C. 232 at 240; and paras 5–011 to 5–014.
[76] *Cavanagh v Bristol and Weston Health Authority* [1992] 3 Med. L.R. 49 at 56, per Macpherson J.
[77] *Penney, Palmer and Cannon v East Kent Health Authority* [2000] Lloyd's Rep. Med. 41 at 46, CA
See also *St-Jean v Mercier* (2002) 209 D.L.R. (4th) 513, SCC, at [55].
[78] [1956] A.C. 613. See S. Bailey, "Causation in negligence: what is a material contribution?" (2010) 30 L.S. 167.

to the damage. The claimant contracted pneumoconiosis from inhaling air which contained silica dust at his workplace. The main source of the dust was from pneumatic hammers for which the employers were not in breach of duty (the "innocent dust"). Some of the dust (the "guilty dust") came from swing grinders for which they were responsible by failing to maintain the dust-extraction equipment. There was no evidence as to the proportions of innocent dust and guilty dust inhaled by the claimant, but such evidence as there was indicated that much the greater proportion came from the innocent source. On the evidence the claimant could not prove "but for" causation, in the sense that it was more probable than not that had the dust-extraction equipment worked efficiently he would not have contracted the disease. Nonetheless, the House of Lords drew an inference of fact that the guilty dust was a contributory cause, holding the employers liable for the full extent of the loss. The claimant did not have to prove that the guilty dust was the sole or even the most substantial cause if he could show, on a balance of probabilities, the burden of proof remaining with the claimant, that the guilty dust had materially contributed to the disease. Anything which did not fall within the principle de minimis non curat lex would constitute a material contribution.[79] Subsequently, in *Nicholson v Atlas Steel Foundry & Engineering Co. Ltd*,[80] on virtually identical facts, the House of Lords held the defendants liable for an employee's pneumoconiosis, even though, in the words of Viscount Simonds, it was "impossible even approximately to quantify" the respective contributions of guilty and innocent dust.

5–034 These cases were significant in easing the claimant's burden of proof for two reasons. First, they were a departure from "but for" causation—the claimants did not have to prove that they would not have suffered the "damage" (i.e. the injury or illness) but for the breach of duty. What had to be proved was redefined as a "material contribution" to the injury or illness, and, notwithstanding this redefinition of the "damage" to which the claimant must establish a causal link in more limited terms than the outcome, the claimant still recovered *damages* for the whole loss, i.e. the outcome, having proved causation in respect of a part only of that loss.[81] Secondly, the courts were willing to draw an *inference* of fact that there had been a material contribution when it was in reality impossible to say whether there had been any such contribution, or even to make a statistical guess.

---

[79] In *Carder v Secretary of State for Health* [2016] EWCA Civ 790; [2017] I.C.R. 392 the defendant conceded that a 2.3 per cent contribution to the claimant's asbestosis was a material contribution, but argued that it made no measurable difference to the symptoms and so damages should not be awarded because the claimant was no worse off. The Court of Appeal held that the defendant's concession was critical and so the judge had been correct to award damages on the basis that the claimant was slightly worse off as a result of the 2.3 per cent exposure. The defendant's argument that the claimant was no worse off could not be reconciled with the concession that the defendant had made a material contribution to the claimant's asbestosis.

[80] [1957] 1 All E.R. 776. See also *Clarkson v Modern Foundries Ltd* [1958] 1 All E.R. 33, applying *Bonnington Castings Ltd v Wardlaw* [1956] A.C. 613. "As long as a defendant is *part* of the cause of an injury, the defendant is liable, even though his act alone was not enough to create the injury. There is no basis for a reduction of liability because of the existence of other preconditions: defendants remain liable for all injuries caused or contributed to by their negligence": *Athey v Leonati* [1997] 1 W.W.R. 97, 103, SCC (original emphasis).

[81] See Stapleton (1988) 104 L.Q.R. 389, 404–405.

Indivisible damage: material contribution test inapplicable   The material   5–035
contribution to damage approach can be used where the claimant's damage is
divisible (or cumulative). However, where the damage is indivisible it is
inappropriate to apply the material contribution to damage approach. In *B v
Ministry of Defence*[82] the claimants were former service personnel who alleged
that they had been exposed to excessive ionising radiation during atmospheric
nuclear tests carried out by the British Government in the Pacific between 1952
and 1958, and as a result had, many years later, developed various forms of
cancer. The Court of Appeal indicated that, though the test in *Bonnington
Castings Ltd v Wardlaw* can be used where negligent and non-negligent causes
have both contributed to the disease but it is not possible to apportion the harm
caused, the claimant can only rely on a material contribution to the condition or
disease:

> "...where the severity of the disease is related to the amount of exposure; further exposure to
> the noxious substance in question is capable of making the condition worse."[83]

Since cancer is not a divisible condition (its severity does not depend on the
extent of the exposure) the exposure to radiation had not made a material
contribution to the disease, only to the risk that it might occur. With regard to
cancer the claimants could not rely on *Bonnington Castings*, which applies:

> "...only where the disease or condition is 'divisible' so that an increased dose of the harmful
> agent worsens the disease... [In *Bonnington Castings* the] tort did not increase the risk of
> harm; it increased the actual harm. Similarly in [*Bailey v Ministry of Defence*[84]], the tort (a
> failure of medical care) increased the claimant's physical weakness. She would have been
> quite weak in any event as the result of a condition she had developed naturally. No one could
> say how great a contribution each had made to the overall weakness save that each was
> material. It was the overall weakness which led to the claimant's failure to protect her airway
> when she vomited with the result that she inhaled her vomit and suffered a cardiac arrest and
> brain damage. In those cases, the pneumoconiosis and the weakness were divisible conditions.
> Cancer is an indivisible condition; one either gets it or one does not. The condition is not
> worse because one has been exposed to a greater or smaller amount of the causative agent."[85]

This view was endorsed in *Heneghan v Manchester Dry Docks Ltd*[86] where Lord   5–036
Dyson MR said that the material contribution to damage test should be applied:

> "...where the court is satisfied on scientific evidence that the exposure for which the
> defendant is responsible has in fact contributed to the injury."

This was readily demonstrated in the case of divisible injuries (such as silicosis
and pneumoconiosis) where the severity of the condition is proportionate to the

---

[82] [2010] EWCA Civ 1317; (2011) 117 B.M.L.R. 101, Smith LJ giving the judgment of the Court.
[83] [2010] EWCA Civ 1317; (2011) 117 B.M.L.R. 101 at [134] (and [149] where the Court of Appeal
accepted the defendants' submissions on this issue).
[84] [2008] EWCA Civ 883; [2009] 1 W.L.R. 1052. See para.5–084 below.
[85] [2010] EWCA Civ 1317; (2011) 117 B.M.L.R. 101 at [150]. This point was not dealt with on
appeal to the Supreme Court: [2012] UKSC 9; [2013] 1 A.C. 78. Smith LJ expressed a similar view,
obiter, in *Dickins v O2 Plc* [2008] EWCA Civ 1144; [2009] I.R.L.R. 58, in the context of claims for
psychiatric harm, on the assumption that psychiatric conditions are indivisible or not "dose-related".
See para.5–044.
[86] [2016] EWCA Civ 86; [2016] 1 W.L.R. 2036 at [46]–[47].

amount of exposure to the causative agent. But where the scientific evidence does not permit a finding that the exposure attributable to a particular defendant contributed to the injury (in this case lung cancer) the court should apply the *Fairchild* test[87] of material contribution to the risk of damage.

(i)   Apportioning causation—(1) defendant's contribution known (divisible harm)

5–037   **Apportion loss where defendant's contribution known**   After *Bonnington Castings Ltd v Wardlaw* it was generally assumed that once the claimant established that the defendant's breach of duty had made a "material contribution to the damage" the defendant was liable for the full loss. The claimant in that case was held to be entitled to compensation for his pneumoconiosis, not just for part of the damage, despite the fact that the defendant was responsible for only part of the silica dust in the atmosphere (the "guilty dust"). In a case involving multiple tortfeasors who have contributed to the same damage it is open to a defendant to seek contribution under the Civil Liability (Contribution) Act 1978 from the third parties whom he alleges are also responsible for the claimant's damage, thereby allocating financial responsibility appropriately, but this is not an option where there is only one culpable defendant. On the other hand, as a general principle of liability a defendant is responsible only for the damage that he has caused, and so where the extent of the defendant's contribution is known, the defendant is liable to that extent and no more.[88] In *Holtby v Brigham & Cowan (Hull) Ltd*[89] the Court of Appeal took the view that where the claimant's case is based on proving a material contribution to the damage the defendant is only responsible for that part of the damage to which his negligence has contributed.

5–038   In *Holtby* the claimant was exposed to asbestos dust over a period of almost 40 years, working for the defendants for about half of that time. For the remainder he worked for other employers doing the same sort of work in similar conditions, in some cases for years and in others for months. He developed asbestosis and sued the defendants, who were held to have been negligent and in breach of statutory duty. The judge held that the defendants were only liable for the damage they had caused, the evidence indicating that if the claimant had only been exposed to asbestos whilst working for the defendants his condition would probably have been less severe. General damages were reduced by 25 per cent. The claimant appealed on the basis that once he established that the defendant's breach of duty materially contributed to his damage he was entitled to recover for the full extent of his loss, applying *Bonnington Castings Ltd v Wardlaw*. Alternatively, he argued that once a claimant has proved that the defendant's conduct had made a

---

[87] *Fairchild v Glenhaven Funeral Services Ltd* [2002] UKHL 22; [2003] 1 A.C. 32; see para.5–050.
[88] See *Thompson v Smiths Shiprepairers (North Shields) Ltd* [1984] Q.B. 405, where the claimant suffered progressive hearing impairment due to industrial noise. The defendants were held liable only for that part of the deafness occurring after the exposure to noise became a breach of duty; *Dillon v Le Roux* [1994] 6 W.W.R. 280 at 300, BCCA, where the claimant had a pre-existing condition that was active and disabling prior to his admission to hospital, and the defendant doctor's negligence increased the damage to the claimant's heart.
[89] [2000] 3 All E.R. 421.

material contribution to the damage the onus shifted to the defendant to prove that someone else was responsible for a specific part of the damage. The Court of Appeal rejected both arguments, upholding the judge's deduction of 25 per cent.[90] Stuart-Smith LJ said that in both *Bonnington Castings* and *McGhee v National Coal Board*[91] the House of Lords had not considered the extent of the defendants' liability because it had not been argued that the defendants' were only liable to the extent of their material contribution—their case had been that they were not liable at all.[92] The onus of proof remained with the claimant to show that the defendant's tortious conduct made a material contribution to the loss, but strictly speaking the defendants were liable only to the extent of that contribution. If the point was never raised or argued by the defendant the claimant would succeed in full, as in *Bonnington Castings* and *McGhee*. But once it became an issue the burden of proof was the claimant's. The effect of *Holtby* is that in a case involving multiple tortfeasors the claimant is left to seek a remedy against each individual tortfeasor who may have contributed to his condition over a working life, placing the risk that one or more defendant employers are untraceable or uninsured on the claimant rather than the defendant, who would have been entitled to claim against the other tortfeasors under the Civil Liability (Contribution) Act 1978.[93] In a claim against a single culpable defendant the defendant is also responsible only for the damage that he has caused, and will be held liable for that proportionate part of the claimant's loss *provided that the damage is divisible* and it is possible to identify that part of the loss, taking a broad brush approach.

It was, perhaps, easier in *Holtby* than in many industrial disease cases to identify the defendant's contribution to the damage since the evidence was that there was a linear progression of the disease depending on the amount of dust inhaled, and so it could be said that all the dust contributed to the final disability. The damage was divisible harm since the severity of asbestosis depends on the cumulative effects of inhaling asbestos, and if there is a correlation between the period of the exposure and the severity of the exposure it is possible, in theory, to calculate the effect of each tortfeasor's breach of duty. In practice, the calculation may not be so straightforward but the problem is addressed (in a somewhat rough and ready manner) by the proposition that when assessing the extent of the defendant's contribution a judge is entitled to take a broad brush approach. The difficulty of

5–039

---

[90] Logically, the defendants in *Holtby* should have been liable for only 50 per cent of the loss, rather than the 75 per cent assessed by the judge, given the period of time the claimant had worked for the defendants. Stuart-Smith LJ explained this as the judge "erring on the side of generosity" to the claimant.

[91] *McGhee v National Coal Board* [1973] 1 W.L.R. 1; see para.5–046.

[92] Note, however, the observation of Lord Uist in *Wright v Stoddard International plc and Novartis Grimsby Ltd* [2007] CSOH 138 at [141] that the apportionment point was not argued in *Bonnington Castings* or *McGhee*: "either because it was never even contemplated or because it was contemplated and considered to be a bad point." Rather the cases established that: "where a pursuer proves that a single defender made a material contribution to his injury or illness, that defender is liable in full to the pursuer for causing the injury, and not just to the extent of his material contribution."

[93] In *Wright v Stoddard International plc and Novartis Grimsby Ltd* [2007] CSOH 138 at [147] Lord Uist declined to apply the approach taken by the Court of Appeal in *Holtby* in Scotland, partly because if the court had a non-statutory power to do what the Court of Appeal had done in *Holtby*, there would have been no need for legislation providing for contribution between tortfeasors.

undertaking the assessment is not a basis for saying that it should not occur.[94] Thus, the court should not be astute to deny claimants relief on the basis that they could not establish with demonstrable accuracy precisely what proportion of their injuries were attributable to the defendant's tortious conduct.[95] Of course, there may be cases where the medical evidence cannot identify such a linear effect and the causal mechanism may be more complex.[96]

(ii) Apportioning causation—(2) defendant's contribution unknown (divisible harm)

5–040   **No apportionment if impossible to attribute particular causes to particular loss**   In *John v Central Manchester and Manchester Children's University Hospitals NHS Foundation Trust*[97] Picken J held that, in a case where proof of causation depends on a material contribution to the claimant's damage, "apportionment is not appropriate where it is not merely difficult but is impossible to allot particular loss to a particular cause". *Holtby* was a case where it was not impossible but "merely difficult to work out what damage had been caused by particular factors" and that was resolved by taking a broad brush approach. The impossibility of attributing causes is not the same as the impossibility of making a precise apportionment. In *John* there were three factors that had all contributed to the patient's brain damage. There was an initial brain injury due to a fall and a non-negligent post-operative infection which caused some brain damage which would have resulted in some degree of cognitive and neuropsychological impairment, and there was also a negligent delay in operating on the claimant which materially contributed to the brain damage. Picken J found that it was impossible, not merely difficult, to attribute particular causes to a particular loss,[98] and since it was impossible to say how much damage each of the three causal factors had caused the defendants were liable for the full loss.

(iii) Apportioning causation—(3) discrete causal events

5–041   **No apportionment if damage attributable to discrete events**   Where the claimant's damage is the product of discrete events, one of which is the

---

[94] *Allen v British Rail Engineering* [2001] EWCA Civ 242; [2001] I.C.R. 942, a case concerning vibration white finger.

[95] [2001] EWCA Civ 242; [2001] I.C.R. 942 at [20].

[96] For example, the defendant's breach may create a "trigger" effect, sparking off an illness that might not otherwise have occurred, and this might be combined with a cumulative effect, e.g. exposure to a toxic agent up to a certain point may be "safe" in that it is unlikely to produce the disease, but after that point the probability of the disease occurring rises significantly. In such a case can D1 who contributes a level of exposure below the trigger level argue that he has not contributed to the disease at all, since the exposure to that point was "safe", whereas D2, who adds to the exposure (possibly adding far less than D1) and thereby takes the claimant over the threshold for the onset of the disease, has materially contributed to the damage? What is the position where it is simply unknown whether the disease is caused by a cumulative effect or a trigger effect or some combination of both?

[97] [2016] EWHC 407 (QB); [2016] 4 W.L.R. 54 at [99].

[98] As also occurred in *Bailey v Ministry of Defence* [2008] EWCA Civ 883; [2009] 1 W.L.R. 1052 and *Williams v The Bermuda Hospitals Board* [2016] UKPC 4; [2016] A.C. 888. See paras 5–084 and 5–087.

negligence of the defendant, it is not appropriate to apportion the loss between the different events. If the defendant's negligence has materially contributed to the loss the defendant is liable in full (subject to any claim for contribution against another negligent defendant under the Civil Liability (Contribution) Act 1978). In *Environment Agency v Ellis*[99] the claimant had symptomless pre-existing degenerative changes in his spine. He suffered an injury to his back in June 1998 due to his employers' negligence, and another injury to his back in May 1999 which was treated as not being the responsibility of his employers. In April 2000 the claimant fell down a flight of stairs at home because his back gave way, causing a serious injury to his right knee. On the basis that the back problem was causative of the fall, the defendants argued that there were three causes of the claimant's loss and that there should be an apportionment between each of them: (i) the pre-existing spinal degeneration (to which they attributed 70 per cent); (ii) the June 1998 accident (to which they attributed 20 per cent); and (iii) the May 1999 accident (to which they attributed 10 per cent). The defendants' alternative argument was that if the pre-existing spinal degeneration should not be taken into account, the accident of June 1998 was responsible for two thirds of the loss and the accident of May 1999 one third. The Court of Appeal held that the pre-existing spinal degeneration was not a cause of the April 2000 accident, and was only relevant when it came to the assessment of damages.[100] Moreover, the 1998 accident was a "but for" cause of 2000 accident, and it was wrong to attribute 10 per cent or a third to the 1999 accident. May LJ commented:

> "It is a commonplace that, if a passenger is injured in a collision between two motor vehicles when each driver's negligence was a material contributing cause of the collision and therefore the injury, the passenger can recover the full amount of his loss from either of the drivers, provided that he does not recover in total more than the full amount of the loss. The two drivers are left to sort out the appropriate contribution between each other under the Civil Liability (Contribution) Act 1978. This is a common illustration of how uncontentious law treats the necessary causation element of the tort of negligence."[101]

On this basis the 1999 accident:

> "...if it had any causative effect, would no more reduce Mr Ellis' damages than would the negligence of a second driver when the injured passenger claimed his full loss against a negligent first driver."[102]

Claimants who satisfy the "but for" test do not have to prove that the defendant's negligence was the only, or chronologically the last, cause of their injuries. The defendants had not argued that the 1999 accident was a full blown intervening event, but merely a "contributory intervening factor". But, said his Lordship, there is:

---

[99] [2008] EWCA Civ 1117; [2009] P.I.Q.R. P5; [2009] L.S. Law Med. 70; discussed by Jones, "Multiple causation" (2008) 24 P.N. 250; McCarthy [2009] J.P.I.L. C30.

[100] In that if a previously symptomless pre-existing condition would have affected the claimant in the future (by producing symptoms) even if there had been no tort, this will reduce the damages attributable to the tort.

[101] [2008] EWCA Civ 1117; [2009] P.I.Q.R. P5 at [1].

[102] [2008] EWCA Civ 1117; [2009] P.I.Q.R. P5 at [37].

"...no free-standing principle which would give apportioning effect to a *contributory* intervening event. The expression appears to have overtones of contributory negligence which is not in point in the present appeal. The single question therefore is whether this case is one where exceptionally the *Holtby* and *Allen* principles should apply."[103]

May LJ concluded that they should not. The apportionment applied in *Holtby v Brigham & Cowan (Hull) Ltd* was limited to industrial disease or injury cases where there had been successive exposure to harm by a number of agencies, where the effect of the harm was divisible, and where it was unjust for an individual defendant to bear the whole of the loss. It did not apply to "single accident" cases, and the accident of April 2000 was, essentially, a single indivisible event.[104]

(iv)   Material contribution to psychiatric harm

5–042   The principle in *Bonnington Castings* can also apply to psychiatric harm. In *Page v Smith (No.2)*[105] the claimant developed a recrudescence of chronic fatigue syndrome (also known as myalgic encephalomyelitis) following a road traffic accident of "moderate severity" in which he suffered no physical injuries. The Court of Appeal accepted that on the evidence there were other possible causes which had contributed to an exacerbation of the claimant's symptoms, but nonetheless considered that the trial judge was entitled to conclude that the accident had materially contributed to the claimant's symptoms, converting his illness from a mild and sporadic state to one of chronic intensity and permanence. This was the position notwithstanding that the claimant's nervous reaction to the accident was "not necessarily proportional to the trauma".

5–043   It would now seem that, in the light of *Holtby v Brigham & Cowan (Hull) Ltd*,[106] defendants are entitled to argue that they are only responsible for that part of the psychiatric condition caused by their breach of duty, so that where it is possible to identify the extent of the contribution made by the defendants' negligence to the claimant's psychiatric damage, the court should make an appropriate apportionment of the damage.[107] Thus, in *Hatton v Sutherland*[108] the Court of Appeal observed that:

---

[103] [2008] EWCA Civ 1117; [2009] P.I.Q.R. P5 at [38].

[104] [2008] EWCA Civ 1117; [2009] P.I.Q.R. P5 at [39].

[105] [1996] 3 All E.R. 272. See also *Vernon v Bosley (No.1)* [1997] 1 All E.R. 577 applying *Bonnington Castings* to psychiatric damage. In *Donachie v The Chief Constable of the Greater Manchester Police* [2004] EWCA Civ 405; *The Times*, 6 May 2004 the Court of Appeal approved the application of *Bonnington Castings* to a case of physical injury (stroke) brought on by increased stress due to an unforeseeable psychiatric reaction.

[106] [2000] 3 All E.R. 421; para.5–038.

[107] See, e.g., *Leigh v London Ambulance Service NHS Trust* [2014] EWHC 286 (QB); [2014] Med. L.R. 134, para.5–089, n.235 where Globe J applied the material contribution to damage test to a claim in respect of post-traumatic stress disorder and dissociative seizures, though the parties had agreed that it was a case involving "cumulative causes" of the damage.

[108] [2002] EWCA Civ 76; [2002] 2 All E.R. 1 at [36] and [41]. In *Barber v Somerset County Council* [2004] UKHL 13; [2004] 1 W.L.R. 1089 at [63] Lord Walker approved the exposition and commentary by the Court of Appeal in *Hatton v Sutherland* at paras [1] to [42] as a valuable

"Many stress-related illnesses are likely to have a complex aetiology with several different causes. In principle a wrongdoer should pay only for that proportion of the harm suffered for which he by his wrongdoing is responsible ...

Hence if it is established that the constellation of symptoms suffered by the claimant stems from a number of different extrinsic causes then in our view a sensible attempt should be made to apportion liability accordingly. There is no reason to distinguish these conditions from the chronological development of industrial diseases or disabilities."

The aetiology of psychiatric harm is notoriously multi-factorial, and therefore it seems likely that there will often be a case for apportioning the loss, though as the Court of Appeal in *Hatton v Sutherland* acknowledged in discussing the apportionment that took place in *Holtby*, this may have to be a somewhat "rough and ready" exercise. Moreover, where the claimant suffered from a pre-disposition to psychiatric illness any assessment of damages should take into account the prospect that the claimant's psychiatric condition would have occurred in any event, resulting in a reduced assessment.[109]

On the other hand, in *Dickins v O2 Plc*[110] the Court of Appeal doubted whether apportionment was appropriate in a case of psychiatric harm, specifically questioning the approach taken by Hale LJ in *Hatton v Sutherland*. This was on the basis that psychiatric harm is an "indivisible injury" to which the material contribution test can be applied. As Smith LJ expressed the point:

5–044

"...if in one breath the judge holds that all that can be said about the effect of the tort is that it made an unspecified material contribution, it is illogical for him, in the next breath, to attempt to assess the percentage effect of the tort as a basis for apportionment of the whole of the damages."[111]

Apportionment was usually carried out only in cases where the injury is divisible, where the seriousness of the medical condition is "dose-related". In that situation the tort has caused only part of the overall injury, and in assessing damages the pragmatic course may be to assess damages for the whole loss and then apportion the loss between the tortious and the non-tortious causes. Such an approach would work, said Smith LJ, in cases such as dust exposure, noise-induced

---

contribution to the development of the law, though not having heard argument on the section dealing with apportionment and quantification of damage (i.e. paras [36] to [42]) thought it better to "express no view on those topics".

[109] "Where the tortfeasor's breach of duty has exacerbated a pre-existing disorder or accelerated the effect of pre-existing vulnerability, the award of general damages for pain, suffering and loss of amenity will reflect only the exacerbation or acceleration. Further, the quantification of damages for financial losses must take some account of contingencies. In this context, one of those contingencies may well be the chance that the claimant would have succumbed to a stress-related disorder in any event": *Hatton v Sutherland* [2002] EWCA Civ 76; [2002] 2 All E.R. 1 at [42]. In *Page v Smith* [1993] P.I.Q.R. Q55 Otton J had reduced the claimant's multiplier in respect of loss of future earnings from 10 to 6 to reflect, inter alia, his previous medical history, his innate vulnerability to episodes of chronic fatigue syndrome which would have continued, and the recurrence of symptoms from the exigencies of life. In *Page v Smith (No.2)* [1996] 3 All E.R. 272 the Court of Appeal approved Otton J's approach to the question of causation, and there was no discussion of his assessment of damages.
[110] [2008] EWCA Civ 1144; [2009] I.R.L.R. 58; discussed by Jones (2008) 24 P.N. 255; Cooksley [2009] J.P.I.L. C15.
[111] [2008] EWCA Civ 1144; [2009] I.R.L.R. 58 at [43].

deafness and hand/arm vibration syndrome, but it was questionable whether it could apply to a case of psychiatric injury where there were multiple causes of the breakdown:

> "I respectfully wish (*obiter*) to express my doubts as to the correctness of Hale LJ's approach to apportionment. My provisional view (given without the benefit of argument) is that, in a case which has had to be decided on the basis that the tort has made a material contribution but it is not scientifically possible to say how much that contribution is (apart from the assessment that it was more than *de minimis*) and where the injury to which that has lead is indivisible, it will be inappropriate simply to apportion the damages across the board. It may well be appropriate to bear in mind that the claimant was psychiatrically vulnerable and might have suffered a breakdown at some time in the future even without the tort. There may then be a reduction in some heads of damage for future risks of non-tortious loss. But my provisional view is that there should not be any rule that the judge should apportion the damages across the board merely because one non-tortious cause has been in play."[112]

This approach rests on the notion that psychiatric illness is an "indivisible harm", though given the medical uncertainty as to the causal mechanisms involved in most psychiatric illness this looks more like a layperson's assumption than medical truth.[113] It may be that for some psychiatric conditions the medical uncertainty is such that it is not possible to say that the defendant's breach of duty has contributed to the illness, as opposed to contributing to the *risk* of developing the illness. If so, a causal analysis based on the decision of the House of Lords in *Fairchild v Glenhaven Funeral Services Ltd*[114] may be more appropriate.

5–045   Of course, if the claimant's psychiatric harm would have eventuated even if there had been no breach of the defendant's specific duty not to cause psychiatric damage the action will fail on the basis that the breach was not a "but for" cause of the claimant's damage. For example, in *Ward v Leeds Teaching Hospitals NHS Trust*,[115] although the defendant's negligence undoubtedly caused the death of the claimant's daughter, it could not be said that it was breach of the duty owed to the claimant, as a "secondary victim", that caused the claimant's psychiatric damage. The overwhelming factor in the claimant's psychiatric illness was the fact of her daughter's death, rather than the events at the hospital that the claimant witnessed, and thus there was no causal connection between the defendant's breach of the specific duty owed to the claimant and the claimant's psychiatric damage.

---

[112] [2008] EWCA Civ 1144; [2009] I.R.L.R. 58 at [46]. See also per Sedley LJ at [53]. See also *B v Ministry of Defence* [2010] EWCA Civ 1317; (2011) 117 B.M.L.R. 101. Contrast *Leigh v London Ambulance Service NHS Trust* [2014] EWHC 286 (QB); [2014] Med. L.R. 134, para.5–089, n.235.

[113] It assumes, for example, that psychiatric conditions are not "dose-related", which may or may not be true. The causes of many psychiatric conditions are shrouded in obscurity which may partly explain why the medical profession consider them to be multi-factorial in their aetiology (with, possibly, the exception of post-traumatic stress disorder, since the condition is *by definition* caused by exposure to traumatic events). In other instances it may be meaningless to think of the relationship between different factors and the patient's psychiatric state as a simple "cause and effect" mechanism.

[114] [2002] UKHL 22; [2003] 1 A.C. 32. See para.5–050.

[115] [2004] EWHC 2106 (QB); [2004] Lloyd's Rep. Med. 530.

(d)   Material contribution to the risk

McGhee v National Coal Board   After *Bonnington Castings Ltd v Wardlaw*[116]   **5–046**
the test for causation could be said to be that the claimant must prove, on the
balance of probabilities, that the defendant's breach of duty caused or materially
contributed to the damage. In *McGhee v National Coal Board*,[117] however, the
House of Lords took this one stage further. The claimant, who worked at the
defendants' brick kilns, contracted dermatitis as a result of exposure to brick dust.
The employers were not at fault for the exposure during working hours, but they
were in breach of duty by failing to provide adequate washing facilities. This
increased the period of time during which the claimant was exposed to contact
with the brick dust while he bicycled home. It was agreed that the brick dust had
caused the dermatitis, but the current state of medical knowledge could not say
whether it was probable that the claimant would not have contracted the disease if
he had been able to take a shower after work. Thus, he could not establish "but
for" causation in respect of the "guilty" exposure. At best it could be said that the
failure to provide washing facilities materially increased the risk of the claimant
contracting dermatitis. The House of Lords held the defendants liable on the basis
that it was sufficient for a claimant to show that the defendants' breach of duty
made the risk of injury more probable even though it was uncertain whether it
was the actual cause.

A majority of their Lordships treated a "material increase in the risk" as   **5–047**
equivalent to a "material contribution to the damage". Lord Simon, for example,
said that:

> "...a failure to take steps which would bring about a material reduction of the risk involves, in
> this type of case, a substantial contribution to the injury."[118]

Lord Wilberforce explicitly recognised that this process involves overcoming an
"evidential gap" by drawing an inference of fact which, strictly speaking, the
evidence does not support (as was done in *Bonnington Castings*), and, moreover,
that this "fictional" inference is drawn for policy reasons. Why, his Lordship
asked, should a man who is able to show that his employer should have taken
certain precautions, because without them there is a risk or an added risk of injury
or disease, and who in fact sustains exactly that injury or disease, have to assume
the burden of proving more? In many cases it is impossible to prove causation
because medical opinion cannot segregate the causes of an illness between
compound causes:

> "And if one asks which of the parties, the workman or the employers, should suffer from this
> inherent evidential difficulty, the answer as a matter of policy or justice should be that it is the
> creator of the risk who, ex hypothesi, must be taken to have foreseen the possibility of
> damage, who should bear its consequences."[119]

---

[116] [1956] A.C. 613.
[117] [1973] 1 W.L.R. 1; [1972] 3 All E.R. 1008.
[118] [1973] 1 W.L.R. 1 at 8; see also per Lords Reid and Salmon at 5 and 11 respectively.
[119] [1973] 1 W.L.R. 1 at 6.

5-048 **Multiple discrete risk factors—*Wilsher v Essex AHA***   In *McGhee* the defendant's breach of duty had resulted in an increase of an existing risk (the risk of contracting dermatitis from brick dust) by extending the period of exposure. In *Wilsher v Essex Area Health Authority*[120] the question was whether *McGhee* could be applied to a case where there were up to five discrete possible causes of the claimant's injury, any one of which might have caused the damage, where the defendants' breach of duty had produced one of the five risk factors. The claimant was a premature baby who, through the defendants' negligence, received an excessive concentration of oxygen. It is known that excess oxygen can damage the retina of a premature baby leading to a condition called retrolental fibroplasia (RLF) which results in blindness.[121] The claimant contracted RLF. However, RLF can occur in premature babies who have not been given additional oxygen and there is evidence of some correlation between RLF and several other conditions from which premature babies can suffer (apnoea, hypercarbia, intraventricular haemorrhage, patent ductus arteriosus), all of which afflicted the claimant. As Mustill LJ put it:

> "What the defendants did was not to enhance the risk that the known factor would lead to injury, but to add to the list of factors which might do so."[122]

The majority of the Court of Appeal held that *McGhee* could apply in these circumstances, recognising that this represented an extension of that case. Mustill LJ expressed the principle in the following terms:

> "If it is an established fact that conduct of a particular kind creates a risk that injury will be caused to another or increases an existing risk that injury will ensue; and if the two parties stand in such a relationship that the one party owes a duty not to conduct himself in that way; and if the first party does conduct himself in that way; and if the other party does suffer injury of the kind to which the risk related; then the first party is taken to have caused the injury by his breach of duty, even though the existence and extent of the contribution made by the breach cannot be ascertained."[123]

Browne-Wilkinson V-C, dissenting, took the view that the position was wholly different from that in *McGhee*:

> "A failure to take preventive measures against one out of five possible causes is no evidence as to which of those five caused the injury."[124]

5-049 The House of Lords reversed the decision of the Court of Appeal on this issue, approving the judgment of the Vice-Chancellor.[125] It was held that *McGhee* did

---

[120] [1987] Q.B. 730.
[121] Retrolental fibroplasia is now known as retinopathy of prematurity. For discussion of medical understanding of its aetiology see Fielder (1997) 3 *Clinical Risk* 47; Clements (1995) 1 *AVMA Medical & Legal Journal* 215.
[122] [1987] Q.B. 730 at 771.
[123] [1987] Q.B. 730 at 771–772; see also per Glidewell LJ at 776.
[124] [1987] Q.B. 730 at 779.
[125] *Wilsher v Essex Area Health Authority* [1988] A.C. 1074. Martin Wilsher's case was subsequently settled: see Kerry (1991) 2 *AVMA Medical & Legal Journal* (No.4) p.12. See also *Murray v Kensington and Chelsea and Westminster Area Health Authority* unreported 11 May 1981, CA, where the claimant failed to establish a causal link between the excess oxygen he had received and RLF.

not establish any new principle of law and did not have the effect of reversing the burden of proof. The burden of proof remained with the claimant throughout, and he must establish that the breach of duty was at least a material contributory cause of the harm, applying *Bonnington Castings v Wardlaw*. What the House of Lords did in *McGhee*, said Lord Bridge, was to adopt a robust and pragmatic approach to the undisputed primary facts of the case and draw a legitimate, common sense, inference of fact that the additional period of exposure to brick dust had probably materially contributed to the claimant's dermatitis.[126]

(i)   *Fairchild v Glenhaven Funeral Services Ltd*

This interpretation of *McGhee*, however, was not accepted by the House of Lords in *Fairchild v Glenhaven Funeral Services Ltd*[127] which involved three consolidated appeals where workers had developed mesothelioma following negligent exposure to asbestos fibres at work. Mesothelioma is an invariably fatal form of cancer which can be latent for up to 40 years. The precise mechanics of the disease are unknown, but the vast majority of cases result from exposure to asbestos (about 1,500 a year in the UK, with only 50 or 60 cases each year where there has been no history of exposure to asbestos dust). Thus, the overwhelming probability was that the employees' mesothelioma was caused by their occupation. The problem in demonstrating causation was that all of the employees had worked for a number of employers where they had been negligently exposed to asbestos, and with the current level of scientific knowledge about the disease the claimants could not identify which employer was responsible because, unlike asbestosis (and pneumoconiosis) which is also caused by exposure to asbestos dust, mesothelioma is not a "cumulative disease". Mesothelioma is an indivisible condition. In the case of a cumulative disease, where the severity of the condition is related to the period of exposure, each negligent employer can be held responsible for a proportionate part of the damage.[128] The *risk* that mesothelioma will occur increases in relation to the total dose of asbestos received, but the severity of the condition and the resulting disability do not vary with the dose. It may be caused by a single fibre, a few fibres, or many fibres.[129] Thus, if there has been more than one employment involving asbestos exposure, there is no means of identifying in which employment the fibre or fibres which caused the disease was inhaled.

5–050

The Court of Appeal[130] had held that the claimants failed to establish causation, because they could not prove on a balance of probabilities that the "guilty" fibres were the result of any particular defendant's breach of duty. There was an "evidential gap". *McGhee* did not assist because in that case there was only one

5–051

---

[126] [1988] A.C. 1074 at 1090.
[127] [2002] UKHL 22; [2003] 1 A.C. 32. See Stapleton (2002) 10 Torts L.J. 276; and Morgan (2003) 66 M.L.R. 277.
[128] See *Holtby v Brigham & Cowan (Hull) Ltd* [2000] 3 All E.R. 421, CA, para.5–038.
[129] This was the effect of the evidence in *Fairchild*. Note however, Lord Phillips' comment in *Sienkiewicz v Greif (UK) Ltd* [2011] UKSC 10; [2011] 2 A.C. 229 at [102] that the "single fibre theory" has been discredited, and that the causal mechanism of mesothelioma is probably more complex.
[130] [2001] EWCA Civ 1881; [2002] 1 W.L.R. 1052.

causative agent (brick dust) and only one possible tortfeasor, and therefore in the light of *Wilsher* (which held that an inference of causation could not be drawn where there was more than one causative agent), it was not possible to rely on *McGhee* where there was more than one tortfeasor in the case of a single, as opposed to a cumulative, cause. The injustice to the claimants in these circumstances was self-evident. Unlike *Bonnington Castings* or *McGhee*, none of the exposure was "innocent"—all the defendants were breach in duty. It was simply that the claimants could not identify which breach of duty had produced the fatal fibre.

5–052   The House of Lords reversed the decision of the Court of Appeal, on the basis that in the special circumstances of this type of case, there should be a relaxation of the normal rule that claimants must prove that but for the defendant's breach of duty they would not have suffered the damage. The possible injustice of imposing liability on a defendant who has not been proved to have caused the claimants' damage had to be weighed against the injustice to claimants. Lord Bingham observed that:

> "… there is a strong policy argument in favour of compensating those who have suffered grave harm, at the expense of their employers who owed them a duty to protect them against that very harm and failed to do so, when the harm can only have been caused by breach of that duty and when science does not permit the victim accurately to attribute, as between several employers, the precise responsibility for the harm he has suffered. … such injustice as may be involved in imposing liability on a duty-breaking employer in these circumstances is heavily outweighed by the injustice of denying redress to a victim."[131]

5–053   Despite the views expressed by Lord Bridge in *Wilsher*, the decision of the House of Lords in *McGhee* did not rest upon a "robust and pragmatic" approach to the drawing of an inference of fact. Rather, said their Lordships in *Fairchild*, *McGhee* decided a question of law which was:

> "…whether, on the facts of the case as found, a pursuer who could not show that the defender's breach had probably caused the damage of which he complained could nonetheless succeed."[132]

The *ratio* of *McGhee*, said Lord Bingham, was:

> "…that in the circumstances no distinction was to be drawn between making a material contribution to causing the disease and materially increasing the risk of the pursuer contracting it."

This was not, said Lord Hoffmann, because the burden of proof was reversed. It would be artificial to treat the employer as having a burden of proof in a case in which ex hypothesi the state of medical knowledge is such that the burden cannot be discharged. Nor was materially increasing the risk equivalent to materially

---

[131] [2002] UKHL 22; [2003] 1 A.C. 32 at [33]. See also Lord Nicholls at [36]: "these appeals should be allowed. Any other outcome would be deeply offensive to instinctive notions of what justice requires and fairness demands"; and Lord Hoffmann at [63].
[132] [2002] UKHL 22; [2003] 1 A.C. 32 at [21] per Lord Bingham.

contributing to the damage, because that was precisely what the expert witnesses were not prepared to say in *McGhee*. Thus, what their Lordships meant in *McGhee* was that:

> "...in the particular circumstances, a breach of duty which materially increased the risk should be treated *as if* it had materially contributed to the disease."[133]

Wilsher still correct   *Wilsher*, however, was also correctly decided on its   **5–054**
facts.[134] It was one thing, said Lord Bingham, to treat an increase of risk as equivalent to the making of a material contribution where a single noxious agent was involved, but another where any one of a number of noxious agents may equally probably have caused the damage. It must questioned, however, whether the distinction between *Wilsher* and *Fairchild* (or *McGhee*) is that there was only one type of noxious agent in *Fairchild* but several in *Wilsher*. For example, what if the claimant in *Fairchild* had been exposed to asbestos dust by employer A, but to a different cancer-producing agent by employer B? If both agents are capable of producing mesothelioma, would the claimant's case fall within *Wilsher* or *Fairchild*? If the relaxation of the causal test is limited to exposure to asbestos dust, then the claim fails, applying *Wilsher*. The injustice that *Fairchild* seeks to address is not, however, limited to a specific noxious agent. It is clear from cases arising in other jurisdictions that similar conceptual problems can arise in very different factual circumstances, the most obvious being the "hunting cases" where a claimant is simultaneously shot by two or more negligent hunters but cannot identify which one shot him.[135] The unfairness to claimants of requiring them to prove the impossible in circumstances where the defendant is in breach of duty is what usually leads the court to relax the normal requirements of proof. Indeed, in *Fairchild* Lord Hoffmann recognised that the distinction between a case involving a single agent and number of different agents was not a principled distinction.[136]

---

[133] [2002] UKHL 22; [2003] 1 A.C. 32 at [65], original emphasis.

[134] See also *Temple v South Manchester Health Authority* [2002] EWCA Civ 1406 where the claimant was unable to prove the causal mechanism for his cerebral oedema produced as a result of developing diabetic ketoacidosis. One theory was that cerebral oedema can be produced if the patient is infused with a below normal concentration of saline solution, and it was on this basis that the defendants were found to have been negligent. But, as in *Wilsher*, the causal mechanism was shrouded in scientific uncertainty, and there were several potential causes which might operate independently or cumulatively. The Court of Appeal upheld the trial judge's conclusion that the claimant had failed to establish the causal link on the balance of probabilities. As Schiemann LJ pointed out, at [64], the layman might be puzzled by a finding that the defendant was in breach of duty for taking a course of action which might cause the very damage which in the event happened, but was held not liable because causation had not been proved. But the state of scientific knowledge was such that it could not be said that giving a low saline solution was ever the cause of cerebral oedema (although, in the circumstances, giving a low saline solution might cause harm and had no significant advantages, and therefore could be characterised as negligent).

[135] In these cases the courts have usually reversed the burden of proof: see *Summers v Tice* 199 P. 2d 1 (1948), Supreme Court of California; *Cook v Lewis* [1952] 1 D.L.R. 1, Supreme Court of Canada.

[136] See [2002] UKHL 22; [2003] 1 A.C. 32 at [71]–[72]: "What if [the claimant] had been exposed to two different agents—asbestos dust and some other dust—both of which created a material risk of the same cancer and it was equally impossible to say which had caused the fatal cell mutation? I cannot see why this should make a difference."

(ii)   The scope of Fairchild

5–055   Defendants are usually held to be in breach of duty precisely because their conduct has created an unreasonable risk of harm. Without caution, the decision in *Fairchild* could be interpreted as creating a general principle that whenever the claimant has difficulty establishing causation, but it can be shown that the defendant's breach of duty increased the risk of harm to the claimant, the rules of causation should be relaxed. In order to avoid this problem their Lordships sought to limit the situations in which the normal requirements of the "but for" test could be dispensed with. Lord Bingham listed six conditions:

> "(1) C was employed at different times and for differing periods by both A and B, and (2) A and B were both subject to a duty to take reasonable care or to take all practicable measures to prevent C inhaling asbestos dust because of the known risk that asbestos dust (if inhaled) might cause a mesothelioma, and (3) both A and B were in breach of that duty in relation to C during the periods of C's employment by each of them with the result that during both periods C inhaled excessive quantities of asbestos dust, and (4) C is found to be suffering from a mesothelioma, and (5) any cause of C's mesothelioma other than the inhalation of asbestos dust at work can be effectively discounted, but (6) C cannot (because of the current limits of human science) prove, on the balance of probabilities, that his mesothelioma was the result of his inhaling asbestos dust during his employment by A or during his employment by B or during his employment by A and B taken together."[137]

If each of these conditions was satisfied, and in "no other case", then his Lordship considered that it was "just and in accordance with common sense" to treat the conduct of A and B in exposing C to a risk to which he should not have been exposed as making a material contribution to the contracting by C of a condition against which it was the duty of A and B to protect him.[138] This conclusion followed even if either A or B was not before the court.

5–056   Lord Hoffmann also limited the principle to circumstances in which there was a duty specifically intended to protect *employees* against being unnecessarily exposed to the risk of (among other things) a particular disease and it is proved that the greater the exposure *to asbestos*, the greater the risk of contracting that disease.[139] In these circumstances, where medical science could not prove whose asbestos was more likely than not to have produced the cell mutation which caused the disease:

> "...a rule requiring proof of a link between the defendant's asbestos and the claimant's disease would, with the arbitrary exception of single-employer cases, empty the duty of content"

with the result that the duty could not effectively exist.[140] In such circumstances, said his Lordship:

---

[137] [2002] UKHL 22; [2003] 1 A.C. 32 at [2].

[138] [2002] UKHL 22; [2003] 1 A.C. 32 at [34].

[139] [2002] UKHL 22; [2003] 1 A.C. 32 at [61].

[140] [2002] UKHL 22; [2003] 1 A.C. 32 at [62]. Though see the comments of Stapleton (2002) 10 Torts L.J. 276, 296 on this, who points out that the duty of employers or occupiers to take reasonable steps not to expose employees or visitors to asbestos would still apply to cases of asbestosis, so that the fact that some claimants (those who developed mesothelioma) could not prove causation would hardly "empty the duty of content". See also Morgan (2003) 66 M.L.R. 277, 282 making a similar point.

"...it would be both inconsistent with the policy of the law imposing the duty and morally wrong for your Lordships to impose causal requirements which exclude liability."[141]

Lord Rodger suggested that certain conditions were necessary, but may not always be sufficient, for applying the *Fairchild* principle: **5–057**

"(1) the principle is designed to resolve the difficulty that arises where it is inherently impossible for the claimant to prove exactly how his injury was caused. It applies, therefore, where the claimant has proved all that he possibly can, but the causal link could only ever be established by scientific investigation and the current state of the relevant science leaves it uncertain exactly how the injury was caused and, so, who caused it. *McGhee* and the present cases are examples.

(2) part of the underlying rationale of the principle is that the defendant's wrongdoing has materially increased the risk that the claimant will suffer injury. It is therefore essential not just that the defendant's conduct created a material risk of injury to a class of persons but that it actually created a material risk of injury to the claimant himself.

(3) it follows that the defendant's conduct must have been capable of causing the claimant's injury.

(4) the claimant must prove that his injury was caused by the eventuation of the kind of risk created by the defendant's wrongdoing. In *McGhee*, for instance, the risk created by the defenders' failure was that the pursuer would develop dermatitis due to brick dust on his skin and he proved that he had developed dermatitis due to brick dust on his skin. By contrast, the principle does not apply where the claimant has merely proved that his injury could have been caused by a number of different events, only one of which is the eventuation of the risk created by the defendant's wrongful act or omission. *Wilsher* is an example.

(5) this will usually mean that the claimant must prove that his injury was caused, if not by exactly the same agency as was involved in the defendant's wrongdoing, at least by an agency that operated in substantially the same way. A possible example would be where a workman suffered injury from exposure to dusts coming from two sources, the dusts being particles of different substances each of which, however, could have caused his injury in the same way...

(6) the principle applies where the other possible source of the claimant's injury is a similar wrongful act or omission of another person, but it can also apply where, as in *McGhee*, the other possible source of the injury is a similar, but lawful, act or omission of the same defendant. I reserve my opinion as to whether the principle applies where the other possible source of injury is a similar but lawful act or omission of someone else or a natural occurrence."[142]

These conditions are clearly at a higher level of generality than those identified by Lord Bingham or Lord Hoffmann. All of their Lordships were clear that in applying *Fairchild* to future cases caution would be essential. There are dangers in over-generalising the principle, which does not apply merely because the claimant has difficulty in discharging the burden of proof.[143] Nonetheless, it was difficult to see how or why the *Fairchild* principle should be restricted to the relationship between employer and employee, still less to the specifics of mesothelioma caused by exposure to asbestos dust. In *Heneghan v Manchester* **5–058**

---

[141] [2002] UKHL 22; [2003] 1 A.C. 32 at [63].

[142] [2002] UKHL 22; [2003] 1 A.C. 32 at [169] to [170]. In *Barker v Corus (UK) plc (formerly Saint Gobain Pipelines plc)* [2006] UKHL 20; [2006] 2 A.C. 572 at [97] Lord Rodger, in a dissenting speech, though not on this point, commented that: "Having reserved my opinion on the point in *Fairchild*, I would now hold that the rule should apply in that situation." See also, per Lord Hoffmann at [16]–[17]; and per Lord Scott at [58]–[59].

[143] [2002] UKHL 22; [2003] 1 A.C. 32 at [43] per Lord Nicholls.

Dry Docks Ltd[144] the Court of Appeal accepted that *Fairchild* applied to a case of lung cancer caused by exposure to asbestos by multiple defendants. Lord Dyson MR commented that:

> "...principle requires that in a situation which is truly analogous to that considered in that case, the *Fairchild* exception should be applied. Otherwise, the law in this area would be inconsistent and incoherent."[145]

The factors which Lord Dyson considered relevant to the imposition of liability in *Fairchild* were that:

> "(i)   all the defendants concede their breach of duty; (ii) all increased the risk that the deceased would contract lung cancer; (iii) all exposed the deceased to the same agency that was implicated in causation (asbestos fibres); but (iv) medical science is unable to determine to which (if any) of the defendants there should be attributed the exposure which actually caused the cell changes which initiated the genetic changes culminating in the cancer."[146]

5–059   **Different types of uncertainty**   The courts are often confronted with uncertainty when seeking to make findings about causation. For example, *Fitzgerald v Lane*[147] involved three discrete possible causes of injury, namely three distinct impacts in a road traffic accident involving a pedestrian and two vehicles. The Court of Appeal accepted that *McGhee* could be applied to hold that the negligence of the second motorist was causally relevant because this had increased the risk of damage to the claimant. This suggested that *McGhee* was not limited to factual uncertainties due to gaps in medical knowledge about the cause of injuries or diseases, but could apply to other types of factual uncertainty.[148] However, in *Sanderson v Hull*[149] the Court of Appeal held that the *Fairchild* principle can only be used to deal with *scientific* uncertainty. It cannot be invoked just because proving the causal link is difficult and depends on the court making primary findings of fact. The cause of the infection was known in *Sanderson* (the claimant transferred bacteria from her hands to her mouth whilst working for the defendants plucking turkeys). The problem was that there were various ways in which she could have picked up the infection, some of which would have been due to a breach of duty and others of which would not. But the uncertainty about causation was a product of the judge failing to make certain findings of fact, it

---

[144] [2016] EWCA Civ 86; [2016] 1 W.L.R. 2036; see R. Geraghty [2016] J.P.I.L. C83.
[145] [2016] EWCA Civ 86; [2016] 1 W.L.R. 2036 at [48]. See also the comments of Lord Hodge (with whom Lord Mance, Lord Clarke and Lord Carnwath agreed) in *International Energy Group Ltd v Zurich Insurance Plc UK* [2015] UKSC 33; [2016] A.C. 509, [98] and [109] that *Fairchild* is not confined to mesothelioma.
[146] [2016] EWCA Civ 86; [2016] 1 W.L.R. 2036 at [47].
[147] [1987] Q.B. 781.
[148] Though note that in *Fitzgerald* the Court also applied the decision of the Court of Appeal in *Wilsher v Essex Area Health Authority* [1987] Q.B. 730 which was later reversed by the House of Lords on the causation issue: [1988] A.C. 1074, para.5–049. In *Fairchild* [2002] UKHL 22; [2003] 1 A.C. 32 at [170] Lord Rodger, without deciding the issue, was inclined to the view that the Court of Appeal had been correct to apply *McGhee* in *Fitzgerald v Lane*.
[149] [2008] EWCA Civ 1211; [2009] P.I.Q.R. P7 at [52].

was not due to scientific uncertainty. The claimant could not rely on *Fairchild* by proving that the breach of duty increased the risk of contracting an infection in these circumstances.[150]

When does *Fairchild* apply?   In what circumstances, then, can the principle in   **5–060**
Fairchild be applied? Professor Stapleton[151] identified a number of factors that *cannot* be freestanding requirements of the *McGhee/Fairchild* principle:

- that the defendant was solely responsible for all the sources of risk to the victim (true in *McGhee*, but not *Fairchild*);
- that all tortfeasors are before the court (all three claimants in *Fairchild* had been exposed to asbestos by parties not before the court);
- that the defendant was the claimant's employer (the claims in *Fairchild* also involved actions against occupiers);
- that the defendant was solely responsible for all the tortious sources of risk to the victim (true in *McGhee*, but not *Fairchild*);
- that there was more than one tortfeasor responsible for tortious exposures (true in *Fairchild*, but not in *McGhee*);
- that the defendant's tortious conduct consisted of a failure to ameliorate a situation that the defendant had earlier created innocently (true in *McGhee*, but not *Fairchild*).

It is difficult to state with precision, however, when the principle *does* apply.[152] Clearly, where there are multiple tortfeasors and they all add to the risk of damage caused by the *same* noxious agent then the principle applies (since that was the decision in *Fairchild* itself); and in the light of their Lordships' approval of *Wilsher* it would seem that where there are four "innocent" possible causes of the claimant's damage, and the defendant adds a fifth "guilty" possible cause, the increase in *overall* risk cannot be equated with a material contribution to the damage, or as Lord Bingham expressed the *Fairchild* principle, cannot be "treated *as if* it had materially contributed to the disease".[153]

Different noxious agents cause damage by the same mechanism   It was   **5–061**
unclear, however, whether the principle applies where there are multiple

---

[150] See also *Clough v First Choice Holidays and Flights Ltd* [2006] EWCA Civ 15; [2006] P.I.Q.R. P22 where the Court of Appeal held that the modified approach to causation adopted in cases such as *McGhee* and *Fairchild* has no application to an ordinary case of personal injury consequent on an individual, specific occasion of negligence for which a single party is responsible. In these cases the court must apply the ordinary "but for" test, on the balance of probabilities.

[151] (2002) 10 Torts L.J. 276,292.

[152] A claimant cannot rely on *Fairchild v Glenhaven Funeral Services Ltd* where it would have the effect of undermining the principle in *Clunis v Camden Islington Health Authority* [1998] Q.B. 978 (see para.11–023) that claimants cannot be compensated for the consequences of their own illegal acts: *O v Ministry of Defence; West v Ministry of Defence* [2006] EWHC 19 (QB). The modified causation test in *Fairchild* was adopted as a matter of justice and fairness, but justice and fairness do not demand a relaxed rule of causation where claimants' damage is partially attributable to their own criminal action (per Owen J at [17]).

[153] See further *Temple v South Manchester Health Authority* [2002] EWCA Civ 1406, para.5–054, n.134.

tortfeasors and they add to the risk of damage caused by *different* noxious agents, but by the same, or broadly the same, mechanism.[154] In *Fairchild* Lord Hoffmann had some difficulty seeing why it should make any difference of principle if a claimant had been:

> "...exposed to two different agents—asbestos dust and some other dust—both of which created a material risk of the same cancer and it was equally impossible to say which had caused the fatal cell mutation."[155]

In *Barker v Corus (UK) plc (formerly Saint Gobain Pipelines plc)*,[156] however, he considered that his own view in *Fairchild* had been wrong, at least in so far as it focused on different types of dust. The true distinction related to the causal mechanism, rather than the specific causal agent. Thus, for Lord Hoffmann it is an essential condition for the operation of the *"Fairchild* exception" that:

> "...the impossibility of proving that the defendant caused the damage arises out of the existence of another potential causative agent which operated in the same way. It may have been different in some causally irrelevant respect, as in Lord Rodger's example of the different kinds of dust, but the mechanism by which it caused the damage, whatever it was, must have been the same. So, for example, I do not think that the exception applies when the claimant suffers lung cancer which may have been caused by exposure to asbestos or some other carcinogenic matter but may also have been caused by smoking and it cannot be proved which is more likely to have been the causative agent."[157]

Similarly, although Lord Scott regarded different types of asbestos as constituting a single agent, his Lordship considered that if the outcome might have been produced by one of a number of different agents and the guilty agent could not be identified (as in *Wilsher*) the *"Fairchild* exception" did not apply.[158] On the other hand, where there are two different noxious agents but the causal mechanism is the same, *Fairchild* will apply.[159]

5–062   **Culpable and innocent contributions to the risk**   It was also uncertain following *Fairchild* whether the principle applies where there is a single tortfeasor who adds to the risk of damage caused by the *same* noxious agent,

---

[154] According to Lord Bingham, no, but according to Lord Hoffmann and Lord Rodger, possibly yes. For further discussion see Stapleton (2002) 10 Torts L.J. 276, 294–298.

[155] [2002] UKHL 22; [2003] 1 A.C. 32 at [72].

[156] [2006] UKHL 20; [2006] 2 A.C. 572.

[157] [2006] UKHL 20; [2006] 2 A.C. 572 at [24]. See also *Amaca Pty Ltd v Ellis* [2010] HCA 5; (2010) 263 A.L.R. 576 where the High Court of Australia applied the traditional "but for" causation test where the issue was whether exposure to asbestos, as opposed to the deceased's smoking habit, had caused his lung cancer.

[158] [2006] UKHL 20; [2006] 2 A.C. 572 at [64].

[159] See the observations of Smith LJ in *Novartis Grimsby Ltd v Cookson* [2007] EWCA Civ 1261 at [72] on the comment of Lord Hoffmann in *Barker* cited in this paragraph: "Although Lord Hoffmann was there saying that the exception would not apply where one causative agent was occupational and the other was smoking, he plainly had in mind that the two agents would act on the body in a different way. In the present case, the evidence was that the amines in cigarette smoke act on the body in the same way as the amines in the occupational exposure. It seems to me that it is highly arguable that the mesothelioma exception [i.e. the principle in *Fairchild*] should apply to bladder cancer and that it would be sufficient if a claimant were to prove that the occupational exposure had made a material contribution to the risk of him developing the disease."

where there is another party who also contributes to the risk by the same mechanism, but that party is "innocent", i.e. not in breach of duty. In *Barker v Corus (UK) plc (formerly Saint Gobain Pipelines plc)*[160] the House of Lords was unanimous that for the "*Fairchild* exception" to apply it was not necessary to prove that all the exposures were tortious (either because, as on the facts of *Barker*, there was a period of exposure for which the claimant was himself culpable, or there was a period of exposure for which no-one was culpable). Indeed, that had been the position in *McGhee v National Coal Board* (where the defendant was responsible for both tortious and non-tortious periods of exposure to brick dust), which their Lordships had approved in *Fairchild*. As Lord Hoffmann put it:

> "...once one accepts that the exception can operate even though not all the potential causes of damage were tortious, there is no logic in requiring that a non-tortious source of risk should have been created by someone who was also a tortfeasor."[161]

It followed that it was:

> "...irrelevant whether the other exposure was tortious or non-tortious, by natural causes or human agency or by the claimant himself. These distinctions may be relevant to whether and to whom responsibility can also be attributed, but from the point of view of satisfying the requirement of a sufficient causal link between the defendant's conduct and the claimant's injury, they should not matter."[162]

This view was endorsed by the Supreme Court in *Sienkiewicz v Greif (UK) Ltd*,[163] where individuals had developed mesothelioma having been exposed to asbestos by only one defendant, but they had also been exposed to asbestos as a result of the background environmental risk. The defendants argued that in these circumstances *Fairchild* did not apply and the claimants had to prove causation on the basis that the defendants' tortious exposure of the deceased to asbestos had "more than doubled the risk"[164] of developing mesothelioma from the background environmental risk. The Supreme Court rejected the argument. The claimants' problems in proving causation arose from the same "rock of uncertainty" that had been identified by Lord Bingham in *Fairchild*, and the same policy considerations applied.[165] There was no justification for distinguishing

---

[160] [2006] UKHL 20; [2006] 2 A.C. 572. Mr Barker had been exposed to asbestos during three material periods. The first two exposures were as a result of breaches of duty by employers. The third exposure was while he was working as a self-employed plasterer when he had failed to take reasonable care to avoid asbestos.

[161] [2006] UKHL 20; [2006] 2 A.C. 572 at [16].

[162] [2006] UKHL 20; [2006] 2 A.C. 572 at [17]; see also, per Lord Scott at [58]–[59]; per Lord Rodger at [99], though note his Lordship's reservation at [100]–[101] in the rare situation where the victim himself was solely responsible for a material exposure to asbestos dust; and, per Lord Walker at [117].

[163] [2011] UKSC 10; [2011] 2 A.C. 229, discussed by J. Stapleton, "Factual causation, mesothelioma and statistical validity" (2012) 128 L.Q.R. 221; S. Steel and D. Ibbetson, "More grief on uncertain causation in tort" [2011] C.L.J. 451.

[164] See *Novartis Grimsby Ltd v Cookson* [2007] EWCA Civ 1261, para.5–064.

[165] [2011] UKSC 10; [2011] 2 A.C. 229 at [142] per Lord Rodger; see also per Lord Phillips at [103].

cases involving multiple tortious exposures from cases of a single tortious exposure by applying a "doubles the risk" test of causation in the case asbestos-induced mesothelioma.

5–063 **What amounts to a "material" contribution to the risk?** The exposure to the risk of harm must be "not insignificant",[166] or the breach of duty must have "contributed substantially to the risk" that the claimant would contract the disease.[167] Their Lordships did not indicate what a *substantial* contribution meant, perhaps not surprisingly given that on any view of the facts in *Fairchild* the defendants' contribution clearly was substantial. Other cases may arise, however, where the only solvent or traceable defendant exposed the claimant to the risk for a relatively short period, where the issue will be important. It will be recalled that in *Bonnington Castings Ltd v Wardlaw* the House of Lords held that anything that did not fall within the principle *de minimis non curat lex* would constitute a material contribution to the claimant's damage, and it would seem that a similar test is appropriate where the breach of duty contributes to the *risk of damage*.[168] So in *Sienkiewicz v Greif (UK) Ltd*[169] the Supreme Court rejected the defendants' argument that in order to constitute a *material* increase in the risk it must be shown that the defendant's tortious exposure of the claimant had more than doubled the environmental, non-tortious risk. An increase in risk of developing mesothelioma as a result of exposure to asbestos of 18 per cent over the background risk constituted a material increase in the risk. If the exposure was de minimis then it would not constitute a material increase in the risk. However, Lord Phillips doubted whether it was possible to define, in quantitative terms, what amounts to de minimis for this purpose. This was a question for the judge on the particular facts of each case.[170]

---

[166] *Fairchild v Glenhaven Funeral Services Ltd* [2002] UKHL 22; [2003] 1 A.C. 32 at [42] per Lord Nicholls.

[167] [2002] UKHL 22; [2003] 1 A.C. 32 at [47] per Lord Hoffmann.

[168] In *Athey v Leonati* [1997] 1 W.W.R. 97 the Supreme Court of Canada held that the defendant's negligence, which the trial judge had concluded was no more than a 25 per cent contributory factor to the claimant's injury, constituted a material contribution to the damage and held the defendant liable for the full loss. Note, however, that in *Cottrelle v Gerrard* (2003) 233 D.L.R. (4th) 45 at [26] the Ontario Court of Appeal pointed out that *Athey* does not mean that the claimant does not have to prove that the defendant's negligence was a cause of the loss: "In *Athey*, the plaintiff proved on a balance of probabilities that the defendants' negligence caused the loss. The defendants sought to escape liability by pointing to other more significant causes for which they were not responsible. It was in that context that *Athey* held that if the defendant's negligence materially contributed to the occurrence of the injury, the defendant could not escape liability by pointing to other causes. However, *Athey* does not excuse the plaintiff from proving on a balance of probabilities that but for the defendant's negligence, the plaintiff would not have suffered the loss." Thus, where the claimant's leg had to be amputated because of an infection and proper treatment might have saved the leg, but the medical evidence was that it was likely that the leg would have been lost in any event, the claimant has simply failed to prove but for causation. On the difficulty of establishing the causal link between negligence and infection see further *Aristorenas v Comcare Health Services* (2006) 274 D.L.R. (4th) 304; (2006) 83 O.R. (3d) 282, Ont CA; *Anderson v Milton Keynes General NHS Trust, Oxford Radcliffe Hospital NHS Trust* [2006] EWHC 2249 (QB); both at para.4–131. See also S. Plowden and H. Volpé, "*Fairchild* and *Barker* in MRSA Cases" [2006] J.P.I.L. 259 arguing that the *McGhee/Fairchild* principle could apply to cases of infection with MRSA.

[169] [2011] UKSC 10; [2011] 2 A.C. 229.

[170] [2011] UKSC 10; [2011] 2 A.C. 229 at [108].

(iii)   Defendant's negligence more than doubles existing risk

In *Novartis Grimsby Ltd v Cookson*[171] the Court of Appeal held that where in the   **5–064**
case of non-divisible harm (cancer of the bladder) the evidence is that the
negligent occupational exposure to a toxic agent (aromatic amines) more than
doubled the risk of the claimant developing the cancer from the risk attributable
to the non-occupational exposure of a toxic agent (smoking), the claimant has
established "but for" causation, and there is no need to consider whether the
negligent exposure materially contributed to the harm or materially contributed to
the risk of developing the harm.[172] Smith LJ commented that:

> "The natural inference to draw from the finding of fact that the occupational exposure was 70%
> of the total is that, if it had not been for the occupational exposure, the respondent would not
> have developed bladder cancer. In terms of risk, if occupational exposure more than doubles
> the risk due to smoking, it must, as a matter of logic, be probable that the disease was caused
> by the former."[173]

Doubling the risk and mesothelioma   In *Sienkiewicz v Greif (UK) Ltd*[174] Lord   **5–065**
Phillips agreed with Smith LJ's proposition, though the issue in *Sienkiewicz* was
whether a statistical approach or the *Fairchild* test for causation should apply in
circumstances where the defendant's breach of duty had the effect of increasing
the deceased's exposure to asbestos by 18 per cent above the background
environmental exposure to asbestos. The defendant argued that in a case
involving a "single exposure" the *Fairchild* test did not apply and the claimant
had to prove that the negligence had more than doubled the environmental risk in
order to establish causation on the balance of probabilities. However, the
Supreme Court held that in a case of mesothelioma caused by exposure to
asbestos *Fairchild* does apply to determine the causation issue and so the
claimant could not be *required* to prove that the defendant's breach of duty had

---

[171] [2007] EWCA Civ 1261.
[172] In other words the line of authority from *Bonnington Castings* to *Fairchild* and *Barker v Corus* is
irrelevant in these circumstances.
[173] [2007] EWCA Civ 1261 at [74]. This view was repeated by Smith LJ in *Sienkiewicz v Greif (UK)
Ltd* [2009] EWCA Civ 1159; [2010] Q.B. 370 at [23]. See also *Jones v Secretary of State for Energy
and Climate Change* [2012] EWHC 2936 (QB) where Swift J used a "doubling of the risk" approach
to the determination of causation of both lung and bladder cancers where the claimants had been
exposed to carcinogenic fumes and dust. Note that in *Williams v The Bermuda Hospitals Board* [2016]
UKPC 4; [2016] A.C. 888 at [48] Lord Toulson, delivering the judgment of the Privy Council,
indicated that the "doubling of risk" test should be used with caution: "But inferring causation from
proof of heightened risk is never an exercise to apply mechanistically. A doubled tiny risk will still be
very small." In *Magill v Panel Systems (DB Ltd)* [2017] EWHC 1517 (QB) the deceased was
scheduled to have surgery for coronary artery disease but he was then diagnosed with mesothelioma
attributable to the defendants' negligence and as a result the surgery was postponed. He died from a
heart attack. Judge Gosnell held that the omission to have the heart surgery doubled the risk of death,
and counsel for the defendants conceded that in those circumstances the defendants had caused or
contributed to an indivisible injury, i.e. arrhythmia, which caused the death. Thus, the defendants were
held liable for the death even though there were other competing causes.
[174] [2011] UKSC 10; [2011] 2 A.C. 229 at [78]: "… as a matter of logic, if a defendant is responsible
for a tortious exposure that has more than doubled the risk of the victim's disease, it follows on the
balance of probability that he has caused the disease…"

more than doubled the risk. It was sufficient that the claimant prove a material increase in the risk of contracting mesothelioma.

5–066　　**Doubling the risk and diseases other than mesothelioma**　　In cases involving diseases other than mesothelioma Lord Phillips could see "no scope for the application of the 'doubles the risk' test" in cases where two agents have operated cumulatively and simultaneously in causing the onset of a disease. In those circumstances *Bonnington Castings Ltd v Wardlaw* would apply, with the consequence that where the disease was indivisible (as with lung cancer) a defendant who had tortiously contributed to the cause of the disease would be liable in full, and where the disease was divisible (as with asbestosis) the tortfeasor would be liable for the share of the disease for which he was responsible.[175] Lord Phillips added that:

> "Where the initiation of the disease is dose related, and there have been consecutive exposures to an agent or agents that cause the disease, one innocent and one tortious, the position will depend upon which exposure came first in time. Where it was the tortious exposure, it is axiomatic that this will have contributed to causing the disease, even if it is not the sole cause. Where the innocent exposure came first, there may be an issue as to whether this was sufficient to trigger the disease or whether the subsequent, tortious, exposure contributed to the cause. I can see no reason in principle why the 'doubles the risk' test should not be applied in such circumstances, but the court must be astute to see that the epidemiological evidence provides a really sound basis for determining the statistical probability of the cause or causes of the disease."[176]

Finally, Lord Phillips suggested that where there were competing alternative (as opposed to cumulative) potential causes of a disease or injury (such as in *Hotson v East Berkshire Area Health Authority*[177]) there was no reason in principle why epidemiological evidence should not be used to show that one of the causes was more than twice as likely as all the others put together to have caused the disease or injury.[178]

5–067　　In *Heneghan v Manchester Dry Docks Ltd*[179] Lord Dyson MR observed that where medical science does not permit determination with certainty of *how* an injury was caused the "doubles the risk" test applies epidemiological data to the question and if the statistical evidence shows that a tortfeasor more than doubled

---

[175] [2011] UKSC 10; [2011] 2 A.C. 229 at [90]. Although the second part of this statement is clearly correct (see para.5–037) it is difficult to reconcile the first part with the proposition that in the case of indivisible harm the material contribution to damage test does not apply (see para.5–035). Moreover, in *Heneghan v Manchester Dry Docks Ltd* [2016] EWCA Civ 86; [2016] 1 W.L.R. 2036, para.5–067, the Court of Appeal held that in the case of lung cancer the *Fairchild* test of material contribution to risk test should apply, and in cases other than mesothelioma this involves apportionment by reference to the defendant's contribution to the risk: see *Barker v Corus (UK) plc* [2006] UKHL 20; [2006] 2 A.C. 572, para.5–072.

[176] [2011] UKSC 10; [2011] 2 A.C. 229 at [91].

[177] [1987] A.C. 750; see para.5–101. *Wilsher v Essex Area Health Authority* [1988] A.C. 1074, para.5–048 would also seem to fit into this category. If there had been epidemiological evidence in *Wilsher* that the risk of developing RLF as a result of exposure to excess oxygen was more than twice the *combined* risk of the other innocent risk factors then the claimant should have succeeded on causation, on the balance of probabilities.

[178] [2011] UKSC 10; [2011] 2 A.C. 229 at [93].

[179] [2016] EWCA Civ 86; [2016] 1 W.L.R. 2036 at [8]; see R. Geraghty [2016] J.P.I.L. C83.

the risk that the victim would suffer the injury "it follows that it is more likely than not that the tortfeasor caused the injury". On the evidence in *Heneghan* this was sufficient to establish that it was probably exposure to asbestos rather than smoking which caused the deceased's lung cancer. This provided the answer to the "what" question, i.e. what toxin probably caused the lung cancer? It was not sufficient, however, to answer the "who" question, which arises in a multiple contributor case, where the issue is which contributor's asbestos caused the claimant's indivisible damage, i.e. lung cancer? In order to attribute causation to each of the multiple tortfeasors the court had to rely on *Fairchild*.[180]

(iv) Distinguishing Wilsher and Fairchild

Fairchild applies where there are multiple defendants in breach of a similar duty because it is unfair or unjust as a matter of policy to deprive a claimant of compensation because he is unable to prove the impossible. But in *Wilsher* the claimant was also faced with having to prove the impossible, namely which of five risk factors, only one of which was attributable to the defendants' negligence, had caused his blindness. It is not clear why the injustice in *Wilsher* was any less than that in *Fairchild*. In *Wilsher* (unlike *Fairchild*) the other potential causes of the damage were "innocent" causes, but in *Barker v Corus (UK) plc*[181] their Lordships held that the fact that the other potential causes were "innocent" was irrelevant to the application of the *Fairchild* principle.

5–068

What, then, is the distinction between *Wilsher* and *McGhee/Fairchild*? On one approach the *McGhee/Fairchild* principle will apply where the *specific risk* which has materialised, for which there is some prima facie evidence, has been enhanced by the defendant's breach of duty, but not where the negligence enhanced a general risk to the claimant, applying a narrow interpretation of the word "risk". So, for example, in *Wilsher* the risk created by the defendants was "RLF caused *by excess oxygen*", not simply an enhancement of an existing risk of RLF from other causes.[182] Until it could be shown that the RLF was caused by

5–069

---

[180] The trial judge in *Heneghan v Manchester Dry Docks Ltd* [2014] EWHC 4190 (QB) at [61] took the view, in a case of multiple tortfeasors who had exposed the deceased to asbestos where the overall contribution of one employer (who had not been sued) to the deceased's asbestos exposure was 56 per cent, that this would have been sufficient to establish causation against that employer on the balance of probabilities. This was not a conclusion primarily based on epidemiology, said Jay J, it was simply "basic arithmetic". On appeal this observation was criticised by counsel, but the Court of Appeal did not consider it necessary to decide whether the criticism was justified: see [2016] EWCA Civ 86; [2016] 1 W.L.R. 2036 at [16] and [55] per Lord Dyson MR and Sales LJ respectively. If Jay J's view is correct, it would seem to produce the odd result that one employer would be liable in full, on the balance of probabilities, for the deceased's cancer applying the traditional "but for" test, and the other employers would be liable to the extent that their breach of duty contributed to the risk of the deceased developing cancer, applying *Fairchild* and *Barker v Corus (UK) plc* [2006] UKHL 20; [2006] 2 A.C. 572, para.5–072 below.
[181] [2006] UKHL 20; [2006] 2 A.C. 572; see para.5–062 above.
[182] In *Kay v Ayrshire and Arran Health Board* [1987] 2 All E.R. 417 the House of Lords made it clear that an overall contribution to "the risk of damage" was insufficient to invoke *McGhee* where the negligence created a risk of a different kind of damage from that which occurred. Lord Mackay (at 425) said that: "In my opinion, it is not right to ask whether [the overdose] materially increased the risk of neurological damage when the evidence available distinguishes between different kinds of neurological damage . . . I cannot accept that it is correct to say that because evidence shows that an

excess oxygen the injury cannot be said to fall squarely within the risk created by the defendants.[183] If it is possible to say that the defendant's negligence enhanced the specific risk which, on the balance of probabilities, has materialised, it is irrelevant that there were other discrete risk factors (as there were in *Wilsher*). In practice, however, the presence of other risk factors will usually make it impossible for claimants to prove exactly which risk has materialised, and they will be unable to overcome the causation hurdle. The claimants in *Fairchild* were in a much better position in being able to argue that the risk which had materialised (the risk of mesothelioma from exposure to asbestos) had probably been increased by the defendants' breach of duty.

5–070   It is not entirely clear why the courts should want to make such fine distinctions when dealing with different types of factual uncertainty. It may be pure chance whether a defendant's negligence enhances an existing risk or adds a new risk factor, even if it is possible to distinguish between such risks. In some cases it may simply be unknown whether an illness is the result of a cumulative effect or of a single event the risk of which has been enhanced by the defendant. In the face of such uncertainty it seems strange to attach such significance to the distinction between cumulative and discrete causes,[184] or "single agent" and "multi-agent" causes. There may be practical reasons for concluding that the *McGhee/Fairchild* principle should be limited to cases involving a single agent, in that it provides a clear boundary and (at least before the decision in *Barker v Corus (UK) plc*[185]) may have reduced the problems associated with contribution between tortfeasors or apportionment of responsibility,[186] but it is certainly not a principled way in which to resolve issues of causal uncertainty arising out of gaps in scientific knowledge.[187]

---

overdose of penicillin increases the risk of particular types of neurological damage found in these cases that an overdose of penicillin materially increases the risk of a different type of neurological damage, namely that which causes deafness when no such deafness has been shown to have resulted from such overdose"; see also per Lord Griffiths at 422.

[183] *Wilsher v Essex Area Health Authority* [1987] Q.B. 730 at 780, per Browne-Wilkinson V-C. Note, however, the comment of Stapleton (2002) 10 Torts L.J. 276, 297–298: "... where the issue of historical connection cannot be established on orthodox principles because of an evidentiary gap, the notion of the sphere of the risk is sufficiently vague to allow manipulation to fit the result desired. ... the claimant in *Wilsher* could have argued that the defendant had created a risk of RLF, and that the injury suffered by the claimant fell squarely within that risk." Of course, the defendant would argue for a narrow formulation of the risk in order to demonstrate that the circumstances of the claimant's injury fell outside that risk.

[184] See Stapleton (1988) 104 L.Q.R. 389, 402 and 406, n.40.

[185] [2006] UKHL 20; [2006] 2 A.C. 572.

[186] Stapleton (2002) 10 Torts L.J. 276, 295.

[187] The suggestion, hinted at by Lord Hoffmann in *Fairchild v Glenhaven Funeral Services Ltd* [2002] UKHL 22; [2003] 1 A.C. 32 at [69], that *Wilsher* turned upon the identity of the defendants (the NHS rather than an employer sued by an employee) and that "the massive increase in the liability of the National Health Service which would have been a consequence of the broad rule favoured by the Court of Appeal in *Wilsher's* case" might justify a different causation rule surely cannot be correct. Of course, the policy issues that medical negligence litigation raises are important and are the subject of much political debate. Whatever the practical solution to these problems, it cannot be right to distort legal principle simply to protect one public sector defendant. See Morgan (2003) 66 M.L.R. 277, 282 making the point that the decision in *Fairchild* had massive financial implications for insurance companies, but that this was not mentioned in any of the speeches.

(v) An evidential base

Even before their Lordships in *Fairchild* had explained that *McGhee* was   **5–071**
authority for a proposition of law, rather than an example of the drawing of an
evidential inference, the Court of Appeal had been careful to stress that there
must be evidence supporting the specific inference that the claimant sought to
persuade the court to draw. A claimant cannot rely on the simple assertion that the
defendant's conduct has increased the risk of harm—there must be specific
evidence to link the defendant's breach of duty to the claimant's harm before an
inference that it has made a material contribution can be drawn (or as expressed
by Lord Bingham in *Fairchild*, "treated *as if* it had materially contributed" to the
claimant's damage). In *Tahir v Haringey Health Authority*[188] the claimant alleged
that the delay in providing medical treatment rendered his condition worse than it
would otherwise have been, on the basis that, in general terms, delay in operating
in his type of case increases the neurological deficit and impairs the prospect of
recovery. The Court of Appeal held that where there has been negligence
resulting in delayed medical treatment it was not sufficient for claimants to show
simply that there was a material increase in the risk or that delay *can* cause
damage. They have to go further and prove that damage was *actually* caused by
the delay. In the absence of findings of fact that identify or quantify the additional
harm, it was not appropriate for a judge to adopt a proportionate approach by
quantifying the total disability and then asking what proportion of that disability
is attributable to the delay.[189]

(e) Apportioning causation—material contribution to the risk

On the facts of *Fairchild* the claimant was entitled to full compensation from the   **5–072**
negligent defendant. There was no question of apportioning the loss proportionately to each potential defendant, with the claimant being entitled to damages
from each defendant in proportion to his exposure to the noxious agent by that

---

[188] [1998] Lloyd's Rep. Med. 104. *Tahir* was applied in *Hussain v Bradford Teaching Hospital NHS
Foundation* [2011] EWHC 2914 (QB); [2013] Med. L.R. 353 where Coulson J held that a culpable
delay of 48 hours in operating on the claimant had not caused the claimant's cauda equine syndrome
or prevented him from making a good recovery; nor had it left him in a generally worse condition than
he would otherwise have been in because that was "an entirely speculative and impressionistic
conclusion" since the expert evidence did not point to any specific aspect of the claimant's symptoms
that would have been improved. The claimant simply had a chance of a better outcome. See also
Oakes v Neininger [2008] EWHC 548 (QB); (2008) 101 B.M.L.R. 68, applying the statement of
principle in *Tahir*, but concluding on the evidence that causation was established (delay in diagnosing
onset of cauda equine syndrome); *Oliver v Williams* [2013] EWHC 600 (QB); [2013] Med. L.R. 344
applying *Tahir* to a delayed diagnosis of ovarian cancer, where the five-and-a-half month delay made
no difference to the staging of the cancer nor to the treatment options; claimant failed to prove on a
balance of probabilities that the delay made a material difference to her life expectancy.
[189] Similarly, in *Brown v Lewisham and North Southwark Health Authority* [1999] Lloyd's Rep. Med.
110 the Court of Appeal held that it is reasonable to draw a common sense inference that an increased
risk of harm must have made a material contribution to the damage where there is some evidence
which supports such an inference. But where there were no objective signs or symptoms of any
aggravation or worsening of the claimant's condition following an allegedly negligently undertaken
journey (between two hospitals) it was not reasonable to draw an inference that the journey
contributed to a deterioration.

defendant. Each defendant was jointly and severally liable for the full loss (though having a right of contribution against the other defendants liable in respect of the same damage under the Civil Liability (Contribution) Act 1978). This approach was challenged by the defendants in *Barker v Corus (UK) plc (formerly Saint Gobain Pipelines plc)*,[190] a case also involving asbestos exposure resulting in mesothelioma, who argued that they should only be responsible to the extent that they contributed to the risk, and should not be held jointly and severally liable for the damage. A majority of their Lordships agreed, and in the process redefined the nature of the damage for which the defendants were to be held responsible. Given that where the *Fairchild* principle applied the creation of a material risk of mesothelioma is sufficient to establish causation, and therefore liability, the damage that the defendant should be regarded as having caused was *the creation of the risk or chance of contracting mesothelioma*, and not the mesothelioma itself. Thus, a defendant would be liable to the extent that he added to the risk. As Lord Hoffmann put it:

> "Consistency of approach would suggest that if the basis of liability is the wrongful creation of a risk or chance of causing the disease, the damage which the defendant should be regarded as having caused is the creation of such a risk or chance. If that is the right way to characterise the damage, then it does not matter that the disease as such would be indivisible damage. Chances are infinitely divisible and different people can be separately responsible to a greater or lesser degree for the chances of an event happening."[191]

This, said his Lordship, would be a fair way to deal with the uncertainties involved. The *"Fairchild* exception" was created because the alternative of leaving the claimant with no remedy was thought to be unfair, but it did not follow that fairness meant the claimant should recover in full from any defendant.[192] On this approach there would normally be no issue of contribution by other defendants or contributory negligence by the claimant, because a

> "...defendant is liable for the risk of disease which he himself has created and not for the risks created by others, whether they are defendants, persons not before the court or the claimant himself."[193]

5–073   **Damages proportionate to risk created by defendant**   Applying *Barker* the claimant is not entitled to full compensation for the mesothelioma, only compensation for the defendant's contribution to the risk of contracting mesothelioma, which it is assumed (for want of a better method) is to be

---

[190] [2006] UKHL 20; [2006] 2 A.C. 572. For comment on *Barker v Corus* see A. Kramer, "Smoothing the Rough Justice of the *Fairchild* Principle" (2006) 122 L.Q.R. 547; G. Turton, "Risk and the damage requirement in negligence liability" (2015) 35 L.S. 75.

[191] [2006] UKHL 20; [2006] 2 A.C. 572 at [35].

[192] "In my opinion, the attribution of liability according to the relative degree of contribution to the chance of the disease being contracted would smooth the roughness of the justice which a rule of joint and several liability creates. The defendant was a wrongdoer, it is true, and should not be allowed to escape liability altogether, but he should not be liable for more than the damage which he caused and, since this is a case in which science can deal only in probabilities, the law should accept that position and attribute liability according to probabilities", per Lord Hoffmann [2006] UKHL 20; [2006] 2 A.C. 572 at [43]; see also per Lord Scott at [62].

[193] [2006] UKHL 20; [2006] 2 A.C. 572 at [47] per Lord Hoffmann; see also, per Lord Scott at [63]; and per Lord Walker at [118].

calculated as a percentage of the damages that would be awarded on a full liability basis for causing mesothelioma, discounted to reflect the defendant's contribution to the overall risk.[194] Nor is the defendant entitled to seek contribution from other defendants, at least in respect of different periods of exposure, since the "damage" they have caused (exposure of the claimant to risk) is not the same. It would be possible, of course, for two defendants to have been negligent with respect to the same period of exposure (for example, an occupier of premises and the employer of an employee working on those premises), in which case a contribution claim would be appropriate. By the same token, it would be possible for a claimant to have been contributorily negligent in a period of exposure for which a defendant was responsible, e.g. by failing to take reasonable precautions against inhalation of asbestos dust. But if the claimant were to be negligent with respect to his own safety during a period of self-employment, that would not fall to be taken into account as reducing the damages payable by a defendant who negligently exposed the claimant to risk during a different period. The claimant's negligence would not have contributed to the same damage for which the defendant was responsible.

Defendant liable only where claimant actually sustains physical harm   If   5–074
the damage is characterised as exposure to the risk of disease, this could, theoretically, open up the possibility of claims by individuals exposed to the risk of harm even though that harm has not yet eventuated. Counsel for the defendants in *Barker v Corus* had expressly declined to characterise the claim as being for the risk of causing disease (as opposed to the disease itself) because he wanted to avoid the possibility that a claim could be made in respect of exposure to the risk of disease when the risk has not materialised. That possibility was prevented, said Lord Hoffmann, because the "*Fairchild* exception" only applies when the claimant has actually contracted the disease against which the defendant should have protected.[195] Outside the exception, the risk of damage or loss of a chance of avoiding damage cannot form the basis of a claim.[196]

Lord Rodger's dissent in *Barker*   In a powerful dissenting speech on the   5–075
question of apportionment Lord Rodger complained that the majority were "not so much reinterpreting as rewriting the key decisions in *McGhee* … and *Fairchild*".[197] For Lord Rodger *Fairchild* had made an explicit connection between proof that the defendants had materially increased the risk of harm and proof that the defendants had caused the claimants' mesothelioma:

---

[194] [2006] UKHL 20; [2006] 2 A.C. 572 at [48] per Lord Hoffmann, and Lord Scott at [62]. So in *Heneghan v Manchester Dry Docks Ltd* [2016] EWCA Civ 86; [2016] 1 W.L.R. 2036 where the evidence was that the deceased's lung cancer was caused by exposure to asbestos and the defendants were responsible for 35.2 per cent of the total exposure to asbestos the claimant recovered 35.2 per cent of the damages that would have been awarded on a full liability basis.

[195] [2006] UKHL 20; [2006] 2 A.C. 572 at [48].

[196] [2006] UKHL 20; [2006] 2 A.C. 572 at [48] per Lord Hoffmann, citing *Gregg v Scott* [2005] 2 A.C. 176; though note that it is arguable that *Gregg v Scott* has not finally determined this issue (see paras 5–121 to 5–124) and Lord Hoffmann's statement is not, in any event, strictly accurate, since loss of chance claims in respect of financial losses are routine in claims against professionals (other than health professionals).

[197] [2006] UKHL 20; [2006] 2 A.C. 572 at [71].

"...by proving that the defendants had materially increased the risk of the victim contracting mesothelioma, the plaintiffs had proved that the defendants had made a material contribution to causing the disease and were accordingly liable for causing it. Reading the speeches as though they were saying something different is unlikely to make an already difficult topic any easier."[198]

Moreover, the new analysis would:

"...tend to maximise the inconsistencies in the law by turning the *Fairchild* exception into an enclave where a number of rules apply which have been rejected for use elsewhere in the law of personal injuries."[199]

The majority were not just on a mission to tidy up the reasoning in *McGhee* and *Fairchild*, but were "spontaneously embarking upon this adventure of redefining the nature of the damage suffered by the victims" in order to enable defendants to be made severally liable for a share of the damages, rather than being jointly liable for the whole of the damages.[200] As his Lordship pointed out, as long as all the possible defendants are solvent or insured, joint and several liability causes defendants and their insurers no difficulty, because a defendant can recover the appropriate contribution from the other defendants and their insurers under the Civil Liability (Contribution) Act 1978. Several liability transfers the risk of the insolvency of potential defendants from solvent defendants and their insurers to claimants, who as a consequence of *Barker v Corus* would have to bring actions against each defendant who exposed the claimant to the risk of harm, and seek to recover damages in respect of that defendant's contribution to the overall risk.

5–076   ***Barker* still correct**   The implications of the combined effect of *Fairchild* and *Barker* for insurers were considered in two Supreme Court decisions. In the first, *Durham v BAI (Run Off) Ltd*[201] the Supreme Court appeared to revise its approach to *Barker* in order to ensure that employers' liability insurance policies would "respond" to the liability being imposed on the employers. Lord Mance, for the majority, concluded that for the purposes of the insurance liability for mesothelioma following exposure to asbestos during an insurance period involved a "weak" or "broad" causal link sufficient for the disease to be regarded as "caused" within the insurance period. It was not accurate to treat the employer's liability as being either solely or strictly for the risk. The reality was that the "employer is being held responsible for the mesothelioma".[202] Lord Clarke, who clearly had reservations as to whether *Barker* was correctly decided, took the view that the injury was the mesothelioma, not the risk of developing mesothelioma, but that:

---

[198] [2006] UKHL 20; [2006] 2 A.C. 572 at [83].
[199] [2006] UKHL 20; [2006] 2 A.C. 572 at [85].
[200] [2006] UKHL 20; [2006] 2 A.C. 572 at [86].
[201] [2012] UKSC 14; [2012] 1 W.L.R. 867 (also known as "the Trigger litigation"); N. McBride and S. Steel "The 'trigger' litigation" (2012) 28 P.N. 285; G. Meggitt "The 'rock of uncertainty'— mesothelioma, insurers and the courts" [2013] J.B.L. 563; Bevan [2012] J.P.I.L. C163.
[202] [2012] UKSC 14; [2012] 1 W.L.R. 867 at [73].

"...by creating the risk of mesothelioma in the future, the employer is *deemed to have caused* the mesothelioma, if it should develop in the future."[203]

It was arguable that *Durham v BAI (Run Off) Ltd* had, in effect, overruled *Barker* on the question of the nature of the damage for which the employer is held responsible, without expressly doing so. That was certainly the interpretation of the Court of Appeal in *International Energy Group Ltd v Zurich Insurance Plc UK*[204] where Toulson LJ said that the decision in *Barker* "has become past history". The damage for which a victim might sue under *Fairchild* was contracting mesothelioma, and the wrongful exposure to asbestos met the causal requirements for him to be entitled to hold the employer responsible in law for his illness.[205] However, the Supreme Court was unanimously of the view that *Durham* had not changed the common law position on causation and that *Barker* still applied (subject to s.3 of the Compensation Act 2006) where a claimant is suing his employer.[206] Lord Mance observed that there had been no challenge to the correctness of *Barker* in *Durham*. It was simply that the court had accepted that within the "*Fairchild* enclave" it was necessary to adopt a "weak" notion of causation, in order to protect victims of mesothelioma, and then held that this weak notion of causation carried through into an insurance context.[207]

(i) Relationship of Barker v Corus to the Fatal Accidents Act 1976

Although the majority of their Lordships in *Barker v Corus* appear to have assumed that redefining the claimant's damage as the defendant's contribution to the risk of harm made no difference to a claim under the Fatal Accidents Act 1976,[208] not least because two of the claimants in the litigation before the House had died, it is not obvious that this approach fits well with the wording of the Fatal Accidents Act. Section 1(1) provides that:

5–077

> "If death is caused by any wrongful act, neglect or default which is such as would (if death had not ensued) have entitled the person injured to maintain an action and recover damages in respect thereof, the person who would have been liable if death had not ensued shall be liable to an action for damages, notwithstanding the death of the person injured."

In *Barker v Corus*, however, the defendants were not held liable for the wrongful act of contributing to the deceased's mesothelioma, which is what killed the deceased, but for *contributing to the risk* of contracting mesothelioma. The

---

[203] [2012] UKSC 14; [2012] 1 W.L.R. 867 at [85], emphasis added. In a dissenting judgment Lord Phillips P insisted that *Barker* created liability only in respect of the risk of the employee developing mesothelioma and that it would be wrong to depart from the reasoning of the majority in *Barker* for the sole purpose of imposing liability on employers' liability insurers ([2012] UKSC 14; [2012] 1 W.L.R. 867 at [137]).

[204] [2013] EWCA Civ 39; [2013] 3 All E.R. 395 at [13].

[205] [2013] EWCA Civ 39; [2013] 3 All E.R. 395 at [28]; see also per Aikens LJ at [48].

[206] *International Energy Group Ltd v Zurich Insurance Plc UK* [2015] UKSC 33; [2016] A.C. 509. For comment see S. Green, "Between a rock of uncertainty and a hard case" (2016) 132 L.Q.R. 25; J. Morgan, "Reinterpreting the reinterpretation of the reinterpretation of *Fairchild*" (2015) 74 C.L.J. 395; J. Fulbrook [2015] J.P.I.L. C188.

[207] [2015] UKSC 33; [2016] A.C. 509 at [49].

[208] See, e.g. Lord Scott [2006] UKHL 20; [2006] 2 A.C. 572 at [63].

majority approach is expressly that the individual defendants had *not* caused the death, merely contributed to the risk of death. But as Lord Rodger pointed out:

> "By any reckoning, death brought on by mesothelioma is indivisible, indeed the classically indivisible injury. Viscount Dunedin once said scornfully of a hypothetical case where two dogs had worried a sheep to death, 'Would we then have to hold that each dog had half killed the sheep ...?': *Arneil v Paterson* [1931] A.C. 560, 565. It is similarly unthinkable that the law would hold that, *vis-à-vis* the claimant, defendant A one-fifth killed the victim of mesothelioma, defendant B one-quarter killed him, defendant C forty per cent killed him and so forth."[209]

Dependants claiming under the Fatal Accidents Act have always been required to prove that *the death* was *caused* by the defendant's wrongful act, and if they establish causation they are entitled to damages in full in respect of their loss of dependency, assessed in accordance with well-established principles under ss.3 and 4 of the Act, subject only to reduction for contributory negligence. There is no provision in the Act allowing for proportionate liability as between claimants and defendant (though defendants can claim contribution from other defendants under the Civil Liability (Contribution) Act 1978). Logically, in a case such as *Barker v Corus*, either the dependants recover in full for their loss of dependency, applying normal principles, on the basis that their Lordships did not purport, and indeed had no power, to amend the Fatal Accidents Act, or the dependants have no claim at all under the Act, on the basis that the damage for which the defendant is held responsible did not cause the death. This issue was not addressed in the majority speeches in *Barker v Corus*, and though the Compensation Act 2006, s.3 now reduces the practical import in the context of asbestos-related mesothelioma, it remains potentially problematic in any other comparable situation of disease resulting in the death of the individual where there are multiple tortfeasors.

(ii) Compensation Act 2003 s.3

5–078 Following the ruling in *Barker v Corus (UK) plc*, an amendment to the Compensation Bill was rapidly introduced to re-establish the principle that defendants are jointly and severally liable for the mesothelioma itself caused by asbestos exposure, and not simply their respective contribution to the risk of contracting mesothelioma. The Compensation Act 2006 s.3 provides that where a "responsible person" (the defendant) has negligently or in breach of statutory duty caused or permitted another person (the victim) to be exposed to asbestos, and the victim has contracted mesothelioma as a result of the exposure, and it is not possible to determine with certainty whether it was that exposure or another exposure which caused the victim to become ill, and the defendant is liable in tort by virtue of the exposure, in connection with damage caused to the victim by the disease (whether by reason of having materially increased a risk or for any other reason), the defendant shall be liable in respect of the whole of the damage caused to the victim by the disease, and that liability is jointly and severally with any other responsible person. The defendant's joint and several liability is

---

[209] [2006] UKHL 20; [2006] 2 A.C. 572 at [69].

irrespective of whether the victim was also exposed to asbestos: (i) other than by the defendant, whether or not in circumstances in which another person has a liability in tort, or; (ii) by the defendant in circumstances in which he has no liability in tort. In other words, the defendant will be jointly and severally liable in a situation such as *Fairchild* itself, where all the other defendants were also liable in tort to the claimant, and where the victim has also been exposed to asbestos non-negligently by another person (as considered in *Barker v Corus*). The defendant will also be jointly and severally liable in circumstances where part of the victim's exposure is attributable to non-negligent conduct by the defendant.[210]

Section 3 of the Compensation Act 2006 has not changed the common law rules on causation. Rather it provides that, in the specific case of asbestos-induced mesothelioma only, if the conclusion is that liability is established applying whatever test of causation is the correct test at common law, the defendant will be jointly and severally liable for the damage itself (i.e. mesothelioma) and not simply severally liable for contributing to the risk of damage.[211] Thus, where *Fairchild* applies *Barker* has the effect of defining the defendant's liability by reference to the risk of damage created by the individual defendant, except that in cases of asbestos-induced mesothelioma the defendant will be jointly and severally liable with any other culpable defendant to the full extent of the claimant's loss attributable to the mesothelioma.

5–079

Damage other than mesothelioma   The general principle of common law established by *Barker v Corus* remains applicable to other forms of personal injury.[212] The general assumption was that *Fairchild* and *McGhee* were part and parcel of the same proposition of law, namely that in some circumstances, not definitively laid out in *Fairchild*, a claimant can rely on the defendant's material contribution to the risk of harm as a means of overcoming scientific gaps in establishing "but for" causation.[213] If the facts of *McGhee* were to recur, *Barker v Corus* would apply, and the claimant would only be entitled to claim in respect of the contribution to the risk of contracting dermatitis that the employer's breach of duty made, and not for the dermatitis itself. By the same token, if a case similar to *Wilsher v Essex Area Health Authority* were to arise where there were, say, only two risk factors, one of which was caused by the defendant's breach of duty and one of which was innocent, then, provided the court could be persuaded that the risk factors operated by way of the same or a similar causal mechanism, the

5–080

---

[210] As, e.g. in *McGhee v National Coal Board* [1973] 1 W.L.R. 1; para.5–046 where the defendant had taken reasonable precautions in respect of part of the claimant's exposure to brick dust, or as where part of the victim's exposure pre-dated the time from which the risks of asbestos exposure became known, so that the defendant was not in breach of duty in respect of that particular period of exposure.

[211] *Sienkiewicz v Greif (UK) Ltd* [2011] UKSC 10; [2011] 2 A.C. 229.

[212] Such as lung cancer: *Heneghan v Manchester Dry Docks Ltd* [2016] EWCA Civ 86; [2016] 1 W.L.R. 2036 (defendants responsible for 35.2 per cent of total exposure to asbestos; claimant recovers 35.2 per cent of the damages that would have been awarded on a full liability basis in respect of deceased's lung cancer).

[213] Lord Hoffmann commented in *Barker v Corus* [2006] UKHL 20; [2006] 2 A.C. 572 at [13] that: "*McGhee* must therefore be accepted as an approved application of the *Fairchild* exception."

Fairchild principle could apply to establish causation but again the defendant's liability would be limited by reference to his contribution to the overall risk of harm, applying *Barker v Corus*.

(f) The "material contribution to damage" test in medical cases

5–081   The uncertainty involved in making difficult judgments about causal relationships in some cases, and the temptation for all concerned, including expert witnesses, to resort to the language of "risk", "risk factors" or "chances" should not obscure the basic proposition that causation is a question of *fact* based on *inferences*[214] from the evidence, and that as a matter of *law* the claimant does not have to prove that the defendant's negligence was the only, or even the main, cause of the damage. He only has to prove a material contribution to the damage, applying *Bonnington Castings Ltd v Wardlaw*.[215] This approach can be seen in a number of cases where the courts have characterised multiple causal factors as *cumulative* causes. It will be recalled that in a case where the claimant's damage is categorised as indivisible the material contribution to the damage test does not apply.[216] A claimant can rely on the material contribution to the damage test in a case involving multiple causes (where one of the causes is the defendant's breach of duty) in the case of divisible damage. If the extent of the defendant's contribution is known (even if this involves a rough and ready calculation) the defendant is liable only to that extent, but if the extent of the defendant's contribution is unknown there will be no apportionment and the defendant is liable in full for the claimant's loss.[217]

5–082   In *Boustead v North West Strategic Health Authority (City Maternity Hospital Carlisle)*[218] the claimant suffered from intraventricular haemorrhage a few hours after his birth resulting in him sustaining brain damage, which he attributed to the negligence of the defendants in delaying proceeding to a Caesarean section. The defendants argued that the intraventricular haemorrhage was due to a number of non-negligent factors, namely the claimant's extreme prematurity, hypoxia at birth secondary to a retroplacental haemorrhage, and respiratory illness due to lung immaturity requiring mechanical ventilation. Intraventricular haemorrhage can occur as a result of prematurity on its own and can also be caused by mechanical ventilation alone, and so, it was said, the claimant may have developed the condition even without the breach of duty. If any hypoxia did occur as a result of the negligence, the defendants argued, it made no difference because the claimant's fate was "sealed" before then by virtue of the presence of other risk factors, predominantly prematurity. The claimant argued that the hypoxia he suffered due to a negligent delay in proceeding to a Caesarean section had probably also made a material contribution to the intraventricular haemorrhage. The medical experts were agreed that more than 50 per cent of babies with this

---

[214] See para.5–030.
[215] [1956] A.C. 613; para.5–033.
[216] See para.5–035. Indivisible damage includes mesothelioma, cancer, death (see para.5–077) and possibly psychiatric harm: see para.5–044.
[217] See para.5–040.
[218] [2008] EWHC 2375 (QB); [2008] L.S. Law Med. 471.

combination of risk factors would develop some degree of intraventricular haemorrhage, but they were unable to identify or quantify the individual causal contribution made by each factor. Mackay J held that these were not competing causes which were mutually exclusive, but were causes which acted cumulatively. Adopting the "robust and pragmatic approach to undisputed primary facts" which Lord Bridge, in *Wilsher v Essex Area Health Authority*,[219] had suggested was the basis of the decision of the House of Lords in *McGhee v National Coal Board*, Mackay J then applied *Bonnington Castings v Wardlaw*, concluding that since there were concurrent *cumulative* causes of the condition, the claimant had satisfied the burden of proving that the defendant's breach of duty had made a material contribution to his disabilities.

In *Telles v South West Strategic Health Authority*[220] a baby developed severe hypoxia one day after her birth, and underwent cardiac surgery two days later. That operation was performed negligently and she continued to suffer from severe hypoxia until she was operated on again three days later. The evidence indicated that she had suffered damage from the hypoxia over the whole period from the onset of the condition to the time of the second operation, but on the scientific evidence it was not possible to apportion the damage sustained from hypoxia between that which occurred before the first operation and that which occurred after it. Saunders J held[221] that the claimant was entitled to recover damages in full for the whole of the damage caused by the hypoxia:

        5–083

> "Medical science is unable at present to answer these questions. On the balance of probabilities I do not think that the damage would have been suffered equally over the whole period. Indeed I think it is extremely unlikely that it was. I do not believe it is possible to apportion the damage and, on the basis of what I understand to be the agreed position in law, the claimant is entitled to recover in full for the PVL."[222]

Bailey v Ministry of Defence   In *Bailey v Ministry of Defence*[223] the claimant underwent a procedure to explore and treat a possible gall stone in her bile duct. Following the procedure her condition deteriorated significantly and there was a period of negligent care which contributed to her deteriorating condition. She also developed pancreatitis, though this was not due to any negligence, but it also caused her overall medical condition to deteriorate. Some two weeks after the original procedure the claimant aspirated her own vomit leading to a cardiac arrest that caused hypoxic brain damage. The causation issue turned on whether the claimant's inability to respond naturally to her vomit was because of weakness due to the severe pancreatitis and/or the weakness due the defendants' negligence. The claimant alleged that as a result of the negligence she became very much more ill after the first procedure than she would otherwise have been, and underwent further procedures that should have been avoided. Although she would probably have developed pancreatitis and renal failure in any event, they

        5–084

---

219 [1988] A.C. 1074 at 1090; see para.5–049.
220 [2008] EWHC 292 (QB); [2013] Med. L.R. 272.
221 On the authority of *Dingle v Associated Newspapers* [1961] 2 Q.B. 169; aff'd at [1964] A.C. 371.
222 [2008] EWHC 292 (QB); [2013] Med. L.R. 272 at [99].
223 [2008] EWCA Civ 883; [2009] 1 W.L.R. 1052; see S. Green, "Contributing to the risk of confusion? Causation in the Court of Appeal" (2009) 125 L.Q.R. 44; G. Turton, "A Case for Clarity in Causation?" (2009) 17 Med. L. Rev. 140.

would have been less severe and she would have been in a much fitter state to combat them. The reason why she aspirated was her extreme weakness as a result of her lengthy illness, caused, or materially contributed to, by the defendant's breach of duty. The defendants argued that the case was governed by *Wilsher* and adding an existing risk to risks which might also have caused harm was not proof of causation, even if the new risk arose from negligence. The trial judge, Foskett J, held that the physical cause of the claimant's aspiration and subsequent cardiac arrest was her weakness and inability to react to her vomit; that there were two contributory causes of that weakness, the non-negligent cause, pancreatitis, and the negligent cause, the lack of care and what flowed from that; and since each "contributed materially" to the overall weakness, and since the overall weakness caused the aspiration, causation was established.[224]

5–085   The Court of Appeal agreed that the judge had applied the correct test. *Bonnington Castings v Wardlaw* was authority for the proposition that in a case involving cumulative causes, where the inadequacies of medical science mean that the relative potency of the causes cannot be established, a claimant merely has to establish that the defendant's breach of duty was a "material" contribution, meaning something more than de minimis.[225] *Wilsher* was distinguished on the basis that it was not a case of causes cumulatively causing injury but a case where there were different distinct causes which operated in a different way and might have caused the injury, where the claimant could not establish which cause either "caused or contributed" to his injury.[226] Waller LJ concluded that:

> "...one cannot draw a distinction between medical negligence cases and others. I would summarise the position in relation to *cumulative cause* cases as follows. If the evidence demonstrates on a balance of probabilities that the injury would have occurred as a result of the non-tortious cause or causes in any event, the claimant will have failed to establish that the tortious cause contributed. *Hotson* exemplifies such a situation. If the evidence demonstrates that 'but for' the contribution of the tortious cause the injury would probably not have occurred, the claimant will (obviously) have discharged the burden. In a case where medical science cannot establish the probability that 'but for' an act of negligence the injury would not have happened but can establish that the contribution of the negligent cause was more than negligible, the 'but for' test is modified, and the claimant will succeed."[227]

5–086   It is respectfully submitted that this analysis is correct. Once the judge had found that the claimant's aspiration of her vomit was caused by her "weakened state" and that her weakened state was caused ("contributed to") by both the defendants' breach of duty and the effects of the (non-negligent) pancreatitis the conclusion that the breach of duty "materially contributed to the damage" was unavoidable. This was a straightforward application of *Bonnington Castings* to a case of medical negligence. Although counsel for the defendant sought to rely on *Wilsher v Essex Area Health Authority* (and also raised in argument the authorities of *Fairchild v Glenhaven Funeral Services Ltd*, *Hotson v East*

---

[224] [2008] EWCA Civ 883; [2009] 1 W.L.R. 1052 at [17] per Waller LJ.

[225] Applying the interpretation of Lord Rodger in *Fairchild v Glenhaven* [2002] UKHL 22; [2003] 1 A.C. 32 at [129] that "in the cumulative cause case such as *Wardlaw* the 'but for' test is modified".

[226] [2008] EWCA Civ 883; [2009] 1 W.L.R. 1052 at [44].

[227] [2008] EWCA Civ 883; [2009] 1 W.L.R. 1052 at [46] (original emphasis). Waller LJ's assertion that the "but for" test is modified when *Bonnington Castings* applies has come in for some criticism: see para.5–088, n.232 below.

Berkshire Area Health Authority and *Gregg v Scott*[228]) this was not a case where the claimant had to rely on the argument that the defendants' negligence had merely increased the *risk* of harm (or reduced the claimant's chances of avoiding harm).[229] She could not prove "but for" causation, in the sense that she could not prove on a balance of probabilities that in the absence of the pancreatitis she would nonetheless have been so weakened by the defendant's negligence that she would have been "unable to respond naturally to her vomit". But she does not have to prove that the negligence was the sole or even the main cause of her weakened state. Applying *Bonnington Castings* she only has to prove that it made a material contribution. There was ample evidence, and consequent findings of fact, to support the conclusion that the negligence had materially contributed to her weakened state. There was no need to draw "robust and pragmatic" inferences, or rely on notions of "increased risk". It is true that *Bonnington Castings* allows the court to overcome evidential gaps due to an inability to say precisely what did cause the damage. So, what was *known* from the evidence in *Bailey* was that the damage was caused by the claimant's inability to respond appropriately to the vomiting; that that was caused by the claimant's weakened state; and the claimant's weakened state was caused by (a) the defendant's negligence *and* (b) pancreatitis. What was *not known* was whether in the absence of (a) the claimant would still have been so weak that she could not respond appropriately; and whether in the absence of (b) she would still have been so weak that she could not respond appropriately. In other words, the scientific gap prevented the claimant from establishing that the weakness arising from the breach of duty probably led to her aspirating her vomit and so caused the heart attack and consequent brain damage. But *Bonnington Castings* permits the court to conclude that it is sufficient to establish causation if (a) made a material contribution to her inability to respond appropriately, and therefore to the damage.

In *Williams v The Bermuda Hospitals Board*[230] the Privy Council accepted that   **5–087** *Bonnington Castings Ltd v Wardlaw* applied to a claim for clinical negligence where there had been a negligent delay in diagnosing and treating the claimant's ruptured appendix. The claimant developed complications after surgery to remove his appendix. The trial judge held that the claimant had not proved on a balance of probabilities that the complications had been caused by the delay, but the Court of Appeal of Bermuda held that the judge had raised the bar "unattainably high". The defendants' breaches of duty had contributed materially to the complications. Giving the judgment of the Privy Council Lord Toulson said that the parallel of *Bonnington Castings* with Mr. Williams' case was "obvious".

---

[228] See para.5–100 et seq., below.

[229] Note that, *by definition*, any breach of duty will necessarily have increased the foreseeable risk of harm to the claimant, otherwise there would not have been a breach of duty, which requires that the defendant has taken an unreasonable risk of causing harm to the claimant. This does not convert all causation problems into arguments about increased causal risk or the loss of a chance.

[230] [2016] UKPC 4; [2016] A.C. 888; discussed by M. Lyons [2016] J.P.I.L. C75; T. Trotman, "Causation in clinical negligence claims after *Williams v Bermuda Hospitals Board*" [2016] J.P.I.L. 154; J. Stapleton and S. Steel, "Causes and contributions" (2016) 132 L.Q.R. 363; and C. Hobson, "*Williams v The Bermuda Hospitals Board*: pro-patient, but for ambiguities which remain" (2017) 25 Med. L. Rev. 126.

It was "immaterial whether the cumulative factors operate concurrently or successively". The sepsis from the ruptured appendix developed incrementally over a period of six hours, progressively causing myocardial ischaemia. Its development and effect on the heart and lungs was a single continuous process. The negligent delay amounted to two hours and 20 minutes and therefore, said Lord Toulson, it was correct to infer on the balance of probabilities that the negligence materially contributed to the process, and that it materially contributed to the claimant's injury. Commenting, obiter, on counsel's criticism of *Bailey v Ministry of Defence* Lord Toulson said that on the facts of *Bailey* the judge had been correct to hold the hospital liable for the consequences of the patient's aspiration of her vomit, but considered that a different rationale applied:

> "As to the parallel weakness of the claimant due to her pancreatitis, the case may be seen as an example of the well-known principle that a tortfeasor takes his victim as he finds her. The Board does not share the view of the Court of Appeal that the case involved a departure from the 'but-for' test. The judge concluded that the totality of the claimant's weakened condition caused the harm. If so, 'but-for' causation was established. The fact that her vulnerability was heightened by her pancreatitis no more assisted the hospital's case than if she had an egg shell skull."[231]

5-088   Despite some criticism,[232] *Bailey v Ministry of Defence* has been applied in a number of subsequent cases. In *Popple v Birmingham Women's NHS Foundation Trust*[233] the Court of Appeal applied *Bailey* to a case of delayed delivery of child which resulted in serious brain damage. Ward LJ (with whom Longmore and Richards LJJ agreed) said:

> "Here the negligent failure to deliver Nathan before 14.44 caused all the damage if this was a 15 minute insult. Medical science cannot establish whether it was a 15 minute insult or a 20 minute insult. If it did take 20 minutes, the damage done in the last five minutes must have made a contribution to the overall harm which was more than minimal. I cannot see why the *Bailey* principle does not apply."[234]

5-089   In *John v Central Manchester and Manchester Children's University Hospitals NHS Foundation Trust*[235] Picken J applied *Bailey* to a case where there were three causal factors involved in the claimant's brain damage. The claimant

---

[231] [2016] UKPC 4; [2016] A.C. 888 at [47]. For discussion of the eggshell skull rule see paras 5–181 et seq.

[232] The criticism tends to focus on the reasoning rather than the outcome: see S. Green "Contributing to the risk of confusion? Causation in the Court of Appeal" (2009) 125 L.Q.R. 44; G. Turton, "A Case for Clarity in Causation?" (2009) 17 Med. L. Rev. 140; J. Stapleton "Unnecessary causes" (2013) 129 L.Q.R. 39 and the discussion of *Bailey* (in the light of Professor Stapleton's analysis) in *Rich v Hull and East Yorkshire Hospitals NHS Trust* [2015] EWHC 3395 (QB); [2016] Med. L.R. 33 at [201]–[211].

[233] [2012] EWCA Civ 1628; [2013] Med L.R. 47.

[234] [2012] EWCA Civ 1628; [2013] Med L.R. 47 at [79]

[235] [2016] EWHC 407 (QB); [2016] 4 W.L.R. 54. See also *Leigh v London Ambulance Service NHS Trust* [2014] EWHC 286 (QB); [2014] Med. L.R. 134 where *Bailey* was applied to a claim in respect of post-traumatic stress disorder and dissociative seizures attributed to the claimant being trapped between seats on a bus due to the dislocation of her knee (the parties had agreed that it was a case involving "cumulative causes" of the damage). The defendants' admitted breach of duty resulted in a 17-minute delay in the arrival of an ambulance. Globe J concluded that it was a case where medical science could not establish the probability that "but for" the negligent delay the PTSD would not have

suffered a head injury in a fall and developed an acute subdural haematoma. There was a negligent six-hour delay in performing a CT scan, with the result that there was a corresponding delay in performing surgery. There had also been a further hour's delay in arranging the claimant's transfer to another hospital for the surgery. The claimant had a seizure in the interim due to raised intra-cranial pressure and a further seizure after the operation. He also developed a non-negligent post-operative infection. He was left with permanent cognitive and neuropsychological impairment. The defendants argued (at least initially) that since the defendants' negligence was merely one of three disparate causal factors, the other two being the head injury and the post-operative infection, the claimant must prove that the breach of duty was the "but for" cause of the damage, and that *Bonnington Castings*, *Bailey* and *Williams v The Bermuda Hospitals Board* did not apply because those cases all involved a "single agency", not multiple causal factors. Picken J rejected the argument, holding that the material contribution to damage approach to causation can apply just much multiple causal factor cases as it does to "single agency" cases. Whether it can be applied in any given case will depend on whether the evidence points to the agency or factor for which the defendant was responsible as a probable contributing factor in causing the claimant's damage. The existence of other, non-negligent factors which may have caused or contributed to the damage *may* prevent the court from inferring that the negligent factor was a contributing cause, but this will depend on the strength of the evidence overall.[236]

Similarly, in *Ingram v Williams*[237] there were three non-negligent causal factors, in addition to the defendant's alleged negligence, implicated in the claimant's damage. The experts' view was that all the causal factors made an unquantifiable material contribution to the claimant's disability. At its highest the experts could say only that if the events alleged to constitute a breach of duty had not occurred there would have been a material but unquantifiable reduction in the degree of disability from which the claimant suffered. Walker J held that on the evidence the claimant's damage was not divisible. The alleged negligence had materially contributed to the damage, and damages would have been awarded in full.[238]

5–090

---

happened, but it was established that the contribution of the negligent delay was more than negligible, and so it made a material contribution to the development of the PTSD. *Leigh* is commented on by Tavares [2014] J.P.I.L. C161.

[236] Note that it is arguable that this is also the position in a case like *Wilsher v Essex Area Health Authority* [1988] A.C. 1074. If, hypothetically, the evidence in *Wilsher* had been that the four non-negligent risk factors that were present only rarely caused damage but the evidence pointed to a very high correlation between excess oxygen (attributable to the defendant's breach of duty) and the damage suffered by the claimant, it might be legitimate to draw the inference that it was probable that the breach of duty did cause the damage applying the "but for" test. The existence of the non-negligent risk factors complicates the assessment, but it all depends on the strength of the evidence about the various risk factors.

[237] [2010] EWHC 758 (QB); [2010] Med. L.R. 255.

[238] The claim failed on the basis that there had been no breach of duty. See also *Barrett v Sandwell and West Birmingham Hospitals NHS Trust* [2015] EWHC 2627 (QB); (2016) 147 B.M.L.R. 151 at [169]–[170] and *Rich v Hull and East Yorkshire Hospitals NHS Trust* [2015] EWHC 3395 (QB); [2016] Med. L.R. 33 [196]–[211] where the actions of the defendants were found not to be in breach of duty, though causation would have been established by applying *Bailey*. In *Gardner v Northampton General Hospital NHS Trust* [2014] EWHC 4217 (QB) at [48] and *Pringle v Nestor Prime Care*

(g) "Material contribution" in other jurisdictions

5–091   **Canada**   In Canada the material contribution to risk test[239] derived from *McGhee v National Coal Board* has had a mixed reception. In *Powell v Guttman*[240] the claimant developed a condition of avascular necrosis following an operation on her leg performed by the defendant orthopaedic surgeon. The defendant negligently failed to advise the claimant to undergo an arthoplasty operation to correct this. When another surgeon performed the operation the claimant sustained a rotary fracture of the femur because the delay had caused the condition of the bone to deteriorate as result of osteoporosis. The question was whether the negligence was a cause of the fracture. The defendant was held liable because his negligence had caused an increase in the osteoporosis which rendered the femur more susceptible to the fracture. This materially increased the risk of the very fracture which did occur. O'Sullivan J.A. applied the principle of *McGhee*:

> "However, I think the law in Canada is that where a tortfeasor creates or materially contributes to a significant risk of injury occurring and injury does occur which is squarely within the risk thus created or materially increased, then unless the risk is spent, the tortfeasor is liable for injury which follows from the risk, even though there are other subsequent causes which also cause or materially contribute to that injury."[241]

5–092   The Saskatchewan Court of Appeal has also applied this principle.[242] On the other hand, in *Wilkinson Estate (Rogin) v Shannon*[243] Anderson J was not convinced that *McGhee* represented the law of Ontario, and in *Wilson v Vancouver Hockey Club*[244] Murray J declined to apply *McGhee* in a case of

---

Services Ltd [2014] EWHC 1308 (QB) at [129] Sir David Eady and Michael Harvey QC, respectively, applied *Bailey* in the alternative, having also found causation established on the balance of probabilities.

[239] The courts have not always drawn a clear distinction between material contribution to risk and material contribution to damage.

[240] (1978) 89 D.L.R. (3d) 180, Man CA.

[241] (1978) 89 D.L.R. (3d) 180 at 192. Though note that in *Meyers v Stanley* 2005 ABCA 114; (2005) 74 D.L.R. (4th) 345 the Alberta Court of Appeal considered this statement of principle to have been overruled by the decision of the Supreme Court of Canada in *Snell v Farrell* (1990) 72 D.L.R. (4th) 289; para.5–092.

[242] *Nowsco Well Service Ltd v Canadian Propane Gas & Oil Ltd* (1981) 122 D.L.R. (3d) 228, a non-medical case. See also *Meyer v Gordon* (1981) 17 C.C.L.T. 1 at 41–42, BCSC where *McGhee* was relied upon as an "additional ground" since the judge had already found that the negligence probably caused the damage. The negligence had "materially increased the risk of injury to the child and materially increased the risk of foetal distress and the resulting hypoxia". In *Wipfli v Britten* (1982) 145 D.L.R. (3d) 80, BCSC; aff'd (1984) 13 D.L.R. (4th) 169, BCCA, the trial judge had relied on *McGhee* to establish causation, but the British Columbia Court of Appeal considered that this was unnecessary, since causation had been established on a balance of probabilities from the evidence. It was a reasonable inference that had the physicians attending the labour known that there were twins the labour would not have been allowed to continue for so long, and this would have avoided or materially lessened the effects of the prolonged labour on the second twin.

[243] (1986) 37 C.C.L.T. 181, Ont HC.

[244] (1983) 5 D.L.R. (4th) 282 at 288; aff'd (1985) 22 D.L.R. (4th) 516, BCCA, citing *Murray v Shaughnessy Hospital* (1982) 15 A.C.W.S. (2d) 389 where Esson J said that he doubted whether *McGhee* applied in British Columbia.

alleged medical negligence. In *Snell v Farrell*[245] the trial judge concluded that *McGhee* shifted the onus of proof to the defendant. The defendant had been "asking for trouble" by operating on the claimant's eye when he knew that his patient had a retrobulbar bleed. The increased risk was followed by injury in the same area of risk, and this was sufficient to establish causation. On appeal to the Supreme Court of Canada,[246] however, it was held that the burden of proof remained with the claimant throughout, applying the interpretation of *McGhee* adopted by the House of Lords in *Wilsher v Essex Area Health Authority*.[247] Nonetheless, though the burden of proof does not change, the court was entitled to draw an inference to establish causation, notwithstanding that causation was not proved by positive evidence:

> "In many malpractice cases, the facts lie particularly within the knowledge of the defendant. In these circumstances, very little affirmative evidence on the part of the plaintiff will justify the drawing of an inference of causation in the absence of evidence to the contrary."[248]

Moreover, the court was entitled to draw such an inference even where there was no firm expert opinion supporting the claimant's theory of causation, since medical experts normally determine causation in terms of certainties whereas the courts deal with the matter on the balance of probabilities.[249]

---

[245] (1986) 40 C.C.L.T. 298, 312–313, NBQB.

[246] (1990) 72 D.L.R. (4th) 289.

[247] See para.5–049.

[248] (1990) 72 D.L.R. (4th) 289 at 300.

[249] In *Meloche v Hotel Dieu Grace Hospital* (1999) 179 D.L.R. (4th) 77, Ont CA, at [34] Carthy JA commented that Sopinka J was saying: "that there is room in some cases, where medical evidence of probability is not likely available, for a trial judge to be more than usually assertive in concluding on a common sense basis that cause led to effect. It is, in effect, a generosity afforded to the victim in circumstances where, through no fault of the plaintiff, the probable cause is not susceptible of proof on a balance of probabilities." However, it would be an unjustified extension of the principle in *Snell v Farrell* to allow the speculation of expert witnesses to associate a delay in diagnosis with the outcome. The trial judge in *Meloche* had not simply filled in a void with common sense pragmatism, but had, impermissibly, challenged the medical opinions with one of his own. See further *Lankenau v Dutton* (1991) 79 D.L.R. (4th) 705, BCCA, where the cause of the claimant's paralysis was known, i.e. compression of the spinal cord during an operation. What was not clear was whether the defendant's negligent failure to make a timely diagnosis made even a partial recovery impossible. In the circumstances of the case, requiring the claimant to prove this was "importing into the concept of the legal burden of proof a requirement that a plaintiff demonstrate scientifically that which is incapable of scientific proof", per Southin JA at 717. Accordingly, this was a case for "a robust and pragmatic approach to the facts". There was sufficient evidence to find that but for the defendant's breach of duty the claimant would not have been in such a hopeless condition. Contrast *Bigcharles v Dawson Creek & District Health Care Society* 2001 BCCA 350; (2001) 5 C.C.L.T. (3d) 157 where the claimant had also sustained paralysis due to spinal cord compression and it was not clear whether this had been an inevitable result of the road traffic accident in which he had been injured or due to a negligent delay in diagnosing a fracture to the spine. A majority of the British Columbia Court of Appeal held that the trial judge had been entitled to conclude that the probabilities were equally balanced and therefore the claimant had not established his case on the balance of probabilities. *Snell v Farrell* did not "permit a trial judge to leap to a conclusion by way of an inference without a full consideration of the evidence during the weighing process" (at [71]). If the weighing of the evidence led to a conclusion that neither party had made out its case on the balance of probabilities, it was open to the trial judge to decline to draw an inference of causation. See also *Pierre v Marshall* [1994] 8 W.W.R. 478 at 506, Alta QB; *Arndt v Smith* [1994] 8 W.W.R. 568 at 579–580, BCSC; aff'd (1997)

(h)   Loss of a chance

5–100   Claimants' complaints in medical negligence actions are frequently, not that doctors have inflicted "additional" injury, but that as a result of defendants' negligence their medical conditions have not been improved or have been allowed to deteriorate. Accordingly, claimants have been deprived of the opportunity of making a full or proper recovery from the illness or injury for which they first sought treatment. Applying the "but for" test of causation, if on the balance of probabilities competent treatment would have prevented the deterioration which has occurred, or produced an improvement, the negligence is causally linked to the damage and the defendant is responsible. Where, however, the patient's prospects of a successful outcome to the treatment were estimated to be less than 50 per cent, the patient cannot satisfy the "but for" test, because even with proper treatment the damage would probably (i.e. more likely than not) have occurred in any event.

(i)   Hotson v East Berkshire Area Health Authority

5–101   An alternative approach to cases involving this type of factual uncertainty is to deal with them in terms of the measure of damages by reference to the chance of loss, rather than determining liability on an all or nothing basis (using the "but for" test). In *Hotson v East Berkshire Area Health Authority*[275] the claimant suffered an accidental injury to his hip in a fall which created a 75 per cent risk that he would develop a permanent disability through avascular necrosis of the femoral epiphysis. Due to negligent medical diagnosis the hip was not treated for five days, and the delay made the disability inevitable. The claimant contended that the doctor's negligence had deprived him of a 25 per cent chance of making a good recovery, whereas the defendant argued that the claimant had failed to prove, on the balance of probabilities, that the negligence caused the disability. The trial judge, Simon Brown J, held that where a "substantial chance" of a better medical result had been lost it was not necessary to prove that the adverse medical result was directly attributable to the breach of duty because the issue was the proper quantum of damage rather than causation. The claimant could prove causation of the lost chance and accordingly he was entitled to damages on the basis of 25 per cent of the value of the claim for the full disability.[276] This approach was upheld by the Court of Appeal, where Sir John Donaldson MR characterised the claim as the loss of the *benefit* of timely treatment, rather than the *chance* of successful treatment. The use of the word "chance" complicated the issue, because it imported probabilities, and opened the way for the defendant's argument. It was also inaccurate, said his Lordship, because it elides the identification of the loss with the valuation of the loss, which are distinct processes. Just as the categories of negligence are never closed, there was no reason why the categories of loss should be closed either.[277]

---

[275] [1987] A.C. 750, CA and HL.
[276] *Hotson v Fitzgerald* [1985] 1 All E.R. 167.
[277] [1987] A.C. 750 at 761.

There was a strong element of policy in the Court of Appeal's decision. Sir John   **5–102**
Donaldson MR commented that:

> "As a matter of common sense, it is unjust that there should be no liability for failure to treat a
> patient, simply because the chances of a successful cure by that treatment were less than 50
> per cent. Nor, by the same token, can it be just that, if the chances of a successful cure only
> marginally exceed 50 per cent, the doctor or his employer should be liable to the same extent
> as if the treatment could be guaranteed to cure. If this is the law, it is high time that it was
> changed …"[278]

The House of Lords reversed the Court of Appeal, however, on the basis that
the judge's finding that there was a high probability, put at 75 per cent, that even
with correct diagnosis and treatment the claimant's disability would have
occurred, amounted to a finding of fact that the accidental injury was the sole
cause of the disability.[279] In other words this was not a "lost chance" case, it was
an all or nothing case—either the fall or the misdiagnosis caused the disability,
and on the balance of probabilities it was the fall. The valuation of a "lost
chance" would only arise once causation had been established. As has been
pointed out, however, this decision fails to address the essence of the claimant's
argument, which was whether a claim formulated as a loss of a chance was
acceptable.[280] If the nature of the damage could be redefined as the loss of a
chance of a successful outcome, rather than the outcome itself (the disability),
then on a traditional causation test the defendants' negligence clearly did cause
the damage (i.e. the lost chance). Logically, the question of whether the
defendant's negligence caused damage is an issue that can only be dealt with
after the nature of the damage has been defined.

---

[278] [1987] A.C. 750 at 759–760. Dillon LJ observed, at 764, that: "If [counsel] is right, and the chance
is lost through a negligent failure of the doctor to examine the patient properly or to diagnose
correctly, with the result that the treatment which alone might have saved the patient is not
undertaken, the patient will have no remedy unless he can show that the chance of the treatment, if
undertaken, proving successful was more than 50 per cent. That to my mind is contrary to common
sense." Some US courts have taken a similar approach. In *Herskovits v Group Health Co-operative of
Puget Sound* 664 P. 2d 474 (1983), Washington SC, H died from cancer. If the tumour had been
diagnosed when it should have been, H had a 39 per cent chance of survival for more than five years.
By the time his tumour was discovered his chance of survival was only 25 per cent. The court allowed
the case to go to the jury on the question of proximate cause, although the "loss" constituted the 14
per cent reduction in the chance of survival, and any damages would be limited to the loss attributable
to the premature death, not the death itself. Dore J commented at 477: "To decide otherwise would be
a blanket release from liability for doctors and hospitals any time there was less than a 50 percent
chance of survival, regardless of how flagrant the negligence." See also *Hicks v United States*, 368 F.
2d 626 (4th Cir.) (1966); *Jeanes v Milner*, 428 F. 2d 598 (USCA 8th Cir.) (1970); *Hamil v Bashline*,
481 Pa. 256 (Pennsylvania SC) (1978); Price (1989) 38 I.C.L.Q. 735. *Herskovits* is discussed by Lord
Mackay in *Hotson v East Berkshire Area Health Authority* [1987] A.C. 750 at 786–789.
[279] [1987] A.C. 750. In the Scottish case of *Kenyon v Bell* 1953 S.C. 125 an infant sustained an
accidental injury to her eye. It was alleged that correct treatment by a casualty officer would have
given the child a "materially greater chance of the eye being saved" and that the loss of a chance of
saving the eye was in itself damage. The argument was rejected by Lord Guthrie as "extravagant and
contrary to principle" because the pursuer would be entitled to damages "although on the evidence the
balance of probability was that the loss of the eye was not caused by the defender". The pursuer had
to show that but for the negligence the eye would have been saved (which he subsequently failed to
do: see *Hotson v East Berkshire Area Health Authority* [1987] A.C. 750 at 784, per Lord Mackay).
[280] Stapleton (1988) 104 L.Q.R. 389, 393. This point was not lost on Sir John Donaldson MR in the
Court of Appeal.

(ii) Statistics

5–103 One of the problems confronting a claimant in this type of case is the courts' attitude to statistical evidence. In *Hotson v East Berkshire Area Health Authority* Croom-Johnson LJ explained the difficulty:

> "If it is proved statistically that 25 per cent of the population has a chance of recovery from a certain injury and 75 per cent do not, it does not mean that someone who suffers that injury and who does not recover from it has lost a 25 per cent chance. He may have lost nothing at all. What he has to do is prove that he was one of the 25 per cent and that his loss was caused by the defendant's negligence. To be a figure in a statistic does not by itself give him a cause of action. If the plaintiff succeeds in proving that he was one of the 25 per cent and that the defendant took away that chance, the logical result would be to award him 100 per cent of his damages and not only a quarter ..."[281]

The claimant's problem, of course, is that by definition he cannot prove that he would have been one of the 25 per cent because if he could, he would be able to show that on a balance of probabilities the defendant did indeed cause the damage. Moreover, he cannot prove this because *as a result of the defendant's negligence* it will never be known whether he would have made a full recovery. It is the defendant's negligence which prevents the claimant from establishing "but for" causation.[282] This in itself might be thought a good policy reason for permitting an action for a lost chance.[283] Lord Bridge acknowledged that in some cases, "perhaps particularly medical negligence cases, causation may be so shrouded in mystery that the court can only measure statistical chances", although "that was not so here".[284]

---

[281] [1987] A.C. 750 at 769; see also Lord Mackay's discussion of statistics at 789; see further Hill (1991) 54 M.L.R. 511 arguing that there is a distinction between the loss of a statistical chance and the loss of a chance that was personal to the claimant; cf. Stapleton (1988) 104 L.Q.R. 389, 399 n.23; Scott (1992) 55 M.L.R. 521. In *Taylor v West Kent Health Authority* [1997] 8 Med. L.R. 251 at 257 Kay J drew a clear distinction between the statistical evidence of average survival rates for patients with breast cancer and evidence particular to the claimant, which indicated that the cancer was particularly aggressive. Although the average patient would have had a greater than 50 per cent prospect of long-term survival, the probability was that even with prompt diagnosis and treatment Mrs Taylor would probably have died at around the time that she did. For discussion of the medical aspects of proving causation in cases of delayed diagnosis of breast cancer see Weisbrod (1997) 3 *AVMA Medical & Legal Journal* 189; and G. Wishart and A. Axon, "Proof of causation: A new approach in cancer cases" (2013) 19 Clinical Risk 130.

[282] This was one compelling reason for the Victoria Court of Appeal's decision in *Gavalas v Singh* [2001] VSCA 23; (2001) 3 V.R. 404 at 417 that the claimant was entitled to claim for loss of a chance where there had been a delayed diagnosis of a brain tumour. However, the High Court of Australia has now ruled that damages should not be awarded for loss of a chance of a better medical outcome: *Tabet v Gett* [2010] HCA 12; (2010) 265 A.L.R. 227.

[283] cf. *Cook v Lewis* [1952] 1 D.L.R. 1, above, para.5–020 where the Supreme Court of Canada considered that this was a good reason for reversing the burden of proof. Note, however, *Benhaim v St Germain* 2016 SCC 48; (2016) 402 D.L.R. (4th) 579 where the Supreme Court of Canada held that there is no rule of law that requires the trier of fact to draw an adverse inference of causation where the defendant's negligence has undermined the claimant's ability to prove causation, even if there is some evidence of causation; rather the question of whether an inference should be drawn should be determined on the evidence as a whole.

[284] *Hotson v East Berkshire Area Health Authority* [1987] A.C. 750 at 782.

In *Laferrière v Lawson*[285] the Supreme Court of Canada took a robust view of statistical evidence, pointing out that the court is not bound to accept statistical evidence at face value but must look to the claimant's particular circumstances to determine whether an inference of causation can be drawn:

> "If one takes, for example, a case in which a doctor neglects to employ a recommended procedure which is said to have a 50 per cent. chance of complete cure, a judge would not necessarily be bound by expert opinion which declined to conclude that application of the procedure to the patient would have avoided the patient's present worsened condition. The judge might well be justified in finding that the procedure in question would probably have benefited the patient, if other factors particular to that plaintiff support that conclusion. The judge's duty is to assess the damage suffered by a particular patient, not to remain paralysed by statistical abstraction.
>
> If one moves then to a procedure which is recommended despite a mere 25 per cent. chance of success according to expert evidence, it is still not a foregone conclusion that the doctor's fault in not using this procedure must be said to have had no causal role in the patient's death or sickness. If the experts are examined properly, a judge might well find that he or she is justified in concluding that the omission of that procedure did not cause the death or sickness, but that it caused other lesser but clearly negative results (e.g., slightly shorter life, greater pain). The doctor's fault could then be judged causal to the extent of the aggravation of what was otherwise an inevitably terminal or morbid condition."[286]

5–104

The question of whether it would ever be possible to claim for loss of a chance in tort was specifically left open by their Lordships in *Hotson*.[287] Lord Mackay took the view that while *McGhee v National Coal Board*[288] was good law it would be unwise to lay down as a rule of law that a claimant could never succeed by proving a loss of a chance in a medical negligence case. A material increase of the risk of a particular result was "equivalent to material decrease in the chance of escaping" the result.[289] Unfortunately, the relationship between *McGhee* and potential lost chance claims has remained unclear. It could be argued that *McGhee* applies where it is impossible to determine the extent of the increased risk,[290] but the lost chance approach when the risk was quantifiable, with the result that the less that was known about the risk the greater the potential award of damages, since under *McGhee* the damages are not necessarily discounted.[291]

5–105

---

[285] (1991) 78 D.L.R. (4th) 609, SCC.

[286] (1991) 78 D.L.R. (4th) 609 at 657.

[287] The Supreme Court of Canada has expressly rejected the loss of chance theory: *Laferrière v Lawson* (1991) 78 D.L.R. (4th) 609, SCC; *Cottrelle v Gerrard* (2003) 233 D.L.R. (4th) 45, Ont CA at [36].

[288] [1972] 3 All E.R. 1008. The House of Lords has subsequently confirmed that *McGhee* is still correct: *Fairchild v Glenhaven Funeral Services Ltd* [2002] UKHL 22; [2003] 1 A.C. 32.

[289] [1987] A.C. 750 at 786. See further the discussion of the decision of the House of Lords in *Gregg v Scott* [2005] UKHL 2; [2005] 2 A.C. 176, below para.5–112.

[290] Provided, of course, that the circumstances were such that the *McGhee/Fairchild* principle of causation could be invoked: see para.5–053 et seq.

[291] In *Seyfert v Burnaby Hospital Society* (1986) 27 D.L.R. (4th) 96, BCSC, McEachern C.J.S.C. adopted a lost chance approach (referring specifically to *Hotson v Fitzgerald*) for this very reason, namely that *McGhee* would place the whole loss upon the defendant. The defendant was negligent in failing to diagnose that the patient had a stab wound which had penetrated the peritoneum, causing a wound to the transverse colon. There were three possible ways of treating this type of injury if diagnosed quickly enough, one of which did not involve a colostomy and delayed recovery. McEachern CJ held that the claimant was: "entitled to recover damages representing the loss of the chance he had of avoiding the risk of a colostomy, a second operation and an extended period of convalescence ... I would fix that chance at 25 per cent., making it necessary that the plaintiff's

On the other hand, in *Barker v Corus (UK) plc*[292] the House of Lords held that, in the context of a claim in respect of mesothelioma following a claimant's exposure to asbestos, when applying the *McGhee/Fairchild* principle, the damage that the defendant should be regarded as having caused is the creation of the risk or chance of contracting mesothelioma, and not the mesothelioma itself. Thus, a defendant would be liable only to the extent that he added to the risk. On this basis there would be little to choose between the *McGhee* approach to causation and a lost chance claim, and it would be difficult to see why in a case such as *Hotson* the claim could not be reformulated in terms of a "material contribution to the damage", or "material contribution to the risk of damage" treating the disability as having two causes, the fall and the negligent delay in treatment.[293]

(iii) Loss of a chance of financial benefit

5–106   It is long established that a lost chance may be actionable in contract.[294] Where, for example, through a solicitor's negligence a client has lost the opportunity to bring proceedings (e.g. because the limitation period has been allowed to expire), the client in an action against the solicitor does not have to prove that he would have won the other case, merely that he has lost "some right of value, some chose in action of reality and substance".[295] Damages are then discounted to reflect his chances of success in the original action. It scarcely seems arguable that the basis of a distinction between *Kitchen* and *Hotson* is that one was a claim in contract and the other in tort, when the duties in each instance are the same, namely a duty to exercise reasonable skill and care. It would lead to the untenable result that, in identical circumstances, a patient who had received treatment privately might have a claim but a patient who received treatment under the National Health Service would not.[296]

---

damages be reduced by 75 per cent" (1986) 27 D.L.R. (4th) 96 at 102. Note that *Seyfert* predates the decision of the Supreme Court of Canada in *Laferrière v Lawson* (1991) 78 D.L.R. (4th) 609 rejecting the loss of chance approach.

[292] [2006] UKHL 20; [2006] 2 A.C. 572; see para.5–072.

[293] See per Lord Bridge at [1987] A.C. 750 at 782. *Hotson* was not argued on this basis. See further para.5–126 below for consideration of the effect of *Barker v Corus* on lost chance claims.

[294] *Chaplin v Hicks* [1911] 2 K.B. 786, on loss of a chance to compete for a prize amongst a limited number of contestants.

[295] *Kitchen v Royal Air Force Association* [1958] 1 W.L.R. 563; *Corfield v DS Bosher & Co.* [1992] 1 E.G.L.R. 163, where damages were awarded on the basis that the claimant had a one-third chance of success.

[296] See *Hotson v East Berkshire Area Health Authority* [1987] A.C. 750 at 760, 764 and 768, per Sir John Donaldson MR, Dillon LJ and Croom-Johnson LJ respectively. See also the comments of Mance LJ in *Gregg v Scott* [2002] EWCA Civ 1471; [2003] Lloyd's Rep. Med. 105 at [65]: "It cannot make all the difference whether such a claim is put in contract or tort, or is against a part of the National Health Service or against a private, contracting hospital." But see *de la Giroday v Brough* [1997] 6 W.W.R. 585, BCCA, where a majority of the British Columbia Court of Appeal accepted that the loss of a chance approach was not available in tort but could apply to breach of a contractual obligation to exercise reasonable care and skill: "Why should a solicitor who misses a limitation period be liable in contract for depriving a client of the opportunity to pursue a cause of action even if the client cannot establish that he would have won his case and a physician who has committed a breach of his contractual obligation by, for instance, not sending his patient to a specialist, not be liable for depriving the patient of the opportunity of prompt, appropriate treatment? In such cases, assessing the

In the House of Lords the analogy of *Kitchen* was dismissed as irrelevant, though it is not entirely clear why it was irrelevant, particularly as their Lordships did not give reasons for this assertion. Lord Bridge thought that the analogy with *Kitchen* was "superficially attractive", but considered that there were "formidable difficulties in the way of accepting the analogy".[297] The trial judge, on the other hand, was unable to see any sensible distinction between the solicitor/client relationship and the doctor/patient relationship in these circumstances.[298]

5–107

An alternative categorisation was suggested by the Court of Appeal in *Allied Maples Group Ltd v Simmons & Simmons*.[299] After the purchase of business property by the claimants, it became apparent that the property carried a contingent liability for which the claimants were responsible. They were unable to reclaim this loss from the vendor under the terms of the sale. They sued the solicitors who had advised them on deal, arguing that if, as it should have been, the risk of the loss had been pointed out to them by the defendants, they would have taken steps to obtain a warranty from the vendor or protect themselves from the loss in some other way. The trial judge found that, on the balance of probability, if asked, the vendor would have agreed to different terms in the contract of sale, giving some form of warranty or protection from the potential liability, and that if the relevant property had not been included in the sale, the whole deal would not have proceeded. In the Court of Appeal Stuart-Smith LJ said[300] that the classification of the causation issue into "all or nothing" on the balance of probabilities or the quantification of the loss of a chance depends upon whether the negligence consists in some positive act or misfeasance, or an omission or nonfeasance.

5–108

(1) In the case of a positive act of misfeasance the question of causation is one of historical fact, which once established on the balance of probability is taken as true. The claimant recovers damages in full.[301] Quantifying claimants' losses, however, may depend upon uncertain future events, such as the degree to which medical conditions will deteriorate or improve, whether they would have continued to earn at the same rate, etc. These

---

damages is not easy but liability is one thing and the measure of damages another", per Southin JA at 599. *de la Giroday* was neither pleaded nor tried as an action for breach of contract. The case was referred for a re-trial.

[297] [1987] A.C. 750 at 782.
[298] [1985] 1 All E.R. 167 at 176; cf. Hill (1991) 54 M.L.R. 511, 519 arguing that *Kitchen* was not a lost chance case.
[299] [1995] 4 All E.R. 907; [1995] 1 W.L.R. 1602.
[300] [1995] 4 All E.R. 907 at 914–916; [1995] 1 W.L.R. 1602.
[301] *Mallett v McMonagle* [1970] A.C. 166 at 176, per Lord Diplock, cited by both Lord Mackay and Lord Ackner in *Hotson* [1987] A.C. 750 at 785 and 792 respectively. See also per Lord Reid in *Davies v Taylor* [1974] A.C. 207 at 212–213. In *Malec v J.C. Hutton Proprietary Ltd* (1990) C.L.R. 638 the High Court of Australia held that the ordinary standard of proof, on the balance of probabilities, applied to the proof of historical facts, whereas for the proof of past hypothetical situations and future possibilities the court should assess the degree of probability that an event would have occurred or might occur and adjust the award of damages to reflect the degree of probability. See also *Poseidon Ltd v Adelaide Petroleum N.L.* (1994) 68 A.L.J.R. 313, HC of Australia, on which see Lunney (1995) 15 L.S. 1.

issues are dealt with on the basis of an assessment of the risk, often expressed in percentage terms, that the event will or will not occur.

(2) Where the defendant's negligence consists of an omission, e.g. to provide proper equipment, or to give proper instructions or advice, causation depends, not upon a question of historical fact, but on the answer to the hypothetical question, what would the claimant have done if the equipment had been provided or the instruction or advice given? This will be a matter of inference to be determined from all the circumstances. Claimants' own evidence that they would have acted to obtain the benefit or avoid the risk, while important, may not be believed by the judge, especially if there is compelling evidence that they would not.[302] Although the question is a hypothetical one, claimants must prove on the balance of probability that they would have taken action to obtain the benefit or avoid the risk, and as with positive acts of misfeasance, if they do establish that, there is no discount of the damages simply because the balance is only just tipped in their favour.[303]

(3) Where, as in *Allied Maples* itself, the claimant's loss depends on the hypothetical action of an independent third party, either in addition to action by the claimant, or independently of it, the claimant does not have to prove on the balance of probability that the third party would have acted so as confer the benefit or avoid the risk to the claimant. Claimants succeed if they show that they had a substantial chance, as opposed to a speculative one, that they would have been successful in negotiating total or partial protection, the evaluation of the substantial chance being a question of quantification of damages. There was "no difference in principle between the chance of gaining a benefit and the chance of avoiding a liability". Nor does it depend upon the claimant proving that the chance of success was over 50 per cent. Provided the chance is substantial it may be less than 50 per cent. This is a two-stage process. First the court must be satisfied that the claimant has lost something of value. An action which was bound to fail or had no substantial prospect of success and was merely speculative was not something of value. It was only if the claim passed that test that the court should evaluate in percentage terms the full value of the lost claim.[304]

---

[302] As, e.g. in *McWilliams v Sir William Arrol & Co. Ltd* [1962] 1 W.L.R. 295; above para.5–008.

[303] In *Bagley v North Hertfordshire Health Authority* (1986) 136 N.L.J. 1014 Simon Brown J awarded damages for negligence which resulted in a stillbirth, and deducted 5 per cent because even without negligence there was a 5 per cent chance that the child would not have survived. This approach was disapproved by Lord Ackner in *Hotson* at [1987] A.C. 750 at 793. See also *Cabral v Gupta* [1993] 1 W.W.R. 648; (1992) 13 C.C.L.T. (2d) 323 where the Manitoba Court of Appeal reversed the trial judge's deduction of 30 per cent of the award of damages which had been made on the ground that there was a 30 per cent risk that even if a foreign body had been detected and removed from the claimant's eye by the defendant ophthalmologist the claimant would nonetheless have had no useful vision in the eye. There was "simply no basis in law for such a deduction".

[304] *Hatswell v Goldbergs (A Firm)* [2001] EWCA Civ 2084; [2002] Lloyd's Rep. P.N. 359 at [48] per Sir Murray Stuart-Smith—where the claimant's action in negligence against a firm of solicitors in respect of allowing a claim for medical negligence to become statute barred under the Limitation Act 1980 was held to have no value, because the medical negligence claim was bound to fail. This rather begs the question, of course, of what the defendant solicitors were doing running a medical negligence claim that was bound to fail. On which see: *Mount v Barker Austin (A Firm)* [1998] P.N.L.R. 493, CA. For discussion of how the court should assess the lost chance of successful litigation see *Pearson v*

The effect of the Court of Appeal's approach in *Allied Maples* is that where   **5–109**
causation depends upon what the claimant himself would have done in a "past"
hypothetical situation the claimant has to establish this on the balance of
probabilities. This most commonly arises in the medical negligence context
where claimants state that if they had been informed about the risks of treatment,
they would not have consented to undergo the treatment and would therefore
have avoided the inherent risk that has materialised.[305] This is also the position
where the question turns upon what the defendant would have done in a "past
hypothetical situation". The claimant must prove that had the defendant not
omitted to act, the hypothetical action would have avoided the damage of which
the claimant complains, or that the defendant's hypothetical action would itself
have been negligent.[306] But where proof of causation depends upon the
independent act of a third party the claimant need only establish that there was a
chance.[307] This could mean that in some cases causation depends upon proof of
both what the claimant or defendant would have done in a hypothetical situation
(on the balance of probabilities) and what an independent third party would have
done (was there a substantial chance?). *Allied Maples*, of course, was a claim
involving concurrent liability to a client in contract and tort, but it is now well
established that this approach should also be applied to cases based exclusively in
tort.[308]

Sanders Witherspoon [2000] P.N.L.R. 110 at 126–135, CA. And for consideration of how to approach
the assessment where there are multiple contingencies, each with its own probability, see *Langford v
Hebran* [2001] EWCA Civ 361; [2001] P.I.Q.R. Q160, applying *Doyle v Wallace* [1998] P.I.Q.R.
Q146, CA.

[305] See paras 7–083 et seq.

[306] See *Bolitho v City and Hackney Health Authority* [1998] A.C. 232; paras 5–011 to 5–014.

[307] cf. the approach of the Supreme Court of Canada in *Walker Estate v York-Finch General Hospital*
(2001) 198 D.L.R. (4th) 193 where the defendants' negligence in screening blood for HIV consisted
of asking potential blood donors general questions about their health rather than asking about
symptom specific conditions and risks. The causation issue depended upon how the potential donors
would have responded to these different questions. The Supreme Court held that the claimants did not
have to prove "but for" causation; nor was the issue analysed as one of a loss of chance; rather the test
was whether the negligence constituted a material contribution to the damage. See further
para.10–056. On the other hand, where the issue was whether an alleged delay in introducing
heat-treated blood products could have avoided the claimants' contracting HIV from an infected blood
transfusion, the claimants had to satisfy the "but for" test, and prove when they became infected on
the balance of probabilities: *Robb Estate v Canadian Red Cross Society* (2001) 9 C.C.L.T. (3d) 131,
Ont CA.

[308] *Stovold v Barlows* [1996] 1 P.N.L.R. 91, CA; *First Interstate Bank of California v Cohen Arnold
& Co.* [1996] 1 P.N.L.R. 17, CA; *Doyle v Wallace* [1998] P.I.Q.R. Q146, CA—prospects of claimant
qualifying and obtaining a job as a drama teacher fell within the third limb of *Allied Maples*, and
therefore had to be assessed on the basis of the chance of her doing so, rather than the probability of
her being successful. See also *Spring v Guardian Assurance plc* [1995] 2 A.C. 296 at 327, a case
involving a negligent employment reference about a former employee, where Lord Lowry said: "Once
the duty of care is held to exist and the defendants' negligence is proved, the plaintiff only has to show
that by reason of that negligence he has lost a reasonable chance of employment (which would have to
be evaluated) and has thereby sustained loss ... He does not have to prove that, but for the negligent
reference, [the third party] *would* have employed him" (original emphasis). See further Stauch (1997)
17 O.J.L.S. 205, 217–224.

5–110   **Applying *Allied Maples* to medical negligence claims**   In *Smith v National Health Service Litigation Authority*[309] the defendants argued that *Allied Maples* did not apply to actions for medical negligence but, rejecting the argument, Andrew Smith J said that *Allied Maples* laid down general principles, and there was no reason to adopt a different approach because the case involved a different category of professional negligence. His Lordship said that when considering the hypothetical actions of the defendant, it is assumed that he would have acted in accordance with his obligations to the claimant, but it is also assumed that he would not have gone beyond his duty. Thus, in *Smith* itself (which concerned allegations that the defendants had failed to examine the claimant at an appropriate time, and thereby had failed to diagnose a congenital problem with her hip which was amenable to treatment), the proper approach to the question of what damage would have resulted from an alleged omission to examine the patient:

> "...would be to assume a properly competent, but not an unusually thorough or able, examination and then to assess the chance that this would have resulted in the claimant not suffering the damage which in the event she has suffered."[310]

5–111   In *Hardaker v Newcastle Health Authority & the Chief Constable of Northumbria*[311] Burnton J, commenting on *Smith*, made it clear that the loss of chance approach could only apply in the medical negligence context where causation depended upon the actions of a third party. Where causation does not depend on the actions of third parties then:

> "...the claimant must establish what injury has been caused, or what aggravation to his injuries has been caused, on the balance of probabilities, by the defendants' negligence. If he succeeds on a probability of 51 per cent., he recovers 100 per cent. of the appropriate compensation for his injury (or aggravation of his injuries); if he establishes only a 49 per cent. probability, he recovers nothing."[312]

(iv)   Loss of a chance of a better medical outcome—Gregg v Scott

5–112   In *Gregg v Scott*[313] the claimant developed non-Hodgkin's lymphoma which presented as a lump under his left arm. His general practitioner diagnosed a lipoma, a benign collection of fatty tissue, and negligently failed to refer him for specialist investigation. As a result of this, the claimant's treatment was delayed by about nine months, and this significantly reduced the claimant's chances of

---

[309] [2001] Lloyd's Rep. Med. 90 at 101.
[310] [2001] Lloyd's Rep. Med. 90 at 102.
[311] [2001] Lloyd's Rep. Med. 512.
[312] [2001] Lloyd's Rep. Med. 512 at [70]. "A chance of a better recovery, unless greater than 50 per cent, and of a specified improvement, is not damage for these purposes", [2001] Lloyd's Rep. Med. 512 at [69].
[313] [2005] UKHL 2; [2005] 2 A.C. 176. For comment on the House of Lords' decision see: J. Stapleton, "Loss of the Chance of Cure from Cancer" (2005) 68 M.L.R. 996; E. Peel, "Loss of a Chance in Medical Negligence" (2005) 121 L.Q.R. 364; Spencer, "Damages for Lost Chances: Lost for Good?" (2005) 64 C.L.J. 282; G. Reid, "*Gregg v Scott* and lost chances" (2005) 21 P.N. 78; S. Maskrey and W. Edis, "*Chester v Afshar* and *Gregg v Scott*: Mixed Messages for Lawyers" [2005] J.P.I.L. 205; Lord Hoffmann, who was one of the judges in *Gregg v Scott*, has expressed his extra-judicial views at (2005) 121 L.Q.R. 592, 600–601.

survival from 42 per cent to 25 per cent.[314] The trial judge, applying *Hotson*, dismissed the claim on the basis that for a person with his condition the chances of a cure were in any event less than 50 per cent, so that as a matter of past fact it was more probable than not that the claimant would have been in his present position even if treatment had started promptly. In other words, the evidence established, as a matter of past fact, that the probability was that the appellant would not have been cured. The Court of Appeal, by a majority, dismissed the claimant's appeal. In the House of Lords the claimant advanced two arguments. First (the "quantification argument"), that the delay in diagnosis had caused physical damage because the claimant's tumour had grown in size causing pain and suffering, and the treatment was more drastic with greater side effects than would have been the case if it had occurred sooner. If the claimant had suffered physical damage he was entitled to compensation for his reduced life expectancy as a matter of assessment of quantum of damage (where future contingencies are measured on the basis of their chances of occurring). Secondly (the "loss of chance argument"), the case was factually different from *Hotson v East Berkshire Area Health Authority*, so that *Hotson* did not preclude a claim based on a reduced prospect of survival; but even if *Hotson* did apply the decision of the House of Lords in *Fairchild v Glenhaven Funeral Services Ltd*[315] permitted the court to depart from it. By a three to two majority the House of Lords rejected the claim. Unfortunately, given the significant disparities in their Lordships' speeches no clear principle has emerged. Despite the majority decision that Mr Gregg's action should be dismissed, it remains arguable that in some circumstances a missed diagnosis could give rise to a claim based on a lost chance of a better medical outcome.

The quantification argument   The argument that the delay in treatment had resulted in physical damage, namely the growth of the tumour, and that the claimant's reduced life expectancy could be dealt with simply as a matter of quantifying his loss was rejected by the majority of their Lordships, though for Lord Hoffmann this was on the basis that it had not been proved that the claimant's likely premature death would be attributable to the growth of the tumour.[316] Baroness Hale apparently took a similar view, on the basis that there was no finding of fact by the trial judge that the delay in treatment caused the "upstaging" (i.e. the growth) of the tumour.[317] Lord Nicholls regarded the argument as superficially attractive, but, without expressly rejecting the argument, considered that it did not get to the heart of the problem.[318] Lord Hope seemed to take a different view of the facts and considered that:

5–113

> "...it was proved on a balance of probabilities that the tumour spread because of the delay in treatment, that this was a physical injury which was caused by the doctor's negligence and that

---

[314] The statistical evidence was problematic. Nonetheless, the Court of Appeal and the majority of the House of Lords proceeded on the basis of these figures. Lord Phillips did not accept the assumptions underlying the assessment of the claimant's chances of survival: see para.5–120.

[315] [2002] UKHL 22; [2003] 1 A.C. 32; paras 5–050 et seq.

[316] [2005] UKHL 2; [2005] 2 A.C. 176 at [68].

[317] [2005] UKHL 2; [2005] 2 A.C. 176 at [202].

[318] [2005] UKHL 2; [2005] 2 A.C. 176 at [58].

this gave [the claimant] a cause of action for the pain and suffering that was caused by that injury and all its other adverse consequences."[319]

His Lordship added:

"The fact that there was a physical injury has been proved on a balance of probabilities. So too has the fact that, in addition to pain and suffering, it caused a reduction in the prospects of a successful outcome. I would hold that, where these factors are present, the way is open for losses which are consequential on the physical injury to be claimed too ... I see the reduction in the prospects of a successful outcome as one element among several in the claim for which there is a single cause—the enlargement of the tumour. This was a physical injury..."[320]

Lord Phillips appears to have agreed with Lord Hope that where a doctor's negligence caused the spread of a patient's cancer the patient can recover for the effect that the spread of the cancer had on his life expectancy, commenting that that "conclusion is not, as a matter of principle, in any way at odds with the current law".[321] However, Lord Phillips considered that it had not been proven on the facts that the defendant's negligent delay had actually reduced the claimant's life expectancy.

5–114   On the other hand, even if it was not demonstrated that the growth of the tumour had reduced the claimant's life expectancy, there could be an award of damages to reflect the fact that the delay could have resulted in more intrusive treatment, and more pain, suffering and distress than would have been experienced had treatment commenced promptly.[322] Baroness Hale said that:

"The defendant is liable for any *extra* pain, suffering, loss of amenity, financial loss and loss of expectation of life which may have resulted from the delay. If, without the delay, the claimant would have achieved a longer gap before more radical treatment became necessary, then he should be entitled to damages to reflect the acceleration in his suffering. If the pain and suffering he would have suffered anyway was made worse by the anguish of knowing that his disease could have been detected earlier, then he should be compensated for that."[323]

It would appear that counsel for the claimant did not pursue this aspect of the claim. The physical, psychological and financial consequences of delayed diagnosis arising from the need for more intrusive or aggressive treatment have always been recoverable.[324] Of course, this would have to be proved on a balance of probabilities.

5–115   **The loss of chance argument**   The loss of chance argument was that the defendant's negligence had reduced the claimant's chances of survival from 42 per cent to 25 per cent; this reduction of prospects was something of value and the claimant was entitled to be compensated for that loss.[325] Despite the majority view refusing the appeal, the effect of the ruling of the House of Lords in *Gregg*

---

[319] [2005] UKHL 2; [2005] 2 A.C. 176 at [96].
[320] [2005] UKHL 2; [2005] 2 A.C. 176 at [117]; see also at [121].
[321] [2005] UKHL 2; [2005] 2 A.C. 176 at [187]; see also at [191].
[322] [2005] UKHL 2; [2005] 2 A.C. 176 at [191] per Lord Phillips.
[323] [2005] UKHL 2; [2005] 2 A.C. 176 at [206] (original emphasis).
[324] See paras 5–129 to 5–130.
[325] The trial judge had calculated the value of the lost chance as 20 per cent of the damages that would have been awarded for the loss of the certainty of a cure: [2005] UKHL 2 at [164].

v Scott on the loss of chance argument is equivocal. Lord Nicholls was strongly supportive of it, and Lord Hope agreed with Lord Nicholls, whilst also accepting the quantification argument. Lord Hoffmann rejected the loss of chance approach, as did Baroness Hale, though she did consider that in some cases there could be a modest claim in respect of "lost years". Lord Phillips agreed that, on the facts, Mr Gregg's appeal should be dismissed, but considered that in certain cases:

> "...there may be a case for permitting a recovery of damages that is proportionate to the increase in the chance of the adverse outcome."[326]

For Lord Nicholls, the loss of a 45 per cent prospect of recovery was just as much a real loss for a patient as the loss of a 55 per cent prospect of recovery. It would be "irrational and indefensible" to deny any remedy to a patient with a 45 per cent chance of recovery whose prospects of recovery were reduced to nil by a negligent diagnosis.[327] Lord Nicholls was well aware of the inherent problem of using statistics to prove what may or may not have happened in a particular case.[328] Despite this it would not be acceptable to reject all statistical evidence out of hand, particularly where the reason why the actual outcome for the individual claimant is not known is that the defendant's negligence has prevented that outcome from becoming known.[329] It would also render the doctor's duty "empty of content". The purpose of a doctor's duty was: "to promote the patients' *prospects* of recovery by exercising due skill and care in diagnosing and treating the patient's condition."[330] If negligent diagnosis or treatment diminished the patient's *prospects* of recovery, a law which did "not recognise this as a wrong calling for redress would be seriously deficient today".[331] Later, Lord Nicholls commented that if a patient's prospects of recovery were to be treated as non-existent whenever they fell short of 50 per cent, the law would "deserve to be likened to the proverbial ass".[332]

5–116

---

[326] [2005] UKHL 2; [2005] 2 A.C. 176 at [190].

[327] [2005] UKHL 2; [2005] 2 A.C. 176 at [3].

[328] See his comments [2005] UKHL 2 at [28].

[329] [2005] UKHL 2; [2005] 2 A.C. 176 at [32]. Contrast *Benhaim v St Germain* 2016 SCC 48; (2016) 402 D.L.R. (4th) 579, para.5–103, n.283 above, on the drawing of adverse causal inferences where the defendant's negligence has prevented the claimant from establishing "but for" causation.

[330] [2005] UKHL 2; [2005] 2 A.C. 176 at [24], original emphasis.

[331] [2005] UKHL 2; [2005] 2 A.C. 176 at [25].

[332] [2005] UKHL 2; [2005] 2 A.C. 176 at [43]. In the Court of Appeal Simon Brown LJ, who coincidentally had been the trial judge in *Hotson* itself, though concluding that the claim in respect of the diminution of life expectancy in *Gregg v Scott* must fail, clearly had reservations. It was: "less than wholly satisfactory to leave the House of Lords speeches in *Hotson* as the final word on the loss of a chance argument. If I consult a doctor about a specific condition and, through the doctor's negligence in diagnosis or treatment, reduce from 49 per cent to 5 per cent my chance of averting an adverse outcome, not everyone would think it 'just and reasonable' that my claim must inevitably fail on the issue of causation. Particularly that may be thought unfair given that in cases where the claimant can prove on the balance of probabilities that, but for the negligence, he would have escaped the adverse consequence of his condition, his damages will nevertheless be discounted to reflect the possibility that this was not so": [2002] EWCA Civ 1471; [2003] Lloyd's Rep. Med. 105 at [101], citing *Smith v Leech Brain and Co. Ltd* [1962] 2 Q.B. 405 and *Judge v Huntingdon Health Authority* [1995] 6 Med. L.R. 223. See also the comments of the Court of Appeal in *Coudert Brothers v Normans Bay Ltd* [2004] EWCA Civ 215; *The Times*, 24 March 2004 on the outcome of the Court of Appeal decision in *Gregg v Scott*. Laws LJ said at [68]: "I am driven to an unhappy sense that the

5–117   Drawing the comparison with claims in respect of loss of a chance of financial benefit, his Lordship considered that since loss of a financial opportunity or chance will give rise to a claim against a negligent professional adviser, justice required that loss of a chance should also constitute actionable damage where what is lost is the chance of health or even life itself.[333] Lord Hope agreed that patients who were already suffering from illness at the date of the doctor's negligence from which they had at that date significant prospects of recovery should have a cause of action for the reduction in those prospects.[334] For Lord Nicholls this view was also supported by the decision of the House of Lords in *Fairchild v Glenhaven Funeral Services Ltd*, which provided an illustration of the court being prepared to adapt the rules of causation "so as to leap an evidentiary gap when overall fairness plainly so requires".[335]

5–118   Lord Hoffmann took the view that for events in the past the law assumes that there is no inherent uncertainty about what happened, nor about whether something which happened in the past will cause something to happen in the future:

> "Everything is determined by causality. What we lack is knowledge and the law deals with lack of knowledge by the concept of the burden of proof."[336]

The progress of the claimant's cancer was not random, but was governed by laws of causality, and an inability to establish that the delay in diagnosis and treatment reduced the claimant's expectation of life could not be remedied by treating the outcome as having been indeterminate.[337] This assumption that past events are determinate (and therefore to be decided upon on an all or nothing basis) is, of course, precisely that: an assumption. His Lordship acknowledged that there are exceptions to this rule, including the relaxation of the "but for" test applied in *Fairchild v Glenhaven Funeral Services Ltd* and the loss of chance approach applied in *Allied Maples Group Ltd v Simmons & Simmons (A Firm)*[338] where the outcome depends on the actions of a third party. He did not, however, attempt to explain the policy basis for these exceptions, other than the suggestion that to extend the *Fairchild* principle, without identifying any control mechanisms to limit its application, would amount to a legislative act and have "enormous consequences" for insurance companies and the National Health Service.[339]

5–119   Baroness Hale agreed that reformulating claims on the basis of loss of a chance would have major consequences. Almost any claim for loss of an outcome could

---

common law has lost its way. If a man's chance of a cure from a potentially fatal cancer has been reduced by another's negligence from 42% to 25%, would not a reasonable jury say that he had been grievously hurt by the negligence?" See also per Waller LJ at [32].
[333] [2005] UKHL 2; [2005] 2 A.C. 176 at [25].
[334] [2005] UKHL 2; [2005] 2 A.C. 176 at [121].
[335] [2005] UKHL 2; [2005] 2 A.C. 176 at [31].
[336] [2005] UKHL 2; [2005] 2 A.C. 176 at [79].
[337] [2005] UKHL 2; [2005] 2 A.C. 176 at [80].
[338] [1995] 1 W.L.R. 1602; see para.5–108.
[339] [2005] UKHL 2; [2005] 2 A.C. 176 at [90]; cf. the reaction of Lord Nicholls at [52] to [56] to the possibility that a ruling in favour of the claimant would increase the financial burden on the NHS or lead to "defensive medicine".

be reformulated as a claim for loss of a chance of that outcome. And if claimants could recover proportionate damages where the chance was less than 50 per cent, why could defendants not argue that where claimants have proved their loss on the balance of probabilities, their liability should be limited to the extent that the claimant has proved loss beyond the 50 per cent hurdle? This form of proportionate liability would increase the complexity of ordinary personal injury claims, and cause "more problems ... than the policy benefits are worth".[340] Baroness Hale also noted the anomalous distinction between the position of solicitors and doctors sued on the basis of a loss of chance:

> "So why should my solicitor be liable for negligently depriving me of the chance of winning my action, even if I never had a better than evens chance of success, when my doctor is not liable for negligently depriving me of the chance of getting better, even if I never had a better than evens chance of getting better? Is this another example of the law being kinder to the medical profession than to other professionals?"[341]

Baroness Hale did not answer this question, other than to observe, somewhat cryptically, that:

> "There is not much difference between the money one expected to have and the money one expected to have a chance of having: it is all money. There is a difference between the leg one ought to have and the chance of keeping a leg which one ought to have."[342]

It is unclear why these differences should mean that the solicitor is held liable but the doctor is not.[343]

Lord Phillips undertook a lengthy analysis of the facts, and the statistics which formed the basis of the findings of fact, and concluded that counsel and the Court of Appeal had misunderstood both the effect of the evidence and the findings made by the trial judge.[344] The view that the claimant's chances of survival had fallen from 42 per cent to 25 per cent was "fallacious".[345] The statistics were based on an assumption that the cohort that made up the statistical model used by the expert witnesses consisted of patients with the same stage of disease as the claimant, but that assumption was questionable, on the evidence. The fact that the claimant had survived to the date of the trial (some five years after treatment had commenced), and indeed to the date of the appeal hearing in the House of Lords (some eight years after treatment had commenced), suggested that applying a

5–120

---

[340] [2005] UKHL 2; [2005] 2 A.C. 176 at [225]. The ordinary rule is that once the claimant has established that an event occurred on the balance of probabilities the law treats it is certain that the event occurred.

[341] [2005] UKHL 2; [2005] 2 A.C. 176 at [218].

[342] [2005] UKHL 2; [2005] 2 A.C. 176 at [220].

[343] Moreover, where a claim is brought by a patient against a doctor on the basis that a negligent diagnosis or prognosis has damaged the patient's opportunity to settle a claim for damages against a third party (such as a negligent motorist) the action against the doctor will proceed on the basis of the patient's lost chance of obtaining a more favourable outcome, applying *Allied Maples*. See paras 2–049 and 2–050. It seems incongruous that patients have a lost chance claim against their doctors for a negligent diagnosis when they are suing in respect of purely financial loss, but not when they are suing for personal injuries arising from the negligent diagnosis.

[344] [2005] UKHL 2; [2005] 2 A.C. 176 at [126].

[345] [2005] UKHL 2; [2005] 2 A.C. 176 at [147].

It would seem that for Lord Phillips it was not so much the principle of awarding damages for loss of chance that concerned him, but the problem of identifying whether the claimant had actually lost anything.

5–124   On this basis, it is arguable that a claimant in a medical negligence action could claim for loss of a chance of a better medical outcome where: (1) there was significant medical uncertainty about the outcome at the time of the alleged negligence (Lord Nicholls); (2) the injury which affected the claimant's prospects lay in the future at the time of the alleged negligence (Lord Hope—query whether this is effectively the same condition as (1)); and (3) the outcome is known (Lord Phillips). Baroness Hale also seemed to contemplate that a modest claim for reduction of life expectancy could arise where the delay in starting treatment had shortened the claimant's life expectancy compared to patients in the claimant's position who received prompt treatment, even if with prompt treatment the patient would probably have died.[354] This involves comparing the median life expectancy of that population of patients and considering to what extent the delayed diagnosis has reduced the claimant's life expectancy. Claimants would be entitled to compensation for that shortening of their (already inevitably shortened) life.

5–125   One issue that was not addressed by the judgments in *Gregg v Scott* is precisely what it is that claimants have to show "as a matter of probability" in a case involving reduced life expectancy. Do they have to demonstrate that the defendant's negligence caused them to lose more than 50 per cent of their chance of a cure, so that if, for example, their prospects of a cure were 80 per cent, but due to the delay they are now only 25 per cent they have lost 55 per cent overall? Or do they merely have to prove that as a result of the defendant's negligence they have moved from the category of patients who would probably have survived (e.g. they had, say, a 60 per cent chance of survival with prompt treatment) into the category of patients who will probably not survive (say, they now have only a 40 per cent chance of survival)? Given that the law treats questions of past fact as proved as a certainty once the claimant establishes that they were more probable than not,[355] in the second situation it is probable, and therefore treated as a certainty, that the patient would have survived.[356] The

---

[354] [2005] UKHL 2; [2005] 2 A.C. 176 at [207]. On which see *JD v Mather* [2012] EWHC 3063 (QB); [2013] Med. L.R. 291 at [44] to [48] (claimant's life expectancy reduced by three years due to delay in diagnosing malignant melanoma); cf. *Oliver v Williams* [2013] EWHC 600 (QB); [2013] Med. L.R. 344 at [42] where the conclusion was that the claimant had not proved on a balance of probabilities that the delay in diagnosing ovarian cancer had affected her life expectancy, distinguishing *JD v Mather* on the basis that in *JD v Mather* "the negligent delay meant that the staging of the melanoma changed and good quality statistical information was available to show the impact of a change in staging on median life expectancy". For discussion of *JD v Mather* and the use of epidemiological data to assess reduced life expectancy in cases of delayed diagnosis of breast cancer see G. Wishart and A. Axon, "Proof of causation: A new approach in cancer cases" (2013) 19 Clinical Risk 130.

[355] *Mallett v McMonagle* [1970] A.C. 166 at 176, per Lord Diplock; *Davies v Taylor* [1974] A.C. 207 at 212–213, per Lord Reid.

[356] See, e.g., *Beldycki Estate v Jaipargas* 2012 ONCA 537; (2012) 222 A.C.W.S. (3d) 1073 where it was held on a balance of probabilities that but for the defendant's negligence the deceased's liver cancer would not have metastasised. The defendant's argument that damages should be reduced to reflect the 30 per cent chance that even if the cancer had been detected and treated the patient would

---

negligence has caused them to move into the category of patients who will probably not survive, and therefore as a matter of past fact it has caused a diminution in life expectancy, not as a matter of lost chances but as a matter of probability. Of course, in assessing the value of that diminution in life expectancy as a matter of quantum, account will be taken of the fact that it was already an impaired life expectancy (there was a 40 per cent chance that they would have died in any event). But this does not affect the question of whether the claimant has proved causation. Although this example is based on a reduction of the claimant's chances by 20 per cent (60 per cent down to 40 per cent), there is no logical reason why much smaller reductions could not be treated in the same way, even as little as two per cent (51 per cent down to 49 per cent). This example illustrates the arbitrary effects of the rule excluding claims based on loss of chance. On the medical evidence, the claimant in *Gregg v Scott* had his chances of survival reduced by 17 per cent and yet he recovered nothing for that loss, whereas a claimant who, fortuitously, starts out with a marginally better than 50 per cent chance of successful treatment may recover damages, applying the balance of probabilities approach, for a significantly smaller reduction in chances.[357]

Moreover, the contrast with the claimants in *Fairchild*, who could not prove that the particular defendants' negligence had caused them any injury whatsoever, but who recovered for the full extent of their harm, is stark.[358] The decision of the House of Lords in *Barker v Corus (UK) plc*[359] that the claims to compensation in a case such as *Fairchild* are based on the defendants' respective contributions to the *risk* of developing harm, and not the harm itself, makes it even more difficult to identify a principled distinction. After all the tort of negligence does not, as a matter of course, distinguish between negligently creating a risk of harm and

5–126

---

not have survived was rejected by the Ontario Court of Appeal. The finding amounted to a conclusion that but for the negligence the deceased would have been cured of cancer: "At law, that he would have been cured was therefore a certainty; that his cancer might still have metastasised was a legal impossibility" (at [84]).

[357] See also Lord Neuberger's extra-judicial comments on *Gregg v Scott*, "Loss of a Chance and Causation" (2008) 24 P.N. 212: "The questions which should have been asked were: what was the claimant's life expectancy without the treatment, and by how much would that expectancy have been increased if he had had the treatment. Your life expectancy is the age which you have a 50% prospect of reaching: you have a less than 50% chance of living any longer and a better than 50% chance of living to any earlier date. So, if the claimant's life expectancy was 43, but would have been 47 if he had had the treatment, one can say that, on the balance of probabilities, he lost 4 years of life. He would have had a 50% chance of living to 47 but, as it is, he only has a 50% chance of living to 43." Lord Neuberger suggested that if the claimant had put his case in this way, "it may well be that at least one of the three in the majority, possibly Lord Hoffmann or Baroness Hale, would have changed sides". In *Wright (A Child) v Cambridge Medical Group* [2011] EWCA Civ 669; [2013] Q.B. 312 at [84] Lord Neuberger MR said that although the reasoning of the House of Lords in *Gregg* did "not conclusively shut out, as a matter of strict logic, this court from applying a loss of a chance approach in this case" his Lordship considered that the Court of Appeal should not expand the loss of a chance doctrine into the realm of clinical negligence, though "the question would be appropriate for reconsideration by the Supreme Court".

[358] Stapleton (2002) 10 Torts L.J. 276, 286 suggests that the claimants in *McGhee* and *Fairchild* recovered for their full loss by default, because the litigants (and the courts) ignored the associated possibility of apportionment.

[359] [2006] UKHL 20; [2006] 2 A.C. 572; see para.5–072.

negligently failing to prevent a risk of harm materialising, otherwise doctors would *never* be held liable for failing to diagnose the patient's condition, even if the diagnosis was straightforward and the failure to intervene was, to a certainty, the cause of the damage.[360] Causing the claimant to lose the chance or opportunity of avoiding harm is just the other side of the same coin of positively creating a risk of harm. If the difference between *Barker v Corus* and *Gregg v Scott* is said to be that in *Barker* (and *Fairchild*) the harm had actually occurred (i.e. the claimants had developed mesothelioma) whereas in *Gregg v Scott* the claimant was still alive and so it could not be proved that he had lost anything, then this would tend to suggest that the loss of chance approach may succeed (applying *Barker*) in a case like *Gregg v Scott* if the claimant had actually died.[361] Otherwise, it is extremely difficult to identify a rational distinction between *Barker v Corus* and *Gregg v Scott*.

5–127   **Australia**   The loss of chance analysis appeared to have been accepted in a number of Australian state decisions.[362] However, in *Tabet v Gett*[363] the High Court of Australia ruled that damages for loss of a chance of a better medical outcome should not be awarded. The judge had held that an exacerbation of the claimant's condition which occurred after the defendant's breach of duty had caused 25 per cent of the claimant's total disability, and that the defendant's breach of duty had caused 40 per cent of the exacerbation, and therefore awarded damages on the basis that the defendant's negligence had caused the claimant to lose a 40 per cent chance of avoiding the exacerbation. Hayne and Bell JJ concluded that the defendant should not be held liable where what is said to have been lost was the possibility (as distinct from the probability) that the brain damage suffered by the claimant would have been less severe than it was:

---

[360] Of course, negligence distinguishes between acts and "pure omissions" when considering whether a duty of care is owed, but once we have concluded that the defendant does owe a duty, he is just as liable for negligent omissions as negligent commissions.

[361] Thus supporting the view expressed above, para.5–124. See also Burrows, "Uncertainty about Uncertainty: Damages for Loss of a Chance" [2008] J.P.I.L. 31 who argues that *Gregg v Scott* involves unexpressed policy concerns to limit claims against medical professionals; and that the "control" mechanisms in *Barker* for limiting claims for loss of chance are: (1) that the damage should have actually materialised; and (2) that the damage must be caused by a single causative agent (as opposed to a multiple causative agent such as occurred in *Wilsher v Essex* [1988] A.C. 1074). Professor Burrows concludes (rightly, it is suggested) that *Gregg v Scott* is a single causative agent case. On this view, if Mr. Gregg had died there would be no material difference between *Gregg v Scott* and *Barker v Corus* (where the mesothelioma had materialised).

[362] *Gavalas v Singh* [2001] VSCA 23; (2001) 3 V.R. 404, at 409 where Callaway JA went so far as to say that: "No advanced system of law could now deny recovery where late diagnosis, in breach of duty to the patient, appreciably reduces the prospects of success of an operation"; *Rufo v Hosking* [2004] NSWCA 391; (2004) 61 N.S.W.L.R. 678; *Halverson v Dobler* [2006] NSWSC 1307 (aff'd [2007] NSWCA 335; (2007) 70 N.S.W.L.R. 151), where it was held that *Rufo v Hosking* applied only where the lost chance was 50 per cent or less, and since the claimant had a 65 per cent chance of avoiding harm he was entitled to full damages.

[363] [2010] HCA 12; (2010) 265 A.L.R. 227; discussed by D. Birch, "*Tabet v Gett*: The High Court's own lost chance of a better outcome" (2011) 19 Tort L. Rev. 76 and S. Holloway, "The legal labyrinth of lost chances: Can a plaintiff recover for loss of a less than even chance in medical negligence cases after *Tabet v Gett*" (2013) 21 Tort L. Rev. 96.

"...the language of loss of chance should not be permitted to obscure the need to identify whether a plaintiff has proved that the defendant's negligence was more probably than not a cause of damage (in the sense of detrimental difference). The language of possibilities (language that underlies the notion of loss of chance) should not be permitted to obscure the need to consider whether the possible adverse outcome has in fact come home, or will more probably than not do so."[364]

Kiefel J added that:

"The requirement of causation is not overcome by redefining the mere possibility, that such damage as did occur might not eventuate, as a chance and then saying that it is lost when the damage actually occurs. Such a claim could only succeed if the standard of proof were lowered, which would require a fundamental change to the law of negligence."[365]

(vi)   Product liability and loss of chance

A claim based on loss of a chance is not appropriate in the context of an action in respect of a defective product under s.3 of the Consumer Protection Act 1987. In *A v The National Blood Authority*[366] Burton J held that the Act, and the European Union Product Liability Directive 1985 (Council Directive (EEC) 85/374) upon which the Act is based, imposes strict liability. The question is whether the product was defective, and if so what damage was caused by that defect. It is not what damage was caused by any conduct, whether wrongful or otherwise, or breach of duty. Questions of what would or might have happened in hypothetical circumstances were simply not relevant.

5–128

(vii)   Recoverable losses in respect of missed diagnosis of cancer

Where it is possible to identify something specific that the claimant has lost as a result of a diagnostic error, rather than a "mere" statistical chance, then the claimant is entitled to compensation for that loss.[367] Their Lordships in *Gregg v Scott* accepted that if a delayed diagnosis had resulted in extra pain, suffering, loss of amenity or financial loss, due for example to the patient having to face more drastic medical intervention than would otherwise have been the case, then compensation for this loss would be payable.[368] Baroness Hale also seemed to accept that a modest claim for reduction of life expectancy could arise where the

5–129

---

[364] [2010] HCA 12; (2010) 265 A.L.R. 227 at [69].
[365] [2010] HCA 12; (2010) 265 A.L.R. 227 at [152]. Loss of chance does not apply when considering compensation under New Zealand's no-fault accident compensation scheme: *Accident Compensation Corporation v Ambros* [2007] NZCA 304 at [46]: "Whatever the future developments in loss of chance in other jurisdictions, the loss of chance analysis seems to us to be incompatible with the accident compensation regime. Under a no fault regime, either there is cover or there is not. There is no ability to discount compensation and in a no fault regime no conceptual need to do so."
[366] [2001] 3 All E.R. 289 at [176]–[180].
[367] Where the evidence is that the defendant's breach of duty actually caused the cancer to spread (as opposed to a missed diagnosis resulting in a delay in treatment allowing the cancer to spread), and had it not spread then on a balance of probabilities the patient would have made a full recovery with standard therapy, the claimant will be entitled to damages on the basis that defendant caused the patient's death: *Bell v Ashford & St Peters Hospital NHS Trust* unreported 27 July 2016, QBD.
[368] As, e.g, in *Hague v Dalzell* [2016] EWHC 2753 (QB)—damages for pain and suffering arising from the fact that the patient's symptoms went untreated for seven months, and the pain and suffering

claimant's life expectancy had been reduced compared to patients in the claimant's position who received prompt treatment, even if the patient was in the category of patients who with prompt treatment would probably have died.[369] In *Philp v Ryan*[370] there was an eight-month delay in diagnosing that the claimant was suffering from prostate cancer. The trial judge awarded damages of €45,000 for the "great anguish and distress" caused by the claimant's reasonable belief that his life expectancy had been reduced,[371] though acknowledging that whether his life had actually been shortened was a matter that could never be known. The judge declined to award damages for loss of life expectancy itself. However, the Supreme Court of Ireland, in a judgment delivered by Fennelly J, increased the damages award by €5,000 to reflect the loss of life expectancy. Fennelly J commented that:

> "I should say that it seems to me to be contrary to instinct and logic that a plaintiff should not be entitled to be compensated for the fact that, due to the negligent diagnosis of his medical condition, he has been deprived of appropriate medical advice and the consequent opportunity to avail of treatment which might improve his condition. I can identify no contrary principle of law or justice. It is commonplace that allowance is made in awards and in settlements for the *risk* that an injured plaintiff *may* in the future develop arthritis in an injured joint. The risk may be high or low—a fifteen percent risk is often mentioned—but damages are paid. I cannot agree that this is any different from what is sought in the present case. It does not matter that the damage suffered by the plaintiff consists of the loss of an opportunity to avail of treatment. It might, with equal logic, be described as an increased risk of shorter life expectancy. It seems to me as illogical to award damages for a probable future injury as if it were a certainty, as to withhold them where the risk is low on the basis that it will not happen at all."[372]

There was no attempt to quantify the claimant's "lost chance". The compensation award was in the form of general damages, and looks not dissimilar from Baroness Hale's suggested "modest claim for reduction of life expectancy".

5–130   In *Sutton v Population Services Family Planning Programme Ltd*[373] McCowan J awarded damages for the premature onset of menopause and four "lost years" to a patient whose cancer was not detected early enough because of the negligence of a nurse. Early detection would not have prevented a recurrence of the cancer because it was of high grade malignancy, but it would have delayed the recurrence by four years, and the claimant would have led a normal life for four more years. There was no award for pain and suffering or for the medical treatment required since the claimant would have had to face the same operations

---

was exacerbated by the anguish of knowing that the cancer could have been detected earlier (although earlier detection would not have prevented her death).
[369] See para.5–124.
[370] [2004] IESC 105; [2004] 4 I.R. 241.
[371] There was no attempt to identify a "recognised psychiatric injury" (see para.2–188). This was an award of general damages for anguish attributable to the claimant's reasonable belief that his life had been shortened.
[372] The Supreme Court also awarded €50,000 aggravated damages for the defendant's deliberate attempt to falsify the medical records in an attempt to improve his prospects of success in the litigation.
[373] *The Times*, 7 November 1981. See also *Judge v Huntingdon Health Authority* [1995] 6 Med. L.R. 223, *Taylor v West Kent Health Authority* [1997] 8 Med. L.R. 251 and *Hague v Dalzell* [2016] EWHC 2753 (QB) on the loss attributable to delay in diagnosing cancer.

and treatment in any event, but four years later.[374] Similarly, in *Laferrière v Lawson*,[375] although the claimant was unable to claim for loss of a chance of a better outcome when the defendant negligently failed to inform her that she had breast cancer or to make any arrangements for appropriate follow-up, she was entitled to compensation for the psychological suffering attributable to her subsequent belief that things might have been different if she had known about her illness earlier and had been treated sooner, which would have exacerbated the pain she experienced as a result of the advance of the disease. She was also entitled to compensation for the fact that earlier treatment would have improved her quality of life in the period during which she survived, although it would not have prevented her death.[376]

2.   CAUSATION IN LAW

The "but for" test excludes those factors which cannot be said to have been *a* cause of the damage, but there may be more than one causal element that satisfies the "but for" test, in which case the court may have to choose which of two or more operative causes are to be treated as the cause *in law* of the claimant's damage. The question is whether the defendant's breach of duty was *the* cause, for the purpose of attributing legal responsibility. The court is not required to find that a single event was the sole legal cause, although there is a tendency for the courts to seek to identify a single cause, at least where the claimant has not been at fault (in which case responsibility will be apportioned under the Law Reform (Contributory Negligence) Act 1945). In practice this can be something of a fiction, and it is important to appreciate that there is an element of judicial policy at work in attributing causal connections.

5–131

"Common sense" is usually said to be the starting point in this process,[377] and judicial common sense is often filtered through a string of metaphors: was the "chain of causation" broken; was the causal link too remote; was the tort a "proximate" or "direct" or "substantial" or "effective" cause, the *causa causans* not merely the *causa sine qua non*? The use of such phrases should not obscure the fact that the court must make a choice, which may be conditioned by common

5–132

---

[374] See also *Gregg v Scott* [2002] EWCA Civ 1471; [2003] Lloyd's Rep. Med. 105 at [60] per Mance LJ: "quite apart from the respondent's negligence, the appellant had cancer, which at least as a matter of statistical probability meant that he was anyway going to suffer a curtailed life, so that there cannot be a simple attribution, to the respondent's negligence, of all the devastating effects on him of his cancer. The extra pain, suffering and distress resulting from the negligence should however be recoverable in damages."

[375] (1991) 78 D.L.R. (4th) 609, SCC.

[376] See also *Pittman Estate v Bain* (1994) 112 D.L.R. (4th) 257, Ont Ct, Gen Div, para.4–060, where the deceased was not informed that a blood transfusion that he had received some years previously had been contaminated with HIV. The transfusion had not been given negligently, but the failure to inform him of his HIV status was negligent. Had he known of his HIV status his death from AIDS could have been delayed. The damage was held to consist of the pain and suffering from his three-week terminal illness, and the loss of two years' life expectancy.

[377] *Cork v Kirby MacLean Ltd* [1952] 2 All E.R. 402 at 407; *Yorkshire Dale Steamship Co. Ltd v Minister of War Transport* [1942] A.C. 691 at 706.

usages of speech and may have only a tenuous connection with scientific notions of logic. As Lord Wright commented in *Liesbosch Dredger v S.S. Edison*:

"In the varied web of affairs, the law must extract some consequences as relevant, not perhaps on grounds of pure logic but simply for practical reasons."[378]

In *Rahman v Arearose Ltd*[379] Laws LJ commented that:

"Once it is recognised that the first principle is that every tortfeasor should compensate the injured claimant in respect of that loss and damage for which he should justly be held responsible, the metaphysics of causation can be kept in their proper place: of themselves they offered in any event no hope of a solution of the problems which confront the courts in this and other areas. The law has dug no deeper in the philosophical thickets of causation than to distinguish between a *causa sine qua non* and a *causa causans*. The latter is an empty tautology. The former proves everything, and therefore nothing: if A kills B by stabbing him, the birth of either of them 30 years before is as much a *causa sine qua non* of the death as is the wielding of the knife. So the law makes appeal to the notion of a proximate cause; but how proximate does it have to be? As a concept, it tells one nothing. So in all these cases the real question is, what is the damage for which the defendant under consideration should be held responsible."

(a)   Successive sufficient causes

5–133   **Successive torts**   Where there are two independent events, each of which were sufficient to have caused the damage sustained by the claimant, the determination of causal responsibility depends on the nature of the events and the order in which they occurred. Thus, where both events are tortious responsibility will be attributed to the tort which occurred first in time.[380] In *Baker v Willoughby*,[381] for example, the claimant sustained an injury to his leg as a result of the defendant's negligence. The claimant was subsequently shot in the same leg during an armed robbery at his place of work, resulting in the amputation of the leg. The defendant argued that the supervening amputation had submerged or obliterated the original injury, and that he should only have to compensate the claimant for the losses up to the date of the shooting. The House of Lords held that the defendant remained responsible for the initial disability even after the amputation. The person who shot the claimant would only have been liable for the *additional* loss that had been inflicted by the shooting, not the whole disability, and so the defendant's argument would have resulted in the claimant being undercompensated because he would have received no compensation at all for the initial disability caused by the defendant after the date of the amputation. It was wrong, said their Lordships,

---

[378] [1933] A.C. 449 at 460. See also *Abbott v Kasza and Ace Construction Co.* [1976] 4 W.W.R. 20 at 28, Alta CA.

[379] [2001] Q.B. 351 at [32]–[33].

[380] *Performance Cars Ltd v Abraham* [1962] 1 Q.B. 33—defendant negligently damaged a motor vehicle which had previously been damaged by the negligence of another motorist; defendant held not liable for the cost of a respray because, having damaged an already damaged car, his negligence was not the cause of the loss. The Court of Appeal applied the same approach to a claim for personal injuries in *Steel v Joy* [2004] EWCA Civ 576; [2004] 1 W.L.R. 3002 at [70], para.5–134.

[381] [1970] A.C. 467.

that the claimant should fall between two tortfeasors, receiving less in damages than he would have received had there been no interval between the torts.[382]

In *Steel v Joy*[383] the claimant suffered an acceleration of symptoms of an underlying congenital condition of seven to ten years as a result of the negligence of D1. Over two years later he suffered a further injury due to D2's negligence which produced an exacerbation of the symptoms of three to six months. If he had not already been injured by D1 the injury caused by D2 would also have produced an exacerbation of the symptoms of seven to ten years (i.e. exactly the same exacerbation as caused by D1's negligence). D1's argument that he was only liable for the exacerbation until the date of the second accident was summarily rejected by the Court of Appeal. D1's second argument that D1 and D2 were liable for causing the "same damage" and that there could be apportionment between the tortfeasors under the Civil Liability (Contribution) Act 1978 was also rejected. *Performance Cars Ltd v Abraham*[384] was still good law, and as a matter of logic and common sense, it was clearly correct. D2 was liable only for the additional losses inflicted by him, not for the consequences of the first injury.[385]

Supervening non-tortious event   On the other hand, where the supervening event is not tortious the defendant's responsibility for the injury ends when the event occurs. In *Jobling v Associated Dairies Ltd*[386] the claimant suffered a back

5–134

5–135

---

[382] An argument accepted as correct by the High Court of Australia in *Wynn v NSW Insurance Ministerial Corporation* (1995) 133 A.L.R. 154 at 163; cf. *Griffiths v Commonwealth* (1985) 72 F.L.R. 260 at 273 applying the preferred solution of the Court of Appeal in *Baker v Willoughby* [1969] 2 W.L.R. 489 that the second tortfeasor is liable for the whole loss, having caused the claimant to "lose" his right of action against the original wrongdoer; Hudson (1987) 38 N.I.L.Q. 190–193. See further *Singh v Aitken* [1998] P.I.Q.R. Q37, County Court where S died of a heart attack, and it was accepted that he would have survived but for the defendants' negligent misdiagnosis of his heart condition. At the time of his death, S had an unanswerable claim for £120,000 against the Motor Insurer's Bureau in respect of a previous accident, but following his death that claim was properly compromised for £20,000. S's dependants brought an action against the defendants under the Fatal Accidents Act 1976 claiming their loss of dependency (on the basis of a 75 per cent dependency claim) in respect of the difference between the original value of the claim against the MIB and the compromise sum. The case was dealt with on the basis that it involved only the assessment of quantum, not a question of causation. It was held that the dependants were entitled to the £75,000 which represented their dependency from the sum that would have been obtained from the MIB by S, but for his death. The defendants had to take S as they found him, namely a man with an unanswerable claim to a large sum of money which was forfeit as a result of their negligence.

[383] [2004] EWCA Civ 576; [2004] 1 W.L.R. 3002, at [55] to [70].

[384] [1962] 1 Q.B. 33, para.5–133, n.380.

[385] "It is true that, but for the first accident, the second accident would have caused the same damage as the first accident. But that is irrelevant. Since the claimant had already suffered that damage, the second defendant did not cause it": [2004] EWCA Civ 576; [2004] 1 W.L.R. 3002 at [70]. See also *Reaney v University Hospital of North Staffordshire NHS Trust* [2015] EWCA Civ 1119; [2016] P.I.Q.R. Q3 (discussed by J. McQuater [2016] J.P.I.L. C14) where the claimant was already in need of a care package due to the fact that she was paraplegic. As a result of the defendants' negligence she needed a much greater package of care. The Court of Appeal, following *Steel v Joy,* held that if the negligence caused a need for care which was substantially of the same kind as the pre-existing needs then the damage caused by the negligence was the additional care needs, whereas if the needs caused by the negligence were qualitatively different from the pre-existing needs, then those needs were caused in their entirety by the negligence.

[386] [1982] A.C. 794.

injury as a result of his employers' negligence, reducing his earning capacity by 50 per cent. Three years later he developed a disease, unconnected with the accident, which rendered him wholly unfit for work. The House of Lords held that the employers were liable for the claimant's reduced earning capacity only for the three-year period. The supervening disease was treated as the sole cause of the claimant's inability to work, although the result was justified, not on the basis of causation, but on the ground of "vicissitudes". When assessing damages for future loss of earnings the award will be discounted for the possibility that other events might have reduced the claimant's earning capacity or working life, even if the tort had not occurred. A subsequent illness is one of these "vicissitudes of life", and, applying the principle that the court will not speculate about future events when the facts are known, the illness must be taken into account. Their Lordships were critical of the decision in *Baker v Willoughby*, while recognising that a different approach could apply where the supervening event consisted of a tort.[387] Lord Keith rationalised the distinction by suggesting that a supervening tort might not be regarded as one of the ordinary vicissitudes of life, and so would not be taken into account, although Lord Wilberforce conceded that there was no logical justification.[388]

5–136   **Chance of second tort occurring in the future**   *Baker v Willoughby* only applies where there are actually two tortious events. In *Heil v Rankin*[389] the Court of Appeal held that when assessing damages for future loss of earnings, where there was a risk that the claimant might have become the victim of a tort in the future which would have caused him to give up work, that risk should be taken into account, thereby reducing the loss of future earnings claim, as would occur with the risk of non-tortious events. The claimant relied on *Baker v Willoughby* on the basis that if an actual second tort did not have the effect of removing the first tortfeasor's liability to compensate the claimant, then a fortiori an hypothetical second tortious event that had not actually occurred should not reduce the level of compensation. If there was no discount for the reality there should be no discount for a chance. The Court of Appeal rejected this argument, applying the vicissitudes approach, on the ground that otherwise the claimant was likely to be overcompensated. If claimants had to be compensated on the basis that they would have continued in employment to retirement, but it was likely that future tortious acts would have caused them to give up employment, then it was "self-evident" that they were being overcompensated.

---

[387] See also *Carslogie Steamship Co. Ltd v Royal Norwegian Government* [1952] A.C. 292 attributing the loss caused by a ship being laid up for repairs following a collision to the need to repair damage caused by a subsequent storm. This principle also applies to claims brought in contract: *Beoco Ltd v Alfa Laval Co. Ltd* [1995] Q.B. 137 at 151, CA.
[388] The claimant's imprisonment as a result of a criminal offence committed by the claimant is also a vicissitude of life that should not be disregarded when considering the effects of the tort on the claimant's earning capacity. So claimants' loss of earning capacity during their imprisonment will be attributed to their incarceration rather than an earlier tort: see *Gray v Thames Trains Ltd* [2009] UKHL 33; [2009] 1 A.C. 1339; para.11–024.
[389] [2001] P.I.Q.R. Q16.

(b) Intervening acts

Where the act of another person, without which the damage would not have occurred, intervenes between the defendant's negligence and the claimant's damage, the court must decide whether the defendant is responsible or whether the intervening act constituted a novus actus interveniens. If the latter, then the act is regarded as having broken the causal connection between the negligence and the damage. This too is treated as a matter of common sense in which metaphor abounds.[390]   **5–137**

There are two broad approaches to this problem. The first asks whether the act was reasonable in the circumstances, which refers to the voluntariness of the act, not whether it was careless. The more voluntary the act the less reasonable it is, and therefore the more likely to be regarded as a novus actus, but even deliberate conduct may be "involuntary" in this sense, where, for example, a person is forced to make some conscious response to a situation brought about by the defendant's negligence.[391] The second approach looks to the foreseeability of the intervention. On this view, even where the intervening act is unreasonable it will not necessarily be treated as breaking the chain of causation. Accordingly, a negligent intervention, negligent medical treatment for example, will not automatically exculpate the original tortfeasor if it is a foreseeable consequence of the defendant's initial negligence.   **5–138**

There is no concept of an "intervening *contributory* event", i.e. an event that does not fully break the causal link between the "but for" cause and the damage, but merely contributes to the damage. If the second event is considered to be an intervening act breaking the causal link between the first event and the damage, then the first event is not regarded as a cause of the damage at all. But if the second event does not break the causal link, the first event remains a cause of damage for which the tortfeasor is fully responsible. There is no basis for apportioning the loss between the two events[392] (subject to the tortfeasor's potential claim for contribution under the Civil Liability (Contribution) Act 1978 against another tortfeasor).   **5–139**

(i)   *Intervening acts of third parties*

Successive acts of negligence   Where there are two successive acts of negligence it may be a nice question whether the second incidence of negligence breaks the chain of causation between the first error and the patient's injury. A   **5–140**

---

[390] So the question may be whether the intervening event was such as to "isolate" or "insulate" or "eclipse" the defendant's negligence, or whether it was merely a "conduit pipe" or "part of a transmission gear set in motion by" the defendant: *Weld-Blundell v Stephens* [1920] A.C. 956 at 986, per Lord Sumner; see also *The Oropesa* [1943] P. 32 at 39, per Lord Wright.

[391] *The Oropesa* [1943] P. 32; *Emeh v Kensington and Chelsea Area Health Authority* [1985] Q.B. 1012, below, para.5–159.

[392] *Environment Agency v Ellis* [2008] EWCA Civ 1117; [2009] P.I.Q.R. P5; [2009] L.S. Law Med. 70; see para.5–041.

subsequent act of negligence may constitute an intervening act.[393] In *Hogan v Bentinck West Hartley Collieries Ltd*[394] the House of Lords held that an operation which had been unreasonably recommended by a doctor broke the chain of causation between the claimant's initial injury sustained at work and the amputation of his thumb. Lord Normand said that:

> "I start from the proposition, which seems to me to be axiomatic, that if a surgeon, by lack of skill or failure in reasonable care, causes additional injury or aggravates an existing injury and so renders himself liable in damages, the reasonable conclusion must be that his intervention is a new cause and that the additional injury or the aggravation of the existing injury should be attributed to it and not to the original accident. On the other hand, an operation prudently advised and skilfully and carefully carried out should not be treated as a new cause, whatever its consequences may be."[395]

5–141   The latter part of Lord Normand's statement makes it clear that where appropriate medical treatment has been properly carried out, the original tortfeasor will be responsible for any complications arising out of the treatment.[396] This result can be justified, if justification were considered necessary, on the basis that: (i) the intervention was reasonable, arising in the ordinary course of events, and so did not break the chain of causation; or (ii) the unforeseeable consequences of a foreseeable and reasonable intervention are within the risk created by the defendant's negligence; or (iii) some complication from medical treatment is foreseeable and it is not necessary to foresee the precise complication which occurred.

5–142   **Intervening medical negligence**   The first part of Lord Normand's statement, on the other hand, suggests that negligence in the performance of corrective treatment will always break the chain of causation. This was never an absolute rule,[397] and in any event can no longer be regarded as correct. Where the intervening event consists of negligent medical treatment it will require a gross act of negligence by the medical staff, amounting to a completely inappropriate response to the patient's condition, to break the causal link.[398] In *Webb v Barclays*

---

[393] Although this will not always be the case: see *Rouse v Squires* [1973] 1 Q.B. 889; and the discussion of this problem in *Knightley v Johns* [1982] 1 All E.R. 851, below, para.5–144. Neither of these cases involved medical negligence.

[394] [1949] 1 All E.R. 588.

[395] [1949] 1 All E.R. 588 at 596.

[396] See *Robinson v Post Office* [1974] 2 All E.R. 737, para.5–186, below; cf. the South African case of *Alston v Marine & Trade Insurance Co. Ltd* 1964 (4) S.A. 112—the claimant suffered a stroke as a result of an interaction between the drug he was prescribed for injuries caused by the defendant's negligence and cheese which he ate. In the light of the medical knowledge at the time it was not unreasonable to eat cheese. Nonetheless, it was held that eating the cheese constituted a novus actus interveniens, even though the claimant acted reasonably.

[397] See, e.g. the comments of Lord du Parcq in *Grant v Sun Shipping Co. Ltd* [1948] A.C. 549 at 563: "If the negligence or breach of duty of one person is the cause of injury to another, the wrongdoer cannot in all circumstances escape liability by proving that, though he was to blame, yet but for the negligence of a third person the injured man would not have suffered the damage of which he complains. There is abundant authority for the proposition that the mere fact that a subsequent act of negligence has been the immediate cause of disaster does not exonerate the original offender."

[398] *Webb v Barclays Bank plc and Portsmouth Hospitals NHS Trust* [2001] EWCA Civ 1141; [2002] P.I.Q.R. P61; [2001] Lloyd's Rep. Med. 500 at [55], citing *Clerk & Lindsell on Torts*, 18th edn (London: Sweet & Maxwell, 2000), para.2–55 (see now *Clerk & Lindsell on Torts*, 22nd edn

Bank plc[399] the Court of Appeal held that there is no rule that where a claimant suffers personal injury due to a defendant's negligence that the defendant's liability ends as a result of negligence by a doctor who treats the original injury but whose negligence makes the claimant's condition worse. Mrs Webb injured an already vulnerable knee in a fall at work for which her employers were found responsible. Subsequently, the surgeon treating her advised Mrs Webb to have an above the knee amputation of her leg, advice which she accepted. That advice was negligent. Her employers settled her claim in full and then brought contribution proceedings against the hospital. The issue was whether the employers' liability in respect of the injuries to the leg included some part of the loss after the amputation, or whether the surgeon's negligent advice broke the causal link between the employers' negligence and the amputation. The Court of Appeal held that the subsequent negligence of a surgeon "did not eclipse the original wrongdoing". The employers were held liable for all the damage attributable to the fall, and 25 per cent of the damage attributable to the amputation. The point was explained by Lord Neuberger MR in *Wright (A Child) v Cambridge Medical Group*:

> "…where there are successive tortfeasors, the contention that the causative potency of the negligence of the first is destroyed by the subsequent negligence of the second depends very much on the facts of the particular case. In many cases where there are successive acts of negligence by different parties, both parties can be held responsible for the damage which ensues, so that the issue is not which of them is liable, but how liability is to be apportioned between them. The mere fact that, if the second party had not been negligent, the damage which subsequently ensued would not have occurred, by no means automatically exonerates the first party's negligence from being causative of that damage."[400]

Thus, if the claimant acts reasonably in seeking or accepting medical treatment, negligence in carrying out the treatment is not necessarily a novus actus interveniens relieving the first tortfeasor from liability for the claimant's subsequent condition. The original injury can be regarded as carrying some risk that medical treatment might be negligently given.[401]

(London: Sweet & Maxwell, 2018), para.2–121 for the same proposition). Note, however, that in *Spencer v Wincanton Holdings Ltd* [2009] EWCA Civ 1404; [2010] P.I.Q.R. P8 the Court of Appeal rejected a test suggesting that where the *claimant's* subsequent conduct is in question it should be capable of being described as "reckless or deliberate" before being regarded as a novus actus interveniens. The issue was said to be whether it was "fair" to hold the defendant responsible for the further damage, and that did not depend on how one characterised the intervening event. See the comments of Sedley LJ in *Spencer* at [15] quoted at para.5–154 below.

[399] [2001] EWCA Civ 1141; [2002] P.I.Q.R. P61; [2001] Lloyd's Rep. Med. 500.

[400] [2011] EWCA Civ 669; [2013] Q.B. 312 at [32]:

[401] *Webb v Barclays Bank plc* [2001] EWCA Civ 1141; [2002] P.I.Q.R. P61; [2001] Lloyd's Rep. Med. 500 at [54], applying a dictum from *Mahoney v Kruschick (Demolitions) Pty Ltd* (1985) 156 C.L.R. 522, HC of Australia. See also *Thefaut v Johnston* [2017] EWHC 497 (QB); [2017] Med. L.R. 319 at [93] per Green J indicating that the same principle would apply to a case involving negligent medical advice (breach of duty to inform patient of risks of surgery; patient requiring revision surgery; strong causal nexus between the initial wrongful advice and any injury attributable to revision surgery in the absence of gross negligence). In *Price v Milawski* (1977) 82 D.L.R. (3d) 130, Ont CA a doctor who negligently failed to identify a fracture of the patient's ankle was held liable for the subsequent negligence of another doctor in the treatment of the patient's condition. It was reasonably foreseeable that once the information generated by the defendant's negligent error got into the hospital records, other doctors subsequently treating the claimant might well rely on the accuracy

5–143   In *Rahman v Arearose Ltd*[402] the claimant was seriously assaulted by two black youths, causing an injury to his right eye. His employers were negligent in failing to take reasonable care to reduce the risk of such assaults. Subsequently, as a result of the negligence of a surgeon, he was rendered blind in the right eye. In addition to the physical injuries, the claimant developed severe psychiatric consequences, including post-traumatic stress disorder, a severe depressive disorder, a specific phobia of Afro-Caribbean people, and enduring personality change. The evidence indicated that the psychiatric reaction was partly due to the assault and partly due to the loss of his eye: (i) the post traumatic stress disorder was due to the loss of the eye; (ii) the phobia was due to the assault and subsequent events; and (iii) the personality change was due to the synergistic interaction between the depression and the post traumatic stress disorder. The Court of Appeal held that a second act of negligence did not necessarily break the causal link between an initial act of negligence and the subsequent damage. Laws LJ commented that:

> "…it does not seem to me to be established as a rule of law that later negligence always extinguishes the causative potency of an earlier tort. Nor should it be. The law is that every tortfeasor should compensate the injured claimant in respect of that loss and damage for which he should justly be held responsible. To make that principle good, it is important that the elusive conception of causation should not be frozen into constricting rules." [403]

The sensible conclusion was that:

---

of that information, i.e. that the X-ray showed no fracture of the ankle. It was also foreseeable that some doctor might do so without checking, even though to do so in the circumstances might itself be a negligent act. It was held that on the particular facts this was a risk that a reasonable doctor would not have brushed aside as far-fetched. See also *Reeves v Carthy* [1984] I.R. 348, Supreme Court of Ireland. Where the defendant's wrongful conduct has generated the very risk of injury resulting from the negligence of another person (whether the claimant or a third party) and that injury occurred in the ordinary course of things, the negligence of the claimant or a third party should not be regarded as a superseding cause: *March v E. & M.H. Stramare Pty Ltd* (1991) 99 A.L.R. 423, HC of Australia; Mullany (1992) 12 O.J.L.S. 431. In *McGroder v Maguire* [2002] NSWCA 261 a doctor who negligently referred the claimant to a chiropractor was held liable for the claimant's injuries following the negligent performance of a manipulation of the claimant's neck by the chiropractor. The claimant's "injuries would not have occurred had he not been treated by a chiropractor. He was only treated by a chiropractor because of [the defendant's] referral. That referral was negligent. His negligence generated the risk of injury by referring him for inappropriate treatment. It is no answer that the treatment was administered negligently", per Beazley JA at [38]. See also the comment of McHugh J in *Bennett v Minister of Community Welfare* (1991) 107 A.L.R. 617 at 632, HC of Australia (not a medical negligence case): "If a doctor has negligently omitted to diagnose a condition which leads to a patient's death, it is no answer to a claim of actionable negligence that subsequently another doctor negligently failed to diagnose the condition at a time when its ultimate consequence could have been avoided. Each negligent omission was a separate and independent cause of the patient's death." cf. *Mitchell v Rahman* (2002) 209 D.L.R. (4th) 621, Man CA, where it was held that negligent misdiagnosis of a dislocated shoulder following a road traffic accident broke the causal link between the accident and the permanent disability which the claimant developed, applying Lord Normand's dictum in *Hogan v Bentinck West Hartley Collieries Ltd* [1949] 1 All E.R. 588 at 596, cited above at para.5–140.
[402] [2001] Q.B. 351.
[403] [2001] Q.B. 351 at [29].

"...while the second defendants obviously (and exclusively) caused the right-eye blindness, thereafter each tort had its part to play in the claimant's suffering."[404]

In *Knightley v Johns*[405] the Court of Appeal said that the question was whether **5–144** the whole sequence of events was a natural and probable consequence of the defendant's negligence, and whether it was reasonably foreseeable, not foreseeable as a mere possibility.[406] In answering this question it was helpful but not decisive to consider which events were deliberate choices to do positive acts and which were mere omissions, which acts and omissions were innocent mistakes or miscalculations and which were negligent. Thus:

"Negligent conduct is more likely to break the chain of causation than conduct which is not; positive acts will more easily constitute new causes than inaction. Mistakes and mischances are to be expected when human beings, however well trained, have to cope with a crisis; What exactly they will be cannot be predicted, but if those which occur are natural the wrongdoer cannot, I think, escape responsibility for them and their consequences simply by calling them improbable or unforeseeable. He must accept the risk of some unexpected mischances."[407]

In deciding which mischances amount to intervening events the court should apply "common sense rather than logic on the facts and circumstances of each case". In *Prendergast v Sam & Dee Ltd*,[408] for example, the Court of Appeal concluded that a pharmacist's negligence in misreading a doctor's prescription, and consequently supplying a patient with the wrong drug, did not break the chain of causation from the doctor's initial negligence in writing an illegible prescription. It was reasonably foreseeable that the prescription could be misread.

---

[404] [2001] Q.B. 351 at [34]. But for criticism of the court's approach in *Rahman v Arearose Ltd* see Weir [2001] C.L.J. 237. *Rahman* was applied in *XP v Compensa Towarzystwo SA* [2016] EWHC 1728 (QB); [2016] Med. L.R. 570, a case in which there were two separate accidents, each of which contributed to the claimant's psychiatric illness, but it was not possible to say with any precision how much each had contributed. In those circumstances, said Whipple J, it was appropriate to adopt a "broad brush approach" to the causal effect of each accident rather than attempting to apply the more precise "but for" approach of *Reaney v University Hospital of North Staffordshire NHS Trust* [2015] EWCA Civ 1119; [2016] P.I.Q.R. Q3 (see para.5–134, n.385).

[405] [1982] 1 All E.R. 851 at 865.

[406] See also per Lord Reid in *Home Office v Dorset Yacht Co. Ltd* [1970] A.C. 1004 at 1030: "Where human action forms one of the links between the original wrongdoing of the defendant and the loss suffered by the plaintiff, that action must at least have been something very likely to happen if it is not to be regarded as *novus actus interveniens* breaking the chain of causation."

[407] [1982] 1 All E.R. 851 at 865, per Stephenson LJ. The difficulty in making categorical statements about the effect of intervening negligence is illustrated by the different results reached by the Court of Appeal in *Knightley v Johns* and *Rouse v Squires* [1973] 1 Q.B. 889, on essentially similar facts. On the other hand, where the intervening conduct can be characterised as reckless, as opposed to merely negligent, it is far more likely to be treated as a novus actus interveniens: *Wright v Lodge* [1993] 4 All E.R. 299; [1993] P.I.Q.R. P31, CA; Jones (1994) 2 Tort L. Rev. 133. See further the comments of Lord Hobhouse in *Reeves v Commissioner of Police for the Metropolis* [2000] 1 A.C. 360 at 392: "Human conduct, which is not entirely reasonable, for example, where it is itself careless, but is within the range of human conduct that is foreseeable and normally contemplated as not unlikely, may add a further cause of the relevant subsequent event but would not normally mean that an earlier relevant event ceased also to be a cause of that later event. Careless conduct may ordinarily be regarded as being within the range of normal human conduct when reckless conduct ordinarily would not."

[408] [1989] 1 Med. L.R. 36, para.4–086.

5–147   **Intervening non-negligent medical treatment**   If subsequent medical negligence does not necessarily break the causal link, it will be even harder to establish a break in the chain of causation where the later medical treatment is found not to be negligent. In *Horton v Evans*[417] a pharmacist who negligently failed to check the dosage of a prescription with the prescribing doctor was held liable for the patient's adverse drug reaction, although another doctor had subsequently repeated the prescription relying only on the information on the label of the medication bottle and what he was told by the patient. Keith J held that it was reasonable for a doctor who is asked for a repeat prescription of a drug to rely on what he saw on the label of the drug bottle provided by the patient and the patient's assurance that she had been on the same dose for years, where the dosage was within known therapeutic limits. Nor was the patient's subsequent adverse reaction to the drug too remote a consequence of the pharmacist's negligence, because a competent pharmacist should reasonably have foreseen that the label on the bottle might be used by a doctor other than the doctor who made the initial prescription error to identify what the initial prescription had been for.

5–148   Similarly, in *O'Gorman v Jermyn*[418] a pathology laboratory mixed up the samples of two patients as a result of which the claimant was diagnosed as having stomach cancer. The claimant subsequently underwent an unnecessary total gastrectomy operation; tests on the removed stomach showed that he did not have cancer. The hospital sought to blame the surgeon who carried out the gastrectomy for the unnecessary surgery, arguing that the surgeon's negligence broke the causal link between laboratory mix up and the gastrectomy. It was argued that the patient's symptoms were inconsistent with a diagnosis of stomach cancer, which in any event was extremely rare in a 21-year-old patient, and that this should have alerted the surgeon to the possibility of a mistake in the histopathological diagnosis. Lavan J held that the surgeon had not been negligent and was entitled to rely on the pathology report:

> "...a surgeon is not expected to be a pathologist, given the sophisticated pathology department which was provided for him by the first defendant (the hospital) which was relied upon by consultant surgeons since the creation of the pathology department."

The judge was clearly influenced in reaching this outcome by the failure of the hospital to lead any evidence as to the normal practice of other surgeons at the hospital in relying on or querying histopathology reports (and possibly by hospital's somewhat breathtaking submission that it bore no responsibility at all, given the surgeon's failure to query the report, for the surgery).

5–149   **No causal link between first act of negligence and claimant's damage** Where the second act of negligence results in damage that cannot be said to be causally linked to the initial negligence, the first tortfeasor is not responsible, not because the later conduct intervened, but because the damage fails to satisfy the "but for" test. In *Yepremian v Scarborough General Hospital*,[419] for example,

---

[417] [2006] EWHC 2808 (QB); [2007] P.N.L.R. 17; [2007] LS Law Med. 212.
[418] [2006] IEHC 398.
[419] (1980) 110 D.L.R. (3d) 513, Ont CA; the action was settled prior to the appeal hearing before the Supreme Court of Canada: (1981) D.L.R. (3d) 341.

doctor G was negligent in failing to diagnose the patient's diabetes. The claimant's subsequent cardiac arrest was caused by the negligent treatment given to the patient by another doctor, R, after the diabetes had been diagnosed. Thus, G's negligence was not a cause in fact of the cardiac arrest. If, however, said the Ontario Court of Appeal, the cardiac arrest had been part of the natural consequences of untreated diabetes, or even of ineffectively treated diabetes, then the subsequent negligence of R would not have prevented G's negligence from being regarded as a cause of the damage. G could not rely on R's failure to rescue the claimant from the consequences of G's negligence.

"Intervening" omissions   This latter point was the basis of the decision in *Thompson v Toorenburgh*[420] where it was held that the failure of a doctor to provide an actus interveniens which would have saved the accident victim's life is not the same as committing an actus interveniens that caused her death. The defendant motorist who caused the deceased's initial injuries was liable, notwithstanding medical "mistreatment".[421] Robertson JA said that: **5–150**

> "Mrs. Thompson would almost certainly have recovered if proper treatment had been applied speedily; the doctors failed to apply that treatment and so failed to save her life, but they did not cause her death. They failed to provide an *actus interveniens* that would have saved her life, but that is not the same as committing an *actus interveniens* that caused her death."[422]

This approach to negligent omissions might be followed in this country.[423] In *Muirhead v Industrial Tank Specialities Ltd*[424] Goff LJ suggested that a negligent failure by a third party to prevent damage caused by the negligence of the defendant would not exonerate the defendant. The defendant could escape responsibility: **5–151**

> "...only where the act or omission of another was of such a nature that it constituted a wholly independent cause of the damage, *i.e.* a *novus actus interveniens*."[425]

On this view it might be argued that a patient's refusal to accept medical treatment on, say, religious grounds does not break the chain of causation either, since, at worst, it represents an "unreasonable" (negligent) failure to intervene to prevent the damage caused by the defendant.[426]

On the other hand, it seems strange to attach significance to the fact that the doctor's negligence consists of an omission to give lifesaving treatment, and so   **5–152**

---

[420] (1973) 50 D.L.R. (3d) 717, BCCA.

[421] The court carefully avoided calling the medical treatment "negligent", although on the facts it is difficult to see how the treatment could not have been negligent.

[422] (1973) 50 D.L.R. (3d) 717 at 721.

[423] In *Panther v Wharton* unreported 29 March 2001, QBD, Peter Heppel QC specifically agreed with the statement of Robertson JA in *Thompson v Toorenburgh*, holding that the subsequent negligence of a consultant physician (in failing to diagnose the claimant's vascular problem) did not break the causal link between the negligence of a general practitioner in failing to refer to the claimant for investigation of her physical symptoms and the resulting damage to her limbs.

[424] [1986] Q.B. 507 at 533.

[425] [1986] Q.B. 507 at 533. This rather begs the question of which acts or omissions are of such a nature that they constitute a wholly independent cause.

[426] See para.5–163, below.

amounts to a failure to provide an actus interveniens rather than constituting a novus actus interveniens, when it is patently clear that if the doctor were sued for negligence he would be held responsible for the death, at least where, on the balance of probabilities the evidence indicates that the patient's life would have been saved by prompt treatment.[427] Where the doctor has a duty of care to treat the patient the courts have no difficulty in regarding an omission to treat as having causative effect. It is submitted that the better approach in this type of case is to treat both the first tort and the subsequent negligently performed medical treatment as causative of the patient's death, and to apportion liability accordingly. Thus, in *Commonwealth of Australia v Martin*[428] M received injuries in a road traffic accident which were such that death was inevitable without proper corrective surgery. The medical treatment was performed negligently and he died four days later. It was held that both the negligent motorist and the negligent doctor had caused the death, and it was not necessary to show that the doctor's negligence constituted a novus actus interveniens before he could be held responsible.

5–153   Where doctors' negligence has increased the susceptibility of the patient to sustaining further injury, they cannot avoid responsibility for a subsequent injury within the risk created by their negligence, even though there are other later causes which also caused or materially contributed to that injury.[429]

(ii)   Intervening act by the claimant

5–154   Medical treatment often depends upon the co-operation of the patient. Where the patient fails to co-operate this may amount to contributory negligence.[430] In an extreme case the patient's conduct may be sufficient to break the chain of causation.[431] The test for an intervening act by the claimant has been said to be whether he acted unreasonably,[432] although it would be open to the court to

---

[427] cf. *Barnett v Chelsea and Kensington Hospital Management Committee* [1968] 1 All E.R. 1068, para.5–005, above.

[428] (1985) 59 A.L.R. 439, Fed Ct of Australia.

[429] *Powell v Guttman* (1978) 89 D.L.R. (3d) 180, Man CA, para.5–091, where the defendant was held liable for a fracture of the patient's leg which occurred in the course of a later operation performed by another doctor. The second doctor was found not to have been negligent.

[430] See paras 11–003 et seq.

[431] *Venner v North East Essex Area Health Authority, The Times*, 21 February 1987; *Murrin v Janes* [1949] 4 D.L.R. 403 at 406, Newfoundland SC—claimant who delayed seeing a doctor to deal with excessive bleeding following extraction of his teeth held to be the sole cause of his misfortune. In *Stevens v Bermondsey and Southwark Group Hospital Management Committee* (1963) 107 S.J. 478 the claimant claimed that a doctor's failure to diagnose the seriousness of his condition following a road traffic accident led to him settling his claim against the third party for a small sum. Paull J dismissed the action against the doctor, partly on the ground that the action against the third party was a novus actus interveniens. This seems doubtful, however, and the decision may be better regarded as a case where there was no duty of care with respect to that particular damage; see paras 2–049 to 2–050.

[432] *McKew v Holland & Hannen & Cubitts (Scotland) Ltd* [1969] 3 All E.R. 1621 at 1623: "if the injured man acts unreasonably he cannot hold the defender liable for injury caused by his own unreasonable conduct. His unreasonable conduct is novus actus interveniens. The chain of causation has been broken and what follows must be regarded as caused by his own conduct and not by the defender's fault or the disability caused by it."

conclude that a claimant who acted unreasonably was guilty of contributory negligence, and apportion responsibility between the claimant and the defendant.[433] In *Spencer v Wincanton Holdings Ltd*[434] Sedley LJ had reservations about a test based solely on whether the claimant's conduct was unreasonable, since it is "a protean adjective. Its nuances run from irrationality to simple incaution or unwisdom". He preferred a formulation based on "fairness". Although fairness might be no more precise than reasonableness, what it did suggest was that:

> "...a succession of consequences which in fact and in logic is infinite will be halted by the law when it becomes unfair to let it continue. In relation to tortious liability for personal injury, this point is reached when (though not only when) the claimant suffers a further injury which, while it would not have happened without the initial injury, has been in substance brought about by the claimant and not the tortfeasor."[435]

In *Spencer* the claimant suffered an accident at work, for which the defendants were responsible, which resulted in an above the knee amputation of his right leg. Some time later, while putting petrol in his car without using a prosthesis or his walking sticks the claimant fell and suffered further injury that resulted in him becoming wheelchair dependent. The Court of Appeal concluded that the claimant's decision not to use a prosthesis or walking sticks did not break the causal link between the original accident and the consequences of the fall, since it was not unfair for the defendant to bear a continuing responsibility for the effects of the original accident. The claimant's conduct was negligent (and therefore "unreasonable") but this did not amount to a novus actus interveniens. Damages were reduced by one third for the claimant's contributory negligence.[436]

The term "unreasonableness" is also used to indicate an element of voluntary conduct by the claimant, and so where the claimant's capacity for rational

5–155

---

[433] As, e.g. in *Sayers v Harlow Urban District Council* [1958] 1 W.L.R. 623, or *The Calliope* [1970] P. 172. See also Millner (1971) 22 N.I.L.Q. 168, 176–179 criticising *McKew v Holland & Hannen & Cubitts (Scotland) Ltd* [1969] 3 All E.R. 1621 for not taking this approach. In *Spencer v Wincanton Holdings Ltd* [2009] EWCA Civ 1404; [2010] P.I.Q.R. P8 at [22] it was pointed out that contributory negligence had not been pleaded in *McKew*. Once it is accepted that defendants owed a duty of care to take reasonable care against negligent conduct by others (including claimants) they cannot assert that the circumstances which gave rise to a breach of that duty constitute a novus actus interveniens: *March v E & MH Stramare Pty Ltd* (1991) 99 A.L.R. 423, HC of Australia; Mullany (1992) 12 O.J.L.S. 431.

[434] [2009] EWCA Civ 1404; [2010] P.I.Q.R. P8 at [11]. The case is commented on by J. McQuater [2010] J.P.I.L. C81.

[435] [2009] EWCA Civ 1404; [2010] P.I.Q.R. P8 at [15].

[436] See also *Dalling v R J Heale & Co Ltd* [2011] EWCA Civ 365 where the claimant's head injury reduced his ability to control his consumption of alcohol. More than three years after the original accident the claimant fell whilst drunk and sustained a further head injury. The Court of Appeal held that the act of getting drunk was not a free and voluntary act, and it was fair to hold the defendants partially responsible for the injuries attributable to the fall whilst the claimant was drunk (damages were reduced by one third for contributory negligence). The case is commented on by McCarthy [2011] J.P.I.L. C208. Cf. *Smith v Youth Justice Board for England and Wales* [2010] EWCA Civ 99 where it was held that a custody officer at a secure training centre who was involved, with two other officers, in the death of a 15-year-old boy from the excessive use of force in applying a restraint technique could not claim damages against her employers in respect of post-traumatic stress disorder. Responsibility for the boy's death, and its effect on the claimant's mental health, lay with the claimant (along with the other officers). Sedley LJ repeated his view that the causal effect of an event comes to an end "when it becomes unfair to let it continue".

judgment has been affected this may remove the necessary voluntary element for an actus interveniens. The less voluntary the claimant's conduct leading to the damage the less unfair it will be to hold the defendant responsible for the consequences of the claimant's actions.[437]

5–156   **Suicide**   It is on this basis that even suicide, which objectively would normally be regarded as an unreasonable act, will not necessarily amount to a novus actus interveniens.[438] At one time it was arguable that the issue turned upon whether at the time of the suicide the deceased was suffering from a disabling mental illness as a result of the injuries inflicted by the defendant.[439] But where the defendant was under a duty to exercise reasonable care to prevent the very event that occurred he cannot complain that the intervention broke the causal link, since that would render the duty ineffective. Thus, in the rare case where the defendant has a duty to protect a person of full understanding from causing harm to himself, it is self-contradictory to say that the breach could not have been a cause of the harm because the victim caused it to himself. In *Reeves v Commissioner of Police for the Metropolis*[440] the deceased hanged himself in a police cell. The defendants were aware that the prisoner was a suicide risk although he had not been diagnosed as suffering from any specific mental disorder. It was conceded that the defendants owed a duty of care, but they denied liability on the basis that the act of suicide constituted a novus actus, breaking the causal link. The House of Lords held that the suicide did not constitute a novus actus. It was not a new act, but the very harm that the defendants were under a duty to try to prevent. Lord Hoffmann said that:

> "...it would make nonsense of the existence of such a duty if the law were to hold that the occurrence of the very act which ought to have been prevented negatived causal connection between the breach of duty and the loss."[441]

Moreover, in *Reeves* the defendant's precise mental state was irrelevant. The duty was owed because the deceased was a known suicide risk, not because of any particular mental state.[442]

---

[437] *Dalling v R J Heale & Co Ltd* [2011] EWCA Civ 365, above; cf. *Wilson v Coulson* [2002] P.I.Q.R. P300, QBD, n.442 below.

[438] *Pigney v Pointer's Transport Services Ltd* [1957] 1 W.L.R. 1121; *Cotic v Gray* (1981) 124 D.L.R. (3d) 641, Ont CA; see paras 4–178 to 4–180; Jones (1990) 6 P.N. 107, 110–112. In *Corr v IBC Vehicles Ltd* [2006] EWCA Civ 331; [2007] Q.B. 46 at [101] Wilson LJ said that *Pigney* was correctly decided, "albeit reached by a route which was incorrect in that it was unrelated to any foreseeability criterion at all".

[439] In *Wright Estate v Davidson* (1992) 88 D.L.R. (4th) 698, BCCA, the deceased's suicide was held to constitute a novus actus interveniens where there was no evidence of disabling mental illness; cf. *Costello v Blakeson* [1993] 2 W.W.R. 562, BCSC, where the claimant suffered from depression amounting to a mental illness, distinguishing it from *Wright Estate v Davidson*.

[440] [2000] 1 A.C. 360.

[441] [2000] 1 A.C. 360 at 367–368.

[442] See also paras 4–181, 4–182, 11–021 and 11–022 on the question of the defences of volenti non fit injuria and ex turpi causa in relation to suicide. On the other hand, a defendant is not responsible for a claimant's voluntary, deliberate and informed decision to use heroin. In *Wilson v Coulson* [2002] P.I.Q.R. P300, QBD the claimant sustained brain damage in a road traffic accident for which the defendant was responsible. Shortly after the accident he started to use heroin, having previously been an occasional user of other drugs, and subsequently sustained additional brain damage following a

In *Reeves* the defendant was aware of the deceased's suicidal state; indeed this, together with the custodial relationship between the deceased and the defendants, was what gave rise to the defendant's duty. But it is clear that in the more typical case of personal injury caused by the defendant's negligence which leads to depression and the victim then taking his own life (or attempting to take his life and suffering injury in the process) the suicide will not necessarily be regarded as breaking the causal link between the defendant's negligence and the death. In *Corr v IBC Vehicles Ltd*[443] an employee sustained physical injury in an industrial accident, subsequently developed depression, and committed suicide six years later. It was held that the claimant's husband's suicide did not break the chain of causation between the negligence and the consequences of the suicide. She did not have to prove that at the time of the accident her husband's suicide was reasonably foreseeable as a type of damage separate from psychiatric and personal injury. The defendant's responsibility for the effects of suicide depended on whether it flowed from a condition for which the defendant was responsible. The claimant founded her claim on the deceased's depression, which was admitted to have been a foreseeable consequence of the defendant's negligence, and the evidence was that suicide is a not uncommon consequence of severe depression. Sedley LJ commented that:

5–157

> "The law of negligence no longer draws any distinction, for purposes of foreseeability and causation, between physical and psychological injury. It was accordingly admitted that the defendants were liable to pay damages both for the physical damage done to Mr Corr and for the depression into which he consequently fell. The question is whether the compensable consequences of the depression include Mr Corr's eventual suicide.
> The answer to such a question is in principle a matter of fact: either the suicide was a product of the depression or it was a discrete event. In practice there will be difficult cases in which the origins of the suicide are complex, throwing up questions of fragile personality and dominant cause. But the suicide in the present case, as a matter of clinical evidence and judgment, was grounded in post-traumatic depression and in nothing else."[444]

His Lordship added that:

> "If a case of suicide is to be excluded, it has to be because the evidence has failed to establish that the judgment and volition of the deceased were overwhelmed by depression consequent on the injury. This is in each case a matter of factual inquiry."[445]

The decision was unanimously upheld by the House of Lords.[446] Lord Bingham indicated that the deceased was not insane, but neither was he fully responsible for his actions. Depression, possibly very severe depression was a foreseeable

5–158

---

heroin overdose. He claimed that the original accident had produced a personality change, which led to him becoming addicted to heroin. Harrison J held that the claimant had not lost the capacity or the power to say no. His action was both unreasonable and illegal: "He was the author of his own misfortune and what followed was caused by his own conduct." Cf. *Dalling v R J Heale & Co Ltd* [2011] EWCA Civ 365.
[443] [2006] EWCA Civ 331; [2007] Q.B. 46.
[444] [2006] EWCA Civ 331; [2007] Q.B. 46 at [67] and [68].
[445] [2006] EWCA Civ 331; [2007] Q.B. 46 at [77].
[446] *Corr v IBC Vehicles Ltd* [2008] UKHL 13; [2008] 1 A.C. 884; discussed by F. McCarthy [2008] J.P.I.L. C63; A. Ritchie and R. McAllister, "Damages for self-harm after suffering tortious injury (suicide and contributory negligence)" [2009] J.P.I.L. 20.

consequence of the defendants' breach of duty. It was not incumbent on the claimant to demonstrate that suicide itself was foreseeable, on the basis that "a tortfeasor who reasonably foresees the occurrence of some damage need not foresee the precise form which the damage may take",[447] but if it were necessary to prove that the suicide was foreseeable, the employers would still have been responsible:

"...a reasonable employer would ... have recognised the possibility not only of acute depression but also of such depression culminating in a way in which, in a significant minority of cases, it unhappily does."

If the victim of a tort took a voluntary, informed decision as an adult of sound mind, making and giving effect to a personal decision about his own future then that could break the chain of causation or "the victim's independent act forms no part of a chain of causation beginning with the tortfeasor's breach of duty".[448] But on the facts of *Corr v IBC Vehicles* the suicide was:

"...not a voluntary, informed decision taken by him as an adult of sound mind making and giving effect to a personal decision about his future. It was the response of a man suffering from a severely depressive illness which impaired his capacity to make reasoned and informed judgments about his future..."[449]

The more unsound the mind of the victim the less likely it is that his suicide will be seen as a novus actus interveniens.[450]

5–159   **Refusing termination of pregnancy following a failed sterilisation**   In *Emeh v Kensington and Chelsea Area Health Authority*[451] the claimant brought an action in respect of the birth of a handicapped child following a negligently performed sterilisation operation. She was about 20 weeks pregnant when she discovered the pregnancy. The trial judge had taken the view that the claimant's decision not to undergo an abortion was so unreasonable as to eclipse the defendants' wrongdoing, and amounted to a novus actus interveniens, and accordingly she was not entitled to damages for the events after she discovered that she was pregnant, except for the expense and pain and suffering of a further sterilisation operation. The Court of Appeal reversed this finding. Purchas LJ said that it was unacceptable that the court should be invited to consider critically the decision of a mother whether to terminate a pregnancy which has been caused by the defendants' negligence. As Slade LJ put it: "By their own negligence, they faced her with the very dilemma which she had sought to avoid by having herself

---

[447] [2008] UKHL 13; [2008] 1 A.C. 884 at [13], applying *Hughes v Lord Advocate* [1963] A.C. 837.
[448] [2008] UKHL 13; [2008] 1 A.C. 884 at [15].
[449] [2008] UKHL 13; [2008] 1 A.C. 884 at [16].
[450] Lord Scott considered ([2008] UKHL 13; [2008] 1 A.C. 884 at [29]) that causation was established on the basis that the defendant must take his victim as he finds him, including his psychiatric condition brought about as a result of the physical injuries caused by the defendants' breach of duty; whereas Lord Neuberger considered that the employers could have foreseen that there was "a substantial risk" of a suicide attempt as a consequence of severe depression brought on by the deceased's physical injuries ([2008] UKHL 13; [2008] 1 A.C. 884 at [56]).
[451] [1985] Q.B. 1012.

sterilised."[452] The fact that she had exercised this particular option in this way did not show that it was an option which she wished to have. His Lordship doubted whether such a decision could ever constitute a novus actus interveniens:

> "Save in the most exceptional circumstances, I cannot think it right that the court should ever declare it unreasonable for a woman to decline to have an abortion, in a case where there is no evidence that there were any medical or psychiatric grounds for terminating the particular pregnancy."[453]

It might be added that if there are no medical or psychiatric grounds for an abortion within the terms of s.1 of the Abortion Act 1967, the abortion would be unlawful, and it could not possibly be unreasonable for a woman to refuse to undergo an unlawful operation. It is unclear, then, what "exceptional circumstances" Slade LJ had in mind which might justify the conclusion that such a refusal was unreasonable. Purchas LJ appeared to suggest that where the sole motivation for the refusal to terminate the pregnancy was "commercial", in that the claimant continued the pregnancy merely in order to increase the damages that would be awarded in the action for the failed sterilisation, that would be a factor to be considered in deciding whether the chain of causation had been broken. Given the multiplicity of medical, social, emotional, moral and economic factors which women take into account when making such a decision, it is highly unlikely that the financial prospects of promoting a civil action for damages could be shown to have been the sole motivation of any woman who decides to continue her pregnancy. Moreover, even in such extreme circumstances a decision that the claimant has acted unreasonably effectively stipulates that she was under a duty to abort in order to reduce the loss otherwise payable by the negligent doctor. The Abortion Act 1967 gives a woman the right to have an abortion in certain circumstances, if she chooses, but there is no law which imposes a duty to abort, and such a duty would appear to violate a principle of public policy upholding the sanctity of human life.[454] Thus, on principle it is submitted that a mother's decision not to undergo an abortion should never be held to constitute to a novus actus interveniens, irrespective of her motives.

5–160

In *McFarlane v Tayside Health Board*[455] the House of Lords confirmed that the failure to undergo a termination of pregnancy or the failure to give the child up for adoption following birth did not break the chain of causation between a negligently performed sterilisation operation or negligent advice as to the success of the sterilisation procedure and the birth.[456] On the other hand, where following a failed sterilisation operation, a claimant knew that she was not sterile, and decided nonetheless to proceed to have sexual intercourse without taking

5–161

---

[452] [1985] Q.B. 1012 at 1024.
[453] [1985] Q.B. 1012 at 1024.
[454] *McKay v Essex Area Health Authority* [1982] Q.B. 1166, see para.2–141.
[455] [2000] 2 A.C. 59 at 74, 104 and 113.
[456] Their Lordships limited the potential damages awarded in such actions on other grounds. See paras 2–055 et seq.; 12–134 et seq.

contraceptive measures, this does break the chain of causation between the negligent performance of the surgery and the subsequent birth of a child.[457]

5–162 **Failing to seek medical treatment**   In *Pidgeon v Doncaster Health Authority*[458] the claimant was negligently advised in 1988 that a smear test for cervical cancer was normal, when it showed pre-cancerous abnormalities. A further test in 1997 resulted in a diagnosis of cervical cancer. In the intervening period the claimant had been spoken to on no less than seven occasions about the need to have a smear test, and had received four letters from the defendants' cervical cancer screening programme about the need to have a smear test. The claimant had not undergone the test because she found it painful and embarrassing, although she was aware that she could develop cervical cancer. The judge held that the claimant's failure to undergo a smear test did not break the causal link between the original negligence and the fact that she had developed cancer, because the claimant did not know of her condition, and had been reassured by the reported result of the 1988 test. Thus, there was:

> "...an important difference between a claimant indulging in behaviour against a background of known vulnerability, whether it be weakness of the leg or ability to conceive, and a claimant failing to take steps which may well reveal a condition, if in fact present, having previously been reassured that it was not present."[459]

However, the claimant's conduct constituted contributory negligence, assessed at two thirds.

5–163 **Refusing to accept medical treatment**   Another situation which could result in a finding that the claimant acted so unreasonably as to break the chain of causation is where the patient refuses further medical treatment which would alleviate his condition or prevent it from deteriorating. It is clear that a claimant has an obligation to mitigate the damage, which may include seeking suitable medical treatment except where there is a substantial risk of further injury or the outcome is uncertain.[460] Mitigation is a principle applied to the assessment of damages, but this stage will not be reached if the refusal of recommended treatment is categorised as an intervening act. In *R. v Blaue*[461] the Court of Appeal held that a patient's refusal to undergo a blood transfusion on religious grounds did not break the chain of causation between a criminal assault and the

---

[457] *Sabri-Tabrizi v Lothian Health Board*, 1998 S.C. 373. See also *Richardson v LRC Products Ltd* [2000] P.I.Q.R. P164, 173; [2000] Lloyd's Rep. Med. 280 at 286 where Ian Kennedy J suggested that a claimant's failure to seek advice about the "morning after pill" to avoid conception following the discovery that a condom had "failed" during sexual intercourse could amount to a failure to mitigate the damage or an intervening cause (the judgment is unclear on this point).

[458] [2002] Lloyd's Rep. Med. 130, County Court.

[459] [2002] Lloyd's Rep. Med. 130 at [23], distinguishing both *McKew v Holland and Hannen and Cubitts (Scotland) Ltd* [1969] 3 All E.R. 1621 and *Sabri-Tabrizi v Lothian Health Board* 1998 S.C. 373; (1998) 43 B.M.L.R. 190 on the basis that in those cases the claimants knew about their particular condition (weakness in the leg and not being sterile, respectively).

[460] See para.12–048.

[461] [1975] 1 W.L.R. 1411.

patient's death, resulting in a charge of manslaughter.[462] It is clear, however, that this decision was based on policy considerations appropriate to the criminal law. Lawton LJ suggested that where the victim brought a civil claim the concept of foreseeability could operate in the wrongdoer's favour, presumably by breaking the chain of causation; and, moreover, the wrongdoer was entitled to expect his victim to mitigate the damage by accepting treatment of a normal kind. It may be argued, however, that a refusal of medical treatment on religious grounds constitutes a failure to provide an actus interveniens that would have avoided the claimant's loss, which is not the same as committing a novus actus interveniens that caused the loss, an argument that has been accepted where a third party fails to intervene.[463] Moreover, the decision to refuse treatment would not necessarily be categorised as "unreasonable", even under the civil law. In *R. v Blaue* Lawton LJ responded to the suggestion that a Jehovah's Witness's decision not to have a blood transfusion was unreasonable:

> "At once the question arises—reasonable by whose standards? Those of Jehovah's Witnesses? Humanists? Roman Catholics? Protestants of Anglo-Saxon descent? The man on the Clapham omnibus?"[464]

In *Maher v Pennine Acute Hospitals NHS Trust*,[465] a decision in the Blackpool   **5–164** County Court, it was held that a decision by a Jehovah's Witness patient to refuse a blood transfusion that would probably have saved her life was not unreasonable and did not break the chain of causation between the defendants' negligence in failing to appreciate that the patient's condition was deteriorating and her death from blood loss. Judge Hinchcliffe QC held that a decision to refuse a blood transfusion would have been unreasonable if it was not based on the patient's religious beliefs, but since the defendants were aware of her religious beliefs, her refusal of blood was not unreasonable.

Of course, *Maher* is not binding authority, and it remains to be seen how the   **5–165** higher English courts would respond to such a case. A decision based on religious beliefs may well be regarded as reasonable because it is considered to be reasonable to conduct one's life according to a religious faith, even if those specific beliefs are not widely accepted within society. This view could be

---

[462] "It does not lie in the mouth of the assailant to say that his victim's religious beliefs which inhibited him from accepting certain kinds of treatment were unreasonable. The question for decision is what caused her death. The answer is the stab wound. The fact that the victim refused to stop this end coming about did not break the causal connection between the act and the death": [1975] 1 W.L.R. 1411 at 1415, per Lawton LJ. See also *R. v Malcherek* [1981] 1 W.L.R. 690; *R. v Cheshire* (1991) 93 Cr. App. R. 251; *R. v Dear* [1996] Crim. L.R. 595.

[463] See above paras 5–150 to 5–151. The distinction between the duty to mitigate and claimants' intervening acts may be the difference between claimants' unreasonable inaction (their failure to minimise loss) and their unreasonable action (their augmenting of the loss), respectively, although the principles are based on the same policy grounds and are sometimes used interchangeably: see Burrows, *Remedies for Torts and Breach of Contract*, 3rd edn (Oxford: Oxford University Press, 2004), p.75.

[464] [1975] 1 W.L.R. 1411, 1415. See also *Malette v Shulman* (1987) 47 D.L.R. (4th) 18; aff'd (1990) 67 D.L.R. (4th) 321, Ont CA, para.6–178, where a doctor who administered a blood transfusion contrary to the patient's instructions was held liable in battery.

[465] Unreported 23 June 2011. See para.6–182. The case is commented on by J. McQuater at [2012] J.P.I.L. C25.

applied both to the question of whether claimants' conduct amounts to a *novus actus interveniens* and to whether they have complied with their obligation to mitigate the damage, which requires claimants only to take reasonable steps in mitigation. It might also be argued that a claimant's refusal of treatment on religious grounds is foreseeable and so did not break the chain of causation, particularly in an action for medical negligence where it could be expected that the doctor would have discussed with the patient in advance what medical treatment would be acceptable. Ultimately, this issue turns upon the courts' assessment of who should bear the burden of the claimant's religious beliefs.

(iii)   Intervening act by the defendant

5–166   A second act of negligence by the defendant cannot break the causal link between an initial act of by the defendant negligence and the claimant's damage. This proposition, which ought to be self-evident, will rarely be of significance in the context of claims for personal injury, since even if the second act did break the causal link the defendant would normally be liable for the loss attributable to the second act of negligence. The argument that the defendant's second act of negligence broke the chain of causation would only be useful to a defendant where there was no liability for the second instance of negligence. But, in any event, the Court of Appeal rejected the proposition in *Normans Bay Ltd v Coudert Brothers*.[466] There were two discrete allegations of negligence against a firm of solicitors. They argued that the second act of negligence broke the causal link between the first act of negligence and the claimants' loss, whilst also contending that the claimants could not rely on the second act of negligence because that was statute barred. The argument, unattractive on its face, seemed to ignore the observation of Lord Browne-Wilkinson in *Bolitho v City and Hackney Health Authority*[467] that a defendant:

> "...cannot escape liability by saying that the damage would have occurred in any event because he would have committed some other breach of duty thereafter."

The Court of Appeal rejected the defendant's argument, on the grounds of public policy. Waller LJ said:

> "Is there a principle which disallows a defendant from relying on a wrong which he has committed in order to reduce the damages that would otherwise flow from a tort or breach of contract? It seems to me that there should be such a principle, and that is what Lord Browne-Wilkinson was recognising. It is quite difficult to say why it should be so, other than that it flows from public policy where it is a principle that a person should not be entitled to rely on their own wrong in order to secure a benefit. It is furthermore not unfair to apply such a principle. Damages would flow from the original act of negligence; why should [the defendants] be allowed to rely on a further act of negligence to reduce that damage?"[468]

Laws LJ agreed that a defendant should not be allowed to rely on his own wrong in order (in whole or part) to break the chain of causation, and that this could be

---

[466] [2003] EWCA Civ 215; *The Times*, 24 March 2004.
[467] [1998] A.C. 232 at 240.
[468] [2003] EWCA Civ 215 at [46].

seen as an application of the general rule of the common law that a party may not rely on his own wrong to secure a benefit. But, in his Lordship's view, the result was also:

"...consonant with modern ideas of causation now being developed in the cases. Authority supports the proposition that the resolution of causation issues, certainly in the law of tort, is by no means merely a fact-finding exercise; in many instances it is an evaluative judgment, concerned to establish the extent to which a defendant should justly be held responsible for what has befallen the claimant. This seems to me to be vouchsafed in particular by the opinions of Lord Bingham and Lord Hoffmann in *Fairchild* [2002] 3 WLR 89 at [10]–[12] and [52]–[54] respectively ..."[469]

3.   REMOTENESS OF DAMAGE

Foreseeability of damage   Rules on remoteness of damage, at least in the tort of negligence, deal with harm which occurs in some freakish or unpredictable fashion. In a system of fault liability, which depends upon foreseeability of the damage as a test of defendants' breach of duty, it may seem unfair to hold defendants responsible for all the damage that their negligence has caused, even where the damage is of a different type or occurred in a different manner from that which would normally be expected. There are two broad approaches to the problem of remoteness. The first takes the view that defendants are liable for all the direct consequences of their negligence, no matter how unusual or unexpected. This treats remoteness as essentially a question of causation. At one time this was thought to be the appropriate rule in the tort of negligence,[470] and it remains the test in actions for trespass to the person.[471] The second approach holds that people are only responsible for consequences that could reasonably have been anticipated, even where they have undoubtedly caused the damage in question. In theory, the test of remoteness in the tort of negligence is now foreseeability of the harm; if the damage was unforeseeable it is too remote.[472] This statement is deceptive, however, because in practice the issue is not that simple. The court must determine precisely what it is that has to be foreseen, and decisions about what falls within the realms of the foreseeable and what may legitimately be ignored in the sequence of events have a vital bearing upon the

5–167

---

[469] [2003] EWCA Civ 215 at [64].

[470] *Re Polemis and Furness, Withy & Co. Ltd* [1921] 3 K.B. 560.

[471] The defendant is liable for all the consequences which are a direct result of the tortious act whether they are foreseeable or not: "In battery, however, any and all damage is recoverable, if it results from the wrongful act, whether it is foreseeable or not. The limitation devices of foresight and remoteness are not applicable to intentional torts, as they are in negligence law", per Linden J in *Allan v New Mount Sinai Hospital* (1980) 109 D.L.R. (3d) 634 at 643.

[472] *Overseas Tankship (UK) Ltd v Morts Dock & Engineering Co., The Wagon Mound* [1961] A.C. 388, PC. It is a matter of some uncertainty whether, and if so how, the test for remoteness of damage differs in the tort of negligence from that applied to actions in contract. It may be that the tests are in effect the same, at least for physical damage, following the decision of the Court of Appeal in *Parsons (Livestock) Ltd v Uttley Ingham & Co. Ltd* [1978] Q.B. 791; see the excellent discussion in Burrows, *Remedies for Torts and Breach of Contract*, 3rd edn (Oxford: Oxford University Press, 2004), pp.83–96. If there is a difference, the test in negligence is more generous to claimants than that in contract (see *The Heron II* [1969] 1 A.C. 350), but this is probably of little or no practical significance in actions for medical negligence since the claimant with a contractual claim will also have a right of action in tort: see para.2–003.

application of the rules on remoteness. Moreover, the courts have not abandoned the general principle that a tortfeasor must "take his victim as he finds him", which in practice means ignoring certain unforeseeable idiosyncrasies in the claimant which may have contributed to the damage. The result is that the limits of actionability set by the rules on remoteness of damage lie somewhere between the two approaches embodied in directness and foreseeability.

5–168 Once it is established that the damage sustained by the claimant was foreseeable, the likelihood that it would occur is irrelevant. In *The Heron II*[473] Lord Upjohn said that:

> "...the tortfeasor is liable for any damage which he can reasonably foresee may happen as a result of the breach however unlikely it may be, unless it can be brushed aside as far-fetched."

The likelihood of the occurrence or the degree of foreseeability relates to the question of whether the defendant acted carelessly in the face of the risk.[474] To some extent this makes the test of remoteness of damage as close to a test based on causation as to one based on foreseeability, because many things which could be regarded as unlikely are foreseeable and yet are not necessarily far-fetched.[475] It is not sufficient, therefore, to say that the test of remoteness of damage is foreseeability. The court has scope to determine the outcome of a case through the definition of what, precisely, must be foreseen. The narrower the range of events or damage that must be anticipated the more difficult it will be for the claimant to overcome the remoteness hurdle. Following *The Wagon Mound* the courts soon came to the view that provided that the type or kind of damage could have been foreseen, it did not matter that its extent or the precise manner of its occurrence could not have been foreseen, and the eggshell skull rule,[476] which was retained after *The Wagon Mound*, is quite explicitly not based on foreseeability.

(a) Manner of the occurrence

5–169 **Precise sequence of events does not have to be foreseen**   The fact that the damage occurred in an unforeseeable way does not necessarily mean that it was not foreseeable. The precise concatenation of events need not be anticipated if the damage is within the general range of what is reasonably foreseeable.[477] In

---

[473] [1969] 1 A.C. 350 at 422.

[474] Although degrees of foreseeability are used in considering whether the chain of causation has been broken by an intervening act: see para.5–144.

[475] In *Emeh v Kensington and Chelsea Area Health Authority* [1985] Q.B. 1012 at 1019 Waller LJ concluded that a risk of between 1 in 200 and 1 in 400 of a pregnant woman giving birth to a child with congenital abnormalities was "clearly one that is foreseeable, as the law of negligence understands it. There are many cases where even more remote risks have been taken to be 'foreseeable'." On variable degrees of foresight applied to both the duty of care in negligence and remoteness see Kidner (1989) 9 L.S. 1.

[476] See para.5–181.

[477] *Stewart v West African Terminals Ltd* [1964] 2 Lloyd's Rep. 371 at 375; *Wieland v Cyril Lord Carpets Ltd* [1969] 3 All E.R. 1006 at 1009; *Sullivan v South Glamorgan County Council* (1985) 84 L.G.R. 415.

Hughes v Lord Advocate[478] some workmen negligently left a manhole open in the street, surrounded by paraffin lamps. Two young boys approached the manhole, out of curiosity, and one of the lamps was knocked into the hole. There was a violent explosion in which one of the boys suffered severe burns. Expert evidence indicated that in these circumstances an explosion was unforeseeable, although burns from a conflagration if the lamp was knocked over could have been anticipated. The House of Lords held that the damage was not too remote. Lord Pearce considered that the accident was simply a "variant of the foreseeable", while Lord Reid took the view that having been caused by a known source of danger, it was no defence that it was caused in an unforeseeable way. Lord Guest concluded that the precise details leading up to the accident do not have to be foreseen; it was sufficient if the accident was "of a type which should have been foreseeable by a reasonably careful person".[479]

To a large extent this issue turns upon how the court frames the question of what has to be foreseen. In *Hughes v Lord Advocate* the question was: "was injury by burning foreseeable?" to which the answer was "yes". If the question had been: "was injury by explosion foreseeable?" the answer would have been "no" and the damage would have been considered to be too remote. This is illustrated by the decision of the Court of Appeal in *Doughty v Turner Manufacturing Co. Ltd*[480] in which an asbestos cover was knocked into a bath of molten liquid. Shortly after, due to a chemical reaction between the asbestos and the liquid which was unforeseeable at the time, there was an eruption of the liquid which burned the claimant who was standing nearby. It was held that burning by an unforeseeable chemical eruption was not a variant of burning by splashing, which was within the foreseeable risk created by knocking the cover into the liquid, distinguishing *Hughes v Lord Advocate*. If the question had been: "was injury by burning foreseeable?" as a consequence of knocking the cover into the liquid then the answer must have been "yes", and the court could have taken the view that the precise manner in which the injury occurred was irrelevant.[481]

5–170

Mechanism of the damage does not have to be foreseen It is not necessary that the precise events be foreseeable provided that they fall within the scope of the risk created by the defendant's breach of duty. In *Wiszniewski v Central*

5–171

---

[478] [1963] A.C. 837.
[479] See also *Spencer v Wincanton Holdings Ltd* [2009] EWCA Civ 1404; [2010] P.I.Q.R. P8—if a relatively minor injury for which the defendant is responsible leads, through medical complications, to an above the knee amputation the defendant can be held responsible for the further consequences of the amputation, such as a fall, even if the claimant has been careless himself. The Court of Appeal rejected the defendants' argument that this was damage of a kind that was not reasonably foreseeable. The consequences that had to be foreseen were not to be narrowly defined. The "kind of consequence" in question was personal injury and the damage resulting from it. If personal injury and its consequences, i.e. amputation, were foreseeable at the time of the initial accident, it followed that personal injury resulting from that amputation was also a consequence that was reasonably foreseeable at the time of the initial accident.
[480] [1964] 1 Q.B. 518.
[481] See also *Tremain v Pike* [1969] 3 All E.R. 1303 and *Crossley v Rawlinson* [1981] 3 All E.R. 674 for examples of how narrowing the scope of the question produces the result that the harm was unforeseeable.

Manchester Health Authority[482] the defendants were held liable in respect of hypoxia suffered by the claimant infant during the course of his birth when the defendants' negligence created a risk of oxygen starvation in the womb, though the actual mechanism by which the claimant sustained the hypoxia was by strangulation because the umbilical cord was looped round his neck and had a knot in it which gradually tightened. The evidence was that a "true knot" in the umbilical cord is very rare, and could not have been foreseen, although a cord being looped around the neck is much more common. The Court of Appeal held that as the damage was of a foreseeable kind, it was irrelevant that the precise mechanism by which the hypoxia occurred was unforeseeable.[483] Similarly, in *Loraine v Wirral University Teaching Hospital NHS Foundation Trust*[484] the defendants' breach of duty created a risk of foetal asphyxia due to a cord prolapse which was both foreseeable and foreseen. However, the claimant suffered asphyxia due to a placental abruption which was an uncommon complication, and not foreseeable in the circumstances. Plender J rejected the defendants' argument that the mechanism of the claimant's asphyxia was unforeseen and therefore the damage was too remote. The damage suffered by the claimant was not different in kind from what was foreseeable:

> "The damage foreseeable in the event of a cord prolapse is precisely the same in kind as the damage suffered by reason of the placental abruption. That damage is cerebral palsy in consequence of foetal asphyxia."[485]

(b) Type of harm

5–172   The damage will be too remote if it is not of the same type or kind as the harm that could have been foreseen. The problem is in defining the "type" of damage that must be foreseen. It would be possible to take a broad view of the classification of harm, dividing it into personal injury, damage to property and financial loss. Thus, if any personal injury were foreseeable the defendant would be liable for any type of personal injuries that occurred. The courts have not done this, although the eggshell skull rule as applied to personal injuries comes close to

---

[482] [1998] Lloyd's Rep. Med. 223, CA.
[483] " . . . it would in my judgment be regarded as an affront to common sense, and the law would look an ass, if we reached any different conclusion", per Brooke LJ [1998] Lloyd's Rep. Med. 223 at 245. See also *Hutchinson v Leeds Health Authority* unreported 6 November 2000 where, relying on *Wiszniewski*, Bennett J held, at [82], that it would also be an affront to common sense if, having established that the defendants were in breach of duty in failing to call in the surgical team to investigate a highly abnormal bowel function in a patient who was very ill, the claimant's action failed because it was not foreseeable that bowel perforation might occur in the posterior rectal wall rather than in some other part of the bowel. In *ST v Maidstone and Tunbridge Wells NHS Trust* [2015] EWHC 51 (QB); [2015] Med. L.R. 70 at [194], Swift J concluded that a foreseeable small risk of cardiac problems leading to brain injury was damage of the same kind as unforeseeable strokes, albeit that the route by which the claimant suffered the damage would not have been the same as the route that was foreseeable.
[484] [2008] EWHC 1565 (QB); [2008] LS Law Med. 573.
[485] [2008] EWHC 1565 (QB); [2008] LS Law Med. 573 at [64]. The defendant was held liable for the asphyxia, applying *Hughes v Lord Advocate* and *Wiszniewski v Central Manchester Health Authority*.

this result.[486] In practice a compromise position seems to have been adopted in which the courts insist that the damage must be of a foreseeable type or kind, whilst giving this term a comparatively wide meaning. In *Draper v Hodder*,[487] for example, Edmund-Davies LJ said that:

> "... the proper test in negligence is not whether the particular type of physical harm actually suffered ought reasonably to have been anticipated, but whether broadly speaking it was within the range of likely consequence."

This is illustrated in *Bradford v Robinson Rentals Ltd*[488] in which the claimant sustained frostbite, having been sent on a journey by his employers in a vehicle without a heater at a time of severe winter weather. Rees J held that frostbite was damage of the same kind as that which was a foreseeable consequence of exposure to extreme cold. On the other hand, in *Tremain v Pike*[489] a farm employee contracted a rare disease transmitted by contact with rats' urine, following an infestation of rats on the farm. Payne J considered that the disease was damage of a different type from the foreseeable damage which could have occurred from rat bites or contamination of food. This decision, it is submitted, takes an unduly myopic view of what may be foreseeable. If the question had been whether illness from some rat-transmitted disease was a foreseeable consequence of an infestation of rats, the answer must surely have been that it was. Very few people would be capable of identifying in advance the specific disease that would be caused.

5–173

In *Sheridan v Boots Co. Ltd*[490] the claimant contracted Stevens-Johnson syndrome, causing blindness, as a side effect of an anti-inflammatory drug, Butazolidin, which was known to have a number of side effects ranging from gastro-intestinal disturbance, gastric ulcers and, in rare cases, blood dyscrazia which could take the form of aplastic anaemia, a very dangerous condition. Stevens-Johnson syndrome was known to be a possible side effect, but this was not widely known. The manufacturer's literature published in the United States mentioned this possibility, but made no mention of it in the literature published in this country. Kenneth Jones J held that the claimant's injury was too remote, because Stevens-Johnson syndrome was not damage of the same type as gastric disturbance. Stevens-Johnson syndrome involved ulceration over a widespread

5–174

---

[486] See paras 5–186 to 5–187. In *Page v Smith* [1996] A.C. 155 the House of Lords held that if physical injury to the claimant was foreseeable the defendant was liable for any psychiatric damage which the claimant sustained as a result of the defendant's negligence, even though physical injury did not in the event occur and the psychiatric damage was itself unforeseeable. This effectively treats psychiatric injury as damage of the same "type" as physical injury. If there is to be no distinction between *physical* injury and *psychiatric* injury, there is little obvious justification for distinguishing between different types of physical injury, at least in the case of personal injuries. In *R. v Croydon Health Authority* [1998] P.I.Q.R. Q26 at 32–33 Kennedy LJ rejected the suggestion that *Page v Smith* had removed the distinction between physical injury and psychiatric injury in this way, though his Lordship did not analyse the speeches in *Page v Smith* and did not give any reasons for his view.
[487] [1972] 2 Q.B. 556 at 573.
[488] [1967] 1 All E.R. 267.
[489] [1969] 3 All E.R. 1303.
[490] Unreported 19 December 1980, QBD.

area of the body, which could affect the eyes. Gastric disturbance, on the other hand, involved localised ulceration in the stomach and does not affect the eyes:

> "It would seem contrary to commonsense to say that a condition involving blindness is of the same kind as one causing gastric ulcer. When examined fully, the two conditions in their symptoms are wholly dissimilar."

5–175   Nor could it be said, his Lordship continued, that they arose through the same mechanism. This case can be contrasted with the decision of the Ontario Court of Appeal in *Graham v Persyko*[491] in which a gastroenterologist was held to have been negligent in prescribing the drug prednisone for the patient's condition. The drug caused avascular necrosis of the femoral heads, which was a rare but known complication. Holland J said that:

> "The complication of necrosis of femoral heads with a short dose of prednisone is known but unusual. There are a number of serious, known and more common side-effects. It may be that the particular side-effect that Mr. Graham suffered was not reasonably foreseeable but damage to Mr. Graham's health was foreseeable and liability results."[492]

5–176   Clearly, treating the type of damage that must be foreseen as "damage to health" takes a very broad view of what must be foreseen, and would be difficult to reconcile with *Sheridan v Boots Co. Ltd*. Given the wide range of adverse effects which were foreseeable in *Graham v Persyko* it would probably not have been difficult to categorise avascular necrosis as simply a variant of one of the foreseeable types of injury. Moreover, necrosis was a known complication "but unusual". It is arguable that this finding made the necrosis foreseeable, since it is well established that for the purpose of remoteness the type of damage need only be foreseeable as a possible risk, it does not have to be likely or reasonably foreseeable.[493] Thus, in *Smith v Brighton and Lewes Hospital Management Committee*[494] a patient who was negligently given 34 instead of 30 injections of streptomycin lost her sense of balance as a result. It was held that the defendant should have appreciated that some injury could be caused by giving an overdose, and she did not have to foresee the quality or extent of the damage. In *Hepworth v Kerr*[495] McKinnon J held that anterior spinal artery syndrome (spinal stroke) was within the range of foreseeable consequences from an experimental hypotensive anaesthetic technique, when the known complications from this procedure included cerebral or cardiac thrombosis. The technique created a

---

[491] (1986) 27 D.L.R. (4th) 699, Ont CA; (1986) 34 D.L.R. (4th) 160, SCC leave to appeal refused; see para.4–139.
[492] (1986) 27 D.L.R. (4th) 699 at 708, citing *Hughes v Lord Advocate* [1963] A.C. 837. The known complications of the drug included: altering the patient's mental state, making some patients suicidal; effects on the cardiovascular system, and retention of salt and water; hypertension; cataracts and glaucoma; peptic ulcer; skin complaints; osteoporosis; reduction of the body's response to infection; diabetes; and, uncommonly, aseptic necrosis of hip joints and other joints.
[493] See para.5–168.
[494] *The Times*, 2 May 1958. In *Reeves v Carthy* [1984] I.R. 348 (Supreme Court of Ireland) it was held that since it was foreseeable that, left untreated, peritonitis leads to circulatory weakness and hypotension, it was also foreseeable that as a consequence of prolonged hypotension the claimant could suffer a stroke. Alternatively, even if the stroke was unforeseeable, it was damage of the same type as the foreseeable harm (circulatory damage and shock) notwithstanding its unforeseeable extent.
[495] [1995] 6 Med. L.R. 139 at 170–171.

foreseeable risk of damage by under-perfusion of major organs of the body, and the injury that occurred was but "a variant of the foreseeable".[496] It was not necessary for the claimant to prove that the defendant must have foreseen that the very mechanism for which the defendant was responsible and which the defendant would have expected to cause a cerebral thrombosis, would be likely to cause a thrombosis in another part of the body closely associated with the brain (the spine).

Similarly, in *Dowson v Sunderland Hospitals NHS Trust*[497] Recorder Burrell QC held that the risk of neonatal stroke through lack of oxygenation, though a rare complication, was nonetheless within the scope of the defendants' duty of care:

    5–177

> "In my judgment, the object of labour management is to take reasonable steps to deliver a properly oxygenated and healthy baby. If the foetus suffers damage in an unexpected way, that can still nevertheless constitute a risk which is within the scope of the duty of care. In this case there is a duty to take reasonable steps to prevent under perfusion to the foetal brain by ensuring, as far as is reasonably possible, a properly oxygenated foetus. If, through lack of cerebral oxygenation, something happens so as to cause or trigger an infarct, then that must be a risk which is within the scope of the duty of care. It is accepted law that if a breach of duty leads to an injury which is of the same type as that which ought to have been foreseen, the defendant does not escape liability because the actual injury occurred in an unforeseen way."[498]

The claim failed, however, because the medical evidence (including extensive medical literature) could not be said to prove that the events relied on during labour which were attributable to the defendants' negligence were in fact known to cause a stroke. Evidence which merely gives rise to a theory or hypothesis on the causal link between hypoxia and stroke does not discharge the burden of proof. It was a legitimate medical and legal conclusion to state that the cause of the claimant's stroke was simply unknown.

In *Kralj v McGrath*[499] an unusual type of loss was said to have been foreseeable. Due to the defendant's negligence one child of twins was born with severe disabilities, and died eight weeks later. The claimant, the child's mother, said that she had always intended to have a family of three children, and as a result of the death she would have to undergo a further pregnancy, which would involve the discomforts involved in the pregnancy (including the fact that it would now have to be delivered by Caesarean section) and additional financial loss. The defendant argued that this was too remote because it was not reasonably foreseeable by the defendant. Woolf J held that it was foreseeable that the claimant might want to have further children following the death of her child, and it was irrelevant that she had not specifically informed the defendant about this.

    5–178

---

[496] Applying *Hughes v Lord Advocate* [1963] A.C. 837.
[497] [2004] Lloyd's Rep. Med. 177, QBD at [19] to [20].
[498] [2004] Lloyd's Rep. Med. 177 at [19].
[499] [1986] 1 All E.R. 54 at 62.

(c)   Extent of the harm

5–179   If the type of harm and the manner of its occurrence were foreseeable it is irrelevant that the physical extent of the damage was unforeseeable.[500] In *Hughes v Lord Advocate* Lord Reid said that:

> "No doubt it was not to be expected that the injuries would be as serious as those which the appellant in fact sustained. But a defender is liable, although the damage may be a good deal greater in extent than was foreseeable. He can only escape liability if the damage can be regarded as differing in kind from what was foreseeable."[501]

This principle applies to all forms of personal injury, including psychiatric harm,[502] and also to property damage.[503]

5–180   Liability for the unforeseeable physical extent of otherwise foreseeable physical harm should be distinguished from the measure of damages required to compensate the claimant's loss. If the defendant injures someone with a high income, or damages a particularly valuable item of property, he must compensate the claimant to the full extent of his loss, and he cannot complain that the damages would have been less if the claimant had a low income or the property was of little value.[504]

(d)   The "eggshell skull" rule

5–181   Where the claimant suffers from a latent physical or psychological predisposition to a particular injury or illness which has been activated by the damage inflicted by the defendant, then defendants are responsible for the additional, unforeseeable damage that their negligence has produced. This is usually referred to as the "thin skull" or the "eggshell skull" rule. If the claimant has an unusually thin skull the defendant cannot complain if the injury is much more serious than would have been the case with a normal person.[505] Provided that some harm was

---

[500] *Smith v Leech Brain & Co. Ltd* [1962] 2 Q.B. 405 at 414, per Lord Parker CJ, stating that this proposition had not been changed by *The Wagon Mound* [1961] A.C. 388.

[501] [1963] A.C. 837 at 845. *Craig v Soeurs de Charité de la Providence* [1940] 3 W.W.R. 336, Sask CA, where the patient suffered more extensive injuries than otherwise foreseeable from a burn by a hot water bottle because he was diabetic; the defendants were held liable for the full loss.

[502] *Brice v Brown* [1984] 1 All E.R. 997. It is irrelevant that the claimant has a predisposition to psychiatric harm which, unknown to the defendant, increases the likelihood of more extensive harm than the ordinary individual would have experienced, provided that it was foreseeable that a person of ordinary fortitude would have sustained psychiatric harm: see para.2–202. See also *Page v Smith* [1996] A.C. 155, HL.

[503] *Vacwell Engineering Co. Ltd v B.D.H. Chemicals Ltd* [1971] 1 Q.B. 88.

[504] *Smith v London & South Western Railway Co.* (1870) L.R. 6 C.P. 14 at 22–23; *The Arpad* [1934] P. 189 at 202. As Fleming, *The Law of Torts*, 8th edn (Sydney, Australia: Law Book Co., 1992), p.206 put it, this is responsibility, not for unexpected consequences, but for the unexpectable cost of expected consequences.

[505] *Owens v Liverpool Corporation* [1939] 1 K.B. 394 at 401; *Dulieu v White & Sons* [1901] 2 K.B. 669 at 679, per Kennedy J: " ... it is no answer to the [plaintiff's] claim for damages that he would have suffered less injury, or no injury at all, if he had not had an unusually thin skull or an unusually weak heart." Distinguish the so-called "crumbling skull" rule—the defendant is not responsible for the debilitating effects of claimants' pre-existing conditions which they would have experienced in

foreseeable, so that it can be said that the defendant was in breach of duty, the defendant is responsible.[506] The same principle has been applied where the claimant had an unusually weak heart,[507] a weak back,[508] and where he was a haemophiliac.[509] In the context of a claim for psychiatric harm, there is no requirement that the defendant be able to foresee either the precise type of psychiatric harm or its extent, provided that psychiatric harm in a person of reasonable fortitude was foreseeable.[510]

The rule even applies where the claimant had an "eggshell personality",[511] although this can produce some outcomes that look distinctly odd. For example, in *Shorey v PT Ltd*[512] the High Court of Australia held that the claimant was entitled to recover for the consequences of a conversion disorder which resulted in paraplegia, although there was no organic cause of the paraplegia, where the defendant's negligence had resulted in the claimant suffering a fall. The physical effects of the fall were probably resolved within about 12 months, but the fall was held to be the cause of the conversion disorder, because it was the trigger or "sentinel event". Kirby J said that:

5–182

> "The principle of law is that a negligent defendant must take its victim as it finds her and must pay damages accordingly. It is not to the point to complain that the injury, in the form of the fall, was trivial in itself and that it would be unfair to burden the [defendants] with the obligation to bear costs consequent upon the fact that the [claimant] was peculiarly susceptible to developing bizarre symptoms inherent in a conversion disorder. If such symptoms were genuine and a consequence of the subject trauma, the apparent disproportion between cause

---

any event. The defendant is liable for any additional damage, but not the pre-existing damage: *Athey v Leonati* [1997] 1 W.W.R. 97 at 107, SCC. But this does not remove the causal effect of the defendant's negligence: "As long as a defendant is *part* of the cause of an injury, the defendant is liable, even though his act alone was not enough to create the injury. There is no basis for a reduction of liability because of the existence of other preconditions: defendants remain liable for all injuries caused or contributed to by their negligence" ([1997] 1 W.W.R. 97 at 103). If there is a risk that a symptomless pre-existing condition would have affected the claimant in the future (by producing symptoms), irrespective of the defendant's negligence, this is taken into account in the assessment of damages: see *Environment Agency v Ellis* [2008] EWCA Civ 1117; [2009] P.I.Q.R. P5; [2009] L.S. Law Med. 70.

[506] *Bourhill v Young* [1943] A.C. 92 at 109, per Lord Wright. See *Hewett v Alf Brown's Transport Ltd* [1992] I.C.R. 530; [1992] P.I.Q.R. P199 where the claimant's injury by lead poisoning was due to her special susceptibility. The damage was held to be unforeseeable; *Moore v Worthing District Health Authority* [1992] 3 Med. L.R. 431, QBD, where bilateral ulnar nerve lesions during the course of a mastoidectomy were attributable, on the facts, to the claimant's abnormal susceptibility to this type of injury.

[507] *Love v Port of London* [1959] 2 Lloyd's Rep. 541.

[508] *Athey v Leonati* [1997] 1 W.W.R. 97, 110, SCC.

[509] *Bishop v Arts & Letters Club of Toronto* (1978) 83 D.L.R. (3d) 107.

[510] *Frazer v Haukioja* 2010 ONCA 249; (2010) 317 D.L.R. (4th) 688; (2010) 101 O.R. (3d) 528, where the claimant developed an anxiety disorder, depression and agoraphobia as a result of the defendant's failure to inform him about a missed diagnosis of an ankle fracture.

[511] *Malcolm v Broadhurst* [1970] 3 All E.R. 508, where the injury aggravated a pre-existing nervous condition; *Page v Smith* [1996] A.C. 155 where the defendant's negligence caused an accident which produced a recrudescence of the claimant's myalgic encephalomyelitis, although the claimant did not sustain any physical injury; *Fryers v Belfast Health and Social Care Trust* [2009] NICA 57; [2010] N.I. 133 at [15]: "If physical injury to the plaintiff is clearly foreseeable, there is no onus on the plaintiff to prove that the Trust should have foreseen psychiatric illness."

[512] [2003] HCA 27; (2003) 197 A.L.R. 410.

and effect is not an exculpation for the negligent party. It does not render the damage 'unforeseeable' or otherwise outside the scope of the damages that may be recovered."[513]

5–183   Similarly, in *Simmons v British Steel*[514] the claimant suffered a head injury at work which produced some minor physical symptoms for a few weeks. Some weeks after the accident he experienced an exacerbation of a pre-existing skin condition, and developed a personality change resulting in a severe depressive illness. The House of Lords held that a causal connection was established between the claimant's anger at his post-accident treatment by his employers (although there was also anger at the fact that the accident had happened) and his psychiatric reaction. Given that he was a "primary victim" (he had actually sustained physical injury, unlike the claimant in *Page v Smith*[515]) it was not necessary to demonstrate that his psychiatric reaction was foreseeable. The defendants had to take their victim as they found him. It was irrelevant whether a psychologically more robust individual would have recovered from the accident.[516] Lord Hope commented that:

> "...there were several causes of the pursuer's anger. It was enough that one of them arose from the fault of the defenders. The pursuer did not need to prove that that cause would of itself have been enough to cause the anger which produced the exacerbation. He was entitled to succeed if it made a material contribution to it."[517]

The defendant does not, however, have to take the claimant's family as he finds them.[518]

5–184   The eggshell skull rule overlaps with the general principle that the extent of the damage need not be foreseeable. Where the claimant's predisposition exacerbates the otherwise foreseeable type of harm then it provides the mechanism by which that principle comes into effect. It is arguable, however, that the eggshell skull rule goes beyond this by allowing recovery for harm of a different type from that which is foreseeable. In *Smith v Leech Brain & Co. Ltd*[519] an employee was burned on the lip by a piece of molten metal. The burn was treated and healed, but due to a premalignant condition the burn promoted a cancerous growth which ultimately led to his death. Lord Parker CJ held the defendants liable for the death:

---

[513] [2003] HCA 27; (2003) 197 A.L.R. 410 at [44]. See also *Degennaro v Oakville Trafalgar Memorial Hospital*, 2011 ONCA 319; (2011) 81 C.C.L.T. (3d) 165—hospital liable for claimant's fibromyalgia which developed four years after she suffered a fall when a hospital bed she was sitting on collapsed, on the basis that the plaintiff was "thin-skulled".

[514] [2004] UKHL 20; 2004 S.C. (HL) 94; [2004] I.C.R. 585.

[515] See para.5–172, n.486.

[516] [2004] UKHL 20; 2004 S.C. (HL) 94; [2004] I.C.R. 585 at [56] per Lord Rodger.

[517] [2004] UKHL 20; 2004 S.C. (HL) 94; [2004] I.C.R. 585 at [26], applying *Bonnington Castings Ltd v Wardlaw* [1956] A.C. 613 and *McGhee v National Coal Board* [1973] 1 W.L.R. 1.

[518] *McLaren v Bradstreet* (1969) 119 N.L.J. 484—claimants could not recover for "family hysteria" resulting from the mother's neurotic reaction to minor injuries to her children caused by the defendant's negligence; cf. *Nader v Urban Transit Authority of New South Wales* [1985] 2 N.S.W.L.R. 501.

[519] [1962] 2 Q.B. 405.

"The test is not whether these [defendants] could reasonably have foreseen that a burn would cause cancer and that [Mr Smith] would die. The question is whether these [defendants] could reasonably foresee the type of injury he suffered, namely, the burn. What, in the particular case, is the amount of the damage which he suffers as a result of that burn, depends upon the characteristics and constitution of the victim."[520]

Lord Parker's reference to the "amount of the damage" suggests that he regarded cancer and death as simply more extensive harm of the same type as the foreseeable harm, the burn. It is difficult, however, to see how these types of damage can be put into the same category. It is respectfully submitted that only if the harm is classified very broadly as "personal injury" could the death be regarded as merely more extensive damage of the same type as the foreseeable injury.   5–185

The eggshell skull rule predates the move to a test of remoteness based on foreseeability, and the reality is that it is extremely difficult to provide a theoretical reconciliation of the two principles. Nonetheless, it has been confirmed on more than one occasion that the eggshell skull rule was not affected by *The Wagon Mound*.[521] In *Robinson v Post Office*[522] the claimant suffered a minor injury as a result of the defendants' negligence, but he suffered a serious allergic reaction to an anti-tetanus injection given by a doctor, causing brain damage. The Court of Appeal held the defendants responsible for the brain damage: 5–186

"...the principle that a defendant must take the plaintiff as he finds him involves that if a wrongdoer ought reasonably to foresee that as a result of his wrongful act the victim may require medical treatment he is, subject to the principle of *novus actus interveniens*, liable for the consequences of the treatment applied although he could not reasonably foresee those consequences or that they could be serious."[523]

There was no suggestion that the *type* of consequences had to be foreseeable, provided that the need for treatment was foreseeable. It may be that the Court regarded "the consequences of medical treatment" as a specific "type" of damage, but since this would cover almost any form of personal injury (provided it is a potential consequence of medical treatment) it is difficult to see how different types of personal injury can be identified as being either foreseeable or unforeseeable consequences of otherwise foreseeable harm. In other words, *Robinson v Post Office* appears to support a very wide categorisation of the type of damage that must be foreseen, an approach that clearly favours claimants. This may be justified by the observation that the eggshell skull rule contains a strong element of policy, particularly in the realm of personal injuries, for as Professor   5–187

---

[520] [1962] 2 Q.B. 405 at 415.
[521] [1961] A.C. 388. See *Oman v McIntyre* 1962 S.L.T. 168; *Warren v Scruttons Ltd* [1962] 1 Lloyd's Rep. 497; *Winteringham v Rae* (1965) 55 D.L.R. (2d) 108 at 112, Ont HC.
[522] [1974] 1 W.L.R. 1176; [1974] 2 All E.R. 737.
[523] See also *Winteringham v Rae* (1965) 55 D.L.R. (2d) 108, Ont HC, where on similar facts a tortfeasor was held liable for the claimant's rare reaction to anti-tetanus serum. Negligent medical treatment may constitute a novus actus interveniens (see paras 5–140 et seq.), though in *Robinson* the doctor had been negligent but his negligence was not a cause of the harm: see para.5–006; cf. *Price v Milawski* (1977) 82 D.L.R. (3d) 130.

Fleming has commented: "Human bodies are too fragile and life too precarious to permit a defendant nicely to calculate how much injury he might inflict."[524]

5–188 It may be arguable that a medical practitioner should be more able to foresee unusual complications arising from negligent medical treatment than other defendants. How many people would appreciate, for example, that if a doctor negligently removed a patient's ectopic kidney believing it to be an ovarian cyst, that this might turn out to be the patient's only kidney, with the result that she would need an organ transplant?[525] Doctors' liability for the consequences of this error can be justified on several grounds: that, as a doctor, this remote risk was foreseeable to them; that the damage was of the same type as the foreseeable harm, although the extent of the damage was unforeseeable; or, that the claimant came within the eggshell skull rule.

5–189 Where defendants' negligence increases the claimant's susceptibility to further injury, and thus effectively renders the claimant thin-skulled, they may be held responsible when further injury is sustained by the claimant.[526]

5–190 On the other hand, the thin skull rule does not require defendant doctors to be held responsible for unforeseeable harm which is unconnected with their breach of duty. In *Brown v Lewisham and North Southwark Health Authority*[527] the defendants admitted that there had been negligence in discharging the claimant from hospital with a chest infection, following a quadruple coronary artery bypass operation. This did not mean, however, that they were to be held liable to the claimant when he developed deep vein thrombosis, resulting ultimately in the loss of his leg, when even if he had stayed in hospital the diagnosis would not have been made any sooner, and the subsequent ambulance journey did not contribute to his developing deep vein thrombosis. Beldam LJ said:

> "I do not see on what policy ground it would be fair or just to hold a doctor to be in breach of duty who failed to diagnose an asymptomatic and undetectable illness merely because he was at fault in the management of a correctly diagnosed but unrelated condition. In short it must be shown that the injury suffered by the patient is within the risk from which it was the doctor's duty to protect him."[528]

---

[524] Fleming, *The Law of Torts*, 8th edn (Sydney, Australia: Law Book Co., 1992), p.206.

[525] *Urbanski v Patel* (1978) 84 D.L.R. (3d) 650, Man QB, see para.2–131.

[526] *Powell v Guttman* (1978) 89 D.L.R. (3d) 180 at 190, Man CA, para.5–091.

[527] [1999] Lloyd's Rep. Med. 110, CA.

[528] [1999] Lloyd's Rep. Med. 110 at 118. *Brown* was distinguished in *ST v Maidstone and Tunbridge Wells NHS Trust* [2015] EWHC 51 (QB); [2015] Med. L.R. 70 at [194], where Swift J applied *Hughes v Lord Advocate* [1963] A.C. 837 in a case where a delay in administering a blood transfusion to a child had allegedly resulted in him suffering a series of strokes. The defendants argued that a stroke was unforeseeable and therefore too remote on the basis that it did not fall within the scope of the defendants' breach of duty. Swift J found that a competent paediatrician should have foreseen that a failure to transfuse promptly would give rise to a small risk of cardiac problems leading to brain injury so that the: "damage would be the same in kind as that which should have been foreseen, although the route by which he suffered the damage would not have been the same as the route that was to be foreseen at the time of the breaches." However, the claim failed on the basis that the claimant's strokes were caused by a focal cerebral arteriopathy which in turn was caused by an upper respiratory tract infection from which he was suffering, which was not attributable to the defendants' breach of duty.

The Court of Appeal applied *Brown v Lewisham and North Southwark Health* **5–191**
Authority in *Thompson v Bradford*[529] in which a child contracted a vaccine strain
of polio (i.e. he developed polio from the vaccination given to him against polio).
The judge held that the defendant general practitioner had been negligent in
failing to advise the parents about the possibility of postponing the vaccination
because the child had a peri-anal abscess (a boil). The reason for considering
postponing the vaccination in these circumstances was because if he needed
surgery for the boil, it might be very uncomfortable for the child if he were to
suffer a reaction to the vaccination to have the discomfort of surgery at the same
time, or possibly because the vaccination might be rendered ineffective, in the
sense of failing to immunise. It was not foreseeable to a reasonably competent
general practitioner that there was any increase in the risk of contracting a
vaccine strain of polio when the child had a boil or might have surgery to remove
the boil. The Court of Appeal held that even if the general practitioner was in
breach of duty in failing to advise the child's parents to postpone the vaccination,
that was not a relevant breach of duty, given the condition which the child
actually developed. Waller LJ commented that:

> "It was not sufficient to hold, as the judge did, that there was 'fault', and then move straight to
> the questions of factual causation i.e. whether the parents if given the choice would have
> postponed, and whether if there had been a postponement [the claimant] would in fact have
> contracted [a vaccine strain of polio] or would have had a reduced chance of doing so."[530]

Since a reasonably competent general practitioner could not have foreseen that if
there was a failure to postpone the vaccination the result would be that the
claimant contracted a vaccine strain of polio, or even an increased risk of this
occurring, there was no relevant breach of duty.

(e) Claimant's impecuniosity

In *Liesbosch Dredger v S.S. Edison*[531] the House of Lords held that a defendant **5–192**
was not responsible for losses which were attributable solely to the claimant's
impecuniosity. This rule was widely regarded as anomalous, and was distinguished on a number of occasions.[532] The anomaly was compounded by the fact
that claimants' impecuniosity will be taken into account in deciding whether they
have fulfilled their duty to mitigate the loss.[533] In practice the rule was rarely

---

[529] [2005] EWCA Civ 1439; [2006] Lloyd's Rep. Med. 95.
[530] [2005] EWCA Civ 1439; [2006] Lloyd's Rep. Med. 95 at [29].
[531] [1933] A.C. 449.
[532] *Martindale v Duncan* [1973] 1 W.L.R. 574; *Jarvis v T. Richards & Co.* (1980) 124 S.J. 793,
holding that the rule was inapplicable where the impecuniosity was caused by the defendant's tort;
Dodd Properties (Kent) Ltd v Canterbury City Council [1980] 1 All E.R. 928, rule inapplicable where
a decision not to effect early repairs to property, because it would lead to financial stringency, was
based on commercial prudence rather than lack of resources; *Mattocks v Mann* [1993] R.T.R. 13, CA;
Alcoa Minerals of Jamaica Inc v Broderick [2002] 1 A.C. 371, PC. See further Coote [2001] C.L.J.
511.
[533] *Dodd Properties (Kent) Ltd v Canterbury City Council* [1980] 1 All E.R. 928 at 935, 941. It
might, on occasion, have been suggested that the claimant's personal injuries could have been reduced
by early medical treatment, which would have been available if the claimant had sought private

relevant in an action for medical negligence, since it was limited to claims in respect of damage to property or pure economic loss. But in *Lagden v O'Connor*[534] the House of Lords held that the rule in *Liesbosch Dredger v S.S. Edison* should no longer be regarded as good law. For Lord Hope the distinction drawn by Lord Wright in the *Liesbosch* between the measure of damage (or remoteness of damage) and mitigation of damage was "a distinction without a difference".[535] It was not necessary to say that the *Liesbosch* was wrongly decided, but the law had moved on, and:

> "...the correct test of remoteness today is whether the loss was reasonably foreseeable. The wrongdoer must take his victim as he finds him ... This rule applies to the economic state of the victim in the same way as it applies to his physical and mental vulnerability. It requires the wrongdoer to bear the consequences if it was reasonably foreseeable that the injured party would have to borrow money or incur some other kind of expenditure to mitigate his damages."[536]

The effect is that defendants must take claimants as they find them, not only with respect to their physical constitution, but also with respect to their financial position.

---

treatment but the claimant was unable to afford the cost of private treatment. In theory the additional damage attributable to the delay is the product of the claimant's impecuniosity, but in practice it was likely that the court would approach this issue as a question of mitigation of damage. Claimants have a duty to take reasonable steps to mitigate their loss, but the court will take account of their financial position in determining what constitutes "reasonable steps". See further para.12–051.

[534] [2003] UKHL 64; [2004] 1 A.C. 1067.

[535] [2003] UKHL 64; [2004] 1 A.C. 1067 at [51].

[536] [2003] UKHL 64; [2004] 1 A.C. 1067 at [61] per Lord Hope. In *Haxton v Philips Electronics UK Ltd* [2014] EWCA Civ 4; [2014] 1 W.L.R. 2721 the Court of Appeal held that a widow whose life expectancy had been curtailed by the defendant's negligence was entitled to recover the diminution in the value of her claim for loss of dependency under the Fatal Accidents Act 1976 arising out of the death of her husband, applying *Lagden v O'Connor*. This head of loss was not too remote since it was "reasonably foreseeable that a curtailment of life may lead to a diminution in the value of a litigation claim and if a claimant has such a claim, the wrongdoer must take the victim as he finds him" (at [23] per Elias LJ). The defendant was responsible for the injuries to both the widow and her deceased husband (asbestos-Induced mesothelioma), and so, said Elias LJ, it must have been foreseeable to the defendant that the claimant would have dependency rights which would be diminished as a result of their negligence, though in any event the position would have been the same if there had been two different tortfeasors.

CHAPTER 6

CONSENT TO TREATMENT

Consent to medical treatment is widely regarded as the cornerstone of the doctor–patient relationship. As a general rule, patients cannot be required to accept treatment that they do not want no matter how painless, beneficial and risk-free the treatment may be and no matter how dire the consequences of a refusal of treatment. This proposition is recognised as both an ethical principle and a legal rule, and is founded, ultimately, on the principle of respect for the patient's autonomy, or, expressed in more compelling terms, on the patient's "right" to self-determination.[1] Thus, the legal requirement for consent expresses respect for the patient's autonomy. In the famous words of Cardozo J:

6–001

> "Every human being of adult years and sound mind has a right to determine what shall be done
> with his own body; and a surgeon who performs an operation without his patient's consent
> commits an assault…"[2]

Patient autonomy is not the only value, however, that the requirement of consent protects. With patients who are unable to exercise autonomous choices, such as children and adults who do not have the relevant capacity to give a valid consent, it serves as a reminder that there must be some lawful justification for a medical procedure which would otherwise constitute the tort of battery. This affirms the ethical principle of respect for persons by giving legal protection to a patient's bodily integrity, irrespective of their mental capacity. There is also some evidence that obtaining the patient's consent may assist in the therapeutic process, by involving the patient in the treatment as an active participant.[3] Moreover,

---

[1] "Even when his or her own life depends on receiving medical treatment, an adult of sound mind is entitled to refuse it. This reflects the autonomy of each individual and the right of self-determination": *St George's Healthcare NHS Trust v S; R. v Collins and Others Ex p. S* [1999] Fam. 26 at 43, CA. "At issue here is the freedom of the patient as an individual to exercise her right to refuse treatment and accept the consequences of her own decision. Competent adults … are generally at liberty to refuse medical treatment even at the risk of death. The right to determine what shall be done with one's body is a fundamental right in our society. The concepts inherent in this right are the bedrock upon which the principles of self-determination and individual autonomy are based. Free individual choice in matters affecting this right should, in my opinion, be accorded very high priority", per Robins JA in *Malette v Shulman* (1990) 67 D.L.R. (4th) 321 at 336, Ont CA. See also *Fleming v Reid* (1991) 82 D.L.R. (4th) 298 at 309–310, Ont CA.

[2] *Schloendorff v Society of New York Hospital* (1914) 211 N.Y. 125 at 126; *Airedale NHS Trust v Bland* [1993] A.C. 789 at 857, 864, 882, 891.

[3] Teff (1985) 101 L.Q.R. 432; Brazier (1987) 7 L.S. 169, 176.

educating patients about their medical care and its limitations results in fewer injuries caused by patients' failure to follow medical advice and a reduction in malpractice litigation.[4]

6–002 This chapter deals with the requirements for consent as a defence to the action for battery and the basis upon which treatment may lawfully be given to a patient who lacks the capacity to consent. The distinct issue of the doctor's duty of care in negligence to supply the patient with information about any proposed treatment or diagnostic procedure is dealt with in Ch.7. Patients' consent must be a "valid" consent, which means that it must be voluntary, patients must have the mental capacity to understand the nature of the procedure to which they are consenting, and they must also have a certain minimal amount of information about the nature of the procedure. Where the patient lacks the relevant capacity to give a valid consent the doctor needs some form of proxy consent, or a court order, or some other lawful justification, which may be either statutory or under the common law. The chapter deals first with the basic principles and requirements for a valid consent, and then goes on to consider the position of adults who lack the capacity to give a valid consent (whether on a permanent basis or temporarily). There is a brief discussion of situations in which patients who are otherwise competent to refuse medical treatment have been compelled to accept treatment contrary to their wishes, and the chapter concludes with a discussion of children as patients.

1. BATTERY

6–003 The tort of battery has generally been regarded as unsuitable as a method of providing compensation for the victims of medical accidents, partly because of its technical limitations, but principally because it is an intentional tort (which can overlap with the criminal offence of assault), and this is considered to be inappropriate in the context of the doctor–patient relationship. Nonetheless the tort is relevant because of the nature of medical practice which often involves physical contact with the patient's body. The courts have been anxious to restrict its application, particularly in the area of information disclosure, and in the interpretation given to the defence of necessity.

6–004 Battery is a form of trespass to the person, and as such it is actionable per se. Damage is not an essential requirement of the tort, although if claimants seek more than nominal damages they will have to establish that they have suffered loss. A battery consists of the infliction of unlawful force on another person.[5] It is an intentional tort, in the sense that the defendant must intend the act which inflicts the force, but an intention to cause injury is not necessary,[6] and the exercise of reasonable care is not a defence. Any direct[7] contact with the

---

[4] Karp (1993) 9 J. of the MDU 26.

[5] *Collins v Wilcock* [1984] 3 All E.R. 374 at 377, CA.

[6] *Wilson v Pringle* [1987] Q.B. 237 at 249.

[7] Note that the requirement of a "touching" (a direct application of force) makes battery unsuitable as a remedy for certain types of treatment where the patient alleges a lack of consent, e.g. drug injuries, where the patient alleges that his consent was invalid because he was given insufficient information,

claimant, no matter how trivial, is sufficient force,[8] and thus the tort protects people not only from physical injury but also their personal dignity from any form of physical molestation.[9] An exception to this principle applies to unavoidable contacts which are generally accepted as a consequence of social life, such as casual jostling in a busy street or touching someone on the shoulder to engage his attention.[10]

Hostility In *Wilson v Pringle*[11] the Court of Appeal said that a touching must be "hostile" in order to constitute a battery. Hostility was said to be a question of fact, but would not be limited to acts of ill-will or malevolence nor "the obvious intention shown in acts like punching, stabbing or shooting". The Court did not indicate, however, what would be considered hostile, except to say that the police officer who, in *Collins v Wilcock*,[12] touched the claimant without any more hostile an intention than to restrain her temporarily was acting in a hostile manner, and therefore unlawfully, because the officer had no power to restrain her.

6–005

This issue is important in the medical context because it would probably be rare that the contact of doctor and patient in the course of an examination or treatment could be regarded as hostile. If hostility is a requirement of the tort, then battery would be largely irrelevant to a medical practitioner's civil liability. It is respectfully submitted that "hostility" is not, and has never been, an element of the tort of battery. In *Re F (Mental Patient: Sterilisation)* Lord Goff addressed the point, doubting the suggestion that a touching must be hostile for the purpose of battery:

6–006

"A prank that gets out of hand, an over-friendly slap on the back, surgical treatment by a surgeon who mistakenly thinks that the patient has consented to it, all these things may transcend the bounds of lawfulness, without being characterised as hostile. Indeed, the suggested qualification is difficult to reconcile with the principle that any touching of another's body is, in the absence of lawful excuse, capable of amounting to a battery and a trespass."[13]

and the drug was taken orally rather than by injection: see *Malloy v Shanahan* 421 A. 2d 803 (1980). The deliberate infliction of harm by indirect means would probably result in liability under the principle in *Wilkinson v Downton* [1897] 2 Q.B. 57; on which see *Wong v Parkside Health NHS Trust* [2001] EWCA Civ 1721; [2003] 3 All E.R. 932; and particularly Lord Hoffmann in *Wainwright v Home Office* [2003] UKHL 53; [2004] 2 A.C. 406 at [36] to [47]. On the meaning of intention under the principle in *Wilkinson v Downton* see *Rhodes v OPO* [2015] UKSC 32; [2016] A.C. 219. For the requirements as to information disclosure for the purposes of battery see paras 6–058 to 6–072.
[8] "The least touching of another in anger is a battery": *Cole v Turner* (1704) 6 Mod. 149, per Holt C.J.
[9] *Collins v Wilcock* [1984] 3 All E.R. 374 at 378, per Goff LJ: "It has long been established that any touching of another person, however slight, may amount to a battery." Thus, battery may take the form of snatching something from the claimant's grasp: *Green v Goddard* (1702) 2 Salk. 641; throwing water at him: *Pursell v Horn* (1838) 8 A. & E. 602; or applying a tone rinse to his hair: *Nash v Sheen* [1953] C.L.Y. 3726.
[10] *Collins v Wilcock* [1984] 3 All E.R. 374 at 378.
[11] [1987] Q.B. 237.
[12] [1984] 3 All E.R. 374.
[13] [1990] 2 A.C. 1 at 73.

6–007   In the Court of Appeal Lord Donaldson MR had observed that prima facie all, or almost all, medical treatment and all surgical treatment of an adult is unlawful, in the absence of consent, however beneficial that treatment might be.[14] Similarly, in *T v T*[15] Wood J commented that the incision of the surgeon's scalpel need not be and is most unlikely to be hostile, but unless a defence or justification is established it falls within the definition of a trespass to the person. This view is consistent with the law in other common law jurisdictions, and provides the whole basis of the proposition that a patient's consent to medical treatment is an essential requirement in law. In *Allan v New Mount Sinai Hospital*, for example, Linden J said that:

> "Battery is the intentional application of offensive or harmful physical contact to a person. Any surgical operation is a battery, unless the patient consents to it."[16]

The requirement for consent means that the patient has the right to make a choice about whether or not to accept medical treatment, and this right of choice necessarily means that the patient has the right to refuse treatment. The right to decline treatment exists:

> "...even where there are overwhelming medical reasons in favour of the treatment and probably even where if the treatment is not carried out the patient's life will be at risk."[17]

In *Airedale NHS Trust v Bland* Lord Mustill commented that:

> "If the patient is capable of making a decision on whether to permit treatment and decides not to permit it his choice must be obeyed, even if on any objective view it is contrary to his best interests. A doctor has no right to proceed in the face of objection, even if it is plain to all, including the patient, that adverse consequences and even death will or may ensue."[18]

---

[14] "This is incontestable": *Re F. (Mental Patient: Sterilisation)* [1990] 2 A.C. 1 at 12.

[15] [1988] Fam. 52 at 67.

[16] (1980) 109 D.L.R. (3d) 634 at 641, Ont HC; see also Cardozo J in *Schloendorff v Society of New York Hospital* (1914) 211 N.Y. 125 at 126, cited above, para.6–001; *Schweizer v Central Hospital* (1974) 53 D.L.R. (3d) 494 at 507, Ont HC; *Parmley v Parmley and Yule* [1945] 4 D.L.R. 81 at 88, SCC; *Marshall v Curry* [1933] 3 D.L.R. 260 at 274.

[17] *Re F (Mental Patient: Sterilisation)* [1990] 2 A.C. 1 at 29, per Neill LJ Lord Donaldson MR, at 19, said that: "The ability of the ordinary adult patient to exercise a free choice in deciding whether to accept or to refuse medical treatment and to choose between treatments is not to be dismissed as desirable but inessential. It is a crucial factor in relation to all medical treatment." See also *Malette v Shulman* (1990) 67 D.L.R. (4th) 321 at 328, Ont CA; *Brightwater Care Group (Inc) v Rossiter* [2009] WASC 229; (2009) 40 W.A.R. 84; *H Ltd v J* [2010] SASC 176; (2010) 107 S.A.S.R. 352. But this principle does not apply to minors. See paras 6–202 to 6–208 on the question of overriding a competent minor's refusal of medical treatment.

[18] [1993] A.C. 789 at 891. See also Lord Keith at 857; Lord Goff at 864; Lord Browne-Wilkinson at 882. Similarly, in *Re T (Adult: Refusal of Treatment)* [1993] Fam. 95, 102, Lord Donaldson MR said that a competent adult has an absolute right to choose whether to consent to medical treatment or to refuse it: "notwithstanding that the reasons for making the choice are rational, irrational, unknown or even non-existent." See also per Butler-Sloss LJ at 116 and Staughton LJ at 120–121; and *Re MB (Medical Treatment)* [1997] 8 Med. L.R. 217; [1997] 2 F.L.R. 426 at 432.

In *St George's Healthcare NHS Trust v S*[19] the Court of Appeal emphasised the   **6–008**
importance of maintaining this principle in the face of perfectly understandable
efforts to save life:

> "When human life is at stake the pressure to provide an affirmative answer authorising
> unwanted medical intervention is very powerful. Nevertheless the autonomy of each
> individual requires continuing protection even, perhaps particularly, when the motive for
> interfering with it is readily understandable, and indeed to many would appear commendable
> ..."

Thus, a competent pregnant woman is entitled to refuse non-consensual
intervention by way of a Caesarean section delivery of the foetus, even if without
the intervention she is likely to die or suffer serious injury, or the foetus is likely
to die.[20]

2. CONSENT AS A DEFENCE TO BATTERY

The patient's consent to medical treatment, or indeed any procedure which   **6–009**
involves a touching of the patient's body, is essential because it renders lawful
what would otherwise constitute the tort of battery, and, indeed, a serious
invasion of the person's bodily integrity.[21] Although battery is said to be an
intentional tort, there is no need for the defendant to have intended to commit a
tort. If, through some oversight, doctors fail to obtain patients' consent to the
procedure in question they will be liable in battery. So, if they perform the wrong
operation,[22] or operate on the wrong limb,[23] or the wrong patient,[24] they commit
a battery. This is the position even where the doctor acts in all good faith, and is
as much the victim of some administrative error as the patient. In *Schweizer v*

---

[19] [1999] Fam. 26 at 46–47.

[20] *St George's Healthcare NHS Trust v S*; *R. v Collins and Others Ex p. S* [1999] Fam. 26; *Re MB (Medical Treatment)* [1997] 8 Med. L.R. 217; [1997] 2 F.L.R. 426. See paras 6–185 to 6–187.

[21] Note that it is not merely the fact of the patient's consent which legitimates the doctor's act, but the fact that it is given within the context of a doctor–patient relationship: *R. v Brown* [1994] 1 A.C. 212 at 258–259, per Lord Mustill. Consent to battery is not the same as the defence of volenti non fit injuria, which is a voluntary agreement by the claimant to absolve the defendant from the legal consequences of an unreasonable risk of harm created by the defendant, where the claimant has full knowledge of both the nature and extent of the risk. The patient who consents to medical treatment does not consent to run the risk of negligence by the doctor: see *Freeman v Home Office* [1984] Q.B. 524 at 557, per Sir John Donaldson MR.

[22] For example, a circumcision instead of a tonsillectomy: see *Chatterton v Gerson* [1981] Q.B. 432 at 443.

[23] *Shaw v Wright* (1993) 4 *AVMA Medical & Legal Journal* (No.2) p.17, where an operation to remove a cataract was performed on the wrong eye. The action was settled for a modest sum, since coincidentally the operation did produce some improvement in the sight of that eye.

[24] Patient misidentification is a widespread problem in the NHS: P. Thomas and C. Evans "An identity crisis? Aspects of patient misidentification" (2004) 10 *Clinical Risk* 18; Giles, S.J., et al, "Experience of wrong site surgery and surgical marking practices among clinicians in the UK" (2006) 15 Qual. Saf. Health Care 363. The National Patient Safety Agency has issued advice to NHS organisations on standardising patient wristbands for patients in hospital (*Standardising wristbands improves patient safety*, July 2007, and *Standardising wristbands improves patient safety: General Guidance, April 2009*, available at *http://www.nrls.npsa.nhs.uk*). The NPSA reported that between February 2006 and January 2007 it had received 24,382 reports of patients being mismatched with their care, and estimated that more than 2,900 of these related to wristbands and their use.

Central Hospital[25] the claimant consented to an operation on his toe, but due to a mix up a spinal fusion operation was performed. The surgeon was held liable in battery.

6–010	**Honest/reasonable mistake no defence**	In *Ashley v Chief Constable of Sussex*[26] the House of Lords held that a defendant's honest mistake as to a state of affairs that would justify, by the defence of self-defence, what would otherwise constitute the tort of battery is not sufficient unless it is also a reasonable mistake. A majority of their Lordships (Lord Scott, Lord Rodger and Lord Neuberger) left open the question of whether even a reasonably held, but mistaken, belief would be sufficient if the defendant was not actually in immediate danger of being attacked.[27] Even if a "reasonable mistake" is a sufficient basis to constitute the defence of self-defence it is doubtful whether the reasoning in *Ashley* could be applied to the defence of *consent* in the medical context, since the court in *Ashley* was concerned with self-defence where the defendant reasonably believed that a suspect was about to use lethal force and the defendant had to make a "split-second decision" whether to shoot him. Where, for example, a surgeon operates on a patient in the mistaken belief that the patient has consented to the procedure (as where surgery takes place at the "wrong site" or on the "wrong patient") it is difficult to see how such a mistake could be categorised as a "reasonable" mistake, irrespective of the surgeon's honest belief that he has the patient's consent. In this situation, there is no need for the surgeon to make a "split-second decision" and it is the surgeon's responsibility to see that he has the patient's consent to the specific procedure before taking the radical step of cutting the patient open.

6–011	**Exceeding the patient's consent**	Clearly, the patient's consent must relate to the procedure that the doctor performs. Just as a complete lack of consent will give rise to an action for battery, a doctor who exceeds the consent given by the patient will also be liable. In *Mulloy v Hop Sang*[28] a patient asked a doctor to repair his injured hand, but not to amputate it, as he preferred to have it looked at in his home town. When the doctor looked at the hand following administration of an anaesthetic he decided that it ought to be amputated, and proceeded to do so. He was held liable in battery because the amputation was contrary to the express objection of the patient. A patient who consents to the administration of a particular type of anaesthetic does not necessarily consent to the administration of a different type of anaesthetic,[29] although it will be a question of fact whether, looking at the matter in broad terms, the consent which the claimant gave was

---

[25] (1974) 53 D.L.R. (3d) 494.

[26] [2008] UKHL 25; [2008] 1 A.C. 962.

[27] See also per Sedley LJ in *Hepburn v Chief Constable of Thames Valley Police* [2002] EWCA Civ 1841 at [24] commenting that an "honest belief in a non-existent state of affairs does not excuse trespass to the person".

[28] [1935] 1 W.W.R. 714, Alta CA.

[29] *Beausoleil v La Communauté des Soeurs de la Charité de la Providence* (1964) 53 D.L.R. (2d) 65, Qué QB Appeal Side.

sufficient to encompass a procedure about which she was not informed.[30] Similarly, a patient who consents to a sterilisation by laparoscopic surgery does not consent to a sterilisation by laparotomy (which involves opening up the abdominal cavity).[31] This is the case even if she has agreed to be "opened up" in the event of an emergency during surgery, such as internal bleeding or an allergic reaction to the gas used to extend the abdomen when conducting laparoscopic surgery, since sterilisation by laparotomy was not a response to a life-threatening emergency, it was merely an alternative method of performing the sterilisation.[32]

Consent limited to a specific limb or site   A patient who consents to a   6–012
procedure being performed on one limb does not consent to the same procedure on another limb, especially where the patient has specifically objected. In *Allan v New Mount Sinai Hospital*[33] the claimant gave an anaesthetist specific directions that he should not touch her left arm because he would "have nothing but trouble there". In the past she had had some difficulty with attempts to find a vein in her left arm. The defendant replied that he knew what he was doing, and did administer the anaesthetic by needle in the claimant's left arm. During the operation the needle slipped out of the arm causing the anaesthetic to leak into the tissues interstitially, instead of through the vein. The normal consequence of this is that the patient has a sore arm for a few days, but the claimant suffered a severe reaction which was entirely unexpected. In the High Court of Ontario Linden J held that although the defendant was not negligent in the way he administered and monitored the anaesthetic, he was liable in battery. The claimant had expressly refused her consent to having the needle inserted into her left arm:

"Without a consent, either written or oral, no surgery may be performed. This is not a mere formality; it is an important individual right to have control over one's body, even where medical treatment is involved. It is the patient, not the doctor, who decides whether surgery will be performed, where it will be done, when it will be done and by whom it will be done."[34]

---

[30] See *Davis v Barking, Havering and Brentwood Health Authority* [1993] 4 Med. L.R. 85; para.6–072, where the patient consented to the administration of a general anaesthetic, and was held to have also consented to a caudal block (a type of epidural anaesthetic) administered by the anaesthetist during the course of the operation. See also *Abbas v Kenney* [1996] 7 Med. L.R. 47, QBD, where the defendant surgeon performed a total pelvic clearance, but the mass which the surgeon believed to be cancer turned out to be endometriosis. The claimant's allegation that she had consented to a laparotomy and oophorectomy but not a total pelvic clearance was rejected on the facts. In *Laing v Sekundiak* 2015 MBCA 72; [2015] 12 W.W.R. 102 the patient consented to a total hip replacement procedure. The defendant surgeon used a new and unproven hip replacement system that was not licensed for use in Canada. It was held that despite this there was a valid consent to the basic nature and character of the operation.
[31] *Candutti v ACT Health and Community Care* [2003] ACTSC 95, Australian Capital Territory Supreme Court.
[32] [2003] ACTSC 95 at [33]. Harper M. commented, at [35], that: "When the problem arose during surgery, there was no reason why the surgery could not have been terminated, and the difficulty explained to the plaintiff. The plaintiff would then have had a number of alternatives available to her."
[33] (1980) 109 D.L.R. (3d) 634; rev'd on a pleading point (1982) 125 D.L.R. (3d) 276.
[34] (1980) 109 D.L.R. (3d) 634 at 642. In *White v Turner* (1981) 120 D.L.R. (3d) 269 at 282–283, Ont HC, aff'd (1982) 12 D.L.R. (4th) 319, Ont CA, Linden J said that the law of battery remains available where there is no consent to the operation, or where the treatment given goes beyond the consent, or where the consent is obtained by fraud or misrepresentation (citing *Reibl v Hughes* (1980) 114 D.L.R. (3d) 1, SCC).

If the defendant had thought that the claimant's view was inadvisable, it was his duty to discuss the matter with her and try to convince her to change her mind.

6–013   A similar issue arose in *Border v Lewisham and Greenwich NHS Trust (formerly South London Healthcare NHS Trust)*[35] but the case was litigated on the basis of an allegation of negligence rather than trespass to the person. The claimant attended an Accident & Emergency department with a suspected fracture of the right humerus. A senior house officer wanted to put a cannula in her arm for the purpose of obtaining intravenous access if it became necessary later. He could not use the right arm, because that was the site of the suspected fracture. The claimant told him not to use the left arm because she had recently had a left mammectomy and axillary node clearance and a cut in that arm carried the risk that she would get an oedema. It was difficult to find a suitable third site for the cannula, and so the doctor inserted it into the claimant's left arm without the patient's consent.[36] The claimant developed an infection at the cannula site, resulting in an oedema and a permanent disability. The argument at trial proceeded on the basis that the issue of consent was unimportant, and centred on whether the doctor had acted in accordance with accepted medical practice. The judge concluded that he had, and that therefore he was not in breach of duty. The Court of Appeal disagreed on the basis that the finding that the procedure was carried out without the claimant's consent should have led the judge to find a breach of duty, even though that was not the way the claimant's case was advanced at trial:

> "A finding of absence of consent to the insertion of the cannula leads inexorably in this case to a finding of breach of duty in inserting it. … The duty to obtain the patient's consent to treatment is a fundamental tenet of medical practice and is inherent in the case-law concerning the duty to take reasonable steps to warn a patient of the risks of treatment so that the patient can make an informed decision about whether to consent to it."[37]

The case was remitted to the trial judge to determine the issue of causation (namely whether the claimant would have consented if the doctor had given her a fuller explanation of the reasons for the insertion of the cannula and of the relative risks of inserting it and of not inserting it) which had not been addressed at trial. In battery this form of causation would have been irrelevant,[38] but the Court of Appeal refused the claimant's application for permission to amend the claim to add a claim of trespass to the person.[39]

6–014   **Withdrawing consent**   Just as a patient may place limits on a consent, so she may also withdraw a consent even though a medical procedure is under way. In

---

[35] [2015] EWCA Civ 8; [2015] Med. L.R. 48.
[36] The judge rejected the doctor's evidence that the claimant positively consented by holding her arm out in a co-operative manner, and preferred the claimant's evidence that she hardly realised what was happening until "Bang, it was done".
[37] [2015] EWCA Civ 8; [2015] Med. L.R. 48 at [24].
[38] See para.7–082. The only issue would have been: did the insertion of the cannula cause the oedema?
[39] This does not alter the basic proposition that a failure to obtain the patient's consent to an injection constitutes battery. The point had been overlooked at first instance.

Ciarlariello v Schacter[40] a patient became agitated during the course of an angiogram, and asked for the test to be stopped. After 10 or 15 minutes the test was resumed and the patient suffered a severe and rare reaction to the procedure. The Supreme Court of Canada stated that where, during the course of a medical procedure, a patient withdraws consent to that procedure, the doctors must halt the process:

> "An individual's right to determine what medical procedures will be accepted must include the right to stop a procedure. It is not beyond the realm of possibility that the patient is better able to gauge the level of pain or discomfort that can be accepted or that the patient's premonitions of tragedy or mortality may have a basis in reality. In any event, the patient's right to bodily integrity provides the basis for the withdrawal of a consent to a medical procedure even while it is underway. Thus, if it is found that the consent is effectively withdrawn during the course of the proceeding, then it must be terminated. This must be the result except in those circumstances where the medical evidence suggests that to terminate the process would be either life-threatening or pose immediate and serious problems to the health of the patient."[41]

The determination of whether or not consent has been withdrawn is a question of fact. The patient may be under the influence of sedatives or other medication which have affected her competence to withdraw consent,[42] or the words used may be interpreted as a cry of pain rather than a withdrawal of consent.[43] On the facts, the patient had withdrawn her consent but had then renewed her consent to the resumption of the test.[44]

Injections   Where a patient consents to the administration of an injection, the consent relates both to the act of inserting the needle and the contents of the syringe. If what is injected is not the substance to which the patient has given consent it is a battery. Thus, in *Potts v North West Regional Health Authority*[45] the claimant agreed to be vaccinated against rubella, but unknown to the claimant the syringe also contained the contraceptive drug Depo-Provera. The defendants were held liable in battery. Consent to the vaccination injection did not amount to consent to anything that the doctors considered to be appropriate being injected into the patient.

6–015

---

[40] (1993) 100 D.L.R. (4th) 609, SCC.

[41] (1993) 100 D.L.R. (4th) 609 at 619, per Cory J delivering the judgment of the court.

[42] See e.g. *Connolly v Croydon Health Services NHS Trust* [2015] EWHC 1339 (QB), where the judge concluded on the evidence that the claimant had not in fact withdrawn her consent, but that in any event the medication she had been given during the course of an angiogram had rendered her incompetent to withdraw her consent (particularly in light of the medical emergency that arose putting her at risk of serious injury or death).

[43] See, e.g. *Mitchell v McDonald* (1987) 40 C.C.L.T. 266.

[44] See para.7–032 for consideration of the information that the patient must be given before a resumption of the procedure. Where persons have consented to the use of gametes for the creation of an embryo for the purpose of infertility treatment by in vitro fertilisation they have an unconditional right to withdraw consent at any time up until the "use" of the gametes, namely the transfer of the embryos into the woman receiving treatment: *Evans v Amicus Healthcare Ltd* [2004] EWCA Civ 727; [2005] Fam. 1; [2004] 3 All E.R. 1025, applying the Human Fertilisation and Embryology Act 1990 Sch.3 para.4(1). The European Court of Human Rights has held that this does not violate the applicant's human rights under the European Convention: *Evans v United Kingdom* (Application No.6339/05) [2007] 2 F.C.R. 5; (2007) 95 B.M.L.R. 107.

[45] Unreported 1983, see *The Guardian*, 23 July 1983, news report.

6–016   **In vitro fertilisation**   By the same token, the agreement of a husband and wife to the use of their gametes for the purpose of in vitro fertilisation and implantation of the resulting embryo into the wife does not amount to a consent to the use of the gametes of a different man. In *Leeds Teaching Hospitals NHS Trust v A*[46] a fertility clinic mistakenly used the sperm of Mr B to create an embryo for implantation into Mrs A. Butler-Sloss P held that the consent of Mr A to the procedure, which he believed involved the use of his own sperm for the creation of the embryo, was vitiated by the clinic's error. This amounted to a fundamental mistake as to the nature of the procedure to which Mr A had consented (although the consequences of this error related to who was to be regarded in law as the father, under the Human Fertilisation and Embryology Act 1990, rather than whether the implantation of the embryo into Mrs A constituted a battery).

6–017   **Non-consensual sterilisation**   In a number of cases women have been sterilised without their consent in the course of other operative procedures, such as Caesarean sections. This may be because the surgeon has taken the view that it would be better for the woman not to have any more children, or it could be that there has been an administrative mix-up. In *Cull v Royal Surrey County Hospital*,[47] for example, an epileptic patient who was pregnant went into hospital for a termination by curettage, but the surgeon performed the major operation of hysterectomy with a view to sterilising her. The patient had specifically refused consent to the sterilisation, and her general practitioner had written to the hospital to make this clear. The letter was mislaid by the hospital staff, although the hospital admission book indicated for "curettage". The jury awarded damages of £120 against the hospital for negligence, and nominal damages for trespass against the surgeon. In *Devi v West Midlands Regional Health Authority*[48] a surgeon performed a sterilisation operation on the claimant in the course of an operation to repair a perforation of the uterus which had been caused during an earlier dilation and curettage. There had been no prior discussion with the claimant about the possibility of sterilisation, the surgeon had simply taken the view that it was in the patient's interests. The defendants admitted liability for battery.[49] Similarly, in *Murray v McMurchy*,[50] a doctor, during the course of a Caesarean section, discovered fibroid tumours in the patient's uterus which he

---

[46] [2003] EWHC 259 (QB); [2003] Lloyd's Rep. Med. 151; [2003] 1 F.L.R. 1091.
[47] [1932] 1 B.M.J. 1195.
[48] Unreported 9 December 1981, CA.
[49] Ormrod LJ questioned whether battery was the appropriate cause of action rather than a claim "on the basis of failure to give proper advice", and said that the case should not be treated as authority on the question of battery, because it had not been discussed in argument. Whatever the status of the case as an authority, it is respectfully submitted that the sterilisation of a competent adult without consent is undoubtedly a battery, and there is no basis for treating it as simply an instance of negligence.
[50] [1949] 2 D.L.R. 442; *Winn v Alexander* [1940] 3 D.L.R. 778; see also *Hamilton v Birmingham Regional Health Board* [1969] 2 B.M.J. 456 in which the claimant was sterilised without her consent during a Caesarean delivery, which was her third Caesarean. She was never asked whether she wanted to be sterilised. Liability was admitted; *Grayson-Crowe v Ministry of Defence* (1992) 3 *AVMA Medical & Legal Journal* (No.3) p.14, where the claimant believed that she was undergoing minor exploratory surgery, but the surgeon performed a hysterectomy because he discovered fibroids. The defendants admitted liability.

believed would be a danger if the patient were to become pregnant again, and so he performed a sterilisation operation. He was held liable in battery. The sterilisation could not be justified under the principle of necessity because there was no immediate threat to the patient's health and it would not have been unreasonable to postpone the operation. It was merely convenient to perform the operation without consent as the patient was already under general anaesthetic.[51] Sterilisation without a competent patient's consent will almost certainly involve a breach of the patient's human rights.[52]

Consent to treatment by a specific doctor   Prima facie the patient's consent   **6–018**
will be limited to procedures to be performed by a particular doctor. Thus, in *Michael v Molesworth*[53] a patient recovered nominal damages for breach of contract when an operation was performed by a doctor other than the doctor whom the patient had anticipated. Similarly, in *Marcoux v Bouchard*[54] LeBel J commented that:

> "Surgery is also based on the principle that the relationship with a physician or surgeon is a deeply personal one. That fact is expressed in the traditional vocabulary of the law, which says that an agreement for medical care must be made *intuitu personae*, with a specific person in mind. A patient will often wish to see a particular physician or to be handled by a particular, clearly identified surgeon. In the case of surgery, the patient is entitled to know who the main actors in the operation will be. However, that obligation would not extend to the usual secondary players who are present during surgery, including anaesthetists, nurses, and physicians in training, such as residents and interns."

Older NHS consent forms contained a clause stating that "No assurance has been given to me that the operation/treatment will be performed or administered by any particular practitioner", a provision which was specifically intended to cover the circumstances of *Michael v Molesworth*. However, such a clause could not be

---

[51] See also *Wells v Surrey Area Health Authority*, *The Times*, 29 July 1978 (news report) in which a Roman Catholic woman was sterilised in the course of a Caesarean operation. She signed the consent form just before she went into the operating theatre. Croom-Johnson J held that she had understood the nature of the operation and therefore consented to the sterilisation, but she had been inadequately counselled as to the implications of the operation. In particular the patient should have been told that there was no medical need for sterilisation, and that there was no urgency about the matter because it could be done at a later stage. The defendants were liable in negligence.

[52] *VC v Slovakia* (18968/07) (2014) 59 E.H.R.R. 29—sterilisation during the delivery of the patient's second child by Caesarean section constituted a breach of art.3 and art.8 of the European Convention on Human Rights. The patient had signed a consent form in the final stages of labour when she was in pain and had been told that if she had another child either she or the baby would die. The European Court of Human Rights held that the circumstances in which the patient had been asked to consent were not compatible with the principles of respect for human dignity and freedom; she had not been fully informed about her health status, the proposed procedure or any alternatives to it. There had been a gross disregard for her right to autonomy and choice as a patient.

[53] [1950] 2 B.M.J. 171.

[54] 2001 SCC 50; (2001) 204 D.L.R. (4th) 1 at [31]. The plaintiff's allegation that she had not consented to a particular surgeon assisting at an operation was rejected on the facts. In *Currie v Blundell* (1992) 10 C.C.L.T. (2d) 288 (Qué SC) a surgeon performing cardiac surgery decided, after the patient was under general anaesthetic, to let a surgical resident perform the surgery under his supervision. The surgeon was held liable for the major complications that arose when the patient's aorta ruptured. The defendant did not have authority to delegate performance of the surgery without the claimant's consent.

taken as an invitation to the whole world to perform surgery upon the patient. For example, if a patient were to consent to surgery being performed by a person whom the patient mistakenly believed to be a registered medical practitioner, but who was in fact unqualified, the consent would be invalid because the qualifications of the person wielding the scalpel go to the *nature* of the transaction.[55] By extension of this argument, it might be said that a patient's consent is not given simply to "a doctor" (any old doctor?) but a doctor whom the patient believes to be qualified and competent to perform the procedure in question. Newly qualified junior doctors, for example, do not, and are not expected to, perform open heart surgery. A patient's signature on a standard consent form could not be taken as consent to such a step.[56] Perhaps to deal with this point, the more recent NHS model consent form states that:

"I understand that you cannot give me a guarantee that a particular person will perform the procedure. The person will, however, have appropriate experience."[57]

6–019 **Burden of proof** It is unclear whether consent is a true defence to an action for battery, or whether the absence of consent is part and parcel of the tort itself. Must claimants prove that they did not consent in order to establish the cause of action, or is it sufficient to prove the direct interference, leaving defendants to justify the act by asserting and proving that the claimants consented? This issue turns, essentially, upon who has the burden of proof. The traditional view has been that consent operates as a defence, and accordingly it is for the defendant to prove that the claimant consented. In *Freeman v Home Office*,[58] however, McCowan J held that the claimant has the burden of proof, a view which effectively redefines battery to mean an "unconsented to interference with another's bodily integrity". On the other hand, in *Collins v Wilcock* Goff LJ appeared to regard consent as a defence,[59] as did Neill LJ in *Re F (Mental Patient: Sterilisation)*,[60] and in *Ashley v Chief Constable of Sussex*[61] Sir Anthony Clarke MR commented that it is "open to debate whether McCowan J.'s

---

[55] Though see *R. v Richardson* [1999] Q.B. 444 and *R v Tabassum* [2000] Lloyd's Rep. Med. 404, CA, paras 6–065 and 6–066.

[56] Where patients have signed a consent form agreeing that trainee surgeons may participate in their treatment and they are aware that the hospital is a teaching hospital it will be difficult for them to establish that they did not consent to the participation of a trainee surgeon: *Clare v Ostolosky* (2001) 300 A.R. 341, Alta QB; *Anderson v Greene* 2010 ABQB 676; (2010) 79 C.C.L.T. (3d) 290.

[57] See, however, *Jones v Royal Devon and Exeter NHS Foundation Trust* unreported 22 September 2015 (Exeter County Court), where the patient had signed a consent form stating that the hospital could not guarantee who would perform her surgery, but on the day of the surgery she discovered that it would be performed by a junior surgeon, not the experienced consultant that she had anticipated (and had been recommended by her general practitioner). There was no failure to warn the patient about the risks of the surgery and no negligence in the performance of the operation, but the hospital were held to have been in breach of duty in negligence for infringement of her right to make an informed choice as to whether and if so when and *by whom* she would be operated on.

[58] [1984] Q.B. 524.

[59] [1984] 3 All E.R. 374 at 378: "Generally speaking, consent is defence to battery"; see also *R. v Brown* [1994] 1 A.C. 212 at 246–247 per Lord Jauncey; *T v T* [1988] Fam. 52 at 66–67; Croom-Johnson LJ in *Wilson v Pringle* [1987] Q.B. 237 at 252 considered that consent was an example of "so-called 'defences'".

[60] [1990] 2 A.C. 1 at 29: "It is apparent therefore that the defence of consent is not a complete answer …" See also *Clerk & Lindsell on Torts*, 22nd edn (London: Sweet & Maxwell, 2018), para.15–93;

conclusion [in *Freeman v Home Office*] on burden of proof is correct".[62] In Canada[63] consent is undoubtedly regarded as a defence, though in Australia there are competing views on the point.[64]

3. FORMS OF CONSENT

(a) Express or implied

Consent may be either express or implied from the claimant's conduct. If a doctor   **6–020**
tells a patient that he wants to give him an injection and the patient silently bares
his arm and holds it out for the needle he will be taken to have consented.[65] If the
doctor reasonably believes that the patient has consented the patient cannot
complain afterwards that there was no consent. Silence by a patient, however, is

---

Dugdale and Stanton, *Professional Negligence*, 3rd edn (London: Butterworths, 1998), para.11.57 placing the onus of proving that the patient has given a valid consent on the doctor; and Trindade (1982) 2 O.J.L.S. 211, 229 to the same effect.

[61] [2006] EWCA Civ 1085; [2007] 1 W.L.R. 398 at [31].

[62] The Court of Appeal held that, whatever the position may be in the context of consent, the burden of proving self-defence in a civil action for battery is on the defendant, a view apparently upheld by the House of Lords: *Ashley v Chief Constable of Sussex* [2008] UKHL 25; [2008] 1 A.C. 962 at [76] per Lord Carswell. It would be somewhat strange if the burden of proving self-defence lay with the defendant, but not the burden of proving consent.

[63] *Beausoleil v La Communauté des Soeurs de la Charité de la Providence* (1964) 53 D.L.R. (2d) 65 at 69; *Hambly v Shepley* (1967) 63 D.L.R. (2d) 94 at 95, Ont CA; *Kelly v Hazlett* (1976) 75 D.L.R. (3d) 536 at 563, Ont HC; *Schweizer v Central Hospital* (1974) 53 D.L.R. (3d) 494 at 510; *Reibl v Hughes* (1980) 114 D.L.R. (3d) 1 at 9, SCC; *Allan v New Mount Sinai Hospital* (1980) 109 D.L.R. (3d) 634 at 641; *Non-Marine Underwriters, Lloyd's of London v Scalera* 2000 SCC 24; (2000) 185 D.L.R. (4th) 1; [2000] 5 W.W.R. 465, SCC; *Laing v Sekundiak* 2015 MBCA 72; [2015] 12 W.W.R. 102 at [74]. See the discussion by Blay (1987) 61 A.L.J. 25.

[64] In *Secretary, Department of Health and Community Services v JWB* [1992] HCA 15; (1992) 106 A.L.R. 385 at 453, HC of Aus, McHugh J observed that lack of consent is not an essential element of the tort of trespass to the person: "The essential element of the tort is an intentional or reckless, direct act of the defendant which makes or has the effect of causing contact with the body of the claimant. Consent may make the act lawful, but, if there is no evidence on the issue, the tort is made out. The contrary view is inconsistent with a person's right of bodily integrity. Other persons do not have the right to interfere with an individual's body unless he or she proves lack of consent to the interference." See also *Dean v Phung* [2012] NSWCA 223 at [64] per Basten JA. Contrast the detailed analysis of Leeming JA (with whom Barrett JA agreed) in *White v Johnston* [2015] NSWCA 18 at [94]–[130] expressly disagreeing with McHugh J and concluding that the absence of consent is an essential element of the tort of battery: "a patient who sues in assault and battery in all cases bears the legal burden of establishing an absence of consent on his or her part" (at [130]), though Leeming JA accepted that in cases where evidence supportive of fraud by the doctor has been adduced, there will be an evidentiary burden placed on the doctor to refute that evidence. On the issue of fraud vitiating a patient's consent see paras 6–063 et seq.

[65] *Allan v New Mount Sinai Hospital* (1980) 109 D.L.R. (3d) 634 at 641; *Glaholt v Ross* 2011 BCSC 1133; (2011) 86 C.C.L.T. (3d) 295 at [191]—[193] (patient who complied with ophthalmologist's request to move her body and eyes in a particular way taken to have consented to the injection of a drug in her eye since by following his instructions the patient led the ophthalmologist to reasonably believe that she consented to the injection). The statement in the text is subject to the proviso that the syringe contains what the patient believed it to contain: *Potts v North West Regional Health Authority* unreported 1983, para.6–015, see *The Guardian*, 23 July 1983, news report.

FORMS OF CONSENT

not necessarily consent; it will depend on the circumstances of the case, and whether the doctor's inference of consent was reasonable.[66]

(b) Consent forms

6–021   Prior to most major surgical procedures the patient will be asked to sign a written consent form. Standard consent forms usually state that the nature and purpose of the operation or treatment have been explained to the patient.[67] But such forms are not conclusive against the patient, they are merely evidence that the patient consented to the procedure in question. In *Chatterton v Gerson* Bristow J said that:

> "...getting the patient to sign a pro forma expressing consent to undergo the operation 'the effect and nature of which have been explained to me' ... should be a valuable reminder to everyone of the need for explanation and consent. But it would be no defence to an action based on trespass to the person if no explanation had in fact been given. The consent would have been expressed in form only, not in reality."[68]

Thus, in *Coughlin v Kuntz*[69] the patient signed consent forms but it was held that he did not understand and appreciate the nature of the procedure and therefore there was no valid consent. The defendant had not informed the patient that the

[66] (1980) 109 D.L.R. (3d) 634 at 641. See also *Schweizer v Central Hospital* (1974) 53 D.L.R. (3d) 494 at 508, per Thompson J: "Consent may be implied where circumstances dictate that it is clearly indicated and it is manifest that the will of the patient accompanies such consent." A lack of objection may not be sufficient for the doctor to infer consent by the patient, a point that becomes significant in the context of the treatment of patients with mental disability: see Gunn (1987) 16 Anglo-American L.R. 242 at 246. See also *Nagy v Canada* 2006 ABCA 227; (2006) 272 D.L.R. (4th) 601 at [52] where the Alberta Court of Appeal stated that "compliance" is not necessarily consent: "the alleged 'consent' arose when a medical doctor was presented with a patient in police custody and asked by the police to conduct what was, on the face of it, a non-medically necessary search of the body of the patient that involved a series of progressively more invasive procedures. In such circumstances, it is incumbent on the doctor to inquire of the patient, in private, whether the patient is consenting to the invasive bodily searches of his or her own free will."
[67] The NHS model consent form 1 included a statement by the health professional concerned that: "I have explained the procedure to the patient." The form then asks the health professional to confirm that the patient has been told about the intended benefits, serious or frequently occurring risks, any extra procedures which may become necessary, what the procedure is likely to involve, the benefits and risks of any available alternative treatments (including no treatment) and any particular concerns of the patient. The model NHS consent forms are available at *http://webarchive.nationalarchives. gov.uk/20130107105354/http://www.dh.gov.uk/en/Publichealth/ Scientificdevelopmentgeneticsandbioethics/Consent/Consentgeneralinformation/DH_4015950.* Where the patient receives treatment privately the contract between doctor and patient may be embodied partly in the written consent form and partly in the oral conversations between doctor and patient prior to the procedure, at which time the nature and effect of the operation should have been explained to the patient: *Eyre v Measday* [1986] 1 All E.R. 488 at 492.
[68] [1981] Q.B. 432 at 443; *Hajgato v London Health Association* (1982) 36 O.R. (2d) 669 at 679; aff'd 40 O.R. (2d) 264, Ont CA: "While the plaintiff signed a standard form of authorisation and consent prior to the operation in which she acknowledged the nature of the operation had been explained to her satisfaction, the existence of that consent does not protect a doctor from liability unless the patient has been informed to the satisfaction of the court." See also *Bickford v Stiles* (1981) 128 D.L.R. (3d) 516 at 520; *Brushett v Cowan* (1987) 40 D.L.R. (4th) 488; rev'd on the facts (1990) 69 D.L.R. (4th) 743, Newfd CA.
[69] (1987) 42 C.C.L.T. 142, BCSC; aff'd [1990] 2 W.W.R. 737, 745, BCCA.

procedure was novel, unique to the defendant, and under investigation by the College of Physicians and Surgeons, who had urged him to undertake a moratorium on the procedure. Conversely, an ineffective signature on the consent form does not necessarily indicate that the patient has not given a valid consent. In *Taylor v Shropshire Health Authority*[70] Popplewell J commented:

> "For my part I regard the consent form immediately before operation as pure window dressing in this case and designed simply to avoid the suggestion that a patient has not been told."

Nonetheless, on the facts, it was held that the patient had in fact been told about the risks involved in a sterilisation operation, and that she had consented.[71]

Forms for refusing consent   Similar principles apply to standard forms used to record a patient's refusal of consent, e.g. where a patient refuses to accept a blood transfusion. In *Re T (Adult: Refusal of Treatment)* Lord Donaldson MR, commenting on the forms used in that case, said that: **6–022**

> "It is clear that such forms are designed primarily to protect the hospital from legal action. They will be wholly ineffective for this purpose if the patient is incapable of understanding them, they are not explained to him and there is no good evidence (apart from the patient's signature) that he had that understanding and fully appreciated the significance of signing it."[72]

In *St George's Healthcare NHS Trust v S*[73] the Court of Appeal said that where a competent patient refuses consent to treatment the advice given to the patient should be recorded:

> "For their own protection hospital authorities should seek unequivocal assurances from the patient (to be recorded in writing) that the refusal represents an informed decision, that is, that she understands the nature of and reasons for the proposed treatment, and the risks and likely prognosis involved in the decision to refuse or accept it. If the patient is unwilling to sign a written indication of this refusal, this too should be noted in writing. Such a written indication is merely a record for evidential purposes. It should not be confused with or regarded as a disclaimer."

Patient sedated when signing consent form   It is not good practice to get patients to sign consent forms just before they have the operation when they have already been sedated. The drug may impair the patient's ability to comprehend,   **6–023**

---

[70] [1998] Lloyd's Rep. Med. 395 at 398. A similar point arises in relation to disclosures about the risks of treatment for the purpose of obtaining "informed" consent: see *Thefaut v Johnston* [2017] EWHC 497 (QB); [2017] Med. L.R. 319 at [78] per Green J (quoted at para.7–006, n.12).

[71] See also *Newbury v Bath District Health Authority* (1998) 47 B.M.L.R. 138 where pre-operative consent to complex spinal surgery was obtained by a house officer with less than six months experience of surgery, but Ebsworth J concluded that the obtaining of the consent had, in any event, to be looked at in the light of the consultations between the surgeon and the patient before the consent form was signed, and before the patient was admitted to hospital. On that basis, the surgeon had informed the patient about the nature of the procedure.

[72] [1993] Fam. 95 at 114. Note that revocation of an "advance directive" refusing certain forms of medical treatment does not require any particular formality. See: *HE v A Hospital NHS Trust* [2003] EWHC 1017 (Fam); [2003] 2 F.L.R. 408 at para.6–027, and the Mental Capacity Act 2005 s.24(3) and (4).

[73] [1999] Fam. 26 at 63.

and render an apparent consent invalid. For example, in *Beausoleil v La Communauté des Soeurs de la Charité de la Providence*[74] the claimant went into hospital for a back operation, and told the surgeon that she wanted a general anaesthetic, not a spinal anaesthetic. On the day of the operation she was sedated and taken to the operating theatre where she told the anaesthetist that she did not want a spinal anaesthetic. The anaesthetist then talked the claimant into accepting the spinal anaesthetic, without examining her or consulting the surgeon. This was administered with reasonable care, but after the operation the claimant was paralysed from the waist down, probably as a result of the spinal anaesthetic. It was held that the claimant had not given a valid consent. Due to the sedation the exchange between claimant and defendant "no longer had any real significance for the plaintiff and … [was] of no legal consequence".[75] Similarly, in *Kelly v Hazlett*[76] the claimant consented to an osteotomy to correct a deformity in her elbow after the administration of a sedative. Morden J commented that the giving of a consent in such circumstances, at the very least, leaves the validity of the consent open to question, although he concluded that, on the facts, the claimant had a sufficient understanding of the basic nature and character of the operation for the consent to be effective.[77] In *Holdsworth v Luton and Dunstable University Hospital NHS Foundation Trust*[78] Judge Freedman rejected the argument that "because the claimant was 'gowned up', she was not in a position to give informed consent." Although there was no specific reference in the consent form signed by the claimant to the risk of persistent or worsening pain following knee replacement surgery the judge accepted the surgeon's evidence that when advising patients about the risks he always made reference to the possibility of ongoing pain.

6–024   **Consent form unsigned**   Just as a signature on a consent form is merely evidence, and not proof, that the patient has consented, the absence of a signature does not necessarily prove the lack of consent. The absence of a signature may, however, when considered with other evidence, indicate that there was no consent or no consent to the extent of the procedure actually carried out. In *Williamson v East London & City Health Authority*[79] the claimant, who had previously had bilateral breast implants, had signed a consent form in January 1994 for a replacement breast prosthesis and right open capsulotomy. Her condition deteriorated between January and April when she was admitted to

---

[74] (1964) 53 D.L.R. (2d) 65, Qué QB Appeal Side.

[75] (1964) 53 D.L.R. (2d) 65 at 76, per Rinfret J. See also *Wells v Surrey Area Health Authority*, *The Times*, 29 July 1978 (news report), n.51, above.

[76] (1976) 75 D.L.R. (3d) 536, Ont HC.

[77] (1976) 75 D.L.R. (3d) 536 at 563. The defendant was held liable in negligence for failing to inform the claimant about the risk of stiffness associated with the operation; see also *Ferguson v Hamilton Civic Hospitals* (1983) 144 D.L.R. (3d) 214 at 237, per Krever J, aff'd (1985) 18 D.L.R. (4th) 638, Ont CA. In *Candutti v ACT Health and Community Care* [2003] ACTSC 95 (SC of the Australian Capital Territory) at [34] Harper M observed: "It is highly undesirable that a plaintiff who has consented months earlier to a surgical procedure should be provided with a last-minute further warning in the operating theatre. The circumstances and timing of such a warning would often leave room for doubt as to whether what followed could truly be described as an informed consent."

[78] [2016] EWHC 3347 (QB); (2017) 154 B.M.L.R. 172.

[79] [1998] Lloyd's Rep. Med. 6; (1998) 41 B.M.L.R. 85, QBD.

hospital. She was examined pre-operatively by the surgeon who discovered lumps in the armpit running down the right arm. The evidence of the surgeon was that she told the claimant that she would now have to remove most of her right breast. The claimant said that she understood that a small portion of breast tissue would have to be removed, and that if she had been told that a mastectomy would be performed she would not have agreed to the procedure, but would have left the hospital and sought a second opinion. The consent form signed in January was amended to reflect the procedure that was actually performed in April, but the amendments were not signed by the claimant. The judge found that, given that the appearance of her breasts was clearly important to the claimant, and the fact that the consent form was not signed by her when it was amended, it was probable that she had not been told about the prospect of a mastectomy. She would have reacted very differently from the way in which the nursing notes had recorded. She would not have been reassured, she would have been horrified and would have expressed that concern. The absence of her signature on the consent form pointed very strongly to the fact that she had not been present when it had been altered. Thus, the claimant had not consented to undergo such an extensive operation.

"Consent" to additional procedures   Some older consent forms included a   **6–025**
clause to the effect that the patient consents to "such further or alternative operative measures or treatment as may be found necessary during the course of the operation or treatment".[80] The effect of such a clause was highly questionable, since if the "further or alternative" treatment was not justified in law under the principle of necessity,[81] it is unlikely that such a blanket consent would protect the doctor because the patient would probably be unaware of the nature of the treatment.[82] The consent form constitutes evidence of consent, but if in fact the

---

[80] MPS General Consent Form, 1988.
[81] See paras 6–167 to 6–171.
[82] cf. Dugdale and Stanton, *Professional Negligence*, 3rd edn (London: Butterworths, 1998), para.11.61, suggesting that such a consent might justify more extensive intervention than would be lawful under the principle of necessity. In *Brushett v Cowan* (1990) 69 D.L.R. (4th) 743, Newfd CA, the claimant signed a consent form authorising a muscle biopsy, and also consented to "such further or alternative measures as may be found to be necessary during the course of the operation". The defendant performed a muscle biopsy and a bone biopsy, and at first instance was held liable in battery in respect of the bone biopsy (see (1987) 40 D.L.R. (4th) 488 at 492). On appeal the decision was reversed, on the basis that the extent of the consent must be judged by looking at all the circumstances, not merely the consent form. The claimant had consented to a diagnostic procedure to determine the cause of her medical problem, and in the circumstances this was a sufficient consent to the bone biopsy. See further *Pridham v Nash* (1986) 33 D.L.R. (4th) 304, Ont HC, where the patient signed a consent form for an investigative laparoscopy, which included a consent to such "additional procedures as may be necessary or medically advisable during the course of" the procedure. It was held that this consent was sufficient to cover the performance of minor surgery during the course of the examination, such as moving and clearing away obstructions, but it would not have justified major surgery; *O'Bonswain v Paradis* (1993) 15 C.C.L.T. (2d) 188, Ont HC. Consent to a breast biopsy is not, however, consent to a mastectomy; *Re P* (1993) 4 *AVMA Medical & Legal Journal* (No.2) p.18, where the claimant had her right breast removed, having consented only to re-excision of a scar on the right breast with lymph node sampling. The action, which appears to have been brought in negligence rather than trespass, was settled.

patient does not understand the nature of the treatment the consent is invalid. The NHS model consent forms do not include such a clause but state that the patient understands:

"...that any procedure in addition to those described on this form will only be carried out if it is necessary to save my life or to prevent serious harm to my health."[83]

At best, this probably amounts to little more than providing information to the patient, since a procedure that was not necessary to save life or to prevent serious harm to the patient's health would not be justified under the common law principle of necessity and, unless there was express consent, would exceed the scope of the patient's consent. The model consent form also stated that:

"I have been told about the additional procedures which may become necessary during my treatment. I have listed below any procedures which I do not wish to be carried out without further discussion."[84]

This wording was an improvement on the previous model consent form since it does at least purport to identify (and thereby place some limit on) the procedures which patients have to indicate they do not wish to undergo. Nonetheless, there is no obligation in law for patients to specify what they do *not* want to have done and the failure to indicate what they do not want to happen is irrelevant. In the absence of a valid justification, such as the patient's consent to the specific procedure that is contemplated, or necessity, all other procedures which involve physical contact with the person are unlawful, as battery. To suggest otherwise, even by implication, as the model consent form appeared to do, misrepresents the true position in law. The solution is simple. If the patient has been told about the additional procedures which may become necessary during the treatment, those procedures should be listed on the form and the patient can then give an express consent to them. Those procedures which the patient does not wish to be carried out can simply be omitted from the form. It may be that listing the procedures which the patient would not want to be carried out is a useful reminder to the medical staff of the limits to the scope of the patient's consent. But the omission of the patient to complete this section of the form does not in itself constitute a consent to those procedures.

(c)   Advance statements—common law

6–026   The ability to give or withhold consent extends to the future, so that individuals may give instructions as to the forms of medical treatment that they will or will not accept in anticipation of the prospect that circumstances may arise in which it will not be possible either to give a valid consent or to refuse consent, because,

---

[83] See NHS model consent form 1 (available at *http://webarchive.nationalarchives.gov.uk/ 20130107105354/http://www.dh.gov.uk/en/Publichealth/Scientificdevelopmentgeneticsandbioethics/ Consent/Consentgeneralinformation/DH_4015950*).
[84] NHS model consent form 1.

for example, of incapacity.[85] Competent patients may even obtain an injunction restraining anyone from performing treatment to which they object.[86] Moreover, there is nothing in the European Convention on Human Rights which alters the right of a competent patient to make a statement refusing life-sustaining medical treatment in the future.[87] But care must be taken to ensure that any advance statement made by the patient covers the circumstances that have arisen. In *Re T (Adult: Refusal of Treatment)*[88] Lord Donaldson MR said that an anticipatory choice made by the patient would bind the doctor "if clearly established and applicable in the circumstances—two major 'ifs'"; and in *St George's Healthcare NHS Trust v S*[89] the Court of Appeal commented that:

> "...if there is reason to doubt the reliability of the advance directive (for example it may sensibly be thought not to apply to the circumstances which have arisen), then an application+ for a declaration may be made."

Since the coming into force of the Mental Capacity Act 2005 any advance statement purporting to refuse life-saving treatment must comply with the formalities set out in s.25(5) and (6).[90]

Revoking an advance statement   The correct approach to the revocation of an advance statement at common law was considered by Munby J in *HE v A Hospital NHS Trust*.[91] The patient, who was 24, was born and, initially, brought up a Muslim, but her parents separated while she was still a child. Subsequently, the patient and her mother both became Jehovah's Witnesses. The patient had a congenital heart problem which she knew would require further surgery as an adult. In February 2001 she signed a pre-printed advance statement, witnessed by two ministers from her church, in which she expressly refused consent to receive blood or primary blood components in any circumstances. The refusal of blood was said to be absolute and not to be overridden in any circumstances by a purported consent of a relative or other person. Clause 2(d) provided that:

6–027

---

[85] *Airedale NHS Trust v Bland* [1993] A.C. 789 at 857, per Lord Keith, and 864, per Lord Goff, who added that: "in such circumstances especial care may be necessary to ensure that the prior refusal of consent is still properly to be regarded as applicable in the circumstances which have subsequently occurred." See also *Malette v Shulman* (1990) 67 D.L.R. (4th) 321 at 330, Ont CA; *Fleming v Reid* (1991) 82 D.L.R. (4th) 298 at 310, Ont CA; *Hunter and New England Area Health Service v A* [2009] NSWSC 761; (2009) 74 N.S.W.L.R. 88. See also the BMA guidance, *Advance decisions and proxy decision-making in medical treatment and research* (2007) (available at *http://www.bma.org.uk/support-at-work/ethics/mental-capacity*); and the GMC guidance, *Consent: patients and doctors making decisions together*, June 2008, paras 57–61 (available at *http://www.gmc-uk.org/static/documents/content/Consent_-_English_1015.pdf*).
[86] *Re C (Adult: Refusal of Treatment)* [1994] 1 W.L.R. 290; para.6–040—where Thorpe J granted an injunction restraining the amputation of the patient's gangrene-infected foot without express consent.
[87] *Re AK (Adult Patient) (Medical Treatment: Consent)* [2001] 1 F.L.R. 129; *Re B (Adult: Refusal of Medical Treatment)* [2002] EWHC 429 (Fam); [2002] 2 All E.R. 449.
[88] [1993] Fam. 95 at 103.
[89] [1999] Fam. 26 at 63.
[90] *W v M* [2011] EWHC 2443 (Fam); [2012] 1 W.L.R. 1653 at [6]. See para.6–030. Though see *Newcastle upon Tyne Hospitals Foundation Trust v LM* [2014] EWHC 454 (COP); [2015] 1 F.C.R. 373; (2014) 137 B.M.L.R. 226, para.6–030 n.105 below.
[91] [2003] EWHC 1017 (Fam); [2003] 2 F.L.R. 408.

"...this advance directive shall remain in force and bind all those treating me unless and until I expressly revoke it in writing."

In April 2003 she fell seriously ill and was rushed to hospital. To have any realistic prospect of survival she needed surgery, and this would be impossible to perform without significant blood loss. She was sedated and unconscious. The patient's mother told the hospital that her daughter objected to the use of blood products. By the time of the court hearing her condition had deteriorated further and the evidence was that it seemed:

"...inevitable that she will die within the next 24 hours with the current treatment that she is receiving, but that blood transfusion might slow or even reverse this deterioration."

The patient's father argued that the advance statement was no longer applicable because the patient was now engaged to a Muslim man, had expressed a commitment to return to the Muslim faith and had not been to her church for some months. Munby J held that the advance statement no longer applied and, as the patient lacked capacity, the doctors could treat her according to her best interests.[92] There were a number of factors, which taken together, were persuasive: (i) she was betrothed to be married to a Muslim and had agreed as a condition of the marriage to revert to being a Muslim; (ii) having promised her fiancé that she would not attend any Jehovah's Witness meetings, she had not done so since the beginning of January 2003; (iii) on a recent occasion she had been in hospital for two days without saying anything about either the advance directive or not having a blood transfusion; (iv) on that occasion she had said that she did not want to die. The most important of these factors was that she had not merely decided to reject her faith as a Jehovah's Witness but had actually implemented that decision, by discontinuing her previously frequent attendance at religious meetings and services. Since the advance statement was founded entirely on her faith as a Jehovah's Witness it did not survive her deliberate, implemented, decision to abandon that faith and to revert to being a Muslim.

6–028   Munby J gave[93] clear guidance on the courts' approach to advance directives.

(1)   The burden of proof is placed:

"...on those who seek to establish the existence and continuing validity and applicability of an advance directive. So if there is doubt that doubt falls to be resolved in favour of the preservation of life."

(2)   The standard of proof requires clear and convincing proof. Although this is still based on the balance of probability, the more grave the matter in issue, the stronger and more cogent must the evidence be:

"Where, as here, life is at stake, the evidence must be scrutinised with especial care. The continuing validity and applicability of the advance directive must be clearly established by convincing and inherently reliable evidence."

---

[92] See paras 6–100 to 6–104.
[93] [2003] EWHC 1017 (Fam); [2003] 2 F.L.R. 408 at [23] to [45].

(3)   The question of whether an advance directive made at some time in the past is still valid and applicable requires especially close, rigorous and anxious scrutiny, bearing in mind any known changes in the patient's circumstances.

(4)   A patient's anticipatory refusal of treatment will not survive a material change of circumstance.

(5)   There are no formal requirements for a valid advance directive. It does not have to be either in or evidenced by writing. An advance directive may be oral or in writing.[94]

(6)   Similarly, there are no formal requirements for the revocation of an advance directive. It does not make any difference whether the advance directive was itself oral or in writing. An advance directive may effectively be revoked either orally or in writing. Thus, a written advance directive can be effectively revoked orally, as can an advance directive executed under seal.

(7)   An advance directive is inherently revocable. An irrevocable advance directive is a contradiction in terms and is therefore a legal impossibility. Any condition in an advance directive purporting to make it irrevocable is contrary to public policy and void.

(8)   Any provision in an advance directive purporting to impose formal or other conditions upon its revocation is also contrary to public policy and void. So, it is contrary to public policy for anyone to stipulate that an advance directive is binding unless and until revoked in writing. (It followed that para.2(d) of the advance directive in this case was void.)

(9)   When a competent adult patient loses both his capacity to decide whether or not to accept medical treatment and any ability to express his wishes and feelings, a previously valid advance directive that has not been revoked in the meantime will in effect become and, at least as long as the patient continues in that condition, will in effect remain irrevocable. This is not because the advance directive has become irrevocable. It is because there is now no one who is able to revoke it. Only the patient himself can revoke his own advance directive.

(10)   But as long as patients remain competent, and so retain the capacity to decide whether or not to accept medical treatment, it is inherent in the very nature of an advance directive that they may revoke it.

(11)   Thus, the question of whether an advance directive has been revoked or has ceased to be operative is a question of fact; and the burden of proof lies on those who assert the continuing validity and applicability of the advance directive. There is an evidential burden on those who assert that an advance directive is no longer operative.

(12)   That evidential burden can be met by pointing to words said to have been written or spoken by the patient; the patient's actions (actions may speak louder than words); or a change in circumstances. Moreover, the longer the time which has elapsed since an advance directive was made, and the greater the apparent changes in the patient's circumstances since then, the

---

[94] Contrast the position under the Mental Capacity Act 2005 s.25(5) and (6) where the advance statement purports to refuse life-sustaining treatment. See para.6–030.

more doubt there is likely to be as to its continuing validity and applicability. And if there is doubt, that doubt will be resolved in favour of the preservation of life.

(d)   Advance decisions—Mental Capacity Act 2005

6–029   The Mental Capacity Act 2005 ss.24–26 gives statutory form to an "advance decision",[95] though the criteria for a valid and applicable advance decision under the Act (particularly for a decision to refuse life-saving treatment) are quite strict.[96] By s.24(1) an advance decision is defined as a decision made by an adult (P) when he has capacity to do so that if, at a later time, and in such circumstances as he may specify, a specified treatment is proposed to be carried out or continued by a person providing healthcare for him, and at that time he lacks capacity to consent to the carrying out or continuation of the treatment, the specified treatment is not to be carried out or continued. The treatment or circumstances may be expressed "in layman's terms".[97] P may withdraw or alter an advance decision at any time when he has capacity to do so, and a withdrawal need not be in writing.[98] An alteration need not be in writing unless s.25(5) (in relation to life-sustaining treatment) applies.[99] An advance decision is not valid if P: (a) has withdrawn the decision at a time when he had capacity to do so; (b) has, under a lasting power of attorney created after the advance decision was made, conferred authority on the donee to give or refuse consent to the treatment to which the advance decision relates; or (c) has done anything else clearly inconsistent with the advance decision remaining his fixed decision.[100] The advance decision does not apply to treatment if at the material time P has capacity to give or refuse consent to the treatment.[101] Nor does the advance decision apply if the treatment is not the treatment specified in the advance decision; if any circumstances specified in the advance decision are absent; or if circumstances

---

[95] Note that in *W v M* [2011] EWHC 2443 (Fam); [2012] 1 W.L.R. 1653 at [84] Baker J said that the judge-made provisions for advance decisions had been superseded by the Act.

[96] See, e.g., C. Johnston, "Advance decision making—rhetoric or reality?" (2014) 34 L.S. 497 who argues that the rhetoric of advance decision-making is not matched by its effectiveness in practice, and that there is a tension between respect for prior patient autonomy and the approach of both medical practitioners and courts to the patient's best interests.

[97] Mental Capacity Act 2005 s.24(2).

[98] Mental Capacity Act 2005 s.24(3) and (4).

[99] Mental Capacity Act 2005 s.24(5).

[100] Mental Capacity Act 2005 s.25(2). Note that in *Re Briggs (Incapacitated Person) (Medical Treatment: Best Interests Decision) (No.2)* [2016] EWCOP 53; [2017] 4 W.L.R. 37 at [22] Charles J, referring to s.25(2)(c) and s.25(3) commented that: "an interpretation of these safety nets based on the sanctity of life or anything else (e.g. the detail of prognosis and alternatives at the time when the question about the treatment arises) that sets a low threshold to rendering an advance decision invalid or inapplicable would run counter to the enabling intention of ss. 24 to 26 of the MCA. In any event, if those provisions did found the view that an advance decision was invalid or inapplicable, and so a best interests test became determinative, I consider that the court would have to take into account the impact of that removal of that person's right of self-determination that he or she has sought to exercise by making an advance decision."

[101] Mental Capacity Act 2005 s.25(3).

exist which were not anticipated at the time of the advance decision and which would have affected P's decision had he anticipated them.[102]

Refusing life-sustaining treatment[103]   An advance decision will not apply to life-sustaining treatment unless P specified that it was to apply to that treatment even if life is at risk, and it is in writing and appropriately signed and witnessed.[104] If the safeguards and formalities of the Act are satisfied the advance decision is binding, but informal statements by the patient made before the illness which resulted in incapacity and which do not address the specific circumstances which have arisen are not binding,[105] and though the court can take them into account in assessing the patient's best interests they will not carry substantial weight.[106] In *A Local Authority v E*[107] Peter Jackson J held that for an advance decision relating to life-sustaining treatment to be valid and applicable, there should be clear evidence establishing on the balance of probability that the decision maker had capacity at the relevant time. Where the evidence of capacity is doubtful or equivocal it is not appropriate to uphold the decision.[108] E had also included in the advance decision a clause stating that: "If I exhibit behaviour seemingly contrary to this advanced directive this should not be viewed as a change of decision." Peter Jackson J took the view that this could not be a binding instruction in light of s.25(2)(c) stating that the advance decision is not valid if P has done anything else clearly inconsistent with the advance decision remaining his fixed decision. On the other hand, in *A NHS Foundation Trust v*

6–030

---

[102] Mental Capacity Act 2005 s.25(4).

[103] Note that where an "advance decision" is taken by the medical staff not to provide potentially life-saving treatment in the form of a "Do Not Attempt Cardio-Pulmonary Resuscitation" notice if the patient should suffer a cardiac arrest the patient is entitled to be consulted about the decision: see *R. (on the application of Tracey) v Cambridge University Hospitals NHS Foundation Trust* [2014] EWCA Civ 822; [2015] Q.B. 543, para.6–163.

[104] Mental Capacity Act 2005 s.25(5) and (6).

[105] *W v M* [2011] EWHC 2443 (CoP); [2012] 1 W.L.R. 1653 at [6] per Baker J. Though see *Newcastle upon Tyne Hospitals Foundation Trust v LM* [2014] EWHC 454 (COP); [2015] 1 F.C.R. 373; (2014) 137 B.M.L.R. 226 where Peter Jackson J held that an oral statement to doctors by a patient who was known to be a Jehovah's Witness, and who had capacity at that time, that she did not want treatment with blood products had to be respected by the doctors. A day later the patient's condition deteriorated to the point where she no longer had capacity, but the judge was satisfied that she had "understood the nature, purpose and effects of the proposed treatment, including that refusal of a blood transfusion might have fatal consequences" and that the decision made "prior to her loss of capacity was applicable to her later more serious condition".

[106] *W v M* [2011] EWHC 2443 (CoP); [2012] 1 W.L.R. 1653 at [6]. Contrast *Re Briggs (Incapacitated Person) (Medical Treatment: Best Interests Decision) (No.2)* [2016] EWCOP 53; [2017] 4 W.L.R. 37 where Charles J placed significant weight on the patient's informal statements as to whether he would wish to have clinically assisted nutrition and hydration continued, given the evidence from the patient's family and former work colleagues.

[107] [2012] EWHC 1639 (Fam); [2012] 2 F.C.R. 523; [2012] Med. L.R. 472 at [55].

[108] [2012] EWHC 1639 (Fam); [2012] 2 F.C.R. 523; [2012] Med. L.R. 472 at [55]. E had a long history of suffering from anorexia nervosa, and had been compulsorily sectioned under the Mental Health Act 1983 on about ten occasions. Peter Jackson J commented at [65]: "Against such an alerting background, a full, reasoned and contemporaneous assessment evidencing mental capacity to make such a momentous decision would in my view be necessary." For comment see Coggon, "Anorexia Nervosa, Best Interests, and the Patient's Human Right to 'A Wholesale Overwhelming of Her Autonomy'" (2014) 22 Med. L. Rev. 119.

X^{109} the patient suffered from severe anorexia and was found to lack capacity with regard to the treatment of her eating disorder, but she also suffered from alcohol dependence and was found to have capacity in relation to treatment of her alcoholism. She had made an advance decision in relation to future treatment of her liver disease (which was caused by her alcohol dependence) refusing specific treatments "even if my life is at risk as a result". Cobb J concluded that the advance decision met the requirements of s.24 of the Mental Capacity Act 2005 and that therefore the advance decision was "entitled to the fullest respect".[110]

6–031 **Defences**   A person who carries out or continues treatment in ignorance of a valid advance decision will not incur any liability.[111] Similarly, a person who withholds or withdraws treatment in the reasonable belief that a valid advance decision applies to the treatment is not liable for the consequences.[112] Where a court is asked to rule on whether a valid advance decision applies in the circumstances, then a person will be able to provide life-sustaining treatment or do anything reasonably believed to be necessary to prevent a serious deterioration in the patient's condition while the ruling is sought, notwithstanding the apparently valid advance decision.[113]

4.   CONSENT MUST BE VALID

6–032   In order to be effective as a defence to a claim in battery the patient's consent must be a valid consent. For this purpose the consent must be "real".[114] There are three elements to this. First, it must be voluntary and uncoerced. Secondly, patients must be capable of understanding the nature of the procedure, i.e. they must have the capacity (or competence) to consent. Thirdly, they must have a

---

[109] [2014] EWCOP 35; [2015] C.O.P.L.R. 11; (2014) 140 B.M.L.R. 41; discussed by J. Coggon (2015) 23 Med. L. Rev. 659; D. Wang (2015) 78 M.L.R. 871.

[110] [2014] EWCOP 35; [2015] C.O.P.L.R. 11; (2014) 140 B.M.L.R. 41 at [34], applying *Airedale NHS Trust v Bland* [1993] A.C. 789, 864 per Lord Goff. This was the case even though this complicated the medical management of her inter-related medical conditions since she had capacity to refuse treatment for some (the effects of her alcoholism), but not other (anorexia) medical conditions. In *X Primary Care Trust v XB* [2012] EWHC 1390 (Fam); (2012) 127 B.M.L.R. 122 Theis J ruled that an advance decision made by a patient with motor neurone disease, by means of communicating his wishes by movement of his eyes, was valid and applicable. A clause in the pro forma document stating "valid until" with a date of 2 May 2012 having been entered did not, on the evidence, place a time limit on the validity of the advance decision but was entered in the context of keeping the advance decision under review.

[111] Mental Capacity Act 2005 s.26(2).

[112] Mental Capacity Act 2005 s.26(3).

[113] Mental Capacity Act 2005 s.26(5). Some care is needed in interpreting this provision. Where a "one-off" medical intervention will resolve the issue, there might be a temptation to apply to the court for a ruling in order to rely on the protection of s.26(5). For example, in the circumstances of a case such as *Malette v Shulman* (1990) 67 D.L.R. (4th) 321, where an unconscious patient in a casualty department of a hospital was found to be carrying a card stating that, as a Jehovah's Witness, she did not wish to have a blood transfusion, the administration of blood was certainly necessary to prevent a deterioration in her condition. She was given a blood transfusion, and survived, thus being presented with a fait accompli. The Ontario Court of Appeal subsequently ruled that the treatment was unlawful, contrary to a valid advance statement on the card. See para.6–178. Section 26(5) would seem to confer protection upon the doctor, provided an application to the court for a ruling was being sought.

[114] *Chatterton v Gerson* [1981] Q.B. 432 at 442.

certain minimum level of information concerning the "nature" of the procedure so that they know what they are consenting to.

(a) Voluntary consent

A person's consent must be voluntary.[115] Consent obtained by coercion or duress is invalid. In *Latter v Braddell*[116] it was held that a housemaid, who, at the insistence of her employer, submitted to a medical examination protesting and sobbing throughout, had consented, even though she mistakenly believed that she was obliged to comply. The majority of the court took the view that the consent would be involuntary only where the claimant submitted through fear of violence. This decision was questionable at the time,[117] and would probably not be followed if the facts were to recur today. Thus, a mistaken belief as to the authority of the defendant may destroy in substance the claimant's freedom to choose.[118]

6–033

In *Freeman v Home Office*[119] it was accepted that in some circumstances a person's apparent consent could be vitiated by the defendant's exercise of authority over him, without any threat of physical violence.[120] The claimant, who was serving a term of life imprisonment, claimed that in the prison context it was impossible for there to be a free and voluntary consent by a prisoner to treatment by a prison medical officer, who was not merely a doctor but a prison officer within the meaning of the Prison Rules who could influence the prisoner's life and his prospects of release on licence. This created an atmosphere of constraint upon an inmate. McCowan J rejected this contention as a proposition of law, taking the view that it is a question of fact in any particular case whether the patient's consent is voluntary. His Lordship added that where, in a prison setting, a doctor has the power to influence a prisoner's situation and prospects a court must be alive to the risk that what may appear, on the face of it, to be a real consent is not in fact so.[121]

6–034

---

[115] *Bowater v Rowley Regis Corporation* [1944] K.B. 476 at 479, per Scott LJ: "A man cannot be said to be truly 'willing' unless he is in a position to choose freely, and freedom of choice predicates, not only full knowledge of the circumstances on which the exercise of choice is conditioned, so that he may be able to choose wisely, but the absence from his mind of any feeling of constraint so that nothing shall interfere with the freedom of his will." This remark was made in the context of the defence of volenti non fit injuria, but it has much force in relation to the defence of consent to battery: see *Freeman v Home Office* [1984] Q.B. 524 at 535–536, 556–557.

[116] (1881) 50 L.J.Q.B. 448, CA.

[117] See the dissent of Lopes J at (1880) 50 L.J.C.P. 166.

[118] *Clerk & Lindsell on Torts*, 22nd edn (London: Sweet & Maxwell, 2018), para.15–98, citing *T v T* [1964] P. 85 at 99, 102; cf. Dugdale and Stanton, *Professional Negligence*, 3rd edn (London: Butterworths, 1998), para.11.60, citing *Latter v Braddell* (1881) 50 L.J.Q.B. 448.

[119] [1984] Q.B. 524.

[120] See also *Nagy v Canada* 2006 ABCA 227; (2006) 272 D.L.R. (4th) 601 where the claimant, who was in police custody, "complied" with a doctor's performance of a non-medically necessary and progressively more invasive search of her body, at the request of the police. It was held that in these circumstances compliance did not constitute consent.

[121] [1984] Q.B. 524 at 542–543; aff'd by the Court of Appeal [1984] Q.B. 524 at 557. See also *Kaimowitz v Michegan Department of Mental Health* 42 U.S.L.W. 2063 (1973) where it was said that the capacity of an involuntarily detained mental patient to consent to psychosurgery was diminished

6–035 **Undue influence of family member** A patient's apparent consent or refusal of consent may be vitiated by the undue influence of a third party, provided it can be demonstrated that the patient's will has been overborne. In *Re T (Adult: Refusal of Treatment)*[122] T was injured in a car accident when she was 34 weeks pregnant. She had been brought up by her mother who was a Jehovah's Witness, although T herself was not a member of the sect. The possibility of a blood transfusion arose. On two occasions, following private conversations with her mother, T told the medical staff that she did not want a blood transfusion. She was informed that there were other options, and that blood transfusions were not normally necessary after a Caesarean section, which was being contemplated. T signed a form of refusal of consent to blood transfusions. Following the operation her condition deteriorated, and she was transferred to intensive care. She remained sedated and in a critical condition until, following an emergency hearing, Ward J granted a declaration that it would not be unlawful for the hospital to administer the blood transfusion. At a second hearing Ward J held that T had neither consented to nor refused consent to a transfusion, and in the emergency situation it was lawful for the doctors to do what they considered to be in T's best interests. The Court of Appeal held that T had not been fit to make a genuine decision due to her debilitated medical condition, and the fact that she had been subjected to the undue influence of her mother, which vitiated her decision to refuse a blood transfusion. In the absence of either a valid consent or a valid refusal of consent the doctors had acted lawfully in giving the transfusion, applying the principle of necessity.[123] Lord Donaldson MR observed that it was wholly acceptable that a patient should receive advice and assistance from others, particularly members of the family, in reaching a decision about whether to accept or reject treatment, and it matters not how strong the persuasion is, as long as it does not overbear the independence of the patient's decision:

"The real question in each such case is: does the patient really mean what he says or is he merely saying it for a quiet life, to satisfy someone else or because the advice and persuasion to which he has been subjected is such that he can no longer think and decide for himself? In other words, is it a decision expressed in form only, not in reality?

When considering the effects of outside influences, two aspects can be of crucial importance. First, the strength of the will of the patient. One who is very tired, in pain or depressed will be much less able to resist having his will overborne than one who is rested, free from pain and cheerful. Second, the relationship of the 'persuader' to the patient may be of crucial importance. The influence of parents on their children or of one spouse on the other can be, but is by no means necessarily, much stronger than would be the case in other relationships. Persuasion based on religious beliefs can also be much more compelling and the fact that arguments based on religious beliefs are being deployed by someone in a very close relationship with the patient will give them added force and should alert the doctor to the possibility—no more—that the patient's capacity or will to decide has been overborne. In other words the patient may not mean what he says."[124]

by the very nature of his incarceration, which through the phenomenon of institutionalisation may strip the individual of the support which enables him to maintain his sense of self-worth.
[122] [1993] Fam. 95.
[123] See paras 6–100 et seq.
[124] [1993] Fam. 95 at 113–114, per Lord Donaldson MR. In *Mrs U v Centre for Reproductive Medicine* [2002] EWCA Civ 565; [2002] Lloyd's Rep. Med. 259 a nurse at an IVF clinic "pressured" the male patient into changing a consent form (to the storage and use of sperm after his death) by suggesting that, if he did not do so, the IVF treatment that he and his wife were undergoing would be

Thus, a doctor has an obligation to consider whether the decision is really that of the patient, though in practice this is more likely to be an issue where the patient is refusing consent since if the patient is agreeing to medically justified treatment recommended by the doctor the normal presumption in favour of an adult patient's competence will apply.

In *R. (on the application of H) v Mental Health Review Tribunal*[125] Holman J held that a conditional discharge from an hospital order under s.73 of the Mental Health Act 1983 which stated that the patient "shall comply" with medication prescribed by a particular doctor did not amount to compulsion. A competent adult patient has an absolute right to refuse medical treatment. Moreover, s.73 did not provide any sanction for a failure to comply with a condition, and the fact that a patient had not complied with a condition was not of itself sufficient for the Secretary of State to exercise a general power of recall under s.73. Although it was possible that if the patient ceased to take his medication he would be recalled, that would not be because he had broken a condition of discharge, but because there was clear medical evidence that if he ceased to take his medication he would pose a serious risk to the safety of others (and so the criteria for detention under the Act would be satisfied). Thus:

6–036

> "...the condition must be read as respecting and being subject to his own final choice, which must be his real or true choice."[126]

(b) Capacity to consent

As a general rule, a person's capacity in law to enter into a transaction depends upon the nature of the transaction, so a person may, at one and the same time, be competent in law for some purposes but not for others.[127] In the context of the doctor–patient relationship, capacity to consent to treatment depends upon the patient's ability to understand the nature of the treatment; it does not depend on

6–037

---

delayed or halted. The Court of Appeal held that, on the facts, the patient's withdrawal of consent to the posthumous use and storage of his gametes had not been vitiated by undue influence. See also *Norberg v Wynrib* (1992) 92 D.L.R. (4th) 449 at 457, SCC, where it was said that the normal presumption that an individual has freedom to consent may be untenable: "A position of relative weakness can, in some circumstances, interfere with the freedom of a person's will. Our notion of consent must, therefore, be modified to appreciate the power relationship between the parties", per La Forest J. Thus, a consent given under the influence of an addiction to drugs may not be valid, where there is an element of exploitation of the doctor–patient relationship by the doctor; cf. *Taylor v McGillivray* (1993) 110 D.L.R. (4th) 64, NBQB, where the consent of a 16-year-old patient to a sexual relationship with a physician was held to be valid, despite the inequality of power between the parties, but the doctor was nonetheless held liable on the basis of a breach of fiduciary duty owed to his patient, applying *Norberg v Wynrib*.
[125] [2007] EWHC 884 (Admin); (2007) 10 C.C.L. Rep. 306.
[126] [2007] EWHC 884 (Admin); (2007) 10 C.C.L. Rep. 306 at [37].
[127] *Masterman-Lister v Brutton & Co. and Jewell and Home Counties Dairies* [2002] EWCA Civ 1889; [2003] 1 W.L.R. 1511 at [27] and [58], approved in *Dunhill v Burgin* [2014] UKSC 18; [2014] 1 W.L.R. 933 at [13]. For example, a person may have sufficient understanding to enter into a contract of marriage but not to make a will: *Re Park's Estate* [1954] P. 89; see also *Re Beaney* [1978] 2 All E.R. 595. See generally *Assessment of Mental Capacity: A Practical Guide for Doctors and Lawyers*, 4th edn, 2015, BMA and Law Society; Grisso and Applebaum, *Assessing Competence to Consent to Treatment*, (Oxford: Oxford University Press, 1998).

an assessment of whether the patient's choice is "correct" or "appropriate".[128] The common law approach now has statutory backing in the form of s.1(4) of the Mental Capacity Act 2005.[129] The question of whether the patient is able to understand the nature of the treatment will be regarded as a question of fact in each case. The starting point is that adult patients are presumed to be competent to give a valid consent, unless the contrary is established,[130] and the burden of proof rests on those asserting incapacity.[131] The important corollary of this presumption is that the vast majority of adult patients are presumed to be competent to *refuse* treatment if they so choose, which is the context in which disputed questions of competence usually arise. When the Law Commission looked at the problem of capacity it recommended legislation to clarify what was regarded as a somewhat confused state of the law.[132] However, by the time that the Mental Capacity Act 2005 was enacted the common law had managed to resolve most of these issues. The result is that there are statutory rules on the meaning of capacity (and hence incapacity) alongside the common law tests. The statutory rules essentially reflect the common law position, so that the common law potentially remains relevant in interpreting the legislation.[133] For example, in *Re SK (vulnerable adult: capacity)*[134] Wood J considered both the statutory test

---

[128] "Legal capacity depends on understanding rather than wisdom; the quality of the decision is irrelevant as long as the person understands what he is deciding": *Masterman-Lister v Jewell and Home Counties Dairies* [2002] EWHC 417 (QB); [2002] Lloyd's Rep. Med. 239 at [19] per Wright J In the Court of Appeal Chadwick LJ said that "what is required is the capacity to understand the nature of that transaction when it is explained": [2002] EWCA Civ 1889; [2003] 1 W.L.R. 1511 at [58]. In *Lindsay v Wood* [2006] EWHC 2895 (QB); [2006] M.H.L.R. 341 a claimant who had suffered brain damage in an accident was found to be unable to weigh up the advantages and risks of accepting an offer of periodical payments or an offer of a lump sum plus periodical payments in settlement of his claim. Stanley Burnton J held that this lack of capacity rendered the claimant unable to manage any complex financial decisions, and therefore a "patient" within the meaning of the Mental Health Act 1983 Pt VII, and the CPR 1998 Pt 21; cf. *Saulle v Nouvet* [2007] EWHC 2902 (QB); [2008] LS Law Med. 201 taking a slightly different approach following the coming into force of the Mental Capacity Act 2005 and a new CPR Pt 21.
[129] See para.6–045 below.
[130] "Every person is presumed to have the capacity to consent to or to refuse medical treatment unless and until that presumption is rebutted": *Re MB (Medical Treatment)* [1997] 2 FLR 426 at 436, per Butler-Sloss LJ; *Re B (Adult: Refusal of Medical Treatment)* [2002] EWHC 429 (Fam); [2002] 2 All E.R. 449, at [28] per Butler-Sloss P. This presumption now has statutory force. See the Mental Capacity Act 2005 s.1(2).
[131] *Masterman-Lister v Brutton & Co. and Jewell and Home Counties Dairies* [2002] EWCA Civ 1889; [2003] 1 W.L.R. 1511 at [17] per Kennedy LJ.
[132] *Mental Incapacity*, Law Com. No.231, (1995) paras 3.14 to 3.21.
[133] See *Local Authority X v MM* [2007] EWHC 2003 (Fam); [2009] 1 F.L.R. 443 at [80]; *Saulle v Nouvet* [2007] EWHC 2902 (QB); [2008] LS Law Med. 201; *Westminster City Council v C* [2008] EWCA Civ 198; [2009] Fam. 11 at [54] per Wall LJ: "I am in no doubt at all that the inherent jurisdiction of the High Court to protect the welfare of incapable adults ... survives, albeit that it is now reinforced by the provisions of the Mental Capacity Act 2005"; *D County Council v LS* [2010] EWHC 1544 (Fam); [2010] Med. L.R. 499 at [29] to [31] per Roderic Wood J noting that: "I have found it useful to consider the common-law provisions, to see what guidance they may offer to me in construing statutory provision." The *Mental Capacity Act Code of Practice* (2007) states (at para.4.33) that: "The Act's new definition of capacity is in line with the existing common law tests, and the Act does not replace them."
[134] [2008] EWHC 636 (Fam); [2008] LS Law Medical 505.

for capacity under s.3 of Mental Capacity Act 2005 and the common law test,[135] concluding that the patient did not have mental capacity to consent to surgery under either test. Moreover, where a person does not meet the statutory test for incapacity (e.g. because their reduced capacity is not a product of an "impairment of, or a disturbance in the functioning of the mind or brain"[136]) the court retains the power to invoke the inherent jurisdiction to protect vulnerable adults[137] to which the common law test will still apply.

(i)   The test for capacity at common law

In the past questions of capacity were generally left to the good sense of the medical profession.[138] There are several possible tests that could be employed: was the patient's decision about whether to accept or reject treatment rational; was the outcome of the choice reasonable; did the patient have "full" understanding; was the patient's decision-making process rational/reasonable irrespective of the outcome? The difficulty with most, if not all, of these tests is that there is a danger of categorising patients as incompetent simply because they have not chosen the medical option that some other person (whether it be the doctor, a relative or the court) would have chosen in the circumstances, and allowing that person to substitute their own paternalistic view of what is in the patient's best interests.[139] Respect for autonomy and self-determination, which are said to be the foundations of the requirement for consent, must allow for patients to make unreasonable, irrational or even silly decisions about their healthcare without the patient immediately being categorised as incompetent. In *Sidaway v Bethlem Royal Hospital Governors*, for example, Lord Templeman said that if a doctor advises a patient to submit to an operation "the patient is entitled to reject that advice for reasons which are rational, or irrational, or for no reason".[140] A test based on the outcome of the individual's decision has never been adopted in English law.[141]

6–038

---

[135] As set out in *Re MB (Medical Treatment)* [1997] 8 Med. L.R. 217; [1997] 2 F.L.R. 426; see para.6–041.

[136] Mental Capacity Act 2005, s.2(1); see para.6–046.

[137] See para.6–149.

[138] Although there is some evidence that, in practice, doctors' interpretations of the legal test for capacity can be somewhat inconsistent: see Shah and Mukherjee, "Ascertaining capacity to consent: a survey of approaches used by psychiatrists" (2003) 43 Med. Sci. Law 231.

[139] There is thus a bias in favour of decisions to accept treatment: Gunn (1987) 16 Anglo-American L.R. 242, 251, citing Roth, Meisel and Lidz (1977) Am. J. of Psych. 279, 281. On the assessment of competence see further: Gunn (1994) 2 Med. L. Rev. 8, commenting on the Law Commission Consultation Paper No.129, *Mentally Incapacitated Adults and Decision-Making: Medical Treatment and Research*, 1993; Jones and Keywood (1996) 2 Med. Law Int. 107; McClelland and Szmukler (2000) 7 E.J.H.L. 47.

[140] [1985] A.C. 871 at 904. See also *Re T (Adult: Refusal of Treatment)* [1993] Fam. 95 at 102, per Lord Donaldson MR, cited above para.6–007, n.18; and *Masterman-Lister v Brutton & Co. and Jewell and Home Counties Dairies* [2002] EWCA Civ 1889; [2003] 1 W.L.R. 1511 at [79] where Chadwick LJ said that a person: "should not be regarded as unable to make a rational decision merely because the decision which he does, in fact, make is a decision which would not be made by a person of ordinary prudence." See further *Smith v Auckland Hospital Board* [1965] N.Z.L.R. 191 at 219 where T.A. Gresson J said: "An individual patient must, in my view, always retain the right to decline operative investigation or treatment however unreasonable or foolish this may appear in the eyes of

6–039   **Understanding the nature of the procedure**   The first guidance from an English court as to the test for capacity in the context of medical treatment came in *Chatterton v Gerson*,[142] where Bristow J was confronted with the question of how much information a patient must be given before the consent can be regarded as valid. His Lordship said that:

> "In my judgment once the patient is informed in broad terms of the nature of the procedure which is intended, and gives her consent, that consent is real, and the cause of action on which to base a claim for failure to go into risks and implications is negligence, not trespass."[143]

Although the case was concerned with the scope of the doctor's duty to provide information to the patient, the ruling had clear implications for the assessment of capacity. If the patient need only be given information in broad terms as to the nature of the intended procedure, it followed that the patient need only understand "in broad terms" the nature of the procedure in order to have sufficient understanding to be considered fully competent to give or withhold consent. This was quite a low level of understanding.

6–040   **Three-stage test**   The issue of the appropriate test for capacity was tangential in *Chatterton v Gerson*, determined only by inference, but in *Re C (Adult: Refusal of Treatment)*[144] it was central. The patient was a 68-year-old man in Broadmoor who was a paranoid schizophrenic. He was diagnosed as having gangrene in the right foot, and it was believed that his chances of survival with conservative treatment were no more than 15 per cent. C refused to consent to a below-the-knee amputation, but did consent to conservative treatment, which was successful. The hospital refused to give an undertaking that it would not amputate in any future circumstances. C sought an injunction restraining the hospital from amputating his leg now or in the future without his express written consent. The medical evidence suggested that the condition of C's foot was such that it would threaten his life again in the future, and that a below-the-knee amputation itself carried a 15 per cent mortality risk. Thorpe J said that the question that had to be addressed was whether it had been established that C's capacity was so reduced by his chronic mental illness that he did not sufficiently understand the nature, purpose and effects of the proffered amputation. The decision-making process

---

his medical advisers"; and *Lepp v Hopp* (1979) 98 D.L.R. (3d) 464 at 470; aff'd (1980) 112 D.L.R. (3d) 67, SCC, where Prowse JA commented that: "Each patient is entitled to make his own decision even though it may not accord with the decision knowledgeable members of the profession would make. The patient has a right to be wrong"; Brazier (1987) 7 L.S. 169, 175.

[141] It follows, of course, that where the outcome of a decision by a patient is apparently rational and reasonable that is not a basis for saying that the patient is competent. So in *Masterman-Lister v Brutton & Co. and Jewell and Home Counties Dairies* [2002] EWCA Civ 1889; [2003] 1 W.L.R. 1511 at [82] Chadwick LJ commented that a person is not to be regarded as having capacity merely because the decision appears rational. Nonetheless, "to my mind, outcomes are likely to be important (although not conclusive) indicators of the existence, or lack, of understanding".

[142] [1981] Q.B. 432.

[143] [1981] Q.B. 432 at 443.

[144] [1994] 1 W.L.R. 290. For comment on *Re C* see Stern (1994) 110 L.Q.R. 541; Gordon and Barlow (1993) 143 N.L.J. 1719; Roberts (1994) 10 P.N. 98. See also *Heart of England NHS Foundation Trust v JB* [2014] EWHC 342 (COP); (2014) 137 B.M.L.R. 232, para.6–052, for a similar case decided under the Mental Capacity Act 2005.

could be analysed in three stages: first, comprehending and retaining treatment information; second, believing it; and, third, weighing it in the balance to arrive at a choice. Applying that test, the presumption that C had the right to self-determination had not been displaced. Although his general capacity was impaired by schizophrenia, it had not been established that he did not sufficiently understand the nature, purpose and effects of the treatment he refused.[145] There was no direct link between C's refusal of amputation and his persecutory delusions. Moreover, he was content to follow medical advice and to co-operate in treatment appropriately as a patient, as long as his rejection of amputation was respected. Despite the fact that C's capacity was reduced by his mental illness, he had understood and had arrived at a clear choice. In the circumstances it was appropriate to grant the injunction restraining any future amputation without C's express consent.[146]

The *Re MB* test   The test established by Thorpe J in *Re C (Adult: Refusal of Treatment)* was adopted and expanded upon in the important decision of the Court of Appeal in *Re MB (Medical Treatment)*.[147] A mother was 40 weeks pregnant when she attended an antenatal class and it was found that the foetus was in the breech position. The risk of serious injury to the child from a natural birth was assessed as 50 per cent though the risk of physical harm to the mother was small. The mother initially agreed to a proposed Caesarean section, but due to an extreme needle phobia she was unable to accept the needles necessary for an anaesthetic and withdrew her consent to the operation. The hospital was granted a declaration that it would be lawful to carry out such treatment as might be necessary and to use reasonable force in the course of such treatment. The Court of Appeal dismissed the mother's appeal on the basis that her needle phobia rendered her temporarily incompetent, so that the principle of necessity

6–041

---

[145] In *Masterman-Lister v Brutton & Co. and Jewell and Home Counties Dairies* [2002] EWCA Civ 1889; [2003] 1 W.L.R. 1511 at [79] Chadwick LJ said that: "a person should not be held unable to understand the information relevant to a decision if he can understand an explanation of that information in broad terms and simple language." His Lordship cited the Law Commission report *Mental Incapacity*, Law Com. No.231, (1995) which, at paras 3.16 and 3.17, effectively adopted Thorpe J's approach. Thus, to be considered competent a person: "should be able both (i) to understand and retain the information relevant to the decision which has to be made (including information about the reasonably foreseeable consequences of deciding one way or another or of failing to make any decision) and (ii) to use that information in the decision making process."

[146] See also *Re AK (Adult Patient) (Medical Treatment: Consent)* [2001] 1 F.L.R. 129, and *Re B (Adult: Refusal of Medical Treatment)* [2002] EWHC 429 (Fam); [2002] 2 All E.R. 449 where patients found to be competent were held entitled to refuse life-sustaining treatment. In *Re W (Adult: Refusal of Medical Treatment)* [2002] EWHC 901 (Fam); [2002] M.H.L.R. 411 a prisoner with a psychopathic disorder was held to be competent to refuse medical treatment for self-inflicted injuries which, if left untreated, could result in septicaemia and death. See also Wicks, E, "The right to refuse medical treatment under the European Convention on Human Rights" (2001) 9 Med. L. Rev. 17. *Re C (Adult: Refusal of Treatment)* confirms the, perhaps trite, proposition that simply because an individual is compulsorily detained in a psychiatric hospital it does not necessarily follow that he is incompetent to make decisions about medical treatment. See also *Fleming v Reid* (1991) 82 D.L.R. (4th) 298 at 310, Ont CA.

[147] [1997] 8 Med. L.R. 217; [1997] 2 F.L.R. 426. Note that in *Local Authority X v MM* [2007] EWHC 2003 (Fam); [2009] 1 F.L.R. 443 at [80] Munby J said that there was no relevant distinction between the test for capacity as formulated in *Re MB* and the test set out in s.3(1) of the Mental Capacity Act 2005.

applicable to incompetent patients governed her situation.[148] Her needle phobia created a state of panic about the surgery so that she was incapable of making a decision and this amounted to such an impairment of her mental functioning as rendered her temporarily incompetent. The Court of Appeal set out a list of factors that have to be taken into account when considering whether a patient is competent to make a decision about medical treatment, though they were not intended to be determinative in every case, because the decision inevitably depends on the particular facts. Nonetheless, it is probably useful to set them out in full:

"(1) Every person is presumed to have the capacity to consent to or to refuse medical treatment unless and until that presumption is rebutted.

(2) A competent woman who has the capacity to decide may, for religious reasons, other reasons, for rational or irrational reasons or for no reason at all, choose not to have medical intervention, even though the consequence may be the death or serious handicap of the child she bears, or her own death. In that event the courts do not have the jurisdiction to declare medical intervention lawful and the question of her own best interests objectively considered, does not arise.

(3) Irrationality is here used to connote a decision which is so outrageous in its defiance of logic or of accepted moral standards that no sensible person who had applied his mind to the question to be decided it [sic.] could have arrived at it. As Kennedy and Grubb *Medical Law* (Butterworths, 2nd edn, 1994) point out, it might be otherwise if a decision is based on a misperception of reality (e.g. the blood is poisoned because it is red). Such a misperception will be more readily accepted to be a disorder of the mind. Although it might be thought that irrationality sits uneasily with competence to decide, panic, indecisiveness and irrationality in themselves do not as such amount to incompetence, but they may be symptoms or evidence of incompetence. The graver the consequences of the decision, the commensurately greater the level of competence is required to take the decision...

(4) A person lacks capacity if some impairment or disturbance of mental functioning renders the person unable to make a decision whether to consent to or to refuse treatment. That inability to make a decision will occur when:

(a) the patient is unable to comprehend and retain the information which is material to the decision, especially as to the likely consequences of having or not having the treatment in question;

(b) the patient is unable to use the information and weigh it in the balance as part of the process of arriving at the decision. If, as Thorpe J observed in *Re C* (above), a compulsive disorder or phobia from which the patient suffers stifles belief in the information presented to her, then the decision may not be a true one. ...

(5) The 'temporary factors' mentioned by Lord Donaldson MR in *Re T* (above) (confusion, shock, fatigue, pain or drugs) may completely erode capacity but those concerned must be satisfied that such factors are operating to such a degree that the ability to decide is absent.

---

[148] For discussion of the treatment of incompetent adult patients at common law see paras 6–100 et seq. On the particular facts, it was held to be in the mother's best interests to have the surgery, given that she wanted the child to be born alive and healthy (she was not opposed in principle to the surgery, it was only the needle phobia that prevented her from consenting) and there was psychiatric evidence that she was likely to suffer significant long-term damage if there was no operation and the child was born handicapped or died. Where an order declaring that it would be lawful to administer treatment to which the patient objects is granted the necessary corollary is that it would also be lawful to use reasonable force in the course of that treatment: [1997] 8 Med. L.R. 217 at 225; [1997] 2 F.L.R. 426 at 439.

(6)   Another such influence may be panic induced by fear. Again, careful scrutiny of the
        evidence is necessary because fear of an operation may be a rational reason for refusal
        to undergo it. Fear may also, however, paralyse the will and thus destroy the capacity
        to make a decision."[149]

In some cases, of which *Re MB (Medical Treatment)* is an example, the condition   **6–042**
from which the patient is suffering may affect his or her competence to make
decisions about treatment of that condition, even though in other respects the
individual is oriented in time and space and appears to be relating to the world in
a meaningful way. This is more likely to be the case with the treatment of certain
mental illnesses or disorders. In *Re W (A Minor) (Medical Treatment: Court's
Jurisdiction)*[150] the Court of Appeal doubted whether a 16-year-old girl suffering
from anorexia nervosa has sufficient understanding to make an informed decision
to refuse treatment, because it is a feature of anorexia nervosa that it is capable of
destroying the ability to make an informed choice. Similarly, in *Re KB (Adult)
(Mental Patient: Medical Treatment)*[151] an 18-and-a-half-year-old patient who
was suffering from anorexia nervosa had been detained under s.3 of the Mental
Health Act 1983. The health authority sought a declaration that naso-gastric
feeding was medical treatment for mental disorder within the meaning of s.63,
which provides that the consent of patients is not required for any medical
treatment given to them for a mental disorder from which they are suffering if the
treatment is given by or under the direction of the responsible medical officer.
Ewbank J held that in the circumstances naso-gastric feeding was treatment
envisaged by s.63, and does not require the consent of the patient. Moreover, K
was not competent to refuse consent. Her condition was such that without food
she would die within the next 14 to 21 days. K did not understand the true
situation; she saw the prospect of death as a long-term or theoretical prospect, and
she was aware that when she got close to death she was likely to be resuscitated
under the emergency provisions of the Act. She suffered from a severe mental
illness, and the treatment she was refusing was related to the mental illness, not to
some unconnected physical condition, as in *Re C.*, where:

"...his mental illness was wholly dissociated from the physical problem that he had and
therefore despite his mental illness he had the capacity to refuse treatment."[152]

Accordingly, K did not have the capacity to refuse consent to treatment.

Misperception of reality   *X NHS Trust v T (Adult Patient: Refusal of Medical*   **6–043**
Treatment)[153] provides a clear example of a patient who lacked competence
because of a misperception of reality. The patient had borderline personality
disorder and in the past had self-harmed by cutting herself, leading at times to

---

[149] [1997] 8 Med. L.R. 217 at 224; [1997] 2 F.L.R. 426 at 436–437. See also the comments of
Butler-Sloss P. in *Re B (Adult: Refusal of Medical Treatment)* [2002] EWHC 429 (Fam); [2002] 2 All
E.R. 449 at [35].
[150] [1993] Fam. 64.
[151] (1994) 19 B.M.L.R. 144.
[152] (1994) 19 B.M.L.R. 144 at 146 per Ewbank J. See also *B v Croydon Health Authority* [1995] Fam.
133, where on facts similar to *Re KB* the Court of Appeal agreed with Ewbank J's assessment that *Re
C* was distinguishable, because "the gangrene was entirely unconnected with the mental disorder".
[153] [2004] EWHC 1279 (Fam); [2005] 1 All E.R. 387; [2004] Lloyd's Rep. Med. 433.

dangerously low haemoglobin levels as result of blood loss. She had received emergency blood transfusions several times. She then signed a purported advance directive refusing consent to blood transfusions because she believed that her blood was evil and contaminated the transfused blood. Charles J held that the patient's references to her blood being evil indicated that she had a misconception of reality, and she was not competent to refuse consent. Similarly, in *Trust A v H (An Adult Patient)*[154] the patient, who suffered from schizophrenia, refused to accept the fact that she already had children and was refusing consent to surgery for an ovarian cyst that could have been cancerous because the treatment would leave her infertile and she wanted to have children in the future. Moreover, she simply did not appreciate the seriousness of her medical condition.

6–044   **Reduced capacity and patient's ambivalence**   Competence is not necessarily a question of all or nothing. The patient's capacity may be reduced in certain respects, for example because of the effects of drugs or the patient's physical condition. In these circumstances the patient's competence can vary with the gravity of the decision that has to be made.[155] Similarly, the patient may be ambivalent about whether or not to accept treatment. Of course, ambivalence may simply be a sign of careful deliberation by a competent individual about a difficult decision. In *Re B (Adult: Refusal of Medical Treatment)*[156] a 43-year-old woman, who was completely paralysed from the neck down, had been put on a ventilator after experiencing respiratory problems. She gave instructions to the hospital that she wanted the ventilator removed, even though she knew that it would almost certainly result in her death. It was suggested on behalf of the hospital that the fact that she had previously agreed to a procedure which involved weaning her from the ventilator over a period of time, although there was a less than 1 per cent chance of independent breathing being achieved, indicated a degree of ambivalence about her decision which undermined her capacity. Butler-Sloss P rejected the proposition, in the face of clear medical evidence that B was competent. The question of ambivalence might be relevant: "if, and only if, the ambivalence genuinely strikes at the root of the mental capacity of the patient."[157]

---

[154] [2006] EWHC 1230 (Fam); [2006] 2 F.L.R. 958. See also *Re PM; Health and Social Services Trust v PM and The Official Solicitor* [2007] NIFam 13—26-year-old patient with advanced kidney failure which, without treatment, would cause him to die within a period of weeks or months refused to accept that he had renal failure and refused to believe that he was at risk of death without treatment. Morgan J held that the patient was delusional and lacked capacity since he was unable to comprehend or retain the information communicated to him as to his condition and the likely consequences of not having treatment. Contrast *Kings College Hospital NHS Foundation Trust v C* [2015] EWCOP 80; [2016] C.O.P.L.R. 50 where a patient refusing dialysis was found to have capacity applying ss.2 and 3 of the Mental Capacity Act 2005.

[155] *Re T (Adult: Refusal of Treatment)* [1993] Fam. 95; see para.6–035 and para.6–173.

[156] [2002] EWHC 429 (Fam); [2002] 2 All E.R. 449.

[157] [2002] EWHC 429 (Fam); [2002] 2 All E.R. 449 at [35] per Butler-Sloss P. In *Re R. (A Minor) (Wardship: Consent to Treatment)* [1992] Fam. 11, a case concerning a 15-year-old girl, it was suggested that the fact that the patient's understanding fluctuated meant that she lacked the relevant capacity to consent. *Re R* was a very different case from *Re B*, with the teenager's mental state fluctuating quite frequently depending upon whether she took the prescribed medication for her mental health problem. Note also that the Mental Capacity Act 2005 s.3(3) specifically allows for the

(ii)   The test for capacity under the Mental Capacity Act 2005

The Mental Capacity Act 2005,[158] which applies only in relation to persons of 16 years or more,[159] provides a statutory definition of what constitutes incapacity. The starting point is that people must be assumed to have capacity unless it is established that they lack capacity.[160] The fact that they make a foolish decision, or a decision that others (such as medical professionals) disagree with, does not establish that they lack capacity. Thus, a "person is not to be treated as unable to make a decision merely because he makes an unwise decision".[161] There is also an emphasis on enabling patients to understand. Section 1(3) provides that:

6–045

> "A person is not to be treated as unable to make a decision unless all practicable steps to help him to do so have been taken without success."

Diagnostic test   The statutory test for capacity involves two stages. The first stage, usually referred to as the "diagnostic test", is set out in s.2(1):

6–046

> "...a person lacks capacity in relation to a matter if at the material time he is unable to make a decision for himself in relation to the matter because of an impairment of, or a disturbance in the functioning of the mind or brain..."

and it is irrelevant whether the impairment or disturbance is permanent or temporary.[162] A lack of capacity cannot be established by reference to people's

---

patient's competence to fluctuate: "The fact that a person is able to retain the information relevant to a decision for a short period only does not prevent him from being regarded as able to make the decision."

[158] See also the *Mental Capacity Act Code of Practice* (2007). Section 42(5) of the Act provides that if a provision of the Code or a failure to comply with the Code is relevant to a question arising in proceedings the court must take that into account in deciding the question. However, the Code provides guidance only, and it is the words of the statute that must be applied: *Mental Health Trust v DD* [2014] EWCOP 11; [2015] 1 F.L.R. 1430; (2014) 140 B.M.L.R. 118 at [156]. See also *RB (A Patient) v Brighton and Hove City Council* [2014] EWCA Civ 561; [2014] C.O.P.L.R. 629 at [64]–[65] and [87] where the Court of Appeal warned against reliance on previous cases when assessing capacity: the court must apply the provisions of the Act, not judicial glosses on the statute. See further D. Allen and C. Ettinger, "An Introduction to Carrying Out Assessments under the Mental Capacity Act" [2015] J.P.I.L. 252; M. Donnelly, "Capacity assessment under the Mental Capacity Act 2005: Delivering on the functional approach?" (2009) 29 L.S. 464; P. Case, "Negotiating the domain of mental capacity: clinical judgement or judicial diagnosis?" (2016) 16 Med. L. Int. 174.

[159] Mental Capacity Act 2005 s.2(5).

[160] Mental Capacity Act 2005 s.1(2).

[161] Mental Capacity Act 2005 s.1(4). In *York City Council v C* [2013] EWCA Civ 478; [2014] Fam. 10 at [53] McFarlane LJ commented that: "the court's jurisdiction is not founded upon professional concern as to the 'outcome' of an individual's decision." This is the case even if the patient's decision will result in their death. So in *Kings College Hospital NHS Foundation Trust v C* [2015] EWCOP 80; [2016] C.O.P.L.R. 50 at [30] MacDonald J said that: "the fact that a decision not to have life-saving medical treatment may be considered an unwise decision and may have a fatal outcome is not of itself evidence of a lack of capacity to take that decision, notwithstanding that other members of society may consider such a decision unreasonable, illogical or even immoral, that society in general places cardinal importance on the sanctity of life and that the decision taken will result in the certain death of the person taking it."

[162] Mental Capacity Act 2005 s.2(2).

age or appearance, or a condition, or an aspect of their behaviour, which might lead others to make unjustified assumptions about their capacity.[163]

6–047   **Functional test**   The second stage, usually referred to as the "functional test", is set out in s.3(1) which provides that people are unable to make decisions for themselves if they are unable:

(a)   to understand the information relevant to the decision;
(b)   to retain that information;
(c)   to use or weigh that information as part of the process of making the decision; or
(d)   to communicate their decision (whether by talking, using sign language or any other means).

Every issue of capacity which falls to be determined under the Act must be evaluated by applying s.3(1) in full and considering each of the four elements of the decision-making process set out at (a) to (d), but the extent to which, on the facts of any individual case, there is a need either for a sophisticated, or for a more straightforward, evaluation of these four elements will vary from case to case.[164] Section 3(1)(c)—the ability to use or weigh information as part of the process of making the decision—is often the critical element in assessing a patient's capacity, but it is important not to confuse a decision by the patient to attach little or no weight to a particular piece of information (e.g. that without medical treatment the prognosis is very poor) with an inability on her part to use and weigh that information.[165] The information relevant to a decision includes: "information about the reasonably foreseeable consequences of (a) deciding one way or another, or (b) failing to make the decision."[166] People cannot be treated as unable to understand the information relevant to a decision if they are able to understand an explanation given in a way that is appropriate their circumstances (using simple language, visual aids or any other means).[167] Any question of

---

[163] Mental Capacity Act 2005 s.2(3).
[164] *Re M (An Adult) (Capacity: Consent to Sexual Relations)* [2014] EWCA Civ 37; [2015] Fam. 61 at [73]. So the question whether an individual has capacity to enter into a sexual relationship will require a less sophisticated analysis than whether she has the capacity to refuse life-saving medical treatment. See [2014] EWCA Civ 37; [2015] Fam. 61 at [71]. This may mean that a different emphasis is given to the elements of s.3(1) depending on the nature of the decision to be made: "It is important to emphasise that s. 3(1)(c) of the Act refers to the ability to use or weigh information as part of the process of making the decision. In some circumstances, having understood and retained relevant information, an ability to use it will be what is critical; in others, it will be necessary to be able to weigh competing considerations", [2014] EWCA Civ 37; [2015] Fam. 61 at [52]. See further on the capacity to consent to sexual relations: *Derbyshire CC v AC* [2014] EWCOP 38 at [28]–[36]; *Tower Hamlets LBC v TB* [2014] EWCOP 53; [2015] C.O.P.L.R. 87; *Luton BC v B* [2015] EWHC 3534 (Fam); [2017] 4 W.L.R. 61; and *London Borough of Southwark v KA* [2016] EWCOP 20; [2016] C.O.P.L.R. 461. For comment on *Re M* see J. Herring and J. Wall, "Capacity to Consent to Sex" (2014) 22 Med. L. Rev. 620.
[165] *Kings College Hospital NHS Foundation Trust v C* [2015] EWCOP 80; [2016] C.O.P.L.R. 50 at [86] per MacDonald J.
[166] Mental Capacity Act 2005 s.3(4).
[167] Mental Capacity Act 2005 s.3(2).

whether a person lacks capacity must be decided on the balance of probabilities.[168] There is no requirement that a person's lack of capacity must be established by psychiatric evidence.[169]

Causal link   Although the statutory test tends to be approached in two stages (s.2(1) and then s.3(1)) in *York City Council v C*[170] McFarlane LJ emphasised that s.2(1) is "the single test, albeit that it falls to be interpreted by applying the more detailed description given around it in ss.2 and 3". This was because there is a danger in structuring the decision by looking to s.2(1) primarily as requiring a finding of mental impairment and nothing more, and then going on to look at s.3(1) as requiring a finding of inability to make a decision: **6–048**

> "The danger is that the strength of the causative nexus between mental impairment and inability to decide is watered down. That sequence—'mental impairment' and then 'inability to make a decision'—is the reverse of that in s.2(1)—'unable to make a decision ... *because of* an impairment of, or a disturbance in the functioning of, the mind or brain'. The danger in using s.2(1) simply to collect the mental health element is that the key words 'because of' in s.2(1) may lose their prominence..."[171]

This does not mean that the impairment of, or disturbance in the functioning of the mind or brain has to be the sole cause of the patient's inability to make a decision, since this would result in the illogical conclusion that where there were other factors the test in s.2 would not apply.[172] The test is:

> "...whether the impairment/disturbance of mind is an effective, material or operative cause. Does it cause the incapacity, even if other factors come into play? This is a purposive construction."[173]

Variable capacity   As at common law, the determination of capacity under the Act is decision specific.[174] An individual may at the same time have capacity to   **6–049**

---

168 Mental Capacity Act 2005 s.2(4). Although considerable importance will attach to the views of independent experts, it is for the court to make the decision about a person's capacity: *WBC v Z* [2016] EWCOP 4 at [69] per Cobb J ("the expert advises and the court decides").

169 *G v E* [2010] EWCA Civ 822; [2012] Fam. 78 at [61]: "Provided there is credible expert evidence upon which the court can be satisfied that the individual concerned lacks capacity that, in our judgment, is sufficient. It would simply be unreal to require psychiatric evidence in every case, quite apart from the fact that it would, in some cases, be irrelevant."

170 [2013] EWCA Civ 478; [2014] Fam. 10 at [56]; P. Skowron, "Evidence and Causation in Mental Capacity Assessments" (2014) 22 Med. L. Rev. 631.

171 [2013] EWCA Civ 478; [2014] Fam. 10 at [58] (emphasis added by McFarlane LJ). On the facts of *York City Council v C* the judge's conclusion that P had capacity to marry (and indeed capacity to undertake most other aspects of daily life, other than to litigate) but lacked capacity to decide to live with her husband was overturned. There was no clear and cogent evidence that she was "unable to make a decision for herself in relation to" re-establishing cohabitation with her husband. The evidence did not explain why she was said to be unable to understand the potential risk that her husband presented and was unable to weigh up the relevant information in relation to cohabiting, but she was able to do so with respect to other aspects of her life.

172 *Norfolk CC v PB* [2014] EWCOP 14; [2015] C.O.P.L.R. 118 at [84] per Parker J.

173 [2014] EWCOP 14; [2015] C.O.P.L.R. 118 at [86].

174 *York City Council v C* [2013] EWCA Civ 478; [2014] Fam. 10 at [35]; *Re M (An Adult) (Capacity: Consent to Sexual Relations)* [2014] EWCA Civ 37; [2015] Fam. 61 at [23].

make one decision but not to make another, more complex, decision. Capacity is also time specific. Section 3(3) of the Act provides that the

> "...fact that a person is able to retain the information relevant to a decision for a short period only does not prevent him from being regarded as able to make the decision."

This allows for those situations where individuals' capacity fluctuates. Provided they have the relevant capacity at the time they make the decision, the fact that at other times they lack capacity is irrelevant to the validity of that decision.[175]

6–050   **The presumption of capacity**   The courts should guard against setting the test of capacity too high because to do so runs the risk of discriminating against persons suffering from a mental disability.[176] The Act places a strong emphasis on the presumption of capacity and seeks to counter the potential prejudices that may lead to false assumptions by those making assessments of a patient's capacity (such as doctors and judges). So, the burden of proof that a patient lacks capacity rests with the person asserting it and patients should be facilitated to make capacitous decisions. A decision to refuse recommended treatment, whether perceived to be reasonable or foolish, is not indicative of a lack of capacity, and a patient suffering from a mental disorder does not necessarily lack capacity.[177] For example, in *Re SB (A patient: capacity to consent to termination)*[178] the patient

---

[175] *A Local Authority v TZ* [2014] EWHC 973 (COP); [2014] C.O.P.L.R. 159 at [25]. Section 2(1) provides that people lack capacity in relation to a matter "if at the material time" they are unable to make a decision for themselves. In a case that is litigated the material time will be the date on which the court is considering capacity: [2014] EWHC 973 (COP); [2014] C.O.P.L.R. 159 at [25] per Baker J.

[176] *PH v A Local Authority* [2011] EWHC 1704 (Fam) at [16xi] per Baker J; *Wandsworth Clinical Commissioning Group v IA* [2014] EWHC 990 (COP); (2014) 139 B.M.L.R. 180 at [37] per Cobb J; *Mental Health Trust v DD* [2014] EWCOP 11; [2015] 1 F.L.R. 1430; (2014) 140 B.M.L.R. 118 at [62] per Cobb J. It will not always be necessary for a person to comprehend all the peripheral detail provided they can comprehend and weigh the salient details relevant to the decision to be made: *L v J* [2010] EWHC 2665 (COP); [2011] 1 F.L.R. 1279 at [24], [58] per Macur J; *CC v KK & STCC* [2012] EWHC 2136 (COP) at [22], [69] per Baker J; *WBC v Z* [2016] EWCOP 4 at [12], [61] per Cobb J. In *A Local Authority v A* [2010] EWHC 1549 (Fam); [2011] Fam. 61. Bodey J held that for the purposes of capacity to consent to contraceptive treatment the patient should have the ability to understand and weigh up the immediate medical issues (including the reason for contraception and what it does; the types available and how each is used; the advantages and disadvantages of each type; the possible side effects of each and how they can be dealt with; how easily each type can be changed; and the generally accepted effectiveness of each). But it did not require an understanding of what bringing up a child would be like in practice, how she would be likely to cope, nor whether any child would be likely to be removed from her care. "To apply the wider test would be to 'set the bar too high' and would risk a move away from personal autonomy in the direction of social engineering" (at [63]). Commenting on this in *RB (A Patient) v Brighton and Hove City Council* [2014] EWCA Civ 561; [2014] C.O.P.L.R. 629 at [42] Jackson LJ noted that: "All long term decisions are made on the basis of peering into an unknown future. Any court applying the test set out in section 3 is imposing an impossible burden if it requires the person to understand and weigh up all information relevant to such decision."

[177] "... the intention of the Act is to allow a protected person as far as possible to make the same mistakes as all other human beings are at liberty to make and not infrequently do": *Re M (An Adult) (Capacity: Consent to Sexual Relations)* [2014] EWCA Civ 37; [2015] Fam. 61 at [88]. Or as Russell J put it in *A London Borough v G* [2014] EWHC 485 (COP); [2014] C.O.P.L.R. 292 at [70]: "People are entitled to mess up their own lives regardless of the opinions of others."

[178] [2013] EWHC 1417 (COP); [2013] 3 F.C.R. 384; (2013) 133 B.M.L.R. 110.

suffered from bi-polar disorder. She stopped taking medication for her condition when she became pregnant and her mental health deteriorated with the result that she developed paranoid or delusional views about her husband and mother. She decided that she wanted to have the pregnancy terminated, but the psychiatric evidence was that her delusional beliefs meant that she lacked capacity to take that decision on the basis that she was unable to use or weigh the information about her family and was not processing information about the reasonably foreseeable consequences of a decision to terminate the pregnancy. Holman J disagreed. Even if, said his Lordship, aspects of the decision-making were influenced by paranoid thoughts in relation to her husband and her mother, she was nevertheless able to describe, and genuinely held, a range of rational reasons for her decision.[179] She had defended and justified her decision when challenged, and maintained her decision for some time. Holman J concluded that it would be a "total affront to the autonomy of this patient" to hold that she lacked capacity to the level required to make the decision.

Adolescents/young adults   The Mental Capacity Act applies to individuals aged 16 and over.[180] Young people have a tendency to take risks that more mature reflection might suggest is unwise, but such behaviour may be "an inherent, inevitable, and perhaps necessary part of adolescence and early adulthood experience".[181] In assessing whether a young person lacks capacity the court should seek to separate out, insofar as it is possible, evidence of the "normal" unhealthy, dangerous, unwise risk-taking of adolescents and young adults from the evidence which points to a lack of capacity.[182]   **6–051**

Refusing amputation   In *Heart of England NHS Foundation Trust v JB*[183] the facts were very similar to those of *Re C (Adult: Refusal of Treatment)*.[184] The 62-year-old patient suffered from paranoid schizophrenia and peripheral vascular disease. Her foot developed gangrene and eventually detached from her leg leaving an unresolved wound. The surgeons considered that an amputation was necessary to allow the wound to be closed and to prevent it becoming infected, though at different times the medical opinion shifted between amputation below the knee, through the knee or above the knee. The patient refused consent to amputation on some occasions, though on others she apparently agreed and had signed a consent form for an above-knee amputation two days before the   **6–052**

---

[179] [2013] EWHC 1417 (COP); [2013] 3 F.C.R. 384; (2013) 133 B.M.L.R. 110 at [44]. Holman J continued: "When I say rational, I do not necessarily say they are good reasons, nor do I indicate whether I agree with her decision, for section 1(4) of the Act expressly provides that someone is not to be treated as unable to make a decision simply because it is an unwise decision." In *A London Borough v G* [2014] EWHC 485 (COP); [2014] C.O.P.L.R. 292 at [76] Russell J, in a case involving the mental capacity of a frail 94-year-old lady, started with the presumption of capacity and so ignored "the wisdom or otherwise of allowing strangers to live in her house and control her finances", though went on to conclude from other evidence that she did lack capacity.

[180] Mental Capacity Act 2005 s.2(5).

[181] *WBC v Z* [2016] EWCOP 4 at [1] per Cobb J.

[182] [2016] EWCOP 4 at [67]. In addition, "naivety, immaturity, diffidence or embarrassment may well not translate into (or necessarily evidence) a lack of capacity": [2016] EWCOP 4 at [41].

[183] [2014] EWHC 342 (COP); (2014) 137 B.M.L.R. 232.

[184] [1994] 1 W.L.R. 290; para.6–040.

application to court. The doctors were unsure whether the patient had capacity and the hospital applied for declaration that the patient lacked capacity, that it would be in her best interests to have a through-knee amputation, and for her to be sedated if she resisted. Peter Jackson J started his judgment with a reminder of the importance of these issues:

> "The right to decide whether or not to consent to medical treatment is one of the most important rights guaranteed by law. Few decisions are as significant as the decision about whether to have major surgery ... Such decisions are intensely personal. They are taken in stressful circumstances. There are no right or wrong answers. The freedom to choose for oneself is a part of what it means to be a human being."[185]

Any temptation to base a judgment of a person's capacity upon whether they seem to have made a good or bad decision, and in particular upon whether they have accepted or rejected medical advice, was absolutely to be avoided. "That would be to put the cart before the horse..."[186] The question was whether the patient could understand, retain, use and weigh the relevant information in coming to a decision. In reaching a view on this, as in *Re C*, what was required was:

> "...that she should understand the nature, purpose and effects of the proposed treatment, the last of these entailing an understanding of the benefits and risks of deciding to have or not to have one or other of the various kinds of amputation, or of not making a decision at all."[187]

This required a broad, general understanding of the kind expected from the population at large. Moreover:

> "...common strategies for dealing with unpalatable dilemmas—for example indecision, avoidance or vacillation—are not to be confused with incapacity. We should not ask more of people whose capacity is questioned than of those whose capacity is undoubted."[188]

JB's tendency at times to be uncommunicative or avoidant and to minimise the risks of inaction were understandable human ways of dealing with her predicament and did not amount to incapacity.[189] Incapacity could not be deduced from isolated instances of eccentric reasoning; nor could it be inferred from her

---

[185] [2014] EWHC 342 (COP); (2014) 137 B.M.L.R. 232 at [1].
[186] [2014] EWHC 342 (COP); (2014) 137 B.M.L.R. 232 at [7], an observation repeated at [27]: "There is a danger that in a difficult case like this the patient is regarded as capable of making a decision that follows medical advice but incapable of making one that does not." In *A Local Authority v TZ* [2014] EWHC 973 (COP); [2014] C.O.P.L.R. 159 at [28] Baker J commented that: "In a case involving a vulnerable adult, there is a risk that all professionals involved with treating and helping that person—including, of course, a judge in the Court of Protection—may feel drawn towards an outcome that is more protective of the adult and thus, in certain circumstances, fail to carry out an assessment of capacity that is detached and objective." Baker J expressed a similar concern in *PH v A Local Authority* [2011] EWHC 1704 (Fam) at [16xiii]. In *Wandsworth Clinical Commissioning Group v IA* [2014] EWHC 990 (COP); (2014) 139 B.M.L.R. 180 the patient had made unwise decisions about his medical treatment in the past, before he had suffered a brain injury, and so they could not be attributed to his acquired cognitive deficit. They did not demonstrate a lack of capacity, but were more reflective of his rather challenging personality (at [69]).
[187] [2014] EWHC 342 (COP); (2014) 137 B.M.L.R. 232 at [24].
[188] [2014] EWHC 342 (COP); (2014) 137 B.M.L.R. 232 at [25].
[189] [2014] EWHC 342 (COP); (2014) 137 B.M.L.R. 232 at [38].

lack of capacity in relation to treatment for her mental illness since there was no necessary correlation between a lack of insight into schizophrenia and incapacity to decide about surgery; nor from the fact that she had changed her position from refusal of all surgery to a willingness to contemplate an operation of some kind.[190] Peter Jackson J concluded that JB undoubtedly had a disturbance in the functioning of her mind in the form of paranoid schizophrenia (as to which she lacked insight), but that it had not been established that she thereby lacked the capacity to make a decision about surgery for herself.

In contrast to *Heart of England NHS Foundation Trust v JB*, in *Surrey and Sussex Healthcare NHS Trust v AB*[191] Keehan J granted a declaration that the patient, JB, lacked capacity to decide whether or not to undergo an above the knee amputation because she had no understanding that the alternative to amputation was death. She had persistent delusional beliefs that the medical staff had caused all of the problems with her foot and that if she were left to her own devices and allowed to go home, all would be well.[192]

6–053

Anorexia nervosa   As with the cases that have arisen for determination at common law, patients suffering from severe anorexia nervosa have invariably been found to lack capacity under the Mental Capacity Act 2005 in respect of decisions to refuse treatment for the condition. For example, in *A Local Authority v E*[193] the patient was a 32-year-old woman suffering from severe intractable anorexia nervosa who was on the verge of death. She also suffered from alcoholism, a personality disorder, and an addiction to medically prescribed opiates. She was being treated under a palliative care regime the purpose of which was to allow her to die in comfort. There were only two options available to the Court: forcible feeding or allowing E to die from starvation. Peter Jackson J noted that there was no doubt that E had an impairment of, or a disturbance in

6–054

---

[190] [2014] EWHC 342 (COP); (2014) 137 B.M.L.R. 232 at [40].

[191] [2015] EWCOP 50.

[192] "She does not accept and does not understand the true nature of her medical condition. She does not accept and does not understand that, absent the proposed surgery, she will die. In the absence of such understanding and acceptance, resulting from her delusional disorder, she is wholly incapable of making a decision about her medical treatment and surgery", [2015] EWCOP 50 at [57]. The judge went on to hold that it was in the patient's best interests to undergo the amputation, though it does not always follow that it is in the best interests of a patient lacking capacity to undergo an amputation, even where the alternative is death: see *Wye Valley NHS Trust v B* [2015] EWCOP 60; [2015] Med. L.R. 552; (2015) 147 B.M.L.R. 187, paras 6–132 and 6–180.

[193] [2012] EWHC 1639 (Fam); [2012] 2 F.C.R. 523; [2012] Med. L.R. 472; commented on by Coggon, "Anorexia Nervosa, Best Interests, and the Patient's Human Right to 'A Wholesale Overwhelming of Her Autonomy'" (2014) 22 Med. L. Rev. 119. See also *NHS Trust v L* [2012] EWHC 2741 (COP)—patient with severe anorexia nervosa (with end stage organ damage) found to lack capacity with regard to medical treatment in the form of nutrition and hydration and the administration of dextrose for hypoglycaemic episodes, though she did have capacity to make decisions about antibiotic treatment for infections, analgesia and treatment for pressure sores; *Re W (Medical Treatment: Anorexia)* [2016] EWCOP 13; (2016) 151 B.M.L.R. 220—28-year-old woman with severe and unremitting anorexia nervosa lacked capacity. In *A NHS Foundation Trust v X* [2014] EWCOP 35; [2015] C.O.P.L.R. 11; (2014) 140 B.M.L.R. 41 Cobb J also concluded that a patient with severe anorexia nervosa lacked capacity to make decisions about the treatment of her anorexia, but did have capacity in relation to the management/treatment of her alcohol dependence disorder. For comment see J. Coggon (2015) 23 Med. L. Rev. 659; D. Wang (2015) 78 M.L.R. 871.

the functioning of, the mind or brain in the form of her anorexia. She was able to understand and retain the information relevant to the treatment decision and could communicate her decision. However, her obsessive fear of weight gain made her incapable of weighing the advantages and disadvantages of eating in any meaningful way: "The need not to gain weight overpowers all other thoughts."[194] She was also subject to strong sedative medication and was in a severely weakened condition. Peter Jackson J concluded that E lacked capacity, whilst also acknowledging that:

"...a person with severe anorexia may be in a Catch 22 situation regarding capacity: namely, that by deciding not to eat, she proves that she lacks capacity to decide at all."[195]

A patient's lack of capacity in respect of treatment for anorexia does not necessarily mean that the patient lacks capacity with respect to the treatment of other, co-morbid conditions.[196]

6–055   **Obstetric care**   Patients with a mental disorder who are also pregnant are not necessarily to be treated as lacking capacity in relation to decisions about their obstetric care, though the courts appear to set the bar quite high in terms of what a pregnant woman must be able to understand and weigh up in reaching such decisions. For example, in *Mental Health Trust v DD*[197] Cobb J considered that in relation to the mode of delivery of the baby a pregnant woman would have to be able to understand, retain and weigh a significant amount of information. This included, but was not necessarily limited to: (i) antenatal care and monitoring, including blood tests to check for anaemia and diabetes; urine tests to check for infections; the benefits of discussion with health services about delivery options; (ii) antenatal monitoring of the foetus; the value of ultrasound imaging; (iii) mode of delivery of the baby, including vaginal delivery, and Caesarean section; (iv) natural and/or induced labour; (v) anaesthesia and pain relief; (vi) the place of delivery—e.g. at home or in a hospital—and the risks and benefits of each option; (vii) the risk of complications, arising from conditions relevant to the mother or the baby; and (viii) postnatal care of mother and baby. The circumstances in which the patient finds herself may, in some instances, also contribute to the conclusion that she is not in a position to weigh the relevant information, even if she understands it.[198]

---

[194] [2012] EWHC 1639 (Fam); [2012] 2 F.C.R. 523; [2012] Med.L.R. 472 at [49].

[195] [2012] EWHC 1639 (Fam); [2012] 2 F.C.R. 523; [2012] Med.L.R. 472 at [53]. The judge also took the view that E had lacked capacity when she had completed advance decisions to refuse life-saving interventions: see para.6–030.

[196] See, e.g., *NHS Trust v L* [2012] EWHC 2741 (COP) and *A NHS Foundation Trust v X* [2014] EWCOP 35; [2015] C.O.P.L.R. 11; (2014) 140 B.M.L.R. 41, n.193 above.

[197] [2014] EWCOP 11; [2015] 1 F.L.R. 1430; (2014) 140 B.M.L.R. 118 at [69].

[198] As, e.g., in *Rochdale Healthcare NHS Trust v C* [1997] 1 F.C.R. 274 where a woman who was refusing a Caesarean section delivery was found to lack capacity when she was in the throes of labour with all the pain and emotional stress that that involved. Johnson J considered that a patient who appeared to be able to accept the inevitability of her own death was not capable of giving full consideration to the options available.

Religious beliefs and capacity   Section 3(1)(c) provides that people will lack   6–056
capacity if they are unable to use or weigh the relevant information as part of the
process of decision-making. However, someone who takes a particular view of
whether or not to accept treatment based on a belief conditioned by religious
convictions may well be unwilling to engage in a process of "weighing" the
information.[199] This is particularly true of, for example, Jehovah's Witness
patients who object to medical treatment with blood or blood products. For
someone who is committed to this religious belief there is simply no weighing to
be done. In *Nottinghamshire Healthcare NHS Trust v RC*[200] Mostyn J said that
this particular aspect of the test for capacity must be applied very cautiously and
carefully when religious beliefs are in play. It would, said his Lordship,

> "...be an extreme example of the application of the law of unintended consequences were an
> iron tenet of an accepted religion to give rise to questions of capacity under the MCA."

As a consequence the judge placed "little emphasis" on the fact that a tenet of the
patient's religious faith prevented him from weighing the advantages of a blood
transfusion.[201]

Coercion or duress   The common law requires that for a valid consent the   6–057
person must both have capacity to consent and consent freely. A patient's consent
may be vitiated by the undue influence of a third party if the evidence
demonstrates that the patient's will has been overborne.[202] Under the Mental
Capacity Act 2005 if there is evidence that a patient is subject to coercion or
duress the court may conclude that he lacks *capacity* on the basis that although,
for the purposes of s.3(1) he can understand and retain the information, he is
unable to use or weigh the information as part of the decision-making process.[203]
However, this can only apply where the diagnostic test of s.2(1) is satisfied, i.e.
there is evidence of impairment of, or a disturbance in the functioning of the
mind or brain. If there is no impairment of, or a disturbance in the functioning of
the mind or brain, there can be no incapacity under the terms of the Act. In those
circumstances, if the patient's will is being overborne by coercion or duress the
court retains an inherent common law jurisdiction for the protection of adults
who are "vulnerable" but who may not lack capacity.[204]

---

[199] Though a patient's unwillingness to attach weight to information does not have to be based on a
religious belief. In *Kings College Hospital NHS Foundation Trust v C* [2015] EWCOP 80; [2016]
C.O.P.L.R. 50 at [38] McDonald J noted that s.3(1)(c) is engaged where a person is *unable* to use and
weigh the relevant information as part of the process of making the decision. If the court is satisfied
that a person is *able* to use and weigh the relevant information, the weight to be attached to that
information in the decision-making process is a matter for the decision maker. Thus: "a person cannot
be considered to be unable to use and weigh information simply on the basis that he or she has applied
his or her own values or outlook to that information in making the decision in question and chosen to
attach no weight to that information in the decision making process."

[200] [2014] EWCOP 1317; [2014] Med. L.R. 260; (2014) 138 B.M.L.R. 147 at [34].

[201] [2014] EWCOP 1317; [2014] Med. L.R. 260; (2014) 138 B.M.L.R. 147 at [35]. The patient was
found to have capacity to refuse treatment with blood products.

[202] *Re T (Adult: Refusal of Treatment)* [1993] Fam. 95, para.6–035.

[203] *A Local Authority v A* [2010] EWHC 1549 (Fam); [2011] Fam. 61 at [66]; *Norfolk CC v PB*
[2014] EWCOP 14; [2015] C.O.P.L.R. 118 at [106].

[204] See para.6–149.

(c) Information

(i) *Information in broad terms about the nature of the procedure*

6–058　　In order to be capable of understanding the nature of the procedure to which they are consenting patients must have some information about the procedure itself.[205] In *Chatterton v Gerson*[206] the claimant suffered from chronic and intractable pain in the area surrounding an operation scar, following a hernia operation. The defendant was a specialist in the treatment of pain, and he administered an intrathecal injection of a solution of phenol and glycerine near the spinal cord with the object of destroying the pain-conducting nerves near the hernia operation site. The operation only relieved the pain temporarily, and the claimant had a second spinal injection given by the same surgeon. This was also unsuccessful in relieving the pain but the claimant's right leg was rendered completely numb, which impaired her mobility. The defendant's practice was to explain to patients that the treatment involved numbness at the site of the pain and a larger surrounding area, and might involve temporary loss of muscle power. The claimant argued that because she had not been informed about the inherent risk of side effects materialising from her treatment, her consent was vitiated and the doctor was liable in battery for all the adverse consequences of her treatment. Bristow J said that in order to vitiate the reality of consent there must be a greater failure of communication between doctor and patient than that involved in a breach of duty if the claim is based on negligence. Accordingly, once the patient was "informed in broad terms of the nature of the procedure which is intended, and gives her consent, that consent is real", and the cause of action on which to base a claim for failure to discuss the risks and implications of a procedure was negligence, not trespass.[207] Miss Chatterton was under no illusion as to the general nature of the proposed procedure, and therefore her consent was not unreal.

6–059　　*Chatterton v Gerson* was the first attempt to introduce into this country the doctrine of informed consent through the action for battery. From the claimant's point of view battery was perceived as having distinct advantages over a claim in negligence (with corresponding disadvantages for defendants). Battery, as a form of trespass, is actionable per se and so does not require proof of damage, although if claimants seek more than nominal damages they will have to establish that the loss was a direct result of the unlawful force. In the absence of consent it is clear that the medical procedure and any complications arising from it are the direct result of the battery. Secondly, once it is established that the patient's consent was invalid, it does not have to be proved that the patient would not have accepted the treatment had he been informed about the inherent risks of the procedure, which

---

[205] See the quotation from *Bowater v Rowley Regis Corporation* [1944] K.B. 476 at 479 cited above, para.6–033, n.115. Patients may be estopped from denying that they have the relevant information if they so act as to lead the defendant reasonably to assume that the information was known to them: *Sidaway v Bethlem Royal Hospital Governors* [1985] A.C. 871 at 894, per Lord Diplock.

[206] [1981] Q.B. 432.

[207] [1981] Q.B. 432 at 443.

is an essential element of a claim based in negligence.[208] Thirdly, medical evidence as to the profession's usual disclosure practice is considered to be irrelevant to a claim based in battery, again because once the consent is vitiated the tort is committed. A final factor, which was clearly influential in the courts' hostility to actions in battery, is the perception of trespass as an intentional tort. It was considered inappropriate that doctors, acting in good faith, should be held liable for an intentional tort.

The view that a failure to discuss or explain the risks of the proposed treatment, or alternatives to that treatment, goes to the doctor's duty of care in negligence, not trespass to the person, was adopted in *Hills v Potter*[209] where it was held that the claimant's undoubted consent to the operation which was in fact performed negatived liability in battery.[210] This approach has been affirmed by the Court of Appeal. In *Sidaway v Bethlem Royal Hospital Governors* Sir John Donaldson MR said that:

6–060

> "I am wholly satisfied that as a matter of English law a consent is not vitiated by a failure on the part of the doctor to give the patient sufficient information before the consent is given."[211]

Once the patient has been informed in broad terms of the nature of the treatment, consent in fact amounts to consent in law.[212] A similar attitude to battery is apparent in the Canadian[213] and Irish[214] courts.

Thus, the courts have drawn a distinction between a lack of information which concerns the *nature* of the procedure (which gives rise to an action in battery) and a lack of information about the risks associated with the procedure (where the action must be based in negligence[215]). It has been forcefully argued that this distinction is untenable: it assumes an inherent difference in terminology and substance between the nature of the treatment and the risks inherent in the treatment.[216] Some risks may be so significant that they relate to the *nature* of the operation itself, so that non-disclosure of the risk would vitiate the consent and lead to liability in battery. It is not self-evident what the "nature" of any particular medical treatment consists of, nor that, for example, a high risk of serious

6–061

---

[208] See para.7–081.

[209] [1983] 3 All E.R. 716 at 728; *Freeman v Home Office* [1984] Q.B. 524 at 537, per McCowan J.

[210] Hirst J said that he deplored reliance on trespass to the person in medical cases of this kind, a dictum that was approved by Lord Scarman in *Sidaway v Bethlem Royal Hospital Governors* [1985] A.C. 871 at 883. See also *The Creutzfeldt-Jakob Disease Litigation* (1995) 54 B.M.L.R. 1, per May J.

[211] [1984] Q.B. 493 at 511; see also per Dunn LJ at 515, and Browne-Wilkinson LJ at 519.

[212] *Freeman v Home Office* [1984] Q.B. 524 at 556, per Sir John Donaldson MR.

[213] *Reibl v Hughes* (1980) 114 D.L.R. (3d) 1 at 10–11, SCC, per Laskin CJC: "I can appreciate the temptation to say that the genuineness of consent to medical treatment depends on proper disclosure of the risks which it entails, but in my view, unless there has been misrepresentation or fraud to secure consent to the treatment, a failure to disclose the attendant risks, however serious, should go to negligence rather than battery." *White v Turner* (1981) 120 D.L.R. (3d) 269 at 283, Ont HC, per Linden J; aff'd (1982) 12 D.L.R. (4th) 319, Ont CA: "The future use of battery is, therefore, limited to cases involving a real lack of consent. Where there has been a basic consent to the treatment, there is no place left for discussions of battery."

[214] *Walsh v Family Planning Services Ltd* [1992] 1 I.R. 496 at 512, 531, Supreme Court of Ireland.

[215] See Ch.7.

[216] Tan (1987) 7 L.S. 149; see also Somerville (1981) 26 McGill LJ 740, 742–52.

consequences is not part and parcel of the "nature" of the procedure.[217] It depends, ultimately, on how one chooses to characterise the nature of any particular activity and the level of abstraction that is adopted.

6–062   Moreover, it is arguable that the Mental Capacity Act 2005 has altered the basis on which the courts should approach this issue. Section 3(1) provides that when assessing a person's capacity a patient is required to understand, retain and use the information relevant to the decision, *in order to be found to have the capacity to make a decision for himself.* Section 3(4) provides that the information relevant to a decision includes "information about the reasonably foreseeable consequences of (a) deciding one way or another, or (b) failing to make the decision". If patients are not actually given this information, it may be difficult to say that they can understand and use it to make a decision, for the purpose of assessing their capacity. Thus, the practical consequence of the Mental Capacity Act 2005 is that patients will have to be given this information, and it is certainly arguable that the reasonably foreseeable consequences of deciding one way or another or failing to make a decision includes some consideration of the risks associated with the treatment options. It is not obvious that this should be limited to information in broad terms about the nature of the procedure.

(ii)   Fraud and misrepresentation

6–063   It is said that if the patient's consent has been obtained by fraud or misrepresentation then it is not a valid consent.[218] Thus, in *Sidaway v Bethlem Royal Hospital Governors* Sir John Donaldson MR said that:

> "It is only if the consent is obtained by fraud or by misrepresentation of the nature of what is to be done that it can be said that an apparent consent is not a true consent. This is the position in the criminal law ... and the cause of action based on trespass to the person is closely analogous."[219]

It is not clear what would constitute fraud or misrepresentation. Must it relate to the nature of the procedure to vitiate consent or will fraud as to the consequences or risks suffice? Sir John Donaldson MR appears to require misrepresentation as to the nature of the procedure: "only if the consent is obtained by fraud or by misrepresentation of the nature of what is to be done". But if the claimant does not consent to the *nature* of what is done the consent is not real, *irrespective of*

---

[217] "In some cases it may be difficult to distinguish, and separate out, the matter of consequential or collateral risks from the basic nature and character of the operation or procedure to be performed ... The more probable the risk the more it could be said to be an integral feature of the nature and character of the operation", per Morden J in *Kelly v Hazlett* (1976) 75 D.L.R. (3d) 536 at 559; cf. the comments of Laskin CJC in *Reibl v Hughes* (1980) 114 D.L.R. (3d) 1 at 9.

[218] "Of course, if information is withheld in bad faith, the consent will be vitiated by fraud", per Bristow J in *Chatterton v Gerson* [1981] Q.B. 432 at 443.

[219] [1984] Q.B. 493 at 511, citing *R. v Clarence* (1888) 22 Q.B.D. 23 at 43 (note, however, that *R. v Clarence* was overruled by the Court of Appeal in *R. v Dica* [2004] EWCA Crim 1103; [2004] Q.B. 1257); see also *Freeman v Home Office* [1984] Q.B. 524 at 537, per McCowan J, and the comment of Sir John Donaldson MR, [1984] Q.B. 524 at 556: "Consent would not be real if procured by fraud or misrepresentation ..."

the reason why.[220] The defendant's motive, whether "fraudulent" or in good faith, is irrelevant. This might suggest that if the exception is to have any meaning it should also include fraud or misrepresentation as to consequences or risks. This certainly appears to have been the view of Laskin CJC delivering the judgment of the Supreme Court of Canada in *Reibl v Hughes*:

> "...unless there has been misrepresentation or fraud to secure consent to the treatment, *a failure to disclose the attendant risks*, however serious, should go to negligence rather than battery."[221]

On this approach misrepresentation as to risks would vitiate the reality of the patient's consent.

Criminal law In the criminal law fraud vitiates consent only where the claimant's mistake concerns the real nature of the transaction.[222] There is no obvious justification, however, for applying the criminal law rule in tort, since it is unduly favourable to the defendant.[223] The consequences of an act are often the crucial factor in the granting of a genuine consent. Except in a dire emergency, no one would consent to major surgery by someone who was not trained to perform it. If the defendant obtained the claimant's consent to an operation by misrepresenting his ability to carry it out, it is difficult to see why the claimant's consent should not be regarded as vitiated by the misrepresentation, even though there is no mistake as to the nature of the act (surgery).[224]

6–064

---

[220] Tan (1987) 7 L.S. 149, 156 makes this point: "There is no magic in the character of the conduct concealing or distorting medical advice for [the] purpose of the defence of consent. The misconduct only gives occasion to the concealment. What is material is the content of the medical advice that is concealed, not the mode of concealment."

[221] (1980) 114 D.L.R. (3d) 1 at 10–11, emphasis added.

[222] For example, persuading a girl to have sexual intercourse by representing to her that it is a surgical operation: *R. v Flattery* (1877) 2 Q.B.D. 410; *R. v Williams* [1923] 1 K.B. 340. The view that the fraud must go to the nature and quality of the act, rather than its consequences, has led to the conclusion that where a woman consented to sexual intercourse, unaware that her partner was suffering from venereal disease, her ignorance of the risk of infection did not invalidate her consent, so that neither a criminal assault (*R. v Clarence* (1888) 22 Q.B.D. 23) nor the tort of battery (*Hegarty v Shine* (1878) 14 Cox C.C. 124 at 145) was committed. However, in *R. v Dica* [2004] EWCA Crim 1103; [2004] Q.B. 1257 the Court of Appeal held that a defendant who, knowing that he was suffering from a serious sexual disease (he was HIV positive) recklessly transmitted it through consensual sexual intercourse could be guilty of inflicting grievous bodily harm, contrary to s.20 of the Offences against the Person Act 1861, and that consent to sexual intercourse could not, in itself, be regarded as consent to the risk of consequent disease (although if the victim did in fact consent to the risk that would be a defence). *R. v Clarence* was overruled. See also *R. v Cort* [2003] EWCA Crim 2149; [2004] Q.B. 388: consent induced by fraud is not a defence to kidnapping (and presumably would not be a defence to the tort of false imprisonment).

[223] In *Hegarty v Shine* (1878) 14 Cox C.C. 124 and 145 the claimant's action against her former lover for infecting her with venereal disease failed because she had consented to the sexual intercourse. The logic of *R. v Dica* [2004] EWCA Crim 1103; [2004] Q.B. 1257 is equally applicable to actions in tort, and it would seem that *Hegarty v Shine* can no longer be regarded as correct. The court in *Hegarty v Shine* also applied the maxim ex turpi causa non oritur actio, and was heavily influenced by the view that the claimant's conduct was unlawful and immoral, a view that would not be persuasive today: see, e.g. the comment of Sopinka J in *Norberg v Wynrib* (1992) 92 D.L.R. (4th) 449 at 483, SCC.

[224] This example is not hypothetical. Persons masquerading as doctors have been convicted of various criminal offences: see Eekelaar and Dingwall [1984] J.S.W.L. 258, 259, n.5. Individuals

6–065 In *R. v Richardson*[225] the Court of Appeal held that the offence of assault, under s.47 of the Offences Against the Person Act 1861 was not committed when a dentist gave treatment to patients while suspended from practice by the General Dental Council. Consent for the purpose of the criminal law was vitiated only where there was a mistake as to the *nature or quality of the act* or the *identity of the person performing it*, not their qualifications or attributes, such as being authorised to provide dental treatment. The prosecution did not argue the case on the basis that the nature or quality of the act was different because the defendant was suspended from practice, but on the ground that the identity of the defendant was different. The assumption was that if the treatment had been given by a person impersonating a dentist it would have been assault, and there was no difference between an unqualified dentist and a dentist suspended from practice. The Crown contended that the concept of the identity of the person should be extended to cover the qualifications or attributes of the dentist on the basis that the patients consented to treatment by a qualified dentist and not a suspended one. This submission was rejected. The patients were fully aware of the identity of the defendant:

> "The common law is not concerned with the question whether the mistaken consent has been induced by fraud on the part of the accused or has been self-induced. It is the nature of the mistake that is relevant, and not the reason why the mistake has been made. In summary, either there is consent to actions on the part of a person in the mistaken belief that he was other than he truly is, in which case it is assault or, short of this, there is no assault."[226]

6–066 By way of contrast, in *R. v Tabassum*[227] the defendant had told three women that he was conducting a survey into breast cancer for the purpose of establishing a database software package, and persuaded the women to allow him to examine their breasts. The women mistakenly believed that he was medically qualified. He was found guilty of indecent assault and the Court of Appeal upheld the conviction on the basis that there was no valid consent. The consent to the touching was given for *medical purposes* and not for any other reason, thus there was consent to the nature of the act but not its quality.

6–067 **Fraud in the context of tort claims** In *Appleton v Garrett*[228] a dentist was held liable in trespass to the person for carrying out unnecessary dental treatment, on a large scale, for profit. In bad faith, he deliberately withheld the information that the treatment was unnecessary because he knew that the claimants would not have consented had they known the true position. Dyson J did not specify the

---

posing as doctors have been convicted of stealing from hospitals: *The Times*, 8 July 1994; and one individual who posed as a locum was known to have put stitches in a head wound, attended a man with a collapsed lung and arranged X-rays. He once tried to help with heart bypass surgery: *The Times*, 5 October 1994; B. Mahandra, "Deception and Self-deception" (2001) 151 N.L.J. 210; "Fake locum doctor sentenced" (*http://www*.cps.gov.uk/news/latest_news/fake_locum_doctor_sentenced); "'Fake' Doctor Allegedly Worked as GP in England" (*http://www*.medicalmistakes.co.uk/news/2015/fake-doctor-worked-as-gp-in-uk-19-03-2015.aspx); "Bogus doctor set up fake surgery" (*http://news.bbc.co.uk/1/hi/england/london/7740329.stm*).

[225] [1999] Q.B. 444.
[226] [1999] Q.B. 444 at 450.
[227] [2000] Lloyd's Rep. Med. 404, CA.
[228] [1996] P.I.Q.R. P1; [1997] 8 Med. L.R. 75.

nature of the procedure to which the claimants had "consented", but appears to
have taken the view that the consent was invalid because the claimants would not
have proceeded had they known the true position (though this is usually also true
of cases where the claimant objects to the consequences, as opposed to the nature,
of the procedure). The implication to be taken from *Appleton v Garrett* is that
where medical treatment is not necessary the "nature" of the treatment is
different. Indeed, it is arguable that it ceases to be "medical treatment", but this
means that the patient's consent must go, not simply to the defendant's act (e.g.
the drilling of a tooth), but also to the context in which the act takes place, i.e.
that the performance of the act is part and parcel of a bona fide decision to
provide appropriate medical treatment. Thus, *R. v Tabassum* and *Appleton v
Garrett* indicate that it is the context which gives the act both its nature and its
quality. On this basis, if in *R. v Tabassum* the defendant had actually been
carrying out a genuine survey into breast cancer and the procedures to which the
women consented were entirely appropriate to that survey, it is arguable that the
fact that he was not medically qualified would have been irrelevant to the nature
and quality of the act to which consent was given, unless a medical qualification
could be said to be crucial to the bona fides of the survey.

In *Dean v Phung*[229] the New South Wales Court of Appeal was faced with similar **6–068**
facts to those in *Appleton v Garrett*. The claimant suffered minor injury to his
front teeth in an accident. Over a period of 12 months the defendant dentist
undertook treatment costing $73,640 during 53 consultations. The claimant
brought proceedings in both negligence and trespass to the person on the basis
that the treatment was unnecessary and ineffective. The dentist admitted liability
in negligence but relied on a defence of consent to the claim in trespass, though
he conceded that the services were unnecessary and inappropriate, and were
carried out solely for the fees. The Court held that the defendant was liable in
trespass because the claimant's consent was vitiated by the defendant's fraud.
Basten JA said that:

> "...the motive of the practitioner in seeking consent to proposed 'treatment' may establish that
> what was proposed was not intended to be treatment at all, so that the nature of the act to
> which consent was ostensibly given was not the act carried out. Thus, although the conduct
> was objectively capable of constituting therapeutic treatment, if it were in fact undertaken
> solely for a non-therapeutic purpose not revealed to the patient, there will be no relevant
> consent."[230]

The defendant's concession that the dental work was unnecessary and
inappropriate meant that any apparent consent did not satisfy the criteria for a
valid consent to treatment, because it was not capable of constituting a
therapeutic response to the patient's condition.[231]

Burden of proving fraud   In contrast to *Dean v Phung*, in *White v Johnston*[232] **6–069**
it was held, on the facts, that some of the dental work done by the defendant

---

[229] [2012] NSWCA 223.
[230] [2012] NSWCA 223 at [63].
[231] [2012] NSWCA 223 at [65] and [66]. Beazley JA agreed with Basten JA.
[232] [2015] NSWCA 18.

dentist was capable of constituting a therapeutic response to the patient's dental state. In those circumstances (i.e. in the absence of the concession made in *Dean v Phung* that the services were unnecessary and inappropriate) an allegation that the patient's ostensible consent was vitiated because the work was undertaken with the undisclosed intention of achieving no therapeutic purpose amounted to an allegation of knowing deceit practised upon the patient, and it was for the patient to prove an allegation of fraud.[233]

6–070   **Lying to the patient**   It is arguable that a deliberate lie in response to a specific question from the patient as to risks could be taken as evidence of bad faith which might vitiate the patient's consent. In *Re T (Adult: Refusal of Treatment)*[234] Lord Donaldson MR said that:

> "...misinforming a patient, whether or not innocently, and the withholding of information which is expressly or impliedly sought by the patient may well vitiate either a consent or a refusal."

This dictum appears to support the view that deliberate lies might vitiate consent, but it would also seem to contradict his Lordship's narrow interpretation of the "fraud or misrepresentation" exception expressed in *Sidaway v Bethlem Royal Hospital Governors*,[235] as being limited to misinformation about the *nature* of the procedure. It seems likely that the courts would seek to deal with deliberate lying as an aspect of the doctor's duty of care in negligence in order to take account of the "therapeutic privilege" argument that disclosure of the information would have been harmful to the patient and, accordingly, the lie was in the patient's "best interests".[236]

---

[233] "I do not accept that a defendant medical practitioner is subject to a legal burden to disprove fraud, or something which is tantamount to fraud, although he or she may become subject to an evidentiary burden to do so", per Leeming JA [2015] NSWCA 18 at [83]. Leeming JA also took the wider view that the burden of proof with respect to an absence of consent lies with the claimant: see para.6–019.

[234] [1993] Fam. 95 at 115.

[235] [1984] Q.B. 493 at 511, para.6–063. See further *Halushka v University of Saskatchewan* (1965) 53 D.L.R. (2d) 436, Sask CA, para.7–130. Note that there is a distinction between fraud, which implies bad faith, and misrepresentation, which does not. A misrepresentation may simply be negligent. In *Ferguson v Hamilton Civic Hospitals* (1983) 144 D.L.R. (3d) 214 at 243–244, aff'd (1985) 18 D.L.R. (4th) 638, Ont CA, it was argued that the non-disclosure of the risks of surgical treatment prior to conducting a diagnostic procedure (which might indicate a need for the treatment) constituted a misrepresentation of the nature of the diagnostic procedure. This argument was rejected, but it was not suggested that the defendant must have acted in bad faith for the "misrepresentation" exception to apply.

[236] See para.7–022. For consideration of the lawfulness of testing patients for HIV antibodies without their knowledge or consent see Sherrard and Gatt (1987) 295 B.M.J. 911; Keown (1989) 52 M.L.R. 790. Minors may be tested for HIV on the direction of the court where the court makes an interim care order or an interim supervision order under s.38(6) of the Children Act 1989: *Re O (Minors) (Medical Examination)* (1992) 15 B.M.L.R. 54; [1993] 1 F.L.R. 860; *Note: Re HIV Tests* [1994] 2 F.L.R. 116. See also *Re C (A Child) (HIV Testing)* [2000] Fam. 48 where the court ordered an HIV test for a newborn baby, despite the parents' opposition, because the medical arguments in favour of testing were "overwhelming". The need for an application to the court is likely to be rare: *President's Direction: HIV Testing of Children* [2003] 1 F.L.R. 1299.

Unlawfully obtained material   The fact that the material used for the   6–071
treatment of the claimant has been obtained unlawfully does not in itself vitiate
the claimant's consent to an otherwise lawful procedure. Thus, an allegation that
the pituitary glands from which was extracted the human growth hormone (HGH)
which had been administered to the claimants had been unlawfully removed from
the bodies of people who had died did not vitiate the claimants' consent to the
injection of the HGH.[237] A tort committed against A cannot be linked to a loss
suffered by B so as to give rise to a claim in tort by B where the tort against A did
not cause B's loss.[238]

(iii)   Consent to a different procedure

Where patients have been told about and given their consent to one procedure it   6–072
may not be entirely clear whether that consent applies to a slightly different
procedure. Ultimately, this will be treated as a question of fact in any given case.
In *Davis v Barking, Havering and Brentwood Health Authority*[239] the claimant
underwent a minor operation for marsupialisation of a cyst. She signed a general
consent form authorising the performance of the operation and the administration
of a general anaesthetic, but during the operation the anaesthetist administered a
caudal block (a type of epidural anaesthetic). After the operation the claimant
discovered that she could not move her legs or control her bladder. She eventually
made a substantial recovery from this condition but was left with a slight
disability. She alleged that since she had not been informed about the possibility
of a caudal block being performed she had not consented to the procedure.
McCullough J concluded that, looking compendiously at what the claimant had
been told about the proposed operation, including the requirement for a general
anaesthetic, she had been informed in sufficient detail to have consented to the
caudal block. It was inappropriate to divide into sections the information required
to be given about the general anaesthetic and information about the caudal block.
A sectionalised approach would encourage the "deplorable" prospect of actions
being brought in trespass rather than negligence:

> "Clearly if it is proposed that a patient should undergo two separate operations it is the duty of
> the doctors to give the patient appropriately full information about each of them. This is so
> whether they are to be performed on two occasions or one. Equally clearly there is no
> obligation to explain every detail of what is proposed. That would be no more in the interests
> of the patient than to inform her of every risk, however remote. The extent of the particularity
> required, whether by way of detail or by way of explanation of risk, must be for the clinical
> judgment of the doctor, and in the event of a dispute about either the court will apply the
> *Bolam* test. Each case must depend on its own facts. Whether a particular aspect of what is
> proposed is a matter of detail or is in reality a matter sufficiently separate to call for separate
> mention is a question of fact and degree."[240]

---

[237] *The Creutzfeldt-Jakob Disease Litigation* (1995) 54 B.M.L.R. 1, per May J. Another example
might be a case where an organ was obtained for transplant contrary to the terms of the Human Tissue
Act 2004. The fact that the donation was unlawful would not in itself vitiate consent to the surgery by
the recipient.
[238] (1995) 54 B.M.L.R. 1.
[239] [1993] 4 Med. L.R. 85.
[240] [1993] 4 Med. L.R. 85 at 90.

There was no realistic distinction, said his Lordship, between omitting to tell a patient that while she is under general anaesthetic a tube will be put into her trachea and omitting to tell her that while she is under a general anaesthetic a needle will be put into her caudal region to provide post-operative analgesia.[241]

5. ADULTS WHO LACK CAPACITY TO CONSENT TO TREATMENT

6–073   This section deals with the position of adults who lack the capacity to consent to medical treatment, both under the Mental Capacity Act 2005 and at common law. It has become apparent since the passage of the 2005 Act that in some circumstances an adult lacking capacity who is in need of medical treatment may fall outside both the Mental Capacity Act and the Mental Health Act 1983, and the courts have had to fill the gap by authorising treatment under the courts' inherent jurisdiction. These cases are considered here. The section ends with a discussion of the difficult issue of withdrawing/withholding medical treatment from incapacitated adults in circumstances where this will probably lead to the death of the patient. The Mental Health Act 1983, which deals with the compulsory detention and treatment of patients suffering from a mental disorder, can apply not only to patients who lack the relevant capacity, but also, in certain circumstances, to individuals who are competent to refuse, and are in fact refusing, consent to treatment for their mental disorder. Thus, it cuts across a categorisation of patients as either having capacity or lacking capacity.[242]

(a)   Treatment under the Mental Health Act 1983

6–074   Most patients who suffer from mental disorder are subject to the same rules with respect to consent to medical treatment as any other adult. Part 4 of the Mental Health Act 1983 (ss.56 to 64), which lays down specific rules for treatment[243]

---

[241] See also *Brushett v Cowan* (1990) 69 D.L.R. (4th) 743, Newfd CA, where a consent to a muscle biopsy was held to cover a bone biopsy on the basis that the claimant had consented to a diagnostic procedure, and in the circumstances this was a sufficient consent to the bone biopsy; *Pridham v Nash* (1986) 33 D.L.R. (4th) 304, Ont HC, where the patient signed a consent form for an investigative laparoscopy, which was held sufficient to cover the performance of minor surgery during the course of the examination; *O'Bonswain v Paradis* (1993) 15 C.C.L.T. (2d) 188, Ont HC, where the claimant consented to a gortex graft for the purpose of providing access for renal dialysis, having been informed that a medically preferable procedure (an arteriovenous fistula (AVF)), with lower risk, would not be feasible because her arteries and veins were too small. When the patient was under general anaesthetic it became apparent that an AVF was possible, and the defendant proceeded to perform that procedure rather than the gortex graft. It was held that the claimant's consent covered the AVF. Both procedures were designed to accomplish the same thing, namely access for dialysis, and the consent for the gortex graft included consent to such "additional or alternative treatment or operative procedure as in the opinion of [the defendant] are immediately necessary". cf. *E v Castro* [2003] EWHC 2066 (QB); (2003) 80 B.M.L.R. 14—a claimant who was not told that he would be catheterised after an operation on his penis, although he had consented to the operation, was entitled to damages for the discomfort caused by his catheterisation for a period of 24 hours.

[242] Nor is the Mental Health Act 1983 limited to adult patients.

[243] A First-tier Tribunal has no jurisdiction over the treatment of patients under the Act; the treatment of patients under the Act is subject to judicial oversight by the courts: *SH v Cornwall Partnership NHS Trust* [2012] UKUT 290 (AAC); [2012] M.H.L.R. 383.

under the Act, both with and without the patient's consent, applies only to certain categories of patient. Section 57,[244] which provides specific protection for a patient where the proposed treatment consists of surgery for destroying brain tissue or for destroying the functioning of brain tissue, or the surgical implantation of hormones for the purpose of reducing the male sex drive, applies to any patient.[245] Apart from this, Pt 4 of the Act applies only to patients liable to be detained under the Act,[246] and to "community patients" who have been recalled to hospital.[247] Thus, it does not apply to patients voluntarily admitted to hospital,[248] to mentally disordered patients who live in the community,[249] to patients subject to guardianship,[250] nor to certain patients who are liable to be detained but who are specifically excluded from Pt 4.[251]

Community treatment orders   Chapter 4 of the Mental Health Act 2007   **6–075** introduced a new regime of "supervised community treatment". Only patients detained in hospital are eligible to be considered for supervised community treatment. Patients are subject to conditions while living in the community, the conditions being for the purpose of ensuring the patient receives medical treatment or to prevent a risk of harm to the patient or others. Patients may be recalled to hospital for treatment, if necessary.[252] "Community patients" are not "detained" or "liable to be detained" for the purposes of Mental Health Act 1983.[253] A community patient is not subject to the provisions of Pt 4 of the Mental Health Act 1983, covering consent to treatment,[254] unless recalled to hospital for treatment. The treatment of patients subject to a community treatment order who have not been recalled to hospital is generally dealt with under a new Pt 4A of the 1983 Act. If recalled, a patient may be given treatment to which ss.58 or 58A of the Mental Health Act 1983 apply,[255] on the basis of a certificate given under Pt 4A of the Mental Health Act 1983.[256] A new s.58A (which covers

---

244 See para.6–087.

245 Mental Health Act 1983 s.56(1).

246 Mental Health Act 1983 s.56(2) and (3).

247 Mental Health Act 1983 s.56(4).

248 With the exception of s.57 (requiring the patient's consent *and* a second opinion where the treatment consists of surgical procedures for destroying brain tissue or the functioning of brain tissue) which is an additional safeguard for patients: Mental Health Act 1983 s.56(1), which provides that s.57, and so far as relevant to that section, ss.59 to 62, apply to any patient. Thus, the protection afforded by s.57 continues to apply to all patients, including voluntary patients. In addition, voluntary patients under the age of 18 are covered by s.58A (applying to electro-convulsive therapy): s.56(5).

249 *R. v Hallstrom Ex p. W. (No.2)* [1986] Q.B. 1090. But patients who are liable to be detained do not cease to be so liable simply because they have been given leave of absence under s.17 of the Act: *Barker v Barking, Havering and Brentwood Community Healthcare NHS Trust* [1999] Lloyd's Rep. Med. 101; also reported as *R. v BHB Community Healthcare NHS Trust Ex p. Barker* [1999] 1 F.L.R. 106; (1999) 47 B.M.L.R. 112, CA.

250 Mental Health Act 1983 s.8(5) providing that a patient received into guardianship ceases to be "liable to be detained".

251 Mental Health Act 1983 s.56(3).

252 Mental Health Act 1983 s.17E.

253 Mental Health Act 1983 s.17D(2)(b).

254 With the exception of s.57 which applies to all patients.

255 See paras 6–088 and 6–089.

256 See Mental Health Act 1983 ss.64A to 64K.

electro-convulsive therapy[257]) in addition to applying to patients who are liable to be detained, also applies to informal patients under the age of 18 years.[258]

6–076　**Treatment of mental disorder only**　The Mental Health Act is concerned only with treatment of the patient's mental disorder, and it cannot be used to authorise treatment for other medical conditions, even in circumstances where the patient lacks the capacity to consent to such treatment.[259] It cannot be used to detain an individual:

> "...against her will merely because her thinking process is unusual, even apparently bizarre and irrational, and contrary to the views of the overwhelming majority of the community at large."[260]

6–077　**The "*Bournewood* gap"**　Where the provisions of the Mental Health Act 1983 do not apply, the power to give treatment now depends upon the Mental Capacity Act 2005 and/or the rules of the common law, which requires either a valid consent given by the patient or justification under the principle of necessity.[261] In *R. v Bournewood Community and Mental Health NHS Trust Ex p. L*[262] the House of Lords held that in the case of a patient admitted to hospital informally under s.131(1) of the Act, where the patient is incapable of consenting to the admission or treatment, the common law principle of necessity could justify both the detention and the treatment of the patient, in his best interests.[263] Subsequently, in *HL v United Kingdom*[264] the European Court of Human Rights held that although the common law defence of necessity could provide a legal basis for detention of a patient lacking capacity, it must be shown that the detention was not arbitrary. Necessity did not provide a set of procedural rules, and so there was no provision for a review of the patient's detention. The contrast between the lack of any fixed

---

[257] See para.6–089.

[258] Mental Health Act 1983 s.56(5).

[259] *Re F (Mental Patient: Sterilisation)* [1990] 2 A.C. 1; *St George's Healthcare NHS Trust v S; R. v Collins and Others Ex p. S* [1999] Fam. 26, CA.

[260] *St George's Healthcare NHS Trust v S; R. v Collins and Others Ex p. S* [1999] Fam. 26 at 51.

[261] "It goes without saying that, unless clear statutory authority to the contrary exists, no one is to be detained in hospital or to undergo medical treatment or even to submit himself to a medical examination without his consent. This is as true of a mentally disordered person as of anyone else", per McCullough J in *R. v Hallstrom Ex p. W (No.2)* [1986] Q.B. 1090 at 1104; cited with approval by the Court of Appeal in *St George's Healthcare NHS Trust v S; R. v Collins and Others Ex p. S* [1999] Fam. 26 at 51.

[262] [1999] 1 A.C. 458.

[263] See para.6–100 et seq. Note, however, that a majority of their Lordships considered that a mental patient in an open, unlocked ward, who appeared to be compliant and made no attempt to leave, was not in fact detained, even though if he had attempted to leave he would have been prevented from doing so by the medical staff, who would then have taken steps to detain him compulsorily under the Mental Health Act 1983. cf. Lord Nolan and Lord Steyn, dissenting on this point. Lord Steyn said that the argument that the patient was free to leave was "a fairy tale". The healthcare professionals had detained him. They intentionally assumed control over him to such a degree (including sedating him with drugs, keeping him under continuous observation, preventing his carers from visiting, and resolving to apply for compulsory admission if he physically resisted) as to amount to a complete deprivation of his liberty. Of course, if the patient is not in fact detained, there was no need for any legal justification for his detention, a point which concerned Lord Nolan, though the hospital clearly would have to justify any treatment given to the patient.

[264] (2005) 40 E.H.R.R. 32; (2005) 17 B.H.R.C. 418; [2005] Lloyd's Rep. Med. 169.

procedural rules by which the admission and detention of compliant incapacitated persons was conducted and the extensive procedural safeguards contained in the Mental Health Act 1983 was "striking".[265] This resulted in the patient's liberty being removed by the hospital's healthcare professionals solely on the basis of their own clinical assessments, completed as and when they considered fit. Judicial review and habeas corpus were not adequate remedies as they did not allow for the resolution of complaints on the basis of incorrect diagnoses and judgments. Thus, L's detention in *R. v Bournewood Community and Mental Health NHS Trust Ex p. L* contravened arts 5(1) and 5(4) of the European Convention on Human Rights (right to liberty and security), and it was irrelevant that he had not resisted his detention. The Court agreed with Lord Steyn in *Bournewood* that, given that the patient was under continuous supervision and control and was not free to leave, the suggestion that he was not detained was "stretching credulity to breaking point" and a "fairy tale".[266] The Court's decision highlighted what came to be known as the "*Bournewood* gap", namely the absence of any procedural safeguards for patients lacking capacity who are informally detained (i.e. detained other than under the compulsory detention provisions of the Mental Health Act 1983). Amendments to the Mental Capacity Act 2005 introduced by the Mental Health Act 2007 sought to address this issue by the introduction of the Deprivation of Liberty Safeguards (DoLS).[267]

(i)   Treatment without consent

Treatment for what?   The Mental Health Act 1983 does not assume that a patient with a mental disorder automatically lacks the capacity to consent to treatment under the Act, since ss.57, 58 and 58A provide for consent by the patient to some forms of treatment. But, by virtue of s.63 the consent of patients is not required for any medical treatment given to them for mental disorders from which they are suffering,[268] not being a form of treatment to which s.57, 58 or 58A applies, if the treatment is given by or under the direction of the approved clinician in charge of the treatment.[269] This permits treatment without consent, or indeed notwithstanding the specific refusal of consent by a patient (except treatment governed by ss.57, 58 or 58A).

6–078

In *R. (on the application of B) v Ashworth Hospital Authority*[270] the Court of Appeal held that the previous version of s.63 only permitted treatment in respect of the mental illness or disorder with which the patient had been classified, with the consequence that if the patient had been classified as suffering from mental illness, and that was the basis on which he was detained or remained liable to be detained, he could not be treated under s.63 for an unrelated mental disorder, unless that disorder was exacerbating the mental illness, so that treatment of the

6–079

---

[265] (2005) 40 E.H.R.R. 32; (2005) 17 B.H.R.C. 418; [2005] Lloyd's Rep. Med. 169 at [120].
[266] (2005) 40 E.H.R.R. 32; (2005) 17 B.H.R.C. 418; [2005] Lloyd's Rep. Med. 169 at [91].
[267] See para.6–120.
[268] But this includes "treatment the purpose of which is to alleviate, or prevent a worsening of, the disorder or one or more of its symptoms or manifestations": Mental Health Act 1983 s.145(4).
[269] For the definition of the approved clinician in charge of the treatment see the Mental Health Act 1983 ss.64(1A) and 145(1).
[270] [2003] EWCA Civ 547; [2003] 1 W.L.R. 1886.

disorder could also be regarded as treatment of the mental illness. However, the House of Lords[271] reversed the Court of Appeal, holding that s.63 could authorise treatment of patients for any mental disorder from which they were suffering, irrespective of whether this fell within the form of disorder from which they were classified as suffering in the application, order or direction justifying their initial detention. Thus, classification has no bearing on treatment. The House of Lords' ruling is in line with amendments to the Mental Health Act 1983 introduced by the Mental Health Act 2007 which removed the different classifications of mental disorder.

(ii)   Meaning of "treatment"

6–080   **Anorexia and force-feeding**   Although s.63 permits treatment without consent, there remains the issue of what constitutes "treatment". In both *Re KB (Adult) (Mental Patient: Medical Treatment)*[272] and *B v Croydon Health Authority*[273] the issue was whether force-feeding an anorexic patient was treatment falling within s.63 for which the patient's consent was not required.[274] In *Re KB* the patient argued that feeding was not treatment of her mental disorder, it was for the physical symptoms. The feeding was to increase her weight and was not being given for her mental disorder. The hospital argued that K was suffering from an eating disorder and relieving the symptoms was just as much a part of the treatment as relieving the underlying cause. If the symptoms were exacerbated by the patient's refusal to eat and drink, the mental disorder became progressively more difficult to treat, and therefore the feeding by naso-gastric tube was an integral part of the treatment of the mental disorder itself. It was also argued that the treatment was necessary in order to make psychiatric treatment of the underlying cause possible at all. Ewbank J accepted that the naso-gastric feeding did fall within s.63.

6–081   Similarly, in *B v Croydon Health Authority* the Court of Appeal agreed that force-feeding an anorexic patient is medical treatment within s.63, since such treatment includes treatment administered to alleviate the symptoms of the disorder as well as treatment to remedy its underlying cause. B suffered from a psychopathic disorder which was incapable of treatment except by psycho-analytical psychotherapy. She argued that giving food might be a prerequisite to a treatment for mental disorder or it might be treatment for the consequences of the mental disorder, but it was not treatment for the disorder itself. Hoffmann LJ considered that this was too atomistic. It required every individual element of the

---

[271] *R. (on the application of B) v Ashworth Hospital Authority* [2005] UKHL 20; [2005] 2 A.C. 278; [2005] 2 All E.R. 289.
[272] (1994) 19 B.M.L.R. 144.
[273] [1995] Fam. 133, CA.
[274] It is assumed that anorexia is a mental illness falling within the terms of the Mental Health Act 1983, although in *B v Croydon Health Authority* the patient suffered from a psychopathic disorder known as borderline personality disorder coupled with post-traumatic stress disorder. Symptoms included depression and a compulsion to self-harm stemming from an irrationally low self-regard. In *Riverside Mental Health Trust v Fox* [1994] 1 F.L.R. 614 the Court of Appeal considered that anorexia may be a mental disorder within the Mental Health Act 1983. See further Fennell (1995) 145 N.L.J. 319.

treatment being given to the patient to be directed to her mental condition. But the test applied to treatment as a whole. Section 145(1) of the Mental Health Act 1983 included within the definition of medical treatment "nursing, care, habilitation and rehabilitation under medical supervision", and so a range of acts ancillary to the core treatment fell within the definition. His Lordship accepted that if there was *no* proposed treatment for B's psychopathic disorder, s.63 could not be invoked to justify feeding her by naso-gastric tube. Indeed, it would not be lawful to detain her at all.[275] But it did not follow that every act which formed part of that treatment within the wide definition in s.145(1) must in itself be likely to alleviate or prevent a deterioration of that disorder:

> "Nursing and care concurrent with the core treatment or as a necessary prerequisite to such treatment or to prevent the patient from causing harm to himself or to alleviate the consequences of the disorder are in my view capable of being ancillary to a treatment calculated to alleviate or prevent a deterioration of the psychopathic disorder."[276]

The Mental Health Act 2007 s.7 amended the definition of medical treatment in s.145(1) of the Mental Health Act 1983, by deleting the words "and also includes care, habilitation and rehabilitation under medical supervision" and substituting "psychological intervention and specialist mental health habilitation, rehabilitation and care". In addition a new s.145(4) provided that:

6–082

> "Any reference in this Act to medical treatment, in relation to mental disorder, shall be construed as a reference to medical treatment the purpose of which is to alleviate, or prevent a worsening of, the disorder or one or more of its symptoms or manifestations."

This wider meaning of medical treatment would certainly encompass the feeding of an anorexic patient (as in *B v Croydon Health Authority*).

Where a patient detained under the Mental Health Act is refusing food but is not suffering from anorexia, force-feeding may not amount to treatment for their mental health condition. In *A NHS Trust v A*[277] the patient was an Iranian doctor who went on hunger strike as a protest at being refused asylum and having his passport taken away by the UK Border Agency. Baker J found that Dr A was suffering from a delusional disorder and that he did not have capacity to make decisions concerning nutrition and hydration. However, Baker J also accepted the

6–083

---

[275] By virtue of s.3(2)(b) of the Mental Health Act 1983, which at that time provided that a patient with a psychopathic disorder could not be detained unless the proposed treatment was "likely to alleviate or prevent a deterioration in his condition". It would still be unlawful to detain a patient under the amended s.3 unless it could be demonstrated that it was "necessary for the health or safety of the patient or for the protection of other persons that he should receive [medical treatment in hospital] which cannot be provided unless he is detained" and such treatment is available. For the amended s.3 see para.2–161.

[276] [1995] Fam. 133 at 138–139. See also *Re JR18's Application for Judicial Review* [2007] NIQB 104; [2008] M.H.L.R. 50 where Weatherup J reached the same conclusion in relation to the Northern Ireland mental health legislation: "It would be somewhat incongruent if this patient could be detained in hospital without her consent for a mental disorder that involved the patient in self-harming and having suicidal ideation and that once detained she could continue to manifest self-harm by resorting to hunger strike, thereby putting her life at risk, but could not be treated for that consequence of her mental disorder without her consent" (at [16]).

[277] [2013] EWHC 2442 (COP); [2014] Fam. 161.

medical professionals' assessment that the administration of artificial nutrition and hydration did not constitute treatment for his mental disorder but for a physical disorder that resulted from Dr A's decision to refuse food. Although the decision to refuse food was flawed, in part because the mental disorder deprived the patient of the capacity to use and weigh information, and therefore the physical disorder was in part a consequence of his mental disorder, it was "not obviously either a manifestation or a symptom of the mental disorder" and so did not fall within the wider definition of medical treatment in s.145 of the Mental Health Act.[278] Baker J added that it was generally undesirable to extend the meaning of medical treatment under the Mental Health Act too far so as to bring about deprivation of liberty in respect of sectioned or sectionable patients beyond what is properly within the ambit of the Mental Health Act.[279]

6–084   **Blood transfusions**   In *Nottinghamshire Healthcare NHS Trust v RC*[280] Mostyn J considered whether the administration of blood products to a patient who was deliberately cutting himself could constitute treatment under the Act. The issue turned upon whether a blood transfusion was treatment for a condition which was a consequence of the patient's mental disorder, which did not fall within s.63, or treatment for a condition which was a symptom or manifestation of the mental disorder, which did fall within s.63, though Mostyn J confessed to "finding the distinction intellectually challenging".[281] His Lordship reasoned that since the act of self-harming was a symptom or manifestation of the underlying personality disorder, treating the wound in any way (such as stitching it up or administering antibiotics to prevent infection) would be treating a manifestation or symptom of the underlying disorder. Low haemoglobin levels are a consequence of bleeding from the wound and so to treat the low haemoglobin by a blood transfusion was just as much treatment of a symptom or manifestation of the disorder as stitching up the wound or administering antibiotics.[282] However, having reached this conclusion, there remained the question of whether the patient should be given a blood transfusion if he were bleeding to death as a consequence of cutting himself. Mostyn J had concluded that, at a time when he had capacity, the patient had executed a valid advance decision to refuse blood products. The doctor had expressed "some ethical difficulty" in overriding a patient's capacitous decision based on religious beliefs and stated that she would choose not to use s.63 to override the advance decision. Mostyn J held that this decision was correct:

"...it would be an abuse of power in such circumstances even to think about imposing a blood transfusion on RC having regard to my findings that he presently has capacity to refuse blood

---

[278] [2013] EWHC 2442 (COP); [2014] Fam. 161 at [79], distinguishing *B v Croydon Health Authority* [1995] Fam. 133 and *R v Collins and Ashworth Hospital Authority Ex p. Brady* [2000] Lloyd's Rep. Med. 355. The judge went on to hold, however, that although the forcible administration of nutrition and hydration could not be authorised under either the Mental Health Act 1983 or the Mental Capacity Act 2005, nonetheless the court could authorise treatment under the inherent jurisdiction of the court, in the patient's best interests. See para.6–150.
[279] [2013] EWHC 2442 (COP); [2014] Fam. 161. at [80].
[280] [2014] EWCOP 1317; [2014] Med. L.R. 260; (2014) 138 B.M.L.R. 147.
[281] [2014] EWCOP 1317; [2014] Med. L.R. 260; (2014) 138 B.M.L.R. 147 at [24].
[282] [2014] EWCOP 1317; [2014] Med. L.R. 260; (2014) 138 B.M.L.R. 147 at [31].

products and, were such capacity to disappear for any reason, the advance decision would be operative. To impose a blood transfusion would be a denial of a most basic freedom."[283]

Accordingly, it would be lawful to withhold any treatment which involved transfusion into the patient of blood or blood components notwithstanding the existence of the doctor's powers under s.63.[284]

Obstetric care   In *NHS Trust 1 v FG*,[285] in the course of setting out guidance for dealing with a pregnant woman with mental health problems who potentially lacks capacity to litigate and to make decisions about her own welfare or medical treatment, Keehan J stated that obstetric care (which includes Caesarean section) may be authorised under s.63 of the Mental Health Act when the primary purpose of the treatment is to alleviate or prevent a worsening in the patient's psychiatric illness or its symptoms. For example, there may be circumstances where early delivery of the baby would enable more effective treatment of the patient's severe mental illness, as where the doctors are reluctant to give appropriate levels of medication for the mental illness, fearing a teratogenic effect on the foetus.[286] If obstetric treatment can be provided under s.63, said Keehan J, then it can be carried out without the patient's consent, using proportionate and necessary restraint.[287]

6–085

Seclusion   In *Colonel Munjaz v Mersey Care NHS Trust; S v Airdale NHS Trust*[288] the Court of Appeal held that the seclusion of a detained patient was capable of being medical treatment falling with s.145, although that did not mean that all uses of seclusion are lawful. Seclusion had to be convincingly shown to be a medical necessity.[289] Seclusion was capable of amounting to a breach of art.3 of the European Convention on Human Rights and also infringes art.8 of the Convention unless it can be justified under art.8(2).[290] This requirement can usually be met by adherence to the rules on seclusion to be found in the Mental Health Act Code of Practice,[291] although a hospital may be able to show good reason for departing from the Code in relation to individual patients or groups of patients.[292] On appeal, the House of Lords held that the decision of Ashworth high security hospital to establish its own policy with respect to the practice of

6–086

---

[283] [2014] EWCOP 1317; [2014] Med. L.R. 260; (2014) 138 B.M.L.R. 147 at [42].

[284] This seems to privilege decisions to refuse treatment based on religious beliefs since s.63 renders lawful treatment of a *competent* patient's mental disorder, and its symptoms or manifestations, despite the patient's refusal of consent. Compulsory treatment of a competent patient without the patient's consent is itself "a denial of a most basic freedom", yet this is precisely what s.63 contemplates.

[285] [2014] EWCOP 30; [2015] 1 W.L.R. 1984 at [85]–[86].

[286] As was the position in *Great Western Hospitals NHS Foundation Trust v AA* [2014] EWHC 132 (Fam); [2014] 2 F.L.R. 1209, though the judge did not rely on s.63 of the Mental Health Act in this case.

[287] [2014] EWCOP 30; [2015] 1 W.L.R. 1984; [2014] Med. L.R. 470 at [86], citing *Tameside and Glossop Acute Services NHS Trust v CH* [1996] 1 F.L.R. 762; [1996] 1 F.C.R. 753; see para.6–185, n.636.

[288] [2003] EWCA Civ 1036; [2004] Q.B. 395; [2003] Lloyd's Rep. Med. 534 at [45].

[289] [2003] EWCA Civ 1036; [2004] Q.B. 395; [2003] Lloyd's Rep. Med. 534 at [48].

[290] [2003] EWCA Civ 1036; [2004] Q.B. 395; [2003] Lloyd's Rep. Med. 534 at [53] and [65].

[291] [2003] EWCA Civ 1036; [2004] Q.B. 395; [2003] Lloyd's Rep. Med. 534 at [74].

[292] [2003] EWCA Civ 1036; [2004] Q.B. 395; [2003] Lloyd's Rep. Med. 534 at [76].

secluding detained patients, which differed in significant respects from the Code of Practice to the Mental Health Act 1983, was not in itself unlawful.[293] Although the Code of Practice should be given great weight, it was guidance rather than instruction. Departure from the Code would require cogent reasons, which should be subject to intense scrutiny by the court. But, properly used, seclusion did not violate a patient's rights under arts 3, 5 or 8 of the European Convention on Human Rights.[294] Lord Bingham considered that "medical treatment" as defined in s.145 of the Mental Health Act 1983 was an expression wide enough to cover the nursing and caring for a patient in seclusion, even though seclusion could not properly form part of a treatment programme.[295]

(iii)   Special rules for particular forms of treatment

6–087   **Surgery for destroying brain tissue and surgical implantation of hormones to reduce male sex drive**   Notwithstanding the effect of s.63 permitting treatment without the patient's consent, some forms of treatment are subject to special safeguards built into the Mental Health Act. Section 57 (treatment requiring consent *and* a second opinion) provides that patients cannot be given any form of medical treatment for mental disorder consisting of a surgical operation for destroying brain tissue or for destroying the functioning of brain tissue (and such other forms of treatment as may be specified in regulations by the Secretary of State[296]) unless they have consented to it, and it has been certified in writing by a registered medical practitioner appointed for the purpose (not being the responsible clinician (if there is one) or the person in charge of the treatment in question) and two other persons (not being registered medical practitioners[297]) who have been professionally concerned with the patient's medical treatment that the patient is capable of understanding the nature, purpose and likely effects of the treatment in question and has consented to it.[298] It must also be certified by

---

[293] *R. (on the application of Munjaz) v Mersey Care NHS Trust* [2005] UKHL 58; [2006] 2 A.C. 148; [2006] 4 All E.R. 736. See further D. Hewitt (2005) 155 N.L.J. 1658.

[294] The European Court of Human Rights agreed: *Munjaz v United Kingdom* [2012] M.H.L.R. 351. This is subject to there being cogent reasons for the practice, appropriate scrutiny of the practice, and that secluded patients be given the most liberal regime compatible with their medical condition.

[295] [2005] UKHL 58; [2006] A.C. 148 at [19]; see also per Lord Hope at [66] and [67].

[296] See the Mental Health (Hospital, Guardianship and Treatment) (England) Regulations 2008 (SI 2008/1184) reg.27(1) (and in Wales the Mental Health (Hospital, Guardianship, Community Treatment and Consent to Treatment) (Wales) Regulations 2008 (SI 2008/2439) reg.38(1)) specifying the surgical implantation of hormones for the purpose of reducing the male sex drive. In *R. v Mental Health Act Commission Ex p. X* (1988) 9 B.M.L.R. 77, DC, it was held that the previous version of these regulations (the Mental Health (Hospital, Guardianship and Consent to Treatment) Regulations 1983 (SI 1983/893)) did not apply to a drug reducing sexual drive which is neither a hormone nor surgically implanted. Other forms of treatment to which s.57 could apply may be specified in a Code of Practice: see Mental Health Act 1983 s.118(2).

[297] One of these persons must be a nurse and one must be neither a nurse nor a registered medical practitioner, and neither of them may be the "responsible clinician (if there is one) or the person in charge of the treatment in question": Mental Health Act 1983 s.57(3). The "responsible clinician" means "the approved clinician with overall responsibility for the case": Mental Health Act 1983 s.64.

[298] In these circumstances the team of one registered medical practitioner and two other persons who are not registered medical practitioners do not owe a private law duty of care to the patient in deciding whether to grant or withhold the certification that the patient is competent to, and has in fact,

the registered medical practitioner that it is appropriate for the treatment to be given.[299] This provision means that competent patients can never be given such treatment without their consent, and the requirement for a second opinion is an additional safeguard.[300] On the face of it s.57 rules out these forms of surgery for patients who are incapable of consenting.[301]

Administration of medicine after three months   Section 58 (treatment requiring consent *or* a second opinion) applies to such forms of treatment for mental disorder as may be specified in regulations made by the Secretary of State, and to the administration of medicine to patients by any means (not being treatment consisting of a surgical operation for destroying brain tissue or for destroying the functioning of brain tissue, which is dealt with by s.57, nor electro-convulsive therapy, which is dealt with by s.58A) at any time during a period for which they are liable to be detained, if three months or more have elapsed since the first occasion in that period[302] when medicine was administered to them by any means for a mental disorder. Originally, s.58 applied to electro-convulsive therapy, but this is now covered by s.58A, and so s.58 is limited to the administration of medicine to detained patients when three or more months have elapsed since the first occasion in that period when medicine was administered to them. Under s.58 patients cannot be given treatment to which the section applies unless: (a) they have consented to it, and either the approved clinician in charge of it or a registered medical practitioner appointed for the purpose has certified in writing that they are capable of understanding its nature, purpose and likely effects and have consented to it; or (b) a registered medical

6–088

consented. Their duties are quasi-judicial, and fall within the field of administrative law. Thus, although a decision that the claimant's treatment fell within s.57 was erroneous, and the decision to refuse to issue a certificate under s.57(2) was *Wednesbury* unreasonable, a private law action for negligence would be struck out as disclosing no reasonable cause of action: *X v A, B and C and the Mental Health Act Commission* (1991) 9 B.M.L.R. 91, QBD.

[299] Mental Health Act 1983 s.57(2)(b). For the purposes of Pt 4 of the 1983 Act (on Consent to Treatment) "it is appropriate for treatment to be given to a patient if the treatment is appropriate in his case, taking into account the nature and degree of the mental disorder from which he is suffering and all other circumstances of his case": Mental Health Act 1983 s.64(3).

[300] "Second opinion" doctors must form their own independent opinions on the existence of the statutory criteria. They should not simply review the responsible medical officer's decision that the criteria are satisfied. At the very least they must act in good faith and with reasonable care in forming their judgments: *R. (on the application of W) v Broadmoor Hospital* [2001] EWCA Civ 1545; [2002] 1 W.L.R. 419 at [71] per Hale LJ. The second opinion doctor must also give written reasons to justify a decision to administer medical treatment to a competent, non-consenting adult patient, and those reasons must be disclosed to the patient by the registered medical officer unless the information would be likely to cause serious physical or mental harm: *R. (on the application of Wooder) v Feggetter* [2002] EWCA Civ 554; [2003] Q.B. 219.

[301] Given the wording of the section it seems extremely doubtful that treatment would be justified under the common law principle of necessity, although the major premise of the decision of the House of Lords in *Re F (Mental Patient: Sterilisation)* [1990] 2 A.C. 1 was that incompetent patients should not be "deprived" of treatment that would otherwise be available to a competent adult.

[302] The three-month period during which the patient is liable to be detained must be a continuous period. Thus, if the patient has been detained and then discharged, but remained in hospital as a voluntary patient, and then detained again and given treatment to which s.58 applies, the three month period (after which treatment under the section requires a "second opinion") commences from the date of the second detention: *McLarnon v Bedford District Care NHS Trust* [2005] Lloyd's Law Rep. Med. 345.

practitioner appointed for the purpose (not being the responsible clinician or the approved clinician in charge of the treatment) has certified in writing that they are not capable of understanding the nature, purpose and likely effects of the treatment or being so capable have not consented to it, but that it is appropriate for the treatment to be given.[303] It is:

> "...appropriate for treatment to be given to a patient if the treatment is appropriate in his case, taking into account the nature and degree of the mental disorder from which he is suffering and all other circumstances of his case."[304]

The person who must certify that the patient has consented to the treatment and is capable of understanding its nature, purpose and likely effects is either "the approved clinician in charge of" the treatment or a registered medical practitioner appointed for the purpose; and the person who, alternatively, must certify that the patient is not capable of understanding the nature, purpose and likely effects of the treatment or has not consented to it is the "responsible clinician or the approved clinician in charge of the treatment in question".[305]

6–089   **Electro-convulsive therapy**   Section 58A of the Mental Health Act 1983 (introduced by s.27 of the Mental Health Act 2007) applies to electro-convulsive therapy and such other forms of treatment as may be specified in regulations.[306] Subject to s.62 (which concerns emergency treatment) patients may not be given treatment to which s.58A applies unless they fall within the criteria set out in subs.(3), (4) or (5). Section 58A(3) provides that the patient must have attained the age of 18 years, have consented to the treatment in question, and either the approved clinician in charge of it or a registered medical practitioner appointed under s.58(3) has certified in writing that the patient is capable of understanding the nature, purpose and likely effects of the treatment and has consented to it. Section 58A(4) applies to patients under 18. It provides that the subsection applies if the patient has not attained the age of 18 years, but has consented to the treatment in question, and a registered medical practitioner appointed under s.58(3) (not being the approved clinician in charge of the treatment) has certified in writing that the patient is capable of understanding the nature, purpose and likely effects of the treatment and has consented to it, and that it is appropriate for the treatment to be given.

6–090   Section 58A(5) applies to electro-convulsive therapy where the patient lacks capacity to consent. It provides that a patient falls within the subsection if a registered medical practitioner appointed under s.58(3) (not being the responsible clinician (if there is one) or approved clinician in charge of the treatment) has

---

[303] Mental Health Act 1983 s.58(3)(b).
[304] Mental Health Act 1983 s.64(3).
[305] Mental Health Act 1983 s.58(3).
[306] Mental Health (Hospital, Guardianship and Treatment) (England) Regulations 2008 (SI 2008/1184) reg.27(3) specifies the administration of medicine as part of electro-convulsive therapy. Reg.27(4) provides that s.58A does not apply to treatment by way of the administration of medicine as part of electro-convulsive therapy where the treatment falls within s.62(1)(a) or (b) (urgent treatment immediately necessary to save the patient's life or prevent a serious deterioration of his condition). In Wales, see the Mental Health (Hospital, Guardianship, Community Treatment and Consent to Treatment) (Wales) Regulations 2008 (SI 2008/2439) reg.38(2) and reg.38(3) respectively.

certified in writing that the patient is not capable of understanding the nature, purpose and likely effects of the treatment, but it is appropriate for the treatment to be given, and that giving the patient the treatment would not conflict with a valid and applicable advance decision made under the Mental Capacity Act 2005,[307] or a decision made by a donee or deputy or by the Court of Protection.[308] Before giving a certificate under s.58A(5) the registered medical practitioner must consult with two other persons who have been professionally concerned with the patient's medical treatment, one of whom must be a nurse, and the other of whom must be neither a nurse nor a registered medical practitioner, and neither of whom are the responsible clinician or the approved clinician in charge of the treatment.[309] Section 58A(7) provides that s.58A cannot by itself confer sufficient authority for patients falling within s.56(5)[310] to be given a form of treatment to which s.58A applies (i.e. electro-convulsive therapy) if they are not capable of understanding the nature, purpose and likely effects of the treatment (and therefore cannot consent to it). The overall effect of s.58A is that *where the patient is competent*, except in an emergency, electro-convulsive therapy (and the administration of medicine as part of electro-convulsive therapy) cannot be given to patients without their consent (unlike s.58 which permits the refusal of consent of a competent patient to be dispensed with in the circumstances set out in the section).

Withdrawing consent   A patient who has consented to any treatment for the purposes of ss.57, 58 and 58A can withdraw this consent at any time before the completion of the treatment.[311] This power to withdraw consent is subject to s.62(2), which provides for the continuation of treatment where, in the view of the approved clinician in charge of the treatment, discontinuance of the treatment would cause serious suffering to the patient.   **6–091**

(iv) Emergencies

In the case of "urgent treatment" s.62 provides that ss.57, 58 and 58A do not apply to any treatment: **6–092**

(a)   which is immediately necessary to save the patient's life; or
(b)   which (not being irreversible) is immediately necessary to prevent a serious deterioration of the condition; or
(c)   which (not being irreversible or hazardous) is immediately necessary to alleviate serious suffering by the patient; or

---

[307] See para.6–029.
[308] See para.6–111.
[309] Mental Health Act 1983 s.58A(6).
[310] Which applies to informal patients (i.e. patients not liable to be detained) under 18 years of age, who are not "community patients".
[311] Mental Health Act 1983 s.60(1). Where patients have given consent but cease to be capable of understanding the nature, purpose and likely effects of treatment before the completion of the treatment they are treated as having withdrawn their consent: s.60(1A) and (1B).

(d)   which (not being irreversible or hazardous) is immediately necessary and represents the minimum interference necessary to prevent patients from behaving violently or being a danger to themselves or to others.[312]

(v)   Guardianship

6–093   Where patients have been received into guardianship, guardians can require them to attend some specified place for the purpose of medical treatment,[313] but guardians cannot require patients to receive treatment, nor can they consent to the giving of treatment to which patients do not themselves consent.[314]

(vi)   The standard for reviewing compulsory treatment decisions and human rights

6–094   In *R. (on the application of W) v Broadmoor Hospital*[315] the Court of Appeal held that challenges to a decision to administer treatment compulsorily under the Mental Health Act 1983 can be made by way of judicial review, an action in the tort of battery, proceedings for a declaration as to the lawfulness of the proposed treatment plan, and proceedings under s.7 of the Human Rights Act 1998 claiming that the hospital was proposing to act in a way that was incompatible with the patient's rights under the European Convention on Human Rights. But whatever procedure is used there must be a full merits review of the decision, with oral evidence and cross-examination, if necessary.[316] The "super-*Wednesbury*" approach[317] to judicial review was not appropriate to a case where the applicant's human rights were in issue.[318] The review will be a "proportionality" review,[319] but given that the intensity of the review depends on

---

[312]   Mental Health Act 1983 s.62. Treatment is irreversible if it has unfavourable irreversible physical or psychological consequences and hazardous if it entails significant physical hazard: s.62(3). Section 62 merely removes the formal requirements for compliance with ss.57, 58 and 58A; it does not itself authorise treatment, which must be justified either under s.63, or at common law by the patient's consent or under the principle of necessity.

[313]   Mental Health Act 1983 s.8(1)(b).

[314]   *R. v Hallstrom Ex p. W (No.2)* [1986] Q.B. 1090 at 1103; *T v T* [1988] Fam. 52, 57. Under the Mental Health Act 1959 s.34(1) a guardian exercised the powers of a father of a child under 14 years of age, which meant that he could consent to treatment on the patient's behalf. The powers of the guardian were amended by the Mental Health (Amendment) Act 1982 ss.8, 65(1), Sch.3 para.66. See generally Fisher [1988] J.S.W.L. 316.

[315]   [2001] EWCA Civ 1545; [2002] 1 W.L.R. 419 at [24], [59] and [62].

[316]   [2001] EWCA Civ 1545; [2002] 1 W.L.R. 419 at [31], [53], [83]; *R. (on the application of N) v Dr M* [2002] EWCA Civ 1789; [2003] 1 W.L.R. 562

[317]   Adopted in *R. v Ministry of Defence Ex p. Smith* [1996] Q.B. 517 and *R. v Collins and Ashworth Health Authority Ex p. Brady* [2000] Lloyd's Rep. Med. 335.

[318]   Applying *Smith and Grady v UK* (1999) 29 E.H.R.R. 493, ECtHR.

[319]   Applying *R. v Home Secretary Ex p. Daly* [2001] UKHL 26; [2001] 2 A.C. 532. Lord Steyn, at [27], said: "… the doctrine of proportionality may require the reviewing court to assess the balance which the decision maker has struck, not merely whether it is within a range of rational or reasonable decisions. Secondly, the proportionality test may go further than the traditional grounds of review in as much as it may require attention to be directed to the relative weight accorded to interests and considerations."

the subject matter in hand,[320] and compulsory medical treatment potentially engages art.2 (the right to life), art.3 (protection against torture or inhuman or degrading treatment) and art.8 (the right to respect for private and family life) of the Convention, this effectively entails a full merits review, with the court reaching its own view as to whether the patient is competent to consent, and whether compulsory treatment is justified. Equally, a decision *not* to treat a patient compulsorily under s.63 where the consequences of the decision not to treat may be life-threatening for the patient should also be brought before the court for a full merits review.[321]

Medical necessity   In *Herczegfalvy v Austria*[322] the European Court of Human Rights, considering whether compulsory treatment could amount to a breach of art.3, said:

6–095

> "While it is for the medical authorities to decide, on the basis of the recognisable rules of medical science, on the therapeutic methods to be used, if necessary by force, to preserve the physical and mental health of patients who are entirely incapable of deciding for themselves and for whom they are responsible, such patients nevertheless remain under the protection of Article 3, the requirements of which permit no derogation. The established principles of medicine are admittedly in principle decisive in such cases; as a general rule, a method which is a therapeutic necessity cannot be regarded as inhuman or degrading. The court must nevertheless satisfy itself that the medical necessity has been convincingly shown to exist."

Thus, the crucial test is whether the medical need for treatment "has been convincingly shown to exist". The Court applied the same test to alleged breaches of the applicant's rights under art.8. In *R. (on the application of W) v Broadmoor Hospital* Hale LJ, commenting on *Herczegfalvy*, said that:

> "One can at least conclude from this that forcible measures inflicted upon an incapacitated patient which are *not* a medical necessity may indeed be inhuman or degrading. The same must apply to forcible measures inflicted upon a capacitated patient."[323]

In other words, compulsory treatment which cannot be convincingly shown to be a medical necessity will amount to a breach of the patient's Convention rights, whether the patient is competent or not. But the fact that there is a responsible body of medical opinion against the proposed treatment is not decisive to determine that medical necessity has not been convincingly shown.[324] The existence of a competing body of medical opinion is relevant to the question of whether treatment is in the patient's best interests or medically necessary, but it is no more than that.[325] The standard is a high one, and the answer to the question whether medical necessity has been convincingly shown depends upon a number of factors, including:

---

[320] [2001] UKHL 26; [2001] 2 A.C. 532 at [28] per Lord Steyn.
[321] *Nottinghamshire Healthcare NHS Trust v RC* [2014] EWCOP 1317; [2014] Med. L.R. 260; (2014) 138 B.M.L.R. 147 at [21] per Mostyn J. The decision in question was whether to administer blood products to a patient who was deliberately self-harming by cutting himself, notwithstanding the patient's capacitous decision to refuse blood products on religious grounds.
[322] (1992) E.H.R.R. 437 at 484 at [82].
[323] [2001] EWCA Civ 1545; [2002] 1 W.L.R. 419 at [79], original emphasis.
[324] *R. (on the application of N) v Dr M* [2002] EWCA Civ 1789; [2003] 1 W.L.R. 562.
[325] [2002] EWCA Civ 1789; [2003] 1 W.L.R. 562 at [27] to [29].

"(a) how certain is it that the patient does suffer from a treatable mental disorder; (b) how serious a disorder is it; (c) how serious a risk is presented to others; (d) how likely is it that, if the patient does suffer from such a disorder, the proposed treatment will alleviate the condition; (e) how much alleviation is there likely to be; (f) how likely is it that the treatment will have adverse consequences for the patient; and (g) how severe may they be."[326]

6–096   In *R. (on the application of PS) v Responsible Medical Officer*[327] Silber J held that the treatment of a competent detained patient with anti-psychotic medication under s.58(3)(b) of the Mental Health Act 1983, contrary to his religious beliefs, did not necessarily involve a breach of art.3 of the European Convention on Human Rights. In order to constitute a breach of art.3, the proposed treatment had to reach a minimum level of severity for ill-treatment, taking into account all the circumstances, including the positive and adverse mental and physical consequences, the nature and context of the treatment, the manner and method of its execution, its duration, and, if relevant, the sex, age and health of the patient. It also had to be established that there was no medical or therapeutic necessity for the treatment, since as a general rule, a method of treatment which is a therapeutic necessity cannot be regarded as inhuman or degrading.[328] Moreover, in order to be in the patient's best interests and a medical necessity, it does not have to be shown that the treatment is necessary to prevent the patient causing harm to others or to protect the patient from serious harm.[329]

6–097   The test of "medical necessity" derived from *Herczegfalvy v Austria* does not require a court considering a challenge to treatment proposed under s.58(3)(b) of the Mental Health Act 1983 to be convinced of each of the individual matters going to the test of medical necessity. There is a single question of medical or therapeutic necessity for the court to address when forcible treatment is challenged. In *R. (on the application of B) v Haddock*[330] the applicant argued that before medical treatment could be administered without the patient's consent under s.58(3) it had to be shown first, that the patient suffered from a particular form of mental disorder, secondly, that the treatment proposed was for that condition, and, thirdly that the appellant would benefit from the treatment. The crucial question was therefore: "what is the relevant diagnosis?" The Court of Appeal rejected this argument, because of the inherent difficulty of making some psychiatric diagnoses, due not least to the possibility of co-morbidity of, for example, some forms of mental illness and psychopathic disorder. Auld LJ commented that:

"...the discipline of psychiatry is one which, notoriously, poses particular difficulties of diagnosis and distinction between mental illness in a clinical sense and personality disorders or other failings. An overly prescriptive or compartmentalised treatment of the processes provided by the Act, with a view to attempting precise and mutually exclusive diagnoses, would bear little relationship to the practicalities of psychiatrists' therapeutic and associated forensic work."[331]

---

[326] [2002] EWCA Civ 1789; [2003] 1 W.L.R. 562 at [19].
[327] [2003] EWHC 2335 (Admin); [2004] M.H.L.R. 1.
[328] [2003] EWHC 2335 (Admin); [2004] M.H.L.R. 1 at [107].
[329] *R. (on the application of B) v S (Responsible Medical Officer, Broadmoor Hospital)* [2006] EWCA Civ 28; [2006] 1 W.L.R. 810; [2006] H.R.L.R. 14.
[330] [2006] EWCA Civ 961; [2006] Lloyd's Rep. Med. 433; [2006] H.R.L.R. 40.
[331] [2006] EWCA Civ 961; [2006] Lloyd's Rep. Med. 433; [2006] H.R.L.R. 40 at [36].

The question of "medical necessity" is composite in nature:

> "It is one to which the answer will always be one of value judgment derived from other value judgments on often difficult and complex questions of diagnosis and prognosis on which there may be some difference of medical opinion."[332]

As to the appropriate standard for determining whether "medical necessity" for compulsory treatment has been established, Auld LJ considered that it could not be expressed in terms of a legal standard of proof, since it involves a professional value judgment about the likelihood of treatment being effective. Although diagnosis may be important to the decision-making process under s.58:

6–098

> "...the clinical reality for psychiatrists is that the precise forms of mental disorder are not always readily diagnosable one from the other; there is overlap and there is often co-morbidity. To require of psychiatrists a state of mind of precision and sureness in matters of diagnosis akin to that required of a jury in a criminal case, even in this fraught context of forcible treatment potentially violating detained patients' human rights, is not sensible or feasible. The same applies to the suggestion of clear and firm attribution of the proposed treatment to a particular form of mental disorder where there is uncertainty as to the boundary line between it and another disorder or where there is co-morbidity. And, as to whether the treatment will do any good, it is unreal to require psychiatrists, under the umbrella of a requirement of medical or therapeutic necessity, to demonstrate sureness or near sureness of success, especially when the Act itself, in section 58(3)(b) hinges the SOAD's certificate on his conclusion as to 'the likelihood' of it benefiting him."[333]

It followed that the requirement for a court to be convinced of medical necessity was not capable of being expressed in terms of a standard of evidential proof. Rather it was a value judgement as to the future, or forecast, to be made by a court in reliance on medical evidence according to a standard of persuasion, and therefore it was doubtful whether it amounted to more than satisfaction of "medical necessity on a balance of probabilities", or as a "likelihood" of therapeutic benefit—the test in s.58(3)(b) for triggering a decision.[334]

(b) Treatment of adult patients who lack capacity at common law[335]

The Mental Health Act 1983 deals with treatment for the patient's mental disorder. It does not authorise treatment for anything other than mental disorder, even where the patient's capacity to give a valid consent is affected by that disorder. It had been generally assumed (or, at least, no one had sought to

6–099

---

332 [2006] EWCA Civ 961; [2006] Lloyd's Rep. Med. 433; [2006] H.R.L.R. 40 at [45].
333 [2006] EWCA Civ 961; [2006] Lloyd's Rep. Med. 433; [2006] H.R.L.R. 40 at [41].
334 [2006] EWCA Civ 961; [2006] Lloyd's Rep. Med. 433; [2006] H.R.L.R. 40 at [42] per Auld LJ.
335 Note that, though the common law principles discussed in the following paragraphs remain relevant, since the Act has not expressly replaced the common law, many of the situations discussed in the cases would now be covered by the Mental Capacity Act 2005. See paras 6–110 et seq. Note also that the court's inherent jurisdiction to protect vulnerable adults who do not fall within the Mental Capacity Act remains available: *DL v A Local Authority* [2012] EWCA Civ 253; [2013] Fam. 1, see para.6–149. For example, a patient's ability to make a competent decision may be impaired by the undue influence of a third party, and not as a result of some "impairment of, or a disturbance in the functioning of, the mind or brain" (s.2(1) of the Act), in which case the Act would not apply.

question it) that doctors were acting lawfully in giving medical treatment to adults who lacked the capacity to consent. The basis for that assumption was not tested in the courts in this country until cases involving the highly controversial issues of abortion and sterilisation of mentally handicapped women arose. In the case of girls under the age of 18 it was clear that the court, in the exercise of the wardship jurisdiction, could authorise an abortion or sterilisation of a minor where it is in her best interests.[336] The wardship jurisdiction is not available, however, once the child reaches the age of majority.

6–100 **Principle of necessity**   In *Re F (Mental Patient: Sterilisation)*[337] the patient was a woman of 36 years who suffered from a serious mental disability. She was a voluntary in-patient at a mental hospital, and had formed a sexual relationship with a male patient. The psychiatric evidence was that F would not understand the meaning of pregnancy, labour or delivery, and would be unable to care for a baby if she had one. From a psychiatric point of view it would have been "disastrous for her to conceive a child". Other contraceptive methods were considered to be unreliable and/or to involve a risk of harm to her physical health. In these circumstances it was thought appropriate that F be sterilised. The House of Lords held that the principle of necessity provided the solution to the problem of patients who lack the capacity to consent. It was axiomatic, said Lord Bridge, that treatment which is necessary to preserve the life, health or wellbeing of the patient may lawfully be given without consent.[338] Lord Goff had no doubt that the common law recognised a principle of necessity which might justify action which would otherwise be unlawful, and Lord Brandon, without referring specifically to a general principle of necessity, said that the common law would be seriously defective if it failed to provide a solution to the problem created by an inability to consent to treatment.

6–101 **Wide statement of patient's "best interests"**   Lord Brandon concluded that an operation or other treatment performed on adult patients who are incapable, for one reason or another, of consenting, would be lawful provided that it is in the best interests of the patient. It will be in their best interests:

> "...if, but only if, it is carried out in order either to save their lives or to ensure improvement or prevent deterioration in their physical or mental health."[339]

This statement of the patient's best interests is extremely wide. Procedures designed to "ensure improvement or prevent deterioration in ... physical or

---

[336] *Re B (A Minor) (Wardship: Sterilisation)* [1988] A.C. 199; *Re P (A Minor)* (1982) 80 L.G.R. 301; *Re D (A Minor) (Wardship: Sterilisation)* [1976] Fam. 185, where the decision went the other way on the facts.
[337] [1990] 2 A.C. 1, CA and HL; Shaw (1990) 53 M.L.R. 91; Jones (1989) 5 P.N. 178. See further the Law Commission Consultation Paper No.129, *Mentally Incapacitated Adults and Decision-Making: Medical Treatment and Research*, 1993; and the Final Report, *Mental Incapacity*, Law Com. No.231, 1995, HMSO. For comment on the Consultation Paper see Gunn (1994) 2 Med. L. Rev. 8 and Freeman (1994) 2 Med. L. Rev. 77; and for comment on the Report see Wilson (1996) 4 Med. L. Rev. 227.
[338] *Re F (Mental Patient: Sterilisation)* [1990] 2 A.C. 1 at 52.
[339] [1990] 2 A.C. 1 at 55.

mental health" would encompass virtually anything that a doctor might ever do to a patient.[340] It would, for example, provide a blanket common law justification for the treatment of mental illness or disorder for which statutory provision is considered necessary in the Mental Health Act 1983, which provides specific safeguards for the patient. His Lordship was clearly concerned not to place constraints on the defence which might otherwise deprive patients of medical care which they need and to which they are entitled.[341]

***Bolam* test of patient's best interests**   Lord Brandon used the same argument to justify adopting the *Bolam*[342] test as the appropriate standard for measuring the patient's best interests: **6–102**

> "If doctors were to be required, in deciding whether an operation or other treatment was in the best interests of adults incompetent to give consent, to apply some test more stringent than the *Bolam* test, the result would be that such adults would, in some circumstances at least, be deprived of the benefit of medical treatment which adults competent to give consent would enjoy. In my opinion it would be wrong for the law, in its concern to protect such adults, to produce such a result."[343]

The difficulty with applying the *Bolam* test to the defence of necessity was that there could well be more than one view, or indeed several views, as to what is in the best interests of the patient and, accordingly, as to what course of conduct in relation to incompetent patients is justified in law. When applied in the context of a negligence action the *Bolam* test effectively means that competing "responsible bodies of medical opinion" cannot be challenged. Following *a* responsible practice means that a defendant is not negligent, even where there are other, and possibly better, responsible practices. Applied to treatment decisions about incapacitated adults this would leave decisions about medical treatment, even controversial treatment such as sterilisation, within the discretion of the medical

---

[340] It clearly covers diagnostic as well as therapeutic procedures: *Re H (Mental Patient)* [1993] 4 Med. L.R. 91; [1993] 1 F.L.R. 28; (1992) 9 B.M.L.R. 71.

[341] [1990] 2 A.C. 1 at 55. See also, at 52, per Lord Bridge, who was worried that a "rigid criterion of necessity" would deprive many patients of treatment which it would be entirely beneficial for them to receive. Lord Goff, at 76, said that in the case of a mentally disordered person the permanent nature of the incapacity calls for a wider range of treatment than would be appropriate in the case of temporary incapacity to be covered by the defence, including routine medical or dental treatment, and even simple care such as dressing and undressing and putting to bed. Indeed, in *R v Bournewood Community and Mental Health NHS Trust Ex p. L* [1999] 1 A.C. 458 the House of Lords held that the principle of necessity could justify the detention and treatment of patients who are admitted to hospital as informal patients under s.131(1) of the Mental Health Act 1983, but lack the capacity to consent to treatment or care. But in *HL v United Kingdom* (2005) 40 E.H.R.R. 32; (2005) 17 B.H.R.C. 418; [2005] Lloyd's Rep. Med. 169 the European Court of Human rights held that such conduct would contravene arts 5(1) and 5(4) of the European Convention on Human Rights, *precisely because* there were no procedural safeguards as checks on the clinical judgment of the health professionals. See para.6–077.

[342] *Bolam v Friern Hospital Management Committee* [1957] 2 All E.R. 118.

[343] *Re F (Mental Patient: Sterilisation)* [1990] 2 A.C. 1 at 68; see also per Lord Bridge at 52.

profession.[344] Patients would have a right to have non-negligent decisions made about their medical treatment, but no right to the "best" decision.

6–103 **Court must choose best option for patient** This concern led the Court of Appeal to emphasise in *Re S (Adult Patient: Sterilisation)*[345] that where the question of appropriate medical treatment comes before a court for decision, while there may be a number of different options which might be lawful in any particular case (since there could be more than one responsible practice), logically there is only one best option, and the court must choose that option in making decisions in the patient's best interests rather than leaving the doctors to choose from the range of lawful options. The issue was whether a 29-year-old woman with severe learning difficulties could lawfully be sterilised despite her lack of capacity because her mother was concerned that she might get pregnant when she moved into a local authority home. The judge held that both contraception (by the insertion of an intra-uterine coil) or surgery were lawful options and had left the decision to the woman's mother in conjunction with the doctors. The Court of Appeal held that the insertion of the intra uterine device was in S's best interests as it was the least invasive option, was not irreversible, and left room for surgical procedures if it proved ineffective. The question for the judge, said Butler-Sloss P, was not whether the proposed treatment fell within the range of acceptable opinion among competent and responsible practitioners, but was it in the best interests of S? Once the judge was satisfied that the range of options was within the range of acceptable opinion among competent and responsible practitioners, the *Bolam* test was irrelevant to the judge's decision.[346]

6–104 **Not just *medical* best interests** In *Simms v Simms; A v A*[347] two young patients were suffering from vCJD, an invariably fatal degenerative disease of the brain. It was proposed that they be subjected to experimental treatment which had a slight, but not non-existent, chance of improving their condition. There was a possibility

---

[344] See *Re W (Mental Patient) (Sterilisation)* [1993] 1 F.L.R. 381, where Hollis J held that sterilisation of a 20-year-old patient, having a mental age of seven, was in her best interests, notwithstanding that there was only a small risk of her becoming pregnant, since a responsible body of medical opinion was in favour of sterilisation.

[345] [2001] Fam. 15. Also reported as *Re SL (Adult Patient) (Medical Treatment)* [2000] Lloyd's Rep. Med. 339; [2000] 2 F.L.R. 389; [2000] 2 F.C.R. 452.

[346] [2001] Fam. 15 at 28 per Butler-Sloss P and at 30 per Thorpe LJ. See also *An NHS Trust v A (An Adult)* [2005] EWCA Civ 1145; [2006] Lloyd's Rep. Med. 29 endorsing *Re S (Adult Patient: Sterilisation)*; *Re A (Medical Treatment: male sterilisation)* [2000] 1 F.L.R. 549; [2000] 1 F.C.R. 193 where the Court of Appeal held that on an application for approval of sterilisation of a mentally incapacitated patient it is the judge, not the doctor, who decides whether it is in the patient's best interests. See further the Law Commission report, *Mental Incapacity*, Law Com. No.231, (1995), para.3.27: "It should be clear beyond any shadow of a doubt that acting in a person's best interests amounts to something more than not treating that person in a negligent manner." For consideration of the courts' approach to the patient's best interests in cases of proposed sterilisation see: (1) where sterilisation was held not to be in the patient's best interests: *Re LC (Medical Treatment: Sterilisation)* [1997] 2 F.L.R. 258; *Re S (Medical Treatment: Adult Sterilisation)* [1998] 1 F.L.R. 944; [1999] 1 F.C.R. 277—risk of pregnancy had to be identifiable rather than speculative; and (2) where sterilisation was held to be in the patient's best interests: *Re X (Adult Sterilisation)* [1998] 2 F.L.R. 1124; *Re ZM and OS (Sterilisation: Patient's Best Interests)* [2000] 1 F.L.R. 523; [2000] 1 F.C.R. 274 (where there were also other therapeutic benefits to the patient having an hysterectomy).

[347] [2002] EWHC 2734 (Fam); [2003] Fam. 83.

of arresting the disease temporarily, and a possibility of prolonging their lives to some extent. An application was made for a declaration that the experimental treatment was in their best interests. Butler-Sloss P observed:

"I have to assess the best interests in the widest possible way to include the medical and non-medical benefits and disadvantages, the broader welfare issues of the two patients, their abilities, their future with or without treatment, the views of the families, and the impact of refusal of the applications. All of these matters have to be weighed up and balanced in order for the court to come to a decision in the exercise of its discretion."[348]

On the evidence, the prospect of a slightly longer life was held to be a benefit worth having for each of the patients. There was sufficient possibility of unquantifiable benefit to hold that it would be in their best interests to have the treatment. The reality was that the patients had very little to lose in the treatment going ahead, and therefore it was a reasonable risk to take.

Male sterilisation   On the other hand, on an application to sterilise a male   **6–105** patient who lacks the capacity to consent, it will be extremely difficult to establish that the procedure is in the best interests of the patient.[349] In *Re A (Medical Treatment: Male Sterilisation)*[350] the Court of Appeal held that it was not in the best interests of a 28-year-old male Down's Syndrome patient to have a vasectomy. Although an assessment of his best interests was not limited to medical interests, and could include medical, emotional and other welfare interests,[351] neither the fact of the birth nor the possible disapproval of his conduct was likely to impinge on a mentally incapacitated man to a significant degree, other than in exceptional circumstances. The question of whether the interests of third parties could ever be taken into account in a case concerned with the best interests of an incapacitated patient was specifically left open.[352]

---

[348] [2002] EWHC 2734 (Fam); [2003] Fam. 83 at [60]. When considering the best interests of a patient the court's duty is "to assess the advantages and disadvantages of the various treatments and management options, the viability of each such option and the likely effect each would have on the patient's best interests and, I would add, his enjoyment of life. On the facts of the present case in particular, any likely benefit of treatment has to be balanced and considered in the light of any additional suffering the treatment option would entail": per Butler-Sloss P in *An Hospital NHS Trust v S* [2003] EWHC 365 (Fam); [2003] Lloyd's Rep. Med. 137 at [47]. See also *An NHS Trust v HM* [2004] Lloyd's Rep. Med. 207; *EP v Trusts A, B & C* [2004] Lloyd's Rep. Med. 211; *Trust A v H (An Adult Patient)* [2006] EWHC 1230 (Fam); [2006] 2 F.L.R. 958—in assessing the best interests of an incompetent patient the court must consider a broad spectrum of medical, social, emotional and welfare issues; the advantages and disadvantages of various treatment and management options, the viability of each option, and its likely effect on the patient (per Sir Mark Potter P.).
[349] Though see *A NHS Trust v DE* [2013] EWHC 2562 (Fam); [2013] Med. L.R. 446; (2013) 133 B.M.L.R. 123, para.6–140 below.
[350] [2000] 1 F.L.R. 549; [2000] 1 F.C.R. 193.
[351] [2000] 1 F.L.R. 549 at 555 per Butler-Sloss P; *An Hospital NHS Trust v S* [2003] EWHC 365 (Fam); [2003] Lloyd's Rep. Med. 137 at [45] per Butler-Sloss P.
[352] [2000] 1 F.L.R. 549 at 556 and 558 per Butler-Sloss P and Thorpe LJ respectively. See generally on the "best interests" test, the Law Commission report, *Mental Incapacity*, Law Com. No.231, (1995) paras 3.24 et seq. The Mental Capacity Act 2005 s.4 now sets out some of the issues that have to be taken into account when deciding what is in a person's best interests.

6–106   **Use of restraint**   In the case of incompetent patients who are refusing consent to surgery which the court rules to be lawful in their best interests, it necessarily follows that if patients resist the attempt to treat them it will be lawful to impose treatment and overcome patients' resistance by sedation and the "moderate and reasonable use of restraint".[353] However, in applying restraint the hospital would have to carefully consider the balance of benefit and disadvantage in giving the proposed treatment and take into account patients' rights not to be subjected to degrading treatment under art.3 of the European Convention on Human Rights.[354]

6–107   **Procedure**   *Re F (Mental Patient: Sterilisation)* raised a procedural problem. The House of Lords concluded that there was no equivalent of the wardship jurisdiction by which the court could exercise a power to consent on behalf of an incompetent adult. The ancient *parens patriae* jurisdiction of the Crown to protect the persons and property of those unable to do so for themselves was no longer available.[355] The court did not have jurisdiction to consent to medical treatment under the Mental Health Act 1983, nor was there any residual inherent jurisdiction (in the absence of the *parens patriae* jurisdiction) to approve or disapprove of a proposed operation. Although it was not essential as a matter of law to obtain the approval of the court to a sterilisation operation on an incompetent adult,[356] nonetheless it would be good medical practice to obtain the "approval" of the court by means of an application for a declaration that the operation would be in the patient's best interests, and this is now the appropriate procedure.[357] Similarly, doctors should seek the guidance of the court, by an application for a declaration, in all cases before withholding life-prolonging treatment from a patient in a persistent vegetative state.[358]

---

[353] *Trust A v H (An Adult Patient)* [2006] EWHC 1230 (Fam); [2006] 2 F.L.R. 958 at [27] per Sir Mark Potter P.

[354] [2006] EWHC 1230 (Fam); [2006] 2 F.L.R. 958 at [27]. Sir Mark Potter P made it clear that the forcible administration of chemotherapy to the patient contrary to her consent or stated wishes was not covered by declaration he granted.

[355] [1990] 2 A.C. 1 at 57–58. For the history of this jurisdiction see Hoggett, "The Royal Prerogative in Relation to the Mentally Disordered: Resurrection, Resuscitation or Rejection", in Freeman (ed.), *Medicine, Ethics and the Law* (London: Sweet & Maxwell, 1988), p.85.

[356] cf. the dissent of Lord Griffiths on this point: [1990] 2 A.C. 1 at 70.

[357] See the speech of Lord Brandon at [1990] 2 A.C. 1 at 65; *J v C* [1990] 3 All E.R. 735. This is now governed by the Court of Protection Practice Direction 9E (supplementing the Court of Protection Rules 2007 Pt 9) *Applications relating to serious medical treatment* (available at *http://www. judiciary.gov.uk/wp-content/uploads/2015/06/copd-pd-9e-serious-medical-treatment.pdf*). Note that from 1 December 2017 the Court of Protection Rules 2007 will be replaced by the Protection Rules 2017 (SI 2017/1035). There is power to grant an interim declaration: see CPR 1998 Pt 25 r.25.1(1)(b) and *X NHS Trust v T (Adult Patient: Refusal of Medical Treatment)* [2004] EWHC 1279 (Fam); [2005] 1 All E.R. 387; [2004] Lloyd's Rep. Med. 433; but a declaration should not be made on an ex parte basis: *St George's Healthcare NHS Trust v S; R. v Collins and Others Ex p. S* [1999] Fam. 26 at 60.

[358] *Airedale NHS Trust v Bland* [1993] A.C. 789; *Frenchay Healthcare NHS Trust v S* [1994] 1 W.L.R. 601; now governed by Court of Protection Practice Direction 9E (supplementing the Court of Protection Rules 2007 Pt 9) *Applications relating to serious medical treatment* (available at *http://www.judiciary.gov.uk/wp-content/uploads/2015/06/copd-pd-9e-serious-medical-treatment.pdf*). From 1 December 2017 the Court of Protection Rules 2007 will be replaced by the Court of Protection Rules (SI 2017/1035). Note also that it is arguable that, in some cases, a declaration of the court is no longer erquired before withdrawing clinically asisted nutrition and hydration from a patient

Cases where declaration is not required   It is not necessary to obtain the   **6–108**
approval of the court prior to performing an abortion on a mentally handicapped
adult provided that the requirements of the Abortion Act 1967 are satisfied and it
is in the patient's best interests.[359] Nor is it necessary to apply for a declaration as
to the lawfulness of a proposed therapeutic operation which would have the
incidental effect of sterilisation of a woman who lacks capacity to consent to the
procedure, where the operation is necessary in order to ensure the improvement
or prevent a deterioration in her health.[360] Similarly, where a proposed invasive
diagnostic procedure (a CT brain scan) is agreed to be in the best interests of the
patient the procedure is lawful and it is not appropriate to grant a declaration to
that effect simply as a "comfort" to the doctors or as protection against the risk of
vexatious litigation in the future by the disgruntled patient.[361] Of course, if an
adult patient is competent to accept or refuse treatment an application to the court
for a declaration where the patient is refusing treatment would be pointless.[362]

Although strictly speaking the court does not exercise a *parens patriae*   **6–109**
jurisdiction when it grants a declaration as to what interventions would or would
not be lawful, in the best interests of an incompetent adult, the distinction is so
theoretical that the court is effectively taking decisions on behalf of the
incapacitated adult.[363]

---

in a vegetative or minimally conscious state: *Re M (WIthdrawal of Treatment: Need for Proceedings)*
[2017] EWCOP 19 (a decision under the Mental Capacity Act 2005).

[359] *Re SG (Adult Mental Patient: Abortion)* [1991] 2 F.L.R. 329; [1993] 4 Med. L.R. 75. The Court of
Protection Practice Direction 9E (supplementing the Court of Protection Rules 2007 Pt 9)
Applications relating to serious medical treatment, para.6(a) indicates that "certain terminations of
pregnancy in relation to a person who lacks capacity to consent to such a procedure" may have to be
brought before the court. The criteria set out by Coleridge J in *An NHS Trust v D* [2003] EWHC 2793
(Fam); [2004] Lloyd's Rep. Med. 107 can probably be taken as a good guide for these purposes.

[360] *Re GF (Medical Treatment)* [1992] 1 F.L.R. 293; [1993] 4 Med. L.R. 77; though if a case falls
near the boundary of what is therapeutically necessary or in the best interests of the patient, it should
be referred to the court for a declaration of lawfulness: *Re S (Adult Patient: Sterilisation)* [2001] Fam.
15 at 32 per Thorpe LJ. For the analogous position where the patient is a minor see: *Re E (A Minor)
(Medical Treatment)* [1991] 2 F.L.R. 585; (1991) 7 B.M.L.R. 117. The Law Commission, *Mental
Incapacity*, Law Com. No.231, (1995), para.6.4 recommended that any treatment likely to render the
patient permanently infertile should require court authorisation, unless it is to treat disease of the
reproductive organs or relieve existing detrimental effects of menstruation.

[361] *Re H. (Mental Patient)* [1993] 4 Med. L.R. 91; [1993] 1 F.L.R. 28; (1992) 9 B.M.L.R. 71.

[362] *St George's Healthcare NHS Trust v S* [1999] Fam. 26 at 63. See also *Re JT (Adult: Refusal of
Medical Treatment)* [1998] 1 F.L.R. 48; [1998] 2 F.C.R. 662 where a declaration that it would be
lawful to abide by the decision of a competent patient to refuse life-saving treatment (kidney dialysis)
was held to be unnecessary. The doctor had "no option but to abide by the patient's decision and he
does not need a declaration from me or from the court that his conduct in so doing is lawful", per Wall
J at 666. The doctors should record the medical advice given to the patient and the patient's refusal of
that advice: see para.6–022.

[363] *Re SA (Vulnerable Adult with Capacity: Marriage)* [2005] EWHC 2942 (Fam); [2006] 1 F.L.R.
867 at [37] per Munby J: "It is now clear ... that the court exercises what is, in substance and reality,
a jurisdiction in relation to incompetent adults which is for all practical purposes indistinguishable
from its well-established *parens patriae* or wardship jurisdictions in relation to children. The court
exercises a 'protective jurisdiction' in relation to vulnerable adults just as it does in relation to wards
of court." See also *Re SK (Vulnerable Adult: Capacity)* [2008] EWHC 636 (Fam); [2008] LS Law
Medical 505 at [67] per Wood J. And see also G. Williams, "The Declaratory Judgment: Old and New
Law in 'Medical Cases'" (2007) 8 Med. Law Int. 277.

(c) Treatment under the Mental Capacity Act 2005

6–110   The Mental Capacity Act 2005 now covers most aspects of the lives of incapacitated adults, including personal welfare and property and financial affairs, but in so far as it provides a statutory process to authorise medical treatment (or indeed, any form of care involving a touching or restraint of the incapacitated adult) the legislation gives individuals a defence to what would otherwise involve trespass to the person. The Act changed the legal basis upon which any treatment or care can be provided for incapacitated[364] patients (provided they are aged 16 or more[365]), whether the incapacity is permanent or temporary, though the basic principles of the patient's "best interests" remain fundamental, and the Act has not changed the courts' approach drastically. Indeed, the common law has not been expressly replaced by the Act which, in some respects, can be seen as simply a statutory codification of common law principles. The provisions of the Act do not apply to medical treatment for mental disorder where such treatment is governed by the Mental Health Act 1983 Pt 4.[366]

(i) Court of Protection

6–111   The Mental Capacity Act created a new Court of Protection which has the power to make declarations as to whether a person has or lacks capacity to make decisions, and declarations as to the lawfulness of an act or omission, or course of conduct, in relation to that person.[367] The court has the power to make decisions on behalf of the person lacking capacity (P) and to appoint a deputy to make decisions on P's behalf.[368] By s.16(3) the power to make decisions is subject to s.1 (setting out the basic principles of the Act) and s.4 (P's best interests). The court's powers include the power to give or refuse consent to the carrying out or continuation of treatment by a person providing healthcare for P[369] and giving a direction that a person responsible for P's healthcare allow a different person to

---

[364] For consideration of the test for capacity under the Act see paras 6–045 et seq.

[365] Mental Capacity Act 2005 s.2(5).

[366] Mental Capacity Act 2005 s.28. See paras 6–074 et seq.

[367] Mental Capacity Act 2005 s.15. The court also has power to make an interim order or give directions if (a) there is reason to believe that P lacks capacity in relation to the matter, (b) the matter is one to which its powers under the Act extend, and (c) it is in P's best interests to make the order, or give the directions, without delay: s.48. The evidence required to invoke this interim jurisdiction is less than that required to rebut the presumption of capacity in a final declaration. The question is whether there is "sufficient evidence to justify a reasonable belief that P may lack capacity in the relevant regard": *Re F* [2010] 2 F.L.R. 28; (2009) 12 C.C.L. Rep. 530; [2009] W.T.L.R. 1309 at [36].

[368] Mental Capacity Act 2005 s.16. Decisions concerning P's welfare or medical treatment must be dealt with under s.16, and so an application concerning whether it is in the best interests of a minimally conscious patient to receive clinically assisted nutrition and hydration cannot be dealt with under s.21A, which is concerned with whether a deprivation of liberty (see paras 6–119 et seq.) is in the patient's best interests: *Re Briggs (Incapacitated Person)* [2017] EWCA Civ 1169 (the fact that applications under s.21A carried an entitlement to non-means-tested legal aid, which was not available in respect of the s.16 procedure in circumstances where a dispute had arisen about the withdrawal of life sustaining treatment may be perturbing to some people, but was not relevant to the scope of s.21A: [2017] EWCA Civ 1169 at [10]).

[369] Mental Capacity Act 2005 s.17(1)(d).

take over that responsibility.[370] The court also has the power to grant declarations as to the lawfulness of acts directed at P insofar as they have impacted on the human rights of members of P's family, and to award damages to P or members of P's family for breach of the Human Rights Act 1998.[371] The powers of deputies are more restricted than the powers of the court.[372]

In *Re P (Adult patient: Consent to Medical Treatment)*[373] Sir Mark Potter P accepted that the provisions granting the court discretion under s.15 to make declarations as to the lawfulness of any act done or yet to be done in relation to P, is a freestanding provision which co-exists with the provisions of the Mental Health Act 1983, and includes the power to make a declaration permitting compulsory removal and detention for the purposes of medical treatment, if found to be in the best interests of P. Such an order would not be in breach of art.5 of the European Convention, provided that: P is incapable of making a decision whether or not to go to the place of treatment and/or to stay within it; that a requirement to go to and remain in the unit would be in his best interests; that the court has declared in advance that it is in the best interests of P to be taken there and to be compelled to remain there by using reasonable and proportionate measures; and that there is a mechanism for timely and ongoing review of P's capacity and best interests with regard to his remaining in the relevant unit. The court may order that, if necessary, it will be lawful to use a reasonable and proportionate degree of force on P if he should resist treatment.[374]

6–112

Court cannot require that treatment be provided   The court will not grant a declaration requiring medical treatment to be carried out if the treating doctor is unwilling to offer that treatment for conscientiously held clinical reasons.[375] Moreover, the power under s.15 to make a declaration does not include the power

6–113

---

[370] Mental Capacity Act 2005 s.17(1)(e).

[371] *YA v A Local Authority* [2010] EWHC 2770 (Fam); [2011] 1 W.L.R. 1505 (claim for breach of art.8 of the ECHR, where it was alleged that the patient, who had been living with his mother, had been taken to hospital by her and when discharged had been placed in a location that was kept from her).

[372] Mental Capacity Act 2005 s.20.

[373] [2008] EWHC 1403 (Fam); [2008] 2 F.L.R. 1196 at [31] and [32]; commented on by Gunn, "Hospital Treatment for Incapacitated Adults" (2009) 17 Med. L. Rev. 274.

[374] [2008] EWHC 1403 (Fam); [2008] 2 F.L.R. 1196 at [25].

[375] *Aintree University Hospitals NHS Foundation Trust v James* [2013] UKSC 67; [2014] A.C. 591 at [18]; *R. (on the application of Burke) v General Medical Council* [2005] EWCA Civ 1003; [2006] Q.B. 273 at [50] and [55]; *United Lincolnshire Hospitals NHS Trust v N* [2014] EWCOP 16; (2014) 140 B.M.L.R. 204; *AVS v An NHS Foundation Trust* [2011] EWCA Civ 7; [2011] 2 F.L.R. 1 at [35]. If another doctor is willing and able to provide treatment the patient can be transferred to that doctor's care, but that does not require a declaration from the court; and "if there is no-one available to undertake the necessary operation the question of whether or not it would be in the patient's best interests for that to happen is wholly academic", [2011] EWCA Civ 7; [2011] 2 F.L.R. 1 at [39]. Contrast *St George's Healthcare NHS Trust v P* [2015] EWCOP 42; [2015] Med. L.R. 463 at [45] where Newton J, having concluded that there was "almost nothing to rebut the very strong presumption that it is in P's best interests to stay alive", ordered and directed that "the renal replacement therapy should continue". As J. Youngs (2016) 24 Med. L. Rev. 99 comments, this "appears to be an instance of the Court of Protection … forcing doctors to provide a treatment". See, however, the response to this by A. Ruck Keene (2016) 24 Med. L. Rev. 286, pointing out that the declaration embodying the court's decision was that it was "lawful, being in [P]'s best interests, for [P] to continue to receive renal replacement therapy", not that it was unlawful for P not to continue to

to require a third party, whether a private individual or a public authority, to provide the resources to fund a particular course of action that would not be available to a person with full capacity.[376] In other words, the court cannot, under the guise of a declaration as to a patient's best interests, obtain the resources for medical treatment or a care package that would not otherwise be available.

(ii)   Lasting power of attorney

6–114   The Act provides the option for an adult who has capacity to grant a "lasting power of attorney" to another adult, conferring on the donee authority to make decisions about the donor's (P's) personal welfare and property and affairs (or specified matters concerning personal welfare or property and affairs) which includes authority to make such decisions when P no longer has capacity.[377] A lasting power of attorney has to be exercised in the best interests of P, and subject to any restrictions specified in the document itself. It cannot authorise the donee of the power to do an act that is intended to restrain P unless: (1) P lacked, or the donee reasonably believed that P lacked, capacity in relation to the matter in question; (2) the donee reasonably believed that it was necessary to do the act in order to prevent harm to P; and (3) the act is a proportionate response to the likelihood of P suffering harm and the seriousness of that harm.[378] "Restraint" means the use, or threat, of force to secure the doing of an act that P resists, or restricting P's liberty of movement, whether or not P resists.[379] This is consistent with the approach of the common law.[380]

6–115   Where a lasting power of attorney authorises the donee to make decisions about P's personal welfare, the authority: (1) does not apply to such decisions unless P lacks, or the donee reasonably believes that he lacks, capacity; (2) is subject to any valid advance decision of P to refuse treatment under ss.24 to 26; and (3) extends to the giving or refusing of consent to the carrying out or continuation of treatment by a person providing healthcare for P (except that this does not authorise the giving or refusing of consent to carrying out or continuing life-sustaining treatment unless the instrument contains an express provision to that effect and is also subject to any conditions or restrictions in the instrument).[381]

---

receive renal replacement therapy. The implication of the hospital's application to the court was that treatment was on offer and would remain on offer if the court concluded that it was in P's best interests to continue to receive treatment.

[376] *Re N (An Adult) (Court of Protection: Jurisdiction)* [2017] UKSC 22; [2017] A.C. 549. Lady Hale DPSC commented, at [1], that: "it is axiomatic that the decision-maker can only make a decision which P himself could have made. The decision-maker is in no better position than P." It followed that "the court can only choose between the 'available options'", [2017] UKSC 22; [2017] A.C. 549 at [35].

[377] Mental Capacity Act 2005 s.9(1).

[378] Mental Capacity Act 2005 ss.11(1) to 11(4).

[379] Mental Capacity Act 2005 s.11(5).

[380] See *Re MB (Medical Treatment)* [1997] 8 Med. L.R. 217; [1997] 2 F.L.R. 426, para.6–041.

[381] Mental Capacity Act 2005 s.11(7) and (8).

(iii)   Lawful care or treatment

Section 5 of the Mental Capacity Act 2005 makes it lawful for any person (D) to   **6–116**
do an act in connection with the care or treatment of another person (P), if before
doing the act D takes reasonable steps to establish whether P lacks capacity in
relation to the matter in question, that D reasonably believes that P lacks capacity
in relation to the matter, and that it will be in P's best interests for the act to be
done.[382] If these conditions are satisfied D does not incur liability in relation to
the act that he would not have incurred if P had capacity to consent and had
consented to D doing the act.[383] D remains potentially liable in tort and in the
criminal law for loss or damage caused by his negligence in performing the
act;[384] and could also be liable for doing an act contrary to a valid advance
decision by P.[385]

Section 5 is subject to two further conditions where D does an act that is intended   **6–117**
to restrain P.[386] First, D must reasonably believe that it is necessary to do the act
in order to prevent harm to P.[387] Secondly, the act must be a proportionate
response to the likelihood of P suffering harm and the seriousness of that harm.[388]
For the purpose of these provisions "restrain" means: (a) the use of, or threats to
use, force to secure the doing of an act which P resists; or (b) restricting P's
liberty of movement, whether or not P resists.[389] Section 5 does not authorise a
person to do an act which conflicts with a decision made by a donee of a lasting
power of attorney granted by P or a deputy appointed for P by the court, provided
the decision by the donee or deputy was made within the scope his authority,[390]
though this latter provision does not prevent a person from providing
life-sustaining treatment or doing any act which he reasonably believes to be
necessary to prevent a serious deterioration in P's condition, while a decision is
sought from the court.[391]

Primacy of Mental Health Act when detaining patient for mental disorder   **6–118**
In *R. (on the application of Sessay) v South London and Maudsley NHS
Foundation Trust*[392] the Divisional Court held that ss.5 and 6 of the Mental
Capacity Act do not confer on police officers authority to remove persons to
hospital or other places of safety for the purposes set out in ss.135 and 136 of the
Mental Health Act 1983. Section 136 permits a constable who finds in a public
place a person who appears to be suffering from mental disorder to remove that
person to a place of safety if necessary to do so in the interests of that person or

---

[382] Section 4 sets out guidance as what must be taken into account when assessing P's best interests;
see paras 6–129 et seq.
[383] Mental Capacity Act 2005 s.5(2). In other words D is not liable in trespass to the person.
[384] Mental Capacity Act 2005 s.5(3).
[385] Mental Capacity Act 2005 s.5(4). See para.6–029.
[386] Mental Capacity Act 2005 s.6(1).
[387] Mental Capacity Act 2005 s.6(2).
[388] Mental Capacity Act 2005 s.6(3).
[389] Mental Capacity Act 2005 s.6(4).
[390] Mental Capacity Act 2005 s.6(6).
[391] Mental Capacity Act 2005 s.6(7).
[392] [2011] EWHC 2617 (QB); [2012] Q.B. 760.

for the protection of others.[393] A person moved to a place of safety under this provision can be detained there for up to 72 hours for the purpose of being examined by a doctor and interviewed by an approved mental health practitioner for the purpose of making any necessary arrangements for treatment or care. In *Sessay* police officers purported to act under ss.5 and 6 of the Mental Capacity Act in detaining and removing the claimant from her home to hospital, who was then detained by the hospital staff in the "section 136 suite" in the mistaken belief that the claimant had been brought to the hospital under the police officers' s.136 powers.[394] The Divisional Court held that the police officers and the hospital did not have lawful authority to detain the claimant.[395] There had been both false imprisonment at common law and a breach of the claimant's art.5 rights under the European Convention on Human Rights. The Court concluded that the Mental Health Act 1983 provides a comprehensive code for the compulsory admission to hospital of non-compliant incapacitated patients believed to be suffering from mental disorder,[396] and the defendants could not rely on the common law defence of necessity[397] or ss.5 and 6 of the Mental Capacity Act to render lawful what would otherwise not be lawful under the Mental Health Act.[398]

(iv) Depriving a patient of liberty

6–119   Initially, s.6(5) of the Mental Capacity Act 2005 provided that D does more than merely "restrain" P if he deprives P of his liberty within the meaning of art.5(1) of the European Convention on Human Rights. This was intended to reflect the human rights jurisprudence which distinguishes between acts which restrict people's liberty of movement and those which deprive people of their liberty within the meaning of art.5. Thus, what s.6(5) effectively did was to provide that

---

[393] Section 135 applies a similar regime to a person in a private place, subject to a warrant having been issued by a justice of the peace.

[394] The claimant was not in a public place when detained by the officers and so a warrant would have been required under s.135 of the Mental Health Act 1983.

[395] It was irrelevant that the hospital could have acted lawfully by detaining the claimant under s.2 (admission for assessment) or s.4 (admission for assessment in cases of emergency) of the Mental Health Act 1983 since they had acted unlawfully in purporting to rely on s.136: [2011] EWHC 2617 (QB); [2012] Q.B. 760 at [54]. On this point see *Lumba v Secretary of State for the Home Department* [2011] UKSC 12; [2012] 1 A.C. 245 at [62], [175], [221] and [239]. Defendants' honest and reasonable beliefs that they had the necessary authority to detain the claimant is irrelevant, if in fact there was no such authority: *R. v Governor of Brockhill Prison, ex p. Evans (No.2)* [2001] 2 A.C. 19.

[396] Applying the approach adopted by the House of Lords in *B v Forsey* 1988 S.C. (H.L.) 28; 1988 S.L.T. 572 to the Mental Health (Scotland) Act 1984.

[397] The defence of necessity provides none of the procedural safeguards found in the Mental Health Act 1983, and so it would fail to satisfy the requirements of the ECHR as set out by the European Court of Human Rights in *HL v United Kingdom* (2005) 40 E.H.R.R. 32; (2005) 17 B.H.R.C. 418; [2005] Lloyd's Rep. Med. 169; see para.6–077.

[398] In addition to a declaration that the detention was unlawful the claimant was also entitled to damages for breach of art.5 and for false imprisonment, to be assessed if not agreed. Note, however, that where there is a procedural error in failing to comply with the requirements of the Mental Health Act when detaining a patient, but the claimant could have been lawfully detained by following a correct procedure the claimant will be entitled to nominal damages only: *Bostridge v Oxleas NHS Foundation Trust* [2015] EWCA Civ 79; [2015] Med. L.R. 113 (applying *Lumba v Secretary of State for the Home Department* [2011] UKSC 12; [2012] 1 A.C. 245 and *R. (on the application of Kambadzi) v Secretary of State for the Home Department* [2011] UKSC 23; [2011] 1 W.L.R. 1299).

a deprivation of liberty within the meaning of art.5 could not be regarded as a mere restriction of movement, and therefore s.6 did not constitute a defence to a breach of art.5. However, s.50 of the Mental Health Act 2007 repealed s.6(5) of the Mental Capacity Act and introduced a complex scheme[399] for determining when it will be lawful to deprive P of his liberty.[400] "Deprivation of a person's liberty" has the same meaning as in art.5(1) of the European Convention on Human Rights, and for this purpose it does not matter whether a person is deprived of his liberty by a public authority or not.[401]

Deprivation of liberty   Apart from interim authority to deprive another person of liberty pending a decision of the court (s.4B), the Mental Capacity Act provides two means by which a deprivation of liberty may be authorised. Section 4A(1) provides that the Act "does not authorise any person ('D') to deprive any other person ('P') of his liberty", but this is subject to the provisions of ss.4A and 4B. Section 4A(3) provides that D may deprive P of his liberty if, by doing so, D is giving effect to a relevant decision of the court, which is a decision made by an order under s.16(2)(a) in relation to a matter concerning P's personal welfare.[402] D may also deprive P of his liberty if the deprivation is authorised by Sch.A1, which applies where P is detained in a hospital or care home.[403]

6–120

Interim authority for deprivation of liberty   Section 4B provides that D is authorised to deprive P of his liberty while a decision as respects any relevant issue is sought from the court, provided three conditions are met:

6–121

(1)   that there is a question about whether D is authorised to deprive P of his liberty under s.4A;

(2)   that the deprivation of liberty
    (a)   is wholly or partly for the purpose of
        (i)   giving P life-sustaining treatment, or
        (ii)   doing any vital act, or
    (b)   consists wholly or partly of
        (i)   giving P life-sustaining treatment, or
        (ii)   doing any vital act; and

(3)   that the deprivation of liberty is necessary in order to
    (a)   give the life-sustaining treatment, or
    (b)   do the vital act.

---

[399] See Law Com. Consultation Paper No.222, *Mental Capacity and Deprivation of Liberty* (2015) pointing to the widespread criticism of the "Deprivation of Liberty Safeguards" (DoLS) for their length and complexity. See further the Law Commission report following the consultation exercise *Mental Capacity and Deprivation of Liberty* (2017) Law Com. 372, ch. 4 (available at *http://www.lawcom.gov.uk/wp-content/uploads/2017/03/lc372_mental_capacity.pdf*). The Law Commission has recommended that the "DoLS should be replaced as a matter of pressing urgency". See generally, R. Jones, *Mental Capacity Act Manual*, 7th edn (London: Sweet & Maxwell, 2016), Pt 2.
[400] In order to comply with the ruling of the European Court of Human Rights in *HL v United Kingdom* (2005) 40 E.H.R.R. 32; (2005) 17 B.H.R.C. 418; [2005] Lloyd's Rep. Med. 169 (see para.6–077).
[401] Mental Capacity Act 2005 s.64(5) and (6).
[402] Mental Capacity Act 2005 s.4A(4).
[403] Mental Capacity Act 2005 s.4A(5).

A vital act is any act which the person doing it reasonably believes to be necessary to prevent a serious deterioration in P's condition.[404]

6–122 **Deprivation of liberty where P is in a hospital or care home**   Schedule A1 of the Mental Capacity Act 2005, which applies to a person (P) who is detained in a hospital or care home in circumstances which amount to a deprivation of liberty, provides a detailed set of procedures and requirements for obtaining a "standard or urgent authorisation".[405] If a standard or urgent authorisation is in force the managing authority of the hospital or care home may deprive P of his liberty by detaining him. Any act done by a person (D) for the purpose of detaining P does not give rise to any liability in relation to the act that he would not have incurred if P had had capacity to consent in relation to D doing the act, and had consented to D doing the act.[406] This effectively provides a defence to what would otherwise be trespass to the person or a breach of art.5 of the European Convention on Human Rights, but it is expressly provided that it is not a defence to civil or criminal liability for negligence, and it is a defence only in respect of acts done for the purpose of the authorisation, and subject to any conditions attached to a standard authorisation.[407] The Schedule applies only to adults who have a mental disorder within the meaning of the Mental Health Act 1983 (but disregarding any exclusion for persons with learning disability, i.e. persons with learning disability fall within the Schedule) and who lack capacity in relation to the question whether or not they should be accommodated in the relevant hospital or care home for the purpose of being given relevant care or treatment.[408] It must, inter alia, be in the best interests of the person to be a detained resident; it must be necessary to prevent harm to him for him to be a detained resident; and it must be a proportionate response to both the likelihood of the person suffering harm and the seriousness of the harm for him to be a detained resident.[409] Section 21A of the Mental Capacity Act 2005 gives the court power to determine issues arising under Sch.A1, including making an order about a person's liability for any act

---

[404] Mental Capacity Act 2005 s.4B(5). Section 4B is concerned with life-sustaining treatment in an emergency, not where there is a full opportunity to have the matter resolved by the court: *A Local Health Board v AB* [2015] EWCOP 31; [2015] C.O.P.L.R. 412 at [49]. The issue in this case was whether an incapacitated patient should have elective heart surgery to reduce the risk of death from an aortic aneurism. If the aneurism ruptured it would be a life or death emergency, but elective surgery to reduce the risk of a rupture was not an emergency.

[405] The details of which amount to over 180 paragraphs in Sch.A1.

[406] Mental Capacity Act 2005 Sch.A1 paras 2 and 3.

[407] Mental Capacity Act 2005 Sch.A1 para.4.

[408] Mental Capacity Act 2005 Sch.A1 paras 13 to 15.

[409] Mental Capacity Act 2005 Sch.A1 para.16. A failure to comply with the procedural requirements of Sch.A1 will give rise to breaches of art.5 and, potentially, art.8: see e.g. *Hillingdon London BC v Neary* [2011] EWHC 1377 (COP); [2011] 4 All E.R. 584; *Re J (An Adult) (Deprivation of Liberty: Safeguards)* [2015] EWCOP 5; [2015] Fam. 291. A local authority also has a duty "to ensure that a person deprived of liberty is not only entitled but enabled to have the lawfulness of his detention reviewed speedily by a court": *Hillingdon London BC v Neary* at [202]. See also *Stanev v Bulgaria* (36760/06) (2012) 55 E.H.R.R. 22; [2012] M.H.L.R. 23; *Červenka v Czech Republic* (62507/12) (ECtHR), discussed at (2017) 24 E.J.H.L. 105 and [2017] E.H.R.L.R. 91.

done in connection with a standard or urgent authorisation before its variation or termination (including an order excluding a person from liability).[410]

Deprivation of liberty where P is not in a hospital or care home Schedule A1 of the Act provides a procedure for authorising a deprivation of liberty for patients in a hospital or care home. Any other patient who is deprived of their liberty requires the approval of the Court of Protection under s.16 of the Act for the deprivation of liberty to be lawful. Clearly, the wider the concept of "deprivation of liberty" the greater the number of cases that will require court approval.

6-123

Meaning of deprivation of liberty In *Cheshire West and Chester Council v P*[411] the Supreme Court adopted a definition of deprivation of liberty which significantly expanded the numbers of patients for whom Court of Protection authorisation is needed. The issue was whether living arrangements made for mentally incapacitated persons living in supervised local authority accommodation or foster care with intensive support amounted to a deprivation of liberty in breach of art.5 of the European Convention on Human Rights. It was common ground, said Baroness Hale,[412] that there were three components of a deprivation of liberty: (a) the objective component of confinement in a particular restricted place for a not negligible length of time; (b) the subjective component of lack of valid consent;[413] and (c) the attribution of responsibility to the state.[414] Only (a)

6-124

---

[410] Note that s.21A cannot be used where there is a dispute about the personal welfare and medical treatment of P. It is limited to resolving the question of whether there is a deprivation of liberty: *Re Briggs (Incapacitated Person)* [2017] EWCA Civ 1169.

[411] [2014] UKSC 19; [2014] A.C. 896. The case is discussed by Y. Amin and R. Horan in "*P v Cheshire West and Chester Council*: What is a deprivation of liberty?" [2014] J.P.I.L. 203.

[412] Applying *Storck v Germany* (61603/00) (2005) 43 E.H.R.R. 6; [2005] M.H.L.R. 211 and *Stanev v Bulgaria* (36760/06) (2012) 55 E.H.R.R. 22; [2012] M.H.L.R. 23.

[413] In *Cheshire West* Lord Kerr noted, at [81], that "The subjective element in deprivation of liberty is the absence of valid consent to the confinement in question—see para 117 of *Stanev*. This must be distinguished from passive acquiescence to the deprivation, particularly where that stems from an inability to appreciate the fact that one's liberty is being curtailed. In para 118(c) the court said that deprivation of liberty occurs when an adult is incapable of giving his consent to admission to a psychiatric institution, even though he had never attempted to leave it." That was the position in *HL v United Kingdom* (2005) 40 E.H.R.R. 32; (2005) 17 B.H.R.C. 418; [2005] Lloyd's Rep. Med. 169; para.6–077 which prompted the deprivation of liberty amendments to the Mental Capacity Act 2005.

[414] In *Storck v Germany* (61603/00) (2005) 43 E.H.R.R. 6; [2005] M.H.L.R. 211 at [89] the European Court of Human Rights held that there were three ways in which the state could be responsible for a deprivation of liberty: (i) direct involvement of public authorities in the applicant's detention; (ii) a violation of art.5(1) by its courts, in compensation proceedings brought by the applicant, failing to interpret the provisions of civil law in the spirit of art.5; and (iii) breach of the state's positive obligation to protect the applicant against interferences with her liberty by private persons. On the attribution of responsibility to the state see: *Staffordshire CC v K* [2016] EWCOP 27; [2016] Fam. 419 (victim of road traffic accident who lacked capacity awarded substantial damages and looked after at home under a regime of care provided by private-sector providers in circumstances that objectively amounted to a deprivation of liberty; a welfare order was required because the court awarding damages and the Court of Protection when appointing a deputy to hold and manage them were aware of K's circumstances: "That knowledge of the courts means that the State has that knowledge (or cannot successfully say that it does not)", per Charles J at [135]). This decision was upheld on appeal: [2016] EWCA Civ 1317; [2017] Fam. 278 (in the absence of a welfare order by the Court of Protection there were "insufficient procedural safeguards against arbitrary detention in a purely

was in issue in *Cheshire West*. It was axiomatic, said Baroness Hale, that "people with disabilities, both mental and physical, have the same human rights as the rest of the human race"[415] including the right to physical liberty, and what it means to be deprived of liberty must be the same for everyone, whether or not they have physical or mental disabilities. It followed that:

> "If it would be a deprivation of my liberty to be obliged to live in a particular place, subject to constant monitoring and control, only allowed out with close supervision, and unable to move away without permission even if such an opportunity became available, then it must also be a deprivation of the liberty of a disabled person. The fact that my living arrangements are comfortable, and indeed make my life as enjoyable as it could possibly be, should make no difference. A gilded cage is still a cage."[416]

It was wrong to compare the life that P was leading with the life which another person with his disabilities might be leading. The person's compliance or lack of objection was not relevant; the relative normality of the placement was not relevant; and the reason or purpose behind a particular placement was also not relevant.[417] The "acid test" was:

> "…whether a person is under the complete supervision and control of those caring for her and is not free to leave the place where she lives."[418]

The fact that the best possible arrangements have been made for P, or that she has as much freedom as possible consistent with her disability, was not the issue.[419] Article 5 required that people should not be deprived of their liberty without proper safeguards, and this involved safeguards which will secure that the legal justifications for the constraints which they are under are made out.[420]

6–125   One effect of *Cheshire West and Chester Council v P* has been that the living arrangements of a much wider range of persons who lack capacity now requires authorisation by the Court of Protection under the Mental Capacity Act s.16, and this has created considerable uncertainty as to the procedural requirements for dealing with a potentially large number of applications.[421]

---

private care regime", at [78]). See also *Haringey LBC v R* [2016] EWCOP 33; [2016] C.O.P.L.R. 476 at [57]–[58] on the imputation of a deprivation of liberty to the state.

[415] [2014] UKSC 19; [2014] A.C. 896 at [45].

[416] [2014] UKSC 19; [2014] A.C. 896 at [46]; applied in *Haringey LBC v R* [2016] EWCOP 33; [2016] C.O.P.L.R. 476 at [54], and it was irrelevant that the individual was content and acquiesced with the arrangements.

[417] [2014] UKSC 19; [2014] A.C. 896 at [50].

[418] [2014] UKSC 19; [2014] A.C. 896 at [54]. Lord Kerr said at [76]: "Liberty means the state or condition of being free from external constraint. It is predominantly an objective state. It does not depend on one's disposition to exploit one's freedom. Nor is it diminished by one's lack of capacity."

[419] Lord Kerr added, [2014] UKSC 19; [2014] A.C. 896 at [82], that: "Benevolence underpinning a regime which restricts liberty is irrelevant to an assessment of whether it in fact amounts to deprivation."

[420] [2014] UKSC 19; [2014] A.C. 896 at [56].

[421] See e.g. *Re X (Deprivation of Liberty)* [2015] EWCA Civ 599; [2016] 1 W.L.R. 227; *Re MOD (Deprivation of Liberty)* [2015] EWCOP 47; *Re NRA* [2015] EWCOP 59; [2015] C.O.P.L.R. 690. For consideration of the circumstances in which an application should be brought under s.21A to

Deprivation of liberty of minors The parents of a 15-year-old autistic boy can **6–126**
consent to a deprivation of his liberty in a hospital adolescent unit[422] but once the
child reaches 16 years a parent cannot consent to his detention, even though it is
both necessary and in his best interests, and this will require the authorisation of
the court.[423] This is the position irrespective of whether the 16 or 17-year-old has
capacity or not.

Where P is ineligible to be deprived of liberty Section 16A(1) limits the **6–127**
power of the court to deprive people of their liberty, providing that if they are
"ineligible to be deprived of liberty" by the Mental Capacity Act 2005, the court
may not include in a welfare order provision which authorises them to be
deprived of their liberty. Similarly, if a welfare order has been made which
includes provision authorising a person to be deprived of his liberty and that
person becomes ineligible to be deprived of liberty under the 2005 Act, the
provision ceases to have effect for as long as the person remains ineligible.[424]
Schedule 1A of the Mental Capacity Act 2005 applies for determining whether or
not P is ineligible to be deprived of liberty by the Act.[425] The rules are complex
and depend on the interaction of the Mental Capacity Act with the Mental Health
Act 1983. In broad terms, the scheme of the Mental Health Act takes precedence
over that of the Mental Capacity Act,[426] though this can give rise to difficulties
where a patient detained (or where the patient could be detained) under the
Mental Health Act requires treatment for a medical condition that cannot be
authorised under that Act (i.e. most treatments for physical as opposed to mental
health conditions) where the treatment will necessarily entail a deprivation of
liberty. In these circumstances if the patient is ineligible to be deprived of liberty
the treatment cannot be authorised under the Mental Capacity Act, and the courts
have had to resort to the inherent jurisdiction to provide lawful authority for
treatment.[427]

---

challenge a deprivation of liberty under a standard authorisation made under Sch.A1, and the different
roles of the relevant person's representative and the independent mental capacity advocate see *Re RD*
[2016] EWCOP 49; [2017] 1 W.L.R. 1723.
[422] *Trust A v X (A Child)* [2015] EWHC 922 (Fam); [2016] 1 F.L.R. 142. But a local authority with
parental responsibility for a child by virtue of an interim care order or a care order cannot consent to
the detention of a child which would otherwise amount to a deprivation of liberty: *Re AB (A Child)*
(Deprivation of Liberty: Consent) [2015] EWHC 3125 (Fam); [2016] 1 W.L.R. 1160 at [29] per
Keehan J.
[423] *Birmingham City Council v D (A Child)* [2016] EWCOP 8; [2016] C.O.P.L.R. 198.
[424] Mental Capacity Act 2005 s.16A(2).
[425] The implications of P being ineligible to be deprived of his liberty for whether it is lawfully
possible to provide medical treatment or care to P are considered below, para.6–150.
[426] See *GJ v Foundation Trust* [2009] EWHC 2972 (Fam); [2010] Fam. 70 at [58]–[65] per Charles J,
as explained by Charles J in *AM v South London & Maudsley NHS Foundation Trust* [2013] UKUT
365 (AAC); [2014] M.H.L.R. 181 at [76]–[79]; *C v Blackburn with Darwen Borough Council* [2011]
EWHC 3321 (Fam); (2012) 15 C.C.L. Rep. 251; [2012] M.H.L.R. 202 at [33]–[35] per Peter Jackson
J; *Northamptonshire Healthcare NHS Foundation Trust v ML* [2014] EWCOP 2; [2014] C.O.P.L.R.
439. See the discussion of *GJ v Foundation Trust* by N. Allen, "The Bournewood gap (as amended?)"
(2010) 18 Med. Law Rev. 78.
[427] See para.6–150.

6-128 **Deprivation of liberty in an intensive care unit** A patient who lacks capacity who is receiving treatment in an intensive care unit of a hospital is not, without more, being compulsorily detained by the state. In *R. (on the application of LF) v HM Senior Coroner for Inner South London*[428] the Court of Appeal considered that, though it was possible for the *Cheshire West* principles to apply in an intensive care setting,[429] on the facts of *LF* the patient was not compulsorily detained, rather she was there to receive life-sustaining treatment:

> "She was physically restricted in her movements by her physical infirmities and by the treatment she received (which for example included sedation) but the root cause of any loss of liberty was her physical condition, not any restrictions imposed by the hospital."[430]

The policy reasons identified in *Cheshire West* for safeguards against a deprivation of liberty did not apply in the case of a physical illness where the treatment a patient of unsound mind is given in good faith and is materially the same treatment as would be given to a person of sound mind with the same physical illness.[431] This approach was endorsed by the Court of Appeal in *Re Briggs (Incapacitated Person)*[432] where King LJ said that:

> "...the question of deprivation of liberty does not arise where a person who lacks capacity is so unwell that they are at risk of dying if they were anywhere other than in hospital and therefore, by virtue of their physical condition, they are unable to leave the hospital. It may be the case however that as the treatment progresses and P's physical condition improves, his or her ongoing care becomes a deprivation of liberty and, at that stage, a standard authorisation or court order will be required if the continued retention of P on the ward is not to become unlawful."

(v)   The patient's best interests

6-129 Section 1(5) of the Mental Capacity Act 2005 provides that an act done, or decision made, for or on behalf of people who lack capacity must be done, or made, in their best interests.[433] Before the act is done or the decision is made, regard must be had to whether the purpose for which it is needed can be as effectively achieved in a way that is less restrictive of people's rights and freedom

---

[428] [2017] EWCA Civ 31; [2017] 3 W.L.R. 382. The issue arose on an application for an inquest into the patient's death following a cardiac arrest to be held with a jury under the Coroners and Justice Act 2009 s.7, which applies, inter alia, where the deceased died while in custody or "otherwise in state detention". The 2009 Act has been amended to make it clear that when a person is deprived of liberty under s.4A(3) or (5) or 4B of the Mental Capacity Act 2005 they are not in "state detention" (thus avoiding the need for an investigation by the coroner on this ground (see s.1(2)(c) of the 2009 Act) every time a person deprived of liberty dies): see the Coroners and Justice Act 2009 s.48(2A), inserted by the Policing and Crime Act 2017 s.178.

[429] Arden LJ gave the example, [2017] EWCA Civ 31; [2017] 3 W.L.R. 382 at [90], of *NHS Trust 1 v FG* [2014] EWCOP 30; [2015] 1 W.L.R. 1984, where a hospital considered that it might have to give obstetric care to a pregnant woman of unsound mind who objected to the treatment.

[430] [2017] EWCA Civ 31; [2017] 3 W.L.R. 382 at [10] per Arden LJ.

[431] [2017] EWCA Civ 31; [2017] 3 W.L.R. 382 at [93].

[432] [2017] EWCA Civ 1169 at [106]. See further the guidance given by King LJ, at [108], as to when an authorisation of a deprivation of liberty will be required for patients receiving medical treatment in hospital for a physical condition.

[433] See H.J. Taylor "What are 'Best Interests'? A Critical Evaluation of 'Best Interests' Decision-Making in Clinical Practice" (2016) 24 Med. L. Rev. 176.

of action.[434] Section 4 sets out criteria for determining whether an act is in the patient's best interests. People making this decision must not make it merely on the basis of (a) patients' age or appearance, or (b) a condition of their, or an aspect of their behaviour, which might lead others to make unjustified assumptions about what might be in their best interests.[435] They must consider all the relevant circumstances, and in particular whether the incapacity is temporary, and if so how long the incapacity will last.[436] They must, so far as reasonably practicable, permit and encourage patients to participate, or to improve their ability to participate, as fully as possible in any act done for them and any decision affecting them.[437] They must also consider, so far as is reasonably ascertainable: (a) patients' past and present wishes and feelings (and, in particular, any relevant written statement made by them when they had capacity); (b) the beliefs and values that would be likely to influence their decision if they had capacity; and (c) the other factors that they would be likely to consider if they were able to do so.[438]

Decision-makers must also take into account, if practicable and appropriate, the views of: (a) anyone named by patients as someone to be consulted on the matter in question or on matters of that kind; (b) anyone engaged in caring for them or interested in their welfare; (c) any donee of a lasting power of attorney granted by them; and (d) any deputy appointed for them by the court, as to what would be in their best interests and, in particular, as to patients' past and present wishes and feelings, and the beliefs and values that would be likely to influence their decision if they had capacity.[439] Where something is done or a decision is made by people other than the court, it is sufficient if, having complied with s.4(1) to (7), they reasonably believe that what they do or decide is in the best interests of the person concerned.[440]   **6–130**

Balance sheet   In assessing the patient's best interests the court should draw up   **6–131**
a balance sheet of the benefits and disadvantages of the proposed course of action. In *Re A (Medical Treatment: male sterilisation)*[441] Thorpe LJ said that:

---

[434] Mental Capacity Act 2005 s.1(6).
[435] Mental Capacity Act 2005 s.4(1).
[436] Mental Capacity Act 2005 s.4(2), (3). Section 4(11) provides that "relevant circumstances" are those (a) of which the person making the determination is aware, and (b) which it would be reasonable to regard as relevant.
[437] Mental Capacity Act 2005 s.4(4). In *Wye Valley NHS Trust v B* [2015] EWCOP 60; [2015] Med. L.R. 552; (2015) 147 B.M.L.R. 187 at [18] this involved the judge seeing the patient face-to-face, rather than relying on medical reports, which gave the patient the opportunity to get his point of view across.
[438] Mental Capacity Act 2005 s.4(6). In *Re Briggs (Incapacitated Person) (Medical Treatment: Best Interests Decision) (No.2)* [2016] EWCOP 53; [2017] 4 W.L.R. 37 at [44] Charles J considered that the provisions of s.4(6) were of "key importance" in the circumstances of that case, where the issue was whether it was in the best interests of the patient to continue clinically assisted nutrition and hydration.
[439] Mental Capacity Act 2005 s.4(7).
[440] Mental Capacity Act 2005 s.4(9). Section 4(5) provides that where the determination relates to life-sustaining treatment the decision-maker must not, in considering whether the treatment is in the best interests of the person concerned, be motivated by a desire to bring about the patient's death. See para.6–156.
[441] [2000] 1 F.L.R. 549 at 560.

"...to make an evaluation of the best interests of a claimant lacking capacity should draw up a balance sheet. The first entry should be of any factor or factors of actual benefit. ... Then on the other sheet the judge should write any counter-balancing dis-benefits to the applicant. ... Then the judge should enter on each sheet the potential gains and losses in each instance making some estimate of the extent of the possibility that the gain or loss might accrue. At the end of that exercise the judge should be better placed to strike a balance between the sum of the certain and possible gains against the sum of the certain and possible losses. Obviously, only if the account is in relatively significant credit will the judge conclude that the applicant is likely to advance the best interests of the claimant."

In *Re SK (Vulnerable Adult: Capacity)*[442] Wood J accepted that this was also the correct way to proceed when considering best interests under s.4 of the Mental Capacity Act 2005.[443] In drawing up the balance sheet some factors have greater weight than others: "The balancing exercise is qualitative rather than merely numerical."[444]

6–132   **The patient's views**   Judgments about what is in a particular patient's best interests are inevitably heavily fact-dependent. A decision about best interests must take into account the patient's welfare in the widest sense; it is not limited to medical issues but includes social and psychological issues.[445] Decision-makers must try to put themselves in the place of individual patients and ask what their attitude to the treatment is or would be likely to be; and they must consult others who are looking after them or are interested in their welfare, in particular for their view of what the patient's attitude would be.[446] Section 4(6) of the Mental Capacity Act requires the court to take into account people's past and present wishes and feelings, and the beliefs and values that would be likely to influence their decision if they had capacity. In *Wye Valley NHS Trust v B*[447] it was argued that the views of a person lacking capacity should be accorded less weight than those of a person with capacity. Peter Jackson J did not accept the premise on which this argument was based. It was true that the views of a person with capacity were, by definition, decisive in relation to any treatment being offered. But once incapacity had been established so that a best-interests decision had to be made, there was:

---

[442] [2008] EWHC 636 (Fam); [2008] LS Law Medical 505 at [71].

[443] See, e.g., the balance sheet added as an Appendix to the judgment of Holman J in *A NHS Trust v K* [2012] EWHC 2922 (COP); [2013] 1 F.C.R. 190.

[444] *M v N* [2015] EWCOP 76; (2015) 148 B.M.L.R. 116 at [46] per Hayden J, citing *Re F (A Child) (International Relocation Cases)* [2015] EWCA Civ 882; [2017] 1 F.L.R. 979; [2016] 2 F.C.R. 368 at [52] where McFarlane LJ observed that a balance sheet "should be no more than an aide memoire of the key factors and how they match up against each other. If a balance sheet is used it should be a route to judgment and not a substitution for the judgment itself. A key step in any welfare evaluation is the attribution of weight, or lack of it, to each of the relevant considerations". See also *Mental Health Trust v DD* [2015] EWCOP 4 at [112] per Cobb J, commenting that the balance sheet approach, though helpful, does not of itself resolve the issues: "my final determination is ultimately informed by the weight put upon the various factors in favour of or against the proposed course of action that are identified therein."

[445] *Aintree University Hospitals NHS Foundation Trust v James* [2013] UKSC 67; [2014] A.C. 591 at [39].

[446] [2013] UKSC 67; [2014] A.C. 591.

[447] [2015] EWCOP 60; [2015] Med. L.R. 552; (2015) 147 B.M.L.R. 187; discussed by L. Series, "The Place of Wishes and Feelings in Best Interests Decisions: *Wye Valley NHS Trust v Mr B*" (2016) 79 M.L.R. 1101.

"...no theoretical limit to the weight or lack of weight that should be given to the person's wishes and feelings, beliefs and values. In some cases, the conclusion will be that little weight or no weight can be given; in others, very significant weight will be due.... the wishes and feelings, beliefs and values of people with a mental disability are as important to them as they are to anyone else, and may even be more important. It would therefore be wrong in principle to apply any automatic discount to their point of view."[448]

The judge gave significant weight to the patient's wishes in concluding that it was not in his best interests to undergo an amputation of his foot, without which he was likely to die shortly.[449] Similarly, in *Newcastle upon Tyne Hospitals Foundation Trust v LM*[450] Peter Jackson J took the view that, if he had not concluded that a Jehovah's Witness had been competent to refuse treatment involving the use of blood products, he would have held that it was not in her best interests to have a blood transfusion: "her wishes and feelings and her long-standing beliefs and values carried *determinative* weight."[451]

On the other hand, in *NHS Foundation Trust v QZ*[452] Hayden J emphasised that the:

6–133

"...wishes and feelings of those who suffer from delusional beliefs are not automatically ... to be afforded the same weight as the beliefs articulated by an individual who has had the fortune to possess the powers of objective reasoning and analysis."

Delusional beliefs should not be discounted merely because they are irrational, since they are real to the individual concerned, but the weight to be attached to the patient's beliefs will differ from case to case.[453] In *Re M (Statutory Will)*,[454] in the context of authorising a statutory will for a person who lacked capacity, Munby J said that in considering the weight and importance to be attached to P's wishes and feelings under s.4(6) of the Act, the court must have regard to all the relevant circumstances. This includes:

---

[448] [2015] EWCOP 60; [2015] Med. L.R. 552; (2015) 147 B.M.L.R. 187 at [10]–[11]; *B v D* [2017] EWCOP 15 at [56].

[449] "I am quite sure that it would not be in Mr B's best interests to take away his little remaining independence and dignity in order to replace it with a future for which he understandably has no appetite and which could only be achieved after a traumatic and uncertain struggle that he and no one else would have to endure. There is a difference between fighting on someone's behalf and just fighting them. Enforcing treatment in this case would surely be the latter", [2015] EWCOP 60; [2015] Med. L.R. 552; (2015) 147 B.M.L.R. 187 at [45]; cf. *Surrey and Sussex Healthcare NHS Trust v AB* [2015] EWCOP 50 at [59]–[61] where the best interests assessment came down in favour of authorising an above the knee amputation.

[450] [2014] EWHC 454 (COP); [2015] 1 F.C.R. 373; (2014) 137 B.M.L.R. 226.

[451] [2014] EWHC 454 (COP); [2015] 1 F.C.R. 373; (2014) 137 B.M.L.R. 226 at [23] (emphasis added). It was also relevant that a transfusion might not have been effective to save her life.

[452] [2017] EWCOP 11 at [31].

[453] On the evidence in *QZ* Hayden J concluded that it was in the patient's best interests to undergo medical investigations to determine whether she had gynaecological cancer (the risk of which was 30–50 per cent) although this would have the almost inevitable effect of exacerbating her mental problems in the short term.

[454] [2009] EWHC 2525 (Fam); [2011] 1 W.L.R. 344 at [35]: "Just as the test of incapacity under the 2005 Act is, as under the common law, 'issue specific', so in a similar way the weight to be attached to P's wishes and feelings will likewise be issue specific."

"(a) the degree of P's incapacity … (b) the strength and consistency of the views being expressed by P; (c) the possible impact on P of knowledge that her wishes and feelings are not being given effect to … (d) the extent to which P's wishes and feelings are, or are not, rational, sensible, responsible and, pragmatically capable of sensible implementation in the particular circumstances; and (e) crucially, the extent to which P's wishes and feelings, if given effect to, can properly be accommodated within the court's overall assessment of what is in her best interests."

6–134   **The views of others**   In many instances the views of members of the patient's close family, though not decisive, will be influential in assessing where the patient's best interests lie. Section 4(7)(b) requires the court to take into account, if practicable and appropriate, the views of "anyone engaged in caring for the person or interested in his welfare".[455] In *A NHS Trust v K*[456] Holman J granted a declaration that it would be lawful for doctors to surgically remove the patient's womb, fallopian tubes and ovaries for the treatment of the patient's endometrial cancer, despite a significant risk of death during or after the surgery due to the patient's comorbid medical conditions. At the time of the hearing her three adult sons supported this course of action and the judge took this into account in reaching a view as to the patient's best interests, bearing in mind that they knew their mother well and each of them would be heavily involved during her recovery and convalescence. Although stressing that the decision as to the patient's best interests is ultimately for the court, Holman J said that he might well have refused to make the declarations if they had raised any reasoned opposition to them. Moreover, he recognised that circumstances could change before the operation (such as the patient's mental state or her likely post-operative compliance) and therefore if any of the patient's sons notified the doctors that he no longer considered the operation should take place there should be a "temporary brake" which would halt the process. This was not an absolute power of veto, since the operation did not require their consent, but there could then be further consideration by the court in light of the changed circumstances.[457]

---

[455] See, e.g., *ZH v Commissioner of Police of the Metropolis* [2013] EWCA Civ 69; [2013] 1 W.L.R. 3021 where the failure of the police to consult the carer of a severely autistic and epileptic 16-year-old, who also suffered from learning disabilities, was unable to communicate by speech, and had a strong aversion to being touched, led the police to over-react to a situation in which the claimant had been standing at the side of a swimming pool for 40 minutes. The failure to consult, amongst other things, resulted in a finding that the police had not been acting in the claimant's best interests when they intervened.

[456] [2012] EWHC 2922 (COP); [2013] 1 F.C.R. 190.

[457] [2012] EWHC 2922 (COP); [2013] 1 F.C.R. 190 at [56] and [57]. See also *Re CS (Termination of Pregnancy)* [2016] EWCOP 10; [2017] 1 F.L.R. 635; (2016) 153 B.M.L.R. 141, where Baker J took into account the views of the patient's mother and sister in deciding whether it was in the best interests of a woman who lacked capacity to have a termination of pregnancy; *Cumbria NHS Clinical Commissioning Group v S* [2016] EWCOP 32; (2016) 153 B.M.L.R. 168 at [13] per Hayden J: "I cannot over-emphasise the importance of listening to the family who ultimately know the patient's personality best. That is not to say that their wishes and views should be determinative, but it is extremely important that they are heard and their observations given appropriate weight"; and *Re Briggs (Incapacitated Person) (Medical Treatment: Best Interests Decision) (No.2)* [2016] EWCOP 53; [2017] 4 W.L.R. 37 on the importance of attaching significant weight to the family's evidence as to the patient's probable choice.

Use of force or covert medication   In some cases what is contemplated being   **6–135**
done to or for patients in their best interests will involve coercion, and where it is
strikingly counter to patients' wishes this could involve the use of physical force
and sedation.[458] In reaching a view as to patients' best interests the court will
have to factor in the negative consequences for them of having their wishes
completely ignored. In *A Local Authority v A*[459] the local authority applied for an
order to force a married woman with a low IQ who had had two previous children
removed from her care at birth to have contraception. Bodey J found that she did
not have capacity to decide whether or not to receive contraception. During the
hearing the local authority had changed its stance, asking the judge simply to
declare that it would be in the interim best interests of A to have contraception, if
she consented.[460] Bodey J declined to make any order about her best interests,
clearly concerned about the impact of compulsion on A and the wider
implications:

> "It is obvious on the facts of this case, that any step towards long-term court imposed
> contraception by way of physical coercion, with its affinity to enforced sterilisation and shades
> of social engineering, would raise profound questions about state intervention in private and
> family life. Whilst the issue of the use of force has not been argued out at this hearing I cannot,
> on these facts, presently see how it could be acceptable."[461]

Analogous to the use of force, in some respects, is the use of covert medication
for patients who are being deprived of their liberty. Covert medication should be
used only in exceptional circumstances, and only after a best interests assessment,
unless the circumstances are urgent.[462]

---

[458] See e.g. *DH NHS Foundation Trust v PS* [2010] EWHC 1217 (Fam); [2010] Med. L.R. 320
(commented on by Mullender, "Involuntary medical treatment, incapacity, and respect" (2011) 127
L.Q.R. 167) where Sir Nicholas Wall P authorised the use of force and sedation so that a 55-year-old
woman who lacked capacity, and had a phobia of hospitals and needles, could undergo surgery for
cancer; *A NHS Trust v K* [2012] EWHC 2922 (COP); [2013] 1 F.C.R. 190—covert sedation lawful
prior to surgery for endometrial cancer in a patient with chronic schizophrenia and delusions
(including the delusion that she was not suffering from cancer); *NHS Trust v Patient* [2014] EWCOP
54—covert sedation and physical restraint authorised in the case of a patient with learning difficulties
and autism who needed surgery for removal of cancerous growth; *W NHS Trust v P* [2014] EWHC
119 (COP); *NHS Foundation Trust v QZ* [2017] EWCOP 11.

[459] [2010] EWHC 1549 (Fam); [2011] Fam. 61.

[460] Though as counsel for A pointed out, such an order was meaningless because if A consented no
order was required; if she did not, the order achieved nothing.

[461] [2010] EWHC 1549 (Fam); [2011] Fam. 61 at [77], having cited in the previous paragraph the
comments of Munby J in *Local Authority X v MM* [2007] EWHC 2003 (Fam); [2009] 1 F.L.R. 48 at
[118] and [120]: "the court must be careful to ensure that in rescuing a vulnerable adult from one type
of abuse it does not expose her to the risk of treatment at the hands of the State which, however well
intentioned, can itself end up being abusive of her dignity, her happiness and indeed of her human
rights ... What good is it making someone safer if it merely makes them miserable?" In *IIBCC v LG*
[2010] EWHC 1527 (Fam) at [39] King J noted that where the incapacitated person is actively
opposed to a course of action "the benefits which it holds for him will have to be carefully weighed up
against the disadvantages of going against his wishes, especially if force is required to do this".

[462] *Re G* [2016] EWCOP 37 at [29]. District Judge Bellamy commented, at [31], that: "The use of
medication without consent or covertly whether for physical health or for mental health must always
call for close scrutiny. It seems to me that there is good reason to pay close regard to the justification
for medication especially if as in this case it potentially impacts upon a person's behaviour or mental
health or is a sedative in effect." In *Re G* the court gave guidance on the procedure that should be
followed where the use of covert medication is being considered.

6–136   **The presumption for life**   In any case where the consequence of a decision about the patient's best interests is that the patient may die there will be a strong presumption that it is in the person's best interests to stay alive.[463] But this is not absolute, and there are cases where it is not in a patient's best interests to receive life-sustaining treatment.[464]

6–137   **Anorexia nervosa**   Adult patients suffering from anorexia nervosa are almost invariably found to lack capacity, at least where the condition is severe and has persisted for some time.[465] It might be thought that it would always be in the best interests of the patient to be force-fed to keep the patient alive, but in severe cases this is not necessarily the outcome. In *NHS Trust v L*[466] the patient had a rare, severe and unremitting form of anorexia nervosa. She had been treated for many years in specialist eating disorder units but there had been no progress in her condition. She was showing signs of irreversible multi-organ failure and her prospects of recovery were approaching zero. In granting a declaration that it would be in L's best interests not to force-feed her, King J acknowledged the "strong presumption" that all steps would be taken to preserve life, save in exceptional circumstances. But force-feeding would be futile given that irreversible organ failure had begun, L could no longer resist infection and she was in imminent danger of cardiac arrest. Force-feeding under sedation would be extremely distressing for L, and even if she could be persuaded to accept a small increase in her nutrient intake her anorexia was so severe and deep-rooted that there was no real possibility of her maintaining co-operation.

6–138   Similarly, in *A NHS Foundation Trust v X*[467] Cobb J held that, notwithstanding the strong presumption in favour of preserving life, it was not in the best interests of a young woman with severe anorexia to authorise force-feeding. This conclusion involved looking at her welfare in the widest sense,[468] and taking into account: the unanimous medical evidence; the restriction on her liberty of forced treatment; the substantial risk (based on her previous behaviour) that forced treatment could lead her to self-harm and suicide attempts; the "paradox" that, though medical treatment is designed to preserve life, but that (as argued by the treating doctors) forced treatment may "be doing no more than facilitating or

---

[463] *Aintree University Hospitals NHS Foundation Trust v James* [2013] UKSC 67; [2014] A.C. 591 at [35] per Baroness Hale DP; see para.6–157.

[464] [2013] UKSC 67; [2014] A.C. 591 at [35]. As, e.g., in *Re R (Serious Medical Treatment)* [2016] EWCOP 60 (in best interests of 40-year-old paranoid schizophrenic not to have treatment for incurable but asymptomatic brain tumour and to be provided with palliative care only).

[465] See para.6–054.

[466] [2012] EWHC 2741 (COP).

[467] [2014] EWCOP 35; [2015] C.O.P.L.R. 11; (2014) 140 B.M.L.R. 41; discussed by J. Coggon (2015) 23 Med. L. Rev. 659; D. Wang (2015) 78 M.L.R. 871. See also *Re W (Medical Treatment: Anorexia)* [2016] EWCOP 13; (2016) 151 B.M.L.R. 220 (in best interests of patient with severe and unremitting anorexia nervosa to be discharged from hospital into community setting, giving her the chance to exercise any control she was capable of over her condition, since continued treatment in specialist unit was unlikely to prolong her life more than any other alternative); *Cheshire and Wirral Partnership NHS Foundation Trust v Z* [2016] EWCOP 56; [2017] C.O.P.L.R. 165 (where Hayden J reached a similar conclusion to that in *Re W* on the particular facts).

[468] Applying *Aintree University Hospitals NHS Foundation Trust v James* [2013] UKSC 67; [2014] A.C. 591 at [39]; see para.6–157.

accelerating the termination of her life"; that forced-feeding may keep her alive but did not treat her condition; that if X was reassured that she would not be force-fed, she would be more likely to engage in the palliative care process; that the process of admitting X and compelling her re-feeding would be highly traumatic to her and cause her considerable distress. Articles 3 and 8 of the ECHR were prominently engaged:

> "...repeated forcible feeding over a long period of time against her clearly expressed wishes, most especially with the use of physical restraint, is likely in my judgment to amount to inhuman or degrading treatment, certainly it would amount to a severe interference with her private life and personal autonomy."[469]

The chance of a successful outcome from force-feeding was less than 5 per cent. It would have required forcible feeding, by restraint if necessary, for a period of up to two years; and, according to the jointly instructed expert, there was "a 95–98% chance that she will spend a miserable time being forcibly fed before she then dies".

In contrast, in *A Local Authority v E*[470] the patient was a 32-year-old woman suffering from severe intractable anorexia nervosa who was being looked after in a community hospital under a palliative care regime the purpose of which was to allow her to die in comfort. Given her physical condition there was a 2–3 per cent mortality risk from the insertion of a PEG line for the purpose of forcible feeding, and she was vulnerable to physical trauma due to her fragile bones. Treatment was likely to take over a year and there was a 20 per cent chance of recovery. As Peter Jackson J noted:

6–139

> "Although the risks of treatment are high and the chances of recovery are low, these are odds that patients and doctors … willingly accept when considering life-saving medical treatment in other circumstances."[471]

The judge came to the conclusion that it was in E's best interests to be forcibly fed. The factors against forcible feeding were that: the people who knew E best (including her parents) did not favour further treatment; treatment entailed bodily intrusion of an intimate kind, and the overbearing of E's will in a way that she considered abusive; the application was brought when E and her family and carers had embarked a long way down the course of palliative treatment and a resumption of treatment deprived E of an imminent and relatively peaceful death; there were significant risks involved in treatment, including a risk to life; the prospects of success were modest and treatment involved the wholesale and prolonged invasion of E's privacy and self-determination. There was also a chance that if E recovered capacity she could make a valid advance decision to refuse future treatment. Against these "weighty factors" was the preservation of E's life. Treatment was not futile since, though burdensome, there was a possibility that it would succeed. Services and funding would be provided that

---

[469] [2014] EWCOP 35; [2015] C.O.P.L.R. 11; (2014) 140 B.M.L.R. 41 at [46].

[470] [2012] EWHC 1639 (Fam); [2012] 2 F.C.R. 523; [2012] Med. L.R. 472; commented on by Coggon, "Anorexia Nervosa, Best Interests, and the Patient's Human Right to 'A Wholesale Overwhelming of Her Autonomy'" (2014) 22 Med. L. Rev. 119.

[471] [2012] EWHC 1639 (Fam); [2012] 2 F.C.R. 523; [2012] Med. L.R. 472 at [79].

were not previously available, and "those who know E best are not in outright opposition to treatment taking place, however sceptical they justifiably feel". The presumption in favour of the preservation of life had not been displaced.

6–140   **Non-therapeutic sterilisation**   Any case which involves a proposal for the non-therapeutic sterilisation of a patient lacking capacity must be taken to the Court of Protection.[472] If, on the facts, there are effective alternative steps that could be taken to reduce the risk of pregnancy (such as contraception and/or appropriate supervision) sterilisation will not be in the patient's best interests since it would be disproportionate and not the least restrictive step to achieve future contraception.[473] In *Re A (Medical Treatment: Male Sterilisation)*[474] the Court of Appeal had concluded that it was not in the best interests of a patient with Down's Syndrome to have a vasectomy since fatherhood and any potential social disapproval would not have a significant impact on his life. However, in *A NHS Trust v DE*[475] the circumstances were somewhat different. DE was a 36-year-old man with learning disabilities who lived with his parents. DE had capacity to consent to sexual intercourse but did not have capacity to understand contraception. He had a long-term relationship with a woman, PQ, who was also learning disabled. Through the efforts of his parents DE had managed to achieve a degree of autonomy in his day-to-day life, though he was heavily dependent on his parents and the local disability services. PQ became pregnant by DE and gave birth to a child. This had a significant impact on DE's life, in that protective measures were put in place to ensure that he and PQ were not left alone, and he was supervised at all times. His relationship with PQ almost broke down. DE was clear that he did not want any more children. King J found that it was in DE's best interests to undergo a vasectomy since this would enable him to continue the relationship with PQ with a significantly reduced risk of another child being born (which was likely to result in the relationship breaking down), would improve his

---

[472] *A Local Authority v K* [2013] EWHC 242 (COP); (2013) 130 B.M.L.R. 195, where at [35] to [37] Cobb J set out the procedure to be followed. See also Court of Protection Practice Direction 9E, *Applications relating to serious medical treatment* (available at *http://www.judiciary.gov.uk/wp-content/uploads/2015/06/copd-pd-9e-serious-medical-treatment.pdf*). Contrast the view of Peter Jackson J in *Re M (Withdrawal of Treatment: Need for Proceedings)* [2017] EWCOP 19 that a declaration of the court is not necessarily required when deciding whether to withdraw treatment from patients in a vegetative or minimally conscious state. Where the proposed treatment is therapeutic and sterilisation is simply an unavoidable consequence of the treatment (such as surgery for suspected cancer) the potential loss of fertility understandably carries much less weight in the balance sheet of the patient's best interests: see e.g. *Cambridge University Hospitals NHS Foundation Trust v BF* [2016] EWCOP 26; [2016] Med. L.R. 314; (2016) 151 B.M.L.R. 166.

[473] [2013] EWHC 242 (COP); (2013) 130 B.M.L.R. 195, applying the Mental Capacity Act 2005 s.1(6). See further *Mental Health Trust v DD* [2014] EWCOP 13; (2014) 142 B.M.L.R. 156; *Mental Health Trust v DD* [2014] EWCOP 44; and *Mental Health Trust v DD* [2015] EWCOP 4 where in the final application of a series of applications concerning the patient's capacity to make decisions about contraception and sterilisation Cobb J held that the patient lacked capacity and it was in the her best interests to be sterilised because a further pregnancy would be life-threatening (the patient had had six children, four of them born by Caesarean section).

[474] [2000] 1 F.L.R. 549; [2000] 1 F.C.R. 193; see para.6–105.

[475] [2013] EWHC 2562 (Fam); [2013] Med. L.R. 446; (2013) 133 B.M.L.R. 123. For discussion see R. Barton-Hanson, "Sterilisation of men with intellectual disabilities: Whose best interests is it anyway?" (2015) 15 Med. Law Int. 49; J. Mead, "Landmark ruling—Male non-therapeutic sterilisation" (2014) 20 Clinical Risk 54.

relations with his parents on whom he was dependent for his physical and emotional welfare, and restore the independence that he had previously been able to enjoy.

Obstetric care   Where a patient who lacks capacity is pregnant the issue of her   6–141
obstetric care may arise, particularly if there is a possibility of her needing a Caesarean section birth. In *Mental Health Trust v DD*[476] Cobb J held that D's impairment of mind (attributable to autistic spectrum disorder, overlaid with a learning disability) prevented her from weighing the information relevant to decisions about her obstetric care. She had given birth on five previous occasions, three of them by Caesarean section, and this was a high-risk pregnancy, with a 1 per cent to 2 per cent chance of a rupture of the previous Caesarean section scars which could cause catastrophic haemorrhaging and would be life-threatening. Cobb J held that it was in the patient's best interests and therefore lawful for her to be conveyed to hospital and to give birth by planned Caesarean section. The applicants were authorised to take such necessary, reasonable and proportionate measures as were in D's best interests, including forced entry into her home, restraint and sedation. Similarly, in *Re AA (Compulsorily Detained Patient: Elective Caesarean)*[477] the patient had been detained under the Mental Health Act 1983 suffering from psychotic episodes and delusional beliefs, and she lacked capacity with respect to her obstetric care. She had had two previous Caesarean sections, and there was a 1 per cent risk of a ruptured womb if she were to have a natural delivery, and on that basis it was held that it was in her best interests to have a planned Caesarean section. Mostyn J authorised the use of reasonable restraint in order to achieve that operation safely and successfully.[478]

Obstetric care and the child's interests   In *Re AA (Compulsorily Detained*   6–142
Patient: Elective Caesarean) Mostyn J noted that the interests of the unborn child were "not the concern of this court" but nonetheless went on to suggest that it was also in the patient's "mental health best interests" that the child should be born alive and healthy, and so there was "a significant mental health advantage in her unborn child not being exposed to risk during his or her birth".[479] That view was supported by the psychiatric evidence. In *Re P*[480] the patient suffered from diabetes and paranoid schizophrenia, and had been compulsorily admitted to a psychiatric hospital. Peter Jackson J granted authorisation for an induced labour and instrumental delivery, and if, in the opinion of the consultant obstetrician, it became medically necessary, authorisation for a Caesarean section. In weighing the patient's best interests Peter Jackson J took into account that: P was strongly

---

[476]   [2014] EWCOP 11; [2015] 1 F.L.R. 1430; (2014) 140 B.M.L.R. 118 at [69].
[477]   [2012] EWHC 4378 (COP); [2014] 2 F.L.R. 237; (2012) 137 B.M.L.R. 123.
[478]   See also *NHS Acute Trust v C* [2016] EWCOP 17; (2016) 152 B.M.L.R. 193 where Theis J made an order under the Mental Capacity Act 2005 authorising a Caesarean section on a patient with long standing bipolar affective disorder who lacked capacity and who was detained under s.2 of the Mental Health Act 1983; *Royal Free NHS Foundation Trust v AB* [2014] EWCOP 50 in which Hayden J granted a declaration authorising a Caesarean section for a patient with a serious psychotic mental illness; *NHS Trust 1 v FG* [2014] EWCOP 30; [2015] 1 W.L.R. 1984; and *Re CA (Natural Delivery or Caesarean Section)* [2016] EWCOP 51; (2016) 154 B.M.L.R. 142.
[479]   [2012] EWHC 4378 (COP); [2014] 2 F.L.R. 237; (2012) 137 B.M.L.R. 123 at [5].
[480]   [2013] EWHC 4581 (COP).

opposed to having a Caesarean section; it was a serious intervention whether or not the patient had capacity, involving the possible need for restraint and sedation followed by major surgery; there were risks associated with a general anaesthetic; and in the case of Caesarean section there could be some threat to the patient's future child-bearing ability. On the other hand, if difficulties arose during labour there was a small, but not insignificant, risk that she would develop serious bleeding as a result of the breakdown of a previous Caesarean scar, and that situation would be potentially life-threatening. Moreover, it was in P's best interests that her baby to be safely delivered:

> "The court cannot be concerned with the interests of the unborn child, but can, and does, have regard to the extremely adverse effect on Mrs. P if unnecessarily her child was not born safely or was born with some avoidable disability as a result of a lack of obstetric care which might have been given."[481]

However, there is clearly a risk that by eliding the mother's psychiatric best interests with avoiding the risk of harm to the child the court is effectively building the child's interests into the assessment of the mother's best interests.[482] It will always be in the best interests of a mother, whether she lacks capacity or not, to give birth to a healthy baby.

6–143   **Obstetric care and patients detained under the Mental Health Act 1983**   In a number of the cases where the court has authorised a Caesarean section under the Mental Capacity Act 2005 the patient was already a detained patient under the Mental Health Act 1983.[483] Where, however, the patient is subject to detention under the 1983 Act and is ineligible to be deprived of her liberty under the Mental Capacity Act (as determined under Sch.1A of the 2005 Act) s.16A(1) of the 2005 Act provides that the court cannot include in a welfare order provisions which authorise P to be deprived of her liberty. It is arguable that in these circumstances unless the Caesarean section can be categorised as treatment for the patient's mental illness under the Mental Health Act 1983, and so can be authorised under s.63 of that Act,[484] the court has no authority to make an order under the 2005 Act for medical treatment that will involve a deprivation of liberty, and will have to fall back on the inherent jurisdiction for the protection of incompetent or vulnerable adults.[485]

6–144   Thus, in *Great Western Hospitals NHS Foundation Trust v AA*[486] a pregnant patient who had bipolar disorder and was suffering from hypomania and puerperal psychosis became highly agitated and uncooperative with almost every

---

[481] [2013] EWHC 4581 (COP) at [17].
[482] As Mostyn J perhaps acknowledged in *Re AA (Compulsorily Detained Patient: Elective Caesarean)* [2012] EWHC 4378 (COP); [2014] 2 F.L.R. 237; (2012) 137 B.M.L.R. 123 at [5] when he commented "I hope not at variance with *Re MB*".
[483] See e.g. *Re AA (Compulsorily Detained Patient: Elective Caesarean)* [2012] EWHC 4378 (COP); [2014] 2 F.L.R. 237; (2012) 137 B.M.L.R. 123; *Re P* [2013] EWHC 4581 (COP); *NHS Trust 1 v FG* [2014] EWCOP 30; [2015] 1 W.L.R. 1984; and *NHS Acute Trust v C* [2016] EWCOP 17; (2016) 152 B.M.L.R. 193.
[484] See para.6–085.
[485] See para.6–150.
[486] [2014] EWHC 132 (Fam); [2014] 2 F.L.R. 1209.

aspect of her obstetric care. She would have been unable to co-operate with an induction of labour. The pregnancy prevented the doctors from giving her the appropriate dose of medication for her mental condition. She was detained under the Mental Health Act 1983. Hayden J concluded that it was in her best interests to undergo an elective Caesarean section under general anaesthetic in view of the unanimous medical evidence that it was the safest option for the patient. However, the declaration had to include an order for restraint of the patient if necessary in order to administer anaesthetic and carry out the surgery, but she was ineligible to be deprived of her liberty under the Mental Capacity Act 2005 because she was a detained patient under the Mental Health Act 1983.[487] Obstetric care was not treatment for the patient's mental disorder and so could not be authorised under the Mental Health Act. Hayden J held that since neither statute could authorise obstetric treatment in the circumstances, the court's inherent jurisdiction could be used to authorise the Caesarean in the patient's best interests.[488] It may be that this is not an interpretation that Parliament intended when passing the amendments to the deprivation of liberty requirements of the Mental Capacity Act 2005, and that further legislation is required to clarify the interaction between the two statutes.[489]

Obstetric care—guidance   In *NHS Trust 1 v FG*[490] Keehan J gave extensive guidance on the steps to be taken when a local authority and/or medical professionals are dealing with a pregnant woman with mental health problems who potentially lacks capacity to litigate and to make decisions about her own welfare or medical treatment.[491] A hospital should apply to the court for orders in relation to P's obstetric care if the case falls within any of the following four categories:

6–145

- category 1—the interventions proposed by the Trust probably amount to serious medical treatment within the meaning of Court of Protection

---

[487] See the Mental Capacity Act 2005 Sch.A1 para.17 and Sch.1A para.2 (Case A).

[488] [2014] EWHC 132 (Fam); [2014] 2 F.L.R. 1209 at [21], applying *A NHS Trust v A* [2013] EWHC 2442 (COP); [2014] Fam. 161 (see para.6–150); see also *NHS Trust 1 v FG* [2014] EWCOP 30; [2015] 1 W.L.R. 1984 at [128] per Keehan J. This point appears not to have been taken in the four cases identified in para.6–143, n.483 above, though it would depend on whether the patient was ineligible to be deprived of liberty applying Sch.A1 para.17 and Sch.1A paras 2 to 5 of the Mental Capacity Act 2005.

[489] See Law Com. Consultation Paper No. 222, *Mental Capacity and Deprivation of Liberty* (2015), ch.10; and the report following the consultation exercise, *Mental Capacity and Deprivation of Liberty* (2017) Law Com. 372, Ch.13 (available at *http://www.lawcom.gov.uk/wp-content/uploads/2017/03/lc372_mental_capacity.pdf*).

[490] [2014] EWCOP 30; [2015] 1 W.L.R. 1984 at [81]–[130], and the Annex to the judgment.

[491] Though the guidance does not apply to every pregnant woman with a diagnosed mental health illness: "No doubt in the vast majority of such cases it will not be necessary to make an application to the Court..." ([2014] EWCOP 30; [2015] 1 W.L.R. 1984 at [82]). In *Re CA (Natural Delivery or Caesarean Section)* [2016] EWCOP 51; (2016) 154 B.M.L.R. 142 Baker J was highly critical of a hospital that had failed to comply with these guidelines (in particular the hospital had started proceedings only two weeks before the baby was due). Baker J added, at [5], that: "Hereafter, all NHS Trusts must ensure that their clinicians, administrators and lawyers are fully aware of, and comply with, the important guidance given by Keehan J in respect of applications of this sort."

Practice Direction 9E, irrespective of whether it is contemplated that the obstetric treatment would otherwise be provided under the MCA or MHA; or

• category 2—there is a real risk that P will be subject to more than transient forcible restraint; or

• category 3—there is a serious dispute as to what obstetric care is in P's best interests whether as between the clinicians caring for P, or between the clinicians and P and/or those whose views must be taken into account under s.4(7) of the MCA; or

• category 4—there is a real risk that P will suffer a deprivation of her liberty which, absent a court order which has the effect of authorising it, would otherwise be unlawful (i.e. not authorised under s.4B of or Sch.A1 to the MCA).

6–146   In a category 1 case an application should be made to the court where (i) delivery by Caesarean section is proposed in circumstances where the merits of that proposal are finely balanced; or (ii) delivery by Caesarean section is proposed and is likely to involve more than transient forcible restraint of P. Keehan J explained that delivery of a baby per se does not amount to serious medical treatment though the medical interventions proposed by the doctors may amount to serious medical treatment. An uncomplicated planned Caesarean section will not of itself amount to serious medical treatment, but may become a case of serious medical treatment where there are factors in P's medical or obstetric history which means she faces a higher risk of complications or because of P's psychiatric condition, the intervention proposed may cause a deterioration in her psychiatric condition which causes her not to be compliant and a degree of force to restrain P is required to carry out the intervention.[492] Moreover:

"A decision to compel a mother, who would otherwise wish to have as natural a birth as possible, to undergo treatment which amounts to SMT is a very serious interference with her human rights as protected by the ECHR. In my judgment such decisions in the case of a P should be brought before the court for permission to undertake the same. Accordingly in this category of case an application should be made to the court irrespective of whether the treatment proposed could be provided pursuant to the provisions of s.5 MCA or as medical treatment under s.63 MHA"[493]

With regard to category 2 cases Keehan J noted that use of more than transient forcible restraint of a mother during labour is so grave an interference with her rights under Arts 3, 5 and 8 of the ECHR that three should be an application to court for authority. There has to be an assessment of the risk of the interference being required at all and the extent and gravity of the potential interference if it were to be undertaken. Where there is no evidence of P having been non-compliant with her care or having been aggressive to medical staff or others it is unlikely that the case would fall within this category.[494]

---

[492] [2014] EWCOP 30; [2015] 1 W.L.R. 1984 at [107]–[112].
[493] [2014] EWCOP 30; [2015] 1 W.L.R. 1984 at [113].
[494] [2014] EWCOP 30; [2015] 1 W.L.R. 1984 at [117]–[119].

Category 3 is reserved for serious disputes about P's obstetric care. Not every **6–147** dispute over P's obstetric care would fall within category 3. "There must be a serious dispute which must have real substance, for instance, based on P's religious beliefs."[495] For category 4, the question of whether proposed obstetric care or the proposed measures used to facilitate it amount to a deprivation of liberty is fact sensitive and has to be considered on a case by case basis, applying the "acid test" from *Cheshire West and Chester Council v P.*[496] If the restraint does not amount to a deprivation of P's liberty, it can be lawful under s.5 of the Mental Capacity Act provided that it is (i) necessary to prevent harm to P and (ii) a proportionate response to the likelihood of P suffering harm and the seriousness of that harm.[497] But if it is likely to amount to a deprivation of liberty and the hospital is unable to rely on Sch.A1 of the Act[498] an order of the court authorising the deprivation must be sought.[499] In those circumstances:

> "Although the Court will not be able to make a welfare order depriving P of her liberty under s.16(2)(a) of the MCA, it will be able to exercise the inherent jurisdiction of the High Court to make such an order provided that it complies with Article 5."[500]

Best interests and access to resources When making a decision as to patients' **6–148** best interests the court can only choose an option that would be available to patients which, if they had capacity, patients could choose themselves. The court cannot insist that a third party, whether a private individual or a public authority, provide resources that would not be available to patients with full capacity.[501] Thus the court is:

> "...confined to choosing between available options, including those which there is good reason to believe will be forthcoming in the foreseeable future."[502]

It can explore a care plan being put forward by a public authority and ask the authority think again, but:

> "...in the final analysis the Court of Protection cannot compel a public authority to agree to a care plan which the authority is unwilling to implement."[503]

---

[495] [2014] EWCOP 30; [2015] 1 W.L.R. 1984 at [123].
[496] [2014] EWCOP 30; [2015] 1 W.L.R. 1984 at [125]. See para.6–124 for the "acid test".
[497] [2014] EWCOP 30; [2015] 1 W.L.R. 1984 at [92], citing s.6(2) and s.6(3).
[498] See para.6–122.
[499] [2014] EWCOP 30; [2015] 1 W.L.R. 1984 at [127].
[500] [2014] EWCOP 30; [2015] 1 W.L.R. 1984 at [128], citing *A NHS Trust v A* [2013] EWHC 2442 (COP); [2014] Fam. 161 at [89]–[96].
[501] *Re N (An Adult) (Court of Protection: Jurisdiction)* [2015] EWCA Civ 411; [2016] Fam. 87; affirmed [2017] UKSC 22; [2017] A.C. 549.
[502] [2015] EWCA Civ 411; [2016] Fam. 87 at [80] per Munby P.
[503] [2015] EWCA Civ 411; [2016] Fam. 87 at [81]. See also *Aintree University Hospitals NHS Foundation Trust v James* [2013] UKSC 67; [2014] A.C. 591 at [18]; para.6–157; *North Yorkshire CC v MAG* [2016] EWCOP 5; [2016] C.O.P.L.R. 346 at [44] per Cobb J.

(d) Treatment under the court's inherent jurisdiction after the Mental Capacity Act 2005

(i) Vulnerable adults

6–149   In *Re L (Vulnerable Adults with Capacity: Court's Jurisdiction) (No.2)*[504] the Court of Appeal rejected an argument that the Mental Capacity Act 2005 constituted a comprehensive statutory provision for the protection of adults and that it was no longer permissible for the High Court to exercise any jurisdiction in relation to the care and protection of adults who fall outside the provisions of the Act. The statute provides a regime for the protection of adults who lack capacity, and s.2(1) provides that:

> "...a person lacks capacity in relation to a matter if at the material time he is unable to make a decision for himself in relation to the matter because of an impairment of, or a disturbance in the functioning of the mind or brain."

Where an adult is unable to make a free choice as a result of undue influence and/or duress the Act will not apply if there is no "impairment of, or a disturbance in the functioning of the mind or brain".[505] In *Re L* the assumed facts were that two elderly adults initially had capacity within the terms of the Act, but the local authority were concerned that they were being abused and controlled by their son, who lived in the same house. This included allegations of physical assaults, threats, preventing them from leaving the house, controlling who could visit them (including health and social care professionals), seeking to coerce his father into transferring ownership of the house into his own name, and pressuring his parents to place his mother into a care home against her wishes. The Court of Appeal held that the court's inherent jurisdiction to protect vulnerable adults had not been removed by the Mental Capacity Act.[506] The jurisdiction applied to those adults whose ability to make decisions for themselves had been compromised by matters other than those covered by the Act, including adults who are (a) under constraint; (b) subject to coercion or undue influence; or for some other reason deprived of the capacity to make the relevant decision or disabled from making a free choice, or incapacitated or disabled from giving or expressing a real and genuine consent.[507] The jurisdiction should only be used where it is necessary

---

[504] [2012] EWCA Civ 253; [2013] Fam. 1.

[505] Note, however, that where the diagnostic test of s.2(1) applies and there is evidence of impairment of, or a disturbance in the functioning of the mind or brain, then duress or coercion may mean that individuals do lack capacity on the basis that they are unable to use or weigh the information as part of the process of making the decision (as required by s.3(1)(c)): *A Local Authority v A* [2010] EWHC 1549 (Fam); [2011] Fam. 61 at [66]; *Norfolk CC v PB* [2014] EWCOP 14; [2015] C.O.P.L.R. 118 at [106].

[506] Applying *Westminster City Council v C* [2008] EWCA Civ 198; [2009] Fam. 11 at [12], [54] (where Wall LJ said: "I am in no doubt at all that the inherent jurisdiction of the High Court to protect the welfare of incapable adults ... survives, albeit that it is now reinforced by the provisions of the Mental Capacity Act 2005"), and approving *Re SA (Vulnerable adult with capacity: marriage)* [2005] EWHC 2942 (Fam); [2006] 1 F.L.R. 867.

[507] [2012] EWCA Civ 253; [2013] Fam. 1 at [54], applying the judgment of Munby J in *Re SA (Vulnerable adult with capacity: marriage)* [2005] EWHC 2942 (Fam); [2006] 1 F.L.R. 867. The list of vulnerable adults could include: "someone who, whether or not mentally incapacitated, and

and proportionate, and cannot be used to undermine the statutory regime of the Mental Capacity Act.[508] The jurisdiction should not be used to impose a decision on an adult with mental capacity, but to facilitate the individual's unencumbered decision-making with a view to re-establishing the individual's autonomy in a manner which enhances, rather than breaches, their ECHR art.8 rights.[509]

(ii) Patients who are ineligible to be deprived of their liberty

Section 16A of the Mental Capacity Act 2005 provides that if people are ineligible to be deprived of liberty by the Act the court cannot include in a welfare order a provision which authorises them to be deprived of their liberty. Schedule 1A para.2 of the Act sets out the circumstances in which people will be ineligible to be deprived of their liberty. Case A of that paragraph applies where the patient is a detained patient under the Mental Health Act 1983. The Mental Health Act provides for the compulsory treatment of a patient's mental disorder, but it does authorise the treatment of a detained patient for a physical medical condition that is unrelated to the mental disorder.[510] The treatment of physical conditions in the case of a patient who lacks capacity is normally authorised under the Mental Capacity Act in the patient's best interests. Where, in order to carry out the treatment, there would have to be some degree of physical or chemical (such as a sedative) restraint of the patient, an order under the Mental Capacity Act, in addition to authorising the treatment, would normally also authorise the medical staff to restrain the patient, which will necessarily involve

6–150

---

whether or not suffering from any mental illness or mental disorder, is or may be unable to take care of him or herself, or unable to protect him or herself against significant harm or exploitation, or who is deaf, blind or dumb, or who is substantially handicapped by illness, injury or congenital deformity", per Munby J in *Re SA (Vulnerable adult with capacity: marriage)* [2005] EWHC 2942 (Fam); [2006] 1 F.L.R. 867 at [82], approved by MacFarlane LJ in *Re L (Vulnerable Adults with Capacity: Court's Jurisdiction) (No.2)* at [23]. This list was said to be descriptive not definitive. The Court clearly considered that a case such as *Re T (Adult: Refusal of Treatment)* [1993] Fam. 95 (where a patient's will was overborne by a combination of her physical condition, her medication, and the undue influence of her mother who objected to her daughter receiving blood products; see para.6–035) would fall within the jurisdiction.

[508] [2012] EWCA Civ 253; [2013] Fam. 1 at [62] and [76] per MacFarlane and Davis LJJ respectively.

[509] [2012] EWCA Civ 253; [2013] Fam. 1 at [67], applying the approach adopted by Macur J in *L v J* [2010] EWHC 2665 (COP); [2011] 1 F.L.R. 1279 at [62]. In *Norfolk CC v PB* [2014] EWCOP 14; [2015] C.O.P.L.R. 118 at [113] Parker J commented that: "The inherent jurisdiction exists to protect, liberate and enhance personal autonomy, but any orders must be both necessary and proportionate." Parker J concluded, at [121], that the inherent jurisdiction extends to orders for residence at a particular place, and that if that constituted a deprivation of liberty then the court could authorise it pursuant to the inherent jurisdiction. It has been argued that the extension of the inherent jurisdiction to "vulnerable" adults does not provide adequate procedural and conceptual safeguards to guarantee that such adults are empowered to make autonomous decisions. The emphasis, however well-intentioned, may be on avoiding risk rather than promoting autonomy: see M. Dunn, I. Clare and A. Holland, "To empower or protect? Constructing the 'vulnerable adult' in English law and public policy" (2008) 28 L.S. 234.

[510] For consideration of what amounts to treatment for the purposes of the Mental Health Act 1983 see paras 6–080 et seq.

depriving the patient of liberty. But s.16A precludes a welfare order from depriving the patient of liberty in this situation. As Baker J put it in *A NHS Trust v A*:

> "...this might make it impossible for someone to be treated in a way that is outwith his 'treatment' under the [Mental Health Act] if that treatment involves a deprivation of liberty. To take a stark example: if someone detained under section 3 is suffering from gangrene so as to require an amputation in his best interests and objects to that operation, so that it could only be carried by depriving him of his liberty, that process could not prima facie be carried out either under the [Mental Health Act] or under the [Mental Capacity Act]. This difficulty potentially opens a gap every bit as troublesome as that identified in the *Bournewood* case itself."[511]

Having concluded that the detained patient in *A NHS Trust v A*, who was refusing nutrition and hydration, could not be force-fed under the Mental Health Act 1983,[512] and that s.16A of the Mental Capacity Act precluded authorising force-feeding under the 2005 Act, Baker J went on to hold that force feeding could be authorised under the court's inherent jurisdiction in the patient's best interests.[513] The inherent jurisdiction was not limited to vulnerable persons but also survived for the benefit of those who lacked capacity where a remedy is not provided by the Mental Capacity Act.[514]

6–151 Similarly, in *A Local Health Board v AB*[515] the patient, who had a learning disability, a diagnosis of autism and schizophrenia, was an in-patient detained under s.3 of the Mental Health Act 1983. She had a heart condition that required surgery. Without surgery she was at an increasing risk of dying from a ruptured aortic aneurism, but with surgery she had good prospects of being restored to a normal life expectancy for a woman with her other medical conditions. The patient did not want surgery, but she lacked capacity to make this decision. Treatment and management of the post-operative period would potentially involve restraint that, in the absence of authorisation, could amount to a breach of her art.5 rights under the European Convention on Human Rights. It was common ground that, as a patient detained under the Mental Health Act 1983, she was ineligible to be deprived of her liberty under the Mental Capacity Act 2005

---

[511] [2013] EWHC 2442 (COP); [2014] Fam. 161 at [67]. Contrast the interpretation of the legislative provisions by Mostyn J in *A Hospital NHS Trust v CD* [2015] EWCOP 74; [2016] C.O.P.L.R. 1; (2015) 149 B.M.L.R. 137 (repeating his own analysis in *An NHS Trust v A* [2015] EWCOP 71; [2016] Fam. 223 at [11]–[14]), concluding that in these circumstances an order could be made by the Court of Protection exercising powers under the Mental Capacity Act 2005 and there is therefore no need to invoke the inherent jurisdiction of the High Court. At the very least these differing interpretations of the statutory provisions have the potential to cause uncertainty and confusion.

[512] See para.6–083.

[513] Applying *Re L (Vulnerable Adults with Capacity: Court's Jurisdiction) (No.2)* [2012] EWCA Civ 253; [2013] Fam. 1 and *Westminster City Council v C* [2008] EWCA Civ 198; [2009] Fam. 11. Baker J noted, [2013] EWHC 2442 (COP); [2014] Fam. 161 at [49], that although the principles to be applied when assessing best interests as set out in s.4 of the Mental Capacity Act 2005 do not, strictly speaking, apply when the court exercises its inherent jurisdiction "they are manifestly applicable in those circumstances because best interests lies at the heart of the inherent jurisdiction".

[514] [2013] EWHC 2442 (COP); [2014] Fam. 161 at [92]–[96], applying *XCC v AA* [2012] EWHC 2183 (COP); [2013] 2 All E.R. 988 at [54] per Parker J. See also *Great Western Hospitals NHS Foundation Trust v AA* [2014] EWHC 132 (Fam); [2014] 2 F.L.R. 1209, para.6–144.

[515] [2015] EWCOP 31; [2015] C.O.P.L.R. 412; *An NHS Trust v HN* [2016] EWCOP 43 is to the same effect.

by virtue of Sch.1A para.2 of the 2005 Act, and that consequently s.16A prevented the court from including in a welfare order a provision authorising the patient's deprivation of liberty. It was also common ground that the heart surgery could not be authorised under the Mental Health Act 1983. Judge Parry granted an order under the court's inherent jurisdiction authorising the surgery and such physical and/or chemical restraint as required to deliver the treatment, applying the approach of Baker J in *A NHS Trust v A*.

(e) Withdrawing or withholding treatment[516]

(i) Common law

Patients in a permanent vegetative state   In the case of a permanently insensate patient (extreme persistent vegetative state) it cannot be said to be in the patient's best interests to continue to receive medication or nourishment which is futile, and therefore the justification for continuing treatment under *Re F (Mental Patient: Sterilisation)*[517] does not apply. Accordingly, it is not unlawful to terminate medical treatment or nourishment for such a patient, even though it is known, and indeed it is the intention, that the consequence will be that the patient will die.[518] The combined effect of *Re F* and *Airedale NHS Trust v Bland* seemed to indicate that the question of whether it was in the patient's best interests to continue to receive treatment was a matter to be determined on the basis of responsible medical opinion, so that provided the doctor's view that further treatment is futile is supported by a responsible body of professional opinion the decision to withdraw treatment will be lawful, despite the existence of a responsible body of professional opinion taking a contrary view. That approach can no longer be considered correct in light of the Court of Appeal's decision in *Re S (Adult Patient: Sterilisation)*[519] that when the court has to rule on a patient's best interests there can logically only be one best option, and the court must choose that option rather than leaving the doctors to choose from the range of

6–152

---

[516] See the GMC guidance, *Treatment and care towards the end of life: good practice in decision making, May 2010*, available at http://www.gmc-uk.org/guidance/ethical_guidance/end_of_life_care.asp. The Court of Appeal held that the previous version of the GMC's guidance was not unlawful: *R. (on the application of Burke) v General Medical Council* [2005] EWCA Civ 1003; [2006] Q.B. 273. In *Aintree University Hospitals NHS Foundation Trust v James* [2013] UKSC 67; [2014] A.C. 591, para.6–157, at [47] Baroness Hale commented that: "there is nothing in this judgment which is inconsistent with the sensible advice given by the General Medical Council in their guidance on *Treatment and care towards the end of life: good practice in decision making*."

[517] [1990] 2 A.C. 1.

[518] *Airedale NHS Trust v Bland* [1993] A.C. 789; *Frenchay Healthcare NHS Trust v S* [1994] 1 W.L.R. 601, CA; *An NHS Trust v D* [2005] EWHC 2439 (Fam); [2006] Lloyd's Rep. Med. 193; (2005) 87 B.M.L.R. 119; *Trust A v M* [2005] EWHC 807 (Fam). See also *Nancy B v Hôtel-Dieu de Québec* (1992) 86 D.L.R. (4th) 385, Qué SC; Dickens (1993) 38 McGill LJ 1053; *Auckland Area Health Board v A.-G.* [1993] 1 N.Z.L.R. 235; [1993] 4 Med. L.R. 239, NZHC. For comment on *Bland* see Finnis (1993) 109 L.Q.R. 337; Hinchliffe and Andrews [1993] Fam. Law 137; Wells [1994] J.S.W.F.L. 65; Lord Goff (1995) 3 Med. L. Rev. 1.

[519] [2001] Fam. 15; para.6–103.

(ii) Mental Capacity Act 2005

6–156   The Mental Capacity Act 2005 has not changed the basic legal principles to be applied to decisions concerning the withdrawal of treatment.[533] The test in the case of a patient who lacks capacity remains the best interests of the patient as set out in s.4. Section 4(5) provides that where the determination relates to life-sustaining treatment the decision-maker must not, in considering whether the treatment is in the best interests of the person concerned, be motivated by a desire to bring about the patient's death. "Life-sustaining treatment" means treatment which in the view of a person providing healthcare for the person concerned is necessary to sustain life.[534] Although the rationale for this provision is self-evident, it may be rather difficult in practice to police the decision-maker's motives where the decision relates to the withdrawal of life-sustaining treatment. This tends to place a premium on the views of the medical staff, since if they agree that it is not in the patient's best interests that treatment continue, the decision-maker's motives will probably not be questioned. If they disagree, however, the position may not be so clear-cut.[535] Ultimately, however, s.4(5) does not require doctors to provide treatment which is not in the patient's best interests.[536]

6–157   The leading case is *Aintree University Hospitals NHS Foundation Trust v James*[537] where Baroness Hale DP set out the basic principles to be applied when an application to withdraw or withhold treatment is before the court. The patient was not in a permanent vegetative state but he was on a ventilator in the critical care unit of a hospital with extremely low prospects of leaving the unit. There was a significant deterioration in his neurological state and the hospital applied for a declaration that in the event of a clinical deterioration it would be in his best interests to withhold invasive support for circulatory problems, renal replacement therapy, and cardiopulmonary resuscitation. Baroness Hale said that the Mental Capacity Act allows a court to do for patients what they could do for themselves if they had capacity, but no more, and thus the court has no greater powers than patients would have if they were of full capacity. A patient cannot insist that a doctor provide a particular treatment, and the court's position is no different.[538]

---

[533] Though note that it is now arguable that, in some cases, a declaration by the court that it is not in the best interests of the patient to receive treatment is no longer required before withholding or withdrawing clinically assisted nutrition and hydration from a patient in a vegetative or minimally conscious state: *Re M (Withdrawal of Treatment: Need for Proceedings)* [2017] EWCOP 19.

[534] Mental Capacity Act 2005 s.4(10). See also s.6(7) authorising people to provide life-sustaining treatment or do any act which they reasonably believe to be necessary to prevent a serious deterioration in P's condition, while a decision is sought from the court.

[535] For discussion of s.4(5) see J. Coggon, "Ignoring the moral and intellectual shape of the law after *Bland*: the unintended side effect of a sorry compromise" (2007) 27 L.S. 110.

[536] *Aintree University Hospitals NHS Foundation Trust v James* [2013] UKSC 67; [2014] A.C. 591 at [29] per Baroness Hale DP, citing and approving paras 5.31–5.33 of the Mental Capacity Act 2005 Code of Practice.

[537] [2013] UKSC 67; [2014] A.C. 591.

[538] [2013] UKSC 67; [2014] A.C. 591 at [18], citing *Re J (A Minor) (Child in Care: Medical Treatment)* [1991] Fam. 33, at 48; *Re J (A Minor)(Child in Care: Medical Treatment)* [1993] Fam. 15, at 26–27; *R v Cambridge District Health Authority, ex p B* [1995] 1 W.L.R. 898; and *R. (on the application of Burke) v General Medical Council* [2005] EWCA Civ 1003; [2006] Q.B. 273 at [50]

The test is *not* whether it is in the patient's best interests to withhold or withdraw treatment but rather whether it is in the patient's best interests to give the treatment, since if it is not in the best interests the court cannot authorise the treatment and it follows that it is lawful to withhold or withdraw treatment, because it will not be lawful to give it.[539] The starting point for the assessment is "a strong presumption that it is in a person's best interests to stay alive", but this is not absolute.[540] Decision-makers should consider the best interests of the particular patient at the particular time of making the decision, and must look at the patient's welfare in the widest sense, medical, social and psychological:

> "...they must consider the nature of the medical treatment in question, what it involves and its prospects of success; they must consider what the outcome of that treatment for the patient is likely to be; they must try and put themselves in the place of the individual patient and ask what his attitude to the treatment is or would be likely to be; and they must consult others who are looking after him or interested in his welfare, in particular for their view of what his attitude would be."[541]

The judge in *James* had been correct to consider whether the proposed treatments would be futile in the sense of being ineffective or being of no benefit to the patient, and the Court of Appeal had set the goal too high by suggesting that treatment is futile unless it has "a real prospect of curing or at least palliating the life-threatening disease or illness from which the patient is suffering".[542] Where the patient suffers from an incurable illness, disease or disability, it is unhelpful to talk of recovering a state of "good health". Resuming a quality of life which the patient would regard as worthwhile is a more appropriate measure.[543] The test is not what the reasonable patient would think; the best interests test considers matters from the patient's point of view, though this does not mean that the patient's or the patient's family's views must be followed:

6–158

> "We cannot always have what we want. Nor will it always be possible to ascertain what an incapable patient's wishes are ... But insofar as it is possible to ascertain the patient's wishes and feelings, his beliefs and values or the things which were important to him, it is those which should be taken into account because they are a component in making the choice which is right for him as an individual human being."[544]

---

and [55]. Note, however, Baroness Hale's comment at [18]: "Of course, there are circumstances in which a doctor's common law duty of care towards his patient requires him to administer a particular treatment, but it is not the role of the Court of Protection to decide that." The point here is that although a common law duty of care may *require* the doctor to treat the patient (e.g. in cases where the failure to treat would be negligent) the Court of Protection will not *order* the doctor to treat. It simply leaves the matter to the civil court (or in an extreme case the criminal court, e.g. for gross negligence manslaughter) to sanction the doctor after the event.

[539] [2013] UKSC 67; [2014] A.C. 591 at [22].

[540] [2013] UKSC 67; [2014] A.C. 591 at [35].

[541] [2013] UKSC 67; [2014] A.C. 591 at [39].

[542] [2013] UKSC 67; [2014] A.C. 591 at [40] and [43].

[543] [2013] UKSC 67; [2014] A.C. 591 at [44].

[544] [2013] UKSC 67; [2014] A.C. 591 at [45]. In *Re Briggs (Incapacitated Person) (Medical Treatment: Best Interests Decision) (No.2)* [2016] EWCOP 53; [2017] 4 W.L.R. 37 at [62] Charles J commented that: "if the decision that P would have made, and so their wishes on such an intensely personal issue can be ascertained with sufficient certainty it should generally prevail over the very strong presumption in favour of preserving life."

6–159   **Diagnosis**   Where it is being contemplated that life-sustaining treatment may be withdrawn from a patient in a permanent vegetative state or a minimally conscious state it is crucial that every step should be taken to diagnose the patient's true condition before any application is made to the court,[545] and in reaching a diagnosis (and any concomitant prognosis) clinicians should follow national guidelines.[546] The difference between a patient in a permanent vegetative state and a patient in a minimally conscious state is important, since patients in a permanent vegetative state have no interests to weigh in the balance[547] and the inevitable conclusion is that it is not in their best interests for life-prolonging treatment to continue. Yet diagnostic errors are not uncommon.[548]

6–160   **Patients in a minimally conscious state**[549]   The concept of a minimally conscious state is not an absolute. It involves a spectrum of levels of consciousness. Decisions about whether it is in a particular patient's best interests to continue (or, in some instances, initiate) life-preserving treatment are extremely fact-sensitive. Unlike the cases of patients with a confirmed diagnosis of permanent vegetative state, the court must undertake a careful assessment of the patient's best interests, using the balance sheet approach, though acknowledging that this is a qualitative rather than a quantitative exercise.[550] In all cases the court will place considerable importance on the preservation of life, to the extent that there will be a presumption in favour of prolonging life, though this is a rebuttable presumption.[551] In considering the patient's best interests the views of

---

[545] *W v M* [2011] EWHC 2443 (Fam); [2012] 1 W.L.R. 1653 at [259]; *Sheffield Teaching Hospitals NHS Foundation Trust v TH* [2014] EWCOP 4; *St George's Healthcare NHS Trust v P* [2015] EWCOP 42; [2015] Med. L.R. 463 at [8] and [49].

[546] *Cwm Taf University Health Board v F* [2015] EWHC 2533 (Fam) where Newton J was highly critical of the failure of a health authority to follow guidelines issued by the Royal College of Physicians, *Prolonged disorders of consciousness: National clinical guidelines*, 2013 (available at: *http://www.rcplondon.ac.uk/guidelines-policy/prolonged-disorders-consciousness-national-clinical-guidelines*), though it was accepted on the evidence that the patient had been in a permanent vegetative state for some years. The guidelines for diagnosis of vegetative state, taken from the RCP document, are set out in *M v N* [2015] EWCOP 76; (2015) 148 B.M.L.R. 116 at [17], and for minimally conscious state at [18]–[20]. Note that the RCP guidelines indicate that a vegetative state arising from hypoxic injury should only be classified as permanent after six months: *St George's Healthcare NHS Trust v P* [2015] EWCOP 42; [2015] Med. L.R. 463 at [21].

[547] *St George's Healthcare NHS Trust v P* [2015] EWCOP 42; [2015] Med. L.R. 463 at [13]. See also para.6–152.

[548] The rate of misdiagnosis can be around 40 per cent: *St George's Healthcare NHS Trust v P* [2015] EWCOP 42; [2015] Med. L.R. 463 at [8].

[549] See R. Huxtable and G. Birchley, "Seeking Certainty? Judicial Approaches to the (Non-)Treatment of Minimally Conscious Patients" (2017) 25 Med. L. Rev. 428.

[550] *M v N* [2015] EWCOP 76; (2015) 148 B.M.L.R. 116 at [46] per Hayden J. The case is discussed by R. Huxtable, "From Twilight to Breaking Dawn? Best Interests, Autonomy, and Minimally Conscious Patients" (2016) 24 Med. L. Rev. 622.

[551] *W v M* [2011] EWHC 2443 (Fam); [2012] 1 W.L.R. 1653; *An NHS Trust v L* [2013] EWHC 4313 (Fam); (2014) 137 B.M.L.R. 141; *United Lincolnshire Hospitals NHS Trust v N* [2014] EWCOP 16; (2014) 140 B.M.L.R. 204; *St George's Healthcare NHS Trust v P* [2015] EWCOP 42; [2015] Med. L.R. 463; *Abertawe Bro Morgannwg University Local Health Board v RY* [2017] EWCOP 2; [2017] C.O.P.L.R. 143; *Re O* [2016] EWCOP 24; (2016) 150 B.M.L.R. 233 at [17] per Hayden J: "The courts must not pursue the principle of respect for life to the point where life has become empty of real content or to a degree where the principle eclipses or overwhelms other competing rights of the patient i.e. in this case simple respect for her dignity."

the patient's family will be taken into account, but will not necessarily be decisive. For example, in *An NHS Trust v L*[552] the patient's family contended that he would have wanted to receive all possible treatment to prolong his life regardless of the likely neurological or physical consequences, and in accordance with his religious beliefs, but nonetheless the court held that, given his profound neurological and physical impairment, it would not be in his best interests to receive active resuscitation in the event of a further cardio-respiratory arrest or other serious deterioration. On the other hand, in *St George's Healthcare NHS Trust v P*[553] Newton J gave effect to the family's view (contrary to that of the hospital) that it was in the patient's best interests to continue to receive renal replacement therapy. Again, in *M v N*[554] Hayden J attached significant weight to the family's view, in this case that the patient would not have wanted to be kept alive in a state where she was profoundly impaired both physically and cognitively due to the progressive, degenerative impact of multiple sclerosis.

Advance decisions Where a patient has executed a valid advance decision which is applicable to the circumstances then a decision-maker, including the court, must respect that decision.[555] The formalities required for an advance decision that involves the refusal of life-sustaining treatment are such that most cases are unlikely to be covered by a valid advance decision. Nonetheless, the effect of s.4(6) of the Mental Capacity Act is that patients' previously expressed views about what they would want to happen if they were in a position where they were unable to express a preference about life-preserving medical interventions should be weighed in determining the patient's best interests. Almost inevitably the patient's views will largely be filtered through the perspective of the family,[556] though in some circumstances the patient may be able to express a preference.[557] Again, the patient's views are important but not

6–161

---

[552] [2013] EWHC 4313 (Fam); (2014) 137 B.M.L.R. 141.

[553] [2015] EWCOP 42; [2015] Med. L.R. 463. In this case the family provided video evidence of the patient's level of interaction with them, which was significantly different from the evidence of the medical staff as to his ability to respond to external stimuli. The clinicians had initially considered that he was in a permanent vegetative state. Newton J was clearly unimpressed by the way in which the Trust's application for a declaration that it was lawful to discontinue treatment had been presented.

[554] [2015] EWCOP 76; (2015) 148 B.M.L.R. 1160. See also *Salford Royal NHS Foundation Trust v Mrs P* [2017] EWCOP 23.

[555] See para.6–030.

[556] "…as to whether or not P would assess his life as being regarded as worthwhile I attach far more weight to the relevant expressions of his articulate and well informed family members and friends who have direct knowledge of P's pre-injury knowledge, understanding and philosophy, in particular those who know about his beliefs and values": *St George's Healthcare NHS Trust v P* [2015] EWCOP 42; [2015] Med. L.R. 463 at [40] per Newton J. See also *Re Briggs (Incapacitated Person) (Medical Treatment: Best Interests Decision) (No.2)* [2016] EWCOP 53; [2017] 4 W.L.R. 37 where Charles J placed significant weight on the family's evidence as to the patient's probable choice to have clinically assisted nutrition and hydration discontinued.

[557] For example, in *United Lincolnshire Hospitals NHS Trust v N* [2014] EWCOP 16; (2014) 140 B.M.L.R. 204 the tube through which the patient had been receiving artificial nutrition had become dislodged and the patient had been physically resistant to all efforts to re-establish a method of providing her with nutrition, and had pulled out a naso-gastric tube and several cannulae. Pauffley J granted a declaration that it was lawful for the hospital to make no further efforts to provide artificial nutrition, to withdraw the provision of intravenous fluids, and to provide appropriate palliative care.

It followed that there was a breach of the patient's art.8 rights in failing to involve the patient in the discussion before the first DNACPR notice was put in her notes. Longmore LJ and Ryder LJ also took the view that the duty to consult was not limited to art.8 considerations. There was also a duty at common law to consult the patient in relation to decisions to treat or not to treat.[570]

6–165 **Patient cannot insist on CPR** The right to be consulted about a DNACPR notice does not mean that the patient or the patient's family are entitled to insist on CPR being provided in the event that the patient has a cardiac arrest.[571] If a doctor's clinical judgment is that CPR is futile or likely to cause further damage there is no ethical or legal duty to provide treatment that is contrary to the doctor's clinical judgment.[572]

6–166 **Incapacitated patients and DNACPR notices** The right to be consulted about a DNACPR notice also applies to an adult patient who lacks capacity under the Mental Capacity Act 2005. Section 4(7) of the Act requires that a decision-maker making a decision in the best interests of the patient must take into account, if practicable and appropriate, the views of "anyone engaged in caring for the person or interested in his welfare". Even if the doctor considers that CPR would be futile, just as *Tracey* makes it clear that this does not obviate the need for consultation with patients who have capacity, the effect of s.4(7) is that consultation about a DNACPR notice is necessary with a carer of an incapacitated patient, unless that is not practical.[573]

6. EMERGENCY (TEMPORARY INCAPACITY)

(a) Common law

6–167 In an emergency, where an otherwise competent patient is unable to consent for some reason, doctors may lawfully proceed to treat the patient without consent. Doctors had been acting on this supposition for years, every time an unconscious patient was wheeled into the casualty department of a hospital, for example. It would be absurd if the law did not provide for this situation. As Lord Bridge observed in *Re F (Mental Patient: Sterilisation)*,[574] doctors and other healthcare

---

[570] [2014] EWCA Civ 822; [2015] Q.B. 543 at [89] and [94] respectively, citing *R. (on the application of Burke) v General Medical Council* [2005] EWCA Civ 1003; [2006] Q.B. 273 at [50]–[55].

[571] *NHS v VT* [2014] C.O.P.L.R. 44—family of Muslim patient in minimally conscious state, with no realistic expectation of recovering any meaningful neurological function, not entitled to require doctors to provide CPR or intensive care if patient's condition deteriorated.

[572] *R. (on the application of Tracey) v Cambridge University Hospitals NHS Foundation Trust* [2014] EWCA Civ 822; [2015] Q.B. 543 at [55]; *R. (on the application of Burke) v General Medical Council* [2005] EWCA Civ 1003; [2006] Q.B. 273 at [50]; *Aintree University Hospitals NHS Foundation Trust v James* [2013] UKSC 67; [2014] A.C. 591 at [18].

[573] *Winspear v City Hospitals Sunderland NHS Foundation Trust* [2015] EWHC 3250 (QB); [2016] Q.B. 691 at [53]. It will not be impractical to consult simply because the decision is taken during the night, when the carer has a telephone and the hospital staff are aware of this: [2015] EWHC 3250 (QB); [2016] Q.B. 691 at [58].

[574] [1990] 2 A.C. 1 at 52.

professionals would otherwise face an intolerable dilemma: if they administer the treatment which they believe to be in the best interests of the patient they might face an action for trespass to the person, but if they withhold that treatment they could be in breach of a duty of care in negligence.

Necessity The basis for justifying emergency treatment of an incapacitated patient without consent is the principle of necessity.[575] The discussion of the defence of necessity in *Re F (Mental Patient: Sterilisation)*[576] proceeded on the assumption that it applied in any situation where an adult was incapable of giving a valid consent to medical treatment, whether the capacity was permanent or temporary. Thus, treatment of temporarily incapacitated patients in an emergency will be lawful if it is in their best interests, that is if, but only if, it is carried out in order either to save their life or to ensure improvement or prevent deterioration in their physical or mental health. Again, this is measured by reference to the *Bolam* test. There are limits, however, to what may be done to the temporarily incapacitated patient. Lord Goff said that officious intervention cannot be justified; nor can intervention be justified when it is contrary to the known wishes of the assisted person. Moreover, Lord Goff explicitly recognised that there was a difference between cases of permanent incapacity and temporary incapacity:

6–168

> "Where, for example, a surgeon performs an operation without his consent on a patient temporarily rendered unconscious in an accident, he should do no more than is reasonably required, in the best interests of the patient, before he recovers consciousness. I can see no practical difficulty arising from this requirement, which derives from the fact that the patient is expected before long to regain consciousness and can then be consulted about longer term measures."[577]

In the Court of Appeal Neill LJ also drew a clear distinction between permanent and temporary incapacity. In an emergency situation treatment should be confined to:

> "...such treatment as is necessary to meet the emergency and such as needs to be carried out at once and before the patient is likely to be in a position to make a decision for himself."[578]

Treatment must be necessary, not merely convenient The Canadian courts distinguish between procedures which it would have been unreasonable to postpone in the circumstances, as opposed to being merely convenient to perform immediately. In *Marshall v Curry*,[579] in the course of a hernia operation being performed under general anaesthetic, the surgeon discovered that his patient had a

6–169

---

[575] An alternative rationale of implied consent (see *Schweizer v Central Hospital* (1974) 53 D.L.R. (3d) 494 at 507; Skegg (1974) 90 L.Q.R. 512) is clearly fictional and invites confusion with situations in which the patient has capacity, refrains from giving an express consent, and yet can be taken to have impliedly consented, for example, by his conduct. It was also suggested, in *Wilson v Pringle* [1987] Q.B. 237 at 252, that urgent surgery on an unconscious patient would not be "hostile" and that accordingly "the surgeon's action is acceptable in the ordinary conduct of everyday life". However, this approach has not been accepted: see *Re F (Mental Patient: Sterilisation)* [1990] 2 A.C. 1 at 73 per Lord Goff, and *T v T* [1988] Fam. 52 at 67 per Wood J (see paras 6–005 to 6–007).
[576] [1990] 2 A.C. 1; see para.6–101.
[577] [1990] 2 A.C. 1 at 77.
[578] [1990] 2 A.C. 1 at 30.
[579] [1933] 3 D.L.R. 260.

diseased testicle. It was held that he was justified in removing the testicle without first bringing the patient round to obtain his consent, because the organ could have become gangrenous and constituted a threat to the patient's life. The circumstances could not have been foreseen before the operation, and the doctor had acted in the best interests of his patient. The removal of the testicle was necessary because it would have been unreasonable to postpone the procedure. On the other hand, in *Murray v McMurchy*,[580] during the course of a Caesarean section, the doctor discovered fibroid tumours in the patient's uterus. He took the view that the tumours would be a danger if the patient were to become pregnant again, and so without reviving the patient from the general anaesthetic he performed a sterilisation operation. The doctor was held liable in battery, because it would not have been unreasonable to postpone the operation. There was no immediate threat to the patient's health; it was merely convenient to perform the operation without consent as she was already under general anaesthetic.[581] Similarly, in the Australian case of *Candutti v ACT Health and Community Care*[582] it was held that when problems arose in performing a laparoscopic sterilisation the doctor was not justified in proceeding to perform a sterilisation by laparotomy (which is much more intrusive surgery involving opening up the abdominal cavity). There was no reason why the surgery could not have been terminated and the problems explained to the patient, who would then have had a number of alternatives to consider (including the sterilisation by laparotomy). Nor did it follow from the fact that the patient had consented to being "opened up" in the event of an emergency during the laparoscopic sterilisation that she had agreed to the laparotomy, since the hypothetical emergency situations that had been explained to her (internal bleeding or an allergic reaction to the gas) were such that it would not have been an option simply to terminate the laparoscopic procedure.

6-170   In *Re F (Mental Patient: Sterilisation)* Lord Goff apparently took the view that the Canadian cases were restricted to the situation where a surgeon, in the course of an operation, discovers some other condition which he believes requires immediate attention although he has not obtained the patient's consent for that. It is not clear why the cases should be limited in this way, since the distinction could apply just as well to the patient who is incapacitated prior to the operation as the patient who is incapacitated during the operation itself. Thus, it is arguable that the measure of what is "reasonably required" under Lord Goff's approach to the temporarily incapacitated patient could be whether it would have been unreasonable to postpone the operation or procedure, as opposed to merely convenient to perform it without consent.[583]

---

[580] [1949] 2 D.L.R. 442.

[581] See also *Parmley v Parmley and Yule* [1945] 4 D.L.R. 81, 89, SCC. For an English case with similar facts to *Murray v McMurchy* see *Devi v West Midlands Regional Health Authority* unreported 9 December 1981, CA, para.6–017.

[582] [2003] ACTSC 95, SC of the Australian Capital Territory.

[583] Whether this would prove, in practice, to be a more stringent test than the *Bolam* test depends upon expert evidence as to what was convenient and what was unreasonable. There is, in theory, a difference between whether it was unreasonable to postpone an operation and whether it was reasonable to proceed. Sometimes it may be reasonable to proceed (and therefore not negligent to do so) but also not unreasonable to postpone the operation until the patient could consent. In other words,

"Consent" of relatives The medical profession appeared to assume for many   **6–171**
years that consent by a spouse or relative will suffice where an adult patient is
incapable of consenting. While it may be "good medical practice" to consult
relatives about a proposed treatment,[584] this has no effect in law.[585] If the
procedure cannot be justified under the principle of necessity, the consent of a
relative offers no protection, other than the practical observation that a patient
may be less likely to litigate if the treatment had the approval of a relative.

(b) Mental Capacity Act 2005

The Mental Capacity Act 2005 has not changed the basic principles to be applied   **6–172**
to patients with temporary incapacity, such as patients who are unconscious due
to an accident or, for example, a heart attack. A person making a decision about
the patient's best interests must take into account (a) whether it is likely that the
person will at some time have capacity in relation to the matter in question and
(b) if so, when that is likely to be.[586] Patients' past and present wishes and
feelings (including in particular any relevant written statements by them when
they had capacity) must be considered, along with the beliefs and values of the
patient that would be likely to influence the decision if they had capacity.[587] The
Act requires a decision-maker to take into account, if practicable and appropriate,
the views of: (a) anyone named by patients as someone to be consulted; (b)
anyone engaged in caring for them or interested in their welfare; (c) any donee of
a lasting power of attorney granted by them; and (d) any deputy appointed for
them by the court, as to what would be in their best interests.[588] The phrase
"anyone ... interested in his welfare" would appear to cover family members in
the case of an emergency, though it remains the case that family members cannot
"authorise" treatment or "consent" on behalf of the unconscious patient, since the
patient's best interests remains the fundamental test (subject to any valid advance
statement by the patient).

---

the test is stricter than in negligence: see Skegg (1974) 90 L.Q.R. 512, 518. Note that since necessity
is a defence the burden of proving that the treatment was necessary must lie with the defendant.

[584] See Lord Goff in *Re F. (Mental Patient: Sterilisation)* [1990] 2 A.C. 1 at 78. See also the Mental
Capacity Act 2005 s.4(7) which provides that where the patient lacks capacity the person making a
decision about the patient's best interests must take into account the views of anyone engaged in
caring for the patient or interested in his welfare; see para.6–134.

[585] *Re T (Adult: Refusal of Treatment)* [1993] Fam. 95 at 103, per Lord Donaldson MR; *Re S.
(Hospital Patient: Court's Jurisdiction)* [1996] Fam. 1 at 19, per Sir Thomas Bingham MR; Skegg,
Law, Ethics and Medicine (Oxford: Oxford University Press, 1988), p.73; see also *Paton v British
Pregnancy Advisory Service Trustees* [1979] Q.B. 276, where it was held that the putative father was
not entitled to intervene to prevent the mother undergoing an abortion. Despite the legal position, *in
practice* family members often play a significant role in the consent process: see R. Gilbar, "Asset or
burden? Informed consent and the role of the family: law and practice" (2012) 32 L.S. 525.

[586] Mental Capacity Act 2005 s.4(3).

[587] Mental Capacity Act 2005 s.4(6).

[588] Mental Capacity Act 2005 s.4(7).

7. REFUSALS OF CONSENT

6–173   The refusal of a competent patient to consent to medical treatment is normally considered to be conclusive. Doctors must respect patients' wishes, no matter how misguided they believe the patient to be, and no matter that they have only the patient's best interests in mind. The doctor who ignores the patient's refusal of consent risks a claim for battery.[589] On the other hand, a doctor must also consider the true scope of a refusal of consent:

> "Was it intended to apply in the circumstances which have arisen? Was it based upon assumptions which in the event have not been realised? A refusal is only effective within its true scope and is vitiated if it is based upon false assumptions."[590]

Moreover, as Lord Donaldson MR pointed out in *Re T (Adult: Refusal of Treatment)*[591] simply because adult patients have a right to choose it does not follow that they have exercised the right. Doctors faced with a refusal of consent should give very careful consideration to the patient's capacity to decide at the time when the decision was made. Patients' capacity may be temporarily reduced, and the doctors should consider whether at the time the decision is made they have the capacity commensurate with the gravity of the decision which they purport to make. The more serious the decision, the greater the capacity required. In cases of doubt about the patient's capacity, said his Lordship, where the withholding of treatment would lead to serious damage to the patient's health or even death, that doubt should be resolved in favour of the preservation of life, since if individuals want to override the public interest in preserving life, they must do so in clear terms. Staughton LJ agreed that an apparent consent or refusal may not be a "true" consent or refusal. Patients' understanding and reasoning powers may be seriously reduced by drugs or other circumstances, although they are not actually unconscious.[592] Conversely, doctors should resist the temptation to conclude that patients are not competent *simply because they have refused treatment*[593]; and, in any event, simply because their capacity is reduced, it does not follow that they are unable effectively to refuse consent.[594] Most patients want their medical condition to improve, if at all possible, and where differences

---

[589] "At common law a doctor cannot lawfully operate on adult patients of sound mind, or give them any other treatment involving the application of physical force however small ... without their consent. If a doctor were to operate on such patients, or give them other treatment, without their consent, he would commit the actionable tort of trespass to the person", per Lord Brandon in *Re F (Mental Patient: Sterilisation)* [1990] 2 A.C. 1 at 55; "There is no doubt that a person of full age and capacity cannot be ordered to undergo a blood test against his will ... [because] English law goes to great lengths to protect a person of full age and capacity from interference with his personal liberty", per Lord Reid in *S v S* [1972] A.C. 24 at 43.

[590] *Re T (Adult: Refusal of Treatment)* [1993] Fam. 95 at 116.

[591] [1993] Fam. 95 at 102.

[592] [1993] Fam. 95 at 122.

[593] "That his choice is contrary to what is to be expected of the vast majority of adults is only relevant if there are other reasons for doubting his capacity to decide. The nature of his choice or the terms in which it is expressed may then tip the balance", [1993] Fam. 95 at 113, per Lord Donaldson MR. The refusal to accept treatment is more likely to lead to a conclusion that the patient is incompetent in the case of minors: see *Re E (A Minor) (Wardship: Medical Treatment)* [1993] 1 F.L.R. 386.

[594] See *Re C. (Adult: Refusal of Treatment)* [1994] 1 W.L.R. 290; para.6–040.

between patient and doctor arise this is likely to be the product of differing assessments of the risks and benefits of the proposed treatment. In some situations, however, the objectives of doctor and patient are at odds.

(a) Hunger strikes

In *Leigh v Gladstone*[595] it was held to be lawful for prison authorities to force-feed a prisoner on hunger strike. The decision was influenced by the fact that suicide, and attempted suicide, was a criminal offence at the time, although it is questionable whether the offence could be committed by omission. The case is now of doubtful authority, and the practice of force-feeding hunger strikers in British prisons has been discontinued.[596] In *Secretary of State for the Home Department v Robb*[597] Thorpe J held that prison officials and medical staff may abide by the decision of a prisoner of sound mind and understanding who goes on hunger strike, and may lawfully abstain from providing hydration and nutrition for so long as the prisoner retains the capacity to refuse them. There was no countervailing state interest which should prevail over the prisoner's right to self-determination. His Lordship said that *Leigh v Gladstone* was "of no surviving application and can be consigned to the archives of legal history".

6–174

On the other hand, in *R v Collins and Ashworth Hospital Authority Ex p. Brady*[598] Kay J held that where the prisoner lacks the relevant mental capacity to make a competent decision, necessity may justify force-feeding. Moreover, Kay J questioned whether there may be circumstances in which state or public interests might prevail over a self-determined hunger strike so as to enable, even if not to require, intervention.[599] His Lordship noted the incongruity of a law that imposes a common law duty to take reasonable care to prevent prisoners committing

6–175

---

[595] (1909) 26 T.L.R. 139.
[596] See Zellick [1976] P.L. 153. See also *Att.-Gen. of British Columbia v Astaforoff* [1984] 4 W.W.R. 385 where the court refused to order treatment of a prisoner on hunger strike; Somerville (1985) 63 Can. Bar Rev. 59. American courts have declined to regard a patient's refusal of life-sustaining medical treatment (including tubal feeding) as equivalent to an attempt to commit suicide: see *Bouvia v Superior Court* 225 Cal. Rptr 297 (1986), Cal CA; *Re Conroy* 486 A. 2d 1209 (1985), New Jersey SC; *Thor v Superior Court* 855 P. 2d 375 (1993), Cal SC. The European Court of Human Rights has held that the forcible feeding of a prisoner on hunger strike does not violate art.3 of the European Convention on Human Rights: *X v Federal Republic of Germany* (1984) 7 E.H.R.R. 152.
[597] [1995] Fam. 127. See also *Airedale NHS Trust v Bland* [1993] A.C. 789 at 859 where Lord Keith commented that the principle of the sanctity of life does not authorise the forcible feeding of prisoners on hunger strike. The New Zealand High Court reached the same conclusion in *Department of Corrections v All Means All* [2014] NZHC 1433; [2014] 3 N.Z.L.R. 404. See also *H Ltd v J* [2010] SASC 176; (2010) 107 S.A.S.R. 352 (competent resident in an "aged care facility" entitled to refuse sustenance and medication, and the motives for the refusal are irrelevant; there is no common law duty to feed oneself and refusal of sustenance and medication is not suicide at common law). However, cf. the approach taken to patients suffering from anorexia nervosa (who will usually be found to lack the capacity to decide to refuse food) in *Re KB (Adult) (Mental Patient: Medical Treatment)* (1994) 19 B.M.L.R. 144, paras 6–042 and 6–080, and *B v Croydon Health Authority* [1995] Fam. 133, para.6–081.
[598] [2000] Lloyd's Rep. Med. 355.
[599] [2000] Lloyd's Rep. Med. 355 at [72]–[73].

suicide or harming themselves,[600] and a rule by which the prison authorities have no power to intervene to prevent prisoners from starving themselves to death. Thus, Kay J observed that:

> "It would be somewhat odd if there is a duty to prevent suicide by an act (for example, the use of a knife left in a cell) but not even a power to intervene to prevent self-destruction by starvation. I can see no moral justification for the law indulging its fascination with the difference between acts and omissions in a context such as this and no logical need for it to do so."[601]

6–176   In *A NHS Trust v A*[602] Baker J acknowledged that:

> "It is not uncommon for people to go on hunger strike in the hope that the Government will be forced to change its policy. Hunger strikes are a legitimate form of political protest. Not all hunger strikers are suffering from a mental disorder."

Nonetheless, although the patient had gone on hunger strike in protest at being refused asylum and having his passport confiscated, he was suffering from a delusional disorder which undermined his capacity to weigh the information when considering whether or not to eat and drink. Baker J held that force-feeding was not treatment for the patient's mental disorder and so could not be administered under the Mental Health Act 1983, but an order authorising force-feeding in the patient's best interests could be made under the court's inherent jurisdiction.[603]

(b)   Suicide

6–177   Where an adult has attempted suicide and is refusing treatment for the effects of the suicide attempt then, in theory, provided the patient is competent to refuse consent to treatment a doctor is not entitled to intervene.[604] The position is, in some respects, analogous to that of a patient refusing treatment because of a religious objection, but since a competent patient is entitled to refuse medical treatment for reasons which are rational, irrational or for no reason at all,[605] the patient who has attempted suicide does not have to justify a refusal of consent. In

---

[600] On which see *Orange v Chief Constable of West Yorkshire Police* [2001] EWCA Civ 611; [2002] Q.B. 347; and *Reeves v Commissioner of Police for the Metropolis* [2000] 1 A.C. 360.

[601] [2000] Lloyd's Rep. Med. 355 at [71]. It seems unlikely that this distinction can rest on the prisoner's mental state, since in *Reeves* it was accepted that the duty of care derives from the fact that the prisoner is a known suicide risk, not from any particular mental state (whether sane or insane).

[602] [2013] EWHC 2442 (COP); [2014] Fam. 161 at [47].

[603] See para.6–150.

[604] cf. Skegg, *Law, Ethics and Medicine* (Oxford: Oxford University Press, 1988), pp.110–112. In *Re F. (Mental Patient: Sterilisation)* [1990] 2 A.C. 1 at 29–30 Neill LJ appeared to leave open the possibility that there may be circumstances in which a doctor is entitled to give treatment in order to save the life of a patient who, having the capacity to make a choice, has refused treatment. Note, also, that in some circumstances a doctor may have a duty to exercise reasonable care prevent suicide attempts: see paras 4–166 to 4–182; but in these circumstances it may be that the patient would not be regarded as competent.

[605] *Sidaway v Bethlem Royal Hospital Governors* [1985] A.C. 871 at 904 per Lord Templeman; *Re T (Adult: Refusal of Treatment)* [1993] Fam. 95 at 102, per Lord Donaldson MR; *Re MB (Medical Treatment)* [1997] 8 Med. L.R. 217 at 224.

practice, however, the difficulty for a doctor in this position is to judge whether the patient does indeed have capacity. It is well-known that not all suicide attempts involve a genuine and fixed intention to die, and in some instances a suicide attempt may itself point to a lack of capacity.[606] Capacity is decision specific and the more serious the decision, the greater the capacity required. It is difficult to think of a decision more serious than refusing life-saving treatment. It seems that in the case of doubt about a patient's capacity a doctor should err on the side of preserving life.[607] Provided that the doctor has taken reasonable steps to establish whether the patient lacks capacity, and reasonably believes both that the patient lacks capacity and that the intervention would be in the patient's best interests the doctor will not liable in trespass to the person.[608] The position is different for minors since the court will authorise treatment of a minor who has attempted suicide even where the minor has capacity.[609]

(c) Religious objections

Jehovah's Witnesses who object on religious grounds to surgical interventions which may involve the use of blood products are entitled to decline treatment. In the Canadian case of *Malette v Shulman*[610] a surgeon administered blood to an unconscious patient admitted into a casualty department after a road accident. He was aware that she carried a card declaring that she was a Jehovah's Witness and that she was not willing to accept blood in any circumstances. Notwithstanding that the operation may well have saved the claimant's life, the defendant was held liable in battery. The claimant was entitled to make a decision to refuse blood prior to and in anticipation of the emergency that arose, and the doctor was obliged to comply with those advance instructions notwithstanding that he had not had an opportunity to dissuade her or explain the risks of refusing a transfusion:

6–178

> "The principles of self-determination and individual autonomy compel the conclusion that the patient may reject blood transfusions even if harmful consequences may result and even if the decision is generally regarded as foolhardy ... To transfuse a Jehovah's Witness in the face of her explicit instructions to the contrary would, in my opinion, violate her right to control her own body and show disrespect for the religious values by which she has chosen to live her life."[611]

---

[606] For example, on the basis that the patient's mental state prevents them from being able to use or weigh information relevant to the decision as part of the process of making the decision: Mental Capacity Act 2005, s.3(1)(c); see para.6–047.

[607] *Re T (Adult: Refusal of Treatment)* [1993] Fam. 95 at 102 per Lord Donaldson MR; see para.6–173.

[608] Mental Capacity Act 2005, s.5(1) and (2).

[609] See *An NHS Foundation Hospital v P* [2014] EWHC 1650 (Fam); [2014] Fam. Law 1249, para.6–205, where Baker J authorised treatment of a competent 17-and-a-half-year old who had taken an overdose of paracetamol (applying *Re W (A Minor) (Medical Treatment: Court's Jurisdiction)* [1993] Fam. 64 and *Re P (Medical Treatment: Best Interests)* [2003] EWHC 2327 (Fam); [2004] 2 F.L.R. 1117). See para.6–204.

[610] (1990) 67 D.L.R. (4th) 321, Ont CA.

[611] (1990) 67 D.L.R. (4th) 321 at 330, per Robins JA. See also the quotation cited above para.6–001, n.1.

It was not for the doctor to second-guess the reasonableness of the decision or to pass judgment on the religious principles which motivated it.[612]

6–179   In *Re T (Adult: Refusal of Treatment)*[613] Butler-Sloss LJ agreed with the principles set out in *Malette v Shulman*, observing that doctors who treat a Jehovah's Witness against his known wishes "do so at their peril".[614] Similarly, in *Nottinghamshire Healthcare NHS Trust v RC*[615] Mostyn J held that it would be "an abuse of power ... even to think about imposing a blood transfusion" on a patient with a mental disorder, but who was regarded as having capacity to refuse consent to a transfusion, notwithstanding that s.63 of the Mental Health Act 1983 would have provided a lawful basis for administering the transfusion.[616] On the other hand, this principle does not apply to Jehovah's Witnesses who object to the administration of blood products to their incompetent minor children, where the treatment is in the best interests of the child.[617]

6–180   **Religious beliefs of patients who lack capacity**   Even where patients lacks capacity to consent, s.4(6) of the Mental Capacity Act 2005 provides that in determining their best interests a decision-maker must consider (a) their past and present wishes and feelings (including any relevant written statement made by them when they had capacity); (b) the beliefs and values that would be likely to influence their decision if they had capacity; and (c) the other factors that they would be likely to consider if they were able to do so. In *Wye Valley NHS Trust v*

---

[612] Damages were assessed at $20,000 for mental distress. In *R. v Blaue* [1975] 1 W.L.R. 1411 the Court of Appeal touched upon this issue indirectly. The defendant had stabbed a young woman who subsequently refused a blood transfusion on religious grounds which would have saved her life. His appeal against a conviction for manslaughter on the ground that her unreasonable refusal of medical treatment broke the chain of causation between the attack and her death was dismissed. Lawton LJ clearly considered that the woman's refusal to consent to a blood transfusion might be considered to be reasonable, although he accepted that there might be a difference between the criminal law and the civil law.

[613] [1993] Fam. 95.

[614] [1993] Fam. 95 at 117. Though the force of this statement is diminished somewhat by Butler-Sloss LJ's comment that: "I do not believe an English court would give damages in those particular circumstances." In *Newcastle upon Tyne Hospitals Foundation Trust v LM* [2014] EWHC 454 (COP); [2015] 1 F.C.R. 373; (2014) 137 B.M.L.R. 226, Peter Jackson J held that an oral statement to doctors by a Jehovah's Witness patient, who had capacity at the time, that she did not want treatment with blood products had to be respected by the doctors when the patient's condition deteriorated to the point where she no longer had capacity. The judge was satisfied that she had "understood the nature, purpose and effects of the proposed treatment, including that refusal of a blood transfusion might have fatal consequences" and that the decision made "prior to her loss of capacity was applicable to her later more serious condition". Query whether, if the hospital had not made an application to court for a ruling on the lawfulness of not giving the patient a blood transfusion, but had gone ahead with a transfusion, the patient would have been entitled to damages for battery, notwithstanding Butler-Sloss LJ's comment in *Re T (Adult: Refusal of Treatment)*. For consideration of the position where the patient may have changed her views about a religious objection to treatment see *HE v A Hospital NHS Trust* [2003] EWHC 1017 (Fam); [2003] 2 F.L.R. 408, discussed at para.6–027.

[615] [2014] EWCOP 1317; [2014] Med. L.R. 260; (2014) 138 B.M.L.R. 147 at [42].

[616] The transfusion would have constituted treatment of a symptom or manifestation of the mental disorder (the patient self-harmed by cutting himself): see para.6–084.

[617] It will invariably be in the best interests of the child where the treatment is life-saving or will avoid serious harm to the child. See para.6–215.

B^{618} the issue was whether it was lawful for doctors to amputate the severely infected foot of a 73-year old man against his wishes. Without surgery he was likely to die quite soon. The patient had a long-standing mental illness (paranoid schizophrenia) and lacked the capacity to make the decision himself. One of the symptoms of his mental illness was that he experienced "angelic voices" telling him whether or not to take his medication. In weighing up the patient's best interests, taking into account the patient's wishes and feelings, and beliefs and values, Peter Jackson J accepted that delusions arising from mental illness may lead to a person's wishes and feelings being given less weight where that is appropriate. However, this could not be:

"...the automatic consequence of the wishes and feelings having a religious component. Mr B's religious sentiments are extremely important to him, even though he does not follow an established religion."[619]

There was a clear conceptual difference between a competent patient who refused a blood transfusion (whose religiously based wishes and feelings must be respected) and an incapable elderly man with schizophrenia who opposed an amputation, but nonetheless it could not:

"...be right that the religiously-based wishes and feelings of the latter must always be overruled. That would not be a proper application of the best interests principle."[620]

Liability in negligence for causing the need for treatment that the patient refuses   The assumption that is generally made when a competent adult Jehovah's Witness refuses blood is that the damage that may be suffered, including death, as a consequence of the refusal is the price that the patient must pay for adhering to religious beliefs. The surgeon does not incur liability for failing to act to preserve the patient's life by giving a blood transfusion. The surgeon's duty is to respect the decision of a competent patient to refuse treatment, and a failure to do so will incur liability, as *Malette v Shulman* demonstrates. An issue that has not yet been resolved is the position where the surgeon is negligent in the course of performing the surgery leading to significant blood loss with the result that the patient dies because the surgical team are unable to provide a transfusion due to the patient's refusal to accept it. The question arose in *Hobbs v Robertson*[621] in which the defendant was negligent in performing a hysterectomy and the patient died as a result of massive blood loss. She would not have died if she had received a blood transfusion, but the patient was a Jehovah's Witness and had signed a form on entering the hospital refusing

6-181

---

[618] [2015] EWCOP 60; [2015] Med. L.R. 552; (2015) 147 B.M.L.R. 187; discussed by L. Series, "The Place of Wishes and Feelings in Best Interests Decisions: *Wye Valley NHS Trust v Mr B*" (2016) 79 M.L.R. 1101.
[619] [2015] EWCOP 60; [2015] Med. L.R. 552; (2015) 147 B.M.L.R. 187 at [14].
[620] [2015] EWCOP 60; [2015] Med. L.R. 552; (2015) 147 B.M.L.R. 187 at [15]. Peter Jackson J took the view that "His religious beliefs are deeply meaningful to him and do not deserve to be described as delusions: they are his faith and they are an intrinsic part of who he is. I would not define Mr B by reference to his mental illness or his religious beliefs. Rather, his core quality is his 'fierce independence', and it is this that is now, as he sees it, under attack" (at [43]). The judge went on to hold that it was not in the patient's best interests to have his foot amputated.
[621] 2006 BCCA 65; (2006) 265 D.L.R. (4th) 537.

to permit a transfusion. The trial judge held that signing the form barred an action against the defendant and that this was not contrary to public policy.[622] The British Columbia Court of Appeal overturned the decision and remitted the case for a further trial on the basis that there was insufficient evidence to resolve the problem of whether there was a contract between the patient and the hospital or the patient and the doctor, to the effect that the patient had waived any claim. One of the questions on which there was insufficient evidence was what would have happened if the patient had refused to sign the form. The judge had proceeded on the basis that the patient would not have been admitted in these circumstances, but it was not clear whether the hospital had the authority to refuse admission for refusal to sign the form or whether this would have been a breach of the patient's rights under the Canadian Charter of Rights and Freedoms.[623]

6–182   The issue has arisen in this country in the unreported County Court decision of *Maher v Pennine Acute Hospitals NHS Trust*.[624] The hospital was aware that the patient was a Jehovah's Witness and would not accept blood products. She underwent an emergency Caesarean section, but two days later died as a result of blood loss. The haemorrhage was not caused by the Caesarean section, but the defendants accepted that the failure to monitor and to identify the patient's deteriorating condition was negligent. By the time the problem was spotted and the patient was transferred to the operating theatre to investigate the cause of the deterioration it was too late and the patient died from blood loss. The patient would have survived with a blood transfusion. Judge Hinchcliffe QC found that had the hospital staff identified the patient's deterioration when they should have she would have been transferred to the operating theatre much sooner and she would probably have survived without the need for a transfusion. The defendants argued that the patient's refusal of blood products was unreasonable and so broke the chain of causation; and that her religious belief in refusing a transfusion should be ignored because the defendants were respecting her rights under the European Convention on Human Rights art.9 (the right to freedom of thought, conscience and religion). Judge Hinchcliffe QC was unwilling to disregard the patient's religious belief: the case was an action in tort, not a claim for breach of her Convention rights under art.9. A decision to refuse a blood transfusion would be unreasonable if not based on religious belief but given that, to the defendants' knowledge, the patient was a Jehovah's Witness, she did not act unreasonably in refusing blood and so it did not amount to an intervening act breaking the causal

---

[622] (2004) 243 D.L.R. (4th) 700, BCSC.

[623] Alternative arguments that might arise in this situation are that: (1) the claim was defeated by the defence of volenti non fit injuria; or (2) the negligence did not cause the death, since the patient's refusal of a blood transfusion broke the chain of causation. The volenti defence would probably be construed narrowly. The argument on behalf of the patient would be that she had agreed to accept the risk of harm ordinarily incidental to surgical complications where a blood transfusion would have prevented that harm, but she did not accept the risk of complications arising from the surgeon's negligence, whether or not a blood a transfusion would have prevented or reduced the harm. See para.11–020. The causation argument is that the claimant's refusal of a transfusion broke the causal link between the negligence and the damage, though this view would not necessarily be accepted by the court. See paras 5–163 to 5–165.

[624] Unreported 23 June 2011. The case is commented on by J. McQuater at [2012] J.P.I.L. C25.

link between the defendants' negligence and the death.[625] This approach appears to privilege religious beliefs when assessing whether a patient is acting "reasonably" when making a decision to refuse medical treatment, the implication being that refusal of a blood transfusion for a non-religious reason would be unreasonable and so break the causal link. The principle applied to issues of *consent* is that a competent patient can refuse medical treatment for reasons that are rational, irrational, or for no reason at all.[626] In *Maher* the different policy issue at stake was who should bear the risk of the consequences of the patient's religious belief, the negligent defendant or the blameless patient? Judge Hinchcliffe concluded that the burden should lay with the defendant who was aware of the patient's views about accepting blood products. But it is arguable that the defendant's awareness of the patient's views is irrelevant, applying the principle that defendants must take their victims as they find them,[627] and it is equally arguable that the reason for the patient's refusal of treatment (whether based on religious belief or otherwise) is also irrelevant, applying the same principle.[628]

(d) Enforced Caesarean section

(i) Patients with capacity

Some American courts have taken the view that it may be justifiable to compel a person to accept medical treatment where this is essential to protect the life or health of a third party, particularly in the case of pregnant women. Thus, a pregnant woman has been ordered to undergo a blood transfusion contrary to her religious beliefs where this was considered necessary to save the life of a foetus of 32 weeks,[629] and women have been compelled to undergo Caesarean deliveries in circumstances where there was a high risk of death both to the child and the mother from a natural birth,[630] and even more disturbingly where the mother was dying from cancer and the operation was clearly contrary to her medical interests.[631]

6–183

---

[625] Applying *Spencer v Wincanton Holdings Ltd* [2009] EWCA Civ 1404; [2010] P.I.Q.R. P8; see para.5–154.

[626] See para.6–038 at n.140.

[627] For example, a defendant must take his victim as found with regard to his propensity to commit suicide following a negligently inflicted injury, unless the deceased took a voluntary, informed decision as an adult of sound mind to take his own life: see *Corr v IBC Vehicles Ltd* [2008] UKHL 13; [2008] 1 A.C. 884, para.5–158.

[628] See the comments of Lawton LJ in *R. v Blaue* [1975] 1 W.L.R. 1411, 1415 quoted at para.5–163.

[629] *Raleigh Fitkin-Paul Morgan Memorial Hospital v Anderson* 201 A. 2d 537 (1964), New Jersey SC.

[630] *Jefferson v Griffin Spalding County Hospital Authority* 274 S.E. 2d 457 (1981), Georgia SC; *Re Madyun* 573 A. 2d 1259 (1986).

[631] *Re AC.* 533 A. 2d 611 (1988). This decision authorising intervention was reversed on appeal, though this was far too late in the day for the mother: 573 A. 2d 1253 (1990), District of Columbia CA.

6–184   The issue first arose in this country in *Re S (Adult: Refusal of Medical Treatment)*,[632] a case where a mature woman of 30 refused, on religious grounds, to consent to a Caesarean section. She had been admitted to hospital with ruptured membranes and in spontaneous labour, and had continued in labour since admission. The baby could not be born alive and there was a serious risk to the mother's life without the operation. Sir Stephen Brown P granted a declaration that it would be lawful to perform the operation and any necessary consequential treatment despite S's refusal of consent, because it was in the "vital interests" of the patient and her unborn child. This decision created a storm of controversy, apparently undermining the normal principle that there is no legal basis for overriding the decision of a competent patient to refuse surgical intervention, even if as a consequence of that decision she will suffer serious injury or die.[633] A foetus has no independent legal personality in law, and only acquires legal personality at birth.[634] Moreover, in *Re F (In Utero)*[635] the Court of Appeal refused to make a foetus a ward of court because of the effect that this would have on the mother's individual liberty. How much greater, then, is the interference with individual liberty of a non-consensual Caesarean section?[636]

6–185   Following *Re S (Adult: Refusal of Medical Treatment)* there were a number of cases in which the courts ordered pregnant women to undergo Caesarean sections, though on each occasion the woman was found to lack capacity.[637] This line of cases was brought to a halt, at least with respect to capacitous women, in

---

[632] [1993] Fam. 123.

[633] See para.6–007. This is subject to any statutory exceptions allowing for compulsory treatment, such as the Mental Health Act 1983.

[634] See *Paton v British Pregnancy Advisory Service Trustees* [1979] Q.B. 276; *C v S* [1988] Q.B 135 at 140.

[635] [1988] Fam. 122; see Morgan [1988] J.S.W.L. 197; cf. *D. v Berkshire County Council* [1987] A.C. 317 allowing a local authority to proceed with care proceedings on an infant on the basis of the mother's behaviour during pregnancy (drug-addiction). In *Winnipeg Child and Family Services (Northwest Area) v G* (1997) 152 D.L.R. (4th) 193 the Supreme Court of Canada came to the same conclusion as the Court of Appeal in *Re F (In Utero)*.

[636] See Stern (1993) 56 M.L.R. 238; de Gama [1993] J.S.W.F.L. 147; Thomson (1994) 2 Med. L. Rev. 127; cf. Wells [1994] J.S.W.F.L. 65, 67–70. Moreover, when weighing the relative claims of mother and foetus it should be remembered that s.1(1)(b) of the Abortion Act 1967 provides that a termination of a pregnancy is not unlawful if it is necessary to prevent grave permanent injury to the physical or mental health of the pregnant woman. In other words, the interests of the mother should prevail over those of the foetus.

[637] *Norfolk and Norwich Healthcare Trust v W* [1996] 2 F.L.R. 613; [1997] 1 F.C.R. 269; (1997) 34 B.M.L.R. 16—where Johnson J held that the patient was incompetent because she was incapable of weighing up the considerations (she had arrived at hospital ready to deliver her baby but in a state of arrested labour and denying that she was pregnant); *Rochdale Healthcare NHS Trust v C* [1997] 1 F.C.R. 274—where the woman had previously had a Caesarean section and said that she would rather die than undergo the same procedure again. The patient was capable of comprehending and retaining information about the proposed treatment and of believing that information, but Johnson J held that she was not competent because she was in the throes of labour with all the pain and emotional stress that that involved. A patient who in those circumstances appeared able to accept the inevitability of her own death was not capable of giving full consideration to the options available; *Tameside and Glossop Acute Services NHS Trust v CH* [1996] 1 F.L.R. 762; [1996] 1 F.C.R. 753—where a paranoid schizophrenic patient, who was detained under the Mental Health Act 1983 s.3, was found to be incompetent because she had a delusional belief that the medical staff wanted to harm both her and the baby. Wall J held that the proposed Caesarean section fell within a broad interpretation of s.63 of the

two important Court of Appeal decisions. In *Re MB (Medical Treatment)*[638] the woman was found to lack capacity on the facts, because she had consented to the Caesarean section, but was refusing the anaesthetic because of an overwhelming needle phobia.[639] This meant that it was open to the court to conclude that a Caesarean section should be authorised, in her best interests. The Court of Appeal made it clear, however, that in the case of a competent pregnant woman the patient has an absolute right to refuse medical intervention. The fact that the baby may be injured or die as result of her refusal of surgery is irrelevant:

> "…we are none the less sure that however desirable it may be for the mother to be delivered of a live and healthy baby, on this aspect of the appeal it is not a strictly relevant consideration. If therefore the competent mother refuses to have the medical intervention, the doctors may not lawfully do more than attempt to persuade her. If that persuasion is unsuccessful, there are no further steps towards medical intervention to be taken. We recognise that the effect of these conclusions is that there will be situations in which the child may die or may be seriously handicapped because the mother said no and the obstetrician was not able to take the necessary steps to avoid the death or handicap. The mother may indeed later regret the outcome, but the alternative would be an unwarranted invasion of the right of the woman to make the decision."[640]

The court simply does not have jurisdiction to take the interests of the foetus into account when a competent woman refuses consent to medical intervention.[641]

In *St George's Healthcare NHS Trust v S; R. v Collins and Others Ex p. S*[642] the applicant was 36 weeks pregnant and was diagnosed as having pre-eclampsia. She was advised that she needed to rest and that labour would have to be induced, otherwise her life and that of the foetus were in danger. S wanted a natural delivery and rejected the advice. She was compulsorily admitted to a mental hospital under s.2 of the Mental Health Act 1983, and shortly afterwards transferred to a general hospital where she continued to refuse to consent to any medical or surgical intervention. The hospital made an emergency ex parte application to a judge who granted a declaration that it was lawful to treat S without her consent, the judge having been informed, incorrectly, that S had been in labour for 24 hours, that without intervention she and the baby would probably die, and that this was an immediately life-threatening situation. A Caesarean section was then performed, and a few days later S was returned to the mental hospital where the detention under the Mental Health Act 1983 was terminated. During her detention under the Act she was not given any treatment for a mental disorder or illness. Subsequently, S appealed against the declaration and applied for judicial review of the decision to apply for her compulsory admission to the mental hospital. The case proceeded on the basis that S had been competent to make decisions about her medical treatment throughout. The Court of Appeal

6–186

Mental Health Act 1983 because a successful pregnancy was a necessary part of the treatment for her psychiatric condition. But see now *St George's Healthcare NHS Trust v S; R. v Collins and Others Ex p. S* [1999] Fam. 26, para.6–186, on this point.

[638] [1997] 8 Med. L.R. 217; [1997] 2 F.L.R. 426.
[639] See para.6–041 above. See also *Bolton Hospitals NHS Trust v O* [2002] EWHC 2871 (Fam); [2003] 1 F.L.R. 824.
[640] [1997] 8 Med. L.R. 217 at 224; [1997] 2 F.L.R. 426 at 438.
[641] [1997] 8 Med. L.R. 217 at 225–226; [1997] 2 F.L.R. 426 at 440–441.
[642] [1999] Fam. 26.

reaffirmed the view expressed in *Re MB (Medical Treatment)* that the court has no jurisdiction to order a competent woman to undergo medical treatment, even where the life of a viable foetus is at risk:

> "In our judgment while pregnancy increases the personal responsibilities of a woman it does not diminish her entitlement to decide whether or not to undergo medical treatment. Although human, and protected by the law in a number of different ways set out in the judgment in *Re MB (An Adult: Medical Treatment)* [1997] 2 F.C.R. 541, an unborn child is not a separate person from its mother. Its need for medical assistance does not prevail over her rights. She is entitled not to be forced to submit to an invasion of her body against her will, whether her own life or that of her unborn child depends on it. Her right is not reduced or diminished merely because her decision to exercise it may appear morally repugnant. The declaration in this case involved the removal of the baby from within the body of her mother under physical compulsion. Unless lawfully justified this constituted an infringement of the mother's autonomy. Of themselves the perceived needs of the foetus did not provide the necessary justification."[643]

In addition, said the Court, the Mental Health Act 1983 did not provide a basis on which to detain a patient in order to perform a non-consensual Caesarean section. A patient may be perfectly rational and outside the ambit of the Act notwithstanding her eccentric thought process.[644] Thus:

> "...a woman detained under the Act for mental disorder cannot be forced into medical procedures unconnected with her mental condition unless her capacity to consent to such treatment is diminished. When she retains her capacity her consent remains an essential prerequisite ..."[645]

It followed that there had been no lawful basis for the non-consensual Caesarean section performed on S, and that surgery amounted to a battery.

6–187 The decisions in *Re MB (Medical Treatment)* and *St. George's Healthcare NHS Trust v S* are correct and entirely in accordance with principle. There is no legal basis for overriding the decision of a competent patient to refuse surgical intervention, except under the Mental Health Act 1983 where the treatment *is for the patient's mental illness or disorder*. In so far as *Re S (Adult: Refusal of Medical Treatment)* purported to authorise the compulsory treatment of a competent patient, it must be taken to have been overruled. Rights only take on significance if they can be exercised when it matters. There is little comfort in the assertion that competent patients have a right to refuse medical treatment, if they are only to be permitted to exercise the right when doctors, or the courts, agree with their judgment. The focus of attention in cases where a pregnant woman refuses medical intervention must be the question of her mental capacity to make

---

[643] [1999] Fam. 26 at 50. See also *CP (A Child) v Criminal Injuries Compensation Authority* [2014] EWCA Civ 1554; [2015] Q.B. 459—mother's excessive alcohol consumption during pregnancy causing damage to the foetus does not constitute the offence, contrary to s.23 of the Offences Against the Person Act 1861, of administering any poison or destructive or noxious thing to "any other person" because the foetus is not regarded as "another person". Lord Dyson MR commented, at [67], that: "save in the exceptional circumstances expressly recognised by Parliament, there should be no criminal liability for what a mother does (or does not do) during pregnancy."

[644] [1999] Fam. 26 at 51, citing Sir Thomas Bingham MR in *Re S-C (Mental Patient: Habeas Corpus)* [1996] Q.B. 599 at 603, and McCullough J in *R. v Hallstrom Ex p. W (No.2)* [1986] Q.B. 1090 at 1104 (see para.6–077, n.261).

[645] [1999] Fam. 26 at 52.

that decision. If she is found to be competent, then that is the end of the matter, no matter how tragic the potential outcome.

(ii) Patients who lack capacity

Where a pregnant woman is found to lack the capacity to make judgments about her obstetric care, and in particular the mode of delivery of the baby, then there are three possibilities.[646] If she is not a detained patient under the Mental Health Act 1983 then it will be possible to authorise a Caesarean section under s.4 of the Mental Capacity Act 2005 if that is in her best interests.[647] If she is a detained patient under the Mental Health Act 1983 and a Caesarean section can be categorised as appropriate treatment for her mental disorder then it can be authorised under s.63 of the of the Mental Health Act.[648] If she is a detained patient under the Mental Health Act 1983 and a Caesarean section cannot be categorised as appropriate treatment for her mental disorder then s.63 cannot be used to authorise the surgery, and it is arguable that the Mental Capacity Act 2005 cannot be used in this situation either because the patient will probably be ineligible to be deprived of her liberty, in which case the court will have to fall back on its inherent jurisdiction to authorise the intervention in the patient's best interests.[649]

6–188

(e) Statutory powers

Mental Health Act 1983 Certain statutory provisions allow for an element of compulsion where "patients" refuse consent. Most prominent of these is the Mental Health Act 1983 which authorises the compulsory admission to hospital of certain patients suffering from mental disorder for assessment or treatment.[650] Patients who are competent to refuse consent can, in some (though not all) circumstances, be compelled to accept treatment for their mental disorder under 1983 Act.

6–189

Public Health (Control of Disease) Act 1984 The Public Health (Control of Disease) Act 1984 s.45G provides that where a justice of the peace is satisfied that a person is or may be infected or contaminated, the infection or contamination is one which presents or could present significant harm to human health, there is a risk that the person might infect or contaminate others, and it is necessary to make an order in order to remove or reduce that risk, an order

6–190

---

[646] For the procedure to be followed when there is serious doubt about the patient's capacity to accept or decline treatment see the Court of Protection Practice Direction 9E (supplementing the Court of Protection Rules 2007 Pt 9) *Applications relating to serious medical treatment* (available at *http://www.judiciary.gov.uk/wp-content/uploads/2015/06/copd-pd-9e-serious-medical-treatment.pdf*). Note that from 1 December 2017 the Court of Protection Rules 2017 will be replaced by the Court of Protection Rules 2017 (SI 2017/1035).
[647] See para.6–141.
[648] See para.6–085.
[649] See paras 6–143 and 6–150.
[650] Mental Health Act 1983 ss.2–6; see para.2–161. For detailed discussion see Hale, *Mental Health Law*, 5th edn (London: Sweet & Maxwell, 2010), Chs 2–4.

imposing restrictions on that person may be made. The order can include: submitting to medical examination, removal to and detention in hospital, being kept in isolation, being disinfected or decontaminated, wearing protective clothing, providing information or answering questions about his health or other circumstances, have his health monitored and the results reported, be subject to restrictions on where he goes or with whom he has contact, and abstaining from working or trading. However, it is notable that s.45G does not include the power to order compulsory medical treatment, and s.45E specifies that regulations made under ss.45B or 45C may not include provisions requiring a person to undergo medical treatment.[651] The power to detain a person for reasons of public health is subject to the Human Rights Act 1998, and in *Enhorn v Sweden*[652] the European Court of Human Rights held that detention to prevent the spread of an infectious disease (in this case HIV) would only be lawful where the disease posed a danger to public health and where the detention was a last resort after other measures had failed.[653]

6–191   **National Assistance Act 1948**   Formerly, s.47 of the National Assistance Act 1948 allowed for the removal to suitable accommodation of persons who are suffering from grave chronic disease or, being aged, infirm or physically incapacitated, are living in insanitary conditions and are not receiving proper care and attention.[654] This provision has been repealed in England[655] but remains in force in Wales. The procedure overlaps to some extent with the procedures for compulsory admission to hospital under the Mental Health Act 1983, but again there is no express power to give medical treatment against the person's wishes.

---

[651] Section 45C confers authority on the appropriate Minister to make regulations for the purpose of preventing, protecting against, controlling or providing a public health response to the incidence or spread of infection or contamination in England and Wales; and s.45B makes similar provision in relation to international travel. See, however, s.13(1)(a) which gives the Secretary of State power to make regulations "with a view to the treatment of persons affected with any epidemic, endemic or infectious disease and for preventing the spread of such diseases". On the exercise of powers under the Public Health (Control of Disease) Act 1984, see S. da Lomba and R. Martin, "Public Health Powers in Relation to Infectious Tuberculosis in England and France: A Comparison of Approaches" (2004) 6 Med. Law Int. 117. On preserving the anonymity of persons compulsorily removed to hospital under the Act see: *Birmingham Post & Mail Ltd v Birmingham City Council* (1993) 17 B.M.L.R. 116.

[652] (56529/00) (2005) 41 E.H.R.R. 30.

[653] In *Greater Glasgow Health Board v W*, 2006 S.C.L.R. 159, Sheriff Court, it was held that it was lawful to detain an individual diagnosed with tuberculosis who had been admitted to the infectious diseases unit at the local hospital, but had absconded on several occasions, under the Public Health (Scotland) Act 1897. Such detention complied with art.5 of the European Convention on Human Rights because it was justified to prevent the spread of an infectious disease that would be dangerous to public health and safety, and it was a last resort, all other options having been considered and rejected for good reasons (applying *Enhorn v Sweden*). A patient could be detained for as long as he remained in an infected condition. Of course, other jurisdictions may have public health legislation permitting both detention *and* treatment of patients who are suffering from serious infectious diseases. See, e.g., *Toronto (City) Associate Medical Officer of Health v McKay* 2007 ONCJ 444; (2007) 286 D.L.R. (4th) 178 where under the authority of the Ontario Health Protection and Promotion Act 1990 the respondent, who was diagnosed with extreme drug-resistant tuberculosis, was ordered to be detained and treated for a second four month period.

[654] For discussion see Hale, *Mental Health Law*, 5th edn (London: Sweet & Maxwell, 2010), pp.139–142.

[655] Care Act 2014, s.46.

8.   CHILDREN

For the purpose of the law of consent, children[656] fall into two categories: either   **6–192**
they have the capacity to make their own decisions about medical treatment, and
can give a valid consent on their own behalf in the same way as an adult; or they
do not have capacity, in which case parental consent will normally be required.
English law takes a different approach, however, when it comes to the decision of
a competent minor to refuse consent. The Court of Appeal has held that parental
consent can be sufficient to protect a doctor from an action in battery where a
competent minor is refusing medical treatment (though a parent cannot veto the
decision of competent minor to accept treatment), and that the court has the
power both to authorise and refuse to authorise treatment, notwithstanding the
views of a competent minor, in the best interests of the child.

(a)   Children with capacity

By s.8(1) of the Family Law Reform Act 1969 children of 16 years or more are   **6–193**
presumed to have the same capacity as an adult to consent to medical
treatment.[657] This does not mean that children under the age of 16 do not have the
relevant capacity. Section 8(3) of the same Act states that: "Nothing in this
section shall be construed as making ineffective any consent which would have
been effective if this section had not been enacted." It was generally assumed that
this subsection was intended to make it clear that the legislation was without
prejudice to the position at common law: if a child below the age of 16 did have
the capacity to consent to medical treatment, s.8 did not change that.

Gillick   This interpretation was challenged in *Gillick v West Norfolk and*   **6–194**
Wisbech Area Health Authority,[658] where the claimant argued that no child under
16 could consent to medical treatment, and that s.8(3) merely preserved the
parental right to consent for children of 16 or 17 years. Although accepted in the
Court of Appeal, this argument was rejected by a majority in the House of Lords.
Lord Fraser said that it was "verging on the absurd" to suggest that a girl or boy
aged 15 could not effectively consent, for example, to have a medical
examination of some trivial injury or even to have a broken arm set. Provided
patients are capable of understanding what is proposed, and of expressing their

---

[656] The Family Law Reform Act 1969 s.1 provides that a person attains "full age" on attaining the age
of 18. Therefore "minors" are those aged below 18, though note that the Mental Capacity Act 2005
applies both to adults and minors aged 16 or 17: Mental Capacity Act 2005 s.2(5).
[657] Section 8(1) provides that: "The consent of a minor who has attained the age of sixteen years to
any surgical, medical or dental treatment which, in the absence of consent, would constitute a trespass
to his person, shall be as effective as it would be if he were of full age; and where a minor has by
virtue of this section given an effective consent to any treatment it shall not be necessary to obtain any
consent for it from his parent or guardian ..." See also Mental Health Act 1983 s.131(2)(3) and (4)
providing that where patients aged 16 or 17 years have capacity to consent to informal admission to
hospital under s.131 their consent is valid even though there are one or more persons who have
parental responsibility for them; and that if they refuse consent to informal admission they cannot be
admitted informally on the basis of parental consent.
[658] [1986] A.C. 112.

own wishes, there was no good reason for holding that they lack the capacity to express them validly and effectively and to authorise the doctor to perform an examination or give treatment.[659]

6–195   Lord Scarman said that as a matter of law a minor child below the age of 16 will have the capacity to consent to medical treatment "when the child achieves a sufficient understanding and intelligence to enable him or her to understand fully what is proposed". This is a question of fact.[660] Lord Templeman agreed that a doctor may lawfully carry out some forms of treatment with the consent of an infant patient, even against the opposition of a parent based on religious or any other grounds.[661] The child must also be capable of understanding the consequences of a failure to treat.[662]

6–196   As with adults the question arises as to how much the patient must understand in order to have the relevant capacity. In *Gillick* their Lordships appeared to require a greater level of understanding from a child under 16 than from an adult, at least with regard to contraceptive advice or treatment.[663] Lord Scarman commented:

> "When applying these conclusions to contraceptive advice and treatment it has to be borne in mind that there is much that has to be understood by a girl under the age of 16 if she is to have legal capacity to consent to such treatment. It is not enough that she should understand the nature of the advice which is being given: she must also have a sufficient maturity to understand what is involved. There are moral and family questions, especially her relationship with her parents; long-term problems associated with the emotional impact of pregnancy and its termination; and there are the risks to health of sexual intercourse at her age, risks which contraception may diminish but cannot eliminate. It follows that a doctor will have to satisfy himself that she is able to appraise these factors before he can safely proceed on the basis that she has at law capacity to consent to contraceptive treatment."[664]

6–197   Given that, on this approach, the patient has to be able to appraise these complex issues before "she has at law capacity to consent to contraceptive treatment" this required a greater degree of understanding than simply the nature of the

---

[659] [1986] A.C. 112 at 169; see also *Johnston v Wellesley Hospital* (1970) 17 D.L.R. (3d) 139, Ont HC; *Ney v A.-G. of Canada* (1993) 102 D.L.R. (4th) 136, BCSC; *Walker v Region 2 Hospital Corp.* (1994) 110 D.L.R. (4th) 477, NBCA; *Van Mol (Guardian ad Litem of) v Ashmore* (1999) 168 D.L.R. (4th) 637, BCCA; *Secretary, Department of Health and Community Services v J.W.B.* [1992] HCA 15; (1992) 106 A.L.R. 385, HC of Aus.

[660] [1986] A.C. 112 at 189.

[661] "The effect of the consent of the infant depends on the nature of the treatment and the age and understanding of the infant. For example, a doctor with the consent of an intelligent boy or girl of 15 could in my opinion safely remove tonsils or a troublesome appendix", [1986] A.C. 112 at 201.

[662] *Re R (A Minor) (Wardship: Consent to Treatment)* [1992] Fam. 11 at 26, per Lord Donaldson MR. See, e.g. *Re E (A Minor) (wardship: medical treatment)* [1993] 1 F.L.R. 386, and *Re S (A Minor) (Consent to Medical Treatment)* [1994] 2 F.L.R. 1065; para.6–200.

[663] The test for capacity in adults has, admittedly, become a little more sophisticated than it was at the time of *Gillick*: see paras 6–037 et seq.

[664] *Gillick v West Norfolk & Wisbech Area Health Authority* [1986] A.C. 112 at 189.

procedure "in broad terms".[665] Speaking specifically about contraceptive advice and treatment, Lord Fraser identified five factors that a doctor would have to consider:

> "...the doctor will, in my opinion, be justified in proceeding without the parents' consent or even knowledge provided he is satisfied on the following matters: (1) that the girl (although under 16 years of age) will understand his advice; (2) that he cannot persuade her to inform her parents or to allow him to inform the parents that she is seeking contraceptive advice; (3) that she is very likely to begin or to continue having sexual intercourse with or without contraceptive treatment; (4) that unless she receives contraceptive advice or treatment her physical or mental health or both are likely to suffer; (5) that her best interests require him to give her contraceptive advice, treatment or both without the parental consent."[666]

Only the first point relates to the girl's *capacity* to consent, the remaining matters being more relevant to the doctor's assessment of whether providing the treatment is in her best interests in the circumstances. Lord Scarman clearly required a higher level of understanding for the purpose of capacity to consent than Lord Fraser,[667] whereas Lord Templeman took the view that a child under the age of 16, although capable of consenting to some forms of treatment, could never have sufficient understanding to have the capacity to consent to contraceptive advice or treatment.[668]

***Gillick* competence**   "*Gillick* competence" is a developmental concept which does not fluctuate on a day-to-day or week-to-week basis. It involves an assessment of mental and emotional age, as contrasted with chronological age, but the test may not be appropriate where, as a result of mental illness, the child's understanding and capacity varies from day-to-day.[669] Moreover, the illness itself may reduce the child's capacity to make a competent decision.[670]   **6–198**

Since the decision of the House of Lords in *Gillick* there has been much greater attention paid to the meaning of and requirements for capacity in adults, both at   **6–199**

---

[665] Logically, it would seem to follow from this that when treating children a doctor has a greater duty to disclose information about the nature of the treatment and, indeed, the risks or consequences of the procedure, at the risk of being held liable in battery for non-disclosure, than is required when treating adults. This point has not been tested.

[666] [1986] A.C. 112 at 174. On the doctor's duty of confidentiality owed to minors see para.8–036. See also the General Medical Council, *0–18 years: guidance for all doctors* (2007) paras 42-52 (available at *http://www.gmc-uk.org/static/documents/content/0-18_years_-_English_1015.pdf*).

[667] See further Jones (1986) 2 P.N. 41.

[668] [1986] A.C. 112 at 204. "I doubt whether a girl under the age of 16 is capable of a balanced judgment to embark on frequent, regular or casual sexual intercourse fortified by the illusion that medical science can protect her in mind and body and ignoring the danger of leaping from childhood to adulthood without the difficult formative transitional experiences of adolescence. There are many things which a girl under 16 needs to practise but sex is not one of them", per Lord Templeman at 201. It is apparent that Lord Scarman's views were also strongly influenced by the fact that the case was concerned with the controversial issue of contraception for girls under 16.

[669] *Re R (A Minor) (Wardship: Consent to Treatment)* [1992] Fam. 11, 25–26, 32, per Lord Donaldson MR and Farquharson LJ respectively. The fact that the minor's mental state was fluctuating meant that she was not competent, since it would be dangerous to the ward if her competence were to be judged purely on her state of mind during a period when her mental illness was in recession. For comment on this case see Bainham (1992) 108 L.Q.R. 194; Douglas (1992) 55 M.L.R. 569; Murphy (1992) 43 N.I.L.Q. 60; Urwin (1992) 8 P.N. 69.

[670] See *Re W (A Minor) (Medical Treatment: Court's Jurisdiction)* [1993] Fam. 64; para.6–042.

common law and in the form of the Mental Capacity Act 2005 (which also applies to minors of 16 or 17 years of age). The test in relation to minors has been modified to reflect that broader understanding of the requirements for capacity. So, for example, in *Re JA (A Minor) (Medical Treatment: Child Diagnosed with HIV)*[671] Baker J said that:

"To be *Gillick* competent, a child must (a) understand the nature and implications of the treatment, which would include the likely effects and potential side effects; (b) understand the implications of not pursuing the treatment, including the nature, likely progress and consequences of any illness that would result from not receiving the treatment; (c) retain the above information long enough for the decision making process to take place and (d) be of sufficient intelligence and maturity to weigh up the information and arrive at a decision."

This formulation teases out some of the issues that the child will have to understand in order to have capacity.[672] As with adult capacity, *Gillick* competence is decision-specific.[673] There is no fixed age at which a child can be said to have the capacity to consent. It is a variable approach which depends upon the maturity of the child and the complexity or seriousness of the procedure required.[674] Even a very young child may have sufficient understanding to have capacity to consent to the dressing of a wound, but, conversely, an older child will probably not be regarded as having sufficient understanding to decline life-saving treatment. In other cases much will depend upon the maturity and understanding of the individual child.[675]

6–200   **No capacity to refuse life-saving treatment**   Whatever the child's level of maturity and understanding it is highly unlikely that a court would conclude that

---

[671] [2014] EWHC 1135 (Fam); [2015] Med. L.R. 26 at [68].

[672] Note that there is no equivalent of the requirement in the Mental Capacity Act 2005 s.2(1) that the inability to make a decision be due to "an impairment of, or a disturbance in the functioning of the mind or brain", presumably on the basis that a child's mind or brain is still developing, and the issue is whether it has developed sufficiently to satisfy the required level of understanding/decision-making.

[673] *Re JA (A Minor) (Medical Treatment: Child Diagnosed with HIV)* [2014] EWHC 1135 (Fam); [2015] Med. L.R. 26 at [69].

[674] So in *Re JA (A Minor) (Medical Treatment: Child Diagnosed with HIV)* [2014] EWHC 1135 (Fam); [2015] Med. L.R. 26 at [76]–[77] Baker J found that a 14-year-old who did not accept his diagnosis that he was HIV positive did not have capacity to refuse anti-retroviral therapy (since this was a complex decision which turned in part on his acceptance of the diagnosis), but he did have capacity to consent to undergoing monitoring, blood tests and chest X-rays, and to accept psychotherapy and peer support, to which he had consented, because these decisions were less complex in that they were not specifically dependent on his acceptance of his diagnosis but rather on the fact that the diagnosis had been given. See also the Children Act 1989 s.44(7) which provides that if a child is of sufficient understanding to make an informed decision he may refuse to submit to a medical or psychiatric examination ordered by the court when making an emergency protection order. Similarly, a supervision order may require a supervised child to submit to a medical or psychiatric examination or treatment, but again the child can refuse consent where he has sufficient understanding to make an informed decision: Children Act 1989 Sch.3 paras 4 and 5; cf., however, *South Glamorgan County Council v B and W* [1993] 1 F.L.R. 574; (1992) 11 B.M.L.R. 162; para.6–207.

[675] So, e.g., one 13-year-old could be *Gillick* competent to decide whether or not to undergo a termination of pregnancy (*An NHS Trust v A* [2014] EWHC 1445 (Fam); [2014] Fam. Law 1229) whereas another 13-year-old may not be *Gillick* competent to make the same decision (*Re X (A Child) (Capacity to Consent to Termination)* [2014] EWHC 1871 (Fam); (2014) B.M.L.R. 143). See para.6–213.

a minor has capacity to refuse life-saving medical treatment. In *Re E (A Minor) (Wardship: Medical Treatment)*[676] Ward J held that a 15-year-old Jehovah's Witness who was refusing consent to a potentially life-saving blood transfusion was not competent because, although he had some concept of the fact that he would die, he had no realisation of the full implications of the process of dying. His Lordship commented that the court "should be very slow to allow an infant to martyr himself".[677] Johnson J adopted a very similar approach in *Re S (A Minor) (Consent to Medical Treatment)*[678] where a 15-and-a-half-year-old girl who had suffered from thalassaemia virtually from birth needed monthly blood transfusions and daily injections. In 1989 her mother joined the Jehovah's Witnesses, and in May 1994 the girl did not attend for her usual transfusion. Both mother and daughter made it clear that they did not want any more transfusions, and the local authority sought an order authorising transfusions. Johnson J granted the order, taking the view that the girl was not competent, relying on Lord Donaldson's comments in *Re R (A Minor) (Wardship: Consent to Treatment)*[679] that to be "*Gillick* competent" a minor requires not merely a full understanding and appreciation of the consequences of the treatment, in terms of intended and possible side effects and, but equally importantly, understanding of the anticipated consequences of a failure to treat. On this basis S had only a very general understanding of some vital matters relating to her treatment and to the consequences for her of that treatment ceasing. She was confused over many details. She did not know how her death would occur. She thought that there might be a miracle and that "God might save me". She did not believe that a refusal to have further transfusions would certainly lead to her death. She was disillusioned with treatment, "fed up with it", and was susceptible to influence from outside:

> "She does not understand the full implications of what will happen. It does not seem to me that her capacity is commensurate with the gravity of the decision which she has made. It seems to me that an understanding that she will die is not enough. For her decision to carry weight she should have a greater understanding of the manner of the death and the pain and the distress."[680]

---

[676] [1993] 1 F.L.R. 386.

[677] This can be contrasted with the position once the minor attains 18 years of age since: (i) a presumption of capacity would apply (Mental Capacity Act 2005 s.1(2)); (ii) it would have to be demonstrated that the patient was unable to make a decision because of "an impairment of, or a disturbance in the functioning of the mind or brain" (Mental Capacity Act 2005 s.2(1)); and (iii) the decisions of adults about their medical treatment based on religious convictions will be respected (see para.6–177). It is understood that when the minor in *Re E (A Minor) (Wardship: Medical Treatment)* reached 18 years of age he persisted in refusing blood products and died as a consequence. In *X v Sydney Children's Hospitals Network* [2013] NSWCA 320; 304 A.L.R. 517, where the court authorised administration of blood products to a competent 17-year-old Jehovah's Witness patient up to the date of his 18th birthday, Basten JA commented at [72]: "The interest of the state is in keeping him alive until that time, after which he will be free to make his own decisions as to medical treatment."

[678] [1994] 2 F.L.R. 1065.

[679] [1992] Fam. 11, 26.

[680] [1994] 2 F.L.R. 1065 at 1075–1076. Johnson J observed, at 1075, that in two-and-a-half years' time the girl would be able to make up her own mind (when she reached 18). See also *Re L (Medical Treatment: Gillick Competency)* [1998] 2 F.L.R. 810; [1999] 2 F.C.R. 524, in which a 14-year-old Jehovah's Witness refused consent to life-saving medical treatment because it would involve blood

6–201   Similarly, in *Re P (Medical Treatment: Best Interests)*[681] Johnson J overrode the wishes of a minor of 16 years and 10 months who was refusing consent to blood products on the basis of his religious faith. Johnson J made no express finding as to whether the minor was competent. There were, said his Lordship, "weighty and compelling reasons" that the order to administer blood if the patient's condition became immediately life-threatening should not be made. Nonetheless, looking at P's interests in the "widest possible sense—medical, religious, social, whatever they be" Johnson J held that the order should be granted subject to the proviso that "no other form of treatment is available".

(b)   The effect of reaching "*Gillick* competence"

6–202   **Parental consent**   At one time the assumption was that a minor who was *Gillick* competent could both give a valid consent to treatment and refuse recommended treatment, just as a competent adult is entitled to decline treatment. In *Gillick v West Norfolk & Wisbech Area Health Authority*[682] it was said that the parental power to consent on the child's behalf is a diminishing one, as the child's understanding and intelligence develops to the stage at which she is capable of making up her own mind and thus acquires the capacity to consent herself. This suggested that as the child developed the capacity to give a valid consent, the power of the parent to consent disappeared, and therefore the competent child effectively had the capacity also to decline proposed treatment. This view was challenged by Lord Donaldson MR in *Re R (A Minor) (Wardship: Consent to Treatment)*,[683] where his Lordship suggested that even where a child is competent, the child's parents have a concurrent power to consent notwithstanding that the child has refused treatment. In his Lordship's view consent was "merely a key which unlocks a door" and there was no difficulty in conceiving of two keyholders, the *"Gillick"* competent' child, whose consent to treatment could not be vetoed by the parents (the situation considered in *Gillick* itself), and the parents whose consent could not be vetoed by the competent child. Thus, parental consent would still protect a doctor from an action in battery despite the child's objection to treatment.

6–203   Although this approach appeared to be inconsistent with *Gillick* (Lord Scarman's speech in particular)[684] it was confirmed by the Court of Appeal in *Re W (A Minor) (Medical Treatment: Court's Jurisdiction)*,[685] where it was held that

---

transfusions. It was held that she was not *Gillick* competent, because her sincerely held beliefs had not been developed through a broad and informed adult experience, but through a sheltered religious upbringing; she knew that she could die without the treatment, but had not been told about the unpleasant manner of her death.

[681] [2003] EWHC 2327 (Fam); [2004] 2 F.L.R. 1117.

[682] [1986] A.C. 112 at 172–173 and 188–189, per Lord Fraser and Lord Scarman respectively.

[683] [1992] Fam. 11 at 23.

[684] See [1992] Fam. 11 at 27–28, per Staughton LJ. Indeed, it appeared to be inconsistent with some provisions of the Children Act 1989: see para.6–199, n.673; but cf. *South Glamorgan County Council v B. and W.* [1993] 1 F.L.R. 574; (1992) 11 B.M.L.R. 162.

[685] [1993] Fam. 64. See Bridgeman (1993) 13 L.S. 69; Eekelaar (1993) 109 L.Q.R. 182; Houghton-James [1992] Fam. Law 550; Lowe and Juss (1993) 56 M.L.R. 865; Mulholland (1993) 9 P.N. 21.

although a competent minor can give a valid consent to medical treatment this does not entail an absolute right to refuse treatment where a parent or person exercising parental responsibility has given a valid consent to treatment.[686] However, Nolan LJ considered that it was axiomatic that where major surgical or other procedures (such as an abortion) were proposed, and the parents were prepared to give consent but the child (having sufficient understanding to make an informed decision) was not, the jurisdiction of the court should always be invoked. On the other hand, the parents have no right to veto treatment to which a competent minor has consented, since this is a clear consequence of *Gillick*.[687] Lord Donaldson MR retreated from his suggestion that consent was the key that unlocked the door, because keys could lock as well as unlock. Rather consent was analogous to a "legal 'flak jacket' which protects the doctor from claims by the litigious". Anyone who gives doctors a flak jacket (i.e. consent) may take it back, but doctors only need one jacket to protect themselves, whether it be given by children, parents,[688] or the court.[689]

Court's power to authorise medical treatment   Whatever the position of a parent or someone exercising parental responsibility, under the wardship or inherent jurisdiction the court has the power to authorise medical treatment of a "*Gillick* competent" minor who is refusing treatment.[690] This is the position whether or not the minor is over 16 years of age. In *Re W (A Minor) (Medical* **6–204**

---

[686] cf. *Walker v Region 2 Hospital Corp.* (1994) 110 D.L.R. (4th) 477, NBCA, where it was held that a 15-year-old who was sufficiently mature to be competent was entitled to refuse medical treatment. The right to consent included the right to refuse treatment. Similarly, in *Van Mol (Guardian ad Litem of) v Ashmore* (1999) 168 D.L.R. (4th) 637 the British Columbia Court of Appeal held that once the child (in that case a 16-year-old) was found to be competent the parents had no right either to consent or to withhold consent. Note, however, that the "mature minor" rule can be overridden by legislation for the protection of minors, and therefore a court can order that it is in the best interests of a competent minor to have blood transfusions despite the objections of the minor or her parents: *U(C) (Next Friend Of) v Alberta (Director of Child Welfare)* (2003) 223 D.L.R. (4th) 662, Alta CA, applying the Alberta Child Welfare Act 1984. Although the court's inherent *parens patriae* jurisdiction for the protection of minors may not be exercisable in the case of a mature minor who is no longer in need of the protection of the court, the legislature's jurisdiction is not so limited (at [33]).

[687] cf. the position of the court, para.6–203; see also *Ney v A.-G. of Canada* (1993) 102 D.L.R. (4th) 136, BCSC.

[688] Some procedures, such as ritual circumcision, require either the consent of *both* parents or a declaration by the court that it is in the child's best interests: *Re J (Specific Issue Orders: Child's Religious Upbringing and Circumcision)* [2000] 1 F.L.R. 571; [2000] 1 F.C.R. 307, CA.

[689] More remarkable, perhaps, than even this narrow view of the role of consent in the context of medical treatment was Lord Donaldson's comment that in the case of a competent *adult* a refusal to give consent would be fully effective as a veto, "but only *because no one else would be in a position to consent*": [1993] Fam. 64 at 77, emphasis added. With respect, this rather puts the cart before the horse. The fundamental proposition is that consent operates as a *defence* to what would otherwise constitute trespass to the person. No one has any claim to invade the bodily integrity of a competent adult without lawful excuse, because the law rightly places such high regard upon the individual's claim to bodily integrity. It is submitted that the notion that the *only* reason that an adult is entitled to reject treatment is because of the happenstance that no one else is in a position to consent is inconsistent with basic principle.

[690] *Re R (A Minor) (Wardship: Consent to Treatment)* [1992] Fam. 11, CA; cf. *Walker v Region 2 Hospital Corp.* (1994) 110 D.L.R. (4th) 477, 488 where a majority of the New Brunswick Court of Appeal held that if a minor is found to be mature, i.e. competent, there was no room for the operation of the court's *parens patriae* jurisdiction (though child protection legislation can be used to override a

Treatment: Court's Jurisdiction)[691] W was a 16-year-old girl who was suffering from anorexia nervosa. Her condition was deteriorating and it was proposed that she be moved to a hospital specialising in the treatment of eating disorders, but she refused to move. On the local authority's application for an order that W be placed in the hospital for treatment and that she be given treatment without her consent if necessary, the judge held that although W had sufficient understanding to make an informed decision, he had the jurisdiction to make such an order and authorised her removal to and treatment at the hospital. The Court of Appeal upheld this decision, on the basis that in the exercise of its inherent jurisdiction to protect the welfare of minors the court can, in the child's own best interests, override the wishes of a mentally competent child who is refusing medical treatment in circumstances where there is a probability of death or severe permanent injury.[692] In reaching a decision as to the minor's best interests, the court will ascertain the wishes of the child and should approach its decision with a strong predilection to give effect to the child's wishes.[693]

6–205   Where, however, the effect of acceding to the minor's wish to refuse treatment is likely to be serious injury or death there is a very high probability that the court will authorise treatment. In *An NHS Foundation Hospital v P*[694] a 17-and-a-half-year old girl with a history of self-harming behaviour had taken an overdose of paracetamol and was refusing to be treated with the antidote. A psychiatrist considered that although she suffered from a personality disorder, she did not lack capacity to make decisions concerning medical treatment, since she was able to understand information and retain it, and also weigh it up and use it. Although the physician at the hospital responsible for treating P's overdose had some doubts about the psychiatrist's opinion Baker J (acting on an emergency application and with limited information) accepted that the presumption of capacity in the Mental

---

competent minor's refusal of potentially life-saving treatment: *U(C) (Next Friend of) v Alberta (Director of Child Welfare)* (2003) 223 D.L.R. (4th) 662).
[691] [1993] Fam. 64; followed in *X v Sydney Children's Hospitals Network* [2013] NSWCA 320; 304 A.L.R. 517.
[692] The effect of s.8(1) of the Family Law Reform Act 1969 (see para.6–193, n.656) was said to be that it enabled the minor to give a valid *consent* to surgical, medical or dental treatment, but this did not entail a right to refuse treatment when parental consent was forthcoming or the court authorised treatment (or, putting it more accurately, the doctor who proceeded to treat in the face of the minor's objections would not be liable in battery). The court also has the power to direct that a 16-year-old girl can be detained in a specialist clinic until completion of her treatment for anorexia nervosa, where her presence in the clinic is an essential part of her treatment and she would otherwise leave if free to do so: *Re C (Detention: Medical Treatment)* [1997] 2 F.L.R. 180; [1997] 3 F.C.R. 49.
[693] See *An NHS Foundation Trust v A* [2014] EWHC 920 (Fam); [2015] 1 F.L.R. 503; (2014) 139 B.M.L.R. 165 at [12] per Hayden J: "a competent young person under the age of 16 years, who is able to understand all the relevant advice and the consequences of that advice, is to be treated as an autonomous individual and respected as such. That of course would not mean her views would be determinative, but they would be given great weight." On the facts the 15-and-a-half year old was found to lack capacity, but Hayden J nonetheless gave "very considerable weight to her strongly expressed resistance" to medical treatment ([2014] EWHC 920 (Fam); [2015] 1 F.L.R. 503; (2014) 139 B.M.L.R. 165 at [15]), though this did not displace the judge's assessment that it was in her best interests to be compulsorily fed and hydrated through a naso-jejunal tube. See also *Re X (A Child) (Capacity to Consent to Termination)* [2014] EWHC 1871 (Fam); (2014) B.M.L.R. 143, para.6–214, on the weight to be attached to the views of a minor who lacked capacity where the proposed treatment was a termination of pregnancy.
[694] [2014] EWHC 1650 (Fam); [2014] Fam. Law 1249.

Capacity Act 2005 had not been displaced. Nonetheless, Baker J granted a declaration that it was lawful, in P's best interests, for treatment for the effects of her overdose to be given (including if necessary sedation or restraint), despite her refusal of treatment.[695] Without treatment she was likely to suffer serious damage to her liver and would probably die.

Court's power to refuse to authorise medical treatment   Just as the court has the power to authorise treatment to which a competent minor is refusing to consent, the same principle must also apply, at least theoretically, where a competent minor has decided to accept medical treatment—the court has the power to refuse to authorise the treatment if it is not in the minor's best interests. In practice, it is difficult to imagine circumstances where this is likely to arise if the treatment is medically justified.

6–206

In *South Glamorgan County Council v B and W*[696] Douglas Brown J held that the Children Act 1989 had not abrogated the powers of the court to override the decisions of even a competent minor, under the court's inherent jurisdiction to safeguard the welfare of minors, applying *Re R (A Minor) (Wardship: Consent to Treatment)* and *Re W (A Minor) (Medical Treatment: Court's Jurisdiction)*. The court's jurisdiction is unlimited.

6–207

Human rights   It remains to be seen whether the approach of the English courts to overriding the refusals of consent of competent minors will withstand a challenge under the European Convention on Human Rights. It is certainly arguable that the non-consensual treatment of competent patients could amount to breach of both art.3 (protection against torture or inhuman or degrading treatment) and art.8 (the right to respect for private and family life) of the Convention. Article 8 is a qualified right, and therefore the court could take into account the provisions of art.8(2),[697] and in particular the qualification "for the protection of health or morals".[698] Article 3 is an absolute right, but in *Herczegfalvy v Austria*[699] it was held that:

6–208

"...as a general rule, a method which is a therapeutic necessity cannot be regarded as inhuman or degrading. The court must nevertheless satisfy itself that the medical necessity has been convincingly shown to exist."

---

[695] Applying *Re W (A Minor) (Medical Treatment: Court's Jurisdiction)* [1993] Fam. 64 and *Re P (Medical Treatment: Best Interests)* [2003] EWHC 2327 (Fam); [2004] 2 F.L.R. 1117.

[696] [1993] 1 F.L.R. 574; (1992) 11 B.M.L.R. 162.

[697] Article 8(2) provides that: "There shall be no interference by a public authority with the exercise of this right except such as is in accordance with the law and is necessary in a democratic society in the interests of national security, public safety or the economic well-being of the country, for the prevention of disorder or crime, for the protection of health or morals, or for the protection of the rights and freedoms of others."

[698] In *An NHS Foundation Hospital v P* [2014] EWHC 1650 (Fam); [2014] Fam. Law 1249, where a competent 17-and-a-half-year old girl was refusing treatment for an overdose of paracetamol, Baker J accepted that art.8 was engaged, but that her rights under art.8 were outweighed by her art.2 right to life.

[699] (1992) E.H.R.R. 437 at [82].

In that case the patient lacked the capacity to consent. It is not clear that the same approach would be applied to a competent patient refusing consent, though the Mental Health Act 1983 contemplates the compulsory treatment of competent patients for their psychiatric illness or disorder, and that would not necessarily involve a breach of Convention rights.[700] On the other hand, no one suggests that competent adults should be treated against their wishes for their physical illnesses, no matter how convincingly the medical necessity has been shown to exist and no matter how serious the consequences for the patient. The right to refuse even life-saving treatment is regarded as fundamental. A distinction based on age (17 years, 364 days as opposed to 18 years?), rather than competence to decide, looks arbitrary and disproportionate to the otherwise legitimate objective of protecting the welfare of minors (the justification for which is, in any event, that minors are often not in a position to exercise an informed decision about their best interests—if this justification is absent on the facts of the case, because the minor is judged to be competent, then the argument for "protecting" the minor's welfare dissolves).

(c) Children lacking capacity

6–209   **Parental consent**   Where a child lacks the relevant capacity to consent to treatment, parental consent will be required unless there is an emergency,[701] though in the case of minors aged 16 or 17 the Mental Capacity Act 2005 will also apply.[702] There must be some limits, however, to the parent's power to give or withhold consent. *Gillick* makes it clear that parental rights to control a child do not exist for the benefit of the parent. They exist for the benefit of the child, and they are justified only in so far as they enable parents to perform their duties

---

[700] See *R. (on the application of W) v Broadmoor Hospital* [2001] EWCA Civ 1545; [2002] 1 W.L.R. 419, para.6–094. Hale LJ commented, at [80]: "I do not take the view that detained patients who have the capacity to decide for themselves can never be treated against their will. Our threshold of capacity is rightly a low one. It is better to keep it that way and allow some non-consensual treatment of those who have capacity than to set such a high threshold for capacity that many would never qualify. Whether the criteria for non-consensual treatment of the capacitated should be limited to treatment which is for their own safety (as opposed to their health) is a difficult and complex question. [Counsel for the applicant] tried to persuade us that there was a developing consensus to that effect. There are indeed indications that the issue of capacity is assuming greater importance in the context of psychiatric treatment. But we have not yet reached the point where it is an accepted norm that detained patients who fulfil the *Re MB* criteria for capacity can only be treated against their will for the protection of others or for their own safety."

[701] *Gillick v West Norfolk & Wisbech Area Health Authority* [1986] A.C. 112 at 173, per Lord Fraser, and 184 and 188 per Lord Scarman; *Ney v A.-G. of Canada* (1993) 102 D.L.R. (4th) 136, BCSC. A local authority may exercise the power of consent to treatment when the child is in care and the authority has acquired parental responsibility: Children Act 1989 s.33(3). Parents do not lose parental responsibility (and therefore the power to consent to treatment) by virtue of the making of a care order (Children Act 1989 s.2), but where there is a conflict between the views of the parents and the local authority, the authority may restrict the extent to which the parents may exercise parental responsibility: Children Act 1989 s.33(3)(b). A person who does not have parental responsibility but has the care of the child may do what is reasonable for the purpose of safeguarding or promoting the child's welfare, which in appropriate circumstances would include giving a valid consent to medical treatment: Children Act 1989 s.3(5).

[702] See para.6–110.

towards the child, and towards other children in the family.[703] Accordingly, the parental power to consent to treatment must be exercised in the best interests of the child.[704] Arguably, this means that a parent may only authorise procedures which are demonstrably for the benefit of the child, indeed parents may owe a *duty* to the child to give or withhold consent in the best interests of the child.[705] In *S v S*,[706] however, the House of Lords considered that a parent would be entitled to require a young child to submit to a blood test for the purpose of determining who was the child's father in a paternity suit, even though the blood test could not be said to be in the child's medical interests and carried some, albeit extremely remote, risk of harm. Lord Reid considered that a parent could take into account the general public interest in the administration of justice and so "would not refuse a blood test unless he thought that would clearly be against the interests of the child".[707] An approach which permits parental consent to procedures which are "not against the child's interests" is clearly wider in its ambit than a test based solely on the child's "best interests", in that it reverses the assessment of the balance of interests, and curiously shifts from *best* interests to simply "interests". The change in emphasis may be significant, however, when considering the question of medical research on children or the transplantation of organs or bodily fluids.[708]

Limits of parental consent   In *Re B (A Minor) (Wardship: Sterilisation)*[709]   **6–210**
Lord Templeman suggested that parental consent would not be sufficient to authorise a doctor to perform a sterilisation operation on a girl under 18 years of age, and that a doctor who relied on parental consent might still be liable in criminal, civil or professional proceedings: a court exercising the wardship jurisdiction was the only authority empowered to authorise such a drastic step

---

[703] [1986] A.C. 112 at 170, per Lord Fraser.

[704] [1986] A.C. 112 at 170 at 200, per Lord Templeman. Note also that some procedures may be unlawful even with parental consent: see the Female Genital Mutilation Act 2003; and also Lord Templeman's comments on sterilisation in *Re B (A Minor) (Wardship: Sterilisation)* [1988] A.C. 199 at 205–206, para.6–210. It would seem that ritual male circumcision remains lawful (*R. v Brown* [1994] 1 A.C. 212 at 231 per Lord Templeman), despite being an irreversible operation which is not medically necessary and which carries physical and psychological risks. But it is a procedure which requires the consent of both parents: *Re J (Specific Issue Orders: Child's Religious Upbringing and Circumcision)* [2000] 1 F.L.R. 571; [2000] 1 F.C.R. 307, CA; *Re S (Children) (Specific Issue Order: Religion: Circumcision)* [2004] EWHC 1282 (Fam); [2005] 1 F.L.R. 236; *Re L (Children) (Specific Issues: Temporary Leave to Remove from the Jurisdiction: Circumcision)* [2016] EWHC 849 (Fam); [2017] 1 F.L.R. 1316. For discussion of the distinctions between male and female circumcision see: *Leeds City Council v M* [2015] EWFC 3; [2015] 1 F.L.R. 905. For consideration of the extreme, and probably unique, circumstances in which the criminal law will permit the defence of necessity to justify the taking of positive steps to end life see: *Re A (Children) (Conjoined Twins: Surgical Separation)* [2001] Fam 147, CA; commented on by Bainham [2001] C.L.J. 49; Burnet (2001) 13 C.F.L.Q. 91; Tausz Smith [2001] Crim. L.R. 400; Rogers [2001] Crim. L.R. 515. The issues are considered in an earlier article by Sheldon and Wilkinson, "Conjoined twins: the legality and ethics of sacrifice" (1997) 5 Med. L. Rev. 149.

[705] *Re J (A Minor) (Wardship: Medical Treatment)* [1991] Fam. 33 at 41, per Lord Donaldson MR.

[706] [1972] A.C. 24.

[707] [1972] A.C. 24 at 44.

[708] See paras 7–139 and 7–155 to 7–156. Note, however, that in *S v S* [1972] A.C. 24 it could be said to be in the child's interests to have the question of paternity determined.

[709] [1988] A.C. 199 at 205–206.

after a full and informed investigation.[710] Although this view was not concurred in by the other members the House, it is now the practice to seek the leave of the High Court in such cases.[711] The approval of the court is not necessary, however, where an operation, such as hysterectomy, is to be performed for therapeutic reasons even though sterilisation would be an incidental result.[712] In these circumstances the parents can give a valid consent. In *R. v Portsmouth Hospitals NHS Trust Ex p. Glass*[713] the Court of Appeal indicated that where doctors and parents cannot agree on the course to be taken in relation to the treatment of a child, and the conflict is of a grave nature, the matter should be brought before the court.[714]

---

[710] See also per Neill LJ in *Re F. (Mental Patient: Sterilisation)* [1990] 2 A.C. 1 at 33, para.7–156 extending this to organ donation by children; and the dissenting speech of Lord Griffiths in *Re F (Mental Patient: Sterilisation)* [1990] 2 A.C. 1 at 70 taking the view that the sterilisation of mentally handicapped adults would only be lawful with the approval of the court.

[711] Either under the Children Act 1989 or the court's inherent jurisdiction. See *Practice Note (Official Solicitor: Appointment in Family Proceedings)* [2001] 2 F.L.R. 155 and *Practice Note (Officers of CAFCASS Legal Services and Special Casework: Appointment in Family Proceedings)* [2001] 2 F.L.R. 151. The House of Lords has held that the court may authorise the sterilisation of a mentally handicapped minor, in her "best interests": *Re B (A Minor) (Wardship: Sterilisation)* [1988] A.C. 199; *Re M (A Minor) (Wardship: Sterilisation)* [1988] 2 F.L.R. 497; cf. the approach of the Supreme Court of Canada in *Re Eve* (1986) 31 D.L.R. (4th) 1 taking the view that non-therapeutic sterilisation of a minor could never be authorised. See further Lee and Morgan (1988) 15 J. of Law and Soc. 229; Brazier (1990) 6 P.N. 25, 26 suggesting that the courts have paid too little attention to the question of whether girls with a mental handicap were competent to refuse consent, before authorising sterilisation under the wardship jurisdiction. In *Secretary, Department of Health and Community Services v JWB* [1992] HCA 15; (1992) 106 A.L.R. 385 the High Court of Australia considered that sterilisation which was not an incidental result of surgery performed to cure a disease or correct some malfunction could not be authorised by a parent, although the procedure could be authorised by the court when it was in the best interests of the minor; *P v P* (1994) 68 A.L.J.R. 449, HC of Aus; Blackwood (1994) 1 J. Law and Med. 252.

[712] *Re E (A Minor) (Medical Treatment)* [1991] 2 F.L.R. 585; (1991) 7 B.M.L.R. 117. See also *Re GF (Medical Treatment)* [1992] 1 F.L.R. 293; [1993] 4 Med. L.R. 77 for the position in the case of an incompetent adult; *Trust A v H (An Adult Patient)* [2006] EWHC 1230 (Fam); [2006] 2 F.L.R. 958—in the best interests of an incompetent patient to undergo a total hysterectomy because she had developed an ovarian cyst that appeared to be cancerous.

[713] [1999] Lloyd's Rep. Med. 367 at 376; [1999] 2 F.L.R. 905, CA. See also *Re J (Specific Issue Orders: Child's Religious Upbringing and Circumcision)* [2000] 1 F.L.R. 571; [2000] 1 F.C.R. 307, CA, which concerned a dispute between the parents about circumcision; *Re C and F (A Child) (Immunisation: Parental Rights)* [2003] EWCA Civ 1148; [2003] 2 F.L.R. 1095; [2003] 3 F.C.R. 156; (2003) 73 B.M.L.R. 152 where there was a dispute between the parents as to whether their children should be immunised. The Court of Appeal upheld the approach of Sumner J authorising the immunisation, given that the medical evidence indicated that for the children concerned the benefits of immunisation outweighed the risks, and it was in the children's best interests. *Re C and F was applied in F v F* [2013] EWHC 2683 (Fam); [2014] 1 F.L.R. 1328, where Theis J held that it was in the best interests of two girls aged 11 and 15 to have an MMR vaccination despite their objections and the objections of their mother. See also *C v A (A Minor)* [2011] EWHC 4033 (Fam) where Theis J authorised MMR vaccinations of children aged 13, 9, 6 and 5 years on an application by the local authority and against the wishes of both parents; *Re M (Children)* [2016] EWFC 69; *Barnet LBC v AL* [2017] EWHC 125 (Fam); [2017] 4 W.L.R. 53.

[714] The European Court of Human Rights subsequently held that, in the absence of court authorisation, the decision of medical staff to administer diamorphine to a child contrary to the express wishes of the child's mother constituted a breach of art.8 of the European Convention on Human Rights: *Glass v United Kingdom* [2004] 1 F.C.R. 553; (2004) 39 E.H.R.R. 15. See also *MAK v United Kingdom* [2010] 2 F.L.R. 451; (2010) 51 E.H.R.R. 14 (blood test and the taking of intimate

Court's power   Under the wardship or the inherent jurisdiction the High Court **6–211**
has the power to authorise or withhold permission for medical treatment of a
minor.[715] At one time the Official Solicitor took the view that the procedural and
administrative difficulties attaching to applications for a specific issue order
under s.8 of the Children Act 1989 were such that the preferred course was to
apply using the court's inherent jurisdiction.[716] Nonetheless, it is clear that the
concept of "parental responsibility" includes the responsibility to bring before a
High Court judge the question whether a child should be sterilised, and
accordingly s.8 can be used where there is a proposal to sterilise a child.[717] In *Re
JM (A Child)*[718] Mostyn J considered that where a final declaration concerning
medical treatment for a minor to which the child's parents did not consent was
being sought an application should be made for a specific issue order under s.8
combined with an application for declaratory relief under the court's inherent
jurisdiction. But, in any event, an application under s.8 is unnecessary where
parental consent to treatment has been given, even where the minor is competent
and has refused consent.[719] Where medical treatment is not urgent and there is no
dispute between the parties the court should leave a decision about whether
treatment should be authorised to whoever is entrusted with the child's long-term
care.[720]

Local authorities   A local authority cannot invoke the wardship jurisdiction of **6–212**
the High Court where a child is the subject of a care order,[721] nor can an authority
apply for a specific issue order under s.8 of the Children Act 1989 with respect to
a child who is in care.[722] This will not normally cause any difficulties in relation
to consent to treatment because the authority will have acquired parental
responsibility and so will be able to give a valid consent. Where, however, a child

photographs of a nine-year-old child suspected of being the victim of sexual abuse, without parental
consent, in circumstances where there was no urgency and no reason to believe that the mother's
consent would not be given when she got to the hospital, held to be a breach of the child's art.8
rights).
[715] Wardship is available only where the child is not in the care of the local authority: Children Act
1989 s.9. The court's inherent jurisdiction with respect to children is wider than the wardship
jurisdiction, and although the use of wardship by local authorities has been curtailed by the Children
Act 1989 this residual jurisdiction is still available: see *S. v McC.* [1972] A.C. 24 at 47–50, per Lord
MacDermott; *Re L. (An Infant)* [1968] P. 119 at 156–157, per Lord Denning MR. Indeed, this is the
assumption made by s.100(4) of the Children Act 1989; see para.6–212.
[716] *Practice Note (Sterilisation: Minors and Mental Health Patients)* [1993] 3 All E.R. 222, para.2.
[717] *Re HG (Specific Issue Order: Sterilisation)* [1993] 1 F.L.R. 587. See also *Re R (A Minor)* (1993)
15 B.M.L.R. 72 where it was held that a specific issue order was appropriate where a local authority
sought the court's authorisation for the use of blood products on a child, contrary to the parents'
objections; cf. *Re O (A Minor) (Medical Treatment)* [1993] 4 Med. L.R. 272; (1993) 19 B.M.L.R 148,
suggesting that the appropriate procedure in such a case was to invoke the court's inherent
jurisdiction, at least on an ex parte application; *Re S (A Minor) (Medical Treatment)* [1993] 1 F.L.R.
376; (1992) 11 B.M.L.R 105.
[718] [2015] EWHC 2832 (Fam); [2015] Med. L.R. 544.
[719] *Re K, W and H (Minors) (Medical Treatment)* (1992) 15 B.M.L.R. 60, applying *Re R (A Minor)
(Wardship: Consent to Treatment)* [1992] Fam. 11, CA; para.6–202.
[720] *Re E (A Child) (Medical Treatment)* [2016] EWHC 2267 (Fam); [2017] 1 F.L.R. 645; (2016) 152
B.M.L.R. 207.
[721] Children Act 1989 s.100(2)(c).
[722] Children Act 1989 s.9(1) and (5).

is in care but the local authority needs a court order to sanction a controversial medical procedure, such as sterilisation, the authority cannot rely on the wardship jurisdiction. In this situation the local authority may apply to the High Court (with the leave of the court) to exercise its inherent jurisdiction over the welfare of children for the purpose of authorising medical treatment provided that the result could not be achieved through an alternative procedure that the authority is entitled to use, and there is reasonable cause to believe that if the inherent jurisdiction is not exercised the child is likely to suffer significant harm.[723]

6–213   **The welfare principle**   In exercising the wardship or the inherent jurisdiction the welfare of the child is the paramount consideration. This welfare principle is also expressed as "the best interests of the child".[724] In *Re J (A Minor) (Wardship: Medical Treatment)*[725] Balcombe LJ said that in determining the child's best interests the court should adopt the standpoint of the reasonable and responsible parent who has the child's best interests at heart. Both Lord Donaldson MR and Taylor LJ appeared to endorse a form of "substituted judgment" test which requires the decision about whether to authorise medical treatment to be taken "from the assumed point of view of the patient".[726] The court may authorise medical treatment of a ward notwithstanding an express refusal of consent by the parents, and may refuse to authorise treatment to which parents have given consent.[727] Moreover, under the wardship or inherent jurisdiction the court may authorise medical treatment even where the child is competent to refuse treatment and has done so.[728]

---

[723] Children Act 1989 s.100(4). This subsection is expressly limited to local authorities and does not apply to a hospital seeking to invoke the court's jurisdiction to resolve a dispute about the medical treatment of a child: *Great Ormond Street Hospital v Yates* [2017] EWCA Civ 410 at [106]–[109].

[724] On the interpretation of the child's "best interests" see: *Re B (A Minor) (Wardship: Medical Treatment)* [1981] 1 W.L.R. 1421; *Re C (A Minor) (Wardship: Medical Treatment)* [1990] Fam. 26, on the appropriate treatment for a terminally ill infant; Roberts (1990) 106 L.Q.R. 218.

[725] [1991] Fam. 33; Wells, Aldridge and Morgan (1990) 140 N.L.J. 1544.

[726] [1991] Fam. 33 at 46, per Lord Donaldson MR. Taylor LJ said, at 55, that: "The test must be whether the child in question, if capable of exercising sound judgment, would consider the life tolerable"; *Airedale NHS Trust v Bland* [1993] A.C. 789 at 833, per Hoffmann LJ: "The patient's best interests would normally also include having respect paid to what seems most likely to have been his own views on the subject. To this extent I think that what the American courts have called 'substituted judgment' may be subsumed within the English concept of best interests." See also per Lord Goff at 872, commenting that the substituted judgment test does not form part of English law, although the best interests test should take account of the patient's personality and preferences; and [1993] A.C. 789 at 895, per Lord Mustill. In *Re Y (Mental Patient: Bone Marrow Donation)* [1997] Fam. 110 at 113 Connell J said that a substituted judgment test was not relevant in this jurisdiction, in the light of Lord Goff's and Lord Mustill's comments in *Bland*.

[727] *Re P (A Minor)* (1982) 80 L.G.R. 301—termination of pregnancy was in the child's best interests, contrary to the wishes of the parents; *Re B (A Minor) (Wardship: Medical Treatment)* [1981] 1 W.L.R. 1421—life-saving medical treatment of newborn baby with Down's Syndrome in child's best interests, notwithstanding parents' refusal of consent; *Re D (A Minor) (Wardship: Sterilisation)* [1976] Fam. 185—sterilisation of an 11-year-old girl with Soto's syndrome held not to be in child's best interests, despite parent's consent; *Re JM (A Child)* [2015] EWHC 2832 (Fam); [2015] Med. L.R. 544—surgery to remove cancerous tumour with 55 per cent to 65 per cent chance of a cure in a ten-year-old child in child's best interests, despite 2 per cent risk of mortality and other consequences; parents' preference for child to be treated with Chinese medicine discounted; *Re AA* [2015] EWHC 1178 (Fam)—implantation of cardioverter defibrillator to avoid further cardiac arrest in best interests of seven-year-old child, despite parents' opposition; the parents had been "overwhelmed really by the

Termination of pregnancy   Where the minor lacks capacity and the proposed   **6–214**
medical treatment is a termination of pregnancy the court will not hesitate to
override the views of the minor's parents and authorise the termination where that
is in the best interests of the minor.[729] Although not necessarily decisive, the
modern approach is to place a strong emphasis on the wishes of the minor. In *Re
X (A Child) (Capacity to Consent to Termination)*[730] a girl of 13 years and 9
months who was pregnant lacked capacity to consent to an abortion. Initially she
was opposed to a termination of the pregnancy, but by the time of the hearing she
had changed her mind. Sir James Munby P, authorising the termination,
commented that even where the child lacks capacity (unless she has so little
appreciation of what is going on as not to be able to express any wishes and
feelings) a vitally important factor in the court's decision will be the wishes and
feelings of the child:

> "Only the most compelling arguments could possibly justify compelling a mother who wished
> to carry her child to term to submit to an unwanted termination. It would be unwise to be too
> prescriptive, for every case must be judged on its own unique facts, but I find it hard to
> conceive of any case where such a drastic form of order—such an immensely invasive
> procedure—could be appropriate in the case of a mother who does not want a termination,
> unless there was powerful evidence that allowing the pregnancy to continue would put the
> mother's life or long-term health at very grave risk. Conversely, it would be a very strong
> thing indeed, if the mother wants a termination, to require her to continue with an unwanted
> pregnancy even though the conditions in section 1 of the 1967 [Abortion] Act are satisfied. A
> child or incapacitated adult may, in strict law, lack autonomy. But the court must surely attach
> very considerable weight indeed to the albeit qualified autonomy of a mother who in relation
> to a matter as personal, intimate and sensitive as pregnancy is expressing clear wishes and
> feelings, whichever way, as to whether or not she wants a termination."[731]

Of course, this is subject to the requirements of the Abortion Act 1967 being met.
The court cannot order a termination of pregnancy in circumstances that did not
satisfy the terms of the Act.[732]

---

intensity of what has happened in the last two months and by the gravity of the decision being asked
of them, with its lifelong consequences", per Bodey J at [16].
[728] *Re R (A Minor) (Wardship: Consent to Treatment)* [1992] Fam. 11, CA; *Re W (A Minor) (Medical
Treatment: Court's Jurisdiction)* [1993] Fam. 64; para.6–204.
[729] *Re P (A Minor)* (1982) 80 L.G.R. 301. *The younger the minor the more readily one may come to
the conclusion that it is in her best interests to have the abortion: Re B (Wardship: Abortion)* [1991] 2
F.L.R. 426 (12-year-old); *Re L (A Minor)* [1992] 3 Med. L.R. 78 (12-year-old).
[730] [2014] EWHC 1871 (Fam); (2014) B.M.L.R. 143. Contrast *An NHS Trust v A* [2014] EWHC 1445
(Fam); [2014] Fam. Law 1229 where a girl who was just 13 was found, on the evidence, to have
sufficient understanding and intelligence to have capacity to decide whether or not to undergo a
termination of pregnancy. She fully understood the implications of the options and the risks that were
involved in relation to each option.
[731] [2014] EWHC 1871 (Fam); (2014) B.M.L.R. 143 at [9]–[10]. See also *Re CS (Termination of
Pregnancy)* [2016] EWCOP 10; [2017] 1 F.L.R. 635; (2016) 153 B.M.L.R. 141, which concerned a
termination of the pregnancy of an incapacitated adult, where Baker J placed considerable emphasis
on the patient's previously expressed intentions to terminate the pregnancy, applying s.4(6) of the
Mental Capacity Act 2005.
[732] [2014] EWHC 1871 (Fam); (2014) B.M.L.R. 143 at [6], following *Re SB (A patient: capacity to
consent to termination)* [2013] EWHC 1417 (COP); [2013] 3 F.C.R. 384; (2013) 133 B.M.L.R. 110,
where an adult with a psychiatric disorder was seeking a termination of pregnancy.

6-215   **Parents' religious beliefs**   Although the courts will respect the decisions of competent adults who decide to refuse medical treatment on the basis of their religious beliefs,[733] they do not take the same approach in the case of minors. The issue tends to crop up most frequently in the context of parents who are Jehovah's Witnesses and object on religious grounds to their child receiving blood products during the course of medical treatment, but the same view is taken where other religious beliefs colour the parents' views of their child's welfare. Although an assessment of the child's best interests includes matters beyond simple physical welfare, when it comes to serious (and potentially life-saving) medical treatment the physical well-being of the child will always take precedence over the parents' religious beliefs.[734] For example, in *NHS Trust v A (A Child)*[735] the court concluded that a bone marrow transplant for a seven-month-old child giving a 50 per cent chance of long-term survival was in the child's best interests where otherwise the child's life expectancy was probably less than 12 months. The parents' faith that God would miraculously cure the child was entirely discounted. Similarly, in *Re E (A Minor) (Wardship: Medical Treatment)*[736] a potentially life-saving blood transfusion to a 15-year-old Jehovah's Witness was held to be in the ward's best interests despite the objections of both the ward and his parents. The English courts consistently authorise the administration of blood or blood products to minors, in the best interests of the minor, despite parental objection based on religious beliefs,[737] an approach also adopted in other jurisdictions.[738]

---

[733] See para.6–178.

[734] This is not confined to the parents' religious beliefs. For example, a parent may have unreasonable and unfounded beliefs in the benefits to be obtained from alternative or complementary therapies. Unless there is evidence ("properly studied, tested, reported on and peer-reviewed") for the efficacy of those therapies as compared to orthodox medical treatment the court will conclude that orthodox treatment is preferable, in the child's best interests: *An NHS Trust v SR* [2012] EWHC 3842 (Fam); [2013] 1 F.L.R. 1297; (2013) 130 B.M.L.R. 119 at [25]. Bodey J authorised the administration of radiotherapy and chemotherapy to a child aged seven, following surgery to remove a brain tumour; the mother's belief that there were alternative therapies which did not involve the side effects of radiotherapy and chemotherapy was irrelevant if there was no clinician willing to take on the care and treatment of the child. And in any event: "To have any realistic prospect of becoming selected by the court … the proposed plan would have to have a prognosis as to probable survival rate not much less than (and preferably equal to) the sort of survival rate achievable through the use of the orthodox treatment universally applied at present by oncologists in this country."

[735] [2007] EWHC 1696 (Fam); [2008] 1 F.L.R. 70; (2007) 98 B.M.L.R. 141.

[736] [1993] 1 F.L.R. 386.

[737] See *Re R (A Minor)* (1993) 15 B.M.L.R. 72; *Re O (A Minor) (Medical Treatment)* [1993] 4 Med. L.R. 272; (1993) 19 B.M.L.R 148; *Re S (A Minor) (Medical Treatment)* [1993] 1 F.L.R. 376; (1992) 11 B.M.L.R. 105; *Re S (A Minor) (Consent to Medical Treatment)* [1994] 2 F.L.R. 1065; *Re L (Medical Treatment: Gillick competency)* [1998] 2 F.L.R. 810; [1999] 2 F.C.R. 524; *Re P (Medical Treatment: Best Interests)* [2003] EWHC 2327 (Fam); [2004] 2 F.L.R. 1117; *Birmingham Children's NHS Trust v B* [2014] EWHC 531 (Fam); (2014) 137 B.M.L.R. 222; *M Children's Hospital NHS Foundation Trust v Y* [2014] EWHC 2651 (Fam); [2014] Fam. Law 1527; *An NHS Trust v B* [2014] EWHC 3486 (Fam); *NHS Foundation Trust v T* [2016] EWHC 2980 (Fam).

[738] As the US Supreme Court put it, in a rather different context from that of medical treatment, parents are not free to make martyrs of their children before they have reached the age of full and legal discretion when they can make that choice for themselves: *Prince v Massachusetts* 321 U.S. 158 at 166 (1944). The Canadian courts take a similar approach to the administration of blood products to minors, at least in the case of minors lacking capacity: see *B(R) v Children's Aid Society of Metropolitan Toronto* (1995) 122 D.L.R. (4th) 1, SCC; *B (SJ) (Litigation Guardian of) v British Columbia (Director of Child, Family & Community Service)* 2005 BCSC 573; (2005) 42 B.C.L.R.

Similarly, the parents' religious beliefs are not factored into the court's approach to decisions to withhold or withdraw treatment from a minor. The parents' religious beliefs are simply not relevant to an objective assessment of what is in the child's best interests.[739]

Parents' lack of capacity   Where a parent lacks capacity to make a decision about the medical treatment of a child the parent's views may still be taken into account in making decisions about the child's best interests. As Peter Jackson J noted in *An NHS Trust v H*,[740] a parent with capacity may be better placed to express views that assist in assessing the child's best interests, but that is a matter of evidence not principle:

6–216

> "Parents who lack capacity may still make telling points about welfare and it would be wrong to discount the weight to be attached to their views simply because of incapacity. It is the validity of the views that matter, not the capacity of the person that holds them."

Withdrawing or withholding treatment   Any decision to withdraw or withhold treatment from a minor must reflect the child's best interests. The cases are highly fact-sensitive, though some general principles set out by Holman J in *An NHS Trust v MB*[741] are often invoked:

6–217

(4th) 321; *Manitoba (Director of Child & Family Services) v C(A)*, 2009 SCC 30; [2009] 7 W.W.R. 379; (2009) 309 D.L.R. (4th) 581. cf., however, *Walker v Region 2 Hospital Corp.* (1994) 110 D.L.R. (4th) 477, NBCA, where a 15-year-old Jehovah's Witness was held to be competent and entitled to reject a blood transfusion; though in *U.(C.) (Next friend of) v Alberta (Director of Child Welfare)* (2003) 223 D.L.R. (4th) 662 (leave to appeal refused: [2003] 2 S.C.R. vi; and [2004] 1 S.C.R. 336), the Alberta Court of Appeal accepted that child protection legislation could override the wishes of a competent 16-year-old who was refusing consent to a blood transfusion. In Ireland see *Children's University Hospital, Temple Street v D* [2011] IEHC 1; [2011] 1 I.R. 665 (parents had constitutional right to raise children according to their own religious and philosophical views, but that right was not absolute; the state's interest in protecting children took precedence over the parents' constitutional rights); and in Australia see *X v Sydney Children's Hospitals Network* [2013] NSWCA 320; 304 A.L.R. 517 (17-year old; court authorised blood transfusions up to the date of the patient's 18th birthday); *Minister for Health v AS* [2004] WASC 286; (2004) 29 W.A.R. 517 (15-year-old); *Hospital v T* [2015] QSC 185 (15-year-old).
[739] *Central Manchester University Hospitals NHS Foundation Trust v A* [2015] EWHC 2828 (Fam); (2015) 148 B.M.L.R. 186 at [19] per Holman J, citing his own judgments in *An NHS Trust v MB* [2006] EWHC 507 (Fam); [2006] 2 F.L.R. 319; [2006] Lloyd's Rep. Med. 323 at [50] and *NHS Trust v A (A Child)* [2007] EWHC 1696; [2008] 1 F.L.R. 70; (2007) 98 B.M.L.R. 141 at [41]: "This case concerns a child who must himself be incapable, by reason of his age, of any religious belief. An objective balancing of his own best interests cannot be affected by whether a parent happens to adhere to one particular belief, or another, or none. I have the utmost respect for the father's faith and belief, and for the faith of Islam which he practises and professes. But I regard it as irrelevant to the decision which I have to take and I do not take it into account at all."
[740] [2013] 1 F.L.R. 1471; [2013] Med. L.R. 70 at [19]. See also *Re Jake (A Child)* [2015] EWHC 2442 (Fam); [2015] Med. L.R. 518 at [44].
[741] [2006] EWHC 507 (Fam); [2006] 2 F.L.R. 319; [2006] Lloyd's Rep. Med. 323 at [16]. Holman J repeated these observations in *Central Manchester University Hospitals NHS Foundation Trust v A* [2015] EWHC 2828 (Fam); (2015) 148 B.M.L.R. 186. See also *NHS Trust v A (A Child)* [2007] EWHC 1696; [2008] 1 F.L.R. 70; (2007) 98 B.M.L.R. 141; *Bolton NHS Foundation Trust v C* [2015] EWHC 2920 (Fam); (2015) 150 B.M.L.R. 161 at [29] per Peter Jackson J; *Re Jake (A Child)* [2015] EWHC 2442 (Fam); [2015] Med. L.R. 518 at [33] per Sir James Munby P; *County Durham and Darlington NHS Foundation Trust v SS* [2016] EWHC 535 (Fam) at [35] per Cobb J.

- It is the duty of the court to exercise its own independent, objective judgment.
- The decision should not be made by reference to the decision judges might make for themselves if, hypothetically, placed in the situation of the patient; nor for a child of the judge if in that situation; nor by reference to whether the respective decisions of the doctors on the one hand or the parents on the other are reasonable decisions.
- The test is the objective best interests of the patient, and this term is used in the widest sense to include every kind of consideration capable of impacting on the decision. These include, non-exhaustively, medical, emotional, sensory (pleasure, pain and suffering) and instinctive (the human instinct to survive) considerations.
- These considerations cannot be weighed mathematically, but the court must do the best it can to balance all the conflicting considerations in a particular case and see where the final balance of the best interests lies.
- Considerable weight must be attached to the prolongation of life because the individual human instinct and desire to survive is strong and must be presumed to be strong in the patient. But it is not absolute, nor necessarily decisive; and may be outweighed if the pleasures and the quality of life are sufficiently small and the pain and suffering or other burdens of living are sufficiently great.
- All cases are very fact specific.
- The views and opinions of both the doctors and the parents must be carefully considered. Where the parents spend a great deal of time with their child, their views may have particular value because they know the patient and how he reacts so well; although the court should be mindful that the views of parents may be coloured by their own emotion or sentiment. It is important to stress that the reference is to the views and opinions of the parents. Their own wishes, however understandable in human terms, are wholly irrelevant to consideration of the objective best interests of the child except to the extent that they may illuminate the quality and value *to the child* of the child/parent relationship.

6–218   The question that must be asked is not whether it is in the best interests of the child to withdraw treatment, but whether it is in the best interests of the child to continue to receive treatment.[742] If the answer to that question is "no" then it will be lawful to withdraw or withhold treatment. The child's best interests must be considered in its widest sense, including medical, emotional, sensory (pleasure,

---

[742] See *Aintree University Hospitals NHS Foundation Trust v James* [2013] UKSC 67; [2014] A.C. 591 at [22] where Baroness Hale DP stated: "Hence the focus is on whether it is in the patient's best interests to give the treatment, rather than on whether it is in his best interests to withhold or withdraw it. If the treatment is not in his best interests, the court will not be able to give its consent on his behalf and it will follow that it will be lawful to withhold or withdraw it. Indeed, it will follow that it will not be lawful to give it." *James* concerned an adult who lacked capacity, but the principle applies equally to minors; *Re A (A Child) (Withdrawal of Medical Treatment)* [2016] EWCA Civ 759; [2016] Med. L.R. 427; (2016) 151 B.M.L.R. 39 at [31].

pain and suffering) and instinctive (the human instinct to survive) considerations.[743] Although there is a strong presumption in favour of preserving life, this is not irrebuttable.[744] Where continued treatment is futile (in the sense of being "pointless or of no effective benefit") there is nothing positive to put into the balance sheet when considering the child's best interests.[745] There are numerous cases where the court has concluded that, on the particular facts, it would not be in a child's best interests to continue medical treatment, or to escalate treatment if the child's condition should deteriorate, with the consequence that it was probable that the child would die.[746] The court order may also provide for palliative care and pain relief, even where the administration of pain relief may have the incidental effect of shortening the child's life.[747] In *Great Ormond Street Hospital v Yates*[748] it was argued that where there was a dispute between the parents and the hospital about discontinuing treatment neither the hospital nor, indeed, the court should interfere with the parents' wish to have alternative treatment abroad unless it could be shown that as a result the child would suffer "significant harm". The Court of Appeal rejected this argument. The child's best interests is:

> "...the established yardstick which applies to all cases and there is no justification for this court now to endorse the creation of a sub-set of cases based upon establishing significant harm."[749]

---

[743] *County Durham and Darlington NHS Foundation Trust v SS* [2016] EWHC 535 (Fam) at [37] per Cobb J, citing *Aintree University Hospitals NHS Foundation Trust v James* [2013] UKSC 67; [2014] A.C. 591 at [39]; *Re A (A Child) (Withdrawal of Medical Treatment)* [2016] EWCA Civ 759; [2016] Med. L.R. 427; (2016) 151 B.M.L.R. 39 at [31]; *Great Ormond Street Hospital for Children Foundation NHS Trust v NO* [2017] EWHC 241 (Fam); (2017) 155 B.M.L.R. 119 (not in best interests of eight-month-old, terminally ill, child to be given invasive interventions which carried a substantial risk of contributing to or causing her death, and would also cause further pain, suffering and distress when the most they might achieve would be to delay death by a short time).

[744] *Kings College Hospital NHS Foundation Trust v Y* [2015] EWHC 1966 (Fam) at [58]; *An NHS Trust v W* [2015] EWHC 2778 (Fam); (2015) 148 B.M.L.R. 169 at [26]; *An NHS Trust v H* [2013] 1 F.L.R. 1471; [2013] Med. L.R. 70 at [25]. Peter Jackson J commented in *An NHS Trust v H* at [35] that "aggressive treatment ... would amount to preserving life for its own sake and ... would be not be in [the child's] best interests".

[745] *Great Ormond Street Hospital v Yates* [2017] EWCA Civ 410 at [49].

[746] See, e.g., *Re B (A Child) (Medical Treatment)* [2008] EWHC 1996 (Fam); [2009] 1 F.L.R. 1264; *An NHS Trust v H* [2013] 1 F.L.R. 1471; [2013] Med. L.R. 70; *Kirklees Council v RE* [2014] EWHC 3182 (Fam); [2015] 1 F.L.R. 1316; *Re AA* [2014] EWHC 4861 (Fam); *Kings College Hospital NHS Foundation Trust v Y* [2015] EWHC 1920 (Fam) and [2015] EWHC 1966 (Fam); *Re Jake (A Child)* [2015] EWHC 2442 (Fam); [2015] Med. L.R. 518; *Central Manchester University Hospitals NHS Foundation Trust v A* [2015] EWHC 2828 (Fam); (2015) 148 B.M.L.R. 186; *An NHS Trust v W* [2015] EWHC 2778 (Fam); (2015) 148 B.M.L.R. 169; *Bolton NHS Foundation Trust v C* [2015] EWHC 2920 (Fam); (2015) 150 B.M.L.R. 161; *Re Y (A Child) (Withholding of Medical Treatment)* [2016] EWHC 206 (Fam); (2016) 151 B.M.L.R. 232; *County Durham and Darlington NHS Foundation Trust v SS* [2016] EWHC 535 (Fam); *An NHS Hospital Trust v GM* [2017] EWHC 1710 (Fam).

[747] *Kings College Hospital NHS Foundation Trust v Y* [2015] EWHC 1920 (Fam) and [2015] EWHC 1966 (Fam); *Re Jake (A Child)* [2015] EWHC 2442 (Fam); [2015] Med. L.R. 518.

[748] [2017] EWCA Civ 410.

[749] [2017] EWCA Civ 410 at [74] per McFarlane LJ, who added, at [95], that the court should evaluate the detail of each option from the child's perspective, and should not prefer any particular option simply because it is put forward by a parent or by a local authority or hospital: "The judge decides what is in the best interests of the child by looking at the case entirely through eyes focused on the child's welfare and focused upon the merits and drawbacks of the particular options that are

6–219   **Professional guidance on withdrawing treatment**   The Royal College of Paediatrics and Child Health publication *Making decisions to limit treatment in life-limiting and life-threatening conditions in children: a framework for practice*[750] provides guidance to doctors on the circumstances in which withholding or withdrawing life-sustaining treatment might be ethically permissible, though emphasises that these are *not* circumstances under which such treatment must certainly be withheld or withdrawn. It describes situations in which individual children should be "spared inappropriate invasive procedures", but again emphasises that it does *not* describe types of children to whom appropriate procedures should be denied. It is apparent that the courts will place considerable weight on this document in reaching a view about a child's best interests. In *Bolton NHS Foundation Trust v C*[751] Peter Jackson J said that the RCPCH guidance was in conformity with previous case law on the withdrawal of life-sustaining treatment and in conformity with art.2 and art.3 of the European Convention on Human Rights. In *County Durham and Darlington NHS Foundation Trust v SS*[752] Cobb J declared that the RCPCH Framework was:

> "…self-evidently an essential basis of practice for the medical profession in dealing with clinical decision-making to limit treatment. It also provides valuable direction for a court when it is required to grapple with the ethical and medical issues in a case such as this."[753]

6–220   **No power to *require* a doctor to provide medical treatment**   The court will not exercise its inherent jurisdiction over minors by ordering a medical practitioner to treat the minor in a manner contrary to the practitioner's clinical judgment, since this would require the doctor to act contrary to the fundamental duty owed to the patient, which, subject to obtaining consent, is to treat patients in accordance with their own best clinical judgment, notwithstanding that other practitioners who were not called upon to treat the patient might have formed quite a different judgment or that the court, acting on expert evidence, might disagree.[754] Nor will the court, in the absence of some very clear and good

---

being presented to the court." An application to the European Court of Human Rights arguing that this involved a breach of the human rights of both the parents and the child was ruled to be inadmissible: *Gard v United Kingdom* (App. No.39793/17).

[750] March 2015 (available at: *http://adc.bmj.com/content/100/Suppl_2/s1.full.pdf+html*).

[751] [2015] EWHC 2920 (Fam); (2015) 150 B.M.L.R. 161 at [28].

[752] [2016] EWHC 535 (Fam) at [22].

[753] See also *Re Jake (A Child)* [2015] EWHC 2442 (Fam); [2015] Med. L.R. 518 at [35] and [42] and *Kings College Hospital NHS Foundation Trust v Y* [2015] EWHC 1920 (Fam) at [38]–[42] and [2015] EWHC 1966 (Fam) at [28]–[51] MacDonald J.

[754] *Re J (A Minor) (Wardship: Medical Treatment)* [1993] Fam. 15, CA, approved in *Aintree University Hospitals NHS Foundation Trust v James* [2013] UKSC 67; [2014] A.C. 591 at [18]. In *Re J* the consultant paediatrician in charge of a 16-month-old child who was profoundly handicapped took the view that it would not be medically appropriate to intervene with intensive therapeutic measures, such as artificial ventilation, if J suffered a life threatening event, and that although ordinary resuscitation with suction, physiotherapy and antibiotics were appropriate, the more intensive measures that would be required if he was unable to breath spontaneously were not. The judge made an order requiring the health authority to use intensive therapeutic measures, including artificial ventilation, for as long as they were capable of prolonging J's life. The Court of Appeal held that this was wrong in law because the court could not order a doctor to treat a patient in a manner which was contrary to the doctor's view of the patient's best interests. It was also erroneous because of the lack of certainty as to what was required of the health authority, and it did not adequately take

reason, stipulate by whom the treatment should or should not be carried out at a particular hospital.[755] It is not entirely clear how the principle that a doctor cannot be ordered to provide a particular treatment is to be reconciled with the view expressed in *Airedale NHS Trust v Bland* that it could be unlawful for a medical practitioner to cease treating an incompetent patient in circumstances where treatment could confer *some* benefit.[756] On this approach, if the treatment could confer "some benefit", in the sense of not being completely futile, the practitioner's clinical judgment as to whether treatment should continue is arguably irrelevant (although, no doubt, it would be a factor in the assessment of whether there was any benefit to be gained from continuing treatment).

Since *Re J (A Minor) (Wardship: Medical Treatment)*[757] the courts have generally refused to dictate to doctors what treatment should be provided for a child, even in cases involving the withdrawal of treatment over the objections of the child's parents.[758] This:

6–221

---

into account whether the authority would have sufficient resources to treat the patient, or whether there were other patients who would be much more likely to benefit from the use of limited resources. The medical staff were free, subject to the appropriate parental consent, to treat J in accordance with their best clinical judgment. See also *County Durham and Darlington NHS Foundation Trust v SS* [2016] EWHC 535 (Fam) at [39].

[755] *Re TM (Medical Treatment)* [2013] EWHC 4103 (Fam); (2014) 136 B.M.L.R. 153 at [23] per Holman J: "neither the mother nor the court should presume to dictate to the hospital by whom medical procedures are carried out at the hospital."

[756] [1993] A.C. 789 at 858–859, per Lord Keith: "… in general it would not be lawful for a medical practitioner who assumed responsibility for the care of an unconscious patient simply to give up treatment in circumstances where continuance of it would confer some benefit on the patient. On the other hand a medical practitioner is under no duty to continue to treat such a patient where a large body of informed and responsible medical opinion is to the effect that no benefit at all would be conferred by continuance." Possibly, the distinction between *Re J* and *Bland* is that while the court will not *order* a doctor to treat, there could be liability for failing to treat if harm results.

[757] [1993] Fam. 15.

[758] See e.g. *Re C (A Minor) (Medical Treatment)* [1998] Lloyd's Rep. Med. 1; [1998] 1 F.L.R. 384; *R. v Portsmouth Hospitals NHS Trust Ex p. Glass* [1999] 2 F.L.R. 905; [1999] Lloyd's Rep. Med. 367, CA; *Royal Wolverhampton Hospitals NHS Trust v B* [2000] 1 F.L.R. 953; [2000] 2 F.C.R. 76; *Kings College Hospital NHS Foundation Trust v Y* [2015] EWHC 1920 (Fam) and [2015] EWHC 1966 (Fam); *Central Manchester University Hospitals NHS Foundation Trust v A* [2015] EWHC 2828 (Fam); (2015) 148 B.M.L.R. 186; *Bolton NHS Foundation Trust v C* [2015] EWHC 2920 (Fam); (2015) 150 B.M.L.R. 161; *County Durham and Darlington NHS Foundation Trust v SS* [2016] EWHC 535 (Fam). Note, however, that in *Glass v United Kingdom* (Application No.61827/00) [2004] 1 F.C.R. 553; (2004) 39 E.H.R.R. 15 the European Court of Human Rights held that the decision by hospital medical staff to impose treatment, in the form of injections of diamorphine, on a disabled child contrary to express (and forceful) parental objection amounted to a breach of the child's art.8 rights under the European Convention on Human Rights. The hospital should have sought court authorisation. The Court declined to rule on the complaint that a "Do Not Resuscitate" (DNR) order had been placed in the child's medical notes without consulting the child's mother (though Judge Casadevall commented that it was difficult to accept that the doctors unilaterally took the serious decision of putting a DNR order in the child's medical notes without the mother's consent and knowledge); and also stressed that it was not its function to question the doctors' clinical judgment with regard to the seriousness of the patient's condition or the appropriateness of the proposed treatment.

"...is subject to the power which the courts always have to take decisions in relation to the child's best interests. In doing so, the court takes fully into account the attitude of medical practitioners."[759]

In *A NHS Trust v D*[760] it was held that a declaration that it was not in the child's best interests that he receive mechanical ventilation, but should receive palliative care, was not inconsistent with the European Convention on Human Rights. There was no breach of art.2, because the declaration was in the child's best interests, and there was no breach of art.3 because in *D v United Kingdom*[761] it was held that art.3 includes the right to die with dignity, and that was what the declaration being granted was seeking to protect. On the other hand, where the doctors are in favour of treating the child, the courts are likely to place great significance on the doctors' views in coming to a conclusion about the child's best interests, even to the extent of concluding that heart transplant surgery should be authorised for a 15-year-old girl.[762]

---

[759] *R. v Portsmouth Hospitals NHS Trust Ex p. Glass* [1999] Lloyd's Rep. Med. 367 at 374 per Lord Woolf MR. On the court's role where there is persisting disagreement between the treating doctors and the parents in the case of a seriously disabled baby see the various applications brought before the court in the case of Charlotte Wyatt: *Portsmouth NHS Trust v Wyatt* [2004] EWHC 2247 (Fam); [2005] 1 F.L.R. 21; (2005) 84 B.M.L.R. 206; *Wyatt v Portsmouth NHS Trust* [2005] EWHC 693 (Fam); [2005] 2 F.L.R. 480; aff'd by *Portsmouth NHS Trust v Wyatt* [2005] EWCA Civ 1181; [2005] 1 W.L.R. 3995; [2005] Lloyd's Rep. Med. 474, where the Court of Appeal held that the best interests of a child in the context of the withholding of medical treatment were not to be determined by the test of whether the child's life, if given the treatment, would be "intolerable". Best interests had to be interpreted more broadly than simply "medical interests" and included emotional and other factors. There was no obligation on the medical profession to give treatment that would be "futile"; *Portsmouth NHS Trust v W* [2005] EWHC 2293 (Fam); [2005] 4 All E.R. 1325; *Re Wyatt* [2006] EWHC 319 (Fam); [2006] 2 F.L.R. 111.

[760] [2000] 2 F.L.R. 677; [2000] Lloyd's Rep. Med. 411. See also *Re L (A Child) (Medical Treatment: Benefit)* [2004] EWHC 2713 (Fam); [2005] 1 F.L.R. 491 where a declaration was granted that it would be lawful not to provide mechanical ventilation to a seriously disabled baby who had only a few weeks or months to live, despite the child's mother wanting to preserve the possibility of mechanical ventilation in an emergency; *King's College Hospital NHS Foundation Trust v T* [2014] EWHC 3315 (Fam); (2015) 143 B.M.L.R. 202—in the best interests of a 17-month-old child to have mechanical ventilation withdrawn given that it was only just sustaining life with no other benefit; *NHS Trust v Baby X* [2012] EWHC 2188 (Fam); (2012) 127 B.M.L.R. 188—in the best interests of a 13-month-old child who had suffered catastrophic brain damage in an accident to have mechanical ventilation withdrawn; X was comatose, probably unaware of any burden in his continued existence but also unconscious of any benefit, and treatment had no chance improving his condition; *Re K (A Child) (Medical Treatment: Declaration)* [2006] EWHC 1007 (Fam); [2006] 2 F.L.R. 883; (2006) 99 B.M.L.R. 98 authorising removal of a feeding tube from a baby with congenital myotonica dystrophy whose condition was so severe that the issue was not whether she would survive but how soon she was likely to die; *Kings College Hospital NHS Foundation Trust v H* [2015] EWHC 1920 (Fam) and [2015] EWHC 1966 (Fam)—lawful, as being in the best interests of a seven-year-old child who suffered from spinal muscular atrophy and whose condition had deteriorated following cardio-respiratory arrest, to withhold intubation and invasive ventilation, withhold cardiopulmonary resuscitation if she went into further cardiac arrest, and to administer pain medication if required, notwithstanding that it might shorten her life.

[761] [1997] 24 E.H.R.R. 423.

[762] *Re M (A Child) (Refusal of Medical Treatment)* [1999] 2 F.L.R. 1097; [1999] 2 F.C.R. 577, where it was said that the risks posed by the operation and by her possible future resentment at her wishes being overridden were both outweighed by the need to preserve her life.

Cases where the parents' views have prevailed over those of the medical profession are rare.[763] In *Re T (A Minor) (Wardship: Medical Treatment)*[764] the doctors treating an 18-month-old child wanted to perform a liver transplant. It was estimated that he would not survive beyond two-and-a-half years without the transplant. The parents were opposed, because the baby had already undergone unsuccessful surgery, which had caused the child pain and distress. The Court of Appeal held that the paramount consideration was the welfare of the child, and not the unreasonableness or otherwise of the parents' refusal to consent. In assessing the child's best interests it was legitimate to take into account the mother's concerns as to the benefits to her son of major invasive surgery and the post-operative treatment, the dangers of failure long-term and short-term, the possibility of the need for further transplants, the likely length of life, and the effect on the child of all of these concerns. It would not be appropriate to coerce the mother into playing the crucial and irreplaceable part in the aftermath of such major surgery, not just during the post-operative treatment, but also throughout her son's childhood. The total commitment of the caring parent was essential to the success of the treatment, and without that commitment it was not in the child's interests to have the surgery:

6–222

> "This mother and this child are one for the purpose of this unusual case ... The welfare of this child depends on his mother."[765]

In *An NHS Trust v MB*[766] Holman J held that it was not in the best interests of a child suffering from severe spinal muscular atrophy to discontinue artificial ventilation with the inevitable result that he would die, since he had age-appropriate cognition, a relationship of value with his family, and other pleasures from sight, touch and sound. The distress and pain that the child suffered did not outweigh those benefits.[767]

(d) Emergencies

In an emergency a doctor will be justified in providing medical treatment to a child who lacks the capacity to consent, without parental consent or the authorisation of the court. The justification is analogous to that which applies to

6–223

---

[763] See the analysis of A. Morris, "Selective Treatment of Irreversibly Impaired Infants: Decision-Making at the Threshold" (2009) 17 Med. Law Rev. 347.

[764] [1997] 1 All E.R. 906; Michalowski (1997) 9 C.F.L.Q. 179.

[765] [1997] 1 All E.R. 906 at 914–915 per Butler-Sloss L.J.

[766] [2006] EWHC 507 (Fam); [2006] 2 F.L.R. 319; [2006] Lloyd's Rep. Med. 323.

[767] Holman J reached this conclusion in the face of a "formidable body of medical evidence of very high quality ... which is all, without exception, to the same effect", namely that ventilation should be withdrawn. Despite acknowledging ([2006] EWHC 507 (Fam); [2006] 2 F.L.R. 319; [2006] Lloyd's Rep. Med. 323 at [90]) that he had no power to require the doctors to provide treatment contrary to their clinical judgment, and declining to make a declaration, a statement by the court that it is in the child's best interests to continue ventilation put the doctors in a very difficult position since their legal duty was to act in the child's best interests, but their clinical judgment was that continued ventilation was not in the child's best interests. For comment on this issue see e.g. *An NHS Trust v L* [2013] EWHC 4313 (Fam); (2014) 137 B.M.L.R. 141 at [116] per Moylan J (a case concerning an incapacitated adult).

patients who are temporarily incapacitated, for example patients who are unconscious following an accident,[768] and is based on the principle of necessity. It may be, however, that in the case of children the concept of emergency is wider than that which would be applied to temporarily incapacitated adults. Thus in *Gillick v West Norfolk and Wisbech Area Health Authority* Lord Scarman commented that:

> "Emergency, parental neglect, abandonment of the child, or inability to find the parent are examples of exceptional situations justifying the doctor proceeding to treat the child without parental knowledge and consent; but there will arise, no doubt, other exceptional situations in which it will be reasonable for the doctor to proceed without the parent's consent."[769]

If, for example, the parents were available but were refusing consent to life-saving treatment, perhaps on religious grounds, a doctor would be justified in performing the treatment, even in the face of an express parental prohibition.[770] In *Gillick* Lord Templeman seemed to have such a situation in mind when he said:

> "I accept that if there is no time to obtain a decision from the court, a doctor may safely carry out treatment in an emergency if the doctor believes the treatment to be vital to the survival or health of an infant and notwithstanding the opposition of a parent or the impossibility of alerting the parent before the treatment is carried out. In such a case the doctor must have the courage of his convictions that the treatment is necessary and urgent in the interests of the patient and the court will, if necessary, approve after the event treatment which the court would have authorised in advance, even if the treatment proves to be unsuccessful."[771]

6–224   Under the Children Act 1989 an emergency protection order may provide for medical or psychiatric examination or other assessment (though not treatment) of the child.[772] While it is in force, however, an emergency protection order gives the applicant (normally the local authority) parental responsibility for the child,[773] which effectively confers the power to consent to medical treatment.

---

[768] See para.6–168.
[769] [1986] A.C. 112 at 189.
[770] See para.6–215.
[771] [1986] A.C. 112 at 200. For an argument that the decision in *Re F (Mental Patient: Sterilisation)* [1990] 2 A.C. 1, para.6–168 provides a justification for routine medical treatment of children (i.e. "non-necessary" but medically desirable in the child's best interests) without parental consent: see Lavery [1990] J.S.W.L. 375. See also Busuttil and McCall Smith [1990] J.S.W.L. 385 for discussion of the problem of medical examination of children who are suspected victims of sexual abuse without parental consent.
[772] Children Act 1989 s.44(6)(b). If the child is of sufficient understanding to make an informed decision he may refuse to submit to the examination or other assessment: s.44(7).
[773] Children Act 1989 s.44(4)(c).

CHAPTER 7

INFORMED CONSENT

Consent to medical treatment involves the exercise of a choice. The power to consent involves also the power to refuse consent, and people cannot make a real choice unless they have information about the options so as to be able to make a reasoned choice. Hence it is said that the consent must be an "informed consent". In law, the question of a patient's *consent* to medical treatment is inextricably linked to the tort of battery,[1] but the courts have stipulated that only a minimal level of information must be conveyed to the patient for this purpose. The failure to go into risks and implications of a proposed treatment is an issue to be considered under the doctor's duty of care in negligence, not battery.[2] Thus, strictly speaking it is a misnomer to speak of "informed consent", since a patient's right to the information which will enable him to make a meaningful choice about treatment options (including the option of no treatment) depends upon the nature of the doctor's duty to exercise reasonable care in performing his professional functions as a doctor. Although the doctor's duty to give the patient information only makes sense in the light of the patient's right to exercise a choice through the power to give or withhold consent,[3] the courts have to a large extent separated these two issues, principally to curtail the use of actions for battery against medical practitioners.[4] The modern approach is to think of a patient's right to information as an aspect of the patient's autonomy, but there is no freestanding cause of action for interference with autonomy.[5] An action for non-disclosure of the risks of treatment will be an action in negligence.

7–001

The duty of care in negligence applies to diagnosis, treatment and advice, and there is no doubt that part of this duty involves giving information to the patient about the diagnosis and the prognosis, in the light of the various treatment options that are available. This inevitably requires some assessment of the prospects that treatment will be successful and the prospects that treatment may be

7–002

---

[1] Though the Court of Appeal has held that carrying out a procedure on a competent patient without consent would constitute a breach of duty in negligence, irrespective of whether the procedure itself conformed with accepted professional practice: see *Border v Lewisham and Greenwich NHS Trust (formerly South London Healthcare NHS Trust)* [2015] EWCA Civ 8; [2015] Med. L.R. 48, para.6–013.

[2] *Chatterton v Gerson* [1981] Q.B. 432 at 443, para.6–058.

[3] See the comments of Lord Scarman in *Sidaway v Bethlem Royal Hospital Governors* [1985] A.C. 871 at 888, approved by the Supreme Court in *Montgomery v Lanarkshire Health Board* [2015] UKSC 11; [2015] A.C. 1430.

[4] The evidence, such as it is, is that cases of informed consent are comparatively few and far between, and successful actions by claimants are even more rare: see Jones (1999) 7 Med. L. Rev. 103.

[5] *Shaw v Kovac* [2017] EWCA Civ 1028; [2017] P.I.Q.R. Q4.

unsuccessful, or may cause additional harm. The crucial question is how much or how little information must be disclosed to satisfy the doctor's duty of care.

7–003   This chapter is divided into three main sections dealing with the principles applied to the duty of disclosure in negligence, the problem of causation, and a final section dealing with three special cases. The section on the duty of disclosure includes discussion of material from several Commonwealth jurisdictions, which may contribute to an understanding of English law. The section on causation covers the torts of both battery and negligence, and serves as a reminder that even where claimants succeed in establishing culpable non-disclosure they may face considerable difficulty in proving that this was a cause of their damage. The final section deals with three special cases, where either the legal requirements for consent and information disclosure may be more extensive than in ordinary cases of treatment (research and transplantation of organs)[6] or the subject has given rise to particular problems in practice (failed sterilisation).

1. THE DUTY OF DISCLOSURE

(a) Introduction

7–004   For almost 60 years the standard applied in English law to a doctor's duty to disclose information to patients about the risks of treatment was the *Bolam* test. A doctor would be found negligent for failing to disclose information only if no responsible body of professional opinion would have failed to disclose it. This was confirmed in the majority decision of the House of Lords in *Sidaway v Bethlem Royal Hospital Governors*.[7] In *Montgomery v Lanarkshire Health Board*[8] the Supreme Court decided that the time had come to follow the lead of Commonwealth jurisdictions and adopt a standard based on a duty to disclose material risks as measured by reference to the risks that an hypothetical reasonable patient (as opposed to a reasonable doctor) would have wanted to have been informed about. This is an important shift in emphasis, though whether it will lead to different outcomes in most cases remains to be seen.[9]

7–005   To date, there have been relatively few cases exploring the implications of *Montgomery* and the case law is overwhelmingly based on *Sidaway*. Where claims for non-disclosure of information have succeeded under *Sidaway* then it would seem highly improbable that a similar claim based on *Montgomery*, with its more patient-focused test, would fail. Those cases will continue to provide guidance on whether, in similar circumstances, a claim for non-disclosure of

---

[6] The issues raised by the topics of research and transplantation of organs straddle the discussion of the law in Ch.6 and this chapter, and so the discussion here is not confined to the duty of disclosure in negligence but also covers the more basic requirements for a valid consent.

[7] [1985] A.C. 871.

[8] [2015] UKSC 11; [2015] A.C. 1430. The case was on appeal from the Scottish Court of Session, but it is clear that the ruling was also intended to represent the law of England and Wales.

[9] Note that failing to involve patients in the choice of medical treatment by not informing them of the risks of the procedure so that they cannot make an informed choice will also involve a breach of the patient's art.8 right to respect for their private life under the European Convention on Human Rights: *Csoma v Romania* [2013] ECHR 8759/05.

information is likely to succeed. Where a claim has failed, applying *Sidaway*, the issue will be more open-textured. It is possible that the claim will succeed on the basis that the defendant has failed to disclose a material risk in circumstances where a responsible body of professional opinion would have supported non-disclosure (and therefore the claim would have failed under *Sidaway*). On the other hand, it is also possible that a case that failed under *Sidaway* would also fail applying the standard requiring the disclosure of material risks. It follows that cases prior to *Montgomery* in which the claimant succeeded on breach of duty will continue to carry some precedential weight, whereas cases in which the claim failed on breach of duty will carry little or no precedential weight. The issue in the latter category of cases will turn on how the courts interpret the duty to disclose material risks. In this context, both the Canadian and Australian cases, which apply a "prudent patient" standard to information disclosure, may provide particularly useful guidance.[10]

In practice, much will continue to depend on the purely factual question of what information the patient was actually given. As with any forensic dispute the credibility of the evidence is important. For defendants this will often depend on the quality of the medical records,[11] though standard clauses in consent forms where patients' signatures purportedly acknowledge that they have been fully informed about the potential risks of treatment will not necessarily be conclusive.[12] For claimants the issue will usually depend on their credibility as a witness, bearing in mind that they will be recalling events some years in the past and they may not have "heard" and absorbed all the information they were given at the time.[13] Claimants' credibility as a witness will also be crucial when it comes to the question of establishing causation, since it has to be proved that had the claimant known about the risks of the medical procedure they would have declined to go ahead at that time.[14] *Montgomery* has not changed the rules on proving causation.

7–006

---

[10] See paras 7–026 et seq.

[11] See para.4–078.

[12] See para.6–021. In *Thefaut v Johnston* [2017] EWHC 497 (QB); [2017] Med. L.R. 319 at [78] Green J commented that: "It is routine for a surgeon immediately prior to surgery to see the patient and to ensure that they remain wedded to the procedure. But this is neither the place nor the occasion for a surgeon for the first time to explain to a patient undergoing elective surgery the relevant risks and benefits. At this point, on the very cusp of the procedure itself, the surgeon is likely to be under considerable pressure of time (to see all patients on the list and get to surgery) and the patient is psychologically committed to going ahead. There is a mutual momentum towards surgery which is hard to halt. There is no 'adequate time and space' for a sensible dialogue to occur and for free choice to be exercised." See also *Dickson v Pinder* 2010 ABQB 269; [2010] 10 W.W.R. 505, para.7–031, n.94 below.

[13] Although if, at the time, it should have been clear to the doctor that the patient did not understand what they were being told the failure to clarify the information for the patient may constitute a breach of duty: see paras 7–069 to 7–072.

[14] See paras 7–090 et seq.

(b) The "prudent doctor" standard

7–007   One aspect of the claimant's case in *Bolam v Friern Hospital Management Committee*[15] was that he had not been warned of the risks involved in electro-convulsive therapy before he received the treatment. In directing the jury, McNair J applied the same test to the question of warning the patient about the risks as applied to treatment, namely whether the defendant fell below the standard of competent professional opinion in deciding whether to warn or not. In effect, a patient was entitled to the information about the risks of treatment that a reasonably prudent doctor would disclose, and, as with alleged breaches of duty in relation to diagnosis and treatment, the patient could only succeed if no responsible body of professional opinion would have failed to divulge the information. Attempts by claimants to challenge this approach to information disclosure in the early 1980s were unsuccessful,[16] and then in 1985 the House of Lords considered the issue in *Sidaway v Bethlem Royal Hospital Governors.*[17] The claimant suffered from persistent pain in her neck and shoulders, and she was advised to have an operation on her spinal column to relieve the pain. The defendant surgeon warned the claimant of the possibility of disturbing a nerve root and the consequences of this, but he did not mention the possibility of damage to the spinal cord, although the operation would be within millimetres of the spinal cord. The overall risk of either of these events materialising was between 1 per cent and 2 per cent, although the risk of spinal cord damage was less than 1 per cent. The potential consequences of these risks ranged from mild to severe, with the most severe consequence of spinal cord damage being partial paralysis. During the course of the operation, which was not performed negligently, the claimant sustained damage to the spinal cord resulting in severe disability from partial paralysis. She alleged that the defendant had been negligent in failing to inform her about this risk, and that had she known the true position she would not have accepted the treatment. The trial judge and the Court of Appeal applied the *Bolam* test, concluding that the defendant had acted in accordance with a practice accepted as proper by a responsible body of medical opinion by not informing the claimant of the risk of damage to the spinal cord.

7–008   In the House of Lords there was some disparity in their Lordships' reasoning. Lord Diplock was clearly in favour of applying the *Bolam* test.[18] Lord Bridge, with whom Lord Keith agreed, accepted that conscious adult patients of sound mind were entitled to decide for themselves whether or not they will submit to a particular course of treatment proposed by a doctor, particularly in the case of surgical treatment under general anaesthesia. However, he was unwilling to adopt the approach taken in the American case of *Canterbury v Spence*[19] which required the disclosure of "material risks" (with the question of what constitutes a material risk to be assessed by reference to the "reasonable patient" rather than the prudent doctor). Lord Bridge appreciated that the *Bolam* test carried the

---

[15] [1957] 2 All E.R. 118; see paras 3–007 to 3–008, 4–164, n.546.
[16] *Chatterton v Gerson* [1981] Q.B. 432 at 443, para.6–058; *Hills v Potter* [1983] 3 All E.R. 716.
[17] [1985] A.C. 871.
[18] [1985] A.C. 871 at 895.
[19] 464 F. 2d 772 (1972), USCA, District of Columbia.

danger of medical paternalism which might not be controlled by the courts.[20] Nonetheless, a decision as to the risks that ought to be disclosed to a patient was primarily a matter of clinical judgment, to which the *Bolam* test should apply. This did not involve handing over to the medical profession the entire question of the scope of the duty of disclosure, including the question whether there had been a breach of that duty, because it remained open to the court to:

"...come to the conclusion that disclosure of a particular risk was so obviously necessary to an informed choice on the part of the patient that no reasonably prudent medical man would fail to make it."[21]

This was the position even in a case where no expert witness condemned the non-disclosure as being in conflict with accepted and responsible medical practice. Lord Bridge cited as an example the Canadian case of *Reibl v Hughes*[22] where the patient was not informed about the 10 per cent risk of suffering a stroke during an operation. In such a case "involving a substantial risk of grave adverse consequences" the surgeon could "hardly fail to appreciate the necessity for an appropriate warning".[23]

Lord Scarman's dissent in *Sidaway*   Lord Scarman, in a strong dissenting **7–009** speech, pointed out that applying the *Bolam* test to the question of how much information a patient is entitled to be given leaves the matter almost entirely to the discretion of the medical profession, which places too much judicial reliance on medical judgment instead of seeing the problem from the patient's point of view:

"If one considers the scope of the doctor's duty by beginning with the right of the patient to make his own decision whether he will or will not undergo the treatment proposed, the right to be informed of significant risk and the doctor's corresponding duty are easy to understand, for the proper implementation of the right requires that the doctor be under a duty to inform his patient of the material risks inherent in the treatment."[24]

---

[20] "To allow expert medical evidence to determine what risks are material and, hence, should be disclosed and, correlatively, what risks are not material is to hand over to the medical profession the entire question of the scope of the duty of disclosure, including the question whether there has been a breach of that duty", per Laskin CJC in *Reibl v Hughes* (1980) 114 D.L.R. (3d) 1, 13, SCC, cited by Lord Bridge at [1985] A.C. 871, 899–900.
[21] [1985] A.C. 871 at 900.
[22] (1980) 114 D.L.R. (3d) 1.
[23] [1985] A.C. 871 at 900. In a somewhat idiosyncratic speech Lord Templeman said that a doctor, making a balanced judgment, had a duty to provide information which was sufficient to enable the patient to reach a balanced judgment about whether to submit to recommended treatment. Patients might make unbalanced judgments because they were deprived of adequate information, but might also make an unbalanced judgments if provided with too much information and were made aware of possibilities which they were not capable of assessing because of their lack of medical training, their prejudices or their personality ([1985] A.C. 871 at 904). It was for the court to decide whether doctors were in breach of their duty with respect to information disclosure, said Lord Templeman, but if they conscientiously endeavoured to explain the arguments for and against the treatment the court would be slow to conclude that they were negligent. In *Pearce v United Bristol Healthcare NHS Trust* [1999] P.I.Q.R. P53 at 58 Lord Woolf MR considered that although Lord Templeman's approach was not precisely that of the majority in *Sidaway*, it did not involve taking a different view from the majority.
[24] [1985] A.C. 871 at 888.

Accordingly, his Lordship preferred a standard of disclosure based on the "reasonably prudent patient" test, which was derived from the American case of *Canterbury v Spence*[25] and the decision of the Supreme Court of Canada in *Reibl v Hughes*.[26] Under this test a doctor must disclose all material risks, and a risk is material:

> "...when a reasonable person, in what the physician knows or should know to be the patient's position, would be likely to attach significance to the risk or cluster of risks in deciding whether or not to forego the proposed therapy."[27]

This requires the doctor to communicate the inherent and potential hazards of the proposed treatment, the alternatives to that treatment, if any, and the likely results if the patient remains untreated. The factors contributing significance to the dangerousness of a medical technique were said to be the incidence of injury and the degree of harm threatened. This standard of disclosure was subject to two exceptions. First, where there is a genuine emergency, e.g. the patient is unconscious; and, secondly, where the information would be harmful to the patient, e.g. where it might cause psychological damage,[28] or where the patient would become so emotionally distraught as to prevent a rational decision. The "therapeutic privilege" defence does not allow the doctor to remain silent about material risks simply because disclosure might prompt the patient to forego treatment that the doctor believes the patient needs in his best interests, otherwise the exception might become so wide as to undermine the requirement of disclosure.

7–010   **The *ratio* of *Sidaway***   Notwithstanding the diversity of the speeches in *Sidaway* it was tolerably clear that the majority of their Lordships adopted the *Bolam* test as the measure of a doctor's duty to disclose information about the potential consequences and risks of proposed medical treatment. This was the view of most commentators,[29] and the Court of Appeal specifically endorsed this interpretation.[30] The objective nature of the test for negligence meant that it was always for the court to determine, ultimately, what constitutes negligence on the basis of the evidence presented. The practices of a profession may be good evidence of

---

[25] 464 F. 2d 772 (1972), USCA, District of Columbia.

[26] (1980) 114 D.L.R. (3d) 1.

[27] 464 F. 2d 772 at 787 (1972).

[28] "Even if the risk be material, the doctor will not be liable if on a reasonable assessment of his patient's condition he takes the view that a warning would be detrimental to his patient's health", per Lord Scarman at [1985] A.C. 871 at 889–890. For an unusual example of this see *Furniss v Fitchett* [1958] N.Z.L.R. 396.

[29] Brazier (1987) 7 L.S. 169 at 182; Norrie (1985) 34 I.C.L.Q. 442 at 450; Tan (1987) 7 L.S. 149 at 161, n.42; Dugdale and Stanton, *Professional Negligence*, 3rd edn (London: Butterworths, 1998), para.17.30; *Jackson & Powell on Professional Liability*, 8th edn (London: Sweet & Maxwell, 2017), para.13–012.

[30] *Gold v Haringey Health Authority* [1988] Q.B. 481; *Blyth v Bloomsbury Health Authority* (1987) reported at (1989) 5 P.N. 167 at 171; [1993] 4 Med. L.R. 151; see also *Worster v City and Hackney Health Authority*, The Times, 22 June 1987, per Garland J; *Moyes v Lothian Health Board* [1990] 1 Med. L.R. 463 at 469.

"reasonable care" but cannot be conclusive.[31] Lord Bridge's "exception" for the non-disclosure of a substantial risk of grave adverse consequences where a doctor could hardly fail to appreciate the necessity for an appropriate warning was arguably just an instance of the "obvious folly" test where it would be appropriate for a court to condemn a common practice as negligent.[32] Similarly, when Lord Bridge said that the issue whether non-disclosure in a particular case should be held to be negligent "is an issue to be decided *primarily* on the basis of expert medical evidence, applying the *Bolam* test", (emphasis added) he was not suggesting that normally the *Bolam* test applied but in exceptional circumstances it could be dispensed with. Rather he was stating the effect of the *Bolam* test itself, which relies *primarily* on expert evidence as to responsible professional practice, but, exceptionally, the court may decline to accept that evidence as a measure of the proper standard in law. Thus, the majority in *Sidaway* consisted of Lords Bridge, Keith and Diplock, who all applied the *Bolam* test.[33]

(c) The "prudent patient" standard

As Lord Scarman noted in *Sidaway*, the rationale for the existence of the doctor's duty of disclosure is that patients have a right to make their own decisions about whether to accept proffered medical treatment, and that "right" is meaningless without the relevant information in order to weigh up the options. *Sidaway* was in many respects a product of its time, paying lip-service to patient autonomy whilst in practice endorsing medical paternalism. Over time, it was seen by many (including some judges) as a lost opportunity for English law to put the patient at the centre of medical decision-making.

7–011

(i) Challenging Sidaway

In *Pearce v United Bristol Healthcare NHS Trust*[34] the Court of Appeal appeared to take the first steps towards a different test. The claimant was pregnant and the delivery of her baby was overdue. She was examined by a doctor who indicated that medical intervention by inducing labour or by proceeding to a Caesarean section was not advisable. The doctor did not inform the claimant that non-intervention carried an increased risk that her baby would be stillborn. A week later the claimant suffered a stillbirth. The risks associated with inducing labour were such that the claimant would not have opted for induction, but she argued that had she known about the risks she would have considered a

7–012

---

[31] See paras 3–026 to 3–047. See in particular *Bolitho v City and Hackney Health Authority* [1998] A.C. 232.
[32] See para.3–036. The court would conclude that no *responsible* body of professional opinion could have failed to disclose that degree of risk: see the comment of Hirst J in *Hills v Potter* [1983] 3 All E.R. 716 at 728 cited at para.3–045.
[33] A view accepted by Lord Woolf MR in *Pearce v United Bristol Healthcare NHS Trust* [1999] P.I.Q.R. P53 at 57 where his Lordship said: "...Lord Diplock also gave a speech which adopted the same approach as that of Lord Bridge. That approach involved applying the *Bolam* test to the giving, or failure to give, advice."
[34] [1999] P.I.Q.R. P53.

Caesarean section. The claimant relied on *Bolitho v City and Hackney Health Authority*[35] where Lord Browne-Wilkinson held that where:

"...professional opinion is not capable of withstanding logical analysis, the judge is entitled to hold that the body of opinion is not reasonable or responsible."

Lord Woolf MR, having considered *Bolitho*, said:

"In a case where it is being alleged that a plaintiff has been deprived of the opportunity to make a proper decision as to what course he or she should take in relation to treatment, it seems to me to be the law ... that if there is a significant risk which would affect the judgment of the reasonable patient, then in the normal course it is the responsibility of a doctor to inform the patient of that significant risk, if the information is needed so that the patient can determine for him or herself as to what course he or she should adopt."[36]

This seemed to combine a prudent patient standard with a reasonable doctor standard—a significant risk affecting the judgment of a reasonable patient would place the onus upon the doctor to disclose that significant risk by virtue of the *Bolam* test. In other words, no reasonable doctor would fail to disclose a risk regarded as significant by a reasonable patient. The Court in *Pearce* considered that, although it was not possible to talk in terms of precise percentages when considering what constituted a significant risk, something in the region of a 10 per cent risk would clearly qualify (consistent with Lord Bridge's speech in *Sidaway*). But an increased risk of stillbirth from non-intervention of 0.1 per cent to 0.2 per cent did not fall into the category of significant risk.

7–013   In *Wyatt v Curtis*[37] a general practitioner negligently failed to warn the claimant about the more serious risks posed to her unborn child of her contracting chickenpox. The general practitioner brought CPR Pt 20 proceedings against a hospital doctor, on the basis that when he saw the claimant, four-and-a-half weeks' later, he too failed to warn the claimant of the same risk. Sedley LJ referred to Lord Woolf's statement in *Pearce*, and commented that:

"Lord Woolf's formulation refines Lord Bridge's test by recognising that what is substantial and what is grave are questions on which the doctor's and the patient's perception may differ, and in relation to which the doctor must therefore have regard to what may be the patient's perception. To the doctor, a chance in a hundred that the patient's chickenpox may produce an abnormality in the foetus may well be an insubstantial chance, and an abnormality may in any case not be grave. To the patient, a new risk which (as I read the judge's appraisal of the expert evidence) doubles, or at least enhances, the background risk of a potentially catastrophic abnormality may well be both substantial and grave, or at least sufficiently real for her to want to make an informed decision about it."[38]

Nonetheless, the Court of Appeal rejected the general practitioner's argument that when the hospital doctor became aware that the patient had been advised about the risks of chickenpox by the general practitioner, it was incumbent upon him to ascertain what advice she had received and to correct it. Sedley LJ accepted that this contention went "well beyond anything laid down in *Sidaway*".

---

[35] [1998] A.C. 232 at 243. See paras 3–034 et seq.
[36] [1999] P.I.Q.R. P53 at 59. Roch and Mummery LJ agreed with Lord Woolf MR.
[37] [2003] EWCA Civ 1779.
[38] [2003] EWCA Civ 1779 at [16].

The question that *Wyatt v Curtis* left unresolved was the precise import of Lord   **7–014**
Woolf's statement in *Pearce*.[39] Sedley LJ touched on its significance in the
quotation above, in that it sought to address the very different perspectives of
doctor and patient when it comes to assessing the significance of any particular
risk, and the need for the doctor to be aware of those different perceptions when
considering what information to give. The language of the judgments was more
in tune with the notion that patients are entitled to be given the information that
enables them to make decisions about their medical treatment, but in practice the
decisions in the cases did not purport to go beyond *Sidaway* in setting the legal
standard for information disclosure.

(ii)   Overturning Sidaway

Montgomery v Lanarkshire Health Board[40]   An important feature of the tort   **7–015**
of negligence is that a defendant's conduct is measured by reference to the
prevailing standards at the time of the alleged breach of duty. This principle is
usually deployed to ensure that defendants are not judged at trial by reference to
more recent standards developed after the relevant events, but it also entails that
professionals must keep up to date with changes in practice. Adherence to
outdated methods risks a finding of negligence.[41] This is clearly evident in
relation to information disclosure by the medical profession.[42] Reflecting
changing attitudes and values, the medical profession has placed much greater
emphasis on providing information to patients over the last few years, as can be
seen from the advice given to the profession by the General Medical Council.[43] In

---

[39] A. Maclean, "Giving the Reasonable Patient a Voice: Information Disclosure and the Relevance of Empirical Evidence" (2005) 7 Med. Law Int. 1 discussed whether *Pearce* had altered the *Sidaway* standard.
[40] The case has provoked extensive comment: T. Elliott, "A break with the past? Or more of the same?" (2015) 31 P.N. 190; C. Hobson, "No (,) more *Bolam* please: *Montgomery v Lanarkshire Health Board*" (2016) 79 M.L.R. 488; R. Bagshaw, "Modernising the doctor's duty to disclose risks of treatment" (2016) 132 L.Q.R. 182; C.P. McGrath, "'Trust me, I'm a patient...': disclosure standards and the patient's right to decide" (2015) 74 C.L.J. 211; R. Heywood, "R.I.P. *Sidaway*: Patient-oriented disclosure—A standard worth waiting for?" (2015) 23 Med. L. Rev. 455; E. Reid, "*Montgomery v Lanarkshire Health Board* and the rights of the reasonable patient" (2015) 19 Edin. L.R. 360; L. Johnston, "Informed consent and the lingering shadow of *Chester v Afshar*" 2015 S.L.T. (19) 81 and 2015 S.L.T. (20) 85; M. Lyons [2015] J.P.I.L. C130; J. Laing, "Delivering informed consent post-Montgomery: implications for medical practice and professionalism" (2017) 33 P.N. 128; R. Heywood and J. Miola, "The changing face of pre-operative medical disclosure: placing the patient at the heart of the matter" (2017) 133 L.Q.R. 296. The journal *Clinical Risk* devoted a whole issue to providing different perspectives on *Montgomery*: see "Patient Consent after *Montgomery*" (2016) 22 *Clinical Risk* 1–41.
[41] See paras 3–074 to 3–078.
[42] Compare, e.g. *Gold v Haringey Health Authority* [1988] Q.B. 481, where it was said that in 1979 there was a responsible body of professional opinion that would not have given a warning about the risk of a sterilisation operation failing, with *Gowton v Wolverhampton Health Authority* [1994] 5 Med. L.R. 432, where the defendants' experts conceded that by 1986 there was no responsible body of opinion which would have omitted to give such a warning.
[43] See para.7–079.

Montgomery v Lanarkshire Health Board[44] the Supreme Court acknowledged that the paradigm of the doctor–patient relationship implicit in *Sidaway* had:

"...ceased to reflect the reality and complexity of the way in which healthcare services are provided, or the way in which the providers and recipients of such services view their relationship."

Patients were more widely regarded as persons holding rights, rather than being passive recipients of medical care, and were often treated as consumers exercising choices. Patients also had much greater access to information about symptoms, investigations, treatment options and risks. The idea that patients were uninformed and unable to understand medical matters was now manifestly untenable. Changes in medical practice meant that doctors were more likely to disclose information and reach consensual decisions with patients about treatment options. Medical paternalism was no longer an appropriate model of the doctor–patient relationship. The Human Rights Act 1998 had also made the courts increasingly conscious of the extent to which the common law reflects fundamental values, which includes the value of self-determination. These changes pointed to an approach to the law which treats patients as adults capable of understanding that medical treatment is uncertain of success and may involve risks, accepting responsibility for the taking of risks affecting their own lives, and living with the consequences of their choices.[45]

7–016   **Reconstructing *Sidaway***   Lord Kerr and Lord Reed embarked on an analysis of the speeches in *Sidaway*, in light of the approach adopted in subsequent cases, and came to the conclusion that both Lord Bridge and Lord Templeman had reached a position "not far distant from that of Lord Scarman",[46] albeit by different routes. Accordingly, it was "wrong to regard *Sidaway* as an unqualified endorsement of the application of the *Bolam* test to the giving of advice about treatment".[47] Lord Diplock's suggestion in *Sidaway* that if the patient wanted more information than would be provided applying *Bolam* it was up to her to ask questions was roundly criticised. It placed the onus of asking questions on the patient who may not know that there is anything to ask about; it led to the drawing of excessively fine distinctions between questioning and expressions of concern falling short of questioning; and it paid no regard to the social and psychological realities of the relationship between a patient and doctor.[48] There was also a logical difficulty in that it was unclear why asking questions should make any difference to the doctor's duty, which under *Bolam* is to provide the

---

[44] [2015] UKSC 11; [2015] A.C. 1430 at [75] per Lord Kerr and Lord Reed (with whom Lord Neuberger, Lord Clarke, Lord Wilson, Lord Hodge and Lady Hale agreed). The case was on appeal from the Scottish Court of Session, but it is clear that the ruling was also intended to represent the law of England and Wales.
[45] See [2015] UKSC 11; [2015] A.C. 1430 at [76]–[81].
[46] [2015] UKSC 11; [2015] A.C. 1430 at [53] and [56].
[47] [2015] UKSC 11; [2015] A.C. 1430 at [57]. On the other hand, if Lord Bridge and Lord Templeman had actually agreed with Lord Scarman's clear preference for a prudent patient standard it is difficult to see why there was any need for a change in the law in *Montgomery*, other than, perhaps, that the lower courts had misunderstood and misapplied *Sidaway* for the last 30 years.
[48] [2015] UKSC 11; [2015] A.C. 1430 at [58].

information that a responsible body of professional opinion would provide. The patient's desire for information would not necessarily change medical opinion. Thus, the exception for patient questions logically undermined the rule. If responsible medical opinion accepted that additional information should be disclosed in response to questions, then there would be no exception to the *Bolam* test.[49]

One of the problems with Lord Bridge's approach in *Sidaway*, said Lord Kerr and Lord Reed, was that some judges had construed the question of when the "disclosure of a particular risk was so obviously necessary to an informed choice on the part of the patient that no reasonably prudent medical man would fail to make it" restrictively, focusing on the specific words used by Lord Bridge to illustrate what he meant ("a substantial risk of grave adverse consequences") or the specific example he gave (a 10 per cent risk of stroke). On the other hand, in some cases the lower courts had "tacitly ceased to apply the *Bolam* test in relation to the advice given by doctors to their patients" and had adopted the approach of Lord Scarman.[50] *Pearce v United Bristol Healthcare NHS Trust*[51] was particularly important. Lord Woolf had been correct in saying that "a significant risk which would affect the judgment of a reasonable patient" would meet that test, and it had nothing to do with the *Bolam* test. In so far as there was a difference between a "significant" risk and a "substantial" risk, "significant" was the more appropriate adjective given that the relevance of a risk to the patient's decision did not depend solely on its magnitude, or on a medical assessment of its significance.[52]

7–017

(iii)   The correct test for disclosure of information about risks

Lord Kerr and Lord Reed emphasised that the doctor's duty to take reasonable care to ensure that a patient is aware of material risks of injury is the counterpart of the patient's right to decide whether or not to incur that risk, and the patient's right to make that decision did not depend exclusively on medical considerations.[53] There was a fundamental distinction between doctors' roles when considering diagnostic or treatment options and their role in discussing with the patient any recommended treatment and possible alternatives, and the risks of injury which may be involved. The doctor's advisory role was not solely an exercise of medical skill, because the risks to health which the patient is willing

7–018

---

[49] [2015] UKSC 11; [2015] A.C. 1430 at [59]. This last point is, perhaps, a little strained. It is perfectly possible to apply a standard based on responsible professional opinion where the amount of information disclosed increases in response to patient questioning, and it would be open to the court to hold that a failure to provide information in these circumstances was such that *no* responsible body of professional opinion would support it.

[50] [2015] UKSC 11; [2015] A.C. 1430 at [63].

[51] [1999] P.I.Q.R. P53, para.7–012.

[52] [2015] UKSC 11; [2015] A.C. 1430 at [66].

[53] [2015] UKSC 11; [2015] A.C. 1430 at [82]. See also at [73] where it was said that "the doctor's duty of care takes its precise content from the needs, concerns and circumstances of the individual patient, to the extent that they are or ought to be known to the doctor" at (approving the decision of the High Court of Australia in *Rogers v Whitaker*; see para.7–034).

to run may be influenced by non-medical considerations. Moreover: "Responsibility for determining the nature and extent of a person's rights rests with the courts, not with the medical professions."[54]

7–019   **Duty to disclose material risks**   It followed that the analysis of the law by the majority in *Sidaway* was unsatisfactory in so far as it applied the *Bolam* test to information disclosure. The correct approach was that of Lord Scarman in *Sidaway* and Lord Woolf MR in *Pearce*:

> "An adult person of sound mind is entitled to decide which, if any, of the available forms of treatment to undergo, and her consent must be obtained before treatment interfering with her bodily integrity is undertaken. The doctor is therefore under a duty to take reasonable care to ensure that the patient is aware of any material risks involved in any recommended treatment, and of any reasonable alternative or variant treatments. The test of materiality is whether, in the circumstances of the particular case, a reasonable person in the patient's position would be likely to attach significance to the risk, or the doctor is or should reasonably be aware that the particular patient would be likely to attach significance to it."[55]

There are two limbs to this test. The first is objective, in that it relies on what the reasonable patient would consider to be a material risk, though taking into account the "patient's position". The patient's position will include, presumably, the patient's age, sex, medical condition(s), the medical options available to diagnose or treat the condition (including the option of not treating) and the likely prospects of success and the risks associated with each option.[56] What the patient would have wanted to know is not strictly relevant to deciding whether a risk was material. The second limb of the test is subjective: if the doctor is aware, or ought reasonably to have been aware in the circumstances, that the patient would consider a particular risk to be material then there is a duty to disclose it, even if the objective reasonable patient would not have attached significance to the risk.

---

[54] [2015] UKSC 11; [2015] A.C. 1430 at [83]. One of the problems of applying the *Bolam* test to information disclosure was said to be that differences in disclosure practice may be "attributable not to divergent schools of thought in medical science, but merely to divergent attitudes among doctors as to the degree of respect owed to their patients": [2015] UKSC 11; [2015] A.C. 1430 at [84].

[55] [2015] UKSC 11; [2015] A.C. 1430 at [87]. Note that the provision of information to patients is not solely for the purpose of enabling the patient to make decisions about proposed treatment. Information may also be important to enable the patient timeously to identify the signs or symptoms of complications from medical treatment that has already been given: *Spencer v Hillingdon Hospital NHS Trust* [2015] EWHC 1058 (QB), see para.4–070.

[56] In *Arndt v Smith* (1997) 148 D.L.R. (4th) 48 at 54 and 55, discussing the "modified objective test" of causation applied in Canada, Cory J said that the "reasonable person in the patient's position" must be "taken to possess the patient's reasonable beliefs, fears, desires and expectations", but "purely subjective fears *which are not related to the material risks* should not be taken into account in applying the modified objective test" (original emphasis). In *Thefaut v Johnston* [2017] EWHC 497 (QB); [2017] Med. L.R. 319 at [55] Green J said that the characteristics of a patient that could be relevant might include the severity of the patient's medical condition, and the patient's tolerance for or stoicism towards pain, or the ability to manage pain. Other, more remote, factors might be "the patient's need to return to work, or the fact that the patient has suffered a recent event in his/her life (such as a bereavement or a divorce) which renders that person unusually fragile and (say) unwilling to take chances at that particular time". Green J added, at [56], that the reference in [89] of *Montgomery* (cited at para.7–045 below) to the effect which the occurrence of the risk would have upon patients' lives suggested that the test would embrace the risk that an adverse outcome could reduce people's mobility and prevent them from engaging in a favourite sport or pastime.

Expressions of concern by the patient or the asking of specific questions should alert the doctor to the fact that the individual patient may consider a risk to be material even though, objectively, a reasonable patient would not. Moreover, the court:

"should not be too quick to discard the second limb ... merely because it emerges that the patient did not ask certain kinds of questions."[57]

The Supreme Court acknowledged that a change in the law may not be welcomed by the medical profession, that it could be argued that the prudent patient standard may result in defensive practices and an increase in litigation; and that the outcome of such litigation may be less predictable. But the General Medical Council had adopted a similar view of doctors' duties some time ago, and the imposition of a duty in law was necessary in order to persuade those doctors who had less skill or inclination for communication with their patients to engage with their responsibilities. It was also arguable that an approach which resulted in patients being more aware that the outcome of medical treatment is uncertain and potentially dangerous would be less likely to encourage recrimination and litigation, in the event of an adverse outcome, leading to a reduction rather than an increase in litigation. Finally, although the outcome of litigation might be less predictable that was a price worth paying for protecting patients from exposure to risks of injury which they would otherwise have chosen to avoid.[58]

7–020

(iv) Exceptions

Emergencies In *Sidaway* Lord Scarman had identified two exceptions to the duty to disclose material risks. The first is where there is a genuine emergency, e.g. where the patient is unconscious. In *Montgomery* the Supreme Court accepted that the doctor is excused from conferring with the patient in circumstances of necessity, such as where the patient requires treatment urgently but is unconscious or otherwise unable to make a decision.[59]

7–021

Therapeutic privilege Lord Scarman's second exception was where the information would be harmful to the patient, for example, where it might cause psychological damage. Again, the Supreme Court accepted that withholding information from a patient is acceptable if the doctor reasonably believes that

7–022

---

[57] [2015] UKSC 11; [2015] A.C. 1430 at [73], approving comments of Gummow J in *Rosenberg v Percival* [2001] HCA 18; (2001) 178 A.L.R. 577 at [79]; see para.7–037.

[58] [2015] UKSC 11; [2015] A.C. 1430 at [93].

[59] [2015] UKSC 11; [2015] A.C. 1430 at [88]. No detail was provided as to precisely when this exception applies, but presumably it would be relevant where the patient lacks capacity to make the decision in question. Bear in mind, however, that under the Mental Capacity Act 2005 a decision to refuse recommended treatment does not in itself mean that a patient lacks of capacity, and a patient suffering from a mental disorder does not necessarily lack capacity (see para.6–050). Even where patients lack capacity, s.4(4) of the 2005 Act provides that so far as reasonably practicable, people making a decision on behalf of patients must permit and encourage them to participate, or to improve their ability to participate, as fully as possible in any act done for them and any decision affecting them (para.6–129). This may involve a dialogue about the risks of treatment, though in the case of an unconscious patient this is clearly impractical.

disclosure would be seriously detrimental to the patient's health.[60] This was also said to have been the case applying the *Bolam* test,[61] but in reality it was not an exception to the rule but rather formed part of the rule itself, given that the *Bolam* test allowed for different levels of disclosure to different patients within the doctor's exercise of clinical judgment. Thus, in *Sidaway v Bethlem Royal Hospital Governors*[62] Lord Templeman commented that a doctor may take the view that a patient would be confused, frightened or misled by detailed information which he would be unable to evaluate at a time when he is suffering from stress, pain and anxiety.

7–023   There is an obvious danger in giving too wide an interpretation to this exception in that it could be used to undermine the patient's right to exercise a choice about whether to accept treatment. The fact that the doctor believes that if the patient were informed about the risks he would decline the treatment which the doctor believes to be in the patient's best interests does not justify withholding the information, otherwise whenever the proposed treatment was medically appropriate, doctors would have no obligation to give patients information about risks. In *Montgomery* the Supreme Court were alert to this possibility and emphasised that the therapeutic exception should not be abused:

> "It is a limited exception to the general principle that the patient should make the decision whether to undergo a proposed course of treatment: it is not intended to subvert that principle by enabling the doctor to prevent the patient from making an informed choice where she is liable to make a choice which the doctor considers to be contrary to her best interests."[63]

(v)   Applying the test to the facts of Montgomery

7–024   In *Montgomery* itself the pursuer, who was pregnant, was diabetic and of small stature. Her consultant obstetrician did not inform her that the risk of shoulder dystocia occurring during the birth of the baby was 9–10 per cent in diabetic patients. There was also a much smaller risk of serious injury to the child (brachial plexus injury 0.2 per cent, and prolonged hypoxia resulting in cerebral palsy or death less than 0.1 per cent). The consultant considered that these risks were low, but that if she told diabetic patients about them they would all opt for an elective Caesarean section, which was not in their interests. During the course of the delivery shoulder dystocia occurred and the baby suffered both a brachial plexus injury and brain damage. The pursuer's claim in respect of non-disclosure of these risks failed in the Court of Session in both the Outer and the Inner House, where, applying *Sidaway*, it was held that the test was whether the defendant had

---

[60] [2015] UKSC 11; [2015] A.C. 1430 at [88].
[61] *Sidaway v Bethlem Royal Hospital Governors* [1984] Q.B. 493 at 521, per Browne-Wilkinson LJ.
[62] [1985] A.C. 871 at 902.
[63] [2015] UKSC 11; [2015] A.C. 1430 at [91]. In *Deriche v Ealing Hospital NHS Trust* [2003] EWHC 3104 (QB) at [50] Buckley J commented that "something more than temporary distress would be needed". In that case, the distress to a pregnant mother from a discussion about the risks to a foetus of the mother contracting chickenpox during pregnancy would be outweighed by the devastation a mother would suffer if the risk materialised and she felt she was not fully warned of it and thus deprived of her right to decide.

conformed to a practice accepted as proper by a responsible body of professional opinion, and that on this issue expert evidence of professional practice was crucial.

The Supreme Court unanimously allowed the pursuer's appeal. Applying the prudent patient standard, the pursuer should have been informed of the risk of shoulder dystocia if she were to proceed to a vaginal delivery, and there should have been a discussion about the alternative of Caesarean section. The risk of shoulder dystocia in her case was 9–10 per cent.[64] Apart from the 0.2 per cent risk of brachial plexus injury to the baby and the smaller risk to the baby of cerebral palsy or death, shoulder dystocia was a major obstetric emergency requiring procedures which were potentially traumatic for the mother. The contrast of the extremely small risk to the mother and virtually non-existent risk for the baby from a Caesarean section was "stark". Although the consultant obstetrician considered that it was not generally in the maternal interest to have a Caesarean section, this was not a situation where the "therapeutic exception" applied. The exception was not intended to enable doctors to prevent their patients from taking an informed decision. It was up to the doctor to explain to the patient why she considered one of the available treatment options was medically preferable to the others, taking care to see that the patient was aware of the considerations for and against each option.[65]

7–025

(d)   The standard applied in other jurisdictions

(i)   Canada

In Canada the Supreme Court established a standard of disclosure based on the "reasonably prudent patient". In *Hopp v Lepp*[66] it was said that a surgeon should answer any specific questions posed by the patient as to the risks involved and should, without being questioned, disclose the nature of the proposed operation, its gravity, any material risks and any special or unusual risks attendant upon the performance of the operation. A risk which is a mere possibility, which ordinarily need not be disclosed, could be regarded as a material risk, requiring disclosure,

7–026

---

[64] In *Jones v North West SHA* [2010] EWHC 178 (QB); [2010] Med. L.R. 90 Nicol J, applying *Pearce v United Bristol Healthcare NHS Trust* [1999] P.I.Q.R. P53, para.7–012, held that the claimant's mother should have been informed of the 10 per cent risk of shoulder dystocia (though the risk of injury was something less than 1 per cent to 2 per cent), but the claim failed on causation.

[65] [2015] UKSC 11; [2015] A.C. 1430 at [95]. It has been suggested that s.1(5) of the Congenital Disabilities (Civil Liability) Act 1976 may impact on the application of *Montgomery* to cases of antenatal advice. Section 1(5) provides that: "The defendant is not answerable to the child, for anything he did or omitted to do when responsible in a professional capacity for treating or *advising the parent*, if he took reasonable care having due regard to then received professional opinion applicable to the particular class of case …" (emphasis added). This is clearly a statutory form of the *Bolam* test. *Clerk & Lindsell on Torts*, 22nd edn (2018), para.10–83, n.545, comments: "Quaere whether this section, which specifically refers to 'advice', precludes the application to cases of antenatal injury in England and Wales of the principle in *Montgomery v Lanarkshire Health Board* [2015] UKSC 11; [2015] A.C. 1430, where the issue was precisely one of negligent advice to the pregnant mother before the birth. The issue did not arise in *Montgomery*, an appeal from Scotland where the 1976 Act does not apply."

[66] (1980) 112 D.L.R. (3d) 67 at 81, SCC.

if its occurrence carries serious consequences such as paralysis or death. Subsequently, in *Reibl v Hughes*[67] the Court explicitly rejected a professional medical standard for determining what are material risks and whether there has been a breach of the duty of disclosure:

"To allow expert medical evidence to determine what risks are material and, hence, should be disclosed and, correlatively, what risks are not material is to hand over to the medical profession the entire question of the scope of the duty of disclosure, including the question whether there has been a breach of that duty ... The materiality of non-disclosure of certain risks to an informed decision is a matter for the trier of fact, a matter on which there would, in all likelihood, be medical evidence but also other evidence, including evidence from the patient or from members of his family."

For example, in *Meyer Estate v Rogers*[68] the Canadian Association of Radiologists had specifically recommended that patients should not be informed of the risks of an allergic reaction to contrast media during an intravenous pyelogram. Nonetheless, it was held that this risk was material, and that the Association's recommendation directly contravened the standard required by *Reibl v Hughes*.

7–027   In *Videto v Kennedy*[69] the Ontario Court of Appeal summarised the effect of *Hopp v Lepp* and *Reibl v Hughes* in the following terms:

(i)   the question of whether a risk is material and whether there has been a breach the duty of disclosure should not be determined solely by the standards of the profession. Professional standards are a factor to be considered;

(ii)   the duty of disclosure embraces what the surgeon knows or ought to know that patients deem relevant to their decision whether or not to undergo the treatment. If patients ask specific questions they are entitled to be given reasonable answers;

(iii)   a risk which is a mere possibility does not ordinarily have to be disclosed, but if its occurrence would have serious consequences it should be treated as a material risk[70];

(iv)   the patient is entitled to be given an explanation of the nature of the operation and its gravity;

(v)   subject to this, other inherent dangers such as the dangers of anaesthetic or the risks of infection do not have to be disclosed[71];

---

[67] (1980) 112 D.L.R. (3d) 67 at 81 at 13, SCC.

[68] (1991) 78 D.L.R (4th) 307, Ont HC.

[69] (1981) 125 D.L.R. (3d) 127, 133–134, Ont CA.

[70] See, e.g. *Lachambre v Nair* [1989] 2 W.W.R. 749; *Meyer Estate v Rogers* (1991) 78 D.L.R (4th) 307 (Ont HC), where a risk of death of between 1 in 40,000 and 1 in 100,000 was held to be a material risk.

[71] See, e.g. *Hajgato v London Health Association* (1982) 36 O.R. (2d) 669 at 680. Note, however, that certain risks of infection, such as the risk of contracting hepatitis from blood products, may be an "unusual or special risk" which should be disclosed: *Kitchen v McMullen* (1989) 62 D.L.R. (4th) 481, NBCA.

(vi) the scope of the duty and whether it has been breached must be decided in the circumstances of each case[72];

(vii) the emotional condition of the patient may in certain cases justify the surgeon in withholding or generalising information which otherwise should be more specific[73];

(viii) the question of whether a particular risk is a material risk and whether there has been a breach of the duty is a matter for the trier of fact.

Meaning of material risk In *White v Turner*[74] Linden J explained that "material risks" are significant risks that pose a real threat to the patient's life, health or comfort. The court must balance the severity of the potential result[75] and the likelihood of its occurring. Even if there is only a small chance of serious injury or death, the risk may be considered material.[76] On the other hand, if there

7–028

---

[72] For example, the patient may already know about the risks from a similar previous experience: *Goguen v Crowe* (1987) 40 C.C.L.T. 212 at 226, NSSC. Where the patient is aware of the risks from a previous operation, but a revision operation carries a threefold increase of risk of complications, that increase in risk is material and should be disclosed: *Semeniuk v Cox* 2000 ABQB 18; [2000] 4 W.W.R. 310 at [18].

[73] See, e.g. *Hajgato v London Health Association* (1982) 36 O.R. (2d) 669 at 680; although it has been held that there is no defence of therapeutic privilege in Canadian law on the ground that the defence undermines the very obligation to disclose material risks: *Meyer Estate v Rogers* (1991) 78 D.L.R (4th) 307, Ont HC; sed quaere. In *Pittman Estate v Bain* (1994) 112 D.L.R. (4th) 257 at 399, Ont Ct, Gen Div, Lang J accepted that there could be cases where a patient is unable or unwilling to accept bad news from a doctor: "In those circumstances, a physician is obliged to take reasonable precautions to ensure that the patient has communicated their desire not to be told, or that the patient's health is *so precarious* that such news will *undoubtedly* trigger an adverse reaction that will cause further unnecessary harm to the patient" (emphasis added).

[74] (1981) 120 D.L.R. (3d) 269 at 284–285, Ont HC; aff'd (1982) 12 D.L.R. (4th) 319, Ont CA.

[75] So "to mention a risk of harm to a nerve without at the same time advising as to the potential consequences to the patient of such harm, is not generally sufficient": *Boschman v Azad* 2002 BCSC 887; (2002) 2 B.C.L.R. (4th) 342 at [29] per Melvin J.

[76] Thus the risk of stroke, however minimal, is a material risk: *Forgie v Mason* (1986) 30 D.L.R. (4th) 548 at 558, NBCA; *Zaiffdeen v Chua* 2005 ABCA 290; (2005) 380 A.R. 200, Alta CA at [25]; *Dickson v Pinder* 2010 ABQB 269; [2010] 10 W.W.R. 505 at [90] and [101]; *Anderson v Queen Elizabeth II Health Sciences Centre* 2012 NSSC 360; (2012) 97 C.C.L.T. (3d) 51 at [316]. It is not sufficient to mention a "stroke". The patient must also be made aware of the potential consequences of a stroke: *Dickson v Pinder* at [101]. Doctors do not satisfy their duty to warn of the risk of stroke by warning of the risk of death and assuming that mentioning the more serious risk, death, comprehended the less serious risk, stroke, because a reasonable patient may be prepared to run the risk of death but not the risk of stroke: *Ferguson v Hamilton Civic Hospitals* (1983) 144 D.L.R. (3d) 214 at 248; aff'd (1985) 18 D.L.R. (4th) 638, Ont CA. The risk of death is a material risk, even when it is extremely small. In *Meyer Estate v Rogers* (1991) 78 D.L.R (4th) 307, Ont HC, it was held that a risk of severe allergic reaction during an intravenous pyelogram of 1 in 2,000 and a risk of death of between 1 in 40,000 and 1 in 100,000 was a material risk; *Brock v Anderson* 2003 BCSC 1359; (2003) 20 C.C.L.T. (3d) 70—small risk of death due to damage to major vessels during laparoscopic surgery was a material risk. The risk of permanent loss or serious impairment of voice is a material risk in the context of the performance a carotid endarterectomy: *Casey v Provan* (1984) 11 D.L.R. (4th) 708, Ont HC. The risk of permanent paralysis to the sciatic nerve being caused during the performance of a pelvic osteotomy, causing foot drop, is a material risk: *Huisman v MacDonald* 2007 ONCA 391; (2007) 280 D.L.R. (4th) 1. A small risk of perforation of the bowel during the course of laparoscopic sterilisation and during a bowel examination by sigmoidoscope has been held not to be a material risk: *Videto v Kennedy* (1981) 125 D.L.R. (3d) 127, Ont CA; *Gonda v Kerbel* (1982) 24 C.C.L.T. 222; cf. *Painter v Rae* [1998] 8 W.W.R. 717, Man QB, where the risk of injury to the bowel during a postpartum tubal ligation was small, but the gravity of the consequences rendered it a material risk;

is a significant chance of slight injury this may also be held to be material.[77] "Unusual or special risks" are risks that are extraordinary or uncommon, but they are known to occur occasionally. Though rare they should be described to a reasonable patient because of their unusual or special character.[78] Thus, where the operation can be described as elective, as e.g. in the case of cosmetic surgery, doctors must be careful to make full disclosure of even remote risks of minor consequences since patients may well decide that they would prefer to live with a blemish than to take the risk.[79] However, in the case of elective surgery a doctor

---

Berezowski-Aitken v McGregor [1998] 8 W.W.R. 322, Man QB, where it was held that a failure to warn of the remote risk of bowel damage leading to infertility, following the performance of a dilatation and curettage ("D&C"), constituted a material risk because of the seriousness of the risk of infertility; *Baksh-White v Cochen* (2001) 7 C.C.L.T. (3d) 138, Ont SC—risk of bowel perforation during performance of hysterectomy constituted a material risk. In *Arndt v Smith* [1994] 8 W.W.R. 568, BCSC, a mother was informed about the most common risks to her foetus of exposure to chickenpox (skin and muscle problems) but was not warned about the most serious, though more remote, risks (cortical atrophy and mental retardation). This was held to be negligent. The more remote risks were material risks, and non-disclosure was "classic medical paternalism". The decision was affirmed by the Supreme Court of Canada on the question of causation: (1997) 148 D.L.R. (4th) 48. In *Krangle v Brisco* (1997) 154 D.L.R. (4th) 707, BCSC, the failure of a general practitioner to advise a 36-year-old pregnant woman to undergo an amniocentesis test for Down's syndrome was held to be negligent. Note that where the risk is very small the claimant is more likely to fail on causation: see para.7-085.

[77] *Rawlings v Lindsey* (1982) 20 C.C.L.T. 301, where a 5 per cent to 10 per cent risk of nerve damage and resultant numbness to the face following wisdom tooth extraction was held to be a material risk; cf. *Diack v Bardsley* (1983) 25 C.C.L.T. 159, BCSC, where the claimant failed on causation. The possibility of partial paraesthesia of the lower side of the face caused by a needle entering the inferior alveolar nerve during the routine administration of local anaesthetic prior to performing root canal work on the patient's teeth is too remote to constitute a material risk: *Schinz v Dickinson* [1985] 2 W.W.R. 673, BCCA; *Mallette v Hagarty* [1994] 7 W.W.R. 402, Alta QB, where Rowbotham J pointed out that the risk of this form of damage was considerably greater where wisdom teeth were being extracted, as in *Rawlings v Lindsey*. See also *Carter v Higashi* [1994] 3 W.W.R. 319, Alta QB, where the risk of fracturing the patient's jaw during extraction of wisdom teeth, put at one in 100,000, was held not to be a material risk; *Thibault v Fewer* [2002] 1 W.W.R. 204, Man QB—a less than 1 per cent risk of developing keratitis, which even if it occurred usually resolved without permanent complication, was not a material or unusual risk of a glycerol rhizotomy procedure.

[78] *Christie v Jason* 2004 MBQB 207; [2005] 5 W.W.R. 163—a 20 to 30 per cent risk of incontinence associated with elective prostate surgery (transurethral prostatectomy for a slightly enlarged but not cancerous prostate) held to be an unusual, significant risk.

[79] *White v Turner* (1981) 120 D.L.R. (3d) 269; aff'd (1982) 12 D.L.R. (4th) 319, Ont CA; *Petty v McKay* (1979) 10 C.C.L.T. 85, BCSC; *Hankins v Papillon* (1980) 14 C.C.L.T. 198 at 203, Qué SC; *Guertin v Kester* (1981) 20 C.C.L.T. 225, BCSC; *MacDonald v Ross* (1983) 24 C.C.L.T. 242; *Hartjes v Carman* (2003) 20 C.C.L.T. (3d) 31, Ont SCJ; cf. *Koller v Colcleugh* (1999) 47 C.C.L.T. (2d) 193, Ont SC, where in a case of elective cosmetic surgery it was held that a 0.3 per cent risk of the "worst case scenario" (extensive abdominal scarring following surgery to remove a vertical abdominal scar) did not constitute a material risk. Browne J concluded that there was not a different standard of disclosure for purely elective surgery; *Perez v Ziesmann* 2005 MBQB 157; [2006] 7 W.W.R. 476 at [17]—risk of loss of the nipple following surgery to correct an inverted nipple, "while extremely rare, was a very serious consequence of the surgery" and should be specifically disclosed. Despite applying the prudent patient test, in a study of Canadian informed consent cases in the 10 years following *Reibl v Hughes* it was found that the claimant's action failed in 82 per cent of cases: Robertson (1991) 70 Can. Bar Rev. 423.

is not negligent simply by failing to make any recommendation for or against the surgery and the non-surgical alternatives.[80]

Alternatives to the recommended treatment   In addition to the risks of treatment a doctor should explain the consequences of leaving the ailment untreated, and the alternative means of treatment and their risks.[81] The duty to disclose the availability of alternatives to the proposed treatment is particularly pressing where more conservative and less risky treatment is available.[82] Lack of negligence in the choice of treatment or the manner in which it is performed does not negate the doctor's duty to inform the patient of the risks of proceeding in one way as opposed to another.[83] So a patient should be informed of a known treatment which other doctors in the same specialty consider to be superior, even if the doctor does not agree;[84] and it is arguable that a patient should be informed that the surgeon is going to use an operative procedure that is unlicensed for use in Canada.[85] Where there are various treatment options, ranging from conservative treatment to radical surgery, the patient should be given sufficient information to place the treatment options in a proper perspective, and so it may be negligent to present drug treatment on an equal footing to surgery, particularly where professional guidelines recommend conservative treatment as the first line of therapy for the patient's condition.[86] In *Van Mol (Guardian ad Litem of) v Ashmore*[87] the British Columbia Court of Appeal held that a 16-year-old patient who was competent to consent should have been informed about the three

7–029

---

[80] *Hill v Victoria Hospital Corp* 2009 ONCA 70; (2009) 174 A.C.W.S. (3d) 1200 at [27]–[29], citing *Zamparo v Brisson* (1981) 32 O.R. (2d) 75 at 84–85 (Ont CA).

[81] *Haughian v Paine* (1987) 37 D.L.R. (4th) 624 at 639 Sask CA; *Schanczi v Singh* [1988] 2 W.W.R. 465, Alta QB; *Seney v Crooks* (1998) 166 D.L.R. (4th) 337, Alta CA; cf. *Bucknam v Kostuik* (1983) 3 D.L.R. (4th) 99 at 111, Ont HC, where Krever J doubted whether a surgeon was under a duty to inform a patient of a less serious alternative procedure which in his own mind was an entirely unreasonable procedure to undertake, even though another school of thought believed the alternative procedure was appropriate for the patient's condition. *Bucknam v Kostuik* was followed on this point in *Moss v Zaw* (2009) 176 A.C.W.S. (3d) 546 (Ont SC) at [141]–[145] (no duty to inform patient of option of performing colonoscopy rather than exploratory bowel surgery because there was overwhelming evidence to support a diagnosis of cancer from the clinical symptoms and a barium enema, though it turned out that the patient did not have cancer). In *McCann v Hyndman* 2004 ABCA 191; [2004] 11 W.W.R. 216, during the course of carrying out surgery, the defendant became aware that two parts of a medical device which were part of an artificial urinary sphincter (a balloon and tubing) had become detached and migrated into the claimant's abdomen. He decided that the risks of attempting to locate and remove them in the course of the surgery were greater than leaving them in the abdominal cavity, but he did not inform the patient about the situation or the risk of a bowel obstruction developing. It was held that this was a material risk, because, though unlikely to occur, the potential consequences were serious, almost always involving further surgery. The defendant was negligent in failing to inform the claimant about this risk, which deprived the patient the opportunity of having the situation monitored by CT scan or MRI and choosing whether or not to undergo further surgery to have the material removed.

[82] *McEachern v University Hospitals Board* 2010 ABQB 253; (2010) 26 Alta. L.R. (5th) 154 at [73].

[83] *Seney v Crooks* (1998) 166 D.L.R. (4th) 337, Alta CA at [54] per Conrad JA.

[84] (1998) 166 D.L.R. (4th) 337, Alta CA at [60]; cf. *Bucknam v Kostuik* (1983) 3 D.L.R. (4th) 99 and *Moss v Zaw* (2009) 176 A.C.W.S. (3d) 546 (Ont SC), n.81 above.

[85] *Laing v Sekundiak* 2015 MBCA 72; [2015] 12 W.W.R. 102 (use of particular type of joint in total hip replacement surgery).

[86] *Zaiffdeen v Chua* 2005 ABCA 290; (2005) 380 A.R. 200, Alta CA at [21].

[87] (1999) 168 D.L.R. (4th) 637, BCCA.

surgical alternatives that were being considered to repair a narrowing of her aorta, and the risks and advantages of each of them. She should also have been informed that she could obtain a second opinion before deciding to proceed with the surgery. Moreover, a general discussion of the risks with the patient's parents was not sufficient to discharge the surgeon's duty.

7–030 **Diagnostic aids** A similar principle applies to diagnostic procedures. The patient is entitled to be informed about diagnostic procedures and their risks where there is uncertainty about the diagnosis and the procedure proposed by the doctor for the presumed diagnosis carries significant risks. In *Cory v Bass*[88] the defendant gastroenterologist diagnosed that the claimant had a high probability of gallstones in the common bile duct. He performed a surgical procedure during which the claimant's duodenum was perforated, giving rise to serious complications. The surgery was performed without negligence, and the expert evidence was in agreement that if there was a high probability of gallstones the surgical procedure carried out by the defendant was the correct option. However, the trial judge accepted the view of the claimant's expert that the presence of gallstones was not probable, but merely a possibility. There were two, low risk, diagnostic procedures that could have been used by the defendant prior to surgery but the defendant did not mention these options to the claimant because he was convinced that his diagnosis on the clinical evidence was correct. The Alberta Court of Appeal upheld the trial judge's conclusion that the defendant had been negligent in failing to inform the claimant about the lower risk diagnostic tests. The surgical procedure undertaken by the defendant carried potentially serious risks, and a patient informed of those risks might reasonably be expected to ask whether the treatment was necessary; how certain was the diagnosis of a high probability of gallstones; and whether it could be made more certain. In order to make:

> "...a fully informed choice, a person in the [claimant's] position would have required information, not only about the significant risks of the [surgery], but also about relevant and low risk tests that might bring more certainty to the need to undergo that risky treatment."[89]

7–031 **Duty to give information in terms the patient can understand** The clarity with which the doctor expresses a warning can, obviously, be crucial to a determination of negligence. In *Bryan v Hicks*[90] a surgeon gave a warning that there was a 1 to 2 per cent risk of "sympathetic pain" following surgery on a ganglion in the wrist. This was the defendant's standard way of telling patients about the risk of reflex sympathetic dystrophy. The British Columbia Court of Appeal held that this was not the same as a warning that there was a risk that the patient's arm could end up being useless. The total risk of reflex sympathetic dystrophy was 3 per cent of all cases, but of these, 95 per cent of patients were left with no symptoms after about a month. The rest (amounting to about three cases in 2,000) developed a severe, permanent form of the condition. It was held that this constituted a material risk, although medical opinion did not consider it

---

[88] 2012 ABCA 136; (2012) 215 A.C.W.S. (3d) 763; (2012) 68 Alta. L.R. (5th) 96.
[89] 2012 ABCA 136; (2012) 215 A.C.W.S. (3d) 763; (2012) 68 Alta. L.R. (5th) 96 at [19].
[90] [1995] 10 W.W.R. 145, BCCA.

necessary to disclose it. A reasonable person would want to know about the risk, particularly given the alternative forms of treatment available. In *Martin v Capital Health Authority*[91] the claimant underwent surgery for the prophylactic internal decompression of a benign cerebellar epidermoid cyst. This was elective surgery; it was not an emergency. The claimant suffered a stroke during the operation, as a result of which he was confined to wheelchair and had difficulty speaking. The risk of some neurological deficit after the procedure was 4 to 5 per cent. Wilson J held that a discussion about the risks took place, but it was ineffective because the claimant did not comprehend the language used by the doctor: "He failed to use laymen's terms that would make it clear to a layman what risk he was facing."[92] A statement that there would be bleeding or a risk of blood vessel damage did not convey to the patient that there was a risk of suffering a stroke. However, the Alberta Court of Appeal reversed this decision on the basis that the patient had been informed about the risks of speech impairment and paralysis, which was the risk that materialised.[93] The trial judge had placed undue emphasis on the use of the word "stroke". There was no obligation to disclose the mechanism of the risk.[94]

Withdrawing consent   Where the patient has been given a full explanation of the risks involved in a procedure, and, having consented, during the course of the procedure withdraws that consent, the duty of disclosure is modified. The doctor is not under an obligation to repeat the full explanation in order to obtain consent to resume the procedure. The obligation is to disclose all facts that a patient would want to know, in the light of any material changes in circumstances since the former explanation, which could alter the assessment of the benefits or disadvantages of continuing the procedure.[95] A patient would want to know of any significant changes in the risks involved or in the need for continuation of the procedure which had become apparent during its course.

7–032

Disclosure of the doctor's health status   Non-disclosure of the treating doctor's own health status has been held not to be negligent where the doctor's condition did not affect the treatment provided to the patient. In *Halkyard v Mathew*[96] a surgeon conducted an hysterectomy, following which the patient's bladder did not function properly. She underwent further surgery to correct the bladder problem, but died as a result of a pulmonary embolism shortly after the second operation. It was argued that she had not given informed consent to the hysterectomy because, although she was informed about the risks of the surgery, including bladder complications, the surgeon had not informed her that he had a

7–033

---

[91] 2007 ABQB 260; (2007) 47 C.C.L.T. (3d) 255; [2007] 8 W.W.R. 328.
[92] 2007 ABQB 260; (2007) 47 C.C.L.T. (3d) 255; [2007] 8 W.W.R. 328 at [66].
[93] *Martin v Capital Health Authority* 2008 ABCA 161; [2008] 7 W.W.R. 30.
[94] This does not undermine the principle that if the patient does not actually understand the risks of the procedure because of the language in which they are explained then the patient's consent is not informed, even if she signs a consent form which refers to the risks: *Dickson v Pinder* 2010 ABQB 269; [2010] 10 W.W.R. 505 at [93], a case where the patient did not understand the full implications of a stroke. See further para.7–069.
[95] *Ciarlariello v Schacter* (1993) 100 D.L.R. (4th) 609, SCC.
[96] [1999] 5 W.W.R. 643, Alta QB.

history of epilepsy, for which he was taking medication. The defendant had not suffered a seizure during the operation, and the medication did not affect the surgeon's ability to carry out the operation. It was held that there was no duty to disclose to the patient the surgeon's personal medical history. It was the duty of the defendant's own physician to determine whether the defendant was fit to continue with surgery, and it was the duty of the hospital employing the surgeon to determine whether a doctor was fit to continue his practice in the hospital. Any doctor also has a personal responsibility to determine whether a physical or mental incapacity would preclude him from continuing to treat patients, but there was no link between the doctor's medical condition and the damage that occurred to the bladder during the operation.[97]

(ii) Australia

7–034   **Rogers v Whitaker**   In Australia the High Court rejected the *Bolam* test as the standard for the disclosure of information by the medical profession, effectively adopting the reasonably prudent patient standard. In *Rogers v Whitaker*[98] the claimant, who was aged 48, was almost totally blind in her right eye following an accident at the age of nine. Her left eye was normal. The defendant ophthalmic surgeon advised that an operation could improve the sight of the right eye. The claimant asked about the possible consequences of the operation, but did not specifically ask whether it could cause damage to the left eye. There was a one in 14,000 chance of sympathetic ophthalmia developing in the left eye, but the defendant did not mention this. If the claimant had known about this risk she would not have agreed to the surgery. Following the operation on the right eye, which was conducted with reasonable skill and care, sympathetic ophthalmia developed and she ultimately lost the sight in her left eye. The claimant had "incessantly" questioned the defendant as to the possible complications. She was, to the defendant's knowledge, keenly interested in the outcome of the procedure, including the danger of accidental interference with her "good" left eye. There was evidence from a body of reputable medical practitioners that, in the circumstances of this case, they would not have warned the claimant of the danger of sympathetic ophthalmia; there was also evidence from similarly reputable medical practitioners that they would have given such a warning. The New South Wales Court of Appeal held[99] that the defendant had been negligent in failing to mention the risk in response to the claimant's general question about possible complications. The High Court of Australia upheld this decision, and an award of damages in excess of $800,000. The question, said the Court, was not

---

[97] The decision was affirmed by the Alberta Court of Appeal: 2001 ABCA 67; [2001] 7 W.W.R. 26, commenting at [11] that: "we do not accept that the law in Canada imposes any liability in negligence on a doctor who fails to disclose his personal medical problems in a case where those medical problems cause no harm to the patient. When harm is caused by the lack of disclosure, liability in negligence may arise. That is not the case here."

[98] (1992) 109 A.L.R. 625; [1993] 4 Med. L.R. 79, HC of Aust; Trindade (1993) 109 L.Q.R. 352; McDonald and Swanton (1993) 67 A.L.J. 145; McSherry (1993) 1 J. Law and Med. 5; Kerridge and Mitchell (1994) 1 J. Law and Med. 239; Jones (1994) 2 Tort L. Rev. 5; Malcolm (1994) 2 Tort L. Rev. 81.

[99] (1991) 23 N.S.W.L.R. 600; [1992] 3 Med. L.R. 331.

whether the defendant's conduct accorded with the practice of the medical profession or some part of it, but whether it conformed to the standard of reasonable care demanded by the law. That was a question for the court, and the duty of deciding it could not be delegated to any profession or group in the community.[100] The nature of the matter to be disclosed, the nature of the treatment, the desire of the patient for information, the temperament and health of the patient and the general surrounding circumstances were all matters to be considered by a medical practitioner in deciding whether to disclose or advise of some risk in a proposed procedure. It followed that a doctor has a duty to warn a patient of a material risk inherent in the proposed treatment. A risk is material if, in the circumstances of the particular case, a reasonable person in the patient's position, if warned of the risk, would be likely to attach significance to it or if the medical practitioner is or should reasonably be aware that the particular patient, if warned of the risk, would be likely to attach significance to it.[101]

The High Court rejected the "somewhat amorphous phrase 'informed consent'" as apt to mislead, since it suggested a test of the validity of a patient's consent, and consent was relevant to actions framed in trespass not in negligence. Nonetheless the Court identified the central problem of such cases in terms of the patient's ability to make a true choice about whether to accept or reject proposed treatment. Except in cases of emergency or necessity, all medical treatment is preceded by the patient's choice to undergo it:

7–035

> "In legal terms, the patient's consent to the treatment may be valid once he or she is informed in broad terms of the nature of the procedure which is intended. But the choice is, in reality, meaningless unless it is made on the basis of relevant information and advice. Because the choice to be made calls for a decision by the patient on information known to the medical practitioner but not to the patient, it would be illogical to hold that the amount of information to be provided by the medical practitioner can be determined from the perspective of the practitioner alone or, for that matter, of the medical profession."[102]

There was a fundamental difference between, on the one hand, diagnosis and treatment and, on the other hand, the provision of advice or information to a patient. Whether a doctor carried out a particular treatment in accordance with the appropriate standard of care was a question in the resolution of which responsible professional opinion would have an influential role to play. But whether the

---

[100] Approving *F v R* (1983) 33 S.A.S.R. 189; *Battersby v Tottman* (1985) 37 S.A.S.R. 524; *Gover v South Australia* (1985) 39 S.A.S.R. 543; *Ellis v Wallsend District Hospital* (1989) 17 N.S.W.L.R 553; *E v Australian Red Cross Society* (1991) 99 A.L.R. 601; [1991] 2 Med. L.R. 303; (1991) 105 A.L.R. 53, Aus Fed CA. In *Rosenberg v Percival* [2001] HCA 18; (2001) 178 A.L.R. 577 at [7], Gleeson CJ commented that *Rogers v Whitaker* makes it clear that professional practice and opinion was relevant, but what the case denied was its *conclusiveness*.
[101] (1992) 109 A.L.R. 625 at 634, per Mason CJ, Brennan, Dawson, Toohey, and McHugh JJ (approved by the Supreme Court in *Montgomery v Lanarkshire Health Board* [2015] UKSC 11; [2015] A.C. 1430 at [73]); *Rosenberg v Percival* [2001] HCA 18; (2001) 178 A.L.R. 577 at [75] per Gummow J.
[102] (1992) 109 A.L.R. 625 at 633. In *Haylock v Morris and Lawrence* [2006] ACTSC 86 it was held that a "remote" or "very remote" risk of paraplegia from an epidural anaesthetic constituted a material risk, notwithstanding medical evidence (including specific guidance from the hospital) that the general practice was not to disclose the risk. The patient should have been advised of the competing risks for epidural and general anaesthesia and permitted to make an informed decision. The action failed on causation.

patient has been given all the relevant information to choose between undergoing and not undergoing the treatment was a question of a different order. It was not a question the answer to which was dependent upon medical standards or practices. Except where the defence of therapeutic privilege might apply, no special medical skill was involved in disclosing information, including the risks attending the proposed treatment. Rather, the skill was in communicating the relevant information to the patient in terms which were reasonably adequate for the purpose having regard to the patient's apprehended capacity to understand that information.[103]

7–036   On the facts of *Rogers v Whitaker*, sympathetic ophthalmia was the only danger whereby both eyes might be rendered sightless. The defendant had acknowledged that, except for death under anaesthetic, it was the worst possible outcome for the claimant. The claimant had incessantly questioned the defendant as to possible complications, including the danger of accidental interference with her good eye, but she did not ask a specific question as to whether the operation on her right eye could affect her left eye. Remarkably, there was a body of professional opinion which considered that an inquiry by a patient should only have elicited a reply dealing with sympathetic ophthalmia if specifically directed to the possibility of the left eye being affected by the operation on the right eye. This view appears to require the claimant to be sufficiently knowledgeable about medical matters to be able to ask the precise question before the doctors consider it appropriate to tell her about the dangers of sympathetic ophthalmia. The High Court described this state of affairs as "curious". The claimant may not have asked the right question, but she had made clear her concern about injury to her one good eye. The risk, although extremely small, was a material risk, because a reasonable person in the claimant's position would be likely to attach significance to the risk, and thus require a warning.[104] It was reasonable, said the Court, for a person with one good eye to be concerned about the possibility of injury to it from a procedure which was elective.

7–037   **Applying *Rogers v Whitaker***   In *Rosenberg v Percival*[105] Gummow J said that in deciding whether a patient was "likely to attach significance to" a particular risk, the extent or severity of the potential injury is of great importance, as is the likelihood of the injury actually occurring.[106] These issues should be considered

---

[103] (1992) 109 A.L.R. 625 at 632–633.

[104] In *F v R* (1983) 33 S.A.S.R. 189 at 191 King CJ said that a risk of harm or of the procedure failing might be so slight in relation to the consequences of not undergoing the proposed treatment that no reasonable person would be influenced by it. The duty to disclose would not extend to such a risk. On the other hand, a small risk of great harm might call for disclosure, although a greater risk of slight harm would not. The more drastic the proposed intervention the more necessary it would be to keep the patient fully informed of the risks and likely consequences. Major surgery calls for special care in this regard. The existence of reasonably available alternative methods of treatment was also an important factor. See also *Chappel v Hart* [1998] HCA 55; (1998) 156 A.L.R. 517; [1999] Lloyd's Rep. Med. 223, HC of Aust, where the failure to disclose the risk of damage to the claimant's vocal cords in the course of an endoscopic division of the pharyngeal pouch was held to be negligent, applying *Rogers v Whitaker*.

[105] [2001] HCA 18; (2001) 178 A.L.R. 577; Kumaralingham Amirthalingham (2001) 117 L.Q.R. 532.

[106] As to which there must be some medical evidence: *Hammond v Heath* [2010] WASCA 6 at [21]. This case concerned whether the patient should have been warned of the risks of leaving Marlex mesh

together: "A slight risk of a serious harm might satisfy the test, while a greater risk of a small harm might not."[107] This should then be weighed against the patient's circumstances, including the patient's need for the operation and the existence of alternative treatments.[108] In *Kerr v Minister for Health*[109] the risk of side effects from the prescription of pethidine was held to be material because the potential injury was severe (a risk of seizure causing injury to body parts and the potential for sudden death), the likelihood of the injury actually occurring was small but not farfetched or fanciful, there were alternatives which were safer and there was no substantial reason for administering pethidine in preference to the alternatives. A patient may be more likely to attach significance to a risk if the procedure is elective rather than life saving.[110] The second, or subjective, limb of the *Rogers* test recognises that the particular patient may not be reasonable. "Unreasonable" fears or concerns will be given full weight under the second limb if the doctor was or should have been aware of them. If the patient asked questions revealing the fear or concern then the doctor would clearly have been aware of them, but that was not the only means of satisfying the second limb, and the courts:

> "...should not be too quick to discard the second limb merely because it emerges that the patient did not ask certain kinds of questions."[111]

Rationale for a strict test of information disclosure In *Rosenberg*[112] Kirby J 7–038 identified a number of reasons, both of principle and policy, to support the strictness of the rule established by *Rogers v Whitaker*:

> "(1)   Fundamentally, the rule is a recognition of individual autonomy that is to be viewed in the wider context of an emerging appreciation of basic human rights and human

---

in place following surgery. Martin CJ said that the duty to warn of the inherent risks of a surgical procedure so that the patient can make an informed decision about whether to proceed was "not a duty to delegate to the patient the responsibility for deciding, in advance of the surgery, the course that should be followed when any of the many contingencies which might arise during a surgical procedure eventuate" ([2010] WASCA 6 at [33]). That was a matter for the surgeon, applying the skill, training and experience of a surgeon.

[107] [2001] HCA 18; (2001) 178 A.L.R. 577 at [77]. In *Hookey v Paterno* [2009] VSCA 48; (2009) 22 V.R. 362 a maxillofacial surgeon informed the patient of the risk of numbness or altered sensation to her face following surgery, and that this could be permanent, but failed to disclose the rare risk of permanent pain. The Victoria Court of Appeal held that this was a material risk that should have been disclosed. The surgeon did not have to itemise every possible symptom, no matter how remote the chance of its occurrence, but he had a duty not to mislead the patient as to the scope of the possible consequences: "to refer to numbness or similar sensation without mentioning the possibility of other neurological consequence was likely to mislead. Such is the natural aversion to pain of most human beings that a patient could well take a different view of the risk of nerve damage according to whether it carried with it even an outside chance of causing permanent pain" ([2009] VSCA 48; (2009) 22 V.R. 362 at [116]).

[108] See, e.g. *Arkinstall v Jenkins* [2001] QSC 421, Qld SC—surgeon who performed breast augmentation held to have been negligent in failing to inform patient about the option of a mastopexy procedure, which would have restored firmness to the patient's drooping breasts without either enlarging or reducing their size.

[109] [2009] WASCA 32.

[110] *Rosenberg v Percival* [2001] HCA 18; (2001) 178 A.L.R. 577 at [78].

[111] [2001] HCA 18; (2001) 178 A.L.R. 577 at [79].

[112] [2001] HCA 18; (2001) 178 A.L.R. 577 at [145].

dignity. There is no reason to diminish the law's insistence, to the greatest extent possible, upon prior, informed agreement to invasive treatment, save for that which is required in an emergency or otherwise out of necessity;

(2)   While it may be desirable to instil a relationship between the healthcare professional and the patient, reality demands a recognition that sometimes (as in the present case) defects of communication demand the imposition of minimum legal obligations so that even those providers who are in a hurry, or who may have comparatively less skill or inclination for communication, are obliged to pause and provide warnings of the kind that Rogers mandates;

(3)   Such obligations have the added benefit of redressing, to some small degree, the risks of conflicts of interest and duty which a provider may sometimes face in favouring one healthcare procedure over another;

(4)   Also, to some extent, the legal obligation to provide warnings may sometimes help to redress the inherent inequality in power between the professional provider and a vulnerable patient; and

(5)   Even those who are dubious about obligations, such as those stated in decisions such as Rogers, commonly recognise the value of the symbolism which such legal holdings afford ... In so far as the law can influence such practice, it should tend, as Rogers does, towards the provision of detailed warnings so that the ultimate choice, to undertake or refuse an invasive procedure, rests, and is seen to rest, on the patient rather than the healthcare provider. To the extent that this result is upheld, it seems likely that recriminations and litigation following disappointment after treatment will be diminished."

7–039   **Therapeutic privilege**   The duty to disclose material risks is subject to the defence of therapeutic privilege, i.e. it is open to doctors to prove that they reasonably believed that disclosure of a risk would be harmful to the patient. A good example of the application of this principle is the case of *Battersby v Tottman*[113] in which the Supreme Court of South Australia held that the defendant was not liable for failing to warn a patient about the risk of blindness associated with the use of a particular drug in high doses because the claimant was incapable by reason of her abnormal mental condition of using the information as the basis for calm or rational decision. She was likely to react hysterically and irrationally and to refuse treatment not on rational grounds or as a result of calm deliberation but as a result of distorted mental processes produced by her mental illness.[114] In *F v R*[115] King CJ said that there may be circumstances where reasonable care for the patient may justify or even require an evasive or less than fully candid answer even to a direct request, and the doctor may reasonably judge that a patient has made an inquiry, not out of a desire for a frank answer, but out of a desire for reassurance.[116] Similarly, doctors can withhold information where they judge on reasonable grounds that the patient's health, mental or physical, might be seriously harmed by the information, or when they reasonably judge that a patient's temperament or emotional state is such that he would be unable to make the information a basis for a rational decision. In *Rogers v Whitaker* Gaudron J

---

[113] (1985) 37 S.A.S.R. 524, SC of S Aus.

[114] (1985) 37 S.A.S.R. 524 at 527, per King CJ; cf. the forthright dissent of Zelling J at 534–535: "In my opinion it is no answer to the claimant's claim to say that the claimant might have had her treatment seriously affected or might have become suicidal if she had been told the truth. In my view no doctor is entitled to give a patient treatment which may blind her or seriously damage her eyesight without first discussing it with the patient and obtaining her consent to the treatment."

[115] (1983) 33 S.A.S.R. 189 at 192, 193, SC of S Aus; see Manderson (1988) 62 A.L.J. 430.

[116] Though this view has now to be considered in the light of the High Court's reaction to questioning by a patient in *Rogers v Whitaker*: see para.7–064.

was anxious to ensure that the defence of therapeutic privilege should not be used to create an exception so wide as to undermine the basic principle requiring disclosure. There was no basis for any defence of therapeutic privilege which was not based in medical emergency[117] or in considerations of patients' abilities to receive, understand or properly evaluate the significance of the information that would ordinarily be required with respect to their condition or the treatment proposed.

(iii)   New Zealand

In *Smith v Auckland Hospital Board*[118] the New Zealand Court of Appeal effectively applied a *Bolam* standard to the disclosure of information to a patient, even in response to a specific request for information by the patient. Barrowclough CJ said that the court would, in most cases, require the assistance of expert medical evidence as to what is generally accepted medical or surgical practice.[119]

7–040

(iv)   Ireland

In *Walsh v Family Planning Services Ltd*[120] Finlay CJ said that there is a clear obligation on a medical practitioner carrying out or arranging for the carrying out of an operation to inform the patient of "any possible harmful consequence arising from the operation, so as to permit the patient to give an informed consent".[121] The extent of this obligation varies with the elective nature of the surgery concerned. There could be instances where notwithstanding substantial medical risks of harmful consequences the carrying out of a particular surgical procedure was so necessary to maintain the life or health of the patient and the consequences of failing to carry it out were so clearly disadvantageous that limited discussion or warning of the possible harmful side effects might be appropriate. But at the other end of the scale, to the extent to which the surgery was elective, the obligation to warn of possible harmful consequences may be more stringent and onerous. The test of negligence for failing to warn of risks was the same as that applied to allegations of negligence in treatment and diagnosis. But where a doctor sought to establish that the warning he gave complied with

7–041

---

[117] As, e.g., in *Hassan v Minister for Health (No.2)* [2008] WASCA 149 where during an induction of labour following a foetal death in utero the claimant experienced a massive haemorrhage and the doctors performed a hysterectomy. The claimant complained that she had not given her consent for the hysterectomy. The Western Australia Court of Appeal held that consent was not needed: "The haemorrhage which followed was in the nature of a major clinical emergency. No consent could be obtained at that point from the patient to proceed to conduct an hysterectomy nor was it necessary. ... the prime consideration was the conservation of the patient's life. In those circumstances, where there is no opportunity to avoid the procedure, consent of that kind is not necessary" (at [211]).

[118] [1965] N.Z.L.R. 191, NZCA.

[119] [1965] N.Z.L.R. 191 at 198; see also per Turner J at 205. Prior to changes introduced to New Zealand's system of no-fault accident compensation in 1992 it was uncertain whether the non-disclosure of risks of treatment fell within the scheme. It is now clear that a negligent failure to obtain informed consent would be covered by the no-fault compensation scheme. See para.1–038.

[120] [1992] 1 I.R. 496, Supreme Court of Ireland.

[121] [1992] 1 I.R. 496 at 510.

general practice, it may be, and certainly in relation to very clearly elective surgery such as a vasectomy, that the court would more readily come to the conclusion that the extent of the warning given or omitted contained inherent defects which ought to have been obvious to any person giving the matter due consideration than it could do in the case of complicated medical or surgical procedures.

7–042   In *Fitzpatrick v White*[122] the patient underwent elective eye surgery to remove a cosmetic defect (a squint). He subsequently had some double vision and headaches, attributable to a rare (less than 1 per cent) complication (slippage of the medial rectus muscle). The patient claimed that in a conversation with the surgeon 30 minutes before the surgery he had not been informed about the risks. The trial judge found that he had been given an appropriate warning, and, on appeal, the patient argued that it was negligent to leave the discussion of risks until just before the surgery when he had already committed himself to having the surgery (though the claimant's evidence at trial was that had he been informed of the risk he would have walked out of the hospital). The Supreme Court of Ireland, clearly having significant doubts about the claimant's credibility, held that the surgeon had not been negligent, in the absence of any evidence that the claimant had actually been disadvantaged by the lateness of the warning or that he was unable to assimilate or properly understand what he was being told. However, in other cases where a warning was given late in the day, particularly where the surgery was elective surgery, "the outcome might well be different". Kearns J, giving the judgment of the Court, stated a clear preference for the prudent patient standard. The "patient centred" approach had been adopted "in virtually every major common law jurisdiction", even, suggested his Honour, in England. This observation was based on the judgment of Lord Woolf M.R. in *Pearce v United Bristol Healthcare NHS Trust* suggesting that if there was a significant risk which would affect the judgment of a reasonable patient, then in the normal course, a reasonable doctor would inform the patient of that significant risk.[123] Kearns J adopted this test, which was, said his Honour, "not dissimilar" from the test adopted in *Rogers v Whitaker*.[124] The words "significant risk" and "material risk" were to be treated as interchangeable. The situation would be different where the doctor was aware that the particular patient, if warned of the risk, would be likely to attach significance to it where another patient might not. The difference was not spelled out by the court but, presumably, where the doctor is aware of the patient's specific concerns, this would increase the duty of disclosure.[125]

---

[122] [2007] IESC 51; [2008] 3 I.R. 551, Supreme Court of Ireland.
[123] See para.7–012, above.
[124] See para.7–034, above.
[125] The Supreme Court came close to adopting a prudent patient standard in *Fitzpatrick v White* and if the issue were to come before it again the tenor of the judgments suggests that the Court would take the next step from *Pearce* to *Montgomery*.

(e) What constitutes a material risk after *Montgomery*?

What, then, constitutes a material risk? Until a body of case law has built up it   **7–043**
will be difficult to predict how the courts will approach the assessment of
material risk. Cases from jurisdictions such as Canada and Australia that have
been using the prudent patient standard for many years may be illustrative of
what could be considered to be a material risk; and cases which pre-date
Montgomery in which claimants have succeeded in establishing a breach of duty
applying the *Bolam* test may also provide some guidance, on the basis that it
seems extremely unlikely that a claimant would succeed applying a prudent
doctor standard but, on the same facts, would fail applying a prudent patient
standard.

(i) The context of the risk

Even under *Sidaway* there were limits to the medical profession's discretion to   **7–044**
withhold information. Thus, Lord Bridge cited *Reibl v Hughes*,[126] in which there
was a 4 per cent risk of death and a 10 per cent risk of stroke in the context of an
operation intended to remove the risk of stroke, as an example of a case where a
court could reasonably conclude that the disclosure of the risk was so obviously
necessary to an informed choice on the part of the patient that no reasonably
prudent doctor would fail to make it, notwithstanding the practice of the
profession. In such a case, where there was a substantial risk of grave adverse
consequences, a doctor could hardly fail to appreciate the necessity for an
appropriate warning.[127] In making this judgment there was an interrelationship
between the chances of a successful outcome and the inherent risks of the
procedure.[128] Similarly, there was a relationship between the nature and severity
of the potential risks and the purpose of the procedure. In the case of minor
surgical operations the court could reasonably require doctors to disclose lower
degrees of risk, whether measured by incidence or severity. Conversely, the more
serious the patient's medical condition the greater the level of risk the doctor
could reasonably omit to disclose. Thus, in the Court of Appeal in *Sidaway*
Browne-Wilkinson LJ commented that:

> "… the materiality of any particular risk must in the ordinary case depend on the relationship
> between the object to be achieved by the operation and the nature of the risks involved. If there
> is a ½ per cent risk of total paralysis, that might well be a material risk in the context of an
> operation designed to get rid of a minor discomfort but not in the context of an operation
> required to avoid death. The decision as to the materiality of a risk does not depend simply on
> the difference between an elective operation and an essential operation: it depends on the
> balancing of benefits and risks."[129]

---

[126] (1980) 114 D.L.R. (3d) 1.

[127] *Sidaway v Bethlem Royal Hospital Governors* [1985] A.C. 871 at 900.

[128] "An operation with a very high success rate and a very low risk of paralysis may, rationally, be
accepted much more readily than one where the prospects of success were more circumscribed,
though the risk of paralysis was still slight", per Kirby P in *Ellis v Wallsend District Hospital* (1989)
17 N.S.W.L.R. 553 at 561, NSWCA.

[129] *Sidaway v Bethlem Royal Hospital Governors* [1984] Q.B. 493 at 521–522. See also *H. v Royal
Alexandra Hospital for Children* [1990] 1 Med. L.R. 297 at 324, NSWSC, per Badgery-Parker J: "The

7–045   There is no reason to think that this type of analysis will not continue to apply to the assessment of what constitutes a material risk under the prudent patient standard. In *Montgomery* the Supreme Court accepted that the issue does not turn simply on the likelihood of the risk materialising:

> "...the assessment of whether a risk is material cannot be reduced to percentages. The significance of a given risk is likely to reflect a variety of factors besides its magnitude: for example, the nature of the risk, the effect which its occurrence would have upon the life of the patient, the importance to the patient of the benefits sought to be achieved by the treatment, the alternatives available, and the risks involved in those alternatives. The assessment is therefore fact-sensitive, and sensitive also to the characteristics of the patient."[130]

7–046   Despite the caveat that the question of whether a risk is material cannot be reduced to percentages there is a strong temptation for courts to focus on the likely incidence of the risk, i.e. how probable it is that the risk will materialise, and to dismiss as immaterial those perceived to have a low incidence. In *A v East Kent Hospitals University NHS Foundation Trust*[131] the claimant mother brought an action for the costs of raising a disabled child who had been born with a chromosomal abnormality. She alleged that following a scan at 28 weeks' gestation the defendants should have alerted her to the possibility that the low growth of the foetus was possibly due to a chromosomal abnormality, and that if she had been alerted to this she would have had an amniocentesis which would have confirmed the condition and that she would then have chosen to have a termination of the pregnancy. Dingemans J held, on the evidence, that the risk was 1 in 1,000 which was "theoretical, negligible or background".[132] If the risk had been between 1 per cent and 3 per cent the judge considered that it should have been raised with the mother, but a reasonable patient in the claimant's position "would have attached no significance to risks at this background level".[133] Although *Montgomery* affirmed the importance of patient autonomy it

---

greater the chance that the risk will eventuate, the more obviously will disclosure be necessary, even though the consequences of the happening of the risk may not be enormous. Conversely, where the possible consequence is disastrous, disclosure may be 'obviously necessary' even though the risk may be quantified as tiny."

[130] *Montgomery v Lanarkshire Health Board* [2015] UKSC 11; [2015] A.C. 1430 at [89]. Note that there is an argument that the Supreme Court elided the risks to the mother and the risks to the child in *Montgomery* (see at [94]). The appeal was concerned with the child's claim. The risk to the child was a 0.2 per cent risk of brachial plexus injury and a less than 0.1 per cent risk of cerebral palsy or death. The Supreme Court considered that the lower courts had been wrong to focus on these risks and ignore the 9 per cent to 10 per cent risk of shoulder dystocia occurring and the consequent harm to the mother. As Lord Stewart pointed out in *Clark v Greater Glasgow Health Board* [2016] CSOH 24 at [31]: "The matter might be tested by figuring a case in which there is a high risk to the baby and a trivial risk to the mother but only the mother is hurt. There may well be an argument for treating the composite risk as the relevant risk in mother-and-baby cases. The Supreme Court does not, however and with respect, provide a rationale for doing so." See R. Bagshaw, "Modernising the doctor's duty to disclose risks of treatment" (2016) 132 L.Q.R. 182 at 186 making the same point: "the claim was on behalf of the injured child, but was being anchored to unreasonable endangerment of his mother. (In England, Wales and Northern Ireland the phrasing of s.1 of the Congenital Disabilities (Civil Liability) Act 1976 might iron away this wrinkle, but this Act does not extend to Scotland.)"
[131] [2015] EWHC 1038 (QB); [2015] Med. L.R. 262.
[132] [2015] EWHC 1038 (QB); [2015] Med. L.R. 262 at [84].
[133] [2015] EWHC 1038 (QB); [2015] Med. L.R. 262 at [89].

was "not authority for the proposition that medical practitioners need to warn about risks which are theoretical and not material".[134]

In *Tasmin v Barts Health NHS Trust*[135] Jay J eschewed describing a risk of 1 in 1000 as "theoretical, negligible or background". Whilst agreeing with Dingemans J that such a risk did not have to be discussed with the parents, he preferred to say simply that "the risk was too low to be material". In *Tasmin* the risk in issue was the risk of permanent neurological damage to the child as a result of hypoxic insult during its delivery and the question was whether the defendant obstetrician should have proceeded to Caesarean section in the light of a pathological CTG trace. It was accepted that the obstetrician had misinterpreted the trace as being suspicious rather than pathological. The Royal College of Obstetricians and Gynaecologists advised that the appropriate response to a pathological trace was to obtain a foetal blood sample, and Jay J held that if this had been done when it should have been done the result would probably have been in the normal range with the consequence that the obstetrician would have recommended continuing with the labour rather than a Caesarean section, and the parents would have accepted this advice. In response to the argument that the parents were not informed about 1 in 1000 risk of permanent neurological damage by continuing with the labour Jay J held that this was not a material risk: "the relevant risk was so low that it was below that borderline."[136] The focus here is clearly on the likely incidence of the risk, and not on the severity of the damage to the child (she suffered a severe brain injury and was seriously disabled). Although the claimant argued that the risk was material because, if it occurred, the effect it would have on the life of the mother and child would be "massive", Jay J appears not to have attempted to weigh the potential severity of the resulting damage against the likelihood of the risk materialising. This may have been because a ruling that the risk was a material risk would have been inconsistent with national guidance from the RCOG and contrary to standard obstetric practice, and the option of a Caesarean section would have to be offered in every similar case even where the result of the foetal blood sample was normal.[137] *Montgomery* could not be used to trump the RCOG guidance and the expert evidence.[138]

7–047

---

[134] [2015] EWHC 1038 (QB); [2015] Med. L.R. 262 at [90]. In comparison, when someone is expecting a good outcome from a chance event it would seem that individuals are willing to take chances on very low odds. For example the chance of winning £100 on the national lottery is approximately 1 in 2180 and the chance of winning the jackpot is 1 in 45 million (*http://playlotto. org.uk/lottery/uklottery_odds.html*). Whether purchasers of lottery tickets are acting as objectively reasonable consumers is, perhaps, another matter.

[135] [2015] EWHC 3135 (QB) at [118].

[136] It will be recalled that In *Pearce v United Bristol Healthcare NHS Trust* [1999] P.I.Q.R. P53, para.7–012, the Court of Appeal held that there was no duty to inform the mother of the 0.1 per cent to 0.2 per cent risk of stillbirth because this did not amount to a "significant risk".

[137] [2015] EWHC 3135 (QB) at [116].

[138] There is more than a hint here of seeking to protect the practices of the medical profession at the expense of a paternalistic view of patients' likely response to being given information about risks. Jay J noted that the reason for the RCOG guidance was that the risks were sufficiently low that it was not regarded as mandatory to spell them out "to labouring mothers and/or to confuse them by routinely offering a [Caesarean section]." The obstetrician in *Montgomery* also had a practice of not informing diabetic pregnant women of the risks of shoulder dystocia because she considered that if she did so

7–048 On the other hand, in *Thefaut v Johnston*[139] Green J focused particularly on the level of the risks that the patient was not informed about, though these were considerably greater than in *A v East Kent Hospitals University NHS Foundation Trust* or *Tasmin v Barts Health NHS Trust*. Having had a conversation with the claimant about the possibility of surgery to alleviate back pain and leg pain, the defendant wrote to the claimant advising her to proceed with the surgery and setting out some of the risks involved. In the conversation the defendant had said that there was a high probability that without surgery the problem would, in any event, resolve in 12 months' time, but made no reference to this in the letter, an omission that Green J considered risked confusing the patient into thinking that because it had not been mentioned as part of the formal advice it was of no real significance or had been overtaken by the formal written advice. The defendant did not tell the claimant that there was an inherent risk of up to 5 per cent that non-negligently performed surgery could cause an exacerbation of her condition. The chances of resolving or improving the claimant's leg pain were about 85 per cent, and the chances of removing or improving the back pain were about 50 per cent, but in the letter the defendant said that the chances of eradicating back pain were not as high as that for the leg (which were said to be at least 90 per cent, though the actual chance was 85 per cent) but were not far off. The defendant told the claimant that the risk of damage to a nerve during surgery was "exceedingly low"; it was actually 1 per cent. Green J concluded, perhaps unsurprisingly, that the letter was a material overstatement of both the risks involved and the chances of a successful outcome. The difference between "at least 90 per cent" and 85 per cent was material because 85 per cent:

> "...is statistically different in a significant manner from an indication of prospects which uses 90 per cent as a minima. The difference between 85 per cent and (say) 95 per cent is 10 per cent which is a potentially important difference."[140]

The failure to mention the up to 5 per cent chance of the procedure causing an exacerbation of the condition was also material. Most significant for Green J, was the cumulative effect of the misrepresentations about the risks, the overestimate of the chances of improvement to the claimant's back pain, and the context that the alternative option of doing nothing would probably have led to a resolution of the claimant's pain in 12 months.[141] A fully informed reasonable patient with the claimant's condition would have declined the surgery or at least deferred it pending a second opinion.

7–049 **Anaesthetic and infection risks** Under the *Bolam* test for the standard of disclosure it was possible to identify some specific matters that either did or did

---

they would all request Caesarean section, but as the Supreme Court concluded, that was a judgment to be made by the patient, not the doctor, albeit with appropriate advice from the doctor.

[139] [2017] EWHC 497 (QB); [2017] Med. L.R. 319.

[140] [2017] EWHC 497 (QB); [2017] Med. L.R. 319 at [73].

[141] [2017] EWHC 497 (QB); [2017] Med. L.R. 319 at [74]: "In particular a combination of a 50:50 chance of success in relation to eradication of back pain in conjunction to a 5 per cent chance of making things materially worse is highly material when compared and contrasted with the counterfactual of no operation and a recovery trajectory of up to 12 months and gradually receding pain."

not fall within the doctor's duty to disclose information. In practice it was easier to identify the information that did not need to be disclosed as opposed to that which ought to have been disclosed. So, it was said that there is no obligation to inform a patient about the risk of death from general anaesthetic,[142] nor about other everyday risks that exist in all surgery, such as bleeding, pain, scars from an incision, or the risk of infection in any surgical procedure, because everyone is expected to know about them.[143] However, in light of the patient-centred approach to information disclosure espoused in *Montgomery v Lanarkshire Health Board*[144] this view is open to debate. Patients may well be aware in general terms that there are risks associated with a general anaesthetic or a risk of contracting an infection following surgery, but not have a clue as to how likely the risks are to materialise or how serious the consequences could be. Who is to say whether the reasonable patient would or would not regard such risks as material? In any event, these risks are likely to vary with the individual circumstances of the patient, such as the patient's age, whether they are overweight, or whether their immune system is compromised in some way. The particular circumstances of the patient may make the risk from anaesthetic or the risk of infection very material indeed.

Other risks There is no duty to advise a patient of possible alternative diagnoses which are reasonably not suspected.[145] Doctors are not under a duty to tell patients that if they are negligent in performing an operation they will cause damage,[146] and the negligent omission to perform the third stage of a three-stage operation does not mean that there has been a failure to disclose the material risks

7–050

---

[142] *Sidaway v Bethlem Royal Hospital Governors* [1984] Q.B. 493 at 522, per Browne-Wilkinson LJ: "It is of course obvious that the doctor is not under any duty give information as to the ordinary risks normally attendant on any operation"; *Sidaway v Bethlem Royal Hospital Governors* [1985] A.C. 871 at 897, per Lord Bridge; cf. Lord Diplock [1985] A.C. 871 at 894; *Considine v Camp Hill Hospital* (1982) 133 D.L.R. (3d) 11 at 39, NSSC. For consideration of consent to, and the disclosure of the risks of, anaesthesia see Nunn (1996) 2 Clinical Risk 74.

[143] *White v Turner* (1981) 120 D.L.R. (3d) 269 at 285, per Linden J, Ont HC; aff'd (1982) 12 D.L.R. (4th) 319, Ont CA. A failure to mention statistics should not be a factor in deciding whether the duty to inform has been breached: *Reibl v Hughes* (1980) 114 D.L.R. (3d) 1 at 13. In some circumstances certain infection risks, such as the risk of contracting AIDS from contaminated blood products, should be disclosed: see *H. v Royal Alexandra Hospital for Children* [1990] 1 Med. L.R. 297 at 324, NSWSC, though the action failed on causation, since, given the balance of risk of infection compared with the risk to the patient, who was a haemophiliac, of not having the treatment the doctors would have gone ahead with the transfusions even if informed of the risk of infection, and the parents would also have given their consent.

[144] [2015] UKSC 11; [2015] A.C. 1430.

[145] *Meiklejohn v St George's Healthcare NHS Trust* [2014] EWCA Civ 120; [2014] Med. L.R. 122 at [62].

[146] "The fundamental assumption is that he knows his job and will do it properly", per Bristow J in *Chatterton v Gerson* [1981] Q.B. 432 at 444; *Holmes v Board of Hospital Trustees of the City of London* (1977) 81 D.L.R. (3d) 67 at 83, Ont HC; *MacDonald v Ross* (1983) 24 C.C.L.T. 242 at 248; *Bloodworth v The South Coast Regional Health Authority (t/a Gold Coast Hospital)* [2004] NSWSC 234 at [142] (no duty to warn of the risk of a rare injury, since the injury was not an inherent risk of the surgery, but rather the result of the surgeon's negligence).

of an operation which omitted the third, crucial stage of the procedure.[147] There is no duty for doctors to disclose their own health status where it does not affect their ability to undertake the treatment.[148] Nor does the duty of disclosure prevent doctors emphasising the need for surgery if that is the surgeon's firm view as to the best course of action:

> "If a doctor, who thinks surgery is strongly called for, tells a patient this and the patient responds, 'do you think an operation is necessary?' the doctor is not to be criticised if he responds, 'well yes, I do,' even if there is some non-operational alternative, so long as the existence and some idea of the merits of the alternative have been conveyed. Nor do I think he was wrong strongly to articulate what he saw as the disadvantages of not operating."[149]

Of course, this is subject to the duty to disclose material risks, and a doctor who minimised the risks in an attempt to persuade the patient to accept a particular treatment may be found to be in breach of duty.[150] The patient should not be "pressurised" to accept the doctor's recommendation. Rather, there should be a dispassionate discussion of the risks and potential consequences.[151]

7–051   A patient is probably entitled to be told that a proposed operation is not in the mainstream of treatment. That was the position under *Sidaway*[152] and it is difficult to see that it should be any different when considering what constitutes a material risk. It has been said in Canada that doctors are not under a duty to inform patients that they are inexperienced in performing a particular procedure,[153] though this is not always the case if the doctor's inexperience raises the risk of harm to the patient significantly.[154]

---

[147] *Correia v University Hospital of North Staffordshire NHS Trust* [2017] EWCA Civ 356; [2017] Med. L.R. 292, a case where there was "no justifiable complaint about the process of consultation and consent up to the moment when the operation began". The negligent omission of the third stage did not negate the patient's consent (at [26]).

[148] *Halkyard v Mathew* [1999] 5 W.W.R. 643; aff'd 2001 ABCA 67; [2001] 7 W.W.R. 26, Alta CA; para.7–033.

[149] *Markose v Epsom & St Helier NHS Trust* [2004] EWHC 3130 (QB); [2005] Lloyd's Rep. Med. 334 at [37] per Judge Harris QC sitting as a Deputy Judge of the High Court. See also *Jones v North West SHA* [2010] EWHC 178 (QB); [2010] Med. L.R. 90 at [59] per Nicol J: the duty to inform patients of significant risks is "not inconsistent with a practice of doctors giving sometimes very firm advice as to what they thought was in their patients' best interests".

[150] This is possibly what Lord Templeman had in mind in *Sidaway v Bethlem Royal Hospital Governors* [1985] A.C. 871 when he said that said that a doctor has a duty to make a "balanced" judgment about information disclosure. See para.7–008, n.23.

[151] *Montgomery v Lanarkshire Health Board* [2015] UKSC 11; [2015] A.C. 1430 at [103] and [104]. These observations were made in the context of a discussion about causation.

[152] So in *Newbury v Bath District Health Authority* (1998) 47 B.M.L.R. 138 at 150 Ebsworth J said that this would obviously be the case "if it involved a method which was entirely new or even relatively untried. I accept that it would be so if the method had fallen out of use because it had been shown to be defective and was not accepted by a responsible body of opinion". However, Ebsworth J held that the evidence in the case had not reached that state, despite the fact that the defendant surgeon had accepted that he was probably the only mainline surgeon using the particular method by 1991.

[153] *Holmes v Board of Hospital Trustees of the City of London* (1977) 81 D.L.R. (3d) 67 at 83 Ont HC; *Huisman v MacDonald* 2007 ONCA 391; (2007) 280 D.L.R. (4th) 1.

[154] *Anderson v Queen Elizabeth II Health Sciences Centre* 2012 NSSC 360; (2012) 97 C.C.L.T. (3d) 51 at [316], where Bourgeois J considered that given the seriousness of the risks associated with the procedure undertaken (insertion of a catheter into an internal jugular vein) the claimant was entitled to be advised of the defendants' degree of experience with the procedure; *Bloodworth v The South Coast*

Alternatives to the proposed treatment   In *Montgomery* the Supreme Court   **7–052**
made it clear that part of the doctor's duty of disclosure extends to disclosing the
existence of any reasonable alternative or variant treatments and the risks
involved in those alternatives.[155] The issue arose in *Birch v University College
London Hospital NHS Foundation Trust*[156] where the claimant underwent a
cerebral angiogram as a diagnostic procedure. She was informed of the 1 per cent
risk of stroke associated with the angiogram and signed a consent form to the
procedure. Unfortunately, following complications she suffered a stroke. The
claimant had not been informed about the comparative risks of the alternative
option of having a non-invasive MRI scan, followed by watchful conservative
treatment. Cranston J held that the duty to inform a patient of the significant risks
would not be discharged unless she was made aware that fewer, or no risks, were
associated with another procedure:

> "...unless the patient is informed of the comparative risks of different procedures she will not
> be in a position to give her fully informed consent to one procedure rather than another."[157]

The fact that the risk associated with the catheter angiography was small was
irrelevant, given that there was no risk of stroke at all from the MRI. The
claimant should have been given a "full and fair" explanation of the risks of both
procedures and why the doctors preferred the catheter angiography.[158]

Regional Health Authority (t/a Gold Coast Hospital) [2004] NSWSC 234 at [152] (where the
evidence was that a surgeon's inexperience in performing laparoscopic surgery specifically increased
the existing risk of that form of surgery, and the risk should have been disclosed). Note also the
curious County Court decision of *Jones v Royal Devon and Exeter NHS Foundation Trust* unreported
22 September 2015 (Exeter County Court) where on the day of the surgery the claimant became aware
that her operation would not be performed by the experienced consultant that she had wanted to
operate but by a more junior surgeon. She felt unable to pull out at such a late stage. The surgery was
not performed negligently but an inherent risk materialised resulting in nerve root damage to her
spine. It was held that the defendants were in breach of duty, apparently on the basis that the claimant
had not been informed who would be operating on her, although she had signed a consent form stating
that the hospital could not guarantee who would perform the surgery. There had not been breach of a
duty to warn the claimant of the risks, but there was an infringement of her right to make an informed
choice as to whether and if so when and *by whom* to be operated on (citing Lord Hope in *Chester v
Afshar* [2004] UKHL 41; [2005] 1 A.C. 134 at [86]; see paras 7–105 et seq.). The surgeon's
inexperience was relevant to one aspect of causation, in that the judge held that the damage would
probably not have occurred if the operation had been performed by the experienced consultant since
there was expert evidence that "experience counts" in reducing the risks of this particular type of
surgery.
[155] *Montgomery v Lanarkshire Health Board* [2015] UKSC 11; [2015] A.C. 1430 at [87] and [89].
[156] [2008] EWHC 2237 (QB); (2008) 104 B.M.L.R. 168.
[157] [2008] EWHC 2237 (QB); (2008) 104 B.M.L.R. 168 at [74]. In *Sem v Mid-Yorkshire Hospitals
NHS Trust* [2005] EWHC 3469 (QB) the claimant underwent a vaginal hysterectomy; the defendants
conceded that the failure to advise the patient about the alternative ways of treating her condition
(surgical and non-surgical) was negligent.
[158] [2008] EWHC 2237 (QB); (2008) 104 B.M.L.R. 168 at [77]. Cranston J added at [78]: "Mrs
Birch's circumstances were unusual. ... Mrs Birch also needed to know there was no risk associated
with this mode of imaging. She needed to know that catheter angiography was more sensitive in
detecting an aneurysm but could not detect cavernous sinus pathology so she would still need an MRI.
She needed to know that while the risk of stroke with catheter angiography was low, there was a slight
increase in risk since she was a poorly controlled, long standing diabetic, with a vascular history.

7–053   In *Meiklejohn v St George's Healthcare NHS Trust*[159] Rafferty LJ appeared to suggest that the approach of Cranston J in *Birch* was confined to the failure to inform the patient about alternative investigations and their risks, "and was not about comparative diagnoses and the risks of different treatments". It is unclear why there should be a difference between investigative procedures and treatments in this respect, and in light of the dicta in *Montgomery* it would seem that the duty to disclose material risks should include disclosing the comparative risks of alternative treatments as well as diagnostic procedures.[160]

7–054   In *Webster v Burton Hospitals NHS Foundation Trust*[161] a consultant obstetrician was negligent in failing to note anomalies on an ultrasound scan and failing to arrange further scans when it was clear that the foetus was small for the gestational age. The issue was what would the further scans have shown and what should have happened as a consequence. The mother was admitted to hospital the day before the due date feeling unwell. The child was delivered 11 days after the due date but had sustained brain damage in the period of two to three days before birth. It was claimed that the mother should have been offered the option of induction of the birth, which she would have accepted, and this would have avoided the child's brain damage. The trial judge, in a judgment that pre-dated the decision of the Supreme Court in *Montgomery*, applied the *Bolam* test and held that a reasonable body of obstetricians would have followed the conservative line of treatment in not proceeding to an induction and that this course of action was neither irrational or illogical (and thus was *Bolitho*-compliant). The Court of Appeal allowed the appeal on the basis that, following *Montgomery*, this was no longer sufficient. In circumstances where there were two options (to take the conservative approach and let nature take its course or induce the birth) the obstetrician's duty was to discuss the options and the risks associated with each course of action with the patient. The child's mother should have been told that there was "emerging but recent and incomplete material showing increased risks of delaying labour in cases with this combination of features".[162] If she had had that information she would have wanted to be delivered on the due date "even if the information had been couched in terms of contrary arguments in favour of non-intervention", and this would have avoided the child's injuries.[163]

Perhaps she should also have been reminded that the most likely cause of her troubles was a benign ischaemic lesion of the type she had suffered previously, and which had spontaneously resolved itself."

[159] [2014] EWCA Civ 120; [2014] Med. L.R. 122; (2014) 137 B.M.L.R. 56.

[160] The duty to disclose alternative treatments is subject, of course, to questions of causation. If the failure to inform the patient of alternatives made no difference to the outcome because the patient would have accepted the recommended treatment the claim will fail: *Barrett v Sandwell and West Birmingham Hospitals NHS Trust* [2015] EWHC 2627 (QB); (2015) 147 B.M.L.R. 151 at [163]–[164].

[161] [2017] EWCA Civ 62; [2017] Med. L.R. 113; (2017) 154 B.M.L.R. 129; discussed by N. Tavares [2017] J.P.I.L. C93.

[162] [2017] EWCA Civ 62; [2017] Med. L.R. 113; (2017) 154 B.M.L.R. 129 at [40].

[163] See also *R v Lanarkshire Health Board* [2016] CSOH 133; 2016 G.W.D. 31–556 where an inexperienced obstetrician failed to follow national guidelines that delivery of a child ought to be expedited when there were indicators of acute foetal compromise. Lord Brailsford said, at [133], that: "at this stage there were two alternative approaches to the management of KR's labour, first to proceed to immediate assisted vaginal delivery or, second, to obtain foetal blood samples and,

Disclosure of treatment options includes the risks of non-intervention   As   **7–055**
the Canadian cases make clear,[164] disclosing the material risks of treatment and
their alternatives includes giving the patient information about the prospects for
recovery, and the risks, by not intervening.[165] It is not uncommon for the
appropriate medical response to be to "wait and see", particularly if the patient's
diagnosis is unclear.[166] This may give rise to certain practical problems for a
doctor in assessing which risks of the various options should be disclosed. Where
there is a recommendation to wait and see if a problem resolves itself without
intervention :

> "...must a doctor now identify the further tests or treatments that *could* be commenced
> immediately, and any significant risks that may be associated with a delay?"[167]

Elective and non-elective procedures   The English courts had been reluctant   **7–056**
to accept a distinction between elective and non-elective procedures. For
example, Sir John Donaldson MR said that the distinction was meaningless to a
patient, because all operations are elective: the patient always has a choice.[168]
Whilst on one level this is patently true, the concept of an elective medical
procedure distinguishes those situations where the patient's condition is such that
there is in reality very little choice (all the evidence points to the treatment being
accepted, possibly in an emergency[169]) from those where the options are more
evenly balanced and there is time for considered reflection. In Canada, for
example, cosmetic surgery has been treated as elective, requiring a greater degree
of information disclosure about inherent risks.[170] The point was made very clear
by McCarthy J in *Walsh v Family Planning Services Ltd*:

---

providing these were satisfactory, proceed to stage two of delivery. In my view these alternatives
should have been explained to KR and the risks associated with each also explained. Had this been
done KR would have been provided with sufficient information to permit her to make an informed
choice as to which course she opted to take. The fact that this approach was not taken renders this case
... fairly within the ratio of *Montgomery*."
[164] See para.7–029.
[165] In *Tasmin v Barts Health NHS Trust* [2015] EWHC 3135 (QB) the defendants argued that
Montgomery did not apply where the doctor is not recommending *treatment*. Jay J held that the
relevant treatment was the recommendation to carry on with labour rather than the option of a
Caesarean section and that the duty to disclose material risks would apply in that situation. It will be
recalled that *Pearce v United Bristol Healthcare NHS Trust* [1999] P.I.Q.R. P53, see para.7–012,
involved a case of non-intervention (leaving the pregnancy to take its course rather than inducing
labour or proceeding to Caesarean section) but the Court of Appeal did not consider that there was no
duty to inform the mother of the risks of stillbirth for this reason; rather a risk of 0.1 per cent to 0.2 per
cent did not amount to a "significant risk" that had to be disclosed.
[166] See para.4–104.
[167] R. Bagshaw, "Modernising the doctor's duty to disclose risks of treatment" (2016) 132 L.Q.R. 182
at 185. The author notes that: "The practical problem here may be that 'non-treatment' is frequently
recommended where there is considerable uncertainty about the cause of a patient's problems, the
severity of any underlying illness, and hence the prognosis, which makes it very difficult to catalogue
and discuss all the possibilities and how, if at all, delay may impinge on their treatment."
[168] *Sidaway v Bethlem Royal Hospital Governors* [1984] Q.B. 493 at 514.
[169] See *Hills v Potter* [1983] 3 All E.R. 716 at 718 where Hirst J observed that it was common ground
in that case that it was not an emergency procedure "but was 'elective' in character, so that it was for
the plaintiff to choose whether or not to undergo it."
[170] *White v Turner* (1981) 120 D.L.R. (3d) 269, Ont HC; aff'd (1982) 12 D.L.R. (4th) 319, Ont CA;
cf. *Gold v Haringey Health Authority* [1988] Q.B. 481 at 489.

"All surgery, in a sense, is elective although the election may have to be implied from the circumstances rather than determined as express ... A patient's condition may be such as to demand surgical intervention as the only hope for survival. Such may be called non-elective surgery. The patient given the choice between enduring pain and having limb replacement surgery or fusion surgery may technically be electing as between the pain and the surgery but the election may be more apparent than real. An extreme of elective surgery would be what is purely cosmetic—simply to improve the natural appearance rather than to remedy the physical results of injury or disease. Even it may have an element of quasi-medical care because of the psychological reaction of the patient to personal appearance. A like argument may be advanced in respect of contraceptive surgery, male or female. Such surgery does not have a direct effect on the health or well being of the patient nor in prolongation of life; it may alleviate marital stress or other domestic pressure and in that sense be therapeutic. Essentially, however, it is for the improvement of the sex life of the couple concerned."[171]

O'Flaherty J commented that where elective surgery which is not essential to health or bodily wellbeing is undertaken, if there is a risk—however exceptional or remote—of grave consequences involving severe pain stretching for an appreciable time into the future and involving the possibility of further operative procedures, the exercise of the duty of care owed by the defendant required that the possible consequences should be explained in the clearest language to the claimant.[172]

7–057 This statement was made in the context of a test for disclosure based on the *Bolam* test, but it applies with even greater force to a test based on the prudent patient. It is arguable that the objective reasonable patient would take into account not only the incidence and severity of any risk, should it materialise, but also the context in which the issue arises, so that procedures which are clearly "elective", as understood by a reasonable patient, will be on a different footing from those where the patient in reality has little option. At its most obvious, an elective procedure such as cosmetic surgery to improve one's appearance should require significantly greater disclosure of the attendant risks than surgery to remove an appendix which is about to rupture, threatening the patient's life.

(ii) The individual patient's knowledge

7–058 **Patient who prefers not to know about the risks** If patients make it clear that they do not want to know about the inherent risks of treatment there is no duty to insist on providing the information.[173] This was the position under *Sidaway* and

---

[171] [1992] 1 I.R. 496 at 517–8, Supreme Court of Ireland.

[172] [1992] 1 I.R. 496 at 535; see also per Egan J at 537. In *Geoghegan v Harris* [2000] 3 I.R. 536 Kearns J regarded *Walsh v Family Planning Services Ltd* as requiring the disclosure of *any* risk which carries the possibility of grave consequences, irrespective of its statistical frequency, in cases of elective surgery. Accordingly, it was held that there was an obligation to warn of a very remote risk of developing neuropathic pain in the patient's lower jaw following surgery for a dental implant, even though all the medical experts were of the view that no warning was necessary. The claim failed, however, on causation.

[173] *Sidaway v Bethlem Royal Hospital Governors* [1984] Q.B. 493 at 521, per Browne-Wilkinson LJ. Sir John Donaldson MR, at 513, suggested that the doctor must identify the patient's "true wishes" and distinguish between patients who want information and patients who are only seeking reassurance.

remains the case after *Montgomery*.[174] In practice it would seem unlikely (though, of course, not impossible) that patients who had very clearly expressed a wish not to be told about the risks of treatment would then litigate on the basis that they should have been informed about material risks. The more likely situation is that a doctor misinterprets the somewhat diffident behaviour of a patient and concludes, incorrectly, that the patient did not want to have information about risks. The issue will turn on the resolution of the factual dispute as to what was said, by whom, and whether it was reasonable for the doctor to have reached that conclusion. It must have been "clear that [the patient] would prefer not to discuss the matter"; ambiguity will not suffice to excuse the failure to disclose the risks that would normally be considered to be significant to a reasonable patient.

Information from other sources   It is not necessarily negligent to omit to give patients information that they have already received from another doctor, since the issue is whether the patient has sufficient information to make an "informed consent", not where the information came from.[175] In theory this could mean that information obtained from any source might be sufficient for the patient to be adequately informed. Many patients now research their own medical conditions on the internet and may well have considerable knowledge about the potential risks of treatment. However, it would be unwise for a doctor to rely on a patient's research as meeting the duty of disclosure. The problems with such a course were outlined by the Saskatchewan Court of Appeal in *Prevost v Ali*:

> "The determination of whether a patient is properly informed by a non-medical source will depend on the circumstances of the particular case. … Internet research can be problematic. It is not always complete or reliable. [The claimant] has a Grade VIII education. There was no evidence before the Court as to the quality of the internet material that he reviewed, and no assurance that what had been reviewed had been fully understood. Further, it is one thing to understand the risk, and an entirely different matter to understand the consequences of the risk should the potential problem come to pass."[176]

Moreover, the patient's research may have focused on one form of treatment but not considered the alternatives and their risks.

Correcting misleading information provided by others   In *Wyatt v Curtis*[177] a general practitioner who had negligently failed to warn the claimant about the more serious risks posed to her unborn child of her contracting chickenpox sought contribution from a hospital doctor, contending that when the hospital

7–059

7–060

---

[174] *Montgomery v Lanarkshire Health Board* [2015] UKSC 11; [2015] A.C. 1430 at [85]: "A person can of course decide that she does not wish to be informed of risks of injury (just as a person may choose to ignore the information leaflet enclosed with her medicine); and a doctor is not obliged to discuss the risks inherent in treatment with a person who makes it clear that she would prefer not to discuss the matter."

[175] *Olbourne v Wolf* [2004] NSWCA 141 at [44]; *Davidson v Connaught Laboratories* (1980) 14 C.C.L.T. 251 at 272, Ont HC. On the other hand, the second doctor may not know precisely what was said to the patient nor whether she understood the information, so it may be a risky strategy for a doctor to rely on what has been said to the patient by others.

[176] 2011 SKCA 50; [2011] 9 W.W.R. 494; (2011) 84 C.C.L.T. (3d) 32 at [38].

[177] [2003] EWCA Civ 1779.

doctor saw the claimant a month later he had also failed to warn the claimant of the same risk. The Court of Appeal rejected the argument that it was incumbent upon the hospital doctor to ascertain what advice the claimant had received and, if necessary, to correct it. The claimant had asked the general practitioner whether the baby would be alright, but no such question was put to the hospital doctor (and it was probably "the false sense of security created by [the general practitioner's] answer which led Miss Wyatt not to ask [the hospital doctor] the same question"[178]). In the absence of any submission that the hospital doctor had a duty to volunteer the risk to the patient the case against him failed. Kay LJ said that:

> "... whatever the precise legal test, I would be reluctant in the extreme to hold that there was any greater duty on the second doctor, whatever his or her status, to do any more than satisfy himself that a warning had already been given by an apparently competent doctor who ought to have had sufficient expertise to give the necessary advice. I am unpersuaded that it would be negligent not to probe the nature of the advice given in such circumstances, although the position would clearly be different if the patient asked for a further opinion as to the risks."[179]

7–061   *Wyatt v Curtis* is, in effect, concerned with the extent of the duty of a second doctor to warn a patient about risks when the doctor is aware that the patient has already been advised by another doctor. As Schiemann LJ commented, such cases are "extremely fact-sensitive". If the patient had sought further information, the hospital doctor's responsibility would have been to provide it, though as Sedley LJ observed:

> "...there is arguably something unreal about placing the onus of asking upon a patient who may not know that there is anything to ask about."[180]

Moreover, *Wyatt v Curtis* clearly cannot be taken as authority for the proposition that a hospital doctor never has a responsibility to check the advice given by a general practitioner. It was important that, as Kay LJ commented: "the evidence showed that a reasonably competent general practitioner should have been capable of adequately advising a patient on this risk."

7–062   In *Deriche v Ealing Hospital NHS Trust*[181] the claimant contracted chickenpox during her pregnancy, and her general practitioner advised a termination of the pregnancy. The claimant was advised by a consultant obstetrician that the risk to her baby was low or very small. The advice was generally reassuring, and that she would not need a termination of the pregnancy, but the severity of the potential damage to the child was neither discussed nor illustrated. The baby was born with severe disabilities. On the basis of the expert medical evidence, Buckley J held that a consultant obstetrician should have satisfied himself that the patient had fully understood the nature of the risks involved, and not simply assumed from a note in the medical records from the Accident & Emergency department of the hospital that the patient had received "full counselling" about the small risk. He should have discussed both the potential severity of any

---

[178]   [2003] EWCA Civ 1779 at [18] per Sedley LJ.
[179]   [2003] EWCA Civ 1779 at [23].
[180]   [2003] EWCA Civ 1779 at [19].
[181]   [2003] EWHC 3104 (QB).

disabilities to the child and illustrated that by reference to some of the four known problems that could occur. The risk of abnormalities was agreed to be two per cent. Buckley J referred to *Wyatt v Curtis* and the proposition that the hospital doctor did not have a duty to volunteer information about risks to the foetus when he knows that the patient has already received such advice. There were important differences from *Wyatt,* however. First, *Wyatt* involved a birth in 1991 as opposed to a birth in 1996, and the expert evidence to the court was different. Unlike *Wyatt* Buckley J had had a submission ("and very clear expert evidence to support it") that, even without being asked, the second doctor had a duty to tell the patient about the risks. Secondly, the consultation with the consultant was at the patient's insistence, and thirdly the question of termination was raised by the patient herself. Thus:

> "It seems that medical practice and opinion may have developed since *Wyatt*. If that is the case, I endorse it. I do not believe it or my conclusions on it are contrary to Kay LJ's views. The experts in my case were, in effect, simply underlining that the second doctor should satisfy himself or herself, otherwise than by simply taking the earlier notes as read. The wisdom of such a course is demonstrated by the findings of fact in *Wyatt* at paragraph 36 and 39 of the trial judge's judgment cited by Sedley L.J. Simple reliance on another's brief note is calculated to give rise to such misunderstanding."[182]

Moreover, "even a small risk of potentially devastating abnormalities is likely to be regarded as highly material to a pregnant woman".[183] This approach would almost certainly be endorsed applying the prudent patient standard of *Montgomery v Lanarkshire Health Board*.

(iii)   The patient who asks questions

Under *Sidaway* a patient was only entitled to the information that a responsible body of professional opinion considered should be volunteered in the circumstances. For patients who wanted more information the solution seemed to be that they should ask questions. Lord Bridge commented that:

7–063

> "... when questioned specifically by a patient of apparently sound mind about risks involved in a particular treatment proposed, the doctor's duty must, in my opinion, be to answer both truthfully and as fully as the questioner requires."[184]

Both Lord Diplock and Lord Templeman appeared to support this proposition.[185] However, in *Blyth v Bloomsbury Health Authority*[186] the Court of Appeal came to

---

[182] [2003] EWHC 3104 (QB) at [48] per Buckley J.
[183] [2003] EWHC 3104 (QB) at [49]. The claim in *Deriche* failed, however, on causation, since Buckley J concluded that it was probable that, even if fully advised about the risks to the foetus, the claimant would not have opted for a termination of the pregnancy.
[184] *Sidaway v Bethlem Royal Hospital Governors* [1985] A.C. 871 at 898.
[185] [1985] A.C. 871 at 895 and 902 respectively.
[186] (1987) reported at (1989) 5 P.N. 167; [1993] 4 Med. L.R. 151. The case was concerned with whether the claimant was given an adequate warning of the potential side-effects of the contraceptive drug Depo-Provera.

the conclusion that the response of a doctor to questions should also be measured against the *Bolam* test. Kerr LJ referred to the dicta of Lord Bridge and Lord Diplock in *Sidaway* and commented:

"The question of what a plaintiff should be told in answer to a general enquiry cannot be divorced from the *Bolam* test, any more than when no such enquiry is made. In both cases the answer must depend upon the circumstances, the nature of the enquiry, the nature of the information which is available, its reliability, relevance, the condition of the patient, and so forth. Any medical evidence directed to what would be the proper answer in the light of responsible medical opinion and practice—that is to say the *Bolam* test—must in my view equally be placed in the balance in cases where the patient makes some enquiry, in order to decide whether the response was negligent or not ... Indeed I am not convinced that the *Bolam* test is irrelevant even in relation to the question of what answers are properly to be given to specific enquiries, or that Lord Diplock or Lord Bridge intended to hold otherwise."[187]

Blyth came as something of a surprise in light of the dicta in *Sidaway*, though there was an (untested) argument that a doctor who did not answer questions truthfully or fully could be held liable in negligence even where there was a practice within the profession not to make full disclosure, on the basis that disclosure was so obviously necessary to an informed choice on the part of the patient that no reasonably prudent doctor would fail to make it.[188]

7–064　The more fundamental problem with this approach to the whole question of information disclosure, which effectively placed the onus on the patient to ask relevant questions, is that the patient may simply be unaware of what questions to ask, or even that there is a need to ask particular questions. As Sedley LJ commented in *Wyatt v Curtis*: "there is arguably something unreal about placing the onus of asking upon a patient who may not know that there is anything to ask about."[189] In *Rogers v Whitaker*[190] the High Court of Australia noted that the problem with applying the *Bolam* test was that even if a patient asked a direct question about the possible risks or complications, the making of that inquiry

---

[187] (1989) 5 P.N. 167 at 173; [1993] 4 Med. L.R. 151 at 157. Neill LJ agreed that the *Bolam* test should apply. In the Court of Appeal in *Sidaway v Bethlem Royal Hospital Governors* [1984] Q.B. 493 at 513, Sir John Donaldson MR suggested that any response to questions from the patient had to take account of the patient's "true wishes", because the expression of a wish for full information either generally or specifically did not necessarily represent the reality of the patient's state of mind, since the patient might simply be seeking reassurance. See also *F v R* (1983) 33 S.A.S.R. 189 at 192 where the Supreme Court of South Australia accepted that there might be circumstances where reasonable care would justify or even require an evasive or less than fully candid answer even to a direct request, and the doctor may reasonably judge that a patient is merely seeking reassurance; *Smith v Auckland Hospital Board* [1965] N.Z.L.R. 191 at 198, NZCA, per Barrowclough CJ: "What is a proper answer will vary according to the circumstances of each case and it cannot always be said—especially when a patient is asking questions of his doctor—that the doctor is bound to give a full, complete and true answer. Much may depend on the effect of the answer on the health of the patient" (though on the facts of *Smith* the failure of the defendant, in response to a direct question, to inform the patient about the risks of aortography fell below the standard of a reasonably competent practitioner).
[188] *Sidaway v Bethlem Royal Hospital Governors* [1985] A.C. 871 at 900, per Lord Bridge; paras 7–008 and 7–010. See also the GMC guidance, *Consent: patients and doctors making decisions together*, June 2008, para.12: "You must answer patients' questions honestly and, as far as practical, answer as fully as they wish."
[189] [2003] EWCA Civ 1779 at [19].
[190] (1992) 109 A.L.R. 625; [1993] 4 Med. L.R. 79; see also *Chappel v Hart* [1998] HCA 55; (1998) 156 A.L.R. 517; [1999] Lloyd's Rep. Med. 223, HC of Aust.

would logically be of little or no significance; medical opinion would still determine whether the risk should or should not be disclosed and the express desire of the patient for information or advice would not alter that opinion or its legal significance. This provided a strong reason for rejecting the *Bolam* test:

> "The fact that the various majority opinions in *Sidaway*, for example, suggest that, over and above the opinion of a respectable body of medical practitioners, the questions of a patient should truthfully be answered (subject to therapeutic privilege) indicates a shortcoming in the *Bolam* approach. The existence of the shortcoming suggests that an acceptable approach in point of principle should recognise and attach significance to the relevance of a patient's questions. Even if a court were satisfied that a reasonable person in the patient's position would be unlikely to attach significance to a particular risk, the fact that the patient asked questions revealing concern about the risk would make the doctor aware that *this patient* did in fact attach significance to the risk. Subject to the therapeutic privilege, the question would therefore require a truthful answer."[191]

In *Montgomery v Lanarkshire Health Board*[192] the Supreme Court acknowledged the problems that *Sidaway* had created for the patient who asked questions and considered it to be "profoundly unsatisfactory". First, approving Sedley LJ's comment in *Wyatt v Curtis*, placing the onus of asking on a patient who may not know that there is anything to ask about was a reversal of logic: **7–065**

> "...the more a patient knows about the risks she faces, the easier it is for her to ask specific questions about those risks, so as to impose on her doctor a duty to provide information; but it is those who lack such knowledge, and who are in consequence unable to pose such questions and instead express their anxiety in more general terms, who are in the greatest need of information. Ironically, the ignorance which such patients seek to have dispelled disqualifies them from obtaining the information they desire."[193]

Second, it led to the drawing of excessively fine distinctions between questioning, on the one hand, and expressions of concern falling short of questioning, on the other. Third, it disregarded:

> "...the social and psychological realities of the relationship between a patient and her doctor. ... Few patients do not feel intimidated or inhibited to some degree."

The Supreme Court also accepted that the High Court of Australia in *Rogers v Whitaker* had been correct in pointing to the logical difficulty inherent in the exception to the *Bolam* test for the questioning patient, in that the patient's questions do not necessarily make any difference to the doctor's duty of care if it   **7–066**

---

[191] (1992) 109 A.L.R. 625; [1993] 4 Med. L.R. 79 at 630–631.

[192] [2015] UKSC 11; [2015] A.C. 1430 at [58].

[193] [2015] UKSC 11; [2015] A.C. 1430 at [58]. On the evidence in *Montgomery* (at [17]) the claimant had expressed concern about the size of the baby and the risk that it might be too big to be delivered vaginally. The defendant obstetrician stated that the claimant had not asked her "specifically about exact risks", and that had she done so the defendant would have advised her about the risk of shoulder dystocia and about the risk of the baby's head becoming stuck. It might be thought that the expression of the claimant's concerns would have triggered a conversation about the risks associated with the baby being too large, and it is a matter for some speculation as to how specific the claimant's questions would have to have been before the defendant would have discussed the risks.

is medical opinion (or responsible professional practice) that determines whether a particular risk should be disclosed.[194] The exception was logically destructive of the supposed rule.

7–067 How, then, should the court respond to the questioning patient under the prudent patient standard adopted in *Montgomery*? Questions by the patient identify specific concerns that the patient may have and so fall under the second, subjective, limb of the prudent patient standard: the risk is material where "the doctor is or should reasonably be aware that the particular patient would be likely to attach significance to it".[195] Expressions of concern by the patient, as well as specific questions, are relevant, and the court should not dismiss the subjective limb of the material risk test merely because the patient did not ask certain kinds of questions.[196] On this approach the asking of questions is incorporated into the issue of what constitutes a material risk, and is not a situation categorised as an exception to the rule.

7–068 This would seem to bring English law into line with the approach adopted in Canada and Australia. In *Hopp v Lepp*[197] Laskin CJC said that where a patient asks specific questions, not by way merely of general inquiry, the questions must be answered, even if they invite answers to merely possible risks. It is a question of fact how specific the questions are. In Ireland it has been said that the strictness of the duty of disclosure is such that there is no room for the operation of an "inquisitive patient" test, because its requirements are subsumed within the broader disclosure rule:

"Current Irish law requires that the patient be informed of any material risk, whether he inquires or not, regardless of its infrequency."[198]

(iv)   Taking into account the patient's knowledge/understanding

7–069 The doctor does not have a duty to make the patient understand; it is a duty to make a reasonable effort to communicate information to the patient.[199] Thus:

---

[194] [2015] UKSC 11; [2015] A.C. 143 at [59]; see para. 7–015 above.

[195] [2015] UKSC 11; [2015] A.C. 143 at [87].

[196] [2015] UKSC 11; [2015] A.C. 143 at [73].

[197] (1980) 112 D.L.R. (3d) 67 at 77, SCC; *Zimmer v Ringrose* (1981) 124 D.L.R. (3d) 214 at 221, Alta CA.

[198] *Geoghegan v Harris* [2000] 3 I.R. 536 at 563 per Kearns J.

[199] See *Kelly v Hazlett* (1976) 75 D.L.R. (3d) 536 at 565, Ont HC, per Morden J stating that it is a duty to be reasonably satisfied that the patient is aware of the risks associated with the treatment of which he should be aware. See also *Stobie v Central Birmingham Health Authority* (1994) 22 B.M.L.R. 135, QBD, where the claimants misunderstood the defendant's advice about failure rates for vasectomy, despite the fact the he "did what he could" to ensure that the claimants did understand that there remained a risk of failure, put at about one in a thousand. In *Murray v NHS Lanarkshire Health Board* [2012] CSOH 123 at [21] Lady Dorrian commented that: "It is of course for the doctors to give the advice, but in the absence of further questions from the patient it is not unreasonable to assume that the advice has been understood, particularly when dealing with matters which are not particularly complicated." Here, the proviso is important. Silence or a lack of questions from the patient cannot necessarily be taken as evidence of understanding. The patient may, as in *Murray* itself, be "a very passive patient" or may be unable to process the information in such a way as to be able to formulate a question.

"Clinicians should take reasonable and appropriate steps to satisfy themselves that the patient has understood the information which has been provided; but the obligation does not extend to ensuring that the patient has understood."[200]

It is not an answer, however, for doctors to say that they do not have the time to give seminars in medicine or that the information is too complicated or technical for the patient to understand. The duty must be to give an explanation in terms which are reasonably comprehensible to a lay person. In *Montgomery v Lanarkshire Health Board*[201] the Supreme Court noted that the doctor has an advisory role which involves dialogue with the patient with the objective of enabling the patient to understand the seriousness of her condition, and the anticipated benefits and risks of the proposed treatment and any reasonable alternatives. The information provided must be comprehensible:

"The doctor's duty is not therefore fulfilled by bombarding the patient with technical information which she cannot reasonably be expected to grasp, let alone by routinely demanding her signature on a consent form."

Of course, there can be no guarantee that the patient will in fact understand the information.[202] Where it is quite apparent to the doctor that the patient has not understood further efforts may need to be made. The Canadian courts, for example, have taken the view that where the patient has language difficulties the doctor is under a special duty to be sure that the patient has understood.[203] But even where the patient's first language is English the language of the medical profession can be confusing:

---

[200] *Al Hamwi v Johnston* [2005] EWHC 206 (QB); [2005] Lloyd's Rep. Med. 309 at [69] per Simon J. The GMC guidance, *Consent: patients and doctors making decisions together*, June 2008, para.11, (available at *http://www.gmc-uk.org/static/documents/content/Consent_-_English_1015.pdf*) states that: "You should check whether patients have understood the information they have been given, and whether or not they would like more information before making a decision."

[201] [2015] UKSC 11; [2015] A.C. 1430 at [90].

[202] See Brazier (1987) 7 L.S. 169 at 177 commenting on the intrinsic difficulty of communicating medical information to patients. One study found that between two and five days after an operation 27 per cent of patients did not know which organ had been operated on, and 44 per cent were unaware of the basic facts relating to the operation, e.g. that a gall bladder had been removed: Byrne, Napier and Cuschieri (1988) 296 B.M.J. 839. See also McMahon, Clark and Bailie (1987) 294 B.M.J. 355 on the provision of drug information to patients. See further Jones (1999) 7 Med. L. Rev. 103, 123–129 where the medical literature on "informed consent" is reviewed; T. Rakow, "Chaos and good order on the assessment and communication of risk" (2004) 10 *Clinical Risk* 97 for a helpful discussion of different approaches to the assessment and communication of risk and probabilities, and the common errors inherent in the perception and understanding of risk.

[203] *Reibl v Hughes* (1980) 114 D.L.R. (3d) 1 at 34; *Schanczi v Singh* [1988] 2 W.W.R. 465 at 474, Alta QB; *Ciarlariello v Schacter* (1993) 100 D.L.R. (4th) 609 at 622–623, SCC. See also the GMC guidance, *Consent: patients and doctors making decisions together*, June 2008, para.21 (available at *http://www.gmc-uk.org/static/documents/content/Consent_-_English_1015.pdf*) which states, amongst other things, that a doctor should: "make sure, wherever practical, that arrangements are made to give the patient any necessary support. This might include, for example: using an advocate or interpreter; asking those close to the patient about the patient's communication needs; or giving the patient a written or audio record of the discussion and any decisions that were made." This advice is reiterated by the GMC in *Good Medical Practice*, March 2013, para.32 (available at *http://www.gmc-uk.org/static/documents/content/GMP_.pdf*): "You must give patients the information they want or need to know in a way they can understand. You should make sure that arrangements are made, wherever possible, to meet patients' language and communication needs."

"The language that medical practitioners use is often a different language, even for those patients who speak English. Thus, a medical practitioner could run a serious risk that their patient does not understand their language when the patient's first language is not English or, if it is English, when the medical practitioner uses medical terminology, Latin or technical terminology."[204]

7–070   In *Lybert v Warrington Health Authority*[205] the Court of Appeal accepted that a doctor has a responsibility to take reasonable steps to ensure that the information given is understood. The claimant had been sterilised at the time of giving birth to her third child by Caesarean section but had not been warned before the operation of the risk that the procedure would fail to achieve sterility. The post-operative warning was inadequate because the timing and the conditions in which it was given were inappropriate, and the warning was not expressed in terms sufficient to impinge upon the claimant's thoughts. An emphatic and clear warning was required, with an assurance that it was being taken in.

7–071   **The patient's response as an indication of misunderstanding**   In *Smith v Tunbridge Wells Health Authority*[206] the claimant underwent a Wells operation (ivalon sponge rectopexy) to repair a rectal prolapse. The surgery was successful in effecting the repair, but due to nerve damage during the surgery the claimant, who was aged 28 at the time of the operation, was rendered impotent and suffered from bladder dysfunction. This is a recognised risk of the operation. Responsible medical opinion, including the defendant surgeon, regarded it as important to explain the particular risks to a patient such as the claimant, i.e. a young, sexually active married man suffering from a condition which was distressing, embarrassing and inconvenient, but which was not life-threatening. He had had the condition for eight years, and was not psychologically vulnerable or mentally unstable. This type of operation was normally performed on elderly women, and it was exceedingly rare on a sexually active man, partly because for anatomical reasons it is a more difficult operation in men. Morland J held the defendants liable on the basis that the surgeon had failed to get across to the claimant the risks involved in the operation:

> "When recommending a particular type of surgery or treatment, the doctor, when warning of the risks, must take reasonable care to ensure that his explanation of the risks is intelligible to his particular patient. The doctor should use language, simple but not misleading, which the doctor perceives from what knowledge and acquaintanceship that he may have of the patient (which may be slight), will be understood by the patient so that the patient can make an informed decision as to whether or not to consent to the recommended surgery or treatment."[207]

The defendant had not been clear in his own mind as to how and to what extent he should explain the risks to the claimant, with the result that his explanation was confused, and the claimant misunderstood the message. If the claimant had been informed of the risk of impotence he would have refused the operation. The

---

[204] *Dickson v Pinder* 2010 ABQB 269; [2010] 10 W.W.R. 505 at [99] per Yamauchi J. The same point also applies to documents, such as a consent form: 2010 ABQB 269; [2010] 10 W.W.R. 505 at [100].
[205] [1996] P.I.Q.R. P45; [1996] 7 Med. L.R. 71.
[206] [1994] 5 Med. L.R. 334, QBD.
[207] [1994] 5 Med. L.R. 334 at 339.

very fact of consent and the speed of consent were indicative, said his Lordship, that a clear warning of the risk of impotence was not communicated to the claimant.[208]

Defendant unaware of patient's misunderstanding   The mere fact that the   7–072
patient has misunderstood information provided by the defendant is not a basis
for a finding of negligence. In *Worrall v Antoniadou*[209] the trial judge concluded
that the defendant had been negligent by unintentionally allowing the patient to
leave a pre-operative consultation with the mistaken impression that a further
procedure would not be necessary until five years after the surgery. The patient
had "got hold of the wrong end of the stick" and the defendant's non-committal
answer had failed to dispel the patient's misunderstanding. The Court of Appeal
reversed the judge's finding of negligence. In these circumstances a doctor should
not be liable:

> "…unless either he/she is responsible for the patient getting hold of the wrong end of the stick
> or, having realised that the patient has or is in danger of getting hold of the wrong end of the
> stick, or in circumstances where the medical professional ought so to have realised, he/she
> takes no step to dispel the misapprehension."[210]

Communication aids   Aids to communication, such as a leaflet explaining the   7–073
procedure and the risks, may be helpful,[211] but there are also dangers in a doctor
relying on leaflets, or even a video, given to the patient prior to surgery as means
of explaining the risks to a patient. In the Canadian case of *Byciuk v
Hollingsworth*[212] the patient was given a video which explained the surgical
procedure he was to undergo and its benefits and risks. The patient remembered
that the video had mentioned some risks but was mainly positive about the
procedure. There was no subsequent discussion between the surgeon and the
patient about the risks of the surgery, nor the patient's comprehension of the
video. McMahon J considered that this form of communication placed a special
burden on the surgeon to ascertain whether the patient had comprehended the
information:

> "… when the physician, for the sake of office efficiency, relies on what can be called remote
> communication by sending the patient a video taped message and some pamphlets to view and
> read at his leisure at home, there is a higher burden on the physician to determine the level of
> the patient's understanding of the message."[213]

---

[208] See also *Dickson v Pinder* 2010 ABQB 269; [2010] 10 W.W.R. 505 at [101], where the patient's
flippant response to being informed about the risk of a stroke was regarded as strong evidence that she
had not understood the risk.

[209] [2016] EWCA Civ 1219; (2017) 153 B.M.L.R. 14.

[210] [2016] EWCA Civ 1219; (2017) 153 B.M.L.R. 14 at [22] per Tomlinson LJ.

[211] For example, the GMC guidance *Consent: patients and doctors making decisions together*, June
2008, para.20 states that: "You may need to support your discussions with patients by using written
material, or visual or other aids. If you do, you must make sure the material is accurate and up to
date." Such aids may be completely unhelpful if they are misleading or confusing: see *Connolly v
Croydon Health Services NHS Trust* [2015] EWHC 1339 (QB) where an information sheet about an
angiogram was misleading but, on the evidence, it was found that the patient had been provided with
sufficient information overall.

[212] 2004 ABQB 370; (2004) 27 C.C.L.T. (3d) 116.

[213] 2004 ABQB 370; (2004) 27 C.C.L.T. (3d) 116 at [33].

That burden was not discharged by merely asking if the patient had watched the video, nor by asking if the patient had any questions about the video.

7–074   **The patient's medical condition**   The doctor will also have to take into account the patient's condition at the time of explaining the risks, since if the patient is debilitated the information may not "get through". In *Smith v Salford Health Authority*[214] the claimant was informed of the risks to his health if he did not have corrective cervical surgery (an occipetal/cervical fusion), but he was not informed of the risks of paralysis or, indeed, death from the surgery itself. Moreover, even if these risks were mentioned, they were not mentioned in terms adequate to register upon the claimant, who at the time was suffering from a headache and the general adverse effects of a recent myelogram. All the experts were agreed that the risks should have been explained, as indeed was the defendant's usual practice, and therefore he had been negligent.

7–075   Similarly, in *McAllister v Lewisham and North Southwark Health Authority*[215] the claimant had a neurological deficit in her left leg which was identified as being attributable to a large arteriovascular malformation (avm), a congenital vascular deformity in the skull. The defendant neurosurgeon recommended an operation to remove the avm. He told the claimant that without the operation her leg would not improve and was likely to get worse in the not too distant future. He also said that there was a 20 per cent chance that the operation itself would make the leg worse, but he made no mention of any of the general risks of brain surgery (such as the possibility of epilepsy and the inevitable consequence that after surgery of this nature she would not be allowed to drive for at least 12 months), and did not inform her that there was any risk that the increased deficit could extend beyond the leg. In particular:

> "...he did not get through to her that there was any risk of the arm becoming impaired, still less of any left-sided hemiplegia. Mr. Strong told me, reciting his general habit in the case of other operable brain conditions, that he thinks he would have mentioned some risk to the left side or arm. If he did so, I can only conclude that he did not do so in any way which was sufficient to enter the plaintiff's consciousness. In fact I rather doubt that he did..."[216]

The claimant was left with the impression that she really "had nothing to lose". This was simply untrue, since the risks associated with the operation were high; indeed the evidence indicated that many neurosurgeons would not even have attempted it in the claimant's circumstances. After the operation the claimant had increased weakness in her leg, and complete hemiplegia on her left side, involving her arm which was completely useless. Rougier J held that to leave the claimant with the impression that there were really no two ways about the operation and that she had nothing to lose constituted negligence. *McAllister v Lewisham and North Southwark Health Authority* demonstrates that a highly selective approach to the disclosure of risk which is positively misleading is

---

[214] [1994] 5 Med. L.R. 321, QBD. The action failed on causation. See also *Lybert v Warrington Health Authority* [1996] P.I.Q.R. P45; [1996] 7 Med. L.R. 71, CA, para.7–070.
[215] [1994] 5 Med. L.R. 343, QBD.
[216] [1994] 5 Med. L.R. 343 at 345, per Rougier J.

likely to result in a finding of negligence, whereas *Smith v Tunbridge Wells Health Authority* indicates that a genuine but ineffective attempt to explain the risks may also be culpable.

The professionally knowledgeable patient   Although when giving informa-   7–076
tion or advice it is appropriate to tailor information to the level of the patient's understanding, a doctor should not make assumptions about the patient's knowledge based on the fact that the patient is professionally qualified. In *Thefaut v Johnston*[217] the patient was a qualified midwife who underwent surgery for the relief of back and leg pain. Green J rejected a suggestion that a surgeon could make assumptions about the pre-existing knowledge of a particular patient and then tailor the advice accordingly. This would render the process arbitrary and subjective. The doctor should "proffer full advice and not shape it according to the patient's perceived state of knowledge".[218]

(v)   Changing standards of disclosure

One consequence of the *Bolam* test was that patients became entitled to more   7–077
information as professional attitudes to the question of information disclosure changed, given that the trend within the profession has been towards greater information disclosure. Indeed, this was part of the Supreme Court's rationale for the change to a prudent patient standard in *Montgomery*.[219] It seems likely that the effect of *Montgomery* will be to accelerate that process. Would any sensible obstetrician now fail to disclose the risks of shoulder dystocia to a pregnant diabetic patient? Whereas under *Bolam/Sidaway* the obstetrician might have been able to adduce evidence of a "responsible" body of professional opinion in favour of non-disclosure, notwithstanding that in a previous case a court had concluded that there was no such evidence presented to it (and thus the defendant had been in breach of duty), if a reasonably prudent patient would have expected disclosure on the basis that the risks were *material* it is difficult to see how in a subsequent case, given evidence of the same risk/benefit ratio, the risks can suddenly become "immaterial". In other words, *Bolam/Sidaway* accommodated a spectrum of differing views within the profession as to what ought to be disclosed, and those in favour of minimum disclosure would not fall foul of the law provided that their view could be said to be reasonable or responsible, even if a substantial majority of the profession were in favour of much fuller disclosure. But once the risks have been categorised by the court as "material risks" that a reasonable patient would want to be informed about, all other things being equal, there is simply no scope for a spectrum of views supporting the disclosure of *less* information. Categorising risks as *material* sets the minimum standard for disclosure, and any doctors within the profession who consider that something less was acceptable practice will simply have to change their ways.

---

[217] [2017] EWHC 497 (QB); [2017] Med. L.R. 319.
[218] [2017] EWHC 497 (QB); [2017] Med. L.R. 319 at [75].
[219] *Montgomery v Lanarkshire Health Board* [2015] UKSC 11; [2015] A.C. 1430 at [77]–[78], [93].

(vi)   The evidential dispute between doctor and patient

7–078   In many cases there will be a straightforward factual dispute as to what the patient was told. Often doctors will have to rely upon their "usual practice", having little direct recollection of an individual patient, whereas patients, for whom the experience is unique, may be better placed to remember the event. On the other hand, patients may be in an emotionally vulnerable state, having to digest both complex medical facts and the implications for their future health, and may recall little detail of what was actually said. In such circumstances the judge will have to draw inferences as to the credibility of the witnesses from the surrounding circumstances. For example, in *Chester v Afshar*[220] there was a dispute between the patient and the doctor as to whether the claimant had been informed about the risk of developing cauda equina syndrome as a consequence of surgery on her spine to deal with back pain. The defendant estimated this risk at 0.9 per cent, and it was common ground that, acting in accordance with good medical practice, the defendant should have warned the claimant of this risk. The question was whether she was in fact informed. The judge held that the claimant's version of events was probably correct, taking into account a number of factors: (1) the claimant was an intelligent and articulate woman whose work (as a journalist) was likely to have developed her abilities to absorb and retain information; (2) for the claimant it was a unique and extremely important event, whereas for the defendant it was one of many; (3) her description of the conversation had the ring of truth about it, and was unlikely to be the product of invention or reconstruction; (4) at an early stage after the operation she was complaining about not having been told about the risks; (5) before the consultation, the claimant was clearly averse to surgery, and anxious to avoid it if possible; (6) the operation was not a matter of urgency; (7) it was extremely improbable that if the claimant had been adequately informed about the risks she would have agreed to the surgery so soon after the consultation (three days later), which effectively prevented her from taking a second or even a third opinion. This was the position, said the judge, whether one applied the subjective test of what this individual claimant would have done, or whether one tested the claimant's subjective evidence against the objective criterion of what a reasonable patient in the claimant's position would have done. The Court of Appeal found the judge's reasoning on this issue "compelling".[221]

(vii)   Codes of practice

7–079   For many years the General Medical Council (GMC) has published advice to doctors about the information that should be given to patients. It was arguable that this guidance represented good evidence of what constitutes good medical practice in the context of information disclosure and that it was therefore

---

[220] [2002] EWCA Civ 724; [2003] Q.B. 356.
[221] On appeal to the House of Lords the issue of whether the defendant had failed to inform the claimant about the risks was not in dispute, since the defendant did not appeal the finding that he had been in breach of duty: see [2004] UKHL 41; [2005] 1 A.C. 134.

evidence of "responsible" medical practice for the purposes of the *Bolam* test.[222] In *Montgomery v Lanarkshire Health Board*[223] the Supreme Court relied, in part, on changes in medical practice since the decision in *Sidaway*, as reflected in the GMC's guidance to the profession, as justification for adopting a standard of disclosure based on the prudent patient. Although the GMC documents do not refer to the disclosure of "material risks", and are expressed at a fairly high level of generality, they probably represent a good starting point for identifying "material information" that ought to be provided to patients.

The model of the doctor–patient relationship that was prevalent in the mid-1980s, in which expert doctors practised their professional skills on passive patients, has given way to a relationship based on "partnership" with patients. In *Good Medical Practice* the GMC states that doctors: **7–080**

> "...must work in partnership with patients, sharing with them the information they will need to make decisions about their care, including: ... their condition, its likely progression and the options for treatment, including associated risks and uncertainties."[224]

More detailed advice as to what doctors should tell their patients is given in para.9 of the GMC document *Consent: patients and doctors making decisions together*[225] which states that doctors must give patients the information they want or need about:

(a)   the diagnosis and prognosis;

(b)   any uncertainties about the diagnosis or prognosis, including options for further investigations;

(c)   options for treating or managing the condition, including the option not to treat;

(d)   the purpose of any proposed investigation or treatment and what it will involve;

(e)   the potential benefits, risks and burdens, and the likelihood of success, for each option; this should include information, if available, about whether the benefits or risks are affected by which organisation or doctor is chosen to provide care;

(f)   whether a proposed investigation or treatment is part of a research programme or is an innovative treatment designed specifically for their benefit;

(g)   the people who will be mainly responsible for and involved in their care, what their roles are, and to what extent students may be involved;

(h)   their right to refuse to take part in teaching or research;

(i)   their right to seek a second opinion;

(j)   any bills they will have to pay;

(k)   any conflicts of interest that you, or your organisation, may have;

---

[222] See Jones (1999) 7 Med. L. Rev. 103 where this argument was developed in more detail.

[223] [2015] UKSC 11; [2015] A.C. 1430; see para.7–015.

[224] GMC, *Good Medical Practice* (2013) para. 49 (available at *http://www.gmc-uk.org/guidance/good_medical_practice.asp*).

[225] June 2008, available at *http://www.gmc-uk.org/static/documents/content/Consent_-_English_1015.pdf.*

(l)   any treatments that you believe have greater potential benefit for the patient than those you or your organisation can offer.

There follows, in paras 28 to 36, detailed statements about the doctor's responsibility to inform the patient about "side effects, complications and other risks". The doctor must provide clear and accurate information about the risks of any proposed investigation or treatment, tailored to the patient's particular circumstances. This includes the adverse outcomes that may result from the proposed options, including the potential outcome of taking no action, and the risk that the intervention may fail to achieve the desired objective. The risks to be disclosed will vary "from common but minor side effects, to rare but serious adverse outcomes possibly resulting in permanent disability or death". There should be no assumptions about a patient's understanding of risk or the importance the patient may attach to different outcomes. Information about risks should be given in a balanced way, avoiding bias, in clear, simple and consistent language. Doctors should also check that the patient understands the terms used, particularly when describing the seriousness, frequency and likelihood of an adverse outcome.

2.   CAUSATION

(a)   Battery and causation

7–081   One of the objections to using the tort of battery as the mechanism for ensuring that doctors disclose information concerning the risks of proposed treatment has been said to be that in battery the claimant does not have to prove causation. Thus, in *Chatterton v Gerson* Bristow J said that:

> "When the claim is based on negligence the plaintiff must prove not only the breach of duty to inform but that had the duty not been broken she would not have chosen to have the operation. Where the claim is based on trespass to the person, once it is shown that the consent is unreal, then what the plaintiff would have decided if she had been given the information which would have prevented vitiation of the reality of her consent is irrelevant."[226]

This is considered to be unfair to defendants because the claimant could in theory succeed in an action where, even if the risks had been disclosed in advance of treatment, the claimant would nonetheless have agreed to proceed and would therefore have sustained the very same injuries as a result of the materialisation of an inherent risk of the treatment.[227] It was this problem that led Bristow J to assert that:

---

[226] [1981] Q.B. 432 at 442–443; cf. *Koehler v Cook* (1975) 65 D.L.R. (3d) 766, BCSC, where the defendant was held liable in trespass for non-disclosure of the risk of loss of smell, and Dryer J went on to consider the causation issue, concluding that the claimant would have declined the operation to cure migraine headaches if she had known about the risk. This case must now be read in the light of *Reibl v Hughes* (1980) 114 D.L.R. (3d) 1.

[227] In *Brushett v Cowan* (1987) 40 D.L.R. (4th) 488 the defendant was held liable in battery for performing a bone biopsy without the patient's consent, although a claim in negligence failed because

"…justice requires that in order to vitiate the reality of consent there must be a greater failure of communication between doctor and patient than that involved in a breach of duty if the claim is based on negligence."[228]

It could be argued, however, that since consent to medical treatment is essentially concerned with patients' rights to exercise a choice about whether to accept or forego a particular treatment, the *reality* of that consent is intrinsically linked to the question of what patients would have chosen to do had they been informed of the risks. If the information would not have altered their decision to accept treatment their consent was "real", whereas if disclosure of the risks would have caused them to change their minds about proceeding with the treatment their consent was not "real" and accordingly should be considered invalid. This approach would build the causation issue into the whole question of the reality of the patient's consent, and thus remove one of the objections to employing the tort of battery in this area. This argument does not appear to have been presented in any case where the problem has arisen, although the courts' clear hostility in this country to the use of actions in battery against doctors would probably lead to its rejection. On the other hand, where the defendant mistakenly fails to obtain the patient's consent, or exceeds the consent given, the present interpretation of "real consent" does not allow the defendant to plead that the patient would, in any event, have consented if he had known the situation.[229]

Remoteness   In battery the test of remoteness of damage is the directness of the damage. The defendant is liable for all the consequences which are a direct result of the tortious act whether they are foreseeable or not. If no damage has been sustained the claimant is still entitled to nominal damages, because battery is actionable per se. Accordingly, in *Allan v New Mount Sinai Hospital*[230] the defendant anaesthetist was held liable for the claimant's rare and unforeseeable reaction to the mishap occasioned by the needle slipping out of the claimant's vein, even though he was not negligent and in negligence the damage would probably have been regarded as too remote.[231]

7–082

---

a reasonable patient would have consented to the biopsy had she been informed about it. The decision on battery was reversed on the facts, without affecting this point: see (1990) 69 D.L.R. (4th) 743, Newfd CA.

[228] *Chatterton v Gerson* [1981] Q.B. 432, 442.

[229] See also Dugdale and Stanton, *Professional Negligence*, 3rd edn (London: Butterworths, 1998), para.11.59 arguing that in any case where the claimant seeks substantial, as opposed to nominal, damages it should be open to the doctor to show that the damage would have been suffered irrespective of the failure to obtain consent.

[230] (1980) 109 D.L.R. (3d) 634, Ont HC; see para.6–012.

[231] "In negligence, the damage that occurs must be within the risk created by the negligent conduct or else there is no responsibility for it because it is too remote. In battery, however, any and all damage is recoverable, if it results from the wrongful act, whether it is foreseeable or not. The limitation devices of foresight and remoteness are not applicable to intentional torts, as they are in negligence law": (1980) 109 D.L.R. (3d) 634 at 643, per Linden J.

(b) Causation in negligence

7–083   Where claimants bring an action in negligence for breach of doctors' duties to provide information they have to establish causation by proving that had they been given a proper warning they would not have accepted the treatment.[232] Although this will normally depend upon evidence given by the claimant, and the court's assessment of claimants' credibility, there is no rule of law that claimants must give evidence personally about what would or would not have happened if they had been properly informed of the facts before making a decision.[233] In both *Chatterton v Gerson*[234] and *Hills v Potter*[235] the claimants failed to convince the court that even if they had been given a fuller explanation about the risks of the procedure they would have declined to undergo it. In each of these cases the court adopted a subjective test for causation: would *this* claimant have accepted the treatment if adequately informed?[236] In Canada a form of objective test for causation is applied, though in practice the two tests do not necessarily result in markedly different outcomes.

(i)   The "modified objective test" of causation—Canada

7–084   In Canada the courts have adopted what has come to be known as a "modified objective test" of causation. The test derives from *Reibl v Hughes*[237] where the Supreme Court of Canada considered that a subjective test was too favourable to claimants, creating the risk of self-serving testimony from patients who, with the benefit of hindsight, would invariably claim that they would have declined treatment had they known about the risks.[238] In order to deal with this perceived problem the Court applied an objective test of causation: would a reasonable person in the claimant's position have declined the treatment? This makes it more difficult for claimants to overcome the causation hurdle, because even where they can demonstrate that they would not have accepted treatment the action will fail if a reasonable person in their position would have gone ahead. The Court recognised that this could place a premium on the doctor's assessment of the

---

[232] See *Bolam v Friern Hospital Management Committee* [1957] 2 All E.R. 118 at 124. Thus, if the claimant already has the knowledge upon which he could base an informed decision about whether to accept treatment, the action will fail for lack of causation, even though he did not receive the information from his own doctor: *Davidson v Connaught Laboratories* (1980) 14 C.C.L.T. 251 at 272, Ont HC.

[233] *Webb v Barclays Bank plc and Portsmouth Hospitals NHS Trust* [2001] EWCA Civ 1141; [2002] P.I.Q.R. P61; [2001] Lloyd's Rep. Med. 500 at [42].

[234] [1981] Q.B. 432 at 445.

[235] [1983] 3 All E.R. 716 at 728.

[236] Leonard J also applied a subjective test in *Blyth v Bloomsbury Health Authority* unreported 1 January 1985, QBD; rev'd on other grounds (1987) CA, reported at (1989) 5 P.N. 167; [1993] 4 Med. L.R. 151. See also *Moyes v Lothian Health Board* [1990] 1 Med. L.R. 463 at 468.

[237] (1980) 114 D.L.R. (3d) 1 at 15–17.

[238] *White v Turner* (1981) 120 D.L.R. (3d) 269 at 286, Ont HC; aff'd (1982) 12 D.L.R. (4th) 319, Ont CA. Note that all testimony given by a claimant or defendant is potentially open to the criticism that it is self-serving. This is not necessarily a reason for adopting an objective test: *Ellis v Wallsend District Hospital* (1989) 17 N.S.W.L.R. 553 at 581, per Samuels JA, NSWCA. Moreover, all reasoning about causation which relies upon the "but for" test is necessarily hypothetical and depends upon the drawing of appropriate inferences from other facts: see para.5–030.

desirability of the treatment being undertaken, but concluded that merely because the recommended treatment was, objectively, medically appropriate it did not necessarily follow that a reasonable person in the claimant's position would agree to it, because the test takes account of the patient's particular situation. Thus in *Reibl v Hughes* the claimant's action succeeded because although without the operation he had a continuing risk of suffering a stroke, the operation itself carried a 10 per cent risk of stroke (which in fact materialised) and a 4 per cent risk of death, and the claimant said that if he had known about these risks he would have delayed the operation in order to earn his full pension benefits at work. There was, moreover, no emergency making the surgery imperative, and the claimant was also under the mistaken impression that the operation would cure his headaches.

More generally, however, the effect of the objective test applied to causation in Canada has been that even where claimants are successful in establishing a breach of the duty of disclosure, the action is much more likely to fail on causation than to succeed.[239] Most of the cases in which claimants have succeeded have involved procedures that could more readily be described as "elective" such as sterilisation[240] or cosmetic surgery,[241] where the balance of risks between the recommended treatment and the alternative treatments (or the alternative of foregoing any treatment) are more finely balanced, and the medical

7–085

---

[239] Robertson (1991) 70 Can. Bar Rev. 423 at 428 points out that even where the claimant succeeds on breach of duty, in 56 per cent of the cases decided in the 10 years following *Reibl v Hughes* the claimant failed to establish causation. See further Dugdale (1986) 2 P.N. 108–111; Jones (1999) 7 Med. L. Rev. 103, 121–123. Actions have failed on the grounds of causation in: *Bickford v Stiles* (1981) 128 D.L.R. (3d) 516, NBSC, where the incidence of vocal cord paralysis from mediastinoscopy was 0.5 per cent and the alternative possible diagnosis was cancer; *Considine v Camp Hill Hospital* (1982) 133 D.L.R. (3d) 11, NSSC, where there was a risk of permanent incontinence of between 1 per cent to 4 per cent in the performance of a prostate operation; *Grey v Webster* (1984) 14 D.L.R. (4th) 706, where evidence of failure rates for tubal ligation ranged from 1 in 300–500, or 2 to 5 per 1,000; *Stamos v Davies* (1985) 21 D.L.R. (4th) 507 at 521, Ont HC, where there was a risk of damage to the spleen during the performance of a lung biopsy, but the provisional diagnosis was of a life-threatening disease with a high mortality rate; *Poole v Morgan* [1987] 3 W.W.R. 217 at 263, Alta QB, where there were risks inherent in laser treatment of the claimant's eye; *Arndt v Smith* [1994] 8 W.W.R. 568, BCSC; aff'd (1997) 148 D.L.R. (4th) 48, SCC, where the fact that the parents did not want an ultrasound scan of the developing foetus indicated "less concern with risks in foresight than in hindsight"; *Petty v McKay* (1979) 10 C.C.L.T. 85, BCSC; *Hajgato v London Health Association* (1982) 36 O.R. (2d) 669 at 680; *Diack v Bardsley* (1983) 25 C.C.L.T. 159 at 170, BCSC, aff'd (1984) 31 C.C.L.T. 308, BCCA; *Ferguson v Hamilton Civic Hospitals* (1983) 144 D.L.R. (3d) 214; aff'd (1985) 18 D.L.R. (4th) 638, Ont CA; *Bucknam v Kostuik* (1983) 3 D.L.R. (4th) 99, Ont HC; *Casey v Provan* (1984) 11 D.L.R. (4th) 708, Ont HC; *Kueper v McMullin* (1986) 30 D.L.R. (4th) 408, NBCA; *Rocha v Harris* (1987) 36 D.L.R. 410, BCCA; *Lachambre v Nair* [1989] 2 W.W.R. 749, Sask QB; *Kitchen v McMullen* (1989) 62 D.L.R. (4th) 481, NBCA; *Ciarlariello v Schacter* (1993) 100 D.L.R. (4th) 609 at 623, SCC, where the statistical risk of a serious adverse reaction to angiography was far less than the risk of death from the non-treatment of a subarachnoid haemorrhage; *Meyer Estate v Rogers* (1991) 78 D.L.R (4th) 307, Ont HC, where there was a risk of severe allergic reaction during an intravenous pyelogram of 1 in 2,000 and a risk of death of between 1 in 40,000 and 1 in 100,000; *Glaholt v Ross* 2011 BCSC 1133; (2011) 86 C.C.L.T. (3d) 295 at [198]–[199], where the risk of blindness if the patient's condition was left untreated was 100 per cent, and the risk of infection from the treatment was 1 per cent; no reasonable patient would have refused treatment.
[240] *Dendaas v Yackel* (1980) 109 D.L.R. (3d) 455; *Painter v Rae* [1998] 8 W.W.R. 717, Man QB, where there was a small but material risk of injury to the bowel during a postpartum tubal ligation.

justification for proceeding is less overwhelming.²⁴² Similarly, it may be easier for a claimant to succeed on causation when the operation was designed to relieve chronic pain, where the claimant's discomfort is highly subjective, particularly where there were other treatment options which carried a lower, or no, risk.²⁴³

7–086 The objective test is open to the criticism that it represents a departure from the principle that the individual patient is entitled to make the decision about whether

---

The claimant succeeded on causation since she had never undergone surgery before, was apprehensive about the anaesthetic, and she knew that there was an alternative, namely that her husband could have a vasectomy.

²⁴¹ *White v Turner* (1981) 120 D.L.R. (3d) 269, Ont HC; aff'd (1982) 12 D.L.R. (4th) 319, Ont CA, on breast reduction surgery; *Normand v Stranc* [1994] 10 W.W.R. 175, Man QB, where the failure to inform the claimant of the risks of infection and scarring following breast reduction surgery was held to be negligent, though the action failed on causation; *Hollis v Dow Corning Corp.* (1993) 103 D.L.R. (4th) 520 at 547, BCCA, where it was held that a reasonable woman in the claimant's position would not have consented to implantation of breast prostheses if warned of the possibility of rupture of the implants inside her body, particularly since the claimant did not require and had not actively sought out the surgery. [The Supreme Court of Canada subsequently held in *Hollis* that in products liability actions a subjective test of causation should apply: (1995) 129 D.L.R. (4th) 609, see para.7–087; *Felde v Vein & Laser Medical Centre* (2003) 68 O.R. (3d) 97; (2003) 21 C.C.L.T. (3d) 81—cosmetic surgery to the patient's lower eyelid, Ont CA; cf. *Petty v McKay* (1979) 10 C.C.L.T. 85, BCSC, where it was held that the claimant, an "exotic dancer", would have gone ahead with the operation (a modified abdominoplasty) even if the risks had been disclosed because she had a desire to attain a state of cosmetic perfection; *Cherewayko v Grafton* [1993] 3 W.W.R. 604, Man QB, where the claimant would have proceeded with breast augmentation even if fully informed about the risks.

²⁴² See, e.g. *Rawlings v Lindsey* (1982) 20 C.C.L.T. 301, in which there was a failure to disclose a 5 to 10 per cent risk of nerve damage and resultant numbness to the face following wisdom tooth extraction; the action succeeded on causation because the teeth were not giving any trouble at the time, they were merely superfluous; cf. *Diack v Bardsley* (1983) 25 C.C.L.T. 159, BCSC, where the teeth were causing problems. In *Berezowski-Aitken v McGregor* [1998] 8 W.W.R. 322, Man QB, there was a negligent failure to warn of the remote risk of bowel damage, leading to infertility, during the performance of a dilatation and curettage (D&C). The claimant succeeded on causation because there was a reasonable alternative to the D&C, namely the conservative option of simply waiting.

²⁴³ *Schanczi v Singh* [1988] 2 W.W.R. 465, Alta QB, where the claimant contracted arachnoiditis (inflammation of one of the membranes sheathing the spinal cord) which was caused by the dye used in the diagnostic myelogram, followed by the surgery (a disectomy performed in the lumbar spine). The option of conservative treatment had not been explored; *Haughian v Paine* (1987) 37 D.L.R. (4th) 624, Sask CA, where there was a small risk (c.1 in 500) of paralysis associated with a laminectomy and discotomy, but the alternative treatment, conservative management, carried no risk; *Forgie v Mason* (1986) 30 D.L.R. (4th) 548 at 559, NBCA; cf. *Thibault v Fewer* [2002] 1 W.W.R. 204, Man QB in which the action failed on causation because the claimant had suffered with constant pain for 20 years and had continued to seek relief from it; she had elected to undergo surgical procedures in the past which carried a higher risk of complications than the procedure in question; the pain had been so bad that she had considered suicide on at least two occasions; and she also continued to take high doses of medication for the pain on a long-term basis, which itself carried serious risk of complications. Similarly, in *Sicard v Sendziak*, 2008 ABQB 690; [2009] 4 W.W.R. 162 the claim failed on causation, the claimant having described his pain as "unbearable"; Verville J concluded that the claimant (or more importantly a reasonable person in his circumstances) would have opted for surgery in an attempt to relieve his debilitating pain, given his disappointing experience with more conservative treatments and his reduced activity. See also the English case of *Newbury v Bath District Health Authority* (1998) 47 B.M.L.R. 138, QBD, where Ebsworth J held that the claimant would have agreed to accept the risk of neurological damage from spinal surgery, put at between 1 and 5 per cent, because she was "was desperate for relief from pain". The operations in the three English cases of *Sidaway v Bethlem Royal Hospital Governors* [1985] A.C. 871, *Chatterton v Gerson* [1981] Q.B. 432 and *Hills v Potter* [1983] 3 All E.R. 716 all involved treatment for chronic pain. Only in *Sidaway* did the claimant succeed on the causation issue.

to accept or reject medical treatment, a principle which the doctor's duty of disclosure is intended to serve.[244] If the success of the claimant's action depends upon what a "reasonable" patient would have done, then it can hardly be said that the patient can reject treatment "for reasons which are rational, or irrational, or for no reason".[245] Moreover, it is doubtful whether the objective test is, strictly speaking, a test of *causation* which, applying the general principles of the tort of negligence, is a question of whether *this* damage would have been suffered by *this* claimant but for the defendant's breach of duty.[246] What, for example, is the position where a reasonable patient in the claimant's position would have declined treatment, but nonetheless the evidence indicates that the claimant would not have declined treatment—does the action fail in these circumstances? What if, as with cosmetic surgery, for example, many reasonable people would refuse surgery when told about the risks but others, arguably equally reasonable, would accept it despite the risks?[247]

Modifying the modified objective test   There have been occasional attempts   7–087
to move away from the objective test in Canada. Thus, in *Buchan v Ortho Pharmaceutical (Canada) Ltd*[248] the Ontario Court of Appeal held that the objective test was "inappropriate" to the disclosure of information by a manufacturer in a products liability case, at least where the product was an oral contraceptive, because the selection of a method of preventing unwanted pregnancy in the case of a healthy woman was a matter, not of medical treatment, but of personal choice, and it was not unreasonable that notice of a serious potential hazard to users of oral contraceptives could influence her selection of another method of birth control. The court considered that a subjective test should be applied. This view was endorsed by the Supreme Court of Canada in *Hollis v Dow Corning Corp.*,[249] a case where the claimant suffered damage following the rupture of a silicone breast implant. Whilst the objective causation test was appropriate to the disclosure of information by doctors to patients, manufacturers were in a different category because they could be expected to act in a more

---

[244] *Ellis v Wallsend District Hospital* (1989) 17 N.S.W.L.R. 553, 560, per Kirby P, NSWCA; *Rosenberg v Percival* [2001] HCA 18; (2001) 178 A.L.R. 577 at [145] per Kirby J, quoted at para.7–038 above.

[245] *Sidaway v Bethlem Royal Hospital Governors* [1985] A.C. 871 at 904, per Lord Templeman. See also per T.A. Gresson J in *Smith v Auckland Hospital Board* [1965] N.Z.L.R. 191 at 219; *Lepp v Hopp* (1979) 98 D.L.R. (3d) 464 at 470, per Prowse JA; aff'd (1980) 112 D.L.R. (3d) 67, SCC.

[246] See, e.g. *McWilliams v Sir William Arroll & Co. Ltd* [1962] 1 W.L.R. 295, para.5–008; Nicholson (1990) 6 P.N. 83 at 84–85.

[247] See *Hollis v Dow Corning Corp.* (1993) 103 D.L.R. (4th) 520 at 525, per Southin JA. A similar problem arises in the context of termination of pregnancy where it may be difficult to find any common or shared values, and there may be more than one reasonable choice. See *Mickle v Salvation Army Grace Hospital* (1998) 166 D.L.R. (4th) 743 at 758–761, Ont Ct, where alleged the negligence concerned non-disclosure of the risk that the foetus carried by a pregnant woman could be handicapped, and the causation issue, applying an objective test, depended not on whether the claimant would have had an abortion, but whether a reasonable woman in her circumstances would have had an abortion. On the facts, it was held that in a case involving relatively minor physical disabilities (asymmetrical limb development) a reasonable woman would not have chosen a termination of a planned pregnancy.

[248] (1986) 25 D.L.R. (4th) 658 at 685–7, Ont CA.

[249] (1995) 129 D.L.R. (4th) 609; Black and Klimchuck (1996) 75 Can. Bar Rev. 355.

self-interested manner. There was a greater likelihood that a manufacturer would overemphasise the value of a product, and underemphasise the risk, and it was therefore highly desirable from a policy perspective to hold manufacturers to a strict standard of warning consumers of the dangerous side effects of their products, by applying a subjective causation test.[250]

7–088   In *Reynard v Carr*[251] it was held that, although ordinarily claimants have the burden of proving that if properly informed they would not have elected for the treatment, where the want of information is due not just to non-disclosure of the risk, but to culpable ignorance of its very existence, claimants do not have to prove that they would not have consented if the doctor had known of the risk and had explained the nature of the risk to them. However, in *Arndt v Smith*[252] the Supreme Court of Canada re-affirmed, by a six to three majority, that the proper test of causation in an action against a medical practitioner was that laid down in *Reibl v Hughes*, namely the "modified objective test" of whether a reasonable person, having the claimant's particular characteristics would have proceeded with the treatment had all material and special risks been disclosed. The "reasonable person" must be "taken to possess the patient's reasonable beliefs, fears, desires and expectations", but:

> "...purely subjective fears *which are not related to the material risks* should not be taken into account in applying the modified objective test."[253]

---

[250] (1995) 129 D.L.R. (4th) 609 at 634, per La Forest J. The reference to the standard of warning is slightly puzzling in this context, given that the issue under consideration was the test to be applied to assessing causation. The explanation can be seen in La Forest J's citation (at 633), with approval, of the reasoning of Robins JA in *Buchan v Ortho Pharmaceuticals (Canada) Ltd* (1986) 25 D.L.R. (4th) 658 at 687: "The suggestion that the determination of this causation issue other than by way of an objective test would place an undue burden on drug manufacturers is answered by noting that drug manufacturers are in a position to escape all liability by the simple expedient of providing a clear and forthright warning of the dangers inherent in the use of their products of which they know or ought to know. In my opinion, it is sound in principle and in policy to adopt an approach which facilitates meaningful consumer choice and promotes market-place honesty by encouraging full disclosure. This is preferable to invoking evidentiary burdens that serve to exonerate negligent manufacturers as well as manufacturers who would rather risk liability than provide information which might prejudicially affect their volume of sales." For discussion of the causation test to be applied to the actions of a "learned intermediary", when the manufacturer has been found to be in breach of a duty to warn, see paras 10–053 et seq.

[251] (1983) 30 C.C.L.T. 42, BCSC. See also *Grey v Webster* (1984) 14 D.L.R. (4th) 706, NBQB, where it was said that a subjective test should be applied to the disclosure of the risk that an operation (sterilisation) might not succeed in its purpose, whereas the objective test applied to the non-disclosure of the risk of additional harm being inflicted by the operation. Nonetheless, the action failed on causation; see para.7–173, n.489.

[252] (1997) 148 D.L.R. (4th) 48, SCC.

[253] (1997) 148 D.L.R. (4th) 48 at 54 and 55 per Cory J (original emphasis). Thus, the honestly held, but idiosyncratic and unreasonable or irrational beliefs of patients are excluded from the equation: (1997) 148 D.L.R. (4th) 48 at 57. For criticism, see Honoré (1998) 114 L.Q.R. 52; Nelson and Caulfied (1998) 32 U.B.C.L. Rev. 353. Clearly, the more willing the court is to take into account the claimant's personal circumstances as part of the "modified objective test" the closer the test comes to resemble a subjective test of what *this* patient would have done: see, e.g. *Huisman v MacDonald* 2007 ONCA 391; (2007) 280 D.L.R. (4th) 1. In *Felde v Vein & Laser Medical Centre* (2003) 68 O.R. (3d) 97; (2003) 21 C.C.L.T. (3d) 81 the Ontario Court of Appeal held that the claimant's financial situation, and her intended career change, fell into the category of "special circumstances" that should be taken into account as part of the modified objective test.

Moreover, questions asked by the patient identify particular concerns that the patient may have, which may then be factored into the assessment of what a reasonable patient, with the patient's reasonable beliefs, fears, desires or expectations, would have done.[254]

Where the defendant's breach of duty consists of a failure to advise the patient, not simply about the risks of the treatment undertaken, but of any alternative procedure and the risks associated with that, claimants will have to prove both that they would have opted for the alternative procedure (applying the "modified objective test") and also that the alternative procedure would probably have produced a better outcome than the treatment they have actually undergone.[255]

7–089

(ii)   The subjective test of causation

The courts in this country have not considered whether an objective test should be applied to cases of non-disclosure,[256] and have been content to apply the subjective test, which asks whether *this* individual patient would have proceeded with treatment if appropriately warned of the risks. It may be, however, that there is little difference in practice between the two approaches, since even under the subjective test the court will not simply accept uncritically claimants' evidence that they would have declined treatment. Judges are alive to the risk that claimants' evidence as to what they would have done may be influenced by hindsight. The court must weigh claimants' evidence against objective criteria in order to assess its credibility, and if a hypothetical reasonable patient would have accepted the treatment, given the balance of risks involved, this may tend to undermine the credibility of the claimants' assertion from the witness box, when it is known that the adverse risk has materialised, that they would have declined the treatment.[257] This point was emphasised by Samuels JA in *Ellis v Wallsend District Hospital*,[258] in which the New South Wales Court of Appeal adopted a

7–090

---

[254] (1997) 148 D.L.R. (4th) 48 at 54.

[255] *Seney v Crooks* (1998) 166 D.L.R. (4th) 337, Alta CA. Though note that Conrad JA suggested, at [99] and [101] that there was a good argument that once the claimant proves that she would have opted for the alternative treatment, the burden of proof should shift to the defendant to establish that it would not have made any difference. *Seney* was applied in *McEachern v University Hospitals Board* 2010 ABQB 253; (2010) 26 Alta. L.R. (5th) 154.

[256] Although see *Hills v Potter* [1983] 3 All E.R. 716 where Hirst J concluded that the claimant's action failed on causation whether the test was subjective or objective.

[257] "I wholeheartedly accept that in retrospect she sincerely believes that she would have so declined. But, having regard to the evidence as to the gravity of her condition, I think it is more likely than not that she would have agreed to go ahead with the operation notwithstanding", per Hirst J in *Hills v Potter* [1983] 3 All E.R. 716 at 728. Similarly in *Chatterton v Gerson* [1981] Q.B. 432 at 445 Bristow J commented that: "... I would not have been satisfied that if properly informed Miss Chatterton would have chosen not to have it. The whole picture on the evidence is of a lady desperate for pain relief." In *Sidaway v Bethlem Royal Hospital Governors* [1985] A.C. 871 the trial judge, Skinner J, did conclude that the claimant would have declined treatment had she known about the risks.

[258] (1989) 17 N.S.W.L.R. 553, NSWCA; Nicholson (1990) 6 P.N. 83. It is clear that in Australia the test of causation is subjective: *Chappel v Hart* [1998] HCA 55; (1998) 156 A.L.R. 517; [1999] Lloyd's Rep. Med. 223, HC of Aust; *Rosenberg v Percival* [2001] HCA 18; (2001) 178 A.L.R. 577 at [24] and [87]. See also *Gover v State of South Australia* (1985) 39 S.A.S.R. 543 at 566; *H v Royal*

subjective test of causation and in *Rosenberg v Percival*[259] McHugh J, in confirming that the subjective test applies in Australia, commented that:

"What a reasonable person would or would not have done in the patient's circumstances will almost always be the most important factor in determining whether the court will accept or reject the patient's evidence as to the course that the patient would have taken. But what a reasonable person would have done is not conclusive. If the tribunal of fact ... accepts the evidence of the patient as to what he or she would have done, then ... that is the end of the matter."

7–091   A number of factors will be taken into account in assessing what the individual claimant would probably have done, and these are set against the backdrop of what the reasonable patient would probably have done in the circumstances. Thus in *Ellis v Wallsend District Hospital*[260] it was said that the court would have regard to evidence about the claimant's temperament, the course of any prior treatment for the same or a similar condition, the nature of the relationship between patient and doctor, including the degree of trust that the patient placed in the doctor, the extent to which the procedure was elective or imposed by circumstantial exigency, and the nature and degree of the risk involved. A similar point was expressed by Hutchison J in *Smith v Barking, Havering and Brentwood Health Authority*[261]:

"However, there is a peculiar difficulty involved in this sort of case—not least for the plaintiff herself—in giving, after the adverse outcome is known, reliable answers as to what she would have decided before the operation had she been given proper advice as to the risks inherent in it. Accordingly, it would, in my judgment, be right in the ordinary case to give particular weight to the objective assessment. If everything points to the fact that a reasonable plaintiff, properly informed, would have assented to the operation, the assertion from the witness box, made after the adverse outcome is known, in a wholly artificial situation and in the knowledge that the outcome of the case depends upon the assertion being maintained, does not carry great weight unless there are extraneous or additional factors to substantiate it. By extraneous or additional factors I mean, and I am not doing more than giving examples, religious or some other firmly held convictions; particular social or domestic considerations justifying a decision not in accordance with what, objectively, seems the right one; assertions made in the immediate aftermath of the operation made in a context other than that of a possible claim for damages; in other words some particular factor which suggests that the plaintiff had grounds for not doing what a reasonable person in her situation might be expected to have done. Of course, the less confidently the judge reaches the conclusion as to what objectively the reasonable patient might be expected to have decided, the more readily will he be persuaded by her subjective evidence."[262]

On this basis, it will probably be rare for a claimant to succeed on the subjective test but fail on the objective test.[263]

Alexandra Hospital for Children [1990] 1 Med. L.R. 297 at 324. In *Smith v Auckland Hospital Board* [1965] N.Z.L.R. 191 the New Zealand Court of Appeal apparently supported a subjective test of causation.

[259] [2001] HCA 18; (2001) 178 A.L.R. 577 at [24].

[260] (1989) 17 N.S.W.L.R. 553 at 581, citing Robertson (1981) 97 L.Q.R. 102, 122.

[261] (1988), [1994] 5 Med. L.R. 285.

[262] (1988), [1994] 5 Med. L.R. 285 at 289.

[263] This did occur in *Considine v Camp Hill Hospital* (1982) 133 D.L.R. (3d) 11, NSSC.

Doctor's advice should be dispassionate   In considering the hypothetical   **7–092**
discussion between doctor and patient when attempting to assess what the patient
would have done if informed about the material risks it should be assumed that
the discussion would have been conducted without the patient being pressurised
to accept the doctor's recommendation. The assumption must be that the patient
was informed of the risks and their potential consequences dispassionately.[264]

Medical evidence as to what patients normally do   In some instances the   **7–093**
court has been prepared to accept medical evidence as to what patients normally
do when advised about the risks. Applying a subjective test of causation, what
other patients may or may not do is not, strictly speaking, the measure of what
this patient would, hypothetically, have done if warned of the risks. However, it
may be a factor in assessing the credibility of the patient's evidence. If most
patients would normally proceed with the treatment there will have to be some
good reason why *this* patient would not. In *Jones v North West SHA*[265] Nicol J
considered that the evidence that:

> "...in 1992 patients would usually take their doctor's advice and it was very rare (if it
> happened at all) for them to go against it"

was a factor that weighed against the claimant. However, this approach should be
treated with some caution. As Sutherland points out, if in the past doctors have
been acting paternalistically and persuading patients to take the option that the
doctor considers best, medical evidence as to what most patients do will be
skewed in favour of accepting the risks.[266]

Where a doctor acts paternalistically because of a concern that with full   **7–094**
information patients would make the "wrong" choice this may work against the
doctor when it comes to causation. In *Montgomery*[267] the defendant obstetrician
gave evidence that it was her practice not to disclose the risks of shoulder
dystocia to diabetic pregnant women:

> "...precisely because most women would elect to have a Caesarean section if informed of the
> risk of shoulder dystocia (contrary, in her view, to their best interests)."

In those circumstances, said the Supreme Court, the only conclusion that could
reasonably be reached was that if the mother had been informed about the risks
and potential consequences she would probably have elected to have a Caesarean
section. It is arguable that in any case where there is evidence of the doctor acting
paternalistically this must be with a view to encouraging or persuading patients to
take the recommended treatment option, probably because of a belief that
otherwise patients would choose the "wrong" option. This would tend to support

---

[264] *Montgomery v Lanarkshire Health Board* [2015] UKSC 11; [2015] A.C. 1430 at [103]–[104].
[265] [2010] EWHC 178 (QB); [2010] Med. L.R. 90 at [56]; see also at [60].
[266] See L. Sutherland, (2015) 126 Rep. B. 6: "The reality is that many members of the medical
profession have been ignoring the GMC guidance, not only in relation to discussion with patients
about the risks of a procedure, but also by actively persuading a patient to follow a course of action
the clinician considers best. The question is not what a patient has done based on inadequate
information, but what would the patient have done if properly advised."
[267] *Montgomery v Lanarkshire Health Board* [2015] UKSC 11; [2015] A.C. 1430 at [101].

the claimant's case that she would have taken the option that would have avoided the risk, because the doctor is to some degree conceding that other patients, if informed, would also not have accepted the recommended treatment (since otherwise there would be no need to conceal information from patients).

7–095 **Patient places trust in the doctor** The assumption tends to be that the greater the trust that a patient has in the doctor the greater the likelihood that the patient would have accepted the doctor's advice to undergo the treatment.[268] However, this should be specific to the individual patient.[269] It would be wrong to reason that patients generally trust their doctor and accept their advice, therefore reasonable patients trust their doctor and so it is probable that the claimant would have trusted her doctor had she been informed of the material risks.[270] This would tend to undermine the whole point of imposing a duty on doctors to disclose material risks, since most claims would then fail on the causation issue.

7–096 **Evidence of what the patient has actually said or done** If the patient has been warned of higher percentage risks of similar harm on two previous occasions and has nonetheless consented to those operations he will have some difficulty persuading the court that he would not have accepted the lower risk associated with a later operation.[271] In *Less v Hussain*[272] it was held that a consultant obstetrician's failure to warn the claimant of the risk of miscarriage and red degeneration would not have changed her decision to conceive a child, even if she had been actively discouraged from attempting to conceive, not least because, following the very difficult pregnancy that she underwent and the death of the baby, she had further meetings with other consultant obstetricians to

---

[268] See e.g. *Meiklejohn v St George's Healthcare NHS Trust* [2014] EWCA Civ 120; [2014] Med. L.R. 122 at [36]: "The hurdle the claimant cannot clear is his attitude to Prof Marsh. He told the judge in terms that he trusted her and would have done what she advised"; *Sem v Mid-Yorkshire Hospitals NHS Trust* [2005] EWHC 3469 (QB) at [54] per Judge Langan QC: "Patients do normally follow the advice of a consultant, and I cannot see in this case any factors which lead me to suppose that [the claimant] would have done otherwise." In *Moyes v Lothian Health Board* [1990] 1 Med. LR 463 at 468 the pursuer failed to establish that she would have declined diagnostic angiography had she been given a full warning of the risks, partly because in her evidence she had emphasised the trust that she had in the neurosurgeon's experience and judgment. Moreover, she appeared to have failed to take into account the risk of not having a potentially serious disease diagnosed if she had declined the angiography.

[269] For example, in *Dickie v Minett* 2012 ONSC 4474; 221 A.C.W.S. (3d) 1010 at [268] the patient had signed but not read a consent form prior to surgery for the removal of wisdom teeth. Bielby J concluded that the failure to read the consent form was evidence of the patient's level of trust in dentists in general, and that regardless of the risks he would have agreed to the extractions on the strength of the dentist's recommendations (there was also evidence that in the past he had trusted his dentists).

[270] This was the approach of Nicol J in *Jones v North West Strategic Health Authority* [2010] EWHC 178 (QB); [2010] Med. L.R. 90 taking the view that in 1992 it would have been "very unusual for a woman in Mrs Jones' position to go against the advice of her consultant", and so the mother would probably have "put her trust in the doctor" (there were also circumstances particular to the mother in this case that pointed to her accepting the medical advice).

[271] *Glancy v Southern General Hospital NHS Trust* [2013] CSOH 35 at [59]. In this case the patient's claim was almost bound to fail on causation, having said in evidence that "he would have done anything" to relieve the pain he was suffering prior to the surgery.

[272] [2012] EWHC 3513 (QB); [2013] Med. L.R. 383; (2013) 130 B.M.L.R. 51.

consider a possible further pregnancy.[273] In some instances where the claimant has agreed to run a risk of serious harm, it may be inferred that she would have been prepared to accept the risk of some lesser injury.[274] For example, in *MacDonald v Stevens*[275] MacKenzie J, applying the Canadian modified objective test for causation, commented that where a claimant had been informed of the risk of brain injury and nonetheless proceeded despite that risk, it was reasonable to infer that he would also have done so if warned of the risk of blindness. This approach requires some caution in categorising a lesser injury. Many patients may consider death to be the worst possible outcome from surgery, whereas others may think that dying on the operating table would be a preferable outcome to living with serious brain damage and/or paralysis. The subjective test of causation should respect both choices.

Specific circumstances applicable to the claimant The more particular to the patient are the circumstances giving rise to the risk, the easier it will be persuade the court that the claimant would have taken an option that avoided the risk. In *Holsgrove v South West London Strategic Health Authority*[276] the claimant sustained brain damage as a result of a delay in her delivery due to shoulder dystocia. Hunt J accepted the evidence of the claimant's parents that if they had been aware of the option of having a Caesarean section the claimant's mother would have taken that option, given that the parents had had a traumatic experience when the claimant's older sister was born because the delivery was difficult due to shoulder dystocia, although the claimant's sister had not suffered any lasting injury. Similarly, in *FM v Ipswich Hospital NHS Trust*[277] Judge McKenna concluded that the claimant's mother would have opted for a Caesarean section, even if advised to proceed with a vaginal birth, because she had had a previous traumatic labour and wanted to avoid a repeat experience at any cost. The judge was persuaded by her statement that what was key for the mother was the identification rather than the quantification of risk, which on the evidence

7–097

---

[273] See also *Prevost v Ali* 2011 SKCA 50; [2011] 9 W.W.R. 494; (2011) 84 C.C.L.T. (3d) 32 where the claimant complained that he had not been fully informed of the risks of surgery on his right wrist for carpal tunnel syndrome, but after issuing proceedings for negligence he underwent the same surgical procedure on his left wrist. The Saskatchewan Court of Appeal held that it could be inferred from this that had he been informed of the material risks and consequences at the time of the first surgery he would nonetheless have proceeded (rejecting the claimant's argument that under the Canadian modified objective test of causation the court cannot rely on the actual actions of the claimant, as opposed to the actions of the reasonable patient, in determining causation).

[274] In *Moyes v Lothian Health Board* [1990] 1 Med. LR 463 at 468 the pursuer accepted in evidence that any general anaesthetic posed a risk, which she estimated (wrongly) was about 5 per cent, when the total risk from the diagnostic angiography that she underwent and the anaesthetic was much lower than this. Given that she was prepared to accept a 5 per cent risk it was difficult to conclude that she would have rejected the angiography procedure had she been informed of the much lower risk associated with it. On the other hand, a willingness to accept medical treatment in the knowledge that it could be a painful process, and could extend over a period of time, is not the same as being willing to accept the risk of permanent pain as consequence of the procedure: *Hookey v Paterno* [2009] VSCA 48; (2009) 22 V.R. 362 at [123].

[275] 2008 BCSC 1018; (2008) 58 C.C.L.T. (3d) 301 at [93].

[276] [2004] EWHC 501 (QB); [2004] All E.R. (D) 445 (Mar).

[277] [2015] EWHC 775 (QB).

"had the ring of truth about it". On the other hand, in *Jones v North West SHA*[278] the claimant's particular circumstances were such that she would probably have accepted medical advice to proceed with a natural birth rather than a Caesarean section because she was a Jehovah's Witness. A Caesarean carried a much higher risk of bleeding and the possible need for a blood transfusion would be correspondingly greater, putting her own life at higher risk (on the assumption that she would refuse to be treated with blood products).[279]

7-098   **Risks or consequences associated with the alternative options**   The assertion by a claimant that he would have opted for an alternative course of action had she been warned of the risks may lack credibility where the risks associated with that alternative are equal to or greater than those of the treatment he has undergone (assuming that the consequences of the risk materialising are of an equivalent nature). In *A v East Kent Hospitals University NHS Foundation Trust*[280] the claimant argued that she should have been warned of the low (1 in 1000) risk that the low growth of the foetus was possibly due to a chromosomal abnormality, and that if she had been given that information she would have had an amniocentesis which would have confirmed the condition and she would then have terminated the pregnancy. But amniocentesis carried a 1 in 100 risk of provoking premature delivery and a premature birth carried risks of significant risk of disability to the child. Dingemans J considered that it would have been illogical for the claimant to opt for a procedure which carried a higher risk of disability in order to exclude or confirm the smaller risk of chromosomal abnormality. The claim failed on causation.[281] Although the judge accepted that someone in the claimant's position did not have to be "logical or internally consistent", clearly when weighing the credibility of a claimant's evidence about what they would have done in a hypothetical situation a lack of logic or consistency will tend to undermine that evidence. On the other hand, where the risks associated with the alternative treatment are lower and the alternative is likely to be equally effective in treating the patient's condition causation can be readily established.[282]

7-099   In *Smith v Barking, Havering and Brentwood Health Authority*[283] the claimant had undergone an operation on her spine at the age of nine to drain a cyst in her spinal cord. This had been causing pain associated with mild quadriparesis. Following the operation the claimant's symptoms abated and she was able to live a normal life for nine years. When she was 18 she began to experience symptoms

---

[278] [2010] EWHC 178 (QB); [2010] Med. L.R. 90.
[279] Nicol J also placed emphasis on the evidence that in 1992 patients would usually take their doctor's advice and it was very rare for them to go against medical advice.
[280] [2015] EWHC 1038 (QB); [2015] Med. L.R. 262.
[281] In addition to the ruling that there was no breach of duty because the risk was not a material risk: see para.7-046. Dingemans J also concluded that on the evidence the claimant would not have proceeded to a termination of the pregnancy at week 32 or 35 of the pregnancy.
[282] As the Western Australia Court of Appeal noted in *Kerr v Minister for Health* [2009] WASCA 32 at [41]: "The veracity of the plaintiff's evidence must be assessed against the objective evidence, such as the availability and effectiveness of alternative treatments. In this case, the evidence is that morphine was much safer and no less advantageous than pethidine. That consideration supports the appellant's evidence that, in effect, she would have asked for a different medication if she had been warned of the risk of side effects from pethidine."
[283] (1988), [1994] 5 Med. L.R. 285.

again. The defendant neurosurgeon considered that a further operation was advisable in the hope of arresting the progress of the condition. Without the operation the claimant's condition would have continued to deteriorate such that within three months she would have been in a wheelchair and within a further six months she would have been tetraplegic. The second operation carried a very real risk of an unsuccessful outcome. In about 50 per cent of cases there was some temporary arrest of the condition, and in the other 50 per cent there was some worsening. The operation was unsuccessful, and the claimant suffered immediate and permanent tetraplegia. It was common ground that the neurosurgeon should have given a warning about the risks involved, and he had failed to do so. Hutchison J, applying a subjective test of causation, concluded that there was nothing that differentiated the claimant from an ordinary reasonable patient. She would have agreed to have the operation because: (a) if nothing was done she would quite quickly become totally disabled; (b) the risk to which the operation exposed her, if unsuccessful, was not a risk of something worse than she was going to have to experience anyway, merely an earlier onset of the condition; (c) the operation held out the prospect of a postponement of the total disability for a significant period; (d) the claimant would have been influenced by the fact that the surgeon, whom she trusted, had concluded that the chances of success were such as to justify attempting the operation.

Seriousness of patient's medical condition   The more serious the patient's medical condition and its potential consequences if left untreated, the more difficult it will be for claimants to persuade the court that they would have done something different had the specific risk been disclosed. In *King v South Eastern Area Health Service*[284] a child received an overdose of chemotherapy for the treatment of cancer and developed quadriplegia as a result of the treatment. Although the doctor had warned the parents of certain catastrophic side effects of the treatment, he had not specifically mentioned quadriplegia as a side effect, though he had indicated that paraplegia or quadriplegia was a risk of progression of the tumour. Newman J rejected the parents' claim that, had they known of the risk of quadriplegia associated with the treatment they would have sought a second opinion, given that it was a life-threatening tumour and that radical therapy was needed in order to save the child's life.

7–100

(iii)   Patient warned of specific risk that materialised but not of other risks

In some instances claimants will have been warned about some, but not all, of the risks associated with a procedure. If the combined, total risk of adverse consequences would have led them to refuse treatment, but they were warned about the specific risk which has materialised, does the action fail on causation on the basis that they were aware of the specific risk and agreed to the procedure? In *Moyes v Lothian Health Board*[285] the pursuer suffered a stroke while undergoing an angiography, which had been recommended to diagnose the cause of a severe

7–101

---

[284] [2005] NSWSC 305.
[285] [1990] 1 Med. L.R. 463, Court of Session, Outer House.

facial pain. This involved injecting a contrast medium into the cerebral blood vessels to render them opaque for the purpose of performing an X-ray. Angiography carries a degree of risk, even in a healthy patient, of about 0.2 per cent to 0.3 per cent of significant neurological symptoms being caused (which included the risk of stroke). If the procedure is carried out under general anaesthetic, there is the additional, though small, risk inherent in the anaesthetic procedure. Specific problems, such as hypersensitivity to the contrast medium may increase the risk. If the patient is known to be hypersensitive the risk of an allergic reaction can be reduced by the administration of premedication. With these precautions the additional risk of neurological complications due to a hypersensitive reaction is about 0.2 per cent to 0.3 per cent, effectively doubling the normal risk. The pursuer claimed that she should have been warned of the risk of stroke inherent in the angiography procedure, a risk which she claimed was increased by her alleged hypersensitivity and her history of migraine. The defender claimed that he did give a general warning about the risk of stroke, but did not warn her of any special risk associated with hypersensitivity or migraine. The medical evidence was that the pursuer's stroke was not caused by an hypersensitive reaction, but by an embolism which was one of the general risks of the procedure. The defender argued that even if it was proved that the pursuer had been hypersensitive it was irrelevant that she had not been warned about the added risk, since it was not this particular risk which had caused the stroke and there was therefore no causal connection between the failure to warn and the injury. The pursuer argued that even if the hypersensitivity did not cause the stroke, since it was one of the factors aggravating the risks she should have been told about it; if she had been told about the cumulative risks she would not have agreed to the angiography and therefore she would not have suffered the stroke (albeit that she was aware of the general risk of stroke associated with angiography). Lord Caplan accepted the pursuer's argument on this point:

"The ordinary person who has to consider whether or not to have an operation is not interested in the exact pathological genesis of the various complications which can occur but rather in the nature and extent of the risk. The patient would want to know what chance there was of the operation going wrong and if it did what would happen. If we were to suppose a situation where an operation would give rise to a one per cent. risk of serious complication in the ordinary case but where there could be four other special factors each adding a further one per cent. to the risk, a patient to whom all five factors applied might have a five per cent. risk rather than the one per cent. risk of the average person. It is perfectly conceivable that a patient might be prepared to accept the risk of one in 100 but not be prepared to face up to a risk of one in 20. If a doctor contrary to established practice failed to warn the patient of the four special risks but did warn the patient of the standard risk and then the patient suffered complication caused physiologically by the standard risk factor rather [than] by one or other of the four special risk factors I do not think the doctor should escape the consequences of not having warned the patient of the added risks which that patient was exposed to. A patient might well with perfect reason consider that if there were five risk factors rather than one then the chance of one or other of these factors materialising was much greater. The coincidence that the damage which occurred was due to the particular factor in respect of which a warning was given does not alter the fact that the patient was not properly warned of the total risks inherent in the operation and thus could not make an informed decision as to whether or not to go through with it… If he had been given due warning he would not have risked suffering adverse complication from that particular operation and the fact that such complication occurred is causal connection enough to found a claim against the doctor."[286]

It would seem to follow from this that where there are cumulative risks some, but not all, of which claimants have been informed, and they would have declined treatment had they known of the total risk, they do not have to prove that the specific risk which has materialised was the one about which they were not informed, i.e. a claimant could succeed on causation even though he was warned about the particular complication that has occurred.

In *Wallace v Kam*[287] this issue came before the High Court of Australia. The defendant surgeon failed to warn the claimant about two distinct material risks of physical injury inherent in proposed surgery. One was the risk of neurapraxia, a temporary condition causing painful local damage to nerves in the legs. The other was a one-in-twenty chance of permanent and catastrophic paralysis caused by damage to nerves in the spine. The first risk materialised, but the second did not. If the claimant had been warned only about the risk of neurapraxia he would have gone ahead with the surgery, but if he had been warned about both risks (as he should have been) he would have declined the surgery and so would not have developed neurapraxia. The High Court accepted that factual causation was established, but held that the scope of the defendant's liability did not extend to the situation where the claimant would have chosen to undergo the surgery had he been warned only of the risk that in fact materialised. The Court accepted that the reasoning in *Moyes v Lothian Health Board* was appropriate where there was a risk of a single physical injury to which there were several contributing factors the combination of which operated to increase the risk of that physical injury occurring:

7–102

> "To fail to warn the patient of one factor while informing the patient of another may in a particular case be to fail to warn the patient of the *extent of the risk* and thereby to expose the patient to a level of risk of the physical injury occurring that is unacceptable to the patient."[288]

But the reasoning in *Moyes* did not apply where what was involved was the materialisation of one of a number of distinct risks of *different* physical injuries. Although warning the patient of one risk and not the other may have exposed the claimant to a level of risk of physical injury that the claimant would not have accepted, the risk of physical injury that materialises is not necessarily the risk of physical injury that was unacceptable to the patient. The fact that the claimant would have declined the treatment (and so avoided the harm) had he been informed about the risk that has not materialised was irrelevant. Although the duty imposed on a doctor to disclose material risks arises by virtue of the patient's right to choose whether or not to undergo a proposed treatment, the policy underlying that duty was neither to protect the right to choose nor to protect the patient from exposure to all unacceptable risks:

---

[286] [1990] 1 Med. L.R. 463 at 467. The pursuer failed on causation for other reasons: see nn.268 and 274, above.
[287] [2013] HCA 19; (2013) 297 A.L.R. 383.
[288] [2013] HCA 19; (2013) 297 A.L.R. 383 at [34] (emphasis added).

"The underlying policy is rather to protect the patient from the occurrence of physical injury the risk of which is unacceptable to the patient. It is appropriate that the scope of liability for breach of the duty reflect that underlying policy."[289]

The defendant was not liable simply for impairing the patient's right to choose whether to accept treatment, nor for exposing him to an unacceptable risk of paralysis that had not occurred. The liability had to be related to the injury that the patient sustained, i.e. the neurapraxia, but the claimant should "not to be compensated for the occurrence of physical injury the risk of which he was prepared to accept".[290]

(iv) The uncertain patient

7–103   It might be thought that if claimants state frankly that they cannot now say what they would have done had they been informed of the risks, given that the risks have materialised and they are being asked to answer an hypothetical question in hindsight, the claim must fail on the basis that they have failed to establish causation, on the balance of probabilities. There are two grounds for saying that this is not necessarily the case. First, where there is other evidence which the court can take into account in assessing what claimants would have done, the proper inference may be that they would have declined to proceed; and second where patients cannot say what they would have done in the longer term but they are clear that they would have deferred the procedure to a later date.

7–104   **Other evidence**   In *McAllister v Lewisham and North Southwark Health Authority*[291] the claimant was not informed about the relatively high risks of serious consequences arising from a particular form of brain surgery. Nor, indeed, was she informed about the dangers of not having the operation, i.e. a cumulative 2 per cent per annum risk of suffering a brain haemorrhage, the consequences of which could be very serious. The claimant said that had she been informed of the risks she would have postponed the operation because she had just got a job which was important to her, and would not have wanted to risk losing it. Beyond that, she was unable to say what she would have done had she been given appropriate information, particularly since she now knew what the result would have been. The defendants argued that in these circumstances the judge had no basis on which to make a finding about whether the claimant would have proceeded or declined the operation after the initial period of postponement, but Rougier J rejected this argument.[292] Looking at all the evidence his Lordship was able to conclude that she would probably have continued to decline the operation: she was a sensible person, and could make a rational judgment; the neurological deficit for which she had first consulted the doctor was not advancing rapidly;

---

[289] [2013] HCA 19; (2013) 297 A.L.R. 383 at [36].

[290] [2013] HCA 19; (2013) 297 A.L.R. 383 at [39]. See also *Waller v James* [2015] NSWCA 232; (2015) 90 N.S.W.L.R. 634, para.2–068, n.220.

[291] [1994] 5 Med. L.R. 343, QBD.

[292] "The fact that the plaintiff herself, fully conscious of the distortion to her thinking likely to be caused by hindsight, is reluctant to hypothesise, should not of itself preclude a judge from the attempt, provided there exists sufficient material upon which he can properly act", [1994] 5 Med. L.R. 343 at 353.

there was a slight chance of the progress of the deficit arresting itself spontaneously; her job, and the independence that it brought, would be just as precious as it had been before; and most importantly, given time to think, and given the fact that this was one of the most important decisions of her life, she would have taken a second opinion, and that second opinion would have been much more keenly aware of the dangers of operating and would not have been in favour of the operation. That would have tipped the balance of the claimant's mind.

Patient would have deferred the procedure: *Chester v Afshar*   The second, more radical ground, applies where claimants establish, on the balance of probabilities, that they would have deferred the decision about whether to proceed. They may be unable in all honesty to say what they would ultimately have decided, given the hypothetical nature of the question, but according to the decision of the House of Lords in *Chester v Afshar*[293] that is irrelevant to the causation question. The claimant underwent spinal surgery for back pain and developed cauda equina syndrome, a recognised risk which she had not been informed about. She had had a consultation with the defendant on a Friday and underwent the surgery on the following Monday. The judge accepted that had she been warned of the risks the claimant would not have consented to the operation taking place on the Monday; she would have a sought a second or a third opinion. There was no urgency, and operating on the Monday did not allow time for a further opinion. The claimant did not argue that she would never at any time or under any circumstances have consented to surgery, and the judge found that it was impossible to say who she would have seen, what advice would have been given, and how she would have acted in response to that advice, although it was improbable that any surgery she might eventually have had would have been identical in circumstances to the operation she actually underwent.

7–105

The Court of Appeal[294] upheld the judge's conclusion that in these circumstances the claimant had established a sufficient causal link between the non-disclosure and the cauda equina syndrome. The defendant argued that the claimant must prove that, if she had been properly advised, she would never have undergone the surgery in question, either on the date on which it was performed or on any subsequent date. If the claimant would have undergone the procedure at some stage in the future then she would have faced the same inherent risks associated with it, and therefore the defendant's negligent failure to inform her of those risks would have been of no causative effect. The alternative view is that the materialisation of a small random risk inherent in a medical procedure producing injury to the claimant is the result of the particular time and circumstances in which the treatment was given (assuming that there is nothing which predisposes the particular patient to this risk), and therefore if treatment had been delayed to another occasion the probability is that the small inherent risk would not have materialised *on that occasion*, and thus the materialisation of the risk is causally linked to the negligent non-disclosure of risk. The defendant's argument seeks to

7–106

---

[293] [2004] UKHL 41; [2005] 1 A.C. 134.
[294] [2002] EWCA Civ 724; [2003] Q.B. 356; commented by J. O'Sullivan, "Causation and non-disclosure of medical risk—reflections on *Chester v Afshar*" (2003) 19 P.N. 370.

define the claimant's damage as exposure to the risk itself, rather than the physical injury caused by the materialisation of the risk, but a willingness to expose oneself to the same potential risk in the future is not proof that the risk would probably have materialised, and therefore the defendant cannot say that his negligence made no difference. Just as defendants are entitled to say that proof that they increased the risk of harm is not normally regarded[295] as proof that they caused the harm (bearing in mind that a careless breach of duty, by definition, involves exposing others to an unreasonable risk, and proof of breach is not treated as equivalent to proof of cause), so too claimants can say that being willing to accept a risk in the future is not proof that damage would probably have occurred on a different occasion. Moreover, if the defendant's argument were correct and the claimant's loss consisted of being exposed to the risk of harm rather than the harm itself, this would also be true of those cases where claimants can establish that they would never at any time have been willing to run the risk, and therefore the measure of damages should, logically, be determined by reference to the risk to which the claimant was exposed not the physical harm that has resulted from the materialisation of the risk. Of course, this is not how quantum is measured in such cases.

7–107 By a bare majority, the House of Lords[296] upheld the decision of the Court of Appeal, applying the majority decision of the High Court of Australia in *Chappel v Hart*.[297] Had she been warned of the 1 per cent to 2 per cent risk of serious complications from spinal surgery the claimant would not have consented to the surgery at that time but would have postponed the decision while she sought a second or a third opinion. She could not say what her ultimate decision would have been, but it was improbable that any surgery she might eventually undergo would have been identical in circumstances to the operation she actually underwent. The issue was whether on this evidence the claimant had established a causal link between the defendant's breach of duty (the negligent failure to warn her about the risks of surgery) and the non-negligent materialisation of the risk during the course of the surgery performed by the defendant.

7–108 **The minority view** In a dissenting speech, Lord Hoffmann said that:

> "Where the breach of duty is a failure to warn of a risk, [the claimant] must prove that he would have taken the opportunity to avoid or reduce that risk. In the context of the present case, that means proving that she would not have had the operation."[298]

---

[295] Except in situations where the principle in *Fairchild v Glenhaven Funeral Services Ltd* [2002] UKHL 22; [2003] 1 A.C. 32, para.5–050 applies.

[296] [2004] UKHL 41; [2005] 1 A.C. 134. For further comment on *Chester v Afshar* see M.A. Jones, "A Risky Business" (2005) 13 Tort L. Rev. 40; J. Stapleton, "Occam's Razor Reveals an Orthodox Basis for *Chester v Afshar*" (2006) 122 L.Q.R. 426; S. Maskrey and W. Edis, "*Chester v Afshar* and *Gregg v Scott*: Mixed Messages for Lawyers" [2005] J.P.I.L. 205; T. Clark and D. Nolan, "A Critique of *Chester v Afshar*" (2014) 34 O.J.L.S. 659.

[297] [1998] HCA 55; (1998) 156 A.L.R. 517; see para.7–114.

[298] [2004] UKHL 41; [2005] 1 A.C. 134 at [29].

His Lordship described the claimant's argument that it was sufficient to show that she would not have had the operation at the time or by the surgeon that she did, even though the risk would have been precisely the same if she had had surgery at another time or by another surgeon, as:

"...about as logical as saying that if one had been told, on entering a casino, that the odds on No 7 coming up at roulette were only 1 in 37, one would have gone away and come back next week or gone to a different casino. The question is whether one would have taken the opportunity to avoid or reduce the risk, not whether one would have changed the scenario in some irrelevant detail."[299]

It is respectfully submitted, however, that this analogy is misleading because it makes the wrong comparison. A patient is seeking to avoid the adverse consequences of a risk materialising; the gambler is hoping that the risk (the chance) will materialise. Moreover, the patient is seeking to establish a causal connection between events that have actually happened (the breach of duty and the materialisation of the risk) not weigh up the comparative risks and benefits of the future alternatives (which is precisely what she was not permitted to do by the defendant's failure to give the relevant information). Though it would be illogical for the gambler to say he would improve his chances of winning by going away and coming back next week or going to a different casino, that was not Miss Chester's complaint. The better analogy would be if two friends, A and B, were at a casino, and A asked B to place a £100 bet for him on number 7 at the next spin of the wheel. Without consulting A, B decides to place the £100 bet on number 14 instead of number 7. B has not changed A's chances of winning. The chances of number 14 coming up are precisely the same as the chances of number 7 coming up. But if number 7 did come up, we would say, in retrospect, that B's actions have *caused* A to lose the bet that he would otherwise have won. It makes no difference that, before the spin of the wheel, A had precisely the same chance of winning with number 14, nor that he would have precisely the same chance of winning (or losing) by placing another £100 bet on another spin of the wheel. Causation is a matter of historical fact, not future risk.

Lord Bingham agreed with Lord Hoffmann that the claimant had not established   **7–109**
"but for" causation, because she had not proved that she would never have undergone the operation, which carried the same risk whenever it was performed, and the doctor's breach of duty had not increased the risk. There are two problems with this approach. First it redefines the nature of the claimant's damage as "an increased exposure to the risk", rather than the physical consequences of the risk materialising. This is not how the courts treat successful claims for non-disclosure of risk. The claimant is compensated for the physical damage arising out of the materialisation of the risk. Moreover, if the damage consisted of an increased exposure to the risk then, on Lord Bingham's approach, a patient who was not informed about the risk and would never have gone ahead with treatment would be entitled to damages for having been exposed to the greater risk, even if the risk did not materialise. Again, this is not how such cases are dealt with. Rather, where the risk does not materialise there is no damage. Lord Hoffmann considered, but then rejected, the possibility of a "modest

---

[299] [2004] UKHL 41; [2005] 1 A.C. 134 at [31].

solatium" in cases where the non-disclosure did not cause the patient any damage, on the basis that it would vindicate the patient's right to choose.[300] Again, this would have involved redefining the claimant's damage as impairment of autonomy, rather than the resulting physical damage. There is no freestanding cause of action for wrongful invasion of a patient's personal autonomy in failing to disclose the risks of treatment.[301] There must be recognised physical harm which is actionable within the traditional framework of an action for negligence.

7–110   The second problem, as the majority speeches in *Chester* indicate, is that a conclusion that in these circumstances there is no causal connection would undermine the very duty owed by the doctor. As Lord Hope put it:

> "...the function of the law is to protect the patient's right to choose. If it is to fulfil that function it must ensure that the duty to inform is respected by the doctor. It will fail to do this if an appropriate remedy cannot be given if the duty is breached and the very risk that the patient should have been told about occurs and she suffers injury."[302]

This is an approach that Lord Hoffmann has taken on a number of other occasions. For example, in *Reeves v Commissioner of Police for the Metropolis*[303] his Lordship said that where the law imposed a duty to guard against suicide attempts by a prisoner:

> "...it would make nonsense of the existence of such a duty if the law were to hold that the occurrence of the very act which ought to have been prevented negatived causal connection between the breach of duty and the loss."

In *Chester* both Lord Hope and Lord Walker drew attention to Lord Hoffmann's previous analysis of causal problems in terms of the scope of a defendant's duty.[304] Lord Walker referred also to *South Australia Asset Management Corp. v York Montague Ltd*[305] and *Kuwait Airways Corpn v Iraqi Airways Co (Nos 4 and 5)*[306] where questions of causation were also linked to the nature and purpose of the defendant's obligation.[307]

---

[300] [2004] UKHL 41; [2005] 1 A.C. 134 at [34].
[301] *Shaw v Kovac* [2017] EWCA Civ 1028; [2017] P.I.Q.R. Q4.
[302] [2004] UKHL 41; [2005] 1 A.C. 134 at [56].
[303] [2000] 1 A.C. 360 at 367–368.
[304] See [2004] UKHL 41; [2005] 1 A.C. 134 at [84] and [91] respectively.
[305] [1997] A.C. 191 at 212–213.
[306] [2002] UKHL 19; [2002] A.C. 883 at 1091, 1106.
[307] See also Lord Hoffmann's observation in *Environment Agency v Empress Car Co. (Abertillery) Ltd* [1999] 2 A.C. 22 at 31 that one cannot give a common sense answer to a question of causation for the purpose of attributing responsibility under some rule without knowing the purpose and scope of the rule. This proposition had been heavily relied on by the Court of Appeal in *Chester* [2002] EWCA Civ 724; [2003] Q.B. 356 at [47]: "The object [of the law requiring doctors to disclose information to patients] is to enable the patient to decide whether or not to run the risks of having that operation at that time. If the doctor's failure to take that care results in her consenting to an operation to which she would not otherwise have given her consent, the purpose of that rule would be thwarted if he were not to be held responsible when the very risk about which he failed to warn her materialises and causes her an injury which she would not have suffered then and there."

The majority view   Lord Hope considered that to leave the patient who would   **7–111**
find the decision about whether to accept medical treatment difficult without a
remedy would render the duty useless. If the claim failed on grounds of causation
it would render the duty:

> "...a hollow one, stripped of all practical force and devoid of all content. It will have lost its
> ability to protect the patient and thus to fulfil the only purpose which brought it into existence.
> On policy grounds therefore I would hold that the test of causation is satisfied in this case. The
> injury was intimately involved with the duty to warn. The duty was owed by the doctor who
> performed the surgery that Miss Chester consented to. It was the product of the very risk that
> she should have been warned about when she gave her consent. So I would hold that it can be
> regarded as having been caused, in the legal sense, by the breach of that duty."[308]

Lord Walker agreed that such a claimant should not be without a remedy
"otherwise the surgeon's important duty would in many cases be drained of its
content".[309]

Despite the majority speeches' reliance on the policy factors underlying the duty   **7–112**
of care as a justification for concluding that causation was satisfied, it is clearly
arguable that if the claimant's damage is considered to be the *physical
consequences* of the materialisation of the risk, rather than simply being exposed
to the risk, "but for" causation was readily established.[310] Lord Hope observed
that: "The 'but for' test is easily satisfied ..."[311]; and Lord Walker commented
that:

> "Bare 'but for' causation is powerfully reinforced by the fact that the misfortune which befell
> the claimant was the very misfortune which was the focus of the surgeon's duty to warn."[312]

Lord Hoffmann's statement that:

> "Where the breach of duty is a failure to warn of a risk, [the claimant] must prove that he
> would have taken the opportunity to avoid or reduce that risk"

is only correct if the damage that forms the gist of the action is "exposure to risk".
But, for example, a claim against an occupier of land in respect of a failure to
warn of a danger on the property, with the result that the entrant suffers an injury
caused by that danger, is not a claim for "exposure to risk"; it is a claim for the
resulting physical injury, whether or not the occupier created or increased the
risk. Similarly, a patient's claim in respect of non-disclosure of risk is for the
physical damage attributable to the materialisation of the risk, not exposure to
risk per se.[313] That is why if the risk does not materialise and no physical damage

---

[308] [2004] UKHL 41; [2005] 1 A.C. 134 at [87].
[309] [2004] UKHL 41; [2005] 1 A.C. 134 at [101]; see also per Lord Steyn at [24] and [25].
[310] See, e.g., *Clerk & Lindsell on Torts*, 22nd edn (London: Sweet & Maxell, 2018) para.10–106,
n.681.
[311] [2004] UKHL 41; [2005] 1 A.C. 134 at [81].
[312] [2004] UKHL 41; [2005] 1 A.C. 134 at [94].
[313] See *Wallace v Kam* [2013] HCA 19; (2013) 87 A.L.J.R. 648 at [9]: "However, consistent with the
underlying purpose of the imposition of the duty to warn, the damage suffered by the patient that the
common law makes compensable is not impairment of the patient's right to choose. Nor is the
compensable damage exposure of the patient to an undisclosed risk. The compensable damage is,

ensues there is no claim. In order to establish causation the *outcome* must be different, but the clear evidence in *Chester v Afshar* was that the outcome was different. As Lord Steyn observed:

> "What is clear is that if she had agreed to surgery at a subsequent date, the risk attendant upon it would have been the same, i.e. 1 per cent–2 per cent. It is therefore improbable that she would have sustained neurological damage."[314]

In other words, notwithstanding the resort to notions of fairness and policy by the majority, *Chester* could have been decided on the simple point that the claimant had established "but for" causation.[315]

7–113   *Chester v Afshar* **applies only in a medical context**   The Court of Appeal has subsequently treated the majority ruling in *Chester v Afshar* as applying an exceptional rule to cases of negligent failure to warn patients about the risks of

---

rather, limited to the occurrence and consequences of physical injury sustained by the patient as a result of the medical treatment that is carried out following the making by the patient of a choice to undergo the treatment" (citing para.2–17 of *Clerk & Lindsell on Torts*, 20th edn (London: Sweet & Maxwell, 2010), and para.7–072 of the 4th edition of this work).

[314] [2004] UKHL 41; [2005] 1 A.C. 134 at [11]. See also *Wallace v Kam* [2013] HCA 19; (2013) 87 A.L.J.R. 648 at [20]: "The better analysis is that it is also a scenario in which a determination of factual causation should be made. Absent the negligent failure to warn, the treatment that in fact occurred would not have occurred when it did and the physical injury in fact sustained when the treatment occurred would not then have been sustained. The same treatment may well have occurred at some later time but (provided that the physical injury remained at all times a possible but improbable result of the treatment) the physical injury that was sustained when the treatment in fact occurred would not on the balance of probabilities have been sustained if the same treatment had occurred on some other occasion." In *Crossman v St George's Healthcare NHS Trust* [2016] EWHC 2878 (QB); (2017) 154 B.M.L.R. 204 the patient underwent a surgical procedure earlier than he would otherwise have done as a result to the hospital's negligence, which was unrelated to the duty to warn about the risks of surgery (the consultant had recommended conservative treatment but the hospital was negligent in listing the patient for early surgery). The patient had been warned about an inherent risk of somewhere between 0.5 per cent and 1 per cent, which materialised. Judge Hughes QC held that the defendants were liable applying the standard "but for" test for causation: "Had he had the operation on a different occasion, he would not have been advised that he was at any greater risk, and, although the risk was in fact higher in his case, it was not one which was more likely than not to be realised. Hence, in my judgment, the claim succeeds on conventional 'but for' causation principles" (at [46]). See also *Thefaut v Johnston* [2017] EWHC 497 (QB); [2017] Med. L.R. 319 at [89] per Green J (if, following a second opinion, the patient would have opted for surgery at a later date the probability was that the damage would not have occurred).

[315] See also *Martin v Capital Health Authority* 2007 ABQB 260; (2007) 47 C.C.L.T. (3d) 255; [2007] 8 W.W.R. 328 where Wilson J, applying *Reibl v Hughes* (1980) 114 D.L.R. (3d) 1, SCC, rejected the defendants' argument that the claimant must establish that he would never have had the surgery. It was not for the claimant "to prove anything more than that he would not have had the operation at that particular time. To say that he must establish that he would never have the operation is in direct contradiction to *Reibl v Hughes*" (at [117]). The claim was for "physical damage and other losses flowing therefrom. Arguments about risk and chance are irrelevant" (at [118]). Wilson J concluded, at [123], that: "Causation will be made out, pursuant to *Reibl v. Hughes*, in any case where a plaintiff establishes that a reasonable person in his position would have declined to proceed at that particular time. Applying this test ... the plaintiffs are entitled to succeed, and the law need not be modified in any way, and not, in particular, by a 'policy'. I do not see why it was necessary to refer to any such 'policy' in [Lord Hope's speech in *Chester v Afshar*]." The case was reversed on appeal on the question of breach of duty, and the Alberta Court of Appeal did not deal with the causation issue: *Martin v Capital Health Authority* 2008 ABCA 161; [2008] 7 W.W.R. 30.

medical treatment. For other claims in respect of negligent advice by professionals the "traditional" causation rules apply, and claimants must normally demonstrate what advice should have been given, and that they would probably have acted on that advice thereby avoiding the loss. In *White v Paul Davidson & Taylor*[316] Arden LJ said that *Chester v Afshar* did not establish a new general rule on causation, but was an application of the principle in *Fairchild v Glenhaven Funeral Services Ltd*[317] that, in exceptional circumstances, rules of causation may be modified on policy grounds. The principle of informed consent to medical procedures had special importance in the law, but there were no particular policy reasons for departing from traditional principles of causation in an ordinary case of solicitors' negligence.[318] In *Beary v Pall Mall Investments (A Firm)*[319] Dyson LJ considered that *Chester* was exceptional and constituted a departure from established principles of causation, justified by the particular policy considerations involved in patients giving informed consent to medical treatment.

Australia   In holding that the defendant was responsible for the claimant's   7–114
partial paralysis in *Chester v Afshar*, the Court of Appeal had relied heavily on the reasoning of the majority of the High Court of Australia in *Chappel v Hart*.[320] The claimant in that case underwent surgery on her throat which carried an inherent risk of damage to her voice. She was not told about this risk, which materialised, despite the defendant exercising reasonable care in carrying out the operation, leaving the claimant with a weak voice. She said that if she had been warned of the risk she would have postponed the surgery, and had it carried out by the most experienced surgeon with a reputation in the field. The defendant argued that there was no causal connection between the failure to warn and the injury because the surgery was inevitable at some point (the claimant's throat condition was gradually deteriorating) and carried the risk which eventuated. Thus, the claimant had not lost a real or valuable chance of the risk being diminished or avoided, and the injury resulted from a random risk that she was willing to accept. It was held that the failure to warn was the cause of the damage to the claimant's voice. The damage consisted of the physical injury resulting in the weak voice; it was not the loss of a chance or an opportunity to avoid that damage by going to a more experienced surgeon. Gaudron J said that:

> "Where there is a duty to inform it is, of course, necessary for a plaintiff to give evidence as to what would or would not have happened if the information in question had been provided. If that evidence is to the effect that the injured person would have acted to avoid or minimise the risk of injury, it is to apply sophistry rather than common sense to say that, although the risk of physical injury which came about called the duty of care into existence, breach of that duty did not cause or contribute to that injury, but simply resulted in the loss of an opportunity to pursue a different course of action."[321]

---

[316] [2004] EWCA Civ 1511; [2005] P.N.L.R. 15 at [40].

[317] [2002] UKHL 22; [2003] 1 A.C. 32.

[318] [2004] EWCA Civ 1511; [2005] P.N.L.R. 15 at [41] to [42].

[319] [2005] EWCA Civ 415; [2005] P.N.L.R. 35 at [38].

[320] [1998] HCA 55; (1998) 156 A.L.R. 517; [1999] Lloyd's Rep. Med. 223; Cane (1999) 115 L.Q.R. 21.

[321] [1998] HCA 55; (1998) 156 A.L.R. 517; [1999] Lloyd's Rep. Med. 223 at [9], cited by the Court of Appeal in *Chester v Afshar* [2002] EWCA Civ 724; [2003] Q.B. 356 at [31]. Some Australian courts treat *Chappel v Hart* as authority for the proposition that evidence of a failure to provide

Kirby J commented that the standard of disclosure in Australian law established by *Rogers v Whitaker*[322] was that the doctor has a duty to warn a patient of material risks, that is those risks to which a reasonable person in the patient's position would be likely attach significance, or if the medical practitioner is or should be reasonably aware that the particular patient, if warned of the risk, would be likely to attach significance to it. Though these standards may be onerous, they are established by law and when not complied with "it should occasion no surprise that legal consequences follow".[323]

(v) Damages for "shock and anxiety" even if the claimant would (hypothetically) have proceeded?

7–115   It is possible that even if claimants fail to prove that if warned about the risk of complications they would have declined the treatment, they may nonetheless be entitled to compensation for the shock and depression consequent upon discovering, without prior warning, that a complication has occurred. In *Smith v Barking, Havering and Brentwood Health Authority*[324] an award of £3,000 general damages was made for the "shock and depression" caused on the claimant discovering, without any prior warning, that she had been rendered tetraplegic immediately following the operation. Similarly, in *Goorkani v Tayside Health Board*[325] it was held that had the pursuer known about the risk of becoming irreversibly infertile as a side effect of drug therapy, he would still have taken the drug because the disease from which he was suffering, for which the drug was prescribed, could lead to blindness. Nonetheless, damages of £2,500 were awarded for the "distress and anxiety" which arose from the pursuer's discovery of the risk of infertility associated with the treatment, and the fact that he was almost certainly infertile. Lord Cameron said that in assessing damages, it was proper to have regard to the concern which the pursuer had about his inability to father children, the frustration and disruption which ignorance about his infertility and the sudden shock of discovery brought to the marital relationship, and the "shock and anger" he experienced.[326] In both of these cases

---

information as to potential risks of the procedure, combined with the materialisation of those risks, is sufficient to establish a prima facie case of causation, which will be accepted by the court in the absence of a more plausible contrary inference: *Elbourne v Gibbs* [2006] NSWCA 127 at [78]; *Shead v Hooley* [2000] NSWCA 362 at [69]; *Hookey v Paterno* [2009] VSCA 48; (2009) 22 V.R. 362 at [334]–[336].

[322] (1992) 175 C.L.R. 479.

[323] [1998] HCA 55; (1998) 156 A.L.R. 517 at [96]. Note that the causation argument was slightly different in *Chappel v Hart* from that in *Chester v Afshar*, because the claimant in *Chappel* argued that had she been informed of the risk she would have postponed the operation and sought out the surgeon with the most experience and best reputation for that type of surgery, thereby reducing the risk of the complication occurring. The argument in *Chester* proceeded on the basis that the risk would have been the same no matter which surgeon carried out the operation.

[324] (1988), [1994] 5 Med. L.R. 285.

[325] [1991] 3 Med. L.R. 33, Court of Session, Outer House.

[326] See further *Laferrière v Lawson* (1991) 78 D.L.R. (4th) 609, SCC, where the claimant was not informed that she had breast cancer and no follow-up treatment was arranged by the defendant. The claimant was held to be entitled to compensation for "psychological damage" attributable to her belief that had she known about the diagnosis earlier something could have been done to prevent the illness from becoming terminal. In *Snider v Henniger* (1992) 96 D.L.R. (4th) 367; [1993] 4 Med. L.R. 211,

the defendants conceded that this head of damage was recoverable, although it may be doubtful whether in the absence of any physical injury for which the defendants are liable, there should be any award for "shock" or "distress" not amounting to a positive psychiatric illness, such as an anxiety neurosis or reactive depression.[327]

3.   SPECIAL CASES

(a)   Research

The fact that a person is the subject of medical research, as a participant in a drug trial for example, may change the nature of the legal requirements for consent.[328] Medical research is normally divided into two broad categories: therapeutic research; and non-therapeutic research. Therapeutic research is an activity which has a therapeutic intention, as well as a research intention, towards the subjects of the research. Thus, the subjects are also patients. Non-therapeutic research is an activity which does not have a therapeutic intention. This research is normally carried out on healthy volunteers, who are not patients. The legal principles applicable to these different categories of research may well differ, although there is a dearth of case law on the subject, and the most comprehensive statements of proper safeguards for research subjects are to be found in national and international ethical codes.[329] It is arguable that these codes of practice provide

7–116

BCSC, the defendant did not inform the claimant that, after a second suture in her cervix to stop bleeding following a miscarriage, there was a risk that if the suture broke down a hysterectomy would probably have to be performed. The evidence indicated that even if the claimant had been informed, the hysterectomy could not have been prevented. The claimant was nonetheless awarded damages for negligence on the ground that the failure to inform her about the risk exacerbated her post-hysterectomy stress and anxiety and adversely affected her recovery from the operation.

[327] Applying *McLoughlin v O'Brian* [1983] 1 A.C. 410 at 431, per Lord Bridge; *Alcock v Chief Constable of the South Yorkshire Police* [1992] 1 A.C. 310 at 409, per Lord Oliver; see para.2–188.

[328] For consideration of the standard of care to be applied to the conduct of research see paras 3–064 to 3–072.

[329] Codes of practice for ethical biomedical research are now very common, both nationally and internationally. There are too many fully to list here, but for some of the more significant documents see: (1) World Medical Association, *Declaration of Helsinki—Ethical Principles for Medical Research Involving Human Subjects* (the most recent version of which is dated October 2013, available at *http://www.wma.net/policies-post/wma-declaration-of-helsinki-ethical-principles-for-medical-research-involving-human-subjects*); (2) Royal College of Physicians, *Guidelines on the Practice of Ethics Committees in Medical Research Involving Human Subjects*, 4th edn, 2007; (3) Royal College of Physicians, *Research Involving Patients*, 1990; (4) the Council for International Organisations of Medical Sciences ("CIOMS") *Guidelines for Biomedical Research Involving Human Subjects*, revised edition 2002 (available at *http://www.cioms.ch/publications/layout_guide2002.pdf*) (these Guidelines are currently under review); (5) the International Conference on Harmonisation, *Guideline for Good Clinical Practice (E6/R1)*, 1996 (available at *http://www.ich.org/fileadmin/Public_Web_Site/ICH_Products/Guidelines/Efficacy/E6/E6_R1_Guideline.pdf*) which deals with the regulation of research involving pharmaceutical products (these Guidelines are currently under review); (6) Council of Europe, *Convention on Human Rights and Biomedicine*, 1997 (available at *http://rm.coe.int/CoERMPublicCommonSearchServices/DisplayDCTMContent?documentId=090000168007cf98*) (for discussion of the background to the Convention see C. Byk, "The European Convention on Bioethics" (1993) 19 J. Med. Ethics 13). The Medical Research Council publishes various guidance, including *Good research practice: Principles and guidelines*, 2012; *Medical*

good evidence of appropriate standards of conduct and information disclosure, although with many, particularly the international codes, the statements of principle tend to be at too high a level of abstraction to be helpful in resolving a specific case. The Medicines for Human Use (Clinical Trials) Regulations 2004 have changed this to some extent in relation to clinical trials on pharmaceutical products because they effectively incorporate into the legal requirements for the conduct of clinical trials on medicinal products the requirements of the *Declaration of Helsinki* and the ICH, *Guideline for Good Clinical Practice*.[330] Thus the failure to comply with these guidelines could constitute a breach of the Regulations and give rise to a criminal offence. The Clinical Trials Regulations cut across the categories of therapeutic and non-therapeutic research, since they apply to both, and they also cover research on competent and incompetent adults, and on minors. For this reason the Regulations are considered in a separate section below,[331] but when considering the discussion of the principles of consent that apply to therapeutic and non-therapeutic research in the following paragraphs the specific regime applied to pharmaceutical clinical trials should be borne in mind.

(i) Distinguish medical treatment from research

7–117   In *Walker-Smith v General Medical Council*[332] Mitting J described the basic distinction between medical treatment and research as:

> "...the aim of medical practice is to benefit the individual patient; the aim of research is to improve the stock of knowledge for the benefit of patients generally."

One of the issues in *Walker-Smith* was whether the definition of "research" involved an objective test or a subjective test. The parties relied on the definition given in the Royal College of Physicians' guidance *Research Involving Patients* (1990):

> "2.2   When an activity is undertaken solely with the intention of benefitting an individual patient, and where there is a reasonable chance of success, the activity may be considered to be part of 'medical practice'. The progressive modification of methods of investigation and treatment in the light of experience is a normal feature of medical practice and is not to be considered as research.

---

research involving children, 2004; and *Medical research involving adults who cannot consent*, 2007 (all available from the MRC website: *http://www.mrc.ac.uk*). See also the GMC guidance, *Good practice in research and Consent to research* (2010) (available at *http://www.gmc-uk.org/static/documents/content/Good_practice_in_research_and_consent_to_research.pdf*). Most of these guidelines assume that a research project has been scrutinised and approved by an ethics committee of some kind. For discussion of the potential liability of research ethics committees see Brazier (1990) 6 P.N. 186; and more generally Kirk (1986) 2 P.N. 186; Teff (1987) 3 P.N. 182; Giesen (1995) 3 Med. L. Rev. 22; Mander (1996) 2 Med. Law Int. 149.

[330] See n.329 above; and the Medicines for Human Use (Clinical Trials) Regulations 2004 (SI 2004/1031) Sch.1 Pt 2, as amended by the Medicines for Human Use (Clinical Trials) Amendment Regulations 2006 (SI 2006/1928) reg.27.

[331] See para.7–140.

[332] [2012] EWHC 503 (Admin); [2013] Med. L.R. 462; (2012) 126 B.M.L.R. 1 at [11]. For comment on *Walker-Smith* see Case, "Treading the line between clinical research and therapy" (2012) 28 P.N. 224.

2.3   In contrast, where an activity involving a patient is undertaken with the prime purpose of testing a hypothesis and permitting conclusions to be drawn in the hope of contributing to general knowledge, this is 'research'. The fact that some benefit expected or unexpected, may result from the activity does not alter its status as research."

However, in para.2.4 the guidance accepted that "The distinction between 'medical practice' and 'research' is often less clear than is suggested above because both are practised simultaneously". A doctor may intend to treat the patient's medical condition while at the same time be hoping to learn something that will contribute to general knowledge. The point was acknowledged in the Royal College of Physicians' guidance *Guidelines on the Practice of Ethics Committees in Medical Research Involving Human Subjects* (1990), para.3.1:

"The definition of research continues to present difficulties, particularly with regard to the distinction between medical practice and medical research. The distinction derives from the *intent*. In *medical practice* the sole intention is to benefit the *individual* patient consulting the clinician, not to gain knowledge of general benefit, though such knowledge may incidentally emerge from the clinical experience gained. In *medical research* the primary intention is to advance knowledge so that *patients in general* may benefit; the individual patient may or may not benefit directly."

Mitting J concluded that the guidance, read as a whole, treated the intention of the person conducting the activity as an essential factor in the determination of the difference between treatment and research.[333] This did not mean that the answer to the question: "treatment or research?" was entirely subjective because the definition of treatment in para.2.2 required that "there is a reasonable chance of success". That test was objective, even though qualified by the *Bolam* test.

The meaning of "research" was important in *Walker-Smith v General Medical Council* because there is a requirement for medical research to be approved and monitored by an ethics committee, and a failure to do so could be categorised as professional misconduct.[334] It is also significant in the context of consent to treatment since it is arguable that the requirements for information disclosure are more extensive in the case of medical research.[335]   **7–118**

(ii)   Therapeutic research

Capacity to consent and voluntariness of consent   Therapeutic research   **7–119**
involves medical treatment of the patient's illness or disability, and on this basis it may be that there is little or no difference in the requirements for an effective consent by the patient, or, indeed as to the doctor's duty to disclose information about the risks of the procedure. Patients' capacity to consent for the purpose of the tort of battery would, be measured by the same criteria as are applied to any form of medical treatment, which depends upon their ability to understand the

---

[333] [2012] EWHC 503 (Admin); [2013] Med. L.R. 462; (2012) 126 B.M.L.R. 1 at [13]. For this purpose, there was no practical difference between "intention" and "purpose" in paras 2.2 and 2.3 of *Research Involving Patients*.
[334] The General Medical Council did not want the issue to turn entirely on the doctor's subjective intentions.
[335] See paras 7–120 et seq. below.

nature of the procedure.[336] Similarly, the voluntariness of the consent would be treated as a question of fact. Just as in a prison setting a court should be alive to the risk that what may appear, on the face of it, to be a real consent is not in fact so,[337] the court should also bear in mind that the stress of illness and the psychological pressures that patients may experience in a "dependent" relationship with their doctors might affect the voluntariness of their consent.[338] Patients may think, for example, that if they were to decline to participate that subsequently they would not be given the best available treatment or the most careful attention of the medical staff.[339] Thus, it is important that patients are aware that they are free to decline to participate, and that this will not affect the treatment that they will receive.

7–120   **Information disclosure**   The final issue concerns the question of how much information the patient must be given. It will be recalled that:

> "...once the patient is informed in broad terms of the nature of the procedure which is intended, and gives her consent, that consent is real."[340]

If the treatment also has a research purpose the question is whether this alters the nature of the procedure, so that a failure to tell patients that they are part of a research study would vitiate the consent. Alternatively, it might be argued that a failure to inform patients constitutes fraud or misrepresentation, on the basis that it involves withholding information in bad faith.[341] Here, everything turns on the meaning that is to be given to the term "nature of the procedure", and, in the absence of authority in this country, the answer must be largely speculative. If the court placed the emphasis on the therapeutic nature of the procedure, the fact that it was also experimental or part of a research project might be regarded as collateral to the therapy, to which consent "in broad terms" had been obtained. On this view the doctor's research intention would be irrelevant to the validity of the patient's consent. On the other hand, it is arguable that the existence of the research intention does indeed change the nature of what is done, irrespective of any additional risk to which the patient may be exposed by virtue of the research

---

[336] See paras 6–037 to 6–057. Children of 16 or 17 years of age will be in the same position as adults by virtue of the Family Law Reform Act 1969 s.8(1). Children under 16 should have capacity if they have sufficient understanding, applying *Gillick v West Norfolk & Wisbech Area Health Authority* [1986] A.C. 112. Query, however, whether a higher degree of understanding would be required for therapeutic research procedures than for simple "therapy", just as a high level of understanding is apparently required for contraceptive advice or treatment; see paras 6–196 to 6–197.

[337] *Freeman v Home Office* [1984] Q.B. 524 at 557; see para.6–034.

[338] In *Kaimowitz v Michegan Department of Mental Health* 42 U.S.L.W. 2063 (1973) it was held that an involuntarily detained mental patient could not give a valid consent to experimental psychosurgery because the process of institutionalisation undermined the voluntary nature of the consent.

[339] The *Declaration of Helsinki* para.27 provides that when obtaining consent the physician should be particularly cautious if the subject is in a dependent relationship with the physician or may consent under duress. In such a case consent should be obtained by a doctor who is not engaged in the research and who is completely independent of this relationship. Para.31 specifies that the refusal of the patient to participate in a study or the patient's decision to withdraw from the study must never interfere with the patient-physician relationship.

[340] *Chatterton v Gerson* [1981] Q.B. 432 at 443, para.6–058.

[341] See paras 6–063 to 6–065.

aspect.[342] It is submitted that the latter approach is correct on principle, on the basis that no one, least of all patients who may be in a particularly vulnerable position, should be the subject of medical research without being aware of the circumstances and consenting to participate.[343]

It has also been suggested that if the consent is to be valid patients must be informed of three further matters: **7–121**

(1)   that they may refuse to participate in the research project or may withdraw at any time from the research, and will suffer no adverse consequences in terms of the treatment they will then receive;

(2)   that they may be a member of a control group in a trial which is intended to evaluate the effectiveness of a new therapy; and

(3)   that the trial is a randomised controlled trial.[344]

The first matter relates to the question of the voluntariness of the consent: if patients do not know that there is no compulsion to participate it may be arguable that their consent was involuntary. The second and third issues relate to patients' knowledge of the treatment that they will receive. Although patients will normally be unaware of which group they will be allocated to, they should be informed of the nature of the treatment which each group will receive, otherwise they cannot consent, even in broad terms, to the nature of the procedure.

Notwithstanding that participation in therapeutic medical research may increase   **7–122**
the inherent risks of injury to a patient, it is unlikely that the courts would regard non-disclosure of risks as vitiating the reality of consent, given the general approach that has been taken to the tort of battery and the non-disclosure of risks.

---

[342] Kennedy & Grubb, *Medical Law*, 3rd edn (London: Butterworths, 2000), p.1710.

[343] The argument that patients should not be informed that they are part of a research study because this would necessarily involve telling them other things about their condition which it would be better for them that they did not know is clearly without substance. If it is in patients' interests not to be informed about their medical condition then this is an argument for excluding them from the study, not failing to inform them about it: see Kennedy, *Treat Me Right* (Oxford: Oxford University Press, 1988) p.223.

[344] Kennedy & Grubb, *Medical Law*, 3rd edn (London: Butterworths, 2000), p.1710. Under a randomised controlled trial two or more groups of research subjects are given different treatments and the results are compared for any statistically significant difference in outcomes; subjects are allocated to the trial groups randomly in order to eliminate any bias in the selection of subjects for particular treatments. It has been found, however, that the majority of patients do not understand the process of randomisation when it is explained to them: see Simes et al. (1986) 293 B.M.J. 1065, 1067. Query whether patients should be informed that the doctor is receiving payment from a pharmaceutical company for enrolling patients in a trial. Earlier guidance from the General Medical Council did not require disclosure of this fact to the patient. The current GMC guidance, *Good practice in research and consent to research* (2010) (available at *http://www.gmc-uk.org/static/documents/content/Good_practice_in_research_and_consent_to_research.pdf*) under a heading "Avoiding conflicts of interest" states that "You must be open and honest in all financial and commercial matters relating to your research and its funding" (para.26), and "You must not allow your judgement about a research project to be influenced, or be seen to be influenced, at any stage, by financial, personal, political or other external interests. You must identify any actual or potential conflicts of interest that arise, and declare them as soon as possible to the research ethics committee, other appropriate bodies, and the participants, in line with the policy of your employing or contracting body" (para.27). Query whether this unequivocally, requires disclosure of financial arrangements.

Clearly, doctors would owe at least the same duty of care to inform a patient about the material risks of treatment as for any other form of treatment, applying *Montgomery v Lanarkshire Health Board*.[345] The question is whether they would be under a duty to volunteer any additional information by virtue of a research intention. It is arguable that a research intention imports a greater responsibility for information disclosure so that doctors come under a duty to disclose all the known risks (not simply "material risks") associated with the therapy.[346] It could be said in reply that patients' need for treatment is the consequence of their medical condition and any question of the potential benefits of research to the public is incidental.

7–123   The *Declaration of Helsinki* states that research subjects:

"...must be adequately informed of the aims, methods, sources of funding, any possible conflicts of interest, institutional affiliations of the researcher, the anticipated benefits and potential risks of the study and the discomfort it may entail."

They should be informed of the right to abstain from participation in the study or to withdraw consent to participate at any time without reprisal. Research subjects should then give a free, informed consent, preferably in writing.[347]

7–124   **Canada**   The Canadian approach to this problem may be instructive. In *Zimmer v Ringrose*[348] the claimant was subjected to a novel and experimental method of sterilisation. At first instance the defendant was held liable because he had failed to inform the claimant that the technique had not been generally accepted by the medical profession, and had not informed her of the failure rate of up to 30 per cent. MacDonald J applied *Halushka v University of Saskatchewan*,[349] a case which was concerned with non-therapeutic research, holding the defendant liable in battery. The Alberta Court of Appeal reversed this decision, taking the view that the standard of disclosure required in *Halushka* was limited to non-therapeutic research:

"In the case of a truly 'experimental' procedure, like the one conducted in *Halushka v University of Saskatchewan*, no therapeutic benefit is intended to accrue to the participant. The subject is simply part of a scientific investigation designed to enhance human knowledge. By contrast, the sterilization procedure performed by the appellant in this case was directed towards achieving a therapeutic end ... [T]he silver nitrate method was experimental only in the sense that it represented an innovation in sterilisation techniques which were relatively

---

[345] [2015] UKSC 11; [2015] A.C. 1430.
[346] Kennedy & Grubb, *Medical Law*, 3rd edn (London: Butterworths, 2000, p.1711 argued that in addition to the information necessary for the purpose of avoiding liability in battery a doctor should be required, in law, to disclose: (i) material risks associated with the research; and (ii) material information necessary to enable the patient to make an "informed decision", e.g. any inconvenience associated with the fact that the patient is a research subject, such as additional hospital visits, additional tests etc.
[347] All at para.26. However, this is qualified under para.30 in the case of research on individuals from whom it is not possible to obtain consent. The Declaration states that the specific reasons for involving research subjects with a condition that renders them unable to give informed consent should be stated in the experimental protocol for consideration and approval of a research ethics committee.
[348] (1978) 89 D.L.R. (3d) 646, Alta SC.
[349] (1965) 53 D.L.R. (2d) 436.

untried ... To hold that every new development in medical technology was 'experimental' in the sense outlined in *Halushka v University of Saskatchewan* would be to discourage advances in the field of medicine."[350]

Nonetheless, the defendant was found to have been negligent in failing to discuss alternative methods of sterilisation because the claimant was given no opportunity to measure the risks involved in the silver nitrate method against those involved in other forms of sterilisation. A reasonable practitioner would also have informed the claimant that the technique had not been approved by the medical profession, since he would realise that this information would be likely to influence the patient's decision whether to undergo the procedure.[351] Similarly, in *Coughlin v Kuntz*[352] the defendant was held liable for failing to disclose that the contemplated operation was novel, unique to the defendant, and under investigation by a professional body, and for failing to inform the claimant that other medical experts had specifically advised against neck surgery.

7–125

Adults who lack capacity   The lawfulness of medical treatment given to adults who lack the capacity to give a valid consent depends upon whether the treatment is in the patient's best interests.[353] Given that the major premise of the decision in *Re F (Mental Patient: Sterilisation)*[354] was that patients who lacked capacity should not be deprived of treatment that would be available to a competent adult the courts would probably take the view that therapeutic research on incompetent adults can be justified if the treatment is in the patient's best interests. Whether treatment which is experimental in nature can be justified as being in the patient's best interests will depend on an assessment of the respective risks and benefits of that treatment compared to the best alternative standard therapy. Thus, where there is no alternative treatment, and the disease from which the incapacitated patient is suffering is progressive and fatal it would be reasonable to:

7–126

"...consider experimental treatment with unknown benefits and risks, but without significant risks of increased suffering to the patient, in cases where there is some chance of benefit to the

---

[350] (1981) 124 D.L.R. 215 at 222–223, per Prowse JA. See also *Cryderman v Ringrose* [1977] 3 W.W.R. 109; aff'd [1978] 3 W.W.R. 481, Alta CA, in which the claimant agreed to be sterilised by the same defendant by the same experimental procedure. The claimant was not informed that the procedure was unreliable or that it might damage the uterus. The trial judge distinguished *Halushka v University of Saskatchewan* (1965) 53 D.L.R. (2d) 436 on the basis that *Halushka* was a case of "pure medical experimentation", where different considerations would apply.

[351] "When an experimental procedure is employed the common law requires a high degree of care and also disclosure to the patient of the fact that the treatment is new and risky", per Stevenson DCJ in *Cryderman v Ringrose* [1977] 3 W.W.R. 109 at 118. The claim for non-disclosure in *Zimmer v Ringrose* failed on the ground that the claimant would have accepted the treatment in any event, although the action succeeded in respect of negligent aftercare.

[352] (1987) 42 C.C.L.T. 142, BCSC; aff'd [1990] 2 W.W.R. 737 at 745, BCCA.

[353] Mental Capacity Act 2005 s.4; see paras 6–129 et seq.

[354] [1990] 2 A.C. 1; see para.6–100.

patient. A patient who is not able to consent to pioneering treatment ought not to be deprived of the chance in circumstances where he would have been likely to consent if he had been competent."[355]

7–127   **Minors who lack capacity**   Therapeutic research on children who lack the relevant capacity will be lawful where parental consent has been obtained, provided the procedure can be said to be in the child's best interests. To the extent that doctors have a duty to disclose additional information to competent patients when the treatment forms part of a research project, the parents would be entitled to a comparable degree of disclosure.

7–128   **Randomised controlled trials and patients' best interests**   Certain forms of research give rise to problems in the case of patients who lack capacity. In a randomised controlled trial, some patients may well receive a treatment which the doctor does not believe to be in their best interests medically. The informed consent of a competent patient to participate may be taken to waive the doctor's duty to act in the patient's best interests, but it is a matter of some doubt whether such a waiver can ever apply where the patient is incapable of consenting.[356]

(iii)   Non-therapeutic research

7–129   As with therapeutic research, the three central issues are the capacity of the research subject to give a valid consent, the voluntariness of the consent, and the appropriate level of information disclosure. With adults, capacity will be treated as a question of fact, namely whether subjects understand the nature of the procedure to which they are consenting. It may be that the test in ss.2 and 3 of the Mental Capacity Act 2005 would apply to assess a volunteer's capacity to consent.[357] Children of 16 or 17 years would not be presumed to be competent by virtue of s.8(1) of the Family Law Reform Act 1969, since that section applies only to "surgical, medical or dental *treatment*",[358] but presumably *Gillick v West Norfolk and Wisbech Area Health Authority*[359] would apply to determine the competence of children to consent to non-therapeutic research. Possibly a higher degree of understanding would be required from a child than in the case of

---

[355] *Simms v Simms; A v A* [2002] EWHC 2734 (Fam); [2003] Fam. 83 at [57] per Butler-Sloss P. On the evidence in *Simms v Simms* it could not be said that treatment was clearly futile, and therefore it satisfied the *Bolam* test. See also *An NHS Trust v HM* [2004] Lloyd's Rep. Med. 207; *EP v Trusts A, B & C* [2004] Lloyd's Rep. Med. 211.

[356] See Kennedy, *Treat Me Right* (Oxford: Oxford University Press, 1988) Ch.10 for extended discussion of the law on randomised controlled trials. See now the Medicines for Human Use (Clinical Trials) Regulations 2004, para.7–145.

[357] See paras 6–045 et seq. If, however, the individual is found to lack capacity under this test, s.4 (best interests test) would not apply: see paras 7–135 to 7–138.

[358] See para.6–193.

[359] [1986] A.C. 112.

medical *treatment*,[360] and the greater the potential risk the greater the understanding that will be required. The voluntary nature of the consent will also be treated as a question of fact.[361]

The argument that the research subject should be fully informed is clearly much stronger in the case of non-therapeutic research. Withholding information about potential risks cannot be justified by reference to the research subject's medical condition or "best interests",[362] and so it is arguable that non-therapeutic research subjects should be given full and complete information about the nature of the research and the inherent risks. In *Halushka v University of Saskatchewan*[363] the claimant was a student who volunteered, for a fee, to undergo an experimental test on a new anaesthetic. He was told that it was a safe test which had been conducted many times before and that there was nothing to worry about. This was untrue, since the anaesthetic had not previously been used or tested by the defendants. The claimant was not told that all anaesthetic agents involve a certain degree of risk, nor was he told that a catheter, which he knew would be inserted into a vein in his arm, would be advanced into his heart. The claimant suffered cardiac arrest, caused by the anaesthetic, and was unconscious for four days. The defendants were held liable in trespass to the person on the basis of a lack of consent, a finding upheld by the Saskatchewan Court of Appeal. Hall JA said that:

> "There can be no exceptions to the ordinary requirements of disclosure in the case of research as there may well be in ordinary medical practice. The researcher does not have to balance the probable effect of lack of treatment against the risk involved in the treatment itself. The example of risks being properly hidden from a patient when it is important that he should not worry can have no application in the field of research. The subject of medical experimentation is entitled to a full and frank disclosure of all the facts, probabilities and opinions which a reasonable man might be expected to consider before giving his consent."[364]

This statement specifies an objective test for disclosure, based upon the information that a "reasonable volunteer" would want to have. Arguably, in the case of non-therapeutic research the test should be subjective (what *this* volunteer would want to know) for the very reasons that Hall JA gives.

Information disclosure   It is not clear whether a lack of information about risks, as opposed to the "nature" of the research procedure, would be treated in this country as relating to the researcher's duty of care in negligence rather than battery. In the context of negligence, in *Gold v Haringey Health Authority*[365] the

7–130

7–131

---

[360] cf. the high level of understanding stipulated by Lord Scarman in *Gillick v West Norfolk and Wisbech Area Health Authority* [1986] A.C. 112 at 189 before a child under 16 could be said to have sufficient capacity to consent to contraceptive advice or treatment: para.6–197.

[361] Where large financial inducements are provided to students or the unemployed this may raise a question mark about the voluntariness of the consent: see, e.g. *The Observer*, 2 October 1988, and *The Times*, 6 October 1986. In 1984 two student volunteers in drug trials died in separate incidents: *The Times*, 30 May 1984, 11 June 1984, and 25 April 1985.

[362] It has been suggested, however, that "informed consent" may bias the results of a clinical trial: Dahan et al. (1986) 293 B.M.J. 363; for criticism of this study see Launer (1986) 293 B.M.J. 627–628.

[363] (1965) 53 D.L.R. (2d) 436, Sask CA.

[364] (1965) 53 D.L.R. (2d) 436 at 443.

[365] [1988] Q.B. 481 at 489.

Court of Appeal refused to draw a distinction between advice given in a therapeutic and a non-therapeutic context, arguing that the *Bolam* test did not depend on the context in which advice was given, but on whether the defendant professed skill or competence in a field beyond that possessed by the man on the Clapham omnibus. On this approach the same standard would apply to a person conducting research as to a doctor providing treatment, which would now mean that a research subject would be entitled to be informed about the material risks that a "reasonable" research subject in that person's position would want to know.[366] It is arguable, however, that a healthy volunteer should be entitled to know more than simply the "material risks" and that disclosure should include all the risks known to the research team, including the very small or remote risks that might not be categorised as "material" in a therapeutic context. The healthy volunteer certainly has an ethical claim to full information about the anticipated risks of the procedure, and this should be reflected in the law.

7–132   Even where volunteers are fully informed about the risks involved in an experimental procedure there may well be some limits to the risks which they can agree to accept, such that if the risks are too great an apparently valid consent might be ineffective.[367]

(iv)   Non-therapeutic research on adults who lack capacity

7–133   Where a potential research subject lacks the capacity to give a valid consent the question arises whether it can ever be lawful for non-therapeutic research to be performed. By definition the research is not in the interests (whether these are categorised as "best interests" or merely "interests") of the research subject, and will normally carry some, albeit remote, risk of harm. On what legal basis could a proxy, whether it be a parent, the court or a doctor "authorise" a procedure that carried risk to the subject but was not intended to have any direct benefit for that person? In *Re F (Mental Patient: Sterilisation)*[368] the House of Lords adopted a wide interpretation of the principle of necessity so as to facilitate the provision of medical treatment to permanently incapacitated adults. The rationale was that adults lacking the capacity to consent should not be in a worse position than competent adults, and should not be deprived of treatment that would be available to them if they were in a position to consent, provided that the treatment could be shown to be in their best interests. The same logic, that they should not be in a worse position than competent adults, would suggest that it would never be lawful to subject an incompetent adult to non-therapeutic research which carried any risk of harm, because otherwise the individual lacking capacity clearly is placed in a worse position than the competent adult who has the right and ability

---

[366] Applying *Montgomery v Lanarkshire Health Board* [2015] UKSC 11; [2015] A.C. 1430.
[367] cf. *Attorney-General's Reference (No.6 of 1980)* [1981] Q.B. 715, where it was held that public policy may dictate that a consent is not valid in law, e.g. in the course of a prize fight. The report of an Institute of Medical Ethics working group recommended that non-therapeutic research procedures on children should not be carried out if they involve "greater than minimal risk": Nicholson, *Medical Research with Children* (Oxford: Oxford University Press, 1986), p.233. For discussion of the problems involved in quantifying acceptable levels of risk in the conduct of research see Nicholson (1986), Ch.5.
[368] [1990] 2 A.C. 1, paras 6–101 to 6–103.

to refuse to participate. Moreover, their Lordships made it clear in *Re F (Mental Patient: Sterilisation)* that the justification for providing treatment did not rest upon a proxy "consent" (which might give the proxy a limited power of choice or discretion) but on the principle of necessity, with the question of "necessity" to be determined, not by the needs of some other person or society in general, but by the best interests of the patient.

This problem was considered by the Law Commission in its report *Mental Incapacity*, where it was recommended that:

    7–134

> "...research which is unlikely to benefit a participant, or whose benefit is likely to be long delayed, should be lawful in relation to a person without capacity to consent if (1) the research is into an incapacitating condition with which the participant is or may be affected and (2) certain statutory procedures are complied with."[369]

The Commission recommended that there should be a statutory Mental Incapacity Research Committee, and a non-therapeutic research procedure should be lawful in relation to a person without capacity only if the committee had approved the research.

Mental Capacity Act 2005 This issue is now governed by the Mental Capacity Act 2005 ss.30–34, and Regulations made under the Act. Section 30(1) provides that intrusive research carried out on, or in relation to, a person who lacks capacity to consent to it is unlawful unless it is carried out (a) as part of a research project which is for the time being approved by the "appropriate body" for the purposes of the Act in accordance with s.31, and (b) in accordance with ss.32 and 33. The "appropriate body" is a committee (a) established to advise on, or on matters which include, the ethics of intrusive research in relation to people who lack capacity to consent to it; and (b) recognised for that purpose by the Secretary of State.[370] Thus, there must be an authorised research ethics committee which has approved the research project, though a clinical trial which is subject to the provisions of the Medicines for Human Use (Clinical Trials) Regulations 2004[371] (or any other regulations relating to clinical trials designated by the Secretary of State) is not to be treated as research for the purposes of s.30,[372] since a clinical trial governed by the Medicines for Human Use (Clinical Trials) Regulations will have to obtain research ethics committee approval under the specific regime for clinical trials. Research is "intrusive" if it is of a kind that would be unlawful if it was carried out (a) on or in relation to a person who had capacity to consent to it, but (b) without his consent.[373]

    7–135

---

[369] Law Com. No.231, (1995), para.6.31. Apparently, the majority of consultees argued that there is an ethical case for conducting non-therapeutic research on incompetent adults, which rested on the desirability of eradicating painful and distressing disabilities, where progress can be achieved without harming research subjects. See also the Law Commission's consultation paper, which preceded the final report, *Mentally Incapacitated Adults and Decision-Making: Medical Treatment and Research*, Law Com. No.129, 1993.

[370] Mental Capacity Act 2005 (Appropriate Body) (England) Regulations 2006 (SI 2006/2810).

[371] See para.7–140.

[372] Mental Capacity Act 2005 s.30(3).

[373] Mental Capacity Act 2005 s.30(2). Section 30(3A) provides that research is not intrusive where it consists of the use of a person's human cells to bring about the creation in vitro, or the subsequent

7–136   An ethics committee may not approve a research project for the purposes of the Mental Capacity Act unless it is satisfied that specific requirements will be met in relation to research carried out on, or in relation to, a person who lacks capacity to consent to taking part in the project ("P").[374] The research must be connected with (a) an impairing condition affecting P, or (b) its treatment.[375] An "impairing condition" means a condition which is (or may be) attributable to, or which causes or contributes to (or may cause or contribute to), the impairment of, or disturbance in the functioning of, the mind or brain.[376] There must be reasonable grounds for believing that research of comparable effectiveness cannot be carried out if the project has to be confined to, or relate only to, persons who have capacity to consent to taking part in it.[377] The research must also (a) have the potential to benefit P without imposing on P a burden that is disproportionate to the potential benefit to P (i.e. therapeutic research), or (b) be intended to provide knowledge of the causes or treatment of, or of the care of persons affected by, the same or a similar condition (i.e. non-therapeutic research).[378] If the research does not have the potential to benefit P without imposing a burden that is disproportionate to the potential benefit to him (and so is justified only by an intention to provide knowledge of the causes or treatment of persons affected by the same or a similar condition) there must be reasonable grounds for believing: (a) that the risk to P from taking part in the project is likely to be negligible, and (b) that anything done to, or in relation to, P will not interfere with P's freedom of action or privacy in a significant way, or be unduly invasive or restrictive.[379]

7–137   Section 32 provides that a person ("R") conducting an approved research project on or in relation to a person ("P") who lacks capacity to consent to taking part in the project must consult a person (who may be the donee of a lasting power of attorney given by P, or P's court-appointed deputy) who is engaged in caring for P or is interested in P's welfare (other than in a professional capacity or for remuneration), and is prepared to be consulted by R, or, if R is unable to identify such a person, he must nominate a person who is prepared to be consulted by R, but has no connection with the project.[380] R must provide the person consulted with information about the project and ask him (a) for advice as to whether P should take part in the project, and (b) what, in his opinion, P's wishes and feelings about taking part in the project would be likely to be if P had capacity in relation to the matter. If, at any time, the person consulted advises R that in his opinion P's wishes and feelings would be likely to lead him to decline to take part

---

storage or use, of an embryo or human admixed embryo. There are special rules applied to the situation where a person has consented to take part in a research project begun before the commencement of s.30, but before the conclusion of the project the person loses capacity to consent to continue to take part in it (see the Mental Capacity Act 2005 s.34, and the Mental Capacity Act 2005 (Loss of Capacity during Research Project) (England) Regulations 2007 (SI 2007/679) and the Mental Capacity Act 2005 (Loss of Capacity during Research Project) (Wales) Regulations 2007 (SI 2007/837)).

[374] Mental Capacity Act 2005 s.31(1).
[375] Mental Capacity Act 2005 s.31(2).
[376] Mental Capacity Act 2005 s.31(3).
[377] Mental Capacity Act 2005 s.31(4).
[378] Mental Capacity Act 2005 s.31(5).
[379] Mental Capacity Act 2005 s.31(6).
[380] Mental Capacity Act 2005 s.32(1)(2)(3) and (7).

in the project (or to wish to withdraw from it) if he had capacity, R must ensure that, if P is not already taking part in the project, he does not take part in it, or if P is taking part in the project, that he is withdrawn from it.[381] However, if R has reasonable grounds for believing that there would be a significant risk to P's health if treatment that P has been receiving as part of the project were discontinued R can continue to provide that treatment.[382] Subsections 32(8)(9) and (10) permit R not to follow the consultation process where treatment is provided as a matter of urgency, but only for so long as it is necessary to take the action as a matter of urgency.

The Act allows P to object to participation in a research project, even though he lacks the capacity to consent to participating.[383] Section 33(2)(a) provides that nothing may be done to, or in relation to, people who lack capacity to consent to which they appear to object (whether by showing signs of resistance or otherwise) except where what is being done is intended to protect them from harm or to reduce or prevent pain or discomfort. Moreover, if they indicate (in any way) that they wish to be withdrawn from the project they must be withdrawn without delay.[384] Similarly, P's previously expressed wishes about participation in research must be respected, so nothing may be done to him which would be contrary to an advance decision of his which has effect, or any other form of statement made by him and not subsequently withdrawn, of which R is aware.[385] At all times the interests of P must be assumed to outweigh those of science and society,[386] and so, for example, R cannot justify continuation of the research on, or in relation to P, simply because withdrawing P might prejudice the validity of the research project. If the person conducting the research has reasonable grounds for believing that one or more of the requirements set out in s.31 is no longer met in relation to research being carried out on P, then P must be withdrawn from the project, without delay,[387] though the provisions requiring that P be withdrawn from the research[388] do not require that treatment that P has been receiving as part of the project be discontinued if R has reasonable grounds for believing that there would be a significant risk to P's health if it were discontinued.[389]

7–138

---

[381] Mental Capacity Act 2005 s.32(5).

[382] Mental Capacity Act 2005 s.32(6).

[383] Although if the research is approved by the research ethics committee then the Human Tissue Act 2004 (Persons Who Lack Capacity to Consent and Transplants) Regulations 2006 (SI 2006/1659) reg.3(2)(c) deems that an incapacitated adult has consented. This applies to an activity involving the storage or use of material for the purposes in Sch.1 of the Human Act Tissue Act 2004 (which includes research in connection with disorders, or the functioning, of the human body) involving material from the incapacitated adult's body where the activity is done for the purpose of intrusive research which is carried out in accordance with the requirements of s.30(1)(a) and (b) of the Mental Capacity Act 2005.

[384] Mental Capacity Act 2005 s.33(4).

[385] Mental Capacity Act 2005 s.33(2)(b).

[386] Mental Capacity Act 2005 s.33(3).

[387] Mental Capacity Act 2005 s.33(5).

[388] Mental Capacity Act 2005 s.33(4) and (5).

[389] Mental Capacity Act 2005 s.33(6).

(v) Non-therapeutic research on minors who lack capacity

7–139   A similar problem arises in the case of non-therapeutic research on children.[390] How can a parent or indeed the court give a valid consent for research which by definition is not in the interests of the child, and may expose him to some risk, however small. The power of parents to exercise consent to medical treatment exists to protect the interests of children and must be exercised in their "best interests".[391] The view that non-therapeutic research on children is unlawful has been widely held by, inter alia, the Medical Research Council, the Medical Defence Union and the Medical Protection Society.[392] In more recent years, however, attitudes seem to have shifted and it has been argued that non-therapeutic research on children would be lawful in certain limited circumstances.[393] It remains to be seen how a court would respond to this question.[394]

(vi) The Medicines for Human Use (Clinical Trials) Regulations 2004

7–140   The Medicines for Human Use (Clinical Trials) Regulations 2004[395] implemented Directive 2001/20/EC[396] on good clinical practice in the conduct of clinical trials on medicinal products for human use. The Regulations apply to clinical trials on medicinal products only. A "clinical trial" is defined as any investigation in human subjects, other than a non-interventional trial,[397] intended (a) to discover or verify the clinical, pharmacological or other pharmacodynamic effects of one or more medicinal products, (b) to identify any adverse reactions to one or more such products, or (c) to study absorption, distribution, metabolism and excretion of one or more such products, with the object of ascertaining the

---

[390] Though bear in mind that the Mental Capacity Act 2005 applies to minors aged 16 or 17.

[391] *Gillick v West Norfolk and Wisbech Area Health Authority* [1986] A.C. 112, para.6–209. The same test is applied to the courts' exercise of the wardship jurisdiction: para.6–213.

[392] See Dworkin (1978) 53 Arch. Disease in Childhood 443.

[393] Dworkin (1978) 53 Arch. Disease in Childhood 443; Dworkin (1987) 13 Monash Univ. L.R. 189. For an extended discussion of this problem see Nicholson, *Medical Research with Children*, 1986, OUP.

[394] See the US case of *Grimes v Kennedy Krieger Institute Inc* (2001) 366 Md 29; 782 A2d 807 holding that there are limits to the parental power to consent to non-therapeutic research on minors, and that it is not in the best interests of healthy children to be put at risk of harm for the benefit to other children in the future.

[395] SI 2004/1031.

[396] The EU Clinical Trials Regulation (EU Regulation No.536/2014) repeals and replaces Directive 2001/20/EC but is not scheduled to come into operation until 2018. Details are available at *http://ec.europa.eu/health/human-use/clinical-trials/regulation/index_en.htm* and on the European Medicines Agency website: *http://www.ema.europa.eu/ema*.

[397] A non-intervention trial is a study of one or more medicinal products which have a marketing authorisation, where (a) the products are prescribed in the usual manner in accordance with the terms of that authorisation, (b) the assignment of any patient involved in the study to a particular therapeutic strategy is not decided in advance by a protocol but falls within current practice, (c) the decision to prescribe a particular medicinal product is clearly separated from the decision to include the patient in the study, (d) no diagnostic or monitoring procedures are applied to the patients included in the study, other than those which are ordinarily applied in the course of the particular therapeutic strategy in question, and (e) epidemiological methods are to be used for the analysis of the data arising from the study.

safety or efficacy of those products. Such trials cannot be conducted unless they have been approved by an ethics committee and authorised by the licensing authority.[398] All clinical trials must be conducted in accordance with good clinical practice[399] the requirements for which are laid down in Sch.1 of the Regulations.[400] The Regulations cover three categories of participant for which specific rules are laid down: (1) competent adults (though an adult means a person who has attained the age of 16); (2) minors; and (3) incompetent adults.

Competent adults   Competent adults include those who gave consent before the onset of incapacity. It is a requirement that research subjects have: (i) had an interview with the investigator, or another member of the investigating team, in which they have been given the opportunity to understand the objectives, risks and inconveniences of the trial and the conditions under which it is to be conducted; (ii) been informed of their right to withdraw from the trial at any time; (iii) given their informed consent to taking part in the trial; and (iv) been provided with a contact point where they may obtain further information about the trial.[401] In addition the research subject may, without being subject to any resulting detriment, withdraw from the clinical trial at any time by revoking their informed consent. People give informed consent to take part in a clinical trial only if their decision: (a) is given freely after that person is informed of the nature, significance, implications and risks of the trial; and (b) either (i) is evidenced in writing, dated and signed, or otherwise marked, by that person so as to indicate their consent, or (ii) if the person is unable to sign or to mark a document so as to indicate their consent, is given orally in the presence of at least one witness and recorded in writing.[402]

7–141

Minors[403] and adults lacking capacity—common principles   In relation to both minors and incapacitated adults there are four common principles, namely: (i) an informed consent given by a person with parental responsibility or a legal representative to a minor or incapacitated adult taking part in a clinical trial represents the research subject's presumed will; (ii) the clinical trial must have been designed to minimise pain, discomfort, fear and any other foreseeable risk in relation to the disease and the minor's stage of development or the adult's cognitive abilities; (iii) the risk threshold and the degree of distress have to be

7–142

---

[398] Medicines for Human Use (Clinical Trials) Regulations 2004 (SI 2004/1031) reg.12. For the meaning of the "licensing authority" see the Human Medicines Regulations 2012 (SI 2012/1916) reg.6.

[399] Medicines for Human Use (Clinical Trials) Regulations 2004 reg.28.

[400] As amended by the Medicines for Human Use (Clinical Trials) Amendment Regulations 2006 (SI 2006/1928) reg.27, the Medicines for Human Use (Clinical Trials) Amendment (No.2) Regulations 2006 (SI 2006/2984) reg.2, and the Medicines for Human Use (Clinical Trials) and Blood Safety and Quality (Amendment) Regulations 2008 (SI 2008/941) reg.4. This includes a requirement to comply with the principles of the Declaration of Helsinki.

[401] Medicines for Human Use (Clinical Trials) Regulations 2004 (SI 2004/1031) Sch.1 Pt 3.

[402] Medicines for Human Use (Clinical Trials) Regulations 2004 Sch.1 Pt 1 para.3.

[403] For the purpose of the Regulations a minor is a person under the age of 16.

specially defined and constantly monitored; and (iv) the interests of the patient must always prevail over those of science and society.[404]

7–143 **Minors** There are then specific requirements[405] for clinical trials using a minor as a research subject, namely: (i) a person with parental responsibility for the minor or, in an emergency a legal representative for the minor, has had an interview with the investigator, or another member of the investigating team, and been given the opportunity to understand the objectives, risks and inconveniences of the trial and the conditions under which it is to be conducted; (ii) that person or legal representative has been provided with a contact point to obtain further information about the trial; (iii) that person or legal representative has been informed of the right to withdraw the minor from the trial at any time; (iv) that person or legal representative has given informed consent to the minor taking part in the trial; (v) the person with parental responsibility or the legal representative may, without the minor being subject to any resulting detriment, withdraw the minor from the trial at any time by revoking the informed consent; (vi) the minor has received information according to his capacity of understanding, from staff with experience with minors, regarding the trial, its risks and its benefits; (vii) the explicit wish of a minor who is capable of forming an opinion and assessing the information to refuse participation in, or to be withdrawn from, the clinical trial at any time is considered by the investigator; (viii) no incentives or financial inducements are given (a) to the minor; or (b) to a person with parental responsibility for that minor or, as the case may be, the minor's legal representative, except provision for compensation in the event of injury or loss; (ix) the clinical trial relates directly to a clinical condition from which the minor suffers or is of such a nature that it can only be carried out on minors; (x) some direct benefit for the group of patients involved in the clinical trial is to be obtained from that trial; (xi) the clinical trial is necessary to validate data obtained (a) in other clinical trials involving persons able to give informed consent, or (b) by other research methods; and (xii) the corresponding scientific guidelines of the European Medicines Agency are followed.

7–144 The Regulations contemplate that a non-therapeutic clinical trial could be undertaken on a minor since the clinical trial must relate directly to a clinical condition from which the minor suffers or "is of such a nature that it can only be carried out on minors". There are no specific provisions, however, governing the basis on which a person with parental responsibility should, or indeed could, give a valid consent (no matter how well "informed") to allow a child to participate in a clinical trial which has no therapeutic benefits for the child, given that the consent would have to be in the best interests of the child. Arguably, this would not be a problem if the child was *Gillick* competent, but where the minor lacks

---

[404] SI 2004/1031 Sch.1 Pt 4 paras 13 to 16, and Pt 5 paras 12 to 15. An exception applies to the requirement to obtain informed consent where treatment is being, or is about to be, provided as a matter of urgency where it is also necessary to take action for the purposes of the clinical trial as a matter of urgency and it is not reasonably practicable to obtain informed consent provided the action taken is carried out in accordance with a procedure approved by an ethics committee at the time when the protocol was approved: Sch.1 Pt 1 para.1(3),(4),(6) and (7).
[405] SI 2004/1031 Sch.1 Pt 4 paras 1 to 12.

capacity precisely the same problem as arises under any other form of non-therapeutic medical research on children would apply.[406]

Adults lacking capacity   In addition to the general principles applicable to both minors and incapacitated adults,[407] there are specific requirements[408] for conducting a clinical trial on adults who lack capacity to consent: (i) the research subject's legal representative has had an interview with the investigator, or another member of the investigating team, in which they have been given the opportunity to understand the objectives, risks and inconveniences of the trial and the conditions under which it is to be conducted; (ii) the legal representative has been provided with a contact point to obtain further information about the trial; (iii) the legal representative has been informed of the right to withdraw the subject from the trial at any time; (iv) the legal representative has given informed consent to the subject taking part in the trial; (v) the legal representative may, without the subject being subject to any resulting detriment, withdraw the subject from the trial at any time by revoking the informed consent; (vi) the subject has received information according to his capacity of understanding regarding the trial, its risks and its benefits; (vii) the explicit wish of a subject who is capable of forming an opinion and assessing the information referred to in the previous paragraph to refuse participation in, or to be withdrawn from, the clinical trial at any time is considered by the investigator; (viii) no incentives or financial inducements are given to the subject or their legal representative, except provision for compensation in the event of injury or loss; (ix) there are grounds for expecting that administering the medicinal product to be tested in the trial will produce a benefit to the subject outweighing the risks or produce no risk at all; (x) the clinical trial is essential to validate data obtained (a) in other clinical trials involving persons able to give informed consent, or (b) by other research methods; (xi) the clinical trial relates directly to a life-threatening or debilitating clinical condition from which the subject suffers.

7–145

The effect of these provisions (which is in marked contrast to those governing minors) is that the research must be of some potential benefit to the incapacitated adult. There must be grounds for expecting that the pharmaceutical product administered "will produce a benefit to the subject outweighing the risks or produce no risk at all" (and it is difficult to envisage a pharmaceutical product that is being tested for its safety or efficacy that will produce "no risk at all"). Moreover, the trial must relate "directly to a life-threatening or debilitating clinical condition from which the subject suffers". Thus, non-therapeutic research on an adult lacking capacity cannot be authorised under the Regulations.

7–146

---

[406] See para.7–139. E. Cave, "Seen but not Heard? Children in Clinical Trials" (2010) 18 Med. L. Rev. 1 discusses the position of minors under the Clinical Trials Regulations.
[407] See para.7–142.
[408] Medicines for Human Use (Clinical Trials) Regulations 2004 (SI 2004/1031) Sch.1 Pt 5 paras 1 to 11. Note that where an activity is done for the purpose of a clinical trial authorised and conducted in accordance with the Clinical Trials Regulations an incapacitated adult is deemed to have consented to the activity which involves material from the incapacitated adult's body: Human Tissue Act 2004 (Persons Who Lack Capacity to Consent and Transplants) Regulations 2006 (SI 2006/1659) reg.3(2)(b).

(vii) Embryo research

7–147   The Human Fertilisation and Embryology Act 1990 s.11, provides for the regulation of research on human embryos and human admixed embryos[409] by a statutory Licensing Authority which may grant licences for the purpose of approved research projects. There are restrictions on the type and purpose of research that may be conducted.[410] Under s.12 one of the conditions for the grant of a licence is that the provisions of Sch.3 concerning consent must be complied with. The consent required is the consent of each person whose gametes or human cells are used for the creation of an in vitro embryo or human admixed embryo, and the consent must specify the purpose for which the embryo may be used, namely treatment services or for the purposes of a project of research.[411] Consent is also required for the storage of gametes, embryos or human admixed embryos, but in any event they may not be stored for more than 10 years.[412] The consent must be in writing and must (normally) be signed. Consent may be varied or withdrawn, but not after the embryo has been used in research.[413] Before people give consent they must be given an opportunity to receive proper counselling about the implications and they must be "provided with such relevant information as is proper", including their right to vary or withdraw consent.[414] In the case of minors and adults who lack capacity to consent, human cells can be used to create an embryo or human admixed embryo for the purposes of a project of research without the consent of the individual whose cells are used in very limited circumstances.[415]

7–148   The Act does not confer any civil remedy for breach of the provisions concerning consent, although failure to comply with the consent requirements would be a breach of the licence conditions stipulated by s.12 and thus would be in contravention of s.3(1), constituting a criminal offence.[416] It might possibly be argued that a breach of the consent requirements should give rise to a tort of breach of statutory duty, although it could be replied that if Parliament had intended to grant a civil remedy for breach of the Act it could easily have made

---

[409] For the definition of human admixed embryo see s.4A(6).

[410] Human Fertilisation and Embryology Act 1990 s.3 (as amended) and Sch.2 paras 3 and 3A. For consideration of what constitutes an embryo see *R. (on the application of Quintavalle) v Secretary of State for Health* [2003] UKHL 13; [2003] 2 A.C. 687.

[411] Human Fertilisation and Embryology Act 1990 Sch.3 para.6 and para.12.

[412] Human Fertilisation and Embryology Act 1990 Sch.3 para.8 and s.14.

[413] Human Fertilisation and Embryology Act 1990 Sch.3 para.1 and para.4. For consideration of the right to withdraw consent under this provision see *Evans v Amicus Healthcare Ltd* [2004] EWCA Civ 727; [2005] Fam. 1 (which concerned fertility treatment rather than research on embryos, on which see also Sch.3 para.4A). The European Court of Human Rights has held that an individual's right to withdraw consent to fertility treatment with an embryo created from his gametes does not violate the other genetic parent's human rights under the European Convention: *Evans v United Kingdom* (Application No.6339/05) [2007] 2 F.C.R. 5; (2007) 95 B.M.L.R. 107.

[414] Human Fertilisation and Embryology Act 1990 Sch.3 para.3. See *Mrs U v Centre for Reproductive Medicine* [2002] EWCA Civ 565; [2002] Lloyd's Rep. Med. 259.

[415] See Human Fertilisation and Embryology Act 1990 Sch.3 paras 15 to 19.

[416] Human Fertilisation and Embryology Act 1990 s.41(2). It is a defence for the person charged to prove that he took all reasonable steps and exercised all due diligence to avoid committing the offence.

express provision to this effect.[417] Alternatively, it might be possible to argue that an action for psychiatric harm should be available, if, for example, a person's gametes or embryos were used for research purposes without his or her consent.[418] This is highly speculative, however, and would depend, inter alia, upon proving that the claimant had suffered from a genuine psychiatric illness as a consequence, not simply emotional distress or grief.

(b) Transplantation

The live donation of organs must be limited to regenerative tissue such as blood or bone marrow, or paired organs such as kidneys, where it is known that the donor can survive with a single organ. Donors cannot give valid consent to the removal of an organ that will result in their death or serious disability.[419] The recipient of an organ transplant will be in the same position as any other patient receiving treatment with regard to consent and information disclosure, bearing in mind the degree of risk associated with the particular form of transplantation.[420] It is arguable, however, that a much stricter standard of information disclosure is required for donors of organs. Their position is analogous to that of volunteers for non-therapeutic research, since the operation is of no medical benefit to the donor, and carries the risk of harm to their health. On this basis, it is submitted that there should be a full and frank disclosure of risks.[421]

7-149

Human Tissue Act 2004   The transplantation of organs and human tissue (the statute refers to "relevant material"[422]) is now governed by the Human Tissue Act

7-150

---

[417] For discussion of the problems surrounding the inference of the tort when Parliament has not expressly dealt with the matter see *Clerk & Lindsell on Torts*, 22nd edn (London: Sweet & Maxwell, 2018) Ch.9.

[418] On psychiatric harm generally, see paras 2–187 et seq. See *Yearworth v North Bristol NHS Trust* [2009] EWCA Civ 37; [2010] Q.B. 1, para.2–242, on the position where the claimants' gametes, which were being stored by the defendants, had been destroyed allegedly as a result of the negligence of the defendants.

[419] *Attorney-General's Reference (No.6 of 1980)* [1981] Q.B. 715; *R. v Brown* [1994] 1 A.C. 212; see generally Dworkin (1970) 33 M.L.R. 353.

[420] Where the patient is incapable of giving a valid consent, for example, in the case of a minor the question is whether the surgery is in the child's best interests: see *An Hospital NHS Trust v S* [2003] EWHC 365 (Fam); [2003] Lloyd's Rep. Med. 137. For a case involving the refusal of a parent to consent to a liver transplant for an 18-month-old child see: *Re T (A Minor) (Wardship: Medical Treatment)* [1997] 1 All E.R. 906, CA, para.6–222; cf. *Re M (A Child) (Refusal of Medical Treatment)* [1999] 2 F.L.R. 1097; [1999] 2 F.C.R. 577, where the court considered that heart transplant surgery should be authorised for a 15-year-old girl, in her best interests.

[421] See Norrie (1985) 34 I.C.L.Q. 442, 452. If doctors' negligence is the cause of the need for the transplantation they may be liable to the donor for the consequences of the donation: *Urbanski v Patel* (1978) 84 D.L.R. (3d) 650, Man QB; para.2–131.

[422] This means material, other than gametes, which consists of or includes human cells, but does not include embryos outside the human body, or hair and nail from the body of a living person: Human Tissue Act 2004 s.53.

2004.[423] The Act confirms that the donation of organs and human tissue is lawful provided it is done with appropriate consent.[424]

7–151   **Live donation**   In the case of live donations, "appropriate consent" means, in the case of an adult, the adult's consent,[425] and in the case a child[426] who has capacity to consent, the child's consent.[427] If the child is alive but is not competent to deal with the issue of consent, or though competent fails to do so, then provided neither a decision of his to consent to the activity, nor a decision of his not to consent to it, is in force, "appropriate consent" means the consent of the person who has parental responsibility.[428] Section 6 makes it lawful to take material from the body of incapacitated adults for the purpose of a transplant in circumstances specified in Regulations, provided that neither a decision of theirs to consent to the activity, nor a decision of theirs not to consent to it, is in force.[429]

7–152   **Live donation—conditions**   Section 33 makes it a criminal offence to remove transplantable material[430] from the body of a living person intending that the material be used for the purpose of transplantation unless the conditions laid down in Regulations are satisfied. These requirements are laid down in reg.11 of the Human Tissue Act 2004 (Persons Who Lack Capacity to Consent and Transplants) Regulations 2006,[431] which provides that a registered medical practitioner with clinical responsibility for the donor must have referred the matter to the Human Tissue Authority; and the Authority must be satisfied that (a) no reward has been or is to be given in contravention of s.32 of the Act, and (b) when the transplantable material is removed (i) consent for its removal for the purpose of transplantation has been given, or (ii) its removal for that purpose is otherwise lawful. Where the referral concerns an organ the referral must state that the doctor (a) is satisfied that the donor's health and medical history are suitable for the purposes of donation; and (b) has (i) provided the donor with the information the donor requires to understand the consequences of donation, and (ii) endeavoured to obtain information from the donor that is relevant to transplantation. Except where the removal of the transplantable material for the

---

[423] The Act is commented on by D. Price (2005) 68 M.L.R. 798.

[424] Though commercial dealing in human material for transplantation is an offence: Human Tissue Act 2004 s.32.

[425] Human Tissue Act 2004 s.3(2).

[426] Note that this means someone who has not attained the age of 18: Human Tissue Act 2004 s.54(1); cf. the Mental Capacity Act 2005 which applies to minors of 16 or 17 years.

[427] Human Tissue Act 2004 s.2(2).

[428] Human Tissue Act 2004 s.2(3).

[429] Section 6 does not apply to transplantation activities in Wales (on which see the Human Transplantation (Wales) Act 2013, s.9).

[430] "Transplantable material" means (a) an organ, or part of an organ if it is to be used for the same purpose as the entire organ in the human body, (b) bone marrow, and (c) peripheral blood stem cells, where that material is removed from the body of a living person with the intention that it be transplanted into another person: Human Tissue Act 2004 (Persons Who Lack Capacity to Consent and Transplants) Regulations 2006 (SI 2006/1659) reg.10(1). But the material referred to in (b) and (c) is transplantable material only where the donor is either an adult who lacks capacity or a child who is not competent to consent: reg.10(3).

[431] SI 2006/1659.

purpose of transplantation is authorised by an order of a court, one or more qualified persons[432] must have conducted separate interviews with (a) the donor, (b) if different from the donor, the person giving consent, and (c) the recipient, and reported to the Authority on the following matters: (a) any evidence of duress or coercion affecting the decision to give consent; (b) any evidence of an offer of a reward; and (c) any difficulties of communication with the person interviewed and an explanation of how those difficulties were overcome. In addition the report of the interview with the donor and, where relevant, the other person giving consent must cover: (a) the information given to the person interviewed as to the nature of the medical procedure for, and the risk involved in, the removal of the transplantable material; (b) the full name of the person who gave that information and his qualification to give it, and (c) the capacity of the person interviewed to understand (i) the nature of the medical procedure and the risk involved, and (ii) that the consent may be withdrawn at any time before the removal of the transplantable material.

Although the Regulations are not explicit about requiring full disclosure of *all* the risks (even remote risks of minor consequences), it is arguable that this is what is required. The Regulations confirm that the donor's fully informed consent is not sufficient to render a transplant lawful, since the Authority must be satisfied that "removal for that purpose is otherwise lawful". As indicated above,[433] as a matter of policy not all donations would be lawful even with consent. Thus, an individual would not be permitted to consent to a procedure that would probably result in his death, even with a view to saving the life of another person.   **7–153**

Donors who lack capacity   The Human Tissue Act 2004 clearly contemplates   **7–154**
that in some circumstances it will be lawful to take material for transplant from a minor who is not competent to consent or an incapacitated adult. In the case of a minor the Act provides for appropriate consent to be the consent of the person who has parental responsibility, but it says nothing about the criteria that should be applied by a person exercising parental responsibility when making a decision whether or not to consent. The normal principle applied to persons exercising parental responsibility is that decisions should be taken in the child's best interests. Regulation 3 of the Human Tissue Act 2004 (Persons Who Lack Capacity to Consent and Transplants) Regulations 2006,[434] in combination with s.6,[435] makes it lawful to take material from incapacitated adults for transplant for certain purposes, provided that neither a decision of theirs to consent to the activity, nor a decision of theirs not to consent to it, is in force. Regulation 3(2) deems that an incapacitated adult has consented to an activity involving the storage or use of material for the purposes in Sch.1 of the Act (which includes transplantation) where the activity is done by people who are acting in what they reasonably believe to be the incapacitated adult's best interests. Neither the Act nor the Regulations specify any criteria for determining the incapacitated adult's

---

[432] As defined in reg.11(10).
[433] Para.7–149.
[434] SI 2006/1659.
[435] Section 6 does not apply to transplantation activities in Wales (on which see the Human Transplantation (Wales) Act 2013, s.9).

best interests (which, presumably, will be governed by the Mental Capacity Act 2005[436]). Thus, the Human Tissue Act has not resolved the question to which the common law had not been able to give any clear answer, which is how it can be in the *best interests* of an incompetent donor to donate an organ or tissue when the process involves risk to the donor, but no obvious benefit.

7–155   The position of incompetent donors appears to be analogous to non-therapeutic research on children and incompetent adults. On one view, this would mean that organs can never be taken from such donors, since donation clearly creates risk to the donor, especially where it involves surgical intervention, and a parent cannot consent to procedures which are contrary to the interests of the child.[437] Some American courts have adopted an extended interpretation of an incompetent donor's "best interests" to include the psychological benefits that would accrue to the donor in order to justify donation between siblings.[438] On the other hand, all Canadian provinces have enacted legislation based on the Uniform Tissue Gift Act,[439] which prohibits minors and mentally incompetent adults from making live donations of non-regenerative tissue.[440] Donation of regenerative tissue such as blood, bone marrow, or skin by minors is left to the common law.

7–156   There are no English cases dealing with organ donation from an incompetent donor, although in *Re F (Mental Patient: Sterilisation)* Neill LJ did touch upon the point:

> "There are, however, some operations where the intervention of a court is most desirable if not essential. In this category I would place operations for sterilisation and organ transplant operations where the incapacitated patient is to be the donor. The performance of these operations should be subject to outside scrutiny. The lawfulness of the operation will depend of course on the question of whether it is necessary or not, but in my view it should become standard practice for the approval of the court to be obtained before an operation of this exceptional kind is carried out."[441]

His Lordship clearly contemplated that organ donation from incompetent donors could be lawful, subject to the supervision of the court,[442] depending upon whether it was "necessary or not". This rather begs the question, however, since the operation may well be necessary from the recipient's point of view, but it might be extremely difficult to claim that it was *necessary* for the incompetent donor's welfare to give up an organ.

---

[436] See para.6–129.

[437] See para.6–209; Norrie (1985) 34 I.C.L.Q. 442, 453.

[438] *Strunk v Strunk* 445 S.W. 2d 145 (1969), Kentucky App; *Hart v Brown* 289 A. 2d 386 (1972), Conn; *Little v Little* 576 S.W. 2d 493 (1979), Texas CA; Dickens (1981) 97 L.Q.R. 462, 476–477; cf. *Re Richardson* 284 So. 2d 388 (1973), Louisiana CA; *Re Pescinski* 226 N.E. 2d 180 (1975), Wisconsin SC; *Curran v Bosze* 566 N.E. 2d 1319 (1990), Ill SC; see Robertson (1976) 76 Columbia Law Rev. 48 discussing the principle of "substituted judgment" under which the decision-maker attempts to make the judgment about donation on behalf of the incompetent donor which the donor would have made if competent.

[439] Except Quebec, which has its own legislative provisions.

[440] Picard and Robertson, *Legal Liability of Doctors and Hospitals in Canada*, 4th edn (Canada: Carswell, 2007), pp.109–110; although a few provinces do permit the inter vivos donation of non-regenerative tissue by minors aged 16 or over, subject to conditions.

[441] [1990] 2 A.C. 1 at 33.

[442] A view which had been taken in *Hart v Brown* 289 A. 2d 386 at 391 (1972).

Regenerative tissue and donors who lack capacity   The argument is   **7–157**
somewhat easier to mount in the case of regenerative tissue, at least where it can
be said that there is some benefit to the donor. In *Re Y (Mental Patient: Bone
Marrow Donation)*[443] the claimant, who was aged 36, needed a bone marrow
transplant for the treatment of non-Hodgkin's lymphoma. There was a strong
likelihood that her condition would progress to acute myeloid leukaemia within
three months. Her sister (the defendant), aged 25, was a suitable donor, but was
severely mentally and physically handicapped, and incapable of consenting. She
had lived in residential accommodation since the age of 10. Her family kept in
touch with her through visits, but the relationship between the sisters was not
particularly strong. The claimant's own ill health had reduced her ability to visit
her sister. The relationship with her mother, who visited regularly, was close, but
the mother was herself now in bad health. The claimant sought an order that two
preliminary blood tests and a bone marrow harvesting operation under general
anaesthetic could lawfully be performed on the defendant, on the basis that they
were in the defendant's best interests. Connell J granted the order. His Lordship
acknowledged that any benefits to the claimant were only relevant in so far as
they had a positive effect on the interests of the defendant. The "substituted
judgment" approach, whereby the court considers what decision the defendant
would have come to had she been capable of consenting, was not relevant.
Connell J accepted that the defendant benefited from the visits of her family. If
the claimant died it would have an adverse effect on the mother, who was already
in ill health, and she would then probably be more restricted in her ability to visit
the defendant by having to look after the claimant's daughter, her only
grandchild. The defendant would then be harmed by the reduction in or loss of
contact with her mother. On the basis of the medical evidence, the physical risks
of the procedure were less than 1 in 10,000 from the general anaesthetic (which
was the same risk as for any healthy patient undergoing a general anaesthetic),
and the defendant had previously had surgery under a general anaesthetic. Thus,
although there were no medical benefits to the defendant, the procedure was to
her "emotional, psychological and social benefit". Connell J was careful to limit
the ambit of his decision to a case involving regenerative tissue:

> "It is doubtful that this case would act as a useful precedent in cases where the surgery
> involved is more intrusive than in this case, where the evidence shows that the bone marrow
> harvested is speedily regenerated and that a healthy individual can donate as much as two pints
> with no long term consequences at all. Thus, the bone marrow donated by the defendant will
> cause her no loss and she will suffer no real long-term risk."[444]

In principle, however, although the medical risks involved in the donation of
bone marrow are probably less than those involved in the donation of a kidney,
there is little to distinguish the two situations. It is a difference of degree rather
than of kind, so that if the balance of advantage in weighing the "emotional,
psychological and social benefit" against the medical risk to the incompetent
donor comes down in favour of the donation, there would seem to be no difficulty

---

[443] [1997] Fam. 110.
[444] [1997] Fam. 110 at 116.

in law in the court granting a declaration that the procedure would be lawful. It is clear that, in such cases, the court must be involved in determining the best interests of the incompetent donor.[445]

7–158   **Cadaver donation**   Cadaver donations are also governed by the Human Tissue Act 2004 in England and Northern Ireland. The removal of an organ from the body of a deceased person for transplantation is lawful if it is done with "appropriate consent". Where the deceased was a child[446] "appropriate consent" means: (a) if a decision of his to consent to the donation of organs, or a decision of his not to consent, was in force immediately before he died, his consent; or (b) if (a) does not apply (i) the consent of a person who had parental responsibility for him immediately before he died, or (ii) where no person had parental responsibility for him immediately before he died, the consent of a person who stood in a qualifying relationship to him at that time.[447] Where the deceased was an adult "appropriate consent" means: (a) if a decision of his to consent to the donation, or a decision of his not to consent, was in force immediately before he died, his consent; or (b) if (a) does not apply and he has appointed a person or persons under s.4 (a nominated representative) to deal after his death with the issue of consent in relation to the donation, consent given under the appointment; or (c) if neither para.(a) nor para.(b) apply, the consent of a person who stood in a qualifying relationship to him immediately before he died.[448] If a nominated representative is not able to give consent the appointment is disregarded; and if it is not reasonably practicable to communicate with a nominated representative within the time available if consent in relation to the activity is to be acted on, he is treated as unable to give consent under the appointment.[449]

7–159   **Cadaver donation in Wales**   From 1 December 2015 the Human Transplantation (Wales) Act 2013 introduced a system of deemed consent under which individuals who lived and died in Wales are presumed to have consented to the donation of their organs for transplantation on death unless they had opted out. The scheme does not apply to minors or adults who lacked capacity, nor to persons who have not voluntarily lived in Wales for more than 12 months. Family

---

[445] Court of Protection, Practice Direction E (supplementing the Court of Protection Rules 2007, Pt 9)—*Applications relating to serious medical treatment* para.5, applying inter alia to organ or bone marrow donation by a person who lacks capacity to consent. Note that from 1 December 2017, the Court of Protection Rules 2007 will be replaced by the Court of Protection Rules 2017 (SI 2017/1035).

[446] This means someone who has not attained the age of 18: Human Tissue Act 2004 s.54(1).

[447] Human Tissue Act 2004 s.2(7). Qualifying relationships are ranked by s.27(4). The views of a person in a higher ranking qualifying relationship take precedence (s.27(6)), and if there is disagreement between persons in a qualifying relationship of equal rank, it is sufficient to obtain the consent of any of them (s.27(7)).

[448] Human Tissue Act 2004 s.3(6). Qualifying relationships are ranked by s.27(4). See *CM v Executor for the Estate of EJ (Deceased)* [2013] EWHC 1680 (Fam); [2013] Med. L.R. 321; (2013) 133 B.M.L.R. 203 for consideration of the meaning of a person in a "qualifying relationship" with the deceased where a third party applies for a blood sample from the deceased for the purpose of testing for a serious blood-borne disease.

[449] Human Tissue Act 2004 s.3(7) and (8).

members cannot veto the deemed consent but they can provide evidence that the deceased objected to donation, in which case the deemed consent provisions do not apply.

Retained organs   The Human Tissue Act 2004 was enacted to provide a detailed statutory framework for the removal, storage and use of human organs and other tissue, in response to the "retained organs" scandal, which was not concerned with organs for transplantation but with organs and tissue retained for research purposes.[450] Although the retention of organs was particularly distressing to the families of the deceased, particularly in the case of parents of young children, the legal basis for any claim that the relatives might have had was somewhat tenuous. The general principle of English law is that there is no property in a corpse,[451] and therefore no general proprietary right to control what happens to a corpse or body parts. In the absence of an intention to cause harm[452] on the part of the persons removing the organs a claim would probably have to be based in negligence for any provable psychiatric harm. The current structure of English law on the recovery of damages for negligently inflicted psychiatric harm is such that this type of claim would be very difficult to establish, given that members of the family may not qualify as "primary" victims and would therefore have to satisfy all the requirements of claims by a "secondary" victim.[453]

7–160

Although the Human Tissue Act 2004 creates criminal offences for breach of its provisions, it does not expressly provide any civil remedy, though it may be that distressed relatives could have an action in respect of breach of the Human Rights Act 1998. *AB v Leeds Teaching Hospital NHS Trust*[454] arose out of claims alleging breaches of the earlier legislation, the Human Tissue Act 1961. The lead claims did not involve the retention of organs for the purpose of research, but Gage J was invited to express a view on an assumed set of facts concerning research. His Lordship concluded that the use of a child's brain acquired by a pathologist following a coroner's post-mortem for research purposes was unlawful, in the sense that it was contrary to the 1961 Act, but it did not give rise

7–161

---

[450] The retention of organs and human tissue following post-mortem without the consent of relatives was found to be a widespread practice after the issue first came to light in the course of the Bristol Inquiry and subsequently at Alder Hey Children's Hospital in Liverpool. See the *Public Inquiry into children's heart surgery at Bristol Royal Infirmary*, 2001 and *The Royal Liverpool Children's Inquiry Report*, 2001, respectively. See further Ellis [2001] J.P.I.L. 264; Austin (2002) 8 *Clinical Risk* 185. For discussion of the ethics of organ retention see Harris (2003) 22 L.S. 527 and Brazier (2003) 22 L.S. 550.

[451] *R. v Kelly* [1998] 3 All E.R. 741 at 749; *Dobson v North Tyneside Health Authority* 1997] 1 W.L.R. 596. See further Grubb, (1998) 3 Med. Law Int. 299; Skegg (1992) 32 Med. Sci. Law 311.

[452] Which, theoretically at least, could give rise to a claim under the principle of *Wilkinson v Downton* [1897] 2 Q.B. 57, though in practice this would be extremely difficult to prove. See the discussion of liability under *Wilkinson v Downton* by Lord Hoffmann in *Wainwright v Home Office* [2003] UKHL 53; [2004] 2 A.C. 406; [2003] 4 All E.R. 969 at [36] to [47]; and *Rhodes v OPO* [2015] UKSC 32; [2016] A.C. 219.

[453] See paras 2–247 et seq. Claims were brought by the relatives of deceased children in respect of the psychiatric distress caused by the removal and retention of organs at the Alder Hey Children's Hospital, but the actions were settled in January 2003 for approximately £5,000 per child: *The Guardian*, 1 and 27 February 2003.

[454] [2004] EWHC 644 (QB); [2005] Q.B. 506. See also the Scottish case of *Stevens v Yorkhill NHS Trust* 2006 S.L.T. 889; (2006) 95 B.M.L.R. 1; and see further para.2–252.

to a cause of action in tort by the parents.[455] However, Gage J agreed with the defendants' concession that the decision to use the brain for research was capable of engaging art.8(1) of the European Convention on Human Rights and constituting a breach of it. Whether the use of the brain in research was capable of justification under art.8(2) would depend upon the facts, but in his Lordship's view it was more likely that it could not be justified:

> "Having concluded that such use would be unlawful my view is that the circumstances in which that use can be justified on grounds of public interest will probably be rare."[456]

(c)   Omission to warn about risk of sterilisation failing[457]

7–162   It is well known within the medical profession that there is a risk that a sterilisation operation will fail to render the patient sterile. The risk can vary with the procedure used and the time at which it is carried out.[458] The existence of this small, but quantifiable, failure rate can make it difficult to prove that there has been negligence in the performance of the operation itself. This has led to a number of cases in which claimants have alleged that the surgeon was negligent in failing to inform them about the failure rate, although, with rare exceptions, these actions have been spectacularly unsuccessful. Following the decision of the House of Lords in *McFarlane v Tayside Health Board*[459] that no duty of care is owed in respect of the cost of raising a healthy child (even where the parent is disabled[460]) these cases are likely to have less significance. However, where the child is born with disabilities it remains possible to claim in respect of the financial costs associated with the disability (even though the child's disabilities are unrelated to the defendant's duty[461]); the parents of a healthy or a disabled child can claim a "conventional sum" of £15,000 for loss of the right to limit the size of one's family[462]; and the mother may also have a claim in respect of her losses.[463]

7–163   **The *Bolam* test**   The early cases were pleaded solely in negligence, relying on the *Bolam* test, with the result that if a responsible body of medical opinion

---

[455] [2004] EWHC 644 (QB); [2005] Q.B. 506 at [296].
[456] [2004] EWHC 644 (QB); [2005] Q.B. 506 at [298].
[457] For guidance on both male and female sterilisation procedures, which includes guidance on the information that patients should be given, see Faculty of Sexual and Reproductive Healthcare Clinical Guidance, *Male and Female Sterilisation*, September 2014 (available at *http://www.fsrh.org/pdfs/ MaleFemaleSterilisation.pdf*).
[458] See, e.g. *Eyre v Measday* [1986] 1 All E.R. 488 at 490–491; *Gold v Haringey Health Authority* [1988] Q.B. 481 at 484; *Videto v Kennedy* (1980) 125 D.L.R. (3d) 612 at 618, Ont HC. The Faculty of Sexual and Reproductive Healthcare Clinical Guidance, *Male and Female Sterilisation*, 2014, estimates the risk to be 0.5 per cent for female sterilisation (laparoscopic tubal occlusion) and 0.15 per cent for male sterilisation.
[459] [2000] 2 A.C. 59. See paras 2–055 et seq.
[460] *Rees v Darlington Memorial Hospital NHS Trust* [2003] UKHL 52; [2004] 1 A.C. 309; see para.2–071.
[461] That is, it was not because of a foreseeable risk of the child being born with disabilities that the defendant was under a duty to warn about the sterilisation failure rate. See paras 2–066 and 2–067.
[462] *Rees v Darlington Memorial Hospital NHS Trust* [2003] UKHL 52; [2004] 1 A.C. 309.
[463] See paras 12–134 et seq.

would not have advised the claimant of the risk that the operation might not succeed in its objective the action failed.[464] There have been several attempts by claimants to circumvent this problem.

Circumventing *Bolam*—contract   In *Eyre v Measday*[465] the claimant entered into a contract with the defendant surgeon to be sterilised. The defendant had emphasised that a sterilisation operation was irreversible, but he did not inform the claimant that there was a less than one per cent risk of pregnancy occurring following such a procedure. The claimant argued that the defendant was in breach of a contractual term that she would be rendered irreversibly sterile, and/or a collateral warranty to that effect which induced her to enter the contract. It was held that the contract was to perform a sterilisation operation, it was not a contract to render the claimant sterile, and there was neither an express nor an implied warranty that the procedure would be an unqualified success. In *Thake v Maurice*[466] the Court of Appeal reached a similar conclusion that, on an objective interpretation, the defendant had not given a contractual guarantee that a vasectomy operation would render the male claimant irreversibly sterile, relying on the observation that medicine is not an exact science and results are to some extent unpredictable. The contractual approach is not entirely ruled out by these decisions; it is simply that it will be extremely difficult to prove that the defendant did in fact guarantee to achieve complete sterility.[467]

7–164

The defendant was, nonetheless, held liable for negligence in *Thake v Maurice*. He had failed to give his usual warning that there was a slight risk that the male claimant might become fertile again. There was no independent evidence called by either party as to the general practice of the profession with regard to warnings at the time of the operation in 1975. The Court of Appeal held that in these circumstances the claimants were entitled to rely on the defendant's own evidence (which was that he considered a warning to be necessary) as indicative of the appropriate standard of care, and that accordingly the defendant was negligent by inadvertently failing to give his usual warning.[468]

7–165

Circumventing *Bolam*—misrepresentation   Where the claimant has not had the operation performed privately the contractual guarantee argument is clearly

7–166

---

[464] *Waters v Park*, The Times, 15 July 1961; *Williams v St Helens and District Hospital Management Committee* unreported 1977, QBD, where the defendant's omission to warn of a risk of failure of 1 in 300 was held not to be negligent where the evidence was that some gynaecologists gave a warning while others did not.
[465] [1986] 1 All E.R. 488; see para.2–017.
[466] [1986] Q.B. 644; see para.2–018.
[467] In *Thake v Maurice* both Pain J and Kerr LJ took the view that the claimant had established this on the evidence. Neill and Nourse LJJ came to a different conclusion.
[468] The defendant had been prevented from leading evidence from expert witnesses by a procedural error. If there had been some evidence that responsible practitioners did not give a warning, the defendant would have escaped liability, notwithstanding that he had inadvertently failed to follow his own usual practice and that he regarded a warning as necessary. See *Moyes v Lothian Health Board* [1990] 1 Med. L.R. 463 at 470; and *Gascoine v Ian Sheridan & Co.* [1994] 5 Med. L.R. 437 at 458, where Mitchell J, commenting on a case of alleged negligent treatment said that: "If on some hit-and-miss basis they treated correctly (or correctly in the opinion of a respected reasonably competent body of thinking in 1978) then liability in negligence could not be established."

not available. In *Worster v City and Hackney Health Authority*[469] the claimant argued that, having signed a consent form which included the words "… and we understand that this means we can have no more children", the surgeon was liable for a negligent misrepresentation under the principle of *Hedley Byrne & Co. Ltd v Heller & Partners Ltd*.[470] The fact that the defendant did not inform her of the risk of the operation failing, it was suggested, combined with the wording of the consent form constituted a representation that sterilisation was certain. Garland J rejected this contention. *Hedley Byrne* did not avail the claimant since that case was concerned with establishing that a duty of care existed when giving gratuitous advice. Once the duty was established the nature of the duty was governed by the *Bolam* test, and applying that test the action failed.[471]

7–167   **Circumventing *Bolam*—therapeutic and non-therapeutic advice**   The third attempt to avoid the implications of the *Bolam* test occurred in *Gold v Haringey Health Authority*.[472] The claimant underwent a sterilisation operation the day after the birth of her third child which failed to render her sterile, and she subsequently had a fourth child. She alleged that the defendants were negligent in failing to warn her of the risks of failure. The evidence was that the failure rate for female sterilisation was in the range 20 to 60 per 10,000, with operations carried out post-partum at the higher end of the range. The failure rate for vasectomy was 5 per 10,000.[473] The trial judge, Schiemann J, found that the defendants did not explain the risk of the operation failing to render the claimant sterile, and did not counsel her and her husband about the possibility of vasectomy, or explain the relative failure rates of the two operations. The medical experts were unanimous that although they themselves would have warned of the risk of failure, nonetheless a substantial body of responsible doctors would not have given any such warning in 1979. Thus, applying the *Bolam* test the claimant's action would fail. Schiemann J drew a distinction, however, between advice given in a therapeutic context and advice given in a contraceptive context.

---

[469] *The Times*, 22 June 1987.

[470] [1964] A.C. 465.

[471] A claim for negligent misrepresentation was also rejected by the Court of Appeal in *Gold v Haringey Health Authority* [1988] Q.B. 481 at 492. The claimant was not entitled to rely on the word "irreversible" as a representation that the operation would succeed, applying *Eyre v Measday* [1986] 1 All E.R. 488. Advice that a sterilisation operation is irreversible, and that there is a risk of the operation failing to achieve sterility, are two different things: *McLennan v Newcastle Health Authority* [1992] 3 Med. L.R. 215 at 216. In *Danns v Department of Health* [1998] P.I.Q.R. P226 the Court of Appeal held that the failure of the Department of Health to publish information in the media about the risks of late re-canalisation following a vasectomy (put at 2,000 to 1) did not give rise to a private law action for breach of the Ministry of Health Act 1919 s.2. The claimants had to show that a decision not to publish information about the known risks to members of the public (the risks had been notified to doctors) was a decision that the Department could not rationally have taken (applying well-known principles of public law). This was not the case on the facts.

[472] [1988] Q.B. 481.

[473] Though see the comment of Roger Clements in (1993) 4 *AVMA Medical & Legal Journal* (No.2) p.19, stating that the failure rates for male and female sterilisation are very similar, and that the claimant's expert evidence in *Gold* was not challenged. But see also *McLennan v Newcastle Health Authority* [1992] 3 Med. L.R. 215, QBD, where the claimant was told that vasectomy had a smaller failure rate than female sterilisation by tubal ligation; and see the guidance from the Faculty of Sexual and Reproductive Healthcare, *Male and Female Sterilisation*, 2014, about the different failure rates for male and female sterilisation, cited above, para.7–162 n.458.

In a therapeutic context there was a body of responsible medical opinion which would not have given a warning, but in a contraceptive context there was no such body of medical opinion. Moreover, even if there had been such a body of opinion, the defendants were still negligent because the *Bolam* test did not apply to advice given in a non-therapeutic context. The Court of Appeal disagreed and allowed the defendant's appeal. Lloyd LJ considered that the distinction between therapeutic and non-therapeutic advice was "elusive", and it was rejected as a departure from the *Bolam* test.[474]

Changing values: medical and legal As attitudes within the medical profession to the disclosure of risk changed so it became easier for claimants to establish negligence, even under the *Bolam* test, on the basis that no reasonable doctor would have failed to disclose the failure rates of male and female sterilisation.[475] The decision of the Supreme Court in *Montgomery v Lanarkshire Health Board*[476] that the standard to be applied to the disclosure of information about the risks of medical treatment should be a requirement to disclose material risks has brought the law into line with prevailing medical values on information disclosure. The test for whether a risk is material is:

> "…whether, in the circumstances of the particular case, a reasonable person in the patient's position would be likely to attach significance to the risk, or the doctor is or should reasonably be aware that the particular patient would be likely to attach significance to it."[477]

In the context of an operation to sterilise a patient (as opposed to a therapeutic procedure, such as a hysterectomy, which has an incidental effect of sterilising the patient) it would seem highly probable that *any* reasonable patient would want to know the likely success/failure rates of a particular procedure, and its alternatives, in terms of achieving complete sterility, and where the patient has a partner the reasonable patient would want to know the comparative success/failure rates of female and male sterilisation. There is simply no compelling reason to fail to give this information to patients.[478]

Risks of sterilisation other than failing to achieve sterility Of course, sterilisation operations may carry other risks, in addition to the risk that the

7–168

7–169

---

[474] [1988] Q.B. 481 at 489–490.

[475] In *Gowton v Wolverhampton Health Authority* [1994] 5 Med. L.R. 432 it was accepted by the defendants' experts that by 1986 it would have been negligent to fail to warn of the risk of recanalisation following a vasectomy operation, a risk put at one in two to three thousand; and in *Newell and Newell v Goldenberg* [1995] 6 Med. L.R. 371 Mantell J acknowledged that there were some doctors who, in September 1985, would not have given a warning against the risk of late recanalisation following a vasectomy, but concluded that common sense and prudence indicated that such a warning ought to have been given, and such doctors could not be considered to be acting reasonably or responsibly.

[476] [2015] UKSC 11; [2015] A.C. 1430.

[477] [2015] UKSC 11; [2015] A.C. 1430 at [87]; see para.7–019.

[478] In *G, PA and C, P v Down* [2009] SASC 217; (2009) 104 S.A.S.R. 332 the Supreme Court of South Australia upheld the trial judge's finding that the defendant was in breach of duty by telling the claimant that the risk of failure for tubal ligation surgery was 1 in 2000 without adding the qualification that this risk was based on his own personal experience, and by failing to tell her that the level of risk as published in the medical literature was between 1 in 500 and 1 in 1000.

procedure may not succeed in achieving sterility. In *Walsh v Family Planning Services Ltd*[479] the Supreme Court of Ireland held that, notwithstanding medical evidence to the contrary from some of the witnesses, there was an obligation to warn a patient about to undergo a vasectomy that very rarely, for no known reason, some patients experience pain for some years after the operation. McCarthy J said that:

> "In determining whether or not to have an operation in which sexual capacity is concerned, it seems to me that to supply the patient with the material facts is so obviously necessary to an informed choice on the part of the patient that no reasonably prudent medical doctor would fail to make it. What then is material? Apart from the success ratio of the operation, what could be more material than sexual capacity after the operation and its immediate sequelae? Whatever about temporary or protracted pain or discomfort, the only information given to the plaintiff and his wife on the score of sexual capacity, upon which they placed so much emphasis, was that contained in the brief paragraph headed 'Does it affect your sex-life? No.' This is not a question merely determining that a particular outcome is so rare as not to warrant such disclosure that might upset a patient but, rather, that those concerned, and this includes the authors of the information sheet, if they knew of such a risk, however remote, had a duty to inform those so critically concerned with that risk. Remote percentages of risk lose their significance to those unfortunate enough to be 100 per cent involved."[480]

Accordingly, the defendants were in breach of their duty for failing to identify the risk of impotence, whether it be functional, due to pain and discomfort, or mechanical, due to some other cause.

7–170   **Causation**   Even if the claimant succeeds in proving that the defendant was in breach of duty in failing to disclose the risk that the operation would not produce sterility, the claimant must still establish causation.[481] Most patients who consider sterilisation for contraceptive purposes would probably undergo the operation even if informed about the remote risk of the procedure failing to achieve sterility, and it would be highly unlikely that they would continue with other contraceptive methods "just in case" the sterilisation had failed,[482] although in

---

[479] [1992] 1 I.R. 496.

[480] [1992] 1 I.R. 496 at 520–521. In *Geoghegan v Harris* [2000] 3 I.R. 536 at 549 Kearns J, commenting on the last two sentences of this quotation, said: "However, the attractiveness of the observation should not occlude the possibility that at times a risk may become so remote, in relation at any rate to the less than most serious consequences, that a reasonable man may not regard it as material or significant. While such cases may be few in number, they do suggest that an absolute requirement of disclosure in every case is unduly onerous, and perhaps in the end counter-productive if it needlessly deters patients from undergoing operations which are in their best interests to have."

[481] It seems unlikely that an argument based on *Chester v Afshar* [2004] UKHL 41; [2005] 1 A.C. 134 (see paras 7–105 et seq.) could succeed in a failed sterilisation operation, at least in the context of the risks of a natural reversal of the procedure (e.g. where there is recanalisation), because in this situation the risk is not specific to the particular procedure at the time of the surgery, but to the individual's body in the future.

[482] *Grey v Webster* (1984) 14 D.L.R. (4th) 706 at 715, NBQB. In *G, PA and C, P v Down* [2009] SASC 217; (2009) 104 S.A.S.R. 332 the claimant should have been told of the 1 in 500 and 1 in 1000 risk that tubal ligation would not achieve sterility but the evidence was that the risk of pregnancy while taking the contraceptive pill was about 1 in 100. The Supreme Court of South Australia, applying a subjective test of causation as measured against objective considerations, held that the claimant had not proved the causal link. What mattered was the relative risk of the two options, and even on the worst odds for the tubal ligation (1 in 500) it was at least five times better to have the operation than to stay on the contraceptive pill. There was no evidence of other viable options, and the

Gowton v Wolverhampton Health Authority[483] the claimants managed to persuade the trial judge that this is what would have happened had they been warned of the risk of a vasectomy operation not producing complete sterility. The couple were determined not to have any further children, and were very fearful of the prospect of a fifth pregnancy. Had she known of the risk of recanalisation following her husband's sterilisation operation it was probable that the female claimant would have continued to take the contraceptive pill, and this would have been sufficient to make it improbable that she would become pregnant.

On the other hand, in *Newell and Newell v Goldenberg*[484] Mantell J did not accept the claimants' contention that had they known about the risk of late recanalisation following a vasectomy, the female claimant would also have undergone sterilisation, reducing the overall risk of pregnancy almost to vanishing point. This was rejected as unpersuasive, despite the claimants' evidence that they were desperate to avoid a further pregnancy, because they had engaged in sexual intercourse between January and November 1992 and in the period between the vasectomy and the second sterile sperm sample using only condoms for protection. There was also evidence from experts that no patient who had been informed of the risk of late failure of vasectomy had declined the operation for that reason or sought additional contraceptive measures. Thus, had the claimants been advised about the failure rate, they would probably have been content to accept the risk without taking any additional precautions. The defendant was held liable, however, for the "anxiety and distress" suffered by the claimants on finding that the female claimant was pregnant, i.e. the distress attributable to the fact the male claimant suspected his wife of having an extramarital affair, since he believed that he could not possibly be the child's father. That could have been avoided had the defendant given a warning about the risk of late recanalisation.[485]

7–171

In *Gold v Haringey Health Authority*[486] the causation point rested on the argument that if the comparative failure rates had been discussed the male claimant would have had a vasectomy, and thus there would have been no difficulty in showing that the claimant would not have proceeded with the operation. In *Thake v Maurice*,[487] on the other hand, the argument was not that if the claimants had known of the risk of recanalisation the male claimant would not have had the vasectomy operation, since on the evidence the failure rate was lower than for female sterilisation. Rather, it was that if they had realised that this was a possibility, the female claimant would have appreciated that she was pregnant earlier in the pregnancy than in fact she did and would have had an

7–172

---

claimant had not alleged that she would have undergone the operation and continued to take the contraceptive pill had she known the relative risks.

[483] [1994] 5 Med. L.R. 432.

[484] [1995] 6 Med. L.R. 371.

[485] Damages were agreed at £500. The law report does not indicate the basis of this agreement, though claims in respect of "anxiety and distress" are not usually maintainable in the tort of negligence unless there is also a genuine psychiatric illness. See para.2–188. The action was brought in both contract and tort.

[486] [1988] Q.B. 481.

[487] [1986] Q.B. 644.

abortion at an early stage. The defendant's claim that this risk was unforeseeable and therefore too remote was rejected by the Court of Appeal.

7–173 Nonetheless, causation will remain a problem in most cases of failure to warn about the risk of the sterilisation not being effective,[488] unless claimants can point to a medically acceptable alternative procedure which carried a lower failure rate,[489] or is in a position to adopt the argument in *Thake v Maurice* that because they were not informed about the remote risk that the sterilisation might be ineffective they did not realise that they might be pregnant until it was too late safely to have an abortion. Where, on the other hand, defendant knows that the sterilisation procedure has failed to render the claimant sterile, but fails to inform the claimant of that fact to give her the opportunity to take alternative contraceptive measures, there will be no difficulty in establishing both negligence and causation.[490] Conversely, where the claimant knows that she is not sterile following a sterilisation operation, but proceeds to have sexual intercourse without taking alternative contraceptive measures, this will break the causal link between the negligence (whether this be in the performance of the surgery or the failure to warn of the risks) and the subsequent birth of a child.[491]

---

[488] See, e.g. *Zimmer v Ringrose* (1981) 124 D.L.R. (3d) 215, Alta CA, where despite the fact that the defendant was held negligent in failing to disclose that his method of sterilisation was experimental, and had not been approved by the profession, the action for non-disclosure failed because a reasonable patient in the claimant's position would have accepted the treatment. The decisive factor in her case was that she wanted to avoid having to go into hospital to be sterilised when she had a young baby at home to look after.

[489] In *Grey v Webster* (1984) 14 D.L.R. (4th) 706, NBQB, the claimant said that if she had known about the failure rate for tubal ligation she would have undergone a hysterectomy to ensure sterility. The medical evidence, however, indicated that hysterectomy was not a medically acceptable procedure merely for sterilisation purposes, and the action failed on causation.

[490] *Cryderman v Ringrose* [1977] 3 W.W.R. 109; aff'd [1978] 3 W.W.R. 481, Alta CA. Note that where the sterilisation operation itself has been performed negligently (see para.4–111), there will be no difficulty in proving causation. The claimant's refusal to undergo an abortion when she discovers that she is pregnant does not amount to a novus actus interveniens: see *Emeh v Kensington and Chelsea Area Health Authority* [1985] Q.B. 1012, para.5–159.

[491] *Sabri-Tabrizi v Lothian Health Board* 1998 S.C. 373.

CHAPTER 8

CONFIDENTIALITY

Doctors owe a duty of confidence in respect of information concerning their patients which they acquire in their capacity as a doctor, whether from the patients themselves or from others. This obligation is widely regarded as one of the cornerstones of the doctor–patient relationship, and this is reflected in a number of international ethical codes.[1] The most important statement of the medical profession's ethical duty is contained in the General Medical Council's guidance *Confidentiality: good practice in handling patient information*[2] which states that:

8–001

> "Trust is an essential part of the doctor–patient relationship and confidentiality is central to this. Patients may avoid seeking medical help, or may under-report symptoms, if they think their personal information will be disclosed by doctors without consent, or without the chance to have some control over the timing or amount of information shared."[3]

The GMC guidance points out that although confidentiality is an important ethical and legal duty it is not absolute. Disclosure of confidential medical information will be justified where:

"a.   The patient consents, whether implicitly for the sake of their own care or for local clinical audit, or explicitly for other purposes...
 b.   The disclosure is of overall benefit to a patient who lacks the capacity to consent...
 c.   The disclosure is required by law ..., or the disclosure is permitted or has been approved under a statutory process that sets aside the common law duty of confidentiality...
 d.   The disclosure can be justified in the public interest..."[4]

---

[1] See, e.g. the *Hippocratic Oath*: "All that may come to my knowledge in the exercise of my profession or outside of my profession or in daily commerce with men, which ought not to be spread abroad, I will keep secret and will never reveal"; *Declaration of Geneva*: "I will respect the secrets which are confided in me, even after the patient has died"; *International Code of Medical Ethics*: "A doctor shall preserve absolute secrecy on all he knows about his patients because of the confidence entrusted in him."

[2] January 2017, available at *http://www.gmc-uk.org/guidance/ethical_guidance/confidentiality.asp*. This guidance came into effect on 25 April 2017. There are various NHS documents emphasising the importance of maintaining patient confidentiality and setting out guidelines, including: *Department of Health, Confidentiality: NHS Code of Practice*, November 2003; Health & Social Care Information Centre (now called "NHS Digital"), *A guide to confidentiality in health and social care*, September 2013; NHS England, *Confidentiality policy*, June 2016; and the *NHS Constitution for England*, July 2015. See also the BMA's *Confidentiality and disclosure of health information tool kit*, and the Medical Defence Union, *Medico-legal guide to Confidentiality*, 2016.

[3] *Confidentiality: good practice in handling patient information*, para.1.

[4] *Confidentiality: good practice in handling patient information*, para.9.

Although the GMC guidance is simply that, i.e. "guidance" not law, it has been developed over the years in light of the developing legal position, and provides a good indication of the probable approach that a court would take to issues of confidentiality in the medical context.[5] For that reason it is referred to frequently in this chapter.

8–002 The justifications for respecting a patient's confidentiality in the information acquired by a doctor arising from the doctor–patient relationship are both ethical and practical. The ethical argument is that the maintenance of confidentiality is concerned with respect for patients' autonomy, and divulging information about patients without their consent threatens their autonomy. Patients must consent to all aspects of the doctor–patient relationship, including the disclosure of information about the patient to others. On this view, confidentiality involves respect for the patient's moral autonomy and is, in some respects, part and parcel of a "right to privacy"—the idea that there are certain aspects of one's being that one is entitled to keep private as an essential element of what it is to be human. The practical, perhaps utilitarian, argument for maintaining medical confidentiality is that without some guarantee of confidentiality patients would not be frank with their doctor because they would be embarrassed if they knew that there was a real prospect that personal information about their medical condition could be released to the world. This would particularly be the case in relation to medical conditions to which a degree of stigma may be attached (such as mental illness or venereal disease), though it would not necessarily be limited to such conditions. If patients could not be frank with their doctor, this would interfere with the doctor's ability to diagnose and treat the patient's condition and so could undermine the practice of medicine. This would not simply be a matter of interfering with the private interests of an individual patient but would not be in the wider public interest.[6]

8–003 In addition to protecting confidentiality through the traditional action for breach of confidence, which is based on the nature of the relationship between the parties, the courts have been developing a wider principle of protection of private information (now termed "misuse of private information") deriving from the jurisprudence of the European Convention on Human Rights. This process is ongoing, and in time may come to replace the conventional action for breach of confidentiality which has a somewhat narrower focus than an approach based on breach of a claimant's human rights.

8–004 One other feature of claims based on breach of confidentiality is that, certainly in the context of the doctor–patient relationship, it is relatively straightforward to establish the existence of a duty. The more contentious issue tends to be: when is it permissible for a defendant to disclose information in breach of that duty? Thus, the real argument is often not did the doctor owe a duty of confidentiality, but was there any lawful justification for breaching the duty undoubtedly owed to the patient? This is reflected in the structure of this chapter which begins with a

---

[5] In *W v Egdell* [1990] Ch. 359 at 390 an earlier version of the GMC guidelines was described by Scott J as "valuable" in showing the approach of the GMC to the breadth of the doctor's duty of confidence; see also per Bingham LJ [1990] Ch. 359 at 420.
[6] See, e.g. *X v Y* [1988] 2 All E.R. 648.

discussion of the traditional claim for breach of confidentiality, considers the developing jurisprudence on the new tort of misuse of private information deriving from the human rights case law, and then addresses the exceptions to the duty of confidentiality (which effectively define the scope of the law on confidentiality). The chapter concludes with a brief consideration of awards of damages.

1. THE LEGAL DUTY TO RESPECT CONFIDENCES

Although there have been relatively few cases where the existence of a duty of medical confidentiality has been in issue, there are numerous dicta stating that medical information is confidential.[7] In *W v Egdell* Scott J said of a psychiatrist who had prepared a medical report on the claimant for use at a Mental Health Review Tribunal:

8–005

> "The question in the present case is not whether Dr Egdell was under a duty of confidence; *he plainly was*. The question is as to the breadth of that duty."[8]

In *Cornelius v De Taranto*[9] it was held that a medico-legal report which contained information about an individual's medical history and private life obtained from an interview and from her medical records, was confidential to the person commissioning the report.

A duty of confidence frequently arises from the relationship between a professional person (such as a lawyer or accountant) and the client. Usually, the duty will derive from the contract, as either an express or implied term. With private patients the duty of confidentiality arises under the contract between doctor and patient, whereas in the absence of a contractual relationship the duty of confidence is imposed by equity. This distinction has little relevance to the nature of the *duty* owed by the doctor, but it does have potential consequences for

8–006

---

[7] "It has always been accepted that information about a person's health and treatment for ill-health is both private and confidential. This stems not only from the confidentiality of the doctor–patient relationship but from the nature of the information itself", per Baroness Hale in *Campbell v MGN Ltd* [2004] UKHL 22; [2004] 2 A.C. 457 at [145] citing the European Court of Human Rights in *Z v Finland* (1997) 25 E.H.R.R. 371; (1997) 45 B.M.L.R. 107 at [95]. "The law has long recognised that an obligation of confidence can arise out of particular relationships. Examples are the relationships of doctor and patient, priest and penitent, solicitor and client, banker and customer", per Lord Keith in *Att.-Gen. v Guardian Newspapers (No.2)* [1990] 1 A.C. 109 at 255; see also *Goddard v Nationwide Building Society* [1987] Q.B. 670 at 685, per Nourse LJ: "The equitable jurisdiction is well able to extend, for example, to the grant of an injunction to restrain an unauthorised disclosure of confidential communications between priest and penitent or doctor and patient"; and *Hunter v Mann* [1974] Q.B. 767 at 772, per Boreham J.

[8] [1990] Ch. 359 at 389, emphasis added. In the Court of Appeal Bingham LJ said, [1990] Ch. 359 at 419, that: "It has never been doubted that the circumstances here were such as to impose on Dr. Egdell a duty of confidence owed to W . . . It is not in issue here that a duty of confidence existed." In *R. v Department of Health, Ex p. Source Informatics* [2001] Q.B. 424 at [19] Simon Brown LJ commented on Bingham LJ's observation that "a dictum from that source is worth many a *ratio decidendi* from another". See also *X v Y* [1988] 2 All E.R. 648, although the breach of confidence at issue in this case was the duty owed by a hospital employee to his employers under a contract of employment, not the duty owed by doctors to their patients.

[9] [2001] E.M.L.R. 12; affirmed [2001] EWCA Civ 1511; (2001) 68 B.M.L.R. 62.

the remedies available, since some doubt has been expressed in the past as to whether there can be an action for damages in respect of a past breach of confidence where the duty is non-contractual.[10] Patients within the NHS do not normally enter into a contractual relationship with their doctor. But equity will intervene to protect confidentiality where three requirements are satisfied, namely: (i) the information must have the necessary quality of confidence about it; (ii) it must have been imparted in circumstances importing an obligation of confidence; and (iii) there must be unauthorised use of that information to the detriment of the person who communicated it.[11] The courts have drawn on the views frequently expressed by the medical profession and the NHS as to the importance of maintaining the confidentiality of medical information. In *R. (on the application of W) v Secretary of State for Health*[12] Lord Dyson MR said that:

> "In our view, all of these documents[13] articulate the same approach to the issue of confidentiality: all identifiable patient data held by a doctor or a hospital must be treated as confidential. The documents have been drafted in expansive terms so as to reflect the reasonable expectations of patients that all of their data will be treated as private and confidential. These publicly available documents inform the expectations of patients being treated in the NHS. They do not seek to distinguish between more or less sensitive categories of patient data."

If information is confidential, the burden lies upon the defendant to establish some justification for disclosure.[14] The private interests of the doctor will rarely, if ever, amount to a sufficient justification for disclosure.[15]

---

[10] See para.8–082. Where the patient has sustained personal injury as a result of the breach of confidence a claim for damages could be based on the tort of negligence: see *Furniss v Fitchett* [1958] N.Z.L.R. 396.

[11] *Coco v AN Clark (Engineers) Ltd* [1969] R.P.C. 41 at 47, per Megarry J; *Stephens v Avery* [1988] Ch. 449 at 452; *Att.-Gen. v Guardian Newspapers (No.2)* [1990] 1 A.C. 109 at 268. There is no duty of confidentiality in respect of information which is trivial: see *Douglas v Hello! Ltd (No.3)* [2007] UKHL 21; [2008] 1 A.C. 1 at [272] and [291] per Lord Walker, and [307] per Baroness Hale (applying observations of Lord Goff in *Att.-Gen. v Guardian Newspapers (No.2)* [1990] 1 A.C. 109 at 282). However, medical information will rarely be regarded as trivial. Perhaps a statement that an individual had contracted a common cold could be considered to be trivial.

[12] [2015] EWCA Civ 1034; [2016] 1 W.L.R. 698 at [39].

[13] The Court referred inter alia, at [38], to the GMC's Standards and Ethics Guidance for Doctors which states that patients have a right to expect that information about them will be held in confidence by their doctors.

[14] *Att.-Gen. v Guardian Newspapers (No.2)* [1990] 1 A.C. 109 at 269 per Lord Griffiths. The public interest in the freedom of the press may, in some circumstances, be sufficient justification. See the discussion by the Court of Appeal in *A v B plc* [2002] EWCA Civ 337; [2003] Q.B. 195 on how the courts should approach the balancing exercise (though this case was somewhat removed from issues of medical confidentiality, since it involved publication of details about the extra-marital affairs of a well-known footballer).

[15] See, e.g., *Re C (A Child)* [2015] EWFC 79; [2015] Med. L.R. 531; [2017] 1 F.L.R. 82 where a psychiatrist applied for disclosure of documents from family court proceedings and a General Medical Council (GMC) fitness to practise panel in order to be able to publicly defend himself from allegations made in the press by a former patient. Sir James Munby PFD refused the application. Even if it were true that the doctor had been "traduced and defamed" by the patient, that did not free the doctor from his continuing duty of confidentiality. See also the GMC guidance *Confidentiality: responding to criticism in the press* (available at *http://www.gmc-uk.org/Responding_to_criticism_in_the_media.pdf_69089850.pdf*).

(a) Must there be a "detriment"?

Medical information imparted in the context of the doctor–patient relationship   **8–007**
clearly has the necessary quality of confidence about it, and is disclosed in
circumstances importing an obligation of confidence, thus satisfying the first two
requirements for the equitable obligation of confidentiality. The question of what
amounts to "detriment" to a patient is, in theory, more problematic and has not
been fully addressed. Do patients who do not base their claim for breach of
confidence on a contractual relationship have to establish that the breach has, or
is likely to, cause financial or physical/psychological harm, or is the disclosure of
the information sufficient in itself to constitute a detriment? Although Megarry J
set out the three requirements for an action for breach of confidence in *Coco v AN
Clark (Engineers) Ltd*, he clearly did not think that some form of detriment would
always be necessary:

> "Some of the statements of principle in the cases omit any mention of detriment; others include
> it. At first sight, it seems that detriment ought to be present if equity is to be induced to
> intervene; but I can conceive of cases where a plaintiff might have substantial motives for
> seeking the aid of equity and yet suffer nothing which could fairly be called a detriment to
> him, as when the confidential information shows him in a favourable light but gravely injures
> some relation or friend of his whom he wishes to protect."[16]

In *Att.-Gen. v Guardian Newspapers Ltd (No.2)*[17] there was a division of opinion   **8–008**
in the House of Lords on this issue, with Lord Griffiths in favour of a requirement
of some detriment, whereas Lord Keith considered that it was a sufficient
detriment to confiders that the information given in confidence is to be disclosed
to persons whom they would prefer not to know of it, even though the disclosure
would not be harmful to them in any positive way. As a general rule, said his
Lordship, it is in the public interest that confidences should be respected, and the
encouragement of such respect may in itself constitute a sufficient ground for
recognising and enforcing the obligation of confidence, even in the absence of
specific detriment. Although Lord Griffiths insisted on some detriment, he did
accept that the court would protect a marital confidence from disclosure on the
ground that this might involve the loss of a friend, "and friends can be
precious".[18] For Lord Keith the invasion of personal privacy in such a case was a
sufficient reason for intervening. The disclosure of confidential medical
information may, of course, result in the loss of a friend, or in extreme cases (as
possibly with HIV and AIDS) substantial financial loss.[19]

The legal protection afforded to medical confidences should not, however,   **8–009**
depend upon this fortuitous and arbitrary circumstance or the artificial
identification of hypothetical or notional losses, and for this reason Lord Keith's

---

[16] [1968] F.S.R. 415 at 421.
[17] [1990] 1 A.C. 109. See also per Lord Goff at 281–282 stating that he would: "wish to keep open
the question whether detriment to the plaintiff is an essential ingredient of an action for breach of
confidence. Obviously, detriment or potential detriment to the plaintiff will nearly always form part of
his case; but this may not always be necessary."
[18] See *Argyll v Argyll* [1967] Ch. 302.
[19] See, e.g. Napier (1989) 18 I.L.J. 84; Wacks (1988) 138 N.L.J. 254, 255.

view is to be preferred. In *Cornelius v De Taranto*[20] Morland J held that the claimant had suffered a detriment because the defendant transmitted a medico-legal report to a psychiatrist and a NHS hospital in breach of contract and in breach of confidence. It mattered not that "no use detrimental to the claimant was made of this report".[21] In *Bluck v Information Commissioner*[22] the Information Tribunal held that:

"...if disclosure would be contrary to an individual's reasonable expectation of maintaining confidentiality in respect of his or her private information, then the absence of detriment is not a necessary ingredient of the cause of action"

and since medical records fell within the meaning of the phrase "private information" an action for breach of confidence would not be defeated by the absence of any detriment (where the records related to a deceased patient).

8–010   It is highly unlikely that a court would refuse to grant an injunction to restrain a threatened breach of medical confidence on the ground that a patient has suffered no detriment. Given that the doctor–patient relationship is often cited as the paradigm example of a confidential relationship, the court would either strain to find something detrimental to the claimant on the facts or would simply accept that the disclosure itself is a detriment. If the patient's complaint concerns a past breach of confidence, however, the arguments may be different since there has been uncertainty about the availability of damages as a remedy for breach of a confidence which is not based on breach of contract, and even here, where the claim is for distress or invasion of privacy, damages may be nominal.[23]

8–011   However, this view may be a product of a rather narrow approach to the nature of the action for breach of confidentiality. The modern approach, particularly in the context of developments arising from the human rights jurisprudence,[24] is that confidential and private information merits appropriate legal protection and that the harm arising from unlawful disclosures is clear. There is undoubtedly a public interest in the preservation of medical confidences, since full disclosure by patients to their doctor of information about their medical condition is an essential requirement for diagnosis and treatment. Patients should not be afraid to

---

[20] [2001] E.M.L.R. 12; affirmed [2001] EWCA Civ 1511; (2001) 68 B.M.L.R. 62.

[21] [2001] E.M.L.R. 12 at [72], citing *X v Y* [1988] 2 All E.R. 648 at 657 where Rose J said that detriment in the use of information about two patients' medical history was not a necessary precondition to injunctive relief: "I respectfully agree with Megarry V.-C. [in *Coco v AN Clark (Engineers) Ltd* [1969] R.P.C. 41 at 48] that an injunction may be appropriate for breach of confidence where the plaintiff may not suffer from the use of the information and that is borne out by more recent observations in the Court of Appeal and the House of Lords ... which contain no reference to the necessity for detriment in use, and indeed point away from any such principle." His Lordship referred to *Lion Laboratories Ltd v Evans* [1985] Q.B. 526; *Schering Chemicals Ltd v Falkman Ltd* [1982] Q.B. 1; and *British Steel Corporation v Granada Television Ltd* [1981] A.C. 1096.

[22] (2007) 98 B.M.L.R. 1; [2008] W.T.L.R. 1 at [15], applying the approach of the Court of Appeal in *McKennitt v Ash* [2006] EWCA Civ 1714; [2008] Q.B. 73 to the effect that trivial information about the claimant's home fell within the protection of art.8 of the European Convention on Human Rights, and if this was protected there was no reason why medical records should not also be protected.

[23] See paras 8–082 to 8–083. This discrepancy may mark a difference between private patients and patients treated under the NHS.

[24] See para.8–020 et seq.

speak frankly about embarrassing matters, or be deterred from obtaining necessary medical assistance by the fear of unauthorised disclosure.[25] This problem is likely to be most acute with illnesses such as venereal disease and AIDS (or HIV infection),[26] and psychiatric disorders.[27] The law also recognises that the private interest of a patient in maintaining the confidentiality of medical information is worthy of protection.

(b) Confidentiality binds subsequent recipients of the confidential information

The duty of confidence binds not only the first recipient of the information, but also anyone else to whom that information is communicated who knows or ought to know that the information which he has received is confidential in character.[28] In *Tchenguiz v Imerman*[29] Lord Neuberger MR said that:

8–012

> "…a claimant who establishes a right of confidence in certain information contained in a document should be able to restrain any threat by an unauthorised defendant to look at, copy, distribute any copies of, or to communicate, or utilise the contents of the document (or any copy), and also be able to enforce the return (or destruction) of any such document or copy."

This principle applies, not only where confidential information is disclosed in breach of an obligation of confidence, but also where the confidential information has been acquired or received without having been disclosed in breach of

---

[25] *X v Y* [1988] 2 All E.R. 648 at 656, per Rose J. See also *I v Finland* (20511/03) (2008) 48 E.H.R.R. 31 where, in the context of a breach of art.8 ECHR, the European Court of Human Rights stressed the importance of maintaining the confidentiality of health data not only to respect the patient's privacy, but also to preserve confidence in the medical profession and in the health services in general.

[26] Venereal disease was the subject of a specific statutory duty of confidence: see the National Health Service (Venereal Diseases) Regulations 1974 (SI 1974/29), but these Regulations were revoked in so far as they applied to England by the Health and Social Care (Miscellaneous Revocations) Regulations 2015 (SI 2015/839) reg.2(2)(a). The Regulations continue to apply in Wales. In *X v Y* [1988] 2 All E.R. 648 at 656 Rose J seemed to assume that the statutory duty applied to AIDS patients. In *H (A Health Care Worker) v Associated Newspapers Ltd* [2002] EWCA Civ 195; [2002] Lloyd's Rep. Med. 210 Lord Phillips MR said, at [27], that: "there is an obvious public interest in preserving the confidentiality of victims of the AIDS epidemic and, in particular, of healthcare workers who report the fact that they are HIV positive." See also *Z v Finland* (1997) 25 E.H.R.R. 371; (1997) 45 B.M.L.R. 107 at [96], ECtHR; *I v Finland* (20511/03) (2008) 48 E.H.R.R. 31.

[27] cf., however, Scott J in *W v Egdell* [1990] Ch. 359 at 393, responding to the suggestion that if patients could not suppress unfavourable psychiatric reports they would not be wholly frank: "I do not think that this answer has much weight. The possibility of a lack of frankness must always be present when a psychiatric examination takes place. An experienced psychiatrist would, I think, expect to be able to detect it. And the lack of frankness itself would constitute material of interest to the psychiatrist."

[28] *Att.-Gen. v Guardian Newspapers Ltd (No.2)* [1990] 1 A.C. 109 at 281–282 per Lord Goff; *Tchenguiz v Imerman* [2010] EWCA Civ 908; [2011] Fam. 116 at [64] per Lord Neuberger MR; *Re General Dental Council's Application* [2011] EWHC 3011 (Admin); [2012] Med. L.R. 204 at [43] and [45].

[29] [2010] EWCA Civ 908; [2011] Fam. 116 at [69].

confidence where the person who acquires the information knows, or has notice, that the information is confidential.[30] As David Richards LJ expressed the point in *Warwickshire CC v Matalia*:

> "While it is true that many of the earlier cases rest on a duty of confidence owed by the defendant to the party that communicated the information to them, that is not now (if it ever was) the sole basis of an actionable duty of confidence or a necessary element of it. The essential element is that the defendant is in possession of information that he knows, or (viewed objectively) ought to know, is confidential."[31]

The obligation on a third party who receives confidential information will vary with the circumstances of the case.[32] Where the confidential information has escaped into the public domain it may not be practical to attempt to restrain everyone with access to the knowledge from making use of it, though a remedy in damages will be available.[33]

(c)   Information in the public domain

8–013   Where information is public knowledge or in the public domain,[34] it no longer has the necessary quality of confidence about it.[35] As Megarry J expressed it in *Coco v AN Clark (Engineers) Ltd*:

> "However confidential the circumstances of communication, there can be no breach of confidence in revealing to others something which is already common knowledge."[36]

---

[30] *Primary Group (UK) Ltd v The Royal Bank of Scotland plc* [2014] EWHC 1082 (Ch); [2014] R.P.C. 26 at [223] per Arnold J, approved by David Richards LJ in *Warwickshire CC v Matalia* [2017] EWCA Civ 991; [2017] E.C.C. 25 at [46]. The question of whether a person has notice "is to be objectively assessed by reference to a reasonable person standing in the position of the recipient" (per Arnold J in *Primary Group (UK) Ltd* at [223]).

[31] [2017] EWCA Civ 991; [2017] E.C.C. 25 at [41]. It is arguable that most forms of medical information about an identifiable individual (excluding the trivial, such as having a cold) are such that, viewed objectively, a reasonable person ought to know that it is confidential.

[32] The breadth and nature of the duty of confidence must be considered separately against each defendant, because "the third party recipient may be subject to some additional and conflicting duty which does not affect the primary confidant or may not be subject to some special duty which does affect the confidant. In such situations the equation is not the same in the case of the confidant and that of the third party and accordingly the result may be different", per Sir John Donaldson MR in *Att.-Gen. v Guardian Newspapers Ltd (No.2)* [1990] 1 A.C. 109 at 183, cited by Scott J in *W v Egdell* [1990] Ch. 359 at 388.

[33] See para.8–014.

[34] The "public domain" means simply that "the information in question is so generally accessible that, in all the circumstances, it cannot be regarded as confidential": *Att.-Gen. v Guardian Newspapers (No.2)* [1990] 1 A.C. 109 at 282 per Lord Goff.

[35] *Saltman Engineering Co Ltd v Campbell Engineering Co Ltd* (1948) 65 R.P.C. 203, 215 per Lord Greene MR; *Seager v Copydex Ltd* [1967] 1 W.L.R. 923, 931 per Lord Denning MR; *H v Tomlinson* [2008] EWCA Civ 1258; [2009] E.L.R. 14 at [27]; *BBC v HarperCollins Publishers Ltd* [2010] EWHC 2424 (Ch); [2011] E.M.L.R. 6; *Ogunkoya v Harding* [2017] EWHC 470 (IPEC).

[36] [1969] R.P.C. 41 at 47.

The original confidential character of information may be lost if it enters the public domain.[37] On the other hand, individuals who, being under the duty of confidence, put the information in the public domain remain bound by the duty. They "cannot by [their] own wrongful act destroy [their] own obligation of confidentiality", and anyone who circulates the information further knowing that it has arisen from a breach of confidence will also remain bound by the duty.[38]

Injunction or damages?   In *Att.-Gen. v Guardian Newspapers (No.2)* there was a difference of view as to whether the original confidant or a third party to whom the information was passed could be restrained from further disclosures when the information had passed into the public domain. Lord Griffiths considered that in some cases it may be appropriate to restrain the original confidant or third party from further disclosure. However, Lord Goff said that once information had been put into the public domain the claimant could not obtain an injunction restraining a defendant from further disclosure even if it was the defendant who had wrongfully destroyed its confidentiality. The defendant may be held liable in damages or required to make restitution for his wrongful act, but the confidential information, as confidential information, has ceased to exist, and with it should go the obligation of confidence.[39] In exceptional circumstances, the law of confidentiality can extend to cover information as to the identity or whereabouts of individuals, where disclosure would place them at risk of serious injury or death, and an injunction may be granted against the whole world.[40]

8–014

(d)   Confidentiality after the patient's death

The practical rationale for a duty of confidentiality, that without it patients may be reluctant to be entirely frank with their doctors, applies with almost as much force to the possibility that information may be disclosed after their death. Although, clearly, a deceased patient cannot experience embarrassment, the question is whether the possibility that disclosures about their medical condition may be made after death would inhibit a living patient from making a full and frank disclosure of relevant information to a doctor. The GMC guidance[41] states that doctors have an obligation to keep personal information confidential after a patient dies, though this may depend on the circumstances.[42] If the patient had asked for information to remain confidential then doctors "should usually abide by their wishes". If the patient had not given specific instructions then the GMC

8–015

---

[37] *Att.-Gen. v Guardian Newspapers (No.2)* [1990] 1 A.C. 109 at 268 per Lord Griffiths and at 282 per Lord Goff.

[38] [1990] 1 A.C. 109 at 284 per Lord Goff.

[39] [1990] 1 A.C. 109 at 286–287. "The subject matter is gone: the obligation is therefore also gone: all that is left is the remedy or remedies for breach of the obligation" (at 287).

[40] *Venables v News Group Newspapers Ltd* [2001] Fam. 430, CA.

[41] *Confidentiality: good practice in handling patient information*, January 2017, para.134.

[42] Thus, disclosure may be required by law, or for the purposes of an inquest or fatal accident inquiry, on death certificates, when a person has a right of access to records under the Access to Health Records Act 1990, or to meet a statutory duty of candour: *Confidentiality: good practice in handling patient information*, January 2017, para.135.

suggest that any request for information should take into account whether the disclosure of information is likely to cause distress to, or be of benefit to, the patient's partner or family; whether disclosure of information about the patient will also disclose information about the patient's family or anyone else; whether the information is already public knowledge or can be anonymised or de-identified; and the purpose of the disclosure.[43]

8–016   The Law Commission took the view that there is no remedy in law in respect of breaches of deceased patients' confidences after their death, e.g. so as to protect friends or relations of the deceased from distress.[44] However, it would seem that this is the perspective of an earlier age. In *Bluck v Information Commissioner*[45] the appellant's daughter died in a hospital at the age of 33. Five years later the appellant discovered that the treatment provided by the hospital had not been satisfactory, and that the hospital had admitted liability for her daughter's death and had paid substantial compensation in settlement of a claim by the daughter's husband and two children of the marriage. The appellant had been attempting to obtain further information about her daughter's death from the hospital, but the hospital refused to divulge the information without the consent of her daughter's husband, as next of kin, which he had refused to give. The appellant made a request for information under the Freedom of Information Act 2000. The hospital declined the request on the basis that the information was confidential and could only be disclosed with the consent of her daughter's widower, and that therefore the information was exempt from disclosure under s.41 of the 2000 Act. The question for the Information Tribunal was whether the obligation of confidentiality survived the death of the patient, and whether the widower, as the deceased daughter's personal representative, had a right to enforce a deceased's entitlement to confidentiality. The tribunal pointed to the "unacceptable practical consequence if the duty did come to an end on death" in that any medical practitioner would be legally entitled to publish information from the records of a deceased patient, possibly for financial gain. Moreover, "those working within palliative care operate on the basis that their patients assume that information about them will not be disclosed to others both before and after they die."[46] The public interest in maintaining confidentiality in the medical records of a deceased patient "outweighs, by some way, the countervailing public interest in disclosure".[47] This view was reinforced by the approach of the European Court of Human Rights in

---

[43] *Confidentiality: good practice in handling patient information*, January 2017, para.136. The GMC guidance, at para.137, then lists a number of situations where a doctor should usually disclose relevant information about a patient who has died, including: under a statutory process; in the public interest to protect others from a risk of death or serious harm; for public health surveillance; when a parent asks about the causes of a child's death; when someone close to an adult patient asks for information about the circumstances of that patient's death; to meet a professional duty of candour; and where necessary to the reporting or investigation of adverse incidents, or complaints, for local clinical audit, or for clinical outcome review programmes. Note, however, para.101 which states that when providing information to relatives of a deceased patient under the doctor's duty of candour the doctor "should still respect the patient's confidentiality". For the GMC's statement of a doctor's professional duty of candour see para.4–054.

[44] Law Com., *Breach of Confidence*, 1981, Cmnd.8388, para.4.107.

[45] (2007) 98 B.M.L.R. 1; [2008] W.T.L.R. 1.

[46] (2007) 98 B.M.L.R. 1; [2008] W.T.L.R. 1 at [21].

[47] (2007) 98 B.M.L.R. 1; [2008] W.T.L.R. 1 at [13].

Z v Finland[48] stressing the importance of medical confidentiality to a person's rights under art.8 of the European Convention, not only to protect a patient's own privacy, but also to preserve confidence in the health services. Without this, patients in need of medical assistance might be deterred from revealing the personal information that may be necessary in order to receive appropriate treatment or even from seeking medical assistance, thereby endangering their own health, and in the case of transmissible disease that of the community. The tribunal concluded that:

> "...such of the older authorities that suggest that personal representatives may not have a right to enforce a deceased's entitlement to confidentiality, should be regarded as having been overruled, at least in relation to medical records, by the more recent cases on private information."[49]

It followed that the hospital had a defence to the disclosure request under the Freedom of Information Act 2000 because the information sought was subject to a duty of confidentiality enforceable by the deceased's husband.[50]

In *Lewis v Secretary of State for Health*[51] Foskett J accepted, without deciding, that it was arguable that the duty of confidentiality survives the patient's death. It was not necessarily a permanent duty: the more intimate and sensitive the type of examination, and the more sensitive the kind of results obtained, the more onerous and prolonged would be the obligation to maintain confidence.[52] Obtaining tissues from a dead body reflected a unique form of intimacy, and the results of any examination that might reveal exposure to ionising radiation made the results extremely sensitive. Such matters were sufficiently sensitive to require a high degree of confidentiality that endured for many years after the death of the individual.[53] In order to justify disclosure of the results of post-mortem examinations of former workers at nuclear installations to a confidential Inquiry the court had to identify a lawful basis for overriding that duty of confidentiality.[54]

8–017

---

[48] (1997) 25 E.H.R.R. 371; (1997) 45 B.M.L.R. 107.

[49] (2007) 98 B.M.L.R. 1; [2008] W.T.L.R. 1 at [28]. See also *Burgess v Wu* (2003) 235 D.L.R. (4th) 341, Ont SCJ, at [128] per Ferguson J: "The defence also submitted that Dr. MacDonald could act as their expert on the ground that since he was no longer treating the deceased or involved in his care he was released from his duties. This is not so. The duty of confidentiality does not die with the patient. It dies with the physician. In my view the other duties survive as well."

[50] Note, however, that there may be specific statutory procedures to authorise disclosure of confidential medical information after the patient's death. See, e.g., *CM v Executor for the Estate of EJ (Deceased)* [2013] EWHC 1680 (Fam); [2013] Med. L.R. 321 (consent of a person in a qualifying relationship under the Human Tissue Act 2004 rendered it lawful for samples to be taken from the body of a deceased person and tested for blood-borne communicable diseases in order to inform doctor who had treated the deceased whether she was at risk of developing a blood-borne disease).

[51] [2008] EWHC 2196 (QB); [2008] LS Law Medical 559 at [18]. In *Re C (A Child)* [2015] EWFC 79; [2015] Med. L.R. 531; [2017] 1 F.L.R. 82 at [17] Sir James Munby PFD commented that: "It is well recognised that, in principle, the duty [of confidentiality] extends beyond the termination of the professional relationship and survives even the death of the patient, client or customer."

[52] [2008] EWHC 2196 (QB); [2008] LS Law Medical 559 at [27].

[53] [2008] EWHC 2196 (QB); [2008] LS Law Medical 559 at [28].

[54] On the facts of this case that justification was the public interest: see para.8–062.

(e)   Anonymised data

8–018   The duty of confidentiality only applies to information relating to identifiable individuals. Thus, if data is anonymised before being released there is no breach. In *R. v Department of Health Ex p. Source Informatics*[55] the Court of Appeal held that pharmacists were entitled to pass on anonymised information concerning drug prescriptions to a commercial organisation which proposed to sell information about doctors' prescribing habits to pharmaceutical companies for marketing purposes. Simon Brown LJ commented that:

> "...the confidant is placed under a duty of good faith to the confider and the touchstone by which to judge the scope of his duty and whether or not it has been fulfilled or breached is his own conscience, no more and no less. One asks, therefore, on the facts of this case: would a reasonable pharmacist's conscience be troubled by the proposed use to be made of patients' prescriptions? Would he think that by entering Source's scheme he was breaking his customers' confidence, making unconscientious use of the information they provide?"[56]

The concern of the law was to protect the confider's personal privacy. The patient had no property in the information and no right to control its use, provided that his privacy was not put at risk, and therefore "the confidence is not breached where the confider's identity is protected".[57] It followed that the:

> "...pharmacists' consciences ought not reasonably to be troubled by co-operation with Source's proposed scheme. The patient's privacy will have been safeguarded, not invaded. The pharmacist's duty of confidence will not have been breached."[58]

8–019   The GMC guidance[59] stresses that where a doctor decides to disclose anonymised information, appropriate controls must be in place to minimise the risk of individual patients being identified. The controls required will depend on the risk of re-identification, and may include signed contracts or agreements containing controls on how the information will be used, kept and destroyed, as well as restrictions to prevent individuals being identified.

---

[55] [2001] Q.B. 424. See also *Department of Health v Information Commissioner* [2011] EWHC 1430 (Admin); [2011] Med. L.R. 363 (anonymised statistical data held by Department of Health about the numbers of abortions in particular categories was not personal data for the purposes of the Data Protection Act 1998 since it would not lead to the identification of a living person).

[56] [2001] Q.B. 424 at [31].

[57] [2001] Q.B. 424 at [34]. Note that the GMC guidance, *Confidentiality: good practice in handling patient information*, January 2017, para.81 adopts the Information Commissioner's Office code of practice approach to "anonymisation", i.e. that data is anonymised "if it does not itself identify any individual, and if it is unlikely to allow any individual to be identified through its combination with other data".

[58] [2001] Q.B. 424 at [35]. For criticism see D. Beyleveld and E. Histed, "Betrayal of Confidence in the Court of Appeal" (2000) 4 Med. Law Int. 276.

[59] GMC, *Confidentiality: good practice in handling patient information*, January 2017, para.86.

2. MISUSE OF PRIVATE INFORMATION

English law has not recognised a freestanding right to privacy, of which a law of confidentiality might be regarded as merely a subsidiary element. As Lord Nicholls put it in *Campbell v MGN Ltd*[60] there is "no over-arching, all-embracing cause of action for 'invasion of privacy'", though the protection of various aspects of privacy has been a fast developing area of the law. The impetus of art.8 of the European Convention for the Protection of Human Rights and Fundamental Freedoms, which provides that "Everyone has the right to respect for his ... family life ...", has led, however, to a new form of tort based on the protection of some aspects of privacy, and the courts are in the process of working out the boundaries of this form of liability. Article 8(2) provides for various exceptions, including:

> "...the interests of national security, public safety or the economic well-being of the country, for the prevention of disorder or crime, for the protection of health or morals, or for the protection of the rights and freedoms of others."

8–020

One of the most important "rights and freedoms of others" is contained in art.10 providing for the right to freedom of expression, though it too is subject to similar exceptions. The Human Rights Act 1998 s.12(4) provides that if a court is considering whether to grant any relief which, if granted, might affect the exercise of the Convention right to freedom of expression the court "must have particular regard to the importance of the Convention right to freedom of expression".

Article 8 and confidentiality It has been clear for some time that the confidentiality of medical records is considered to be a central aspect of the requirement of art.8 of the European Convention on Human Rights, providing the right to respect for private and family life. In *Z v Finland*[61] the European Court of Human Rights stated that:

8–021

> "... the protection of personal data, not least medical data, is of fundamental importance to a person's enjoyment of his or her right to respect for private and family life as guaranteed by article 8 of the Convention. Respecting the confidentiality of health data is a vital principle in the legal systems of all the Contracting Parties to the Convention. It is crucial not only to respect the sense of privacy of a patient but also to preserve his or her confidence in the medical profession and in the health services in general.
> Without such protection, those in need of medical assistance may be deterred from revealing such information of a personal and intimate nature as may be necessary in order to receive appropriate treatment and, even, from seeking such assistance, thereby endangering their own health and, in the case of transmissible diseases, that of the community."[62]

---

[60] [2004] UKHL 22; [2004] 2 A.C. 457 at [11], citing *Wainwright v Home Office* [2003] UKHL 53; [2004] A.C. 406. See also *Ash v McKennitt* [2006] EWCA Civ 1714; [2008] Q.B. 73 at [8] per Buxton LJ.
[61] (1997) 25 E.H.R.R. 371; (1997) 45 B.M.L.R. 107 at [95].
[62] See also *MS v Sweden* (1997) 28 E.H.R.R. 313; (1997) 3 B.H.R.C. 248 at [41]; *I v Finland* (20511/03) (2008) 48 E.H.R.R. 31; *Szuluk v United Kingdom* (36936/05) (2009) 50 E.H.R.R. 10; [2009] LS Law Medical 438.

But as with the law of confidentiality, this right is not absolute. The interests of a patient and the community in protecting the confidentiality of medical information may be outweighed by other interests, such as the prosecution of criminal offences or the publicity of court proceedings.[63] Any interference with the claimant's art.8 rights must be necessary in a democratic society and proportionate to the legitimate aims pursued.[64]

8–022   **Development of misuse of private information**   The issue came to prominence in the UK in *Campbell v MGN Ltd*[65] in which a newspaper published details of the claimant's treatment for drug addiction at a self-help group (Narcotics Anonymous), plus covert photographs of her leaving the premises. The House of Lords held that this constituted an interference with the claimant's right to respect for private life. The information that she was receiving therapy from a self-help group was equated with disclosure of the clinical details of medical treatment. Lord Nicholls explained how the action for breach of confidence had developed:

> "A breach of confidence was restrained as a form of unconscionable conduct, akin to a breach of trust. Today this nomenclature is misleading. The breach of confidence label harks back to the time when the cause of action was based on improper use of information disclosed by one person to another in confidence. To attract protection the information had to be of a confidential nature. But the gist of the cause of action was that information of this character had been disclosed by one person to another in circumstances 'importing an obligation of confidence' even though no contract of non-disclosure existed: see the classic exposition by Megarry J in *Coco v AN Clark (Engineers) Ltd* [1969] RPC 41, 47–48. The confidence referred to in the phrase 'breach of confidence' was the confidence arising out of a confidential relationship.
> This cause of action has now firmly shaken off the limiting constraint of the need for an initial confidential relationship. In doing so it has changed its nature. ... Now the law imposes a 'duty of confidence' whenever a person receives information he knows or ought to know is fairly and reasonably to be regarded as confidential. Even this formulation is awkward. The continuing use of the phrase 'duty of confidence' and the description of the information as 'confidential' is not altogether comfortable. Information about an individual's private life would not, in ordinary usage, be called 'confidential'. The more natural description today is that such information is private. The essence of the tort is better encapsulated now as misuse of private information."[66]

8–023   Lord Hoffmann pointed out that two developments in the law had changed the courts' approach. First, an acknowledgement that distinguishing between confidential information obtained through the violation of a confidential relationship and similar information obtained in some other way was artificial; and secondly the acceptance, influenced by the European Convention, of the privacy of personal information as something worthy of protection in its own right.[67] Human rights law identified private information as something worth protecting as an aspect of human autonomy and dignity:

---

[63] (1997) 25 E.H.R.R. 371; (1997) 45 B.M.L.R. 107 at [97]. See also *MS v Sweden* (1997) 28 E.H.R.R. 313; (1997) 3 B.H.R.C. 248, para.8–057.
[64] See e.g. *Re General Dental Council's Application* [2011] EWHC 3011 (Admin); [2012] Med. L.R. 204; para.8–057.
[65] [2004] UKHL 22; [2004] 2 A.C. 457.
[66] [2004] UKHL 22; [2004] 2 A.C. 457 at [13] and [14].
[67] [2004] UKHL 22; [2004] 2 A.C. 457 at [46].

"...the new approach takes a different view of the underlying value which the law protects. Instead of the cause of action being based upon the duty of good faith applicable to confidential personal information and trade secrets alike, it focuses upon the protection of human autonomy and dignity—the right to control the dissemination of information about one's private life and the right to the esteem and respect of other people."[68]

His Lordship added that the extent to which information about one's state of health, including drug dependency, should be communicated to other people was plainly something which individuals were entitled to decide for themselves.[69]

Baroness Hale observed that an individual's "reasonable expectation of privacy"[70] is "not the end of the story". It is a threshold test which brings the balancing exercise into play. If the information is found to be "private" the court must then balance the claimant's interest in keeping the information private against the countervailing interest of the recipient in publishing it. It had always been accepted that information about a person's health and treatment for ill health is both private and confidential, and that this arises not only from the confidentiality of the doctor–patient relationship but from the nature of the information itself.[71] However, not every statement about a person's health will necessarily be confidential or risk harm to the person's physical or moral integrity:

8–024

> "The privacy interest in the fact that a public figure has a cold or a broken leg is unlikely to be strong enough to justify restricting the press's freedom to report it. What harm could it possibly do? Sometimes there will be other justifications for publishing, especially where the information is relevant to the capacity of a public figure to do the job."[72]

In *McKennitt v Ash*[73] Buxton LJ explained that in developing a right to protect privacy the courts have "shoehorned" the human rights jurisprudence into the tort of breach of confidence, and this has resulted in the action for breach of confidence being employed where there was no pre-existing relationship of confidence between the parties, but the "confidence" arose from the defendant having acquired by unlawful or surreptitious means information that he should have known he was not free to use. One solution to this apparent difficulty was to employ Lord Nicholls' terminology and rechristen the action as the tort of "misuse of private information". Thus:

8–025

> "...in order to find the rules of the English law of breach of confidence we now have to look in the jurisprudence of articles 8 and 10 ... [which] are the very content of the domestic tort that the English court has to enforce."[74]

---

[68] [2004] UKHL 22; [2004] 2 A.C. 457 at [51].
[69] [2004] UKHL 22; [2004] 2 A.C. 457 at [53], citing *Z v Finland* (1997) 25 E.H.R.R. 371 at [95].
[70] On the interpretation of this term see also *McKennitt v Ash* [2006] EWCA Civ 1714; [2008] Q.B. 73 and *Browne v Associated Newspapers Ltd* [2007] EWCA Civ 295; [2008] Q.B. 103—this requires a detailed examination of the circumstances on a case-by-case basis, including the nature of the information and the circumstances in which it has been imparted or obtained. The mere fact that the information was imparted in the course of a relationship of confidence does not necessarily create an expectation of privacy.
[71] [2004] UKHL 22; [2004] 2 A.C. 457 at [145].
[72] [2004] UKHL 22; [2004] 2 A.C. 457 at [157].
[73] [2006] EWCA Civ 1714; [2008] Q.B. 73.
[74] [2006] EWCA Civ 1714; [2008] Q.B. 73 at [11].

There is a two-stage test: first is the information "private" within the meaning established by art.8; and secondly, if so, in all the circumstances, must the interest of the owner of the private information yield to the right of freedom of expression conferred on the publisher by art.10? This balancing exercise involves weighing the public and private interests in maintaining privacy against the public interest in disclosure in a process that is not dissimilar to identifying the limits to the duty of confidentiality by reference to exceptions to the rule.

8–026   In *Douglas v Hello! Ltd (No.3)*,[75] Lord Nicholls summarised the position:

> "As the law has developed breach of confidence, or misuse of confidential information, now covers two distinct causes of action, protecting two different interests: privacy, and secret ('confidential') information. It is important to keep these two distinct. In some instances information may qualify for protection both on grounds of privacy and confidentiality. In other instances information may be in the public domain, and not qualify for protection as confidential, and yet qualify for protection on the grounds of privacy. Privacy can be invaded by further publication of information or photographs already disclosed to the public. Conversely, and obviously, a trade secret may be protected as confidential information even though no question of personal privacy is involved."

In the context of medical information it is apparent that disclosure of a patient's medical records may fall under *both* (what is now categorised as a tort of) breach of confidentiality, arising from the nature of the relationship between doctor and patient, and the tort of misuse of private information which does not depend upon a specific relationship but arises where the court holds that there is a "reasonable expectation of privacy" and the balancing exercise comes down in favour of maintaining privacy against the public interest in disclosure.

8–027   **Distinguish breach of confidentiality and misuse of private information**   In *Vidal-Hall v Google Inc*[76] the Court of Appeal considered that it was now an uncontroversial proposition that the law of confidentiality had been developed and adapted to protect one aspect of invasion of privacy, the misuse of private information, in order to give appropriate effect to the right to respect for private and family life embodied in art.8 ECHR. But the actions for breach of confidentiality and misuse of private information were not the same and protected different interests. They are now two separate and distinct causes of action.[77] The action for misuse of private information is now regarded as a tort.[78] In *Vidal-Hall v Google Inc* the Court of Appeal was unequivocal. There was no:

---

[75] [2007] UKHL 21; [2008] 1 A.C. 1 at [255].
[76] [2015] EWCA Civ 311; [2016] Q.B. 1003 at [19]. *Vidal-Hall* is commented on by J. Folkard, "Privacy and conflicts in the Court of Appeal" (2016) 132 L.Q.R. 31.
[77] [2015] EWCA Civ 311; [2016] Q.B. 1003 at [21].
[78] See e.g. *Murray v Big Pictures (UK) Ltd* [2008] EWCA Civ 446; [2009] Ch 481 at [24] per Sir Anthony Clarke MR: "Although the origin of the cause of action relied upon is breach of confidence, since information about an individual's private life would not, in ordinary usage, be called 'confidential', the more natural description of the position today is that such information is private and the essence of the tort is better encapsulated now as misuse of private information"; *Imerman v Tchenguiz* [2010] EWCA Civ 908; [2011] Fam. 116 at [65] per Lord Neuberger MR: following the decision of the House of Lords in *Campbell v MGN Ltd* "there is now a tort of misuse of private information".

"...satisfactory or principled answer to the question why misuse of private information should not be characterised as a tort for the purposes of service out of the jurisdiction."[79]

Misuse of private information was "a civil wrong without any equitable characteristics". The law of confidentiality protects secret or confidential information where the focus is on the duty of good faith, whereas the tort of misuse of private information focuses on privacy and the protection of human autonomy and dignity.[80] The Court cited Lord Nicholls' observations in *Douglas v Hello! Ltd (No.3)*[81] that it was important to keep the two causes of action distinct, though in some cases information could "qualify for protection both on grounds of privacy and confidentiality". In others, information could be in the public domain, and so not qualify for protection as confidential, and yet qualify for protection on the grounds of privacy.

The main difference between the tort of misuse of private information and breach of confidentiality is that the former can still apply where the information is in the public domain, whereas confidentiality is usually lost once the information is public. As a consequence a claimant may not be able to obtain an injunction to prevent further disclosures of confidential information,[82] and will be left to a remedy in damages. The focus of misuse of private information is on the intrusion into the claimant's private life,[83] and the fact that information has been put into the public domain does not necessarily mean that further publication does not constitute an additional intrusion. A claimant in this situation may be able to obtain an injunction to prevent that further invasion of privacy.[84] In practice, many of the cases brought for misuse of private information have involved celebrities being harassed by the media, often, though not always, in relation to a newspaper's wish to publish details of a claimant's sexual "misconduct". But as the Supreme Court pointed out in *PJS v News Group Newspapers Ltd*[85] as a general rule there is no public interest in the disclosure of purely private sexual encounters, even if they involve adultery or more than one person at the same time, and such disclosure will on the face of it constitute the tort of invasion of privacy. Moreover, unlike confidentiality, repetition of such a disclosure is capable of constituting a further tort of invasion of privacy, even in

8–028

---

[79] [2015] EWCA Civ 311; [2016] Q.B. 1003 at [43]; see also at [51]; endorsed by the Court of Appeal in *Gulati v MGN Ltd* [2015] EWCA Civ 1291; [2017] Q.B. 149 at [88]. On misuse of private information as a tort see: *Axon v Ministry of Defence* [2016] EWHC 787 (QB); [2016] E.M.L.R. 20 at [72]; *Burrell v Clifford* [2016] EWHC 294 (Ch); [2017] E.M.L.R. 2 at [149]; *DB v General Medical Council* [2016] EWHC 2331 (QB); (2016) 152 B.M.L.R. 106 at [50] per Soole J: "Misuse of private information is now a distinct cause of action in tort which reflects the common law's absorption of Article 8 into the established cause of action for breach of confidence."

[80] [2015] EWCA Civ 311; [2016] Q.B. 1003 at [25].

[81] [2007] UKHL 21; [2008] 1 A.C. 1 at [255].

[82] *Att.-Gen. v Guardian Newspapers (No.2)* [1990] 1 A.C. 109; see para.8–014.

[83] "... the modern law of privacy is not concerned solely with information or 'secrets': it is also concerned importantly with intrusion", per Eady J in *CTB v News Group Newspapers Ltd* [2011] EWHC 1326 (QB) at [23].

[84] See *Douglas v Hello! Ltd (No.3)* [2007] UKHL 21; [2008] 1 A.C. 1 per Lord Nicholls at [255], quoted at para.8–026 above.

[85] [2016] UKSC 26; [2016] A.C. 1081 at [32] per Lord Mance (with whom Lord Neuberger, Lady Hale and Lord Reed agreed).

relation to persons to whom disclosure or publication was previously made.[86] A further important difference between the two causes of action is that the level of damages awarded for the misuse of private information tends to be greater than for breach of confidentiality.[87]

8–029   **The medical context**   Medical information about an individual almost invariably qualifies as confidential (subject to a number of exceptions), and it is arguable that disclosure of such information should also qualify for the protection of the tort of misuse of private information.[88] Medical information is undoubtedly considered to be private information, and maintaining its confidentiality is justified as much by the protection of the patient's right to human autonomy and dignity as it is in enforcing a "duty of good faith". If the publication of photographs, taken in a public place, of the children of "celebrities" can qualify for protection as the misuse of private information,[89] it is difficult to see how the publication of information about a claimant's medical condition could fail to receive similar protection. Moreover, both causes of action are underpinned by the art.8 ECHR right to respect for private and family life.[90] Thus, although the two causes of action have different conceptual foundations[91] and protect different interests, in the specific context of medical information both actions could have a role to play. This is potentially important for claims based on the misuse of medical information awards of damages may be higher.

3.   SCOPE OF THE DUTY OF CONFIDENCE—EXCEPTIONS TO THE RULE

8–030   Even where the disclosure of the information would affect the privacy of an identifiable individual, the duty of confidence is not absolute, and it is only by looking at the circumstances in which a breach of confidence can be justified in law that the scope of the duty can be appreciated. The General Medical Council, while emphasising the importance of maintaining confidentiality, sets out a number of circumstances in which information about a patient may be

---

[86] [2016] UKSC 26; [2016] A.C. 1081 at [32]. See also the observations of Lord Neuberger (with whom Lady Hale, Lord Mance and Lord Reed agreed) at [58]–[61] on the distinction between confidentiality and misuse of private information, and the significance of the concept of intrusion to the latter.

[87] See paras 8–085 et seq.

[88] See, e.g., in a different context, the comments of Lord Neuberger MR in *Imerman v Tchenguiz* [2010] EWCA Civ 908; [2011] Fam. 116 at [67]–[68] pointing to the interrelationship and overlap of the two causes of action.

[89] See *Murray v Express Newspapers Plc* [2008] EWCA Civ 446; [2009] Ch. 481; *Weller v Associated Newspapers Ltd* [2015] EWCA Civ 1176; [2016] 1 W.L.R. 1541.

[90] On the application of art.8 to claims for breach of confidentiality see *MS v Sweden* (1997) 28 E.H.R.R. 313; (1997) 3 B.H.R.C. 248; *Z v Finland* (1997) 25 E.H.R.R. 371; (1997) 45 B.M.L.R. 107; *I v Finland* (20511/03) (2008) 48 E.H.R.R. 31. And on the application of art.8 to claims for invasion of privacy based on the publication of photographs taken in a public place, i.e. the equivalent of the tort of misuse of private information, see: *Von Hannover v Germany* (59320/00) (2005) 40 E.H.R.R. 1.

[91] *Vidal-Hall v Google Inc* [2015] EWCA Civ 311; [2016] Q.B. 1003 at [25].

disclosed.[92] Some of these circumstances correspond to exceptions to the duty of confidentiality in law, and most of them do not give rise to difficulty.[93]

(a)   Consent by the patient[94]

Consent by a patient with capacity[95] to the disclosure of medical information is a valid defence. The right to confidentiality is the patient's, not the doctor's or the hospital's. Thus, a hospital is not entitled to object to a patient's solicitor seeing the patient's medical records where the patient has granted the solicitor a signed and dated form of authority.[96] Consent does not have to be in writing to be valid and may be express or implied.[97]

8–031

(b)   Sharing information with others providing the patient's care[98]

Doctors working in hospital and general practice are usually working in a healthcare team, some of whose members may need access to confidential information about the patient in order to perform their duties. The General Medical Council (GMC) states that express consent is not usually needed before relevant personal information is shared to enable the treatment to be provided, since most patients will understand and expect that information has to be shared

8–032

---

[92] Confidentiality: good practice in handling patient information, January 2017, paras 9, 10 and 80.

[93] In Lewis v Secretary of State for Health [2008] EWHC 2196 (QB); [2008] LS Law Medical 559 at [19] Foskett J observed that: "The content of an obligation imposed upon a professional by his profession is not, of course, necessarily coterminous with the obligation imposed by law in similar circumstances although it may be a useful indicator of the perceived values by which the relationship of the professional to his client (in this case, patient) are to be judged."

[94] See Confidentiality: good practice in handling patient information, January 2017 at paras 8f, 13–14, 62 and 95. Para.115 provides that where a third party such as a patient's insurer or employer, or a government department, or an agency assessing a claimant's entitlement to benefits, asks for personal information about a patient the doctor should, inter alia, be satisfied that the patient has sufficient information about the scope, purpose and likely consequences of the examination and disclosure, and the fact that relevant information cannot be concealed or withheld, and obtain or have seen written consent to the disclosure from the patient or a person authorised to act on the patient's behalf. See further GMC, Disclosing information for employment insurance and similar purposes, 2017.

[95] The starting presumption is that an adult patient has the capacity to make decisions about the disclosure of their personal information: Confidentiality: good practice in handling patient information, January 2017, para.41. See also the Mental Capacity Act 2005 s.1(2); para.6–045.

[96] Re NR's Application for Judicial Review [2015] NIQB 35, where the patient was a detained mental patient who had applied to the mental health review tribunal for a review of the lawfulness of his detention, but the principle is the same whether or not the patient is a detained patient.

[97] Hunter v Mann [1974] Q.B. 767 at 772. Though in cases where it is sought to argue that patients in general may be taken to have impliedly consented to the use of information for a particular purpose, it may be better to deal with the situation as part of the wider public interest defence: R. v Department of Health Ex p. Source Informatics [2001] Q.B. 424 at [51]. This avoids the problem of seeking to rely on the implied consent of those individuals who may expressly refuse consent. Implied consent will most commonly arise where information is shared amongst health professionals for the purpose of providing treatment to the patient. See para.8–032.

[98] GMC, Confidentiality: good practice in handling patient information, January 2017 at paras 26–33.

with others in the healthcare team and consent can usually be implied.[99] Doctors must make it clear to members of the team who receive the information that it is given to them in confidence.[100] Clearly, all the members of the healthcare team come under a corresponding duty of confidentiality with regard to the information communicated to them about the patient. Similarly, public bodies, such as NHS Trusts, have a responsibility to take appropriate steps to preserve the confidentiality of medical records when transmitting them to another public body.[101]

8-033   The sharing of medical information for the purpose of treatment would probably be regarded by a court as an instance of implied consent by the patient, although in *W v Egdell*[102] Scott J considered that the disclosure of an independent psychiatrist's report to the hospital where the claimant was detained was justified under this provision, even though the patient had expressly refused his consent. The Court of Appeal doubted whether this exception applied,[103] however, because the psychiatrist did not have a continuing professional relationship with the claimant, although the circumstances of the disclosure fell within the letter of the exception. If Scott J's view were correct then implied consent could not be the basis for the exception. The circumstances that arose in *W v Egdell* would clearly not be covered by the current GMC guidance.

(c)   Medical emergency

8-034   The GMC guidance provides for situations, such as a medical emergency, where a patient cannot be informed about the sharing of information. In these cases the doctor should pass relevant information promptly to those providing the patient's care.[104]

(d)   Sharing information with the patient's family

8-035   Members of the patient's family or those close to the patient will often want to have information about the patient's condition, diagnosis and prognosis, and in most instances the patient will probably be content for that information to be shared. Nonetheless, the medical information remains confidential and doctors should obtain the patient's consent to disclose it to family members. If the patient

---

[99] This is subject to information being readily available to patients explaining how their information will be used and that they have the right to object, and that the doctor has no reason to believe the patient has objected: GMC, *Confidentiality: good practice in handling patient information*, January 2017, para.28. If the patient objects to sharing information for their direct care the doctor should not disclose the information unless it would be justified in the public interest or it is of overall benefit to a patient who lacks the capacity to make the decision: para.30. If patients with capacity continue to object to disclosure it should be explained to them that they cannot be referred or have arrangements made for their treatment without also disclosing the information: para.31.

[100] GMC, *Confidentiality: good practice in handling patient information*, January 2017, at para.28d.

[101] *A Health Authority v X* [2001] 2 F.L.R. 673; [2001] Lloyd's Rep. Med. 349 at [57] per Munby J; aff'd [2001] EWCA Civ 2014; [2002] 2 All E.R. 780.

[102] [1990] Ch. 359 at 392; see paras 8–063 to 8–064 for the facts of this case.

[103] [1990] Ch. 359 at 420–421, per Bingham LJ.

[104] *Confidentiality: good practice in handling patient information*, January 2017, para.32.

refuses then doctors may encourage the patient to reconsider the decision if sharing the information could be beneficial to the patient's care and support, but ultimately the patient's wishes should be respected unless disclosure is justified in the public interest.[105] The GMC suggest that where a patient lacks capacity to make the decision:

> "it is reasonable to assume the patient would want those closest to them to be kept informed of their general condition and prognosis, unless they indicate (or have previously indicated) otherwise."[106]

(e) Children

The same duties of confidentiality apply to minors as to adults, with the consequence that identifiable information should only be disclosed: if it is necessary to achieve the purpose of the disclosure (otherwise the information should be anonymised); the patient (or, if appropriate, those with parental responsibility for the patient) has been informed about the possible uses of their information; the patient (or someone with parental responsibility) has consented (unless an exception applies); and the disclosure is kept to the minimum necessary.[107] Disclosure without consent may be lawful if there is an overriding public interest, disclosure is required by law, or where disclosure is in the best interests of a child or young person who lacks capacity to make a decision about disclosure.[108]

8–036

Refusals of consent   The default position is that where minors have capacity to consent to disclosure they should be asked for their consent to do so.[109] Where a minor with capacity refuses to consent, the public interest may justify disclosure to an appropriate person or authority if this is necessary to protect the child or young person, or someone else, from the risk of death or serious harm, such as: where children or young persons are at risk of neglect or sexual, physical or emotional abuse; behaviour that might put them or others at risk of serious harm (such as serious addiction, self-harm or joy-riding); or the information would help in the prevention, detection or prosecution of serious crime.[110]

8–037

---

[105] *Confidentiality: good practice in handling patient information*, January 2017, paras 36 and 37. On the public interest defence see para.8–059.

[106] *Confidentiality: good practice in handling patient information*, January 2017, para.38.

[107] GMC, *0–18 years: guidance for all doctors*, 2007, paras 42–43 (available at *http://www.gmc-uk. org/static/documents/content/0_18_years.pdf*).

[108] GMC, *0–18 years: guidance for all doctors*, 2007, at para.46. See also GMC, *Protecting children and young people: the responsibilities of all doctors*, 2012, paras 31 and 36 (available at *http://www.gmc-uk.org/static/documents/content/Protecting_children_and_young_people_-_English_ 1015.pdf*). Note that these principles apply to *justify* the disclosure, i.e. they operate as a defence to what would otherwise be a breach of the duty of confidentiality. There are some situations where the doctor may be under a positive *duty* to disclose, either at common law (see e.g. *Brown v University of Alberta Hospital* (1997) 145 D.L.R. (4th) 63, Alta QB, para.2–043 and *JD v East Berkshire Community Health NHS Trust* [2005] UKHL 23; [2005] 2 A.C. 373, paras 2–044 and 2–099–2–100) or by statute (see e.g. the Female Genital Mutilation Act 2003 s.5B).

[109] GMC, *Protecting children and young people: the responsibilities of all doctors*, 2012, para.35.

[110] GMC, *0–18 years: guidance for all doctors*, 2007, para.49. See also GMC, *Protecting children and young people: the responsibilities of all doctors*, 2012, paras 32 and 37.

8–038   **Disclosures to parents**   Where children who lack capacity ask a doctor not to disclose information about their condition or treatment to a third party, such as a parent, the GMC guidance indicates that the doctor should try to persuade them to allow an appropriate person to be involved in the consultation. If the patient refuses and the doctor judges that it is necessary, in their best interests, he may disclose relevant information to a parent or an appropriate authority.[111] The doctor should tell the patient before disclosing any information.[112] On the other hand, where a child has sufficient maturity and understanding to have capacity the doctor must normally respect the confidentiality of the doctor–patient relationship. Only where the public interest defence applies (e.g. if the doctor suspected that a request for contraceptive or abortion advice was as a consequence of sexual abuse) would disclosure contrary to the competent minor's wishes be justified, but in this respect children are probably in no different position from that of adults.[113]

8–039   In *R. (on the application of Axon) v Secretary of State for Health*[114] Silber J held that guidance to health professionals issued by the Department of Health in 2004 on giving advice and treatment to patients under the age of 16 on sexual matters which recommended that doctors follow the criteria set out in *Gillick* was not unlawful. *Gillick* had held that the interests of the parents and the importance of family life did not override the duty of confidentiality owed by a doctor to a child under 16. Nor was there any difference between advice on contraception and advice on abortion or sexually transmitted disease. Withholding information from the parents of a patient under 16 relating to the advice or treatment of the patient on sexual matters did not infringe the parents' rights under art.8(1) of the European Convention on Human Rights, and even if it did satisfy the criteria under art.8(1), such interference would be justified under art.8(2).

---

[111] GMC, *0–18 years: guidance for all doctors*, 2007, para.51. This modified guidance is derived from the decision of the House of Lords in *Gillick v West Norfolk and Wisbech Area Health Authority* [1986] A.C. 112, on which see paras 6–193 et seq. On the child's right to confidentiality see J. Loughrey, "Medical information, confidentiality and a child's right to privacy" (2003) 23 L.S. 510.

[112] GMC, *0–18 years: guidance for all doctors*, 2007 para.51. Note that there may be rare circumstances in which there could be a duty of care not to reveal facts about the patient's condition to the patient. *Furniss v Fitchett* [1958] N.Z.L.R. 396 provides an unusual example. The Data Protection Act 1998 s.30 and the Data Protection (Subject Access Modification) (Health) Order 2000 (SI 2000/413) exempts from the general right of access to information conferred by that Act information as to the physical or mental health of a data subject, where, inter alia, access would be likely to cause serious harm to the physical or mental health of the data subject. See *Roberts v Nottinghamshire Healthcare NHS Trust* [2008] EWHC 1934 (QB); [2008] LS Law Medical 586; [2008] M.H.L.R. 294. See also Senior Courts Act 1981 ss.33 and 34 under which disclosure of medical records can be limited to the applicant's legal advisers and/or any medical or other professional adviser of the applicant; see further paras 13–038, 13–043, 13–058.

[113] See para.8–040, n.115, below.

[114] [2006] EWHC 37 (Admin); [2006] Q.B. 539; [2006] 2 F.L.R. 206.

(f)   Adults at risk of abuse or neglect

Adult patients who have capacity are entitled to make their own decisions about   **8–040**
the disclosure of personal medical information to others where the failure to
disclose may put them at risk of harm.[115] An adult patient's lack of capacity does
not mean that the rules of confidentiality do not apply, but respect for the patient's
dignity and privacy (including the patient's previously expressed preferences and
what is known about the patient's wishes, feelings, beliefs and values) have to be
considered in the context of the treatment and care that the patient requires.[116]
However, where the patient lacks capacity and the doctor believes that the patient
may be the victim of neglect or physical, sexual or emotional abuse, or any other
kind of serious harm, the doctor should disclose information promptly to an
appropriate responsible person or authority, where disclosure is in the patient's
best interests.[117] In law, this exception would probably be justified under the
"public interest" defence. In some instances the doctor may be under a statutory
duty to report concerns about a vulnerable adult.[118]

(g)   Statutory obligations

A doctor "must disclose information if it is required by law".[119] There are a   **8–041**
number of statutes under which the disclosure of information is compulsory, and
doctors are not exempt from these requirements.[120] The GMC suggest that before

---

[115] Where the risk is of harm to others, the position is potentially different: see para.8–059. The GMC
guidance acknowledges that there may be rare exceptions to the principle that competent adults are
entitled to take their own decisions affecting their own welfare: "In very exceptional circumstances,
disclosure without consent may be justified in the public interest to prevent a serious crime such as
murder, manslaughter or serious assault *even where no one other than the patient is at risk*. This is
only likely to be justifiable where there is clear evidence of an imminent risk of serious harm to the
individual, and where there are no alternative (and less intrusive) methods of preventing that harm":
Confidentiality: good practice in handling patient information, January 2017, para.59, n.19 (emphasis
added).

[116] See *Confidentiality: good practice in handling patient information*, January 2017, paras 44–47.

[117] *Confidentiality: good practice in handling patient information*, January 2017, para.55. This
exception is slightly at odds with the guidance given by the GMC in para.49 that where patients have
indicated that they do not want the information to be disclosed but the doctor considers that "it would
be of overall benefit to the patient and you believe they lack capacity to make that decision, you may
disclose relevant information to an appropriate person or authority". This is a simple "best interests"
test and if a doctor is justified in disclosing information where it is in patients' best interests it is not
clear why para.55 would require "neglect or physical, sexual or emotional abuse, or any other kind of
serious harm". Best interests involves weighing the balance of benefits between disclosure and
non-disclosure and would not necessarily require the prospect of "serious harm" to the patient.

[118] See GMC, *Confidentiality: key legislation*, 2017 (available at *http://www.gmc-uk.org/Key_
legislation.pdf_69089457.pdf*).

[119] *Confidentiality: good practice in handling patient information*, January 2017, paras 88, 53.

[120] See, e.g., Public Health (Control of Disease) Act 1984 ss.45C, 45F and the Health Protection
(Notification) Regulations 2010 (SI 2010/659) (duty to notify suspected cases of disease, infection or
contamination); Abortion Act 1967 s.2 and the Abortion Regulations 1991 (SI 1991/499) as amended;
Road Traffic Act 1988 s.172(2) (on which see *Hunter v Mann* [1974] 1 Q.B. 767); Misuse of Drugs
Act 1971 s.23; Terrorism Act 2000 s.19; National Health Service Act 2006 s.269 and (in England) the
National Health Service and Public Health (Functions and Miscellaneous Provisions) Regulations
2013 (SI 2013/261) Part 3 and (in Wales) the National Health Service (Notification of Births and

complying with a request for information the doctor should: be satisfied that personal information is needed and that the disclosure is *required* by law; only disclose information relevant to the request and in the required manner; tell patients about such disclosures whenever practicable unless it would undermine the purpose of the disclosure to do so; and abide by patient objections if there is provision for objection.[121]

(h) Clinical audit

8–042   Clinical audit is defined by the GMC as: "the evaluation of clinical performance against standards or through comparative analysis, to inform the management of services."[122] Its objective is to improve patient safety or services, and can take the form of health care staff meeting to discuss the cases of particular patients, often with a view to learning from mistakes. If the audit is undertaken by the team that provided the patient's care identifiable information may be disclosed on the basis of implied consent, if it is not practicable to use anonymised information, provided that patients have access to information explaining that their medical information may be disclosed for clinical audit and that they have the right to object, and they have not objected.[123]

8–043   If the audit is to be undertaken by a team other than the one that provided the care, or those working to support them, the GMC state that the information should be anonymised, and if it is not practicable to anonymise the information the patient's express consent must be obtained or there must be some other legal basis for breaching confidentiality.[124] In *R. v Department of Health Ex p. Source Informatics*[125] it was suggested that the use of identifiable data for the purpose of

Deaths) Regulations 1982 (SI 1982/286). For consideration of the extent to which it is possible to prevent publication of the name and address of a person against whom an order for the compulsory removal to hospital of a person with a notifiable disease has been made under the Public Health (Control of Disease) Act 1984, see: *Birmingham Post & Mail Ltd v Birmingham City Council* (1993) 17 B.M.L.R. 116. (A broader power to order health measures in relation to persons who are or may be infected or contaminated is now contained in the Public Health (Control of Disease) Act 1984 s.45G.)
[121] *Confidentiality: good practice in handling patient information*, January 2017, para.88. Where a statute permits, but does not require, the disclosure of confidential medical information the doctor must be careful to see that there is a legal basis for breaching confidentiality, such as patient consent or the public interest: para.19.
[122] *Confidentiality: good practice in handling patient information*, January 2017, para.96, n.35. For consideration of confidentiality in the context of the education and training of health professionals see GMC, *Confidentiality: disclosing information for education and training purposes*, 2017. The basic proposition is that anonymised information will often be sufficient for these purposes and, if that is not possible, the patient's explicit consent should be obtained before disclosing it to anyone who is not part of the team providing the patient's direct care. Doctors in training or medical students who are part of the team providing care will need access to the patient's information in the same way as other members of the healthcare team.
[123] *Confidentiality: good practice in handling patient information*, January 2017, para.96. The GMC guidance is somewhat opaque as to the position where the patient does object, stating that they should be removed from the audit "if practicable" and if it is "not practicable" this should be explained to the patient "along with any options open to them": para.97. Query whether one option would be to bring a claim for breach of confidentiality?
[124] *Confidentiality: good practice in handling patient information*, January 2017, at para.98.
[125] [2001] Q.B. 424 at [53].

audit, provided the use was "very strictly controlled", would be acceptable, either because it falls within the public interest defence or because the scope of the duty of confidentiality is circumscribed to accommodate it.

(i) Financial audit or administrative purposes

These activities may involve disclosure of information about individuals for purposes other than the patient's healthcare. If the information is in a form which does not enable individuals to be identified, there is no question of a breach of confidence.[126] The GMC states that doctors should provide such information in an anonymised form, if practicable, and that if identifiable information is needed the doctor must be satisfied that there is a legal basis for breaching confidentiality.[127] In some instances financial audit and health service management may be covered by s.251 of the National Health Service Act 2006 and the Health Service (Control of Patient Information) Regulations 2002.[128]

8–044

In *R. (on the application of W) v Secretary of State for Health*[129] the applicants were four non-UK residents who had been or were liable to be charged in excess of £1,000 for NHS services, and were liable to immigration sanctions if they failed to pay the charges. The Home Office could refuse an application for leave to remain if NHS debts totalling at least £1,000 had been incurred. The NHS bodies where the applicants had received treatment passed information to the Secretary of State for Health, who in turn passed it to the Home Office, which included the name, date of birth and gender of the patient, current address, the nationality and travel document number with expiry dates, and the amount and date of the debt. The information did not include any reference to the patient's clinical history, medical condition, treatment or prognosis, though the identity of the NHS body making the charge was in some cases enough to indicate the nature of the patient's illness. The applicants challenged the lawfulness of passing the information to the Home Office on the grounds that it was private and confidential, that the NHS bodies did not have the power to pass it to the Secretary of State who also did not have the power to pass it to the Home Office, and that disclosure of the information constituted a breach of their art.8 ECHR rights. The Court of Appeal accepted that the information was inherently private information in that it revealed information about the health of the applicants, i.e. that they were unwell to the extent that they had to seek medical care. The fact that the disclosure was less intrusive than disclosure of detailed information about an individual's medical condition and treatment did not mean that it was not intrusive or that the information was not private. Rather, it meant that it was likely to be easier to justify disclosure.[130] The Court concluded that since

8–045

---

[126] See *R. v Department of Health Ex p. Source Informatics* [2001] Q.B. 424.
[127] *Confidentiality: good practice in handling patient information*, January 2017, para.99. A legal basis for breaching confidentiality would be that the disclosure is required by law, the patient has given express consent, there is a statute authorising the disclosure (such as the National Health Service Act 2006 s.251) or disclosure is justified in the public interest: para.80.
[128] See para.8–048 below.
[129] [2015] EWCA Civ 1034; [2016] 1 W.L.R. 698.
[130] [2015] EWCA Civ 1034; [2016] 1 W.L.R. 698 at [34]–[35].

overseas visitors were informed before being treated that if they incurred charges in excess of £1,000, and did not pay, their information could be passed to the Home Office for immigration purposes they could not have any, still less any reasonable, expectation that the information would not be passed on.[131] The judge had been correct to find that the information was not private vis-à-vis the Secretary of State and the Home Office.[132] Similarly, any interference with the applicants' art.8 rights was modest and was justified under art.8(2).

(j)   Adverse incident reporting

8–046   Adverse incident reporting schemes are designed to enable health service organisations to learn from errors and "near miss" incidents with a view to improving future patient safety. In some instances there is an organisational duty of candour placed on the provider of healthcare services to notify the patient "or a person lawfully acting on their behalf" of a notifiable safety incident.[133] Usually this will mean reporting the incident to the patient, but in some instances it will involve informing someone other than the patient (such as relatives where the patient has died). The GMC guidance states that where the law requires personal information to be disclosed for these purposes the doctor must comply.[134] For non-statutory incident reporting schemes the doctor should seek the patient's consent to disclose personal information unless it is not appropriate or practicable to do so.[135] In some instances the public interest may justify disclosure without consent.

(k)   Medical research and epidemiology

8–047   Some of the earlier versions of the GMC's advice on confidentiality and medical research made no reference to the patient's consent, and it was at least arguable that a legal justification for the exception could derive from the public interest defence, in that it is in the public interest that properly regulated medical research should be conducted and that the results should be available to the scientific community.[136] On the other hand, research should not normally be conducted

---

[131] [2015] EWCA Civ 1034; [2016] 1 W.L.R. 698 at [44].

[132] [2015] EWCA Civ 1034; [2016] 1 W.L.R. 698 at [45]. The Court acknowledged that there might be exceptions such as where the patient was unconscious, or vulnerable and unable to speak English.

[133] See the Health and Social Care Act 2008 (Regulated Activities) Regulations 2014 (SI 2014/2936) reg.20; see para.4–055.

[134] *Confidentiality: good practice in handling patient information*, January 2017, para.102, subject to the doctor being satisfied that personal information is needed and the disclosure is required by law, and that the information is relevant and supplied in the way required by the law: para.88.

[135] *Confidentiality: good practice in handling patient information*, January 2017, para.102.

[136] Researchers may not be able to maintain the confidentiality of their data, even where it is supplied to them on a confidential basis. In the litigation concerning claims that some children have sustained brain damage as a reaction to pertussis vaccine, the defendants sought access to the data contained in the National Childhood Encephalopathy Study, which had been provided to the researchers on a confidential basis by doctors and hospitals. Stuart-Smith J held that the interests of justice outweighed both the interests of patients in maintaining confidentiality of their records and the public interest in conducting research, which could be damaged if doctors and patients who co-operated in research projects believed that the information they supplied would not be kept confidential. It was ordered

without the patients' consent, and if the doctor can reasonably practicably obtain consent to conducting the research there would seem to be no reason for not obtaining consent to disclosure of the results at the same time. Previous guidance issued by the GMC suggested that where a research project depended on using identifiable information, and it was not practical to contact patients to seek their consent, this should be drawn to the attention of a research ethics committee so that it could consider whether the likely benefits of the research outweighed the loss of confidentiality. But as the GMC acknowledged, although the views of a research ethics committee would, no doubt, be taken into account by a court if a claim for breach of confidentiality were made, the court would make its own assessment of whether the public interest was served in determining whether the breach of confidentiality was justified.[137] The default position is that express consent from the patient is usually needed before the disclosure of identifiable information for research purposes and patients must be given enough information on which to base their decision.[138] The situation where obtaining consent is impracticable and anonymised information cannot be used is governed by the National Health Service Act 2006 s.251.

National Health Service Act 2006 s.251   There is statutory provision covering   **8–048**
situations where the consent of the patient to the use of health records cannot practically be obtained, and anonymised information is insufficient. Research projects may involve tens of thousands of patients where contact would be impracticable, but it may be judged that the essential nature of the research is such that the public interest outweighs issues of privacy. Some patients are not capable of giving consent, but the health service may still need to know about them and their medical conditions. Moreover, sometimes excluding those who refuse consent could bias data collection to the extent that it loses all value. In order to deal with the potential problem that these situations create, s.251 of the National Health Service Act 2006[139] allows the Secretary of State to make regulations to permit the processing of prescribed patient information for medical purposes where it is considered necessary or expedient (a) in the interests of improving patient care, or (b) in the public interest.[140]

Section 251(4) provides that regulations may not make provision requiring the   **8–049**
processing of confidential patient information for any purpose if it would be reasonably practicable to achieve that purpose otherwise than pursuant to such regulations, having regard to the cost of and the technology available for achieving that purpose, in other words if it would be reasonably practicable to obtain the patient's consent or anonymise the information. Nor may regulations

---

that the data be produced, with patient anonymity preserved by referring to patients by number: *Kinnear v Wellcome Foundation Ltd; Loveday v Renton*, both unreported on this point. On the relationship between research, access to records and confidentiality see Thomson (1993) 1 J. Law and Med. 95.

[137] *Confidentiality: Protecting and Providing Information*, June 2000, para.31.
[138] That the consent must be informed flows logically from the Supreme Court's ruling in *Montgomery v Lanarkshire Health Board* [2015] UKSC 11; [2015] A.C. 1430; see para.7–015 et seq.
[139] Formerly s.60 of the Health and Social Care Act 2001. See also the Health and Social Care (Control of Data Processing) Act (Northern Ireland) 2016.
[140] See the Health Service (Control of Patient Information) Regulations 2002 (SI 2002/1438).

provide for requiring the processing of confidential patient information solely or principally for the purpose of determining the care and treatment to be given to particular individuals[141]; or permit the processing of prescribed patient information in a manner inconsistent with the Data Protection Act 1998.[142] The Health Service (Control of Patient Information) Regulations 2002 cover essentially: (1) the information held by and activities of cancer registries (medical purposes related to the diagnosis or treatment of neoplasia); (2) the diagnosis and control of communicable diseases and other risks to public health (including monitoring and managing the delivery, efficacy and safety of immunisation programmes, adverse reactions to vaccines and medicines, and risks of infection acquired from food or the environment); (3) medical research; and (4) the audit, monitoring and analysing of the provision made by the health service for patient care and treatment.[143] The processing of confidential patient information in accordance with the regulations is not unlawful, despite any obligation of confidence owed by that person in respect of it.[144]

8–050   The GMC guidance states that doctors:

"…should only disclose personal information for research if there is a legal basis for the disclosure and the research has been approved by a research ethics committee",[145]

which imposes the additional requirement to obtain ethical approval. However, the only "legal basis" for disclosure of non-anonymised information is patient consent or an application under the Health Service (Control of Patient Information) Regulations 2002.[146] Approval by a research ethics committee does not, in itself, create a defence in law. It would seem highly unlikely that a court

---

[141]   National Health Service Act 2006 s.251(6).

[142]   National Health Service Act 2006 s.251(7).

[143]   The Regulations probably do not apply to confidential patient information generated outside the NHS: *Lewis v Secretary of State for Health* [2008] EWHC 2196 (QB); [2008] LS Law Medical 559 at [46]–[49]. In this case the issue was whether the disclosure of the results of post-mortem examinations of former workers at nuclear installations to a confidential inquiry could be authorised. Foskett J doubted that the removal of tissues from a deceased person for the purposes of analysis formed part of "care and treatment", and also doubted that the inquiry would be engaged in the "audit, monitoring and analysing of the provision made by the health service" for patient care and treatment (see the Health Service (Control of Patient Information) Regulations 2002 (SI 2002/1438) Sch.1 para.5). It followed that the Regulations did not provide authority for the disclosure to the inquiry of the results of the post-mortem examinations, though Foskett J acknowledged that the converse view was at least reasonably arguable.

[144]   National Health Service Act 2006 s.251(2)(*c*); and Health Service (Control of Patient Information) Regulations 2002 (SI 2002/1438) reg.4. For the definition of "patient information" and "confidential patient information" see National Health Service Act 2006 s.251(10) and (11). Before making regulations under s.251 the Secretary of State must consult the Care Quality Commission: s.252. See further P. Case, "Confidence Matters: the Rise and Fall of Informational Autonomy in Medical Law" (2003) 11 Med. L. Rev. 208 for a detailed discussion of confidentiality in the context of medical research, and the implications of what is now s.251 of the National Health Service Act 2006 (previously s.60 of the Health and Social Care Act 2001) and the Health Service (Control of Patient Information) Regulations 2002.

[145]   *Confidentiality: good practice in handling patient information*, January 2017, para.113.

[146]   An application for access to patient information without consent must be made to the Confidentiality Advisory Group of the NHS Health Research Authority (*http://www.hra.nhs.uk/ resources/confidentiality-advisory-group*).

would accept that the wider public interest defence[147] should apply where there has been a disclosure of identifiable patient information falling outside these requirements. If Parliament has provided a mechanism for lawfully conducting research involving the disclosure of identifiable patient information then it should not be for the courts to create a further exception to the duty of confidentiality.[148]

(l)   Disclosure to a court or in connection with litigation[149]

A doctor must comply with an order of a court to disclose confidential medical information. Examples include the direction of a judge that a doctor must give evidence in court either orally or by producing documents,[150] and an order under ss.33 or 34 of the Senior Courts Act 1981,[151] though in most cases the applicant seeking disclosure under these provisions will be the patient who will effectively have consented to the disclosure.[152] The GMC cautions that, unless the patient

8–051

---

[147] See para.8–059 below.

[148] See also GMC, *Confidentiality: good practice in handling patient information*, January 2017, para.107. As the guidance points out the Confidentiality Advisory Group of the Health Research Authority will not usually authorise disclosures under reg.5 of the 2002 Regulations to which the patient has objected: para.105, n.40.

[149] *Confidentiality: good practice in handling patient information*, January 2017, paras 90–93. Doctors do not enjoy a privilege equivalent to legal professional privilege: *Att-Gen v Mulholland and Foster* [1963] 2 Q.B. 477 at 484. See also Matthews (1984) 1 L.S. 77.

[150] In *Wakefield v Channel Four Television Corporation* [2006] EWHC 3289 (QB); (2007) 94 B.M.L.R. 1 the GMC objected to an order for the inspection of medical records provided to the GMC as part of a disciplinary investigation of a doctor, who subsequently brought libel proceedings against Channel Four Television. The GMC had provided the records to the doctor as part of the disciplinary process, and Channel Four sought inspection of the records as being relevant to its defence of the libel action. The GMC argued that the public interest that litigants be given access to potentially relevant materials was outweighed by the damage to the public interest that would flow from an order for disclosure or inspection, the GMC having given assurances to patients that the records would only be used for the purposes of investigating and/or prosecuting the doctor. Patients would be reluctant to make complaints against doctors, or to support them, if they had legitimate cause for concern that their confidential medical records might be disclosed in litigation which had no bearing upon their own welfare. Eady J rejected the GMC's argument. Inspection should not be ordered unless it was necessary and proportionate to the litigation, and patient confidentiality was a relevant factor to take into account, but the public interest in the administration of justice, and the limited, proportionate nature of disclosure and inspection (there was no need for any patient to be identified) were such that standard disclosure and inspection were appropriate.

[151] See paras 13–053 to 13–058, 13–072. See, e.g. *Australian Red Cross Society v BC* [1992] 3 Med. L.R. 273 SC of Vict, App Div; *PD v Australian Red Cross Society (New South Wales Division)* (1993) 30 N.S.W.L.R. 376, NSWCA; *Sharpe Estate v Northwestern General Hospital* (1991) 76 D.L.R. (4th) 535, Ont Ct Gen Div, aff'g (1990) 74 D.L.R. (4th) 43, in which courts have ordered the defendants to disclose the identity of blood donors to the claimant, because the public interest in the administration of justice outweighed the public interest in preserving the privacy and confidentiality of blood donors; cf. *AB v Glasgow and West of Scotland Blood Transfusion Service* (1989), 1993 S.L.T. 36; 15 B.M.L.R. 91. See further paras 13–094 to 13–096.

[152] Contrast *R. (on the application of B) v Stafford Combined Court* [2006] EWHC 1645 (Admin); [2007] 1 W.L.R. 1524 where the Crown Court, on the defence application for disclosure of the medical records of B, a 14-year-old girl who was to be the principal witness in a trial of W who was charged with sexual offences against B, ordered an NHS Trust to disclose B's medical records. B had not been given notice of the application and had not had an opportunity to make representations. The

has consented to disclosure[153] or a formal court order has been made for disclosure, information should not be disclosed merely in response to demands from other persons such as a solicitor, police officer or an official of the court.[154]

8–052 A judge has a discretion to allow a doctor to decline to answer a question when giving evidence in court. In *Hunter v Mann*[155] Widgery CJ said that:

> "... if a doctor, giving evidence in court, is asked a question which he finds embarrassing because it involves him talking about things which he would normally regard as confidential, he can seek the protection of the judge and ask the judge if it is necessary for him to answer."

The judge's exercise of this discretion clearly depends on the relevance and significance of the potential answer to the issues being tried.

8–053 **Adoption proceedings: interests of the child** In *Re C (A Minor) (Evidence: Confidential Information)*[156] a mother, who had looked after her child for only four days after its birth, refused consent to the child being adopted. The mother's general practitioner voluntarily provided to the applicants information about the mother's medical condition which the applicants sought to introduce as evidence in the adoption proceedings. The mother sought to exclude the evidence on the basis that it had been provided by her general practitioner in breach of confidence. The Court of Appeal had some doubts as to whether a breach of confidence had actually occurred, but nonetheless held that, if it had, the breach was justified. The public interest in the court dealing with the adoption proceedings in the child's best interests in full possession of the relevant information outweighed the public interest in preserving confidentiality between doctor and patient. Moreover, the doctor had not disclosed the information to the world at large, but only for the restricted purpose of the adoption proceedings.

8–054 **Personal injury claims** Claimants who bring actions in which the state of their health is in issue do not thereby automatically waive confidentiality in their medical records. They are entitled to maintain confidentiality, even where the medical records have been compiled by servants or agents of the defendants themselves.[157] The defendant in the litigation must either obtain the claimant's

---

Divisional Court held that, on these particular facts, the court had breached B's rights under art.8 of the ECHR. See also *Wakefield v Channel Four Television Corporation* [2006] EWHC 3289 (QB); (2007) 94 B.M.L.R. 1 above, n.150.

[153] As where a patient grants written authority to a solicitor acting on his behalf to obtain a copy of his medical records; a hospital cannot deny the solicitor access to the records on grounds of "data protection": *Re NR's Application for Judicial Review* [2015] NIQB 35. This proposition is so startlingly obvious that the need for litigation to establish the point seems extraordinary.

[154] *Confidentiality: good practice in handling patient information*, January 2017, para.93.

[155] [1974] 1 Q.B. 767 at 775. See also *Confidentiality: good practice in handling patient information*, January 2017, para.91.

[156] [1991] 2 F.L.R. 478.

[157] In *Shaw v Skeet* [1996] 7 Med. L.R. 371, QBD, it was suggested that in bringing a personal injury action claimants waive their rights to confidentiality, a view also taken in *Hay v University of Alberta Hospital* (1990) 69 D.L.R. (4th) 755; [1991] 2 Med. L.R. 204, Alta QB. However in both *St Louis v Feleki* (1990) 75 D.L.R. (4th) 758, Ont HC and *Burgess v Wu* (2003) 235 D.L.R. (4th) 341, Ont SCJ, this approach was rejected.

waiver of confidentiality or an order of the court for their disclosure.[158] In *Nicholson v Halton General Hospital NHS Trust*[159] the Court of Appeal held that where a claimant brings an action for personal injuries the court will not compel the claimant to waive the right of confidentiality of medical records, although in an appropriate case it can order that the action be stayed until he consents to waive the right. It is submitted that the correct approach in this situation is that claimants retain the right to insist on the confidentiality of the medical records and do not automatically waive their entitlement to confidentiality, subject to the requirement that the defendant is entitled to such access to the records as is required to deal with the litigation fairly.[160] A defendant is entitled to such access to the medical records as the court orders in the course of the litigation through the process of discovery and, if necessary, on subpoena, in order fairly to dispose of the issues in dispute between the parties.[161]

(m) Disciplinary proceedings

A doctor must comply with an official request to disclose personal information from a statutory regulatory body for any of the healthcare professions, where it is necessary in the interests of justice and for the safety of other patients.[162] If a doctor is considering referring concerns about another doctor to the GMC for investigation, the patient's consent must be obtained before disclosing identifiable information, where practicable. Even if the patient objects to the disclosure there may be exceptional cases where it is justified. This would probably be on the basis that the public interest defence applies.[163]

8–055

There is clearly a public interest in the proper regulation of the healthcare professions which will normally justify the disclosure of otherwise confidential information to a professional regulatory agency. In *Woolgar v Chief Constable of Sussex Police*[164] the Court of Appeal held that the disclosure of information about a nurse by the police to the United Kingdom Central Council for Nursing,

8–056

---

[158] *Dunn v British Coal Corporation* [1993] P.I.Q.R. P275, CA.

[159] [1999] P.I.Q.R. P310.

[160] *Burgess v Wu* (2003) 235 D.L.R. (4th) 341 at [76], applying *M(A) v Ryan* (1997) 143 D.L.R. (4th) 1, SCC.

[161] See *Richards v Kadian* [2005] NSWCA 328; (2005) 64 N.S.W.L.R. 204—commencing proceedings for medical negligence did not amount to a waiver of the confidentiality of the doctor–patient relationship between the claimant and his treating physician. The defendant had other means of obtaining information about the patient's medical condition (including obtaining the medical records on subpoena; and discovery of documents), and therefore the court would not permit the defendant to interview the claimant's treating medical specialists.

[162] Medical Act 1983 s.35A (as amended) gives the GMC power to require doctors to supply any document or information which appears relevant to the discharge of the GMC's functions in respect of a practitioner's fitness to practise, provided that the disclosure is not prohibited by other legislation (the most relevant of which will be the Data Protection Act 1998). On s.35A see *R. (on the application of Nakash) v Metropolitan Police Service* [2014] EWHC 3810 (Admin); [2015] A.C.D. 36 (evidence excluded from doctor's criminal trial for sexual assault of patient on the basis that it was inadmissible was relevant to GMC's investigation; police justified in disclosing the evidence, even though it had been obtained unlawfully, to enable the GMC to protect public health and safety).

[163] See paras 8–059 et seq.

[164] [2000] 1 W.L.R. 25.

Midwifery and Health Visiting (the UKCC[165]) was justified both under the law of confidentiality and art.8 of the European Convention on Human Rights:

"... where a regulatory body such as the UKCC, operating in the field of public health and safety, seeks access to confidential material in the possession of the police, being material which the police are reasonably persuaded is of some relevance to the subject matter of an inquiry being conducted by the regulatory body, then a countervailing public interest is shown to exist which, as in this case, entitles the police to release the material to the regulatory body on the basis that save in so far as it may be used by the regulatory body for the purposes of its own inquiry, the confidentiality which already attaches to the material will be maintained."[166]

Although art.8(1) of the Convention provides that everyone has the right to respect for their family lives, art.8(2) allows for exceptions in the interests of national security, public safety or the economic wellbeing of the country, for the prevention of disorder or crime, for the protection of health or morals, or for the protection of the rights and freedoms of others, provided it can be said that the interference was also necessary in a democratic society. The police were justified in reporting information to the UKCC:

"...in the interests of ... public safety ... or for the protection of health or morals, or for the protection of the rights and freedoms of others."

Indeed, the police were free to pass on confidential information even if there was no request from the regulatory body, which in their reasonable view, in the interests of public health or safety, should be considered by a professional or regulatory body.[167]

8–057   In *Re General Dental Council's Application*[168] Sales J held that the General Dental Council (GDC) could lawfully pass patient records onto its investigating committee and, if necessary, to its practise committee, as part of a disciplinary investigation against a dentist. The disclosure would satisfy art.8(2) because it pursued legitimate objectives, being "in the interests of ... public safety", "for the protection of health and morals" and "for the protection of the rights and freedoms of others"; it was "in accordance with the law", because it was pursuant to the clear statutory regime in the Dentists Act 1984; and it was "necessary in a democratic society", given that it was proportionate to the important public

---

[165] Now the Nursing and Midwifery Council: Nursing and Midwifery Order 2001 (SI 2002/253) (as variously amended—see in particular the Nursing and Midwifery (Amendment) Order 2008 (SI 2008/1485)).

[166] [2000] 1 W.L.R. 25 at 36.

[167] [2000] 1 W.L.R. 25 at 36. On the other hand, where the issue is whether an expert report obtained by the GMC for the purpose of investigating a patient's complaint about a doctor's professional competence should be disclosed to the patient the court should weigh the private interests of the patient against the private interests of the doctor: *DB v General Medical Council* [2016] EWHC 2331 (QB); (2016) 152 B.M.L.R. 106. Soole J held that the balance came down in favour of not disclosing the report. The GMC should have started with a presumption against disclosure and should have given weight to the doctor's express refusal of consent and his privacy right as a data subject (under the Data Protection Act 1998). The fact that the sole or dominant purpose of the patient's request for disclosure was to use the report in litigation weighed heavily against disclosure, given that CPR Pt 31 provided the patient with a more appropriate procedure which was a less restrictive interference with the doctor's privacy right.

[168] [2011] EWHC 3011 (Admin); [2012] Med. L.R. 204.

interest which was being promoted by the professional proceedings and was subject to appropriate safeguards. There was no obligation on the GDC to seek a court order before proceeding without the patients' consent to the disclosure. The case was analogous, said Sales J, to the decision of the European Court of Human Rights in *MS v Sweden*[169] in which the applicant sustained a back injury and objected to the disclosure of medical records to the Social Insurance Office for the purpose of assessing her compensation claim. It was held that there were relevant and sufficient reasons for the communication of the medical records and this was not disproportionate to the legitimate aim pursued. This justified what would otherwise have been a breach of the applicant's rights under art.8(1) of the European Convention on Human Rights.

Similarly, in *A Health Authority v X*[170] the Court of Appeal held that disclosure by a local authority, following a public law case in the Family Division, of general practitioner records to a health authority for the purpose of the authority carrying out its regulatory function, was justified provided that there were effective safeguards of the patients' confidentiality and anonymity. There was, said the Court, a high public interest, analogous to the public interest in the administration of justice, in the proper administration of professional disciplinary hearings, particularly in the field of medicine. The question was whether the public interest in effective disciplinary procedures for the investigation and eradication of medical malpractice outweighed the confidentiality of the records, but as Thorpe LJ observed: "The balance came down in favour of production *as it invariably does*, save in exceptional cases."[171] In *Re General Dental Council's Application*[172] Sales J placed great emphasis on this point, observing that:

8–058

"...other than in cases of extremely trivial allegations, any allegation of impairment of fitness to practise on the part of a dentist will be a serious matter, because of the strength of the public interest in maintaining high standards on the part of medical practitioners, including dentists, so as to maintain public confidence in health services."

Even where patients have expressly refused their consent to the disclosure of medical records to a professional body exercising disciplinary functions, the public interest in the investigation of allegations against dentists and other medical practitioners of impairment of fitness to practise is so strong as to override the private interests of patients in preserving confidentiality.[173]

---

[169] (1997) 28 E.H.R.R. 313; (1997) 3 B.H.R.C. 248.
[170] [2001] EWCA Civ 2014; [2002] 2 All E.R. 780. *A Health Authority v X (No.2)* [2002] EWHC 26; [2002] 1 F.L.R. 383; [2002] Lloyd's Rep. Med. 145 concerned an unopposed application to vary an order granting permission to disclose documents from care proceedings to certain official and professional bodies, including the GMC.
[171] [2001] EWCA Civ 2014; [2002] 2 All E.R. 780 at [20] (emphasis added). See also *Re A (A Minor) (Disclosure of Medical Records to the General Medical Council)* (1998) 47 B.M.L.R. 84; [1999] 1 F.C.R. 30—the court has the power to attach conditions protecting the confidentiality of patients to an order directing the release of case papers in Children Act proceedings to a third party.
[172] [2011] EWHC 3011 (Admin); [2012] Med. L.R. 204 at [57].
[173] [2011] EWHC 3011 (Admin); [2012] Med. L.R. 204 at [48]. It is good practice (though not a legal obligation) to inform the patients in advance about what the disciplinary body proposes to do with the records, so that patients have an opportunity to consider whether to make objections and if need be apply to court to raise those objections: [2011] EWHC 3011 (Admin); [2012] Med. L.R. 204 at [48]. Sales J considered that the same principle applied to the patients' rights under the European

(n) Disclosure in the public interest: protecting third parties

8–059 Although the law of confidentiality appears to focus on an individual's privacy rights and protection from private information being tossed around the public domain, the legal and ethical principles underpinning confidentiality rely heavily on notions of the public interest. In the medical context there is said to be a strong public interest in preserving confidentiality because without it many patients would be reluctant to seek medical treatment, or would do so without being entirely frank with their doctors, and this would have negative consequences for public health. Not only would individual patients suffer unnecessarily from treatable conditions, but the practice of medicine would become more expensive,[174] and for some medical conditions there would be a greater likelihood of the spread of the disease or illness. On the other hand, in some circumstances a strict adherence to confidentiality may put others at risk of harm or prevent otherwise wholly beneficial practices (such as medical research or clinical audit) from taking place. In these cases, in the absence of consent by the patient or a specific legal provision either requiring or authorising the disclosure of the information, the public interest may justify disclosure without the patient's consent or, in some instances, even in the face of an express refusal of consent by the patient. Most of the exceptions to the duty of confidentiality identified by the GMC in *Confidentiality: good practice in handling patient information* rest, in effect, on an assessment of the public interest.[175] Any disclosure which is said to be justified in the public interest must involve a weighing of the competing public interests: the importance of maintaining confidences has to be balanced against the potential benefit (or harm avoided) from breaching the duty of confidentiality.

8–060 The GMC guidance states that where disclosure of confidential information is intended to protect others the doctor should ask for the patient's consent unless it is not safe or practicable to do so, or the information is required by law. If it is not practicable then disclosure may be justified in the public interest without the patient's consent, and in exceptional cases where a patient has withheld consent:

> "...if failure to do so may expose others to a risk of death or serious harm. The benefits to an individual or to society of the disclosure must outweigh both the patient's and the public interest in keeping the information confidential."[176]

Convention on Human Rights, and that the GDC "would only have to take reasonable steps to identify and notify the patients concerned. It would not be obliged to do so if that was impracticable … or undesirable for some reason of the public interest": [2011] EWHC 3011 (Admin); [2012] Med. L.R. 204 at [65] (applying *General Dental Council v Rimmer* [2010] EWHC 1049 (Admin)).

[174] Doctors would have less information with which to make a diagnosis and so have to undertake a more expensive range of diagnostic testing, and patients would probably receive treatment at a later stage of their illness (being reluctant to seek treatment until their medical condition gave them little choice but to seek help) which could also be more expensive.

[175] Para.9 of the document identifies only four situations where doctors may disclose personal information without breaching duties of confidentiality, namely: consent (express or implied) by the patient; where the patient lacks the capacity to consent and disclosure is in the patient's interests; disclosure is required or authorised by the law; and, disclosure can be justified in the public interest. The other categories are merely instances of these four cases.

[176] *Confidentiality: good practice in handling patient information*, January 2017, para.64.

Examples include: disclosures necessary for the prevention, detection or prosecution of serious crime, especially crimes against the person; where a patient is not fit to drive; or has been diagnosed with a serious communicable disease; or poses a serious risk to others through being unfit for work.[177]

The balancing exercise   In some instances making the judgment whether to disclose confidential information will be relatively easy. For example, a person who has developed epilepsy and is suffering from significant seizures is clearly not fit to drive a motor vehicle, and to continue to do so would put both the patient and others at risk of serious injury or death. If the patient persisted in driving and refused to notify the DVLA of his medical condition, it would not take a great deal of reflection by a doctor to conclude that it was in the public interest to disclose the patient's condition to the DVLA. Other situations may be less clear cut. In considering whether the public interest would justify disclosure the GMC suggests that doctors should take into account:

8–061

> "a.   the potential harm or distress to the patient arising from the disclosure – for example, in terms of their future engagement with treatment and their overall health
> b.   the potential harm to trust in doctors generally – for example, if it is widely perceived that doctors will readily disclose information about patients without consent
> c.   the potential harm to others (whether to a specific person or people, or to the public more broadly) if the information is not disclosed
> d.   the potential benefits to an individual or to society arising from the release of the information
> e.   the nature of the information to be disclosed, and any views expressed by the patient
> f.   whether the harms can be avoided or benefits gained without breaching the patient's privacy or, if not, what is the minimum intrusion."[178]

If a failure to disclose the information would "leave individuals or society exposed to a risk so serious that it outweighs patients' and the public interest in maintaining confidentiality" the doctor "should disclose relevant information promptly to an appropriate person or authority".[179] Patients should be informed before disclosing the information "if it is practicable and safe to do so" even if the intention is to disclose without their consent.

Public interest: the law   The law has long recognised that disclosures of confidential information may be justified in the public interest. It has been said

8–062

---

[177] *Confidentiality: good practice in handling patient information*, January 2017, paras 65–66. See also paras 8–038 and 8–040. The guidance notes state that there is no agreed definition of what constitutes "serious crime" (para.63, n.23). The GMC provides additional guidance on the last three cases: *Confidentiality: Patients' fitness to drive and reporting concerns to the DVLA or DVA*, 2017; *Confidentiality: disclosing information about serious communicable disease*, 2017; and *Confidentiality: disclosing information for employment, insurance and similar purposes*, 2017. See also *Confidentiality: reporting gunshot and knife wounds*, 2017. All of these documents are available at *http://www.gmc-uk.org/guidance/news_consultation/30319.asp*. See also Department of Health, *Confidentiality: NHS Code of Practice, Supplementary Guidance: Public Interest Disclosures*, November 2010.
[178] *Confidentiality: good practice in handling patient information*, January 2017, para.67. See also paras 106–111 on "public interest disclosures for health and social care purposes".
[179] *Confidentiality: good practice in handling patient information*, January 2017, at para.68.

that "there is no confidence as to the disclosure of iniquity",[180] though the iniquity rule is itself only part of the wider principle of public interest which may justify disclosure. This inevitably involves the weighing of competing interests, as Lord Goff observed in *Att.-Gen. v Guardian Newspapers (No.2)*:

> "...although the basis of the law's protection of confidence is that there is a public interest that confidences should be preserved and protected by the law, nevertheless that public interest may be outweighed by some other countervailing public interest which favours disclosure ... It is this limiting principle which may require a court to carry out a balancing operation, weighing the public interest in maintaining confidence against a countervailing public interest favouring disclosure."[181]

In *Lewis v Secretary of State for Health*[182] Foskett J held that the public interest justified the disclosure to a confidential inquiry of the results of post-mortem examinations of former workers at nuclear installations. The inquiry, which was sponsored by two Secretaries of State, was into the circumstances in which organs and tissue had been removed for analysis to determine the presence, if any, of radionuclide content of the organs. There was a public interest in determining what had happened and why, and this outweighed the public interest in maintaining the confidentiality of medical records and information, provided that proper safeguards were in place to ensure that inappropriate information did not become public. The fact that the inquiry was sponsored by two Secretaries of State answerable to Parliament was itself compelling evidence of the public interest in enabling the inquiry to have the fullest facilities to carry out its functions.[183]

(i)   *Potentially dangerous patients*

8–063   **Detained psychiatric patients**   The scope of the public interest defence in the specific context of the doctor–patient relationship was considered in *W v Egdell*,[184] where the question was whether a psychiatrist who had prepared a medical report on a patient was entitled to disclose the contents of the report both to the hospital where the patient was detained and to the Home Secretary. W was detained as a patient in a secure hospital without limit of time following a conviction for manslaughter of five neighbours on the grounds of diminished responsibility. He was diagnosed as suffering from paranoid schizophrenia. Ten years after his detention he applied to a Mental Health Review Tribunal for a transfer to a regional secure unit with a view, ultimately, to obtaining a conditional discharge. W's solicitors instructed Dr Egdell, a consultant psychiatrist, to produce an independent psychiatric report for the purpose of the Tribunal hearing. Dr Egdell referred to the possibility that W was suffering from a paranoid psychosis rather than paranoid schizophrenia, which meant that

---

[180] *Fraser v Evans* [1969] 1 Q.B. 349 at 362, per Lord Denning MR citing Page Wood V-C in *Gartside v Outram* (1856) 26 L.J. Ch. 113 at 114.
[181] [1990] 1 A.C. 109 at 282.
[182] [2008] EWHC 2196 (QB); [2008] LS Law Medical 559 at [58].
[183] [2008] EWHC 2196 (QB); [2008] LS Law Medical 559 at [59].
[184] [1990] Ch. 359.

medication would be less effective in protecting against a relapse. Moreover, there was a possibility that W might have a psychopathic deviant personality.

In view of the report W's solicitors withdrew the application to the Tribunal. Dr   **8–064**
Egdell then sent the report to the hospital, also urging the hospital to forward a copy to the Home Secretary. Subsequently the Home Secretary referred W's case to the Mental Health Review Tribunal under s.71(2) of the Mental Health Act 1983, and sent a copy of the report to the Tribunal. W sought an injunction restraining the defendants from using or disclosing the contents of the report, and damages (including aggravated damages) against the hospital board and the Home Secretary. Scott J held that Dr Egdell's duty to W was not his only duty, since W was not an ordinary member of the public. He was a detained patient in a secure hospital subject to a regime whereby decisions concerning his future were to be taken by public authorities. In taking those decisions W's interests would not be the only or even the main criterion. The safety of the public would be the main criterion. In those circumstances Dr Egdell had a duty to the public to place the result of his examination before the proper authorities, if, in his opinion, the public interest so required. The public interest in disclosure outweighed W's private interest.[185]

The Court of Appeal agreed that Scott J had struck the correct balance between   **8–065**
the public interest in patients being able to make full and frank disclosure to their doctors in reliance on the doctors' obligation of confidence, and the public interest in the safety of members of the public who might be at risk if W were released:

"Where a man has committed multiple killings under the disability of serious mental illness, decisions which may lead directly or indirectly to his release from hospital should not be made unless the responsible authority is properly able to make an informed judgment that the risk of repetition is so small as to be acceptable. A consultant psychiatrist who becomes aware, even in the course of a confidential relationship, of information which leads him, in the exercise of what the court considers a sound professional judgment, to fear that such decisions may be made on inadequate information and with a real risk of consequent danger to the public is entitled to take such steps as are reasonable in all the circumstances to communicate the grounds of his concern to the responsible authorities."[186]

---

[185] The actions against the other defendants also failed, though Scott J considered that even if the case against Dr Egdell had succeeded the other defendants would have had a valid public interest defence in view of the nature of the statutory scheme created by the Mental Health Act 1983. The claims against the other defendants were not pursued on appeal. An argument that Dr Egdell's report was the subject of legal professional privilege was rejected by Scott J, and dismissed almost peremptorily by the Court of Appeal.

[186] [1990] Ch. 359 at 424. See also *R. v Crozier* (1990) 8 B.M.L.R. 128, CA, where a psychiatrist instructed by the appellant acted reasonably and responsibly in showing his report on the appellant to prosecuting counsel, since he believed that the appellant suffered from a psychopathic disorder which made him a danger to the public. The public interest in disclosure outweighed the duty of confidence owed to the appellant. In *Smith v Jones* (1999) 169 D.L.R. (4th) 385 a psychiatrist instructed by the defence to provide a forensic assessment on an individual accused of aggravated sexual assault on a prostitute formed the view that the accused was dangerous and likely to commit further offences involving the kidnap and murder of prostitutes. When he discovered that his concerns would not be brought to the attention of the sentencing judge, he issued an application for a declaration that he was entitled to disclose his opinion, and the statements made to him by the accused, in the interests of public safety. The Supreme Court of Canada held that the safety of the public may justify the disclosure of information even though the solicitor-client privilege, which attaches to communications

8-066   **Voluntary psychiatric patients**   Where a psychiatric patient has not been detained following conviction for an offence of violence, but the doctor nonetheless considers that the patient is a potential danger to others, it is probable that a court would conclude that disclosure could be justified in the public interest.[187] However, this must be a question of degree. It is recognised that, in the context of the therapeutic relationship, some patients may express a desire to harm others which they have no intention of ever acting upon. But in other instances it will be difficult to predict whether a patient is likely to act upon threats made known to a doctor. The GMC guidance on when disclosure is appropriate (which is not limited to psychiatric patients) refers to the prevention, detection or prosecution of serious crime, especially crimes against the person, but acknowledges that there is no agreed definition of what constitutes serious crime.[188] The seriousness of the potential crime is, in any event, only one factor. Just as important is a judgment as to the likelihood that a patient will proceed to carry out threats of harm to others. Inevitably this involves a balancing exercise.[189] Provided that the doctor has undertaken the balancing exercise in good faith, possibly also involving colleagues in the assessment process, it is difficult to see a court retrospectively second-guessing a decision to breach the patient's confidentiality.[190]

8-067   **Infectious patients**   Precisely same issues as with potentially dangerous psychiatric patients arise with patients who have infectious medical conditions. Patients are entitled to expect that information about their medical condition will remain confidential, but if there are others at risk of infection from contact with them and they refuse to inform the third parties and take appropriate precautions to prevent the infection spreading it is likely to be in the public interest for the doctor to inform those at risk. The GMC advises that in these circumstances a doctor may disclose information:

---

between clients and experts retained by their lawyer for the purpose of preparing a defence, would normally apply (i.e. legal professional privilege, see para.13–076). Disclosure would be justified where there was a clear, imminent risk of serious bodily harm or death to an identifiable person or group.

[187] As the Supreme Court of California expressed this in *Tarasoff v Regents of the University of California*, 551 P. 2d 334; Sup., 131 Cal. Rptr. 14 (1976) the "protective privilege ends where the public peril begins". See para.2–166. The issue in *Tarasoff* was whether a psychotherapist owed a duty of care in negligence to a former girlfriend of a patient. Clearly, if the court concludes that the doctor does owe a duty of care to a third party there can be no duty of confidence owed to the patient since otherwise the doctor would be placed in the impossible position of owing conflicting duties to different parties.

[188] *Confidentiality: good practice in handling patient information*, January 2017, para.63, n.23, referring to *Confidentiality: NHS Code of Practice Supplementary Guidance: Public Interest Disclosures* (Department of Health, 2003) which provides examples including: crimes causing serious physical or psychological harm to individuals (such as murder, manslaughter, rape and child abuse); crimes that cause serious harm to the security of the state and public order; and crimes that involve substantial financial gain or loss. Examples of crimes suggested to not be serious enough to warrant disclosure without consent are listed as: theft, fraud, and damage to property where loss or damage is less substantial.

[189] See para.8–061 above.

[190] As Neils Bohr is reputed to have pointed out, in a very different context: "Prediction is very difficult, especially if it's about the future."

"to a person who has close contact with a patient who has a serious communicable disease if you have reason to think that: (a) the person is at risk of infection that is likely to result in serious harm; (b) the patient has not informed them and cannot be persuaded to do so."[191]

(ii) Potentially dangerous health professionals

In *Saha v General Medical Council*[192] the appellant doctor was diagnosed with hepatitis B but did not inform his employers and continued to perform procedures on patients which involved a risk of transmitting the condition. This was contrary both to NHS guidance and GMC guidance,[193] which also provided that where another doctor became aware of such a situation that doctor should inform an appropriate person in the healthcare worker's employing authority. It was discovered that the appellant was hepatitis B positive. He was instructed not to perform any more exposure prone procedures and the case was referred to the GMC. The appellant argued that the disclosure of information about his medical condition to the GMC constituted a breach of the duty of confidentiality and of his rights under art.8 of the ECHR. The judge, Stephen Morris QC, held that there was no relevant breach of confidentiality, which was not an absolute right, but necessarily involved a balancing of competing public interests. The public interest in patient safety and welfare was an extremely important consideration. Nor was there a breach of the appellant's art.8 rights since interference with the right to confidentiality could be justified by reference to other interests, including public safety, protection of health or protection of rights and freedoms of others.[194] Moreover, the NHS and GMC guidance made it clear that where there was reason to believe that a hepatitis B-infected health worker had not followed advice, and so had put patients at risk, other healthcare workers would have a duty to inform an appropriate person, and doctors had a corresponding duty to refer a recalcitrant doctor to the GMC.[195]

8–068

(iii) Disclosing genetic information

GMC guidance Where a patient has a genetic condition it may be indicative of a similar condition in a blood relative. Usually patients will agree to disclosure of this type of information to relatives, which, depending on the nature of the genetic condition, may enable the relative to seek treatment or at least be aware of the prospect of developing symptoms in the future. The GMC guidance is less

8–069

---

[191] GMC, *Confidentiality: disclosing information about serious communicable diseases*, 2017, para.13. At para.2, n.2, a serious communicable disease is said to be "any disease that can be transmitted from human to human and that can result in death or serious illness. It particularly applies to, but is not limited to, HIV, tuberculosis, and hepatitis B and C".

[192] [2009] EWHC 1907 (Admin); [2009] LS Law Medical 551.

[193] See now GMC, *Confidentiality: disclosing information about serious communicable diseases*, 2017, para.6.

[194] [2009] EWHC 1907 (Admin); [2009] LS Law Medical 551 at [67], [68], distinguishing *Z v Finland* (1997) 25 E.H.R.R. 371; (1997) 45 B.M.L.R. 107 where infringement of art.8 was found in relation to the *public* disclosure of medical records. The judge also considered that it was highly relevant to whom the disclosure was made: "disclosure to a person who is aware of the confidentiality and who has a role in its consideration or evaluation (such as a health care worker) is to be distinguished from general disclosure or publication."

[195] [2009] EWHC 1907 (Admin); [2009] LS Law MEdical 551, at [69], [70].

than informative on what should be done if the patient refuses consent to disclosure of the information to relatives, stating that disclosure might be "justified in the public interest if failure to disclose the information leaves others at risk of death or serious harm" and that the doctor will need to:

> "...balance your duty to make the care of your patient your first concern against your duty to help protect the other person from serious harm."[196]

This statement is a little disingenuous. It fails to point out an important distinction between the circumstances in which the public interest defence is usually invoked to justify disclosure to protect others from a risk of death or serious harm and the case of genetic information. Where the patient has a psychiatric condition or an infectious disease and is potentially dangerous to others, it is the patient who would, in theory, cause harm to the third party. In the case of a genetic condition the patient presents no risk of injury to the third party, it is the condition itself which will cause the harm. The knowledge that the patient has the condition *may* be of some benefit to the third party, but in weighing the balance of interests the fact that the patient is not the cause of the harm must strengthen the patient's claim to have medical information remain confidential. Nor is it entirely obvious that the doctor actually has a *duty* "to help protect the other person from serious harm". The GMC guidance does not attempt to identify either the source or the nature of this duty to someone who is not the doctor's patient. A joint report of the Royal College of Physicians, the Royal College of Pathologists and the British Society of Human Genetics, *Consent and Confidentiality in Genetic Practice*[197] does not take the matter further since it cites the GMC guidance for the proposition that there may be a duty to disclose information.

8–070   **Duty of care in negligence**   The issue of the disclosure of genetic information was considered in the context of the tort of negligence in *ABC v St George's Healthcare NHS Foundation Trust*.[198] The claimant's father was diagnosed with Huntington's disease, a genetic condition with a 50 per cent chance that it will be transmitted to a child. Huntington's is progressive and invariably fatal. The father refused consent to informing the claimant, who was pregnant, and the medical staff complied with his wishes. After the baby was born the claimant was inadvertently informed about her father's condition and she was subsequently diagnosed with the disease. She brought a claim against the hospital, arguing that they owed her a duty of care to inform her about her father's condition, and that if she had known she would have been tested and diagnosed with Huntington's disease and she would then have terminated the pregnancy. Her damage was said to be psychiatric harm and the prospect that if her child was diagnosed with the

---

[196] *Confidentiality: good practice in handling patient information*, January 2017, para.75.

[197] *Consent and Confidentiality in Genetic Practice: Guidance on Genetic Testing and Sharing Genetic Information*, 2011 (available at *http://www.bsgm.org.uk/media/678746/consent_and_confidentiality_2011.pdf*).

[198] [2015] EWHC 1394 (QB); [2015] P.I.Q.R. P18; [2015] Med. L.R. 307; discussed by R. Gilbar and C. Foster, *"Doctors' Liability to the Patient's Relatives in Genetic Medicine: ABC v St George's Healthcare NHS Trust"* (2016) 24 Med L. Rev. 112; V. Chico, "Non-disclosure of genetic risks: The case for developing legal wrongs" (2016) 16 Med. Law Int. 3; M. Fay, "Negligence, genetics and families: a duty to disclose actionable risks" (2016) 16 Med. L. Int. 115.

disease she would be put to additional expense. Nicol J held that in these circumstances the claimant was not owed a duty of care and so the action was struck out as disclosing no reasonable cause of action.[199]

The Court of Appeal reversed Nicol J's decision to strike out the claim.[200] Irwin LJ (giving a judgment with which Gloster VP and Underhill LJ agreed) considered each of the nine factors advanced by the defendants as to why imposing a duty of care would be problematic,[201] coming to the conclusion that it could not be said that the claimant's case was "unarguable" and therefore it should not have been dismissed on a strike-out application. Irwin LJ (without reaching a concluded view) appeared to reject the defendants' arguments against imposing a duty to breach the patient's confidentiality, and in particular the risk of imposing conflicting duties on doctors (the duty of confidentiality owed to the patient and the duty of care owed to a third party). This must be because when the duty of care, if any, arises breach of the duty of confidence is justified in the public interest. In effect, a patient would have no right to confidentiality in respect of genetic information.

8–071

The Quebec Court of Appeal came to a similar conclusion to that of Nicol J in *ABC* in *Liss v Watters*,[202] holding that a doctor was not under a duty of care to inform members of a child's extended family about the genetic risk of developing a neurological disorder which the doctor had diagnosed in the child.[203] A duty of care in negligence would have potentially negative social consequences, with doctors being required to seek out and inform all third persons within a radius of contact, beyond the patient, whether or not the doctor had met them or knew their names and irrespective of foreseeability of risk. This could result in doctors being reluctant to undertake medical work in fields where genetic risks were present. Such a duty to warn could transform the doctor–patient relationship. Imposing a duty of care would also involve a breach of confidentiality, which would have had implications for the present, and future consequences of the patient's autonomy and private life. Care had to be taken not to overstate the exceptions to the fundamental duty of confidentiality a physician owes to his patient. There was a narrow category of exception whereby non-consensual disclosure could be

8–072

---

[199] On the basis that it would not be fair, just or reasonable to impose a duty of care owed to the claimant, applying the third limb of the *Caparo* tripartite test for a duty of care. See para.2–034. See also *Smith v University of Leicester NHS Trust* [2016] EWHC 817 (QB) where Judge McKenna held that the defendants' genetic counselling service did not owe a duty of care to two second cousins of a patient to diagnose the patient's genetic condition promptly (though there was no issue of confidentiality in *Smith* because the patient would have brought the diagnosis to the attention of his wider family).

[200] *ABC v St George's Healthcare NHS Foundation Trust* [2017] EWCA Civ 336; [2017] P.I.Q.R. P15; [2017] Med. L.R. 368; para.2–128. The Court of Appeal decision is discussed by R. Geraghty [2017] J.P.I.L. C125.

[201] See para.2–127.

[202] 2012 QCCA 257; (2012) 92 C.C.L.T. (3d) 1.

[203] As in *ABC v St George's Healthcare NHS Foundation Trust*, the loss to the claimant was said to arise from a lost opportunity to terminate a pregnancy (in 2002), although it was argued that the doctor should have informed the extended family members in the 1970s, notwithstanding that "he had never met them and likely did not even know their names" (2012 QCCA 257; (2012) 92 C.C.L.T. (3d) 1 at [67]).

justified by considerations of public health, urgency or imminent danger, but those exceptions did not apply in *Liss*.[204]

(iv) Limits to the public interest

8–073 **Distinguish "interesting to the public"** The public interest defence to a breach of confidence is potentially very wide in its scope, but it is possible to identify certain limitations on the application of the defence. First, it is well settled that there is a distinction between what is interesting to the public and what is in the public interest. It does not follow that simply because information would be of interest to the public that it is in the public interest to disclose it.[205]

8–074 **Limited/appropriate disclosure** Secondly, the public interest defence justifies disclosure to the "proper authorities" not necessarily to the world at large.[206] If, for example, Dr Egdell had sold his report to the newspapers he would undoubtedly have been in breach of his duty of confidence.[207] By the same token, in order to satisfy the requirements of art.8 of the European Convention on Human Rights, any disclosure which the defendant seeks to justify under art.8(2) must be the minimum necessary to meet the defendant's legitimate objective, i.e. it must be proportionate.[208] So a disclosure which goes beyond what is necessary for the proper protection of individuals will not be justified. For example, in *Peters-Brown v Regina District Health Board*[209] the claimant had infectious hepatitis B, but recovered after two months, and thereafter tested negative. For the protection of its staff, the defendant hospital made a list of patients who had infectious blood or bodily fluids. The list was circulated in its laboratories and taped to a computer in a private room in its emergency department. The claimant subsequently found a copy of the list posted in the staff room at her place of work. The Saskatchewan Court of Appeal held that, although the defendant was entitled to notify its staff, who were also subject to a duty of confidentiality, it had been negligent in the manner of posting the information, which should have been loaded on the computer rather than being taped to the computer. It was entirely foreseeable that ambulance crew, police and other unauthorised persons would see the list, even in the private room, causing the claimant mental distress.

---

[204] 2012 QCCA 257; (2012) 92 C.C.L.T. (3d) 1 at [111].
[205] *X v Y* [1988] 2 All E.R. 648. See further *H (A Health Care Worker) v Associated Newspapers Ltd* [2002] EWCA Civ 195; [2002] Lloyd's Rep. Med. 210 where the Court of Appeal acknowledged that a public debate about the procedures to be adopted by a health authority when a healthcare worker was diagnosed as HIV positive would raise some issues of public interest.
[206] *W v Egdell* [1990] Ch. 359, 392; *Att.-Gen. v Guardian Newspapers (No.2)* [1990] 1 A.C. 109 at 282 per Lord Goff; *Re C (A Minor) (Evidence: Confidential Information)* [1991] 2 F.L.R. 478; *Saha v General Medical Council* [2009] EWHC 1907 (Admin); [2009] LS Law Medical 551 at [67].
[207] [1990] Ch. 359 at 389 and 419 per Scott J and Bingham LJ respectively.
[208] *Z v Finland* (1997) 25 E.H.R.R. 371; (1997) 45 B.M.L.R. 107 at [105]; *MS v Sweden* (1997) 28 E.H.R.R. 313; (1997) 3 B.H.R.C. 248 at [44]; *Szuluk v United Kingdom* (36936/05) (2009) 50 E.H.R.R. 10; [2009] LS Law Medical 438.
[209] [1996] 1 W.W.R. 337; aff'd [1997] 1 W.W.R. 638, Sask CA.

Real risk of harm to others   Thirdly, the risk of danger to the public must be a   8–075
"real risk".[210] It is not clear what constitutes a real risk, though on the facts of *W
v Egdell* a possibility of danger rather than a probability appeared to be sufficient.
It is for the court to determine whether the doctor's assessment of the risk is
sound.[211]

"Public" interest   A further issue concerns the meaning of the word "public".   8–076
In *W v Egdell* both Scott J and the Court of Appeal spoke of the danger *to the
public* as the criterion which justified disclosure. Although it might be argued that
danger to a single individual does not constitute danger to the public, the public
interest is broader in conception than simply "danger to the public". It is
submitted that, on principle, even where the danger is merely to a single
individual the public interest in protecting that individual from physical harm
would justify disclosure.[212]

This could be relevant not only in the case of psychiatric patients who constitute   8–077
a danger to others, but also patients with a serious communicable disease who,
despite counselling,[213] refuse either to tell those at risk of contracting the disease
from them about their condition or to change their behaviour so as to minimise
the risk of spreading the infection. Few would doubt that disclosure in these
circumstances would be justified in law, in the public interest, even if only one
individual was at risk.[214]

---

[210] *W v Egdell* [1990] Ch. 359 at 424, per Bingham LJ.

[211] "Where, as here, the relationship between doctor and patient is contractual, the question is
whether the doctor's disclosure is or is not a breach of contract. The answer to that question must turn
not on what the doctor thinks but on what the court rules. But it does not follow that the doctor's
conclusion is irrelevant. In making its ruling the court will give such weight to the considered
judgment of a professional man as seems in all the circumstances to be appropriate": [1990] Ch. 359
at 422, per Bingham LJ.

[212] For example, in *Schering Chemicals Ltd v Falkman Ltd* [1982] Q.B. 1 at 27 Shaw LJ said that: "If
the subject matter is something which is inimical to the public interest or *threatens individual safety*,
a person in possession of knowledge of that subject matter cannot be obliged to conceal it . . ."
(emphasis added). See also Barrowclough CJ in *Furniss v Fitchett* [1958] N.Z.L.R. 396 at 405–406:
"Take the case of a doctor who discovers that his patient entertains delusions in respect of another, and
in his disordered state of mind is liable at any moment to cause death or grievous bodily harm to that
other. Can it be doubted for one moment that the public interest requires him to report that finding to
someone?"

[213] Note that the vast majority of patients, when counselled about their HIV status and the risk of
transmission of HIV to a sexual partner, will either inform their sexual partner themselves or consent
to the information being disclosed. See the medical evidence in *BT v Oei* [1999] NSWSC 1082 and
Harvey v PD [2004] NSWCA 97; (2004) 59 N.S.W.L.R. 639. See paras 2–148 to 2–152 for further
discussion of these cases.

[214] The GMC accepts that disclosure may be made in exceptional circumstances, where the failure to
disclose may expose others to a risk of death or serious harm provided that the benefits to an
individual or to society of the disclosure would outweigh both the patient's and the public interest in
keeping the information confidential. See the GMC guidance, *Confidentiality: good practice in
handling patient information*, January 2017, para.64. For consideration of the position where a
healthcare worker is infected with HIV see Mulholland (1993) 9 P.N. 79; and *Saha v General Medical
Council* [2009] EWHC 1907 (Admin); [2009] LS Law Medical 551; para.8–068 (doctor infected with
hepatitis B).

8–078   **Detained or voluntary psychiatric patient**   A final question concerning the limits of the public interest defence, which arises from *W v Egdell*, is whether different considerations apply to patients who are compulsorily detained under the provisions of the Mental Health Act 1983.[215] Scott J expressly based his decision on the circumstances in which the psychiatric report had been commissioned, including the fact that W was subject to a restriction order under the Act. This, his Lordship concluded, placed W and persons like him:

> "…in a position in which the duty of confidence owed by their psychiatrists is less extensive than the duty that would be owed by psychiatrists to ordinary members of the public."[216]

The limitation on W's rights was justified by the need that the hospital, the Home Secretary and the Tribunal should be fully informed about W when considering his clinical management and possible discharge. However, Bingham LJ said that restricted patients under the Mental Health Act 1983 should not enjoy different rights from any other patient with respect to the duty of confidence, except in so far as a breach of confidence could be justified in the public interest. In W's circumstances decisions about his release from hospital should not be made unless the responsible authority was able to make an informed judgment that the risk was so small as to be acceptable. That consideration weighed the balance of public interest decisively in favour of disclosure.[217]

8–079   The problem for a doctor with a patient who is not subject to a restriction order lies in the difficulty of assessing the risk. With a patient in W's position then, arguably, the evidence of the potential danger is more readily apparent, and those to whom disclosure should be made are more readily identified, namely persons who have some degree of control over W's future conduct. It does not necessarily follow that the duty of confidence owed by psychiatrists varies with different types of patient, except to the extent that each patient is different and accordingly the psychiatrist's professional judgment as to the risk presented to the public varies.

(v)   Discretion or duty?

8–080   In *W v Egdell* Scott J's judgment was ambiguous about whether doctors who form the view that their patient constitutes a potential risk to others merely has a discretion to breach the confidentiality of the doctor–patient relationship (which would give them a defence to a claim for breach of confidence by the patient) or whether they come under a duty to disclose the information. At one point Scott J said that a doctor in Dr Egdell's position:

---

[215] Mental Health Act 1983 ss.37 and 41. These provisions apply where a person has been convicted of a criminal offence, as was the case in *W v Egdell*. The civil process for compulsory admission to hospital of patients suffering from mental disorder is governed by Pt II of the 1983 Act.

[216] [1990] Ch. 359 at 393.

[217] The hospital, the Secretary of State and the tribunal were all engaged in public law functions in the exercise of statutory powers which placed a strong emphasis on public safety and, bearing in mind W's history, his status as a detained patient was, almost inevitably, a significant factor to be weighed in assessing the public interest.

> "…owes a duty not only to his patient but also a duty to the public. His duty to the public would require him, in my opinion, to place before the proper authorities the result of his examination if, in his opinion, the public interest so required."[218]

The Court of Appeal indicated that the defendant was justified in disclosing the report, but the decision does not suggest that he was under a duty to disclose it. This would seem to be the better view.[219]

4. DAMAGES

(a) Damages for breach of confidence

Although there is no doubt that a legal duty of confidence exists between doctor and patient, the remedies available for the enforcement of that duty are somewhat limited in the particular context of the doctor–patient relationship. If patients become aware that a doctor is about to make an unauthorised disclosure of confidential information then they are entitled to an injunction to restrain the disclosure, and in a case such as *W v Egdell*[220] the return of any medical reports disclosed to third parties. But if the breach of confidence has already taken place an injunction may be pointless, and patients may well seek damages for the disclosure itself.

8–081

There was some doubt, however, about the availability of damages as a remedy for a past breach of confidence which is not based on a breach of contract.[221] Claims brought by patients in the NHS would not be founded on contract. Moreover, even where the claim is based in contract it was doubtful that damages would be awarded for the mental distress occasioned by the disclosure of personal information. The general rule is that damages will not be awarded in contract for the mental distress, injury to feelings or annoyance resulting from a breach of contract,[222] unless the contract was itself a contract to provide peace of

8–082

---

[218] [1990] Ch. 359 at 392.

[219] It is unlikely that it would be a criminal offence to withhold such information, in the absence of a specific statutory requirement for disclosure (as, e.g. in *Hunter v Mann* [1974] Q.B. 767). Similarly, it is difficult to see how such a duty could arise in equity or by whom it would be enforced. Possibly Scott J considered that Dr Egdell was under some "quasi public law duty" to disclose the report to the relevant authorities, in view of the particular circumstances under which the report was prepared. In this sense it might be argued that Dr Egdell was engaged in a "public" function, even though the report had been prepared at W's request and for the purpose of supporting his application to the tribunal. Possibly Scott J had a duty of care in negligence in mind when he referred to Dr Egdell's duty, but this is also doubtful given the context in which the words were used, particularly the reference to a duty owed to the public. Duties of care are normally expressed in much more restricted terms than this, being owed to persons who are foreseeable as likely to be directly affected by the defendant's failure to exercise reasonable care.

[220] [1990] Ch. 359; see para.8–063.

[221] See the Law Commission Report No.110, *Breach of Confidence*, 1981, Cmnd.8388, paras 4.75 to 4.77. See, however, Capper (1994) 14 L.S. 313, arguing that in an appropriate case equitable compensation or damages under Lord Cairns' Act (the Chancery Amendment Act 1858) should be available for breach of an equitable duty of confidentiality. See also L. Clarke, "Remedial responses to breach of confidence: the question of damages" (2005) 24 C.J.Q. 316.

[222] *Addis v Gramophone Co Ltd* [1909] A.C. 488; *Bliss v South East Thames Regional Health Authority* [1987] I.C.R. 700 at 717–718. Similarly, in the absence of physical injury, there is no

mind or freedom from distress.[223] This was the view taken by Scott J in *W v Egdell*. If W's claim had succeeded he would not have been entitled to damages in contract for shock and distress (except for nominal damages for the breach), and, his Lordship concluded, there was no reason why equity should not follow the law on this point.[224]

8–083   In *Cornelius v De Taranto*[225] the defendant passed a medico-legal report that had been commissioned and paid for by the claimant to a psychiatrist and a NHS hospital, in breach of contract and in breach of confidence. The report, for which the claimant had paid £630, contained information about the claimant's medical history and private life, which she had tried, unsuccessfully, to retrieve from the NHS. Morland J referred to art.8 of the European Convention on Human Rights, which provides for the right to respect for private and family life, and pointed out that it would be a "hollow protection" of that right if in a case involving breach of confidence in which details of the confider's private and family life were disclosed to others, the only remedy that English law allowed was nominal damages.[226] An injunction or order for delivery up of all copies of the report would have been of little use in this case, because the damage had already been done. In his Lordship's view, to refuse recovery of damages for mental distress caused by breach of confidence, when no other substantial remedy was available, would illustrate that something was wrong with the law.[227] Although Morland J appreciated that awarding damages for mental distress caused by breach of a duty of confidence was contrary to the view expressed by Scott J in *W v Egdell*, nonetheless he concluded that he should award damages for injured feelings: "Although it is a novel instance of such a remedy, it is in accord with the movement of current thinking."[228] Even so, damages for the mental distress sustained should be modest, said his Lordship. They were assessed at £3,000.[229] In *Archer v Williams*[230] Jackson J accepted, on the basis of *Cornelius v De Taranto* and *Campbell v Mirror Group Newspapers Ltd*,[231] that:

> "…where a breach of confidence causes injury to feelings, this court has power to award general damages. General damages for injury to feelings should be kept to a modest level and should be proportionate to the injury suffered. Such awards should be well below the level of general damages for serious physical or psychiatric injury."

---

liability in tort for mental distress falling short of psychiatric illness: *Hinz v Berry* [1970] 2 Q.B. 40 at 42; *McLoughlin v O'Brian* [1983] 1 A.C. 410 at 431; see para.2–188.

[223] *Jarvis v Swan Tours Ltd* [1973] Q.B. 233; *Heywood v Wellers* [1976] Q.B. 446.

[224] [1990] Ch. 359 at 398. This point was not considered by the Court of Appeal in *W v Egdell* [1990] Ch. 359, in view of the result on liability.

[225] [2001] E.M.L.R. 12; (2001) 68 B.M.L.R. 62.

[226] [2001] E.M.L.R. 12; (2001) 68 B.M.L.R. 62 at [65].

[227] [2001] E.M.L.R. 12; (2001) 68 B.M.L.R. 62 at [69].

[228] [2001] E.M.L.R. 12; (2001) 68 B.M.L.R. 62 at [77].

[229] The Court of Appeal upheld Morland J's finding on liability on the basis that there had been no express consent to the report being sent to the claimant's general practitioner and a consultant psychiatrist. But the question damages for mental distress was not discussed in the Court of Appeal: [2001] EWCA Civ 1511; [2002] E.M.L.R. 6; (2002) 68 B.M.L.R. 62.

[230] [2003] EWHC 1670 (QB); [2003] E.M.L.R. 38 at [76].

[231] [2002] EWHC 499 (QB); [2002] E.M.L.R. 30; [2002] H.R.L.R. 28.

Damages of £2,500 were awarded in respect of the disclosure of private information from the claimant's diaries to the press. The action was based on breach of contract, though Jackson J accepted that there was also breach of an equitable duty of confidence.

Although the trend of the decisions on damages is to award modest damages for breach of confidence, even where the claim is not brought in respect of breach of contract, the result for patients is not entirely satisfactory. There are conflicting first instance decisions on the point, and if the views of Scott J in *W v Egdell* were applied a past breach of confidence would give rise to a claim for damages only if the patient could establish substantive damage which flowed from the breach, and possibly this would only apply to contractual breaches of confidence.[232] The Law Commission recommended that the action for breach of confidence should take the form of a statutory tort and that damages for mental distress caused by a past breach should be available,[233] but this recommendation has not been implemented.

8–084

(b)   Damages for misuse of private information

The somewhat parsimonious approach to the award of damages for breach of confidence in disclosing medical information may have to be reconsidered in light of the more generous damages awards that have been made in actions for misuse of private information. Moreover, in cases where there is an overlap between the two actions the claim for misuse of private information may provide a route to a more substantial award of damages.

8–085

In *Cooper v Turrell*[234] the defendant engaged in a malicious internet campaign against a public company and one of its directors, alleging dishonesty and criminal conduct, and making damaging statements about the director's health and his fitness to do his job. Tugendhat J found that the defendant was liable both in libel and misuse of private information, awarding the company £30,000 for the libel and £10,000 for the breach of confidence, and the director £50,000 for the libel and £30,000 for the misuse of his private information. The awards for the libel and misuse of private information were distinct because damages for defamation are a remedy to vindicate a claimant's reputation from the damage done by the publication of false statements, whereas damages for misuse of private information are to compensate for the damage, and injury to feelings and distress, caused by the publication of information which may be either true or false.[235] For Tugendhat J the fact that the subject of the words complained of in

8–086

---

[232] Though if the breach of confidence leads to foreseeable physical harm to the patient this may amount to a breach of the doctor's duty of care in negligence to his patient: see *Furniss v Fitchett* [1958] N.Z.L.R. 396, where the facts were somewhat unusual.

[233] Law Commission Report No.110, *Breach of Confidence*, Cmnd.8388 (1981), paras 6.5 and 6.114.

[234] [2011] EWHC 3269 (QB). See also *Mosley v News Group Newspapers Ltd* [2008] EWHC 1777 (QB); [2008] E.M.L.R. 20, where Eady J awarded the claimant, a well-known public figure, £60,000 in respect of the publication of details of his private sexual activities, "albeit unconventional", with a number of prostitutes.

[235] [2011] EWHC 3269 at [102].

awards are unknown. However, in *PJS v News Group Newspapers Ltd*[249] Lord Mance pointed out that the issue remains open for determination at appellate level, and Lord Toulson observed that Eady J's decision in *Mosley* that exemplary damages cannot be awarded for breach of privacy, was not necessarily the final word on the subject. His Lordship added that:

> "Proportionality is essential, but I would not rule out the possibility of the courts considering such an award to be necessary and proportionate in order to deter flagrant breaches of privacy and provide adequate protection for the person concerned."

(c) Damages for breach of the Data Protection Act 1998

8–089 A breach of confidence or the misuse of private information may also, on appropriate facts, amount to a breach of the Data Protection Act 1998.[250] Section 13(1) of the Act provides that:

> "An individual who suffers damage by reason of any contravention by a data controller of any of the requirements of this Act is entitled to compensation from the data controller for that damage";

and s.13(2) adds that:

> "An individual who suffers distress by reason of any contravention by a data controller of any of the requirements of this Act is entitled to compensation from the data controller for that distress if (a) the individual also suffers damage by reason of the contravention, or (b) the contravention relates to the processing of personal data for the special purposes."[251]

Where there has been a breach of the data protection principles,[252] the data subject will be entitled to damages where the claimant can establish a loss due to the breach, or to nominal damages for the breach itself and substantive damages for proven distress.[253] In *Vidal-Hall v Google Inc*[254] the issue was whether a claimant could recover damages for distress in circumstances where he had not suffered any "damage" (i.e. pecuniary loss) within the meaning of s.13(1), despite the wording of s.13(2)(a). The Court of Appeal held that s.13(2) was incompatible with art.23 of the Directive 95/46/EC (the 1998 Act had been

---

[249] [2016] UKSC 26; [2016] A.C. 1081 at [42] and [92] respectively.

[250] See, e.g., the County Court decision of *Grinyer v Plymouth Hospital NHS Trust* (2012) 125 B.M.L.R. 1 (Plymouth County Court) where the claimant obtained substantive damages under the Act against the defendant NHS Trust in respect of unauthorised access to his medical records by one of its employees who had been in a relationship with the claimant in circumstances where there was almost certainly a breach of medical confidentiality. The breach produced an exacerbation of the claimant's pre-existing paranoid personality disorder.

[251] The Data Protection Act 1998 s.3 provides that the special purposes are (a) the purposes of journalism, (b) artistic purposes, and (c) literary purposes.

[252] See s.4(4) and Schs 1 to 4 of the 1998 Act.

[253] *Halliday v Creation Consumer Finance Ltd* [2013] EWCA Civ 333; [2013] 3 C.M.L.R. 4; *AB v Ministry of Justice* [2014] EWHC 1847 (QB) (breach of the subject access provisions of s.7); *CR19 v Chief Constable of Northern Ireland* [2014] NICA 54.

[254] [2015] EWCA Civ 311; [2016] Q.B. 1003.

enacted in order to implement this Directive). It followed that in, order to comply with EU law, s.13(2) should be disapplied and damages for distress could be awarded even in the absence of other damage.[255]

---

[255] "Since what the Directive purports to protect is privacy rather than economic rights, it would be strange if the Directive could not compensate those individuals whose data privacy had been invaded by a data controller so as to cause them emotional distress (but not pecuniary damage). It is the distressing invasion of privacy which must be taken to be the primary form of damage ... and the data subject should have an effective remedy in respect of that damage", [2015] EWCA Civ 311; [2016] Q.B. 1003 at [77].

CHAPTER 9

LIABILITY OF HOSPITALS AND CONTRIBUTION

In theory there are two grounds upon which a hospital authority[1] may be held responsible for injury to patients. The first, and by far the most common, is by virtue of an employer's vicarious liability for the torts of an employee committed during the course of employment. Although in the past hospital authorities had an effective immunity from liability for the negligence of professional staff, for over 60 years now hospitals have been in the same position as other employers with respect to vicarious liability. The only lingering uncertainty concerns precisely which staff are considered to be employees.   9–001

The second, and in some respects more speculative, ground is the concept of direct liability, by which a hospital is held liable not for the tort of an employee but for breach of its own duty owed directly to the patient. This may be the result of some organisational error, where, for example, there is an inadequate system for co-ordinating the work of staff which has put patients at risk. Alternatively, it may be that a hospital owes a primary, non-delegable duty to patients. Breach of such a duty renders the hospital liable to the patient whether it is occasioned by the conduct of an employee or of someone who is not an employee, such as an independent contractor. Thus, there can be some overlap between vicarious liability and a non-delegable duty. These two forms of liability are conceptually quite distinct, though in reality the purpose of imposing a non-delegable duty is simply to establish the responsibility of an "employer" for the negligence of independent contractors.   9–002

This chapter considers both the vicarious liability of a hospital authority and its potential direct liability to patients and others. It then discusses the rules on contribution between tortfeasors, which though not frequently an issue in medical negligence litigation, can be relevant in this context. The chapter concludes with a brief section on NHS Indemnity, the practical consequences of which can occasionally render the precise legal position of a defendant irrelevant.   9–003

---

[1] The organisation of the NHS seems to change on a regular basis, no matter what the political orientation of the government of the day. One consequence is that the body legally responsible for the consequences of harm to patients and others changes from time to time. Previously it was "health authorities", now usually NHS Trusts or NHS Foundation Trusts, and in some circumstances the NHS Litigation Authority. The Health and Social Care Act 2012 abolished primary care trusts and created clinical commissioning groups in their place. The term "hospital authority" is used in this chapter in a generic sense to refer to the body responsible in law for damage arising out of the provision of healthcare.

1. VICARIOUS LIABILITY

9–004   An employer is vicariously liable for torts committed by employees acting in the course of their employment.[2] Thus, in the paradigm case the focus is on two stages: (1) was there a true relationship of employer–employee between D2 and D1; and (2) was D1 acting in the course of his employment when he committed the tortious act?[3] Vicarious liability arises from the nature of the relationship, it does not depend upon any personal fault by the employer. Liability is imposed on the employer, not for a breach of the employer's duty to the claimant, but for the employee's breach of a duty owed by the employee to the claimant. This can be distinguished from the situation in which the employee's act results in the breach of a primary duty owed by the employer to the claimant.[4]

(a)   For whose acts is an employer responsible?

9–005   The traditional approach to vicarious liability was that an employer could be held vicariously liable for the torts of employees, but not the torts of others, such as an independent contractor (except for comparatively rare cases of liability for breach of the employer's non-delegable duty). Thus, the initial focus of the enquiry was on the nature of the relationship between the tortfeasor and the employer. This involved looking for a test to distinguish the employer–employee relationship from other relationships. Various factors may be taken into account such as the intention of the parties,[5] the degree of control exercised by the employer over the individual,[6] the degree to which the individual is integrated within the business,[7] and the allocation of financial risk,[8] but none of them are conclusive. Each can be

---

[2] See generally *Clerk & Lindsell on Torts*, 22nd edn (London: Sweet & Maxwell, 2018), Ch.6.

[3] *Various Claimants v Institute of the Brothers of the Christian Schools* [2012] UKSC 56; [2013] 2 A.C. 1 at [19] per Lord Phillips, who also commented that the "law of vicarious liability is on the move", recognising that the typical example of an employer's vicarious liability for an employee's torts is not the only relationship that can give rise to vicarious liability.

[4] See e.g. *Hudson v Ridge Manufacturing Co. Ltd* [1957] 2 Q.B. 348 where an employee was injured as a result of a "practical joke" by another employee. The employer was held liable, not on the basis of vicarious liability, but for breach of the employer's primary duty to exercise reasonable care for the health and safety of employees, one aspect of which involves an obligation to select competent fellow employees. The employer had been aware of the employee's persistent practical joking. Streatfeild J concluded that if an employee: "by his habitual conduct, is likely to prove a source of danger to his fellow employees, a duty lies fairly and squarely on the employers to remove that source of danger." Contrast *Harrison v Michelin Tyre Co. Ltd* [1985] 1 All E.R. 918, where the employer was held to be vicariously liable for an isolated act of horseplay by an employee and *Graham v Commercial Bodyworks Ltd* [2015] EWCA Civ 47; [2015] I.C.R. 665; [2015] P.I.Q.R. P15 where the employer was held not to be vicariously liable for the reckless behaviour of an employee (the issue in these cases being whether the acts were "in the course of employment").

[5] *Ferguson v Dawson Partners (Contractors) Ltd* [1976] 1 WLR 1213; *Young & Woods Ltd v West* [1980] I.R.L.R. 201; *Massey v Crown Life Insurance Co.* [1978] 1 W.L.R. 676.

[6] An employer "not only order or require what is to be done, but how it shall be done": *Collins v Hertfordshire County Council* [1947] K.B. 598, 615 per Hilbery J.

[7] *Stevenson Jordan & Harrison Ltd v Macdonald & Evans* [1952] 1 T.L.R. 101 at 111; *Bank voor Handel en Scheepvart NV v Slatford* [1953] 1 Q.B. 248, 290.

[8] *Montreal v Montreal Locomotive Works Ltd* [1947] 1 D.L.R. 161 at 169; *Market Investigations Ltd v Minister of Social Security* [1969] 2 Q.B. 173, 184; *Lee Ting San v Chung Chi-Keung* [1990] 2 A.C. 374 at 382.

criticised as failing to provide a clear-cut test, either by assuming what they seek to prove or simply begging the question (e.g. how much control, how much integration?).

Other relationships   It is now clear that vicarious liability can extend beyond the employment relationship. In *Cox v Ministry of Justice*[9] Lord Reed expressed the obligation at a higher level of generality than the employment relationship: **9–006**

> "Vicarious liability in tort is imposed upon a person in respect of the act or omission of another individual, because of his relationship with that individual, and the connection between that relationship and the act or omission in question."

This re-examination of the nature of the relationships that can give rise to vicarious liability has been driven, in part, by the spate of claims arising from historic sexual and physical abuse, cases which have also had to address the nature of the conduct for which "employers" may be held responsible. In *Various Claimants v Institute of the Brothers of the Christian Schools*[10] the Supreme Court held that a religious order could be vicariously liable for sexual abuse allegedly perpetrated by members of that order who worked as teachers at a residential school for boys, although the religious order did not manage the school and the Christian brothers who taught there had contracts of employment with the managers of the school. Lord Phillips, giving the only judgment of the court, referred to the policy objective underlying vicarious liability, which was:

> "...to ensure, in so far as it is fair, just and reasonable, that liability for tortious wrong is borne by a defendant with the means to compensate the victim. Such defendants can usually be expected to insure against the risk of such liability, so that this risk is more widely spread."[11]

There were a number of policy reasons that usually made it fair, just and reasonable to impose vicarious liability on the employer when the following were criteria are satisfied:

> "(i) the employer is more likely to have the means to compensate the victim than the employee and can be expected to have insured against that liability; (ii) the tort will have been committed as a result of activity being taken by the employee on behalf of the employer; (iii) the employee's activity is likely to be part of the business activity of the employer; (iv) the employer, by employing the employee to carry on the activity will have created the risk of the tort committed by the employee; (v) the employee will, to a greater or lesser degree, have been under the control of the employer."[12]

---

[9] [2016] UKSC 10; [2016] A.C. 660 at [15].
[10] [2012] UKSC 56; [2013] 2 A.C. 1.
[11] [2012] UKSC 56; [2013] 2 A.C. 1 at [34].
[12] [2012] UKSC 56; [2013] 2 A.C. 1 at [35]. Though Lord Phillips acknowledged, at [36], that "the significance of control today is that the employer can direct what the employee does, not how he does it". See also *Cox v Ministry of Justice* [2016] UKSC 10; [2016] A.C. 660 at [21] per Lord Reed on this point. In *Various Claimants v Barclays Bank Plc* [2017] EWHC 1929 (QB) Nicola Davies J applied these five criteria to claims for sexual assaults committed by a doctor on job applicants and existing employees required to undergo a medical assessment with a doctor nominated by the defendant bank. The bank argued that the doctor was an independent contractor, not an employee. The judge, following a detailed consideration of each of the five criteria, held that the relationship was akin to a relationship of employment (at [45]).

His Lordship concluded that where there was no contract of employment between the defendant and the tortfeasor but their relationship had the same incidents:

"...that relationship can properly give rise to vicarious liability on the ground that it is 'akin to that between an employer and an employee'."[13]

The relationship between the Christian brothers and the Institute had many of the elements, and all the essential elements, of the relationship between employer and employees, and in so far as the relationship differed from that of employer–employee those differences were not material.[14]

9–007   In *Cox v Ministry of Justice*[15] the Supreme Court held that the prison service, an executive agency of the Ministry of Justice, could be vicariously liable for the negligence of a prisoner in the course of his work in a prison kitchen. Applying *Christian Brothers*, Lord Reed said that:

"...a relationship other than one of employment is in principle capable of giving rise to vicarious liability where harm is wrongfully done by an individual who carries on activities as an integral part of the business activities carried on by a defendant and for its benefit (rather than his activities being entirely attributable to the conduct of a recognisably independent business of his own or of a third party), and where the commission of the wrongful act is a risk created by the defendant by assigning those activities to the individual in question."[16]

The defendant does not have to be carrying on activities of a commercial nature, and the benefit derived from the tortfeasor's activities did not have to take the form of a profit. It was sufficient that the defendant was carrying on activities in the furtherance of its own interests, and that the individual for whose conduct the defendant may be vicariously liable carried on activities assigned to him by the defendant as an integral part of its operation and for its benefit. By assigning those activities to him the defendant must have created a risk of his committing the tort.[17] Lord Reed pointed out that the approach taken in *Christian Brothers* had resulted in an extension of the scope of vicarious liability beyond the traditional employer–employee relationship and this maintained previous levels

---

[13] [2012] UKSC 56; [2013] 2 A.C. 1 at [47]. See also *E v English Province of Our Lady of Charity* [2012] EWCA Civ 938; [2013] Q.B. 722 (relationship between catholic priest and bishop akin to one of employment).

[14] [2012] UKSC 56; [2013] 2 A.C. 1 at [56]–[58]. The defendants were vicariously liable notwithstanding that another organisation employed the Christian brothers and was also vicariously liable for the same tort.

[15] [2016] UKSC 10; [2016] A.C. 660. For discussion of *Cox* see J. Plunkett, "Taking stock of vicarious liability" (2016) 132 L.Q.R. 556; P. Morgan, "Certainty in vicarious liability: a quest for a chimaera?" (2016) 75 C.L.J. 202; and R. Geraghty [2016] J.P.I.L. C64.

[16] [2016] UKSC 10; [2016] A.C. 660 at [24].

[17] [2016] UKSC 10; [2016] A.C. 660 at [30]. See also *Armes v Nottinghamshire County Council* [2017] UKSC 60 where the Supreme Court applied *Cox* to the relationship between a local authority and foster carers. The local authority were held vicariously liable for abuse perpetrated by foster carers on the children placed in their care by the authority on the basis that: the abuse was committed in the course of an activity carried out for the benefit of the authority; the placement rendered the children particularly vulnerable to abuse; there was no parallel in ordinary family life for the local authority's powers and the authority exercised a significant degree of control over what the foster parents did and how they did it; and local authorities were in a better position to compensate the victims of abuse.

of protection for the victims of torts, notwithstanding changes in the legal relationships between enterprises and members of their workforces:

"...which may be motivated by factors which have nothing to do with the nature of the enterprises' activities or the attendant risks."[18]

On the facts of *Cox* the Prison Service was vicariously liable because prisoners working in the prison kitchens were integrated into the operation of the prison, and the activities assigned to them formed an integral part of the activities carried on in the furtherance of its aims, namely the activity of providing meals for prisoners. It would be unjust, said Lord Reed, if the claimant's ability to obtain compensation for an injury suffered at work should depend on whether the member of the catering team who had been negligent happened to be a prisoner or a civilian member of staff.[19]

(i)   Hospital authorities

At one time it was thought that hospital authorities were not vicariously liable for the negligence of their "professional" staff, whether doctors or nurses, in the performance of their professional duties. This stemmed from the ruling of the Court of Appeal in *Hillyer v Governors of St. Bartholemews Hospital*,[20] which was based to some extent on the view that when acting on a professional judgment doctors exercised a discretion which the hospital authority could not control, and in the absence of control they were not employees.[21] The authority's responsibility was limited to exercising reasonable care in the selection of competent staff (which was a primary duty) and to vicarious liability for the performance of:

9–008

---

[18] [2016] UKSC 10; [2016] A.C. 660 at [29]. Thus: "defendants cannot avoid vicarious liability on the basis of technical arguments about the employment status of the individual who committed the tort", at [31]. This pre-empts arguments that, e.g., there was no employment relationship because the tortfeasor was an unpaid intern, or had a "zero hours" contract. See also *Mohamud v WM Morrison Supermarkets Plc* [2016] UKSC 11; [2016] A.C. 677 at [55] per Lord Dyson, attributing developments in the law as to the type of relationship that has to exist between an individual and a defendant for vicarious liability to be imposed to a response to changes in the legal relationships between enterprises and members of their workforces and the increasing complexity and sophistication of the modern organisation of enterprises.

[19] [2016] UKSC 10; [2016] A.C. 660 at [42].

[20] [1909] 2 K.B. 820; see also *Evans v Liverpool Corp* [1906] 1 K.B. 160 which was followed by the Court of Appeal in *Hillyer*; *Hall v Lees* [1904] 2 K.B. 603, where a nursing association undertook to supply competent nurses, not to nurse the patient, and so were not liable for a nurse's negligence. In *Gold v Essex County Council* [1942] 2 K.B. 293 at 301 Lord Greene MR said that in *Hall v Lees* the contract was a special one "and the case has nothing to do with hospitals or nursing homes".

[21] In *Cassidy v Ministry of Health* [1951] 2 K.B. 343 at 361 Denning LJ suggested that the decision in *Hillyer* was attributable "to a desire to relieve the charitable hospitals from liabilities which they could not afford"; see also the comments of Lord Cooper in *MacDonald v Board of Management for Glasgow Western Hospitals* 1954 S.C. 453 at 476. Lord Denning returned to this theme, but this time as a champion of financially beleaguered NHS hospitals, on a number of occasions: see para 3–134, n.348, and para.4–177.

"…purely ministerial or administrative duties, such as … attendance of nurses in the wards, the summoning of medical aid in cases of emergency, the supply of proper food and the like."[22]

9–009   The "control test" is no longer considered adequate as a determinant of the employer–employee relationship in modern economic conditions, where employers often do not have the technical expertise to supervise and control the manner in which skilled employees perform their work.[23] There is no single test: the question depends upon weighing a number of possibly conflicting factors in order to decide whether the work is performed under a contract of service or a contract for services,[24] though this distinction is itself no longer determinative in light of the Supreme Court decision in *Cox v Ministry of Justice*,[25] since, in addition to those employed under a contract of service, an employer can be vicariously liable where the relationship is akin to an employment relationship.[26]

9–010   The move away from the consequences of *Hillyer* began in *Gold v Essex County Council*,[27] where the Court of Appeal refused to accept the distinction between purely administrative duties and professional duties, holding the hospital authority vicariously liable for the negligence of a qualified radiographer employed under a contract of service. Lord Greene MR approached the question in terms of the obligation to the patient undertaken by a hospital. It was not a duty simply to provide suitable equipment and facilities, and to take reasonable care in selecting competent staff. It was a duty to treat the patient with the apparatus provided, and this could not be avoided by employing someone to discharge the duty, irrespective of whether the procedure involved the use of skill. MacKinnon and Goddard LJJ simply took the view that since the radiographer was employed under a contract of service, and was therefore an employee, the hospital authority were vicariously liable for his negligence. The position of the hospital in the case of negligence by a doctor was left unresolved. Goddard LJ considered that the hospital would be responsible for the negligence of doctors on the permanent staff, provided they were employed under a contract of service, although visiting surgeons and physicians were not employed under a contract of service, but rather a contract for services.[28] This was applied by Hilbery J in *Collins v*

---

[22] [1909] 2 K.B. 820 at 829. *Hillyer* was followed in *Strangeways-Lesmere v Clayton* [1936] 2 K.B. 11; *Dryden v Surrey County Council* [1936] 2 All E.R. 535; and *Marshall v Lindsey County Council* [1935] 1 K.B. 516, CA. The House of Lords in *Lindsey County Council v Marshall* [1937] A.C. 97 did not consider whether *Hillyer* was correctly decided.

[23] A point made by Kahn-Freund (1951) 14 M.L.R. 504.

[24] *Ready Mixed Concrete (South East) Ltd v Minister of Pensions and National Insurance* [1968] 2 Q.B. 497; *Market Investigations Ltd v Minister of Social Security* [1969] 2 Q.B. 173; *O'Kelly v Trusthouse Forte plc* [1983] I.R.L.R. 367. See paras 9–005 to 9–007 above.

[25] [2016] UKSC 10; [2016] A.C. 660; para.9–007.

[26] As, e.g., in *Various Claimants v Barclays Bank Plc* [2017] EWHC 1929 (QB)—bank vicariously liable for sexual assaults committed by doctor appointed to carry out medical assessments of prospective and actual employees of the bank; and *Armes v Nottinghamshire County Council* [2017] UKSC 60 (see n.17 above).

[27] [1942] 2 K.B. 293.

[28] [1942] 2 K.B. 293 at 313 and 310. See also Lord Greene MR at 302 commenting that with consultants the nature of the work and their relationship with the hospital is such that the hospital does not undertake responsibility for their negligence. His Lordship expressly left open the position of a resident house surgeon.

Hertfordshire County Council,[29] holding a hospital authority vicariously liable for the negligence of a resident junior house surgeon (employed on a temporary, but full-time basis). On the other hand, the authority was not responsible for the conduct of a visiting surgeon, although he had been engaged on similar written terms (but part-time) to the resident junior houseman.[30]

In *Cassidy v Ministry of Health*[31] the Court of Appeal confirmed that a hospital authority will be held vicariously liable for the negligence of all staff, nurses and doctors alike, employed under a contract of service as part of the permanent staff of the hospital. Denning LJ was clear that a hospital is in the same position as any other employer with respect to the torts of employees:

9–011

> "In my opinion authorities who run a hospital, be they local authorities, government boards, or any other corporation, are in law under the selfsame duty as the humblest doctor; whenever they accept a patient for treatment, they must use reasonable care and skill to cure him of his ailment. The hospital authorities cannot, of course, do it by themselves: they have no ears to listen through the stethoscope, and no hands to hold the surgeon's knife. They must do it by the staff they employ; and if their staff are negligent in giving the treatment, they are just as liable for that negligence as is anyone else who employs others to do his duties for him."[32]

The position of a consultant surgeon or physician who is not an employee of the hospital was, however, expressly distinguished by Somervell and Singleton LJJ.[33] Somervell LJ suggested that a patient who is treated by a consultant is in much the same position as a private patient who has arranged to be operated upon by a specific doctor. Denning LJ went further than the majority, taking the view that a hospital is under a non-delegable duty to treat patients, a duty which cannot be discharged by delegating its performance to a consultant under a contract for services. If this is correct the basis on which consultants are engaged, whether as employees or independent contractors, is, in practice, irrelevant: the hospital will be liable for their negligence.[34]

Subsequently, in *Roe v Minister of Health*[35] the Court of Appeal considered the question of a hospital authority's responsibility in respect of a part-time anaesthetist, and concluded that there would be vicarious liability, although on

9–012

---

[29] [1947] 1 K.B. 598 at 614–620.
[30] [1947] 1 K.B. 598 at 619. In *Cassidy v Ministry of Health* [1951] 2 K.B. 343, 352 Somervell LJ described the relationship between the visiting surgeon and the hospital in *Collins* as "obscure".
[31] [1951] 2 K.B. 343. The same view has been taken in Scotland: *MacDonald v Board of Management for Glasgow Western Hospitals* 1954 S.C. 453; *Fox v Glasgow South Western Hospitals* 1955 S.L.T. 337; Ireland: *O'Donovan v Cork County Council* [1967] I.R. 173; *Byrne v Ryan* [2007] IEHC 207; [2009] 4 I.R. 542; Australia: *Samios v Repatriation Commission* [1960] W.A.R. 219; and in Canada: *Fleming v Sisters of St. Joseph* [1938] S.C.R. 172; *Fraser v Vancouver General Hospital* (1951) 3 W.W.R. 337 at 340, 347, BCCA, aff'd [1952] 3 D.L.R. 785, SCC; *Martel v Hotel-Dieu St.-Vallier* (1969) 14 D.L.R. (3d) 445, SCC; *Toronto General Hospital v Aynsley* (1971) 25 D.L.R. (3d) 241, SCC.
[32] [1951] 2 K.B. 343 at 360.
[33] [1951] 2 K.B. 343 at 351 and 358 respectively.
[34] See paras 9–038 to 9–040. There is, however, a possible difference between vicarious liability for employees and liability under a non-delegable duty for the acts of independent contractors, in that the employer is not liable for the "collateral negligence" of an independent contractor; see para.9–052.
[35] [1954] 2 Q.B. 66.

the facts there had been no negligence. Denning LJ repeated the view he had expressed in *Cassidy v Ministry of Health*, apparently conflating the question of vicarious and primary liability:

> "...the hospital authorities are responsible for the whole of their staff, not only for the nurses and doctors, but also for the anaesthetists and the surgeons. It does not matter whether they are permanent or temporary, resident or visiting, whole-time or part-time. The hospital authorities are responsible for all of them. The reason is because, even if they are not servants, they are the agents of the hospital to give the treatment. The only exception is the case of consultants or anaesthetists selected and employed by the patient himself."[36]

Morris LJ, relying on the judgment of Lord Greene MR in *Gold v Essex County Council*, said that the question depended upon what the hospital had undertaken to provide, and that this was a question of fact in each case. On the facts the anaesthetists in *Roe* "were members of the 'organisation' of the hospital: they were members of the staff engaged by the hospital to do what the hospital itself was undertaking to do."[37] On this basis the principle of *respondeat superior* applied. It would seem that both Lord Greene MR and Morris LJ considered that the hospital's "undertaking" was the basis for imposing *vicarious liability*, not as giving rise to a non-delegable duty. Under a non-delegable duty the hospital would be responsible for the conduct of a consultant (unless the consultant was privately engaged by the patient) but the consultant was specifically excluded from the hospital's responsibility by Lord Greene.

9–013 The cumulative effect of these cases is that a hospital authority will be vicariously liable for the negligence of all full-time or part-time employees.[38] At one time was arguable that visiting consultants did not fall into the category of employees,[39] although in *Razzel v Snowball*[40] Denning LJ said that since the introduction of the National Health Service the term "consultant" did not denote a particular relationship between a doctor and a hospital. Rather, it was simply a title denoting a place in the hierarchy of the hospital staff:

> "He is a senior member of the staff but nevertheless just as much a member of the staff as the house surgeon."[41]

This view has not had to be tested in the courts since in practice, whatever the legal niceties may be, hospital authorities within the NHS do not argue the point

---

[36] [1954] 2 Q.B. 66 at 82.
[37] [1954] 2 Q.B. 66 at 91.
[38] *Gold v Essex County Council* [1942] 2 K.B. 293 (radiographer); *Collins v Hertfordshire County Council* [1947] 1 K.B. 598 (resident house surgeon and pharmacist); *Cassidy v Ministry of Health* [1951] 2 K.B. 343 (assistant medical officer); *MacDonald v Board of Management for Glasgow Western Hospitals* 1954 S.C. 453 (resident medical officer); *Roe v Minister of Health* [1954] 2 Q.B. 66 (anaesthetist); *Fox v Glasgow South Western Hospitals* 1955 S.L.T. 337 (nurses). An employer will be vicariously liable for injury to an employee caused by the negligence of an occupational medical officer: *Stokes v Guest, Keen and Nettlefold (Bolts and Nuts) Ltd* [1968] 1 W.L.R. 1776, para.4–009.
[39] This was the view of Hilbery J. in *Collins v Hertfordshire County Council* [1947] 1 K.B. 598 at 619–620; see also *MacDonald v Board of Management for Glasgow Western Hospitals* 1954 S.C. 453 at 478, 485; *Higgins v North West Metropolitan Hospital Board* [1954] 1 W.L.R. 411 at 417.
[40] [1954] 1 W.L.R. 1382.
[41] [1954] 1 W.L.R. 1382 at 1386.

that a consultant is not an employee when engaged on NHS work. Consultants clearly fall within the terms of HC (89)34 which introduced "NHS Indemnity", on the assumption that they are members of staff for whom the hospital authority or NHS Trust will be vicariously liable.[42] This is also true of staff supplied to the hospital by outside agencies. It is arguable that an agency nurse, for example, remains the employee of the agency and does not become an employee of the hospital authority for the purpose of vicarious liability,[43] though the Court of Appeal has held that it is possible to make a finding of "dual" vicarious liability on the basis that the employee has two employers and both can be vicariously responsible.[44] The hospital authority will accept responsibility for the negligence of agency staff, however, under the terms of NHS Indemnity.[45] The fact that NHS hospital authorities accept vicarious responsibility for consultants and agency staff removes much of the practical import of the arguments about whether a hospital is under a non-delegable duty to patients. In any event, it is probable that any attempt by a hospital to escape vicarious responsibility would now be met by Lord Reed's proposition in *Cox v Ministry of Justice*[46] that vicarious liability can apply to any relationship where harm is wrongfully caused by an individual carrying on activities as an integral part of the business activities of the defendant and for its benefit:

"...and where the commission of the wrongful act is a risk created by the defendant by assigning those activities to the individual in question."

The one exception could be where it is clear that the patient has engaged the doctor privately and the hospital is merely providing "hotel facilities" to enable the treatment to be carried out.

Surgeons do not normally employ the nurses in the operating theatre or on the ward and will not be responsible for their negligence in carrying out the instructions that have been given with regard to the patient's treatment.[47] Nursing staff remain the employees of the hospital, and if the hospital is not liable for the conduct of a nurse who is acting under the instructions of the surgeon or doctor the reason is:

9–014

---

[42] See paras 9–081 to 9–082.

[43] For the effect of transferring employees between employers see *Mersey Docks and Harbour Board v Coggins & Griffith (Liverpool) Ltd* [1947] A.C. 1; *Bhoomidas v Port of Singapore Authority* [1978] 1 W.L.R. 189; *Gibb v United Steel Companies Ltd* [1957] 1 W.L.R. 668; *Morris v Breaveglen Ltd* [1993] I.C.R. 766; *Nelhams v Sandells Maintenance Ltd* [1996] P.I.Q.R. P52; *Hawley v Luminar Leisure Ltd* [2006] EWCA Civ 18; [2006] P.I.Q.R. P17; [2006] I.R.L.R. 817. Note, however, that staff supplied by an employment agency may not be employees of the agency: see *Ironmonger v Movefield Ltd* [1988] I.R.L.R. 461.

[44] *Viasystems (Tyneside) Ltd v Thermal Transfer (Northern) Ltd* [2005] EWCA Civ 1151; [2006] Q.B. 510.

[45] See HC(89)34, para.8 and Annex A, para.18. The Circular was updated by HSG (96)48 and *NHS Indemnity—Arrangements for Clinical Negligence Claims in the NHS*, NHS Executive, 1996 (available at *http://www.nhsla.com/claims/Documents/NHS%20Indemnity.pdf*) (see App.1).

[46] [2016] UKSC 10; [2016] A.C. 660 at [24].

[47] *Perionowsky v Freeman* (1866) 4 F. & F. 977; *Morris v Winsbury-White* [1937] 4 All E.R. 494, 498.

"...not that *pro hac vice* she ceases to be the servant of the hospital, but that she is not guilty of negligence if she carries out the orders of the surgeon, however negligent those orders may be."[48]

(ii)   General practice

9–015   General practitioners offering primary care services are not employees,[49] and so a claim for negligence against a general practitioner (or a general dental practitioner) would have to be pursued against the individual doctor.[50] General practitioners will be vicariously liable for the negligence of their employees, such as nurses or receptionists.[51] The position of a locum tenens is unclear. It seems likely that a deputising doctor would not be considered to be an employee, but would be categorised as an independent contractor.[52] On the other hand, it is

---

[48] *Gold v Essex County Council* [1942] 2 K.B. 293 at 299, per Lord Greene MR; *Johnston v Wellesley Hospital* (1970) 17 D.L.R. (3d) 139, 152, Ont HC. Note, however, that a nurse does not necessarily act with reasonable care by mechanically following a doctor's orders. If the instruction was obviously incorrect the nurse would have a duty to seek confirmation from the doctor: per Goddard LJ at [1942] 2 K.B. 293 at 313; see para.4–097.

[49] In *Wadi v Cornwall and Isles of Scilly Family Practitioner Committee* [1985] I.C.R. 492 the Employment Appeal Tribunal held that the relationship between general practitioners and a Family Health Service Authority was not contractual but statutory; and in *Roy v Kensington and Chelsea and Westminster Family Practitioner Committee* [1992] 1 A.C. 624 the House of Lords doubted, without deciding, whether the relationship between a general practitioner and the NHS was contractual in nature. There were "contractual echoes in the relationship". Nonetheless, a general practitioner has private law rights against the health authority, arising from the legislation (now the National Health Service Act 2006, the National Health Service (General Medical Services Contracts) Regulations 2015 (SI 2015/1862) and the National Health Service (Personal Medical Services Agreements) Regulations 2015 (SI 2015/1879)).

[50] The National Health Service (General Medical Services Contracts) Regulations 2015 (SI 2015/1862) reg.91 and the National Health Service (Personal Medical Services Agreements) Regulations 2015 (SI 2015/1879) reg.83 make professional indemnity insurance compulsory for general practitioners in the NHS. The Medical Act 1983 s.44C (which applies to doctors in private practice as well as in the NHS) requires a person who holds a licence to practise as a medical practitioner to have in force an indemnity arrangement which provides appropriate cover for practising as such. This could be a policy of insurance or an arrangement (e.g. with an employer) made for the purposes of indemnifying a person, or a combination of both. "Appropriate cover" means cover against liabilities that may be incurred in practising as a medical practitioner which is appropriate, having regard to the nature and extent of the risks of practising as such (Medical Act 1983 s.44C(3)). See also GMC's guidance, *Good Medical Practice*, 2013, para.63 (available at *http://www.gmc-uk.org/guidance/good_medical_practice.asp*): "You must make sure you have adequate insurance or indemnity cover so that your patients will not be disadvantaged if they make a claim about the clinical care you have provided in the UK." A failure to insure can lead to the doctor being struck off the register: *Irvine v General Medical Council* [2017] EWHC 2038 (Admin). See also the National Health Service Act 2006 s.166 in relation to indemnity cover for NHS pharmacists.

[51] See, e.g. *Lobley v Nunn* unreported 9 December 1985, CA, where an action against a receptionist failed on the facts; *T (A) v Mah* 2012 ABQB 777; [2013] 9 W.W.R. 648, where a physician was held vicariously liable for the negligence of a receptionist in giving a patient the wrong appointment date; *Hancke v Hooper* (1835) 7 C. & P. 81, where a surgeon was held liable for the negligence of an apprentice.

[52] This was the conclusion of Osler J in *Rothwell v Raes* (1988) 54 D.L.R. (4th) 193 at 262, Ont HC, who emphasised the independence of the locum's professional judgment. The locum's freedom of action as a medical practitioner was not circumscribed in any way, other than financial. There are restrictions on the ability of a general practitioner in the NHS to sub-contract clinical services: see the National Health Service (General Medical Services Contracts) Regulations 2015 (SI 2015/1862)

possible that in light of the Supreme Court's more flexible approach to the relationships that can give rise to vicarious liability a general practitioner might be held vicariously liable for the conduct of a locum.[53] It is doubtful whether a general practitioner would be under a non-delegable duty with respect to the negligence of a locum. Staff directly employed by a Clinical Commissioning Group or a local authority (e.g. as a public health doctor or a district nurse) clearly are employees for whose negligence the employer can be vicariously liable. Clinical Commissioning Groups are eligible to participate in the Clinical Negligence Scheme for Trusts,[54] and guidance issued by the NHS Litigation Authority as to who is eligible for indemnity cover under the scheme renders much of the debate about who is an employee redundant.[55]

(iii) Private treatment

Where patients have received treatment privately they could sue the hospital or clinic, which will be vicariously liable for the negligence of their employees, but, in practice, the doctor may not be employed by the hospital or clinic. Unless the hospital has held the doctor out to the patient as an employee,[56] it will not be liable for negligence and the patient will have to sue the doctor individually. This may depend upon the construction placed on the contract between the hospital and patient. On the other hand, it is arguable that where the patient's contract is with the hospital then the hospital undertakes a non-delegable duty, at least where the contract is to provide treatment as opposed to merely providing facilities for

9–016

Sch.3 Pt 5 paras 44 and 45, and the National Health Service (Personal Medical Services Agreements) Regulations 2015 (SI 2015/1879) Sch.2 Pt 5 para.43. The general practitioner must be satisfied, inter alia, that it is reasonable in all the circumstances to sub-contract and that the person is qualified and competent to provide the service. The Regulations are silent on the question of the general practitioner's responsibility for actions of a locum, though they provide that the general practitioner may not sub-contract obligations to provide clinical services unless satisfied that the sub-contractor has appropriate professional indemnity cover (National Health Service (General Medical Services Contracts) Regulations 2015 reg.91(2) and National Health Service (Personal Medical Services Agreements) Regulations 2015 reg.83(2)). In any event these provisions regulate the general practitioner's position under the terms of service with the NHS, and they would not necessarily be conclusive in law vis-à-vis the patient.

[53] See paras 9–006–9–007.

[54] See para.9–087.

[55] See *NHS Indemnity—Arrangements for Clinical Negligence Claims in the NHS*, para.7: "NHS Indemnity covers the actions of staff in the course of their NHS employment. It also covers people in certain other categories whenever the NHS body owes a duty of care to the person harmed, including, for example, locums, medical academic staff with honorary contracts, students, those conducting clinical trials, charitable volunteers and people undergoing further professional education, training and examinations. This includes staff working on income generation projects. GPs or dentists who are directly employed by Health Authorities, e.g. as Public Health doctors (including port medical officers and medical inspectors of immigrants at UK air/sea ports), are covered." The term "employment" also includes formal secondment to a Primary Care Trust from a partner organisation. This is an old document but it remains available at *http://www.nhsla.com/claims/Documents/NHS%20Indemnity.pdf* (also under a link to "NHS Indemnity" at *http://www.nhsla.com/Claims/Pages/Handling.aspx*). See Appendix 1.

[56] See, e.g. *Rogers v Night Riders* [1983] R.T.R. 324, CA, where a minicab hire firm were held to be under a non-delegable duty with regard to the safety of vehicles, although the vehicle drivers were independent contractors.

treatment to be given by an independent doctor. This view derives some support from an observation by Morris LJ in *Roe v Minister of Health*:

> "While the requisite standard of care does not vary according as to whether treatment is gratuitous or on payment, the existence of arrangements entitling the plaintiffs to expect certain treatment might be a relevant factor when considering the extent of the obligation assumed by the hospital."[57]

9–017   Where a doctor who is not employed by the hospital has been engaged directly by the patient the hospital will not be liable for the doctor's negligence, and the patient's claim will be against the doctor personally. This applies both to vicarious liability and non-delegable duties.[58] If staff employed by the hospital, such as nurses, are involved in assisting the doctor to provide treatment, then the hospital is potentially vicariously liable for their negligence in the usual way, whether the hospital is private or NHS.

(b)   For what acts is an employer responsible?

(i)   Acts in the course of employment

9–018   The vicarious liability of an employer applies to the torts of employees or someone in a comparable relationship[59] who is acting in the course of their employment. This tends to be treated as a question of fact in each case. Provided that employees are still engaged on the tasks they were employed to do, albeit they are doing it in a wrongful and unauthorised manner, they will be acting in the course of employment. Sometimes the question is phrased in terms of whether employees were acting within "the scope of his employment"? The older cases tended to focus on whether employees were still engaged on the employer's business when the tort occurred, as opposed to having gone off "on a frolic of his own".[60] But the answer to these questions depended on how widely the court defined "the scope" of the particular employment, and in some instances employees could be found to be acting within the scope of their employment even when doing something specifically prohibited by their employer[61] or which involved a criminal offence.[62] This aspect of vicarious liability does not appear to have created problems in the context of medical negligence actions. In theory

---

[57] [1954] 2 Q.B. 66 at 89.
[58] See Denning LJ in *Cassidy v Ministry of Health* [1951] 2 K.B. 343 at 362 and *Roe v Minister of Health* [1954] 2 Q.B. 66 at 82; *Johnston v Wellesley Hospital* (1970) 17 D.L.R. (3d) 139 at 152–153, Ont HC; *Crits v Sylvester* (1956) 1 D.L.R. (2d) 504 at 508, Ont CA; aff'd (1956) 5 D.L.R. (2d) 601, SCC, holding that a hospital authority is not liable if a doctor employed by the patient, not the hospital, fails to use the equipment available; the hospital is not required to oversee the use of appliances by a privately engaged doctor.
[59] See para.9–006.
[60] *Joel v Morison* (1834) 6 C. & P. 501, 503 per Parke B.
[61] As e.g. in *Rose v Plenty* [1976] 1 W.L.R. 141 (prohibition on driver giving lifts to third parties); *Canadian Pacific Railway Co. v Lockhart* [1942] A.C. 591 (prohibition on driving an uninsured vehicle); *Limpus v London General Omnibus Co.* (1862) 1 H. & C. 526 (prohibition on bus driver from racing against buses of rival companies).
[62] *Lloyd v Grace, Smith & Co.* [1912] AC 716; *Morris v C.W. Martin & Sons Ltd* [1966] 1 Q.B. 716.

surgeons who perform operations beyond sphere of their experience could be considered to be acting outside the scope of employment, but this is a question of degree, and the circumstances would probably have to be quite extreme before this would become a live issue.[63] Liability will not necessarily be limited to acts in the course of providing treatment itself, so, for example, the hospital may be responsible for negligence which leads to the patient falling out of bed.[64]

The traditional test for what constitutes the "course of employment" is whether the employee's conduct was a wrongful and unauthorised mode of doing some act authorised by the employer.[65] Although this test has not generally been a problem in the context of medical negligence claims, there are certain situations, particularly where the employee's conduct is an intentional wrong, where there is a tendency to blur the distinction between the employee's duty and the employer's duty to the claimant. Intentional wrongs are comparatively rare in the healthcare setting but they can occur,[66] and an issue may then arise as to whether the NHS Trust employing the individual would be vicariously liable. It is difficult to fit intentional wrongs into the traditional "course of employment" test because, generally speaking, employers do not employ individuals to commit intentional wrongs, particularly criminal offences. The response of the courts has been to develop a test based on the closeness of the "connection" between the employee's wrongful conduct and the employer's business.

9–019

(ii) "Close connection" test

In *Lister v Hesley Hall Ltd*[67] the warden of a boarding house attached to a school for children with emotional and behavioural difficulties systematically sexually abused the claimants who were resident in the boarding house. The question was whether the warden's employers were vicariously liable for the sexual abuse (a claim that there had been negligence by the school in appointing and supervising the warden having been abandoned). The traditional test for the course of employment does not provide a ready solution to cases involving intentional conduct. Indeed, as a general rule the more egregious the conduct, the less likely

9–020

---

[63] HC(89)34, Annex A, para.12 stated that "actions in the course of NHS employment" should be interpreted liberally.

[64] *Smith v Lewisham Group Hospital Management Committee, The Times*, 21 June 1955; *Beatty v Sisters of Misericorde of Alberta* [1935] 1 W.W.R. 651.

[65] See *Clerk & Lindsell on Torts*, 22nd edn (London: Sweet & Maxwell, 2018), para.6–28, citing *Salmond & Heuston on the Law of Torts*, 21st edn (London: Sweet & Maxwell, 1996) p.443.

[66] The Beverley Allitt case would be one example. See Appleyard (1994) 308 B.M.J. 287; Dyer (1993) 306 B.M.J. 1431. Another would be the doctor who uses the opportunity of examining patients as a means of committing sexual assaults. See *R. v Tabassum* [2000] Lloyd's Rep. Med. 404, CA, although the defendant in that case was not a doctor. See also *Weingerl v Seo* (2005) 256 D.L.R. (4th) 1 where the Ontario Court of Appeal held that a private clinic was vicariously liable for sexual assault committed by an ultrasound technician on a patient (videoing patient getting dressed and undressed in a temporary changing room and unauthorised tests of lower abdominal area). Vicarious liability was justified because the technician's wrongful act was so closely related to authorised conduct (applying the decision of the Supreme Court of Canada in *Bazley v Curry* (1999) 174 D.L.R. (4th) 45; [1999] 8 W.W.R. 197).

[67] [2001] UKHL 22; [2002] 1 A.C. 215; Feldthusen (2001) 9 Tort L. Rev. 173; Glofcheski (2004) 12 Tort L. Rev. 18.

it is that the test will be satisfied, because it becomes difficult to categorise it as merely an "unauthorised mode" of performing an "authorised" act. The warden was responsible for the care of the children, and the abuse could hardly be called an unauthorised mode of doing some act authorised by the employers. It was the very antithesis of what he was authorised to do. Nonetheless, the House of Lords unanimously held the school to be vicariously liable for the warden's conduct, placing some emphasis on the fact that the school had undertaken the care and safekeeping of the boys. Lord Steyn said that the question was:

> "...whether the warden's torts were so closely connected with his employment that it would be fair and just to hold the employers vicariously liable. On the facts of the case the answer is yes. After all, the sexual abuse was inextricably interwoven with the carrying out by the warden of his duties..."[68]

Lord Clyde said that the sufficiency of the connection could be gauged by asking whether the wrongful acts could be seen as ways of carrying out the work which the employer had authorised. There had to be some greater connection between the tortious act of the employee and the circumstances of his employment than the mere opportunity to commit the act which has been provided by the access to the premises which his employment has permitted.[69] Thus, as Lord Millett pointed out, the fact that the employment provided access to the premises would not be sufficient, because the same would have been true of a groundsman or the school porter. It was the employee's position as warden and the close contact with the boys which that work involved which created a sufficient connection between the acts of abuse and the work he had been employed to do. His general duty was to look after the claimants. The fact that he performed that function in a way which was an abuse of his position and a negation of his duty did not sever the connection with his employment.[70]

9–021   In *Various Claimants v Institute of the Brothers of the Christian Schools*[71] Lord Phillips had suggested that it was not easy to identify from *Lister* the precise criteria that will give rise to vicarious liability for sexual abuse, because the

---

[68] [2001] UKHL 22; [2002] 1 A.C. 215 at [28]. See also *Various Claimants v Barclays Bank Plc* [2017] EWHC 1929 (QB) at [46]—sexual assaults committed by a doctor on job applicants and existing employees required to undergo a medical assessment with a doctor nominated by the defendant bank were inextricably interwoven with the carrying out by the doctor of his duties pursuant to his engagement by the bank, and so satisfied the close connection requirement.

[69] [2001] UKHL 22; [2002] 1 A.C. 215 at [45]. In *Balfron Trustees Ltd v Peterson* [2001] I.R.L.R. 758 at [33] Laddie J suggested that the focus should be on the relationship between the employer and the victim of the employee's tort, combined with a normative judgment as to whether the employer *ought* to be held liable in the circumstances.

[70] [2001] UKHL 22; [2002] 1 A.C. 215 at [82]. See further *Mattis v Pollock (trading as Flamingo's Nightclub)* [2003] EWCA Civ 887; [2003] 1 W.L.R. 2158 where the Court of Appeal held that a nightclub was vicariously liable for a revenge attack on a customer by a "bouncer", applying *Lister*. See also *Majrowski v Guy's and St Thomas's NHS Trust* [2006] UKHL 34; [2007] 1 A.C. 224, where the House of Lords held that the defendant NHS Trust was vicariously liable under the Protection from Harassment Act 1997 s.3, for harassment committed by one of its employees in breach of s.1 of the Act, applying *Lister*. *Majrowski* is commented on by Stevens (2007) 123 L.Q.R. 30.

[71] [2012] UKSC 56; [2013] 2 A.C. 1 at [74].

"close connection" test says nothing about the nature of the connection. However, in *Mohamud v WM Morrison Supermarkets Plc*[72] Lord Toulson considered that there was a:

"...risk in attempting to over-refine, or lay down a list of criteria for determining, what precisely amounts to a sufficiently close connection to make it just for the employer to be held vicariously liable. Simplification of the essence is more desirable."

The court has to consider two matters: (1) the nature of the employee's job; and (2) whether there was sufficient connection between the position in which he was employed and his wrongful conduct to make it right for the employer to be held liable.[73] There was nothing wrong with the approach in *Lister*, said Lord Toulson, and the law would not be improved by a change of vocabulary. Lord Dyson agreed that the *Lister* test was imprecise, but that was inevitable: "To search for certainty and precision in vicarious liability is to undertake a quest for a chimaera."[74] On the facts of *Mohamud v WM Morrison Supermarkets Plc* the defendant employers of a petrol kiosk attendant who had subjected a customer to an unprovoked assault were held vicariously liable for the assault. Lord Toulson accepted that it was a gross abuse of the employee's position:

"...but it was in connection with the business in which he was employed to serve customers. His employers entrusted him with that position and it is just that as between them and the claimant, they should be held responsible for their employee's abuse of it."[75]

(c)   Employer's right to indemnity

There is an implied term in employees' contracts of employment that they will exercise reasonable care when performing their duties. Where an employee's negligence leads to the employer's vicarious liability then at common law the employer is entitled to be indemnified for the loss attributable to the employee's breach of contract. In *Lister v Romford Ice & Cold Storage Co. Ltd*[76] an employee negligently injured his father, who was also employed by the same company. The employers' insurers met the father's claim against the company for the negligence of the son, and then sued the son in the company's name, exercising their right of subrogation under the contract of insurance. By a

9–022

---

[72] [2016] UKSC 11; [2016] A.C. 677.
[73] [2016] UKSC 11; [2016] A.C. 677 at [44]–[45], applying a principle of social justice going back to Holt C.J. in the late 17th and early 18th centuries.
[74] [2016] UKSC 11; [2016] A.C. 677 at [54]. His Lordship added, at [56], that the changes to the test for when an employee was acting in the course of employment had been prompted by the aim of producing a fairer and more workable test.
[75] [2016] UKSC 11; [2016] A.C. 677 at [47]. The employee's motive was irrelevant. It looked obvious that he was motivated by personal racism rather than a desire to benefit his employer's business, but that was "neither here nor there", [2016] UKSC 11; [2016] A.C. 677 at [48]. Contrast *Bellman v Northampton Recruitment Ltd* [2016] EWHC 3104 (QB); [2017] I.C.R. 543 (employer not vicariously liable for assault by one employee on another employee after a work Christmas party). For discussion of *Mohamud* see J. Plunkett, "Taking stock of vicarious liability" (2016) 132 L.Q.R. 556; P. Morgan, "Certainty in vicarious liability: a quest for a chimaera?" (2016) 75 C.L.J. 202; and J. Fulbrook [2016] J.P.I.L. C69.
[76] [1957] A.C. 555.

majority the House of Lords held that the son was liable to indemnify the employers, and hence the insurers. This case led to some concern at the prospect of insurers enforcing employers' rights against employees with detrimental consequences for industrial relations. Employers' liability insurers subsequently entered into a "gentlemen's agreement" not to pursue such claims unless there was evidence of collusion or wilful misconduct.[77]

9-023   In *Jones v Manchester Corporation*[78] an inexperienced anaesthetist negligently administered an overdose of anaesthetic, the consequence of which was that the patient died. The hospital board was also found to have been negligent in allowing the anaesthetist to give the anaesthetic without supervision from a more experienced colleague. The issue before the Court of Appeal was the allocation of responsibility between the doctor and the health board. Hodgson LJ, in a dissenting judgment, would have granted a hospital board a full indemnity against the anaesthetist on the basis that there had been a breach of the implied term in the contract between the hospital board and the doctor that she would exercise reasonable skill and care. Denning LJ doubted whether such a term should be implied into the contract, and Singleton LJ held that the right to indemnity from an employee under the contract of employment does not apply where the employer has himself contributed to the damage or if the employer bears some part of the responsibility, where, for example, a more senior employee's negligence has contributed to the damage.[79] The employer is then limited to claiming contribution from the negligent employee under the Civil Liability (Contribution) Act 1978.

9-024   The issue does not arise in England in a case where the negligent doctor is employed by a NHS hospital, because since the introduction of NHS Indemnity[80] it has been accepted that the NHS does not require doctors to carry professional indemnity insurance and that the NHS would accept responsibility for paying any compensation to a patient injured by the doctor's negligence.[81] However, the point could arise in a case where the NHS, whether a NHS Trust or a Clinical Commissioning Group, contracts with a third party provider of healthcare for the provision of specific health services. An employee of the third party provider who is negligent in the course of performing their professional duties could find that their employer's insurer, having compensated the injured patient on the basis that the employer was vicariously liable for the employee's negligence, may seek an

---

[77] Gardiner (1959) 22 M.L.R. 552. See also *Morris v Ford Motor Co. Ltd* [1973] Q.B. 792 where a majority of the Court of Appeal held that in an industrial setting it was unacceptable to allow subrogation to the employers' right of indemnity. An employee of Ford negligently injured an employee of a firm of cleaners, and under the terms of their contract with Ford the cleaners were contractually bound to indemnify Ford in respect of the damages paid to the injured employee. The cleaners (who were not bound by the insurers' "gentlemen's agreement") claimed to be subrogated to Ford's right of indemnity against the negligent employee, but by a majority the Court of Appeal disagreed (not least because the cleaners had been advised to insure against their potential liability under the indemnity clause). The decision is difficult to reconcile with *Lister*.

[78] [1952] 2 Q.B. 852.

[79] [1952] 2 Q.B. 852 at 865

[80] See para.9-081.

[81] This had been the position for many years in the case of other professionals, such as nurses or physiotherapists, even before NHS Indemnity.

indemnity from the employee (the insurer being subrogated to the rights of the employer by virtue of the contract of insurance).

This issue was at the heart of the Scottish case of *Bell v Alliance Medical Ltd*.[82] Alliance Medical were contracted by Forth Valley Health Board to carry out MRI scanning at Falkirk hospital and were responsible for the management and operation of the MRI scanning unit. A radiographer employed by Alliance Medical was found to have been negligent in the cannulation of the patient's arm. Alliance Medical claimed an indemnity from the radiographer on the basis of an implied term in her contract of employment. Lord Boyd held that *Lister v Romford Ice & Cold Storage Co. Ltd* was still good law in Scotland and that Alliance Medical were entitled to the indemnity. The judge also held that the Health Board owed a non-delegable duty of care to the patient on the basis of the Supreme Court's ruling in *Woodland v Swimming Teachers Association*[83] but that the radiographer was not entitled to an indemnity from the Health Board because it would "be wrong in principle to allow the [radiographer] to rely on her own negligence to secure a contribution from the [Health Board]".[84] Lord Boyd added, somewhat laconically, that the:

9–025

"...decision may have consequences for the relationship between medical staff, whether or not employed by a health board or by contractors to it, and the NHS."[85]

The radiographer in *Bell v Alliance Medical Ltd* was insured as a consequence of her membership of the Society of Radiographers, and it is possible that the insurers of Alliance Medical sought to enforce the indemnity precisely because she was insured.[86] But as Lord Boyd noted the radiographer was not obliged to be a member of the Society, and there was no obligation for her to be insured against professional liability either as a condition of her contract of employment or any statutory provision. There was nothing, in theory, to stop Alliance Medical seeking an indemnity even if she was not insured.[87] This could leave health professionals who are not employed directly by a NHS body open to the risk of personal claims for indemnity by the liability insurers of their employers exercising their rights of subrogation under the policy of insurance.[88]

9–026

---

[82] [2015] CSOH 34; 2015 S.C.L.R. 676.
[83] [2013] UKSC 66, [2014] A.C. 537; see para.9–044.
[84] [2015] CSOH 34; 2015 S.C.L.R. 676 at [119].
[85] [2015] CSOH 34; 2015 S.C.L.R. 676 at [119].
[86] Though there is nothing in the law report to suggest this.
[87] [2015] CSOH 34; 2015 S.C.L.R. 676 at [109].
[88] Note that since April 2013, in England, third party providers of healthcare who have contracted with a NHS body to provide healthcare to NHS patients have been entitled to join the Clinical Negligence Scheme for Trusts (CNST) and therefore to be indemnified for their liabilities arising out of the NHS care they provide. See para.9–087. It is highly unlikely that the NHS Litigation Authority, as administrator of CNST, would seek to enforce the employer's right to indemnity against a negligent employee of the third party healthcare provider who was a member of CNST, particularly since this would not be done in the case of a NHS employee. Nonetheless, the possibility of case similar to *Bell v Alliance Medical Ltd* arising in England must remain where the third party provider of healthcare has a commercial insurer.

2. DIRECT LIABILITY

9–027 The concept of the direct liability of a hospital authority is used in two distinct ways. First, where the authority is itself at fault in the manner in which it has performed its functions, although it may not be possible to identify any particular employee who was negligent. This may be categorised as a form of organisational failure. Secondly, direct liability is also used to describe the imposition of a non-delegable duty, for the purpose of establishing the authority's responsibility for the negligence of an independent contractor. As a general rule people are not liable for the torts of an independent contractor, unless they authorised or ratified the tort,[89] or unless they themselves have been negligent in selecting an incompetent contractor, or employing an inadequate number of employees for the job,[90] or they have interfered with the manner in which the work was performed so causing the damage.[91] If employers discover that the contractor's work is being done in a foreseeably dangerous fashion they may be liable if they condone the negligence.[92] In each of these instances the employer is personally at fault. There are, however, a number of circumstances in which people may be liable for the negligence of an independent contractor without fault on their part. Here employers are said to be under a non-delegable duty, which means that they may delegate the performance of the duty to another, but not the responsibility for the manner in which the duty is performed. If the contractor is negligent it is the employer's primary duty to the claimant that is broken.[93] In this situation there is no "personal" fault by employers, and the concept of non-delegable duty simply means that they are liable for non-performance of the duty: it is no defence to show that they delegated the performance to another person, whether their employee or not, whom they reasonably believed to be competent to perform it.[94] The circumstances in which a non-delegable duty will be imposed are relatively fixed, but there is little in the way of guiding principle which determines precisely how and when such a duty arises.[95]

(a) Organisational errors

9–028 The notion that a hospital authority may be directly liable for negligence in the organisation of its services is not new. Actions have in the past been formulated in this way in order to overcome the argument that the hospital were not vicariously liable for the negligence of their professional staff. Thus, in *Vancouver General Hospital v McDaniel*[96] the claimant went into a hospital for infectious diseases

---

[89] *Ellis v Sheffield Gas Consumers Co* (1853) 2 E. & B. 767.
[90] *Pinn v Rew* (1916) 32 T.L.R. 451.
[91] *McLoughlin v Pryor* (1842) 4 M. & G. 48.
[92] *D & F Estates Ltd v Church Commissioners for England* [1989] A.C. 177 at 209.
[93] Sometimes referred to as a duty to see that care is taken, as opposed to a duty to exercise reasonable care: cf. *The Pass of Ballater* [1942] P. 112 at 117; and *Stennett v Hancock* [1939] 2 All E.R. 578.
[94] *McDermid v Nash Dredging and Reclamation Co Ltd* [1987] A.C. 906 at 919, per Lord Brandon.
[95] For discussion see McKendrick (1990) 53 M.L.R. 770. Though see *Woodland v Swimming Teachers Association* [2013] UKSC 66; [2014] A.C. 537, para.9–044.
[96] (1934) 152 L.T. 56.

for the treatment of diphtheria, and contracted smallpox. She claimed that the defendants were negligent in the system of infection control that they adopted, namely the juxtaposition of smallpox patients to the claimant, and the attendance on the claimant by nurses who also nursed smallpox patients. Lord Alness observed that the claimant had not alleged negligence on the part of an employee of the hospital:

> "The complaint is that the technique was adopted by the appellants, not that it failed in its execution. In other words, the case made against the appellant is one, not of vicarious, but of direct responsibility."[97]

This type of direct liability may take a number of forms. A hospital will be under a primary liability if it fails to provide suitable medical facilities or equipment,[98] or if it has been negligent in selecting incompetent staff.[99] A hospital also owes a duty to establish adequate procedures to safeguard patients from cross-infection,[100] and from the risk of errors in the administration of drugs.[101] In *Bull v Devon Area Health Authority*[102] the health authority were held liable for

9–029

---

[97] (1934) 152 L.T. 56 at 57.

[98] *Vuchar v Trustees of Toronto General Hospital* [1937] 1 D.L.R. 298 at 321, Ont CA, a case which applied *Hillyer v Governors of St. Bartholemews Hospital* [1909] 2 K.B. 820; *Goodwin v Olupona* 2013 ONCA 259; (2013) 228 A.C.W.S. (3d) 524 at [38]: "maintaining the physical plant and equipment at a level capable of meeting the patients' needs is the hospital's responsibility." *Denton v South West Thames Regional Health Authority* unreported 26 November 1980, QBD, on failing to have a system to check the safety of equipment. The provision of equipment clearly involves a duty to maintain the equipment in a safe working order: see e.g. *Stockford v Johnston Estate* 2008 NBQB 118; (2008) 57 C.C.L.T. (3d) 135—hospital liable for consequences of a failed sterilisation operation because it did not have the equipment used in the procedure calibrated, as recommended by the manufacturer.

[99] *Wilsher v Essex Area Health Authority* [1987] Q.B. 730 at 775, per Glidewell LJ. This was the limit of the hospital's duty in *Hillyer v Governors of St. Bartholemews Hospital* [1909] 2 K.B. 820. In *Brus v Australian Capital Territory* [2007] ACTSC 83 a hospital was held to be under a duty of care to ensure that the doctors that it engaged were are adequately and appropriately qualified to perform the services offered to patients. The hospital were in breach of that duty by holding out a doctor as a level 3 registrar when it knew that she was a level 2 registrar who had been rated as unsatisfactory for surgical skills at level 2. They had allowed the doctor "to perform a procedure that was clearly beyond the capacity of a second year trainee with adverse training assessments for surgical skills" (at [59]). Connolly J rejected the contention that "there is a general duty of care on a public hospital to in effect provide public patients with a choice of doctor, or to appraise a patient as to the academic standing of a registrar. However, there is a duty on a hospital to ensure that it provides patients with suitably qualified staff" (at [62]).

[100] *Vancouver General Hospital v McDaniel* (1934) 152 L.T. 56; *Lindsey County Council v Marshall* [1937] A.C. 97.

[101] *Collins v Hertfordshire County Council* [1947] 1 K.B. 598, where a hospital failed to bring to the attention of an unqualified junior medical officer the requirements of their routine procedures for having a written prescription signed by a qualified person. Hilbery J commented, at 614, that: "If they had had a proper system in operation, this solution could not have arrived at the theatre, let alone arrived at the body of the unfortunate patient." There may also be an obligation to have a system for informing patients about the side effects of drugs: see the discussion of *Blyth v Bloomsbury Health Authority* (1987), (1989) 5 P.N. 167; [1993] 4 Med. L.R. 151, CA, by Montgomery (1987) 137 N.L.J. 703.

[102] (1989), [1993] 4 Med. L.R. 117, CA; para.4–154. See also *Robertson v Nottingham Health Authority* [1997] 8 Med. L.R. 1 at 13, CA—systems of communication between staff are "essentially management as opposed to clinical matters"; para.9–040. For discussion of the duty with regard to hospital Accident & Emergency departments see paras 3–097 and 4–006.

instituting an unreliable system for calling expert assistance to an obstetric emergency. It was unclear precisely why the communication system had broken down, but the inference was that either there had been negligence in the operation of the system, or it was inadequate to cope with even minor hitches which it should have been possible to anticipate. This illustrates the point that a safety system may be either poorly designed or poorly implemented. Moreover, the stronger the evidence that the system is adequate to cope with all eventualities, the more compelling will be the inference that there must have been some negligence on the part of the hospital staff in implementing the procedure, for which the hospital authority will be vicariously liable.[103] The failure to enforce its own rules and regulations can amount to negligence on the part of the hospital.[104]

9–030   A hospital authority may be negligent by providing an inadequate number of staff to care safely for the patients,[105] or in permitting an inexperienced doctor to administer anaesthetics without proper supervision.[106] Similarly, employing too many inexperienced staff can amount to negligence by the hospital. In *Wilsher v Essex Area Health Authority* Browne-Wilkinson V-C said that:

> "In my judgment, a health authority which so conducts its hospital that it fails to provide doctors of sufficient skill and experience to give the treatment offered at the hospital may be directly liable in negligence to the patient. Although we were told in argument that no case has ever been decided on this ground and that it is not the practice to formulate claims in this way, I can see no reason why, in principle, the health authority should not be so liable if its organisation is at fault."[107]

---

[103] See Nathan, *Medical Negligence* (London: Butterworths, 1957), p.102; *Voller v Portsmouth Corporation* (1947) 203 L.T.J. 264. In practice it may be impossible to identify whether the system was inadequate or whether individuals have been careless in implementing it: see, e.g. *Cassidy v Ministry of Health* [1951] 2 K.B. 343 at 359, per Singleton LJ. This has the effect of blurring the distinction between the hospital's primary liability for organisational errors and vicarious liability.

[104] *Bergen v Sturgeon General Hospital* (1984) 28 C.C.L.T. 155, Alta QB, on inconsistency between the hospital's policy on the keeping of accurate notes and records and what happened in practice; *Bernier v Sisters of Service* [1948] 2 D.L.R. 468, Alta SC.

[105] *Laidlaw v Lions Gate Hospital* (1969) 8 D.L.R. (3d) 730, BCSC, where the hospital had provided a sufficient number of nurses per patient, but had failed to correct a lackadaisical attitude which had arisen among the nurses as to how many should be present in the post-anaesthesia recovery room; *Krujelis v Esdale* (1971) 25 D.L.R. (3d) 557, BCSC, where the hospital was held vicariously liable for the negligence of nurses, when three out of five on duty in the post-anaesthesia recovery room went for their coffee break together. Employing insufficient staff may mean that existing staff have to work excessive hours. If this results in harm to an employee's health the health authority may be liable in its capacity as an employer: see *Johnstone v Bloomsbury Health Authority* [1992] Q.B. 333.

[106] *Jones v Manchester Corporation* [1952] Q.B. 852; *Goodwin v Olupona* 2013 ONCA 259; (2013) 228 A.C.W.S. (3d) 524— error of inexperienced nurse on an obstetric ward attributable in part to hospital's failure to train and supervise its nurses; *Gottstein v Maguire and Walsh* [2004] IEHC 416; [2007] 4 I.R. 435—hospital held to be negligent in failing to have any staff in the intensive care unit who were trained to replace a tracheostomy tube if it became dislodged, despite the fact that such an occurrence was not uncommon and constituted an emergency; cf. *Hinfey v Salford Health Authority* [1993] 4 Med. L.R. 143, where it was held that the defendants were not negligent to permit an allegedly inexperienced obstetrician deliver a baby unsupervised.

[107] [1987] Q.B. 730 at 778 citing *McDermid v Nash Dredging and Reclamation Co Ltd* [1987] A.C. 906 a case in which the House of Lords subsequently applied the principle that an employer's duty with respect to the safety of employees is non-delegable. Glidewell LJ agreed, at 775: "that there seems to be no reason in principle why, in a suitable case different on its facts from this, a hospital management committee should not be held directly liable in negligence for failing to provide sufficient qualified and competent medical staff."

An individual patient could face considerable difficulty, however, in proving negligence on this basis, a point that Browne-Wilkinson V-C acknowledged:

"To what extent should the authority be held liable if (*e.g.* in the use of junior housemen) it is only adopting a practice hallowed by tradition? Should the authority be liable if it demonstrates that, due to the financial stringency under which it operates, it cannot afford to fill the posts with those possessing the necessary experience? But, in my judgment, the law should not be distorted by making findings of personal fault against individual doctors who are, in truth, not at fault in order to avoid such questions."[108]

(i)   Failure to provide adequate resources

In *Bull v Devon Area Health Authority*[109] Slade LJ considered that an allegation about inadequate levels of staffing would have to be judged according to professional standards at the time, applying the *Bolam* test,[110] and Dillon LJ simply commented that the level of staffing should be "reasonably sufficient for the foreseeable requirements of the patient".[111] Mustill LJ had some reservations, however, about the argument that the hospital authority could not be expected to do more than their best, allocating their limited resources as favourably as possible. Although public medicine might not be precisely analogous to other public services, there was a danger in assuming that it was sui generis, and that it was necessarily a complete answer to say that even if the system in any hospital was unsatisfactory, it was no more unsatisfactory than those in force elsewhere.[112] Similarly, in *Re HIV Haemophiliac Litigation*[113] Ralph Gibson LJ said that although it was difficult to prove negligence when the defendant was required to exercise discretion and form judgments on the allocation of public resources, that was not sufficient to make it clear that there could be no claim in negligence.

9–031

An action in negligence against a hospital authority which alleges that the claimant sustained injury through an inadequate provision of resources, whether it be staff, equipment, or funds for drugs, would have to prove that the lack of resources was a consequence of negligence in the *organisation* of the hospital

9–032

---

108 [1987] Q.B. 730 at 778.

109 (1989), [1993] 4 Med. L.R. 117, CA.

110 On the differences in the standards of care that can be expected at different hospitals see: *Koerber v Trustees of the Kitchener-Waterloo Hospital* (1987) 62 O.R. (2d) 613, Ont HC; *Bateman v Doiron* (1993) 18 C.C.L.T. (2d) 1, NBCA, para.4–154, n.520.

111 Though the fact that an emergency is foreseeable does not necessarily mean that it is negligent to fail to take precautions against it. In *Garcia v St Mary's NHS Trust* [2006] EWHC 2314 (QB); [2011] Med. L.R. 348 at [94]–[96] it was held that the hospital was not negligent in failing to have a surgical registrar on site to deal with a cardiac emergency following coronary bypass surgery when such an emergency was rare (one in a thousand), given the resources available at the hospital. The case is commented on by Beswick, "A First Class Service? Setting the Standard of Care for the Contemporary NHS" (2007) 15 Med. L. Rev. 245.

112 See para.4–154. See also *Knight v Home Office* [1990] 3 All E.R. 237 at 243, para.4–152 where Pill J said that the lack of resources to provide a better staff/patient ratio was not necessarily a complete defence. Lack of funds would not justify a failure to provide *any* medical facilities for prisoners in a large prison.

113 (1990), [1996] P.I.Q.R. P220; see also *Brown v Alberta* [1994] 2 W.W.R. 283, Alta QB.

itself.[114] It is not sufficient simply to point to the lack of resources, since this may well be a consequence of resource allocation decisions over which the hospital has no control. Moreover, challenges on public law grounds to decisions about resource allocation made by the Secretary of State or individual health authorities have been notably unsuccessful.

(ii) Public law challenges to resource allocation decisions

9–033   An earlier version of s.3 of the National Health Service Act 2006, which itself was derived from s.3 of the National Health Service Act 1977, placed a duty on the Secretary of State to provide throughout England, to such extent as he considered necessary to meet all reasonable requirements, inter alia, hospital accommodation; medical, dental, ophthalmic, nursing and ambulance services; services for the diagnosis and treatment of illness; facilities for the prevention of illness, the care and aftercare of persons suffering from illness and facilities for the care of expectant and nursing mothers and young children. Amendments to the 2006 Act introduced by the Health and Social Care Act 2012 now place this s.3 duty on Clinical Commissioning Groups, bodies corporate established by 2012 Act. The duty has been held to be limited by reference to the resources made available to the National Health Service in order to meet the healthcare needs of the population. It does not provide a "blank cheque" for patients who believe that resources should be allocated to deal with their particular medical condition. In *R. v Secretary of State for Social Services, Ex p. Hincks*[115] four patients, who had been waiting for orthopaedic operations for some years, sought to challenge a decision to postpone the expansion of a local hospital due to the cost, relying on s.3. The application for judicial review failed. Lord Denning MR said that additional words had to be implied into s.3(1) which should read: "to such extent as he considers necessary to meet all reasonable requirements *such as can be provided within the resources available*." Bridge LJ commented that there must be some limitation on the resources available to finance the health service and that limitation must be determined in the light of the current government economic policy. That was an implication which must be read into s.3(1). Similar wording is to be found in the current version of s.3.[116]

9–034   This approach was followed in two cases where parents sought to require a hospital to provide the facilities and staff necessary to perform heart surgery on

---

[114] In *Wilsher v Essex Area Health Authority* [1987] Q.B. 730 at 778 Browne-Wilkinson V-C said: "... I can see no reason why, in principle, the health authority should not be so liable *if its organisation is at fault*" (emphasis added). See Montgomery (1987) 137 N.L.J. 703 at 705 who comments that: "To hold health authorities liable for inadequate systems would provide a mechanism whereby managers can be made accountable for the effects which their activities have on patient care."

[115] (1979) 123 S.J. 436; aff'd (1980) 1 B.M.L.R. 93, CA.

[116] Section 3(1) provides that: "A clinical commissioning group must arrange for the provision of the following *to such extent as it considers necessary to meet the reasonable requirements of* the persons for whom it has responsibility ..." (emphasis added).

two young children. Both applications for judicial review were unsuccessful. In *R. v Central Birmingham Health Authority Ex p. Walker*[117] Sir John Donaldson MR said that:

> "It is not for this court, or indeed for any court, to substitute its own judgment for the judgment of those who are responsible for the allocation of resources. This court could only intervene where it was satisfied that there was a prima facie case, not only of failing to allocate resources in the way in which others would think that resources should be allocated, but a failure to allocate resources to an extent which was *Wednesbury* unreasonable ... [T]he jurisdiction does exist. But it has to be used extremely sparingly."

Subsequently, in *R. v Central Birmingham Health Authority Ex p. Collier*[118] Stephen Brown LJ considered that this would be the position even if the medical evidence were to establish that there was immediate danger to the child's health. Ralph Gibson LJ commented that the courts have no role as a general investigator of social policy and of the allocation of resources. Rather, the court's jurisdiction was limited to dealing with breaches of duty under law, including decisions made by public authorities which are shown to be unreasonable.

These cases make it clear that an action which alleges that the failure to provide adequate resources constitutes negligence would be unlikely to succeed. Decisions about the allocation of resources are made under statutory powers which confer a broad discretion on decision-makers. A claim that such a decision has been taken negligently must first establish that the discretion was exercised ultra vires the statutory power, applying public law principles,[119] but the courts are reluctant to make such a finding in the context of health resources.[120] Where,

9–035

---

[117] (1987) 3 B.M.L.R. 32 at 35–36, CA.
[118] Unreported 6 January 1988, CA. See also *R. v Cambridge Health Authority Ex p. B.* [1995] 1 W.L.R. 898, CA; *R. (on the application of Longstaff) v Newcastle NHS Primary Care Trust* [2003] EWHC 3252 (Admin); [2004] Lloyd's Rep. Med. 400; *R. (on the application of K) v West London Mental Health NHS Trust* [2006] EWCA Civ 118; [2006] 1 W.L.R. 1865 at [56] where Dyson LJ commented: "The duty of the Secretary of State [under s.3 of the NHS Act] is to provide hospital accommodation etc to such extent as *he* considers necessary to meet all reasonable requirements. These words are clear and unequivocal. It is for the Secretary of State to make a judgment of what is necessary to meet all reasonable requirements. That involves taking into account resource implications (see paras 46 and 47 above). It also involves establishing priorities (comparing the respective needs of patients suffering from different illnesses and determining the respective strengths of their claims to treatment) as well as the proven success or otherwise of the proposed treatment and the seriousness of the condition that the treatment is intended to relieve" (original emphasis). Note that the duty under s.3 of the NHS Act 2006 now applies to clinical commissioning groups (CCG) rather than the Secretary of State (following amendments introduced by the Health and Social Care Act 2012) though a CCG must act consistently with the discharge by the Secretary of State of the duties imposed by s.1 of the 2006 Act.
[119] See *Anns v Merton London Borough Council* [1978] A.C. 728 at 754; *Dorset Yacht Co Ltd v Home Office* [1970] A.C. 1004 at 1067; *X (Minors) v Bedfordshire County Council* [1995] 2 A.C. 633 at 736–737, though Lord Browne-Wilkinson said that it was not a question of whether the decision was ultra vires, but whether it was outside the ambit of the public authority's discretion. See further para.10–017 for discussion of the distinction between policy and operational decisions.
[120] A decision to refuse funding for a medical procedure where there is little evidence of clinical benefit will be lawful, given that the defendants had a statutory responsibility to break even in each financial year, and had to make very difficult choices as to what procedures to fund: *R. (on the application of C) v Berkshire West Primary Care Trust* [2011] EWCA Civ 247; [2011] Med. L.R. 226; (2011) 119 B.M.L.R. 135. On the other hand, a health authority cannot refuse to provide treatment

however, it can be proved that the health authority has failed to establish any policy about the allocation of resources for a particular treatment or has adopted a blanket policy which is applied rigidly, without reference to the circumstances of the particular case, it is more likely that the authority will be held to have acted ultra vires.[121]

9–036   **Human rights**   It is arguable that where the decision challenged by an applicant for judicial review engages the applicant's rights under the European Convention on Human Rights, the court should undertake a full "merits review" of that decision, and not limit itself to considering whether the decision fell within the range of reasonable decisions that a reasonable public authority could take (as would be required under a *Wednesbury* review). This seems to be the effect of the decision of the Court of Appeal in *R. (on the application of W) v Broadmoor Hospital*,[122] although the standard of review is dependent upon the context in which the decision has been taken.[123] But in *North West Lancashire Health Authority v A, D and G*[124] the Court of Appeal was critical of the applicants' resort to arguments about human rights. The suggestion that the failure to provide medical treatment as part of a general policy of setting

---

that would be provided to other patients merely because the patient has the means to pay for the treatment privately out of an award of damages: *R. (on the application of Booker) v NHS Oldham* [2010] EWHC 2593 (Admin); [2011] Med. L.R. 10 (see also National Health Service Act 2006 s.1(4), stating that "services provided as part of the health service in England must be free of charge except in so far as the making and recovery of charges is expressly provided for by or under any enactment").

[121] See *R. v North Derbyshire Health Authority Ex p. Fisher* [1997] 8 Med. L.R. 327—failure of a health authority to establish a policy for the provision of a drug (beta-interferon) for the treatment of multiple sclerosis in accordance with guidance issued by the Department of Health; *North West Lancashire Health Authority v A, D and G* [2000] 1 W.L.R. 977; [1999] Lloyd's Rep. Med. 399—a policy to accord cases of transsexualism lower priority in the allocation of funding than other medical conditions, and refuse treatment save in exceptional cases, was not irrational, but such a policy must have genuine regard for individual clinical needs and recognise the possibility of exceptional cases. Each request for treatment should be considered on its individual merits; *R. (on the application of Rogers) v Swindon NHS Primary Care Trust* [2006] EWCA Civ 392; [2006] 1 W.L.R. 2649; [2006] Lloyd's Rep. Med. 364—policy of refusing to fund a drug for treatment of early stage cancer except in exceptional circumstances held unlawful because in practice it was a blanket policy; *R. (on the application of Ross) v West Sussex Primary Care Trust* [2008] EWHC 2252 (Admin); (2008) 106 B.M.L.R. 1—policy of refusing to treat patient's application for exceptional funding for drug treatment of cancer where a patient was "representative of a group of patients" held to be unlawful because the policy was self-contradictory in that it effectively required the patient to be "unique" rather than exceptional; *R. (on the application of Rose) v Thanet Clinical Commissioning Group* [2014] EWHC 1182 (Admin); (2014) 138 B.M.L.R. 101—clinical commissioning group did not have to follow NICE guidelines when making a decision about funding treatment in exceptional circumstances but had to give clear reasons for any general policy that did not follow it, and could not refuse to follow the guidelines simply because it disagreed with the medical or scientific evidence on the effectiveness of the treatment.

[122] [2001] EWCA Civ 1545; [2002] 1 W.L.R. 419 at [24], [59] and [62]. See the discussion at para.6–094.

[123] See *R. v Secretary of State for the Home Department Ex p. Daly* [2001] UKHL 26; [2001] A.C. 532.

[124] [2000] 1 W.L.R. 977; [1999] Lloyd's Rep. Med. 399. See also *R. (on the application of Condliff) v North Staffordshire Primary Care Trust* [2011] EWCA Civ 910; [2012] 1 All E.R. 689—defendants entitled to reject application from morbidly obese patient for funding of gastric bypass surgery since its policy of considering only clinical need, and refusing to take into account non-clinical, social factors was not a breach of art.8.

priorities for healthcare constituted a breach of art.3 of the Convention (prohibiting torture and inhuman or degrading treatment) trivialised that article and the important values that it protects. And though art.8 (the right to respect for private and family life) could be engaged in such a case, the jurisprudence on art.8 did not suggest that there was a positive obligation on states to provide medical treatment.

(b)   Non-delegable duty[125]

There are two grounds for suggesting that a hospital authority owes a non-delegable duty to patients in the hospital, the first deriving from the common law and the second from statute.

9–037

(i)   Common law

In *Cassidy v Ministry of Health*[126] Denning LJ asserted that hospital authorities were under a primary, non-delegable duty to patients, at least where doctors or surgeons, whether consultants or not, were employed and paid, not by patients but by the hospital authorities. It was irrelevant whether the contract under which they were employed was a contract of service or a contract for services; the hospital authorities were liable for their negligence in treating patients:

9–038

"...the hospital authorities accepted the plaintiff as a patient for treatment, and it was their duty to treat him with reasonable care. They selected, employed, and paid all the surgeons and nurses who looked after him. He had no say in their selection at all. If those surgeons and nurses did not treat him with proper care and skill, then the hospital authorities must answer for it, for it means that they themselves did not perform their duty to him. I decline to enter into the question whether any of the surgeons were employed only under a contract for services, as distinct from a contract of service. The evidence is meagre enough in all conscience on that point. But the liability of the hospital authorities should not, and does not, depend on nice considerations of that sort. The plaintiff knew nothing of the terms on which they employed their staff: all he knew was that he was treated in the hospital by people whom the hospital authorities appointed; and the hospital authorities must be answerable for the way in which he was treated."[127]

His Lordship repeated this view in both *Roe v Minister of Health*[128] and in *Jones v Manchester Corporation*.[129] The authority of this proposition remained uncertain, since the majority of the Court of Appeal in both *Cassidy* and *Roe* proceeded on the basis that the doctors concerned were employees for whom the health authority would be vicariously liable.[130] But in *X (Minors) v Bedfordshire County Council* Lord Browne-Wilkinson appeared to confirm Lord Denning's approach when he said that:

9–039

---

[125] See P. Giliker, "Non-delegable duties and institutional liability for the negligence of hospital staff: fair, just and reasonable?" (2017) 33 P.N. 109.

[126] [1951] 2 K.B. 343 at 362–365.

[127] [1951] 2 K.B. 343 at 365.

[128] [1954] 2 Q.B. 66 at 82.

[129] [1952] Q.B. 852 at 869.

[130] See the comments of Lord Jauncey in *Esso Petroleum Co Ltd v Hall Russell and Co Ltd* [1989] A.C. 643 at 686–687.

"It is established that those conducting a hospital are under a direct duty of care to those admitted as patients to the hospital (I express no view as to the extent of that duty). They are liable for the negligent acts of a member of the hospital staff which constitute a breach of that duty, whether or not the member of staff is himself in breach of a separate duty of care owed by him to the plaintiff."[131]

In *Woodland v Swimming Teachers Association*[132] Lord Sumption said that:

"..the time has come to recognise that Lord Greene in *Gold* and Denning LJ in *Cassidy* were correct in identifying the underlying principle",

and Baroness Hale agreed, observing that this provided a "ready answer to the examples of the agency nurse and the supply teacher".[133]

9–040   In *Robertson v Nottingham Health Authority*[134] the Court of Appeal held that a hospital has a "non-delegable duty" to establish a proper system of care, just as much as it has a duty to engage competent staff and a duty to provide proper and safe equipment and safe premises: "A health authority owes its patient a duty to provide her with a reasonable regime of care at its hospital."[135] A reasonable regime of care meant:

"…a regime of a standard that can reasonably be expected of a hospital of the size and type in question—in the present case a large teaching centre of excellence."[136]

The problem in *Robertson* concerned a breakdown in communications between staff. As in *Bull v Devon Area Health Authority*,[137] the Court of Appeal held that a hospital authority owes a duty to a patient to provide her with a reasonable regime of a standard that can reasonably be expected of a hospital of the size and type in question. If there was an effective system in place, then the hospital would be vicariously liable for the negligence of any member of staff who did not take reasonable care to see that that the system worked efficiently; whereas if there was no effective system in place, the hospital would be directly liable in negligence for the lacuna. Thus:

"…if a patient is injured by reason of a negligent breakdown in the systems for communicating material information to the clinicians responsible for her care, she is not to be denied redress merely because no identifiable person or persons are to blame for deficiencies in setting up and monitoring the effectiveness of the relevant communication systems. She is entitled to say, like the successful plaintiff in *Bull*: 'You, the health authority were responsible for my care: you are responsible if there is a breakdown, reasonably attributable to improper practice, in the

---

[131] [1995] 2 A.C. 633 at 740, citing *Gold v Essex County Council* [1942] 2 K.B. 293 at 301, per Lord Greene; *Cassidy v Ministry of Health* [1951] 2 K.B. 343, per Denning LJ; *Roe v Minister of Health* [1954] 2 Q.B. 66; *Wilsons & Clyde Coal Co Ltd v English* [1938] A.C. 57; and *McDermid v Nash Dredging and Reclamation Co Ltd* [1987] A.C. 906.
[132] [2013] UKSC 66; [2014] A.C. 537 at [23].
[133] [2013] UKSC 66; [2014] A.C. 537 at [37].
[134] [1997] 8 Med. L.R. 1, CA.
[135] [1997] 8 Med. L.R. 1 at 13, citing *Gold v Essex County Council* [1942] 2 K.B. 293, *Roe v Minister of Health* [1954] 2 Q.B. 66, and *Cassidy v Ministry of Health* [1951] 2 K.B. 343.
[136] [1997] 8 Med. L.R. 1 at 13.
[137] (1989), [1993] 4 Med. L.R. 117, CA.

systems used at your hospital for communicating material information to the clinicians responsible for my care: and I was injured as a result of this negligence.'"[138]

The application of the principle of a non-delegable duty can be seen in the county court decision of *M v Calderdale & Kirklees Health Authority*.[139] The claimant was sent by her general practitioner to a private clinic for a termination of pregnancy which was carried out negligently, with the result that she subsequently gave birth to a healthy child. The defendants argued that the limit of their duty was to exercise reasonable care to select a competent private clinic. That view was rejected (though on the facts, it was arguable that they had failed even in that respect—the defendants had no idea whether the clinic had insurance, no up-to-date information about the competence of staff at the clinic, and could not produce the contract with the clinic). The judge held that the NHS is under a non-delegable duty and therefore was responsible for the negligence of the clinic.[140] The health authority had a duty to bring about the effective provision of services, either by providing the services themselves or securing others to provide them on their behalf. The claimant had "never left the care of" the health authority. She had not had an opportunity to divert from the route of treatment arranged on her behalf, and should not be in a worse position than a patient who remained "in-house". Thus, her rights and remedies should be the same.

9–041

In *A (A Child) v Ministry of Defence*[141] Bell J was critical of the decision in *M v Calderdale & Kirklees Health Authority*, suggesting that it had gone much further than anything said in *Gold* or *Cassidy*. In the Court of Appeal in *A v Ministry of Defence*[142] Lord Phillips MR agreed with Bell J's view:

9–042

"This finding [in *Calderdale*] did not represent the current state of English law. It seems to have been based on the observations of Lord Greene MR in *Gold* and of Denning LJ in *Cassidy*, although in neither instance did these represent the reasons for the decision of the majority of the court."

---

[138] [1997] 8 Med. L.R. 1 at 13. See also *Collins v Mid-Western Health Board* [2000] 2 I.R. 154, Supreme Court of Ireland, discussed at para.3–123, a case concerning a systems failure in the admission of a patient to hospital. In *A v Ministry of Defence* [2004] EWCA Civ 641; [2005] Q.B. 183 at [32] Lord Phillips MR described the non-delegable duty found in *Robertson v Nottingham Health Authority* as an "organisational duty", i.e. a "duty to use reasonable care to ensure that the hospital staff, facilities and organisation provided are those appropriate to provide a safe and satisfactory medical service for the patient". This was distinct from a non-delegable duty to: "ensure that the treatment administered by the hospital to the patient is administered with reasonable skill and care. This duty will be broken if one of the hospital staff, however competent, commits an isolated act of negligence in the treatment of the patient." In *Farraj v King's Healthcare NHS Trust* [2009] EWCA Civ 1203; [2010] 1 W.L.R. 2139 at [79] Dyson LJ suggested that the statement of Brooke LJ in *Robertson v Nottingham Health Authority* that the hospital owed a non-delegable duty was probably obiter, and that the ratio of the decision was Brooke LJ's statement that "if a patient is injured by reason of a negligent breakdown in the systems for communicating material information to the clinicians responsible for her care, she is not to be denied redress merely because no identifiable person or persons are to blame".
[139] [1998] Lloyd's Rep. Med. 157, Huddersfield County Court.
[140] Again, applying *Gold v Essex County Council* [1942] 2 K.B. 293 and the dictum of Denning LJ in *Cassidy v Ministry of Health* [1951] 2 K.B. 343 at 365.
[141] [2003] EWHC 849 (QB); [2003] Lloyd's Rep. Med. 339; [2003] P.I.Q.R. P607 at [53].
[142] [2004] EWCA Civ 641; [2005] Q.B. 183 at [52].

On the other hand, later in his judgment Lord Phillips appeared to accept the a hospital could owe a non-delegable duty in respect of the treatment that it provided in the hospital itself, so that it would be irrelevant whether the professional who was negligent was engaged as an employee or an independent contractor:

> "It seems to me that there are strong arguments of policy for holding that a hospital, which offers treatment to a patient, accepts responsibility for the care with which that treatment is administered, regardless of the status of the person employed or engaged to deliver the treatment. Lord Browne Wilkinson in *X v Bedfordshire* proceeded on the premise that this is established English law."[143]

M v Calderdale & Kirklees Health Authority had gone too far in suggesting that there could be a non-delegable duty in respect of the treatment provided by another organisation (such as the private clinic in that case), though the hospital would be under a duty to exercise reasonable care in selecting another organisation to provide medical care.

9–043   In *Farraj v King's Healthcare NHS Trust*[144] Dyson LJ, having reviewed these cases, was prepared to assume (without deciding) that English law had reached the stage that it could be said that a hospital owes a non-delegable duty to ensure that its patients are treated with due skill and care:

> "I shall assume that a hospital generally owes a non-delegable duty to its patients to ensure that they are treated with skill and care regardless of the employment status of the person who is treating them. As explained in *Kondis*,[145] the rationale for this is that the hospital undertakes the care, supervision and control of its patients who are in special need of care. Patients are a vulnerable class of persons who place themselves in the care and under the control of a hospital and, as a result, the hospital assumes a particular responsibility for their well-being and safety. To use the language of *Caparo Industries plc v Dickman* [1990] 2 A.C. 605, 618A it is therefore fair just and reasonable that a hospital should owe such a duty of care to its patients in these circumstances."

In *Farraj* a hospital (KCH) was asked by a hospital in Jordan to undertake a DNA test on foetal cells for an inherited blood disorder. KCH sent the sample to a private cytogenetics laboratory (CSL) which, for a fee, cultured the cells and returned them to KCH for DNA analysis. A technician at CSL had doubts about whether the sample sent for culture contained foetal cells, but those doubts were not communicated to KCH and KCH did not query whether the sample was satisfactory. The cultured sample was tested at KCH and the parents were informed that the test for the disease was negative. After the birth it was discovered that the child had the disease. The parents brought an action for wrongful birth. The trial judge found that both KCH and CSL had been negligent, but on appeal it was held that KCH was not negligent in that it was entitled to rely on a clearly understood arrangement, namely that it would be assumed that the

---

[143] [2004] EWCA Civ 641; [2005] Q.B. 183 at [63].
[144] [2009] EWCA Civ 1203; [2010] 1 W.L.R. 2139 at [88]; discussed by Lyons [2010] J.P.I.L. C9; R. Nayer, "Outsourcing genetic and diagnostic services: a consideration of the principles for establishing a hospital's non-delegable duty and why it matters" [2011] J.P.I.L. 61; R. Heywood "Non-delegable duties and hospitals" (2010) 26 P.N. 49. For comment by the respective lawyers involved in this case see Gillings (2010) 16 Clinical Risk 119 and Shaw (2010) 16 Clinical Risk 157.
[145] *Kondis v State Transport Authority* (1984) 55 A.L.R. 225.

sample was satisfactory unless CSL informed it otherwise. It followed that CSL was solely responsible. The claimants also argued that KCH owed them a non-delegable duty of care in conducting the test and that KCH was therefore also liable for the negligence of CSL. The Court of Appeal rejected the argument. Even assuming that a hospital owes a non-delegable duty to its patients the parents were not patients of KCH; they had not been admitted to KCH for treatment. KCH provided diagnostic and interpretative services but those services could have been provided by a specialist laboratory. There was a significant difference between providing a testing service for someone who was not a patient and carrying out tests on samples which are provided by a patient. Dyson LJ was prepared to accept that:

> "...if a patient who is admitted to hospital for treatment has tests carried out in the hospital, then the non-delegable duty of care, which for present purposes I am assuming to exist, would extend to the carrying out of the tests. But that is because the conducting of the tests is part of the treatment that the patient is receiving in the hospital."[146]

The general rule, said Dyson LJ, is that duty to take reasonable care may be discharged by entrusting the performance of a task to an apparently competent independent contractor, and any departure from the general rule must be justified on policy grounds. On the facts of *Farraj* there were no policy reasons for departing from the general rule.

Criteria for a non-delegable duty   In *Woodland v Swimming Teachers Association*[147] Lord Sumption considered that the decision of the Court of Appeal in *Farraj* was correct. In *Woodland* itself the Supreme Court held that a school owed a non-delegable duty with respect to the safety of its pupils and though performance of the school's educational functions could be delegated to others, responsibility for negligence in carrying out those functions could not. Lord Sumption took the opportunity to identify some of the criteria for the existence of a non-delegable duty. Putting to one side cases involving "extra-hazardous" activity and dangers on the highway, the remaining cases were said to be characterised by the following defining features:

9–044

---

146 [2009] EWCA Civ 1203; [2010] 1 W.L.R. 2139 at [92]. See further *S v Lothian Health Board* [2009] CSOH 97; 2009 S.L.T. 689 where Lady Stacey allowed a proof before answer in a case where a pregnant woman was offered a screening test for cystic fibrosis which was reported as negative but she subsequently gave birth to a boy who suffered from cystic fibrosis. The test was carried out as part of a research study being conducted by the University of Edinburgh, was not funded by the health board or the hospital, and was performed by an employee of the University of Edinburgh, not the hospital. On the other hand, the pursuer had been referred to the hospital for standard antenatal care and had been given a leaflet at the hospital inviting her to have the test. There was nothing in the leaflet indicating that the analysis would be carried out by anybody other than the hospital. The leaflet also stated that if the test was positive the hospital would arrange further testing and may offer the patient a termination of pregnancy. There was nothing in the leaflet suggesting that the offer of the test was unusual or some type of "extra" that was not normally offered in maternity care at the time. It was at least arguable that the hospital had assumed responsibility for the wellbeing of the patient and that it would be fair, just and reasonable to impose a duty of care.
147 [2013] UKSC 66, [2014] A.C. 537 at [24].

"(1)   The claimant is a patient or a child, or for some other reason is especially vulnerable or dependent on the protection of the defendant against the risk of injury.[148] Other examples are likely to be prisoners and residents in care homes.

(2)   There is an antecedent relationship between the claimant and the defendant, independent of the negligent act or omission itself, (i) which places the claimant in the actual custody, charge or care of the defendant, and (ii) from which it is possible to impute to the defendant the assumption of a positive duty to protect the claimant from harm, and not just a duty to refrain from conduct which will foreseeably damage the claimant. It is characteristic of such relationships that they involve an element of control over the claimant, which varies in intensity from one situation to another, but is clearly very substantial in the case of schoolchildren.

(3)   The claimant has no control over how the defendant chooses to perform those obligations, i.e. whether personally or through employees or through third parties.

(4)   The defendant has delegated to a third party some function which is an integral part of the positive duty which he has assumed towards the claimant; and the third party is exercising, for the purpose of the function thus delegated to him, the defendant's custody or care of the claimant and the element of control that goes with it.

(5)   The third party has been negligent not in some collateral respect but in the performance of the very function assumed by the defendant and delegated by the defendant to him."[149]

9–045   **Lack of control of environment irrelevant**   Control of the environment in which the injury was sustained is not an essential element. Defendants are liable under a non-delegable duty not because they have control of the environment but in spite of the fact that they may have none. The essential element is "control over the claimant for the purpose of performing a function for which the defendant has assumed responsibility".[150] In *Woodland* the claimant was a 10-year-old pupil who sustained severe brain damage in the course of a swimming lesson arranged by the school but provided and supervised by an independent contractor. The school owed a non-delegable duty because it exercised control over pupils, who were both vulnerable and highly dependent on the observance of proper standards of care by those in control, so that when a school delegated control to a third party it was reasonable that the school should be answerable for the careful exercise of that control. The duty applies only where an independent contractor is performing functions which the school has *assumed* a duty to perform. The swimming lessons were an integral part of the school's teaching function and the negligence occurred in the course of the very functions which the school had assumed an obligation to perform and had delegated to its contractors.[151]

9–046   **Assuming duty to vulnerable claimant**   In *GB v Home Office*[152] Coulson J held that the Home Office had undertaken a non-delegable duty in relation to the provision of medical care to detainees held in an immigration removal centre.

---

[148] As Giliker points out: "The express reference to patients ... indicates that, at the very least, it will impose on hospitals a non-delegable duty to ensure that a patient receives treatment administered with reasonable care and skill": P. Giliker, "Non-delegable duties and institutional liability for the negligence of hospital staff: fair, just and reasonable?" (2017) 33 P.N. 109, 115.

[149] [2013] UKSC 66, [2014] A.C. 537 at [23].

[150] [2013] UKSC 66, [2014] A.C. 537 at [24].

[151] For comment on *Woodland* see J. Morgan, "Liability for independent contractors in contract and tort: duties to ensure that care is taken" (2015) 74 C.L.J. 109; R. George, "Non-delegable duties of care in tort" (2014) 130 L.Q.R. 534; Fulbrook [2014] J.P.I.L. C1.

[152] [2015] EWHC 819 (QB).

The centre was run by Serco on behalf of the Home Office. The claimant was prescribed an anti-malarial drug by a local general practitioner because the Home Office was proposing to return her to Nigeria, and the rules required the prescription of anti-malarial drugs to detainees who might be sent back to countries where malaria is commonplace. It was alleged that the claimant suffered a psychosis triggered by the anti-malarial drug. Coulson J applied *Woodland v Swimming Teachers Association*. The claimant was vulnerable. Lord Sumption had referred to prisoners as an example of a vulnerable group, and there was no meaningful distinction to be drawn between a prisoner and a detainee in an immigration removal centre. Both were held against their will and cannot leave the place where they are detained. Detainees are dependent on the protection of the defendant. There was a significant element of control. The claimant was obliged to accept the medical treatment she was given. There was no free choice. The provision of medical care was an integral part of the positive duty owed by the defendant to the claimant, the performance of which had been delegated to Serco. The claimant argued that it should make no difference to the defendant's duty that the defendant had chosen to outsource the running of the detention centre to an independent contractor. Coulson J agreed:

"The out-sourcing should be irrelevant in law. Rather, it should not be for GB to have to try and work out which private contractor or individual doctor might be liable for which failure, and then litigate on the basis of that assessment. She was detained by the defendant; she was in the defendant's control; she was entitled to look to the defendant for proper protection. If she did not receive it, the defendant was in breach of its duty. Accordingly, for all these reasons, I conclude that the imposition of a non-delegable duty in this case is fair, just and reasonable."[153]

The defendant had decided to detain the claimant and so had clear responsibilities for her treatment as a detainee. It would not be just, fair or reasonable to conclude that those responsibilities disappeared simply because of an outsourcing decision.[154]

On the other hand, in *NA v Nottinghamshire CC*[155] the Court of Appeal concluded   **9–047**
that a local authority did not owe a non-delegable duty in respect of decisions to place the claimant with foster parents, and so was not responsible for alleged physical and sexual abuse while the claimant was placed with two foster families. Tomlinson LJ considered that to be non-delegable a duty must relate to a function which the delegator has assumed a duty to perform, but fostering is not something that can be done by a local authority. Accordingly, by arranging the foster placement the local authority had discharged rather than delegated its duty to provide accommodation and maintenance for the child.[156] Burnett LJ took the

---

[153] [2015] EWHC 819 (QB) at [42].
[154] [2015] EWHC 819 (QB) at [43]. Coulson J recognised that he was differing from the decision of Supperstone J in *Morgan v Ministry of Justice* [2010] EWHC 2248 (QB) (no non-delegable duty owed by Ministry of Justice in respect of medical care provided by the local NHS primary care trust to a prisoner detained in prison) and that the facts of *Morgan* were too close to the facts in *GB* to be sensibly distinguished. But *Morgan* had not survived the decision of the Supreme Court in *Woodland*.
[155] [2015] EWCA Civ 1139; [2016] Q.B. 739; S. Tofaris, "Vicarious Liability and Non-Delegable Duty for Child Abuse in Foster Care: A Step Too Far?" (2016) 79 M.L.R. 884.
[156] [2015] EWCA Civ 1139; [2016] Q.B. 739 at [24].

view that the cases on non-delegable duties were all about negligence, not assault. It was difficult to envisage circumstances in which the court could conclude that there was no vicarious liability for an assault but then go on to fix a defendant with liability for breach of a non-delegable duty not to assault the claimant. Black LJ was more sanguine about the possibility of a non-delegable duty in relation to assault in circumstances where the defendant was not vicariously liable for the assault, but concluded that in *NA* imposing a non-delegable duty on a local authority would be unreasonably burdensome. It would have the effect of scarce resources being used in an attempt to ensure that nothing went wrong and would lead to defensive practice in relation to the placement of children with foster parents. The Supreme Court agreed that a local authority does not owe a non-delegable duty in respect of the abuse of childen placed with foster parents.[157] A non-delegable duty might create a conflict between the authority's interests in avoiding potential liabilty, and would amount to a form of state insurance for the actions of the child's family members.

9–048   **Australia**   The view that the liability of a hospital to a patient is based on a personal non-delegable duty has been approved, obiter, on two occasions by the High Court of Australia.[158] In *Ellis v Wallsend District Hospital*,[159] the one Australian case which has had to decide the issue, the New South Wales Court of Appeal was divided as to whether a non-delegable duty arose on the facts. The majority (Samuels and Meagher JJA) distinguished between a hospital which functions merely as a provider of facilities pursuant to an arrangement between the doctor and the hospital, and a hospital which functions as a place where a person in need of treatment goes to obtain treatment.[160] In the latter case a non-delegable duty could arise,[161] but such a duty:

"...does not extend to treatment which is performed by a doctor pursuant to a direct engagement with the patient, and not on behalf of the hospital."[162]

The basis for establishing a non-delegable duty lies in the nature of the relationship between the patient and the hospital. Where the patient goes directly

---

[157] *Armes v Nottinghamshire County Council* [2017] UKSC 60. Note, however, that the Supreme Court held that the local authority could be *vicariously* liable for the abuse of children placed in the care of foster parents. See para.9-007, n.17

[158] *Commonwealth v Introvigne* (1982) 56 A.L.J.R. 749 at 755; *Kondis v State Transport Authority* (1984) 55 A.L.R. 225 at 234. The possibility of establishing a personal non-delegable duty owed by a hospital to a patient was accepted by the New South Wales Court of Appeal in *Albrighton v Royal Prince Alfred Hospital* [1980] 2 N.S.W.L.R. 542 at 561–562, although this would depend upon the facts proved. See further Whippy (1989) 63 A.L.J. 182.

[159] (1989) 17 N.S.W.L.R. 553, CA; Nicholson (1990) 6 P.N. 83.

[160] Relying on the judgment of Houlden JA in *Yepremian v Scarborough General Hospital* (1980) 110 D.L.R. (3d) 513 at 581, Ont CA.

[161] Thus, accounting for the dicta in *Albrighton v Royal Prince Alfred Hospital* [1980] 2 N.S.W.L.R. 542 at 561–562, which was a case where the patient had gone directly to the hospital for treatment.

[162] (1989) 17 N.S.W.L.R. 553 at 604. Denning LJ would have agreed that where the patient himself selects and employs the doctor or surgeon, the hospital authorities are not liable for his negligence, because he is not employed by them: *Cassidy v Ministry of Health* [1951] 2 K.B. 343 at 362.

to the hospital for advice and treatment, the hospital, by accepting the patient, undertakes to make available all the therapeutic skill and devices which it is reasonably able to deploy:

"If the hospital's response is to open the door and admit the patient to the benefits of the medical and surgical cornucopia within it remains responsible to ensure that whatever treatment or advice the horn disgorges is given with proper care; its duty cannot be divested by delegation."[163]

The patient had been treated by a doctor who was an "honorary medical officer" with privileges at the hospital. She had approached the doctor herself and he had arranged for her admission to the hospital and performed the surgery. In these circumstances a non-delegable duty did not arise. The hospital was merely a provider of the facilities for the treatment. Kirby P, dissenting, took the view that the hospital was not a "mere venue" for the performance of private medical procedures, it was an integrated institution and an honorary medical officer was part of it.[164] In his Honour's opinion the hospital was vicariously liable for all its staff, whether the position was "honorary" or not, and directly liable by virtue of a non-delegable duty.

9-049

Canada   The courts in Australia have accepted that a hospital may come under a non-delegable duty to its patients, albeit that there is a difference of opinion as to precisely when the duty arises. On the other hand, in *Yepremian v Scarborough General Hospital*[165] the majority of a five-judge Ontario Court of Appeal held that in Canada a hospital does not undertake a non-delegable duty to patients, whether they present themselves directly at the door of the hospital or not.[166]

9-050

(ii)   Statute

The second ground for suggesting that under the NHS a hospital authority is under a non-delegable duty to provide medical services to the patient derives from the statutory obligation placed on a health authority under the National Health Service Act 2006, through the duty placed on the Secretary of State. In *Razzel v Snowball*[167] the Court of Appeal held that the duty placed on the Minister of Health by s.3(1)(c) of the National Health Service Act 1946 was not limited to merely providing competent specialists, but extended to providing

9-051

---

[163] (1989) 17 N.S.W.L.R. 553 at 605, per Samuels JA.

[164] "He was integrated into the discipline and direction of the hospital. What he did in his rooms was his affair. But when he came into the hospital, he was part of the hospital. When working on its premises he was part of its integrated medical team": (1989) 17 N.S.W.L.R. 553 at 566.

[165] (1980) 110 D.L.R. (3d) 513, Ont CA. The action was settled before an appeal to the Supreme Court of Canada was heard: (1981) 120 D.L.R. (3d) 341.

[166] cf. *Aynsley v Toronto General Hospital* (1969) 7 D.L.R. (3d) 193 at 209, Ont CA; aff'd (1971) 25 D.L.R. (3d) 241, SCC where Aylesworth JA said that a hospital was liable for the negligence of a doctor even if he had been employed under a contract for services. This suggests that the hospital was under a non-delegable duty, since the negligence would have been that of an independent contractor. This was a case of private medicine, however, and a contractual relationship between the hospital and the patient may well create a non-delegable duty.

[167] [1954] 1 W.L.R. 1382; see also *Higgins v North West Metropolitan Hospital Board* [1954] 1 W.L.R. 411.

treatment by means of their services. The effect of this particular ruling was that the defendant doctor was to be regarded as carrying out the Minister's duty and therefore he was entitled to claim the benefit of a one year period of limitation that applied to acts done in pursuance or execution of any Act of Parliament or any public duty under s.21 of the Limitation Act 1939. It is arguable that the consequence of this is that the equivalent provision in s.3(1) of the National Health Service Act 2006 creates a non-delegable statutory duty to provide treatment services which is not discharged by the appointment of competent staff, whether as an employee or an independent contractor, such as a consultant.[168] This argument has not been tested in the courts, and it remains to be seen how the proposition would be received if advanced by a claimant.[169] The Health and Social Care Act 2012 amended the National Health Service Act 2006 with the effect that the duty contained in s.3 of the 2006 Act is now placed on Clinical Commissioning Groups, rather than the Secretary of State, though s.3(1F) provides that in exercising its functions a CCG must act consistently with the discharge by the Secretary of State of the duties imposed by s.1 of the 2006 Act (i.e. the duty to promote a comprehensive health service, a duty which is now shared with the National Health Service Commissioning Board[170]). Arguably, this change in the allocation of the duties under the National Health Service Act 2006 does not affect the point arising from *Razzel v Snowball*, though it could affect the identity of the defendant subject to such a duty.

(iii)   Collateral negligence

9–052   Even where a non-delegable duty is established the employer is not liable for acts of collateral negligence by an independent contractor. This is negligence which is not committed in the performance of the very work which has been delegated, although in practice it can be very difficult to distinguish between collateral acts and acts which are simply a manner of performing the delegated work.[171] The distinction was accepted by Denning LJ in *Cassidy v Ministry of Health*,[172] but was said to be unimportant in that case:

---

[168] Dugdale and Stanton, *Professional Negligence*, 3rd edn (London: Butterworths, 1998), para.22.20, who state that "it is undoubtedly the case that the effect of basing this duty on statute is to ensure that it is non-delegable in its nature".

[169] One unusual feature of the case was that it was the claimant who argued that the Minister's duty was merely to provide the specialists and not the treatment, whereas it was the defendant who was claiming that he was performing the Minister's non-delegable duty. In *Yepremian v Scarborough General Hospital* (1980) 110 D.L.R. (3d) 513 at 565 Blair JA considered that the liability of hospitals in the United Kingdom "now rests on a clear statutory foundation", relying on *Razzel v Snowball* [1954] 1 W.L.R. 1382. There is authority for the view that where a statute imposes an "absolute" duty, responsibility for its performance cannot be delegated: *Smith v Cammell Laird & Co Ltd* [1940] A.C. 242; *The Pass of Ballater* [1942] P. 112. Whether a duty is "absolute" depends upon the construction of the statute, but it can apply to a duty to use "due diligence": *Riverstone Meat Co Pty Ltd v Lancashire Shipping Co Ltd* [1961] A.C. 807.

[170] National Health Service Act 2006 s.1H(2).

[171] See *Padbury v Holliday & Greenwood Ltd* (1912) 28 T.L.R. 494; *Holliday v National Telephone Co* [1899] 2 Q.B. 392.

[172] [1951] 2 K.B. 343 at 365.

"...because we are not concerned with any collateral or casual acts of negligence by the staff, but negligence in the treatment itself which it was the employer's duty to provide."

There is no comparable restriction on an employer's vicarious liability, provided the employee's negligence occurred in the course of employment or is sufficiently closely connected to the employment.

(iv) Rationale for non-delegable duties

The underlying justification for imposing a non-delegable duty on hospital authorities rests on patient expectations.[173] Patients know nothing about the terms upon which the hospital engages its staff. They go to hospital for treatment and if they suffer injury in the course of that treatment their entitlement to damages should not turn upon whether the negligence was inflicted by an employed nurse or an agency nurse, a house surgeon or a visiting consultant.[174] In *Yepremian v Scarborough General Hospital*[175] Arnup JA was critical of the notion of non-delegable duties because it seemed to be a case of saying: "In all the circumstances, the hospital *ought* to be liable." This, however, is the very point, and it is as true of the principle of vicarious liability, and indeed most tort duties.

9–053

In *Woodland v Swimming Teachers Association*[176] Lord Sumption suggested that non-delegable duties were part of the long-standing policy of the law to protect those who are both inherently vulnerable and highly dependent on the observance of proper standards of care by those with a significant degree of control over their lives. Part of the rationale was that the imposition of a non-delegable duty was a reasonable response to the modern trend of public authorities to "outsource" their services. In the past, in a case such as *Woodland*, education authorities would have been vicariously liable to claimants injured during a swimming lesson (on the assumption that a teacher would have been in charge of the lesson) and so a non-delegable duty was not adding a new source of potential liability.[177] Lord Sumption also pointed out that the responsibilities of fee-paying schools are already non-delegable because they are contractual. There was:

9–054

"...no rational reason why the mere absence of consideration should lead to an entirely different result when comparable services are provided by a public authority. A similar point can be made about the technical distinctions that would otherwise arise between privately funded and NHS hospital treatment."[178]

---

[173] Though note that in *Farraj v King's Healthcare NHS Trust* [2009] EWCA Civ 1203; [2010] 1 W.L.R. 2139 at [91] Dyson LJ said that to ask what the expectations of the claimant patient would have been does not provide the answer to the question whether the hospital owes a non-delegable duty of care. Rather, the question was one of policy for the courts to determine by reference to what is fair, just and reasonable.

[174] See Whippy (1989) 63 A.L.J. 182, 201. This point has been made by McKendrick (1990) 53 M.L.R. 770 in the wider context of employers' vicarious liability. Given the elusiveness of the distinction between a contract of service and a contract for services, and the difficulty that the courts have in identifying it, there is no obvious reason why an employer's responsibility should hang on this particular issue.

[175] (1980) 110 D.L.R. (3d) 513 at 532, Ont CA.

[176] [2013] UKSC 66, [2014] A.C. 537 at [25](1).

[177] [2013] UKSC 66, [2014] A.C. 537 at [25](4); see also per Baroness Hale at [40].

[178] [2013] UKSC 66, [2014] A.C. 537 at [25](5).

9–055 The policy that has been adopted with regard to negligent treatment given in NHS hospitals of, in effect, ignoring the distinction between employees and independent contractors provided that the claimant's injury was caused in the course of receiving NHS treatment, has rendered much (but not all[179]) of the argument about non-delegable duties redundant. The hospital authority will accept vicarious liability for the negligence of consultants and agency staff irrespective of whether they are engaged under a contract of service or a contract for services. Moreover, even with private medical treatment, in practice it will rarely matter to the claimant whether the hospital owes a non-delegable duty since if the doctor is proved to have been negligent the patient will have a claim against him, and if he is not an employee but an independent contractor he should have insured against liability through a medical defence organisation.[180] If the doctor is not negligent there would not in any event have been an action against the hospital for breach of its non-delegable duty. The issue becomes of practical importance to the claimant if the doctor has no, or limited, insurance cover,[181] or where the claimant has chosen to sue only the hospital and not the doctor.[182] The effect of imposing a non-delegable duty on a hospital is to make the hospital a guarantor of the independent contractor's solvency, or rather to place the risk of the contractor's insolvency or lack of insurance cover on the hospital rather than the claimant. If the contractor is negligent the hospital will have either a contractual claim for indemnity or a right to contribution under the Civil Liability (Contribution) Act 1978.

(v) Responsibility for treatment overseas

9–056 The question of whether a hospital owes a non-delegable duty to its patients does have potential practical significance where patients are sent overseas, at NHS expense, to have treatment. If patients are injured as a result of the negligence of the treating hospital, they will want to be able to sue the health authority or NHS Trust that referred them in this country. The existence of a non-delegable duty would make that course much simpler to pursue. The practical importance of this is illustrated by *A v Ministry of Defence*.[183] The claimant suffered serious brain damage during the course of his birth in 1998 in a German obstetric unit as a result of negligence by a German doctor. A's father was in the Army, and his mother was provided with obstetric services on the basis of arrangements entered into by the Ministry of Defence (MoD) to provide healthcare for members of the armed forces and their families while posted to Germany. Until 1996 secondary healthcare was provided in Germany in British military hospitals staffed by Army and RAF doctors and nurses or civilian health professionals employed by the MoD, for whose negligence the MoD was vicariously liable. During the mid-1990s arrangements for medical care for service personnel and their families were changed. As part of that change, the MoD subcontracted to Guy's and St

---

179 See paras 9–039 to 9–040.
180 See the Medical Act 1983 s.44C.
181 As was the case in *Ellis v Wallsend District Hospital* (1989) 17 N.S.W.L.R. 553 at 569.
182 As occurred in *Yepremian v Scarborough General Hospital* (1980) 110 D.L.R. (3d) 513, Ont CA.
183 [2003] EWHC 849 (QB); [2003] Lloyd's Rep. Med. 339; [2003] P.I.Q.R. P607.

Thomas Hospital NHS Trust (GST) the procurement of secondary hospital care in five German hospitals. A was born in one of these hospitals. Negligence by the German doctor was admitted. The issue was whether A could sue the MoD or GST in England under English law, or whether he would have to bring a claim in Germany under German law. The answer to that question depended upon the nature of the duty undertaken by the MoD and GST to the claimant, who were clearly not vicariously liable for the doctor's negligence. Had either the MoD or GST undertaken a non-delegable duty to ensure that medical treatment in the German hospital was provided with reasonable care and skill, or was it limited to exercising reasonable care in the selection of appropriate German providers of hospital care and the supervision of standards in those hospitals? Bell J concluded that the defendants' responsibility was limited to exercising reasonable care in selecting and supervising standards in the German hospitals. They had not undertaken a non-delegable duty for the provision of healthcare to Army personnel and their families in Germany, and therefore were not responsible for the doctor's negligence.

Bell J identified the rationale for imposing a non-delegable duty on hospitals in the relationship between the parties which gives rise to a special responsibility— the hospital undertakes the care, supervision and control of patients who are in special need of care, and has assumed responsibility in circumstances where the claimant could reasonably expect that reasonable care will be exercised.[184] On the facts of *A v Ministry of Defence*, the MoD was generally responsible for the wellbeing of service personnel, civilian employees and their dependants, while residing in another country, and encouraged the feeling that "the Army will look after you". But the MoD had informed service personnel of the changed arrangements for the provision of healthcare, and there was no justification for any assumption by A's parents that the Army itself was continuing to provide hospital care. The MoD was under a duty to provide access to an appropriate regime of healthcare in Germany. It had not assumed responsibility for treating service personnel or their dependants and had not accepted them as patients for the purposes of hospital care. It had assumed an obligation to provide access to an appropriate system of hospital care provided by a third party. This was a duty, said Bell J, to exercise reasonable care in selecting and putting into action appropriate providers, and it discharged that duty by contracting with GST to procure German hospitals and to manage their contracts. Similarly, when it came

9–057

---

[184] See the judgment of Mason J in *Kondis v State Transport Authority* (1984) 55 A.L.R. 225, cited by Bell J, [2003] EWHC 849 (QB); [2003] Lloyd's Rep. Med. 339; [2003] P.I.Q.R. P607 at [59], and the judge's comment at [69] that: "in so far as those features lead in the Australian cases to a duty to ensure the safety of the claimant, they go further than the English cases." Sed quaere, in light of Lord Browne-Wilkinson's dictum in *X (Minors) v Bedfordshire County Council* and the Court of Appeal's judgment in *Robertson v Nottingham Health Authority*, para.9–040. Indeed, Bell J acknowledged, at [68], that: "What Lord Greene MR said in *Gold*, has great force, to my mind, but his wider personal, non-delegable duty still depends upon the hospital's acceptance of the patient for treatment, or advice, by itself." In *Gold v Essex County Council* [1942] 2 K.B. 293 at 304 Lord Greene had said: "It is clear therefore, that the powers of the defendants include the power of treating patients . . . If they exercise that power, the obligation which they undertake is an obligation to treat, and they are liable if the persons employed by them to perform the obligation on their behalf act without due care. I am unable to see how a body invested with such a power and to all appearance exercising it can be said to be assuming no greater obligation than to provide a skilled person and proper appliances."

to the legal position of GST, it was never envisaged that GST would itself provide medical services directly to service personnel or their families in Germany. GST's duty of care had to be seen in the context of what GST contracted to do. It did not contract to treat British patients in German hospitals. It did not contract to manage the German hospitals, as opposed to managing its contracts with the German hospitals. It followed that there was no basis for a non-delegable duty on GST to ensure that reasonable care and skill were used in hospital treatment in Germany. The duty was to exercise reasonable care in the selection of German hospitals to provide particular forms of treatment and to manage the contract with the hospital in such a manner as would avoid an unsafe hospital regime.[185]

9–058　The Court of Appeal affirmed the decision of Bell J.[186] The Ministry of Defence did not undertake the business of treating patients in hospital in Germany, but simply arranged for treatment to be provided by others. It was not under a non-delegable duty to ensure that German hospitals exercised reasonable skill and care when treating British servicemen and their dependants. Although, said Lord Phillips MR, there were:

> "...strong arguments of policy for holding that a hospital, which offers treatment to a patient, accepts responsibility for the care with which that treatment is administered, regardless of the status of the person employed or engaged to deliver the treatment",[187]

the Ministry of Defence was not running hospitals in Germany, and the fact that it once did run its own hospitals, and would have been under a non-delegable duty in respect of treatment provided in those hospitals at that time, did not mean that it continued to be under a non-delegable duty in respect of treatment provided by German hospitals after the change in 1996.

9–059　In *A v Ministry of Defence* Lord Phillips commented that:

> "...hitherto a non-delegable duty has only been found in a situation where the claimant suffers an injury while in an environment over which the defendant is in control"[188]

and the MoD was not in control of the German doctor. However, in *Woodland v Swimming Teachers Association*[189] Lord Sumption, whilst agreeing that the decision in *A v Ministry of Defence* was correct, disagreed with Lord Phillips' view that control of the environment in which injury is caused was an essential element for a non-delegable duty of care in such cases:

> "The defendant is not usually in control of the environment in which injury is caused by an independent contractor. That is why as a general rule he is not liable for the contractor's negligence. Where a non-delegable duty arises, the defendant is liable not because he has control but in spite of the fact that he may have none. The essential element in my view is not control of the environment in which the claimant is injured, but control over the claimant for the purpose of performing a function for which the defendant has assumed responsibility."

---

[185] "Even the Australian cases require acceptance of the claimant as the hospital's own patient for treatment, before the duty to ensure safe care arises": [2003] EWHC 849 (QB) at [69] per Bell J.
[186] *A v Ministry of Defence* [2004] EWCA Civ 641; [2005] Q.B. 183.
[187] [2004] EWCA Civ 641; [2005] Q.B. 183 at [63].
[188] [2004] EWCA Civ 641; [2005] Q.B. 183 at [47].
[189] [2013] UKSC 66; [2014] A.C. 537 at [24].

The correct reason for the decision in *A v Ministry of Defence*, said Lord Sumption, was that there was no delegation of any function which the Ministry had assumed personal responsibility to carry out, and no delegation of any custody exercised by the Ministry over soldiers and their families.

There is a world of difference, of course, between the position of military personnel and their families posted abroad, who are (or should be) aware of the arrangements put in place for their medical treatment while abroad, and the position of a NHS patient who is referred to a NHS hospital for treatment, and is then invited to have that treatment abroad at the NHS's expense as part of a scheme for reducing NHS waiting lists or waiting times. The NHS, unlike the MoD, is in the business of providing healthcare to its patients. Those patients go to a NHS hospital with a view to receiving treatment at that or another NHS facility. The hospital has undertaken a responsibility to provide treatment to the patient (as Lord Greene in *Gold* and Denning LJ in *Cassidy* indicated). It would be unfortunate, to say the least, if the consequence of referring patients abroad for treatment in order to meet particular political or financial objectives in the NHS were that injured patients would have to undertake the litigation process abroad, against the hospital that actually carried out the treatment, with all the practical and financial impediments that this would create for a claimant. The simple solution in this situation is that the NHS hospital should be regarded as having undertaken to provide treatment to the patient and should be under a non-delegable duty to see that care is taken. The standard required to discharge this duty is still a negligence standard. The NHS is not subject to strict liability. To cover the risk of negligently inflicted injury in the course of treatment, the NHS hospital should simply obtain an indemnity from the overseas provider of treatment against their liability to patients for breach of this non-delegable duty, as part of the contract with that hospital to provide the treatment services.

9–060

Older Department of Health guidance on overseas treatment for NHS patients pointed out that the law on the liability of the NHS for clinical issues "is not wholly clear" and that the courts:

9–061

"...may regard NHS bodies as having a duty of care that cannot be delegated, despite the fact that treatment was being provided by a non-UK provider. Patients would therefore be able to sue the NHS in the English courts, rather than having to take a case through foreign courts. This approach is in line with the Government's policy preference, which states that patients travelling abroad for treatment should have the same rights and remedies as patients receiving treatment in the UK."[190]

The Clinical Negligence Scheme for Trusts covers treatment abroad, and the expectation of the Department of Health was that "a patient wishing to sue for medical negligence would sue the NHS in England" though claims may focus on alleged negligent selection of foreign providers.[191] More recent guidance

---

[190] Department of Health, *Treating More Patients and Extending Choice: Overseas Treatment for NHS Patients, Guidance for Primary Care and Acute Trusts*, November 2002, para.6.1 (this document is no longer available; this paragraph was cited in *A v Ministry of Defence* [2004] EWCA Civ 641; [2005] Q.B. 183 at [50]).
[191] Department of Health, *Treating More Patients and Extending Choice: Overseas Treatment for NHS Patients, Guidance for Primary Care and Acute Trusts*, November 2002, at para.6.5.

provided by NHS England where *patients* seek NHS funding for treatment abroad is that the NHS is not liable for errors in the treatment received.[192] So in *S2 and Directive routes: guidance for commissioners* it is said that:

> "NHS clinicians and commissioners cannot be held liable for any failures in treatments organised by the patient and undertaken in another EEA country. Their role is strictly limited to helping facilitate this if that is the patient's expressed wish."[193]

Of course, NHS guidance is not definitive and in any event it is arguable that there is a distinction between a *patient* who seeks NHS funding for treatment abroad and a decision by an NHS Trust that, for its own purposes, it is appropriate to send a patient abroad for treatment that the Trust would otherwise have provided.

9–062   The decision in *A v Ministry of Defence* may point to the conclusion that a non-delegable duty would not be imposed on the NHS in relation to simple medical negligence by an overseas provider, and that any claim against the NHS would have to be on the basis that it had been negligent in selecting the overseas provider. On the other hand, in *A v Ministry of Defence* Lord Phillips distinguished between the position of the NHS and the Ministry of Defence, commenting that even if it were correct to hold that an NHS Trust owes a non-delegable duty to ensure that a patient sent overseas for treatment receives careful treatment "it would not follow that the same was true of the MoD in this case".[194] Thus, the decision in *A v Ministry of Defence* is not necessarily conclusive in relation to overseas treatment commissioned by the NHS, which, unlike the MoD, is in the "business" of providing healthcare.[195]

3.   JOINT LIABILITY AND CONTRIBUTION

(a)   Civil Liability (Contribution) Act 1978

9–063   Where two or more tortfeasors[196] are liable for the same damage[197] they will be entitled to claim contribution from each other under the Civil Liability (Contribution) Act 1978.[198] The Act allows for the apportionment of damages[199]

---

[192] *NHS Choices: revised information for patients*, 1 May 2016, p.9 (available at *http://www. england.nhs.uk/wp-content/uploads/2016/03/nhs-revsd-info-pats.pdf*).

[193] March 2016, para.66 (available at *http://www.england.nhs.uk/wp-content/uploads/2016/03/s2-directv-guid-comms-mar16.pdf*).

[194] [2004] EWCA Civ 641; [2005] Q.B. 183 at [54].

[195] See C. Guthrie and H. Volpe, "Overseas Treatment for NHS Patients" [2006] J.P.I.L. 12 for discussion of some of the complexities involved in such cases, including potential conflict of laws problems.

[196] Where the alleged defendant does not owe a duty of care to the claimant then clearly there can be no claim for contribution. Thus, a defendant sued in respect of damage to a child cannot seek contribution from the child's mother in respect of her alleged pre-natal negligence, which may have contributed to the child's damage, because the mother does not owe a duty of care to the foetus that she carries: *Preston v Chow* (2002) 211 D.L.R. (4th) 758, Man CA. The Congenital Disabilities (Civil Liability) Act 1976 s.1(1) specifically excludes the child's mother as a potential defendant, except where the injury is attributable to her negligent driving of a motor vehicle: Congenital Disabilities (Civil Liability) Act 1976 s.2.

between the respective defendants, it does not operate as a defence to the claimant's claim. Similarly, judgment against one defendant is not a bar to a subsequent action against other defendants.[200] If the first judgment remains unsatisfied the claimant can sue the other tortfeasors, subject to a possible penalty in costs.[201] Where the claimant does not sue all the persons responsible for the damage a defendant may join the others in third party proceedings.[202]

Effect of settlement in full and final satisfaction of C's claim   Although the Act specifically preserves the claimant's right to bring later proceedings against another defendant, in some circumstances the settlement of his action against one defendant may preclude a subsequent action against another defendant. In *Jameson v Central Electricity Generating Board*[203] the House of Lords held that where a claimant enters into a settlement with a concurrent tortfeasor,[204] D1, which is expressed to be in "full and final settlement" of the claim, he cannot then claim against a second concurrent tortfeasor, D2, in respect of the same damage.[205] It follows that if D2 is no longer liable to the claimant there can be no claim for contribution under the Act by D2 against D1 (since D2 will no longer have any need for contribution against D1).[206] Whether the agreement can be said to have "satisfied" the claim for damages depends on the wording of the

9–064

---

[197] See para.9–074 for discussion of this term. Note that where the court is in a position to apportion the causal contribution made by each defendant's tortious conduct, as in *Holtby v Brigham & Cowan (Hull) Ltd* [2000] 3 All E.R. 421, the Civil Liability (Contribution) Act 1978 does not come into play, because each defendant is liable to the claimant only to the extent of his contribution to the damage. The claimant cannot sue one defendant for the full extent of his loss, leaving that defendant to obtain contribution from other defendants under the Act. The claimant is effectively forced to sue each and every defendant for that part of the damage caused by each defendant. See paras 5–037—5–038. See also Weir [2001] C.L.J. 237, 239 for critical comment. The same principle will apply where the claimant has relied on the *Fairchild/McGhee* principle to establish causation, so that the defendant has materially increased the risk of harm to the claimant. The defendant is held liable only to the extent that he contributed to the risk, applying *Barker v Corus (UK) plc (formerly Saint Gobain Pipelines plc)* [2006] UKHL 20; [2006] 2 A.C. 572: see para.5–072. There is no room for the application of the Civil Liability (Contribution) Act 1978 in such a case.

[198] See Dugdale (1979) 42 M.L.R. 182.

[199] The apportionment can include a payment reasonably made under a settlement agreement in respect of the defendant's liability to meet the claimant's costs: *BICC Ltd v Cumbrian Industrial Ltd* [2001] EWCA Civ 1621; [2002] Lloyd's Rep. P.N. 526.

[200] Civil Liability (Contribution) Act 1978 s.3.

[201] Civil Liability (Contribution) Act 1978 s.4.

[202] CPR Pt 20.

[203] [2000] 1 A.C. 455.

[204] As opposed to a joint tortfeasor. The defendants are "joint tortfeasors" where they have participated in some common enterprise, where a person has authorised another to commit a tort, and where an employer is vicariously liable for the torts of his employees. Where, however, their independent actions coincide to produce the same damage they are "several concurrent tortfeasors" (e.g. the negligence of two drivers causes a road accident which injures a third party).

[205] Though note that in *McGill v Sports and Entertainment Media Group* [2016] EWCA Civ 1063; [2017] 1 W.L.R. 989 at [91] the Court of Appeal considered that: "The doctrine is not confined to concurrent tortfeasors, and the true question which has to be answered is whether, by settling the earlier action, the claimant has fixed the full measure of his loss, so that he has no remaining loss to recover from anybody else."

[206] Though D1 can still claim contribution from D2 by virtue of s.1(2) and s.1(4) of the Civil Liability (Contribution) Act 1978; see para.9–071.

settlement. If it is not expressed to be in full and final satisfaction, or if the claimant specifically reserves the right to maintain a claim against other concurrent tortfeasors, it will not have the effect of extinguishing those claims.

9–065   In *Jameson* itself, J. contracted mesothelioma from exposure to asbestos at work. He brought an action against his former employers (D1), and settled the claim for substantially less than its full value. After his death, his widow brought an action for loss of dependency under the Fatal Accidents Act 1976 against the Central Electricity Generating Board (D2), the occupiers of the premises where he had been exposed to asbestos. The claim against D2 was worth substantially more than the sum for which J. had settled his claim against D1. Both defendants were in breach of a duty to J, in respect of the same damage (the mesothelioma) and under the Civil Liability (Contribution) Act 1978 s.1(3), the employers, D1, would have been liable to make contribution to D2, notwithstanding the settlement. Their Lordships held, however, that the settlement by a claimant of an action against one concurrent tortfeasor could have the effect of barring a further claim against another concurrent tortfeasor. In these circumstances the Act becomes irrelevant because D2 then has no liability to C, and therefore no need to seek contribution from D1. The solution to this potential problem for claimants is expressly to reserve the right to claim against other potential defendants when accepting a settlement from one defendant.[207]

9–066   Subsequently, in *Heaton v Axa Equity & Law Assurance Society plc*[208] the House of Lords explained that the decision in *Jameson* was based on the proposition that where the claimant has entered into an agreement with D1 under which he accepts a sum as full compensation for the damage suffered, an action by the claimant against D2 cannot proceed because if the compensation is in full satisfaction of the damage sustained it reflects the claimant's full loss and thereby extinguishes it.[209] It is not that the agreement between the claimant and D1 was intended to confer some benefit on D2, but that the claimant no longer has any loss which requires compensation. Conversely, as Lord Bingham pointed out:

> "While it is just that [the claimant] should be precluded from recovering substantial damages against [D2] in a case where he has accepted a sum representing the full measure of his estimated loss, it is unjust that [the claimant] should be so precluded where he has not."[210]

The primary focus in deciding whether the claimant has received full compensation for his loss will be the terms of the settlement agreement, but even so, said Lord Bingham, a number of factors have to be taken into account:

---

[207] Although D1 may be reluctant to agree to such a reservation because it leaves open the possibility of a contribution claim under the Act from D2 if the claimant brings a further action against D2. The better option might be for the claimant to agree to indemnify D1 against any potential liability to make contribution that D1 has.

[208] [2002] UKHL 15; [2002] 2 A.C. 329.

[209] [2002] UKHL 15; [2002] 2 A.C. 329 per Lord Mackay at [41] and Lord Rodger at [80].

[210] [2002] UKHL 15; [2002] 2 A.C. 329 at [5]. As to whether the test for determining whether the claimant "has accepted a sum representing the full measure of his estimated loss" is purely objective, or includes a subjective element, see *McGill v Sports and Entertainment Media Group* [2016] EWCA Civ 1063; [2017] 1 W.L.R. 989 at [100]: "...fairness requires that the court should be able to take [the claimant's] motivation into account as part of the factual matrix relevant to the issue whether the claimant has indeed accepted a sum representing the full measure of his estimated loss."

(1)   the release of one concurrent tortfeasor does not have the effect in law of releasing another concurrent tortfeasor;

(2)   an agreement made between the claimant and D1 will not affect the claimant's rights against D2 unless either: (a) the claimant agrees to forgo or waive rights which he would otherwise enjoy against D2, in which case his agreement is enforceable by D1; or (b) the agreement falls within the limited class of contracts which either at common law or by virtue of the Contracts (Rights of Third Parties) Act 1999 is enforceable by D2 as a third party;

(3)   the use of clear and comprehensive language to preclude the pursuit of claims and cross-claims as between the claimant and D1 has little bearing on the question whether the agreement represents the full measure of the claimant's loss. The more inadequate the compensation agreed to be paid by D1, the greater the need for D1 to protect himself against any possibility of further action by the claimant to obtain a full measure of redress;

(4)   an express reservation by the claimant of his right to sue D2 will fortify the inference that the claimant is not treating the sum recovered from D1 as representing the full measure of his loss, but the absence of such a reservation is of less significance, since there is no need for the claimant to reserve a right to do that which he is ordinarily fully entitled to do without any such reservation;

(5)   if D1, on compromising the claimant's action, wishes to protect himself against any claim against him by D2 for contribution, he can achieve that end either (a) by obtaining an enforceable undertaking by the claimant not to pursue any claim against D2 relating to the subject matter of the compromise, or (b) by obtaining an indemnity from the claimant against any liability to which D1 may become subject relating to the subject matter of the compromise.[211]

Settlements in the context of medical negligence   In *Rawlinson v North Essex Health Authority*[212] Mitchell J applied *Jameson v Central Electricity Generating Board* to a medical negligence action. In 1995 the claimant had settled his action for negligence against a pharmaceutical company in respect of damage attributable to the use of the drug myodil in the performance of a myelogram. In 1997 the claimant issued proceedings against the health authority alleging negligent treatment in respect of the manner in which the myodil was used and of a failure to aspirate. This was similar to the allegation of negligence that was made against the pharmaceutical company, in that it was alleged that aspiration of the myodil would have eliminated or substantially reduced the risk of the claimant contracting arachnoiditis. The claimant accepted that the settlement had been in full and final satisfaction of any claim or cause of action that he may have had against the pharmaceutical company in respect of the use of myodil. Mitchell J held that the settlement barred a subsequent claim against the hospital. The loss on which the claimant relied was identical to that which had been the subject of the settlement. The question was not whether the claimant has received the full

9–067

---

[211] [2002] UKHL 15; [2002] 2 A.C. 329 at [9].
[212] [2000] Lloyd's Rep. Med. 54.

value of his claim, but whether the sum he received in settlement of it was intended to be in full satisfaction of the tort.

9–068   In *Appleby v Northern Devon Healthcare NHS Trust*[213] the claimant was involved in a road traffic accident in which he sustained injuries to his leg. He was treated at the defendant hospital, but ultimately his leg had to be amputated. He settled a claim for damages against the other driver on the basis of a 60 per cent reduction of the award for his contributory negligence, then brought a claim against the hospital for clinical negligence. The hospital argued that the settlement extinguished the claimant's action against the hospital on the basis that the damage was the same in both actions. Sir Robert Nelson held that the test was whether the sum in the settlement represented the full measure of the estimated loss. The two claims were different with different tortfeasors liable in respect of essentially the same damage but, through different causes of action, with a different route to their liability and different extents of liability. The settlement of the road traffic accident claim did not represent the full measure of the claimant's loss. It would, therefore, be wrong to preclude the claimant from continuing his action against the hospital.

9–069   Similarly, in *Wright v Barts Health NHS Trust*[214] the claimant was injured at work due to the negligence of CCRL Ltd, and was taken to the defendant hospital. The treatment he received was allegedly negligent. The claimant brought an action for the whole of the loss (in excess of £3 million) against CCRL. That claim was settled on the basis of an 80 per cent reduction of the damages for the claimant's contributory negligence. Before the settlement the claimant wrote to the defendants alleging clinical negligence, but did not attempt to identify what elements of the loss caused by the accident would have been avoided by non-negligent treatment. The defendants argued that the claim was an abuse of process on the basis that the claimant had accepted a settlement in the action against CCRL for the injuries which formed the subject matter of the claim against the hospital, or alternatively that the settlement had extinguished the claimant's loss, relying on *Jameson v CEGB* and *Heaton v AXA Equity and Law Life Assurance Society plc*. Edis J noted that the case concerned concurrent tortfeasors, i.e. parties who commit separate tortious acts which cause or contribute to the same damage, and that *Heaton* is authority for the proposition that the rule that the release of one joint tortfeasor operates as a release for all does not apply to concurrent tortfeasors. CCRL and the hospital were liable in respect of the same damage, but that damage was only part of the claimant's loss. There was the damage that occurred before the alleged clinical negligence and the loss which occurred after the clinical negligence but which would have occurred in any event, for which only CCRL was liable:

> "After the clinical negligence there is the additional loss which would not have occurred but for the clinical negligence. The hospital is liable for this, as also is CCRL. CCRL is only liable for the proportion of this part of the loss which remains due after the reduction for clinical [sic] negligence. The hospital is liable for all of it. It follows that if one action had been

---

[213] [2012] EWHC 4356 (QB).
[214] [2016] EWHC 1834 (QB); [2016] Med. L.R. 545; commented on by N. Tavares [2016] J.P.I.L. C230.

initiated against both tortfeasors and if judgment had been given against them both, those judgments would have been in different sums. This is because each made a contribution to that part of the loss by a different tortious act in breach of different duties to the claimant. They are concurrent tortfeasors, not joint tortfeasors."[215]

The claimant had not been fully compensated for his loss. With regard to the loss for which both tortfeasors were liable CCRL was not liable for the whole loss because of the discount for the claimant's contributory negligence, whereas the hospital was liable to compensate the claimant for the whole of that loss if the negligence claim succeeded. The hospital was not liable for that part of the loss which was not caused by the alleged clinical negligence, and CCRL had neither paid nor purported to pay the whole loss caused by the hospital. It was impossible, said Edis J, to construe the agreement between CCRL and the claimant as providing full compensation for the loss claimed against the hospital. The substantial discount for contributory negligence in the settlement with CCRL was a sufficient basis for the decision, but the facts of the case illustrated:

"...a general principle which is that a settlement with one concurrent tortfeasor does not release the others unless it is clear that it was intended to have that effect, or unless the payment clearly satisfies the whole claim."[216]

Same damage, different cause of action   The Civil Liability (Contribution) Act 1978 applies to any type of action; the defendants' liability need not be based on breach of the same obligation. So a defendant who is in breach of contract may seek contribution from a defendant who is in breach of a duty of care in tort, provided that both contributed to the claimant's damage.[217]

9–070

Settlement of a doubtful claim   A settlement of the claimant's action before judgment by one defendant does not remove the right to seek contribution from another defendant, irrespective of whether he is or ever was liable in respect of the damage, provided, however, "that he would have been liable assuming that the factual basis of the claim against him could be established".[218] Thus, settlement of a doubtful claim does not prejudice the defendant's claim to

9–071

---

[215] [2016] EWHC 1834 (QB); [2016] Med. L.R. 545 at [17]. Query whether Edis J meant to refer to the "reduction for *contributory* negligence" rather than the "reduction for clinical negligence".

[216] [2016] EWHC 1834 (QB); [2016] Med. L.R. 545 at [19]. Edis J considered that "Nelson J. was right in *Appleby* for the reasons which he gave": [2016] EWHC 1834 (QB); [2016] Med. L.R. 545 at [21].

[217] Civil Liability (Contribution) Act 1978 s.6(1). But defendants' liability to make contributions to another defendant under the Act depends upon their being liable to the claimant. If by virtue of a contract between the claimant and D1, D1 is not liable to the claimant, D2 cannot claim contribution from D1: *Co-operative Retail Services Ltd v Taylor Young Partnership* [2002] UKHL 17; [2002] 1 W.L.R. 1419, where architects and consulting engineers, who were allegedly negligent in respect of a fire, were not entitled to claim contribution from the main contractor or an electrical sub-contractor, even though their share of responsibility for the loss was comparatively minor.

[218] Civil Liability (Contribution) Act 1978 ss.1(2) and 1(4). See *WH Newson Holding Ltd v IMI Plc* [2016] EWCA Civ 773; [2017] Ch. 27—where D1 makes a bona fide settlement or compromise with the claimant the effect of s.1(4) on a contribution claim by D1 against D2 is that there can be no investigation into whether D1 was actually liable to the claimant. All that D1 has to show is that, assuming that the factual basis of the claim against him could be established, that factual basis would have disclosed a reasonable cause of action against him making him liable in law to the claimant in respect of the damage.

contribution provided the doubts concern issues of fact. Where the settlement is based on uncertainty about the law defendants may have to prove that they were liable to the claimant in order to maintain the claim for contribution.[219] In these circumstances they may have to submit to judgment in order to protect their right to contribution.

9–072   **Effect of expiry of C's limitation period against D**   Where defendants cease to be liable to a claimant they are nonetheless still subject to a claim for contribution by another defendant, unless they ceased to be liable to the claimant by virtue of the expiry of a limitation period which extinguished the claimant's right of action against them.[220] Most limitation periods, including those applying to actions for personal injuries, do not extinguish claimants' right of action but merely bar their remedy. Thus, the fact that defendants would not be liable to the claimant because the claimant's limitation period has expired against them does not prevent another defendant bringing a contribution claim against them.[221] If the claimant has sued the defendant to judgment, s.1(5) of the Civil Liability (Contribution) Act 1978 provides that the judgment is conclusive in contribution proceedings "as to any issue determined by that judgment" in favour of the person from whom contribution is sought. There is a potential conflict here between s.1(3) and (5), since if the claimant's action failed because it was statute barred by the Limitation Act 1980 then s.1(5) appears to preclude a contribution claim by another defendant. This provision was intended to apply to a determination of the issue on the merits, not on a procedural point.[222]

9–073   **Rights of indemnity**   The Act does not affect an express or implied contractual or other right to indemnity, or an express contractual provision regulating or excluding contribution.[223] Thus, a defendant who is liable to make a contribution under the Act may recover this sum from another defendant in contract.[224]

---

[219] Dugdale (1979) 42 M.L.R. 182, 184.

[220] Civil Liability (Contribution) Act 1978 s.1(3).

[221] Similarly, where a defendant (D1) has settled the claimant's (C's) action against him he may still be liable to make contribution to another defendant (D2): *Logan v Uttlesford District Council* (1984) 136 N.L.J. 541; *Jameson v Central Electricity Generating Board* [1998] Q.B. 323, CA. This point was not appealed to the House of Lords in *Jameson* but was assumed to be correct by Lord Hope: [2000] 1 A.C. 455, 471. This is subject to the proviso that D2 remains liable to C. In the light of the decision of the House of Lords in *Jameson v Central Electricity Generating Board*, if D1's settlement extinguishes D2's liability to C, D2 will have no need to claim contribution from D1. The limitation period for contribution proceedings under the Civil Liability (Contribution) Act 1978 is two years from the date of judgment or compromise: Limitation Act 1980 s.10. This is the judgment or award which ascertains the quantum, and not merely the existence, of the tortfeasor's liability: *Aer Lingus plc v Gildacroft Ltd* [2006] EWCA Civ 4; [2006] 1 W.L.R. 1173.

[222] *Clerk & Lindsell on Torts*, 22nd edn (London: Sweet & Maxwell, 2018), para.4–21. See, however, *Nottingham Health Authority v Nottingham City Council* [1988] 1 W.L.R. 903 at 906 where, without reference to s.1(5), Balcombe LJ assumed that a defendant who was held not liable due to a successful limitation plea would still be liable to make contribution; and *RA Lister & Co Ltd v EG Thomson (Shipping) Ltd (No.2)* [1987] 1 W.L.R. 1614 at 1623, holding that a stay in proceedings or dismissal of an action for want of prosecution, which are procedural not substantive issues, do not fall within s.1(5) and so do not preclude contribution proceedings.

[223] Civil Liability (Contribution) Act 1978 s.7(3).

[224] *Sims v Foster Wheeler Ltd* [1966] 1 W.L.R. 769, CA; *Greenwich Millennium Village Ltd v Essex Services Group plc* [2014] EWCA Civ 960; [2014] 1 W.L.R. 3517. An employer has no right to

The "same damage"   A claim for contribution can only be brought against a   **9–074**
person liable in respect of the "same damage". This phrase has given rise to some
difficulties of interpretation. In *Eastgate Group Ltd v Lindsey Morden Group
Inc*[225] the Court of Appeal held that a claim against a person in breach of contract
falls to be reduced by a payment made by a person liable for breach of a
professional duty. The normal rule is that any actual diminution of claimants'
losses should be brought into account in assessing their claim for damages. The
fact that the claimant might recover different sums by way of *damages* from D1
and D2 did not mean that D1 and D2 were not liable for the same *damage*.

There are a number of situations where the claims have been found not to be in   **9–075**
respect of the same damage. In *Royal Brompton Hospital NHS Trust v
Hammond*[226] a distinction was drawn between the damage caused by primary
claims and secondary claims. A secondary claim arises from the loss or
devaluation of a primary claim, for example where a solicitor handling a personal
injuries claim is negligent, resulting in the loss of the claim against the original
tortfeasor. The claim against the negligent solicitor is not for the same damage as
the original action of the client against the tortfeasor. Thus, a claim against an
architect for negligence resulting in a weakening of the client's claim for breach
of contract against the main contractor under a building contract was not for the
same damage as the client's claim against the main contractor for delay in
performing the contract. The architect's negligence had not led to any delay in
performing the contract. Similarly, where D1 and D2 are liable to different parties
the claim is not in respect of the same damage.[227]

In *Rahman v Arearose Ltd*[228] the claimant was seriously assaulted by two black   **9–076**
youths, causing an injury to his right eye. His employers were held liable in
negligence for failing to take reasonable care to reduce the risk of such assaults.
Subsequently, as a result of the negligence of a surgeon, the claimant was
rendered blind in the right eye. In addition to the physical injuries, the claimant
developed severe psychiatric consequences, including post-traumatic stress
disorder, a severe depressive disorder, a specific phobia of Afro-Caribbean
people, and an enduring personality change. The psychiatric evidence indicated
that the post-traumatic stress disorder was due to the loss of the eye; the phobia
was due to the assault and subsequent events; and the personality change was due
to the synergistic interaction between the depression and the post-traumatic stress
disorder. One of the issues for the Court of Appeal was whether there could be an
apportionment of responsibility between the claimant's employers and the

---

indemnity from an employee under the contract of employment if the employer has contributed to the
damage or bears some part of the responsibility, where, for example, a more senior employee's
negligence has contributed to the damage: *Jones v Manchester Corporation* [1952] Q.B. 852 at 865,
per Singleton LJ. Clearly, this rule does not apply to a claim for contribution under the Civil Liability
(Contribution) Act 1978.
[225] [2001] EWCA Civ 1446; [2002] 1 W.L.R. 642; distinguishing *Howkins & Harrison (A Firm) v
Tyler* [2001] P.N.L.R. 27; [2001] Lloyd's Rep. P.N. 1, CA.
[226] [2002] UKHL 14; [2002] 1 W.L.R. 1397.
[227] *Birse Construction v Haiste Ltd* [1996] 1 W.L.R. 675, CA, where D2 was liable to D1 (in respect
of a claim by the claimant) but could not claim contribution from D3, even though D1 could have
claimed contribution from D3 on the basis that D3 was liable to the claimant.
[228] [2001] Q.B. 351.

hospital in respect of the claimant's psychiatric condition. Laws LJ pointed out that tortfeasors are concurrent when their wrongful acts or omissions cause a single indivisible injury. Each tortfeasor is then liable in full to compensate the claimant for the whole of the damage: "The characteristic of such torts is the *logical* impossibility of apportioning the damage among the different tortfeasors."[229] The expression the "same damage" in the 1978 Act meant (and meant only) the kind of single indivisible injury as arises at common law in a case of concurrent torts.[230] The clearest example of concurrent torts was:

> "...one where the injury in question would not have occurred but for both torts: where, if only one had been committed, the injury would not have occurred at all ... [For example] two assailants, not acting in concert, shoot a man who dies in consequence; but the expert evidence is that either shot on its own, while causing grave injuries, would not have been fatal. The death is entirely and only the result of both shots."[231]

In this situation, both defendants are fully liable for the death. A second example of concurrent tortfeasors was where each of two causes was necessary to produce the damage, e.g. where two persons independently shoot at a person at the same time, with both shots being fatal. Again, both are fully liable for the death. But where each tortfeasor caused some part of the damage, but neither caused the whole, and some part of the damage (but not all) would therefore have occurred if only one tort had been committed, but on the evidence it is impossible to identify with precision what part of the damage has been caused by which defendant, the defendants are not concurrent tortfeasors. Laws LJ said that it would plainly be unjust to proceed on the footing that defendants are responsible for the whole of the claimant's damage when, demonstrably, they are not. Once the case is categorised as one of concurrent torts then the rule is that each tortfeasor is liable for the whole of the damage in question. But where the court knows that the initial stage of the damage was caused by A (and not B) and that the latter stage was caused by B (and not A), it is not obliged to proceed contrary to the true facts on the assumption that each has caused the whole of the damage. The difficulty of apportioning responsibility between A and B was not a reason to hold both liable for the whole. Thus, on the facts of *Rahman v Arearose Ltd* it was not a case of concurrent torts. The respective torts were causes of distinct aspects of the claimant's overall psychiatric condition, neither caused the whole of it, and therefore the Civil Liability (Contribution) Act 1978 did not apply.[232]

9–077   **Contribution to the risk of damage**   Where defendants are held liable on the basis that their negligence has materially contributed to the *risk* of the claimant's damage (and that damage has actually occurred), in circumstances where the court is unable to conclude that the negligence materially contributed to the claimant's *damage*, defendants are only liable to the extent that their negligence contributed to the risk; they are not liable for the whole of the damage.[233] Thus,

---

[229] [2001] Q.B. 351 at [17], original emphasis.
[230] [2001] Q.B. 351 at [18].
[231] [2001] Q.B. 351 at [19].
[232] For criticism of this decision see Weir [2001] C.L.J. 237.
[233] See *Barker v Corus (UK) plc (formerly Saint Gobain Pipelines plc)* [2006] UKHL 20; [2006] 2 A.C. 572. See para.5–072.

where there are multiple defendants who have each contributed to the risk of harm, they are severally liable in respect of that part of the risk that they have contributed, and there is no scope for contribution between the tortfeasors under the Civil Liability (Contribution) Act 1978.

Apportionment   Section 2(1) of the 1978 Act provides that the amount of contribution shall be: 9–078

"...such as may be found by the court to be just and equitable having regard to the extent of that person's responsibility for the damage in question."

This wording is similar to that of s.1 of the Law Reform (Contributory Negligence) Act 1945 and it is not surprising that the courts should take a similar approach to apportioning responsibility under the two statutes.[234] In assessing the respective responsibilities of the parties the court may have regard both to the causative potency of the fault of a party and also the blameworthiness of the party, though causative responsibility is likely to be the most important factor in the assessment of contribution.[235] Section 2(1) of the 1978 Act involves a semi-structured discretion which directs the court to attach most weight to the defendant's causal responsibility for the damage in question, and if non-causative material is brought into account, it will have only a limited role (being given less weight than material showing the defendant's responsibility for the act in question).[236] In any event, the order for contribution must be just and equitable within s.2(1), and so there must be a sufficient relationship between any non-causative material and the damage in question.[237]

The court's discretion is limited by s.2(3) which provides that where the claimant's damages would be subject to any limitation (imposed by statute or agreement) or any reduction because of contributory negligence the contribution award should not exceed this amount. In other words defendants cannot be required to pay more by way of contribution than they would have been liable to pay to the claimant. There is no rule of law that parties who have been merely negligent cannot be required to make contribution to a party found guilty of fraud,[238] although the discrepancy in their conduct will clearly be relevant when assessing the amount of contribution, even to the extent of assessing a nil   9–079

---

[234] See, e.g. *J (A Child) v Wilkins* [2001] P.I.Q.R. P179. The claimant was a two-year-old child who was held on her mother's knee in the front passenger seat of a car being driven by her aunt. The defendant negligently collided with the car, causing serious injuries to the claimant which could have been wholly avoided if she had been restrained in an approved child seat. The defendant joined the claimant's mother and aunt as CPR Pt 20 defendants. The Court of Appeal upheld the judge's assessment that liability should be apportioned 75 per cent to the defendant and 25 per cent to the mother and aunt, applying the well-known approach adopted in *Froom v Butcher* [1976] Q.B. 286 to the assessment of contributory negligence in cases involving a failure to wear a seat belt.
[235] *Brian Warwicker Partnership plc v HOK International Ltd* [2005] EWCA Civ 962; [2005] Lloyd's Rep. Med. 464; [2006] P.N.L.R. 5 at [42] per Arden LJ, applying *Re-Source America International Ltd v Platt Site Services Ltd* [2004] EWCA Civ 665; (2004) 95 Con. L.R. 1.
[236] [2005] EWCA Civ 962; [2005] Lloyd's Rep. Med. 464; [2006] P.N.L.R. 5 at [45].
[237] [2005] EWCA Civ 962; [2005] Lloyd's Rep. Med. 464; [2006] P.N.L.R. 5 at [45].
[238] For example, in *Downs v Chappell* [1996] 3 All E.R. 344 at 363 a negligent defendant was required to contribute equally with a fraudulent defendant on the basis that the negligence had a greater causative impact.

contribution.[239] But the personal innocence of an employer held vicariously liable for the fraud of an employee is not a relevant consideration when determining apportionment between the employer and another defendant.[240] The correct approach is to determine the respective responsibilities of the defendants who are personally responsible, and the employer is then vicariously responsible for the employee's contribution.

9–080   **NHS Indemnity and contribution**   The effect of NHS Indemnity and the arrangements for pooling claims brought against the NHS (considered below) is that, in practice, contribution claims under the Civil Liability (Contribution) Act 1978 tend to be limited to actions arising out of private medicine,[241] disputes between general practitioners and hospitals,[242] and disputes between general practitioners and pharmacists.[243] Of course, it is always open to any defendants to seek to agree their respective responsibilities without recourse to the legislation.

4. NHS INDEMNITY

9–081   Although the contribution legislation has been used in medical negligence litigation,[244] its significance was greatly reduced in actions against NHS hospital doctors in 1954 when Circular HM(54)32 was introduced. This established a

---

[239] *K v P (J, Third Party)* [1993] Ch. 140, where it was held that the common law maxim ex turpi causa non oritur actio did not apply as a defence to a claim for contribution under the 1978 Act.

[240] *Dubai Aluminium Co Ltd v Salaam* [2002] UKHL 48; [2003] 2 A.C. 366.

[241] *Trustees of London Clinic v Edgar* unreported 19 April 2000, QBD, is an example of a contribution claim between the private clinic responsible for the negligence of the nursing staff and the consultant surgeon.

[242] *Wyatt v Curtis* [2003] EWCA Civ 1779 provides an example of a dispute between a general practitioner and a hospital as to who was responsible for a failure to warn a pregnant woman who had contracted chickenpox about the risk of serious abnormalities being caused to her unborn child. In *Maguire v North West Strategic Health Authority* [2012] EWHC 3272 (QB) (also referred to as "McGuire" in the transcript) a general practitioner sought contribution from a hospital on the basis that the hospital's advice to the parents of a two-year-old child on discharging him from hospital, and/or the failure to arrange an earlier follow-up appointment, had been negligent. It was claimed that the parents should have been advised to take the child straight to hospital in the event of a recurrence of symptoms, rather than taking him to the general practitioner. The argument was rejected on the basis that it implied that the hospital should not have trusted the competence of a general practitioner to make a correct diagnosis and refer the child back to hospital. Consultants had to be able to trust general practitioners to do their job. The case was rare, but not complex, and the general practitioner did not have to treat the condition, merely evaluate it. The general practitioner's negligence was the sole cause of the damage.

[243] See, e.g. *Dwyer v Roderick, The Times*, 12 November 1983, CA, where a general practitioner negligently prescribed too high a dosage of a drug, and the pharmacist negligently failed to spot the error in the prescription. On appeal, liability was apportioned 45 per cent to the general practitioner and 55 per cent to the pharmacist; *Prendergast v Sam and Dee Ltd* [1989] 1 Med. L.R. 36, CA, where liability was apportioned 25 per cent to the doctor who negligently wrote a prescription which could be misread, 75 per cent to the pharmacist who misread the prescription and supplied the patient with the wrong drug.

[244] See, e.g. *Jones v Manchester Corporation* [1952] Q.B. 852 where the issue concerned the respective responsibilities of a junior and inexperienced anaesthetist whose negligence resulted in the death of a patient, and the hospital authority which failed to provide appropriate supervision. The

private arrangement between doctors' defence organisations and the Department of Health by which payment to the claimant was apportioned between the defendants by agreement amongst themselves in each case, or in the absence of agreement in equal shares. This provided a formal, though not legally binding, mechanism which would reduce defendants' costs and at the same time present a united front to the claimant in the conduct of the litigation. The arrangement was replaced from 1 January 1990 with the introduction of "NHS Indemnity" under which health authorities assumed responsibility for claims of medical negligence and ceased to require their medical and dental staff to subscribe to a defence organisation,[245] though general practitioners working in primary care were never covered by these arrangements. NHS Indemnity was introduced as a result of substantial increases in the subscription rates of the medical defence organisations in the 1980s, and the growing pressure to relate subscription rates to the doctor's specialty, with high risk specialties paying a higher rate. It was considered that this could lead to distortion in pay and recruitment to the medical profession.[246]

Since NHS Indemnity was first introduced the administrative structure of the NHS has changed considerably. Health authorities no longer manage NHS hospitals (all NHS hospitals are now NHS Trusts or NHS Foundation Trusts) and Clinical Commissioning Groups have replaced Primary Care Trusts (which had previously replaced health authorities) as the bodies responsible for commissioning healthcare services.[247] A special health authority, the NHS Litigation Authority, manages all claims for clinical negligence against NHS employees, and administers risk pooling schemes for clinical negligence, the first of which was established in 1995 (the Clinical Negligence Scheme for Trusts (CNST)). Thus, the question of who is covered by NHS Indemnity tends to resolve into the issue of who is covered by CNST.

9–082

Court of Appeal, taking the view that the hospital should bear the brunt of the responsibility, allocated 80 per cent to the hospital and 20 per cent to the doctor; *Collins v Hertfordshire County Council* [1947] 1 K.B. 598 at 623–625.

[245] See *Claims of Medical Negligence Against NHS Hospital and Community Doctors and Dentists*, HC(89)34, HC(89)(FP) 22. This was updated by HSG(96)48 and *NHS Indemnity—Arrangements for Clinical Negligence Claims in the NHS*, NHS Executive, 1996, available at *http://www.nhsla.com/ Claims/Documents/NHS%20Indemnity.pdf* (see App.1). On the original Health Circular see Brazier (1990) 6 P.N. 88; Tingle (1991) 141 N.L.J. 630. The NHS was unusual as an employer, in requiring doctors employed in NHS hospitals to subscribe to a medical defence organisation (the Medical Defence Union, the Medical Protection Society, or the Medical and Dental Defence Union of Scotland) as part of the term of the contract of employment.

[246] Similar concerns are now being expressed about increases in the subscription rates to defence organisations for general practitioners. The government has introduced a scheme to protect general practitioners from rises in subscriptions in 2016–2018, allocating funding to cover annual inflationary increases in indemnity costs: Department of Health, *GP Indemnity Review* (2016) (available at *http://www.england.nhs.uk/wp-content/uploads/2016/07/gp-indemnity-rev-summary.pdf*). The scheme will be reviewed in 2018.

[247] CCGs are responsible for commissioning the majority of NHS services for patients in their population area, including: primary care services, hospital services (such as elective hospital care, urgent and emergency care) and most community services, including district nurses, learning disability services and mental health services.

9–083　**Who is covered by NHS Indemnity?**　NHS Indemnity applies to hospital authority responsibilities, namely a hospital's vicarious liability for the negligence of staff acting in the course of their employment, including consultants and staff provided by external agencies, irrespective of the precise legal relationship between these individuals and the hospital (i.e. whether or not they are in law employees or independent contractors).[248] HSG(96)48 and the accompanying documentation[249] updated the guidance given in HC(89)34 and takes the view that in addition to staff acting in the course of their NHS employment, NHS Indemnity covers locum doctors, medical academic staff with honorary contracts, students, researchers conducting clinical trials, charitable volunteers and people undergoing professional education, training and examinations, "whenever a NHS body owes a duty of care to the person harmed". Any work which is outside the scope of a hospital doctor's employment (e.g. reports for insurance companies or locum work for a general practitioner) is not covered, and the doctor will have to rely on subscription to a defence organisation for indemnity. A "Good Samaritan" act of assisting at an accident, although apparently excluded from coverage under the Guidance, appears now to fall within the coverage of CNST.[250]

9–084　NHS Indemnity does not apply to general practitioners except where the general practitioner has a contract of employment (e.g. as a clinical assistant at a hospital or as a public health doctor) with a NHS Trust and the treatment is being given under that contract. Claims against general practitioners will normally be handled by their defence organisation.[251] If a hospital is essentially providing only hotel services and the patient remains in the general practitioner's care, the hospital authority will not be responsible, and the claim will be dealt with by the general practitioner's defence organisation. Where a case involves a claim against both a

---

[248] Of course, this does not resolve the legal issues, but simply specifies how hospital authorities are to deal with them in practice. NHS Indemnity did not change the law as to whose conduct a hospital authority is responsible for, and theoretically it would still be open to take a vicarious liability point in a particular case involving, say, agency staff who are probably not employees. This is not done in practice, and, indeed, health authorities did not take the vicarious liability point for agency staff and consultants before 1990.

[249] *NHS Indemnity—Arrangements for Clinical Negligence Claims in the NHS*, NHS Executive, 1996. This is an old document but it remains available at *http://www.nhsla.com/claims/Documents/ NHS%20Indemnity.pdf* (also under a link to "NHS Indemnity" at *http://www.nhsla.com/Claims/ Pages/Handling.aspx*). (See also App.1, below.)

[250] *NHS Indemnity—Arrangements for Clinical Negligence Claims in the NHS*, para.19 provides that: "'Good Samaritan' acts are not part of the healthcare professional's work for the employing body. Medical defence organisations are willing to provide low-cost cover against the (unusual) event of anyone performing such an act being sued for negligence. Ambulance services can, with the agreement of staff, include an additional term in the individual employee contracts to the effect that the member of staff is expected to provide assistance in any emergency outside of duty hours where it is appropriate to do so."

[251] The Medical Defence Union, the Medical Protection Society, or the Medical and Dental Defence Union of Scotland. All doctors are required to have indemnity cover: Medical Act 1983 s.44C. Doctors working in a NHS hospital will be covered by NHS Indemnity, and will only need to subscribe to a defence organisation to cover work outside the scope of their employment (such as private work or work as a locum general practitioner). The defence organisations will also provide assistance with other professional matters, such as handling complaints and disciplinary issues, and so most doctors subscribe to one of the defence organisations.

NHS Trust and a general practitioner the possibility of a contribution claim exists, but the guidance emphasises that, as previously, NHS defendants should seek to reach agreement out of court as to the proportion of their respective liabilities, and to co-operate fully in the formulation of the defence.

NHS Indemnity does not apply to private hospitals[252] or private work performed by a consultant in a NHS hospital. But where junior medical staff are involved in the care of private patients in NHS hospitals, they would normally be doing so as part of their contract with the hospital authority or NHS Trust. To the extent that NHS employees participate in the treatment, the hospital will be vicariously liable for their negligence.

9–085

The NHS Litigation Authority[253]   In November 1995 the NHS Litigation Authority, a special health authority, was established with the responsibility for administering schemes set up under what is now s.71 of the National Health Service Act 2006 permitting NHS bodies to pool the costs of injury, loss or damage to property and liabilities to third parties arising out of their NHS activities.[254] The NHS Litigation Authority was formerly responsible for determining standards of risk management but, from March 2013, the Litigation Authority ceased assessing risk management standards and introduced a "Safety and Learning Service" to support its members to build a safety and learning culture. The Litigation Authority's primary role centres on claims handling for members of the risk pooling schemes and the payment of damages in the case of successful claims. The Authority administers two principal[255] schemes: (i) the Clinical Negligence Scheme for Trusts (CNST); and (ii) the Existing Liabilities Scheme (ELS).

9–086

The Clinical Negligence Scheme for Trusts (CNST)   CNST covers liabilities for clinical negligence where the adverse event occurred on or after 1 April 1995.[256] The scheme, which applies to England only,[257] applies to any liability in

9–087

---

[252] Although third party providers of NHS healthcare are now eligible to join CNST which will provide indemnity coverage in respect of claims arising out of that NHS healthcare.

[253] Note that the operating name of NHS Litigation Authority since April 2017 is now "NHS Resolution", though the NHSLA's formal status has not changed.

[254] *NHS Litigation Authority Framework Document*, 2013 (available at: *http://www.nhsla.com/Pages/ Publications.aspx?library=aboutus%7cframeworkdocument*).

[255] The NHS Litigation Authority also has responsibility for miscellaneous residual medical negligence liabilities of certain special health authorities and the Regional Health Authorities (which were abolished from 1 April 1996). The Ex-Regional Health Authorities Scheme covers the liabilities of the hospitals and other services formerly managed at a regional level, prior to the abolition of regional health authorities. The authority also administers two other risk pooling schemes in respect of non-clinical claims.

[256] See the NHS (Clinical Negligence Scheme) Regulations 2015 (SI 2015/559), which came into force on 1 April 2015, replacing and consolidating the amended NHS (Clinical Negligence Scheme) Regulations 1996 (SI 1996/251).

[257] The functions of the Secretary of State under s.126(4) of the National Health Service Act 1977 and s.21 of the National Health Service and Community Care Act 1990 were transferred to the National Assembly for Wales under the National Assembly for Wales (Transfer of Functions) Order 1999 (SI 1999/672) art.2 and Sch.1, as amended by s.66(5) of the Health Act 1999. In Wales the Welsh Risk Pool Services reimburses losses over £25,000 incurred by Welsh NHS bodies arising out of negligence. The Welsh Risk Pool Services is a mutual organisation funded through the NHS Wales

tort under the law of England and Wales which a member of the scheme owes to a third party in respect of or consequent upon personal injury or loss arising out of or in connection with any breach of a duty of care which: (a) the member owes to any person in connection with the diagnosis of any illness or the care or treatment of any patient; and (b) is in consequence of any act or omission on the part of (i) a person employed or engaged by the member in connection with any relevant function of the member; or (ii) an employee or agent of a person engaged by the member in connection with any such function.[258]

9–088   The scheme is funded by contributions from the organisations who are members of the scheme, NHS Trusts, NHS Foundation Trusts and (prior to their abolition) NHS primary care trusts. Since April 2013 clinical commissioning groups and independent sector providers of NHS healthcare have been entitled to join CNST to be indemnified for the NHS care they provide. It is not an insurance fund, but a "pay as you go" scheme which only collects enough money each year in contributions to cover the actual costs which fall into that year, plus a small margin to form a contingency reserve and cover administrative expenses. CNST operates on a "claims paid" basis, which means that it will provide cover if the member is a member of the scheme continuously at the date of the adverse event which subsequently gives rise to the claim and the date of settlement. The object is to permit members of the scheme to spread the cost of claims. From April 2002 the NHS Litigation Authority took over from NHS Trusts the handling and management of all clinical negligence claims against NHS Trusts in England, although the NHS Trust remains the legally responsible defendant.[259]

9–089   **The Existing Liabilities Scheme (ELS)**   ELS covers incidents of clinical negligence which occurred before 1 April 1995.[260] It is funded by the Secretary of State, through the NHS Litigation Authority. From 1 April 2000, the NHS

Healthcare budget (*http://www.wales.nhs.uk/sitesplus/955/page/58513*). A similar, but not identical, scheme operates in Scotland (the Clinical Negligence and Other Risks Insurance Scheme (CNORIS) covering clinical negligence in the NHS and integrated health and social care boards in Scotland (*http://clo.scot.nhs.uk/our-services/cnoris.aspx* and *http://www.sehd.scot.nhs.uk/dl/DL(2015)23.pdf*). In Northern Ireland there is a Clinical Negligence Central Fund (CNCF).

[258] NHS (Clinical Negligence Scheme) Regulations 2015 (SI 2015/559) reg.8. Similar wording, with appropriate amendments, applies to the Existing Liabilities Scheme which indemnifies eligible bodies with respect to liability for clinical negligence arising out of or in connection with a breach of duty before 1 April 1995: NHS (Existing Liabilities Scheme) Regulations 1996 (SI 1996/686) reg.4. Reg.10 of the NHS (Clinical Negligence Scheme) Regulations 2015 provides for indemnity in respect of certain liabilities arising where health services were being provided by non-members of the scheme under commissioning or sub-contracting arrangements. There is no reference in the Regulations to claims arising from failures to obtain consent, which give rise to actions in trespass to the person rather than negligence, which technically do not involve breach of a duty of care. This is probably an oversight and the NHS Litigation Authority do not take the point.

[259] Prior to this change there were complicated rules about the levels of "excess", which ranged from £10,000 to £500,000, that had to be met by the individual NHS Trust before it could claim indemnity from CNST. These excess levels were abolished from 1 April 2002, so that the whole cost of indemnity is met from the CNST.

[260] NHS (Existing Liabilities Scheme) Regulations 1996 (SI 1996/686); as amended by NHS (Existing Liabilities Scheme) (Amendment) Regulations 1997 (SI 1997/526); NHS (Existing Liabilities Scheme) (Amendment) Regulations 1999 (SI 1999/1275); NHS Liabilities Schemes Amendment Regulations 2005 (SI 2005/604).

Litigation Authority assumed responsibility for recording, handling and accounting for payments under the scheme, although legal responsibility remained with the relevant NHS body. From the same date, health organisations no longer make, or account for, any part of the payment, and the NHS Litigation Authority undertakes all the administration arrangements.

CHAPTER 10

DEFECTIVE PRODUCTS

It was the tragedy of thalidomide that first brought to public attention the   **10–001**
problems confronting the victims of defective drugs in obtaining compensation
for their injuries. This provided the stimulus for tighter control of drug marketing
by the Medicines Act 1968, and ultimately led to the setting up of the Pearson
Commission to look into the system of compensation for personal injuries.
Actions in respect of defective drugs are probably the most common form of
medical product liability claims, but they are not the only product which could
give rise to litigation in a healthcare setting. Claims have been made in respect of
defective heart valves,[1] intra-uterine devices,[2] contaminated blood products,[3]
human growth hormone,[4] breast implants,[5] tampons[6] and hip joints,[7] and it would
not be difficult to think of other products which could provoke litigation if
defective.[8]

---

[1] *Sunday Times*, 10 March 1985 reporting on deaths linked to a faulty valve, the Bjork-Shiley valve,
manufactured in the US by a subsidiary of Pfizer; [1990] 32 Law Soc. Gaz. 7; *Shaw v Medtronic
Corevalve LLC* unreported 20 January 2017.
[2] Claims against A.H. Robins, the American pharmaceutical company that marketed the Dalkon
Shield, led to that company going into voluntary liquidation with an estimated liability of $US 2.5
billion. See Ferrell (1988) 62 A.L.J. 92.
[3] *A v National Blood Authority* [2001] 3 All E.R. 289; *Re HIV Haemophiliac Litigation* (1990),
[1996] P.I.Q.R. P220; *Brown v Alberta* [1994] 2 W.W.R. 283, Alta QB. See also *H v Royal Alexandra
Hospital for Children* [1990] 1 Med. L.R. 297, NSWSC; *E. v Australian Red Cross Society* (1991) 99
A.L.R. 601; [1991] 2 Med. L.R. 303, Fed Court of Aust; (1991) 105 A.L.R. 53, Aust Fed CA; *PQ v
Australian Red Cross Society* [1992] 1 V.R. 19, Vict SC; *Pittman Estate v Bain* (1994) 112 D.L.R.
(4th) 257, Ont Ct, Gen Div; *Kitchen v McMullin* (1989) 62 D.L.R. (4th) 481, NBCA. On defective
blood bags see (1995) 311 B.M.J. 145.
[4] *The Creutzfeldt-Jakob Disease Litigation, Plaintiffs v United Kingdom Medical Research Council*
(1996) 54 B.M.L.R. 8; [1996] 7 Med. L.R. 309; para.3–069.
[5] *Foster v Biosil* (2000) 59 B.M.L.R. 178; *Hollis v Dow Corning Corp.* (1995) 129 D.L.R. (4th) 609,
SCC; *Bendall v McGhan Medical Corp.* (1993) 106 D.L.R. (4th) 339, a case dealing with the
procedural issue of whether a class action should be instituted in Ontario; *Attis v Canada (Minister of
Health)*, 2008 ONCA 660; (2009) 300 D.L.R. (4th) 415. See Balen (2002) 8 *Clinical Risk* 177.
[6] *Worsley v Tambrands Ltd* [2000] P.I.Q.R. P95; *Thompson v Johnson and Johnson Pty Ltd* [1992] 3
Med. L.R. 148; [1991] 2 V.R. 449, SC of Victoria, App Div; see (1990) 301 B.M.J. 257.
[7] *Wilkes v Depuy International Ltd* [2016] EWHC 3096 (QB); [2017] 3 All E.R. 589; *Jones v Zimmer
GmbH* 2013 BCCA 21; [2013] 4 W.W.R. 257; (2013) 358 D.L.R. (4th) 499. Indeed, any artificial joint
could potentially be defective: *Drady v Canada (Minister of Health)* 2008 ONCA 659; (2008) 300
D.L.R. (4th) 443 (temporomandibular joint implant).
[8] For example: heart pacemakers (as in *Boston Scientific Medizintechnik GmbH v AOK
Sachsen-Anhalt – Die Gesundheitskasse (C-503/13)* EU:C:2015:148; [2015] 3 C.M.L.R. 6; (2015)
144 B.M.L.R. 225); donated organs (see *Sumners v Mid-Downs Health Authority and South East
Thames Health Authority* discussed at (1989) 298 B.M.J. 1544; *Sumners v Mid Downs HA & Brighton*

10–002   The same legal principles apply whatever the product in question, although drug injuries do appear to create their own special problems.[9] All drugs have some inherent risk. They are designed to interfere with the body's chemistry, and some patients will have idiosyncratic reactions. Many drugs cannot be made completely safe for their intended or ordinary use even when they are properly manufactured and are not impure. Notwithstanding the medically recognisable risk of harm that they present, the marketing of such drugs may be justified by their utility.[10] Thus, it can be difficult to come to a judgment about what is a "defective" drug, since the risk of side effects for a minority of patients may be acceptable in view of the benefits for the majority of patients.[11] Where, on the other hand, an alternative, safe, option is available a product which carries inherent risk may be categorised as defective.[12]

10–003   A further problem stems from the difficulty of proving causation. This arises at two levels. First, it must be shown that the drug in question is capable of causing the type of harm from which the claimant is suffering. This will depend upon

---

HA [1996] C.L.Y. 2366 on the assessment of damages); contaminated or defective donated sperm (*ter Neuzen v Korn* (1995) 127 D.L.R. (4th) 577, SCC). In *A v National Blood Authority* [2001] 3 All E.R. 289 it was held that human blood amounted to a "product", for the purposes of the Consumer Protection Act 1987 and it would seem to follow that other bodily fluids or organs would also fall within the terms of the Act. In any event, so far as the tort of negligence is concerned liability turns on the foreseeability of the risk of harm from contamination, rather than categorisation as a "product" or otherwise.

[9] See R. Goldberg, *Medicinal Product Liability and Regulation* (Oxford: Hart Publishing, 2013).

[10] *Buchan v Ortho Pharmaceutical (Canada) Ltd* (1986) 25 D.L.R. (4th) 658 at 668, Ont CA; *XYZ v Schering Health Care Ltd* [2002] EWHC 1420 (QB); (2002) 70 B.M.L.R. 88. Surprisingly, perhaps, there is no reported case in this country in which a court has had to make a finding of liability against a drug manufacturer. Claims have been made in respect of, inter alia, thalidomide, opren, debendox, myodil, pertussis vaccine, neomycin, benzodiazepine, epilim and seroxat but the actions have either settled or failed for want of proof of causation: see *Davies v Eli Lilly & Co* (1987) 137 N.L.J. 1183 and Dyer (1988) 296 B.M.J. 109 on the Opren settlement; Orme (1985) 291 B.M.J. 918 on Debendox; and *The Times*, 1 August 1995 on the myodil settlement. The group actions in the benzodiazepine litigation gave rise to numerous procedural difficulties and were eventually struck out as an abuse of process, and for want of prosecution: see *AB v John Wyeth & Brother Ltd and Roche Products Ltd* [1992] 3 Med. L.R. 190; [1992] P.I.Q.R. P437; [1992] 1 W.L.R. 169, CA; *AB v John Wyeth & Brother Ltd* [1993] 4 Med. L.R. 1; *AB v John Wyeth & Brother Ltd* [1994] P.I.Q.R. P109; [1994] 5 Med. L.R. 149, CA; *AB v John Wyeth & Brother Ltd* [1997] P.I.Q.R. P385; [1997] 8 Med. L.R. 57. See also *Bailey v GlaxoSmithKline (UK) Ltd* [2016] EWHC 178 (QB) (a case-management hearing in litigation concerning the antidepressant seroxat). For discussion of some of the difficulties faced by claimants suing in respect of drug injuries 30 years after the thalidomide disaster see Ferguson [1992] J.R. 226; and in respect of claims arising from the side effects of the contraceptive pill, see Ferguson (1995) 145 N.L.J. 846.

[11] This is the logic of the limited no-fault compensation available under the Vaccine Damage Payments Act 1979 for individuals who suffer vaccine damage, since they bear the brunt of the cost of a scheme that is intended to benefit the population at large. The sums available are comparatively small in relation to the harm suffered, and there may still be problems in proving causation: see *Loveday v Renton* [1990] 1 Med. L.R. 117. For discussion of the Act see Dworkin [1978–79] J.S.W.L. 330; R. Goldberg, "Vaccine damage and causation—social and legal implications" (1996) 3 J.S.S.L. 100; R. Tindley, "A critical analysis of the vaccine damage payments scheme" (2008) 19 E.B.L. Rev. 321; and para.1–049.

[12] *Nicholson v John Deere Ltd* (1986) 34 D.L.R. (4th) 542 at 549, per Smith J, Ont HC: "A manufacturer does not have the right to manufacture an inherently dangerous article when a method exists of manufacturing the same article without risk of harm. No amount of or degree of specificity of warning will exonerate him from liability if he does."

scientific evidence, which may be difficult to obtain and may be equivocal in its conclusions.[13] Where, for example, there is a substantial delay in the injuries becoming manifest, as can be the case with teratogenic injuries,[14] and/or where the adverse reactions constitute an addition to the background risk so that it is extremely difficult, if not impossible, to distinguish drug injuries from other, often unknown, causes, the difficulties of proving causation may be insurmountable.[15] Secondly, even where it is accepted that the drug is capable of causing the type of injury concerned, claimants must still prove that *their* injury was attributable to the drug in question and not some other factor, such as illnesses for which they were being treated, or an unforeseen interaction between a number of drugs taken at the same time. Where generic drugs or drugs from different manufacturers have been used over a number of years, there may be difficulties simply in identifying a defendant.[16]

Donoghue v Stevenson[17] established that, in addition to any liability in contract, **10–004** there could also be liability in the tort of negligence for defective products, but, in spite of some cases which suggested that in certain circumstances a high standard of care would be required, the action has remained fault-based. The English courts have not followed the American example where strict liability in tort was established.[18] In the 1970s a number of law reform bodies recommended that strict liability for defective products should be introduced and following a European Community initiative the United Kingdom has a form of strict liability by virtue of the Consumer Protection Act 1987. Thus, liability for damage caused by defective products is a combination of liability in contract, the tort of negligence and under Pt I of the Consumer Protection Act 1987.

---

[13] Or may even demonstrate that the drug does not have the adverse effects which are alleged: see Goldberg (1996) 4 Med. L. Rev. 32, discussing the distorting effect of litigation on the scientific evidence in cases where it was alleged that the drug Debendox caused birth defects.

[14] See, e.g. *Sindell v Abbott Laboratories* 607 P. 2d 924, (1980) below, para.10–070

[15] *Kay v Ayrshire and Arran Health Board* [1987] 2 All E.R. 417, where the claimant failed to prove that an overdose of penicillin could cause deafness; *Loveday v Renton* [1990] 1 Med. L.R. 117, where the claimant failed to prove, on a balance of probabilities, that pertussis vaccine could cause brain damage in young children, although it was "possible" that there was a causal link; see also *Rothwell v Raes* (1988) 54 D.L.R. (4th) 193; aff'd (1990) 76 D.L.R. (4th) 280, Ont CA on the pertussis vaccine and causation; cf. the more robust approach of the Supreme Court of Ireland to the question of the causal link between a defective batch of pertussis vaccine and brain damage in children in *Best v Wellcome Foundation Ltd* [1994] 5 Med. L.R. 81; [1993] 3 I.R. 421; (1992) 17 B.M.L.R 11. See also the *Royal Commission on Civil Liability and Compensation for Personal Injury*, Cmnd.7054 (1978), Vol.I, para.1364.

[16] See, e.g., *Mann v Wellcome Foundation Ltd* unreported 20 January 1989, QBD; cf. the approach adopted to this type of problem by the California Court of Appeal in *Sindell v Abbott Laboratories* 607 P. 2d 924, (1980), para.10–070, below.

[17] [1932] A.C. 562.

[18] See *Restatement, Torts (Second)*, § 402A (1965). The American Law Institute's *Restatement (Third) of Torts: Products Liability* (1998) removed the "consumer expectations" test from the concept of what is defective and distinguished between three types of defect: manufacturing defects, design defects and marketing defects (essentially inadequate instructions for use or warnings). It involved a switch to a form of liability that is arguably closer to negligence than strict liability.

1. CONTRACT

10–005   The ultimate consumer of a product will rarely be in a contractual relationship with the manufacturer, and this is particularly true of medicinal products. However, a defective product sold by a retailer may give rise to an action for breach of contract, which through the contractual chain of supply may be traced back to the manufacturer in the form of indemnity claims. The contractual action is limited, by the doctrine of privity of contract, to the purchaser of the product and it is of no value to, for example, a member of the purchaser's family injured by the product. This is the major drawback of the claim in contract.

10–006   Where a contractual remedy is available it will often be more advantageous to the claimant than a claim in tort. A purchaser of goods will have the benefit of implied terms as to the satisfactory quality and fitness for purpose of the goods,[19] which in the case of "consumer" transactions cannot be excluded.[20] Liability is strict, in the sense that it does not have to be shown that the defect was attributable to the vendor's fault, and the exercise of reasonable care is not a defence. Moreover, the contractual action is available for products which are defective in quality, though not dangerous, if the defect is such as to constitute a breach of warranty. This type of claim is not available in the tort of negligence.

10–007   Thus, non-prescription products sold by retail pharmacists over the counter may be the subject of a contractual action if the purchaser sustains injury, as would drugs supplied on private (i.e. non-NHS) prescription. Products supplied under NHS prescriptions, on the other hand, are not supplied under a contract between the pharmacist and the consumer, but by virtue of the of the patient's statutory right to demand the product on payment of the prescription charge and the Minister's statutory obligation to supply it.[21] The result is that, in practice, contractual claims arising from defective drugs are likely to be extremely rare.[22]

---

[19] Consumer Rights Act 2015 ss. 9 and 10 (for consumer contracts); Sale of Goods Act 1979 s.14 and Supply of Goods and Services Act 1982 s.4 (for non-consumer contracts) and s.9 (for non-consumer contracts of hire). *Baxter v Barnes* [2015] EWHC 54 (QB) defendant in breach of s.9(2) of the Supply of Goods and Services Act 1982 (platform supplied by the defendant was not of a satisfactory quality). Note that what is satisfactory quality or fit for its purpose will be a matter of degree in the case of drugs which may have known side effects; it does include, however, the packaging and instructions for use, so that if the instructions are wrong or misleading the goods are not of satisfactory quality or fit for their purpose: *Wormell v RHM Agriculture (East) Ltd* [1986] 1 All E.R. 769.

[20] Consumer Rights Act 2015 s.31.

[21] *Pfizer Corpn v Ministry of Health* [1965] A.C. 512; *Appleby v Sleep* [1968] 2 All E.R. 265 at 269.

[22] And in any event, the mere fact that a drug carries inherent risks from side effects does not necessarily mean that it is not of satisfactory quality or not fit for its purpose: *Merck Sharp & Dohme (Australia) Pty Ltd v Peterson* [2011] FCAFC 128; (2011) 284 A.L.R. 1 at [173]–[174], where the Full Court of the Federal Court of Australia observed that "it cannot be presumed in law, and it is not obvious in fact, that the patient impliedly makes known to the dispensing pharmacist that he or she is acquiring the product that is dispensed for purposes which include some generalised purpose of safety or absence of adverse side-effects ... prescription medications are rarely risk free. No doubt that is why they are available only on prescription".

In some circumstances a NHS body may enter into a contractual relationship with a patient, for example, for the sale of a piece of equipment.[23]

Retailers sued in contract by the purchaser of defective goods will normally have a contractual claim for indemnity against their own vendor (wholesaler or distributor), and so on, up the contractual chain to the manufacturer who produced the defective goods, subject to any valid exemption clauses. In this way, in theory at least, liability will rest with the person responsible for the defect. This contractual chain may break down if, for example, one link is missing, having gone into liquidation or is simply untraceable through lack of records.[24] The doctrine of privity of contract then prevents any further claims along the contractual chain.[25] From the claimant purchaser's point of view this will be irrelevant, unless it is the retailer who is no longer available to be sued, in which case the purchaser's contractual claim will be useless. This will leave the purchaser in the same position as all other claimants injured by a defective product, having to rely on a claim in tort for negligence or under the Consumer Protection Act 1987. **10–008**

2. TORT

(a) Manufacturers' duty

In *Donoghue v Stevenson*[26] the House of Lords held that the manufacturers of a defective product owed a duty of care in negligence to the ultimate consumer of the product, notwithstanding the absence of any contractual relationship between the consumer and the manufacturer.[27] In the course of his speech Lord Atkin expressed the duty in these terms: **10–009**

> "A manufacturer of products which he sells in such a form as to show that he intends them to reach the ultimate consumer in the form in which they left him, with no reasonable possibility

---

[23] See, e.g., *SE Wood v Days Health UK Ltd* [2016] EWHC 1079 (QB) where a NHS Trust had supplied a motorised wheelchair free of charge as an NHS service, but the patient paid £500 to the Trust for a "seat riser" as an add-on unit. The patient alleged that she suffered injury when the seat riser malfunctioned. Laing J granted the claimant summary judgment in contract against the Trust on the basis that there had been a breach of the terms implied by ss.13 and 14 of the Sale of Goods Act 1979, and/or of an express obligation to repair and maintain the wheelchair. The Trust's argument that there was no contract because it had not made a profit and that it was merely ordering the riser from the supplier on behalf of the claimant was rejected on the evidence.

[24] As occurred in *Lambert v Lewis* [1982] A.C. 225.

[25] There may be a claim, however, under the Civil Liability (Contribution) Act 1978. In addition, it has been held that economic loss suffered by a distributor in a chain of supply which consists of a liability to pay damages to the ultimate consumer for physical injuries, or to indemnify a distributor lower in the chain for liability to the consumer for physical injuries, may be recoverable from the manufacturer under the principle of *Donoghue v Stevenson* [1932] A.C. 562: see *Lambert v Lewis* [1982] A.C. 225 at 277–278; *Virgo Steamship Co. SA v Skaarup Shipping Corpn.* [1988] 1 Lloyd's Rep. 352.

[26] [1932] A.C. 562.

[27] So removing the so-called "privity of contract" fallacy, which argued that the claimant was seeking to take the benefit of a contract (between manufacturer and wholesaler or retailer) to which he was not a party, attributed to *Winterbottom v Wright* (1842) 10 M. & W. 109. For discussion of the privity of contract fallacy see *Dutton v Bognor Regis Urban District Council* [1972] 1 Q.B. 373 at 392–393.

of intermediate examination, and with the knowledge that the absence of reasonable care in the preparation or putting up of the products will result in injury to the consumer's life or property, owes a duty to the consumer to take that reasonable care."[28]

Lord Thankerton said that the defendant brought himself into a direct relationship with the consumer by placing his product upon the market in a form which precluded interference with or examination of the product by any intermediate handler, with the result that the consumer was entitled to rely on the exercise of reasonable care by the manufacturer to secure that the product should not be harmful.

10–010   The manufacturer's duty has been given a broad interpretation. "Product" includes almost any item capable of causing damage, such as underpants,[29] motor cars,[30] hair dye,[31] lifts[32] and chemicals.[33] Similarly, "ultimate consumer" means anyone foreseeably harmed by the defective product. This includes the user of the product, such as a donee, a member of the purchaser's family, including a foetus in utero,[34] or an employee of the purchaser,[35] someone who handles the product, such as a storeman or a shopkeeper,[36] and a bystander.[37]

(i)   Defendants

10–011   The range of potential defendants has also been extended to include not only manufacturers, but also repairers[38] and assemblers.[39] Suppliers of goods, such as retailers or wholesalers, may be liable if the circumstances are such that they ought reasonably to have inspected the goods or tested them.[40] Distributors who obtain goods from suppliers of doubtful reputation ought to test them,[41] and a fortiori when the manufacturers' instructions state that the product should be tested.[42] The duty does not arise in all cases of supply, only where the

---

[28] [1932] A.C. 562 at 599. This duty applies to personal injuries and physical damage to other property, including economic loss consequential on the physical damage, applying the usual principles of the tort of negligence. Pure economic loss, which includes physical damage to the product itself, is not recoverable: *Murphy v Brentwood District Council* [1991] 1 A.C. 398; *Muirhead v Industrial Tank Specialities Ltd* [1986] Q.B. 507.

[29] *Grant v Australian Knitting Mills Ltd* [1936] A.C. 85.

[30] *Herschtal v Stewart & Arden Ltd* [1940] 1 K.B. 155.

[31] *Watson v Buckley, Osborne Garrett & Co Ltd* [1940] 1 All E.R. 174.

[32] *Haseldine v Daw & Son Ltd* [1941] 2 K.B. 343.

[33] *Vacwell Engineering Co. Ltd v B.D.H. Chemicals Ltd* [1971] 1 Q.B. 88.

[34] Congenital Disabilities (Civil Liability) Act 1976; see paras 2–135 to 2–144.

[35] *Davie v New Merton Board Mills Ltd* [1959] A.C. 604.

[36] *Barnett v H. and J. Packer & Co. Ltd* [1940] 3 All E.R. 575.

[37] *Stennett v Hancock* [1939] 2 All E.R. 578.

[38] *Stennett v Hancock* [1939] 2 All E.R. 578; *Haseldine v Daw & Son Ltd* [1941] 2 K.B. 343 at 379.

[39] *Howard v Furness Houlder Argentine Lines Ltd* [1936] 2 All E.R. 781.

[40] *Andrews v Hopkinson* [1957] 1 Q.B. 229; cf. *Hurley v Dyke* [1979] R.T.R. 265. See also *Good-Wear Treaders Ltd v D & B Holdings Ltd* (1979) 98 D.L.R. (3d) 59, holding that a supplier owes a duty not to supply a product to a purchaser whom he knows intends to misuse the product, thereby endangering the safety of third parties.

[41] *Watson v Buckley, Osborne Garrett & Co.* [1940] 1 All E.R. 174.

[42] *Kubach v Hollands* [1937] 3 All E.R. 907.

circumstances indicate that an inspection or test is reasonably required. Clearly, if the dangerous defect was in fact known to the supplier he ought, at least, to give a warning to the recipient.

(ii)   Regulatory agencies as potential defendants

An issue that arises in the context of pharmaceutical products is the possible liability of statutory regulatory agencies. Under the Human Medicines Regulations 2012 the "licensing authority" is responsible for the grant, renewal, variation, suspension and revocation of licences, authorisations, certificates and registrations under the Regulations.[43] The licensing authority is advised by the Commission on Human Medicines, an advisory non-departmental public body sponsored by the Department of Health, which must give advice with respect to the safety, quality and efficacy of medicinal products and promote the collection and investigation of information relating to adverse reactions.[44] The Medicines & Healthcare products Regulatory Agency is an executive agency of the Department of Health which is responsible for the regulation of medicines and medical devices.[45]

10–012

The effect is that pharmaceutical products and medical devices distributed in the United Kingdom will have been scrutinised for safety by an independent public body. If the product is found to have a design defect it is at least arguable that the regulator should be responsible along with the manufacturer, for allowing a defective product to be marketed. The Medicines Act 1968 does not confer any general civil right of action for breach of its terms, nor does it grant any immunities from any action that would otherwise be available.[46] The Human Medicines Regulations 2012 are silent in respect of civil liability, except that

10–013

---

[43] Human Medicines Regulations 2012 (SI 2012/1916) reg.6(1). The licensing authority consists of the Secretary of State and Minister for Health, Social Services and Public Safety: reg.6(2),(6). The Regulations apply to a "medicinal product", which is defined in reg.2.

[44] Human Medicines Regulations 2012 reg.10(3). An "adverse reaction" means a response to a medicinal product that is noxious and unintended: reg.8.

[45] See *http://www.gov.uk/government/organisations/medicines-and-healthcare-products-regulatory-agency*. In addition to the Human Medicines Regulations 2012 see also the Medical Devices Regulations 2002 (SI 2002/618) (as amended), which governs the supply and use of medical devices, implementing three European Directives, 90/385/EEC (on active implantable medical devices); 93/42/EEC (on medical devices); and 98/79/EC (on in vitro diagnostic medical devices). See further Directive 2007/47/EC amending Directives 90/385/EEC and 93/42/EEC (and Directive 98/8/EC on the placing of biocidal products on the market). Regulation (EU) 2017/745 repeals and replaces Directives 90/385/EEC and 93/42/EEC, subject to an 18-month transitional period. The Medicines for Human Use (Clinical Trials) Regulations 2004 (SI 2004/1031) (as amended) implement the European Clinical Trials Directive, 2001/20/EC, which lays down standards for the manufacture, import and labelling of investigational medicinal products. The Directive requires member states to set up inspection systems for good manufacturing practice and good clinical practice. It also provides for safety monitoring of patients/volunteers in trials, and sets out procedures for reporting and recording adverse drug reactions and events. The Regulations provide, inter alia, that a clinical trial may be conducted only if it has been authorised by the licensing authority and an ethics committee has approved it. The EU Clinical Trials Regulation (EU Regulation No.536/2014) repeals and replaces Directive 2001/20/EC but is not scheduled to come into operation until 2018. Details are available at *http://ec.europa.eu/health/human-use/clinical-trials/regulation/index_en.htm* and on the European Medicines Agency website: *http://www.ema.europa.eu/ema*.

[46] Medicines Act 1968 s.133(2).

where the licensing authority makes a recommendation or requirement in response to the suspected or confirmed spread of (a) pathogenic agents; (b) toxins; (c) chemical agents; or (d) nuclear radiation, which may cause harm to human beings, then the holder of an authorisation for the product, the manufacturer of the product, any officer, servant, employee or agent of the holder of an authorisation or the manufacturer, or any healthcare professional cannot be subject to civil liability for any loss or damage resulting from the use of the product in accordance with the recommendation or requirement,[47] though this immunity does not apply to liability under s.2 of the Consumer Protection Act 1987 (liability for defective products).[48]

10–014 **Claims against regulatory agencies generally** In a number of cases it has been held that certain regulatory authorities do not owe a duty of care to members of the public when performing their statutory functions.[49] Most, though not all,[50] of these cases were concerned with pure economic loss, rather than personal injuries and thus may not be directly relevant to actions in respect of alleged negligence in the regulation of medicines or medical devices. Various other factors have been taken into account, however, in denying the existence of a duty of care, some of which would be relevant in this context. All deal with liability for the conduct of third parties, where the question will frequently be: what degree of control did the defendant have over the third party's conduct? The mere fact that the regulatory body could register or de-register the third party and thus had some control over whether the third party could continue the operations which caused the claimant's loss is not a ground for imposing a duty of care.[51] It has been said that the imposition of a duty of care might lead to a conflict of duties, in which the regulatory agency adopts an unusually conservative or defensive approach to its functions because of the fear of liability, a practice which may not be in the public interest.[52] Where the claimant would have an

---

[47] Human Medicines Regulations 2012 reg.345.
[48] Human Medicines Regulations 2012 reg.345(4).
[49] See *Yuen Kun-yeu v Att.-Gen. of Hong Kong* [1988] A.C. 175; *Davis v Radcliffe* [1990] 1 W.L.R. 821; *Rowling v Takaro Properties Ltd* [1988] A.C. 473; *Minories Finance Ltd v Arthur Young* [1989] 2 All E.R. 105; *Mills v Winchester Diocesan Board of Finance* [1989] Ch. 428; *Murphy v Brentwood District Council* [1991] 1 A.C. 398.
[50] cf. *Hill v Chief Constable of West Yorkshire* [1989] 1 A.C. 53 and *Smith v Chief Constable of Sussex* [2008] UKHL 50; [2009] 1 A.C. 225 (allegations that the police owed a duty to the victim of a criminal offence to prevent the offender from causing injury to the claimants). See also *X (Minors) v Bedfordshire County Council* [1995] 2 A.C. 633 where the House of Lords concluded that a social services authority should not owe a duty of care in negligence in respect of the manner in which it performed its statutory child protection functions, whether by wrongly taking a child into care whereby the child suffered psychiatric damage or by negligently failing to take steps to protect children at risk of abuse or neglect. Lord Browne-Wilkinson commented, at 751, that: "the courts should proceed with great care before holding liable in negligence those who have been charged by Parliament with the task of protecting society from the wrongdoings of others." The decision in *X (Minors)* was reversed in *JD v East Berkshire Community Health NHS Trust* [2005] UKHL 23; [2005] 2 A.C. 373, discussed at paras 2–099 et seq.
[51] *Yuen Kun-yeu v Att.-Gen. of Hong Kong* [1988] A.C. 175; *Davis v Radcliffe* [1990] 1 W.L.R. 821.
[52] *Yuen Kun-yeu v Att.-Gen. of Hong Kong* [1988] A.C. 175, 198; *Rowling v Takaro Properties Ltd* [1988] A.C. 473 at 502; *Hill v Chief Constable of West Yorkshire* [1989] 1 A.C. 53 at 63; *X (Minors) v Bedfordshire County Council* [1995] 2 A.C. 633 at 750. On the risk of "defensive licensing" of pharmaceutical products see Teff (1984) 47 M.L.R. 303 at 310–311.

alternative remedy, even against another defendant,[53] or where the claimant is merely a member of a large unascertained class of potential claimants the courts may deny the existence of a duty of care.[54]

In *Yuen Kun-yeu v Att.-Gen. of Hong Kong*[55] the Privy Council took the view that since the statutory framework which established the particular regulatory system did not provide for compensation, it would be "strange" for the courts to superimpose a common law duty of care. Similarly, in *Murphy v Brentwood District Council*[56] Lord Oliver pointed to the absence of any specific provision in the legislation creating a private law right of action for breach of statutory duty, as one reason for not imposing a duty of care on the local authority in exercising its statutory powers to ensure that new buildings comply with building regulations.   **10–015**

In response it might be argued that most of these cases have been concerned with actions for pure economic loss, and that different considerations apply where a public body can be said to owe a statutory duty to the public with regard to public health and safety, as is arguably the position under the Medicines Act 1968 and/or the Human Medicines Regulations 2012. Thus, where a regulatory agency has been established with the specific objective of protecting the public from dangerous practices then, arguably, it should be easier to find a duty of care owed to individual members of the public injured or killed as a result of the agency's negligent failure to regulate. For example, in the Canadian case of *Swanson v The Queen in Right of Canada*[57] it was held that an agency with responsibility for regulating the safety of commercial airlines was liable for negligently permitting an airline to continue unsafe practices, having issued warnings to the airline but failed to take any further enforcement proceedings to require compliance with safety standards. Similarly, in *Perrett v Collins*[58] the Court of Appeal held that the Civil Aviation Authority could owe a duty of care to a passenger injured in an air accident in respect of a negligently issued certificate of airworthiness.[59]   **10–016**

Claims against regulatory agencies in the medical context   In *Department of Health and Social Security v Kinnear*[60] claims were brought against the Department of Health and Social Security (DHSS) in respect of injuries alleged   **10–017**

---

[53] *La Banque Financière de la Cité SA v Westgate Insurance Co. Ltd* [1988] 2 Lloyd's Rep. 513 at 563; *Simaan General Contracting Co. v Pilkington Glass Ltd (No.2)* [1988] Q.B. 758 at 786.

[54] *Hill v Chief Constable of West Yorkshire* [1989] 1 A.C. 53 at 62.

[55] [1988] A.C. 175 at 195.

[56] [1991] 1 A.C. 398 at 490.

[57] (1991) 80 D.L.R. (4th) 741, Fed CA.

[58] [1998] 2 Lloyd's Rep 255; [1999] P.N.L.R. 77. See also *Health and Safety Executive v Thames Trains Ltd* [2003] EWCA Civ 720; (2003) 147 S.J.L.B. 661 where Court of Appeal took the view that it was at least arguable that the Health and Safety Executive (HSE) could owe a duty of care in negligence to the victims of a train crash which may have been caused by a faulty signalling system, on the basis that the HSE had failed to prohibit the use of the track with a signalling system which it should have known was unsafe.

[59] Contrast cf. *Philcox v Civil Aviation Authority*, *The Times*, 8 June 1995 where the Court of Appeal held that the CAA did not owe a duty of care to the owner of an aircraft that crashed because it was the owner's responsibility to maintain the aircraft, and the CAA's supervisory role was for the protection of the public against an owner's failures.

[60] *The Times*, 7 July 1984.

to have been caused by reaction to whooping cough vaccine. The DHSS adopted a policy of promoting immunisation against whooping cough in the bona fide exercise of a statutory discretion under the National Health Service Act 1946 s.26. Stuart-Smith J held that since the policy was within the limits of the discretion it could not give rise to a cause of action.[61] Even allegations of negligence on the part of the department's servants, e.g. in failing to submit relevant reports to the persons taking the policy decisions prior to and leading up to the formulation of the policy, could not found a cause of action against the department. On the other hand, claims that the DHSS had given negligent or misleading advice to health authorities regarding the circumstances in which inoculations should be performed, and the factors to be applied in determining whether particular individuals should be inoculated, were not struck out as disclosing no reasonable cause of action. It was at least arguable that the alleged negligent advice fell within the operational category, in which negligence in the performance of a statutory power could give rise to a duty of care.[62]

10–018   In *Re HIV Haemophiliac Litigation*[63] the Court of Appeal had to consider whether haemophiliacs who had been infected with the HIV virus as a result of receiving contaminated blood products, had a prima facie case in negligence against, inter alia, the Department of Health, the Licensing Authority under the Medicines Act 1968 and the Committee on the Safety of Medicines (CSM),[64] in the course of proceedings for discovery of documents. Ralph Gibson LJ commented that although it was difficult to prove negligence when the defendant was required to exercise discretion and form judgments on the allocation of public resources, that was not sufficient to make it clear that there could be no

---

[61] Applying *Anns v Merton London Borough Council* [1978] A.C. 728 at 754; *Dorset Yacht Co. Ltd v Home Office* [1970] A.C. 1004 at 1067. See also *Bonthrone v Secretary of State for Scotland* 1987 S.L.T. 34; *Ross v Secretary of State for Scotland* [1990] 1 Med. L.R. 235. In *Danns v Department of Health* [1998] P.I.Q.R. P226, the Court of Appeal held that the failure of the Department of Health to publish information in the media about the risks of late re-canalisation following a vasectomy (put at 2,000 to 1) did not give rise to a private law action for breach of the Ministry of Health Act 1919 s.2.
[62] Adopting the operational/policy dichotomy used by Lord Wilberforce in *Anns v Merton London Borough Council* [1978] A.C. 728. Similarly, in *Rothwell v Raes* (1988) 54 D.L.R. (4th) 193 at 346, Ont HC; it was held that the Ontario Ministry of Health did owe a duty of care with regard to the implementation of a policy decision to establish a system for pertussis vaccination, although the Ministry had not been negligent on the facts. The trial judge relied on *City of Kamloops v Neilsen* (1984) 10 D.L.R. (4th) 641, in which the Supreme Court of Canada had adopted Lord Wilberforce's operational/policy dichotomy. *Anns v Merton London Borough Council* was overruled by the House of Lords in *Murphy v Brentwood District Council* [1991] 1 A.C. 398 on the question of the *type of loss* which may be recoverable for acts of negligence, but the distinction between operational and policy decisions, which was relied on by Lord Diplock in *Home Office v Dorset Yacht Co. Ltd* [1970] A.C. 1004, has continued to be used by the courts as a basis for determining negligence in the performance of statutory powers. In *X (Minors) v Bedfordshire County Council* [1995] 2 A.C. 633 at 736–737, Lord Browne-Wilkinson suggested that the public law doctrine of ultra vires was not a suitable test; rather, where it is sought to make a public body liable at common law for negligence in the exercise of a discretion the first requirement is to show that the decision was outside the ambit of the discretion altogether, but where the factors relevant to the exercise of the discretion include matters of policy the court cannot adjudicate on such policy matters, and thus a common law duty of care in relation to the taking of decisions involving policy matters cannot exist.
[63] (1990), [1996] P.I.Q.R. P220.
[64] Now the Commission on Human Medicines (*http://www.gov.uk/government/organisations/commission-on-human-medicines*).

claim in negligence. This interlocutory decision appears simply to assume, without deciding the issue, that a duty of care could exist.[65]

In *Smith v Secretary of State for Health*[66] it was alleged that the CSM[67] had been negligent in delaying a public announcement warning of the risk that aspirin could cause serious harm to children. The claimant was a six-year-old child who contracted chicken pox in May 1986. She was given aspirin for relief of symptoms, in accordance with recommended doses for children. She developed Reye's syndrome, and sustained seriously disabling injury. Less than a month later the Department of Health issued a general public warning advising that children under 12 should not be given aspirin in any form, and required pharmacists to remove all junior aspirin from their shelves. This was as a result of advice from the CSM that in some cases aspirin had been linked to children developing this condition. The CSM had been monitoring the potential problem before it concluded at a meeting in March 1986 that the evidence of a causal link between aspirin and Reye's syndrome in children was overwhelming. It recommended that a general warning on the use of aspirin in children should be given without delay. Shortly after that meeting the Department of Health held a meeting in April 1986 with representatives of the aspirin industry where it became apparent that the manufacturers would probably be willing to withdraw paediatric aspirin from sale voluntarily. It was judged that this would be a much more effective means of dealing with the problem than invoking the statutory mechanisms under the Medicines Act 1968. The Department therefore decided to postpone the CSM recommendation to publish an immediate warning. Following further meetings with the industry, the manufacturers agreed to the voluntary withdrawal from sale of paediatric aspirin and to participate in a campaign of public education. The CSM met again at the end of May and the Department made a public announcement on 10 June 1986. The claimant argued that the decision to delay a public announcement after the meeting of the CSM in March 1986 was negligent.

10–019

Causation was not seriously contested. Morland J found that had the warnings about the danger been prominently publicised in the media before the claimant became unwell, her mother would have become of aware of them and would not have given aspirin. The defendants accepted that the administration of aspirin was

10–020

---

[65] See also *Brown v Alberta* [1994] 2 W.W.R. 283, Alta QB, where, on similar facts, the court refused to strike out the claimant's claims against the Crown as disclosing no reasonable cause of action, on the ground that claims should not be struck out unless it could be said that the actions were doomed to fail on the facts, which would not be the case unless the issue was beyond doubt, clear and unambiguous. It was alleged that the Crown had failed to pass regulations and adopt policies relating to the collection and distribution of blood products, and had failed to provide funding for the implementation of blood testing. In *Robb Estate v Canadian Red Cross Society* (2001) 9 C.C.L.T. (3d) 131 the Ontario Court of Appeal held that the Canadian Red Cross Society had not been negligent in failing to take positive steps to accelerate the regulatory process to allow heat-treated blood products (as a means of destroying the HIV virus) to be used for the treatment of haemophiliacs. In passing, the Court commented, at [66], that the regulatory agency was "required to take reasonable steps to abide by its own regulatory processes. It had no obligation to, nor in our view could it, dispense with the regulatory requirements . . ."

[66] [2002] Lloyd's Rep. Med. 333.

[67] In 2005 this committee became the Commission on Human Medicines. The functions of the Commission are set out in the Human Medicines Regulations 2012 (SI 2012/1916) reg.10.

a contributing cause of the claimant's Reye's syndrome. Thus, the two substantive issues were whether the decision to postpone the publication of the warning was negligent and whether the defendants owed a duty of care to a member of the public in reaching a decision about such a warning in its role as regulator. Morland J found for the defendants on both issues. First, on the question of breach of duty, although there was a real risk of grave or fatal injury to two or three children created by the delay in issuing the warning, this had to be balanced against the:

> "...undoubted benefit of a coherent co-ordinated comprehensive campaign including the withdrawal of paediatric aspirin with the full weight of the Department of Health, the CSM and the industry behind it thus giving a clear definitive unambiguous message to both professionals and the general public."[68]

Without a postponement of the warning there was a risk that the positive co-operation of the industry, and the benefits to the campaign that that created, might be lost. In the circumstances, his Lordship concluded that the postponement was reasonably justifiable, and therefore the defendants had not been negligent.

10–021 With regard to the duty of care, Morland J held that it could not be said that the Secretary of State or the CSM could never owe a duty of care to an individual member of the public from a failure to exercise or an improper exercise of statutory powers and duties. For example, decisions that were irrational or reached in bad faith could give rise to a duty.[69] Moreover, there was "no blanket immunity from a common law suit if the special circumstances demand a remedy."[70] But where the CSM was making discretionary or policy decisions its conduct was not justiciable in private law, and it would be contrary to the public interest to allow those decisions to form the basis of a duty of care. Although there could be a narrow line between discretionary/policy decisions and operational decisions, the decision to postpone the CSM's final recommendation until the May meeting and the decision to advise against an interim warning were clearly on the discretionary/policy side of the line. So were a number of other decisions that the CSM had to make in relation to the warnings, such as the upper age limit of children; the mode of issuing the warning (whether by a general media warning or a warning to doctors only); whether to delay the warning until the pharmaceutical industry had agreed fully to co-operate; whether or not paediatric aspirin should be withdrawn; and the details of labelling.[71] It followed that no common law duty was owed by the CSM or the Secretary of State in respect of these decisions because they were matters of discretion or policy and so not justiciable.

---

[68] [2002] Lloyd's Rep. Med. 333 at [106].
[69] [2002] Lloyd's Rep. Med. 333 at [95]. His Lordship gave the examples of a decision to delay an announcement for political reasons or a decision to delay a meeting to avoid a clash with a sporting event.
[70] [2002] Lloyd's Rep. Med. 333 at [95].
[71] [2002] Lloyd's Rep. Med. 333 at [91] to [94].

Canada The Canadian courts have had to consider the position of the regulator **10–022** of medicinal products and medical devices on a number of occasions. In *Baric v Tomalk*[72] Pierce J refused to strike out as disclosing no reasonable cause of action an allegation that the Canadian medical devices regulatory agency owed a private law duty of care to individual patients when implementing its regulatory policy concerning approvals for medical devices imported into Canada. The agency's role was the pre-market investigation, monitoring, approval, testing, and regulation of medical devices, including imported devices. It was relevant, said Pierce J, that the agency was:

> "...the only regulator of medical devices, with full powers to inspect, analyze, seize, warn and prevent sale of medical devices available in Canada that may cause harm. No other agency or individual in Canada is invested with these powers. It is evident that the purpose of the statutory scheme and the administration based on it is to minimize risks to patients receiving medical devices. Thus, it is arguable that the plaintiffs would rely on Health Canada to screen medical devices; to remove from distribution any medical devices it knew were available for implantation in Canada and likely to be harmful; and to warn them of any danger. The plaintiffs might ask: 'If we cannot rely on the Bureau of Medical Devices, then on whom do we rely? Who else has the expertise?' It is at least arguable that the oral surgeons did not have the resources to investigate medical devices; neither did the hospital."[73]

In response to the defendants' argument that they were engaged in policy-making, taking into account the wider public interest, the judge commented that the "line between making policy and implementing it is a fine one, and fact specific". It was at least arguable that once Parliament had established a screening programme for medical devices and equipped the regulator with the means to undertake that task, the public will rely on that regulatory jurisdiction.[74] It was also arguable that:

> "...the role of Health Canada went beyond making policy about medical devices. The allegations in the pleadings suggest that policy, once made, was purposefully implemented with the end-users of devices in mind. Once a government chooses to occupy a regulatory field, it must do so without negligence."[75]

This approach has not been followed in subsequent cases. In *Klein v American* **10–023** *Medical Systems Inc.*[76] a claim was brought against, inter alia, Health Canada (an agency of the Canadian federal government that regulates the sale and marketing of medical devices), in respect of a medical device designed to alleviate or cure female incontinence. It was held that Health Canada did not owe a duty of care to patients allegedly injured by a defective medical device. The relevant Regulations did not impose an explicit duty on Health Canada to assess the safety of a

---

[72] (2006) 38 C.C.L.T. (3d) 300, Ont SCJ.
[73] (2006) 38 C.C.L.T. (3d) 300 at [64].
[74] (2006) 38 C.C.L.T. (3d) 300 at [84].
[75] (2006) 38 C.C.L.T. (3d) 300 at [86]. The pleadings alleged facts which, if proved at trial, would have constituted a gross dereliction of the regulator's responsibilities (whether or not those responsibilities were owed to individuals or only to the public at large). It may be that Pierce J was persuaded by this to at least allow the claimant to establish the facts. The judge also rejected an argument that the claim was advocating a new form of regulatory liability not previously recognised by the courts, citing the decision of the Supreme Court of Canada in *Barreau du Québec v McCullock-Finney* (2004) 240 D.L.R. (4th) 410; see para.2–258.
[76] (2006) 278 D.L.R. (4th) 722; (2006) 44 C.C.L.T. (3d) 47 (Ont SCJ).

product, and the role performed by Health Canada in exercising administrative discretion in the public interest was incompatible with a private law duty of care. Recognising a duty of care would create a spectrum of unlimited liability to an unlimited class, and would effectively create an insurance scheme for medical devices funded by taxpayers. A duty of care might also have a negative impact on the government's ability to balance all relevant interests when making regulatory decisions regarding medical devices. Public health involved placing considerations of collective risk and benefit to a population above consideration as to the possible effects on individuals. The proper defendant in such cases was the manufacturer who is responsible for the careful monitoring and long term safety of the drug or device.[77]

10–024   The Ontario Court of Appeal took a similar view in *Drady v Canada (Minister of Health)*,[78] a case concerning temporomandibular joint implant and *Attis v Canada (Minister of Health)*,[79] which concerned breast implants. In *Drady* the claimant alleged that scientific staff at Health Canada knew about the danger posed by the joint implants and had been negligent in failing to prohibit test, assess, monitor and warn the public and users about the risks of the devices. Lang JA held that though Health Canada owed a public law duty of care to the residents of Canada generally, breach of such a public law duty did not give rise to a private law cause of action. Given that there was no private law duty of care arising out of the statutory framework of regulation, the issue was whether Health Canada had assumed a proximate relationship with the claimant based on the interactions between the parties. The pleadings contained allegations that Health Canada had made general statements to the public which amounted to representations about the safety of the devices, but there was no specific representation or reliance on Health Canada regarding the safety of the implant. In those circumstances it was plain and obvious that the claimant could not establish a direct and close relationship of proximity making it just and fair to impose a private law duty of care on Health Canada, and accordingly the claim was struck out as disclosing no reasonable cause of action.

10–025   In *Attis* similar allegations were made concerning the failure of Health Canada to regulate breast implants, specifically in failing to: issue a ban or warning about the devices; seize, monitor or test the devices; remediate the consequences of the failed devices; and enforce the regulations against the manufacturers and distributors; and that there had been negligence in applying a risk-benefit analysis to the implants. The claimants relied on *Baric v Tomalk*,[80] but Lang JA considered that, to the extent that it recognised a form of government liability for negligence in the context of the medical device regulatory regime, *Baric* had

---

[77] (2006) 278 D.L.R. (4th) 722; (2006) 44 C.C.L.T. (3d) 47 (Ont SCJ) at [37]. Chapnik J. noted, at [33], that: "Health Canada is only one player in the complex regulatory and delivery scheme governing medical devices in Canada. It has no direct role in the commercial transaction or the medical decision-making that leads to individual use. The duties of care toward the patient or consumer are qualitatively different from any public duty owed by Health Canada as the government regulator."
[78] 2008 ONCA 659; (2008) 300 D.L.R. (4th) 443.
[79] 2008 ONCA 660; (2009) 300 D.L.R. (4th) 415 at [66].
[80] (2006) 38 C.C.L.T. (3d) 300, Ont SCJ; para.10–022.

effectively been overruled by *Klein v American Medical Systems Inc.*[81] Again, the Ontario Court of Appeal concluded that the statutory scheme indicated that the government's duty was owed to the public as a whole, not to an individual consumer. The statutory duty in relation to the safety of devices was explicitly placed on the manufacturer and the distributor, not the government:

> "...there was no obligation on Health Canada to undertake safety and efficacy testing, or to engage any other compliance or enforcement mechanism. The regulations simply authorized Health Canada to enforce the various aspects of the compliance requirements if it chose to do so. Thus, Health Canada was akin to an overseer or watchdog, able to employ discretionary, but not mandatory, enforcement of the legislative scheme."[82]

The government was dependent on the manufacturer to ensure product safety, as much as the consumer. On the other hand, direct communication or interaction between the regulatory agency and the individual in the operation or implementation of a policy could give rise to a private law duty of care, "particularly where the safety of the individual is at risk".[83] Lang JA gave the example of a decision by a government agency to issue a warning about a specific danger or to make representations about the safety of a product. The government could be liable for the manner in which the warning was issued, or the content of the representations, especially where the government had disseminated the warning or representation knowing that the individual consumer would rely on its contents and the individual does so.[84]

On the claimants' pleaded case in *Attis* Health Canada had not provided any direct service to the claimants and had not had any contact with them. Health Canada did not keep, and was not required to keep, any record of individuals who received implants, and there was no mechanism to notify individuals about product defects or recalls. Those responsibilities were placed on the manufacturer. The statutory regime placed the duty on the medical device industry to ensure the safety of its products, to track product complaints, to recall dangerous products, and to warn consumers, and the claimants' expectations and reliance would have been on their medical advisors, the hospital, the manufacturer and the distributor of the device. Health Canada had been acting within its statutory role in exercising its discretion regarding the enforcement of the regulatory regime, and the absence of any direct interaction with the claimants it was plain and obvious that the claimants had failed to frame a cause of action capable of establishing a proximate relationship with Health Canada for the purposes of a establishing duty of care in negligence.

10–026

In any event, Lang JA considered that there were strong policy reasons to reject such a duty of care, including the risk of indeterminate liability which could result in the government becoming the virtual insurer of medical devices, and the potential chilling effect on public health if Health Canada was held to owe a private law duty of care to the individual consumer. In making regulatory decisions Health Canada had to weigh the need of some individuals to obtain

10–027

---

[81] (2006) 278 D.L.R. (4th) 722; (2006) 44 C.C.L.T. (3d) 47 (Ont SCJ).
[82] *Attis v Canada (Minister of Health)*, 2008 ONCA 660; (2009) 300 D.L.R. (4th) 415 at [57].
[83] 2008 ONCA 660; (2009) 300 D.L.R. (4th) 415 at [66].
[84] 2008 ONCA 660; (2009) 300 D.L.R. (4th) 415 at [66].

relief from suffering (and sometimes death), despite the risks of a particular device, with the desire of others to avoid all risk. In making such decisions the regulator had to consider the needs of the public at large in determining whether a device met the minimum requirements for sale and distribution. The risk of liability would distract it from its mandate of establishing public health priorities, and this would be contrary to public health principles and detrimental to the collective public interest. Finally, imposing liability on the regulator could result in decreased vigilance by the manufacturer, importer and distributor of the product, and diminished deterrence for a regulated industry was to be avoided particularly when it was the industry, not the regulator, that held critical knowledge regarding product safety.

10–028   *Taylor v Canada (Attorney General)*[85] was another class action against Health Canada alleging regulatory negligence, in respect of temporomandibular joint implants. The parties accepted the approach adopted in *Drady v Canada (Minister of Health)*[86] and *Attis v Canada (Minister of Health)*[87] to the analysis of the statutory regulatory regime. The question was whether the pleadings had alleged sufficient interaction between Health Canada and the claimant to establish a finding of proximity sufficient for the purposes of a prima facie duty of care. There was a distinction, said Doherty JA, between representations made specifically to a claimant and relied on by that claimant, which could create a direct connection between the regulator and the claimant, and general representations made by the regulator to the public and relied on by the claimant as a member of the public which, standing alone, did not create a direct relationship. However, general representations and reliance on those representations could, in combination with other factors, create a relationship that was sufficiently close and direct to render it fair and just to impose an obligation to be mindful of the claimant's legitimate interests. The pleadings alleged that Health Canada had repeatedly misrepresented the safety of the implants that the claimants had received by wrongly representing that the implants had received a notice of compliance under the regulatory regime, and that when Health Canada became aware of its misrepresentation it failed to correct it despite the knowledge that the implants were being improperly imported and sold in Canada and that there was strong evidence that the implants were unsafe. Those allegations described a relationship between Health Canada and the users of the implants that was different from the relationship that existed between Health Canada and consumers of medical devices at large. On an application to strike out the claims as disclosing no reasonable cause of action Doherty JA concluded that it was not plain and obvious that the claim was bound to fail for want of a private law duty of care, and therefore the actions should not be struck out at that stage.[88]

---

[85] 2012 ONCA 479; (2012) 352 D.L.R. (4th) 690.
[86] 2008 ONCA 659; (2008) 300 D.L.R. (4th) 443.
[87] 2008 ONCA 660; (2009) 300 D.L.R. (4th) 415.
[88] The action was allowed to proceed, but it remained for the claimants to establish the factual basis for the claimed duty of care, and even if the claimants succeeded in this, the policy arguments against the imposition of a duty of care articulated by Lang JA in *Attis v Canada (Minister of Health)* would tend to point against finding that the regulator owed a duty of care.

(b) Intermediate inspection

The manufacturer's duty applies to products which are intended to "reach the ultimate consumer in the form in which they left him, with no reasonable possibility of intermediate examination".[89] The article need not reach the ultimate consumer in a sealed package for the duty to apply. It is sufficient if it was subject to the same defect as it had when it left the manufacturer, and the consumer used it as it was intended to be used.[90] The mere opportunity for inspection of the product after it has left the hands of the manufacturer will not excuse the defendant.[91] Lord Atkin's term "reasonable possibility" of intermediate inspection has been interpreted to mean "reasonable probability" of intermediate inspection.[92] Thus, manufacturers are liable if they have no reason to contemplate that an intermediate examination will occur, whether by a third party or the consumer. The question is whether a reasonable person would anticipate an examination before use which would avoid injury to the user.[93]

10–029

Warnings and intermediate inspection Where manufacturers have given a warning, for example, to test a product before use, this may be sufficient to discharge their duty.[94] The effect of the warning will depend upon its terms. For example, the suggestion that the product be tested before use creates a reasonable probability of intermediate inspection, whereas a warning against using the product in certain circumstances (e.g. contra-indications for use of a drug) limits what can be regarded as ordinary use. Ignoring the warning might constitute a misuse of the product. It is clear that the warning need not necessarily be addressed to the ultimate consumer. A warning to an intermediary, such as a prescribing doctor or pharmacist, may be sufficient.[95]

10–030

Causation The question of intermediate examination is closely related to the concepts of causation and contributory negligence. It has been held that there is

10–031

---

[89] *Donoghue v Stevenson* [1932] A.C. 562 at 599, per Lord Atkin.
[90] *Grant v Australian Knitting Mills Ltd* [1936] A.C. 85.
[91] *Herschtal v Stewart & Arden Ltd* [1940] 1 K.B. 155; *Griffiths v Arch Engineering Co. Ltd* [1968] 3 All E.R. 217.
[92] *Paine v Colne Valley Electricity Supply Co. Ltd* [1938] 4 All E.R. 803 at 808–809; *Buckner v Ashby and Horner Ltd* [1941] 2 K.B. 321 at 333; *Haseldine v Daw & Son Ltd* [1941] 2 K.B. 343 at 376.
[93] *Gallagher v N. McDowell Ltd* [1961] N.I. 26 at 42. In *Aswan Engineering Establishment Co. v Lupdine Ltd* [1987] 1 All E.R. 135 at 153–154 Lloyd LJ said that there is no independent requirement for the claimant to show that there was no reasonable possibility of intermediate examination. Rather, this is merely a factor, usually an important factor, which the court must consider when determining whether the damage was reasonably foreseeable.
[94] See further paras 10–042 to 10–049. In *Holmes v Ashford* [1950] 2 All E.R. 76 the manufacturers of a hair dye were held not liable when a hairdresser disregarded an instruction to test the product before using it on a customer; *Kubach v Hollands* [1937] 3 All E.R. 907 the manufacturer of a chemical was held not liable to a schoolgirl injured in an explosion, having warned the retailer to examine and test the chemical before use. The retailer did not test the chemical or warn the teacher who purchased it that it should be tested.
[95] See paras 10–043 to 10–046, below.

no liability if the claimant knew of the danger and ignored it,[96] nor if a third party knew of the danger, and, being under a duty to remove the product from circulation, failed to do so.[97] These cases can be explained in terms of causation rather than intermediate examination. The defendant's negligence was not the cause of the damage because the intervening conduct of the claimant or the third party broke the chain of causation.[98]

10-032 **Apportion liability**   It is arguable, however, that a defendant who has created a dangerous situation should not be excused merely because someone else, whether an intermediary or the claimant, has failed to remove the danger. If both have been at fault then both should be held responsible. In the case of a negligent intermediary this could be achieved by apportioning liability between the manufacturer and the intermediary under the Civil Liability (Contribution) Act 1978. If it is the claimant who has failed to use a reasonable opportunity to examine the goods, then it is a case of contributory negligence, for which damages can be apportioned.[99] Knowledge of the danger will be irrelevant, however, if there were no practical steps that the claimant could take to avoid it.[100] In *Rimmer v Liverpool City Council* the Court of Appeal said that an opportunity for inspection by the claimant will not exonerate the defendant unless the claimant:

> "…was free to remove or avoid the danger in the sense that it was reasonable to expect him to do so, and unreasonable for him to run the risk of being injured by the danger."[101]

The circumstances in which a patient could be said to have a realistic opportunity for intermediate inspection of a medicinal product must be rare indeed.

10-033 **Misuse of the product**   If the consumer misuses the product in an unforeseeable fashion the defendant will not be liable. This is not because of contributory negligence or causation, but because the manufacturer is responsible

---

[96] *Farr v Butters Bros & Co.* [1932] 2 K.B. 606; *Howmet Ltd v Economy Devices Ltd* [2016] EWCA Civ 847; [2016] B.L.R. 555 at [92] per Jackson LJ: "Once the end user is alerted to the dangerous condition of a chattel, if he voluntarily continues to use it thereby causing personal injury or damage, he normally does so entirely at his own risk. I say 'normally' rather than 'always', because (as Arden LJ explains) there are some situations in which the claimant may have no choice but to continue using the chattel as before." Arden LJ, at [122], drew attention to the reservations of Sir Donald Nicholls V-C in *Targett v Torfaen Borough Council* [1992] 3 All E.R. 27 at 37 (quoted at para.10–032, n.101 below).
[97] *Taylor v Rover Co. Ltd* [1966] 1 W.L.R. 1491.
[98] *Grant v Australian Knitting Mills Ltd* [1936] A.C. 85 at 105.
[99] See, e.g. *McCain Foods Ltd v Grand Falls Industries Ltd* (1991) 80 D.L.R. (4th) 252, NBCA.
[100] *Denny v Supplies and Transport Co. Ltd* [1950] 2 K.B. 374.
[101] [1985] Q.B. 1 at 14. In *Targett v Torfaen Borough Council* [1992] 3 All E.R. 27 at 37 Sir Donald Nicholls V-C said that: "Knowledge of the existence of a danger does not always enable a person to avoid the danger. In simple cases it does. In other cases, especially where buildings are concerned, it would be absurdly unrealistic to suggest that a person can always take steps to avoid a danger once he knows of its existence, and that if he does not do so he is the author of his own misfortune… Knowledge, or opportunity for inspection, does not by itself always negative the duty of care or break the chain of causation. Whether it does so depends on all the circumstances. It will do so only when it is reasonable to expect the plaintiff to remove or avoid the danger and unreasonable for him to run the risk of being injured by the danger."

only for dangers arising from a product's contemplated use. If misused, the product cannot be said to be "defective", so there is no breach of duty.[102] On the other hand, where the misuse is foreseeable there will at least be an obligation to give a warning not to use the product in this manner, and in some instances there may be a duty not to supply a product which it is known will be misused.[103]

(c) What is "defective"?

Defects may arise in the manufacture or design of the product, or in its presentation with inadequate warnings or instructions for use. The standard of care required is the usual standard in all actions for negligence: reasonable care in all the circumstances of the case.

10–034

(i) Manufacturing defects

Examples of manufacturing defects include construction faults, contamination of the product, errors in mixing compounds, and faulty packaging which cause the product to deteriorate. Manufacturers are almost invariably held liable for this type of error,[104] although they may escape responsibility where the defect could have been identified by intermediate inspection. Since the product fails to conform to the manufacturer's own design specification it is easier for the claimant to prove negligence. In *Best v Wellcome Foundation Ltd*[105] the defendants were held liable for brain damage to the claimant caused by the administration of a defective batch of pertussis vaccine. The batch was excessively high in both potency and toxicity, and had failed the "mouse weight gain test" by a considerable margin, but was nonetheless released for use without further testing. Given that the manufacturers were aware of the possibility of serious reaction in small children to the vaccine by way of brain damage, however rare:

10–035

> "...they owed a duty to exercise a high degree of care in regard to the testing, before issue of such a vaccine where they knew, or must have known, that it would be injected into children on a general or universal basis, at a very young age, and with the recommendation of the medical profession and of national health authorities."[106]

The defect must have arisen while under the defendant's control; intermeddling by a third party at a later stage will exculpate the manufacturer, unless the intermeddling ought reasonably to have been foreseen and guarded against.[107] For example, the manufacturer is not liable if the product has been stored improperly by a retailer causing it to deteriorate, or (in the context of an

---

[102] *Aswan Engineering Establishment Co. v Lupdine Ltd* [1987] 1 All E.R. 135 at 154.
[103] See, e.g. *Good-Wear Treaders Ltd v D & B Holdings Ltd* (1979) 98 D.L.R. (3d) 59.
[104] See para.10–066.
[105] [1994] 5 Med. L.R. 81; [1993] 3 I.R. 421; (1992) 17 B.M.L.R 11, Supreme Court of Ireland.
[106] [1994] 5 Med. L.R. 81 at 98, Supreme Court of Ireland, per Finlay CJ.
[107] See also the Consumer Protection Act 1987 s.4(1)(d) which provides a defence where the defect arose after the supply by the defendant.

allegation of a failure to warn) if consumer information leaflets have been removed from the package after it left the manufacturer's control.

(ii) Design defects

10–036 Where the product has a design defect it conforms to the manufacturer's specification but causes injury from ordinary use in a manner that was not anticipated at the time of design or manufacture. The product is intrinsically unsafe. Manufacturers undoubtedly have a duty to exercise reasonable care in the design of a new product,[108] which includes an obligation to be careful in conducting the research which goes into the design.[109] The courts are generally reluctant, however, to impose liability for negligent design. One of the difficulties is that the defect may not have been apparent before the product was marketed. For liability in negligence the defect must have been foreseeable at the time of design and manufacture: if the risk was unforeseeable in the light of the scientific and technical knowledge at the time there is no negligence.[110] Whilst a manufacturer is under a duty to keep abreast of medical and scientific discoveries,[111] the courts are wary of making judgments with the benefit of hindsight.[112]

10–037 On the other hand, manufacturers cannot automatically rely on the innovative nature of their product, claiming that they were engaged on a "venture into the unknown" where the risks were unforeseeable because they were operating at the frontiers of human knowledge. In *Independent Broadcasting Authority v EMI*

---

[108] *Hindustan Steam Shipping Co. Ltd v Siemens Bros & Co. Ltd* [1955] 1 Lloyd's Rep. 167.

[109] *Vacwell Engineering Co. Ltd v BDH Chemicals Ltd* [1971] 1 Q.B. 88 at 99, per Rees J: "...it was the duty of BDH to have established and maintained a system under which adequate investigation and research into the scientific literature took place in order to discover, *inter alia*, what hazards were known before a new, or little known, chemical was marketed"; see also at 109.

[110] For an example of this in the context of a medical product liability action see *Mann v Wellcome Foundation Ltd* unreported 20 January 1989, QBD, where it was held that the risk of deafness from the application of neomycin spray to burns was unforeseeable in the light of the medical and scientific knowledge. Unforeseeable reactions may also be held to be too remote a consequence of the breach of duty: see *Sheridan v Boots Co Ltd* unreported 1980, QBD in which the claimant contracted Stevens-Johnson syndrome as a side effect of an anti-inflammatory drug, which was known to cause gastric ulcers. The injury was held to be too remote, because Stevens-Johnson syndrome was not damage of the same type as gastric disturbance. See further para.5–174.

[111] *Stokes v Guest, Keen & Nettlefold (Bolts & Nuts) Ltd* [1968] 1 W.L.R. 1776 at 1783; *Cartwright v GKN Sankey Ltd* [1972] 2 Lloyd's Rep. 242 at 259; *Bolam v Friern Hospital Management Committee* [1957] 2 All E.R. 118 at 122.

[112] See, e.g. the comments of Mustill J in *Thompson v Smiths Shiprepairers (North Shields) Ltd* [1984] Q.B. 405 at 422 on the question of the time at which employers became negligent in failing to take precautions against hearing loss, given the knowledge within the industry: "One must be careful, when considering documents culled for the purpose of a trial, and studied by reference to a single isolated issue, not to forget that they once formed part of a flood of print on numerous aspects of industrial life, in which many items were bound to be overlooked. However conscientious the employer, he cannot read every textbook and periodical, attend every exhibition and conference, on every technical issue which might arise in the course of his business; nor can he necessarily be expected to grasp the importance of every single item which he comes across." *Mann v Wellcome Foundation Ltd* unreported 20 January 1989, QBD provides a similar example in the context of product liability; cf. also the "development risks" defence under the Consumer Protection Act 1987 s.4(1)(e), para.10–122, below.

Electronics Ltd and BICC Construction Ltd[113] the House of Lords held that the designers of a new type of television mast were negligent, even though it was the first such mast to be constructed anywhere in the world. Lord Edmund-Davies said that, although judgment with hindsight has to be avoided, the designers had a duty to identify and think through the problems presented by their lack of empirical knowledge so that the dimensions of the venture into the unknown could be adequately assessed:

> "And it is no answer to say ... 'it wasn't obvious because it hadn't been considered'. The learned trial judge held that it should have been, and in my judgment he was right in saying so."[114]

The graver the danger, the greater the need for special care, and in some instances the risks may be so great or their elimination may be so difficult to ensure with reasonable certainty that the only reasonable course is to abandon the project altogether. "The law requires even pioneers to be prudent."[115]

Relative risk The difficulty with medicinal products, and particularly drugs, is that most if not all are recognised as carrying some degree of risk, from side effects, allergic reactions or other unforeseen consequences. The question of what is safe is inevitably a relative concept, particularly in this field. It is a question of whether a reasonable person would consider the relative risk acceptable given the objective desired in using the product, and the risks associated with alternative treatments or non-treatment. The risks that would be acceptable in producing a new analgesic would be far less than the risks attached to a new drug for the treatment of, say, cancer or AIDS. Provided that the risk–benefit ratio is acceptable, and provided the manufacturer has taken all reasonable care to eliminate risks (e.g. by proper scientific research, including volunteer and clinical trials, and full reference to published literature) it is not negligent to market the drug. Where the reaction is rare, but severe, it will be unlikely that studies will reveal this before marketing.[116] On the other hand, where a manufacturer had sold 20 million bottles of corn solvent to the public, it was said that one aspect of the danger to the public arose from the wide variation in tolerance by different individuals of the kerotolytic substance when applied to the skin as distinct from corns. Accordingly:

10–038

> "...one must have in contemplation pretty well the whole scope of human variation in that vast market. There was a duty on the defendants to give some warning and to secure the bottle in some better way..."[117]

In *XYZ v Schering Health Care Ltd*[118] the claimants suffered from a number of cardiovascular complications, including deep vein thrombosis, strokes and pulmonary embolisms after taking third generation combined oral contraceptives.

10–039

---

[113] (1980) 14 Build. L.R. 1.
[114] (1980) 14 Build. L.R. 1 at 31.
[115] (1980) 14 Build. L.R. 1 at 28, per Lord Edmund-Davies.
[116] See, e.g. Newdick (1985) 101 L.Q.R. 405 at 418–9.
[117] *Devilez v Boots Pure Drug Co. Ltd* (1962) 106 S.J. 552, per Elwes J.
[118] [2002] EWHC 1420 (QB); (2002) 70 B.M.L.R. 88.

They alleged that third generation combined oral contraceptives were defective on the basis of their increased risk of such side effects over the second generation contraceptives. The issue was not whether there was a risk attached to the drug (there clearly was), but whether the relative risk of the third generation contraceptives was more than twice that of the second generation contraceptives. Following a detailed analysis of epidemiological evidence and consideration of the most appropriate method of calculating the risk, Mackay J held that the most likely figure for the increase in relative risk was 1.7, which meant that, on the balance of probabilities, there was no increase in the relative risk of the third generation of combined oral contraceptives to the second generation.[119]

10–040 The difficulty of proving negligence will be even greater where the claimant has sustained injury while taking part in a programme of research, whether in the form of pre-clinical or clinical trials. Adverse reactions are more likely to be regarded as unforeseeable and so unavoidable with the exercise of reasonable care. A claimant would probably have to establish negligence in the conduct of the research.[120]

(iii) Marketing defects

10–041 It is not necessarily enough for a manufacturer simply to produce an article that has a "safe" design and conforms to its design specification. There is an obligation to supply adequate information to consumers to allow them to use the product safely. At its simplest this involves informing consumers how the product should be used, and where necessary warning against improper and potentially dangerous misuse. A warning may allow users to avoid the danger altogether. Moreover, some products have an inherent and irreducible element of risk in their use, and a warning may give users the opportunity to make an informed decision whether to expose themselves to that risk. This is more likely to be the position in the case of drugs.

(d) Warnings

10–042 An adequate warning may be sufficient to discharge the manufacturer's duty of care, as may a warning that in its existing condition a product is unsafe,[121] though it may be that there is no duty to warn of known hazards.[122] The explicitness of

---

[119] The relative risk would have to have been greater than 2.0 before it could be said that the increase in relative risk had probably caused the claimants' damage. Although this issue went to the question of whether there was a causal link between third generation contraceptives and venous-thromboembolism the defendants accepted that if the causal link was established the claimants would also succeed on the question of whether the drugs were defective within the meaning of s.3 of the Consumer Protection Act 1987 because the women and their prescribers were entitled to be told of a doubling of the risk (even if the overall risk was very low in absolute terms) before making their decisions or giving advice, and they were not told: [2002] EWHC 1420 (QB); (2002) 70 B.M.L.R. 88 at [20] per Mackay J.

[120] See para.3–064. An ex gratia payment of compensation may be available to a healthy volunteer or a patient who sustains injury during the course of a drug trial: see para.3–073.

[121] *Kubach v Hollands* [1937] 3 All E.R. 907; *Holmes v Ashford* [1950] 2 All E.R. 76. See the example of Goddard LJ in *Haseldine v Daw & Son Ltd* [1941] 2 K.B. 343 at 380. In *Hurley v Dyke*

the warning will vary with the danger likely to be encountered in the ordinary use of the product,[123] although where a method exists of manufacturing the same product without risk of harm then no amount of or degree of specificity of warning will exonerate the manufacturer of an inherently dangerous article.[124]

(i)   The learned intermediary

It is not necessary that the warning be addressed directly to the consumer where a product is intended to be used under the supervision of experts. A warning given to the expert will normally be sufficient to discharge the manufacturer's duty of care.[125] In the case of prescription products the prescribing doctor is clearly in the position of an intermediary. In *Buchan v Ortho Pharmaceuticals (Canada) Ltd* Robins JA commented that: **10–043**

> "... the manufacturer of drugs, like the manufacturer of other products, has a duty to provide consumers with adequate warning of the potentially harmful side-effects that the manufacturer knows or has reason to know may be produced by the drug ... In the case of prescription drugs, the duty of manufacturers to warn consumers is discharged if the manufacturer provides prescribing physicians, rather than consumers, with adequate warning of the potential danger."[126]

Prescription drugs are available only on prescription and prescribing doctors are in a position to take into account the propensities of the drug and the susceptibilities of the patient. They have a duty to inform themselves of the benefits and potential dangers of the drugs they are prescribing, and they have to exercise an independent judgment as a medical expert based on their knowledge of the patient and the drug.[127] The duty to supply full information to the medical profession about prescription drugs is greater than the doctor's duty to give   **10–044**

[1979] R.T.R. 265 the House of Lords apparently accepted that a warning that a second hand car was sold "as seen and with all its faults" might have been sufficient to fulfil the defendant's duty even if he had known of a specific defect but had failed to advise the purchaser of the danger; cf. *Andrews v Hopkinson* [1957] 1 Q.B. 229.

[122] *McTear v Imperial Tobacco Ltd*, 2005 2 S.C. 1, Court of Session (OH) at [7.172] et seq., where it was said that the dangers of smoking were already well known to the public. Sed quaere whether the public truly appreciates the seriousness of the risk.

[123] *Lambert v Lastoplex Chemical Co.* (1971) 25 D.L.R. (3d) 121, SCC. There is no duty to warn of an obvious danger which is known to the ultimate consumer: *Deshane v Deere & Co.* (1993) 106 D.L.R. (4th) 385, Ont CA.

[124] *Nicholson v John Deere Ltd* (1986) 34 D.L.R. (4th) 542, 549, Ont HC; see also *Good-Wear Treaders Ltd v D & B Holdings Ltd* (1979) 98 D.L.R. (3d) 59, where it was held that a warning may be inadequate where the manufacturer knows that the product will be used in a dangerous manner.

[125] *Holmes v Ashford* [1950] 2 All E.R. 76; *Kubach v Hollands* [1937] 3 All E.R. 907.

[126] (1986) 25 D.L.R. (4th) 658 at 669, Ont CA. See also *H v Royal Alexandra Hospital for Children* [1990] 1 Med. L.R. 297, NSWSC, on warnings about the risks of infection with HIV from blood products.

[127] Under the Human Medicines Regulations 2012 regs 294, 295 and 297 medicinal products cannot be promoted to persons qualified to prescribe or supply the products unless they have been supplied with the information specified in those regulations and Sch.30 of the Regulations. On the duty to provide patients with information about medicines see the Human Medicines Regulations 2012 Pt 13 Ch.1 and Schs 24–27. See also the Medicines (Data Sheet) Regulations 1972 (SI 1972/2076) (as amended). The data sheet must inform the doctor of the contra-indications, any warnings that should be given and the necessary precautions for safe administration. The information that has to be given to

information to a patient, since the manufacturer's disclosure does not intrude upon the practice of medicine or the doctor–patient relationship, and doctors need the information so that they can properly assess the situation.[128]

10–045
This principle is known as the "learned intermediary rule".[129] Generally, it applies where a product is highly technical in nature and is intended to be used only under the supervision of experts, or where the nature of the product is such that the consumer will not realistically receive a direct warning from the manufacturer before using the product.[130] Thus, the rule was held to apply to silicone breast implants by the Supreme Court of Canada in *Hollis v Dow Corning Corp.*,[131] since direct warnings to the consumer are not feasible, given the need for intervention by a surgeon. The rule presumes that the intermediary is fully apprised of the risks associated with the use of the product, and therefore the manufacturer can only discharge its duty to the consumer when the intermediary's knowledge approximates to that of the manufacturer:

> "To allow manufacturers to claim the benefit of the rule where they have not fully warned the physician would undermine the policy rationale for the duty to warn, which is to ensure that the consumer is fully informed of all risks."[132]

Accordingly, the onus on the manufacturer to be forthcoming with information to the medical profession was "extremely high", as information about unexplained ruptures of the implants became available to the defendants, even if they did not consider the developments to be conclusive. They had to take into account the seriousness of the risk posed by the potential rupture of the implants.

10–046
The "learned intermediary rule" has been held to be inapplicable to the manufacturers of oral contraceptives in some jurisdictions in the United States of America, where it has been held that, to be effective, a warning must reach the consumer/patient.[133] The rationale for this approach is that in the case of the contraceptive pill there is heightened participation of patients in the decision to

---

patients in product leaflets is governed by the Medicines (Leaflets) Regulations 1977 (SI 1977/1055) (as amended). See also the Medicines (Labelling) Regulations 1976 (SI 1976/1726) (as frequently amended).

[128] *Davidson v Connaught Laboratories* (1980) 14 C.C.L.T. 251 at 276, Ont HC—manufacturer of a rabies vaccine held negligent in failing to supply information to doctors about the risks associated with the vaccine. The action failed for lack of causation: see para.10–050. There is, of course, no guarantee that the doctor will pass on the information to the patient, though the doctor is under a duty to disclose "material risks" to a patient: *Montgomery v Lanarkshire Health Board* [2015] UKSC 11; [2015] A.C. 1430, para.7–015 et seq.

[129] For discussion and criticism of the learned intermediary rule see Ferguson (1992) 12 O.J.L.S. 59; Peppin (1991) 70 Can. Bar Rev. 473.

[130] *Hollis v Dow Corning Corp.* (1995) 129 D.L.R. (4th) 609 at 623, SCC.

[131] (1995) 129 D.L.R. (4th) 609 at 623 at 624.

[132] (1995) 129 D.L.R. (4th) 609 at 623 per La Forest J. For comment on *Hollis* see Black and Klimchuck (1996) 75 Can. Bar Rev. 355.

[133] *MacDonald v Ortho Pharmaceutical Corp.* 475 N.E. 2d 65 (1985), Mass; *Odgers v Ortho Pharmaceutical Corp.* 609 F. Supp. 867 (1985), DC Mich; *Stephens v G. D. Searle & Co.* 602 F. Supp. 379 (1985), Mich; *Lukaszewicz v Ortho Pharmaceutical Corp.* 510 F. Supp. 961 (1981), Wis, holding that the manufacturer of oral contraceptives has a duty to provide the consumer with written warnings conveying reasonable notice of the nature, gravity, and likelihood of known or knowable side effects, and advising the consumer to seek fuller explanation from the prescribing physician.

use the drug; there may be substantial risks associated with its use; it is feasible for the manufacturer to give warnings direct to the user; there is frequently limited participation by the physician in the decision to take the pill; and there is a real possibility that patients may not be fully informed by their doctors. This view was followed obiter by the Ontario Court of Appeal in *Buchan v Ortho Pharmaceuticals (Canada) Ltd*,[134] where it was said that manufacturers of oral contraceptives should be obliged to warn the ultimate consumer as well as prescribing physicians about the risks associated with the pill.

(ii) What is an "adequate" warning?

An adequate warning should be communicated clearly and understandably in a manner calculated to inform the user of the nature of the risk and the extent of the danger; it should be in terms commensurate with the gravity of the potential hazard, and it should not be neutralised or negated by collateral efforts on the part of the manufacturer.[135] For example, promotional literature which seeks to minimise any suggestion of risk or promote the drug as "completely safe" would tend to negate the effectiveness of a warning.[136] The location and prominence of a warning may be a significant factor.[137] In *Buchan v Ortho Pharmaceuticals (Canada) Ltd* Robins JA said that:

10–047

"Whether a particular warning is adequate will depend on what is reasonable in the circumstances. But the fact that a drug is ordinarily safe and effective and the danger may be rare or involve only a small percentage of users does not necessarily relieve the manufacturer of the duty to warn. While a low probability of injury or a small class of endangered users are factors to be taken into account in determining what is reasonable, these factors must be balanced against such considerations as the nature of the drug, the necessity for taking it, and the magnitude of the increased danger to the individual consumer. Similarly where medical evidence exists which tends to show a serious danger inherent in the use of a drug, the manufacturer is not entitled to ignore or discount that information in its warning solely because it finds it to be unconvincing; the manufacturer is obliged to be forthright and to tell the whole story. The extent of the warning and the steps to be taken to bring the warning home to physicians should be commensurate with the potential danger—the graver the danger, the higher the duty."[138]

The defendant manufacturers in that case were held liable in negligence on the basis of a failure to give sufficient information to the medical profession about the risks of oral contraceptives. The fact that the manufacturers were aware that warnings had been circulated to the profession by the Canadian Food and Drugs Directorate on the instructions of the relevant Minister did not relieve them of

10–048

---

[134] (1986) 25 D.L.R. (4th) 658 at 688–689, Ont CA.

[135] *Buchan v Ortho Pharmaceuticals (Canada) Ltd* (1986) 25 D.L.R. (4th) 658 at 667.

[136] On misleading advertising campaigns by pharmaceutical companies see *The Times*, 25 March 1985, p.8, which also suggested that regulation of advertising by the DHSS was ineffective; see also Teff (1984) 47 M.L.R. 303, 314. For the provisions regulating the contents of drug advertisements see the Human Medicines Regulations 2012 (SI 2012/1916) Pt 14.

[137] *Lambert v Lastoplex Chemical Co.* (1971) 25 D.L.R. (3d) 121, SCC.

[138] (1986) 25 D.L.R. (4th) 658 at 678–679, Ont CA. See also *Rothwell v Raes* (1988) 54 D.L.R. (4th) 193 at 341–342, Ont HC, on inadequate warnings by the manufacturers of pertussis vaccine to the medical profession. The action failed on the ground that the vaccine did not cause the claimant's injuries (aff'd (1990) 76 D.L.R. (4th) 280).

their legal duty to warn the profession.[139] Thus, the duty to warn doctors cannot be delegated. The manufacturer cannot justify a failure to warn on the ground that doctors were in a position to learn about the risks inherent in the product from other sources. In *Davidson v Connaught Laboratories* Linden J observed that:

> "A drug company cannot rely upon doctors to read all the scientific literature outlining the specific dangers involved in the many drugs they have to administer each day ... They have little time for deep research into the medical literature. They rely on the drug companies to supply them with the necessary data."[140]

In *Buchan* a significant factor in the conclusion that the defendants had negligently failed to give adequate warning to consumers was the fact that the defendants' associated companies in other countries (including the United Kingdom) had given a much more comprehensive warning.

10–049　**New knowledge**　Where there have been developments in the state of the manufacturer's knowledge there is an obligation to keep the medical community advised of those developments. Thus, in *Hollis v Dow Corning Corp.*[141] the manufacturers of breast implants became aware of the fact that an implant could rupture for a variety of reasons, including normal use, and that the life expectancy of implants was unpredictable, before the claimant received her implant in October 1983, but did not update their warning to surgeons until 1985. The statistical risk of rupture was less than 0.1 per cent, though the consequences for the patient were serious. The manufacturers were held liable for failing to pass on this new information to doctors. It was not an obligation to issue a new warning each time a rupture occurred, but it was not expecting too much to require the manufacturers to issue updated information to the medical community on a yearly basis, or sooner if the circumstances warranted it.[142]

---

[139] "The report of the advisory committee cannot be considered determinative of the nature and extent of the legal duty imposed on drug manufacturers to warn the medical profession. The duty to warn of a risk so grave as stroke ... arose long before the report ... The report did not release Ortho from its common law duty, limit its ability to discharge the duty, or fix a standard of disclosure to the medical profession": (1986) 25 D.L.R. (4th) 658 at 680–651, per Robins JA; *Thompson v Johnson and Johnson Pty Ltd* [1992] 3 Med. L.R. 148; [1991] 2 V.R. 449, SC of Victoria, App Div—manufacturers of tampons held not liable for failing to warn users of the risk of toxic shock syndrome at the time when the claimant's injury occurred, given the significant differences between the situation in North America and that in Australia, the different attitudes of the health authorities, and the fact that at the time there had been no case of toxic shock syndrome associated with the use of tampons in Australia despite extensive use over a considerable period of time.

[140] (1980) 14 C.C.L.T. 251 at 276, Ont HC. In the UK doctors' other sources of drug information, in addition to the manufacturers, include the *British National Formulary*, produced jointly by the BMA and the British Pharmaceutical Society, *MIMS* (the *Monthly Index of Medical Specialities*), and *Prescriber*.

[141] (1993) 103 D.L.R. (4th) 520, BCCA; aff'd (1995) 129 D.L.R. (4th) 609, SCC.

[142] (1993) 103 D.L.R. (4th) 520 at 544, per Prowse JA: "A manufacturer should not be too coy about revealing the risks associated with its product and then expect to avoid liability by placing the full burden of those risks on either the medical community or the patient." In the Supreme Court of Canada, La Forest J indicated that in the case of medical products "the standard of care to be met by manufacturers in ensuring that consumers are properly warned is necessarily high. Medical products are often designed for bodily ingestion or implantation, and the risks created by their improper use are obviously substantial": (1995) 129 D.L.R. (4th) 609 at 619.

(e) Failure to warn and causation

Where the alleged negligence consists of a failure to warn either the consumer or   **10–050**
an intermediary, such as a prescribing doctor, about the side effects or
contra-indications of a drug, for example, claimants still have to prove that had
the warning been given they would not have taken the drug. In other words they
must demonstrate that the negligent omission caused or contributed to the
damage. In the case of prescription drugs or medical devices the causation issue
is complicated by the effect of the "learned intermediary rule". Strictly, claimants
would have to prove not only that they would have declined the treatment or
procedure had they been informed about the risks, but also that the intermediary,
who will usually be the doctor, would have acted differently had a suitable
warning been given. Thus, in *Davidson v Connaught Laboratories*[143] the
manufacturer of a rabies vaccine was found to have given an inadequate warning
to doctors in its literature accompanying the vaccine. The manufacturer did not
mention myelitis or neuritis; nor the possibility of paralysis or death; nor were
there any figures relating to the risks, nor any source material. The defendants
had known of these dangers for a long time. The manufacturer was held not
liable, however, because:

(i)   the information would not have changed the doctors' decision to
        recommend use of the vaccine, because of the grave danger associated with
        rabies (it is often fatal); and,
(ii)   the claimant had been given full information about the risks, in any event,
        by another doctor.[144]

Accordingly, there are two causation issues that arise in these cases: (1) what
would the doctor have done had the manufacturer complied with its duty to
provide appropriate information; and (2) what would the claimant have done had
the doctor passed on the relevant information about the associated risks?

Test for causation is subjective   In principle, since determining causation is   **10–051**
essentially a factual enquiry,[145] the test in both cases should be subjective. In
other words, it depends on whether *this* patient would have taken the drug in
question or accepted the use of the relevant medical device[146]; and where
causation depends upon what the prescribing doctor would have done had he
been given an adequate warning by the manufacturer, the test should also be
subjective to *that* doctor and should not be determined by what a reasonable

---

[143] (1980) 14 C.C.L.T. 251, Ont HC.
[144] See also *H v Royal Alexandra Hospital for Children* [1990] 1 Med. L.R. 297, NSWSC, where it
was held that the failure of the manufacturers of blood products in 1983 to warn doctors of the risk
that the products could transmit HIV was negligent, but that such a warning would have had no effect
on the decision of the doctors to use the products for the treatment of a haemophiliac with a joint
bleed, given the perception of the relative risks of treatment and non-treatment.
[145] Notwithstanding that this enquiry is sometimes infused with policy questions: see paras 5–019,
5–047, 5–050 et seq.
[146] See paras 7–081 et seq. in the context of actions against health professionals in respect of
non-disclosure of the risks of treatment.

doctor would have done in the circumstances. Thus, in *The Creutzfeldt-Jakob Disease Litigation, Straddlers Group A and C v Secretary of State for Health*,[147] the causation question depended on whether clinicians treating patients with human growth hormone would have stopped the treatment had they been informed about the small risk of transmitting to the patient the agent that causes CJD. Morland J held that this issue was to be determined simply on the balance of probabilities as to how the treating clinicians would have responded to the information, though the evidence was that the clinicians probably would have halted the treatment programme. On the other hand, it is at least arguable that where the causation question depends upon the hypothetical conduct of an independent third party, the analysis should proceed on the basis of the loss of a chance of avoiding the harm.[148] As between the defendant manufacturer and the injured patient, the treating doctor would seem to be "an independent third party". This point has not yet been tested in the English courts.

10–052   **Canada**   By contrast, the Canadian courts take a different approach to these issues. The normal rule in Canada for the non-disclosure of risks associated with medical treatment is that the test is objective, i.e. the action fails if a reasonable patient in the claimant's position would have proceeded had she been informed about the risks.[149] In *Hollis v Dow Corning Corp.*[150] a majority of the Supreme Court of Canada held that in the context of a product liability claim the test of causation should be subjective not objective. Although a different, subjective, test of causation in cases of failure to warn where the action was against a manufacturer (as opposed to the objective reasonable patient test when the action was against a doctor or hospital) might seem anomalous, the justification, said La Forest J, was to be found in the different circumstances in which the relevant duties arise. The duty of the doctor was to give the best medical advice to a particular patient in a specific context. The manufacturer, on the other hand, could be expected to act in a more self-interested manner:

> "In the case of a manufacturer, therefore, there is a greater likelihood that the value of a product will be overemphasised and the risk underemphasised. It is, therefore, highly desirable from a policy perspective to hold the manufacturer to a strict standard of warning consumers of dangerous side-effects to these products."[151]

10–053   **Presumption that learned intermediary would have warned patient**   Moreover, for similar policy reasons the Canadian courts have taken a highly relaxed view of the first causation issue in a case involving a learned intermediary, namely what would the intermediary have done had the manufacturer complied with its duty to provide a warning to the intermediary? In *Buchan v Ortho Pharmaceuticals (Canada) Ltd*[152] the Ontario Court of Appeal held that it ought not to be incumbent on a claimant to prove as part of her case what her doctor might or might not have done had he been adequately warned. One could assume

---

[147] (1998) 54 B.M.L.R. 104.
[148] See *Allied Maples Group Ltd v Simmons & Simmons* [1995] 4 All E.R. 907, para.5–108.
[149] *Reibl v Hughes* (1980) 114 D.L.R. (3d) 1, SCC. See para.7–084.
[150] (1995) 129 D.L.R. (4th) 609, SCC.
[151] (1995) 129 D.L.R. (4th) 609 at [46].
[152] (1986) 25 D.L.R. (4th) 658 at 682 and 686–688.

that a doctor would not ignore a proper warning or fail to disclose a material risk or otherwise act negligently. Moreover, even if the evidence indicated that the doctor was negligent, the manufacturer would not be shielded from liability if the negligence was a foreseeable consequence of the manufacturer's breach of duty to warn. This was said to be a rebuttable presumption. In *Hollis v Dow Corning Corp.*,[153] however, the Supreme Court of Canada went a step further and held that, in effect, what the intermediary would have done in a hypothetical situation was irrelevant to the causation issue. The claimant was in a position of great informational inequality with respect to both the manufacturer and the doctor, and the defendant's argument would require her to prove a hypothetical situation relating to her doctor's conduct, a hypothetical situation that had been brought about by the defendant's own failure to perform its duty. Justice dictated that she should not be penalised for the fact that had the manufacturer actually met its duty to warn, the doctor might still have been at fault and failed to pass on the information.[154] La Forest J, giving the majority judgment, explained the basis for this conclusion:

> "Simply put, I do not think a manufacturer should be able to escape liability for failing to give a warning it was under a duty to give, by simply presenting evidence tending to establish that even if the doctor had been given the warning, he or she would not have passed it on to the patient, let alone putting an onus on the claimant to do so. Adopting such a rule would, in some cases, run the risk of leaving the claimant with no compensation for her injuries. ... As I see it, the claimant's claim against the manufacturer should be dealt with in accordance with the following rationale. The ultimate duty of the manufacturer is to warn the claimant adequately. For practical reasons, the law permits it to acquit itself of that duty by warning an informed intermediary. Having failed to warn the intermediary, the manufacturer has failed in its duty to warn the claimant who ultimately suffered injury by using the product. The fact that the manufacturer would have been absolved had it followed the route of informing the claimant through the learned intermediary should not absolve it of its duty to the claimant because of the possibility, even the probability, that the learned intermediary would not have advised her had the manufacturer issued it. The learned intermediary rule provides a means by which the manufacturer can discharge its duty to give adequate information of the risks to the claimant by informing the intermediary, but if it fails to do so it cannot raise as a defence that the intermediary could have ignored this information."[155]

This reverses the effect of the decision in *Davidson v Connaught Laboratories* to the extent that causation rested on what the doctor would have done, and appears to convert what the Ontario Court of Appeal in *Buchan v Ortho Pharmaceuticals (Canada) Ltd* regarded as a rebuttable presumption into an irrebuttable presumption. It would seem that the second basis for the decision in *Davidson*, namely that the claimant had already received full information from another source, remains intact, since if the claimant was aware of the risk (from whatever source) but nonetheless chose to proceed with the treatment this must be clear evidence of what she subjectively would have done had the manufacturer complied with its duty to warn.[156]

10–054

---

[153] (1995) 129 D.L.R. (4th) 609, SCC.

[154] (1995) 129 D.L.R. (4th) 609 at [55] and [57] per La Forest J.

[155] (1995) 129 D.L.R. (4th) 609 at [60] and [61].

[156] Note also that establishing what subjectively claimants would have done in an hypothetical situation often involves testing the credibility of their subjective assertions against objective criteria. See para.7–091.

10–055 **Contrast English approach** It is unlikely that an English court would take so generous a view of the causation issue in relation to the actions of a learned intermediary, and that the test will continue to be subjective (i.e. what would this intermediary have done?). Whether that should be resolved on an "all or nothing" basis, on the balance of probabilities, or on the basis of a lost chance, with the question turning on whether there was substantial chance (which might be less than 50 per cent) of the intermediary passing on the warning, remains to be seen.

10–056 **Material contribution to the damage** Another alternative would be to ask whether the negligence made a material contribution to the damage. This involves a departure from the "but for" test, without resorting to the lost chance analysis. In *Walker Estate v York-Finch General Hospital*[157] the Canadian Red Cross Society was held to have been negligent in the manner in which it screened potential blood donors for HIV, in that it had asked potential donors about their general health instead of asking about symptom specific conditions and risks. Whether a properly conducted screening method would have elicited the relevant information and enabled the defendants to screen out high risk donors depended upon how the potential donors would have reacted to more specific questioning. The Supreme Court of Canada held that the claimant could not rely on the presumptive causation test established in *Hollis* because *Walker* did not involve the "learned intermediary" rule.[158] This left the question of what approach should be taken to establishing causation where the causal link depended on the actions of a third party. It was held that the correct approach was not to apply the "but for" test, but to ask whether the negligence constituted a material contribution to the damage:

> "In cases of negligent donor screening it may be difficult or impossible to prove hypothetically what the donor would have done had he or she been properly screened by the C.R.C.S. The added element of donor conduct in these cases means that the but-for test could operate unfairly, highlighting the possibility of leaving legitimate plaintiffs uncompensated. Thus, the question in cases of negligent donor screening should not be whether the C.R.C.S.'s conduct was a necessary condition for the plaintiff's injuries using the 'but-for' test, but whether that conduct was a sufficient condition. The proper test for causation in cases of negligent donor screening is whether the defendant's negligence 'materially contributed' to the occurrence of the injury."[159]

10–057 It would certainly be open to an English court to adopt this approach, applying *Bonnington Castings Ltd v Wardlaw*[160] and *Fairchild v Glenhaven Funeral Services Ltd*,[161] though their Lordships in *Fairchild* were careful to limit the application of this more relaxed causation test. Although there is nothing in principle to prevent it, it is not clear that the *Fairchild* principle would be applied

---

[157] (2001) 198 D.L.R. (4th) 193, SCC.

[158] (2001) 198 D.L.R. (4th) 193 at [86].

[159] (2001) 198 D.L.R. (4th) 193 at [88]. On the other hand, where the issue was whether an alleged delay in introducing heat-treated blood products could have avoided the claimants' contracting HIV from an infected blood transfusion, the claimants had to satisfy the "but for" test, and prove when they became infected on the balance of probabilities: *Robb Estate v Canadian Red Cross Society* (2001) 9 C.C.L.T. (3d) 131, Ont CA.

[160] [1956] A.C. 613.

[161] [2002] UKHL 22; [2003] 1 A.C. 32. See the discussion at paras 5–050 et seq.

to circumstances where the causal uncertainty rests on the hypothetical conduct of individuals, as opposed to scientific uncertainty about the causal mechanism of a disease. The decision of the Court of Appeal in *Allied Maples Group Ltd v Simmons & Simmons*[162] would suggest that where the causal outcome depends upon the hypothetical actions of an independent third party the correct approach is to assess the chances that, in the absence of negligence by the defendant, the third party would have acted in way which would have avoided the claimant's damage, with damages being assessed on the basis of the value of the lost chance.

(f) Continuing duty

Negligence depends upon foreseeability of injury. If at the time that a product was put onto the market the defect was unknown the manufacturer was not negligent. If a danger becomes apparent (or ought to have been discovered) it will be negligent to continue to produce the same unmodified product, or at least to do so without attaching a warning.[163]   **10–058**

In addition, the manufacturer is under a continuing duty in respect of products already in circulation which are now known to be defective. The manufacturer must take reasonable steps either to warn users of the danger or recall the defective products.[164] In *Hobbs (Farms) Ltd v Baxenden Chemical Co. Ltd*[165] Sir Michael Ogden QC said that: **10–059**

> "... a manufacturer's duty of care does not end when the goods are sold. A manufacturer who realises that omitting to warn past customers about something which might result in injury to them must take reasonable steps to attempt to warn them, however lacking in negligence he may have been at the time the goods were sold."[166]

Moreover, where a product has not been recalled and there is strong evidence to suggest that problems in the manufacture of the product have been concealed to avoid the commercial repercussions that a recall would entail, the court will more readily infer that a defect was due to negligence in the manufacturing process.[167]

In *Buchan v Ortho Pharmaceuticals (Canada) Ltd*[168] the Ontario Court of Appeal applied the principle of a continuing duty to the manufacturer of oral contraceptives with respect to warnings of side effects to be given to doctors who prescribed the drug. Robins JA expressed the proposition in these terms: **10–060**

---

[162] [1995] 4 All E.R. 907.

[163] *Wright v Dunlop Rubber Co. Ltd* (1972) 13 K.I.R. 255 at 272.

[164] *Rivtow Marine Ltd v Washington Iron Works* (1973) 40 D.L.R. (3d) 530 at 536, SCC; *Buchan v Ortho Pharmaceuticals (Canada) Ltd* (1986) 25 D.L.R. (4th) 658 at 667, Ont CA; *Hollis v Dow Corning Corp.* (1995) 129 D.L.R. (4th) 609 at 618, SCC.

[165] [1992] 1 Lloyd's Rep. 54 at 65.

[166] This continuing duty to warn only applies to *dangerous* defects. Thus, a manufacturer's knowledge that an engine was likely to fail much sooner than indicated in the manual did not give rise to a duty to warn users to have the engine checked more frequently so as to avoid the risk of damage to the engine itself, which is a form of economic loss: *Hamble Fisheries Ltd v Gardner & Sons Ltd, The "Rebecca Elaine"* [1999] 2 Lloyd's Rep. 1, CA.

[167] *Carroll v Fearon* [1998] P.I.Q.R. P416, CA.

[168] (1986) 25 D.L.R. (4th) 658.

"A manufacturer of prescription drugs occupies the position of an expert in the field; this requires that it be under a continuing duty to keep abreast of scientific developments pertaining to its product through research, adverse reaction reports, scientific literature and other available methods. When additional dangerous or potentially dangerous side-effects from the drug's use are discovered, the manufacturer must make all reasonable efforts to communicate the information to prescribing physicians. Unless doctors have current, accurate and complete information about a drug's risks, their ability to exercise the fully informed medical judgment necessary for the proper performance of their vital role in prescribing drugs for patients may be reduced or impaired."[169]

10–061 **Continuing duty to monitor adverse drug reactions** A new drug which produces a high incidence of adverse reactions (c.1 in 300) should be spotted in pre-clinical or clinical trials. Less common reactions may only become apparent when the drug is in widespread use. It is almost inevitable, then, that some drug injuries will only be identified after the product has been marketed. The exercise of reasonable care clearly requires that manufacturers have an effective system for monitoring adverse reactions and for the recall of defective products, both for manufacturing defects (to identify faulty batches, for example) and for design defects, which may involve removing the product from the market altogether.[170] In a suitable case an appropriate warning may be sufficient to satisfy the manufacturer's duty. In this country it is a condition of the grant of a product licence for pharmaceutical products that such a procedure exists,[171] but nonetheless there could be negligence in implementing the recall procedure.[172]

(g) Common practice

10–062 Where manufacturers have complied with the standards normally adopted within the industry, this will usually be taken as good evidence that they have acted with reasonable care, just as a departure from common practice may be evidence of

---

[169] (1986) 25 D.L.R. (4th) 658 at 678.

[170] In the past, the "yellow card scheme" (see now *http://yellowcard.mhra.gov.uk*), in which doctors submitted reports on adverse reactions to the CSM, was not particularly effective in identifying adverse reactions: see Teff (1984) 47 M.L.R. 303, 315. The anti-arthritis drug, Opren, was not suspended by the Licensing Authority under the Medicines Act 1968 until after more than 3,500 reports of adverse reactions, including 61 fatalities: Teff, (1984) 47 M.L.R. 303, 304, n.5. See further *The Lancet*, 5 November 1988, pp.1059, 1060 on the withdrawal of "Merital" (nomifensine), suggesting that undue reliance on the yellow card scheme may result in insufficient emphasis on other preventive measures. The CSM put pressure on the manufacturers to withdraw the drug following a sharp increase in reports under the scheme in 1985, but there had been suspicions about adverse reactions since 1979. See also *The Lancet*, 31 January 1987, p.287, reporting the withdrawal of "Dorbanex" (danthron).

[171] See the Human Medicines Regulations 2012 Pt 11, "Pharmacovigilance"; Medicines (Standard Provisions for Licences and Certificates) Regulations 1971 (SI 1971/972) Sch.1 para.6, as amended; and in respect of medical devices see the Medical Devices Directive (Directive 93/42/EEC) art.10 (which is effectively implemented by the Medical Devices Regulations 2002 (SI 2002/618) reg.13) imposing a requirement to report adverse events arising from the use of medical devices. Reports should be made to the Medicines & Healthcare products Regulatory Agency (*http://www.gov.uk/government/organisations/medicines-and-healthcare-products-regulatory-agency*).

[172] See, e.g. *Nicholson v John Deere Ltd* (1986) 34 D.L.R. (4th) 542. The defendants "had a duty to devise a programme that left nothing to chance", per Smith J at 549. The defendants' efforts to warn were deficient in that they were doomed to failure with respect to the vast majority of users; *McCain Foods Ltd v Grand Falls Industries Ltd* (1991) 80 D.L.R. (4th) 252.

negligence.[173] Neither, however, is necessarily conclusive of the issue,[174] In the case of pharmaceutical products manufacturers must comply with the statutory requirements of the Medicines Act 1968 and the Human Medicines Regulations 2012. Compliance will not be conclusive, but it will undoubtedly constitute strong evidence of the exercise of reasonable care. If an independent body, such as the Commission on Human Medicines (CHM),[175] has reached the same view as the manufacturer on the safety of a product or the adequacy of warnings this will inevitably influence the court's assessment of whether there has been negligence, assuming that the same information was available to both the CHM and the manufacturer, and assuming, of course, that the CHM has not been negligent.[176] In *Thompson v Johnson and Johnson Pty Ltd*[177] it was said that the attitude, advice and response of the Australian Department of Health and the Public Health Advisory Committee of the National Health and Medical Research Council to a reported case of toxic shock syndrome caused by tampons was a significant factor to take into account when considering whether the manufacturers had been negligent in failing to give warnings of the risk to the public:

> "Whether or not the N.H.M.R.C. recommended that a warning be given was not determinative of the question of reasonable care, for to accept that proposition would permit the respondents to abrogate the duty of reasonable care owed by them. It is not the response of such a body which determines whether a person in the position of the respondent is or is not negligent. That is for the courts to decide. However, it is a relevant fact to be taken into account when determining whether reasonable care has been exercised."

In *Budden v BP Oil Ltd and Shell Oil Ltd*[178] it was alleged that children had sustained injuries attributable to inhaling petrol fumes containing lead, and they brought an action against the oil companies. The levels of lead in petrol complied with statutory regulations, and these levels had been set by the Secretary of State, having received expert advice. The Court of Appeal took the view that in these circumstances the decision about lead levels must be presumed to be in the public interest, and accordingly the manufacturers or suppliers of petrol could not be said to be negligent if the limit to which they adhered was one which they were entitled reasonably to believe to be consistent with the public interest. It could not be said that:

10–063

> "...a reasonable person, with the knowledge which the oil companies had or should have had, objectively weighing all relevant considerations, had failed in his duty owed to the children in

---

[173] See paras 3–021 to 3–054.

[174] Thus, in *Merck Sharp & Dohme (Australia) Pty Ltd v Peterson* [2011] FCAFC 128; (2011) 284 A.L.R. 1 at [161] the Full Court of the Federal Court of Australia commented that: "It may be accepted that the legislation is concerned to establish minimum safety standards for the availability and use of regulated medicines in the public interest. We are unable to discern in the legislation an intention to abrogate the common law rights of individual consumers."

[175] *http://www.gov.uk/government/organisations/commission-on-human-medicines/about*.

[176] See *Buchan v Ortho Pharmaceuticals (Canada) Ltd* (1986) 25 D.L.R. (4th) 658 at 672–673, where the issue was raised, but not decided, whether compliance by the manufacturer with the requirements of the Canadian Food and Drug Directorate as to the warnings to be given directly to the users of oral contraceptives absolved them from liability. The trial judge had held that the statement required by the FDD "amounted to no warning at all".

[177] [1992] 3 Med. L.R. 148 at 171–172; [1991] 2 V.R. 449, SC of Victoria, App. Div.

[178] [1980] J.P.L. 586.

complying with the requirements prescribed by the Secretary of State and approved, impliedly, by Parliament, after the investigation which had been made of the very matters which were relevant for the companies' decisions."[179]

10–064   The grant of product licences under the Human Medicines Regulations 2012 does not depend upon express approval by Parliament, but nonetheless the logic of *Budden v BP Oil Ltd and Shell Oil Ltd* could well be applied to pharmaceutical products licensed by the Licensing Authority.[180] On the other hand, in *Best v Wellcome Foundation Ltd*[181] a manufacturer of pertussis vaccine was held to have been negligent in releasing a batch of the vaccine which tests had shown to have a high level of potency, which it was known could be linked with high levels of toxicity, although the relevant regulations laid down only minimum not maximum levels of potency. The batch had also failed the "mouse weight gain test", a test routinely carried out, but not mandatory under the regulations. Finlay CJ considered that, in the circumstances, compliance with minimum criteria was inadequate:

> "Merely to comply, in my view, with mandatory or minimum requirements imposed by national health authorities in the area in which the vaccine was manufactured, or merely to rely on one particular point of view in a debated question concerning the risks involved, would not necessarily, in any given case, constitute a sufficient degree of care to discharge the legal duty of a manufacturer of vaccine in these circumstances."[182]

Moreover, where a manufacturer has failed to comply with the provisions of the Human Medicines Regulations 2012 concerning the safety of a pharmaceutical product this must put the onus on the defendant to justify its conduct, although breach is not negligence per se.[183]

(h)   Proof

10–065   The burden of proving negligence rests with the claimant. In *Donoghue v Stevenson*[184] Lord Macmillan said that there was no presumption of negligence nor any justification for applying the maxim res ipsa loquitur in such a case. Where, however, a defect has arisen in the course of construction it will be

---

[179] [1980] J.P.L. 586 at 587. The court was worried that if it were to make a finding of negligence there would be a constitutional anomaly, because the court would effectively be declaring a decision of Parliament to be unlawful: "The authority of Parliament must prevail."

[180] cf. also Consumer Protection Act 1987 s.4(1)(a), para.10–114, below, providing a defence to strict liability under that Act where the defect was attributable to compliance with any statutory requirement or a European Community obligation. For further discussion see Newdick (1992) 47 Food and Drug L.J. 41.

[181] [1993] 3 I.R. 421; [1994] 5 Med. L.R. 81; (1992) 17 B.M.L.R 11, Supreme Court of Ireland.

[182] [1994] 5 Med. L.R. 81, 98.

[183] The Human Medicines Regulations 2012 do not confer any civil right of action for damages for breach, nor do they confer any immunity from such claims except in limited circumstances (see para.10–013). See also Medicines Act 1968 s.133(2).

[184] [1932] A.C. 562.

virtually impossible for a claimant to show by affirmative evidence what went wrong. In *Grant v Australian Knitting Mills Ltd*[185] this difficulty was recognised. Lord Wright said that:

> "[The manufacturing] process was intended to be foolproof. If excess sulphites were left in the garment, that could only be because someone was at fault. The appellant is not required to lay his finger on the exact person in all the chain who was responsible or to specify what he did wrong. Negligence is found as a matter of inference from the existence of the defects taken in connection with all the known circumstances."[186]

The effect of this is that in cases of manufacturing defects the claimant will normally establish negligence by proving the existence of the defect, and that this was probably not a result of events that occurred after the product left the manufacturer's possession.[187] The possibility of intermediate deterioration or tampering with the product will be taken into account in terms of the degree of likelihood that the defect was present when it left the manufacturer.[188] It is irrelevant whether the inference of negligence is called res ipsa loquitur or not, because in some instances it amounts in practice to a form of strict liability. The greater the danger the greater the precautions that will be required to discharge a duty of care.[189] Defendants may rebut the inference by proving how the defect occurred and showing that this was not due to lack of care on their part, but this may be difficult. Ironically, the stronger the evidence that manufacturing systems were "foolproof", the stronger is the inference that the defect arose as a result of carelessness by one of their employees, for whose negligence they will be held vicariously liable.[190]

10–066

Proof of defective design   The claimant will have greater difficulty in proving negligence where the product is defective in design rather than manufacture. It is easier to demonstrate that a product is defective if it does not meet the manufacturer's own standards because something has gone wrong during manufacture. Where, however, a product performs as it was designed and intended there is no obvious standard against which to compare it.[191] The design may have been the result of a conscious compromise between cost and safety, or

10–067

---

[185] [1936] A.C. 85.

[186] [1936] A.C. 85 at 101.

[187] *Mason v Williams & Williams Ltd* [1955] 1 W.L.R. 549. In *Carroll v Fearon* [1998] P.I.Q.R. P416 at 422 the Court of Appeal commented that: "once it was established that the tyre disintegrated because of an identified fault in the course of its manufacture the judge had to decide whether this fault was the result of negligence at Dunlop's factory. He did not have to identify any individual or group of employees or the acts or omissions which resulted in [the defect]. If the manufacturing process had worked as intended this defect should not have been present." See also *Divya v Toyo Tire and Rubber Co Ltd* [2011] EWHC 1993 (QB) (cause of accident was sudden and unexpected loss of a tyre's tread; reasonable inference was that there was a manufacturing defect in the construction of the tyre).

[188] See, e.g. *Evans v Triplex Safety Glass Co. Ltd* [1936] 1 All E.R. 283.

[189] *Wright v Dunlop Rubber Co. Ltd* (1972) 13 K.I.R. 255 at 273–274.

[190] *Grant v Australian Knitting Mills Ltd* [1936] A.C. 85; *Hill v James Crowe (Cases) Ltd* [1978] 1 All E.R. 812 at 816, criticising *Daniels v White & Sons Ltd* [1938] 4 All E.R. 258 where carbolic acid used in washing bottles contaminated lemonade, and the defendants were held not liable on proving the effectiveness of the system.

[191] Unless specifically governed by statute; see, e.g. Consumer Protection Act 1987 s.11.

between efficacy and safety.[192] In the case of a drug, if the risk was a known risk it may be treated as an unavoidable side effect which was acceptable because of the otherwise beneficial effects of the drug, either for the claimant or other users. Side effects are simply part of the cost-benefit analysis undertaken when considering whether a drug has a safe design.

10–068 On the other hand, if a particular risk was unforeseeable it is not possible to take reasonable precautions against it by amending the design. This is especially true of products such as drugs, where, despite extensive pre-marketing research, it may not be possible to predict all the potential reactions that may occur in a large population. In addition to the problem of proving causation, this will make it difficult to prove that the manufacturer was negligent because at the time when the product was marketed the risk was unknown.[193] Thus, although design defects can be negligent, the courts are more reluctant to hold defendants liable in such cases.[194]

(i) Causation in fact

10–069 In addition to any questions of causation which may arise from intermediate examination, claimants have to prove that the defective product in fact caused the injury of which they complain, applying the usual principles of causation.[195] This will tend to be more difficult with defective drugs.[196] There may be difficulty in isolating drug-induced harm from the background incidence of such injuries. Merely proving an increased risk of injury does not in itself establish causation. The question is whether one can a infer a causal link. In *Best v Wellcome Foundation Ltd*[197] the Supreme Court of Ireland was prepared to make an assumption that if there was a temporal connection between the child's first convulsion and the administration of the pertussis vaccine manufactured by the defendants then causation was established. It was accepted in this case that there was a possibility that pertussis vaccine could, in rare cases, cause brain damage. The only alternative explanation was that the claimant had suffered from "infantile spasms, cause unknown", which, as O'Flaherty J pointed out, was a description rather than a diagnosis of the claimant's condition. *McGhee v National Coal Board*[198] was never a complete solution to the problem of separating drug-induced injuries from the background incidence of such harm.

---

[192] "Most, if not all, drugs cannot be effective unless they are also powerful enough to be potentially harmful": Teff (1984) 47 M.L.R. 303, 309.
[193] *Mann v Wellcome Foundation Ltd* unreported 20 January 1989, QBD. See also Newdick (1985) 101 L.Q.R. 405; and on the thalidomide tragedy see Teff and Munro, *Thalidomide: The Legal Aftermath*, 1976.
[194] Newdick (1987) 103 L.Q.R. 288, 300–304.
[195] See para.5–005 et seq.
[196] See Newdick (1985) 101 L.Q.R. 405, 420; Stapleton (1985) 5 O.J.L.S. 248, 250 discussing the difficulties of proving causation with certain types of disease; and *Kay v Ayrshire and Arran Health Board* [1987] 2 All E.R. 417; *Loveday v Renton* [1990] 1 Med. L.R. 117; *Rothwell v Raes* (1988) 54 D.L.R. (4th) 193; aff'd (1990) 76 D.L.R. (4th) 280, Ont CA; cf. *Best v Wellcome Foundation Ltd* [1994] 5 Med. L.R. 81; [1993] 3 I.R. 421; (1992) 17 B.M.L.R 11. See generally paras 5–022 et seq.
[197] [1994] 5 Med. L.R. 81; [1993] 3 I.R. 421; (1992) 17 B.M.L.R 11.
[198] [1972] 3 All E.R. 1008; see para.5–046.

There, it was known that excess exposure to brick dust could cause dermatitis; the only question was whether on the particular facts it was the negligent period of exposure that had caused the claimant's dermatitis. Where it is not known whether a drug can cause a particular reaction this approach cannot assist the claimant.[199] Nor does it solve the problem of multiple potential defendants in cases of generic prescribing, where it may be impossible for a claimant to say which manufacturer was responsible for the drug he took, especially if it was taken over a long period of time.[200]

Multiple defendants and proportionate loss This issue was addressed by the California Court of Appeal in *Sindell v Abbott Laboratories*,[201] where, due to the very long delay in the teratogenic effects of the drug DES (diethylstilboestrol) becoming apparent, it was impossible for the claimant to identify the particular manufacturers of the drug taken by her mother during pregnancy. The court reversed the burden of proof, requiring the manufacturers to show that their product was not used, and in the absence of proof, damages were apportioned between the various defendants on the basis of their market share of sales of the drug.[202]   **10–070**

It seemed unlikely that this was an approach that would be followed by the English courts, though the decision of the House of Lords in *Fairchild v Glenhaven Funeral Services Ltd*[203] does open up this possibility. In *Fairchild*, according to the scientific evidence, the overwhelming probability was that the claimants' mesothelioma was caused by occupational exposure to asbestos fibres, but because mesothelioma is not a cumulative condition, and can be caused by a few or even one asbestos fibre, it was impossible to say which of a number of exposures during a working life caused the claimants' disease. This made it impossible to identify which of a number of defendants (employers and/or occupiers) was responsible for the mesothelioma. Their Lordships held that in the special circumstances of the case, there should be a relaxation of the normal rule that claimants must prove that but for the defendant's breach of duty they would not have suffered the damage. Although this involved potential injustice by imposing liability on a defendant who had not been proved to have caused the claimants' damage, that had to be weighed against the injustice to the claimants of being denied a claim because they were unable to pin responsibility on a specific defendant, in circumstances where the defendants were in breach of duty and the very high probability was that the illness was caused by the breach of at least one of the defendants. Thus, in the particular circumstances of the case, a   **10–071**

---

[199] As, e.g. in *Loveday v Renton* [1990] 1 Med. L.R. 117, and *Rothwell v Raes* (1988) 54 D.L.R. (4th) 193; aff'd (1990) 76 D.L.R. (4th) 280, Ont CA. Though cf. the more robust approach of the Supreme Court of Ireland to this issue in *Best v Wellcome Foundation Ltd* [1994] 5 Med. L.R. 81; [1993] 3 I.R. 421; (1992) 17 B.M.L.R 11.

[200] For an example of this type of problem see *Mann v Wellcome Foundation Ltd* unreported 20 January 1989, QBD.

[201] 607 P. 2d 924 (1980).

[202] For discussion of this case see Newdick (1985) 101 L.Q.R. 405 at 427–429; Teff (1982) 31 I.C.L.Q. 840; and see further *Hymowitz v Eli Lilly & Co.* 73 N.Y. 2d 487 (1989) applying *Sindell* even where the defendants could prove that the claimant had not used their product.

[203] [2002] UKHL 22; [2003] 1 A.C. 32. See the discussion at paras 5–050 et seq.

defendant's breach of duty which materially increased the risk of the claimant contracting mesothelioma should be treated *as if* it had materially contributed to the disease.[204] Although their Lordships were careful in seeking to limit the application of this principle,[205] the analogy with *Sindell v Abbott Laboratories* is self-evident. If a noxious agent (a "defective" drug) can be proved to be the cause of a claimant's damage, but it is impossible for the claimant to prove which of a number of defendants manufactured the particular drug that that he took, it would be no less unjust to the claimant to deny him a remedy against the manufacturers than it would have been to deny the claimants in *Fairchild* a remedy. The only real difference between the two cases is that in *Sindell* the defendants were held liable for a proportion of the damage only, based on their market share, rather than each defendant being held fully responsible for the claimant's loss, with the defendants left to sort out their respective shares of responsibility through contribution proceedings under the Civil Liability (Contribution) Act 1978.[206]

10–072 The perceived unfairness to defendants of a solution that rendered them liable in full when they had contributed only a part of the risk of harm led the House of Lords to adopt a proportionate share test. In *Barker v Corus (UK) plc (formerly Saint Gobain Pipelines plc)*[207] a majority of their Lordships held that where, applying the approach in *Fairchild*, a defendant is held to have caused the claimant's loss on the basis that his negligence has materially contributed to the *risk* of the claimant's damage (and that damage has actually occurred), in circumstances where the court is unable to conclude that the negligence materially contributed to the claimant's *damage*,[208] defendants are liable only to the extent that their negligence contributed to the risk; they are not liable for the whole of the damage. Thus, where there are multiple defendants who have each contributed to the risk of harm, they are severally liable in respect of that part of the risk that they have contributed, and there is no scope for contribution between the tortfeasors under the Civil Liability (Contribution) Act 1978. The effect of *Barker* was immediately reversed by the Compensation Act 2006 s.3, in relation to asbestos-related mesothelioma[209] (which was the form of damage at issue in both *Fairchild* and *Barker*), but *Barker* continues to apply to other forms of damage, and so opens up the possibility of "proportionate loss" claims analogous to *Sindell v Abbott Laboratories*.

---

[204] Applying *Bonnington Castings Ltd v Wardlaw* [1956] A.C. 613.

[205] See the discussion at paras 5–054 to 5–069.

[206] See paras 9–063 et seq. Note that Stapleton (2002) 10 Torts L.J. 276, 286 suggests that the claimants in *Fairchild* recovered for their full loss by default, because the litigants (and the court) ignored the possibility of apportionment. A decision that the claimant was only entitled to proportionate damages from each defendant would put the onus on the claimant to sue all the relevant defendants, and it would also place the risk of a defendant being insolvent or uninsured on the claimant, rather than the other defendants.

[207] [2006] UKHL 20; [2006] 2 A.C. 572. See para.5–072.

[208] In which case *Bonnington Castings Ltd v Wardlaw* [1956] A.C. 613 would apply, see para.5–033.

[209] See para.5–078.

3. CONSUMER PROTECTION ACT 1987

Although in cases of manufacturing defects the liability of manufacturers in   **10–073**
negligence amounts, in effect, to a form of strict liability, the action for
negligence remains essentially fault-based and subject to all the vagaries
associated with such actions. Some claimants simply fall through the compensation net due to an inability to prove negligence, particularly if the risk of injury
was unforeseeable. Iatrogenic and teratogenic drug injuries are often in this
category, and it was one of the most prominent and poignant examples of drug
injuries, the thalidomide tragedy, which prompted calls for reform. Both the Law
Commission and the Pearson Commission recommended the introduction of
strict liability for defective products.[210] The Strasbourg Convention on Products
Liability in regard to Personal Injury and Death 1977, and two draft European
Community Directives, led finally to the European Community Directive on
Liability for Defective Products 1985,[211] which required member states to
implement its terms within three years. This was done by Pt I of the Consumer
Protection Act 1987 which came into force on 1 March 1988 and applies to
damage caused by products which were put into circulation by the producer after
that date.[212] Section 1(1) states that Pt I of the Act:

> "...shall have effect for the purpose of making such provision as is necessary in order to
> comply with the product liability Directive and shall be construed accordingly."

In the light of s.1(1), it is arguable that where there is a conflict between the Act
and the Directive then the Directive should prevail. Indeed, in *A v The National
Blood Authority*[213] Burton J considered that in view of s.1(1) and the decision of
the European Court of Justice in *Commission of the European Communities v
UK*,[214] the Act had to be interpreted consistently with the Directive and therefore
it was simpler to "go straight to the fount" and apply the wording of the
Directive.

In theory the Act introduces a regime of strict liability for injuries inflicted by   **10–074**
defective products, but the very concept of a product which is "defective"
involves resorting to much the same approach as when deciding whether there
has been negligence, particularly where it is alleged that a product is defective in
design.[215] This is even more apparent with the development risks defence, which
would seem to exclude liability for unforeseeable design defects. Moreover, the
problem of proving causation remains intractable. Given that liability in
negligence for most construction defects comes close to strict liability, since
negligence tends to be inferred from the defect itself, it was considered unlikely
that the Consumer Protection Act would produce a marked change from the

---

[210] Law Com. No.82, Cmnd.6831 (1977); *Royal Commission on Civil Liability and Compensation for Personal Injury*, Cmnd.7054 (1978), Vol.I, Ch.22.
[211] Dir. 1985 No.374.
[212] Consumer Protection Act 1987 s.50(7); SI 1987/1680.
[213] [2001] 3 All E.R. 289 at 297.
[214] (C300/95) [1997] All E.R. (EC) 481; [1997] 3 C.M.L.R. 923.
[215] Clark (1985) 48 M.L.R. 325; Stapleton (1986) 6 O.J.L.S. 392.

action in negligence apart from the reversal of the burden of proof in one area.[216] Indeed, it has been doubted whether the victims of thalidomide, who provoked the initial cry for reform, would be in any better position under the Act than in the tort of negligence.

10–075 The decision of Burton J in *A v The National Blood Authority*[217] to interpret the Product Liability Directive as creating a regime of truly strict liability required a reassessment of the effect of the legislation. Burton J concluded that the purpose of the Product Liability Directive had been to remove the need for a claimant to prove that the defendant had been negligent, and therefore the defendants' argument that they had exercised all reasonable care to avoid transmitting the Hepatitis C virus through blood products was irrelevant. His Lordship made the not unreasonable observation that if both the Directive and the Act were to be interpreted as simply a variant of negligence there would have been no point to enacting the legislation. Similarly, in *Abouzaid v Mothercare (UK) Ltd*[218] the Court of Appeal had no difficulty with the notion that a product could be defective within the meaning of the Act, even though the defendant was not liable in negligence at common law because the risk of injury, although identifiable (and therefore not entirely unforeseeable), was very small.

10–076 The Act has not replaced the common law; it is an additional remedy.[219] If for any reason the Act does not apply (if, for example, the special limitation periods under the Act have expired, or the product which caused the damage was put into circulation before the Act came into force on 1 March 1988) a claim for negligence may still be available.[220]

(a) Claimants

10–077 Section 2(1) provides that:

> "...where any damage is caused wholly or partly by a defect in a product, every person to whom subsection 2 below applies shall be liable for the damage."

---

[216] See Stapleton (1986) 6 O.J.L.S. 392; Newdick (1987) 103 L.Q.R. 288; Newdick [1988] C.L.J. 455; Stoppa (1992) 12 L.S. 210. For discussion of some of the difficulties involved in bringing claims under the Act see: C. Johnston, "A Personal (and Selective) Introduction to Product Liability Law" [2012] J.P.I.L. 1; D. Body, "Product liability claims under the Consumer Protection Act 1987: some practical problems" [2012] J.P.I.L. 79.

[217] [2001] 3 All E.R. 289; see para.10–091.

[218] [2000] All E.R. (D) 2436; *The Times*, 20 February 2001.

[219] Consumer Protection Act 1987 s.2(6).

[220] The Consumer Protection Act 1987 Pt II lays down general requirements for the safety of certain consumer goods and gives the Secretary of State power to make specific safety regulations (see, e.g. the Medical Devices Regulations 2002 (SI 2002/618)). Breach of these regulations is a criminal offence, and by s.41 an individual injured by an infringement of a safety regulation (but not the general safety requirement) can bring an action for breach of statutory duty. This right of action appears not to have been widely used, though see *Howmet Ltd v Economy Devices Ltd* [2016] EWCA Civ 847; [2016] B.L.R. 555 at [102]–[105] where a claim for breach of s.41 failed on causation.

This section confers a right of action on *any* person who suffers damage as a result of a defective product.[221] There is no need to establish that the claimant was foreseeable as likely to be affected by the defect, nor that the defendant was negligent. Proof that the product was "defective" and that the defect caused the damage puts the onus on the defendant to establish one of the specific defences.

(b) Defendants

Section 2 imposes liability on four categories of defendant: (i) the producer of the product; (ii) anyone who holds themselves out as the producer; (iii) an importer; and (iv) in certain circumstances, the supplier.[222] This creates the possibility of suing multiple defendants under the Act for a single injury.

10–078

The producer A "producer" is the manufacturer of the product, or the person who won or abstracted a substance which has not been manufactured, or the processor where the "essential characteristics" of a product are attributable to an industrial or other process.[223] "Producer" also includes the manufacturer of a component part.[224] The component manufacturer will be liable together with the manufacturer of the finished product if the damage caused by the finished product is attributable to a defect in the component. On the other hand, it would seem that the component manufacturer is not liable for damage caused by the finished product if the component was not defective. This is the position where the defect in the finished product was wholly attributable to the design of that product, because s.4(1)(f) provides a specific defence for the component manufacturer. The Act does not deal with the position of the component manufacturer where the defect in the finished product is a construction defect or the result of a defective component supplied by another manufacturer, but under the Directive people are liable only for products which they have supplied, and the component manufacturer does not supply the finished product.

10–079

The definition of producer is wide enough to encompass, not only a large pharmaceutical company, but also the individual pharmacist or doctor who mixes small amounts of product to produce a compound or mixture, or the doctor who modifies an appliance, or uses an additive in an intravenous solution.

10–080

Holding oneself out as the producer People who hold themselves out as the producer of the product "by putting his name on the product or using a trade mark or other distinguishing mark in relation to the product".[225] Whereas a retail supplier will not normally be liable, retailers who adopt the practice of putting

10–081

---

[221] Including antenatal injuries: Consumer Protection Act 1987 s.6(3). But the Act has no territorial effect beyond the United Kingdom, European Union or European Economic Area (EEA). Consumers who suffer damage outside the EEA, who have no connection with the EEA, and where marketing and supply of the defective product was outside the EEA are not within the scope of the Act: *Allen v Depuy International Ltd* [2014] EWHC 753 (QB); [2015] 2 W.L.R. 442.

[222] Consumer Protection Act 1987 s.2(2), 2(3).

[223] Consumer Protection Act 1987 s.1(2). "Essential characteristics" are not defined by the legislation.

[224] This is by virtue of the definition of "product" in s.1(2).

[225] Consumer Protection Act 1987 s.2(2)(b); the "own-brander".

their own brand name on goods produced by others will be liable for defects in those goods. This is now a common practice with large retail chain stores in the United Kingdom. Supermarkets and retail chemists who supply non-prescription medicines under their own brand name will be treated as the producer. However, it is not thought that simply attaching a name and address to a product, which pharmacists and dispensing doctors are required to do by law, constitutes holding oneself out as the producer.

10–082   **The importer**   Importers of a product are liable if they imported it from a place outside the European Community into a member state in the course of any business of theirs, to supply it to another.[226] The importer from another member state into the United Kingdom is not liable under this subsection. So the importer of a defective product from Japan is liable for damage caused by the defect, but not the importer of a product from France. If the Japanese product had first been imported to France and then imported to the United Kingdom, the French importer would be liable, but not the UK importer.

10–083   **The supplier**   Suppliers of goods, whether retailers or intermediate distributors, are not normally liable under the Act. Suppliers will be liable, however, if they fail, within a reasonable period of receiving a request from the person who suffered the damage, to identify either the producer, "own-brander", or importer, or the person who supplied the product to them.[227] Suppliers are not liable under s.2(3) merely because they cannot identify who provided the component parts or raw materials in a finished product supplied to them[228]; rather it is the producer or supplier of the finished product that they must identify. The claimant's request must be made within a reasonable period after the damage occurs, and at a time when it is not reasonably practical for the claimant to identify them. This section is intended to give claimants an identifiable defendant and puts the onus on suppliers, such as retail pharmacists and dispensing general practitioners, to keep accurate records of their own sources of supply. This may be a particular problem for pharmacists dispensing generic drugs. If suppliers comply with the request they are not liable under the Act, even if the claimant cannot pursue a remedy against the identified defendants, e.g. because they are in liquidation. The liability of suppliers in the tort of negligence is potentially wider than this.

10–084   **Parallel systems of compensation**   A service provider, such as a hospital providing medical treatment which, in the course of providing treatment to a patient, uses a defective product of which it was not the producer does not fall within the scope of Directive 1985/374 (and so would not be subject to liability under the Consumer Protection Act 1987). In *Centre Hospitalier Universitaire de Besancon v Dutrueux*[229] a patient suffered burns during surgery which were caused by a defect in the temperature-control mechanism of a heated mattress. The hospital was strictly liable to the patient under French domestic law. The

---

[226] Consumer Protection Act 1987 s.2(2)(c).
[227] Consumer Protection Act 1987 s.2(3); on the meaning of "supply" see s.46.
[228] Consumer Protection Act 1987 s.1(3).
[229] (C-495/10) [2012] 2 C.M.L.R. 1; (2012) 127 B.M.L.R. 1.

European Court of Justice held that the hospital could not be considered to be an operator in the production and marketing chain of the mattress, to which the definition of "producer" related, nor could it be treated as the supplier of the product (and thus it was not the producer, importer or supplier of the mattress). But there was no objection to a parallel system of compensation in domestic law, said the Court, provided that it did not adversely affect the system of product liability established by the Directive. As long as it remained possible for the liability of the producer of the defective product to be put in issue when the conditions of the Directive were met it was irrelevant that a domestic scheme of no-fault liability applied to service providers, since this was additional to producer liability and could enhance consumer protection. The possibility of a product liability claim against the producer by both the patient and the service provider (e.g. by way of third party proceedings) had to remain open.

(c)   Products

"Product" means any "goods or electricity" and includes a product which is comprised in another product whether as a component part or raw material.[230] There was some doubt as to whether human organs or bodily fluids, such as blood, should be treated as "products" under the Act, though this doubt has now been resolved in favour of treating them as products to which the Act does apply.[231]

10–085

Agricultural produce and game were excluded unless it had undergone an industrial process,[232] although there is no definition of an "industrial process". The processor was only liable as a producer if the "essential characteristics" of the product were attributable to an industrial or other process.[233] This requirement does not apply to other potential defendants in respect of processed products, the "own-brander", the importer or the supplier. Nor was it necessary that the defect in the product was the result of the industrial process itself. For example, food that was contaminated prior to processing could give rise to liability under the Act, once processed, whereas the same contaminated food sold to consumers unprocessed was not within the Act. This could be a relevant distinction with some forms of herbal remedy. The exception for agricultural products was

10–086

---

[230] Consumer Protection Act 1987 s.1(2). "Goods" includes substances, growing crops and things comprised in land by virtue of being attached to it, and any ship, aircraft or vehicle: s.45.
[231] *A v National Blood Authority* [2001] 3 All E.R. 289; the Pearson Commission recommended that organs and blood should be subject to a strict liability regime: Cmnd.7054, (1978), Vol. I, para.1276. See Lee and Morgan, *Human Fertilisation & Embryology* (Oxford: Blackstone Press, 2000), p.261, discussing whether embryos or gametes could be regarded as "products". See also Stern (1994) 2 Med. L. Rev. 261, 262. In *E v Australian Red Cross Society* (1991) 99 A.L.R. 601; [1991] 2 Med. L.R. 303 at 326, Fed Court of Aust, Wilcox J considered, without resolving, the question of whether blood could amount to "goods".
[232] Consumer Protection Act 1987 s.2(4). Agricultural produce means "any produce of the soil, of stock-farming or of fisheries": s.1(2).
[233] Consumer Protection Act 1987 s.1(2).

removed by EU Directive 99/34 which extends the 1985 Product Liability Directive to agricultural produce, but only in respect of products put into the market after 4 December 2000.[234]

(d) Defects

10–087 Liability under the Consumer Protection Act 1987 is strict, not absolute. Claimants do not succeed simply by showing that the product caused damage; they must prove that the damage was caused by a defect in the product. By s.3(1) a product has a defect "if the safety of the product is not such as persons generally are entitled to expect". Safety includes safety with respect to component parts, and with respect to property damage as well as personal injury. The crucial question is: what are persons generally entitled to expect by way of safety? The answer, almost inevitably, must be: it all depends on the circumstances of the case.[235]

10–088 **Consumer expectations**   Persons generally are entitled to expect that food and drink will not be contaminated with decomposed snails or acid, that clothes and hair dye will not contain skin irritants, that motor cars will not have defective steering, that dangerous chemicals will be adequately labelled, and so on. But they are not necessarily entitled to expect that drugs will have no adverse side effects, that all motor cars will be as safe as modern technology can make them, nor that hot drinks will not burn skin if the drink is spilled.[236] The seriousness of the potential injury is a factor relevant to what persons are entitled to expect.[237] Safety, like risk, is a relative concept, and this is just as true in determining what is "defective" as it is in deciding whether a manufacturer has been negligent. It is a question of degree, in which levels of safety are traded off against both cost and the usefulness of the product, although this is more likely to be an intuitive judgment than a strict cost–benefit analysis.[238] The question of what persons generally are entitled to expect has to be measured objectively and not by reference to the actual expectations of an actual or even a notional individual or group of individuals: it is a matter of law, not actual individual or even general expectation.[239] Accordingly, in deciding whether a product has a defect, it is for the court to:

---

[234] See O'Rourke (1999) 149 N.L.J. 1106.

[235] In *Abouzaid v Mothercare (UK) Ltd* [2000] All E.R. (D) 2436 at [40] Chadwick LJ said that the question of whether the safety of a product was such as persons generally were entitled to expect is a question of fact.

[236] *B v McDonald's Restaurants Ltd* [2002] EWHC 490 (QB).

[237] *Abouzaid v Mothercare (UK) Ltd* [2000] All E.R. (D) 2436 at [27] where Pill LJ considered that the seriousness of an injury to the eye would affect the expectations of members of the public, whereas expectations would be lower if the worst that could happen was the risk of striking a hand with an elasticated strap.

[238] See Clark (1985) 48 M.L.R. 325. In *G v Fry Surgical International Ltd* (1992) 3 *AVMA Medical & Legal Journal* (No.4) p.12 an action under the Consumer Protection Act 1987 against the importers of a pair of arthroscopy scissors which fractured during the course of an operation, leaving a fragment in the claimant's knee, was settled by the defendants on the basis that the scissors were defective.

[239] *Wilkes v Depuy International Ltd* [2016] EWHC 3096 (QB); [2017] 3 All E.R. 589 at [69].

"...assess the appropriate level of safety ... taking into account the information and the circumstances before it, whether or not an actual or notional patient or patients, or indeed other members of the public, would in fact have considered each of those factors and all of that information."[240]

All the circumstances to be considered   Section 3(2) provides that in   **10–089**
determining what persons generally are entitled to expect "all the circumstances shall be taken into account", including:

"(a)   the manner in which, and purposes for which, the product has been marketed, its get-up, the use of any mark in relation to the product and any instructions for, or warnings with respect to, doing or refraining from doing anything with or in relation to the product;
(b)   what might reasonably be expected to be done with or in relation to the product; and
(c)   the time when the product was supplied by its producer to another;
and nothing in this section shall require a defect to be inferred from the fact alone that the safety of a product which is supplied after that time is greater than the safety of the product in question."

In *Richardson v LRC Products Ltd*[241] it was held that, though the natural   **10–090**
expectation of consumers would be that a condom would not fail, this was not something that persons generally were entitled to expect, particularly since the defendants did not claim that their product would be 100 per cent effective. Thus, the fact that a condom had failed did not prove that it was defective under s.3(1).[242] It is not clear why a condom which is proved to have failed as a result of a rupture is not defective. In *Richardson* Kennedy J stated that:

"Naturally enough the users' expectation is that a condom will not fail. There are no claims made by the defendants that one will never fail and no-one has ever supposed that any method of contraception intended to defeat nature will be 100 per cent. effective. This must particularly be so in the case of a condom where the product is required to a degree at least to be, in the jargon, 'user friendly'."[243]

With respect, this fails to address the statutory test as to what is defective. The suggestion that the fact that the manufacturer has not claimed that his products will never fail should be taken into account in assessing what is defective is misplaced. Few, if any, manufacturers would make such an inflated claim, but

---

[240] [2016] EWHC 3096 (QB); [2017] 3 All E.R. 589 at [72] per Hickinbottom J.
[241] [2000] P.I.Q.R. P164; [2000] Lloyd's Rep. Med. 280.
[242] In *Foster v Biosil* (2000) 59 B.M.L.R. 178, Central London County Court, it was held that in a claim in respect of allegedly defective silicone breast implants, which ruptured and leaked silicone, the claimant must prove both that the implant was defective under s.3 and the cause of the defect, applying *Richardson v LRC Products Ltd*. The claimant had to prove that there was a defect in the product, not merely that the product failed in circumstances which were unsafe and contrary to what persons generally are entitled to expect. This she failed to do, on the balance of probabilities, in the face of evidence from the manufacturer that there had been no other implant from the particular batch which had been reported as defective, and statistics showing that failures were very rare. On the other hand, as Balen (2002) 8 *Clinical Risk* 177, 184 comments: "To give protection to consumers it should be sufficient to demonstrate that a product was not as safe as expected (as per the wording of the Act and Directive) without having to identify the precise cause of the defect." See also Freeman [2001] J.P.I.L. 26.
[243] [2000] Lloyd's Rep. Med. 280 at 285.

that tells us nothing about whether any particular product is defective.[244] Most failures of condoms are probably due to consumer misuse and lack of skill in using the condom may be a risk that consumers must accept, but it is entirely unclear why consumers must accept that some condoms will fail through manufacturing defects, simply because the manufacturers have never claimed that their products are 100 per cent safe. What if, instead of pregnancy, the consequence of the failure was that one of the parties transmitted HIV to the other. Would the consumer expectation test suggest that the condom was not defective in these circumstances?

10–091   In contrast, in *A v National Blood Authority*[245] Burton J held that consumers are entitled to expect that blood products would be 100 per cent safe, and therefore the supplier of blood infected with the virus hepatitis C had supplied a product which was defective. The claimants were infected with the hepatitis C virus through blood transfusions which had used blood from infected donors. Although the risk of infection with hepatitis C in this manner was known, at the time when the claimants were infected it was impossible to avoid, either because the virus had not been discovered or because there was no test for the virus in blood products. The defendants accepted that liability under art.6 of the European Union Product Liability Directive 1985 was strict, in the sense that it did not depend on the proof of fault by the claimant. Nonetheless, they argued that in determining whether the blood was defective under art.6 (which corresponds to s.3 of the 1987 Act) the fact that the risk was unavoidable should be taken into account. Blood was an inherently risky product, and therefore the infected blood should not be regarded as a non-standard product, that is a product which fell below the levels of safety to be expected in a standard product, where the harmful (non-standard) characteristic had caused the claimants' damage. The blood supplied by the defendants was provided as a service to society, and the defendants had no alternative but to supply it to hospitals.

10–092   In a robust judgment, Burton J held that blood infected with hepatitis C virus was defective under the Product Liability Directive. Article 6 states that a product is defective if it does not provide a level of safety which a person is entitled to expect, irrespective of whether that lack of safety could have been avoided by the manufacturer. The argument that the public were only entitled to expect that level of safety which could have been achieved by the exercise of reasonable precautions was rejected. The consumer had an expectation, and was entitled to expect, that blood used in transfusions would be 100 per cent safe and would not be infected with hepatitis C. The Directive was intended to eliminate proof of fault or negligence in order to make it easier for claimants to prove their case. Not only do consumers not have to prove that producers did not take reasonable steps, or all reasonable steps, to comply with their duty, but also they do not have to show that producers did not take all legitimately expectable steps either. The infected blood products were non-standard products because they were different

---

[244] For example, in *Grant v Australian Knitting Mills Ltd* [1936] A.C. 85 at 95 it was said that 4,737,600 garments had been manufactured by a similar process, without any complaint from consumers, before the product in question was worn by the claimant. That, however, did not prevent the Privy Council from holding the defendants liable in negligence.
[245] [2001] 3 All E.R. 289.

from the norm which the producer intended for use by the public.[246] The fact that the risk of viral infection is inherent in blood, as a natural product, was irrelevant. Moreover, the question of whether the defendants could have avoided the damage to the claimants was not one of the circumstances to be taken into account within art.6. It was not a relevant circumstance since it was beyond the purpose of the Directive and had it been intended, would have been included as a derogation from it. Also excluded from consideration were the impracticability, cost or difficulty of identifying the potentially harmful agent and taking preventive measures, and the potential social benefits of the product.[247] As Burton J commented:

> "This is obviously a tough decision for any common lawyer to make. But I am entirely clear that this was the purpose of the Directive, and that without the exclusion of such matters (subject only to the limited defence of Article 7(e) [the 'development risks' defence]) it would not only be toothless but pointless."[248]

In other words, if the Directive and the 1987 Act are interpreted in such a manner as to be little different from the law of negligence, there was no point to the legislation. This strengthened Burton J's conclusion that, on the wording of the Directive, it was clear that a true form of strict liability had been enacted.

Foreseeability irrelevant   Similarly, in *Abouzaid v Mothercare (UK) Ltd*[249]   **10–093**
Chadwick LJ said that the question under s.2(1) of the Act is how was the damage caused; it is not was the cause of the damage foreseeable? The question of whether the manufacturer might have been expected to discover the defect, given the state of scientific and technical knowledge at the time, though relevant to the defence under s.4(1)(e), was not relevant to the issue to be addressed under s.3, which is what degree of safety are persons generally entitled to expect?[250] Thus, Chadwick LJ observed:

> "…in the context of the test to be applied under sections 2(1) and 3(1) it is irrelevant whether the hazard which causes the damage has come, or ought reasonably to have come, to the attention of the producer before the accident occurs. To hold otherwise is, to my mind, to seek

---

[246] 99 out of 100 bags of blood were not infected and would cause no injury, but the defendants' argument, rejected by Burton J, was that all of the bags of blood were standard because they all carried the *risk* of infection, in the sense that, without a test, it was possible that any individual bag carried the virus. Note that in *Wilkes v Depuy International Ltd* [2016] EWHC 3096 (QB); [2017] 3 All E.R. 589 at [94] Hickinbottom J considered that the categorisation of defects into "standard"/"non-standard" was "unnecessary and undesirable" and that treating the distinction as a rigid categorisation was "positively unhelpful and potentially dangerous". His Lordship added, at [96], that: "I appreciate that, where a particular specimen of a product is out of specification (or otherwise "non-standard"), then risk-benefit of an in-specification product is unlikely to have much, if any, weight: but I would not advocate a rule of law that it must have none. In assessing the safety of a product, the court should consider the relevant circumstances, in a suitably flexible way: no more and no less."

[247] But see para.10–105 below.

[248] [2001] 3 All E.R. 289 at [69]. For comment on *A v The National Blood Authority* see Howells and Mildred (2002) 65 M.L.R. 95; Hodges (2001) 117 L.Q.R. 528; Goldberg (2002) 10 Med. L. Rev. 165; Brown (2001) 7 *Clinical Risk* 144; Melville Williams [2001] J.P.I.L. 238.

[249] *The Times*, 20 February 2001; [2000] All E.R. (D) 2436 at [38], CA.

[250] *The Times*, 20 February 2001; [2000] All E.R. (D) 2436 at [43], CA.

to reintroduce concepts familiar in the context of a claim in negligence at common law into a statutory regime which has been enacted in order to give effect to the Product Liability Directive …"[251]

10–094 **Consumer expectations of medicinal products**   The types of defect which can arise fall into the same categories as are found with the tort of negligence, namely defects in the manufacture, design, or the presentation of the product with inadequate warnings or instructions for use. "Consumer expectations" are treated as a measure of defectiveness, but medicinal products almost invariably carry some risk of adverse reactions, even if in only a small minority of consumers. Thus, although the decision in *A v National Blood Authority* indicates that consumers are entitled to expect that blood used for transfusion will not be contaminated with a dangerous virus, it is arguably still the case that they are not necessarily entitled to expect that other medical products will be entirely risk-free. The risks have to be weighed against the anticipated benefits, and indeed against the "costs" of not using the product, such as the harm associated with the disease, and the risks and anticipated benefits of alternative treatments. This process is familiar from the assessment of what constitutes negligence.

10–095 In *Wilkes v Depuy International Ltd*[252] the claimant underwent hip-replacement surgery. The artificial hip was made from metal components which included a steel femoral shaft (C-Stem) produced by the defendant manufacturer. Three years after the surgery the C-Stem fractured. The claimant alleged, inter alia, that the C-Stem was defective under s.3 of the Consumer Protection Act on the basis that its safety was not such as persons generally were entitled to expect. Hickinbottom J noted that the C-Stem fell within the scope of the Medical Devices Directive[253] as implemented in the UK by the Medical Devices Regulations 2002.[254] This meant that medical devices cannot be marketed unless the risks associated with the device were "acceptable", and the acceptability of risks had to be seen in the context of the potential benefits that the device will bring:

> "Given that no medicinal product is free from risk, and thus 'safety' in this field is inherently and necessarily a relative concept, a medical device will only be allowed onto the market if the product is assessed as having a positive risk-benefit ratio."[255]

This view translated to Hickinbottom 's approach to consumer expectations for the purpose of deciding whether a product was defective under s.3. Since no medicinal product, if effective, could be absolutely safe there could:

---

[251] *The Times*, 20 February 2001; [2000] All E.R. (D) 2436 at [44], CA.
[252] [2016] EWHC 3096 (QB); [2017] 3 All E.R. 589; discussed by M. Harvey [2017] J.P.I.L. C128; and J. Eisler, "One step forward and two steps back in product liability: the search for consistency in the identification of defects" [2017] C.L.J. 230.
[253] Directive 93/42/EEC.
[254] SI 2002/618.
[255] [2016] EWHC 3096 (QB); [2017] 3 All E.R. 589 at [13].

"…not be a sensible expectation that any medicine or medicinal product is entirely risk-free …
the potential benefits (including potential utility) of such a product have to be balanced against
its risks."[256]

Given that a medicine or medical device would almost always involve design
compromises the effect of eliminating or reducing a particular risk had to be seen
in the context of any adverse consequences in the form of increased risks of a
different sort or reduced benefit and utility.[257]

Hickinbottom J concluded that the C-Stem did not fall below the safety persons
were generally entitled to expect at the time it was put into circulation.[258] On the
evidence, a change in the design to reduce the risk of fracture to zero would have
had some negative consequences, which included a financial cost to hospitals and
the potentially "disastrous" risk of mismatching (if the particular stem had been
mistakenly used with a ceramic head). The C-Stem "complied with all relevant
mandatory standards" and satisfied all of the regulatory requirements, including
those imposed to ensure that the product was "acceptably" safe. It was true that
there was a small risk of fatigue failure at the neck of the C-Stem, but there was
no evidence that any other design had no such risk or that the risk was higher than
other models. The proviso to s.3(2) of the Act (stating that a defect is not to be
inferred from the fact that a later product is safer than the safety of the product in
question) also suggested that the fact that a safer design could be envisaged did
not mean that a current product is defective. The risk of stem fracture was
small,[259] and the instructions for use supplied with the C-Stem warned of the
precise risk. The claimant had been informed about other, higher, risks of failure
of the hip-replacement surgery, each of which would have resulted in a revision
procedure (which was the consequence of the C-Stem fracture). In assessing the
safety of the product, said Hickinbottom J, the court should take into account
both the chance of the adverse event happening and the consequences if the
adverse event occurred. The risk of C-Stem fracture was small and the
consequence was a revision operation to replace the artificial hip, which though
"unpleasant and debilitating" was "relatively limited".[260] The approach of
Hickinbottom J to determining what constitutes a defective product under the
Consumer Protection Act is almost identical to the analysis that would be
undertaken with a claim framed in the tort of negligence, and provides a stark
contrast to the decision of Burton J in *A v National Blood Authority*.[261]

Added risk of product failure can constitute a defect   In *Medtel Pty Ltd v
Courtney*[262] the Full Court of the Federal Court of Australia held that a product
which carried a "superadded risk" of failure, over and above the background risk,
was defective even though it had not actually failed. Mr Courtney had a heart

10–096

10–097

[256] [2016] EWHC 3096 (QB); [2017] 3 All E.R. 589 at [65].
[257] [2016] EWHC 3096 (QB); [2017] 3 All E.R. 589 at [82].
[258] See [2016] EWHC 3096 (QB); [2017] 3 All E.R. 589 at [117]–[132].
[259] The defendants had experienced a stem fracture failure rate of 0.195 per cent, and a stem neck
fracture (which is what occurred in the claimant's case) rate of 0.004 per cent: [2016] EWHC 3096
(QB); [2017] 3 All E.R. 589 at [48].
[260] [2016] EWHC 3096 (QB); [2017] 3 All E.R. 589 at [132].
[261] [2001] 3 All E.R. 289; see para.10–091.
[262] [2003] FCAFC 151; (2003) 198 A.L.R. 630.

pacemaker implanted. It was subsequently discovered that, due to the process of manufacture (which involved the use of a particular type of solder) there was a risk of premature battery failure. It was not possible to identify the precise risk, but the minimum figure was that 5.5 per cent of the pacemakers manufactured with this type of solder failed prematurely. Following a "hazard alert" about this risk, the claimant was advised by his doctor to have his pacemaker explanted. He brought an action (in relation to the additional surgery that this necessitated) under the Australian Trade Practices Act 1974 which entitles consumers to obtain compensation for loss or damage they suffer if they acquire goods which are not of merchantable quality or fit for the purpose for which they were sold. The evidence at trial was that the claimant's pacemaker had at all times functioned normally, and that had it remained place it would not have ceased to function prematurely due to battery depletion (i.e. it was one of the 90 per cent or more of pacemakers subject to the hazard alert that, despite the use of the particular type of solder, did not suffer premature battery failure, though this could not have been known at the time when the claimant was advised to have the surgery to remove the pacemaker). Nonetheless it was held that the pacemaker was not of merchantable quality or fit for purpose, because at the time of implantation it was subject to a risk of premature failure over and above the background or random risk of failure that affects all pacemakers. Reasonable consumers (in this case patients having heart pacemakers implanted) would not expect their pacemakers to be manufactured in such a way as to be subject to a superadded risk of premature failure. Although the language of the Trade Practices Act 1974 is different from that of the Consumer Protection Act 1987, the test of merchantable quality is based on reasonable consumer expectations, just as the test of what is defective under s.3 of the 1987 Act is based on consumer expectations of safety. In effect, the court concluded that the pacemaker was defective because of uncertainty about its reliability caused by a particular process of manufacture (going beyond the normal, small, risks of failure associated with such devices) in circumstances where reliability is absolutely crucial.[263]

10–098   A similar approach was taken by the European Court of Justice in *Boston Scientific Medizintechnik GmbH v AOK Sachsen-Anhalt – Die Gesundheitskasse*[264] where it was held that a medical device implanted in the human body (pacemakers and implantable cardioverter defibrillators) could be found to be defective under Directive 1985/374, even though no defect had been detected in the specific device implanted, where other devices in the same product group had a significantly increased risk of failure. In the light of the function of pacemakers and implantable cardioverter defibrillators, and the particularly vulnerable situation of patients using such devices, the safety requirements for those devices

---

[263] See O. Melnitchouk and S. Pearl, "Hazard Alerts and Product Liability: Can a Normally Functioning Medical Device be a Defective Product?" (2004) 6 Med. Law Int. 87 for discussion of *Medtel Pty Ltd v Courtney* in the context of the Consumer Protection Act 1987 and the decision of Burton J in *A v National Blood Authority* [2001] 3 All E.R. 289.
[264] (C-503/13) EU:C:2015:148; [2015] 3 C.M.L.R. 6; (2015) 144 B.M.L.R. 225. This case was combined with *Boston Scientific Medizintechnik GmbH v Betriebskrankenkasse RWE* (C-504/13).

which such patients are entitled to expect are particularly high, given the abnormal potential for damage which the products might cause to the patients concerned.[265] It followed that where:

"...products belonging to the same group or forming part of the same production series, such as pacemakers and implantable cardioverter defibrillators, have a potential defect, such a product may be classified as defective without there being any need to establish that that product has such a defect."[266]

Compensation for the damage attributable to the defect had to cover, inter alia, the costs relating to the replacement of the defective product, including the costs of any necessary surgical operations.

Compliance with regulatory requirements In *Wilkes v Depuy International Ltd*[267] Hickinbottom J noted that:

10–099

"...every aspect of the design, testing, promotion and marketing of medicines and medicinal products, including medical devices such as prosthetic components, is now closely regulated; and regulated on the basis of the precautionary principle. Broadly, the relevant regulatory authority, applying its own scientific and medical expertise, will only allow a product to be put (and, thereafter, maintained) on the market if it is satisfied that the product meets appropriate standards of safety, efficacy and quality."

What is the consequence of a defendant's product meeting, or failing to meet, standards of safety, efficacy and quality laid down by a regulator? The formal position of the courts is that non-compliance with statutory standards will provide *evidence* that the product is defective, but is not conclusive. Similarly, compliance with those standards is *evidence* that the product is not defective.[268] In practice, however, compliance with statutory standards for safety will make it extremely difficult for a claimant to demonstrate that the product was defective because that would effectively amount to a challenge to the conclusions of the regulator. In *Wilkes* the product had satisfied all of the regulatory requirements, including those imposed to ensure that the product was "acceptably" safe. For Hickinbottom J it was important that the regulators "acting in the public interest and on the basis of full information" had assessed the C-Stem to be acceptably safe. Though it was not an automatic defence:

"...the fact that the regulator has made such an assessment is powerful evidence that the level of safety of the product was that which persons generally were entitled to expect."[269]

---

[265] (C-503/13) EU:C:2015:148; [2015] 3 C.M.L.R. 6; (2015) 144 B.M.L.R. 225 at [39]–[40].
[266] (C-503/13) EU:C:2015:148; [2015] 3 C.M.L.R. 6; (2015) 144 B.M.L.R. 225 at [43].
[267] [2016] EWHC 3096 (QB); [2017] 3 All E.R. 589 at [7].
[268] [2016] EWHC 3096 (QB); [2017] 3 All E.R. 589 at [97], [101].
[269] [2016] EWHC 3096 (QB); [2017] 3 All E.R. 589 at [124]. Contrast *XYZ v Schering Health Care Ltd* [2002] EWHC 1420 (QB); (2002) 70 B.M.L.R. 88 at [19] per Mackay J: "I note with respect and interest the conclusions of the regulators who looked into this matter, but am in no way bound by them, nor indeed am I strongly influenced by them in the end."

10–100 **Warnings**   Consumer expectations may be limited by any warnings or contra-indications given by the manufacturer, either directly to the consumer[270] or to an intermediary such as the prescribing physician.[271] It does not make sense, however, to speak of warnings against dangers which were unknown or unforeseeable by the producer, and once the question of foreseeability arises the concept of reasonable care is reintroduced.[272] A warning contained in a legible and unambiguous leaflet will normally suffice. A manufacturer cannot be expected to cater for lost leaflets or consumers who choose not to replace a lost leaflet.[273]

10–101 **Misuse by the consumer**   Misuse of the product by the consumer will be taken into account. If the product is used in a way which could not reasonably be expected then, as with negligence, it cannot be considered defective. Foreseeable misuse will make the product defective, subject to a possible defence of contributory negligence.[274]

10–102 **Deterioration of the product over time**   Section 3(2)(c) takes account of the time at which the product was supplied by the producer (not when supplied to the consumer) in assessing whether it was defective. The product may have deteriorated since it left the producer's hands, as a result of the passage of time, or repeated use, or misuse or mishandling. A product which has deteriorated in this way is not necessarily defective, though it is not necessarily safe either. It will depend upon the nature of the product, how much time has elapsed, how much use it has had, and so on. Keeping and using drugs after their expiry date may be an example of contributory negligence, but it may also indicate that the drugs were not even defective if the consumer was not entitled to expect that they would not deteriorate. But the mere passage of time, during which period a danger in a product has become apparent, does not mean that consumer

---

[270] Warnings "qualify the expectation that the public generally are entitled to expect of a particular product, and thus go to the issue of whether that product is defective": *Wilkes v Depuy International Ltd* [2016] EWHC 3096 (QB); [2017] 3 All E.R. 589 at [103].

[271] In *Wilkes v Depuy International Ltd* [2016] EWHC 3096 (QB); [2017] 3 All E.R. 589 at [108] Hickinbottom J noted that the fact that there is a learned intermediary does not provide a complete or automatic defence for a producer of a medicinal product, but "particularly in respect of a product such as a prosthesis (in respect of which there is no obligation upon a producer to give any information direct to the patient) [it was] unarguable that the fact that there is a learned intermediary (who has chosen a particular prosthesis for a particular patient and has available, not only his general professional knowledge, but also the specific [instructions for use] including warnings)" could be other than a relevant consideration for the purposes of s.3.

[272] Clark (1987) 50 M.L.R. 614 at 617. Notwithstanding the introduction of strict product liability in the United States, defective design cases and cases of failure to warn are treated as equivalent to actions in negligence: see *Feldman v Lederle Laboratories* 479 A. 2d 374 (1984); *Brown v Superior Court* 751 P. 2d 470 (1988). On the other hand, a product which could have been rendered "safe" by an appropriate warning can nonetheless be held to be defective even though the producer was unaware of the danger associated with its design because there had been no previous reports of accidents with the product: *Abouzaid v Mothercare (UK) Ltd* [2000] All E.R. (D) 2436, CA.

[273] *Worsley v Tambrands Ltd* [2000] P.I.Q.R. P95.

[274] See e.g. *Palmer v Palmer* [2006] EWHC 1284 (QB) where a device designed to enable an inertia reel seat belt in a motor vehicle to be used with a young child was held to be defective because the design and instructions made it likely to be misused by the introduction of too much slack in the seat belt.

expectations have changed. The question of what consumers can reasonably expect does not depend on whether a manufacturer could reasonably have been expected to be aware of the hazard at the time. The product is to be judged by the expectations of the public at large, as determined by the court, and the passage of time does not necessarily alter public expectations as to the safety of a product.[275]

Effect of products supplied later being safer   The proviso to s.3(2) states that   **10–103**
the defectiveness of a product is not to be inferred simply from the fact that products which are supplied at a later date are safer than the product in question. In negligence, of course, carelessness is measured by reference to the knowledge and standards applicable at the time of the accident, ignoring subsequent improvements,[276] and the proviso appears to apply a similar standard. This must go to the question of proof, however, rather than creating a rule of law, otherwise all unforeseeable defects would be excluded from the ambit of the Act, as in negligence. Presumably, a case such as *Roe v Minister of Health*[277] is just the type of situation which ought to be covered by strict liability, since persons generally are entitled to expect that anaesthetics will not be contaminated with paralysing agents.[278] Once an improved product becomes available this may be relevant to whether the old product is defective if the supply of the old product is *continued*, as in negligence, but this begs the question of what is meant by "improved". A new drug may have fewer side effects, but be less effective, or it may be more effective, but have more side effects. At what point can it be said that the drug is "improved"? This is all a matter of degree, and also depends upon knowledge about the new product, which it may take some time to acquire through clinical use.[279]

No "continuing duty"   Moreover, it would appear that there is no equivalent   **10–104**
under the Act of a "continuing duty" parallel to that in the tort of negligence, requiring the manufacturer to recall products which were not known to be defective at the time of supply, where it has subsequently been discovered that the product does create an unacceptable risk of harm. Although the supply of similar products after the date of knowledge could result in the conclusion that they are defective, there is nothing in s.3 to indicate how a product that was "safe" at the time of supply can subsequently become defective, unless it can be said that some obligation to recall products forms part of consumer expectations. Indeed, there is

---

[275] *Abouzaid v Mothercare (UK) Ltd* [2000] All E.R. (D) 2436 at [43] and [25] per Chadwick and Pill LJJ respectively.
[276] *Roe v Minister of Health* [1954] 2 Q.B. 66, para.3–079, but the duty does at least extend beyond the date of putting the product into circulation, requiring a manufacturer to warn about any subsequently discovered dangers or in an appropriate case to recall the product; see para.10–059.
[277] [1954] 2 Q.B. 66.
[278] See, however, the development risks defence, paras 10–122 to 10–129, below.
[279] Drugs which are supplied as part of a clinical trial probably do fall within the ambit of the Act, but the fact the product is still under research would have a bearing on whether it could be said to be defective. Moreover, the development risks defence would apply, effectively excluding the manufacturer's responsibility for unforeseeable reactions: para.10–122. See further paras 3–068 et seq.

a specific defence where defendants can show that the defect did not exist in the product when they supplied it to another.[280]

10–105   **Relevance of cost of product and avoidability of risk**   The Act does not mention the cost of the product as a factor in determining defectiveness. Where the defect is a construction defect or a failure to warn or provide adequate instructions for use then cost is probably irrelevant, but it may well be a significant feature where it is claimed that the product is defective in design.[281] In *A v National Blood Authority*[282] Burton J held that the impracticability and the cost or difficulty of identifying the potentially harmful agent and taking suitable precautions, were to be ignored when considering whether blood products contaminated with the hepatitis C virus were defective. However, in *Wilkes v Depuy International Ltd*[283] Hickinbottom J commented, obiter, that:

> "…without inappropriately moving the focus from the product to the acts and omissions of the producer and/or others, cost too must be potentially relevant."

This was linked to the question of whether the "avoidability" of the risk had to be taken into account. Hickinbottom J conceded that there was a danger of focusing on the acts or omissions of the designer/producer, which is impermissible since the question is whether the product has a defect not whether the producer has acted reasonably or carefully, but nonetheless considered that:

> "…the ease with which and extent to which, a risk might be avoided, may, in appropriate cases, be a circumstance that is relevant to the question of level of safety and therefore defect under the Act."[284]

Avoidability could not be considered in a vacuum and would not be determinative of whether the product was defective, but in an appropriate case:

> "…the ease and extent to which a risk can be eliminated or mitigated may be a circumstance that bears upon the issue of the level of safety that the public generally is entitled to expect."[285]

10–106   **Exercise of reasonable care is not a defence**   Once it is established that the product was defective, liability is strict, in the sense that it is not a defence for producers to show that they exercised reasonable care. It is arguable, however, that, notwithstanding *A v National Blood Authority*, many of the factors taken into account in deciding whether a manufacturer has discharged a duty of care in negligence are relevant to the decision-making process about whether a product is defective under the Act.[286]

---

[280] See para.10–118.
[281] See Stapleton (1986) 6 O.J.L.S. 392, 404; Newdick (1987) 103 L.Q.R. 288, 300–304.
[282] [2001] 3 All E.R. 289.
[283] [2016] EWHC 3096 (QB); [2017] 3 All E.R. 589 at [83]; see M. Harvey [2017] J.P.I.L. C128.
[284] [2016] EWHC 3096 (QB); [2017] 3 All E.R. 589 at [85].
[285] [2016] EWHC 3096 (QB); [2017] 3 All E.R. 589 at [89].
[286] See *Wilkes v Depuy International Ltd* [2016] EWHC 3096 (QB); [2017] 3 All E.R. 589; para.10–095.

(e)   Types of loss

The Act is designed to protect consumer expectations in the safety of products, **10–107** and therefore there is no liability in respect of pure economic loss, damage to commercial property or damage to the product itself, even if the product is potentially dangerous. For the purpose of liability under s.2, damage means "death or personal injury or any loss of or damage to any property (including land)".[287] Loss of or damage to the product itself is specifically excluded, as is loss of or damage to a product caused by a defective component product which had been supplied with the product.[288]

By s.5(3) property damage claims are limited to property which is: (a) ordinarily **10–108** intended for private use, occupation and consumption; and (b) intended by the people suffering the loss or damage mainly for their own private use, occupation or consumption. This excludes damage to business property.[289] Actions in respect of property damage (but not personal injury) below £275 are also excluded.[290]

(f)   Causation

The claimant has the burden of proving that the product was defective and that **10–109** the damage was caused "wholly or partly" by the defect,[291] though if the claimant proves that the product was defective it is not necessary to demonstrate the cause of the defect.[292] The difficulty of proving factual causation in some instances is just as great as in the tort of negligence, although there is no requirement to prove that the damage was of a foreseeable type, as in negligence. In *A v The National Blood Authority*[293] Burton J held that a claim based on loss of a chance is not appropriate in the context of an action for breach of s.3 of the Act. Both the Act, and the Product Liability Directive 1985, impose strict liability. The question is whether the product was defective, and if so what damage was caused by that defect. It is not what damage was caused by any conduct, whether wrongful or

---

[287] Consumer Protection Act 1987 s.5(1). The words "death or personal injury" must be given a broad interpretation: *Boston Scientific Medizintechnik GmbH v AOK Sachsen-Anhalt – Die Gesundheitskasse* (C-503/13) EU:C:2015:148; [2015] 3 C.M.L.R. 6; (2015) 144 B.M.L.R. 225 at [47]. Thus, where a heart pacemaker or an implantable cardioverter defibrillator was found to be defective the damage included the losses attributable to a surgical operation to replace the defective product, if such an operation was necessary to overcome the defect in the product: EU:C:2015:148; [2015] 3 C.M.L.R. 6; (2015) 144 B.M.L.R. 225 at [55].

[288] Consumer Protection Act 1987 s.5(2). But in the case of defective silicone breast implants that have to be removed the patient is entitled to recover the cost of an operation to replace the implants, including the cost of the replacement implants themselves: *Hems v Poly Implants Prosthesis* [2007] C.L.Y. 1063, Nottingham County Court.

[289] *Renfrew Golf Club v Motocaddy Ltd* [2016] CSIH 57; 2016 S.C. 860; 2016 S.L.T. 781 (golf clubhouse was not property ordinarily intended for private use or occupation).

[290] Consumer Protection Act 1987 s.5(4).

[291] Consumer Protection Act 1987 s.2(1).

[292] *Ide v ATB Sales Ltd* [2008] EWCA Civ 424; [2008] P.I.Q.R. P13 at [19]; *Baker v KTM Sportmotorcycle UK Ltd* [2017] EWCA Civ 378 at [35]; *Wilkes v Depuy International Ltd* [2016] EWHC 3096 (QB); [2017] 3 All E.R. 589 at [73].

[293] [2001] 3 All E.R. 289.

otherwise, or breach of duty. Thus, questions of what would or might have happened in hypothetical circumstances are not relevant.[294]

10–110   The Act makes it clear that the producer remains liable where the damage is caused partly by the defect and partly by some other event. The other event may be entirely innocent or it may be the "faulty" conduct of a third party, for example, the failure of a third party to examine or test the product or heed warnings in the manufacturer's instructions for use. It will be recalled that so far as the tort of negligence is concerned the failure to take advantage of a reasonable opportunity for intermediate inspection may be treated as breaking the chain of causation. It is arguable that this is not the position under the Act, because the damage is "partly" caused by the defective product and "partly" by the failure of the intermediate examination. The manufacturer and the third party will be jointly and severally liable, and their respective responsibilities can be apportioned under the Civil Liability (Contribution) Act 1978. On the other hand, it is possible that where the manufacturer has good grounds for contemplating that an intermediate inspection will occur or that an intermediary will follow instructions then the product will not be categorised as defective. Section 3(2) provides that instructions, warnings, and "what might reasonably be expected to be done with or in relation to the product" can be taken into account in determining what is defective. Thus, the effects of intermediate examination may simply have been shifted from the causation stage of the inquiry to the earlier point of deciding whether the product was unsafe in all the circumstances. If the product is categorised as defective, then the omission of an intermediate examination should not defeat the action on grounds of causation.

10–111   Logically, the same approach should apply to "faulty" conduct by claimants. If they misuse the product in an unforeseeable fashion or disregard a warning the conclusion may simply be that the product was not defective. If it is found to be defective, claimants' conduct should be treated as contributory negligence.

(g)   Defences

10–112   Once the claimant proves that the product was defective and caused the damage the onus shifts to the defendant to establish one of the specific defences provided in s.4. One potential defence is expressly prohibited. By s.7 liability cannot be "limited or excluded by any contract term, by any notice or by any other provision". This prevents the manufacturer excluding liability under the Act to the injured consumer.[295] It does not, however, affect possible exclusion or limitation clauses in the contracts which constitute the chain of supply from

---

[294] It follows that the "but for" test for factual causation (see para.5–005 et seq.) has no application to a claim under the Consumer Protection Act 1987: C. Johnston, "A Personal (and Selective) Introduction to Product Liability Law" [2012] J.P.I.L. 1 at 12.

[295] An exclusion of liability for personal injuries caused by negligence will be invalid by virtue of the Consumer Rights Act 2015 s.65(1); see para.11–033.

manufacturer to distributor to retailer. Such clauses would not necessarily be caught by the Unfair Contract Terms Act 1977.[296]

(i) Miscellaneous defences[297]

Section 4 sets out six defences available to a defendant sued under the Act. Most are quite straightforward but one, the "development risks" defence, requires more detailed analysis.[298] In each case the burden of proof is on the defendant,[299] and the defence must be pleaded.[300]   **10–113**

Compliance with statutory requirement   Section 4(1)(a) provides a defence   **10–114** where the defect was attributable to compliance with any statutory requirement or European Community obligation. Compliance with the Human Medicines Regulations 2012 or regulations made under the Medicines Act 1968 should not be an automatic defence, but this may be good evidence that the product conformed to what persons generally are entitled to expect by way of safety, as in the case of negligence.[301]

No supply by the defendant   It is a defence if the defendant never supplied the   **10–115** product to another.[302] In *Veedfald v Arhus Amtskommune*,[303] a fluid used for flushing kidneys prior to transplantation was defective so that a kidney donated by the claimant's brother for transplantation to the claimant was damaged and could not be used. The fluid was manufactured at a laboratory owned and managed by the defendant for use at another hospital owned and managed by the defendant, a public body which was a non-profit making organisation. The defendant argued that the product had not been put into circulation. The European Court of Justice held that the fact that it had not left the defendant's premises did not mean that it had not been put into circulation. A defective product was put into circulation when it was used during the provision of a specific medical service, consisting of preparing a human organ for transplantation, and the damage caused to the organ resulted from that preparatory treatment (applying art.7(a) of Council Directive 85/374/EEC).

The European Court of Justice had another opportunity to clarify the meaning of   **10–116** "put into circulation" in *O'Byrne v Sanofi Pasteur MSD Ltd (formerly Aventis*

---

[296] See *Thompson v T Lohan (Plant Hire) Ltd* [1987] 1 W.L.R. 649; cf. *Phillips Products Ltd v Hyland* [1987] 1 W.L.R. 659. Of course, exclusion clauses in the chain of supply are irrelevant to the consumer's action.
[297] Note that special rules in respect of limitation periods apply to claims brought under the Consumer Protection Act 1987: see para.11–158.
[298] See paras 10–122 et seq.
[299] Section 4(1) states that "it shall be a defence for [the defendant] to show…"
[300] *Abouzaid v Mothercare (UK) Ltd* [2000] All E.R. (D) 2436 at [10], CA.
[301] With the probable being result that the product is not defective under s.3 of the Act: *Wilkes v Depuy International Ltd* [2016] EWHC 3096 (QB); [2017] 3 All E.R. 589 at [124] (compliance with safety standards set by a regulatory authority "powerful evidence" of no defect); para.10–099.
[302] Consumer Protection Act 1987 s.4(1)(b), e.g. if it was stolen from him.
[303] (C-203/99) (2001) 66 B.M.L.R. 1; Bright (2002) 8 *Clinical Risk* 67.

Pasteur MSD Ltd).[304] The claimant brought an action in respect of a vaccine which had been produced by a French company, S, and sent to its wholly owned UK subsidiary company, M, for distribution in September 1992, and sold to the NHS in October 1992. It was important for the purposes of the limitation period to know whether the vaccine had been put into circulation when it was sent to M or when it had been sold to the NHS. It was held that a product is "put into circulation" when it is taken out of the manufacturing process operated by the producer and enters a marketing process in the form in which it is offered to the public in order to be used or consumed. Where an entity in the distribution chain is closely linked to the producer, as in the case of a wholly owned subsidiary of the producer, it is necessary to establish on the facts whether the link is so close that the subsidiary is in reality involved in the manufacturing process so that "producer" included the subsidiary and, consequently, a transfer of the product from the producer to the subsidiary did not amount to putting into circulation.[305]

10–117 **Supply was not in the course of a business** Section 4(1)(c) provides that it is a defence where the only supply by the defendant was otherwise than in the course of a business, and if he is a producer, "own-brander" or importer that this is by virtue only of things done by him otherwise than with a view to profit. Thus, free samples would not be within the defence, since they are distributed with a view, ultimately, to profit. In the *Veedfald* case[306] the defendant also argued that the product had not been manufactured for an "economic purpose" (within the meaning of art.7(c) of Council Directive 85/374/EEC) as the laboratory and hospital were entirely publicly funded. Again, the European Court of Justice rejected the defendant's argument. The exemption from liability where an activity has no economic or business purpose does not extend to the case of a defective product which has been manufactured and used in the course of a specific medical service which is financed entirely from public funds and for which the patient is not required to pay directly.

10–118 **Defect did not exist at the time of supply** It is a defence that the defect did not exist in the product when the defendant supplied it to another.[307] If the defendant is a supplier, as opposed to a producer, an "own-brander" or an importer, it is a defence to show that the defect did not exist, not when *he* supplied it, but when it was last supplied by the producer, "own-brander" or importer.[308]

---

[304] (C-127/04) [2006] 1 W.L.R. 1606; (2006) 91 B.M.L.R. 175.

[305] This ruling was to "to avoid the possibility of the limitation period starting to run as a result of internal transactions within the group, even though the product had not yet left the producer's sphere of control": *Aventis Pasteur SA v OB* (C-358/08) [2010] 1 W.L.R. 1375 at [52].

[306] (2001) 66 B.M.L.R. 1.

[307] Consumer Protection Act 1987 ss.4(1)(d),(2)(a). In *Piper v JRI (Manufacturing) Ltd* [2006] EWCA Civ 1344; (2006) 92 B.M.L.R. 141 the defendants demonstrated, on the evidence, that a hip replacement prosthesis was not defective at the time that it was supplied to the hospital for implantation into the claimant. *Piper* is commented on by M. Mildred [2007] J.P.I.L. C5.

[308] Consumer Protection Act 1987 s.4(2)(b).

Component manufacturer   A component manufacturer is not liable for a   **10–119**
defect in the finished product which was wholly attributable to the design of the
finished product (e.g. where the component product is normally safe in its
contemplated use but is misused in the design of the finished product); nor where
the defect is due to the compliance by the component manufacturer with
instructions given by the manufacturer of the finished product.[309]

Contributory negligence   Contributory negligence is a partial defence.[310] Of   **10–120**
course, misuse of the product by the claimant may be relevant to the question of
whether the product was defective at all, or whether an otherwise defective
product caused the claimant's damage. Conceptually these are distinct issues—if
the product was defective, and if it was a cause, even a partial cause, of the
damage the defendant is liable, and the claimant's fault is relevant only to
apportionment of the damages. In practice, however, it may be difficult to
separate these questions.

In theory problems could arise as to the basis on which damages should be   **10–121**
apportioned since the claimant is at fault and the defendant in breach of a strict
duty which may not involve any negligence on his part. In such circumstances
what is the "claimant's share in the responsibility for the damage"?[311] This is not
likely to be a major obstacle, however, because the courts have considerable
experience of apportionment in other areas where the defendant may have been in
breach of a strict statutory duty (e.g. employers' liability) and the claimant has
been negligent.

(ii)   The "development risks" defence

Under s.4(1)(e) of the Consumer Protection Act 1987 it is a defence to prove that: **10–122**

> "…the state of scientific and technical knowledge at the relevant time was not such that a
> producer of products of the same description as the product in question might be expected to
> have discovered the defect if it had existed in his products while they were under his control."

The "relevant time" is the time when the defendant supplied the product to
another which is, in effect, when it was put into circulation.[312]

This so-called development risks defence was one of the most controversial   **10–123**
aspects of both the European Community Directive and the Consumer Protection
Act 1987. Its effect is to excuse a defendant who can show that the defect was
unknown and unforeseeable when he put the product into circulation, the
justification being that if defendants were held responsible for unknown and
unknowable risks this might deter the development of new products which might
be beneficial to the public at large. The objection to the defence is that it
represents a policy of allowing individual consumers to bear these development
risks should they materialise, when the possibility of loss spreading through

---

[309] Consumer Protection Act 1987 s.4(1)(f).
[310] Consumer Protection Act 1987 s.6(4).
[311] Law Reform (Contributory Negligence) Act 1945 s.1(1); see paras 11–003 to 11–019.
[312] Consumer Protection Act 1987 s.4(2)(a).

insurance and the price mechanism was readily available. It amounts to a retreat into negligence theory at precisely the point that strict liability is most useful.[313]

10–124   Both the Law Commission and the Pearson Commission recommended that this defence should not be available. Pearson, for example, commented that it would "leave a gap in the compensation cover, through which, for example, the victims of another thalidomide disaster might easily slip".[314] Indeed, the pharmaceutical industry could be one of the principal beneficiaries of this defence. There is a public policy argument in favour of the development and marketing of new drugs which are intended to save life and reduce pain and suffering, even where the drugs carry risks to the public. The central issue, however, is who should carry the burden of these development risks. If it is in the public interest then maybe the public should bear the risks, either through strict liability and the market mechanism (whereby producers insure against the risk and include the cost of insurance in the price of the product) or through a no-fault compensation scheme.[315]

10–125   **Contrast s.4(1)(e) and art.7(e)**   The wording of the defence invites comparison with the scientific and technical knowledge of a hypothetical producer of "products of the same description as the product in question". This is a subjective test of knowledge, by reference to the knowledge of the industry concerned, not general scientific and technical knowledge. The Act seemed to differ significantly from the Directive on this point. Article 7(e) of the Directive confers the defence where:

> "…the state of scientific and technical knowledge at the time when he put the product into circulation was not such as to enable the existence of the defect to be discovered."

This version of the defence appeared to be narrower than s.4(1)(e) of the Act, since it is easier to prove that no producer of similar products could have discovered the defect, than to prove that no one, considering the state of scientific and technical knowledge, could have discovered the defect.[316] Thus, it had been argued that s.4(1)(e) effectively excused defendants when they had not been negligent in failing to discover the defect, and amounted to little more than a reversal of the burden of proving negligence.[317] The discrepancy between art.7(e) and s.4(1)(e) was referred to the European Commission on the basis that the Act did not fully implement the Directive, and the Commission took the issue to the European Court of Justice. The Court concluded, however, that there was no

---

[313] Although see Stapleton (1986) 6 O.J.L.S. 392, 408–413 arguing that even without a development risks defence the same considerations have to be taken into account in a scheme which bases liability on defectiveness; Stoppa (1992) 12 L.S. 210.

[314] *Royal Commission on Civil Liability and Compensation for Personal Injury*, Cmnd.7054 (1978), Vol.I, para.1259.

[315] On no-fault compensation for drug injuries see Fleming (1982) 30 Am. J. Comp. Law 297.

[316] Crossick (1988) 138 N.L.J. 223; cf. Newdick [1988] C.L.J. 455, 459–60 who argues that the Directive is ambiguous and that s.4(1)(e) is the correct interpretation of the ambiguity.

[317] Newdick [1988] C.L.J. 455, 460, 475. See also Newdick (1985) 101 L.Q.R. 405, 406 commenting that: "…a state of the art defence would be sufficient to undermine the entire policy of a scheme of strict liability so far as it applied to drug damage."

conflict between art.7(e) and s.4(1)(e). The UK courts would be able to achieve the purpose of art.7(e) in interpreting s.4(1)(e).[318] Moreover, s.1(1) states that Pt I of the Act:

"...shall have effect for the purpose of making such provision as is necessary in order to comply with the product liability Directive and shall be construed accordingly",

and thus it is arguable that if there is any discrepancy between the Act and the Directive a domestic court should interpret provisions in the Act in accordance with the Directive. Indeed, in *A v The National Blood Authority*[319] Burton J simply applied the provisions of the Directive, as directly applicable in English law, effectively bypassing any potential conflict with the Consumer Protection Act 1987.

Meaning of "scientific and technical knowledge"   A major problem in applying s.4(1)(e) is the interpretation of the words "scientific and technical knowledge". It is not clear when "information" becomes "knowledge". This could be when it is accepted as scientific fact; or when it is published in a scientific journal as a hypothesis[320]; or when a researcher in a laboratory considers it to be a remote possibility. Where there are conflicting views within the scientific community, then which view must the manufacturer follow? How discoverable must the defect be? With the expenditure of moderate or reasonable or extensive resources? Indeed, is cost a relevant consideration at all? If the defect could have been discovered from existing information but the appropriate intellectual "connections" have not been made by researchers, is this "knowledge" from which the defect might be expected to have been discovered?[321]   **10–126**

In *Abouzaid v Mothercare (UK) Ltd*[322] the claimant was struck in the eye by an elasticated strap used to attach an accessory to a child's pushchair. The Court of Appeal rejected the defendants' argument that the absence of any accident records for similar types of accident meant that they did not have the relevant   **10–127**

---

[318] *Commission of the European Communities v UK* (C300/95) [1997] All E.R. (EC) 481; for discussion of this case and its implications for the development risks defence see C. Hodges (1998) 61 M.L.R. 560 and M. Mildred and G. Howells (1998) 61 M.L.R. 570.

[319] [2001] 3 All E.R. 289 at 297.

[320] See *Merck Sharp & Dohme (Australia) Pty Ltd v Peterson* [2011] FCAFC 128; (2011) 284 A.L.R. 1 at [203]–[208] where the Full Court of the Federal Court of Australia drew a distinction between a *hypothesis* that Vioxx tablets materially increased the risk of patients suffering a myocardial infarction and scientific *knowledge* or knowledge at the "scientific level" that there was an increased risk of a myocardial infarction. The defendants did not acquire the relevant knowledge until they had knowledge at the "scientific level". (By amendment to the Trade Practices Act 1974 Australia introduced a regime of strict liability for defective products, including the development risks defence, based on the EC Directive on Liability for Defective Products 1985/374.)

[321] In *Independent Broadcasting Authority v EMI Electronics Ltd and BICC Construction Ltd* (1980) 14 Build. L.R. 1 at 36 Lord Fraser commented that: "The error arose not from difficulty of calculation but from the omission of what seems to me to have been a simple piece of reasoning about known facts"; cf. where the primary information has not been discovered. For discussion of what is meant by "knowledge" in the context of development risks see Newdick (1991) 20 Anglo-Am. L.R. 127; C. Pugh and M. Pilgerstorfer, "The Development Risks Defence—Knowledge, Discoverability and Creative Leaps" [2004] J.P.I.L. 258.

[322] [2000] All E.R. (D.) 2436.

scientific or technical knowledge, within the meaning of s.4(1)(e). Pill LJ said that the defence contemplated scientific and technical advances which throw additional light, for example, on the propensities of materials and allow defects to be discovered.[323] Chadwick LJ said that the question of whether the defendants could have discovered the defect in 1990 before the accident to the claimant occurred had nothing to do with the state of scientific or technical knowledge at that time. There was a simple, practical test which could have been carried out. No advance in scientific or technical knowledge was required to enable the test to be carried out, and the only reason that it had not been carried out before 1990 was that the defendants had not thought of doing so. Thus, the defence under s.4(1)(e) was "simply not engaged in the present case".[324]

10–128   In *Commission of the European Communities v UK*[325] the European Court of Justice indicated that for the defence to be overcome the relevant knowledge must have been accessible at the time when the product was put into circulation. In *A v The National Blood Authority*[326] Burton J held that the defence in art.7(e) of the European Union Product Liability Directive (on which s.4(1)(e) of the 1987 Act is based) does not apply where the existence of a generic defect was known, or should have been known, in the light of accessible information. Burton J concluded that a risk ceases to be a development risk and becomes a known risk, not if and when the producer in question has the requisite knowledge, but if and when such knowledge is accessible anywhere in the world "outside Manchuria".[327] The reference to Manchuria was meant to deal with the situation where the relevant knowledge was available, but only to scientists in an unknown research laboratory in an inaccessible part of the world. In such circumstances it would not be treated as "accessible" knowledge. But once the existence of the defect was known, there was a risk of that defect materialising in any particular product, and it was immaterial that the known risk was unavoidable in the particular product. In those circumstances a producer continued to produce and supply the product at its own risk. It would be inconsistent with the purpose of the Directive if producers, in the case of a known risk, continued to supply products simply because they were unable to identify in which of their products that defect would occur, or, where they were obliged to supply, continued to supply without accepting the responsibility for any injuries resulting. The purpose of art.7(e) was to avoid discouraging innovation and to exclude development risks, hence it protected a producer in respect of the unknown. The effect was not that non-standard products (i.e. products which were different from the norm which the producer intended for use by the public) were excluded from falling within art.7(e), since they could qualify where the problem was not known. However, once the problem was known, by virtue of accessible information, then a non-standard product would no longer qualify for protection under art.7(e).

---

[323] [2000] All E.R. (D.) 2436 at [29].
[324] [2000] All E.R. (D.) 2436 at [46]. Note also that if the defendants' argument were accepted it would mean that the first victim of a defective product would have considerable difficulty in establishing liability.
[325] (C300/95) [1997] All E.R. (EC) 481.
[326] [2001] 3 All E.R. 289.
[327] [2001] 3 All E.R. 289 at [76].

Thus, in the case of contaminated blood products, where the risk was known but the there were no means of avoiding the risk, art.7(e) provided no defence.

Manufacturing defects   At one time it was unclear whether the defence **10–129** applied to manufacturing defects. On the face of it the defence is concerned with producers' knowledge of the possibility that the defect might exist, and excuses them from liability if they could not have known about the risk. Thus, it appears to be concerned with design defects rather than construction defects. However, it was arguable that the defence might also apply to construction defects which it is known can occur but the state of technical knowledge is such that it is impossible to devise a quality control system that would detect all defective items in the production line.[328] In *Richardson v LRC Products Ltd*[329] Ian Kennedy J took a narrow view of the development risks defence. It did not apply unless the evidence showed that "there was a defect of whose possible existence the leading edge of available scientific knowledge was ignorant". The test was not what the defendants knew but what they could have known if they had consulted those who might be expected to know the state of research and all available literature sources. The defence did not apply in the case of:

"...a defect of a known character merely because there is no test which is able to reveal its existence in every case."[330]

This indicates that the defence does not apply to construction defects, a view which is supported by the decision of Burton J in *A v The National Blood Authority*.[331]

---

[328] See Newdick [1988] C.L.J. 455, 469–473.
[329] [2000] P.I.Q.R. P164; [2000] Lloyd's Rep. Med. 280.
[330] [2000] P.I.Q.R. P164; [2000] Lloyd's Rep. Med. 280 at 285.
[331] [2001] 3 All E.R. 289.

CHAPTER 11

DEFENCES AND LIMITATION

This chapter deals with general defences to an action for negligence[1] and the question of limitation periods. It is comparatively rare for such general defences to be raised in the context of medical negligence actions, principally because the circumstances in which medical treatment occurs are unlikely to create much scope for the type of "misbehaviour" by claimants which typically gives rise to a specific defence. Thus, in practice, the expiry of the limitation period is much more likely to be raised as a "defence" by the defendant. The overall balance of the chapter between general defences and limitation reflects this.

1. DEFENCES

Where claimants fail to establish the necessary elements of the tort of negligence (duty of care, breach of that duty, and the causal link to the damage), their action will fail, and in a sense the defendant's "defence" has succeeded. Claimants lose because they have failed to establish that a tort was committed. But even where they succeed in proving the required elements of the tort of negligence, they will still lose if the defendant can rely on a general defence (though in the case of contributory negligence the effect is that the damages are reduced).[2]

(a) Contributory negligence

In many instances a doctor needs the patient's co-operation in order to make an accurate diagnosis or for the purpose of administering the treatment. Sometimes this will be absolutely vital. For example, the doctor will need reasonably

11–001

11–002

11–003

---

[1] Given that consent is a defence to an action for trespass to the person, the whole of Ch.6 is, in one sense, a discussion of defences.

[2] Note that, in addition to general defences, there are sometimes specific immunities available to particular categories of defendant. The Crown Proceedings Act 1947 s.10 conferred immunity on the Crown in respect of death or injury to a member of the armed forces who "at the time when that thing was suffered" was on duty or who, though not on duty, was on any service property. This immunity has been repealed in respect of causes of action accruing from 15 May 1987. In *Derry v Ministry of Defence* [1999] P.I.Q.R. P204 a soldier alleged that a military doctor had been negligent in failing to diagnose cancer. He argued that the defendants could not rely on s.10 where there was a negligent failure to diagnose a pre-existing medical condition, but the Court of Appeal held that the immunity applied. The "thing suffered" was the misdiagnosis, which occurred on each occasion he was examined at the military hospital, and therefore fell within that subsection. The House of Lords has also held that s.10 was not incompatible with art.6 of the European Convention on Human Rights: *Matthews v Ministry of Defence* [2003] UKHL 4; [2003] 1 A.C. 1163.

accurate information regarding the patient's symptoms, and/or medical history (e.g. the patient may forget to mention an allergy to penicillin). Similarly, the co-operation of the patient may be essential in implementing a treatment regime, for example, with regard to taking medication in the right quantity and at the right times of day, or returning for further treatment or tests. If patients fail to follow proper instructions and this is a cause of their injuries then it will be possible to argue that they have been contributorily negligent, or in an extreme case that their conduct is the sole cause of the damage.[3] Alternatively, where patients have failed to communicate the nature of the symptoms from which they are suffering the conclusion may simply be that the doctor was not negligent in failing to make the correct diagnosis on the basis of the available information.[4] This may also be the outcome where the patient has refused to engage with treatment or the diagnostic process. For example, in *Malone v Greater Glasgow and Clyde Health Board*[5] the patient, without plausible explanation, failed to attend three appointments for an echocardiogram recommended by the defendant and so was discharged from the clinic. It was held that there was no breach of duty by the consultant haematologist, who had ruled out any haematological explanation for the patient's anaemia, and had wanted the patient to undergo an ECG to rule out other possible causes.

(i) General

11-004 Where damage is attributable partly to the fault of the defendant and partly to the fault of the claimant then the award of damages may be reduced by reason of the claimant's contributory negligence.[6] The reduction will be to such extent as the court thinks just and equitable having regard to the claimant's share in responsibility for the damage.

11-005 **Scope of contributory negligence** Fault means:

---

[3] *Venner v North East Essex Area Health Authority, The Times*, 21 February 1987; *Murrin v Janes* [1949] 4 D.L.R. 403 at 406, Newfd SC, where a claimant's delay in seeing a doctor to deal with excessive bleeding following extraction of his teeth was held to be the sole cause of his misfortune.

[4] *Gordon v Wilson* [1992] 3 Med. L.R. 401, Court of Session (Outer House); *Morrison v Forsyth* [1995] 6 Med. L.R. 6, Court of Session, where a general practitioner was found not liable for failing to visit a patient because the seriousness of the patient's condition was not made clear in the course of a telephone conversation; *Friedsam v Ng* [1994] 3 W.W.R. 294, BCCA, where the patient's omission to inform a general practitioner of isolated instances of chest pains and incontinence meant that the defendant had not been negligent in failing to embark upon a more detailed inquiry; *Baird v Sinclair* (1997) 162 N.S.R. (2d) 386, Nova Scotia SC, where the patient failed to inform an emergency doctor of the circumstances and full extent of an injury to his leg and the treatment was held to be appropriate and to the standard reasonably to be expected of an emergency doctor.

[5] [2017] CSOH 31.

[6] Law Reform (Contributory Negligence) Act 1945 s.1. The defence must be specifically pleaded: *Fookes v Slaytor* [1978] 1 W.L.R. 1293; see also CPR r.16.5. In *Brown v Merton, Sutton and Wandsworth Area Health Authority* [1982] 1 All E.R. 650 at 652 counsel for the defendants intimated that he would rely on the defence of inevitable accident. This defence is generally regarded as limited to actions in trespass, and in any event it is confined to accidents that could not have been avoided by the exercise of reasonable care. Thus, in an action for negligence a plea of inevitable accident is, in effect, a denial of negligence.

"...negligence, breach of statutory duty or other act or omission which gives rise to a liability in tort or would, apart from this Act, give rise to the defence of contributory negligence."[7]

The legislation clearly applies to the tort of negligence. There had been some uncertainty as to whether it also applies to actions for battery, though there was some authority for the view that it could apply to actions in trespass to the person.[8] However, in *Co-operative Group (CWS) Ltd v Pritchard*[9] the Court of Appeal held that contributory negligence could not be relied upon in an action for trespass to the person. The word "fault" as applied to a claimant in the Law Reform (Contributory Negligence) Act 1945 could only be taken into account if the conduct gave rise to a defence of "contributory negligence" at common law before the passing of the Act. Since there was no case before the Act which held that contributory negligence constituted a defence to assault and battery the Act could not be relied on to reduce a claimant's damages for assault and battery.[10] It follows that in any claim by a patient for battery, on the basis that she has not given a valid consent to medical treatment, the defence of contributory negligence will not apply.[11]

Contract   There has also been some controversy about the extent to which the Act applies to actions in contract. The Act is open to different interpretations and this has produced conflicting authorities.[12] It has now been held that where the defendant's negligent breach of contract would have given rise to liability in the tort of negligence independently of the existence of the contract, damages may be apportioned for the claimant's contributory negligence.[13] This means that the defence will be available in virtually all actions arising out of private medical treatment, since the obligations imposed by the contract are normally the same as the duty to exercise reasonable care in the tort of negligence.[14] On the other hand,

11-006

---

[7] Law Reform (Contributory Negligence) Act 1945 s.4.

[8] *Barnes v Nayer*, The Times, 19 December 1986, CA; *Wasson v Chief Constable of the Royal Ulster Constabulary* [1987] 8 N.I.J.B. 34; *Murphy v Culhane* [1977] Q.B. 94; cf. *Lane v Holloway* [1968] 1 Q.B. 379; Hudson (1984) 4 L.S. 332.

[9] [2011] EWCA Civ 329; [2012] Q.B. 320; J. Goudkamp, "Contributory negligence and trespass to the person" (2011) 127 L.Q.R. 519; J. Fulbrook [2011] J.P.I.L. C197.

[10] [2011] EWCA Civ 329; [2012] Q.B. 320 at [62] per Aikens LJ. Cases since the 1945 Act suggesting that it could be used to reduce a claimant's damages in the torts of assault and battery were inconsistent with statements of principle made in two House of Lords decisions, namely *Standard Chartered Bank v Pakistan National Shipping Corp (No.2)* [2002] UKHL 43; [2003] 1 A.C. 959 and *Reeves v Commissioner of Police for the Metropolis* [2000] 1 A.C. 360. *Pritchard* was applied in *Hicks v Young* [2015] EWHC 1144 (QB).

[11] Although not specifically mentioned by Aikens LJ it would seem that false imprisonment, which is an action for trespass to the person, would also be covered by the ruling in *Co-operative Group (CWS) Ltd v Pritchard*. This is potentially relevant where a patient has been detained or physically restrained without lawful authority (e.g. where the defendant purports to detain the patient under the Mental Health Act 1983, but the provisions of that Act are not satisfied).

[12] See Burrows, *Remedies for Torts and Breach of Contract*, 3rd edn (Oxford: Oxford University Press, 2004), pp.136–143.

[13] *Forsikringsaktieselskapet Vesta v Butcher* [1988] 3 W.L.R. 565, CA, approving the analysis of Hobhouse J at [1986] 2 All E.R. 488 at 508.

[14] The concurrent duty of care in tort to exercise reasonable skill and care owed by a professional to a client under the contract of retainer will normally fall into this category, so that the negligent professional can rely on contributory negligence as a defence: *UCB Bank plc v Hepherd Winstanley &*

where (a) liability does not depend on negligence but arises from breach of a strict contractual duty; or (b) liability arises from breach of a contractual obligation which is expressed in terms of exercising reasonable care, but does not correspond to a common law duty of care which would exist independently of the contract; apportionment under the Act is not available.[15] Thus, if a patient was able to establish that the doctor had given a contractual warranty to achieve a particular result, this would fall into category (a) and the damages could not be apportioned for contributory negligence.[16] In the context of the relationship between doctor and patient, it is difficult to imagine contractual duties expressed in terms of exercising reasonable care which would not correspond to duties in the tort of negligence (category (b)), particularly since the courts have stressed that patients who receive treatment under the NHS should not be placed at a disadvantage, in terms of their legal rights, in comparison with patients who receive treatment privately.[17]

11-007   **Medical negligence**   Although, in theory, there is no reason why contributory negligence should not apply in a claim for medical negligence, as with any other type of action for negligence, in practice the defence is rarely invoked successfully, and this is reflected in a comparative dearth of cases.[18] It may be that, as a general rule, the plea is considered to be inappropriate in an action for medical negligence, given the inequality between the respective positions of doctor and patient. Patients do not usually question the advice or conduct of their doctors, at least initially, even when they are aware that their conditions are deteriorating or not improving.[19] Contributory negligence is measured by the standard of the reasonable, prudent person, which is meant to be the same standard of care as that applied to defendants.[20] In practice the courts tend to

---

Pugh (A Firm) [1999] Lloyd's Rep. P.N. 963, CA; *Platform Home Loans Ltd v Oyston Shipways Ltd* [2000] 2 A.C. 190; see also *Barclays Bank plc v Fairclough Building Ltd (No.2)* [1995] P.I.Q.R. P152; (1995) 76 B.L.R. 1.

[15] *Forsikringsaktieselskapet Vesta v Butcher* [1988] 3 W.L.R. 565; *Barclays Bank plc v Fairclough Building Ltd (No.1)* [1995] Q.B. 214, CA.

[16] For the difficulties of proving this see para.2–017. If, in the case of a strict contractual warranty, the claimant has been guilty of "contributory" fault there is a risk that the court will conclude that the defendant's breach was not a *cause* of the loss, in which case the claim fails entirely: see, e.g. *Lambert v Lewis* [1982] A.C. 225.

[17] See para.2–011.

[18] See Giesen, *International Medical Malpractice Law* (Netherlands: Martinus Nijhoff Publishers, 1988), para.236; Picard and Robertson, *Legal Liability of Doctors and Hospitals in Canada*, 4th edn (Canada: Carswell, 2007), pp.368–373.

[19] In *Montgomery v Lanarkshire Health Board* [2015] UKSC 11; [2015] A.C. 1430 at [58] Lord Kerr and Lord Reed noted that: "... an approach which requires the patient to question the doctor disregards the social and psychological realities of the relationship between a patient and her doctor, whether in the time-pressured setting of a GP's surgery, or in the setting of a hospital. Few patients do not feel intimidated or inhibited to some degree." In *Crossman v St George's Healthcare NHS Trust* [2016] EWHC 2878 (QB); (2017) 154 B.M.L.R. 204 at [32] a patient who had been told by a surgeon that he wanted to try conservative treatment (physiotherapy) for three months before considering surgery was found not to have been at fault in failing to question why he had been listed for early surgery by the negligent hospital. When the patient phoned the hospital he had been told that if he did not keep his appointment he would "go to the bottom of the queue" and so it was unsurprising that his reaction was not to question what was happening.

[20] *Jones v Livox Quarries Ltd* [1952] 2 Q.B. 608 at 615.

require less from claimants in the way of prudence for their own safety than from defendants, and this is likely to be even more apparent with patients, who rely heavily on the skills and knowledge of medical practitioners.[21]

By raising the plea of contributory negligence the defendant may highlight the extent of the doctor's duty to take special care in giving the patient instructions, and making sure that the patient understands both the instructions and the importance of strictly adhering to them.[22] In *Marshall v Rogers*,[23] for example, the defendant alleged that the claimant's injury was caused by his own negligence in failing to follow the instructions that he had been given and to report his symptoms. It was held, however, that where a dangerous remedy was being attempted the doctor was negligent in delegating his own professional duty of deciding the true meaning of the patient's progressive symptoms to the patient himself, especially given that the patient had to make a subjective assessment of his symptoms. The defendant should have conducted daily tests.

11–008

(ii) Failing to follow medical advice

If patients ignore doctors' advice (for example, by discharging themselves from hospital contrary to medical advice or failing to return for further treatment) it may be easier to establish contributory negligence. It would have to be shown that a reasonable person would have been aware of the significance of the advice, which could depend upon the nature of the advice given by the doctor and whether the advice, and the consequences of failing to follow it, was clear to the patient.[24] In *Spencer v Hillingdon Hospital NHS Trust*[25] the claimant underwent surgery for an inguinal hernia. Some time after his discharge from hospital he developed bilateral pulmonary emboli. On discharge he had been told that if he had any problems he should contact the hospital or his general practitioner, but he had not been informed that he could suffer a deep vein thrombosis or pulmonary embolism as a consequence of the surgery; nor was he given any information as to the signs and symptoms that he might suffer in the event of developing a deep vein thrombosis or pulmonary embolism. In the days after the operation the claimant experienced pain in both calf muscles, but he attributed this to his lack of exercise while he had been recovering from the operation, rather than to the operation itself. The defendants were held to have been negligent in failing to

11–009

---

[21] On the other hand, doctors rely on patients to be truthful about their medical history and the failure to provide crucial information about previous visits to hospital and the diagnosis and medical advice given to the patient may constitute contributory negligence, or in an extreme case undermine the claimant's case on causation: see *Zeb v Frimley Health NHS Foundation Trust* [2016] EWHC 134 (QB) where, notwithstanding the defendants' admission of breach of duty, the claimant's application for an interim payment was refused on the basis that the claimant's action could fail on causation and/or contributory negligence.

[22] See paras 4–063 to 4–073. See Karp (1993) 9 J. of the MDU 26, who points out that educating patients results in fewer injuries, and better compliance with medical advice.

[23] [1943] 4 D.L.R. 68 at 77.

[24] *Munday v Australian Capital Territory Health and Community Care Service* [2004] ACTSC 134 (Supreme Court of the Australian Capital Territory) at [85] and [102]—claimant informed that it was preferable to remain in hospital, but "the absence of a note of discharge contrary to advice" supported the view that the medical advice was no stronger than that.

[25] [2015] EWHC 1058 (QB).

give the claimant information about the small risk of developing deep vein thrombosis or pulmonary embolism post-operatively. They argued that the claimant had been contributorily negligent in failing to follow the instructions to report on "any problems" he experienced, namely the calf pain. The argument was rejected since the calf pain arose several days after the operation, in an area of his body that had not been operated on, and after he had recovered from the procedure. He believed that the calf pain was due to his inactivity and he could not reasonably have foreseen that by not seeking medical attention for the calf pain he would suffer deep vein thrombosis and a pulmonary embolism—this was precisely what the defendants should have warned the claimant about.

11–010   In some circumstances there may well be a responsibility upon the doctor to adopt a system for following up patients who do not comply with advice to re-attend for further treatment or tests.[26] The one English reported case in which the claimant's conduct was held to have been negligent is *Pidgeon v Doncaster Health Authority*[27] where a claimant who developed cervical cancer, having been told that the results of a smear test were negative, was held to have been two thirds contributorily negligent in failing to have a further smear test despite frequent reminders. In *Sims v MacLennan*[28] a claim in respect of the death of a patient in 2011 from a stroke failed on both breach of duty and causation, but Judge Simpkiss went on to consider, hypothetically, contributory negligence, concluding that if liability had been established damages should have been reduced by 25 per cent to reflect the patient's negligence in failing to follow his general practitioner's advice in 2007 to make an appointment to have his blood pressure checked (the patient having been aware that his blood pressure had been high in the past).[29]

11–011   **Canada**   Some Canadian courts have made findings of contributory negligence against careless patients on the basis that the patient had sufficient knowledge about her medical condition that she should have sought further medical advice, or that the risk she was taking was obvious. In *Brushett v Cowan*[30] the claimant was contributorily negligent in engaging in ordinary activities without crutches following a bone biopsy on her leg, because she had failed to ask for clear instructions regarding the use of the crutches. A failure to have a post-operative

---

[26] Scott (1993) 4 *AVMA Medical & Legal Journal* (No.3) p.7.

[27] [2002] Lloyd's Rep. Med. 130, Doncaster County Court.

[28] [2015] EWHC 2739 (QB).

[29] See also *Turner v Carver*, Chelmsford County Court, 6 July 2016, a claim arising out of revision surgery some six months after cosmetic breast augmentation surgery. Following the revision surgery the claimant developed a haematoma at the operation site and required emergency surgery. Judge Moloney QC held that there had been no breach of duty on the part of the defendant, but that if breach of duty had been established the claimant would have been found 66 per cent contributorily negligent for "engaging in vigorous gym exercises within two weeks of that operation in defiance of a clear warning to leave a much longer period after the operation".

[30] (1987) 40 D.L.R. (4th) 488; aff'd (1990) 69 D.L.R. (4th) 743, Newfd CA. In *Vancouver General Hospital v McDaniel* (1934) 152 L.T.R. 56 it was suggested that the failure to be vaccinated against smallpox might constitute contributory negligence in a claim for infecting the patient with the disease, but this allegation was not pursued.

check-up, as suggested by the doctor, has been held to be negligent,[31] as has the failure to pursue physiotherapy when advised to do so.[32] In *Crossman v Stewart*[33] a patient who obtained prescription drugs from an unorthodox source, and continued to use the drugs on a prolonged basis without obtaining prescription renewals and without consulting the "prescribing" physician, was described as "foolhardy in the extreme". She was held to be responsible for two thirds of the damage to her eyesight caused by the side effects of the drug. In *Zhang v Kan*[34] the defendant doctor declined to refer a 36-year-old pregnant patient for an expedited amniocentesis. This was negligent, given her age and the risk of the baby having a genetic defect. However, the patient (and her husband) were held to have been contributorily negligent, since the patient had researched the topic of amniocentesis and knew that at her age she was at high risk of bearing a Down's Syndrome child. She had already discussed the need for an amniocentesis with another doctor, and she had doubted the defendant's advice that it was too late in the pregnancy for the test. She could have consulted another doctor, which she actually did two months later. Her husband had told her to trust the defendant because he was a doctor, but the couple were aware that there might be a problem if there was no amniocentesis. Contributory negligence was assessed at 50 per cent.

Australia   Similarly, Australian courts have found patients who failed to follow medical advice to be contributorily negligent. In *Almario v Varipatis (No.2)*[35] a   **11–012**

---

[31] *Fredette v Wiebe* [1986] 5 W.W.R. 222, BCSC; *Rupert v Toth* (2006) 38 C.C.L.T. (3d) 261, Ont SCJ.

[32] *Ibrahim v Hum* 2004 ABQB 420; [2005] 6 W.W.R. 564, Alta QB. The patient was also negligent in failing to volunteer to the defendant that she had been treated by other doctors for her condition, depriving the defendant of the opportunity to obtain relevant medical records from those doctors. See also *McLintock v Alidina* 2011 ONSC 137; (2011) 80 C.C.L.T. (3d) 289 at [171]–[173] (patient contributorily negligent by failing to bring an abnormality in her breast to the attention of her doctor in a timely fashion and by failing to book regular physical examinations and mammograms, as advised); *Lodge v Fitzgibbon* 2010 NBQB 63; (2010) 919 A.P.R. 100; (2010) 356 N.B.R. (2d) 100 at [218] (patient contributorily negligent having delayed seeking medical attention when a melanoma recurred, contrary to medical advice to seek attention if she noticed discoloration in the area of previous excisions; damages were reduced by 10 per cent: 2011 NBQB 226; (2011) 973 A.P.R. 202; (2011) 378 N.B.R. (2d) 202 at [152]); *Bennett v Landecker* 2011 ONSC 6168; (2011) 88 C.C.L.T. (3d) 314 (patient, who had seen an ophthalmologist complaining of loss of vision in the upper visual field of his left eye, was contributorily negligent when shortly after he suffered a total loss of vision in his left eye but did not report this either to the ophthalmologist or to his general practitioner for several weeks; damages were reduced by 40 per cent).

[33] (1977) 82 D.L.R. (3d) 677 at 686, BCSC. It is also possible that unreasonable behaviour by patients after the defendant's negligent conduct could be characterised as a failure to mitigate their loss: see para.12–048. In *Brain v Mador* (1985) 32 C.C.L.T. 157, Ont CA, a patient who failed to take steps to seek further medical advice following a vasectomy which had developed complications was held to have acted unreasonably, and his damages were reduced by 50 per cent for failing to mitigate the loss. On the other hand, in *Saint-Clair v Spiegel* (2001) 31 C.C.L.T. (3d) 119, Ont SCJ, the claimant's refusal to undergo a mastectomy, as advised, and withdrawing from a programme of chemotherapy before completion of the treatment were held not to be contributory negligence in a case of missed diagnosis of breast cancer. The decision to forego radical mastectomy was not unreasonable where alternative treatments were available and given that the claimant had consented to surgery to remove the tumour.

[34] 2003 BCSC 5; (2003) 15 C.C.L.T. (3d) 1.

[35] [2012] NSWSC 1578.

general practitioner was held to have been negligent in failing to refer a morbidly obese patient to a bariatric surgeon for consideration for surgery or, alternatively, to refer the patient to an obesity clinic to be seen by a specialist in obesity management. It was not sufficient simply to outline the options to the patient and advise him to lose weight when the patient had a history of unsuccessful attempts to lose weight. On the other hand the patient's failure to accept medical advice to manage his obesity by dieting and exercising constituted contributory negligence. Although the claimant was not advised of the risk of the specific health condition which he developed (progressive liver disease leading to cancer of the liver) nonetheless there was a foreseeable and not insignificant risk of serious illness unless he reduced his weight. It followed that:

> "...a reasonable person in the position of the plaintiff would have taken the precaution of dieting given there was a relatively high degree of probability that serious illness would overtake him unless his obesity was overcome and that that harm could well be grave."[36]

In *Young v Central Australian Aboriginal Congress Inc*[37] the patient, who was 26, died as a result of a coronary thrombosis attributable to long-standing coronary artery disease. It was held that his failure to keep appointments, the failure to follow up recommended tests, and the failure to mention to hospital doctors the concerns that had previously been expressed by another doctor about his medical condition amounted to contributory negligence.[38]

(iii)   Smoking and other addictions

11–013   In *Badger v Ministry of Defence*[39] a claimant who had continued to smoke cigarettes, knowing that this created a risk of damaging his health, was held to have been contributorily negligent in a claim in respect of lung cancer caused by the defendants' negligent exposure of the claimant to asbestos. "A reasonably prudent man," said Stanley Burnton J, "warned that there is a substantial risk that smoking will seriously damage his health, would stop smoking."[40] The judge noted that the evidence indicated that:

> "...by 1971, when the first health warnings were put on cigarette packets, it was reasonably foreseeable by a reasonably prudent man that if he smoked he risked damaging his health."[41]

His Lordship accepted that the claimant must have had some degree of freedom to choose to avoid the risk that was partly responsible for the harm, but rejected

---

[36] [2012] NSWSC 1578 at [168] per Campbell J. Damages were reduced by 20 per cent.
[37] [2008] NTSC 47. See also *Locher v Turner* (1995) Aust. Torts Rep. 81–336, Qd CA, where a patient reported rectal bleeding to her doctor, who examined her and concluded that the source of the bleeding was piles. The claimant did not report further episodes of bleeding to her doctor when she saw him, because she thought that this was also attributable to her piles, but it turned out to be caused by colon cancer. The doctor was found negligent in failing to review the initial diagnosis, but the claimant was held 20 per cent contributorily negligent for failing to report the further episodes of rectal bleeding.
[38] Damages were reduced by 50 per cent.
[39] [2005] EWHC 2941 (QB); [2006] 3 All E.R. 173.
[40] [2005] EWHC 2941 (QB); [2006] 3 All E.R. 173 at [48].
[41] [2005] EWHC 2941 (QB); [2006] 3 All E.R. 173 at [44].

the argument that the deceased was so addicted to tobacco that he could not reasonably have been expected to stop smoking.[42] Damages were reduced by 20 per cent. In *Dumais v Hamilton*[43] the claimant, a smoker, was repeatedly told by the defendant surgeon that she must not smoke for at least a week after surgery (a "tummy tuck" operation). She ignored the instruction and the post-operative smoking contributed to skin necrosis attributable to the surgery. The Alberta Court of Appeal held that the claimant was contributorily negligent although she was not aware of the nature and character of the potential injuries that could result from smoking. The test was whether she took reasonable care of herself in the circumstances, and by persisting in smoking after the operation, despite clear and repeated advice from the surgeon that she should not do so, her behaviour was not reasonable. Damages were reduced by 50 per cent.

In *St George v Home Office*[44] the claimant suffered serious brain damage following an epileptic seizure, having fallen from an upper bunk while in prison. The prison authorities were aware that he was an intravenous heroin user, that he drank heavily and that he had been having fits. MacKay J held that he was contributorily negligent, reducing the award of damages by 15 per cent, on the basis that he was at fault:

11–014

> "…in relation to the choices he had made in his life prior to the events of this night. That fault has caused or contributed to the dreadful injuries in this way, not because they have put him in prison, but because he was knowingly risking injury to his health by doing what he was doing, even if he did not know how it would happen. This is so as much as if he had wandered abroad in a drug-induced state of intoxication and walked into the path of a negligently driven car."[45]

This view took a rather sweeping approach to the nature of contributory fault. Many individuals "knowingly risk injury to their health" from lifestyle choices, such as drinking alcohol, overeating or even engaging in risky activities such as mountaineering or sky diving. MacKay J's approach opened up the possibility of a contributory negligence defence to any subsequent negligence claim where, for example, a doctor negligently failed to diagnose cirrhosis of the liver due to alcohol consumption, or diabetes attributable to obesity, or even where a surgeon was negligent in operating on a broken leg which had been caused by the patient engaging in an activity that involved "knowingly risking injury to his health". The Court of Appeal reversed the ruling on contributory negligence.[46] Dyson LJ accepted that the judge was entitled to hold that the claimant was at fault in becoming addicted to drugs and alcohol, and to infer that the claimant must have known that the abuse of drugs and alcohol on the scale necessary to lead to

---

[42] [2005] EWHC 2941 (QB); [2006] 3 All E.R. 173 at [46]. See also *Blackmore v Department for Communities and Local Government* [2017] EWCA Civ 1136 at [38] approving Stanley Burnton J's approach to the assessment of contributory negligence due to the claimant's smoking, taking into account both the causative effect and the blameworthiness of the parties in applying a percentage reduction for contributory negligence (in this case 30 per cent); *Horsley v Cascade Insulation Services Ltd* [2009] EWHC 2945 (QB) where the claimant suffered from asbestosis as a result of exposure to asbestos; damages reduced by 20 per cent for contributory negligence in smoking.

[43] (1998) 219 A.R. 63.

[44] [2007] EWHC 2774 (QB).

[45] [2007] EWHC 2774 (QB) at [58].

[46] [2008] EWCA Civ 1068; [2009] 1 W.L.R. 1670; discussed by McQuater [2009] J.P.I.L. C34.

addiction was dangerous to his health. It was also correct that but for the addiction, the claimant would not have suffered a withdrawal seizure and would not have fallen from the top bunk and suffered the head injury:

> "In that sense his injury was the result partly of his addiction. But in my view the addiction was not a potent cause of the injury."[47]

The injury triggered by the fall was too remote in time, place and circumstance and was not sufficiently connected with the negligence of the prison staff to be properly regarded as a cause of the injury.[48] Dyson LJ rejected the analogy with a person in a drug-induced state of intoxication walking into the path of a negligently driven car. The closer analogy was:

> "...with the case of a claimant who seeks medical treatment for a condition from which he is suffering as a result of his own fault and sustains injury as a result of negligent treatment. Examples of such a condition are lung cancer caused by smoking or cirrhosis of the liver caused by excessive consumption of alcohol."[49]

In such a case the claimant's fault in smoking or consuming excessive alcohol was not a potent cause of the injury suffered as a result of the negligent medical treatment. The fault was not sufficiently closely connected with the defendant's negligence. Rather, it was simply part of the claimant's history.[50]

11–015   In *Preston v Chow*[51] a pregnant teenager contracted herpes through unprotected sexual intercourse. The defendant doctor was negligent in failing to diagnose herpes, and the child suffered serious disabilities as a result of contracting herpes during the course of the birth. The defendant could not claim that the child's damages should be reduced as a result of the mother's alleged negligence in engaging in unprotected sexual intercourse because the mother does not owe a duty of care to the child,[52] but argued that contributory negligence applied to the mother's claim for damages in respect of her loss of earnings. Greenberg J rejected the argument. Although there could be contributory negligence by a patient that related to the diagnosis or treatment of a disease (for example by delaying seeking medical attention or failing to follow medical advice) there was no authority for the proposition that a patient who has been negligent in contracting a disease or suffering an accidental injury could be regarded as contributorily negligent where the doctor has negligently failed to diagnose or treat it:

---

[47] [2008] EWCA Civ 1068; [2009] 1 W.L.R. 1670 at [51].
[48] [2008] EWCA Civ 1068; [2009] 1 W.L.R. 1670 at [56].
[49] [2008] EWCA Civ 1068; [2009] 1 W.L.R. 1670 at [58].
[50] [2008] EWCA Civ 1068; [2009] 1 W.L.R. 1670 at [58]. See also *Calvert v William Hill Credit Ltd* [2008] EWCA Civ 1427; [2009] Ch. 330 at [70]—the fact that the claimant was a pathological gambler due to lifestyle choices made before the defendant bookmakers undertook a duty to prevent him from gambling with them on the telephone for a period of six months was not a basis for a finding of contributory negligence.
[51] 2007 MBQB 318; [2008] 3 W.W.R. 47; (2007) 54 C.C.L.T. (3d) 49.
[52] See *Preston v Chow* (2002) 211 D.L.R. (4th) 758, Man CA; para.2–135, n.431.

"Is the patient who smokes contributorily negligent where a doctor negligently misses a diagnosis of lung cancer? Can a doctor avoid liability for negligently treating the victim of a car accident who was not wearing a seat belt?"[53]

The implicit answer to these rhetorical questions was: no.

It would seem that where the patient's history of addiction or poor lifestyle choices have led to the need for medical treatment, that conduct *in itself* cannot be regarded as contributory negligence if there is negligence by a doctor in diagnosis or treatment of the condition. By the same token, if patients ignore specific medical advice to change their pattern of behaviour (such as stop smoking, reduce alcohol consumption or take steps to reduce body weight) this would not be contributory negligence where the doctor's negligence related to the diagnosis or treatment of the resulting medical problem, since it should make no difference to diagnosis and treatment whether patients' lung cancer, liver disease or diabetes was self-inflicted or caused by environmental or genetic factors. On the other hand, where the failure to follow medical advice is causally linked to the damage which the patient attributes to the doctor's breach of duty this can constitute contributory negligence. So in *Almario v Varipatis (No.2)*[54] a morbidly obese patient was regularly advised to lose weight by his general practitioner and failed to do so, but the doctor's negligence consisted of failing to take reasonable steps to assist the patient to lose weight by either referring him to a bariatric surgeon to consider surgery or referring him to an obesity clinic. The resulting medical complications from the patient's obesity were the product of *both* the doctor's negligence and the patient's contributory negligence in failing to take steps to reduce his weight. Similarly, in *Dumais v Hamilton*[55] the claimant was told by the defendant surgeon that she must not smoke for at least a week after surgery, but he did not explain why and the claimant ignored the instruction. Skin necrosis developed in the surgical area. There was clear evidence that the post-operative smoking contributed to the necrosis. In this situation the claimant's unreasonable conduct was causally linked to the damage attributable to the defendant's negligence.

11–016

(iv)   Suicide attempts

It would also be possible for a plea of contributory negligence to apply in cases where the claimant attempts suicide and a claim is brought against medical staff on the basis of a negligent failure to prevent the suicide attempt. In *Reeves v Commissioner of Police for the Metropolis*,[56] a similar type of claim brought against the police, the deceased was held 50 per cent contributorily negligent because he was partially responsible for his death, which was the result of the combination of the failure of the police to protect a prisoner who was a known suicide risk from harming himself and his own deliberate decision to end his life. Possibly, where the deceased was of unsound mind his suicide would not give rise to the defence of contributory negligence, by analogy with the position of

11–017

---

[53] 2007 MBQB 318; [2008] 3 W.W.R. 47; (2007) 54 C.C.L.T. (3d) 49 at [199].
[54] [2012] NSWSC 1578; para.11–012.
[55] (1998) 219 A.R. 63; para.11–013.
[56] [2000] 1 A.C. 360.

young children who are not of full understanding.[57] In this situation the court is comparing the negligence of the defendant against the intentional conduct of the claimant, but it is not simply a matter of assessing relative blameworthiness, but the parties' respective "responsibility for the damage". Thus, the Act requires the court to apportion:

> "...not merely degrees of carelessness but 'responsibility' and... an assessment of responsibility must take into account the policy of the rule, such as the Factories Acts, by which liability is imposed. A person may be responsible although he has not been careless at all, as in the case of breach of an absolute statutory duty. And he may have been careless without being responsible, as in the case of 'acts of inattention' by workmen."[58]

11–018   In *Corr v IBC Vehicles Ltd*[59] the deceased committed suicide, having developed clinical depression after an accident at work. The House of Lords were divided as to whether contributory negligence should apply. Lord Bingham and Lord Walker considered that it was inappropriate to attach any blame to the deceased given that his judgment was impaired by the severe depression brought about by the defendants' negligence. Lord Scott accepted that the deceased's suicidal tendencies had been caused by the employers' negligence, but:

> "...he was not an automaton. He remained an autonomous individual who retained the power of choice. The evidence that clinical depression leads often to suicidal tendencies and that between 1 in 10 and 1 in 6 persons succumb to those tendencies is evidence also that between 9 in 10 and 5 in 6 persons do not."[60]

His Lordship would have reduced the damages by 20 per cent. Lord Mance and Lord Neuberger considered that contributory negligence could apply in principle to such a case, though no deduction should be made because the issue had not been dealt with in detail at any earlier stage of the proceedings. Lord Mance commented that:

> "...a conclusion that a person suffering from depressive illness has no responsibility at all for his or her own suicide, and is in effect acting as an automaton, may be open to question in law, at least when the person's capacity to make a reasoned and informed judgment is described as 'impaired' rather than eliminated... It may be right, not only to consider more closely with the benefit of expert evidence what is involved in 'impairment' but also, as Lord Hope suggested in *Reeves* at p.385A, to identify differing degrees of impairment and responsibility. It may also be relevant if other factors were also operating on the claimant, independently of the accident and the consequent depression—for example, impending exposure of lack of probity, financial ruin or matrimonial breakdown."[61]

(v)   Apportionment

11–019   If the claimant has been found to contributorily negligent s.1(1) of the Law Reform (Contributory Negligence) Act 1945 provides that the court should reduce the claimant's damages:

---

[57] [2000] 1 A.C. 360 at 372 per Lord Hoffmann.
[58] [2000] 1 A.C. 360 at 371.
[59] [2008] UKHL 13; [2008] 1 A.C. 884.
[60] [2008] UKHL 13; [2008] 1 A.C. 884 at [31].
[61] [2008] UKHL 13; [2008] 1 A.C. 884 at [51]. See also per Lord Neuberger at [64]–[69] for discussion of the relationship between the deceased's mental state and contributory negligence.

"...to such extent as the court thinks just and equitable having regard to the claimant's share in the responsibility for the damage."

The phrase "just and equitable" confers a broad discretion on the court, which has to weigh both the causative potency of the conduct of the defendant and claimant as well as their respective blameworthiness. In *Jackson v Murray*[62] Lord Reed observed that:

"It is not possible for a court to arrive at an apportionment which is demonstrably correct. The problem is not merely that the factors which the court is required to consider are incapable of precise measurement. More fundamentally, the blameworthiness of the pursuer and the defender are incommensurable. The defender has acted in breach of a duty (not necessarily a duty of care) which was owed to the pursuer; the pursuer, on the other hand, has acted with a want of regard for her own interests. The word 'fault' in section 1(1), as applied to 'the person suffering the damage' on the one hand, and the 'other person or persons' on the other hand, is therefore being used in two different senses. The court is not comparing like with like."

This means that apportionment of responsibility is inevitably a rough and ready exercise and a variety of possible answers can legitimately be given.[63] For that reason an appellate court should be slow to interfere with an apportionment fixed by the trial judge. It is only where there is an identifiable error, such as an error of law, or a difference of view as to the apportionment of responsibility which exceeds the ambit of reasonable disagreement that warrants the conclusion that the court below has gone wrong.[64] An apportionment should not be changed merely because the appellate court disagreed as to the precise figure, but it could be altered if it was "outside the range of reasonable determinations". Nor is it simply a matter of how large the difference of view is. There is a

"qualitative difference between a finding of 60% contribution and a finding of 40% which was not so apparent in the quantitative difference between 40% and 20%."[65]

(b) Volenti non fit injuria

Volenti non fit injuria consists of a voluntary agreement by the claimant to absolve the defendant from the legal consequences of an unreasonable risk of harm created by the defendant, where the claimant has full knowledge of both the

11–020

---

[62] [2015] UKSC 5; [2015] 2 All E.R. 805; [2015] P.I.Q.R. P16 at [27]. The case is commented on by Tavares [2015] J.P.I.L. C152. In *Blackmore v Department for Communities and Local Government* [2017] EWCA Civ 1136 the Court of Appeal rejected the defendants' argument that where a claimant who had contracted lung cancer following exposure to asbestos was guilty of contributory negligence by smoking apportionment should be based solely on the respective causative contribution of asbestos and smoking to the cancer. The court should also take into account the relative blameworthiness of the defendant in exposing employees to asbestos and that of the employee in smoking. On that basis, there was no reason to interfere with the judge's assessment of a 30 per cent reduction for contributory negligence.

[63] [2015] UKSC 5; [2015] 2 All E.R. 805; [2015] P.I.Q.R. P16 at [28].

[64] [2015] UKSC 5; [2015] 2 All E.R. 805; [2015] P.I.Q.R. P16 at [35].

[65] [2015] UKSC 5; [2015] 2 All E.R. 805; [2015] P.I.Q.R. P16 at [38]. Lord Reed considered, at [44], that the "view that parties are equally responsible for the damage suffered by the pursuer is substantially different from the view that one party is much more responsible than the other. Such a wide difference of view exceeds the ambit of reasonable disagreement, and warrants the conclusion that the court below has gone wrong".

nature and extent of the risk. This should not be confused with *consent* to medical treatment which provides a defence to what would otherwise be the tort of battery. The patient who consents to medical treatment does not thereby agree to run the risk of negligence by the doctor.[66]

11–021 The one situation where the volenti defence could plausibly apply to a medical negligence action is in the case of suicide by a patient in circumstances where the doctor was under a duty to take reasonable precautions to prevent a suicide attempt. The point had been touched upon by the Court of Appeal in *Kirkham v Chief Constable of Greater Manchester Police*,[67] though it was said that the defence would only arise where the person was "of sound mind". But in *Reeves v Commissioner of Police for the Metropolis*[68] the House of Lords held that volenti does not apply where the claimant's act was the very thing that the defendant was under a duty to take reasonable care to prevent, irrespective of the suicide's mental state. If the defendants owed a duty of care to prevent a suicide attempt they cannot argue that the act which they were under a duty to prevent gave rise to the defence of volenti, because that would undermine the point of imposing a duty of care.[69]

(c)   Illegality

11–022 The fact that the claimant was involved in committing a criminal offence at the time of sustaining damage may, in some instances, constitute a defence.[70] This is usually expressed in the Latin maxim *ex turpi causa non oritur actio* (an action cannot be founded on a base cause). Of course, it will be extremely rare for a claimant in a medical negligence action to be involved in illegality which is directly linked to the treatment, although in *Kirkham v Chief Constable of Greater Manchester Police* the Court of Appeal accepted that the ex turpi causa defence is not confined to criminal conduct, but could apply to illegal or immoral conduct by the claimant if in all the circumstances an award of damages would be

---

[66] See *Freeman v Home Office* [1984] Q.B. 524 at 557, per Sir John Donaldson MR.

[67] [1990] 2 Q.B. 283.

[68] [2000] 1 A.C. 360.

[69] See also the discussion of the relevance of the deceased's mental state when he committed suicide in *Corr v IBC Vehicles Ltd* [2006] EWCA Civ 331; [2007] Q.B. 46 (deceased committed suicide, having developed clinical depression after an accident at work). The House of Lords affirmed this decision: [2008] UKHL 13; [2008] 1 A.C. 884, but only Lord Bingham's speech touched upon the volenti defence, which was rejected as having "no independent validity" given that the deceased's suicide was not something to which he had "consented voluntarily and with his eyes open but an act performed because of the psychological condition which the employer's breach of duty had induced" (at [18]).

[70] Although this is sometimes viewed as being a matter of public policy, rather than a defence. See Lord Sumption in *Les Laboratoires Servier v Apotex Inc* [2014] UKSC 55; [2015] A.C. 430 [23], and *Jetivia SA v Bilta (UK) Ltd* [2015] UKSC 23; [2015] A.C. 430 at [62] and [100], commenting that ex turpi causa, though described as a defence, is in reality "a rule of judicial abstention", and that the public interest may require the court to take the point of its own motion. In *O v Ministry of Defence; West v Ministry of Defence* [2006] EWHC 19 (QB) Owen J held that illegality was not a defence, as such, and therefore the burden of establishing that it applied did not rest with the defendant.

an affront to the public conscience.[71] Awarding damages following a suicide would not affront the public conscience, at least where there was medical evidence that the suicide was "not in full possession of his mind".[72] Farquharson LJ said that an action could hardly be said to be grounded in immorality where "grave mental instability" on the part of the victim has been proved, although "the position may well be different where the victim is wholly sane".[73] In the context of a claim following a suicide attempt it would appear that there is considerable overlap between the ex turpi causa defence and the volenti defence.[74] But in *Reeves v Commissioner of Police of the Metropolis*[75] the Court of Appeal held that ex turpi causa does not apply in a case where the claimant's conduct was the very act that the defendant was under a duty of care to prevent, whether or not the claimant was of sound mind.[76]

In *Clunis v Camden & Islington Health Authority*[77] the claimant was a mental patient, with a history of seriously violent behaviour, who had been compulsorily detained under the Mental Health Act 1983. Three months after his discharge from hospital the claimant killed a stranger in an unprovoked attack, and he was subsequently convicted of manslaughter on the ground of diminished responsibility. The claimant brought an action against the health authority claiming that if he had received appropriate aftercare he would not have committed the crime and would not therefore have been detained in a special hospital, or at least would not have been detained for as long (if the aftercare had involved compulsory admission to hospital under the Mental Health Act). The Court of Appeal struck out the claim, inter alia, on the ground that the action was based on the claimant's own illegal act, and therefore the maxim ex turpi causa non oritur actio applied. Although the claimant's mental responsibility was impaired, a plea of diminished responsibility did not remove liability for his criminal act. He must have known what he was doing and that it was wrong, and therefore the claim was contrary to public policy. The court would not aid a litigant who relied on his own criminal or

11–023

---

[71] [1990] 2 Q.B. 283 at 291, per Lloyd LJ. Note, however, that the "public conscience" test has been criticised as granting too much discretion to the court. For an extended discussion see *Clerk & Lindsell on Torts*, 22nd edn (London: Sweet & Maxwell, 2018), paras 3–02 to 3–56.

[72] [1990] 2 Q.B. 283 at 291 per Lloyd LJ; see also *Funk Estate v Clapp* (1986), 68 D.L.R. (4th) 229 and (1988) 54 D.L.R. (4th) 512.

[73] The meaning of the phrases "grave mental instability" and "wholly sane" is a matter of some conjecture. Query whether a person who is not insane, but whose judgment is impaired by an emotional, as opposed to a psychological, disturbance falls into the category of "not wholly sane".

[74] In *Hyde v Tameside Area Health Authority* (1981), (1986) 2 P.N. 26 at 29–30 Lord Denning MR was opposed to allowing actions based on suicide or attempted suicide, a view that was clearly based on considerations of policy, and in particular his Lordship's belief that "'medical malpractice' cases should not get out of hand here as they have done in the United States of America". In *Kirkham v Chief Constable of Greater Manchester Police* [1990] 2 Q.B 283 at 292–293 Lloyd LJ did not share this view.

[75] [1999] Q.B. 169.

[76] [1999] Q.B. 169 at 185, per Buxton LJ. There was no appeal on the issue of ex turpi causa in the House of Lords, but the reasoning of their Lordships in relation to the argument that the deceased's suicide constituted a novus actus interveniens or that the deceased was volenti is entirely consistent with the Court of Appeal's approach to ex turpi causa.

[77] [1998] Q.B. 978.

immoral act.[78] On the other hand, it would seem that where a claimant "did not know the nature and quality of his act or that what he was doing was wrong"[79] public policy would not necessarily preclude a claim against a health authority in these circumstances (provided that the claimant can establish that the defendants owed him a duty of care). In *Hunter Area Health Service v Presland*[80] a majority of the New South Wales Court of Appeal, on very similar facts to *Clunis*, held that the negligent hospital authority did not owe a duty of care to a psychiatric patient who had been prosecuted for murder but found not guilty by reason of insanity. Although the plaintiff lacked moral culpability by reason of his insanity, his act remained an unlawful and wholly unreasonable act. It was not "justifiable homicide" but unlawful homicide for which he was not criminally responsible.[81]

11–024　　**Two forms of ex turpi causa**　　In *Gray v Thames Trains Ltd*[82] the claimant developed a personality change after sustaining injuries caused by the defendants' negligence and some two years later attacked and killed a stranger. He pleaded guilty to manslaughter on the grounds of diminished responsibility and was ordered to be detained in hospital under the Mental Health Act 1983. The defendants accepted that they were liable in principle for the claimant's losses, including loss of earnings before the killing, but denied responsibility in respect of loss of earnings after the killing on the basis of ex turpi causa. The claimant did not claim damages for the consequences of being detained in a mental hospital (a claim that would have been rejected on the authority of *Clunis v Camden and Islington Health Authority*), but claimed to be entitled to the loss of earnings attributable his developing post-traumatic stress disorder, including the

---

[78] This includes refusing to compensate claimants for the consequences of their illegal drug abuse. In *Wilson v Coulson* [2002] P.I.Q.R. P300, QBD, the claimant suffered brain damage in an accident caused by the defendant's negligence. He alleged that this had produced a personality change which led him to start using heroin. Harrison J, applying *Clunis*, held that there was no action in respect of further brain damage caused by an overdose of heroin, because the claimant's decision to use heroin was voluntary, deliberate and informed, and he had not lost the capacity or the power to say no. His action was both unreasonable and illegal and he should not be allowed to profit from his own actions. Similarly, in *B v Chief Constable of X* [2015] EWHC 13 (QB); [2015] I.R.L.R. 284 an undercover police officer who voluntarily misused drugs (cocaine) was not entitled to damages for his psychiatric injury because the condition was a product of the fact that he had been confronted with his own misconduct in disciplinary proceedings, and the consequences of those disciplinary proceedings: "to allow him to bring a claim for psychiatric injury caused by (or, if relevant, inextricably linked with) such misconduct would compromise the integrity of the legal system. It would award him damages for the consequences of his own voluntary misuse of drugs", per Males J at [23]. See also *AB v Royal Devon and Exeter NHS Foundation Trust* [2016] EWHC 1024 (QB) (claimant not entitled to cost of professional management of a large award of damages where his incapacity to manage it himself, if it occurred, would be because he had reverted to the abuse of illegal drugs); for comment see N. Tomkins [2016] J.P.I.L. C144.
[79] [1998] Q.B. 978 at 989.
[80] [2005] NSWCA 33; (2005) 63 N.S.W.L.R. 22.
[81] The case was dealt with on the basis of an absence of a duty of care, rather than the defence of ex turpi causa. See also *Ellis v Counties Manukau District Health Board* [2007] 1 N.Z.L.R. 196, where a health authority was held not liable to a psychotic patient for failing to take steps to prevent him killing his father. The absence of control over the patient precluded a duty of care. In the criminal prosecution the claimant had been held not guilty of killing his father by reason of insanity, and Potter J held that ex turpi causa should not apply.
[82] [2009] UKHL 33; [2009] 1 A.C. 1339.

loss of earnings after the date of the killing. The House of Lords held that ex turpi causa applied and the claimant was not entitled to the loss of earnings after the date of the offence. Lord Hoffmann explained that there are two forms of the ex turpi causa rule of public policy:

> "In its wider form, it is that you cannot recover compensation for loss which you have suffered in consequence of your own criminal act. In its narrower and more specific form, it is that you cannot recover for damage which flows from loss of liberty, a fine or other punishment lawfully imposed upon you in consequence of your own unlawful act. In such a case it is the law which, as a matter of penal policy, causes the damage and it would be inconsistent for the law to require you to be compensated for that damage."[83]

The claim for loss of earnings fell within the narrow form. The claimant's loss of earnings (and any claim for general damages for his detention, conviction and damage to reputation) after his conviction for manslaughter was a consequence of the conviction, and the claimant could not be compensated for the consequences of a sentence imposed by the criminal law. The claimant had also sought an indemnity against any claims which might be brought by dependants of the person he had killed, and a claim for general damages for feelings of guilt and remorse consequent upon the killing. This, said Lord Hoffmann, fell within the wider form of ex turpi causa. The claimant's liability to compensate the dependants of the person he had killed was an immediate "inextricable" consequence of his having intentionally killed him, and the same was true of his feelings of guilt and remorse. Accordingly, the wider form of the rule applied and the claimant was not entitled to damages in respect of those heads of damage either.[84]

The correct "test" for ex turpi causa   Over the last 20 years or so there has been considerable controversy over the conceptual basis of ex turpi causa which has played out in the House of Lords and the Supreme Court.[85] At its broadest the dispute has been between some judges who want to apply a simple, rule-based test and others who prefer a more flexible approach that can be tailored to the very different circumstances that can arise across a range of factual situations and causes of action. For some time the leading case was *Tinsley v Milligan*[86] where

11–025

---

[83] [2009] UKHL 33; [2009] 1 A.C. 1339 at [29].

[84] In *British Columbia v Zastowny* 2008 SCC 4; [2008] 4 W.W.R. 381; (2008) 290 D.L.R. (4th) 219 the Supreme Court of Canada held that ex turpi causa barred the claimant from recovering damages for time spent in prison. Compensation for periods of unemployment due to incarceration for conduct which the criminal law determined worthy of punishment would create a clash between the criminal and civil law, compromising the integrity of the justice system. Moreover, where a claimant's principal source of income is criminal activity the court is likely to discount heavily any award of damages for future loss of earnings (or in the case of a fatal accident a dependant's claim for loss of dependency): *Burns v Edman* [1970] 2 Q.B. 541; *Hunter v Butler* [1996] R.T.R. 396; *Beljanski v Smithwick* 2006 BCCA 399; [2006] 11 W.W.R. 274; (2006) 275 D.L.R. (4th) 116.

[85] See *Tinsley v Milligan* [1994] 1 A.C. 340; *Hounga v Allen* [2014] UKSC 47; [2014] 1 W.L.R. 2889; *Les Laboratoires Servier v Apotex Inc* [2014] UKSC 55; [2015] A.C. 430; *Jetivia SA v Bilta (UK) Ltd* [2015] UKSC 23; [2016] A.C. 1; and *Patel v Mirza* [2016] UKSC 42; [2017] A.C. 467. The Law Commission has also attempted, without success, to identify a consistent approach to the application of ex turpi causa in different situations: see *The Illegality Defence*, Law Com. No.320, March 2010.

[86] [1994] 1 A.C. 340.

the House of Lords held that for ex turpi causa to apply the claimant had to, somehow, need to *rely* on the illegality in order to frame the cause of action. This was true of *Clunis v Camden & Islington Health Authority* where the claimant was effectively relying on his own unlawful of act of manslaughter in order to assert a claim for damages against the health authority for the consequences of that unlawful act, but in other cases it was less obvious whether the claimant had to *rely* on his illegal conduct even though it was obvious that he was engaged in illegal activity at the time of sustaining the damage.[87] There was agreement that ex turpi causa is based on public policy and that underpinning this is the recognition of the inherent contradiction in asserting that for the purposes of the criminal law the claimant was legally responsible for his actions, whereas under the law of tort he was not responsible, but the defendants were, for the personal and financial consequences of the offence. An award of damages to the offender creates an appearance that the civil law is condoning the criminal offence, and this potential conflict between the outcomes in the criminal and the civil proceedings would tend to undermine confidence in the integrity of the legal system. Preservation of the integrity of the legal system is now the generally accepted rationale for ex turpi causa,[88] but against this background there is considerable scope for disagreement as to what is required in order to preserve that integrity. Should it apply as a rigid rule of law removing any discretion from the court or can the court consider the wider picture and weigh competing policies that would point to imposing liability on the defendant notwithstanding the claimant's illegal conduct?

11–026   The issue finally came to a head in the decision of the Supreme Court in *Patel v Mirza*[89] where the majority favoured a "test" in which the court should weigh a variety of factors.[90] Lord Toulson said that because questions of fairness and policy were different in different cases and led to different rules, one could not simply extrapolate rules applicable to one situation and apply them to another. There were simply too many variables.[91] The underlying policy reasons for the defence of illegality were that people should not be allowed to profit from their own wrongdoing and the law should be coherent and not self-defeating. In reaching a view as to whether a claim tainted by illegality was harmful to the integrity of the legal system the court should:

---

[87] Compare, e.g., *Delaney v Pickett* [2011] EWCA Civ 1532; [2012] 1 W.L.R. 2149 and *Joyce v O'Brien* [2013] EWCA Civ 546; [2014] 1 W.L.R. 70.

[88] See e.g. *Hounga v Allen* [2014] UKSC 47; [2014] 1 W.L.R. 2889 at [44] per Lord Wilson.

[89] [2016] UKSC 42; [2017] A.C. 467; discussed by J. Goudkamp, "The end of an era? Illegality in private law in the Supreme Court" (2017) 133 L.Q.R. 14.

[90] For the majority a test based on the claimant having to rely on the illegality depended on a procedural question of whether the claimant had to plead the illegal act, which was arbitrary, and had led to uncertain case law about what constitutes reliance. *Tinsley v Milligan* should no longer be followed ([2016] UKSC 42; [2017] A.C. 467 at [110]). Note that although *Patel v Mirza* was a case in contract and unjust enrichment there was no suggestion that the same approach should not be applied to tort claims.

[91] [2016] UKSC 42; [2017] A.C. 467 at [92]. The variables included the seriousness of the illegality, the knowledge and intentions of the parties, the centrality of the illegality, the effect of denying the defence and the sanctions which the law already imposes.

(a)   consider the underlying purpose of the prohibition which has been transgressed and whether that purpose will be enhanced by denial of the claim;

(b)   consider any other relevant public policies which may be rendered ineffective or less effective by denial of the claim; and

(c)   consider whether denial of the claim would be a proportionate response to the illegality, bearing in mind that punishment is a matter for the criminal courts.[92]

In *Henderson v Dorset Healthcare University NHS Foundation Trust*[93] Jay J considered whether, in the light of *Patel v Mirza*, *Clunis v Camden and Islington HA* and *Gray v Thames Trains Ltd* were still good law. The facts of *Henderson* were almost identical to those of *Clunis*. The claimant suffered with paranoid schizophrenia and during a period of psychosis killed her mother. She pleaded guilty to a charge of manslaughter by reason of diminished responsibility. The defendant NHS Trust admitted that but for its breach of duty in failing to respond adequately to the claimant's condition the killing would not have occurred. The claimant sought general damages for a depressive disorder and PTSD consequent on the killing of her mother, for her loss of liberty caused by compulsory detention in hospital, and for loss of amenity, and damages in respect of her lost inheritance (due to the operation of the Forfeiture Act 1982), and future loss in the form of the cost of psychotherapy and of a care manager/support worker. Jay J came to the conclusion that, although, in view of the criminal judge's sentencing remarks, there was some debate as to whether the claimant's personal responsibility was less than that of the claimant in *Clunis*, he was bound by both *Gray* and *Clunis* and thus none of the heads of damage were recoverable. Both *Gray* and *Clunis* were "*Patel*-compliant" on their particular facts, being cases where the claimants' personal responsibility could not be regarded as insignificant.[94]

11–027

Unlawful medical procedures   In some cases the medical treatment which claimants allege they should have received is unlawful because there is a statutory prohibition. In *Rance v Mid-Downs Health Authority*[95] a mother had

11–028

---

[92] [2016] UKSC 42; [2017] A.C. 467 at [101] and [120]. Various factors were relevant to whether it would be disproportionate to apply ex turpi causa but there was no definitive list because of the infinite variety of cases.

[93] [2016] EWHC 3275 (QB); [2017] 1 W.L.R. 2673.

[94] [2016] EWHC 3275 (QB); [2017] 1 W.L.R. 2673 at [99]. There had been some debate in *Gray* as to whether, in a case where the claimant's offending behaviour had played no part in the decision to impose the hospital order, "the hospital order should be treated as being a consequence of the defendant's mental condition and not of the defendant's criminal act" (per Lord Phillips in *Gray v Thames Trains Ltd* [2009] UKHL 33; [2009] 1 A.C. 1339 at [15]; see also per Lord Rodger at [83] and Lord Brown at [103]). Lord Hoffmann had considered that the sentence for manslaughter must be assumed to be what the criminal court regarded as appropriate to reflect the personal responsibility for the crime he had committed ([2009] UKHL 33; [2009] 1 A.C. 1339 at [41]). In *Henderson* Jay J noted that in *Clunis* the Court of Appeal had not distinguished between degrees of personal responsibility. A plea of guilty to the offence of manslaughter must be treated as conclusive proof that the claimant possessed the mental pre-requisites of criminal responsibility, namely the ability to form the intention to kill or seriously injure her mother.

[95] [1991] 1 Q.B. 587.

negligently been denied the opportunity to have an abortion, but the period of gestation was such that, as the law then stood,[96] a termination of the pregnancy would probably not have satisfied the requirements of Abortion Act 1967 and therefore would not have been lawful. Her claim for damages was denied on policy grounds, since the claimant could not have taken advantage of the lost opportunity to terminate the pregnancy without breaking the law. Similarly, a claim for damages in respect of rendering the claimant infertile cannot include the cost of procedures connected with surrogate motherhood if those procedures would be in breach of the Surrogacy Arrangements Act 1985.[97] Thus, claims arising out of the negligent performance of procedures which are unlawful are likely to be barred on the grounds of policy.[98] However, the claimant's illegal conduct is not a defence to a claim under the Human Rights Act 1998.[99]

(d) Exclusion of liability

11–029   It is highly unlikely that a doctor or hospital in the NHS would seek to limit or exclude liability for negligence though it is theoretically possible, even in the absence of a contract with the patient, by means of an exclusionary notice. However, attempts to exclude or limit liability are regulated by statute. There are now two statutory regimes applying to exclusion clauses and notices: the Unfair Contract Terms Act 1977 and the Consumer Rights Act 2015. Although the precise wording of these statutes differs, with regard to attempts to exclude liability the effect of the legislation is similar. In practice, the exclusion of liability to consumers is regulated by the 2015 Act, and the exclusion of liability to non-consumers continues to be regulated by the 1977 Act (whereas before the Consumer Rights Act 2015 came into force the Unfair Contract Terms Act 1977 applied both to non-consumers and consumers).

11–030   Under s.2(1) of the Unfair Contract Terms Act 1977 people who act in the course of a business (whether their own or another's) cannot by a contractual term or by notice exclude or restrict liability for death or personal injury resulting from negligence; and any attempt to exclude or restrict liability for other forms of loss

---

[96] Following amendment of the Abortion Act 1967 by the Human Fertilisation and Embryology Act 1990 s.37, there is no time limit where the termination is necessary to prevent grave permanent injury to the health of the woman, where the pregnancy involves risk to her life, or where there is a substantial risk that the foetus would be seriously handicapped. Where any of these grounds applied the causation issue in *Rance* would be irrelevant. The time limit under s.1(1)(a) of the Abortion Act 1967 is 24 weeks.

[97] See *Briody v St Helens and Knowsley Area Health Authority* [2001] EWCA Civ 1010; [2002] Q.B. 856; para.12–070.

[98] Another example would be a claim arising out of an unlawful organ transplant operation contrary to the Human Tissue Act 2004 (see s.32). In *Norberg v Wynrib* (1992) 92 D.L.R. (4th) 449 the Supreme Court of Canada held that ex turpi causa did not apply to an action where the defendant doctor had supplied drugs to a patient who was addicted to painkillers and tranquillisers in exchange for sexual contact. The patient had also been obtaining drugs from other doctors, and was convicted of the offence of "double-doctoring". The illegality was not causally linked to the harm suffered by the claimant.

[99] *Al Hassan-Daniel v Revenue and Customs Commissioners* [2010] EWCA Civ 1443; [2011] Q.B. 866.

or damage resulting from negligence is subject to a test of reasonableness.[100] The term "business" is not defined, but it is broad enough to include the provision of healthcare whether privately or under the NHS.[101] The Consumer Rights Act 2015 governs exclusion clauses between a "consumer" and a "trader". The 2015 Act amends s.2 of the Unfair Contract Terms Act 1977, stipulating that it does not apply to a consumer contract or a consumer notice, so that the Unfair Contract Terms Act 1977 will apply only to non-consumer contracts and notices, provided that the defendant is acting in the course of a business.

Part 2 of the Consumer Rights Act 2015 regulates unfair terms in consumer   **11–031** contracts and consumer notices. A consumer contract is a contract between a trader and a consumer.[102] A consumer notice is a notice that relates to rights or obligations as between a trader and a consumer or purports to exclude or restrict a trader's liability to a consumer, and includes an announcement, whether or not in writing, and any other communication or purported communication.[103] A trader is

"...a person acting for purposes relating to that person's trade, business, craft or profession, whether acting personally or through another person acting in the trader's name or on the trader's behalf",[104]

and "business" includes the activities of any government department or local or public authority.[105] Again this is clearly broad enough to include the provision of healthcare, under the NHS or privately. A consumer is "an individual acting for purposes that are wholly or mainly outside that individual's trade, business, craft or profession"[106] and this would clearly cover patients, members of their family and other third parties who might fall within the scope of a duty of care owed by a medical professional or hospital.

An unfair term of a consumer contract or an unfair consumer notice is not binding   **11–032** on the consumer.[107] A term or notice is unfair if, contrary to the requirement of good faith, it causes a significant imbalance in the parties' rights and obligations under the contract to the detriment of the consumer.[108] These provisions are broadly the equivalent of s.2(2) of the Unfair Contract Terms Act 1977 which subjects contract terms and notices seeking to exclude or restrict liability for damage other than death or personal injury caused by negligence to a test of reasonableness.

Section 65 is, in broad terms, the equivalent of s.2(1) of the 1977 Act. Section   **11–033** 65(1) provides that:

---

[100] Unfair Contract Terms Act 1977 s.2(2).
[101] Unfair Contract Terms Act 1977 s.1(3)—s.14 provides that "business" includes a profession and the activities of any government department or local or public authority.
[102] Consumer Rights Act 2015 s.61(1), (3).
[103] Consumer Rights Act 2015 s.61(4), (7), (8).
[104] Consumer Rights Act 2015 s.2(2).
[105] Consumer Rights Act 2015 s.2(7).
[106] Consumer Rights Act 2015 s.2(3).
[107] Consumer Rights Act 2015 s.62(1), (2).
[108] Consumer Rights Act 2015 s.62(4), (6). Sch.2, with s.63(1), of the Act contains an indicative and non-exhaustive list of terms of consumer contracts that may be regarded as unfair.

"...a trader cannot by a term of a consumer contract or by a consumer notice exclude or restrict liability for death or personal injury resulting from negligence."

As with the Unfair Contract Terms Act 1977 "negligence" covers a contractual or tortious duty to take reasonable care or exercise reasonable skill.[109] In addition, Sch.2 of the Consumer Rights Act 2015 provides that a contract term which has the object or effect of excluding or limiting the trader's liability in the event of the death of or personal injury to the consumer resulting from an act or omission of the trader may be regarded as unfair (and therefore not binding on the consumer under s.62(1)). Given that s.65(1) prevents the exclusion or restriction of liability for death or personal injury resulting from *negligence*, this provision leaves it open for the court to declare terms restricting or excluding liability for breach of a stricter obligation than negligence to be non-binding where the consumer has suffered personal injuries or death.

11–034   As with the 1977 Act, a defendant cannot rely on an exclusionary contract term or notice to invoke the defence of volenti non fit injuria. Section 65(2) of the 2015 Act provides that where a term of a consumer contract, or a consumer notice, purports to exclude or restrict a trader's liability for negligence, a person is not to be taken to have voluntarily accepted any risk merely because the person agreed to or knew about the term or notice.

11–035   The overall effect of the statutory regime is that in the unlikely event that a doctor or hospital attempted to exclude liability for negligence causing personal injury or death to a patient the exclusion clause or notice would be invalid. Attempts to exclude negligence liability for other forms of loss (damage to property or pure economic loss) are subject to a test of reasonableness (under the Unfair Contract Terms Act 1977) or fairness (under the Consumer Rights Act 2015).

2.   LIMITATION

11–036   Periods of limitation, within which claimants must commence their action or find it barred, are entirely the creation of statute, now mostly consolidated in the Limitation Act 1980. The basic rule governing an action in tort is that claims cannot be brought more than six years from the date on which the cause of action accrued.[110] In torts actionable per se, such as trespass to the person, the cause of action normally accrues at the date of the defendant's wrong, whereas with torts actionable only on proof of damage, such as negligence, the action accrues when damage occurs. This will usually be at the same time as the defendant's act or omission, but not necessarily so. In contract the limitation period is also six years from the accrual of the action,[111] which normally occurs at the date of the breach of contract.

11–037   **Rationale**   The rationale for limitation periods is that they protect defendants from stale claims, they encourage claimants to proceed without unreasonable

---

[109] Consumer Rights Act 2015 s.65(4).
[110] Limitation Act 1980 s.2. The six-year period was first introduced by the Limitation Act 1623.
[111] Limitation Act 1980 s.5.

delay, and they provide finality so that people can feel confident after a certain period of time that potential claims against them are closed and they can arrange their affairs accordingly.[112] On the other hand, claimants should not be penalised for failing to institute proceedings at a time when they were unaware that they had sustained any damage or that it was attributable to the defendant, or were simply not in a position to institute proceedings. The difficulty is to reach a reasonable balance between the interests of claimants and those of defendants. This has been achieved by grafting onto the basic limitation periods special rules for cases of personal injuries, claimants under a disability, latent damage, and fraud or concealment of the cause of action by the defendant. In broad terms, the effect of these special statutory provisions is to postpone the operation of the limitation period whilst the claimant is unaware of facts conferring a right of action, though ignorance of the law does not prevent time from running. Medical negligence actions are usually, though not exclusively,[113] concerned with claims for personal injuries or death, and this section will concentrate largely on the special rules applying to this form of action.[114]

Reform   The Law Commission recommended reform of the law on limitation periods to introduce a single, core limitation regime, applying, as far as possible, to all claims for a remedy for a wrong, claims for the enforcement of a right and claims for restitution.[115] The core regime would consist of a primary limitation period of three years starting from the date on which the claimant knows, or ought reasonably to know: (a) the facts which give rise to the cause of action; (b) the identity of the defendant; and (c) if the claimant has suffered injury, loss or damage or the defendant has received a benefit, that the injury, loss, damage or benefit was significant. There would be a longstop limitation period of 10 years, starting from the date of the accrual of the cause of action or (for claims in tort where damage is an essential element of the cause of action, or claims for breach of statutory duty) from the date of the act or omission which gave rise to the cause of action. This core regime would apply to the majority of tort claims, but would be modified in the case of claims in respect of personal injuries. For personal injuries (and claims under the Law Reform (Miscellaneous Provisions) Act 1934 and the Fatal Accidents Act 1976 arising out of personal injury to the deceased person) the court would have a discretion to disapply the primary limitation period (as under the current law), with no longstop limitation period. This would apply to all personal injury actions, whatever the cause of action, except that for claims under the Consumer Protection Act 1987 the longstop would be an absolute bar and would run from a different starting date. The core

11–038

---

[112] *Report of the Committee on Limitation of Actions in Cases of Personal Injury* (1962), Cmnd.1829, para.17; *Birkett v James* [1978] A.C. 297 at 331.

[113] Any action which gives rise to a claim for pure economic loss will be subject to the ordinary six-year period of limitation, unless it can be said to cause latent damage; see para.11–161. On the possible claims in respect of economic loss which could be made against a medical practitioner see paras 2–049 to 2–051, 2–052 et seq., 2–085, 2–108 to 2–111, 2–179 to 2–186.

[114] For a more detailed discussion see: A. McGee, *Limitation Periods*, 6th edn (London: Sweet & Maxwell, 2013).

[115] Law. Com. No.270, *Limitation of Actions*, 2001.

regime would also apply to claims by a subsequent owner of damaged property and claims for contribution or an indemnity. The Law Commission's recommendations have not been enacted.

(a) Personal injuries and death

11–039 Limitation of action in cases involving personal injuries or death is governed, as a general rule,[116] by the provisions of the Limitation Act 1980 ss.11–14 and 33. The basic scheme provides for a three-year limitation period which runs from either (a) the date on which the cause of action accrued, or (b) if later, the date of knowledge of the existence of a cause of action.[117] This is subject to the court's discretion to allow the action to proceed notwithstanding the expiry of the three-year period.[118] The three-year period applies to:

> "...any action for damages for negligence, nuisance or breach of duty... where the damages claimed by the plaintiff... consist of or include damages in respect of personal injuries to the plaintiff or any other person."[119]

This expressly includes breach of a contractual duty.

11–040 **Trespass to the person** In *Stubbings v Webb*[120] the House of Lords held that s.11(1) of the Limitation Act 1980, which was in identical terms to and bore the same meaning as s.2(1) of the Law Reform (Limitation of Actions) Act 1954, had been intended by Parliament to be limited to personal injury resulting from accidents caused by negligence, nuisance or breach of a duty of care. Injuries arising from deliberate assault, including indecent assault and rape, were intended to be subject to the six-year limitation period of s.2 of the Limitation Act 1980, under which there was no discretionary power to allow the action to proceed once the six-year period had elapsed.[121] *Letang v Cooper*,[122] in which the Court of

---

[116] The Limitation Act 1980 does not apply where a period of limitation is prescribed by other legislation: s.39. Special rules apply to accidents occurring in the course of international travel (Carriage by Air Act 1961 ss.1(1), 5(1), Sch. art.29; Merchant Shipping Act 1995 s.190) and nuclear incidents (Nuclear Installations Act 1965 s.15). See also Consumer Protection Act 1987 Sch.1, in respect of claims under that Act, amending the Limitation Act 1980, below, para.11–158. Claims brought under the Consumer Protection Act 1987 are subject to a three-year limit from the date the cause of action accrued or the claimant's date of knowledge. This is capable of being extended but is subject to a 10-year "longstop". Claims under the Human Rights Act 1998 are subject to a one-year limitation period which runs from the date on which the act complained of took place, with a discretion for the court to extend the period if it is equitable to do so: Human Rights Act 1998 s.7(5). See para.11–178.

[117] Limitation Act 1980 s.11(3) and (4). The date of accrual will often be the same as the date of the claimant's knowledge; see para.11–052. The fact that the Limitation Act 1980 is a consolidating statute means that earlier case law on the interpretation of its provisions remains authoritative. The present scheme covering personal injuries was introduced by the Limitation Act 1975, adding new ss.2A–2D to the Limitation Act 1939.

[118] s.33; see paras 11–121 et seq.

[119] Limitation Act 1980 s.11(1).

[120] [1993] A.C. 498.

[121] Subject to the effect of s.28 postponing the *commencement* of the limitation period during the claimant's minority or incapacity; see para.11–152.

[122] [1965] 1 Q.B. 232.

Appeal had held that the wording of the statute was broad enough to apply to actions for trespass to the person and therefore the three-year limitation period applied, was overruled on this point. The words "breach of duty" did not include within the section all actions in which damages for personal injuries were claimed. There was a distinction between breach of a duty of care not to cause personal injury, and an obligation not to infringe any legal right of another person. It followed that cases of "deliberate assault" such as rape or indecent assault were not actions for breach of duty within the meaning of s.11(1).

This lead to what Lord Hoffmann in *A v Hoare*[123] identified as the "most remarkable example of the anomaly" which arose in *S v W (Child Abuse: Damages)*[124] where the claimant sued both her father and her mother for sexual abuse by the father. The claim was not commenced until almost 10 years after the last act of abuse and accordingly the claim against the father for intentional assault was struck out, applying *Stubbings v Webb*. There was a six-year limitation period with no discretion to disapply. However, the claim against the mother was in negligence for failing to protect the claimant from her father. Because the claim was framed in negligence it was governed by s.11 and therefore subject to the discretionary provisions of s.33. The judge permitted the claim to proceed under s.33 and the Court of Appeal upheld this decision. The action against the mother for failing to protect her daughter was therefore permitted to proceed while the action against the actual abuser was statute-barred. Sir Ralph Gibson in the Court of Appeal remarked that this result was "illogical and surprising" and deserving of the attention of the Law Commission. The Law Commission also referred to the effect of *Stubbings* as "anomalous" and recommended reform.   **11–041**

In *A v Hoare*[125] the House of Lords reviewed the legislative history and considered how the previous statutory provisions had been interpreted. Their Lordships concluded that it would be right to depart from *Stubbings* and reaffirmed the law laid down by the Court of Appeal in *Letang v Cooper*. The reference to breach of duty in s.11(1) should be construed broadly enough to include trespass to the person. The three-year time limit for personal injury claims applied in claims arising both in negligence and in trespass to the person.   **11–042**

Implications in the medical context   The decision of the House of Lords in *A v Hoare* plainly has important implications in abuse and other intentional assault claims, but is also of significance in the field of medical malpractice litigation. Whilst the vast majority of medical claims arise in the tort of negligence, trespass to the person can also be relevant. For example, where a surgeon operates on a competent patient without having obtained the patient's consent he is liable in battery. Sometimes this may be the result of a conscious decision by the doctor to proceed without full consent, but more commonly it is the result of a careless mix-up, and the surgeon performs the wrong operation or operates on the wrong limb or even the wrong patient. Previously, as a consequence of the decision in   **11–043**

---

[123] [2008] UKHL 6; [2008] 1 A.C. 844 at [23].
[124] [1995] 1 F.L.R. 862.
[125] [2008] UKHL 6; [2008] 1 A.C. 844; see S. Brown, "Limitation—still something of a lottery" [2008] J.P.I.L 176.

Stubbings, a patient who alleged that a doctor had undertaken a procedure involving bodily contact without a valid consent had to bring the action for trespass to the person within six years, without any possibility of the court's discretion to allow the action to proceed under s.33 being available. Following the decision in *A v Hoare*, such an action will be treated as one of personal injury within s.11(1) and the patient must bring the action within three years. Although this is a shorter period the patient will have the opportunity of taking advantage of both the knowledge provisions of s.14 and, more importantly, the discretionary provisions of s.33.

11–044   **Personal injuries**   "Personal injuries" includes any disease and any impairment of a person's physical or mental condition.[126] Where the breach of duty does not itself cause the personal injuries, but deprives the claimant of a chance of receiving compensation for the injuries the three-year period does not apply. For example, a solicitor's negligence which results in his client's claim for personal injuries becoming statute-barred gives rise to a claim for financial loss which is subject to the ordinary six-year limitation period under s.2 (tort) or s.5 (contract) of the Limitation Act,[127] although this is now subject to specific provisions on latent damage. So where a patient suffers purely financial loss due to a doctor's negligence (e.g. giving up work following a negligent misdiagnosis[128]) the six-year period will apply.

11–045   **"Wrongful birth"—personal injury or economic loss?**   The question of the nature of the loss where a claim is made in respect of the costs of raising a child following negligence on the part of medical staff is problematic. In *Pattison v Hobbs*[129] the Court of Appeal held that the financial loss resulting from the birth of a healthy child following a negligently performed sterilisation operation did not involve a claim for personal injuries, and therefore s.2 applied. The significance of this is that within the six-year period the claimant has an absolute right to bring an action, but if the claim is for personal injuries there is no absolute right after three years, and the claimant must rely on the court exercising its discretion to allow his claim to proceed. Thus, it was arguable that in some "wrongful birth" cases, where the action had not been commenced within three

---

[126] Limitation Act 1980 s.38(1).

[127] See, e.g. *Ackbar v Green & Co. Ltd* [1975] 1 Q.B. 582, where insurance brokers who failed to obtain insurance against the risk of personal injury were subject to the six-year period, although the claim materialised when the claimant sustained personal injury. Croom-Johnson J gave the example of a claim against a solicitor.

[128] See *Hedley Byrne & Co. Ltd v Heller & Partners Ltd* [1964] A.C. 465 at 517, per Lord Devlin, para.2–050; see also *Stevens v Bermondsey and Southwark Group Hospital Management Committee* (1963) 107 S.J. 478, para.2–049.

[129] *The Times*, 11 November 1985. In *Allen v Bloomsbury Health Authority* [1993] 1 All E.R. 651 at 658; [1992] P.I.Q.R. Q50, a case of a negligent failure to diagnose that the claimant was pregnant, where the claimant would have had a termination if she had known about the pregnancy early enough, Brooke J said: "I realise that if Parliament does not intervene this is likely to mean that different limitation periods may apply to the two types of claim, since it is hard to see how s.11 of the Limitation Act 1980 would apply to a claim limited to the financial costs associated with the upbringing of the unwanted child since this would be, on the facts of a case like the present, a straightforward *Hedley Byrne & Co. Ltd v Heller & Partners Ltd* type of claim for foreseeable economic loss caused by negligent advice or misstatement."

years, it might be preferable for the claimant to forego the claim for personal injuries (e.g. the pain and suffering of pregnancy or of a repeat sterilisation operation), since the bulk of the damages reflect the financial costs of rearing the child.[130]

In *Walkin v South Manchester Health Authority*,[131] however, the Court of Appeal held that a claim for the economic loss attributable to the birth of a child following a failed sterilisation operation fell within s.11, as a claim for "damages in respect of personal injuries". The unwanted conception was a personal injury because the physical change to the claimant's body was an unwanted condition which she had sought to avoid by being sterilised. Auld LJ observed that:

11–046

> "Post-natal economic loss may be unassociated with 'physical injury' in the sense that it stems from the cost of rearing a child rather than any disability in pregnancy or birth, but it is not unassociated with the cause of both, namely the unwanted pregnancy giving rise to the birth of a child. In my view, claims in such circumstances for pre-natal pain and suffering and post-natal economic costs arise out of the same cause of action."[132]

Although the claim for the costs of raising the child depended on the birth of the child, rather than the pregnancy, the birth was not an intervening event: it was caused by the personal injury, namely the unwanted pregnancy. *Pattison v Hobbs*, said Auld LJ, was a decision of a two-judge Court of Appeal which turned on a point of pleading. The question whether an action was for damages in respect of personal injuries was a matter of substance, not pleading.[133]

---

[130] See paras 12–134 et seq. See, however, the comments of Nicholls LJ in *Howe v David Brown Tractors (Retail) Ltd (Rustons Engineering Co Ltd, third party)* [1991] 4 All E.R. 30 at 41, pointing out that in an ordinary claim for personal injuries which includes a claim for the financial loss resulting from the physical injury, such as loss of future earnings: "the claim for financial loss is as much a claim for 'damages in respect of personal injuries' as is the claim for damages in respect of the physical injury itself. The plaintiff could not step outside the three-year limitation period prescribed by s.11 by abandoning any claim for damages in respect of the physical injury and claiming only damages in respect of his loss of earnings."

[131] [1995] 1 W.L.R. 1543; *Saxby v Morgan* [1997] P.I.Q.R. P531; [1997] 8 Med. L.R. 293, CA.

[132] [1995] 1 W.L.R. 1543 at 1549.

[133] See also *Bennett v Greenland Houchen & Co. (A Firm)* [1998] P.N.L.R. 458 in which the claimant brought an action against the defendant firm of solicitors in respect financial loss alleged to have been caused by the defendants' negligence, but also alleged that he suffered clinical depression arising out of the defendants' negligent handling of his case against his former employers. The Court of Appeal applied *Walkin*, holding that it was an action which included a claim for personal injuries, and therefore subject to a three-year limitation period. Similarly, where a former client sues a solicitor for financial loss arising from negligence in the handling of her divorce ancillary relief claim and includes a claim for "anxiety and stress" the three-year limitation period applies: *Oates v Harte Reade & Co. (A Firm)* [1999] 1 F.L.R. 1221; and a claim against the owner of a motor vehicle for permitting a driver to use the vehicle without insurance (under the principle of *Monk v Warbey* [1935] 1 K.B. 75), which on the face of it seems to be a claim for financial loss, nonetheless falls within s.11 rather than s.2: *Norman v Aziz* [2000] P.I.Q.R. P72, CA. cf. *Pounds v Eckford Rands (A Firm)* [2003] Lloyd's Rep. P.N. 195, QBD—claimant was entitled to amend a claim in respect of solicitors' alleged professional negligence in handling her ancillary relief proceedings by deleting all reference to her claim for personal injury, because the defendants had not previously raised the limitation defence and the vast bulk of the claim was for economic loss, not personal injury. See also *Shade v Compton Partnership* [2000] P.N.L.R. 218, QB. In both of these cases the personal injury element formed only a modest part of the overall claim.

11–047   This issue has been complicated by the ruling of the House of Lords in *McFarlane v Tayside Health Board*[134] that no duty of care is owed to the parents in respect of the financial cost of bringing up a healthy child following negligent advice about, or the negligent performance of, a sterilisation operation. Subsequently, in *Parkinson v St James and Seacroft University Hospital NHS Trust*[135] the Court of Appeal held that the parents of a disabled child born following a negligently performed sterilisation operation were entitled to the additional costs of raising that child, i.e. the additional costs attributable to the disability itself. Thus, such claims are in any event limited to cases involving a disabled child.[136] But the decision in *McFarlane* has cast some doubt on the status of *Walkin*, because their Lordships drew a clear distinction between the *mother's* claim in respect of the pain, suffering and consequential losses associated with the pregnancy, and the *parents'* claim in respect of the financial costs of the raising the child, apparently categorising the parents' claim as one for pure economic loss.[137]

11–048   In *Greenfield v Irwin*,[138] the Court of Appeal treated *McFarlane* as deciding that the nature of the parents' claim for the costs of childrearing was purely economic, a view which led Laws LJ to comment[139] that if the Court of Appeal's reasoning in *Walkin* was at variance with *McFarlane* then it was impliedly disapproved by *McFarlane*. In the one case which has had to consider this issue in the limitation context, Leveson J held that he was bound by the Court of Appeal's decision in *Walkin*.[140] It was clear that the mother's claim was a claim for personal injuries. The question was whether the claim which was made for the costs incurred in looking after a disabled child also represented part of the claim in respect of personal injuries or was a separate claim for economic loss, based on the tort of negligent misrepresentation.[141] Leveson J did not regard Laws LJ's observation in *Greenfield v Irwin* "as appellate encouragement to reach the conclusion that *Walkin* is no longer good law". The question posed by Auld LJ in *Walkin* was whether the claim in respect of the childrearing costs was an action for damages:

> "…consisting of or including damages in respect of personal injuries. That is or at least could be different from the question whether the claim for the cost of upbringing of a child is pure or consequential economic loss."[142]

---

[134] [2000] 2 A.C. 59. See paras 2–055 et seq.

[135] [2001] EWCA Civ 530; [2002] Q.B. 266; see para.2–061.

[136] Though following *Rees v Darlington Memorial Hospital NHS Trust* [2003] UKHL 52; [2004] 1 A.C. 309 the parents are entitled to a conventional award of £15,000 for loss of the right to limit the size of one's family. This head of damage applies whether the child is healthy or disabled. See paras 2–072–2–074.

[137] This was the approach of Lord Slynn and Lord Hope. Lord Steyn and Lord Millett refused to treat the distinction between economic loss and physical damage as relevant to the outcome in *McFarlane*, Lord Millett suggesting that the distinction between pure or consequential was "technical and artificial if not actually suspect".

[138] [2001] EWCA Civ 113; [2001] 1 W.L.R. 1279.

[139] [2001] EWCA Civ 113; [2001] 1 W.L.R. 1279 at [53].

[140] *Godfrey v Gloucestershire Royal Infirmary NHS Trust* [2003] EWHC 549 (QB); [2003] Lloyd's Rep. Med. 398.

[141] [2003] EWHC 549 (QB); [2003] Lloyd's Rep. Med. 398 at [21].

[142] [2003] EWHC 549 (QB); [2003] Lloyd's Rep. Med. 398 at [35].

It followed that s.11 of the Act applied, which meant that the limitation period was three years from the date of the claimant's knowledge, but with the discretionary power to disapply the limitation period.

Calculating the three-year period   In computing the three-year period the date on which an accident occurred is ignored. In *Marren v Dawson Bentley & Co. Ltd*[143] the claimant's accident occurred on 8 November and he issued his claim form in court on 8 November three years later. Havers J ruled that the claim was in time confirming that the limitation period starts to run on the day after the cause of action accrues. The expiry of the limitation period is fixed by reference to something the claimant has to do. Bringing the claim to the court with a request that it be issued is something that the claimant has to do. The time at which the request is complied with by the court is not within his control. In *St Helens MBC v Barnes*[144] the Court of Appeal confirmed that if the claim form is delivered to the court before the expiry of the limitation period, but the court issues the claim form after the expiry of the limitation period, the action has been brought within the limitation period. If the court office is closed for the whole of the last day of the period, it is extended until the next day on which the court office is open.[145]

11–049

As a general rule, once the period has started to run it cannot be suspended; only the issue of the claim form stops time running.[146] The parties may agree, expressly or impliedly, to extend the time, but the mere fact that negotiations towards a settlement were in progress when the three-year period expired will not constitute such an agreement, unless the defendant's conduct is such that he is estopped from relying on the defence.[147] For these purposes it is only safe to rely on an express admission of liability or an express statement that the defendant will not take the limitation point. The Limitation Act 1980 provides the defendant with a time bar defence. If the defence is not pleaded the claim can continue to judgment.[148] The right to rely on the defence under the Act may be waived by the

11–050

---

[143] [1961] 2 Q.B. 135.
[144] [2006] EWCA Civ 1372; [2007] 1 W.L.R. 879. See also *Page v Hewetts Solicitors* [2012] EWCA Civ 805; [2012] C.P. Rep. 40; and *Dixon v Radley House Partnership (A Firm)* [2016] EWHC 2511 (TCC); [2017] C.P. Rep. 4 (payment of incorrect fee for the issue of proceedings does not invalidate the proceedings).
[145] *Pritam Kaur v Russell & Sons Ltd* [1973] Q.B. 336; *Yadly Marketing Co Ltd v Secretary of State for the Home Department* [2016] EWCA Civ 1143; [2017] 1 W.L.R. 1041. This principle applies only where the court office is closed during the whole of the last day of the period.
[146] Once the claim form has been issued it must normally be served on the defendant within four months of the date of issue: CPR r.7.5(1). There is generally little point in delaying service of the claim form, particularly since interest on general damages runs from the date of service (see para.12–047) and the Civil Procedure Rules are based on the premise that proceedings will be conducted with reasonable dispatch. The court has a power to extend the time for serving the claim form for periods of up to four months at a time (CPR r.7.6), but once the period permitted for service has expired the court can only extend the time for service in limited circumstances: see CPR r.7.6(3).
[147] *Deerness v John Keeble & Son Ltd* [1983] 2 Lloyd's Rep. 260, where the House of Lords declined to infer such an agreement from continuing negotiations and an interim payment; *K Lokumal & Sons (London) Ltd v Lotte Shipping Co. Pte. Ltd* [1985] 2 Lloyd's Rep. 28.
[148] CPR r.16.5 and *Ronex v John Laing* [1983] 1 Q.B. 398, CA. See CPR 16PD.13.1 which provides that "The defendant must give details of the expiry of any relevant limitation period relied upon".

defendant[149] and further a defendant can be estopped from relying on the defence.[150] Section 36(2) of the 1980 Act specifically preserves equitable remedies in limitation cases and the Court of Appeal has confirmed that the provisions of the Act can be overridden by e.g. contract, waiver, estoppel or unconscionable conduct.[151]

(b) Commencement of the three-year period

11–051   Time begins to run from either the date on which the cause of action accrued or the date of the claimant's knowledge, if later. The claimant's knowledge may be actual or constructive.

(i)   Accrual of the cause of action

11–052   **Accrual of cause of action in negligence**   A cause of action is simply a factual situation entitling a person to a remedy.[152] In negligence the action accrues when damage occurs, which is usually but not always at the same time as the defendant's breach of duty. The action will accrue even though the damage is undiscoverable.[153] In the case of minor or trivial harm it will be a question of fact whether the claimant has sustained "damage" sufficient for the cause of action to accrue. If it falls within the principle de minimis non curat lex it will be ignored, but not otherwise.[154] In cases of progressive damage resulting from a *continuing* breach of duty a fresh cause of action arises so long as the wrongful act continues (as, e.g. in industrial deafness cases). Claimants are entitled to claim for so much of the damage as was caused in the three years immediately preceding the issue of the claim form. They may be able to claim for earlier damage if the court exercises its discretion under s.33 of the Limitation Act 1980, provided that the earlier damage was attributable to the defendant's breach of duty.[155] If, as a question of fact, the subsequent deterioration of the claimants' conditions are attributable to events which occurred more than three years before the issue of the claim form the claim is out of time.

---

[149] *Lubovsky v Snelling* [1944] K.B. 44.
[150] *Co-operative Wholesale v Chester Le Street* [1998] R.V.R. 202 and *Ellis v Lambeth* (2000) 32 H.L.R. 596, CA.
[151] *Co-operative Wholesale v Chester Le Street* [1998] R.V.R. 202.
[152] *Letang v Cooper* [1965] 1 Q.B. 232 at 242–243, per Diplock LJ.
[153] *Cartledge v Jopling & Sons Ltd* [1963] A.C. 758.
[154] [1963] A.C. 758. Asymptomatic, minor physiological damage had in the past been held to be sufficient to give rise to a cause of action: see *Church v Ministry of Defence* (1984) 134 N.L.J. 623; *Sykes v Ministry of Defence, The Times*, 23 March 1984; *Patterson v Ministry of Defence* [1987] C.L.Y. 1194. But see now the discussion of this issue by the House of Lords in *Rothwell v Chemical & Insulating Co Ltd* [2007] UKHL 39; [2008] 1 A.C. 281, para.12–001, n.1.
[155] See, e.g. *Thompson v Smiths Shiprepairers (North Shields) Ltd* [1984] Q.B. 405. If the earlier damage cannot be attributed to the defendant's breach of duty, nonetheless the award of damages for the later, actionable damage may be proportionately greater because additional harm to a person who has an existing disability may have more catastrophic consequences than the initial injury: *Paris v Stepney Borough Council* [1951] A.C. 367; *Berry v Stone Manganese & Marine Ltd* [1972] 1 Lloyd's Rep. 182 at 196.

Claims in contract   In simple contract[156] the cause of action accrues at the date   **11–053**
of breach of contract, although it is possible that where there is an omission to
perform a contractual duty this may constitute a "continuing breach of contract"
up to the point at which it is no longer possible to perform the duty, with the
cause of action accruing at that date.[157] On this basis it is arguable that an
omission to give a warning to avoid certain activities which might be dangerous
to the patient during the course of treatment could give rise to a continuing duty
to give the appropriate advice. However, in *Capita (Banstead 2011) Ltd v RFIB
Group Ltd*[158] the Court of Appeal preferred the approach of the Court of Appeal
in *Bell v Peter Browne & Co*, taking the view that there was usually no
continuing duty to correct a mistake after the giving of negligent advice, so that a
fresh cause of action did not accrue every day after the mistake had been made
until it was corrected.

Date of accrual *or* date of knowledge   There is a practical advantage to the   **11–054**
claimant in issuing the claim form within three years of the accrual of the cause
action, since no question of having to establish the precise date of knowledge will
then arise. But if more than three years have elapsed since the date of accrual of
the action, the primary limitation period will not necessarily have expired. Time
does not run unless and until the claimant acquires the relevant "knowledge",
which can occur at the date of accrual or later, but never before the action has
accrued.

(ii)   Date of knowledge

By s.14(1) references to people's date of knowledge are references to the date on   **11–055**
which they first had knowledge of the following facts:

> "(a)   that the injury in question was significant; and
> (b)   that the injury was attributable in whole or in part to the act or omission which is
>   alleged to constitute negligence, nuisance or breach of duty; and
> (c)   the identity of the defendant; and
> (d)   if it is alleged that the act or omission was that of a person other than the defendant, the
>   identity of that person and the additional facts supporting the bringing of an action
>   against the defendant . . ."

These provisions are conjunctive: if claimants do not have the knowledge
specified in any of these paragraphs then they do not have "knowledge" for the
purpose of starting the limitation period running (though para.(d) only applies in

---

[156] See *West Bromwich Albion Football Club Ltd v El Safty* [2006] EWCA Civ 1299; [2007] P.I.Q.R.
7, for a consideration of the respective contractual and tortious duties arising where an orthopaedic
surgeon provided medical treatment under the terms of a BUPA insurance policy to a footballer
employed by the football club. See paras 2–008 to 2–010, and 2–185 to 2–186.
[157] *Midland Bank Trust Co. Ltd v Hett, Stubbs & Kemp* [1979] Ch. 384; cf. *Bell v Peter Browne &
Co.* [1990] 2 Q.B. 495, CA.
[158] [2015] EWCA Civ 1310; [2016] Q.B. 835. See also *Rayner v Wolferstans (A Firm)* [2015] EWHC
2957 (QB) at [120]–[123].

certain circumstances). On the other hand, s.14(1) is also exhaustive: no knowledge of any further facts is required.[159]

11–056 **Meaning of "knowledge"** There are two aspects to determining whether a claimant had the relevant knowledge for the purpose of s.14. The first is what is it that the claimant must "know"? This is laid out in s.14(1), namely that the injury was significant, that it was attributable to the defendant's breach of duty, the identity of the defendant, and, if relevant, the facts which would justify proceedings against the defendant where the breach of duty was committed by someone other than the defendant (i.e. in cases of vicarious liability or breach of a non-delegable duty). "Significant injury" is defined in s.14(2), and has been the subject of some judicial debate.[160] Whether the injury was attributable to the defendant's breach of duty involves knowledge of the causal link, and this has proved to be particularly troublesome, especially in cases of medical negligence.[161]

11–057 The second aspect of determining whether the claimant had "knowledge" lies in identifying the basis on which and the degree of conviction with which a claimant must hold a belief about the relevant facts. Knowledge depends on the acquisition of accurate information, but the quality and quantity of information required before claiming to "know" something as a "fact" will vary from person to person. Some (A) may claim to know something to be correct on the basis of very little information, or on information of doubtful accuracy, and express a strong belief in the truth or correctness of that information, where others (B) would be more cautious in coming to a conclusion about the information. B might say "I suspect that X is true, but I do not know"; or B might say "I believe that X is true but I cannot know it is true until I have further verification"; whereas A might say "I know for sure that X is true", where the statement is based on little more than suspicion and/or repeated rumour. The point at which information becomes "knowledge" of a "fact" can be highly subjective, depending on the degree of scepticism and analytic rigour that the individual brings to the process. Is there any way to apply an objective test to a claimant's state of knowledge?

11–058 In *Halford v Brookes*[162] Lord Donaldson MR said that the word knowledge:

> "...has to be construed in the context of the purpose of the section, which is to determine a period within which a plaintiff can be required to start any proceedings. In this context 'knowledge' clearly does not mean 'know for certain and beyond possibility of contradiction'. It does, however, mean 'know with sufficient confidence to justify embarking on the preliminaries to the issue of the writ, such as submitting a claim to the proposed defendant, taking legal and other advice and collecting evidence'. Suspicion, particularly if it is vague and unsupported, will indeed not be enough, but reasonable belief will normally suffice. It is

---

[159] *Dobbie v Medway Health Authority* [1994] 1 W.L.R. 1234 at 1247, per Steyn LJ. Where a defendant applies to strike out an action *in limine* on the ground that the date of the claimant's knowledge of the relevant facts was more than three years before the issue of the claim form, the court should not grant the application unless the issue is clear and obvious and the contrary unarguable: *Davis v Ministry of Defence*, *The Times*, 7 August 1985, CA, per May LJ.

[160] See paras 11–073–11–081.

[161] See paras 11–082–11–099.

[162] [1991] 1 W.L.R. 428 at 443. This statement was approved by Lord Wilson in *AB v Ministry of Defence* [2012] UKSC 9; [2013] 1 A.C. 78 at [12].

probably only in an exceptional case such as *Davis v Ministry of Defence* that it will not, because there is some other countervailing factor."

In *Nash v Eli Lilly & Co.*,[163] in which the claimants alleged that they had suffered adverse reactions to the drug Opren, the Court of Appeal held that "knowledge" is a condition of mind which imports a degree of certainty:

"...and... the degree of certainty which is appropriate for this purpose is that which, for the particular plaintiff, may reasonably be regarded as sufficient to justify embarking upon the preliminaries to the making of a claim for compensation such as the taking of legal or other advice."

This is a two-stage process involving: (i) the nature of the information received, the extent to which claimants pay attention to the information as affecting them, and their capacity to understand it; and (ii) evaluation of the information that has been received and understood, e.g. it may be regarded as unreliable or uncertain. Therefore the court must assess the intelligence of claimants, consider and assess their assertions as to how they regarded such information as they had, and determine whether they had knowledge of the facts by reason of their understanding of the information.[164]

In *North Essex District Health Authority v Spargo*[165] Brooke LJ set out a number of propositions, taken from previous authorities, about the meaning of the word "knowledge" for the purpose of s.14:

    11–059

"(1)   The knowledge required to satisfy section 14(1)(b) is a broad knowledge of the essence of the causally relevant act or omission to which the injury is attributable;

(2)   'Attributable' in this context means 'capable of being attributed to' in the sense of being a real possibility[166];

(3)   A plaintiff has requisite knowledge when she knows enough to make it reasonable for her to begin to investigate whether or not she has a case against the defendant. Another way of putting this is to say that she will have such knowledge if she so firmly believes that her condition is capable of being attributed to an act or omission which she can identify (in broad terms) that she goes to a solicitor to seek advice about making a claim for compensation[167];

(4)   On the other hand she will not have the requisite knowledge if she thinks she knows the acts or omissions she should investigate but in fact is barking up the wrong tree; or if her knowledge of what the defendant did or did not do is so vague or general that she cannot fairly be expected to know what she should investigate; or if her state of mind is such that she thinks her condition is capable of being attributed to the act or omission alleged to constitute negligence, but she is not sure about this, and would need to check it with an expert before she could be properly said to know that it was."

In an area of the law where judicial comment is quite frequent, and not always consistent, Brooke LJ's statement has been treated as particularly authoritative,

---

[163] [1993] 1 W.L.R. 782 at 792, CA.

[164] [1993] 1 W.L.R. 782 at 792, CA. See also *Skitt v Khan and Wakefield Health Authority* [1997] 8 Med. L.R. 105, CA.

[165] [1997] P.I.Q.R. P235 at 242; [1997] 8 Med. L.R. 125 at 129–130.

[166] Approved in *AB v Ministry of Defence* [2012] UKSC 9; [2013] 1 A.C. 78 at [2], [79].

[167] This paragraph was criticised by Lord Kerr in his dissenting judgment in *AB v Ministry of Defence* [2012] UKSC 9; [2013] 1 A.C. 78 at [204] on the basis that it conflates the claimant's knowledge and belief: "Knowing is not believing. To know something to be true is different from believing it to be so."

and it has been said that the *Spargo* principles were intended not simply as guidelines, but as binding rules.[168] However, in *AB v Ministry of Defence*[169] Lord Walker said that:

> "…short summaries like that of Brooke LJ in *Spargo* (which Lord Phillips rightly describes as a 'valiant attempt') may be unhelpful if treated as if they were statutory texts. The words of the 1980 Act themselves must be the starting-point, illuminated where necessary by judicial exposition…"

11–060   **The distinction between "knowledge" and "belief"**   The distinction between knowledge and belief was at the heart of the Supreme Court decision in *AB v Ministry of Defence*[170] which involved claims by veteran servicemen who alleged that they had been exposed to radiation during the testing of thermonuclear devices in the atmosphere in the 1950s and that the radiation was responsible for the various medical conditions from which they suffered. Most of the claims had been issued in 2005, but the claimants argued that they did not acquire knowledge for the purposes of s.14(1) until they received an expert report in 2007 which provided some evidence of exposure to radiation. The defendants denied that there was a causal link between any exposure to radiation and the claimants' damage, whilst at the same time asserting that the claimants had knowledge for the purposes of s.14(1)(b) "that the injury was attributable in whole or in part to the act or omission which is alleged to constitute negligence" long before receipt of the expert report.[171] The Supreme Court divided sharply on the question of what would suffice as "knowledge" for the purposes of s.14. The minority (Lords Phillips and Kerr, and Lady Hale) took the view that s.14 expressly requires that claimants must have knowledge of the facts that make up the essential elements of their claim to start the limitation period running, and that since it was common ground that when the claimants issued proceedings "there were no known facts capable of supporting a belief that the veterans' injuries were attributable to exposure to ionising radiation" then in so far as they believed that their injuries were attributable to radiation "that belief was not reasonable".[172] The claimants' subjective belief, without any scientific evidence to support it, that exposure to radiation had caused their damage was not "knowledge" of the "fact" that their

---

[168] *Griffin, Lawson and Williams v Clywd Health Authority* [2001] EWCA Civ 818; [2001] P.I.Q.R. P420; *Corbin v Penfold Metallising Company Ltd* [2000] Lloyds Rep. Med. 247 at 249, CA: the Court: "intended to lay down, not merely guidelines, but authoritative statements of how section 14 should be interpreted."

[169] [2012] UKSC 9; [2013] 1 A.C. 78 at [68].

[170] [2012] UKSC 9; [2013] 1 A.C. 78.

[171] Defendants who deny that there is causal link between any breach of duty and the claimant's damage will invariably find themselves in the inconsistent position of arguing that for the purposes of limitation the claimant knew about a causal connection which they themselves are denying existed. See e.g. *Ali v Courtaulds Textiles Ltd* [1999] Lloyd's Rep. Med. 301 at 303 per Henry LJ (a case of alleged industrial deafness): "At the same time as the defendants allege that the claimant 'knew that his deafness was attributable to exposure to noise' they were relying on their own expert's report that, subject to further tests, there was nothing in the pattern of his pure tone audiometry to suggest noise exposure as a cause of the deafness, and that the 'genuine conductive loss' originated from childhood otitis media . . ."

[172] [2012] UKSC 9; [2013] 1 A.C. 78 at [139] per Lord Phillips.

damage was attributable to the acts or omissions of the defendants.[173] A claimant had to have a reasonable belief before it could amount to knowledge, and a reasonable belief had to be based to some degree on known facts.[174] Lord Kerr pointed out that s.14 did not provide that the claimant would have statutory knowledge

> "when he *believed* (or even firmly believed) that the injury was attributable to the defendant's act or omission. The natural meaning of the language used was that the plaintiff needed to *know it* rather than to believe it and that he needed *to know it as a fact.*"[175]

Lord Kerr acknowledged that the concepts of belief and knowledge might be inherently subjective, but that did not make them interchangeable.[176]

The majority in *AB v Ministry of Defence* (Lords Wilson, Walker, Brown and Mance) held that the claims were statute-barred since it was: **11–061**

> "...a legal impossibility for a claimant to lack knowledge of attributability for the purpose of section 14(1) at a time after the date of issue of his claim."[177]

The statement of truth that claimants must make when issuing claim forms is that they believe the facts stated in it are true. This, said Lord Wilson, could be regarded as an explicit recognition by claimants that they then have knowledge of attributability for the purpose of s.14(1).[178] There is clearly a risk that this comes close to establishing a legal fiction, for policy reasons. Lord Brown observed that on Lord Phillips' approach the more hopeless the claim the more likely it would be that a claimant could defeat the limitation defence no matter how long ago the alleged cause of action arose, and that this could not have been Parliament's intention.[179] Discerning the intention of Parliament is no easy task, of course, and in his dissenting judgment Lord Kerr pointed out that if Parliament had intended

---

[173] [2012] UKSC 9; [2013] 1 A.C. 78 at [136].

[174] [2012] UKSC 9; [2013] 1 A.C. 78 at [137]. See also per Lady Hale at [169]: "Like it or not, time does not begin to run until the claimant has 'knowledge' of the essential 'facts' ... The strength of a claimant's subjective belief is not a sensible basis for deciding who does, and who does not, have an absolute right to pursue his action."

[175] [2012] UKSC 9; [2013] 1 A.C. 78 at [185] (original emphasis).

[176] [2012] UKSC 9; [2013] 1 A.C. 78 at [194]: "I know something to be true because I have a factual foundation for my knowledge of its truth. I may believe something to be true without any basis in practical reality whatever. And simply because I assert the truth of a particular proposition, I cannot be taken to *know* (as opposed to *believe*) it to be so" (original emphasis); "knowledge depends on factual information rather than simple belief, however fervently held", [2012] UKSC 9; [2013] 1 A.C. 78 at [202].

[177] [2012] UKSC 9; [2013] 1 A.C. 78 at [3] per Lord Wilson.

[178] [2012] UKSC 9; [2013] 1 A.C. 78 at [3]. See also per Lord Walker at [67], Lord Brown at [71] and Lord Mance at [84]. Lord Wilson, at [6], considered that it was: "heretical that a claimant can escape the conventional requirement to assert his cause of action for personal injuries within three years of its accrual by establishing that, even after his claim was brought, he remained in a state of ignorance entirely inconsistent with it."

[179] [2012] UKSC 9; [2013] 1 A.C. 78 at [72]. See also Lord Walker at [67] arguing that Parliament cannot have intended that claimants with a belief that they had suffered personal injuries through the fault of another "but with no real prospect of proving legal liability on the balance of probability, would be able to keep their claims on ice, as it were, for an indefinite period, in the hope that one day the right evidence might turn up". Lady Hale, at [174], acknowledged that there was "a very good case for the law being different. But I do not think that we should translate our view of what a sensible

the start of the limitation period to depend on the claimant's belief the repeated use of the word "knowledge" in s.14 was "mystifying". It would have been a simple task, said his Lordship, for Parliament to have specified that claimants need only have a belief in the matters set out in s.14(1) if that had been their intention. Moreover, it was:

> "...inherently unlikely that that Parliament could ever have intended that claimants should be encouraged to commence litigation when all that they had to go on was a belief, however strongly held."[180]

11–062 **Strength of claimant's belief** Lord Wilson accepted that the concepts of "belief" and of "knowledge" are inherently subjective. Nonetheless a claimant was "likely to have acquired knowledge of the facts specified in section 14 when he first came reasonably to believe them".[181] His Lordship accepted Lady Hale's view (in her dissenting judgment) that:

> "...it is difficult to see how an unreasonable belief in attributability can amount to 'knowledge of the fact' of attributability. It clearly does not. It amounts to an unreasonable belief. Only when there is some reasonable basis in evidence or objective fact for that belief can it be turned into something approaching knowledge."[182]

But he rejected the view that claimants lack knowledge until they have the evidence with which to substantiate their belief in court.[183] The degree of confidence with which a belief should be held before it amounts to knowledge is such as

> "...to justify embarking on the preliminaries to the issue of a writ, such as submitting a claim to the proposed defendant, taking legal and other advice and collecting evidence."[184]

Lord Mance considered that use of the words "reasonable belief" involves focusing not on whether the belief is evidence-based but on whether the belief was held with a sufficient degree of confidence to justify embarking on the preliminaries to making a claim, including collecting evidence.[185]

11–063 **Distinguish belief and suspicion** The position is probably different where claimants merely have a "suspicion" that their damage was caused by an act or omission of the defendant, though distinguishing between an individual's "suspicions" and "beliefs" might test the skills of a psychologist or a linguistic philosopher. In *Halford v Brookes*[186] Lord Donaldson MR distinguished between suspicion, "particularly if it is vague and unsupported", which would not be

---

law of limitation would say into our view of what it does say. Knowledge and belief are different concepts and there is no reason to believe that Parliament intended to equate the two".
[180] [2012] UKSC 9; [2013] 1 A.C. 78 at [188].
[181] [2012] UKSC 9; [2013] 1 A.C. 78 at [12].
[182] [2012] UKSC 9; [2013] 1 A.C. 78 at [170].
[183] [2012] UKSC 9; [2013] 1 A.C. 78 at [11].
[184] [2012] UKSC 9; [2013] 1 A.C. 78 at [12], citing Lord Donaldson MR in *Halford v Brookes* [1991] 1 W.L.R. 428.
[185] [2012] UKSC 9; [2013] 1 A.C. 78 at [83].
[186] [1991] 1 W.L.R. 428 at 443.

sufficient for the purposes of s.14, and reasonable belief which would normally suffice. In *Stephen v Riverside Health Authority*[187] Auld J held that even a deep-rooted suspicion on the part of the claimant that an incompetently conducted X-ray had caused her symptoms did not amount to knowledge, when she had been assured by several highly qualified doctors that the dose of radiation she had received was not high and could not have caused her symptoms. It was not until she was informed by a medical expert that the symptoms were indicative of a radiation dosage high enough to increase the risk of cancer that the claimant acquired knowledge, notwithstanding that a protective claim form had been issued some eight years before. However, it would seem that, following the majority ruling in *AB v Ministry of Defence*, by issuing the protective claim form the claimant in *Stephen* would now be deemed to have had sufficient knowledge at that point in time.

The significance of consulting a lawyer The third *Spargo* principle[188]   **11–064**
(namely that claimants have the requisite knowledge when they know enough to make it reasonable for them to begin to investigate whether or not they have a case against the defendant) appears to treat any claimant who goes to a solicitor as having the requisite degree of knowledge. What, though, if the claimant is simply unsure, and is seeking advice/information? It cannot be suggested that simply by going to a solicitor the claimant necessarily has knowledge of all the relevant *facts*, e.g. as to the identity of the defendant. In *Sniezek v Bundy (Letchworth) Ltd*[189] the Court of Appeal said that there was nothing in the Limitation Act to suggest that any special consequences must or should be deemed to arise from the claimant seeking legal advice. The question remains the individual's state of knowledge of the relevant facts, rather than his lawyer's opinion about the prospects of success in legal proceedings. Applying the third *Spargo* principle, there was a distinction to be drawn between claimants who have a firm belief that they have a significant injury attributable to their working conditions (especially a belief that takes them to a solicitor for advice about a claim), a belief that they retain whatever contrary advice they receive, and claimants who believes that they may have, or even probably have, a significant injury which is attributable to their working conditions, but are not sure and feel it necessary to have expert advice on those questions. The former has knowledge of significant injury and attribution for the purposes of s.14, but the latter does not.[190] Once time starts to run, it is not postponed even if claimants sensibly think, on the basis of legal and/or medical advice, that they should not proceed to litigation.[191]

---

[187] [1990] 1 Med. L.R. 261.
[188] See para.11–059.
[189] [2000] P.I.Q.R. P213.
[190] See also *Secretary of State for Trade and Industry v Mackie* [2007] EWCA Civ 642 where the claimant was adjudged to have known he had a significant injury (industrial deafness) following a hearing test, notwithstanding that he had received negative advice from a union official as to the prospects of a claim. By contrast see *Kew v Bettamix Ltd* [2006] EWCA Civ 1535; [2007] P.I.Q.R. P16 where the claimant was adjudged not to have knowledge until he was told by a doctor that his working conditions, as opposed to old age, might account for his symptoms. cf. *Cartledge v Jopling* [1963] A.C. 758 and see *Ali v Courtaulds Textiles Ltd* (1999) 52 B.M.L.R. 129, CA, para.11–067.
[191] *Sniezek v Bundy (Letchworth) Ltd* [2000] P.I.Q.R. P213 at 230, per Judge LJ.

11–065   In *AB v Ministry of Defence*[192] Lord Wilson pointed out that where the claimant's belief was held "with sufficient confidence to justify embarking on the preliminaries to the issue of a writ" such as to amount to knowledge for the purpose of s.14 it is likely that the claimant will have conducted an investigation with the assistance of lawyers, and this may include a search for evidence, including the evidence of experts. But the focus has to be on "the moment when it is reasonable for the claimant to embark on such an investigation". It is possible for claimants to approach a lawyer before their belief is held with sufficient confidence and carries sufficient substance to make it reasonable for them to do so, and so consulting a lawyer does not *automatically* mean that claimants have acquired the relevant knowledge, though "such an inference may well be justified".[193] There is a distinction between claimants' beliefs, held with sufficient confidence to justify embarking on the preliminaries to the issue of the claim (which therefore constitutes "knowledge") and the assembly by the claimant and their legal team, with the help of experts, of the evidence justifying the commencement of proceedings with a reasonable prospect of success.[194]

11–066   **The significance of consulting an expert**   In *O'Driscoll v Dudley Health Authority*[195] Stuart-Smith LJ said that the fourth *Spargo* principle[196]

> "…must be read as postulating a situation antithetical to that covered by the third principle; i.e. the fourth principle postulates a state of mind short of a firm belief which takes a potential claimant to a solicitor."

The reference in principle (4) to "the need to check with an expert" was a reference to the need for an expert's opinion before even the claimant can be said to know that the attributability of her condition to a particular "act or omission" was a real possibility:

> "That is not the same investigation as is referred to in the first limb of principle three; this latter is an investigation into whether the plaintiff 'has a case against the defendant'—what Brooke LJ later in his judgment called 'enquiry whether the identified injury was indeed probably caused by the identified omission and whether the omission (identified initially in broad terms) amounted to actionable negligence'—an investigation which must be carried out whilst the limitation clock is ticking."[197]

---

[192] [2012] UKSC 9; [2013] 1 A.C. 78 at [12].

[193] [2012] UKSC 9; [2013] 1 A.C. 78 at [12]. See also per Lord Walker at [54]–[55].

[194] [2012] UKSC 9; [2013] 1 A.C. 78 at [58] per Lord Walker. Though as Lord Walker acknowledged there can be real difficulty in the practical application of the distinction between knowledge of the "essence" of a claim and the evidence necessary to prove it to the requisite legal standard. But, as Lord Wilson observed at [25]: "once the requisite knowledge has arisen, the difficulty of actually establishing the claim confers no right thereunder to a further, open-ended, extension of the time within which the action must be brought."

[195] [1998] Lloyd's Rep. Med. 210 at 221. See also *Roberts v Winbow* [1999] P.I.Q.R. P77; [1999] Lloyd's Rep. Med. 31, CA, for discussion of the distinction between Brooke LJ's principles (3) and (4).

[196] See para.11–059.

[197] [1998] Lloyd's Rep. Med. 210 at 221–222.

Thus, consulting an expert is also not necessarily conclusive that the claimant has the relevant knowledge. For example, in *Ali v Courtaulds Textiles Ltd*[198] the question was whether the claimant knew that deafness in a man in his 60s was caused by the ageing process or by noise at work. The claimant knew he was deaf. He knew that exposure to noise could cause deafness. He also knew that the ageing process could cause deafness. But, said the Court of Appeal, he could not know whether his deafness had been caused by ageing or noise until he received an expert's report to that effect. The judge had held that the mere fact that he sought that advice by going to a solicitor fixed him with constructive knowledge. That conclusion flew in the face of the proviso to s.14(3).[199] Knowledge as to whether his deafness was noise-induced or age-induced was ascertainable only with the help of expert medical advice, and he had taken all reasonable steps to obtain that advice once he became aware that his deafness could be noise-induced. Thus, the case fell within the third category of principle 4 of Brooke LJ's categories in *Spargo*, i.e. he thought that his condition was capable of being attributed to the act or omission alleged to constitute negligence, but he was not sure about this, and needed to check it with an expert before he could properly be said to know that it was.

11–067

In *AB v Ministry of Defence*[200] Lord Wilson accepted that consulting an expert is not a conclusive indication that the claimant had the relevant knowledge. The court should have regard to the confidence with which the claimant held the belief and the substance which it carried, before consulting the expert, the reasons which induced the claimant to consult the expert, and, if the conclusion is that at that prior stage the claimant lacked belief of the requisite character, the effect on the claimant's belief of receipt of the expert's report.

11–068

Changes in the claimant's beliefs   The distinction between "belief" and "knowledge" may be particularly difficult to draw in the case of claimants who initially have a firm belief that their injuries are due to the default of the defendant, but on making appropriate inquiries are informed by expert opinion that they are mistaken. If, subsequently, their initial beliefs are confirmed by further expert opinion, at what point did they acquire "knowledge", thereby setting the limitation period running? In *Davis v Ministry of Defence*[201] the Court of Appeal held that the claimant's strong belief that his dermatitis had been caused by his working conditions and that he had a good claim for damages against the defendants did not amount to "knowledge" where his medical and legal advisers took a different view of the cause of the dermatitis, namely that it was constitutional. The claimant accepted this advice until, following a subsequent severe attack of dermatitis, he received different expert advice that it was indeed attributable to his working conditions. May LJ said that the words "act or omission which is alleged to constitute negligence, nuisance or breach of duty" of s.14(1)(b) could be compendiously described as the defendants' failure

11–069

---

[198] [1999] Lloyd's Rep. Med. 301, CA. See also *Harrild v Ministry of Defence* [2001] Lloyd's Rep. Med. 117, QBD.
[199] Which deals with constructive knowledge. See para.11–105.
[200] [2012] UKSC 9; [2013] 1 A.C. 78 at [13].
[201] *The Times*, 7 August 1985.

to provide the claimant with *safe* working conditions. Thus, the question that had to be asked was when did the claimant first know that his dermatitis was attributable in whole or in part to his employers' failure to provide safe working conditions? On the facts, he did not acquire knowledge until he received expert advice which confirmed his suspicions.

11–070 Commenting on *Davis* in *Nash v Eli Lilly & Co.*,[202] however, the Court of Appeal said that:

> "The decision does, however, appear to regard as arguable the contention that, if a claimant is shown to have had knowledge, as we understand the meaning of that word in this context, that his injury is attributable to the act or omission of the defendant, the subsequent obtaining of expert advice for the purpose of legal proceedings which says that the injury is not so attributable, could retrospectively cause him never to have had such knowledge. We do not accept that that contention is arguable. It seems to us to be in conflict with the words of the statute."

On the other hand, the Court explained:

> "... whether a claimant has knowledge depends both upon the information he has received and upon what he makes of it.[203] If it appears that a claimant, while believing that his injury is attributable to the act or omission of the defendant, realises that his belief requires expert confirmation before he acquires such a degree of certainty of belief as amounts to knowledge, then he will not have knowledge until that confirmation is obtained."[204]

In other words, if claimants have acquired "knowledge" they cannot subsequently lose it simply because they receive expert advice which tends to undermine their belief. But claimants' state of mind may not be such as to be categorised as "knowledge", even where they hold a strong belief that their injuries are attributable to the defendant's breach of duty. Everything would seem to hang upon the degree of conviction with which claimants hold their belief, and whether they appreciate that they required expert confirmation. It seems likely that where claimants have a strong belief, issue proceedings against the defendant and then receive negative expert advice leading them to discontinue the action, that initial belief will be treated as knowledge for the purpose of s.14. They could not claim that they only acquired knowledge on receipt of further expert advice confirming their original belief.[205] This view is consistent with the majority decision in *AB v*

---

[202] [1993] 1 W.L.R. 782 at 795, CA.

[203] In *AB v Ministry of Defence* [2012] UKSC 9; [2013] 1 A.C. 78 at [47] Lord Walker commented that this statement "can no longer be accepted, at any rate without a lot of qualification" because the claimant's date of knowledge should be "ascertained in the same way for all claimants, without regard to their personal characteristics". On the other hand, the majority decision in *AB v Ministry of Defence* relates claimants' knowledge to the firmness with which they hold their belief and the substance attached to that belief. If claimants' characteristics are irrelevant to the state of their "knowledge" then s.14(1) would apply an entirely objective standard, and in that case it would be difficult to see the need for s.14(3) which sets out the requirements for constructive knowledge.

[204] [1993] 1 W.L.R. 782 at 795.

[205] On this approach, *Davis v Ministry of Defence*, where a protective a claim form had been issued, would appear to have been wrongly decided. In *Sniezek v Bundy (Letchworth) Ltd* [2000] P.I.Q.R. P213 at 219, CA, Bell J said that *Davis* had not survived *Nash*, and in *AB v Ministry of Defence* the majority judgments were critical of *Davis*. Lord Walker said that he found the judgment of May LJ in *Davis* "quite puzzling".

Ministry of Defence that it is a legal impossibility for claimants to lack knowledge of attributability for the purpose of s.14(1) at a time after the date of issue of their claim.[206]

Claimant was "barking up the wrong tree"   In *Spargo v North Essex District Health Authority v Spargo*[207] one of the circumstances falling within Brooke LJ's fourth principle was that a claimant: **11–071**

> "...will not have the requisite knowledge if she thinks she knows the acts or omissions she should investigate but in fact is barking up the wrong tree."

Section 14(1)(b) requires that the claimant have knowledge:

> "...that the injury was attributable in whole or in part to the act or omission which is alleged to constitute negligence, nuisance or breach of duty."

In some cases claimants may have a firm belief, even a conviction, that their injuries were caused in a particular way, but it subsequently turns out that they were mistaken and their injuries were caused by some other "act or omission" of the defendant. In these circumstances they were "barking up the wrong tree" and on the wording of s.14(1)(b) do not have the required knowledge until they discover their mistake, notwithstanding the possibility that a claim form has already been issued.[208]

In *Martin v Kaisary (No.2)*[209] Hodge J held that the claimant was barking up the wrong tree because he initially thought that post-operative complications were associated with the use of the drug heparin. It was not until he received a report in 2003 that his cardiac arrest was due to haemorrhaging from the operation site that he realised he should have been investigating a possible claim against the hospital in addition to a claim against the surgeon. Similarly, in *Harrison v Isle of Wight NHS Primary Care Trust*[210] a patient underwent unsuccessful surgery to relieve pain in her right shoulder. Her solicitors sent a letter of claim to the Trust alleging that her ongoing symptoms were due to an excessive excision of bone from her right clavicle and acromion. It was subsequently discovered that her symptoms   **11–072**

---

[206] [2012] UKSC 9; [2013] 1 A.C. 78 at [3] per Lord Wilson.
[207] [1997] P.I.Q.R. P235 at 242; [1997] 8 Med. L.R. 125 at 129–130. The phrase was originally used in the limitation context by Hoffmann LJ in *Broadley v Guy Clapham & Co.* [1994] 4 All E.R. 439.
[208] *Rowbottom v Royal Masonic Hospital* [2002] EWCA Civ 87; [2002] Lloyd's Rep. Med. 173; [2003] P.I.Q.R. P1, where the claimant believed that complications arising from a wound infection following surgery for a hip replacement, leading eventually to amputation of his leg, were due to the failure of a drain inserted into his leg. He believed that he had been given prophylactic antibiotics. He did not acquire knowledge that he had not been given prophylactic antibiotics until he received confirmation from a medical expert that it was reasonable to assume that if there was no record of antibiotics having been given then he probably had not received any. See also *Driscoll-Varley v Parkside Health Authority* [1991] 2 Med. L.R. 346, and the comments of Hoffmann LJ on this case in *Broadley v Guy Clapham & Co.* [1994] 4 All E.R. 439 at 449, para.11–088; *Khan v Ainslie* [1993] 4 Med. L.R. 319; *North Essex District Health Authority v Spargo* [1997] P.I.Q.R. P235; [1997] 8 Med. L.R. 125 at 130 per Brooke LJ; *Baig v City & Hackney Health Authority* [1994] 5 Med. L.R. 221 at 224; para.11–099.
[209] [2005] EWHC 531 (QB).
[210] [2013] EWHC 442 (QB); [2013] Med. L.R. 334.

were due to the deltoid muscle having become detached from the acromion during the surgery. Judge McKenna held that the essence of the claim was the detachment of the deltoid muscle, not the removal of an excessive amount of bone, and in making the initial allegation the claimant had been barking up the wrong tree.[211] On the other hand, in *Rayner v Wolferstans (A Firm)*[212] Wilkie J held that a patient who suffered pain immediately on being given an epidural injection had a broad knowledge of the essence of the causally relevant act or omission to which the injury was attributable. She had a firm belief that her injuries had been caused by something that had gone wrong in the administration of the epidural, and it was irrelevant that she did not know the precise mechanism by which the injury occurred or the precise form of negligence which it was later alleged must have caused the injury.[213] It would seem that whether the court accepts that the claimant had been barking up the wrong tree will depend on the degree of particularity that is attributed to the defendant's "act or omission". For example, it should not be sufficient in a medical negligence context for the claimant simply to believe that the damage was "due to the operation". Section 14 requires more a precise identification of the act or omission in question.

11–073   **Section 14(1)(a)—knowledge that the injury was significant**   Section 14(1)(a) of the Limitation Act 1980 requires that the claimant had knowledge of the fact that the injury in question was "significant", and s.14(2) provides that an injury is significant if the person whose date of knowledge is in question would reasonably have considered it sufficiently serious to justify his instituting proceedings for damages against a defendant who did not dispute liability and was able to satisfy a judgment. At one time, this was considered to be a combined subjective/objective test,[214] and so it was a question of what a reasonable person of the claimant's age, with the same background, intelligence and disabilities would reasonably have known.[215]

11–074   However, this partly objective and partly subjective test was rejected by the Court of Appeal in *McCoubrey v Ministry of Defence*[216] and by the House of Lords in *A v Hoare*.[217] In *McCoubrey* Neuberger LJ said:

---

[211] "I do not accept, on the facts of this case, that the fact that the claimant had instructed solicitors, that they had sent a letter of claim or indeed that they had entered into correspondence about extensions to the limitation period demonstrates that the claimant had acquired the necessary knowledge for the purposes of s.11 since throughout the period in question the claimant and her advisers were pursuing a line of enquiry which proved abortive, that is to say they were barking up the wrong tree": [2013] EWHC 442 (QB); [2013] Med. L.R. 334 at [51].

[212] [2015] EWHC 2957 (QB).

[213] Wilkie J, [2015] EWHC 2957 (QB) at [114], distinguished *Harrison v Isle of Wight NHS Primary Care Trust* on the basis that in *Harrison* there was "there was a lack of certainty on the part of the claimant from the outset. The cause of the injury from which the claimant suffered was substantially different from that which had previously been considered at the earlier stage of the investigation".

[214] "Taking *that* plaintiff, with *that* plaintiff's intelligence, would he have been reasonable in considering the injury not sufficiently serious to justify instituting proceedings for damages?" per Geoffrey Lane LJ in *McCafferty v Metropolitan Police District Receiver* [1977] 1 W.L.R. 1073 at 1081.

[215] *Davis v City and Hackney Health Authority* [1991] 2 Med. L.R. 366.

[216] [2007] EWCA Civ 17; [2007] 1 W.L.R. 1544.

[217] [2008] UKHL 6; [2008] 1 A.C. 844.

"...the question of whether an injury is 'significant' within section 14(1)(a), as expanded in section 14(2), must be decided by reference to the seriousness of the injury, and not by reference to its effect, let alone its subjectively perceived effect, on the claimant's private life or career."[218]

Thus, the proper approach to the question raised by s.14(2) was to consider, on the hypothesis stated in the subsection:

"...the reaction to the injury (as opposed to its possible consequences) of a reasonable person in the objective circumstances of the actual claimant, while disregarding his actual personal attributes, such as intelligence aspirations aggressiveness and the like."[219]

In *A v Hoare*[220] their Lordships held that in light of the decision of the House of Lords in *Adams v Bracknell Forest Borough Council*[221] that the test for constructive knowledge in s.14(3) of the Limitation Act 1980 is objective, the same approach should be taken to s.14(2) in relation to whether claimants knew that they had suffered significant injury. Lord Hoffmann stated that the test as to the significance of an injury is: **11–075**

"...external to the claimant and involves no inquiry into what he ought reasonably to have done. It is applied to what the claimant knew or was deemed to have known but the standard itself is impersonal. The effect of the claimant's injuries upon what he could reasonably have been expected to do is therefore irrelevant."[222]

The claimant is therefore assumed to be a reasonable person who has suffered injury and the question whether the injury is "significant" or not is to be considered objectively without considering the claimant's own character and intelligence.[223]

Test for significance of psychological harm   It had previously been suggested   **11–076**
that where there was some difficulty in determining when a claimant first knew that an injury was significant, because the injury consisted of psychological damage and the claimant had put the relevant events to the back of the mind, or tried to block or suppress the events, this should be taken into account.[224] In *A v*

---

[218] [2007] EWCA Civ 17; [2007] 1 W.L.R. 1544 at [39].
[219] [2007] EWCA Civ 17; [2007] 1 W.L.R. 1544 at [52]. His Lordship disapproved, at [38], the combined subjective/objective approach of Geoffrey Lane LJ in *McCafferty*.
[220] [2008] UKHL 6; [2008] 1 A.C. 844.
[221] [2004] UKHL 29; [2005] 1 A.C. 76; and see para.11–110.
[222] [2008] UKHL 6; [2008] 1 A.C. 844 at [39].
[223] "You ask what the claimant knew about the injury he had suffered, you add any knowledge he had about the injury which may be imputed to him under s.14(3) and you then ask whether a reasonable person with that knowledge would have considered the injury sufficiently serious to justify his instituting proceedings for damages against the defendant who did not dispute liability and was able to satisfy a judgment..." per Lord Hoffmann, [2008] UKHL 6; [2008] 1 A.C. 844 at [34]. But this approach does not require the court to attribute to claimants knowledge of facts that they did not actually possess: *Field v British Coal Corporation* [2008] EWCA Civ 912 (applying *Hoare* to a claim for industrial deafness).
[224] *KR v Bryn Alyn Community (Holdings) Ltd (In Liquidation)* [2003] EWCA Civ 85; [2003] Q.B. 1441; and also *Young v Catholic Care (Diocese of Leeds)*, one of the six composite cases considered by the House of Lords in *A v Hoare*, where the claimant's evidence was that he had put his memories "in a box with a tightly sealed lid".

Hoare Lord Hoffmann noted that the fact that the claimant may have been in denial was something that might be of interest to a psychologist but was not relevant to s.14(2) which "assumes a practical and relatively unsophisticated approach to the question of knowledge".[225] The claimant's subjective reasons and beliefs may, however, be relevant to the court's exercise of discretion under s.33.

11-077   The Court of Appeal applied *A v Hoare* in *Albonetti v Wirral MBC*,[226] another case involving historic sexual abuse, concluding that the "injury in question" for the purposes of s.14 must be the injury which the claimant knew about at the material time. In other words, the immediate effect of the abuse, namely the pain, distress and humiliation which the claimant experienced at the time. People who had been severely sexually abused must know that they had suffered not only a grave wrong but also a significant injury. Whilst claimants may not know themselves whether or not it is worth bringing an action, they would at least know enough to make it reasonable to expect them to consult a solicitor. Had they done so, they would have discovered that substantial damages could be awarded for such abuse.

11-078   **Initial injury seems trivial**   Where an injury initially appears to be trivial but subsequently turns out to be serious, time does not run until the claimant knows that the injury is in fact serious. However, s.14(2) appears to make most injuries significant in monetary terms, since it may not take much to justify instituting proceedings against a solvent defendant who admits liability. Thus, where the injury, though minor, is sufficiently serious to institute proceedings, and the claimant subsequently discovers a far more serious injury caused by the same accident, time will run from the date of the first injury known to be significant. An action in respect of the second injury commenced more than three years after knowledge of the first injury will be barred,[227] though the claimant's appreciation of the seriousness of an injury may well depend upon the medical advice received.[228]

---

[225] [2008] UKHL 6; [2008] 1 A.C. 844 at [43].

[226] [2008] EWCA Civ 783. See also *B v Nugent Care Society* [2008] EWCA Civ 795; *JL v Bowen* [2017] EWCA Civ 82; [2017] P.I.Q.R. P11.

[227] *Bristow v Grout, The Times*, 3 November 1986; *Roberts v Winbow* [1999] P.I.Q.R. P77; [1999] Lloyd's Rep. Med. 31, CA; see also *Miller v London Electrical Manufacturing Co. Ltd* [1976] 2 Lloyd's Rep. 284 at 287, and the comments of Butler-Sloss LJ on *Miller* in *Harding v Peoples' Dispensary for Sick Animals* [1994] P.I.Q.R. P270 at 273.

[228] In *Harding v Peoples' Dispensary for Sick Animals* [1994] P.I.Q.R. P270 the claimant sustained a back injury in 1988 which resulted in her being off work for seven weeks. The Court of Appeal held that she did not acquire knowledge that the injury was significant until 1990 when it became apparent that the injury was considerably more serious than had initially been appreciated. She had undergone an inconclusive X-ray, and her general practitioner did not suggest that there were any serious symptoms. She was led to the view that the injury would resolve itself in due course, and thus was entitled to view her injury as not being significant, even though it was painful, "because the issue was whether it was of sufficient significance to institute proceedings, not whether it was of discomfort or pain to her in circumstances in which it would not occur to any reasonable person to bring proceedings". See also *Sir Robert Lloyd & Co Ltd v Hoey* [2011] EWCA Civ 1060—claimant unaware that chest pain and breathlessness suffered in 1985, symptoms which had fully resolved by January 1986, were caused by diffuse pleural thickening following exposure to asbestos, and so was unaware of any injury or disability which might cause a reasonable person to issue proceedings until 2008 when he received a medical report.

Risk of future deterioration   At one time it was arguable that where the initial   **11–079**
injury was not significant but there was a medically recognised risk of
deterioration in the future, knowledge of the risk was enough to start time
running, provided the risk itself was sufficiently serious.[229] This argument is no
longer tenable in light of the decision of the House of Lords in *Rothwell v
Chemical & Insulating Co Ltd*[230] that symptomless minor physiological changes
to the body do not constitute actionable damage, and that knowledge that such
changes create a risk of significant damage developing in the future is not
sufficient to constitute actionable damage either.[231]

Exacerbation of existing injury   Where an existing injury or disability has   **11–080**
allegedly been exacerbated by the defendant's negligence, the relevant
knowledge for the purpose of s.14 is claimant's knowledge of the exacerbation,
not knowledge of the original injury.[232]

Side effects of prescribed medication   In *Nash v Eli Lilly & Co*.[233] the   **11–081**
claimants alleged that they had suffered side effects from the use of the
prescription drug Opren. Since many drugs carry a risk of unwanted side effects
which a patient may be prepared to tolerate, given the benefits that the drug
confers in treating the ailment, the issue arose as to the point at which it could be
said that they had suffered "significant injury". The Court of Appeal accepted that
there was a valid distinction between an expected, or accepted, side effect, which
would not constitute "significant injury", and an injurious or unacceptable
consequence. Time would not begin to run until the claimants had knowledge that
the side effects were injurious or unacceptable. However, in *Briggs v Pitt-Payne
& Lias*[234] the Court of Appeal held that the question of balancing side effects
against the overall beneficial effects of a drug was "simply not relevant" to the
question of whether the claimant is aware that he is suffering from "significant
injury".

Section 14(1)(b)—knowledge of causation[235]   Section 14(1)(b) of the Act   **11–082**
provides that the claimant must have knowledge that the injury was attributable
in whole or in part to the "act or omission which is alleged to constitute

---

[229] Symptomless, minor physiological damage has in the past been held to be actionable, particularly
where it carried a slight risk of future damage, and/or gave rise to anxiety in the claimant: *Church v
Ministry of Defence* (1984) 134 N.L.J. 623; *Sykes v Ministry of Defence, The Times*, 23 March 1984.
[230] [2007] UKHL 39; [2008] 1 A.C. 281; para.12–001, n.1.
[231] So in *Preston v BBH Solicitors* [2011] EWCA Civ 1429 it was held that a claimant who knows
that he has developed pleural plaques in the lungs and is aware of the *possibility* that he may have
asbestosis does not have knowledge that he has a significant injury until he receives a diagnosis of
asbestosis, since pleural plaques do not constitute actionable injury, applying *Rothwell v Chemical &
Insulating Co Ltd* [2007] UKHL 39; [2008] 1 A.C. 281.
[232] *McManus v Mannings Maine Ltd* [2001] EWCA Civ 1668.
[233] [1993] 1 W.L.R. 782, CA.
[234] [1999] Lloyd's Rep. Med. 1.
[235] Note that most of the cases which consider the meaning of "knowledge" for the purpose of s.14(1)
are concerned with the claimant's knowledge of causation. See paras 11–056 to 11–072 above. See in
particular the discussion of *AB v Ministry of Defence* [2012] UKSC 9; [2013] 1 A.C. 78.

negligence". This refers to the claimant's knowledge of *factual* causation.[236] The claimant's ignorance of causation in law is irrelevant.[237] Once claimants have the broad knowledge that injuries are attributable to the defendant's acts or omissions they have sufficient knowledge for the purpose of s.14(1)(b), even if they do not know the specific acts or omissions and are not in a position to draft a fully particularised statement of claim.[238] Moreover, claimants will be taken to know that their injuries were "attributable" to the defendant's act or omission if they knew that it was "capable of being so attributed".[239]

11–083　　In *North Essex District Health Authority v Spargo*[240] Brooke LJ said that:

> "The test is a subjective one: what did the plaintiff herself know? It is not an objective one: what would have been the reasonable layman's state of mind in the absence of expert confirmation?"

This must still be the case, given that s.14(1) is concerned with the claimant's *actual* knowledge, and the question of what an objective, reasonable claimant ought to have known is dealt with as a matter of constructive knowledge in s.14(3). The issue is what will be accepted as evidence of the claimant's actual state of mind. A strong, but irrational, belief in a causal connection does not amount to "knowledge", even after the decision of the Supreme Court in *AB v Ministry of Defence*,[241] but a reasonable belief, i.e. a belief based on some objective criteria, probably does constitute "knowledge", even if that belief requires confirmation by an expert. Mere "suspicion" of a causal link, however, does not constitute knowledge. Nor does the strength of the claimant's belief, in itself, constitute evidence that the claimant had knowledge, because that belief may have been mistaken.[242] If the claimant has taken the step of issuing proceedings *AB v Ministry of Defence* indicates that the claimant must have had knowledge at the latest when proceedings were issued. But even this proposition must be subject to the caveat that where the claimant has issued proceedings on the mistaken basis that it was the defendant's act, X, that caused the damage

---

[236] *Dobbie v Medway Health Authority* [1994] 1 W.L.R. 1234 at 1247, per Steyn LJ. See, e.g. *Marston v British Railways Board* [1976] I.C.R. 124.

[237] Limitation Act 1980 s.14(1) specifically provides that: "...knowledge that any acts or omissions did or did not as a matter of law involve negligence ... is irrelevant."

[238] *Wilkinson v Ancliff (BLT) Ltd* [1986] 1 W.L.R. 1352 at 1365, CA; *Hayward v Sharrard* (1998) 56 B.M.L.R. 155 at 165, CA. See, however, the cases where the claimant was "barking up the wrong tree", para.11–071 above.

[239] [1986] 1 W.L.R. 1352 at 1365, CA. "Capable of being so attributed" means attributable as a real, not a fanciful, possibility, but it does not have to be a *probable* cause of the injury. "One is dealing here with knowledge, actual or imputed, and not with proof of liability": *Guidera v NEI Projects (India)* unreported 30 January 1990, CA, per Sir David Croom-Johnson. "To 'attribute' means 'to reckon as a consequence of'": *Halford v Brookes* [1991] 1 W.L.R. 428 at 443, per Lord Donaldson MR.

[240] [1997] P.I.Q.R. P235; [1997] 8 Med. L.R. 125 at 131.

[241] [2012] UKSC 9; [2013] 1 A.C. 78; see paras 11–060–11–062.

[242] As where the claimant was "barking up the wrong tree": see para.11–071.

when in reality it was the defendant's act, Y, that caused the damage it is at least arguable that the claimant did not have the relevant knowledge when the first proceedings were issued.[243]

Knowledge of causation in the context of medical treatment There has been   **11–084**
some difficulty in identifying precisely what patients must know about their medical treatment for the purpose of s.14(1)(b). Can it be said that claimants' knowledge that an injury was attributable to "medical treatment" is knowledge in "broad terms",[244] that it was attributable to an act or omission which is alleged to constitute negligence in circumstances where they cannot identify, let alone particularise, the relevant acts or omissions? It is strongly arguable that knowledge that an injury was caused by, say, an operation is not necessarily knowledge for the purpose of s.14, given that injury following an operation may arise without negligence as an unavoidable complication of the procedure, or the operation may simply have been unsuccessful in preventing claimants' medical conditions from deteriorating as a consequence of the original disease or injury which was being treated.[245] Moreover, most people would not regard *successful* medical treatment as constituting an *injury*, so that if patients are informed that surgery was successful they would not even consider that they had been injured, let alone address their mind to the question of which acts or omissions had caused the "injury". Thus, the minimum knowledge that a claimant would require is knowledge that "something has gone wrong" with the treatment in order to distinguish those injuries which were unavoidable consequences of the procedure and those which are attributable to the "act or omission which is alleged to constitute negligence". This, indeed, has been the approach taken in a number of cases.

In *Bentley v Bristol and Weston Health Authority*[246] Hirst J held that a claimant's   **11–085**
knowledge that an injury which she had suffered was attributable in whole or in part to an operation did not arise until she became aware of some act or omission which could have affected the safety of the operation. Broad knowledge that the injury was caused by the operation per se did not set the limitation period running, since the operation is not the act or omission which is itself alleged to constitute negligence. The crucial issue was knowledge of the act or omission alleged to constitute negligence, namely some conduct or failure which could affect the safety of the operation:

---

[243] Again, on the basis that the claimant was "barking up the wrong tree". In *Whitfield v North Durham Health Authority* [1995] 6 Med. L.R. 32 at 37 the Court of Appeal held that it was wrong to treat the issue of a protective claim form as determinative, by itself, of the question of knowledge under s.14. In *AB v Ministry of Defence* [2012] UKSC 9; [2013] 1 A.C. 78 at [84] Lord Mance noted that, though it was unnecessary to decide the point, the position may be different from that in *AB*: "if the claimant has issued proceedings which he is no longer pursuing and in relation to which no limitation issue can therefore arise (as was the case in *Whitfield v North Durham Health Authority* [1995] 6 Med. L.R. 32)."

[244] Applying *Wilkinson v Ancliff (BLT) Ltd* [1986] 1 W.L.R. 1352 at 1365, CA.

[245] See, e.g. *Harrington v Essex Area Health Authority*, *The Times*, 14 November 1984, where it was held that knowledge by the claimant that he had contracted an infection in the operating theatre, was not knowledge that the infection was attributable to an act or omission constituting negligence, since an infection can be contracted without negligence on the part of anyone.

[246] [1991] 2 Med. L.R. 359.

"... the performance of a surgical operation (*i.e.* an act invasive to the plaintiff's body to which the plaintiff has consented) is not the act or omission which is itself alleged to constitute negligence. The act or omission which *is* alleged to constitute negligence in operation cases is some conduct or failure which can affect the safety of the operation. Knowledge of such act or omission will frequently depend on information derived by the plaintiff from expert opinion ..."[247]

11–086   In *Nash v Eli Lilly & Co.*[248] Hidden J adopted the approach of Hirst J in *Bentley v Bristol and Weston Health Authority*, commenting that there must be a degree of specificity, not a mere global or catch-all character about the act or omission which is alleged to constitute negligence. Attributing the injury to vague and generalised conduct such as "the operation at the hospital" was not enough. The claimant must know some specific fact in relation to the conduct of the operation. Moreover, the fact of which the claimant must have knowledge is the fact which is the basis of the allegation of negligence upon which the action is founded. That did not mean, however, that the claimant must have knowledge of every act or omission set out in the statement of claim, which in *Nash* amounted to 60 pages of pleadings. The crucial issue in that case, which dealt with a number of late claims in the Opren litigation, was the definition of the relevant acts or omissions of the defendants. Hidden J held that these consisted of exposing the claimants to a drug which was unsafe in that it was capable of causing persistent photosensitivity and/or in failing to take reasonable steps to protect the claimants from such a condition. The Court of Appeal accepted that this was the appropriate degree of "specificity" with which the defendants' act or omission must be identifiable by the claimant:

"It was not, in our judgment, the intention of Parliament to require for the purposes of section 11 and section 14 of the Act proof of knowledge of the terms in which it will be alleged that the act or omission of the defendants constituted negligence or breach of duty. What is required is knowledge of the essence of the act or omission to which the injury is attributable."[249]

---

[247] [1991] 2 Med. L.R. 359 at 364 (original emphasis); cf. *Hendy v Milton Keynes Health Authority* [1992] 3 Med. L.R. 114; [1992] P.I.Q.R. 281 where Blofeld J concluded that, while a claimant's date of knowledge that an injury was attributable in whole or in part to an operation could well have depended on the date when she had received an expert's report, in a less complicated case the date of knowledge arose when she appreciated in general terms that her problems were attributable to the operation, even if the precise terms of what had gone wrong were not known.

[248] [1991] 2 Med. L.R. 169. See also *Driscoll-Varley v Parkside Health Authority* [1991] 2 Med. L.R. 346 where Hidden J held that the test to be applied in s.14(1)(b) was not "was there some negligence in the treatment at St. Mary's Hospital which cannot be properly identified but which must have happened?" The Act refers to knowledge that the injury was attributable to "the act or omission which is alleged to constitute negligence" and thus the relevant knowledge was of an act or omission alleged in the claimant's statement of claim to constitute negligence, namely premature mobilisation following a fractured leg. An awareness that the leg was not healing properly and a belief that this was attributable to post-operative care was not "knowledge".

[249] *Nash v Eli Lilly & Co.* [1993] 1 W.L.R. 782 at 799, CA. See also *Whiston v London SHA* [2010] EWCA Civ 195; [2010] 1 W.L.R. 1582 at [28]–[30], where it was held that the claimant's knowledge that he was delivered by the use of forceps was not knowledge of the essence of his claim; the essence of the claim was that the obstetrician had persisted with the attempt to deliver the claimant by forceps for too long, had used the wrong type of forceps, and had delayed seeking assistance from a more experienced obstetrician. "These three elements of the claimant's case were not mere details of his case. They *were* his case stripped to its essentials", per Dyson LJ at [30].

In *Broadley v Guy Clapham & Co.*,[250] however, the Court of Appeal held that the **11–087** approach adopted by Hirst J in *Bentley* was inconsistent with the proviso to s.14(1)(b) that:

> "...knowledge that any acts or omissions did or did not, as a matter of law, involve negligence ... or breach of duty is irrelevant."[251]

Bentley required knowledge on the claimant's part of all matters necessary to establish negligence or breach of duty, and this was too high a test. The claimant in *Broadley* underwent an operation to remove a foreign body from her knee and for at least seven months after the operation she needed two sticks in order to walk. It was held that by then she must have considered that something was significantly wrong and that she was suffering from something other than a direct and inevitable consequence of the operation. She had constructive knowledge of a potential cause of action because a reasonable person in her position would have sought further medical assistance or made further enquiries of the doctor. The claimant argued that she did not have knowledge until she knew of:

> "...some act or omission which could adversely affect the safety of the operation or proper recovery from the operation, such as unreasonable interference with the nerve or failure reasonably to safeguard it from damage, or failure properly to investigate and/or repair the nerve lesion in time."

In response to this Leggatt LJ commented that:

> "The use of the words 'unreasonable', 'reasonably' and 'properly' would only be justified if section 14(1)(b) required knowledge that the injury was attributable to negligence. It is plain from the concluding words of section 14(1) that 'knowledge that any acts or omissions did or did not, as a matter of law, involve negligence' is irrelevant. In my judgment the only function of the words 'which is alleged to constitute negligence ...' is to point to the relevant act or omission to which the injury was attributable."[252]

Accordingly, the decision in *Bentley* was wrong, since it required a too detailed **11–088** knowledge on the part of the claimant. Mrs Bentley knew that her injuries were attributable to damage caused in the sciatic nerve in the course of a hip replacement operation, and she knew soon afterwards that one way in which nerves can be damaged in the course of an operation is when they are retracted to keep them out of the way while the surgeon is working on the hip joint. What she did not know was that the retraction in her case might have been *excessive*. In holding that until then she did not have sufficient knowledge for the purposes of s.14(1) Hirst J was requiring knowledge that the surgeon had fallen short of some

---

[250] [1994] 4 All E.R. 439; [1993] 4 Med. L.R. 328, CA.
[251] See para.11–102.
[252] [1994] 4 All E.R. 439 at 447; [1993] 4 Med. L.R. 328 at 333. See also per Hoffmann LJ at 448 and 333 respectively: "...the words 'which is alleged to constitute negligence, nuisance or breach of duty' serve to *identify* the facts of which the plaintiff must have knowledge without implying that he should know that they constitute a breach of a rule, whether of law or some other code of behaviour. Section 14(1)(b) requires that one should look at the way the plaintiff puts his case, distil what he is complaining about and ask whether he had in broad terms knowledge of the facts on which that complaint is based."

standard of care, and this was not required by the Act.[253] *Driscoll-Varley v Parkside Health Authority*[254] was different, said Hoffmann LJ, because there the claimant was "barking up the wrong tree". The claimant thought that the complications from which she suffered had been caused by the way the operation on her leg had been done, and only later did she discover that the real cause was not the operation but the subsequent removal of her leg from traction.[255] Thus, *Driscoll-Varley* was concerned with identification of the act which caused the injury and not with appreciation of whether the act was capable of being attributable to negligence or fault.[256] Balcombe LJ referred to four heads under which the required knowledge for the purpose of s.14 could be considered:

> "(1) Broad knowledge. Carrying out the operation to her knee in such a way that something went wrong, namely that it caused foot drop (an injury to her foot) . . .
> (2) Specific knowledge. Carrying out the operation in such a way as to damage a nerve thereby causing foot drop (an injury to her foot) . . .
> (3) Qualitative knowledge. Carrying out the operation in such a way as unreasonably to cause injury to a nerve (unreasonably to expose a nerve to a risk of injury).
> (4) Detailed knowledge (which I take to be knowledge sufficiently detailed to enable the plaintiff's advisers to draft a statement of claim)."[257]

Qualitative or detailed knowledge went beyond the standard necessary for the purposes of s.14, said his Lordship.

11–089 In *Dobbie v Medway Health Authority*[258] the claimant issued a claim form in 1989 in respect of the removal of her breast during the course of a breast biopsy operation performed in 1973. Although the surgeon believed a lump in the breast to be malignant, subsequent pathological examination revealed that it was benign. The claimant was told by medical staff that the breast had been removed to be safe rather than sorry; that the hospital did not have facilities for testing breast lumps while the patient was under anaesthetic; and that she should be grateful that she did not have cancer. She subsequently suffered severe psychological problems attributable to the loss of her breast. It was argued that since the claimant had been told at the time that she had received the appropriate treatment, she did not know that she should not have had her breast removed until either she received an expert's report to this effect in 1990, or at the earliest in 1988 when she heard about a successful claim in a similar case. Otton J held that in 1973 the claimant had broad knowledge of sufficient facts to conclude that her breast had been unnecessarily removed, that something had gone wrong, and that this was attributable to the defendants' negligence and/or that her breast had been removed

---

[253] [1994] 4 All E.R. 439 at 449, per Hoffmann LJ.
[254] [1991] 2 Med. L.R. 346.
[255] In *AB v Ministry of Defence* [2012] UKSC 9; [2013] 1 A.C. 78 at [38] Lord Walker considered that *Driscoll-Varley v Parkside Health Authority* was: "a rather marginal example of barking up the wrong tree, since the plaintiff's misapprehension was in relation to the causative event in a single course of treatment, although the real complaint was about the after-care rather than the operation itself."
[256] See also *Khan v Ainslie* [1993] 4 Med. L.R. 319; *Baig v City and Hackney Health Authority* [1994] 5 Med. L.R. 221 at 224; para.11–099.
[257] [1994] 4 All E.R. 439 at 446–447; [1993] 4 Med. L.R. 328 at 332.
[258] [1994] 1 W.L.R. 1234, CA. Leave to appeal refused: [1994] 1 W.L.R. 1553.

without her consent.[259] She may not have had sufficient knowledge to enable counsel to draft a fully particularised statement of claim, but she knew that her injuries were capable of being attributable to what could compendiously be called the defendants' fault. This was sufficient knowledge to set time running against her in both negligence and trespass to the person. This decision was upheld by the Court of Appeal, except that Sir Thomas Bingham MR suggested that the judge had been wrong to refer to the breast being "unnecessarily" removed, to something going wrong and to the health authority's negligence. These matters were irrelevant under s.14. It could not plausibly be suggested that the words "act or omission" import any requirement that the act or omission should be actionable or tortious, since that would stultify the closing words of subs.14(1) and would flout the recommendation[260] on which the legislation was founded:

> "... it is customary in discussing tortious liability to refer to acts and omissions, and I do not think the meaning of section 14(1)(b) would be any different had the reference been to conduct. Time starts to run against the claimant when he knows that the personal injury on which he founds his claim is capable of being attributed to something done or not done by the defendant whom he wishes to sue. This condition is not satisfied where a man knows that he has a disabling cough or shortness of breath but does not know that his injured condition has anything to do with his working conditions. It is satisfied when he knows that his injured condition is capable of being attributed to his working conditions, even though he has no inkling that his employer may have been at fault."[261]

The claimant argued that the word "injury" should be interpreted in a way which distinguished between the normal or expected consequences of successful medical treatment and the consequences of faulty treatment. The man in the street, it was suggested, would not regard himself as "injured" by a successful operation. He would only regard himself as injured if he suffered consequences other than those normally attributed to the treatment. Beldam LJ rejected this argument because it could not be reconciled with the definition of personal injuries in s.38(1):

11–090

> "The interpretation of 'personal injuries' in section 38(1), though plainly not exhaustive, does indicate that 'injury' cannot be qualified by the addition of words implying its source or aetiology. Nor is there any need to import the perception of the reasonable patient."[262]

The implication of refusing to draw a distinction between successful and unsuccessful surgery, however, would seem to be that everyone who undergoes a surgical operation is, by definition, "injured" and know that they have suffered injury immediately. The fact that the patient does not know that the surgery has gone wrong would be irrelevant to the running of the limitation period. This conclusion seems so bizarre that the proposition must be open to serious question. Consider, for example, a patient who has an appendix removed. She would not consider, and reasonably so, that she had suffered any injury at the hands of the

11–091

---

[259] [1992] 3 Med. L.R. 217, QBD.
[260] i.e. the Law Reform Committee's Twentieth Report, *Interim Report on Limitation of Actions in Personal Injury Claims*, (1974) Cmnd.5630.
[261] [1994] 1 W.L.R. 1234 at 1240.
[262] [1994] 1 W.L.R. 1234 at 1246. The Limitation Act 1980 s.38(1) provides that: "'personal injuries' includes any disease and any impairment of a person's physical or mental condition, and 'injury' and cognate expressions shall be construed accordingly."

doctor. Appendectomy is a potentially lifesaving procedure. The pain and suffering involved in the surgery, and the resultant scar, though clearly "caused" by the surgeon's knife would not normally be thought of as an "injury" when the operation is undertaken on reasonable grounds. If, however, the operation was totally unnecessary on the clinical signs, then a patient would reasonably consider that she had been damaged by having to undergo a needless operation. If the fact that the operation was unnecessary only became apparent much later, the patient only acquired knowledge that she had suffered an *injury* at that time. It is the decision to undertake the operation itself, rather than the performance of the operation (which may have been technically perfect) that is the gist or the "essence" of her complaint.[263] But the decision to perform the operation can only be characterised as an "injury" if the decision was mistaken, and therefore the claimant can only acquire knowledge that she has suffered an injury when she learns that the decision was mistaken. She need not know that it was a careless or negligent mistake, but she has to know that there *was* a mistake, i.e. that there was an error or that "something had gone wrong", before she can have knowledge that she has even suffered an injury.

11-092   In *Dobbie* the Court of Appeal was concerned not to reach a position where the claimant could effectively postpone the running of the limitation period by asserting that she did not know that she had a cause of action in law.[264] With great respect, this interpretation appears to confuse the question of whether the claimant knew that the facts would give her a cause of action in law, which is excluded by the proviso, with the question of the claimant being able to identify the relevant act or omission of the defendant as a cause of her injuries. Knowledge that the defendant's acts or omissions have or have not caused the claimant's injuries is knowledge about a *fact*, not about the law. The question is *which facts* must the claimant have knowledge of, given that s.14(1)(b) clearly does *not* state that it is sufficient to know that the injury was attributable to the defendant's *conduct* (notwithstanding Sir Thomas Bingham MR's statement to the contrary). Although in most cases reference to the defendant's conduct would not make any difference, in some cases the wording is crucial. The subsection focuses attention on the specific conduct of the defendant which it is

---

[263] See, e.g. *Gascoine v Ian Sheridan & Co.* [1994] 5 Med. L.R. 437, a case where judgment was delivered (three months) after, but without reference to, the Court of Appeal's decision in *Dobbie*. Mitchell J, at 442, defined the "act" alleged to constitute negligence to which the claimant's injury was attributable as neither the manner of administering the treatment (external pelvic irradiation) nor the dosage, but the decision to treat her with external pelvic irradiation at all, thereby exposing her unnecessarily to the inherent risks of that procedure. The validity of the decision to treat was an "act" quite independent from the "act" constituting the conduct of the treatment. Although the claimant knew that she was ill, she did not acquire knowledge for the purpose of s.14 until she became aware not only that the immediate cause of her injuries was irradiation, but also that it was the decision to treat unnecessarily which caused the injuries.

[264] " . . .in so far as it has been suggested that the judgments in some cases imply that the plaintiff must have some indication of fault or error in his treatment before he is aware that he has suffered injury, such a requirement is inconsistent with the clear words of section 14," per Beldam LJ at [1994] 1 W.L.R. 1234 at 1246. Steyn LJ said, at 1248, that: "Stripped to its essentials counsel's argument is simply an attempt to argue that the injured party must know that he has a possible cause of action. That is not a requirement of section 14(1)." See also the comment of Hoffmann LJ in *Broadley v Guy Clapham & Co.* [1994] 4 All E.R. 439 at 448, cited above, para.11–087, n.252.

subsequently alleged by the claimant constitutes negligence, nuisance or breach of duty. The claimant need not be aware that this conduct would in law give rise to an action for damages, but must have *some* knowledge of the relevant acts or omissions.[265] In an ordinary road traffic or work accident this is relatively straightforward. In a medical negligence action, however, because, as is frequently stressed when considering whether a defendant is in breach of duty, the fact that "injury" has occurred following surgical intervention cannot itself indicate that there has even been an error, let alone negligence, the claimant needs more than simply knowledge that the injury was attributable to the operation.

This point was made clear by the Court of Appeal in *Hallam-Eames v Merrett*,[266] which was concerned with the interpretation of the analogous provision in s.14A of the Limitation Act 1980 in respect of claims for economic loss. Hoffmann LJ said that:

    11–093

> "If all that was necessary was that a plaintiff should have known that the damage was attributable to an act or omission of the defendant, the statute would have said so. Instead, it speaks of the damage being attributable to 'the act or omission which is alleged to constitute negligence.' In other words, the act or omission of which the plaintiff must have knowledge must be that which is causally relevant for the purposes of an allegation of negligence. There may be many acts, omissions or states which can be said to have a causal connection with a given occurrence, but when we make causal statements in ordinary speech, we select on common sense principles the one which is relevant for our purpose . . ."[267]

The words "which is alleged to constitute negligence" served to identify the facts of which the claimant must have knowledge. It was not sufficient for the claimant to know merely that the relevant damage had been caused by *an* act or omission of the defendant. Commenting on *Dobbie*, Hoffmann LJ said that Mrs Dobbie had to know more than that her breast had been removed. She had to know that a healthy breast had been removed. That was the essence of what she was complaining about. Nor did this require knowledge of fault or negligence:

> "The plaintiff does not have to know that he has a cause of action or that the defendant's acts can be characterised in law as negligent or as falling short of some standard of professional or other behaviour . . . He must have known the facts which can fairly be described as constituting the negligence of which he complains. It may be that knowledge of such facts will also serve to bring home to him the fact that the defendant has been negligent or at fault. But that in itself is not a reason for saying that he need not have known them."[268]

---

[265] In *Baig v City and Hackney Health Authority* [1994] 5 Med. L.R. 221 at 224, Rougier J commented that the words of s.14(1)(b) "admit of no interpretation other than" that the knowledge required is "knowledge, at any rate in general outline, of just what it was that the defendant had either done or failed to do which had caused the damage". Rougier J did not refer to *Dobbie*, although his Lordship's judgment was given a month after the Court of Appeal's decision.

[266] [1996] 7 Med. L.R. 122.

[267] [1996] 7 Med. L.R. 122 at 125–126.

[268] [1996] 7 Med. L.R. 122 at 126. See also *Ostick v Wandsworth Health Authority* [1995] 6 Med. L.R. 338, Mayor's and City of London Court, where it was held that it was not sufficient that the claimant knew she had received an injury that had not healed. It was necessary to know that there was a causal link between the treatment or lack of treatment and the subsequent physical disability, i.e. the fact that the injury had not healed.

In *Haward v Fawcetts (A Firm)*[269] the House of Lords approved the approach in *Hallam-Eames v Merrett Syndicates Ltd* that, for the purposes of s.14A(8) of the Limitation Act 1980, the relevant knowledge was knowledge of the facts constituting the essence of the complaint of negligence.

11–094   This approach now seems to be accepted in cases of medical negligence. In *Forbes v Wandsworth Health Authority*[270] a claimant who was unaware of the acts or omissions of the defendants constituting negligence did not have the relevant knowledge, notwithstanding that it might mean that he would not acquire knowledge until he also knew of the negligence. He had no cause to suspect that anything had gone wrong, other than that the operation had not been a success. Accordingly, he had no reason to believe that the amputation of his leg was due to an act or omission of the defendants until he received an expert's report 10 years after the operation.[271]

11–095   **Knowledge of an omission to treat the patient**   The point is at its most obvious where the alleged negligence consists of an omission to treat. Claimants must know more than the mere fact that they have not been treated. In *Smith v West Lancashire Health Authority*[272] the claimant had been told that the initial treatment had not worked and that there was nothing further that could be done. He presumed that he had received proper treatment, but in fact the operation had been performed too late to achieve full recovery. Russell LJ said that the alleged negligence consisted of the omission to operate promptly, together with the failure properly to diagnose his condition. The reality was that the claimant did not know that there had been an omission to operate at all until he received advice to that effect from his own expert witness:

> "True, he knew that he had not had an operation on or about 12 November 1981, but that knowledge cannot, in my judgment, be knowledge of an omission 'which is alleged to constitute negligence'. One cannot know of an omission without knowing what it is that is omitted. In this case, that was an operation to reduce the fracture dislocations, as opposed to conservative treatment. Simply to tell the plaintiff that the first course of treatment had not worked, is not the same as imbuing the plaintiff with the knowledge of an omission to operate."[273]

---

[269] [2006] UKHL 9; [2006] 1 W.L.R. 682; [2006] P.N.L.R. 25.

[270] [1997] Q.B. 402.

[271] Although the Court of Appeal did consider that he had constructive knowledge when, following an unsuccessful heart bypass operation, he had his leg amputated. See para.11–107.

[272] [1995] P.I.Q.R. P514, CA.

[273] [1995] P.I.Q.R. P514 at 517. See also *Parry v Clwyd Health Authority* [1997] P.I.Q.R. P1; [1997] 8 Med. L.R. 243; *Hind v York Health Authority* [1998] P.I.Q.R. P235; [1997] 8 Med. L.R. 377—a claimant who was repeatedly assured by medical staff that her incontinence was a natural consequence of the birth process, had nothing to do with any medical intervention, and in time would correct itself, did not have knowledge of the causally relevant omission, namely the failure to repair a tear immediately after the birth. Similarly, in *James v East Dorset Health Authority* (1999) 59 B.M.L.R. 196 the Court of Appeal held that a patient whose condition had deteriorated following an operation and who inferred that it had not been a success, nonetheless did not acquire knowledge within s.14 when there was nothing to alert him to the fact that he had suffered an injury during the operation. A claimant must know that he has suffered an injury before he can have knowledge that it was a significant injury. Sedley LJ commented, at 201, that: "I do not believe that in enacting s.14

Similarly, in *Bates v Leicester Health Authority*[274] it was held that the claimant's **11–096** knowledge that his disability was caused by the duration of his mother's labour when he was born was not sufficient to give him knowledge of the omission alleged to constitute negligence, i.e. the doctors' failure to intervene in a protracted labour. The claimant had to know that the failure to intervene was avoidable, as opposed to knowing that the failure to intervene was negligent, which is irrelevant. Moreover, in determining a claimant's knowledge the court must take into account any advice she has received, because "until someone or some incident directly challenges the advice, you continue reasonably to assume it was correct".[275]

Knowledge that something has "gone wrong" with treatment In *Broadley v* **11–097** *Guy Clapham & Co.*,[276] Hoffmann LJ said that s.14(1)(b) required that:

"…one should look at the way the plaintiff puts his case, distil what he is complaining about and ask whether he had in broad terms knowledge of the facts on which that complaint is based."

In the context of complications arising from medical treatment the claimant's "complaint" is not that there has been a complication which is attributable to treatment as such, since he can have no complaint about that per se, but that the complication was attributable *to the act or omission of defendant which is now alleged to constitute negligence*. That knowledge cannot be derived from the knowledge that the defendant performed the operation, but only from the knowledge, in broad terms, that "something has gone wrong affecting the safety of the operation".[277] This is why many of the cases, including several Court of Appeal decisions, refer to the claimant having to have knowledge of some error by the defendant before s.14(1)(b) is satisfied, despite Beldam LJ's suggestion that this is inconsistent with the clear words of the subsection. For example, in both *Davis v Ministry of Defence*[278] and *Wilkinson v Ancliff (BLT) Ltd*[279] the Court of Appeal considered that an employee had to know that his injuries were

---

Parliament intended to reward those alert to assume that every misfortune is someone else's fault and to place at a disadvantage those who do not assume the worst when there is nothing to alert them to it."

[274] [1998] Lloyd's Rep. Med. 93.

[275] *Oakes v Hopcroft* [2000] Lloyd's Rep. Med. 394 at [33] per Lord Woolf CJ. As Clarke LJ commented, at [49]: "It is not easy to identify what a claimant must know about an omission in order to have knowledge that her loss is capable of being attributed to it." Thus, where a claim was brought in respect of allegedly negligent medical advice as a result of which the claimant settled an action against a third party for much less than the true value of the claim, the question was whether she was aware of "the essence of the omission which had caused the original settlement to be too low, i.e. that there had been a misdiagnosis; not … whether that misdiagnosis had been negligent but simply whether there had been a misdiagnosis": [2000] Lloyd's Rep. Med. 394 at [41] per Waller LJ. *Oakes v Hopcroft* is a decision on the virtually identically worded provisions in s.14A concerned with latent damage.

[276] [1994] 4 All E.R. 439; [1993] 4 Med. L.R. 328, CA.

[277] Note that even in *Broadley v Guy Clapham & Co.* [1994] 4 All E.R. 439 at 446, Balcombe LJ appeared to accept that "broad knowledge" was required, and that this involved knowledge "that something went wrong". See para.11–088.

[278] *The Times*, 7 August 1985.

[279] [1986] 1 W.L.R. 1352 at 1365, CA.

attributable to the defendant's failure to provide *safe* working conditions.[280] Similarly, in *Nash v Eli Lilly & Co.*[281] the Court of Appeal accepted that the relevant acts or omissions of the defendants consisted of exposing the claimants to a drug which was *unsafe*. Knowledge that their symptoms were simply attributable to taking a drug could not constitute knowledge by the claimants of any relevant act or omission on the part of the defendant manufacturers. The reference to "safety" clearly requires that the claimant know more than simply that the defendant's *conduct* caused the injury. It is submitted that she must either know, or have constructive knowledge, that "something has gone wrong" sufficiently to consider investigating the circumstances.

11–098 **Patient misinformed about treatment by defendant** In any event, where claimants are informed at the time by medical staff involved that nothing has gone wrong, and that their treatment was consistent with good medical practice, they do not know that they have suffered an injury because there is no basis for challenging either the performance of the treatment itself or the decision to proceed with the treatment. When Mrs Dobbie was informed that she was lucky to be alive, she was not simply being advised that the surgery to remove her breast had been technically competent, she was being advised that the decision to remove her breast was not an error or a mistake. On that information, she did not know that she had suffered an injury. In *Scuriaga v Powell*[282] the defendant performed an unsuccessful abortion on the claimant, but the doctor lied, telling the claimant that the operation had failed because she had a physical defect. She did not know that the failure to terminate the pregnancy was due to the doctor's negligence until she received a consultant's report more than three years after the failed operation. It was held that time did not begin to run until the claimant discovered that the failure was due to the doctor's conduct of the operation.

11–099 **Patient misunderstands the cause of symptoms** Moreover, the cases where claimants mistakenly believed that injuries were attributable to a particular aspect of their treatment[283] in which it has been held that this did not constitute knowledge for the purpose of s.14, also indicate that knowledge that an injury was attributable simply to "the treatment" or "the defendant's conduct" is not sufficient. For example, in *Khan v Ainslie*[284] the claimant initially believed, incorrectly, that eye drops put into his eye for the purpose of a test in 1983 were the cause of the loss of sight in his left eye. He was not aware, until he received an expert's report in 1989, that the problems with his eye were attributable to the omission to refer him for immediate treatment. Despite the fact that the claimant clearly believed that his eye problems were attributable to the defendants' conduct, it was held that the relevant date was 1989 when the report was obtained, because until that stage the claimant had no knowledge of the

---

[280] See also *Farmer v National Coal Board*, *The Times*, 27 April 1985, CA, where Griffiths LJ said that if the claimant is told that the cause of an injury has been the *faulty operation* of a complicated process by an employer, that was sufficient knowledge of an act or omission to start time running.
[281] [1993] 1 W.L.R. 782 at 799.
[282] (1979) 123 S.J. 406; aff'd, unreported 24 July 1980, CA.
[283] i.e. the claimant was "barking up the wrong tree": see para.11–071.
[284] [1993] 4 Med. L.R. 319.

attributability of his disability to delay, and was ignorant of the link to the act or omission on which he now relied as being negligent. Similarly, in *Baig v City & Hackney Health Authority*[285] Rougier J commented that though a sufficiently firm conviction will suffice for the purpose of knowledge, the conviction must be right, in the sense that it accords with the way in which the case is ultimately advanced in reliance on specialist opinion:

> "It seems to me to be a travesty of language to hold that somebody who approaches his case in a wholly erroneous belief—however strong—as to the cause of his injury could ever have the requisite knowledge. On the contrary, he has the reverse."[286]

Thus, contrasting these cases with *Dobbie*, the claimant may be in a better position for limitation purposes to adopt a belief which turns out to be incorrect than to have no belief at all about medical treatment.[287]

Section 14(1)(c)—knowledge of the defendant's identity   This will not normally be a problem in cases of medical negligence, although the claimant may not know which individual in a team caused the injury.[288] This is irrelevant, however, since where the claimant knows that the injuries were caused by one or other of two defendants, but not both, and does not know which defendant is responsible the claimant would be expected to sue both in the alternative.[289]   **11–100**

Section 14(1)(d)—knowledge of vicarious liability   Section 14(1)(d) refers to the circumstances required to establish an employer's vicarious liability for the torts of employees committed in the course of employment, though the wording is wide enough to cover liability for the conduct of independent contractors where the defendant is under a relevant "non-delegable" duty. The precise identity of the employee is irrelevant if the claimant is aware that the damage was caused by one or more of the defendant's employees acting in the course of employment.[290] The claimant does not have to know that on the facts the defendant would be held vicariously liable in law.   **11–101**

Claimant's ignorance of the law   It is claimants' knowledge of *facts* that governs the commencement date. Section 14(1) specifically provides that claimants' ignorance that, as a matter of law, the facts would give them a cause of   **11–102**

---

[285] [1994] 5 Med. L.R. 221, QBD.

[286] [1994] 5 Med. L.R. 221 at 224. See also *Driscoll-Varley v Parkside Health Authority* [1991] 2 Med. L.R. 346, and the comments of Hoffmann LJ on this case in *Broadley v Guy Clapham & Co.* [1994] 4 All E.R. 439 at 449, para.11–088.

[287] See also *Martin v Kaisary (No.2)* [2005] EWHC 531 (QB).

[288] As, e.g. in *Cassidy v Ministry of Health* [1951] 2 K.B. 343. For the problems a claimant may encounter in identifying a corporate defendant see: *Simpson v Norwest Holst Southern Ltd* [1980] 1 W.L.R. 968; *Cressey v E. Timm & Son Ltd* [2005] EWCA Civ 763; [2005] 1 W.L.R. 3926, where the claimant was misled as to the correct defendant by his payslips identifying an entity other than his employer as his employer.

[289] *Halford v Brookes* [1991] 1 W.L.R. 428 at 437, per Lord Donaldson MR.

[290] Since, where the defendant is responsible in law for all the staff who played some role in the claimant's treatment, it is unnecessary for the claimant to identify the particular employee who was at fault in order to establish vicarious liability: *Cassidy v Ministry of Health* [1951] 2 K.B. 343.

action is irrelevant.[291] This is the case even where the claimant has received incorrect advice about the legal position, whether from a lawyer or not.[292] Care has to be taken, however, to distinguish clearly between ignorance of facts which would be relevant to the potential success of the claim and ignorance of the law. For example, in *Jones v Liverpool Health Authority*[293] Glidewell LJ said that if claimants are informed by a medical expert that they probably do not have a valid claim, and years later they are advised by another medical expert, on the same facts, that they probably do have a valid claim, they cannot claim that they did not have knowledge until they received the later opinion. With respect, this rather assumes that it is the function of medical experts to advise about the law, which, clearly, it is not. If the first expert advised that in his opinion there was no causal connection between the relevant acts or omissions and the claimant's injury, then the advice concerns a fact, notwithstanding that the conclusion would also be that no claim in law would be sustainable because the injury could not be attributed to the defendant's acts or omissions. If this was the only information claimants had then they would only acquire the relevant knowledge when informed by the second expert that there was a causal connection.

11–103   In *Rowe v Kingston upon Hull City Council*[294] the judge found that the claimant was aware that he suffered from dyslexia and that remedial steps could have been taken, before his 18th birthday, but he did not know that he had suffered an "injury" until the position was brought home to him by a decision of the High Court in *Phelps v Hillingdon London Borough Council*.[295] The Court of Appeal accepted that "injury" could include a failure to mitigate the adverse consequences of a congenital defect, but on the judge's findings of fact the claimant was aware that he had suffered an injury before his 18th birthday. The fact that he was unaware, until the decision in *Phelps*, that he might be able to sue the education authority in respect of that injury was irrelevant, and the primary limitation period, therefore, expired on his 21st birthday. The claimant's argument that a reasonable person would not have regarded what the claimant had experienced as an injury until the *Phelps* case had been decided was described by Keene LJ as "mere semantics". The knowledge referred to in s.14(1):

> "...is of certain facts, not of whether in law those facts amounted to an 'injury'. The claimant knew that he could have been helped by the education authorities and he knew that he had not been, with the result that his condition had not been ameliorated. That latter aspect is the injury, whether the claimant knew that it could be called an 'injury' or not."[296]

---

[291] The nature of the claimant's ignorance of the law is also irrelevant. So it does not matter whether the claimant's ignorance relates to whether there has been a breach of duty by the defendant or whether the defendant owed the claimant a duty of care: *Bowie v Southorns* [2002] EWHC 1389 (QB); [2003] P.N.L.R. 7.

[292] See *Farmer v National Coal Board, The Times*, 27 April 1985, CA, where erroneous legal advice by a union official that the claimant's action had no chance of success did not prevent time running against the claimant, since from facts ascertainable by her she could reasonably have acquired the necessary knowledge.

[293] [1996] P.I.Q.R. P251 at 266.

[294] [2003] EWCA Civ 1281; [2004] P.I.Q.R. P16.

[295] [1997] 3 F.C.R. 621.

[296] [2003] EWCA Civ 1281; [2004] P.I.Q.R. P16 at [21] per Keen LJ.

Nor did the restrictions imposed by ss.11 and 14 of the Limitation Act 1980 involve a breach of art.6 of the European Convention on Human Rights. The mere fact that people may not realise that they have a good claim until a decision in the courts clarifies the matter did not provide a justification for interpreting the Act differently.[297]

Although ignorance of the law is irrelevant to the question of the claimant's knowledge for the purpose of s.14, it is relevant to the court's exercise of discretion under s.33.[298]

11–104

(iii) Constructive knowledge

A person's knowledge includes constructive knowledge, which by virtue of s.14(3) means:

11–105

> "...knowledge which he might reasonably have been expected to acquire—
> (a)   from facts observable or ascertainable by him; or
> (b)   from facts ascertainable by him with the help of medical or other appropriate expert advice which it is reasonable for him to seek;
> but a person shall not be fixed under this subsection with knowledge of a fact ascertainable only with the help of expert advice so long as he has taken all reasonable steps to obtain (and, where appropriate, to act on) that advice."

The constructive knowledge provisions of s.14(3) are an important part of the Limitation Act and seek to ensure that the right balance is struck between achieving fairness for claimants and avoiding stale claims and unnecessary prejudice for defendants.

A subjective or objective test?   It is for the defendant to establish the case of constructive knowledge on the balance of probabilities.[299] There had been a degree of conflict between the relevant authorities as to the correct test to apply. It appeared that constructive knowledge was a combination of a subjective and an objective test. The application of s.14(3) and the overlap between the objective and subjective elements of the test had led to some disagreement as to how constructive knowledge should be imputed to claimants in practice. In *Nash v Elli Lily & Co*[300] Purchas LJ said that:

11–106

> "... the proper approach is to determine what this plaintiff should have observed or ascertained, while asking no more of him than is reasonable. The standard of reasonableness in connection with the observations and/or the effort to ascertain are therefore finally objective but must be qualified to take into consideration the position, and circumstances and character

---

[297] [2003] EWCA Civ 1281; [2004] P.I.Q.R. P16 at [24] per Keen LJ.
[298] Limitation Act 1980 s.33(3)(a) and (e); *Brooks v Coates (UK) Ltd* [1984] 1 All E.R. 702 at 713; *Coad v Cornwall and Isles of Scilly Health Authority* [1997] 1 W.L.R. 189, CA.
[299] *Miller v Thames Valley Strategic Health Authority* [2005] EWHC 3281 (QB) per Butterfield J.
[300] [1993] 1 W.L.R. 782 at 799, CA. See also *Colegrove v Smyth* [1994] 5 Med. L.R. 111 at 114 per Buckley J (applying *McCafferty v Metropolitan Police District Receiver* [1977] 1 W.L.R. 1073, CA): "It boils down to this, that the test is objective but it is applied to the particular plaintiff in the particular circumstances in which he found himself, so to that extent it does involve a subjective element."

of the plaintiff... In considering whether or not the inquiry is, or is not, reasonable, the situation, character and intelligence of the plaintiff must be relevant."

11–107 However, in *Forbes v Wandsworth Health Authority*[301] the Court of Appeal had some difficulty in seeing how the individual character and intelligence of the claimant in a personal injury case could be relevant to the question of constructive knowledge (doubting the view expressed by Purchas LJ in *Nash v Eli Lilly & Co.*). The claimant had his leg amputated in 1982 following an unsuccessful heart bypass operation. He did not consult a solicitor until 1991, and obtained a report from a vascular surgeon in 1992 indicating that delay in treating him after the first operation had caused the damage that resulted in the amputation. The Court of Appeal held that, although the claimant had no actual knowledge, he did have constructive knowledge. He expected the operation to be successful and it was not, and a reasonable man would have sought advice reasonably promptly. He should have sought expert medical advice some 12 to 18 months after he came out of hospital, by which time he would have had time to overcome his shock at losing his leg and take stock of his disability and its consequences. On the question of whether it was reasonable for the claimant to take expert advice, Stuart-Smith LJ said that two alternative courses of conduct may both be perfectly reasonable. Accepting the situation, and saying "It was just one of those things. The doctors probably did their best" may be reasonable, just as taking a second opinion as to whether there was any lack of care may be reasonable. But a claimant who takes the first option is making a choice. A reasonable person in the claimant's position, who knew that the operation had been unsuccessful, and that he had suffered a major injury which would seriously affect his enjoyment of life in the future would take advice reasonably promptly:

> "It does not seem to me that the fact that a plaintiff is more trusting, incurious, indolent, resigned or uncomplaining by nature can be a relevant characteristic, since this too undermines any objective approach."[302]

11–108 In *O'Driscoll v Dudley Health Authority*[303] Otton LJ commented that it was not easy to reconcile *Nash* and *Forbes* on this point:

> "Applying the *Forbes* test a person who is too incurious, indolent, resigned or uncomplaining to do anything about it would be unreasonable if he allowed a potential claim to lapse through effluxion of time. I would see no reason to exclude a person who is too trusting. It would not be unreasonable to expect him to take reasonable steps to obtain advice, if only to verify whether his trust was not misplaced."[304]

---

[301] [1997] Q.B. 402.

[302] [1997] Q.B. 402 at 414. See also *Slevin v Southampton and South West Hampshire Health Authority* [1997] 8 Med. L.R. 175, QBD, applying *Forbes*: the claimant knew that she should have been delivered by Caesarean section and that if she had been she would not have suffered her injury; she knew that her injury occurred at the hands of the defendant in the course of a breech delivery; this was sufficient to give her constructive knowledge that the injury was attributable to the act or omission alleged to constitute negligence.

[303] [1998] Lloyd's Rep. Med. 210 at 217.

[304] [1998] Lloyd's Rep. Med. 210 at 218.

The problem with this is that it may be very difficult for even a reasonable person to know whether he is being "too trusting" particularly if there is nothing to put him on notice that he should make enquiries. For example, if a patient is informed after surgery that the injury he sustained in the course of the operation was an inherent risk of the treatment, is he entitled to accept that statement face value? At what point must patients question what they are told in order to verify whether their trust is misplaced?[305]

In *Smith v Leicester Health Authority*[306] the Court of Appeal regarded *Nash* and **11–109** *Forbes* as conflicting decisions, and concluded that the claimant's individual characteristics, which might distinguish her from the reasonable person should be disregarded. Constructive knowledge involved an objective test which does not take account of the claimant's individual characteristics (such as her forbearance, or unwillingness to criticise) but does take account of her individual circumstances, such as what she has been told by medical staff. The claimant in *Smith* was told and accepted that the cyst which rendered her tetraplegic was congenital, and that the operation in question had saved her life. She had no reason to suppose that the earlier diagnoses were wrong. In the case of an omission what the claimant has to know is that there was a lost opportunity to prevent the injury:

> "If the decision in *Forbes* is being read as saying that every time a patient has an operation and, following the operation is significantly disabled, the patient has some 12 to 18 months to decide consciously or unconsciously whether to investigate a possible claim against those who operated, then in our view the decision in *Forbes* is being misinterpreted and misapplied. The question posed by s.14(3) with respect to the seeking of medical or other appropriate expert advice is the simple one whether it was reasonable for the plaintiff to seek such advice. Whether it was reasonable for the plaintiff to seek such advice depends on the facts and circumstances of each case, but excluding the character traits of the individual plaintiff."[307]

The objective test The conflict between *Forbes* and *Nash* on the subjective/ **11–110** objective test for constructive knowledge was resolved by the House of Lords in *Adams v Bracknell Forest Borough Council*.[308] Their Lordships concluded that the objective approach to constructive knowledge adopted in *Forbes* was to be preferred. Lord Hoffmann accepted the argument that the existence of the court's discretion to disapply the primary limitation period (under the Limitation Act 1980 s.33) had altered the balance between claimants and defendants, so that there was no need to construe the constructive knowledge provisions in a way that was particularly favourable to claimants. The test is whether a reasonable claimant, having suffered the injury in question, ought reasonably to have known the relevant facts. The claimant's particular character or intelligence is irrelevant. Thus, Lord Hoffmann observed that:

---

[305] See the comment of Lord Woolf CJ in *Oakes v Hopcroft* [2000] Lloyd's Rep. Med. 394 at [33]: "until someone or some incident directly challenges the advice, you continue reasonably to assume it was correct."
[306] [1998] Lloyd's Rep. Med. 77.
[307] [1998] Lloyd's Rep. Med. 77 at 87.
[308] [2004] UKHL 29; [2005] 1 A.C. 76.

"It is true that the plaintiff must be assumed to be a person who has suffered the injury in question and not some other person. But, like Roch LJ in *Forbes* [1997] QB 402, 425 I do not see how his particular character or intelligence can be relevant. In my opinion, section 14(3) requires one to assume that a person who is aware that he has suffered a personal injury, serious enough to be something about which he would go and see a solicitor if he knew he had a claim, will be sufficiently curious about the causes of the injury to seek whatever expert advice is appropriate."[309]

On the other hand, if the injury itself would reasonably inhibit a claimant from seeking advice, that is a factor which must be taken into account.[310] Lord Scott agreed that the claimant's personal characteristics, such as shyness or embarrassment, which may have inhibited the claimant from seeking advice but which would not be expected to have inhibited others with a similar disability, should be left out of the equation: "It is the norms of behaviour of persons in the situation of the claimant that should be the test."[311] Lord Walker agreed that the distinction between circumstances and personal characteristics was intelligible and helpful in many cases, but considered that there were bound to be some cases in which the distinction is elided (for example, where a claimant has suffered serious head injuries this may raise an issue as to whether he has the legal capacity either to commence or to compromise legal proceedings on his own).[312] Baroness Hale observed that it would be reasonable for potential claimants to seek advice when they have good reason to do so. This will depend on the situation in which they find themselves, which includes the consequences of the accident, illness or other injury they have suffered. But, "Rarely, if ever, will it depend on his personal characteristics".[313] If it was reasonable to seek advice, the fact that the claimant was reluctant to make a fuss or embarrassed to talk to the doctor, though understandable, does not take the case outside s.14(3). Baroness Hale speculated that there may be a difference between personal characteristics which affect claimants' abilities to acquire information and those which affect their reaction to what they did know, and therefore did not entirely rule out consideration of claimants' personal characteristics, and Lord Walker agreed that this distinction may be useful in some cases.

11–111   In *Whiston v London SHA*[314] Dyson LJ concluded that *Adams* is authority for the proposition that s.14(3) requires an objective (or mainly objective) test to be applied to constructive knowledge. However, Lord Hoffmann's statement at para.[47] of *Adams*[315] was not part of the ratio of the case. There was no *rule* that a claimant who has knowledge that he has suffered a significant injury is fixed with knowledge of the facts that he would have ascertained if he made enquiries about the cause of the injury; in other words the:

---

[309] [2004] UKHL 29; [2005] 1 A.C. 76 at [47].
[310] [2004] UKHL 29; [2005] 1 A.C. 76 at [49].
[311] [2004] UKHL 29; [2005] 1 A.C. 76 at [71].
[312] [2004] UKHL 29; [2005] 1 A.C. 76 at [77].
[313] [2004] UKHL 29; [2005] 1 A.C. 76 at [88].
[314] [2010] EWCA Civ 195; [2010] 1 W.L.R. 1582 at [54].
[315] Quoted at para.11–110 above.

"...subsection does not provide that actual or constructive knowledge that the injury is significant is determinative of the constructive knowledge issue."[316]

It might be a "normal expectation" that claimants who have suffered an injury serious enough to be something about which they would go and see a solicitor would also be sufficiently curious about the causes of the injury to seek appropriate expert advice, but ultimately what was reasonably to be expected of claimants would depend on all the circumstances of the case.[317] This was not to overlook the fact that the court must apply an objective test, and that in *Adams* the House of Lords intended to tighten up the requirements for constructive knowledge, given that s.33 provided the court with a discretion to permit the action to proceed: the court would "expect a heightened degree of curiosity of the reasonable claimant than it would do absent section 33".[318]

Distinguish "personal characteristics" and "personal circumstances" The   **11–112**
effect of *Adams* seems to be that much depends upon what is meant by a "personal characteristic" of the claimant. If the court is required to look objectively at the reasonableness of the claimant's conduct, taking into account personal circumstances (including the effects of the accident), there is a distinct possibility, as Lord Walker suggested, that the subjective and the objective may be elided. If, for example, as a result of the injury the claimant develops depression and is then unable to deal with various aspects of daily living, including summoning the intellectual and emotional energy to embark on investigating the causes of the injury, is this lack of drive a subjective "personal characteristic" of the claimant (to be ignored) or is it an objective "personal circumstance" (to be taken into account)? And why should it make the slightest difference whether or not the depression is the result of the injury itself? It may be that the objective "reasonable claimant" is deemed not to suffer from depression, but if the claimant had serious, pre-existing, physical disabilities which impaired his ability to investigate a claim, is this not a personal circumstance rather than a personal characteristic? In both *Whiston v London SHA*[319] and *Johnson v Ministry of Defence*[320] the Court of Appeal drew a

---

[316] [2010] EWCA Civ 195; [2010] 1 W.L.R. 1582 at [58].
[317] [2010] EWCA Civ 195; [2010] 1 W.L.R. 1582 at [58]. See also *Johnson v Ministry of Defence* [2012] EWCA Civ 1505; [2013] P.I.Q.R. P7 at [24] per Dame Janet Smith: "what Lord Hoffmann must have meant was that there would be an assumption that a person who had suffered a significant injury would be sufficiently curious to seek advice unless there were reasons why a reasonable person in his position would not have done. Such a reason might be that the condition, although in law significant, was something that the claimant had become so used to it (for example because it had been present from birth or childhood) that a reasonable person would not be expected to be curious about its cause"; *Platt v BRB (Residuary) Ltd* [2014] EWCA Civ 1401; [2015] P.I.Q.R. P7 at [19] and [28].
[318] [2010] EWCA Civ 195; [2010] 1 W.L.R. 1582 at [59]; *Johnson v Ministry of Defence* [2012] EWCA Civ 1505; [2013] P.I.Q.R. P7 at [28]. See also *Collins v Secretary of State for Business Innovation and Skills* [2014] EWCA Civ 717; [2014] P.I.Q.R. P19; and *Platt v BRB (Residuary) Ltd* [2014] EWCA Civ 1401; [2015] P.I.Q.R. P7.
[319] [2010] EWCA Civ 195; [2010] 1 W.L.R. 1582.
[320] [2012] EWCA Civ 1505; [2013] P.I.Q.R. P7.

distinction between an adult who had suffered an unexpected injury[321] and a claimant who had lived with a disability from birth or early childhood who would not necessarily be curious about the cause of the disability, having lived with it for most of their life, such that the disability has become a part of who they are. This would seem to be a "personal characteristic" rather than a mere circumstance, but would nonetheless be a relevant consideration. Dame Janet Smith also considered that the age and mental capacity of the claimant were part of the "essential characteristics" of the claimant which should be taken into account in assessing whether they had acted reasonably for the purposes of s.14(3).[322]

11–113   *Adams* was applied in *Miller v Thames Valley Strategic Health Authority*,[323] a case involving a 61-year-old man and an alleged failure to diagnose a brain tumour when he was 19. In 1969 he had had a brain tumour removed. By that time he had lost virtually all the vision in his right eye and a substantial part of the useful vision in his left eye. In 2000 he learned from his medical records that a neurologist who had examined him in 1963 had suspected he had a tumour. The claimant maintained that had the condition been diagnosed and treated in 1963 or 1964, his loss of vision would, in all probability, have been averted. The defendant contended that although the claimant did not have actual knowledge of the failure to diagnose the tumour and the consequences of that failure for his vision, he did have constructive knowledge from about 1969. Butterfield J said:

> "It is for the defendant to establish the case of constructive knowledge on the balance of probabilities. The defendant must establish that the claimant, as a reasonable man of moderate intelligence, should have appreciated in all the relevant circumstances that there was a real possibility that the defendant had failed to diagnose his brain tumour when it should have done in 1963 or 1964. Further, the defendant must establish on the balance of probabilities that this failure had caused or contributed to the claimant's loss of vision."[324]

He went on to find that the defendant had failed to establish this on the balance of probabilities. The doctors had never suggested to the claimant that they could have made their diagnosis earlier than they did and there was no reason why he should have reached a different conclusion. No reasonable man of moderate intelligence would have made the connection between his condition in 1963 to 1966 and the condition as it was found in the operation three years later.

11–114   **Disability from birth is different from injury later in life**   In *Khairule v North West Strategic Health Authority*[325] Cox J considered the application of the *Adams* objective test in the case of a claimant with cerebral palsy and drew a distinction between someone who had lived with such disability from birth and someone who had suffered injury in his later years. The claimant was, objectively, in the position of the person contemplated in s.14(3). Whilst the test was objective, that did not prevent the claimant's objective circumstances being

---

[321] "The unexpected removal of a leg on the operating table would be expected to excite a high and immediate degree of curiosity": [2012] EWCA Civ 1505; [2013] P.I.Q.R. P7 at [24].
[322] [2012] EWCA Civ 1505; [2013] P.I.Q.R. P7 at [24].
[323] [2005] EWHC 3281 (QB).
[324] [2005] EWHC 3281 (QB) at [27].
[325] [2008] EWHC 1537 (QB); commented on by Lyons [2008] J.P.I.L. C207.

taken into account in asking when a reasonable person in his circumstances, suffering from athetoid cerebral palsy and with the same level of disability and intellect, would have had the curiosity to begin investigating with expert help whether his injury could be considered capable of being attributed to something the hospital staff did or did not do at the time of his birth. Though the claimant's personal, subjective characteristics were to be disregarded, those characteristics personal to him that were a direct result of his injury were to be taken into account. The claimant's condition could not be regarded as a trigger for fixing the date of knowledge of attributability. His cerebral palsy was part of him and he had lived with it for as long as he could remember.[326] However, on the facts, gradually over time he gained independence, experience and, by the end of 2002, unrestricted access to the internet. As a result, pursuant to s.14(3), taking into account the claimant's circumstances he had constructive knowledge of attributability by the end of 2002 and his claim was statute-barred unless it could be saved by s.33.

Other examples   As with actual knowledge, mere suspicion does not amount to **11–115** knowledge.[327] Where claimants refused further tests to assist diagnosis and discharged themselves from hospital when they knew that the diagnosis was provisional, they acted unreasonably and had constructive knowledge of the diagnosis that the tests would probably have revealed.[328] A failure to take up an opportunity to inspect records which would have revealed relevant information has been held to be unreasonable.[329] Constructive knowledge does not include the knowledge of a child's parents during the child's minority.[330] Moreover, an ordinary person of average intelligence and average understanding of medical matters is not expected to infer from the fact that a child is born with cerebral

---

[326] In *Whiston v London SHA* [2010] EWCA Civ 195; [2010] 1 W.L.R. 1582 at [60] Dyson LJ agreed with the approach of Cox J in *Khairule* that a distinction should be drawn between people who have lived with a disability and its effects all their lives (who are more likely to be accepting of their disability) and people who suffer injuries following an adverse incident which occurs in adulthood. Nonetheless, there will come a time, where the disability becomes more serious as the claimant reaches adulthood, when it would be reasonable for a claimant who knew that his disability was in some way related to the circumstances of his delivery (rather than, say, a genetic disorder) to ask questions about the circumstances of his birth (on the facts the claimant's mother, who was a nurse, would have been able to give him information about the relevant facts): [2010] EWCA Civ 195; [2010] 1 W.L.R. 1582 at [63]. See also *Johnson v Ministry of Defence* [2012] EWCA Civ 1505; [2013] P.I.Q.R. P7 at [24].

[327] *Wilkinson v Ancliff (BLT) Ltd* [1986] 1 W.L.R. 1352; *Stephen v Riverside Health Authority* [1990] 1 Med. L.R. 261.

[328] *Denford v Redbridge and Waltham Forest Health Authority* [1996] 7 Med. L.R. 376.

[329] *Pierce v Doncaster MBC* [2008] EWCA Civ 1416; [2009] 1 F.L.R. 1189 at [33]: "It is true that it will be relevant ... to consider any disability or difficulty which the claimant had in pressing his request or in seeking expert advice. This claimant was a damaged personality and it may be that he was somewhat inhibited by the suggestion that the contents of the file might be distressing. But even assuming that were so, on the agreed facts set out there can only be one answer to this question. He knew where the file was. He wanted it. He was offered access to it. He could clearly have gone to Doncaster to obtain it."

[330] *Parry v Clwyd Health Authority* [1997] P.I.Q.R. P1; [1997] 8 Med. L.R. 243; *Appleby v Walsall Health Authority* [1999] Lloyd's Rep. Med. 154; cf. *O'Driscoll v Dudley Health Authority* [1998] Lloyd's Rep. Med. 210 at 220, where Sir Christopher Slade treated the parents' actual knowledge as imputed to the child, so that her actual knowledge commenced at age 18.

palsy that there was a real possibility that an act or omission of the medical staff was the cause of the injury.[331] A reasonable person obeys the law, and therefore claimants who did not seek advice because they were concerned that this might lead to their own illegal conduct being referred to the police were fixed with constructive knowledge of facts which the expert would have ascertained.[332]

11–116 **Failure to consult a lawyer** A failure to seek legal advice will give rise to constructive knowledge of the facts which would have been discovered after the date at which it would have been reasonable to seek such advice.[333] Where the question is whether it was reasonable for claimants to seek expert advice, even applying an objective test it would seem that their personal circumstances should be taken into account, so that it may well be reasonable for claimants who are seriously ill or dying not to seek legal advice,[334] though this is a question of degree.[335] Similarly, it may be reasonable for claimants to delay seeking legal advice where they were still receiving treatment and did not wish to sour relations with the doctors who were treating them.[336] Some account will also be taken of the limited resources available to claimants by way of advice, where, e.g. their solicitors could only seek expert advice to the extent that they were authorised to do so by the Legal Aid Board.[337]

---

[331] *Parry v Clwyd Health Authority* [1997] P.I.Q.R. P1; [1997] 8 Med. L.R. 243. See also *De Martell v Merton and Sutton Health Authority* [1995] 6 Med. L.R 234 where it was held that the claimant had acted reasonably in not inquiring into the circumstances of his birth, because his mother had become pregnant by her uncle and was reluctant to talk about it.

[332] *Coban v Allen* [1997] 8 Med. L.R. 316, CA, where the claimant did not pursue his action because of his illegal immigration status. This was a decision on the latent damage provisions contained in s.14A(10) of the Limitation Act 1980, which is in identical terms to s.14(3).

[333] *Hills v Potter* [1984] 1 W.L.R. 641 at 653.

[334] *Newton v Cammell Laird & Co. (Shipbuilders and Engineers) Ltd* [1969] 1 W.L.R. 415. In *Davis v City and Hackney Health Authority* [1991] 2 Med. L.R. 366 it was held that it was appropriate to look at the difficulties faced by the particular claimant, including any physical disability from which he suffered, the fact that his parents, on whom he had been largely dependent, had discouraged him from seeking to pursue a claim arising from injuries sustained at the time of his birth, and the fact that the prospect of seeing a solicitor alone intimidated him. See also *Bates v Leicester Health Authority* [1998] Lloyd's Rep. Med. 93 where the claimant had significant communication difficulties and relied heavily on his mother who was forcefully dismissive of his chances of a claim and therefore he acted reasonably in not pursuing the matter sooner.

[335] So in *Forbes v Wandsworth Health Authority* [1997] Q.B. 402 the Court of Appeal took the view that where a claimant has had his leg amputated following heart bypass surgery he should have sought expert medical advice some 12 to 18 months after he came out of hospital, by which time he would have had time to overcome his shock at losing his leg and take stock of his disability and its consequences.

[336] *Ostick v Wandsworth Health Authority* [1995] 6 Med. L.R. 338—the claimant was justified in waiting to see if her treatment was successful before seeking legal advice; *Driscoll-Varley v Parkside Health Authority* [1991] 2 Med. L.R. 346 at 357 where the claimant had been warned by her solicitors that commencing litigation against the hospital might alienate the surgeon. It was not unreasonable to fail to take the matter further at an earlier stage, given her concern not to antagonise the consultant who had the continued care of her and in whom she had confidence.

[337] *Khan v Ainslie* [1993] 4 Med. L.R. 319. On the other hand, in *Skitt v Khan and Wakefield Health Authority* [1997] 8 Med. L.R. 105 the Court of Appeal held that though lack of funds to obtain an expert's report could be a factor, that has to be weighed against the seriousness of the injury and its consequences for the claimant in deciding whether objectively it was reasonable to seek expert medical advice. On the facts it was understandable that the claimant did not seek such advice, but it was not reasonable.

Expert fails to discover or disclose a relevant fact   The proviso to s.14(3)   **11–117**
prevents a claimant from being fixed with constructive knowledge where an
expert has failed to discover or disclose a relevant fact that ought to have been
revealed.[338] It will only apply, however, to facts which are "ascertainable *only*
with the help of expert advice". Where claimants themselves could have
discovered the information then they are fixed with any knowledge that the
expert acting on their behalf ought to have acquired,[339] provided that it was
information which claimants could reasonably be expected to acquire.[340]

Claimant's expert a lawyer   Particular problems arise when the claimant's   **11–118**
"expert" is a lawyer. First, by virtue of the proviso to s.14(1), where a claimant
receives erroneous advice about the law (e.g. that the facts do not disclose a cause
of action) this is irrelevant and does not prevent time running.[341] Secondly, where
legal "advice" consists of a failure to discover relevant facts, or a failure to
suggest a line of enquiry that would have revealed the facts, then in theory the
proviso to s.14(3) applies, and the claimant is not fixed with constructive
knowledge.[342] But in *Leadbitter v Hodge Finance Ltd*[343] a very narrow view was
taken of the facts which are ascertainable *only* with the help of expert advice. In
that case an accident victim was expected to be capable of obtaining a police

---

[338] See, e.g. *Marston v British Railways Board* [1976] I.C.R. 124, where the expert dealt only with
the hardness of a metal hammer, not its defective condition; see also *Stephen v Riverside Health
Authority* [1990] 1 Med. L.R. 261, where the claimant had been assured by a "chorus of highly
qualified experts" that her symptoms could not have been caused by the dose of radiation that she had
received; *Davis v Ministry of Defence, The Times*, 7 August 1985, CA. In *Baig v City and Hackney
Health Authority* [1994] 5 Med. L.R. 221 at 225, Rougier J suggested that it would be inappropriate to
impute the necessary knowledge to the claimant by reason of an expert's report which was "puzzling
and ambiguous in its terms". In *Hepworth v Kerr* [1995] 6 Med. L.R. 135 the claimant suffered
paraplegia following an operation under general anaesthetic and, despite a suggestion in the medical
notes that his condition might have been attributable to the operation, he was assured on several
occasions by the neurosurgeon who subsequently treated him for the paralysis that the operation had
not caused his condition. A report by the neurosurgeon to the claimant's solicitors came to the same
conclusion. The defendants argued that the claimant had constructive knowledge because a competent
solicitor should have realised that the neurosurgeon was the wrong expert and had not indicated that
he had read the hospital medical notes. This argument was rejected by Latham J. To require the
claimant or his solicitor to question whether the expert had obtained sufficient information from the
notes or to question whether or not he was the appropriate expert was "asking for a startling degree of
scepticism". Some solicitors might have been sceptical, but that did not mean that it was something
that any reasonably competent solicitor would have done.
[339] *Leadbitter v Hodge Finance Ltd* [1982] 2 All E.R. 167 at 174–175; *Halford v Brookes* [1991] 1
W.L.R. 428 at 434. This includes any knowledge about facts that his solicitors ought to have acquired:
Henderson v Temple Pier Co. Ltd [1998] 1 W.L.R. 1540.
[340] In *Fowell v National Coal Board, The Times*, 28 May 1986, Parker LJ said that the missing facts
(namely that workmen were not employed by the defendant but by an independent contractor) were
ascertainable by the claimant, because he could have simply written to the National Coal Board, but
this was knowledge which he could not himself have been reasonably expected to acquire; cf. the
investigative skills expected of the claimant in *Leadbitter v Hodge Finance Ltd* [1982] 2 All E.R. 167,
para.11–118.
[341] *Farmer v National Coal Board, The Times*, 27 April 1985, CA.
[342] See *Central Asbestos Co. Ltd v Dodd* [1973] A.C. 518 at 555–556, per Lord Salmon commenting
on the effect of the earlier legislation, the Limitation Act 1963, and distinguishing between legal
advice which leaves the claimant in ignorance of material facts, and legal advice that on the facts he
has no remedy in law.
[343] [1982] 2 All E.R. 167 at 174–175.

report, making inquiries of the fire brigade and local residents, and interviewing potential witnesses. This raises a question as to precisely what facts would be treated as ascertainable only with legal assistance. For example, would a patient be expected to seek and obtain his own medical records?

11–119   Thirdly, it is possible that s.14(3)(b) does not apply to *any* form of legal advice. In *Fowell v National Coal Board*[344] the Court of Appeal doubted, without deciding the point, that a party's solicitor was an "expert" within the meaning of the subsection, which was directed to experts in the sense of expert witnesses.[345] If correct, this would mean that a claimant is not constructively fixed with the knowledge of his solicitor *by virtue of s.14(3)*.[346] It would seem, however, that under the general law of agency a claimant is fixed with the knowledge that the solicitor actually has,[347] and in *Simpson v Norwest Holst Southern Ltd*[348] it appears to have been assumed by the Court of Appeal that a claimant will also be fixed with knowledge which the solicitor ought reasonably to have acquired.[349] Presumably this would be the position even where the claimant could not reasonably have acquired the knowledge. Thus, a claimant who has no actual or constructive knowledge may be caught by the solicitor's constructive knowledge and will be unable to rely on the proviso to s.14(3)(b). In this situation time will run against the claimant who may have to apply to the court to allow the action to proceed under s.33.

11–120   In *Nash v Eli Lilly & Co.*,[350] on the other hand, Hidden J observed that the discussion of this question in *Fowell* was obiter and that there was no binding authority as to whether facts ascertainable by a claimant with the help of legal advice fall within the terms of s.14(3)(b). His Lordship doubted whether ordinarily they do, but could envisage circumstances where they might: if, for example, the identification of a potential defendant turned upon the construction of legislation. Moreover, Hidden J came to the conclusion that a claimant may be fixed with constructive knowledge of facts that the solicitor knows or ought reasonably to have known, because this falls within s.14(3)(a) as a fact

---

[344] *The Times*, 28 May 1986; *Khan v Ainslie* [1993] 4 Med. L.R. 319 at 325.

[345] cf. s.33(3)(f): in exercising its discretion to allow the action to proceed the court will consider the steps taken by the claimant to obtain expert advice, including legal advice.

[346] *Fowell v National Coal Board* was cited on this point by Russell LJ in *Halford v Brookes* [1991] 1 W.L.R. 428 at 434, with apparent approval.

[347] *Khan v Ainslie* [1993] 4 Med. L.R. 319 at 325, per Waterhouse J: "There are, of course, reasons why [s.14(3)] could and should be interpreted narrowly, on the basis that 'him' simply means a plaintiff and not his legal adviser. But my impression is that the balance of the argument is in favour of including the agent of the plaintiff within the scope of 'him'." On the other hand, for the purpose of the exercise of discretion under s.33 there is no rule that anything done by the lawyers must be visited on the client: *Das v Ganju* [1999] P.I.Q.R. P260, 268; [1999] Lloyd's Rep. Med. 198 at 204, CA; *Corbin v Penfold Metallising Company Ltd* [2000] Lloyds Rep. Med. 247 at 251, CA; *Steeds v Peverel Management Services Ltd* [2001] EWCA Civ 419; *The Times*, 16 May 2001, CA.

[348] [1980] 1 W.L.R. 968 at 974.

[349] See the discussion in *Fowell v National Coal Board*, *The Times*, 28 May 1986, where Parker LJ specifically left this point open.

[350] [1991] 2 Med. L.R. 169.

"ascertainable by him".[351] Thus, "ascertainable" would include facts ascertainable by claimants personally and by others (including lawyers and doctors) ascertaining facts for them. On this interpretation it is not clear why there is any need for s.14(3)(b), which would appear to be subsumed within s.14(3)(a). This view would also seem to restore the application of the proviso to legal advice, at least if legal advice can be said to be "expert advice".[352]

(c) Court's discretion

Claimants have an indefeasible right to bring an action within the primary three-year limitation period. Where that period has expired claimants may still be able to proceed if they can persuade the court to exercise its discretion under s.33 in their favour.

11–121

(i) Availability of the discretion

In *Firman v Ellis*[353] the Court of Appeal said that the court's discretion under s.33 was unfettered. It was not restricted to a residual category of exceptional cases. This view was approved by the House of Lords in *Thompson v Brown Construction (Ebbw Vale) Ltd*,[354] and again by the House of Lords in *Horton v Sadler*.[355] Previous editions of this work have had to grapple with the House of Lords' decision in *Walkley v Precision Forgings Ltd*[356] where their Lordships drew a distinction between a claimant who had not issued any proceedings within the primary three-year limitation period, who could invoke s.33, and a claimant who had issued a claim form within the limitation period but who had not proceeded with the action, who could not. A second claim form issued out of time would be statute-barred. The ratio of *Walkley* was that the claimant had been prejudiced not by the application of s.11 but by the failure to proceed with the first action. This led to a number of attempts by the courts to distinguish *Walkley* and to limit it to its particular facts in order to ameliorate the manifest unfairness

11–122

---

[351] A view supported, obiter, by Buckley J in *Colegrove v Smyth* [1994] 5 Med. L.R. 111. See also the comments of Waterhouse J in *Khan v Ainslie* [1993] 4 Med. L.R. 319 at 325, cited above, para.11–119, n.347.

[352] The Court of Appeal could "see no reason to depart from" Hidden J's general approach to this issue, merely commenting that: "where constructive knowledge is under consideration through the channel of a solicitor, this can only be relevant where it is established that the plaintiff ought reasonably to have consulted a solicitor at all. Thus it is for the defendant to establish not only that a solicitor whom the plaintiff might consult would have the necessary knowledge but also that it was reasonable to expect the plaintiff to consult him." See *Nash v Eli Lilly & Co.* [1993] 1 W.L.R. 782 at 800, CA.

[353] [1978] Q.B. 886.

[354] [1981] 1 W.L.R. 744; see also *Donovan v Gwentoys Ltd* [1990] 1 W.L.R. 472 at 477, per Lord Griffiths.

[355] [2006] UKHL 27; [2007] 1 A.C. 307; see K. Patten "Limitation and Discretion in the House of Lords—A Farewell to *Walkley*" [2006[J.P.I.L 295.

[356] [1979] 1 W.L.R. 606.

of the decision for claimants.[357] The restrictions on a claimant's entitlement to invoke the court's discretion under s.33 established by *Walkley*, and the exceptions to those restrictions, are no longer relevant because in *Horton v Sadler* the House of Lords overruled *Walkley*. Lord Bingham commented that:

> "...the reasoning of [*Walkley*] was unsound, that it has given rise to distinctions which disfigure the law in this area and that the effect has been to restrict unduly the broad discretion which Parliament conferred."[358]

The result is that the court has an unfettered discretion to disapply the limitation period where it is equitable to do so, which means "no more (but also no less) than fair".[359]

(ii)   Exercise of the discretion

11–123   The court's discretion under s.33 is completely unfettered.[360] Section 33(1) provides that the court may direct that the three-year period specified by ss.11, 11A and 12 shall not apply if it would be equitable to allow the action to proceed, having regard to the degree to which (a) those sections prejudice the claimant, and (b) the decision to allow the action to proceed would prejudice the defendant.[361] The court has to balance the degree of prejudice to the claimant caused by the operation of the primary limitation period against the prejudice to the defendant if the action were to be allowed to proceed. The stronger the claimant's case is on the merits the greater the prejudice to him, and conversely, the weaker his case the less he is prejudiced.[362] On the other hand, if defendants

---

[357] See, e.g. *Thompson v Brown Construction (Ebbw Vale) Ltd* [1981] 1 W.L.R. 744; *Shapland v Palmer* [1999] P.I.Q.R. P249; *Piggott v Aulton (Deceased)* [2003] EWCA Civ 24; [2003] P.I.Q.R. P22; *Adams v Ali* [2006] EWCA Civ 91; [2006] 1 W.L.R. 1330; [2006] P.I.Q.R. P20.

[358] [2006] UKHL 27; [2007] 1 A.C. 307 at [28].

[359] [2006] UKHL 27; [2007] 1 A.C. 307 at [32] per Lord Bingham. An attempt to resurrect the effect of *Walkley* where the claimant has issued a first claim form within the limitation period but had then failed to serve it on the defendant in the four months allowed for service was rejected by the Court of Appeal in *Aktas v Adepta* [2010] EWCA Civ 1170; [2011] Q.B. 894. The defendant argued that issuing a second claim form outside the limitation period constituted an abuse of process, and so should be struck out, because the claimant was attempting to avoid the effect of the Civil Procedure Rules requiring service within four months. The Court of Appeal, applying *Horton*, concluded that this was an attempt circumvent the will of Parliament by preventing a claimant from seeking to rely on the s.33 discretion. There should be no fetter on the availability of the discretion.

[360] *Thompson v Brown Construction (Ebbw Vale) Ltd* [1981] 1 W.L.R. 744; *Donovan v Gwentoys Ltd* [1990] 1 W.L.R. 472 at 477. See K. Patten, "Judicial Discretion to Extend the Limitation Period—Policy, Principle and Application" [2004] J.P.I.L. 306; K. Patten, "Windfalls and corrective justice—discretion to extend the limitation period in personal injury cases" (2017) 33 P.N. 8.

[361] The word "equitable" is not a term of art, it is simply another way of saying "fair and just" as between the parties: *Ward v Foss*, *The Times*, 29 November 1993, CA, per Hobhouse LJ. Where the claimant has been untruthful and sought to mislead the court on key issues, it is unlikely that the court will consider it equitable to disapply the limitation period: *Long v Tolchard* [2001] P.I.Q.R. P18, CA; cf. *Davis v Jacobs and Camden & Islington Health Authority and Novartis Pharmaceuticals (UK) Ltd* [1999] Lloyd's Rep. Med. 72 at 87–88, where it was alleged that as a result of the defendants' negligence the claimant's personality was substantially altered by the drugs he was prescribed as part of a clinical trial.

[362] "Plainly it is more prejudicial to a plaintiff to be deprived of a cause of action when it is almost bound to succeed . . . than one that looks highly speculative. Equally, although it is always prejudicial

have a good case on the merits there is probably less prejudice to them in allowing the action to proceed, although in *Thompson v Brown Construction (Ebbw Vale) Ltd*[363] Lord Diplock said that it was still highly prejudicial to defendants to allow the action to proceed even where they have a good defence on the merits.

Meaning of "prejudice"   It has been argued, and indeed apparently accepted in   **11–124**
some cases, that the prejudice to defendants is at its greatest when they have no defence on the merits since they have been deprived of a cast-iron (limitation) defence. This is not an attractive argument, however, since it undermines the whole rationale of giving the court a discretion to override the primary limitation period.[364] "Prejudice" to the defendant must mean more than simply the removal of the limitation defence. Why, it might be asked, should the court be concerned with the cogency of the evidence and its effect on defendants' ability to establish a defence on the merits when the prejudice to defendants is greater if they have no such defence? This point was acknowledged by Leggatt LJ in *Hartley v Birmingham City District Council*:

> "The defendants' approach produces the bizarre, if logical, result that the prejudice to the defendants is greatest when they have no defence to the merits of the claim, because not disapplying the limitation provision affords them a defence on liability which they would not otherwise have had. But a decision not [sic. query delete the "not"] to allow the action to proceed would cause the defendants to suffer no injustice whatever in being required to meet a claim of which they had had prompt notice and which they had had every opportunity of preparing themselves to meet. Equity need not be concerned to afford adventitious protection to a tortfeasor who has not been deprived of any opportunity to defend himself."[365]

Parker LJ suggested that in nearly all cases the prejudice to the claimant by the operation of the limitation period and the prejudice to the defendant if the limitation period is disapplied will be equal and opposite. The stronger the claimant's case against the defendant the greater the prejudice to him from the operation of the limitation period and the greater the prejudice to the defendant if the provision is disapplied. Similarly, the weaker the claimant's case the less he will be prejudiced by the operation of the limitation period and the less the defendant is prejudiced if the provision is disapplied. This led his Lordship to the conclusion that the loss of the defence *as such* was of little importance. What was of paramount importance was the effect of the delay on the defendant's ability to

---

to a defendant to be deprived of a defence under the Limitation Act, it may be less inequitable or unfair where the plaintiff has a strong case and more unfair where he has a weak one. But where as here the limitation issue is tried and determined before the merits of the claim, the court cannot and should not attempt to determine the merits on affidavit evidence. All that can be done and should be done is for the judge to take an overall view of the prospects of success . . ." per Stuart-Smith LJ in *Dale v British Coal Corporation* [1992] P.I.Q.R. P373, 380, CA; *Forbes v Wandsworth Health Authority* [1997] Q.B. 402 at 418: "The court can, of course, only take a broad view of the matter at this stage." In *AB v Ministry of Defence* [2012] UKSC 9; [2013] 1 A.C. 78 at [27] Lord Wilson observed that it was "undesirable" for a court considering an exercise of the discretion under s.33 to "have detailed regard to the evidence with which the claimant aspires to prove his case at trial".
[363] [1981] 1 W.L.R. 744 at 750.
[364] See Jones (1985) 1 P.N. 159 at 162.
[365] [1992] 1 W.L.R. 968 at 982.

defend.[366] Thus, where there was a short delay after the expiry of the primary limitation period, which was not caused by the claimant's fault but was entirely the fault of his solicitors, and the delay did not affect the defendant's ability to defend the action on the merits, the court was justified in exercising the discretion in favour of the claimant under s.33 even though he would have a cast-iron action against his solicitors if the action were not allowed to proceed.

11–125   In *Ward v Foss*[367] Hobhouse LJ considered the "paradox" postulated by Parker LJ in *Hartley v Birmingham City Council* but concluded that the paradox does not exist:

> "The prejudice to the plaintiff is indeed the prejudice which would result from being de-barred from pursuing his action. But the prejudice to the defendant is not the prejudice of meeting a liability but of having to defend, or otherwise deal with, a stale claim. This prejudice to the defendant may well be no less, indeed it may be greater, where the claim is unmeritorious. I agree with Parker LJ and Leggatt LJ when they stressed the importance of the 'effect of the delay upon the defendant's ability to defend' and whether the defendant is still 'properly equipped to meet' the claim notwithstanding the delay that has occurred."

But it was not inequitable, said his Lordship, that a defendant should meet his liabilities in accordance with the laws of this country, nor did a requirement that he should meet his legal liabilities show, without more, that he would suffer relevant prejudice within the meaning of s.33:

> "For the purposes of s.33, if a defendant is to say that he is prejudiced, he must show something more than merely that he is going to be required to meet his legal liabilities. The prejudice must arise from some other additional element—some change of his position which would not have occurred if the action had been brought within time—some belief by the defendant that he was not going to be troubled with the claim—some alteration in his financial position or some failure to make provision for the claim—the loss of relevant evidence—some difficulty in having a fair trial after the lapse of time. No list can be exhaustive and the statute requires the court to have regard to all the circumstances of the case. But it must be some factor over and on top of the legal liability of the defendant which creates the prejudice."[368]

It is respectfully submitted that the approach of Hobhouse LJ is correct. In the same case Simon Brown LJ said that s.33 was concerned with prejudice to the defendant *caused by the delay*. This was plain both from the express terms of s.33 and on the authorities. It would seem, then, that whereas from the claimant's perspective the inability to continue the action as a result of the operation of the Limitation Act does constitute prejudice, loss of the limitation defence in itself cannot constitute relevant prejudice to the defendant, and in exercising the discretion conferred by s.33 the court should balance the prejudice to the claimant

---

[366] [1992] 1 W.L.R. 968 at 980.

[367] *The Times*, 29 November 1993, CA.

[368] *The Times*, 29 November 1993, CA. See also *McEvoy v AA Welding and Fabrication Ltd* [1998] P.I.Q.R. P226 at 273 where Pill LJ commented that: "An important feature of the present case is *the lack of prejudice to the defendants* by reason of the fact that they have, subject to their limitation defence, admitted liability" (emphasis added). In *Shapland v Palmer* [1999] 1 W.L.R. 2068, CA, the only prejudice to the defendant was being deprived of the limitation defence, and accordingly the Court exercised the discretion in the claimant's favour.

of *losing the right to bring an action* with the prejudice to the defendant of having to face a *late claim*, not the prejudice of having to face a claim at all after the expiry of the primary limitation period.

The interpretation given in *Hartley v Birmingham City Council* was fully endorsed by the Court of Appeal in *Cain v Francis*[369] which laid down the definitive approach to apply in cases where the defendant has no defence on the merits. There was concern that judges at first instance were taking diametrically opposed views of the meaning of prejudice to the defendant. There should be consistency of approach, said Smith LJ, between judges on an issue as fundamental as whether the loss of a limitation defence amounts to real prejudice in a case where the defendant had no defence to liability on the merits. The issue could be tested by asking what were the rights of the parties before the operation of s.11. The claimant had the right to pursue his cause of action which he lost by the operation of s.11, whereas the defendant had an obligation to pay the damages due; his right was the right to a fair opportunity to defend himself against the claim. Section 11 gives the defendant a complete procedural defence which removes the obligation to pay. But:

11–126

> "In fairness and justice, he only deserves to have that obligation removed if the passage of time has significantly diminished his opportunity to defend himself (on liability and/or quantum). So the making of a direction, which would restore the defendant's obligation to pay damages, is only prejudicial to him if his right to a fair opportunity to defend himself has been compromised."[370]

Parliament could not have intended that that financial prejudice, as such, should be taken into account, said Smith LJ, because, in fairness and justice, defendants ought to pay the damages if, having had a fair opportunity to defend themselves, they are found liable.[371] Claimants are in a different position because the effect of s.11 is that they have been prejudiced by the loss of the right to enforce their cause of action. Thus, when it comes to exercising the discretion:

> "...the basic question to be asked is whether it is fair and just in all the circumstances to expect the defendant to meet this claim on the merits, notwithstanding the delay in commencement. The length of the delay will be important, not so much for itself as to the effect it has had. To what extent has the defendant been disadvantaged in his investigation of the claim and/or the assembly of evidence, in respect of the issues of both liability and quantum? But it will also be important to consider the reasons for the delay. Thus, there may be some unfairness to the defendant due to the delay in issue but the delay may have arisen for so excusable a reason, that, looking at the matter in the round, on balance, it is fair and just that the action should proceed."[372]

It cannot always be said, however, that where the ability of a defendant to defend on the merits has not been affected by the delay, the benefit of the limitation

11–127

---

[369] [2008] EWCA Civ 1451; [2009] Q.B. 754; the case is discussed by Stockwell [2009] J.P.I.L. C99.
[370] [2008] EWCA Civ 1451; [2009] Q.B. 754 at [69].
[371] [2008] EWCA Civ 1451; [2009] Q.B. 754 at [70]. See also the observation of Sir Andrew Morritt C at [81] that the loss of a limitation defence of itself could not be regarded as a head of prejudice to the defendant at all: "it is merely the obverse of the disapplication of s.11 which is assumed."
[372] [2008] EWCA Civ 1451; [2009] Q.B. 754 at [73].

defence must be regarded as a "windfall". In *Nash v Eli Lilly & Co.*[373] the Court of Appeal held that there may be significant and relevant prejudice to a defendant even if it is shown that the claimant's claim is a poor case lacking in merit, since by disapplying the primary limitation period the defendants are put to the expense of defending a poor case, which may well cost far more to defend than the case would be held to be worth. Allowing the action to proceed may simply enable a dilatory claimant to claim from the defendants a sum in settlement which reflects the risk in costs to the defendants rather than the fair value of the claim.

11–128   When considering the degree of prejudice to the parties the court is required by s.33(3) to:

"...have regard to all the circumstances of the case, and in particular to:
(a)   the length of and reasons for the delay on the part of the plaintiff;
(b)   the extent to which, having regard to the delay, the evidence... is likely to be less cogent...;
(c)   the conduct of the defendant after the cause of action arose, including the extent (if any) to which he responded to requests reasonably made by the plaintiff for information or inspection for the purpose of ascertaining facts which were or might be relevant to the plaintiff's cause of action against the defendant;
(d)   the duration of any disability of the plaintiff arising after the date of the accrual of the cause of action;
(e)   the extent to which the plaintiff acted promptly and reasonably once he knew whether or not the act or omission of the defendant, to which the injury was attributable, might be capable at that time of giving rise to an action for damages;
(f)   the steps, if any, taken by the plaintiff to obtain medical, legal or other expert advice and the nature of any such advice he may have received."

11–129   **All the circumstances of the case**   It has been stressed by both the Court of Appeal and the House of Lords that the court should consider *all* the circumstances of the case, not simply the issues identified by s.33(3).[374] Provided this has been done, the Court of Appeal will be reluctant to interfere with the trial judge's exercise of discretion,[375] though it has been said that the fact that the judge did not specifically have regard to the degrees of prejudice to the claimant and the defendant respectively, but went straight to the circumstances mentioned in paras (a) to (f) of s.33(3) does not necessarily mean that the judgment is flawed. The prejudice to each side may be "obvious" and not have to be expressly considered.[376]

---

[373] [1993] 1 W.L.R. 782 at 808.
[374] *Taylor v Taylor, The Times*, 14 April 1984, CA; *Donovan v Gwentoys Ltd* [1990] 1 W.L.R. 472; *KR v Bryn Alyn Community (Holdings) Ltd (In Liquidation)* [2003] EWCA Civ 85; [2003] Q.B. 1441 at [74].
[375] *Conry v Simpson* [1983] 3 All E.R. 369; *Bradley v Hanseatic Shipping Co. Ltd* [1986] 2 Lloyd's Rep. 34. The court will overturn a judge's exercise of discretion only if it can be shown that he has "gone very wrong indeed", per Lawton LJ at 38. And see Clarke LJ in *Burgin v Sheffield City Council* [2005] EWCA Civ 482 at [16]: "This court will only interfere with the exercise of a judge's discretion where he has erred in principle or made a decision which is plainly wrong."
[376] *Yates v Thakeham Tiles Ltd* [1995] P.I.Q.R. P135 at 139, per Nourse LJ, CA. But where a judge is minded to grant a long "extension" he should take meticulous care in giving reasons for doing so: *KR v Bryn Alyn Community (Holdings) Ltd (In Liquidation)* [2003] EWCA Civ 85; [2003] Q.B. 1441 at [74].

Length of and reasons for the delay—s.33(3)(a)   "Delay" in s.33(3)(a) and   **11–130**
(b) refers to the period between the expiry of the primary limitation period and
the issue of the claim form, not the period between the accrual of the action or the
claimant's "knowledge" and the issue of the claim form.[377] However, in *Donovan
v Gwentoys Ltd*[378] the House of Lords, whilst agreeing with this interpretation of
s.33(3), held that in weighing the degree of prejudice to the defendant the court
was entitled to take into account the whole period of delay, including that within
the primary limitation period, as part of all the circumstances of the case. The
delay which their Lordships had in mind appears to be the delay between the
commencement of the limitation period and notification to the defendant of the
claim, rather than the issue of the claim form, the object being to bar "thoroughly
stale claims".[379] Lord Griffiths said that:

> "... it must always be relevant to consider when the defendant first had notification of the
> claim and thus the opportunity he will have to meet the claim at the trial if he is not to be
> permitted to rely on his limitation defence."[380]

Thus, there will be a distinction between cases where the defendant was notified
of the claim fairly promptly, and so had an opportunity to give it full
consideration, but the limitation period has expired through an oversight by the
claimant's solicitors,[381] and cases such as *Donovan v Gwentoys Ltd*, where the
defendant first heard of the claim some five years after the accident and was not

---

[377] *Thompson v Brown Construction (Ebbw Vale) Ltd* [1981] 1 W.L.R. 744 at 751; *Eastman v London
County Bus Services Ltd, The Times*, 23 November 1985, CA; *T v Boys and Girls Welfare Service*
[2004] EWCA Civ 1747.
[378] [1990] 1 W.L.R. 472; applied in *Cain v Francis* [2008] EWCA Civ 1451; [2009] Q.B. 754 at [74];
McDonnell v Walker [2009] EWCA Civ 1257; [2010] P.I.Q.R. P5; *Davidson v Aegis Defence Services
(BVI) Ltd* [2013] EWCA Civ 1586; [2014] 2 All E.R. 216.
[379] In *Collins v Secretary of State for Business Innovation and Skills* [2014] EWCA Civ 717; [2014]
P.I.Q.R. P19 the Court of Appeal held that it was also appropriate to take into account the elapse of
time between the defendant's breach of duty and the *start* of the limitation period as one of the factors
to be considered in all the circumstances of the case under s.33(3). However, Jackson LJ commented,
at [65], that: "Loss of cogency of evidence during the limitation period must be a factor which carries
more weight than (a) the disappearance of evidence before the limitation clock starts to tick or (b) the
loss of cogency of evidence before the limitation clock starts to tick."
[380] [1990] 1 W.L.R. 472 at 479. His Lordship added that to the extent that *Eastman v London County
Bus Services Ltd, The Times*, 23 November 1985, appears to cast doubt on this proposition, it should
not be followed.
[381] As occurred in *Thompson v Brown Construction (Ebbw Vale) Ltd* [1981] 1 W.L.R. 744; *Cain v
Francis* [2008] EWCA Civ 1451; [2009] Q.B. 754; see also *Simpson v Norwest Holst Southern Ltd*
[1980] 1 W.L.R. 968 at 977 where the claim was only 14 days out of time and the defendants had had
an early opportunity of investigating the claim and getting their evidence together. In *Godfrey v
Gloucestershire Royal Infirmary NHS Trust* [2003] EWHC 549 (QB); [2003] Lloyd's Rep. Med. 398
Leveson J commented, at [38], that since the claimant's complaint about the management of her
pregnancy had been put into writing very quickly, giving the defendants the opportunity to obtain
information from the medical staff almost contemporaneously with events, and they were put on
notice that proceedings were being contemplated, it could not be "suggested that the claim has come
out of the blue many years after the events".

in a position to investigate it until six years after the events.[382] In *Ward v Foss*[383] there was a delay of over four years after the expiry of primary limitation period, but there had been prompt notification of the claims and within two years of the accident the defendant's solicitors had been instructed to negotiate a settlement, which implied an appropriate degree of investigation. The early notification of the claim made the case more like *Thompson v Brown Construction (Ebbw Vale) Ltd* than *Donovan v Gwentoys Ltd*. In contrast, Stuart-Smith LJ pointed out in *Dale v British Coal Corporation*[384] that where the existence of a claim and sufficient particulars of it are given so late that it is virtually impossible for the defendants to investigate it a defendant will be gravely prejudiced if s.11 is disapplied, because he is almost powerless to defend the case on its merits. Such a case would require exceptional circumstances to outweigh that prejudice, and to bring the scales down in favour of the claimant.

11–131   In *T v Boys and Girls Welfare Service*[385] the Court of Appeal noted that by the time that the claim was brought, 28 years had passed since the events that gave rise to the action, and the service of the claim was the first notice that the defendant had of the allegations. The Court held that it was no answer to say that the prejudice had only been marginally increased by the fact that the claim was made two years after the limitation period had expired. Parliament had determined in s.11 and s.14 of the Act where the balance of prejudice should normally be struck. It followed that s.33 was only available in special cases and it was for the claimant in any particular case to establish that his claim was one of those special cases. The mere fact of being asked to deal with a stale claim was itself prejudice, and the staler the claim the greater the prejudice. The policy of the law was to permit people and organisations to arrange their affairs on the basis that there came a time when they should not be asked to meet such claims.

11–132   A short delay probably causes little prejudice to the defendant,[386] indeed, a very short delay (of one day) causes no prejudice at all, particularly where the defendant was notified about the claim at an early stage.[387] It has been suggested

---

[382] [1990] 1 W.L.R. 472 at 479, per Lord Griffiths; cf. the position where the claimant is under a disability; the defendant may be seriously prejudiced in his ability to produce evidence, but this is irrelevant: see para.11–152, and *Bull v Devon Area Health Authority* (1989), [1993] 4 Med. L.R. 117, CA.

[383] *The Times*, 29 November 1993, CA.

[384] [1992] P.I.Q.R. P373 at 385, CA.

[385] [2004] EWCA Civ 1747.

[386] *Firman v Ellis* [1978] Q.B. 886; *Simpson v Norwest Holst Southern Ltd* [1980] 1 W.L.R. 968 at 977; *Atha v ATV Network* unreported 28 June 1983, QBD; *Grenville v Waltham Forest Health Authority* unreported 18 November 1992, CA; *Adams v Ali* [2006] EWCA Civ 91; [2006] 1 W.L.R. 1330; [2006] P.I.Q.R. P20—delay of 13 months but the defendant was notified of the claim within days of the accident and liability was admitted; *Johnston v Chief Constable of Merseyside* [2009] EWHC 2969 (QB); [2009] M.H.L.R. 343—delay of two-and-a-half months, but defendant aware of claim because an earlier claim had been submitted within limitation period, but that claim was a nullity because the claimant had not applied for leave under s.139(2) of the Mental Health Act 1983, a point that had been raised by the defendant days before the expiry of the limitation period; cf. *Davis v Soltenpar* (1983) 133 N.L.J. 720 where the claim form was 24 days late, the defendant's case was "wholly without merit" but the discretion was not exercised in the claimant's favour.

[387] *Hartley v Birmingham City District Council* [1992] 1 W.L.R. 968; *Cain v Francis* [2008] EWCA Civ 1451; [2009] Q.B. 754 at [74] per Smith LJ: "If, as here, a defendant has had early notification of

that a delay of five or six years could raise a rebuttable presumption of prejudice,[388] though the Court of Appeal has indicated that a presumption of prejudice is not justified because it would "impermissibly cut down the wide discretion" in s.33 cases,[389] though as a general proposition the longer the delay the more likely it is that the balance of prejudice will swing against disapplying the primary limitation period.[390]

Reasons for the delay   The length of the delay is probably of less significance than the reasons for the delay and the effect on the cogency of the evidence. Reasons for the delay will vary considerably, and whereas claimants' subjective beliefs may be irrelevant to the question of their knowledge under s.14 they are relevant to the court's exercise of discretion.[391] Claimants may have been unaware of their legal rights[392]; or the injury may not have seemed so serious at first[393]; or they may have felt that they were "sponging" if they sued and may have wanted to maintain good relations with the defendant[394]; or they may have been in a debilitated physical and mental state throughout the relevant period;[395];   **11–133**

a claim and every possible opportunity to investigate and to collect evidence, some delay after the expiry of three years will have had no prejudicial effect." See also *Hendy v Milton Keynes Health Authority* [1992] 3 Med. L.R. 114; [1992] P.I.Q.R. P281, where there was a delay of nine days, but no effect on the cogency of the evidence, and no prejudice to the defendants.

[388] *Buck v English Electric Co. Ltd* [1977] 1 W.L.R. 806, where there was a nine-year delay, but the defendants were not seriously prejudiced because in that period they had dealt with many similar claims and evidence was available; *Pilmore v Northern Trawlers Ltd* [1986] 1 Lloyd's Rep. 552, another case involving a nine-year delay; cf. *Cornish v Kearley* (1983) 133 N.L.J. 870, where there was a three-year delay, but the reasons for the delay were reasonable, the cogency of the evidence was affected but not greatly, and, in the circumstances, it was not unreasonable for the claimant to have delayed taking legal advice.

[389] *KR v Bryn Alyn Community (Holdings) Ltd (In Liquidation)* [2003] EWCA Civ 85; [2003] Q.B. 1441 at [79].

[390] [2003] EWCA Civ 85; [2003] Q.B. 1441 at [80]; *Rowe v Kingston upon Hull City Council* [2003] EWCA Civ 1281; [2004] P.I.Q.R. P16.

[391] *Buck v English Electric Co. Ltd* [1977] 1 W.L.R. 806; *McCafferty v Metropolitan Police District Receiver* [1977] 1 W.L.R. 1073; *Coad v Cornwall & Isles of Scilly Health Authority* [1997] 1 W.L.R. 189; *Skerratt v Linfax Ltd (t/a Go Karting for Fun)* [2003] EWCA Civ 695; [2004] P.I.Q.R. P10 at [26]. But even an honest subjective belief held by the claimant may be blameworthy, and something to be taken into account in weighing the balance of prejudice: at [31].

[392] *Brooks v Coates (UK) Ltd* [1984] 1 All E.R. 702 at 713, where the delay was 15 years, but the claimant's ignorance was not unreasonable; *Coad v Cornwall & Isles of Scilly Health Authority* [1997] 1 W.L.R. 189; cf. *Dobbie v Medway Health Authority* [1994] 1 W.L.R. 1234, CA, where there was a gap of 16 years between the claimant's operation and the issue of the claim form. The Court of Appeal held that the delay was too great, despite the fact that the claimant had been unaware of her right to bring an action. If one of the reasons for delay is the claimant's failure to take legal advice this should be taken into account as a relevant circumstance under s.33(3)(f): *Skerratt v Linfax Ltd (t/a Go Karting for Fun)* [2003] EWCA Civ 695; [2004] P.I.Q.R. P10 at [31].

[393] *McCafferty v Metropolitan Police District Receiver* [1977] 1 W.L.R. 1073.

[394] *Buck v English Electric Co. Ltd* [1977] 1 W.L.R. 806; *McCafferty v Metropolitan Police District Receiver* [1977] 1 W.L.R. 1073. A patient's natural reluctance to upset the doctor/patient relationship by engaging in litigation will be relevant here.

[395] *Mills v Dyer-Fare* unreported 9 March 1987, QBD; *Birnie v Oxfordshire Health Authority* (1982) 2 *The Lancet* 281, QBD; *Pearse v Barnet Health Authority* [1998] P.I.Q.R. P39; *Godfrey v Gloucestershire Royal Infirmary NHS Trust* [2003] EWHC 549 (QB); [2003] Lloyd's Rep. Med. 398 at [41], where the claimant had to "cope with a severely disabled baby which will have imposed its own emotional physical and financial constraints on the single minded pursuit of this litigation". In

or the defendant may have contributed to the delay by withholding information from the claimant.[396] Generally, where claimants' conduct has not been personally blameworthy this will carry considerable weight in persuading the court to exercise the discretion in their favour.[397] On the other hand, where the delay is inexcusable and has caused forensic prejudice to the defendant the court is much less likely to exercise the discretion in favour of the claimant.[398]

11–134   **Effect of delay on the cogency of the evidence—s.33(3)(b)**   Usually it is the effect of the delay on the cogency of the evidence which is most significant. If documents have been destroyed or witnesses have disappeared this is a different situation from cases where there is little real dispute about the facts, since the defendant's ability to defend the case has clearly been prejudiced.[399] The essential question under s.33 is whether, given the passage of time, the court can fairly try

---

Sanderson v Bradford MBC [2016] EWHC 527 (QB) at [31] Judge Walden-Smith gave a list of reasons explaining why the deceased, who had died of mesothelioma, had not brought an action sooner, including the shock of the unexpected diagnosis, the effects of the treatment he had undergone, a period of unexpected remission during which he sought to keep life as normal as possible, his desire not to leave his family with legal debts, and the "perfectly understandable human reaction to such catastrophic news that there were more important things than bringing a claim for damages". These factors, combined with the fact that the post-limitation period of delay was 10 weeks weighed heavily in favour of granting an extension of time.

[396] *Drury v Grimsby Health Authority* [1997] 8 Med. L.R. 38.

[397] *Brooks v Coates (UK) Ltd* [1984] 1 All E.R. 702; *Bates v Leicester Health Authority* [1998] Lloyd's Rep. Med. 93 at 102; *Ashe Construction Ltd v Burke* [2003] EWCA Civ 717; [2004] P.I.Q.R. P11—claimant not personally blameworthy, and the delay was largely attributable to the conduct of his lawyers; the action was allowed to proceed despite a substantial delay (over seven years), because the issues at trial would largely turn on the safety of the "system of work" adopted by the defendants rather than a dispute as to what had actually happened. In *Whiston v London SHA* [2010] EWCA Civ 195; [2010] 1 W.L.R. 1582 the claimant suffered from cerebral palsy caused by brain damage sustained at birth in 1974; his condition worsened in 2005 and he issued proceedings in 2006. Although "he did not exhibit the curiosity of the reasonable person in his circumstances" he was not to be criticised, because he had been coping well despite his disabilities and he had just wanted to get on with his life.

[398] *McDonnell v Walker* [2009] EWCA Civ 1257; [2010] P.I.Q.R. P5; commented on by Cooksley [2010] J.P.I.L. C49. Where claimants offers no explanation for the delay they are unlikely to persuade the court to disapply the primary limitation period: *Berry v Calderdale Health Authority* [1998] Lloyd's Rep. Med. 179, CA; *Buckler v Sheffield City Council* [2004] EWCA Civ 920; [2005] P.I.Q.R. P3—no disapplication of the primary limitation period where there was a delay of nine years after expiry of limitation period, when the claimant had taken a conscious decision not to do anything about bringing a claim, and his medical condition in 2001 was no worse than in 1991.

[399] "In my judgment where the existence of a claim and sufficient particulars of it are given so late that it is virtually impossible for the defendants to investigate it, either because witnesses cannot be traced, memories will inevitably have faded or vital documents are lost, a defendant is gravely prejudiced if section 11 of the Act is disapplied, because he is almost powerless to defend the case on its merits. In such a case it will require exceptional circumstances to outweigh the prejudice and to bring the scales down in favour of the plaintiff," per Stuart-Smith LJ in *Dale v British Coal Corporation* [1992] P.I.Q.R. P373 at 385, CA; *Sayers v Lord Chelwood* [2012] EWCA Civ 1715; [2013] 1 W.L.R. 1695 at [63]; cf. *Brooks v Coates (UK) Ltd* [1984] 1 All E.R. 702, 713–714. On the other hand, where there is a long limitation period, as in the case of minors, delay after expiry of the limitation period may have no real effect on the cogency of the evidence, since the delay during the primary limitation period may have done all the damage to the cogency of the evidence that is going to occur: see *Doughty v North Staffordshire Health Authority* [1992] 3 Med. L.R. 81 at 85, per Henry J; *Colegrove v Smyth* [1994] 5 Med. L.R. 111 at 118, per Buckley J.

the claim that the defendant was negligent.[400] The defendant is not required to adduce evidence of specific prejudice as a result of delay, since the court is entitled to draw an inference that there has been prejudice caused by delay as a result of impairment of witnesses' recollections.[401] Cases which are based on allegations about failures in systems of work are likely to be better documented than "one off" accidents.[402] Similarly, where the defendants have had to investigate and prepare to meet another case on liability arising out of the same facts, the cogency of the evidence may not be affected by the delay.[403] Cases of medical negligence should be reasonably well documented in the medical records[404]; although this is not always the case. In *Forbes v Wandsworth Health Authority*[405] the Court of Appeal declined to exercise the discretion under s.33 in

---

[400] *Rowe v Kingston upon Hull City Council* [2003] EWCA Civ 1281; [2004] P.I.Q.R. P16 at [35] per Keene LJ. A short delay is unlikely to affect the cogency of the evidence so that it will probably remain possible to fairly try the claim: *Johnston v Chief Constable of Merseyside* [2009] EWHC 2969 (QB); [2009] M.H.L.R. 343. Contrast *Albonetti v Wirral MBC* [2008] EWHC 3523 (QB) (though cited by Westlaw as [2009] EWHC 832 (QB)): an "understandable" delay of almost 40 years had made it impossible to hold a fair trial into allegations that a local authority had been negligent in permitting a third party to perpetrate sexual abuse on the claimant.

[401] *Price v United Engineering Steels Ltd* [1998] P.I.Q.R. P407.

[402] See, e.g. *Cotton v General Electric Co. Ltd* (1979) 129 N.L.J. 73; *Pilmore v Northern Trawlers Ltd* [1986] 1 Lloyd's Rep. 552; *Buck v English Electric Co. Ltd* [1977] 1 W.L.R. 806, where the evidence was no less cogent due to the delay because the defendants had dealt with a number of similar claims; *Kew v Bettamix Ltd (formerly Tarmac Roadstone Southern Ltd)* [2006] EWCA Civ 1535; [2007] P.I.Q.R. P16.

[403] *Bowers v Harrow Health Authority* [1995] 6 Med. L.R. 16—claim brought by a mother in respect of her psychological injury where the defendants had already investigated the case on liability brought by the estate of a young child; *Richardson v Watson* [2006] EWCA Civ 1662; [2007] R.T.R. 21; [2007] P.I.Q.R. P18—the fact that the defendant would have to defend claims under the Fatal Accidents Act 1976 by children of the deceased on precisely the same issues was an important factor in permitting an action by the deceased's spouse to proceed, disapplying s.12 of the Limitation Act 1980; *Johnston v Chief Constable of Merseyside* [2009] EWHC 2969 (QB); [2009] M.H.L.R. 343 at [46]—claimant's action for false imprisonment not out of time (being governed by s.2 of the Limitation Act 1980) and claimant's action for assault, which was only two-and-a-half months out of time, turned on precisely the same facts; s.11 disapplied.

[404] See, e.g. *Bentley v Bristol and Weston Health Authority* [1991] 2 Med. L.R. 359; *Farthing v North East Essex Health Authority* [1998] Lloyd's Rep. Med. 37, CA; *Smith v Leicester Health Authority* [1998] Lloyd's Rep. Med. 77, CA, where the case on liability turned almost entirely on X-rays taken in 1954 and 1955 which did not come to light until 1995; *Godfrey v Gloucestershire Royal Infirmary NHS Trust* [2003] EWHC 549 (QB); [2003] Lloyd's Rep. Med. 398 at [40]. In *Pearse v Barnet Health Authority* [1998] P.I.Q.R. P39 it was held that there was no prejudice to the defendants from a delay between 1991 and 1994 in dealing with a case based on events in 1970 which would inevitably turn on the (virtually complete) medical records; see also *Ward v Foss, The Times*, 29 November 1993, CA; cf. *Bull v Devon Area Health Authority* unreported 9 April 1987, QBD; aff'd [1993] 4 Med. L.R. 117, CA. In *Hills v Potter* [1984] 1 W.L.R. 641 at 653–654 Hirst J said that if the defendant's evidence was accepted then he had suffered no prejudice as a result of the delay. Since the defendant's evidence was accepted, and particularly having regard to the gravity of the claimant's injuries, it was proper to disapply the limitation bar. But see *KR v Bryn Alyn Community (Holdings) Ltd (In Liquidation)* [2003] EWCA Civ 85; [2003] Q.B. 1441 at [74] where the Court of Appeal said that where judges determine the s.33 issue along with the substantive issues in a case, they should take care not to determine the substantive issues, including liability, causation and quantum, before determining the issue of limitation and, in particular, the effect of delay on the cogency of the evidence: "To rely on his findings on those issues to assess the cogency of the evidence for the purpose of the limitation exercise would put the cart before the horse."

[405] [1997] Q.B. 402.

the claimant's favour having regard to the prejudice to the defendants after a long delay, caused by an inability now to locate medical records and witnesses, fading memories, the difficulty that experts would have in dealing with the appropriate standards of practice of 14 years earlier, and the fact that the claimant's case was supported by scanty evidence and had only modest prospects of success.

11–135   In *Rayner v Wolferstans (A Firm)*[406] Wilkie J took the view that where the claimant alleges that injuries were caused by inadvertent negligence, and that at trial res ipsa loquitur will be relied on, the prejudice to the defendant of any delay is probably less significant because it is highly unlikely that the medical staff present will be in a position to add to the matters noted in the medical records at the time, and the main burden of the debate before the court would be undertaken by medical experts on the basis of the medical records. It would also be open to the hospital to adduce evidence of their systems, procedures and protocols, to answer the claimant's contention that contamination of the contents of an epidural injection must have occurred through negligence.

11–136   In *Nash v Eli Lilly & Co.*[407] Hidden J said that it was not simply a matter of assessing the effect of delay on the cogency of the *defendant's* evidence when assessing prejudice to the defendant, because a lack of cogency in the claimant's evidence due to delay may be used to the advantage of the claimant, for example, in an attempt to explain away or mitigate the effects of omissions or contradictions in that evidence. This approach was rejected, however, by the Court of Appeal.[408] There was no basis in s.33(3) for the concept that lack of cogency in the claimant's case could inure to the benefit of the claimant's case and thereby prejudice the defendant. This was logically unsustainable because it depended upon an assumption that the trial judge would not be able properly to assess the evidence led on behalf of the claimant.

11–137   On the other hand, in *Hammond v West Lancashire Health Authority*[409] the defendants had destroyed the claimant's X-rays because they did not consider them to be part of the patient's medical record (sic). They claimed to have suffered prejudice. The Court of Appeal considered that the prejudice, if anything, was to the claimant and upheld the judge's decision to disapply the limitation period. Similarly in *Whiston v London SHA*[410] the claimant suffered brain damage due to lack of oxygen at birth and issued proceedings more than 30 years later. The CTG trace had gone missing (though the other medical records were still available). Dyson LJ rejected the defendants' argument that they had been prejudiced by the absence of the CTG trace. The argument assumed that it would have contained material favourable to the defendant, but there was no

---

[406] [2015] EWHC 2957 (QB) at [152]–[155].
[407] [1991] 2 Med. L.R. 169.
[408] [1993] 1 W.L.R. 782 at 807. In any event, damage to the cogency of the evidence may be prejudicial to the claimant's case. In *Adams v Ali* [2006] EWCA Civ 91; [2006] 1 W.L.R. 1330; [2006] P.I.Q.R. P20, a case where the defendant had admitted liability, Ward LJ commented, at [39], that: "I am not persuaded that the defendant will suffer any greater prejudice than the claimant in this respect; perhaps the deficiencies in mounting the claim for pecuniary damage will redound to the defendant's advantage and there is no great problem about marshalling the medical evidence."
[409] [1998] Lloyd's Rep. Med. 146.
[410] [2010] EWCA Civ 195; [2010] 1 W.L.R. 1582.

reason to suppose that it would have favoured the defence case more than the claimant's case, and it might have been neutral. Given that the burden of proof at trial would be on the claimant, there was no basis for concluding that the defendant has been prejudiced more than the claimant.[411]

Conduct of the defendant—s.33(3)(c)   Section 33(3)(c) refers specifically to   **11–138** the extent to which the defendant responded to reasonable requests for information or inspection for the purpose of ascertaining facts which were or might be relevant to the claimant's cause of action. Potential defendants do not have a duty to volunteer information but they should not obstruct the claimant in obtaining information.[412] This includes the conduct of defendants' solicitors and their insurers. Defendants' conduct is relevant even where they have made an honest mistake in giving misleading information.[413] Delay in responding to notification of the claim will be relevant.[414] The defendant's conduct before the intimation of proceedings can also be relevant to the exercise of the discretion.[415]

Duration of claimant's disability—s.33(3)(d)   If claimants are under a   **11–139** disability at the date at which the cause of action accrued the commencement of the limitation period is postponed until they cease to be under a disability,[416] but supervening disability does not stop time running. It will be taken into account, however, in the exercise of the discretion. Since minority can never supervene, s.33(3)(d) applies only to supervening mental incapacity. Although there are some cases in which claimants' physical disability has been considered to be

---

[411] See also *Khairule v North West SHA* [2008] EWHC 1537 (QB) at [122] where Cox J considered that the loss of CTG trace was "unfortunate" but the courts were: "used to dealing with birth injury cases where the CTG is missing, either in whole or in part, or where its presence is not as helpful as might be hoped due to failures in the time-keeping mechanism." The absence of the CTG was not a factor which would prevent a fair trial, given the available evidence, which was the crucial question.
[412] *Thompson v Brown Construction (Ebbw Vale) Ltd* [1981] 1 W.L.R. 744 at 751. A serious delay in providing the claimant's medical records may be a relevant consideration: *Mills v Dyer-Fare* unreported 9 March 1987, QBD; *Atkinson v Oxfordshire Health Authority* [1993] 4 Med. L.R. 18, QBD, where a failure to tell the claimant or his mother what had happened during the course of an operation meant that to a large extent the delay was of the defendants' own making.
[413] *Marston v British Railways Board* [1976] I.C.R. 124; a fortiori where the defendant has deliberately misled the claimant: see, e.g. *Scuriaga v Powell* (1979) 123 S.J. 406, para.11–098, a case where the defendant's conduct prevented the claimant from acquiring knowledge of the relevant facts under s.14.
[414] *Leeson v Marsden* [2008] EWHC 1011 (QB); [2008] LS Law Med. 393; (2008) 103 B.M.L.R. 49 where a doctor failed to serve a letter of response to the letter of claim; *Sanderson v Bradford MBC* [2016] EWHC 527 (QB) where there was an unexplained delay of three months (contrary to the relevant Pre-Action Protocol) between receipt of the letter of claim and notifying insurers, who then instructed solicitors; defendants' contention that had they received notification sooner (the claim was issued 10 weeks outside the limitation period) they would have investigated it quickly given little weight.
[415] *Kew v Bettamix Ltd (formerly Tarmac Roadstone Southern Ltd)* [2006] EWCA Civ 1535; [2007] P.I.Q.R. P16 (occupational physician, having examined the claimant and suspected the possibility of the claimant having developed hand arm vibration syndrome, recommended a review medical examination in 12 months' time, but though the report was forwarded to the employers, no further medical examination, which may well have alerted the claimant to the possibility of an action, was carried out).
[416] Limitation Act 1980 s.28; see para.11–152.

relevant under this paragraph,[417] it is submitted that the better view is that s.33(3)(d) is restricted to supervening mental incapacity which is of sufficient degree to satisfy the requirements of s.38(2), i.e. the claimant lacks capacity to conduct legal proceedings.[418] The claimant's physical disabilities can be considered under s.33(3)(a), as part of the reasons for the delay, or as part of "all the circumstances of the case".[419] The House of Lords reiterated this in *A v Hoare*,[420] a case concerning sexual abuse. Whether the actual claimant, taking into account his psychological state in consequence of the injury, could reasonably have been expected to start proceedings, was not a factor relevant under s.14(2) but was a factor to be dealt with under s.33. Their Lordships confirmed that this was the right place to consider it until Parliament decided whether to give effect to the Law Commission's recommendation of a more precise definition of psychological incapacity suffered by victims of sexual abuse. The House of Lords also confirmed that the approach to the exercise of discretion remained as described in *Horton v Sadler*[421] and commented on the sort of considerations which ought clearly to be in mind in historic sexual abuse cases.[422]

11–140   **Extent to which claimant acted promptly—s.33(3)(e)**   The date at which the claimant became aware of the existence of a cause of action is not necessarily the

---

[417] *Wood v SFK (UK) Ltd* unreported 7 April 1982, QBD; *Hart v British Leyland Cars Ltd* unreported 22 March 1983, QBD; *Pilmore v Northern Trawlers Ltd* [1986] 1 Lloyd's Rep. 552 at 554; *Bater v Newbold* unreported 30 July 1991, CA.

[418] See *Cornish v Kearley and Tonge Ltd* (1983) 133 N.L.J. 870; *Yates v Thakeham Tiles Ltd* [1995] P.I.Q.R. P135, CA; *Thomas v Plaistow* [1997] P.I.Q.R. P540, CA (all applying the old test for a claimant under a disability, namely whether the claimant was of "unsound mind", which was satisfied if he was a person who, by reason of mental disorder, was incapable of managing and administering his property and affairs; see para.11–152).

[419] *Pearse v Barnet Health Authority* [1998] P.I.Q.R. P39. The fact that the claimant's physical disabilities have been mistakenly considered under s.33(3)(d) does not detract from the exercise of the overall discretion: *Yates v Thakeham Tiles Ltd* [1995] P.I.Q.R. P135. Moreover, to the extent that the claimant suffers psychological damage falling short of incapacity to conduct legal proceedings, her psychological condition can be taken into account under s.33(3)(a) as part of the reasons for the delay: *Jones v City and Hackney Health Authority* unreported 1993, QBD.

[420] [2008] UKHL 6; [2008] 1 A.C. 844.

[421] [2006] UKHL 27; [2007] 1 A.C. 307.

[422] See also *B v Nugent Care Society (formerly Catholic Social Services (Liverpool))* [2008] EWCA Civ 795 where the Court of Appeal remitted the question of the exercise of the s.33 discretion back to the High Court because the judge had failed, in the light of *A v Hoare* [2008] UKHL 6; [2008] 1 A.C. 844, to take into account the now admissible impact of any inhibition to complain or bring proceedings. Nor, in the context of s.33, had he dealt with the causative effect of the abuse on any psychological condition that the claimants might now suffer. Further, the judge had not considered the parties' difficulties of examining that question at what was a late stage. He had not dealt with any difficulties that the claimants might have in dealing with the fact of the abuse. See further for the correct approach to the exercise of the s.33 discretion in cases of historic sexual abuse: *B v Nugent Care Society* [2009] EWCA Civ 827; [2010] 1 W.L.R. 516; *B v Nugent Care Society (formerly Catholic Social Services (Liverpool))* [2010] EWHC 1005 (QB); (2010) 116 B.M.L.R. 84; *Raggett v Society of Jesus Trust 1929 for Roman Catholic Purposes* [2010] EWCA Civ 1002; [2010] C.P. Rep. 45; *RE v GE* [2015] EWCA Civ 287; *A v Trustees of the Watchtower Bible and Tract Society* [2015] EWHC 1722 (QB); *GH v Catholic Child Welfare Society (Diocese of Middlesbrough)* [2016] EWHC 3337 (QB); [2017] E.L.R. 136; *JL v Bowen* [2017] EWCA Civ 82; [2017] P.I.Q.R. P11; and in cases of historic physical abuse: *XA v YA* [2010] EWHC 1983 (QB); [2011] P.I.Q.R. P1.

same as the date of "knowledge" for the purpose of s.14, and may well be later.[423] It had been considered to be a general proposition that if claimants had acted promptly and reasonably once they became aware of the cause of action then it was not to be counted against them that their lawyers had been dilatory and allowed the primary limitation period to expire.[424] However, in *Horton v Sadler*[425] Lord Carswell commented that:

"In *Das v Ganju* [1999] Lloyd's Rep. Med. 198 at 204 and *Corbin v Penfold Metallising Co Ltd* [2000] Lloyd's Rep. Med. 247 at 251 the Court of Appeal expressed the view that there was no rule that the claimant must suffer for his solicitor's default. If this is interpreted, as it was in *Corbin*, as meaning that the court is not entitled to take into account against a party the failings of his solicitors who let the action go out of time, that could not in my view be sustained and the criticism voiced in the notes to the reports of *Das* and *Corbin* would be justified. The claimant must bear responsibility, as against the defendant, for delays which have occurred, whether caused by his own default or that of his solicitors, and in numerous cases that has been accepted: see, e.g., *Firman v Ellis* [1978] Q.B. 886, *Thompson v Brown* [1981] 1 W.L.R. 744 and *Donovan v Gwentoys Ltd* [1990] 1 W.L.R. 472. The reason was articulated by Ward LJ in *Hytec Information Systems Ltd v Coventry City Council* [1997] 1 W.L.R. 1666, a case of striking out, when he said, at p 1675: 'Ordinarily this court should not distinguish between the litigant himself and his advisers. There are good reasons why the court should not: first, if anyone is to suffer for the failure of the solicitor it is better that it be the client than another party to the litigation; secondly, the disgruntled client may in appropriate cases have his remedies in damages or in respect of the wasted costs; thirdly, it seems to me that it would become a charter for the incompetent (as Mr McGregor eloquently put it) were this court to allow almost impossible investigations in apportioning blame between solicitor and counsel on the one hand, or between themselves and their client on the other.'"

In *Yates v Thakeham Tiles Ltd*[426] the claimant consulted solicitors after the expiry of the primary limitation period, and the solicitors did not notify the defendants of a potential claim until a year later. The Court of Appeal held that this was proper where the solicitors were obtaining all the relevant information to support the claim, such as advice from counsel, and obtaining legal aid. On the other hand, if the claimant has a potential claim against solicitors as a result of delay, this may reduce the degree of prejudice suffered by the claimant.

11–141

Steps taken by claimant to obtain expert advice—s.33(3)(f) This includes legal advice and whether it was favourable or unfavourable.[427] Thus, while

11–142

---

[423] *Eastman v London County Bus Services Ltd, The Times,* 23 November 1985, CA.
[424] *Thompson v Brown Construction (Ebbw Vale) Ltd* [1981] 1 W.L.R. 744 at 752; *Das v Ganju* [1999] P.I.Q.R. P260; [1999] Lloyd's Rep. Med. 198, CA; *Corbin v Penfold Metallising Company Ltd* [2000] Lloyds Rep. Med. 247 at 251, CA; *Steeds v Peverel Management Services Ltd* [2001] EWCA Civ 419; *The Times,* 16 May 2001, CA; s.33(3)(e) is concerned only with the conduct of the claimant, not his advisers: *Davis v Jacobs and Camden & Islington Health Authority and Novartis Pharmaceuticals (UK) Ltd* [1999] Lloyd's Rep. Med. 72 at 86, per Brooke LJ; cf. constructive knowledge under s.14(3) where the claimant is fixed with the knowledge about facts that his lawyers ought reasonably to have discovered: *Henderson v Temple Pier Co. Ltd* [1998] 1 W.L.R. 1540; *Hayward v Sharrard* (1998) 56 B.M.L.R. 155.
[425] [2006] UKHL 27; [2007] 1 A.C. 307 at [53].
[426] [1995] P.I.Q.R. P135, CA.
[427] *Jones v G.D. Searle & Co. Ltd* [1979] 1 W.L.R. 101. The claimant can be required to disclose the nature of the advice he received. See also *Halford v Brookes* [1991] 1 W.L.R. 428, where the delay was attributable to the claimant being advised that her only civil remedy was against the Criminal Injuries Compensation Board. As soon as she was advised that there was another remedy she acted promptly in issuing a claim form. See too *Thompson v Brown Construction (Ebbw Vale) Ltd* [1981] 1

erroneous legal advice will not prevent time running under the three-year limitation period, it is relevant to the exercise of discretion.

11–143 **Other factors: availability of an alternative remedy** The availability of an alternative remedy (e.g. against the claimant's negligent solicitors) is a "highly relevant consideration", but it is not conclusive against the exercise of the discretion in the claimant's favour.[428] Even where claimants would have a cast-iron case against their solicitors they will suffer some prejudice, even if only minor, in having to find and instruct new solicitors, additional delay, and a possible personal liability for costs up to the date of the court's refusal of the application.[429] In addition, any damages recovered in the action against the solicitors will be assessed on the basis of the claimant's lost chance of recovering damages against the initial defendant rather than the full value of the claim against that defendant, and so litigation against the claimant's former solicitors will almost always be "second best".[430] Nonetheless, it is something which the court can, and usually should, take into account in weighing the overall balance of prejudice.[431]

11–144 The fact that claimants would have a cast-iron case against their solicitors is not necessarily a reason to use the occasion to teach the solicitors a lesson, particularly where the delay after the expiry of the limitation period was short and had caused the defendants no material prejudice.[432] Where there is any real dispute about the solicitors' liability in negligence then the chances of the

---

W.L.R. 744 at 751–752, per Lord Diplock, and *Bentley v Bristol and Weston Health Authority* [1991] 2 Med. L.R. 359. The failure of claimants to seek legal advice, even if based on an honest subjective belief that they did not have a claim, may be culpable and count against the exercise of discretion in the claimant's favour: see *Skerratt v Linfax Ltd (t/a Go Karting for Fun)* [2003] EWCA Civ 695; [2004] P.I.Q.R. P10 at [46]. The position may be different if the claimant has been misled by the defendants as to whether or not there was a cause of action: *Skerratt v Linfax Ltd (t/a Go Karting for Fun)* [2003] EWCA Civ 695.

[428] *Cain v Francis* [2008] EWCA Civ 1451; [2009] Q.B. 754 at [72] per Smith LJ: prejudice to the claimant "is greatly reduced if he has a good claim over against his solicitor. In a case where the defendant has suffered some forensic or procedural prejudice, which will diminish his ability to defend himself, it will be relevant to consider that the claimant has another remedy. But the fact that the claimant has a claim over will not necessarily mean that the direction should be refused. It might still be fair and just that the defendant remains in the frame".

[429] *Thompson v Brown Construction (Ebbw Vale) Ltd* [1981] 1 W.L.R. 744 at 750. He might prefer to sue the real tortfeasor, said Lord Diplock, rather than his former solicitors. Query, however, why the claimant's *preferences* should have any bearing on the balance of prejudice between claimant and defendant. See also *Ramsden v Lee* [1992] 2 All E.R. 204 at 212, a case where the defendant had been notified of the claim within a month of the accident, and there was no dispute on liability; there had been two interim payments, but the claim form was issued six months out of time. The Court of Appeal held that the judge had exercised his discretion correctly in allowing the action to proceed. Part of the prejudice to the claimant consists of being forced to change from bringing an action against a tortfeasor, who may know little or nothing of the weak points of the claimant's case, to bringing an action against his solicitor, who will know a great deal about his case: *Hartley v Birmingham City District Council* [1992] 1 W.L.R. 968 at 980, CA.

[430] *Davidson v Aegis Defence Services (BVI) Ltd* [2013] EWCA Civ 1586; [2014] 2 All E.R. 216; *Leeson v Marsden* [2008] EWHC 1011 (QB); [2008] LS Law Med. 393; (2008) 103 B.M.L.R. 49; *Rayner v Wolferstans (A Firm)* [2015] EWHC 2957 (QB) at [132].

[431] [2013] EWCA Civ 1586; [2014] 2 All E.R. 216 at [13] per Longmore LJ.

[432] *Steeds v Peverel Management Services Ltd* [2001] EWCA Civ 419; *The Times*, 16 May 2001, CA.

claimant having an alternative remedy should be largely disregarded.[433] Nor should the seriousness of the claimant's solicitors' error weigh in the balancing exercise under s.33, which should assess the prejudice to the respective parties.[434]

Where claimants have already changed solicitors there is less prejudice to them if the discretion is not exercised, even in the case of a short delay,[435] and a fortiori where claimants have already commenced proceedings against their former solicitors.[436] In *Conry v Simpson*,[437] however, the Court of Appeal refused to interfere with the trial judge's exercise of discretion in favour of the claimant, although the claim form had been issued three years and ten months out of time and an action against the former solicitors had been commenced. Stephenson LJ commented that it is very seldom that a remedy against a solicitor can be as satisfactory as a remedy against the original tortfeasor. On the other hand, in *Donovan v Gwentoys Ltd*[438] Lord Griffiths said that the claimant would suffer "only the slightest prejudice" if she were required to pursue her remedy against her solicitors, although in that case there was severe prejudice to the defendant caused by the delay in notification of a claim.

11–145

Other factors: miscellaneous Other factors may also be relevant to the court's exercise of discretion. The weakness of the claimant's case on liability is clearly relevant to the balance of prejudice, since the weaker the case the less the claimant has to lose by the operation of s.11.[439] The court should also take into account the likely value of the claim, if successful.[440] It is legitimate to take into account the insurance position of both defendant and claimant, as part of all the circumstances of the case.[441] The court will not apply different principles to

11–146

---

[433] *Firman v Ellis* [1978] Q.B. 886 at 916, per Geoffrey Lane LJ, who added that it was undesirable that there should be any detailed enquiry into the question of the solicitors' negligence; *Das v Ganju* [1999] P.I.Q.R. P260 270; [1999] Lloyd's Rep. Med. 198, 205, CA; see generally Jones (1985) 1 P.N. 159; Steiner (1990) 6 P.N. 183.

[434] *Horton v Sadler* [2006] UKHL 27; [2007] 1 A.C. 307 at [56] per Lord Carswell.

[435] *Straw v Hicks* unreported 13 October 1983, CA.

[436] *Mills v Ritchie* unreported 12 November 1984, QBD.

[437] [1983] 3 All E.R. 369.

[438] [1990] 1 W.L.R. 472; cf. *Ramsden v Lee* [1992] 2 All E.R. 204 where, having been notified of the claim at an early stage and admitted liability, the only prejudice to the defendant was the loss of the "windfall" limitation defence.

[439] *B v Ministry of Defence* [2010] EWCA Civ 1317; (2011) 117 B.M.L.R. 101 (inequitable to disapply the limitation period because the claims were so weak on causation); affirmed *AB v Ministry of Defence* [2012] UKSC 9; [2013] 1 A.C. 78 at [27], [65], [89]. The Court of Appeal decision is commented on by McCarthy [2011] J.P.I.L. C30.

[440] *Cairns-Jones v Christie Tyler South Wales West Division Ltd* [2010] EWCA Civ 1642 at [8], applying *Robinson v St. Helens MBC* [2002] EWCA Civ 1099; [2003] P.I.Q.R. P128 at [33] (quoted at para.11–147 below); *Whiston v London SHA* [2010] EWCA Civ 195; [2010] 1 W.L.R. 1582 at [84]. The lower the value of the claim the less the claimant is prejudiced by the claim not being allowed to proceed, and conversely the higher the value of the claim the greater the prejudice to the claimant.

[441] *Firman v Ellis* [1978] Q.B. 886 at 916; *Liff v Peasley* [1980] 1 W.L.R. 781 at 789. In *Horton v Sadler* [2006] UKHL 27; [2007] 1 A.C. 307 at [56] Lord Bingham commented that: "recognising the reality of insurance, the courts have routinely and rightly taken account of the parties' insurance rights". Since it is legitimate, when considering prejudice to the claimant, to take into account the fact that the claimant will have a claim against his solicitors, it is also legitimate to take into account the fact that the defendant is insured and that if he is deprived of his fortuitous limitation defence he will have a claim on his insurers: *Hartley v Birmingham City District Council* [1992] 1 W.L.R. 968 at 980,

multi-party litigation, however, from the principles applied to ordinary, single claimant actions when exercising the discretion. The merits of each case must be considered individually.[442] The moral culpability of the defendant is not a matter to be taken into account.[443] It has been suggested that the fact that a medical negligence action is a claim for professional negligence may be an additional factor in the defendant's favour when the court considers the exercise of discretion, because such actions have more serious consequences for defendants and should be prosecuted without delay.[444] In *Biss v Lambeth Health Authority*[445] the Court of Appeal held, in the somewhat analogous context of an application to strike out an action for want of prosecution, that there was prejudice to the defendants in the worry that professional staff would suffer with the action hanging over them like the "sword of Damocles", although it would be exceptional to treat the "mere sword of Damocles, hanging for an unnecessary period" as a sufficient reason in itself to strike out.[446] In *Dobbie v Medway Health Authority*,[447] a case in which there was a 13-year delay after the expiry of the primary limitation period, Otton J applied this reasoning to the exercise of discretion under s.33:

> "There must come a time when the Sword of Damocles must be removed from above the head of a professional man and he can either continue with his professional work or retire from it with the knowledge that his conduct (whatever it may be) will not continue to haunt him. That time has surely come in this case. Likewise for the hospital and the health authority."[448]

This was a "potent factor" which tipped the balance substantially in favour of the defendants. In the Court of Appeal, however, Beldam LJ disagreed with the decision to take into account the sword of Damocles argument, commenting that he could not see how such a consideration could apply to doctors who do not

---

CA. In *Kelly v Bastible* [1997] 8 Med. L.R. 15 the Court of Appeal held that the fact that the defendant is insured was one of the factors that could be placed in the scales when weighing prejudice to the parties under s.33, but if, treating the defendant and insurer as a composite unit, the delay had seriously prejudiced their ability to defend the action, and if the court would not have allowed the action to proceed had the defendant not been insured, the weight to be given to the mere fact that the defendant was insured should be nil. In *Sayers v Lord Chelwood* [2012] EWCA Civ 1715; [2013] 1 W.L.R. 1695 at [67] the Court of Appeal considered that an important factor in refusing to disapply the limitation period was that, due to the delay in instituting proceedings, the defendants had lost insurance documents and so were exposed to personal liability in respect of a quarter of the claim.
[442] *Nash v Eli Lilly & Co.* [1991] 2 Med. L.R. 169; aff'd [1993] 1 W.L.R. 782 at 810, CA.
[443] *GH v Catholic Child Welfare Society (Diocese of Middlesbrough)* [2016] EWHC 3337 (QB); [2017] E.L.R. 136 at [56]–[57]. If moral culpability were relevant "it would be difficult to see how a defendant could ever succeed on the section 33 issue when attempting to defend an allegation of child sexual abuse. There would always be a high level of moral culpability attached to the allegations", per Judge Gosnell (a point which the judge repeated in *AB v Catholic Child Welfare Society* [2016] EWHC 3334 (QB) at [56] and *CD v Catholic Child Welfare Society* [2016] EWHC 3335 (QB) at [59]).
[444] *Jackson & Powell on Professional Liability*, 8th edn (London: Sweet & Maxwell, 2017), para.5–126.
[445] [1978] 1 W.L.R. 382.
[446] *Department of Transport v Chris Smaller (Transport) Ltd* [1989] A.C. 1197 at 1209–1210, per Lord Griffiths.
[447] [1992] 3 Med. L.R. 217.
[448] [1992] 3 Med. L.R. 217 at 224.

know that any action is contemplated against them.[449] It would seem that the issue could only be relevant where doctors had had a claim intimated but there had been a long delay in issuing the claim form.[450]

The financial consequences for the defendant of the delay itself is a relevant consideration (as opposed to the mere fact that removal of the limitation defence may result in the defendant being required to pay damages). Thus, in *Smith v Leicester Health Authority*[451] the judge took into account the defendants' changed financial arrangements, which meant that the defendants would have to bear some £100,000 more than if the action had been brought before January 1990. But in balancing the prejudice between the parties the judge did not refer at all to the financial loss that the claimant would suffer if s.11 was not disapplied (she had succeeded on liability). The Court of Appeal pointed out that the claimant's financial loss, if the action was statute barred, was likely to have been 10 times greater than the additional financial prejudice to the defendants, and this was an important factor in exercising the discretion in her favour. On the other hand, the court must also consider the question of proportionality in the exercise of the discretion under s.33. Thus:

11–147

"...courts should be slow to exercise their discretion in favour of a claimant in the absence of cogent medical evidence showing a serious effect on the claimant's health or enjoyment of life or employability. The likely amount of an award is an important factor to consider, especially if... they are likely to take a considerable time to try."[452]

(d) Death

(i) Fatal Accidents Act 1976

In an action for loss of dependency under the Fatal Accidents Act 1976 if the death occurred before the expiry of the deceased's three-year limitation period, then a new three-year period commences in favour of the dependants. This period runs from the date of death or the date of the dependants' "knowledge", whichever is later.[453] If there is more than one dependant and their dates of

11–148

---

[449] [1994] 1 W.L.R. 1234 at 1246.

[450] In *Birnie v Oxfordshire Area Health Authority* (1982) 2 *The Lancet* 281, QBD, Glidewell J considered that it was a relevant point in the case of an individual defendant doctor that he had had the claim hanging over him since it was first intimated to him; and also that he was not insured. See further *Slevin v Southampton and South West Hampshire Health Authority* [1997] 8 Med. L.R. 175 at 181 and *Sims v Dartford and Gravesham Health Authority* [1996] 7 Med. L.R. 381 on the "sword of Damocles" point.

[451] [1998] Lloyd's Rep. Med. 77. See also *McHugh v Gray* [2006] EWHC 1968 (QB); [2006] Lloyd's Rep. Med. 519—the court is entitled to take into account the prejudice to those with financial responsibility for claims such as this (a claim against a psychiatrist commenced some seven years after expiry of the primary limitation period) where uncertainty persists because claims are not made and dealt with promptly (per Beatson J at [26]).

[452] *Robinson v St. Helens MBC* [2002] EWCA Civ 1099; [2003] P.I.Q.R. P128 at [33]. This comment was approved by Lord Hoffmann in *Adams v Bracknell Forest Borough Council* [2004] UKHL 29; [2005] 1 A.C. 76 at [54].

[453] Limitation Act 1980 s.12. "Knowledge" is defined in s.14; see para.11–055.

knowledge are different, time runs separately against each of them.[454] If the Fatal Accidents action is not commenced within three years of the death or the date of knowledge of the dependants the action is barred.[455] The court may "disapply" the provisions of s.12, however, by virtue of its discretion under s.33, in which case the guidelines of s.33(3) have effect as if references to the claimant (usually the personal representative) included references to the dependants.

11–149 If the deceased's three-year limitation period had expired before he died then in theory he could not have maintained an action at the date of his death and the dependants' action is barred by s.12(1). For this purpose no account is taken of the possibility that the deceased might have made a successful application to override the fixed period under s.33. However, s.33 applies to the Fatal Accidents Act and the court can exercise its discretion and direct that s.12(1) of the Limitation Act 1980 and s.1(1) of the Fatal Accidents Act 1976 shall not apply. In exercising its discretion the court must have regard to the length of and reasons for the delay on the part of the deceased.[456] The court may disapply s.12 only where the reason why the deceased could no longer maintain an action was because of the time limit in s.11.[457] If he could no longer maintain an action for any other reason the court has no discretion to allow the dependants' action to proceed.

(ii)   Law Reform (Miscellaneous Provisions) Act 1934

11–150 The position in the case of an action on behalf of the estate of a deceased person under the Law Reform (Miscellaneous Provisions) Act 1934 is similar to that which applies to Fatal Accident Act claims. If the deceased died before the expiry of his three-year limitation period, a new three-year period commences which runs from either the date of death or the date of the personal representative's knowledge, whichever is later.[458] If there is more than one personal representative and their dates of knowledge are different, time runs from the earliest date.[459] If this period expires the personal representative may invoke s.33 requesting the court to exercise its discretion to override the effect of s.11(5).

11–151 Where the deceased died after the expiry of the three-year limitation period an action by the personal representative is barred by s.11(3), but the court can exercise its discretion under s.33 in favour of the personal representative, again having regard to the length of and the reasons for the delay by the deceased.[460]

---

[454] Limitation Act 1980 s.13(1).

[455] Limitation Act 1980 s.12(2).

[456] Limitation Act 1980 s.33(4).

[457] Limitation Act 1980 s.33(2).

[458] Limitation Act 1980 s.11(5).

[459] Limitation Act 1980 s.11(7); cf. the position with dependants under the Fatal Accidents Act, where time runs separately against each dependant: s.13(1).

[460] An argument that any damages awarded to the deceased's estate constituted a "windfall" to the beneficiaries of the estate and that this should be taken into account when considering the s.33 discretion was rejected as having no merit in *Nicholas v Ministry of Defence* [2013] EWHC 2351 (QB), given that the law allows the estate to benefit from damages awarded in respect of the deceased's tortious injuries.

(e) Persons under a disability

People are under a disability while they are infants (i.e. under 18[461]) or if they **11–152**
lack capacity (within the meaning of the Mental Capacity Act 2005) to conduct
legal proceedings.[462] If people to whom a right of action accrues are under a
disability at the date when the action accrued, time does not run until they cease
to be under a disability or dies, whichever occurs first.[463] Thus, an infant has an
indefeasible right to bring an action for personal injuries at any time before the
age of 21,[464] and people who lack capacity to conduct legal proceedings have
three years from the date they acquire capacity. The fact that a defendant may
suffer prejudice from a long delay is immaterial.[465] There is, of course, nothing to
stop a person under a disability bringing an action while still under the disability.
If the accident itself caused immediate incapacity time will not begin to run.[466]

If the claimant was not under a disability when the action accrued, supervening **11–153**
incapacity will not prevent time running.[467] This applies even where the

---

[461] Family Law Reform Act 1969 s.1.

[462] Limitation Act 1980 s.38(2). This definition was substituted (from 1 October 2007) by the Mental
Capacity Act 2005 for an earlier test, namely, that claimants were under a disability if they were of
unsound mind, and they were of unsound mind if they were people who, by reason of mental disorder
were incapable of managing and administering their property and affairs. In *Masterman-Lister v
Jewell and Home Counties Dairies* [2002] EWCA Civ 1889; [2003] 1 W.L.R. 1511 the Court of
Appeal concluded that capacity should be judged in relation to the decision or activity in question, not
globally, a view approved by the Supreme Court in *Dunhill v Burgin* [2014] UKSC 18; [2014] 1
W.L.R. 933 at [13]. In *Dunhill* Lady Hale thought (at [14]) that it was unlikely that there were any
differences between the old and the new law and concluded that "the test of capacity to conduct
proceedings for the purpose of CPR Part 21 is the capacity to conduct the claim or cause of action
which the claimant in fact has, rather than to conduct the claim as formulated by her lawyers" (at
[18]). Note that under the old test mental illness did not necessarily mean that claimants were
incapable of managing their affairs, and if they were capable of managing their affairs they were not
under a disability: *Dawson v Scott-Brown* unreported 18 October 1988, CA. The same principle
applies to mental capacity under the Mental Capacity Act 2005. A claimant suffering from mental
illness or disorder does not necessarily lack capacity under the Act, which is decision-specific. For
discussion of the test for capacity in the 2005 Act see paras 6–045 et seq.

[463] Limitation Act 1980 s.28(1) and (6). This assumes, of course, that claimants have the relevant
"knowledge" under s.14. If not, then time will not run until they acquire knowledge. If people under
a disability die the primary limitation period starts to run, and there can be no further extension under
s.28, even if the people to whom the cause of action accrues are themselves under a disability: s.28(3).

[464] *Tolley v Morris* [1979] 1 W.L.R. 592.

[465] If Parliament had intended prejudice to be a material consideration under s.28, it would have said
so, as it did elsewhere in the Limitation Act 1980: *Headford v Bristol and District Health Authority*
[1995] P.I.Q.R. P180 at 184; [1995] 6 Med. L.R. 1 at 4, per Rose LJ, CA.

[466] *Kirby v Leather* [1965] 2 Q.B. 367, CA. This applies if the incapacity arises at any time before the
end of the day on which the accident occurred; *Boot v Boot* unreported 7 May 1991, CA; *Turner v WH
Malcolm Ltd* (1992) 15 B.M.L.R. 40, CA. As Glidewell LJ observed, at 48, in this case "Parliament
has in effect provided that there is no limitation period for a plaintiff who is under a permanent
disability".

[467] *Purnell v Roche* [1927] 2 Ch. 142. Hence where it is alleged that the accident which is the subject
of the litigation caused the incapacity to conduct legal proceedings it may be crucial to know whether
this was immediate or whether there was a period of time during which the claimant was not under a
disability: see, e.g. *Boot v Boot* unreported 7 May 1991, CA.

supervening disability arose before the claimant's date of knowledge under s.14.[468] The apparent harshness of this rule may be mitigated by the court's exercise of discretion under s.33(3)(d).

(f) Deliberate concealment

11–154   Where any fact relevant to the claimant's right of action has been deliberately concealed by the defendant, the limitation period does not begin to run until the claimant has discovered the concealment or could with reasonable diligence have discovered it.[469] This provision is not limited to fraud in a technical sense, but includes the deliberate commission of a breach of duty in circumstances in which it is unlikely to be discovered for some time.[470] This includes the commission of a wrong knowingly or recklessly, but mere negligence is not sufficient. In a novel interpretation of s.32, the Court of Appeal held that concealment was deliberate if the defendant had intentionally committed an act or omission which involved a breach of duty in circumstances in which it was unlikely to be discovered for some time, even though the defendant had no knowledge or intention of concealment.[471] This interpretation meant that defendants must simply intend the act or omission which resulted in a breach of duty; they did not have to intend to commit a breach of duty. The result was that many instances of "ordinary negligence" by professionals fell with s.32 (since professionals normally intend to act in performing their job), apparently rendering many other provisions of the Limitation Act redundant. The House of Lords reversed this ruling in *Cave v Robinson Jarvis & Rolf (A Firm)*.[472] Lord Millett said that concealment and non-disclosure, though different concepts, both required knowledge of the fact which is to be kept secret, and someone could "not sensibly be said either to conceal or to fail to disclose something of which he is ignorant". Accordingly, his Lordship concluded that:

> "…section 32 deprives a defendant of a limitation defence in two situations: (i) where he takes active steps to conceal his own breach of duty after he has become aware of it; and (ii) where he is guilty of deliberate wrongdoing and conceals or fails to disclose it in circumstances where it is unlikely to be discovered for some time. But it does not deprive a defendant of a

---

[468] Except that in a case of latent damage which does not involve a claim for personal injuries, where the claimant was under a disability at the "starting date" (as defined in s.14A(5) of the Limitation Act 1980) the limitation period is extended to three years from the date when the claimant ceased to be under a disability or died (whichever occurred first), subject to the overall longstop specified in s.14B of 15 years from the date of breach of duty: Limitation Act 1980 s.28A.

[469] Limitation Act 1980 s.32(1). "Defendant" includes the defendant's agent and any person through whom the defendant claims. For (obiter) discussion of the position where there are two separate losses, the first of which is concealed by the defendant but the second of which is known to the claimant, who then allows the limitation period in respect of the second loss to expire, see: *Williams v Lishman Sidwell Campbell & Price Ltd* [2010] EWCA Civ 418; [2010] P.N.L.R. 25.

[470] Limitation Act 1980 s.32(2).

[471] *Cave v Robinson Jarvis & Rolf (A Firm)* [2001] EWCA Civ 245; [2002] 1 W.L.R. 581, applying the earlier Court of Appeal decision in *Brocklesby v Armitage & Guest (Note)* [2002] 1 W.L.R. 598.

[472] [2002] UKHL 18; [2003] 1 A.C. 384.

limitation defence where he is charged with negligence if, being unaware of his error or that he has failed to take proper care, there has been nothing for him to disclose."[473]

In *Skerratt v Linfax Ltd (t/a Go Karting for Fun)*[474] the claimant was injured in an accident at the defendants' indoor go-karting track. Before using the track he signed a disclaimer, which he believed meant that he rode on the go-karts at his own risk. After the three-year limitation period had expired the claimant was contacted by solicitors who had acted for another claimant who had also sustained injury at the track, suggesting that the claimant might have a claim in respect of his injuries. The claimant issued proceedings almost five years after his accident. When the defendants raised a limitation defence, the claimant sought to rely on s.32. He argued that the disclaimer amounted to a deliberate representation by the defendants that even if they were negligent the claimant would have no cause of action; that by virtue of the Unfair Contract Terms Act 1977 s.2, that representation was false in so far as the claim was based on negligence; and that he had relied on the representation once he had the accident, since that was the reason he had not brought a claim until contacted by the solicitors. The Court of Appeal held that there was no concealment falling within the terms of s.32. The defendants did not make a representation merely by asking the clamant to sign a disclaimer. There was no suggestion that the defendants had deliberately, in the knowledge that it was untrue, made a representation that there was no cause of action. Moreover, everything relied upon by the claimant occurred before the accident, before he had a cause of action. There was, said Waller LJ:

11–155

> "...nothing to show that the defendants either made any representation post-accident or conducted themselves in any way as to show that they were continuing to make some form of representation that they had made prior to the accident. In my view, it is difficult to conceive of a case of concealment unless that concealment takes place either at the very time that the cause of action is accruing, or unless it takes place after the cause of action has accrued . . ."[475]

His Lordship also doubted whether the existence or otherwise of a cause of action is a *fact* relevant to the claimant's right of action.

In most cases of "deliberate concealment" in an action involving personal injuries the claimant will simply not have the knowledge required under s.14 of the Limitation Act 1980 to start the limitation period running.[476] Deliberate concealment under s.32 might possibly be relevant where the claim for medical negligence is not categorised as an action for personal injuries, since the

11–156

---

[473] [2002] UKHL 18; [2003] 1 A.C. 384 at [25]. The non-disclosure to the claimant of a medical report prepared by the defendant for the claimant's employers does not amount to deliberate concealment: *Dawson v Scott-Brown* unreported 18 October 1988, CA. On the other hand, a failure by a firm of solicitors to inform the claimant of an offer of £100 compensation by potential defendants, because that might have revealed their own earlier negligence, was held to be deliberate concealment: *Kitchen v Royal Air Force Association* [1958] 1 W.L.R. 563, CA (a decision under the Limitation Act 1939).
[474] [2003] EWCA Civ 695; [2004] P.I.Q.R. P10.
[475] [2003] EWCA Civ 695; [2004] P.I.Q.R. P10 at [20].
[476] See *Scuriaga v Powell* (1979) 123 S.J. 406; aff'd, unreported 24 July 1980, CA, para.11–098. Claims under the Fatal Accidents Act 1976 are specifically excluded from the provisions of s.32: Limitation Act 1980 s.12(3).

limitation period runs from the date of accrual of the cause of action not the claimant's date of knowledge, unless the damage is latent. In *Sheldon v RHM Outhwaite (Underwriting Agencies) Ltd*[477] the Court of Appeal held that deliberate concealment of a cause of action which occurs after the cause of action has accrued does not suspend or postpone the running of the limitation period until discovery of the concealment, because the wording of s.32(1)(b) did not have the effect of interrupting a limitation period that had already started to run. The Latent Damage Act 1986 was intended to fill any unjust lacuna in which claimants in non-personal injury actions could lose their cause of action before they knew of its existence. This decision effectively permitted defendants to reap the fruits of their own unconscionable conduct (subject to the latent damage provisions), and, as Sir Thomas Bingham MR acknowledged, deprived the subsection of much practical substance. By a bare majority the House of Lords reversed the decision of the Court of Appeal.[478] Section 32(1)(b) operated to postpone the running of the limitation period in every case where there was deliberate concealment by the defendant of facts relevant to the claimant's cause of action, regardless of whether the concealment was contemporaneous with or subsequent to the accrual of the cause of action. Thus, subsequent concealment has the effect of bringing s.32 into play, thereby excluding ss.2 and 5, and the claimant has a full six years from the date of discovery of the concealment in which to bring the action.

11–157   In *Williams v Fanshaw Porter & Hazelhurst (A Firm)*[479] the Court of Appeal gave further consideration to the effect of s.32(1)(b) of the Limitation Act 1980. A trainee legal executive, B, who was handling the claimant's clinical negligence claim, agreed to a consent order whereby a doctor, against whom the claimant had issued proceedings, ceased to be a party to the proceedings, erroneously believing that the claim against the doctor could be reinstated at a later date. He subsequently applied to rejoin the doctor, but the application was dismissed. He did not inform the claimant of either the consent order or the failed attempt to rejoin the doctor, because he was embarrassed by the mistake. A year later B issued fresh proceedings on behalf of the claimant against the doctor, but the proceedings were struck out as an abuse of process, and an appeal against the strike out was unsuccessful. At that point B advised the claimant that she should consult other solicitors. More than six years after the mistaken consent order, but

---

[477] [1994] 3 W.L.R. 999, CA, Staughton LJ dissenting. See, however, *Kitchen v Royal Air Force Association* [1958] 1 W.L.R. 563, a case where subsequent concealment appears to have been treated as precluding reliance on the limitation period.

[478] [1996] 1 A.C. 102. In *Westlake v Bracknell District Council* (1987) 282 E.G. 868 it was held that an assurance to the claimant by the defendant that there was "nothing to worry about" when the claimant raised a query about facts which could indicate that the defendant has been negligent might constitute deliberate concealment, or, alternatively, the defendant would be estopped from raising the limitation defence. But if the claimant is aware of the relevant *facts* during the period preceding the concealment, the subsequent acts of the defendant cannot conceal those facts from the claimant: *Sheldon v RHM Outhwaite (Underwriting Agencies) Ltd* [1996] 1 A.C. 102 at 144; *Ezekiel v Lehrer* [2002] EWCA Civ 16; [2002] Lloyd's Rep. P.N. 260. In *Markes v Coodes* [1997] P.N.L.R. 252, QBD, it was held that a solicitor's failure to inform a client of a possible claim in negligence by the client against the solicitor, or at least to advise the client to seek independent legal advice, amounted to deliberate concealment within s.32(1)(b).

[479] [2004] EWCA Civ 157; [2004] 1 W.L.R. 3185.

less than six years after the claimant was informed about the consent order, the claimant issued proceedings against the firm of solicitors. The question was whether B had deliberately concealed any fact relevant to the claimant's right of action against the solicitors within the meaning of s.32(1)(b), thereby postponing the commencement of the limitation period. The Court of Appeal held that B's conduct did fall within s.32(1)(b). Park J said that there were four points to be noted about the wording of s.32(1)(b).[480] First, it does not provide that the right of action must have been concealed from the claimant; only that a fact relevant to the right of action should have been concealed from the claimant. Second, although the concealed fact must have been relevant to the right of action the subsection does not require that the defendant must have known that the fact was relevant to the right of action (although in most cases defendants probably will have known that the fact or facts which they concealed were relevant). The fact must have been one which the defendant knew, because otherwise it could not have been concealed, but it is not necessary that the defendant knew that the fact was relevant to the claimant's right of action. Third, the subsection only requires that any fact relevant to the right of action is concealed. It does not require that all facts relevant to the right of action are concealed. Fourth, the fact must be "deliberately concealed". For concealment to be deliberate, the defendant must have considered whether to inform the claimant of the fact and decided not to. Moreover, the fact which the defendant decides not to disclose must either be one which it was his duty to disclose, or one which would ordinarily have been disclosed in the normal course of the relationship with the claimant but he has consciously decided to depart from what he would normally have done and kept quiet about it. By taking a conscious decision not to inform the claimant about the fact that he had agreed to the consent order and the fact that the consent order had been made, B deliberately concealed facts relevant to the claimant's right of action against the solicitors. It was irrelevant that B's motive for concealing the facts was to avoid embarrassment and not to conceal from the claimant the possibility that she might have a claim in negligence against the solicitors: "What is relevant to s.32(1)(b) is the fact of concealment, not the reason or motive for it."[481] Where defendants have deliberately concealed a fact realising that it was relevant (or reckless as to whether or not it was relevant) to an actual or a potential claim against them, the fact that they believed that any potential claim would, if pursued against them, fail, does not prevent their conduct from falling with s.32(1)(b).[482]

---

[480] [2004] EWCA Civ 157; [2004] 1 W.L.R. 3185 at [14].
[481] [2004] EWCA Civ 157; [2004] 1 W.L.R. 3185 at [16] per Park J.
[482] [2004] EWCA Civ 157; [2004] 1 W.L.R. 3185 at [38] per Mance LJ. See also the discussion, at [35] to [39], by Mance LJ of the two possible interpretations of the mental element required under s.32(1)(b).

(g) Defective products

11–158 Special rules in respect of limitation periods apply to claims brought under the Consumer Protection Act 1987.[483] The claimant has three years within which to bring an action, running from either the date on which the action accrued (i.e. when the damage occurred) or, if later, the date of "knowledge".[484] Knowledge is defined in similar terms to that for ordinary personal injuries claims, to include the fact that the damage was significant, that it was caused by the defect and the identity of the defendant.[485] The claimant's ignorance that as a matter of law the product was defective is irrelevant and does not prevent time running.

11–159 These rules apply both to personal injuries and property damage claims brought under the Consumer Protection Act 1987. In the case of personal injuries, however, the court has a discretion under the Limitation Act 1980 s.33 to override the three-year limit and allow the action to proceed. But these limitation periods are subject to an overall longstop which expires 10 years after the product was put into circulation by the defendant.[486] The longstop is an absolute bar, even in cases where there has been deliberate concealment or the claimant was under a disability, and the court has no discretion to override this limit in personal injuries cases, even where the damage had not occurred by the end of the 10-year period. A claimant caught by the longstop (a situation which could arise with certain types of drug injury) will have to sue in negligence in order to invoke the court's discretion, since other forms of action are not subject to this longstop.

11–160 In *O'Byrne v Sanofi Pasteur MSD Ltd (formerly Aventis Pasteur MSD Ltd)*[487] the claimant was vaccinated in the UK in 1992 with a vaccine produced by S which had been sent to its wholly-owned UK subsidiary company M for distribution in September 1992. In October 1992, M sold the vaccine to the Department of Health. In November 2000, the claimant brought a claim against M under the Consumer Protection Act 1987 in the mistaken belief that M was the producer of the vaccine. In October 2002 the claimant brought a second claim against S, who argued that the action was out of time since it was brought more than 10 years after the vaccine was put into circulation. The claimant argued that the vaccine had not been put into circulation until it was supplied by M to the Department of Health (which was less than 10 years before the claim against S). The claimant sought an order in the action against M that S be substituted for M as the defendant. The High Court referred the matter to the European Court of Justice, which held that a product was regarded as having been put into circulation when it was taken out of the manufacturing process operated by the producer and entered a marketing process in the form in which it was offered to the public in order to be used or consumed. It was not important whether the sale was made directly by the producer to the user or consumer, or was carried out as part of a distribution process involving one or more operators. Where an entity in the distribution chain was closely linked to the producer, as in the case of a wholly

---

[483] Consumer Protection Act 1987 Sch.1, amending the Limitation Act 1980.
[484] Limitation Act 1980 s.11A(4).
[485] Limitation Act 1980 s.14(1A); cf. s.14(1).
[486] Limitation Act 1980 s.11A(3).
[487] (C127/04) [2006] 1 W.L.R. 1606; (2006) 91 B.M.L.R. 175.

owned subsidiary of the producer, it was necessary to establish on the facts whether the link was so close that that entity was in reality involved in the manufacturing process so that "producer" included the entity and consequently a transfer of the product from the producer to the entity did not amount to putting into circulation. The European Court also held that where an action was brought in respect of defective products and the claimant made an error as to the identity of the producer it was a question for national procedural law whether one party could be substituted for another as defendant, subject to the party falling into the category of potential defendants specified in the Product Liability Directive.[488]

(h) Latent damage—financial loss or property damage

The vast majority of medical negligence actions involve claims in respect of personal injuries, but in some circumstances a doctor's negligence may cause purely financial loss.[489] In this situation the ordinary six-year limitation period under s.2 (tort) or s.5 (contract) of the Limitation Act 1980 would normally apply. Where, however, claimants are unaware that they have sustained any damage or loss they may be able to rely on an extended limitation period applicable to cases of latent damage. If, for example, as a result of a negligent diagnosis the doctor wrongly advised the patient that he was medically unfit to carry out a particular type of work and the patient took a lower paid job, he would have suffered a continuing loss of earnings. If more than six years later the patient discovered the error he might be faced with the argument that the six-year limitation period has already expired.[490]

11–161

---

[488] Council Directive 85/374/EEC. See, however, paras 11–170–11–173 for the limits on substituting a new party in a claim under the Consumer Protection Act 1987.

[489] See paras 2–049–2–080, 2–179–2–186.

[490] This example could raise problems, however, as to precisely when the cause of action accrued, since it involves a continuing loss. In *Midland Bank Trust Co. Ltd v Hett, Stubbs & Kemp* [1979] Ch. 384 Oliver J held that the failure of a solicitor to register an option to purchase a farm as estate contract gave rise to a continuing breach of duty to the client until the point at which the option was defeated by the sale of the farm. However, *Midland Bank* was doubted by the Court of Appeal in *Capita (Banstead 2011) Ltd v RFIB Group Ltd* [2015] EWCA Civ 1310; [2016] Q.B. 835 on the basis that, usually, the failure to correct negligent advice does *not* give rise to a continuing duty of care with a new cause of action accruing on each day that the advice remains uncorrected. In cases of negligent professional advice the courts have tended to the view that claimants sustain damage when they act in reliance on the advice by entering into the particular transaction, not when the subsequent financial loss occurs, the damage consisting of a contingent liability to future loss for which they could have sued immediately: see *Forster v Oughtred & Co.* [1982] 1 W.L.R. 86; *DW Moore & Co. Ltd v Ferrier* [1988] 1 W.L.R. 267; *Bell v Peter Browne & Co.* [1990] 2 Q.B. 495; *Byrne v Hall, Pain & Foster* [1999] 1 W.L.R. 1849; *Nouri v Marvi* [2010] EWCA Civ 1107; [2011] P.N.L.R. 7. In *Law Society v Sephton and Co.* [2006] UKHL 22; [2006] 2 A.C. 543 the House of Lords held that a contingent liability is not damage until the contingency occurs. The possibility of an obligation to pay money in the future is not of itself damage. So where there is a purely contingent obligation no actual damage is sustained until the contingency is fulfilled and the loss becomes actual. See also *Berney v Saul (t/a Thomas Saul & Co)* [2013] EWCA Civ 640; [2013] P.N.L.R. 26—claimant's action against negligent solicitors accrued when she settled her personal injuries claim at an undervalue, not when the risk of this occurring first arose.

11–162   The Latent Damage Act 1986 introduced a special extension of the ordinary six-year limitation period in tort[491] in cases of latent damage (other than personal injuries). The claimant has three years from the date on which he discovered or ought reasonably to have discovered significant damage, subject to an overall "longstop" which bars all claims brought more than 15 years from the date of the defendant's negligence.[492] The limitation period is six years from the date on which the action accrued or three years from the "starting date", whichever expires later.[493] The starting date is the earliest date on which the claimant (or any person in whom the cause of action was vested before him) first had both a right to bring the action, and knowledge of (a) the material facts about the damage, (b) that the damage was caused by the defendant's negligence, (c) the identity of the defendant, and (d) if the negligence was that of a person other than the defendant, the identity of that person and the facts supporting an action against the defendant.[494] Material facts are such facts about the damage as would lead a reasonable person who had suffered such damage to consider it sufficiently serious to justify instituting proceedings for damages against a defendant who did not dispute liability and was able to satisfy a judgment.[495] As with the scheme for personal injuries claimants' ignorance that as a matter of law they have a cause of action does not prevent time running,[496] and claimants will be fixed with constructive knowledge, including the knowledge of experts.[497]

---

[491] The provisions do not apply to claims in contract: *Iron Trade Mutual Insurance Co. Ltd v J.K. Buckenham Ltd* [1990] 1 All E.R. 808; *Société Commerciale de Réassurance v ERAS (International) Ltd (Note)* [1992] 2 All E.R. 82. Where, however, the defendant owes concurrent duties in contract and tort the claimant is entitled to pursue the action which will give him a practical advantage on the question of limitation: *Henderson v Merrett Syndicates Ltd* [1995] 2 A.C. 145 at 191 per Lord Goff.

[492] Latent Damage Act 1986 s.1, inserting new ss.14A and 14B into the Limitation Act 1980.

[493] Limitation Act 1980 s.14A(3) and (4).

[494] Limitation Act 1980 s.14A(5), (6) and (8). It is clear that the courts' approach to s.14A closely mirrors that taken to the analogous provisions in s.14: see *Spencer-Ward v Humberts* [1995] 06 E.G. 148, CA; *Hallam-Eames v Merrett* [1996] 7 Med. L.R. 122, CA; *Oakes v Hopcroft* [2000] Lloyd's Rep. Med. 394. For discussion of the meaning of knowledge under s.14, see paras 11–055 et seq. See especially *Haward v Fawcetts (A Firm)* [2006] UKHL 9; [2006] 1 W.L.R. 682; [2006] P.N.L.R. 25 where the House of Lords held that for the purposes of s.14A(8) the relevant knowledge was knowledge of the facts constituting the essence of the complaint of negligence, approving *Hallam-Eames v Merrett Syndicates Ltd.* This was not when the claimant first knew that he might have a claim for damages, but the earlier date when the claimant first knew enough to justify setting about investigating the possibility that the defendant's advice was defective.

[495] Limitation Act 1980 s.14A(7). See *Horbury v Craig Hall & Rutley* (1991) 7 P.N. 206; *Hamlin v Edwin Evans* (1996) 80 B.L.R. 85, CA—negligent house survey report gives rise to one single cause of action accruing when damage was suffered for the first time, and later, more serious, damage is not relevant; *Blakemores LDP (In Administration) v Scott* [2015] EWCA Civ 999; [2016] C.P. Rep. 1; *Eagle v Redlime Ltd* [2011] EWHC 838 (QB); (2011) 136 Con. L.R. 137—claimant was aware that there had been subsidence to a building, causing the drainage system to sink and cracking to the walls, and that was enough to lead a reasonable person to consider it sufficiently serious to justify commencing proceedings for damages. The fact that he did not know the true cause of the damage until he received a structural report was irrelevant.

[496] Limitation Act 1980 s.14A(9). This refers to ignorance that as a matter of law the claimant has a cause of action against the current defendant. The word "negligence" in s.14A(9) "does not embrace the negligence of some third party in an adversarial relationship with the defendant now being sued": *Chinnock v Veale Wasbrough* [2015] EWCA Civ 441; [2015] P.N.L.R. 25; [2015] Med. L.R. 425 at [88]. Thus, where the claimants' action is against lawyers for alleged negligence in failing to advise that they had a viable claim for clinical negligence claimants would have to know (either actually or constructively) that the advice they received was wrong (in that they actually did have a cause of

Section 14B provides that an action for damages for negligence (other than for personal injuries) shall not be brought more than 15 years from the date of the act or omission which is alleged to constitute negligence. This overrides s.14A, and it is irrelevant that the cause of action may not yet have accrued (i.e. no damage has occurred) or that the starting date has not yet occurred (i.e. the damage is still latent).[498]

11-163

(i) Contribution proceedings

In contribution proceedings the limitation period is two years from the date of judgment or settlement, even if the claimant's claim against the defendant would be statute-barred.[499] In *Aer Lingus plc v Gildacroft Ltd*[500] the Court of Appeal held that the relevant judgment for the purpose of setting the two-year limitation period running under s.10 of the Limitation Act 1980 against a tortfeasor who is claiming contribution from another defendant under the Civil Liability (Contribution) Act 1978 is a judgment or award which ascertains the quantum, and not merely the existence, of the tortfeasor's liability, and therefore the limitation period does not commence until quantum has been ascertained, either by judgment or award or agreement.[501]

11-164

In *Knight v Rochdale Healthcare NHS Trust*[502] a surgeon settled proceedings brought against him by a patient, agreeing to pay damages to the patient, on 24 October 2000. The agreement was embodied in a consent order on 8 November 2000. On 1 November 2002 the surgeon issued contribution proceedings against the defendants. Where a person becomes entitled to bring contribution proceedings by virtue of a "judgment", s.10(3) of the Limitation Act provides that the right of action accrues on the date on which the judgment was given. Section 10(4) provides that in any case not falling within s.10(3) the right of action accrues on the earliest date on which the amount of compensation is agreed.

11-165

---

action against the medical practitioner but had been advised that they did not) in order for the limitation period against the lawyers to start running.

[497] Limitation Act 1980 s.14A(10). Claimants will not be fixed with knowledge of a fact ascertainable only with the help of expert advice so long as they have taken all reasonable steps to obtain, and where appropriate act on, that advice: Limitation Act 1980 s.14A(10). See *Chinnock v Veale Wasbrough* [2015] EWCA Civ 441; [2015] P.N.L.R. 25; [2015] Med. L.R. 425 on constructive knowledge under s.14(10).

[498] The provisions in s.32 concerning deliberate concealment are not, however, subject to the longstop. Limitation Act 1980 ss.14A and 14B do not apply to actions commenced or claims barred before they came into force on 18 September 1986.

[499] Limitation Act 1980 s.10. Where, however, the expiry of the claimant's limitation period extinguishes the claimant's right of action against the defendant the right to contribution is lost: Civil Liability (Contribution) Act 1978 s.1(3). Most limitation periods do not extinguish claimants' rights, but merely bar their remedy. An exception is the 10-year longstop applied to claims for defective products under the Limitation Act 1980 s.11A(3) which does bar claimants' rights of action. See further para.9–072.

[500] [2006] EWCA Civ 4; [2006] 1 W.L.R. 1173.

[501] An interim payment, whether voluntary or court ordered, is not sufficient to start the limitation period; the words "the amount to be paid" in s.10(4) refer to the final overall figure, not agreement of sums towards a final figure: *Spire Healthcare Ltd v Brooke* [2016] EWHC 2828 (QB); [2017] 1 W.L.R. 1177.

[502] [2003] EWHC 1831 (QB); [2004] 1 W.L.R. 371.

Crane J held that the right to contribution accrued, and the two-year limitation period therefore started to run, when a firm agreement was reached, unless the agreement required the making of a consent order before it took effect. It followed that, on the facts, the limitation period for the contribution proceedings had expired.

11–166   In *Chief Constable of Hampshire v Southampton City Council*[503] the Court of Appeal considered that the decision in *Knight v Rochdale Healthcare NHS Trust* had been correct.[504] On 4 November 2010 the original claim against the Chief Constable (D1) was compromised by acceptance of a CPR Pt 36 offer, but on 15 December 2010 there was a consent order embodying the settlement agreement. The claim against the local authority (D2) for contribution was commenced on 3 December 2012. The Court of Appeal held that s.10(4), not s.10(3), of the 1978 Act applied. The consent order did not constitute a "judgment" by which the D1 was "held liable". It followed that the right to contribution accrued, and the limitation period commenced, when the Pt 36 offer was accepted. Nor did the fact that an agreement about the costs in the original claim was reached much later alter the position. Despite the fact that costs paid to the claimant in the original action can be the subject of a claim for contribution, the word "damage" in s.10(4) refers to the actual damage which has been wrongfully caused to or inflicted upon the claimant. The claimant's right to recover costs from D1 is not part of the claimant's "damage", but is an ancillary entitlement, subject to the discretion of the court.[505] It followed that D1's claim for contribution was statute-barred.

(j)   New claims in pending actions

11–167   As a general rule, new claims which are outside a relevant limitation period cannot be brought by addition to or amendment of existing proceedings since this would have the effect of depriving a defendant of an otherwise valid limitation defence.[506] Section 35 of the Limitation Act 1980 allows for limited exceptions to this rule, in combination with CPR rr.17.4 and 19.5, which deal with amendments to statements of case and the addition or substitution of new parties after the end of a relevant limitation period respectively. A new claim made in the course of any action is deemed to be a separate action and to have been commenced, in the case of a CPR Pt 20 claim, on the date on which that claim was commenced, and in the case of any other new claim, on the same date as the original claim.[507] A "new claim" is any claim by way of set-off or counter-claim, any claim involving the addition or substitution of a new cause of action or a new party, and a claim

---

[503] [2014] EWCA Civ 1541; [2015] P.I.Q.R. P5.

[504] Although Jackson LJ, at [31], had some reservations about the reasoning of Crane J in *Knight*.

[505] [2014] EWCA Civ 1541; [2015] P.I.Q.R. P5 at [42]–[43].

[506] If the limitation period has not expired at the date when the application to amend is heard the court has an unrestricted discretion to allow the amendments: CPR r.19.2; *Welsh Development Agency v Redpath Dorman Long Ltd* [1994] 1 W.L.R. 1409 at 1416, CA. For criticism of this decision see James (1995) 14 C.J.Q. 42.

[507] Limitation Act 1980 s.35(1). C. Thomas, "Amending Proceedings after the expiry of the Limitation period: A Review of Section 35 of the Limitation Act 1980" [2005] J.P.I.L. 351.

made in or by way of a Pt 20 claim.[508] By s.35(3) of the Limitation Act 1980 the court cannot allow a new claim, other than an original set-off or counter-claim,[509] to be made in a pending action after the expiry of a limitation period which would affect a new action to enforce that claim. The court has no discretion to allow amendments to add or substitute a new cause of action[510] or a new party to an existing claim, except in three situations: first, where the court exercises its discretion under s.33 to disapply the provisions of ss.11 or 12 in a personal injuries action[511]; secondly, in the case of a claim involving a new party, if the relevant limitation period was current when the proceedings were started and the addition or substitution of the new party is necessary[512]; and thirdly, where the claim involves the addition or substitution of a new claim, if the new claim arises out of the same or substantially the same facts in respect of which the party applying for permission has already claimed a remedy in the proceedings.[513]

---

[508] Limitation Act 1980 s.35(2) and (1)(a). The Civil Procedure Rules replaced the term "third party proceedings" with "Part 20 claim". The old terminology is still to be found in the Limitation Act 1980. "Third party proceedings" means any proceedings brought in the course of any action by any party to the action against a person not previously a party to the action, other than proceedings brought by joining any such person as a defendant to any claim already made in the original action by the party bringing the action: Limitation Act 1980 s.35(2). Thus, a claim for contribution between existing defendants to an action does not constitute third party proceedings (because "third party proceedings" involve bringing somebody in who is not already a party to the action), and they are deemed by s.35(1)(b) to have been commenced on the same date as the original action: *Kennett v Brown* [1988] 1 W.L.R. 582.

[509] A claim is an original set-off or an original counterclaim if it is a claim made by way of set-off or by way of counterclaim by a party who has not previously made any claim in the action: Limitation Act 1980 s.35(3). Thus, a defendant sued within the limitation period may claim once in respect of a set-off or counterclaim even though they are not pleaded until after the limitation period has expired. However, for this to apply the set-off or counterclaim must not have been time-barred when the original action was commenced: *Al-Rawas v Hassan Khan and Co (A Firm)* [2017] EWCA Civ 42; [2017] 1 W.L.R. 2301. On the meaning of an "original counterclaim" see *Law Society v Wemyss* [2008] EWHC 2515 (Ch); [2009] 1 W.L.R. 2254.

[510] A claim in negligence against a motorist is a different cause of action from a claim based on statute against an insurer: *Nemeti v Sabre Insurance Co Ltd* [2013] EWCA Civ 1555; [2014] P.I.Q.R. P12, applying s.35(3).

[511] Limitation Act 1980 s.35(3); CPR r.19.5(4). The s.33 application must be made before or at the same time as the application for leave to amend, because the effect of making the amendment to add a new party or a new claim is that the amendment relates back to date of issue of the claim form, thereby defeating the limitation defence: *Welsh Development Agency v Redpath Dorman Long Ltd* [1994] 1 W.L.R. 1409, CA, overruling *Kennett v Brown* [1988] 1 W.L.R. 582 on this point. See also *Howe v David Brown Tractors (Retail) Ltd (Rustons Engineering Co Ltd, Third Party)* [1991] 4 All E.R. 30, where *Kennett v Brown* had been distinguished. For criticism of the effects of *Welsh Development Agency v Redpath Dorman Long Ltd* see James (1995) 14 C.J.Q. 42.

[512] Limitation Act 1980 s.35(5)(b); CPR r.19.5(2).

[513] Limitation Act 1980 s.35(5)(a); CPR r.17.4(2). A statement of case can be amended after the expiry of the limitation period to add a new claim which is founded on the defendant's version of the facts rather than those in the claimant's existing claim: *Goode v Martin* [2001] EWCA Civ 1899; [2002] 1 W.L.R. 1828. The court may also allow an amendment to a statement of case to correct a mistake as to the name of a party, but only where the mistake was genuine and not one which would cause reasonable doubt as to the identity of the party: CPR r.17.4(3). Similarly, an amendment to alter the capacity in which a party claims may be permitted if the new capacity is one which that party had when the proceedings started or has since acquired: CPR r.17.4(4). And see *Adelson v Associated Newspapers* [2007] EWCA Civ 701; [2008] 1 W.L.R. 585 where the Court of Appeal held that when interpreting the provisions of the CPR in respect of the substitution of parties, which closely followed the form of the relevant parts of the Limitation Act 1980 s.35, it was necessary to have regard to the

11–168   **Procedure**   Where a claimant seeks to add a new claim by amendment to the existing proceedings and the defendant objects that the new claim falls outside the limitation period the court can deal with it either as a conventional application for an amendment or direct that the question of limitation be determined as a preliminary issue. If it opts for the former it should not descend into factual issues which are seriously in dispute, but consider whether the defendant has a "reasonably arguable case on limitation", and if so it should refuse the claimant's application.[514] It is open to the claimant to issue separate proceedings in respect of the new claim, to which the defendant can plead its limitation defence, and the limitation issue will then be determined at trial. If there is no reasonably arguable case on limitation the court has a discretion to allow the amendment if it sees fit in all the circumstances.[515] The second option is for the court to determine the question of limitation as a preliminary issue at the same time as considering whether to give permission to amend, but in practice this course will seldom be appropriate.[516]

11–169   **Adding a new party**   The addition or substitution of a new party will be "necessary" only if the court is satisfied that: (a) the new party is to be substituted for a party who was named in the claim form in mistake for the new party; (b) the claim cannot properly be carried on by or against the original party unless the new party is added or substituted as claimant or defendant[517]; or (c) the original party has died or had a bankruptcy order made against it and interest or liability has passed to the new party.[518]

---

jurisprudence in relation to RSC Ord.20 r.5 (*Morgan Est (Scotland) Ltd v Hanson Concrete Products Ltd* [2005] EWCA Civ 134; [2005] 1 W.L.R. 2557 doubted). The Court also gave guidance on the detailed application of r.19.5(3)(a) and what needs to be established in order to satisfy the court that there had been a mistake. See further *Lockheed Martin Corp v Willis Group Ltd* [2010] EWCA Civ 927; [2010] C.P. Rep. 44; [2010] P.N.L.R. 34 on the correct approach following *Adelson v Associated Newspapers*.

[514] *Chandra v Brooke North (A Firm)* [2013] EWCA Civ 1559; [2014] T.C.L.R. 1; (2013) 151 Con. L.R. 113 at [66]–[67].

[515] [2013] EWCA Civ 1559; [2014] T.C.L.R. 1; (2013) 151 Con. L.R. 113 at [66]–[67], applying *Welsh Development Agency v Redpath Dorman Long Ltd* [1994] 1 W.L.R. 1409.

[516] [2013] EWCA Civ 1559; [2014] T.C.L.R. 1; (2013) 151 Con. L.R. 113 at [70]. See also *Bellinger v Mercer Ltd* [2014] EWCA Civ 996; [2014] 1 W.L.R. 3597.

[517] See, e.g. *Merrett v Babb* [2001] EWCA Civ 214; [2001] Q.B. 1174, where a claim was mistakenly brought by one co-owner of property against a valuer in respect of a negligent valuation for the whole of the financial loss attributable to the negligence. The Court of Appeal held that the other co-owner could be added as a claimant, even though by that time the limitation period had expired. In *Roberts v Gill & Co* [2010] UKSC 22; [2011] 1 A.C. 240 the Supreme Court held that in a claim for negligence brought by a residuary beneficiary of an estate against the solicitors instructed by the administrator of the estate it was not "necessary" to add the administrator to the action brought in the claimant's personal capacity. It followed that the administrator could not be added to the claim after the limitation period had expired, although the claimant wanted to continue the action in a representative capacity (on behalf of the estate) and it was necessary to add the administrator to the representative action.

[518] Limitation Act 1980 s.35(6); CPR r.19.5(3). CPR r.17.4(3) requires that the mistake as to the name of a party be genuine, but CPR r.19.5(3)(a) states simply that a new party may be substituted for a party who was named in the claim form by mistake. However, in *International Distillers and Vinters Ltd v JF Hillebrand (UK) Ltd, The Times*, 25 January 2000, QBD, it was held that it would be unlikely for an application for substitution of a new party under CPR r.19.5(3)(a) to succeed unless the original mistake was genuine. For discussion of the meaning of a mistake in identity see *The Al Tawwab*

Adding new party to product liability claim under Consumer Protection Act   **11-170**
1987   In *O'Byrne v Aventis Pasteur MSD Ltd*[519] the claimant sought permission
to substitute out of time a new defendant for the defendant against whom
proceedings had originally been issued. The claimant alleged that he suffered
brain damage as a result of a vaccine produced by D2 which had been sent to its
wholly owned UK subsidiary company, D1, for distribution, and sold to the
Department of Health. Under the Consumer Protection Act 1987 there is a
10-year longstop limitation period from the date when the product was put into
circulation.[520] The claimant issued proceedings against D1 within the 10-year
period, believing that D1 was the manufacturer of the vaccine. D1 filed a defence
stating that it was merely the distributor of the vaccine. In June 2002, before the
10-year limitation period expired, the claimant's solicitors invited D2 to consent
to being joined to the action, which it did, but on the understanding that its
consent would be withdrawn if it transpired that it had a limitation defence. In
2003 D2's joinder to the action was set aside, prompting the claimant's
application under s.35 of the Limitation Act 1980. D2 argued, first, that a party's
name is not given "in mistake" where the claimant, even though under a mistake
at the time when the action was commenced, was not under any mistake about the
identity of the party against whom it was intending to proceed at the time when
the relevant limitation period expired. Teare J rejected this argument as contrary
to the express wording of s.35(6). D2's argument would also produce the odd
result that the jurisdiction to substitute a party:

> "...did not exist where a claimant had mistakenly named a person as defendant but then by
> diligent inquiry discovered the truth before the limitation period expired, whereas the
> jurisdiction to substitute a party did exist where a claimant had mistakenly named a person as
> defendant but then negligently failed to inquire further. Thus the more negligent the claimant
> had been the more likely it would be that the jurisdiction existed."[521]

D2's second argument was that in such a situation the substitution of a new party
after the expiry of the limitation period cannot be regarded as "necessary"; the
application to substitute has come about, not because of the mistake initially
made by the claimant, but because of the claimant's election to proceed against
the original defendant after there was no longer any mistake. Teare J also rejected
this argument on the basis that the true construction of s.35(4) to (6) is that:

[1991] 1 Lloyd's Rep. 201 at 205–206; *Evans Construction Co. Ltd v Charrington & Co. Ltd and
Bass Holdings Ltd* [1983] Q.B. 810; *The Hibernian Dance Club v Murray* [1997] P.I.Q.R. P46, CA;
Horne-Roberts v Smithkline Beecham plc [2001] EWCA Civ 2006; [2002] 1 W.L.R. 1662; *Lockheed
Martin Corp v Willis Group Ltd* [2010] EWCA Civ 927; [2010] C.P. Rep. 44; [2010] P.N.L.R. 34; *The
Insight Group Ltd v Kingston Smith (a firm)* [2012] EWHC 3644 (QB); [2014] 1 W.L.R. 1448;
American Leisure Group Ltd v Olswang LLP [2015] EWHC 629 (Ch); [2015] P.N.L.R. 21. The
provision is not limited to the correction of mere "misnomers", but relates to the "identity" of the
intended defendant by reference to a description which is specific to the particular case, e.g. "the
landlord", "the employers", "the manufacturer of the product". And see *Adelson v Associated
Newspapers* [2007] EWCA Civ 701; [2008] 1 W.L.R. 585 on the application of the test laid down in
The Al Tawwab [1991] 1 Lloyd's Rep. 201, CA.
[519] [2006] EWHC 2562 (QB); [2007] 1 W.L.R. 757.
[520] On which see *O'Byrne v Sanofi Pasteur MSD Ltd (formerly Aventis Pasteur MSD Ltd)* (C127/04)
[2006] 1 W.L.R. 1606; (2006) 91 B.M.L.R. 175, para.11–160.
[521] [2006] EWHC 2562 (QB); [2007] 1 W.L.R. 757 at [18].

"... where the new party is to be substituted for a party whose name had been given in a claim in the original action in mistake for the new party's name substitution is to be regarded as necessary for the determination of the original action."[522]

That construction was consistent with CPR r.19.5(3)(a) and with *Morgan Est (Scotland) Ltd v Hanson Concrete Products Ltd.*[523] On this basis the conclusion that the name of D1 was given in a claim made in the original action in mistake for the name of D2 necessarily meant that the substitution of D2 for D1 was to be regarded as "necessary for the determination of the original action".[524] Thus, the court had jurisdiction to substitute D2 for D1.

11–171 The Court of Appeal[525] upheld the judge's decision to substitute D2 for D1. However, on further appeal, the House of Lords[526] concluded that the judgment of the European Court of Justice[527] was not so clear and obvious as to leave no scope for any reasonable doubt as to its application. The matter was referred back to the European Court for clarification as to whether it was consistent with the Product Liability Directive that proceedings started against someone described as the producer of a product should count as having been started against the real producer, where the claimant had mistakenly named as a defendant someone who was not the producer.

11–172 The European Court of Justice held that, although the Product Liability Directive did not prescribe the procedural rules that applied when a claimant had made a mistake as to the identity of the producer, which was therefore a matter for national law, the general rule under the Directive is that after the 10-year longstop has expired it is not permissible to add the producer as a defendant to proceedings brought within the limitation period against another person.[528] However, the Court added that the Directive did not preclude a national court from holding that, in the proceedings instituted within the longstop period against the wholly-owned subsidiary (D1) of the "producer", that producer (D2) can be substituted for D1 if the court found that the putting into circulation of the product in question was, in fact, determined by D2. It was a matter for the national court to assess whether the putting into circulation of the product in question was, in fact, determined by the parent company which manufactured it.[529]

---

[522] [2006] EWHC 2562 (QB); [2007] 1 W.L.R. 757 at [20].
[523] [2005] EWCA Civ 134; [2005] 1 W.L.R. 2557 at [39] per Jacob LJ.
[524] [2005] EWCA Civ 134; [2005] 1 W.L.R. 2557 at [21].
[525] [2007] EWCA Civ 966; [2008] 1 W.L.R. 1188.
[526] [2008] UKHL 34; [2008] 3 C.M.L.R. 10.
[527] In *O'Byrne v Sanofi Pasteur MSD Ltd (formerly Aventis Pasteur MSD Ltd)* (C127/04) [2006] 1 W.L.R. 1606; para.11–160.
[528] *Aventis Pasteur SA v OB* (C-358/08) [2010] 1 W.L.R. 1375. That is the position even where the claimant made a genuine mistake and, intending to sue the person he believed to be the manufacturer, issued proceedings within the 10-year longstop period against the wrong person: [2010] 1 W.L.R. 1375 at [48].
[529] [2010] 1 W.L.R. 1375 at [51]–[53]. The Court also pointed out (at [54]–[59]) that where the claimant was not reasonably able to identify the producer before making a claim against the supplier of the product, the supplier could be treated as a producer for the purposes of the Directive if it did not inform the claimant, on its own initiative and promptly, of the identity of the producer or its own supplier. A mere denial by the supplier that it is a producer is insufficient. The subsidiary had bought

The case came back to the Supreme Court in *O'Byrne v Aventis Pasteur MSD*   **11–173**
Ltd.[530] The claimant accepted that the ruling of the European Court prevented the
addition of a new party under s.35 of the Limitation Act after the expiry of the
10-year longstop, but argued that D1 was the wholly owned subsidiary of D2 and
that D2 had determined the putting into circulation of the vaccine when it
supplied it to D1 (thus bringing the case within the qualification identified by the
European Court of Justice). The Supreme Court rejected the argument, explaining
that the European Court had *not* ruled that the mere fact that D1 was the wholly
owned subsidiary of D2 could be a reason for allowing D2 to be substituted for
D1 after the expiry of the 10-year period. Rather it was simply one factor to be
taken into account by the court when assessing how closely the subsidiary was
involved with its parent's business as a producer. If D2 was actually in a position
to decide when the product was to be distributed, then D1 would be integrated
into the manufacturing process and so tightly controlled by D2 that proceedings
against D1 could properly be regarded as proceedings against the parent
company, D2. The claimant objected that if the European Court's judgment was
interpreted in such a narrow way it would mean that substitution would be
possible only where the D1 could, in any event, itself be sued as a producer (on
the basis that it was possible to show that the subsidiary was so closely integrated
into the parent's business that the subsidiary could be treated as a producer under
the Directive). But the Supreme Court concluded that that was indeed the
position, pointing out that if there was no advantage to suing the manufacturer in
substitution for the supplier the claimant would not do so.[531]

Adding a NHS hospital to a claim against a surgeon   In *Martin v Kaisary*[532]   **11–174**
the Court of Appeal held that it was not necessary to add a NHS Trust to an action
brought against a surgeon who had carried out a private operation at the Trust
hospital because in order to determine the surgeon's liability at trial the court
would have to examine the actions of the medical staff at the hospital (what the
staff did, what information they conveyed to the surgeon, whether the surgeon
asked for further information and what he did with the information that was
provided to him) but not their liability.

Adding a new cause of action—the same or substantially the same facts   **11–175**
Section 35(5) permits a claim involving a new cause of action to be added if the
new cause of action arises out of the same facts or substantially the same facts as
are already in issue on any claim previously made in the original action. The
question of what constitutes "the same or substantially the same facts"[533] has

---

the vaccine directly from the parent company and so clearly knew the identity of the producer at the
time when the claimant brought proceedings against it. See the Consumer Protection Act 1987 s.2(3);
para.10–083.
[530] [2010] UKSC 23; [2010] 1 W.L.R. 1412.
[531] [2010] UKSC 23; [2010] 1 W.L.R. 1412 at [34]–[35]. The Supreme Court pointed out that there
might be an advantage if, say, the supplier were insolvent.
[532] *(No.1)* [2005] EWCA Civ 594; [2006] P.I.Q.R. P5.
[533] Note that "'the same or substantially the same' is not synonymous with 'similar'. The word
'similar' is often used in this context, but it should not be regarded as anything more than a convenient
shorthand": *Bellinger v Mercer Ltd* [2014] EWCA Civ 996; [2014] 1 W.L.R. 3597 at [37] per
Tomlinson LJ.

been said to be "substantially a matter of impression".[534] In *Sayer v Kingston & Esher Health Authority*[535] it was held that where the claimant had pleaded negligence in the performance of a Caesarean section operation, and subsequently sought to include allegations in respect of events leading up to the operation and the post-operative treatment, the amendments arose out of substantially the same facts as were already in issue. Mann LJ commented that the facts were the "facts relating to the birth of the plaintiff's second child" and it was unreal to compartmentalise that single event into a number of discrete parts. Similarly, in *Grewal v National Hospital for Nervous Diseases*[536] the claimant sought to add an allegation of trespass to the person in a medical negligence action, on the basis that the defendants had exceeded the consent given by the claimant by performing a laminectomy on the spine when all that had been consented to was a biopsy. Dunn LJ said that, although the legal issue was a different one, the question was whether the cause of action arose out of the same or substantially the same facts. That involved a consideration of the evidence which would be likely to be led in support of the new cause of action. Since it would be necessary to lead substantially the same evidence as would have been necessary to support the statement of claim as originally pleaded, the claim in trespass arose out of substantially the same facts. It was artificial to distinguish between what had happened in the ward, as opposed to what had happened in the operating theatre.[537] Where the court has jurisdiction to permit an amendment after the relevant period of limitation has expired it must still exercise a discretion as to whether to allow the amendment.[538]

---

[534] *Welsh Development Agency v Redpath Dorman Long Ltd* [1994] 1 W.L.R. 1409 at 1418, CA. In the case of a fatal accident, a claim on behalf of the deceased's dependants under the Fatal Accidents Act 1976 will usually arise out of the same facts or substantially the same facts as a claim on behalf of the estate under the Law Reform (Miscellaneous Provisions) Act 1934: *Booker v Associated British Ports* [1995] P.I.Q.R. P375, CA.

[535] Unreported 9 March 1989, CA; *Booker v Associated British Ports* [1995] P.I.Q.R. P375, CA—the facts in issue in a Fatal Accidents Act claim were substantially the same facts as were already in issue in the claim being conducted on behalf of the deceased employee's estate under the Law Reform (Miscellaneous Provisions) Act 1934.

[536] (1982) 132 N.L.J. 1149, CA.

[537] See further, on this issue: *Dornan v JW Ellis & Co. Ltd* [1962] 1 Q.B. 583; *Hay v London Brick Co Ltd* [1989] 2 Lloyd's Rep. 7; *Adam v Hemming* unreported 8 March 1991, CA; *Sion v Hampstead Health Authority* [1994] 5 Med. L.R. 170. A claim for breach of the claimant's art.3 and art.8 rights under the European Convention on Human Rights is not necessarily based on the same or substantially the same facts as a common law claim in negligence: *Henderson v Dorset Healthcare University NHS Foundation Trust* [2016] EWHC 3032 (QB); [2017] Med. L.R. 57 (claimant refused permission to amend claim to add claims under the Human Rights Act 1998 to existing negligence action).

[538] Under the old Rules of the Supreme Court the test was whether it was "just to do so", which was a matter of balancing the prejudice to the claimant and the prejudice to the defendant. See *Hancock Shipping Co Ltd v Kawasaki Heavy Industries Ltd, The Casper Trader* [1992] 1 W.L.R. 102. The court was not required to treat a claimant seeking permission to amend in the same way as a claimant seeking the court's exercise of discretion under s.33 of the Limitation Act 1980: *Adam v Hemming* unreported 8 March 1991, CA, per Ralph Gibson LJ. The exercise of the discretion is now subject to the overriding objective "to deal with cases justly": CPR r.1.1. In *Henderson v Dorset Healthcare University NHS Foundation Trust* [2016] EWHC 3032 (QB); [2017] Med. L.R. 57 Warby J refused permission to add a human rights claim to an existing claim for common law negligence because there had been unreasonable delay by the claimant and adding the new claim would result in an adjournment of the trial. The potential value to the claimant of the amendments had to be assessed in

(k)   Burden of proof

Defendants must plead the limitation period in their defence if they seek to rely   **11–176**
on it,[539] though they are not obliged to take the point and the court will not do so
if they omits it.[540] There is some uncertainty concerning who has the burden of
proof as to whether the action is or is not statute barred. Logically, if limitation is
considered to be a defence, the burden of proving that the claim is out of time
should rest with defendants. This view has been adopted on more than one
occasion.[541] On the other hand, the Court of Appeal has also stated that the
burden of proof lies with claimants.[542] In *Fowell v National Coal Board*,[543] a case
involving personal injuries, Parker LJ said that as limitation is a matter of
defence, it must be for the person setting up limitation to assert and prove that the
claim is time barred, which, in the first instance, requires no more than proof that
the three-year period has elapsed. If this period has elapsed but claimants wish to
argue that the date of knowledge was later, it is for them to assert and give
evidence that they first had knowledge of the relevant facts under s.14(1) of the
Act on a date later than the accrual of the cause of action.[544] If, however,
defendants wish to displace this by asserting an earlier date of knowledge, it is for
them to do so.

the context of the litigation overall and the overriding objective. The new claims were put forward
five years out of time; unconscionably late in the proceedings; when a trial was imminent; and when
the defendant had been proceeding on the basis that no human rights claims were being pursued.

[539] CPR 16PD.13.1. If defendants consider that they have a good limitation defence their proper
course is either to plead the defence and seek a trial of the defence as a preliminary issue, or, in a very
clear case, to apply to strike out the claim on the ground that it is frivolous and vexatious and an abuse
of the process of the court, but they cannot seek to strike out the claim on the ground that it discloses
no reasonable cause of action: *Ronex Properties Ltd v John Laing Construction Ltd* [1983] Q.B. 398.
Given the availability of the discretion under s.33 of the Limitation Act 1980, it will rarely be
possible, in a personal injuries action, to say that the case is "very clear". The claimant may, but is not
required to, stay silent about the limitation issue in the statement of claim, leaving the defendant to
raise it as a matter of defence. The claimant may, however, simply plead that the action is not
statute-barred: see *Driscoll-Varley v Parkside Health Authority* [1991] 2 Med. L.R. 346 at 358.
Wherever it is feasible a judge should decide the limitation point by a preliminary hearing by
reference to the pleadings and written witness statements and the extent and content of disclosure: *KR
v Bryn Alyn Community (Holdings) Ltd (In Liquidation)* [2003] EWCA Civ 85; [2003] Q.B. 1441 at
[74].

[540] See *Kennett v Brown* [1988] 1 W.L.R. 582.

[541] *Darley Main Colliery Co. v Mitchell* (1886) 11 App. Cas. 127 at 135; *O'Connor v Isaacs* [1956] 2
Q.B. 288 at 364; *The Pendrecht* [1980] 2 Lloyd's Rep. 56 at 60.

[542] See *Cartledge v Jopling & Sons Ltd* [1962] 1 Q.B. 189; *London Congregational Union Inc. v
Harriss & Harriss* [1988] 1 All E.R. 15; *Crocker v British Coal Corporation* (1996) 29 B.M.L.R. 159,
QBD; see also *Nash v Eli Lilly & Co.* [1991] 2 Med. L.R. 169, QBD, where it was said that the
preliminary burden of establishing that a case falls within the limitation period rests with the claimant,
but thereafter, in relation to the question of a claimant's constructive knowledge, the burden falls upon
the defendant; see also *Driscoll-Varley v Parkside Health Authority* [1991] 2 Med. L.R. 346 at 357, to
the same effect.

[543] *The Times*, 28 May 1986. See also *Nash v Eli Lilly & Co.* [1993] 1 W.L.R. 782 at 796, CA.

[544] See also *Haward v Fawcetts* [2006] UKHL 9; [2006] 1 W.L.R. 682 at [106] per Lord Mance in
relation to s.14A: "Under section 14A the onus is on a claimant to plead and prove that he first had the
knowledge required for bringing his action within a period of three years prior to its bringing." The
point was reiterated by Lord Mance in *AB v Ministry of Defence* [2012] UKSC 9; [2013] 1 A.C. 78 at

11–177   Where the claimant makes an application under s.33 to disapply the primary limitation period the burden of proving that it is just and equitable to allow the action to proceed is the claimant's.[545] It is not helpful in the abstract to describe this burden as a "heavy burden" or a "light burden" since the issue is fact-specific and so the burden will vary from case to case.[546]

(l)   Human Rights Act claims

11–178   Proceedings under the Human Rights Act 1998 are subject to a one-year limitation period running from the date on which the act complained of took place, or such longer period as the court considers equitable having regard to all the circumstances.[547] In *Rabone v Pennine Care NHS Foundation Trust*[548] Lord Dyson said that it will often be appropriate to take into account factors of the type listed in s.33(3) of the Limitation Act 1980[549] when considering whether it is equitable to grant an extension of time under s.7(5), though the wording of s.7(5) should be applied. It would be wrong, said his Lordship, to interpret it as if it contained the language of s.33(3). Lord Dyson pointed to several factors in *Rabone* which strongly militated in favour of an extension of time, namely that: the required extension was short (four months); the defendant NHS Trust had suffered no prejudice by the delay; the applicants had acted reasonably in delaying proceedings whilst waiting for a report of the findings of an internal investigation into the circumstances of their daughter's death; and "most important of all" they had a good claim for breach of art.2.[550]

---

[84] in relation to personal injuries: "Once an issue of knowledge is identified as arising under sections 11(4)(b) and 14(1), the onus lies upon the claimant to make good his case on knowledge…" See also per Lord Phillips in *AB* at [144].

[545] *Thompson v Brown Construction (Ebbw Vale) Ltd* [1981] 1 W.L.R. 744 at 752; see para 11–096.

[546] *Sayers v Lord Chelwood* [2012] EWCA Civ 1715; [2013] 1 W.L.R. 1695 at [53]–[55], applying *AB v Ministry of Defence* [2010] EWCA Civ 1317; (2011) 117 B.M.L.R. 101 at [96].

[547] Human Rights Act 1998 s.7(5). On the distinction between the "act complained of" and the consequences of the act see *O'Connor v Bar Standards Board* [2016] EWCA Civ 775; [2016] 1 W.L.R. 4085.

[548] [2012] UKSC 2; [2012] 2 A.C. 72 at [75].

[549] See paras 11–128 et seq.

[550] [2012] UKSC 2; [2012] 2 A.C. 72 at [79]; see also per Baroness Hale at [108]. The burden of establishing that it would be equitable in all the circumstances to grant an extension of time lies with the claimant: *M v Ministry of Justice* [2009] EWCA Civ 419; (2009) 159 N.L.J. 860. A claimant seeking an extension of time has to make that clear, both to the court and the opposing party, and set out the grounds and evidence on which they rely: *O'Connor v Bar Standards Board* [2016] EWCA Civ 775; [2016] 1 W.L.R. 4085. See also *Cameron v Network Rail Infrastructure Ltd* [2006] EWHC 1133 (QB); [2007] 1 W.L.R. 163 (not equitable to extend limitation period where claimant was a solicitor who was aware of the possibility of a claim under the 1998 Act for a considerable time before he did anything to investigate the legal position).

CHAPTER 12

DAMAGES

Most actions against medical practitioners are claims in respect of personal injuries or death, and the consequential financial loss, and there is no difference in the principles applied to the assessment of damages in medical negligence cases from other actions for personal injuries.[1] Injunctive relief is rarely relevant, with the possible exception of actions for breach of confidence. Accordingly, this chapter concentrates largely on the principles adopted by the courts in the assessment of damages for personal injuries and death.[2]

12–001

---

[1] Note that not all physiological changes to the body will necessarily give rise to an action for damages. In *Rothwell v Chemical & Insulating Co Ltd* [2007] UKHL 39; [2008] 1 A.C. 281 the House of Lords held that pleural plaques, which are localised areas of fibrous tissue in the pleura around the lungs caused by exposure to asbestos, did not constitute actionable damage. Plaques are usually symptomless and only detectable on X-rays, though they are evidence of exposure to asbestos and are markers for an increased risk of developing more serious asbestos-related diseases such as asbestosis, lung cancer and mesothelioma. Nor, said their Lordships, did the risk of future illness or a claimant's anxiety about the possibility of that risk materialising constitute actionable damage, even if the anxiety causes a recognised psychiatric illness. By the same token, individuals who due to the defendant's negligence have been exposed to a sensitising agent without developing any symptoms, and who would not develop symptoms unless they were further exposed to that sensitising agent have not suffered actionable personal injury: *Greenway v Johnson Matthey plc* [2016] EWCA Civ 408; [2016] 1 W.L.R. 4487, where employees had been sensitised to platinum salts and therefore were no longer able to work in conditions where they were likely to come into contact with platinum salts. The financial loss they sustained as a result of no longer being able to work with platinum salts constituted pure economic loss which did not fall within the scope of their employers' duty to exercise reasonable care for the health, safety and welfare of employees. No doubt the position would have been different if they were likely to come into contact with a sensitising agent commonly encountered in daily life and so develop symptoms on a regular basis.

[2] It is not possible to give more than an outline of the law on damages for personal injuries here. For detailed discussion see *Kemp & Kemp, The Quantum of Damages* (London: Sweet & Maxwell), and *McGregor on Damages*, 19th edn (London: Sweet & Maxwell, 2014). Strictly speaking, claims in respect of certain financial losses arising out of "wrongful conception" or "wrongful birth" may not be categorised as actions for personal injuries but they are nonetheless included in this chapter. It is arguable that such claims, at least in respect of the costs associated with raising a child, constitute pure economic loss, but in practice the courts have not drawn a sharp distinction between these categories of loss in such cases: see *Greenfield v Irwin* [2001] EWCA Civ 113; [2001] 1 W.L.R. 1279, applying *McFarlane v Tayside Health Board* [2000] 2 A.C. 59, HL.

1. GENERAL PRINCIPLES

(a) Types of damages

(i) Fundamental principles

12–002 The fundamental principle applied to the assessment of an award of damages in tort is that claimants should be fully compensated. They are entitled to be restored to the position that they would have been in had the tort not been committed, in so far as this can be done by the payment of money. The classic statement of this proposition was by Lord Blackburn in *Livingstone v Rawyards Coal Company*:

> "Where any injury is to be compensated by damages, in settling the sum of money to be given for reparation or damages you should, as nearly as possible, get that sum of money which will put the party who has been injured, or who has suffered, in the same position as he would have been in if he had not sustained the wrong for which he is now getting his compensation or reparation."[3]

This statement was echoed by Lord Lloyd in *Wells v Wells*:

> "The task of the court in assessing damages for personal injury is to arrive at a lump sum which represents, as nearly as possible, full compensation for the injury which the plaintiff has suffered."[4]

In contract claimants are entitled to be placed in the position they would have been in had the contract been performed, but in practice this is unlikely to produce a different measure of damages in contract and tort in an action for personal injuries.

12–003 **Non-pecuniary loss** In the case of non-pecuniary loss the principle of restoring claimants to their pre-accident position is inappropriate. No amount of money can restore a lost limb or take away the experience of pain. Here the principle applied by the courts is that damages for non-pecuniary loss should be "fair" or "reasonable". This is patently unhelpful, because it simply begs the question of what is a fair or reasonable sum. The award is inevitably an arbitrary one. In practice, the courts adopt a tariff or "going rate" for specific types of injury in an

---

[3] *Livingstone v Rawyards Coal Co.* (1880) 5 App. Cas. 25 at 39. In torts actionable *per se*, such as trespass to the person, a claimant could be awarded nominal damages where it is clear that a tort has been committed but the claimant has suffered no loss (see e.g. *Bostridge v Oxleas NHS Foundation Trust* [2015] EWCA Civ 79; [2015] Med. L.R. 113 where the claimant was detained under the Mental Health Act 1983 but there had been a procedural error; he was entitled to nominal damages only for the tort of false imprisonment because he could have been lawfully detained under the Act if the error had been drawn to the defendants' attention and therefore he had suffered no loss justifying substantial damages (applying *Lumba v Secretary of State for the Home Department* [2011] UKSC 12; [2012] 1 A.C. 245 and *R. (on the application of Kambadzi) v Secretary of State for the Home Department* [2011] UKSC 23; [2011] 1 W.L.R. 1299*). Similarly, in contract nominal damages may be awarded where there has been a breach of contract but no loss. In the tort of negligence damage is the gist of the action, and some substantive damage must be proved for the action lie. These distinctions will rarely, if ever, be relevant to claims in respect of personal injuries.
[4] [1999] 1 A.C. 345 at 363.

attempt to achieve some degree of consistency between claimants with similar injuries and to provide a basis for the settlement of claims.[5]

General and special damages   Inexact or unliquidated losses are compensated by an award of "general damages". In an action for personal injuries this includes the non-pecuniary losses which are compensated under the heads of pain and suffering, and loss of amenity. It also includes prospective pecuniary losses such as future loss of earnings and medical expenses. "Special damages" are the losses that are capable of being calculated with reasonable accuracy, and will normally consist of accrued pecuniary losses, such as loss of earnings and other expenses incurred from the date of the injury to the date of assessment.[6] The distinction is important for the purpose of determining the appropriate rate of interest, since different rates apply to special damages and general damages for non-pecuniary loss, and no interest will be awarded in respect of future pecuniary loss.[7] Although the court will assess damages under these broad heads, the court should also have regard to the appropriateness of the total award in order to avoid any overlapping of the different heads of damage, though it is doubtful whether there can be any overlap between pecuniary and non-pecuniary losses.[8]

12–004

(ii)   Aggravated damages

Where damages are at large, that is where the award is not limited to the pecuniary loss that can be specifically proved,[9] the court may take into account the manner in which the tort was committed in assessing damages. If it was such as to injure the claimant's proper feelings of dignity and pride then aggravated damages may be awarded.[10] Aggravated damages are compensatory, but they are higher than would normally be the case to reflect the greater injury to the claimant.[11]

12–005

---

[5] See the Judicial College, *Guidelines for the Assessment of General Damages in Personal Injury Cases*, 14th edn (Oxford: Oxford University Press, 2017) for a summary of the range of awards by injury type; and see also *Kemp and Kemp, The Quantum of Damages* (London: Sweet & Maxwell) for a more detailed analysis of the case law giving rise to the Guidelines.
[6] Though "special damage" has sometimes been used to refer simply to pecuniary loss, and "general damages" to non-pecuniary loss: *R. (on the application of Greenfield) v Secretary of State for the Home Department* [2005] UKHL 14; [2005] 1 W.L.R. 673 at [11], [12].
[7] CPR 16PD para.4.3 provides that claimants in an action for personal injuries must attach to or serve with their particulars of claim a medical report about the personal injuries which they allege in their claim. There must also be a schedule of details of any past and future expenses and losses which they claim: CPR 16PD para.4.2. On the payment of interest see para.12–046.
[8] *Lim Poh Choo v Camden and Islington Area Health Authority* [1980] A.C. 174 at 191, 192.
[9] *Rookes v Barnard* [1964] A.C. 1129 at 1221. This includes loss of reputation, injured feelings, pain and suffering or loss of amenity: *Broome v Cassell & Co. Ltd* [1972] A.C. 1027 at 1073.
[10] *Jolliffe v Willmett & Co.* [1971] 1 All E.R. 478—an "insolent and high-handed trespass" by a private investigator.
[11] The Law Commission recommended that aggravated damages should be renamed "damages for mental distress" and that it should be made clear that such awards are compensatory and are not intended to punish the defendant: Law Com. No.247, *Aggravated, Exemplary and Restitutionary Damages*, 1997.

12–006 **Personal injuries** In *Kralj v McGrath*[12] Woolf J held that aggravated damages should not be awarded in an action for negligence against a doctor, notwithstanding that the medical evidence indicated that the claimant's treatment had been "horrific". If, on the other hand, the particular treatment increased the claimant's pain and suffering this should be reflected in a higher award under this head. This approach was approved by the Court of Appeal in *AB v South West Water Services Ltd*.[13] Thus, in a case of personal injuries the measure of compensatory damages should include all the injuries that have been suffered, physically, psychologically and mentally, and to the extent that these effects have been exacerbated by distress and anxiety caused by the defendant's conduct, this will be reflected in the ordinary measure of compensatory damages. On the other hand, mere indignation and anger aroused by the defendant's conduct is not a proper subject for compensation, since it is neither pain nor suffering.[14]

12–007 In *Appleton v Garrett*[15] the defendant dentist had carried out large-scale, unnecessary treatment in order to increase his income. He deliberately, and in bad faith, withheld from the claimants the information that the treatment was unnecessary because he knew that they would not have consented to the treatment had they known the true position. The defendant was held liable in trespass to the person, and Dyson J took the view that there was contumelious conduct or motive on the part of the defendant, having deliberately caused pain and damage to his patients, taken advantage of their young age, and abused his position of trust. He had "wilfully damaged teeth on a massive scale". Dyson J distinguished *AB v South West Water Services Ltd* on the basis that, first, the tort in that case was a negligently committed nuisance, whereas in *Appleton v Garrett* it was a case of trespass to the person. In *AB v South West Water* the Court of Appeal appeared to have accepted that indignation aroused by a defendant's conduct can increase the claimant's damages in defamation cases because "injury to the plaintiff's feelings and self-esteem is an important part of the damage for which compensation is awarded". There was no reason in principle, said Dyson J, why awards of aggravated damages should not be made for feelings of anger or indignation in other causes of action such as trespass to the person, where injury to feelings is an important part of the damage for which compensation is awarded:

> "To say that the law permits recovery of aggravated damages where the relevant conduct has caused injury to feelings, insult, indignity, humiliation and a heightened sense of injury or grievance, but not where it has caused anger or indignation, is very difficult to justify in terms of principle or common sense."[16]

The observations of the Court of Appeal should be understood as being restricted to cases where injury to a claimant's feelings and self-esteem were not an important part of the damage for which compensation is awarded. Secondly, and in any event, in addition to feelings of anger and indignation, all the claimants

---

[12] [1986] 1 All E.R. 54.
[13] [1993] Q.B. 507.
[14] [1993] Q.B. 507 at 528, 532.
[15] [1996] P.I.Q.R. P1.
[16] [1996] P.I.Q.R. P1 at 7.

had suffered mental distress and injury to their feelings, as well as a heightened sense of injury or grievance, when they learned that the treatment they had undergone was unnecessary. Assessing the aggravated damages on a "moderate basis" Dyson J held that they should be assessed at 15 per cent of the sum awarded in each case for general damages for pain, suffering and loss of amenity.

It is submitted that, as a matter of principle, there is no reason why doctors should be specifically excluded from the ambit of aggravated damages, which are compensatory not punitive, although in practice it will be unlikely that mere negligence would be sufficient for such an award.[17] In *Broome v Cassell & Co. Ltd*[18] Lord Reid said that the commission of a tort in a malicious, insulting or oppressive manner may aggravate the claimant's injury. It is arguable that some forms of medical treatment could be regarded as oppressive or insulting: sterilisation of a competent adult without consent, for example.[19] In *Barbara v Home Office*[20] a remand prisoner was forcibly injected with a tranquillising drug by prison officers, and the defendants admitted liability for trespass to the person. The claimant was awarded £100 general damages and £500 aggravated damages, but a claim for exemplary damages was rejected. Mere negligence, it was said, did not justify an award of exemplary damages simply because it resulted in a trespass to the person which from the claimant's point of view could be regarded as oppressive.

Aggravated damages simply part of general damages In practice the issue of aggravated damages may no longer arise in the context of medical negligence cases. In *Richardson v Howie*[21] the Court of Appeal held that, in cases of assault, it was no longer appropriate to characterise an award of damages for injury to feelings as aggravated damages, except possibly in a wholly exceptional case.

12–008

12–009

---

[17] Although the door is not completely closed. Note the comment of Lord Neuberger in respect of aggravated damages being awarded in negligence in *Ashley v Chief Constable of Sussex* [2008] UKHL 25; [2008] 1 A.C. 962 at [102]: "Aggravated damages are awarded for feelings of distress or outrage as a result of the particularly egregious way or circumstances in which the tort was committed, or in which its aftermath was subsequently handled by the defendant. If that is so, I cannot see why such damages should not logically be recoverable in some categories of negligence claims. In the present case, for instance, it must have been reasonably foreseeable (the normal tort test) that a negligently mishandled armed police raid could result in just the sort of mental distress or shock that aggravated damages are intended to reflect. It appears to me that it would be reminiscent of the bad old days of forms of action if the court held that the Ashleys' claim could result in aggravated damages if framed in battery, but not if framed in negligence. In my view, there is a strong enough case for saying that aggravated damages would be recoverable for the instant negligence for the point to have been validly conceded by the Chief Constable."

[18] [1972] A.C. 1027 at 1085.

[19] See para.6–017. In *Devi v West Midlands Regional Health Authority* unreported 9 December 1981, CA, compensatory damages of £4,000 were awarded in a case of non-consensual sterilisation, without any reference to aggravated damages. In *Muir v The Queen in right of Alberta* (1996) 132 D.L.R. (4th) 695, Alberta QB, the court awarded very substantial aggravated damages (of $125,000 in addition to $250,000 for pain and suffering) in respect of the claimant's unlawful sterilisation following her wrongful detention at the age of 10 in an institution for "mental defectives" (for which a further $250,000 compensatory award was made).

[20] (1984) 134 N.L.J. 888. A similar allegation failed on the facts in *Freeman v Home Office* [1984] Q.B. 524.

[21] [2004] EWCA Civ 1127; [2005] P.I.Q.R. Q3.

That element of compensatory damages should be taken into account as part of general damages. The case involved a very serious assault. The trial judge awarded £10,000, £5,000 of which was aggravated damages, but failed to give reasons for his award. The Court of Appeal noted that the agreed appropriate compensatory award was in the bracket of £2,000 to £7,500. Whilst it was appropriate in such cases to award damages for:

> "...injury to feelings including the indignity, mental suffering, humiliation or distress that might be caused by such an attack, as well as the anger or indignation arising from the circumstances of the attack",

such damages were compensatory in nature. A court should not characterise the award of damages for injury to feelings that might be caused by such an attack as aggravated damages. Injury to feelings should be compensated as part of the general damages awarded. Such damages could not properly be characterised as "aggravated".[22] Save possibly in a wholly exceptional case, there should be no additional award beyond that required to compensate the claimant. The case did not approach being "wholly exceptional" and it was therefore wrong in principle to make a distinct award for aggravated damages. The Court of Appeal concluded that the appropriate compensatory award, taking into account Ms Richardson's admitted injury to feelings from the vicious nature of the attack, was £4,500. No guidance was given on what would amount to a "wholly exceptional" case in which an additional award of aggravated damages would be justified. However, if even on the facts of this particularly vicious assault aggravated damages were not justified, then in practice it is difficult to see in what circumstances an award may now be made. Given that such damages appear very unlikely to be awarded for negligence and are unlikely to be awarded for assault it is now difficult to foresee circumstances where aggravated damages would be available in a medical negligence case. That is not to say that claimants will be uncompensated. The Court of Appeal made it clear that the aggravating factors should be compensated through the award of general damages. In practice this is likely to result in awards towards the top end of the appropriate bracket for general damages, if not slightly above.[23]

---

[22] See also *Martins v Choudhary* [2007] EWCA Civ 1379; [2008] 1 W.L.R. 617 at [20] per Smith LJ: "...where damages fall to be awarded for injury to feelings, the quantum of damage should reflect the aggravating features of the defendant's conduct as they have affected the claimant. As 'aggravated damages' are supposed to be compensatory, that seems to me to be the most satisfactory way of dealing with them. If a separate award of 'aggravated damages' is made, it looks like a punishment; in other words it looks like exemplary damages." Nonetheless, the judge had been entitled to make separate awards of damages for psychiatric harm and injury to feelings in a harassment case.

[23] Cases involving the physical and/or sexual abuse of children may have an element of the award of general damages which are in substance, if not in form, aggravated damages. See e.g. *RAR v GGC* [2012] EWHC 2338 (QB); *JXL v Britton* [2014] EWHC 2571 (QB); *BDA v Quirino* [2015] EWHC 2974 (QB); *R v Scout Association* [2016] EWHC 587 (QB). Clearly, such cases are at some considerable remove from medical negligence cases.

(iii)   Exemplary damages

Aggravated damages should be distinguished from exemplary damages. **12–010**
Exemplary damages are punitive in nature and are awarded in addition to
compensatory damages in order to teach the defendant that "tort does not pay". In
other words, exemplary damages aim to punish the wrongdoer. English common
law limits the circumstances in which exemplary damages may be awarded to
two categories of case, namely: (i) oppressive, arbitrary or unconstitutional action
by servants of the government; and (ii) where the defendant's conduct has been
calculated to make a profit which may well exceed the compensation available.[24]

Cause of action "test"   In *AB v South West Water Services Ltd*[25] the Court of   **12–011**
Appeal held that, in addition to these restrictions, exemplary damages should
only be available in torts which were recognised before the decision in *Rookes v
Barnard* as establishing a claim for exemplary damages. This effectively
excluded such awards in actions for negligence, including medical negligence,
although they are a feature in malpractice claims against doctors in some
American and Commonwealth jurisdictions.[26] In *Kuddus v Chief Constable of
Leicestershire Constabulary*,[27] however, the House of Lords held that this "cause
of action" test was not good law (overruling *AB v South West Water* on this
point). The question to be considered was the nature of the defendant's conduct
and whether it fitted into Lord Devlin's categories in *Rookes v Barnard*, not the
basis of the cause of action.

Reform   Although the issue did not arise for decision in *Kuddus*, Lord Nicholls   **12–012**
even suggested that the restrictions inherent in Lord Devlin's categories ought to
be reconsidered.[28] With regard to the second category, the "key", said his

---

[24] *Rookes v Barnard* [1964] A.C. 1129; *Broome v Cassell & Co. Ltd* [1972] A.C. 1027. What is
required is knowledge by defendants that what they propose to do is against the law or a reckless
disregard for whether it is legal or illegal. Carelessness alone, however extreme, is not enough: *John
v Mirror Group Newspapers Ltd* [1997] Q.B. 586 at 618 per Sir Thomas Bingham MR. An attempt by
the defendant to conceal the commission of a tort with the object of limiting the amount of damages
payable to the claimant, though reprehensible, does not fall into the second category: *AB v South West
Water Services Ltd* [1993] Q.B. 507 at 526.
[25] [1993] Q.B. 507.
[26] See, e.g. *Backwell v AAA* [1997] 1 V.R. 182, Vict CA, where having inseminated the claimant with
semen from a donor of an incompatible blood type, the defendant doctor persuaded the claimant to
have a termination of the resulting pregnancy, contrary to her beliefs, by making false threats that if
she had a miscarriage her identity might be revealed in the ensuing publicity, that this might force the
donor insemination programme to close, and that it might be difficult for the claimant receive donor
insemination in the future. See also the discussion by Lord Nicholls in *A v Bottrill* [2002] UKPC 44;
[2003] 1 A.C. 449 at [41] to [49]. In *Steinkrauss v Afridi* 2013 ABCA 417; (2013) 5 Alta. L.R. (6th)
210 the Alberta Court of Appeal accepted that it was arguable that exemplary damages could be
awarded in a claim under the Fatal Accidents Act where a doctor had altered a deceased patient's
medical records in order to divert responsibility from himself.
[27] [2001] UKHL 29; [2002] 2 A.C. 122.
[28] [2001] UKHL 29; [2002] 2 A.C. 122 at [66]: "Whatever may have been the position 40 years ago,
I am respectfully inclined to doubt the soundness of this distinction today. National and international
companies can exercise enormous power. So do some individuals. I am not sure it would be right to
draw a hard-and-fast line which would always exclude such companies and persons from the reach of
exemplary damages. Indeed, the validity of the dividing line drawn by Lord Devlin when formulating

Lordship, should be outrageous conduct on the part of the defendant. There was no obvious reason why, if exemplary damages were to be available "the profit motive should suffice but a malicious motive should not".[29] The Law Commission has recommended that the power to award exemplary damages should be retained, while being put on a more rational basis, with the test laid down in *Rookes v Barnard* being abolished.[30] This would open up the possibility of such awards in clinical negligence actions, though only in respect of conscious wrongdoing by a defendant which is outrageous, or where disregard of the claimant's rights is contumelious. Clearly, this would be a rare case, although the facts of *Appleton v Garrett*[31] might be thought to fall into such a category.

12–013   In *A v Bottrill*[32] the Privy Council considered the extent of the jurisdiction to award exemplary damages in New Zealand for negligent conduct. The case arose out of the "wholesale misreading of cervical smears" by the defendant pathologist. The defendant's false reporting rate was 50 per cent or higher. The majority of the Privy Council (in an opinion delivered by Lord Nicholls) considered that the rationale for exemplary damages was to punish the defendant for his outrageous conduct, to mark the court's disapproval of such conduct and to deter him from repeating it.[33] Thus, in principle a court's jurisdiction to award exemplary damages should extend to all cases of tortious wrongdoing where the defendant's conduct satisfied the criterion of outrageousness, because otherwise some types of outrageous conduct would fall within the jurisdiction and others would not.[34] Cases satisfying the test of outrageousness would usually involve intentional wrongdoing with, additionally, an element of flagrancy or cynicism or oppression; something additional, rendering the wrongdoing or the manner or circumstances in which it was committed particularly appalling. These were the features rendering the defendant's conduct outrageous. Overwhelmingly, in cases of negligence, an award of exemplary damages would be appropriate only where the defendant's wrongdoing was intentional or consciously reckless.[35] There could be rare cases, however, where:

---

his first category is somewhat undermined by his second category, where the defendants are not confined to, and normally would not be, government officials or the like."

[29] [2001] UKHL 29; [2002] 2 A.C. 122 at [67].

[30] Law Com. No.247, *Aggravated, Exemplary and Restitutionary Damages*, 1997, para.5.41: "...there appears to be no sound reason why outrageously wrongful conduct should not attract a punitive award even if it is not committed by a servant of the government."

[31] See para.12–007 above.

[32] [2002] UKPC 44; [2003] 1 A.C. 449; Manning (2003) 119 L.Q.R. 24; Todd (2004) 12 Tort L. Rev. 8.

[33] Citing Lord Devlin in *Rookes v Barnard* [1964] A.C. 1129 at 1228.

[34] [2002] UKPC 44; [2003] 1 A.C. 449 at [22]. New Zealand, of course, has a no-fault accident compensation scheme for persons who suffer personal injury by accident, and someone who qualifies for compensation under the statutory scheme has no claim for damages at common law for personal injuries arising out of the accident. This bar to action does not, however, preclude a claim for exemplary damages: *Donselaar v Donselaar* [1982] 1 N.Z.L.R. 97, NZCA. And see also *L v Robinson* [2000] 3 N.Z.L.R. 499 where exemplary damages were awarded against a psychotherapist for engaging in sexual misconduct with a patient who was in a particularly vulnerable position, having approached the defendant for therapy because of previous sexual abuse.

[35] [2002] UKPC 44; [2003] 1 A.C. 449 at [24].

"...the defendant departed so far and so flagrantly from the dictates of ordinary or professional precepts of prudence, or standards of care, that his conduct satisfies this test even though he was not consciously reckless."[36]

The ultimate touchstone was the outrageous conduct of the defendant which called for punishment. However, in *Couch v Attorney General (No.2)*[37] the Supreme Court of New Zealand exercised its new power as the final appellate jurisdiction in New Zealand to depart from decisions of the Privy Council, holding that although exemplary damages were not limited to intentional torts they should not be awarded unless the defendant had a conscious appreciation of the risk of causing harm and had run that known risk. In other words, it was not sufficient that the defendant's conduct was objectively recklessness even if it was outrageous; exemplary damages could only be awarded for subjective and outrageous recklessness.

A v Bottrill remains of persuasive authority in English law.[38] The different views   **12–014**
on exemplary damages evident in the House of Lords in *Kuddus v Chief Constable of Leicestershire Constabulary* and the difference of opinion in the Privy Council in *A v Bottrill*[39] suggest that there is room for debate at the highest judicial level as to the role of exemplary damages. Lord Nicholls, for example, seemed to favour the Law Commission's position that the restrictive test laid down in *Rookes v Barnard* should be abolished.[40] The significance of *A v Bottrill* for English law lies in the marker it lays down for potential future developments.

(b)   The form of the award: lump sum or periodical payments

(i)   A single claim and the lump sum

Claimants can only bring one action in respect of a single tort. They cannot bring   **12–015**
a second action based on the same facts simply because the damage turns out to be more extensive than was first anticipated.[41] Damages are normally assessed

---

[36] [2002] UKPC 44; [2003] 1 A.C. 449 at [26].
[37] [2010] NZSC 27; [2010] N.Z.L.R. 149.
[38] See *Willers v Joyce* [2016] UKSC 44; [2016] 3 W.L.R. 534, holding that, on common law issues, any Privy Council decision should normally be regarded by any judge of England and Wales as being of great weight and persuasive value.
[39] Lord Hutton and Lord Millett dissented on the basis that exemplary damages should only be awarded in cases where defendants were subjectively aware of the risk to which their conduct exposed the claimant and deliberately or recklessly took that risk: [2002] UKPC 44; [2003] 1 A.C. 449 at [73]. This was the view adopted by the Supreme Court of New Zealand in *Couch v Attorney General (No.2)* [2010] NZSC 27; [2010] N.Z.L.R. 149.
[40] His Lordship commented, [2002] UKPC 44; [2003] 1 A.C. 449, at [41], that: "Their Lordships also consider that past experience, as expressed in observations or decisions of the higher courts in New Zealand and elsewhere in the common law world, supports the broader approach. Leaving aside England, still toiling in the chains of *Rookes v Barnard* [1964] A.C. 1129, courts in common law countries have remained true to the underlying rationale of the exemplary damages jurisdiction."
[41] *Fetter v Beale* (1701) 1 Ld Raym. 339 at 692; *Bristow v Grout, The Times*, 9 November 1987, CA; cf. *Brunsden v Humphrey* (1884) 14 Q.B.D. 141 where the claimant was held to be entitled to bring two separate actions in respect of damage to property and personal injuries arising out of the same events, because they are two distinct rights. There cannot be two actions, however, for two separate forms of personal injury arising from a single negligent act, even where one of the injuries only comes

once-and-for-all. A limited exception may apply where there is evidence of a change of circumstances after the trial of an action, but before an appeal. In these circumstances the Court of Appeal may admit the new evidence to mitigate the consequences of the lump sum system.[42] As a general rule, however, once the time limit for an appeal has expired an appeal out of time on the basis of changed circumstances will not be permitted.[43] The common law approach has always been that damages should be awarded in the form of a lump sum, both for accrued and prospective losses.[44] However, the court now has a statutory power in cases involving personal injuries to require a defendant to make periodical payments, and in certain specified circumstances to review the award at a later date if the estimate of the claimant's loss turns out to be either too low or too high.

12–016   When assessing damages in the form of a lump sum the court will make an estimate of the chances that a particular event will or would have happened, and reflect those chances in the amount of damages awarded, irrespective of whether the chance was more or less than even.[45] The question is whether the chance is substantial. If it is a mere possibility or speculative it must be ignored, although the question of whether the chance is substantial or speculative should be decided without regard to legal niceties, but on a consideration of all the facts in proper perspective.[46]

---

to light after damages for the first injury have been recovered: see *Bristow v Grout, The Times*, 9 November 1987. In *Crawford v Dally and Royal Marsden Hospital* [1995] 6 Med. L.R. 343, QBD, the claimant issued a counterclaim to an action for payment of fees in respect of private medical treatment, alleging negligence in the treatment, but limited to the further medical expenses arising out of the treatment. A subsequent claim in respect the serious personal injury allegedly caused by the original treatment was barred by the principle of res judicata, applying *Talbot v Berkshire County Council* [1994] Q.B. 290. The rule can produce real injustice: see *Wain v F. Sherwood and Sons Transport Ltd* [1999] P.I.Q.R. P159. In *Johnson v Gore Wood & Co (a firm)* [2002] 2 A.C. 1 the House of Lords held that *Henderson* should not be rigidly applied. The court should take a broad, merits-based approach which takes account of all the facts of the case and focuses on whether, in bringing a claim or raising a defence in later proceedings, a party is misusing or abusing the process of the court. See *Toth v Ledger* [2002] P.I.Q.R. P1, CA, where a claim for bereavement damages under the Fatal Accidents Act 1976 was settled, but the claimant was entitled to continue with his common law claim for psychiatric damage.

[42] *Mulholland v Mitchell* [1971] A.C. 666; *Lim Poh Choo v Camden and Islington Area Health Authority* [1980] A.C. 174. The Court may permit a party to argue a point that was not raised at trial where there has been a change in the law in the interim: see, e.g. *McCamley v Cammell Laird Shipbuilders Ltd* [1990] 1 W.L.R. 963 at 975, but the principle remains that fresh evidence will not normally be received: *Briody v St Helens and Knowsley Area Health Authority* [2001] EWCA Civ 1010; [2002] Q.B. 856 per Judge LJ at [47]. The principles of *Ladd v Marshall* [1954] 1 W.L.R. 1489 continue to apply under the Civil Procedure Rules: [2002] Q.B. 856 at [50] per Judge LJ.

[43] The time limits for filing a notice of appeal are very short; see CPR r.52.4. On the extension of time in which to appeal see *R. (on the application of Hysaj) v Secretary of State for the Home Department* [2014] EWCA Civ 1633; [2015] 1 W.L.R. 2472.

[44] *Fournier v Canadian National Railway* [1927] A.C. 167 at 169; *British Transport Commission v Gourley* [1956] A.C. 185 at 212; *Burke v Tower Hamlets Health Authority, The Times*, 10 August 1989.

[45] *Mallett v McMonagle* [1970] A.C. 166 at 176, per Lord Diplock.

[46] *Davies v Taylor* [1974] A.C. 207 at 212, per Lord Reid.

(ii) Periodical payments

The rule that damages may only be awarded as a lump sum had the potential to cause particular problems in cases of serious personal injuries, especially where the medical prognosis was uncertain. This was because the court had to assess damages based on assumptions about what would happen to the claimant in the future and those assumptions were unlikely to be correct. The claimant's condition may have become worse than could have been anticipated at the trial or it may have improved. He may live longer than his predicted life expectancy and the damages awarded may therefore be inadequate; or he may die sooner, with the result that the damages will not be used for their intended purpose and will result in a windfall for the beneficiaries of his estate. This was noted by Lord Scarman in *Lim Poh Choo v Camden and Islington Area Health Authority*:

> "Knowledge of the future being denied to mankind, so much of the award as is attributed to future loss and suffering will almost surely be wrong. There is really only one certainty: the future will prove the award to be either too high or too low."[47]

12–017

Structured settlements A structured was a private arrangement between the claimant and the defendant's liability insurer under which the normal lump sum damages award could be varied or "structured" over a period of time. The settlement could include a lump sum element plus periodic payments intended to meet the claimant's future losses. The payments could be for a fixed period or until the claimant's death, and they could be index-linked. The payments were financed by the purchase of an annuity by the liability insurer with the money, or part of it, that would have been paid to the claimant as a lump sum. The annuity was held by the insurer on behalf of the claimant and the payments were not taxable as income in the claimant's hands. Moreover, the insurer was not liable to tax on the annuity either. The result was that for large awards, where the tax liability on the income generated by investment of the lump sum damages would be high, the value of the arrangement to both claimant and insurer was substantially greater than the traditional lump sum award. The possibility of index-linking also addressed the problem of inflation eroding the value of the award, though it could not eliminate this problem entirely when certain costs (such as the cost of care) increased at a higher rate than the chosen index.

12–018

Structured settlements were advantageous to some claimants who had sustained serious personal injury and who would have a substantial claim for future pecuniary loss.[48] They did not, however, constitute the form of periodic payments recommended by the Pearson Commission in order to remove some of the

12–019

---

[47] [1980] A.C. 174 at 183. See also *Wells v Wells* [1999] 1 A.C. 345 at 363–364 per Lord Lloyd.

[48] For discussion of structured settlements in the context of medical negligence claims see: Lewis (1993) 56 M.L.R. 844; and R. Lewis, *Structured Settlements: The Law and Practice* (London: Sweet & Maxwell, 1993), Ch.16. There were significant differences in structured settlements in the context of NHS clinical negligence claims because there was no liability insurer involved, and it was possible to structure a settlement without purchasing an annuity from a life insurer.

uncertainties in assessing future pecuniary losses.[49] They depended upon agreement between the parties; the court had no power to order a defendant to accept this form of settlement. The periodic payments were only varied over time in accordance with the terms agreed at the outset; they could not take account of unanticipated events affecting the claimant's future pecuniary expenditure. The absence of any provision enabling the court to impose a structured settlement, a shortage of life companies willing to provide such annuities coupled with low annuity rates, and the reluctance of parties to embrace them as an option, meant that lump sum settlements tended to be preferred, although a significant number of structured settlements were set up in cases of the most serious injury.

12–020   **Statutory periodical payments**   Following a consultation exercise by the Lord Chancellor's Department it became evident that there was widespread support for periodical payments to compensate for future loss and care costs, and that the courts should have the power to order periodical payments without consent.[50] The Courts Act 2003 ss.100 and 101 introduced significant amendments to the Damages Act 1996. A new s.2 of the Damages Act 1996, which came into force on 1 April 2005, provides that a court awarding damages for future pecuniary loss in respect of personal injury may order that the damages are wholly or partly to take the form of periodical payments, and must consider whether to make that order.[51] If the parties consent, a court awarding other damages in respect of personal injury may order that the damages are wholly or partly to take the form of periodical payments.[52] Thus:

(1)   the court must consider[53] whether to make a periodical payments order in respect of future pecuniary loss;

---

[49] *Royal Commission on Civil Liability and Compensation for Personal Injury*, Cmnd.7054 (1978), Vol.I, para.573; cf. Law Com. No.56, HC 373, 1973, para.28 rejecting the introduction of periodical payments.

[50] LCD, *Damages for Future Loss*, CP 01/02, and LCD, *Responses to Consultation on Damages for Future Loss*, CP (R) 01/02, November 2002.

[51] Damages Act 1996 s.2(1), as amended. See also CPR Pt 41 rr.41.4 to 41.10 and Practice Direction 41B. See more generally: R. Lewis "The Politics and Economics of Tort Law: Judicially Imposed Periodical Payments of Damages" (2006) 69 M.L.R. 418; R. De Wilde, "Periodical Payments—a Journey into the Unknown" [2005] J.P.I.L. 320; N. Bevan and H. Gregory, "Periodical Payments" (2005) 155 N.L.J. 565, 907 and 980; N. Martin, "The Two-tier Damages Regime—Traditional Settlements or Periodical Payments" [2010] J.P.I.L. 219; C. Malla, "PPOs in Catastrophic Injury Claims" [2013] J.P.I.L. 169; R. Weir "Periodical Payments Orders—Where Are We Now?" [2014] J.P.I.L. 16.

[52] Damages Act 1996 s.2(2). Where parties consent to a periodical payments order made by the court they are bound by the order and cannot withdraw their consent: *Bennett v Stephens* [2012] EWHC 58 (QB); [2012] R.T.R. 27; Ettinger [2012] J.P.I.L. C108.

[53] This obligation applies even where the parties have reached agreement, e.g. that a periodical payments order should be made. The court is not required to give effect to the parties' contract: *Morton v Portal Ltd* [2010] EWHC 1804 (QB); cf. *Gilliland v McManus* [2013] NIQB 127 at [5]. Referring to the court's power to impose a periodical payments order on the parties without their consent Gillen J said: "it does not appear to me that such a power can be exercised by the court when the parties are of full age, have legal capacity and have *consented* to a settlement. In such a case they can agree any order they wish and such consent order is beyond the jurisdiction of the court to consider save for the enforcement of its terms. However in all cases where the court *makes an award*

(2)   the court may impose such an order on the parties[54]; and

(3)   with the consent of the parties the court may award damages other than future pecuniary loss by periodical payments.

Payments must be reasonably secure   Before making such an order the court must be satisfied that the continuity of payment under the order is reasonably secure,[55] but continuity of payment is deemed to be reasonably secure if, inter alia, the source of payment is a government or health service body.[56] In *YM v Gloucestershire Hospitals NHS Foundation; Kanu v King's College Hospital Trust*[57] an issue arose as to whether an order for periodical payments against a NHS Foundation Trust would be "reasonably secure" because, unlike ordinary NHS Trusts, there is no statutory requirement[58] for the liabilities of a Foundation Trust that gets into financial difficulties to be transferred to the Secretary of State. The "obligation" to transfer liabilities is discretionary. In order to resolve this problem, the NHS Litigation Authority agreed to be named as the source of the periodical payments and to be made legally responsible for payments to the claimants. An Appendix to the report of *YM* includes a Model Form of Order. Since then, the problem has been resolved in favour of security of payments through collateral agreements made between the NHS Litigation Authority and the Secretary of State for Health.[59]

12–021

There is greater uncertainty regarding the position of the medical defence organisations. They are not protected by the Financial Services Compensation Scheme (FSCS).[60] The FSCS does not cover self-funded payments which is the

12–022

---

including where a court has to approve settlements and compromises made in respect of infants and patients the requirement arises" (original emphasis).

[54] Where there is a substantial reduction of the damages award due to the claimant's contributory negligence a periodical payments order may be less appropriate because the claimant will never achieve full compensation and a lump sum may provide greater flexibility in meeting the claimant's future needs: *Gilliland v McManus* [2013] NIQB 127; cf. *Sarwar v Ali* [2007] EWHC 1255 (QB); [2007] LS Law Med. 375 where Lloyd Jones J considered that a periodical payments order would be more likely to secure the claimant's position and come close to covering the full cost of his care, taking into account a reduction of 25 per cent for contributory negligence.

[55] Damages Act 1996 s.2(3). See E. Tomlinson and H. Smith, "Periodical Payments Orders" [2016] J.P.I.L. 243.

[56] Damages Act 1996 s.2(4)(c). See the Damages (Government and Health Service Bodies) Order 2005 (SI 2005/474) designating the National Health Service Litigation Authority (NHSLA) as a health service body for this purpose, in England.

[57] [2006] EWHC 820 (QB); [2006] P.I.Q.R. P27; [2006] Lloyd's Rep. Med. 309.

[58] This was under the terms of National Health Service (Residual Liabilities) Act 1996. See now the National Health Service Act 2006 s.70.

[59] The collateral agreements provide that in the event of the insolvency of a Foundation Trust in circumstances where the NHSLA does not have the necessary funds to meet the periodical payment, the Secretary of State will put the NHSLA in funds to do so. There is also the added security of s.70 of the National Health Service Act 2006 under which the NHSLA (unlike Foundation Trusts) is a special health authority within the meaning of the Act. If it ceases to exist the Secretary of State must ensure that its financial liabilities are met.

[60] Damages Act 1996 s.2(4)(b) provides that the continuity of payment will be deemed to be secure if it is protected by a scheme under s.213 of the Financial Services and Markets Act 2000. The FSCS provides such protection. See *Billingsley v UPS Ltd* [2013] R.T.R. 30 (QBD) (foreign insurer covered by the FSCS, therefore continuity of payment under a periodical payments order was reasonably secure).

basis on which payments by, for example, the Medical Defence Union and the Medical Protection Society are made. If periodical payments are to be ordered against these organisations, another form of security will need to be provided and the court will want evidence of the nature and extent of that security.[61]

12–023   **Indexation of awards**[62]   Section 2(8) of the Damages Act provides that an order for periodical payments shall be treated as providing for the amount of payments to vary by reference to the retail prices index (RPI), though s.2(9) permits that an order may include provision (a) disapplying s.2(8), or (b) modifying the effect of s.2(8). In *Flora v Wakom (Heathrow) Ltd*[63] the defendant argued that s.2(8) represented the default position, and that the court could only depart from indexation by reference to the retail prices index in exceptional circumstances.[64] The Court of Appeal rejected this submission, on the basis that there was nothing in the language of the subsections which called for this conclusion, and it could have the effect of failing to provide full compensation for future losses where the RPI did not maintain parity with alternative indexes, such as the average earnings index (AEI). Parliament cannot have intended to provide lower compensation through periodical payments than would be appropriate when applying the "100 per cent principle" that the victim of a tort was entitled to be compensated as nearly as possible in full for all pecuniary losses.[65] Brooke LJ concluded that the Court of Appeal should hear a number of cases in order to determine the issue of indexation.[66]

12–024   In *Tameside and Glossop NHS Trust v Thompstone*[67] the Court of Appeal dealt comprehensively with the issue of indexation in four conjoined appeals involving seriously injured young claimants with significant claims for future care costs.[68] At issue in each case was whether periodical payments should be indexed by reference to the RPI or by reference to an arguably more suitable earnings index. In all four cases the first instance judges, rather than indexing care costs by reference to the AEI or the annual survey of hours and earnings median earnings level index (ASHE), had accepted a modified ASHE index, namely the annual

---

[61] For further discussion see Peter Andrews QC, *Kemp & Kemp, The Quantum of Damages* (London: Sweet & Maxwell), Ch.23.

[62] See E. Tomlinson and R. Potts, "Valuing Periodical Payments in a Post-*Thompstone* World" [2007] J.P.I.L. 173; V. Wass, "The Indexation of Future Care Costs" [2007] J.P.I.L. 247; H. Trusted, "Periodical Payments after the Court of Appeal decision in *Thompstone*" [2008] J.P.I.L 44; R. Lewis, "The indexation of periodical payments of damages in tort: the future assured?" (2010) 30 L.S. 391.

[63] [2006] EWCA Civ 1103; [2007] 1 W.L.R. 482; [2006] 4 All E.R. 982.

[64] The phrase "exceptional circumstances" emanated from guidance provided by the Department of Constitutional Affairs which stated: "The provisions in the Act on indexation of periodical payments were merely intended to reflect the current position, where lump sums are linked to RPI in the great majority of cases. But it would remain open to the court to adopt a different index (or none) in a particular case if there were particular exceptional circumstances which justified its doing so." The guidance was expressly rejected by the Court of Appeal in *Flora*.

[65] [2006] EWCA Civ 1103; [2007] 1 W.L.R. 482 at [28] per Brooke LJ.

[66] [2006] EWCA Civ 1103; [2007] 1 W.L.R. 482 at [33]. Sir Mark Potter and Moore Bick LJ agreed.

[67] [2008] EWCA Civ 5; [2008] 1 W.L.R. 2207.

[68] The four conjoined cases were *Thompstone*, along with *Corbett v South Yorkshire Strategic Health Authority* [2007] L.S. Law Med. 430; *RH v United Bristol Healthcare NHS Trust* [2007] EWHC 1441 (QB); [2007] L.S. Law Med. 535; and *South West London Strategic Health Authority v De Haas* unreported 24 November 2006, QBD.

survey of hours and earnings: occupational earnings for care assistants and home carers index (ASHE 6115),[69] as more accurately reflecting the increasing cost of care over the years. It was found to be the most precise measure available, since it was authoritative, as it came from the Office of National Statistics, and it was accessible and statistically reliable. Nor was there any difficulty in using different indexes for different heads of claim within the same case, such as the AEI for future loss of earnings and the ASHE 6115 for future care costs.[70]

The Court of Appeal rejected the defendants' appeals. Waller LJ pointed out that **12–025** in *Flora v Wakom (Heathrow) Ltd*[71] (which was binding authority) the Court had made it clear that the power under s.2(9) of the 1996 Act to disapply or modify the use of RPI was not confined to exceptional circumstances. A periodical payments order was quite different in character from a lump sum award. Periodical payments took the investment risk and the problems of trying to manage a large capital sum away from claimants, and it was unnecessary to make the kind of guesses about the future that are needed when calculating a lump sum for future losses. The compensatory principle was that claimants are entitled to be compensated in full for their losses and if a different index from RPI was more likely to achieve full compensation it should be used. The defendants, who were all funded by the NHS, argued that even if ASHE 6115 provided a more accurate calculation of compensation for the injured claimants, the additional costs imposed on the NHS made periodical payments too expensive and therefore unfair: the Court should balance justice for the claimants against that the wider public interest of preserving NHS funds to benefit the health care of the wider community. The Court of Appeal concluded, correctly it is suggested, that concepts of distributive justice have no role to play once liability has been established and the court is assessing the claimant's financial loss. At that point corrective justice should be the prevailing principle.[72]

Nor does a claimant have a legal burden of proof to persuade a judge to consider **12–026** another index in place of RPI. Under the Damages Act the court has an inquisitorial role and it was entirely appropriate for a judge to decide which of

---

[69] Strictly, ASHE 6115 is not an index. Dr Victoria Wass, the Cardiff University labour economist who gave expert evidence for the claimants proposed that the weighted average of the claimant's cost of care be matched to the appropriate percentile of ASHE 6115 and thereafter the cost of the care be tracked to that percentile which would have the effect of reflecting changes in the costs of care as accurately as possible.

[70] *Sarwar v Ali* [2007] EWHC 1255 (QB); [2007] L.S. Law Med. 375.

[71] [2006] EWCA Civ 1103; [2007] 1 W.L.R. 482; [2006] 4 All E.R. 982.

[72] *Thompstone v Tameside and Glossop Acute Services NHS Trust* [2008] EWCA Civ 5; [2008] 1 W.L.R. 2207 at [47]. In *RH v United Bristol Healthcare NHS Trust* [2007] EWHC 1441 (QB); [2007] L.S. Law Med. 535 at [97] Mackay J had rejected the same argument, pointing out that even if in cases concerned with novel extensions to the duty of care in negligence it may be appropriate to appeal to notions of "distributive justice" by reference to the reaction of the man on the London underground (see the comments of Lord Steyn in *McFarlane v Tayside Health Board* [2000] A.C. 83 quoted at para.2–055, n.167) that was no basis for applying it in the context of the assessment of damages: "If that same man were asked whether, if there were two identically injured claimants, one as a result of a road accident and the other by clinical negligence, the second should have his compensation reduced by several hundred thousand pounds to help pay for the running of the NHS and the first should receive full compensation, I suspect the answer would be a short and unfavourable one."

several indices best provided for the claimant's needs.[73] It is suggested this is also correct. If the court has the power to impose periodical payments then it should also have an obligation to consider the most suitable way to provide those payments. It is not for a claimant to satisfy the court on the balance of probabilities that there is a more appropriate index than RPI, simply that there are alternatives. The Court also gave guidance on the evidence that will normally be required to assess whether periodical payments should be ordered, and if so, on what basis. It is appropriate for the claimant to obtain and submit to the court independent, expert financial advice to assist the court but it will rarely be appropriate for the defendant to adduce its own independent expert evidence on this issue.

12–027   The Court sought to draw a firm line under this issue, pointing out that all of the defendants' objections to using ASHE 6115 as the basis for indexing future care costs had failed in the courts below and in the Court of Appeal:

> "We hope that as a result of these proceedings the National Health Service, and other defendants in proceedings that involve catastrophic injury, will now accept that the appropriateness of indexation on the basis of ASHE 6115 has been established after an exhaustive review of all the possible objections to its use, both in itself and as applied to the recovery of costs of care and case management. It will not be appropriate to reopen that issue in any future proceedings unless the defendant can produce evidence and argument significantly different from, and more persuasive than, that which has been deployed in the present cases. Judges should not hesitate to strike out any defences that do not meet that requirement."[74]

Despite this, there is always the possibility of new circumstances arising where the use of ASHE 6115 is not considered to be appropriate.[75]

---

[73] [2008] EWCA Civ 5; [2008] 1 W.L.R. 2207 at [67], approving the approach taken by Swift J in *Thompstone* at first instance: "We cannot express these fundamental propositions better than they were put by Swift J in paragraph 52 of her judgment in *Thompstone*: 'My task is to decide what form of order will best meet the claimant's needs, and so far as section 2(8) and (9) is concerned, to determine what is appropriate, fair and reasonable. These matters do not lend themselves to determination by the burden of proof. Insofar as the claimant does bear any burden, it seems to that this is an evidential burden, i.e. an obligation to adduce evidence sufficient to establish a case that the RPI is an inappropriate measure of indexation and there is at least one alternative, more appropriate, measure that the court might adopt.'"

[74] [2008] EWCA Civ 5; [2008] 1 W.L.R. 2207 at [100]. The appellants sought permission to appeal to the House of Lords. Limited permission was granted by the House of Lords, but in July 2008 the NHSLA withdrew the appeal. One of the agreed terms of the withdrawal of the appeal was that the cases of *Thompstone*, *Corbett* and *RH* be remitted back to the High Court to determine the final form of order that should apply in each case which would then form a model to be used in future NHS cases. On this see *Thompstone v Tameside Hospital NHS Foundation Trust* [2008] EWHC 2948 (QB); [2009] P.I.Q.R. P9; and *RH v University Hospitals Bristol NHS Foundation Trust (formerly United Bristol Healthcare NHS Trust)* [2013] EWHC 299 (QB); [2013] P.I.Q.R. P12 (which dealt with changes to the model order necessitated by a change in the methodology used by the Office of National Statistics for calculating ASHE 6115). On the right of an insurer making periodical payments to have regular updates on the claimant's medical condition and confirmation that the claimant is still alive see: *Wallace v Follett* [2013] EWCA Civ 146; commented on by Ettinger [2013] J.P.I.L. C212.

[75] See for example *Mealing v Chelsea & Westminster Healthcare NHS Trust* [2008] EWHC 1664 (QB) where Teare J on an appeal of a case management decision had to consider the appropriate earnings index in France and permitted both sides to call expert evidence on this issue. See also *A v Powys Local Health Board* [2007] EWHC 2996 (QB) where Lloyd Jones J considered it appropriate to make an award for future care costs by way of a lump sum rather than by way of periodical

Varying orders for periodical payments   Section 2B of the Damages Act **12–028**
1996 empowers the Lord Chancellor to introduce secondary legislation,
permitting a court to vary an existing order for periodical payments, if the order
expressly permits a party to apply for a variation. The Damages (Variation of
Periodical Payments) Order 2005[76] art.2 states that:

> "If there is proved or admitted to be a chance that at some definite or indefinite time in the
> future the claimant will—
> (a)   as a result of the act or omission which gave rise to the cause of action, develop some
>   serious disease or suffer some serious deterioration, or
> (b)   enjoy some significant improvement, in his physical or mental condition, where that
>   condition had been adversely affected as a result of that act or omission,
> the court may, on the application of a party, with the agreement of all the parties, or of its own
> initiative, provide in an order for periodical payments that it may be varied."

Article 5 of the Order provides that when the court makes a variable order: (a) the   **12–029**
damages must be assessed or agreed on the assumption that the disease,
deterioration or improvement will not occur; (b) the order must specify the
disease or type of deterioration or improvement; (c) the order may specify a
period within which an application for it to be varied may be made; (d) the order
may specify more than one disease or type of deterioration or improvement and
may, in respect of each, specify a different period within which an application for
it to be varied may be made; (e) the order must provide that a party must obtain
the court's permission to apply for it to be varied, unless the court otherwise
orders. These provisions are comparable to the requirements that apply to awards
of provisional damages.[77]

A party may make only one application to vary a variable order in respect of each   **12–030**
specified disease or type of deterioration or improvement (art.7), but where the
order has specified a period within which an application for it to be varied may be
made, a party may make more than one application to extend the period and this
does not count as an application to vary a variable order (art.6). Once the
specified period has expired a party may not apply for the variable order to be
varied (art.6(b)). Article 9 provides for the variation of an agreement between the
parties as to periodical payments (as opposed to an order of the court, covered by
art.2).

By art.13, when the court is faced with an application for the variation of a   **12–031**
variable order or a variable agreement, if it is satisfied that the disease,
deterioration or improvement specified in the order or agreement has occurred,
and that it has caused or is likely to cause an increase or decrease in the pecuniary
loss suffered by the claimant, it may order:

---

payments where the claimant lived in Ireland. There was currently no earnings series appropriate to
use as a means of indexing carers' earnings in Ireland and it was inappropriate to use an index that
measured price inflation in the United Kingdom to upgrade future care costs that would be incurred in
Ireland. Moreover, the claimant's own preference was for a lump sum and the defendant was neutral
as to the form of award.
[76] SI 2005/841. This came into force on 1 April 2005.
[77] See para.12–033 below.

"(i) the amount of annual payments to be varied, either from the date of the application for permission or from the date of the application to vary if the order did not require the permission of the court for an application to vary, or from such later date as it may specify in the order;

(ii) how each payment is to be made during the year and at what intervals;

(iii) a lump sum to be paid in addition to the existing periodical payments."

12–032 **Alternatives to periodical payments** Periodical payments give the court (and the parties) considerably more flexibility than the rigidity of the previous mandatory lump sum approach. Before periodical payments were introduced, the law had developed other mechanisms in an attempt to mitigate some of the problems caused by awarding damages only in the form of a lump sum. These remain relevant, notwithstanding the availability of periodical payments, and can assist in ameliorating those problems although not removing them entirely. The mechanisms are the possibility of claiming provisional damages and separate trials on liability and quantum.

(c) Provisional damages[78]

12–033 Section 32A of the Senior Courts Act 1981 introduced a procedure for the award of provisional damages in cases where there is a "chance" that as a result of the tort claimants will develop some serious disease or suffer some serious deterioration in their condition. In such cases claimants may be awarded provisional damages assessed on the basis that the disease or deterioration will not occur. If the event subsequently materialises the claimant can then make an application for further damages in order to compensate for the loss that has now occurred. This procedure should produce assessments of damages which more accurately reflect the loss that claimants have sustained, since they will not be compensated for a risk that may never materialise, and moreover, if the risk does materialise the claimant will receive fuller compensation, instead of damages heavily discounted under the lump sum system on the basis that there is only a small risk that the loss may occur.

12–034 Under CPR Pt 41 a claim for provisional damages must be pleaded by the claimant,[79] and when making an order the court must specify the disease or type of deterioration which will entitle the claimant to make a further application for damages, and the period of time within which the second application should be made.[80] The claimant must apply for further damages within the specified period

---

[78] J. Chamberlayne and L. Morgan, "Provisional Damages Awards: Exceptions to the Principle of 'Full & Final Settlement'" [2012] J.P.I.L. 112.

[79] See CPR r.16.4(1)(d). The information that must be included in the particulars of claim is specified in CPR 16PD para.4.4. See also CPR 41APD.

[80] CPR r.41.2(2). The claimant may make more than one application to extend the period within which the application for further damages must be made: r.41.2(3). The court may also order that there should be no limit of time within which the application must be made, where there is no medical or other scientific evidence upon which any limit could sensibly be based: *Thurman v Wiltshire and Bath Health Authority* [1997] P.I.Q.R. Q115, where the order concerned the recurrence of cancer secondary to cancer of the cervix; *A v National Blood Authority* [2001] 3 All E.R. 289 at [211], where Burton J ordered that the duration of the period within which claimants in the "hepatitis C litigation" could make an application should be the life of each claimant.

(or such period as extended by the court[81]), giving the defendant (and the defendant's insurer, if known) 28 days' notice of intention to apply, and only one application for further damages can be made in respect of each disease or type of deterioration specified in the award of provisional damages.[82]

Type of deterioration Provisional damages are not appropriate in all, or even most, cases.[83] Since the disease or type of injury for which the claimant is entitled to seek further damages must be specified when the claimant applies for provisional damages, the procedure does not cover a general deterioration in the claimant's condition, nor an unforeseen complication. "Serious deterioration" in the claimant's condition means "something beyond ordinary deterioration" and this is a question of fact depending on the circumstances of the case, including the effect of the deterioration on the claimant.[84]

12–035

"Chance" cases must be distinguished from cases where the medical evidence can forecast with a reasonable degree of certainty that the claimant's condition will deteriorate causing a reasonably probable degree of disability. A typical example of this situation occurs where it is possible to predict that over the years arthritis is likely to develop in a damaged joint. Here damages should be assessed on the single lump sum basis, discounting the award for the chance that arthritis will not occur. In *Willson v Ministry of Defence*[85] it was held that the development of arthritis to the point at which surgery is required, or which requires the claimant to change his employment, did not fall within the definition of serious deterioration, rather it was "simply an aspect of a progression of this particular disease". Similarly, the chance that due to a disabling injury the claimant may sustain a further injury, even if that injury could be severe, did not call for provisional damages. The risk of a serious injury was not to be equated with a serious deterioration in the claimant's physical condition.

12–036

Meaning of "chance" The term "chance" can cover a wide range between something that is de minimis and something that is a probability, but it must be measurable rather than fanciful. Provided the chance is measurable it can fall within the procedure for provisional damages, however slim the chance may be.[86]

12–037

---

[81] Where a provisional damages order was made under the old Rules of the Supreme Court Ord.37, before the CPR came into effect, the CPR govern any application to the court to extend the period for the making of an application for further damages after the expiry of the period set by the original order: *Blythe v Ministry of Defence* unreported 25 November 2013, CA; see Tomkins [2014] J.P.I.L. C32.

[82] CPR r.41.3. Though if there is more than one event or trigger identified in the order, there can be an application in respect of each trigger event that occurs: *A v National Blood Authority* [2001] 3 All E.R. 289 at [211]. An offer by a defendant to make a payment of provisional damages necessarily involves an admission of liability: *Boyd v Gates (UK) Ltd* [2015] CSOH 100; 2015 S.L.T. 483 (a case dealing with the equivalent scheme for provisional damages in Scotland).

[83] An award of provisional damages is discretionary. The court will weigh up the possibility of doing justice by a once-and-for-all assessment against the possibility of doing better justice by reserving the claimant's right to return at a future date: *Willson v Ministry of Defence* [1991] 1 All E.R. 638 at 645.

[84] *Willson v Ministry of Defence* [1991] 1 All E.R. 638 at 642.

[85] [1991] 1 All E.R. 638 at 642 and 643.

[86] [1991] 1 All E.R. 638 at 642, per Scott Baker J. See also *Wan v Fung* [2003] 7 C.L. 113, QBD, discussing the award of provisional damages in respect of a risk of developing epilepsy put at between

But this does not mean that where it is not possible to express the chance in percentage terms it must regarded as fanciful. In *Woodward v Leeds Teaching Hospitals NHS Trust*[87] the defendants had been negligent in delaying the diagnosis and treatment of a tumour on the claimant's pituitary gland which caused the claimant to suffer classic acromegalic gigantism. Judge Stuart Baker made an order for provisional damages in respect of the "real risk" that the tumour would recur causing a significant increase in the claimant's symptoms and requiring extensive medical treatment. The fact that the claimant's condition was rare so that there was little statistical data or clinical experience by which to assess or measure the risk did not mean that the risk was not present or that it was negligible, minimal or fanciful.

12-038   In *Davies v Bradshaw*[88] Wilkie J declined to make an award for provisional damages in respect of a claimant who had an increased risk of developing syringomyelia, relying upon the principle that courts should be slow to invoke the concept of provisional damages where they are in a position to make a judgment on future developments of the injury for which damages were being assessed. He found that the future risk was insufficiently distinct from the types of cases referred to in *Willson* for an award of provisional damages to be appropriate. On the other hand, in *Kotula v EDF Energy Networks (EPN) Plc*[89] Irwin J held that the risk of developing syringomyelia could not be said to be fanciful. Not only was the chance measurable, but it had been measured and agreed. Of individuals in the claimant's position about 1 per cent would probably develop a clinically significant syringomyelia, and 0.1 per cent would have serious effects from developing a syrinx. There was a clear-cut event which could have serious consequences for the claimant. This was:

> "...precisely the kind of rare but highly damaging contingency which Parliament must be taken to have in mind, when permitting damages awards to be provisional, and permitting the variation of periodical payments."[90]

12-039   **Triggering a claim for further damages**   Provisional damages are limited to cases where there is a clear-cut event, or events,[91] which will trigger an entitlement to further compensation, i.e. cases where there would be little room for later dispute whether or not the contemplated deterioration had actually

---

1 per cent and 2 per cent; *Farrugia v Burtenshaw* [2014] EWHC 1036 (QB); [2014] Med. L.R. 153 (provisional periodical payments order to reflect the 2 per cent risk of the claimant developing uncontrolled epilepsy); *Loughlin v Singh* [2013] EWHC 1641 (QB); [2013] Med. L.R. 513 (provisional damages order for 2–3 per cent risk of developing epilepsy, with 0.6 per cent risk of it being uncontrolled epilepsy); *Yale-Helms v Countess of Chester Hospital NHS Foundation Trust* unreported 13 February 2015, QBD (3 per cent risk of developing epilepsy and 20 per cent chance that if epilepsy developed it would become severe and uncontrolled).
[87] [2012] EWHC 2167 (QB) at [167] to [175].
[88] [2008] EWHC 740 (QB).
[89] [2011] EWHC 1546 (QB).
[90] [2011] EWHC 1546 (QB) at [48].
[91] In *A v National Blood Authority* [2001] 3 All E.R. 289 at [211] Burton J specified five possible "triggers", any one of which would entitle a claimant to make an application for further damages.

occurred.[92] The claimant still has to establish causation when making the application for further damages, i.e. that the damage of which he now complains is causally linked to the defendant's tort. But where a defendant had agreed to "an award of immediate damages on a full liability basis" and also agreed that:

"...damages which may fall to be assessed in the future under the terms of the Order [for provisional damages], shall also fall to be assessed on the same basis as the immediate award"

the effect was that it was not open to the defendant to argue that it was not his breach of duty which caused the damage.[93] Thus, defendants must be careful about the terms of any agreement when settling orders for provisional damages.

Death of the claimant and Fatal Accidents Act claims   It was previously the case that where claimants had received an award of provisional damages to reflect the chance that their condition might deteriorate, but they subsequently died as a result of that deterioration, their dependants could not bring an action for their loss of financial dependency under the Fatal Accidents Act 1976 (because a claim under that Act requires that the deceased had a subsisting claim against the defendant at the time of death). There was no mechanism for granting a declaration, as part of the claim for provisional damages, that the surviving dependants should be entitled to claim under the Fatal Accidents Act 1976 if claimants should subsequently die.[94] Now, s.3 of the Damages Act 1996 provides that an award of provisional damages to a claimant shall not operate as a bar to an action in respect of that person's death under the Fatal Accidents Act 1976 where the claimant subsequently dies as a result of the act or omission which gave rise to the cause of action for which the damages were awarded. If the deceased had received any damages in respect of pecuniary loss which, in the event, falls after the death, this must be taken into account in assessing the loss of dependency claim under the Fatal Accidents Act.

12–040

In *Molinari v Ministry of Defence*[95] the claimant was suffering from leukaemia, and the question arose whether provisional damages should be awarded on the basis of the risk of a relapse in his medical condition, in circumstances where there was a substantial chance that if a relapse were to occur the claimant would die. The procedure for awarding provisional damages appears to assume that a

12–041

---

[92] *Willson v Ministry of Defence* [1991] 1 All E.R. 638 at 644; *Patterson v Ministry of Defence* [1987] C.L.Y. 1194. Thus, they are appropriate for cases with "a clear and severable risk rather than a continuing deterioration, as is the typical osteoarthritic picture": [1991] 1 All E.R. 638 at 644; *Allott v Central Electricity Generating Board* unreported 19 December 1988, QBD. The fact that there is disagreement in the medical evidence, however, about the risk of the claimant contracting cancer in the future does not preclude the court from making an award of provisional damages: *Hurditch v Sheffield Health Authority* [1989] 2 All E.R. 869.

[93] *Green v Vickers Defence Systems Ltd* [2002] EWCA Civ 904; *The Times*, 1 July 2002. Provided that the claimant established that he had developed a condition specified in the order, it was irrelevant that he could not prove which of several defendants had exposed him to the relevant asbestos. The specific point on which the defendants were seeking to rely in this case (concerning the development of mesothelioma after exposure to asbestos by multiple defendants) is no longer open, following the ruling of the House of Lords in *Fairchild v Glenhaven Funeral Services Ltd* [2002] UKHL 22; [2003] 1 A.C. 32, paras 5–050 et seq.

[94] *Middleton v Elliott Turbomachinery Ltd*, *The Independent*, 16 November 1990, CA.

[95] [1994] P.I.Q.R. Q33, QBD.

deterioration in the claimant's condition could only result in an increase in the global damages recoverable by him; but this may not be the case where the deterioration leads to death. In an extreme case, said the judge, where there was a risk of a deterioration leading to a decrease in the loss, the proper course might be for the court to refuse to award provisional damages on the ground that the potential injustice to the defendants far outweighed the potential injustice to the claimant of a traditional award. On the facts, however, it was held that provisional damages should be awarded, since any injustice to the defendants of making a provisional award was more than outweighed by the potential injustice to the claimant of making a lump-sum award on the traditional basis.

12–042   **Future medical treatment**   In *A v The National Blood Authority (Hepatitis C Litigation)*[96] Burton J considered that it was not clear that the undergoing of treatment in the future, and the consequential damage that might ensue, fell within the court's jurisdiction to make an order for provisional damages under s.32A of the Senior Courts Act 1981.[97] But in any event, the court's wide case-management powers under the Civil Procedure Rules were such that the court could make an order under CPR r.3.1(2) for the separate trial of any issue of damages arising out of future treatment, and adjourn the trial of such issue generally. This effectively creates an alternative procedure akin to that for provisional damages, but without the specific restrictions that s.32A and CPR Pt 41 impose.

12–043   **Where medical treatment improves claimant's condition**   The approach of Burton J in *A v The National Blood Authority (Hepatitis C Litigation)* can be contrasted with that of Eady J in *Adan v Securicor Custodial Services Ltd*.[98] As a result of a road traffic accident for which the defendants were responsible the claimant suffered brain damage and subsequently developed a psychosis which resulted in him being detained under the Mental Health Act 1983. As long as he was detained as a patient, his care costs were nil, but if he were discharged from hospital he would require specialist care. He was likely to remain a detained patient for the foreseeable future. The claimant sought an order that he should have liberty to apply for further damages if in the future his mental health improved sufficiently for him to be discharged from hospital, because he would then incur the relevant care costs. It was conceded that the rules on provisional damages did not cover his circumstances, since the contingency was that his medical condition might improve, not that it would deteriorate. Eady J refused the claimant's application. It was in the interests of justice that there should be finality in litigation, and though Parliament had created an exception in the statutory scheme for provisional damages, that did not cover the circumstances of

---

[96] [2002] Lloyd's Rep. Med. 487.
[97] But see *Chewings v Williams* [2009] EWHC 2490 (QB); [2010] P.I.Q.R. Q1 where Slade J made an order for provisional damages where the risk was that the injury to the claimant's leg could deteriorate and that the claimant would undergo a fusion operation on his ankle. There was a risk of complications developing from the surgery which could lead to the need for a below the knee amputation. The chance of amputation occurring after such an infection was small but not negligible. Slade J put the risk at 2 per cent.
[98] [2004] EWHC 394 (QB); [2005] P.I.Q.R. P6.

the case. The prospect of the defendant's insurers remaining exposed to an uncertain liability, potentially measured in seven figures, for an indefinite period of time was inherently undesirable and oppressive. The prospect of a significant improvement in the claimant's mental health was largely speculative, and the claimant could not discharge the burden of proof in respect of future care and accommodation. Thus, the continuing potential liability and uncertainty for the defendants' insurers was out of all proportion to any corresponding benefit to the claimant. *A v The National Blood Authority and Others (Hepatitis C Litigation)* was different because there the parties had agreed to the order for a separate trial and an adjournment generally in relation to the possibility of claimants needing medical care in the future. Eady J observed that Burton J had commented[99] that:

> "...on any future application to take this course, absence of consent on one side or the other may be, if not a total bar, certainly a factor rendering it unlikely that the course will be followed."

(d) Split trial and interim payments

Split trial   The Civil Procedure Rules provide for separate trials on liability and damages, so that the assessment of damages can be made at a later date when the medical prognosis is more certain.[100] The court may at any stage of the proceedings, and of its own motion, direct a separate trial of any issue. This procedure is of value where the claimant's medical condition is unstable and needs time to settle, and it may be particularly useful in the case of young children where it may be very difficult to assess the extent of the long-term disability when the child is still developing.[101]

12–044

Interim payments   The procedure can be combined with the power to seek an interim payment to meet the claimant's immediate needs, which is then deducted from the final award.[102] An interim payment may be obtained where the defendant has admitted liability, or the claimant has obtained judgment for damages to be assessed, or if the claim went to trial, the claimant would obtain judgment for a substantial amount of money against the defendant from whom the interim payment is sought, whether or not that defendant is the only defendant

12–045

---

[99] [2002] Lloyd's Rep. Med. 487 at 493.
[100] CPR Pt 3 r.3.1(2)(i).
[101] See e.g. *Cook v Cook* [2011] EWHC 1638 (QB); [2011] P.I.Q.R. P18 (order that assessment of damages of a claimant aged 10 years be limited to the loss up to age 16, with another assessment of quantum at that time, because the long-term outcomes were so uncertain and speculative).
[102] CPR Pt 25 rr.25.6 to 25.9 and PD25B. On the court's exercise of discretion as to whether to order an interim payment and the effect on the ultimate assessment of quantum see *Campbell v Mylchreest* [1999] P.I.Q.R. Q17, CA.

or one of a number of defendants to the claim.[103] The court must not order an interim payment of more than a reasonable proportion of the likely amount of the final judgment.[104]

(e) Interest

12–046 Where damages for personal injuries or death exceeding £200 are awarded the court must award interest unless there are special reasons for not doing so.[105] In the case of special damages for accrued pecuniary loss interest will normally be awarded at half the special account rate on money paid into court, running from the date of the accident to the date of trial, the reasoning being that part of the loss will have occurred immediately after the tort and part immediately before the assessment.[106] Interest at half the rate is a compromise. If, however, there are special circumstances which would make it unfair to apply this rule it may be possible to obtain interest at the full rate on certain items of special damage which have been incurred shortly after the accident.[107] Where the defendant has

---

[103] CPR Pt 25 r.25.7(1)(a)–(c); see also r.25.7(1)(e) for claims in which there are two or more defendants and the order is sought against any one or more of those defendants. On the interpretation of r.25.7(1)(e) see *Berry v Ashtead Plant Hire Co Ltd* [2011] EWCA Civ 1304; [2012] P.I.Q.R. P6.

[104] CPR Pt 25 r.25.7(4). This should take into account any contributory negligence and any relevant set-off or counterclaim: r.25.7(5). The leading case is *Eeles v Cobham Hire Services Ltd* [2009] EWCA Civ 204; [2010] 1 W.L.R. 409 where the Court of Appeal gave guidance on the principles to be applied, particularly in a case where the final award is likely to include an order for periodical payments. See R. Weir, "Interim Payments: Life After *Eeles*" [2011] J.P.I.L. 19. *Eeles* has been followed on numerous occasions: *P v Taunton and Somerset NHS Trust* [2009] EWHC 1965 (QB); [2009] LS Law Medical 598; (2009) 110 B.M.L.R. 164; *FP v Taunton and Somerset NHS Trust* [2011] EWHC 3380 (QB); [2012] Med. L.R. 195; *Mabiriizi v HSBC Insurance (UK) Ltd* [2011] EWHC 1280 (QB); [2011] Med. L.R. 379; *PZC v Gloucestershire Hospitals NHS Trust* [2011] EWHC 1775 (QB); [2011] P.I.Q.R. P17; *Oxborrow v West Suffolk Hospitals NHS Trust* [2012] EWHC 1010 (QB); [2012] Med. L.R. 297; *Sedge v Prime* [2012] EWHC 3460 (QB); (2013) 129 B.M.L.R. 37; *Beasley v Alexander* [2013] EWHC 4739 (QB); *Smith v Bailey* [2014] EWHC 2569 (QB); [2015] P.I.Q.R. P3; [2014] Med. L.R. 408; *Grainger v Cooper* [2015] EWHC 1132 (QB); *AC v St Georges Healthcare NHS Trust* [2015] EWHC 3644 (QB); *LAT v East Somerset NHS Trust* [2016] EWHC 1610 (QB); [2016] Med. L.R. 438; *Sellar-Elliott v Howling* [2016] EWHC 443 (QB); [2016] P.I.Q.R. P13; *Zeb v Frimley Health NHS Foundation Trust* [2016] EWHC 134 (QB) (no interim payment where the defendant arguably had a complete defence); *C v Nottingham University Hospitals NHS Trust* unreported 20 September 2016, QBD (no interim payment award where the defendant has not had a proper opportunity to investigate quantum).

[105] Senior Courts Act 1981 s.35A; County Courts Act 1984 s.69—ss.35A(2) and 69(2) respectively require that interest "shall be" awarded by the court in personal injury cases unless there are "special reasons to the contrary". A claim for interest must be specifically pleaded: CPR Pt 16 r.16.4(1)(b). The interest is not taxed as income: Income Tax (Trading and Other Income) Act 2005 s.751.

[106] *Jefford v Gee* [1970] 2 Q.B. 130 at 146; *Cookson v Knowles* [1979] A.C. 556. In the case of a split trial in a personal injuries action, where liability is agreed or determined first with damages to be assessed later, interest on the damages awarded under s.17 of the Judgments Act 1838 will run from the date of judgment on damages and not from the date of judgment on liability: *Thomas v Bunn* [1991] 1 All E.R. 193, HL.

[107] *Ichard v Frangoulis* [1977] 1 W.L.R. 556. Private medical fees are one possible example: see *Dexter v Courtalds Ltd* [1984] 1 All E.R. 70 at 73. In the "generality of personal injury cases", however, the principles laid down in *Jefford v Gee* [1970] 2 Q.B. 130 should be applied: [1984] 1 All E.R. 70 at 74, per Lawton LJ. A claim for the full rate of interest must be pleaded.

failed to beat a CPR Pt 36 offer, interest may be awarded at an enhanced rate.[108] No deduction is made to allow for the receipt of social security benefits by the claimant.[109] Interest is not awarded on future pecuniary loss, such as prospective loss of earnings or medical expenses, because the loss has not yet accrued.[110] In Fatal Accident Act cases interest should be awarded only on that part of the dependency that relates to the period between death and trial at half the special account rate.[111]

Simple interest[112] on damages for non-pecuniary loss (pain and suffering and loss of amenity) is awarded at a modest rate, currently 2 per cent, for the period from the date of service of the claim form to the date of trial.[113] This low rate is attributable to the fact that a large proportion of nominal interest rates is represented by inflation, and inflation is taken into account when the court assesses the damages for non-pecuniary loss by a general uprating of the tariffs or bands applied to different types of injury.[114] Interest at 2 per cent represents an approximate real rate of return for the claimant not having the use of his money.[115] The fact that interest runs from the date of service of the claim form

12–047

---

[108] For discussion of the principles to be applied to the assessment of this enhanced rate, see *Petrotrade Inc. v Texaco Ltd* [2001] 4 All E.R. 853, CA.

[109] *Wisely v John Fulton (Plumbers) Ltd* [2000] 1 W.L.R. 820—thus, recoverable social security benefits should not be deducted from damages for loss of earnings when calculating interest; see also *Davies v Inman* [1999] P.I.Q.R. Q26, CA—claimant entitled to interest on his loss of earnings even though his employer continued to pay him, the claimant having undertaken to repay the employer from any damages he received.

[110] *Cookson v Knowles* [1979] A.C. 556; *Joyce v Yeomans* [1981] 1 W.L.R. 549.

[111] *Cookson v Knowles* [1979] A.C. 556, HL. Applied in *A Train & Sons Ltd v Fletcher* [2008] EWCA Civ 413; [2008] 4 All E.R. 699 where the Court of Appeal held that the trial judge had been bound to follow the guidelines given by the House of Lords in *Cookson* to the effect that interest on damages for loss of financial dependency should be at half rates and limited to the period between the death and the date of the trial. The respondent had argued that the decision in *Cookson* was not a rule of law or binding principle but a practice that was open to the instant court to revise. However, the Court of Appeal said that to depart from the method of calculation prescribed in *Cookson* would be to depart from the clearly stated underlying principle.

[112] The Law Commission report, *Pre-Judgment Interest on Debts and Damages*, Law Com. No.287 (2004), recommended that there should be a right to compound interest in some circumstances. The Commission considered that the main cost increase of their proposals would be in clinical negligence claims, where a high proportion of money is spent on claims where the gap between the loss and payment is 15 years or more.

[113] *Birkett v Hayes* [1982] 2 All E.R. 710; [1982] 1 W.L.R. 816; *Wright v British Railways Board* [1983] 2 A.C. 773. Personal injury cases seem to be in a special category, since interest on damages for non-pecuniary loss will not be awarded in actions for deceit or false imprisonment: *Saunders v Edwards* [1987] 2 All E.R. 651; *Holtham v Commissioner of Police of the Metropolis*, The Times, 28 November 1987. See also Andrew Ritchie, *Kemp and Kemp, The Quantum of Damages* (London: Sweet & Maxwell), Ch.26, for an interesting discussion about the possibility of interest running from the date of the letter before action in cases where quantification is straightforward. However, this argument is unlikely to succeed in medical negligence cases.

[114] It is arguable that this low rate should not apply to damages for bereavement under the Fatal Accidents Act 1976 s.1A (see para.12–167), because the amount of the award is fixed by statute and does not increase when tariffs are uprated: see *Prior v Bernard Hastie & Co.* [1987] C.L.Y. 1219; *Sharman v Sheppard* [1989] C.L.Y. 1190.

[115] It was arguable that the rate should be increased to 3 per cent in the light of the decision of the House of Lords in *Wells v Wells* [1999] 1 A.C. 345—see the comments of Lord Lloyd on *Wright v British Railways Board* at 371–372; *Burns v Davies* [1999] Lloyd's Rep. Med. 215 at 217 where Connell J applied a rate of 3 per cent; cf. *Lawrence v Chief Constable of Staffordshire* [2000] P.I.Q.R.

provides a very good reason for both issuing and serving a claim form early, even where negotiations are proceeding, since interest can amount to a substantial sum (notwithstanding the low interest rate) where the award of damages for non-pecuniary loss is likely to be high and the delay between initiating a claim and trial is likely to be lengthy, which may well be the case in a medical negligence action. Moreover, where the claimant has delayed in bringing a claim to trial the judge has a discretion to disallow interest on pre-trial damages.[116] Prompt issue and service of the claim form also avoids problems with limitation periods and the time limits for service.

(f) Mitigation of damage

12–048   Claimants are under a duty to mitigate the damage caused by the defendant's tort, although they commit no wrong against the defendant if they fail to do so.[117] If they have lost a job as a result of the injury they should seek alternative employment, if they are capable of working. If they take a lower paid job they can only recover from the defendant the difference between their previous and present earnings. Claimants should also seek medical attention which will improve their medical condition, although they will not be required to undergo a medical procedure where there is a substantial risk of further injury or the outcome is uncertain. The test is whether in all the circumstances, including particularly the medical advice received, the claimant acted reasonably in refusing the treatment.[118] Where the medical advice is conflicting, or the treatment involves some risk and the doctors prefer to leave the final decision to the claimant, a refusal of treatment will be considered to be reasonable.[119] The

---

Q349, where the Court of Appeal said that there was no reason to depart from the 2 per cent rate, a view which is more in tune with current low levels of general interest rates.

[116] *Birkett v Hayes* [1982] 2 All E.R. 710 at 717; [1982] 1 W.L.R. 816; *Spittle v Bunney* [1988] 1 W.L.R. 847; [1988] 3 All E.R. 1031; *Corbett v Barking Havering and Brentwood Health Authority* [1991] 2 Q.B. 408; *Read v Harries* [1995] P.I.Q.R. Q34.

[117] *Darbishire v Warran* [1963] 1 W.L.R. 1067 at 1075. See M. Underhill "Mitigation of Loss: The Duty to Mitigate" [2013] J.P.I.L. 234.

[118] *Selvanayagam v University of West Indies* [1983] 1 All E.R. 824 at 827; [1983] 1 W.L.R. 585, PC; *Marcroft v Scruttons Ltd* [1954] 1 Lloyd's Rep. 395; *McAuley v London Transport Executive* [1957] 2 Lloyd's Rep. 500; cf. the more subjective approach of the Australian courts in *Glavonjic v Foster* [1979] V.R. 536 and *Karabotsos v Plastex Industries Pty Ltd* [1981] V.R. 675 where the test was said to be whether a reasonable man in the claimant's particular circumstances and subject to the various factors that affected the claimant, would have refused the treatment; see further Hudson (1983) 3 L.S. 50. In *Marcroft v Scruttons Ltd* [1954] 1 Lloyd's Rep. 395 the Court of Appeal clearly had some sympathy for the claimant's subjective response to the recommended treatment, which was electro-convulsive therapy, but nonetheless applied an objective test.

[119] *Savage v T. Wallis Ltd* [1966] 1 Lloyd's Rep. 357; *McAuley v London Transport Executive* [1957] 2 Lloyd's Rep. 500 at 505; *Selvanayagam v University of West Indies* [1983] 1 All E.R. 824; [1983] 1 W.L.R. 585. There is no obligation upon a claimant who has become pregnant following a negligently performed sterilisation operation to undergo an abortion to mitigate the loss: *Emeh v Kensington and Chelsea Area Health Authority* [1985] Q.B. 1012; *McFarlane v Tayside Health Board* [2000] 2 A.C. 59 at 81, 105, 112–113; paras 5–159 to 5–161. See also *Richardson v LRC Products Ltd* [2000] P.I.Q.R. P164 at 173; [2000] Lloyd's Rep. Med. 280 at 286—a claimant's failure to seek advice about the "morning after pill" to avoid conception following the discovery that a condom had "failed" during sexual intercourse could amount to a failure to mitigate the damage or an intervening cause. In *Edmonds v Lloyds TSB Group plc* [2004] EWCA Civ 1526 the claimant's decision to refuse three

burden of proving that the claimant acted unreasonably in failing to mitigate the loss is the defendant's.[120] The defendant must plead the allegation of failure to mitigate with sufficient particularity to enable the claimant to meet it.[121]

Claimant loses job taken in mitigation of loss of earnings   In *Morris v Richards*[122] the Court of Appeal held that where a claimant loses her job as a result of the injuries sustained in an accident, takes up a new job in mitigation of the loss of earnings, but then loses her new job the defendant may have a responsibility for the claimant's loss of earnings after the loss of the new job. Obtaining a new job does not necessarily break the causal link between the defendant's tort and the loss of earnings. Keene LJ said that: **12–049**

> "The liability of a tortfeasor is not to be reduced because the injured party, having lost employment because of the injury, takes a different job in an attempt to mitigate his or her damage but loses that job because it is beyond his or her capabilities."[123]

Schiemann LJ indicated that the crucial question was whether the claimant was at fault in losing her new job; if so, then she will have difficulty in recovering for loss of earnings after the loss of the new job. On the other hand:

> "If she was not at fault then in general she will recover. . . . bearing in mind that it was the wrongful act of the defendant which put the claimant in the position of having to find a new job and that therefore she should not be judged too harshly."[124]

Claimant unreasonably refusing medical treatment   If the claimant has acted unreasonably in refusing medical treatment a question arises as to how damages should be assessed where the treatment cannot guarantee an improvement in the claimant's condition. In *Janiak v Ippolito*[125] the mitigating operation which the claimant had unreasonably refused to undergo had a 70 per cent chance of success. The Supreme Court of Canada held that, rather than assuming (on the basis of the balance of probabilities) that the operation would succeed, the 30 per cent chance of the operation failing to alleviate the claimant's condition should be taken into account in assessing damages for prospective loss   **12–050**

---

epidural injections into her lower back under general anaesthetic was held to be reasonable, given the advice of her general practitioner, the lack of any guarantee of success, and a consultant's opinion that her refusal was reasonable.
[120] *Steele v Robert George & Co. (1937) Ltd* [1942] A.C. 497; *Richardson v Redpath, Brown & Co. Ltd* [1944] A.C. 62, HL. A dictum to the contrary effect in *Selvanayagam v University of West Indies* [1983] 1 All E.R. 824; [1983] 1 W.L.R. 585 would seem to be incorrect (see McGregor (1983) 46 M.L.R. 758; Kemp (1983) 99 L.Q.R. 497) a view which has now been accepted by the Privy Council: *Geest plc v Lansiquot* [2002] UKPC 48; [2002] 1 W.L.R. 3111 at [14]. If the defendant intends to contend that a claimant has failed to act reasonably to mitigate the claimant's damage, notice must be clearly given to the claimant long enough before the hearing to enable the claimant to prepare to meet it: [2002] UKPC 48; [2002] 1 W.L.R. 3111 at [16].
[121] *Geest plc v Monica Lansiquot* [2002] UKPC 48; [2002] 1 W.L.R. 3111.
[122] [2003] EWCA Civ 232; [2004] P.I.Q.R. Q30.
[123] [2003] EWCA Civ 232; [2004] P.I.Q.R. Q30 at [21].
[124] [2003] EWCA Civ 232; [2004] P.I.Q.R. Q30 at [16].
[125] (1985) 16 D.L.R. (4th) 1, SCC; aff'g (1981) 126 D.L.R. (3d) 623, Ont CA. The same principles apply to the claimant's refusal to take medical tests: *Engel v Kam-Ppelle Holdings Ltd* [1993] 2 W.W.R. 373, SCC.

of earnings. It is unclear how the English courts would approach this problem because, although an action for the loss of a less than 50 per cent chance of a successful medical outcome has not yet been accepted,[126] the courts have no difficulty in taking into account even small chances of future events when assessing damages. It is suggested that the chance of the treatment failing to achieve its purpose should be taken into account, particularly since it may well be this factor which persuades the claimant to refuse the treatment and notwithstanding that objectively the refusal is considered to be unreasonable.[127]

12–051 **Claimant's impecuniosity**   Where the claimant is unable, through impecuniosity, to mitigate the damage, the defendant is liable for the full loss.[128] There is now no difference between the rule applied to mitigation and the rule applied where the damage itself is the product of the claimant's impecuniosity. In both cases defendants must take claimants as they find them with respect to their financial resources.[129]

2. PERSONAL INJURIES: PECUNIARY LOSSES

12–052 A claimant who sustains personal injuries will normally suffer two distinct types of loss, pecuniary and non-pecuniary loss. Pecuniary loss is the damage that is capable of being directly calculated in monetary terms, whether accrued or prospective. It includes, for example, loss of earnings and pension rights, medical expenses, travelling expenses, the cost of special equipment and the cost of employing someone to carry out domestic duties which the claimant is no longer able to perform.[130] Following *Jefford v Gee*[131] damages in a personal injuries action must be particularised under at least three broad heads for the purpose of calculating interest, namely special damages, prospective pecuniary loss, and

---

[126] See paras 5–100 et seq.

[127] In *McAuley v London Transport Executive* [1957] 2 Lloyd's Rep. 500 at 505, Jenkins LJ said that: "damages ought to be assessed as they would properly have been assessable if [the claimant] had, in fact, undergone the operation and secured the degree of recovery to be expected from it." This permits the defendant to benefit from an assumption that a particular event would have occurred as a certainty, whereas claimants normally have their future losses discounted for the chance that particular events might not have occurred, e.g. that they might not have continued working until retirement age. It is not clear why defendants should be in better position than claimants in this respect. Thus, where the claimant has reasonably refused to undergo an operation in the short term, but might choose to accept treatment in the future, there will be a discount of the award of damages which reflects the chance both that the claimant might have the treatment and that it might be successful; it should not be assumed in the defendant's favour that there will be an operation and that it would be successful: *Thomas v Bath District Health Authority* [1995] P.I.Q.R. Q19, CA. See also *Dudarec v Andrews* [2005] EWHC 155 (QB). The Court of Appeal allowed the defendant's appeal in *Dudarec* ([2006] EWCA Civ 256; [2006] 1 W.L.R. 3002) but did not interfere with the trial judge's findings on the mitigation issue.

[128] *Clippens Oil Co. v Edinburgh & District Water Trustees* [1907] A.C. 291 at 303; *Dodd Properties (Kent) Ltd v Canterbury City Council* [1980] 1 All E.R. 928 at 935, 941; [1980] 1 W.L.R. 433; *Eaton v Johnston* [2008] UKPC 1.

[129] See para.5–192.

[130] For a review of cases on non-pecuniary loss in serious injury cases see J. Rowley, "Serious Personal Injury Litigation—a Quantum Update" [2008] J.P.I.L 109.

[131] [1970] 2 Q.B. 130.

non-pecuniary damages, though in practice distinct items of loss are particularised in much greater detail. Care should be taken when identifying these items of loss to avoid overlap or duplication in the total assessment.

(a) Medical and other expenses

(i) Medical and care costs

Claimants are entitled to recover medical and other expenses (such as additional housing and travel costs) which are reasonably incurred.[132] Accrued expenses will be awarded as part of the special damages, whereas future medical expenses will be estimated by the multiplier method and awarded as general damages in the form of a lump sum or as periodical payments.[133] The possibility of avoiding medical expenses, or part of them, by taking advantage of NHS facilities is disregarded.[134] Thus, claimants can insist on damages to cover the cost of private medical treatment at the defendant's expense, although the court does not exercise any control over how they use the award (except where they are a minor or an adult who lacks capacity as defined by the Mental Capacity Act 2005). If it seems likely that claimants will be unable to receive privately all the treatment or care that they need, and will eventually have to enter a publicly funded facility, a deduction from the award for future medical expenses will be made to allow for this.[135] Indeed, if, on the balance of probabilities, private medical treatment is not going to be used, *for whatever reason*, claimants are not entitled to claim for an

12–053

---

[132] He is not entitled to the cost of an operation which he would have had to undergo in any event: *Cutler v Vauxhall Motors Ltd* [1971] 1 Q.B. 418. There is no strict test that, for the cost of non-medical therapies to be recoverable, they had to have been recommended by a medical practitioner: *Jones v Royal Devon and Exeter NHS Foundation Trust* [2008] EWHC 558 (QB); (2008) 101 B.M.L.R. 154. The appropriate test is whether such treatment is reasonable, not remote and is proportionate.

[133] For discussion of the "multiplier method" in the context of future loss of earnings see paras 12–079 et seq. When dealing with future nursing care or domestic assistance the multiplier may be higher than for the loss of earnings claim because the period during which nursing care is needed may well exceed the claimant's pre-accident working life expectancy. For the approach to be applied to assessing the life expectancy of a seriously disabled child see: *The Royal Victoria Infirmary & Associated Hospitals NHS Trust v B (A Child)* [2002] EWCA Civ 348; [2002] Lloyd's Rep. Med. 282; [2002] P.I.Q.R. Q10. See also Strauss and Shavelle, "Life expectancy: what lawyers need to know" (1999) 5 *AVMA Medical & Legal Journal* 25; Hermer and Pickering [2002] J.P.I.L. 377 on the approach to multipliers in cases involving very serious injuries; L. Rosenbloom, "Estimating life expectancy in children with neurological disabilities" (2004) 10 *Clinical Risk* 13; R. Miles, "Life expectancy estimation in cerebral palsy—a paediatrician's approach" (2008) 14 *Clinical Risk* 130; E-A. Gumbel, "Calculating life expectation, periodical payments and developments since *Royal Victoria Infirmary & Associated Hospitals NHS Trust v B (A Child)*" (2008) 14 *Clinical Risk* 133. For examples of how statistical evidence has been used in first instance decisions see also *Lewis v Royal Shrewsbury Hospital NHS Trust* [2007] EWHC 1054 (QB); *Sarawar v Motor Insurers Bureau* [2007] EWHC 274 (QB); *Arden v Malcolm* [2007] EWHC 404 (QB); and *Burton v Kingsbury* [2007] EWHC 2091 (QB).

[134] Law Reform (Personal Injuries) Act 1948 s.2(4). The Pearson Commission recommended repeal of this provision: *Royal Commission on Civil Liability and Compensation for Personal Injury*, Cmnd.7054 (1978), Vol.I, para.342.

[135] *Lim Poh Choo v Camden and Islington Area Health Authority* [1980] A.C. 174; *Housecroft v Burnett* [1986] 1 All E.R. 332 at 342.

expense which they are not going to incur.[136] Where claimants have in fact used NHS facilities for medical treatment they cannot recover what they would have paid had they received private treatment.[137] Any saving to claimants which is attributable to their maintenance wholly or partly at public expense in a hospital, nursing home or other institution will be set off against any income they have lost as a result of their injuries.[138] A similar rule applies to claimants who make savings in domestic expenditure while being looked after in a private institution.[139]

12–054 If claimants have to live in a special institution, such as a nursing home, or receive attendance or care at home, they are entitled to the cost of that, provided that it is reasonably necessary.[140] Where there is a choice as to where the claimant is cared for it is not necessarily a question of which option is the cheapest. Thus, a claimant who needs constant nursing care may be entitled to be cared for at home rather than in an institution, even if this is more expensive, provided it is reasonable in the circumstances.[141] Where the cost of care at home is substantially greater than that of care in an institution the burden of proving that it is reasonable to incur this expense is the claimant's.

(ii)   Accommodation costs

12–055 Claimants can recover the cost of adapting accommodation to their special needs resulting from their disabilities,[142] subject to a deduction for the added capital value of the property which would be recoverable on a sale.[143] If it is not possible to adapt existing accommodation damages will be awarded in respect of the purchase of special accommodation,[144] but they will be assessed, not on the basis of the capital cost of the property, but by reference to the additional annual cost

---

[136] *Woodrup v Nicol* [1993] P.I.Q.R. Q104 at 114 CA, per Russell LJ, citing *Harris v Brights Asphalt Contractors* [1953] 1 Q.B. 617 and *Cunningham v Harrison* [1973] Q.B. 942 at 957.

[137] *Harris v Brights Asphalt Contractors Ltd* [1953] 1 Q.B. 617 at 635; *Lim Poh Choo v Camden and Islington Area Health Authority* [1980] A.C. 174 at 188.

[138] Administration of Justice Act 1982 s.5.

[139] *Lim Poh Choo v Camden and Islington Area Health Authority* [1980] A.C. 174.

[140] *Shearman v Folland* [1950] 2 K.B. 43. See Browne and Gardiner [2002] J.P.I.L. 369.

[141] *Rialas v Mitchell*, The Times, 17 July 1984; *Ahsan v University Hospitals Leicester NHS Trust* [2006] EWHC 2624; [2007] P.I.Q.R. P19—the religious beliefs of the claimant and the wishes of the family should be taken into account in assessing what is reasonable.

[142] Which, in appropriate cases, can include adaptations designed to treat the claimant's disability, such as a hydrotherapy pool: *A (A Child) v University Hospitals of Morecambe Bay NHS Foundation Trust* [2015] EWHC 366 (QB); [2015] P.I.Q.R. Q3; [2015] Med. L.R. 204.

[143] *Roberts v Johnstone* [1989] Q.B. 878. See G. Jones, "Accommodation Claims: *Roberts v Johnstone*" [2011] J.P.I.L. 71; W. Waldron and I. Gunn, "I'll Huff and I'll Puff ...: *Roberts v Johnstone*" [2012] J.P.I.L. 231. Where the claimant is a child and the parents are separated it may be reasonable to recover the cost of purchasing and adapting homes for both parents so that the child can stay with each of them: *Manna (A Child) v Central Manchester University Hospitals NHS Foundation Trust* [2017] EWCA Civ 12; [2017] P.I.Q.R. Q2; discussed by C. Ettinger [2017] J.P.I.L. C97.

[144] Or, in an appropriate case, the demolition of an existing property and building new accommodation adapted for the claimant's disability: *Robshaw v United Lincolnshire Hospitals NHS Trust* [2015] EWHC 923 (QB); [2015] Med. L.R. 339, where Foskett J took the view that the immediate capital cost of demolition and rebuild could achieve a considerable saving in annual costs in the future.

over the claimant's lifetime of providing that accommodation, as compared with ordinary accommodation. This is because the award is intended to compensate for the claimant's loss; it should not enhance the capital value of the claimant's estate after death.[145]

(iii) Relationship between care costs and public provision of care

Where the claimant receives services provided by a local authority, such as accommodation and/or care as a consequence of disabilities caused by the tort, then the claimant may or may not be liable to pay for those services depending upon the statutory basis upon which they have been provided. In some, but not all, instances the authority is entitled to make a reasonable charge for those services. In some cases the local authority must "disregard" funds attributable to compensation for personal injury when assessing whether the claimant is liable to be charged, and there may be differences between funds classified as capital and funds classified as income. If the authority is entitled to charge, or may become entitled to charge in the future, then the claimant will want damages or an indemnity[146] from the defendant to cover that potential cost. If the claimant is receiving, or will receive, the services free of charge the defendant may argue either that the claimant has suffered no loss under this head of damage or that the

12–056

---

[145] *Roberts v Johnstone* [1989] Q.B. 878 at 893. Damages "are notionally intended to be such as will exhaust the fund, contemporaneously with the termination of the plaintiff's life expectancy". The Court of Appeal applied a rate of 2 per cent of the capital value as the annual cost. This was then multiplied by the appropriate multiplier for the claimant's life expectancy. In *Iqbal v Whipps Cross University Hospital NHS Trust* [2006] EWHC 3111 (QB); [2007] LS Law Med. 97; [2007] P.I.Q.R. Q5 Sir Rodger Bell held that it would be inappropriate to make any deduction from the claimant's award allowing for the savings that parents would make in not having to pay rent on their own property as a result of living rent free in the accommodation purchased for the claimant. It was "not just to deprive parents of the incidental benefit of living rent free, when there are so many sacrifices on their part, most obviously the detriment to their quality of life, which must go uncompensated under our law of tort, however high the award in their child's favour" (at [83]). See also the discussion of this issue by Swift J in *Whiten v St George's Healthcare NHS Trust* [2011] EWHC 2066 (QB); [2012] Med. L.R. 1 at [456] to [472], and by Warby J in *A (A Child) v University Hospitals of Morecambe Bay NHS Foundation Trust* [2015] EWHC 366 (QB); [2015] P.I.Q.R. Q3; [2015] Med. L.R. 204 at [143]–[152]. Contrast this with the approach of HHJ MacDuff in *Lewis v Royal Shrewsbury Hospital NHS Trust* [2007] EWHC 1054 (QB) that where parents rent out their old home some allowance should be made for the benefit of the rental income they receive. *Iqbal* was considered by the Court of Appeal ([2007] EWCA Civ 1190; [2008] P.I.Q.R. P9) but this point was not dealt with.

[146] As in *Avon County Council v Hooper* [1997] 1 W.L.R. 1605; [1997] 1 All E.R. 532 where the costs of maintaining the patient in a residential home were wholly met by the local authority in discharge of its duties under the National Assistance Act 1948 s.29 and the National Health Service Act 1977 Sch.8. The settlement of the patient's claim for medical negligence against the health authority provided for the cost of keeping the patient at the home from the date of the settlement, and an indemnity to the patient (and his estate) against any liability to the local authority for the cost of care at the home prior to that date. Following the patient's death, the local authority sought to recover the cost of the provision of services to him prior to the settlement. The Court of Appeal held that since the patient/estate had a right to an indemnity, he had the "means" to pay for them and so it was reasonable to charge for the services. Thus, the health authority were liable to meet the costs of the past care by virtue of the indemnity. Contrast *Thrul v Ray* [2000] P.I.Q.R. Q44 and *Firth v Geo. Ackroyd Junior Ltd* [2001] P.I.Q.R. Q27, in both of which the court came to the conclusion that the claimants were not entitled to an indemnity from the defendants.

claimant has a duty to mitigate the loss by accepting the gratuitous services. In either case, the defendant will argue that it is not liable to compensate the claimant for that particular loss.

12–057 There are a number of policy issues that intersect in these cases. The most obvious policy is that the tortfeasor should pay for the full financial consequences of the tort, but if the court accepts that the claimant has suffered no loss the saving to the defendant represents a pure windfall—the loss, in effect, falls on public funds rather than on defendants or their insurers.[147] In *Crofton v National Health Service Litigation Authority*,[148] for example, the Court of Appeal noted that there was:

> "...much to be said for the view that the tortfeasor should pay, and that the state should be relieved of the burden of funding the care of the victims of torts and that its hard-pressed resources should be concentrated on the care of those who are not the victims of torts ... It does not seem right, particularly where the care costs are very large, that they should be met from the public purse rather than borne by the tortfeasor."

A second issue is the effect of provisions in some of the relevant legislation for disregarding funds derived from compensation for personal injury. In theory, claimants could receive "double compensation" if they are entitled to damages from the defendant for the cost of care but then receives those services free of charge from the local authority. In practice, there are ways of avoiding this risk. An issue that will be of critical concern to claimants is that where damages are assessed on the basis that they will benefit from free statutory services for the rest of their life there is no guarantee that those services will actually continue to be provided. Government or local authority policy may change in the future, for example in response to the increasing demands for social care services placed on the state by an ageing population. Services may be withdrawn or means testing extended. There is no good reason why the risk of such detrimental changes should be borne by the claimant rather than the defendant. Moreover, claimants may have little or no control over the manner in which their needs are met by local authority care services. The standard of care may fall over time in response to financial pressures placed on local authorities, whereas an award of damages gives them some degree of control over the services that are purchased to meet their reasonable needs.

12–058 **Meeting the claimant's "reasonable needs"** In *Sowden v Lodge; Crookdale v Drury*[149] the Court of Appeal held that the test is whether the care and accommodation chosen and claimed for was reasonable by reference to an assessment of the nature and extent of the claimant's needs, and not whether objectively it was reasonable as measured by the claimant's "best interests". Generally, the approach should be to compare what a claimant reasonably requires with what a local authority, having regard to inevitable uncertainties, is

---

[147] Of course, in the context of medical negligence litigation this will usually be a dispute between two different public bodies (a local authority and the NHS) as to who should bear the loss, but at the end of the day it will be taxpayers' money, albeit coming from different pots of taxation.
[148] [2007] EWCA Civ 71; [2007] 1 W.L.R. 923 at [88].
[149] [2004] EWCA Civ 1370; [2005] 1 W.L.R. 2129; [2005] 1 All E.R. 581.

likely to provide in the discharge of its duty under the National Assistance Act 1948 s.21. If the likely public provision fell short of the claimant's reasonable requirements, the defendant had to pay for those reasonable requirements. This was subject to the argument that public provision under s.21 could be augmented by a "top-up" contribution from the defendant which would meet the claimant's reasonable needs.[150] Pill LJ stressed the need for cogent evidence as to how the proposed care and accommodation regimes will operate in practice. Once claimants have demonstrated what their reasonable needs for future care are, the onus is on the defendant to show that the local authority could wholly or partially satisfy those reasonable needs.[151] If there is little or no evidence about the local authority's eligibility criteria, how and to what extent the local authority discharges its statutory duty, the type of accommodation which the local authority would consider to be suitable, or the amount they would usually expect to pay, the defendant will not have discharged the evidential burden.[152] The local authority's interest in the outcome of a case (in terms of whether, following an award of damages, it will be permitted to charge for accommodation and/or care provided to the claimant) means that it may be appropriate for the authority to be joined as a party to the litigation.[153]

Security of public provision in the future   Judges have shown some   **12–059** understandable scepticism as to whether local authority provision will actually meet a claimant's reasonable needs, particularly when policy on public provision can change as a result of resource constraints. In *Godbold v Mahmood*[154] Mitting J said that:

> "I have no confidence that the duty currently imposed by ministerial direction will exist at a time relevant to this claimant's needs. The duty is imposed not by primary legislation or even by secondary legislation, but by a combination of primary legislation and ministerial direction. The ministerial direction can be changed or withdrawn at any time without recourse to Parliament. It is notorious that the burden of providing for the elderly and disabled, which since 1990 has fallen on local authorities, has increased and is increasing. It is not beyond question that local authorities will persuade a future Secretary of State that the burden is insupportable and should be modified, reduced or even in certain circumstances withdrawn."

In *Freeman v Lockett*[155] Tomlinson J pointed out that no local authority could ever give any guarantee or undertaking as to what its policy for future care funding would be. It was impossible for the court to undertake the exercise of

---

[150] See also *Coombs v Dorset NHS Primary Care Trust* [2013] EWCA Civ 471; [2014] 1 W.L.R. 111 where the Court of Appeal held that there was nothing in principle to prevent a patient who was compulsorily detained in hospital under the Mental Health Act 1983 from purchasing "top-up" care, provided it was consistent with the recommendations of the responsible clinician. That meant that the patient could include an element for additional care in a claim for damages against the defendant NHS Trusts.

[151] [2004] EWCA Civ 1370; [2005] 1 W.L.R. 2129; [2005] 1 All E.R. 581 at [99] per Longmore LJ; *Walton v Calderdale Healthcare NHS Trust* [2005] EWHC 1053 (QB); [2006] P.I.Q.R. Q3 at [18] per Silber J. See further G. Martin, "Nine reasons not to be afraid of *Sowden*" [2006] J.P.I.L. 162.

[152] *Godbold v Mahmood* [2005] EWHC 1002 (QB); [2006] P.I.Q.R. Q5.

[153] *Nottinghamshire CC v Bottomley* [2010] EWCA Civ 756; [2010] Med. L.R. 407; see Lyons [2010] J.P.I.L. C207.

[154] [2005] EWHC 1002 (QB); [2006] P.I.Q.R. Q5 at [26].

[155] [2006] EWHC 102 (QB); [2006] P.I.Q.R. P23; [2006] Lloyd's Rep. Med. 151.

estimating what the claimant might receive from the local authority in the future, and therefore no deduction should be made from the award of damages to reflect the possible continued availability to her of direct payments from the local authority. The defendant had failed to prove that the local authority would continue to contribute to the claimant's care costs in the future, and neither the defendant nor his insurers were prepared to offer an indemnity to cover the risk that the claimant's local authority funding might be withdrawn or reduced in the future.[156] Similarly, in *Peters v East Midlands Strategic Health Authority*[157] the Court of Appeal concluded that the trial judge had been correct to have regard to the possibility of legislative change as a relevant factor in deciding whether it was reasonable for the claimant to opt for private funding rather than rely on the provision of accommodation and care free of charge by the local authority.

12–060   **Residential care and domiciliary care**[158]   In *Crofton v National Health Service Litigation Authority*[159] at the date of the trial the claimant, who had suffered severe brain damage shortly after birth, was living in supervised accommodation where his carers were paid for by the local authority. The judge held that the local authority would make yearly direct payments towards the claimant's care costs, which should be deducted from the total care costs. On appeal, one of the issues was whether there should be a deduction from the award of damages in respect of the claimant's care costs of the direct payments made to the claimant under the National Assistance Act 1948 s.29. Section 21 of that Act gives rise to a local authority's duties to provide residential accommodation to persons aged 18 and over who by reason of age, illness disability or any other circumstances are in need of care and attention which is not otherwise available to them. Section 22 authorises local authorities to charge for that accommodation. However, the National Assistance (Assessment of Resources) Regulations 1992 provide that capital and income deriving from compensation for personal injuries administered by the court shall be disregarded in assessing the person's resources. Section 29 of the Act permits the local authority, under ministerial guidance, to

---

[156] See also *Tinsley v Sarkar* [2005] EWHC 192 (QB); [2006] P.I.Q.R. Q1—primary care trust had a duty under s.117 of the Mental Health Act 1983 to provide aftercare to the claimant free of charge, with no power of recoupment, but the duty was not open-ended and the trust's available resources were relevant; the claimant had no right to choose how his needs would be met and there was no provision for top-up of funds. Leveson J held that the Trust's resources did not extend to a regime that was reasonable to meet the claimant's needs, and so awarded damages for future care costs on the basis of the claimant's reasonable needs.

[157] [2009] EWCA Civ 145; [2010] Q.B. 48 at [87]. See also *Crofton v National Health Service Litigation Authority* [2007] EWCA Civ 71; [2007] 1 W.L.R. 923 at [108]: "It is by no means far-fetched to suggest that, at some time in the future, the ministerial policy of ring-fencing personal injury damages and/or the Council's approach to that policy will change."

[158] For discussion of the two different approaches applied to residential care and domiciliary care in relation to statutory disregards of compensation payments see A. Thornton, "Personal Injury Disregards and the Form of Award: Risks and Reform" [2013] J.P.I.L. 182. Note that the different treatment of residential care services and direct payments for domiciliary care in relation to the statutory disregard in the National Assistance (Assessment of Resources) Regulations 1992, considered in *Crofton v National Health Service Litigation Authority*, has been removed by the Care Act 2014 from, at the latest, 1 April 2016. See A. Thornton "Care Act 2014: Changes to the Means Testing of Personal Injury Damages and their Implications for the Form of Award" [2015] J.P.I.L. 91.

[159] [2007] EWCA Civ 71; [2007] 1 W.L.R. 923; [2007] P.I.Q.R. Q3.

make direct payments for promoting the welfare of persons in their own homes, but payments under s.29 do not fall within the National Assistance (Assessment of Resources) Regulations. The Court of Appeal concluded, however, that under policy guidelines, the capital sum represented by an award of damages which is administered by the Court of Protection would be disregarded. But the treatment of income under the guidance was "far from clear". The Court held that:

> "...the judge was right to hold that the council could and would make direct payments to meet the claimant's care needs despite the award of damages, and that these payments should be taken into account in the assessment of damages."[160]

Commenting on the approach of Tomlinson J in *Freeman v Lockett*[161] to the uncertainties surrounding future local authority provision, the Court of Appeal accepted that there may be cases where the possibility of a claimant receiving direct payments was so uncertain that they should be disregarded altogether in the assessment of damages, though if the court found that a claimant will actually receive direct payments that finding should be taken into account in the assessment, and the correct way to reflect the uncertainties is to discount the multiplier.[162] On the facts of *Crofton* the Court considered that the judge had been wrong to apply the agreed whole-life multiplier to the direct payments. The uncertainties surrounding future provision of direct payments should have led him to conclude that a substantial discount to the multiplier was necessary:

12–061

> "It is by no means far-fetched to suggest that, at some time in the future, the ministerial policy of ring-fencing personal injury damages and/or the council's approach to that policy will change."[163]

However, there was so little evidence available to the Court on this issue that they were unable to determine the correct multiplier, and the case was remitted to the judge for further consideration of the evidence.

Claimant's entitlement to damages from the tortfeasor as of right   In *Peters v East Midlands Strategic Health Authority*[164] the claimant was living in a local authority funded care home. The defendant NHS Trust argued that the local authority had a statutory obligation under the National Assistance Act 1948 s.21 to provide for her care, and that the local authority was not entitled to seek a contribution from the claimant towards the costs of her care because under the Income Support (General) Regulations 1987 Sch.10 para.44 the whole amount of damages awarded to the claimant for personal injury was to be disregarded as

12–062

---

[160] [2007] EWCA Civ 71; [2007] 1 W.L.R. 923; [2007] P.I.Q.R. Q3 at [87].
[161] [2006] EWHC 102 (QB); [2006] P.I.Q.R. P23; [2006] Lloyd's Rep. Med. 151.
[162] [2007] EWCA Civ 71; [2007] 1 W.L.R. 923 at [96].
[163] [2007] EWCA Civ 71; [2007] 1 W.L.R. 923 at [108]. For comment on *Crofton v National Health Service Litigation Authority* see E. Gumbel and H. Witcomb, "Public Provision of Care and Accommodation in PI after *Crofton v NHSLA*" [2007] J.P.I.L. 160; S. Brown, "*Crofton v NHSLA*: Something for Everyone—but No Real Practical Guidance" [2007] J.P.I.L. 168; and A. Jeffreys "Local Authority Funding of Care and Accommodation in Catastrophic Claims" [2008] J.P.I.L. 209.
[164] [2009] EWCA Civ 145; [2010] Q.B. 48. *Peters* is commented on by Fulbrook [2009] J.P.I.L. C89; D. Coldrick and A. Thornton, "The Recovery of Damages for Care and the Provision of Statutory Care Services—A Deputy's Perspective" [2011] J.P.I.L. 30.

capital available to meet the costs of care provided by the local authority. The claimant had a "place for life" at the care home and would continue to be cared for at the public expense regardless of any award of damages. On this basis, the Trust argued that she had suffered no loss under the heading for accommodation and care. The Court of Appeal upheld the judge's decision that the statutory disregard applied to the whole of the damages award, including any award for care needs. That, however, was not the end of the matter. The Court held that the claimant was entitled to recover damages from the defendant as a matter of right, irrespective of her statutory right to have the loss made good in kind by the provision of services by a public authority. There was:

"...no reason in policy or principle which requires us to hold that a claimant who wishes to opt for self-funding and damages in preference to reliance on the statutory obligations of a public authority should not be entitled to do so as a matter of right. The claimant has suffered loss which has been caused by the wrongdoing of the defendants. She is entitled to have that loss made good, so far as this is possible, by the provision of accommodation and care."[165]

Provided that there was no real risk of double recovery, there was no reason in principle why the claimant should give up her right to damages to meet her wish to pay for her care needs herself rather than to become dependent on the State.[166] As for double recovery, where a claimant had been awarded 100 per cent of the care costs required to meet her needs there was no duty on a deputy acting on behalf of the claimant to seek full public funding. Where the Court of Protection was involved in administering the claimant's affairs, the risk of double recovery could be dealt with by providing the Court of Protection with a copy of the judgment in the personal injuries claim and seeking an order that no application for public funding of the claimant's care under the National Assistance Act 1948 should be made without further order. The order should also provide for the defendants to be notified of an application for permission to apply for public funding.[167]

12–063   Although not strictly necessary, given the conclusion that the claimant was entitled to damages for her care needs as of right, the Court of Appeal went on to consider whether the claimant was acting reasonably in opting for private funding of her care needs, rather than relying on the local authority to provide services for free. As the Court noted, there are many cases where the courts have awarded a

---

[165] [2009] EWCA Civ 145; [2010] Q.B. 48 at [53], applying *The Liverpool (No.2)* [1963] P. 64, where it was held that a claimant who has a right of action against both a wrongdoer and an innocent party for compensation is entitled to choose against whom to enforce his right. In *Peters* it was irrelevant that the claimant had a common law right to compensation against the NHS Trust and a statutory right against the local authority to have the loss made good in kind, rather than by payment of compensation: [2009] EWCA Civ 145; [2010] Q.B. 48 at [54]. *Peters* was applied on this point in *Harman (A Child) v East Kent Hospitals NHS Foundation Trust* [2015] EWHC 1662 (QB); [2015] P.I.Q.R. Q4, where, at [26], Turner J rejected the defendants' suggestion that the offer of a capped indemnity to cover for the risk of public funding being withdrawn or reduced was sufficient: "The right of recovery against the tortfeasor in this category of case cannot be diluted by the offer of an indemnity."

[166] [2009] EWCA Civ 145; [2010] Q.B. 48 at [56].

[167] [2009] EWCA Civ 145; [2010] Q.B. 48 at [63]–[65]. See also *Harman (A Child) v East Kent Hospitals NHS Foundation Trust* [2015] EWHC 1662 (QB); [2015] P.I.Q.R. Q4 at [26], providing for an appropriately worded indemnity from the claimant's deputy to preclude double recovery.

claimant care costs as a head of loss, not on the grounds that the claimant is entitled to the costs as of right, but because local authority care has been ruled out as inadequate, uncertain or unavailable.[168] It was unsurprising, then, when the Court held that the possibility of legislative change to the provisions for free care was a relevant factor in deciding whether it was reasonable to opt for private funding rather than rely on the local authority.[169] The risk of such a change may be low, but there was:

"...no reason why the claimant should take the risk that the policy of ring-fencing personal injury damages is changed and with immediate effect."[170]

That made it entirely reasonable for the claimant to opt for self-funding through the award of damages rather than seek provision of care and accommodation at public expense.

Position of the public authority after an award of damages has been made   **12–064**
In *Peters*, addressing the question of possible double recovery, the Court of Appeal said that where a court has awarded 100 per cent of the care costs that are necessary to meet a claimant's needs there could be no duty on the claimant's case manager or deputy to seek full public funding so as to achieve a double recovery. There was "no basis in law, fairness or common sense for such a duty".[171] A question then arises as to the position of the local authority or health authority faced with an application for care services or treatment which would normally be free to the applicant where the authority is aware that there has been an award of damages to cover the cost of those services. The short answer is that the authority must apply the criteria that would be applied to any other applicant. The authority cannot rely on the principle that the "tortfeasor pays" or on the possibility of double recovery when making a decision about access to services. In *R. (on the application of Booker) v NHS Oldham*[172] Judge Pelling QC held that *Peters* was not authority for the proposition that a health authority is entitled to refuse treatment or services to an individual who would otherwise meet the criteria for treatment or services just because they have received an award of damages for personal injuries. The NHS is a comprehensive health service free at the point of delivery and a patient who has received a damages award is in no different position from a patient who is independently wealthy or who is insured in relation to medical expenses who would also be able to afford the cost of treatment.

Similarly, in *Tinsley v Manchester City Council*[173] the claimant had received an   **12–065**
award of damages which included the full cost of meeting his future care needs,[174] and since then had paid for the cost of his accommodation and care

---

168 [2009] EWCA Civ 145; [2010] Q.B. 48 at [36].
169 [2009] EWCA Civ 145; [2010] Q.B. 48 at [87], citing *Crofton v National Health Service Litigation Authority* [2007] EWCA Civ 71; [2007] 1 W.L.R. 923 at [108].
170 [2009] EWCA Civ 145; [2010] Q.B. 48 at [88].
171 [2009] EWCA Civ 145; [2010] Q.B. 48 at [61].
172 [2010] EWHC 2593 (Admin); [2011] Med. L.R. 10.
173 [2016] EWHC 2855 (Admin); [2017] Med. L.R. 28.
174 See *Tinsley v Sarkar* [2005] EWHC 192 (QB); [2006] P.I.Q.R. Q1, para.12–059, n.156 above.

needs. The claimant's deputy took the view that the claimant could not sustain the cost of funding his existing care arrangements and applied to the local authority to provide after-care services under s.117 of the Mental Health Act 1983. The local authority refused to provide the service on the basis that the claimant could afford the cost himself, and to provide the service free of charge would amount to "double recovery". Judge Stephen Davies held that the local authority could not refuse to supply a service to which a person was otherwise entitled under s.117 on the ground that the claimant had received of damages for personal injury which included the cost of such care. The local authority, relying on the statement from *Peters* that there was "no basis in law, fairness or common sense" for a duty to be imposed on a deputy to seek double recovery, argued that the application for services should be dismissed on the basis that a deputy seeking to obtain double recovery was acting unlawfully and in breach of duty. However, the judge accepted the claimant's argument that it was wrong to elevate the dictum from *Peters* into a freestanding rule of law in order to prevent people who were otherwise entitled from making a claim under s.117 to enforce their right to do so. The rule against double recovery was a common law concept applied to the assessment of damages, and it had no relevance to a claim for a statutory entitlement in circumstances where a person was entitled to make such a claim regardless of his financial circumstances.[175] Nor could it be said that a deputy owes duties to the local authority or to the defendant in the personal injury action. Moreover, it was unclear how the Administrative Court on an application for judicial review was to assess whether the deputy was in breach of his duty to the client. The Court was in no position to judge whether as a result of unwise financial decisions by the deputy the claimant was in need of s.117 services. Did the deputy have to wait until all the personal injuries damages had been exhausted before applying for support, or could he apply if all the funds awarded for future care were exhausted but the claimant still had substantial funds left over from other elements of the damages award?[176] If an exception to the statutory right to free after-care services under s.117 was to be applied to claimants who have received damages for personal injuries that was something that Parliament should address by amending the legislation.[177]

12–066   **Complexity of the rules**   The relationship between awards of damages for the cost of care and public provision of care can be extremely complex. In *Crofton v National Health Service Litigation Authority* the Court of Appeal lamented the difficulties that this can create:

"We cannot conclude this judgment without expressing our dismay at the complexity and labyrinthine nature of the relevant legislation and guidance, as well as (in some respects) its

---

[175] "It does not seem to me to be possible to deny a remedy to a claimant, otherwise entitled to complain that the relevant authority has refused to provide aftercare services under s.117 by wrongfully relying on his receipt of personal injury damages, on the basis that his deputy ought not to be entitled to advance this claim because it would offend a common law rule as to the assessment of damages which has no role to play in the assessment under s.117", [2016] EWHC 2855 (Admin); [2017] Med. L.R. 28 at [36].
[176] [2016] EWHC 2855 (Admin); [2017] Med. L.R. 28 at [37].
[177] [2016] EWHC 2855 (Admin); [2017] Med. L.R. 28 at [38].

obscurity. Social security law should be clear and accessible. The tortuous analysis in the earlier part of this judgment shows that it is neither."[178]

In theory, where a claimant receives 100 per cent compensation for the cost of future care the claimant should have no need for support from public services or funds. But as *Tinsley v Manchester City Council* illustrates, there is no guarantee that the assumptions that are made when calculating future losses will actually turn out to be correct, and there is always a risk that what at the time appears to be "full" compensation will in practice prove to be insufficient to meet the claimant's needs. Moreover, it seems probable that in many cases where a settlement is negotiated, even on a "full liability" basis, there will be some discount of the damages award to reflect the litigation risk, and where liability is contested the discount will be greater. The consequence is that for many claimants the funds to pay for future care will be insufficient, and they will have to resort to assistance from public services or funds. In this situation the interaction between common law principles of full compensation but no double recovery and entitlement to both means-tested and non-means tested benefits/ services becomes critical from the claimant's perspective. Despite some changes introduced by the Care Act 2014 and the Care and Support (Charging and Assessment of Resources) Regulations 2014,[179] that interaction remains extremely complex.[180]

(iv) Other expenses and losses

Where a claimant suffers from a major disability as a result of injuries the items of additional expense can be numerous. They may include the cost of adapting a car; the extra costs of running a household such as higher costs attributable to having to run larger accommodation or accommodation adapted to the claimant's disability; additional laundry bills; the cost of clothes which may wear out more frequently; the expense of maintaining a car[181] or house[182] which the claimant will no longer be able to do; the cost of special equipment such as wheelchairs, and nursing or medical appliances; physiotherapy and other forms of rehabilitative therapy; the additional costs of going on holiday; and, where claimants are incapable of managing their affairs, the cost of administration of the damages fund by the Court of Protection.[183] The claimant is entitled to travelling expenses incurred in obtaining medical treatment, and also the travelling expenses

12–067

---

[178] [2007] EWCA Civ 71; [2007] 1 W.L.R. 923 at [111].

[179] SI 2014/2672.

[180] See in particular A. Thornton, "Care Act 2014: Changes to the Means Testing of Personal Injury Damages and Their Implications for the Form of Award" [2015] J.P.I.L. 91.

[181] There is potentially a degree of overlap in the award of damages if claimants receive a large sum for loss of earnings from which they may have purchased and run a car in any event. If they are claiming the cost of specially adapted transport there will clearly be an element of overlap which should be taken into account.

[182] See Snell, "Damages for DIY and Gardening" [2002] J.P.I.L. 385.

[183] *Jones v Jones* [1985] Q.B. 704; *Rialas v Mitchell, The Times*, 17 July 1984.

attributable to relatives' visits to claimant, provided the visits are of benefit to the claimant in mitigating the damage (but not where the sole justification is the claimant's comfort or pleasure).[184]

12–068 **Loss of ability to perform household tasks or care for another** Where non-earners, such as housewives, are injured then, clearly, they cannot claim for the earnings that they would have lost had they been in paid employment. But people who are deprived of their ability to look after their families suffer a real loss, even though other members of the family now perform the tasks that they used to do, and they are entitled to compensation for this loss.[185] For the future this loss is estimated on the basis of the cost employing domestic help, irrespective of whether a housekeeper will be employed. Past loss, on the other hand, is compensated as an addition to the award of general damages if a housekeeper has not been employed.[186] Claimants are also entitled to damages for care which, as a result of the defendant's negligence, they are no longer able to give to a relative, spouse or partner living as part of the same household, where that care goes beyond the ordinary interaction of members of a household. To the extent that another member of the family has mitigated the loss by providing additional care, the claimant would hold the damages on trust for that member of the family.[187]

12–069 **Divorce and marriage prospects** Where claimants' injuries lead to the break up of their marriage the financial consequences of the divorce are not recoverable, either on the basis that the loss is too remote or on the ground of public policy.[188] On the other hand, loss of marriage prospects may be the subject of an award of general damages for pain and suffering.[189]

12–070 **Loss of fertility** In the "wrongful birth" cases the claimant is complaining that the defendants have failed to prevent the birth of a child.[190] But the converse situation can also arise: the negligence may interfere with a claimant's fertility, giving rise to a claim for damages for that loss. The question then may be: to what lengths is the claimant allowed to go, at the defendant's expense, in an effort

---

[184] *Hunt v Severs* [1994] 2 A.C. 350 at 356–357. This curious head of damage stems from a dictum of Diplock J in *Kirkham v Boughey* [1958] 2 Q.B. 338 at 343, and now appears to be well established, although strictly speaking it is not the claimant's loss. The expenses are normally agreed, as, e.g. in *Donnelly v Joyce* [1974] Q.B. 454 and *Thomas v Wignall* [1987] Q.B. 1098.

[185] *Daly v General Steam Navigation Co. Ltd* [1981] 1 W.L.R. 120.

[186] This approach is criticised as illogical by Burrows, *Remedies for Torts and Breach of Contract*, 3rd edn (Oxford: Oxford University Press, 2004), p.279; and the Law Commission in its report *Damages for Personal Injury: Medical, Nursing and Other Expenses; Collateral Benefits*, Law Com. No.262, 1999.

[187] *Lowe v Guise* [2002] EWCA Civ 197; [2002] Q.B. 1369, CA—claimant who looked after his disabled brother full-time was no longer able to do so after sustaining injuries caused by the defendant's negligence.

[188] *Pritchard v JH Cobden Ltd* [1988] Fam. 22, CA, disapproving *Jones v Jones* [1985] Q.B. 704. Subsequently in *Pritchard v J.H. Cobden Ltd* [1987] 2 F.L.R. 56 the same court held that the legal costs of the divorce *were* recoverable from the tortfeasor on the particular facts of the case.

[189] See para.12–128.

[190] See paras 12–134 et seq.

to redress the loss? In *Briody v St Helen's & Knowsley Health Authority*[191] as a result of the defendant's negligence the claimant underwent a sub-total hysterectomy, which left her ovaries intact, but rendered her sterile. Ebsworth J held that she was not entitled to the cost of a surrogacy arrangement as part of her loss. It was contrary to public policy to award damages to enable a party to enter into a contract which under English law was unenforceable.[192] Moreover, the chances of a successful conception were so low as to make it unreasonable to require the defendant to fund the treatment. Ebsworth J did not exclude the possibility that, on different facts (for example, a younger claimant with a higher prospect of success using her eggs; and an arrangement that fell within English law, i.e. non-commercial), the costs of surrogacy might be a recoverable head of damage where the claimant's fertility had been affected by the defendant's negligence. This decision was upheld by the Court of Appeal.[193] The facts had changed slightly by the time of the appeal, in that the claimant had successfully had her own eggs artificially fertilised by her partner's sperm, and the frozen embryos were in storage. However, the prospects of a successful pregnancy arising from the use of the embryos were extremely small (put at 1 per cent by one expert witness and much less than 1 per cent by another), so "vanishingly small" that it was not reasonable to expect the defendants to pay the expense of such a slim chance.[194] An alternative proposal to use donor eggs was more likely to succeed, but it would not restore the claimant to her position before the negligent act. Neither the child nor the pregnancy would be hers, and it could be compared to adoption, the costs of which it would not be reasonable to expect the defendants to meet. The Court did not rule out the possibility, on appropriate facts, that damages in respect of the costs of surrogacy might be recoverable, though Hale LJ expressed the tentative view that this might be a step too far.[195]

In *XP v Compensa Towarzystwo SA*[196] the claimant, who was aged 40 at the date of the damages assessment, suffered a miscarriage as a consequence of a road

12–071

---

[191] [2000] P.I.Q.R. Q165; [2000] Lloyd's Rep. Med. 127.

[192] See the Surrogacy Arrangements Act 1985.

[193] *Briody v St Helens and Knowsley Area Health Authority (Claim for Damages and Costs)* [2001] EWCA Civ 1010; [2002] Q.B. 856.

[194] [2001] EWCA Civ 1010; [2002] Q.B. 856 at [22] per Hale LJ.

[195] In *XX v Whittington Hospital NHS Trust* [2017] EWHC 2318 (QB) Sir Robert Nelson held that the claimant was entitled to the cost of surrogacy, using her own eggs. The chances of a successful procedure were significantly better than in *Briody* (the prospects of success were "reasonable if not good"), and it was not contrary to public policy to use an agency to find and use a surrogate mother provided it was on a non-profit basis. The Court of Appeal had not ruled out such an award in *Briody*, though the costs of a commercial surrogacy arrangement in California were irrecoverable because such contracts remain illegal in the UK; nor were the costs a procedure using donor eggs recoverable (applying *Briody*).

[196] [2016] EWHC 1728 (QB); [2016] Med. L.R. 570. See also *Finnie v South Devon Healthcare NHS Foundation Trust* [2014] EWHC 4333 (QB) (claimant developed a recto-vaginal fistula following a negligent operation on her rectum, thereby reducing her fertility; held that she was entitled to damages for the cost of assisted conception for one child, but not for a second child because by that stage she would probably have required assisted conception in any event because of her partner's low fertility). Where the injury to the claimant is such that she or he will never be able to become a genetic parent, even with assisted conception, an award of general damages should be made to compensate for the claimant's lost fertility, but putting a value on this can be difficult. See C. Thorne, "What price parenthood? The value we place on a family" [2016] J.P.I.L. 95.

traffic accident, and went on to develop post-traumatic stress disorder and depression. Whipple J held that she was entitled to claim the cost of fertility treatment. She had split up with the father of the child before the miscarriage, but had planned to continue the pregnancy and raise the child as a single parent. She had not had another relationship since the split. The defendants argued that the claimant remained fertile and that her problem was her lack of a partner, not the accident that caused the miscarriage. Whipple J rejected the argument. The claimant was merely seeking to be put into the position she would have been before the accident. Her fertility was reducing with age:

"Time is pressing and she cannot afford to wait for a partner, or for better circumstances or health, before trying to become pregnant naturally."[197]

The fact that the claimant had not met anyone and so had been unable to mitigate her loss by becoming pregnant naturally was not to be held against her, particularly given that her ill health since the accident was part of the problem in finding a new partner.

(v) Gratuitous care provided by a third party

12–072 In many instances a third person, such as a relative or friend, bears part of the cost of the claimant's injury, either in the form of direct financial payments or by providing gratuitous services, such as nursing assistance. A spouse or relative may give up paid employment to look after the claimant, but the third party has no direct claim in tort against the defendant. Claimants can recover this cost, however, from the defendant, irrespective of whether they are under any legal or moral obligation to reimburse the third party. In *Donnelly v Joyce*[198] the Court of Appeal held that this expense was the claimant's loss, and consisted of the need for nursing services or special equipment, not the expenditure of the money itself. The question of who provided the service or purchased equipment, or whether the claimant was under an obligation to repay, were said to be irrelevant to the defendant's liability. The measure of the loss is the "proper and reasonable cost" of supplying the claimant's needs. In the case of a relative who has given up paid employment this will be at least the relative's loss of earnings, subject to a ceiling of the commercial rate for supplying those services to the claimant.[199] It would seem that, normally, the full commercial rate should not be applied unless the relative has given up paid employment, the assumption being that where relatives look after the claimant out of love or a sense of duty the commercial rate is inappropriate.[200] Awards in respect of gratuitous care are not reserved for very

---

[197] [2016] EWHC 1728 (QB); [2016] Med. L.R. 570 at [125].
[198] [1974] Q.B. 454.
[199] *Housecroft v Burnett* [1986] 1 All E.R. 332. In *Croke v Wiseman* [1981] 3 All E.R. 852; [1982] 1 W.L.R. 71 the claimant's mother had given up her employment to look after him. Her loss of earnings included loss of pension rights in the job she had given up. An award under this head can be made even though the carer has not lost wages of her own in order to look after the claimant: *Mills v British Rail Engineering Ltd* [1992] P.I.Q.R. Q130, CA.
[200] *McCamley v Cammell Laird Shipbuilders Ltd* [1990] 1 W.L.R. 963 at 966–967, CA; see *Almond v Leeds Western Health Authority* [1990] 1 Med. L.R. 370, where half the commercial rate was awarded for past care; cf. *Van Gervan v Fenton* (1992) 109 A.L.R. 283, where the High Court of Australia held

serious cases. Provided that the claimant's illness or injury was sufficiently serious to give rise to a need for care and attendance significantly over and above that which would be given anyway in the ordinary course of family life, an award should be made.[201]

In *Drake v Foster Wheeler Ltd*[202] it was held that the value of the palliative care in a hospice provided by a charitable foundation free of charge to the deceased was recoverable by the deceased's estate, for the benefit of the foundation. This was sufficiently analogous to gratuitous care provided at home by a relative or friend, in circumstances where the deceased's health, pain levels and support needs had reached a point where it was no longer possible, appropriate or practicable for him to remain at home.

12–073

Damages held on trust for provider of voluntary care   In *Hunt v Severs*[203] the House of Lords accepted that the basis of the claimant's claim consisted of his need for services, but disapproved the suggestion in *Donnelly v Joyce* that the question of what source the claimant's needs have been met from was irrelevant to the assessment of damages. The underlying rationale of the law is to enable voluntary carers to receive proper recompense for their services, and thus the injured claimant who recovers damages under this head should hold them on trust for the voluntary carer.[204]

12–074

that the reasonable value of a carer's services should be the market cost. In practice the loss will usually be assessed on the basis of the carer's net loss of earnings, even where the commercial rate is higher and the carer is providing 24-hour-a-day care and had previously been employed for five days a week for eight hours a day: *Fitzgerald v Ford* [1996] P.I.Q.R. Q72, CA; *Evans v Pontypridd Roofing Ltd* [2001] EWCA Civ 1657; [2002] P.I.Q.R. Q61; *Willbye v Gibbons* [2003] EWCA Civ 372; [2004] P.I.Q.R. P15; *Massey v Tameside & Glossop Acute Services NHS Trust* [2007] EWHC 317 (Admin).
[201] *Giambrone v JMC Holidays Ltd (formerly Sunworld Holidays Ltd) (No.2)* [2004] EWCA Civ 158; [2004] 2 All E.R. 891.
[202] [2010] EWHC 2004 (QB); [2011] 1 All E.R. 63; [2010] P.I.Q.R. P19. See Cooksley [2010] J.P.I.L. C203 and S. Glynn, "Gratuitous Care Claims for Third Parties" [2011] J.P.I.L. 175.
[203] [1994] 2 A.C. 350; Reed [1994] J.P.I.L. 139, 215; *Willbye v Gibbons* [2003] EWCA Civ 372; [2004] P.I.Q.R. P227.
[204] Approving *Cunningham v Harrison* [1973] Q.B. 942 at 952. For criticism of this approach see Matthews (1994) 13 C.J.Q. 302; Kemp (1994) 110 L.Q.R. 524; Hoyano (1995) 3 Tort L. Rev. 63; Reed (1995) 15 O.J.L.S. 133; Matthews and Lunney (1995) 58 M.L.R. 395. The Australian High Court has declined to follow *Hunt v Severs*, preferring instead the approach of the Court of Appeal in *Donelly v Joyce*, while taking a more robust view of the practical realities in such cases, including the insurance position: see *Kars v Kars* (1996) 141 A.L.R. 37; Luntz (1997) 113 L.Q.R. 201; Vines (1997) 5 Tort L. Rev. 93; Degeling (1997) 71 A.L.J. 882. The court must take steps to see that the terms of the trust are fulfilled: *H v S* [2002] EWCA Civ 792; [2003] Q.B. 965 at [30]. If the carer dies before the damages are received the relevant part of the damages will be held on trust for the carer's estate: *Hughes v Lloyd* [2007] EWHC 3133 (Ch); [2008] W.T.L.R. 473. For discussion of the nature of the *Hunt v Severs* trust and the implications for claimants and their advisers see Watson and Barrie (2003) 19 P.N. 320. In *Drake v Foster Wheeler Ltd* [2010] EWHC 2004 (QB); [2011] 1 All E.R. 63; [2010] P.I.Q.R. P19 at [43], although the sum recovered by the deceased's estate was technically held for the hospice that had provided gratuitous palliative care to the deceased, Judge Anthony Thornton QC held that under the Civil Procedure Rules the court can direct that a trust need not be established, and that the defendant should be directed to pay the sum directly to the hospice and then provide the estate with a copy of the receipt for the payment.

12–075 **Value of certain gratuitous services not recoverable** It followed from the reasoning of their Lordships in *Hunt v Severs*[205] that where the gratuitous services are provided by the defendant tortfeasor the claimant cannot recover the cost of the services by way of damages.[206] There can be no claim for gratuitous services provided by a spouse to the claimant's business as a result of the injury. This is in a different category from caring services.[207]

(b) Loss of earnings

12–076 Loss of earnings will be calculated over two periods: the loss up to the date of assessment and the prospective loss. Where the claimant's working life expectancy has been reduced the prospective loss of earnings will have to be further divided into the period during which the claimant is expected to survive, and the period during which he would have been employed but is not now expected to survive (the "lost years"), because the basis of the calculation is different in these periods.

(i) Past loss of earnings

12–077 Calculating the loss of earnings up to the date of assessment is usually a reasonably precise exercise, intended to measure claimants' actual loss over the period that they have been unable to work. This is the net loss, after deducting the claimant's income tax[208] and national insurance contributions,[209] and the claimant's contributions to a compulsory pension scheme.[210] Any loss of pension rights resulting from the contributions not having been paid is calculated separately.[211] All forms of earnings are included, such as perquisites.[212] If the claimant's rate of pay would have changed during this period, then this is taken into account.[213] The accrued loss of earnings to the date of trial form part of the

---

[205] [1994] 2 A.C. 350.

[206] Overruling *Donnelly v Joyce* on this point. The rationale can be seen from Lord Bridge's observation ([1994] 2 A.C. 350 at 363) that: "there can be no ground in public policy or otherwise for requiring the tortfeasor to pay to the plaintiff, in respect of the services which he himself has rendered, a sum of money which the plaintiff must then repay to him." The Law Commission recommended legislation to reverse this effect of *Hunt v Severs*, though approving much of the reasoning in the case: *Damages for Personal Injury: Medical, Nursing and Other Expenses; Collateral Benefits*, Law Com. No.262, 1999. See also *Hayden v Hayden* [1992] 1 W.L.R. 986, where the Court of Appeal held that in a claim under the Fatal Accidents Act 1976 the gratuitous services of the tortfeasor could be taken into account as reducing the claimant's loss and were not a "benefit" accruing as a result of the death which, under s.4, would have to be disregarded.

[207] *Hardwick v Hudson* [1999] 3 All E.R. 426, CA.

[208] *British Transport Commission v Gourley* [1956] A.C. 185. For criticism of this principle see Bishop and Kay (1987) 104 L.Q.R. 211.

[209] *Cooper v Firth Brown Ltd* [1963] 1 W.L.R. 418.

[210] *Dews v National Coal Board* [1988] A.C. 1.

[211] *Auty v National Coal Board* [1985] 1 All E.R. 930; [1985] 1 W.L.R. 784; *Brown v Ministry of Defence* [2006] EWCA Civ 546; [2006] P.I.Q.R. Q9.

[212] *Kennedy v Bryan, The Times*, 3 May 1984—company car.

[213] *Cookson v Knowles* [1979] A.C. 556 at 569, a Fatal Accidents Act case.

special damages. Claimants must give credit for the expenses they would have incurred had they been at work; for example, the cost of travel to and from work should be deducted.[214]

(ii) Prospective loss of earnings

Calculating claimants' future loss of earnings can cause real problems because the court will have to prophesy both what will happen to them, in the future and what would have happened if they had not been injured, in order to estimate the difference. This involves considering their life expectancy, earnings, the chance that they may have increased their earnings through promotion or reduced them through redundancy or illness, and what financial benefits they will now receive.

12–078

Multiplier method   If the damages award is to be made as a lump sum the court will use the multiplier method to calculate prospective loss of earnings (though it is always open to the court to make, or for the parties to agree, a periodical payments order in respect of future loss[215]). The starting point is to work out the claimant's net annual loss of earnings, as at the date of assessment, not the date of injury.[216] The net annual loss is known as the "multiplicand". This will be adjusted to take account of the claimant's individual prospects of a future increase in income (for example, through a promotion[217]), but no allowance will be made for a general rise in real average earnings. This sum is then multiplied by a "multiplier" which is based on the number of years that the loss is likely to continue. The multiplier is discounted, however, to take account of the uncertainty of the prediction (e.g. the claimant might have lost a job in any event through redundancy or illness in the future), and the fact that the claimant receives the money immediately as a capital sum, instead of in instalments over the rest of his working life.[218] The Ogden Tables are used as a guide to selecting the correct multiplier.[219] The claimant is then expected to invest the award of damages and use both the income and part of the capital over the expected period of the loss, so that at the end of that period the whole award will be exhausted

12–079

---

[214] Though the court should not spend an inordinate time on calculating insignificant amounts of travel expenses where the court is attempting to assess damages in a broad way: *Eagle v Chambers (No.2)* [2004] EWCA Civ 1033; [2004] 1 W.L.R. 3081; [2005] 1 All E.R. 136 at [68], citing Lord Griffiths in *Dew v National Coal Board* [1988] A.C. 1 at 13. In *HS v Lancashire Teaching Hospitals NHS Trust* [2015] EWHC 1376 (QB) at [40] William Davis J declined to make any deduction for travelling expenses to and from work, commenting that *Eagle v Chambers (No.2)* had not established a principle that a deduction should be made; rather the Court of Appeal had declined to interfere with the decision of the judge to deduct 15 per cent from the calculation of past earnings for travel costs on the basis that it was not wrong in law.

[215] See paras 12–020 et seq.

[216] *Cookson v Knowles* [1979] A.C. 556.

[217] *Roach v Yates* [1938] 1 K.B. 256; *Robertson v Lestrange* [1985] 1 All E.R. 950.

[218] No reduction is made for the fact that the claimant does not have to "earn" the money. For discussion of the multiplier to be applied to future loss of earnings where there was a chance that a young woman in employment would have given up that employment to have children see *Hughes v McKeown* [1985] 3 All E.R. 284; [1985] 1 W.L.R. 963 and *Housecroft v Burnett* [1986] 1 All E.R. 332 at 345 stating that this chance should be ignored; cf. the alternative approach in *Moriarty v McCarthy* [1978] 2 All E.R. 213.

[219] See para.12–081.

(although part of the living expenses may have included provision for retirement). Thus, the claimant is compensated on an annuity basis.

12–080 **Loss of chance of higher earnings** In some cases where the claimant's prospects of having improved earnings in the future have been fairly speculative the courts have resorted to a "loss of chance" approach to the assessment, based on the likely actions of third parties, rather than adopting the more traditional multiplier method (which, of course, is also concerned with assessing the chances that something might or might not have happened).[220] In *Herring v Ministry of Defence*[221] Potter LJ suggested that the loss of chance approach might be suitable where the chance to be assessed was the chance that the career of a claimant would take a particular course leading to significantly higher overall earnings than those which it was otherwise reasonable to take as the baseline for calculation. But in a case where the career model adopted by the judge had been chosen because it was itself the appropriate baseline, and/or was one of a number of alternatives likely to give more or less similar results, then it was neither necessary nor appropriate to adopt the loss of chance approach in respect of the possibility that the particular career may not, after all, be followed. Rather the multiplier method was appropriate, with the multiplier or multiplicand within the career model being adjusted to the circumstances of the particular claimant. The starting point was to form a view as to the most likely future working career ("the career model") of the claimant had he not been injured. If at the time of the accident, the claimant was in an established job in which he was likely to have remained but for the accident, the working assumption is that he would have done so and the conventional multiplier/multiplicand method of calculation is adopted, taking into account any reasonable prospects of promotion or movement to a better paid field of work. If a job change is unlikely significantly to affect the level of future earnings, it should be ignored in the multiplicand/multiplier exercise.[222] It was generally appropriate to make a discount in the multiplier in respect of contingencies or "the vicissitudes of life".[223] The discount for the general vicissitudes of future illness or unemployment was generally around 10 per cent.[224] A higher discount by virtue of additional future contingencies would

---

[220] See *Doyle v Wallace* [1998] P.I.Q.R. Q146, CA; *Langford v Hebran* [2001] EWCA Civ 361; [2001] P.I.Q.R. Q160; *XYZ v Portsmouth Hospital NHS Trust* [2011] EWHC 243 (QB); (2011) 121 B.M.L.R. 13 (applying the "chance" approach to the assessment of a business's future turnover and profit margin). This approach applies *Allied Maples Group Ltd v Simmons & Simmons* [1995] 4 All E.R. 907; [1995] 1 W.L.R. 1602; para.5–108, which is more usually relevant to questions of causation rather than the assessment of quantum. See also *Appleton v El Safty* [2007] EWHC 631 (QB).

[221] [2003] EWCA Civ 528; [2004] 1 All E.R. 44 at [25] and [26]. See also *Brown v Ministry of Defence* [2006] EWCA Civ 546; [2006] P.I.Q.R. Q9.

[222] It is not always appropriate to use the multiplier method to assess a claimant's loss of earning capacity, particularly where the disability is minor and the claimant is still in employment: see *Billett v Ministry of Defence* [2015] EWCA Civ 773; [2016] P.I.Q.R. Q1, para.12–098, n.275. *Billett* is discussed by N. Poole and L. Collignon, "Calculating Future Loss of Earnings Using Ogden Tables A–D" [2017] J.P.I.L. 26.

[223] [2003] EWCA Civ 528; [2004] 1 All E.R. 44 at [23] per Potter LJ.

[224] [2003] EWCA Civ 528; [2004] 1 All E.R. 44 at [38] per Potter LJ: "The Tables in the Notes to the Ogden Tables make plain that on an 'average' basis the discount appropriate to be allowed for the possibility that illness and unemployment will interrupt a claimant's earning career is a small one as compared with levels which have been traditionally applied. In my view that is a matter which should

only be justified if there were tangible reasons relating to the personality or likely future circumstances of the claimant going beyond the purely speculative.[225]

Ogden Tables   The 6th edition of the Ogden Tables[226] introduced a   **12–081**
significantly different approach to discounting the multiplier. The multiplier has already been discounted for mortality so no further deduction should be made for this. The Tables already reflect life expectancy. After mortality, the principal contingencies are unemployment and illness. The 6th edition was based on academic research which had demonstrated that the key factors which determine whether claimants will work in the future are their pre-accident work records, their pre-accident educational achievements and their disabilities. It provided a more accurate method for assessing the prospects for an individual claimant as opposed to the more general rule of thumb discount that was applied previously.[227] Three categories of educational attainment are set out (broadly "good", "medium" and "low"). Tables A to D then set out the discount rates to be applied to the conventional Ogden multiplier to reflect the lifetime risks of unemployment. The tables are further subdivided by reference to whether the claimant was in work or out of work at the date of trial or assessment, gender and level of disability. Proper application of the criteria can make a significant difference to outcome compared to the previous conventional discount approach.[228]

Use of this approach does not preclude a judge from making a further discount   **12–082**
based on the facts of a particular case. The purpose of the Tables is to enable a judge to calculate an initial adjustment to the multiplier to reflect the claimant's employment status, disability status, and educational attainment. It remains open to a judge to make a further discount to take account, for example, of a particular claimant's employment history or previous medical history or particular type of employment, and the Notes to the Tables give various examples of discounts for further contingencies that could be made.[229]

---

be borne in mind by judges when considering the level of discount to be made for contingencies generally." The trial judge in *Herring v Ministry of Defence* had applied a 25 per cent discount for general contingencies.
[225] [2003] EWCA Civ 528; [2004] 1 All E.R. 44 at [31].
[226] April 2007. In particular the approach set out in Section B of the Explanatory Notes. The Ogden Tables were originally produced in 1984 by a joint working party of lawyers and actuaries as a helpful means of selecting the correct multiplier.
[227] See H. Trusted, "The Sixth Edition of the Ogden Tables" [2007] J.P.I.L 262; V. Wass, "Discretion in the Application of the New Ogden Six Multipliers" [2008] J.P.I.L 154; C. Melton, "Ogden Six—Adjustments to Working Life Multipliers" [2009] J.P.I.L. 66. The Ogden Tables are currently in their 7th edition (2011).
[228] *Connor v Bradman* [2007] EWHC 2789 (QB).
[229] See Ch.10 of *Kemp & Kemp, The Quantum of Damages* (London: Sweet & Maxwell). The 7th edition of the Ogden Tables is available at *http://www.gov.uk/government/uploads/system/uploads/attachment_data/file/245859/ogden_tables_7th_edition.pdf*. Supplementary Tables to the 7th edition are available at *http://www.gov.uk/government/uploads/system/uploads/attachment_data/file/599837/Actuarial_tables_for_use_in_personal_injury_and_fatal_accident_cases_7th_edition_Supplementary_Tables.pdf*.

12–083   **Where multiplicand is too uncertain to use multiplier method**   Where there is no, or an uncertain, pre-accident record of the claimant's earnings the claim for prospective loss of earnings can be more speculative, and the court may decide not to use the multiplier method and may simply award a lump sum for loss of earning capacity.[230] This will often be the position where young children suffer serious injury. Such an award is not "calculated" arithmetically but is largely impressionistic, and the sum will often be discounted quite heavily to allow for its inherent uncertainty. Where possible, however, the court will attempt to make an assessment of the loss of earnings using the multiplier method, even if that involves relying on national average earnings figures to establish the multiplicand.[231] So in *Ward v Allies and Morrison Architects*[232] the Court of Appeal said that:

> "...the multiplicand/multiplier methodology and the Tables and guidance in the current edition of Ogden should normally be applied when making an award of damages for future loss of earnings, unless the judge really has no alternative."

But the burden is on claimants to provide evidence of the likely pattern of both their future earnings if they had not been injured, and their future earnings given that they have now been injured, to enable the judge to make the calculation. If there are too many imponderables concerning the claimant's future loss of earnings, and the court should follow the *Blamire* approach.

12–084   **Correct "discount" rate for selecting the multiplier**   In the past the courts selected multipliers based on the assumption that a person who invested a capital sum would receive a return of approximately 4.5 per cent after the effects of tax

---

[230] *Blamire v South Cumbria Health Authority* [1993] P.I.Q.R. Q1, where there was great uncertainty about the future lost earnings of a 21-year-old nurse, Steyn LJ said: "It seems to me that the judge carefully assessed the prospects and the risks for the plaintiff. He had well in mind that it was his duty to look at the matter globally and to ask himself what was the present value of the risk of future financial loss. Inevitably, one is driven to the broad brush approach. He had in his mind that there was no perfect arithmetical way of calculating compensation in such a case. The law is concerned with practical affairs and, as Lord Reid said in *BTC v Gourley* [1956] A.C. 185 at 212, very often one is driven to make a very rough estimate of the damages." This approach was approved by the Court of Appeal in *Ronan v Sainsbury's Supermarkets Ltd* [2006] EWCA Civ 1074 where it was said that the approach in *Blamire* may be appropriate where the uncertainties of a case made the multiplier/multiplicand approach unworkable. See para.12–097 for the distinction between a *Blamire* award being a lump sum to represent lost future *earnings* and a *Smith v Manchester* award being a lump sum to represent loss of future *earning capacity*.

[231] In *Herring v Ministry of Defence* [2003] EWCA Civ 528; [2004] 1 All E.R. 44, at [24], Potter LJ commented: "In the situation of a young claimant who has not yet been in employment at the time of injury but is still in education or has otherwise not embarked on his career, or (as in this case) one who has taken time out from employment in order to acquire a further qualification for a desired change of direction, it may or may not be appropriate to select a specific career model in his chosen field. In this connection the court will have regard to the claimant's previous performance, expressed intentions and ambitions, the opportunities reasonably open to him and any steps he has already taken to pursue a particular path. In many cases it will not be possible to identify a specific career model and it may be necessary simply to resort to national average earnings figures for persons of the claimant's ability and qualifications in his likely field(s) of activity. In other cases, however, it may be possible with confidence to select a career model appropriate to be used as the multiplicand for calculating loss."

[232] [2012] EWCA Civ 1287; [2013] P.I.Q.R. Q1 at [20].

and inflation had been taken into account.[233] It had long been argued that that assumption was unrealistic, with the result that the multipliers were too low and claimants were being under compensated.[234]

Effect of inflation   This problem is greater in periods of high inflation, but the courts refused to make any allowance for future inflation eroding the value of an award.[235] Protection against inflation was to be sought by careful investment, the assumption being that some capital appreciation of the money invested will offset increases in the cost of living.[236] In *Lim Poh Choo v Camden and Islington Area Health Authority*[237] it was accepted, however, that in an exceptional case some allowance might be made if on the particular facts an award which ignored inflation would not result in fair compensation, although Lord Scarman commented that claimants who receive a lump sum award "are entitled to no better protection against inflation than others who have to rely on capital for their support".[238] His Lordship added that attempts to take inflation into account sought a perfection in the assessment of damages which was beyond the inherent limitations of the system.

12–085

Index-linked securities   This approach to calculating the multiplier was challenged in *Wells v Wells*,[239] on the basis that the advent of index-linked government securities provided a much fairer solution to the problem of protecting claimants from the effects of inflation. The advantage of index-linked government securities from the claimant's perspective is that they are a virtually risk-free investment and the return can be calculated with some precision. The same sum invested in equities might produce a much higher return, but might equally produce a significantly lower return. Shares are an inherently volatile investment, particularly in the short term. That volatility creates a serious risk because claimants have to sell part of the investment at regular intervals to meet their income needs. If claimants have to sell in a period when the stock market is depressed, they will have to realise a larger part of the underlying investment to produce the same sum, and as Lord Lloyd observed, "the depleted fund may never recover". What is prudent for an ordinary investor (i.e. investing in a spread of equities and more secure bonds and gilts), said Lord Lloyd, is not necessarily

12–086

---

[233] *Cookson v Knowles* [1979] A.C. 556 at 577, per Lord Fraser; *Auty v National Coal Board* [1985] 1 All E.R. 930; [1985] 1 W.L.R. 784; *Robertson v Lestrange* [1985] 1 All E.R. 950.

[234] See Kemp (1985) 101 L.Q.R. 556; Luckett and Craner [1994] J.P.I.L. 139; *Read v Harries* [1995] P.I.Q.R. Q25 at 28, per Morland J. The higher the assumed rate of return the lower the lump sum awarded.

[235] See *Taylor v O'Connor* [1971] A.C. 115; *Mitchell v Mulholland (No.2)* [1972] 1 Q.B. 65; *Cookson v Knowles* [1979] A.C. 556; *Lim Poh Choo v Camden and Islington Area Health Authority* [1980] A.C. 174.

[236] *Taylor v O'Connor* [1971] A.C. 115 at 143, per Lord Pearson.

[237] [1980] A.C. 174.

[238] This view is inconsistent with the basic principle in assessing tort damages of restoring claimants to their pre-accident positions, because if they would have had better protection from inflation if they were in employment then they are worse off as a result of the tort by now being forced to rely on investment income. This point was acknowledged by Lords Lloyd and Hutton in *Wells v Wells; Thomas v Brighton Health Authority; Page v Sheerness Steel Co. Ltd* [1999] 1 A.C. 345, hereafter *"Wells v Wells"*.

[239] [1999] 1 A.C. 345. See Goldrein (1998) 148 N.L.J. 1149.

prudent for a claimant, because an ordinary investor may be able to take a long-term view and "ride out" falls in the market until the value of equities has recovered, whereas:

> "...what the prudent plaintiff needs is an investment which will bring him the income he requires without the risks inherent in the equity market."

The House of Lords held that the claimants were entitled to be compensated on the assumption that they would invest in index-linked government securities, a view which had been recommended by the Law Commission.[240]

12–087 Claimants are not required to invest in index-linked government securities. Except for claimants who fall within the jurisdiction of the Court of Protection, the courts do not exercise a supervisory role, and claimants are normally free to spend damages awards as they see fit. But in *assessing* the level of compensation, the calculation is not to be made on the assumption that they are obliged to invest in equities. Since the average return on index-linked government securities in 1998 was approximately 3 per cent (as opposed to the assumed return of 4.5 per cent upon which the traditional approach was based) their Lordships in *Wells v Wells* indicated that, as a matter of guidance rather than precedent,[241] the appropriate discount rate (i.e. the assumed rate of return) should be 3 per cent. This would require a larger initial lump sum, which is reflected in a higher multiplier. The consequence of this change was that for seriously injured claimants awards of damages in respect of future pecuniary losses increased significantly. The rationale of investing in index-linked government securities is reflected in the Ogden Tables (now in their 7th edition) which are regularly relied upon when valuing claims and, though they have not been formally adopted by the courts, the practice was endorsed in *Wells v Wells*.[242]

12–088 **Lord Chancellor's guidance on the "discount" rate** The Damages Act 1996 s.1 permits the Lord Chancellor to give general guidance on rates of return, though leaving discretion to the courts to apply different rates where appropriate. The Damages (Personal Injury) Order 2001[243] prescribed 2.5 per cent as the rate of return that the courts should apply to calculations of future pecuniary loss (reflecting the fall in general interest rates since the decision in *Wells v Wells*). Section 1(2) of the Damages Act 1996 permits the court to adopt a different rate in special circumstances, but the Court of Appeal has made it clear such cases will be rare.[244] In *Cooke v United Bristol Health Care; Sheppard v Stibbe; Page*

---

[240] *Structured Settlements and Interim and Provisional Damages*, Law Com. No.224, 1994, paras 2.25–2.28.

[241] Different economic circumstances might justify a change to the guide figure in the future.

[242] [1999] 1 A.C. 345 at 347D, per Lord Lloyd: "The [actuarial] tables should be regarded as the starting point, rather than a check. A judge should be slow to depart from the relevant actuarial multiplier on impressionistic grounds, or by reference to a 'spread of multipliers in comparable cases', especially where the multipliers were mixed before actuarial tables were widely used." Use of the Tables was supported by the Law Commission, *Structured Settlements and Interim and Provisional Damages*, Law Com. No.224, 1994, para.2.15.

[243] SI 2001/2301.

[244] *Warriner v Warriner* [2002] EWCA Civ 81; [2002] 1 W.L.R. 1703—the set rate will only be departed from if the case falls into a category that the Lord Chancellor had not considered when

v Lee[245] the claimants sought to introduce expert evidence to the effect that earnings, care and medical costs, rise at a greater rate than the retail price index, and therefore the conventional method of assessing future loss seriously underestimates the future cost of care. The expert evidence suggested that to overcome this problem the court should adopt revised multiplicands with stepped increases over time. The Court of Appeal held that this evidence should not be introduced because it constituted an attempt to subvert the assumed rate of return set by the Lord Chancellor for the multiplier. A direct challenge to the discount rate had been rejected by the Court of Appeal in *Warriner v Warriner*[246] and it followed that an indirect attempt to challenge that rate, which undermined the operation of the Damages Act 1996 s.1, should also be rejected. The effects of inflation in claims for future loss must be catered for solely by means of the multiplier, as reflected in the discount rate. Thus, the multiplicand must be treated as an indication of the current costs at the date of trial.

In *Page v Plymouth Hospitals NHS Trust*[247] Davis J rejected the claimant's claim for the costs of investment advice and fund management charges incurred in the management of his damages on the basis that, again, it was an indirect attack on the Damages (Personal Injury) Order 2001. The discount rate had been set by reference to index-linked, gilt-edged stock and not a mixed portfolio of stocks and shares. Investment costs were in substance to be regarded as within the territory of the applicable discount rate, and thus it was inherent in the Lord Chancellor's reasons for the 2001 Order that the costs of investment advice were taken into account in setting the discount rate.[248]   **12–089**

Different discount rates for different heads of loss?   It seems highly probable   **12–090**
that but for the Damages (Personal Injury) Order 2001 the courts would have departed from the 3 per cent guidance given by the House of Lords in *Wells v Wells*. In *Simon v Helmot*[249] the Privy Council dismissed an appeal from the Court of Appeal of Guernsey (where the Damages (Personal Injury) Order 2001 does not apply) which had adopted different discount rates for different heads of loss (to reflect the evidence that different rates of inflation would apply to earnings-related future losses and for costs that were not earnings related) and included a "negative" discount rate of minus 1.5 per cent to the earnings-related losses, with a discount rate of 0.5 per cent for non-earnings related losses. The effect of the negative discount rate is that in arriving at the multiplier there should

---

recommending the rate and/or had special features shown not to have been taken into account. In *Harries v Stevenson* [2012] EWHC 3447 (QB) Morgan J held that the fact the defendant was insured by the Medical Defence Union, which could not provide reasonable security for payments under a periodical payments order, did not amount to a special circumstance that was not contemplated by the Lord Chancellor when setting the discount rate in 2001, and therefore *Warriner* applied.
[245] [2003] EWCA Civ 1370; [2004] 1 W.L.R. 251; [2004] 1 All E.R. 797.
[246] [2002] EWCA Civ 81; [2002] 1 W.L.R. 1703.
[247] [2004] EWHC 1154 (QB); [2004] 3 All E.R. 367; [2004] P.I.Q.R. Q6; [2004] Lloyd's Rep. Med. 337.
[248] See also *Eagle v Chambers (No.2)* [2004] EWCA Civ 1033; [2004] 1 W.L.R. 3081; [2005] 1 All E.R. 136, holding that panel brokers' fees charged by the Court of Protection for investment advice were not recoverable.
[249] [2012] UKPC 5; [2012] Med. L.R. 394; (2012) 126 B.M.L.R. 73.

be an addition to the number of years rather than a reduction.[250] In response to the question whether it was acceptable in principle for there to be different discount rates for different heads of loss or to apply a discount rate which is not a discount rate at all, but an adjustment of the lump sum in the reverse direction, Lord Hope said that the answer was to be found in the premise that the victim of a tort is entitled to be fully compensated.[251]

12–091   **Lord Chancellor's revised guidance on the discount rate**   Since the Lord Chancellor prescribed a discount rate of 2.5 per cent in 2001 there has been a significant change in economic conditions, including the collapse of financial markets in 2008–2009 and a prolonged period of low interest rates. In 2010 the Lord Chancellor announced that the Ministry of Justice would undertake a review of the discount rate, and Consultation Papers were issued in August 2012 and February 2013. By the Damages (Personal Injury) Order 2017[252] the Lord Chancellor set the discount rate at minus 0.75 per cent, which has had the effect of producing a substantial increase in the calculation of future losses.[253] In light of the 2017 Order the Government Actuary's Department has published supplementary tables to the Ogden Tables[254] which contain multipliers calculated at minus 0.75 per cent.

12–092   **Effect of taxation**   A problem similar to that of accounting for future inflation arises in connection with the effect of taxation. The award of damages in a personal injuries action is not itself liable to tax,[255] but the income produced by investing the award is taxable. Where claimants receive a very large award it is possible that the income generated will be subject to higher rate tax, with the

---

[250] [2012] UKPC 5; [2012] Med. L.R. 394; (2012) 126 B.M.L.R. 73 at [14].

[251] [2012] UKPC 5; [2012] Med. L.R. 394; (2012) 126 B.M.L.R. 73 at [52]. See also per Lady Hale at [60]: "The only principle of law is that the claimant should receive full compensation for the loss which he has suffered as a result of the defendant's tort, not a penny more but not a penny less"; and Lord Dyson at [118].

[252] SI 2017/206. The Order came into force on 20 March 2017.

[253] A challenge to the process by which the Lord Chancellor's decision was reached was rejected in *R. (on the application of Association of British Insurers) v Lord Chancellor* [2017] EWHC 106 (Admin); [2017] A.C.D. 34. Note, however, that following extensive lobbying the government has undertaken a consultation exercise on how the discount rate should be set in future. The government intends to introduce legislation setting out the methodology for the Lord Chancellor to set the rate by reference to expected rates of return on a low risk diversified portfolio of investments rather than very low risk investments; taking into account the actual investment practices of claimants and the investments available to them. After an initial review when the legislation comes into force the rate would be reviewed at least every three years. See the Ministry of Justice response to the consultation exercise, *The Personal Injury Discount Rate: How it should be set in future*, 7 September 2017 (available at *https://www.gov.uk/government/uploads/system/uploads/attachment_data/file/642810/ discount-rate-response-consultation-web.pdf*).

[254] See para.12–081. The Ogden Tables can be found at *http://www.gov.uk/government/uploads/ system/uploads/attachment_data/file/245859/ogden_tables_7th_edition.pdf* and the Supplementary Tables are at *http://www.gov.uk/government/uploads/system/uploads/attachment_data/file/599837/ Actuarial_tables_for_use_in_personal_injury_and_fatal_accident_cases_7th_edition_ Supplementary_Tables.pdf*.

[255] *British Transport Commission v Gourley* [1956] A.C. 185. Income tax is not payable in respect of periodical payments of personal injury damages: Income Tax (Trading and Other Income) Act 2005 s.731.

effect that the combined fund of capital and income from which claimants must meet their annual loss may be inadequate. In *Hodgson v Trapp*[256] the House of Lords held that it was not permissible, having selected a multiplier on the conventional basis, then to increase the multiplier to take account of the effects of higher rates of tax. Lord Oliver reiterated that the process of assessing future pecuniary loss cannot, by its nature, be a precise science. Future taxation was just as uncertain as future inflation, and so predicting what might happen to future political, economic or fiscal policies required not the services of an actuary or an accountant, but those of a prophet. There was no justification for singling out taxation for special treatment when it was merely one of the many imponderables that have to be taken into account in the conventional method of assessing damages.[257]

As in *Lim Poh Choo*, their Lordships accepted that there might be very exceptional cases where special allowance might have to be made for inflation and taxation,[258] although Lord Oliver observed that it was difficult to envisage circumstances in which something so inherently uncertain could be proved to the satisfaction of the court. Possibly it could tip the balance in favour of the selection of a higher multiplier as part of the assessment of all the uncertain factors that have to be taken into account, but it would not be proper to make a specific addition to the multiplier on account of this one factor. Moreover, when considering the effect of higher rate tax on the damages award the court must be careful to look only at the damages awarded for future loss (whether for prospective loss of earnings or the cost of future care) to which the multiplier method is appropriate. Only the income from that fund would be relevant to the question of higher rate taxation. If, for example, the claimant chose to invest the damages awarded for non-pecuniary loss in order to supplement his income, and this put him into a higher tax bracket, that would not be a reason for increasing the award for loss of future earnings and future care.

12–093

(iii)   The lost years

Where the claimant's life expectancy has been reduced by his injuries this may well have reduced the period during which he would have been earning in the future. In *Oliver v Ashman*[259] the Court of Appeal held that the losses incurred in these "lost years" (the period between his expected date of death and the date that he would have stopped working but for the tort) were not recoverable, on the basis that a claimant cannot suffer a loss during a period when he will be dead. This rule created a problem for claimants with dependants because of the

12–094

---

[256] [1989] A.C. 807.
[257] [1989] A.C. 807 at 835.
[258] A point which was accepted in *Wells v Wells* [1999] 1 A.C. 345—see the speech of Lord Steyn. See *Van Oudenhoven v Griffin Inns Ltd* [2000] 1 W.L.R. 1413, CA, where an argument that higher rates of taxation in Holland justified either a higher multiplier or a reduced discount rate was rejected on the facts. In any event, said the Court of Appeal, where it was argued that the incidence of foreign taxation made the case exceptional, the court would also take into account corresponding advantages in the country concerned, such as a lower cost of living or lower indirect taxation, or the possibility of a higher rate of return on investments.
[259] [1962] 2 Q.B. 210.

interrelationship with the Fatal Accidents Act. Normally, where victims of a tort die as a result of injuries their dependants have a claim against the tortfeasor for their financial loss under the Fatal Accidents Act 1976. Such a claim is only available, however, where at the date of the death the victim would have had a right of action against the tortfeasor. If, while still alive, the deceased had obtained a judgment against the tortfeasor or settled the claim, then on death there is no subsisting right of action and the dependants have no claim under the Act. Thus, *Oliver v Ashman* penalised the claimant's dependants, since their dependency in the lost years would generally have been met from the claimant's earnings during that period. It was this consideration which led the House of Lords to overrule *Oliver v Ashman in Pickett v British Rail Engineering Ltd.*[260] Damages for prospective loss of earnings will be awarded for the whole of the claimant's pre-accident working life expectancy, subject to a deduction for the money that the claimant would have spent on his own (not his dependants') living expenses during the lost years. His own living expenses will not be incurred and therefore they are not a real loss.[261]

12–095 Although the objective of *Pickett v British Rail Engineering Ltd* was, in effect, to protect the interests of dependants, where a lump sum award is made there is no way of ensuring that the claimant does in fact use the damages to make provision for his dependants. However, following the introduction of the periodical payments regime the court has the option of making an order directing that payment be made to dependants after a claimant's death.[262] With a lump sum payment claimants are also entitled to an award covering the lost years even if they have no dependants. Where the claimant has an established pattern of earnings it will be easier to make an appropriate calculation. There would appear to be no reason in principle why the loss of a pension should not also be recoverable on the basis of the ruling in *Pickett*.[263]

12–096 **Young children** In the case of a young single person the award is likely to be modest to reflect the high degree of speculation involved.[264] Exceptionally a young child may have a claim for loss of earnings in the lost years,[265] but though in principle the loss is recoverable the speculative nature of the loss will often

---

[260] [1980] A.C. 136.

[261] See *Harris v Empress Motors Ltd* [1983] 3 All E.R. 561; [1984] 1 W.L.R. 212 and *Phipps v Brooks Dry Cleaning Services Ltd* [1996] P.I.Q.R. Q100 on the calculation of the living expenses; *White v London Transport Executive* [1982] Q.B. 489; *Adsett v West* [1983] Q.B. 826; *Wilson v Stag* (1986) 136 N.L.J. 47; Evans and Stanton (1984) 134 N.L.J. 515, 553; Kelly [2000] J.P.I.L. 137.

[262] CPR r.41.8(2). This may be used, for example, to provide for school fees but otherwise may, in practical terms, be of limited use in comparison to the desirability of a lump sum.

[263] *JR v Sheffield Teaching Hospitals NHS Foundation Trust* [2017] EWHC 1245 (QB); [2017] P.I.Q.R. Q3 at [22] per William Davis J.

[264] *Harris v Empress Motors Ltd* [1983] 3 All E.R. 561; [1984] 1 W.L.R. 212; *Adsett v West* [1983] Q.B. 826. It may be that where the lost years claim is highly speculative, it is better simply to make a small adjustment to the multiplier (adding 1 or a half) as applied to the full multiplicand, rather than attempting to speculate on notional earnings and notional living expenses: *Housecroft v Burnett* [1986] 1 All E.R. 332 at 345, per O'Connor LJ.

[265] *Gammell v Wilson* [1982] A.C. 27 at 78.

result in an assessment of nil damages.[266] In *Iqbal v Whipps Cross University Hospital NHS Trust*[267] the Court of Appeal held that though *Pickett v British Rail Engineering Ltd* did not in principle restrict a claim for the lost years to adults, with or without dependants, a view reinforced by *Gammell v Wilson*,[268] the trial judge was not entitled to ignore the ruling of the Court of Appeal in *Croke v Wiseman* that in the case of young children the uncertainty of assessing the award should result in a nil assessment unless there were exceptional circumstances. The judge's attempt to distinguish *Croke* on the basis that actuarial science had moved on since 1981 was misplaced. Although *Croke* was not consistent with the decisions of the House of Lords in *Pickett* and *Gammell*, the judge (and the Court of Appeal) were bound to follow *Croke*, and it was for the House of Lords to correct any error.[269] In *JR v Sheffield Teaching Hospitals NHS Foundation Trust*[270] Davis J distinguished *Croke v Wiseman* on the basis that the claimant was not a catastrophically injured child, but a 24-year-old man who could engage with others. Thus, pure speculation was not required in order to assess the lost years claim. Davis J rejected the defendants' argument that, given that his injuries were caused at birth, the claimant could have litigated when he was seven years old (the age of the claimant in *Croke*) or nine (the age of the claimant in *Iqbal v Whipps Cross University Hospital NHS Trust*) and the mere fact that he was now an adult should not change the position. The claimant's adulthood was not arbitrary, but a fact which should not be ignored. There was no reason not to apply the principles in *Pickett v British Rail Engineering Ltd*, and it was not necessary to show that a claimant has or will have dependants to establish a lost years claim.[271]

(iv) Loss of earning capacity

Where people suffer permanent disabilities which affect their ability to earn in the future at the same rate as they earned before the injuries, then they may or may not suffer a loss of earnings. The loss may be total if they are unable to work at all, or partial if they are able to take a less remunerative job. In some instances, although the injuries have affected their ability to earn, they suffer no loss of earnings because their employer continues to employ them at the same rate of pay. In these circumstances claimants are entitled to damages for their loss of

12–097

---

[266] *Croke v Wiseman* [1981] 3 All E.R. 852; [1982] 1 W.L.R. 71; *Connolly v Camden and Islington Area Health Authority* [1981] 3 All E.R. 250.
[267] [2007] EWCA Civ 1190; [2008] P.I.Q.R. P9; [2008] LS Law Med. 22.
[268] [1982] A.C. 27, HL.
[269] [2007] EWCA Civ 1190; [2008] P.I.Q.R. P9; [2008] LS Law Med. 22 at [64]. See also *Totham v King's College Hospital NHS Foundation Trust* [2015] EWHC 97 (QB); [2015] Med. L.R. 55 where, despite serious reservations, Laing J applied *Croke v Wiseman*. *Totham* is discussed by J. McQuater [2015] J.P.I.L. C155.
[270] [2017] EWHC 1245 (QB); [2017] P.I.Q.R. Q3; discussed by C. Ettinger [2017] J.P.I.L. C166.
[271] [2017] EWHC 1245 (QB); [2017] P.I.Q.R. Q3 at [33]–[37]. Davis J also rejected the defendants' argument that the decision would give young claimants an incentive to delay issuing proceedings until adulthood, pointing out that the claimant's parents had struggled to look after him in inadequate accommodation without any real assistance for over 20 years, and no-one in their position would delay issuing proceedings to the child's adulthood in order to obtain a lost years claim "of relatively modest proportions". The decision is currently under appeal.

earning capacity if there is a real risk (as opposed to a fanciful or speculative risk) that they could lose their existing employment in the future, because their capacity to find a job with equivalent remuneration has been reduced, and they are now at a disadvantage in the labour market.[272] If the court makes a separate assessment for loss of earning capacity and loss of future earnings, care must be taken to avoid any duplication in the award.[273]

12–098   It has been said that there is no real difference between damages for loss of earning capacity and damages for future loss of earnings.[274] A reduction in the claimant's present earning capacity is ultimately likely to have some impact on the level of future earnings. In practice, however, awards for loss of earning capacity are more impressionistic and less susceptible to the multiplier method of calculation, though in an appropriate case the multiplier method can be used.[275] This will involve using the Ogden Tables which, since the 6th edition, have included Tables which in addition to life expectancy and early receipt of the money also adjust for claimants' pre-accident work record, their pre-accident educational achievements and their disabilities. Where, however, the disabilities are minor and the claimant is still in employment, the Tables are likely to give an incorrect assessment and the court should:

> "...make a broad assessment of the present value of the claimant's likely future loss as a result of handicap on the labour market, following the guidance given in *Smith v Manchester* and *Moeliker*."[276]

12–099   The assessment of loss of earning capacity is particularly speculative in the case of children where there may be little or no evidence about what the child may

---

[272] *Smith v Manchester Corporation* (1974) 17 K.I.R. 1; *Moeliker v Reyrolle & Co. Ltd* [1977] 1 All E.R. 9; Ritchie [1994] J.P.I.L. 103. This is a two-stage test: (1) was there a substantial or real risk that the claimant would lose his present job at some time before the end of his working life? and (2) if so, what is the present value of that future risk? A risk can be real even though it is unlikely, and substantial does not mean that it is likely to happen on the balance of probabilities: *Robson v Liverpool City Council* [1993] P.I.Q.R. Q78, CA. It is good practice to plead expressly a claim for *Smith v Manchester* damages, but where sufficient facts about the claimant's medical condition are pleaded to make it clear that, in the eyes of most potential employers, the claimant's value as an employee has been reduced, that will be sufficient: *Thorn v Powergen plc* [1997] P.I.Q.R. Q71, CA.

[273] *Clarke v Rotax Aircraft Equipment Ltd* [1975] 1 W.L.R. 1570; *Ronan v Sainsbury's Supermarkets Ltd* [2006] EWCA Civ 1074.

[274] *Foster v Tyne and Wear County Council* [1986] 1 All E.R. 567, 571–572; *Tait v Pearson* [1996] P.I.Q.R. Q92; *Royal Commission on Civil Liability and Compensation for Personal Injury*, Cmnd.7054 (1978), Vol.I, para.338.

[275] *Dhaliwal v Personal Representatives of Hunt (Deceased)* [1995] P.I.Q.R. Q56 at 59; *Tait v Pearson* [1996] P.I.Q.R. Q92. For an argument that the courts should adopt a formulaic approach to assessing the loss, rather than an "impressionistic" approach see Chippindall [2001] J.P.I.L. 37.

[276] *Billett v Ministry of Defence* [2015] EWCA Civ 773; [2016] P.I.Q.R. Q1 at [99] per Jackson LJ. The award for loss of earning capacity in *Billet* was reduced from £99,000 (calculated by reference to the Ogden Tables) to £45,000 as consequence of this approach, on the basis that this represented two years' loss of earnings. See V. Wass, "*Billett v Ministry of Defence*: a second bite" [2015] J.P.I.L. 243; N. Poole and L. Collignon, "Calculating Future Loss of Earnings Using Ogden Tables A–D" [2017] J.P.I.L. 26. *Billett* was applied in *Murphy v Ministry of Defence* [2016] EWHC 3 (QB) where the disability was "modest" and the claimant was in secure employment.

eventually do for a living.[277] The solution is to award only moderate sums in this situation, although there is no tariff or conventional award for loss of earning capacity and each case must be considered on its own facts.[278] In *Foster v Tyne and Wear County Council*,[279] for example, an award of £35,000 to an adult claimant under this head was upheld by the Court of Appeal.[280] Where an assessment of loss of earning capacity is made in respect of claimants' contribution to the profits of a business in which they are a partner, the loss should be assessed on the basis of their actual contribution to the running of the business, not the internal arrangements in the accounts agreed with the Inland Revenue for tax purposes.[281]

(c) Deductions[282]

A person who suffers personal injury may receive financial support from a number of sources other than tort damages.[283] The most common source is social security benefits, but others include sick pay, pensions, private insurance and charitable donations. The compensatory principle applied to the assessment of tort damages should mean that, in theory, any receipt of financial assistance from

12–100

---

[277] See *S v Distillers Co. (Biochemicals) Ltd* [1970] 1 W.L.R. 114; *Joyce v Yeomans* [1981] 1 W.L.R. 549; *Croke v Wiseman* [1981] 3 All E.R. 852; [1982] 1 W.L.R. 71; *Mitchell v Liverpool Area Health Authority*, The Times, 17 June 1985. In *Cronin v Redbridge London Borough Council*, The Times, 20 May 1987 the Court of Appeal complained that this was an exercise in unsatisfactory guesswork. See Denyer [1992] Fam. Law 207 and Denyer [1997] J.P.I.L. 244 on the calculation of loss of earnings for injured children.
[278] *Page v Enfield and Haringey Area Health Authority*, The Times, 7 November 1986. The court may be willing to use the multiplier method for assessment of loss of earnings of even a young child, based on a multiplicand of the national average wage: see *Croke v Wiseman* [1981] 3 All E.R. 852; [1982] 1 W.L.R. 71; *Moser v Enfield and Haringey Area Health Authority* (1983) 133 N.L.J. 105. In *Aboul-Hosn v Trustees of the Italian Hospital* (1987) 137 N.L.J. 1164 an 18-year-old with four "A" Levels and a place at university was held to have a good prospect of earning £18,000 per annum, plus a company car.
[279] [1986] 1 All E.R. 567.
[280] See also *Morgan v UPS Ltd* [2008] EWCA Civ 375. Although the Court of Appeal accepted that a Recorder's award for loss of earning capacity (*Smith v Manchester*) had been generous, and was difficult to reconcile with some of his findings about the claimant's aptitude and appetite for work, the award was not so generous that it should be interfered with. It was stressed that the appropriate approach to future loss of earnings varied with the circumstances of each particular claimant. It was also said that the fair assessment of damages in such cases would be enhanced if awards called *Smith v Manchester* were confined to situations analogous to those in that case.
[281] *Ward v Newalls Insulation Co. Ltd* [1998] 2 All E.R. 690; [1998] 1 W.L.R. 1722, CA, where the claimant, W, contributed 50 per cent with his other partner, E, but for tax purposes it was declared that there were four partners, W, E and their respective spouses.
[282] See generally, R. Lewis, *Deducting Benefits from Damages for Personal Injury* (Oxford: Oxford University Press, 1999).
[283] The Pearson Commission found that the tort system provided about 25 per cent of the total compensation paid out to the victims of personal injury: *Royal Commission on Civil Liability and Compensation for Personal Injury*, Cmnd.7054 (1978), Vol.I, para.44.

another source is deducted in full from the award of damages, since they reduce the claimant's loss. There are, however, a number of competing policy factors which may justify non-deduction.[284]

(i)   Social security benefits[285]

12–101   In principle, benefits paid by the state in the form of social security should be deducted from damages awards on the basis that damages are meant to be compensatory and claimants should not be in a better financial position than they would have been but for the tort. By 1988, although there were statutory exceptions, the common law had essentially reached the position that most social security benefits should be fully deducted. The Social Security Act 1989, however, introduced a scheme for recoupment by the state from tortfeasors of certain social security benefits paid to claimants.[286] This system was significantly amended by the Social Security (Recovery of Benefits) Act 1997, but the pre-1989 common law rules remain potentially relevant to any case which is not covered by the 1997 Act.[287]

12–102   Under the pre-1989 rules the extent of deduction of benefits depended to a large extent upon whether the case was governed by statute or the common law. By s.2(1) of the Law Reform (Personal Injuries) Act 1948[288] half the value of certain benefits was deducted from the damages for loss of earnings, up to five years after the accident.[289] Where the matter was free from statutory regulation the courts had increasingly taken the view that benefits should be fully deducted in order to avoid double recovery by the claimant.[290] Most benefits have been held to be fully deductible, including attendance allowance and mobility allowance,[291] statutory sick pay,[292] unemployment benefit,[293] reduced earnings allowance,[294]

---

[284] For an analysis of the policy issues see R. Lewis, *Deducting Benefits from Damages for Personal Injury* (Oxford: Oxford University Press, 1999), pp.15–47, also at Lewis (1998) 18 L.S. 15; Law Commission Consultation Paper No.147, *Damages for Personal Injury: Collateral Benefits*, 1997; Law Commission Report, *Damages for Personal Injury: Medical, Nursing and Other Expenses; Collateral Benefits*, Law Com. No.262, 1999.

[285] See also Ch.5 of *Kemp and Kemp, The Quantum of Damages* (London: Sweet & Maxwell).

[286] The recoupment provisions of the Social Security Act 1989 were subsequently incorporated into Pt IV of the Social Security Administration Act 1992.

[287] Over time the names of some benefits have changed, and some have been abolished or replaced by new benefits. Where the rules on deductions are governed by a statutory provision then changes to the benefits will have to be reflected in the legislation in order for those rules to apply; but where the common law applies the courts will look to the nature of the benefit in assessing whether the principle of deductibility applies. For example, the renaming of supplementary benefit as income support made no difference to the common law principle of deductibility.

[288] This provision was repealed by the Social Security (Recovery of Benefits) Act 1997 Sch.3 para.1.

[289] But after five years these benefits were not deducted at all: *Jackman v Corbett* [1988] Q.B. 154; *Almond v Leeds Western Health Authority* [1990] 1 Med. L.R. 370.

[290] *Hodgson v Trapp* [1989] A.C. 807 at 823, per Lord Bridge. The Pearson Commission also recommended that there should be no overlap between tort damages and social security payments: *Royal Commission on Civil Liability and Compensation for Personal Injury*, Cmnd.7054 (1978), Vol.I, para.482.

[291] *Hodgson v Trapp* [1989] A.C. 807, overruling *Bowker v Rose* (1978) 122 S.J. 147.

[292] *Palfrey v Greater London Council* [1985] I.C.R. 437.

past receipts of income support and family credit,[295] and, in a claim for the cost of maintaining a child following a failed sterilisation operation, child benefit.[296] State retirement pension may be an exception to the principle of full deductibility.[297]

Recoupment of benefits Under the "recoupment" rules the amount of any "relevant benefit" paid or likely to be paid to or for the claimant in respect of the accident, injury or disease was disregarded in assessing damages in respect of an accident, injury or disease.[298] In other words, the benefit was *not* deducted in calculating damages payable by the defendant. The person paying compensation (the "compensator") in respect of an accident, injury or disease suffered by the "victim" was not allowed to make the payment until the Secretary of State had furnished him with a certificate of the total benefit. The compensator then deducted from the payment a sum equal to the gross amount of any relevant benefits paid or likely to be paid to or for the victim during the "relevant period" in respect of that accident, injury or disease. That deduction was then paid to the Secretary of State. Even where the damages were reduced to take account of the claimant's contributory negligence the whole of the "relevant benefits" had to be deducted. The "relevant period" was five years from the date of the accident or injury, or in the case of a disease five years from the first claim for a relevant benefit consequent upon the disease, but a payment of compensation in final discharge of the claim before the end of the five years brought the "relevant period" to an end. After the relevant period the recoupment provisions did not apply, but under the legislation the relevant benefits were still to be disregarded in assessing damages and so were not deducted. This produced double recovery in any case where the claimant's entitlement to relevant benefits continued after the settlement of the damages claim (indirectly encouraging early settlement) and in any case where the entitlement to benefit exceeded five years (which would tend to be the more serious cases).

12–103

On the other hand, the recoupment rules could work hardship for claimants. Certain compensation payments were exempted, most notably "small payments"

12–104

---

[293] *Nabi v British Leyland (UK) Ltd* [1980] 1 All E.R. 667; *Westwood v Secretary of State for Employment* [1985] A.C. 20.
[294] *Flanagan v Watts Blake Bearne & Co. plc* [1992] P.I.Q.R. Q144.
[295] *Lincoln v Hayman* [1982] 2 All E.R. 819; [1982] 1 W.L.R. 488; *Gaskill v Preston* [1981] 3 All E.R. 427. Supplementary benefit and family income supplement were replaced by income support and family credit respectively by the Social Security Act 1986 ss.20–22. The possibility of future receipts of these benefits should be ignored because an award of damages for prospective loss of earnings will probably remove the claimant's entitlement to the benefit: *Gaskill v Preston*, above.
[296] *Emeh v Kensington and Chelsea Area Health Authority* [1985] Q.B. 1012 at 1022. Note that following the decision in *McFarlane v Tayside Health Board* [2000] 2 A.C. 59 that parents cannot claim for the cost of raising a healthy child the issue of deducting child benefit is redundant. Where the claim is for the cost of raising a disabled child (in which the ordinary costs of raising a healthy child are deducted from the damages award) child benefit is not deducted: see *Rand v East Dorset Health Authority (No.2)* [2001] P.I.Q.R. Q1; [2000] Lloyd's Rep. Med. 377, para.12–149, where the point was conceded by the defendants.
[297] *Hewson v Downs* [1970] 1 Q.B. 73. It is doubtful, however, whether this decision can survive the reasoning in *Hodgson v Trapp* [1989] A.C. 807.
[298] Social Security Administration Act 1992 s.81(5).

(payments under £2,500). Under the recoupment rules any relevant benefit could be recouped against the whole award of damages. Thus, a claimant's non-pecuniary losses could be set against benefits received, with the result that in some cases claimants received no damages at all. In many instances, insurers would make an offer of settlement under £2,500 which the claimant would effectively be forced to accept because a higher settlement would mean that all the damages would be recouped. This meant that claimants did not receive an award of damages that reflected their true loss under normal tort rules, and the Secretary of State did not recoup any social security benefits either, with a resulting windfall to insurers. Moreover, once the level of benefits reached the point at which they equalled or exceeded the damages, that was the limit of the compensator's liability to repay to the Secretary of State the benefits paid as a result of the accident/disease.

12–105   Another problem could arise where the claimant was unemployed and in receipt of benefits prior to the accident, and the benefits became "recoupable" by virtue of the accident, even though there was no loss of earnings claim against the defendant because the claimant was unemployed with little prospect of obtaining employment.[299] This effectively allowed the compensator to set off the social security benefits (which the claimant would probably have received in any event) against any damages for non-pecuniary loss. The solution devised by the courts to this situation was for the claimant to claim as part of the special damages the loss of "non-recoupable benefit" to which the claimant had been entitled prior to the accident.[300]

12–106   **Recovery of benefits**   The Social Security (Recovery of Benefits) Act 1997[301] made important changes to this system. Benefits are no longer "recouped" they are "recovered" from the compensator. Any "recoverable benefits" paid to the victim of an accident, injury or disease in respect of the accident, injury or disease in the "relevant period" are recoverable from the compensator. The two most significant changes were that: (1) only certain specified benefits are recoverable against specified heads of damages; and (2) the compensator is liable to pay to the Secretary of State an amount equal to the total amount of the recoverable benefits, which can exceed the amount that would have been payable as compensation.[302]

---

[299] *Hassall v Secretary of State for Social Security* [1995] 3 All E.R. 909; [1995] 1 W.L.R. 812, CA.
[300] [1995] 3 All E.R. 909; [1995] 1 W.L.R. 812, CA; *Neal v Bingle* [1998] Q.B. 466, CA, a decision on the construction of s.81(5) of the Social Security Administration Act 1992. This problem does not arise under the system of recovery of benefits introduced by the Social Security (Recovery of Benefits) Act 1997 where there is no loss of earnings claim because benefits received in respect of loss of income can only be recovered against loss of earnings. If there is no loss of earnings there can be no deduction under that head.
[301] The Act applies retrospectively to all settlements made or judgments given on or after 6 October 1997: s.2. The Act is discussed in detail by Dismore [1998] J.P.I.L. 14. For the procedure on appeals see the Social Security (Recovery of Benefits) Act 1997 ss.10–14 (as amended), and the Social Security and Child Support (Decisions and Appeals) Regulations 1999 (SI 1999/991).
[302] Social Security (Recovery of Benefits) Act 1997 s.6.

Heads of loss from which specified benefits are recoverable   Schedule 2 of   **12–107**
the 1997 Act sets out the heads of damages against which the specified benefits[303]
can be recovered. There has been an attempt to relate the benefits to the nature of
the loss for which the damages have been awarded. Thus, the following benefits
can be recovered only against that part of the award of compensation relating to
loss of earnings during the relevant period: universal credit, disablement pension;
employment and support allowance; incapacity benefit; income support;
invalidity pension and allowance; jobseeker's allowance; reduced earnings
allowance; severe disablement allowance; sickness benefit; statutory sick pay[304];
unemployability supplement; and unemployment benefit. The following benefits
are recoverable only against the compensation for the *cost of care* incurred during
the relevant period: attendance allowance; daily living component of personal
independence payment; care component of disability living allowance; and
disablement pension increase. Where care is provided gratuitously the claimant is
normally entitled to recover as special damages the reasonable value of that care,
the damages being held on trust for the person providing the care.[305] The
compensator is entitled to offset the benefits reimbursed to the Secretary of State
under this heading against the liability to the claimant in respect of the damages
for gratuitous care.[306] Finally, the following benefits are recoverable only against
the compensation for *loss of mobility* during the relevant period: mobility
allowance[307]; mobility component of personal independence payment; mobility
component of disability living allowance.

In the absence of agreement between the parties, the court has to specify the   **12–108**
amount of the damages attributable to "earnings lost during the relevant period",
the "cost of care incurred during the relevant period" and "loss of mobility during
the relevant period".[308] The first two heads are normally calculated separately,

---

[303] Note that some of the benefits listed in Sch.2 have been replaced and are no longer payable.
[304] Only 80 per cent of payments of statutory sick pay paid between 6 April 1991 and 5 April 1994 is
recoverable, and none is recoverable from 6 April 1994: Social Security (Recovery of Benefits) Act
1997 Sch.2 para.2.
[305] See *Hunt v Severs* [1994] 2 A.C. 350, paras 12–074–12–075.
[306] *Griffiths v British Coal Corporation* [2001] EWCA Civ 336; [2001] 1 W.L.R. 1493.
[307] Which ceased to be paid from 6 April 1992.
[308] Social Security (Recovery of Benefits) Act 1997 s.15. In *Chatwin v Lowther* [2003] EWCA Civ
729; [2003] P.I.Q.R. Q5 the Court of Appeal considered the meaning of the term "loss of earnings" in
the context of recovery of benefits. The claimant was self-employed, but making a loss prior to the
accident, and was rendered unable to work as a result of the accident. She reasonably continued to
incur an expense of the business for a period after the accident (rent on commercial premises) and was
therefore awarded a sum in partial compensation for this expense (five sevenths). The Court of Appeal
held (Hale LJ dissenting) that the defendant was entitled to offset relevant benefits in respect of "loss
of earnings" (namely severe disablement allowance) against the award for the rent. As Brooke LJ
observed, at [48], the damages award allowed the claimant to recover that part of her earnings which
would have been available to go towards the rent, and "by this route she was entitled to recover the
annual sums she would have earned which would have covered five-sevenths of her rent liability".
That was to be regarded as compensation for earnings lost within the meaning of that expression in
Sch.2 of the Social Security (Recovery of Benefits) Act 1997. Wilson J said, at [42], that: "I consider
that the law applies the same principle when it compensates for an increase in business loss from
£2,000 p.a. to £7,000 p.a. as when it compensates for a reduction in business profit from £5,000 to nil.
Yet, were the claimant's contentions valid, the amount of severe disablement allowance (and other
state benefits) received in respect of the accident would fall to be deducted from the amount payable

but compensation for loss of mobility could include pecuniary losses (e.g. walking aids, adaptations to vehicles, etc.) and non-pecuniary loss (e.g. loss of amenity from the inability to get around as easily). The intention behind the amendments, however, was that benefits should not be deducted from awards for non-pecuniary loss.

12–109   **Where recoverable benefit exceeds claimant's loss**   If the amount of recoverable benefit is greater than the amount deductible from the compensation payment, the compensator is liable to repay the additional amount to the Secretary of State. For example, say the claimant has losses of £12,000 in respect of lost earnings, and £10,000 in respect of pain and suffering, and has received £15,000 in employment and support allowance and £5,000 in respect of the daily living component of personal independence payment as a result of the injuries he received. The claimant's compensation for loss of earnings will be reduced to nil, because the employment and support allowance is a benefit listed against loss of earnings and can be set off against the lost earnings element. Neither the balance of £3,000 employment and support allowance (£15,000 minus £12,000) nor the £5,000 daily living component of personal independence payment can be deducted from the compensation for pain and suffering. The claimant therefore receives £10,000 for pain and suffering. The compensator is liable to pay £20,000 of recoverable benefit to the Secretary of State. Thus, the compensator pays in total £30,000, of which the claimant receives £10,000 and the Secretary of State £20,000. This exceeds the total compensation (£22,000 for loss of earnings and pain and suffering) that would have been payable to the claimant in the absence of social security benefits.

12–110   **Exempted payments**   The 1997 Act provides that certain compensation payments are exempted payments.[309] Although the Act provides for small payments to be exempted no figure has been prescribed in Regulations. The small payments limit had been used by insurers to drive down offers of settlement under the old recoupment system.

12–111   **Ignore specified benefits when assessing damages**   The listed benefits under the compensation recovery scheme are disregarded when assessing damages,[310]

---

to the claimant by the defendant only in the latter case; and in the former case the conjunction of state benefits and unreduced payment to her by the defendant would put the claimant in a better position than she would have enjoyed in the absence of the accident."

[309] Social Security (Recovery of Benefits) Act 1997 Sch.1; and Social Security (Recovery of Benefits) Regulations 1997 reg.2 (SI 1997/2205). These include, inter alia: small payments; awards under the criminal injuries compensation scheme; payments under the Powers of Criminal Courts (Sentencing) Act 2000 s.130; payments made in respect of Fatal Accidents Act 1976 claims; payments under the Vaccine Damage Payments Act 1979; payments under accident insurance policies entered into by the victim before the accident; any redundancy payments taken into account in assessing damages; payments from certain trusts; contractual sums paid by employers to their employees in respect of a period of incapacity for work; and, so much of the payment as is referable to costs.

[310] Social Security (Recovery of Benefits) Act 1997 s.17. Thus, where a defendant makes a payment into court setting out the gross figure for compensation, and identifying the recoverable benefits payable to the Secretary of State, and the claimant accepts the payment into court, but the amount of recoverable benefit is subsequently reduced to nil following an appeal, the claimant is entitled to the

and there is no recovery of benefits paid after the date of settlement or after five years, whichever is the sooner,[311] thus retaining the advantage of early settlement for claimants, and the element of overcompensation for those claimants who continue to receive benefits in respect of the accident after settlement. This overcompensation is also reflected in the assessment of interest on damages since in *Wisely v John Fulton (Plumbers) Ltd; Wadey v Surrey County Council*[312] the House of Lords held that by virtue of s.17 receipt of benefit is to be disregarded when calculating interest. Thus, a claimant is entitled to interest on past loss of earnings, without bringing into account the fact that some of that loss of earnings was met by receipt of benefits. Where, however, the claimant has received recoverable benefits which exceed the damages payable under a particular head of damages, such as loss of earnings, with the result that the defendant is required to reimburse the Secretary of State for benefits paid to the claimant which exceed the damages for which the defendant would otherwise have been liable, the defendant is entitled to offset the liability to pay the claimant interest on that head of damages against the "excess" benefits repaid to the Secretary of State.[313]

Causal link   There has to be a causal link between the claimant's entitlement to the relevant benefits and the accident, injury or disease which gives rise to the claim for compensation, for recovery of benefits to apply.[314] The causal link does not have to be a "but for" cause. Provided that the accident, injury or disease was *a* cause of the payment of benefit then the benefit has been paid "in respect of" the accident, injury or disease. Where the claimant was in receipt of benefits before the accident and continues to receive the same benefits after the accident, the benefit may be attributable to the accident.[315] The causation issue not infrequently gives rise to disputes between the Secretary of State and defendants

12–112

---

gross amount of the payment into court. The defendant cannot amend the notice of payment into court in order to delete any reference to the recoverable benefits: *Hilton International Hotels (UK) Ltd v Smith* [2001] P.I.Q.R. P197, QBD. Social Security (Recovery of Benefits) Act 1997 s.17 precludes the defendant from insisting that any of the benefits set out in Sch.2 of the Act should be used to mitigate the claimant's loss, and so a claimant is not obliged to invest receipts of mobility allowance in the Motability scheme: *Eagle v Chambers (No.2)* [2004] EWCA Civ 1033; [2004] 1 W.L.R. 3081; [2005] 1 All E.R. 136. For consideration of the complex interaction between the rules on recovery of benefits and CPR Pt 36 payments where the claimant has been found to have been contributorily negligent and the question arises as to whether the claimant has beaten the defendant's Pt 36 payment for the purpose of assessing costs; see *Williams v Devon County Council* [2003] EWCA Civ 365; [2003] P.I.Q.R. Q4.

[311] Social Security (Recovery of Benefits) Act 1997 s.3, which defines the "relevant period".

[312] [2000] 1 W.L.R. 820; [2000] 2 All E.R. 545.

[313] *Griffiths v British Coal Corporation* [2001] EWCA Civ 336; [2001] 1 W.L.R. 1493.

[314] This is the effect of Social Security (Recovery of Benefits) Act 1997 s.1(1)(b).

[315] *Hassall v Secretary of State for Social Security* [1995] 3 All E.R. 909; [1995] 1 W.L.R. 812, CA—income support paid to the claimant who was unemployed at the date of the accident and already in receipt of income support was paid "in respect of" the accident. So where a claimant accepts a sum from the defendant in respect of loss of earnings over a shorter period than the certificate of relevant benefit covers, the benefit is nonetheless recoverable provided that it was paid in consequence of the accident, injury or disease giving rise to the claim for compensation. The fact that the claimant reluctantly accepted a "reduced" payment into court because he was under financial pressure is irrelevant where the benefit he has received is all related to the injuries he sustained in the accident: *Re R (Social Security Claimant)* [1993] P.I.Q.R. P254 (a decision under the old "recoupment" rules).

and their insurers. Where, for example, benefit has been paid to the claimant as a result of incapacity for work arising out of an accident for a period of, say, three years, but the medical evidence in the civil action indicates that the claimant was unfit for work for only six months, the Secretary of State will often have issued a certificate of recoverable benefits to cover the three-year period. The defendant will dispute the total amount of the recoverable benefit stated on the certificate, but although the amount can be reviewed by the Secretary of State,[316] in practice this will commonly lead to an appeal to a first-tier tribunal which can only take place after the claim has been finally disposed of and the recoverable benefits paid to the Secretary of State.[317] If the tribunal concludes that the accident, injury or disease was not actually the cause of the disablement in respect of which benefit (such as disablement benefit following an industrial accident) has been paid, or that the accident, injury or disease did not cause the claimant to be incapable of work (where benefits have been paid in respect of that incapacity) the benefits are not recoverable.[318] In other words, if benefit has been mistakenly paid to the claimant and included in the certificate of recoverable benefits, it is open to the compensator to appeal the certificate on the grounds of lack of causation.

12–113   A further complication[319] arising from a decision of a tribunal that the benefit, or part of it, contained in the Secretary of State's certificate of recoverable benefit is not recoverable (for example because there is no causal link between the payment of benefit and the defendant's tort) is: what happens to the overpaid benefit? The Secretary of State is liable to repay the overpaid benefit to the compensator, who is then liable to pass on the repayment to the claimant.[320] In *Bruce v Genesis Fast Food Ltd*,[321] however, the defendants claimed that they were not liable to repay the claimant. There was an agreed settlement of some £155,000 but since the claimant was a patient, and sued by a litigation friend, this settlement required the approval of the court. The court order reflected the agreement and included provision for the defendants to withhold some £33,000 to pay a CRU certificate of recoverable benefit. Subsequently the figure for the recoverable benefit was reduced by a tribunal to £878 (and a second certificate of recoverable benefit in this amount was issued). The Secretary of State repaid to the compensator over £39,500 (allowing for a previous payment of recoverable benefit by the compensator to the Secretary of State). When the defendants refused to pay this to the claimant, the claimant issued an application to the court in the original action for an order requiring the defendants to hand the sum over. The defendants argued that: (i) the express provisions of the agreement, which were reflected in

---

[316] Social Security (Recovery of Benefits) Act 1997 s.10.

[317] Social Security (Recovery of Benefits) Act 1997 s.11(3).

[318] See the decisions of the tribunal of Social Security Commissioners R(CR) 1/02 and R(CR) 2/02. See Axon [2001] J.P.I.L. 411.

[319] Though not the only one. For discussion of the meaning of a CPR Pt 36 offer to settle a claim for £x "net of CRU" see *Crooks v Hendricks Lovell Ltd* [2016] EWCA Civ 8; [2016] 1 Costs L.O. 103, where a subsequent reduction of the recoverable benefits meant that the claimant had beaten the defendants' Pt 36 offer with consequent implications for liability for costs. The case is discussed by J. McQuater [2016] J.P.I.L. C105.

[320] See the Social Security (Recovery of Benefits) Regulations 1997 reg.11(5).

[321] [2003] EWHC 788 (QB); [2004] P.I.Q.R. P9.

the court order, overrode the effect of the Social Security (Recovery of Benefits) Act 1997 s.8 and reg.11(5) of the 1997 Regulations; (ii) the benefit of the defendants' CRU appeal was independent from the judgment sum and the claimant was not a party to the CRU appeal and therefore had no locus standi; (iii) repayment of the benefits to the claimant would represent double recovery of the compensation award and state benefits; and (iv) the defendants would be entitled to rectification of the court order to reflect the true intentions of the parties.

McKinnon J rejected the defendants' arguments. The parties to litigation could not contract out of the legislative regime, and the court order had to be construed accordingly. It followed that the claimant was entitled to the repayment. A sum had been withheld under the order in order meet the first CRU certificate. If the revised figure for the second certificate had been known at the date of the court order, then the deduction would not have been made. The claimant had locus standi, and was correct to have brought the application within the original proceedings. There was no double recovery by the claimant, because the tribunal had concluded that the benefits received by the claimant were not related to the accident for which the defendants had been required to pay compensation. Finally, rectification of the order was not appropriate because the parties had not proceeded on a misunderstanding of the effects of the legislation. The defendants had made a unilateral mistake as to the effects of the legislation, and the consequences of that were not to be laid at the claimant's door. One consequence of this ruling, which, with respect, is entirely correct, is that it would seem that there will now be little incentive for defendants to appeal CRU certificates in cases where the recoverable benefit has been wholly set off against the damages award, because the consequence of a reduction in the certificate is that the sum should be fully reimbursed to the claimant. Where the recoverable benefits have exceeded the damages award, or where not all of the benefits can be set off against the relevant heads of the compensation payment, defendants will continue to have an interest in appealing the CRU certificate. **12–114**

Only personal injury claims   The recovery of benefits only applies to actions for personal injuries. So where the claim is based on the financial losses resulting from a negligent misrepresentation, not personal injury suffered by the claimants, any benefits paid to the claimants are not recoverable under the 1997 Act.[322] **12–115**

Rationale   The justification for the recovery of social security benefits is relatively simple to state. The pre-1989 method of deducting benefits meets the compensation principle by reflecting the claimant's actual loss. It ignores, however, the consequences for defendants, or more realistically their insurers, which is that the damages are reduced and they are better off by an amount equivalent to the benefits paid by the State and funded by the taxpayer. Recovery merely puts the loss where it belongs, with the defendant's insurers rather than the taxpayer, reducing public expenditure and contributing to economic efficiency by internalising this cost to the activity generating the risk of injury. **12–116**

---

[322] *Rand v East Dorset Health Authority (No.2)* [2001] P.I.Q.R. Q1; [2000] Lloyd's Rep. Med. 377; see para.12–150 below.

Whatever the logic of this proposition (and it is by no means clear that those who effectively have to pay the insurance premiums which fund the tort system are a significantly different group from taxpayers[323]) it clearly makes no sense in relation to medical negligence claims which are met from NHS funds, also provided by the taxpayer. Recovery in this context simply means shifting taxpayers' money from one government department to another government department, while adding to administrative costs, although it would seem that the unit cost of administering the system is low.[324]

12–117 **Non-recoverable benefits** Benefits which are not subject to the statutory regime of recovery are dealt with on the basis of common law rules, which prior to the introduction of recoupment in 1989, had effectively reached the point of full deductibility. Thus, in assessing loss of earnings any housing benefit received by the claimant as a result of the tort should be deducted.[325]

(ii) Recovery of the cost of NHS treatment

12–118 The Health and Social Care (Community and Health Standards) Act 2003 Pt 3 introduced a revised scheme for the recovery of NHS charges where a person makes a compensation payment to an injured person in consequence of the injury (including psychological injury but excluding disease, unless the disease is itself attributable to the injury). This applies where the injured person has received NHS treatment at a health service hospital, been provided with NHS ambulance services as a result of the injury for the purposes of taking him to hospital for NHS treatment (unless he was dead on arrival at the hospital), or both. Private treatment at NHS premises is excluded, as is primary medical and dental services (i.e. general practitioner and dental services). A compensation payment means any payment by or on behalf of a person who is or who is alleged to be liable to any extent in respect of the injury or in pursuance of a compensation scheme for motor accidents (thus including compensation payable by the Motor Insurers Bureau). The format of the scheme, in broad terms, follows that for recovery of social security benefits, though there are some important differences. The purpose of the scheme is to require liability insurers to pay the cost to the NHS of treating in hospital individuals injured by tortfeasors, and there is provision for payment to be passed on to the NHS hospital or ambulance service that provided the treatment. This has implications for clinical negligence claims since it would be circular for a NHS Trust hospital responsible for negligently injuring a patient, which then provides treatment to that patient, to have to pay the cost of that treatment in order to have that cost reimbursed to itself. Accordingly, under Sch.10 para.5 of the Act a compensation payment which would be made by the responsible body of the health service hospital to whom the payment would

---

[323] See the comments of Lord Bridge in *Hodgson v Trapp* [1989] A.C. 807 at 823 on the significant overlap between those groups that effectively fund the tort system and taxpayers. Nor is it clear that the taxpayer should benefit from the recovery of contributory benefits which are paid for wholly by employees' and employers' national insurance contributions, and are arguably analogous to private insurance purchased by the claimant; see paras 12–120 to 12–121.

[324] Dismore [1998] J.P.I.L. 14, 33 suggested that this was, on average, £10 per case.

[325] *Clenshaw v Tanner* [2002] EWCA Civ 1848; [2002] All E.R. (D) 412 (Nov).

subsequently be passed is an "exempt payment" and not subject to recovery under the scheme (the same rule applies to a relevant ambulance trust to whom the payment would subsequently be passed). This exemption only applies, however, where the treatment (or ambulance service) is provided by the defendant. If the injured person receives treatment at another NHS hospital as a result of injuries sustained at the defendant NHS hospital, the recovery scheme applies to that treatment. Other exempted compensation payments include, inter alia, payments in consequence of an action under the Fatal Accidents Act 1976 (which reflects the position under the recovery of social security benefits). The scheme came into force on 29 January 2007.[326]

(iii) Other collateral benefits

Where the claimant has received compensation or pecuniary benefits from a source other than social security, the question of deduction depends upon the nature of the benefit and the source. Prima facie, the recoverable loss is the net loss, and so financial gains accruing to claimants which they would not have received but for the accident should be taken into account in mitigation of his loss.[327]

12–119

Personal accident insurance and charitable payments   There are two well-established exceptions to the deduction of financial gains accruing to the claimant. First, the proceeds of a personal accident insurance policy taken out by the claimant are ignored, on the basis that otherwise the claimant's foresight and thrift would benefit the defendant rather than himself.[328] Secondly, gratuitous payments to the claimant from charitable motives are not deducted, again on the basis that the donor intended to benefit the claimant, not the defendant.[329] On the other hand, an ex gratia payment to the claimant by the tortfeasor does not normally fall within the "benevolence exception" to the fundamental principle that a claimant is entitled to recover the full extent of the *net* loss, and no more, even if the payment had been made from motives of benevolence.[330]

12–120

---

[326] See further the Personal Injuries (NHS Charges) (General) and Road Traffic (NHS Charges) (Amendment) Regulations 2006 (SI 2006/3388), as amended, and the Personal Injuries (NHS Charges) (Amounts) Regulations 2015 (SI 2015/295), as amended.

[327] *Hussain v New Taplow Paper Mills Ltd* [1988] A.C. 514 at 527, per Lord Bridge; *Hodgson v Trapp* [1989] A.C. 807 at 819E per Lord Bridge. A tax rebate under the PAYE system due to the fact that the claimant is not earning is deductible from the loss of earnings: *Hartley v Sandholme Iron Co. Ltd* [1975] Q.B. 600. Savings attributable to the fact that the claimant is being maintained in a public or private institution should be deducted from the loss of earnings claim: Administration of Justice Act 1982 s.5; *Lim Poh Choo v Camden and Islington Area Health Authority* [1980] A.C. 174. Any savings from expenses which are no longer being incurred, such as travelling expenses to and from work, should be deducted (though see para.12–077, n.213 above).

[328] *Bradburn v Great Western Railway Co.* (1874) L.R. 10 Ex. 1; *Parry v Cleaver* [1970] A.C. 1 at 14, per Lord Reid.

[329] *Redpath v Belfast and County Down Railway* [1947] N.I. 167; *Parry v Cleaver* [1970] A.C. 1, 14; *Hussain v New Taplow Paper Mills Ltd* [1988] A.C. 514 at 527.

[330] *Gaca v Pirelli General plc* [2004] EWCA Civ 373; [2004] 1 W.L.R. 2683, holding that *McCamley v Cammell Laird Shipbuilders Ltd* [1990] 1 W.L.R. 963 (CA) had been wrongly decided on this point. The position may be different if the tortfeasor made an ex gratia payment and explicitly said that the payment was a gift made on the basis that it would not be deducted from any damages that may be

12–121   **Occupational pensions**   In *Parry v Cleaver*[331] the House of Lords held, by a bare majority, that an occupational disability pension should not be deducted from lost earnings, whether the pension was contributory or non-contributory. The majority of their Lordships took the view that the nature of a pension makes it analogous to private insurance effected by the claimant.[332]

12–122   **Sick pay**   Occupational sick pay will be deducted if it is paid as a term of the claimant's contract of employment, and this is the case whether or not the employer has taken out a policy of insurance to cover the contractual commitment to pay sick pay, and irrespective of the fact that the entitlement to sick pay applies to long-term incapacity for work.[333] It has been argued, however, that where there is some direct or indirect link between the benefits received by the claimant and wages foregone, as part of the overall wage structure, for example, then the position is closer to *Parry v Cleaver* in the sense that the claimant has "purchased" the benefits himself.[334] There would seem to be little in logic to justify the different approaches to occupational sick pay and occupational pensions, though in practice everything turns upon how the payment is characterised: if it is a "pension" it is not deducted, if it is "sick pay" it is deducted.

12–123   **Non-deductible sick pay**   Where claimants are under a contractual obligation to repay to their employer any payments of sick pay if they are successful in an

---

awarded if litigation ensued: [2004] EWCA Civ 373 at [31] per Dyson LJ. Moreover, the fact that the payment made by the defendant (who was the claimant's employer) was the product of an insurance policy paid for by the defendant did not bring the case within the "private insurance" exception to full deduction of collateral benefits. An employee was not to be treated as having paid for, or contributed to the cost of, insurance merely because the insurance has been arranged by his employer for the benefit of his employees. The insurance monies must be deducted unless the claimant paid or contributed to the insurance premium directly or indirectly, and this will not be inferred simply from the fact that the claimant is an employee for whose benefit the insurance has been arranged: [2004] EWCA Civ 373 at [56] per Dyson LJ.

[331] [1970] A.C. 1.

[332] Lord Morris, dissenting, pointed out that in reality there is no difference between receipt of sick pay and receipt of a pension. The true loss of earnings in each case is the difference between what claimants received prior to injury and what they now receive by virtue of a contract of employment. Nor is it an answer to say that they "earned" their pension entitlement by their own efforts, since if they obtain alternative employment the claimant must account for their new earnings in mitigation of their lost earnings, notwithstanding that these receipts are "earned". In *Smoker v London Fire and Civil Defence Authority* [1991] 2 A.C. 502 the House of Lords affirmed that *Parry v Cleaver* was correctly decided, on the basis that pension benefits constitute deferred remuneration in respect of the claimant's past work, and the tortfeasor cannot appropriate the fruit of the claimant's past service. Where, however, the injury leads to a reduction of claimant's retirement pension under an occupational pension scheme, because he is prevented from making full contributions, then disability pension payments which will be received after the claimant would have retired should be taken into account as mitigating the loss of pension: *Parry v Cleaver* [1970] A.C. 1 at 20–21, per Lord Reid.

[333] *Hussain v New Taplow Paper Mills Ltd* [1988] A.C. 514, HL, distinguishing *Parry v Cleaver* [1970] A.C. 1. Lord Bridge commented, at 530, that sick pay is "a partial substitute for earnings and . . . the very antithesis of a pension, which is payable only after employment ceases".

[334] Anderson (1987) 50 M.L.R. 963, 970. This argument is open to the objection that all "benefits" under a contract of employment form part of the wage or salary structure, which the employee "purchases" by working under the terms of the contract.

action for damages, then sick pay should not be from the award.[335] Similarly, gratuitous payments of sick pay should not be deducted since they are analogous to charitable payments.[336]

Pre-retirement incapacity pension   In *Longden v British Coal Corporation*[337]   **12–124**
the claimant was unable to work following an accident at work. He was awarded an incapacity pension under his occupational pension scheme which he would continue to receive after his normal retirement age of 60, though it was lower than the pension he would have received had he continued to work to age 60. The defendants sought to deduct the incapacity pension that would be received to age 60 from the claim in respect of loss of pension rights from age 60 (the disability pension payable *after* age 60 was clearly deductible from the sum claimed in respect of lost retirement pension). The House of Lords held that (with the exception of a lump sum received on accepting the disability pension) such payments received before the normal retirement age did not have to be brought into account. Lord Hope said that the claimant could not reasonably be expected to set aside the sums received as incapacity pension during the period when he is unable to earn wages because of his disability in order to make good his loss of pension after his normal retirement age. It would be:

"...unjust if the plaintiff's claim for loss of pension after his normal retirement age were to be extinguished by capitalising sums paid to him before that age as an incapacity pension to assist him during his disability."[338]

Redundancy payments   If claimants are made redundant as a result of their   **12–125**
injuries, in the sense that their disability makes them a more likely candidate for redundancy, any redundancy payment should be deducted.[339] But if they would have been redundant regardless of the accident the payment will not be deducted,[340] although this will clearly be a factor in calculating the loss of earnings attributable to the tort since it is known that the claimant would not have continued in that employment. A compensation payment from a statutory compensation scheme for workers who developed an industrial disease (pneumoconiosis) is fully deductible from damages awarded in respect of the same illness.[341] There was no reason why the normal principle against over-compensation should not apply.

---

[335] *Browning v War Office* [1963] 1 Q.B. 750 at 759, 770; see also *Dennis v London Passenger Transport Board* [1948] 1 All E.R. 779 where the claimant was under a moral but not a legal obligation to repay and Denning J held that where others have made up the claimant's wages in the expectation of being repaid the tortfeasor should not be permitted to reduce the damages payable. The award should be held by the claimant on trust for the employer: *Mosson v Spousal (London) Ltd* [2016] EWHC 53 (QB); [2016] 4 W.L.R. 28 at [54]. The sum to be repaid to the employer will normally be net of income tax and national insurance contributions: *Franklin v British Railways Board* [1994] P.I.Q.R. P1.

[336] *Parry v Cleaver* [1970] A.C. 1 at 4; *Cunningham v Harrison* [1973] Q.B. 942; [1973] 3 All E.R. 463, CA.

[337] [1998] A.C. 653.

[338] [1998] A.C. 653 at 669.

[339] *Colledge v Bass Mitchells & Butlers Ltd* [1988] 1 All E.R. 536.

[340] [1988] 1 All E.R. 536 at 540.

[341] *Ballantine v Newalls Insulation Co. Ltd* [2001] I.C.R. 25; [2000] P.I.Q.R. Q327, CA.

3.   PERSONAL INJURIES: NON-PECUNIARY LOSSES

12–126 Non-pecuniary losses consist of the pain and suffering caused by the injury itself, and the loss of amenity which is consequent upon any disability attributable to the injury. Here restoring claimants to their pre-accident position is clearly impossible, and the guiding principle is said to be that the award should be fair or reasonable.

(a)   Pain and suffering

12–127 The claimant is entitled to damages for actual and prospective pain and suffering caused by the injury, by a neurosis resulting from the injury, or attributable to any necessary medical treatment for the injury. This includes any discomfort, humiliation, or disfigurement suffered by the claimant. The mere fact that life expectancy has been reduced does not give rise to a damages award.[342] On the other hand, people who suffer mental anguish because they are aware that their life expectancy has been reduced can recover for that anguish.[343] In *Kadir v Mistry*[344] the deceased should have been diagnosed with stomach cancer in June 2007 whereas the tumour was not diagnosed until March 2008 and she died in August 2008. Treatment would probably have delayed a fatal outcome to July or August 2010. Laws LJ said that awareness that one's life expectancy has been reduced does not require certain knowledge. Section 1(1)(b) applies if :

> "...the claimant or deceased has good objective reason to fear that his expectation of life has been reduced. As a matter of ordinary humanity, it seems to me plain that if some good objective reason to fear is shown, then a subjective fear and the anguish that surely follows it will ordinarily be liable to be inferred."[345]

12–128 Similarly, people who are physically or mentally incapacitated by their injuries and are capable of appreciating the condition to which they have been reduced

---

[342] Administration of Justice Act 1982 s.1(1)(a), abolishing the common law claim for loss of expectation of life. An attempt to get around this in a case involving the failure to obtain the patient's consent to treatment was rejected in *Shaw v Kovac* [2017] EWCA Civ 1028; [2017] P.I.Q.R. Q4, a case where the patient died on the operating table. There is no freestanding claim for damages for negligently depriving a claimant of the opportunity to give informed consent, and no separate head of loss for an unlawful invasion of the patient's personal right to personal autonomy. If, however, a patient's suffering is increased by knowing that personal autonomy has been invaded through an absence of informed consent, that can be reflected in the award of compensatory general damages for injury to feelings, including mental suffering, distress, humiliation, anger or indignation: [2017] EWCA Civ 1028 at [70].

[343] Administration of Justice Act 1982 s.1(1)(b).

[344] [2014] EWCA Civ 1177.

[345] [2014] EWCA Civ 1177 at [15]. An award of £3,500 was made for the mental suffering resulting from the deceased's awareness for the last three months of her life that her life expectation had been reduced. For comment on *Kadir* see M. Lyons [2014] J.P.I.L. C165. See also *Brown v Hamid* [2013] EWHC 4067 (QB) where the deceased's knowledge that his expectation of life had been reduced by about a year due to a failure to diagnose pulmonary hypertension and prescribe treatment was taken into account in assessing general damages for pain and suffering (though no specific sum for this was identified in the overall award of £8,500).

are entitled to be compensated for the anguish that this creates.[346] However, if the claimant is permanently unconscious or for some other reason is incapable of subjectively experiencing pain, there will be no award for pain and suffering.[347] If the claimant's marriage prospects have been affected, the award will include an element to compensate for the loss of comfort and companionship which marriage might have brought, although disregarding the economic aspect of loss of marriage prospects.[348]

A claimant who sustains psychiatric harm in the form of a recognised psychiatric illness is entitled to be compensated for that illness, but not for mere sorrow or grief.[349] If, however, the claimant's mental distress or grief at the death of a loved one exacerbates the pain and suffering which the claimant sustained in the same incident, preventing the claimant from making a recovery as quickly as would otherwise have occurred, this will be reflected in the award of damages for pain and suffering. In *Kralj v McGrath*[350] the claimant suffered physical injuries due to the defendant doctor's negligent treatment in the course of delivering a baby. She also suffered shock as a result of being told about the baby's injuries and seeing the child for the eight weeks that it survived. No award was made for the claimant's grief at the death of the child, but allowance was made for the fact that her experience of her own injuries was more drastic than it would otherwise have been because of the grief which she suffered at the same time in relation to the death of the child. Conversely, if the child had been healthy this would probably have reduced the impact of the claimant's injuries, because she would have had the joy of motherhood to console her. In a number of cases awards have included an element for a reactive depression suffered by a patient following negligent medical treatment.[351]

12–129

---

[346] *H West & Son Ltd v Shephard* [1964] A.C. 326.

[347] *Wise v Kaye* [1962] 1 Q.B. 638.

[348] *Moriarty v McCarthy* [1978] 2 All E.R. 213; *Hughes v McKeown* [1985] 3 All E.R. 284; [1985] 1 W.L.R. 963; *Morgan v Gwent Health Authority, The Independent*, 14 December 1987 CA—breakup of the claimant's engagement as a result of a negligently administered blood transfusion which would have caused serious complications to a foetus conceived with her fiancé. The chances that the claimant would find a husband with whom there would be no complications if she conceived were 17 per cent.

[349] *Hinz v Berry* [1970] 2 Q.B. 40 at 42; *McLoughlin v O'Brian* [1983] 1 A.C. 410 at 431, per Lord Bridge; *Alcock v Chief Constable of the South Yorkshire Police* [1992] 1 A.C. 310 at 409, per Lord Oliver.

[350] [1986] 1 All E.R. 54; see also *Bagley v North Hertfordshire Health Authority* (1986) 136 N.L.J. 1014 and cf. *Kerby v Redbridge Health Authority* [1993] 4 Med. L.R. 178; [1994] P.I.Q.R. Q1 on the assessment of damages following a stillbirth. This can include the mother's loss of earnings in having to undergo another pregnancy to complete her planned family: *Kralj v McGrath* [1986] 1 All E.R. 54; and damages for "the rigours of an additional pregnancy" that she will have to undergo: *Kerby v Redbridge Health Authority* above. See further Burrows, *Remedies for Torts and Breach of Contract*, 3rd edn (Oxford: Oxford University Press, 2004), p.292.

[351] *Biles v Barking Health Authority* [1988] C.L.Y. 1103 (discussed by Puxon and Buchan (1988) 138 N.L.J. 80)—clinical depression and sexual dysfunction following unnecessary sterilisation and probable permanent sterility; *Ackers v Wigan Area Health Authority* [1991] 2 Med. L.R. 232—severe depression after an operation under general anaesthetic where the claimant was awake; *Phelan v East Cumbria Health Authority* [1991] 2 Med. L.R. 419—£15,000 in respect of "awareness" during surgery under general anaesthetic; *Grieve v Salford Health Authority* [1991] 2 Med. L.R. 295 reactive depression following a stillbirth; *Kerby v Redbridge Health Authority* [1993] 4 Med. L.R. 178; [1994] P.I.Q.R. Q1—depression following the death of one twin, three days after the birth; *Wheatley v*

(b) Loss of faculty and amenity

12–130   The injury itself represents loss of faculty whereas the consequences of the injury on the claimant's activities represents loss of amenity. This includes inter alia loss of job satisfaction (which is also referred to as loss of congenial employment),[352] loss of leisure activities and hobbies, and loss of family life. It is rare for the courts to distinguish between these separate heads of damage since normally a single global award is made to cover all the claimant's non-pecuniary losses.[353] An award of damages will be made for loss of amenity even where the claimant is permanently unconscious and unable to appreciate the condition.[354] This treats loss of amenity as an "objective" loss which the fact of unconsciousness does not change.[355]

12–131   **The tariff system**   The courts operate a "tariff" system with a view to obtaining some degree of uniformity between claimants with comparable injuries, and to facilitate the settlement of claims. The tariff is not precisely fixed. There is a band or range of figures for particular injuries which allows the court to take account

---

Cunningham [1992] P.I.Q.R. Q100—loss of a child in early pregnancy by miscarriage (not a medical negligence case); *G v North Tees Health Authority* [1989] F.C.R. 53—general damages of £5,000 each to a six-year-old child and mother, where the child was wrongly identified as a victim of sexual abuse as a result of a mix up with a vaginal swab, and the mother had become depressed and suicidal, until the error was discovered; *Smith v Barking, Havering and Brentwood Health Authority* (1988), [1994] 5 Med. L.R. 285, where general damages of £3,000 were awarded to a patient for shock and depression caused by discovery, without any prior warning of the risk, that she had been rendered tetraplegic following an operation. The claimant would have progressed to this condition within six to nine months in any event, and the claim in respect of an omission to disclose the risk failed on causation; *Goorkani v Tayside Health Board* [1991] 3 Med. L.R. 33—£2,500 awarded for the "distress and anxiety" which arose from the pursuer's discovery of the risk of infertility associated with drug therapy and the fact that he was almost certainly infertile. Query, however, whether in the absence of any physical injury for which the defendants were liable, there should be any award for "shock" or "distress" not amounting to a positive psychiatric illness: *McLoughlin v O'Brian* [1983] 1 A.C. 410 at 431, per Lord Bridge; *Alcock v Chief Constable of the South Yorkshire Police* [1992] 1 A.C. 310 at 409, per Lord Oliver; para.2–188.

[352] *Willbye v Gibbons* [2003] EWCA Civ 372; [2004] P.I.Q.R. P15 at [11]; *Evans v Virgin Atlantic Airways* [2011] EWHC 1805 (QB) at [30]; *Dudney v Guaranteed Asphalt Ltd* [2013] EWHC 2515 (QB) at [28]; *Davison v Leitch* [2013] EWHC 3092 (QB) at [61]; *Murphy v Ministry of Defence* [2016] EWHC 3 (QB) at [187]. See S. Allen, "Loss of Congenial Employment" [2009] J.P.I.L. 135.

[353] Where the claimant has sustained multiple injuries the judge should approach the assessment by having separate figures in mind for each of the injuries and then stepping back and considering whether the aggregate sum is reasonable compensation for the totality of the injury, rather than identifying a global sum and then breaking the award down: *Sadler v Filipiak* [2011] EWCA Civ 1728, applying *Brown v Woodall* [1995] P.I.Q.R. Q36 (CA).

[354] *Wise v Kaye* [1962] 1 Q.B. 638; *H West & Son Ltd v Shephard* [1964] A.C. 326; *Lim Poh Choo v Camden and Islington Area Health Authority* [1980] A.C. 174.

[355] In *H West & Son Ltd v Shephard* [1964] A.C. 326 at 341 Lord Reid, dissenting, commented that: "...there is something unreal in saying that a man who knows and feels nothing should get the same as a man who has to live with and put up with his disabilities, merely because they have sustained comparable physical injuries. It is no more possible to compensate an unconscious man than it is to compensate a dead man." The Pearson Commission recommended that damages for non-pecuniary loss should not be recoverable in cases of permanent unconsciousness: *Royal Commission on Civil Liability and Compensation for Personal Injury*, Cmnd.7054 (1978), Vol.I, paras 397–398. In *Lim Poh Choo v Camden and Islington Area Health Authority* [1980] A.C. 174 the House of Lords were unwilling to reverse *H West & Son Ltd v Shephard*, preferring to leave the issue to legislation.

of subjective factors which may exacerbate, or reduce, the impact of a particular injury on the claimant. The Law Commission Report on *Damages for Personal Injury: Non-Pecuniary Loss*[356] suggested that awards for non-pecuniary loss were too low, at least in serious cases. In *Heil v Rankin*[357] a specially constituted five-judge Court of Appeal accepted the thrust of the Law Commission's proposals, whilst not accepting that there should be an "across the board" increase in awards for non-pecuniary loss. The Court held that there should be a tapered increase in awards, with an increase of about a third for the most serious injuries, but no increase at all for awards which were currently assessed at under £10,000. The bracket for the most serious injuries should start at £150,000 rising to £200,000 for the very worst cases, with £175,000 being appropriate for an "average" case of tetraplegia. These figures are meant to increase in line with the retail prices index (RPI), although the Court accepted that part of the argument for the tapered increase that they applied was that, over time, the RPI does not fully reflect the general increase in prosperity. The public might reasonably expect that such awards bear some relationship to levels of income and wealth in society, particularly since assessing the level of damages was essentially a "jury function".

In *Simmons v Castle*[358] the Court of Appeal declared that from 1 April 2013, in all civil claims the level of general damages for (i) pain and suffering, (ii) loss of amenity, (iii) physical inconvenience and discomfort, (iv) social discredit, or (v) mental distress, should be 10 per cent higher than previously. The increase was made to compensate claimants funding their actions by a conditional fee agreement for the loss of the right to recover, as part of the costs of the action, the success fee from defendants. This was part of the reform of civil litigation costs following recommendations by Sir Rupert Jackson.[359] The only exception to the 10 per cent increase was for claimants who had entered into a conditional fee agreement before 1 April 2013, and so fell into the exception provided in s.44(6) of the Legal Aid, Sentencing and Punishment of Offenders Act 2012 permitting the award of a success fee.[360]

12–132

Guidelines   Whilst authoritative judicial guidelines as to the appropriate band or range of figures for particular injuries are set by the Court of Appeal,[361] in

12–133

---

[356] Law Com. No.257, 1999. See also Law Com. No.225, *Personal Injury Compensation: How Much is Enough?*, 1994, making the same point. For cogent criticism of awards of damages for pain and suffering and loss of amenity in general, and of the Law Commission's approach in particular, see Lewis, "Increasing the Price of Pain: Damages, The Law Commission and *Heil v Rankin*" (2001) 64 M.L.R. 100.

[357] [2001] Q.B. 272; Lewis (2001) 64 M.L.R. 100.

[358] [2012] EWCA Civ 1039 and [2012] EWCA Civ 1288; [2013] 1 W.L.R. 1239.

[359] *Review of Civil Litigation Costs: Final Report*, December 2009.

[360] The exception is clearly a transitional provision, and there are no other exceptions. The 10 per cent increase in general damages must be applied even if the claimant was not being funded by a conditional fee agreement: *Summers v Bundy* [2016] EWCA Civ 126; [2016] P.I.Q.R. Q6, where the claimant was legally aided.

[361] *Wright v British Railways Board* [1983] 2 A.C. 773 at 785 per Lord Diplock: "The Court of Appeal, with its considerable case-load of appeals in personal injury actions and the relatively recent experience of many of its members in trying such cases themselves is, generally speaking, the tribunal best qualified to set the guidelines for judges currently trying such actions."

practice the introduction of the Judicial College *Guidelines for the Assessment of General Damages in Personal Injury Cases*[362] has proved invaluable. The Guidelines provide a useful summary of the relevant range of figures for each type of injury. They are based on composite practical experience and reported case law, and they are commonly used in practice and widely accepted to be the first point of reference for assessing a likely award.[363]

4. WRONGFUL BIRTH

12–134 Claims for wrongful birth refer to actions by parents in respect of their losses arising out of the birth of a child which it is alleged would not have been born but for the defendant's negligence. The act of negligence may arise prior to conception, as for example with a failed sterilisation operation,[364] an omission to warn about the risks of a sterilisation operation failing to achieve its purpose,[365] or negligent genetic counselling about the risks of having a child with a congenital disability.[366] Some commentators have categorised these actions as claims for "wrongful conception" to distinguish them from the situation where the negligence occurs after conception, a category of case labelled as "wrongful birth", which essentially consists of failing to offer a pregnant woman the opportunity to have a lawful termination of pregnancy or to carry out the termination carefully. Thus, "wrongful birth" would cover negligence in the performance an abortion operation,[367] failing to detect that the claimant was pregnant in circumstances where, if the pregnancy had been diagnosed earlier, the mother would have had an abortion,[368] and a failure to advise a mother known to be pregnant of the risk that the foetus may be born with serious disabilities thus depriving her of the opportunity to have an abortion under the Abortion Act 1967.[369] Although the distinction between "wrongful conception" and "wrongful birth" may be descriptively accurate, the courts have concluded that conceptually there is no real distinction between them, at least for the purpose of identifying the defendant's duty of care.[370]

12–135 The question of what damages are recoverable in such cases has been the subject of appellate scrutiny in three decisions, two by the House of Lords and one by the Court of Appeal. In the context of assessing damages, the factual differences between the circumstances of each type of case can give rise to some distinctions of significance, particularly in the light of the decision of the House of Lords in

---

[362] 14th edn (Oxford: Oxford University Press, 2017).

[363] As a general rule practitioners would use the Guidelines as the starting point and then refer to a more detailed reference to tailor the likely award to the facts of their case. Almost inevitably, this would be *Kemp and Kemp, The Quantum of Damages* (London: Sweet & Maxwell).

[364] See para.4–111.

[365] See paras 7–162 et seq.

[366] *Anderson v Forth Valley Health Board*, 1998 SLT 588; (1997) 44 B.M.L.R. 108, Court of Session, Outer House.

[367] See para.4–061.

[368] *Allen v Bloomsbury Health Authority* [1993] 1 All E.R. 651.

[369] *McKay v Essex Area Health Authority* [1982] Q.B. 1166; para.2–141; *Salih v Enfield Health Authority* [1990] 1 Med. L.R. 333, QBD.

[370] See para.2–052.

McFarlane v Tayside Health Board[371] that the parents are not entitled to recover the financial cost of raising a healthy child. The typical "wrongful conception" case, a failed sterilisation, is likely to result in the birth of a healthy child (though as a matter of random chance, the child could be disabled) though an allegation of negligent genetic counselling will probably be focused on the fact that the parents have a disabled child, or at least a child with the congenital condition which they sought to avoid. On the other hand, the typical "wrongful birth" case, the failure through appropriate testing to identify the fact that the foetus has or is at risk of having a serious disability, will result in the birth of a disabled child, though the negligent performance of an abortion which fails to terminate the pregnancy or the negligent failure to detect the pregnancy early enough for a lawful abortion could result in the birth of healthy child. Thus, the distinction between "wrongful conception" and "wrongful birth" is not analytically useful in this context. Rather, it is the factual context of the negligent act or omission that is important to the assessment of the parents' loss (was the child wanted or unwanted? is it healthy or disabled?), not whether it was prior or subsequent to the conception.

Until the decision of the House of Lords in *McFarlane v Tayside Health Board*, the assessment of damages in wrongful birth cases had not given rise to particular problems. The general principles of compensation in tort actions were applied, although the nature of the loss—whether economic or personal injuries—had not been seriously addressed.[372] After some initial hesitation about awarding damages for the financial consequences of a wrongful birth, at least where the child was healthy,[373] the Court of Appeal came to the conclusion in *Emeh v Kensington and Chelsea and Westminster Area Health Authority*[374] that since a sterilisation operation is lawful, and the avoidance of pregnancy and birth was the object of the operation undergone by the claimant, the compensatable loss extended to any reasonably foreseeable financial loss directly caused by the unexpected pregnancy. Moreover, there were no good policy reasons for denying the claim for the financial loss, regardless of whether the child was healthy or disabled. Following the decision in *Emeh*, claims for the costs of bringing up either healthy or disabled children were accepted as valid. However, the view that parents could recover for the financial cost of raising an unwanted healthy child was rejected by the House of Lords in *McFarlane v Tayside Health Board*.[375] Their Lordships distinguished the parents' claim for the financial consequences of the existence of a healthy child (which was not recoverable) from the mother's claim in respect of the pregnancy itself, and any adverse consequences for her of

12–136

---

[371] [2000] 2 A.C. 59. See para.2–055.

[372] See *Allen v Bloomsbury Health Authority* [1993] 1 All E.R. 651 at 658, per Brooke J.

[373] *Udale v Bloomsbury Area Health Authority* [1983] 2 All E.R. 522, Jupp J, who interestingly dismissed the claim for the cost of the "unwanted" child's upbringing on clear public policy grounds that would be broadly adopted subsequently by the House of Lords; cf. the decision of Pain J in *Thake v Maurice* [1986] Q.B. 644.

[374] [1985] Q.B. 1012, preferring the view of Pain J in *Thake v Maurice* [1986] Q.B. 644.

[375] [2000] 2 A.C. 59. See para.2–055. It follows that some of the cases which pre-date *McFarlane* have to be treated with caution, and those which are concerned exclusively with the assessment of loss in respect of the cost of raising a healthy child are no longer relevant.

the pregnancy (for which damages remained recoverable).[376] Subsequently, the Court of Appeal in *Parkinson v St James and Seacroft University Hospital NHS Trust*[377] held that *McFarlane* did not have the effect of precluding the parents' claim for the additional financial loss incurred in respect of a disabled child. The House of Lords then revisited matters in *Rees v Darlington Memorial Hospital NHS Trust*[378] (probably) upholding *Parkinson* and going on to rule that there can be no claim for the cost of raising a healthy child where the parent is disabled (though the right to claim for the additional costs of raising a disabled child remains). Their Lordships in *Rees* also confirmed that the parents of a healthy or a disabled child can now claim a "conventional sum" of £15,000 for loss of the right to limit the size of one's family. In broad terms, there are three aspects to consider in the light of these cases: (a) the healthy child; (b) the disabled child; and (c) the disabled mother.

(a) The healthy child—the mother's claim

12–137 Following *McFarlane* there can be no claim for the costs of caring for or the losses incurred as a result of bringing up a healthy child. With regard to the mother's claim, although their Lordships were in general agreement in *McFarlane* that the mother had a claim for damages, they were far from unanimous in their views as to which losses were compensatable. Lord Slynn considered that Mrs McFarlane was entitled to general damages for the pain, discomfort and inconvenience of the unwanted pregnancy and birth, and to special damages consisting of: (1) any extra medical expenses, (2) clothes for herself, (3) equipment on the birth of the baby, and (4) "in principle" compensation for loss of earnings due to the pregnancy and birth. Lord Steyn agreed that Mrs McFarlane had suffered personal injury as a consequence of the birth and was entitled to damages for that, including loss of earnings during the later stages of pregnancy. Lord Hope characterised the unwanted conception as a harmful event to the mother—it was the very thing that she had been told would not happen after the vasectomy. Objections to her claim on moral or religious grounds must be rejected since this was an area of family life where freedom of choice may properly be exercised. The claim for solatium and financial loss attributable to the pregnancy did not terminate at the birth—she might have suffered physical or emotional problems after the birth or sustained a loss of income due to the effects upon her of the pregnancy, applying the normal rules of remoteness of damage. But Lord Hope excluded the costs of the child's layette as being part of the child's rearing costs. Lord Clyde agreed that the mother was entitled to general damages by way of solatium, but excluded the costs of rearing the child, including the layette and any loss of earnings by the mother "as a result

[376] This is the "distinction between damage attributable to the effects of pregnancy and confinement and alleged damage attributable to the existence of the healthy child that is born": *Greenfield v Irwin* [2001] EWCA Civ 113; [2001] 1 W.L.R. 1279 at [52] per Laws LJ.
[377] *Parkinson v St James and Seacroft University Hospital NHS Trust* [2001] EWCA Civ 530; [2002] Q.B. 266; approved by the Court of Appeal in *Groom v Selby* [2001] EWCA Civ 1522; [2002] P.I.Q.R. P201; [2002] Lloyd's Rep. Med. 1; see para.2–061.
[378] [2003] UKHL 52; [2004] 1 A.C. 309; paras 2–062 and 2–071.

of the birth of the child" (though this appears not to exclude loss of earnings during the pregnancy). Lord Millett would have excluded the mother's claim for the pain and distress of the pregnancy and delivery: they were the "price of parenthood" and the fact that this particular price was paid by the mother alone was irrelevant. On the other hand, his Lordship would have awarded general damages to both Mr and Mrs McFarlane for the fact that their autonomy has been breached because they had lost the freedom to limit the size of their family. This should be a conventional sum, not exceeding £5,000. The expense of the child's layette was not recoverable.[379]

Loss of the right to limit the size of one's family   At the time Lord Millett's views were clearly in the minority in respect of what the mother was entitled to claim. However, a seven-judge House of Lords subsequently reconsidered *McFarlane* in *Rees v Darlington Memorial Hospital NHS Trust*[380] and a bare majority of the House held that the parents of a healthy or a disabled child were entitled to claim a "conventional sum" of £15,000 for loss of the right to limit the size of one's family. This is in addition to the mother's claim in respect of losses associated with the pregnancy itself.   **12–138**

Mother's pain and suffering   Logically, in any case where but for the defendant's negligence the mother would not have become pregnant (such as a failed sterilisation or pre-conception negligent genetic counselling) she should be entitled to damages for the pain and suffering associated with the pregnancy and birth itself, which she would otherwise have avoided, and, in the case of a failed sterilisation the pain and suffering attributable to a further sterilisation operation. In the case of post-conception negligence (which may consist of simply failing to identify that the mother is pregnant or of a failure in the screening process for foetal abnormality) the mother would not be entitled to damages for the pregnancy itself, though insofar as she has continued with the pregnancy after the date at which she would have opted for a termination there may be additional losses, such as the inconvenience and distress associated with the later stages of pregnancy, the pain and suffering of the birth itself, and possibly loss of earnings.[381] Against this may be offset the inconvenience, pain and suffering associated with the termination of the pregnancy which she did not undergo.[382] There should be no offset, however, against the award for the pain and distress suffered by the mother during the pregnancy and birth on account of the happiness that a healthy child will bring after the birth.[383]   **12–139**

---

[379] Unless, as a result of the incorrect information, the McFarlanes had disposed of equipment previously purchased for other children which they would have kept had they known that they would have another child. This was "a direct and foreseeable consequence of the information they were given being wrong."

[380] [2003] UKHL 52; [2004] 1 A.C. 309.

[381] In *Scuriaga v Powell* (1979) 123 S.J. 406; aff'd unreported 24 July 1980, CA, the award included a sum for diminution of the claimant's marriage prospects following a failed abortion operation.

[382] *Thake v Maurice* [1986] Q.B. 644 at 682; *Allen v Bloomsbury Health Authority* [1993] 1 All E.R. 651, at 657.

[383] [1986] Q.B. 644 at 682.

12–140 **Mother's pecuniary losses**   With regard to pecuniary losses, in the case of a failed sterilisation the mother is entitled to the cost of a second sterilisation operation.[384] Any claim in respect of the mother's loss of earnings must be limited to losses during the pregnancy and, presumably, in respect of a period after the birth when it would not be reasonable to expect her to return to work.[385] She is not entitled to loss of earnings attributable to giving up work simply to look after the child, since this is regarded as part of the cost of raising a healthy child.[386] If, however, the mother sustains injury in the course of the pregnancy, or develops a condition, such as postnatal depression, which is causally linked to the pregnancy, which prevents her from returning to work then she should be entitled to loss of earnings under the normal principles applied to any personal injuries action.[387]

(b)   The disabled child

12–141   Where the child is disabled there are three aspects to the assessment of the damages: (1) the mother's claim in respect of losses flowing from the pregnancy or its continuation, which includes pecuniary losses and general damages in respect of pain and suffering and loss of amenity; (2) the parents' claim for general damages arising from the shock of discovering that the child is disabled; and (3) the parents' claim in respect of the financial loss flowing from the child's disability.

(i)   The mother's claim where the child is disabled

12–142   The mother is entitled to damages in respect of the pregnancy on a similar basis as if the child were born healthy, including general damages for pain and suffering,[388] and special damages for any additional medical expenses or clothing, and loss of earnings during the pregnancy, where the negligence resulted in the pregnancy itself.[389] Where the child was wanted, and the negligence consisted of a failure to diagnose the child's disabilities during the pregnancy thereby depriving the mother of an opportunity of having an abortion, the damages must be limited to the consequences of the failure to terminate the

---

[384] As had been conceded in *Emeh v Kensington and Chelsea Area Health Authority* [1985] Q.B. 1012.

[385] There would be some logic in linking this period to the statutory provisions on a woman's right to maternity leave.

[386] *Groom v Selby* [2001] EWCA Civ 1522; [2002] P.I.Q.R. P201; [2002] Lloyd's Rep. Med. 1.

[387] See *Ahern and Ahern v Moore and The Southern Health Board* [2013] IEHC 72; [2013] 1 I.R. 205 where the child was born with serious disabilities and died at the age of six months. Ryan J held that the mother's claim for damages was not limited to the period up to the birth. Agreeing with Lord Hope's analysis in *McFarlane*, Ryan J held that the principle to be applied was remoteness of damage, not a specific timescale. On that basis the postnatal six-month period was included, both in respect of pecuniary and non-pecuniary losses.

[388] Which includes both the physical and psychological effects of the pregnancy: *Taylor v Shropshire Health Authority* [2000] Lloyd's Rep. Med. 96, a failed sterilisation case decided before *McFarlane; Rand v East Dorset Health Authority* [2000] Lloyd's Rep. Med. 181.

[389] *Hardman v Amin* [2000] Lloyd's Rep. Med. 498; *Lee v Taunton and Somerset NHS Trust* [2001] 1 F.L.R. 419, QBD.

pregnancy, rather than the pregnancy itself, though in reality it is probable that any loss of earnings would be towards the end of the pregnancy and therefore that loss is related to the continuation of the pregnancy. General damages will cover the inconvenience of the pregnancy and childbirth and the shock of the mother's realisation that she had given birth to a disabled child.[390]

Against the general damages should be offset the pain and suffering associated **12–143** with a termination of the pregnancy which the mother did not undergo.[391] If as a consequence of the birth of the disabled child the mother chooses not to have a further child that she would otherwise have had there may be an additional offset in respect of the further pregnancy that she will not now experience.[392] In addition, if the evidence establishes that had the mother had a termination of the pregnancy she would have subsequently become pregnant again in an attempt to have a healthy child, there should be an offset in relation to the loss and expense of that hypothetical future pregnancy and childbirth. Such a set-off may reduce the claim under this head to nil.[393] On the other hand, in *Rand v East Dorset Health Authority*[394] Newman J awarded *additional* general damages in respect of a further pregnancy to a mother who claimed that she went on to have a third child, after the birth of the disabled child, in order to "prove" to herself and her family that she was able to have a healthy child.[395]

(ii)   General damages to the parents

Before *McFarlane* precluded claims in respect of the costs of raising a healthy **12–144** child, it was the standard practice to offset the parents' claim for general damages in respect of loss of amenity for the time and trouble involved in raising the child against the parents' happiness and joy in having the child. That offset was not applied in the case of a disabled child, however, thereby recognising the additional stress, anxiety and burdens involved in bringing up a disabled child.[396] This head of loss has continued to be recognised in cases involving disabled

---

[390] *Hardman v Amin* [2000] Lloyd's Rep. Med. 498; *Lee v Taunton and Somerset NHS Trust* [2001] 1 F.L.R. 419. The assumption is that the shock of discovering that the child is disabled at the birth, rather than at the time of the scan during the pregnancy, is more traumatic for the mother: *Rand v East Dorset Health Authority* [2000] Lloyd's Rep. Med. 181 at 200.

[391] *Rand v East Dorset Health Authority* [2000] Lloyd's Rep. Med. 181.

[392] *Salih v Enfield Health Authority* [1991] 3 All E.R. 400, CA.

[393] *Hardman v Amin* [2000] Lloyd's Rep. Med. 498 at 501. In *Lee v Taunton and Somerset NHS Trust* [2001] 1 F.L.R. 419 at 429 Toulson J commented that: "...in attempting to draw a balance sheet which shows a true and fair view of the injured party's loss, credit items can only be taken into account which are commensurable with the debits claimed. You can offset apples against apples, and pears against pears, but not apples against pears."

[394] [2000] Lloyd's Rep. Med. 181 at 200.

[395] The causal link between the defendant's negligence in failing to inform the parents of the results of a routine pregnancy scan which disclosed the risk that the mother was carrying a Down's Syndrome baby, and the further pregnancy, is somewhat tenuous in this case. The mother's evidence was that she wanted to prove that she could have another healthy baby and wanted her first child to have a "normal" brother or sister. Arguably, this would still have been the case even if the defendants had not been in breach of duty and the mother had had an abortion.

[396] *Emeh v Kensington and Chelsea Area Health Authority* [1985] Q.B. 1012 at 1028–1029; *Allen v Bloomsbury Health Authority* [1993] 1 All E.R. 651 at 657.

children. In *Rand v East Dorset Health Authority*[397] Newman J awarded general damages of £30,000 to the mother and £5,000 to the father for loss of amenity, namely the real and physical experience of looking after a disabled child with all its consequences for their private life.[398] The argument that this involved an award of general damages for pain and suffering and loss of amenity as a consequence of economic loss rather than personal injury to the parents was rejected. Similarly, in *McLelland v Greater Glasgow Health Board*[399] an award of £5,000 to the father was upheld on appeal. This was compensation for the shock and distress of discovering, soon after the birth, and contrary to the expectation that the defendants had created, that the child was affected by Down's Syndrome. It also reflected the "stress and wear and tear" of bringing up a child with the Syndrome.[400] Lord Prosser rejected the defendants' argument that the father was a "secondary victim" (a categorisation derived from claims in respect of psychiatric damage[401]). Nor was the distinction between ordinary emotional reactions and a positive psychiatric illness drawn in cases involving pure psychiatric damage relevant in the context of this type of claim. The parents are also entitled to a "conventional sum" of £15,000 for loss of the right to limit the size of one's family.[402]

(iii) Financial loss arising from the child's disability

12–145 In addition to the mother's claim to financial loss stemming from the pregnancy or the continuation of the pregnancy, and general damages to both the mother and father in respect of the shock of discovering that the child is disabled and the

---

[397] [2000] Lloyd's Rep. Med. 181.

[398] "The defendant is not liable for the disability but liable for having failed to protect the claimants from the consequences of the disability. The burdens are consequential upon the failure of the defendant to take reasonable steps to protect the claimants from having to suffer the burdens. It is obvious that the birth of a disabled child will dramatically affect the quality of life of both parents and it is to be inferred that a reason why they would have terminated the pregnancy was to avoid such a loss of amenity in their lives. As the law stands they cannot recover for any distress which causes no injury, but the loss of amenity caused by being required to expend time caring for a disabled child is a real and physical consequence. I have no doubt that it has sometimes led to exhaustion. In my judgment the law can recognise a claim for a continuing loss of amenity where a breach of duty has caused physical consequences giving rise to the loss of amenity", [2000] Lloyd's Rep. Med. 181 at 201, per Newman J.

[399] 2001 S.L.T. 446, Court of Session, Extra Div.

[400] See also *Allen v Bloomsbury Health Authority* [1993] 1 All E.R. 651 at 657–658 where Brooke J described this as "general damages for the burden of bringing up a handicapped child" and stressed that "this head of damages is different in kind from the typical claim for anxiety and stress associated with and flowing from an injured person's own personal injuries". For other examples see *Taylor v Shropshire Health Authority* [2000] Lloyd's Rep. Med. 96; *Hardman v Amin* [2000] Lloyd's Rep. Med. 498.

[401] See paras 2–195 et seq. Contrast *Ahern and Ahern v Moore and The Southern Health Board* [2013] IEHC 72; [2013] 1 I.R. 205 at [82] where Ryan J held that a father (unlike the mother) was not entitled to damages for "severe distress and emotional anguish" following the birth of a baby with severe physical defects which died at six months of age. There could be no damages for distress in the absence of a defined psychiatric injury. Nor could the father recover any financial expenses, since that was pure economic loss, unconnected to any physical harm to the father.

[402] *Rees v Darlington Memorial Hospital NHS Trust* [2003] UKHL 52; [2004] 1 A.C. 309; para.12–138.

"wear and tear" of raising a disabled child, the parents are entitled to recover the costs of caring for the child associated with the disability. The House of Lords had left this open following *McFarlane* but it was confirmed by the Court of Appeal in *Parkinson v St James and Seacroft University Hospital NHS Trust.*[403] Hale LJ came to the conclusion that the essence of the five speeches in *McFarlane* was the concept of "deemed equilibrium". In her analysis the ratio of *McFarlane* was that the benefits of healthy children outweigh the financial burdens of their upkeep and maintenance. Damages for the financial cost of raising a disabled child did not treat a disabled child as "worth" less than a healthy child, but simply recognised that a disabled child costs more in terms of upkeep and maintenance. Such claims were confined to children with "significant" disabilities which would be a matter to be considered on a case-by-case basis.[404] *Parkinson* was considered by the House of Lords in *Rees*, but their Lordships' decision was far from a ringing endorsement of Hale LJ's judgment.[405] Nevertheless, the decision that the parents are entitled to compensation for the costs associated with the child's disability remains good law.

Mother's loss of earnings   Whilst *Parkinson* upheld the principle of damages being awarded, case law after *McFarlane* established the nature and scope of the damages recoverable. In *Hardman v Amin*[406] the defendant conceded that the mother was entitled to claim for her loss of earnings due to having to give up work to look after her disabled child. On the other hand, in the case of a healthy child a mother is not entitled to claim her lost earnings when she gives up work to look after the child, since that is treated as part of the childrearing costs.[407] Since the basis of the claim in respect of the disability is limited to the additional costs attributable to the child's disability,[408] it would seem that there should be some deduction from the award in respect of a disabled child of those childrearing costs that would have been incurred in any event, if the child had been healthy, i.e. the basic maintenance costs.[409] Thus, if the mother would have given up work to look after a healthy child it is difficult to see how she could recover for the identical loss simply because the child is disabled.   **12–146**

Cost of gratuitous services provided to the child   A further issue in *Hardman v Amin* was whether the mother was entitled to recover for the cost of gratuitous   **12–147**

---

[403] *Parkinson v St. James and Seacroft University Hospital NHS Trust* [2001] EWCA Civ 530; [2002] Q.B. 266; approved by the Court of Appeal in *Groom v Selby* [2001] EWCA Civ 1522; [2002] P.I.Q.R. P201; [2002] Lloyd's Rep. Med. 1.
[404] See para.2–065.
[405] Of the seven Law Lords who heard the case and gave judgment, three thought *Parkinson* was correctly decided. Two would have overruled it, expressly disagreeing with the "deemed equilibrium" concept. One did not express a view and one would have limited its application. See paras 2–062 to 2–063.
[406] [2000] Lloyd's Rep. Med. 498 at 508.
[407] *Greenfield v Irwin* [2001] EWCA Civ 113; [2001] 1 W.L.R. 1279; Grubb (2001) 9 Med. L. Rev. 54.
[408] Applying *Parkinson v St James and Seacroft University Hospital NHS Trust* [2001] EWCA Civ 530; [2002] Q.B. 266.
[409] See *McLelland v Greater Glasgow Health Board* 2001 S.L.T. 446, Extra Div.

services provided to the disabled child, following *Housecroft v Burnett*[410] (provided that there was no overlap between the loss of earnings and the cost of care[411]). The defendant argued that the mother could not claim the cost of gratuitous services to the child, because the claim was for economic loss by the mother, not for physical injury sustained by the child. This approach was rejected by Henriques J. Compensation for the mother's time spent caring for the child was to be assessed on the basis of *Housecroft v Burnett*, for which the measure of damages should be the "commercial cost" of the care, less 25 per cent.[412] Alternatively, if the claim for the loss calculated in accordance with *Housecroft v Burnett* was wrong, Henriques J held that the mother was entitled to damages for the loss of amenity consisting of the stress, anxiety and disruption of her life resulting from the obligation to bring up a disabled child.[413]

12–148   **Offsetting financial savings to the parents**   In *Salih v Enfield Health Authority*[414] the Court of Appeal held that where the parents decide not to have further children because of the problems they face in bringing up a handicapped child, this would produce a saving in expenditure which would otherwise have been incurred and this saving must be brought into account in assessing the cost of providing for the handicapped child. Logically, this approach appears to be correct and there is nothing in *McFarlane* or *Parkinson* which would suggest that *Salih* is wrong. It would seem to be somewhat rough justice, however, if parents who had wanted to have, say, two children, decide that the emotional and financial cost of raising their one disabled child is such that they will not have a second child, and are then told that the financial saving they will make in not having the second child will reduce the defendants' liability to contribute to the cost of their child's disability.[415]

12–149   **Child benefit not deductible**   In principle any other benefits or savings arising out the defendants' negligence should be brought into account in reducing the parents' financial loss. For example, before *McFarlane* it had been accepted that child benefit must be deducted from the cost of maintaining the child.[416] Child benefit is not a "relevant benefit" for the purpose of the recovery of social

---

[410] [1986] 1 All E.R. 332.

[411] In *Fish v Wilcox* (1993) 13 B.M.L.R. 134; [1994] 5 Med. L.R. 230, CA, it was held that an award of damages in respect of the birth of a handicapped child should not include an amount in respect of the mother's lost earnings *in addition* to a sum for the services she was rendering in caring for the child. She cannot make a profit by being compensated for doing two jobs.

[412] [2000] Lloyd's Rep. Med. 498 at 509.

[413] [2000] Lloyd's Rep. Med. 498 at 510: "To retreat to a position where claimants who sustain stress or psychological damage without compensation in circumstances such as this would not only be insensitive but would constitute a failure to compensate in manifestly meritorious circumstances." See also *Taylor v Shropshire Health Authority* [2000] Lloyd's Rep. Med. 96 where, before the decision in *McFarlane*, it had been held that in addition to general damages for the physical and psychological effects of the pregnancy, the mother was entitled to damages for the additional burden of bringing up a disabled child.

[414] [1991] 3 All E.R. 400.

[415] cf. *McLelland v Greater Glasgow Health Board* 2001 S.L.T. 446, declining to follow *Salih* on this point.

[416] *Emeh v Kensington and Chelsea Area Health Authority* [1985] Q.B. 1012.

security benefits under the Social Security (Recovery of Benefits) Act 1997,[417] and therefore the principle of full deductibility from the assessment of the damages applied. But now that the compensatable financial loss is limited to the costs attributable to the child's disability, rather than the full costs of raising the child, it would seem that receipts of child benefit should not be deducted. In *Rand v East Dorset Health Authority (No.2)*[418] the defendants conceded, rightly it is submitted, that child benefit was not deductible because it was not paid by reason of the child's disability. Child benefit is a contribution to the cost of raising every child, healthy or disabled, and it would be wrong to offset a benefit that was not linked to the basis of the defendants' liability, namely the child's disability.

Other social security benefits   In *Rand* Newman J also held that recovery of benefits under the Social Security (Recovery of Benefits) Act 1997 did not apply to a claim made by parents against a health authority in respect of the additional cost of raising a disabled child, where the negligence consisted of failing to inform the parents of the risk that the child would be born disabled thereby denying the parents the option of having a termination of the pregnancy. That was a claim for financial loss resulting from negligent misrepresentation not personal injury suffered by the claimants. But the 1997 Act only applies to actions for personal injuries. Accordingly, recovery of benefits does not apply. That means that the common law rules on deduction of benefits applies, which in most instances means that the full value of benefits paid in consequence of the tort should be deducted. However, receipt of invalid care allowance by the parents of the child should not be deducted because that is awarded in respect of the care of the child, whereas the parents were compensated by the defendants, not for caring for the child, but for their reasonable expenditure in connection with the child's disability.[419] Moreover, any benefits paid to the child in respect of disabilities do not reduce the loss to the parents, since the benefits were for the child who was not compensated by the defendants, and therefore they should not be deducted from the damages award.[420]   **12–150**

Three further issues in relation to the assessment of the financial loss associated with the child's disability have arisen, namely: (i) can the costs of raising the disabled child extend beyond age 18; (ii) can the loss exceed what the parents could afford to spend; and (iii) does s.2(4) of the Law Reform (Personal Injury) Act 1948 apply?   **12–151**

Can the costs of raising the disabled child extend beyond age 18?   The costs associated with the child's disability beyond the age of 18 are recoverable.[421] This is because the normal principles of foreseeability apply to the assessment of   **12–152**

---

[417] See paras 12–106 et seq.

[418] [2001] P.I.Q.R. Q1; [2000] Lloyd's Rep. Med. 377.

[419] [2001] P.I.Q.R. Q1; [2000] Lloyd's Rep. Med. 377. It is not clear how this view sits with the approach of Henriques J in *Hardman v Amin* where it was held that the mother was entitled to recover the cost of gratuitous services provided to the disabled child: see para.12–147.

[420] [2001] P.I.Q.R. Q1; [2000] Lloyd's Rep. Med. 377. These benefits were Disability Living Allowance, and from age 18, Income Support and Severe Disablement Allowance.

[421] *Rand v East Dorset Health Authority* [2000] Lloyd's Rep. Med. 181; *Nunnerley v Warrington Health Authority* [2000] P.I.Q.R. Q69, QBD. Although *Nunnerley* predates *McFarlane* leave to appeal

the loss, and in any event it cannot be said that the parents' responsibility towards a disabled child ends at the child's 18th birthday.[422]

12–153 **Can the loss exceed what the parents could afford to spend?** The claim for the economic loss attributable to the child's disability is not limited to the amounts which a claimant would have been able to contribute to such costs in the absence of an award of damages to meet them. An argument to limit damages in this way had been accepted in *Rand v East Dorset Health Authority*.[423] Newman J considered that this followed from the categorisation of the loss as economic loss. But in *Hardman v Amin*[424] Henriques J rejected this view, accepting the claimant's argument that categorisation of a claim as one for economic loss identified the criteria to be satisfied before a duty and its scope are established, but has nothing to do with the quantification of damages once a breach of duty is shown to have resulted in loss of a type which the defendant was under a duty to avoid.[425] As Henriques J commented, the effect of the defendant's argument would be that:

> "The poorer the claimant, the less she will be able to spend on her disabled child. Indeed, it might deny the claim of the poorest parent unable to buy in any care or equipment."

The measure of the loss was the reasonable needs of the disabled child, and was not limited by reference to what the claimant would, but for the award, have been able to afford to spend on care.

12–154 In *Lee v Taunton and Somerset NHS Trust* Toulson J agreed with Henriques J on this point.[426] Similarly, in *Roberts v Bro Taf Health Authority*[427] Turner J considered that the approach adopted by Henriques J in *Hardman* was correct:

---

on the question of whether damages should be limited to the date of the child's 18th birthday was subsequently refused, *sub nom. Gaynor N v Warrington Health Authority* [2003] Lloyd's Rep. Med. 365.

[422] As Hale LJ commented in *Gaynor N v Warrington Health Authority* [2003] Lloyd's Rep. Med. 365, at [16]: "the argument that damages should be limited up to the age of eighteen was based on a very narrow view of what might or might not be the responsibilities of parents towards children, particularly those children who sadly suffer a disability. There is a great deal in family law to indicate that liabilities not only towards those children, but also to the parent who is looking after those children (should there have been a marriage as there was in this case), may indeed endure long beyond the age of eighteen. But in any event I would have thought that there is no basis for departing from the normal principles of reasonable foreseeability of the loss in question in this case." See also R. Glancey QC, "Damages for Wrongful Birth—Where do they end?" [2006] J.P.I.L. 271, arguing that the parents' financial loss extends beyond the child's 18th birthday, and that damages may even cover a period beyond the parents' life expectancy.

[423] [2000] Lloyd's Rep. Med. 181 at 194: "The claimants may only recover such losses as they have in fact sustained, or will probably sustain, in the future. Their own means, as opposed to Katy's needs, are determinative of this issue. In my judgment, this must follow as a matter of law from the categorisation of the claim as a claim for pure economic loss."

[424] [2000] Lloyd's Rep. Med. 498 at 506–508.

[425] See also *Taylor v Shropshire Health Authority* [2000] Lloyd's Rep. Med. 96 at 103; *Anderson v Forth Valley Health Board* (1997) 44 B.M.L.R. 108 at 139.

[426] [2001] 1 F.L.R. 419 at 433: "I do not see why the quantification of her loss under this head should be affected by her means. Her need exists, whether she has the means to meet it or not. It is quantifiable. It was caused by the defendants' negligence. In principle she should therefore be entitled

"It would be inconsistent with the *rationale* [of *Parkinson*] that the *needs* of the family in connection with extra expenditure should be rationed by the economic circumstances in which the family found itself."[428]

Moreover, as Turner J pointed out, in this type of case the mother also has a claim to substantial damages in respect of the pregnancy itself. If she were to expend this sum on providing care for the child then the claim in respect of that care becomes "self-funding at the defendants' expense".[429] In other words the mother would become richer in any event and so can afford the care for the child, and therefore the defendants have to pay for that care.[430]

Does s.2(4) of the Law Reform (Personal Injury) Act 1948 apply?   There is   **12–155** some uncertainty as to how the financial loss attributable to the child's disability should be categorised. In principle, it would appear to be a claim for pure economic loss. There are statements in *McFarlane* to the effect that the costs of raising a healthy child constitutes pure economic loss,[431] and in most actions since *McFarlane* the claim in respect of the costs of raising a disabled child has been characterised as one for pure economic loss. The issue is significant in the context of a number of statutory provisions where the legislation makes the outcome turn upon whether the claimant's action is one for personal injuries.

In *Hardman v Amin*[432] the defendant argued that the claimant had not suffered   **12–156** personal injuries, and therefore s.2(4) of the Law Reform (Personal Injuries) Act 1948, which requires the court to disregard the possibility that the claimant can avoid expenses by taking advantage of facilities under the NHS, did not apply. The consequence, said the defendant, was that the claimant must mitigate her loss by taking advantage of facilities under the NHS. Henriques J considered *Walkin v South Manchester Health Authority*,[433] where, in the context of the Limitation Act 1980, the Court of Appeal treated a wrongful conception claim as an action for personal injuries, and the comments of their Lordships in *McFarlane*, and held that the claim was an action for personal injuries:

---

to recover the cost of it. It would be invidious if two mothers in Mrs. Lee's situation, each having the same needs, differed in their ability to recover the cost of meeting those needs, because one possessed independent means and the other did not."

[427] [2002] Lloyd's Rep. Med. 182.
[428] [2002] Lloyd's Rep. Med. 182 at [15], original emphasis.
[429] [2002] Lloyd's Rep. Med. 182 at [16].
[430] See further Whitfield (2002) 18 P.N. 234 at 246.
[431] *McFarlane v Tayside Health Board* [2000] 2 A.C. 59 at 75 per Lord Slynn: "It is to be remembered on this part of the case that your Lordships are concerned only with liability for economic loss"; at 79 per Lord Steyn: "the father's part of the claim for the cost of bringing up the unwanted child is undoubtedly a claim for pure economic loss. Realistically, despite the pregnancy and child birth, the mother's part of the claim is also for pure economic loss." See also per Lord Hope at 89; per Lord Clyde at 102; and per Lord Millett at 109. Note, however, that not all of their Lordships considered that the categorisation of the loss as pure economic loss or consequential economic loss was determinative of the outcome.
[432] [2000] Lloyd's Rep. Med. 498.
[433] [1995] 1 W.L.R. 1543; [1995] 4 All E.R. 132; see para.11–000.

"It would be an anomaly for a wrongful conception claim to be an action for damages for personal injuries whilst a wrongful birth case was not."[434]

The continuation of a pregnancy which should not have been continued could amount to a personal injury. While the logic of treating the unnecessary continuation of a pregnancy as personal injury to the mother is obvious, it is not so clear that the financial costs of raising a disabled child are part and parcel of that injury, so as to be treated as consequential loss. Indeed, their Lordships in *McFarlane* drew a distinction between the mother's claim in respect of her losses during and shortly after the pregnancy and the parents' claim in respect of the costs of raising the child, the latter being treated as pure economic loss; and in *Rand v East Dorset Health Authority (No.2)*[435] Newman J held that recovery of benefits under the Social Security (Recovery of Benefits) Act 1997 did not apply because the parents' claim for the cost of raising a disabled child was not an action for personal injuries. If the mother's loss and the parents' loss are distinct claims, it would seem that the costs of raising a disabled child should not be covered by s.2(4) of the Law Reform (Personal Injuries) Act 1948.[436] That is not the end of the matter, of course, since the defendant would have to demonstrate that the parents had failed to mitigate their loss by not taking advantage of facilities for free treatment for the child under the NHS, and that is a question of whether they acted unreasonably in insisting on private medical care.

(c) The disabled parent

12–157   In *Rees v Darlington Memorial Hospital NHS Trust*[437] the mother was almost blind and was concerned that her lack of sight would prevent her properly caring for a child. She therefore underwent a sterilisation procedure at the defendant's hospital. The procedure was negligently performed and she subsequently gave birth to a healthy child. She brought a claim seeking the full cost of bringing up the child. At issue was whether her circumstances should constitute an exception to the general principle laid down by the House of Lords in *McFarlane* that there could be no claim for the financial costs of raising a healthy child. The Court of Appeal[438] accepted that, in principle, a mother who was herself disabled was entitled to bring an action in respect of the additional costs of raising the child

---

[434] [2000] Lloyd's Rep. Med. 498 at 501. Note that for the purpose of the Limitation Act 1980 it makes sense to have a single commencement point for the running of the limitation period, and *Walkin* can be seen as an attempt by the Court of Appeal to prevent claimants opting for either the longer six-year period in cases not involving personal injuries (but without a discretion to extend to the period) or the three-year period plus a discretion to disapply the primary limitation period in cases involving personal injuries, depending upon whichever option suited the circumstances of the claimant's case. Moreover, it remains to be seen whether *Walkin* can survive the reasoning in *McFarlane*. See para.11–046.

[435] [2001] P.I.Q.R. Q1; [2000] Lloyd's Rep. Med. 377; see para.12–150 above.

[436] See *Lee v Taunton and Somerset NHS Trust* [2001] 1 F.L.R. 419 at 431 per Toulson J suggesting, provisionally, that s.2(4) did not apply to the financial costs of raising a disabled child.

[437] [2003] UKHL 52; [2004] 1 A.C. 309; para.2–069.

[438] [2002] EWCA Civ 88; [2003] Q.B. 20.

attributable to her disability. It was fair, just and reasonable that she recover the additional costs she would incur as a consequence of her disability, in bringing up the child.

A seven-judge House of Lords allowed the hospital's appeal. By a majority of four to three their Lordships held that no exception to the general principle of *McFarlane* should be made for a disabled mother who gives birth to a healthy child. Of course, the disabled mother is entitled to claim in respect of the same losses associated with the pregnancy itself as the healthy mother. By a majority of four to two (with one not expressing a view) they took up the suggestion of Lord Millet in *McFarlane* and held that the parents of a child born following a negligently performed sterilisation procedure or as a consequence of negligent contraceptive advice should receive a "conventional" award of £15,000 to compensate for the loss of their ability to limit the size of their family. This head of damages applies whether or not the child or the parent is healthy or disabled.

12–158

(d)   Wrongful life

In contrast to claims for wrongful birth or wrongful conception, wrongful life claims concern claims by children for damages in respect of their own disabilities where they are born in circumstances where but for the negligence of the doctors, the mother would have been advised to have a termination of pregnancy. Such claims were considered to be contrary to public policy by the Court of Appeal in *McKay v Essex Area Health Authority*.[439]

12–159

5.   DEATH

At common law people's deaths extinguished any cause of action that may have existed against them and any cause of action that the deceased may have had against another. Moreover, a person's death did not confer any common law right of action on another person against the person who had caused the death, which meant that the dependants of someone killed by another's negligence had no action in respect of their loss of financial support by the deceased. Both of these rules have been changed by legislation: the Law Reform (Miscellaneous Provisions) Act 1934 and the Fatal Accidents Act 1976 (consolidating previous Fatal Accidents Acts) respectively.[440]

12–160

---

[439] [1982] 2 Q.B. 1166; para.2–141. The Court noted that it would be unable to place a value on damages for non-existence and that in any event for births occurring after 22 July 1976 such claims would be contrary to the Congenital Disabilities (Civil Liability) Act 1976. The Act provides a remedy for children whose claims arise as a result of injuries tortiously inflicted prior to birth. See para.2–135.

[440] See generally the Law Commission Report, *Claims for Wrongful Death*, Law Com. No.263, 1999.

(a) Survival of actions

12–161   The Law Reform (Miscellaneous Provisions) Act 1934 s.1(1) provides that on the death of any person all causes of action (except defamation) subsisting against or vested in them survive against, or, as the case may be, for the benefit of, their estate. The Act does not create a cause of action; it merely allows for the survival of existing actions, except that where, as a result of an act or omission by the deceased, damage has been suffered which would have given rise to a cause of action had the person not died before or at the same time as the damage suffered, s.1(4) deems that the cause of action shall subsist as if they had died after the damage was sustained.

12–162   An action brought by the estate of a deceased claimant is dealt with on the same basis as for a living claimant, and the measure of damages will generally be the same. The estate can recover any expenses incurred or any loss of earnings attributable to the tort up to the date of death, but not after the death.[441] Similarly, pain and suffering and loss of amenity up to the date of death are recoverable,[442] including any suffering attributable to the deceased's knowledge that life expectancy has been reduced.[443] Where the death was caused by the act or omission which gives rise to the cause of action, damages are calculated without reference to any loss or gain consequent upon the death, except that a sum in respect of funeral expenses may be included.[444] Thus, gains to the estate, such as the proceeds of a life insurance policy, and losses, such as the loss of a life interest under a trust, are ignored. Where a patient has died following private surgery, the estate cannot claim the cost of the surgery (on the basis that the surgery was rendered futile by the negligence of the surgeon), because the cost of the surgery did not flow from the negligence but from the deceased's promise to pay the hospital for the operation.[445]

(b) Fatal accidents

12–163   The Fatal Accidents Act 1976 s.1(1) confers upon the dependants of a deceased person a cause of action in respect of their loss of financial dependency, provided that the deceased would have had an action in tort in respect of the injuries that caused his death.[446] The dependants have a cause of action in their own right in

---

[441] Claims in respect of loss of earnings in the "lost years" do not survive for the benefit of the estate: Law Reform (Miscellaneous Provisions) Act 1934 s.1(2)(a) (as amended by the Administration of Justice Act 1982 s.4(2)), reversing the effect of *Gammell v Wilson* [1982] A.C. 136. Thus, lost years claims are only available to living claimants, or where the death occurred before 1 January 1983.

[442] In *Hicks v Chief Constable of South Yorkshire Police* [1992] 2 All E.R. 65 however, the House of Lords held that damages for pain and suffering in the few minutes between an injury and death are not recoverable under the Law Reform (Miscellaneous Provisions) Act 1934.

[443] *Kadir v Mistry* [2014] EWCA Civ 1177; para.12–127.

[444] Law Reform (Miscellaneous Provisions) Act 1934 s.1(2)(c).

[445] *Batt v Highgate Private Hospital* [2004] EWHC 707 (Ch); [2005] P.I.Q.R. Q1.

[446] Fatal Accidents Act 1976 s.2(3) provides that: "Not more than one action shall lie for and in respect of the same subject matter of complaint." In *Cachia v Faluyi* [2001] EWCA Civ 998; [2001] 1 W.L.R. 1966 the Court of Appeal held that the word "action" should be interpreted to mean "served process". Thus, where a writ had been issued in a Fatal Accidents Act claim on behalf of three young

respect of financial loss[447] irrespective of any claim that might be made on behalf of the deceased's estate under the Law Reform (Miscellaneous Provisions) Act 1934. The dependants' action is derivative, in that it can be maintained only if the defendant would have been liable to the deceased, and it is subject to any defences, such as contributory negligence or volenti non fit injuria, that the defendant could have raised against the deceased.[448] If for any reason the deceased could not have maintained an action at the moment of death, if, for example, he has sued the defendant to a judgment or settled the claim while still alive, the dependants have no claim.[449]

An award of damages under the Fatal Accidents Act may consist of (i) damages for bereavement (ii) damages for the dependants' actual and prospective pecuniary loss, and (iii) if the dependants have in fact incurred funeral expenses they are entitled to be reimbursed.[450] Financial dependency has to be established, but this in itself is not sufficient to qualify for compensation. First, the claimant must fall within the list of dependants set out in the Act.

12–164

(i) Who qualifies as a dependant?

The class of dependants who can bring a claim under the Fatal Accidents Act 1976 is exhaustively defined in s.1 to include: a spouse, former spouse, civil

12–165

---

children, but never served, there was nothing to prevent a further writ being issued and served provided the children's claims were not barred by a limitation period. This was because s.2(3) was a "procedural quirk" which did not have any legitimate aim, and therefore an interpretation which restricted the children's right to claim would be in breach of art.6 of the European Convention on Human Rights, by restricting access to the courts.

[447] There can be no award under the Act in respect of a claimant's emotional dependency: *Thomas v Kwik Save Stores Ltd, The Times*, 27 June 2000, CA. The only exception is entitlement to damages for bereavement (para.12–167), but this is a fixed statutory sum and does not depend on proof of damage in the form of grief or psychiatric harm.

[448] An apportionment will be made where the death was caused partly by the negligence of the dependant: *Mulholland v McRae* [1961] N.I. 135; but this does not affect the claims of other dependants: *Dodds v Dodds* [1978] Q.B. 543.

[449] The House of Lords assumed that this was the position in *Pickett v British Rail Engineering Ltd* [1980] A.C. 136. Where the deceased's action was statute-barred under the Limitation Act 1980 the dependants can request the court to exercise its discretion to allow the action to proceed under s.33: see para.11–149. In *Thompson v Arnold* [2007] EWHC 1875 (QB); [2008] P.I.Q.R. P1; [2008] LS Law Med. 78 the deceased settled an action for personal injuries before her death, having failed to make any claim in respect of the "lost years". Langstaff J held that a subsequent claim under the Fatal Accidents Act on behalf of the deceased's dependants could not be maintained, applying *Read v Great Eastern Railway Co* (1867–68) L.R. 3 Q.B. 555. The Human Rights Act 1998 had not changed the court's approach to this issue. The position is different, however, where the personal injuries claim is compromised or discontinued after the death of the deceased. The Fatal Accidents Act claim accrues at the date of the death and is a separate action from the personal injuries or Law Reform Act claim, and so is not affected by discontinuance of the personal injuries action after the death: *Reader v Molesworths Bright Clegg Solicitors* [2007] EWCA Civ 169; [2007] 1 W.L.R. 1082; [2007] 3 All E.R. 107.

[450] Fatal Accidents Act 1976 s.3(5). Except that funeral expenses should not be awarded in a case where the defendant's breach of duty merely accelerated the symptoms of a pre-existing condition by a relatively short period of time: *Brown v Hamid* [2013] EWHC 4067 (QB) at [40]. The cost of a wake is not recoverable under the Act: *Jones v Royal Devon and Exeter NHS Foundation Trust* [2008] EWHC 558 (QB); (2008) 101 B.M.L.R. 154 at [135].

partner, former civil partner, or "cohabitee"[451] of the deceased; any parent or other ascendant, any child or other descendant, or any person treated by the deceased as a parent or as a child; and any person who is, or is the issue of, a brother, sister, uncle or aunt of the deceased. A relationship by marriage or civil partnership is treated as a relationship by blood, and a relationship by half-blood as a relationship of the whole blood. The stepchild of any person is treated as a child, and an illegitimate person is treated as the legitimate child of the mother and reputed father or, in the case of a person who has a female parent by virtue of s.43 of the Human Fertilisation and Embryology Act 2008, the legitimate child of the mother and that female parent. An action will normally be instituted by the personal representative of the deceased person's estate on behalf of the dependants, but if an action is not commenced within six months any dependant can sue on behalf of all the dependants.[452]

12–166 **Excluded dependants and the Human Rights Act**[453] In *Swift v Secretary of State for Justice*[454] the claimant had been living with the deceased as husband and wife for about six months before he was killed in an accident at work. Their child was born after his death and had a claim for loss of dependency under the Act. The claimant did not qualify as a dependant because she had not been living with the deceased as husband and wife for at least two years. She argued that s.1(3)(b) of the Act was incompatible with her rights under art.14 in combination with art.8 of the European Convention on Human Rights. The Court of Appeal held that the different treatment of claimants under the Fatal Accidents Act based on the length of their cohabitation was not incompatible with her Convention rights. Lord Dyson expressed the view that:

> "Parliament was entitled to decide that there had to be some way of proving the requisite degree of permanence and constancy in the relationship beyond the mere fact of living together as husband and wife. It was entitled to take the view that there cannot be a presumption in the case of short-term cohabitants, unlike that of married couples (section 1(3)(a)) or parents and their children (section 1(3)(e)) that the relationship is or is likely to be one of permanence and constancy."[455]

---

[451] i.e. a person who was living as the husband, wife or civil partner of the deceased in the same household immediately before the date of the death, and had been so living for at least two years: Fatal Accidents Act 1976 s.1(3)(b). On the meaning of "living in the same household" see *Pounder v London Underground Ltd* [1995] P.I.Q.R. P217. A divorced woman who remarries, but who subsequently returns to live with her first husband, is capable of being a dependant, as a former wife, and does not have to satisfy the residence requirements of s.1(3)(b): *Shepherd v Post Office, The Times*, 15 June 1995, CA. See further *Kotke v Saffarini* [2005] EWCA Civ 221; [2005] 2 F.L.R. 517; [2005] P.I.Q.R. P26 on the meaning of "living in the same household". There is a distinction between intending to live in the same household, planning to do so and actually doing so. So where the deceased retained his own home, leaving his wardrobe and possessions there, and living out of an overnight bag at the claimant's house, he had not been living in the same household. Nor did the sharing of shopping expenses when the claimant and the deceased were together at her house establish that there was a joint household.

[452] Fatal Accidents Act 1976 s.2.

[453] For detailed consideration of the impact of the Human Rights Act on Fatal Accident Act claims and in particular the class of dependants entitled to claim see R. Davison, "The Fatal Accidents Act 1976—Does it mean what it says?" [2007] J.P.I.L. 297.

[454] [2013] EWCA Civ 193; [2014] Q.B. 373.

[455] [2013] EWCA Civ 193; [2014] Q.B. 373 at [36].

It was a proportionate means of pursuing a legitimate aim, which was:

"...to confer a right of action on dependants of primary victims of fatal wrongdoing to recover damages in respect of their loss of dependency, but to confine the right to recover damages to those who had relationships of some degree of permanence and dependence."[456]

(ii)   Damages for bereavement

Damages for bereavement were introduced by the Administration of Justice Act 1982 s.3, creating a new s.1A of the Fatal Accidents Act 1976. This is a fixed sum of £12,980 for deaths on or after 1 April 2013[457] awarded to the spouse or civil partner of the deceased or the parents of a deceased unmarried[458] minor child (though only the mother in the case of an illegitimate child).[459] Where both parents of a child claim damages for bereavement the award will be divided equally between them. The award does not require proof of any financial dependency, and there is no inquiry into the extent of the claimant's grief; the award is a conventional sum which may be increased by regulations but not by the courts. A claim for bereavement damages does not survive for the benefit of the spouse's or parent's estate.[460] Where young children are killed damages for bereavement plus funeral expenses will commonly be the only sum payable by the defendant.

12–167

Human rights   In *Cameron v Network Rail Infrastructure Ltd*[461] it was held that the restrictions on who can claim damages for bereavement under s.1A of the Fatal Accidents Act 1976 are not incompatible with the European Convention on

12–168

---

[456] [2013] EWCA Civ 193; [2014] Q.B. 373 at [23].

[457] Damages for Bereavement (Variation of Sum) (England and Wales) Order 2013 (SI 2013/510). The sum had previously been: £11,800 for actions accruing on or after 1 January 2008 (Damages for Bereavement (Variation of Sum) (England and Wales) Order 2007 (SI 2007/3489)); £10,000 for actions accruing on or after 1 April 2002 (Damages for Bereavement (Variation of Sum) (England and Wales) Order 2002 (SI 2002/644)); £7,500 for actions accruing on or after 1 April 1991 (Damages for Bereavement (Variation of Sum) (England and Wales) Order 1990 (SI 1990/2575)).

[458] Or a minor who was not in a civil partnership.

[459] Damages for bereavement will not be awarded to the parents of a stillborn child, although a mother will be entitled to general damages for the loss of satisfaction of bringing her pregnancy to a successful conclusion, and where appropriate, for being unable to complete her planned family: *Bagley v North Hertfordshire Health Authority* (1986) 136 N.L.J. 1014. Damages under these heads should be not less than the statutory sum awarded for bereavement; cf. *Kerby v Redbridge Health Authority* [1993] 4 Med. L.R. 178; [1994] P.I.Q.R. Q1, where Ognall J held that there should be no award for the "dashed hopes" of bringing a pregnancy to a successful conclusion, because this was either the same as bereavement, or an award for grief, sorrow or distress attendant on the loss of a loved one, which is not actionable in negligence (applying *McLoughlin v O'Brian* [1983] 1 A.C. 410 at 431; see para.2–188). His Lordship also doubted whether distress associated with fact that the claimant is unable to achieve her planned size of family is a head of damage recognised by law. This latter issue did not arise on the facts in *Kerby*, since the claimant was willing and able to attempt further pregnancies, and on this basis she was entitled to damages for "the rigours of an additional pregnancy" that the she would now have to undergo to achieve her planned size of family (assessed at £1,500).

[460] Law Reform (Miscellaneous Provisions) Act 1934 s.1(1A).

[461] [2006] EWHC 1133 (QB); [2007] 1 W.L.R. 163. See also *Swift v Secretary of State for Justice* [2013] EWCA Civ 193; [2014] Q.B. 373, para.12–166, on the question of whether the categorisation of dependants under the Act is compliant with European Convention rights.

Human Rights, and that therefore children of the deceased had no claim. Similarly, in *Smith v Lancashire Teaching Hospitals NHS Trust*[462] an argument that excluding cohabitees who are not married or in a civil partnership from the remit of s.1A amounted to a breach of Convention rights was rejected, though Edis J was highly critical of the rationale for limiting awards of bereavement damages and considered that the "current law is in need of reform".[463] On the other hand, in *Rabone v Pennine Care NHS Foundation Trust*[464] the Supreme Court held that the parents of a deceased adult child, a mental patient who committed suicide due to the defendants' negligence, qualified as "victims" for the purpose of maintaining a claim under the Convention arising out of their adult daughter's death. They had not lost their victim status by settling a negligence action on behalf of their daughter's estate. The parents were awarded £5,000 each as financial redress for breach of their art.2 rights, though they would not have been entitled to damages for bereavement under the Fatal Accidents Act 1976 because their daughter was no longer a minor.[465]

12-169 When bereavement damages were introduced it was recognised that it was not possible to quantify appropriate financial compensation to reflect the loss of a loved one. A bereavement award could only represent an acknowledgment of the loss and not true compensation. Nevertheless, in practice claimants do see such awards in these terms. They consider them to be derisory and an insult, and considerable concern has been caused by the narrow categories of people entitled to claim. The Law Commission's report *Claims for Wrongful Death* noted the problem.[466] Indeed, the Law Commission had considered the option of abolition, acknowledging the arguments against a bereavement award that grief cannot be expressed in monetary terms and that such awards were in any event subsidiary to compensation for pecuniary losses. Ultimately, however, the Law Commission concluded that bereavement damages were now part of English law and should remain.

(iii)   Loss of financial dependency

12-170 Damages for loss of financial dependency upon the deceased will be awarded in proportion to the injury resulting from the death to the dependants respectively.[467] This is determined by the multiplier method. The purpose of the award is to provide the dependants with a capital sum[468] which with prudent management will be sufficient to provide material benefits of the same standard and duration

---

[462] [2016] EWHC 2208 (QB); [2017] P.I.Q.R. P4; J. Fulbrook [2017] J.P.I.L. C31.
[463] [2016] EWHC 2208 (QB); [2017] P.I.Q.R. P4 at [109]–[112].
[464] [2012] UKSC 2; [2012] 2 A.C. 72.
[465] For criticism of this "outflanking" of the Fatal Accidents Act see A. Tettenborn, "Wrongful Death, Human Rights and the Fatal Accidents Act" (2012) 128 L.Q.R. 327.
[466] Law Commission, *Claims for Wrongful Death*, Law Com. No.263, 1999.
[467] Fatal Accidents Act 1976 s.3(1). See H. Trusted, "The meanings of dependency: Problems arising from section 3(1) of the Fatal Accidents Act 1976" [2015] J.P.I.L 149.
[468] The Court now also has power in certain circumstances to order periodical payments in Fatal Accident Act claims: see CPR r.41.8(2), and 41BPD.2.1 explaining that an order may be made under this rule where a dependant would have had a claim under s.1 of the Fatal Accidents Act 1976 if the claimant had died at the time of the accident. See generally para.12–020 et seq.

as would have been provided for them out of the deceased's earnings had he lived.[469] The starting point is the amount of the deceased's wages, less an amount for his own personal and living expenses. This provides a basic figure for estimating the dependency.[470] The length of the dependency must then be estimated.[471] This involves consideration of the deceased's pre-accident life expectancy, discounted for the contingency that he might not have lived or continued working for that long in any event. The multiplier must then be modified to take account of the dependant's future prospects. With dependent children the dependency would not normally extend beyond the end of their full time education.[472] A dependent spouse's life expectancy will be taken into account in determining the multiplier, and where the dependant has died before the trial damages will be awarded only for the period of survival after the deceased's death.[473] The multiplier should be calculated from the date of the assessment, not the date of the deceased's death.[474] Pecuniary losses between the date of death and the date of assessment should be calculated in the same way as for claims in non-fatal cases, with the multiplier being the number of years between the date of death and the date of the assessment. The court can take into account any changes in that period that materially affect the calculation.

Prospects of widow's remarriage ignored   In assessing damages payable to a   **12–171** widow in respect of the death of her husband, the prospects of remarriage or, indeed, the fact of remarriage is not taken into account.[475] This rule relieves the court from having to make what were regarded as distasteful assessments of a widow's prospects of remarriage, although it departs from the compensatory

---

[469] *Mallett v McMonagle* [1970] A.C. 166 at 174, per Lord Diplock.

[470] *Davies v Powell Duffryn Associated Collieries Ltd* [1942] A.C. 601 at 617. The multiplicand will be based upon what the deceased would have been earning at the date of assessment not the date of death: *Cookson v Knowles* [1979] A.C. 556 at 573, 575.

[471] For discussion of the factors to be taken into account in arriving at an appropriate multiplier see *Corbett v Barking Havering and Brentwood Health Authority* [1991] 2 Q.B. 408 at 421–423, per Purchas LJ.

[472] Where there is a chance that a child will proceed to higher education, this chance should be reflected in the multiplier and should not be discounted completely: *Corbett v Barking Havering and Brentwood Health Authority* [1991] 2 Q.B. 408, CA, applying *Davies v Taylor* [1974] A.C. 207.

[473] *Whittome v Coates* [1965] 1 W.L.R. 1285, where the dependant's reduced life expectancy was taken into account; *Williamson v John I Thornycroft & Co. Ltd* [1940] 2 K.B. 658, where the dependant died. Where the dependant's reduced life expectancy or death is itself due to a tort she (or her estate if she has died) is entitled to recover from the second tortfeasor the diminution in the value of her claim for loss of dependency under the Fatal Accidents Act 1976 arising out of the death of the primary victim: *Haxton v Philips Electronics UK Ltd* [2014] EWCA Civ 4; [2014] 1 W.L.R. 2721. Elias LJ, at [23], said that it was: "reasonably foreseeable that a curtailment of life may lead to a diminution in the value of a litigation claim and if a claimant has such a claim, the wrongdoer must take the victim as he finds him." *Haxton* is discussed by Bevan [2014] J.P.I.L. C88.

[474] *Knauer v Ministry of Justice* [2016] UKSC 9; [2016] A.C. 908 overruling *Cookson v Knowles* [1979] A.C. 556 and *Graham v Dodds* [1983] 1 W.L.R. 808 on this point.

[475] Fatal Accidents Act 1976 s.3(3). In *Owen v Martin* [1992] P.I.Q.R. Q151 the Court of Appeal held that in assessing the spouse's dependency the court should take account of the possibility that a married couple might divorce, since what has to be valued is the dependant's expectation of continuing dependency on the deceased had he or she lived; *D and D v Donald* [2001] P.I.Q.R. Q44, QBD; cf. *Wheatley v Cunningham* [1992] P.I.Q.R. Q100, QBD, where it was held that mere statistics as to the prevailing divorce rate should not be taken into account where the evidence was that the claimant and the deceased were happily married.

principle of assessing damages, particularly where the widow has in fact remarried and is being supported by her new husband. On the other hand, the prospects of remarriage of a widower, a former spouse and a "cohabitee" are taken into account, and even a widow's prospects of remarriage may have to be considered in relation to her children's claim for loss of dependency.[476] Section 3(4) of the Fatal Accidents Act provides that when assessing the dependency of a "cohabitee"[477] the fact that the dependant had no enforceable right to financial support by the deceased as a result of their living together should be taken into account. This will be reflected in a lower multiplier.

12–172   **Reasonable expectation of pecuniary advantage in the future**   Dependants must establish a pecuniary loss resulting from the death, but need not prove that they had received a pecuniary advantage from the deceased before the death. A reasonable expectation of pecuniary benefit in the future had the deceased lived is sufficient.[478] This will usually arise where parents had some expectation of financial support from a child. With young children, however, the prospect of any pecuniary benefit will normally be too speculative.[479]

12–173   The benefit lost must be the product of the relationship between the dependant and the deceased, not, for example, as a consequence of a contractual obligation.[480] The claimant cannot claim for the loss of an appreciating asset. So there was no claim in respect of the capital appreciation of a property that the claimant had been planning to purchase with the deceased as a family home but had not done so as a result of the death.[481] The loss of a speculative capital gain was distinct from a loss of dependency:

---

[476] *Thompson v Price* [1973] Q.B. 838. cf. *De Sales v Ingrilli* [2002] HCA 52; (2002) 193 A.L.R. 130 at [46], [161], [169] where a majority of the High Court of Australia held that normally, no deduction should be made on account of the contingency that a surviving partner (whether widow or widower) will remarry, whether as a separate deduction, or as an item added to the deduction for the vicissitudes of life.

[477] Defined in s.1(3)(b) of the Act; see para.12–165 n.450.

[478] *Taff Vale Railway Co. v Jenkins* [1913] A.C. 1; *Kandalla v British European Airways* [1981] Q.B. 158; *Singh v Aitken* [1998] P.I.Q.R. Q37, Middlesbrough County Court, where the expected benefit consisted of a share of the damages that the deceased would have received from a previous tortfeasor had he not died as a result of the defendants' negligence. In *Davies v Taylor* [1974] A.C. 207 the claimant widow had left her husband five weeks before he was killed in a road accident. The House of Lords held that she did not have to prove that it was more probable than not that there would have been a reconciliation, merely that there was a substantial, as opposed to speculative, chance that she would have returned to him and thereby benefited from his survival. Lord Reid said that if the chance was substantial it must be evaluated, but if it was a mere possibility it must be ignored. On the facts the chance of a reconciliation was speculative.

[479] *Barnett v Cohen* [1921] 2 K.B. 461.

[480] *Malyon v Plummer* [1964] 1 Q.B. 330. See also *Rupasingh v West Hertfordshire Hospitals NHS Trust* [2016] EWHC 2848 (QB); [2017] P.I.Q.R. Q1—mother not entitled to claim for her reduced earnings following the death of her husband as a result of having to return to Sri Lanka so that her young children could be looked after by her parents; the dependency claim based on the loss of the father's services had already been valued and compromised on the basis of commercial and gratuitous care.

[481] *Batt v Highgate Private Hospital* [2004] EWHC 707 (Ch); [2005] P.I.Q.R. Q1 (intended purchase of property for £94,000; property valued at £205,000 at the date of trial).

"You cannot have, by definition, a dependency on the outcome of speculative risk because it may yield nothing (or a loss) on which to be dependent. The value of the dependency has to be freeze-framed at the point of death and without the benefit of hindsight that a trial brings."[482]

Dependency on deceased's illegal earnings   If the deceased's earnings came **12–174** entirely from the proceeds of criminal activity there can be no claim for loss of dependency, since the claim will be ex turpi causa.[483] Similarly, where the deceased's earnings were obtained from "moonlighting", whereby he did not disclose his earnings while drawing social security benefits at the full rate, his widow was not entitled to claim for loss of dependency under the Fatal Accidents Act.[484] Such a claim was contrary to public policy because: (1) it assumed that someone who had committed fraud in the past would continue to do so in the future, ignoring the possibilities of repentance or detection; and (2) it treated the proceeds of illegally concealed earnings as a valid head of damages. To support a claim for loss of dependency under s.3(1) the deceased's income must have been honestly earned or received[485]; although if the earnings are from a lawful source, collateral illegality (such as the failure to pay tax or national insurance contributions) will not prevent recovery in respect of lost earnings.[486] Conversely, the loss of social security benefits on the death of a spouse can constitute loss of financial dependency, though this will depend upon the type of benefit lost.[487]

Loss of gratuitous services provided by deceased   The pecuniary advantage **12–175** lost as a result of the death must be capable of being calculated in monetary terms, but need not be merely financial. It includes gratuitous services rendered

---

[482] [2004] EWHC 707 (Ch); [2005] P.I.Q.R. Q1 at [66] per Judge Darlow. In addition, the increase in capital value post-dated the death but was not as a result of the death. It was the result of market forces and had nothing to do with the death.

[483] *Burns v Edman* [1970] 2 Q.B. 541, where the judge rejected the possibility that the deceased, who was aged 32, might reform and adopt a lawful lifestyle as entirely speculative and unproven to the point of improbability. In *Beljanski v Smithwick* 2006 BCCA 399; [2006] 11 W.W.R. 274; (2006) 275 D.L.R. (4th) 116 the British Columbia Court of Appeal allowed for the possibility that a "career criminal" might reform on achieving greater maturity, and so made a "modest" award of $10,000 to each dependant.

[484] *Hunter v Butler* [1996] R.T.R. 396, CA.

[485] *Hunter v Butler* [1996] R.T.R. 396 at 403, per Waite LJ.

[486] *Newman v Folkes and Dunlop Tyres Ltd* [2002] P.I.Q.R. Q13, QBD, which was not a Fatal Accidents Act case. Garland J explained that the difference between *Newman* and *Hunter v Butler* was that in *Hunter v Butler* the claimant was equally guilty with her deceased husband of a fraud on the social security system. In *Hewison v Meridian Shipping PTE* [2002] EWCA Civ 1821; [2003] I.C.R. 766; [2003] P.I.Q.R. P17 the Court of Appeal held that where the claimant's future employment had depended on a continuing deceit of his employers that he did not have epilepsy, the deceit was essential to the claim for loss of future earnings. The claim was based substantially on an unlawful act, so that public policy could exclude the claim. In *Major v Ministry of Defence* [2003] EWCA Civ 1433; (2003) 147 S.J.L.B. 1206 the Court of Appeal distinguished *Hewison* on the basis that in *Hewison* the claimant had obtained his employment by deception (a lie about his medical condition) and his entitlement to future earnings in that job depended upon a continuing deception. In *Major* the claimant had also told a lie in order to obtain her employment with the defendants, but the injury for which she was claiming compensation occurred before she obtained her employment (per Chadwick LJ at [18]), or she was put in the position of being unable to work by the defendants' tort, and the fact that in order to gain employment she would have to behave deceitfully was a matter that she was entitled complain of in respect of the defendants' tort (per Buxton LJ at [12]).

[487] *Cox v Hockenhull* [2000] 1 W.L.R. 750; [1999] 3 All E.R. 577, CA.

by a member of the family, such as a wife or mother.[488] This will be assessed not merely on the basis of the physical tasks that a mother would perform, and so damages are not necessarily limited to the cost of hiring a housekeeper but take into account the whole of a good mother's care of her family.[489] Conversely, where the deceased mother was unreliable and may not have been available to provide steady parental support had she lived, the dependent child's award should be discounted to allow for the real possibility that the mother would not have stayed with her family.[490] Where the court assesses the loss of a parent's services on the basis of the commercial cost of hiring a nanny to look after a child, the award will be reduced to take account of the fact that as children get older and become more independent they will be less in need of the services of a nanny.[491] In the case of the death of a spouse an award will be made for loss of services around the home previously provided by the spouse and which will now have to be paid for, such as cleaning, gardening, DIY etc.[492]

---

[488] *Regan v Williamson* [1976] 1 W.L.R. 305. The fact that those services are now being provided gratuitously by another member of the family does not affect the dependant's claim to compensation: *Hay v Hughes* [1975] Q.B. 790, where it was held that dependant children were entitled to the cost of future care following the death of their parents even though they had been, and would continue to be, cared for by their grandmother.

[489] *Hay v Hughes* [1975] Q.B. 790; *Mehmet v Perry* [1977] 2 All E.R. 529, where a father gave up his job to look after the children and damages were assessed as his loss of earnings; *Cresswell v Eaton* [1991] 1 W.L.R. 1113; [1991] 1 All E.R. 484. See also *K v JMP Co. Ltd* [1976] Q.B. 85 in relation to claims by three illegitimate children in respect of their father's death. Part of the award to the children included an element for their mother's financial loss, because this affected her ability to provide for the children. For consideration of the principles involved in assessing the value of a mother's lost services see: Exall [2003] J.P.I.L. 51; Leech (1994) 144 N.L.J. 1438.

[490] *Stanley v Saddique* [1992] Q.B. 1. In these circumstances the multiplier method of assessment will be inappropriate, and damages should be assessed on the basis of a jury award.

[491] *Spittle v Bunney* [1988] 1 W.L.R. 847; [1988] 3 All E.R. 1031; see also *Corbett v Barking Havering and Brentwood Health Authority* [1991] 2 Q.B. 408 at 419 where Purchas LJ said that the method of establishing an infant dependant's loss of its mother's services by taking the net wages of a notional nanny as the basis for the multiplicand was a crude and approximate instrument, acceptable only because there is no better means of approaching this almost unquantifiable aspect of dependency. For the effect of adoption on a child's claim for loss of dependency see *Watson v Willmott* [1991] 1 Q.B. 140.

[492] There is a difference of view as to whether, in addition to the value of the deceased's lost services, a sum should be awarded for loss of the intangible benefit of having those services provided by a spouse or partner as contrasted with the inconvenience of having to find and choose commercial providers of those services: see *Mosson v Spousal (London) Ltd* [2016] EWHC 53 (QB); [2016] 4 W.L.R. 28 (where Garnham J refused to make such an award) and *Wolstenholme v Leach's of Shudehill Ltd* [2016] EWHC 588 (QB) (where Judge McKenna considered that this was a well-established head of loss; as did Judge Chamberlain QC in *Grant v Secretary of State for Transport* [2017] EWHC 1663 (QB)). In *Magill v Panel Systems (DB Ltd)* [2017] EWHC 1517 (QB); [2017] Med.L.R. 440 Judge Gosnell declined to make an award in respect of the claimant's loss of her deceased husband's care and attention because this was the loss that an award of bereavement damages was intended to compensate.

(iv) Deductions

Any benefits which have accrued or will or may accrue to any person from the deceased's estate or otherwise as a result of death are disregarded.[493] Thus, any insurance money, pension,[494] social security benefits[495] or inheritance from the deceased's estate (including any damages awarded to the estate under a Law Reform (Miscellaneous Provisions) Act 1934 claim[496]) are ignored in calculating the financial loss.

12–176

Gratuitous benefits provided to the dependant "Benefits" are not restricted to direct pecuniary benefits, and so in assessing a child's loss of dependency following the death of a mother the fact that the child will have a better home and receive a higher standard of motherly services from a stepmother than from the natural mother, had she lived, is to be disregarded by virtue of s.4.[497] On the other hand, in *Hayden v Hayden*[498] the Court of Appeal held that gratuitous services provided by the tortfeasor could be taken into account as reducing the dependant's loss. The defendant was the father of the infant claimant who was claiming in respect of the loss of her mother's services following a fatal car accident. The defendant had given up work to look after the claimant. It was held that the father's services were not a benefit which had accrued to the claimant as a result of the death and so did not fall to be disregarded under s.4. Rather they could be taken into account as diminishing the claimant's loss under s.3(1). This appears to be inconsistent with the approach taken in *Stanley v Saddique*, or alternatively with the view adopted in *Hay v Hughes*[499] that gratuitous services

12–177

---

[493] Fatal Accidents Act 1976 s.4, as substituted by the Administration of Justice Act 1982 s.3. On the relationship between establishing the loss of dependency under s.3(1) and disregarding benefits accruing from the death see: *Wood v Bentall Simplex Ltd* [1992] P.I.Q.R. P332; *Cape Distribution Ltd v O'Loughlin* [2001] EWCA Civ 178; [2001] P.I.Q.R. Q8; *Welsh Ambulance Services NHS Trust v Williams* [2008] EWCA Civ 81 at [50] (benefits brought to family business by children after the death of their father were not to be taken into account in assessing their loss of dependency, not because the benefits had to be ignored under s.4, but "because that financial benefit was irrelevant to the assessment of the dependency under section 3. ... nothing that a dependant (or for that matter anyone else) could do after the death could either increase or decrease the dependency. The dependency is fixed at the moment of death; it is what the dependants would probably have received as benefit from the deceased, had the deceased not died. What decisions people make afterwards is irrelevant"). See Cooksley [2008] J.P.I.L. C128, for comment on *Welsh Ambulance Services NHS Trust v Williams*.

[494] *Pidduck v Eastern Scottish Omnibuses Ltd* [1990] 1 W.L.R. 993; [1990] 2 All E.R. 69, CA, where it was held that a widow's allowance payable to the claimant from the deceased's pension scheme on his death should be disregarded by virtue of s. 4 in calculating her loss of dependency.

[495] Damages awarded under the Fatal Accidents Act 1976 are specifically excluded from the rules on recovery of social security benefits: Social Security (Recovery of Benefits) Regulations 1997 (SI 1997/2205) reg.2(2)(a).

[496] Since a claim for loss of earnings in the lost years does not survive for the benefit of the estate (Law Reform (Miscellaneous Provisions) Act 1934 s.1(2)(a)) the Law Reform Act damages will be limited to any pecuniary loss, including loss of earnings, prior to the death, and an award for pain and suffering and loss of amenity during the period in which the deceased survived. Before the amendment of s.4 of the Fatal Accidents Act 1976 in 1982, Law Reform Act damages passing to a dependant under the estate would have been deducted from the dependency claim.

[497] *Stanley v Saddique* [1992] Q.B. 1.

[498] [1992] 1 W.L.R. 986.

[499] [1975] Q.B. 790.

provided by the dependant's grandmother should be disregarded on the basis that the services did not result from the death but from the generosity of the grandmother. Nonetheless, the approach adopted in *Hayden v Hayden* would seem to be consistent with that applied by the House of Lords to the question of gratuitous services provided to a claimant by the tortfeasor in non-fatal accident cases.[500]

12–178   In *R. v Criminal Injuries Compensation Board Ex p. K (Minors)*[501] the Divisional Court said that *Hayden v Hayden* did not establish any general principles of law applicable to the valuation of claims by children. It was a case where the father who took on additional parental responsibilities was also the tortfeasor, and there was no third party who stepped in to look after the orphaned child, as had occurred in *Stanley v Saddique and Hay v Hughes*. Where, as in *Ex p. K* itself, a third party provides replacement services, insofar as those services were a benefit they must be disregarded when assessing damages. Thus, it could not be said that the children had suffered no loss, because to say this would involve taking into account something which s.4 said the court should not take into account.[502]

12–179   **Benefits from an employer's retirement or death in service scheme**   In *McIntyre v Harland & Wolff plc*[503] the claimant's husband died from mesothelioma as a result of the defendants' negligence. Had he not died he would have received retirement benefits under the defendants' provident fund scheme. Because his employment was terminated before his death (due to his absence as a result of his illness) he was entitled to a payment under the same scheme in respect of the termination of his employment. This sum was paid, after his death, to his estate. The claimant sought to recover as part of her loss of dependency the retirement benefits under the scheme that her husband would have received had he lived. The defendants objected that this would lead to double recovery, i.e. recovery of both the retirement benefits and the termination of employment benefits. The Court of Appeal held that the claimant was entitled to recover the retirement benefits, since this was part of the loss attributable to the defendants' tort (but for the breach of duty resulting in the death, the deceased would have lived and would therefore have received the retirement benefits). The termination of employment benefits paid to the estate fell to be disregarded under s.4 of the Fatal Accidents Act 1976, because that payment was made to the deceased, not to the claimant, and the claimant only received that payment as the beneficiary of

---

[500] See *Hunt v Severs* [1994] 2 A.C. 350, paras 12–074–12–075. See further Kemp (1993) 109 L.Q.R. 173.

[501] [2000] P.I.Q.R. Q32.

[502] See further *L (A Child) v Barry May Haulage* [2002] P.I.Q.R. Q35, QBD; and *H v S* [2002] EWCA Civ 792; [2003] Q.B. 965 where the Court of Appeal held that children whose divorced mother was killed in an accident were entitled to compensation for loss of her services, and the services now provided by their father (who had previously contributed nothing to their welfare) were to be disregarded by virtue of s.4. The damages can only be awarded on the basis that they are used to reimburse the voluntary carer for the services. They are held on an enforceable trust for the carer ([2002] EWCA Civ 792; [2003] Q.B. 965 at [30]). On the other hand, a father has parental responsibilities to provide care and support for his children. It seems odd, to say the least, that a father who has been avoiding his legal duties to his children should then be paid for providing the very services it was his responsibility in law to provide.

[503] [2006] EWCA Civ 287; [2006] 1 W.L.R. 2577; [2007] 2 All E.R. 24.

the deceased's estate (which s.4 says should be disregarded). If this resulted in double recovery that was because s.4 of the Act allows for the possibility of double recovery.

The Court of Appeal clarified the application of s.4 in *Arnup v MW White Ltd*[504]   **12–180**
where a widow received two payments in respect of her husband's death. The first payment (of £129,600) was from the employers' "death benefit scheme" under which the employers had taken out a policy of insurance for the benefit of its employees which paid four times the deceased's salary following death in service. The second payment (of £100,000) had been paid in respect of benefits received under a life policy from the employers' "employee benefit trust" which had been established by the employers with independent trustees. The trustees had taken out a life policy covering each of the employers' employees in the sum of £100,000. The employers argued that both payments should be taken into account in assessing the claimant widow's loss of dependency. The claimant argued that both should be disregarded under s.4 of the Fatal Accidents Act. At first instance Judge Richard Seymour QC held that neither payment fell within s.4 because neither payment became payable to the claimant on the death of her husband; the death was the occasion for making the payments, but not what caused them to accrue. However, he then went on to distinguish between the two payments. He held that the £129,600 payable under the "death benefit scheme" was deductible because it was effectively an insurance policy. It could not be said that the £129,600 payment fell within the rule that the proceeds of an insurance policy to which the claimant (or deceased in this case) had contributed were to be disregarded in the assessment of damages because there was no evidence that the deceased had made any contribution to the cost of the insurance (e.g. through accepting a reduced salary). On the other hand, the payment of £100,000 fell within the exception for gratuitous payments made from charitable motives and should not be taken into account. The trustees had an unfettered discretion as to how to deal with assets within the trust fund, and were totally independent from the company. Thus, the payment constituted a gratuitous sum paid by a third party.

The Court of Appeal allowed the claimant's appeal, holding that once the judge   **12–181**
had concluded that the payments did not result from the death, so that s.4 did not apply, he should then have adopted the common law position that benefits which did not result from the death were equally to be disregarded because of that very lack of relationship with the death. Where they were not received as a result of the death, they were completely irrelevant to the whole question of assessment of damages. In any event, all benefits which came to the claimant as a result of the death were to be disregarded. The Court of Appeal stated that the expression "or otherwise as a result of his death" in s.4 was wide enough to cover benefits in kind which accrued as a result of the death and any other kind of benefit which might not yet have been identified. It was quite clear that Parliament's intention in amending the 1976 Act was to continue and complete the trend towards disregarding receipts so as to ensure that all benefits coming to the dependant as a result of the death were to be left out of account. The issue of causation was no

---

[504] [2008] EWCA Civ 447; [2008] I.C.R. 1064; commented on by N. Cooksley [2009] J.P.I.L. C28.

longer a matter of any great importance in cases of this kind. The statutory disregard provisions covered all benefits which accrued as a result of the death, and so it no longer mattered whether a benefit accrued as a result of the death; it could not be deducted in any event.

CHAPTER 13

PRACTICE AND PROCEDURE

1. INTRODUCTION

Medical negligence claims are within the genus, but are a particular species, of personal injury litigation. Whilst medical negligence claims have much in common with personal injury actions there are important distinctions. In particular:

- pre-action disclosure will nearly always be required, as early access to the relevant medical records is vital in determining whether or not there has been sub-standard treatment;
- expert evidence is essential to establish liability (both breach of duty and causation) as well as quantum;
- causation is often of far more significance in medical negligence claims than in personal injury claims; and
- claimants often have broader objectives than simply the recovery of damages, such as an explanation, an apology, further treatment and, sometimes, a wish to see systemic changes which will avoid a repetition of what has occurred.

13–001

Whilst the Pre-action Protocol for Personal Injury Claims[1] governs many types of personal injury claim there is a specific Protocol applicable for clinical negligence claims; the Pre-Action Protocol for the Resolution of Clinical Disputes[2] ("The Protocol"), as updated in 2015, which has the general aims of helping to maintain or restore the patient/healthcare provider relationship, as well as resolving disputes without litigation, and a number of specific objectives which include:

13–002

- greater openness between the parties when something has gone wrong with a patient's treatment to encourage early communication of the perceived problem;
- sufficient disclosure of information to encourage early resolution of a dispute;
- ensuring that relevant medical records are provided on request to patients or their representatives;

---

[1] Pre-Action Protocol for Personal Injury Claims: *Civil Procedure 2017* (London: Sweet & Maxwell, 2017), Vol.1, section C2.
[2] See App.2, and *Civil Procedure 2017* (London: Sweet & Maxwell, 2017), Vol.1, para.C3–001.

- where resolution is not achievable laying the ground for litigation to proceed on a reasonable timetable at a reasonable and proportionate cost;
- discouraging the prolonged pursuit of unmeritorious claims and the prolonged defence of meritorious claims; and
- ensuring that the parties are aware of the options available to pursue and resolve disputes.

13–003　This is not a book on how to sue health professionals or the NHS, and this chapter cannot hope to provide a comprehensive guide to all the procedural issues that arise in the conduct of medical negligence litigation.[3] It does not attempt to do so but, rather, focuses on some of the more substantial issues that are likely to arise. This chapter seeks to address those key differences between general personal injury actions and medical negligence claims, with the intention of providing useful guidance for practitioners, as well as outlining the timed sequence of steps provided for by the Protocol which reflect good practice in the conduct of medical negligence claims.

2.　COMPLAINT

13–004　Medical negligence claims will often be about more than simply obtaining compensation. Clients can be motivated by the need to understand what has gone wrong and why. They may want to obtain an apology or recognition of their suffering. They may wish to see that steps are taken to ensure that what happened to them does not happen to anyone else. They may be seeking further or alternative treatment. It is vital, when taking initial instructions, to identify what it is the client seeks to achieve. That will allow the practitioner to map out clients' objectives from the outset, manage their expectations appropriately and advise them accordingly. Making a complaint using the NHS Complaints Procedure may sometimes achieve, and on other occasions help to achieve, the client's objectives.

13–005　The NHS Complaints Procedure is designed to be used by individuals rather than by lawyers. Clients will, often, have pursued a complaint before approaching a solicitor and, if so, the investigation and the response may provide some helpful information which will assist the solicitor in giving advice. If the client has not yet pursued a complaint it is important to consider whether the NHS Complaints Procedure should be utilised before commencing a legal claim.

13–006　Using the NHS Complaints procedure will result at the very least in an explanation and occasionally an acknowledgment that what has occurred was unacceptable. A complaint can often prompt a change in hospital practice or procedure and can also result in an apology. Clients should appreciate that these are outcomes that are unlikely to be available through a medical negligence claim where the court simply has the power to award compensation.

13–007　The NHS Complaints Procedure covers complaints made by a person about any matter connected with the provision of NHS services by NHS organisations or

---

[3] For detailed guidance see *Civil Procedure 2017* (London: Sweet & Maxwell, 2017) Vol.1.

primary care practitioners (general practitioners, dentists, opticians and pharmacists). The procedure also covers treatment provided overseas or by the private sector where the NHS has paid for it. Where the NHS organisation concerned is a Foundation Trust they will have their own system for dealing with complaints and they should be contacted directly for details.

A complaint should normally be made within 12 months of the date of the relevant treatment or the date of knowledge. However, NHS complaints managers and primary care practitioners do have a discretion to waive this time limit if there are good reasons why the complaint could not be brought earlier. **13–008**

The complaints process provides for a three-tier approach. The first tier is that of "local resolution". The complaint will be dealt with by the NHS Trust or primary care provider involved and the formal response will usually be from the chief executive of the Trust or the primary care provider. The aim of the local resolution process is to resolve complaints as quickly and sensibly as possible. The complaint should be responded to by the primary care provider within 10 working days of receipt and by an NHS Trust within 25 working days of receipt, although these deadlines can be extended by agreement. **13–009**

If the client is not satisfied with that response then the next step is to escalate the complaint to the second tier known as "independent review". This involves contacting the Care Quality Commission, an independent body established to promote improvements in healthcare. The Commission will carry out an independent review of the complaint, usually by appointing an independent consultant from another Trust to review the treatment provided and to respond. **13–010**

If after the independent review the client remains unhappy with the response, the third and final tier of the complaints procedure is to refer the complaint to the Health Service Ombudsman, which is independent of both the NHS and the government. **13–011**

If clients want help with the complaints process they can contact the Patient Advice and Liaison Service (PALS). PALS have been established in every NHS Trust and Clinical Commissioning Group. PALS are not part of the complaints process but they are able to help clients and may even be able to resolve complaints informally. In addition to PALS, there is also the NHS Complaints Advocacy Service which provides independent advice and support to people who want to complain about the NHS.[4] **13–012**

Clients who have cases where quantum is modest and where there may be difficult issues on breach of duty and causation may be advised that the complaints process is a more appropriate remedy than a civil claim. Clients who have claims where quantum is significant and there may be a need for care and assistance may wish to proceed straight to litigation without spending unnecessary time using the complaints process. For cases where there may be some dispute as to what happened or where the facts are unclear and the claim is **13–013**

---

[4] Information about the NHS Complaints Advocacy Service can be found at *http://www. healthwatch.co.uk/sites/healthwatch.co.uk/files/complaints_advocacy.pdf*. See also *http://www.nhs.uk/ NHSEngland/complaints-and-feedback/Pages/nhs-complaints.aspx*.

not financially very significant, then the complaints process may be of value in finding out more about the claim before submitting an application for legal aid.

3.   FUNDING

13–014   One of the features that distinguishes medical negligence claims from more general personal injury claims relates to funding. Legal aid, though only for very specific types of claim,[5] remains available in addition to the, now more widely used, conditional fee agreements. Another feature of medical negligence work is the specialism of practitioners, recognised by accreditation schemes which are run by the Law Society, Action against Medical Accidents (AvMA) and the Association of Personal Injury Lawyers (APIL).

(a)   Private

13–015   The client may wish to fund the claim privately. In order to ensure compliance with the Solicitors Code of Conduct 2011 it will normally be necessary for the practitioner to advise the client about the range of potential funding arrangements available and provide appropriate advice to the client so that the client can make an informed decision.

13–016   Unlike personal injury claims, where a practitioner can often form a fairly good view on the issue of liability at the stage of taking initial instructions, medical negligence claims may need significant investigation of the medical treatment received before a sensible view on the merits of the case can be formed. It may therefore be necessary to undertake initial investigations on a private basis, with a view to subsequently entering into a conditional fee agreement at a later stage.

(b)   Insurance

13–017   The client who proceeds on a private basis may be entitled to an indemnity for costs incurred, and protection against the opponent's costs, under a legal expenses insurance policy which may be a policy specifically for that purpose or part of another policy such as motor, home or household contents. It is very important to discuss this with the client initially and to investigate the availability of "before the event" (BTE) legal expenses insurance. If appropriate insurance cover is available this may be an effective way of funding the case. There are, however, some potential drawbacks which need to be borne in mind.

13–018   First, the insurer may insist on one of their panel firms being instructed, at least for the initial investigation. It may be possible, particularly in higher value claims, to persuade the insurer that the client should have freedom of choice, although the insurer is likely to want confirmation that the firm instructed has at the very least got a member of one of the recognised accreditation schemes. Once

---

[5] See para.13–021.

the case is at the point where court proceedings are required, the insurer is obliged to give effect to the client's freedom of choice of solicitor.[6]

Secondly, it is important to establish at the outset what the level of indemnity under the policy is. Significant costs can be incurred even in modest clinical negligence claims, particularly when both sides' costs are taken into account. It is important to recognise that if there is an indemnity limit of, for example, £50,000 that the policy effectively provides cover for both sides' costs. It is therefore good practice to treat the policy as providing an indemnity of £25,000 for the client's own costs with the other £25,000 of the indemnity being earmarked in respect of indemnity against the possibility of an adverse costs order for the defendant's costs. If the indemnity is not sufficient, and it can prove difficult to subsequently "top up" the cover by having the indemnity limit increased, there is a very real risk that clients will not be able to utilise the policy and to take their case through to trial if necessary. It may be that insufficient indemnity under the policy is a sufficient reason on its own to advise a client that use of their BTE policy is not appropriate.

13–019

(c) Legal Aid

Notwithstanding the withdrawal of legal aid for personal injury claims in 2000, legal aid remains available for some medical negligence claims, provided the firm has a legal aid agency franchise for clinical negligence. Legal aid was, traditionally, the most significant source of funding for medical negligence claims, but now, whilst some claims are still funded by legal aid, restrictions on the scope of legal aid mean that the majority of claims are pursued on the basis of conditional fee agreements. To obtain legal aid a claim must (1) be within scope, (2) satisfy the merits test, (3) meet the costs/benefit analysis and (4) the client must be eligible financially.

13–020

Scope   The scope of legal aid is now defined by the provisions of the Legal Aid, Sentencing and Punishment of Offenders Act 2012. Schedule 1 Pt 1 para.23 of the Act provides that legal aid may be available for a claim for damages in respect of clinical negligence which caused a neurological injury to an individual ("V") as a result of which V is severely disabled,[7] where the negligence occurred while V was in his mother's womb, or during or after V's birth[8] but before the end of the following period: (i) if V was born before the beginning of the 37th week of pregnancy, the period of eight weeks beginning with the first day of what would have been that week; or (ii) if V was born during or after the 37th week of

13–021

---

[6] See the Insurance Companies (Legal Expenses Insurance) Regulations 1990 (SI 1990/1159) and the associated EU Directive (Legal Expenses Insurance Directive (87/344/EEC)) along with the decision of the Financial Ombudsman in the case of *Mrs A v B Insurance Co.*, Complaint Reference 1000326959/AYC/33.

[7] "Disabled" means physically or mentally disabled: para.23(5).

[8] "Birth" means the moment when an individual first has a life separate from his or her mother: para.23(5).

pregnancy, the period of six weeks beginning with the day of V's birth. The legal services must be provided to V, or if V has died they must be provided to V's personal representative.[9]

13–022   **Merits test and costs/benefit criteria**   The merits test is laid down in the Civil Legal Aid (Merits Criteria) Regulations 2013.[10] The rules for the "merits criteria" are complex and readers should refer to the Regulations and specialist works. The costs/benefit criteria are also set out in the Regulations[11]:

- if the prospects of success of the case are very good (an 80 per cent or more chance of obtaining a successful outcome), the Director must be satisfied that the likely damages exceed likely costs;
- if the prospects of success of the case are good (a 60 per cent or more chance, but less than an 80 per cent chance, of obtaining a successful outcome), the Director must be satisfied that the likely damages exceed likely costs by a ratio of two to one; or
- if the prospects of success of the case are moderate (a 50 per cent or more chance, but less than a 60 per cent chance, of obtaining a successful outcome), the Director must be satisfied that the likely damages exceed likely costs by a ratio of four to one.

13–023   **Financial eligibility**   The Civil Legal Aid (Financial Resources and Payment for Services) Regulations 2013[12] deal with financial eligibility. Whilst legal aid is subject to financial eligibility, children are assessed on their own income and outgoings, and are therefore almost always going to be financially eligible. If a client is likely to be eligible for public funding it will normally be appropriate to seek public funding, or at least advise the client fully on that option.

13–024   **Funding**   There are two levels of legal aid funding that can be awarded to pursue a medical negligence claim:

- investigative representation: granted when it is not clear whether a case will succeed. This representation is limited to the strength of contemplated proceedings—this will aim to enable clients to obtain medical notes, obtain one medical record per specialism and includes the issuing and conduct of proceedings but only so far as necessary;
- full representation: granted only when the cost/benefit criteria and merits criteria are met. The prospects of success must not be poor or borderline.

13–025   Legal aid will be subject to appropriate costs conditions. The fact that a case could be brought by way of a conditional fee agreement does not prevent the grant of legal aid.

---

[9] Para.23 is subject to exclusions which would be unlikely ever to be relevant to a birth injury claim: para.23(4).
[10] SI 2013/104.
[11] See SI 2013/104 regs 5, 42, 43.
[12] SI 2013/480.

(d)   Conditional fee agreements

Whilst conditional fee agreements have been commonplace in personal injury claims since 2000, it has taken longer for medical negligence lawyers to embrace conditional fee agreements. However, as the proportion of the population financially eligible for legal aid has reduced, and the scope of legal aid for such claims been restricted, the use of conditional fee agreements for medical negligence cases has become more widespread.   **13–026**

Unlike the vast majority of personal injury claims, the difficulty with clinical negligence work is in accurately assessing the risk at the outset. Nevertheless, in appropriate cases, it should be possible to assess risk and enter a conditional fee agreement at an early stage. Ideally, the conditional fee agreement will need to be supported by "after the event" (ATE) insurance which will cover disbursements and, if proceedings are commenced, the opponent's costs.   **13–027**

It is essential that any conditional fee agreement complies with the statutory requirements found in s.58 of the Courts and Legal Services Act 1990 and also complies with the Conditional Fee Agreements Order 2013.[13] A success fee payable under a conditional fee agreement has not, since 2013, been recoverable as part of the costs of the claim and, accordingly, is a cost which the successful claimant will need to meet out of damages, subject to the protection afforded by the 2013 Regulations. Many claimants pursing a medical negligence claim funded by a conditional fee agreement will wish to take out ATE insurance. With medical negligence claims part of the premium payable for ATE insurance (related to the cost of obtaining reports on breach of duty and causation) remains recoverable, as part of the costs of the claim under the Recovery of Costs Insurance Premiums in Clinical Negligence Proceedings (No.2) Regulations 2013.[14]   **13–028**

4.   ACCESS TO HEALTH RECORDS

It has long been recognised that doctors owe a duty of confidence with respect to information concerning patients arising out of the doctor–patient relationship, so that patients can restrain the unauthorised disclosure of their medical records to third parties. However, the courts have been reluctant to establish a common law right for patients to demand access to their own medical records.[15] Patients now have statutory rights of access to their records, principally through the Data Protection Act 1998, the Access to Health Records Act 1990 and the Access to Medical Reports Act 1988. This legislation is essentially concerned with the right of patients to know what is contained in their medical records and to permit the correction of inaccurate records, but it is also highly relevant in the context of medical negligence litigation for discovering what went wrong with the patient's treatment. A specific objective of the Protocol is to ensure that relevant medical records are provided promptly by the healthcare provider to the patient, or the   **13–029**

---

13 SI 2013/689.
14 SI 2013/739.
15 See, however, paras 13–064 to 13–068.

representative of the patient. In most medical negligence claims that is an essential step as a preliminary to obtaining expert evidence.

(a) Data Protection Act 1998

13–030   The Data Protection Act 1984 gave individuals a right of access to information, including medical records, held about them in computerised form for the first time. Subsequently, the Access to Health Records Act 1990 granted patients a right of access to non-electronic health records. The Data Protection Act 1998 replaced the 1984 Act and most of the 1990 Act, bringing electronic and non-electronic records under the same statutory regime. The only part of the Access to Health Records Act 1990 still in force relates to access to a patient's medical records after his death.

13–031   The Data Protection Act 1998 gives individuals a right of access to information held about them. Section 1(1) provides that "data" means information which: (a) is being processed by means of equipment operating automatically in response to instructions given for that purpose; (b) is recorded with the intention that it should be processed by means of such equipment; (c) is recorded as part of a relevant filing system or with the intention that it should form part of a relevant filing system; or (d) does not fall within (a), (b) or (c) but forms part of an accessible record as defined by s.68. Section 68 defines an "accessible record" as, inter alia, a health record, which means any record which (a) consists of information relating to the physical or mental health of an individual, and (b) has been made by or on behalf of a health professional in connection with the care of that individual. "Health professional" is widely defined in s.69. "Personal data" means data which relate to a living individual who can be identified from that data or from that data and other information in the possession of, or likely to come into the possession of the data controller, and includes any expression of opinion about the individual and any indication of the intentions of the data controller or any other person in respect of that individual.[16] Information as to the physical or mental health or condition of the data subject is "sensitive personal data".[17] "Data controller" means a person who determines the purposes for which and the manner in which any personal data are processed; and "data processor" means any person, other than an employee of the data controller, who processes the data on behalf of the data controller. "Data subject" means an individual who is the subject of personal data.

(i) Personal data

13–032   In *Durant v Financial Services Authority (Disclosure)*[18] the court was asked to consider what constituted "personal data" within s.1(1) of the Data Protection Act. Following unsuccessful litigation against a bank the claimant sought

---

[16] It does not include anonymised statistical information: *Department of Health v Information Commissioner* [2011] EWHC 1430 (Admin); [2011] Med. L.R. 363.
[17] Data Protection Act 1998 s.2.
[18] [2003] EWCA Civ 1746; [2004] F.S.R. 28.

disclosure of various records relating to the dispute held about him by the Financial Services Authority. He made two requests to the FSA under s.7 of the Act for disclosure of his personal data in both manual and electronic files. The FSA provided him with copies of documents held in computerised form that went beyond his entitlement under the Act but refused his request for information held on manual files on the ground that the information sought was not "personal" within the definition of "personal data" in s.1(1) of the Act. The claimant contended that the wide and inclusive definition of "personal data" in s.1(1) covered any information retrieved as a result of a search under his name, anything on file which had his name on it or from which he could be identified or from which it was possible to discern a connection with him. The court disagreed, holding that not all information retrieved from a computer against an individual's name or unique identifier was personal data within the Act. Mere mention of the data subject in a document did not necessarily amount to personal data. It depended on where such mention fell in a continuum of relevance or proximity to the subjects, as opposed to matters in which they were involved to a greater or lesser degree. Two measures of relevance or proximity were whether it was significantly biographical, and whether the data subject was the focus of attention. The information must have affected the subject's privacy in personal, family, business or professional life. The purpose of the relevant legislation was to apply the same standard of accessibility to personal data in manual filing systems as to computerised records, and the protection was aimed at the data and not the documents. The data must be readily accessible for reasons of practicality. The legitimate interests of third parties identifiable from a data subject's personal data were highly relevant to, but not determinative of, the reasonableness of any decision to disclose the personal data where the third party's consent had not been sought. A court's discretion under s.7(9) was generalised and untrammelled. In this case, the mere fact that a document was retrievable by the claimant's name did not make it personal data and just because information about his complaint to the FSA emanated from him did not make it his own personal data. The court considered that the claimant's claim was a misguided attempt to use the Act as a means of third party discovery with a view to litigation and suggested that those contemplating or advising in such proceedings should carefully scrutinise the present judgment for guidance.

(ii) Processing personal data

In *Johnson v The Medical Defence Union Ltd*[19] the Court of Appeal was asked to consider how data was "processed". The appellant consultant orthopaedic surgeon appealed against a decision of Rimer J[20] that although the defendant had unfairly processed his personal data, the unfair processing had been of such a minor and inconsequential nature that he was not entitled to compensation. The MDU in turn cross-appealed against the finding that its treatment of the appellant's data fell within the remit of the Data Protection Act 1998 and that if the "processing" of it had been fair, the outcome would have been different. The

13–033

---

[19] [2007] EWCA Civ 262; (2007) 96 B.M.L.R. 99.
[20] [2006] EWHC 321; (2006) 89 B.M.L.R. 43; (2006) Info. T.L.R. 47.

dispute between the parties arose after the MDU terminated the appellant's membership which included discretionary professional indemnity cover. The appellant had never been the subject of a claim for alleged professional negligence, although complaints had been made against him. The MDU conducted a risk assessment review, following which the decision was made to terminate his membership. The risk management policy was not dependent on any allegation against the appellant being well founded. Rather, it depended simply on the fact that the allegation had been made. A significant part of the information relied upon by the risk manager had been held on computer, and in order to access the information, she had had to process it in the sense of retrieving the information up onto her computer screen. The remainder of the exercise had involved her summarising the files and making observations about selected files. The appellant had commenced legal action on the basis that the process carried out by the risk manager was intrinsically unfair. The judge had determined that the risk assessment had involved the "processing of data" within the meaning of the Act, and that such "processing" had been unfair, though only in a minor respect. He had furthermore found that if the data processing had been fair, the MDU's decision to terminate the appellant's membership would probably not have been made and an entitlement to damages would have arisen. On appeal, the main area of disagreement centred on the extent to which the whole of the dealing with the appellant's case constituted a continuous and single operation of "processing", even if not all of it was performed by automatic means, and the extent to which the mental process of selection and analysis of information fell within the terms of the Act. The Court of Appeal held (Arden LJ dissenting) that the judge had erred in finding that the risk manager's selection of data amounted to processing of data within the terms of the Act. First, it was necessary to be very cautious about construing the Council Directive 95/46 art.2(b) in a manner that allowed the words "whether or not by automatic means" to effectively override the scheme of the rest of the Directive. Secondly, although the risk manager's selection and analysis of the material had been only one step in a more lengthy operation, it was the only part about which the appellant had complained. On the facts, the selection of information was not even "partly by automated means" because it had not involved any automated means at all and therefore the scope of the Directive to the instant case was limited by art.3.1 of the Directive. The manual selection process operated by the risk manager had amounted to "processing" for the purposes of the Act because the Directive applied to the selection of personal data which, following such selection, was to be placed on a computer. The court had a duty to interpret s.1(2)(a) of the Act so far as possible in accordance with the Directive. The expression "personal data" in s.1(2)(a) included information which would constitute "personal data" when both the act of obtaining the information and the act of inputting it into a computer were complete.

(iii)   Right of access to the data

13–034   Section 7(1) of the Act confers a right of access to personal data by the data subject. A request to supply the information must be in writing and the data controller may charge a fee (subject to a maximum fee).[21] The data controller is not obliged to comply with the request for access where the request cannot be complied with, without disclosing information relating to another individual[22] who can be identified from the information unless: (a) the other individual consents; or (b) it is reasonable in all the circumstances to comply with the request without the consent of the other individual.[23] Where information can be communicated without disclosing the identity of the other individual (e.g. by omitting names or other identifying particulars) the exception in s.7(4) does not apply.[24] In the case of information as to the physical or mental health or condition of the data subject, s.7(4) is modified by the addition of another subparagraph, so that (in addition to the situations in (a) and (b) above) where the data controller cannot comply with the request without disclosing information relating to another individual who can be identified from the information, the data controller is not obliged to comply with that request unless the information is contained in a health record and the other individual is a health professional who has compiled or contributed to the health record or has been involved in the care of the data subject in the capacity of a health professional.[25] The data controller is not excused from supplying as much of the information sought by the request as can be communicated without disclosing the identity of the other individual concerned, whether by omitting names or identifying particulars or otherwise.[26]

A data subject has a right to prevent processing likely to cause damage or distress. Under s.10 individuals can give written notice to a data controller to cease, or not to begin, processing personal data of which they are the data subject on the ground that it is likely to cause substantial damage or substantial distress to them or another person, and that the damage would be unwarranted. This right does not apply if: (1) the data subject has given consent to the processing; (2) the processing is necessary for the performance of a contract to which the data subject is a party or for the taking of steps at the request of the data subject with a view to entering into a contract; (3) the processing is necessary for compliance with any legal obligation to which the data controller is subject, other than a contractual obligation; or (4) the processing is necessary to protect the vital interests of the data subject. The Secretary of State may prescribe other cases to which s.10(1) does not apply.

13–035

---

[21] Data Protection Act 1998 s.7(2). The maximum fee under the Act is £50 which must cover the cost of producing all records, X-rays, scans and CTG traces: *Hubble v Peterborough NHS Trust* unreported 21 March 2001. Note: this maximum fee does not apply to applications for records made under the Access to Health Records Act 1990 (see below) although arguably it provides a guideline for what is a reasonable fee for such requests.

[22] This includes a reference to information identifying that individual as the source of the information sought by the request: Data Protection Act 1998 s.7(5).

[23] Data Protection Act 1998 s.7(4). As to when it may be reasonable to comply without consent see s.7(6).

[24] Data Protection Act 1998 s.7(5).

[25] Data Protection (Subject Access Modification) (Health) Order 2000 (SI 2000/413) art.8(a).

[26] Data Protection Act 1998 s.7(5).

(iv)   Remedies

13–036   If the court is satisfied that the data controller has failed to comply with the request for access to information, in contravention of the Act, the court can order the data controller to comply with the request.[27] This provision is modified, however, in relation to personal data consisting of information as to the physical or mental health or condition of the data subject to permit any other person to whom serious harm to the subject's physical or mental health or condition would be likely to be caused by compliance with the request, in contravention of the Act, to request that the court order the data controller not to comply with the request.[28] This permits the court to rule one way or the other on the question of whether disclosure of the information to the data subject is potentially dangerous to another person (an issue that is most likely to arise in the context of psychiatric patients).[29]

13–037   Individuals are entitled to compensation for any damage by reason of any contravention by the data controller of any requirements of the Act.[30] Individuals are also entitled to compensation for any distress if they also suffer damage by reason of the contravention, or the contravention relates to processing personal data for "special purposes".[31] Special purposes are the purposes of journalism, artistic or literary purposes.[32] This means that, effectively, in the context of health records there is no compensation for distress if there is no damage, unless health records are processed for special purposes.[33] It is a defence for defendants against whom compensation is sought to prove that they exercised reasonable care to comply with the requirements of the Act.[34] An individual may apply to a court for rectification, blocking, erasure or destruction, of inaccurate data, including an expression of opinion which is based on inaccurate data.[35] A similar order can be made where data subjects have suffered damage by reason of contravention of the Act entitling them to compensation under s.13 where there is a substantial risk of further contravention of the Act in respect of that data.[36]

---

[27]   Data Protection Act 1998 s.7(9).

[28]   Data Protection (Subject Access Modification) (Health) Order 2000 (SI 2000/413) art.8(b).

[29]   See *Re R (A Child)* (also known as *S v W Primary Care Trust*) [2004] EWHC 2085 where the court had to balance the public and private interests in maintaining the confidentiality of the information about the child's mother contained in the child's medical records and the public and private interests in permitting or requiring their disclosure for the purpose of assessing whether the child had a claim for medical negligence.

[30]   Data Protection Act 1998 s.13(1).

[31]   Data Protection Act 1998 s.13(2).

[32]   Data Protection Act 1998 s.3.

[33]   e.g. journalism, where the newspaper is in breach of s.10, there could be a claim for distress alone if it is "substantial" distress, though there is a "public interest" defence for data processed for "special purposes": s.32.

[34]   Data Protection Act 1998 s.12(3).

[35]   Data Protection Act 1998 s.14(1).

[36]   Data Protection Act 1998 s.14(4).

(v) Exemptions

The Secretary of State has power to exempt from the subject information **13–038** provisions, or modify those provisions, in relation to personal data consisting of information as to the physical or mental health or condition of the data subject.[37] The Data Protection (Subject Access Modification) (Health) Order 2000[38] exempts from the subject information provisions of the Act personal data processed by a court consisting of information supplied in a report or other evidence given to the court in proceedings involving children where the relevant rules of court permit information to be withheld by the court in whole or in part from the data subject.[39] Article 5 provides that the access provisions under s.7 of the Data Protection Act do not apply where access "would be likely to cause serious harm to the physical or mental health of the data subject or any other person". Data controllers who are not health professionals must not withhold information to which the Order applies on this ground unless they first consult the person who appears to be the appropriate health professional on the question whether or not the exemption applies with respect to the information.[40]

Conversely, a data controller who is not a health professional must not **13–039** communicate information as to the physical or mental health or condition of the data subject in response to a request without first consulting the person who appears to be the appropriate health professional on the question of whether or not the exemption in art.5(1) applies.[41] This does not apply where the request relates to information which the data controller is satisfied has previously been seen by the data subject or is already within the knowledge of the data subject,[42] nor where the data controller has consulted the appropriate health professional prior to receiving the request and obtained in writing from that health professional an opinion that the exemption on art.5(1) does not apply with respect to all the information which is the subject of the request.[43]

Where the data subject is a child and the application for access is made by a **13–040** person having parental responsibility, or the data subject is incapable of managing his own affairs and the application for access is made by a person appointed by the court to manage his affairs, then the data is exempt from access under s.7 to the extent to which it would involve disclosure of information: (a) provided by the data subject in the expectation that it would not be disclosed to the person making the request; (b) obtained as a result of any examination or

---

[37] Data Protection Act 1998 s.30.
[38] SI 2000/413.
[39] SI 2000/413 art.4.
[40] SI 2000/413 art.5(2). This provision does not apply if the data controller has consulted the appropriate health professional before receiving the request for access, and obtained in writing from that health professional an opinion that the exemption in art.5(1) applies with respect to all the information which is the subject of the request: art.7(1). That opinion must have been obtained within six months prior to the request for information, or if it was obtained within six months and it is reasonable in all the circumstances to re-consult the appropriate health professional the data controller must consult the health professional: art.7(2).
[41] SI 2000/413 art.6(1).
[42] SI 2000/413 art.6(2).
[43] SI 2000/413 art.7(3).

investigation to which the data subject consented in the expectation that the information would not be so disclosed; or (c) which the data subject has expressly indicated should not be so disclosed.[44]

(b) Access to Health Records Act 1990

13–041 The Data Protection Act 1998 repealed almost the whole of the Access to Health Records Act 1990 which previously conferred a right of access to non-computerised records. The one exception relates to applications for access to health records where the patient has died, and therefore the 1990 Act is now exclusively concerned with access where the patient has died. By s.1(1) a "health record" means a record which (a) consists of information (including an expression of opinion) relating to the physical or mental health of an individual who can be identified from that information, or from that and other information in the possession of the holder of the record; and (b) has been made by or on behalf of a health professional[45] in connection with the care of that individual. Under s.3(1)(f) of the Access to Health Records Act 1990, where the patient has died, an application for access to a health record may be made to the holder of the record by the patient's personal representative and any person who may have a claim arising out of the patient's death. The holder of the record, within a maximum period of 40 days, must give access to the record by allowing the applicant to inspect the record (or an extract), or if the applicant so requires by supplying a copy of the record or extract.[46] Where any information is expressed in terms which are not intelligible without explanation, an explanation of those terms must be provided.[47]

13–042 The right of access is not absolute; there are a number of exceptions. On an application after the patient has died by the patient's personal representative or any person who may have a claim arising out of the patient's death, access shall not be given if the record includes a note, made at the patient's request, that access should not be given on such an application.[48] Section 5(4) excludes access in the case of an application made by someone other than the patient (or on the patient's authority) to any part of the record which, in the opinion of the record holder, would disclose information provided by the patient in the expectation that it would not be disclosed to the applicant, or information obtained as a result of any examination or investigation to which the patient consented in the expectation that the information would not be disclosed. In addition, access does not have to be given to any part of the record which, in the opinion of the holder of the record, would disclose information which is not relevant to any claim which may arise out of the patient's death.[49]

---

[44] SI 2000/413 art.5(3).

[45] For the definition of "health professional" see Access to Health Records Act 1990 s.2(1) specifying that "health professional" has the same meaning as in the Data Protection Act 1998 (see s.69 of the 1998 Act).

[46] Access to Health Records Act 1990 s.3(2) and (5).

[47] Access to Health Records Act 1990 s.3(3).

[48] Access to Health Records Act 1990 s.4(3).

[49] Access to Health Records Act 1990 s.5(4).

Section 5(1) contains two significant restrictions on the right of access. Where, in **13–043** the opinion of the holder of the record, access to any part of a health record would disclose: (i) information likely to cause serious harm to the physical or mental health of the patient or of any other individual; or (ii) information relating to or provided by an individual, other than the patient, who could be identified from that information (unless the individual concerned consents or the individual is a health professional who has been involved in the care of the patient[50]), access shall not be given. Furthermore, s.5(1)(b) excludes any part of a health record which was made before the commencement of the Act, namely 1 November 1991,[51] except, and to the extent that, in the opinion of the holder of the record, the giving of access is necessary in order to make intelligible any part of the record to which access is required to be given.[52]

People who consider that any information contained in a health record to which **13–044** they have been given access is inaccurate may apply to the holder of the record to have the record corrected.[53] The holder of the record must either make the necessary correction, or, if not satisfied that the information is inaccurate, make a note in the record of the matters which the applicant considers to be inaccurate, and in either case, supply the applicant with a copy of the correction or note. There is no remedy in damages, however, in respect of damage or distress suffered as a result of inaccuracy in the health record. The only remedy available under the Act is an application to the court for an order requiring the holder of a health record to comply with any requirement of the Act.[54] For the purpose of determining this issue the court may require the record to be available for its own inspection, but shall not require the record to be disclosed to the applicant or his representatives whether by disclosure or otherwise.[55]

The Act clearly contemplates applications for access to health records in advance **13–045** of litigation, and to this extent it may supplement the provisions of s.33(2) of the Senior Courts Act 1981 for pre-action disclosure.[56] It cannot entirely replace this procedure, however, because there are several drawbacks. First, a "health record" is defined as information relating to the physical or mental health of an individual who can be identified from that information, and has been made by or on behalf of a health professional *in connection with the care of that individual*. It is doubtful whether this would apply to all the documents (an accident report, for example) that might be relevant to the conduct of litigation, and which are subject to disclosure under the procedure for pre-action disclosure. Secondly, the Access to Health Records Act applies only to health records made after 1 November 1991, except to the extent that access is necessary to an earlier record to make intelligible access to a record made after that date. No such restriction applies to the procedure for pre-action disclosure. Thirdly, information may be withheld if,

---

[50] Access to Health Records Act 1990 s.5(2).
[51] Access to Health Records Act 1990 s.12(2).
[52] Access to Health Records Act 1990 s.5(2).
[53] Access to Health Records Act 1990 s.6(1). "Inaccurate" means incorrect, misleading or incomplete: s.6(3).
[54] Access to Health Records Act 1990 s.8(1).
[55] Access to Health Records Act 1990 s.8(4).
[56] See paras 13–053 to 13–059.

in the opinion of the holder of the record, it is likely to cause serious harm to the physical or mental health of the patient or of any other individual, or if the information would, in effect, break another person's confidence. Again, no such restriction applies to disclosure under the Senior Courts Act 1981, although an order may direct that disclosure be limited to the applicant's legal advisers or legal and medical advisers. Finally, it would seem inappropriate to allow the holder of the record, who may be a potential defendant, to determine which information is or is not relevant to any claim which may arise out of the patient's death, as is possible under s.5(4), although, admittedly, under s.33(2) of the Senior Courts Act the documents sought by the applicant must be "relevant to an issue arising or likely to arise out of that claim".

13–046   The Access to Health Records Act 1990 may have at least one advantage over the Senior Courts Act 1981 in respect of pre-action disclosure against a party who is not likely to be a party to the proceedings. It is not possible to obtain an order for pre-action disclosure against someone who is not likely to be a party to proceedings, although disclosure against third parties is possible once an action has been commenced. Where, however, a third party holds documents which constitute a "health record" within the meaning of s.1(1) the claimant will be able to make an application for access to that record under the 1990 Act.

(c)   Access to Medical Reports Act 1988

13–047   The Access to Medical Reports Act 1988 s.1 grants an individual a right of access to any medical report relating to the individual which is to be, or in the previous six months has been, supplied by a medical practitioner, who is or has been responsible for the clinical care of the individual, for employment or insurance purposes. The Act does not apply to a report prepared by a doctor who had not previously been responsible for the individual's clinical care, e.g. a doctor instructed by employers or prospective employers on an ad hoc basis. The individual must consent to any application to a medical practitioner for a medical report on the individual for employment or insurance purposes, and when giving consent can state that the individual wishes to have access to the report before it is supplied. Access means making the report or a copy of it available for the individual's inspection or supplying a copy.[57] Where an individual has been given access to a report it should not be supplied to the applicant unless the individual consents, and the individual may request the doctor to amend any part of the report which is considered to be incorrect or misleading.[58]

13–048   Under s.7 there are exceptions to the right of access where disclosure would be likely to cause serious harm to the physical or mental health of the individual or others, or would be likely to reveal information about another person, or to reveal the identity of another person who has supplied information to the practitioner about the individual (unless that person consents, or the person is a health professional who has been involved in the care of the individual and the

---

[57] Access to Medical Reports Act 1988 s.4(4). The doctor may charge a reasonable fee for supplying a copy.
[58] Access to Medical Reports Act 1988 s.5(1) and (2).

information relates to or has been provided in that capacity). Where the exceptions apply to a part but not the whole of a medical report the individual's right of access applies to the remainder, and where the exceptions apply to the whole report, the doctor must not supply the report unless the individual consents.

There is no remedy in damages for a failure to comply with the terms of the Act, but where people have failed or are likely to fail to comply with any requirement of the Act an individual may apply to the court for an order that they comply with that requirement.

13–049

(d) Using medical records in evidence

Medical records are important evidence in medical negligence claims, as those records are intended to ensure that patients are treated effectively and appropriately by providing relevant information to treating clinicians. The records, therefore, are likely to be the best evidence of crucial matters such as history, examination, investigations, referral, follow-up, diagnosis, treatment and advice/consent. Consequently, evidentially, the records are likely to play a much more important role in a clinical negligence claim than a personal injury claim, at least so far as liability is concerned. In personal injury claims, and sometimes in clinical negligence claims, problems can arise when entries in medical records are treated as evidence of the background facts, as opposed to simply evidence of the history taken. Difficulties can also arise if there is an issue about whether the entries in the records accurately reflect what was said.

13–050

In *Denton Hall Legal Services v Fifield*[59] the Court of Appeal considered what approach to take where the note made by a doctor in the notes was not consistent with what the claimant had said in her witness statement. What the doctor wrote down in the notes as having been told him by the patient, as opposed to the opinion that he expressed on the basis of those statements, was not evidence of the making of the statement that he recorded. Where the record was said to contradict the evidence as to fact given by the patient, the record was of a previous inconsistent statement allegedly made by the patient. As such the record itself was hearsay. It might however be proved as evidence that the patient did indeed speak as alleged in two ways: first, if the statement was put to the witness, she might admit to having made it; alternatively, if she did not distinctly so admit, the statement might be proved under the Criminal Procedure Act 1865 s.4; second, by the Civil Evidence Act 1995 s.6(5) those provisions did not prevent the statement being proved as hearsay evidence under s.1 of the 1995 Act. If the court concluded that such inconsistent statement had been made, that went only to the credibility of the witness; the statement itself could not be treated as evidence of its contents. In this case the Court of Appeal held that none of those steps had been taken and the trial had proceeded on the erroneous basis that the medical records were evidence, without analysis of what if anything they proved. The Court of Appeal went on to confirm how this situation should be approached.

13–051

---

[59] [2006] EWCA Civ 169; [2006] Lloyd's Rep. Med. 251, and see D. Sanderson, "Inconsistent statements in medical records" [2006] J.P.I.L 207.

Once the defendant had identified a potential inconsistent statement in the records they should plead their positive case in the defence or counter schedule. A note should be inserted to the effect that they intend to rely on the records referred to but that it is not intended to call the maker of the note as they cannot reasonably be expected to recollect anything beyond what has been recorded. The onus then shifts to the claimant to indicate the extent to which he disputes the accuracy or completeness of the record. At trial the inconsistent record should be put to the claimant in cross-examination. If the claimant does not admit making the statement, the cross-examiner must ensure that particulars of the occasion on which the statement is alleged to have been made are put to the claimant. If the claimant still does not admit having made it, the statement can be admitted under s.2 of the Civil Evidence Act 1995 or a witness (the doctor) can be called to give oral evidence on the previous inconsistent statement.

5. DISCLOSURE AND THE PROTOCOL

13–052 In the past the adversarial nature of civil proceedings was regarded as justification for allowing the parties to a civil action to conceal the nature of their case from each other. This was particularly true of actions for medical negligence. The modern approach, however, is to conduct litigation with "cards on the table" so that the parties can assess the relative strengths and weaknesses of their respective cases and where appropriate, settle the action. Consequently, reflecting the more open approach, access to medical records, in order to identify whether a claim has any prospects of success, should no longer present the hurdle that it once did.[60] The statutory provisions allowing access to medical records are reflected by the terms of the Protocol, the general aims of which are to maintain/restore the relationship between the patient and health care provider and to resolve disputes, if possible, without litigation.

(a) Pre-action disclosure

(i) Against a potential defendant

13–053 Access to patients' medical records is essential to enable their legal and medical advisers to determine whether an action for negligence has any prospect of success. Section 33(2) of the Senior Courts Act 1981 in the High Court and s.52(2) of the County Courts Act 1984 in the County Court along with CPR r.31.16 provide a procedure by which a potential claimant may apply for disclosure of relevant documents from a potential defendant before proceedings have started.[61] As Lord Denning MR has observed, one of the objects of the provision is to enable claimants to find out whether or not they has a good cause

---

[60] See S. Burn, "Obtaining and Disclosing the Claimant's Medical Records" [2004] J.P.I.L. 297.
[61] This procedure was formerly limited to actions involving claims in respect of personal injuries or death. That restriction was removed by the Civil Procedure (Modification of Enactments) Order 1998 (SI 1998/2940) art.5.

of action before they issue proceedings.[62] It is designed to facilitate settlements and to avoid fruitless actions.[63] Before considering an application to court, the claimant should make a written request for voluntary disclosure in accordance with the Protocol (Annex B), providing the appropriate format of consent form, under the Data Protection Act 1998, as published by the Law Society and the British Medical Association. A Protocol for Obtaining Hospital Medical Records includes standard forms to facilitate the process.[64] This procedure, and the more open climate to litigation, means that applications to court should rarely be required in medical negligence litigation. Records should be disclosed within 40 days. Failure to comply with this part of the Protocol should lead to a complaint to the Information Commissioner, for non-compliance with the Data Protection Act 1998, or an application for pre-action disclosure to the Court.

Claimants' solicitors should not accept disclosure of the medical records to a nominated medical expert, but should insist on disclosure to themselves in order to organise the records into chronological order, check them against the claimant's statement, identify missing documents, and identify the relevant issues for consideration and/or clarification by the medical experts and/or counsel. Orders under s.33(2) of the Senior Courts Act 1981 and s.52(2) of the County Courts Act 1984 can exclude production to patients themselves but not to their legal advisers, and if an NHS Trust persists in seeking to limit disclosure to a medical expert an application will have to be made. It is now rare for NHS defendants to refuse voluntary disclosure, provided that it is made clear in the letter of request that there is some basis for the request and that it is not purely speculative.[65]

13–054

The Senior Courts Act 1981[66] permits a person who has not issued a claim form to make an application for disclosure of documents from a person who is likely to be a party to the proceedings. Section 33(2) provides that:

13–055

> "On an application, in accordance with rules of court, of a person who appears to the High Court to be likely to be a party to subsequent proceedings in that court the High Court shall, in such circumstances as may be specified in the rules, have power to order a person who appears to the court to be likely to be a party to the proceedings and to be likely to have or to have had in his possession, custody or power any documents which are relevant to an issue arising or likely to arise out of that claim—
> (a)   to disclose whether those documents are in his possession, custody or power; and

---

[62] *Dunning v Board of Governors of the United Liverpool Hospitals* [1973] 2 All E.R. 454, 457; *Shaw v Vauxhall Motors Ltd* [1974] 1 W.L.R. 1035 at 1039.

[63] *Lee v South West Thames Regional Health Authority* [1985] 2 All E.R. 385 at 387.

[64] See App.2. The courts always did encourage voluntary disclosure, even under the old Rules of the Supreme Court. See the comments of Lord Denning MR in *Shaw v Vauxhall Motors Ltd* [1974] 1 W.L.R. 1035 at 1039.

[65] Note, however, that patients who make a request to see their health records under the Data Protection Act 1998 do not have to give any reason or justification for the request. In *Hall v Wandsworth Health Authority* (1985) 129 S.J. 188 Tudor Price J said that a period of six weeks for the health authority to comply with a request for voluntary disclosure was a reasonable period: "If in a particular case for a particular reason it is insufficient the defendants ... should request more time, preferably with an explanation ... [I]f there is a prompt answer and a promise of discovery is given at an early stage there will be no need for plaintiffs to threaten or issue section 33 proceedings."

[66] County Courts Act 1984 s. 52(2) is the relevant section for pre-action disclosure orders in the County Court and is in similar terms.

    (b)   to produce such of those documents as are in his possession, custody or power to the applicant or, on such conditions as may be specified in the order—
        (i)   to the applicant's legal advisers; or
        (ii)   to the applicant's legal advisers and any medical or other professional adviser of the applicant; or
        (iii)   if the applicant has no legal adviser, to any medical or other professional adviser of the applicant."[67]

Applications under s.33(2) of the Senior Courts Act 1981 must be supported by evidence. An order may be made only where the respondent is likely to be a party to subsequent proceedings; the applicant is also likely to be a party to those proceedings; if proceedings had started the respondent's duty by way of standard disclosure under CPR r.31.6 would extend to the documents or classes of documents of which the applicant seeks disclosure[68]; and disclosure before proceedings have started is desirable in order to dispose fairly of the anticipated proceedings, assist the dispute to be resolved without proceedings, or save costs.[69] An order must specify the documents or the classes of documents which respondents must disclose and require them to specify any of the documents which are no longer in their control or in respect of which they claim a right or duty to withhold inspection.[70] In a medical negligence action there should be little difficulty in establishing the relevance of the medical records to a potential claim.

13–056   In dealing with applications for pre-action disclosure the court has to ask itself two questions, the first jurisdictional, the second as to the exercise of discretion.[71] The jurisdictional question is resolved by considering whether there is a real

---

[67] See also Senior Courts Act 1981 s.33(1) which provides that the court may make an order providing for the inspection, photographing, preservation, custody and detention of property, the taking of samples of property and the carrying out of any experiment on or with any property which may become the subject matter of subsequent proceedings in the High Court.

[68] Pre-action disclosure can only take place when the issues in dispute have been sufficiently identified and can only extend to those documents which are liable to be disclosed at the stage in proceedings when the general obligation of disclosure arises. This is a matter for the discretion of the judge: *Bermuda International Securities Ltd v KPMG (A Firm)* [2001] EWCA Civ 269; [2001] Lloyd's Rep. P.N. 392, CA. In *Hutchinson 3G UK Ltd v O2 (UK) Ltd* [2008] EWHC 55 it was held that the threshold requirements for an application for pre-action disclosure were not met where the applicant failed to establish that the documents were likely to fall within standard disclosure and that pre-action disclosure was likely to dispose of the dispute or save costs. It was said that it was inappropriate for the respondents to be required to identify which documents were within the scope of standard disclosure. An application for pre-action disclosure had to be highly focussed, either in supporting or undermining an issue that was likely to be pleaded.

[69] CPR r.31.16(3). For discussion of the meaning of the word "likely" in this context see: *Medisys plc v Arthur Andersen (A Firm)* [2002] P.N.L.R. 538; [2002] Lloyd's Rep. P.N. 323, QBD and *Smith v Secretary of State for Energy and Climate Change* [2013] EWCA Civ 1585; [2014] 1 W.L.R. 2283. See also *Burns v Shuttleworth Ltd* [1999] 1 W.L.R. 1449, CA, concerning the interpretation of the words "in which a claim for personal injuries is likely to be made" which were in the differently worded RSC Ord.24 r.7A. See also *Northumbrian Water Ltd v British Telecommunications plc* [2005] EWHC 2408; [2006] B.L.R. 38 and *Briggs & Forrester Electrical Ltd v Southfield School for Girls* [2005] EWHC 1734; [2005] B.L.R. 468.

[70] CPR r.31.16(4).

[71] *Black v Sumitomo Corp* [2001] EWCA Civ 1819; [2002] 1 W.L.R. 1562; *Harris v Newcastle Health Authority* [1989] 2 All E.R. 273 at 278, per Mann LJ. See also *OCS Group Ltd v Wells* [2008] EWHC 919; [2009] 1 W.L.R. 1895; para.13–063, below and *Smith v Secretary of State for Energy and Climate Change* [2013] EWCA Civ 1585; [2014] 1 W.L.R. 2283.

prospect of the order being fair to the parties if litigation was commenced, or of assisting the parties to avoid litigation, or of saving costs in any event.[72] The words "likely to be a party to proceedings" mean likely to be involved if proceedings are issued, and "likely" means no more than "might well". Prospective claimants do not have to show that they have a "reasonable basis" for making the claim against the prospective defendant.[73] There is no minimum level of arguability necessary to establish jurisdiction, though this factor may be a relevant consideration when the court is considering the discretionary stage of the test.[74] The procedure is not simply about providing evidence for a claimant to bring an action. When the claimant obtains disclosure this may well indicate that there is truly no basis for an allegation of negligence, and it is in the public interest that litigation which has no prospect of success should not be initiated.[75]

Relevance of a possible limitation defence In *Harris v Newcastle Health Authority*[76] the defendants declined the claimant's request for pre-action disclosure on the ground that the action was statute-barred, the events giving rise to the claim having occurred over 20 years before. Both the district registrar and, on appeal, the judge refused the claimant's application because the strength of the limitation defence was such that the action was doomed to fail. In the Court of Appeal Kerr LJ said that if it was plain beyond doubt that a defence of limitation would be raised and would succeed, then the court was entitled to take that matter into account. However, a claimant in a personal injuries action can always make an application to override the limitation period under s.33 of the Limitation Act 1980, and that must also be taken into account before it can be said that the action is clearly bound to be defeated by the limitation defence. Kerr LJ accepted that in the normal run of cases:

13–057

> "…even where a defence of limitation has a strong prospect of success, like here, it is very difficult for a court, on limited material, before pleadings and discovery, to conclude at that stage that the situation is such that the proposed action is bound to fail and therefore frivolous, vexatious or otherwise ill-founded. So in general I would accept … that issues relevant to limitation should not enter into consideration on applications for pre-trial discovery."[77]

---

[72] [2001] EWCA Civ 1819.
[73] [2001] EWCA Civ 1819. Under the old RSC it was said that the court would not permit "fishing expeditions": *Shaw v Vauxhall Motors Ltd* [1974] 1 W.L.R. 1035 at 1040, per Buckley LJ. But that did not mean that the applicant had to prove that he had a good cause of action: "One of the objects of the section is to enable a plaintiff to find out—before he starts proceedings—whether he has a good cause of action or not. This object would be defeated if he had to show—in advance—that he had already got a good cause of action before he saw the documents", per Lord Denning MR in *Dunning v Board of Governors of the United Liverpool Hospitals* [1973] 2 All E.R. 454 at 457; see also *Shaw v Vauxhall Motors Ltd* [1974] 1 W.L.R. 1035 at 1039.
[74] *Jet Airways (India) Ltd v Barloworld Handling Ltd* [2014] EWCA Civ 1311; [2015] C.P. Rep. 4.
[75] Figures from the Legal Services Commission for 1999–2000 indicated that 60 per cent of legally aided clinical negligence litigation was not pursued beyond the initial investigation, although more recent figures from the NHSLA suggest overall success rates for claimants of over 40 per cent: see para.1–015.
[76] [1989] 2 All E.R. 273.
[77] [1989] 2 All E.R. 273 at 277. Sir John Megaw said, at 279, that: "…it cannot be said with any certainty that on discovery facts would not emerge which would be relevant to the issue of limitation."

Accordingly, since it was likely that proceedings would be instituted regardless of the outcome of the application for disclosure, and since it could not be said that the proceedings were doomed to failure because pre-trial disclosure might reveal facts which would be relevant to the success or otherwise of the limitation defence, the court would exercise its discretion to order disclosure of the hospital records.

13–058   **To whom must disclosure be made?**   Under ss.33(2) and 34(2) of the Senior Courts Act 1981 the court can order disclosure to the applicant's legal advisers, plus any medical or other professional adviser of the applicant, or if the applicant has no legal adviser, to any medical or other professional adviser. This permits the court to order that disclosure exclude the patient (though not the patient's legal adviser). In *Davies v Eli Lilly & Co.*[78] the Court of Appeal held that in exceptional circumstances the court would permit a person who is neither a party's legal adviser, nor an employee of a legal adviser, nor a professional expert to undertake the inspection of documents if the person's assistance was essential in the interests of justice and the court was satisfied that there would be no breach of the duty of confidentiality.[79] Accordingly inspection by a "scientific co-ordinator" in the Opren litigation was authorised, even though the defendants objected on the ground that he was a journalist who had been critical of the pharmaceutical industry. This decision concerned inspection of documents after an action had been commenced, but there is no reason in principle why it should not also apply to pre-trial disclosure provided that the person qualifies as a "professional adviser".

13–059   **Costs**   The general rule is that the court will award the person against whom the order is sought the costs of the application and of complying with any order made on the application.[80] But the court has a discretion to make a different order, having regard to all the circumstances, including the extent to which it was reasonable to oppose the application and whether the parties have complied with any relevant pre-action Protocols.[81] Under the old Rules of the Supreme Court, where the defendant had no reasonable excuse for failing to comply with a written request for disclosure of documents before an application for disclosure was made, the defendant could be ordered to pay the applicant's costs.[82] In view of the greater emphasis now placed on patients' entitlement to see their medical records, and the Department of Health's policy on the disclosure of records, which is reflected in the Pre-Action Protocol for the Resolution of Clinical Disputes, there is generally no good reason for a NHS Trust to refuse a voluntary

---

[78] [1987] 1 W.L.R. 428.
[79] This was under the provisions of the old RSC Ord.24 r.9.
[80] CPR r.46.1(2).
[81] CPR r.46.1(3). See *Bermuda International Securities Ltd v KPMG (A Firm)* [2001] EWCA Civ 269; [2001] Lloyd's Rep. P.N. 392, CA.
[82] *Hall v Wandsworth Health Authority* (1985) 129 S.J. 188; see also *Jacobs v Wessex Regional Health Authority* [1984] C.L.Y. 2618, where the claimant's solicitors had pointed out in correspondence with the defendants that an application would result in needless public expense, since the claimant was legally aided. The defendants were ordered to pay the claimant's costs.

request for the disclosure of medical records, and failure to do so, in accordance with the Protocol, may well result in an order for costs in favour of the applicant.[83]

Congenital disabilities   The Congenital Disabilities (Civil Liability) Act 1976   **13–060** confers a right of action on a child who is born alive and disabled in respect of the disability, if it is caused by an occurrence which affected either parent's ability to have a normal healthy child, or affected the mother during pregnancy, or affected the mother or child in the course of its birth, causing disabilities which would not otherwise have been present.[84] It is possible for a father, though generally not the mother, to be a defendant to an action brought under the Act by a child. Sections 27–29 of the Human Fertilisation and Embryology Act 1990 deal with the status of the "parents" of children born as a consequence of in vitro fertilisation or artificial insemination, with the consequence that a child's mother or father may, in law, not be the same person as his genetic mother or father. Under s.35(1) of that Act, where for the purpose of instituting proceedings under the Congenital Disabilities (Civil Liability) Act 1976 it is necessary to identify a person who would or might be the parent of a child but for ss.27–29 of the Human Fertilisation and Embryology Act 1990, the court may on the application of the child make an order requiring the Human Fertilisation and Embryology Authority to disclose any information contained in the register kept in pursuance of s.31 identifying that person. The court must be satisfied that the interests of justice require it to make the order.[85]

(ii)   Against third parties

An order for pre-action disclosure can only be made under s.33(2) of the Senior   **13–061** Courts 1981 against a person who is "likely to be a party to the proceedings". Thus, if claimants need disclosure of documents from some other person, then, in the absence of voluntary disclosure, they will normally have to issue the claim form and apply for disclosure against the other person under s.34 of the Senior Courts Act 1981.[86] Voluntary disclosure, however, should be regarded as the norm. In *Walker v Eli Lilly & Co.*[87] Hirst J stated that health authorities and doctors who are not likely to be defendants should respond readily and promptly to requests for disclosure to avoid unnecessary expense and delay. This point is reinforced by the Data Protection Act 1998 (and the Access to Health Records Act 1990 in relation to requests following the death of a patient) which gives patients a right of access to their health records irrespective of the possibility of litigation. These statutes may be of some value in seeking disclosure against a doctor or health authority who is not a potential defendant, but there are some restrictions on their effectiveness for this purpose.[88] Moreover, the Protocol for

---

[83] *Sharp v Leeds City Council* [2017] EWCA Civ 33; [2017] 4 W.L.R. 98.
[84] See paras 2–135 et seq.
[85] Human Fertilisation and Embryology Act ss.34(2) and 35(3) 1990 (as amended by the Human Fertilisation and Embryology Act 2008).
[86] See Dijendra Basu, "Obtaining disclosure from non parties" [2005] J.P.I.L 198.
[87] (1986) 136 N.L.J. 608.
[88] See para.13–045.

Obtaining Hospital Medical Records (Annex B to the Pre-Action Protocol for the Resolution of Clinical Disputes), applies equally to third parties as it does to potential defendants. The Protocol is approved by the Department of Health, whose policy is that patients are entitled to see their records.

13–062   A further possibility to consider when seeking disclosure from a third party is the court's inherent power to order a person to disclose information under the principle in *Norwich Pharmacal Co. v Commissioners of Customs and Excise*.[89] Where a person through no fault of his own, and whether voluntarily or not:

> "...has got mixed up in the tortious acts of others so as to facilitate their wrongdoing he may incur no personal liability but he comes under a duty to assist the person who has been wronged by giving him full information and disclosing the identity of the wrongdoers."[90]

This allows a potential claimant to examine third party documents to identify a wrongdoer and establish a cause of action, including "fishing" for the names of wrongdoers.[91] The principle applies even though without the information sought claimants cannot ascertain whether an unidentified third party has in fact committed a tort against them; nor is it necessary that the tort committed against them be criminal in nature.[92] Disclosure under the *Norwich Pharmacal* principle is only available, however, where the third party has been involved in the wrongdoing in some way. It will not be ordered against a "mere witness".[93] For the purpose of disclosure under *Norwich Pharmacal* there is no requirement that the people against whom the proceedings had been brought should be a wrongdoer. It is sufficient if they have become involved in the wrongdoing. If they were involved it is irrelevant that they were innocent and in ignorance of the wrongdoing by the person whose identity was sought by the applicant. Nor is there a requirement that disclosure be for the purpose of enabling civil proceedings being brought against the wrongdoer.[94] The real question is likely to be whether the third party is a mere witness or more than a mere witness.[95]

---

[89] [1974] A.C. 133.

[90] [1974] A.C. 133 at 175, per Lord Reid. See also *Koo Golden East Mongolia v Bank of Nova Scotia* [2007] EWCA Civ 1443; [2008] Q.B. 717 although on the facts the Court declined to make an order due to state immunity.

[91] *Loose v Williamson* [1978] 1 W.L.R. 639.

[92] *P v T Ltd* [1997] 1 W.L.R. 1309. The *Norwich Pharmacal* principle can also apply to contractual disputes: *Carlton Film Distributors Ltd v VCI plc* [2003] EWHC 616; [2003] F.S.R. 47.

[93] *Ricci v Chow* [1987] 1 W.L.R. 1658; *AXA Equity & Law Life Assurance Society plc v National Westminster Bank plc* [1998] C.L.C. 1177, CA. An employee or agent of a corporation which is party to the proceedings is not to be regarded as a mere witness and can be required to give disclosure on behalf of the corporation: *Harrington v North London Polytechnic* [1984] 3 All E.R. 666. The court's jurisdiction under *Norwich Pharmacal* is a remedy of last resort. The jurisdiction can only be exercised against innocent third parties if they are the only practicable source of information: *Mitsui & Co. Ltd v Nexen Petroleum UK Ltd* [2005] EWHC 625; [2005] 3 All E.R. 511.

[94] *Ashworth Hospital Authority v MGN Ltd* [2002] UKHL 29; [2002] 1 W.L.R. 2033, where a newspaper was ordered to disclose the name of an intermediary, who had received from an employee of Ashworth Hospital, details of the medical records of a patient at the hospital. The hospital wanted to discover the name of the employee in order to dismiss him, rather than to bring civil proceedings against him. For consideration of the order for costs on a *Norwich Pharmacal* application see *Totalise plc v Motley Fool Ltd* [2001] EWCA Civ 1897; [2002] 1 W.L.R. 1233. As a general rule costs should be recovered from the wrongdoer rather than the innocent party. In a normal case the applicant for a *Norwich Pharmacal* order should be ordered to pay the costs of the party making the disclosure,

(iii)   Against a potential claimant

In *OCS Group Ltd v Wells*[96] the court had to consider a pre-action application for   **13–063**
disclosure of the claimant's medical records by the defendants in a personal
injury claim. The relevant Protocol was the Personal Injury Pre-Action Protocol
rather than the Pre-Action Protocol for the Resolution of Clinical Disputes but the
case is nonetheless worthy of note. The claimant had been injured in an accident
at work and one of the issues was the extent to which the claimant's injuries
affected her earning capacity and future loss. The claimant's solicitors had
obtained the medical records but no medical evidence had been obtained
notwithstanding the agreement of the parties as to the instruction of an
appropriate expert. After a period of considerable delay by the claimant's
solicitors coupled with a refusal to give any disclosure to support the claimant's
claim, the defendant made an application for pre-action disclosure under s.52(2)
of the County Courts Act 1984 and CPR rr.31.16 and 31.6. The court had to
consider the relevant jurisdictional threshold tests to be applied and then go on to
consider whether its discretion to make such an order should be applied. First, the
parties were likely to be parties to subsequent proceedings if brought
(r.31.16(3)(a)(b)). Second, the claimant's medical records would be documents
falling within standard disclosure if proceedings had started (r.31.16(3)(c)) in that
they were relevant to the issue of earning capacity.[97] However, on the third test as
to whether disclosure before proceedings have started is desirable either to
dispose fairly of the anticipated proceedings or to assist the dispute to be resolved
without proceedings (r.31.16(3)(d)) Nelson J considered that the defendants were
unable to establish this. He noted that the application of this third threshold test
tended to merge into the exercise of discretion and had regard to the Personal
Injury Protocol which does not provide for disclosure of medical records by a
claimant to a defendant. The judge was mindful of the fact that the records were
private and confidential and that the claimant should not be required to disclose
them prematurely. Just because they would become disclosable once proceedings

---

including the costs of the disclosure. *Norwich Pharmacal* applications are akin to proceedings for
pre-action disclosure, where costs are governed by CPR r.48.2. cf. *Ackroyd v Mersey Care NHS Trust*
[2003] EWCA Civ 663; [2003] Lloyd's Rep. Med. 379; (2003) 73 B.M.L.R. 88 where the Court of
Appeal held that it was at least arguable that the investigative journalist who had provided details of
the medical records of the patient detained at Ashworth hospital to the newspaper had a public interest
defence to a claim by the hospital that he should identify the hospital employee who had divulged the
medical records. It was arguable that the public interest in the protection of a journalist's sources
could override the public interest in preserving the confidentiality of medical records. If the
journalist's source could invoke a public interest defence, then a *Norwich Pharmacal* claim would not
be established for want of a "wrongdoer". In *Mersey Care NHS Trust v Ackroyd (No.2)* [2007] EWCA
Civ 101; [2007] H.R.L.R. 19; (2007) 94 B.M.L.R. 84 the Court of Appeal upheld the decision of the
judge to refuse to order the journalist to disclose the name of his source. It could not be said to be both
necessary, in the sense of there being an overriding interest amounting to a pressing social need, and
proportionate. The facts were significantly different from those in the action against the newspaper.
[95] *Various Claimants v News Group Newspapers Ltd* [2013] EWHC 2119 (Ch); [2014] Ch. 400.
[96] [2008] EWHC 919; [2009] 1 W.L.R. 1895, Nelson J on appeal from the Clerkenwell and
Shoreditch County Court.
[97] It is well established that once proceedings have been issued medical records are disclosable in
personal injury cases, certainly where there is a claim for loss of earnings or impaired earning
capacity: *Dunne v British Coal Corporation* [1993] I.C.R. 591.

were issued was not a sufficient ground to order pre-action disclosure. The judge went on to consider the exercise of discretion notwithstanding his finding that the defendant had failed to establish the third threshold test. The judge was critical of the claimant's delay and recognised that this had caused prejudice to the defendant who had been unable to value the claim or to seek to resolve it expeditiously. However, the sanction for delay lay in costs, not the disclosure of private medical records. Disclosure of the claimant's medical records to the defendant should be made only at the appropriate time once proceedings had been issued and not before.

(iv)   A common law duty of disclosure?

13–064   It is possible that the courts could develop a common law duty requiring doctors to inform patients about what has happened in the course of a treatment or procedure that has gone wrong. Sir John Donaldson MR has expressed strong views on this issue. In *Lee v South West Thames Regional Health Authority*, his Lordship referred to the doctor's duty to answer the patient's questions about proposed treatment following *Sidaway v Bethlem Royal Hospital Governors*,[98] and commented:

> "Why, we ask ourselves, is the position any different if the patient asks what treatment he has in fact had? Let us suppose that a blood transfusion is in contemplation. The patient asks what is involved. He is told that a quantity of blood from a donor will be introduced into his system. He may ask about the risk of AIDS and so forth and will be entitled to straight answers. He consents. Suppose that, by accident, he is given a quantity of air as well as blood and suffers serious ill effects. Is he not entitled to ask what treatment he in fact received, and is the doctor and hospital authority not obliged to tell him, 'in the event you did not only get a blood transfusion. You also got an air transfusion'? Why is the duty different before the treatment from what it is afterwards?
>
> If the duty is the same, then if the patient is refused information to which he is entitled, it must be for consideration whether he could not bring an action for breach of contract claiming specific performance of the duty to inform. In other words, whether the patient could not bring an action for discovery, albeit on a novel basis."[99]

13–065   Subsequently, in *Naylor v Preston Area Health Authority*[100] his Lordship returned to this theme, suggesting that in professional negligence cases, and in particular in medical negligence cases, there is a duty of candour resting on the professional man:

> "In this context I was disturbed to be told during the argument of the present appeals that the view was held in some quarters that whilst the duty of candid disclosure, [referred to in *Lee v South West Thames Regional Health Authority*], might give rise to a contractual implied term

---

[98] [1985] A.C. 871.
[99] [1985] 2 All E.R. 385 at 389–390. Mustill LJ agreed with this statement. The difficulty of obtaining information from medical staff when something has gone wrong was illustrated in *Bayliss v Blagg* (1954) 1 B.M.J. 709, in which there had been a long delay by the hospital staff in telling parents about a deterioration in their child's medical condition, and the court concluded that there had been a deliberate attempt by the hospital to conceal and misrepresent to the family the condition of the child. Stable J observed: "I would like to know if this is the system under our State medical service. The parent has a right to know—this isn't Russia." Counsel for the *defendants* replied: "One can't get facts from hospitals. They are grossly impertinent when you ask."
[100] [1987] 2 All E.R. 353 at 360.

and so benefit private fee-paying patients, it did not translate into a legal or equitable right for the benefit of national health service patients. This I would entirely repudiate. In my judgment, still admittedly and regretfully *obiter*, it is but one aspect of the general duty of care, arising out of the patient/medical practitioner or hospital authority relationship and gives rise to rights both in contract and in tort. It is also in my judgment, not obiter, a factor to be taken into account when exercising the jurisdiction under Ord. 38 with which we are concerned."

In *McInerney v MacDonald*[101] the New Brunswick Court of Appeal held that patients do have a contractual right of access to their medical records, even when the records in the hands of the treating doctor have not been created by the doctor herself. On appeal, the Supreme Court of Canada was not convinced by arguments based on contract.[102] Nonetheless, it was held that patients are entitled to have access to their records, on the basis that the doctor–patient relationship is a fiduciary relationship and that certain equitable duties arise between doctor and patient. Medical records consist of information that is highly private and personal, information that goes to the personal integrity and autonomy of the patient. The trust-like "beneficial interest" of the patient in the information indicated that as a general rule the patient should have a right of access to it and the doctor should have a corresponding obligation to provide it. This principle also applied when the information was conveyed to another doctor who then becomes subject to the duty to afford the patient access to that information. La Forest J pointed out that:

13–066

"...one of the duties arising from the doctor-patient relationship is the duty of the doctor to act with utmost good faith and loyalty. If the patient is denied access to his or her records, it may not be possible for the patient to establish that this duty has been fulfilled. As I see it, it is important that the patient have access to the records for the very purposes for which it is sought to withhold the documents, namely, to ensure the proper functioning of the doctor-patient relationship and to protect the well-being of the patient. If there has been improper conduct in the doctor's dealings with his or her patient, it ought to be revealed. The purpose of keeping the documents secret is to promote the proper functioning of the relationship, not to facilitate improper conduct."[103]

The equitable nature of the remedy gives the court discretion to refuse access to the records where non-disclosure is appropriate, if, for example, it is in the patient's best interests to deny access, the onus being on the doctor to justify an exception to the general rule of access.[104]

---

[101] [1991] 2 Med. L.R. 267; (1990) 66 D.L.R. (4th) 736.
[102] (1992) 93 D.L.R. (4th) 415, SCC.
[103] (1992) 93 D.L.R. (4th) 415 at 425–426. See Dickens (1994) 73 Can. Bar Rev. 234. In *Parslow v Masters* [1993] 6 W.W.R. 273, Sask QB, it was held that the claimant was entitled to see a medical report and the doctor's entire medical file concerning her where the report was prepared for the purposes of an insurance company, on the basis that the physician–patient relationship is a fiduciary relationship. Although the insurer paid for the report the insured disclosed private information about herself to enable the doctor to prepare the report, and this created the doctor–patient relationship.
[104] It is clear that the denial of access to information was to be regarded as exceptional, where for example there was real potential for harm to the patient or a third party. Paternalistic assumptions about the patient's "best interests" were inappropriate, since non-disclosure itself could affect the patient's wellbeing; and, moreover, the patient's wellbeing had to be balanced with the patient's right to self-determination: "In short, patients should have access to their medical records in all but a small number of circumstances. In the ordinary case, these records should be disclosed upon the request of

13–067 In *R. v Mid-Glamorgan Family Health Services Authority Ex p. Martin*[105] Popplewell J took the view that, since in *Sidaway v Bethlem Royal Hospital Governors* both the Court of Appeal and the House of Lords had rejected the notion that the doctor–patient relationship was fiduciary in nature, the basis on which the Supreme Court proceeded in *McInerney v MacDonald* could not be accepted in English law.[106] The applicant sought to know why, in 1969, he had been committed under the Mental Health Act 1959 and what the basis of his treatment had been. A consultant psychiatrist considered that the records contained information that it would be detrimental for the claimant to see, and the health authority claimed an absolute right, as owners of the records, to control access to them. They had offered to give conditional disclosure, to a medical expert nominated by the applicant. Popplewell J drew a distinction between the information conveyed by a patient for the benefit of the doctor's consideration and the conclusion which the doctor comes to, based on that information:

> "The opinion of the doctor is wholly the property of the doctor. It does not seem to me that the fact that the patient provides the original information entitles him subject to exceptions, to see the conclusions of the doctors based on that information …"[107]

Accordingly, there was no right at common law to access to any medical records which predated the coming into force of the Access to Health Records Act 1990. Indeed, the existence of this legislation, together with the Data Protection Act 1984 and the Access to Medical Reports Act 1988, supported the view that there was no common law right of access, said his Lordship, since this legislation would have been unnecessary if the right had existed at common law.[108] Moreover, art.8 of the European Convention for the Protection of Human Rights and Fundamental Freedoms, providing for a right to respect for private and family life, did not assist the applicant's argument for access. Although his Lordship commented that the logic behind Lord Donaldson MR's observations in *Lee v South West Thames Regional Health Authority* and *Naylor v Preston Area Health Authority* could scarcely be doubted, even so there might be:

---

the patient unless there is a *significant likelihood of a substantial adverse effect* on the physical, mental or emotional health of the patient or harm to a third party", per La Forest J, at (1992) 93 D.L.R. (4th) 415 at 430, emphasis added.

[105] [1993] P.I.Q.R. P426; [1994] 5 Med. L.R. 383.

[106] See *Sidaway v Bethlem Royal Hospital Governors* [1984] Q.B. 493 at 515 and 518–519, per Dunn and Browne-Wilkinson LJJ respectively, and per Lord Scarman in the House of Lords: [1985] A.C. 871 at 884. In *Breen v Williams* (1996) 138 A.L.R. 259 the High Court of Australia held that property in medical records remains that of the doctor, and there was no implied contractual right to access to the record. Declining the invitation to apply *McInerny,* it was held that the doctor–patient relationship is not fiduciary in character, but based on the doctor's contractual or tortious duty to exercise reasonable care. It was not permissible to use the law of fiduciary obligations to provide relief which would have the effect of imposing a novel positive obligation on a doctor to maintain and furnish medical records to a patient. For discussion of this case see Nolan (1997) 113 L.Q.R. 220.

[107] [1993] P.I.Q.R. P426 at 438.

[108] If the existence of legislation on a subject demonstrated that there was no equivalent common law right prior to the passage of the legislation the Court of Appeal could not have concluded in *Burton v Islington Health Authority* [1993] Q.B. 204 that a duty of care in negligence could be owed to a child born injured as a consequence of the defendant's negligence where the injuries were inflicted while the child was in utero, following the passage of the Congenital Disabilities (Civil Liability) Act 1976.

"...a difference between the doctor generally explaining what has happened and the patient being provided with the detailed written records which it was never intended for his eyes to see. Thus a doctor may be perfectly willing to give factual information but be disinclined to allow the patient to see opinions for instance expressed about the reliability or otherwise or the sanity or otherwise of that patient."[109]

On appeal, the Court of Appeal accepted that a doctor, and likewise a health authority, as the owner of the patient's medical records, might deny access to them if it was in the patient's best interests to do so, for example if disclosure would be detrimental to the patient's health.[110] In the light of the health authority's offer, that was a complete answer to the case. But, whereas Popplewell J considered that the issue was whether, at common law, patients had an unconditional right of access to their medical records, Nourse LJ preferred to state the issue in terms of whether a doctor or health authority, as owner of the patient's medical records, was entitled to deny access to them on the ground that their disclosure would be detrimental to the patient. A public body was in no different position from that of a private doctor whose relationship with his patient was governed by contract. There was no absolute right to deal with medical records in any way that a health authority chose. The doctor's duty, like the authority's, was to act at all times in the best interests of the patient. This involves a duty to keep the records confidential, and to hand them on to the patient's next doctor or make them available to the patient's legal advisers if they are reasonably required for the purpose of legal proceedings in which the patient is involved:

13–068

"The respondents' position seems to be that no practical difficulty could arise in such circumstances, but that they would act voluntarily and not because they were under a legal duty to do so. If it ever became necessary for the legal position to be tested, it is inconceivable that this extreme position would be vindicated."[111]

Evans LJ said that there was no good reason for doubting that a right of access to medical records does exist, or that it was qualified where disclosure would harm the physical or mental health of the patient:

"The record is made for two purposes which are relevant here: first, to provide part of the medical history of the patient, for the benefit of the same doctor or his successors in the future; and secondly, to provides a record of diagnosis and treatment in case of future inquiry or dispute. These purposes would be frustrated if there was no duty to disclose the records to medical advisers or to the patient himself, or his legal advisers, if they were required in connection with a later claim. Nor can the duty to disclose for medical purposes be limited, in

---

[109] [1993] P.I.Q.R. P426 at 437. It is not clear, however, why the doctor's willingness or disinclination to provide information to the patient should be relevant to the question of whether the patient has a legal *right* to information. Note that a failure to tell the patient that something has gone wrong with treatment may be relevant when the court considers an application to disapply the three-year primary limitation period under the Limitation Act 1980 s.33: see *Atkinson v Oxfordshire Health Authority* [1993] 4 Med. L.R. 18, QBD.

[110] [1995] 1 All E.R. 356; [1995] 1 W.L.R. 110; Grubb (1994) 2 Med. L. Rev. 354; Feenan (1996) 59 M.L.R. 101.

[111] [1995] 1 All E.R. 356; [1995] 1 W.L.R. 110 at 363–364, per Nourse LJ.

my judgment, to future medical advisers. There could well be a case where the patient called for them in order to be able to give them to a future doctor as yet unidentified, e.g. in case of accident whilst travelling abroad."[112]

(v) A statutory duty of disclosure

13–069 A duty of candour has now been given statutory status by reg.20 of the Health and Social Care Act 2008 (Regulated Activities) Regulations 2014.[113] The duty of candour is considered in Ch.4.[114]

(vi) An ethical duty of disclosure?

13–070 Clinicians have an ethical duty to inform patients, or their relatives, when something has gone wrong with their treatment which could be regarded as encompassing a duty to give disclosure.[115]

(b) Post-action disclosure

(i) Between the parties to the action

13–071 Once a claim has been commenced the normal rules on disclosure between the parties apply.[116] CPR r.31.6 provides for standard disclosure, which requires parties to the action to disclose only the documents[117] on which they rely, the documents which adversely affect their own or another party's case or support another party's case, and the documents which they are required to disclose by a relevant practice direction.[118] The duty of disclosure is limited to documents which are or have been in a party's control,[119] but the duty of disclosure continues throughout the proceedings.[120] The Court may also make an order for specific disclosure or specific inspection of documents under CPR r.31.12.[121]

---

[112] [1995] 1 All E.R. 356; [1995] 1 W.L.R. 110 at 365.

[113] SI 2014/2936.

[114] See para.4–055.

[115] The General Medical Council advises doctors that they "must be open and honest with patients if things go wrong. If a patient under your care has suffered harm or distress, you should: (a) put matters right (if that is possible); (b) offer an apology (c) explain fully and promptly what has happened and the likely short-term and long-term effects": *Good Medical Practice* (2013) para.55 (available at *http://www.gmc-uk.org/guidance/good_medical_practice/communicate_effectively.asp*). See para.4–054. Note that the Compensation Act 2006 s.2 provides that: "An apology, an offer of treatment or other redress, shall not of itself amount to an admission of negligence or breach of statutory duty."

[116] See the CPR Pt 31.

[117] "Document" means anything in which information of any description is recorded: CPR r.31.4.

[118] CPR r.31.10 sets out the procedure for standard disclosure.

[119] CPR r.31.8.

[120] CPR r.31.11.

[121] For discussion of the court's power to order specific disclosure under CPR r.31.12 see: *Bennett v Compass Group UK & Ireland Ltd* [2002] EWCA Civ 642; [2002] I.C.R. 1177.

(ii)   Against third parties

Once an action has been commenced a person who is not a party to the action   **13–072**
may be ordered to disclose documents under s.34(2) of the Senior Courts Act
1981 and CPR r.31.17. Section 34(2) is expressed in almost identical terms to
s.33(2), except that the court has the power to order disclosure and production of
documents by a person who is not a party to the proceedings. An application must
be supported by evidence. The court may make an order for disclosure only
where the documents are likely to support the case of the applicant or adversely
affect the case of one of the other parties to the proceedings, and disclosure is
necessary in order to dispose fairly of the claim or to save costs.[122]

The jurisdiction to make an order against a non-party must be exercised with   **13–073**
caution, reflecting the need for confidentiality and reflecting the terms of the CPR
rather than the Data Protection Act 1998.[123] Before making an order, the court
must be satisfied that the requirements of CPR r.31.17(3) were satisfied and that
the documents do in fact exist. The non-party, who has no access to the pleadings
or the evidence, should not be left to determine whether the documents satisfy
r.31.17(3). Thus the court must be satisfied that (i) there were documents falling
within the specified classes and (ii) that those documents were, not might be,
documents the disclosure of which would support the applicant's case or
adversely affect the case of another party to the proceedings.[124]

There is, of course, nothing to stop voluntary disclosure. In *Walker v Eli Lilly &*   **13–074**
Co.[125] the claimant applied under s.34(2) for disclosure of her hospital medical
records from a health authority which was not a party to the proceedings. The
authority was reluctant to disclose the records voluntarily. Hirst J said that where
no special consideration of confidentiality is invoked, the court will "almost
certainly" order disclosure if an application should become necessary, and so
health authorities and medical practitioners should respond readily and promptly
to any requests for disclosure in such cases, so that unnecessary expense and
delay can be avoided. The health authority had been anxious that any documents
disclosed might subsequently be used against them. His Lordship pointed out,
however, that there is an implied undertaking by a party seeking disclosure in
legal proceedings that documents so obtained will be used only for the purpose of
those proceedings and for no other purpose. Where it is the defendant seeking
disclosure of the claimant's medical records from a third party, the usual practice
would be for the claimant to consent to production of the relevant documents to
the defendant's medical advisers. If the claimant unreasonably withholds consent
then rather than making an application under s.34 the defendant can apply for a
stay of the proceedings until the claimant does consent. This is quicker and
cheaper than a s.34 application.[126]

---

[122] CPR r.31.17(3).
[123] *Re Howglen Ltd* [2001] 1 All E.R. 376 at 382; *A v X and B (Non-Party)* [2004] EWHC 447 (QB)
and *Durham County Council v Dunn* [2012] EWCA Civ 1654; [2013] 1 W.L.R. 2305.
[124] [2001] 1 All E.R. 376 at 382–383.
[125] (1986) 136 N.L.J. 608.
[126] *Dunn v British Coal Corporation* [1993] P.I.Q.R. P275 at 280, where the Court of Appeal held
that if claimants claim that they have suffered an injury causing permanent loss of earnings and loss of

(c) Privilege

13–075   There is no obligation to produce for inspection a privileged document, although it should normally be disclosed as in the party's possession if it is relevant to the action.[127] The claim for privilege should be made in the party's list of documents, with a statement of the grounds on which privilege is claimed.[128] The ground of privilege which will most commonly be relevant to medical negligence actions is legal professional privilege, though public interest immunity may, on rare occasions, apply.[129]

(i) Legal professional privilege

13–076   **Communications with client**   Legal professional privilege can take two forms. First, confidential communications between solicitors acting in their professional capacity and their clients for the purpose of obtaining legal advice and assistance are privileged, whether or not in contemplation of litigation.[130] This will be construed broadly. Where information is passed by solicitors or clients to the other as part of a continuing process aimed at keeping both informed so that advice may be sought and given, privilege will attach.[131] Legal advice is not limited to advice about the law, but can include advice about what should prudently and sensibly be done in the relevant legal context. Privilege does not extend, however, to all communications between solicitor and client on matters within the ordinary business of a solicitor.[132] In *Three Rivers District Council v Governor and Company of the Bank of England (No.6)*[133] the Court of Appeal

---

earning capacity, they must prove that the loss of future earnings or earning capacity was caused by the accident. The onus is upon them, and therefore they have to prove that they were in normal health. Accordingly, all their medical records should be disclosed to the defendant, not merely those relating to the injury which is the subject of the litigation. If they would reveal an unrelated but embarrassing condition, disclosure should be limited to the defendant's medical advisers, except in so far as it is necessary to refer to matters relevant to the litigation. Where, however, the application is made under s.34 of the Senior Courts Act 1981 or s.53 of the County Courts Act 1984 disclosure will not be limited to the defendant's medical advisers, but will extend to legal advisers: *Hipwood v Gloucester Health Authority* [1995] P.I.Q.R. P447; [1995] 6 Med. L.R. 187, CA.

[127] CPR r.31.3.

[128] CPR r.31.19(3),(4).

[129] Privilege also applies to documents which will expose a party to criminal proceedings or a penalty: Civil Evidence Act 1968 s.14; and to communications conducted on a "without prejudice" basis for the purpose of settling a dispute. "Without prejudice" privilege applies to the substance of the communication rather than the form, so that a document marked "without prejudice" may not be privileged if its purpose is not to reach a compromise, and, conversely privilege may attach even where the words are not used: *Buckinghamshire County Council v Moran* [1990] Ch. 623; *South Shropshire District Council v Amos* [1986] 1 W.L.R. 1271.

[130] Though note that legal advice privilege does not apply to legal advice given by someone other than a member of the legal profession: *R. (on the application of Prudential Plc) v Special Commissioner of Income Tax* [2013] UKSC 1; [2013] 2 A.C. 185.

[131] *Balabel v Air India* [1988] Ch. 317, CA.

[132] [1988] Ch, 317; see, e.g. *Conlon v Conlons Ltd* [1952] 2 All E.R. 462. Privilege applies to communications between an "in-house" salaried lawyer and his employer: *Alfred Crompton Amusement Machines Ltd v Commissioners of Customs and Excise (No.2)* [1974] A.C. 405; and to communications with counsel: *Curtis v Beaney* [1911] P. 181.

[133] [2004] EWCA Civ 218; [2004] Q.B. 916.

held that legal advice privilege did not apply to advice about the preparation and presentation of evidence to a public inquiry in the way least likely to attract public criticism. However, the House of Lords reversed this ruling.[134] Legal advice privilege was not simply an extension of litigation privilege; rather legal professional privilege is a single integral privilege, with subheads of legal advice privilege and litigation privilege. Litigation privilege was restricted to proceedings or anticipated proceedings in a court of law. The Court of Appeal had adopted too narrow an approach to the scope of legal advice privilege in holding that the privilege was "an aid to litigation" and applied only where the client's legal rights and liabilities were at stake. Legal advice privilege covered advice and assistance in relation to public law rights, liabilities and obligations as well as private law rights. Legal advice privilege was not limited to advice involving informing the client about the law but included advice as to what should prudently and sensibly be done in the relevant legal context.[135] The House of Lords made it plain that there are firm policy grounds for retaining legal professional privilege. Lord Scott said:

> "...it is necessary in our society, a society in which the restraining and controlling framework is built upon a belief in the rule of law, that communications between clients and lawyers, whereby the clients are hoping for the assistance of the lawyer's legal skills of their (the clients') affairs, should be secure against the possibility of any scrutiny from others, whether police, the executive, business competitors, inquisitive busybodies or anyone else."[136]

Their Lordships stressed that there must be a "relevant legal context" for advice to attract legal professional privilege. They reiterated that the principle laid down in *Minter v Priest*[137] remained good law:

> "...all communications between a solicitor and his client relating to a transaction in which the solicitor has been instructed for the purpose of obtaining legal advice will be privileged, notwithstanding that they do not contain advice on matters of law or construction, provided that they are directly related to the performance by the solicitor of his professional duty as legal adviser of his client."[138]

Once it is established that it applies, legal professional privilege is absolute.[139] No exceptions are permitted whereby the court balances the conflict of interest between the solicitor's client in maintaining the privilege against the damage to someone else, or indeed the public interest, if the evidence is not made

13–077

---

[134] [2004] UKHL 48; [2005] 1 A.C. 610; [2005] 4 All E.R. 948.
[135] For comment on *Three Rivers* see C. Tapper (2005) 121 L.Q.R. 181; A. Ruck Keene, "Privilege Returns?" [2005] J.P.I.L. 91.
[136] [2004] UKHL 48; [2005] 1 A.C. 610 at [34].
[137] [1929] 1 K.B. 655; [1930] A.C. 558.
[138] [2004] UKHL 48; [2005] 1 A.C. 610 at [111] per Lord Carswell.
[139] There is, however, a fraud exception to legal professional privilege. *Kuwait Airways Corp v Iraqi Airways Co.* [2005] EWCA Civ 286; [2005] 1 W.L.R. 2734. The Court of Appeal confirmed that the fraud exception could apply where there was a claim to litigation privilege as much as where there was a claim to legal advice privilege. In cases where the issue of fraud was one of the issues in the action, the exception could only be used where there was a very strong prima facie case of fraud. Where the issue of fraud was not one of the issues in the action, a prima facie case of fraud might suffice.

available.[140] In *General Mediterranean Holdings SA v Patel*[141] Toulson J held that the Civil Procedure Act 1997 did not delegate power to restrict the right to legal confidentiality and therefore the Civil Procedure Rules could not abrogate a "fundamental substantive right" to legal professional privilege. The only circumstance in which the right to legal confidentiality could be questioned was where a client attempted to use the solicitor and client relationship for illegal purposes. And in *Linstead v East Sussex, Brighton and Hove Health Authority*[142] Forbes J held that the same principle applied to the second category of legal professional privilege, which applies to a witness statement prepared in the course of litigation, where the sole or dominant purpose for which it came into existence was for obtaining legal advice in relation to contemplated proceedings. The coming into force of the Civil Procedure Rules, with the overriding objective of dealing with cases justly, and the Human Rights Act 1998 had not changed the rules on legal professional privilege, which remained absolute if it was not waived or abrogated. Legal professional privilege was not subject to any balancing exercise of weighing competing public interests.

13–078 **Communications with third parties** The second form of legal professional privilege applies to communications between a solicitor and a third party, either directly or through an agent, which arise after litigation is contemplated or commenced and the communication is made with a view to that litigation. Such communication is privileged if its purpose is to obtain or give advice on the litigation, or obtain evidence to be used in it.[143] Where documents have a dual purpose, the test is whether the dominant purpose of the document was for legal advice in contemplation of litigation. Thus, an accident report will not be privileged unless the sole or dominant purpose for which it was prepared was for

---

[140] *R. v Derby Magistrates Court Ex p. B* [1996] A.C. 487. The rule applies even if it may prejudice a defendant's defence to a charge of murder. Lord Taylor CJ said, at 507, that: "The principle which runs through all these cases, and the many other cases which were cited, is that a man must be able to consult his lawyer in confidence, since otherwise he might hold back half the truth. The client must be sure that what he tells his lawyer in confidence will never be revealed without his consent. Legal professional privilege is thus much more than an ordinary rule of evidence, limited in its application to the facts of a particular case. It is a fundamental condition on which the administration of justice as a whole rests." In *Paragon Finance plc v Freshfields (A Firm)* [1999] 1 W.L.R. 1183, CA, Lord Bingham CJ said that *R. v Derby Magistrates Court Ex p. B* made it plain that in the context of legal professional privilege there was no balance to be drawn between the requirements of fairness and justice against any legitimate interest a claimant might have in maintaining the confidentiality of a confidential relationship, though his Lordship did exclude cases "where client and legal adviser have abused their confidential relationship to facilitate crime or fraud". In this situation the privilege probably does not arise, rather than criminal activity constituting an exception.

[141] [2000] 1 W.L.R. 272.

[142] [2001] P.I.Q.R. P356.

[143] *Anderson v Bank of British Columbia* (1876) 2 Ch. D. 644. In wardship proceedings the court has power, in an appropriate case, to override the legal professional privilege attaching to documents, where it is necessary to achieve the best interests of the child: *Re A (Minors: Disclosure of Material)* (1991) 7 B.M.L.R. 129; *Re D and M (Minors)* (1993) 18 B.M.L.R. 71, CA. In *Re L (Police Investigation: Privilege)* [1997] A.C. 16 the House of Lords held that though communications between solicitor and client were absolutely privileged, communications between a solicitor and a third party in contemplation of litigation were not absolute, at least in the context of non-adversarial proceedings brought under the Children Act 1989, where the child's welfare was the paramount consideration.

submission to a legal adviser for advice in the light of anticipated or existing proceedings.[144] Accident reports are often prepared as a matter of course in order to find out the cause of the accident and avoid future occurrences. In this situation it will be difficult for the report to satisfy the dominant purpose test. The court will look to the substance of the matter. Defendants will be unable to claim privilege by dressing up reports to appear as though the dominant or sole purpose was the collection of evidence in contemplation of litigation, if in reality the report had a dual purpose.[145]

The dominant purpose of a document is not necessarily to be determined by the intention of the person who created the document, and so privilege could attach to a letter written by a party to his insurers to inform them about circumstances giving rise to a claim on an indemnity policy which subsequently led to litigation, even though it was the insurers, rather than the party, who wanted the document for the purpose of obtaining legal advice.[146] It is not necessary for a decision to have been made to instruct solicitors before it can be said that proceedings are contemplated. The test is that if litigation is reasonably in prospect, documents brought into existence for the purpose of enabling solicitors to advise whether a claim should be made or resisted are privileged, provided that this was their dominant purpose when they were created.[147]

13-079

Waiving privilege The privilege belongs to the client, not to the solicitor[148] and can be waived by the client but not by the solicitor.[149] Clients can expressly waive their legal professional privilege by electing to disclose communications which the privilege would entitle them not to disclose, though where the disclosure is partial, an issue as to the scope of the waiver may arise. There is no rule that a party who waives privilege in relation to one communication is taken to waive privilege in relation to all communications,[150] but privilege may not be

13-080

---

[144] *Waugh v British Railways Board* [1980] A.C. 521. The time for determining the purpose of a document is when it was brought into being. Thus, the mere fact that litigation was reasonably in prospect and that the documents are subsequently used to obtain legal advice does not necessarily mean that the documents will be privileged where, at the time they were brought into being, there was another dominant purpose: *Alfred Crompton Amusement Machines Ltd v Commissioners of Customs and Excise (No.2)* [1974] A.C. 405. See also *Komori v Tayside Health Board* [2010] CSOH 30; 2010 S.L.T. 387 (documents created by a health board in the course of an investigation into a patient's complaint were not covered by privilege).

[145] *Lask v Gloucester Health Authority* (1985) 2 P.N. 96 at 100; [1991] 2 Med. L.R. 379 at 383, per O'Connor LJ: "Once the second purpose is shown to be a purpose of the document, it seems to me that it is impossible to say that the judge was wrong to say that it was an equal purpose because by itself I would have thought that the prevention of similar accidents must be, in a hospital of all places, at least of equal importance as the provision of material for the solicitor." The prevention of future accidents was expressly stated to be a purpose of hospital accident reports in the NHS Circular H.M. (55)66; cf. *McAvan v London Transport Executive* (1983) 133 N.L.J. 1101.

[146] *Guinness Peat Properties v Fitzroy Robinson Partnership* [1987] 1 W.L.R. 1027.

[147] [1987] 1 W.L.R. 1027.

[148] *Goddard v Nationwide Building Society* [1987] Q.B. 670.

[149] *Al-Fayed v Commissioner of Police of the Metropolis (No.1)* [2002] EWCA Civ 780; *The Times*, 17 June 2002, approved in *Watts v Oakley* [2006] EWCA Civ 1905.

[150] *Fulham Leisure Holdings Ltd v Nicholson Graham & Jones (A Firm)* [2006] EWHC 158; [2006] 2 All E.R. 599. The claimant had made voluntary disclosure of an attendance note of a consultation and the instructions given for that consultation that would otherwise have been privileged. The

waived in such a partial and selective manner that unfairness or misunderstanding may result.[151] When a former client sues a solicitor the claimant impliedly waives any right to legal professional privilege in relation to any communication between them so far as necessary for the just determination of his claim. But the implied waiver does not apply to communications to which the solicitor was not privy, and the solicitors are not entitled to disclosure of communications between their former client and their new solicitors, instructed for the purpose of continuing the transaction that the defendant solicitors had originally been instructed to deal with.[152]

13–081   **Inadvertent disclosure and waiver**   Where there has been inadvertent disclosure and inspection of a privileged document the question of whether the party making the inadvertent disclosure has waived privilege depends upon whether the recipients realised that they had been permitted to see the privileged document only by reason of an obvious mistake. Where it would have been evident to a reasonable person with the qualities of the recipient that there had been a mistake, the court may restrain by injunction the recipient from using the document in the proceedings, even though the mistake was not in fact evident to the recipient.[153] The onus is on the party seeking the injunction to satisfy the court that the mistake was obvious and that the recipient ought to have realised this. But in any event, parties who have inspected a privileged document which has been inadvertently passed to them may only use it or its contents with the permission of the court.[154]

---

defendant contended that as a result the claimant had waived privilege in the whole category of documents relating to legal advice, thus opening them up to disclosure and inspection. It was held that it was open to a party to disclose some, but not all, of the documents falling within a privileged category. The issue was whether the documents disclosed constituted the "transaction" in relation to which disclosure had been given. The court had to consider whether proper disclosure had been given in relation to that transaction. The starting point was to identify the "transaction" in respect of which the disclosure had been made. That transaction might be identifiable simply from the nature of the disclosure made, for example, advice given by counsel on a single occasion. However, it might be apparent from the material available that the transaction was wider than that which was immediately apparent. If it was, then the whole of the wider transaction must be disclosed. When that had been done, further disclosure would be necessary if it was required in order to avoid unfairness or misunderstanding of what had been disclosed. On consideration of the disclosure, there was no basis for saying that the material was being deployed unfairly and the claimant was entitled to draw the waiver line more or less where it had drawn it.

[151] *Paragon Finance plc v Freshfields (A Firm)* [1999] 1 W.L.R. 1183, CA.

[152] [1991] 1 W.L.R. 1183.

[153] See *Pizzey v Ford Motor Company Ltd* [1994] P.I.Q.R. P15, CA; *Goddard v Nationwide Building Society* [1987] Q.B. 670, CA; *Guinness Peat Properties v Fitzroy Robinson Partnership* [1987] 1 W.L.R. 1027, CA; *Derby & Co. Ltd v Weldon (No.8)* [1991] 1 W.L.R. 73, CA. In *ISTIL Group Inc v Zahoor* [2003] EWHC 165; [2003] 2 All E.R. 252 Lawrence Collins J accepted that where a privileged document has been seen by the opposing party the court can intervene on equitable grounds to grant an injunction restraining that party from using the privileged document, but held that where the party to whom the document belongs has committed a forgery and sought to put forward misleading evidence (particularly where the forgery was produced for the purpose of the litigation) the equitable jurisdiction to restrain a breach of confidence gave way to the public interest in the proper administration of justice. Thus, the court could exercise its discretion to refuse the claimants' application for an injunction. The claimants did not have an absolute right to rely on litigation privilege.

[154] CPR r.31.20.

Reference to documents in expert witness reports In *Clough v Tameside &*   **13–082**
Glossop Health Authority[155] Bracewell J held that where a report or statement
which would otherwise be privileged is referred to in an expert witness report
produced on behalf of a party and disclosed to the other party, with the intention
of relying on that expert report, service of the report waived privilege in respect
of the statement or document. The duties of an expert witness included the duty to
state the facts or assumptions upon which the opinion was based. An essential
element in the process was for a party to know and to be able to test in evidence
the information supplied to experts in order to ascertain whether the opinion is
based on a sound factual basis or on disputed matters or hypothetical facts yet to
be determined by the court. Thus, the court would exercise its discretion to order
production of the document.[156] However, in *R. v Davies*[157] the Court of Appeal
doubted whether passing reference in an expert's report to another document
would necessarily amount to a waiver of privilege in that document by the client.
The Civil Procedure Rules now provide that an expert's report must state the
substance of all material instructions, whether written or oral, on the basis of
which the report was written[158]; and that the instructions are not privileged from
disclosure, but the court will not order disclosure of any specific document or
permit any questioning in court, other than by the party who instructed the expert,
unless it is satisfied that there are reasonable grounds to consider the statement of
instructions to be inaccurate or incomplete.[159] Moreover, an expert instructed
within the terms of CPR Pt 35 owes an overriding duty to the court,[160] so it could
be argued that the expert may have to disclose otherwise privileged information.
On the other hand, privilege protects the client's interests and if it exists must be
protected unless the client waives the privilege. Thus, it is arguable that it cannot
be part of a witness's duty to the court to override the client's privilege without
the client's consent. Moreover, given that privilege is a matter of substantive law,
indeed a fundamental right, it is difficult to see how rules of procedure can
abrogate the client's privilege.[161]

In *Lucas v Barking, Havering and Redbridge Hospitals NHS Trust*[162] the   **13–083**
claimant produced two experts' reports with his particulars of claim. Both reports
referred to a witness statement of the claimant, and one report referred to a
previous expert's report. The defendant sought inspection of those documents,
relying on CPR r.31.14(2) which permits a party to apply for an order for
inspection of any document mentioned in an expert's report which has not
already been disclosed in the proceedings. CPR r.31.14(2) is subject, however, to
CPR r.35.10(4), which allows a party to resist disclosure unless the court is
satisfied that there are reasonable grounds to consider the statement of

---

[155] [1998] 1 W.L.R. 1478.
[156] This was a decision under the old RSC Ord.24 r.10(1).
[157] [2002] EWCA Crim 85.
[158] CPR r.35.10(3).
[159] CPR r.35.10(4).
[160] CPR r.35.3. For the purpose of the CPR an "expert witness" is an expert who has been instructed
to give or prepare evidence for the purpose of court proceedings: CPR r.35.2.
[161] See *General Mediterranean Holdings SA v Patel* [2000] 1 W.L.R. 272 and *Linstead v East Sussex,
Brighton and Hove Health Authority* [2001] P.I.Q.R. P356, above, para.13–077.
[162] [2003] EWCA Civ 1102; [2004] 1 W.L.R. 220; [2003] 4 All E.R. 720.

instructions to the expert to be inaccurate or incomplete. The issue in the Court of Appeal was whether the word "instructions" should be given a narrow interpretation (thereby applying only to what the expert was told) or a broad interpretation (thereby covering material supplied to the expert as the basis on which he had been asked to advise). Waller LJ said that the appeal raised "a quite fundamental question as to what effect the new CPR were intended to have on the issue of privilege".[163] It was unlikely, however, that "the CPR would have intended to abolish privilege at a stroke under r.31.14(1) without expressly saying so".[164] The Court of Appeal held that "instructions" should be given a wide interpretation. CPR r.35.10(3):

> "...compels disclosure of what would otherwise be privileged material, and indeed compels that material to be referred to in such a way that under the common law there would be held to be waiver of all other privileged material relevant to showing there was no 'cherry picking' at least where that material was deployed at a hearing."[165]

But because a party is compelled to disclose material instructions, CPR r.35.10(4) provides some protection where an expert complies with that requirement. It is:

> "...designed primarily to give protection to a party who would otherwise have waived privilege by being compelled to set out matters in an expert's report. It is also designed so far as possible to prevent lengthy arguments as to whether there has been a waiver of privilege either prior to the trial or indeed at trial leading to an entitlement to further disclosure."[166]

It followed that the claimant's witness statement and the previous expert's report fell within the protection of r.35.10(4). Normally:

> "...material supplied by the instructing party to the expert as the basis on which the expert is being asked to advise should ... be considered as part of the instructions and thus subject to r.35.10(4)."[167]

13–084 *Lucas v Barking* was considered in *Expendable Ltd v Rubin*[168] where the Court of Appeal addressed the fundamental conflict between privilege and disclosure. A witness statement made and served by one of the parties in a bankruptcy case made reference to a letter which had not been disclosed. At issue was whether the reference to the letter contained in the words "he wrote to me" was a direct and specific reference in accordance with CPR r.31.14 and, if so, whether CPR r.31.14 provided for the automatic and absolute waiver of privilege as a result. The Court of Appeal confirmed that the document had to be either specifically mentioned (i.e. in a letter dated ...) or directly alluded to and that the test was not a difficult one. The form of the words used was a direct allusion to the making of the document itself and it had therefore been mentioned in the witness statement and was thus within CPR r.31.14. However, the Court of Appeal took exception to the appellant's contention that simply because the letter had been mentioned in

---

163 [2003] EWCA Civ 1102; [2004] 1 W.L.R. 220; [2003] 4 All E.R. 720 at [12].
164 [2003] EWCA Civ 1102; [2004] 1 W.L.R. 220; [2003] 4 All E.R. 720 at [24].
165 [2003] EWCA Civ 1102; [2004] 1 W.L.R. 220; [2003] 4 All E.R. 720 at [27] per Waller LJ.
166 [2003] EWCA Civ 1102; [2004] 1 W.L.R. 220; [2003] 4 All E.R. 720 at [31].
167 [2003] EWCA Civ 1102; [2004] 1 W.L.R. 220; [2003] 4 All E.R. 720 at [34].
168 [2008] EWCA Civ 59; [2008] 1 W.L.R. 1099.

the witness statement that CPR r.31.14 provided for the automatic and absolute waiver of privilege. They considered that this would be a significant change from the previous law and that there was no good reason or explanation for such a change. Such a fundamental change in the law whereby the protection of privilege would be lost merely by the mention of a document should not be inferred from an interpretation of a provision of the CPR. Privilege was a fundamental right that could not be overridden by general words. Rule 31.19 (claim to withhold inspection or disclosure of a document) should be read as having general application and r.31.14 (right to inspect documents mentioned in statements of case, etc.) should be seen as simply an adjunct to r.31.3 (right of inspection of a disclosed document). What appeared at first blush to be an absolute right to inspect for the purposes of r.31.14 was in fact a qualified right by reference to r.31.3. Whilst the letter had been mentioned, privilege had not been lost.

Joint selection of experts   The Protocol makes no express provision for the **13–085** joint selection of experts, in the way that the Pre-Action Protocol for Personal Injury Claims (the PI Protocol) does, but, on the basis of the general provisions found in the Practice Direction—Pre-Action Conduct and Protocols[169] joint selection should be considered where this may be appropriate. Whilst each party is likely to unilaterally obtain expert evidence dealing with breach of duty and causation there may be expert evidence on quantum where, before proceedings are commenced, it is worth the claimant exploring joint selection by nomination of potentially suitable experts. In *Carlson v Townsend*,[170] in accordance with the PI Protocol, the claimant supplied a list of three potential experts to the defendant, who objected to one of the names on the list. The claimant instructed one of the other two experts to provide a report, but did not disclose that report. The claimant then instructed another expert who was not on the agreed list and appended a copy of that report to the particulars of claim. The defendant claimed that the originally selected expert was jointly instructed and therefore he was entitled to see a copy of that report. The Court of Appeal held that there had been joint selection of the expert, but not joint instruction. The claimant had not waived privilege in the first report by agreeing to joint selection in accordance with the PI Protocol, and therefore was entitled to refuse to disclose the report. Whilst failure to disclose the report did not amount to non-compliance with the PI Protocol the instruction of a second expert, without giving the defendant an opportunity to object, was non-compliance. Accordingly, the claimant would have to obtain the court's permission to call the second expert to give evidence and the defendant was likely to be given permission to rely on corresponding expert evidence (which might not have been appropriate had there been joint selection).[171]

[169] https://www.justice.gov.uk/courts/procedure-rules/civil/rules/pd_pre-action_conduct.
[170] [2001] EWCA Civ 511; [2001] 1 W.L.R. 2415.
[171] See also *Nicholson v Halton General Hospital NHS Trust* [1999] P.I.Q.R. P310 where the Court of Appeal held that a claimant was entitled to maintain the right of confidentiality between a treating doctor and patient, and it was for the claimant to waive that right. The court would not compel him to waive the right, but in an appropriate case it could order that the action be stayed until he consented to waive the right of confidentiality (to enable the defendant to have access to relevant information in the

13–086   Where there has been joint selection of an expert and the evidence of that expert is not disclosed or if the claimant needs permission from the court to change the expert on whose evidence permission to rely has been given the court may make any subsequent order, giving permission to rely on a further expert, conditional upon the party agreeing to waive privilege and produce the earlier evidence which is proposed be discarded. In *Beck v Ministry of Defence*[172] the defendants sought to substitute one expert for another expert without having to disclose the first expert's report. The defendants had had the claimant examined by a consultant psychiatrist, but although the report was said to be favourable to the defence on liability, the defendants lost confidence in him as an expert witness and wanted to instruct a second consultant psychiatrist. The claimant refused to attend a second psychiatric assessment. The Court of Appeal held that the defendants should be permitted to have a new expert examine the claimant, but only on condition that the report of the first expert be disclosed to the claimant. This was in order to discourage the practice of expert shopping. Lord Phillips MR said that:

> "...a claimant can reasonably object to having to be examined again if this is, or may be, because the conclusions reached by the first expert have proved more favourable to him than the defendants had anticipated. I do not consider that the court should order a second examination or stay proceedings pending a second examination by a new expert if this is a possibility. So to order would be to permit the possibility of expert shopping which is undesirable. In this case ... it is not said that [the first expert's] conclusions are unfavourable to the defendants, but that the form or manner in which those conclusions have been expressed in the report that he has prepared are so unsatisfactory as to have resulted in a loss of confidence in him as an expert."[173]

A claimant should not have to take such an assertion on trust, and therefore any permission to instruct a new expert should be on terms that the report of the previous expert be disclosed.

13–087   The Court of Appeal considered and approved *Beck in Hajigeorgiou v Vasiliou*.[174] In that case Dyson LJ drew a clear distinction between permission to call an expert (which was required under CPR Pt 35) and permission to instruct an expert (which was not). The defendant had been given permission to call an expert. The fact that it had obtained a report from one expert did not preclude it from instructing and relying on the report of a second expert. Had the defendant required permission then it would have been right to give it on condition that the first report was disclosed, following *Beck*. *Hajigeorgiou* concerned the valuation of a restaurant business and it may be possible to draw a distinction between personal injury cases where the claimant would be required to undergo a second medical examination and those where, e.g. all that is needed is to permit an expert access to a restaurant.

---

claimant's medical records). In *Kapadia v London Borough of Lambeth* (2000) 57 B.M.L.R. 170, the Court of Appeal held that a claimant who consents to a medical examination requested by the defendant also consents to the disclosure of the report resulting from that examination to the defendant. He cannot insist on seeing the report first or vetoing its disclosure.
[172] [2003] EWCA Civ 1043; [2004] P.I.Q.R. P1.
[173] [2003] EWCA Civ 1043; [2004] P.I.Q.R. P1 at [32] to [33].
[174] [2005] EWCA Civ 236; [2005] 1 W.L.R. 2195 (Brooke, Dyson and Gage LJJ).

The approach to conditional orders, granting permission to rely on expert **13–088** evidence, outlined in *Beck* and *Hajigeorgiou* was confirmed by the Court of Appeal in *Edwards-Tubb v JD Wetherspoon Plc.*[175] This decision confirmed that where a party did not yet have permission to rely on expert evidence but had obtained, and was proposing to discard, evidence from a jointly selected expert, the court had power to make a conditional order requiring waiver of privilege, and production of the evidence, as a condition of granting permission. That decision highlights the risk of joint selection, particularly in contentious areas such as liability, and why this process will often be suited only to experts dealing with issues such as quantum, and even then in areas where there is unlikely to be significant controversy.

Watts v Oakley[176] concerned the question of privilege in relation to a draft **13–089** medical report obtained by the claimant in a road traffic accident claim. The parties had obtained their own psychiatric reports. The defendant's psychiatric expert suggested that the claimant's symptoms were exaggerated and, at least partly, deliberately exaggerated. The claimant sought permission to obtain a further report from a neuropsychologist. At a case management hearing the District Judge gave the claimant permission, making an order by consent that "The claimant shall file and serve the [neuropsychologist's] report by" a particular date. At issue was whether the claimant had thereby agreed to waive privilege in that report[177] or whether the claimant retained privilege and could then make a choice as to whether or not to rely on the report once it was obtained. In other words, if the claimant chose to rely on it, then it should be filed and served in accordance with the order but if the claimant chose not to rely on it, it remained privileged and did not need to be disclosed in accordance with the terms of the order. The claimant chose not to rely on the report and the defendant raised the matter at the next hearing. The District Judge considered the terms of the order to be mandatory, relying on the use of the word "shall", and ordered disclosure. The order for disclosure was upheld on appeal before the circuit judge. The matter was appealed to the High Court where it was heard by Sir Igor Judge. He noted:

> "...the general principle that such reports are privileged from disclosure, unless they are to be used at the hearing or unless privilege in them has been waived... The principle is clear. The report of an expert instructed by one of the parties is normally a privileged document and nothing in the CPR, nor in the pre-action protocols, nor in any authority that has been drawn to our attention disapplies the principle."[178]

He then went on to consider whether privilege had been waived and concluded that there was no evidence that the claimant had intended to waive privilege in the report nor was any precise reason for waiver demonstrated. The judge concluded that it was unlikely in the extreme that a solicitor would waive

---

[175] [2011] EWCA Civ 136; [2011] 1 W.L.R. 1373.
[176] [2006] EWCA Civ 1905.
[177] See *Al-Fayed v Commissioner of Police of the Metropolis* [2002] EWCA Civ 780; *The Times*, 17 June 2002, and in particular at [16.ii], which indicates that a solicitor acting as an advocate is clothed with ostensible authority, if not implied or express authority, to waive privilege.
[178] [2006] EWCA Civ 1905 at [20]–[21].

privilege in a document which he had not yet seen because it had not come into existence. If the claimant chose to rely on it then it should be disclosed in accordance with the terms of the order. If the claimant chose not to rely on it then the provision in the order was superfluous. The judge noted that such difficulties could have been avoided if the words "if relied on" or similar were used in the order but doubted that even that was necessary.

13–090   In *Stallwood v David and Adamson*[179] Teare J confirmed that there were circumstances under CPR Pt 35 where a party dissatisfied with an amended opinion from their expert after the experts' discussion could obtain permission to rely on evidence adduced from an additional expert. The claimant had instructed an expert but after the experts' meeting her expert had changed his opinion such that her prospects of succeeding on recovering in respect of her inability to work were significantly reduced. The claimant sought to adduce evidence from a second expert but this was refused by the judge. Teare J upheld her appeal against his decision stating that under the note to CPR r.35.12(1) any party who believed that an expert had stepped outside his expertise or had acted incompetently in reaching agreement could argue that any agreement should not be accepted by the court. Further, a court was able to allow a party to adduce further expert evidence if there was good reason to suppose that the first expert had modified his opinion for reasons that could not properly and fairly support his revised decision; and such a procedure was "reasonably required to resolve the proceedings". On the facts there was an exceptional reason why the application should be reheard (given the conduct of the judge) and the overall justice of the case required that the claimant be permitted to call a second expert.

13–091   The Court of Appeal in *Jackson v Marley Davenport Ltd*[180] confirmed that draft experts' reports prepared either on an advisory basis or for a conference with lawyers are privileged.

13–092   Since privilege belongs to the client, it cannot normally be relied upon by a third party. In *Lee v South West Thames Regional Health Authority*,[181] however, the Court of Appeal held that a memorandum prepared by a third party at the request of a potential defendant for the purpose of enabling the potential defendant to obtain legal advice was privileged, and the third party would not be required to disclose the memorandum to the claimant on an application for pre-action disclosure under s.33(2) of the Senior Courts Act 1981, even though the third party was not at the time that the memorandum was prepared a potential defendant and was in effect sheltering under another potential defendant's privilege. The infant claimant was taken to hospital for treatment of burns. He developed respiratory problems and was put on a ventilator, and then he was transferred from a hospital under the responsibility of Hillingdon Area Health Authority to another hospital under North East Thames Area Health Authority. The transfer was carried out by the ambulance service provided by South West Thames Regional Health Authority. The claimant sustained brain damage, either

---

[179] [2006] EWHC 2600; [2007] 1 All E.R. 206. See also *Guntrip v Cheney Coaches Ltd* [2012] EWCA Civ 392; [2012] C.P. Rep. 26.
[180] [2004] EWCA Civ 1225; [2004] 1 W.L.R. 2926.
[181] [1985] 2 All E.R. 385.

in hospital or in transit. Hillingdon, for the purpose of obtaining legal advice, requested and obtained a report by the ambulance crew from South West Thames. Subsequently, South West Thames refused to allow the claimant to inspect the memorandum on the ground that it was privileged. It was held that a defendant should be free to seek evidence without being obliged to disclose the results of his researches to his opponent, and that since Hillingdon had not waived their claim to privilege, and it would be impossible in the circumstances for matters to be arranged so that the document could be used against one defendant (South West Thames) and not the other (Hillingdon), inspection should not be ordered.[182]

(ii) Public interest immunity

Documents do not have to be disclosed where disclosure would damage the public interest.[183] This immunity does not depend upon a party objecting to disclosure, but can be raised by the court if necessary. The proper approach where there is a question of public interest immunity is to weigh the two public interests, that of the nation or public service in non-disclosure and that of justice in the production of the documents. The court will consider the importance of the documents in the litigation, and whether their absence will result in a denial of justice to one or other of the parties.[184] In *Campbell v Tameside Metropolitan Borough Council*[185] Ackner LJ said that there is a heavy burden on the party seeking to justify non-disclosure of relevant documents. The confidential nature of the communication is not of itself a sufficient ground if disclosure would assist the court to ascertain facts relevant to the action:

13–093

> "The private promise of confidentiality must yield to the general public interest, that in the administration of justice truth will out, unless by reason of the character of the information or the relationship of the recipient of the information to the informant a more important public interest is served by protecting the information or identity of the informant from disclosure in a court of law."[186]

---

[182] Sir John Donaldson MR said that the Court had reached this conclusion "with undisguised reluctance, because we think that there is something seriously wrong with the law if Marlon's mother cannot find out what exactly caused this brain damage": [1985] 2 All E.R. 385 at 389. This prompted his Lordship's comments about a doctor's common law duty to inform patients when something has gone wrong with the treatment: see paras 13–064 to 13–065.

[183] Senior Courts Act 1981 s.35(1); *Conway v Rimmer* [1968] A.C. 910; *Burmah Oil Co. Ltd v Bank of England* [1980] A.C. 1090; *D v NSPCC* [1978] A.C. 171; *Air Canada v Secretary of State for Trade (No.2)* [1983] 2 A.C. 394. CPR r.31.19(1) provides that people may apply without notice for an order permitting them to withhold disclosure of a document on the ground that disclosure would damage the public interest. CPR r.31.19(8) provides that Pt 31 of the CPR does not affect any rule of law permitting a document to be withheld from disclosure or inspection on the ground that disclosure or inspection would damage the public interest.

[184] Though the strength of the claimant's case is not a relevant consideration: *D v NSPCC* [1978] A.C. 171 at 216, per Lord Diplock; *Sharpe Estate v Northwestern General Hospital* (1991) 76 D.L.R. (4th) 535 at 540, Ont Ct Gen Div.

[185] [1982] Q.B. 1065.

[186] [1982] Q.B. 1065 at 1075, citing Lord Diplock in *D v NSPCC* [1978] A.C. 171 at 218. It may be that in an appropriate case it would be possible for the court to order production of part only of a document which was otherwise subject to the immunity: *Goodwill v The Chief Constable of Lancashire Constabulary* [1993] P.I.Q.R. P187 at 193, per Evans LJ.

The Court of Appeal held that confidential psychiatric reports held by an education authority on a pupil were not protected by public interest immunity in an action for negligence against the authority brought by a teacher who had been assaulted by the boy. Lord Denning MR commented that he could see no:

> "...difference between this case and the ordinary case against a hospital authority for negligence. The reports of nurses and doctors are, of course, confidential; but they must always be disclosed..."[187]

Once the court has engaged in the balancing exercise by weighing the public interest in preserving the immunity against the public interest that all relevant information which might assist a court to adjudicate should be before the court and concluded that public interest immunity applies, there is no further discretion. The material to which the immunity applies must be excluded from the case.[188]

13–094   Public interest immunity will rarely be relevant to medical negligence litigation. The issue was raised in *Re HIV Haemophiliac Litigation*[189] in which haemophiliacs and their families who had been infected with HIV as a result of treatment with contaminated blood products imported from the United States were suing, inter alia, the Department of Health, the licensing authority under the Medicines Act 1968, and the national Blood Products Laboratory. The Department of Health claimed public interest immunity in respect of certain documents on the basis that they related to the formulation of policy by ministers or were briefings for ministers about whether a policy of self-sufficiency in blood products should be established, the resources necessary for such a policy, and the role and organisation of the Blood Products Laboratory and the National Blood Transfusion Service. The claimants conceded that public interest immunity arose, but argued that the public interest in the fair trial of the proceedings outweighed the public interest in preserving the immunity. The Court of Appeal accepted the claimants' argument that it was very likely that the documents contained material which would give substantial support to their contentions in the action and that without them the claimants might be deprived of the means of proper presentation of their case.[190]

13–095   In *Australian Red Cross Society v BC*[191] the Supreme Court of Victoria ordered the defendants to disclose the identity of a blood donor to the claimant on the basis that the public interest in the administration of justice outweighed the public interest in preserving the privacy and confidentiality of blood donors. Although not treated as a ground for the decision the court noted that legislation in Victoria made it an offence for a blood donor to make a false statement when supplying information to the defendants in the prescribed form, and this represented a deliberate public policy that information given to the Red Cross by donors would not necessarily be kept in confidence, since it could be the subject of criminal

---

[187] [1982] Q.B. 1065 at 1074.
[188] *Powell v Chief Constable of North Wales Constabulary, The Times*, 11 February 2000, CA.
[189] [1996] P.I.Q.R. P220.
[190] Applying the test of Lord Fraser in *Air Canada v Secretary of State for Trade (No.2)* [1983] 2 A.C. 394.
[191] [1992] 3 Med. L.R. 273, SC of Vict, App Div.

prosecution.[192] In *Sharpe Estate v Northwestern General Hospital*[193] the claimant, a haemophiliac, was seeking access to Canadian Red Cross records in an attempt to identify whether any of the donors from whom he had received blood was HIV positive at the time of the donation. Without this evidence his action against the Red Cross Society was bound to fail on causation. There were about 1,250 donors from whom the blood and blood products came. Again the argument was that without confidentiality the supply of donated blood would be reduced. There was no evidence that donors demanded or expected confidentiality of their records, though it was the perception of the Red Cross that this was the case. It was held that the interests of the claimant should take precedence. Given that, following the introduction of HIV testing of blood donors, cases such as the claimant's were now unlikely to occur, the small possibility of the undesirable effects of disclosure on the donors was:

"…insignificant when measured against the overwhelming need of society to have all legitimate tools available in the search for truth in the trial process."[194]

In *AB v Glasgow and West of Scotland Blood Transfusion Service*,[195] on the other hand, it was held that a material risk of a national deficiency in the supply of blood for transfusion was sufficient public interest to override the petitioner's claim to know the identity of a blood donor for the purpose of bringing an action in negligence against the donor. The existence of such a material risk was assumed, however, on the basis that the claim to public interest immunity was made by a Minister of the Crown. Lord Morison indicated that the position would have been different in the absence of a ministerial objection to disclosure, in that the court would assess the merits of the defendants' objection on the available evidence, in order to determine whether the petitioner's interest should prevail over the objection.[196] Moreover, his Lordship suggested that the risk to the blood supply was perhaps a little overstated, commenting that:

13–096

---

[192] This point was central to the decision of the New South Wales Court of Appeal in *PD v Australian Red Cross Society (New South Wales Division)* (1993) 30 N.S.W.L.R. 376. The defendants had undertaken a survey which purported to show that a substantial number of donors would not donate blood again if they knew that their name and information about them could be made available to a person who developed an infection after a transfusion of the donor's blood. The court acknowledged that any significant diminution in the level of blood donations would be a serious matter. The process of balancing the public interest in the proper administration of justice, and non-disclosure in the public interest of preserving an adequate blood supply did not have to take place, however, because since 1985 the Red Cross had been under a statutory obligation to obtain a certificate from donors relating to their medical suitability before accepting a donation. A person who signed a certificate containing a statement which to that person's knowledge was false or misleading committed a criminal offence. The certificates could not be withheld from the police or from the legal advisers of intending claimants or the courts. Legislation also authorised the courts to order the Red Cross to disclose information enabling a blood donor who had given HIV contaminated blood to be identified and traced. In these circumstances the blanket public interest immunity claimed by the Red Cross could not be supported.
[193] (1991) 76 D.L.R. (4th) 535, Ont Ct Gen Div, aff'g (1990) 74 D.L.R. (4th) 43.
[194] (1991) 76 D.L.R. (4th) 535 at 540, per Haley J.
[195] (1989), 1993 S.L.T. 36; 15 B.M.L.R. 91, Court of Session, Outer House.
[196] See further Grubb and Pearl (1991) 141 N.L.J. 897 and 938. Public interest immunity might also be raised with respect to the disclosure of raw data in research projects, on the ground that patients and doctors might be unwilling to participate in research if they thought that confidential information

"It is not immediately apparent to me why [donors acting from altruistic motives] would be deterred from pursuing these motives by an apprehension that they might be unjustifiably sued. If on the other hand there are any persons who give blood without due regard to their responsibilities, the public interest would plainly be served if they were discouraged from doing so."

6.   THE ROLE OF EXPERTS

13–097   An expert's duty is to the court. CPR r.35.3(1) provides: "It is the duty of an expert to help the court on matters within his expertise..." CPR r.35.3(2) continues: "This duty overrides any obligation to the person from whom he has received instructions or by whom he is paid..." This was confirmed by Lord Woolf MR, the architect of the Civil Procedure Rules, in *Stevens v Gullis*.[197] Lord Woolf referred to CPR PD35 and Cresswell J's judgment in *National Justice Compania Naviera SA v Prudential Life Assurance Co. Ltd "The Ikarian Reefer"*.[198]

13–098   The duties and responsibilities of expert witnesses were summarised with particular clarity by Cresswell J in *"The Ikarian Reefer"*.[199] Those principles have been expanded upon in the CPR Pt 35, and in particular the Practice Direction that supplements CPR Pt 35 and more recently the *Guidance for the Instruction of Experts in Civil Claims* published by the Civil Justice Council in December 2014.[200]

13–099   **Conflicts of interest**   The question of experts and potential or actual conflicts of interest was considered by the Court of Appeal in *Toth v Jarman*.[201] A party who wishes to call an expert with a potential conflict of interest should disclose details of that conflict at as early a stage in the proceedings as is possible. *Toth* was a clinical negligence case against a general practitioner in which the trial judge preferred the evidence of the defendant's expert on causation and the claim failed. On appeal new evidence was adduced showing that the defendant's expert was a member of the Cases Committee of the Medical Defence Union who had acted for the defendant. The claimant alleged an undisclosed conflict of interest between the expert's duty of objectivity and his interest in assisting the defence of a member of the MDU. The Court of Appeal stated that the presence of a conflict of interest did not automatically disqualify an expert. The key question was whether the expert's opinion was independent. The expert's expression of opinion had to be independent of the parties and the pressures of litigation (*Ikarian Reefer*). Moreover, the need for an expert to give an independent opinion flowed from his duty to the court under CPR r.35.3 to assist the court in relation to matters that fell within his expertise. However, where an expert had a material or

---

would have to be disclosed in the course of litigation. On the other hand, confidentiality could be protected by maintaining anonymity of the research subjects, if possible.

[197] [2000] 1 All E.R. 527.
[198] [1993] 2 Lloyd's Rep. 68.
[199] [1993] 2 Lloyd's Rep. 68 at 81–82, QBD. See para.3–190.
[200] Available at *https://www.judiciary.gov.uk/wp-content/uploads/2014/08/experts-guidance-cjc-aug-2014-amended-dec-8.pdf*.
[201] [2006] EWCA Civ 1028; [2006] 4 All E.R. 1276 (Note); [2006] Lloyd's Rep. Med. 397.

significant conflict of interest the court was likely to decline to act on his evidence or indeed to give permission for his evidence to be adduced. Thus it was important that a party who wished to call an expert with a potential conflict of interest should disclose details of that conflict at as early a stage in the proceedings as possible. The time for disclosing the existence of a possible conflict of interest was when the report of the expert was first served on the other parties. If, however, the conflict only arose after that time, the appropriate time for disclosure was the first practicable date thereafter. Experts should produce their curriculum vitaes when providing their reports, which should give details of any employment or activity that raised a possible conflict of interest. In this case, the expert had been a member of the committee and the committee had responsibility for the case. He was therefore in principle subject to a conflicting duty. That information should have been made available to the claimant and to the court. However, in view of the practice of the committee to exclude any committee member who was an expert in a case from deliberations in respect of that case and given that the expert had not in fact been a member of the committee at the relevant time, even if his conflict of interest had earlier been a disqualifying interest, it became immaterial. Similarly, where the defendant relied on an expert who had been his mentor that interest should have been disclosed and the failure to do so affected the weight, and potentially the admissibility, of the expert's evidence.[202]

Managing expert witnesses   CPR Pt 35 was regarded as a significant plank in the Woolf reforms, and lays down detailed rules for managing the use of expert witnesses, in an attempt to reduce cost and delay in litigation. Expert evidence should be restricted to that which is reasonably required to resolve the proceedings.[203] Experts have an overriding duty to the court. Experts' duties are to help the court on matters within their expertise,[204] and this duty overrides any obligation to the person who instructed them or by whom they are paid.[205] Expert evidence should generally be given in the form of a written report.[206] An expert's report must state the substance of all material instructions, whether written or oral, on the basis of which the report was written.[207] The instructions are not privileged from disclosure, but the court will not order disclosure of any specific document or permit any questioning in court, other than by the party who instructed the expert, unless it is satisfied that there are reasonable grounds to consider the statement of instructions to be inaccurate or incomplete.[208]

13–100

---

[202] *EXP v Barker* [2017] EWCA Civ 63; [2017] Med. L.R. 121; (2017) 155 B.M.L.R. 18; see para.3–191.
[203] CPR r.35.1.
[204] CPR r.35.3(1).
[205] CPR r.35.3(2). Where a party's expert witness completely disregards the CPR and orders of the court, the expert witness may be barred from giving evidence on behalf of that party, even though this may result in the party losing the case: *Stevens v Gullis* [2000] 1 All E.R. 527, CA.
[206] CPR r.35.5(1).
[207] CPR r.35.10(3).
[208] CPR r.35.10(4). See para 3–083.

13–101   **Court's permission**   One of the key principles underlying CPR Pt 35 is that no party may call an expert or put in evidence an expert's report, without the Court's permission (reflecting the case management role of the Court).[209] This has led to the court in practice limiting the number of expert witnesses to one for each party in any given speciality. As Brooke LJ observed in *ES v Chesterfield and North Derbyshire NHS Trust*[210] "it will only be in a really exceptional case that more than one expert in any particular specialty will be permitted". In that case the claimant sought permission to call a second expert witness in obstetrics, on the basis that two of the defendants' witnesses of fact were also consultant obstetricians, and they would inevitably have to explain their conduct by reference to their experience and the practice of others in the field of obstetrics. Together with the defendants' expert witness, that would mean that the claimant's expert would be faced with three "expert witnesses" and therefore the claimant would not be able to present her case on an equal footing (one of the factors to considered under the overriding objective of the CPR: see CPR r.1.1(2)(a)). The Court of Appeal accepted this argument. Having regard to the importance of the case to the parties, the high value of the claim (estimated to be around £1.5 million), the complexity of the case, and the financial position of the parties (both of whom were publicly funded), they would not have been on an equal footing if the claimant were limited to a single obstetric expert. The extra time and expense of an additional expert was not disproportionate in a case of such high monetary value and importance to the parties. Holman J commented that:

> "When a court is considering what practices may be adopted by a responsible body of medical opinion, it seems to me impossible to exclude evidence given by two doctors, now both of consultant status, of their own experience, however much they may be labelled and confined as 'witnesses of fact'. The reality is that they have and profess expertise and, if credible, their evidence based on their experience and expertise cannot be ignored. So in my view there *is* an issue of equality of footing if the claimant is permitted to call one obstetric expert while the defendants can rely upon two consultants plus an expert."[211]

Similarly, Kennedy LJ said that:

> "In response to any criticisms which may be made by the appellant's expert the respondents will be able to deploy three consultant obstetricians and it is no sufficient answer to say that two of them are witnesses as to fact. If the case is contested they are bound to seek to justify what they did or omitted to do by reference to the practice of others of which they are aware."[212]

Brooke LJ cautioned that:

> "Nothing in this judgment must be taken to give any sort of green light to the calling of two experts in a single discipline in any case which does not have exceptional features. On this appeal the presence of three consultants on the defendants' side constitutes such an exceptional feature."[213]

---

[209] CPR r.35.4.
[210] [2003] EWCA Civ 1284; [2004] Lloyd's Rep. Med. 90 at [14].
[211] [2003] EWCA Civ 1284; [2004] Lloyd's Rep. Med. 90 at [32] (original emphasis).
[212] [2003] EWCA Civ 1284; [2004] Lloyd's Rep. Med. 90 at [37].
[213] [2003] EWCA Civ 1284; [2004] Lloyd's Rep. Med. 90 at [27].

In addition to this feature, Kennedy LJ emphasised that the case was exceptional because it was very substantial and of great importance to the parties; the additional costs likely to be incurred were not significant in the context of the size of the claim, and there was no reason to believe that the order would delay the trial (the claimant had already instructed a second obstetric expert).[214]

Written reports and the expert literature   As noted above, a general principle of expert evidence is that expert evidence should be given in the form of a written report unless the court directs otherwise.[215] In medical negligence cases it is commonplace for the expert's written report to refer to appropriate medical literature. In *Wardlaw v Farrar*[216] Brooke LJ commented that:

13–102

> "The standard form of order made by the High Court masters in the Queen's Bench Division in clinical negligence cases now contains these provisions: 'Any unpublished literature upon which any expert witness proposes to rely shall be served at the same time as service of his statement together with a list of published literature and copies of any unpublished material. Any supplementary literature upon which any expert witness proposes to rely shall be notified to all other parties at least one month before trial. No expert witness shall rely upon any publications that have not been disclosed in accordance with this direction without leave of the trial judge on such terms as he deems fit ... Parties to agree the trial bundle ... not less than 7 days before the hearing.'
> Now that so many relatively heavy clinical negligence actions in the multi-track are being conducted in county courts, in addition to district registries of the High Court, it is essential that best practice should be followed throughout the country in relation to case management directions in the multi-track in this specialist field. If these directions had been made in the present case, the medical literature would have been handled in a more orderly manner."[217]

Written questions   A party may put written questions about an expert's report to an expert instructed by another party or a single joint expert appointed under CPR r.35.7,[218] but written questions may only be put once, within 28 days of service of the expert's report and for the purpose of clarification only, unless the court gives permission or the other party agrees.[219] Answers to these questions are then treated as part of the expert's report. If the expert does not answer a

13–103

---

[214] See also *Kirkman v Euro Exide Corp (CMP Batteries Ltd)* [2007] EWCA Civ 66; [2007] C.P. Rep. 19—claimant entitled to call his treating orthopaedic surgeon as a witness of fact to give evidence as to whether he would have needed surgery on his knee but for the accident; *DN v Greenwich LBC* [2004] EWCA Civ 1659; [2005] 1 F.C.R. 112—defendant psychologist's evidence as to why he considered that his conduct had not fallen below the standard of reasonable care was admissible; the fact that it might lack the objectivity of an independent expert went to the issue of cogency, not admissibility; *Beaumont v Ministry of Defence* [2009] EWHC 1258 (QB) where it was held that a defendant obstetrician relying on his own expertise when giving factual evidence, in addition to calling an independent obstetrician as an expert, was not sufficient to justify granting the claimant permission to call two experts.
[215] CPR r.35.5(1).
[216] [2003] EWCA Civ 1719; [2004] Lloyd's Rep. Med. 98; [2004] P.I.Q.R. P289; [2003] 4 All E.R. 1358 (Note).
[217] [2003] EWCA Civ 1719; [2004] Lloyd's Rep. Med. 98; [2004] P.I.Q.R. P289; [2003] 4 All E.R. 1358 at [23] to [24]. See also *Breeze v Ahmed* [2005] EWCA Civ 223; [2005] C.P. Rep. 29 where the Court of Appeal emphasised that where an expert witness relies on medical literature to support his opinion, that medical literature should be made available to the court.
[218] CPR r.35.6(1).
[219] CPR r.35.6(2). For discussion of the meaning of "clarification" see *Mutch v Allen* [2001] EWCA Civ 76; [2001] P.I.Q.R. P26.

written question the court may order that the party who instructed the expert may not rely on the evidence of that expert and/or that the party may not recover the fees and expenses of that expert from any other party.[220]

(a) Single joint experts

13–104   The court has the power to direct that evidence be given by a single joint expert.[221] If the parties cannot agree who should act as the expert the court may select from a list prepared or identified by the instructing parties or direct that the expert be selected in such other manner as the court may direct.[222] This creates the possibility that one of the parties may not be happy with a report of the single joint expert. In *Daniels v Walker*[223] the defendant was unhappy with the report obtained from a jointly instructed expert. He wanted to obtain his own expert's report, and permission for that expert to interview the claimant. The Court of Appeal held that where the parties agree a joint expert, the fact of agreement does not preclude a party from obtaining a report from a different expert, or if appropriate from relying on the evidence of another expert. The joint instruction of an expert was the first step, but if having obtained the joint expert's report a party, for reasons which were not fanciful, wanted to obtain further information before deciding whether to challenge part or the whole of the joint report, they should normally be allowed to obtain that evidence. But if the claim for damages was modest, the court might refuse the instruction of a second expert and merely permit the dissatisfied party to put questions to the expert who had already prepared the report, to ensure proportionality in the conduct of the litigation.

13–105   In *Layland v Fairview New Homes plc*[224] Neuberger J said that the effect of Lord Woolf's analysis in *Daniels v Walker*, coupled with the overriding objective, is that where the court has ordered a report from a single expert pursuant to CPR r.35.7 and one of the parties wishes to call their own expert the position is that: (i) the court has a discretion whether to accede to the application; (ii) whether it will accede to the application depends on all the circumstances, including the value of the claim and the grounds on which the applicant seeks to challenge the single expert's view; (iii) even where there may be grounds for permitting parties to call their own expert the court may well require further steps to be taken first; (iv) the court will normally permit parties to call their own expert if they have reasonable grounds for doing so. Moreover, where a single joint expert's view is adverse to the claimant this does not necessarily mean that the claimant is effectively bound by the expert's conclusion, and therefore it is inappropriate to grant summary judgment under CPR Pt 24 if there is a prospect that the expert, through cross-examination, or the court, through submissions, may be persuaded to reach a different conclusion. Nor should a claim be dismissed under Pt 24 merely because it is for a small sum, looks weak and is being pursued unattractively or ineptly.

---

[220] CPR r.35.6(4).
[221] CPR r.35.7(1).
[222] CPR r.35.7(3).
[223] [2000] 1 W.L.R. 1382.
[224] [2002] EWHC 1350; [2003] C.P.L.R. 19; [2003] B.L.R. 20.

In *Peet v Mid-Kent Healthcare NHS Trust*[225] the claimant's parents wanted to have a conference with jointly instructed experts in the absence of any representative of the defendants, who objected. The Court of Appeal held that to have an experts' conference, including lawyers, without a representative of the defendants was inconsistent with the concept of a single joint expert. There was nothing wrong, subject to both sides being present, with having a discussion with joint experts in order for the lawyers to understand and test the views of each individual expert, but the idea that one side should be able to test the views of an expert in the absence of the other party was not permissible. Thus, a party cannot have unilateral access to a joint expert without the consent of the other jointly instructing party.

13–106

In *Wright v Sullivan*[226] the Court of Appeal clarified the approach to be taken with regard to case managers. In cases of serious injury the claimant often appoints a case manager whose duties can include being responsible for setting up and managing the claimant's care regime along with assisting with accommodation and equipment needs. The defendant had contended for the joint instruction of the case manager arguing that the case manager should effectively be accorded the status of a single joint expert. The Court of Appeal rejected this approach holding that the case manager is appointed solely to assist the injured claimant. The case manager's duty can only be to the injured claimant. The case manager must act in the best interests of the claimant and joint instruction would be inappropriate. Should it be necessary to call the case manager to give evidence, their status would be as a witness of fact, not an expert witness.

13–107

In practice it will be very rare to have a single joint expert dealing with liability or causation in medical negligence cases. Given the nature of the *Bolam* test and the differences of professional opinion that often arise on causation, a single expert would effectively be determining the outcome of the case. Thus, in *Oxley v Penwarden*[227] the Court of Appeal took the view that in clinical negligence claims the parties should have an opportunity of investigating causation through an expert of their own choice:

13–108

> "It is inevitable in a case of this class that parties will find the greatest difficulty in agreeing on the appointment of a single expert. That burden would then be cast upon the court and would, in turn, lead to the judge selecting an expert, if there be more than one school of thought on this issue, from one particular school of thought and that would effectively decide an essential question in the case without opportunity for challenge."[228]

Again, in *Simms v Birmingham Health Authority*[229] the Court of Appeal confirmed that the parties in a complex clinical negligence claim should be able to plead their own case on breach of duty and causation fully, with the assistance of their own expert evidence.

---

[225] [2001] EWCA Civ 1703; [2002] 1 W.L.R. 210.
[226] [2005] EWCA Civ 656; [2006] 1 W.L.R. 172; [2006] P.I.Q.R. Q4.
[227] [2001] Lloyd's Rep. Med. 347, CA.
[228] [2001] Lloyd's Rep. Med. 347 at [8] per Mantell LJ.
[229] [2001] Lloyd's Rep. Med. 382.

13–109   On the other hand, a single joint expert is now expected on issues of quantum. In *Peet v Mid-Kent Healthcare NHS Trust* Lord Woolf indicated that:

> "The starting point is: unless there is reason for not having a single expert, there should be only a single expert. If there is no reason which justifies more evidence than that from a single expert on any particular topic, then again in the normal way the report prepared by the single expert should be the evidence in the case on the issues covered by that expert's report. In the normal way, therefore, there should be no need for that report to be amplified or tested by cross-examination. If it needs amplification, or if it should be subject to cross-examination, the court has a discretion to allow that to happen. The court may permit that to happen either prior to the hearing or at the hearing. But the assumption should be that the single joint expert's report is the evidence. Any amplification or any cross-examination should be restricted as far as possible. Equally, where parties agree that there should be a single joint expert, and a single joint expert produces a report, it is possible for the court still to permit a party to instruct his or her own expert and for that expert to be called at the hearing. However, there must be good reason for that course to be adopted. Normally, where the issue is of the sort that is covered by non-medical evidence, as in this case, the court should be slow to allow a second expert to be instructed."[230]

That is why, when the need for this evidence is established at an early stage before proceedings have been commenced, the prospect of joint selection should be explored before obtaining expert evidence on quantum, at least evidence that is not likely to be controversial.

(b)   Meetings of experts

13–110   The court may, at any stage, direct a discussion between experts for the purpose of requiring the experts to: (a) identify and discuss the expert issues in the proceedings; and (b) where possible, reach an agreed opinion on those issues.[231] This is now standard practice in medical negligence cases. The court may also direct that following a discussion between experts they must prepare a statement for the court showing: (a) those issues on which they agree; and (b) those issues on which they disagree and a summary of their reasons for disagreeing.[232] In *H, H and R v Lambeth, Southwark & Lewisham Health Authority, West Kent Health Authority and Bexley & Greenwich Health Authority*[233] the claimant objected to an order that the expert witnesses of both sides meet, because it was said that without lawyers present at the meeting, her expert might waver under pressure from experts for the defence (given that it was a small area of medical specialisation, where everybody knew everybody else, and the defendant was a particularly eminent practitioner). This, said the claimant, would be unfair. The Court of Appeal held that a meeting to narrow the medical issues before trial was valuable in meeting the overriding objective of the Civil Procedure Rules, by permitting active case management.[234] CPR r.1.4 required the court to further the overriding objective by actively managing cases. This included identifying issues

---

[230] [2001] EWCA Civ 1703; [2002] 1 W.L.R. 210 at [28].
[231] CPR r.35.12(1).
[232] CPR r.35.12(3).
[233] [2001] EWCA Civ 1455; [2002] P.I.Q.R. P152.
[234] See CPR r.1.4(2), which sets out the objectives of case management, including, amongst others, identifying the issues at an early stage, deciding promptly which issues need full investigation at trial and disposing summarily of the others, and helping the parties to settle the whole or part of the case.

at an early stage and encouraging the parties to co-operate with one another. The power in CPR r.35.12 to order a meeting of experts was designed to further this objective. Even if both parties objected the court could make such an order. The general approach should be that a meeting should usually occur where there has been an exchange of experts reports. Some very good reason for not having a meeting would have to be shown.[235] CPR r.35.12(4) provides that the content of such discussions would not be referred to at trial, unless by agreement between the parties, and where the experts reach agreement on an issue it is not binding, unless the parties agree. This gave the claimant some protection. The Court of Appeal also refused an order permitting the parties' lawyers to be present at the meeting.[236] The lawyers could draw up the agenda. The meeting could be recorded so that if anything improper occurred, or there was any misunderstanding of the legal issues, it would be apparent.

Although the content of the discussion between the experts cannot be referred to at trial unless the parties agree,[237] there is nothing to prevent cross-examination of experts at trial on an issue discussed at the experts' meeting. So if experts concede a point in discussion, they are likely to concede it again in the witness box. Any agreement between the experts at the discussion does not bind the parties unless the parties expressly agree to be bound by the agreement,[238] although this rule does not affect the admissibility of the experts' joint statement. **13–111**

The status of the joint statement of the experts following a meeting was considered by the Court of Appeal in *Aird v Prime Meridian*.[239] Where a joint statement of experts is prepared pursuant to CPR r.35.12 the statement is not privileged, nor does it acquire "without prejudice" status just because it has been used in a "without prejudice" mediation. **13–112**

7. USING THE PROTOCOL

The Protocol reinforces the best practice of investigating potential medical negligence claims by, first, obtaining the medical records and then seeking expert evidence on liability (breach of duty and causation). **13–113**

The Protocol goes on to describe the procedure that will usually be followed, prior to issue of proceedings, which should help to ensure, where possible, that the general aims of the Protocol can be achieved. **13–114**

---

[235] [2001] EWCA Civ 1455; [2002] P.I.Q.R. P152 at [17] and [18] per Tuckey LJ.
[236] See the view expressed in the Protocol for the Instructions of Experts to give Evidence in Civil Claims para.18.8: "The parties' lawyers may only be present at discussions between experts if all parties agree or the court so orders. If lawyers do attend, they should not normally intervene except to answer questions put to them by the experts or to advise about the law."
[237] CPR r.35.12(4).
[238] CPR r.35.12(5).
[239] [2006] EWCA Civ 1866; [2007] B.L.R. 105.

(a) Letter of notification

13–115   The Protocol provides the claimant with an opportunity to send a letter of notification. Such a letter may be sent as and when the claimant has obtained positive expert evidence and may be a relevant consideration if the defendant subsequently seeks additional time in which to respond to the letter of claim. A letter of notification should be acknowledged within 14 days of receipt.

(b) Letter of claim

13–116   Whether or not a letter of notification has been sent the claimant will need to send a letter of claim. The letter of claim should deal with a number of matters in order to comply with the requirements of the Protocol including:

- a clear summary of the facts on which the claim is based, including the alleged adverse outcome, and the main allegations of negligence;
- a description of the claimant's injuries, and present condition and prognosis;
- an outline of the financial loss incurred by the claimant, with an indication of the heads of damage to be claimed and the scale of the loss, unless this is impracticable;
- confirmation of the method of funding and whether any funding arrangement was entered into before or after April 2013; and
- the discipline of any expert from whom evidence has already been obtained.

13–117   The letter of claim should refer to any relevant documents, including health records, and if possible enclose copies of any such documents which will not already be in the possession of the potential defendant (the Protocol giving the example of relevant general practitioner records if the claim is brought against a hospital). The claimant may choose to provide the defendant with a complete bundle, so the parties can work from the same pagination, and other documentation, such as a chronology, which may assist.

13–118   It is important to note that there is no requirement to send a medical report with the letter of claim, as disclosure of reports is optional. If expert evidence is to be disclosed that should, at this stage, usually relate only to condition and prognosis. Unilateral disclosure of expert evidence dealing with liability, whether this is breach of duty and/or causation, will not normally be appropriate. Occasionally, however, if the case is very strong on liability such evidence might be disclosed, on a without prejudice basis, just to confirm the strength of the case.

13–119   If the expert evidence on quantum is not complete, at the stage of the letter of claim, this is a useful opportunity to suggest experts with a view to joint instruction or, at least, joint selection by analogy with the Pre-action Protocol for Personal Injury Claims and/or identifying an agreed expert in accordance with the Practice Direction—Pre-action Conduct and Protocols.

Whilst the letter should identify the main heads of the claim for expenses and losses a schedule, at this stage, is usually optional. It may be possible to provide a schedule, if the expenses and losses are fairly limited and the evidence to access these is already available, in which case that may facilitate settlement. Otherwise an indication of the main heads of claim will have to suffice. **13–120**

The Protocol confirms the claimant may want to make an offer to settle the claim at this early stage by putting forward an offer in respect of liability and/or an amount of compensation and may wish to do so in accordance with CPR Pt 36. If such an offer is made that should generally be supported by a medical report, dealing with condition and prognosis, and by a schedule of expenses and losses with supporting documentation (although the Protocol recognises a medical report may not be necessary where there is no significant continuing injury, nor may a detailed schedule be necessary in a low value case). **13–121**

Paragraph 3.14 of the Protocol provides that any letter of claim sent to an NHS Trust or Independent Sector Treatment Centre should be copied to NHS Resolution. Proceedings should not be issued until after four months from the letter of claim unless, for example, there is a limitation issue. Meanwhile, further investigations can be carried out to help assess quantum where appropriate. **13–122**

(c) Acknowledgement

The defendant should acknowledge the letter of claim within 14 days of receipt and identify who will be dealing with the matter. **13–123**

(d) Response

Within four months of the letter of claim there should be a reasoned answer, in the form of a letter of response, by the healthcare provider which, to comply with the Protocol, should deal with the following matters: **13–124**

- if the claim is admitted, say so in clear terms;
- if only part of the claim is admitted, make clear which issues of breach of duty and/or causation are admitted and which are denied and why;
- state whether it is intended that any admissions will be binding;
- if the claim is denied, include specific comments on the allegations of negligence and, if a synopsis or chronology of relevant events has been provided and is disputed, the defendant's version of those events;
- if supportive expert evidence has been obtained, identify which disciplines of expert evidence have been relied upon and whether they relate to breach of duty and/or causation;
- if known, state whether the defendant requires copies of any relevant medical records obtained by the claimant (to be supplied for a reasonable copying charge);
- provide copies of any additional documents relied upon, e.g. an internal protocol;

- if not indemnified by the NHS, supply details of the relevant indemnity insurer;
- inform the claimant of any other potential defendants to the claim.

(e) ADR

13–125 The Protocol confirms the parties should consider whether some form of ADR would be more suitable than litigation and, if so, endeavour to agree which form to adopt. The Protocol identifies potential forms of ADR as including:

- discussion and negotiation;
- early neutral evaluation;
- mediation; and
- the NHS complaints procedure.

APPENDIX 1

NHS INDEMNITY

ARRANGEMENTS FOR CLINICAL NEGLIGENCE CLAIMS IN THE NHS

Executive summary

Introduction

This is a summary of the main points contained within *NHS Indemnity Arrangements for clinical negligence claims in the NHS*, issued under cover of HSG 96/48. The booklet includes a Q&A section covering the applicability of NHS indemnity to common situations and an annex on sponsored trials. It covers NHS indemnity for clinical negligence but not for any other liability such as product liability, employers liability or liability for NHS trust board members.

Clinical Negligence

Clinical negligence is defined as "a breach of duty of care by members of the health care professions employed by NHS bodies or by others consequent on decisions or judgements made by members of those professions acting in their professional capacity in the course of their employment, and which are admitted as negligent by the employer or are determined as such through the legal process".

The term health care professional includes hospital doctors, dentists, nurses, midwives, health visitors, pharmacy practitioners, registered ophthalmic or dispensing opticians (working in a hospital setting), members of professions allied to medicine and dentistry, ambulance personnel, laboratory staff and relevant technicians.

Main Principles

NHS bodies are vicariously liable for the negligent acts and omissions of their employees and should have arrangements for meeting this liability.

NHS Indemnity applies where

(a)   the negligent health care professional was:
    (i)   working under a contract of employment and the negligence occurred in the course of that employment;
    (ii)   not working under a contract of employment but was contracted to an NHS body to provide services to persons to whom that NHS body owed a duty of care;
    (iii)   neither of the above but otherwise owed a duty of care to the persons injured.

[1323]

(b)   persons, not employed under a contract of employment and who may or may not be a health care professional, who owe a duty of care to the persons injured. These include locums; medical academic staff with honorary contracts; students; those conducting clinical trials; charitable volunteers; persons undergoing further professional education, training and examinations; students and staff working on income generation projects.

Where these principles apply, NHS bodies should accept full financial liability where negligent harm has occurred, and not seek to recover their costs from the health care professional involved.

Who is Not Covered

NHS Indemnity does not apply to family health service practitioners working under contracts for services, eg GPs (including fundholders), general dental practitioners, family dentists, pharmacists or optometrists; other self employed health care professionals eg independent midwives; employees of FHS practices; employees of private hospitals; local education authorities; voluntary agencies. Exceptions to the normal cover arrangements are set out in the main document.

Circumstances Covered

NHS Indemnity covers negligent harm caused to patients or healthy volunteers in the following circumstances: whenever they are receiving an established treatment, whether or not in accordance with an agreed guideline or protocol; whenever they are receiving a novel or unusual treatment which, in the judgement of the health care professional, is appropriate for that particular patient; whenever they are subjects as patients or healthy volunteers of clinical research aimed at benefitting patients now or in the future.

Expenses Met

Where negligence is alleged, NHS bodies are responsible for meeting: the legal and administrative costs of defending the claim or, if appropriate, of reaching a settlement; the plaintiff's costs, as agreed by the two parties or as awarded by the court; the damages awarded either as a one-off payment or as a structured settlement.

NHS Indemnity

Clinical Negligence—Definition

1.   Clinical negligence is defined as:

> "A breach of duty of care by members of the health care professions employed by NHS bodies or by others consequent on decisions or judgements made by members of those professions acting in their professional capacity in the course of employment, and which are admitted as negligent by the employer or are determined as such through the legal process."*

---

* The NHS (Clinical Negligence Scheme) Regulations 1996, which established the Clinical Negligence Scheme for Trusts, defines clinical negligence in terms of " . . .a liability in tort owed by a

2. In this definition "breach of duty of care" has its legal meaning. NHS bodies will need to take legal advice in individual cases, but the general position will be that the following must all apply before liability for negligence exists:

   2.1 There must have been a duty of care owed to the person treated by the relevant professional(s);

   2.2 The standard of care appropriate to such duty must not have been attained and therefore the duty breached, whether by action or inaction, advice given or failure to advise;

   2.3 Such a breach must be demonstrated to have caused the injury and therefore the resulting loss complained about by the patient;

   2.4 Any loss sustained as a result of the injury and complained about by the person treated must be of a kind that the courts recognize and for which they allow compensation; and

   2.5 The injury and resulting loss complained about by the person treated must have been reasonably foreseeable as a possible consequence of the breach.

3. This booklet is concerned with NHS indemnity for clinical negligence and does not cover indemnity for any other liability such as product liability, employers liability or liability for NHS trust board members.

Other terms

4. Throughout this guidance:

   4.1 The terms "an NHS body" and "NHS bodies" include Health Authorities, Special Health Authorities and NHS Trusts but excludes all GP practices whether fundholding or not, general dental practices, pharmacies and opticians' practices.

   4.2 The term "health care professional" includes:

   Doctors, dentists, nurses, midwives, health visitors, hospital pharmacy practitioners, registered ophthalmic or registered dispensing opticians working in a hospital setting, members of professions supplementary to medicine and dentistry, ambulance personnel, laboratory staff and relevant technicians.

Principles

5. NHS bodies are legally liable for the negligent acts and omissions of their employees (the principle of vicarious liability), and should have arrangements for meeting this liability. NHS Indemnity applies where:

   5.1 the negligent health care professional was working under a contract of employment (as opposed to a contract for services) and the negligence occurred in the course of that employment; or

   5.2 the negligent health care professional, although not working under a contract of employment, was contracted to an NHS body to provide services to persons to whom that NHS body owed a duty of care.

6. Where the principles outlined in paragraph 5 apply, NHS bodies should accept full financial liability where negligent harm has occurred. They should not seek to

---

member to a third party in respect of or consequent upon personal injury or loss arising out of or in connection with any breach of a duty of care owed by that body to any person in connection with the diagnosis of any illness, or the care or treatment of any patient, in consequence of any act or omission to act on the part of a person employed or engaged by a member in connection with any relevant function of that member".

recover their costs either in part or in full from the health care professional concerned or from any indemnities they may have. NHS bodies may carry this risk entirely or spread it through membership of the Clinical Negligence Scheme for Trusts (CNST—see EL(95)40).

Who is Covered

7. NHS Indemnity covers the actions of staff in the course of their NHS employment. It also covers people in certain other categories whenever the NHS body owes a duty of care to the person harmed, including, for example, locums, medical academic staff with honorary contracts, students, those conducting clinical trials, charitable volunteers and people undergoing further professional education, training and examinations. This includes staff working on income generation projects. GPs or dentists who are directly employed by Health Authorities, eg as Public Health doctors (including port medical officers and medical inspectors of immigrants at UK air/sea ports), are covered.

8. Examples of the applicability of NHS Indemnity to common situations are set out in question and answer format in Annex A.

Who is not Covered

9. NHS Indemnity does not apply to general medical and dental practitioners working under contracts for services. General practitioners, including GP fundholders, are responsible for making their own indemnity arrangements, as are other self-employed health care professionals such as independent midwives. Neither does NHS Indemnity apply to employees of general practices, whether fundholding or not, or to employees of private hospitals (even when treating NHS patients) local education authorities or voluntary agencies.

10. Examples of circumstances in which independent practitioners or staff who normally work for private employers are covered by NHS Indemnity are given in Annex A. The NHS Executive advises independent practitioners to check their own indemnity position.

11. Examples of circumstances in which NHS employees are not covered by NHS Indemnity are also given in Annex A.

Circumstances Covered

12. NHS bodies owe a duty of care to healthy volunteers or patients treated or undergoing tests which they administer. NHS Indemnity covers negligent harm caused to these people in the following circumstances:
   12.1 whenever they are receiving an established treatment, whether or not in accordance with an agreed guideline or protocol;
   12.2 whenever they are receiving a novel or unusual treatment which in the clinical judgement of the health care professional is appropriate for the particular patient;
   12.3 whenever they are subjects of clinical research aimed at benefiting patients now or in the future, whether as patients or as healthy volunteers. (Special arrangements, including the availability of no-fault indemnity apply where research is sponsored by pharmaceutical companies. See Annex B.)

Expenses Met

13. Where negligence is alleged NHS bodies are responsible for meeting:
    13.1 the legal and administrative costs of defending the claim and if appropriate, of reaching a settlement, including the cost of any mediation;
    13.2 where appropriate, plaintiff's costs, either as agreed between the parties or as awarded by a court of law;
    13.3 the damages agreed or awarded, whether as a one-off payment or a structured settlement.

Claims Management Principles

14. NHS bodies should take the essential decisions on the handling of claims of clinical negligence against their staff, using professional defence organizations or others as their agents and advisers as appropriate.

Financial Support Arrangements

15. Details of the Clinical Negligence Scheme for Trusts (CNST) were announced in EL(95)40 on 29 March 1995.
16. All financial arrangements in respect of clinical negligence costs for NHS bodies have been reviewed and guidance on transitional arrangements (for funding clinical accidents which happened before 1 April 1995), was issued on 27 November 1995 under cover of FDL(95)56. FDL(96)36 provided further guidance on a number of detailed questions.

ANNEX A

Questions and Answers on NHS Indemnity

Below are replies to some of the questions most commonly asked about NHS Indemnity.

1. **Who is covered by NHS Indemnity?**
   NHS bodies are liable at law for the negligent acts and omissions of their staff in the course of their NHS employment: Under NHS Indemnity, NHS bodies take direct responsibility for costs and damages arising from clinical negligence where they (as employers) are vicariously liable for the acts and omissions of their health care professional staff.

2. **Would health care professionals opting to work under contracts for services rather than as employees of the NHS be covered?**
   Where an NHS body is responsible for *providing* care to patients NHS Indemnity will apply whether the health care professional involved is an employee or not. For example a doctor working under a contract for services with an NHS Trust would be covered because the Trust has responsibility for the care of its patients. A consultant undertaking contracted NHS work in a private hospital would also be covered.

3. **Does this include clinical academics and research workers?**
NHS bodies are vicariously liable for the work done by university medical staff and other research workers (eg employees of the MRC) under their honorary contracts, but not for pre-clinical or other work in the university.

4. **Are GP practices covered?**
GPs, whether fundholders or not [and who are not employed by Health Authorities as public health doctors], are independent practitioners and therefore they and their employed staff are not covered by NHS indemnity.

5. **Is a hospital doctor doing a GP locum covered?**
This would not be the responsibility of the NHS body since it would be outside the contract of employment. The hospital doctor and the general practitioners concerned should ensure that there is appropriate professional liability cover.

6. **Is a GP seeing a patient in hospital covered?**
A GP providing medical care to patients in hospital under a contractual arrangement, eg where the GP was employed as a clinical assistant, will be covered by NHS Indemnity, as will a GP who provides services in NHS hospitals under staff fund contracts (known as "bed funds"). Where there is no such contractual arrangement, and the NHS body provides facilities for patient(s) who continue to be the clinical responsibility of the GP, the GP would be responsible and professional liability cover would be appropriate. However, junior medical staff, nurses or members of the professions supplementary to medicine involved in the care of a GP's patients in NHS hospitals under their contract of employment would be covered.

7. **Are GP trainees working in general practice covered?**
In general practice the responsibility for training and for paying the salary of a GP trainee rests with the trainer. While the trainee is receiving a salary in general practice it is advisable that both the trainee and the trainer, and indeed other members of the practice, should have appropriate professional liability cover as NHS indemnity will not apply.

8. **Are NHS employees working under contracts with GP fundholders covered?**
If their employing NHS body has agreed a contract to provide services to a GP fundholding practice's patients, NHS employees will be working under the terms of their contracts of employment and NHS Indemnity will cover them. If NHS employees themselves contract with GP fundholders (or any other independent body) to do work outside their NHS contract of employment they should ensure that they have separate indemnity cover.

9. **Is academic General Practice covered?**
The Department has no plans to extend NHS Indemnity to academic departments of general practice. In respect of general medical services, Health Authorities' payments of fees and allowances include an element for expenses, of which medical defence subscriptions are a part.

10. **Is private work in NHS hospitals covered by NHS Indemnity?**
NHS bodies will not be responsible for a health care professional's private practice, even in an NHS hospital. However, where junior medical staff, nurses or members

of professions supplementary to medicine are involved in the care of private patients in NHS hospitals, they would normally be doing so as part of their NHS contract, and would therefore be covered. It remains advisable that health professionals who might be involved in work outside the scope of his or her NHS employment should have professional liability cover.

11. **Is Category 2 work covered?**
Category 2 work (eg reports for insurance companies) is by definition not undertaken for the employing NHS body and is therefore not covered by NHS Indemnity. Unless the work is carried out on behalf of the employing NHS body, professional liability cover would be needed.

12. **Are disciplinary proceedings of statutory bodies covered?**
NHS bodies are not financially responsible for the defence of staff involved in disciplinary proceedings conducted by statutory bodies such as the GMC (doctors), UKCC (nurses and midwives), GDC (dentists) CPSM (professions supplementary to medicine) and RPSGB (pharmacists). It is the responsibility of the practitioner concerned to take out professional liability cover against such an eventuality.

13. **Are clinical trials covered?**
In the case of negligent harm, health care professionals undertaking clinical trials or studies on volunteers, whether healthy or patients, in the course of their NHS employment are covered by NHS Indemnity. Similarly, for a trial not involving medicines, the NHS body would take financial responsibility unless the trial were covered by such other indemnity as may have been agreed between the NHS body and those responsible for the trial. In any case, NHS bodies should ensure that they are informed of clinical trials in which their staff are taking part in their NHS employment and that these trials have the required Research Ethics Committee approval. For non-negligent harm, see question 16 below.

14. **Is harm resulting from a fault in the drug/equipment covered?**
Where harm is caused due to a fault in the manufacture of a drug or piece of equipment then, under the terms of the Consumer Protection Act 1987, it is no defence for the producer to show that he exercised reasonable care. Under normal circumstances, therefore, NHS indemnity would not apply unless there was a question whether the health care professional either knew or should reasonably have known that the drug/equipment was faulty but continued to use it. Strict liability could apply if the drug/equipment had been manufactured by an NHS body itself, for example a prototype as part of a research programme.

15. **Are Local Research Ethics Committees (LRECs) covered?**
Under the Department's guidelines an LREC is appointed by the Health Authority to provide independent advice to NHS bodies within its area on the ethics of research proposals. The Health Authority should take financial responsibility for members' acts and omissions in the course of performance of their duties as LREC members.

16. **Is there liability for non-negligent harm?**
Apart from liability for defective products, legal liability does not arise where a person is harmed but no one has acted negligently. An example of this would be unexpected side-effects of drugs during clinical trials. In exceptional circumstances (and within the delegated limit of £50,000) NHS bodies may consider whether an

ex-gratia payment could be offered. NHS bodies may not offer advance indemnities or take out commercial insurance for non-negligent harm.

17. **What arrangements can non-NHS bodies make for non-negligent harm?**

Arrangements will depend on the status of the non-NHS body. Arrangements for clinical trials sponsored by the pharmaceutical industry are set out in Annex B. Other independent sector sponsors of clinical research involving NHS patients (eg universities and medical research charities) may also make arrangements to indemnify research subjects for non-negligent harm. Public sector research funding bodies such as the Medical Research Council (MRC) may not offer advance indemnities nor take out commercial insurance for non-negligent harm. The MRC offers the assurance that it will give sympathetic consideration to claims in respect of non-negligent harm arising from an MRC funded trial. NHS bodies should not make ex-gratia payments for non-negligent harm where research is sponsored by a non-NHS body.

18. **Would health care professionals be covered if they were working other than in accordance with the duties of their post?**

Health care professionals would be covered by NHS Indemnity for actions in the course of NHS employment, and this should be interpreted liberally. For work not covered in this way health care professionals may have a civil, or even, in extreme circumstances, criminal liability for their actions.

19. **Are health care professionals attending accident victims ("Good Samaritan" acts) covered?**

"Good Samaritan" acts are not part of the health care professional's work for the employing body. Medical defence organizations are willing to provide low-cost cover against the (unusual) event of anyone performing such an act being sued for negligence. Ambulance services can, with the agreement of staff, include an additional term in the individual employee contracts to the effect that the member of staff is expected to provide assistance in any emergency outside of duty hours where it is appropriate to do so.

20. **Are NHS staff in public health medicine or in community health services doing work for local authorities covered? Are occupational physicians covered?**

Staff working in public health medicine, clinical medical officers or therapists carrying out local authority functions under their NHS contract would be acting in the course of their NHS employment. They will therefore be covered by NHS Indemnity. The same principle applies to occupational physicians employed by NHS bodies.

21. **Are NHS staff working for other agencies, eg the Prison Service, covered?**

In general, NHS bodies are not financially responsible for the acts of NHS staff when they are working on an individual contractual basis for other agencies. (Conversely, they are responsible where, for example, a Ministry of Defence doctor works in an NHS hospital.) Either the non-NHS body commissioning the work would be responsible, or the health care professional should have separate indemnity cover. However, NHS Indemnity should cover work for which the NHS body pays the health care professional a fee, such as domiciliary visits, and family planning services.

22. **Are former NHS staff covered?**

NHS Indemnity will cover staff who have subsequently left the Service (eg on retirement) provided the liability arose in respect of acts or omissions in the course of their NHS employment, regardless of when the claim was notified. NHS bodies may seek the co-operation of former staff in providing statements in the defence of a case.

23. **Are NHS staff offering services to voluntary bodies such as the Red Cross or hospices covered?**

The NHS body would be responsible for the actions of its staff only if it were contractually responsible for the clinical staffing of the voluntary body. If not, the staff concerned may wish to ensure that they have separate indemnity cover.

24. **Do NHS bodies provide cover for locums?**

NHS bodies take financial responsibility for the acts and omissions of a locum health care professional, whether "internal" or provided by an external agency, doing the work of a colleague who would be covered.

25. **What are the arrangements for staff employed by one trust working in another?**

This depends on the contractual arrangements. If the work is being done as part of a formal agreement between the trusts, then the staff involved will be acting within their normal NHS duties and, unless the agreement states otherwise, the employing trust will be liable. The NHS Executive does not recommend the use of ad hoc arrangements, eg a doctor, in one trust asking a doctor in another to provide an informal second opinion, unless there is an agreement between the trusts as to which of them will accept liability for the "visiting" doctor in such circumstances.

26. **Are private sector rotations for hospital staff covered?**

The medical staff of independent hospitals are responsible for their own professional liability cover, subject to the requirements of the hospital managers. If NHS staff in the training grades work in independent hospitals as part of their NHS training, they would be covered by NHS Indemnity, provided that such work was covered by an NHS contract of employment.

27. **Are voluntary workers covered?**

Where volunteers work in NHS bodies, they are covered by NHS Indemnity. NHS managers should be aware of all voluntary activity going on in their organizations and should wherever possible confirm volunteers' indemnity position in writing.

28. **Are students covered?**

NHS Indemnity applies where students are working under the supervision of NHS employees. This should be made clear in the agreement between the NHS body and the student's educational body. This will apply to students of all the health care professions and to school students on, for example, work experience placements. Students working in NHS premises, under supervision of medical academic staff employed by universities holding honorary contracts, are also covered. Students who spend time in a primary care setting will only be covered if this is part of an

NHS contract. Potential students making preliminary visits and school placements should be adequately supervised and should not become involved in any clinical work. Therefore, no clinical negligence should arise on their part.

In the unlikely event of a school making a negligent choice of work placement for a pupil to work in the NHS, then the school, and not NHS indemnity, should pick up the legal responsibility for the actions of that pupil. The contractual arrangement between the NHS and the school should make this clear.

29. **Are health care professionals undergoing on-the-job training covered?**
Where an NHS body's staff are providing on-the-job training (eg refresher or skills updating courses) for health care professionals, the trainees are covered by NHS Indemnity whether they are normally employed by the NHS or not.

30. **Are Independent midwives covered?**
Independent midwives are self-employed practitioners. In common with all other health care professionals working outside the NHS, they are responsible for making their own indemnity arrangements.

31. **Are overseas doctors who have come to the UK temporarily, perhaps to demonstrate a new technique, covered?**
The NHS body which has invited the overseas doctor will owe a duty of care to the patients on whom the technique is demonstrated and so NHS indemnity will apply. NHS bodies, therefore, need to make sure that they are kept informed of any such demonstration visits which are proposed and of the nature of the technique to be demonstrated. Where visiting clinicians are not formally registered as students, or are not employees, an honorary contract should be arranged.

32. **Are staff who are qualified in another member state of the European Union covered?**
Staff qualified in another member state of the European Union, and who are undertaking an adaptation period in accordance with EEC directive 89/48EEC and the European Communities (Recognition of Professional Qualifications) Regulations 1991 which implements EEC Directive 89/48/EEC) and EEC Directive 92/51/EEC, must be treated in a manner consistent with their qualified status in another member state, and should be covered.

ANNEX B

Indemnity for Clinical Studies Sponsored by Pharmaceutical companies

Section One

1. Clinical research involving the administration of drugs to patients or non-patient human volunteers is frequently undertaken under the auspices of Health Authorities or NHS Trusts.
2. When the study is sponsored by a pharmaceutical company, issues of liability and indemnity may arise in case of injury associated with administration of the drug or other aspects of the conduct of the trial.

3.   When the study is not sponsored by a company but has been independently organised by clinicians, the NHS body will carry full legal liability for claims in negligence arising from harm to subjects in the study.

4.   The guidance in Section 2 and the Appendix has three purposes:

- to ensure that NHS bodies enter into appropriate agreements which will provide indemnity against claims and proceedings arising from company-sponsored clinical studies;

- to ensure that NHS bodies, where appropriate, use a standard form of agreement (Appendix) which has been drawn up in consultation with the Association of the British Pharmaceutical Industry (ABPI);

- to advise Local Research Ethics Committees (LRECs) of the standard form of agreement.

Section Two

1.   A wide variety of clinical studies involving experimental or investigational use of drugs is carried out within NHS bodies. This includes studies in patients (clinical trials) and studies in healthy human volunteers. They may involve administration of a totally new (unlicensed) drug (active substance or 'NAS') or the administration of an established (licensed) drug by a novel route, for a new therapeutic indication, or in a novel formulation or combination.

2.   Detailed guidance on the design, conduct, and ethical implications of clinical studies is given in:

HSG(91)5: Local Research Ethics Committees (with accompanying booklet). NHS Executive: 1991;

Guidelines for Medical Experiments in non-Patient Human Volunteers, ABPI:1988, amended 1990;

Research Involving Patients, Royal College of Physicians of London: 1990;

Guidelines in the Practice of Ethics Committees in Medical Research, 2nd edition; Royal College of Physicians of London: 1990;

Clinical Trial Compensation Guidelines ABPI: 1991

3.   The Medicines Act 1968 provides the regulatory framework for clinical studies involving administration of drugs to patients. Drugs which are used in a sponsored* clinical study in patients will be the subject of either a product licence (PL), a clinical trial certificate (CTC), or clinical trial exemption (CTh) which is held by the company as appropriate. A non-sponsored study conducted independently by a practitioner must be notified to the Licensing Authority under the Doctors and Dentists Exemption (DDX) scheme. Studies in healthy volunteers are not subject to regulation under the Medicines Act and do not require a CTC, Cm, or DDX. Further particulars of these arrangements are provided in Medicines Act leaflet $M_1 11\ 30: A$ guide to the provisions affecting doctors and dentists (DHSS: 1985).

4.   Participants in a clinical study may suffer adverse effects due to the drug or clinical procedures. The appendix to this annex is a model form of agreement between the company sponsoring a study and the NHS body involved, which indemnifies the authority or trust against claims and proceedings arising from the study. The model agreement has been drawn up in consultation with the Association of the British Pharmaceutical Industry (ABPI).

---

*   A sponsored study may be defined as one carried out under arrangements made by or on behalf of the company who manufactured the product, the company responsible for its composition, or the company selling or supplying the product.

5.   This form of indemnity will not normally apply to clinical studies which are not directly sponsored by the company providing the product for research, but have been independently organised by clinicians. In this case, the NHS body will normally carry full legal liability for any claims in negligence arising from harm to subjects in the study.

6.   The NHS body will also carry full legal liability for any claims in negligence (or compensation under the indemnity will be abated) where there has been significant non-adherence to the agreed protocol or there has been negligence on the part of an NHS employee, for example, by failing to deal adequately with an adverse drug reaction.

7.   The form of indemnity may not be readily accepted by sponsoring companies outside the UK or who are not members of the ABPI. NHS bodies should, as part of their risk management, consider the value of indemnities which are offered and consider whether companies should have alternative arrangements in place.

8.   Several health authorities and trusts have independently developed forms of indemnity agreement. However, difficulties have arisen when different authorities have required varying terms of indemnity and this has, on occasion, impeded the progress of clinical research within the NHS. Particular difficulties may arise in large multi-centre trials involving many NHS bodies when it is clearly desirable to have standardised terms of indemnity to provide equal protection to all participants in the study.

9.   Responsibility for deciding whether a particular company-sponsored research proposal should proceed within the NHS rests with the Health Authority or Trust within which the research would take place, after consideration of ethical, clinical, managerial, financial, resource, and legal liability issues. The NHS body is responsible for securing an appropriate indemnity agreement and should maintain a register of all clinical studies undertaken under its auspices with an indication whether it is a company-sponsored study and, if so, with confirmation that an indemnity agreement is in place. If for any reason it is considered that the model form of indemnity is not appropriate or that amendments are required, the NHS body involved should seek legal advice on the form or amendments proposed.

10.   Even when the model form of indemnity is agreed, the NHS body should satisfy itself that the company sponsoring the study is substantial and reputable and has appropriate arrangements in place (for example insurance cover) to support the indemnity. The NHS body will carry full liability for any claims in negligence if the indemnity is not honoured and there is not supporting insurance.

11.   Where a clinical study includes patients or subjects within several NHS bodies, for example in a multi-centre clinical trial, it is necessary for each Authority or Trust to complete an appropriate indemnity agreement with the sponsoring company.

12.   Where independent practitioners, such as general medical practitioners, are engaged in clinical studies, Health Authorities should seek to ensure that such studies are the subject of an appropriate indemnity agreement. It is good practice for the GP to notify the Health Authority of his participation in any clinical study.

13.   Clinical investigators should ensure that details of any proposed research study are lodged with the appropriate NHS body and should not commence company-sponsored research unless an indemnity agreement is in place.

14.   Local Research Ethics Committees (LRECs) provide independent advice to NHS and other bodies and to clinical researchers on the ethics of proposed research projects that involve human subjects [HSG(91)5]. Clinical investigators should not commence any research project involving patients or human volunteers without LREC agreement. Acceptance of the ABPI guidelines and the terms of the model

indemnity agreement should normally be a condition of LREC approval of any pharmaceutical company sponsored project.

ANNEX B: APPENDIX

Form of Indemnity for Clinical Studies

To: [Name and address of sponsoring company] ("the Sponsor")

From: [Name and address of Health Authority/Health Board/NHS Trust] ("the Authority")

Re: Clinical Study No [ ] with [name of product]

1.   It is proposed that the Authority should agree to participate in the above sponsored study ("the Study") involving [patients of the Authority] [non-patient volunteers] ("the Subjects") to be conducted by [name of investigator(s)] ("the Investigator") in accordance with the protocol annexed, as amended from time to time with the agreement of the Sponsor and the Investigator ("the Protocol"). The Sponsor confirms that it is a term of its agreement with the Investigator that the Investigator shall obtain all necessary approvals of the applicable Local Research Ethics Committee and shall resolve with the Authority any issues of a revenue nature.

2.   The Authority agrees to participate by allowing the Study to be undertaken on its premises utilising such facilities, personnel and equipment as the Investigator may reasonably need for the purpose of the Study.

3.   In consideration of such participation by the Authority, and subject to paragraph 4 below, the Sponsor indemnifies and holds harmless the Authority and its employees and agents against all claims and proceedings (to include any settlements or ex-gratia payments made with the consent of the parties hereto and reasonable legal and expert costs and expenses) made or brought (whether successfully or otherwise):

    (a)   by or on behalf of Subjects taking part in the Study (or their dependants) against the Authority or any of its employees or agents for personal injury (including death) to Subjects arising out of or relating to the administration of the product(s) under investigation or any clinical intervention or procedure provided for or required by the Protocol to which the Subjects would not have been exposed but for their participation in the Study.

    (b)   by the Authority, its employees or agents or by or on behalf of a Subject for a declaration concerning the treatment of a Subject who has suffered such personal injury.

4.   The above indemnity by the Sponsor shall not apply to any such claim or proceeding:

    4.1   to the extent that such personal injury (including death) is caused by the negligent or wrongful acts or omissions or breach of statutory duty of the Authority, its employees or agents;

    4.2   to the extent that such personal injury (including death) is caused by the failure of the Authority, its employees, or agents to conduct the Study in accordance with the Protocol;

    4.3   unless as soon as reasonably practicable following receipt of notice of such claim or proceeding, the Authority shall have notified the Sponsor in writing of it and shall, upon the Sponsor's request, and at the Sponsor's cost, have permitted the Sponsor to have full care and control of the claim or proceeding using legal representation of its own choosing;

4.4 if the Authority, its employees, or agents shall have made any admission in respect of such claim or proceeding or taken any action relating to such claim or proceeding prejudicial to the defence of it without the written consent of the Sponsor such consent not to be unreasonably withheld provided that this condition shall not be treated as breached by any statement properly made by the Authority, its employees or agents in connection with the operation of the Authority's internal complaint procedures, accident reporting procedures or disciplinary procedures or where such statement is required by law.

5. The Sponsor shall keep the Authority and its legal advisers fully informed of the progress of any such claim or proceeding, will consult fully with the Authority on the nature of any defence to be advanced and will not settle any such claim or proceeding without the written approval of the Authority (such approval not to be unreasonably withheld).

6. Without prejudice to the provisions of paragraph 4.3 above, the Authority will use its reasonable endeavours to inform the Sponsor promptly of any circumstances reasonably thought likely to give rise to any such claim or proceeding of which it is directly aware and shall keep the Sponsor reasonably informed of developments in relation to any such claim or proceeding even where the Authority decides not to make a claim under this indemnity. Likewise, the Sponsor shall use its reasonable endeavours to inform the Authority of any such circumstances and shall keep the Authority reasonably informed of developments in relation to any such claim or proceeding made or brought against the Sponsor alone.

7. The Authority and the Sponsor will each give to the other such help as may reasonably be required for the efficient conduct and prompt handling of any claim or proceeding by or on behalf of Subjects (or their dependants) or concerning such a declaration as is referred to in paragraph 3(b) above.

8. Without prejudice to the foregoing if injury is suffered by a Subject while participating in the Study, the Sponsor agrees to operate in good faith the Guidelines published in 1991 by The Association of the British Pharmaceutical Industry and entitled "Clinical Trial Compensation Guidelines" (where the Subject is a patient) and the Guidelines published in 1988 by the same Association and entitled "Guidelines for Medical Experiments in non-patient Human Volunteers" (where the Subject is not a patient) and shall request the Investigator to make clear to the Subjects that the Study is being conducted subject to the applicable Association Guidelines.

9. For the purpose of this indemnity, the expression "agents" shall be deemed to include without limitation any nurse or other health professional providing services to the Authority under a contract for services or otherwise and any person carrying out work for the Authority under such a contract connected with such of the Authority's facilities and equipment as are made available for the Study under paragraph 2 above.

10. This indemnity shall be governed by and construed in accordance with English/Scottish* law.

* Delete as appropriate

APPENDIX 1: NHS INDEMNITY

SIGNED on behalf of the Health
Authority/
Health Board/NHS Trust

....
Chief Executive/District General Manager

SIGNED on behalf of the Company

....

Dated...

Note: © NHS Litigation Authority. This version of the guidance on NHS Indemnity is taken from the NHS Litigation Authority's website (*http://www.nhsla.com/Claims/Documents/NHS%20Indemnity.pdf*) with permission.

APPENDIX 2

PRE-ACTION PROTOCOL FOR THE RESOLUTION OF CLINICAL DISPUTES

1 INTRODUCTION

1.1 This Protocol is intended to apply to all claims against hospitals, GPs, dentists and other healthcare providers (both NHS and private) which involve an injury that is alleged to be the result of clinical negligence. It is not intended to apply to claims covered by—

(a) the Pre-Action Protocol for Disease and Illness Claims;

(b) the Pre-Action Protocol for Personal Injury Claims;

(c) the Pre-Action Protocol for Low Value Personal Injury Claims in Road Traffic Accidents;

(d) the Pre-Action Protocol for Low Value Personal Injury (Employers' Liability and Public Liability) Claims; or

(e) Practice Direction 3D—Mesothelioma Claims.

1.2 This Protocol is intended to be sufficiently broad-based and flexible to apply to all sectors of healthcare, both public and private. It also recognises that a claimant and a defendant, as patient and healthcare provider, may have an ongoing relationship.

1.3 It is important that each party to a clinical dispute has sufficient information and understanding of the other's perspective and case to be able to investigate a claim efficiently and, where appropriate, to resolve it. This Protocol encourages a cards-on-the-table approach when something has gone wrong with a claimant's treatment or the claimant is dissatisfied with that treatment and/or the outcome.

1.4 This Protocol is now regarded by the courts as setting the standard of normal reasonable pre-action conduct for the resolution of clinical disputes.

1.5

1.5.1 This Protocol sets out the conduct that prospective parties would normally be expected to follow prior to the commencement of any proceedings. It establishes a reasonable process and timetable for the exchange of information relevant to a dispute, sets out the standards for the content and quality of letters of claim and sets standards for the conduct of pre-action negotiations.

1.5.2 The timetable and the arrangements for disclosing documents and obtaining expert evidence may need to be varied to suit the circumstances of the case. Where one or more parties consider the detail of the Protocol is not appropriate to the case, and proceedings are subsequently issued, the court will expect an explanation as to why the Protocol has not been followed, or has been varied.

Early Issue

1.6

    1.6.1 The Protocol provides for a defendant to be given four months to investigate and respond to a Letter of Claim before proceedings are served. If this is not possible, the claimant's solicitor should give as much notice of the intention to issue proceedings as is practicable. This Protocol does not alter the statutory time limits for starting court proceedings. If a claim is issued after the relevant statutory limitation period has expired, the defendant will be entitled to use that as a defence to the claim. If proceedings are started to comply with the statutory time limit before the parties have followed the procedures in this Protocol, the parties should apply to the court for a stay of the proceedings while they so comply.

    1.6.2 The parties should also consider whether there is likely to be a dispute as to limitation should a claim be pursued.

Enforcement of the Protocol and sanctions

1.7   Where either party fails to comply with this Protocol, the court may impose sanctions. When deciding whether to do so, the court will look at whether the parties have complied in substance with the Protocol's relevant principles and requirements. It will also consider the effect any non-compliance has had on any other party. It is not likely to be concerned with minor or technical shortcomings (see paragraph 4.3 to 4.5 of the Practice Direction on Pre-Action Conduct and Protocols).

Litigants in Person

1.8   If a party to a claim does not seek professional advice from a solicitor they should still, in so far as is reasonably possible, comply with the terms of this Protocol. In this Protocol "solicitor" is intended to encompass reference to any suitably legally qualified person.

    If a party to a claim becomes aware that another party is a litigant in person, they should send a copy of this Protocol to the litigant in person at the earliest opportunity.

2   THE AIMS OF THE PROTOCOL

2.1   The **general** aims of the Protocol are—
    (a)   to maintain and/or restore the patient/healthcare provider relationship in an open and transparent way;
    (b)   to reduce delay and ensure that costs are proportionate; and
    (c)   to resolve as many disputes as possible without litigation.

2.2   The **specific** objectives are—
    (a)   to encourage openness, transparency and early communication of the perceived problem between patients and healthcare providers;
    (b)   to provide an opportunity for healthcare providers to identify whether notification of a notifiable safety incident has been, or should be, sent to the

claimant in accordance with the duty of candour imposed by section 20 of the Health and Social Care Act 2008 (Regulated Activities) Regulations 2014;

(c)   to ensure that sufficient medical and other information is disclosed promptly by both parties to enable each to understand the other's perspective and case, and to encourage early resolution or a narrowing of the issues in dispute;

(d)   to provide an early opportunity for healthcare providers to identify cases where an investigation is required and to carry out that investigation promptly;

(e)   to encourage healthcare providers to involve the *National Health Service Litigation Authority* (NHSLA) or their defence organisations or insurers at an early stage;

(f)   to enable the parties to avoid litigation by agreeing a resolution of the dispute;

(g)   to enable the parties to explore the use of mediation or to narrow the issues in dispute before proceedings are commenced;

(h)   to enable parties to identify any issues that may require a separate or preliminary hearing, such as a dispute as to limitation;

(i)   to support the efficient management of proceedings where litigation cannot be avoided;

(j)   to discourage the prolonged pursuit of unmeritorious claims and the prolonged defence of meritorious claims;

(k)   to promote the provision of medical or rehabilitation treatment to address the needs of the claimant at the earliest opportunity; and

(l)   to encourage the defendant to make an early apology to the claimant if appropriate.

2.3   This Protocol does not—

(a)   provide any detailed guidance to healthcare providers on clinical risk management or the adoption of risk management systems and procedures;

(b)   provide any detailed guidance on which adverse outcomes should trigger an investigation; or

(c)   recommend changes to the codes of conduct of professionals in healthcare.

3   THE PROTOCOL

3.1   An illustrative flowchart is attached at Annex A which shows each of the stages that the parties are expected to take before the commencement of proceedings.

Obtaining health records

3.2   Any request for records by the **claimant** should—

(a)   **provide sufficient information** to alert the defendant where an adverse outcome has been serious or has had serious consequences or may constitute a notifiable safety incident;

(b)   be as **specific as possible** about the records which are required for an initial investigation of the claim (including, for example, a continuous copy of the CTG trace in birth injury cases); and

(c)   include a request for any relevant guidelines, analyses, protocols or policies and any documents created in relation to an adverse incident, notifiable safety incident or complaint.

3.3 Requests for copies of the claimant's clinical records should be made using the Law Society and Department of Health approved **standard forms** (enclosed at Annex B), adapted as necessary.

3.4

    3.4.1 The copy records should be provided **within 40 days** of the request and for a cost not exceeding the charges permissible under the Access to Health Records Act 1990 and/or the Data Protection Act 1998. Payment may be required in advance by the healthcare provider.

    3.4.2 The claimant may also make a request under the Freedom of Information Act 2000.

3.5 At the earliest opportunity, legible copies of the claimant's medical and other records should be placed in an indexed and paginated bundle by the claimant. This bundle should be kept up to date.

3.6 In the rare circumstances that the defendant is in difficulty in complying with the request within 40 days, the **problem should be explained** quickly and details given of what is being done to resolve it.

3.7 If the defendant fails to provide the health records or an explanation for any delay within 40 days, the claimant or their adviser can then apply to the court under rule 31.16 of the Civil Procedure Rules 1998 ('CPR') for an **order for pre-action disclosure**. The court has the power to impose costs sanctions for unreasonable delay in providing records.

3.8 If either the claimant or the defendant considers **additional health records are required from a third party**, in the first instance these should be requested by or through the claimant. Third party healthcare providers are expected to co-operate. Rule 31.17 of the CPR sets out the procedure for applying to the court for pre-action disclosure by third parties.

Rehabilitation

3.9 The claimant and the defendant shall both consider as early as possible whether the claimant has reasonable needs that could be met by rehabilitation treatment or other measures. They should also discuss how these needs might be addressed. An immediate needs assessment report prepared for the purposes of rehabilitation should not be used in the litigation except by consent.

    (A copy of the Rehabilitation Code can be found at: http://www.iua.co.uk/IUA_Member/Publications)

Letter of Notification

3.10 Annex C1 to this Protocol provides a **template for the recommended contents of a Letter of Notification**; the level of detail will need to be varied to suit the particular circumstances.

3.11

    3.11.1 Following receipt and analysis of the records and, if appropriate, receipt of an initial supportive expert opinion, the claimant may wish to send a Letter of Notification to the defendant as soon as practicable.

    3.11.2 The Letter of Notification should advise the defendant that this is a claim where a Letter of Claim is likely to be sent because a case as to breach of duty and/or causation has been identified. A copy of the Letter of Notification should also be sent to the NHSLA or, where known, other relevant medical defence organisation or indemnity provider.

3.12

   3.12.1 On receipt of a Letter of Notification a defendant should—

      (a)   acknowledge the letter within 14 days of receipt;

      (b)   identify who will be dealing with the matter and to whom any Letter of Claim should be sent;

      (c)   consider whether to commence investigations and/or to obtain factual and expert evidence;

      (d)   consider whether any information could be passed to the claimant which might narrow the issues in dispute or lead to an early resolution of the claim; and

      (e)   forward a copy of the Letter of Notification to the NHSLA or other relevant medical defence organisation/indemnity provider.

   3.12.2 The court may question any requests by the defendant for extension of time limits if a Letter of Notification was sent but did not prompt an initial investigation.

Letter of Claim

3.13 Annex C2 to this Protocol provides **a template for the recommended contents of a Letter of Claim**: the level of detail will need to be varied to suit the particular circumstances.

3.14 If, following the receipt and analysis of the records, and the receipt of any further advice (including from experts if necessary – see Section 4), the claimant decides that there are grounds for a claim, a letter of claim should be sent to the defendant as soon as practicable. Any letter of claim sent to an NHS Trust should be copied to the National Health Service Litigation Authority.

3.16 This letter should contain—

      (a)   a **clear summary of the facts** on which the claim is based, including the alleged adverse outcome, and the **main allegations of negligence**;

      (b)   a description of the **claimant's injuries**, and present condition and prognosis;

      (c)   an outline of the **financial loss** incurred by the claimant, with an indication of the heads of damage to be claimed and the scale of the loss, unless this is impracticable;

      (d)   confirmation of the method of funding and whether any funding arrangement was entered into before or after April 2013; and

      (e)   the discipline of any expert from whom evidence has already been obtained.

3.17 The Letter of Claim **should refer to any relevant documents**, including health records, and if possible enclose copies of any of those which will not already be in the potential defendant's possession, e.g. any relevant general practitioner records if the claimant's claim is against a hospital.

3.18 **Sufficient information** must be given to enable the defendant to **focus investigations** and to put an initial valuation on the claim.

3.19 Letters of Claim are **not** intended to have the same formal status as Particulars of Claim, nor should any sanctions necessarily apply if the Letter of Claim and any subsequent Particulars of Claim in the proceedings differ.

3.20 **Proceedings should not be issued until after four months from the letter of claim.**

     In certain instances it may not be possible for the claimant to serve a Letter of Claim more than four months before the expiry of the limitation period. If, for any reason, proceedings are started before the parties have complied, they should seek to agree to apply to the court for an order to stay the proceedings whilst the parties take steps to comply.

3.21 The claimant may want to make an **offer to settle** the claim at this early stage by putting forward an offer in respect of liability and/or an amount of compensation in accordance with the legal and procedural requirements of CPR Part 36 (possibly including any costs incurred to date). If an offer to settle is made, generally this should be supported by a medical report which deals with the injuries, condition and prognosis, and by a schedule of loss and supporting documentation. The level of detail necessary will depend on the value of the claim. Medical reports may not be necessary where there is no significant continuing injury and a detailed schedule may not be necessary in a low value case.

Letter of Response

3.22 Attached at Annex C3 is a template for the suggested contents of the **Letter of Response**: the level of detail will need to be varied to suit the particular circumstances.

3.23 The defendant should **acknowledge** the Letter of Claim **within 14 days of receipt** and should identify who will be dealing with the matter.

3.24 The defendant should, **within four months** of the Letter of Claim, provide a **reasoned answer** in the form of a **Letter of Response** in which the defendant should—

(a)   if the **claim is admitted**, say so in clear terms;

(b)   if only **part of the claim is admitted**, make clear which issues of breach of duty and/or causation are admitted and which are denied and why;

(c)   state whether it is intended that any **admissions will be binding**;

(d)   if the **claim is denied**, include specific comments on the allegations of negligence and, if a synopsis or chronology of relevant events has been provided and is disputed, the defendant's version of those events;

(e)   if supportive expert evidence has been obtained, identify which disciplines of expert evidence have been relied upon and whether they relate to breach of duty and/or causation;

(f)   if known, state whether the defendant requires copies of any relevant medical records obtained by the claimant (to be supplied for a reasonable copying charge);

(g)   provide copies of any additional documents relied upon, e.g. an internal protocol;

(h)   if not indemnified by the NHS, supply details of the relevant indemnity insurer; and

(i)   inform the claimant of any other potential defendants to the claim.

3.25

3.25.1 If the defendant requires an extension of time for service of the Letter of Response, a request should be made as soon as the defendant becomes aware that it will be required and, in any event, within four months of the letter of claim.

3.25.2 The defendant should explain why any extension of time is necessary.

3.25.3 The claimant should adopt a reasonable approach to any request for an extension of time for provision of the reasoned answer.

3.26 If the claimant has made an offer to settle, the defendant should respond to that offer in the Letter of Response, preferably with reasons. The defendant may also make an offer to settle at this stage. Any offer made by the defendant should be made in accordance with the legal and procedural requirements of CPR Part 36 (possibly including any costs incurred to date). If an offer to settle is made, the defendant should provide sufficient medical or other evidence to allow the claimant to properly consider the offer. The level of detail necessary will depend on the value of the claim.

3.27 If the parties reach agreement on liability, or wish to explore the possibility of resolution with no admissions as to liability, but time is needed to resolve the value of the claim, they should aim to agree a reasonable period.

3.28 If the parties do not reach agreement on liability, they should discuss whether the claimant should start proceedings and whether the court might be invited to direct an early trial of a preliminary issue or of breach of duty and/or causation.

3.29 Following receipt of the Letter of Response, if the claimant is aware that there may be a delay of six months or more before the claimant decides if, when and how to proceed, the claimant should keep the defendant generally informed.

4   EXPERTS

4.1 In clinical negligence disputes separate **expert opinions** may be needed—
- on breach of duty;
- on causation;
- on the patient's condition and prognosis;
- to assist in valuing aspects of the claim.

4.2 It is recognised that in clinical negligence disputes, the parties and their advisers will require flexibility in their approach to expert evidence. The parties should co-operate when making decisions on appropriate medical specialisms, whether experts might be instructed jointly and whether any reports obtained pre-action might be shared.

4.3 Obtaining expert evidence will often be an expensive step and may take time, especially in specialised areas of medicine where there are limited numbers of suitable experts.

4.4 When considering what expert evidence may be required during the Protocol period, parties should be aware that the use of any expert reports obtained pre-action will only be permitted in proceedings with the express permission of the court.

5   ALTERNATIVE DISPUTE RESOLUTION

5.1 Litigation should be a last resort. As part of this Protocol, the parties should consider whether negotiation or some other form of alternative dispute resolution ('ADR') might enable them to resolve their dispute without commencing proceedings.

5.2 Some of the options for resolving disputes without commencing proceedings are—
(a) discussion and negotiation (which may or may not include making Part 36 Offers or providing an explanation and/or apology);
(b) mediation, a third party facilitating a resolution;
(c) arbitration, a third party deciding the dispute;
(d) early neutral evaluation, a third party giving an informed opinion on the dispute; and
(e) Ombudsmen schemes.

5.3 Information on mediation and other forms of ADR is available in the *Jackson ADR Handbook* (available from Oxford University Press) or at—
- http://www.civilmediation.justice.gov.uk/
- http://www.adviceguide.org.uk/england/law_e/law_legal_system_e/law_taking_legal_action_e/alternatives_to_court.htm

5.4 If proceedings are issued, the parties may be required by the court to provide evidence that ADR has been considered. It is expressly recognised that no party can or should be forced to mediate or enter into any form of ADR, but a party's silence in response to an invitation to participate in ADR might be considered unreasonable by the court and could lead to the court ordering that party to pay additional court costs.

6 STOCKTAKE

6.1

6.1.1 Where a dispute has not been resolved after the parties have followed the procedure set out in this Protocol, the parties should review their positions before the claimant issues court proceedings.

6.1.2 If proceedings cannot be avoided, the parties should continue to co-operate and should seek to prepare a chronology of events which identifies the facts or issues that are agreed and those that remain in dispute. The parties should also seek to agree the necessary procedural directions for efficient case management during the proceedings.

ANNEX A

An Illustrative Flowchart

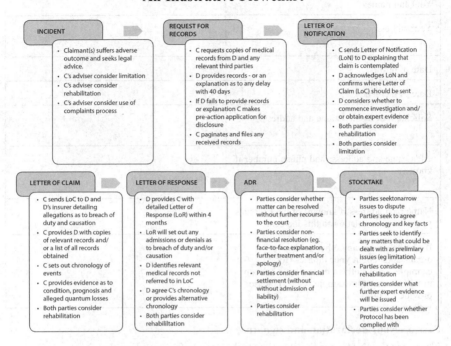

INCIDENT
- Claimant(s) suffers adverse outcome and seeks legal advice.
- C's adviser consider limitation
- C's adviser consider rehabilitation
- C's adviser consider use of complaints process

REQUEST FOR RECORDS
- C requests copies of medical records from D and any relevant third parties
- D provides records - or an explanation as to any delay with 40 days
- If D fails to provide records or explanation C makes pre-action application for disclosure
- C paginates and files any received records

LETTER OF NOTIFICATION
- C sends Letter of Notification (LoN) to D explaining that claim is contemplated
- D acknowledges LoN and confirms where Letter of Claim (LoC) should be sent
- D considers whether to commence investigation and/ or obtain expert evidence
- Both parties consider rehabilitation
- Both parties consider limitation

LETTER OF CLAIM
- C sends LoC to D and D's insurer detailing allegations as to breach of duty and causation
- C provides D with copies of relevant records and/ or a list of all records obtained
- C sets out chronology of events
- C provides evidence as to condition, prognosis and alleged quantum losses
- Both parties consider rehabilitation

LETTER OF RESPONSE
- D provides C with detailed Letter of Response (LoR) within 4 months
- LoR will set out any admissions or denials as to breach of duty and/or causation
- D identifies relevant medical records not referred to in LoC
- D agree C's chronology or provides alternative chronology
- Both parties consider rehabililtation

ADR
- Parties consider whether matter can be resolved without further recourse to the court
- Parties consider non-financial resolution (eg. face-to-face explanation, further treatment and/or apology)
- Parties consider financial settlement (without without admission of liability)
- Parties consider rehabilitation

STOCKTAKE
- Parties seek to narrow issues to dispute
- Parties seek to agree chronology and key facts
- Parties seek to identify any matters that could be dealt with as preliminary issues (eg limitation)
- Parties consider rehabilitation
- Parties consider what further expert evidence will be issued
- Parties consider whether Protocol has been complied with

ANNEX B

Form For Obtaining Health Records

Consent form

(Releasing health records under the Data Protection Act 1998)

About this form

In order to proceed with your claim, your solicitor may need to see your health records. Solicitors usually need to see all your records as they need to assess which parts are relevant to your case. (Past medical history is often relevant to a claim for compensation.) Also, if your claim goes ahead, the person you are making the claim against will ask for copies of important documents. Under court rules, they may see all your health records. So your solicitor needs to be familiar with all your records.

Part a – your, the health professionals' and your solicitor's or agent's details

Your full name:	
Your address:	
Date of birth:	
Date of incident:	
Solicitor's or agent's name and address:	
GP's name and address (and phone number if known):	
Name (and address if known) of the hospitals you went to in relation to this incident:	
If you have seen any other person or organisation about your injuries (for example, a physiotherapist) or have had any investigations (for example, x-rays) please provide details.	

Part b – your declaration and signature

Please see the 'Notes for the client' over the page before you sign this form.

To health professionals

I understand that filling in and signing this form gives you permission to give copies of all my GP records, and any hospital records relating to this incident, to my solicitor or agent whose details are given above.

Please give my solicitor or agent copies of my health records, in line with the Data Protection Act 1998, within 40 days.

Your signature: . . . .   Date:.../....../...

Part c – your solicitor's or agent's declaration and signature

Please see the 'Notes for the solicitor or agent' over the page before you sign this form.

To health professionals

I have told my client the implications of giving me access to his or her health records. I confirm that I need the full records in this case. I enclose the authorised fee for getting access to records.

Solicitor's
or agent's signature: . . . .   Date: .../....../...

Notes for the client

Your health records contain information from almost all consultations you have had with health professionals. The information they contain usually includes:

- why you saw a health professional;
- details of clinical findings and diagnoses;
- any options for care and treatment the health professional discussed with you;
- the decisions made about your care and treatment, including evidence that you agreed; and
- details of action health professionals have taken and the outcomes.

By signing this form, you are agreeing to the health professional or hospital named on this form releasing copies of your health records to your solicitor or agent. During the process your records may be seen by people who are not health professionals, but they will keep the information confidential.

If you are making, or considering making, a legal claim against someone, your solicitor will need to see copies of all your GP records, and any hospital records made in connection with this incident, so he or she can see if there is anything in your records that may affect your claim. Once you start your claim, the court can order you to give copies of your health records to the solicitor of the person you are making a claim against so he or she can see if any of the information in your records can be used to defend his or her client.

If you decide to go ahead with your claim, your records may be passed to a number of people including:

- the expert who your solicitor or agent instructs to produce a medical report as evidence for the case;
- the person you are making a claim against and their solicitors;
- the insurance company for the person you are making a claim against;
- any insurance company or other organisation paying your legal costs; and
- any other person or company officially involved with the claim.

You do not have to give permission for your health records to be released but if you don't, the court may not let you go ahead with your claim and, in some circumstances, your solicitor may refuse to represent you.

If there is very sensitive information in the records, that is not connected to the claim, you should tell your solicitor. They will then consider whether this information needs to be revealed.

Notes for the solicitor or agent

Before you ask your client to fill in and sign this form you should explain that this will involve his or her full health records being released and how the information in them may be used. You should also tell your client to read the notes above.

If your client is not capable of giving his or her permission in this form, this form should be signed by:

- your client's litigation friend;
- someone who has enduring power of attorney to act for your client; or
- your client's receiver appointed by the Court of Protection.

When you send this form to the appropriate records controller please also enclose the authorised fees for getting access to records.

If you find out at any stage that the medical records contain information that the client does not know about (for example, being diagnosed with a serious illness), you should discuss this with the health professional who provided the records.

Unless your client agrees otherwise, you must use his or her health records only for the purpose for which the client signed this form (that is, making his or her claim). Under the Data Protection Act you have responsibilities relating to sensitive information. The entire health record should not be automatically revealed without the client's permission and you should not keep health records for any longer than you need them. You should return them to the client at the end of the claim if they want them. Otherwise, you are responsible for destroying them.

Notes for the medical records controller

This form shows your patient's permission for you to give copies of his or her full GP record, and any hospital records relating to this incident, to his or her solicitor or agent. You must give the solicitor or agent copies of these health records unless any of the exemptions set out in The Data Protection (Subject Access Modification) (Health) Order 2000 apply. The main exemptions are that you must not release information that:

- is likely to cause serious physical or mental harm to the patient or another person; or

- relates to someone who would normally need to give their permission (where that person is not a health professional who has cared for the patient).

Your patient's permission for you to release information is valid only if that patient understands the consequences of his or her records being released, and how the information will be used. The solicitor or agent named on this form must explain these issues to the patient. If you have any doubt about whether this has happened, contact the solicitor or agent, or your patient.

If your patient is not capable of giving his or her permission, this form should be signed by:

- a 'litigation friend' acting for your patient;

- someone with 'enduring power of attorney' to act for your patient; or

- a receiver appointed by the Court of Protection.

You may charge the usual fees authorised under the Data Protection Act for providing the records.

The BMA publishes detailed advice for doctors on giving access to health records, including the fees that you may charge. You can view that advice by visiting www.bma.org.uk/ap.nsf/Content/accesshealthrecords.

This form is published by the Law Society and British Medical Association. (2nd edition, October 2004)

ANNEX C

Templates for Letters Of Notification, Claim and Response

C1 Letter of Notification

To

Defendant

Dear Sirs

Letter of Notification

Re: [Claimant's Name, Address, DoB and NHS Number]

We have been instructed to act on behalf of [Claimant's name] in relation to treatment carried out/care provided at [name of hospital or treatment centre] by [name of clinician(s) if known] on [insert date(s)].

The purpose of this letter is to notify you that, although we are not yet in a position to serve a formal Letter of Claim, our initial investigations indicate that a case as to breach of duty and/or causation has been identified. We therefore invite you to commence your own investigation and draw your attention to the fact that failure to do may be taken into account when considering the reasonableness of any subsequent application for an extension of time for the Letter of Response.

Defendant

We understand that you are the correct defendant in respect of treatment provided by [name of clinician] at [hospital/surgery/treatment centre] on [date(s)]. If you do not agree, please provide us with any information you have that may assist us to identify the correct defendant. Failure to do so may result in costs sanctions should proceedings be issued.

Summary of Facts and Alleged Adverse Outcome

[Outline what is alleged to have happened and provide a chronology of events with details of relevant known treatment/care.]

Medical Records

[Provide index of records obtained and request for further records/information if required.]

Allegations of Negligence

[Brief outline of any alleged breach of duty and causal link with any damage suffered.]

Expert Evidence

[State whether expert evidence has been obtained or is awaited and, if so, the relevant discipline.]

Damage

[Brief outline of any injuries attributed to the alleged negligence and their functional impact.]

Funding

[If known, state method of funding and whether arrangement was entered into before or after April 2013.]

Rehabilitation

As a result of the allegedly negligent treatment, our client has injuries/needs that could be met by rehabilitation. We invite you to consider how this could be achieved.

Limitation

For the purposes of limitation, we calculate that any proceedings will need to be issued on or before [date].

Please acknowledge this letter by [insert date 14 days after deemed receipt] and confirm to whom any Letter of Claim should be sent. We enclose a duplicate of the letter for your insurer.

Recoverable Benefits

The claimant's National Insurance Number will be sent to you in a separate envelope.

We look forward to hearing from you.

Yours faithfully,

C2 Letter of Claim

To Defendant

Dear Sirs

Letter of Claim

[Claimant's name] -v- [Defendant's Name]

We have been instructed to act on behalf of [Claimant's name] in relation to treatment carried out/care provided at [name of hospital or treatment centre] by [name of clinician(s) if known] on [insert date(s)]. Please let us know if you do not believe that you are the appropriate defendant or if you are aware of any other potential defendants.

Claimant's details

Full name, DoB, address, NHS Number.

Dates of allegedly negligent treatment

• include chronology based on medical records.

Events giving rise to the claim:

• an outline of what happened, including details of other relevant treatments to the client by other healthcare providers.

Allegation of negligence and causal link with injuries:

• an outline of the allegations or a more detailed list in a complex case;

• an outline of the causal link between allegations and the injuries complained of;

• A copy of any supportive expert evidence (optional).

[1352]

The Client's injuries, condition and future prognosis

• A copy of any supportive expert report (optional);

• Suggestions for rehabilitation;

• The discipline of any expert evidence obtained or proposed.

Clinical records (if not previously provided)

We enclose an index of all the relevant records that we hold. We shall be happy to provide copies of these on payment of our photocopying charges.

We enclose a request for copies of the following records which we believe that you hold. We confirm that we shall be responsible for your reasonable copying charges. Failure to provide these records may result in costs sanctions if proceedings are issued.

The likely value of the claim

• an outline of the main heads of damage, or, in straightforward cases, the details of loss;

• Part 36 settlement offer (optional);

• suggestions for ADR.

Funding

[State method of funding and whether arrangement was entered into before or after April 2013.]

We enclose a further copy of this letter for you to pass to your insurer. We look forward to receiving an acknowledgment of this letter within 14 days and your Letter of Response within 4 months of the date on which this letter was received. We calculate the date for receipt of your Letter of Response to be [date].

Recoverable Benefits

The claimant's National Insurance Number will be sent to you in a separate envelope.

We look forward to hearing from you.

Yours faithfully

C3 Letter of Response

To

Claimant

Dear Sirs

Letter of Response

[Claimant's name] -v- [Defendant's Name]

We have been instructed to act on behalf of [defendant] in relation to treatment carried out/care provided to [claimant] at [name of hospital or treatment centre] by [name of clinician(s) if known] on [insert date(s)].

The defendant [conveys sympathy for the adverse outcome/would like to offer an apology/denies that there was an adverse outcome].

Parties

It is accepted that [defendant] had a duty of care towards [claimant] in respect of [details if required] treatment/care provided to [claimant] at [location] on [date(s)].

However, [defendant] is not responsible for [details] care/treatment provided to [claimant] at [location] on [date(s)] by [name of clinician if known].

Records

We hold the following records...

We require copies of the following records...

Failure to provide these records may result in costs sanctions if proceedings are issued.

Comments on events and/or chronology:

We [agree the chronology enclosed with the Letter of Claim] [enclose a revised chronology of events].

We enclose copies of relevant [records/Protocols/internal investigations] in respect of the treatment/care that [claimant] received.

Liability

In respect of the specific allegations raised by the claimant, the defendant [has obtained an expert opinion and] responds as follows:-

[each allegation should be addressed separately. The defendant should explain which (if any) of the allegations of breach of duty and/or causation are admitted and why. The defendant should also make clear which allegations are denied and why].

Next Steps

The defendant suggests...

[e.g. no prospect of success for the claimant, resolution without admissions of liability, ADR, settlement offer, rehabilitation].

Yours faithfully,

GLOSSARY OF MEDICAL TERMS

Abdominoplasty	plastic surgery on the abdomen.
Abduction	movement away from the mid-line.
Acceleration injury	diffuse shearing injury to the brain substance.
Acute myeloid leukaemia	a form of leukaemia in which the type of blood cell that proliferates abnormally originates in the blood forming (myeloid) tissue of the bone marrow. Can involve any of the cells produced by the marrow. Myeloid leukaemia may be acute or chronic, depending on the rate of progression of the disease.
Adduction	movement towards the mid-line.
Adrenaline	hormone secreted by the adrenal gland, having effects on the circulation, muscles and sugar metabolism.
Agnosia	inability to recognise familiar complex auditory, visual or tactile stimuli, despite intact sensory input to the brain.
Agraphia	inability to express thoughts in writing.
AIDS	acquired immune deficiency syndrome; an illness (often if not always fatal) in which opportunistic infections or malignant tumours develop as a result of the severe loss of cellular immunity, which is itself caused by earlier infection with a retrovirus, HIV, transmitted in sexual fluids and blood.
Akinesia	inability to start a movement.
Alexia	loss of power to grasp meaning of written or printed words and sentences.
Amenorrhoea	absence or suppression of menstrual discharge.
Amnesia	disorders of memory; literally without (a) memory (mnesis). May be an imprinting deficit for new material, or a memory retrieval deficit for old material.
Amniocentesis	the process whereby a needle is inserted in the sac which surrounds the foetus in the uterus (the amnion) and some of the contained amniotic fluid is withdrawn. The procedure as a great potential for antenatal diagnosis.
Aneurism	swelling in the wall of an artery.
Angiography	X-ray of the blood vessels.
Ankylosis	obliteration of a joint by fusion, either bony or fibrous.

[1357]

Anosmia	loss of sense of smell. May also affect the perceived taste of liquid and solid foodstuffs.
Anoxia	deficiency in oxygen supply to the brain, if profound, causes permanent brain damage.
Anterior colporrhaphy	stitching of the vagina in order to reduce laxity in a case of prolapse of the bladder.
Anterior spinal artery syndrome	spinal stroke, caused by interruption of the flow of blood to the spine
Anterograde amnesia	loss of memory for events occurring subsequent to amnesia causing trauma; patient is unable to acquire or learn new information.
Anticonvulsant	a drug used to reduce the incidence of epileptic fits, for example valproate (Epilim), carbamazepine (Tegretol), phenytoin (Epanutin).
Aorta	the major artery of the body from which all other systemic arteries derive; it originates in the left ventricle of the heart and ends by dividing into the common iliac arteries which are destined to supply blood to the legs.
Aortography	radiographic examination of the aorta, usually by insertion of a catheter into the femoral artery.
Aortoplasty	operation to repair aorta.
Aphasia	absence of the capacity for language comprehension, or expression, in the absence of any defect in the voice, sight or hearing.
Aphonia	inability to make sounds.
Apnoea	suspension or cessation of breathing.
Aplastic anaemia	anaemia (lack of haemoglobin) caused by poor or absent production of blood cells in the bone marrow.
Appendicectomy	surgical removal of the appendix.
Apraxia	loss of ability to carry out skilled voluntary movements, in the absence of limb paralysis.
Arachnoid mater	a water-tight meningeal membrane forming the outer boundary of the subarachnoid space that contains cerebrospinal fluid.
Arachnoiditis	an inflammatory response of the arachnoid, one of three coverings, or meninges, that envelop the brain and spinal cord, which may result from infection, including syphilis and tubercular meningitis, or trauma (including that resulting from surgery, lumbar puncture and spinal anaesthesia).
Arteriography	X-ray examination of an artery that has been outlined by the injection of a radio-opaque contrast medium.
Arteriovascular malformation	variation in the normal physical structure of the arteriovascular system.
Arteriovenous fistula	an abnormal communication between an artery and a vein.
Arthoplasty	surgical remodelling of a diseased joint.

Arthrodesis	surgical fusion of a joint.
Arthroplasy	surgical reconstitution or replacement of a joint.
Arthroscopy	inspection by means of an arthroscope of the cavity of a joint.
Artificial insemination	introduction of semen into the vagina by means of an instrument in order to achieve conception.
Aseptic necrosis	the death of cells in an organ or tissue caused by disease, physical or chemical injury or interference with the blood supply, in aseptic conditions (i.e. the absence of bacteria, fungi, viruses or other organisms that could cause disease).
Aspiration	sucking out fluid (e.g. from a joint or cavity) through a hollow needle.
Astereognosis	inability to recognise objects by touching them alone.
Ataxia	loss of coordination and precision of movement of torso, head or limbs due to a defect in the cerebellum, vestibular or proprioceptive system.
Atrophy	a state of wasting due to some interference with tissue nutrition.
Attention	the active selection of information, with concurrent inhibition of other, competing information.
Audiometry	the assessment and quantification of hearing function.
Avascular necrosis	death of tissue through deprivation of blood supply; refers particularly to bones—e.g. head of femur following fracture of neck of femur.
Babinski reflex	extension of the great toe on scratching the sole, indicating an upper motor neurone lesion.
Basal ganglia	clusters of nerve cells (grey matter), deep in each cerebral hemisphere, relaying motor and sensory impulses.
Behcet's disease	a rare, chronic inflammatory disorder, the cause of which is unknown; symptoms include recurrent ulcers in the mouth and on the genitals, and eye inflammation. The disorder may also cause various types of skin lesions, arthritis, bowel inflammation, meningitis and cranial nerve palsies. Behcet's disease may involve all organs and affect the central nervous system, causing memory loss and impaired speech, balance and movement.
Benzodiazepine	a group of pharmacologically active compounds used as minor tranquillisers and hypnotics.
Bilateral carotid arteriogram	a picture of the arteries on either side of the neck which supply blood to the head. The examination of the arteries is effected by means of radiology after injection of a radio-opaque material.
Bilirubin encephalopathy	see *kernicterus*.
Biopsy	sample of tissue taken from the living body for microscopic examination.

Bitemporal hemianopia	loss of the outer halves of both visual fields.
Bi-valve	removal of a plaster cast by cutting along each side of its length, permitting replacement if required.
Bradykinesia	slowness in movement.
Brachial palsy	a condition characterised by a weak, numb or paralysed arm. Often caused by injury to the brachial plexus of nerves which arise from the neck to supply the arm (e.g. as a result of a road traffic accident).
Brachial plexus	a network of nerves arising from the spine at the base of the neck, from which arise the nerves supplying the arm, forearm and hand, and part of the shoulder.
Brain stem	posterior part of the brain comprising the midbrain, pons and medulla containing vital centres, ascending and descending tracts, nuclei of cranial nerves and the reticular formation.
Broca's area	an area for speech in the dominant, frontal lobe of the brain.
Bulbar	concerning the medulla.
Burr-hole	hole drilled in the skull.
Bursa	a cyst-like sac between a bony prominence and the skin, e.g. prepatellar bursa, inflammation in which constitutes "housemaid's knee".
Callus	the cement-like new bone formation which produces union of the fragments of a fracture.
Capsulotomy	an incision into the capsule of the eye lens.
Cardiac	pertaining to the heart.
Carotid endarterectomy	operation on the carotid artery (in the neck) to remove debris blocking the artery and hence reduce the risk of a stroke.
Carpal tunnel	the channel in the wrist through which the median nerve passes.
Cataract	opacity in the lens of the eye, resulting in blurred vision.
Catheter	a tube for insertion into a narrow opening so that fluids may be introduced or removed.
Cauda equina syndrome	impairment of the nerves in the cauda equina (the bundle of spinal nerve roots that arise from the lower end of the spinal cord), resulting in low back pain, unilateral or usually bilateral sciatica, saddle sensory disturbances, bladder and bowel dysfunction, and variable lower extremity motor and sensory loss.
Caudal block	a type of epidural anaesthesia which is particularly suitable for operations on the anus, the vagina and the urethra.
Central nervous system (CNS)	comprising the spinal cord and brain, the latter containing the cerebrum, cerebellum, mid-brain, pons and medulla. Excludes peripheral nerves that run outside the spinal cord.
Cephalic	pertaining to the head.
Cerebral	pertaining to the brain.

Cerebral palsy	any of various non-progressive forms of paralysis caused by damage to motor areas of the brain before or during birth, manifested in early childhood by weakness and imperfect control of the affected muscles.
Cerebral thrombosis	clotting in a blood vessel in the brain.
Cervical	pertaining to the neck.
Cervical laminectomy	an operation to remove a prolapsed spinal disc from the neck.
Chondral	pertaining to the cartilage.
Crohn's disease	inflammation of the bowel.
Chronic adhesive arachnoiditis	inflammation of the lining of the brain and spinal cord.
Circumflex artery	an artery of curved or winding form, or which bends around others; example—the circumflex iliac artery.
Cirrhosis	a condition in which the liver responds to injury or death of some of its cells by producing interlacing strands of fibrous tissue between which are nodules of regenerating cells.
Claudication	lameness, applied particularly to pain in the calf muscles resulting from defective blood supply owing to arterial disease.
Cognition	mental functions of attention, memory, thinking, perception and intellectual activity.
Colon	main part of the large intestine.
Colostomy	the operation of making an artificial opening into the colon (the greater portion of the large intestine) through the abdominal wall.
Coma	absence of awareness of self and environment even when the subject is externally stimulated. Defined on the Glasgow Coma Scale as a score of eight or less.
Comminuted	a type of fracture of a bone in which there are more than two fragments.
Concussion	a reversible disturbance of consciousness following head trauma.
Confabulation	filling in gaps in memory with invented and often improbable stories or facts which the patient accepts as true.
Congenital disabilities	a disabling condition recognised at birth or believed to have been present since birth, whether inherited or caused by an environmental factor.
Consciousness	state of awareness of the self and the environment, the opposite of coma.
Contusion	bruising of neural tissue.
Cord prolapse	downward displacement of the umbilical cord.
Corneal reflex	normal blinking on touching the cornea of the eye.
Corpus callosum	a large bank of nerve fibres connecting the two cerebral hemispheres.

[1361]

Cortex	the outer layer of a structure, e.g. the "shell" of a bone; the surface layer (grey matter) of the cerebral and cerebellar hemispheres of the brain.
Cortical atrophy	thinning of cortical tissue.
Costal	pertaining to the ribs.
Cranial nerves	the nerves of the brain, twelve on each side, arising directly from the brain and the brain stem.
Craniectomy	opening in the skull where the bone is not replaced.
Craniotomy	opening in the skull where the bone is replaced.
Crepitus	a creaking or grating, found in osteo-arthritic joints; also in recent fractures and with inflammation of tendons and their sheaths (tenosynovitis).
Creutzfeldt-Jakob Disease	a rare, degenerative, fatal brain disorder, which causes rapid, progressive dementia and associated neuromuscular disturbances.
Cryoprecipitate	a component of blood used to aid coagulation.
Curettage	scraping of the internal surface of an organ or body cavity by means of a spoon-shaped instrument.
CSF	cerebrospinal fluid, which covers the surface of the brain and spinal cord and circulates inside the ventricles of the brain.
CT (Computed Tomography)	a scan which uses a finely collimated moving X-ray beam and a computer to construct pictures of a part of the body, which show internal structure as though the organ examined had been sliced open.
Cyanosis	blueness from deficient oxygenation of the blood.
Cytology	the study of the structure and function of cells.
Deceleration injury	see *Acceleration injury*.
Deep vein thrombosis	a blood clot (thrombus) that develops in a deep vein, usually in the leg; this can happen if the vein is damaged or if the flow of blood slows down or stops
Degeneration	death of tissue.
Dementia	deterioration of intellect, involving a diffuse reduction in cognitive functions, and changes in personality.
Demyelination	loss of the myelin that sheathes nerve fibres.
Denial	a defence mechanism whereby unacceptable ideas or facts are not perceived or allowed into full conscious awareness.
Depo-Provera	injectible contraceptive hormone.
Dermatitis	inflammation of the skin caused by an external agent.
Diabetes insipidus	passage of uncontrolled amounts of dilute urine.
Diabetes mellitus	passage of uncontrolled amounts of urine containing too high a concentration of glucose.
Diffuse injury	pattern of brain injury following rapid acceleration or deceleration of the head, as in some falls or road traffic accidents.

Dilatation and Curettage (D and C)	scraping the inside of the womb; this procedure is often performed in cases of excessive bleeding.
Diphtheria	an acute contagious infection caused by the bacterium corynebacterium diphtheriae.
Diplopia	double vision.
Disarticulation	amputation through a joint.
Disc, intervertebral	fibro-cartilaginous "cushion" between two vertebrae.
Discotomy	surgical incision into a spinal disc.
Disorientation	a state of mental confusion with respect to time, place, identity of self, or other persons or objects.
Distal	farthest point from the centre (opposite to proximal).
Dominant hemisphere	the cerebral hemisphere or side of the brain controlling speech. The left hemisphere in most people.
Dorsal spine	that part of the spine to which the ribs are connected; known also as the "thoracic" spine.
Dorsiflexion	movement of a joint in a backward direction.
Dorsum	back or top, e.g. back of hand, top of foot;
Duodenal ulcer	an ulcer in the duodenum caused by the action of acid and pepsin on the lining of the duodenum.
Dupuytren's contracture	thickened fibrous tissue in the palm of the hand causing contracture of the fingers.
Dura mater	outer layer of the meninges that are the membranous coverings of the brain. Closely applied to the inner surface of the skull and spinal canal in the vertebrae.
Dys-	prefix meaning difficult, defective, painful, e.g. dyspnoea, meaning shortness of breath.
Dyscrasia	an abnormal state of the body or part of the body, especially one due to abnormal development or metabolism.
Dysarthria	disturbance of speech articulation. Pronunciation, intonation and metre of spoken word defective.
Dyslexia	a reading disability.
Dysphagia	disturbance of swallowing.
Dysphasia	disturbance of communication. Receptive component in which the written or spoken word is not perceived correctly. Expressive component in which the patient cannot find the correct word to express themselves.
Dysplasia	malformation, abnormal development of tissue.
-ectomy	suffix meaning surgical excision—e.g. patellectomy, removal of the patella.
EEG (electroencephalography)	recording the amplified spontaneous electrical activity of the brain from surface electrodes.
Effusion	extravasation of fluid in a joint (or any cavity), e.g. "water on the knee" (i.e. synovitis).

Electrocardiogram (ECG)	a tracing which represents the passage of the nervous electrical discharge through the muscle of the heart. The technique involves recording from the leads placed on the limbs and on specified parts of the chest wall. Its main use is to follow the progress of a myocardial infarction (ischaemic death of portions of heart muscle) or to assist in the diagnosis in the event of uncertainty: indigestion is, for example, notorious for mimicking cardiac disease.
Electroconvulsive therapy (ECT)	an accepted treatment for particularly, depressive psychosis. It consists of the passage of an electric current through the frontal lobes of the brain.
ELISA test	enzyme linked immunosorbent assay test; an initial screening test for detecting HIV antibodies.
EMG	(electromyography) recording of muscle and nerve electrical activity.
Embolism	blockage of a blood vessel by a clot which has migrated.
Emphysema, surgical	collection of air in the tissues through puncture of the lung by a fractured rib.
Encephalopathy	brain damage due, to various (e.g. toxic) causes.
Encephalitis	inflammation of the brain. A potentially fatal viral or bacterial disease that damages the brain and brainstem bilaterally.
Endocartis	inflammation of the lining of the heart cavity and valves.
Endometriosis	the presence of membranous material of the kind lining the womb at other sites within the cavity of the pelvis.
ENT	ear, nose and throat.
Enuresis	urinary incontinence during the night.
Epidural	an injection of anaesthetic into the epidural space of the spine, used especially to control pain during childbirth by producing a loss of sensation below the waist without affecting consciousness.
Epilepsy	an episodic disturbance of brain activity following abnormal spontaneous electrical discharges within the brain, leading to a fit.
Epiphyseal line	the cartilaginous plate near the end of a bone at which the bone grows in length.
Epiphysis	the end of a bone during the period of growth.
Erythema	superficial blush or redness of the skin, e.g. as from a very slight burn or scald.
Erythrocyte	red blood corpuscle.
Eschar	crust of dead skin.
ESR	erythrocyte sedimentation rate. A laboratory test upon the blood to detect the presence of an inflammatory process in the body.

Evoked response	(or potential) an electrical response recorded in some part of the nervous system (e.g. visual cortex); evoked or elicited by stimulation elsewhere (e.g. eyes—visual evoked responses).
Extension	moving a joint into the straight position (opposite to flexion).
Extensor plantar response	see *Babinski reflex*.
External	outer side, syn, lateral (opposite to medial).
Factor VIII	a protein found in blood which aids coagulation. Deficiency of this factor results in haemophilia A. Produced from plasma by fractionation.
Fascia	a fibrous membrane.
Fibro-cartilaginous embolism (FCE)	a rare occurrence whereby emboli locate themselves in the arteries and/or veins supplying the cervical cord causing loss of blood supply to the spinal cord, and resulting in paralysis or death. An embolus consists of material, such as a blood clot, fat, air, amniotic fluid or a foreign body that is carried from one point in the blood circulation to lodge at another.
Flaccidity	loss of normal tone in muscles leaving them abnormally limp.
Flexion	moving a joint into the bent position (opposite to extension).
Flexor plantar response	the normal downward movement of the big toe when the sole is scratched.
Flexor spasm	painful contraction of muscles in spastic limbs.
Focal injury	injury to a circumscribed area of brain.
Foetal hypoxia	hypoxia of the foetus (see *Hypoxia*).
Fossa	anatomical term for a depression or furrow.
Fractionation	a biochemical process of separating out certain blood components, such as factor VIII, from plasma.
Frontal	at the front of the brain, or the skull.
Frontal lobes	the brain's anterior portions lying above the eyes.
Gangrene	total death of a structure through deprivation of blood supply.
Genu	the knee joint.
Gestational diabetes	glucose intolerance of variable degree with onset or first recognition during pregnancy, which affects about 4 per cent of all pregnant women.
Glasgow Coma Scale (GCS)	numerical scale from three (total unresponsiveness) to 15 (normal consciousness).
Glaucoma	a condition in which loss of vision is caused by an abnormally high pressure in the eye.
Gliosis	scar tissue replacement of damaged brain tissue.
Gluteal	pertaining to the buttock.

Grand mal epilepsy	epilepsy involving loss of consciousness and generalised convulsions, often associated with urinary incontinence and tongue biting during the fits.
Grey matter	neural tissue largely comprising nerve cell bodies and dendrites constituting the cerebral cortex, the brain nuclei and central columns of the spinal cord.
Gyri	convolutions on the cortical surface of the brain, representing folds of the cerebral cortex.
Haemarthrosis	effusion of blood in a joint.
Haematoma	an accumulation of blood within the tissues which clots to form a solid swelling.
Haemophilus influenza type b	a bacterial infection which can cause meningitis, epiglottitis, pneumonia, septic arthritis, infection of tissues under the skin, infected lining of the heart, pus in the lungs and infection of bone. Despite its name, it is not related to influenza. It is the leading cause of acute bacterial meningitis in infants and children under five.
Heamorrhage	blood that has escaped from a blood vessel. An extradural haemorrhage becomes an extradural haematoma when the blood begins to clot.
Hallux	the great toe.
Hemianopia	loss of half of the visual field. If vision is lost on the same side in both eyes, the hemianopia is termed homonymous.
Hemiparesis	unilateral motor weakness, affecting face, arm and/or leg.
Hepatitis	infection of the liver. Hepatitis A, known as infective hepatitis, is spread by ingestion through faecal transmission, and is thus very common in institutions. Hepatitis B, or serum hepatitis, spreads from blood or blood products to blood; it requires either to be injected or to be applied to open breaches in the skin—thus, drug addicts, haemophiliacs and the like are particularly at risk. The third principal variant of the disease is known as hepatitis non-A, non-B and is diagnosed by exclusion of the other recognisable types.
Heterotopic ossification	(calcification) the formation of extraneous bone in muscle tissue, causing painful and often severely restricted movement.
HIV	human immuno-deficiency virus; this is the virus which causes Aids.
Hodgkin's disease	a malignant disease of lymphatic tissues.
Human growth hormone	a hormone essential for bone and organ growth in youth; too little causes dwarfism, too much causes gigantism.
Hydrocephalus	accumulation of excessive cerebrospinal fluid in the ventricles of the brain.
Hyper-	prefix meaning increase above the normal.

Hypercarbia	abnormally high concentration of carbon dioxide in the blood.
Hyperphagia	pathological overeating.
Hypo-	prefix meaning decrease below the normal; anatomical term for below.
Hypoglycaemia	a deficiency of glucose in the bloodstream causing muscular weakness and lack of co-ordination, mental confusion and sweating.
Hypotension	low blood pressure.
Hypoxia	the condition of the body when it is supplied with insufficient oxygen for its needs.
Hysterectomy	excision of the uterus.
Hysterosalpingogram	radiogram of the Fallopian tubes.
Hysterosalpinogram	radiogram of the interior of the womb and the Fallopian tubes following injection of a radio-opaque fluid.
Iatrogenic	induced unintentionally by a physician through his diagnosis, manner or treatment; of or pertaining to the induction of (mental or bodily) disorders, symptoms etc., in this way.
Ictal	a symptom or sign during an epileptic fit, causally related to the fit.
Idiopathic	of unknown cause.
Illeum	the lower half of the small intestine.
Illium	the main bone of the pelvis.
Induration	hardening of a tissue.
Infarct	a wedge-shaped area of non-viable tissue, produced by loss of the blood supply.
Inguinal	pertaining to the groin.
Intelligence	those aspects of cognitive function which are measured by an intelligence test; may reflect the ability to learn from experience, think in abstract terms and deal effectively with one's environment.
Intercostal	between the ribs.
Intracranial hypertension	high tissue pressure inside the skull, not high blood pressure.
Intercranial shunt	a passage within the skull connecting two anatomical channels and diverting blood from one to the other.
Intramedullary nail	a device used to align and stabilise fractures of the long bones, such as the tibia or femur.
Intraventricular haemorrhage	a collection of blood within the ventricular system, commonly associated with intracerebral haematoma or subarachnoid haemorrhage.
Intravenous pyelogram	a succession of X-ray films of the urinary tract following the injection into a vein of a radio-opaque substance, used to test kidney function.

[1367]

Intubation	the introduction of a tube into part of the body for the purpose of diagnosis or treatment.
Ipsilateral	on the same side.
IQ (intelligence quotient)	a statistically derived average of verbal, non-verbal and general ability from one or many test performances which comprise a standardized intelligence test (e.g. see *Wechsler Adult Intelligent Scale (WAIS)*). An individual, performance is compared to the average for a particular age group.
Ischaemia	a reduced or insufficient amount of blood being supplied to a region of the brain or body.
-itis	suffix meaning inflammation, e.g. osteitis, inflammation of a bone.
Ivalon sponge rectopexy (Wells operation)	a surgical procedure to correct, a rectal prolapse.
Keloid	a scar which is thickened and deep pink in colour.
Kernicterus (bilirubin encephalopathy)	damage to the brain of a neonate by an excess of bilirubin (bile pigment) in the blood.
Kyphosis	posterior convexity of the spine.
Laceration	tearing of tissue.
Laminectomy	excision of one or more of the posterior arches of the vertebrae (each arch being formed by the junction of two laminae), especially as a method of access to the spinal canal.
Laparoscopy	visual examination of the interior of the peritoneal cavity by means of a laparoscope inserted into it through the abdominal wall or vagina.
Laparotomy	a cutting through the abdominal walls into the cavity of the abdomen.
Lateral	outer side, or external (opposite to medial).
Lesion	a structural change in a tissue caused by disease or injury.
Leucocyte	white blood corpuscle.
Leukaemia	any of a group of malignant diseases in which the blood-forming organs produce increased numbers of white blood cells (leucocytes).
Lipoma	a common benign tumour composed of well-differentiated fat cells.
Lipping	ridge of adventitious bone at joint edges in arthritis (syn. osteophytic formation).
Lobectomy	excision of diseased or traumatised lobe of the brain.
Logynon	an oral contraceptive pill.
Long-term memory	the relatively permanent component of memory, one's previously acquired knowledge, as opposed to the more fluid short-term memory.
Lordosis	anterior convexity of spine.

Lumbar	the "small" of the back, i.e. situated between the dorsal (thoracic) and sacral levels.
Lumen	the cavity of a tubular structure.
Macro-	prefix meaning abnormally large size.
Malar	pertaining to the cheek.
Mallet finger	inability actively to straighten the terminal joint of a finger.
Mandible	the lower jaw.
Marsupiliasation	an operative technique for curing a cyst.
Mastectomy	surgical removal of a breast.
Mastoidectomy	an operation to clear out infection in the bony protuberance behind the ear.
Maxilla	the upper jaw and cheek bones.
Measles	a highly infectious viral disease, mainly affecting children.
Medial	inner side, or internal (opposite to lateral).
Mediastinoscopy	procedure to view the organs of the mediastinum. The mediastinum is in the central chest and contains the heart, windpipe (trachea) and gullet (oesophagus).
Medullary cavity	the soft interior of a bone.
Memory	the process through which we retain learned knowledge, in a form that can be recalled later.
Memory span	the number of items (digits, words) that are correctly recalled after a single presentation.
Meningitis	inflammation of the membranes of the brain or spinal cord.
Meniscus	the semilunar cartilage of the knee.
Mesothelioma	a cancer of the pleura (the linings of the inner chest wall and outside surface of the lungs) which is associated with asbestos inhalation.
Micro-	prefix meaning abnormally small size.
Migraine	hemicranial headache due to a disturbance in the normal calibre of the cranial blood vessels. May be precipitated by trauma, and has a number of clinical variants.
Minoxidil	a drug for the treatment of high blood pressure.
Motor	pertaining to movement (applied particularly to muscle action).
MRI (magnetic resonance image)	a scan which uses signals emitted from water in tissue placed in a strong magnetic field and a computer to construct pictures that are presented as apparent slices through the body in any plane. Can detect subtle tissue abnormalities.
Mumps	a common viral infection, mainly affecting children between the ages of 5 and 15.

[1369]

Myalgic encephalomyelitis (ME)	also referred to as chronic fatigue syndrome; a neurological disease which affects the brain at a physical, mental and emotional level. The first symptoms are similar to flu, but they do not resolve and may become worse. Symptoms include poor memory and concentration, sleep disorders, mood swings, extreme fatigue, muscle pain and stomach pains. ME is still not generally accepted as a "disease" because there is no accepted test for it and the same condition may result from a number of different causative factors.
Myelination	formation of fatty substance around nerve fibres or axons, important for nerve impulse conduction, the white matter of the brain and spinal cord.
Myelo-	prefix meaning pertaining to the spinal cord.
Myelography	radiography of; the spinal cord after injection of a contrast medium (radio opaque liquid) into the subarachnoid space.
Myeloid leukaemia	a virulent species of white cell cancer.
Myo-	prefix meaning pertaining to muscle.
Myocardial infarction	death of part of the heart, following interruption of its blood supply.
Myodil	a contrast medium injected into the back to improve X-ray images of the spine.
Myopericarditis	inflammation of the muscular wall of the heart and of the enveloping pericardium.
Necrosis	death of tissue, end stage of infarction.
Neomycin	an anti-bacterial drug.
Neural function	the electrical and chemical activity of nerve cells and fibres.
Non-Hodgkin's lymphoma	any malignant tumour of lymph nodes, excluding Hodgkin's disease.
Nystagmus	rhythmic involuntary oscillatory movement of the eyes.
Obtundation	reduction in alertness accompanied by a lowered awareness of the environment, slower psychological responses to stimulation, and increased hours of sleep, often with drowsiness in between.
Occipital lobes	the brain's posterior portions.
Oculo-vestibular reflex	eye movement reflex that is elicited in comatose patients with an intact brain stem, by initiating convection currents in the vestibular apparatus by syringing ice cold water into the external auditory meatus.
Oculomotor	concerned with eye movement.
Oedema	accumulation of fluid in tissues, usually following tissue damage.
Olfactory	pertaining to the sense of smell.
Oligo-	prefix meaning few or lack of.
Oophorectomy	surgical removal of an ovary.

Opren	a drug for the treatment of arthritis.
Orthopaedic	relating to the muscular-skeletal system.
Osteitis	inflammation of bone.
Osteomyelitis	inflammation of the bone marrow due to infection.
Osteophyte	ridge of adventitious bone at joint edges in arthritis (syn. "lipping").
Osteoporosis	loss of mineral salts from bones, the result of lack of use owing to injury or disease, reducing the mechanical strength of the bone.
Osteotomy	dissection of the bones (anat.); cutting of a bone in order to correct a deformity (surg.).
Outcome	function at a specified interval after an insult or therapeutic intervention.
Ovarian cyst	a fluid-filled sac in the ovary.
Paget's Disease	a disease which affects chiefly the elderly and is often symptomless, being characterised by the localised alteration of tissue in one or more bones (most often in the spine, skull or pelvis), which becomes thickened and may undergo fracture or bending.
Paired associate learning	the learning of stimulus-response pairs. When the first member of a pair (stimulus) is presented, the patient must give the second member (response).
Palmar flexion	moving the wrist in the direction that the palm faces (syn. flexion).
Para-	prefix meaning by the side of, near, through, abnormality.
Paresis	incomplete paralysis.
Parietal lobes	area of brain midway between the front and back of the head.
Patent ductus arteriosis	the ductus arteriosis is a blood vessel adjacent to the heart which allows blood to bypass the lungs while a foetus is in the womb. At birth it should close. If it remains patent it can result in a "blue baby" and require an operation to tie it off.
Pelvic thrombosis	Thrombosis in the pelvis (see *Thrombosis*).
Peptic ulcer	a breach of the lining (mucosa) of the digestive tract produced by digestion of the mucosa by pepsin and acid.
Periarthritis	inflammation round a joint, due to infection or injury, causing pain and restricted movement.
Perinatal asphyxial damage	damage attributable to suffocation producing oxygen deprivation, in the perinatal period (the period from about three months before to one month after birth).
Peritoneum	the double serous membrane which lines the cavity of the abdomen.
Peritonitis	inflammation of the peritoneum, or of some part of it.
Pertussis	whooping cough.

Petit mal epilepsy	a form of epilepsy involving a momentary alteration in consciousness.
Phenytoin	anticonvulsant drug (trade name: Epanutin).
Pia mater	inner layer of the meninges that are the membranous coverings of the brain. Closely applied to the surface of the brain and the spinal cord.
Pituitary fossa	the bony cavity at the base of the skull where the pituitary gland (which has an important influence on growth and bodily functions) is situated.
Plantar flexion	flexing the foot, pointing the toes downwards.
-plegia	suffix meaning paralysis.
Plasticity	the modifiability of a substrate, enabling functional change.
Pneumoconiosis	a disease of the lungs; this condition is often manifested by miners who have been exposed to coal dust.
Pneumohorax	air in the pleural cavity, e.g. from puncture of the lung by a fractured rib—and causing collapse of the lung.
Poly-	prefix meaning much or many.
Porencephaly	cavities in the brain substance due to tissue loss after severe brain damage.
Post traumatic amnesia	absence of memory for events surrounding the insult. May occur despite apparently normal levels of arousal.
Post traumatic stress disorder	the development of characteristic symptoms following a psychologically distressing event or situation of an exceptionally threatening or catastrophic nature. The characteristic symptoms include persistent re-experiencing of the traumatic event; persistent avoidance of stimuli associated with the trauma and "psychic numbing"; and persistent symptoms of anxiety or increased arousal.
Pre-eclampsia	a condition that can affect women at an advanced stage of pregnancy, marked by high blood pressure, swelling of the ankles and protein in the urine; can develop into the more serious condition of eclampsia, involving convulsions.
Prefrontal	the most anterior portion of the frontal lobe.
Primacy effect	(in memory) the tendency for initial words in a list to be recalled more readily than those from the middle or end of the list.
Proactive interference	the interference of earlier learning with the learning and recall of new material.
Prolapse	extrusion or protrusion, of a structure.
Pronation	twisting the forearm, the elbow being fixed, to bring the palm of hand facing downwards (opposite to supination).
Proximal	nearest the centre (opposite to distal).
Psychomotor epilepsy	a form of epileptic seizure in which the individual loses contact with the environment but appears conscious and performs some routine, repetitive act, or engages in more complex activity.

[1372]

Psychosocial	areas of psychological and social functioning, which may include family status, emotional adjustment, interpersonal skills and adjustment employment or other activity, financial status and acceptance of disability.
Ptosis	drooping of the eyelid.
Puerperal Fever	infection of the vagina and uterus consequent on childbirth.
Pulmonary	pertaining to the lung.
Quadriplegia	paralysis of all four limbs.
Rabies	an acute virus disease of the central nervous system that can affect all warm-blooded animals; usually transmitted to people by a bite from an infected dog.
Reaction time	the time between the presentation of a stimulus and the occurrence of a response.
Recency effect	(in memory) the tendency for the last few words on a list to be recalled more readily than words elsewhere from the list.
Recognition	the correct association of an item with a category.
Reduction	restoration to a normal position, e.g. of a fractured bone or a dislocated joint.
Reflex sympathetic dystrophy	a chronic condition characterised by severe burning pain, pathological changes in bone and skin, excessive sweating, tissue swelling and extreme sensitivity to touch. The syndrome is a nerve disorder that occurs at the site of an injury (most often to the arms or legs), but it can occur without apparent injury.
Reflux oesophagitis	inflammation of the oesophagus due to frequent regurgitation of acid and peptic juices from the stomach.
Repex	an automatic response to a stimulus.
Rena	pertaining to the kidney.
Retinoplasty of prematurity	see retrolental fibroplasia.
Retrieval	locating and reproducing information from memory.
Retro-	prefix meaning behind or backward.
Retroactive interference	the interference in recall of something earlier learned by something subsequently learned.
Retrobulbar bleed	bleeding which occurs behind the eyeball.
Retrograde amnesia	loss of memory for information acquired prior to the event that causes amnesia.
Retrolental fibroplasia	the abnormal proliferation of fibrous tissue immediately behind the lens of the eye, leading to blindness. It was formerly seen in newborn premature infants due to over-administration of oxygen.
Reye's syndrome	involves brain damage (encephalopathy) and liver damage of an unknown cause. It is associated with the use of aspirin in children to treat chickenpox or influenza.
Rigidity	increased tone in limb or trunk.

Rocky Mountain Spotted Fever	a disease of rodents and other small animals in the USA caused by the micro-organism rickettsia rickettsii, transmitted to people by ticks.
Romberg's sign	pathological increase of body sway when the patient stands erect with toes and heels touching and eyes closed; unsteadiness occurs if test positive. A test of balance and proprioception.
Rotational injury	diffuse shearing injury to brain substance magnified by rotatory forces.
Rubella	German measles.
Saggital split osteostomy	a surgical procedure performed on the jaw with the object of bringing forward the lower mandible.
Sclerosis	increased density, e.g. of a bone, owing to disease or injury.
Scoliosis	lateral (i.e. sideways) curvature of the spine.
Sensory	pertaining to sensation.
Septicaemia	destruction of tissues due to absorption of disease-causing bacteria or their toxins, from the blood stream. Sometimes used to refer simply to blood poisoning.
Sequestrum	a fragment of dead bone.
Short-term memory	the component of the memory system that has limited capacity and will maintain information for only a brief time.
Shoulder dystocia	difficult delivery arising from the shoulders of the foetus failing to negotiate the inlet of the pelvis.
Sigmoidoscope	a speculum for examining the lower bowel and for assisting in minor operations therein.
Sinus	a track leading from an infected focus, e.g. in a bone—to an opening on the surface of the skin.
Slough	tissue, usually skin, dead from infection.
Smallpox	an acute infectious virus disease causing high fever and a rash that scars the skin, generally transmitted by direct contact with an infected person.
Sodium valproate	anticonvulsant drug (trade name: Epilim).
Somatosensory area	regions in the parietal lobes of the brain which register sensory experiences such as heat, cold, pain and touch.
Spasmodic torticollis	a rheumatic seizure of the muscles of the neck in which it is so twisted as to keep the head turned to one side; also known as wryneck.
Spina bifida	a developmental defect in which the newborn baby has part of the spinal cord and its coverings exposed through a gap in the backbone; symptoms can include paralysis of the legs, incontinence and mental retardation from the commonly associated brain defect hydrocephalus.
Spleen	a large ovoid organ on the left side of the body, below and behind the stomach, which forms a major part of the reticuloendothelial system.

Spondylolisthesis	a forward shift of one vertebra upon another, due to a defect of the joints that normally bind them together; may be congenital or develop after injury.
Spondylosis	degenerative changes in the spine.
Status epilepticus	epileptic fits following each other in continuous rapid succession.
Stevens-Johnson syndrome	an illness characterised by a severe widespread rash and mouth ulcers, often caused by an allergic reaction to a drug.
Stupor	unconscious state, but arousable.
Subarachnoid haemorrhage	bleeding into the subarachnoid space surrounding the brain, causing severe headache with stiffness of the neck.
Subclavian vein	part of a major vein of the upper extremities or forelimbs that passes beneath the clavicle and is continuous with the axillary vein.
Subcortical	beneath the cortex.
Subdural haemorrhage	bleeding, usually due to trauma, between the dura mater and the brain.
Sulci	grooves on the surface of the brain separating cerebral gyri or convolutions.
Supination	twisting the forearm, the elbow being flexed, to bring palm of hand facing upwards (opposite to pronation).
Suxamethonium	a muscle relaxant drug.
Sympathetic ophthalmia	an auto-immune disease in which a penetrating injury to one eye produces inflammation in the fellow, non-injured eye, usually associated with loss of uveal tissue or uveal prolapse.
Syndrome	characteristic collection of signs and symptoms.
Synovitis	inflammation of the lining membrane of a joint.
Syphilis	a chronic venereal disease, caused by the bacterium treponema pallidum, resulting in the formation of lesions throughout the body.
Tachycardia	racing of the heart; increased pulse rate.
Tegretol	anticonvulsant drug.
Temporal lobes	the portions of the brain behind the eyes.
Teratogenic	pertaining to teratogenesis—any substance, agent or process that induces the formation of developmental abnormalities in a foetus.
Test battery	a collection of tests used to appraise individual abilities.
Tetanus	an acute, infectious disease affecting the nervous system, caused by the bacterium Clostridium tetani.
Thalidomide	a drug formerly used as a sedative, which if taken in the first three months of pregnancy could cause foetal abnormalities.
Therapeutia	pertaining to treatment, the application of a remedy.
Thorax, thoracic	the chest, pertaining to the chest.

Thrombosis	clotting (thrombus) in a blood vessel or in the heart.
Tissue	anatomically a complex of similar cells and fibres forming a structure within an organ of the body.
Toxic shock syndrome	a rare type of blood poisoning caused by the common bacteria staphylococcus aureus, which normally live harmlessly on the skin and in the nose, armpit, groin or vagina of one in every three people. Half the reported cases of toxic shock syndrome are associated with women using tampons; half result from localised infections.
Tracheotomy	operative opening into the trachea (windpipe) to bypass laryngeal or pharyngeal obstruction to the airway.
Traction	method by which fractures are realigned by applying linear force at right angles to the displacement of the bone fragments.
Tinnitus	ringing in the ears.
Tone	the tension present in a muscle at rest.
Tubal ligation	the tying off of the fallopian tubes; sterilisation procedure.
Tuberculosis	an infectious disease caused by the bacillus mycobacterium tuberculosis, characterised by the formation of nodular lesions (tubercles) in the tissues.
Upper respiratory tract infection	infection of the upper respiratory tract (the nose, nasal cavity, larynx, trachea, and some of the sinuses and air cells). Upper respiratory tract infections include the common cold, influenza, laryngitis, pharyngitis, sinusitis, tonsillitis and croup (in children).
Ureteric damage	damage to the ureter.
Valgus	outward deviation, e.g. genu valgum knock-knee (the tibia deviates outwards from the knee).
Varicosity	dilatation of veins.
Varus	inward deviation, e.g. genu varum bow-leg (the tibia deviates inwards from the knee).
Vasectomy	sterilisation of the male by division of each vas deferens which connects each testis to the urethra; the operation can be carried out under local anaesthesia and on an out-patient basis.
Vegetative state	a condition after severe brain injury, involving a return of wakefulness accompanied by an apparent total lack of cognitive function and awareness of the environment.
Vena cava	either of the two main veins, conveying venous (blue) blood from the other veins to the heart.
Ventricles	interconnected cavities in the brain containing CSF, comprising the two lateral ventricles, and the third and fourth ventricles.
Ventricular dilatation	an increase in the size of the lateral ventricles of the brain.
Vertigo	unpleasant sensation of abnormal rotation.

Vestibular	concerned with the inner ear labyrinth and its cerebral connections, particularly in the brainstem.
Visual fields	area perceived by each eye.
Wechsler Adult Intelligent Scale (WAIS)	a set of 11 tests designed to assess general intellectual ability in adults. Latest revision published in 1981, known as the WAIS-R.
Wells operation	See *ivalon sponge rectopexy.*
Whiplash injury	injury to cervical structures when the head moves violently in one direction and then bounding back in the reverse direction, as when occupants in a vehicle without head restraints are struck from behind.
White matter	the part of the brain and spinal cord that contains myelinated fibres.
Whooping cough	an acute contagious disease, primarily affecting children, due to infection of the mucous membranes lining the air passages by the bacterium haemophilus pertussis.
Xanth-	prefix meaning yellow.

INDEX

LEGAL TAXONOMY
FROM SWEET & MAXWELL

This index has been prepared using Sweet and Maxwell's Legal Taxonomy. Main index entries conform to keywords provided by the Legal Taxonomy except where references to specific documents or non-standard terms (denoted by quotation marks) have been included. These keywords provide a means of identifying similar concepts in other Sweet and Maxwell publications and online services to which keywords from the Legal Taxonomy have been applied. Readers may find some minor differences between terms used in the text and those which appear in the index. Suggestions to *sweetandmaxwell.taxonomy@tr.com*.

All references are to paragraph number

INDEX